P9-EED-152

THE CQ Researcher

formerly Editorial Research Reports

JANUARY — DECEMBER 1996

Published by Congressional Quarterly Inc. 1414 22nd Street, N.W., Washington, D.C. 20037
Congressional Quarterly offers a complete line of publications and research services.
For subscription information, call (202) 887-6279 or (800) 432-2250 ext. 279.

ISBN 1-56802-253-0
ISSN 1056-2036

s of The CQ Researcher

erly Editorial Research Reports)

Subscribers to *The CQ Researcher* receive 48 reports per year. Each report provides background on a current topic of widespread interest. Designed as a starting place for research, the reports define the issues and include a chronology and extensive bibliographies. A feature called "At Issue," which quotes opposing viewpoints from two experts, also is a part of each report.

The publication is available in various formats.

The Report

The report, about 12,000 words in length, is issued on Friday four times a month. Each report treats a subject that is in the news or likely to be in the news in the near future.

Bound Reports

The weekly reports are bound into quarterly paperback editions and an annual hardbound cumulation.

Index

A subject index to the reports is published each quarter and cumulated annually. The latest index may be found (in the blue pages) at the back of this volume.

Citation

Recommended format for citing these reports in a bibliography, based on The Modern Language Association of America's *Handbook for Writers of Research Papers,* 3rd edition, follows.

Clark, Charles S. "The Obscenity Debate." *The CQ Researcher* 20 Dec. 1991: 969-992.

THE CQ Researcher

formerly Editorial Research Reports

CONTENTS **JANUARY - DECEMBER 1996**

THE CQ Researcher®

PUBLISHED BY CONGRESSIONAL QUARTERLY INC.

Emergency Medicine

Is it a vital safety net or a drain on health resources?

The United States boasts the world's most advanced emergency medical system. But over-reliance on the emergency room for non-emergency needs — particularly by the poor and uninsured — has long prevented the specialty from being a hospital profit center. The movement toward managed care has prompted health insurers to seek cost savings by steering patients away from the emergency room except in true emergencies. Specialists worry that their prerogatives in defining such emergencies may be superseded by non-specialists reviewing cases after the fact. They also argue that emergency departments deserve ongoing financial support because, without universal health insurance, the emergency room will remain the only source of health care for many Americans.

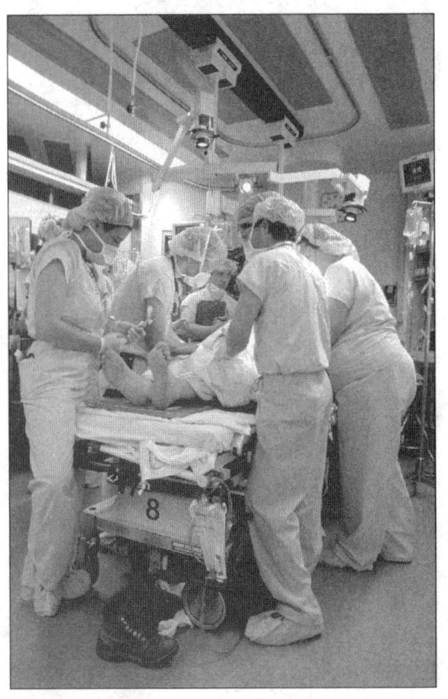

INSIDE

THIS ISSUE

CQ Jan. 5, 1996 • Volume 6, No. 1 • Pages 1-24

Formerly Editorial Research Reports®

EMERGENCY MEDICINE

THE ISSUES

BACKGROUND

CURRENT SITUATION

OUTLOOK

SIDEBARS AND GRAPHICS

FOR FURTHER RESEARCH

COVER: A PATIENT IN THE EMERGENCY ROOM AT THE SHOCK TRAUMA CENTER AT THE UNIVERSITY OF MARYLAND MEDICAL CENTER. (© 1990 KENNETH JARECKE, CONTACT PRESS IMAGES, PICTURE NETWORK INTERNATIONAL LTD.)

Jan. 5, 1996
Volume 6, No. 1

The CQ Researcher (ISSN 1056-2036). Formerly Editorial Research Reports. Published weekly (48 times per year, not printed the first Friday of any month with five Fridays) by Congressional Quarterly Inc., 1414 22nd St., N.W., Washington, D.C. 20037. Rates are furnished upon request. Second-class postage paid at Washington, D.C. POSTMASTER: Send address changes to The CQ Researcher, 1414 22nd St., N.W., Washington, D.C. 20037.

Emergency Medicine

BY CHARLES S. CLARK

THE ISSUES

A young pregnant woman suddenly experiences abdominal pain. Like many in her predicament, she considers making a dash for the emergency room. But first, she dials the 800 number she was given by her health insurance plan. Instantly, she is talking to a trained nurse — not one in her hometown of Pittsburgh, but one of the 60 or so nurses in Chicago, Sacramento or Phoenix who operate round-the-clock "teleservice" centers for a company called Access Health Inc.

On hearing the young woman's symptoms, the nurse asks a series of questions and reads from a set of physician-approved protocols that appear on her computer screen. They guide the nurse and the caller in determining the proper treatment, time frame and appropriate home-care measures.

"Often, when our nurses say 'Let's talk about it,' the caller's anxiety level goes down palpably over the phone," says Maureen Gill, a registered nurse who is vice president for clinical services at the Sacramento-based company. "People ask how can we do this when we can't see the patient. But once they know how it works, they see that we don't diagnose. We just establish categories: emergent [life- or limb-threatening], urgent, non-urgent or watchful waiting, each with a time frame for physician evaluation."

The practice of "telephone triage," which Access Health has been performing since 1986, is now available to 6 million customers in its contracting companies and managed-care organizations.

Many in medicine welcome such services. "People rely on the medical system both for information and reassurance," says Susan VanDevanter Brennan, an emergency room nurse at the Reston Hospital Center in Fairfax County, Va. "Telephone-triage nurses are the gatekeepers for correct information and are licensed to provide that reassurance. It may be difficult for consumers to understand that in the health care of the 1990s, the goal is to provide appropriate medical care *and* limit hospitalization and cut expenses. It's not appropriate to run a CAT scan for every headache."

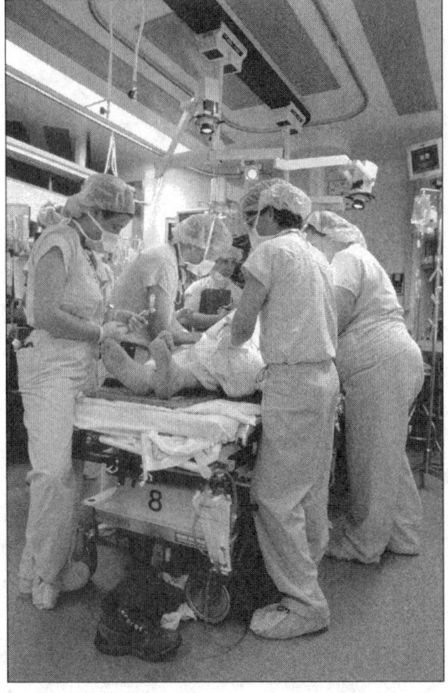

Others urge caution. The effectiveness of telephone triage "depends on the patient, their ability to respond, their education level and whether or not they are language-impaired," says Diane Rowland, executive director of the Kaiser Commission on the Future of Medicaid.

"If done carefully and properly, it can be useful for certain patients," says Dr. Gregory Henry, president of the American College of Emergency Physicians (ACEP). "But much of the published literature shows that it is less than satisfactory."

Debates over what is or is not satisfactory are unfolding across the health-care landscape as the nation continues its transition from traditional fee-for-service medicine to the brave new world of managed care. And few specialties will feel the effects as dramatically as emergency medicine.

Some 56 million Americans are now enrolled in health maintenance organizations (HMOs), which require patients to see a "gatekeeper" or primary-care doctor who oversees their medical care. Most plans tell patients that a "failure to contact the primary-care physician prior to emergency treatment may result in denial of payment."

The reason? In 1993, there were 97.4 million visits to emergency rooms in the United States, up from 65.9 million in 1973. (*See graph, p. 4.*) A significant portion — estimates usually range from 30-55 percent — probably could have been handled less expensively in doctors' offices or clinics. Some analysts say emergency care costs two-to-three times as much as the same care elsewhere, burdening hospitals and health-insurance plans with an estimated $5 billion in unnecessary expenses. [1]

Factors contributing to the increase in emergency room visits include the estimated 41 million Americans who lack health-insurance coverage; the elderly's growing use of emergency services; and the increasing prevalence of more serious illnesses and social problems. [2] (*See chart, p. 4.*) Cocaine-related emergency room visits rose 15 percent in 1994 after leveling off in 1993, according to a survey released in November by the federal Substance Abuse and Mental Health Services Administration.

For decades, the costs of maintaining an emergency room and trauma facility in every community were accepted as a given, with most hospitals covering the sizable expenses through add-ons to bills for other hospital services. Such cost-shifting forced private insurers and patients to pay an average of 29 percent over hospitals' reported costs for their care in 1993 to make up for deficient payments

Emergency Room Visits on the Rise

Visits to emergency departments rose by almost 50 percent from 1973-1993. The most commonly cited factors were the number of people without health insurance, especially those seeking non-urgent care; the elderly's growing use of emergency services; and the increasing prevalence of more serious illnesses and social problems.

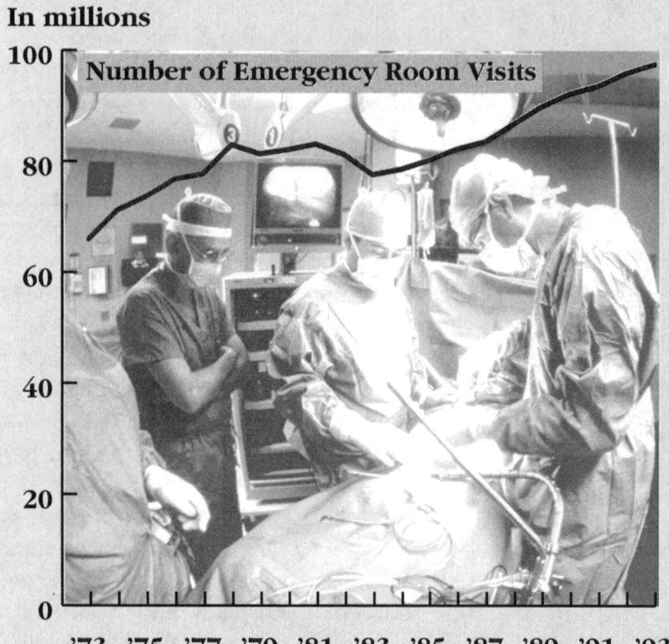

Factors Increasing ER Visits Since 1985

	Percent of hospitals reporting
Uninsured people seeking non-urgent health care	81%
People who are 65 years or older	80
People without health insurance	79
Severity of illness	79
People who do not have a regular physician	71
People who are unemployed	67
Alcohol-related illness or injuries	64
Violence-related injuries	63
Illegal drug-related medical problems	61
Insured people seeking non-urgent care	54
AIDS-related illnesses	51

Sources: American Hospital Association, Hospital Statistics, Annual Survey of Hospitals (line graph figures); General Accounting Office, Emergency Departments Unevenly Affected by Growth and Change in Patient Use, *January 1993.*

from Medicare, Medicaid and uninsured patients. [3] Cost-shifting is high on the list of what managed-care boosters want to curb.

Recent crackdowns by HMO gatekeepers on emergency room use have provoked a backlash among emergency physicians. Doctors, mainly in the New York City area, complained to reporters last year about "retrospective denials," a kind of Monday-morning quarterbacking in which insurance companies decline to reimburse health-care providers or patients after a decision is made — days or weeks later — that a treatment performed in the emergency room could have been referred to a primary-care provider. [4]

The ACEP publicized a number of instances where patients treated in emergency rooms for chest pains, seizures and breathing difficulties were later denied reimbursement. In Washington, the Health and Human Services Department official in charge of managed care, Rodney C. Armstead, reportedly sent a letter to 164 HMOs that do business with Medicare reminding them of their obligations to provide emergency care. [5]

And last February, a family in Fulton County, Ga., won a $45 million medical malpractice award because their six-month-old son had to have his legs and hands amputated after his HMO, Kaiser Permanente of Georgia, decided to send him to a hospital 42 miles from his house. The boy's heart stopped during the ambulance ride. He was revived, but circulation ceased to his extremities and he later developed gangrene, the *Atlanta Journal* reported. [6] Kaiser Permanente is appealing the court ruling.

The problem of retrospective denials goes to the heart of emergency medicine, then-ACEP President Richard V. Aghababian said last July. "According to the Centers for Disease Control, the No. 1 complaint of people presenting to the emergency department is abdominal pain," he said. That "can indicate many different conditions with varying degrees of severity. It could be very serious conditions such as cholecystitis, appendicitis, pancreatitis, ectopic pregnancy, dissection of the aorta, or it could be less serious conditions such as gastroenteritis, a urinary tract infection or constipation. The problem is that on the front end you simply don't know whether it's serious or non-urgent." [7]

Emergency medicine carries several distinctions. It's a young specialty, officially recognized by the American Medical Association only in 1979. It became one of the fastest growing medical fields in the 1980s as what formerly were called emergency rooms (ERs) were upgraded to emergency departments (EDs).

Today, the U.S. emergency medicine system is looked upon as a model by countries around the world. "Internationally, emergency medicine as we know it doesn't exist," says Robert Shesser, interim chairman of the Department of Emergency Medicine at George Washington University Medical Center. "It's pretty good in Anglophone countries, and developed countries have ambulances with doctors on board, but they don't have hospitals with integrated triage and a screening area. Their systems don't work as well with patients who have multi-system diseases or unclear diseases, so they have high hospital admissions and patients who fall between the cracks."

Emergency medicine practitioners are the only medical specialists required by federal and state law to see and screen all patients who present themselves, regardless of their ability to pay (*see p. 14*). A disproportionate share of publicly insured and uninsured patients utilize emergency departments. In 1990, one survey reported, 20 percent of emergency room visits were billed to Medicare and 17 percent to Medicaid, compared with only 13 percent and 10 percent of over-all hospital care. Fourteen percent of Americans were without health insurance in 1990, but the uninsured represented more than 19 percent of ED patients. [8]

Many emergency medicine practitioners take pride in being part of the social safety net. "We're in a prime position to teach physicians social activism and train physicians in social policy," says Charlotte Yeh, chief of emergency medicine at New England Medical Center in Boston. "We really have a direct link to the community. We're not ensconced in the fortress of the hospital." [9]

That's why many in the field are worried about possible changes in the Medicare and Medicaid programs, changes that could threaten the viability of emergency departments attached to many urban public hospitals.

But managed-care advocates argue that the equation could evolve as citizens — including the indigent — become more knowledgeable health-care consumers who understand emergency medicine's appropriate role. "We need to see emergency rooms close because as a health-care system, we can't afford so many," says Joanne Wilkinson, physician coordinator for emergency services at the Harvard Community Health Plan in Boston. "With managed care, we've seen a greatly reduced reliance on the ER. We believe health care for the poor will not suffer, but will improve."

As the public becomes more aware of the issues surrounding emergency care — stimulated by NBC's "ER" and other TV medical dramas (*see story, p. 8*) — the specialty's conundrums are likely to rise in visibility. As former Surgeon General Joycelyn Elders put it, "Emergency medicine is part of the health-care system that the majority of us seldom think about, hope never to use and yet expect to have available 24 hours [a day] when the need arises." [10]

Here are some of the key questions being asked:

Are emergency rooms used too much for primary care?

With its soothing night lamps and doors that open 24-hours each day, the emergency room attracts Americans with all types of ailments and all types of health plans. But it is the indigent who depend on it most heavily.

"The psych patient and the homeless person want to stay in the ER to get seen immediately," says a clinical specialist in the emergency department of Denver General Hospital. "He doesn't want to get put out in the waiting room or the walk-in clinic, where the wait could be two, four, five hours. And he knows from experience that the likelihood of getting a real bed upstairs is much greater if he comes in through the emergency room than the walk-in clinic." [11]

It's not just the indigent who feel their medical problems are more urgent than their doctors will eventually say. In one recent study, 89 percent of ER patients thought they needed to be seen immediately; but only 43 percent required care within 24 hours, according to physician review. [12]

Some studies have found that members of minority groups are particularly dependent on emergency room care. Hispanics are twice as likely and African Americans are three times as likely as whites to identify a hospital outpatient department or emergency department as their usual source of care, according to a recent study. African Americans and Hispanics also were slightly more likely than whites to visit an ER for non-urgent medical problems. [13]

Larry Gage, president of the National Association of Public Hospitals, argues that the ER-dependency of minorities is really "an artifact of poverty. It has to do with whether you're uninsured and whether you're in an inner-city area with no clinics or doctors with private offices," he says. "Minorities don't enjoy the ER any more than the ERs enjoy treating them. The inner-city ERs are often busy, unpleasant or even unhealthy, and patients don't get treated fast unless they're a real emergency."

Patients who are uninsured "know that eventually they will get seen at the ER," says Shesser at the GW Medical Center. "Many of them are

Many ER Visits Are for Non-Urgent Conditions

Many of those who visit emergency departments have conditions that don't require immediate care, and probably could have been treated in a doctor's office or clinic. But the exact proportion is subject to dispute. Estimates usually range from 30-55 percent. The urgency of a patient's injury or illness may be difficult to assess unless the person is seen by trained medical staff. And many of those who seek help for non-urgent conditions don't have a primary health-care provider.

GAO Estimate of Non-Urgent Use

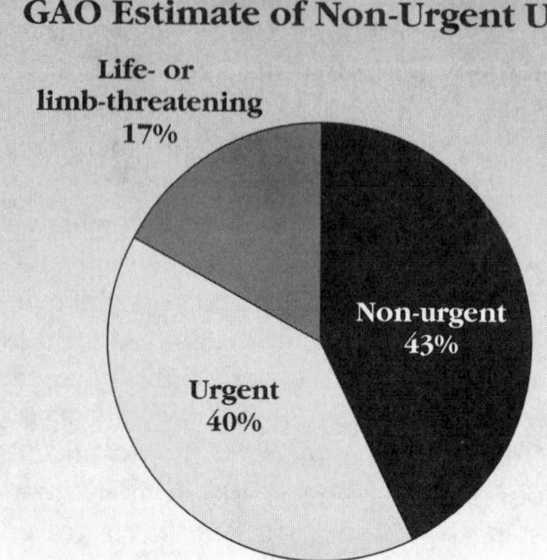

Reasons for Non-Urgent Use

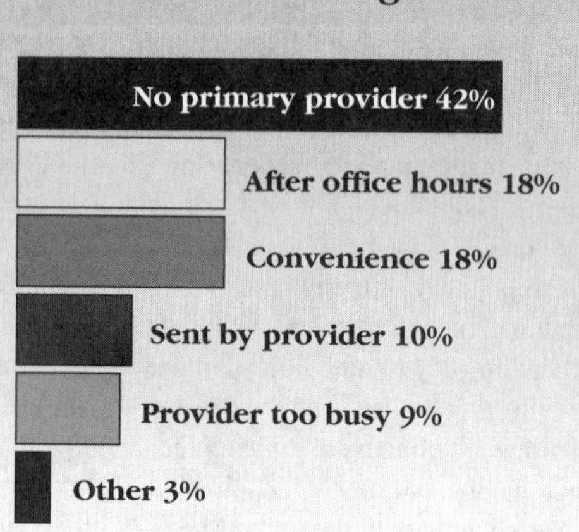

Source: General Accounting Office, Emergency Departments Unevenly Affected by Growth and Change in Patient Use, *January 1993*

working people. A janitor, for example, doesn't have the liberty to go to a doctor's appointment at an inconvenient time."

At GW, "we try to convince patients of the need for access to primary care, but many ask us why?" says Dr. Keith Ghezzi, medical director and chief operating officer for the GW Medical Center. Because of laws requiring that all patients coming to emergency departments be screened, attempts to curb ED use may not save as much money as reformers think, Ghezzi adds. "In person hours, it costs as much to screen patients as to treat them."

Efforts to channel more ER patients to primary care require a delicate balancing of factors, says Elinor Walker, a health scientist administrator at the federal Agency for Health Care Policy and Research. "You have to consider how accurate the discrimination is between emergency and non-emergency cases; how realistic is it for a trauma center to maintain a high level of technology just for rare emergencies; and what is the source of its revenue, especially if many of its patients are uninsured?"

In recent years, Walker notes, research has made it clear that in cases of myocardial infarction (heart attack), "there can be improved outcomes if the patients are treated in the first hour. But when we get chest pain, we don't all immediately call 911. If the system has let you know that it may resist your emergency, you're likely to delay even more."

Emergency physicians point to other areas in which providing primary care in the ER may actually have advantages. Mammograms and prostate exams provided by ER personnel to patients who lacked a primary-care physician were found to be effective as preventive-care measures and logistically easy for emergency departments to administer, a recent study noted. [14]

Another example is asthma. ACEP's Henry says "emergency departments can now treat [asthma] in four to six hours, whereas in the old days, the patient would have had to be admitted." In fact, he says, "with proper use of emergency care, the number of hospital beds could be cut in half."

Supporters of managed care often criticize the lack of continuity in emergency care, but ER practitioners defend their specialty. "Where is the evidence that acute, episodic care is deleterious or inferior to continuous primary care?" ask emergency physicians Gary P. Yount and David Sklar. "Few studies compare intermittent care with continuous care, and the results have been mixed. . . . Whether the additional expertise of emergency physicians in acute care will balance their lack of continuity experience with a particular patient is situation-specific." [15]

Emergency physicians also defend the ER on budgetary grounds. They say the cost analyses put forward by health reformers often ignore hidden expenses, such as the costs of forwarding a patient to a doctor's office or another hospital and the startup costs of building alternative clinics. [16]

"We all want to reduce costs," says Henry, "but emergency medicine represents only 1.5 percent of the health-care dollar in the United States. We have fixed costs, so we might as well be utilized. The misconception is that we are high-cost. In truth, we're only high charge, because 60-80 percent of our patients don't pay the full charge. Some would like to point to a hospitals' books and show you that the emergency room loses money, but it's actually a principal revenue generator. Fifty percent of admissions come from the ER. At an average hospital, at 365 patients a year, that alone adds $1.8 million in revenues."

Nor is emergency medicine fraught with unnecessary costs, says Robert M. Williams, a professor of emergency medicine at the University of Michigan. He challenges studies showing that ER treatment costs two-to-three times as much as the same care elsewhere. He says the average costs of non-urgent ED visits are similar to private physician office charges, $62 vs. $50. By that estimate, the potential savings of diverting non-urgent cases from the ER are much closer to $0.5 billion than the critics' $5 billion estimate, Williams says.

Emergency physicians point out that there will always be a need for someone to provide unscheduled care. "The ER is the only place open 24 hours a day, seven days a week," Henry says. "At 2 a.m. on Christmas Eve, it will look at your kid, and you don't have to put down your first dime. We're bound by our Hippocratic oath, and we are the network between the general masses and the health-care system."

But as managed care and other health reforms advance, debate over the value of emergency care is likely to hinge on marketplace issues of who can deliver most frugally. "Emergency physicians have been trying to have it both ways," says Charles Lucey, director of Unisys-Lousiana Medicaid in Baton Rouge. "Emergency physicians have differentiated themselves from primary care practitioners, and are making it a high-paying specialty, pricing themselves higher than primary care." [17]

And nearly everyone agrees that patients will be asked to take on more of the burden for proper use of the health-care system. A doctor in Portland, Ore., brought this point home in a recent letter to *The New York Times*: "A patient who has had a rash for two weeks goes to the emergency room at 11:30 on a Saturday night to be evaluated and becomes irate when I suggest that he be seen during regular office hours." [18]

Will the transition to managed care harm emergency medicine?

The general premise behind managed care is that "care should be coordinated with a primary physician," says Dr. Art Levin, a specialist in public health and preventive medicine with Prudential Insurance Co. of America, which operates many HMOs. "If members are going helter-skelter to the ER for episodic and uncoordinated care, you do not have a very desirable situation."

HMO officials admit that honest people can disagree over what constitutes an emergency situation. "There are always gray areas," Levin says, citing the example of a man with chest pains who goes to the ER and learns that he has indigestion. But there are also cases in which patients simply fail to assume proper responsibility, he adds, such as the woman who experiences uterine bleeding for a month, and then suddenly runs to the ER when it worsens.

"Most insurers would pay for something where a reasonable person would think his ailment is an emergency," Levin says. Most often, "it's an issue not of emergent vs. non-emergent but whether the care is appropriate or needed for the condition. It will always be more economical, for example, to do tests on an elective, rather than on an emergent basis."

Critics of managed care who work in emergency medicine do not argue with the over-all concept. "ERs want to work cooperatively with managed care because it's the future," says ACEP President Henry. "There will be changes, and we need strong physician influence while going into this world or it will be done the antagonistic way."

Managed care should not be viewed "as a monolith," Henry adds. "There are wonderful providers, and certain HMOs are very strongly doctor-influenced. There is the 50-60 percent that do it with intelligence and compassion. But as in any competitive market, there are those that are less scrupulous."

What bothers many emergency physicians are the retrospective denials of patients' emergency claims. (*See "At Issue," p. 17.*) Denial rates range from 1 percent to 15 percent among HMOs, according to the Oklahoma City-based Emergency Physicians Billing Service. [19]

In the ER, "we treat symptom comments and complaints," Henry says. "Is it appendicitis or stomach flu? How do we know until there's been an exam and some observations and some time. For HMOs to take the final diagnosis and then say they won't pay is immoral. We're made to look like bad guys because we must then send a bill back to the patient. Payment should be decided not on the final diagnosis but on the presenting complaint."

There are signs that the public may also be wary of HMOs. A survey of 3,348 adults in three cities in 1994, taken by Louis Harris Associates for the Commonwealth Fund philan-

Continued on p. 9

TV Portrayals Add Glamour to the ER

Hectic schedules and night shifts leave little time for emergency medical professionals to lounge in front of their televisions. Even so, it's hard to find a doctor, nurse or ambulance crew member who's unaware of the huge public relations boost they've gotten from TV's No. 1-rated show, NBC's "ER," and other medical dramas.

"'ER' is very realistic and does a good job of presenting the diversity of the population and the incidents we face day to day," says Susan VanDevanter Brennan, an emergency room nurse at the Reston Hospital Center in Fairfax County, Va. "It captures the full emotional range of what we deal with, both with patients and among our colleagues."

"'ER' carries the message that doctors are just people, but really are dedicated to excellence," says Dr. Gregory Henry, president of the American College of Emergency Physicians. "It boils it down to 'We're there, we care.' Because it's entertainment, they have to take some poetic license, but they do a wonderful job of capturing the intensity and decency of ER personnel."

Courtesy of Warner Bros. Television

The cast of NBC's "ER"

One reason "ER" is so realistic, Henry says, is that its chief writer, Lance A. Gentile, is an emergency physician who often consults with other professionals for story ideas. "Most of the stories you see were solicited from the field," Henry says.

The same is true for "Rescue 911," now shown on cable's Family Channel. "'Rescue 911' helps us by exposing the community to an aspect of public safety they were heretofore unaware of," says Steve Souder, administrator of the Emergency Communications Center in Arlington, Va. "It's not only a valuable crash course on the role of 911, it's also an education in life-saving techniques and common-sense practices."

A precursor of "Rescue 911" was a 1970s TV show called "Emergency." It was one of "the great things that catapulted firefighters into becoming providers of life-saving emergency medical services," says Doug Brown, director of federal relations for the International Association of Fire Chiefs. This was particularly true, he says, of paramedics who served in the Vietnam War and were seeking new civilian careers.

Trade journals for the emergency medicine profession contain proud testimony from members who have shared their expertise with TV producers seeking realism. Several years ago, a propmaster from the ABC hit series "NYPD Blue" contacted New York City's Emergency Medical Services about renting an ambulance and equipment. The result was a consulting partnership that regularly allows trained emergency medical technicians and paramedics to play roles that otherwise would have gone to actors.

"In the story line, [Detective Andy] Sipowicz receives several gunshot wounds to the back," read one account of life on the "NYPD Blue" set. "He loses a great deal of blood and falls unconscious. Here's where the technical advice began. The [New York emergency medicine public information office] had to explain in detail the medical conditions that would cause the detective to lose consciousness. After a quick lesson in hypovolemia [blood loss] and shock management, everyone agreed that Sipowicz would need an IV, [military anti-shock] trousers, a collar and long board and an endrotracheal tube, all of which had to be simulated, yet look realistic." [1]

Inevitably, emergency medical professionals spot technical errors in such shows. "ER" should get credit for realistically showing trauma, cases of social neglect and AIDS, says Dr. B. Tilman Jolly, an assistant professor and attending physician at the emergency room of the George Washington University Hospital. "But no patient ever has to wait on 'ER'," he says. "And they sometimes show mistakes that are not portrayed as mistakes. One example was [a show about a] pregnant woman. Because there were no beds in the labor and delivery department, she was put through a 12-hour labor in the ER. That's malpractice." In the real world, he explains, "there are other hospitals in town. And while I'm board-certified in emergency medicine and have delivered babies, I'm not qualified to induce labor for 12 hours. The show finally did reveal it as a bad outcome, and the staff got in trouble. But that wasn't seen until the end."

The entertainment world clashes with the realities of medicine in other ways, too. A recent issue of a nurses magazine reprinted an exchange that appeared after the popular gossip magazine *Us* last April ran a feature on George Clooney, the heartthrob actor who plays one of the lead characters on "ER." The accompanying photograph showed him surrounded by sexy nurses in near-pornographic poses.

"Nurses are professional, caring and dedicated to quality patient care," roared a letter to *Us*' editor from the director of nursing in the emergency department at a hospital in Greensboro, N.C. "They should not be portrayed as sex-starved, half-dressed individuals with thermometers stuck in their gartered nylons."

The show's executive producer, John Wells of Warner Brothers Television, sent a reply explaining that the photo in question was the responsibility of Clooney and *Us* magazine. "'ER' tries scrupulously to present the work of nurses in a serious and honest way," he wrote. "We have no control over the publicity undertaken by the individual actors." [2]

---

1 "NYPD Blue," *Emergency Medical Services,* May 1994, p. 43.

2 *Journal of Emergency Nursing,* August 1995, p. 276.

Continued from p. 7

thropy, found greater dissatisfaction levels among managed-care enrollees than those still in fee-for-service health plans. Access to emergency care was rated as only fair or poor by 12 percent of managed-care patients compared with only 5 percent of those in fee-for-service plans. [20]

There has been a steady drumbeat of complaints in recent years about how managed-care companies have plunged into the effort to win contracts with states to treat their low-income Medicaid patients. Some 13 states have been given special waivers from the federal Health Care Financing Administration (HCFA) to contract out Medicaid coverage, with mixed results.

"Managed care is like the little girl with a curl — when it's good its very, very good, but when it's bad, it's horrid," says Stan Dorn, the health division director of the Children's Defense Fund in Washington. "The good ones offer regular doctors, appropriate care and preventative care, are open 24 hours a day and offer Medicaid patients the same care as the middle class."

But Dorn cites cases in New York, Florida, California and Tennessee in which HMOs moved so rapidly to take over Medicaid cases that many eligible patients were not aware of their new status and continued to show up at public emergency rooms, some of which were in financial straits. In some cases, failure to record a citizen's name in a computer meant that care was denied. In others, aggressive sales staff exaggerated the range of benefits and made appointments for patients for which no doctor was available. There were also instances of money skimming by HMO officers.

"You have to remember that the financial incentive is the opposite of what it is in fee-for-service," Dorn says. "Managed care seeks to collect as many fees as possible while providing as little service as possible. That means they must be set up carefully so that natural incentives don't harm care."

The Group Health Association of America, the Washington trade group for HMOs, disputes the notion of widespread public dissatisfaction. The Commonwealth Fund poll of just three cities was too narrow, it argues, and concentrated on low-income people who are more apt to be dissatisfied. The association points to other polls, such as one from the Lincoln, Neb.,-based National Research Corp., showing satisfaction levels higher among managed-care patients than others. And it cites a literature analysis covering 16 studies from 1980-94, showing that quality of care in HMOs was better than or equal to results in fee-for-service plans on 14 of 17 quality-of-care measures. [21]

Addressing the problems that occurred in some states when Medicaid plans switched to managed care, Carmella Bocchino, the GHAA's director of medical services, attributes them to the fact that "the Medicaid population that is now in managed care hasn't been educated. With lots of new outreach, we believe it will continue to improve."

Rowland at the Kaiser Commission expresses similar views. "The more you develop infrastructure and patient education, the more likely it is to be successful," she says. "The [Medicaid] experiences of Arizona and Oregon show that it can take time to smooth out the wrinkles both on the provider side and beneficiary side. But you can't expect to go overnight from fee-for-service to managed care, and from ERs to not using ERs, without some people falling through the cracks."

Managed care has helped Massachusetts keep state Medicaid expenditures down, according to a recent article in *The Boston Globe*. Costs are growing at a rate of about 3 percent annually, one-third the national pace. About 95 percent of the state's Medicaid recipients who are eligible for managed care — basically, those who are not elderly, institutionalized or have another health insurer — are enrolled in HMOs or other primary-care programs. Nationally, the proportion enrolled in managed care is about 10 percent. [22]

The transition to managed care in Massachusetts has been successful largely "because we have educated our participants and changed the culture on how to use the ER," says Wilkinson at the Harvard Community Health Plan. "A primary-care doctor is what the poor need most in order to hook up with a health system," she adds.

Others are more skeptical that current versions of health-care reform will produce better coverage for the indigent. In a scathing essay about the "social Darwinism" of managed care, New York City emergency physician Lewis R. Goldfrank recently complained that "those who see physicians and nurses as 'providers,' our patients as 'consumers,' the treatment of a patient as a 'delivery of service,' and the ED as the 'marketplace' have designs on the future of emergency medicine that represent an attack on medical practice, quality, education and medial altruism." [23]

Others hope emergency doctors will do more than simply look out for their own specialty. Walker at the Agency for Health Care Policy and Research says emergency physicians complain, but they don't always do much to support the preventative, long-range, home-based approaches to health care that are associated with family doctors and health plans. "Asthmatics, for example, are not well served if they have to come to the brink of suffocation to get care, and asthma is an area where there are lots of new approaches to teaching patients to manage their breathing," she says. "I'm not suggesting that ERs consciously seek out a higher patient load, but they're trained to get in and get out quickly."

GW's Shesser says the issue is how to align different payment mechanisms embodied in both managed care and fee-for-service. "If you work, say, in Washington, D.C. but you live in Fredericksburg, Va., the system should allow you to come to an emergency department that's more convenient to your work. Once we make a commitment to install facilities for all emergencies in a geographical catchment area and then staff up, we will get a lot of ambulatory, unscheduled care that would be disruptive in a doctor's office stream of scheduled patients. Patients formulate relationships with us. HMOs feel this is anathema to their mission, even though creatively we can often provide better feedback to a primary-care doctor. Emergency medicine needs to be integrated. We need to define ourselves better to show how much of a resource we are." ■

BACKGROUND

Birth of a Specialty

Baron Dominique-Jean Larrey, the chief physician in Napoleon's army, is credited with creating, in 1797, the first pre-hospital system for assigning priorities for medical treatment and moving the wounded from battlefields to first-aid stations.

Such techniques were notably absent during the American Civil War, though the first U.S. ambulance services appeared in Cincinnati in 1865 and in New York in 1869. The first trained rescue squad reportedly was formed in Roanoke, Va., in the 1920s.

The term *triage,* meaning "to sort out according to quality," first appeared in the 18th century in connection with the wool trade, and later was applied to coffee beans. It was first used in reference to the handling of injured people in the 1930s. [24]

The notion of an emergency phone line for police, fire and medical services dates back to the 999 code used in England beginning in the late 1930s — a practice that made an impression on the American troops stationed there during World War II. In 1957, the National Association of Fire Chiefs recommended a universal emergency phone number, and AT&T began offering all communities the service in 1968. (It is currently available in 75 percent of U.S. cities and towns, covering about 35 percent of the country.)

Public awareness of techniques such as mouth-to-mouth resuscitation and closed cardiac massage were spreading by the 1950s, as were concerns about non-urgent use of hospital emergency rooms. Data from the American Hospital Association show that emergency room visits rose by 175 percent from 1954-64, faster than those for outpatient visits or admissions.

Yet this care was often provided by nurses or moonlighting physicians from a hodgepodge of specialities in poorly equipped rooms. A 1955 report in the *Bulletin of the American College of Surgeons* called emergency rooms the hospital field's "weakest link." Rescue service was informal during this period, with as many as half of patients arriving at hospitals in vehicles run by mortuary companies. [25]

In 1966, the *Journal of the American Medical Association* estimated that 42-46 percent of patient emergency room visits were "non-emergent," or not life- or limb-threatening. That same year, the National Academy of Sciences published a landmark report, *Accidental Death and Disability: The Neglected Disease of Modern Society,* that was influential in publicizing society's lack of preparedness for handling accident victims. Its recommendations influenced the 1966 Highway Safety Act that established the Department of Transportation and required states to develop Emergency Medical Services Systems. In 1973, the Emergency Medical Services Systems Act provided federal guidelines and funding for such systems.

Battle for Recognition

The first physicians to specialize in emergency care came together at a community hospital in Alexandria, Va. in the mid-1960s. "A group of family practitioners decided that they liked what had been a rotation for all doctors, in which you worked in the ER and then referred patients to yourself," says GW's Shesser. "They agreed, for a fee, to refer patients to other specialists as backups and for follow-up, in return for seeing them first in the ER. So the 'Alexandria Plan' spread to become the norm."

At the time many hospitals didn't have ERs, and though some state laws required public hospitals to provide emergency care, many had low standards. In 1968, eight doctors in South Lansing, Mich., launched the American College of Emergency Physicians. The organization's goals were to educate and train physicians in emergency medicine and to provide quality emergency care in the nation's hospitals. [26]

The first emergency residency program was launched at the University of Cincinnati. (By 1975, the number of residency programs had risen to 32; it's now up to 112.) In the early 1970s, a group of Southern California doctors led by Alex Bannister organized a corporation called Emergency Physicians Group Inc., which became the first major private franchise.

Business boomed. "Some increase was due to the rise in traffic and leisure-time accidents, and their tendency to occur outside doctors' regular office hours," write journalist Edith Alston and physician David Cutler. "Some was due, after the introduction of Medicare and a Medicaid during the mid-1960s, to doctors defending themselves against a slow reimbursement system by restricting their practices to patients able to pay. Whatever was stimulating the flow, the public looked more and more to the emergency room as the gateway to

Continued on p. 14

Chronology

1960s *Public and professionals become increasingly aware of the need to plan for delivery of emergency medical services.*

1966
National Academy of Sciences publishes influential report *Accidental Death and Disability: The Neglected Disease of Modern Society.* Highway Safety Act requires states to develop regional Emergency Medical Services (EMS) Systems.

1968
American College of Emergency Physicians is founded in South Lansing, Mich. AT&T enables phone companies to offer communities 911 service.

1969
Department of Transportation establishes 81-hour course for emergency medical technicians, eventually adopted by all states. First residency program for physicians in emergency medicine is launched at the University of Cincinnati.

1970s *Emergency medicine is recognized as a profession.*

1971
"Emergency" TV series popularizes paramedics profession.

1973
Congress passes Emergency Medical Services Systems Act to spawn network of offices in every area to measure need for emergency services.

1974
President Gerald Ford signs presidential proclamation designating Emergency Medical Services Week, now held annually in May.

1976
College of Emergency Physicians issues handbook outlining principles of emergency practice.

1979
American Medical Association accepts emergency medicine as a specialty.

1980s *Emergency medicine becomes one of the fastest growing specialties; ERs become overcrowded with indigent patients; rise of managed care.*

1980
First board certification exams in emergency medicine.

1981
Assassination attempt on President Ronald Reagan puts emergency medicine in spotlight. Research and education institute later named for him at George Washington University Medical Center.

1982
Tax Equity and Fiscal Responsibility Act first permits health maintenance organizations (HMOs) to accept Medicare patients.

1983
Texas enacts law requiring all general hospitals to provide emergency services to persons in need. Definition of emergency services expands to include prevention of disfigurement, organ impairment and active labor.

1985
National Research Council publishes *Injury in America: A Continuing Public Health Problem.*

March 20, 1986
Congress clears previous year's reconciliation measure called Consolidated Omnibus Budget Reconciliation Act (COBRA) containing Emergency Medical Treatment and Labor Act, which requires emergency rooms to see and screen all patients regardless of ability to pay.

1990s *Health reforms debated nationally; debates over impact of managed care.*

1990
Trauma Care Systems and Planning Act encourages trauma systems run by local EMS authorities to identify patients and match with resources.

September 1993
Health Care Financing Administration study on retrospective denials of ER care by HMOs raises issue of whether government definitions of true emergencies need changing. Clinton administration unveils ill-fated health-care reform plan.

July 1995
Access to Emergency Medical Services Act introduced by Reps. Benjamin L. Cardin, D-Md., and Marge Roukema, R-N.J., would require insurers to cover emergencies as defined by "prudent layperson."

September 1995
Republican Congress unveils Medicare and Medicaid reform proposals.

One Night in a Washington Emergency Room . . .

The call comes in at about 6 p.m. A man who looks to be in his 60s is en route with a scalp laceration, probably the result of a fall. He is confused and his blood-sugar level may be low, the ambulance crew reports.

"Could be a diabetic," says Dr. B. Tilman Jolly as he instructs his team of medical residents, nurses and trauma technologists.

It is Sunday evening and Jolly is on the home stretch of his 12-hour shift as the physician in charge of the emergency room at George Washington University Hospital in Washington D.C. Though both his trauma bays are vacant, Jolly can see from constantly updated notations in colored marker on the unit's display board that most of his nine exam rooms are in use. The complaints range from an infected leg, to flu-like symptoms, back and shoulder pain, a drug overdose ("non-lethal but needs psychiatric evaluation") and a stroke that required admission to the hospital.

The board bears a column indicating each patient's health insurance carrier. In 20-25 percent of the cases, the space reads "uninsured."

Insurance coverage "is becoming an issue because of health maintenance organizations," Jolly says. "It used to be that we would simply say, 'OK, admit him.' But now we say things like, 'He's with Kaiser, and they don't have a contract with us.' So if we can stabilize him, we transfer him to a contract hospital."

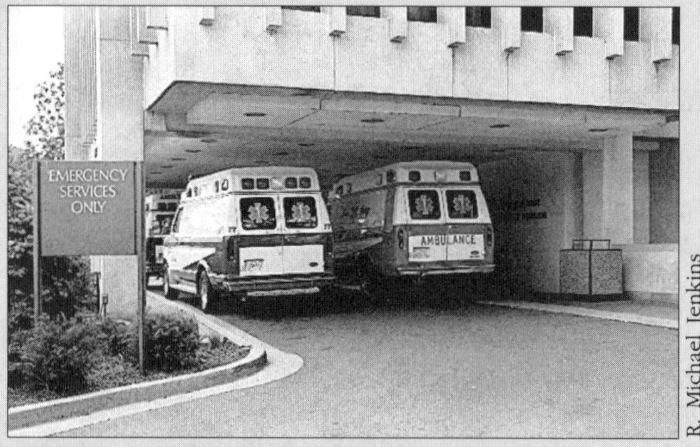

R. Michael Jenkins

The GW unit is famous as the site where President Ronald Reagan was treated after he was shot by a would-be assassin in March 1981.

The GW unit is famous as the site where President Ronald Reagan was treated after he was shot by a would-be assassin in March 1981. It also is a key facility in a city with soaring numbers of indigent patients and a reputation as the nation's "murder capital." GW's physicians treat 500 trauma patients a year, 40 percent of which have suffered bullet or knife wounds, as opposed to injuries from falls or car accidents.

"We're the receiving area for Members of Congress, the White House, embassies and the State Department, as well as tourists and many of the homeless," Jolly says. Though the trauma unit at Washington's public hospital, D.C. General, is closer to the neighborhoods where most assaults and homicides occur, its long waits and financial troubles have forced patients and city dispatchers to rely increasingly on GW. Designed to handle 20,000 cases a year, GW's emergency unit takes in 50,000, its patients on gurneys often lining the hallways.

Minutes after tonight's alert, paramedics wheel in a white, elderly male. Trauma technologists wearing light blue scrubs and nurses in darker blue cut off his clothing with trauma scissors. He is bleeding from the back of his head. "Can you remember what happened today?" asks the resident in charge of the case. All he can recall is his name.

The paramedic tells Jolly that the patient was combative and pulled out and bent the needle and catheter that had been inserted in his arm to measure his blood-sugar level. The measurement taken en route to the hospital shows that the patient is low on sugar (hypoglycemic). Jolly orders a blood-alcohol test, continued use of the special collar that was applied to immobilize his neck and a CAT scan to check for brain injury.

No one knows who called the ambulance in this case. Probably a frightened neighbor who saw the man sprawled in his apartment building hallway, says the paramedic. To guard against spine injury, the crew had to place a board between the patient's back and the stretcher, which made negotiating the elevator difficult.

"No one makes house calls anymore," Dr. Jolly tells his visitor. "But if the paramedic tells us that the home is a dump, with old wasted food on the floor, we can tell that perhaps the patient needs to be admitted to protect him" and that social services should visit his home. The resident tells Jolly that the man clearly smells of alcohol.

Communication with family members can be vital in such cases. The emergency department's secretary says the patient's sister is expected soon in the lobby. This must be noted at the registration desk at the unit's entranceway, where the triage nurse, a social worker and a volunteer aide have stations across from the waiting room. Soon, Jolly will meet the patient's sister and brother in a conference room to discuss the man's drinking habits.

It is the attending physician's lot to juggle many cases at once, which means an unceasing blur of demands for his attention. "We're a teaching hospital," Jolly says. "The residents and medical students all have patients, and they show them to me as needed, unless they're very sick. I see every patient, but it would be superfluous to do everything for every patient if you've got a good resident."

The attending doctor has backup teams of cardiologists, orthopedic surgeons and other specialists available within minutes from other departments. And as a Level-I trauma center, GW has multi-million-dollar radiology, CAT-scan and

. . . A Safety Net for a 'Collection of Humanity'

ultra-sound equipment (to help diagnose problem pregnancies) running 24 hours a day. "We're spoiled here," Jolly says. "At other hospitals, the patients might have to take their chances and wait until the next day."

After being briefed by a resident, Jolly examines a 27-year-old African-American woman who was knocked unconscious when a cabinet fell on her shoulder. The woman's mother said she was out for five minutes, but when Jolly presses, they agree it was more like a few seconds. He listens to a nurse's report about a patient who has left the hospital without permission. He confirms a resident's interpretation of an X-ray showing a bicyclist's broken thumb. And he chats with a GW student complaining of a cold and congestion. The student is making a reluctant visit to the ER because he has no regular doctor.

One of the most common complaints seen in the ER is asthma. Jolly applies his stethoscope to the rib cage of a 43-year-old African-American woman whose usual self-treatment with a nebulizer has not eased her problem breathing. She says she likes the GW emergency room because her primary care doctor doesn't work Sundays, and because the triage nurse takes her right away.

"Asthma patients can get really sick very fast," Jolly says, adding that he seldom wastes time questioning whether his patients truly belong in the emergency room. "They're already here, and we're already here," he says. 'We have high fixed costs, but our cost per patient is relatively low. And if someone is sick and they don't know how sick, their doctor doesn't want to get up at 3 a.m. to see them." GW has directories of hundreds of health-plan providers they can refer patients to, "but we can't guarantee that our patients will follow up on it," he says.

Jolly is well aware of how managed-care groups can retrospectively deny coverage for his patients' claims. "It's easy to tell retrospectively whether a certain treatment was needed, but I'm not permitted to turn anyone down."

Next, Jolly examines a Moroccan woman who is breathing at an alarmingly fast 26 times per minute. Her friend and neighbor, acting as translator, explains that she gets colds and rapid breathing about three times a year. She has been in the country for two years and has no regular doctor. They had been on their way to the public hospital but got lost and ended up at GW. As Jolly orders a chest X-ray, he mentions that the rising number of immigrants has required GW to compile a directory of bilingual hospital staff. The Moroccan woman is admitted after tests show pneumonia and low oxygen levels.

An attending physician's authority often spills into non-medical areas. On this night, an obese woman with difficulty walking has come for an X-ray. Jolly decides there is no reason to admit or treat the wheelchair-bound, Eastern European woman. He decides she can go home in an ambulance, which Medicaid should cover. "The problem is, taxi drivers can't help take a patient inside their home, so you have to rely on private ambulances," he says. Too many people use the D.C. ambulance system as a transport system, he adds, even for a sprained ankle.

Suddenly the woman in the wheelchair is heard shrieking. Nurses tell Jolly that she has absconded with a datebook belonging to another patient. She demands to be taken to a neighboring hospital. She wants the staff to call 911. Jolly instructs the staff to call hospital security.

"She's socially maladjusted, and you can't reason with her," Jolly confides. "Non-medical people don't realize the collection of humanity we have to deal with. You have to stand them down with a combination of logic and whatever you think works." The woman is finally wheeled out by a D.C. police officer.

On this night, it turns out that the only person who is "really sick," in Jolly's words, is the sixty-something man with the scalp laceration. Though the blood around his neck has properly clotted, his wound has not yet been closed pending an X-ray of his neck. His blood test reveals an alcohol level three times the legal limit.

The radiologist has had trouble getting the right angle on his X-ray because the man will not cooperate. He has fought off his heart monitor, refused to urinate in a bottle and is demanding a cup of coffee. "I'm leaving as soon as I can and I'm going to sue you," he shouts at the resident who gave him a rectal exam. "You are intoxicated, sir," Jolly tells him.

As staff prepare to treat his scalp wound, Jolly decides to admit the elderly man overnight for observation. It will take a team of five to turn him over to delicately remove his collar brace. "The trauma technologists do the suturing and splinting even better than a plastic surgeon," Jolly says. "If you had to hire doctors for that, things would get bogged down."

In supervising ambitious staffers who work lengthy shifts and get few breaks for meals, Jolly tries to let his people do things as they see fit. Only occasionally is he prompted to step in and correct a technique. "Our people know what role they play, who is supposed to be talking and who's not," he says. "They believe in the hierarchy. And if there's a disagreement, someone at the faculty level can come in and say how it'll be done."

The frustration of emergency room work is that there is little sense of closure. Staffers who've moved on to the next emergency find themselves wondering how their previous patients made out.

"There's no automatic follow-up, but if a patient has been admitted to the hospital, the computer will show us their discharge papers," Jolly says. "We want to know the result of what we did."

A Tour of the Communications Center ...

"Arlington County 911, what is your emergency?" As soon as the caller starts to speak, the computer screen lights up with a Cadillac version of "caller I.D.," providing the household's phone number, address, the date and time, and, in some jurisdictions, a code indicating which fire, police or ambulance service should respond.

"The caller might say something like, 'My child is turning blue, and I don't know what to do. Hurry, hurry, hurry,'" says Steve Souder, administrator of the Emergency Communications Center in Arlington, Va. "Our call-taker then enters the code for a choking child," and instantly forwards the computer file to a second computer run by a dispatcher.

Lisa Thompson

A staffer at the Emergency Communications Center operates the computers that speed up both call-taking and dispatching.

This state-of-the-art communications system is known as "enhanced 911." But it takes more than sophisticated technology to calm the fears of citizens worried about news accounts of 911 calls that were met with costly, even deadly delays.

Avoiding situations like what happened in Philadelphia in November 1994 — when tapes revealed a call-taker arguing rudely with someone trying to report a mob fatally beating a 16-year-old boy — requires "training and culture," Souder says. "The mindset is one of caring and giving and asserting, coupled with solid training and protocols."

Souder says Arlington has the advantage of being a "clean operation," in which publicly run police, fire and ambulance services are jointly dispatched by civilian staffers. "There are no multiple agencies or different levels of authority and protocols, with all the associated difficulties," he says.

Emergency calls and dispatches in Arlington County, a suburb of Washington, D.C., are handled round-the-clock by some 50 employees who've been through an 18-month training period that includes cross-training in performing one another's jobs.

Since 1971, Arlington has been a member of a Northern Virginia consortium that shares fire and ambulance services among three jurisdictions. Regardless of where the emergency is, the communications center that gets the call does the dispatching. That means the Arlington center could dispatch an ambulance from neighboring Alexandria or Fairfax County. "A parent [with an injured child] doesn't care what's written on the side of the truck," Souder says.

What is often not clear to panicked callers is that dispatching gets underway right away, via an electronic signal to a fire station. "We tell this to the frantic father or mother and ask them to pay attention while we give them our pre-arrival protocol instructions," Souder says. "Otherwise, they're likely to shout about why we are asking all these questions."

The dispatcher's computer automatically provides information on the in-service unit closest to the caller, as well as alternative

Continued from p. 10

medical care, and by 1975, the stream of patients had swelled to 50 million a year. . . .The emergency room . . . was evolving into the most highly utilized area in many an institution; it was the McDonald's of medicine, totting up it's patient-care increase at a rate of about 10 percent a year." [27]

Still, professional acceptance as a medical specialty was slow. As recently as 1981, *The New England Journal of Medicine* editorialized that "Anyone who has rotated through busy, varied intern services should be comfortable with all the procedures performed in ERs. It is true that one must know a little of everything, but the requisite knowledge need not be more than shallow. It is in essence the knowledge required for the first few moments of general practice." [28]

Anti-Dumping Laws

By the 1980s, emergency rooms — particularly those in cities — had become severely overcrowded. Public hospitals in many cities became the dumping grounds for indigent and uninsured patients whom private hospitals were declining to treat. In March 1986, as part of a mammoth budget bill called the Consolidated Omnibus Budget Reconciliation Act (COBRA), Congress passed the Emergency Medical Treatment and Labor Act. It imposes a unique requirement on all U.S. emergency rooms that receive Medicare and Medicaid funds, mandating that they screen and stabilize every patient who presents himself, regardless of ability to pay. Violations of the statute can result in civil monetary penalties of up to $50,000.

Since the law took effect, "There have been fines in probably two dozen cases," says Gage of the public hospital group, "but some private hospitals simply closed their ERs."

Crowded conditions worsened in cities such as New York, Boston and Los

... From the Folks Who Answer When You Call 911

units in descending order of proximity, in case the first is already in use. The dispatch made, the dispatcher then forwards the computer file to a second dispatcher at a neighboring console who will maintain contact with the emergency crew for the duration of the incident.

The initial call-taker, meanwhile, continues talking to the caller. This procedure, called "bridging the gap," involves reading from a set of pre-written medical cards, marked by topics such as choking, that contain medically certified first-aid instructions. There is no attempt to diagnose an ailment, but the call-taker can ask questions and offer the caller advice on techniques such as the Heimlich maneuver and cardiopulmonary resuscitation. Any information gleaned about the victim, such as his medical history or his location within the house, is immediately passed to the rescue crew.

Arlington is fortunate, Souder adds, because all of its ambulances have Advanced Life Support status, meaning they are staffed by paramedics who have training and skills a step above emergency medical technicians. "In the past 15 years, paramedics have reached a much higher level of training. So doctors now have a higher level of confidence in their giving uncoached care in the pre-hospital phase," Souder says.

And more often than not, the ambulance is accompanied by a fire truck staffed by fire fighters trained as emergency medical technicians. This is a sensible use of fire equipment and crews that might otherwise be idle, Souder says, and if the crew is not needed to help with the victim, it can be dispatched elsewhere from that site.

"If all goes well, within four minutes or less from the time of the call, a medic is knocking at the victim's door," Souder says. "In cases where pre-arrival instruction is provided by the call-taker, we don't hang up or let the caller hang up until we have confirmation of arrival through the ambulance radio, and again when the medic gets on the phone and says, 'We're on it.'" The well-briefed medics can quickly treat or transport the patient to the closest hospital, the name of which is transmitted back to the dispatcher's computer.

The Arlington center has a back-up power system and a set of manual procedures at the ready in case its computers break down. The wonders of technology permit all calls to be taped for possible review, and provide a special keyboard that call-takers can use with the deaf. Non-English-speaking callers are handled by pushing a button that instantly patches in a third-party organization in Monterey, Calif., that has staff translators for 157 languages.

The center also has special lines to handle calls from mobile phones, whose owners are asked to disclose their current location. Cellular phones "add a whole new dimension" to 911, Souder says. They allow much more rapid reporting of traffic accidents, the only downside being that a single accident might prompt 40 calls.

Souder's staff is accustomed to a heavy flow. The Arlington center gets about 400 calls a day, with peak hours usually Friday and Saturday nights, before area bars close. They handle prank calls from children, misdials from people calling overseas and nasty, sometimes racially tinged, calls from a few irate citizens. They are specially trained to diffuse tension in people who are impatient or in violent situations. [1]

"To someone whose house is burning, two minutes feels like a week," Souder says. "Our people must have three ears and eyes in back of their heads, to be able to hear conversations across the room and know how it impacts what they're doing. If there's any doubt, if the trouble is unknown, we just go."

[1] Studies show that only about 3-4 percent of callers might be described as "hysterical." See Marie Nordberg, "Dispatch Disasters," *Emergency Medical Services*, August 1995, p. 38.

Angeles. In 1989, 40 percent of hospital ERs were overcrowded, an ACEP survey noted. From 1985-90, 85 percent of hospitals reported an increase in the number of patients with non-urgent conditions being treated in the ER; more than half of the ERs requested, at least once during the year, that ambulances temporarily be diverted elsewhere. [29]

Some think the overcrowding problem has been exaggerated. "The media focused on inner-city overcrowding, which is true in large cities of the Northeast, but there is no overcrowding nationally," says GW's Shesser. "In fact, ERs in the suburbs are trying to bring in patients."

Indeed, in recent years emergency room crowding appears to have eased, and one key reason, say officials at HMOs, is the rise of managed care. ■

CURRENT SITUATION

Health-Care Reform

The beginning of the Clinton administration in 1993 spawned intensive debates over proposals for national health-care reform. With the prospects of redressing longstanding flaws came fears of losing ground. "It appeared that emergency medicine had reached the third stage and was beginning to be accepted as a necessary specialty, until health-care reform," complained emergency physician Peter Rosen. "While health-care reformers appeared to demote emergency medicine to the first stage in their recent proposals, it actually seemed more like they wished the specialty did not exist at all." [30]

The comprehensive overhaul initially proposed by the Clinton administration would have offered all Americans inpatient, outpatient and emergency room services, with a $25 co-payment if an emergency room was used in a non-emergency. [31] But Clinton's plan also would have taken steps to discourage what some said was a glut of medical specialties in order to encourage primary care and family practices. [32] And it came at a time when emergency physicians were issuing warnings of coming shortages of trained emergency personnel.

With the Republican takeover of Congress after the 1994 elections (fueled largely, many said, by the failure of Clinton's health-care plan), the agenda quickly switched to budget balancing and proposals for vast changes in Medicare and Medicaid. The GOP plan is to slow Medicare spending by offering senior citizens alternatives in private health insurance, as well as cut Medicaid spending by devolving responsibility for care of the poor to state governments.

Many in emergency medicine agree on the need to reduce the federal budget deficit, and many hold out hopes that moving more indigent patients into managed care will ultimately be good for the country. But advocates for the poor worry that millions will lose their access to health care.

A recent analysis by the Consumers Union and the National Health Law Program warns that cuts in projected federal Medicaid spending could be more devastating than comparable cuts in Los Angeles in the early 1980s. In response to a 1982 budget shortfall, California cut projected state Medicaid spending by 18 percent, or $524 million. As a result, the study says, "Los Angeles County's trauma care system, formerly a national model, collapsed under the strain of providing expensive emergency care to many uninsured patients. Eleven out of 23 trauma-care centers closed, leaving more than 800,000 county residents without access to necessary trauma care." [33]

"The grim results of California's cutbacks suggest the harm that could ensue nationally if congressional proposals are enacted," the study concludes.

The GOP's proposal to freeze Medicare payments to ambulance crews for seven years drew a protest from the American Ambulance Association, the National Association of State EMS Directors and the National Association of EMS Physicians. In a full-page ad in *The Washington Post* on Nov. 27, the groups warned that the freeze would "undermine the readiness and stability of our EMS system, and hurt those we are directly charged with caring for."

David Nevins, president of the Sacramento-based ambulance association, says the freeze would force "reductions in timely response, standards of care and training" because ambulance systems rely on Medicare for 30 percent of their funding. "Everyone in emergency medicine says they're the safety net, but we truly are," he says. "We get there first, and we're the patients' first contact. If we can't move them to the ER, they don't get there."

But most parties are resigned to some level of cutbacks. Even President Clinton's budget proposals would cut payments currently going to states with hospitals that take a "disproportionate share" of uninsured, non-paying patients. Congress has agreed to help states whose Medicaid budgets are disproportionately impacted by illegal immigrants who flock to emergency rooms but have little money to pay for services. A special fund over the next five years will provide money to, in descending order, California, New York, Texas, Florida, Illinois, New Jersey, Arizona, Massachusetts, Virginia, Washington, Georgia, Maryland, Colorado, Oregon and New Mexico. [34]

The Prudent Layperson

Of direct concern to emergency medicine is a proposed change in the law that determines which emergency treatment is required to be covered by managed-care plans — those that average people perceive to be an emergency condition, or those that experts later deem are true emergencies.

Last July, Reps. Benjamin L. Cardin, D-Md., and Marge Roukema, R-N.J., introduced the Access to Emergency Medical Services Act. Among other things, it would have established a uniform definition of an emergency based on symptoms; banned requirements of prior authorization for emergency care; required authorizations of emergency treatment to be produced within 30 minutes; banned policies that discourage use of 911; and required plans to offer 24-hour access. It was backed enthusiastically by the ACEP, as well as groups such as Public Citizen, Citizen Action, the American Heart Association, the American Academy of Pediatrics, the International Association of Fire Fighters, the National Association of EMS Physicians and the Emergency Nurses Association.

This fall, a "prudent layperson" provision introduced by Sen. Bob Graham, D-Fla., cleared the Senate as part of its Medicare reform package. When the House Commerce Committee approved its Medicare provisions, it included a similar provision introduced by Rep. Greg Ganske, R-Iowa, a physician. That version, however, was dropped before the full House voted on the Medicare overhaul.

During the conference, the Senate provision was dropped in favor of the House position, which made no change in current law, a position backed by insurance and HMO industry groups. The ACEP was furious, and sent a letter to House Speaker Newt Gingrich, R-Ga., vowing to discourage senior citizens from joining managed-care plans if they deny payment for unauthorized emergency care.

Opponents in managed care view the prudent layperson definition as an impediment to their goal of reducing

Continued on p. 18

At Issue:

Should a "prudent layperson" definition of a medical emergency be adopted by all health-care plans?

Richard V. Aghababian
Then-President, American College of Emergency Physicians

FROM TESTIMONY PREPARED FOR HOUSE WAYS AND MEANS HEALTH SUBCOMMITTEE AND COMMERCE HEALTH AND ENVIRONMENT SUBCOMMITTEE, JULY 27, 1995.

yes

The No. 1 complaint of people presenting to the emergency department is abdominal pain. [A]bdominal pain can indicate many different conditions with varying degrees of severity. It could be very serious conditions such as cholecystitis, appendicitis, pancreatitis, ectopic pregnancy, dissection of the aorta or it could be less serious conditions. . . .The problem is that on the front end you simply don't know whether it's serious or non-urgent.

[That is why we have] advocated that a prudent layperson definition of emergency be adopted for all health-care plans, including the Medicare program. The definition says: "Emergency health-care services are those . . . that are provided in a hospital emergency facility after the sudden onset of a medical condition that manifests itself by symptoms of sufficient severity, including severe pain, that the absence of immediate medical attention could reasonably be expected by a prudent layperson, who possesses an average knowledge of health and medicine to result in: (1) placing the patient's health in serious jeopardy; (2) serious impairment to bodily functions; or (3) serious dysfunction of any bodily organ or part. . . .

The effect of adopting the definition would be to shift the focus of any disputed service from a review of the patient's discharge diagnosis to a review of the patient's presenting symptoms. The adoption of this definition does not take away the managed-care plan's ability to review these cases. It simply directs that the focus of the review should be appropriately on the patient's presenting symptoms and whether, from a lay perspective, the patient acted prudently. . . .

Increasingly, emergency physicians are being pressured by managed-care plans to transfer patients to plan hospitals or to discharge patients for economic reasons and against the advice of the treating physicians. . . .

Plans today routinely deny payment for emergency medical services if the patient did not obtain prior authorization to go to seek care in the emergency department. Coverage is frequently denied for emergency services simply because the patient was unable to reach the patient's primary-care physician. In many instances, these denials are issued regardless of the patient's condition and regardless of whether the primary-care physician was available. . . .

Patients who believe they are experiencing a medical emergency should not delay seeking treatment because they are uncertain whether those services will be covered.

BlueCross BlueShield Association
FROM POSITION PAPER, DECEMBER 1995.

no

We believe that this definition is unnecessary. Current requirements are both clear and sufficient to assure access to necessary emergency medical care. The additional elaboration of requirements included in the proposals would not offer any clearer guidance to health plans, health-care providers or beneficiaries. It may lead beneficiaries to believe, wrongly, that any services provided in a hospital emergency room will be covered by their health plan.

Convincing evidence has not been presented that the denial of appropriate care for bona fide emergencies is more than an isolated problem that can be solved within the framework of existing legislative and regulatory requirements. Studies have shown that more than half of all emergency room visits in 1992 were for non-urgent care. . . .

If legislation clarifying the requirement that health plans cover emergency services is necessary, then it is essential that such legislation clearly indicate that:

- the health plan is required to establish procedures through which a subscriber can obtain authorization to obtain emergency care outside the network or timely access to medical treatment from a health-plan provider;
- the health plan is required to cover only that medical care that is needed to stabilize the patient until the patient is transferred to the care of a health-plan provider. This will ensure that treatment occurs in the most efficient, appropriate setting;
- the health plan is required to pay the provider at the lesser of the amount that would have been paid under Part A or Part B of the Medicare program or the amount that the health plan would have paid if the services had been provided by a member of the health plan's provider network;
- the health plan may require the beneficiary to pay the co-insurance that would have been required under Part A or Part B of the Medicare program;
- and the health plan may deny coverage if the health plan concludes on the basis of a physician's review of the patient's medical record that the condition did not require immediate treatment, and the subscriber did not attempt to contact the plan or their provider prior to seeking care outside the network provided in a non-emergency situation;
- or the subscriber could have obtained care from a health plan provider that was equally accessible as the provider that provided the emergency services;
- or the subscriber had been experiencing symptoms for more than 24 hours.

FOR MORE INFORMATION

American College of Emergency Physicians, 1111 19th St. NW, Suite 650, Washington, D.C., 20036; (202) 728-0610. Founded in 1968, this group of 18,000 doctors monitors legislation, regulation and intra-professional training issues on behalf of emergency medicine.

Group Health Association of America, 1129 20th St. NW, Suite 600, Washington, D.C., 20036. (202) 778-3200. This trade association for health maintenance organizations monitors legislation and regulations, provides legal counsel and conducts educational programs.

National Association of EMS Physicians, 230 McKee Place, Suite 500, Pittsburgh, Pa., 15213; (412) 578-3222. This professional association for out-of-hospital emergency medical-care providers includes 1,500 nurses, paramedics, physicians, administrators, education specialists and researchers.

National Health Law Program, 1815 H St. NW, Suite 705, Washington, D.C., 20006; (202) 887-5310. This nonprofit public-interest law center founded in 1969 specializes in health issues affecting low-income Americans, including Medicaid and hospital emergency care.

unnecessary emergency room use. It "creates a spurious precision without really adding anything," says Henry Bachofer, executive director for legislative policy for the Blue Cross and Blue Shield Association. "Medicare law already requires us to be available 24-hours, seven days a week. And it's untrue that we have complete latitude to deny payments," he says, noting the appeal process that the federal government offers. "We do apply a retroactive test of reasonableness. Say hospital A is one-tenth of a mile closer than hospital B, but hospital B participates in our plan. If you simply went into the nearest ER, why should you be completely protected by a doctor on call within 30 minutes? You should have known where to go based on material we sent you when you joined."

Wilkinson at the Harvard Community Health Plan echoes this sentiment. The prudent layperson definition, coupled with existing laws requiring that ERs screen all patients, would virtually "require open access to the ER," she says. "It does not make medical or economic sense."

Levin of Prudential says that no HMO will refuse to "pay for procedures or diagnostic tests if they were performed in good faith. In an ideal world, you would have no retrospective denials, but there will probably always be some. HMOs are certainly aware of the potential liabilities, so they don't micromanage; they generally advise you go to the nearest ER or call 911."

Dr. Jeffrey Kang, chief medical officer in the office of managed care at HCFA, notes that even with a prudent layperson definition, an "imprudent person of good faith," say, someone who made a mistake in choosing to come to the ER, is made to pay for a lack of expertise."

Kang also sees a possible middle ground: "We could actually get managed care in all situations to pay for the screening and stabilization [not necessarily the treatment]. Then we could continue to educate patients, and any that slip through the cracks, the plans could go ahead and pay for."

Another possible compromise is a new service in which trained emergency doctors contract with managed-care groups to oversee emergency care at out-of-network hospitals. One such service, Bethesda, Md.-based Acucare, reportedly saved Kaiser Permanente over $1 million for emergency services in the Washington, D.C., area during 1991 alone.[35]

"As a patient, I'm not prudent. I hurt and I want intelligent care, meaning nurse triage based on protocols," says Acucare President Casey Jason. "I want to be an informed patient, but to expect a patient who hurts to decide is unrealistic and punitive. If the patient is unable to get a quick intelligent triage from a health plan, then the plan should suffer the consequences. It should be a positive experience for the patient and the provider, not a battlefield." ■

OUTLOOK

Taking Care of the Poor

People who aspire to be emergency physicians are "action-oriented types, who want questions answered quickly, make rapid decisions and are interested in acute aspects of stabilizing patients, not the chronic aspects," says Ghezzi at the GW Medical Center. "Many like the lifestyle: when you're on duty, you're dedicated; when you're off, your time is your own, either for family or academics. You also get a taste of all the different disciplines, obstetrics, orthopedics, radiology, without having to focus on one."

The success of an emergency department is not measured in dollars alone. Ghezzi says some hospital emergency departments use quality indicators that compare nationwide data on such issues as the number of patients who have longer-than-six-hour stays, the number discharged but later readmitted and the number of discrepancies between a radiograph reading by an attending physician and changes in patient treatment after a follow-up reading by a radiologist.

But many in the field and out will measure the success of emergency medicine on the quality of care given to those who lack the means to pay for it. Though the goal of universal health coverage has lost favor in the current debate, it may return to the agenda if the prospect of seeing publicly financed hospitals overburdened and closing becomes a reality. Says Gage of the public hospital group: "We'd be delighted with universal coverage." Emergency-room care of the indigent "is not a franchise we want to hold onto. We're looking for ways to share the burden."

"If everyone is cost-cutting, and there's no more cost-shifting, then the uninsured aren't going to get served," says HCFA's Kang. "The progressive states have bad debt compensation pools funded through tax revenues, but you will see pressures on these funds. Eventually, we all pay unless we're willing to literally throw people out the door and let them die on the street."

Rick Pollack, vice president of the American Hospital Association, says: "Hospitals are at a crossroads. They have to decide what they want to do when they grow up. They're either going to be a vendor selling discounted rates to employers and insurance companies, or they can become a partner in a health plan and take responsibility for providing the full range of services, competing to move up the food chain."

"This is a social problem," says ACEP's Henry. "If some child is hit by a bus, do you want some place where he can go? If a poor hospital closes, where will those patients go? With certain hospitals in richer areas, it begs the question. Should there be a tax on these hospitals to care for indigents? I've asked managed-care people, I've asked industry, I've asked insurance people. They all say it's a problem but not our problem."

The poor represent "the soft underbelly of society," Henry adds. And it's the emergency medical community that "looks after these people every night." ■

Notes

[1] Laurence C. Baker and Linda Schuurman, "Excess Cost of Emergency Department Visits for Non-Urgent Care," *Health Affairs,* winter 1994, pp. 162-171. Some analysts say the excess-cost figure is higher than $5 billion. A private consulting firm put it at $14.1 billion, or $5.6 million per hospital. See the Advisory Board Company, "Redefining the Emergency Department: Five Strategies for Reducing Unnecessary Visits," 1993.

[2] See General Accounting Office, *Emergency Departments: Unevenly Affected by Growth and Change in Patient Use,* January 1993, p. 19.

[3] Prospective Payment Assessment Commission, "Medicare and the American Health Care System: Report to the Congress," June 1995. Established under the Social Security Act Amendments of 1983, the commission advises Congress and the secretary of the Department of Health and Human Services on Medicare payments to hospitals and other facilities. Also see Lewin-ICF for the Health Care Financial Management Association, "Cost-Shifting: A Self-Limiting Process," April 1992. Medicare is the federal health program for the elderly; Medicaid is the joint federal-state health program for the poor and disabled.

[4] *The New York Times,* July 9, 1995.

[5] *Ibid.*

[6] *Atlanta Journal,* Feb. 4, 1995.

[7] Testimony prepared for the House Ways and Means Health Subcommittee and Commerce Health and Environment Subcommittee, July 27, 1995.

[8] General Accounting Office, *op. cit.,* p. 26.

[9] Quoted in American College of Emergency Physicians, *America's Health Care Safety Net: Emergency Medicine: 1968-1993 and Beyond,* 1993, p. 22.

[10] Quoted in "Non-Urgent Emergency Department Needs," editorial, *Journal of the American Medical Association,* June 22/29, 1994, p. 1953.

[11] Quoted in Eugene Richards, *The Knife and Gun Club: Scenes from an Emergency Room* (1989), p. 72.

[12] David W. Baker, Carl D. Stevens and Robert H. Brook, "Determinants of Emergency Department Use by Ambulatory Patients at an Urban Public Hospital," *Annals of Emergency Medicine,* March 1995, p. 311.

[13] Marsha Lillie-Blanton and Ana Alfaro-Correa, "In the Nation's Interest: Equity in Access to Health Care," Joint Center for Political and Economic Studies, 1995, pp. 18, 22. Also see Shelley I. White-Means and Michael C. Thornton, "What Costs Savings Could Be Realized by Shifting Patterns of Use From Hospital Emergency Rooms to Primary Care?" *American Economic Review, Papers and Proceedings,* May 1995, p. 138.

[14] Robert Rodriguez, William J. Kreider and Larry J. Baraff, "Need and Desire for Preventive-Care Measures in Emergency Department Patients," *Annals of Emergency Medicine,* November 1995, p. 615.

[15] Gary P. Yount and David Sklar, "Health Care Reform and Emergency Medicine," *Annals of Emergency Medicine,* May 1995, p. 666.

[16] See Carole Bullock, "Does Primary Care Belong in the ED?' *Emergency Medicine News,* June 1995, p. 1.

[17] Quoted in Bullock, *op. cit.,* p. 34.

[18] *The New York Times,* July 13, 1995.

[19] *USA Today,* Aug. 22, 1995.

[20] Poll released July 19, 1995.

[21] Robert H. Miller and Harold S. Luft, "Managed Care Plan Performance Since 1980: A Literature Analysis," *Journal of the American Medical Association,* May 18, 1994, p. 1512.

[22] *The Boston Globe,* Nov. 21, 1995.

[23] Editorial, *Annals of Emergency Medicine,* May 1995, p. 692.

[24] Edward Ziegler, with Lewis R. Goldfrank, M.D., *Emergency Doctor* (1987), p. 2.

[25] See American College of Emergency Physicians, *op. cit.,* p. 6.

[26] *Ibid.,* p. 5.

[27] Edith Alston and David Cutler, *Emergency Room: Confessions of an E.R. Doctor* (1984), p. 31.

[28] American College of Emergency Physicians, *op. cit.,* p. 7.

[29] General Accounting Office, *op. cit.,* p. 34.

[30] Quoted in Josiah Macy Foundation, *The Role of Emergency Medicine in the Future of American Medical Care,* Proceedings of a Conference, chaired by L. Thompson Bowles, 1995, p. 77.

[31] See "Health Care's Hour," *CQ Weekly Report Special Report,* Sept. 25, 1993.

[32] For background, see "Primary Care," *The CQ Researcher,* March 17, 1995, pp. 217-240.

[33] Jeanne Finbert and Stan Dorn, "Unraveling the Mystery of Medicaid Block Grants: Proposed Cuts Threaten Consumers of All Income Levels," National Health Law Program and Consumers Union, July 1995, updated October 1995.

[34] See the *CQ Weekly Report,* Nov. 18, 1995, p. 3539.

[35] See Brian McCormick, "Managed Care M*A*S*H," *American Medical News,* Nov. 6, 1995, p. 3.

Bibliography

Selected Sources Used

Books

Alston, Edith, and David Cutler, M.D., *Emergency Room: Confessions of an E.R. Doctor,* Harcourt Brace Jovanovich, 1984.

A journalist recounts her year spent observing life in the emergency room. She discusses the "ER High" that reporters and other visitors often experience as they marvel at the drama and the skills of professional medical staff.

Richards, Eugene, *The Knife and Gun Club: Scenes from an Emergency Room,* Atlantic Monthly Press, 1989.

A photographer who also writes and teaches provides vivid photos and in-depth testimony from staff at the Denver General public hospital in Colorado. The text waxes philosophical about poverty and medical altruism.

Shohen, Saundra and Ann Loring, *Emergency!: Stories from the Emergency Department of a New York Hospital,* St. Martin's Press, 1989.

An emergency room administrator and a TV producer describe life in overburdened Roosevelt Hospital in New York City, where former Beatle John Lennon was pronounced dead after he was assassinated in 1980.

Ziegler, Edward, with Lewis R. Goldfrank, M.D., *Emergency Doctor,* Harper & Row Publishers, 1987.

An author teamed up with the director of Emergency Medical Services for New York's Bellevue Hospital Center to describe the impact of AIDS, alcoholism and drug abuse on the daily routine. The doctor also discusses his life in medical school.

Articles

Cunningham, Peter J., Carolyn M. Clancy, Jowel W. Cohen and Melissa Wilets, "The Use of Hospital Emergency Departments for Non-urgent Health Problems: A National Perspective," *Medical Care Research and Review,* December 1995, p. 453.

A team of health-finance analysts evaluate past studies on the overuse of emergency medicine while offering new analysis of 1987 data from the National Medical Expenditure Survey.

Reports and Studies

The Advisory Board Company, *Redefining the Emergency Department: Five Strategies for Reducing Unnecessary Visits,* 1993.

A private, health consulting firm in Washington, D.C., assembled original research for this analysis of emergency health-care expenditures, highlighting cost-saving opportunities in chronic care management, substance abuse screening and counseling, off-site centers for the homeless, primary care liaison and collaborative clinics.

American College of Emergency Physicians, *America's Health Care Safety Net: Emergency Medicine: 1968-1993 and Beyond,* 1993.

The professional organization for emergency physicians offers a history and overview of the issues it confronts, among them overcrowding, uncompensated care, the transition to managed care and shortages in training.

General Accounting Office, *Emergency Departments: Unevenly Affected by Growth and Change in Patient Use,* January 1993.

Requested by the Senate Finance Subcommittee on Health for Families and the Uninsured, this survey of 1,025 hospitals measures crowding, cost-shifting and non-urgent uses of the nation's emergency rooms.

Killie-Blanton, Marsha, and Ana Alfaro-Correa, *In the Nation's Interest: Equity in Access to Health Care,* Joint Center for Political and Economic Studies, 1995.

A Washington research group explores the health-care needs of Hispanics and African Americans, examining differences in spending patterns and offering proposals to improve access.

Josiah Macy Jr. Foundation, *The Role of Emergency Medicine in the Future of American Medical Care,* 1995.

These proceedings of a 1994 conference lay out the mainstream views among emergency medicine physicians. It offers a history of the profession and policy prescriptions, and warns of a shortage of fully trained EM doctors

Transportation Department, National Highway Traffic Safety Administration, *EMS System Development: Results of the Statewide EMS Assessment Program,* April 1995.

Results of a state-by-state survey from 1988-94 conclude that there is inadequate coordination and funding for emergency medical services among state governments in seeking to assure coverage of all population areas.

Transportation Department, National Highway Traffic Safety Administration, *Final Administrative Summary Rural Preventable Mortality Study,* December 1992.

A study of emergency response results to preventable-death trauma cases in the rural state of Montana shows that inappropriate care was provided in some 15 percent of pre-hospital care, 62 percent of emergency room care and 21 percent in later care.

The Next Step

Additional information from UMI's Newspaper & Periodical Abstracts database

Definition of an "Emergency"

Clark, Jane Bennett, "Protecting your emergency rights," *Kiplinger's Personal Finance Magazine,* August 1995, pp. 98-100.
Patients could pay dearly if their emergency room claim is rejected by their insurer. The importance of researching emergency room use guidelines and knowing which hospital to go to for treatment is addressed.

Pear, Robert, "H.M.O.'s refusing emergency claims, hospitals assert," *The New York Times,* July 9, 1995, p. 1.
As enrollment in HMOs soars, hospitals across the country report that HMOs are increasingly denying claims for care provided in hospital emergency rooms. Such denials create obstacles to emergency care for HMO patients and can leave them responsible for thousands of dollars in medical bills.

911 Emergency Communications

Abbinanti, C.A., "911 dispatchers soon will dispense first-aid advice," *Chicago Tribune,* Dec. 27, 1994, p. L2.
"Help is on the way" will soon take on a new meaning in three Lake County, Ill., communities, as police and fire dispatchers gear up to offer emergency medical assistance over the phone. Dispatchers will not only send ambulances but dispense first-aid advice in the minutes before a paramedic arrives.

"Arbiter rules for dispatchers in 911 case," *The New York Times,* April 8, 1995, p. A6.
The American Arbitration Association has granted back the jobs of six police dispatchers in Philadelphia who were dismissed or transferred for their handling of calls alerting them to what proved to be the fatal beating of a teenager in November 1994.

Bell, Rhonda, "911 suit has wrong number," *Times-Picayune,* Aug. 25, 1995, p. A1.
Alex Dufrene of Des Allemands, La., lost his suit against the St. Charles Parish 911 emergency system. Dufrene charged that the system discriminated against rural residents by changing their street addresses.

Boyd, Richard, "911 panel recommends one emergency service," *Times-Picayune,* March 30, 1995, p. B4.
The emergency medical services subcommittee of St. Tammany Parish, La., 911 Board voted to recommend that the board institute a single-provider system and scrap the current system, which is under fire for alleged response delays in rural areas.

Charles, Alfred, "Firemen to handle 911 calls," *Times-Picayune,* March 3, 1995, p. B1.
In an effort to reduce the time New Orleans residents must wait to receive emergency medical treatment, the city will experiment with a system under which New Orleans firefighters will help EMS teams respond to emergency calls, the City Council was told.

Ferris, Jan, "In some suburbs, calling 911 gets wrong number," *Chicago Tribune,* Oct. 17, 1994, p. C2.
There are at least a dozen Chicago suburbs that do not have access to a 911 service. Four percent of the state's population must dial seven numbers to reach police, firefighters and paramedics.

Marcazzo, Regina, "New 911 to aid all of Suffolk in 1997," *The New York Times,* Nov. 19, 1995, p. L8.
Under the new enhanced 911 system that is being installed in Suffolk County, N.Y., people needing emergency help should be able to obtain it even if they cannot speak or do not know their precise whereabouts. The new system is examined.

Martin, Andrew, "911 answers some with deadly quiet," *Chicago Tribune,* Nov. 10, 1995, p. 1.
A telephone blackout is one in a series of problems plaguing the $217 million 911 communications system in Chicago. Some police officers fear that a major breakdown could jeopardize the safety of police and residents.

Pfeiffer, Sacha, "911 system creates tough choices," *Boston Globe,* Nov. 5, 1995, p. W1.
Enhanced emergency 911 telephone service in suburbs west of Boston is examined, focusing on the greater security the system offers as well as the increased liabilities. It focuses on the investigation of all "hang up," or "abandoned" calls, which are automatically traced and must be investigated.

Strausberg, Chinta, "Barrow calls for probe of 911," *Chicago Defender,* Nov. 13, 1995, p. 5.
Operation PUSH Chair Willie Barrow is calling for a Chicago City Council probe into the death of the chair of her tape ministry division, Ben Cleveland Jennings, who was allegedly refused 911 service.

Wetzel, Dan, "Teens map the city for 911 center," *Chicago Tribune,* Oct. 11, 1994, p. C2.

Chicago's state-of-the-art, $213 million, 911 emergency center is giving 13 disadvantaged Whitney Young High School seniors an opportunity to help program the complex system. The students take old paper maps of the city and computerize them.

Emergency Rooms

Bass, Frank, "Emergency room care drives up costs: Doctors," *The Houston Post*, Jan. 23, 1994, p. A26.
Pediatricians meeting in Dallas on Jan. 22, 1994, said that the emergency room costs of caring for sick children whose problems could have been headed off with regular medical care results in a higher health care tab, which in turn means higher health insurance costs and less available health care for poor families.

Bindman, Andrew B., "Triage in accident and emergency departments," *British Medical Journal* (International), Aug. 12, 1995, p. 404.
Modern emergency room triage practices are discussed in an editorial. The focus is usually on finding patients who may not actually need emergency care.

"Drugs tied to 500,000 emergency room visits in '94," *Boston Globe*, Nov. 8, 1995, p. 4.
A half-million Americans went to hospital emergency rooms with drug-related problems in 1994, including a record number with cocaine-related episodes.

Ellis, Ralph, "New hospital center to ease emergency room load," *Atlanta Constitution*, Jan. 5, 1995, p. 1.
A new community care center at Southern Regional Medical Center is expected to unclog the emergency room and provide quicker service to patients with non-urgent ailments. The opening of the Riverdale, Ga., facility in late January or early February 1995 may even save money.

"Emergency-room nurses," *The Wall Street Journal*, Sept. 19, 1995, p. A1.
Emergency-room nurses staged a sickout at County-USC Medical Center in Los Angeles, forcing the huge hospital to turn away ambulances. The nurses apparently were angered at Los Angeles County's decision to issue 6,700 layoff, demotion and transfer notices to health-care workers.

Ferris, Jan, "New Medicaid clinic aims to cure emergency room overcrowding," *Chicago Tribune*, Sept. 15, 1994, p. 8.
Central DuPage Hospital is set to open DuPage County, Ill.'s first Medicaid clinic in Bloomingdale, aimed at patients who often have to turn to emergency rooms for care because private physicians won't treat them.

Fracassa, Anne, "Hospital expands emergency room," *Detroit News*, Jan. 12, 1995, p. B6.
Macomb Hospital Center in Warren, Mich., has invested $1.27 million to renovate its emergency center. With most of the construction complete, the new emergency facility officially opened in January 1995.

McCarthy, Michael, "Consent and U.S. emergency room studies," *Lancet*, April 30, 1994, p. 1093.
A report by the staff of the U.S. House Subcommittee on Regulation, Business Opportunities and Technology has found that mentally incapacitated patients are often being treated with experimental drugs and unapproved medical devices in U.S. emergency rooms without patient consent or the approval of their next-of-kin. The report says that federal regulations governing exceptions to informed consent are too vague.

McClellan, Bill, "Emergency room visits with kids can be touchy," *St. Louis Post-Dispatch*, Feb. 22, 1995, p. B1.
Bill McClellan relates taking his son to the emergency room after the boy broke his ankle.

"Medicare use of hospital outpatient clinics and emergency rooms: Selected CYs 1980-91," *Healthcare Financing Review*, February 1995, pp. 102-103.
The use of outpatient clinics and emergency rooms by Medicare beneficiaries has risen since the 1980s. The rise in outpatient clinic and emergency room visits is examined.

Meyer, Josh, "Cuts deal blow to emergency room services," *Los Angeles Times*, Sept. 17, 1995, p. A1.
In the scramble to shrink Los Angeles County's vast health-care system, so many trauma-care nurses were handed pink slips that the quality of treatment in the region's emergency rooms could be jeopardized, public-health workers said on Sept. 16, 1995.

Olson, Erik J., "No room at the inn: A snapshot of an American emergency room," *Stanford Law Review*, January 1994, pp. 449-501.
The emergency rooms of U.S. hospitals have become the principal suppliers of non-urgent primary care to the under- and uninsured. The demographics of the U.S. emergency room are examined, its finances are analyzed and a system of primary care clinics created through a public/private partnership between municipalities and existing private health care providers is proposed.

Opatrny, Dennis J., "St. Luke's closes emergency room," *San Francisco Chronicle*, July 24, 1994, p. B5.
St. Luke's Hospital in San Francisco's Mission District closed its emergency room on July 23, 1994, 10 days before a strike deadline set by nurses and health care workers.

Range, Peter Ross, "ER: A view from the emergency room," *TV Guide*, Nov. 19, 1994, p. 22.
According to real-life emergency room doctors and nurses, the NBC drama "ER" is professionally inaccurate. Some examples of inaccurate procedures performed in "ER" that would never be conducted in a real emergency room are discussed.

Sklar, David P., "Emergency medicine," *JAMA: The Journal of the American Medical Association,* June 1, 1994.
The present emergency department environment has been created by access for all, 24-hour availability, primary care, critical care, social services and care for indigent patients. Violence against physicians, nurses and emergency medical technicians and the appropriate timing of the termination of pre-hospital efforts are discussed.

Proposed Medicaid Overhaul

Vobejda, Barbara and Judith Havemann, "Medicaid changes will lead to emergency room closings, study says," *The Washington Post,* Oct. 25, 1995, p. A8.
Consumers Union testified that the huge spending bill before the Senate would strip 12 million Americans of health coverage and close numerous emergency rooms and trauma centers across the country. The group told Democratic senators that the proposed overhaul of Medicaid would harm consumers.

Training and Certification in Trauma Care

Friend, Tim, "Emergency room care troubling," *USA Today,* Sept. 8, 1994, p. A1.
A new report indicates that many emergency room patients would be better off being treated by paramedics, who are likely to have more emergency care training than most doctors.

"Study finds lack of emergency specialists at many hospitals," *The New York Times,* Sept. 8, 1994, p. A19.
A report from a panel chaired by L. Thompson Bowles, president of the National Board of Medical Examiners, strongly condemns a practice in which medical residents supplement their incomes by working part time at night in emergency rooms. The report, to be released Sept. 12, 1994, says that many "moonlighters" lack training and adequate experience. Only about half of the nation's 25,000 jobs in emergency medicine are filled by doctors certified to provide emergency care.

Tobin, James, "Receiving's staffers will be trained on stress disorder," *Detroit News,* Nov. 10, 1995, p. D1.
In a program believed to be the first of its kind, officials will soon train the staff of Detroit Receiving Hospital in the perils of post-traumatic stress disorder, not only among patients, but among the doctors and nurses who must cope with daily exposure to the victims of crime, cruelty and disaster.

Using Emergency Rooms for Primary Care

Colburn, Don, "Emergency room care not always necessary," *The Washington Post,* March 14, 1995, p. W5.
A study of patients in the emergency room of a large Los Angeles County, Calif., public hospital has suggested three reasons patients end up in hospital emergency rooms for costly treatment of non-urgent conditions such as sore throats and chronic backache.

Dunea, George, "Emergency room medicine: 1," *British Medical Journal* (International), Aug. 26, 1995, p. 574.
In the U.S., many people use hospital emergency rooms for all medical needs. This results in higher costs because doctors unfamiliar with patients and problems will order more tests than are needed. It also leads to overcrowding of emergency rooms.

Ellis, Ralph, "Clinic to offer quick care for non-emergencies," *Atlanta Constitution,* March 23, 1995, p. 1.
South Fulton Medical Center is opening a new clinic to provide faster and cheaper treatment for people who visit the emergency room for routine care.

Gonzalez, David, "Emergency room option: Free ride to hospital's clinic," *The New York Times,* July 16, 1995, p. 1.
In order to reduce the burden on its emergency room, Columbia-Presbyterian Medical Center in New York City has opened an urgent care clinic in the inner city, several blocks east of the hospital. It is the first such center in the city, and possibly in the U.S., that emphasizes linking poor and working people with primary care physicians, and that physically takes them there from the hospital.

Lozano, Paula, Frederick A. Connell and Thomas D. Koepsell, "Use of health services by African-American children with asthma on Medicaid," *JAMA: The Journal of the American Medical Association,* Aug. 9, 1995, pp. 469-473.
A historical cohort study using Medicaid claim data was conducted to determine whether African-American children with asthma use more emergency department (ED) and inpatient medical services and fewer preventive services than white children with similar insurance coverage and family income. African-American children were more likely than white children to make ED visits or be hospitalized for asthma.

Back Issues

Great Research on Current Issues Starts Right Here...Recent topics covered by The CQ Researcher are listed below. Before May 1991, reports were published under the name of Editorial Research Reports.

JUNE 1994
Education and Gender
Gun Control
Public Land Policy
Nuclear Arms Cleanup

JULY 1994
Dietary Supplements
Public Opinion and Foreign Policy
Crime Victims' Rights
Birth Control Choices

AUGUST 1994
Genetically Engineered Foods
Electing Minorities
Prozac Controversy
College Sports

SEPTEMBER 1994
Home Schooling
Welfare Experiments
Courts and the Media
Regulating Tobacco

OCTOBER 1994
Historic Preservation
Religion and Politics
Arts Funding
Economic Sanctions

Back issues are available for $5.00 (subscribers) or $8.00 (non-subscribers). Quantity discounts apply to orders over ten. To order, call Congressional Quarterly Customer Service at (202) 887-8621.

Binders are available for $18.00. To order call 1-800-638-1710. Please refer to stock number 648.

NOVEMBER 1994
Sex on Campus
Blood Supply Safety
Testing Term Limits
Religion in America

DECEMBER 1994
Farm Policy
Arms Sales
Earthquake Research
The Future of Television

JANUARY 1995
Treating Addiction
Child Custody and Support
Parents and Schools
Non-Proliferation Treaty at 25

FEBRUARY 1995
Cracking Down on Immigration
The Business of Sports
Reinventing Government
Housing Discrimination

MARCH 1995
Death Penalty Debate
Primary Care
Democracy in Africa
Environmental Movement at 25

APRIL 1995
Abortion Clinic Protests
Dieting and Health
Combating AIDS
Rethinking Affirmative Action

MAY 1995
Assisted Suicide Controversy
Overhauling Social Security
Learning to Read
Mandatory Sentencing

JUNE 1995
Combating Infectious Disease
Property Rights
Repetitive Stress Injuries
Regulating the Internet

JULY 1995
War Crimes
Highway Safety
Combating Terrorism
Preventing Teen Drug Use

AUGUST 1995
Job Stress
Organ Transplants
United Nations at 50
Advances in Cancer Research

SEPTEMBER 1995
Catholic Church in the U.S.
Northern Ireland Cease-Fire
High School Sports
Teaching History

OCTOBER 1995
Quebec's Future
Revitalizing the Cities
Networking the Classroom
Indoor Air Pollution

NOVEMBER 1995
The Working Poor
The Jury System
Sex, Violence and the Media
Police Misconduct

DECEMBER 1995
Teens and Tobacco
Gene Therapy's Future
Global Water Shortages
Third-Party Prospects

Future Topics

- ***Punishing Sex Offenders***
- ***Bilingual Education***
- ***Helping the Homeless***

THE CQ Researcher

PUBLISHED BY CONGRESSIONAL QUARTERLY INC.

Punishing Sex Offenders

Will the courts overturn tough new laws?

Violent assaults on children in several highly publicized incidents have spurred states to pass new laws cracking down on sex offenders. A majority of states now notify residents of communities where a sex offender has been released. Some detain especially dangerous sex criminals for an indefinite term of mental treatment once their sentences expire. These laws are being challenged in the courts by those who charge they punish individuals for the same crime twice. Moreover, some treatment experts say the laws are based on a misconception about who commits sex crimes. Most convicted sex offenders are relatives or friends of their victims. With therapy, many can learn to control their sexual obsessions, some clinicians maintain. But the mental health profession remains divided over whether rehabilitation works.

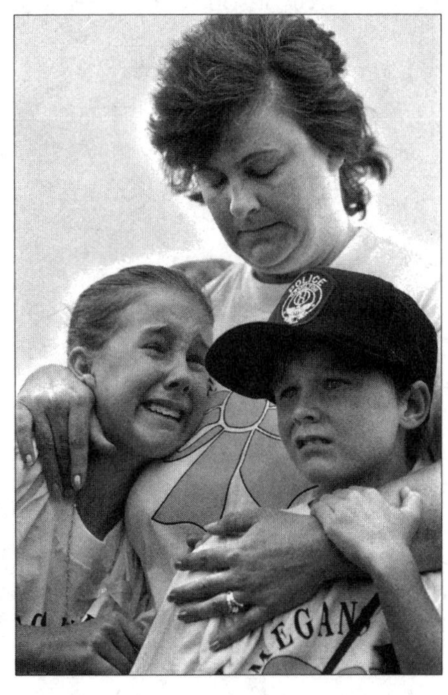

INSIDE THIS ISSUE

CQ | Jan. 12, 1996 • Volume 6, No. 2 • Pages 25-48

Formerly Editorial Research Reports

THE ISSUES

BACKGROUND

CURRENT SITUATION

OUTLOOK

SIDEBARS AND GRAPHICS

FOR FURTHER RESEARCH

COVER: MAUREEN KANKA HUGS HER TWO SURVIVING CHILDREN AT AN ANTI-CRIME RALLY IN HAMILTON, N.J., TWO DAYS AFTER HER 7-YEAR-OLD DAUGHTER MEGAN WAS SLAIN. HER DEATH LED TO PASSAGE OF "MEGAN'S LAW," WHICH REQUIRES COMMUNITIES TO BE NOTIFIED ABOUT DANGEROUS SEX OFFENDERS WHO MOVE INTO THE AREA. (PHOTO COURTESY OF *THE TRENTON TIMES.*)

The CQ Researcher

Jan. 12, 1996
Volume 6, No. 2

PUBLISHED BY
Congressional Quarterly Inc.

The CQ Researcher (ISSN 1056-2036). Formerly Editorial Research Reports. Published weekly (48 times per year, not printed the first Friday of any month with five Fridays) by Congressional Quarterly Inc., 1414 22nd St., N.W., Washington, D.C. 20037. Rates are furnished upon request. Second-class postage paid at Washington, D.C. POSTMASTER: Send address changes to The CQ Researcher, 1414 22nd St., N.W., Washington, D.C. 20037.

Punishing Sex Offenders

By Sarah Glazer

The Issues

Shortly before convicted child molester Earl Shriner was scheduled to be released from a Washington state prison in 1988, prison officials faced an awful dilemma. They knew Shriner had drawn pictures and written in his diary about torturing children once he was free, but he had served his sentence and had to be released. Prison officials tried to have Shriner committed to a mental institution, but a judge ruled that he was not mentally ill under the law.

Five months after his release, Shriner raped and sexually mutilated a 7-year-old boy. *

The case raised an outcry in Washington state and led to the passage of a comprehensive legislative package aimed at stopping another Earl Shriner. One statute permits police to notify residents when a recently released sex offender moves into the neighborhood. Another permits the state to hold "sexually violent predators" indefinitely in a mental-treatment wing of the state prison.

Since then, dozens of states have passed similarly tough statutes, often following horrifying sexual crimes in their own backyards. As of December 1995, 30 states had passed community-notification laws. (*See map, p. 28.*)

But the laws have been challenged by civil libertarians as attacks on the rights of prisoners who have served the full sentence for their crimes. In New Jersey, a federal judge has declared the state's notification law unconstitutional, saying it amounts to a second punishment on offenders who committed their crimes before the law took effect Jan. 1, 1995.

* Shriner forced the boy off his bike in woods near Tacoma, Wash., raped and stabbed him, cut off his penis and left him for dead. The boy survived and identified Shriner as his attacker.

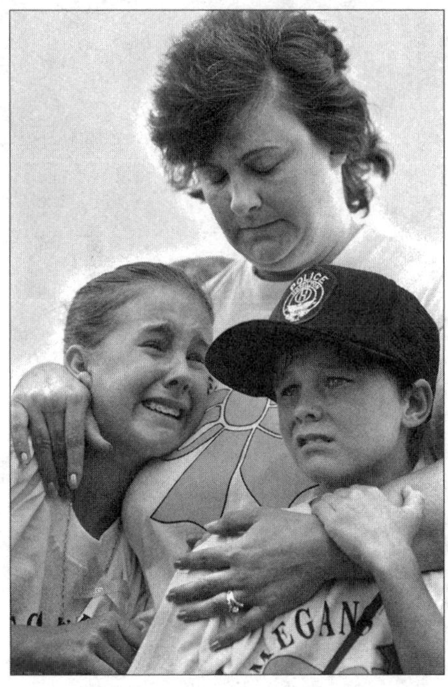

Laws that permit dangerous sexual predators to be detained beyond their sentences have been challenged in five states — Washington, Wisconsin, Kansas, Minnesota and Iowa. Minnesota passed its statute in 1994, joining a growing number of states that detain sex offenders with mental disorders who are "likely to engage" in future sexual crimes. The law was prompted by the scheduled release of 54-year-old Dennis Linehan, a rapist and murderer. Linehan is challenging the law as unconstitutional. *

"It's a long stretch from our system of due process and the standard of proof beyond a reasonable doubt to this prediction of future dangerousness," says attorney Kathleen Milner of the Minnesota Civil Liberties Union, which filed an amicus brief on behalf of Linehan. "Conceivably, after sex offenders they'll move on to other areas: 'Well, you're likely to shoplift again, so we're going to hold you.'"

* Linehan is appealing a lower court ruling upholding his commitment. Oral arguments were heard by the Minnesota Court of Appeals on Nov. 17, 1995. A decision is expected in February.

The tough anti-predator laws raise basic questions about how sex offenses should be viewed: Are they caused by mental illnesses that can be treated with therapy? Or are they crimes, plain and simple, that should be punished?

The mental health profession is divided over the issue. And there is vigorous debate over which, if any, treatments are effective in rehabilitating sex offenders. (*See story, p. 32.*)

The Washington State Psychiatric Association is among those challenging the state's sexual predator law, under which the state currently is holding 32 sex offenders beyond their sentences. "These are merely criminals," says Seattle psychiatrist James D. Reardon, an association spokesman. "There is no scientifically based effective treatment for sex offenders. We couldn't find any research [showing] that treating is any more effective than incarcerating."

But some experts who work with sex offenders insist they have found therapies that work, among them Fred S. Berlin, director of the National Institute for the Study, Prevention and Treatment of Sexual Trauma in Baltimore, Md. "I don't think the majority [of sex offenders] have a condition that's curable," he says, "but I do think that many of them have a psychiatric disorder and can, like alcoholics, learn to control themselves and live safely in the community."

"There are probably sex offenders who are criminals and some who are mentally ill," says Roxanne Lieb, associate director of the Washington State Institute for Public Policy at Evergreen State College in Olympia, Wash. "It's not black and white, as it's been posed in this debate." Certain therapies may help specific types of sex offenders but have little effect on others who are more likely to reoffend, Lieb says.

"Incest offenders are in a very different category from a compulsive pedophile who targets little boys, has

How States Keep Tabs on Sex Offenders

Forty-seven states (shaded blue) require sex offenders to register with local police whenever they move into a community. Thirty states (diagonal lines) require some type of community notification about sex offenders, such as police going door-to-door to alert residents or posting notices in the neighborhood.

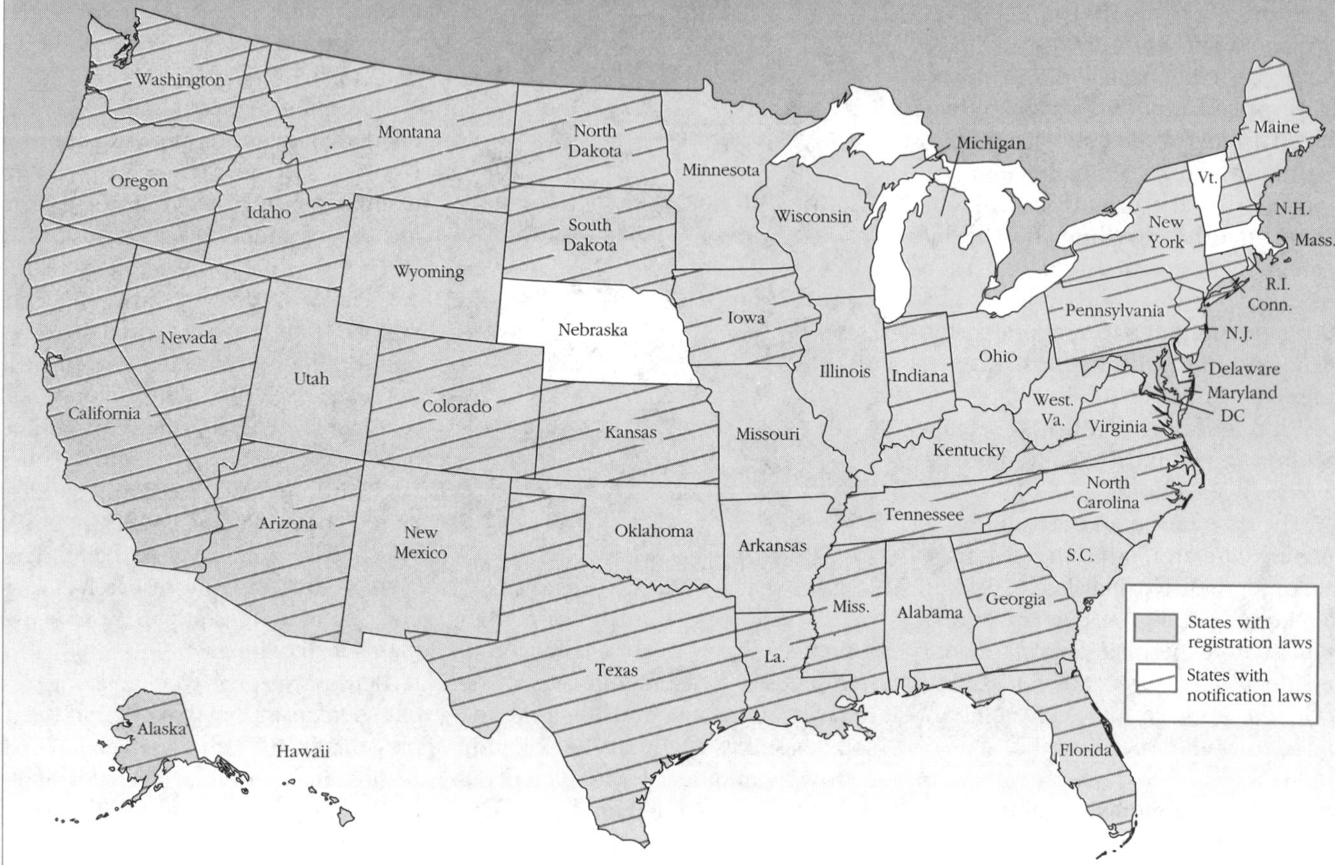

Note: Sex offender registration statutes are likely to be considered and passed this year in Massachusetts, Nebraska and Washington, D.C. The legislation has little apparent support in Vermont.

Source: National Center for Missing and Exploited Children, January 1996

done it 20 times and will do it 20 times more," says Lieb. "With an incest offender violating his daughter, it's not sexual drive; it's more typically issues of power and control." Incest offenders — usually fathers, stepfathers and uncles — are also the least likely of all sex offenders to commit sex crimes again — particularly outside the family. (*See table, p. 30.*)

The most well-publicized cases tend to focus on violence by strangers. Yet rape-murders constitute fewer than 3 percent of all sex offenses, and sadistic sex offenders are equally uncommon, according to Robert E. Freeman-Longo of the Safer Society Foundation in Brandon, Vt., which tracks sex-offender treatment programs nationwide and provides treatment referral.

In almost 90 percent of the molestation cases leading to convictions, the children know their abuser, according to the federal Bureau of Justice Statistics (BJS). In almost half the cases, the abuser is a parent or relative. Similarly, adults are more likely to be raped by someone they know than by strangers; acquaintances, boyfriends or family members represent about 60 percent of convicted rapists. [1]

"The public always hates the sex offenders it doesn't know and believes they should all go to prison forever," says Lucy Berliner, research director at the Harborview Sexual Assault Center in Seattle, which treats assault victims. "The one they do know — their brother, their son, their pastor

— they want to have the opportunity to get rehabilitated."

Berliner served on the task force that drafted Washington state's pioneering sex predator law. She defends the law against assaults by civil libertarians, arguing that it's narrowly drawn to get at a few hard-core, repetitive offenders like Shriner.

For policy-makers, it comes down to a balancing act between the rights of ex-offenders and the rights of potential victims. "Is the state helpless?" asks Alexander D. Brooks, professor of law emeritus at Rutgers Law School in Newark, N.J. "Must the state release such a person and say it can't do anything until he commits another crime?"

Initially, Brooks expected to oppose the Washington state law on civil liberties grounds, but he changed his mind after contemplating the legal impasse Washington state faced in the Shriner case.

"Which interest are you more concerned about protecting?" he asks. "Keeping dangerous offenders on the street, where they will commit sexual offenses against women and children, or protecting women and children by committing the most dangerous offenders with the hope of treating them?"

As courts and legislatures debate how to deal with sex offenders, here are some of the questions being asked:

Should citizens be informed of sex offenders living in their community?

In July 1994, in a suburb of Trenton, N.J., 7-year-old Megan Kanka walked across the street to see a neighbor's puppy. She never came home. Jesse Timmendequas, a neighbor and twice-convicted sex offender, has been charged with murdering Megan. Jury selection in his long-delayed trial is set to begin in February.

Unbeknown to the neighborhood, Timmendequas had spent six years in Avenel, New Jersey's treatment-prison for sex offenders, for molesting and attempting to kill another little girl. Within weeks of Megan's death, more than 200,000 New Jerseyans had signed a petition demanding that government officials notify communities when sex offenders move into the neighborhood.

In October 1994, Republican Gov. Christine Todd Whitman signed a package of 10 bills, which came to be called "Megan's Law." The most controversial provision requires released sex offenders to register with local police.

In addition, neighborhoods must be told the identity, criminal record and address of sex offenders who prosecutors think pose a high risk of reoffending. If the risk is low, only law enforcement officers are notified. If the risk is moderate, organizations such as schools and day-care organizations are notified. If the risk is high, all residents of the offender's neighborhood must be notified through such methods as distributing handbills or door-to-door visits.

Although New Jersey has had relatively little experience with the law so far, there already have been some problems with it, according to Edward Martone, executive director of the American Civil Liberties Union of New Jersey.

Shortly after the law took effect in January 1995, a father and son in Phillipsburg, N.J., broke into a house where a recently paroled sex offender was living. They beat up a man sleeping on the couch whom they mistook for the parolee.

Vigilantism is one of the major arguments that has been raised against notification laws. In Washington state, which in 1990 became the first state to approve notification, a sex offender's house was burned down after his community was notified. In the law's first three years, there were approximately 14 incidents against sex offenders ranging from insults to rock-throwing, according to the Institute for Public Policy.

The law's advocates respond that the vigilantism has been minimal considering that communities were notified about 176 sex offenders during the period. Berliner also points out that before the law the public often learned of neighbors charged with repellent crimes through weekly records of arrests printed in local newspapers.

Catherine Broderick, who heads a unit in the Morris County, N.J., prosecutors office responsible for implementing Megan's Law, says that each notification her office makes will include a warning that vigilante activities will be prosecuted. Broderick notes that the Phillipsburg men who mistakenly attacked a neighbor have been prosecuted. "The idea is not to punish people further for offenses," she says. "The idea is to educate the public as a tool to prevent future victims."

But critics doubt the laws will work. They point to a recent study in Washington state which found no difference in rearrest rates among sex offenders since passage of the community notification law five years ago. [2]

In Camden County, N.J., a sex offender whose community had been notified raped a child at a fast-food restaurant in a neighboring town. The incident shows the bill "is an incentive to get out of town, to hide," Martone says. "It's cruelly ironic that the notification bill is causing people to seek anonymity. It's the worst way to deal with repetitive and compulsive sex offenders. It gives them reason to avoid family, treatment, detection and take it on the lam."

Advance publicity won't necessarily deter sex offenders within their own neighborhood, either, Martone adds. He cites the recent case of a 15-year-old Lakewood, N.J., boy who was raped in the apartment of a released sex offender despite warnings about the man sent to area residents, including the boy's parents. The law, Martone asserts, "doesn't provide protection. It says, 'Here's a picture of a guy we think is a time bomb. Have a nice day.'"

Freeman-Longo at the Safer Society

When Sex Offenders Commit New Crimes

*Recidivism rates vary widely among different types of sex offenders. Exhibitionists and child molesters are most likely to commit new offenses, according to a survey of international research findings. * Incest offenders are the least likely to reoffend.*

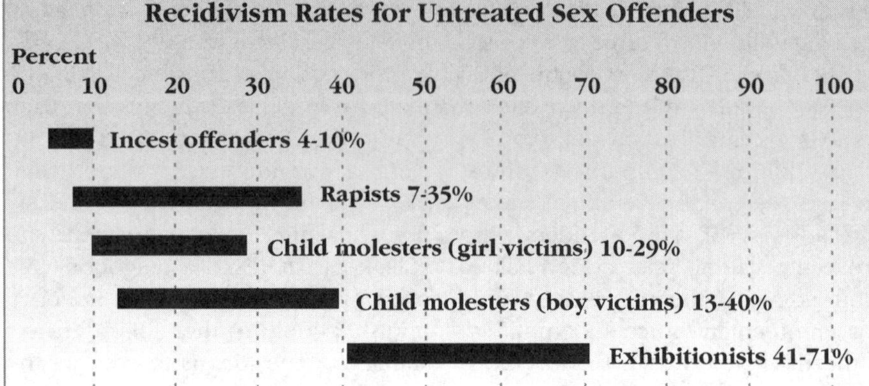

* *The survey tracked the most frequently cited studies of recidivism by offenders not treated by mental health professionals for sexual deviancy. Recidivism is defined as a rearrest, a reconviction or a return to prison.*

Source: W. L. Marshall and H.E. Barbaree, Handbook of Sexual Assault *(1990), in Lin Song and Roxanne Lieb, "Adult Sex Offender Recidivism: A Review of Studies," Washington State Institute for Public Policy, January 1994*

Foundation also opposes notification laws. In New Jersey, some incest victims now fear reporting their abuse because of the public humiliation that could be created by the public notification law, he said in a recent report. "If notification prevails, how fair is it for a child to go to school and hear others talk about his or her brother, father or grandfather, the sexual offender?" [3]

"We know low self-esteem and lack of an ingrained social structure are factors that feed into [abusive] behavior," he says. "Public notification will worsen some of the problems."

Broderick concedes that the notification laws "will not eliminate child abuse." She admits, "Quite frankly, for this really to work, it would have to become a national program." But she says notification still provides a sense of relief to parents and has educated families to the dangers of sexual abuse.

When Broderick has knocked on doors to inform residents that a sex offender is living in their neighborhood, she says there's usually a double reaction — shock followed by calm. "The second reaction is a kind of confidence. 'At least I know this and can work with my child and any other member of the family that needs to know.'"

Alerting neighbors means some sex offenders are caught earlier in the cycle of recidivism. In Washington state, offenders identified by community notification were arrested for new crimes much earlier than similar offenders released before the notification law — a median of about two years vs. five years for the comparison group. [4]

Often, the re-arrests are for more minor charges, such as communicating with a minor for immoral purposes, according to Lieb of the Institute for Public Policy, which conducted the study. Detectives in some counties have been assigned to offenders targeted by community notification and may be giving them intensified scrutiny, she suggests.

Berliner says the law was drafted not so much to reduce crime but in response to citizens who say they have a right to be informed. "If a person who has raped and molested numerous children . . . moves in next-door and you have young children, do you want to know about it?" Berliner asks. "Citizens do."

Should sex offenders be kept in confinement after they have served their prison sentences?

Washington state changed the nation's legal landscape in 1990 when it broadened its laws confining sexual criminals once their prison sentences had expired. Traditionally, Washington and other states permitted the involuntary hospitalization of mentally ill persons considered dangerous through civil commitment procedures. Washington's law was so narrowly drawn that convicted molester Shriner could not be detained after completing his sentence.

But the 1990 law targeted a new class of offender, the "sexually violent predator." The law defined a predator as someone charged or convicted of a crime of sexual violence who suffers from a "mental abnormality or personality disorder" which makes the person likely to commit future predatory sexual acts. Offenders deemed by a court to fit that definition can be confined at a prison treatment facility indefinitely — until considered safe to be released into the community.

A federal judge has declared such confinement unconstitutional because it punishes the same crime twice. In an opinion issued Aug. 25, 1995, John C. Coughenour, a U.S. District Judge in Seattle, called the law "an unconstitutional second punishment," violating the Constitution's ex post facto and double jeopardy clauses as well as the offender's due-process rights. [5]

The state of Washington has appealed the decision and is expected to take it to the Supreme Court if necessary. *

Because Shriner had told a cellmate about his plans to attack small children on his release, prison officials sought to commit him to a mental hospital under Washington's law for sexual psychopaths. But a judge turned down their request. Shriner did not fit the definition of a mentally ill person under the narrowly drawn statute and had not committed a recent overt act proving he was dangerous.

"Generally, the interpretation of [the psychopath law] is they are psychotic and out of touch with reality," Berliner explains, "so our [predator] bill and the ones adopted in the states since then have used a different definition of what is wrong with these people."

Washington's new legislation was intended "to fill the gap in our sentencing structure to cover people who have completed their sentences and are still dangerous" but may not be crazy under a strict definition, Berliner says. There are "people in prison fantasizing about going out and raping and killing children. Well, people [in Washington state] said, 'We don't accept that there's nothing you can do about that situation.' "

Berliner argues that the new law, which has become a model for several other states, was narrowly drawn, thus limiting the impact on most prisoners' civil liberties. In fact, only 32 offenders, less than 1 percent of all imprisoned sex offenders in the state, have been confined under the new statute.

But the law's opponents contend that the state is detaining sex offenders who aren't mentally ill under the guise of mental health treatment. "You can't put someone who is not mentally ill in an institution," says Robert C. Boruchowitz, an attorney in the Seattle Public Defender's office who represents eight of the 32 offenders. "And the state is basically pretending our guys are mentally ill to get around the due-process problem."

One of Boruchowitz's clients is Andre Brigham Young, a three-time convicted rapist, who has challenged his commitment under the predator statute as unconstitutional. His case will be heard before the Ninth Circuit Court of Appeals later this year.

Boruchowitz argues that the Legislature was trying to find a "pseudo-mental definition" to get around the rights of released prisoners. "Mental abnormality" is not a clinically recognized term, he notes. And the term "personality disorder," which generally refers to a person's history of maladaptive behavior, is so broad that it encompasses "virtually everyone in prison," he argues.

Psychiatrist Reardon agrees. "These people deliberately decide to commit a crime. To say illness causes them to commit a crime is ridiculous." Though Reardon agrees the behavior is abnormal and may even be compulsive, he asserts, "to say someone who has this compulsion is mentally ill is stretching the boundaries of mental illness."

Reardon also views the treatment offered in prison as essentially a sham. "All the surveys show there is no treatment being done. The [staff] are not trained. The program is not organized."

Boruchowitz says his clients feel more like prisoners in the mental wing than they did behind conventional bars. "It's a maximum security facility," he says. "There's barbed wire all around it. The guards are instructed to shoot anyone who tries to escape."

In a highly critical 1992 evaluation of the treatment program, Canadian psychologist Vernon L. Quinsey noted that offenders being held were "embittered" by the additional confinement and that only three were actively engaged in treatment. He also pointed out an apparent contradiction in the new law. The statute is directed at those offenders unlikely to be "cured," yet it requires them to receive treatment — with their release conditional on a court or jury decision that they are no longer a threat.

The program's lack of any procedure for releasing offenders on a gradual or temporary basis into the community is a "fatal problem," Quinsey concluded. Without it, staff had only the offender's behavior in the "artificial" environment of the prison on which to base predictions of future dangerousness. [6]

Four years later, the state still has not introduced a gradual-release program for these specially designated sex offenders, Boruchowitz says, and not a single offender has been declared safe enough by staff to be released permanently.

"There is no question there have been problems," Berliner concedes. But she argues the treatment program could be improved in the future and that new treatments may be developed to render this class of sex offenders less dangerous. "The law shouldn't be found unconstitutional because it's a crummy treatment program," she argues.

But civil libertarians say the law sets a dangerous precedent for detaining other kinds of lawbreakers on the basis of what they might do in the future. Eric S. Janus, a professor at William Mitchell College of Law in St. Paul, Minn., says a Minnesota law modeled on Washington's statute "is pure preventive detention." Potentially, warns Janus, "The principle underlying it would swallow the entire criminal justice system."

Janus is one of the attorneys representing rapist-murderer Linehan, who at age 24 strangled a 14-year-old babysitter who resisted his advances. Trial testimony revealed that in addition to the babysitter, Linehan assaulted several women before being caught and imprisoned. In 1975, Linehan escaped from prison and fled to Michigan, where he was imprisoned for assaulting a 12-year-old girl. In 1983, at the completion of his Michigan sentence, he was returned

---

* Judge Coughenour has agreed to let the state keep the 32 prisoners committed under the law incarcerated until an appeals court decides the first challenge.

Combining Group Therapy and Drugs . . .

Eight men sit around an oval table discussing their struggles with addiction. But these are not drug addicts or alcoholics. They are sex offenders — child molesters, exhibitionists, a cross-dresser and a peeping Tom. For the most part, they are white, affluent and well-educated.

The men are participants in group therapy at the National Institute for the Study, Prevention and Treatment of Sexual Trauma in Baltimore, Md. In essence, the institute borrows the techniques of alcoholism treatment in making clients confront their crimes while assuring them they are not alone in their fantasies.

"The child is to the pedophile what the bottle is to the alcoholic," says institute Director Fred S. Berlin, a psychiatrist at Johns Hopkins University. "When people have intense cravings, and satisfying these cravings brings pleasure, it's hard to deny themselves." Like alcoholism, Berlin believes, sex offending is a life-long disease that can be managed but not "cured."

The treatment regimen consists primarily of weekly group therapy for a year, followed by another year of occasional sessions. The aim is to make offenders accept responsibility for their acts, find remorse for the people they have hurt and develop strategies to avoid repeating their crimes, such as avoiding situations associated with their temptations. The institute currently treats 130 sex offenders.

Bob, a baby-faced child molester, clutches his coat to his chest as he describes how he recently accompanied a child on an amusement park ride — violating a court order barring him from contact with minors.* Bob was arrested two years ago and attends group therapy as a condition of probation — as do half the group members.

Bob was on a church outing when a parent who was terrified of roller coasters asked him to ride with her 6-year-old child. "I felt sorry for the kid. He had no way of getting on the rides," Bob explains. He insists he was not sexually attracted to the boy.

The other group members are skeptical of Bob's rationale, asking why he participated in an excursion that would inevitably include children. "Let's be real," says Associate Director Kate Thomas, an attractive woman with waist-long blond hair who leads the therapy session. "If the church tells you to do something harmful, it's like friends getting you into a bar."

It's hard to square Bob's gentle demeanor with his revelations of past crimes. While working as a nurse, he says he sexually assaulted several comatose adults. He recalls reading a pornographic story when he was 13 about a nurse who would similarly "relieve" her patients. "It stuck with me [that] I was helping them," he says. "But in my head, I knew I wasn't."

Thomas says offenders typically minimize their responsibility for their crimes. More than once she has heard a child molester say: "I shouldn't have been doing it, but she came on to me."

There's also an element of escapism in the men's acts. David, a distinguished-looking middle-aged man with a neat, gray beard, describes his recent arrest for hugging a strange woman from behind as she bent over her car in a parking lot. He has a history of "froitteurism," touching or rubbing up against strangers, and of exposing himself.

"I've exchanged normal heterosexual relations with my wife for this," David says sadly. "Your wife is a real person," observes John, who identifies himself as a pedophile. "These people are anonymous."

Though their obsessions vary, the men in the room agree that it is hard to control their behavior.

"I never intended to hurt any of these kids," says Bob, who met most of the children he molested through church activities. "The opportunity arose, and I did it. I didn't have enough control to stop it."

Bob gets weekly injections of Depo-Provera, a drug that lowers the hormone testosterone, thus reducing desire for sexual activity. About one-quarter of the men treated at the institute take testosterone-lowering drugs — all voluntarily. Although the drugs lower sex drive, Thomas says, patients on it can still have intercourse.

One group member, a medical student, was suspended from school for peeping at women in public bathrooms several times a day. He has found the medication helpful in controlling his voyeurism yet still maintains a sexual relationship with his girlfriend.

"They're tired of being so driven by sexuality that they can't do much else with their lives," Thomas says of the men on drugs.

Patients treated with the drugs also participate in the institute's standard treatment regimen of group therapy. In

* The men's names have been changed to protect their privacy.

to Minnesota and incarcerated.

On May 15, 1992, Linehan was scheduled to be released. Instead, he was committed to a state mental hospital under Minnesota's "psychopathic personality" law. However, the state Supreme Court overturned Linehan's commitment in June 1994, saying he did not fit the law's definition of a psychopath as someone unable to control his sexual impulses.

Under a new law, passed in August 1994 in response to Linehan's imminent release, prosecutors need only prove that someone is unwilling to control his or her sexual impulses. The new statute permits the commitment of "sexually dangerous persons" who have a history of past harmful sexual conduct, are likely to repeat the conduct in the future and have a personality disorder.

Linehan was committed under the new law, which he challenged on

. . . Helps Sex Offenders Deal With Compulsions

a 1991 study of 626 patients treated by the clinic, Berlin reported that five years after they had been treated, fewer than 10 percent had committed sexual offenses again. Among the most compliant patients, fewer than 5 percent committed new sexual offenses. [1]

The hormonal treatment aims to accomplish in a reversible form the same testosterone-lowering goal as surgical castration — which removes the testes. In studies, castration appears to be the most effective treatment in reducing repeat crimes among sex offenders. One study of 121 castrated sex offenders in Switzerland found a 7.4 percent recidivism rate compared with a 52 percent rate 10 years later for men not undergoing the procedure. [2] A recent review of the literature also found hormonal treatments effective in reducing repeat sex offenses. [3] *(See "At Issue," p. 41.)*

However, Depo-Provera plagues some patients with side effects, including weight gain, high blood pressure, nightmares, cold sweats and lethargy. About half of those who begin the hormonal treatment discontinue it. [4]

A drug preferred for its limited side effects is Depo-Lupron, but according to Thomas, it costs $400-$500 for each monthly injection, compared with $40 for each weekly injection of Depo-Provera.

Because of the expense and side effects, drugs are not widely used. Less than 20 percent of adult sex offender treatment programs use them, according to a national survey by the Safer Society Foundation in Brandon, Vt. "I don't know of any correctional systems that use it," says survey co-author Robert E. Freeman-Longo. "It's seen as still experimental."

Ethical and legal issues have been raised over whether sex offenders can be forced to take the drug. In a 1983 Michigan case, Judge John Fitzgerald sentenced Roger Gauntlett, who had pleaded no-contest to molesting his 14-year-old stepdaughter, to five years of treatment with Depo-Provera. On appeal, the Michigan Appeals Court ruled Gauntlett couldn't be forced to take the drug, saying it isn't widely accepted as a safe and reliable treatment for sex offenders. [5]

"There's always the issue of whether prisoners are really consenting or not," says Stephen Huot, director of sex offender and chemical dependency services for the Minnesota Department of Corrections, which does not offer Depo to sex offenders. "I'd hate to pressure or encourage someone to go on Depo and have them say, 'They forced me to go on it, and now I've got cancer.' We've shied away from it."

Also controversial is whether lowering the sex drive really gets to the root of sex offender behavior. Berlin sees sex offending, particularly pedophilia, as "occurring in response to a powerful biological drive that recurrently craves satiation." In his view, hormonal drugs work as an "appetite suppressant."

But victim advocates take issue with the institute's view of sex offending as biologically driven. "By defining the problem as one of sexual preference, and innate, they've tended to argue that the social policy of treating these people as criminals is somewhat unfair. That's where it's controversial," says Lucy Berliner, research director at the Harborview Sexual Assault Center in Seattle, which treats sexual-assault victims. She sees punishment as well as treatment as important.

Some experts suggest hormonal drugs may help individuals oppressed by persistent sexual fantasies but not those with primarily sadistic motivations.

The men who meet for group therapy at the Baltimore institute bear little resemblance to the serial murderers who make the headlines. But they are actually more representative of the majority of sex offenders, according to experts.

"Most people involved with children sexually are not dirty old men who pull children into a back alley," says Thomas. "They're people who like kids, and kids like them." Statistically, the child molester is far more likely to be the child's father, step-father, uncle or family friend than a stranger.

Dangerous sexual predators who prey on children they don't know constitute a small minority of the sex offender population. They're also the least likely to bare their souls in group therapy.

"It's the silent ones, the ones we're not hearing from, who are the real scaries," says a group member.

---

[1] Fred S. Berlin et al., "A Five-Year Plus Follow-Up Survey of Criminal Recidivism Within a Treated Cohort of 406 Pedophiles, 111 Exhibitionists and 109 Sexual Aggressives: Issues and Outcome," *American Journal of Forensic Psychiatry*, Vol. 12, No. 3, 1991, p. 5.

[2] Fred S. Berlin, "The Case for Castration: Part 2," *The Washington Monthly*, May 1994, p. 28.

[3] Gordon C. Nagayama Hall, "Sexual Offender Recidivism Revisited: A Meta-Analysis of Recent Treatment Studies," *Journal of Consulting and Clinical Psychology*, 1995, p. 802.

[4] *Ibid.*, p. 807.

[5] Anthony Schmitz, "A Shot in the Dark," *Health*, January-February 1993, p. 22.

---

constitutional grounds. In July 1995, a district judge upheld Linehan's indefinite commitment, saying, "Commitment is necessary for the protection of the public." But the real test will come in the appellate courts in the months ahead. Meanwhile, Linehan remains in a state mental hospital. [7]

"One of the reasons we think this law is so destructive is it puts therapists and courts in the position of gazing into a very cloudy crystal ball and predicting the future," says Janus. He describes Linehan, who has spent 27 years in prison, as "no different from any other criminal."

"What could Linehan do to show he's not dangerous?" Janus asks. "He's had 20 years of good behavior [in prison] and that's not good enough. He's gone through treatment and that's not enough."

Some psychologists say they've developed good instruments for predicting who is dangerous. Quinsey has developed a prediction tool, based largely on the offender's past history, which is "as good or slightly better than short-term weather forecasting," predicting accurately in 75 percent of cases, he says.

But that confidence is by no means unanimously shared in the field. "You can flip a coin and get a better prediction than by clinical evaluation," Reardon maintains.

Seattle University School of Law Professor John Q. La Fond asks how many harmless former offenders would be mistakenly detained on the side of caution. People tend to over-predict violence, he says, particularly when "the prosecution parades the [assault] victims in front of a jury and says, 'Do you want to be responsible for this [offender] recommitting a crime?' "

Can sex offenders be rehabilitated?

There is vigorous debate within the psychological community over which, if any, treatments keep sex offenders from committing new crimes.

Psychologist Quinsey, who represents the more skeptical wing, says most studies are poor and don't show evidence of treatment effects. "I would argue we don't know enough to establish effectiveness," he says. "We don't have a lot of treatment studies with follow-ups."

Some sex offenders, such as child molesters, may assault another child as long as 20 years after their first conviction. But studies may not capture those later offenses because they don't follow sex offenders long enough.

In addition, most treatment efforts are directed at lower-risk offenders — those who are living in the community on probation or parole and receiving therapy on an outpatient basis. "So it's hard to tell whether treatment's making a difference, because their rates of recidivism are already very low," says Berliner. The most dangerous offenders, those who would likely have the highest rates of reoffending, may get screened out of research studies, may not volunteer or may reside in prisons without treatment programs, she notes.

Complicating the study of treatment is the fact that sex offenders differ so much in their motives and modus operandi. For example, one type of child molester has primarily sadistic motives and seeks out children who are strangers exclusively for sex. Another type shows a sustained interest in an individual child and has primarily non-genital sexual relations with children. [8]

"I think we need to look at different forms of treatment for different types of offenders," says Judith V. Becker, a University of Arizona professor of psychology and psychiatry. She concludes in a recent article that the research literature "provides definite grounds for optimism" for some segments of the offender population. [9] "The majority of individuals who want to work on their behavior can do it, but there is no treatment that is 100 percent effective for everybody."

On the other hand, for the small number of dangerous offenders who have committed murder along with sexual crimes, most treatment experts agree with Quinsey that, "If you're a clinician and treating these guys, you'd have to be a fool to say we should let them go. The data on effectiveness of treatment doesn't support it."

One of the most extensive reviews of sex-offender treatment research, published in 1989, concluded after looking at 42 studies that "There is as yet no evidence that clinical treatment reduces rates of sex re-offenses in general." [10]

But Kent State University psychologist Gordon C. Nagayama Hall says that the review surveyed treatment programs from the 1960s and '70s that would now be considered "rather dated." In an analysis of 12 more recent studies of treatment programs, he found that treatment was on balance effective. About 19 percent of the sex offenders who attended treatment programs committed sexual offenses again, compared with 27 percent for untreated sex offenders. [11]

Surgical castration, which removes the testes, the body's testosterone-producing organ, is the most effective way of reducing recidivism, according to Hall's analysis of a German study. (Hall's analysis included no such studies from the U.S., where castration is widely viewed as unethical by the medical profession and criminal justice system.)

The most effective treatments after surgical castration, Hall found, are testosterone-lowering hormonal treatments and cognitive-behavioral treatments. Drugs that reduce testosterone, the hormone responsible for sexual drive, achieve nearly the same effect as surgical castration but have the advantage of being reversible. (*See "At Issue," p. 41.*)

Cognitive-behavioral treatments use group and individual therapy to confront the distorted thinking that leads to sex offenders' behavior. For example, a group-therapy leader will challenge a child molester's assertion that his fondling of a child is an educational initiation into sex.

Least effective, Hall found, were pure behavioral treatments. This kind of therapy generally aims to discourage or interrupt inappropriate sexual arousal. One behavioral treatment lets the patient reach a point of sexual excitement while looking at pictures of children, then gives him a strong whiff of ammonia. This approach gets temporary results but wears off over time, Hall says.

Experts emphasize that recidivism rates vary among different kinds of sex offenders. For example, rapists tend to be the most criminally versatile, repeating sexual and other crimes in higher proportions than child molesters. Incest offenders tend to have the lowest recidivism rates, probably because their interest is concentrated within the family.

An 'Unlikely' Sex Offender

By the late 1970s, Wayne had rebuilt his life. In the small Midwestern community he had moved to he was a respected citizen, editor of the local newspaper and a youth league baseball coach. *

Few people in town knew he had served time in prison for sexually molesting an 8-year-old boy. No one knew he hadn't stopped.

Unlike the serial pedophiles who get headlines for their savage attacks, Wayne says he never threatened or physically harmed his victims. Rather, he says, he built up their trust and manipulated it. The young boys he knew were flattered by the friendly editor's invitation to stay overnight at his house.

Typically, Wayne would invite a boy into his house to look at his *Playboy* magazines. Wayne would become sexually aroused, leading to oral sex or masturbation. Wayne likens his method to the childhood game of "playing doctor." He says he never engaged in penetration or rape.

In never physically harming his victims, Wayne is similar to most other child molesters, according to Kate Thomas, associate director of the National Institute for the Study, Prevention and Treatment of Sexual Trauma in Baltimore, Md. Few pedophiles "do something physically painful," she says. "Not a lot make verbal threats." Children often go along, psychologists say, because they don't recognize inappropriate fondling as abuse.

Wayne's double life ended in 1983, when an 11-year-old boy who had been given the overnight treatment broke the secret. Wayne was arrested and pleaded guilty.

Knowing that he faced a tough prison sentence because it was his second molestation conviction, Wayne and his lawyer cast about for an alternative treatment plan. A friend told Wayne he had seen the institute's director, Johns Hopkins University psychiatrist Fred S. Berlin, on the Phil Donahue show. Berlin had described his treatment of rapists and pedophiles with Depo-Provera, a testosterone-lowering drug that reduces interest in sex.

As part of a pre-sentence evaluation approved by the court, Wayne flew to Baltimore and entered Berlin's program for three months, receiving weekly injections of Depo-Provera and attending group therapy sessions. Wayne says Depo-Provera helped him control his obsessive desire for young boys. While he was on the drug, a 14-year-old boy attending a class with him caught his attention.

"In the past in that situation, my mind would have been constantly rolling, wondering if I can work my way to visit him," Wayne recalls. "Now it wasn't. I realized that I was attracted, but I went no further."

However, the judge presiding over Wayne's case rejected his attorney's proposal that he stay in treatment in Baltimore as an alternative to prison. Wayne had to serve five years in prison, where he was not permitted to use Depo-Provera. But he says the therapy he received there was helpful.

At first, Wayne attended a prison drug/alcohol treatment program and was told to think about his sexual addiction every time participants talked about drugs and alcohol. He says he realized the addictions were similar and that he had to go through the same feelings of remorse and concern for others that are the basic building blocks of Alcoholics Anonymous.

Later, in a prison group therapy program for sex offenders, Wayne met other victims of childhood sexual abuse, including a young man serving a life sentence for killing his abuser. For the first time, Wayne says, he realized the young boys he had molested were victims, too, not equal social partners. "In this abusive behavior, I wasn't putting faces on these people," he says. "This was an object meeting my needs, and now all of a sudden I was putting a face on it."

In 1989, after getting out of prison, Wayne returned to Baltimore and attended weekly group therapy sessions at the sexual trauma institute as a condition of his parole. He finished parole in 1992, but he has continued to attend group therapy at the institute at his own expense.

"This is the most honest one and a half hours I have all week," says Wayne, who is convinced group therapy "works" as treatment.

Today, at 47, Wayne looks and talks like the white-collar professional he is. Since leaving prison, he has entered the hotel business. Moreover, he has come to grips with the fact that he is gay and is starting to feel attracted to adult men.

He traces his attraction to young boys to his own adolescence. In junior high school, he had been popular until his family moved away, and he became introverted. Apparently, he says, "I just froze at that juvenile age." Wayne estimates he has abused 75 boys in his lifetime.

Like the treatment experts at the institute, Wayne sees his pattern with young boys as a craving that, like alcoholism, cannot be "cured" but can be managed with vigilance.

"I will always be attracted" to young boys he says, "but I don't feel that desire to take it further."

* Wayne's last name has been withheld to protect his privacy.

Most people are surprised to discover that except for exhibitionists, a minority of sex offenders offend again. On average, about 17 percent of rapists commit sexual offenses within four years after release while about 11 percent of child molesters do, according to an analysis of the research by R. Karl Hanson, a senior research officer for Canada's solicitor general.

When it comes to committing other kinds of crimes, "rapists look a lot more like your general criminal," Hanson notes. About 23 percent of them commit some kind of violent, non-sexual crime, according to his analysis of studies from around the world. Only 8 percent of child molesters get involved in non-sexual crimes. [12]

Rapists also appear more difficult to treat. Some studies report successfully lowering recidivism rates with child molesters, says skeptic Quinsey, "but there aren't any with rapists."

According to official statistics, sex offenders actually have lower recidivism rates than criminals who commit crimes for economic gain. In the United States, more than half the inmates in state prisons for car theft are arrested again for some kind of property crime within three years of their release. By contrast, fewer than 8 percent of rapists in U.S. prisons are rearrested for rape. [13]

Of course, rape and other sexual assaults are notoriously underreported, researchers caution. Psychologist Becker cites one estimate that less than 10 percent of U.S. rapes are ever reported to police. Moreover, sex offenses are often plea-bargained down to lesser infractions and may not show up as sex crimes in official records, Becker notes. [14]

Public concern focuses on the small group of offenders who commit sexual assault repeatedly. Some child molesters may have 100 victims over a lifetime, experts say, but may only be convicted for abusing one or two. ■

BACKGROUND

Focus on Punishment

From the beginning, American society has punished sex offenses harshly. The nation's first recorded execution of a youth involved a 17th-century Massachusetts farmboy who engaged in sexual play with one of his pet animals. [15]

But at various times in American history, sexual deviancy has been viewed as a disease to be treated. Between 1937 and 1972, 25 states and the District of Columbia passed laws that permitted sex offenders who were considered psychopaths to be institutionalized. [16] These statutes, writes law Professor La Fond, "reflected the buoyant therapeutic optimism of that period." [17]

Generally, such offenders were hospitalized in lieu of imprisonment. But by 1990, most of those laws had been repealed. "The treatment was not successful," explains Brooks at Rutgers. "Many people became very disillusioned with those statutes and said, 'We'll rely on punishment.' "

In Washington state, for example, a major legislative study on the sexual psychopath program confirmed the critics' view that the programs did not work. In a 1985 audit of Washington's sex offender treatment program, the Legislature's Budget Committee found that the recidivism rate of offenders in treatment was about the same as that for offenders imprisoned without treatment.

Some state legislatures came to believe that offenders were being released prematurely under the statutes, posing a danger to public safety. In addition, some critics charged that many sex offenders were manipulating the programs to avoid prison. [18]

In the 1970s, many states introduced "determinate sentencing," which set minimum sentences for violent crimes. This approach reflected the general disillusionment with rehabilitation and increasing public insistence on punishing violent criminals. In the late '70s and early '80s, rehabilitation programs in prisons across the country were dramatically curtailed.

Washington Gets Tough

Ironically, determinate sentences have now been blamed by some observers for incarcerating sex offenders for relatively short periods. On average, rapists served just over five years in prison in 1992, the latest year for which BJS statistics are available. In Washington, Berliner says determinate sentencing forced the release of rapist Shriner because he had met good-behavior requirements in prison.

Shriner's subsequent savage assault on a 7-year-old boy prompted the passage in 1990 of the first of a new wave of state "sexual predator" laws. These laws aimed to confine sex offenders who meet a broader definition of mental abnormality than the old laws. If a prosecutor can persuade a judge or jury that a prisoner eligible for release is still dangerous and suffers from a mental disorder, the prisoner can be detained until the state determines he is rehabilitated.

The Washington statute was part of a broad law aimed at sex offenders, known as the Community Protection Act. Another pioneering statute in the act requires communities to be notified about newly released sexual offenders in the area. Components of the comprehensive Washington legislation that have received less national attention, but which Berliner considers equally important, include:

- Treating victims of sexual assault and children with sexual behavior problems;
- Treating juvenile sex offenders; and
- Establishing standards for professionals who treat sex offenders.

Since 1990, several states have used Washington's predator statute as a model, including Minnesota, Kansas, California, Arizona and Nevada. Law Professor Janus believes that the laws have sprung up largely in response to public sentiment that sentences are generally too short for violent offenders.

La Fond says the new trend toward involuntary therapy for sexual offenders recalls the thinking behind the early psychopath laws, when it was widely believed that sexual deviancy was a treatable illness."You're getting a resurgence from the psychology camp saying, 'This may not be mental illness, but it's a behavioral problem.'"

Child Abuse Reporting Laws

In the 1960s and '70s, growing

Continued on p. 38

Chronology

1930s ***In an era optimistic about the powers of psychotherapy, states begin passing laws permitting involuntary commitment of sex criminals to mental hospitals in lieu of prison.***

1937
Minnesota becomes one of the first states to enact a "sexual psychopath" law, authorizing the government to place a sex offender in a psychiatric institution for treatment instead of prison.

—— • ——

1960s ***By the late 1960s, well over half the states have enacted "sexual psychopath" laws permitting the state to commit sex criminals indefinitely for mental treatment. Federal government pushes states to adopt laws requiring reporting of child abuse.***

1963
U.S. Children's Bureau drafts model legislation for states to require physicians to report suspected child abuse. Within three years, all states enact reporting laws.

—— • ——

1970s ***Crime increases at alarming rates, raising questions about the goal of rehabilitation for criminals. Between 1971 and 1980, the violent crime rate increases almost 50 percent, according to the FBI. Rise in reported cases of child abuse prompts academic studies and the first federal abuse legislation.***

1974
President Richard M. Nixon signs Child Abuse Prevention and Treatment Act establishing federal Center on Child Abuse and Neglect.

—— • ——

1980s ***As the national mood turns away from criminal rehabilitation and toward punishment, states begin repealing their sexual psychopath laws and adopting "determinate sentencing" laws to ensure prison sentences for violent crimes. All but a handful of states repeal their sexual psychopath laws by 1990.***

1981
California Legislature repeals its Mentally Disordered Sex Offender legislation, stating that sex offenses are not the product of "mental disease."

1984
Washington state passes legislation phasing out its sexual psychopath law and adopting a determinate-sentencing scheme.

1989
Psychologist Lita Furby publishes review of 42 treatment studies finding no evidence that clinical treatment reduces recidivism among sex offenders.

—— • ——

1990s ***Responding to crimes committed by released sex offenders with histories of violent sexual assault, states pass laws to detain sex offenders longer for mental treatment and to warn communities about released sex offenders.***

1990
Washington passes pioneering Community Protection Act, permitting the state to detain dangerous "sexual predators" in mental treatment indefinitely after their prison sentences expire.

1994
President Clinton signs federal crime bill urging states to pass sex offender registration statutes by 1997 and encouraging passage of community notification laws.

October 1994
Following the murder of 7-year-old Megan Kanka, allegedly by a released sex criminal, New Jersey enacts "Megan's Law" requiring communities to be notified about dangerous sex-offenders who move into the area; it is considered the toughest law of its kind.

Feb. 28, 1995
A federal judge in Newark, N.J., declares the notification provision of "Megan's Law" unconstitutional. The state is appealing the case, which is expected to reach the U.S. Supreme Court.

Aug. 25, 1995
A federal judge declares Washington state's sexual predator law unconstitutional on the grounds that it punishes the same crime twice. The state is appealing the decision, which is also expected to reach the Supreme Court.

Continued from p. 36

awareness of child abuse prompted the federal government to pass legislation encouraging the reporting of such offenses. In 1964, the U.S. Children's Bureau drafted model legislation requiring physicians to report suspected child abuse. Within three years, all states had enacted such reporting laws. [19]

Some of these laws had the unintended effect of driving sex offenders underground, some treatment experts charge. For example, in 1988, Maryland expanded its reporting law to require treatment professionals to report disclosures by adult patients about their abuse of children while they were in treatment. In 1989, all patient disclosures, even about abuse that occurred before treatment, became reportable in Maryland.

Since the reporting change in 1989, the number of adult patients voluntarily coming to the Johns Hopkins University Sexual Disorders Clinic (now the National Institute for the Study, Prevention and Treatment of Sexual Trauma) has dropped from approximately seven per year to zero, according to clinic Director Berlin.

"The law that's intended to make society safer is actually deterring undetected people with pedophilia from getting treatment that would enable them to be less risk to the community," Berlin says.

The 'Typical' Offender

Sex offenders come from all classes of society. But in contrast to most criminals, those in state prisons for rape or sexual assault are "primarily older white males," notes Allen J. Beck, a BJS statistician.

Unlike youths arrested for stealing cars or TV sets, whose criminal activity usually decreases as they age, sex offenders can be remarkably persistent. While sex offenders account for only one out of 10 state prison inmates, they represent one of every four prisoners over age 54, Beck says.

Reuters

Reginald Muldrew, also known as the "pillowcase rapist," was released from a California prison in December.

Nevertheless, treatment experts say it is becoming increasingly clear that most adult offenders commit their first sexual crimes before reaching adulthood. According to one study, 60-80 percent of adult sex offenders began their deviant behavior as teenagers. [20]

In one national study of 1,600 youths referred to treatment programs, sexual offenders ranged in age from 5-19, with a median age between 14 and 15. Over 90 percent of the juvenile offenders had victimized a relative or acquaintance. The most common scenario involved a victim age 7 or 8. [21]

Numerous theories explain why people become sex offenders. They range from the biological — offenders have higher testosterone levels and thus stronger sex drives — to the environmental. Freeman-Longo at the Safer Society Foundation says the children and teens he sees have been victims of childhood abuse themselves. "We see kids 4-6 who have been sexually abused. They act it out on other kids at the same ages."

"A lot of these kids are masturbating to thoughts of sexually abusing and molesting people," says Freeman-Longo. "We believe this behavior in most cases is learned, and we believe we can help them unlearn the behavior."

Another theory views sex offenders, especially pedophiles, as never having acquired the social skills necessary for normal adult relationships. In American society, "we have a very definite pressure for people to succeed socially," Freeman-Longo says. "For someone who comes up short," a less threatening form of behavior, like a relationship with a child or flashing in front of strangers, "is an option." ■

CURRENT SITUATION

Tracking Offenders

Despite statistics indicating that many sex criminals do not repeat their crimes, the public is not convinced. Over the past three years, as a result, states have been busy enacting a variety of laws to track sex offenders after they leave prison. As of November 1995, 47 states had laws requiring offenders to register with law enforcement authorities whenever they move into a community; in 1993, only 24 states had such registration laws.

Generally, these laws require offenders to provide their name, address, place of employment and sex convictions for up to 10 years after leaving prison. In most states, the registration information is available only to police. Registration helps police enforce court orders forbidding child molesters from working around children — such as in day-care centers or nursery schools. It also gives police a headstart if, for example, a parent calls with concerns about a neighbor who happens to be registered, according to Teresa Klingensmith, manager of legislative affairs at the National Center for Missing and Exploited Children in Arlington, Va.

"With registration, police can say, 'Ma'am, it's probably not a good idea for your child to be alone with this individual,'" even though they can't give explicit information, Klingensmith says. "Meanwhile, they send a squad car to check things out."

The 1994 omnibus anti-crime bill gave states additional impetus to enact registration laws. States that don't pass them by 1997 lose a portion of their federal crime-fighting funds under the sweeping $30.2 billion legislation. The law also encourages the state to enact community notification laws. [22]

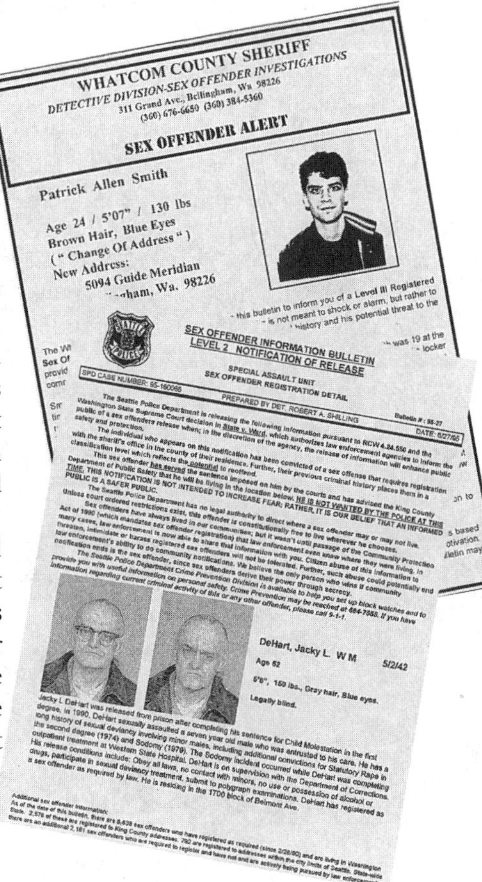

WHATCOM COUNTY SHERIFF
DETECTIVE DIVISION-SEX OFFENDER INVESTIGATIONS
311 Grand Ave., Bellingham, Wa 98226
(360) 676-6650 (360) 384-5360

SEX OFFENDER ALERT

Patrick Allen Smith

Age 24 / 5'07" / 130 lbs
Brown Hair, Blue Eyes
(" Change Of Address ")
New Address:
5094 Guide Meridian
...gham, Wa. 98226

...this bulletin to inform you of a Level III Registered ...is not meant to shock or alarm, but rather to ...history and his potential threat to the ...

SEX OFFENDER INFORMATION BULLETIN
LEVEL 2 NOTIFICATION OF RELEASE

SPECIAL ASSAULT UNIT
SEX OFFENDER REGISTRATION DETAIL

SPD CASE NUMBER: 95-160066 | PREPARED BY DET. ROBERT A. SHILLING | Bulletin #: 95-27 | DATE: 6/27/95

The Seattle Police Department is releasing the following information pursuant to RCW 4.24.550 and the Washington State Supreme Court decision in State v. Ward, which authorizes law enforcement agencies to inform the public of a sex offenders release when; in the discretion of the agency, the release of information will enhance public safety and protection.

The individual who appears on this notification has been convicted of a sex offense that requires registration with the sheriff's office in the county of their residence. Further, their previous criminal history places them in a classification level which reflects the potential to reoffend.

This sex offender has served the sentence imposed on him by the courts and has advised the King County Department of Public Safety that he will be living in the location below. HE IS NOT WANTED BY THE POLICE AT THIS TIME. THIS NOTIFICATION IS NOT INTENDED TO INCREASE FEAR; RATHER, IT IS OUR BELIEF THAT AN INFORMED PUBLIC IS A SAFER PUBLIC.

The Seattle Police Department has no legal authority to direct where a sex offender may or may not live. Unless court ordered restrictions exist, this offender is constitutionally free to live wherever he chooses.

Sex offenders have always lived in our communities; but it wasn't until passage of the Community Protection Act of 1990 (which mandates sex offender registration) that law enforcement even knew where they were living. In many cases, law enforcement is now able to share that information with you. Citizen abuse of this information to threaten, intimidate or harass registered sex offenders will not be tolerated. Further, such abuse could potentially end law enforcement's ability to do community notifications. We believe the only person who wins if community notification ends is the sex offender, since sex offenders derive their power through secrecy.

The Seattle Police Department Crime Prevention Division is available to help you set up block watches and to provide you with useful information on personal safety. Crime Prevention may be reached at 684-7555. If you have information regarding current criminal activity of this or any other offender, please call 9-1-1.

DeHart, Jacky L. W M 5/2/42
Age 52
5'8", 150 lbs., Gray hair, Blue eyes.
Legally blind.

Jacky L DeHart was released from prison after completing his sentence for Child Molestation in the first degree, in 1990. DeHart sexually assaulted a seven year old male who was entrusted to his care. He has a long history of sexual deviancy involving minor males, including additional convictions for Statutory Rape in the second degree (1974) and Sodomy (1979). The Sodomy incident occurred while DeHart was completing outpatient treatment at Western State Hospital. DeHart is on supervision with the Department of Corrections. His release conditions include: Obey all laws, no contact with minors, no use or possession of alcohol or drugs, participate in sexual deviancy treatment, submit to polygraph examinations. DeHart has registered as a sex offender as required by law. He is residing in the 1700 block of Belmont Ave.

Additional sex offender information:
As of the date of this bulletin, there are 8,638 sex offenders who have registered as required (since 2/28/90) and are living in Washington State. 2,576 of these are registered to King County addresses. 782 are registered to addresses within the city limits of Seattle. State-wide there are an additional 2,181 sex offenders who are required to register and have not and are actively being pursued by law enforcement.

Notification Laws

As of December 1995, 30 states had gone a step further, passing laws requiring communities to be notified about dangerous sex offenders. Both registration and notification laws have been challenged in the courts. Though some decisions have limited the scope of registration laws, they have generally withstood constitutional challenges. The legal status of the notification laws is less clear.

New Jersey's notification law has been challenged on constitutional grounds. Because of lower-court rulings halting the notifications, the state has had barely six weeks of experience with the law since it took effect Jan. 1, 1995. New Jersey's Supreme Court ruled in July 1995 that the law was constitutional but ordered the state to give sex offenders more due-process rights, including the right to appeal their notification status before a judge. New Jersey prosecutors were preparing to resume enforcing the law again under the new procedures in December.

Meanwhile, a federal district court judge in Newark has declared the notification law unconstitutional because of its retroactive nature. New Jersey's law, the nation's toughest, covers anyone who has ever, at any time, committed a sex crime. (Washington state's law, by contrast, applies only to offenders about to be released or on probation or parole.)

However, the New Jersey Supreme Court decision upholding the statute takes precedence, and thus the notification law remains enforceable pending resolution of the appeals in federal courts. But most experts agree the constitutional questions will cast a shadow over such laws until the issue is eventually resolved by the United States Supreme Court.

The challenge to the law in federal court was brought by a man who was found guilty of sodomy in 1971 and sentenced to 20 years in state prison. After his release, Megan's Law was enacted and applied retroactively to him. The man, Alexander Artway, argued that because he had already served his time, community notification amounted to a second punishment.

Federal District Judge Nicholas H. Politan found that the law violated the U.S. Constitution's ex post facto clause, which forbids laws that change the punishment attached to a crime after the crime has been committed. He likened the notification law to the "Scarlet Letter" in Colonial America and the Star of David that Jews were forced to wear in Nazi Germany. Public notification could affect an individual's ability to be employed and to return to a normal, law-abiding life in the community, the judge said, thus constituting a second punishment. [23]

"The judge is saying, 'You didn't tell people [about notification] when they pleaded guilty two decades ago, and so it's unfair to say now, 'Here's another punishment,'" says Martone of the ACLU, which filed an amicus brief challenging the law.

The state of New Jersey has appealed the federal decision to the Third Circuit, arguing that the notification is merely regulatory, not a punishment. A decision is expected early this year. The losing side is expected to appeal to the Supreme Court.

In addition to its constitutional problems, New Jersey's law faces a practical hurdle. Some 2,100 sex offenders have registered so far, but the number eligible could be in the tens of thousands. "One of the failures is the only way notification works is if you have a universe of honest, compliant sex offenders," says Martone.

But sex offenders have been inventive in evading the laws. In Washington state, offenders have given vacant lots as their addresses. In New Jersey, released prisoners have embarrassed innocent citizens by giving their addresses.

Klingensmith estimates that 15 states have followed Washington state in enacting sexual predator laws permitting violent and mentally ill offenders to be held for treatment after completing their prison sentences. The constitutionality of such laws has been challenged in five states. Most eyes are trained on Washington state, which has appealed a federal ruling that the law is unconstitutional. Oral arguments are set for March in the Ninth Circuit Court of Appeals.

Harsher Sentences

Harsher sentences being meted out today reflect the increased public anxiety over violent sex crimes. Reported rapes, for example, grew by 14 percent between 1988 and 1994. But experts say the main reason for the harsher sentences (and resulting rise in the prison population) is that judges are doing what the public wants — locking up sex criminals for longer periods.

In 1980, 20,500 men and women were in state prisons for sex offenses. By 1993, the number had quadrupled to 80,000, growing faster than the general prison population, which tripled in the same period, according to the BJS.

Between 1988 and 1992, the average time rapists served in prison rose from 48 months to 57 months. On average, rapists served 50.4 percent of their sentences, while first-time murderers went free after serving only 41 percent of their sentences. [24]

The numbers disguise the fact that sentences are all over the board for sex offenders. In some states, a molester with numerous victims may get just four years; in others the same offender may receive 20 years, according to the Center for Missing Children.

At the same time, funding for treatment in prisons has been drying up. In the past year, Alabama, Virginia, Oregon and California have shut down their programs, according to the Safer Society Foundation. "Most sex offenders in prison do not get treatment," says Freeman-Longo. "You have to go to private clinics, and not every state has one."

One reason for the closed programs is expense. In Washington, institutionalized sex offenders cost the state $100,000 per person annually, about four times the cost of regular imprisonment. Another reason is undoubtedly the current get-tough-on-crime climate. "Since politicians are unwilling to pay for treatment in prison, there's very little rehabilitation," says Klingensmith. "The public is thinking, 'Let's just incapacitate them.'"

Treatment Approaches

In a 1994 national survey, the Safer Society Foundation counted 1,784 public and private sex-offender treatment programs nationwide, 710 of them for adults. The most popular single treatment approach is the behavioral-cognitive approach, which seeks to change sex offenders' warped thinking about their crimes through such means as group therapy. The next most popular approach, known as relapse prevention, combines therapy for sex offenders with monitoring by counselors trained to recognize when offenders are falling into old behavior patterns. [25]

The nation's most extensive relapse prevention program, set up in Arizona in 1987, allows lifelong probation for sex offenders considered likely to reoffend. According to psychologist Becker, virtually all convicted child molesters in the state are put into the program — either instead of prison or upon release from prison for a second molestation conviction. Participants must attend two hours of outpatient group therapy per week for at least 18 months. Probation officers and specially trained "surveillance" officers make unannounced visits to those probationers considered most likely to commit another crime. [26]

Arizona is the only state with lifelong probation. But the idea of using probation and parole with mandated treatment as an alternative to prison is becoming "more and more common" nationwide, according to Freeman-Longo. Part of the motivation is avoiding the cost and overcrowding of prisons.

"We can't put everyone that commits a crime in prison," says probation officer Randy Walker, who works with sex offenders in Maricopa County, Ariz. "Otherwise we'd have to put a chain-link fence around Arizona." Arizona's toughened probation program, including mandatory therapy, costs the state $3,500 per individual annually, compared to $16,000 for keeping a prisoner behind bars, according to Lori Scott, supervisor of the sex offender unit for Maricopa County Adult Probation in Phoenix.

Under the Arizona law, lifetime probationers must meet 17 conditions on their lifestyle, including living at an approved residence, generally one not located near a school or playground, and are generally prohibited from dating women with children, possessing pornographic material or patronizing topless bars or adult bookstores.

In Arizona, a sex offender who violates any of these conditions can have his probation revoked and be returned to jail. Probation officers can also use intermediate steps like im-

Continued on p. 42

At Issue:

Is "chemical castration" an acceptable way to treat sex offenders?

Douglas J. Besharov
Resident scholar, American Enterprise Institute

FROM *ABA JOURNAL,* JULY 1992.

yes

On humanitarian and civil liberties grounds, most experts now oppose [surgical castration] and it is unlikely that many courts will turn to it as an alternative to incarceration — especially since there is a better option.

First tried more than 25 years ago, the use of hormone suppressors — also known as "chemical castration" — has proven highly effective for certain sex offenders. The most common drug used is medroxyprogesterone acetate, a synthetic progesterone originally developed as a contraceptive marketed as Depo-Provera. . . .

Carefully conducted research indicates that hormone therapy works — when coupled with appropriate counseling — for most paraphiliacs (sex offenders driven by overwhelming sexual fantasies). Recidivism rates are under 5 percent.

Just as in surgical castration, the subject can still have erections, and many successfully impregnate their wives. For this reason, hormone treatment does not work for anti-social personalities or for those who sex offenses are motivated by feelings of anger, violence or power. The treatment does not reach the causes of their harmful behavior. Thus, proper diagnosis is essential.

Some may argue that hormone treatment as an alternative to incarceration is too lenient for serious sex crimes. First, it is possible to combine treatment with incarceration. But more importantly, we should remember how frequently serious offenders serve very short sentences. Nationally, convicted rapists serve less than six years in jail, and that does not include all those who plead guilty to a lesser offense. For too many offenders, the sexual abuse and violence in prisons merely heightens their propensity to commit further crimes. . . .

Others will oppose using these drugs because, even though they work, they are an invasion of bodily integrity and reproductive freedom. (Side effects include weight gain, hot flashes and hypertension.) But it is more accurate to see them as equivalent to the psychotropic drugs, which include antidepressants, antipsychotics and tranquilizers, now routinely used to treat many mental disorders.

Some would even deny defendants the right to accept the treatment in lieu of imprisonment because the choice is inherently coercive. Perhaps it is. But the question is this: When faced with the certainty of incarceration, wouldn't we all want to be able to make such a choice? To ask the question is to answer it.

After all the sensationalism, the use of hormone-suppressing drugs, in certain cases, holds great promise for reducing the level of sexual violence against women and children. As a voluntary alternative, it is in both the defendant's and society's interest.

Andrew Vachss
Juvenile justice advocate and crime novelist

FROM *ABA JOURNAL,* JULY 1992.

no

As a criminal justice response to the chronic, dangerous sexual psychopath, castration of any kind is morally pernicious and pragmatically impotent. Even if we could ignore the implications of mutilation-as-compensation for criminal offenses, castration must be rejected on the most essential of grounds: The "cure" will exacerbate the "disease." . . .

Violent sex offenders are not victims of their heightened sex drives. Rapists may be "expressing their rage." Predatory pedophiles may be "replaying their old scripts." But any sexual sadist, properly interviewed, will tell you the truth: They do what they do because they want to do it. Their behavior is not the product of sickness — it is volitional.

Castration will not remove the source of a violent sex offender's rage — only one single instrument of its expression. . . . The castration remedy implies some biological cause for sexual offenses. Once fixed, the offender ceases to be a danger. This is nonsense — the motivation for sexual assault will not disappear with the severed genitalia or altered hormones. . . .

Even the most liberal of Americans have become suspicious of a medical model to explain sex offenders. Such offenders may plot and plan, scheme and stalk for months, utilize the most elaborate devices to avoid detection, even network with others and commercially profit from their foul acts.

But some psycho-apologist can always be found to claim the poor soul was deep in the grip of irresistible impulse when he was compelled to attack. Imagine the field day the expert-witness fraternity will have explaining how the castrated child molester who later killed his new victims was rendered insane as a result of the castration itself.

Sex offender treatment is the growth industry of the 1990s. Chemical castration already looms as a Get-Out-of-Jail-Free Card. Castration validates the sex offender's self-portrait: He is the victim; he can't help himself. It panders to our ugliest instincts, not the least of which is cowardice — the refusal to call evil by its name.

Nor can castration be defended because the perpetrator chooses it. Leaving aside the obvious issue of coercion, under what theory does a convicted criminal get to select his own (non-incarcerative) sentence?

America loves simple solutions to complex problems, especially solutions with political utility, like boot camp for youthful offenders. The last thing our cities need is muggers in better physical shape. When it comes to our own self-interest (and self-defense), the greatest sickness is stupidity. Castration qualifies . . . on all counts.

FOR MORE INFORMATION

The Association for the Treatment of Sexual Abusers, 10700 S.W. Beaverton-Hillsdale Highway, Suite 26, Beaverton, Ore. 97005-3035; (503) 643-1023. This nonprofit organization for professionals in the field of sex offender treatment is devoted to the development of professional standards and the dissemination of research.

CURE-SORT (Citizens United for the Rehabilitation of Errants — Sex Offenders Restored Through Treatment), P.O. Box 7782, Baltimore, Md. 21221-0782. CURE is a national organization founded by families of prisoners in 1972. This chapter, which represents sex offenders, lobbies for treatment of imprisoned sex offenders and alternatives to incarceration.

National Center for Missing and Exploited Children, 2101 Wilson Blvd., Suite 550, Arlington, Va. 22101-3052; (703) 235-3900. The center closely tracks state legislation affecting child abuse.

Safer Society Foundation, P.O. Box 340, Brandon, Vt. 05733-0340; (802) 247-3132. The foundation provides information on treating sexual abusers, conducts a nationwide survey every two years of treatment programs for sex offenders and provides a service that refers sex offenders to treatment.

National Center for Prosecution of Child Abuse, 99 Canal Center Plaza, Suite 510, Alexandria, Va. 22314; (703) 739-0321. The center tracks legislation and court cases related to sex offenders and assists prosecutors with their cases.

Continued from p. 40

posing a curfew.

Since May 1993, only 10 of the 800 sex offenders on probation in Maricopa County have committed new sex offenses, a recidivism rate of less than 1 percent, according to Scott. About 10 percent have committed technical violations like consorting with children.

Emphasis on Prevention

Increasingly, child abuse experts are urging more emphasis on improving prevention programs.

A recent report by the American Psychological Association says that traditional school programs that try to teach children to avoid sexually abusive situations "don't work very well," because children can't be expected to know what is, or isn't, appropriate touching in every situation. Instead, the report urges, programs should be expanded to target adults perpetrators. [27]

In Vermont, the Safer Society Foundation is pioneering a confidential telephone hotline called "Stop it Now!" to encourage molesters and potential offenders to seek treatment. Organizers also hope that offenders will turn themselves in to criminal authorities, noting that someone who does so is likely to receive more lenient treatment than someone arrested.

Other experts are working to root out sexual abusers even earlier. Since 1988, the C. Henry Kempe National Center for Prevention and Treatment of Child Abuse and Neglect in Denver, Colo., has been training teachers in 12 states to identify sexually abusive children. A curriculum developed by the center teaches educators to confront children about the behavior and to know when to refer them to counseling.

Gail Ryan, director of the center's Perpetration Prevention Project, says sexually abusive teens treated by the center often start their behavior in preschool and elementary school — with no adverse consequences from adults. "If we can interrupt the behavior and get it back on a more normal course," she says, "that's the only way we'll slow the tide." ■

OUTLOOK

Legal Skirmishes

Activists on both sides of the sex-offender debate are looking to the Supreme Court for resolution of key issues. Yet even if the high court upholds state efforts to detain sex criminals beyond their sentence, the struggles in courtrooms and legislatures won't necessarily stop.

Klingensmith predicts further legal skirmishes as civil libertarians in some states charge that incarcerated sex offenders are not receiving meaningful counseling. "You can't just house them in what is really a prison — with a mental-hospital name," she says. "The court is still going to say, 'In application, that's punishment even though your law in spirit is constitutional.' "

If the Supreme Court strikes down sexual-predator laws as unconstitutional, state legislators are likely to crack down on sex offenders with harsher sentences.

According to Rutgers law Professor Brooks, the attacks on Washington state's sexual-predator statute already have fostered a get-tough attitude among many legislators. Brooks says the local sentiment is, "What we really ought to do is enact statutes like 'two strikes and you're in for life.' Forget treatment. Let's just punish these bastards." That approach would be "dreadful," in Brooks' view, because it would take in many sex offenders who could otherwise be successfully treated.

California has already moved in that direction. During the 1994 gubernatorial campaign, Republican Gov. Pete Wilson signed a so-called "one-strike" bill. It calls for 25 years to life for a first-time sexual assault involving torture, mayhem, kidnaping or burglary with the intent to commit rape. [28]

During the campaign, Wilson also signed legislation to commit repeat sex offenders to secure mental health facilities before their scheduled release from prison. He emphasized that he saw the bill as a way to incapacitate sex criminals with mental disorders. "They'll only see the light of day when a jury is convinced they won't prey on innocent citizens," Wilson said. "For some, that should be a very long, long time." [29]

California's crackdown gained national attention recently when a notorious rapist was released from prison in December. Both of California's recently enacted sex-offender laws had been signed too late to affect Reginald Muldrew.

Known as the "pillowcase rapist" because he put pillowcases over his victims' heads, Muldrew has been linked to 200 sex crimes in the Los Angeles area from 1976-78. In 1978, he was convicted of four rapes and 13 related sex, burglary and robbery offenses. He was sentenced to 25 years but eventually had nine years shaved off for good behavior.

"He is one of a handful of very high-profile cases where the Department of Corrections has no leeway to keep them in prison any longer than their prison sentence," says Christine May, a spokeswoman for the California Department of Corrections. Psychiatrists diagnosed Muldrew as having a mental disorder that still makes him dangerous, she said.

Three demonstrators from the Women's Coalition in Pasadena held pillowcases as they protested Muldrew's release from Vacaville State Prison on Dec. 5. Muldrew flew to Las Vegas and has not been heard from since, according to May.

Some of Washington state's older sex-crime prisoners also could go free if the state's ground-breaking mental-commitment law is struck down. After the state passed the law in 1990, it enacted a "three strikes and you're out" law which sends criminals to prison for life after committing three serious offenses. In the future, many of the repeat sex offenders originally targeted by the 1990 mental-commitment law would be locked up for life under the three strikes law, according to Lieb at the Institute for Public Policy.

In fact, the debate over Washington's mental-commitment law could become moot if the Legislature passes a "one-strike" law covering most serious sex offenders, according to Berliner.

But Berliner cautions that such a law will take effect too late to apply to the 32 controversial sex offenders currently being held for mental-health therapy in Washington's prison system. If the sexual-predator law that put them there is declared unconstitutional by the Supreme Court, she says, "32 extremely dangerous people will be released all at once." ■

Sarah Glazer is a Washington, D.C., writer who specializes in health and social-policy issues.

Notes

[1] For background, see "Violence Against Women," *The CQ Researcher,* Feb. 26, 1993, pp. 169-193.

[2] Donna D. Schram and Cheryl Darling Milloy, "Community Notification: A Study of Offender Characteristics and Recidivism," Washington State Institute for Public Policy, October 1995.

[3] Robert E. Freeman-Longo, "Public Notification of Sexual Offender Release: Prevention or Problem," Safer Society Foundation, 1995, p. 3.

[4] Schram and Milloy, *op. cit.*

[5] *Andre Brigham Young v. David Weston,* U.S. District Court, Western District of Washington at Seattle, Aug. 25, 1995.

[6] *Review of Sexual Predator Program,* Washington State Institute for Public Policy, February 1992, pp. 3-4 of appendix by Vernon L. Quinsey, Queens University, Ontario.

[7] See Lisa Grace Lednicer, "Linehan Confined Under New State Statute," *St. Paul Pioneer Press,* July 28, 1995, p. 1A.

[8] See Judith V. Becker, "Offenders: Characteristics and Treatment," *The Future of Children,* summer/fall 1994, p. 181.

[9] *Ibid.,* p. 189.

[10] L. Furby, M. Weinrott and L. Blackshaw, "Sex Offender Recidivism: A Review," *Psychological Bulletin,* Vol. 105, No. 1, 1989, pp. 3-30.

[11] Gordon C. Nagayama Hall, "Sexual Offender Recidivism Revisited: A Meta-Analysis of Recent Treatment Studies," *Journal of Consulting and Clinical Psychology,* October 1995, pp. 802-809.

[12] Hanson presented his unpublished data in September 1995 to a conference in Cambridge, England, on sex offenders. It is based on 77 studies encompassing some 24,000 offenders in the U.S., Canada and Europe. Publication is scheduled in the May 1996 issue of *Forum on Corrections Research,* published by the Correctional Service of Canada.

[13] Allen J. Beck, "Recidivism of Prisoners Released in 1983," *Bureau of Justice Statistics Special Report,* April 1989, p. 6. This is the most recent year for which national recidivism rates are available.

[14] Becker, *op. cit.,* p. 183.

[15] See Jerome G. Miller, "Why the Scarlet 'A' Works Against Us," *Los Angeles Times,* Oct. 19, 1994, p. B7.

[16] Becker, *op. cit.,* p. 185.

[17] John Q. La Fond, "Washington's Sexually Violent Predator Law," *University of Puget Sound Law Review,* spring 1992, p. 661.

[18] *Ibid.,* pp. 668-69.

[19] The Children's Bureau is part of the Health and Human Services Department. For background, see "Child Sexual Abuse," *The CQ Researcher,* Jan. 15, 1993, pp. 25-48.

[20] Becker, *op. cit.,* p. 179.

[21] *Ibid.*

[22] *1994 Congressional Quarterly Almanac,* pp. 273-294. President Clinton signed the bill on Sept. 13, 1994.

[23] *Artway v. New Jersey,* Feb. 28, 1995.

[24] See Andre Henderson, "Corrections: The Scariest Criminal," *Governing,* Aug. 1, 1995, p. 34.

[25] *1994 Nationwide Survey of Treatment Programs and Models Serving Abuse-Reactive Children and Adolescent and Adult Sex Offenders,* Safer Society Foundation, 1994, p. 12.

[26] Becker, *op. cit.,* p. 192.

[27] American Psychological Association news release, "Psychologists Call for Overhaul of Child Protection System," Dec. 22, 1995, and "Psychological Issues Related to Child Maltreatment: Working Group Reports of the APA Coordinating Committee on Child Abuse and Neglect," *Journal of Clinical Child Psychology,* December 1995, p. 19.

[28] Amy Wallace and Eric Bailey, "'One Strike' Rape Bill is Signed by Wilson," *Los Angeles Times,* Sept. 9, 1994, p. 3.

[29] Press release from Gov. Pete Wilson, Oct. 10, 1995.

Bibliography

Selected Sources Used

Books

Allison, Dorothy, *Bastard Out of Carolina,* Plume, 1993 (paperback).
This novel, a National Book Award finalist in 1992, contains some unbearable descriptions of child abuse by an author who was abused herself as a child.

Vachss, Alice, *Sex Crimes,* Random House, 1993.
Former prosecutor Vachss tells the story of what it's like to prosecute sex offenders in New York.

Articles

Becker, Judith V., "Offenders: Characteristics and Treatment," *The Future of Children,* summer/fall 1994, pp. 176-197.
Becker, a professor of psychology and psychiatry at the University of Arizona, summarizes the research on treatments and causes of child molestation and concludes there's room for optimism.

Decter, Midge, "Megan's Law and *The New York Times,*" *Commentary,* October 1994, p. 61.
Decter responds to criticisms of Megan's Law, arguing that, "Life imprisonment without parole for the sexual assaulter of a little girl is not only the one truly safe decision from the point of view of society; it might, ironically, be an act of kindness to the rapist as well."

Henderson, Andre, "Corrections: The Scariest Criminal," *Governing,* Aug. 1, 1995, p. 34.
A review of how states are responding to sex offenders and the constitutional cloud over the laws they are passing.

Kaihla, Paul, "Sex Offenders: Is there a Cure?" *MacLeans,* Feb. 13, 1995, pp. 56-57.
Kaihla quotes several prominent Canadian researchers in reviewing the debate over whether treatment reduces recidivism among sex offenders.

Popkin, James, et al., "Natural Born Predators," *U.S. News & World Report,* Sept. 19, 1994, p. 64.
Popkin looks at what communities have done to protect themselves against sex offenders.

McQuay, Larry Don, "The Case for Castration, Part I," *The Washington Monthly*, May 1994, p. 26.
Texas inmate McQuay, imprisoned for child molestation, argues that he should be castrated. "Without the right treatment, I believe that eventually I will rape, then murder my victims to keep them from reporting me," he writes. (See response to McQuay, below).

Berlin, Fred S., "The Case for Castration, Part II," *The Washington Monthly,* May 1994, p. 28.
Psychiatrist Berlin responds that chemical castration, lowering testosterone through hormonal injections, is a better idea.

Wright, Lawrence, "A Rapist's Homecoming," *The New Yorker,* Sept. 4, 1995, pp. 56-69.
Wright describes the release of convicted rapist Donald Arthur Chapman from New Jersey's Avenel treatment facility for sex offenders. The warning of his therapist to county prosecutors that he was likely to commit another crime and the frightened response of his home town inspired the expansion of New Jersey's civil commitment statute under Megan's Law.

Reports and Studies

Schram, Donna D., and Cheryl Darling Milloy, "Community Notification: A Study of Offender Characteristics and Recidivism," Washington State Institute for Public Policy, October 1995.
This widely cited study found that community notification made little difference in sex offender recidivism.

"1994 Nationwide Survey of Treatment Programs and Models Servicing Abuse-Reactive Children and Adolescents and Adult Sex Offenders," Safe Society Foundation, 1994.
This nationwide survey is conducted every two years by the Brandon, Vt.,-based foundation.

The Next Step

Additional information from UMI's Newspaper & Periodical Abstracts database

Chemical Castration

Basheda, Valarie, "Measure seeks chemical castration of rapists," *Detroit News,* May 12, 1994, p. A1.
Chemical castration could be used to prevent twice-convicted rapists from committing the crime again under a measure that passed the Michigan House.

"Castration bill in Florida," *The New York Times,* March 31, 1994, p. A14.
The Florida Senate approved legislation March 30, 1994, that would allow judges to order the chemical castration of twice-convicted rapists by having them take a synthetic female hormone.

"Chemical castration: Whoa," *Detroit News & Free Press,* May 15, 1994, p. B2.
An editorial discusses the Michigan House of Representatives having approved legislation allowing a judge to order a sex-drive inhibiting drug for twice-convicted sex offenders. It says that the provision is probably a bad idea that, at the very least, deserves a much closer look by the Michigan Senate.

Vaillancourt, Meg, "Chemical castration mulled for sex crimes," *Boston Globe,* April 13, 1995, p. 31.
Freshman legislator John Locke urged Massachusetts lawmakers to consider voluntary "chemical castration" for sexual offenders, but civil libertarians and prisoners' rights advocates called the proposal "political grandstanding."

Williams, Mike, "Nudity, castration steal the spotlight," *Atlanta Constitution,* April 6, 1994, p. A3.
They have clamored for the chemical castration of repeat rapists. With only days remaining in their two-month session, however, Florida lawmakers have yet to pass a budget or tackle the much-publicized crisis in the state's juvenile justice system.

"Megan's Law"

Bernstein, Andrea, "Should you be told that your neighbor is a sex offender?" *Ms.,* November 1995, pp. 24-26.
Many states are adopting laws that allow police officials to notify residents and community organizations if a repeat sex offender is moving into the neighborhood. Opposition to this type of law argues that these measures only provide the illusion of safety and that public officials do not need to concern themselves with the private sphere.

Fein, Bruce and Edward Martone, "Megan's Law," *ABA Journal,* March 1995, pp. 8-39.
Whether or not there should be laws to inform communities when convicted sex offenders more into the area is discussed. Some say this will help cut down on crime, while others believe it creates a climate of vigilante justice.

Hanley, Robert, "Sex-offender disclosure law hitting snags in New Jersey," *The New York Times,* Jan. 9, 1995, p. A1.
Megan's Law, which requires community notification of the presence of those convicted of sexual crimes, is hitting snags in New Jersey much like similar programs attempted in several other states. Logistical and legal problems have popped up, slowing the Legislature's plan to make entire towns aware of sexual predators and prevent attacks like the one on Megan Kanka, after whom the law has come to be known.

Jerome, Richard, Maria Eftimiades, Nick Gallo and Stephen Sawicki, "Megan's legacy," *People Weekly,* March 20, 1995, pp. 46-51
Seven-year-old Megan Kanka was brutally murdered, and her family is fighting for a law that would let other parents know when a sex offender moves in next door. Kanka's ghastly death at the hands of a child molester and the fight for legislation to alert parents to the danger of an offender in their neighborhood are discussed.

Peterson, Iver, "Mix-ups and worse arising from sex-offender notification," *The New York Times,* Jan. 12, 1995, p. B1.
New Jersey's new sex-offender law, named for Megan Kanka, has caused mix-ups and mishaps that have sent officials scrambling to correct shortcomings. The law requires county prosecutors to determine whether a convicted sex offender about to be released poses a low, medium or high threat, and such offenders are required to register with the police when they settle in the state.

Plesa, David, "Law would notify sex offenders' neighbors," *The Houston Post,* Jan. 5, 1995, p. A19.
Texas Sen. Florence Shapiro is proposing legislation that would help make communities aware of sex offenders who are released from prison into their neighborhoods. The bill follows the example of "Megan's Law" in New Jersey, which was passed in 1994 in the wake of the slaying of 7-year-old Megan Kanka, allegedly by a convicted sex offender living across the street from her home.

"Sex offender laws require notification," *News Media & the Law,* spring 1995, pp. 4-6.
New Jersey passed "Megan's Law," which authorizes prosecutors to notify community members when released sex offenders move into their neighborhood, after the murderer

of 7-year-old Megan Kanka turned out to be a neighbor with a record of child molestation. "Megan's Law" and affirmative disclosure in various states are discussed.

Sullivan, Joseph F., "A crackdown on sex offenders in New Jersey," *The New York Times,* Oct. 21, 1994, p. B6.
The New Jersey Assembly on Oct. 20, 1994, gave final passage to six bills that tighten supervision of sex offenders and impose tougher sentences in certain cases. The package of legislation is known collectively as "Megan's Law," after Megan Kanka of Hamilton Township. Highlights of the new legislation are discussed.

Sullivan, Joseph F., "Whitman approves stringent restrictions on sex criminals," *The New York Times,* Nov. 1, 1994, p. B1.
New Jersey Gov. Christine Todd Whitman on Oct. 31, 1994, signed into law a nine-bill package intended to keep a tight rein on sex offenders, making them subject to lifetime supervision. Critics say the legislation, which was spurred by the assault and killing in July of 7-year-old Megan Kanka by a convicted sex offender, contains more symbolism than substance and is headed for a certain constitutional challenge.

"Suspect's lawyers want an alias for Megan's law victim," *The New York Times,* Oct. 25, 1995, p. B5.
Defense lawyers representing Jesse K. Timmendequas, the man who is accused of brutally raping and then killing 7-year-old Megan Kanka in New Jersey, want the girl's name excluded from their client's capital murder trial, with Megan and her family, who are potential witnesses, identified to jurors by an alias. The case led to the creation of a law bearing Megan's name.

Wharton, Joseph, "Court upholds Megan's Law," *ABA Journal,* October 1995, p. 6.
New Jersey's Supreme Court has upheld Megan's Law , a law requiring government officials to notify communities of the presence of sexual offenders at the time of their release from prison. The bill had first been approved last fall by the state legislature.

Sex Offenders

Davis, Laura, Marilyn D. McShane and Frank P. Williams III, "Controlling computer access to pornography: Special conditions for sex offenders," *Federal Probation,* June 1995, pp. 43-48.
Computers have given child molesters access to a plethora of pornographic material. Vital information that probation officers who are preparing presentence investigations on sex offenders and who are supervising them should know about computer access to pornography is discussed.

Denson, Bryan, "Castration bill no help for jailed sex offender," *The Houston Post,* March 27, 1995, p. A13.
Texas inmate Larry McQuay will not receive his wish to be castrated by the state as medical treatment for his urge to molest children even if a bill that would allow imprisoned pedophiles to be voluntarily castrated goes through as expected. Under the bill, only offenders with two convictions are eligible for castration, and McQuay only has one conviction.

Leo, John, "Dealing with career predators," *U.S. News & World Report,* April 11, 1994, p. 19.
The U.S. appears to be growing numb to the folly of a justice system that keeps putting dangerous sexual offenders and other criminals back on the streets. The social cost of letting career predators go is discussed.

Nordheimer, Jon, "New look at jail unit housing sex offenders," *The New York Times,* Nov. 2, 1994, p. B6.
A New Jersey task force on Nov. 1, 1994, toured the Adult Diagnostic and Treatment Center in Avenel, which houses violent rapists and child molesters with compulsive disorders who are often driven to commit more crimes once in the outside world unless their behavior can be modified before their prison time runs out. The visit came one day after Governor Christine Todd Whitman signed a package of bills that will keep a tight rein on sex offenders once they're released from prison.

Schultz, Pamela D., "Sex offender law not the answer," *Chicago Tribune,* April 2, 1995, p. 6.
Schultz explores why sex-offender notification policies are not the way to protect children from sexual exploitation; they just force criminals to move from one community to another.

"Sex offenders: Double jeopardy?" *The Economist,* Sept. 2, 1995, pp. 24-25.
Federal Judge John Coughenour has ruled that Washington State's sexual-offender center is little more than a jail in disguise. The state has apparently violated constitutional provisions guaranteeing a fair trial and barring two prison terms for one crime.

Smolowe, Jill, "Not in my backyard!" *Time,* Sept. 5, 1994, p. 59.
Citizens are determined to keep paroled murderers and sex offenders from settling in their communities. The crusade to keep criminals out and the demand for notification laws are discussed.

Sex Offender Registration

"Children's Express — Assessing Megan's Law: Kids hold court to fight sex offenders," *Amsterdam News,* Sept. 9, 1995, p. 20.
A Children's Express article discusses "Megan's Law," which forces convicted sex offenders to register with the state. Megan Kanka was a 7-year-old New Jersey girl who was abused and murdered by a convicted sex felon.

Johnson, Ted, "Sex offenders arrested for violating registration law," *Los Angeles Times,* July 26, 1995, p. B3.
A police task force arrested seven convicted sex offenders in the San Gabriel Valley and Whittier, Calif., for violating a state law that requires them to register their addresses with city authorities. The sweep came after the murder of a West Covina woman by a paroled sex offender.

Rojas, Aurelio and Thaii Walker, "Sex offender registration system failing," *San Francisco Chronicle,* April 4, 1994, p. A1.
A special report examines the failure of California's Sex Offender Registration Act, a 47-year-old law requiring convicted sex offenders to inform police every time they move. Justice Department officials say 80 percent of offenders routinely ignore registration requirements.

Tierney, Tim, "Police are gearing up to track sex offenders — All of them," *Chicago Tribune,* Dec. 1, 1995, p. S5.
Stricter registration laws for paroled sex offenders will take effect Jan. 1, 1996, so officials at the South Suburban Association of Chiefs of Police meeting in Crestwood, Ill., took advantage of a state police training session to prepare.

Sex Offender Treatment Programs

Bonapace, Ruth, "Can sex offenders really be cured?" *The New York Times,* Aug. 21, 1994, p. N1.
The recent arrest of convicted sex offender Jesse Timmendequas in the murder of a 7-year-old Hamilton Township, N.J., girl, Megan Kanka, has raised concerns about the effectiveness of treatment programs for those who commit sex crimes.

Lakey, Joyce F., "The profile and treatment of male adolescent sex offenders," *Adolescence,* winter 1994, pp. 755-761.
The most prominent characteristics of male adolescent sex offenders are described. Treatment includes and mandates accountability and correcting of thinking errors in such offenders, while building a foundation of morality, remorse and empathy for victims.

Lester, Thomas L., "Sex offender facility committed to change and rehabilitation," *Corrections Today,* April 1995, pp. 168-171.
Ninety-eight percent of the population at Oregon's Snake River Correctional Institution are sex offenders. The other 2 percent are there for gang management purposes or have the skills to maintain the physical plant.

Marx, Gary, "Getting help to sex offenders," *Chicago Tribune,* Dec. 18, 1994, p. C2.
A group therapy session is one part of a new sex-offender treatment program at the Big Muddy River Correctional Center in far southern Illinois, which officials hope will help rapists, pedophiles and other sex offenders across the nation. The program is examined.

Miller, Jerome G., "The folly of not treating sex offenders," *The Washington Post,* Jan. 10, 1995, p. A17.
Jerome G. Miller criticizes Virginia Gov. George Allen's proposal to end funding for all treatment programs for sex offenders in state prisons on the premise that treating them does not work. Miller says that the sex offender ex-convict released to the streets after years without treatment is a disaster waiting to happen.

Slattery, Ryan, "Bill would OK drug treatment, study of Massachusetts sex offenders," *Boston Globe,* Dec. 8, 1994, p. 39.
Proposals to correct 1994's ballot problems and to offer voluntary chemical treatment to sex offenders are among the thousands of bills filed for consideration by the Massachusetts Legislature in 1995.

Smith, Mark, "Therapists assail controversial self-help plan for sex offenders," *Houston Chronicle,* April 23, 1995, p. E1.
A proposal in the Texas Legislature to allow released sex offenders to seek treatment from other sex offenders in volunteer self-help groups is drawing heavy criticism from licensed therapists, who feel they should be the primary providers of treatment .

Worling, James R., "Adolescent sibling-incest offenders: Differences in family and individual functioning when compared to adolescent non-sibling sex offenders," *Child Abuse & Neglect,* May 1995, p. 633-635.
Adolescent male sex offenders who assaulted younger siblings were compared to those who offended against non-sibling children. The etiology and treatment of adolescent sibling-incest offenders are discussed.

Back Issues

Great Research on Current Issues Starts Right Here...Recent topics covered by The CQ Researcher are listed below. Before May 1991, reports were published under the name of Editorial Research Reports.

JULY 1994
Dietary Supplements
Public Opinion and Foreign Policy
Crime Victims' Rights
Birth Control Choices

AUGUST 1994
Genetically Engineered Foods
Electing Minorities
Prozac Controversy
College Sports

SEPTEMBER 1994
Home Schooling
Welfare Experiments
Courts and the Media
Regulating Tobacco

OCTOBER 1994
Historic Preservation
Religion and Politics
Arts Funding
Economic Sanctions

NOVEMBER 1994
Sex on Campus
Blood Supply Safety
Testing Term Limits
Religion in America

DECEMBER 1994
Farm Policy
Arms Sales
Earthquake Research
The Future of Television

JANUARY 1995
Treating Addiction
Child Custody and Support
Parents and Schools
Non-Proliferation Treaty at 25

FEBRUARY 1995
Cracking Down on Immigration
The Business of Sports
Reinventing Government
Housing Discrimination

MARCH 1995
Death Penalty Debate
Primary Care
Democracy in Africa
Environmental Movement at 25

APRIL 1995
Abortion Clinic Protests
Dieting and Health
Combating AIDS
Rethinking Affirmative Action

MAY 1995
Assisted Suicide Controversy
Overhauling Social Security
Learning to Read
Mandatory Sentencing

JUNE 1995
Combating Infectious Disease
Property Rights
Repetitive Stress Injuries
Regulating the Internet

JULY 1995
War Crimes
Highway Safety
Combating Terrorism
Preventing Teen Drug Use

AUGUST 1995
Job Stress
Organ Transplants
United Nations at 50
Advances in Cancer Research

SEPTEMBER 1995
Catholic Church in the U.S.
Northern Ireland Cease-Fire
High School Sports
Teaching History

OCTOBER 1995
Quebec's Future
Revitalizing the Cities
Networking the Classroom
Indoor Air Pollution

NOVEMBER 1995
The Working Poor
The Jury System
Sex, Violence and the Media
Police Misconduct

DECEMBER 1995
Teens and Tobacco
Gene Therapy's Future
Global Water Shortages
Third-Party Prospects

JANUARY 1996
Emergency Medicine

Back issues are available for $5.00 (subscribers) or $8.00 (non-subscribers). Quantity discounts apply to orders over ten. To order, call Congressional Quarterly Customer Service at (202) 887-8621.

Binders are available for $18.00. To order call 1-800-638-1710. Please refer to stock number 648.

Future Topics

- ***Bilingual Education***
- ***Helping the Homeless***
- ***Reforming the CIA***

THE CQ Researcher

PUBLISHED BY CONGRESSIONAL QUARTERLY INC.

Debate Over Bilingualism

Should English be the nation's official language?

Large-scale immigration from Latin America and Asia in recent years has convinced many Americans that English should be made the official language of the United States. They argue that a common culture is what holds a nation together, and that a common language is needed to convey and preserve that culture. Consequently, they want bilingual-education programs to focus on teaching English, and programs that reinforce newcomers' native languages to be reformed or abolished. Bilingual-education advocates argue that cultural and language diversity are national strengths that should be nurtured. They view official English as unnecessary, and probably unconstitutional, and oppose legislation designed to make English the national language and, in one case, to abolish bilingual education outright.

INSIDE THIS ISSUE

CQ Jan. 19, 1996 • Volume 6, No. 3 • Pages 49-72

Formerly Editorial Research Reports

Debate Over Bilingualism

COVER: BARBARA SASSA-DANIELS

The CQ Researcher

Jan. 19, 1996
Volume 6, No. 3

The CQ Researcher (ISSN 1056-2036). Formerly Editorial Research Reports. Published weekly (48 times per year, not printed the first Friday of any month with five Fridays) by Congressional Quarterly Inc., 1414 22nd St., N.W., Washington, D.C. 20037. Rates are furnished upon request. Second-class postage paid at Washington, D.C. POSTMASTER: Send address changes to The CQ Researcher, 1414 22nd St., N.W., Washington, D.C. 20037.

Debate Over Bilingualism

BY CRAIG DONEGAN

THE ISSUES

A Texas judge outraged supporters of bilingual education last summer when he ruled that the mother of a 5-year-old girl was abusing her daughter by speaking to her only in Spanish. "If she starts first grade with the other children and cannot even speak the language that the teachers and the other children speak . . . you're abusing that child and you're relegating her to the position of house maid," said District Judge Samuel C. Kiser. [1]

In a year that saw large cuts in federal funding for bilingual education and several congressional proposals to make English the nation's official language, Kiser's comments grabbed national headlines and exposed raw nerves.

The National Council of La Raza, the nation's leading Hispanic organization, and the National Association for Bilingual Education (NABE) demanded an immediate apology. [2] The Congressional Hispanic Caucus condemned Kiser for "labeling the Spanish language as abuse." [3]

Even the organization U.S. English, a leader of the official-English movement, termed Kiser's statement "well-intentioned, but misguided."

Two weeks after his controversial ruling, Kiser apologized to the nation's housekeepers, whom "I hold . . . in the highest esteem." Yet he emphatically defended his ruling, adding that it actually would help the little girl "to be truly bilingual."

To many observers, the episode was but the latest indication of growing nativism in the U.S. In fact, some think that it's motivated by ethnic and racial prejudice and that support for official English and opposition to bilingual education provide the movement's leaders with a socially acceptable cover.

"It is certainly more respectable to discriminate by language than by race," says education writer James Crawford, author of the 1993 book *Hold Your Tongue: Bilingualism and the Politics of "English Only."* "Most people are not sensitive to language discrimination in this nation, so it is easy to argue that you're doing someone a favor by making them speak English."

To the degree that official English succeeds, he says, "we'll be a much more divided society in which newcomers are at a perpetual disadvantage."

A month after the Texas flap, Senate Majority Leader Bob Dole, R-Kan., the leading Republican presidential candidate, endorsed official English. Addressing the American Legion, Dole said that U.S. schools must teach immigrant children English and "stop the practice of multilingual education as a means of instilling ethnic pride or as a therapy for low self-esteem or out of elitist guilt over a culture built on the traditions of the West." [4]

House Speaker Newt Gingrich, R-Ga., writes in his 1995 book *To Renew America* that "Without English as a common language, there is no [American] civilization."

Such statements make bilingual-education advocates see red. They charge that proponents of official English and cutting bilingual programs don't understand the difference between common language and common values, and blindly support the outmoded idea of a cultural melting pot.

The campaign against multilingualism is "mean-spirited," said Rep. Jose E. Serrano, D-N.Y. "It's being done for cheap political trickery to get your so-called angry white male even angrier now." [5] Last summer, Serrano introduced an "English-Plus" resolution calling for recognition of English as the nation's common language but supporting bilingual education and multilingualism.

"The agenda of English only is hard-core anti-immigrant," says Crawford, citing a U.S. English survey that revealed "pretty openly anti-Hispanic attitudes" among the group's members.

Official-English backers are comparable to "Nazis, the Klan, skinheads and other boosters of the master race," writer Andrew Ward noted in *The Washington Post* recently. Their message to immigrants is "that they are not welcome here until they have ceased to discomfit the rest of us with their strangeness." [6]

In response to Ward, Dole wrote that, "Promoting English as our national language is not an act of hostility but a welcoming act of inclusion." Dole argued that some leaders of the bilingual establishment have corrupted the intent of the 1968 Bilingual Education Act, which sought to make children with limited English proficiency (LEP) fluent in English. Today, Dole noted, bilingualism supporters are pressing for "long-term exercises in native-language instruction." And that means "thousands of children [are] failing to learn the language, English, that is the ticket to the American dream." [7]

Official-English supporters say their adversaries are liberal elitists who want

States Where English Is the Official Language

Nearly half the states (in blue) have laws designating English as their official language, and many others are considering such measures. In addition, several bills in Congress urge adoption of English as the federal government's official language.

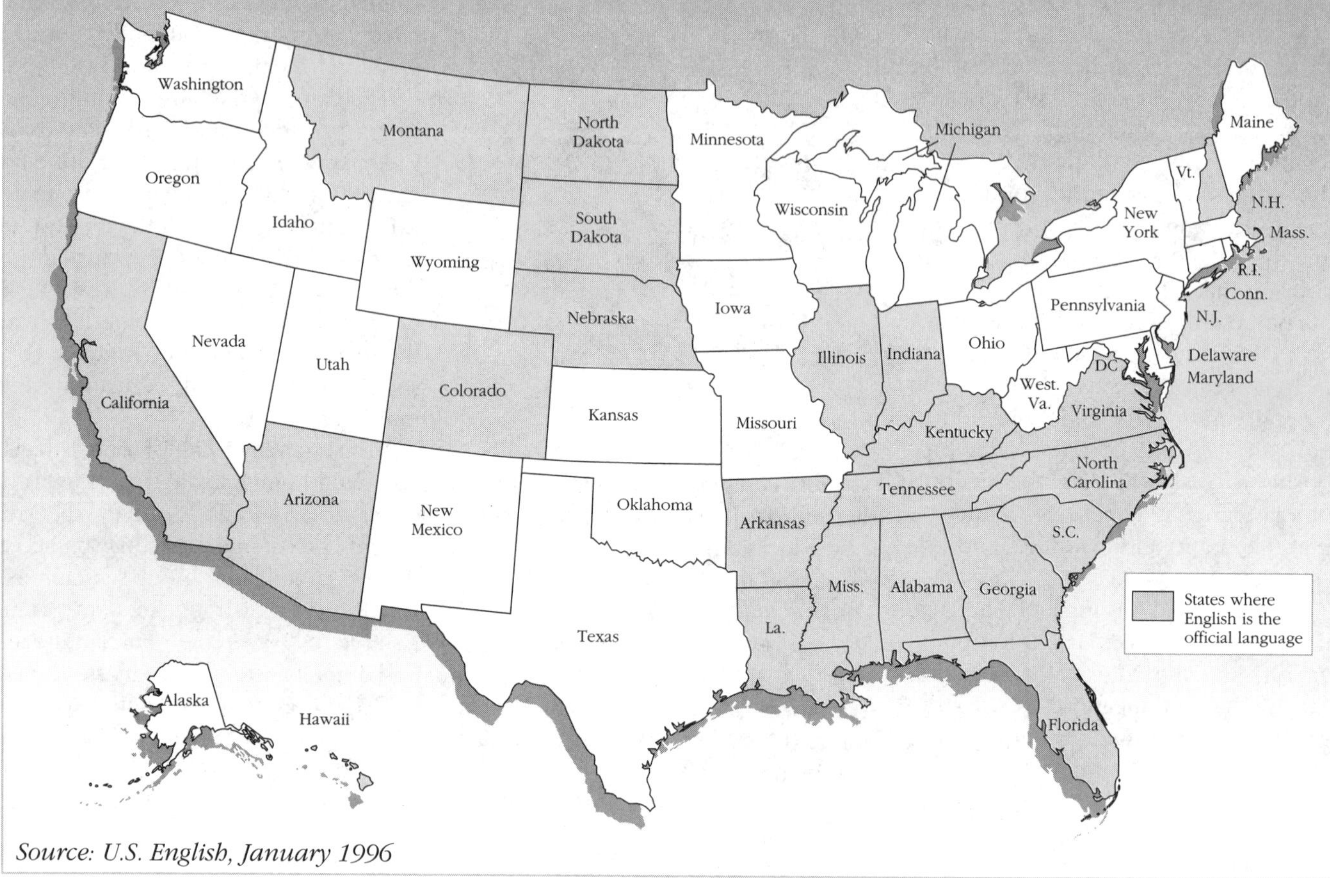

Source: U.S. English, January 1996

to separate Americans into warring ethnic camps, confined to language ghettos, isolated from economic opportunity and contemptuous of U.S. culture. They also accuse the bilingual camp of wanting to explode the cultural melting pot that has made the United States a relatively peaceful society derived from many cultures.

"Only those who are ripping off . . . government programs, like bilingual education . . . are opposed" to official English, says Rep. Toby Roth, R-Wis., sponsor of an official-English bill. [8]

Already, 22 states have passed laws or constitutional amendments making English their official language. Yet in Arizona, the 9th U.S. Circuit Court of Appeals on Oct. 5, 1995, upheld a lower court ruling that the state's official-English provision violates the U.S. Constitution's First Amendment (*see p. 63*).

At the national level, at least six official-English bills and one constitutional amendment have been proposed in the House and Senate (*see p. 63*). Congressional action is expected after hearings in January.

Most official-English supporters also want to reform or abolish bilingual education. "It's a disaster now," says Sally Peterson, a kindergarten teacher in Los Angeles and former bilingualism advocate. "It's not a bilingual-education program. It's a Spanish-development program." [9]

At the Center for Equal Opportunity (CEO), which backs official English, Communications Director Jorge Amselle says, however, that "Official English is pointless without reforming bilingual education and other bilingual policies. Of the 22 states with official-English laws, only Alabama actually reduces [official] multilingualism" by offering driver's license exams in English only.

"The flip side is California, which has an official-English constitutional amendment but sees multilingualism continuing to increase," Amselle adds. "If that's all that's going to happen, then what's the point" of passing such laws?

Yet even when bilingual programs do work, critics claim that total immersion in English-language classrooms is pedagogically more sound and culturally more desirable.

Proponents of bilingualism counter that long-term studies now prove that quality bilingual instruction works better than other methods for teaching LEP students. Also, they say, two-way classes — in which half the children speak English — work best of all and even should be used to promote bilingualism among native English-speakers.

They also argue that eliminating bilingualism could wipe out advances — such as bilingual ballots — in civil rights and voting-rights legislation over the past 30 years.

In response, the Congressional Hispanic Caucus has introduced English-plus legislation, and the San Antonio, Texas, City Council recently adopted a similar resolution. (*See story, p. 60.*)

Still, the forces of bilingualism may be losing ground. Last summer, Congress cut $38.5 million from the $195.2 million fiscal 1995 bilingual-education budget. In proposals for fiscal 1996, the House only offered $53 million for the program, and the Senate Appropriations Committee proposed $123 million; the White House has asked for about $200 million. At least two official-English bills before Congress propose eliminating the Department of Education's Office of Bilingual Education and Minority Language Affairs. That would leave bilingual education to state and local governments and rob bilingualism of the federal commitment proponents say it should have.

As lawmakers and education experts debate the issue, here are some of the questions being asked:

Does bilingual education hamper a student's ability to learn English and move into the mainstream?

It is one thing to say bilingual education does or does not work. It is another to prove it.

Measuring success in the world of bilingual education is a relatively new art. And that means researchers are just now amassing enough data to analyze students' long-term performance.

To complicate matters, opponents differ about how to measure failure or success. Are student exit rates from bilingual, immersion or ESL (English as a second language) programs after just three years reliable indicators of how well a program works? * Is English proficiency a good gauge of success? Must researchers follow LEP students over years of schooling to measure not just how well they learn English but how well they learn other subjects?

The varieties of bilingual education offer another challenge to researchers seeking the best teaching methods. (*See story, p. 54.*)

Bilingual proponents cite research being done by Virginia Collier and Wayne P. Thomas of George Mason University in Fairfax, Va. They are completing an analysis of studies that examined 42,000 students over the past 13 years to discover which ways of teaching English to non-English-speaking children work best.

So far, they say, their findings confirm earlier studies that show two-way classes are superior. Such classes help students gain knowledge in complex subjects while developing fluency in a second language over seven to 10 years. After about the fourth grade, students in two-way classes even outperform native-English speakers in English-only classes.

"During the Spanish part of the day, Spanish-speaking students explain lessons to native-English peers," Collier says. "During the English part of the day, the roles reverse. There is constant peer tutoring going on."

Collier stresses that unlike some traditional bilingual programs, two-way programs never segregate students from the kids who speak English. Rather, they encourage students to depend on one another for help, which fosters respect for each other's language and culture.

Opponents of bilingualism, however, say the new studies are not comprehensive enough to show that bilingual education works better than other methods of teaching English to LEP students. That's partly because the notion of native-language instruction is misconceived, says Amselle of the CEO.

"It is true that people already literate in one language become literate in a second language faster," he says. "But bilingual education's methodology has turned this truth on its head by taking students literate in no language and making them literate in their native language, and then making them literate in English. Approaches that focus almost entirely on native-language instruction are crippling the children's educational opportunities."

The spring 1995 issue of *The American Experiment,* the CEO's quarterly newsletter, highlights recent studies that flunk bilingual-education programs. One, a four-year New York City study released in 1994, found that ESL students achieved English proficiency and left their programs faster than those enrolled in bilingual classes.

A two-year California study by the Little Hoover Commission, a state watchdog agency, reported similar findings and noted that "native-language instruction has been divisive, wasteful and unproductive."

Finally, the CEO cited an El Paso, Texas, study showing that LEP students in English-immersion classes enter the educational mainstream in three to four years compared with six to seven years for bilingual students and score better on tests in subjects other than English proficiency.

Critics also say that many bilingual-education programs perpetuate the students' original language and promote non-native cultures at the expense of English.

---

* Under federal guidelines, students are expected to be mainstreamed into all-English classes after three years of bilingual education.

Teaching English to Non-English Speakers . . .

The primary goal of bilingual education in the United States is to teach English to students who don't speak English or have limited English proficiency (LEP). Several approaches are used to teach LEP students, some of which borrow methodology from or overlap with others:

Transitional bilingual education (TBE) aims to move LEP students into mainstream classes within two or three years. Such programs teach students subject matter in their native language as needed for them to keep up with their English-speaking peers while enrolling them in special classes that teach them ***English as a second language*** (ESL). Teacher skills and program designs determine how much native-language instruction students receive.

Most bilingual classes are taught using the ***transitional method***, which does not aim to preserve or enhance students' native language while teaching them English. But bilingual proponents who prefer ***developmental bilingual education*** (DBE) call the transitional approach "subtractive" because it doesn't maintain a student's native language. Such critics prefer DBE because it is designed to increase the student's native-language skills by teaching the student in his or her native language plus English at least through the sixth grade. The idea, they say, is to teach ***additive bilingualism***, which makes students fluent in two languages while making them more nimble learners.

Educators who prefer this approach argue that it is the best way to help students achieve what is called cognitive-academic language proficiency over a period of five to seven years. Supporters say this method is superior to learning basic interpersonal communication skills ("playground English"), which they argue is essentially what students learn in transitional classes.

The most sophisticated developmental approach is called ***two-way bilingual education.*** It mixes non-native English-speaking students with roughly an equal number of native-English speakers in the same classroom where, generally, students are taught in one language in the morning and the other language in the afternoon. This approach aims to make both sets of students bilingual at levels of fluency that allow each to advance to or above grade level in learning languages and other subjects. Such programs are rare, but where they exist, and where they have well-trained bilingual teachers (teachers fluent in both languages and who use interactive or group-learning techniques), most researchers and observers say that students perform better at every level of learning than their peers, no matter what kind of instruction the non-two-way students receive.

Immersion education sits near the other end of the bilingual-teaching spectrum. In these classes — broadly known as ***special alternative instructional programs,*** the most popular of which is ***structured immersion*** — students learn their second language from instructors who teach them subject matter presented in the new language. Teaching is geared toward the child's ability to comprehend the lessons based on clues instructors give to coax the students through their lessons. Ideally, the students absorb or learn grammar as well as vocabulary in the process. While immersion is based on instruction in the student's second language, it is not what is generally called "sink-or-swim" — in which teachers offer no special help in learning the new language and which the U.S. Supreme Court, in *Lau v. Nichols* (1974), declared a violation of federal civil rights law.

One popular offshoot of immersion education is called ***alternate immersion*** — also known as ***sheltered English*** or ***sheltered subject-matter instruction.*** In sheltered classes, children learn their second language first by studying subjects,

"When bilingual education was being considered by Congress, it had a limited mission: to teach children of Mexican descent in Spanish while they learned English," writes CEO President Linda Chavez. "Instead, it has become an expensive behemoth, often with a far-reaching political agenda: to promote Spanish among Hispanic children — regardless of whether they speak English or not, regardless of their parents' wishes and even without their knowledge." [10]

Bilingualism's defenders respond that the New York, California and El Paso studies are flawed and, in some ways, dishonest.

"In the New York study, there was no attempt to account for variables such as the children's socio-economic status," says Crawford. Children from families with more education, higher income and better living conditions will naturally do better than children with fewer advantages, he says.

Moreover, says Crawford, the studies do not consider the need for "long-term academic achievement and life chances for kids who come to school speaking little or no English. How fast they learn English is not important for long-term achievement. Academic research shows that cognitive academic language is more complex and takes longer [than three years] to learn," he says.

NABE Executive Director Bill Lyons agrees. "Leaders of English First and U.S. English are myopic in their concentration on speed over content," Lyons says. "When it comes to interest and achievement, speed kills."

Collier is particularly critical of the New York study, which has gotten more publicity than the others. In addition to using exit rates to measure academic success, she says the New York report did not reveal that students with the most formal education were placed in ESL classes while those with less education were shunted into bilingual classes. "If you were to choose one key

... Offers a Wide Range of Techniques

such as math, that are less language-intensive. As they learn more English, they move to more language-intensive subjects such as social studies. This approach sometimes involves the ***preview-review method,*** in which a lesson is taught once in the first language and then again in the second language (frequently by a different teacher) with a lag between the two lessons of as much as a full day.

Concurrent translation is a popular alternative to sheltered English, although researchers have found that its effectiveness is limited. That's because, they say, children tend only to absorb what is said in their first language and teachers tend to favor one language over the other, which causes the instruction to be unbalanced.

Because there is a severe shortage of qualified bilingual teachers, and because in some schools the variety of languages students speak is so great, ***ESL*** instruction — which generally means offering "pull-out classes" for language minority students a few times a week — is used widely.

The most basic ESL instruction encourages students to learn grammar and translation through memorization, writing and other drills. Another approach, ***communication-based ESL,*** emphasizes learning language in context at a level where the student is most likely to comprehend the teacher's speech when combined with physical cues about the content of the lesson being taught. In communication-based ESL, teachers ease students toward an understanding of their second language by creating a non-threatening classroom atmosphere and involving reluctant students gradually.

When Congress reauthorized the Bilingual Education Act in 1994, it also collapsed its 1984 definition of transitional bilingual and developmental bilingual education into a single category and added a provision for special alternative instructional programs as well.

Gone is a TBE provision mandating that teachers in schools that receive federal bilingual funds "incorporate the cultural heritage of [LEP] children and of other children in American society," since the new wording focuses on language alone.

Under the 1994 provisions, bilingual education instructs LEP students in English and their native languages; is geared toward making them proficient in English while mastering subject matter at the appropriate grade level; allows for development of native or ancestral languages of LEP students along with special groups of people including American Indians, Alaska Natives and Native Hawaiians; and sanctions two-way bilingual programs.

Congress also added ***special alternative instructional programs*** (SAIP) for LEP students, which allow English-only instruction in schools where there are few such students or students speak many different languages, or where there is a shortage of qualified bilingual education teachers. [1]

As these final changes suggest, the trend in federal bilingual-education legislation has evolved from simply guaranteeing equal access to public education to ensuring native-language instruction and the teaching of LEP students' cultural heritage to approval of a wider variety of approaches. These allow for, among other things, English-only instruction, teaching LEP students' in both English and their native languages and encouraging language maintenance and bilingual learning among LEP and native-English speakers enrolled together in two-way classes.

---

[1] James Crawford, *Bilingual Education: History, Politics, Theory and Practice* (1995), 3d Edition, pp. 243-48.

predictor of how well students will do in these settings, it would be how much formal schooling they have had before they entered the program," says Collier. "Consequently, they were comparing apples and oranges."

The El Paso study, Collier says, followed one ESL and one bilingual class, but students in both classes received the same amount of native-language instruction. The difference between them was that the bilingual class was taught in traditional lecture style and the ESL was built around interactive learning, which stacked the deck in favor of the ESL students.

Even then, she says, "One study tells you nothing. You must have 100 empirical studies to know there is a strong pattern of success or failure in a particular method of teaching or learning. That's because humans themselves are so variable."

Collier adds that, among the studies she has reviewed, students receiving bilingual education consistently do best in the long run. This, she says, is because non-English-speaking students taught mainly in English fall behind in content learning. That leaves them to play catch-up in the later grades. Bilingual learners, she says, do not have that handicap.

Opponents counter that bilingual education frequently segregates students during the school day, which slows assimilation and throws up barriers between different language groups. Immersion classes are superior in part because, when students are segregated, it is for brief periods of time. Moreover, opponents argue, immersion students are fully competent to understand lessons in English after three years of instruction, which allows them to move more quickly than bilingual students into the mainstream of English-language learning.

Should Congress eliminate federal funding for bilingual

How Americans Feel About Bilingual Education

Which of these three statements comes closest to your views on bilingual education?

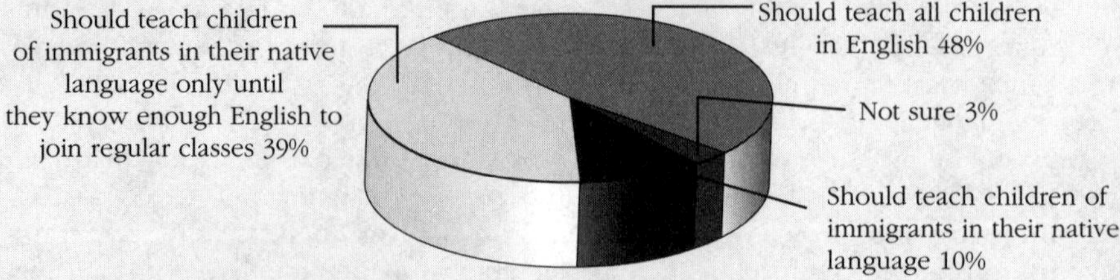

Are you strongly in favor of bilingual education, somewhat in favor of it, somewhat opposed to it or strongly opposed to it?

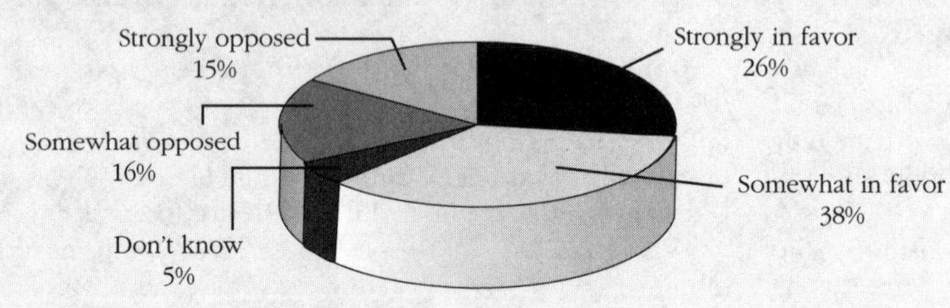

Do you think there should be a law making English the official language of the U.S.?

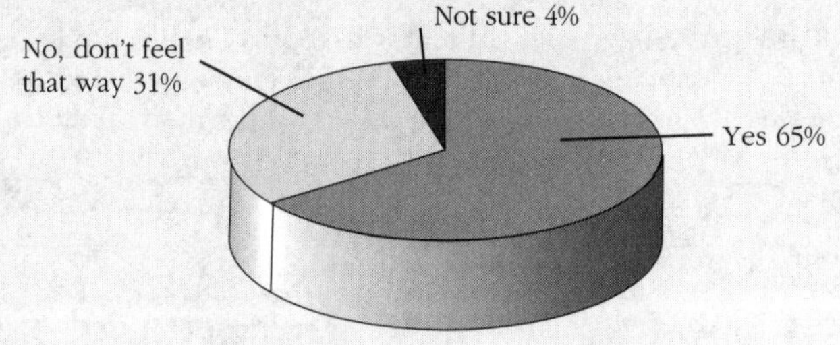

Sources: Roper Center for Public Opinion Research; Time/*CNN/Yankelovich Partners, September 1995 (questions 1 and 3); National Opinion Research Center, January-May 1994 (question 2)*

education in the schools?

In a Feb. 23, 1995, letter to his House colleagues, Rep. Peter T. King, R-N.Y., explained why he thinks bilingualism has gone too far. "Since the late 1960s, with bilingual education, bilingual ballots [and] bilingual signs on government buildings, we have been encouraging immigrants not to learn English," he wrote. "In fact, we are giving them the false security of their native tongue and confining them to permanent ghettos." [11]

Two days before sending his letter, King introduced the National Language Act of 1995 — the most sweeping official-English legislation submitted so far in the 104th Congress. In addition to calling for English as the nation's official language, King's bill would repeal the Bilingual Education Act, terminate the Office of Bilingual Education and excise bilingual provisions that have been added to the Voting Rights Act of 1965. It also would override existing state laws and regulations that involve the government in multilingualism or mandate bilingual education. [12]

English First prefers King's bill and similar House legislation introduced by Rep. Roth. On the other hand, U.S. English Chairman Mauro Mujica prefers what he calls the "rational" Language of Government legislation introduced by Sen. Richard C. Shelby, R-Ala., and Rep. Bill Emerson, R-Mo. It advocates use of official English by the federal government only and does not suggest changes in bilingual education or the Education Department. Such matters, says Mujica, are better kept separate from the official-English debate.

King's bill reflects actions Congress already has taken to scale back federal funding for bilingual education. The cuts have come for a variety of reasons, including the belief among critics that bilingual education has failed both to turn LEP children into English readers, writers and speakers and to cut the drop-out rate among Hispanic students.

"Bilingual education started out in 1968 as a modest $7.5 million pilot program to help Mexican-American children learn English. Today it's a $5 billion boondoggle [including federal, state and local funds] that actually prevents kids from acquiring the language that will determine their economic and social success as adults," writes Rosalie Pedalino Porter, author of the 1990 book *Forked Tongue: The Politics of Bilingual Education* and chairman of the Institute for Research in English Acquisition and Development (READ). [13]

Federal funding is only a small fraction of the total amount spent on bilingual education today. "Let us be clear at the outset that the federal subsidy of bilingual education is small (6 percent of all funds spent on programs for limited-English students) and that the federal government has not imposed a mandate on any school district to provide a certain type of program," says a READ report prepared for U.S. English in 1995. [14]

Nevertheless, says READ, the Office of Bilingual Education has "vigorously promoted programs of native-language instruction over any other educational approach." Indeed, 75 percent of all bilingual federal funds go to native-language instruction. Because the very name Bilingual Education Act gives de facto official support to native-language instruction, READ and U.S. English propose renaming it as the English Learners Act and making more funds available to a wider variety of programs.

"Instead of eradicating all the funds for children who don't speak English, we advocate block grants to schools so they can determine the best methods for teaching these children," said Daphne Magnuson, a spokeswoman for U.S. English.[15]

While bilingual-education supporters generally say that schools should be allowed to choose programs, they argue that by cutting bilingual funds Congress undermines grants needed to start new bilingual programs, train bilingual teachers and finance studies in the field. Rather than scrap programs whose weaknesses are dictated by local circumstances, such as shortages of qualified teachers or misclassification of LEP students, they say bolster what works — the teaching methods Collier and Thomas describe.

Ultimately, then, the fight over funding hinges on whether bilingual education works. Rep. Roth says it not only has failed but also has damaged the students it purports to serve. "There is nothing that harms youngsters or holds them back, makes them second-class citizens as much as bilingual education," Roth told his House colleagues in July.[16]

Proponents of cuts also note that polls show immigrant families want their children to learn English first and complain that children often are railroaded into bilingual classes where they do not belong. Dominga Sanchez, for example, recalled that when her son Javier was a third-grader, he was moved into classes where he was taught in Spanish, though he spoke English fluently.

When Sanchez, a Puerto Rican by birth, begged the teacher to let her son return to regular classes, she was rebuffed with this question: "Why? Don't you feel proud to be Hispanic?"[17]

Bilingual-education opponents say such examples are proof that bilingual education no longer is a language program but a vehicle for divisive multiculturalism whose goal is teaching the Spanish language and transmitting Hispanic culture.

Official-English supporters say U.S. culture is blowing apart at the seams and that the unifying force of a common language — English — is threatened by multilingualism's tendency to separate and alienate U.S. citizens from one another.

Writer Crawford disagrees. "Immigrants are learning English more rapidly than ever," he says. "Minority languages are the ones that are threatened by English — not the other way around."

As to the wisdom of cutting federal support for bilingual education, "It would be a disaster," George Mason's Collier says. "That's because the state's wouldn't take up the responsibility. They're overwhelmed already."

Should Congress declare English the nation's official language?

At one level, the debate over official English seems largely symbolic. With the exception of Alabama, the states with official-English laws continue to do business as usual. At another level, the debate is substantive: Official-English laws eventually could change the way the government communicates with citizens and how citizens exercise their rights.

Official-English supporters say U.S. culture is blowing apart at the seams and that the unifying force of a common language — English — is threatened by multilingualism's tendency to separate and alienate U.S. citizens from one another.

"The purveyors of political correctness have been successful in instituting big-government programs to actively dissuade new immigrants from learning English," said Rep. King.[18] "Current law actually mandates multilingual programs and services. The U.S. Department of Education requires bilingual classes be provided to schoolchildren."

King notes that city and state governments sanction public signs in various languages; that driver's license tests in New York City are administered in 21 languages and schools are taught in 115 languages besides English; and that ballots in Los Angeles are in six languages.

Rep. Emerson charged in December that the "federal government has sanctioned and promoted what amounts to unofficial multilingualism."[19] If Congress doesn't quit supporting multilingualism and start promoting English, he said, the government will have created a "linguistic welfare" system.

Jim Boulet Jr., executive director of English First, noted that during the 1960s the federal government "turn[ed] its back on two centuries of successful assimilation of immigrants" by making "bilingual education, bilingual ballots and other forms of multilingual mandates . . . the law of the land."[20]

Boulet, who said that official-English legislation should abolish bilingual ballots, called bilingual education "unique among federal programs in that it makes no one happy. It doesn't work, immigrants oppose it and taxpayers despise it."

Beyond that, says Stanley Diamond, chairman of the National English Campaign and the California English Campaign, all immigrants to the United States "have a duty . . . to understand and respect our system, including our language. And our duty as citizens is to provide facilities, opportunities, encouragement and funding for the integration and Americanization of immigrants."

Official-English would halt the "tribalization" of U.S. culture, diminish separatism and reinforce the shared values of a common culture, supporters say. Some point to the secession movement in Quebec, Canada, and the fragmentation of the former Yugoslavia to show how official bilingualism or multilingualism can tear a nation apart.

All the talk about tribalism and the unifying power of language angers defenders of bilingualism. English is the language of 97 percent of U.S. citizens, they say, as well as the dominant language of commerce, technology and diplomacy worldwide.

Despite their anger, bilingualism proponents on occasion have used humor and ridicule to answer their critics. In Texas, they describe their monolingual adversaries as "bi-ignorant." U.S. House Del. Robert A. Underwood, D-Guam, in October threatened to propose a ketchup-only bill after news reports said salsa had become America's most popular condiment. [21]

More seriously, Collier says that attempts to legislate official English are rooted in the mistaken assumption that immigrants are not learning English fast enough. But, she says, "socio-linguistic studies show that acquisition of English and loss of the first language occur in the second generation for most immigrant groups," even among Spanish speakers, the group most frequently cited as anti-assimilationist.

Also, says Collier, whether young students learn English through native-language bilingual instruction or through ESL classes, by the fourth grade they know that English is the language of power and adopt it regardless of what their teachers want them to do.

Raul Yzaguirre, president of La Raza, notes that official-English supporters actually are pushing policies that end up doing what they accuse bilingualists of doing. "This legislation is divisive and discriminatory, and it invites frivolous litigation," says Yzaguirre. "We already have a common language, and it is English. Let's spend our energies, therefore, in truly helping people to learn English rather than debating this unnecessary legislation." [22]

As to what holds the nation together, NABE's Lyons says it is not language, but "American ideals of freedom, democracy and tolerance." [23]

Lyons also contends that the "English-only" debate isn't about the importance of English. Rather it is about "new government regulations on language use," he says.

Crawford agrees. "Inherent in the idea of legalizing a single language for public use [is] the restriction, to a greater or lesser extent, of other languages," he writes. "However one [tries] to dress this up, it [is] a program of exclusion and coercion." [24]

Lyons argues that multilingualism should be treated as a natural resource since it is essential for success in international markets, where producers must understand the customs and the cultures of their customers.

Moreover, Lyons says, it is odd that Rep. Roth, as chair of the Congressional Travel and Tourism Caucus, should be so enthusiastic about making English the nation's official language. With foreign travelers expected to have spent approximately $535 billion in the United States in 1995, Lyons says he is puzzled by "English-only legislation" that would mandate removal of foreign-language signs designed to help tourists. [25]

Ultimately, opponents say, official English would damage U.S. traditions of ethnic and cultural diversity protected by the Constitution. And, they warn, it would show the world that the United States had become a frail and quaking giant immobilized by fear in a rapidly shrinking world. ■

Background

Early Concerns

When the first European settlers arrived in North America, they brought a diversity of cultures and languages — from Spanish-speaking Roman Catholics to English, French and Dutch Protestants, Catholics and Quakers. Eager to convert the Native Americans they encountered, Catholics in the South and Puritans in the North combined bilingual education with evangelism to communicate and transmit their religion and culture. The Puritans even built bilingual schools to provide instruction to the native populations in Massachusetts and Rhode Island.

Depending upon one's point of view, the new settlers either wanted to share their culture with others or obliterate the culture of people they did not understand, and whom they feared. Either way, the new settlers sought to survive not only physically but also culturally. Common language was deemed essential.

During the Revolutionary period, some Colonials entertained notions of making German, French, Greek, Hebrew, or even an entirely new tongue the official language of the emerging nation. Roger Sherman, a member of

Continued on p. 60

Chronology

Early 1900s

State and federal laws limit immigration and require schoolchildren to learn English.

1906
Congress requires immigrants to speak English in order to become naturalized citizens.

1917
Wartime hostility toward Germany sparks state legislation to limit or ban German-language instruction in schools.

1923
U.S. Supreme Court rules in *Meyer v. Nebraska* that the state's interest in fostering "a homogeneous people with American ideals" is not adequate justification for outlawing foreign-language instruction in the public schools.

May 26, 1924
Congress passes the Immigration Quota Act primarily to reduce the number of immigrants from Eastern and Southern Europe.

1960s-1990s

The rise of the bilingual-education movement sparks an ongoing battle in the courts and Congress.

1963
Dade County, Fla., institutes bilingual public school program for Cuban refugees, sparking similar programs in Texas, California and other states.

Oct. 30-31, 1966
National Education Association launches the bilingual-education movement at a conference in Tucson, Ariz.

1968
Congress passes the Bilingual Education Act (Title VII of the Elementary and Secondary Education Act) to help stem the high dropout rate among Hispanics.

Jan. 21, 1974
U.S. Supreme Court rules unanimously in *Lau v. Nichols* that schools denying special instructional materials to limited-English-proficiency (LEP) students may be violating the 1964 Civil Rights Act.

1975
Congress extends the 1965 Voting Rights Act to include language minorities and to require bilingual voting procedures in areas where a significant number of voters do not speak English.

1980
Dade County prohibits use of public funds for teaching in languages other than English.

1984
New York state education reforms include foreign-language requirements for all students and allow non-native English speakers academic credit for proficiency in their native language.

1984
Congress extends the Bilingual Education Act through 1988 creating new programs to help students maintain their native languages after learning English.

1984
California voters approve Proposition 38 opposing the federal Voting Rights Act's provision for bilingual ballots. In *Soberal-Perez v. Heckler,* the 2nd U.S. Circuit Court of Appeals rules that non-English speakers can't compel government to provide information in languages other than English.

Sept. 26, 1985
Education Secretary William Bennett calls the Bilingual Education Act "a bankrupt course" in which "too many children have failed to become fluent in English."

1986
California voters overwhelmingly approve Proposition 63, the first official-English measure passed by ballot initiative.

1993
Scholars at Stanford University create a "Blueprint for the Second Generation" endorsing equal opportunity for language-minority students and the right of all U.S. students to acquire proficiency in more than one language.

1994
President Clinton endorses the Stanford Working Group's "Blueprint." Congress passes the Improving America's Schools Act, which changes federal grant provisions for the Bilingual Education Act and Emergency Immigration Education Act.

1995
At least six bills are introduced in Congress to make English the official U.S. language or abolish government-mandated bilingual education. On July 13, Rep. Jose E. Serrano, D-N.Y., introduces his "English-Plus Resolution" to counter the official-English bills. In the fall, Sen. Bob Dole, R-Kan., and Speaker of the House Newt Gingrich, R-Ga., declare support for official English and warn that multilingualism threatens the nation's cultural unity and political stability. On Oct. 5, in a 6-5 ruling, the 9th U.S. Circuit Court of Appeals rules in *Yniguez v. Mofford* that Arizona's official-English law violates the free-speech provision of the First Amendment.

Texas Acknowledges Its Unique Hispanic Heritage . . .

Sixty-one percent of Texans surveyed in October 1995 agreed that the Lone Star State needs a law similar to California's Proposition 187, which bars illegal or undocumented aliens from receiving government services.

However, The Texas Poll also found that 53 percent thought that certain public school classes should be bilingual while 45 percent thought that they should be in English only, and 44 percent said they support passage of an English-only law. [1]

Republican Gov. George W. Bush, who has said the state will keep its commitment to bilingual education, said that Texas should "enforce the border," but it should not deny schooling to any child who seeks it. "I believe we ought to educate the children," he said.

Speaking a month before a federal court ruled that California may not deny elementary or high school education to the children of illegal aliens, Bush warned that Texas does not want the "harsh isolationist rhetoric" of the 1996 presidential campaign to damage his state's relations with Mexico or any other Latin American nation. [2]

Bush's position is supported by San Antonio Mayor Bill Thornton and City Councilman Juan Solis 3d, who on Nov. 9, 1995, got unanimous approval from the council for a resolution "supporting citizens' right to live and prosper in a multilingual society."

The resolution, which cites San Antonio's multicultural history and its ties to Mexico and the rest of Latin America, declares that "legislation, initiatives, or resolutions designed to make English the official language would only serve to undermine the business, social and cultural traditions upon which this city was founded."

Citing San Antonio's desire for openness and flexibility, the resolution adds that the city "will encourage and support a multilingual environment (English-Plus) wherein persons of all ethnicities and races will not be discouraged from speaking the languages of their forefathers."

The resolution will have no direct effect on the city's independent school districts, which are directed by elected school boards, not city hall.

San Antonio — the 10th largest city in the United States — is more than 60 percent Hispanic, the majority Mexican-American. Solis, whose council district is 94 percent Hispanic, says 70 percent of the entire city will be Hispanic by the year 2020.

Since Congress approved the North American Free Trade Agreement (NAFTA) in 1993, local civic and business leaders have promoted San Antonio (which is 150 miles from Laredo on the Texas/Mexico border) as the United States' gateway not just to Mexico but to Latin America.

The city was stunned last spring by military budget cuts and the federal government's decision to close the maintenance depot at Kelly Air Force Base, and Thornton now wants San Antonio to move aggressively on the trade front so it can "join the fraternity of world-trade centers," such as Hong Kong, Singapore, Amsterdam and Miami. [3]

"I was surprised when [Senate Majority leader and Republican presidential candidate] Bob Dole began talking about English, only because that made me realize this could become a national issue like Proposition 187 in California," says Thornton, "and I did not want that to happen in San Antonio."

Thornton and Solis sought input and support for their resolution from organizations including the Mexican American Legal Defense and Education Fund, the Lawyers Guild for Civil Rights, the American G.I. Forum, a Hispanic veterans group, and San Antonio's chambers of commerce.

Having solidified broad support from among such diverse groups, the Thornton/Solis initiative went unopposed — even by the city's conservative radio talk-show hosts — to the City Council.

"Our resolution is a counterbalance to California, which has told the rest of the world to check your culture and your language at the door,' " says Solis. "We ask them not to check their cultures at the border or to put their languages

Continued from p. 58

the Continental Congress from Connecticut, spoke for many when he said, sarcastically: "It would be more convenient for us to keep the language as it is and make the English speak Greek." [26]

In 1780, John Adams suggested creating an American academy to safeguard the purity of the English language — an idea that was quickly swept aside.

Out of necessity, bilingualism — and even multilingualism — remained the norm in North America throughout most of the 19th century. Before 1800, private schools for German-English bilingual education were common in the United States. French-language schools sprang up in the Northeast, and Dutch-language schools in the middle states.

Not everyone was sanguine about catering to the newcomers' needs. Thomas Jefferson, for instance, warned that European arrivals would bring anti-democratic principles and "with their language . . . transmit [these principles] to their children."

After the U.S. bought the Louisiana Territory from France, the territorial governor appointed by Jefferson declared English the language of local government in New Orleans. French-speaking residents were not pleased, and Jefferson told the governor to end the policy. "I think it visible that most of whatever discontent exists among the French inhabitants arises from the introduction of our language too suddenly," he wrote. [27]

Official-English Laws Prove Largely Symbolic

When Louisiana joined the union in

. . . and Gives Support to Bilingual Education

into their pockets. We ask them to bring their cultures and their dollars with them when they come to San Antonio."

"I want San Antonio to be a model for a future where business decisions are made in a world without borders," he adds.

Solis, who is secretary-treasurer of the Hispanic Elected Local Officials of the National League of Cities, says the nonpartisan group agreed during its annual meeting in Phoenix in December to promote San Antonio-style English-plus resolutions in cities and towns across the country. The aim is to counteract the local and state advances U.S. English has made in recent years.

Instead of being divisive, says Thornton, San Antonio's resolution "will bring social rest as opposed to social conflict, whereas English-only would bring out the worst qualities in people and would lead nowhere."

"I'm not trying to create a Tower of Babel," he says. "I'm simply recognizing the reality that San Antonio is a community of two languages — English and Spanish. If I lived in Seattle, Vancouver or Portland, I might be encouraging Japanese."

Yet such talk raises red flags among official-English supporters. Linda Chavez, president of the Center for Equal Opportunity (CEO), notes that Josué Gonzalez, who served as director of bilingual education in the Jimmy Carter administration, has written that Spanish "should no longer be regarded as a 'foreign' language."

Moreover, she says that Eugene E. Garcia, head of bilingual education at the U.S. Department of Education, has declared that "the border for many is nonexistent. For me, for intellectual reasons, the border shall be nonexistent."

During the National Association for Bilingual Education's annual meeting in February, Chavez writes, "several speakers challenged the idea of U.S. sovereignty and promoted the notion that the Southwest and Northern Mexico form one cultural region, which they dub La Frontera." There, according to some advocates, non-citizens should be allowed to vote in U.S. elections.[4]

CEO Communications Director Jorge Amselle takes Chavez' criticism a few steps further, suggesting secession is a possibility. Although bilingual advocates deny it, he says the division in Canada sparked by the secession movement in Quebec could repeat itself in the Southwestern United States.

"Both Quebec and the Southwest are conquered territories with distinct linguistic and cultural institutions and traditions," he says. "In Canada, 15 years after establishment of official bilingualism, Quebec began trying to separate. If we become officially bilingual in the Southwest, there might also be separatist tendencies.

"Already, the border is disappearing, with those on the political left fearing the effects of NAFTA and those on the right fearing cultural disintegration."

Also, he says, "there are political movements in Mexico saying that children born in the United States to Mexican citizens should retain Mexican citizenship, which would make them dual citizens of the United States and Mexico." The Mexican government, he adds, supports bilingual education in the Southwest.

Solis, however, says not to worry — that the children must be educated to make them productive citizens and that bilingual education will make them doubly productive and twice as valuable to an economy that relies increasingly on ties to Latin America.

"We're all patriots," he adds. "We're all Americans."

---

[1] The poll was conducted by the University of Texas Office of Survey Research for Harte-Hanks Communications Inc.

[2] Maria F. Duran, "Poll Shows Most Texans Favor a Law Like Prop 187," *San Antonio Express-News,* Nov. 4, 1995, p. 1A.

[3] Loydean Thomas, *San Antonio Express-News,* Nov. 1, 1995.

[4] Linda Chavez, "One Nation, One Common Language," *Reader's Digest,* August 1995.

1812, it made English the official language for all laws and official records. However, this did not stop the practice of publishing statutes and other public documents in French, too. In Louisiana's case, as in most others, declaring English the official language was a symbolic gesture with little impact.

In fact, throughout most of the 19th century, pragmatism in language laws as well as teaching practices ruled the day. Between 1839 and 1880, teachers used German, French and Spanish in schools in Ohio, Louisiana, New Mexico and elsewhere.

In the 1830s, the Republic of Texas printed laws in English and Spanish. The California constitution of 1849 required that laws be printed in English and Spanish. In 1851, a Los Angeles ordinance provided that "all the rudiments of the English and Spanish language shall be taught" in public schools. The Colorado territory in 1867 mandated bilingual teaching in all schools with 25 or more non-English-speaking students.

Yet in 1841 Texas changed its policy on bilingualism, abolishing the printing of laws in Spanish.

At the national level, the Indian Peace Commission of 1868 reported that American Indians remained resistant to U.S. culture partly because tribes clung to their native tongues. The commission's solution: "Schools should be established, which children should be required to attend; their barbarous dialects should be blotted out and the English language substituted."[28]

Immigration Intensifies Concerns About Assimilation

By century's end, the vast numbers of

Southern and Eastern European immigrants had made the issue of assimilation critical. The old Jeffersonian fears soon made their way into federal legislation that restricted immigration and imposed quotas, following World War I.

In 1919, *The New York Times* editorialized against teaching German to schoolchildren. Some states banned teaching any foreign language in the elementary schools, but the Nebraska Legislature passed the most restrictive language policy of the time when it outlawed teaching German under any circumstances. At war's end, 15 states declared English the basic language for teaching.

In 1923, however, the U.S. Supreme Court declared the Nebraska law unconstitutional. Relying on the 14th Amendment's due-process clause, the court ruled that the state's interest in fostering "a homogeneous people with American ideals" did not justify the Legislature's interference with the students' right to acquire knowledge, the teachers' right to practice their profession and the parents' right to shape the schooling of their offspring. [29]

From World War I through the early 1950s, bilingual education lay dormant while a number of states passed laws forbidding the use of languages other than English at school. In Texas, where until the 1960s most Hispanic students attended segregated schools, it was against the law to teach the lower grades in any language but English. After integration, and until the late 1960s, many districts forbade children to speak Spanish anywhere on school property.

Courts, Congress Act

Following World War II, the sudden discovery that American children had fallen behind their Russian counterparts, particularly in math and science, prompted Congress to pass the National Defense Education Act (1958), which included funds for teaching foreign languages. Soon after, Fidel Castro overthrew the Batista government in Cuba, after which thousands of refugees fled to Florida. Many gravitated to Dade County, changing the ethnic mix and making Miami the nation's bilingual capital.

In Texas, where until the 1960s most Hispanic students attended segregated schools, it was against the law to teach the lower grades in any language but English. After integration, and until the late 1960s, many districts forbade children to speak Spanish anywhere on school property.

The refugees revitalized bilingual education but changed its emphasis. Rather than being a transitional tool to help immigrants assimilate into U.S. culture, the Cubans wanted to preserve their native tongue and perpetuate their native culture. That was because the refugees wanted to go home — to Cuba — if only Castro would disappear.

Bilingual Education Act of 1968

At the same time, the civil rights movement prompted concern in the Southwest about high dropout rates among Mexican-Americans and hope that bilingual education might turn the numbers around. To that end, Sen. Ralph W. Yarborough, D-Texas, sponsored the Bilingual Education Act of 1968 (actually Title VII of the Elementary and Secondary Education Act). Yarborough's legislation was rooted in the Civil Rights Act of 1964, which outlawed discrimination based on a student's limited ability to use English.

Yet if the idea was to help Spanish-speaking students compete with their English-speaking peers, Yarborough made clear that the Mexican-American presence in South Texas was unique. For most immigrants, the "decision to come here carried with it a willingness to give up their language, everything," he said. "That wasn't true in the Southwest. We went in and took the people over, took over the land and culture. They had our culture superimposed on them. They did not consent to abandon their homeland and to come here and learn anew." [30]

Yarborough's 1968 proposal followed a series of state statutes that had established bilingual education in Massachusetts, New Mexico, Texas, California and other states.

Immigration reform also became a hot issue in the 1960s. Led by liberals such as Sen. Edward M. Kennedy, D-Mass., Congress passed immigration reforms that resulted in a flood of immigrants from Latin America, the Caribbean and Asia. Newcomers overwhelmed school districts with non-English-speaking students in need of instruction.

The U.S. Supreme Court re-entered the picture in 1974. In *Lau v. Nichols,* the court ruled that LEP children have the right, under the Civil Rights Act, to special help in learning English. Congress moved swiftly, passing legislation that same year that required native-language instruction for non-English-speaking students in school districts that applied for federal bilingual-education grants.

In 1975, Congress extended the 1965 Voting Rights Act to include language minorities, requiring bilingual voting assistance for people who need it and placing a permanent ban on literacy tests for voting.

To further improve educational opportunities for language-minority students, the 5th U.S. Circuit Court of Appeals in 1981 established a three-pronged test that LEP programs had to pass to satisfy the requirements of the Equal Educational Opportunities Act of 1974. The court held, in *Castaneda v. Pickard,* that programs for LEP students must be based on sound educational theory, that schools must make good-faith efforts to help the programs succeed and that they must monitor outcomes to determine whether they are successful.

National Mood Changes

The national mood toward accommodating language minorities began to change in the early 1980s, however, with the launch of President Ronald Reagan's conservative revolution. Political correctness on college campuses became a national symbol of liberal multiculturalism gone haywire, as legal and illegal immigrants from war-torn Central America and impoverished Mexico put unprecedented demands on U.S. schools, hospitals and social-service agencies.

For Americans alarmed by such developments, language became a symbol, and an issue. Since 1981, every session of Congress has considered at least one constitutional amendment to make English the official language. And in 1983, Sen. S.I. Hayakawa, R-Calif., a Japanese-American linguistics expert, responded by founding U.S. English. A year later, Dade County made English its official language.

To date, the toughest and most publicized reaction to the increase in language minorities is California's Proposition 187, approved by voters in 1994. The landslide vote echoed the 73 percent majority that passed Proposition 63 in 1986, making English the state's official language.

Although Proposition 187 sought to end most government services to illegal or undocumented aliens, in November 1995 a federal court ruled that the state could not deny public education to resident children regardless of their status.[31]

The court's ruling, coupled with the 1990 Native American Language Act, which helps preserve indigenous languages, signals the hardiness of the pro-bilingual movement. Dade County, for example, in 1993 repealed its 1984 ordinance declaring English the official language. In addition, the Congressional Hispanic Caucus has submitted an English-plus resolution to Congress, and last November the San Antonio City Council unanimously opposed official English. ■

CURRENT SITUATION

Test Case in Arizona

The debate over official English and bilingual education is nothing if not emotional, but adversaries ultimately must deal with serious legal issues. Nowhere is this clearer than in Arizona, where the official-English law required legislators, judges and other state employees to conduct official business in English. But in its October ruling, the 9th Circuit called the law unconstitutional and inefficient. (On Dec. 20, an organization called English Language Advocates petitioned the Supreme Court to review the circuit court's ruling.)

The court ruled that the law's wording was not narrow or specific enough to permit non-English speech "when reasonable to facilitate the day-to-day operation of the government." That, according to the court, made the state government less efficient than it would be without the law.

There also was a "realistic danger," the judges said, that the state's "sweeping English-only mandate" might have a "chilling" effect on the First Amendment "speech rights of all . . . state and local employees, officials and other officers."[32]

U.S. English disagrees, arguing that official English does not violate free-speech rights but "merely limits the circumstances where the government provides services in languages other than English." Moreover, the group says, official English "promotes unity, streamlines government and . . . empowers immigrants. U.S. English advocates allowing the use of other languages "for public health and safety, judicial proceedings (although actual trials are conducted in English), foreign-language instruction and tourism."[33]

Opposition Legislation

The official-English legislation proposed by Rep. Emerson and Sen. Shelby follows the U.S. English model. Considered the least radical of such proposals pending in Congress, the legislation would apply only to government use of language and recommends that savings generated by an official-English law should be used to teach English to LEP students.

Opponents, however, see the legislation as a threat not only to free speech but also to bilingual education. "They say they're not out to eliminate bilingual education," says Crawford, "but there is no obvious loophole for bilingual."

In the last Congress, he says, similar legislation exempted "anything educational or informational, but that dropped out this time, and they put in its place a narrower loophole for foreign-language instruction."

Rep. Roth's bill meets bilingual education head-on. It proposes to abolish bilingual education and bilingual ballots altogether while requiring the government to promote the use of English. The bill also would limit all naturalization ceremonies to English and require enforcement of existing English-proficiency standards for immigrants.

Legislation sponsored by Rep. King goes further. It would abolish the Office of Bilingual Education, eliminate bilingual ballots and return to the Treasury all unspent funds granted under the Bilingual Education Act.

The most sweeping proposal, by Rep. John T. Doolittle, R-Calif., would amend the Constitution to make English the nation's official language.

Funding Cut for Bilingual Education

Depending on whom one listens to, official English is either flying high or is lost amid the more sweeping budget matters being considered in Congress. Yet while lawmakers remain unclear about what they will do with official English, they have been more decisive about funding bilingual education.

Funding for bilingual education fell nearly 50 percent in the 1980s. During the 1995 budget-rescission process, Congress cut $38.5 million from programs. That, say critics, worsens existing difficulties such as teacher shortages and underserved LEP populations.

The cuts also take funds from some new programs that the Improving America's Schools Act of 1994 created when it modified the Bilingual Education Act and the 1984 Emergency Immigrant Education Act. According to the Congressional Research Service (CRS), proposed cuts in fiscal 1996 appropriations for Labor, Health and Human Services and Education would amplify the effect of the 1995 cuts on projects to improve bilingual training and education programs.

Department of Education figures also show that while bilingual instructional services aided 300,000 students in fiscal 1994, and 425,000 in 1995, they would serve only 200,000 children under the House's 1996 appropriations request or 700,000 if Congress funded President Clinton's request.

Angry Parents, Teachers

While bilingual-education defenders say the programs need more money to thrive, some teachers in California and parents in New York say they are fed up with a system that has treated them poorly. In Westminster, Calif., where at least one school has a non-English-speaking student population of 78 percent, administrators last fall told teachers they could be transferred if they refused to take classes to learn Spanish or Vietnamese.

The teachers rebelled, their union put sympathetic new members on the school board and the new board has said it will phase out bilingual classes.

"It is unconstitutional to force American citizens to learn a foreign language in order to keep their job," said Michael Verringia, the new school board president. [34]

Last year the California Board of Education also took action against bilingual education. On July 14, 1995, it adopted a new policy that advocates moving LEP students into English-language classes as quickly as possible. If a district can show that LEP students will learn English and not fall behind academically, the board promises to grant waivers exempting such students from classes that use native-language instruction. [35]

NABE's Lyons says the California teachers' opposition is related to job security or ego, not good teaching practices. "Language acquisition is the only area where we expect students to outperform teachers," he says. "Some high schools and junior high schools have to depend on students to maintain their computer networks. With bilingual education it is sometimes the same. The students, not the teachers, are bilingual."

In New York City, parents are leading the opposition to some bilingual-education practices. The Bushwick Parents Organization, which represents 150 Brooklyn families, has sued the state education commissioner for allegedly allowing tens of thousands of students to "languish" in bilingual classes well beyond the normal three years. "For a lot of kids, bilingual education becomes a prison," said lawyer Robert Smith, who represents the families. "They don't learn the English they need, and they can't get out." [36]

The parents say that students with Hispanic surnames and low test scores on an English-language test are funneled into native-language bilingual classes even if the children speak English and want to remain in all-English classes. "In New York, all kids with Hispanic surnames have to be assessed for language proficiency, and that is no doubt the cause of some problems with assignment of students," says pro-bilingual writer Crawford. "The idea is that kids [who need bilingual education] might slip through the cracks" unless the schools can identify them.

While some critics complain that education bureaucrats claim to know more about the children's needs than do their parents, Crawford says that if the schools "have an objective test, then they do know more than the parents about the kids' language abilities."

In Washington, D.C., Cooke Elementary School in the multi-cultural Adams-Morgan neighborhood was told it could

Continued on p. 66

At Issue:

Should English be the official language of the United States?

MAURO E. MUJICA
Chairman/CEO, U.S. English

FROM TESTIMONY BEFORE THE HOUSE ECONOMIC AND EDUCATIONAL OPPORTUNITIES SUBCOMMITTEE ON EARLY CHILDHOOD, YOUTH AND FAMILIES, NOV. 1, 1995.

yes

As an immigrant myself, I know firsthand how important it is to know English to succeed in the United States. . . . [It] is incomprehensible to me that anyone would not support the designation of English as the official language of this great country. Individuals who are not English proficient are more often than not relegated to second-class citizenship, and vulnerable to being isolated by language barriers that render them dependent on the government for assistance. . . . [B]y framing a language policy for the federal government, Congress will be taking a giant step in the direction of solving this problem. . . .

Everybody seems to agree, even the staunchest opponents of official-English legislation, . . . that English is the language of this country. Everybody also seems to agree that immigrants want and need to learn English. . . .

Thus, I am baffled by the fact that there are some people in this country opposed to the designation of English as our official language. Don't these individuals understand that money spent on superfluous foreign-language publications and services is money better spent on the teaching of English?. . .

Eighty-six percent of Americans and 81 percent of immigrants want to make English the official language of this country. It should be noted that generally speaking we are the exception to the rule, in that 69 other sovereign nations have official-language policies. The vast majority of citizens in this country are fed-up with the present-day situation, which has fostered linguistic welfare, poly-lingual education that prevents the rapid acquisition of English by students in our public schools and the rapid growth of costly foreign-language governing. With millions of new immigrants and millions more of illegal immigrants, we in this country must have a common means of communication. . . .

More than any other form of government, democracies require interaction between the people and the governing bodies, constant interaction that provides a barometer for those governing to use in determining the impact of their decisions upon the governed. A shared method of communication — a common language — is essential for this dynamic. . . .

When we talk about one common language, we are not asking people to stop using or to forget their first language. U.S. English promotes the idea that people should speak many languages. . . . [But] maintaining one's original language is the responsibility of the individual, not of the government. We strongly believe that immigrants coming to this country have an obligation to learn the common language of this country — English — as soon as possible.

ROBERT A. UNDERWOOD
U.S. delegate from Guam (D)

FROM TESTIMONY BEFORE THE HOUSE ECONOMIC AND EDUCATIONAL OPPORTUNITIES SUBCOMMITTEE ON EARLY CHILDHOOD, YOUTH AND FAMILIES, NOV. 1, 1995.

no

I come before you today to express my strong feelings regarding legislation that would make English the official language of the United States. I feel that such legislation is unnecessary for the workings of American government, ill-advised and counterproductive. As officials of the federal government, we must recognize that it is unnecessary since it solves no problem in the operation and management of the federal government. It is ill-advised because it will contribute to a climate of nativism and communicates to speakers of languages other than English that they are somehow less a part of this country than others and that their ability to use another language is seen as potentially damaging to the core of our social unity. Lastly, it is counterproductive because it sends a negative and regressive message about the nation's development of language resources at a time when we need our people to learn more languages and when we need to cultivate existing linguistic resources. . . .

English is the de facto official language of this country. . -. . Some might then argue that since this is the case, what would be the objection to declaring English the official language of the federal government. The easy answer is that if this were the case, there is no need to declare English the official language. But many people still feel a need to send a message. The question then is what is that message and who is this message for. Obviously, this message is not being sent to people who speak only English. . . . [It's] being sent to speakers of non-English languages. . . .

The ill-advised message seems to be that we are less than those who can speak only English; that there is something foreign about our maintenance of a tongue different than most. I know many will say . . . that no such affront is intended. But in light of the reality that there is no problem with the official use of English, any effort to coerce English-only at this time must be seen as giving life to the social forces of resentment. This resentment could stem from the rise of "foreign accents" in our day-to-day lives and the increasing use of languages other than English on the radio and television. . . . This kind of resentment is not based on a need to improve communication, it is based on a fear of being subsumed by a growing "foreignness" in our midst.

This may not be the intended result, but I submit that it will be the real result. And the fact that such resentment is based on attitudes which need adjusting rather than with the policies which need fixing ought to reveal to us how ill-advised this type of legislation really is.

FOR MORE INFORMATION

English First, 8001 Forbes Place, Suite 102, Springfield, Va. 22151; (703) 321-8881. Founded in 1986, English First lobbies for official English and against bilingual education.

National Association for Bilingual Education, 1220 L St. N.W., Suite 605, Washington, D.C. 20005-4018; (202) 898-1829. NABE works to improve educational programs for non-English-speaking students and to promote bilingualism among English-speaking American students.

U.S. Department of Education, Office of Bilingual Education and Minority Languages Affairs, 330 C. St. S.W., Washington, D.C. 20202-6510; (202) 205-5463. Provides school districts and state education agencies with grants to establish, operate and improve programs for people with limited English proficiency and administers assistance programs for refugee and immigrant children.

U.S. English, 1747 Pennsylvania Ave., N.W., Suite 1100, Washington, D.C. 20006-4600; (202) 833-0100. Founded in 1983, U.S. English promotes legislation to make English the official language of the U.S. government and bilingual-education reform.

Continued from p. 64

have a $1 million federal grant if it created a two-way bilingual program at the school. But many black parents and teachers were furious over the funding targeted for Hispanics. Even Hispanic parents were split on whether it is good to teach all students 80 percent in Spanish and 20 percent in English through the first three grades. [37]

There also is the matter of choice. "Any program where you have to force students to participate is doomed to fail," says the CEO's Amselle. "Parents tell us their children are being forced to participate in dual-immersion programs. They tell us that if you're an Hispanic parent, and your child gets put into one, you can get him out. But if you're an Anglo, you're stuck."

George Mason's Collier says she is not aware of schools where children are forced into two-way programs, although she has heard that one district has considered it. "I think it would be very dangerous to mandate [two-way classes]," she says. "It needs to be a community decision, as was the case at Oyster Elementary" — a Washington, D.C., school widely cited as a model for two-way bilingual education. ■

OUTLOOK

Battle Lines Drawn

In the United States, public opinion polls show strong approval for English as the official language. But they also reveal doubt among Americans when asked if bilingual education should be abolished. *(See poll, p. 56.)* Given Americans' ambivalence on bilingual education, most official-English backers say the Emerson/Shelby legislation is the most likely to succeed.

But bilingual-education advocates Lyons and Serrano say the White House has promised that President Clinton will veto any official-English legislation Congress passes. Along with other opponents of such legislation, they say there are more than ideological and pedagogical reasons for a veto.

According to Edward M. Chen, an attorney with the American Civil Liberties Union of Northern California, official-English laws "deny fair and equal access to government, violate the First Amendment rights of elected officials and public employees" and "foster anti-immigrant bigotry and intolerance and exacerbate ethnic tensions." [38]

Another difficulty with official English, critics say, is that legislation cannot distinguish clearly between official and unofficial government business. That leaves a large gray area where official English may or may not apply, and thus will invite constant challenge.

Similarly, critics say, legislation that abolishes bilingual education would undoubtedly continue to undergo challenge or change. "The ideal model from our perspective is developmental bilingual," says Lyons, citing successful two-way schools such as Oyster Elementary and Coral Way Elementary in Coral Gables, Fla.

For such programs to work, says Collier, schools must have well-qualified bilingual teachers who engage students in cooperative learning. And that means the federal government must continue to fund and support innovative bilingual education and teacher development.

U.S. English and READ, however, want government and schools to return to the original intent of Title VII — a transitional program to make non-English speakers fluent in English as quickly as possible. Among other things, they recommend moving responsibility for preservation of Native American languages to the Bureau of Indian Affairs and funneling 75 percent of Title VII funds to local school districts for LEP instruction. But first, they say, all federal money for "English-learner programs" should be distributed in block grants for the states to allocate. Finally the two groups suggest changing the name of the Bilingual Education Act to the English Learners Act.

The two organizations also want to rename the National Clearinghouse for Bilingual Education as the National Clearinghouse on English Learner Education and have it collect data to identify the most effective ways of teaching

English to non-English speakers. "The allocation of funds for instructional-materials development in the native language should be eliminated in this act, with materials development for Native Americans and other specifically protected groups funded by different agencies," they suggest.[39]

To illustrate how far off course bilingualism has gone, CEO President Chavez cites the Los Angeles Unified School District's *Bilingual Methodology Study Guide*. "The guide advises teachers 'not to encourage minority parents to switch to English in the home, but to encourage them to strongly promote development of the primary language,' " she says. "Incredibly, it also declares that 'excessive use of English in bilingual classrooms tends to lower students' achievement in English.' "[40]

Some of the reforms sought by Chavez and others have already begun at the state level. In Massachusetts, for example, Republican Gov. William F. Weld has recommended to the legislature a bilingual-education reform plan that requires bilingual-education teachers to be fluent in English, limits student participation in special language programs to three years and gives parents a choice in whether their children enroll in LEP or mainstream classes.

"Gov. Weld believes that in an incredibly competitive work environment, the mastery of English is essential, and that this proposal provides the best way for students to become successful competitors," says Terry Ann Knopf, a spokeswoman for Massachusetts' Executive Office of Education.

But Rick Lopez, NABE's legislative policy director, questions the motives behind Weld's proposals. Deciding how many years students receive bilingual education "should be a pedagogical question, not a political one," Lopez says. Moreover, "Teachers need to be proficient in a lot of things," he adds, "and singling out English proficiency for bilingual teachers seems like cynical grandstanding more than anything else." ■

Notes

[1] *The New York Times,* Aug. 30, 1995, p. 12A.
[2] *Education Week,* Sept. 13, 1995.
[3] Press release, Congressional Hispanic Caucus, Sept. 7, 1995.
[4] *The Washington Post,* Sept. 22, 1995, p. A3.
[5] *The Dallas Morning News,* Sept. 18, 1995. Action has yet to be taken on Serrano's resolution.
[6] Andrew Ward, "What's So American About English?" op-ed column, *The Washington Post,* Dec. 6, 1995.
[7] Bob Dole, "Ticket to the American Dream," *The Washington Post,* Dec. 19, 1995, p. A15.
[8] *Congressional Record,* Nov. 13, 1995, p. H12132.
[9] Quoted in Carol Innerst, "Differences Prevent Debate on Bilingual Education," *The Washington Times,* Sept. 19, 1995, p. 10A.
[10] Linda Chavez, "One Nation, One Common Language," *Reader's Digest,* August 1995. Chavez is a former staff director of the U.S. Commission on Civil Rights.
[11] "Reporters Briefcase," *Washington Alert,* Feb. 23, 1995.
[12] Joyce Price, "English-Only Advocates Sense Momentum: See Passing Chance for Proposed Bills," *The Washington Times,* Sept. 7, 1995, p. 2A.
[13] Rosalie Pedalino Porter, "Bilingual Ed Flunks Out," *The American Experiment,* spring 1995, published by the Center for Equal Opportunity.
[14] Institute for Research in English Acquisition and Development (READ), "Rewriting the Bilingual Education Act: Title VII of the Elementary and Secondary Education Act," February 1995.
[15] Price, *op. cit.*
[16] *Congressional Record,* July 10, 1995, p. H6726.
[17] Susan Headden, "Tongue-tied in the Schools: Bilingual Education Began as a Good Idea. Now it Needs Fixing," *U.S. News & World Report,* Sept. 25, 1995, p. 44.
[18] Testimony before House Economic and Educational Opportunities Subcommittee on Early Childhood, Youth and Families, Oct. 18, 1995.
[19] Testimony submitted to the Senate Governmental Affairs Committee, Dec. 6, 1995.
[20] Testimony before Senate Governmental Affairs Committee, Dec. 6, 1995.
[21] *Congressional Monitor,* Oct. 20, 1995.
[22] Press release, National Council of La Raza, Dec. 6, 1995.
[23] Testimony submitted to the Senate Governmental Affairs Committee, Dec. 6, 1995.
[24] James Crawford, *Hold Your Tongue: Bilingualism and the Politics of "English Only"* (1993), pp. 111-112.
[25] Testimony submitted to Senate Governmental Affairs Committee, Dec. 6, 1995.
[26] Crawford, *op. cit.,* p. 28.
[27] *Ibid.,* pp. 39-41.
[28] *Ibid.,* pp. 43-44.
[29] James Crawford, ed., *Language Loyalties: A Source Book on the Official English Controversy* (1992), pp. 226 and 235-7. See also Steven R. Aleman et al, "English as the Official Language of the United States: An Overview," Congressional Research Service, Oct. 20, 1995.
[30] Crawford, *Hold Your Tongue, op. cit.,* p. 75.
[31] Jean Pasco and John Gittelsohn, "Save Our State Founders See No SOS," *The Orange County Register,* Nov. 11, 1995, p. 5A.
[32] Charles V. Dale and Mark Gurevitz, "Legal Analysis of Proposals to Make English the Official Language of the United States Government," Congressional Research Service, Oct. 17, 1995, pp. 11-12.
[33] "Facts and Issues: Questions and Answers About Official English," Position paper, U.S. English.
[34] Margot Hornblower, "Should Bilingual Schooling Be Silenced?" *Time,* Oct. 9, 1995, p. 41.
[35] Lynn Schnailberg, "Board Relaxes Bilingual-Ed. Policy in Calif.," *Education Week,* Aug. 2, 1995, p. 1.
[36] Jacques Steinberg, "State Is Accused of Overuse of Bilingual Classes," *The New York Times,* Sept. 19, 1995.
[37] John Leo, "Bilingualism: Qué Pasa?" *U.S. News & World Report,* Nov. 7, 1995, p. 22.
[38] Testimony before the House Economic and Educational Opportunities Subcommittee on Early Childhood, Youth and Families, Nov. 1, 1995.
[39] Institute for Research in English Acquisition and Development (READ), *op. cit.*
[40] Chavez, *op. cit.*

Bibliography

Selected Sources Used

Books

James Crawford, *Bilingual Education History, Politics, Theory and Practice,* 3d Edition, revised and expanded, Bilingual Educational Services, 1995.

This history of the development and debate over teaching English to non-native English speakers is a gold mine of information.

James Crawford, *Hold Your Tongue: Bilingualism and the Politics of "English Only,"* Addison-Wesley, 1992.

Crawford, a proponent of bilingual education, discusses the development of bilingual education and the movement to make English the United States' official language. He sees the debate as one between minorities insistent upon legitimate language rights pitted against the tyranny of the majority whose attempts to coerce national unity will backfire and create a balkanized United States.

James Crawford, *Language Loyalties: A Source Book on the Official English Controversy,* Addison-Wesley, 1992.

This companion to Crawford's *Hold Your Tongue* collects speeches, essays and arguments for and against official English from the 18th century to 1991.

Rosalie Pedalino Porter, *Forked Tongue: The Politics of Bilingual Education,* Basic Books, 1990.

Porter passionately discusses what she sees as the decline of bilingual education from its original goal of teaching English to a program driven by multicultural purists who value preservation of native culture and language over mastery of English. Porter is director of the Institute for Research in English Acquisition and Development (READ).

Articles

Chavez, Linda, "One Nation, One Common Language," *Reader's Digest,* August 1995.

A stinging indictment of bilingual education by the head of the Center for Equal Opportunity (CEO).

Collier, Nancy, "A Synthesis of Studies Examining Long-Term Language Minority Student Data on Academic Achievement," *Bilingual Research Journal,* winter/spring 1992, pp. 187-212.

Collier, a professor at George Mason University in Fairfax, Va., looks at studies that examine the academic achievements of language-minority students over at least four years. She concludes that instruction in the students' first language, balanced with instruction in a second language, results in higher achievement than programs that teach LEP students only in the second language.

Collier, Nancy, "Acquiring a Second Language for School," *Directions in Language Education,* fall 1995, pp. 1-12.

An overview of the results of 25 years of bilingual-education research in which the author concludes that two-way bilingual education in elementary school is the best model for long-term academic success.

Headden, Susan, "Tongue-tied in the Schools: Bilingual Education began as a good idea. Now it needs fixing," *U.S. News & World Report,* Sept. 25, 1995, pp. 44-46.

A brief critical discussion of what the author finds to be bilingual education's shortcomings.

Hornblower, Margaret, "Putting Tongues in Check: Should bilingual schooling be silenced?" *Time,* Oct. 9, 1995, pp. 40-50.

Hornblower summarizes the most recent criticisms of bilingual education and then provides overviews of current research that appear to show such criticism is either premature or ill-founded.

Reports and Studies

Aleman, Steven R., et al, "English as the Official Language of the United States: An Overview," *A CRS Report for Congress,* Oct. 20, 1995.

This Congressional Research Service (CRS) report includes a brief overview of the issue, a history of recent congressional action and a discussion of some of the legal, educational and immigration issues.

Choya, Wilson L., et al, "The Title VII Academic Excellence Program: Disseminating Effective Programs and Practices in Bilingual Education," Policy Studies Associates and SRI International, 1994.

Sponsored by the Department of Education, this study includes an overview of federal involvement in bilingual education and descriptions of various programs for limited-English proficiency populations.

Dale, Charles V., and Mark Gurevitz, "Legal Analysis of Proposals to Make English the Official Language of the United States Government," *A CRS Report for Congress,* Oct. 17, 1995.

This CRS report provides detailed discussion of constitutional issues that have some bearing on official-English laws. The report includes a discussion of proposed federal legislation and an addendum listing provisions of state official-English laws.

The Next Step

Additional information from UMI's Newspaper & Periodical Abstracts database

Bilingual education

Chavez, Linda, "Bilingual education gobbles kids, taxes," *USA Today,* June 15, 1994, p. A15.
Chavez contends that bilingual education in the U.S. has become an unruly behemoth costing local, state and federal governments billions each year. Chavez argues that there is no scientifically valid research that proves that teaching immigrant students in their native language is the best way to teach them English.

Cohen, Muriel, "Bilingual education," *Boston Globe,* Dec. 4, 1994, p. B1.
The continuing controversy over bilingual education is examined.

Cohen, Muriel, "Bilingual education badly flawed, author says," *Boston Globe,* Nov. 19, 1995, p. A49.
Rosalie Porter's warnings against the concept of bilingual education are discussed.

Colvin, Richard Lee, "Bilingual education groups protest changes," *Los Angeles Times,* Dec. 8, 1994, p. A3.
A change in California's policy that, if adopted, would allow local school districts to teach some students in English rather than their native languages has outraged supporters of bilingual education, prompting them to organize a protest at the State Board of Education meeting on Dec. 8, 1994.

Colvin, Richard Lee, "Bilingual education rift divides state teachers union," *Los Angeles Times,* June 5, 1995, p. A3.
The re-examination by Californians and their leaders of efforts to educate the rapidly rising population of children not fluent in English spread to the California Teachers Association on June 4, 1995, with a display of disharmony over bilingual education.

"DPS should look to ESL as alternative to bilingual ed," *Denver Post,* June 10, 1994, p. B6.
An editorial comments that it may be more sensible to de-emphasize bilingual education and strengthen the English as a second language (ESL) program as Denver-area schools are hard-pressed to find teachers for the bilingual program.

Gunnison, Robert B., "Report hits state policy on bilingual education," *San Francisco Chronicle,* July 10, 1993, p. A15.
The Little Hoover Commission, a state watchdog agency, declared on July 9, 1993, that bilingual education in California's public schools is a failure.

Howe, Peter J., "House rejects change in bilingual education," *Boston Globe,* April 12, 1995, p. 31.
The Massachusetts House overwhelmingly rejected Gov. William F. Weld's proposed reform of bilingual-education programs in a test-run vote.

Merl, Jean, "Bias charged in meeting on bilingual education," *Los Angeles Times,* Jan. 20, 1993, p. A14.
Amid accusations that it stacked the deck in inviting testimony, the Little Hoover Commission on Jan. 19, 1993, conducted a tense public hearing that further fueled the hot debate over bilingual education.

Moore, Teresa, "State expands schools' choices on bilingual education," *San Francisco Chronicle,* July 15, 1995, p. A15.
On July 14, 1995, California's Board of Education adopted a policy that will allow school districts greater freedom to choose from several approaches to bilingual education.

Moroney, Tom, "Speaking up for bilingual education," *Boston Globe,* Oct. 1, 1995, p. SW1.
Immigrants in Brockton, Mass., said they agree, in part, that anyone coming to the U.S. should learn English as quickly as possible. But many also said that the schools should provide help for children and that other agencies should be given more money to provide more instruction for adults.

Pack, William, "Future appears secure for bilingual education," *The Houston Post,* Feb. 27, 1993, p. A13.
The Clinton administration's positive attitude toward bilingual education has made the National Association for Bilingual Education optimistic and enthusiastic about the future. Bilingual experts sense that the general public is more receptive toward bilingual education and the idea that a second language is an important skill to learn.

Pyle, Amy, "Pressure grows to reform bilingual education in state," *Los Angeles Times,* May 22, 1995, p. A1.
In the first article of an occasional series, the campaign to reform bilingual education in California is discussed. The state's system spends about $400 million annually to educate 1.2 million children who speak little or no English, and reformers claim that the program is not working.

Pyle, Amy, "English fluency moves up the priority ladder," *Los Angeles Times,* July 31, 1995, p. B1.
As part of her series on bilingual education, Pyle discusses the Los Angeles Board of Education's plans to revise its nationally acclaimed bilingual-education program. A new state policy gives schools more power to choose how they teach students who do not speak English.

Small, Rick, "English language is strong enough without attacks on bilingual education," *Boston Globe,* Oct. 8, 1995, p. SW2.

Small comments on the ignorance associated with the view that the English language is under threat, including a discussion of linguistic aspects of the language, bilingual education and the cultural skirmish over English.

Smith, Leo, "High hopes," *Los Angeles Times,* June 28, 1995, p. E1.

Nidia Calles, a 25-year-old Los Angeles resident who came to the U.S. from the Honduras at the age of 16, is profiled. Calles teaches English as a second language to about 175 students at Los Angeles High School.

Thomas, Kimberly, "Bilingual education opposed," *Detroit News,* May 25, 1995, p. E3.

The Dearborn, Mich., public school district has withdrawn its earlier support of a bilingual-education program and jeopardized its chances for $5 million in federal grants to teach children with a limited knowledge of English, about one-quarter of the district's students.

Tucker, Jill, "Golden think tank: Drop bilingual education," *Denver Post,* April 2, 1995, p. A15.

Eliminating bilingual education and reforming welfare as ways to slow legal and illegal immigration in Colorado have been recommended by the Independence Institute, a conservative think tank in Golden, Colo.

Welsh, Patrick, "Our Classroom Barrios: For Hispanic Students, American Schools Can Be a Nightmare," *The Washington Post,* Sept. 8, 1991, p. C1.

Welsh discusses the difficulty Hispanic students have in American classrooms due to isolatation from other students into English as a Second Language classes and from jealousy, suspicion and class snobbery among Hispanics themselves.

West, Woody, "Bilingual education spells failure in any language," *Insight on the News,* May 1, 1995, p. 40.

West argues that bilingual-education programs, which began following a 1972 California Supreme Court decision, are abject failures. Bilingual education penalizes the children of immigrants because they fail to assimilate.

Wong, Doris Sue, "Opponents protest Weld bill to revise bilingual education," *Boston Globe,* March 31, 1995, p. 31.

At a packed and raucous hearing at the State House, students, teachers, parents and union officials charged that a bill filed by Gov. Weld would lead to the demise of transitional bilingual education in Massachusetts.

Funding Issues

Hornbeck, Mark, "Pupils may lose guarantee of aid in native tongue," *Detroit News,* Dec. 1, 1995, p. D1.

Michigan's mandatory bilingual-education program, where English is a second language, costs the state $4.2 million annually, and now a growing number of lawmakers want to let local boards of education decide whether new arrivals can continue using native languages in school while they learn English.

Instruction Methods

Gersten, Russell, and John Woodward, "A Longitudinal Study of Transitional and Immersion Bilingual Education Programs in One District," *Elementary School Journal,* January 1995, pp. 223-239.

A longitudinal evaluation of two approaches to the education of language-minority students — transitional bilingual education and bilingual immersion — in El Paso, Texas, is described. Bilingual immersion was favored in language and reading in grades 4-6.

Hansen, Ellen, "Tutoring Program Shortens the Wait for English Course at Josiah Quincy School," *Boston Globe,* Dec. 22, 1991, p. 63.

The TAG, or Take and Give, program at Josiah Quincy Elementary School in Boston's Chinatown neighborhood allows graduates of the school's adult English as a Second Language program to tutor elementary school students who have not yet had ESL courses.

Housel, Debbie, "Newspapers muy bien in bilingual instruction," *The Houston Post,* March 2, 1993, p. A3.

Maida Feliciano, who teaches English as a second language at Paul Revere Middle School, said she has taught her students to read and to understand American customs with the help of *The Houston Post.* In Texas, 450 schools are using the paper through the Newspaper in Education program.

Official English Proposals

Amselle, Jorge, "HUD's battle against English only," *The Wall Street Journal,* Aug. 21, 1995, p. A8.

Amselle accuses the Department of Housing and Urban Development (HUD) of harassing Allentown, Penn., over an ordinance passed by the City Council urging the mayor to issue all documents exclusively in English. The ordinance was brought to HUD's attention in the first place because HUD Secretary Henry Cisneros' sister lives in the area. Amselle argues against multilingualism in the U.S. and supports a pending amendment in the agency's appropriations bill, which bars HUD from interfering with local official-English laws.

Amselle, Jorge, "Urgent: Reform bilingual education," *The Christian Science Monitor,* Dec. 26, 1995, p. 22.

Amselle says that reforming bilingual education is more important than passing symbolic official-English legislation.

Boulet, Jim Jr., "A Trojan horse," *Atlanta Journal,* April 6, 1995, p. A15.

In a letter to the editor, Jim Boulet Jr. of English First says that anyone who calls the official-English bill on Georgia Gov. Zell Miller's desk a victory for official English is fooling themselves; they should encourage Miller to veto it.

Hopwood, William J., "A new tower of Babel," *The Wall Street Journal,* Nov. 1, 1995, p. A15.
Hopwood responds to the Oct. 18, 1995, commentary "The Bilingual Ed Trap." Hopwood says that the official-English movement seeks only to assure that the business of our government is conducted in one common language so as to avoid the Balkanization and tribalism so evident in most strife-torn, officially multilingual countries throughout the world.

"In English, please," *The Christian Science Monitor,* Nov. 2, 1995, p. 20.
An editorial examines the "official-English" bills pending in Congress in late 1995, and notes the arguments by proponents of the bills, who claim that a common language will promote unity and political stability, and critics of the bill, who say that such bills foster anti-immigration sentiment.

Mark, Cynthia, "Keep momentum for official English," *Chicago Tribune,* Sept. 28, 1995, p. 16.
In a letter to the editor, Mark of English First argues for making English the official language in the U.S.

Mujica, Mauro E., "English unites the nation," *USA Today,* April 6, 1995, p. A12.
Mujica, chairman and CEO of U.S. English, argues that the passage of official-English language legislation will promote unity, cut wasteful spending and empower immigrants.

"Open letter," *National Review,* Nov. 6, 1995, pp. 14-16.
An open letter to House Speaker Newt Gingrich, R-Ga., and Senate Majority Leader Bob Dole, R-Kan., from the editors of *National Review* urges them to propose a constitutional amendment declaring English as the official language of the U.S.

Robison, Clay, "Official English only is preying on fear," *Houston Chronicle,* Sept. 10, 1995, p. C2.
Robison comments that many politicians, such as Bob Dole and Pat Buchanan, support making English the official language of the U.S. not because of any threat to the language but to make political points based on fear and divisiveness.

Seligman, Daniel, "The comeback of English," *Fortune,* April 3, 1995, p. 141.
Seligman discusses a bill that has been introduced in Congress called the National Language Act of 1995 that would terminate all federal support for bilingual education and declare English to be the official language of the U.S.

Soto, Lucy, "Backers of official English face vote Today," *Atlanta Constitution,* Feb. 27, 1995, p. B2.
A controversial state Senate bill that would make English the official language of Georgia is scheduled to be voted on in a House committee. The legislation, which has prompted allegations of bigotry and xenophobia, states that all public records, meetings and official documents could be published only in English and that state services could be provided only in English.

Urban Issues

Constable, Pamela, "A new accent on education: Rise of immigrants means schools must navigate a sea of diversity," *The Washington Post,* April 2, 1995, p. B1.
After a decade of massive foreign immigration to the Washington D.C., area, there are more than 20,000 public school students who were either born abroad or are studying English as a foreign language. The ways in which schools deal with the diverse student population are examined.

Dillon, Sam, "Report faults bilingual education in New York," *The New York Times,* Oct. 20, 1994, p. A1.
In a first step toward re-examining bilingual education in New York City, the Board of Education on Oct. 19, 1994, released a study concluding that the current efforts to educate tens of thousands of students in their native languages are flawed.

Leff, Lisa, "Where bilingual education is a two-way street," *The Washington Post,* March 13, 1994, p. B1.
Washington D.C.'s Oyster Bilingual School, where a multicultural student body evenly divides its time between English and Spanish, is featured. The new breed of bilingual-education programs cropping up in area schools is discussed.

Robinson, Lauren, "2M Sought for Bilingual Education," *Boston Globe,* Dec. 4, 1992, p. 44.
School Superintendent Lois Harrison-Jones has asked the Boston School Committee to consider spending about $2 million in 1993 to improve bilingual education by reopening a West Roxbury school and limiting class sizes in 44 other schools.

"Teaching Taxi English as a Second Language," *The New York Times,* Oct. 6, 1991, p. A7.
Efforts to teach New York City taxicab drivers English are discussed. Over 90 percent of drivers are immigrants.

Yardley, Jonathan, "The hard lessons of bilingual education," *The Washington Post,* Oct. 24, 1994, p. B2.
Yardley discusses the bilingual-education program of New York City, which has had negative results, and comments that bilingual education lets educators avoid the tough job of teaching English to a wave of immigrant students.

Back Issues

Great Research on Current Issues Starts Right Here...Recent topics covered by The CQ Researcher are listed below. Before May 1991, reports were published under the name of Editorial Research Reports.

JULY 1994
Dietary Supplements
Public Opinion and Foreign Policy
Crime Victims' Rights
Birth Control Choices

AUGUST 1994
Genetically Engineered Foods
Electing Minorities
Prozac Controversy
College Sports

SEPTEMBER 1994
Home Schooling
Welfare Experiments
Courts and the Media
Regulating Tobacco

OCTOBER 1994
Historic Preservation
Religion and Politics
Arts Funding
Economic Sanctions

NOVEMBER 1994
Sex on Campus
Blood Supply Safety
Testing Term Limits
Religion in America

Back issues are available for $5.00 (subscribers) or $8.00 (non-subscribers). Quantity discounts apply to orders over ten. To order, call Congressional Quarterly Customer Service at (202) 887-8621.

Binders are available for $18.00. To order call 1-800-638-1710. Please refer to stock number 648.

DECEMBER 1994
Farm Policy
Arms Sales
Earthquake Research
The Future of Television

JANUARY 1995
Treating Addiction
Child Custody and Support
Parents and Schools
Non-Proliferation Treaty at 25

FEBRUARY 1995
Cracking Down on Immigration
The Business of Sports
Reinventing Government
Housing Discrimination

MARCH 1995
Death Penalty Debate
Primary Care
Democracy in Africa
Environmental Movement at 25

APRIL 1995
Abortion Clinic Protests
Dieting and Health
Combating AIDS
Rethinking Affirmative Action

MAY 1995
Assisted Suicide Controversy
Overhauling Social Security
Learning to Read
Mandatory Sentencing

JUNE 1995
Combating Infectious Disease
Property Rights
Repetitive Stress Injuries
Regulating the Internet

JULY 1995
War Crimes
Highway Safety
Combating Terrorism
Preventing Teen Drug Use

AUGUST 1995
Job Stress
Organ Transplants
United Nations at 50
Advances in Cancer Research

SEPTEMBER 1995
Catholic Church in the U.S.
Northern Ireland Cease-Fire
High School Sports
Teaching History

OCTOBER 1995
Quebec's Future
Revitalizing the Cities
Networking the Classroom
Indoor Air Pollution

NOVEMBER 1995
The Working Poor
The Jury System
Sex, Violence and the Media
Police Misconduct

DECEMBER 1995
Teens and Tobacco
Gene Therapy's Future
Global Water Shortages
Third-Party Prospects

JANUARY 1996
Emergency Medicine
Punishing Sex Offenders

Future Topics

- ***Helping the Homeless***
- ***Reforming the CIA***
- ***Campaign Finance Reform***

THE CQ Researcher

PUBLISHED BY CONGRESSIONAL QUARTERLY INC.

Helping the Homeless

Will cuts in welfare spending cause hardships?

Fifteen years after homelessness emerged as a national issue, experts still disagree on how many people are homeless, what causes homelessness and whether other Americans are losing sympathy for the homeless because of "compassion fatigue." Local ordinances targeting the homeless suggest that sympathy is indeed declining. At the same time, opinion polls show strong support for publicly funded programs to help homeless people get back on their feet. The Republican-controlled Congress, meanwhile, seems intent on overhauling the nation's welfare system in ways that could add to the woes of the homeless. Some welfare-reform advocates argue that private caregivers could make up for reduced public aid. But churches and charities say their resources already are stretched to the limit.

INSIDE THIS ISSUE

CQ Jan. 26, 1996 • Volume 6, No. 4 • Pages 73-96

Formerly Editorial Research Reports

Helping The Homeless

COVER: JIM HUBBARD

Jan. 26, 1996
Volume 6, No. 4

Published By
Congressional Quarterly Inc.

Bibliographic records and abstracts included in The Next Step section of this publication are from UMI's Newspaper and Periodical Abstracts database, and are used with permission.

The CQ Researcher (ISSN 1056-2036). Formerly Editorial Research Reports. Published weekly (48 times per year, not printed the first Friday of any month with five Fridays) by Congressional Quarterly Inc., 1414 22nd St., N.W., Washington, D.C. 20037. Rates are furnished upon request. Second-class postage paid at Washington, D.C. POSTMASTER: Send address changes to The CQ Researcher, 1414 22nd St., N.W., Washington, D.C. 20037.

Helping the Homeless

By Richard L. Worsnop

The Issues

Visitors to Washington, D.C., often remark on the beauty of Luther Place Memorial Church, a neo-Gothic, red sandstone structure built in 1870 to commemorate the end of the Civil War. Today, Luther Place is fighting a civil war of its own. Because the church operates several programs for the homeless, it faces periodic attacks from zoning and licensing agencies, historic preservationists and neighborhood residents worried about erosion of property values.

"We've been involved in this kind of thing for years," says Senior Pastor John Steinbruck. "It has cost us hundreds of thousands of dollars to defend ourselves in court. Our opponents harass us, play games with us, drag everything out. And, of course, that's the plan — to exhaust us in every way, not the least being financially."

Still, the church has no intention of abandoning its efforts on behalf of the homeless. Steinbruck describes the buildings housing Luther Place's feeding, shelter and counseling programs as "a village" or "an enclosed, self-supporting kind of campus."

"In that environment of love and care, healing can take place," Steinbruck says. "People are shown how to reach a better place in life. We try to provide an exit route from homelessness to independence. It's not our goal to provide just three 'hots' and a cot."

The homeless people who live and receive counseling in the Luther Place complex "aren't straggling around outside, nor are they a problem to the community," Steinbruck adds. "Our block is . . . probably the most drug-free block in Washington. We know who's doing what on the street, and we will give [drug dealers] no peace if they're in our territory."

Even so, years of experience have taught Steinbruck that further attempts to rein in the Luther Place homeless programs are likely. "Anytime you work for justice, you're going to encounter opposition," he says. "So Jesus said, and so it has always been."

In Steinbruck's opinion, the skirmishes are fed largely by the Nimby ("Not in my back yard!") syndrome and gentrification of the Luther Place neighborhood in the last 15 years.[1] "When new people move in and decide that our work with the homeless conflicts with their vision of the area, then they will do what they can to terminate our programs." He notes that objections from neighbors forced Luther Place to lop two stories off a 10-story building offering affordable housing for the homeless, now under construction on the site of a former church parking lot.

The Luther Place story is by no means unusual. All across the country, providers of services for the homeless report concerted efforts to curb their activities. At the same time, local governments have enacted ordinances against panhandling, sleeping or sitting in public places and other behavior associated with the homeless. "What we're seeing is the criminalization of homelessness," Steinbruck says.

Two recently issued reports cast additional light on the trend. In a survey of 36 local jurisdictions nationwide, the National Law Center on Homelessness and Poverty concluded: "The prevalence of Nimby reactions to housing and services for homeless people indicates that many localities might be more interested in moving homeless people than in eradicating homelessness." "Not only does this [approach] exact a horrible human toll on those who cannot obtain services," the center added, "it merely serves to perpetuate the problem proponents of Nimbyism seek to avoid: people living on our cities' streets."[2]

The second report, by the U.S. Conference of Mayors, is the 11th in an annual series aimed at gauging the extent of homelessness and hunger in the United States by surveying the demand for emergency food and shelter services in selected cities. The ability of local service providers to meet that demand also comes under scrutiny.[3]

The 1995 report, like those that preceded it, found that homeless people's demands outstripped available public and private resources in most survey jurisdictions. Nonetheless, St. Louis Mayor Freeman R. Bosley Jr. took heart from the finding that demand for services by hungry and homeless people declined during the year in three areas — Minneapolis-St. Paul, Alexandria, Va., and Norfolk, Va. This could mean, he said, that "we may be seeing the first glimmers of light at the end of this very long and dark tunnel we know as hunger and homelessness in America. We may finally be seeing the results of some extraordinary efforts of public and private agencies, churches and individuals who have dedicated them-

The Changing Homeless Population

Families with children comprised more than a third of the homeless population in 29 major cities surveyed by the U.S. Conference of Mayors in 1995. The number of homeless families has increased significantly in the past decade.

Composition of the Homeless Population

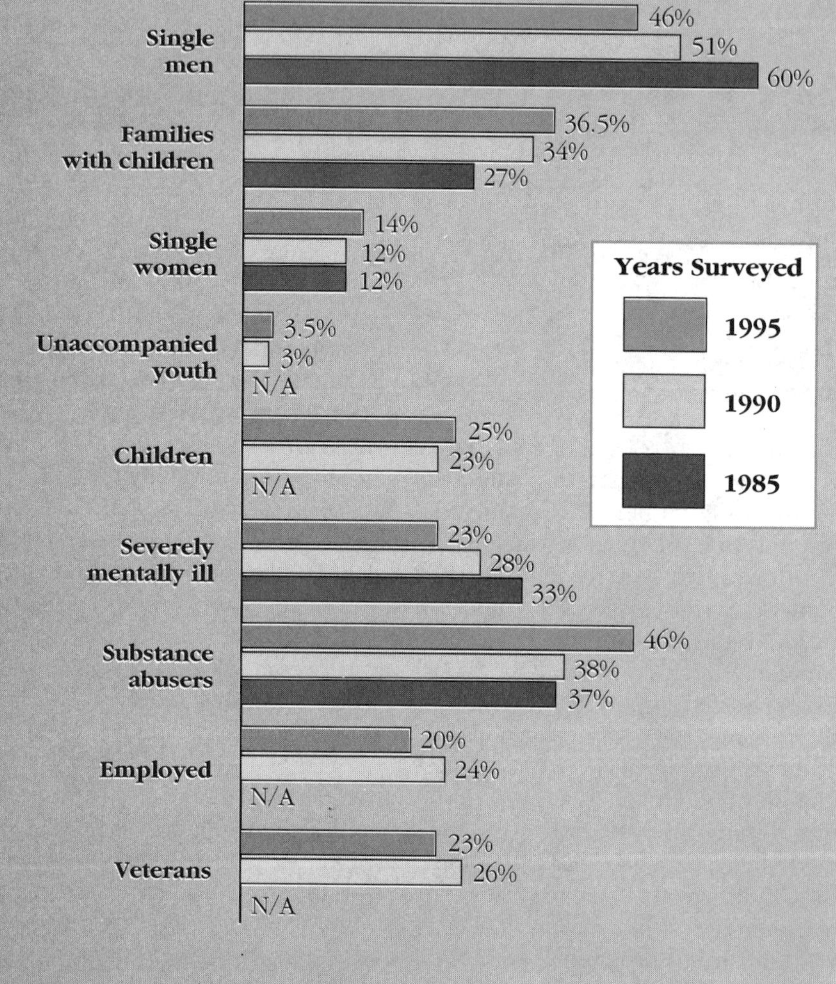

Source: U.S. Conference of Mayors, A Status Report on Hunger and Homelessness in America's Cities: 1995, *December 1995*

selves to aiding and comforting those among us for whom life's most basic elements, food and shelter, appear out of reach." [4]

However, Bosley cautioned that possible cuts in federal welfare spending could plunge the tunnel into total gloom once again. "It doesn't take much imagination to project the cumulative impact of the massive cuts expected in welfare, Medicaid, housing assistance, food stamps, the earned income tax credit and a variety of social services," he said. "These are the programs and services that we know can help keep people out of soup kitchens and homeless shelters. Take them away — we know what will happen."

The ongoing federal budget clash between Congress and the White House will help determine whether the programs and services cited by Bosley survive in viable form. But even as that conflict rages, other uncertainties make it hard to assess the current status, let alone the future, of homelessness in America. These are some of the key questions being asked:

Is the U.S. homeless population growing?

Since homelessness emerged as a national problem in the early 1980s, experts have been unable to agree on how many homeless people there are and on whether or not the total is rising. Estimates range from a few hundred thousand to as many as several million. Lack of consensus on this basic policy issue is understandable; individuals and families without a permanent address often are hard to find.

To arrive at a more accurate estimate, head counters of the homeless often apply a statistical "fudge factor" to their raw data. Inevitably, though, the resulting figures come under fire for understating or overstating the true size of the homeless population, locally or nationally. (*See story, p. 78.*)

Even providers of services to the homeless differ on whether or not the number of people without shelter is growing. Steinbruck believes the total is climbing, and he attributes much of the increase to deinstitutionalization of the mentally ill. "We now have at least one or two generations that have never been in mental institutions," he says. "They've been on the streets. When I first started my ministry, people who showed symptoms of mental illness usually were institutionalized. That doesn't happen anymore. So you've got paranoid schizophrenics on the streets talking to telephone poles, and hearing voices no one else can hear."

Mentally ill homeless people "aren't dangerous; they're just pitiful," Steinbruck adds. "We haven't provided them with the community-based residential facilities or mental health services they need. And I believe that is unconscionable."

John Wimberly, the pastor of Washington's Western Presbyterian Church, which operates a breakfast program for the homeless, says the number of people served " has stayed about the same for about 10 years." He notes, however, that "the homeless population has changed in terms of who is homeless. When we started our program 12 years ago, a high percentage of the participants were mentally ill, or had drug or alcohol problems. Now, a high percentage are just what I would call poor people."

A typical example, he says, is "a guy who drops out of school at 15 and quickly gets into trouble with the law. After a series of run-ins, he serves time in [prison]. He's 20 years old when he gets out, and he has no high school diploma, no skills. As a result, he ends up homeless. Folks like him generally are eager to work and eager to learn. But they made a mistake when they were 15, and that's that."

Another common scenario cited by Wimberly involves "a married couple living in public housing. They get divorced, which means that everybody in the family ends up homeless. They were able to scrape by on two marginal incomes, but they find out they can't make ends meet when they're by themselves."

Wimberly believes "the homeless population [as a whole] is becoming younger. They're people who, with job training, could take care of themselves. The trouble is, those programs aren't widely available. In some ways, I think, the changing nature of the homeless population is more significant than the numbers."

Thomas L. Kenyon, president of the National Alliance to End Homelessness, a Washington-based advocacy group, believes the country's homeless population has been "fairly stable for the last three to four years." The reason, he says, is that "existing programs to aid the homeless have been working. People have had places where they could go to reclaim their lives, and then move back out into the community."

Salvation Army

Homeless men crowd into a Salvation Army soup kitchen in Seattle, Wash., for a hot meal.

Sister Connie Driscoll, president of the St. Martin de Porres House of Hope, a residence for homeless women and their children on Chicago's South Side, agrees with Kenyon that many homeless people have made the difficult transition to independent living. Some homeless advocates, she says, "just repeatedly claim 'homelessness is rising,' without ever mentioning how many homeless people have moved back into the work force, moved into their own apartments, retrieved their children from state custody."

Sister Connie, who also heads the Chicago Task Force on Homelessness, believes the number of homeless people is declining both in her city and elsewhere. [5] "Chicago has 5,500 shelter beds, and it has the capacity to add more, if necessary," she says. "But last winter, when we were at 40 to 50 below zero with wind chill, we still had empty beds in the system."

According to Sister Connie, the unused beds didn't mean homeless people were afraid to sleep in shelters. "You read all the time that shelters are dangerous, but it isn't true," she says. "In this city, if shelters are found to be unsafe, the Department of Human Services shuts them down and refuses to fund them. The department employs monitoring teams to make sure people in shelters are treated properly. Whenever abuses come to light, Human Services gets new people to run the facilities."

She acknowledges that some homeless people steer clear of shelters regardless of weather conditions: "We try to coax them inside, but sometimes they won't go in because they're mentally ill. Or, they prefer to live the way they want to live. We can't force them to come in out of the cold."

Is lack of housing the main cause of homelessness?

The term "homeless" suggests that all would be well if people without a fixed address could be moved into affordable housing. But homeless-care providers generally say that, while housing is important, it isn't a cure-all.

When the House of Hope began its transitional shelter and substance-

How Many Americans Are Homeless?

Nailing quicksilver to the wall might be easier than conducting a census of the homeless. But despite the inherent difficulties of the task, the quest for an accurate head count persists at all levels of government. Policy-makers need to know how many people require emergency food, shelter and other services before they can devise ways of meeting those needs.

The 1995 annual report of the National Alliance to End Homelessness, a Washington-based advocacy group, touched on some of the pitfalls of enumerating people without a permanent place to live. On any given night, the alliance estimated, some 750,000 Americans will be homeless. It further estimated that between 1.3 million and 2 million persons will experience homelessness over the course of a year.

"This is the number of people who live on the streets, in emergency or transitional shelters, in cars and in campgrounds," the group stated in explaining its enumeration criteria. "It does not include the several million people estimated to be doubled up — staying temporarily with family and friends, but with no housing of their own. Nor does it include people housed in prisons, mental hospitals or in other institutions, but without an independent home.

"Similarly, it does not reflect the millions of people who are precariously housed, paying such a large percentage of their incomes for rent that any unforeseen medical expense, or temporary job loss, could dislodge them. However, all these people make up the pool from which people cycle in and out of homelessness." [1]

René I. Jahiel, an adjunct professor of health services research and policy at the New School for Social Research in New York, pointed to several potential sources of counting error. "Homeless people must be enumerated directly, as opposed to counting the number of [shelter] beds (the number of homeless people may be greater or less than the number of beds), or the number of meals served (one person may be served more than once)," he noted. "The timing of the enumeration is important, since at certain times of night the homeless people may not have arrived or may have already left." [2]

Double-counting may be the chief bugaboo of people who enumerate the homeless. This can occur, Jahiel observed, "when a homeless person meets the enumerators twice in the same area or when a homeless person spends part of the night in a shelter and part on the street and is counted in both places." To hold duplication error to a minimum, Jahiel advises census-takers to identify homeless persons by name and then check for duplicated names. The problem is, many homeless persons give fictitious names to interviewers.

Despite 15 years of experience, estimates of the nation's homeless population still span a broad spectrum. In a December 1994 professional journal article that attracted much comment, Bruce G. Link and a group of colleagues at Columbia University's School of Public Health stated that about 8.5 million Americans experienced homelessness between 1985 and 1990. The estimate was based on a telephone survey of representative U.S. households. Respondents were asked, "Have you ever had a time in your life when you considered yourself homeless?" Affirmative replies elicited follow-up questions.

Christopher Jencks, a Northwestern University sociology professor, is skeptical of multimillion-person estimates of the nation's homeless. "From all the studies I have seen," he wrote in 1994, "I would guess — no one can do more than that — that the homeless population grew from about 125,000 in 1980 to around 400,000 in 1987-1988 and then fell to around 325,000 in 1990." [3]

As for what the future may hold, Jencks offered these thoughts: "If no one drank, took drugs, lost touch with reality or had trouble holding a job, homelessness would be rare. But if America had a system of social welfare comparable to that of Sweden or Germany, homelessness would also be rare. In those countries job training is far better, unskilled jobs pay better, benefits for the unemployed are almost universally available and the mental health system does much more to provide housing for the mentally ill. It is the combination of widespread individual vulnerability and collective indifference that leaves so many Americans in the streets." [4]

---

[1] National Alliance to End Homelessness, *Annual Report 1995*, p. 4.

[2] René I. Jahiel, "The Size of the Homeless Population," *Homelessness: A Prevention-Oriented Approach* (1992), p. 338.

[3] Christopher Jencks, "The Homeless," *The New York Review of Books*, April 21, 1994, p. 22.

[4] *Ibid.*, p. 27.

abuse recovery programs for homeless women 13 years ago, Sister Connie says, "We had the same liberal bent as everybody else: 'These poor people; we've got to do something to help them.' " Experience altered that perception. "After a while, you find yourself saying, 'Wait a minute. Housing isn't the issue here. The issue is personal responsibility and accountability. You've got to get your life together. We can't do this for you, we can only give you the tools. You've got to do it.' "

After working with the homeless, Sister Connie says, "You become more conservative in your thinking on what the problem really is. Many people have been evicted from their apartments not because they *couldn't* pay their rent, but because they *didn't* pay it. Some spent the rent money on drugs, of course, while others used it to buy big-ticket items. And still others thought, 'Nobody's ever going to evict me.' "

She has found that many newly homeless people assumed someone else was always going to take care of them. "Well, that kind of thinking has to stop," she says. "The monthly welfare check is not always going to be there, and now I think many people are realizing that."

In Sister Connie's view, "enormous job-training programs" offer the best hope of reducing homelessness. "Private agencies can do that better than government," she says, because "government can't practice love, either tough or soft. It's incapable of doing that."

Contributing Editor Pete Hamill of *New York* magazine agrees that lack of shelter is a symptom of homelessness, not the underlying cause. "This is not a housing problem," he wrote. "It is a health problem. Not another abstract conflict between the dogmas of liberalism and conservatism. It is an emergency. A health emergency. Thousands of homeless men are sick and dying. And they are passing their diseases on to others." [6]

Hamill added, "Some advocates claim that the homeless are drunk, stoned or insane because they don't have one-bedroom apartments; but the truth is more likely that they are on the streets because they are drunks, crackheads or crazies."

Kenyon recalls that, "Years ago, when this problem first arose, all of us advocates kept talking about nothing but housing, housing, housing." Now, he says, there is general agreement that housing "is what homeless people ultimately need, but only after the systemic causes of their homelessness are addressed."

"You can't expect someone who's lived on the street for eight months to consult the job bank and then apply for a job the very next day," Kenyon says. "That's just not going to happen. If you've been on the street that long, you're so down, so beaten, that you need a period of rebirth or rejuvenation to rebuild your self-confidence. You need to work with professionals who can help you do that before you would have any realistic chance of finding employment."

Steinbruck believes lack of housing is one of two interrelated causes of homelessness. The other is the growing shortage of jobs paying enough to enable individuals and families to afford a permanent dwelling.

"When I started in ministry, I used to visit many elderly in my parish who lived in an old hotel," he says. "Those people got by on Social Security and a hot plate. They lived simply, but they could live. But those old hotels have disappeared; very cheap garden apartments have gone, too." The type of housing being pushed today, he adds, is "$500,000, million-dollar homes. That's where the market is; not affordable housing. You'd go broke if you tried to build affordable housing in this country. And now government has decided to get out of the business" of providing it.

A similar transformation has taken place in the job market, he notes. "When I grew up in North Philadelphia, there were major industries all around us — Philco, RCA, Heinz, textile mills. These companies offered jobs that could last a lifetime. But those jobs aren't there anymore."

Are Americans losing sympathy for the homeless?

Anecdotal evidence suggests Americans are turning their backs on the homeless. For example, the recent National Law Center report cites 61 examples, dating from 1993, of local government and resident opposition to the siting or operation of homeless services.

Of these, the report said, "21 proposed projects were halted (34 percent), six existing facilities were forced to close (10 percent), two existing facilities were forced to move (3 percent), five government-run facilities were closed by the jurisdiction running them (8 percent) and 18 service providers were able to establish the opposed program largely intact (30 percent)." In the nine remaining cases (15 percent), the outcome was adjudged "ambiguous" or "ongoing." [7]

Other observers contend that Americans are suffering from a collective case of "compassion fatigue." New Yorkers, journalist Hamill wrote, "don't want to hear much about the homeless anymore. . . . They don't want to read interviews with men who live in cardboard boxes. They don't want to hear about Vietnam from men who were 15 the year the war ended or who don't know where I Corps was. They don't want to hear any more prison-yard raps. They don't want to listen to any more sad songs." [8]

Sister Connie says "there's no doubt" that popular sympathy for the homeless is receding. She blames the trend on homeless advocates, who she feels go too far in accentuating the negative. "Many major foundations have moved away from homelessness and gone in an entirely different direction," she says. "I've heard foundation officials say, in effect, 'We've been pumping millions of dollars into this over the last 10 or 12 years, and now you're telling us our money hasn't done any good?' You can't blame them for thinking, 'If our money isn't helping to solve the problem, why should we continue supporting these programs?' "

Steinbruck has a somewhat different take on the compassion issue. "Basically, people are decent," he says. "But we have become somewhat numbed in the 1990s. I believe there's something in our culture which makes us think that if a problem can't be solved in 10 years, then we should declare it to be illegal. People get weary, they crawl into their cul-de-sacs, and what's out of sight slips out of mind."

It's not difficult for Americans to remain "oblivious to the tragedies around them," Steinbruck feels. "In the morning, you can get into your air-conditioned car, drive down an expressway, park in an underground garage, take an elevator to your office in a climate-controlled high rise and never

Homelessness in U.S. Cities, 1995

To assess the status of homelessness and hunger in U.S. cities in 1995, the U.S. Conference of Mayors surveyed major cities whose mayors are members of its Task Force on Hunger and Homelessness. Here are some of the major findings of the 29-city survey:

■ Requests for emergency shelter increased by an average of 11 percent in 1995, with 63 percent of the survey cities registering an increase. Requests for shelter by homeless families alone increased by 15 percent, with 71 percent of the cities reporting an increase.

■ Nineteen percent of the requests for emergency shelter by homeless people overall and 24 percent of the requests just by homeless families were unmet last year.

■ People in the survey cities remain homeless an average of six months. Sixty-two percent of the cities said that the length of time people are homeless increased last year.

■ The number of emergency shelter beds increased overall in the survey cities by an average of 3 percent. Transitional housing units increased by an average of 6 percent, single-room occupancy (SRO) units by 5 percent.

■ All of the cities said they expected the demand for emergency shelter to increase in 1996.

Source: U.S. Conference of Mayors, A Status Report on Hunger and Homelessness in America's Cities: 1995, *December 1995.*

have to breathe the air that people on the street breathe. You can live that indifferently if you choose to."

Wimberly, in contrast, sees "no evidence" that Americans are losing sympathy for the homeless. "I sense we may be becoming less compassionate toward the poor in general, but I haven't sensed that attitude toward the homeless," he says. "In fact, a part of me thinks there may be a slightly increased sensitivity [to the plight of the homeless]. The reason is that so many people are feeling vulnerable in their own lives because of what's going on in the economy."

Wimberly concedes there is mounting impatience "with some of the more aggressive and obnoxious homeless people." On the other hand, he says, contributions to Western Presbyterian "indicate that people are still very concerned" about the homeless people the church serves. Moreover, "The level of volunteer involvement — our program is staffed primarily by volunteers — remains very high. College students are still interested in coming over here and working with us."

If Americans seem less compassionate toward the homeless than they did a decade ago, Kenyon says, it's because homelessness "is no longer the cause du jour." He believes that, "on a personal basis, one to one, Americans are still extremely compassionate about homeless people. But because the problem still exists, most people don't appreciate that solutions do exist and that they are working. If they weren't working, there would be even more homeless people on the street."

Public opinion polls taken in recent years have generally found a high level of support for programs to aid poor, hungry and homeless individuals and families. For example, the almost 16,000 households surveyed recently for the Food Research and Action Center, a Washington-based group that seeks more effective policies to eradicate domestic hunger and malnutrition, were asked, "How important do you consider the issue of alleviating hunger and poverty in the upcoming presidential and congressional campaigns?" Ninety-five percent of those questioned rated the issue "extremely important," "very important" or "important," while only 5 percent said it was "not very important" or "not at all important." [9] Other surveys have consistently shown majority support for tax increases earmarked for programs benefiting the homeless. [10]

Maria Foscarinis, executive director of the National Law Center, feels the survey results show that Nimbyism directed at homeless shelters and services flies in the face of popular opinion. "It's indicative of a system that allows small groups of people to act on their irrational fears," she says. "Anti-homeless Nimbyism receives attention disproportionate to its actual support among the public."

When the responses to surveys about the homeless are broken down by respondents' age, a generation gap emerges. The data clearly show that older people are more sympathetic than younger people toward the homeless. Advocates for the homeless aren't surprised.

"Many of us who are 55 and older had parents who went through the Great Depression," notes Kenyon. "Younger people, who haven't gone through a major upheaval like the Depression or World War II, tend to think homelessness is a deliberate lifestyle choice. That's why they often disdain the people they see living on the streets."

As Sister Connie sees it, young people's attitudes toward the homeless "are just part of the '90s syndrome," which by her definition includes breakdown of the traditional family structure. "If young people don't have a stable family situation at home, why should they care about somebody on the street? In fact, they don't care. They're worried about their own lives." ■

BACKGROUND

Vagrants and Vagabonds

The only thing really new about homelessness in the United States is the term used to describe it. Vagrancy and begging have been marginal features of American life since the early days of the Republic.

Over the years, though, perceptions of the jobless and homeless poor have changed. In the past, Alice S. Baum and Donald W. Burnes wrote in a 1993 study of the problem, "the public was willing to admit that social isolation, alcoholism, drug abuse and mental illness were closely associated with homelessness, and from time to time reformers have designed programs intended to address these problems, some punitive, some generous." Today, in contrast, "fearful of blaming the victim, most people prefer to deny these conditions and view homelessness as a single problem: being without a home." [11]

Borrowing from British experience, Americans of a century ago drew a sharp distinction between poverty and pauperism — that is, between the "deserving" and the "undeserving" poor. The deserving poor comprised incurably ill and physically handicapped persons, widows and orphans, and men unable to care for their families because of sudden job loss. For the most part, the term pauper was reserved for able-bodied men who refused any work. Though little assistance for the poor was available, virtually all of it went to individuals and families whose condition was deemed beyond their control. Paupers received only contempt.

As Baum and Burnes noted, some of the most romantic figures of 19th-century America were, in essence, persons without steady employment or fixed addresses. The list included "hunters, trappers, fur traders, Indian scouts, explorers and cowboys, who were always on the move, pushing the frontier westward." Admired to this day for their rugged individualism, "these loners were, nevertheless, first and foremost social isolates — unmarried men, detached from family and friends, members of no communities except the temporary societies they formed with their wandering comrades." [12]

Meanwhile, the social and economic upheavals of the time left deep scars. Many wounded Civil War veterans, unable to regain their bearings, joined the ranks of the itinerant poor. Widows and orphans of men killed in the conflict often suffered a similar fate.

The depressions that periodically shook the economy in the post-Civil War era plunged thousands of families into sudden indigence. Temple University historian Kenneth L. Kusmer noted that the "increasing number of homeless men during the very period when the United States was emerging as an industrial nation was no coincidence. The new vagrancy was an indigenous aspect of a country in rapid transition from an agricultural and small-town society to one centered in great cities." [13]

Government Helps Out

Before the 1930s, private charities and local governments furnished the bulk of services for poor, jobless and homeless people. But the Great Depression that followed the stock market crash of October 1929 produced a social crisis that overwhelmed the resources of traditional caregivers. As the nationwide unemployment rate rose into double-digit figures, breadlines and soup-kitchen queues grew steadily longer. At the same time, shantytowns derisively called "Hoovervilles" sprang up in large cities — even in the middle of New York's Central Park.

Soon after Franklin D. Roosevelt took office as president in 1933, the federal government began to assume a major role in combating poverty and homelessness — though chiefly on a temporary, emergency basis, and with some strings attached. For instance, the Works Progress Administration (WPA) was created in 1935 to provide jobs for the unemployed. However, applicants had to meet strict residency requirements to qualify for the jobs.

Most of the emergency relief programs established in the early years of the New Deal were discontinued with the advent of World War II. With war-production plants operating at peak capacity, civilian unemployment virtually vanished. Joblessness remained at low levels after peace returned, especially during the 1950s. By that time, homelessness seemed confined to the alcoholic and mentally disturbed single men who frequented neighborhoods like lower Manhattan's Bowery, with its abundance of cheap bars and flophouses.

Before long, though, homelessness resurfaced as a national concern. Social historians date the turnabout from February 1963, when President John F. Kennedy asked Congress to adopt a "bold new approach" to the mentally ill, a request that was to have unforeseen consequences. Kennedy urged the creation of a nationwide network of community mental health centers to replace existing facilities for treating the mentally ill. A shift to community-based care was widely seen as humane, since numerous abuses of patients had come to light at state-operated institutions.

Congress acceded to Kennedy's request to localize treatment of the mentally ill. From the outset, though, it was clear that many recently released patients were not receiving the aftercare they needed to function in a non-institutional setting. As a result, many mental patients ended up on the streets. [14]

Court Rulings Affecting the Homeless

The 1970s saw the courts become embroiled in the homelessness issue for the first time. In January 1972, the U.S. Supreme Court unanimously upheld lower court rulings barring one-year welfare residency laws in New York and Connecticut. The following month, the high court struck down as unconstitutionally vague a Jacksonville, Fla., ordinance used to punish persons as vagrants if they violated laws against loafing, "nightwalking" or avoiding work. The decision was framed in broad enough language to void many of the vagrancy laws on the books in other cities and states.

Callahan v. Carey, the nation's first right-to-shelter lawsuit, was filed in New York State Supreme Court in October 1979 by homeless advocate Robert M. Hayes. In a ruling handed down that Dec. 7, Justice Andrew R. Tyler ordered New York City and New York state to create 750 new beds for the "helpless and homeless men of the Bowery."

Matters did not end there, however. Although New York agreed in a 1981 consent decree to improve conditions in its shelters, homeless advocates had to obtain 19 additional court orders to force full compliance.

The Public Takes Notice

It was around this time — it's impossible to fix a precise date — that panhandlers and shabbily dressed people sleeping on outdoor steam grates began to attract the anxious notice of city residents and the news media. At first, the development was blamed on the 1981-82 recession and federal budget cuts made by the Reagan administration. Once the economy improved, it was assumed, the number of homeless people would drop.

But that failed to happen, forcing social commentators to look for other, more deep-seated causes of homelessness. The introduction of highly addictive crack cocaine in the mid-1980s obviously was a major factor. But changes in the work force and in housing availability may have been even more disruptive.

Homeless advocates pointed out that the unskilled day-labor jobs transients had long relied on were rapidly disappearing, as was much of the nation's stock of low-rent housing. Many apartments in public housing complexes were being boarded up because of vandalism or lack of maintenance. And in some cities, entire high-rise public housing projects were being demolished as uninhabitable. The combination of fewer bottom-tier jobs and fewer affordable-housing units evidently tipped thousands of poor people out of their homes and into the streets.

Loss of privately owned shelter for low-income people compounded the problem. Rooming houses, once a common residential option in big cities, have become an endangered housing species. Many of the structures, especially those in gentrified neighborhoods, have been returned to single-family use and sold at a handsome profit by their owners.

The supply of single-room occupancy (SRO) hotels has fallen sharply for the same reason. From the 1950s until well into the 1970s, SROs provided decent shelter for thousands of Americans suffering from mental or emotional disorders or drug dependency. Neighborhood residents often campaigned to have the buildings shut down, arguing that the persons who lived in them made too much noise and engaged in petty crime.

As in the case of rooming houses, however, economic forces were the controlling ones. Since the 1970s, numerous SRO buildings have been transformed into multi-room apartments for the upscale rental or condominium market. Others have been torn down as unsalvageable.

Christopher Jencks, a sociology professor at Northwestern University, feels that construction of "cubicle hotels" modeled on the flophouses of yore could do much to alleviate homelessness. He acknowledges that cubicle housing would "provoke opposition in some neighborhoods." On the other hand, they "would also cost far less to build and maintain than regular SRO rooms." Finally, he says, "Such a program would sharply reduce both the number of people sleeping in public places and the number wandering the streets during the day." [15]

But assuming cubicle housing was built, how much of it would be needed? There is no consensus on this point, since government officials and homeless-care providers offer widely divergent estimates of the number of Americans without shelter. The debate dates at least from 1980, when Mitch Snyder, a homeless activist with

Continued on p. 84

Chronology

19th Century

The Civil War, massive immigration and westward expansion create a vast and variegated army of the homeless — including such romantic figures as cowboys, Indian scouts and gold seekers.

1890
New York enacts the first law under which a state government assumes full responsibility for all of the "insane poor."

—— • ——

1930s ***After the stock market crash of 1929, shantytowns of the homeless spring up in cities across the nation.***

1933-1935
The Federal Emergency Relief Administration (FERA) supplies shelter, food, medical care, clothing, cash and jobs to the homeless.

1935
FERA is replaced by programs targeting individual needs. The Works Progress Administration (WPA) creates jobs on but requires applicants to meet strict residency tests.

—— • ——

1960s ***A law hailed initially as humane causes homelessness to swell after years of seeming remission.***

1963
At the behest of President John F. Kennedy, Congress passes the Community Health Centers Act, which deinstitutionalizes an estimated 430,000 mentally ill people.

1970s ***The courts rule on homelessness for the first time.***

1972
The Supreme Court decriminalizes vagrancy and declares that laws making residency a condition for receiving public assistance are unconstitutional.

Dec. 7, 1979
Ruling in *Callahan v. Carey,* New York Supreme Court Justice Andrew R. Tyler declares that the state and the city must provide "clean bedding, wholesome food and adequate supervision and security" for the homeless.

—— • ——

1980s ***The nation awakens to the problems of homelessness just as the supply of affordable housing for the poor begins to shrink.***

September 1982
The Community for Creative Non-Violence, a homeless-advocacy group in Washington, D.C., estimates that 2.2 million Americans lack shelter.

October 1982
A 55-city survey by the U.S. Conference of Mayors reports that only 43 percent of the demand for emergency services for the homeless is met.

July 22, 1987
President Ronald Reagan signs into law the Stewart B. McKinney Homeless Assistance Act, which provides for emergency shelters, job training and other programs.

1990s ***Increasingly, homelessness is perceived as a complex condition resistant to quick or easy remedies.***

May 1992
The Census Bureau issues the results of a nationwide 1990 survey of homeless people. Some 459,000 persons are tallied in shelters and on the street. Homeless advocates assail the count as far too low.

May 17, 1994
The Interagency Council on the Homeless outlines a strategy to trim the number of homeless Americans by one-third. The council recommends a "continuum of care" approach offering individuals and families a variety of services.

Dec. 6, 1995
President Clinton vetoes the balanced budget bill approved by Congress. The measure would have cut federal welfare spending by $81.5 billion and eliminated the preference for homeless-assistance groups in the disposal of surplus federal property, as provided by the McKinney Act.

Dec. 13, 1995
The National Law Center on Homelessness and Poverty issues a report analyzing Nimby ("Not in my backyard!") opposition to services for homeless people in 36 jurisdictions across the U.S.

Dec. 19, 1995
A U.S. Conference of Mayors survey notes that "An estimated 19 percent of the requests for emergency shelter by homeless people overall and 24 percent of the requests by homeless families alone are estimated to have gone unmet during the last year."

Can Homelessness Be Prevented?

The adage about "an ounce of prevention . . ." applies as surely to homelessness as to any other aspect of life. If a person can be identified as "at risk" of becoming homeless, conventional wisdom holds, he or she can be spared the trauma of living for weeks or months on the streets — and society will be spared the cost of living with or undoing the damage.

Thomas L. Kenyon, president of the National Alliance to End Homelessness, notes that many prevention efforts originate "in faith-based groups, community centers or close-knit neighborhoods." If a family's house burns down, or the chief breadwinner is thrown out of work, "There's a network in place that can say, 'All this family needs is such-and-such,' and they'll do their best to provide it."

The Rental Assistance Program (RAP) in New York City, administered by the National Coalition for the Homeless, provides up to $200 a month to help people pay the rent. Though geared primarily to people on the streets, in homeless shelters or coming out of drug rehabilitation, the privately funded program also covers persons squeezed into small apartments with family members or friends. Experience shows that many of these people end up homeless.

New York's Chase Manhattan Corp. offers bank accounts to homeless veterans in the city. In many cases, having a secure haven for their money enables the vets to rent an apartment after months or years of homelessness.

The Life Skills Program, operated nationwide by the Alliance to End Homelessness, teaches daily living skills to persons who have never learned them. Subjects include setting goals, parenting, budgeting and being a good tenant.

Many local governments also operate programs to forestall homelessness. Sister Connie Driscoll, president of the St. Martin de Porres House of Hope, a women's shelter on Chicago's South Side, notes that the city operates numerous hotlines to prevent minor personal crises from escalating into major ones: "Say there's no heat in the apartment. Or the tenant can't pay that month's rent. Or maybe there's some other kind of landlord-tenant dispute. The city of Chicago's hotlines are set up to handle situations like that — situations that could easily lead to homelessness if untreated. And that's a good, solid way to go about it."

A limited amount of homelessness-prevention assistance is available at the federal level as well. For example, the Gateway Program, a demonstration program included in the 1990 amendments to the Stewart B. McKinney Homeless Assistance Act, provided for education, job training and various supportive services for public-housing residents.

But such programs were assailed by Alice S. Baum and Donald W. Burnes, authors of *A Nation in Denial: The Truth About Homelessness,* as "the ultimate creaming mechanism." Baum and Burnes maintain that the programs focus resources on that segment of the "at risk" population that is least at risk. "[P]revention programs are targeted to people who are not disaffiliated or disabled by alcoholism, drug addiction or mental illness, and who are therefore not homeless," they write. "These may be good and necessary programs, but they are not programs to help the homeless." [1]

A 1990 report by the U.S. General Accounting Office stated that homelessness-prevention programs "are not intended for the mentally ill or substance abusers who are at risk because their problems go beyond a short-term financial crisis. These people require much more in the way of support services, including long-term professional help and drug abuse treatment." [2]

In any event, much of the discussion about homelessness prevention is academic, Kenyon says. That's because "there are very few funds available for prevention. Until it's a crisis, an in-your-face situation, people just don't want to spend money on it."

[1] Alice S. Baum and Donald W. Burnes, *A Nation in Denial: The Truth About Homelessness* (1993), pp. 85-86.

[2] U.S. General Accounting Office, *Homelessness: Too Early to Tell What Kinds of Prevention Assistance Work Best* (1990), p. 11, cited in *ibid.*, p. 86.

the Community for Creative Non-Violence (CCNV) in Washington, D.C., began to draw frequent media coverage. In a 1982 report, "Homelessness in America: A Forced Watch to Nowhere," Snyder and a colleague, Mary Ellen Hombs, estimated that 2.2 million people lacked shelter nationwide and predicted that the number would reach 3 million or more in 1983.

"Lacking better figures, others repeated this guess, usually without attribution," Jencks noted. "In due course, it became so familiar that many people treated it as a well-established fact." [16] Today, experts still debate not only the size of the homeless population but also the proper methodology to use in counting it. (*See story, p. 78*).

McKinney Act

Snyder played a pivotal role in pressuring Congress to approve the Stewart B. McKinney Homeless Assistance Act, still the most important law of its kind on the federal statute books.* The measure was introduced Jan. 8, 1987, bringing to an end a seven-week protest at the Capitol by advocates of increased aid to the homeless. CCNV members had camped out near the

* The man for whom the law is named was a Republican House member from Connecticut who died of complications from AIDS on May 7, 1987, before the measure cleared Congress. It was noted at the time that McKinney contracted his final illness — pneumonia — after sleeping overnight with several congressional colleagues on outdoor heating grates to dramatize the plight of the homeless.

Capitol's East Front since Thanksgiving Day 1986 next to a homemade statue honoring the homeless. Snyder had defied police and court orders to remove the figure.

House approval of the homeless bill early that March came just two nights after a highly publicized "Grate American Sleep-Out," in which a dozen members of Congress joined a small crowd of movie stars and activists to spend a bitterly cold night on the streets of Washington. The event was organized by Snyder and actor Martin Sheen, who had portrayed Snyder in a television program about the homeless.

As signed into law by President Ronald Reagan on July 22, 1987, the McKinney Act authorized $443 million in homeless aid for fiscal 1987 and an additional $616 million for fiscal 1988. Among other provisions, it established an Interagency Council on the Homeless, comprising the heads of 15 federal agencies or persons designated by them, to coordinate federal programs to assist the homeless and to report to Congress and the president on the extent of the nation's homeless problem. *

The nearly 20 programs covered by the measure included emergency food and shelter, medical and mental-health care, permanent housing, education and job training. In addition, the law directed the secretary of the Department of Housing and Urban Development (HUD) to identify underused federal buildings and make them available for housing homeless individuals and families.

When Congress extended the McKinney Act in 1993, it authorized $150 million to develop and renovate single rooms for the homeless — the approach Jencks was to endorse the following year. At the same time, Congress chose not to fund the Interagency Council on the Homeless. However, the council resurfaced later that year as a working group under the direction of the White House.

Salvation Army

Carrying all their wordly possessions, a homeless family walks the streets in Phoenix, Ariz.

Clinton Administration Tackles the Problem

A tragedy that occurred toward the end of 1993 prodded the Clinton administration to step up its efforts on behalf of the homeless. HUD Secretary Henry G. Cisneros voiced dismay when a homeless woman, Yetta M. Adams, 43, was found dead on a bus shelter bench on the street outside his office early on Nov. 29. The low temperature that morning had been 34, two degrees above the threshold that triggers Washington's emergency-shelter program. Cisneros said that Adams' death was "an indictment of a system that evolved haphazardly to treat the symptom of homelessness and failed to address its underlying causes." [17]

Cisneros showed his concern by advancing several hundred thousand dollars to the Washington city government in early December to upgrade its homeless-outreach efforts. He also announced that HUD, which is primarily responsible for federal programs for the homeless, would tap a special-assistance fund to distribute $25 million to other cities for similar purposes. At the end of the month, the Clinton administration announced grants of $411 million to fund 187 homeless-assistance programs in 44 states. California was the primary beneficiary, with almost $75 million; New York, with some $40 million, was second.

Then, in May 1994, the Clinton administration issued a blueprint for trimming the U.S. homeless population by one-third. The report, called "Priority: Home! The Federal Plan to End Homelessness," proposed $900 million in new HUD spending for homeless aid, bringing the total to a record $2.15 billion in fiscal 1995.

To achieve its aims, the report recommended a "continuum of care" combining shelter, education, substance-abuse counseling, job training and medical treatment. Many private caregivers already had decided that homeless people require several types of assistance, tailored to individual need, to get back on their feet.

Cities Crack Down

As federal concern about the homeless mounted in 1994, city govern-

Continued on p. 87

* The number of agencies was later expanded to 17.

How Hollywood Views the Homeless

The road is your estate,
The earth your little dinner plate;
It's spring, you hobo, sing,
"Hallelujah, I'm a bum again!"

Is it fun to be homeless? The easy answer — seemingly the only answer — is no. But Hollywood often says yes.

To be sure, many movies affirm the conventional wisdom that homelessness is one station stop short of hell. Director John Ford's 1939 film version of John Steinbeck's novel *The Grapes of Wrath* heads the list. Less familiar, though just as powerful in its way, is "Wild Boys of the Road," a 1933 Warner Bros. drama about jobless youths who ride the rails, panhandle and steal.

However, the prototypical homeless character in film is Charlie Chaplin's Little Tramp, never more poignant than in "City Lights" (1931). The story begins as the Tramp buys a flower from a blind girl (Virginia Cherrill) with his last cent. To pay for an operation to restore her sight, he takes jobs as a street sweeper and a boxer. Finally, using money supplied by a millionaire he has saved from drowning, the Tramp arranges for the surgery, which is successful. All the while, the girl can only guess at the identity of her benefactor.

The film ends as she sees him for the first time. James Agee, the late film critic, described the scene as follows: "She recognizes who he must be by his shy, confident, shining joy as he comes silently toward her. And he recognizes himself, for the first time, through the terrible changes in her face. The camera just exchanges a few quiet close-ups of the emotions which shift and intensify in each face. It is enough to shrivel the heart to see, and it is the greatest piece of acting and the highest moment in movies." [1]

Later movies were to spin variations on the "City Lights" scenario. Prominent among them is "Hallelujah, I'm a Bum," a social-fable musical of 1933. Initially, the film focuses on homeless men camped out in New York's Central Park. Implausibly cheerful, they converse among themselves in rhymed couplets and repeatedly break into song. (The excellent score is by Richard Rodgers and Lorenz Hart.)

Bumper (Al Jolson), the park's self-styled "mayor," is anything but downcast about his hand-to-mouth existence. At one point, indeed, he rhapsodizes in song about the rootless life:

Your home is always near;
The moon's your chandelier;
Your ceiling is the sky,
Way up high.

The dramatic tension in "Hallelujah, I'm a Bum" springs from Bumper's entanglements with the mayor of New York (Frank Morgan) and the mayor's mistress (Madge Evans). As with "City Lights," the film concludes on a bittersweet note.

In "My Man Godfrey" (1936), a ditsy Manhattan society girl (Carole Lombard) wins a scavenger hunt by corralling a "forgotten man" (William Powell) at the East River garbage dump he calls home. ("A scavenger hunt is exactly like a treasure hunt," she explains. "Except in a treasure hunt, you try to find something you want, and in a scavenger hunt, you try to find something that nobody wants.")

Godfrey becomes the indispensable manservant of the girl's rich but addled family and also saves it from financial ruin. He manages to do this because, it turns out, he's not a feckless vagabond at all but a well-heeled Boston blueblood temporarily down on his luck. Despite the shaky premise of its denouement, "Godfrey" remains a screwball comedy classic.

Another comedy, "Sullivan's Travels" (1941), depicts homelessness as unflinchingly as any "serious" film. The title character is a director of hugely popular Hollywood fluff like "So Long, Sarong," "Hey, Hey, in the Hayloft" and "Ants in Your Pants of 1939." Deep down, though, Sullivan (Joel McCrea) yearns to make an epic about down-and-outers called "Oh Brother, Where Art Thou?" — a "true canvas of the suffering of humanity," as he puts it. Sullivan's studio reluctantly humors him. What follows, as the director's illusions about homelessness are shattered, is a heady blend of slapstick and melodrama.

Hollywood still turns out films about homelessness, though not so many as in the old days. Now as before, the situation typically is played for laughs. A prime example is "Down and Out in Beverly Hills" (1983), in which Nick Nolte plays Jerry Baskin, a derelict who tries to drown himself in the heated backyard pool of an affluent Beverly Hills couple, the Whitemans (Richard Dreyfuss and Bette Midler). After being rescued, Jerry does more than ingratiate himself with the Whitemans — he takes over their household, with often hilarious results. [2]

In 1991, actor-director Mel Brooks explored homelessness in "Life Stinks." Starring as Goddard Bolt, an obnoxious billionaire, Brooks bets a rival tycoon that he can survive on the streets of Los Angeles for a month without money. Amid its typically Brooksian barrage of gags, the film strives to make some sort of meaningful statement about homelessness. But most critics felt the jokes and the message both fell flat. "[T]hin at best, tasteless at worst," was the verdict of the anonymous reviewer in *Leonard Maltin's Movie and Video Guide*.

---

[1] James Agee, "Comedy's Greatest Era," *Agee on Film* (1958), p. 10.

[2] "Down and Out in Beverly Hills" is an updated version of a 1932 French film, "Boudou Saved From Drowning."

Continued from p. 85

ments were adopting harsher policies. That May, for example, New York Mayor Rudolph W. Giuliani announced that in order to qualify for shelter and other services, homeless persons would have to be willing to participate in job training, drug treatment and other self-help programs. Moreover, he said the city would begin denying shelter to families who turn down more than three apartments offered by the city.

The Giulani approach seemed positively benign compared with some adopted by other cities that year. In a survey of 49 cities released in December 1994, the National Law Center on Homelessness and Poverty found that 42 "pursued efforts to criminalize activities associated with homelessness," while the remaining seven "adopted alternative approaches." [18]

Of the 42 cities that engaged in anti-homeless activities in 1994, the center found that 62 percent enacted or enforced anti-panhandling ordinances; 26 percent enacted or enforced restrictions on occupying public spaces; 24 percent conducted police sweeps of homeless persons; 24 percent selectively enforced laws rarely applied to the non-homeless; and 21 percent enacted or enforced curbs on providers of services to the homeless.

Arguing that such laws and policies are unfair, the center declared: "In the absence of sufficient shelter space, homeless people literally have nowhere else to go — or be — than the streets and other public places. In the absence of sufficient jobs or income, homeless people may literally have no means to meet basic survival needs other than begging for change. Cities that punish their homeless residents for these activities essentially punish them for being homeless."

The center conceded that "Some concerns about the use of public space are legitimate: Ultimately, no city resident — homeless or housed — wants people living and begging in the streets. But criminalizing these activities is not the solution. Instead of attacking homeless people, cities should attack homelessness." [19] ■

CURRENT SITUATION

Good News, Bad News

Despite a handful of positive developments, 1995 brought few improvements in the condition of America's homeless. For instance, this December's report by the National Law Center on Homelessness and Poverty found a rising tide of Nimbyism across the country (*see pp. 76, 84*).

Of the 36 jurisdictions covered in the latest survey, five were named the "most exclusionary" — Eureka and Roseville, Calif.; Huntsville, Ala.; Collier County, Fla. (Naples); and Cleveland, Ohio. According to the report, Roseville "refused to open its armory as a shelter for the winter of 1994-95 as it had each of the previous six years, despite local churches' offer to pay the cost." In addition, "the city began dismantling encampments, discarding property and issuing citations to homeless people living — by necessity — in public places." [20]

Five other communities were singled out for having the "meanest streets" — Atlanta, San Francisco, * Seattle, Santa Ana, Calif., and Santa Monica, Calif. According to the report, Atlanta "discriminatorily enforces a variety of ordinances against homeless people, including its ban on 'remaining' in a parking lot, with an eye toward clearing the streets for the Summer Olympics." [21]

Foscarinis, the law center's executive director, isn't surprised by the apparent increase in antipathy toward the homeless in some cities. "Certain systemic problems contribute to Nimbyism," she says. "For example, the zoning process in many cities is one that presumptively excludes services for the homeless — and is designed in many cases to set up confrontations. So what we end up with is a very vocal — albeit very small — group of people who wield enormous power in leading opposition to these kinds of programs."

Rick Herz, the law center's civil rights monitor, notes that "All services for the homeless tend to get painted with the brush of those homeless people who local residents most fear. For instance, residents will be as vociferously opposed to shelters for families as they are to shelters for mentally ill single men."

Similarly, adds Herz, "Well-run group homes for recovering substance abusers or mentally ill people virtually always face opposition at first. But after a year or two, [group homes] come to blend in with the neighborhood, and may even be seen as community assets."

To illustrate his point, he cites what happened after residents of the Briarwood neighborhood in Queens, N.Y., learned that the city planned to open a homeless shelter nearby. "They fought the idea," says Herz. "But after it became apparent the shelter was going in, the neighbors got together and said, 'OK. We're going to work with this facility to make it the best it can be. That will help the shelter residents, and it'll also help us.' And that's just what happened."

As the National Law Center report pointed out, however, caregivers often must take legal action to secure their right to operate programs benefiting the homeless. One such court

* San Francisco's new police chief, Fred Lau, said Jan. 11 that he plans to disband the city's program to rid city streets and parks of the homeless and panhandlers. Lau, chosen by new Democratic Mayor Willie Brown, said sleeping in parks and urinating in public remain illegal, but that police would no longer go out of their way to target violators.

case was *Western Presbyterian Church v. [District of Columbia] Board of Zoning Adjustment.* Western Presbyterian had served breakfast to homeless people on its property in downtown Washington for about 10 years. When it announced plans to move to a residential neighborhood about 10 blocks away in April 1994, it said it would continue feeding the homeless. After neighbors objected, the city zoning administrator ruled against Western Presbyterian, stating that the breakfast program was not an "accessory use . . . customarily incidental to" use of a church building.

On the eve of the move, Western Presbyterian obtained a temporary U.S. District Court injunction blocking enforcement of the zoning ordinance. The court subsequently ruled that "this well-run and necessary effort to minister to the less fortunate residents of this city ought not be arbitrarily restricted and relegated to the less desirable areas of the city because of the unfounded or irrational fears of certain residents." On Sept. 9, 1994, the court made the injunction permanent.

The city government, then headed by Mayor Sharon Pratt Kelly, appealed the September ruling. But the appeal was dropped after Marion Barry succeeded Kelly as mayor in January 1995.

Wimberly, Western Presbyterian's pastor, is pleased that the District Court decision "has some precedental value in terms of protecting other churches and synagogues that might be working with the homeless." He also believes Western Presbyterian has been made to feel welcome in its new home.

By the time the court fight ended, he says, "the number of people opposed to us was very small. I would never say they've given up in the sense that they now like the program. But clearly, the neighborhood not only accepts what we do for the homeless; I think many people actually embrace it."

Wimberly recalls that, about six months after the move, he was approached by a woman he knew "had been very upset about the feeding program being here." She wanted to know when it was to begin. "When I told her it had been running for the past six months, she was stunned. She couldn't believe we could feed the homeless without causing a problem. And we haven't [caused a problem]."

One of the most important judicial rulings bearing on homelessness issues was handed down May 15, 1995, by the U.S. Supreme Court. At issue in *City of Edmonds [Wash.] v. Oxford House Inc.* was a local zoning ordinance barring more than five unrelated individuals from occupying a single-family dwelling; no such restriction applied to the number of related persons who could live in such a home.

The city government cited the law in an effort to bar the operation of a group residence for recovering substance abusers housing 10 to 12 persons. Oxford House, a national organization, said the ordinance violated 1988 amendments to the 1968 Fair Housing Act that outlawed housing discrimination based on race, religion, sex, family status, national origin or disability. Challenging that interpretation, Edmonds said the zoning standard fell within an exemption to the 1988 amendments. The exemption provided that the federal statute does not "limit the applicability of any reasonable . . . restrictions regarding the maximum number of occupants permitted to occupy a dwelling."

Justice Ruth Bader Ginsburg, writing for the court majority, held that cities could limit the number of occupants in a home to prevent overcrowding. They could not, however, place restrictions on who could live in a home, she wrote. The zoning provisions invoked against Oxford House, Ginsburg declared, "are classic examples of a use restriction and complementing family composition rule. These provisions do not cap the number of people who may live in a dwelling. In plain terms, they direct that dwellings be used only to house families."

Further court challenges to local curbs on providers of services to the homeless are expected. The National Law Center, for instance, has called on the Justice Department and other federal agencies to work with it in determining whether efforts to exclude such services violate civil rights laws.

Paul Hancock, housing section chief of the Justice Department's Civil Rights Division, says he "can't say" at present whether the department will conduct an investigation of the kind sought by the center. He notes, however, that "we do have some authority to enforce laws that prohibit certain types of discrimination. And sometimes those laws can be used to prevent discrimination against people who are homeless."

The housing section has limited freedom to maneuver because its jurisdiction "doesn't directly address homelessness," Hancock explains. He adds, however, that the section did enter a Philadelphia housing case which touched on the issue. "We felt the proposed housing was under attack because the people who were going to live in it were mentally ill and formerly homeless," he says. "So we alleged discrimination on the basis of disability."

Studies and News Reports Underscore the Problem

A week after the National Law Center released its latest survey, the U.S. Conference of Mayors issued a status report on hunger and homelessness in 29 cities of varying size across the country. Although the focus was somewhat different, the tone of the conference's report also was generally downbeat. Among other things, it found that:

- Sixty-three percent of the people seeking emergency food assistance in survey cities in 1995 were members of families — parents and their children.
- Requests for emergency shelter by families rose by 15 percent over 1994. At the same time, about 24 percent of family shelter requests went unmet.
- An estimated 46 percent of home-

Continued on p. 90

At Issue:

Do anti-panhandling ordinances violate the civil rights of homeless people?

yes

U.S. DISTRICT JUDGE ROBERT W. SWEET
Decision in* Loper v. New York City Police Department, *challenging the constitutionality of New York City's anti-begging statute, Sept. 30, 1992.

The difference between giving a dollar to a homeless beggar . . . and [to] the Coalition for the Homeless is largely semantic. Both are charitable acts intended to provide someone with food, clothing or shelter. The organized charity will take some amount off the top for administrative expenses. It no doubt will also spend some of the dollar to publicize the fact that homeless people do exist and need help. This message, though, is the exact same message the homeless beggar conveys. . . .

One can readily imagine scenarios in which the government could permissibly ban some begging. For example, a ban on aggressive begging would probably survive scrutiny, as would a ban on begging immediately outside ATMs. A regulation prohibiting all solicitation in a 10-block radius from Grand Central Station during the rush hour no doubt might constitute a reasonable time, place and manner restriction. But . . . the statute [in question] cuts off all means of allowing beggars to communicate their message of solicitation. . . .

The speaker's primary interest is that of being able to call something to the attention of a wide audience. In this case, the speaker's interest is the impoverished person's interest in calling his condition to the attention of the general public, and in directly soliciting funds on his own behalf from anyone who will listen. The beggar's personal message also contains a broader social message even when it is not explicitly presented to his audience. . . . It is the message that social and economic conditions and opportunities and governmental services are such that many people are unable to support themselves and must rely on the freely given alms of others in order to eke out an existence while living on the streets of New York. This, too, is a critical message that the beggar has a genuine and legitimate interest in presenting to the public at large. . . .

Here, the court is presented with a statute that imposes a blanket ban on conduct with an expressive component entitled to some First Amendment protection. It does this in a manner directed at the content of that expression by allowing the organized charity to solicit on the street while preventing the unorganized beggar from doing so. While the government has a valid interest in preventing fraud, preserving public order and protecting and promoting the interests of audiences and bystanders, the interest in permitting free speech and the message begging sends about our society predominates. [The New York City anti-begging statute] is therefore unconstitutional under the First Amendment to the United States Constitution, as applied to the states.

(This ruling was upheld in 1993 by the Second Circuit U.S. Court of Appeals.)

no

GREGORY P. KANE
Reporter

FROM *THE BALTIMORE SUN*, SEPT. 19, 1994.

Is there a right so silly that the American Civil Liberties Union won't defend it?

Apparently not. U.S. District Court Judge Frederic N. Smalkin ruled last month that Baltimore's ordinance against aggressive panhandling violated the Constitution. It unfairly singled out the homeless, the good judge reasoned. Local ACLU lawyers reacted as if the ruling were the second coming of the First Amendment free-speech guarantee.

Before Judge Smalkin and civil libertarians get too ecstatic, perhaps someone should point out what the law did. It actually protected panhandlers — from themselves, mainly.

In July of 1993, a panhandler named Benjamin Chapman Jr. was stabbed to death in front of tourists in downtown Baltimore. He asked someone for money, got turned down, and, according to witnesses, stupidly and recklessly made some nasty remark in protest. He took a knife in the chest for his trouble.

For civil libertarians, Mr. Chapman was simply exercising his right to free speech. I say he was engaging in sheer idiocy. Those of us who walk Baltimore's streets on a regular basis know we can't say anything to anyone at any time we please. To do so courts disaster. We realize that having a right to free speech and knowing when and where to use it are two entirely different matters.

Panhandlers, on the other hand, seem incapable of making that distinction. Months before Mr. Chapman's death, I predicted that such an ugly incident would occur. Panhandlers were no longer taking "no" as an answer to requests for money. They were getting surly, bilious, argumentative. They were acting, in short, as though they were entitled to our money.

Predictably, this attitude rubbed some people the wrong way. I saw several incidents in which panhandlers nearly came to blows with guys tired of the aggressive panhandling some people now regard as a right. . . .

Those begging for money in the streets clearly have no . . . family and friends. The question, of course, is why. The answer is because their families and friends know them. They know that the person cannot be trusted either to stay with them or to be given money. So panhandlers turn to complete strangers, whom they can con into believing that they're genuinely homeless, or that they're simply looking for a meal when in reality they are looking for the next hit of crack or scrounging up the price of some cheap booze.

The crack or the booze may be the reason the panhandler is on the street asking for handouts in the first place. Giving money only subsidizes the panhandlers' habits and feeds their illusion that they can simply abrogate responsibility for their own lives and shift it to the rest of us.

FOR MORE INFORMATION

National Alliance to End Homelessness, 1518 K St. N.W., Washington, D.C. 20005; (202) 638-1526. The alliance seeks to form a public-private partnership to abate problems of the homeless.

National Law Center on Homelessness and Poverty, 918 F St. N.W., Suite 412, Washington, D.C. 20004-1406; (202) 638-2535. The center is a legal advocacy group that monitors legislation affecting the homeless.

U.S. Conference of Mayors, Task Force on Hunger and Homelessness, 1620 Eye St. N.W., 4th floor, Washington, D.C. 20006; (202) 293-7330. The task force studies trends in hunger, homelessness and community programs that address homelessness and hunger in U.S. cities.

U.S. Department of Housing and Urban Development, Special Needs Assistance Programs, HUD Building, Room 7262, Washington, D.C. 20410; (202) 708-4300. HUD promotes cooperation among federal agencies on homelessness issues.

Continued from p. 88

less people were substance abusers, 23 percent were mentally ill, 21 percent were veterans and 20 percent were employed. In addition, 8 percent suffered from AIDS or HIV-related illness. [22]

Commenting on the report's findings, Mayor Patricia Ticer of Alexandria, Va., said: "It's never a pretty picture. But it may be as good as it's going to get for some time." [23]

Holiday-period news stories about homelessness, which have become a media staple over the years, underscored Ticer's point. On Dec. 19, Chicago police stumbled upon two squalid, virtually uninhabitable apartments containing a total of 13 children. According to the Rev. Paul Jakes Jr., who runs a homeless shelter in the neighborhood and had recently baptized the mother of two of the children, the tragedy is that abjectly poor people "will make the lifestyle which is abnormal a normal life and will just continue to dwell in that." He added, "For many people who are homeless, having some semblance of a home, having a door and apartment, as long as they have four walls, they feel secure, even if it is a deplorable situation." [24]

The day after the Chicago story broke, *The Washington Post* reported that small children, some only weeks old, were routinely shuttled between overnight shelters in the city and forced onto the streets with their parents in the morning. "A government that keeps its mayor's official family toasty warm . . . can surely find the resources to maintain a 24-hour facility for high-risk babies and their families in the dead of winter," the paper commented in a Dec. 21 editorial. A week later, the city opened two shelters for such families. ■

OUTLOOK

Fear of Budget Cuts

When homeless advocates gaze into their crystal balls, they find a giant cloud blocking their view. It is there courtesy of Congress and the White House, locked in combat over balancing the federal budget. The fate of hundreds of government programs hangs in the balance, including those that benefit the homeless as well as poor and hungry people generally. There seems little doubt that federal welfare spending faces deep cuts; the question is how deep the cuts will be.

The balanced-budget package vetoed by President Clinton on Dec. 6 contained much to make homeless advocates wince. Besides trimming welfare spending by $81.5 billion over seven years, the measure would have converted the Aid to Families with Dependent Children (AFDC) program from an entitlement to a block grant. States also would have received a limited option to convert the federal food stamp program into a block grant, with funding cut significantly.

Another provision of the vetoed bill would have eliminated the McKinney Act's preference for homeless-assistance groups in the disposal of surplus federal property, such as vacant military bases. However, the measure also would have established a program through which the General Services Administration could turn over property it manages to homeless-assistance groups.

Clinton vetoed a revised version of welfare reform on Jan. 9, asserting that the bill "does too little to move people from welfare to work." Designed to save about $58 billion over seven years, the measure would have expanded state control of welfare programs and ended the longstanding guarantee of welfare payments to eligible low-income women and children. In addition, it would have imposed time limits and work requirements on persons receiving welfare.

Because House and Senate Democrats voted overwhelmingly against the welfare-overhaul bill, Republicans had no chance of overriding Clinton's veto. Once again, then, the fate of proposals to overhaul the welfare system apparently hinges on broader budget-balancing negotiations between Congress and the White House.

Alluding to the budget battle's implications for hungry and homeless Americans, Ticer declared that "the future is pretty bleak." Echoing her sentiments, St. Louis Mayor Bosley said: "In the face of what Congress is proposing, officials in our cities fear increased hunger and homelessness [in 1996], increased stress on families and communities, fewer housing options, fewer jobs, less child care — less of everything we need to turn these problems around." [25]

Detroit officials estimate that demand for emergency shelter beds will triple this year if only 1 percent of the city's current AFDC recipients lose benefits because of welfare reform. Similarly, Denver's youth shelter fears being overwhelmed as teenagers are kicked out of their homes "due to increased stress and domestic violence as families struggle to survive with ever-decreasing resources." [26]

Some members of Congress and private advocates of welfare reform suggest that churches and foundations could step up their support of the homeless and accomplish more with less than the federal government has done. "We must replace the welfare state" with a "strategy of dramatically increasing private charities," House Speaker Newt Gingrich, R-Ga., said last year. He suggested that homelessness could be greatly reduced if "every church and synagogue in America" were to "adopt one homeless person." [27]

Homeless advocates say this is wishful thinking. Private charities already "are paddling as fast as they can," says Ticer, adding: "They can't pick up this kind of slack." Kenyon of the National Alliance to End Homelessness agrees. He foresees "an implosion of more people at risk, and a [caregiving] system that's going to be overcrowded and underfunded."

Overall, Kenyon is "very, very pessimistic" about what the future holds for aid to the homeless and other needy people. "I saw some figures that said if the private sector picked up the federal funding slack in this area over the seven years of this budget, corporate and foundation giving would have to increase 40 times. That's just never going to happen; it couldn't possibly happen. I know how hard I have to work to get corporate and foundation money to support our organization. It's not that businesses and foundations aren't willing to contribute; but they have other social causes to take care of besides homelessness."

Sister Connie says she agrees with many, though not all, of the welfare changes sought by Congress. Nonetheless, she hopes the lawmakers "use a lot of compassion and heart" in making the spending cuts. "They shouldn't just look at it as a numbers crunch, and say, 'We can lop this off, we can lop that off.' We've got to remember, really deep down in our hearts, that all the homeless people out there are our brothers and our sisters. Their children are our children. We have got to find a way for them to survive in a better life. That's the bottom line." ■

Notes

[1] For background see "Not In My Backyard!" *Editorial Research Reports,* June 9, 1989, pp. 305-320.

[2] National Law Center on Homelessness and Poverty, *No Room for the Inn,* December 1995, p. iii.

[3] U.S. Conference of Mayors, *A Status Report on Hunger and Homelessness in America's Cities: 1995,* December 1995.

[4] Prepared remarks at a news conference held to release the report on Dec. 19, 1995. Bosley is a former co-chair of the Conference of Mayors' task force on hunger and homelessness.

[5] The task force is a unit of the Chicago Department of Human Services.

[6] Pete Hamill, "How to Save the Homeless — and Ourselves," *New York,* Sept. 20, 1993, p. 36.

[7] National Law Center, *op. cit.,* p. i.

[8] Hamill, *op. cit.,* p. 35.

[9] The survey was released Dec. 19, 1995. It was conducted in late September and October by the A.C. Nielsen Consumer Information Services Panel.

[10] See "The Homeless," *The CQ Researcher,* Aug. 7, 1992, pp. 665-688.

[11] Alice S. Baum and Donald W. Burnes, *A Nation in Denial: The Truth About Homelessness* (1993), p. 91.

[12] *Ibid.,* p. 94.

[13] Quoted by Rick Beard in *On Being Homeless: Historical Perspectives* (1987), p. 23.

[14] See Bob Prentice, "Homelessness and Public Policy," in *Nursing and Health Care for the Homeless,* Juanita K. Hunter, ed. (1993), p. 21.

[15] Christopher Jencks, "Housing the Homeless," *The New York Review of Books,* May 12, 1994, p. 43.

[16] Christopher Jencks, "The Homeless," *The New York Review of Books,* April 21, 1994, p. 20. Jencks' two articles for the *New York Review* were adapted from his 1994 book, *The Homeless.*

[17] Writing in *The Washington Post,* Dec. 5, 1993.

[18] National Law Center on Poverty and Homelessness, *No Homeless People Allowed,* December 1994, p. i.

[19] *Ibid.,* pp. ii, vi.

[20] National Law Center, *No Room for the Inn, op. cit.,* p. iv.

[21] *Ibid.,* p. v.

[22] U.S. Conference of Mayors, *op. cit.,* pp. 1-2.

[23] Prepared remarks at U.S. Conference of Mayors news conference, Dec. 19, 1995. Ticer, who also served as co-chair of the conference's task force on hunger and homelessness, resigned as mayor Jan. 5 to take the Virginia Senate seat to which she was elected last November.

[24] Quoted in Dec. 19, 1995, Associated Press dispatch.

[25] Prepared remarks at U.S. Conference of Mayors news conference, Dec. 19, 1995.

[26] U.S. Conference of Mayors *Status Report, op. cit.,* p. 85.

[27] Quoted by Andrew Stark in *The New York Times,* Feb. 5, 1995, p. E17. Also see "Can Charity Fill the Gap?" *Time,* Dec. 4, 1995, pp. 44-53.

Bibliography

Selected Sources Used

Books

Baum, Alice S., and Donald W. Burnes, *A Nation in Denial: The Truth About Homelessness,* Westview Press, 1993.

Baum and Burnes dismiss claims that homelessness results from "lack of affordable housing, poverty, declining social benefits, and the nature of America's political and economic systems." Instead, they argue, it is "a condition of disengagement from ordinary society — from family, friends, neighborhood, church, and community; perhaps most important, it is a loss of self."

Jahiel, René I., ed., *Homelessness: A Prevention-Oriented Approach,* The Johns Hopkins University Press, 1992.

Jahiel and his fellow contributors examine three approaches to preventing homelessness: "primary (preventing homelessness from occurring or recurring), secondary (returning homeless people to a stable existence in homes of their own as soon as possible), or tertiary (preventing or minimizing the damage done by homelessness to the individual."

Snow, David A., and Leon Anderson, *Down on Their Luck: A Study of Homeless Street People,* University of California Press, 1993.

The authors contend that "any serious attempt to alleviate the problem of homelessness in the United States must move beyond a perspective based on individual pathology." They add that, "To focus on treating the homeless without changing the sociopolitical and economic contest in which they are embedded is to perpetuate a revolving-door policy that uses resources inefficiently, results in repeated failures, and engenders alienation and hopelessness among the homeless."

Articles

Driscoll, Sister Connie, "Chicago's House of Hope: Tough, Loving Methods of Helping the Homeless," *Policy Review,* summer 1993.

Sister Connie, a firm believer in the "tough love" approach to treating the homeless, describes the operations of the St. Martin de Porres House of Hope, a residence for homeless women and their children on Chicago's South Side. She writes, "Our experience has convinced us that, while the housing supply is a factor [in homelessness], the deeper problem is a lack of personal responsibility on the part of homeless people themselves."

Hamill, Pete, "How to Save the Homeless — and Ourselves," *New York,* Sept. 20, 1993.

Hamill describes why many New Yorkers no longer feel much sympathy for the homeless people in their midst. Asserting that homelessness is basically a public health crisis, he sets forth 11 proposals to combat it.

Jencks, Christopher, "The Homeless" and "Housing the Homeless," *The New York Review of Books,* April 21, 1994 and May 12, 1994.

In this two-part article adapted from a book published the same year, Jencks tries to make sense of the wildly varying estimates of the U.S. homeless population issued over the years by advocacy groups and governmental bodies. He also suggests ways in which affordable housing could be made available to the homeless at a cost acceptable to taxpayers.

Link, Bruce G., et al., "Lifetime and Five-Year Prevalence of Homelessness in the United States," *American Journal of Public Health,* December 1994.

Link and his colleagues at Columbia University's School of Public Health conclude that "The magnitude of the problem of homelessness is much greater than most previous attempts to enumerate homeless people have led us to believe." Indeed, they estimate that 8.5 million Americans experienced homelessness between 1985 and 1990.

Reports and Studies

National Law Center on Homelessness and Poverty, *No Homeless People Allowed,* December 1994.

The report focuses on local ordinances barring or limiting activities associated with homeless people, such as panhandling and sitting or sleeping in public places for extended periods.

National Law Center on Homelessness and Poverty, *No Room for the Inn,* December 1995.

Though it covers some of the same ground as the 1994 report, the recent survey focuses on local efforts to use zoning ordinances to limit the availability of shelters, feeding programs and other services for the homeless. The report also looks at relevant court cases.

United States Conference of Mayors, *A Status Report on Hunger and Homelessness in America's Cities: 1995,* December 1995.

In this 29-city survey, the conference reports isolated instances of progress in alleviating homelessness. For the most part, though, demand for services still exceeds supply in most areas. And given the budget-balancing fight raging in Congress, the conference sees little to look forward to in 1996.

The Next Step

Additional information from UMI's Newspaper & Periodical Abstracts database

City Ordinances and the Homeless

Barras, Jonetta Rose, "District to Track Homeless," *The Washington Times,* Oct. 21, 1992, p. B1.
Washington, D.C., Mayor Sharon Pratt Kelly approved the use of voucher cards to help stop aggressive panhandling and moved to fully implement a three-year-old law designed to identify persons using the city's homeless shelters.

Hill-Holtzman, Nancy, "Santa Monica tangles with homeless issue," *Los Angeles Times,* March 29, 1994, p. B6.
The Santa Monica, Calif., City Council will consider a new plan to get tough on the homeless by, among other things, confiscating shopping carts and curtailing panhandling. Dozens of city residents had shown up at a previous meeting to issue complaints on the issue.

"Homeless advocates fault Hartford's ban on begging," *The New York Times,* April 26, 1995, p. B6.
The Hartford, Conn., City Council has passed an ordinance that bans aggressive panhandling. Advocates for the homeless have vowed to appeal the ban in the courts and to protest it in the streets with a "day of begging" and a daylong boycott of city merchants.

Lawson, Phil, "Drop Matrix program and help the homeless," *San Francisco Chronicle,* Jan. 4, 1994, p. A17.
Lawson argues that San Francisco's Matrix program should be dropped and that all people of faith should help the homeless through housing programs, job training and support services.

Government Funding

Bardwell, S. K., "Homeless parolees heading for streets," *Houston Chronicle,* June 29, 1995, p. A29.
More than 2,000 homeless, jobless parolees at halfway houses, many not finished with their drug-addiction treatments, will be released in Texas because of a funding problem stemming from an investigation into the Texas Commission on Alcohol and Drug abuse.

Brown, DeNeen L., "20 million HUD plan eyed skeptically by some homeless advocates," *The Washington Post,* Sept. 22, 1993, p. D4.
HUD's $20 million proposal to eliminate homelessness in Washington, D.C., which calls for permanent housing units, job-training slots and substance-abuse treatment for drug addicts, drew skeptical reactions from some homeless people and advocates for the homeless who said the plan's provisions are inadequate to meet the needs of the District's estimated 10,000 homeless individuals and families.

Browne, J. Zamgba, "Homeless have a friend in HUD, Cisneros makes award," *Amsterdam News,* Nov. 26, 1994, p. 4.
HUD Secretary Henry G. Cisneros announced he has allocated $8.7 million to ensure counseling for placement, job training, health care and substance abuse for homeless persons in New York City.

Food, Shelter and Health-Care Programs

Aliotta, Jerome, "Project extends health care help to homeless," *Detroit News,* Oct. 14, 1994, p. B7.
The Homeless Health Care Project, part of Downriver Community Services in Algonac, Mich., helped more than 3,300 people in 1993 find medical care and help for emergency dental, optical, prescription and substance-abuse problems. The program is funded with $450,000 from HHS and local donations.

Dugger, Celia W., "City weighs rent charges for homeless in shelters," *The New York Times,* May 3, 1994, p. B3.
In an effort to prod homeless people to seek treatment or training, New York City and New York state are considering charging those who refuse help a "modest" rent for remaining in a city shelter. The rules, which would apply to single adults and not to families, would most sharply affect homeless people who suffer from mental illness or addiction.

Ferrell, David, "Forcing the homeless to help themselves," *Los Angeles Times,* Aug. 28, 1994, p. A1.
The Salvation Army's homeless shelter in Bell, Calif., is seen by some experts as a model approach to combating homelessness. The warehouse shelter runs on a system of small rewards and well-applied discipline. Boarders must be sober and must attend school or job-training classes.

Greenwood, Tom, "Macomb churches put out welcome mat for homeless," *Detroit News,* April 14, 1995, p. B4.
For the homeless of Macomb County, Mich., there are 46 havens between them and living in the street. They are turning to McRest, Macomb County Rotating Emergency Shelter Team, a nonprofit group of churches that take in the homeless for a week at a time on a rotating basis. The churches offer food, beds, laundry services, medical and psychological counseling, transportation and morale-building, non-judgmental support.

Larrabee, John, "Helping Boston's homeless, with coupons," *USA Today,* May 31, 1994, p. A2.

To separate the hungry from the hustlers panhandling on downtown streets, some of Boston's downtown merchants, churches and volunteer groups will begin selling coupons worth 25 cents apiece that can be redeemed in stores and restaurants for food and other essentials. The coupons will not buy alcohol, tobacco or lottery tickets.

McRoberts, Flynn, "Program offers homeless time, place to heal," ***Chicago Tribune,*** **Oct. 19, 1994, p. C1.**
Edward Buckner, the first alumnus of Chicago's Interfaith House, will join a host of dignitaries to mark its official opening as the Midwest's first facility for homeless men and women to recover from hospitalization. Interfaith House is another example of how policy-makers and advocates for the homeless are changing the way America fights homelessness, from simply providing food and shelter to coordinating a whole range of services.

Robinson, James, "Sanctuary for the homeless," ***Houston Chronicle,*** **Aug. 17, 1995, p. A34.**
The Daybreak homeless shelter, sponsored by St. John's United Methodist Church, was opened on Aug. 16, 1995. The shelter will provide food, showers, laundry facilities and medical care for the homeless in the downtown Houston area.

Rubin, Bonnie Miller, "Group aids homeless night, day," ***Chicago Tribune,*** **Jan. 11, 1995, p. SW2.**
Homeless advocates throughout the Chicago area, whose efforts for years have included providing meals and a place to sleep, are now channeling their energy into more long-term solutions. They say they want to attack homelessness at its roots: unemployment, substance abuse and job training.

Sibley, Celia, "Homeless find little shelter as cold wave hits county," ***Atlanta Constitution,*** **Jan. 6, 1995, p. XJ1.**
All over Gwinnett County, Ga., telephones jangled as people sought help as the coldest weather of the year hit the metro area. Workers at several social-service agencies, cooperative ministries and shelters scrambled to find blankets, coats, food, utility money, propane and sleeping bags to keep them going.

"Strong-arming the homeless," ***The New York Times,*** **April 15, 1995, p. A18.**
An editorial calls for an investigation into disturbing evidence that an outreach program run by the Grand Central Partnership has evolved into a vigilante operation against New York City's homeless. The editorial says that the outreach workers are supposed to offer referrals for food, shelter and clothing, but according to four former workers, the workers resorted to strong-arm tactics to get the homeless to move.

Toolen, Tom, "Port Authority's homeless policy called a success," ***The New York Times,*** **Jan. 23, 1994, p. N1.**
The success in New Jersey of the Port Authority of New York and New Jersey's two-year-old Operation Alternative, which attempts to keep bus, train and airport terminals free of homeless loiterers and panhandlers while offering food, clothing, shelter or medical attention to those who are in need, is examined.

White, Roxanne, "Homeless teens need help to find a way off streets," ***Denver Post,*** **Nov. 20, 1995, p. B7.**
As part of a series of articles on the agencies and people who benefit from funding by Denver's Mile High United Way, Roxanne Hart, the executive director of Urban Peak, discusses how her organization provides counseling, food, clothing, shelter and medical assistance for runaways and other youths.

Williams, Terri, "Homeless group might be moved off street and into old fire station," ***The Houston Post,*** **Feb. 17, 1994, p. A29.**
Houston Councilwoman Sheila Jackson Lee is working out a plan to house a group of about 30 homeless people at Fire Station No 5, which is currently being used as a storage facility. Lee said on Feb. 16, 1994, that she is trying to get a nonprofit organization to lease the station and provide mental-health as well as job-training programs there.

Wolcott, Jennifer G., "Boston cooking program puts homeless in kitchens," ***Christian Science Monitor,*** **Feb. 16, 1995, p. 13.**
The food-service training program for homeless people started by Roger Wellington in Boston is discussed. Wellington selected several residents of the Pine Street Inn shelter for his program, which includes field internships and responsibility for helping to cook more than 1,500 meals a day for shelter residents.

Zorn, Eric, "Homeless shelters no place of refuge," ***Chicago Tribune,*** **Jan. 20, 1994, p. C2.**
Zorn says that many of Chicago's homeless people are reluctant to stay at overnight shelters for the homeless because the shelters are increasingly filled with the mentally ill and substance abusers and beset by theft, disease and gang activity.

Job Training

Henneberger, Melinda, "Assessing the needs of New York's homeless," ***The New York Times,*** **April 2, 1993, p. A1.**
New York City's efforts to assess the needs of homeless families so that they can be better served are examined. The city is trying to determine which people need only housing and which people need other services such as drug-abuse treatment or job training.

Hubler, Shawn, "Homeless Tell of Need for Job Skills, Programs," ***Los Angeles Times,*** **Dec. 15, 1992, B1.**
In what is believed to be the nation's first systematic

"homeless poll," a Gallup Organization survey of Skid Row has found that, more than affordable housing or free food, Los Angeles' street people most want job training, women's programs and treatment for substance abuse.

Wong, Dean K., "Powell to address homeless vets," *Boston Globe,* May 29, 1993, p. 47.
During his whirlwind June 1993 visit to the Boston area to deliver the commencement address at Harvard University, Colin Powell will also address the first graduating class of the New England Shelter for Homeless Veterans' automated accounting job

Public Opinion

McGrory, Mary, "Helping — and Hating — the Homeless," *The Washington Post,* Jan. 5, 1992, p. C1.
McGrory discusses the fear of homeless people felt by most Americans and the opinion of Patrick J. Buchanan and others that there is something wrong with homeless people. Buchanan thinks people who do not quit panhandling should be jailed.

Stein, Ben, "Cities Must Reclaim Streets from Homeless," *USA Today,* Dec. 24, 1990, p. A10.
Guest columnist Ben Stein maintains that homeless people are a threat to society and to themselves and says that laws must be enacted and enforced to put an end to vagrancy, loitering and panhandling

Substance Abuse and the Homeless

Adams, John Carter, "Goal for homeless," *Chicago Tribune,* Feb. 9, 1994, p. 18.
In a letter to the editor, John Carter Adams of Olive Branch Mission says he is devoting efforts to working himself out of a job as a shelter director; he wants to direct a program of transitional housing with job training, substance abuse treatment and ultimately affordable housing.

Faciane, Valerie, "Homeless to get Christmas in July," *Times-Picayune,* July 3, 1994, p. OT1.
New Orleans' Bridge House, a nonprofit substance-abuse treatment center, is featured.

Kaufman, Michael T. "From homeless addict to the comeback route," *The New York Times,* Feb. 2, 1994, p. B2.
The story of Angel Perez, a homeless man in New York City who was helped by a New York City police officer, is recounted. Perez was sent to a sobering-up station run by the city, then to a month in a detoxification center in Yonkers, and then to the Good Samaritan Hospital in Suffern. Perez has been living for six months in a residential treatment program of Enter and so far has managed to stay away from liquor and drugs.

Leal, Susan, "The homeless wait as studies pile up," *San Francisco Chronicle,* Sept. 23, 1994, p. A27.
Leal, a member of the San Francisco Board of Supervisors, comments on problems with San Francisco's federally financed substance-abuse programs, and says that the city has taken steps to begin fixing the system, noting the focus must be on services to people in need and not providers.

Moore, Kimberly C., "Tipper Gore seeks to aid mentally ill homeless," *Boston Globe,* Oct. 17, 1993, p. 16.
As the mental health adviser to President Clinton's health-care task force, Tipper Gore already has accomplished her first undertaking with the administration by ensuring that mental health and substance abuse treatment would be covered by insurance under the proposed health-care reform package.

Murdoch, Joyce, "Montgomery's homeless get a sobering message," *The Washington Post,* June 21, 1993, p. D1.
Montgomery County, Md.'s refusal since January 1993 to put a roof over the heads of alcoholics who do not want treatment is part of a philosophical shift away from housing the homeless on a first-come, first-serve basis.

Sampson, Michele, "Drug Center Saves Homeless Addicts," *Times-Picayune,* July 22, 1992, p. B1.
Seven people have graduated from a rehabilitation project sponsored by Tulane University and The New Orleans Homeless Substance Abuse Project. The federally financed, nonprofit program provides long-term residential care for the homeless and their families, and all the adults in the program have been diagnosed as alcoholics, drug addicts or mentally ill.

Williams, Leslie, "Grant will help N.O. homeless," *Times-Picayune,* Jan. 19, 1994, p. B1.
A $1.7 million grant from HUD to help New Orleans-area homeless people recovering from substance abuse may be used to buy an apartment building or old hotel to renovate. There are approximately 7,000 to 10,000 homeless people in New Orleans.

Young, Cathy, "Denial obscures truth about homeless," *Detroit News,* March 8, 1994, p. A9.
Young comments on the denial of the truth about problems of mental illness and substance abuse among the homeless that prevent honest discussion of ways to solve the problem.

Back Issues

Great Research on Current Issues Starts Right Here...Recent topics covered by The CQ Researcher are listed below. Before May 1991, reports were published under the name of Editorial Research Reports.

JULY 1994
Dietary Supplements
Public Opinion and Foreign Policy
Crime Victims' Rights
Birth Control Choices

AUGUST 1994
Genetically Engineered Foods
Electing Minorities
Prozac Controversy
College Sports

SEPTEMBER 1994
Home Schooling
Welfare Experiments
Courts and the Media
Regulating Tobacco

OCTOBER 1994
Historic Preservation
Religion and Politics
Arts Funding
Economic Sanctions

NOVEMBER 1994
Sex on Campus
Blood Supply Safety
Testing Term Limits
Religion in America

DECEMBER 1994
Farm Policy
Arms Sales
Earthquake Research
The Future of Television

JANUARY 1995
Treating Addiction
Child Custody and Support
Parents and Schools
Non-Proliferation Treaty at 25

FEBRUARY 1995
Cracking Down on Immigration
The Business of Sports
Reinventing Government
Housing Discrimination

MARCH 1995
Death Penalty Debate
Primary Care
Democracy in Africa
Environmental Movement at 25

APRIL 1995
Abortion Clinic Protests
Dieting and Health
Combating AIDS
Rethinking Affirmative Action

MAY 1995
Assisted Suicide Controversy
Overhauling Social Security
Learning to Read
Mandatory Sentencing

JUNE 1995
Combating Infectious Disease
Property Rights
Repetitive Stress Injuries
Regulating the Internet

JULY 1995
War Crimes
Highway Safety
Combating Terrorism
Preventing Teen Drug Use

AUGUST 1995
Job Stress
Organ Transplants
United Nations at 50
Advances in Cancer Research

SEPTEMBER 1995
Catholic Church in the U.S.
Northern Ireland Cease-Fire
High School Sports
Teaching History

OCTOBER 1995
Quebec's Future
Revitalizing the Cities
Networking the Classroom
Indoor Air Pollution

NOVEMBER 1995
The Working Poor
The Jury System
Sex, Violence and the Media
Police Misconduct

DECEMBER 1995
Teens and Tobacco
Gene Therapy's Future
Global Water Shortages
Third-Party Prospects

JANUARY 1996
Emergency Medicine
Punishing Sex Offenders
Bilingual Education

Back issues are available for $5.00 (subscribers) or $8.00 (non-subscribers). Quantity discounts apply to orders over ten. To order, call Congressional Quarterly Customer Service at (202) 887-8621.

Binders are available for $18.00. To order call 1-800-638-1710. Please refer to stock number 648.

Future Topics

- ***Reforming the CIA***
- ***Campaign Finance Reform***
- ***Academic Politics***

THE CQ Researcher

PUBLISHED BY CONGRESSIONAL QUARTERLY INC.

Reforming the CIA

Is the spy agency a dinosaur in today's world?

After World War II, the Central Intelligence Agency emerged as a key weapon in the Cold War with the Soviet Union. The Soviet empire's collapse radically altered the nature of foreign threats to the United States. Today, some critics say, the CIA is ill-suited for a world where economic secrets and international criminal plots rival military conspiracies in importance. Some critics even call for dismantling the agency, especially in the wake of the recent Aldrich Ames spy scandal. Others say the agency has a role in the new world order but must be extensively changed, along with the entire intelligence community. As he seeks to retool the CIA, the agency's new director, John M. Deutch, must confront low staff morale and an ever-tightening budget.

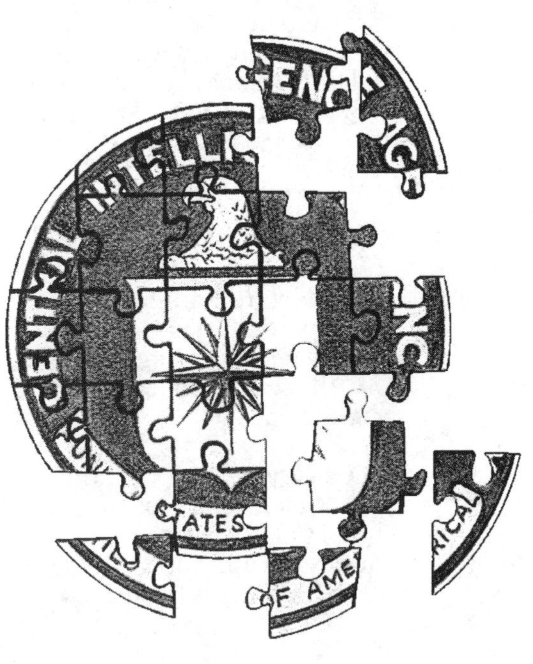

INSIDE THIS ISSUE

CQ | Feb. 2, 1996 • Volume 6, No. 5 • Pages 97-120

Formerly Editorial Research Reports

Reforming The CIA

Cover: Barbara Sassa-Daniels

Feb. 2, 1996
Volume 6, No. 5

Bibliographic records and abstracts included in The Next Step section of this publication are from UMI's Newspaper and Periodical Abstracts database, and are used with permission.

The CQ Researcher (ISSN 1056-2036). Formerly Editorial Research Reports. Published weekly (48 times per year, not printed the first Friday of any month with five Fridays) by Congressional Quarterly Inc., 1414 22nd St., N.W., Washington, D.C. 20037. Rates are furnished upon request. Second-class postage paid at Washington, D.C. POSTMASTER: Send address changes to The CQ Researcher, 1414 22nd St., N.W., Washington, D.C. 20037.

Reforming the CIA

BY MARY H. COOPER

THE ISSUES

When Aldrich "Rick" Ames was sentenced to life in prison in 1994, the worst spy scandal in CIA history finally seemed over. The treasonous ex-agent would sell no more top-secret information to the former Soviet Union or Russia, but he hadn't finished talking. Before he was hustled away in chains, he leveled a final blast at the agency he had betrayed.

"The espionage business, as carried out by the CIA and a few other American agencies, was and is a self-serving sham, carried out by careerist bureaucrats who have managed to deceive several generations of American policy-makers and the public about both the necessity and the value of their work," Ames said. "There is and has been no rational need for thousands of . . . agents working around the world, primarily in and against friendly countries . . . Frankly, these spy wars are a sideshow which [has] had no real impact on our significant security interests over the years." [1]

Many CIA and government officials dismissed Ames' diatribe, coming as it did from such a notorious traitor. But many critics of the U.S. intelligence community felt that Ames, of all people, had spoken the truth — or close to it. One thing was certain: As a 31-year veteran of the fabled agency, he had had ample opportunity to assess its effectiveness and competency.

As counterintelligence chief of the CIA's Soviet branch, Ames had worked with the top spymasters at CIA headquarters in Langley, Va. From his privileged perch in the secretive directorate of operations, Ames had made millions of dollars selling America's secrets. Over the course of nine years, Ames had exposed the identities of scores of Soviet citizens on the CIA payroll, at least 10 of whom were executed for treason.

Today, in the wake of the scandal, sweeping re-examinations of U.S. intelligence operations are under way by congressional committees, a special presidential commission and the CIA itself. "It is evident that the most difficult intelligence activity to manage is human intelligence, clandestinely collected intelligence by our men and women," CIA Director John M. Deutch acknowledged during recent House committee hearings on the agency's future. "We are in a time of transition. This is a period like the era after World War II, where key decisions will be made that will shape the strength of the U.S. intelligence community for years to come." [2]

After World War II, the Central Intelligence Agency and a dozen other American spy organizations emerged as key weapons in the Cold War pitting the U.S. against the Soviet Union and its allies around the world. (*See story, p. 102.*) In a war without tanks and guns, the combatants attacked and counterattacked using espionage, disinformation and covert political action to achieve their objectives.

The demise of the Soviet Union radically altered the nature of foreign threats to the United States. Suddenly, the world's most notorious and efficient espionage agency — the KGB — was greatly weakened and, in any case, no longer under the direction of a hostile superpower. Many Third World governments that had represented Soviet interests, such as Angola and Afghanistan, no longer were perceived as threats to the United States. The overthrow of anti-U.S. governments in several former Soviet allies further eroded the threat. The East German intelligence agency Stasi, second only to the KGB as the CIA's most effective adversary, ceased to exist altogether after German reunification in 1990.

The Cold War's end, coupled with the Ames debacle and other problems, made the CIA and the other spy agencies natural targets during congressional efforts to reduce the federal budget deficit. In fact, in 1990, long before budget cutters capped spending by other federal agencies, the CIA imposed its own 3 percent ceiling on agency budget increases. Although the cost of running U.S. intelligence agencies is buried in the classified portion of the Pentagon's budget, word got out that it amounted to some $28 billion in 1994. [3] The CIA received only about $3.1 billion of the total, with the remainder largely going to intelligence operations run by the Defense Department. These include the National Security Agency, which gathers "signals intelligence" using satellites and ground stations, and the Central Imagery Office, which provides reconnaissance data to military commanders in the field.

But the CIA's pre-emptive budget cutbacks did not stave off criticism of the beleaguered agency. It had never recovered public esteem after the 1986 Iran-contra scandal (*see p. 111*). Then, in February 1994, came the Ames scandal, which prompted CIA Director R. James Woolsey's abrupt resignation at the end of the year. Antagonism toward the agency continued to mount last year, when it was revealed that CIA officials had covered up the involvement of a paid CIA informant in the 1992 murder of a Guatemalan guerrilla leader married to American lawyer Jennifer Harbury.

By early last year, the CIA's prestige had dropped so low that when President Clinton asked then-Deputy Defense Secretary Deutch to find a new CIA director, there were so few candidates interested in that post that Deutch was persuaded to take the job himself. By the time he assumed the post in May, morale at the agency was at rock bottom.

"The thing that really tickles me, in a cynical sort of way, is that half of the press criticism is about the ineffectualness of the intelligence agencies," says David Whipple, executive director of the Association of Former Intelligence Officers. "The other half involves raising the red flag of alarm over the possibility of creating a monolithic organization which would be too effective. You just can't win."

A few critics say the record of American intelligence is so poor that the government should get out of the spy business entirely. Sen. Daniel Patrick Moynihan, D-N.Y., has submitted legislation that would dismantle the CIA and the other agencies engaged in espionage and limit information gathering to the State Department's diplomatic sources. "Secrecy is a disease," he said. "It causes hardening of the arteries of the mind. It hinders true scholarship and hides mistakes." [4] (*See "At Issue," p. 113.*)

But most experts and legislators say that intelligence gathering is a vital function of government, especially for the world's greatest power. "The focus of the CIA's operations has changed," says Adm. William O. Studeman, CIA acting director in early 1995. "But the mission of the agency hasn't changed at all. And I don't think either the organization or its mission should change."

The role of intelligence may be even more vital today, some experts say, than during the Cold War. In the place of a clearly identifiable menace — the Soviet bloc — the main threats to American security often come from small, transnational groups that require even sharper intelligence capabilities to identify and track before they can harm U.S. interests. "There are a lot of circumstances, when it comes to terrorism and narcotics, [arms] proliferation and other threats, where the American government is going to need to be able to act secretly," says Robert M. Gates, director of central intelligence from 1991-1993. "So I think that capability needs to be a strong one."

Reuters

Soviet spy Aldrich H. Ames pleaded guilty to espionage in 1994 and agreed to cooperate with investigators in exchange for a life term in prison and lenient treatment for his wife, Rosario. She was sentenced to five years.

To cope with the changing nature of threats to U.S. national security, many experts are calling for a fundamental redesign of the intelligence community. They differ widely, however, in their suggestions on how the CIA and other agencies should deal with the new international environment. Last February, President Clinton named former Defense Secretary Les Aspin to head the independent Commission on the Roles and Capabilities of the United States Intelligence Community. The panel of 17 presidential and congressional appointees was asked to study the intelligence community's needs in the post-Cold War era and recommend possible reforms to the CIA and other spy agencies.

Although the commission suffered a setback with Aspin's death last summer, it has continued its work under Harold Brown, also a former Defense secretary, and is scheduled to present its recommendations on March 1. [5] As part of their oversight responsibilities, the congressional intelligence committees also have been holding a series of hearings on ways to prepare the intelligence community for the 21st century.

"Nobody knows what recommendations they will be making," Whipple says. "However, this is a healthy exercise."

As former and current intelligence officers and lawmakers consider the nation's future intelligence needs, these are some of the issues they face:

Should an intelligence "czar" be appointed to oversee the entire intelligence community?

Since the CIA was created under the 1947 National Security Act, the director of the CIA has also held the title of director of central intelligence (DCI), with responsibility for collecting and analyzing all the nation's intelligence data for the National Security Council (NSC) and the president.[6]

Over the years, however, critics have complained that the DCIs have focused most of their attention on the CIA and not paid sufficient attention to the intelligence community as a whole. "With the exception of [Adm.] Stansfield Turner back in the 1970s, nobody has really made a very serious effort" to provide such oversight, Whipple says, "which is the director of central intelligence's responsibility under the law. Considering that Adm. Turner tried and failed, and that Deutch is trying to do it now, it's going to be fascinating to see how Deutch is going to fare."

One of Deutch's first undertakings upon becoming CIA director last May, in fact, was to hand over much of the agency's day-to-day administration to his deputies (*see p. 112*). The shift has allowed the new director to dedicate more time to matters involving the community as a whole, including testifying before the congressional committees now studying the role of intelligence in U.S. foreign policy.

Even if Deutch eventually proves more successful than his predecessors at wearing the two hats conferred on him by law — oversight of the CIA and the intelligence community — some experts say the dual role is intrinsically too burdensome to carry out effectively. Senate Intelligence Committee Chairman Arlen Specter, R-Pa., has proposed amending the 1947 law to create a new position: director of national intelligence. Like the drug "czar," who coordinates the nation's war on drugs, the "intelligence czar" would oversee the entire intelligence community, with direct links to the White House. Under such an arrangement, CIA directors would have no more authority than the heads of the other intelligence agencies.

Some military intelligence officers, particularly those who have chafed under the CIA's dominance of the community, like the idea. Retired Air Force Lt. Gen. James R. Clapper, a former director of the Defense Intelligence Agency, recalled a certain "CIA-centric point of view" when dealing with the directors of central intelligence. "There is an understandable bias that creeps into the decisions they make that I think subtly, and not so subtly, favors the agency," Clapper said. "I think it would be better to have someone who can preside over the community Solomon-like and look at it objectively, particularly when issues arise within the agency which consume the DCI's time and energies, as we had with the Ames case."[7]

"We are in a time of transition. This is a period like the era after World War II, where key decisions will be made that will shape the strength of the U.S. intelligence community for years to come."

— CIA Director James M. Deutch

To Gates, the potential benefits of an intelligence czar depend on how the role is defined. "The idea of strengthening the power of the director of central intelligence to truly manage the intelligence community is a good idea," he says. "The idea of creating a director of national intelligence completely separate from CIA, where there's a different person who is the director of CIA, is a terrible idea."

The problem boils down to power and money, Gates says. "In Washington, if you don't have troops, you don't count," he says. "I've worked in the National Security Council and at the White House under four presidents, as well as at CIA, and I can tell you that's how it works." An intelligence czar with no independent base would have to have authority over the entire intelligence budget to be effective, he explains.

"When you consider that 85 percent of that budget is under the Defense Department," Gates continues, "there's no way any secretary of Defense is going to give up that kind of control over organizations for which he has ultimate responsibility. So you automatically have a situation in which the new intelligence czar sitting over in the Old Executive Office Building has no significantly greater budgetary or management authority than the current director of central intelligence. At the same time, because he does not head CIA he has been stripped of all of his organizational base and independence. That kind of position is guaranteed to fail."

A better way to enhance the director's ability to manage the intelligence community, in Gates' view, would be to allow the director to

A Baker's Dozen of Spy Agencies

The 1947 National Security Act created the Central Intelligence Agency as the core of a network of government agencies responsible for collecting overseas information of interest to policy-makers. The law called for a director of central intelligence to head the CIA and also to coordinate the activities of the intelligence community as a whole. The director is appointed by the president, subject to Senate approval. The intelligence community today is comprised of 13 departments or agencies, eight of them within the Defense Department, which receives about 90 percent of the inteligence budget:

Central Intelligence Agency — The CIA is an executive branch agency made up of four directorates, or departments. The directorate of administration oversees the agency's day-to-day operations. One of its functions is counterintelligence, protecting the agency's security and preventing infiltration by double agents such as Aldrich Ames. The directorate of intelligence employs experts in many fields to evaluate the mountains of data — known as HUMINT, or human intelligence — that are collected in the field by overseas agents. Scientists in the directorate of science and technology assess foreign technological advances and devise equipment and processes designed to counter the use of those advances against American interests. The directorate of operations conducts covert operations overseas using some 5,000 agents.

The eight Defense Department intelligence agencies are:

Defense Intelligence Agency — The DIA is the military counterpart to the CIA, collecting information of use to the military services and coordinating the activities of all Defense Department intelligence agencies.

National Security Agency — From its headquarters at Fort Meade, Md., the highly secretive NSA collects SIGINT, or signals intelligence, from spy satellites and sophisticated bugging equipment that enables officers to listen in on conversations and peek at virtually any spot on the globe. Although it is not well known, the NSA employs far more people and uses much more money than the CIA. The NSA is Maryland's largest employer, with about 20,000 employees, and with its $8 billion budget is the biggest spender of all the intelligence agencies. [1]

Army, Air Force, Naval and Marine Corps Intelligence Agencies — The four branches of the armed services each collect intelligence relevant to their particular needs.

National Reconnaissance Office — Coordinates the collection and analysis of information from airplane and satellite reconnaissance by the military services and the CIA.

Central Imagery Office — Coordinates the dissemination of satellite and air reconnaissance data to military commanders during combat. The office was set up in 1992 after the military complained about delays in getting key intelligence data during the Persian Gulf War.

In addition to the Defense Department agencies, four other executive branch departments and agencies collect intelligence information:

State Department — Seeks a wide range of information affecting U.S. foreign policy.

Energy Department — Collects data on nuclear energy, including the possible diversion of civilian nuclear materials for weapons.

Treasury Department — Collects information that may affect U.S. fiscal or monetary policy.

Federal Bureau of Investigation — Seeks information for cases involving international crime.

[1] See Scott Shane Gericke and Tom Bowman, "America's Most Secret Spy Agency," *The Baltimore Sun*, Jan. 7, 1996.

move personnel and funds among the various agencies at his discretion and to wield veto power over high-level intelligence appointments. "We should enhance the DCI's authority to manage the community and American intelligence, rather than ripping him up by the roots and plunking him down in the Old Executive Office Building in a very grand suite but without any real power," Gates says.

Other critics say creating a new intelligence czar runs counter to ongoing efforts by businesses and public agencies to downsize their operations by trimming unnecessary jobs. "I do not support an intelligence czar," says Studeman. "I think it's quite honestly just another layer. It creates bureaucracy and is neither required nor desired. The director of central intelligence is more than capable of dividing his time between the issues associated with the management of the Central Intelligence Agency and those associated with the management of the intelligence community, provided that he organizes himself to do that."

Deutch agrees with both his predecessors on the need to maintain the CIA director's authority over the entire intelligence community. "I believe that the director of central intelligence must put a priority on his or her role as head of the community," he testified at a recent hearing. "It is a community of different organizations with one organization still at the hub of the wheel, independent of the policy departments and with a hand in every [type of] intelligence, and by that I refer to the Central Intelligence Agency." [8]

Deutch also acknowledged the difficulties CIA directors will face if, as he proposes, Congress expands their budgetary authority over the other intelligence agencies. How will the other agency chiefs respond to such a change? Deutch said, "They'll go out of their minds."

Should some law enforcement and intelligence agencies merge?

The 1947 National Security Act drew

clear boundaries separating the CIA's intelligence-gathering function from the investigative role of the Federal Bureau of Investigation (FBI) and other law-enforcement agencies. It also specifically barred CIA from conducting police activities.

But those lines have been blurred since the end of the Cold War and the preoccupation with Soviet military power. Now a number of other threats to national security have emerged as priorities for American intelligence, among them proliferation of nuclear, biological and chemical weapons; the potential for aggression by "rogue" nations; narcotics trafficking; international crime syndicates; and illegal-alien smuggling.

Because many of these threats involve groups of criminals working overseas as well as in the United States, the line separating the law enforcement and intelligence communities has become less distinct. At no time has this been more apparent than following the February 1993 bombing of the World Trade Center in New York City. More timely information from overseas intelligence outposts, some critics say, might have helped U.S. law enforcement agents stop the bombers before they could act.

The bombing sparked calls for closer collaboration between the CIA and FBI. "The resulting overlap in the concerns and activities of the intelligence and law enforcement communities has prompted some people to suggest that we should simply merge the two communities in an effort to achieve greater efficiency in the fight against international crime," said Deputy Attorney General Jamie S. Gorelick. "We believe this would be a serious mistake. There are ample reasons, grounded in history and constitutional principles, to maintain a clear demarcation between the missions and authorities of the two communities."[9]

Gorelick and other critics of a law enforcement-intelligence merger, which has been proposed periodically since 1947, say it invites abuse of power. Among other things, they say, a superagency could become a monolithic nightmare capable of evading congressional oversight.

Studeman calls the merger idea "patently ridiculous. . . . It is very important to recognize that the '47 act specifically bars CIA from having police powers," he says. "They are not desired, and they would get the agency into activities that in my view it doesn't need to be engaged in."

"The idea of creating a director of national intelligence completely separate from CIA, where there's a different person who is the director of CIA, is a terrible idea."

— Former CIA Director Robert M. Gates

Another obstacle to a merger is their fundamental clash in missions. "Law enforcement wants to identify bad guys and put them in jail," says Gates. "Intelligence wants to identify bad guys and follow them or recruit them, so they can keep getting information from them. These are very different cultures, and trying to merge them creates all kinds of potential problems."

According to Studeman, past experience working with law enforcement agencies overseas suggests that the bigger threat would come from the law enforcement side of such a merger. "The law enforcement guys are increasingly trying to go overseas, but they don't want to play as a team in the overseas environment," he says. "If a crime has been conducted, their view is that they have unambiguous authority, and that they don't need to check in with anybody. But when you're operating in an overseas environment, you do need to deal with the chief of mission and with other people on the country team so that you don't end up doing something wrong."

In Latin America and Southeast Asia, in particular, where the Drug Enforcement Agency (DEA) has pursued narcotics traffickers, Studeman says the failure of law enforcement agents to play by the rules has been "a source of continuous tension."

Many experts say that merging the law enforcement and intelligence communities is not the best way to coordinate their efforts. "We have been working over the last year to build a connection," says Studeman. He cites the creation last March of the Intelligence-Law Enforcement Policy Board, which he co-chaired with Gorelick. "What we need to do in the modern world is create matrix organizations like this to deal with overlapping roles while keeping the missions and charters of the various organizations apart and separate," he says. "This way, we can continue to protect our sources and methods while providing a lot of information to law enforcement, which they can then use, applying their own methods, to build their cases. It's really the best way to do it."

Deutch agrees that intelligence and law enforcement should be kept separate. "Good spies make bad cops," he testified last December, "and I also believe that good cops make bad spies. Accordingly, I believe the intelligence-gathering components of the United States government's attack on [international terrorism, crime and narcotics] should be in the hands of the intelligence community rather than through an expanded law enforcement presence overseas." [10] At the same time, Deutch has continued Studeman's active promotion of the policy board, recently noting that CIA and FBI representatives now meet twice a week.

At the same time, Deutch acknowledged that the tensions between law enforcement and intelligence are unlikely to go away. "I don't have a magic solution to give you on this," he said at the December hearing. "I will say that at a practical, working level, the cooperation is improving every day and is much better in the areas of terrorism and counternarcotics, especially between the bureau and the CIA," he said. "But I do think that it continues to need some attention because of the changing nature of the threat."

Should the CIA continue to conduct covert political action?

The CIA was originally conceived as an intelligence-gathering organization. But the National Security Act left vague the limits of this essentially passive function. Following the KGB's example, the CIA soon after its creation began to act on the information it collected, attempting to influence events in foreign countries.

Conducted by the directorate of operations, covert political action has been the most controversial feature of U.S. intelligence. At its most effective, the public has not even been aware of its work. "The covert actions which have succeeded, in my own experience, have been very important and very unpublicized," says Whipple, who served as CIA station chief in such hot spots as Vietnam, Burma and Cambodia during his 35-year career. "If a covert action goes wrong, you're apt to hear about it, and there will be lots of criticism. If a covert action goes right, you don't hear about it at all because part of its success is that it was not exposed."

"The law enforcement guys are increasingly trying to go overseas, but they don't want to play as a team in the overseas environment."

— Admiral William O. Studeman
Former Acting CIA Director

Covert operations that have turned out well by most standards — and which have been publicized — include the CIA's role in arresting Carlos the Jackal, an international terrorist who had eluded capture for two decades until his 1994 arrest in Sudan. The CIA also helped track down Arab terrorist Ramzi Yousef, who was charged with masterminding the Trade Center bombing.

But when covert operations have failed, they have sometimes revealed questionable methods used to reach equally questionable ends. During the 1961 Bay of Pigs fiasco, for example, the agency trained an improbably small force of Cuban exiles to invade Cuba and assassinate Fidel Castro. In retrospect, critics said the operation had been doomed to failure and never should have been undertaken under any circumstances.

Today, with the KGB and its dirty tricks apparently out of the picture, some say the United States should get out of the business of secretly manipulating events overseas. "Covert action has been overused as an instrument of foreign policy, and the reputation of the United States has suffered," writes Roger Hilsman, an assistant secretary of State for intelligence and research in the 1950s. "And while one action, taken in isolation, might seem worth the cost of slightly tarnishing the national image, the cumulative effect of several hundred blots has been to blacken it entirely, thus corroding one of America's major political assets — a belief abroad in American intentions and integrity. Covert political action is not only something the United States can do without in the post-Cold War world, it is something the United States could have done without during the Cold War as well." [11]

CIA officials counter that covert action is sometimes necessary to gain friendly foreign governments' support for U.S. policies, such as the pursuit of drug lords or terrorists in countries where such criminals are at least as powerful as government officials. "There are a lot of situations in which other countries won't cooperate with us if their cooperation is openly acknowledged," says Studeman. "There are a lot of circumstances in which they know there will be leaks, but as long as it's not officially confirmed they're willing to work with us."

The spread of transnational threats to U.S. security makes a strong covert-action capability as necessary as ever, in the view of many intelligence officials. "Covert action is a legitimate policy arm that falls between conventional defense and conventional diplomacy," Gates says. "It is something that countries like ours, faced with proliferation and other threats, must execute."

Although he declines to elaborate on the details, Gates says the directorate of operations already has in hand a strategic plan that would "streamline" its covert and political action. But the biggest obstacle to the plan's implementation, Gates says, is the CIA bureaucracy itself. "There are people in the directorate of operations who feel that if everybody would just go away, they could simply go back to business as usual. They should not ever be allowed to go back to business as usual. They need to get on and execute the strategic plan to better allow them to execute their foreign intelligence mission and their covert action mission."

Should the CIA be in the business of gathering economic intelligence?

Over the past two decades, the United States has seen its postwar dominance of the world economy erode as Japan and Western European countries have become increasingly formidable competitors. As global economic competition heats up, violations of international trade agreements and pacts governing copyrights and patents are assuming growing importance. As a result of these trends, the economy has moved closer to the top of U.S. national security concerns.

Economic-intelligence gathering poses special diplomatic risks because many of the targets are longstanding American allies. Two embarrassing incidents occurred last year alone. In February, the French government expelled CIA agents for trying to steal government documents related to General Agreement on Tariffs and Trade (GATT) negotiations. And it was reported that the CIA had eavesdropped on Japanese negotiators during bilateral auto talks in Geneva in June.[12]

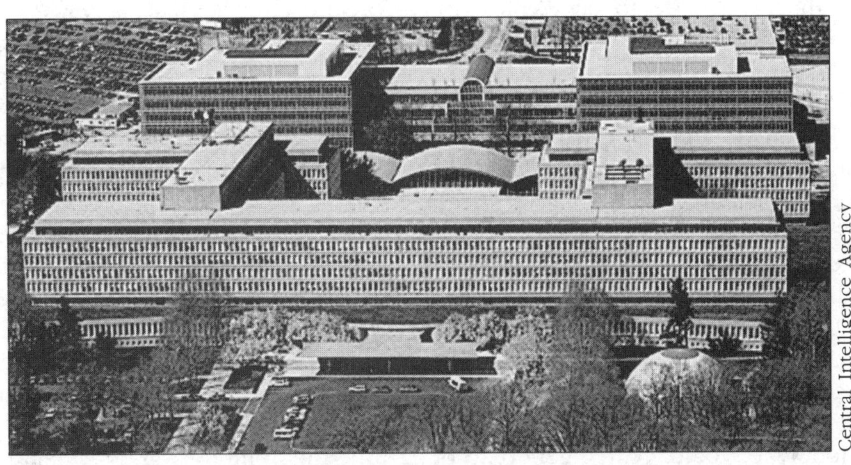

Central Intelligence Agency

CIA headquarters is located on a 258-acre campus in Langley, Va., about eight miles from downtown Washington, D.C.

Advocates of a smaller role for the CIA say the rewards of economic intelligence are not worth such diplomatic setbacks. "If the world's major trading powers begin viewing each other with suspicion, hoarding economic breakthroughs like atomic secrets and monitoring each other like enemies," wrote former Rep. Dave McCurdy, D-Okla., "the world could easily slide into an economic version of the Cold War."[13]

Some critics suggest that the government agencies that use intelligence data to make economic policy are perfectly capable of collecting the information on their own. But Gates says the CIA is gathering economic intelligence at the request of those selfsame government agencies. "The fact is that the office of the U.S. Trade Representative, the Treasury Department and the Commerce Department can collect a great deal of overtly available information," he says. "But if a foreign government is cheating on some arrangement with the United States, those guys are not likely to find out about it except through intelligence."

Gates equates economic-intelligence gathering to monitoring compliance with arms control agreements. "Finding out what the other guys are doing, what they're bringing to the table, whether they are behaving themselves — these have been viewed by the policy community as legitimate and desirable roles for CIA to play for 30 years or more," he says.

Studeman says the intelligence agencies also help protect U.S. businesses overseas, saving them billions of dollars a year. "We try to detect people who are not playing by the rules, who are doing bribes or kickbacks or who are illegally [supporting] projects overseas in competition with Americans," he says. "Then the government moves to stop abuses from occurring."

Intelligence officers generally support the CIA's role in economic-information gathering. The only controversial issue, in their view, is the use of that information once they have it. "The intelligence community has always collected economic intelligence," says Whipple. "The issue really is whether the dissemination of that intelligence should be provided directly from an intelligence agency to a private corporation. That I would be against for a variety of reasons."

Studeman says that the CIA has conducted three internal studies on the agency's potential role in economic espionage and that all three reached the same conclusion: "The intelligence community should not use its instruments for the conduct of industrial espionage," collecting economic data overseas that would then be given to private industries.

Gates agrees. "I don't know any intelligence officer who thinks that we ought to be collecting contract information or proprietary technology information to give to U.S. companies," he says. "I think the key role for CIA in this arena is to support U.S. government policy-making, not in direct support of U.S. business."

Industrial espionage poses a host of problems. For one thing, the international ties of many U.S. companies make it hard to determine what constitutes an American company. Then there is the fairness issue. "If you did acquire such information, who would you give it to?" Studeman asks. "If it's aerospace information, do you give it to Northrop-Grumman and not to Boeing?" The potential for political corruption is obvious, he adds, making today's concerns over campaign contributions "pale in insignificance."

American businesses appear to agree that industrial espionage is a bad idea, and many would eliminate all CIA involvement in economic fact-finding as well. "The plain fact is that spying on allies is neither an ethical nor an efficient means of gathering economic information," concludes an editorial in *Business Week* magazine. "For a fraction of the sum spent on spying, Washington can gather data by hiring foreign-speaking analysts to comb public documents." [14]

In any event, critics in the business community say, American companies don't need the CIA to compete in the global marketplace. "To sell U.S. automobiles in Japan, the Big Three don't need spooks trying to infiltrate the Japanese government," writes *Fortune* columnist Rob Norton. "The intelligence they need is more basic, such as the insight that you should put the steering wheel on the right-hand side of the car if you expect to sell it in Japan — something U.S. carmakers are only beginning to do. . . . [T]he notion that [the CIA should] be permitted to preserve itself in the name of 'economic warfare' should be terminated, as the cinematic spoofs like to say, with extreme prejudice." [15] ■

BACKGROUND

The Black Chamber

In 1882, the Navy created the nation's first spy service, the Office of Naval Intelligence, to determine the ability of foreign countries to engage U.S. ships at sea. Three years later, the Army set up an analogous service, the Military Information Division. [16]

The shortcomings of these early spy operations became evident during World War I, when the Army set up a more sophisticated spy group, known as MI-8, to detect enemy agents, primarily by intercepting and decoding German correspondence. After the war, the Army disbanded MI-8. But the group's work continued to be carried out by the so-called "Black Chamber," the country's first civilian spy agency. Soon after its founding in 1919, the small and highly secretive State Department operation had broken the diplomatic codes of most of America's allies and foes alike.

Intelligence activities were controversial from the start. Newly appointed Secretary of State Henry L. Stimson unceremoniously disbanded the Black Chamber in 1929, noting that, "Gentlemen do not read each other's mail." The business of gathering intelligence on other countries was handed over to the State Department's normal diplomatic channels.

As Europe edged closer to World War II, President Franklin D. Roosevelt called on World War I hero William "Wild Bill" Donovan to help improve the quality of intelligence reaching Washington. Over the strong objections of FBI Director J. Edgar Hoover and the heads of military spy groups fearful of losing power, the president in 1941 appointed Donovan to head the new office of the Coordinator of Information, which was to collect and analyze all data of interest to national security.

In 1942, after the U.S. entry into the war, Donovan's fledgling group was renamed the Office of Strategic Services (OSS), with responsibility for both military and diplomatic intelligence. The agency received valuable help in perfecting its methods from the respected British secret service, MI-6.

Despite its successes during the war, President Harry S Truman bowed to public pressure from Hoover and congressional critics and disbanded the OSS in 1945.

CIA's Heyday

Less than a year later, Truman reversed his OSS decision in order to deal with the sudden onset of the Cold War. Closed out of the Soviet Union in the aftermath of World War II, American policy-makers had no reliable information on which to base U.S. policy toward the wartime ally turned adversary. By contrast, covert action had been an integral part of Soviet foreign policy since the USSR was founded in 1922.

To counter Stalin's KGB, Truman decided the United States needed a permanent, peacetime intelligence capability.

Continued on p. 108

Chronology

1940s-1950s

The Central Intelligence Agency is created to help stop the expansion of the Soviet Union and, during the heyday of covert operations, orchestrates several overseas coups.

Sept. 18, 1947
The National Security Act creates the CIA and the position of director of central intelligence to head the new agency and oversee all other agencies comprising the U.S. intelligence community.

1953
The CIA supports the ouster of Mohammad Mossadeq, the leftist premier of Iran, and the installation of the pro-American shah.

1954
U.S. intelligence officers bring about the ouster of Guatemalan leader Jacobo Arbenz Guzman after he threatens to appropriate the U.S.-owned United Fruit Co.

1960s-1970s

The CIA, after enjoying free rein in the early days of the Cold War, comes under growing scrutiny.

1960
The U-2 spy plane piloted by American pilot Francis Gary Powers is shot down on a reconnaissance flight over the Soviet Union.

April 17, 1961
The CIA's first major, public fiasco occurs when a CIA-backed invasion of Cuba by 1,400 U.S.-trained Cuban exiles is thwarted at the Bay of Pigs.

1962
The CIA's discovery of Soviet nuclear missile sites in Cuba sparks the Cuban missile crisis, prompting President John F. Kennedy to demand, and eventually obtain, the withdrawal of the missiles and end the Cold War's most dangerous crisis.

1965
The CIA again falls into disfavor following the disclosure of its covert operations to shore up the anti-communist government of South Vietnam. Criticism grows with the escalation of U.S. involvement in the Vietnam War.

1972
Hostility toward the CIA mounts when it is revealed that former agency employees working for the Republicans broke into Democratic Party headquarters in Washington's Watergate complex. The scandal launches congressional investigations that uncover numerous violations of the CIA's 1947 mandate.

1980s

The intelligence community expands as a result of President Ronald Reagan's campaign to "rearm America."

1987
Public support for the CIA plummets with the Iran-contra scandal, involving the illegal sale of arms to Iran to fund the agency's secret support of anti-government rebels in Nicaragua.

1990s

The demise of the Soviet Union and resulting end of the Cold War prompt a re-examination of U.S. intelligence needs.

1991
U.S. military commanders complain of delays in receiving vital intelligence data during the Persian Gulf War, the first major military conflict of the post-Cold War era.

February 1994
CIA officer Aldrich H. Ames is arrested for selling secrets to Soviet authorities over nearly a decade, damaging U.S. national security and leading to the executions of at least 10 CIA informants in the Soviet Union.

Jan. 9, 1995
CIA Director R. James Woolsey resigns in the wake of the Ames scandal. Adm. William O. Studeman becomes acting director.

Feb. 2, 1995
President Clinton calls on former Defense Secretary Les Aspin to head a bipartisan commission to study the intelligence requirements of the post-Cold War era. Following Aspin's death in May, former Defense Secretary Harold Brown is appointed to head the Commission on the Roles and Capabilities of the U.S. Intelligence Community. At about the same time, congressional intelligence committees also begin hearings on possible reforms in U.S. intelligence gathering.

March 1995
President Clinton nominates Deputy Defense Secretary John M. Deutch to become the director of central intelligence.

March 1, 1996
The Brown commission is scheduled to report its findings to the president.

Continued from p. 106

Dispelling fears that a new intelligence service could be used to spy on Americans, he persuaded Congress to pass the National Security Act, which he signed into law Sept. 18, 1947. In addition to the CIA, the law created the National Security Council (NSC) to oversee all intelligence activities and a director of central intelligence to manage these operations.

The CIA's legal mandate was to collect, analyze and distribute foreign intelligence to appropriate government officials and to advise the NSC on national security. It was barred from participating in domestic operations, which the law clearly placed under FBI authority. The law also empowered the CIA to carry out "services of common concern" and to "perform such other functions and duties related to intelligence affecting the national security as the NSC will from time to time direct." This ambiguous language would later enable the new agency to engage in covert action. It also provided the flexibility to accommodate reforms called for in later years.

The deepening of the Cold War and the onset of the Korean War in 1950 intensified the demand for intelligence. By 1953, just six years after it was created, the CIA employed more than 10,000 people in the United States and in its stations, or offices, around the world. Under the leadership of Allen Dulles, President Dwight D. Eisenhower's director of central intelligence, the CIA enjoyed a period of widespread support from the American public, which viewed it as a key defense against communism.

It was in these years that the CIA engaged in some of its best-known — and most controversial — covert operations. In 1953, the CIA masterminded the ouster of leftist Premier Mohammad Mossadeq in Iran and the installation of the pro-American shah, whose friendly regime gave the United States a foothold in the Middle East. The following year, the agency engineered the ouster of Guatemalan leader Jacobo Arbenz Guzman, who had threatened to appropriate the U.S.-owned United Fruit Co.

American U-2 pilot Francis Gary Powers testifies during his espionage trial in Moscow in August 1960. As the Cold War intensified during the 1950s, the CIA turned increasingly to high-altitude flights and other advanced technology to gather intelligence. Powers was released in exchange for a convicted Soviet spy in 1962.

Technological advances in the 1950s greatly improved the CIA's ability to collect intelligence. The high-altitude U-2 spy plane, in particular, enabled the United States to photograph Soviet military installations without endangering the lives of agents on the ground. With the U-2 and sophisticated eavesdropping technologies, the CIA could rely more heavily on signals — as opposed to human — intelligence. Even after Soviet missiles managed to shoot down the U-2 piloted by Francis Gary Powers in 1960, public support for the agency and its high-tech missions ran high.

Crisis Years

The CIA's high approval rating with the American public abruptly plummeted on April 17, 1961, when 1,400 CIA-trained Cuban exiles invaded Cuba to overthrow Fidel Castro. The small force was easily routed by Cuban soldiers, and the incident drew worldwide criticism. In the United States, the CIA would never fully recover the public support it had once enjoyed.

The incident led President John F. Kennedy to restructure the CIA, curtailing its paramilitary operations and concentrating on intelligence gathering. The agency's discovery of Soviet missile sites in Cuba in 1962 led to the Cuban missile crisis, enabling the president to demand, and eventually obtain, the withdrawal of the missiles and end the Cold War's most dangerous crisis.

Following a brief period of support, the CIA again fell into disfavor in 1965 following the disclosure of its covert operations to shore up the anticommunist government of South Vietnam. As U.S. involvement in the Vietnam War escalated, so did opposition to the war, including CIA covert operations. Hostility toward the agency peaked in 1972, when the public learned that former CIA employees had broken into Democratic headquarters in the Watergate complex.

Shortly after President Richard M.

Nixon appointed William E. Colby as CIA director in 1973, an internal CIA investigation into unethical or illegal agency activities was leaked to the press. The list of violations, dubbed the "Family Jewels," included instances of illegal wiretapping, break-ins and surveillance aimed at American citizens, in clear violation of the 1947 law. The list prompted the first of what would become a series of investigations into the agency's activities.

The Rockefeller Commission, set up by President Gerald R. Ford, found in 1975 that the CIA had kept files on more than 7,500 Americans and infiltrated the antiwar movement, among other abuses. The revelations prompted Congress to establish oversight committees in both houses to investigate CIA activities throughout the world.

Under the direction of Sen. Frank Church, D-Idaho, and Rep. Otis G. Pike, D-N.Y., the Senate and House intelligence committees uncovered a number of CIA plots to assassinate foreign leaders, including Castro, Rafael Trujillo of the Dominican Republic and Patrice Lumumba of Zaire, as well as creating the upheaval in Chile that led to President Salvador Allende's assassination. The committees' findings prompted Ford to reorganize the CIA, specifically forbidding it from participating in assassination attempts and restricting its intelligence-gathering methods.

With the Ayatollah Khomeini's overthrow of the shah in 1979 and subsequent taking of 66 American hostages in Teheran, public attitudes toward the CIA again shifted. Fearful that reform efforts had gone too far during the administration of President Jimmy Carter, American voters in 1980 picked Ronald Reagan to usher in a more aggressive foreign policy, including a reinvigorated CIA.

Under the direction of Reagan appointee William J. Casey, the CIA hired thousands of new staffers, expanded its headquarters and increased covert action, including paramilitary operations in Soviet outposts such as Angola, Afghanistan and Nicaragua. Congress increased funding for intelligence, reportedly raising the CIA's budget by the mid-1980s to more than $3 billion a year, about the same amount as the current budget.

Shortly after President Richard M. Nixon appointed William E. Colby as CIA director in 1973, an internal CIA investigation into unethical or illegal agency activities was leaked to the press. The list of violations, dubbed the "Family Jewels," included instances of illegal wiretapping, break-ins and surveillance aimed at American citizens, in clear violation of the 1947 law.

In 1987, however, the agency faced yet another scandal when congressional investigators revealed that the CIA had illegally supported Nicaraguan "contra" rebels by giving them money made from secret arms sales to Iran. Casey died from cancer before he could testify on the Iran-contra affair.

Three years later, the Soviet Union collapsed, ending the Cold War. With the disappearance of the main rationale for its existence, the CIA once again became the focus of intense scrutiny, as policy-makers and legislators began debating the role of intelligence in the post-Cold War era. ■

CURRENT SITUATION

Overhauling the Agency

The FBI's arrest of Aldrich Ames in 1994 led to perhaps the most damaging scandal in the CIA's turbulent history. Ames' treasonous work had gone unchecked for nine years. If the spy agency couldn't even detect such activities among its own staff, critics asked, how could it be effective in the rest of the world?

The Ames scandal continued to take its toll on the CIA's credibility in late 1995, when it was revealed that for eight years the agency had knowingly handed over to three presidents, and to the Pentagon, intelligence that had come from double agents who worked for both the CIA and the KGB. Moreover, the CIA had not said anything about the double agents. [17]

Intelligence officials acknowledged their failure to detect Ames' treason. "There is a reluctance to accept the fact that somebody inside this organization, who had gone through all of those things that I had gone through and others had gone through, really would be a traitor," said former Deputy CIA Director Richard J. Kerr. "All I can say is, I didn't ask the right questions." [18]

Together with the radically altered international environment of the post-Cold War era, the Ames scandal prompted the most thorough review of U.S. intelligence needs since the CIA's founding. Alternatives being considered by the Brown commission and congressional committees range from abolish-

Continued on p. 111

Breaking Through the CIA's Glass Ceiling

The intelligence community has gained a reputation as one of the least inviting workplaces for women in the federal government. The military, which accounts for about 90 percent of the intelligence budget, has a long tradition of male dominance. Only in recent years have the services consistently promoted women to higher ranks.

But the civilian branch of the U.S. intelligence system also has been known as inhospitable to women who seek advancement. If anything, the "glass ceiling" barring the promotion of women (and minorities) to senior positions has been more firmly in place at the Central Intelligence Agency than at any other government agency.

The international spy community also has a long history of dominance by men. Britain's MI-6, the elite spy agency that served as a model for the CIA, was portrayed as an exclusive club of Cambridge- and Oxford-educated white men in Ian Fleming's spy novels glorifying dashing James Bond — Agent 007. As popularized by a series of movies since the 1960s, first starring Sean Connery, spying had little room for women, except as sex objects who merely underscored the masculine nature of espionage.

CIA Executive Director Nora Slatkin

A similar tone was set in the CIA's early days just after World War II, when the first spymasters came from a small and tightly knit community of Eastern-educated young men from wealthy families. Bored by their jobs on Wall Street, they were drawn to the adventure and sense of mission the agency provided in its quest to conquer communism.

"Secretive, elitist and seemingly above partisan politics, the CIA seemed to be the kind of organization made for an independent spirit like [Richard] Bissell," writes *Newsweek* journalist Evan Thomas of one of the early agency directors. " 'There was a feeling of esprit,' [Bissell] said, 'a sense that you could accomplish things.' "[1]

After decades of offering few professional opportunities for women, the CIA found itself the target of a class-action sexual discrimination suit last year brought by nine women in the agency's top-secret directorate of operations. The case, which was settled out of court, followed on the heels of a sexual-harassment lawsuit that revealed a seamier side to gender discrimination at the agency. Former CIA station chief Janine Brookner had charged the agency with falsely accusing her of sexual promiscuity after she reported a fellow employee for beating his wife. In December 1994, the CIA agreed to settle the case for $410,000.[2]

Actually, the CIA has been a hard place to make a career for anyone who isn't a white male. In 1990, an internal study found, only 7 percent of senior officers were women, and 1.7 percent were African-Americans. Hispanics and other minorities were even more poorly represented.

Since 1991, however, programs to recruit and promote more women, minorities and people with disabilities have had some success. The percentage of women among senior officers has doubled, to 14.4 percent, the agency reports, and the percentage of African-Americans has almost doubled, to 3.2 percent. "We are determined to break any glass ceiling and to ensure that the most qualified candidates — to include women and minority officers — continue to be assigned to the agency's senior positions," said the agency's top female, Executive Director Nora Slatkin.[3]

Slatkin's appointment itself was a CIA first. Slatkin had been an assistant secretary of the Navy when she was hired in May by newly sworn in Director John M. Deutch to oversee the agency's day-to-day operations. But her goal of opening more senior positions to women, minorities and disabled people is hampered by the agency's need to pare its work force because of budgetary constraints. "If I could pin our lack of progress in work force demographics on one thing, it would be [downsizing]," she said. "There is no way that, with the large number of people leaving annually and the small numbers of people coming in, we can show much improvement."

The CIA's hiring goals also have been stymied by resistance from the white males who continue to dominate the agency. A 1994 internal survey intended to measure morale found that white male officers expressed feelings that ranged from "worried" to "angry," which they attributed to such new programs as sexual-harassment prevention workshops and diversity training, as well as downsizing. "We will continue to monitor the concerns of white male employees," Slatkin testified. "Our goal is to provide a fair and equitable work environment for all employees."

Deutch has promised to continue improving the CIA's spotty record in hiring practices. "I am determined that the intelligence community include its emphasis on diversity in its work force," Deutch told the House Select Intelligence Committee Dec. 19. "It is important for our mission that we take advantage of the unique background of all of our citizens."

---

[1] Evan Thomas, *The Very Best Men* (1995), p. 99.

[2] See Elaine Shannon, "Skirts and Daggers," *Time*, June 12, 1995, pp. 46-47.

[3] Testimony before the House Select Intelligence Committee, Nov. 29, 1995.

Continued from p. 109

ng the CIA altogether to giving it greater powers than it has enjoyed since the CIA's heyday under Dulles.

Clinton's Goals

The bipartisan, 17-member Brown commission, appointed last February by President Clinton and the congressional leadership, was given a year, under the fiscal 1995 intelligence authorization act, to present its recommendations. "During the Cold War, U.S. intelligence agencies focused their activities principally on monitoring and analyzing the activities of the Soviet Union and its Warsaw Pact allies," the commission's work plan states. "With the disintegration of the Soviet Union and Warsaw Pact, is this intelligence apparatus still needed? If so, what are the continuing objectives served by such an apparatus? How should it be organized? What should it cost?" [19]

The Brown commission is but one element of President Clinton's attempt to redefine the intelligence community's mission. Last March, the president signed a classified order outlining his priorities for CIA operations in coming years. The directive established a committee of senior officials from agencies that use intelligence data and charged them with defining the kinds of information they want to receive from the CIA and other spy agencies. By authorizing the CIA's "customers" to order the data they want, Clinton greatly curtailed the agency's freedom to act independently.

As the intelligence community's most important customer, the president has for the past year held the key to the agency's future, pending completion of the Brown commission's review next month. Clinton's list of intelligence priorities reportedly has focused on "rogue" nations — chiefly Iran, Iraq and North Korea — which have been implicated in terrorism and nuclear proliferation; Islamic fundamentalist groups involved in terrorism; and sources of future threats to U.S. security. Economic-intelligence gathering, a controversial mission for the spy agencies, came lower on the president's list. [20]

Since deciding to send American troops to help enforce the recent Dayton peace accord ending hostilities in Bosnia, Clinton has focused the intelligence community's activities on providing military data to support Pentagon strategy. Since the 1991 Persian Gulf War, when military commanders complained that they did not receive the intelligence they needed fast enough, the Defense Department has tried to wrest control over intelligence matters from the CIA. The ensuing turf war has colored the debate over intelligence missions for the future.

"The military under Defense Secretary [William J.] Perry are very much concerned that their role is being undermined," says Whipple, whose organization represents former officers of both the military and civilian side of the intelligence community. "On the other hand, I think everybody would expect to see the CIA director try to enforce his role."

Deutch Takes Over

In the eight months since he became the 17th director of central intelli-

Photographs by Murry H. Sill

The Iran-Contra Scandal

Under CIA Director William Casey, the CIA increased its covert action, including paramilitary operations in Soviet outposts such as Angola, Afghanistan and Nicaragua. In 1987, however, the agency faced yet another scandal when congressional investigators revealed that the CIA had illegally supported Nicaraguan contra rebels (above) in the 1980s by giving them money raised from secret arms sales to Iran. Casey died from cancer before he could testify on the Iran-contra affair.

gence, Deutch has taken a number of steps to help shape the community's future direction. As soon as he took office, he ordered a shake-up of CIA personnel, replacing top managers who were deemed tainted by the Ames scandal. In an effort to more effectively carry out his role over the community as a whole, he appointed Nora Slatkin as the agency's executive director and George J. Tenet as deputy director in charge of day-to-day operations and administration.*

While he has refrained from more sweeping organizational changes, Deutch has taken steps to more closely coordinate the activities of military and civilian intelligence operations. He has proposed the merger of two offices to jointly run the management and acquisition of military and intelligence satellites. The Joint Space Management Board would be co-directed by Deutch and his former superior, Defense Secretary Perry, with whom Deutch reportedly continues to enjoy a close relationship. "This is an important step forward that will lead to a cost savings in the long run," Deutch told lawmakers. [21]

A more controversial proposal put forward by Deutch would consolidate the military and civilian offices that analyze and distribute geo-locational data into a single National Imagery and Mapping Agency. "The motivation for this change," the director explained, "is primarily to meet the military's need for dominant battlefield awareness and, as the Gulf war illustrated, the need for imagery to be distributed in a timely fashion to battlefield commanders." [22] Concerned that Congress had not yet received sufficient information on the proposed new agency, lawmakers prohibited the CIA and the Defense Department from creating the agency as part of the fiscal 1996 intelligence authorization bill. [23]

Deutch's proposals have earned praise from former intelligence officials. "I certainly approve of the move to create a national imagery agency since it was my task force in 1992 that recommended it in the first place," says Gates, adding that he failed to win the support of then-Defense Secretary Dick Cheney and Joint Chiefs of Staff Chairman Colin Powell. "Taking advantage of the special relationship between Deutch and Perry to implement that recommendation is a good idea and a step forward," Gates says.

While giving the new director high marks for taking on the task of overseeing the intelligence community at a time of rapid change, former Acting Director Studeman is more wary than some observers about Deutch's personnel changes. "As someone who came from the old days, I think it's unfair to portray the image that the people in the old days couldn't do anything right and that these new people will be saviors," Studeman says. "One administration connects to the next, and everybody builds on what others have done."

Studeman also worries about the high profile Deutch has assumed, in contrast to the established CIA culture, which calls for officials to assume a less visible role. "I think the intelligence community worries a little bit about the emergence of a cult of personality," he says. "I think John thinks it's great that he's been on the cover of *Parade* magazine, but most people in the intelligence community are a little more reclusive. At the same time, we recognize that we have to be more willing to explain to the American public where their dollars are going, for what kinds of operations and why these are important. As long as they are not used to glorify individuals, demystification and openness in intelligence are important." ■

* Before their appointments at CIA, Slatkin was an assistant secretary of the Navy, and Tenet was senior director for intelligence programs at the National Security Council.

OUTLOOK

Deutch's Challenges

As the Clinton administration and lawmakers await the Brown commission's final recommendations, scheduled for release in early March, former intelligence officials point to several obstacles that stand in the way of effective reform of the CIA and other spy agencies.

An important constraint is money. If, as most observers predict, effective intelligence gathering will require ever more sophisticated technology, the intelligence community stands to suffer disproportionately from budget cutbacks. Congress refused to include money for Deutch's proposed mapping and imagery office in its most recent budget. "There are objections in the current environment in Washington to creating a whole new and very large agency," Gates says. It is up to the administration, he adds, "to prove why it will save money and make the overall effort more efficient. That case can be made and made strongly."

At the same time, Deutch enjoys some advantages that his predecessors lacked. Even if policy-makers decide not to create a new intelligence czar, the current CIA director has positioned himself well, by delegating some of his CIA responsibilities, to carrying out his dual role more effectively. "He is spending more of his attention on community matters," says Whipple. "He has much more chance of succeeding in [overseeing the community] than any director the agency's had before because of his relationship with the man who really controls the intelligence budget, Mr. Perry."

Deutch's ability to get what he wants from the staff of the various intelligence agencies, however, is

Continued on p. 114

At Issue:

Should the CIA be abolished?

yes

SEN. DANIEL PATRICK MOYNIHAN, D-N.Y.
FROM SENATE REMARKS, JAN. 4, 1995.

It is no secret that a serious re-examination of our intelligence needs is in order. Since 1991 . . . I have endeavored to bring the shortcomings of the intelligence community to public light. Not to denigrate our intelligence efforts, but to improve them. . . . [Today I propose] the transfer of the functions of the Central Intelligence Agency to the Department of State.

The scrutiny that has now visited the intelligence community in the aftermath of the exposure of Aldrich Ames . . . increases the likelihood that some long-needed reassessments will be made. I do not relish these circumstances, for to a great extent the Ames case merely distracts from some of the most fundamental defects of the CIA. . . .

Speaking before the Boston Bar Association in 1993, [author] John Le Carré . . . questioned the contributions of spies to the winning of the Cold War. In his remarks he stated: "You see, it wasn't the spies who won the Cold War. I don't believe that in the end the spies mattered very much at all. Their capsuled isolation and their remote theorizing actually prevented them from seeing, as late as 1987 or '88, what anybody in the streets could have told them 'It's over. We've won. . . .' "

If covert operations failed to have an impact . . . what of our intelligence analysis? How did that serve us in the Cold War? I believe I have fully laid out to the Senate on previous occasions my assessment and those of numerous respected individuals on the performance of the CIA in this regard. The defining failure of the CIA was their inability to predict the collapse of the Soviet Union. . . .

Today we hear some revisionist rumblings that the CIA did in fact see the Soviet collapse emerging after all. If some individual CIA analysts were more prescient than the corporate view, their ideas were filtered out in the bureaucratic process; and it is the corporate view that counts because that is what reaches the president and his advisers. On this one, the corporate view missed by a mile. . . .

After World War II, it was originally intended that intelligence would be coordinated by the secretary of State. The maneuvering of some of the more powerful assistant secretaries in the State Department at the time prevented that from being implemented, and the independent Central Intelligence Agency was soon formed. Dean Acheson, who was present at the creation, doubted the wisdom of such a move. "I had the gravest forebodings about this organization and warned the president that, as set up, neither he, the National Security Council, nor anyone else would be in a position to know what it was doing or to control it," [Acheson said]. The State Department must function as the primary agency in formulating and conducting foreign policy. Any other arrangement invites confusion.

no

R. JAMES WOOLSEY
Former CIA director

FROM TESTIMONY BEFORE THE HOUSE PERMANENT SELECT COMMITTEE ON INTELLIGENCE, MAY 22, 1995.

Allegations that the intelligence community has not been adapting to deal with the issues of the post-Cold War era are nonsense. The proliferation of weapons of mass destruction, terrorism rogue states and other such post-Cold War issues have for some years been given substantial prominence by my predecessors and by the superb professionals of the intelligence community. . . . At the same time we must all realize that just because the Cold War has ended does not mean that we can now afford to ignore, for example, Russia. The stresses inside the Russian military, the effectiveness of Russian custody of fissionable material, their advanced weapons technology, which may be increasingly sold to other countries, and the complex and troubling partnerships between Russian business, organized crime and the power ministries, including Russian intelligence, are all important subjects on which we need to continue to collect intelligence. . . .

I believe that there are two main reasons why some have not understood how thoroughly and continuously the intelligence community has been adapting to the post-Cold War world.

First, because the [intelligence] networks with worldwide reach . . . existed during the Cold War and continue to exist, albeit in changed form, this is sometimes thought to indicate an unwillingness by the intelligence community to adapt to the new era. The reality is that these networks must continue to exist and exhibit at least a worldwide reach if the United States is to continue to be a world power. We cannot afford to close any one of them down as then-Secretary of State [Henry L.] Stimson closed down the State Department's code-breaking in the 1920s, remarking that "gentlemen don't read one another's mail."

If we, for example, shut down the CIA as Sen. Moynihan has proposed, the virtual destruction of our ability to conduct espionage would make us essentially blind and deaf to the plans and activities of terrorists and the proliferators of nuclear, chemical and bacteriological weapons around the world. Secretary Stimson and the rest of the world were quite lucky that in the interwar years the U.S. Navy and British intelligence were both being less than gentlemanly with respect to Japanese and German mail, and the codes that protected them. Without intelligence, at many crucial turning points World War II could have gone in very different directions. If we, as a nation, make a Stimson-like mistake by closing down a vital intelligence capability, then the next time we need a crucial item of intelligence there may well be no one else to cover for us.

FOR MORE INFORMATION

Association of Former Intelligence Officers, 6723 Whittier Ave., Suite 303A, McLean, Va. 22101; (703) 790-0320. Representing former military and civilian officers, the association promotes increased public support for intelligence agencies.

Center for National Security Studies, 2130 H St. N.W., Suite 701, Washington, D.C. 20006; (202) 994-7060. Sponsored by the Fund for Peace, the center monitors intelligence activities of the CIA and the FBI; its library is open to the public by appointment.

Central Intelligence Agency, Langley, Va. (mailing address: Washington, D.C. 20505); (703) 482-7676. The CIA provides limited information to the public on its activities and missions.

Federation of American Scientists, 307 Massachusetts Ave. N.E., Washington, D.C. 20002; (202) 546-3300. This research group monitors a broad array of national security issues involving intelligence, including arms control compliance and defense policy.

National Security Archive, 2130 H St. N.W., Suite 701, Washington, D.C. 20006; (202) 994-7000. This research institute maintains a collection of declassified and unclassified documents related to U.S. foreign policy and national security affairs.

open to debate, observers say. "He's going to have to deal with the group of people he brought in who, by and large, have limited or no intelligence operations experience," says Whipple. "Are they going to be effective managers of the future, or is their lack of operational experience going to hinder them from gaining the confidence of the people they're supposed to supervise? I think that's an open question at this point." ■

Notes

[1] Quoted in Caleb Carr, "Aldrich Ames and the Conduct of American Intelligence," *World Policy Journal,* fall 1994, p. 20. Ames made the statement on April 28, 1994.

[2] Testimony before the House Select Intelligence Committee, Dec. 19, 1995.

[3] See "The New CIA," *The CQ Researcher,* Dec. 11, 1992, pp. 1073-1096; and "$28 Billion Spying Budget Is Made Public by Mistake," *The New York Times,* Nov. 5, 1994.

[4] Sen. Moynihan addressed the Senate Jan. 4, 1995.

[5] At the Brown commission's only public hearing, in Washington on Jan. 19, 1996, six intelligence experts testified, including former Deputy CIA Director Bobby Ray Inman, former Defense Secretary Frank C. Carlucci and former Attorney General William Barr.

[6] For background, see Sen. Moynihan addressed the Senate Jan. 4, 1995 and "National Security Council," *Editorial Research Reports,* Jan. 16, 1987, pp. 17-28.

[7] Clapper testified Nov. 16, 1995, before the House Select Intelligence Committee.

[8] Deutch testified Dec. 19, 1995, before the House Select Intelligence Committee.

[9] Gorelick testified Oct. 25, 1995, before the Senate Select Intelligence Committee.

[10] From testimony before the Dec. 19, 1995 House Select Intelligence Committee hearing.

[11] Roger Hilsman, "Does the CIA Still Have a Role?" *Foreign Affairs,* September/October 1995, p. 112.

[12] See David E. Sanger and Tim Weiner, "Emerging Role for the CIA: Economic Spy," *The New York Times,* Oct. 15, 1995, p. A1.

[13] Dave McCurdy, "Glasnost for the CIA," *Foreign Affairs,* January/February 1994, p. 129.

[14] "Let's Just Fire the Spies," *Business Week,* Oct. 30, 1995, p. 178.

[15] Rob Norton, "The CIA's Mission Impossible," *Fortune,* Oct. 2, 1995, p. 55.

[16] Information in this section is based on Rafaela Ellis, *The Central Intelligence Agency* (1988).

[17] See Walter Pincus, "Tainted Moscow Data Swayed U.S., CIA Says," *The Washington Post,* Dec. 9, 1995.

[18] Kerr testified Nov. 16, 1995, before the House Select Intelligence Committee.

[19] From the commission's work plan, submitted June 7, 1995, to the House and Senate Select Intelligence Committees.

[20] See Walter Pincus, "Control Tightened On Spy Agencies," *The Washington Post,* March 10, 1995.

[21] From Dec. 19 testimony before the House Select Intelligence Committee.

[22] *Ibid.*

[23] See Donna Cassata, "Spy Budget Cleared for Clinton; Plan for New Agency Curbed," *Congressional Quarterly Weekly Report,* Dec. 23, 1996, pp. 3894-3895.

Bibliography

Selected Sources Used

Books

Grose, Peter, *Gentleman Spy: The Life of Allen Dulles*, Houghton-Mifflin, 1994.
During his eight years as CIA director, Allen Dulles oversaw the agency's early covert operations, including the overthrow of leftist governments in Iran and Guatemala. The author focuses on the rivalry between Dulles and his brother, John Foster Dulles, who served during the same period as President Dwight D. Eisenhower's secretary of State.

Richelson, Jeffrey T., *A Century of Spies: Intelligence in the Twentieth Century*, Oxford University Press, 1995.
This chronology of spy operations since 1900 demonstrates the continuing use of espionage as a vital weapon of diplomacy and war. Even with the development of satellite imagery and electronic eavesdropping, intelligence gathering by covert agents in the field continues to play a key role in spy agencies around the world.

Thomas, Evan, *The Very Best Men: The Early Years of the CIA*, Simon & Schuster, 1995.
Thomas, Washington bureau chief of *Newsweek*, focuses on the careers of four early spymasters — Frank Wisner, Richard Bissell, Tracy Barnes and Desmond FitzGerald. With their inherited wealth, glamorous private lives and impeccable educations, they helped shape the old boys' network that came to characterize the CIA.

Articles

Carr, Caleb, "Aldrich Ames and the Conduct of American Intelligence," *World Policy Journal*, fall 1994.
In the wake of the Ames spy scandal, the author calls for the elimination of most U.S. spy agencies. Rather than conducting covert operations, he writes, they should limit their activities to analyzing public information they obtain from overseas.

Cogan, Charles G., "Partners in Time," *World Policy Journal*, summer 1993.
A former officer in the CIA's secretive operations directorate describes the agency's role in helping Afghan rebels drive Soviet troops from their country in 1989, hastening the end of the Cold War. The agency failed, however, to accurately assess the United States' ability to influence political events in Afghanistan after the Soviet withdrawal.

Duffy, Brian, "The Cold War's Last Spy," *U.S. News & World Report*, March 6, 1995.
Aldrich Ames sold U.S. secrets to the Soviet Union for years before the FBI finally caught up with him. Ames wreaked untold damage on U.S. national interests and identified at least 10 Soviet nationals on the CIA payroll who were later executed for treason.

Hilsman, Roger, "Does the CIA Still Have a Role?" *Foreign Affairs*, September/October 1995.
Intelligence is not worth the money and effort that go into it, writes Hilsman, a former State Department official. The United States gets too little valuable information, he claims, to justify the blows to its international reputation caused by spy scandals.

Maas, Peter, "Is He the CIA's Last, Best Hope?" *Parade Magazine*, Nov. 19, 1995.
This cover story focusing on the career, record and aspirations of CIA Director John M. Deutch has attracted criticism from fellow intelligence officers for violating the intelligence community's unwritten code of conduct requiring them to shirk publicity.

McCurdy, Dave, "Glasnost for the CIA," *Foreign Affairs*, January/February 1994.
The author, a former Democratic representative from Oklahoma and chairman of the House Intelligence Committee, supports creating the position of director of national intelligence to oversee a "leaner, more integrated, and above all more open U.S. intelligence community."

Pipes, Richard, "What to Do About the CIA," *Commentary*, March 1995.
The author, a Harvard University history professor, defends the role of an independent, streamlined Central Intelligence Agency as an essential source of information for policy-makers.

Schweizer, Peter, "The Growth of Economic Espionage," *Foreign Affairs*, January/February 1996.
The United States has become the leading target of foreign intelligence agencies eager to procure American technological secrets and other information of potential benefit to their economies. According to the author, a visiting scholar at the Hoover Institution, economic espionage will soon eclipse military espionage as the main focus of spy agencies.

Weiner, Tim, "The CIA's Most Important Mission: Itself," *The New York Times Magazine*, Dec. 10, 1995.
The Cold War's end and the Aldrich Ames spy scandal have forced the CIA to re-examine its mission. John M. Deutch, the agency's director since last May, has reorganized much of its operations but is facing pressure from critics to make further changes.

The Next Step

Additional information from UMI's Newspaper & Periodical Abstracts database

Aldrich Ames Spy Scandal

Deutch, John, "Moving beyond Ames," *The Washington Post,* Nov. 5, 1995, p. C7.

John M. Deutch, director of the CIA, comments on the damage inflicted by Aldrich Ames on U.S. intelligence and security interests, noting the good things that were done by the CIA in that time and expressing a need to move forward.

Risen, James, "CIA chief gives new details on damage done by Ames," *Los Angeles Times,* Dec. 9, 1995, p. A1.

CIA Director John M. Deutch revealed on Dec. 8, 1995, that Russian President Boris Yeltsin continued to reap the benefits of Aldrich Ames' treason against the U.S. long after the collapse of the Soviet Union by using information from the spy to make it difficult for the U.S. to guess his foreign policy moves.

Risen, James, "CIA still reeling from Ames ties to Soviet agents," *Los Angeles Times,* Nov. 27, 1995, p. A1.

The Soviet Union's double-agent network in the late 1980's was so successful that the CIA apparently did not figure out that it was dealing with double agents for two or three years after the network was created. Details of the CIA's investigation of Aldrich Ames and his espionage are examined.

Risen, James, "Gates says aides failed to tell him about Ames," *Los Angeles Times,* Nov. 2, 1995, p. A1.

Former CIA Director Robert M. Gates said on Nov. 1, 1995, that senior agency officials were convinced in 1992 that Aldrich Ames was a Russian mole but did not tell Gates of their suspicions. Ames remained in place as a spy for nearly two more years.

Taubman, Philip, "Mr. Angleton and Mr. Ames," *The New York Times,* Dec. 17, 1995, p. 12.

Taubman says that the story of James Jesus Angleton, who as head of counterintelligence at the CIA terrorized the organization in a ceaseless search for Russian spies, and Aldrich Ames, who for 10 years sold Moscow nearly every secret about American espionage activities in Russia, is the story of the failure of the CIA. Taubman adds that both Angleton and Ames gravely damaged the CIA in their relentless pursuits.

Disband the CIA?

Alterman, Eric, "A view to a kill," *Rolling Stone,* March 23, 1995, pp. 48-54.

The data the CIA collects are available for the price of a bus ticket in Turkmenistan, Alterman writes. The question of why U.S. taxpayers should continue to shell out billions to pay for it is discussed. The CIA's very existence is being questioned by Congress.

Cassata, Donna, "Experts: CIA needs reform but not a czar," *Congressional Quarterly Weekly Report,* May 27, 1995, p. 1.

The question of whether the CIA has outlived its usefulness is discussed. Several in the intelligence community have embraced legislation sponsored by Sen. Daniel Patrick Moynihan, D-N.Y., to break up the CIA.

Holt, Pat M., "Cabinet rank for CIA would distort its role," *Christian Science Monitor,* April 6, 1995, p. 19.

Holt criticizes the idea of giving Cabinet rank to John Deutch, President Clinton's nominee to be the director of the CIA.

Pipes, Richard, "What to do about the CIA," *Commentary,* March 1995, pp. 36-43.

The CIA is fighting for its life for the second time since its creation in 1947. The charge that the CIA has consistently provided the government with faulty assessments and tolerated inexcusable security breaches in its ranks and that it has become redundant is examined.

Risen, James, "U.S. played key role in arrest of drug lord, sources say," *Los Angeles Times,* June 13, 1995, p. A7.

U.S. intelligence officials played a hidden but crucial role in the June 9, 1995, arrest of Gilberto Rodriguez Orejuela, the most powerful drug lord in Colombia, sources said on June 12. Officials refused to provide detailed accounts of the role of the CIA and DEA in tracking and locating Rodriguez.

Economic Espionage

Anthes, Gary H., "Feds limit info warfare role," *Computerworld,* Sept. 18, 1995, p. 24.

Senior intelligence and law enforcement officials with the CIA and FBI are said to be more willing to help businesses outside the military arena since the end of the Cold War. They are more aggressively alerting U.S. companies about industrial espionage threats.

Lane, Charles, "Why spy?" *The New Republic,* March 27, 1995, p. 10.

President Clinton has defined national security to include economic security. The CIA's effort at economic intelligence gathering is a redundant activity that dilutes the agency's focus and stretches its resources.

Lesher, Richard L., "Coming in from the cold (war)," *Chicago Defender,* Dec. 2, 1995, p. 10.
Dr. Richard L. Lesher criticizes the CIA for committing itself to expanded international economic intelligence-gathering, feeding confidential Japanese trade positions in the auto negotiations to U.S. Trade Representative Mickey Kantor.

Moore, Martha T., "CIA discovers new role since Cold War," *USA Today,* Oct. 25, 1995, p. B1.
Intense international economic competition has supplanted political-military rivalry between superpowers in the 1990s. As the CIA looks for a new role following the end of the Cold War, economic intelligence gathering has come to be central to the agency's mission.

Sanger, David E., and Tim Weiner,"Emerging role for the C.I.A.: Economic spy," *The New York Times,* Oct. 15, 1995, p. 1.
Spying on allies for economic advantage is a crucial new assignment for the CIA now that American foreign policy is focused on commercial interests abroad.

Covert Operations

Blum, Andrew, "Ex-spy says U.S. indicted him for role in Pan Am case," *National Law Journal,* Sept. 25, 1995, p. A11.
Former Mossad agent Juval Aviv told Pan Am's insurers a rouge CIA unit protecting a Syrian heroin-smuggling ring permitted the bombing of Pan Am Flight 103. Aviv's indictment for mail fraud, which he claims is motivated by the CIA's obsession with getting back at him, is discussed.

Cassata, Donna, "Drive to reform CIA intensifies as Ames case fallout worsens," *Congressional Quarterly Weekly Report,* Nov. 4, 1995, p. 3.
After finding out that Aldrich Ames' treachery allowed sullied information to reach the top echelons of the U.S. government during the Cold War, the congressional oversight committee is even more determined to see far-reaching reforms at the CIA.

"CIA chief states case for covert action," *The New York Times,* Sept. 13, 1995, p. A12.
The CIA will maintain, and perhaps increase, its covert operations abroad and continue to hire informers from terrorist cells, military governments and drug syndicates, the new director, John M. Deutch, said on Sept. 12, 1995.

"CIA inquiry into own role in Guatemala a grim joke," *National Catholic Reporter,* Aug. 11, 1995, p. 28.
An editorial contends that the CIA's attempt to police itself in regard to its operations in Guatemala is an insult. Since the mid-1950s, the CIA has supported some of Central America's bloodiest dictators.

"Details emerge on CIA's role in coverup of Guatemala killings," *San Francisco Chronicle,* March 24, 1995, p. A12.
A day after the disclosure by U.S. Rep. Robert Torricelli, D-N.J., of the CIA's link to the deaths of a Guatemalan guerrilla and an American innkeeper, the case of Col. Julio Roberto Alpirez was provided on March 23, 1995, by several officials from the White House.

Lane, Charles, "Get smarter," *The New Republic,* April 24, 1995, p. 15.
The Guatemalan Army's swank School of Intelligence, designed and built by the CIA in the 1980's, is discussed, as is alleged U.S. hypocrisy for supporting the army's human rights atrocities. An investigation into CIA activity in Guatemala will soon be conducted.

Mann, Jim, "CIA keeping historians in the dark about its Cold War role in Japan," *Los Angeles Times,* March 20, 1995, p. A5.
During the first few months of 1995, the CIA has been quietly doing its utmost to prevent some of the most important classified information about America's role in the Cold War from coming to light. The agency has refused to declassify files that show what it was doing in Japan during the Cold War.

Priest, Dana, and Smith, R Jeffrey, "Defense Dept. to investigate U.S. military role in Guatemala," *The Washington Post,* April 1, 1995, p. A2.
Deputy Defense Secretary John M. Deutch announced an investigation into the U.S. military's activities in Guatemala from the early 1980s to the present. The U.S. has been accused of playing a role in the slayings of American innkeeper Michael DeVine and guerrilla leader Efrain Bamaca Velasquez, which were allegedly ordered by paid CIA informer Col. Julio Roberto Alpirez.

Risen, James, "Congress OKs House plan to fund covert action in Iran," *Los Angeles Times,* Dec. 22, 1995, p. A18.
House Speaker Newt Gingrich, R-Ga., has won his behind-the-scenes battle in mid-December 1995 to provide secret funding for a new CIA covert-action program in Iran. The Clinton administration and the CIA had opposed the plan.

Risen, James, "3 ex-CIA directors blamed for agency role in misdeeds," *The Los Angeles Times,* Nov. 1, 1995, p. A1.
The CIA's inspector general has charged that three former agency directors and nine other former and current officials should be held accountable because some disinformation from Soviet double agents was knowingly passed to the President, the CIA reported to Congress on Oct. 31, 1995.

Robbins, Carla Anne, "CIA's Guatemala scandal turns up

pressure for quick, broad reform of intelligence services," ***The Wall Street Journal,*** **April 11, 1995, p. A22.**
Hard decisions on CIA reform may have been hastened in the wake of the most recent scandal. Charges have been made that the CIA deliberately covered up its links to the murders of a U.S. innkeeper in Guatemala and a Guatemalan rebel leader married to a U.S. citizen.

Smith, R. Jeffrey, "Deutch cites concerns on CIA failings," ***The Washington Post,*** **June 22, 1995, p. A15.**
CIA Director John M. Deutch said he is concerned about allegations that the agency's operatives were involved in committing human rights abuses in Guatemala and took part in covert activities there that violated government policies.

Smith, R Jeffrey, "Expansion of covert action eyed," ***The Washington Post,*** **Sept. 13, 1995, p. A7.**
CIA Director John M. Deutch and other senior intelligence officials raised the possibility that the Clinton administration may soon decide to expand the use of covert action, or clandestine operations, by U.S. intelligence agencies to try to influence activities in foreign countries.

Weiner, Tim, "C.I.A. says agents deceived superiors on Guatemala role," ***The New York Times,*** **July 26, 1995, p. A1.**
An internal CIA investigation into the agency's conduct in Guatemala concludes that CIA officers there failed to disclose their clandestine activities to two U.S. ambassadors, to Congress and to the agency itself, intelligence officials said on July 25, 1995.

"World wire: Probe of CIA role in car talks," ***The Wall Street Journal,*** **Oct. 18, 1995, p. A17.**
The U.S. promised Japan that it will investigate reports of CIA spying during car trade talks in which information was allegedly leaked to U.S. Trade Representative Mickey Kantor during June 1995 talks in Geneva. Kantor was seeking better access to Japanese markets for U.S. cars and parts.

CIA Director John M. Deutch

"An interview with CIA Director John Deutch," Morning Edition — National Public Radio, June 19, 1995.
Martha Raddatz spent the day with CIA Director John Deutch, who has already made some changes in the agency since taking office a month ago. He advocates declassifying information concerning American history.

Black, Chris, "Deutch vows change, takes CIA post Today," ***Boston Globe,*** **May 10, 1995, p. 3.**
With a unanimous vote in the U.S. Senate and a mandate to shake up the CIA, John M. Deutch will take over as its sixth director in 10 years.

"CIA Director Deutch," ***The Wall Street Journal,*** **Sept. 25, 1995, p. A1.**
A CIA official said CIA Director John M. Deutch ordered changes at a government organization that manages the U.S. spy satellite program after learning it had built up a huge cash reserve without telling overseers. By charging Congress in advance for programs, the National Reconnaissance Organization apparently accumulated some $1 billion.

"Deutch deserves praise for shaking up the CIA," ***Denver Post,*** **May 21, 1995, p. D2.**
An editorial applauds John Deutch for keeping his promise to shake up the CIA if confirmed as its new director.

Pincus, Walter, "CIA's spies watching Deutch's disciplinary decision on Paris station chief," ***The Washington Post,*** **Dec. 27, 1995, p. A6.**
CIA Director John M. Deutch faces a major disciplinary decision in January 1996 that could provide an important test of the influence of the agency's clandestine directorate of operations. Deutch's decision concerns the fate of the agency's chief of station in Paris, who has accepted responsibility for errors that led to French counterintelligence uncovering a CIA economic espionage operation.

Pincus, Walter, "Deutch under pressure to punish CIA agents," ***The Washington Post,*** **July 31, 1995, p. A6.**
Congressional pressure is building for CIA Director John M. Deutch to take strong action against individuals involved in the agency's failure for more than three years to disclose to Congress an intelligence report that implicated Guatemalan Col. Julio Roberto Alpirez, a CIA-paid informant, in the 1990 murder of a U.S. citizen.

Quinn-Judge, Paul, "Answering the call for reform," ***Boston Globe,*** **April 27, 1995, p. 11.**
John Deutch's forceful promises of swift changes and new leadership at the CIA showed that he had learned from James Woolsey's unhappy tenure.

Ricks, Thomas E., and Rick Wartzman, "John Deutch, new nominee to head CIA, faces challenges at the troubled agency," ***The Wall Street Journal,*** **March 13, 1995, p. A7.**
John Deutch, President Clinton's new nominee to head the CIA, brings to the job a reputation for being whip-smart and sometimes abrasive, but able to work well with Congress and the administration. Clinton agreed to raise the post to Cabinet status to get Deutch to accept the nomination.

"98-0 Senate vote puts Deutch atop CIA," ***Chicago Tribune,*** **May 10, 1995, p. 16.**
By 98-0, the Senate voted on May 9, 1995, to install John Deutch as the new CIA director. A chemist by training, Deutch will try to restore the spy agency's lost luster.

Schorr, Daniel, "Deutch, Freeh learn a hard lesson,"

***Christian Science Monitor,* Sept. 1, 1995, p. 19.**
Schorr discusses the difficult positions of CIA Director John Deutch and FBI Director Louis Freeh as they try to deal with problems created before they arrived at their respective agencies.

Smith, R. Jeffrey, "CIA director pledges swift reform," *The Washington Post,* May 16, 1995, p. A15.
The CIA's new director, John M. Deutch, predicted that a report of the spy agency's performance in Guatemala will conclude it took improper actions there and also vowed swift internal repairs to prevent a recurrence of any mistakes.

Smith, R. Jeffrey, "Deutch orders speedup in Balkan atrocities data," *The Washington Post,* Nov. 17, 1995, p. A36.
Responding to complaints that Washington, D.C., has been too slow in providing data to a U.N. tribunal probing war crimes in the former Yugoslavia, CIA Director John M. Deutch ordered all U.S. intelligence agencies to make supporting the tribunal "a high priority."

Smith, R. Jeffrey, "Deutch outlines plan to centralize control of intelligence community," *The Washington Post,* Dec. 20, 1995, p. A23.
CIA Director John M. Deutch outlined before a House committee his aim to strengthen the CIA director's ability to coordinate most intelligence community activities, and eliminate waste created by poor budget choices by centralizing the drafting of the U.S. intelligence budget within the CIA.

Smith, R. Jeffrey, and Walter Pincus, "Deutch leaving no doubt who's in charge of intelligence," *The Washington Post,* Dec. 10, 1995, p. A6.
As the first CIA director since William Casey to be appointed to the Cabinet, John M. Deutch has taken on a novel role as superior to the heads of all intelligence-gathering operations, including the Defense Intelligence Agency and the National Security Agency.

Reform Proposals

Corn, David, "Deutch uncle," *The Nation,* May 22, 1995, pp. 709-710.
Statements by CIA Director-nominee John Deutch at his confirmation hearing concerning comprehensive reform of the agency are discussed in an editorial. The CIA is a bureaucratic beast that should be downsized dramatically, it says.

Hilsman, Roger, "Does the CIA still have a role?" *Foreign Affairs,* September 1995, pp. 104-116.
The CIA should stick to its strengths—analysis for policy-makers and high-tech surveillance and analysis for policy-makers. Cloak-and-dagger foreign policy has been unsuccessful.

Landay, Jonathan S., "Deutch cleans spy house, hires new trench coats," *Christian Science Monitor,* May 17, 1995, p. 3.
On May 16, 1995, less than a week after becoming the director of the CIA, John Deutch announced a new top management team of mostly outsiders at the agency. Deutch said that the appointments would provide an indication of some of the changes he plans to institute at the CIA, and stated that improving the agency's relations with Congress would be one of his top priorities.

"Mr. Deutch's auspicious debut," *The New York Times,* May 22, 1995, p. A14.
An editorial asserts that CIA Director John Deutch has "set a new tone of responsibility and accountability" at the CIA since taking office in May 1995. The editorial approves Deutch's appointment of a strong team of outsiders and his rejection of the "agency nostrum" that only experienced intelligence executives can understand and run the CIA.

"Mr. Deutch's message," *The New York Times,* April 28, 1995, p. A32.
An editorial says that CIA Director John Deutch's emphatic commitment to cleanse and redesign the CIA could herald a watershed in the history of the troubled agency. The editorial adds that Deutch's testimony before the Senate Intelligence Committee on April 26, 1995, put the agency on notice that its next director has no tolerance for immoral, illegal or incompetent intelligence activities and will dismiss anyone who does.

Nelson, Anna Kasten, "The unfortunate exclusion of scholars from debate over the future of the CIA," *The Chronicle of Higher Education,* March 31, 1995, p. A44.
Scholars and the rest of the public are being excluded from an assessment of the CIA and its future by not being able to examine information necessary to participate. The CIA has been highly selective in releasing documents.

Smith, R. Jeffrey., "If confirmed, Deutch intends to reform CIA, officials say," *The Washington Post,* April 26, 1995, p. A2.
John M. Deutch, President Clinton's nominee to direct the CIA, wants to restructure how the U.S. performs its intelligence gathering and intends to move quickly to reform the agency's covert action program, which is plagued with scandal.

Back Issues

Great Research on Current Issues Starts Right Here...Recent topics covered by The CQ Researcher are listed below. Before May 1991, reports were published under the name of Editorial Research Reports.

JULY 1994
Dietary Supplements
Public Opinion and Foreign Policy
Crime Victims' Rights
Birth Control Choices

AUGUST 1994
Genetically Engineered Foods
Electing Minorities
Prozac Controversy
College Sports

SEPTEMBER 1994
Home Schooling
Welfare Experiments
Courts and the Media
Regulating Tobacco

OCTOBER 1994
Historic Preservation
Religion and Politics
Arts Funding
Economic Sanctions

NOVEMBER 1994
Sex on Campus
Blood Supply Safety
Testing Term Limits
Religion in America

Back issues are available for $5.00 (subscribers) or $8.00 (non-subscribers). Quantity discounts apply to orders over ten. To order, call Congressional Quarterly Customer Service at (202) 887-8621.

Binders are available for $18.00. To order call 1-800-638-1710. Please refer to stock number 648.

DECEMBER 1994
Farm Policy
Arms Sales
Earthquake Research
The Future of Television

JANUARY 1995
Treating Addiction
Child Custody and Support
Parents and Schools
Non-Proliferation Treaty at 25

FEBRUARY 1995
Cracking Down on Immigration
The Business of Sports
Reinventing Government
Housing Discrimination

MARCH 1995
Death Penalty Debate
Primary Care
Democracy in Africa
Environmental Movement at 25

APRIL 1995
Abortion Clinic Protests
Dieting and Health
Combating AIDS
Rethinking Affirmative Action

MAY 1995
Assisted Suicide Controversy
Overhauling Social Security
Learning to Read
Mandatory Sentencing

JUNE 1995
Combating Infectious Disease
Property Rights
Repetitive Stress Injuries
Regulating the Internet

JULY 1995
War Crimes
Highway Safety
Combating Terrorism
Preventing Teen Drug Use

AUGUST 1995
Job Stress
Organ Transplants
United Nations at 50
Advances in Cancer Research

SEPTEMBER 1995
Catholic Church in the U.S.
Northern Ireland Cease-Fire
High School Sports
Teaching History

OCTOBER 1995
Quebec's Future
Revitalizing the Cities
Networking the Classroom
Indoor Air Pollution

NOVEMBER 1995
The Working Poor
The Jury System
Sex, Violence and the Media
Police Misconduct

DECEMBER 1995
Teens and Tobacco
Gene Therapy's Future
Global Water Shortages
Third Party Prospects

JANUARY 1996
Emergency Medicine
Punishing Sex Offenders
Bilingual Education
Helping the Homeless

Future Topics

- ***Campaign Finance Reform***
- ***Academic Politics***
- ***College Admissions***

The CQ Researcher

Published by Congressional Quarterly Inc.

Campaign Finance Reform

Are tighter laws needed to police the system?

Money has been called the mother's milk of politics. Today, candidates need more and more of it to run for office. It typically costs $500,000 to run for a seat in the House of Representatives, and Senate campaigns run into the millions. And this year's presidential candidates have raised $125 million besides the money they get from public campaign financing. Candidates spend much of their time raising money, and a large part of their funds come from special interest groups known as political action committees (PACs). Many members of Congress want to control spending and tighten limits on contributions from individuals and PACs. But opponents say contribution and spending limits hamper political competition and hurt rather than help the political system.

Inside This Issue

CQ Feb. 9, 1996 • Volume 6, No. 6 • Pages 121-144

Formerly Editorial Research Reports

CAMPAIGN FINANCE REFORM

COVER: BARBARA SASSA-DANIELS

THE CQ Researcher

Feb. 9, 1996
Volume 6, No. 6

The CQ Researcher (ISSN 1056-2036). Formerly Editorial Research Reports. Published weekly (48 times per year, not printed the first Friday of any month with five Fridays) by Congressional Quarterly Inc., 1414 22nd St., N.W., Washington, D.C. 20037. Rates are furnished upon request. Second-class postage paid at Washington, D.C. POSTMASTER: Send address changes to The CQ Researcher, 1414 22nd St., N.W., Washington, D.C. 20037.

Campaign Finance Reform

BY KENNETH JOST

THE ISSUES

Linda Smith and Bill Bradley seem as different as two members of Congress could be. Smith is a freshman Republican from Washington state who won her House seat with support from religious conservatives and anti-tax groups. Bradley, set to retire at the end of his third term as a senator from New Jersey, is a liberal Democrat with a reputation for thoughtful work on complex, low-profile issues.

Despite their different political backgrounds, however, Bradley and Smith do agree on one issue: Both lawmakers say money has too much influence in Washington and that sweeping changes are needed to reform the system.

"Money not only determines who is elected, it determines who runs for office and it determines what government accomplishes — or fails to accomplish," Bradley said in a speech to Harvard University's John F. Kennedy School of Government last month. "Real reform of democracy must begin by completely breaking the connection between money and politics."

For her part, Smith has angered her own party's leadership by pressing for action on legislation to set new limits on fundraising and create voluntary spending limits in congressional campaigns. She complains that House Speaker Newt Gingrich, R-Ga., has been too slow to act on the issue.

"What we need is not more study of the problem of money and politics in Washington," Smith wrote in an op-ed article in *The New York Times* in November. "What we need is to end the problem."

Lobbying groups that have pushed for tougher laws on campaign finances echo the refrain. "The American people are deeply concerned about this issue," says Ann McBride, president of the citizens' group Common Cause. "They understand that their voices can't compete with the increasing influence of money on Capitol Hill."

The concern about the impact of money on politics has increased in recent years with the rising cost of campaigns, the growing fundraising burdens on incumbents and challengers alike and the increasing proportion of funds contributed by special-interest groups through political action committees (PACs). (*See graphs, p. 128.*) Despite widespread dissatisfaction with the current system, however, lawmakers, advocates and experts differ sharply on how to change it.

The traditional reform groups — including Common Cause, the League of Women Voters and Ralph Nader's Public Citizen — continue to call for tighter limits on contributions by individuals and PACs and so-called voluntary spending limits tied to some form of public support for the costs of campaigns. But some groups, including the American Civil Liberties Union (ACLU) on the left and the Cato Institute on the right, oppose spending limits as infringements on freedom of speech. And many of the groups that help finance campaigns, as well as some academic experts, argue that current laws have actually hurt the political process.

Bradley Smith, a professor at Capital University Law Center in Columbus, Ohio, says campaign laws have "stifled third-party activity, helped entrench incumbents, limited the number of candidates and the type of candidates we've gotten and in many ways driven out the candidates we'd most like to have."

"The ability to raise money has become a much more important attribute because of the contribution limits," says Smith, who recently authored a critique of campaign finance laws. [1]

The disagreements among advocacy groups and experts stem in part from differing diagnoses of the current system's problem. Traditional reform groups strongly contend that campaigns cost too much and that better-financed candidates have an inordinate advantage against their opponents. "Right now, money is what drives the system," says Becky Cain, national president of the League of Women Voters. "The more you have, the better chance you have of winning."

But opponents of more restrictive campaign finance laws insist that the reform groups exaggerate the power of money to determine election outcomes. "Money can only get a candidate's message out," Edward H. Crane III, president of the Cato Institute, told the House Oversight Committee last November. " There is no guarantee that people will like what they hear."

Rather than tighten existing laws, these groups want to raise or eliminate contribution limits, which they say hamper political competition and in any event encourage complex arrangements aimed at evading the restrictions. Some, but not all, of the

The Rising Cost of Campaigning

Spending on elections rose from less than $150 million in 1952 to more than $3 billion in 1992. Inflation accounted for part of the rise, along with increased competition and the use of high technology. About $2.2 billion was spent at the national level for presidential and congressional candidates and party committees; the rest went for local and state candidates and ballot issues.

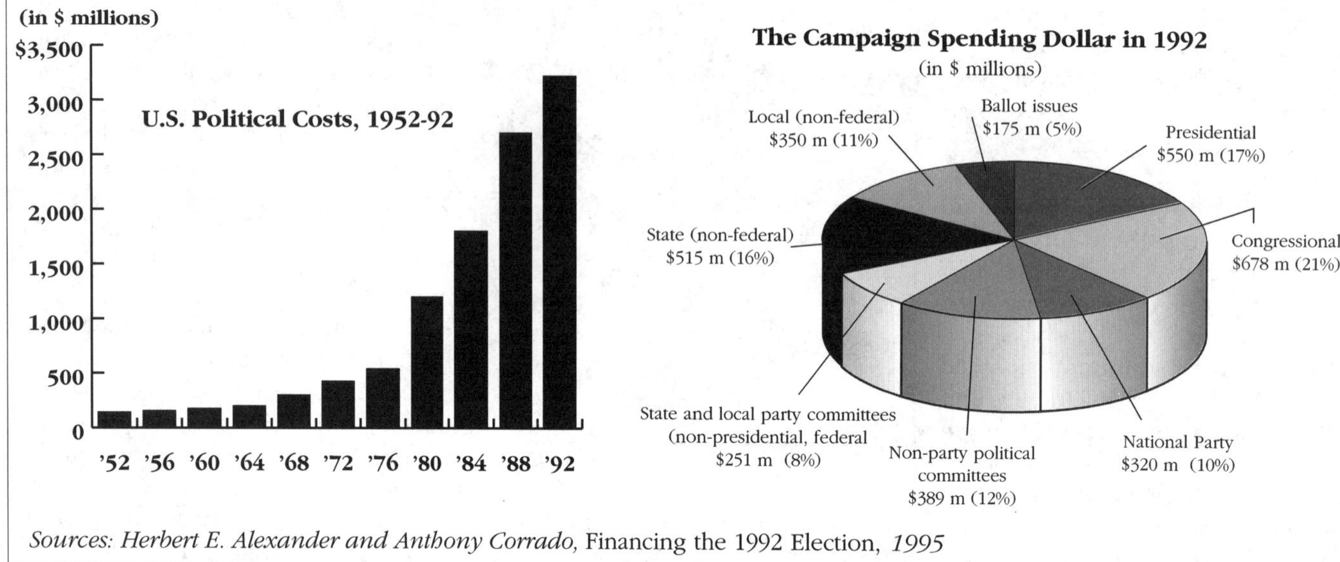

Sources: Herbert E. Alexander and Anthony Corrado, Financing the 1992 Election, *1995*

groups and experts who oppose contribution limits also oppose public campaign financing, which traditional reform groups continue to favor despite strong political opposition to direct taxpayer funding for candidates.

Public support for tighter campaign finance laws has peaked over the years at times of political scandal. The current federal campaign finance law — enacted in 1974 — was a direct outgrowth of the 20th century's greatest political scandal: Watergate (*see p. 132*). The law limited contributions and spending for all federal elections and, in particular, tried to insulate presidential politics from the effects of campaign fundraising by providing for full public funding of general election campaigns as well as partial public funding for primary races.

Supporters call the presidential campaign financing scheme a success. "It's been a success in increasing competitiveness, in controlling spending and in reducing the influence of special interests," says McBride at Common Cause.

Critics acknowledge some benefits from the presidential system but disagree with reform groups on extending public financing to other races. "At the presidential level, the funding levels are substantial and the issues are well known," says law Professor Smith. "At lower levels, I think it's agreed that public financing would tend to help incumbents."

In any event, the effects of the 1974 law were blunted by a Supreme Court decision only two years later striking down mandatory spending limits on First Amendment grounds. The result has been to leave congressional candidates with no ceiling on expenditures. Presidential candidates who decline public funding also are exempt from spending limits — a legal gap that opened the way for Ross Perot in 1992 and Malcolm S. "Steve" Forbes Jr. today to finance multimillion-dollar campaigns out of their own pockets.

Proposals to tighten the campaign finance laws in one way or another have been introduced almost continuously since the 1976 Supreme Court ruling, but only minor revisions have been enacted into law. In the past decade, Republicans and Democrats have fought to a stalemate on the issue in each successive Congress. Democrats generally favored spending limits and public financing; Republicans generally opposed those steps but supported limits on PACs.

Hope for breaking that deadlock rose last summer when President Clinton and House Speaker Gingrich shook hands at a joint appearance in Claremont, N.H., and agreed to a bipartisan commission on campaign and lobbying reform. But the two leaders never agreed on the details, and the plan is now considered dead.

The issue is very much alive on Capitol Hill, however, with dozens of bills introduced by members of both parties in both the House and the Senate. Reform groups have now rallied around companion bills introduced with bipartisan support in both chambers.

The two measures would either ban PACs altogether — a constitutionally dubious proposition — or substantially lower the contribution limits for PACs in congressional races. They also provide for spending limits in congressional races tied to reduced-cost broadcast advertising and mailings.

Perot joined with McBride, Cain and Joan Claybrook, president of Public Citizen, in a letter in December urging lawmakers to enact the measure. The letter called the bill "a major breakthrough in the fight to clean up the discredited and unfair campaign finance system in Congress."

But opponents continued to insist that the reform groups' proposals would make the political system worse, not better. "The reforms they support will do nothing but enhance the power of millionaires, incumbents and the media," Crane told the House Oversight Committee in November. "They will restrict, if not cut off, the free flow of information to the voters."

The bills faced uncertain prospects, given the complexity of the issues and the distractions of a presidential campaign. But Rep. Smith, a lead sponsor of the House bill, says supporters will try to force a floor vote on the measure if Gingrich does not make what her spokeswoman calls a "genuine effort" on the issue early this year.

As the debate simmers on Capitol Hill, here are some of the questions that are being asked:

Is too much money spent on political campaigns?

Political campaign spending began rising sharply with the 1968 elections and has continued to increase, although at a slower pace, in the most recent elections. For the 1991-1992 election cycle, national, state and local candidates spent a total of $3.2 billion, according to the nation's leading campaign finance scholar, Herbert E. Alexander. [2]

Congressional campaign spending has been part of that increase. Spending for elections to the House of Representatives totaled $347 million in 1994, four times as much as in 1978. Today, the average House candidate spends about $440,000, while the average Senate race costs $4.4 million. [3]

Critics say these costs strain officeholders and candidates alike. "A senator must raise, from the day when he or she arrives in the Senate, $15,000 a week, every week, month in and month out, year in and year out, for the entire term," says McBride of Common Cause. "There is no question that spending is out of control."

Simultaneously, the critics say, the current system shuts out challengers who cannot compete with incumbents' ability to raise funds. "It deters good candidates from participating in the process," says League of Women Voters President Cain. "Ordinary folks who might want to get into the system just look at that and say it's overwhelming."

The public generally shares the reformers' view that campaign spending is too high. Many of the leading political scientists who have studied campaign financing, however, disagree. "There's not too much money in politics for the number of elections we have and the amount of information that voters are expected to sift," says Michael J. Malbin, director of the Rockefeller Institute of Government at the State University of New York, Albany.

"It's hard to argue that you're spending too much money on congressional elections when half the voters can't name the candidates the day after they voted," says Gary Jacobson, chairman of the political science department at the University of California, San Diego.

These academic experts view campaign spending just as the Supreme Court does — as political speech, a way of getting valuable information to voters. "The amount of information that voters have and the turnout directly relate to the amount of money spent," Malbin says.

The overall spending, defenders of campaign spending like to point out, amounts to less than the country's two largest advertisers — Procter & Gamble and Philip Morris — spend promoting their products in any given year. [4]

"The amounts are large," retorts McBride. Comparing campaign expenditures to commercial advertising budgets, she adds, "is to compare apples and oranges."

Defenders of campaign spending also contend that critics overstate the impact of big campaign budgets on the outcome of elections. The candidate who spends more money may not always emerge as the winner. As examples, Malbin notes that the two biggest spenders in the 1994 congressional elections both lost: Republican Michael Huffington, who spent more than $28 million of his own money in a losing Senate race in California, and Republican Oliver L. North, who raised and spent $21 million in a failed Senate campaign in Virginia. "The more they spent, the more voters knew about them, the more unpopular they became," Malbin says. [5]

Advocates and experts on both sides of the campaign finance reform issue do agree on one point: Challengers need to spend money to get their names, and their platforms, before voters in order to compete with well-known, and well-entrenched, incumbents. But they draw different conclusions.

Defenders of the current system insist that the campaign spending limits favored by reformers will end up limiting challengers' ability to compete. "Any spending limit low enough to hurt, on balance hurts the challenger," says Malbin, who supports some changes in current law, but not spending limits.

Reformers, however, contend that current campaign finance laws contribute to challengers' money problems and that realistic spending limits — $600,000 for House races is the current legislative proposal — would help reduce overall spending without

Is the Federal Election Commission a Toothless Watchdog?

As the ranking Republican on the House Elections Subcommittee in 1993, Rep. Robert L. Livingston wanted the Federal Election Commission (FEC) to have more money to enforce federal campaign finance laws. But the Louisiana lawmaker changed his tune after the FEC began writing regulations later that year to prevent members of Congress from spending campaign funds for personal use.

In 1994, Livingston cited the personal use rules as an example of "overregulation" when he led an unsuccessful effort to cut the agency's $27 million budget by more than 10 percent. Then, after becoming chairman of the House Appropriations Committee, Livingston threw his weight last February behind a 10 percent cut again. Later, with the personal use rules officially in effect, Livingston dispatched a team of investigators to examine FEC operations.

The budget cut Livingston sought was finally reversed, but Livingston did succeed in earmarking $1.5 million for purposes other than enforcement. For advocates of campaign finance laws, the episode illustrates the inherent contradiction that the FEC faces in carrying out its duties.

"The FEC's budget, structure and personnel are controlled by the very people that it is supposed to regulate," says Elizabeth Hedlund, editor of *FEC Watch*, a newsletter published by the Center for Responsive Politics. "You could say," Hedlund adds, "that the personal use rules cost the FEC $1.5 million." [1]

Congress has kept the FEC on a short leash since creating the agency as part of the post-Watergate campaign finance act in 1974. Initially, the law provided for the six members of the commission to be appointed by Congress itself. The Supreme Court ruled that procedure violated separation of powers principles, but the law still requires the president to appoint an equal number of members from the two major parties — effectively giving each party veto power over policy or enforcement initiatives.

In addition, members of Congress pay closer attention to FEC proceedings than those of other agencies. After the agency instituted a policy of random audits of campaign accounts a few years ago, lawmakers protested — and the FEC quickly dropped the practice. Last year, several lawmakers of both parties criticized the personal use rules during the FEC's budget hearings.

With short funding, the agency has also been chronically overworked. Campaign audits take years to complete. As a result, campaign law violations are likely to be detected, if at all, only long after an election is over and the winner securely in office.

Stuck with the reputation of a toothless watchdog, the agency has improved its image somewhat among advocates of campaign finance laws in the past few years.

Former Chairman Trevor Potter, a Republican appointed by President George Bush, broke with the other GOP commissioners to give the three Democratic appointees a fourth vote on enforcement matters and some controversial new regulations. [2] One result was an increase in civil penalties collected by the FEC — from $225,000 in 1992 to $1.7 million in 1994.

Hedlund and others cite the FEC's suit against GOPAC, the political action committee once headed by House Speaker Newt Gingrich, R-Ga., as an example of the agency's tougher enforcement approach. The commission's suit, filed in 1994, claims GOPAC was helping Gingrich and other Republican candidates for Congress before registering as a federal political action committee. Gingrich and lawyers for GOPAC deny the charges, saying the group was helping Republicans at the state and local levels but not in congressional elections.

But critics of stricter campaign finance laws say the FEC has been overstepping its authority in recent years. "It's incongruous that we would be talking about adding on regulation in the area of campaign finance when we are talking about reducing the role of the federal government in practically every other area," says Brent Thompson, executive director of the Fair Government Foundation. The foundation was formed and is headed by Sen. Paul Coverdell, R-Ga., who paid a $32,000 fine last year for campaign finance violations. [3]

For her part, Hedlund says the agency today 'is not doing well" because of the budget pressure from Congress and a delay by President Clinton in making three appointments to the commission. (Potter resigned last spring, and the terms of two other commissioners have expired.) She says Clinton's failure to make the appointments casts doubt on his commitment to campaign finance reform.

"It's sending a message that the FEC simply isn't that important, and that conflicts with what he has said repeatedly, that campaign reform is a high priority for him," Hedlund says. "His actions just aren't matching his words."

[1] For coverage of the episode, see *Roll Call,* Feb. 27, 1995, p. 1; *The Washington Post,* March 18, 1995, p. A18, and May 21, 1995, p. C7.

[2] See *Legal Times,* Dec. 11, 1995, p. 1. For earlier examinations of the agency, see *National Journal*, April 2, 1994, pp. 775-778; *Rolling Stone,* April 21, 1994, pp. 37-40.

[3] See *Roll Call,* May 22, 1995, p. 17.

---

hurting challengers. "The current system isn't helping that challenger one bit right now," says Cain. "It's not leveling the playing field — in fact quite the opposite."

Under the Supreme Court's 1976 ruling in *Buckley v. Valeo,* however, campaign spending limits can be imposed only as a condition of receiving public funding. As a result, reformers have to tie the two proposals together — and public funding proposals face strong political opposition (*see p. 128*).

Moreover, many experts contend

that spending limits simply cannot be effective. "They don't work, they won't work," says Larry Sabato, a political science professor at the University of Virginia who has followed campaign finance issues for a decade.

Candidates and their supporters will find some way to circumvent any spending ceilings, critics of the proposals contend. As one example, they point to the use of "independent expenditures" from a candidates' own pocket, which cannot be limited under the Supreme Court's ruling (*see p. 134*).

Still, reform groups say spending limits are essential in any campaign finance bill. "If you don't cap the amount that can be spent, then there is a never-ending search for money, and it just completely raises the stakes higher and higher," says McBride.

Do interest groups gain too much influence through campaign contributions?

Campaign contribution limits have reduced the importance of "fat cat" donors, but a new vehicle for special interests has taken their place: political action committees. PACs were created as a mechanism for organized labor to get around the ban on direct union contributions to political campaigns. But the nearly 4,000 PACs registered today with the Federal Election Commission (FEC) represent virtually every imaginable corporate, labor or ideological interest.

PACs have become a major source of campaign contributions. All told, PACs contributed more than $189 million to congressional candidates in the 1993-1994 election cycle — three times as much as in 1979-1980. [6] (*See graph, p. 128.*)

For Democrats, PAC contributions have amounted to almost half of the funds raised in past congressional elections. But PAC contributions began shifting toward Republicans as the 1994 elections neared, and the GOP share of PAC donations has continued to increase since the Republican takeover of Congress. Republicans received about two-thirds of the $35 million in PAC funds contributed to members of Congress in the first six months of 1995, according to the Center for Responsive Politics (CRP). [7] In the process, GOP lawmakers have become more dependent on PAC money. A Common Cause study found that PAC contributions amounted to 45 percent of the money raised by freshman House Republicans in the first half of 1995. [8]

To critics, including many lawmakers in both parties, PACs are both the symbol and substance of what is wrong with the present system of financing campaigns. "PACs are one of the key problems where you have to pay to play," says Joshua Goldstein, the CRP's research director, "and they are paying a lot of money to influence elections and the legislative process in Washington."

A leading advocate for business-oriented PACs concedes that the political climate is favorable for imposing new restrictions on their contributions. "The situation is one of jeopardy for PACs," says lobbyist Steven Stockmeyer, executive director of the National Association of Business PACs. "Right now, there seems to be a political imperative [to curb PACs] unless it's changed."

Stockmeyer concedes that PACs use their contributions to further their political interests, but he contends reformers have distorted the issue by focusing solely on PACs. "If they were looking at the totality of the system," he says, "they wouldn't pick on PACs because all the studies have shown that individual contributors are just as self-interested."

Many academic experts also accuse campaign reform groups of exaggerating the impact that PACs have on the political process. "Anybody who controls campaign resources is going to have some kind of influence," says the University of California's Jacobson. But he adds, "The evidence of wholesale buying and selling of policy just isn't there."

Defenders of PACs cite a 1989 article as evidence that PAC contributions are less important in congressional voting than reformers — or the public — generally believe. [9] The author, political consultant Janet M. Grenzke, correlated PAC contributions to House members with their roll-call votes from 1975-1982. She said she found "little evidence" that the contributions "affected" the members' voting patterns.

Grenzke's study, however, was limited in many ways. For example, the 10 PACs she studied included six union-affiliated PACs but no corporate PACs. She explained the gap by saying that no corporate PAC that contributed to House members during the period provided a list of issues on which they were particularly interested. [10] In addition, the study covered an early period in the growth of PACs. Total PAC contributions for 1981-1982 came to $88 million; the amounts continued to rise through the rest of the decade.

More broadly, reformers emphasize that PACs have their greatest impact in less visible ways than floor votes. "PAC influence does not come simply in terms of votes," Fred Wertheimer, the longtime president of Common Cause until his retirement last year, wrote in a law journal article. "It takes more subtle forms as well." Wertheimer quoted former Sen. William Proxmire, D-Wis., who noted that PACs get their "payoff" in many forms, ranging from "a speech not delivered" or "a colleague not influenced" to "a witness not invited to testify" or "a minor change in one paragraph in a 240-page bill." [11]

Sabato at the University of Virginia agrees with PAC defenders that reformers exaggerate the issue. But he also says that PACs get "plenty" for their money. "Access alone is a very substantial item," Sabato says. "Particularly on technical items, they can get their way and they always will. It's

Total PAC Spending, 1979-94

Spending by PACs more than tripled between 1979 and 1994. In 1993-94, business PACs gave about the same amount to Republicans and Democrats, but most of the labor money went to the Democrats. Most PAC money goes to incumbents — about 75 percent in 1994. At the end of 1994, there were 3,954 registered PACs, compared with 608 in 1974.

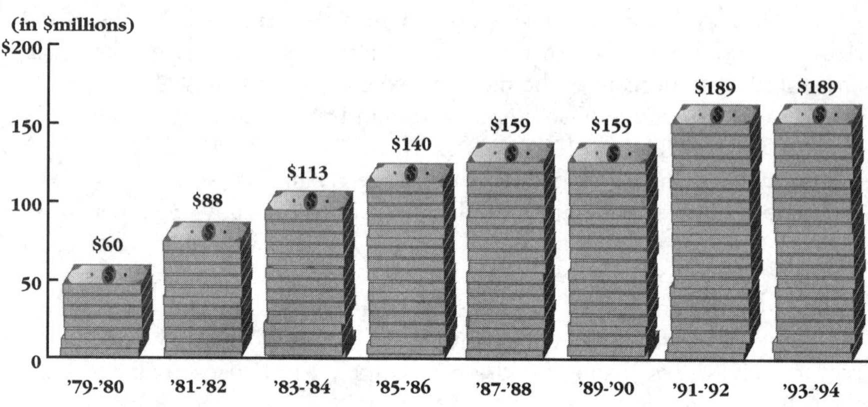

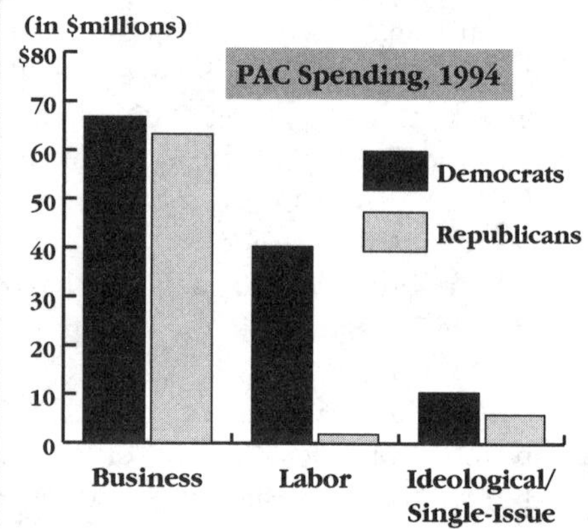

How PACs Operate

PACs typically represent business, labor or ideological/single-issue groups and can give congressional and presidential candidates up to $5,000 per election. A PAC gets its money not from the sponsoring group itself but from its members or employees, which allows PACs to bypass the ban on direct contributions from companies or unions.

Source: Larry Makinson, The Price of Admission: Campaign Spending in the 1994 Elections, *The Center for Responsive Politics, 1995.*

those little subcommittee technical amendments that matter, that affect one company or one industry where you may not have an opposing PAC working the issue."

Current law allows an individual PAC to give up to $5,000 to an individual candidate in a federal election. The bipartisan legislation being pushed by reformers in Congress would abolish PACs altogether or, if that provision is held unconstitutional, lower the contribution limit to $1,000. In addition, the bill would seek to reduce the role of PAC contributions by providing that congressional candidates can receive no more than 25 percent of their funds from contributions of more than $250.

Defenders of PACs say the outright ban would certainly be struck down as an unconstitutional limitation on political speech. "I don't see how, under the First Amendment, you can show any pressing government need for preventing people from pooling their resources for political benefit," says Stockmeyer. "That's just anathema to the First Amendment."

As for the contribution limits, Stockmeyer argues they would simply encourage individuals to find other ways of making contributions that would be harder to identify and regulate. "Our position is get it all on the table," says Stockmeyer.

Supporters of the legislation say the bill would guard against that possibility by limiting lobbyist contributions to $100 and setting an overall limit for candidates on large contributions. But they insist that PAC contributions are central to any reform. "You have to limit PACs as any part of a campaign finance bill, both to reduce their dominance in the process and to reduce the negative impact they have on legislative decisions after the election," McBride says.

Should Congress approve public campaign financing or other subsidies for congressional candidates?

For more than 30 years, advocates of campaign finance reform have argued that the most effective way of cleaning up the current system is some form of public campaign financing. Today, reform groups still hope to extend public funding beyond presidential campaigns to congressional races. But in the face of political opposition and budget constraints, they have lowered their immediate goal to providing some "public resources" to candidates in the form of free or reduced-cost media advertising and postage or a tax credit for small campaign contributions.

"Public financing is a proven way to get resources to candidates," says McBride. "But you don't have to have public money to get real resources to candidates."

Opponents attack public campaign financing on both political and fiscal grounds. Law Professor Smith writes that public financing is "a serious boondoggle" that could end up costing $260 million per congressional election for

House candidates alone. [12]

Smith also called public financing "undemocratic" because of public opposition and because of the impact on political parties. He said campaign funding tends to favor incumbents at the expense of challengers and third parties, but simultaneously does channel some tax moneys to fringe candidates or parties with little public support.

The public view of public financing is a subject of dispute among lawmakers, advocates and experts. Supporters maintain that the public approves of public campaign financing. As evidence, they cite polls taken periodically by the Gallup organization since 1973 showing majority or plurality support for public funding, with one exception in 1982. [13] But, Professor Smith noted, two 1990 polls found the public opposed to the idea. An NBC News/*Wall Street Journal* survey found 55 percent opposed and 38 percent in favor of public financing, while an ABC News/*Washington Post* poll registered 20 percent in favor, 31 percent opposed and 49 percent undecided. [14]

An examination of the polls suggests that the framing of the question strongly affects the response. The Gallup Poll asks respondents whether it would be "a good idea" for the federal government to provide "a fixed amount of money" for congressional candidates and to prohibit all private contributions. The polls cited by Smith asked the question in a more straightforward way: "Would you favor or oppose public financing of congressional elections?"

Most recently, a poll commissioned by a pro-reform group, Campaign America, found narrow public support for partial public financing of campaigns with questions framed in a positive manner. A question tying public campaign financing to "limiting the influence of special interests" found 50 percent in favor and 43 percent opposed. A second question tying campaign spending limits to partial public funding produced a similar result, 48 percent in favor and 40 percent opposed. But the survey, directed by Democratic pollster Mark Mellman and Republican pollster William D. McInturff, also indicated that voters could be swayed by negative arguments that public campaign funding was a wasteful use of tax dollars and would only go to pay for negative campaigns anyway. [15]

Whatever the polls show, reformers concede that Congress is not going to approve public campaign financing in the near future. "The question of public financing is really off the table, because of the budget situation," McBride says.

Instead, the legislation that reform groups are pushing would give candidates a small break on media costs. Candidates who agree to abide by spending limits would be given 30 minutes of free television time and would be able to purchase additional television time at a 50 percent discount. Candidates would also be allowed two mailings during the campaign at reduced postal rates.

Supporters say this proposal would ease fundraising pressures somewhat and benefit challengers by helping ensure some access to media advertising. But broadcasters are virtually certain to oppose the idea.

Ironically, many of the academic experts who are skeptical of most campaign finance reform proposals embrace the idea of some form of public financing or subsidies for candidates. Malbin says he favors public financing without spending limits — so-called "floors without ceilings" — as a way to try to help challengers to compete. Sabato, among others, calls for restoring the tax credit for small campaign contributions by individuals that was established in 1971 but repealed in 1986 as part of the effort to simplify the tax code.

"If you look at what makes people unhappy about the funding status quo — interested money, the absence of spending limitations and the problem of funding challengers — the only way you solve those three problems is with public funding," says Frank Sorauf, a University of Minnesota political scientist. "All the rest of it is tinkering."

But Sorauf concedes that Congress is unlikely to enact public campaign funding anytime soon. "In the present political climate," he says, "it doesn't have a snowball's chance in hell." ■

BACKGROUND

The Evils of Money

Money has tainted American politics since the early days of the Republic, when some candidates rewarded their supporters with whiskey. The spread of popular democracy in the 19th century brought with it greater demands for campaign money that were met first by the patronage-based "spoils system" and then after the Civil War by fundraising from corporations and wealthy industrialists.

The efforts to control those abuses have been partly successful. But the skyrocketing cost of campaigning in the era of television politics has increased candidates' need for money and spawned new campaign financing practices that have proved more resistant to legal controls. [16]

Early campaigns cost little money, and candidates themselves paid most of their expenses. But Jacksonian democracy in the 1830s made campaigns more expensive by broadening the electorate and introducing modern electioneering. To pay for campaigns, the Democratic Party began assessing government employees, who owed their jobs in the days before civil service to political patronage alone. The practice eventually became widespread under both Democrats and Republicans.

The post-Civil War era of railroad building and industrialization gave rise to huge corporations that, along with the individuals who controlled them, became the dominant source of campaign money by the end of the 19th century. Some industrialists supported the Democratic Party, but most business money went to Republicans. In 1888, the GOP's national chairman raised about 40 percent of the cost of the presidential campaign from manufacturers in his home state of Pennsylvania. In 1896, the legendary party Chairman Mark Hanna made the GOP's fundraising more systematic by assessing banks and corporations based on their financial worth. [17]

Early Reforms

The practice of assessing government employees spawned the first campaign finance reform bill: a Whig proposal in 1839 to bar political contributions by federal officers. It did not pass. But the calls for civil service reform increased after the Civil War and gained urgency with the assassination of President James A. Garfield by a disappointed job-seeker in 1881.

Two years later, a chastened Congress enacted the nation's first civil service law. The Pendleton Act is best known for establishing competitive examinations for federal jobs, but it also sought to reform campaign fundraising by prohibiting the solicitation of political contributions from federal workers covered by the law.

The growing role of business money in political campaigns brought calls for reforms beginning in the 1890s. Democrats blamed their defeat in the 1896 election on the corporate funds raised for the Republican nominee, William McKinley. A year later, four states that had backed Democrat William Jennings Bryan banned campaign contributions by corporations. After new revelations of contributions from insurance companies and other corporations to GOP coffers in 1900 and 1904, Congress was moved to act. With support from Democrats and reformist Republicans, Congress in 1907 barred banks and corporations from making political contributions to candidates for federal office — Congress or the presidency.

Congress passed the first federal campaign disclosure law in 1910, but the weak Publicity Act required disclosure only after the election. Amendments a year later added campaign spending limits of $5,000 and $10,000 for House and Senate candidates, respectively. In 1921, the Supreme Court weakened the law by ruling that Congress had no power to regulate party primaries. To comply with the decision, Congress in 1925 repealed the disclosure requirements for primary elections. The Corrupt Practices Act — enacted in the wake of the Teapot Dome Scandal — also raised the spending limits for Senate races in high-population states to $25,000. Candidates for president and vice president remained outside the law.

The early bans on assessments of government employees and corporate contributions reduced, but did not eliminate, those practices. But the campaign finance disclosure and spending limits were completely ineffective. As Alexander notes, the law required candidates to report spending made with their "knowledge or consent." Most candidates interpreted the provision narrowly and did not disclose expenditures by their campaign committees. And they circumvented the spending limits by establishing multiple campaign committees.

Contributors similarly avoided the $5,000 limit on individual contributions, added to the law in 1940, by making multiple donations to separate campaign committees. [18] With that background, it is perhaps not surprising that there is no record of anyone ever having been prosecuted under the Corrupt Practices Act before it was replaced by a new federal campaign finance law in 1971.

Increased Spending

Political campaigns were still relatively inexpensive as late as 1950. Republicans spent more than $3 million in their 1896 and 1900 campaigns, but their spending fell in the next three elections. Campaign spending rose in the 1920s: Herbert Hoover spent $6.3 million to Al Smith's $5.3 million in the 1928 presidential race. But the use of radio actually allowed spending to drop in the next election: Hoover and Franklin D. Roosevelt each spent less than $3 million in 1932. [19] And Alexander Heard, in his study of campaign financing in 1960, concluded that after allowing for inflation and the larger electorate, the overall cost of national campaigning did not increase between the 1920s and '50s. [20]

The introduction of television advertising in the 1950s, however, began to change the picture of campaign costs. Dwight D. Eisenhower spent $6.6 million in his 1952 race — more than three times the amount spent by the Republican nominee four years earlier. In 1960, Richard M. Nixon and John F. Kennedy each spent roughly $10 million. Nixon's next two campaigns set new records for presidential campaign spending: $25.4 million in 1968 and a whopping $61.4 million in 1972. Democrats could not keep pace with Republican fundraising, but their spending rose, too. Hubert H. Humphrey spent $11.6 million in 1968; George McGovern spent $30 million four years later.

Congressional campaign spending rose as well, mocking the evidently unrealistic limits prescribed by law. Moreover, the law's disclosure provisions proved of little use. Congress had en-

Continued on p. 132

Chronology

1800s Modern politics meets its need for money first by assessing government workers and then by raising funds from corporations and wealthy individuals. Abuses produce calls for reforms.

1883
Pendleton Act establishes the federal civil service and prohibits soliciting covered workers for political contributions.

Early 1900s Congress passes campaign finance laws, but disclosure provisions and spending limits go unenforced.

1907
Tillman Act prohibits banks or corporations from contributing to candidates for federal office.

1910
Publicity Act requires House candidates to disclose campaign expenditures and receipts. The law is amended a year later to cover Senate candidates and to add campaign spending limits.

1925
Corrupt Practices Act re-enacts campaign disclosure provisions and raises spending limits for Senate races in larger states.

1950-1960s Television advertising raises the cost of campaigning. Pressure for revising federal campaign laws grows.

1966
Public financing for presidential elections is approved as attachment to unrelated bill. Congress suspends provision in 1967.

1970s Watergate scandal leads to overhaul of campaign finance laws, but Supreme Court rules major portions unconstitutional.

1971
Congress re-enacts public financing for presidential campaigns, but at President Richard M. Nixon's insistence delays system until after the 1972 election. Lawmakers also approve Federal Election Campaign Act (FECA), strengthening campaign disclosure and contribution limits.

Feb. 7, 1972
Nixon signs FECA into law. Nixon's re-election committee conducts a fundraising blitz before the law takes effect on April 7.

Aug. 9, 1974
Nixon resigns to avoid impeachment on charges that include illegal use of campaign contributions to finance Watergate break-in and obstructing investigations of the burglary.

Oct. 15, 1974
FECA amendments are signed into law by President Gerald R. Ford. Act sets spending limits for congressional races and individual contribution limits; it also creates Federal Election Commission (FEC) to enforce law.

Jan. 30, 1976
Supreme Court rules mandatory campaign spending limits violate First Amendment free speech provision. But decision upholds contribution limits and public financing for presidential candidates (*Buckley v. Valeo*).

1979
Congress approves package of FECA amendments, including "soft money" provision to allow state and local parties to underwrite voter registration drives on behalf of presidential candidates.

1980s Campaign spending rises along with the number of political action committees (PACs).

February 1988
Democrats in Senate withdraw bill to establish public financing for congressional races.

1990s Partisan deadlock persists on campaign finance overhaul.

August 1990
House and Senate approve bills with voluntary spending limits and restrictions on PACs. Conferees fail to meet to resolve differences.

May 9, 1992
President George Bush vetoes Democrat-backed bill to provide partial public financing and set congressional spending limits.

Sept. 30, 1994
Democrats fail to break Republicans' filibuster in Senate against new public financing/spending limits bill for congressional races. Common Cause says House Democrats share blame for bill's failure.

June 11, 1995
President Clinton and House Speaker Gingrich promise to create a bipartisan commission on campaign finance reform.

Rising Presidential Spending . . .

Spending on presidential elections rose steadily from 1960-1992, with a 65 percent increase from 1984 to 1988, when no incumbent was running and the presidency was wide open for the first time in 20 years. In 1992, with George Bush seeking re-election, prenomination costs were lower than in 1988. *

* Spending figures reflect actual expenditures not adjusted for inflation.

Source: Herbert E. Alexander and Anthony Corrado, Financing the 1992 Election, *1995*

Continued from p. 130

trusted its own officers — the House clerk and Senate secretary — with the job of maintaining campaign contributions and spending reports. Heard, writing in 1960, found the reports to be "of little value." [21] But the lawmakers failed to approve various proposals offered during the late 1940s and '50s to strengthen the law by creating an independent agency to take over the job.

A new call for reform came in 1962 from a presidential commission headed by Heard, who had served as a Democratic staff member in the Senate in the 1950s and gone on to become a professor at the University of North Carolina. The Commission on Campaign Costs called for raising spending limits, establishing an independent agency to implement the law and providing "matching" public funds to presidential candidates. President Kennedy gave the report little support, and Lyndon B. Johnson initially showed little interest in the subject after he became president.

Johnson did submit a campaign finance bill in 1966 that called for strengthening disclosure requirements and contribution limits and repealing spending limits. The House passed the bill, but it was bottled up in the Senate. Meanwhile, however, Sen. Russell Long, a Louisiana Democrat known for parliamentary wizardry, managed to get a public-financing provision for presidential campaigns enacted into law by attaching it to an unrelated, end-of-session measure. A year later, though, opponents from both parties succeeded in suspending the provision before it could take effect for the 1968 campaign.

Aftermath of Watergate

The pressure to strengthen federal campaign finance laws continued after Nixon's election to the presidency in 1968. In 1971, the Democratic-controlled Congress passed two measures embodying reforms long urged by critics of the law. The Federal Election Campaign Act strengthened disclosure provisions by requiring reports from political committees, not just candidates, and by requiring identifying information from political contributors. It also limited federal candidates to spending 10 cents per voter on "communications media." Nixon signed the bill into law on Feb. 7, 1972.

Meanwhile, the Revenue Act of 1971 resuscitated public campaign financing for presidential candidates, with funds to come from a $1 checkoff on income tax returns. The bill also provided for a tax credit or deduction to encourage political contributions. Nixon reluctantly signed the measure, but only after forcing Democrats to agree that public financing was not to take effect until after the 1972 campaign.

Nixon also acted to undercut the effect of the strengthened disclosure requirements by conducting a fund-raising blitz in the weeks before the new law was to take effect on April 7. Democrats agreed to voluntarily disclose contributions received before that date, but Nixon did so only after being sued by Common Cause. The partial disclosure shortly before the November election showed that the Committee to Re-elect the President had raised $11.4 million in the month before the law took effect, almost half of it within the 48 hours immediately before the effective date. [22]

Meanwhile, the first of the Watergate investigations produced evidence before the November election that the president's campaign committee had used a secret fund — consisting of illegal, laundered, corporate contributions and some legal but undisclosed contributions — to finance the break-in at the Democratic National Committee headquarters. Investigations after Nixon's re-election showed that campaign funds had also been used to pay hush money to the Watergate burglars. The political convulsions from these disclosures resulted in a fortified federal campaign finance law, signed by President Gerald R. Ford two months after the scandals had forced Nixon's resignation.

The new disclosure law sought to reduce the influence of major contributors by limiting individuals to giving $1,000 per candidate per election or an aggregate total of $25,000 to all candidates, national party committees or political action committees. It also sought to cap spending on congressional races — $140,000 for House races and ceilings for Senate races ranging upwards from $250,000 for the smallest states. The act also set up public financing for presidential campaigns, with full public funding for the general election and matching funds for candidates during party primaries.

The law, which also created the FEC, moved through Congress with bipartisan support. Despite reservations, Ford signed it into law, saying that "the times demand this legislation." But a few opponents of the law quickly took advantage of a provision designed to authorize and expedite a constitutional challenge to the act. And less than two years later, the Supreme Court ripped a gaping hole in the intricate structure Congress had built to control campaign spending.

The Limits of Reform

Two decades after its enactment, campaign finance reform has produced less change than its supporters had hoped. The effort to keep private funds out of presidential elections has been undercut by the growing use of so-called soft money. (*See graph, p. 134.*) The act's limits on congressional campaign spending were thrown out by the Supreme Court on First Amendment grounds. And if the effort to limit the influence of "fat cat" contributors in congressional races has been partly successful, the law also paved the way for special interests to expand the use of a different mechanism, the political action committee, to gain access and influence in Washington.

The Supreme Court's blow to campaign finance reform came in a case brought by unlikely political bedfellows: James L. Buckley, who had been elected to the Senate from New York on the Republican and Conservative party tickets; Eugene J. McCarthy, the former anti-war Democratic senator from Minnesota; and Stewart Mott, the General Motors heir who bankrolled McCarthy's 1968 campaign. The plaintiffs claimed that the restrictions on individual contributions and on overall campaign spending violated the rights to freedom of speech and political association. They named Francis R. Valeo, the secretary of the Senate, as the lead defendant.

The court's ruling in *Buckley v. Valeo* on Jan. 30, 1976, left major parts of the law intact. The justices ruled that the limits on individual contributions to candidates are a permissible means of preventing the risk of corruption. They rejected First Amendment and equal-protection challenges to public financing for presidential candidates. But they struck down candidate spending limits as an unjus-

. . .Rising Congressional Spending

Congressional campaign spending rose gradually from 1970 through 1990 and then jumped in the 1991-1992 election cycle with an increased number of candidates and rising public discontent with Congress. The drop in spending for the 1994 elections may reflect the fact that it was an "off year" election (no presidential contest), or that the cost of congressional campaigns has plateaued.

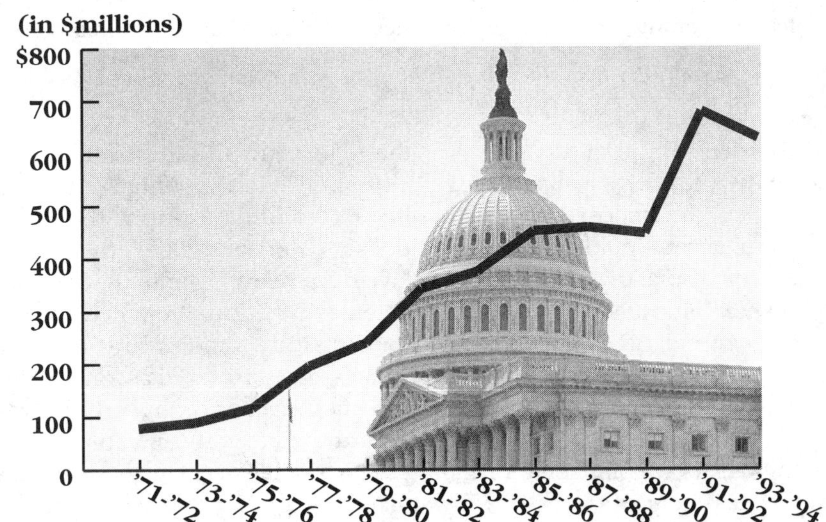

Sources: Herbert E. Alexander and Anthony Corrado, Financing the 1992 Election, 1995; *Vital Statistics on Congress, 1996*

Top Soft Money Contributors to Political Parties

The big soft money contributors to Republican Party committees in the first half of 1995 were the oil and gas industry and tobacco interests. Democrats' top soft money benefactors were lawyers, organized labor and the entertainment industry.

Top Contributors to Republicans

Philip Morris	tobacco	$729,749
RJR Nabisco	tobacco	286,450
Brown & Williamson	tobacco	260,000
Atlantic Richfield (ARCO) *	oil and gas	215,900
Archer Daniels Midland (ADM)	agriculture	205,000
News Corp (Rupert Murdoch) *	communications	201,500
Forstmann, Little & Co.	securities	175,000
Reliance Group Holdings	insurance	170,000
The Seagram Co. *	liquor	165,000
US Asia Commercial Development	international trade	150,000
American Financial Corp.	insurance	140,000

Top Contributors to Democrats

The Seagram Co. *	liquor	$375,000
Harold Nix & Associates	lawyers	260,000
Milberg, Weiss, Bershad, Hynes & Lerach *	lawyers	180,000
Johnny Chung	electronics	175,000
The Yucaipa Companies *	food	156,500
Bernard L. Schwartz	aerospace	120,000
Service Employees International Union	labor	115,000
Abex Inc. *	aerospace	110,000
Entergy Corp.	energy	110,000
Walt Disney Co.	entertainment	103,000
United Food & Commercial Workers Union International	labor	100,500

What Is Soft Money?

Under current law, corporations and labor unions can't contribute to federal elections, and individuals and political action committees (PACs) are subject to federal limits. But donations are exempt from the federal contribution limits if they are given to state and local party committees for general voter registration or mobilization activities and are not aimed at influencing federal elections.

Such donations are known as soft money. Campaign finance reform advocates say national party officials raise soft money clearly to influence presidential and congressional elections and that the practice evades the federal limits. But officials in both parties say soft money is an important, and legal, mechanism for strengthening state and local party organizations.

* Includes contributions from subsidiaries and/or executives/partners

Sources: Herbert E. Alexander and Anthony Corrado, Financing the 1992 Election, *1995; Common Cause, Nov. 2, 1995.*

tified burden on political speech. Nonetheless, the court said that spending limits can be imposed on candidates who accept public financing. The decision also allowed individuals to spend unlimited amounts on "independent expenditures" in political races. Finally, the court held that the FEC violated separation of power principles because the law provided for Congress to appoint some of the commission's members.

Congress moved quickly to re-establish the FEC by providing for the president to appoint all of its voting members. But the other gaps left by the high court's ruling could not be closed. By allowing unlimited spending by candidates from their own pockets, the court paved the way for lavish spending by millionaire candidates. In addition, it opened the way for individuals and groups to spend whatever they wanted as long as they kept their electioneering separate from the candidates' official campaign.

Two other major gaps in the law that emerged in the next decade stemmed from decisions by Congress itself. The provision in the 1974 law to allow federal contractors to establish PACs led to an enormous growth in their number, size and influence. PAC contributions to congressional candidates rose from $34.1 million in 1978 to $178.8 million in 1994. Corporate PACs showed the greatest growth — increasing their contributions more than sevenfold during the period from $9.5 million to $64.1 million. Labor PACs also increased their giving, but at a slightly slower rate — from $9.9 million to $40.7 million. [23]

Meanwhile, Congress opened a new gap in the law in 1979 by exempting from federal contribution limits any sums given to state and local party committees for general voter registration or mobilization activities as long as they were not aimed at influencing federal elections. The use of this "soft money" was pioneered by Ronald Reagan in his 1980 campaign and has grown in importance with each succeeding election. In 1988, Democrats raised about $23 million in soft money, Republicans about $22 million. For the 1991-1992 election cycle, the figures soared to $117.8 million for Republicans and $95.7 million for Democrats. [24]

Critics said that national party officials were raising the money with the clear purpose of influencing presidential and congressional elections. They also contended that the practice allowed wealthy individuals and businesses to evade the federal limits on contributions as well as the ban on corporate contributions. But officials in both parties said the practice complied with the law and served the goal of strengthening state and local party organizations.

Partisan Deadlock

Campaign finance reform fell off the congressional agenda in the early 1980s with Republicans in control of the White House and the Senate. But when Democrats recaptured the Senate in 1986, they revived the issue with proposals to provide public financing and spending limits. Republicans countered with proposals to eliminate or restrict PACs, which were proving more lucrative for Democrats than Republicans. The competing partisan interests produced deadlock.

Democrats brought a bill to the Senate floor in 1988 but failed to break a Republican filibuster. In 1990, the House and the Senate passed somewhat similar Democratic-backed bills late in the session, but with little time and continuing disagreements lawmakers never met to try to resolve the differences. Two years later, Democrats did get legislation through Congress, but President George Bush vetoed the measure, and the effort to override the veto fell nine votes short in the Senate.

Clinton's election in 1992 raised the hopes that legislation would be enacted with a Democratic majority in Congress and a Democrat in the White House. But Clinton did not make the issue a priority, and House Democrats moved at a snail's pace. They waited until Nov. 22, 1993, to move the bill through the House and then until August 1994 to appoint conferees to try to work out the substantial differences with a bill passed by the Senate in June 1993. With adjournment nearing, Senate Republicans used a parliamentary maneuver to block a conference. [25]

Hopes to resolve the stalemate were raised again on June 11, 1995, when Clinton and Gingrich made their handshake promise in New Hampshire to create a bipartisan commission to overhaul campaign finance laws. But the hopes were quickly dashed. Within a week Clinton proposed creating a commission whose recommendations would be sent to Congress for an up-or-down vote without amendment. Gingrich called it a "gimmick" but waited until November to offer his alternative — a less powerful commission without a fast-track vote procedure. By year's end, reformers were conceding the commission idea had died. ■

CURRENT SITUATION

Gingrich's 'Heresy'

In November, when Gingrich finally laid out his thoughts on campaign finance issues, his views dramatically departed from those of the lawmakers and groups backing reform legislation. Appearing before the House Oversight Committee on Nov. 2, Gingrich differed with reformers not only on the timing and structure of the proposed study commission but also on the underlying substantive issues, including limits on spending and contributions and restrictions on PACs. [26]

"We need a very profound overhaul of our political system," Gingrich said. But he challenged what he called the "myth" that campaigns cost too much. "The political process, in fact, is not overfunded, but underfunded," Gingrich declared.

The speaker rejected spending limits, saying that in his own case restrictions would hurt his ability to respond to unfavorable press coverage. "I would guess that over half of the money I raise is spent offsetting the weight of" the *Atlanta Journal-Constitution,* he said. As for PACs, Gingrich dropped his previous calls for abolishing them and instead called only for limiting their contributions to $1,000. At the same time, he said individual-contribution limits should be raised from $1,000 to $5,000.

Gingrich drew compliments from Democratic leaders who followed him at the hearing. Minority Leader Richard A. Gephardt of Missouri called Gingrich's proposal for a bipartisan commission "a good idea" and said the members should "open their mind to new thinking and new ideas that are out there."

Two weeks later, Gingrich also won praise from David Broder, the respected political reporter for *The Washington Post.* Gingrich was "dead-right to challenge the conventional wisdom on this subject and urge politicians and pundits to think again before they saddle the country with another batch of ill-considered 'reforms,'" Broder wrote. The column bore the headline "Gingrich's Heresy." [27]

Supporters of the reform measures, however, sharply criticized Gingrich's statements. McBride called the commission proposal "a phony." Rep. Smith said the timetable calling for the group to report around May 1 amounted to reneging on Gingrich's previous promise to bring campaign finance legislation to the House floor in January. "The old boys and the old establishment came up with the best solution they could — to . . . stall for time," Smith told reporters.

FEC Investigates GOPAC

In his comments to the committee, Gingrich also criticized the FEC, calling its enforcement policies "profoundly restrictive" and "adversarial." His comments came while the FEC was investigating a PAC that Gingrich once headed, GOPAC.

GOPAC was founded in 1979 to help Republicans running for state and local offices. But the FEC claims that Gingrich, who took over the organization in 1986, changed its focus to helping elect Republican House members. PACs seeking to influence federal elections are required to register with the FEC and disclose contributions, but GOPAC did not register until 1991.

The commission sued GOPAC in April 1994, contending that the group had become involved in federal elections before registering as a PAC. Gingrich denounced the suit as a "power grab" and insisted the group had done nothing wrong. "We were talking about campaigns in general and to Congress in general, and none of the money went to federal campaigns," Gingrich said. [28]

To buttress its case, the FEC filed new documents in late November that sought to link GOPAC's contributions directly to Gingrich's closely fought bid for re-election in 1990. The filing — based on internal GOPAC documents — claimed that Gingrich received at least $250,000 in support from the group in 1990, before it had registered as a political action committee for federal elections. Gingrich won re-election that year by 974 votes. [29]

A spokeswoman for Gingrich called the FEC's allegations "bogus" and insisted the expenditures cited in the filings were all proper. "These were legitimate travel expenses for strategy and planning sessions for GOPAC," Lauren Sims told reporters. But McBride said the charges "raise serious questions about the speaker and GOPAC violating the campaign finance laws to get him elected."

Search for Alternatives

The House Oversight Committee forged ahead with its campaign finance hearings in November and December but showed no signs of moving toward a consensus on legislation. Chairman Bill Thomas, a California Republican and Gingrich loyalist, conducted the sessions more like a college seminar than a hearing on specific legislative proposals.

The committee's witness lists also showed a bias against reform proposals. Witnesses at the Nov. 16 session on political action committees included representatives from the ACLU, the Cato Institute and corporate and labor union PACs — all opposed to further restrictions. At the committee's Dec. 12 hearing on the role of political parties, the chairmen of the two major parties, along with a panel of four political scientists, all called for allowing national parties to give more money to congressional candidates.

Shut out of the normal legislative channels, the sponsors of the major reform bills said they would try to find other routes to push the proposals. In the House, Rep. Smith was joined by fellow Republican Christopher Shays of Connecticut and several Democrats in sponsoring a bill they called the Bipartisan Clean Congress Act of 1995. The parallel Senate measure — the Senate Campaign Finance Reform Act of 1995 — was being put together by Republican John McCain of Arizona and Democrat Russell D. Feingold of Wisconsin, joined by freshman Republican Fred Thompson of Tennessee.

In the House, Smith vowed to use a so-called discharge petition to pry the bill out of committee and onto the House floor. But the procedure requires signatures by a majority of House members and rarely succeeds. Smith was riding a wave of national publicity with her outspoken support for campaign finance reform. But opponents of the legislation said she was burning her bridges with Gingrich and other Republican leaders. "Linda Smith has so alienated herself from her own leadership that she's out in the cold," says Stockmeyer.

Supporters of the legislation saw a more promising scenario in seeking action first in the Senate, where procedural rules make it easier for bills to be attached to unrelated legislation. "We try to get a time agreement" to force a vote in the Senate, says McBride, "and then put the pressure and the spotlight on the House. It's going to be very difficult to stonewall."

But Stockmeyer predicted that Republicans would thwart the reformers' goals in the Senate, too. "It's extreme wishful thinking for Common Cause to think that McCain-Feingold might be passed," he says. "Any attempt at public financing and any attempt at spending limits will not pass. Republicans will just not support that. That just ain't what Republicans are all about." ■

OUTLOOK

Flight From Congress

With another election year approaching, more and more members of Congress have been deciding to call it quits. By late January, 13

Continued on p. 139

At Issue:

Have campaign finance laws improved the political process?

Ann McBride
President, Common Cause

WRITTEN FOR *THE CQ RESEARCHER*, FEB. 9, 1996

yes

Federal campaign finance laws enacted in the wake of the Watergate scandal have unquestionably improved the political process by establishing a system of timely and comprehensive disclosure that gives voters information about where candidates get their money and how they spend it. And the presidential campaign finance system that was another part of the Watergate reforms also initially met its goal to reduce the influence of special interests and eliminate corruption in the election for our country's highest office.

For the first decade of its existence, the presidential system reduced the role of special-interest influence money in presidential campaigns and made presidential elections more competitive by equalizing spending between candidates. Presidential candidates who choose to accept public funds also agree to adhere to spending limits in both the primary and general elections. All but two of the 66 major party candidates since 1976 have opted into this system.

This reform also has restrained spending: In 1972, the Nixon campaign spent $60 million, the equivalent of over $200 million in inflation-adjusted dollars. By contrast, spending by each of the candidates in 1992 was about $90 million, well below the rate of spending prior to the reform.

Unfortunately, the integrity of the presidential system has been undermined by the "soft money" loophole — money raised outside the federal contribution limits and disclosure requirements. The use of the soft-money loophole since the 1980s has resulted in huge corporate donations and $100,000-plus individual contributions again being raised by national political leaders and by the political parties.

Congress' failure to enact comprehensive reforms for its own elections has resulted in a spiral of campaign spending and fundraising. The Supreme Court's decision to strike down spending limits has resulted in an explosive increase in campaign spending and an ever-growing fundraising burden on congressional candidates. This, in turn, has made candidates more dependent on special-interest campaign contributions, including money from political action committees, or PACs.

The congressional system also heavily favors incumbents, who receive 10 times as much PAC money as challengers and, on average, over 2.5 times as much money overall as challengers. It is often impossible for challengers to amass the resources necessary to compete effectively against well-funded incumbents.

Bipartisan legislation pending in both houses of Congress would go far toward removing the gaps in the law. The bills would limit PACs, eliminate the soft-money loophole and establish voluntary spending limits for congressional candidates. Congress should enact this legislation this year to ensure that the post-Watergate reforms achieve their full potential.

Edward H. Crane III
President, The Cato Institute

WRITTEN FOR *THE CQ RESEARCHER*, FEB. 9, 1996

no

Congress enacted the current federal campaign finance law in the wake of government abuses of power in the Vietnam War and the Watergate affair. Perversely, the law actually enhanced government power by chilling political debate and making it significantly more difficult for challengers to defeat incumbents. Not only were strict contribution limits placed on federal campaigns, the 1974 act also limited spending to just $70,000 for House races and $100,000, or eight cents per voter, for Senate races.

Fortunately, the Supreme Court struck down the spending limits as an infringement on the First Amendment right to free speech. Unfortunately, the court upheld the contribution limits, as though money raised has no relationship to money spent.

In any event, it is clear from any objective standard that we spend far too little on federal campaigns in the first place. Total direct spending for all congressional races in the 1994 election cycle was just $3 per eligible voter. Americans spend more money on yogurt each year than they spend on federal elections. Studies have always demonstrated that the more money that is spent on campaigns, the more knowledgeable voters are about the issues addressed in those campaigns.

The hysteria that groups like Common Cause bring to the campaign finance reform debate is based on the faulty assumption that money buys candidates. But as Bradley A. Smith, author of a Cato Institute study on the subject writes, "Every systemic study conducted of legislative voting behavior has concluded that campaign contributions have little or no effect on that behavior." Ideology, voter sentiment and party discipline are correlated much more closely to voting behavior than sources of campaign contributions.

Furthermore, why should those with the capacity to enhance political discourse through significant campaign contributions be denied that option when we allow others to spend all they want, just because they chose the favored profession of the media or being a candidate? Whether or not one agrees with Ross Perot or Steve Forbes, it is hard to deny that they have enhanced democracy through their efforts. And who would deny that the millions of dollars of free publicity that a Gary Trudeau, a Rush Limbaugh or a Katherine Graham can give their favorite causes is not a healthy part of a free society?

Americans rightly oppose federal funding of federal elections. The best thing we can do to shake up our stagnant electoral process is eliminate limits on campaign contributions altogether, have full disclosure and thereby open up the political process to a diversity of candidates now precluded from seeking office.

Groups Look to States for Campaign Finance Overhaul

With campaign finance legislation stymied in Congress, reform groups are pushing proposals at the local and state levels to try to limit the influence of money in politics.

Supporters won approval in 1994 of statewide voter initiatives in Missouri, Montana and Oregon establishing contribution limits for state races well below the $1,000 limit for federal elections — typically, $100 for legislative races and $500 or less for statewide contests.

This year, reform groups are gathering signatures for similar $100-limit proposals in five more states: Alaska, Arkansas, California, Colorado and Maine. In California, separate coalitions of public interest groups are sponsoring competing initiatives and exchanging harsh accusations about which measure is tougher.

Donna Edwards, director of the Center for New Democracy, a Washington-based group that provides technical assistance to the state organizations, says the proposals being considered in Washington lag far behind the restrictions being enacted in the states. "They don't even come close to what people are willing to do in the states," says Edwards. "People here in Washington just underestimate the power of this issue."

The $100-limit proposals debuted in the District of Columbia, where voters approved a ballot initiative by a nearly 2-to-1 margin in 1992. Two years later, voter initiatives passed with substantial majorities in Missouri (77 percent), Montana (63 percent) and Oregon (72 percent). Colorado voters, however, narrowly defeated a similar measure — 54 percent to 46 percent.

The new proposals are being pushed by state and local public interest research groups or PIRGs — the grassroots organizations associated with consumer activist Ralph Nader. Supporters lace their appeals with populist rhetoric. Wendy Wendladt, an official of the California PIRG serving as campaign coordinator for its initiative, refers to the $100 limit for legislative races as "a contribution that ordinary people can afford." The measure would allow contributions up to $200 for statewide contests.

The rival California initiative — being sponsored by the state chapters of Common Cause and the League of Women Voters along with Ross Perot's United We Stand, America — also limits contributions to $100 for state Assembly contests, but sets higher limits for state Senate races ($250) and statewide elections ($500).

The Common Cause measure would double the campaign contribution limits, however, for any candidate who agrees to abide by spending limits. The ceilings, for primary and general elections combined, would be $300,000 for the state Assembly, $600,00 for the state Senate and $12 million for the gubernatorial election.

The California PIRG initiative seeks to impose spending limits with a mandatory provision — directly challenging the U.S. Supreme Court's 1976 decision in *Buckley v. Valeo* overturning mandatory spending limits. "Most reformers would agree that the time has come to challenge that decision," says Wendladt.

Supporters of the other initiative, however, say the Supreme Court is not going to overturn *Buckley*. Ruth Holton, executive director of the state's Common Cause organization, calls the California-PIRG measure "a fraud. It's the Trojan horse that opponents of reform will use to kill our measure," she says.

Wendladt is similarly critical of the Common Cause initiative. She says the provision's variable limits "institutionalize a system of fat-cat contributors. That's not returning politics to the grass roots."

California currently has no contribution or spending limits for state elections, even though it pioneered state campaign finance laws with a voter initiative in 1974 that imposed contribution and spending limits and disclosure requirements. But the spending limits were struck down after *Buckley*.

The state's voters in 1988 approved two new campaign finance initiatives containing contribution limits and other provisions. Under California law, the initiative with the higher number of votes went into effect, but federal courts struck down its major provisions. "We ended up with essentially nothing," says Daniel Loewenstein, a law professor at the University of California, Los Angeles, and former head of the state's Fair Political Practices Commission.

Some experts expect both initiatives to be approved this year as well. "Californians seem to be very concerned" about campaign finance issues, says Robert Stern, director of the private Center for Governmental Studies in Los Angeles, who helped write the Common Cause initiative and advised on the drafting of the California-PIRG measure. "People have really awakened to the problem of money and are ready to impose drastic restrictions."

Bruce Cain, associate director of the Institute of Governmental Studies at the University of California, Berkeley, agrees that it is "quite possible" that both measures could be adopted. But he also predicts that politicians and contributors will find ways to evade the restrictions.

Cain says that the courts are certain to strike down mandatory spending limits if they are enacted and that contingent spending limits "don't work" because wealthy candidates can spend unlimited sums out of their own pockets. As for the contribution limits, he predicts they would result in "a proliferation of PACs that will bundle together the smaller contributions."

"Everything we saw at the federal level," Cain concludes, "will just come true in California."

Continued from p. 136

senators — a record — and some 27 representatives had announced they were not seeking re-election in November. Their reasons ranged from the personal — spending more time with family — to the substantive — growing doubt about the ability of Congress to make a difference. But one complaint was heard time and time again: the never-ending need to raise more and more money for the next campaign.

"What has changed is the enormous amount of money in the system," retiring Republican Sen. Nancy Landon Kassebaum told radio talk show host Diane Rehm on Dec. 14. "I'm not one of those who think you're bought, but it's the time and energy that are drained." Kassebaum added that she was "aghast that it takes $2 million to run for the Senate in Kansas."

Illinois Democrat Paul Simon, appearing with a panel of other retiring senators on CBS' "60 Minutes" on Dec. 17, recalled that he spent $8.4 million in his last campaign, in 1990. "It has a corrupting influence on all of us," Simon said of the fundraising burdens. Do contributors feel you owe them something because they gave you money? correspondent Ed Bradley asked. "Some of them do," Simon answered.

Presidential candidates still raise large sums of campaign money, too, despite the public financing system established in the post-Watergate law. President Clinton and the Republican presidential hopefuls collectively raised $125 million by the end of 1995, according to the Center for Responsive Politics. President Clinton had the biggest war chest — just under $27 million through Sept. 30 — while Senate Majority Leader Bob Dole and Texas Sen. Phil Gramm had raised the largest amounts among the Republicans, with $26 million and $21 million, respectively. [30]

"We're seeing more money raised earlier than we've ever seen in a presidential race," says the center's Goldstein. "The reason is that money wins elections, and [the candidates] want to win. You've got a lot of candidates who are attempting to win the nomination through strength of money."

In its own report on presidential candidates' fundraising, another watchdog group, the Center for Public Integrity, sought to link campaign contributions to the candidates' current or past policy positions. In a new book provocatively titled *The Buying of the President,* the center said that Dole had supported a tax break and an agricultural program that benefited one of his biggest donors, the Ernest and Julio Gallo winemaking family. As another example, the book implied that the Clinton administration had tailored its telecommunications policies to benefit major telephone and entertainment companies whose officers were among Clinton's major contributors. [31]

Dole and the administration both denied any link between the contributions and the policies. But Charles Lewis, the center's executive director, said the book showed that the presidential campaign was "not so much a horse race or a beauty contest, but instead a giant auction in which multimillion-dollar interests compete to influence and gain access to the candidates." [32]

The inside-the-Beltway lawyers and lobbyists who are the targets of the lawmakers' fundraising solicitations have their own complaints about the system. Stockmeyer calls for prohibiting fundraisers outside a member's state or district while Congress is in session. "In effect, you'd eliminate the Washington fund-raiser," he says. "We'd all see more of our families, and our livers would all function better."

President Clinton added his voice to the calls for reform in his State of the Union address on Jan. 23. After praising the lawmakers for strengthening lobbyist disclosure and banning gifts and meals from lobbyists, Clinton said he wanted to "challenge Congress to go further: to curb special interest influence in politics by passing the first truly bipartisan campaign finance reform bill in a generation." After pausing for applause, Clinton continued, "You, the Republicans and Democrats alike, can show the American people that we can limit spending and open the airwaves to all candidates."

Outside observers voice doubt, however, that the growing discontent

FOR MORE INFORMATION

The Cato Institute, 1000 Massachusetts Ave. N.W., Washington, D.C. 20001; (202) 842-0200. The libertarian think tank, founded in 1977, opposes campaign contribution and spending limits and public campaign financing.

Center for Responsive Politics, 1320 19th St. N.W., Suite 700, Washington, D.C. 20036; (202) 857-0044. The center, founded in 1983, serves as an information clearinghouse on campaign contribution and spending disclosure reports.

Common Cause, 2030 M St., N.W., Washington, D.C. 20036-3380; (202) 833-1200. The citizens' group has been the leading advocacy organization supporting stronger campaign disclosure laws, contribution and spending limits and public financing since its founding in 1970.

National Association of Business PACs, 801 N. Fairfax St., Suite 215, Alexandria, Va. 22314; (703) 836-4422. Steven Stockmeyer, executive director. The organization, founded in 1977, opposes additional limits on PACs but supports a number of other changes in campaign finance laws.

with the campaign finance system, both inside Washington and in the country at large, will goad Congress into action. "It's not a hot issue for voters," says American University political science Professor Candice Nelson. "Members of Congress don't have voters calling them up and asking, 'What are you going to do about campaign finance reform?' "

But some of the experts take heart from the likelihood that broad reform measures may fail once again this year. "I don't think that a Common Cause-style bill would be good for the country," Malbin of the Rockefeller Institute told the House Oversight Committee in December. But Malbin nonetheless has his own list of recommended changes, including a ban on federal candidates' raising soft money and an increase in individual and political party contribution limits.

For her part, Common Cause President McBride remains determined that some form of campaign finance legislation will be enacted this year. "I don't think the Congress can go back home and not pass a bill," she says. "The issue is whether they're going to pass real and effective reform or something that's not real."

Most experts, however, simply forecast no action. "It looks like stalemate forever," says the University of California's Jacobson. "I think of this as less a problem than a situation. Problems have solutions. Situations you just live with." ■

Notes

[1] See Bradley A. Smith, "Campaign Finance Regulation: Faulty Assumptions and Undemocratic Consequences," Cato Institute, Sept. 13, 1995.

[2] Herbert E. Alexander and Anthony Corrado, *Financing the 1992 Elections* (1995), p. 3. Alexander says the amount increased by about 19 percent from the figure for the 1987-1988 election cycle — about the same increase as the consumer price index (18.7 percent).

[3] Michael J. Malbin, "Campaign Finance," in Norman J. Ornstein, Thomas E. Mann and Michael J. Malbin, Vital *Statistics on Congress, 1995-1996* (1996), p. 81.

[4] See Alexander and Corrado, *op. cit.*

[5] *Ibid.*, pp. 76-77. Malbin notes that North's financial reports exaggerate the impact of his spending since much of the money went to direct-mail solicitations to raise funds through small individual contributions.

[6] Larry Makinson, "The Price of Admission: Campaign Spending in the 1994 Elections," Center for Responsive Politics, August 1995, p. 10.

[7] "Capital Eye," Center for Responsive Politics, Nov. 1, 1995, p. 1.

[8] Common Cause, "Shake Up or Shake Down?" Aug. 15, 1995. See *The Washington Post*, Aug. 15, 1995, p. A15 and July 23, 1995, p. A8.

[9] Janet M. Grenzke, "PACs and the Congressional Supermarket: The Currency Is Complex," *American Journal of Political Science*, Vol. 33, No. 1, February 1989, pp. 1-24.

[10] *Ibid.*, p. 5.

[11] Fred Wertheimer and Susan Weiss Manes, "Campaign Finance Reform: A Key to Restoring the Health of Our Democracy," *Columbia Law Review*, Vol. 94, No. 4, May 1994, p. 1140.

[12] Smith, *op. cit.*, p. 25. Smith based his calculation on $300,000 — "the minimum needed for an effective campaign" — to each of 870 candidates for the House of Representatives.

[13] David B. Magelby and Candice J. Nelson, *The Money Chase: Congressional Campaign Finance Reform* (1990), pp. 153-154.

[14] Smith, *op. cit.*, p. 24, citing Frank Sorauf, *Inside Campaign Finance: Myths and Realities* (1990), pp. 145-146.

[15] The Mellman Group, "Campaign for America: Summary of Key Findings," September 1995.

[16] For historical background, see Herbert E. Alexander, *Financing Politics* (1992), pp. 9-49; and Robert E. Mutch, *Campaigns, Congress, and Courts: The Making of Federal Campaign Finance Law* (1988), pp. 1-52.

[17] Mutch, *op. cit.*, pp. xvi-xvii.

[18] Alexander, *op. cit.*, pp. 25-26. Mutch notes that the contribution limit was amended on the last day of congressional debate to exempt contributions to state and local political committees. See Mutch, *op. cit.*, pp. 34-35.

[19] For a complete table of costs of presidential general elections, 1860-1988, see Alexander, *op. cit.*, pp. 80-81. The figures in the table, and those cited in the article, are not adjusted for inflation.

[20] Alexander Heard, *The Costs of Democracy* (1960), pp. 402-403.

[21] *Ibid.*, cited in Mutch, *op. cit.*, p. 26.

[22] Alexander, *op. cit.*, p. 31. Among the contributions disclosed were the two largest ever made: $2 million by insurance magnate W. Clement Stone and $1 million by Mellon heir Richard Mellon Scaife. Mutch, *op. cit.*, pp. 45-46.

[23] See Malbin, *op. cit.*, p. 107.

[24] See Alexander, *op. cit.*, pp. 115-117 (1988 figures); *The Wall Street Journal*, March 4, 1993, p. B2 (1992 figures).

[25] See *1994 Congressional Quarterly Almanac*, pp. 32-34; *1992 Congressional Quarterly Almanac*, pp. 63-70; *1990 Congressional Quarterly Almanac*, pp. 59-71.

[26] See *The New York Times*, Nov. 3, 1995, p. A26; *The Washington Post*, Nov. 3, 1995, p. A21; *Congressional Quarterly Weekly Report*, Nov. 4, 1995, p. 3351.

[27] *The Washington Post*, Nov. 14, 1995, p. A19.

[28] See *The Washington Post*, May 11, 1994, p. A14.

[29] See *The Washington Post*, Nov. 30, 1995, p. A1; *The New York Times*, Nov. 30, 1995, p. A1.

[30] Center for Responsive Politics, "The First Primary: Early Fund-Raising in the 1996 Presidential Election," January 1996. The report found a total of $94 million raised through Sept. 30; end-of-year filings raised the total for all candidates to $124.5 million, according to Goldstein. The total included $18 million for GOP candidate Forbes, $16.5 of it in the form of a personal loan from the candidate to his campaign.

[31] Charles Lewis and the Center for Public Integrity, *The Buying of the President* (1996).

[32] Quoted in *The Washington Post*, Jan. 12, 1996, p. A13.

Bibliography

Selected Sources Used

Books

Alexander, Herbert E., *Financing Politics: Money, Elections, and Political Reform* [4th ed.], Congressional Quarterly, 1992.
Alexander, the dean of campaign finance scholars, provides an overview of the history of campaign finance reform and current issues relating to the 1974 campaign finance law. The book includes a seven-page bibliography. Alexander, who heads the Citizens' Research Foundation at the University of Southern California, Los Angeles, has also authored or co-authored quadrennial books since 1960 on the financing of U.S. elections, most recently, *Financing the 1992 Election* (M.E. Sharpe, 1995), co-authored with Anthony Corrado.

Heard, Alexander, *The Costs of Democracy,* University of North Carolina Press, 1960.
This important work, written before passage of strong federal disclosure requirements, examines campaign fundraising and expenditures, evaluates then-existing campaign finance laws and recommends some policy changes, including public financing and communications subsidies or tax credits for political contributions.

Lewis, Charles, and the Center for Public Integrity, *The Buying of the President,* Avon, 1996.
Lewis details the financial support received by President Clinton and nine Republican presidential candidates and cites instances in which some of them have taken actions that benefited their contributors. Lewis is executive director of the center, which he helped found in 1989.

Magelby, David B., and Candice J. Nelson, *The Money Chase: Congressional Campaign Finance Reform,* Brookings Institution, 1990.
Magelby, a professor of political science at Brigham Young University, and Nelson, a professor at American University, give an overview of campaign finance issues and seek to evaluate the effects of proposed revisions in campaign finance laws.

Mutch, Robert, E., *Campaigns, Congress and the Courts: The Making of Federal Campaign Finance Laws,* Praeger, 1988.
Mutch, who has taught political science at several colleges, traces the history of federal campaign finance laws from the earliest proposals in the 1800s through the post-Watergate 1974 reform and the debate over the effects of the law.

Sorauf, Frank, *Inside Campaign Finance: Myths and Realities,* Yale University Press, 1992.
Sorauf, a professor at the University of Minnesota, Minneapolis, gives an historical overview and survey of contemporary campaign finance issues from a viewpoint skeptical of "reform" positions.

Articles

Malbin, Michael J., "Campaign Finance," in Norman J. Ornstein, Thomas E. Mann, and Michael J. Malbin, *Vital Statistics on Congress, 1995-1996,* American Enterprise Institute/Congressional Quarterly, 1995.
Malbin, director of the Rockefeller Institute of Government at the State University of New York in Albany, finds that congressional campaign spending and PAC contributions remained largely steady in the 1994 election and that Republican challengers were relatively well-financed in comparison to challengers of either party in years past.

Wertheimer, Fred, and Susan Weiss Manes, "Campaign Finance Reform: A Key to Restoring the Health of Our Democracy," *Columbia Law Review*, Vol. 94, No. 4, May 1994, pp. 1126-1159.
Wertheimer, then president of Common Cause, and Manes, formerly the organization's vice president for issue development, strongly argue that campaign finance laws should be tightened to restrict the influence of political action committees and to strengthen the enforcement powers of the Federal Election Commission.

Reports and Studies

Goldstein, Joshua, *PACs in Profile: Spending Patterns in the 1994 Elections,* Center for Responsive Politics, May 1995.
This detailed, 98-page report shows that PAC contributions in the 1994 elections totaled $189.2 million and that business PACs and, to a lesser extent, labor and ideological PACs, gave most of their money to incumbents.

Larry Makinson, *The Price of Admission: Campaign Spending in the 1994 Elections,* Center for Responsive Politics, August 1995.
This detailed, 250-page report documents, state by state and race by race, campaign contributions and expenditures in Senate and House elections in 1994.

Smith, Bradley A., *Campaign Finance Regulation: Faulty Assumptions and Undemocratic Consequences,* Cato Institute, Sept. 13, 1995.
Smith, an assistant professor at Capital University Law Center in Columbus, Ohio, strongly argues that current campaign finance laws have hampered public participation in the political system and reduced political competitiveness.

The Next Step

Additional information from UMI's Newspaper & Periodical Abstracts database

Campaign Finance Reform

Berke, Richard L., "Debate on campaign finance laws generates a scramble for donations," ***The New York Times,*** **Aug. 13, 1993, p. A18.**

Legislators, fearful that the passage of a campaign finance reform bill would hamper their ability to raise money, have begun pressuring lobbyists and PACs for early donations. Fundraising efforts of particular Congressmen are detailed.

Corn, David, and Amy Shefrin,"Campaign finance earns interest," ***The Nation,*** **Oct. 2, 1995, pp. 352-354.**

Efforts by Sen. Russell Feingold, D-Wis., and Sen. John McCain, R-Ariz., to curb the excesses of the present campaign finance system are discussed. Feingold watered down his original proposal in favor of a weaker one that has some chance of passing.

"Inside Congress — Issue: Campaign finance," ***Congressional Quarterly Weekly Report,*** **Jan. 6, 1996, p. 20.**

The entry summarizes the status of legislation at the start of the 104th Congress, second session.

Shillinger, Kurt, "Drive to change campaign finance gains in Congress," ***The Christian Science Monitor,*** **Nov. 2, 1995, p. 1.**

Congress has produced a bipartisan campaign finance reform bill in early November 1995. The bill includes voluntary spending limits, free and reduced-rate TV time, restrictions on PAC contributions and the abolition of soft money from corporations and unions.

Wines, Michael, "House Democrats scuttle revolt on campaign finance measure," ***The New York Times,*** **Nov. 22, 1993, p. A1.**

Leaders of the Democrats in the House on Nov. 21, 1993, narrowly overcame an internal revolt against a plan to overhaul campaign spending laws, but the passage of the measure is still up in the air. Even if the House passes a version of campaign reform on Nov. 22, it will have to be mated with a wholly different version that passed the Senate in June.

Zuckman, Jill, "Senate kills campaign finance bill," ***Boston Globe,*** **Oct. 1, 1994, p. 3.**

The Senate killed legislation to revamp campaign financing rules as the session of Congress that many new members had vowed would be known as the Reform Congress prepared to adjourn.

Editorials

"Campaign-finance: Clinton should decline soft money, set a new standard," ***Detroit News & Free Press,*** **June 25, 1994, p. A8.**

An editorial says incumbent lawmakers need to embrace political campaign finance reform, and President Clinton needs to lead the effort.

"Campaign-finance reform falters," ***St. Louis Post-Dispatch,*** **April 1, 1993, p. C2.**

An editorial criticizes President Clinton's delay of a campaign finance reform bill and states that PAC contributions must be curbed.

"Fine-Tuning for Campaign Finance," ***The New York Times,*** **Dec. 13, 1989, p. A30.**

An editorial commends New York City's new public campaign financing system, which was designed to reduce reliance on big contributions and discourage political favoritism.

"A Sneaky Blow at Campaign Finance," ***The New York Times,*** **May 16, 1995, p. A20.**

An editorial criticizes a Republican proposal to abolish the public campaign financing system for presidential candidates.

Political Action Committees

"Campaign finance reform," ***The Christian Science Monitor*****, p 2, col 1 Nov. 23, 1993, p. 2.**

House Democratic leaders will get a vote on their campaign finance bill, which limits overall PAC donations to $200,000 per election, in November 1993. House Republicans and maverick Democrats plan to block the leadership bill and offer their own bill, which they claim offers true reforms.

Dewar, Helen, and Kenneth J. Cooper, "Campaign finance reform mired in gulf between House and Senate," ***The Washington Post,*** **May 28, 1994, p. A8.**

Swift passage of legislation to overhaul congressional campaign financing laws has been jeopardized because the House and Senate remain sharply divided over limits on contributions from PACs.

Dewar, Helen, "Campaign-finance reform may prove the test of Republican resolve to change Washington," ***The Washington Post,*** **June 27, 1994, p. A5.**

Legislation to overhaul Congress' campaign financing rules hangs by a thread as Democratic leaders in the House and Senate edge warily toward a showdown over the critical issue of limits on contributions from PACs.

Smith, Linda, "Reform campaign finance now," *The Christian Science Monitor,* Nov. 28, 1995, p. 20.
Rep. Linda Smith, R-Wash., argues that House Speaker Newt Gingrich should lead the campaign to reform political finance in late 1995, and notes the negative influence that PACs may have on candidates' interests.

Wartzman, Rick, "Campaign finance showdown nears," *The Wall Street Journal,* Nov. 18, 1994, p. A20.
Now that the GOP has taken control of the House and Senate and PAC money is starting to increasingly flow to Republicans, the approach Republicans take toward campaign finance reform will go to the heart of how much the GOP is really willing to shake up Washington.

Soft Money

"Abolish soft money now," *St. Louis Post-Dispatch,* Sept. 13, 1995, p. B6.
The editorial describes soft money as the campaign finance system's biggest loophole, one that almost invites candidates and their friends to break the law.

Babcock, Charles R., "Democratic soft money scorecard," *The Washington Post,* Nov. 3, 1995, p. A21.
A list of donations to national Democratic committees from Jan. 1-June 30, 1995, is given. The Democratic soft money scorecard is examined.

Babcock, Charles R., and Kenneth J. Cooper, "Clinton campaign finance plan would eliminate soft money," *The Washington Post,* March 26, 1993, p. A11.
President Clinton's advisers are drafting campaign finance overhaul proposals that would eliminate national parties' acceptance of millions of dollars in large "soft money" donations, but would cushion the blow by allowing individuals to double their annual contributions to candidates and parties to $50,000.

Bates, James, "Hollywood is a major player in political soft money game," *The Los Angeles Times,* April 29, 1994, p. D5.
A Common Cause report says the entertainment industry is one of the heavyweights to give "soft money" to national political party committees.

Edsall, Thomas B., "Corporations favor Republican Party with soft money," *The Washington Post,* Sept. 14, 1995, p. A4.
The GOP has surged ahead in the competition to raise "soft money" from the politically active corporate community. The pattern of giving in the first half of 1993, 1994 and 1995 shows an upward trend in large contributions to GOP committees.

Farrell, John Aloysius, "Soft money diary entry brings Gramm rough patch," *Boston Globe,* Sept. 9, 1995, p. 4.
Sen. Phil Gramm's presidential campaign hit a sudden patch of turbulence over an entry in former Oregon Sen. Bob Packwood's diaries suggesting the two Republicans worked to evade federal election law and direct $100,000 of political "soft money" toward Packwood's 1992 re-election.

Melton, R.H., "Corporate contributions pour into the RNC," *The Washington Post,* April 6, 1995, p. A19.
Dozens of U.S. companies and individuals with interests before the new Republican-controlled Congress were among those who gave more than $7.2 million in "soft money" to the GOP's national committee during the first two months of 1995, according to a study issued by Common Cause.

Schorr, Daniel, "What soft money can buy," *The Christian Science Monitor,* Sept. 15, 1995, p. 19.
Schorr discusses the revelations in former Sen. Bob Packwood's diary about his close relationships with lobbyists. Schorr states that Packwood's dramatization of influence-peddling in Congress may be the greatest service he has ever performed.

State Campaign Finance Laws

Gavin, Jennifer, "NRA on both sides of campaign-finance talk," *Denver Post,* Aug. 27, 1995, p. A12.
The impact that money donated to Colorado legislators by the NRA has had on the support for firearm legislation in the state Legislature is examined.

Gillam, Jerry, "Campaign finance reform bill is vetoed," *The Los Angeles Times,* Oct. 1, 1994, p. A22.
California Gov. Pete Wilson vetoed a campaign finance reform bill that would have limited contributions and spending by candidates for the state Legislature and provided for partial public financing.

Wardlaw, Jack, "Campaign finance proposal may bar PAC contributions," *Times-Picayune,* March 14, 1995, p. B3.
An ad hoc Louisiana Senate committee is studying far-reaching changes in the state's campaign finance law that would bar contributions from PACs, labor unions or corporations.

Back Issues

Great Research on Current Issues Starts Right Here...Recent topics covered by The CQ Researcher are listed below. Before May 1991, reports were published under the name of Editorial Research Reports.

AUGUST 1994
Genetically Engineered Foods
Electing Minorities
Prozac Controversy
College Sports

SEPTEMBER 1994
Home Schooling
Welfare Experiments
Courts and the Media
Regulating Tobacco

OCTOBER 1994
Historic Preservation
Religion and Politics
Arts Funding
Economic Sanctions

NOVEMBER 1994
Sex on Campus
Blood Supply Safety
Testing Term Limits
Religion in America

DECEMBER 1994
Farm Policy
Arms Sales
Earthquake Research
The Future of Television

JANUARY 1995
Treating Addiction
Child Custody and Support
Parents and Schools
Non-Proliferation Treaty at 25

FEBRUARY 1995
Cracking Down on Immigration
The Business of Sports
Reinventing Government
Housing Discrimination

MARCH 1995
Death Penalty Debate
Primary Care
Democracy in Africa
Environmental Movement at 25

APRIL 1995
Abortion Clinic Protests
Dieting and Health
Combating AIDS
Rethinking Affirmative Action

MAY 1995
Assisted Suicide Controversy
Overhauling Social Security
Learning to Read
Mandatory Sentencing

JUNE 1995
Combating Infectious Disease
Property Rights
Repetitive Stress Injuries
Regulating the Internet

JULY 1995
War Crimes
Highway Safety
Combating Terrorism
Preventing Teen Drug Use

AUGUST 1995
Job Stress
Organ Transplants
United Nations at 50
Advances in Cancer Research

SEPTEMBER 1995
Catholic Church in the U.S.
Northern Ireland Cease-Fire
High School Sports
Teaching History

OCTOBER 1995
Quebec's Future
Revitalizing the Cities
Networking the Classroom
Indoor Air Pollution

NOVEMBER 1995
The Working Poor
The Jury System
Sex, Violence and the Media
Police Misconduct

DECEMBER 1995
Teens and Tobacco
Gene Therapy's Future
Global Water Shortages
Third-Party Prospects

JANUARY 1996
Emergency Medicine
Punishing Sex Offenders
Bilingual Education
Helping the Homeless

FEBRUARY 1996
Reforming the CIA

Back issues are available for $5.00 (subscribers) or $8.00 (non-subscribers). Quantity discounts apply to orders over ten. To order, call Congressional Quarterly Customer Service at (202) 887-8621.

Binders are available for $18.00. To order call 1-800-638-1710. Please refer to stock number 648.

Future Topics

- ***Academic Politics***
- ***College Admissions***
- ***Preventing Youth Violence***

THE CQ Researcher

PUBLISHED BY CONGRESSIONAL QUARTERLY INC.

Academic Politics

Is political correctness a problem on college campuses?

Five years after news accounts raised the specter of U.S. campuses awash in "political correctness," academics and political activists are still battling over the direction of higher education. The academic community, said to be dominated by liberals, has provoked a conservative backlash that is reaching new degrees of mobilization. Some critics charge that many professors try to indoctrinate students rather than educate them, and that tenured faculty superstars do little teaching. Others complain about the rise of multicultural studies and campus anti-harassment codes. In the face of such challenges, academics accustomed to a significant say in the governance of colleges and universities are revisiting age-old debates about the limits of academic freedom.

INSIDE THIS ISSUE

CQ | Feb. 16, 1996 • Volume 6, No. 7 • Pages 145-168

Formerly Editorial Research Reports

ACADEMIC POLITICS

COVER: GEORGETOWN UNIVERSITY, WASHINGTON, D.C. (CREDIT: R. MICHAEL JENKINS)

The CQ Researcher

Feb. 16, 1996
Volume 6, No. 7

The CQ Researcher (ISSN 1056-2036). Formerly Editorial Research Reports. Published weekly (48 times per year, not printed the first Friday of any month with five Fridays) by Congressional Quarterly Inc., 1414 22nd St., N.W., Washington, D.C. 20037. Rates are furnished upon request. Second-class postage paid at Washington, D.C. POSTMASTER: Send address changes to The CQ Researcher, 1414 22nd St., N.W., Washington, D.C. 20037.

Academic Politics

By Charles S. Clark

The Issues

When recruiters for Oberlin College held an open house recently in Washington, D.C., a parent raised an issue that would have been unimaginable a decade earlier. After viewing a film stressing the Ohio school's history as the first U.S. college to admit women and blacks, the father of a high school senior stood and asked, "Is there much political correctness on the campus?"

Yes, it is a problem, particularly in certain departments, an alumnus replied, noting that there are even separate dormitories for black students who desire them. The parent came away suspecting that Oberlin is perhaps "too bent on changing the world and not intent enough on understanding it. That may not be fair," he adds, "but I didn't think it was the right place for my daughter."

College officials resist the suggestion that incoming freshmen — and the parents who foot their bills — should be wary of the atmosphere on today's campuses. "Oberlin is a self-selecting place, where people come for intellectual rigor and commitment to social change," says school Vice President Young Dawkins. Nonetheless, he says that when he asked Oberlin students about political correctness on campus, "I was surprised at the uniformity of the answers: There *is* a small pocket of political correctness, as there is at any school, but it has downsurged. Students now are much more concerned about financial aid."

It has been five years since a flurry of newspapers and magazines trumpeted the arrival of political correctness, bringing its alleged epidemic of leftist campus "thought police," speech codes, sensitivity training and politicized professors pushing multicultural curricula.

And while the term "PC" has grown stale from overuse, the political clashes that spawned it persist. (*See story, p. 152.*) A chief reason, observers argue, is demographics: While students in the 1990s have been increasingly conservative and career-minded, their counterparts from the 1960s, an era when U.S. campuses erupted in radical protest, have assumed their places as tenured faculty.

Also altering the landscape are increases in the number of faculty who are female and minority. Only 43 percent of newly hired faculty are U.S.-born, male and white, compared with 59 percent of senior faculty, according to a recent Education Department survey. [1]

To many, the effect of all these changes can be worrisome. When it comes to curricula, "there aren't many rules now," says Stephen H. Balch, president of the National Association of Scholars (NAS), an academic-reform group. "Back in the 1960s, there were [required] core courses, with only two to three classes to choose among, so there was a common experience. Nowadays, it's a smorgasbord."

To make matters worse, Balch says, "Over the past 20 years, more and more academics have taken up advocacy positions. As more minority students attend college, many of these professors see them as political fodder to create a mass of alienated people. It's a disservice" to education.

David Horowitz, a onetime Marxist who is now a noted conservative critic of academia, recalls that higher education in the late 1950s "embraced a self-defined, disinterested pursuit of learning. Today, it embraces social transformation," he complains. "Professors have this Rousseauist idea that we're here to end war, racism and discrimination, and all that is required is changing social construction. 'What prevents this?' they ask themselves. The answer is bad attitudes and ideas, which is why liberals can't tolerate dissent on such issues as gay or women's studies."

Evidence for such charges is anecdotal. Conservative advocacy groups such as Accuracy in Academia circulate "exposés" of professors such as Vassar College's Wendy Graham, whose American literature course puts what critics deride as an overbearing emphasis on homoerotic interpretations of works by F. Scott Fitzgerald and Ernest Hemingway. [2] Conservatives also have criticized Cornell University for investigating plant pathology Professor James R. Aist, a born-again Christian who angered gay rights activists by posting flyers on campus announcing that "Homosexuals can change." [3]

Conservative students concerned about political bias have taken to poring over voter registration rolls to check the party affiliations of their professors. A tabulation of liberal arts faculty at Cornell and Stanford found only 17 Republicans and 163 Democrats at Stanford and 171 Democrats and only 7 Republicans at Cornell. On both campuses, the most lopsided

How College Students View Political Correctness on Campus

Slightly more than half of 749 college students surveyed last year agreed that students are concerned with being politically correct, and more than 60 percent said this concern had affected their behavior.

Most students on your campus are concerned about being politically correct:

Total Population

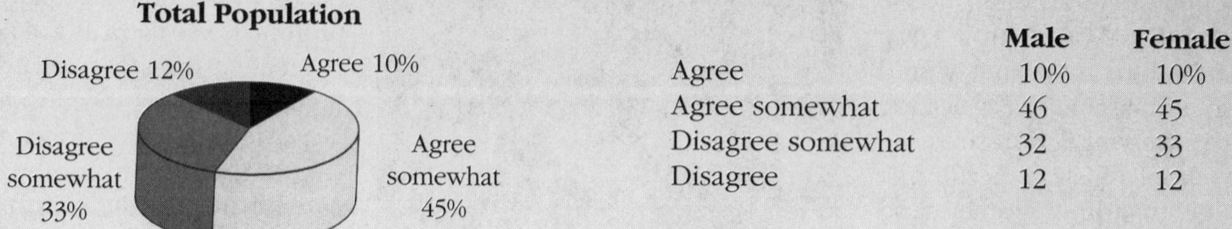

	Male	Female
Agree	10%	10%
Agree somewhat	46	45
Disagree somewhat	32	33
Disagree	12	12

Students sometimes censor their language and adjust their behavior because of political correctness:

Total Population

Disagree 19%
Agree 21%
Disagree somewhat 19%
Agree somewhat 41%

	Male	Female
Agree	21%	22%
Agree somewhat	39	43
Disagree somewhat	20	19
Disagree	21	17

Political correctness has been constructive on your campus:

Total Population

Disagree 19%
Agree 6%
Disagree somewhat 33%
Agree somewhat 43%

	Male	Female
Agree	5%	6%
Agree somewhat	40	46
Disagree somewhat	33	32
Disagree	22	16

Political correctness is just a passing fad:

Total Population

Disagree 14%
Agree 11%
Disagree somewhat 38%
Agree somewhat 38%

	Male	Female
Agree	14%	7%
Agree somewhat	38	38
Disagree somewhat	37	38
Disagree	11	17

There has been a rebellion/backlash against political correctness:

Total Population

Disagree 10%
Agree 17%
Disagree somewhat 33%
Agree somewhat 40%

	Male	Female
Agree	20%	15%
Agree somewhat	39	42
Disagree somewhat	32	34
Disagree	10	10

Source: Playboy, *June 1995; poll conducted by Maritz Research among 749 students on 50 campuses.*

departments were English, women's studies and African-American studies, where in some cases there were no registered Republicans.[4]

Critics of academia also charge that professors don't teach enough, that lifetime tenure for many is an excuse to be lazy or to build a political empire. (*See story, p. 158.*)

The National Review College Guide, a listing of some 60 colleges deemed hospitable to conservatives, also notes what it considers the worst offenders in higher education. Its "academic gulag" consists of Amherst, Brown, the University of California at Berkeley, Michigan, Harvard, Dartmouth, Duke, Pennsylvania, Stanford, Smith, Wesleyan and Yale. They were chosen, the guide explains, because "they do a poor job of teaching undergraduates (or they ignore them altogether); they have eviscerated or abandoned their graduation requirements and academic standards; or they have succumbed to attempts to impose an ideological orthodoxy on the intellectual life of the university."[5]

The reported pressure on today's campus to toe a leftist line is traced to a combination of influences, among them overly opinionated teachers, freshman orientations that seek to alter social attitudes and, of course, the students themselves. Militant groups of students, unchecked by academe's notoriously pliable administrators, are said to create an atmosphere of intimidation that even threatens professors who fail to conform.

"It gets worse as you move from the elite campuses down the academic ladder toward city and community colleges," says sociologist Nathan Glazer, a professor emeritus at Harvard. "At schools with large populations of minorities, it's a particularly bad situation because student leadership is less modulated and less sophisticated, and the press is less likely to cover the events. The professors watch their words, but the students don't have to watch theirs, so that on racial issues things proceed from misunderstood statements to outrage very quickly."

Beyond the anecdotes, there is evidence that the American campus has changed substantially in the past quarter-century, at least partly in the direction so lamented by conservative critics. More than 300 colleges have racial or sexual speech codes," according to the Freedom Forum First Amendment Center. And 85 percent of colleges have redesigned courses to "increase multicultural awareness," according to a recent American Council on Education survey.[6]

But the notion that U.S. campuses have been hijacked by dangerous ideologues strikes many as a stretch. "At some schools, there will always be some young person whose psyche is so fragile that he shouldn't be exposed to certain things," says Jordan E. Kurland, associate general secretary of the American Association of University Professors (AAUP). "But the whole purpose of higher education is to get tossed into the fray. I would like to think that the large majority of people admitted to college with [solid] academic credentials will benefit and not be victimized."

Stuart O. Landry, a retired professor of zoology at the State University of New York, Binghamton, pooh-poohs the idea that young students' minds are "tabula rasas" — blank slates. Charges of indoctrination are a "bum rap," he says. "There may be some professors who want to put something across, but in such courses the students usually say nothing in response. Any course in which the professor is an activist or has a point of view automatically means easy grades. So if all the student has to do is say, 'Yes, I'm in favor of that,' it's the professor who would get manipulated."

To many in the academic community, the barrage of conservative charges about PC-dominated campuses is part of a nationally orchestrated effort to set up a strawman and knock it down, an effort to roll back the clock on progressive scholarship. "It began in the 1950s with William F. Buckley Jr. and the Young Americans for Freedom," says Ellen Messer-Davidow, an associate professor of English at the University of Minnesota. "By the '70s, the [conservative] movement had built numerous think tanks, training institutes, legal centers, advoacy groups and foundations to become a huge social and cultural infrastructure."

"They've been brilliant in pulling together different strains, such as the Christian right, neoconservatives and libertarians," she adds. "And now they have organized conservative alumni and trustees and the coordinated archipelago of conservative student newspapers to target progressive trends and bring pressure on college presidents to hire and fire and change policies. That's who invented political correctness."

Scott Jaschik, deputy managing editor of *The Chronicle of Higher Education,* which regularly reports on PC controversies, says the number of alleged incidents seems quite small given that there are 3,300 colleges and universities, including "many in more conservative parts of the country where ideological norms are different from those at Northeastern colleges. In recent years," he says, "there have been more accusations, but it's hard to tell whether there are more incidents or just more people on the right who see going to the press as a way of dealing with it." What is clear, he adds, is that "we have not seen signs that fewer students are applying to elite schools such as Harvard, Yale or Stanford because of stories about political correctness."

The direction the debate is likely to take next will hinge largely on the following questions:

Is political correctness a threat on today's campus?

"PC: Alive and Entrenched," reads a chapter heading in a recent book by

How Professors View the Campus 'Climate'

Women professors and faculty of color are treated fairly on campus, according to more than 80 percent of the teachers responding to a national survey on higher education. However, less than half thought that many courses included minority and feminist perspectives.

Agree "strongly" or "somewhat" with the following statements	Percentage of faculty responding
Faculty of color are treated fairly here	86%
Women faculty are treated fairly here	82
Faculty are committed to welfare of the institution	82
Faculty are strongly interested in academic problems of undergraduates	80
Faculty are interested in students' personal problems	77
Most faculty here are sensitive to the issues of minorities	73
Administrators here act in good faith	64
Student affairs staff have the support and respect of faculty	60
Many courses include minority group perspectives	40
There is little trust between minority student groups and campus administrators	37
Many courses include feminist perspectives	32
People here don't treat each other with enough respect	31
Faculty feel that most students are well-prepared academically	25
There is a lot of campus racial conflict here	14

Source: The American College Teacher: National Norms for the 1992-93 HERI Faculty Survey, Higher Education Research Institute, University of California, Los Angeles, May 1993. The survey includes the responses of 29,771 faculty at 289 two-year and four-year colleges and universities.

Lynne V. Cheney, the conservative former chair of the National Endowment for the Humanities (NEH). She makes her case with a string of anecdotes, beginning with the tale of a University of Michigan sophomore who got into trouble over the way he began an essay on why people brush-off pollsters. He used what Cheney agrees was an immature approach: "Let's say Dave Stud is entertaining three beautiful ladies in his penthouse when the phone rings. . . ." But the female teaching assistant who graded his paper called it "offensive" and threatened to file formal sexual harassment charges if future writings took the same tack.[7] (*See story, p. 162.*)

To Neil Hamilton, a professor at the William Mitchell College of Law in St. Paul, Minn., the tell-tale PC issue is affirmative action.[8] He wrote his 1995 book, *Zealotry and Academic Freedom,* after campus officials investigated him in response to a memo he wrote criticizing affirmative action in admissions and hiring, which a colleague had leaked to some black students.

"The charges are moral turpitude, which is how [Sen. Joseph] McCarthy began his charges" about Communists in the 1950s, Hamilton says. "I'm not saying things are as repressive as they were during the McCarthy era, when there were firings. But [now] there is an institutionalized apparatus for investigation and tribunal. Intellectuals tend to be leftists, and faculty tend to be more ideological than the general population. [Campus officials] view disagreement as heresy. Though only a small subset of professors are true radicals," he adds, "the others tend to do nothing about it, which feeds the zealotry."

Christina Hoff Sommers, a professor of philosophy at Clark University in Worcester, Mass., and author of the 1994 book *Who Stole Feminism?*, says: "You can't overstate the politicization of campuses. It would be hard to find an English Department in any kind of university that doesn't focus on the political meaning of books — if they acknowledge there is such a thing as great books."

While Marxism and the literary theory known as deconstructionism have been discredited, she says, "feminism is going strong. It's nearly impossible to get a job if you can't pass the feminist litmus test. And whereas traditional scholars thought it was fair to include at least one professor with a different point of view — one Marxist or one deconstructionist — nowadays the feminists who have power don't feel at all obligated to bring in a traditionalist."

To Balch of the NAS, proof of PC's widespread influence is "the extracurricular sideshow, the residential life programs and sensitivity sessions that instruct [conservative] students on their 'troglodyte' prejudices. Freshman orientation is no longer just how to get to the health center, etc., but how to change your attitudes on race, sex and homophobia," he says.

Take a look at the speakers invited to campuses, adds Horowitz, president of the Center for the Study of Popular Culture in Studio City, Calif. "You get a conservative about once every three to four years. I've visited about 60 campuses, and only twice was I invited by the administration with campus funding. There's not one university where I'm welcome." What's more, Horowitz says, the students he meets have nearly all read books by liberals such as Noam Chomsky, but few have even heard of classic conservative thinkers such as Friedrich von Hayek or Ludwig von Mises.

To many in academia, such fears are not to be taken seriously. "The term political correctness is used as indiscriminately as Dunkin' Donuts," says Catherine R. Stimpson, who holds the title of "university professor" at Rutgers University and is currently director of fellows at the John D. and Catherine T. MacArthur Foundation. "But if we define the term to mean having rigid attitudes, then it is as minor now as it always was."

"There are important underlying demographic and intellectual changes going on on campus," she says. "Like America itself, it is becoming a different, more inclusive society. The blathering of fools from all points on the ideological spectrum is as much with us as death or taxes. But for every person who wishes to punish someone for a racial epithet, there is someone else who would stop women's studies in its tracks. There are people who simply want no changes."

Harvard's Glazer, while agreeing that there is an atmosphere of intimidation on campuses, points out that conservatives today are well represented, too. "The conservative journal is an established tradition, and though an outspoken conservative professor may have difficulty getting hired, there are conservative departments, at Boston University, for example."

Kurland of the AAUP rejects both the view that political correctness is widespread and that it is not cause for concern. "Where the truth resides depends on which day you ask me," he says. "But when you look at the whole of the academic community, you see that any trend or fad or zealotry or movement can be red-hot at particular institutions while others haven't even heard of it."

A survey of 30,000 college teachers across the country shows slightly liberal political leanings. Four percent describe themselves as being on the far left; 39 percent say they're liberal;

Continued on p. 153

How Professors View Campus Priorities

Recruiting minorities and promoting multiculturalism were considered high-priority institutional issues by slightly more than half of the professors responding to a national survey on higher education. But less than a third of the faculty members thought their schools put a high priority on teaching students how to change society.

Institutional Priorities Rated "Highest" or "High"	Percentage of faculty responding
Promote students' intellectual development	79%
Increase or maintain institutional prestige	69
Enhance institution's national image	58
Help students examine and understand their personal values	52
Recruit more minority students	52
Create a diverse multicultural campus environment	51
Develop a sense of community among students and faculty	48
Hire more minority faculty and administrators	47
Develop leadership ability among students	44
Hire more women faculty and administrators	42
Promote student involvement in community service activities	31
Help students learn how to bring about change in American society	28
Hire faculty "stars"	20

Source: The American College Teacher: National Norms for the 1992-93 HERI Faculty Survey, Higher Education Research Institute, University of California, Los Angeles, May 1993. The survey includes the responses of 29,771 faculty at 289 two-year and four-year institutions.

'Political Correctness' Wasn't Born Yesterday

Careful conversationalists have an easy way to throw a safety net under a risky opinion nowadays. They simply add the preface: "This may not sound politically correct, but. . . ."

Yet in the five years since the term swooped onto mainstream America's radar screen, "political correctness" has become an irony wrapped in an insult wrapped in a joke.

The phrase was first used commonly among 1930s Stalinists to evoke, in sociologist Todd Gitlin's phrase, "a sense of historical certitude." [1] In the 1980s, it was expropriated by conservative campus activists to conjure up an Alice-in-Wonderland world of ultimate unreason, in which sentencing comes before trial and words mean whatever one wishes.

Beginning with a reference in a well-noted *New York Times* article by Richard Bernstein in October 1990, [2] the term "political correctness" was popularized in stories about campus intolerance in *New York* magazine, *Newsweek, The New York Review of Books* and *The Atlantic*. A Nexus database search of periodicals shows that the phrase or its variants appeared only 28 times in 1988, 48 times in 1989 and 102 times in 1990. Then it took off, appearing 619 times in 1991, 963 times in 1992, 1,512 times in 1993, 1,549 times in 1994 and 1,428 times in 1995.

The phrase arrived on the best-seller list in 1994 with James Finn Garner's satirical *Politically Correct Bedtime Stories*. Its variant, "Politically Incorrect," has been the subject of a copyright dispute between comedian Jackie Mason and the producers of a popular Comedy Central television show. And more recently on campus, its use has spiraled to obscure rhetorical levels — a mysterious organization at the University of Maryland calls itself the Politically Incorrect Coalition Against Feminazis.

Historically, the first known reference is traced to a 1793 Supreme Court case, in which a justice is on record as noting: "This is not politically correct." [3]

Definitions of the term are still evolving. Author Dinesh D'Souza, whose 1991 book *Illiberal Education* did much to launch the debate on the issue, cites a recent dictionary entry describing political correctness as "marked by or adhering to a typically progressive orthodoxy on issues involving especially race, gender, sexual affinity or ecology." [4]

Bernstein of the *Times* has noted that political correctness is "a sort of unofficial ideology of the university." [5] University of Massachusetts sociologist Paul Hollander favors a definition that speaks of "the drive to cast all matters of culture and intellect in political terms." [6]

At elite universities, political correctness is "a form of snobbery that is easily made fun of by the right," says *Time* magazine's liberal essayist Barbara Ehrenreich. [7] "How can anyone defend an expression that sounds so prim, narrow and inquisitorial?" wonders Harvard English Professor Robert Brustein. [8]

Hardly anyone does defend it, liberals hasten to point out. That's because it is nearly always the conservatives who invoke the phrase. "Politically correct was originally an approving phrase on the Leninist left to denote someone who steadfastly toed the party line," writes Paul Berman, editor of *Debating PC: The Controversy Over Political Correctness on College Campuses*. "Then it evolved into 'PC', an ironic phrase among wised-up leftists [in the 1960s and '70s] to denote someone whose line-toeing was too much to bear. Only in conjunction with the PC debate itself did the phrase get picked up by people who had no fidelity to radicalism at all, but who relished the nasty syllables for their twist of irony." [9]

John Wilson, a University of Chicago graduate student who works with the liberal group Teachers for a Democratic Culture, says that conservatives who rail against "PC" seem to miss the point that the original leftists used the phrase self-mockingly. "The conservatives' distaste for radicals is such that they refuse even to acknowledge stealing political correctness from leftists," he writes. "To admit this would suggest the presence of critical elements (and a sense of humor) on the left." [10]

There are signs that many are growing weary of the term. At a conference on advocacy in the classroom last June, a professor requested that speakers banish the phrase because it "came from hate-filled people who defended the status quo and were trying to stifle debate." [11]

Luther Keith, assistant managing editor at the *Detroit News,* recently took his fellow journalists to task for "tossing the phrase willy-nilly into all manner of 'objective' news stories apparently without realizing — or not caring — that doing so fuels the fires of racial and gender intolerance." [12]

Neil Hamilton, a professor at the William Mitchell Law School in St. Paul, Minn., says, "Political correctness has been given so many meanings that it has become meaningless." He offers a more precise alternative: "faculty fundamentalism from the radical academic left."

---

[1] Todd Gitlin, *The Twilight of Common Dreams* (1995), p. 169.

[2] Richard Bernstein, "The Rising Hegemony of the Politically Correct," *The New York Times,* Oct. 28, 1990.

[3] See John Wilson, *The Myth of Political Correctness* (1995), p. 3.

[4] Dinesh D'Souza, *Illiberal Education* (revised 1992), p. xiv.

[5] Bernstein, *op. cit.*

[6] Paul Hollander, " 'Imagined Tyranny': Political Correctness Reconsidered," *Academic Questions,* fall 1994, p. 51.

[7] Barbara Ehrenreich, "The Challenge for the Left," in Paul Berman, ed., *Debating PC: The Controversy Over Political Correctness on College Campuses* (1992), p. 335.

[8] Robert Brustein, "Dumbocracy in America," *Partisan Review,* fall 1993, p. 527.

[9] Berman, *op. cit.,* p. 5.

[10] Wilson, *op. cit.,* p. 5.

[11] Thomas Reeves, "Partisan Revelry at the Advocacy Conference," *Academe,* fall 1995, p. 53.

[12] Luther Keith, "That Troubling Term: 'Political Correctness,' " *Editor & Publisher,* Dec. 23, 1995, p. 40.

Continued from p. 151

35 percent say middle of the road; 21 percent say conservative; and 0.5 percent say they're on the far right, according to 1992-93 data from the University of California, Los Angeles (UCLA). Only 45 percent of the teachers overall say that "influencing social values" is a personal goal (female faculty members were slightly higher, at 55 percent). [9]

Among students, a survey for *Playboy* magazine published last June found 55 percent saying that most students on campus were concerned about being politically correct, while 57 percent said there had been a rebellion or backlash against political correctness. But last April, in a survey confined to 600 randomly selected students and faculty at Carleton College, in Northfield, Minn., 73 percent agreed that "political correctness interferes with honest discussion of diversity."

Christopher Long, vice president of the Intercollegiate Studies Institute, which promotes conservative ideas on campus, says that investigators of PC need look no further than the college course catalogues, which demonstrate a preoccupation with issues of race, gender, class and sex. At Yale, the "crazy courses" that Long's group derides include Elizabeth Wilson's English course, "The Story of Incest," and Jessica Branch's "Constructing Lesbian Identities."

The most conspicuous target of anti-PC attacks is the Modern Language Association (MLA), a century-old group of humanities professors who meet annually to share new research. They were ridiculed last year by *The New Criterion,* a conservative journal of the arts, for offering workshops that focused less on the classics of the literary canon than on newly fashionable gay liberation studies, with titles such as "The Epistemology of the Queer Classroom: A Roundtable." [10]

MLA members, long accustomed to such criticism, point out that their organization of 32,000 is a "big tent," and that literature from time immemorial has evoked passion and controversy. Phyllis Franklin, the group's executive director, points out that professors are "under major pressure to see things in a new way, to innovate. For each generation, professors must make the material come alive or it becomes hard to teach and make it vital to young people." The rising interest in race, class and gender over the past 20 years simply "introduces that approach and adds it to all that existed before," she explains. "It's not like science, where we drop an incorrect view once it has been succeeded."

Gay themes, she continues, have emerged in studies of literature just as gay issues have "emerged throughout society — in the workplace, the armed forces and churches. How could you have the classroom be isolated from society?"

Franklin, whose organization runs a job bank for professors, is skeptical of reports that political conservatives have trouble getting hired. "It's a shocking statement," she says. "If such a scholar really knows his business, he should be able to come to an interview and talk knowledgeably about all these new approaches and then explain why he wouldn't use them."

Peter Gay, a professor emeritus in history at Yale, says he believes many of the horror stories about political correctness. "But as a liberal," he says, "I am sorry that liberals let PC [get out of control] and allowed the protection of good sense and objectivity to get into the hands of the right wing." Why, Gay adds, should conservatives "be so mad that academia is full of liberals when it's the conservatives who are running the country?"

Are professors meeting their obligations to students?

Last year's MLA conference, held in Chicago in December, offered the usual workshops with attention-grabbing titles, such as "Cinema's Anal Compulsions" and "The Medieval Fetish." To those worried over dwindling requirements that students study Shakespeare, such pursuits reflect an academic community that is not merely searching for fresh approaches but out of touch with its mission.

Such topics "are chosen not to attract students but to impress other professors," says Balch. "This preoccupation with sex and pleasure is a form of decadence. Many professors who are tenured live a comfortable life, and some almost regard the job as a form of a pension. They are more apt to be absorbed with self-fulfillment. The result is a prurience that carries sex to an unwholesome extreme of intellectualization."

Critics have long charged that professors spend their time avoiding undergraduates and publishing in abstruse, low-circulation, ultra-specialized journals. The debate over political correctness has brought new pressures for change, and at public universities there are new pressures from state legislatures. [11]

Senior faculty report spending fewer than 10 hours teaching and eight hours advising students every week, according to the UCLA survey. The number of students assigned to each faculty member has shrunk from 9.8 per professor in 1976 to 8.3 in 1991, note two conservative critics. [12] What's more, faculty whose teaching represents less than half their total work actually earned more than those professors who spend the most time with students. The absence of strong teaching requirements is most notable at major research universities, such as Harvard and Yale.

Indeed, senior faculty's reliance on teaching assistants (TAs) to teach courses was a major issue in the graduate students' strike at Yale that was settled last month. As one striker put it, the university doesn't want to publicize how much teaching the TAs do because it "wants parents to keep believing they pay all this tuition to have their children taught by renowned professors, not lowly teaching assistants." [13]

Laziness does not appear to be the

reason for the limited amount of teaching by professors. As many as 34 percent of the college teachers responding to the UCLA survey reported being under extreme stress, citing time pressures and lack of personal time. And while 99 percent said they wanted to be good teachers, only 10 percent said that faculty on their campus were rewarded for good teaching.

"There are professors who neglect students but whom the university administrators like because they write great books," says Yale's Gay. "We're supposed to be evaluated equally for teaching, research and service to the department, but everyone knows that's not true." Furthermore, the oft-conflicting duties of publishing, teaching at the graduate level and teaching undergraduates each require differing talents, he adds.

SUNY's Landry denies the existence of "a tug-of-war between teaching and research. Teaching and research blend together, particularly when you move up the academic scale," he says. "If you're a student listening to a famous historian, he isn't going to stop to explain things in words of one syllable — if you're not prepared, you won't appreciate it. Bad lecturing does happen. But if a professor is enthusiastic about a subject, it will come through in good teaching."

Landry also cautions college students not to expect the kind of spoon-feeding and detailed instructions that one finds at the elementary and high school levels. "I tell my students that at age 50 I had to teach myself matrix algebra, and if I didn't understand it, I simply went over it again. Many of the students simply don't want to grow up. They need to get to the point where it is all [independent] learning and no teaching."

Glazer of Harvard points out that professors are really like small business operators. "They run their own shops, do research, go to conferences, work with graduate students. I wouldn't know how to change this at the major research universities, where there is little access to professors for undergrads. If you force them to teach, many of the big names will leave."

The interests of scholars are not always the same as the interests of the university, says Balch, noting that many professors' workloads are protected by union contracts. "It would be good for many to be exposed to more undergraduates," he says, "but some of the research is also very important," particularly at the upper-tier schools. "It's not a matter than can be put into some formula."

The charge that many academics sit in intellectual ghettos and spin out insubstantial scholarship has been challenged in strong terms. "To be specialized is not to be trivial," a group of humanities scholars has written. "What may seem obscure and narrow to one not versed in a field may be crucial: The study of the inherited characteristics of fruit flies sounds like an amazingly specialized and pointless subject, until one knows that such studies shed light on fundamental genetic mechanisms. The study of Balinese cockfighting sounds exceedingly recondite, but Clifford Geertz's work on this subject is now a famous piece of ethnography, a central example in the debates about understanding of another culture and the interpretation of ways not our own." [14]

As for the alleged preoccupation with sex, the MLA's Franklin says: "Sex is an important aspect of human life. Poets and novelists have long written about it, so it seems inevitable that scholars would deal with it. It is true that earlier in the century, the scholarship on it was not as explicit and forthright. But that's not just in the academy. Outside in society, on television, things are said today that wouldn't have been said in public before."

Is there too much advocacy in the college classroom?

At Mount Holyoke College in South Hadley, Mass., many students reportedly were put off when a feminist professor railed against heterosexual marriage. Among other things, the professor gave an exam that asked students to discuss the assertion that marriage is a license to abuse women. Many felt their grades would suffer if they disagreed with the premise. "There were no such complaints about politicized grading back when I was writing Marxist papers at Columbia," Horowitz says, "and that was during the McCarthy period."

Sommers says she was "shocked" when she interviewed radical scholars for her book. "I'd always assumed you presented both sides of an argument," says the philosophy professor. "It never occurred to me to offer my view as correct. These professors use the class to indoctrinate, and the classroom gets compromised. I'd say about 10-20 percent of the young women they teach turn into angry feminists. The other 80 percent leave simply ignorant of their ethnic and cultural heritage."

Besides women's studies, the most politicized departments on campus are English composition and history, according to Balch. "In many introductory composition classes, which are required, the professors are much less concerned with how students write, and more with how they think about ethnic or gay studies. A traditional liberal education is intended to get students to think, and while traditional professors may have their own views, their object is not to turn their students into their clones."

The notion that professors commonly seek to indoctrinate students seems a "straw-woman" to Susan McGee Bailey, executive director of the Wellesley College Center for Research on Women. "I don't think I can recall any woman who worked with us as having grown angered or disillusioned with the importance of the issues we work with. It is critically important that perspectives of gender, race and class be brought to bear. Previously, the people in history, economics and political science assumed that all questions were being asked. Women's and ethnic studies have since showed that not all perspectives were being included."

Asked why English courses are sometimes taught with political texts, Rutgers' Stimpson says: "Good writing, good reading and good thinking are inseparable. You don't learn grammar only by rules of punctuation in a vacuum. You learn with good arguments, dialogue and critical thinking. You learn to write in an authentic voice while also mastering competency in our common language. There are a thousand ways to skin this particular cat. The end we seek can be reached through a variety of honorable means."

Yale's Gay believes indoctrination is improbable. "You have to make distinctions between what courses students *can* take and what they *need* to take," he says. "At Brown, there is extreme freedom from [academic] requirements. Yale, too, has an open program, a smorgasbord. As the students network during the shopping-around period, they collect syllabi and try to calculate whether there's less work in course A or course B. So the idea that you can force them into a right- or left-wing cookie-cutter approach is unlikely."

"Personally, I've been very good about my politics," Gay continues. "It's no secret I'm a liberal Democrat, but I keep that out of it, unlike a friend of mine at the University of Colorado, who once joked to a class, 'It's so simple, even a Republican can understand it.' During President [Ronald] Reagan's first term, I made an anti-Reagan joke that seemed appropriate. But the kids hissed me, and I said, 'You're absolutely right. I wouldn't wear a political button to class.' "

"Still, my guess is we all inject something," Gay continues. "The positive view I take of the French Revolution is today not fashionable. But my position would come out. We're only human. And if a student objects, I must think of how to react. If I had an extreme right-winger on my hands, I would be put off, but I wouldn't penalize him."

Any indoctrination is too much, whether left or right, says the AAUP's Kurland. "Some people want to sell something to a captive audience, but that's not what they're getting paid to do." Kurland cautions, however, that "the number of actual cases in which professors had to be removed or thwarted is happily minuscule. When a dean hears a complaint from alumni or a concerned parent, he should make the professor aware that someone is out there monitoring the situation. But it would be out of order to tell the professor that he has to shut up or the student will quit, and the alumni won't give money."

Last June, the MLA joined with 15 other groups to sponsor a conference in Pittsburgh on advocacy in the classroom. Some 300 academics attended sessions on such topics as "Is advocacy inevitable?" and "Feminism in the academy." Conferees also reviewed the AAUP's 1940 manifesto on tenure, which declared that "teachers are entitled to freedom in the classroom in discussing their subject, but they should be careful not to introduce to their teaching controversial matter which has no relation to their subject."

That statement was expanded in 1970 to note: "The intent of this statement is not to discourage what is 'controversial.' Controversy is at the heart of the free academic inquiry which the entire statement is designed to foster. The passage serves to underscore the need for teachers to avoid persistently intruding material which has no relation to their subject."

Also heard at the conference was a statement from Nadine Strossen, president of the American Civil Liberties Union. She noted that a teacher's own judgment forms a part of academic material, "which should include presentation of divergent opinions and doctrines" delivered "without the assumption that they are settled in advance or that there is only one 'right' answer." Also quoted was a former AAUP general counsel, who has noted that "evidence is not to be distorted," and that professors should "treat with respect the students who disagree."

Gerald Graff, a University of Chicago English professor who heads the liberal group Teachers for a Democratic Culture, questioned whether it is possible or even attractive to have balance within a single class, and suggested that a better approach would be encouraging the student to seek balance in the over-all courses and perspectives offered on campus.

Michael Olivas, the current AAUP general counsel, noted that some accusations of "advocacy in the classroom often turn upon characteristics ascribed by students to their teachers (e.g. that women teachers are feminists, favor women and are 'soft on social issues,' or that black professors are 'too sensitive' on issues of race." [15]

Overall, there was "almost unanimous agreement that indoctrination is unacceptable," says the MLA's Franklin. "There is no doubt that there have been some cases of poor judgment, but I was stunned by the consensus at this meeting."

Less impressed was Thomas C. Reeves, a professor of history at the University of Wisconsin, Parkside, who faulted conference planners for not inviting more conservatives and mocked some speakers for dismissing well-known critics of PC as merely "angry, anti-intellectual and nostalgic." [16] ■

BACKGROUND

Protecting Professors

The stereotype of professors as pampered and isolated goes back at least to economist Adam Smith, who noted in the *Wealth of Nations* that he had abandoned Oxford University in the 1740s because the professors had "given up altogether even the pretence of teaching." [17]

Ridicule of esoteric research by MLA members goes back to the group's founding in 1883. "It was kinder and gentler back then," notes Franklin, in contrast with today's critics of political correctness, who bring a "take-no-prisoners tone to the debate." In times of high unemployment, she says, the academy always comes in for criticism, particularly from writers and poets who resent people who appear to have cushy jobs while they have to live off their sales. "A lot depends on what is going on outside in society."

It was the acerbic H.L. Mencken who wrote early in this century that "the professor must be an obscurantist or he is nothing. He has a special unmatchable talent for dullness; his central aim is not to expose the truth clearly but to exhibit his profundity — in brief to stagger the sophomores and other professors." [18]

The academy, however, also has fostered debate over dead-serious issues. In his history of academic zealotry, law Professor Hamilton identifies six waves of persecution that occurred before the current controversies: the 19th-century fights over Darwinism and evolution; criticism of the academy from Gilded Age industrialists; the fights over patriotism during World War I; anti-communism before World War II; the McCarthy period; and the New Left radicalism of the 1960s.

It was for the protection of academe's ivy-covered walls that the AAUP was founded in 1915, with celebrated educator John Dewey of Columbia University as president. Its declaration of principles, based on the writings of Johns Hopkins Professor A.O. Lovejoy, stated that a university "should be an intellectual experiment station, where new ideas may germinate and where their fruit, though still distasteful to the community as a whole, may be allowed to ripen until finally, perchance, it may become a part of the accepted intellectual food of the nation or of the world." [19]

Five years later, the AAUP declared, "faculty should be the legislative body for all matters concerning the educational policy of the university." It was a bitter pill for college presidents, regents and alumni. Indeed, it was a direct challenge to a system in which a socialist professor could be fired from a major state university for criticizing the use of child labor by coal-mining companies.

The McCarthy Uproar

While the AAUP was successful at creating the modern tenure system in 1940, it was less adept at defending the scores of professors who would lose their posts during the anti-communist hysteria of the late 1940s and early '50s. (A 1955 survey identified at least 126 professors whose jobs had been threatened, most of them at elite schools. [20])

The AAUP held meetings and drafted statements, but historians agree that it failed to respond to McCarthyism forcefully. "What can any college president do when the Un-American Activities Committee, or anyone else, phones him to say that Professor X is a card-carrying member of the [Communist] Party?" read a proposed policy statement. "He can say, 'I'm not interested,' and hang up. If a college is to protect the freedom by which alone it exists in the tradition of democratic education, it has got to run the risk" of hanging up. [21]

It would require new AAUP leadership in the mid-1950s to get the organization to take a tougher stand. By this time, a young conservative named William F. Buckley Jr., author of a 1951 attack on the academy called *God and Man at Yale,* had helped to galvanize an organized conservative movement. In a 1956 essay, he made his now-famous gibe about the academy's reputation for liberalism: "I would rather be governed by the first 2,000 names in the Boston telephone directory than by the 2,000 members of the faculty at Harvard University." [22]

Though the 1950s are often remembered as a peaceful, conformist era, they brought signs of the coming dispute over the sanctity of the Western literary canon. "With the new generation of students, Milton declines in the curriculum, even Shakespeare has lost heavily; Homer and Virgil are practically gone," wrote poet and Kenyon College Professor John Crowe Ransom in 1958. "The literary interest of the students today is 90 percent in literature of their own age." [23]

An Age of Divisions

In the economic boom years of the 1960s, a stream of federal research grants gave thousands of American academics new jobs and the accompanying academic freedom. Many threw themselves into the race to "publish or perish." A Brookings Institution survey of 3,000 professors early in the decade showed that up to two-thirds of the courses at big universities were being taught by teaching assistants, and that most senior professors wanted to reduce their teaching time even further. [24]

When campuses exploded over civil rights and the Vietnam War, professors found themselves on the hot seat. Many watched with mixed loyalties as students took over administration buildings and police arrived to quell rioting. A 1969 survey of 60,000 professors by the Carnegie Commission on Higher Education found that 3 percent approved of the demonstrations unreservedly, 40 percent approved with reservations, 42 percent disapproved with reservations and 16 percent unreservedly disapproved. [25]

Continued on p. 159

Chronology

1900-1940s

U.S. professors organize to govern American colleges and universities, copying the German model of "academic villages"; McCarthyism tests professors.

1915
Formation of American Association of University Professors (AAUP).

1940
Release of AAUP statement on academic freedom, tenure and due process.

1949
AAUP drafts statements but fails to respond forcefully to McCarthy-period charges that many professors are communists.

1950s-1960s

Conservatives begin challenging the educational establishment; student unrest rocks campuses, prompts new studies in race, class and gender.

1951
Conservative Yale student William F. Buckley Jr. attacks higher education in *God and Man at Yale.*

1953
Formation of the conservative Intercollegiate Studies Institute.

1960
University of Illinois Professor Leo Koch is fired after his letter condoning premarital sex is printed in a student newspaper.

1969
Black power advocate Angela Davis is fired from the University of California for being a member of the Communist party.

1970s-1980s

Marxism, feminism and a theory of literary analysis known as "deconstructionism" transform the academy. Conservative backlash arises against perceived leftist domination of campus.

1970
AAUP defends the academic freedom of Angela Davis, charged with aiding black militant prisoner George Jackson.

1980
Supreme Court says professors' "authority in academic matters is absolute."

1985
Accuracy in Academia is founded to investigate alleged indoctrination by professors.

1987
National Association of Scholars seeks to "resist the ideological misuse of teaching and scholarship"; Stanford University broadens traditional Western curriculum in wake of protests by black students.

1990s ***Rise of debate over "political correctness."***

Oct. 28, 1990
Richard Bernstein's *New York Times* article on campus intolerance launches debate on political correctness.

1991
Publication of Dinesh D'Souza's *Illiberal Education;* AAUP releases tentative statement on political correctness, accusing critics of opposing equal opportunity.

May 4, 1991
President George Bush criticizes political correctness in speech at the University of Michigan.

1992
American Academy for Liberal Education is founded as new accrediting body focusing on Western traditions.

September 1994
Court reverses suspension of veteran University of New Hampshire teacher J. Donald Silva for classroom comments deemed sexually harassing by students.

March 1995
Yale University returns $20 million donation to Texas billionaire Lee Bass after professors disagree on his proposed Western Civilization curriculum; National Alumni Forum launched.

June 1995
Modern Language Association conference explores charges of advocacy in the classroom.

October 1995
Supreme Court lets stand lower court ruling that City University of New York acted fairly in demoting Leonard Jeffries from chairmanship of black studies after he allegedly made racist and anti-Semitic remarks; conference on "Zealotry and Academic Freedom" is held at William Mitchell College of Law in St. Paul, Minn.

Tenure: An Idea Whose Time Has Come and Gone?

Whenever the Ivory Tower comes under siege, critics of academia, as well as members of the public, complain that the nation's elite of tenured professors live in a tweedy, protective bubble.

"Tenure corrupts, enervates and dulls higher education," conservative author Charles J. Sykes writes in his 1988 book *ProfScam*. "It is, moreover, the academic culture's ultimate control mechanism to weed out the idiosyncratic, the creative, the nonconformist. The replacement of lifetime tenure with fixed-term renewable contracts would, at one stroke, restore accountability, while potentially freeing the vast untapped energies of the academy that have been locked in the petrified grip of a tenured professoriate." [1]

The university is "the most pervasive socialist institution in our free-market society," says David Horowitz, co-editor of *Heterodoxy* magazine and a critic of political correctness. [2] "There's no bottom line like there is in business, where you can go bankrupt, or in science, where your research can fail. Radicals understand that, so I say get rid of tenure so that everyone has to perform."

Scholar Martin Anderson of the conservative Hoover Institute proposes "grandfathering out" the tenure system. "Professors who are good don't need tenure, and those who need tenure usually aren't very good," he writes. [3]

The idea of lifetime tenure dates back to the Middle Ages, when scholars who were funded by powerful princes and barons felt the need to be protected against retaliation from patrons who disapproved of a learned work's conclusions. It was institutionalized during the 19th century in the "academic village" universities of Germany, from which the American academy borrowed heavily.

The U.S. system, formally instituted in 1940, was a reaction against instances in which professors were dismissed for taking stands. Someone who advocated, say, restrictions on Chinese immigration, could be fired by an industrialist like Leland Stanford or his wife, co-founders of the university bearing their name, and whose railways were built using Chinese labor. Or an economist advocating New Deal reforms in the 1930s might be threatened by a state university president who favored free-market economics.

The legal framework for tenure was based on the freedom principles outlined in a 1938 report to the American Association of University Professors (AAUP) and the Association of American Colleges. It called for a system based on "freedom of teaching, of research and of extra-mural activities" and "a sufficient degree of economic security to make the profession attractive to men and women of ability." The report further proposed that professors who survived a probationary period be presumed permanent, and "that the services of the teacher or investigator in question can be terminated by the institution only for adequate cause and after a fair hearing, except in the case of retirement for age." [4]

Tenured professors can still be fired for malfeasance and incompetence. And in recent years, fiscal crises have prompted some financially strapped institutions to consider dismissing tenured professors as part of restructuring plans. Some were actually let go at Bennington College in Vermont, and dismissals were narrowly averted at California's San Diego State University. The process has been carefully monitored by the university professors association. [5]

As professors increasingly stay on the job longer into old age, college administrators rely more on untenured graduate students, associates and adjunct professors to avoid expensive commitments to tenure.

"There is always talk about abolishing tenure, and many colleges don't have it," says Nathan Glazer, a Harvard University sociologist emeritus. "But not having it is actually more expensive. You have to review people every five years and have more meetings. The alternative to tenure is having a strong administration. But this is unthinkable because of the power of the professors as a union. The professoriate is an integral part of university government, and that is hard to change."

What's more, not all critics of the politicized campus agree that killing tenure will advance their cause. "If you abolish tenure, the first ones to go would be the conservatives, because we're in the minority," says Christina Hoff Sommers, a professor of philosophy at Clark University in Worcester, Mass.

Stuart O. Landry, a retired professor of zoology at the State University of New York, Binghamton, notes that "tenure and job security are not the same thing. Tenure is supposed to be awarded cautiously, not just because someone has tried for seven years. It is also a privilege that confers upon you an obligation to do things such as serve on committees and, when appropriate, to stand up in the faculty Senate and say, 'Mr. President, you don't know what you're talking about.' "

"People within academia don't always appreciate their extraordinary opportunity to speak forthrightly," adds Todd Gitlin, a sociologist at New York University, "while people on the outside don't always appreciate the importance of academic freedom."

The university professors association views tenure as a way to enhance educational quality. Jordan E. Kurland, the group's associate general secretary, says "abolishing tenure has been an issue since the invention of tenure. But there is little chance of it happening at major universities. Courts have made it legally impossible to abolish existing tenure, only prospective tenure. So institutions must deal with fitness in individual cases."

---

[1] Charles J. Sykes, *ProfScam: Professors and the Demise of Higher Education* (1988), p. 258.

[2] *Heterodoxy*, published by the Center for the Study of Popular Culture, Studio City, Calif., covers freedom-of-speech issues.

[3] Martin Anderson, *Impostors in the Temple* (1992), p. 121.

[4] American Association of University Professors, "75 Years: A Retrospective on the Occasion of the Seventy-Fifth Annual Meeting," *Academe*, May-June 1989, p. 10.

[5] See *Academe*, March-April 1993, p. 94, and March-April 1995, p. 91.

Continued from p. 156

By the 1970s, many newly hired professors in sociology, history, economics and political science departments were combining academic work with political organizing. It was a sharp contrast to the fear-ridden McCarthy era. Barbara Foley, for example, a Marxist professor at the University of Chicago, was busy recruiting students for a group called the International Committee Against Racism and selling newspapers for the Progressive Labor Party. [26]

But the most prominent example of the professor as pied piper was Yale "deconstructionist" Paul de Man. Though his literary theories were tough to follow, his charisma charmed students and faculty alike. "At the literature lectures, everyone on the faculty watched de Man's face, to gauge his reaction," writes academic memoirist Alice Kaplan. She and her friends described deconstructionism as "when you figure out that a story or a poem is in the wrong — not because the author is lying but because there is something inherently deceitful about language. . . . It's the deconstructive critic's job to find the places where language breaks down, by looking up close and finding language's sleight of hand." [27]

Traditionalists were put off by de Man's belief that an author's intended meaning is less important than the effect of his text. His reputation suffered a few years after his death, when in 1987 it was revealed that as a young Belgian in the 1940s he had written for pro-Nazi newspapers.

Conservative Backlash

By the mid-1980s, with the Reagan administration in power, conservatives had launched a new attack on academia's perceived drift away from traditional Western education.

In 1984, NEH chairman and later Education Secretary William J. Bennett wrote an indictment called "To Reclaim a Legacy: A Report on Humanities in Higher Education." He was followed in 1987 by University of Chicago classicist Allan Bloom, whose book *The Closing of the American Mind* blasted the rise of "cultural relativism" in the academy. "There is no vision, nor is there a set of competing visions, of what an educated human being is," Bloom complained. "The question has disappeared, for to pose it would be a threat to the peace." [28]

As the seeds of a campaign against "political correctness" were being sown, a seminal event took place at Stanford University on Jan. 15, 1987. According to news accounts picked up later in dozens of books and articles, some 500 mostly minority students and faculty launched a protest march to demand a new "rainbow" curriculum designed to make the traditional Western curriculum more multicultural. Their chant: "Hey hey, ho ho, Western culture's got to go!"

The intimidating image was featured by conservative writer Dinesh D'Souza in the 1991 book that became a key text in the PC debate, *Illiberal Education: The Politics of Race and Sex on Campus*. Two Stanford graduates also recounted the anecdote in the opening chapter of their 1995 book *The Diversity Myth,* one of the most recent conservative attacks on PC. [29]

Critics, however, would fault D'Souza and others who repeated the story for factual errors. New York University sociologist Todd Gitlin called D'Souza's work "sloppy and amateurish" because it portrayed the students' demands as a proposal to drop Western culture altogether, when in fact the new curriculum that was eventually adopted offered a choice of eight subsections, all of them including traditional Western readings.

"In one of the eight," Gitlin writes, "the reading list included *I, Rigoberta Menchu* by the Guatemalan Indian who was shortly to win the Nobel Peace Prize. D'Souza declared arbitrarily that this, one of more than 40 assigned texts in the course, was 'perhaps the text which best reveals the premises underlying the new Stanford curriculum,' and devoted two pages to trashing it. What he devoted no pages to mentioning was that all eight courses assigned the Old and New Testament, Freud, Marx, Shakespeare and Aristotle." [30]

Similarly, John Wilson, author of the 1995 book *The Myth of Political Correctness,* points in particular to the impression given by D'Souza, Bennett and others that civil rights leader Jesse Jackson was directing the students in the ominous chant. In fact, as Bennett later acknowledged, Jackson tried to quiet the chant, and was quoted as saying, " The issue is not that we don't want Western culture. We're from the West." [31]

D'Souza, a fellow at the American Enterprise Institute, replies that when his book came out, "all six universities I had written about did internal [fact-checking], and none came up with errors of fact. One or two minor errors were pointed out by well-meaning critics on things for which I had relied on newspaper accounts."

As for the charges of distortions, D'Souza acknowledges that "the whacky courses are only a part of the new curriculum, and Shakespeare is still in. But in writing, one tends to focus on what is changing and what is wrong. If four airplanes have crashed in the past six months, you're obligated to mention that hundreds land safely every day, but you write mostly about the four." ■

CURRENT SITUATION

Critics Organize

From his perch at the pinnacle of power in Congress, House Speaker

Newt Gingrich, R-Ga., is among those raining criticism on liberal academics. He wrote recently that "college and university faculties have developed a game in which they have lots of petty power with very little accountability." [32]

Last March, Yale University stunned the academic community when it announced that it was returning a $20 million donation given by alumni Lee Bass. The billionaire Texas businessman had made the offer on condition that the money be used to hire new, full-time professors to teach classic Western civilization. The Yale faculty, however, in the midst of preparing for layoffs, could not agree on how to restructure its budget. There was also disagreement over whether Bass was demanding approval of the professors, or whether he simply wanted to endorse certain selections. Conservatives, both on and off campus, took the rejection of Bass' gift as a sign of ideological rigidity that was denying Yale new opportunities.

Within days of Yale's announcement, a group of conservatives led by former NEH Chair Cheney announced the formation of the National Alumni Forum to give alumni more say in campus policies and to counter political correctness. "It comes down to the question of who owns the university," Cheney said at the time.

"It's always interesting when a highly politicized group gets together and says it wants to eliminate political influence," replied David Merkowitz, a spokesman for the American Council on Education. [33]

The alumni forum joins another new group, the American Academy for Liberal Education, a college-accrediting organization that focuses on the traditional Western liberal arts education. Recently recognized by the Education Department, the accrediting group aims to promote "high standards of teaching, including direct contact between senior faculty and students."

Among professors, a new group of humanities specialists, the Association of Literary Scholars and Critics, held its first annual meeting last October in Minneapolis. Headed by Boston University Professor Roger W. Shattuck, the 1,400-member group seeks to counter what it sees as academia's obsession with the ethnicity and sexual orientation of authors rather than narrative style and technique. [34]

Conservatives' Tactics

Established critics of academia have also been active. The Wilmington, Del.-based Intercollegiate Studies Institute is now channeling foundation money to support 58 conservative student newspapers, with 10 more applying, says Vice President Long. "We consider ourselves at a high point because the papers are regularly published, and high quality. Whereas five years ago they were only at elite schools such as Dartmouth and Vassar, now we have them at public schools such as East Missouri State and Wabash College."

The papers are intended as a balance to campus papers supported by student-activity fees that the institute believes merely perpetuate academia's role as "leftism's last redoubt." The institute's founder, former Reagan domestic policy adviser T. Kenneth Cribb Jr., says that countering liberalism on campus has huge national importance because it lays the groundwork for political change years later. "By the time the political battle is joined in Washington," he says, "it's [simply] a question of generalship. The correlation of forces has been determined decades beforehand."

Accuracy in Academia distributes its *Campus Report* to 1,500 colleges and high schools, excoriating professors deemed too PC. Originally, the group had planned to recruit outsiders to visit campuses to monitor professors' lectures but abandoned the tactic after critics characterized it as spying.

"It's mainly students who contact us with problems," says Executive Director Peter LaBarbera. "It's one way to hold professors accountable when tenure puts them out of reach. It's hard to get at the truth in that closed environment. We try to have more than one source, but it's hard because students fear for their grades. We always call a professor in question, and we go out of our way to get both sides."

Kurland of the AAUP says he does not hesitate to "declare war" on Accuracy in Academia, whose tactic of "encouraging students to secretly snitch on professors is terribly unwholesome."

English Professor Messer-Davidow, a cross-disciplinary scholar who is studying conservative organizing, says, "Watch what they do, not what they say. The National Association of Scholars, for example, presents itself as a purely academic organization, but two leaders of its California chapter are spearheading a statewide ballot initiative to curb affirmative action in public agencies and universities." Many of these groups, she adds, "are leading the attack on the academy for its liberalizing trends that, in fact, seek to enhance education and employment opportunities for all."

Defenders of affirmative action have themselves been organizing professors and alumni. Angered that Harvard's tenured faculty is only 11 percent women (less than half the national average), a group called the Committee for the Equality of Women at Harvard was formed in December. It has called upon alumni to boycott Harvard's $2 billion fundraising campaign and to put their donations instead into an escrow account, pending changes in hiring practices. [35] ■

OUTLOOK

Swings of the Pendulum

The news bulletins from academia continue thick and fast:

Continued on p. 162

At Issue:

Is political correctness a major problem at American colleges and universities?

Peter A. Thiel
***Co-author of* The Diversity Myth**

FROM REMARKS AT A DEBATE AT ACCURACY IN ACADEMIA'S 10TH ANNIVERSARY CONFERENCE, OCT. 14, 1995.

yes

If you are white or male or heterosexual or able-bodied or wealthy, then you are already more guilty than you can possibly imagine. I just wanted to get everyone's attention. I did not actually make this up. This was the welcome that was given at Stanford Law School a couple of years ago to the incoming students.

Even though I did not think it was a particularly good introduction to the American legal system, I thought it might be a good place to start a debate on political correctness, which I'm going to define very simply as a very harsh intolerance with people whose politics are incorrect, which in the context of our college campuses means an intolerance for people whose views do not fit the agenda of the American Left, which dominates on the campus scene.

Now, there's been a great deal of talk about how conservative students and faculty are mistreated. . . . Certainly, people who are objectively not within a certain left-wing mold do get singled out, but I want to focus on another dimension of the problem, which is sort of relative intolerance — an intolerance for people who are often quite liberal but who do not necessarily fit the party line on every single issue. . . .

I think you can even be quite radical and be subject to political correctness. . . . [Take] the case of Jan Kerkhoven. He was a third-year doctoral candidate in the school of education and was, by any standard, quite a politically correct person. Nel Noddings, Jan's adviser, explained that Kerkhoven was so interested in feminist studies that he had even participated in a special reading. But even this sort of ideological commitment was not enough.

Jan attempted to enroll in a class entitled "Feminist Methodology and the Social Sciences," an upper division feminist studies course. He was the only male in the class, and the class basically revolved around the oppression of women. Jan agreed that women were terribly oppressed, but he also thought that other people were oppressed as well. The course instructor, however, believed that only women were oppressed. Some students in class agreed with the instructor and complained about Jan's disturbing views.

Of course, instead of confronting the disturbing views, they had a somewhat easier recourse. They could get rid of the disturbing person instead. The instructor threw him out of class on the basis that he was insufficiently prepared. . . .

[T]oday we see this very broad coalition of conservatives and liberals — a very unusual coalition of people from across the political spectrum who are saying that we've had enough of the intolerance, close-mindedness and incivility.

John K. Wilson
***Author of* The Myth of Political Correctness**

FROM REMARKS AT A DEBATE AT ACCURACY IN ACADEMIA'S 10TH ANNIVERSARY CONFERENCE, OCT. 14, 1995.

no

I am not here to defend political correctness or to defend the particular examples that Peter cited, which quite frankly are pretty tame. I've heard much worse. Why I am here is to deny the existence of political correctness. You may wonder how can I say this. I will concede to you that if American colleges and universities were controlled by a cadre of totalitarian leftists who were suppressing students' freedom of expression by speech codes and who were forcing or coercing faculty to toe the liberal line or face being dismissed, if indeed political correctness were alive and thriving on American campuses, I would be sitting right there. But I don't think that's true.

When I refer to political correctness as a myth, I'm not saying that these examples are untrue and that there are no examples of liberal or leftist intolerance on campus. . . . [But] political correctness has to mean more than just a few anecdotes or a few examples. It has to mean a pervasive intolerance on college campuses against a particular group, a particular ideology, in this case being conservatives. . . .

A lot of the anecdotes that are told about political correctness do not in fact show what I feel is a necessary degree of intolerance or suppression to count as something that is a violation of academic freedom, whether it's the academic freedom of students or professors. In many cases, in fact, a lot of what is called political correctness is criticizing conservatives. . . . But criticism, in and of itself, does not count as intolerance, does not count as suppression of free speech. . . .

What's more, you can't look at political correctness without also looking at conservative correctness . . . the intolerance directed against leftists and liberals on college campuses. So when you talk about the right-wing students who are being censored, the faculty who are brought up on harassment charges, the intimidation of dissenting views in the classroom, the false accusations of racism and sexism, the conservative newspapers that are trashed and defunded, I say to you, "Welcome to the real world."

I also say to you, "What about the left-wing students who are punished for their views, the professors who are dismissed for being feminists, the gay and lesbian groups that are banned from some campuses, the professors who express liberal views who get criticized and attacked?"

What we need to do is find a more consistent defense of academic freedom, to recognize that there are examples of leftist intolerance, and you can call them political correctness, but there is not a movement of political correctness. . . .

Professors Once Shielded by Academic Freedom...

J Donald Silva lectured to his students in the manner he had grown accustomed to in 30 years at the University of New Hampshire. But in 1992, the words of the tenured professor and part-time pastoral counselor would reverberate nationally in debates over sexual harassment.

For a good example of a simile, Silva offered his technical-writing class the following: "Belly dancing is like jello on a plate with a vibrator under the plate." In an earlier lecture, he had tried to explain why good writing requires focus: "I will put focus in terms of sex, so you can better understand it. Focus is like sex. You seek a target. You zero in on your subject. You move from side to side. You close in on the subject. You bracket the subject and center on it. Focus connects language and centers on it. Focus connects language and experience. You and the subject become one." [1]

Nine female students filed complaints against Silva. They cited these comments from his lectures and various private conversations that made them uncomfortable. Following an investigation by the university, Silva was required to announce that any of his students could transfer to an alternative course. (Some 26 did so.) Silva was also reprimanded. This required him to reimburse the university for the cost of the alternative courses, undergo weekly counseling for a year, avoid retaliating against students who complained and apologize in writing "for creating a hostile and offensive academic environment."

When Silva refused to bow to the reprimand, he was suspended. The campus sexual-harassment review system was then set in motion, and investigators from the American Association of University Professors (AAUP) were brought in. Silva, meanwhile, filed a lawsuit to overturn the suspension. The investigation found that the case had merit because his comments in class were unrelated to his subject, and that due process had been followed. But on Sept. 15, 1994, Silva won his court case and was reinstated.

The Silva case became fodder in the debates over political correctness. For years, campuses have sought to thwart overt sexual harassment — when a professor seeks sex from a student in return for good grades, for example. [2] But here was an instance that went straight to the heart of a professor's teaching, and many in academia greeted the case with alarm.

"The whole idea that a remark made to a class, one not even directed at one person in the class, but a simple sexual reference, can mean you get brought up on charges makes me wonder, who can be safe?" says Stephen H. Balch, president of the National Association of Scholars (NAS). "It defeats the whole purpose of a free, open class."

"This notion of creating a hostile environment comes from those who are chronically offended, who are not a majority," adds Christina Hoff Sommers, a professor of philosophy at Clark University and author of the 1994 book *Who Stole Feminism?* "They have this attitude that no male professor should be alone with a female undergraduate, and that professors should scrupulously avoid all humor. . . . They're turning every case into an occasion for litigation, acrimony and divisiveness."

Nan Stein, an expert on sexual harassment in schools at the Wellesley College Center for Research on Women, was on the New Hampshire campus the day Silva was exonerated. "What the general public learned about that case isn't everything that happened," she says, citing a charge that Silva had also made suggestive comments to a woman in the library stacks. "A lot of it couldn't be printed in the paper or broadcast on the radio" because of the language used, she said. "You had to read it in an amicus brief."

What is clear is that many in academia have had to alter their styles in light of the sexual-harassment risk. In a landmark California case decided last April, a tenured professor of English and film studies at San Bernardino Valley College unsuccessfully defended his "confrontational" and aggressive methods, which included assigned readings from *Playboy* and *Hustler* magazines.

The case revolved around Professor Dean Cohen, who had flunked a female student who had demanded an alternative to his assignment to define pornography. Acting on her complaint, the school required Cohen to provide a syllabus of all readings at the start of each course; attend a sexual-harassment seminar within 90 days; undergo a formal performance evaluation; and modify his teaching strategy to avoid creating a climate that impedes learning. [3]

Professors can also be taken to task for behavior outside the classroom. At Syracuse University last year, Stephen Dobyns, a tenured creative writing professor, was suspended without pay for two years after a student complained that, at a social gathering, he had thrown a drink in her face after she confronted him for speaking to another man about her breasts. [4]

Many campuses have taken steps to head off harassment cases before they occur. When Harvard Law School adopted its "Sexual Harassment Guidelines" last April, commentators complained that there wasn't a demonstrated need for them.

Continued from p. 160

• A course in "white racism" proposed by a black sociologist at the University of Connecticut is rejected by school officials as offensive for singling out one group.

• In California, state senators demand the firing of the president of the University of California at Santa Cruz for appointing famed 1960s radical Angela Davis to a special chair.

• Georgetown University announces that it will no longer require English majors to study Chaucer, Shakespeare and Milton.

Kurland of the AAUP accepts such events as inevitable in the evolutionary process that shapes higher education. "I

. . . Now Risk Charges of Sexual Harassment

"The discussion is a sign of the times, as is the need perceived among students that we have to discuss this or be seen as uncaring of their concerns," Dean Robert Clark told *The Wall Street Journal.* [5]

At the University of Massachusetts, a harassment code under consideration would punish any verbal conduct that "may include, but is not limited to, epithets, slurs, negative stereotyping, threatening language or written or graphic material that serves to harass an individual or group of individuals." Already at U. Mass, professors receive an orientation on the school's hostile-environment policy forbidding "leering, explicit jokes, offensive remarks and posters." [6]

Cornell University has implemented a set of review procedures that authorize faculty members to serve as "harassment counselors." These officials are assigned to keep files of student complaints about individual professors, who have no chance to see the files or know when a complaint has been added to them. [7] Several well-publicized charges of sexual harassment — including one in which an accused professor is suing the school for $1.5 million — have prompted Cornell to consider putting enforcement in the hands of administrators, not faculty.

"We oppose separate procedures of due process on sexual harassment," says Jordan E. Kurland, associate general secretary of the AAUP. "At its most extreme, almost everything can be called sexual harassment, and there's an hysteria and unfairness. We have no use for sexual harassment, but there is an awful lot wrong in the world — thievery, murder — and sexual harassment is not all by itself the lowest level of hell."

In a statement initially released in 1984 (updated in 1995), the professors' group sought to balance its goals of academic freedom and respect for a non-threatening learning environment. It defined sexual harassment, in part, as speech or conduct that is "reasonably regarded as offensive and substantially impairs the academic or work opportunity of students, colleagues or co-workers. If it takes place in the teaching context, it must also be persistent, pervasive and not germane to the subject matter. The academic setting is distinct from the workplace in that wide latitude is required for professional judgment in determining the appropriate content and presentation of academic material." [8]

The National Association of Scholars in February 1995 asked members to submit complaints about harassment charges and new campus requirements such as "sensitivity training." The NAS was reacting to the release in 1994 of guidelines designed to curb campus racial harassment written by the Education Department's Office of Civil Rights (OCR). The NAS called them "an unhealthy combination of broadly defined 'harassment' offenses and still broader federal enforcement powers." It encouraged professors to write to Washington in protest and warned members that a similar set of guidelines was in the works for sexual harassment.

Last May, Norma Cantu, assistant Education secretary for civil rights, wrote to the scholars group rebutting the assertion that her office was broadening its powers. "The racial-harassment guidelines follow well-established legal principles," she wrote, noting that her office's concept of "hostile environment" harassment stems from a compendium of court cases as well as federal civil rights laws. [9] "OCR recognizes and respects academic freedom and the free-speech rights of individuals," she added. She also noted that her office is still deciding whether to issue new guidance on sexual harassment.

Observers acknowledge that society is still groping for a proper balance between academic freedom and the handling of sexual harassment. "The existence of all these procedures and campus committees are evidence of a lot of confusion," says Stein at Wellesley. "I wish so much vigor would be applied to sex discrimination. I care about the First Amendment, but academic freedom is not a constitutional right. Being able to go to school unimpeded *is.*"

---

[1] The facts in this case are taken from a report by an investigative committee appointed by the American Association of University Professors, published as "Academic Freedom and Tenure: University of New Hampshire," *Academe,* November-December 1994, p. 70.

[2] For background, see "Sex on Campus," *The CQ Researcher,* Nov. 4, 1994, pp. 961-984.

[3] Michael A. Olivas, "Fear and Loathing in the Classroom: Faculty and Student Rights in Comparative Context," draft report by the general counsel of the American Association of University Professors, June 30, 1995.

[4] See Francine Prose, "Bad Behavior," *The New York Times Magazine,* Nov. 26, 1995.

[5] Harvey A. Silverglate, "Harvard Law Caves In to the Censors," *The Wall Street Journal,* Jan. 8, 1996.

[6] See Daphne Patai, "What Price Utopia?: In Academe's Brave New World, a Discouraging Word Need Never Be Heard?" *The Chronicle of Higher Education,* Oct. 27, 1995, p. A56.

[7] See Jeremy Rabkin, "Briefing for a Descent Into Hell: Today's Campus," *The Weekly Standard,* Jan. 15, 1996, p. 28.

[8] American Association of University Professors, *Policy Documents and Reports,* 1995 edition, p. 171.

[9] See "Hate Crimes," *The CQ Researcher,* Jan. 8, 1993, p. 18.

---

do not fear for the long-term future of the Western canon," he says. "In actuality, it has not suffered that much. In a few places, there are fewer requirements, but I don't think the humanities classes that undergraduates take today are that different from those of their parents. The wave crests and recedes, but things don't go back to where they were. It's usually for the better."

Others are more alarmed. Accuracy in Academia's LaBarbera says: "People have realized that the future of the country is at stake. It's not just college, but high school and elementary school. All this emphasis on race, gender and class has only divided society as it thinks more about race,

FOR MORE INFORMATION

Accuracy in Academia, 4455 Connecticut Ave. N.W., Suite 330, Washington, D.C. 20008; (202) 364-3085. Founded in 1985 by conservative media critics, this group publishes a monthly newspaper reporting on professors and incidents that it says threaten academic freedom.

American Association of University Professors, 1012 14th St. N.W., Suite 500, Washington, D.C. 20005; (202) 737-5900. Founded in 1915 to press for academic freedom, this 44,000-member group is the chief policy-making body and union for college teachers.

Modern Language Association, 10 Astor Place, New York, N.Y. 10003; (212) 475-9500. Founded in 1883, the 32,000-member MLA provides opportunities for academics to share scholarly findings in the humanities. It publishes numerous newsletters and periodicals and maintains a job bank.

National Association of Scholars, 575 Ewing St. Princeton, N.J. 08540; (609) 683-7878. Formed in the mid-1980s, this group of 4,000 academics seeks to counter trends in the academy that favor multicultural curricula, affirmative action and ideology in the classroom.

gender and class. There's now more racism on campus than ever before."

Balch of the NAS says the real problem is that there is little real education, that standards have gotten low. "Employers are yelling about no basic literacy skills, a lack of basic knowledge of history even among people from the best schools," he says. "If we don't understand how this exceptional society came to exist, we will lose it."

Rutgers' Stimpson attributes much of the friction to the fact that the younger generation of scholars is facing "a terrible job market. And," she adds, "so many of our political leaders are reluctant to sustain this magnificent education system that America built — the best in world."

The threat of political correctness, says Horowitz, "is uppermost on every parents' mind. I'm asked about it all the time. But these colleges are huge. You can still get a good education if you stay in the sciences, economics or political science. America is a hard country to take over."

To Franklin of the MLA, the nation's academy is, and must remain, "both a product of society and protected from society. It reflects society, but it also maintains some distance. It's a unique institution." ■

Notes

[1] See *The Chronicle of Higher Education,* Feb. 2, 1996.

[2] Accuracy in Academia, *Campus Report,* September 1995, p. 1.

[3] Center for the Study of Popular Culture, *Heterodoxy,* November 1995, p. 13.

[4] "Our Monotone Universities," *The American Enterprise,* September-October 1995.

[5] Charles J. Sykes and Brad Miner, eds., *The National Review College Guide* (updated 1993), p. 239.

[6] See "What Should College Students Be Taught?" *Editorial Research Reports,* Jan. 5, 1990, pp. 1-16.

[7] Lynne V. Cheney, *Telling the Truth* (1995), p. 57.

[8] See "Rethinking Affirmative Action," *The CQ Researcher,* April 28, 1995, pp. 375-398.

[9] Eric L. Dey, Claudia E. Ramirez, William S. Korn and Alexander W. Astin, "The American College Teacher," Higher Education Research Institute, University of California at Los Angeles, May 1993.

[10] Hilton Kramer and Roger Kimball, "Farewell to the MLA," *The New Criterion,* February 1995, p. 5.

[11] An AAUP report in January said that 21 states in recent years have enacted mandates regarding faculty workloads. The association argues that "direct intervention in, and regulation of, the academic community from outside are more likely to diminish the role of public education than to result in 'better' teaching, research and service." See AAUP, "The Politics of Intervention: External Regulation of Academic Activities and Workloads in Public Higher Education," January-February, 1996.

[12] Chester E. Finn Jr. and Bruno V. Manno, "Behind the Curtain," *Wilson Quarterly,* winter 1996, p. 44.

[13] Quoted in *The Washington Post,* Feb. 4, 1996.

[14] George Levine et al, "Speaking for the Humanities," American Council of Learned Societies, 1989, p. 6.

[15] *MLA Newsletter,* fall 1995.

[16] Thomas C. Reeves, "Partisan Revelry at the Advocacy Conference," *Academic Questions,* fall 1995, p. 53.

[17] Peter Ackroyd, "Pence and Sensibility," *The New Yorker,* Jan. 16, 1996, p. 70.

[18] Quoted in Charles J. Sykes, *ProfScam: Professors and the Demise of Higher Education* (1988), p. 4.

[19] American Association of University Professors, "75 Years: A Retrospective on the Occasion of the Seventy-Fifth Annual Meeting," *Academe,* May-June 1989, p. 9.

[20] Hamilton, *op. cit.,* p. 29.

[21] American Association of University Professors, *op. cit.,* p. 28.

[22] John Judis, *William F. Buckley Jr.: Patron Saint of the Conservatives* (1988), p. 217.

[23] Quoted in James Atlas, *The Battle of the Books* (1989), p. 122.

[24] Sykes, *op. cit.,* p. 34.

[25] See Everett Carll Ladd Jr. and Seymour Martin Lipset, *The Divided Academy* (1975), pp. 203, 206. Percentages don't add to 100 percent because of rounding.

[26] Sykes, *op. cit.,* p. 142.

[27] Alice Kaplan, *French Lessons: A Memoir* (1993), p. 148.

[28] Allan Bloom, *The Closing of the American Mind* (1987), p. 337.

[29] David O. Sacks and Peter A. Thiel, *The Diversity Myth: Multiculturalism and the Politics of Intolerance at Stanford* (1995), p. 1. For background, see "Racial Tensions in Schools," *The CQ Researcher,* Jan. 7, 1994, pp. 1-24.

[30] Todd Gitlin, *The Twilight of Common Dreams* (1995), p. 172.

[31] John Wilson, *The Myth of Political Correctness* (1995), p. 64. Wilson is a University of Chicago graduate student.

[32] Newt Gingrich, *To Renew America* (1995), p. 219.

[33] Quoted by The Associated Press, March 17, 1995.

[34] *The Chronicle of Higher Education,* Oct. 6, 1995, p. A21; "ALSC Newsletter," fall 1995.

[35] See *Newsweek,* Dec. 11, 1995, p. 81.

Bibliography

Selected Sources Used

Books

Anderson, Martin, *Imposters in the Temple,* Simon and Schuster, 1992.
A former Reagan administration official now at the Hoover Institute blasts recent trends toward the politicization of academe.

Atlas, James, *The Battle of the Books,* W.W. Norton, 1990.
A *New York Times* writer explores recent changes in the academic curriculum.

Berman, Paul, ed., *Debating P.C.: The Controversy Over Political Correctness on College Campuses,* Dell Publishing, 1992.
A noted liberal commentator compiled these key essays on campus politics.

Bernstein, Richard, *Dictatorship of Virtue: Multiculturalism and the Battle for America's Future,* Alfred A. Knopf, 1994.
A *New York Times* writer, the first to popularize the term "political correctness," examines U.S. cultural and political trends.

Bloom, Allan, *The Closing of the American Mind,* Simon and Schuster, 1987.
The late University of Chicago classicist indicts "cultural relativism" in higher education.

Cheney, Lynne V., *Telling the Truth: Why Our Culture and Our Country Have Stopped Making Sense — And What We Can Do About It,* Simon & Schuster, 1995.
The former chair of the National Endowment for the Humanities says campus PC is "alive and entrenched."

Collier, Peter, and David Horowitz, *The Heterodoxy Handbook: How to Survive the PC Campus,* Regnery Gateway Publishing, 1994.
Two 1960s radicals-turned-conservatives assembled this compendium of reportedly outrageous events at U.S. colleges and universities.

D'Souza, Dinesh, *Illiberal Education: The Politics of Race and Sex on Campus,* Vintage Books, Revised 1992.
A conservative fellow at the American Enterprise Institute wrote this seminal work on political correctness.

Gitlin, Todd, *The Twilight of Common Dreams: Why America is Wracked by Culture Wars,* Henry Holt, 1995.
A New York University sociologist offers a leftist perspective on political correctness and other academic issues.

Hamilton, Neil, *Zealotry and Academic Freedom: A Legal and Historical Perspective,* Transaction Publishers, 1995.
A professor at William Mitchell College of Law in St. Paul, Minn., traces the roots of "academic fundamentalism of the left."

Kimball, Roger, *Tenured Radicals: How Politics Has Corrupted Our Higher Education,* Harper & Row, 1990.
An editor at *The New Criterion* criticizes academic trends away from the traditional Western canon.

Ladd, Everett Carll Jr., and Seymour Martin Lipset, *The Divided Academy,* Carnegie Foundation for the Advancement of Teaching, 1975.
A top pollster and a top political scientist analyze results of a landmark survey of 60,000 academics.

Sacks, David O., and Peter A. Thiel, *The Diversity Myth: Multiculturalism and the Politics of Intolerance at Stanford,* The Independent Institute, 1995.
Two recent Stanford graduates indict the university for incidents of political correctness.

Sykes, Charles J., *ProfScam: Professors and the Demise of Higher Education,* Regnery Gateway Publishing, 1988.
A conservative author blasts academe for neglecting traditional teaching and indulging in politics.

Wilson, John, *The Myth of Political Correctness,* Duke University Press, 1995.
A University of Chicago graduate student says charges of rampant political correctness reflect exaggerations by conservatives.

Reports and Studies

Levine, George, et al, *Speaking for the Humanities,* American Council of Learned Societies, Occasional Paper No. 7, 1989.
A panel of top humanities professors defends current literature and language studies against criticism that they are politicized and out of touch.

"The Politics of Political Correctness," *Partisan Review,* Special Issue, fall 1993.
Twenty-seven intellectuals respond to an editor's invitation to gauge the importance of political correctness.

The Next Step

Additional information from UMI's Newspaper & Periodical Abstracts database

Academic Freedom

"Ideas Beat Ideology at D.U.," *Denver Post,* Jan. 9, 1991, p. B6.
An editorial praises the University of Denver's decision to allow guest professors Charles Murray and Richard Herrnstein to teach in 1991 in spite of their controversial reputations as a step that will strengthen the school's tradition of academic freedom.

Jaschik, Scott, "GOP presidential candidates bring out long knives when higher-education programs are on the table," *The Chronicle of Higher Education,* May 5, 1995, pp. A28-A29.
The positions of the 1996 GOP presidential candidates on higher education issues are discussed. Five of the nine candidates have pledged to eliminate the Education Department, and six of the nine have vowed to eliminate affirmative action initiatives on college campuses.

Kriegel, Leonard, "Academic Freedom and Racial Theories," *The New York Times,* May 3, 1990, p. A27.
Kriegel comments on the issues of race at City College of New York and states that those professors who have mouthed intellectual nonsense dealing with the issue deserve to have their freedom of speech protected even if their blather only goes skin deep.

Lowi, Theodore J., "Media fascination with self-styled public intellectuals," *The Chronicle of Higher Education,* Jan. 27, 1995, p. B1.
The self-styled new public intellectuals are neither new nor very public, but the press is giving them a lot of attention. These days, rather than the weight of their arguments, a favorable political or cultural climate is often key to public intellectuals' success. The media's fascination with them and the conservative attack on academe are discussed.

Sowell, Thomas, "Good teachers need not apply," *Forbes,* June 19, 1995, p. 67.
The academic world regards teaching awards as the kiss of death, Sowell writes. Publish or perish still holds true in academic circles. Academia needs to kick its research addiction cold turkey.

Wilson, Robin, "Flash point at Rutgers U.," *The Chronicle of Higher Education,* Feb. 24, 1995, pp. A21-A23.
Despite his apologies for a racial comment, hundreds of minority students have joined protests in an effort to force Francis L. Lawrence to resign as president of Rutgers University. The reactions of the students and those who support Lawrence are discussed.

Multicultural Curriculum

Cribb, T. Kenneth Jr., David Sacks and Peter Thiel, "Alumni to the rescue," *National Review,* Sept. 25, 1995, pp. 44-48.
Education changed when radicals entered school systems and redesigned traditional curricula, revamped reading lists and subverted the traditional mission of the university. Alumni influence may be the only thing that causes schools to get back on the track and depoliticize education.

Sacks, David, and Peter Thiel, "College sticker price: $100,000 (education optional)," *Policy Review,* fall 1995, pp. 48-52.
Multicultural activists have largely succeeded in killing the core humanities curriculum at California's Stanford University, generally on the grounds that its promotes "Western Culture," which the activists oppose. The average undergraduate education at a top college now costs $100,000 — a lot of money for admission into a politically correct fun park, the authors write.

Wilson, John K., "Many of the most vocal critics of political correctness simply want to impose their own version," *The Chronicle of Higher Education,* July 28, 1995, p. B3.
Some conservative groups that complain about college speech codes are leading efforts to censor campus life, especially by restricting the activities of gays and lesbians. Examples of such attempts at censorship are discussed.

"Political Correctness"

Abramowitz, Michael, "Literature Professors Look Inward and Find Scant Evidence of PC," *The Washington Post,* Jan. 3, 1992, p. A3.
Literature professors who have come under fire for being among the chief purveyors of the new, leftish orthodoxy known derisively as political correctness contend that much of the criticism is unfair, hyped by the media and a gross caricature of what is happening on campus.

DePalma, Anthony, "In Campus Debate on New Orthodoxy, a Counteroffensive," *The New York Times,* Sept. 25, 1991, p. A1.
Liberal professors and administrators are planning a counteroffensive to the conservative attack on "political correctness" on U.S. college campuses that right-wing intellectuals waged in 1991. The academics claim that the whole "PC" controversy was a smokescreen to an effort to roll back affirmative action plans and multicultural programs.

Friedman, Debra, "The academy," *Contemporary Sociology,* November 1995, pp. 744-748.

Articles from *Daedalus* and *Partisan Review* on the structure and context of U.S. universities and the politics involved with political correctness are discussed, and two books on universities and sociology are reviewed.

Hentoff, Nat, "Whitewashing Political Correctness," *The Washington Post,* Sept. 21, 1991, p. A23.

Hentoff criticizes the "Statement on the Political Correctness Controversy" released by the American Association of University Professors for being a "whitewash" of the politically correct movement at U.S. colleges.

Laird, Michael J., "The constitutionality of political correctness," *Communications & the Law,* Sept. 1994, pp. 43-55.

Laird examines whether colleges and universities need a code of conduct or regulations attempting to outline acceptable conduct, verbal or written communication, visual displays, or other expressive behavior.

Parenti, Michael, "The myth of the liberal campus," *Humanist,* September 1995, pp. 20-23.

Conservative critics say U.S. universities are in the grip of politically correct left-wingers who have stifled academic discourse. A look at who controls universities' purse strings reveals a different kind of censorship.

Parks, Ward, "Political Correctness and Higher Education," *The Washington Times,* Nov. 30, 1992, p. E4.

Parks argues that efforts in colleges and universities to promote multiculturalism are simply a means of forcing students to adopt the liberal attitudes and beliefs of their professors.

"PC at Hampshire College," *The Wall Street Journal,* Jan. 4, 1991, p. A6.

An editorial says if the *The Wall Street Journal* made year-end awards for Political Correctness, Hampshire College in Amherst, Mass., would surely rank among the finalists. The examples of two professors who weren't reappointed are detailed.

Radin, Charles A., "An ivory cower," *Boston Globe,* Jan. 20, 1993, p. 1.

While the uproar over speech codes and other formal attempts to regulate opinion on U.S. college campuses has died down, pressure on faculty and students to stay within "politically correct" bounds is increasingly restricting course content and classroom discussions, many professors say.

"Should a Writing Class Teach Social Diversity?" *The New York Times,* Feb. 3, 1991, p. 43.

English professors at the University of Massachusetts at Amherst, responding to criticism over their decision to include issues of racial and social diversity in freshman writing classes, say they are teaching students how to write, not how to be "politically correct."

Wilson, Robin, "From opposite poles, new books examine political correctness," *The Chronicle of Higher Education,* Oct. 27, 1995, p. A21.

A book by David O. Sacks and Peter A. Thiel entitled *The Diversity of Myth: Multiculturalism and the Politics of Intolerance at Stanford* examines multiculturalism curricula changes at Stanford University. The book covers many issues dealing with political correctness on campus.

Sexual Harassment

Wilson, Robin, "A fractured department," *The Chronicle of Higher Education,* Jan. 13, 1995, pp. A14-A15.

Three professors in the history department on California State University's Chico campus are engaged in a fight that involves a range of bizarre accusations. The battle, which started with an off-color memo and sex-harassment charges and has led to a lawsuit, is discussed.

Wilson, Robin, "Whose rights are protected?" *The Chronicle of Higher Education,* Sept. 8, 1995, pp. A25-A27.

The sexual harassment charges against Cornell University Professor James B. Maas are examined. Maas was found guilty by the university, but he is suing, saying his rights were not protected.

Tenure

Cage, Mary Crystal, "A test case for tenure," *The Chronicle of Higher Education,* Dec. 8, 1995, pp. A17-A19.

Florida Atlantic University Professor Cecilia Campoverde received tenure based not on any traditional scholarship but on her work in the classroom and the community. Campoverde's situation has become a test case on how colleges award tenure, but her experience has touched a nerve and raised questions at Florida Atlantic about the standards for tenure.

Greenberg, Milton, "Considering tenure — It's not holy writ: Can we talk?" *Educational Record,* fall 1995, pp. 35-36.

The vast majority of tenured college and university professors are white males between the ages of 35 and 55 who have unlimited time to serve in their positions. Untenured and part-time faculty is largely made up of women and minorities.

Magner, Denise K., "Men on the firing line," *The Chronicle of Higher Education,* Oct. 20, 1995, pp. A17-A19.

St. Bonaventure University in New York faced serious financial problems, and administrators knew cutbacks were in order. Twenty-two male professors were fired, eighteen of whom were tenured, which caused massive controversy over the role of affirmative action at the school.

Back Issues

Great Research on Current Issues Starts Right Here...Recent topics covered by The CQ Researcher are listed below. Before May 1991, reports were published under the name of Editorial Research Reports.

AUGUST 1994
Genetically Engineered Foods
Electing Minorities
Prozac Controversy
College Sports

SEPTEMBER 1994
Home Schooling
Welfare Experiments
Courts and the Media
Regulating Tobacco

OCTOBER 1994
Historic Preservation
Religion and Politics
Arts Funding
Economic Sanctions

NOVEMBER 1994
Sex on Campus
Blood Supply Safety
Testing Term Limits
Religion in America

DECEMBER 1994
Farm Policy
Arms Sales
Earthquake Research
The Future of Television

Back issues are available for $5.00 (subscribers) or $8.00 (non-subscribers). Quantity discounts apply to orders over ten. To order, call Congressional Quarterly Customer Service at (202) 887-8621.

Binders are available for $18.00. To order call 1-800-638-1710. Please refer to stock number 648.

JANUARY 1995
Treating Addiction
Child Custody and Support
Parents and Schools
Non-Proliferation Treaty at 25

FEBRUARY 1995
Cracking Down on Immigration
The Business of Sports
Reinventing Government
Housing Discrimination

MARCH 1995
Death Penalty Debate
Primary Care
Democracy in Africa
Environmental Movement at 25

APRIL 1995
Abortion Clinic Protests
Dieting and Health
Combating AIDS
Rethinking Affirmative Action

MAY 1995
Assisted Suicide Controversy
Overhauling Social Security
Learning to Read
Mandatory Sentencing

JUNE 1995
Combating Infectious Disease
Property Rights
Repetitive Stress Injuries
Regulating the Internet

JULY 1995
War Crimes
Highway Safety
Combating Terrorism
Preventing Teen Drug Use

AUGUST 1995
Job Stress
Organ Transplants
United Nations at 50
Advances in Cancer Research

SEPTEMBER 1995
Catholic Church in the U.S.
Northern Ireland Cease-Fire
High School Sports
Teaching History

OCTOBER 1995
Quebec's Future
Revitalizing the Cities
Networking the Classroom
Indoor Air Pollution

NOVEMBER 1995
The Working Poor
The Jury System
Sex, Violence and the Media
Police Misconduct

DECEMBER 1995
Teens and Tobacco
Gene Therapy's Future
Global Water Shortages
Third-Party Prospects

JANUARY 1996
Emergency Medicine
Punishing Sex Offenders
Bilingual Education
Helping the Homeless

FEBRUARY 1996
Reforming the CIA
Campaign Finance Reform

Future Topics

- ***College Admissions***
- ***Preventing Youth Violence***
- ***The British Monarchy***

THE CQ Researcher

PUBLISHED BY CONGRESSIONAL QUARTERLY INC.

Getting Into College

Why is the competition for admission so fierce?

A college degree is no longer seen as a luxury reserved mainly for the rich and well-connected. The increasingly tight job market has made higher education a virtual prerequisite for career advancement, while sharpening the competition for admission to top-ranked colleges. At the same time, the declining number of traditional applicants has forced colleges to recruit older students and students from overseas, as well as members of underrepresented minority groups. With tuition and related expenses rising faster than the overall inflation rate, attending college often stretches the financial reserves of even middle-class families to the limit. But now many institutions are offering honors programs, merit scholarships and tuition discounts to high-achieving applicants to improve the schools' academic reputations.

INSIDE THIS ISSUE

CQ Feb. 23, 1996 • Volume 6, No. 8 • Pages 169-192

Formerly Editorial Research Reports

GETTING INTO COLLEGE

COVER: DAVIDSON COLLEGE, DAVIDSON, N.C. (WILLIAM R. GIDUZ)

Feb. 23, 1996
Volume 6, No. 8

PUBLISHED BY
Congressional Quarterly Inc.

The CQ Researcher (ISSN 1056-2036). Formerly Editorial Research Reports. Published weekly (48 times per year, not printed March 1, May 31, Aug. 30, Nov. 29, 1996) by Congressional Quarterly Inc., 1414 22nd St., N.W., Washington, D.C. 20037. Rates are furnished upon request. Second-class postage paid at Washington, D.C. POSTMASTER: Send address changes to The CQ Researcher, 1414 22nd St., N.W., Washington, D.C. 20037.

Getting Into College

BY RICHARD L. WORSNOP

THE ISSUES

In a tense ritual played out every spring, high school seniors across the country suddenly turn into compulsive mail-watchers. They're looking for fat envelopes — not thin ones — from the colleges to which they have applied. As all college-bound students know, thick envelopes bear a coveted acceptance letter and the necessary admissions documents. A thin envelope merely contains one of those painfully perfunctory rejection letters: "We've had many good applicants this year, and we're sorry . . ."

More than 12.2 million undergraduates were enrolled in college in 1994 — a near record — underscoring how highly Americans prize a college degree. A generation ago, a secondary school diploma often sufficed as an entry-level job credential. Today, however, employers increasingly expect job seekers to have an undergraduate degree. The more demanding job market helps explain why college enrollment remained high, even as the smaller "baby-bust" generation came of age in the 1980s and early '90s.

During the post-baby boom period, colleges compensated for the dip in the traditional pool of students by introducing new programs and more aggressive recruiting to reach out to potential students long underrepresented on campus. They launched efforts to recruit African-Americans, Asian-Americans, Hispanics, Native Americans and prospective students over 25 — once thought too old to attend college. They developed marketing campaigns that often included financial incentives like merit scholarships and tuition discounts. And they even reached out to affluent students overseas, where an American sheepskin is especially coveted — and usually paid for in cash.

At Stanford University, as at many

institutions of higher education, the changes over the years were dramatic. Jean H. Fetter, a former dean of undergraduate admissions at Stanford, notes in her recent memoir that the 1948 Stanford yearbook "contains no more than a handful of non-white faces, and all of those are Asian. In 1993, almost half of the undergraduate population [was] non-white."

In 1948, moreover, women had to undergo a separate admissions process to get into Stanford, and many of them studied to be nurses or teachers. In 1993, Fetter notes, almost half of the university's undergraduates were women, and they were enrolled "in all disciplines." [1]

Despite the changes on campus, some things have largely remained the same. Getting into school still depends, to a large extent, on grades and test scores. (*See table, p. 172.*) And while some schools must beat the bushes to fill the next freshman class, top-rated institutions continue to get droves of applicants. Unsuccessful applicants sometimes blame their rejection on affirmative action, saying schools favor lackluster minority candidates over those with superior academic credentials. [2]

But admissions officials explain that grades and test scores, while critical, are by no means the only factors weighed during the application-review process. At many schools, sought-after athletes often receive special consideration, as do the children of alumni or applicants from distant states. And yes, top schools acknowledge, they will take a chance on minority students who show promise but didn't have the advantages enjoyed by more affluent applicants.

"Once we factor in criteria beyond the academic record," Fetter writes, "the process becomes . . . more complex. What could have been a scientific selection process, based on tables with weighted quantitative measures of academic achievement, now becomes a scientific art."

Fetter notes that "the dilemma of unequal opportunities so apparent in the academic criterion is ever-present in these considerations, too. Students from economically disadvantaged classes have many fewer opportunities to engage in extracurricular activities and, in many cases, time outside of class needs to be spent on essentials — such as supplementing the family income." [3]

Richard Shaw, dean of admissions and financial aid at Yale University, views admissions decisions as the end product of numerous mini-decisions. "We look at just about every piece of information a student submits," he says. "The essay that accompanies the application is part of it. So are teacher and school recommendations and activities outside the classroom.

"No single factor makes or breaks a candidate. But all the factors, in combination, do make a difference. For example, if students don't engage the essay seriously, that's going to count against them."

In short, there is no one way, let

Joan Q. Student
Class of 2000

How Colleges Weigh Academic Achievement

High school grade-point average (GPA) or class rank is the most important academic factor in admissions decisions, according to a national survey. Admissions test scores and the difficulty of high school coursework are next in importance.

H.S. TRANSCRIPT
S.A.T. SCORE

Average Importance of Factor in 1992

	Public institutions	Private institutions
High school GPA or rank	4.0	4.0
Admissions test scores	3.6	3.4
Achievement test scores	1.6	1.9
Letters of recommendation	1.9	3.0
Interviews	1.7	2.7
Essays	1.7	2.6
Health statement	1.4	1.4
State of residence	1.8	1.2
Portfolios, auditions, etc.	1.7	1.9
High school coursework	2.9	3.3
College-level work in high school	2.7	2.9
Declaration of major	1.8	1.7
Minority group membership	2.2	1.8
Gender	1.2	1.4
Disability group membership	1.4	1.2
Financial need	1.2	1.3

Average importance was computed as the mean where:

1 = Not considered
2 = A minor factor
3 = A moderately important factor
4 = A very important factor
5 = The single most important factor

Source: American Association of Collegiate Registrars and Admissions Officers, Challenges in College Admissions: A Report of a Survey of Undergraduate Admissions Policies, Practices and Procedures, *1995. The survey was taken in 1992 and included responses from 2,000 two-year and four-year institutions.*

alone a shortcut, to get into the college of one's dreams. But the endless stream of books and computer software offering tips on submitting a winning application underscores how intense the competition for higher education has become. (*See story, p. 180.*)

For increasing numbers of college-bound students, getting accepted by a college is only the first of two difficult steps toward a degree. Many families find that putting enough money together can stretch their financial reserves to the limit, or even beyond. When that happens, the family usually seeks grants or loans from federal, state and school sources. In the 1994-95 academic year, The College Board reported, $46.8 billion in such aid was available, an 8 percent increase from the previous year. [4]

Demand for loans and grants seems likely to mount in coming years, because annual increases in college costs continue to rise at a higher rate than the Consumer Price Index. The trend has dimmed the college hopes of many high school students. According to a recent national survey, 53 percent of the high school students who responded said they would have more trouble paying for college than their parents did. [5] And the National Center for Education Statistics has reported that 58 percent of the full-time undergraduates in colleges or vocational and technical schools in 1992-93 obtained financial help. [6]

The affordability issue is of particular concern to students hoping to attend Ivy League and other highly selective institutions. After Yale announced last May that the cost for the 1995-96 year would rise to a breathtaking $27,630, the *Yale Daily News* complained: "The university's administrators must pursue other avenues that will enable them to stabilize the increase in the term bill, or at least keep it consistent with the inflation rate. At this pace, our children may only hear stories about the Yale experience and education, since by the time they are of college age, a four-year Yale education will cost a mere $240,000." [7]

Yale's Shaw is well aware of the money woes facing families of prospective college students — and not just low-income families. Like many schools, Yale admits students on a "need-blind" basis — without considering a student's ability to pay. "We meet the full demonstrated need of students who apply to the institution," Shaw says. "We see more and more families in the $80,000 to $100,000-and-better [income] range that really have not, for whatever reason, had the ability to save for college."

Robert Chernak, vice president of student and academic support services at George Washington University (GW), in Washington, D.C., notes that inflation has forced changes in saving strategies for college. In the 1960s, he recalls, the rule of thumb was that you saved for four years, paid college bills until you had to take out a loan, and then had maybe four years of loan repayments. "Today," he says, "families start saving earlier, if they can, and take longer to work down the loan debt. You're looking at 15 to 18 years, just as a guess, as the average [loan] payout period."

Roger Swanson, associate executive director of the American Association of Collegiate Registrars and Admissions

Officers, points to "the difficulties that can arise when a college student amasses a significant amount of loan debt." To make matters worse, if two students with college bills get married, "they've got double the amount of debt, and if they both go on to graduate school, they're looking at an even heavier burden."

Despite the crushing cost of attending a highly selective college, many students and parents regard it as money well spent. According to educators Philip J. Cook and Robert H. Frank, "Many of our best and brightest high school seniors know what most of our higher-education leaders have been reluctant to admit: An increasingly small number of colleges and universities have become the gatekeepers of society's top-paying jobs." [8]

Cook and Frank, who authored a 1995 book on the widening gap between rich and poor Americans, *The Winner-Take-All Society,* pointed out that 59 percent of the finalists in the Westinghouse Science Talent Search in the 1980s attended one of just seven institutions — Cornell, Harvard, Princeton, Stanford, Yale, California Institute of Technology and Massachusetts Institute of Technology. Today, an estimated 75 percent of all college-bound seniors apply to only 25 percent of the country's colleges and universities. [9]

As this year's crop of high school seniors sets its sights on college, these are some of the questions being asked:

Is rising competition for top students good for higher education?

Just as many high school seniors are struggling to get into selective colleges, many colleges are competing for the most scholastically gifted students. The aim is to boost the institution's academic ranking, ideally to the elite level. One popular strategy is to award merit scholarships, issued on the basis of academic performance rather than financial need. Some colleges offer tuition discounts on the same basis.

W. Patrick Hinely/Washington and Lee University

Washington and Lee University began admitting women in 1985. Tuition at the 1,600-student school in Lexington, Va., will be $15,280 in fall 1996, up 5 percent from the previous year.

GW instituted a merit-aid program several years ago to boost its number of coveted National Merit Scholarship finalists. The program succeeded beyond expectations, at which point the school capped the amount of aid offered. "It was an intentional decision," says Chernak, "because we're now at the level where we wanted to be all along — accepting roughly 40 National Merit finalists in each freshman class of about 1,300."

More significantly, GW's scholarship initiative seems to have affected overall applications. "Applications increased from about 6,000 in 1988 to a record 10,400 last year," Chernak reports. "The average SAT scores and high school class ranking of our incoming freshmen also have continued to rise. Of course, to convert those accepted applicants into GW students, we've had to be a little more generous with them in terms of merit aid than we had been in the past."

Large state universities often choose a different approach to lure top students. Many have established highly selective honors programs that give students a small-college experience amid the big-campus setting. One of the oldest such programs is operated by the University of Colorado at Boulder. The 600 students in the Colorado honors program may choose among 30 or so courses per semester, with enrollment limited to 15 students per course. "What we really offer are seminars," says program director Dennis Van Gerven.

His ultimate aim is to convert the honors program to a full-fledged honors college that could tap the resources of the entire university. The program currently focuses on the arts and sciences, with some work offered in engineering and business.

Honors colleges are becoming an increasingly effective way to attract top students, Van Gerven says, in part because "parents are becoming very careful shoppers. They don't want to send an outstanding young man or woman to an institution that can't provide something more than the tradi-

How Personal Qualities Affect Admissions Decisions

Private institutions emphasize personal qualities in admissions decisions far more than public colleges and universities, according to a national survey of four-year schools.

	Percentage that considered personal quality important	
Personal quality	**Public institutions**	**Private institutions**
Leadership ability	45%	76%
Extracurricular activities	45	73
Community and church activities	34	74
Motivation and initiative	48	86
Work experience	34	51
Compatibility with school's philosophy	42	84

Source: American Association of Collegiate Registrars and Admissions Officers, Challenges in College Admissions: A Report of a Survey of Undergraduate Admissions Policies, Practices and Procedures, *1995. The survey was taken in 1992 and included responses from 2,000 two-year and four-year institutions.*

tional kind of large-lecture-format experience. They don't want to think of their children wandering about a campus with 25,000 other students." Honors programs, in contrast, provide "a neighborhood experience, a small community environment for undergraduates." And the cost is often less than half that of a high-level, private institution.

Van Gerven believes that "the flagship institutions of state systems can no longer afford to be inattentive to the curricular needs, the quality-teaching needs, of the undergraduates they serve. Parents are rebelling at the idea of faculty who don't teach but do research. We have to make it clear that we're committed to quality undergraduate education in addition to the research mission of the institution."

Shaw acknowledges that state university honors programs draw from the same applicant pools that selective private institutions use. "Having been admissions director at the University of Michigan, which has a strong honors program, I know those are attractive programs to students," he says. "They're trying to capture what we do [at Yale] as a matter of course in smaller microcosms of their campus environments."

Critics of merit scholarships, public university honors programs and other incentives say they benefit a relatively small percentage of college applicants. "A college is going to make aid more available to students who bring to it something the college wants," says Swanson of the registrars' association. "For instance, the lucky student could be a National Merit scholar, an outstanding tuba player or a Native American." On the other hand, "the average middle-class student" without unusual credentials may be left in the cold.

Current trends in admissions policies also trouble two economics professors who often address student-aid issues. "Intensifying competition for students, especially for affluent students with strong academic credentials, raises difficult policy questions for colleges and universities and society," Michael S. McPherson and Morton Owen Schapiro wrote recently. "Individual institutions must weigh the potential gains in prestige and student recruitment that may result from a successful merit scholarship program against the risks of getting caught up in a self-destructive, zero-sum competition with other institutions for the same small set of students." [10]

Chernak says GW considered the zero-sum hazard when it launched its merit-aid program, but he says the university dodged the bullet. "Sometimes you need a booster rocket to improve the quality of entering freshmen," he says. "The National Merit finalist program helped us do that. Eventually, though, you have to wean yourself off that kind of major financial commitment, and hope that it translates into a better applicant pool over the long term.

"There can be a halo effect when you penetrate certain high schools in areas where you weren't strong before. You hope the students from those schools who attend GW act as role models for other kids in their communities. And that's how it has worked out for us."

Can the pool of college applicants be broadened?

For years, conventional wisdom

among educators held that nationwide college enrollment totals were hostage to demographic trends. As a result, foreboding gripped the higher education community as the 1970s drew to a close. That's when the last members of the baby-boom generation were entering college, leaving behind a much smaller baby-bust cohort. The Census Bureau projected an 18 percent drop in the country's college-age population during the 1980s, with most of the decrease — an estimated 11 percent — likely to occur during the first half of the decade. Most observers said the U.S. college-student population faced significant shrinkage and that some small institutions would have to close.

But the gloomy predictions were far off the mark, according to *Challenges in College Admissions,* the 1995 report on a recent national survey. "Between 1979 and 1992, the number of 18-year-olds in the United States decreased by 1 million, and the number of 18-year-old high school graduates decreased by over half a million," the report states. "Yet total enrollment in higher education increased substantially." In addition, the 1985-1992 period saw hefty increases in applications to four-year institutions and in the average number of applicants per enrolled freshman. [11]

These counter-intuitive developments, the report suggests, grew out of aggressive marketing. Colleges spent more on such traditional recruiting tools as campus visits by prospective students and their families, visits to high schools by college admissions staffers and direct-mail appeals. But the greatest increases in recruiting activity were more narrowly focused, targeting racial and ethnic minorities, academically talented students, international students and adults. Toward the end of the decade, moreover, a majority of institutions responding to the survey said they had expanded their geographic recruiting ranges.

One such college was GW. "From 1988 to 1994, we invested considerable time and money to reach out west of the Mississippi," says Chernak. "We felt we were perceived primarily as an Eastern school. We're now getting a pretty good applicant flow from areas where we weren't well represented before. In 1988, maybe 10 percent of our incoming freshmen came from west of the Mississippi. Now it's probably closer to 30 percent."

Recruiting drives during the 1980s paid off for U.S. higher education as a whole, as well as for individual schools. Although the number of U.S. high school graduates fell by about 500,000 between 1980 and 1985, first-time college enrollments fell by fewer than 300,000. The reason, according to *Challenges in College Admissions,* is that "the proportion of high school graduates going directly on to college or university increased from 50 to 58 percent during this period." [12]

The trend continued through the rest of the decade. "Between 1985 and 1990, the number of high school graduates decreased by [an additional] 300,000, making the total decline since 1980 almost three-quarters of a million students. But the proportion of high school graduates going directly on to college increased from 58 to 60 percent . . . and first-time freshman enrollment decreased by only 29,000 students." By 1992, 62 percent of high school graduates were heading to college. [13]

The 1980s showed that unfavorable demographic trends can be blunted or even neutralized by expanding the pool of qualified college applicants. The National Center for Education Statistics expects undergraduate enrollment to increase steadily over the next 10 years, reaching a peak of almost 14 million students by the year 2005. For both public and private institutions, growth of full-time enrollment is projected to outpace part-time enrollment by a substantial margin.

Electronic technology may push the potential market for higher education

An Academic Profile of Undergraduates

More than a quarter of the nation's undergraduates needed remedial English and math in 1994, according to a national survey. Fewer than 10 percent had earned college credits while in high school.

Percentage of undergraduates who. . .	
Needed financial aid	63%
Needed remedial math	33%
Needed remedial English	27%
Earned college credits in high school	9%
Are degree-seeking	81%

Source: Elaine El-Khawas, *Campus Trends,* 1995, American Council on Education. The 1995 survey included responses from 407 two-year and four-year public and private colleges and universities.

Monitoring Changes in Enrollment

More than 40 percent of U.S. colleges and universities reported enrollment gains among African-Americans, Hispanics and students age 25 and older in 1994.

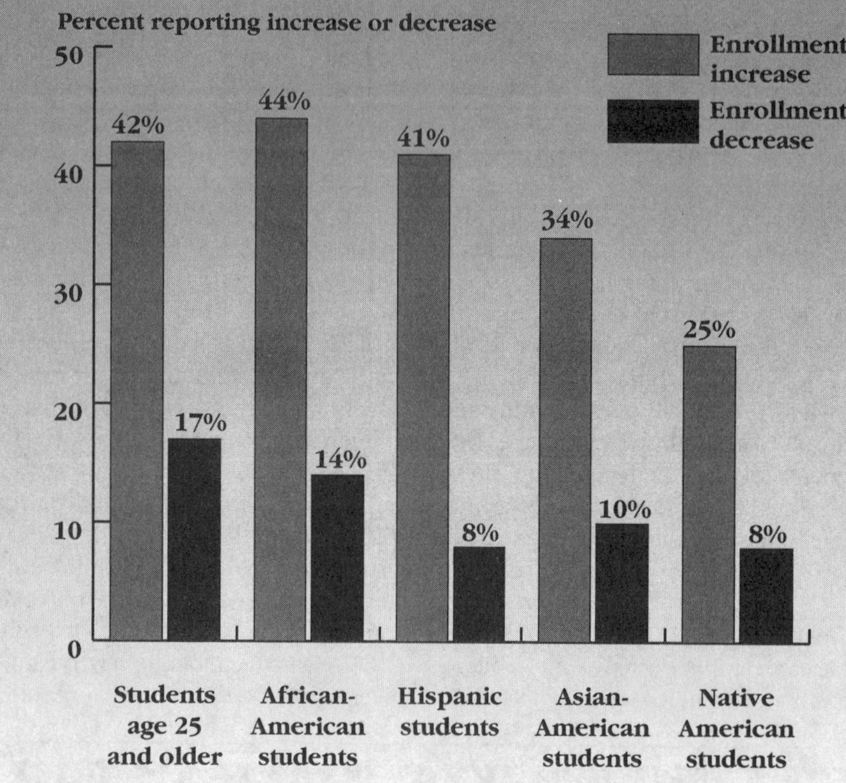

Note: Totals do not add up to 100 because percentages for "no change" were not included.

Source: Elaine El-Khawas, Campus Trends, *1995, American Council on Education. The 1995 survey included responses from 407 two-year and four-year public and private colleges and universities.*

well beyond current projections (*see p. 187*). The list of possibilities includes interactive video, CD-ROM instruction packages and, possibly, breakthroughs not yet on the horizon. As these new options emerge, degree-certification standards could undergo substantial change.

Will minorities be penalized by the University of California Board of Regents' decision to prohibit affirmative action?

The most dramatic development in college admissions policy in recent years was last summer's decision by the University of California (UC) Board of Regents to bar affirmative action in admissions, hiring and contracting (*see p. 183*). Preliminary projections by the university indicate that, under the new guidelines, the number of black students attending UC's nine campuses could drop by as much as 50 percent and the number of Hispanic students by as much as 24 percent. At the same time, the number of Asian students may rise by up to 25 percent, with white enrollment remaining basically unchanged. *

The fight against affirmative action was led by UC Regent Ward Connerly, who attracted wide media notice because he is an African-American. In his view, affirmative action is a polite term for racial bias. "It's interesting that the university community is probably the only government institution fighting to preserve the right to discriminate on the basis of race," he said shortly before the regents voted on his proposal. "I'm saying, 'Let's take a new look at this. . . . [W]hy aren't we out there trying to figure out how to create an inclusive university community without taking race into account?' "[14]

Carl C. Jorgensen, an African-American Harvard graduate who is now an associate sociology professor at the University of California, Davis, feels the ban on affirmative action could have unanticipated results. By the year 2002, he writes, "white or Asian-American graduates of some UC campuses may have much less personal knowledge of black and brown people and their perspectives than did graduates in 1992."[15]

In Jorgensen's opinion, moreover, "Ending affirmative action is not particularly in business' interest. Most businesses now want a diverse work force so that they can sell to diverse communities. So, I'm sure a lot of business people are pressuring the regents to change [their decision]. It's hard to tell what will happen, but I wouldn't be surprised to see some modification" of the new policy.

But some observers believe the new policy leaves enough "wiggle room" for campus administrators to maintain a

* According to statistics released Feb. 13, 1996, a record 45,939 high school students applied for the fall semester at UC, but applications from American Indians and Latinos dropped 9.8 percent and 2.3 percent, respectively, and applications from African-Americans rose just 0.6 percent. By comparison, applications from all three groups rose by several percentage points in the previous two years.

racially diverse student body. It does so by allowing admissions officials to consider an economically disadvantaged student's background, provided they do so in a race-neutral way. This approach would have the effect of "providing affirmative action preferences to the disadvantaged of all races," writes Richard D. Kahlenberg. "Defining beneficiaries by class, not race, would restore fairness to a system that has strayed far from the goals of the early proponents of affirmative action." [16]

Swanson feels that Californians and other Americans still support action to help members of underrepresented groups gain admission to college — "but not in the particular way that affirmative action spelled out." While further retreat from preferential admissions practices may occur, he doesn't sense "any withdrawal of commitment to the spirit" of helping disadvantaged students better themselves through higher education. ■

BACKGROUND

Diverse Standards

Until the late 19th century, criteria for admission to American colleges varied widely from institution to institution. Consequently, many colleges operated preparatory academies to help students acquire the academic background they needed. If a college lacked such a program, prospective students often either enrolled in another academy or hired a private tutor.

Entrance exams typically consisted of the college president and several faculty members testing the applicant's knowledge of Latin, Greek and mathematics — the essential building blocks of a classical education. The interrogation often lasted from dawn to dusk, with only a short break for lunch.

According to education historian Harold S. Wechsler, "the decision to admit a student . . . was determined by the quality of his answers, the college's financial picture and not infrequently on the kindliness of a faculty member." [17] When subjects such as geography, English grammar and history became entrance requirements, many colleges replaced the oral exams with a battery of written tests.

Davidson College

Davidson College students Jin Chang, a Korean-American from Charlotte, N.C., and Arsiyanti Ardie, from Jakarta, Indonesia.

Colleges sought to secure their status in American society by portraying themselves as "capstones" of a system from which the next generation of national leaders was sure to emerge. To succeed, they sought cooperation from private academies and, later, public high schools in tailoring the secondary school curriculum to fit college requirements. But the diversity of college entrance standards made the task difficult. Wilson Farrand, headmaster of Newark Academy, touched on the problem in a speech in 1895: "Princeton and Columbia call for six books of the *Aeneid;* Yale requires, in addition, the *Ecologues*. These do not count for maximum standing at Princeton unless combined with the *Georgics*. . . . Princeton requires Latin of candidates for one course, but not for others. Yale demands it of all, Columbia of none." [18]

Certificate System Launched at University of Michigan

While colleges and high schools in the East continued to bicker over entrance requirements, the University of Michigan in the early 1870s pioneered a new approach — admitting all graduates of high schools in the state that had been accredited by a team of inspectors. The policy was modeled on the German system of secondary schools, the gymnasia. Many of those who supported admission by a certificate, Wechsler wrote, saw it as a "potential solution for solving a basic problem faced by most American colleges in the 19th century — the need to maintain and, if possible, to increase enrollments." [19]

Only 5 percent of American 17-year-olds graduated from high school in 1890, and only a fraction of that group went on to college. Many institutions adopted the certificate system with the expectation that more students would seek admission once demanding entrance exams were dropped. As more colleges joined the movement, regional associations were formed to inspect and accredit secondary schools.

By the turn of the century, the

certificate system had become the most popular method of regulating college admissions. Not surprisingly, it gained broadest acceptance in the Midwest, where the movement began. Resistance was strongest among the older, elite colleges of the New England and Middle Atlantic states.

"Such institutions," Wechsler wrote, "opposed certification because it was new and they revered traditions; because it threatened their domination of the high schools . . . and because it implied that they were in competition for students, something their high enrollments did not support in fact and their high self-estimate did not allow in principle." [20] Over time, however, all of the Ivy League schools except Harvard, Princeton and Yale adopted the system.

Standardized Exams

The elite colleges were never comfortable with certification, but neither were they satisfied with widely divergent standards for college entrance. For this reason, presidents Nicholas Murray Butler of Columbia and Charles W. Eliot of Harvard led a campaign to bring about closer cooperation between institutions of higher learning and secondary schools, while keeping the final decision on admissions with the colleges. Their efforts culminated in the creation of the College Entrance Examination Board in 1900.

The College Board supplied standardized entrance examinations to its members. Only 12 schools joined at the outset: Barnard, Bryn Mawr, Columbia, Cornell, Johns Hopkins, New York University, University of Pennsylvania, Rutgers, Swarthmore, Union, Vassar and Women's College of Baltimore. Gradually the board attracted more members, who saw in it the chance to reach a larger and more varied group of students. Examinations soon were available to students throughout the nation. By 1910, even the "Big Three" — Harvard, Yale and Princeton — had joined the fold.

In the 1919-20 academic year, almost 600,000 students in search of credits or degrees attended the country's 1,041 institutions of higher learning. Many were World War I veterans. "As was to be demonstrated repeatedly in later decades, military service undoubtedly had alerted veterans to the value and need of college training and stimulated their re-enrollments, as well as initial entry, into college," wrote Garland G. Parker, an authority on college enrollment patterns. [21]

During the 1920s Americans came to place an increasingly high value on education, including higher education. "There was a strong feeling among parents generally, especially immigrants, that educational advancement offered a sure outlet from ghetto life and a high road to success for their children," Parker wrote. "The colleges largely were populated by the offspring of the well-to-do, but many thousands of lower-middle-class students from urban, as well as rural, areas found their way onto college campuses. The nation was on the threshold of the greatest experiment in mass education at the collegiate level that the world had yet seen." By the end of the decade, the number of college students had doubled to 1.1 million.

In the 1930s, the Depression exerted the major influence on higher education. Enrollments held steady or even continued to rise through 1931, fell off noticeably from 1932 to 1934 but climbed significantly in the next two years and maintained an upward curve through the balance of the decade. The rise in enrollment during the middle and late 1930s stemmed in part from New Deal legislation, which included federal aid to needy college students. "Despite the throes of the Depression," Parker observed, "the American people continued to have faith in higher education as a stepping stone to success for themselves and their children. Even though times got harder, every effort was made to support their sons, especially, in school as long as financial resources permitted."

Meanwhile, changes were occurring in standardized college entrance examinations. The original College Board tests had been essay exams, but educators began to question whether that was the best way to identify candidates who would succeed in college. After World War I, the College Board became interested in testing programs developed by the government to measure soldiers' ability to perform various assignments.

Aptitude Tests Introduced

In 1926, the board administered its first aptitude test, the Scholastic Aptitude Test (SAT), a multiple-choice exam covering a wide array of topics. The aim was to measure "future ability" rather than "past mastery," to reveal the broad expanse of a student's knowledge, not the minute details of his preparation. Colleges generally preferred the new SAT, and most of the older exams were dropped during World War II, never to return.

By 1946, the College Board had expanded its testing program far beyond college entrance examinations. Among its clients were the State Department, the U.S. Naval Academy and the National Administrative Board for Pepsi-Cola Scholarships. But many board members felt the board had strayed too far from its original mandate, and on Dec. 19, 1947, the board, in cooperation with the Carnegie Foundation for the Advancement of Teaching and the American Council on Education, established the Educational Testing Service (ETS). The new organization was given responsibility for developing all the tests formerly handled by the board itself.

A report published by the President's Commission on Higher Education in 1946 noted that only a fraction of those who could benefit from higher educa-

Continued on p. 180

Chronology

1800s-1920s

Individual colleges set their own admission standards until the late 19th century, when higher education becomes more widely available and uniform standards for admission begin to win acceptance.

1900
The College Entrance Examination Board — now known as the College Board — is established to provide standardized tests to member institutions.

1926
The College Board administers its first Scholastic Aptitude Test (SAT) as an alternative to traditional essay exams.

1940s

Higher education undergoes explosive growth after World War II as returning G.I.s jam campuses across the country.

1944
President Franklin D. Roosevelt signs the Servicemen's Readjustment Act (the G.I. Bill), the largest college scholarship program in the nation's history.

Dec. 19, 1947
The College Board, in cooperation with the Carnegie Foundation for the Advancement of Teaching and the American Council on Education, establishes the Educational Testing Service (ETS) to develop the tests formerly handled by the board itself.

1950s-1970s

College cost increases outstrip rises in the Consumer Price Index, stirring alarm among parents of college-age children.

1959
The American College Testing Program (ACT) is founded in Iowa City, Iowa.

Nov. 8, 1965
President Lyndon B. Johnson signs into law the Higher Education Act, which provides aid to needy college students through grants, Guaranteed Student Loans and work-study programs.

June 28, 1978
The U.S. Supreme Court rules in *University of California Regents v. Bakke* that institutions of higher learning may weigh race as a factor in admissions policies but may not designate a set number of places for minority applicants.

1990s

Student aid and preferential admissions policies stir controversy among higher education officials and the families of students planning to attend college.

July 23, 1992
President George Bush signs the Higher Education Act Amendments of 1992, making federal aid more widely available to college students from middle-income families.

Aug. 10, 1993
President Clinton signs the Student Loan Reform Act, which provides direct federal loans to college students. The new loan program largely replaces the existing system, which provided costly subsidies to the commercial banks that acted as middlemen in loan transactions.

July 1995
University of California (UC) Board of Regents votes to end racial preferences in hiring and contracting by January 1996 and in student admissions by January 1997.

Jan. 23, 1996
UC President Richard Atkinson announces that the ban on using race and gender as factors in undergraduate admissions decisions will not take effect until January 1998.

Jan. 23, 1996
In his State of the Union address, President Clinton proposes "a tax deduction for all education and training [expenses] after high school" as part of his Middle-Class Bill of Rights.

Jan. 28, 1996
Atkinson concedes he overstepped his authority in changing the regents' timetable on implementing the affirmative action ban.

Feb. 15, 1996
University of California regents compromise and agree to end preferences beginning with the spring 1998 term.

Feb. 21, 1996
The required number of signatures must be gathered by this date to put the California Civil Rights Initiative 1996 on the state ballot in November. The initiative seeks approval of a ban on racial preferences in state colleges and universities, public employment and government contracting.

Annual College Rankings Find Ready Market

Given the high premium placed on a college education, it's little wonder that rankings of colleges by academic distinction, affordability and myriad other criteria have found a ready market. So, too, have books and magazines offering advice on selecting the right college, and getting in.

The rising cost of college is in large part responsible for the popularity of such publications. With many institutions charging between $10,000 and $25,000 a year for tuition and other services, students and their families are determined to get maximum value for their money. Annual college rankings are published by such periodicals as *Barron's*, *Money* and *U.S. News & World Report*. Admissions tips are offered by such guides as *Playing the Selective College Admissions Game* and *Scaling the Ivy Wall in the '90s*.

The *U.S. News* survey is probably the best-known of the magazine rankings. It divides the country's 1,400 accredited, four-year colleges and universities with more than 200 students into four categories — national universities, regional universities, national liberal arts colleges and regional liberal arts colleges. Each institution then is judged in terms of how it rates in terms of reputation, selectivity, faculty, student retention, financial resources and student satisfaction. The school's ranking in each area is then weighted in accordance with a statistical formula.[1] After these six sub-scores are added together, the schools are listed in descending order of combined score.

Campus officials often complain about the methodology used in college rankings, saying some factors receive either too little or too much consideration. For their part, survey-takers accuse certain administrators of handling their data in a way that produces a higher survey ranking than is justified. Last spring, for instance, *The Wall Street Journal* reported that a number of colleges had inflated the composite SAT score of their freshman class by tossing out the scores of foreign students, student athletes and other low academic achievers.[2]

Such practices lend support to the claim that schools are becoming increasingly competitive for students, and that as a result higher education is becoming more of a buyer's than a seller's market. Mel Elfin, the editor in charge of the *U.S. News* college survey, thinks a shakeout among colleges is overdue. In his opinion, "We should be closing one school a week."[3]

[1] Reputation and selectivity each count for 25 percent, faculty for 20 percent, student retention for 15 percent, financial resources for 10 percent and student satisfaction for 5 percent.

[2] *The Wall Street Journal*, April 5 1995, p. A1.

[3] Quoted by Bill Gifford, "The Arbiter," *Lingua Franca*, January-February 1995, p. 42.

Continued from p. 178

tion actually were enrolled in colleges. "American colleges must envision a much larger role for higher education in the national life," the commission stated. "They can no longer consider themselves merely the instrument for producing an intellectual elite; they must become the means by which every citizen, youth and adult, is enabled and encouraged to carry his education, formal and informal, as far as his native capacities permit."

Enrollment Skyrockets

As it happened, American colleges and universities experienced unparalleled growth and expansion over the next 20 years. This new era in higher education had been launched by the Servicemen's Readjustment Act of 1944 — the G.I. Bill — the largest scholarship program in the nation's history. Veterans who were enrolled as full-time students were provided with living allowances, while the government made direct payments to their institutions for tuition, fees and other normal school costs.

The coming of the generation born after World War II — the baby boom — boosted college enrollment to unprecedented levels in the 1960s. Between 1959-1960 and 1969-1970 enrollment more than doubled, rising from 3.5 million to 8 million. Not only was there a hefty increase in the number of college-age students, but the proportion actually attending college rose also. By 1970, 34 percent of the 18-21 age group were enrolled in degree or credit programs in higher education, compared with 23 percent in 1960, 15 percent in 1950 and 11 percent in 1940.

Social pressure to go to college increased enormously during the 1960s. One reason was that higher education was seen as the most likely path to economic success and individual fulfillment. In addition, a steady rise in per capita income throughout the decade meant that more parents could afford to send their children to college than ever before. And as more and more persons obtained degrees, employers began recruiting college graduates for jobs that formerly had gone to high school graduates.[22]

Around this time, however, a college degree became more difficult to obtain. As enrollments soared in the late 1950s and the '60s, many private institutions, and some public ones, began to limit the size of their student bodies and raise admission standards. Greater stress was placed on national college aptitude tests, including the SAT. So pressing was the demand for tests to screen students that the American College Testing Program (ACT) was founded in 1959 in Iowa City, Iowa. (*See story, p. 182.*)

One of the key developments in higher education during this period was the growth of two-year community colleges. Vocationally oriented junior colleges had been around since the mid-19th century, but they remained a minor feature of American postsecondary education until the late 1950s. By the mid-1960s, these colleges, now called community colleges, were opening at the rate of about one a week.

In the 1959-1960 school year, some 640,500 students were enrolled in two-year colleges. A decade later, the number had grown to almost 2 million full- and part-time students, or nearly 30 percent of all U.S. undergraduates. The rapid advance of community colleges was attributed to their open-admission policies, their wide geographic distribution and their low tuition fees. In addition, two-year institutions generally offered night courses for working students.

Aid From Congress

As the community college boom proceeded, families across the country were starting to worry that they could not afford to send their children to college. Tuition and other fees were rising at a higher rate — often substantially higher — than the Consumer Price Index (CPI).

Congress addressed this concern by passing the Higher Education Act, signed into law by President Lyndon B. Johnson on Nov. 8, 1965. Title IV of the far-reaching measure established several programs offering grants and loans to college students on the basis of family income. They included grants, which recipients did not have to repay (now known as Pell Grants); Guaranteed Student Loans, later known as Stafford Loans, which students had to repay after graduation; and work-study programs, which enabled students to pay for part of their education by working during the school year at on-campus or public-sector jobs.

Davidson College

Professor William Mahony takes his class in Asian religious thought outdoors at Davidson College, near Charlotte, N.C. Tuition at the 1,400-student school will be $18,954 in fall 1996, up 5.3 percent from the previous year.

By today's standards, the amount of aid provided by the 1965 law was modest: $70 million annually in fiscal years 1966-1968 for first-year scholarships as well as the money needed to continue each scholarship beyond the first year. Moreover, the law required that scholarship funds be distributed in accordance with each state's proportionate share of the U.S. college student population. For their part, colleges were required to encourage needy high school students to seek a college education.

Though the education act relieved some of the financial burden on lower- and middle-income families, increases in tuition and other charges continued to outstrip the overall inflation rate. Congress provided more relief when it reauthorized the act in 1992.

The revised law made federal aid available to more middle-income students by allowing them to deduct the value of the equity in their families' home or farm from calculations to determine the students' eligibility for aid. It also increased the amount of money that lower-income, full-time students could obtain through Stafford Loans.

The most controversial provision of the reauthorization bill called for issuing the federal loans to students directly through their college, bypassing the commercial banks and guarantee agencies that typically had acted as middlemen. The banks objected to being frozen out, and President George Bush also complained. After the direct-loan provision was changed

Standardized Tests Take Differing Approaches

When college admissions officers evaluate applicants, high school grades and class standings count for much. But academic standards at the nation's thousands of secondary schools vary widely, making valid comparisons difficult. Thus, many institutions also consult standardized test scores to provide a more rounded picture of a candidate's ability to handle college work.

The two most widely used college-entrance exams are the Scholastic Assessment Test (SAT), dating from 1926, and the American College Testing Program (ACT), introduced in 1959. Although both are widely used, they differ somewhat in approach.

The SAT (now called the SAT I: Reasoning Test) is a three-hour, two-part exam that measures academic aptitude in terms of verbal and mathematical reasoning. Each of the two sections is scored on a scale ranging from 200 to 800 (students earn 200 points just by signing their name), and the two scores then are added together. In addition to SAT I, some students take one or more SAT II: Subject Tests in such fields as literature, biology, American history and French.

Starting this year, SAT I scores will be reported on a scale "recentered" at 500, the midway point between 200 and 800. The change was made in response to the long downward drift in SAT scores. Last year, the nationwide average score was 428 on the verbal portion and 482 on the mathematical portion. Even if this year's scores turn out to be precisely the same, they will appear to be some 75 points higher because of recentering.

According to the College Board, "recentering does not affect the way test-takers compare to each other within the test-taking pool, and therefore will cause no student to either gain or lose a seat in college." The board further notes that, "As the unwavering performance percentiles will show, the new scores do not mean that students are suddenly performing at a higher level."[1] In any case, the maximum total SAT I score will remain 1,600.

ACT Assessment, the American College Testing counterpart of SAT I, comprises separate multiple-choice exams in English, mathematics, reading and science reasoning. All are graded on a scale of 1 to 36, with fractional scores converted to the nearest whole number. The numbers then are added together and divided by four to produce a composite score.

There is one further scoring difference between the ACT and SAT I. ACT scores are based solely on the number of correct answers, with no penalty imposed for guessing. With SAT I, in contrast, incorrect answers are subtracted from the final score and additional points are taken off to compensate for possible guesses. (SAT I test-takers are allowed to use calculators on the math test, but ACT test-takers are not.)

The SAT I tends to be the college entrance exam of choice on the East Coast and West Coast, while the ACT tends to be more popular in the Middle West and Far West. But overall, "The trend these days is toward accepting either," says Kelley Hayden, corporate communications director for American College Testing. According to Hayden, institutions generally use the higher score, "depending upon which one looks best for the individual student."

[1] The College Board, "The New SAT," May 1995, p. 1.

to a four-year demonstration program, Bush withdrew his veto threat and signed the measure.

Congress returned to the student-loan issue after Bill Clinton became president in 1993. Under the 1993 omnibus budget-reconciliation bill, direct loans were to be phased in over four years, reaching 60 percent of total new loan volume in the 1998-1999 academic year. The measure also lowered the interest-rate cap on both direct loans and guaranteed student loans from 9 percent to 8.25 percent. Students, moreover, were given several options for repaying their loans. Direct-loan advocates said the changes would save $4.6 billion over five years.

Affirmative Action

In recent decades, affirmative action has rivaled the availability of student aid as a hot-button issue among students and educators alike. Supporters of affirmative action say race- and gender-conscious remedies are designed to ensure that otherwise fully qualified minorities have access to institutions — in this case, places of higher learning — that historically had excluded them. Opponents, by contrast, argue that affirmative action is a politically correct euphemism for quota systems that often admit unqualified applicants.

Two Supreme Court cases in the 1970s showed how divisive affirmative action could be. In *DeFunis v. Odegaard,* plaintiff Marco DeFunis, a white Phi Beta Kappa graduate of the University of Washington, charged that in 1971 he was denied admission to the university's law school so that a less-qualified minority student could be accepted. The law school, which had received 1,600 applications for 150 openings, acknowledged that 36 minority candidates had been admitted with grades and test scores lower than DeFunis'. By a 5-4 vote, the court refused to decide the case because DeFunis had been allowed to attend the law school while the case was being adjudicated.

In *University of California Regents v. Bakke,* a 1978 case similar to *DeFunis,* two closely divided rulings were handed down by the high court. Allen Bakke, a white college graduate, had sought admission to 13 medical schools in 1972 and '73, only to be rejected by all of them. Applying to the University of California, Davis, for the second time in 1974, Bakke again was turned down. On both occasions, 16 minority applicants were admitted to Davis under affirmative action programs. Bakke sued the university, saying his grades and test scores were better than those of most of the minority applicants who were admitted.

This time, also by a 5-4 margin, the court held that state universities may not set aside a fixed quota of seats in each class for minority group members, denying white applicants the opportunity to compete for those places. But at the same time, the court — in yet another 5-4 vote — held that it is constitutionally permissible for admissions officers to consider race as one of the many factors that determine which applicants are accepted.

With these guidelines in mind, UC officials began crafting a quota-less affirmative action policy for the system's nine campuses. In its current form, the policy provides that 60 percent of UC applicants are admitted solely on the basis of high school grades and test scores. The remaining 40 percent are admitted on grade points and test scores, with supplemental points awarded for such factors as residency, veteran's status, disability, community service, underrepresented minority and economically disadvantaged status.

UC's admissions formula is credited with giving the university one of the nation's most racially and ethnically diverse student bodies. Almost 4 percent of the 162,000-plus students are black, 25 percent are Asian-American and 12 percent are Hispanic. According to *New Republic* Associate Editor Hanna Rosin, the California approach is a "workable model" that has "achieved what the convulsive national debate on affirmative action has been seeking: the elusive middle ground." [23] ■

CURRENT SITUATION

California Controversy

Many educators share Rosin's high regard for UC-style affirmative action. But the feeling is far from unanimous, as shown by last July's 14-10 decision by the university Board of Regents to bar racial and gender preferences in admissions, effective Jan. 1, 1997. A month earlier, Republican Gov. Pete Wilson had issued an executive order curbing affirmative action programs that gave special consideration to women and minorities in state hiring and contracts. The regents' vote and Wilson's order were widely viewed as efforts to jump-start the governor's brief campaign for the 1996 Republican presidential nomination.

Wilson, however, insisted he acted out of belief that individual merit should be the controlling factor in college admissions. "Racial preferences are by definition racial discrimination," he wrote in the *San Francisco Chronicle.* "They were wrong 30 years ago when they discriminated against African-Americans. And they're wrong today, when they discriminate against Asian- or Caucasian-Americans." The best way to build a diverse student body, he added, "isn't to grant special preferences in admissions to some students at the expense of others, it's to ensure that every student receives the elementary and secondary education that will allow them to compete for admissions to UC . . . regardless of the color of their skin, their race, ethnicity or gender." [24]

Connerly, the regent who proposed the affirmative action ban, voiced similar thoughts. "People have consciously, in the academic world, bought . . . the notion that groups ought to be represented, that there ought to be parity," he said. "It is a fundamentally different view than the one I grew up with, of individuals working hard to move up that ladder on the basis of individual effort." [25]

But Regent Roy T. Brophy, who opposed the ban, saw "no need to act so abruptly and unilaterally." *(See "At Issue," p. 185.)* In his opinion, the policy shift "put the university at the center of a political debate and set the regents against UC's administration, faculty and students — including those students who someday might want to attend our campuses." Instead, he argued, the regents should have conducted a study "to identify equitable options that would have preserved what worked well about affirmative action and addressed what needed attention." [26]

Brophy's misgivings apparently echoed the feelings of many college students and faculty members, both in California and elsewhere. For instance, the faculty senates of all nine UC campuses have publicly opposed the ban. Moreover, a recent nationwide survey of 240,082 college freshmen conducted by UCLA's Higher Education Research Institute found that 70 percent of the respondents felt race should receive at least "some special consideration" by college admissions officers. On the other hand, opinion was evenly split among respondents as to whether "affirmative action in college admissions should be abolished."

The seemingly contradictory responses on affirmative action prompted the survey's associate director, Linda J. Sax, to note: "This discrepancy highlights the fact that people are willing to support the consideration of race in admissions, but are less willing to commit themselves to the more politically loaded phrase, 'affirmative action.' "[27]

The UC admissions controversy heated up again Jan. 23, when University President Richard C. Atkinson said the ban on factoring race and gender into admissions decisions would be postponed until fall 1998. Wilson and Connerly immediately accused Atkinson of foot-dragging and said they would accept no change in the regents' 1997 timetable. Atkinson beat a partial retreat Jan. 25, informing Wilson and the UC regents by letter that the delay in implementing the ban would apply only to undergraduate admissions. Full capitulation came Jan. 28, as Atkinson conceded he had overstepped his authority. On Feb. 15, 1996, the Regents compromised and voted unanimously to eliminate preferences in undergraduate admissions beginning with students applying for the spring 1998 term.

At least one additional chapter in the California affirmative-action saga remains to be written. It centers on the California Civil Rights Initiative, which Wilson and Connerly hope to place on the Nov. 5 ballot. If approved by voters, the initiative would amend the state constitution to abolish preferences based on race, gender or ethnic origin in state employment and contracting as well as admissions to public institutions of higher learning. Feb. 21 is the deadline for collecting the required number of signatures.

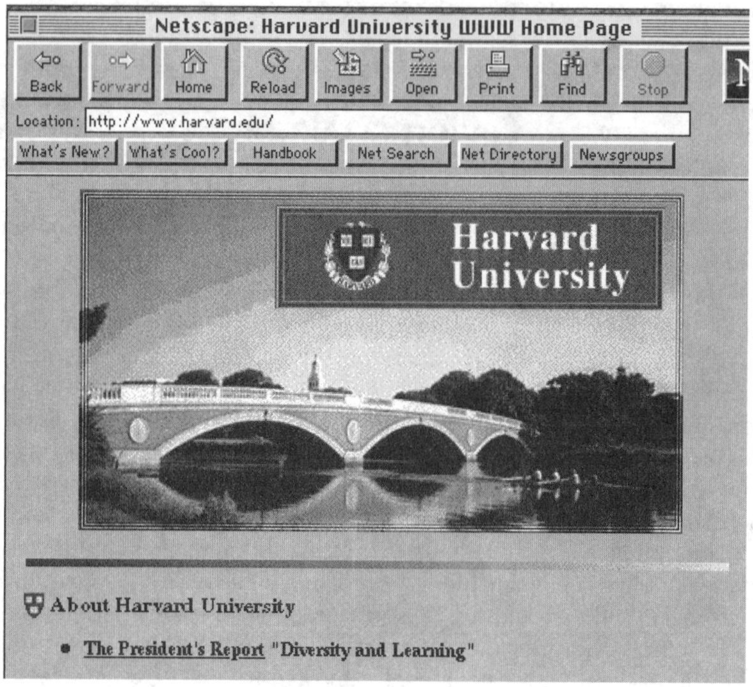

Financial Aid

College students in California and across the country seem at least as concerned about the cost of college as they are about affirmative action. The recent UCLA survey, the 30th in an annual series, reported that a record 71.4 percent of respondents said they worried about having enough money to complete their education. The previous high, 64.9 percent, was recorded in 1966. In addition, 39.5 percent of those questioned said they believed they would have to take a job to help pay for college expenses.

Harvard University is among many higher education institutions that are providing information to applicants via the World Wide Web.

The cause for concern is real. Tuitions have risen 6 percent at public and private universities each year for the past three years; costs this year are expected to rise 4-5 percent at many schools.[28]

Financially pinched students no doubt applauded the student-aid initiatives President Clinton proposed in his Jan. 23 State of the Union address to Congress. They included $1,000 merit scholarships to the top 5 percent of graduating seniors in every American high school and expansion of the federal work-study program from the current 700,000 students to 1 million by the year 2000. In addition, the president repeated earlier proposals for a $300 increase this year (to $2,620) in the size of the maximum Pell Grant, and for a tax deduction of up to $10,000 for money spent on college tuition or job training. "Higher education is more important today than ever before," he declared.

Not surprisingly, college admissions officials welcomed Clinton's proposals. "People should acknowledge that higher education is an expenditure that will benefit the country in the long term," says Yale's Shaw. "If families can be encouraged to put up the money to send their children to college, and receive some tax relief in return, it would be sort of like getting a federal loan, wouldn't it? It's a way to encourage families to give kids the kind of quality education that they often have earned — and deserve."

Few educators expect the Republican-controlled Congress to embrace tax deductions for tuition outlays. Indeed, GOP leaders have called for cuts of more than $10 billion in student aid over the next seven years. Reports of widespread abuse of student loan and grant programs lent substance to the demands for reform.

On Jan. 22, however, the Education Department announced that the rate at which college students default on their loans fell from 22.4 percent in 1990 to 11.6 percent in 1993. Moreover, the department said it had collected more than $2 billion in overdue loans. Education Secretary Richard W. Riley credited more vigorous action

Continued on p. 186

At Issue:

Was the University of California Board of Regents justified in ending affirmative action preferences for admissions?

YES

GOV. PETE WILSON, R-CALIF.
FROM *THE SAN FRANCISCO CHRONICLE*, JAN. 18, 1996.

Last July, the University of California's Board of Regents decided . . . that every high school graduate in California should have an equal opportunity to compete for admissions to the UC system based on individual merit, regardless of race.

It was the right decision then. It's the right decision now.

Racial preferences are by definition racial discrimination. They were wrong 30 years ago when they discriminated against African-Americans. And they're wrong today, when they discriminate against Asian- or Caucasian-Americans.

Abolishing them . . . was not only necessary to meet the University of California's mission as an institution of higher learning committed to the fundamental American principles of equal opportunity and individual merit, it was critical to maintaining for the university support and credibility among the millions of hard-working Californians whose taxes finance this institution.

Admission to UC isn't an entitlement that should be distributed based on some quota. It's something to be earned — based on hard work and individual excellence.

Ending racial preferences in admissions at UC was also necessary to comply with the law of the land as articulated by the U.S. Supreme Court. In a series of decisions last spring, the court made it abundantly clear that classifying individuals by race, except in the narrowest circumstances, is unconstitutional. . . .

Rather than constantly revisiting this decision, we must get on with implementing it and making the other changes necessary to ensure that every Californian has the opportunity to pursue the world-class education offered by all nine UC campuses. In the past five years, we've more than doubled the student aid available to California's college students. And this year, an expanding economy has allowed us to keep student fees from increasing.

But we cannot ignore the failure of a K-12 system that has allowed so many Californians to graduate from high school unprepared for college. The best way to ensure diversity at UC isn't to grant special preferences in admissions to some students at the expense of others; it's to ensure that every student receives the elementary and secondary education that will allow them to compete for admissions to UC based on individual merit, regardless of the color of their skin, their race, ethnicity or gender. . . .

Today, we must renew our commitment to fundamental fairness. The regents must fulfill their obligation to set policy for this institution and continue moving forward to equal opportunity for all Californians by rejecting motions to retreat from last July's principled decision — a retreat which, however well-intended, would commit this university system to a morally indefensible policy of explicit racial and gender preferences.

NO

ROY T. BROPHY
Member and past chairman of the University of California Board of Regents

FROM *THE SAN DIEGO UNION-TRIBUNE*, NOV. 14, 1995.

It was a mistake for the University of California Board of Regents to abolish affirmative action practices at UC — a mistake that needs fixing. This was clear to me when the regents acted last July. That's why I voted against the action. . . . I believe there's a better way to proceed. It centers on two key factors: a proposed ballot measure called the California Civil Rights Initiative (CCRI) and UC's traditional respect for the principle of "shared governance."

If passed by voters, the CCRI would amend the state Constitution to eliminate preferences based on race, gender or ethnicity in state employment, public contracting and college and university admissions. The backers of the initiative are currently far short of collecting enough signatures to qualify it for the November 1996 ballot. They have until Feb. 21 to do so. If they succeed, the voters will decide the future of affirmative action as we know it in this state and within the University of California.

The Board of Regents could have waited for this to play out. We could have used the time to consult with faculty and students, administrators, staff and others who have a stake in this issue. The regents could have taken a vote, but held off final adoption of any changes pending the fate of the CCRI. We could have conducted a study . . . to identify equitable options that would have preserved what worked well about affirmative action and addressed what needed attention. I proposed an amendment to this effect at the July regents' meeting. It was defeated 14-10. If CCRI fails to qualify for the ballot, I fully intend to raise the issue again. I will formally propose to the regents that they reconsider their vote of last July, examine this most sensitive issue more carefully and fairly and, in so doing, revive the principle and practice of shared governance.

Shared governance is one of the qualities that has made UC one of the world's great universities. Put simply, it means that the regents, in governing the university, delegate the implementation of policy to the president and the chancellors, and entrust to the faculty academic matters such as academic policy, hiring and promotions and the conditions for admission.

At the heart of shared governance is the idea of communication and consultation. This is especially important in matters that affect the role of the faculty and the educational experience we provide to students. The regents, by voting as they did last July, broke from this valued tradition. . . .

What the regents did was wrong. How they did it was wrong. We need to work together, all of us at UC, to make it right.

Setting Academic Standards for Athletes

At many colleges, the most closely watched admissions decisions are those involving student athletes. Jean H. Fetter, former dean of undergraduate admissions at Stanford University, put it this way: "[W]hen the Stanford team does well, the coach gets a lot of credit; when the team performs badly, the dean of undergraduate admissions is held responsible." [1]

At Stanford, one of the nation's most selective private universities, students who want to participate in intercollegiate athletics are considered "through fundamentally the same admissions process as every other applicant for the freshman and transfer classes," Fetter noted. But many other institutions hold incoming student athletes to lower academic standards than other freshmen must meet.

The current standards, approved in 1983 by the National Collegiate Athletic Association (NCAA), require incoming athletes at Division I schools to have at least a 2.0 high school grade-point average (out of 4.0) in a core curriculum of 11 courses. They also must score at least 700 points (out of a possible 1,600) on the combined Scholastic Achievement Tests (SATs) or average 15 points (out of 36) on each of the four parts of the American College Testing Program (ACT).

In 1992, however, the NCAA tightened the standards. Under the revised rules, which take effect Aug. 1, 1996, freshman athletes will be ineligible for Division I teams unless they have a high school grade-point average (GPA) of 2.5 in 13 core courses. In addition, they must get at least 700 on the SATs, as before, or average 17 on the ACT. [2] A new sliding scale allows athletes to gain eligibility with a core GPA as low as 2.0, provided they offset it with substantially higher standardized test results.

Also starting Aug. 1, athletes who fall short of the new academic requirements but meet other minimum standards can practice and receive athletic aid as freshmen. Such athletes, called partial qualifiers, can meet a sliding scale that allows for a combined SAT score as low as 600 (or an ACT average score of 15) if it is offset by a core GPA of at least 2.75. These athletes retain three years of eligibility.

On Jan. 8, 1996, Division I delegates to the NCAA's annual convention in Dallas, Texas, narrowly defeated a proposal to eliminate standardized-test scoring requirements for student athletes with solid grades in high school core courses. The 163-161 vote mirrored a longstanding split in NCAA Division I ranks between institutions determined to hold athletes to some minimum academic-performance standards and those who say such rules discriminate against youngsters from low-income families. [3]

---

[1] Jean H. Fetter, *Questions and Admissions: Reflections on 100,000 Admissions Decisions at Stanford* (1995), p. 152.

[2] The NCAA is now adding together individual ACT scores to yield a combined total. Thus, starting Aug. 1, incoming freshmen athletes must score at least 68 points (out of 144) on the four segments.

[3] For background, see "High School Sports," *The CQ Researcher,* Sept. 22, 1995, pp. 825-848, and "College Sports," *The CQ Researcher,* Aug. 26, 1994, pp. 745-768.

against defaulters by the Clinton administration and a healthier national economy. "These significant default reductions and loan collections should quiet critics who claim we aren't up to the task, and therefore shouldn't be entrusted to manage the direct-loan program," Riley declared. [29]

Competition for Students

Top colleges say that students are so worried about getting into good schools that the number of applications has increased at least 50 percent in the last decade. At Georgetown University, for example, the number of applications grew from 6,500 in 1991 to more than 10,000 this year. [30]

To gain an edge in attracting the top students, many selective colleges and universities are turning to binding early-admissions programs, in which applications typically are due by Nov. 1 of the high school senior year. Such programs are open to students who promise to attend the school if admitted.

When Yale switched from non-binding to binding early admissions last fall, the number of early applicants dropped by 31 percent. "It wasn't a surprise to us; we kind of anticipated that," Shaw says. At the same time, he adds, "Our overall applications are up. More students are using the regular application process, which is something we feel perfectly comfortable with." According to the College Board, 471 institutions had early-admission programs last year, compared with 371 in 1990.

Meanwhile, a U.S. college education is becoming increasingly sought by students abroad. And foreign students, in turn, are prized because, typically, they pay higher fees than U.S. students and are ineligible for financial aid. Although students from abroad usually seek degrees from four-year universities, many initially enroll in a two-year community college to improve their English and stretch their financial resources.

In the United States, competition for students now extends well beyond traditional recruiting territories. Some institutions have opened recruiting offices in neighboring or distant states in an effort to build student bodies that are geographically or ethnically more diverse. Others have gone electronic, making glossy campus "tours" available via CD-ROM.

Such promotions are beyond the reach of many small, private colleges. These institutions often turn to private recruiting firms to drum up applicants

— a practice deplored by many education officials. "How can a salesperson who is quota-driven be thinking about the best interest of the kids as opposed to themselves?" asked William McClintick, vice president of admission practices at the National Association of College Admission Counselors. [31] ■

OUTLOOK

Continued Growth?

As they chart the future, college educators foresee continued growth of U.S. higher education. Part of it will come in the traditional way — expansion of existing campus facilities. Swanson notes, however, that some institutions have neither the space nor the desire to expand. That's particularly true, he says, of "smaller, liberal arts colleges that feel they have reached a size that's right for them."

Swanson also believes community colleges will assume a more significant role in coming years, since they often have a flexibility that many four-year institutions lack. "If the local fire department wants to offer a fire-science course, for instance, the community college can send some of its faculty to teach it at the firehouse. Community colleges aren't necessarily tied to specific locations."

Electronic instruction may hold the greatest potential of all for fueling higher education's growth. "With distance learning, you can offer a course at several sites simultaneously and have two-way communication between faculty and students," says Swanson. "We're also going to see more packaging of education through various electronic media, from the Internet to CD-ROM."

Elaine El-Khawas, vice president for policy analysis and research at the American Council on Education, notes that it's possible even now to obtain a college degree entirely by electronic means. At this point, however, the opportunity exists only "in very specific areas — a master's degree in certain engineering technology fields, for instance. But that kind of thing is going to advance further."

Mixing classroom and electronic instruction raises the question of who decides whether a student has qualified for a college degree. According to El-Khawas, "Most universities will require some minimum amount of coursework taken in their facilities to obtain a degree from them. That's the practice today. If you transfer into a college with a good number of credits toward a bachelor's degree, you may still have to take, say, one-quarter of your total courses at that institution. That kind of requirement is likely to remain in place."

So-called proprietary institutions could witness substantial growth in the future. "We tend to think of those as being very skill-specific — Connecticut School of Horseshoeing, or something like that," says Swanson. "But many of them offer bona fide transfer courses as well. Students may enroll primarily to take a certain skill course, but they can also take general-studies courses that can help them gain admission to another institution."

Because proprietary schools usually operate on a for-profit basis, adds Swanson, "they're looking very actively at expanding their markets." Victims of corporate downsizing could be particularly receptive to what the proprietaries have to offer: "Increasingly, people will need retraining in their original field or an entirely different field."

The celebrated baby-boom generation, which triggered the college enrollment boom of the 1960s and '70s, may come to higher education's rescue again. "Large numbers of baby boomers are going to be early-retiring

FOR MORE INFORMATION

American Association of Collegiate Registrars and Admissions Officers, 1 Dupont Circle N.W., Suite 330, Washington, D.C. 20036-1171; (202) 293-9161. AACRAO develops admissions and registration policies and conducts institutional research.

American College Testing, 2201 N. Dodge St., P.O. Box 168, Iowa City, Iowa 52243; (319) 337-1000. ACT prepares the ACT Assessment, a college-entrance exam taken by more than 1.5 million students a year.

American Council on Education, 1 Dupont Circle N.W., Suite 800, Washington, D.C. 20036-1193; (202) 939-9300. This organization for colleges, universities, education associations and students with disabilities conducts research on a number of topics in higher education.

The College Board, 45 Columbus Ave., New York, N.Y. 10023; (212) 713-8000. The board and its more than 2,900 member institutions promote high learning standards, equity of opportunity and financial support for needy college students.

Educational Testing Service, Rosedale Road, Princeton, N.J. 08541; (609) 921-9000. ETS, the world's largest private organization devoted to education measurement, is best known as the source of the Scholastic Achievement Test (SAT), one of the two leading U.S. college-entrance exams.

National Association of College Admission Counselors, 1631 Prince St., Alexandria, Va. 22314; (703) 836-2222. NACAC members help students make the transition from high school to college.

in their 50s," says Swanson. "These people are going to have a lot of time on their hands, and they are not known for sitting around doing nothing. So I think they'll be in the market for additional kinds of career training, or simply personal or cultural development: 'I've always wanted to take Latin.' We're seeing a bit of this already in certain areas of the country — Florida, Arizona and California in particular — and we're going to see a lot more of it in the next decade."

Besides phasing in new instruction technology, GW's Chernak believes that "schools will have to figure out more cost-efficient ways of managing themselves." That likely means that such thorny issues as tenure "will come up for debate and be challenged, maybe even abolished."[32] Another possibility is that "three-year baccalaureate programs will become more popular to cut out a year of cost and get students into the labor market earlier. Schools are not going to be able to sustain the continued increases in tuition beyond what the American public can afford."

El-Khawas agrees. "The world of higher education is changing, and the ability to project from the past no longer holds," she says. "My guess is that colleges will continue to be [priced] somewhat ahead of inflation for the next five to 10 years. To survive, colleges will have to find a market for whatever price they charge. Those that don't find a market will close, while those that do find one will be able to thrive." ■

Notes

[1] Jean H. Fetter, *Questions and Answers: Reflections on 10,000 Admissions Decisions at Stanford* (1995), p. 253.

[2] See "Rethinking Affirmative Action," *The CQ Researcher,* April 18, 1995, pp. 375-398.

[3] Fetter, *op. cit.,* p. 250.

[4] The College Board, *Trends in Student Aid 1985 to 1995,* September 1995. See "Paying for College," *The CQ Researcher,* Nov. 20, 1992, pp. 1001-1024.

[5] The survey by *Who's Who Among American High School Students,* released Jan. 17, 1996, was sent last summer to 8,000 high school juniors and seniors. Of the 3,351 respondents, 98 percent were planning to go to college.

[6] National Center for Education Statistics, *National Post-Secondary Student Aid Study,* 1995.

[7] "How High Is Too High?" *Yale Daily News,* March 1, 1995.

[8] Philip J. Cook and Robert H. Frank, "The Economic Payoff of Attending an Ivy League Institution," *The Chronicle of Higher Education,* Jan. 5, 1996, p. B3. Cook teaches public policy at Duke University; Frank teaches economics at Cornell University.

[9] Laura Elliott, "Getting In," *The Washingtonian,* October 1993, p. 69.

[10] Michael S. McPherson and Morton Owen Schapiro, "Pricing and Financial Aid in a Shifting Environment," *The College Board Review,* spring 1995, p. 21.

[11] Hunter M. Breland, et al., *Challenges in College Admissions: A Report of a Survey of Undergraduate Admissions Policies, Practices and Procedures* (1995), p. x. The report was sponsored by the American Association of Collegiate Registrars and Admissions Officers, American College Testing, The College Board, Educational Testing Service and the National Association of College Admission Counselors.

[12] *Ibid.,* p. 3.

[13] *Ibid.,* p. 5.

[14] Quoted by Kit Lively, "Man Behind Cal. Proposal Has Felt Racism's Sting," *The Chronicle of Higher Education,* July 28, 1995, p. A27.

[15] Carl C. Jorgensen, "The Consequences in California," *The Chronicle of Higher Education,* Aug. 11, 1995, p. B2.

[16] Richard D. Kahlenberg, "Affirmative Action by Class," *The Washington Post,* July 17, 1995, p. A19. Kahlenberg recently authored a book on affirmative action due to be published in May.

[17] Harold S. Wechsler, *The Qualified Student* (1977), p. 7.

[18] From "The Reform of College Entrance Requirements," Farrand's inaugural address as president of the Schoolmaster's Association of New York and Vicinity, Oct. 12, 1895, quoted in Wechsler.

[19] Wechsler, *op. cit.,* p. 20.

[20] *Ibid.,* p. 57.

[21] Garland G. Parker, *The Enrollment Explosion: A Half Century of Attendance in U.S. Colleges and Universities* (1971), p. 23.

[22] See "Jobs in the '90s," *The CQ Researcher,* Feb. 28, 1992, pp. 181-204.

[23] Hanna Rosin, "Race Matters," *The New Republic,* Oct. 23, 1995, p. 21.

[24] Pete Wilson, "Why Racial Preferences Must End," *San Francisco Chronicle,* Jan. 18, 1996, p. A21.

[25] Quoted by Lively, *op. cit.,* p. A27.

[26] Roy T. Brophy, "Regents Erred on Affirmative Action," *San Diego Union-Tribune,* Nov. 14, 1995, p. B7.

[27] UCLA Public Information Office news release, Jan. 8, 1996.

[28] *USA Today,* Feb. 20, 1996, p. 1D.

[29] Quoted in "Big Drop in Student-Loan Defaults Disclosed by Education Department," *The Chronicle of Higher Education,* Feb. 2, 1996, p. A25.

[30] "The Top Colleges Are Reporting Record Numbers of Applications," *The New York Times,* National Edition, Feb. 18, 1996, p. 35.

[31] Quoted by Steve Stecklow, "Some Small Colleges Hire Recruiters to Get Bigger Freshman Class," *The Wall Street Journal,* Sept. 5, 1995, p. A1.

[32] See "Academic Politics," *The CQ Researcher,* Feb. 16, 1996, pp. 145-168.

Bibliography

Selected Sources Used

Books

Fetter, Jean H., *Questions and Admissions: Reflections on 100,000 Admissions Decisions at Stanford,* Stanford University Press, 1995.

Fetter, a former dean of undergraduate admissions at Stanford University, concludes: "One hundred thousand applications later, I am somewhat sadly . . . resigned to the fact that I made many more young people unhappy than happy with the decisions for which I was responsible. . . . I am older (certainly), wiser (probably) and humbler (unquestionably) — and persuaded that no one, including admissions officers, will ever master the art of human assessment. And that is probably a very good thing."

Greene, Howard, and Robert Minton, *Scaling the Ivy Wall in the '90s,* Little, Brown, 1994.

The authors of this guide write, "Our underlying philosophy . . . is that a determined student in the upper quarter of his or her secondary school can be offered admission to at least one of the [76] selective colleges we list." They caution, however, that "We say *can be,* not necessarily *will be.*" To help applicants get into the college of their choice, the authors lay out a 12-step strategy, including "Excel Outside Class," "Make the Most of Campus Visits" and "Write an Exciting Essay."

Moll, Richard, *Playing the Selective College Admissions Game,* Penguin Books, 1994.

Moll, a former dean of admissions at Bowdoin College, Vassar College and the University of California-Santa Cruz, offers a wealth of tips on how to make a winning admissions application. His touch throughout is light.

Articles

Elliott, Laura, "Getting In," *The Washingtonian*, October 1993.

Elliott goes behind the scenes to find out how one selective private institution — Georgetown University — puts together an incoming freshman class. As might be expected, the hardest decisions come after the truly outstanding applicants are chosen and the obviously unqualified ones are rejected.

Lewis, Stephen R., "Ensuring Access, Strengthening Institutions," *The College Board Review,* spring 1995.

"The month of April has become a vast, national 'used car lot' for admitted students," says Lewis, president of Carleton College in Northfield, Minn. "A decade ago students received an offer of financial aid and made a decision to accept it or reject it. Now the father or mother calls the financial aid officer and says, in effect, 'Your letter was an interesting first offer. What are you really going to do for us?'"

McPherson, Michael S., and Morton Owen Schapiro, "Pricing and Financial Aid in a Shifting Environment," *The College Board Review*, spring 1995.

"In many states, the public community colleges have held tuitions down, while state four-year colleges and universities are increasing tuition rapidly, which often puts them out of reach for economically disadvantaged students," McPherson and Schapiro write. "It is especially disturbing that public colleges and universities are increasing their spending on merit scholarships faster than they are increasing spending for need-based aid."

Tully, Shawn, "Finally, Colleges Start to Cut Their Crazy Costs," *Fortune,* May 1, 1995.

"Shielded by a web of laws, traditions and folkways, colleges have long proceeded at their own rhythms, blithely piling on costs and programs," Tully writes. "Productivity, a religion in the boardroom, has been heresy on campus." Now, however, economic realities are turning higher education into a buyer's market. Tully describes what colleges are doing to make their product more affordable.

Reports and Studies

American Association of Collegiate Registrars and Admissions Officers, *Challenges in College Admissions*, 1995.

The main challenge examined in this study is the sharp drop in the U.S. college-age population over the past 15 years. Despite widespread expectations of an enrollment crisis, colleges continued to thrive by adopting innovative and aggressive marketing strategies.

American Council on Education, *Campus Trends 1995*, July 1995.

Noting that "Active learning, uses of electronic technology and other changes are on the way," this report states that "Colleges and universities would be well-advised to maintain close ties with high schools and with educators in their communities, both to stay abreast of changing student needs and expectations and to keep in touch with the often substantial changes being made by the school systems themselves."

University of Colorado at Boulder, *Honors Program Self-Study,* spring 1996.

This internal study describes how the university's highly regarded honors program operates and how it compares with similar programs at other institutions. It ends with a review of plans for expansion and restructuring.

The Next Step

Additional information from UMI's Newspaper & Periodical Abstracts database

Affirmative Action

Ayres, B. Drummond Jr., "On affirmative action, Wilson's moderate path veered quickly to right," *The New York Times,* Aug. 8, 1995, p. A10.

Gov. Pete Wilson, R-Calif., has made the fight to eliminate affirmative action programs based on sex and race the center of his presidential bid, but this is a 180-degree turn for the politician, who for nearly 30 years has strongly supported affirmative action programs in hiring, contracting and college admissions.

Baumann, Marty, "What Voters Say on Affirmative Action, Preference," *USA Today,* March 2, 1992, p. A9.

The results of a *USA Today*/CNN/Gallup poll are presented. Voters in general and Southern white voters in particular were asked if they would be more or less likely to vote for a presidential candidate who favors strengthening affirmative action laws for all minorities or giving blacks preference for jobs and college admissions.

Bunzel, John H., "Race and college admissions," *Public Interest,* winter 1996, pp. 49-58.

University officials have failed to explain how the quest for racial diversity is balanced against other factors. The admission process at elite universities is discussed.

Dembner, Alice, "Academic leaders uphold affirmative action," *Boston Globe,* July 22, 1995, p. 1.

Struggling against California's power as a trendsetter, academic leaders across the nation vowed not to abandon affirmative action policies in hiring and admissions.

"Minority initiative remains top priority," *Educational Record,* spring 1995, pp. 95-98.

The "Minority Initiative" of the American Council on Education guides a substantial portion of the council's work on behalf of U.S. colleges and universities and is geared toward advancing minority participation and success in higher education at every level. The initiative and the council's activities are detailed.

"Regent softens stance on affirmative action," *The New York Times,* June 21, 1995, p. A14.

Ward Connerly, the University of California regent who touched off a statewide debate early in 1995 by calling for an end to affirmative action in college admissions, now says he sees merit in some cases of preferential treatment for black and Hispanic students.

"Rescind U.C. vote on affirmative action," *San Francisco Chronicle,* Jan. 13, 1996, p. A18.

An editorial calls for a closer look at the import and long-term ramifications of the 1995 University of California Board of Regents vote abolishing affirmative action. The vote represents a breach of academic respect and cooperation and should be rescinded, the editorial says.

Wallace, Amy, "4 U.C. regents seek meeting on affirmative action vote," *Los Angeles Times,* Dec. 6, 1995, p. A3.

Four University of California regents have called for a special board meeting in December 1995 to discuss allegations that the Board of Regents ignored the views of its faculty when voting to roll back affirmative action in the summer of 1995.

Athletics and Admissions Policies

Carmody, Deirdre, "Colleges Bend Admissions for More Than Athletes," *The New York Times,* Jan. 25, 1989, p. B6.

The NCAA's Proposition 42, which raises scholarship standards for freshman athletes, has been met with criticism from those who contend the rule discriminates against poor blacks and brings to light a college admissions principle of bending the rules in certain circumstances, such as when students' talents lie solely in science or the dramatic arts or if their parents are generous donors.

Kelly, Dennis, "Students Say Sports Is Key to College Aid," *USA Today,* Nov. 26, 1990 p. A1.

More high school students think their best chance for a college scholarship will come from athletics rather than academics or other special skill areas, according to a study conducted by the National Research Center for College and University Admissions.

MacFarquhar, Neil, "High grades, hoop dreams," *The New York Times,* June 5, 1995, p. B1.

In 1995 for the third year in a row, every graduating senior at St. Anthony High School in Jersey City, N.J., has been accepted at a college. The 47 seniors collecting diplomas on June 5 have amassed more than $1 million in financial aid. There is no question that the school's statistics are boosted by its champion basketball team and the fact that its players win full college scholarships, but those outside the team succeed as well.

Sperber, Murray, "Affirmative action for athletes," *Education Digest,* December 1995, pp. 57-59.

Sperber comments on what he calls the illogic and hypocrisy of the special-admissions loophole for college athletes. Admissions inevitably will be denied to large numbers of minority applicants who present considerably higher grades and test scores — and much greater potential for academic achievement — than many athletes.

Efforts to Recruit Students

Biemiller, Lawrence, "Banners, brochures, small talk: An admissions director works college night at Bishop McDevitt," *The Chronicle of Higher Education,* Nov. 3, 1995, p. A67.

Mark Lapreziosa's work as admissions and financial aid director at Beaver College, Glen side, Pa., is described. Lapreziosa competes against Boston College and other schools during college night at high schools.

Curtis, Diane, "Early College Admissions — Many Schools Leery," *San Francisco Chronicle,* Feb. 12, 1990, p. A1.

The growing trend of expanded early college admissions programs has sparked debate among educators on the collegiate and high school levels. The controversy over whether it benefits the student is discussed.

Mathews, Jay, "New college rush: Signing high school seniors early," *The Washington Post,* Jan. 4, 1996, p. A19.

New university admissions policies have been putting pressure on American high school students to pick their college in the first weeks of their senior year, a change that some educators say is rushing what should be a longer, more thoughtful process.

Sanoff, Alvin P., and Kukula Glastris, "The consulting game," *U.S. News & World Report,* Sept. 18, 1995, pp. 119-122.

Many colleges, faced with dwindling enrollments and ballooning financial-aid budgets, are operating much more like corporate America, turning to consultants for sophisticated advice on a variety of issues. As a result, college fairs are out and sophisticated marketing is in. The techniques used by the University of Virginia and DePaul University to attract enrollees are discussed.

Stecklow, Steve, "Peddling schools: Some small colleges hire recruiters to get bigger freshman class," *The Wall Street Journal,* Sept. 5, 1995, p. A1.

Many colleges, scrambling for students at a time when tuition has risen too high for many families to afford, are taking extreme measures to recruit students. Bethany College in Scotts Valley, Calif., has outsourced its entire admission operation to D.H. Dagley Associates Inc. Other techniques include telemarketing, direct mailing, geodemographic research and computerized-inquiry tracking.

Stepp, Diane R., "Out-of-state schools losing to HOPE," *Atlanta Journal Constitution,* Jan. 21, 1996, p. D1.

As college admissions offices make last-minute pitches for the 1996-97 school year's freshmen class, out-of-state colleges are finding it tougher to attract students from Georgia, which is due mainly to the Helping Outstanding Students Educationally scholarship fund.

Tips on Applying

Arenofsky, Janice, "Do grades tell the whole story?" *Career World,* November 1995, pp. 6-12.

Some researchers believe that grades don't always represent a student's knowledge or skill level and that high grades are not the only thing that can lead to success. Extracurricular activities and volunteer experiences can help an average student in the college admissions process.

Daniels, Charlene D., "Do Your Application Legwork," *USA Today,* Oct. 27, 1992, p. D4.

Three members of *USA Today's* 1991 All-USA Academic Team, who have been through the college admissions and financial aid process and are now college sophomores, offer advice to future college students.

Hill, James, "ACT making a career for itself, opens office in Vernon Hills mall," *Chicago Tribune,* May 24, 1995, p. L2.

ACT, a nonprofit organization known nationally for its college admissions testing, now provides a wide range of assessments and related services in college financial aid, scholarship and recognition programs.

Ordovensky, Pat, "Early applicants get financial aid," *USA Today,* Oct. 27, 1994, p. D4.

Answers to some of the questions received from callers to *USA Today's* College Admissions/Financial Aid Hot Line are given.

Pina, Phillip, "Early lessons for the college-bound," *USA Today,* Nov. 15, 1995, p. D6.

Asking everything from how to pay for college to where to send applications, 1,400 employees and their children attended college planning seminars sponsored by communications giant GTE Corp. GTE originated the teleconference from four major plants and broadcast it live to 18 of the company's buildings across the country on Nov. 4, 1995.

Roberts, Raequel, "The Admissions Maze," *The Houston Post,* June 25, 1989, p. F1.

The world of modern-day college and university admissions process is examined.

Back Issues

Great Research on Current Issues Starts Right Here...Recent topics covered by The CQ Researcher are listed below. Before May 1991, reports were published under the name of Editorial Research Reports.

AUGUST 1994
Genetically Engineered Foods
Electing Minorities
Prozac Controversy
College Sports

SEPTEMBER 1994
Home Schooling
Welfare Experiments
Courts and the Media
Regulating Tobacco

OCTOBER 1994
Historic Preservation
Religion and Politics
Arts Funding
Economic Sanctions

NOVEMBER 1994
Sex on Campus
Blood Supply Safety
Testing Term Limits
Religion in America

DECEMBER 1994
Farm Policy
Arms Sales
Earthquake Research
The Future of Television

Back issues are available for $5.00 (subscribers) or $8.00 (non-subscribers). Quantity discounts apply to orders over ten. To order, call Congressional Quarterly Customer Service at (202) 887-8621.

Binders are available for $18.00. To order call 1-800-638-1710. Please refer to stock number 648.

JANUARY 1995
Treating Addiction
Child Custody and Support
Parents and Schools
Non-Proliferation Treaty at 25

FEBRUARY 1995
Cracking Down on Immigration
The Business of Sports
Reinventing Government
Housing Discrimination

MARCH 1995
Death Penalty Debate
Primary Care
Democracy in Africa
Environmental Movement at 25

APRIL 1995
Abortion Clinic Protests
Dieting and Health
Combating AIDS
Rethinking Affirmative Action

MAY 1995
Assisted Suicide Controversy
Overhauling Social Security
Learning to Read
Mandatory Sentencing

JUNE 1995
Combating Infectious Disease
Property Rights
Repetitive Stress Injuries
Regulating the Internet

JULY 1995
War Crimes
Highway Safety
Combating Terrorism
Preventing Teen Drug Use

AUGUST 1995
Job Stress
Organ Transplants
United Nations at 50
Advances in Cancer Research

SEPTEMBER 1995
Catholic Church in the U.S.
Northern Ireland Cease-Fire
High School Sports
Teaching History

OCTOBER 1995
Quebec's Future
Revitalizing the Cities
Networking the Classroom
Indoor Air Pollution

NOVEMBER 1995
The Working Poor
The Jury System
Sex, Violence and the Media
Police Misconduct

DECEMBER 1995
Teens and Tobacco
Gene Therapy's Future
Global Water Shortages
Third-Party Prospects

JANUARY 1996
Emergency Medicine
Punishing Sex Offenders
Bilingual Education
Helping the Homeless

FEBRUARY 1996
Reforming the CIA
Campaign Finance Reform
Academic Politics

Future Topics

- ***Preventing Youth Violence***
- ***The British Monarchy***
- ***Tax Reform***

PUBLISHED BY CONGRESSIONAL QUARTERLY INC.

The British Monarchy

Will the royal family be replaced by a republic?

The prolonged collapse of the marriage of Prince Charles and Lady Diana has brought the British monarchy embarrassment and ridicule at home and abroad. Critics say the sordid details behind the failed marriage have destroyed the royal family's image as an exemplar of stability and propriety. They also contend that the monarchy undermines governmental accountability and democratic processes. But supporters say the monarchy promotes national unity, preserves historic traditions and acts as a check against political abuse. Critics want a national referendum on abolishing the monarchy and establishing a republic after Queen Elizabeth's death. But no major politician has taken up the issue. And polls indicate that most Britons favor keeping the monarchy — even though they also doubt its long-term survival.

INSIDE THIS ISSUE

March 8, 1996 • Volume 6, No. 9 • Pages 193-216

Formerly Editorial Research Reports

THE BRITISH MONARCHY

COVER: LADY DIANA AND PRINCE CHARLES DURING A VISIT TO SOUTH KOREA IN NOVEMBER 1992. PAGE 195: QUEEN ELIZABETH II. (REUTERS)

March 8, 1996
Volume 6, No. 9

PUBLISHED BY
Congressional Quarterly Inc.

The CQ Researcher (ISSN 1056-2036). Formerly Editorial Research Reports. Published weekly (48 times per year, not printed March 1, May 31, Aug. 30, Nov. 29, 1996) by Congressional Quarterly Inc., 1414 22nd St., N.W., Washington, D.C. 20037. Rates are furnished upon request. Second-class postage paid at Washington, D.C. POSTMASTER: Send address changes to The CQ Researcher, 1414 22nd St., N.W., Washington, D.C. 20037.

The British Monarchy

BY KENNETH JOST

THE ISSUES

He was a handsome prince. She was a shy kindergarten teacher. Their romance began after a polo match and blossomed quickly. One year later, they were married in a 300-year-old cathedral, amid pomp and pageantry, with the whole world watching.

But the fairy tale marriage of Prince Charles, heir to the British throne, and Lady Diana Spencer soon turned into a dreary royal soap opera.* He was never at home. She had trouble adjusting to her new life. He was aloof. She was emotional. They quarreled over trips. They quarreled over the children. And there was another woman: Charles' longtime friend Camilla Parker-Bowles, wife of one of his polo-playing friends.

Now the marriage is over. In a private 45-minute meeting on Feb. 28, the Princess of Wales informed Prince Charles that she would agree to a divorce. It was, her lawyer, Anthony Julius, told reporters, "an exceptionally difficult decision" — but an inevitable one. Two months earlier — in the week before Christmas — Queen Elizabeth II had written to her son and daughter-in-law to say that she, and her husband Prince Philip, the Duke of Edinburgh, favored "an early divorce" for the couple. In a statement to the press at that time, Prince Charles said he agreed.

Diana's agreement to a divorce leaves several questions yet to be answered about the royal couple. But beyond the difficulties for Charles and Diana, the breakup of their marriage has raised serious questions about the very survival of the 1,200-year-old monarchy.

Polls show that an increasing number of Britons — about one-sixth — want to abolish the monarchy. Half of those surveyed do not expect that it will last another 100 years. (*See chart, p. 196.*)

Meanwhile, details of the divorce must be worked out. One, of course, is money. Diana is believed to be seeking a financial settlement in the neighborhood of 15 million pounds (about $22.5 million), enough to provide a net annual income of about 500,000 pounds ($750,000) to cover her somewhat lavish personal needs and pay for an office and staff.

In addition, Diana has been pressing to retain her title and ensure a continuing public role after the divorce. Her lawyers reportedly lost one battle when they failed to persuade Buckingham Palace to allow her to keep the title "Her Royal Highness," which will be dropped from her name after the divorce. Diana said she would retain the title "Princess of Wales," would continue to live at Kensington Palace in London and have offices at St. James's Palace. Diana also said she would "be involved in all decisions" relating to the couple's children, the Princes William, 13, and Harry, 11, who stand second and third in the line of succession to the throne.

But Buckingham Palace issued a statement saying those questions have yet to be decided. And a palace spokesman insisted that Diana made the decision to drop "Her Royal Highness" without any pressure from the queen or Prince Charles. [1]

"The royal soap opera has done the monarchy enormous damage because it has portrayed itself throughout the 20th century as a model family," says author Anthony Holden, who has written a critical biography of Prince Charles and an account of the breakup sympathetic to Lady Diana. [2]

Even supporters of the monarchy concede that the royal family's difficulties — Princess Andrew is separated from his wife, Sarah Ferguson; Princess Anne is divorced; and Prince Philip is said to have an eye for the ladies — have shattered its carefully cultivated image as an exemplar of British stability and propriety.

"There is a sense in which the monarchy has been dethroned already," says Anthony King, a professor of government at Essex University. "Neither the monarchy as an institution nor the royal family as a group of people is held in the high esteem in which it once was."

The criticisms of the monarchy extend beyond the peccadilloes of the royal family. Critics also have attacked the costs of the monarchy — estimated at 50 million pounds per year (about $75 million) — its property holdings and the tax exemptions granted to the queen and some members of her family. Those criticisms have had some effects. The queen and Prince Charles agreed in late 1992 to pay taxes. Payments for the expenses of the royal family under the so-called "Civil List" are now limited to the queen, Prince Philip and the queen mother. And the royal yacht *Britan-*

* Diana's proper title is Lady Diana, Princess of Wales. It is incorrect to refer to her as Princess Diana because she was not born into a royal family.

Future of the British Monarchy

Attitudes toward the royal family have become more negative in recent years, according to a survey conducted for The Independent on Sunday. *Half of those polled do not expect the monarchy to last another 100 years.*

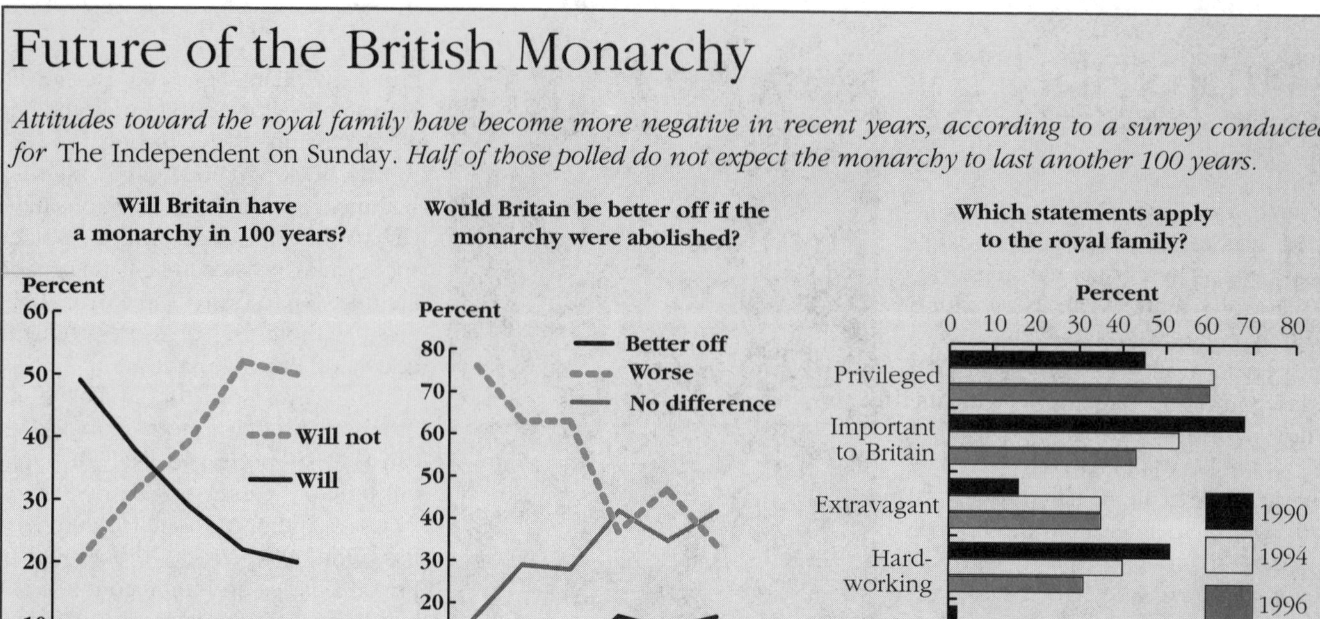

Source: Survey of 1,165 adults conducted by Market & Opinion Research International (MORI) on behalf of The Independent on Sunday, *Feb. 7-9, 1996.*

nia will be decommissioned sometime next year.

Such steps have not quieted those who criticize the monarchy on broader grounds. Some critics say the monarchy props up a secretive and unaccountable governmental system that hampers individual freedom and discourages individual initiative. "The existence of the monarchy acts as a giant cloak under which government can get away with lots of things, which is why the government is very keen on preserving the monarchy," says Andrew Puddephat, director of Charter 88, a constitutional-reform organization that takes its name from England's "Glorious Revolution" of 1688.

"The class system still pervades this country," says Edgar Wilson, a professor of philosophy at Manchester Metropolitan University and editor of the pro-republican journal *The Republic*. "The monarchy dignifies a system of privilege that cannot otherwise be justified."

Supporters of the monarchy often respond by stressing the limited role that the monarch plays in making government policy. "The convention has been clear that the monarch does not exercise his or her political will in matters of political controversy," says David Starkey, a constitutional historian at the London School of Economics.

But some supporters of the monarchy are calling for a more active role for the queen — or king. Writing in his new book, *The Monarchy and the Constitution,* Vernon Bogdanor, a political scientist at Oxford University, says the monarchy "must, while retaining its political neutrality, involve itself even more with society than it has in the past." Bogdanor cites Prince Charles' involvement in work for the inner city poor, ethnic minorities and other disadvantaged Britons as an example of what he calls "the practical employment of [the monarchy's] symbolic influence." [3]

The criticisms of the monarchy have produced the most substantial movement for replacing the monarchy with a republic since the 1870s. One group, the Republican, founded in 1983, directly calls for replacing the monarchy with a republic, headed by an elected head of state, after the end of Queen Elizabeth's reign. Puddephat's group simply calls for a national referendum on the monarchy. "In a mature democracy, one should consent to the governing arrangement," he explains.

Some supporters of the monarchy agree on giving Britons a chance to vote on its future. "I think that the time will come in the very near future when the public is given a chance to make a decision," says Harold Brooks-Baker, publishing director of *Burke's Peerage,* the genealogical reference service. "If you had a referendum today, the monarchy would win very narrowly. If you didn't have the queen there and you had Prince Charles, I think a republic would be voted in."

Other supporters of the monarchy, however, say it still enjoys the backing of the vast majority of the British public. "The monarchy is going to persist, for two very simple reasons," says Jonathan Dimbleby, a television journalist and author of an admiring authorized biography of Prince Charles. [4] "There is no head of steam for its downfall, and there is no significant politician who advocates its demise. And that is because the overwhelming majority of the public wants the monarchy to persist."

As Britons continue to ponder the monarchy's future, here are some of the questions being asked:

Will Prince Charles become king — and will his divorce limit his role if he does?

It was 60 years ago this year that King Edward VIII yielded to pressure from the British government and the Church of England and gave up his throne for the woman he loved — an American divorcee, Wallis Warfield Simpson. Public and official attitudes toward divorce have changed since then. Today, supporters of the monarchy say they see no reason why a divorced Prince Charles cannot accede to the throne after the death of his mother.

"There is no constitutional bar to his becoming king," says Starkey at the London School of Economics. "The constitution is what public opinion will wear. In the 1930s, it was quite clear that the public would not [tolerate] a monarch wed to a divorcee. Today, opinion polls are showing 80-90 percent [of the public] in favor of a royal divorce."

Despite the change in public opinion, however, the Church of England — which Charles would head as king — still maintains an official prohibition against divorce or remarriage within the Church. Princess Anne had to remarry in the Church of Scotland to skirt the ban. And Church leaders have given mixed signals about how they view the breakup of Charles' and Diana's marriage.

Even some critics of the monarchy, however, say they see no problem from a divorce. "I don't think there are" any constitutional issues, says Wilson at Manchester Metropolitan University. "Henry VIII founded the Church of England precisely so that he could divorce his wife."

Still, many of the monarchy's critics view a divorce as irreconcilable with the monarch's position as Supreme Governor of the National Church. Writing shortly after Charles' and Diana's separation, novelist A.N. Wilson said that a divorced king "would surely put the Church and the Crown in an impossible situation." [5] He predicted that a divorce would finally lead to a separation between Church and monarchy and the disestablishment of the Church.

Holden, however, predicts that the Church eventually will pose no obstacle to Charles becoming king after a divorce. "The Church keeps making different noises," Holden says. "The establishment can keep moving the goalposts to accommodate the monarchy, which of course is the cornerstone of the establishment."

Charles himself has raised the issue of changing the relationship between the Crown and the Church of England. While still a member of the Church, he has adopted beliefs in mysticism that, as biographer Dimbleby says, stretch his bonds to the Church "to the limit." [6] And he has declared that he wishes to reign not as "Defender of the Faith," but more broadly as "Defender of Faith."

Some experts suggest that Britain's growing secularization and its changing demographics may make disestablishment inevitable anyway. While most Britons are nominally members of the Church of England, no more than 2 percent attend church services regularly. And recent immigration has brought an increase in the size of other religious communities, including Hindus and Muslims. Even some leaders of the Church of England have hinted that the Church itself would benefit from a separation from the Crown.

Even if Church doctrine does not bar Charles from the throne, some critics believe that his accession is threatened by his personal unpopularity. These critics talk of "skipping a generation" and looking to Charles' elder son, Prince William, to succeed Queen Elizabeth. The most recent poll found Britons closely divided on the idea — with 43 percent in favor of Prince William becoming king in Charles' stead and 46 percent opposed. [7]

Charles' admirers believe that his present unpopularity is both exaggerated and unfair. "I think that his residual popularity is far higher than you would imagine from reading the newspaper," Dimbleby says.

"Most people don't understand the importance of the things he's interested in," says Brooks-Baker of *Burke's Peerage*. "He is a very modern monarch."

Charles' critics warn that he would stretch public tolerance past the breaking point if he decided to marry Camilla Parker-Bowles after the divorce is final. But some supporters of the monarchy say even that step would not bar Charles from the throne. "Public opinion may not [support] remarriage," says Starkey. "It certainly won't [support] remarriage now. But let them get used to the fact. After about five years, why not make it official?"

Given the queen's apparent good health, both Charles and the British public will likely have many years to get used to the divorce. Critical observers warn that the interim will not be pleasant for the monarchy.

"It seems a reasonable prediction that these matters will not be settled overnight," says David Cannadine, a leading British historian now teaching at Columbia University in New York. "And the media being as prurient and sensationalistic as it is, this will cause a lot more attention and publicity for the royal family."

But supporters say that, ultimately, time is on the monarchy's side — and Charles'. "There is a feeling that he is heir to the throne," says Dimbleby, "that he has weathered the storm, that he will be king and that he will be

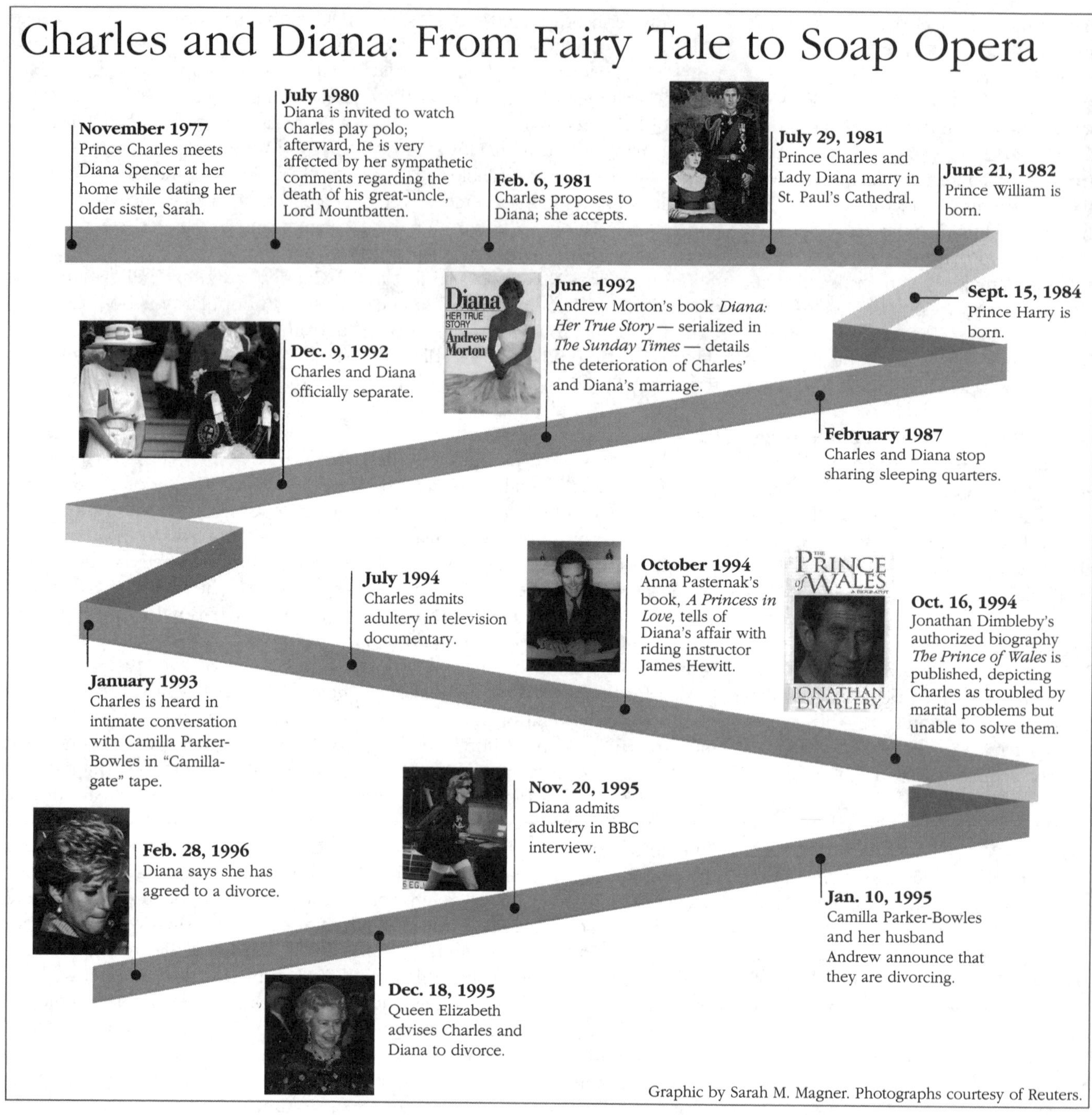

Graphic by Sarah M. Magner. Photographs courtesy of Reuters.

regarded with respect and affection when that happens."

Will Lady Diana play a public role after the divorce?

When he announced Charles' and Diana's separation in December 1992, Prime Minister John Major said the breakup posed no obstacle to Diana's being crowned queen "in due course." But, according to journalist Andrew Morton, whose revelation-packed books documented the demise of Charles' and Diana's marriage, Diana herself believed even before the separation that she would never become queen. [8]

Nonetheless, Diana has fought to retain a royal title and maintain some public role for herself after the divorce. Her supporters believe she is entitled to both. "She remains and always will remain an object of complete fascination and admiration — admiration for taking on the system and admiration for behaving in public like a princess," Holden says.

Diana's critics, however, believe that

after the divorce, she will have no claim on any official role. "Other than being a mother of a possible future monarch or two, I don't see any official role," says Brooks-Baker. Professor Starkey agrees. "In constitutional law, she's just a vehicle through which the royal gene has passed," he says.

The question of Diana's title is important in a system based on protocol. The loss of the honorific "Her Royal Highness" — bestowed on the children of the sovereign and their sons, the eldest son of the eldest son of the Prince of Wales and their wives — was a setback for Diana's legal team. Her new title — if finally confirmed by the queen — will be "Diana, Princess of Wales" — a subtle but unmistakable demotion from "the Princess of Wales."

Diana has also sought a role as a sort of roving ambassador for Britain. She reportedly discussed the idea with Prime Minister Major in December. Major has supported the idea, but Starkey says the queen might balk at any such arrangement. "Ambassadors are formally appointed by the queen, and the queen is not in a mood to do her any favors at the moment," he says.

Still, Holden believes Diana would present a positive image for Britain around the world as "a country looking to its future rather than coasting on its past." Within Britain, she remains a popular figure and presumably will continue to be sought after for charitable causes and the like even after the divorce.

Moreover, the monarchy's laws of succession mean that Diana cannot be completely removed from the royal stage. "Diana will be the mother of the next king of England" after Charles, says historian Cannadine. "One of these days it is not inconceivable that she will be the presiding matriarch of her son's reign."

Should Britain abolish the monarchy?

When asked once to defend the monarchy, Prince Philip remarked that anything that had lasted more than 1,000 years must have some good to it. Other supporters of the monarchy also cite its longevity as one of its principal justifications. And many defend it as a working constitutional arrangement that promotes national unity and guards against governmental abuse.

"In this country there hasn't been a dictatorship since [Oliver] Cromwell," says Brooks-Baker, referring to the anti-monarchist 17th-century leader. "No politician can run away with power because the queen will step in. That is the type of government that every country needs."

Oxford's Bogdanor stresses that under a monarchy, "the head of state is free from party ties." With government policy affecting more aspects of national life, he continues, it "remains . . . of inestimable value" that "the symbol of the state should remain uncontaminated by political controversy." [9]

Critics of the monarchy, however, contend that the Crown no longer serves its major purposes well. These critics — including republicans who would abolish the monarchy and reformers who would merely reduce its size and powers — argue that the Crown has now become a source of divisiveness instead of unity and a cause of governmental abuse instead of a barrier to it.

"There's a very strong feeling that the royal trappings of the family — the size of the Civil List, the tax arrangements and the way it is used as a cover by government — is very much now heavily under criticism," says Puddephat of Charter 88.

The marital problems between Prince Charles and Lady Diana are one explanation that critics give for the divisions over the monarchy. "There are his and her parties in the country," says Wilson at Manchester Metropolitan University. "Half the country thinks Diana is a wonderful person who has been wronged by a rather foppish person, and the other half thinks she's a manipulative hysteric who he never should have married in the first place."

For the most part, Queen Elizabeth herself remains above these criticisms. "The queen herself has not done any political harm," says King at Essex University. When a new biography of the queen appeared in January, one reviewer described her as "the most honest, dutiful, decent, professional and genuinely Christian monarch ever to sit on the British throne." [10]

The classic definition of the monarch's political role comes from the 19th-century journalist Walter Bagehot, who, in his book, *The English Constitution,* said the monarch had the right to be consulted, to advise and to warn. Queen Elizabeth has avoided political harm by largely staying out of partisan politics. But she is not free of political views and, apparently, sometimes communicates them to the prime minister in their private weekly meetings.

In his new book, *The Hidden Wiring: Unearthing the British Constitution,* Peter Hennessy, a professor of contemporary history at Queen Mary and Westfield College, University of London, cites accounts that the queen had some influence on Britain's policies toward the former state of Rhodesia in its transition to black-majority rule in the 1960s. More recently, she reportedly disagreed with some of Prime Minister Margaret Thatcher's domestic policies during the 1980s. But the queen has never stated these views publicly. [11]

Supporters of the monarchy see this role of private counsel and caution as its major strength. "That is what constitutional monarchs are for," Hennessy writes. Opponents, however, say it gives the government too much power at the expense of democratic processes. "The queen gets to see the prime minister literally once a week," says Stephen Haseler, a professor of government at London's Guildhall University and chairman of the Republican. "That's bound to give her quite substantial power."

Leaders of the republican movement also say that the monarch has more power than commonly believed — not only ordinary powers, such as dismissing a government or issuing proclamations and regulations, but also the power to declare a state of emergency. "Farfetched as it may seem in these peaceful times, it's still true that an unelected, unrepresentative leader has these powers," says philosophy Professor Wilson. [12]

But supporters of the monarchy say that these powers, unexercised in recent times, could become more important in the near future. They note that the recent emergence of a third party, the Liberal Democrats, could give the monarch a more important role in shaping a new government than under a two-party system.

Moreover, the monarch remains as head of the Commonwealth and the recognized head of state of 15 of its member nations, including Canada and Australia. In addition, the pressure in Wales and Scotland for greater autonomy could enhance the monarch's role in maintaining some unity of Britain's component parts. "If the structure of the United Kingdom comes apart at the seams," says historian Starkey, "the whole position of the monarchy would become a matter of central importance."

These broad political questions matter less in the short-term than the controversies about the costs and privileges of the monarchy and the size of the royal family's holdings. A poll by *The Guardian* newspaper in early 1995 showed that a majority of Britons — 53 percent — want the monarchy's expenses to be cut. The same percentage also favored reducing the number of taxpayer-financed palaces to two from the current number, five. [13]

For some observers, the public attitude reflects a needed adjustment to the realities of Britain's present conditions, as a country with reduced diplomatic and economic strength. "The real problem is that Britain has still got a grand imperial, great power monarchy, but Britain is no longer a grand imperial, great power," says historian Cannadine. "There is a need for less ostentation, less secrecy and a court bureaucracy that is more attuned to the social structure of the nation as a whole."

Political scientist King makes a similar diagnosis, but he also predicts that the monarchy will adjust — just as it has adjusted for more than 1,000 years. "People are less sympathetic to the upper-class sentiment and outlook of the royal family," King says. "If the royal family want the monarchy to continue, they'll just have to change with the times." ■

BACKGROUND

Pragmatic Monarchy

Queen Elizabeth II can trace her ancestry to King Egbert, who ruled the kingdom of Wessex in the ninth century. Since then, the monarchy has reigned over England — and now Scotland, Wales and Northern Ireland — through domestic and foreign wars, imperial conquests and decolonization, and economic growth and decline. It has survived, with only an 11-year interruption in the 17th century, by adapting to changing conditions and by accepting limits on its power with the rise of new political forces. [14]

The English kings of the ninth and 10th centuries — notably, Alfred the Great (871-899) — succeeded in unifying the kingdom and repelling the Viking invaders from the north. In the 11th century, however, William, duke of Normandy, crossed the Channel to claim the throne. He defeated his cousin Harold II at the Battle of Hastings in 1066 and ruthlessly brought England under his control over the next two decades.

William's successors included kings skilled in statecraft — notably, Henry II (1154-1189), who issued a charter of liberties and established royal courts to protect them. But Henry's sons — Richard and John, rival claimants to the throne — were failures as kings. Richard ignored England for the Crusades. At his death, John acceded to the throne, adopting vindictive policies that made enemies at home and abroad. His legacy, however, is the cornerstone of English constitutional law: the Magna Carta, the historic affirmation of the supremacy of law over royal power that feudal barons forced on John in 1215.

Over the next three centuries, England's Plantagenet kings waged war at home and abroad. Edward I's conquest of Scotland in 1305 was reversed a decade later by Robert the Bruce. The Hundred Years' War in France, unpopular at home, ended in inglorious defeat in 1453. Two rival houses — the Yorks and Lancasters — then fought a civil war from 1455 to 1485 that ended with the victory of Henry, Earl of Richmond, at Bosworth Field and his accession as Henry VII, the first of the great Tudor monarchs.

Henry's son, Henry VIII, continued the centralization of power his father had begun. But he staked his monarchy on a showdown with the papacy over his desire to divorce the first of his six wives, Catherine of Aragon. Pope Clement VII's refusal to permit the divorce enraged Henry, who broke with the Church, confiscated the monasteries and had Parliament in 1534 declare him the "only Supreme Head of the Church in England."

Catholic and Protestant England were to be at war for the next 150 years. Elizabeth, who succeeded her Catholic half-sister Mary in 1558, sought to adopt a policy of religious tolerance within the established

Continued on p. 202

Chronology

1000-1699 *England is ruled in turn by Norman, Plantagenet, Tudor and Stuart dynasties. The monarchy is toppled during the English Civil War, restored and then limited in its powers by a bloodless revolution in 1688.*

1066
William, Duke of Normandy, defeats Harold II at the Battle of Hastings, beginning 150 years of Norman rule of England.

1534
Henry VIII completes his break with the Roman Catholic Church through legislation from Parliament recognizing the king as "supreme head" of the Church of England.

1603
Queen Elizabeth I dies without an heir after a long and glorious reign. She is succeeded by King James VI of Scotland, the first of the Stuart dynasty, who reigns as James I in England.

1688
"The Glorious Revolution" enthrones William, duke of Orange, and his wife Mary as limited monarchs, with a Bill of Rights guaranteeing Parliament's supremacy over the Crown.

1700-1899 *The monarchy's political powers are reduced.*

1887
Queen Victoria celebrates her 50th year on the throne with a Jubilee Celebration marking new public popularity for the monarchy.

1900-1949 *The monarchy gains visibility and popularity during two world wars and survives an abdication.*

1936
Edward VIII abdicates to marry an American divorcee, Wallis Warfield Simpson; his brother accedes to the throne as George VI.

1950-1979 *The royal family becomes more visible and more popular.*

June 2, 1953
The coronation of Elizabeth II is the first to be televised. The celebration is held 16 months after she acceded to the throne following her father's death.

1969
Queen Elizabeth takes viewers on a guided tour of Buckingham Palace in a BBC television documentary, "The Royal Family."

1980s *The marriage of Prince Charles and Lady Diana Spencer turns from fairy tale to soap opera.*

July 29, 1981
Prince Charles, 33, marries Diana Spencer, 20, in a wedding viewed by a global TV audience of more than 700 million people.

1990s *The monarchy comes under increasing criticism; Charles and Diana separate and move toward divorce.*

1992
Queen Elizabeth's 40th year on the throne is marked by controversies and hardships; four days after a fire at Windsor Castle, she describes the year in a Nov. 24 speech as "annus horribilis."

Nov. 26, 1992
Prime Minister John Major announces that the queen and Prince Charles have agreed to pay taxes and that the government will no longer pay expenses for most members of the royal family.

Dec. 9, 1992
Major tells Parliament that Charles and Diana have decided to separate.

May 22, 1993
Charter 88, a constitutional-reform group, convenes an unprecedented formal conference on the future of the monarchy.

Dec. 5, 1994
The Labor Party's shadow home secretary calls for reducing the monarchy's size and powers, but no legislation is introduced.

January 1995
A poll finds that 28 percent of Britons want to abolish the monarchy immediately or after the queen's death and that a majority want to reduce public support for the royal family.

Dec. 18, 1995
Queen Elizabeth advises Charles and Diana that she favors "an early divorce."

Feb. 28, 1996
Diana announces that she will give Charles a divorce.

Continued from p. 200

Church, but Puritans and Catholics remained unreconciled. Nonetheless, Elizabeth was able to carry out an energetic foreign policy and promote benevolent policies at home — notably, the adoption of the poor law in 1601 requiring local parishes to care for the needy.

When Elizabeth died without an heir in 1603, the crown passed to King James of Scotland, a fourth-generation descendant of Henry VII. The century of Stuart rule witnessed a continuing clash between the Crown and Parliament, complicated by religious battles and the uncertain union between England and Scotland.

James' son, Charles I, gave his reluctant assent to Parliament's passage of the Petition of Right in 1628, prohibiting all forms of taxation without Parliament's consent. A year later, Charles dissolved Parliament and sought to govern without Parliament for the next 11 years. But the costs of fighting a war in Scotland forced Charles to convene a new Parliament, which in 1641 passed a law requiring the summoning of Parliament every three years with or without the king's initiative.

The clash between Crown and Parliament led to civil war in 1642 and again in 1648, culminating in Charles' execution in 1649. The republican Commonwealth was quickly transformed into dictatorship under Oliver Cromwell, who styled himself Lord Protector of England, Scotland and Ireland. He died in 1658; a year later, his son, Richard, yielded power. From exile, Charles II issued a declaration describing Parliament as "a vital part of the constitution." Thus reassured, parliamentarians welcomed the Restoration when Charles returned to English soil in May 1660.

Religious issues continued to fester and fed into the battle for power between the monarchy and Parliament, which passed laws in the 1660s limiting rights of religious dissenters. After Charles died in 1685, his Catholic brother James II tried to secure freedom of worship for Catholics. His efforts produced a revolt in Parliament, which declared the throne vacant and offered the crown to William, the Protestant duke of Orange and husband of James' daughter Mary.

The "Glorious Revolution" installed William and Mary as king and queen for life. More important, it enacted the Declaration of Right, which called for "frequent" meetings of Parliament and prohibited the monarch from making or suspending laws without Parliament's consent. The charter also fortified parliamentary power to levy taxes and authorize an army, safeguarded parliamentary debate and elections, and guaranteed jury trials. "The result," *The Oxford Illustrated History of the British Monarchy* concludes, "was an important and permanent shift in the balance of power between monarchy and Parliament." [15]

After Mary's death, William ruled alone until he died in 1702, when he was succeeded by Anne II, James' second daughter. When she died without an heir in 1714, the crown passed to a new dynasty — the Protestant House of Hanover, the Germanic house that James I's granddaughter had married into. But the three kings George, who ruled in succession until 1820, saw their power wane as Cabinet government was strengthened and parliamentary opposition enshrined. And royal power declined further as Britain approached the transition from an aristocratic to a democratic society in the 19th century.

The clearest demonstration of the monarch's new, subordinate role came with the parliamentary reform crisis in the first years of the short reign of William IV (1830-1837). Thanks to a system of "pocket boroughs" — where individual patrons chose representatives to Parliament — and "rotten boroughs" — where members were chosen by bribery — no more than one-third of the members of the House of Commons could be viewed as freely elected.

William and the pro-royalist Tories opposed efforts to change the system, but the pro-reform Whigs triumphed in successive elections in 1830 and 1831. After the House of Commons passed the Reform Act, however, the House of Lords refused its assent. With the country on the verge of civil war, William reluctantly acceded to the advice of the Whig leader Earl Grey to persuade the Tory lords to let the bill become law. [16]

The Popular Monarchy

The popularity of the monarchy has fluctuated dramatically through history, but the personal esteem of the king or queen has been largely irrelevant to political events. The political, social and cultural democratization of the 19th and 20th centuries, however, made public opinion an important political force and the monarch a more familiar figure. Ironically, though, this new democratic era has seen the British monarchy become more popular rather than less so.

This advancing royal popularity began in the latter decades of the record 63-and-a-half-year reign of Queen Victoria, who acceded to the throne in 1837 after her uncle, William IV, died without an heir. Initially, the teenaged queen was hesitant about her duties. Then, for a decade after the death of her beloved husband Prince Albert in 1861, Victoria became a recluse, pleading fatigue and illness in avoiding all public engagements. By the time of the national celebration of her Golden Jubilee in 1887, however, Victoria had emerged as a beloved figure, the symbol of stable government at home and expanding empire abroad.

With her powers limited by the centuries of constitutional tradition, political leaders had no reason to resist this idolization of the queen — and, indeed, some reason to promote it.

The traditionally royalist Tories viewed the monarchy, as British historian Linda Colley notes, as an aid in appealing to working-class voters and countering socialism. [17] For their part, neither the Liberal Party nor, later, the Labor Party saw any political benefit in opposing the monarchy. Labor leader Ramsay MacDonald, writing in 1911, described the cause of republicanism as "of abstract interest only." [18]

The heart of the monarchy's new appeal lay in what Colley, who now teaches at Yale University, labels "the cult of royal domesticity." The monarchy was no longer an austere, imposing presence. Victoria was instead the head of "a cosy royal family." The transformation was recognized at the time: Bagehot wrote that the idea of a royal family gave the monarchy influence to compensate for the loss of its formal powers. In the 20th century, the image has been carefully cultivated by Victoria's most successful descendants: the two kings George and the current Queen Elizabeth.

Victoria's immediate successor, however, put the image of royal domesticity to the test. In contrast to his introverted mother, King Edward VII showed evident delight in his public duties and relish in his private pleasures. But the Oxford history of the monarchy suggests that his notorious extramarital liaisons only served to enhance his popularity. "His womanizing was, by most of his subjects, regarded amiably as a sign of manliness and spirit," the authors write. [19]

George V, who acceded to the throne after Edward's death in 1910, was a more dour king, but he, too, made the monarchy more popular in his quarter-century reign. He set an example for wartime Britain in 1915 by banning alcohol from all palaces for the duration. Two years later, he changed the royal family's name from that of Prince Albert's Germanic house, Saxe-Coburg-Gotha, to the thoroughly English name of Windsor. His personal popularity survived largely intact despite his role in granting Irish home rule and in resolving three-way splits between Conservative, Liberal and Labor parties in the 1920s and '30s.

George V's death on Jan. 20, 1936, left as the heir to the throne his oldest son David, who shared his grandfather's love for life rather than his father's devotion to royal duties. He chose to rule under his grandfather's name as Edward VIII, but he had no choice on how his reign ended. He loved an American woman, Wallis Warfield Simpson, who was his constant companion before and during his brief reign. In October 1936, Simpson filed for a divorce against her husband. The Tory prime minister, Stanley Baldwin, bluntly warned the king that the monarchy's power depended on its reputation and integrity. Labor and Liberal party leaders echoed the understood warning that Simpson was unacceptable as queen. The king gave his answer on Nov. 16, telling Baldwin that he was prepared to abdicate to marry his love.

Many thought the abdication dealt a mortal blow to the monarchy. But Edward began the rehabilitation process in his broadcast message to the nation by introducing his younger brother, the new king, as a man with "a happy home with his wife and children." Although inexperienced, George VI devoted himself to his duties and won the public's admiration and respect.

The outbreak of World War II underlined his role as national leader. Significantly, he remained in Buckingham Palace in London rather than seek refuge from German bombing. His daughter, Princess Elizabeth, showed her own sense of duty by joining the Auxiliary Territorial Service when she turned 18. The image of a perfect royal family was reinforced after the war with Elizabeth's marriage to Prince Philip in 1947 and the birth of a son, Charles, one year later. By the time of the king's death on Feb. 6, 1952, the abdication crisis was history.

As queen, Elizabeth II has shown a 20th-century sense of how to preserve the monarchy's prestige. She decided to allow television coverage of her coronation. The event, on June 2, 1953, showed off the British monarchy at its ceremonial best for her subjects in Britain and the Commonwealth and for millions of others around the world. Two decades later, the queen achieved another public-relations masterstroke by agreeing in 1969 to take the British public in a behind-the-scenes tour of the Palace in the BBC television documentary, "The Royal Family."

In her official roles, Elizabeth has been the very model of a modern limited monarch. She followed party leaders' advice in designating a new prime minister at two moments of uncertain succession in 1957 and 1963. She dutifully read the official papers delivered in the monarch's "boxes," but she voiced no public opinions and gave no interviews.

The royal family's image suffered with the breakup of the marriage of her sister, Princess Margaret, from photographer Anthony Armstrong-Jones in 1976. But as Elizabeth celebrated her Silver Jubilee in 1977, the monarchy seemed more secure than ever. And on the eve of her jubilee, biographer Robert Lacey ended an account of her reign by noting "the blossoming of her son," Prince Charles. [20]

Charles and Diana

Charles did, in fact, develop late in life. [21] He had done well but not brilliantly in his studies at his father's former prep school and Cambridge University and in five years' service in the Navy. After he left the Navy in 1976, some thought was given to looking for "a real job" for him. But it was decided that he should devote himself to royal duties even though his mother's good health meant he had

Continued on p. 206

Some Monarchs Hold On in Democratic Era . . .

The 20th century has not been kind to the world's monarchs. Two world wars, the rise of communism and nationalism, and the spread of democracy have combined to end most hereditary monarchies around the world and to leave most surviving monarchs with relatively limited powers.

Still, more than two dozen monarchs continue to reign today in Europe, Asia, Africa and the Middle East. And defenders continue to see a useful role for them in maintaining national unity, shoring up democracy and containing partisan political conflict.

"I don't think there's any prejudice against monarchy today because all the monarchies are constitutional," says Harold Brooks-Baker, editor of *Burke's Peerage,* the bible of the British aristocracy. "America supposedly has checks and balances. A monarchy endeavors to have the same kind of strength. What most monarchies have developed in recent years is a forced slowdown on some decisions."

The kings, queens, princes, emperors, sultans and emirs of today rule in some of the world's smallest countries, like the European mini-states of Liechtenstein and Luxembourg, the Himalayan kingdom of Bhutan and the tiny Pacific island nation of Tonga. But monarchs also reign in two of the world's wealthiest and most important powers — Japan and Saudi Arabia. Monarchs also reign in seven of the countries in the North Atlantic Treaty Organization (NATO) and in neutral Sweden.

For the most part, today's monarchs coexist quite comfortably with democratic government. But several of the rulers of Islamic states continue to resist democratization. Still, the United States maintains close ties with Arab monarchs, viewing them as critical players in Mideast diplomacy and bulwarks against the advance of Islamic fundamentalism.

In Europe, most of the 10 monarchs play limited roles. Like the British monarch, they retain formal powers to dissolve the national legislature, designate a new head of government and sign legislation into law, but defer to political leaders in playing those roles. In 1990, Belgium's late king, Baudouin, stepped down for one day rather than block a liberal abortion law that he said he could not sign because of religious objections.

Saudi Arabia's King Fahd is one of nine monarchs in Islamic countries and, along with Jordan's King Hussein, a powerful ruler and a major figure in Mideast diplomacy. The emirs of smaller Gulf states — Bahrain, Kuwait, Oman and Qatar — follow Fahd's example in running their oil-rich countries like family corporations. "Our monarchs don't reign, they rule — sometimes with an iron hand," says Mark Hudson, a professor at Georgetown University's Center for Contemporary Arab Studies.

Democracy is making some advances, however, in the Arab world. Jordan's King Hussein and Morocco's King Hassan II both moved their countries toward democracy with parliamentary elections in 1993, the first in 40 years for Jordan and 10 years for Morocco. The Kuwaiti emir, Sheik Jabir Ahmed Sabah, yielded to U.S. pressure after the war with Iraq to reconvene the country's parliament. But political parties are still banned, and parliament has struggled against the ruling family to try to assert its powers.

Japan's Emperor Akihito remains an important and beloved figure, but has virtually no political role. The Constitution imposed by the United States after World War II stripped the emperor of all political powers, even the formal

Monarchies Around the World

Europe	
Belgium	King Albert II
Denmark	Queen Margrethe II
Liechtenstein	Prince Hans Adam II
Luxembourg	Grand Duke Jean
Monaco	Prince Rainier III
Netherlands	Queen Beatrix
Norway	King Harald V
Spain	King Juan Carlos I
Sweden	King Carl XVI Gustaf
United Kingdom	Queen Elizabeth II
Islamic world	
Bahrain	Emir Isa bin Salman Al Khalifa
Brunei	Sultan Hassanal Bolkiah
Jordan	King Hussein
Kuwait	Emir Jabir al-Ahmad al-Jabir al Sabah
Malaysia	Paramount Ruler Tuanku Ja'afar ibn Al-Marhum Tuanku Abdul Rahman
Morocco	King Hassan II
Oman	Sultan Qaboos ibn Said Al Said
Qatar	Emir Hamad ibn Khalifa Al Thani
Saudi Arabia	King Fahd ibn Abd al-Aziz Al Saud
Asia (non-Islamic countries)	
Bhutan	King Jigme Singye Wangchuck
Cambodia	King Norodom Sihanouk
Japan	Emperor Akihito
Nepal	King Birendra Bir Bikram Shah Dev
Thailand	King Bhumibol Adulyadej
Africa (south of the Sahara)	
Lesotho	King Letsie III
Swaziland	King Mswati III
Oceania	
Tonga	King Tupou IV, Taufa'ahau

Source: Central Intelligence Agency, Chiefs of State and Cabinet Members of Foreign Governments: A Directory, *November 1995.*

. . . But Most Have Limited Powers

role held by most constitutional monarchs to designate the prime minister.

Four of Asia's other non-Islamic countries have hereditary rulers. Thailand's King Bhumibol Adulyadej is a popular and, in recent years, occasionally outspoken leader; he is also the world's longest-ruling monarch, now in his 50th year on the throne. He has heart problems, however, and his son has been forced to deny accusations of involvement in organized crime.

In neighboring Cambodia, King Norodom Sihanouk, who was ousted from the throne in the 1950s by a rightist coup, was restored to power in 1993 as part of a United Nations-brokered accord to end the country's bloody civil war. But the opposition Khmer Rouge remain unreconciled, and Sihanouk himself is aging and has been treated for cancer.

In the Himalayan kingdom of Bhutan, King Jigme Singye Wangchuck rules as an absolute monarch, allowing little power to the national parliament, ordering all Bhutanese to wear traditional dress and supporting an ethnic-cleansing campaign against Nepalese-speaking southerners. Nepal's King Birendra, on the other hand, has won praise for allowing democratic elections in 1990 and then refusing to block the installation of a communist-led government in 1994 after the Communist Party led in parliamentary balloting.

Sub-Saharan Africa has only two national monarchies, in tiny Lesotho and in Swaziland. Swaziland's King Mswati III rules his country like a traditional monarch, allowing little power to parliament and maintaining the ban on political parties. Lesotho's King Letsie III, who acceded after the death of his father in an automobile accident in January, took over a country with democratic forms but influential roles for the military and the monarchy. Some of Africa's sub-national ethnic groups also have hereditary kings, such as the Zulus in South Africa.

With its colonial history, the Western Hemisphere never had much use for monarchs, and there are no hereditary rulers in North or South America today. Some dictators, however, have tried to pass their mantle on to their offspring — for example, Haiti's François Duvalier, who ruled with terror and corruption for 14 years and designated his son, Jean-Claude, to succeed him.

Today's monarchs are generally more familiar and less austere than the kings and emperors of the past. The Scandinavian rulers have been dubbed "bicycling monarchs" because they shun most royal ostentations. Denmark's Queen Margrethe does, in fact, bicycle about the countryside unaccompanied. Spain's Juan Carlos motorcycles, also without security. Once, he rescued an out-of-gas motorist, his identity concealed until he lifted his visor at the end of the incident to accept his countryman's thanks.

Some monarchs, however, still keep a royal distance from their subjects. Japan's Emperor Akihito is rarely seen in public, except for the ritualistic annual greetings at the Imperial Palace on his birthday. Saudi's King Fahd lives in regal ostentation, though the royal family maintains the practice of holding regular meetings where ordinary people can come to present grievances.

The idea of kingship is as old as recorded history, according to Richard Rose, an expert on monarchy at the University of Strathclyde in Scotland. [1] But the earliest kings gained their positions through battle, choice of elders or popular acclaim. Hereditary monarchy developed much later, Rose says, primarily as a way to end disputes about leadership. The doctrine of divine rule, which has undergirded monarchies in Europe and Asia, developed first in the East; it took hold in Europe only in the 15th and 16th centuries.

The French and American revolutions were both aimed at ending monarchical rule. But the backlash against the French Revolution and the Napoleonic empire actually helped strengthen European monarchies. Ironically, the nationalist revolutions in Europe in the 19th and early 20th centuries also were a boon time for monarchs, since the newly formed countries typically recruited a nobleman to serve as king in order to gain national unity and international legitimacy.

World War I marked the beginning of the end for the monarchical era, with the defeat of the German, Austro-Hungarian and Ottoman empires and the toppling of the tsar in the Russian Revolution. The end of World War II brought the rejection of the Italian monarchy and the displacement of Eastern Europe's monarchies by communist governments. In the decades after the war, nationalist and fundamentalist movements toppled several conservative monarchs in Islamic countries, including Egypt (1952), Iraq (1958), Yemen (1962), Libya (1969) and Iran (1979).

No new monarchies have been created in recent years. But Spain restored its monarchy after the death of the dictator Francisco Franco. And Cambodia installed Norodom Sihanouk as king to try to end a bloody civil war. In both countries, the newly installed king was viewed as the most likely leader to reunify a badly divided nation. But, despite a flurry of speculation, the former communist countries of Eastern Europe have shown no inclination to restoring monarchical rule since the end of the Cold War.

Rose predicts that no new monarchies will be created in the future. He also warns that existing monarchies, including Britain's, risk their survival if they become too involved in politics. "The way in which a country goes from monarchy to republic is that the king or queen gets caught up in politics, tries to influence events and takes sides," Rose says. "Sooner or later, you're going to be on the losing side."

---

[1] See Richard Rose, "Monarchy, Constitutional," in *The Encyclopedia of Democracy* (1995), pp. 843-847.

Continued from p. 203

many years, if not decades, ahead of him as Prince of Wales.

In his biography, Dimbleby says that Charles quickly showed a seriousness of purpose. He founded a new charity, the Prince's Trust, aimed at the inner city. He complained in a 1978 memo about the "ceaseless round of official engagements" and asked about spending more extended periods in a factory, farm and immigrant areas "in less artificial circumstances."

But thanks to his very public interest in playing polo and dating attractive women, Charles also developed the image of a playboy. Dimbleby says that the image — and the substance — worried his friends and his family, including his father, Prince Philip, and his great-uncle Lord Mountbatten. In a letter in 1978, Mountbatten chided Charles for showing "no signs that you were pulling yourself together." [22]

As he entered his 30s, Charles' own sense of duty combined with the pressure from his family and the public to move him toward marriage. By 1980, public attention, as well as Charles', was focused on Diana Spencer, the attractive teenaged daughter of a prominent aristocratic family. Charles had met Diana in 1977 while dating her older sister. He was drawn by her easygoing manner and touch of irreverence; he was won over by touching comments she made to him after the death of Lord Mountbatten, who was killed by an Irish Republican Army bomb in 1979. Dimbleby says Charles told friends in fall 1980 that he "did not yet love her," but "was sure that he could." Prince Philip counseled him to make a decision, for her sake. He proposed in February 1981, and the wedding was set for July.

The wedding — viewed by a worldwide television audience of 700 million or more — was a sight to behold. [23] Charles was regal in the full dress uniform of a Royal Navy commander. Diana, now 20, was resplendent in an ivory silk taffeta dress encrusted with sequins and pearls. The hour-long ceremony, held in St. Paul's Cathedral, was conducted by the Archbishop of Canterbury, who pronounced the royal couple "man and wife together." Charles did not kiss Diana in the cathedral. But they gave every other appearance of complete happiness as they waved to the cheering crowds from a magnificent horse-drawn carriage — festooned with a bouquet of balloons — on their return ride to Buckingham Palace.

Reuters

The Duchess of York, separated from Prince Andrew, has tried to improve her public image through her work with children's charities.

In fact, however, the relationship between Charles and Diana was troubled from the start, according to later accounts in Morton's books and elsewhere. Diana took a family trip to Australia after the engagement was announced and was bothered that Charles never telephoned her. She also felt anxious about Charles' feelings toward Camilla Parker-Bowles after discovering, on the eve of the wedding, that he was giving her an expensive, engraved bracelet; Diana took no reassurance from his protestations that they were just friends.

After the marriage, Charles and Diana argued "continually," according to Morton. The bickering combined with the pressure of her new duties to bring on attacks of the eating disorder bulimia nervosa and then a number of half-hearted suicide attempts. In the first, Diana threw herself down the stairs in 1982, while she was pregnant with their first child, William.

Prince William's birth on June 21, 1982, provided reprieve from the troubles, Morton writes, but it did not last long. Meanwhile, the royal press was already finding and reporting evidence of marital difficulties. The reports grew through the decade, but were consistently denied by the Palace. [24]

Eventually, however, the evidence was in plain view for all to see: Diana turning away a public buss from Charles after a polo match in April 1992; Diana, photographed conspicuously alone at the Pyramids in Egypt and the Taj Mahal in India during official visits later that year; and, most tellingly, Charles and Diana standing side by side during a state visit to South Korea in November 1992, unmistakable mutual antipathy written on their faces.

Despite the marital difficulties, Diana was winning over the British and worldwide public as a modern-day "people's princess." She devoted herself to comforting deprived children and people suffering from AIDS, cancer and leprosy. Charles, meanwhile, was drawing intense public criticism for delivering outspoken views on such topics as alternative medicine and organic agriculture (which he favored) and modern architecture (which he opposed). At the time of their wedding, Charles was the second most popular member of the royal family, after the queen. By the early 1990s, Diana had displaced him in the public's esteem.

'Annus Horribilis'

The year 1992 — the 40th anniversary of the queen's accession to the throne — brought events to a head for Charles and Diana as well as the royal family.[25]

The troubles began in January with reports of compromising pictures of Prince Andrew's wife, Sarah, the Duchess of York, and a male admirer. The Palace announced the couple's separation in March; the pictures, finally published in August, showed "Fergie" sun-bathing topless as her male friend sucked her toes.

In June, *The Sunday Times* began publishing excerpts from Morton's first book, depicting Diana as the victim of beastly neglect from her husband and the royal family. Diana's image suffered in August with the broadcast and publication of the "Squidgy" tapes: a recorded telephone conversation between Diana and a male friend, James Gilbey, who repeatedly called her "darling" or "Squidgy" as she described her marriage as "real, real torture."[26] In September, tabloids reported that Diana had enjoyed a "physical" relationship with Major James Hewitt, her children's riding instructor.

The damage to Diana's image did nothing to rehabilitate Charles'. In November, the first reports came of what came to be called the "Camillagate" tapes, which eventually became public in January. The prince was heard on the recorded phone call telling his "friend" Camilla, "I love you, I adore you," and expressing the hope — as Morton put it — "that he could be turned into a Tampax tampon so that he could be constantly joined with the wife of one of his closest friends."[27]

Meanwhile, the queen herself had been drawn into a bruising public controversy over the royal finances. In a thoroughly documented book, journalist Philip Hall estimated her personal wealth at 400 million pounds ($600 million) and the total value of the Crown's jewelry, property and other holdings at 1.2 billion pounds ($1.8 billion).[28] Hall also documented the relatively recent decisions exempting the royal family from taxation. A Conservative member of Parliament bluntly described the queen as "stinking rich," and calls came for the queen to make some form of tax payments.

Later in the year, Windsor Castle sustained millions of dollars of uninsured damage from a Nov. 20 fire ignited by a spotlight trained on a curtain. In a speech four days later, the queen somberly described the year in Latin as "annus horribilis." She asked for sympathy, but made no offer to pay for the restoration of the family's beloved castle. On Nov. 26, however, Prime Minister Major announced that the queen and Prince Charles had agreed in principle to pay income tax. In addition, he said the government would no longer pay the tab for any members of the royal family except the queen, the queen mother and Prince Philip.

Two weeks later, Major again rose in Parliament to deal with the royal family's problems — this time, announcing the separation of the Prince and Princess of Wales. Major sought to minimize the impact of the announcement. He said Charles and Diana had "no plans to divorce" and maintained that their constitutional positions, including "the succession to the throne," were "unaffected." "There is no reason," he continued, "why the Princess of Wales should not be crowned queen in due course."

Holden says Major decided on his own to state publicly remarks that the Palace was distributing as background guidance for journalists.[29] Whatever the origin of the addendum, it strained credulity. "Gasps were heard in the chamber," author Wilson writes.[30] As time went on, the incredulity only grew.

The Queen Intervenes

For the next three years, the British press, broadcasters and publishers deluged the British and worldwide publics with more and more details of Charles' and Diana's marital difficulties in a form of "he said, she said" conducted first through surrogates and then by the principals themselves.

Diana's accusations in Morton's book — attributed to friends but gradually accepted as reflecting the princess' views — were most fully answered in Dimbleby's June 1994 television documentary about Charles and the biography that appeared in October. Dimbleby stressed that he was doing a serious biography of the heir to the throne, not a gossipy account of a broken marriage. But the book allowed Charles and his admirers to depict the prince as a husband who was troubled by his wife's difficulties but unable to help her and as a father who loved his children and strained to spend time with them while maintaining a busy official schedule.

The documentary — broadcast on the British network ITV — made the biggest news, however, with Charles' pained admission that he had cheated on his wife beginning at least six years before their separation. Were you faithful to Diana, Dimbleby asked. "Yes," Charles replied, adding after a pause, "until it became irretrievably broken down, us both having tried." Despite the admission, Dimbleby said reaction to the documentary was overwhelmingly positive. The prince's office counted 6,000 letters of support and fewer than 50 of criticism.[31]

In the meantime, Diana announced in December 1993 that she was withdrawing from all official duties to devote more time to the couple's two children, Princes William and Harry. The decision did not free her from public attention; reporters and photographers continued to dog her steps and plumb the details of her life. Then, last fall, she decided herself to lift the veil on her life by agreeing to a lengthy interview on the BBC program "Panorama."

Diana acknowledged in the Nov. 20 broadcast that she had been in love with Hewitt — and felt betrayed when he told of their romance in the book *Princess in Love.*[32] But she devoted most of her comments to describing her feelings of helplessness in the marriage to Charles and her resentment of his continuing to see Camilla. "There were three of us in this marriage," Diana told the interviewer, "so it was a bit crowded."

In the interview, Diana turned aside the suggestion of a divorce. "I don't want a divorce, but obviously we need clarity," she said. A month later, the queen acted to clarify the situation by, in effect, commanding the couple to divorce. "The queen has written to both the Prince and Princess of Wales after considering the present situation," a Palace spokesman said in confirming the Dec. 18 letters two days later. "It is her view, which is supported by the duke, that an early divorce is desirable."[33]

The Palace statement said Prince Charles also agreed on the need for an early divorce and ended with an assurance that the queen and Prince Philip "will continue to do all they can to support the princess and particularly the children." The statement made no reference to Diana's views; the princess was to hold her counsel for another 10 weeks, until her decision late last month to agree to an official end of a marriage that had long since been over. ■

CURRENT SITUATION

Sounds of Silence

With the opposition Labor Party well ahead of Prime Minister Major's Conservative Party in the polls, Labor leader Tony Blair called last month for a broad-ranging election debate over constitutional reform issues. Blair's Feb. 7 speech reaffirmed the Labor Party's commitment to reforming the House of Lords to eliminate voting rights for hereditary peers. He also called for greater self-government for Scotland and Wales and for home rule for the city of London.[34]

Blair left one important constitutional issue untouched, however: the monarchy. Despite steadily increasing public and press criticism of the royal family in the past several years, Blair made no proposal for reducing the size of the monarchy or the powers of the Crown.

The issue had been broached a little over a year earlier by one of the prospective Cabinet members of a Labor government: Shadow Home Secretary Jack Straw. In an interview on "Panorama" in December 1994, Straw called for cutting in half — from 40 to 20 — the members of the royal family entitled to be called His or Her Royal Highness, with only five or six to perform official duties. Straw also called for limiting the power of the government to use the royal prerogative to force legislation through Parliament.

In the wake of sharp criticism from Tory leaders, Blair stood by Straw's remarks at the time, saying that he had approved the comments. But today, an aide to Blair insists that the comments were only personal, not party policy. "Labor has no policy about the monarchy in the sense of changing its current position or status," says the aide, who asked not to be quoted by name. "We have policies for constitutional reform, which of course might have tangential effects, but nothing that would directly touch on the monarchy."

For its part, the governing Conservative Party has delighted, both then and now, in depicting Straw's and Blair's positions as a threat to Britain's constitutional system and, in particular, to the monarchy. Tory Party Chairman Brian Mawhinney blasted Blair last month for proposing "an entirely new constitutional order based on fashionable left-wing prejudices in defiance of the wisdom of the ages." He said the Conservative Party "will fight tooth and nail for Britain's constitution" in the coming election, which must be called by May 1997.

Haseler, chairman of the Republican, praises Blair's renewed support for reforming the House of Lords, but says he is not surprised at the Labor leader's decision to pass over the issue of the monarchy. "There are a lot of politicians, Conservative as well as Labor, even Thatcherites, who privately think this institution is ludicrous for a country purporting to be modern," Haseler says. "The problem is with politicians who want to become peers and knights and so forth. They're much more tied in with the system."

Still, the anti-monarchist cause received a boost on Feb. 18 when *The Independent on Sunday* became the first national newspaper in recent times to editorialize in favor of abolishing the monarchy. "The Crown's survival," the newspaper declared, "reinforces the impression that British society is like a pyramid and that, at its apex, birth counts for more than merit."

Along with the editorial, the newspaper published a new poll indicating the monarchy's declining hold on the British public. Only 34 percent of those surveyed thought Britain would be

Continued on p. 210

At Issue:

Should Britain abolish the monarchy?

YES

The Independent On Sunday
From an editorial, Feb. 18, 1996.

Abolition of the monarchy would be an undertaking so far-reaching, so drastic, so controversial that it would daunt any politician. That, however, is precisely why the subject needs to be addressed. The Crown is part of the fabric of British life. . . .

If Britain's identity is indeed bound up with the monarchy, we have tied our future to an institution that looks increasingly frail. Hardly a day goes by without at least one newspaper . . . headlining some new "royal" controversy. . . . Royal coverage is like drugs or pornography: Once the appetite is whetted, higher and harder fixes are needed. . . .

The royals, partly through their own actions, have become part of the show-business industry. . . . Some may blame the tabloids for intrusion. But monarchy has always depended on popular fascination. . . . We are expected to dance with joy at the romance of a royal wedding; we cannot then be expected to avert our eyes when the romance turns sour. . . .

The truth is that, though the queen herself has no political power, Britain is still governed by royal prerogative, exercised on the monarch's behalf by her ministers. The result is that, in many areas, ministers have near-dictatorial powers which cannot be checked or even properly scrutinized by Parliament. . . .

Can these prerogative powers be abolished, or at least reduced, without abolishing the monarchy itself? Can Britain become republican in its politics while still preserving the fun, glamour and glitter of princes and princesses? Yes, in theory. In reality, however, republicanism and democracy go beyond written constitutions and bills of rights. They also require an attitude of mind, a belief that every citizen has the right to a hearing, a sense that no doors are closed to talent and energy. . . . The Crown's survival reinforces the impression that British society is shaped like a pyramid and that, at its apex, birth counts for more than merit. . . .

The defenders of the monarchy fall back on the argument that, if nothing else, it is a tourist attraction. So it is, but it is hard to believe that tourists would cease their pilgrimages to Buckingham Palace, the Mall, the Tower or Windsor Castle simply because a monarch no longer rules. . . .

The stronger argument is that the monarchy connects us to our history. . . . Yet it has become almost a commonplace of post-war political debate that Britain is too weighed down by history. . . . In any case, British history should not be about the glories of its kings and queens; rather, it should be about how the people wrested and defended their liberties from the Crown. . . . Would it not connect us to a different, but better, strain of our history if we were to abolish the monarchy and proclaim the final triumph of the people?

NO

H.B. Brooks-Baker and C. L. Cameron
Publishing director and editor of *Burke's Peerage*

Written for *The CQ Researcher*, March 8, 1996

Winston Churchill often described parliamentary democracy and constitutional monarchy as being imperfect systems, but systems that were, nonetheless, the best that man had yet devised.

It is human nature to require that there be a leader at the helm. In our century we have looked to our heads of state for this leadership. Apart from the numerous ceremonial duties that they are required to carry out, a head of state should foster and maintain the notion of political accountability, whilst remaining at all times above politics. Yet in a republic it is usually an ex-politician who becomes head of state, one who tries hard to shake off old political allegiances but who generally fails.

The British system of constitutional monarchy, however, aptly demonstrates why a monarchy is a more successful figurehead than a president. In Britain, the monarchy remains very much at the heart of the constitution, a fact that gives continuity and pride to the nation. This is true despite any problems that the monarch or other members of the royal family may have.

Queen Elizabeth II keeps unto herself powers that may surprise. She has the power to choose a prime minister, dissolve parliament and declare war. Yet, in reality, she waives these residual powers and is bound by tradition to accept the advice of parliament. Moreover, she must always consult her ministers and receive their approbation before issuing a command. It is a system that prevents politicians from easily usurping power and that has prevented a dictator from ruling Great Britain since Oliver Cromwell.

The real font of power, technically at Buckingham Palace, is in reality now divided between Downing Street and Westminster. Advice, however, from the palace can act as a restraining influence on governments in Great Britain and the Commonwealth, which, together, represent almost one-third of the people in the world today. If one were to jettison the monarchy, these organs would be turned upside down, and any replacements instituted only at vast cost to the people.

British monarchy has served both the Empire and the Commonwealth with great distinction, but it is threatened because the idea of republicanism seems more democratic and less overtly hierarchical. It is widely accepted that monarchy is one of the most enduring and stable forms of government. In Great Britain it derives its legitimacy and continuity from an unwritten constitution that provides a solid foundation for society.

America's Favorite Soap Opera

Americans fought to be free of the British monarchy 200 years ago, but now they can't get enough of "the Royals." Americans have avidly followed every twist and turn in the soap opera lives of Britain's royal family for the past 15 years — from the fairy tale wedding of Prince Charles and "Princess Di" to the sunbathing antics of the Duchess of York, from Prince Andrew's porn-star girlfriend to Elizabeth's somber stoicism.

What's the fascination in a story about a fabulously wealthy family with a record of broken marriages that lives across the Atlantic Ocean and has nothing to do with the daily lives of average Americans?

"It's really Diana that captivated everyone," says Landon Jones, managing editor of *People* magazine, which has put the glamorous princess on its cover a record 38 times since 1981. "You had the fairy tale princess myth, and then things came into conflict. In Britain, you marry for duty; and you stay married for duty and obligation — or do you? These are dilemmas that most Americans are not familiar with."

With the couple's conflicts becoming more and more evident, the story's appeal became simpler to define. "It's a soap opera," Jones says. "It's family life writ large: the woman who marries for dreams and finds out he's philandering."

Some observers fault the focus on a sordid tale, the fascination with the spectacle of the high and mighty brought low. "It's part of the international, white-trash, soap-opera, tabloid business," says Christopher Hitchens, a British journalist in the United States who writes for *Vanity Fair* and *The Nation*.

Indeed, as *Washington Post* reporter Roxanne Roberts noted last year in *The Guardian*, "The British monarchy is America's favorite soap opera, a real-life 'Dynasty.' If the hysterics and adultery and ballgowns weren't enough, now there's drilling for oil on the grounds of Windsor Castle. If you kick them out of London, they'd feel right at home in Dallas." [1]

But Jones makes no apologies for covering the story so thoroughly. And he notes that if *People* has dealt with the seamy side of the story, it also has covered the constitutional issues raised by Charles' and Diana's marital difficulties. "I think we do that better than the British press," Jones says. "They tend to skip that."

Jones says Americans have a feeling of "residual nostalgia" about the British monarchy. Diana Nicholson, executive director of the English-Speaking Union in Washington, agrees. "It's something with a lot of pageantry and tradition, which the United States doesn't have," says Nicholson, a Briton who has lived in the United States since 1965.

Hitchens says that if Britain were to abolish the monarchy, it would have little effect on the United States. But Jones says Americans would not want to see the royal family go. "Americans think it's quaint and charming that Britain has the monarchy," he says.

"And Americans appreciate a good show," adds Roberts, "which is why we view the British monarchy with a kind of indulgent affection typically reserved for, say, a fabulously extravagant aunt."

[1] Roxanne Roberts "The View From Abroad: Citizens for Soap," *The Guardian*, Jan. 10, 1995.

worse off without the monarchy — down from 77 percent in 1984 and from 50 percent in 1992. Seventeen percent thought the country would be better off, while 42 percent said it would make no difference.

But supporters of the monarchy say that neither the opponents nor the public at large have offered a clear alternative. "None of these people have a clear idea of what a replacement would be," says Brooks-Baker. "There's a considerable amount of anti-monarchy feeling, but it's balanced by a great deal of indifference, tremendous indifference."

Waiting Period

As the debate over constitutional reform resumed, Prince Charles and Lady Diana were both staying out of the headlines for the most part. Behind the scenes, lawyers for the two royals began negotiating the details of a divorce, but the process was neither quick nor easy.

Both Charles and Diana are taking their public standing into account in the process, according to Geoffrey Waters, a matrimonial lawyer with the London firm of Wedlake Bell Solicitors. "Neither of them will want to be seen as cast in the mold of being the mean person, she in the form of being too grasping and he in the form of being too mean," Waters says.

British law allows a couple to obtain a divorce after two-years' separation without proof of other grounds — such as adultery — as long as both parties consent. By withholding consent, Diana was thought to be trying to use it as a bargaining chip on other issues. But with many key questions still unresolved after last month's announcement, the strategy appears to have failed, at least in part.

The financial settlement Diana is reportedly seeking will be beyond Prince Charles' means and thus will require some contribution from Queen Elizabeth herself. The prince reportedly has an annual income of 4.5 million pounds (about $7 million) from his 125,000-acre Duchy of Cornwall estate, not enough to pay the settlement. [35]

Diana's choice of lawyers indicates the importance of the financial aspects of the divorce. After the death of her first lawyer, Paul Butner, she turned to a senior commercial lawyer, Lord Mischon, with a reputation as a hard-nosed negotiator. Prince Charles is being represented by Farrar & Co., the queen's solicitors.

Custody arrangements are unlikely to pose a serious problem, Waters says. "Both of them will obviously want to maximize their access to the children," Waters says. "But as the children become older, inevitably they'll be wanting to spend less time with their parents."

Charles is the third of the queen's children to have a failed marriage. Besides Prince Andrew's separation, Princess Anne, the Princess Royal, was divorced in April 1992 from Mark Phillips after a 19-year marriage. Eight months later, she married Tim Laurence, with whom she had been romantically involved at least since 1989. The queen's youngest son, Prince Edward, is still single, but some palace-watchers have said that he plans to marry his longtime girlfriend, Sophie Rhys-Jones, sometime this year.

The prince and princess left their Feb. 28 meeting without speaking to reporters. Charles spoke later that night at a Hindu temple and declined to comment. Diana was so distraught that she pulled out of an official dinner the next night. "The princess would prefer a few days of quiet before she picks up her public engagements again," her spokeswoman, Jane Atkinson, said. "Any woman would." ■

OUTLOOK

'Long to Reign Over Us'

Queen Elizabeth will mark two personal milestones in the coming months. She celebrates her 70th birthday on April 21. Seven weeks later — on June 12 — she will surpass the 44-year, 127-day reign of her namesake, Elizabeth I, to become Britain's fifth-longest-reigning monarch ever.

Supporters and opponents of the monarchy alike are already anticipating a more remarkable achievement. If the queen's longevity matches that of the still active, 95-year-old queen mother, Elizabeth could even surpass Queen Victoria's record 63-and-a-half-year reign. That day, one admiring reviewer calculated earlier this year, will come on Sept. 9, 2015. [36]

For supporters of the monarchy, the queen's popularity and longevity provide comfort that the current troubles will pass and will pose no bar to Prince Charles' accession to the throne in due course. "Charles has got time to play for," says historian Starkey. "Everything suggests that keeping a relatively low profile, letting events take their course, will diminish whatever opposition there is at the moment."

Opponents of the monarchy, however, believe that time is on their side. Very deliberately, they propose postponing the demise of the monarchy until "after the queen goes" — as they delicately phrase it — but beginning now to plan for the establishment of a new British republic. "We're basically saying this should be Elizabeth the Last," says Haseler of the Republican. "It's a clean break. It's a sensible time to make the break."

Supporters of the monarchy minimize the current agitation for a republic. "There has been scarcely any increase in pro-republican sentiment," says political scientist King. "You would find it hard to mount a demonstration in London or elsewhere for republicanism."

But the advocates of constitutional reform think that popular support for other changes — such as an elected House of Lords — will produce a new public view of the monarchy as well. "The wind's behind us," says Puddephat of Charter 88. "All the opinion polls show that there's 60-80 percent support for the package of constitutional reforms. Once the changes are in the air, it will be very difficult for the monarchy to justify its position."

The obstacles to changing the monarchy, however, are formidable. As *The Independent* noted in its editorial calling for abolition, the monarchy is "part of the fabric of British life" — from the national anthem ("Long Live the Queen") and governmental nomenclature ("Her Majesty's Government") to the royal presence at countless sporting, charitable and official functions. The parliamentary work needed to unravel that fabric, historian Hennessy says in his new book, "would paralyze the legislative timetable of any government that introduced it." And, he adds, "it would split the country from top to bottom." [37]

If he does become king, Prince Charles will have had one of the longest periods of preparation of any British monarch. His biographer Dimbleby thinks that time will erase his current unpopularity and ease the public criticism of Charles for the breakup of his marriage. "People will come to see that he should not be hounded for the failure of his marriage," Dimbleby says.

Charles' admirers predict that he would be a modern monarch, more informal and more accessible than

FOR MORE INFORMATION

Charter 88, Exmouth House, 3-11 Pine St., London EC1R 0JH, United Kingdom; (44) 171-833-1988. This constitutional-reform organization, founded in 1988, advocates a nationwide referendum on the monarchy.

Embassy of the United Kingdom of Great Britain and Northern Ireland, 3100 Massachusetts Ave., N.W., Washington, D.C. 20008; (202) 462-1340. The embassy's press and public information section provides information about the British government and government policies.

English-Speaking Union, 15 Dupont Circle, N.W., Washington, D.C. 20036; (202) 234-4602. The organization, founded in Britain in the 1920s, promotes Anglo-American relations through a variety of activities, including scholarships and cultural exchanges.

The Republican, P.O. Box 2698, London W14 9ZT, United Kingdom; (44) 181-875-9854. The organization, founded in 1983, favors replacing the monarchy with a republic, headed by an elected president.

Queen Elizabeth. "Despite the naval uniforms and the entourage he has and the big house he lives in, his instinct is to be close to the people," says King at Essex University.

But, as historian Cannadine points out, there are no guarantees. "The point about monarchy is that you buy the whole deal," he says. "You don't have any choice about who gets the job next." A long preparation is no guarantee either, Cannadine adds. The century's best monarchs were not born with the expectation of reigning: George V acceded after the early death of his brother Edward VII, while George VI and Elizabeth came into the line of succession only because of Edward VIII's abdication.

In the end, the British monarchy's durability perhaps defies rational explanation. For centuries, it has been, in Bogdanor's phrase, "the magical monarchy." To continue to survive, Bogdanor advises that it change with the times into a more "practical monarchy." "Today, it needs not only to be seen," he writes. "It has also to do."[38]

The monarchy's 1,200-year history demonstrates its capacity for change. So the question for the immediate future is whether the current royal family will change enough to accommodate Britons' restiveness about its trappings. But even critical observers doubt the prospects for abolishing it. "It's here because it's here," says Cannadine. And, he adds, "it's going to remain around." ■

Notes

[1] See *The Times* (of London), Feb. 29, 1996, p. 1; *The New York Times,* March 1, 1996, p. A3.

[2] See Anthony Holden, *King Charles III* (U.S. title, 1988) and *The Tarnished Crown: Diana and the House of Windsor* (1993).

[3] Vernon Bogdanor, *The Monarchy and the Constitution* (1995), p. 308.

[4] See Jonathan Dimbleby, *The Prince of Wales: A Biography* (1994).

[5] A.N. Wilson, *The Rise and Fall of the House of Windsor* (1993), pp. 141-142.

[6] Dimbleby, *op. cit,* p. 246.

[7] The Gallup Organization, December 1995. The poll was conducted in November 1995.

[8] Andrew Morton, *Diana: Her True Story* (1992), p. 6. See also Andrew Morton *Diana: Her New Life* (1994).

[9] Bogdanor, *op. cit.,* p. 307.

[10] Andrew Roberts, "Daylight and Magic," *The Times* (of London), Jan. 25, 1996.

[11] Peter Hennessy, *The Hidden Wiring: Unearthing the British Constitution* (1996), p. 70. Hennessy was quoting from a memoir by Lord Callaghan, foreign secretary and later prime minister, and a television interview by former Australian Prime Minister Bob Hawke. When *The Sunday Times* reported in 1986 that the Queen disagreed with a wide range of Thatcher's domestic and foreign policies, her private secretary wrote a letter saying the story was without substantiation. See Holden, *op. cit.,* pp. 215-217, and Wilson, *op. cit.,* pp. 22-23.

[12] See Edgar Wilson, "The Power of the Royals," *The Guardian,* Jan. 9, 1995, p. T6.

[13] *The Guardian,* Jan. 10, 1995, p. 2.

[14] For historical background, see John Cannon and Ralph Griffiths, *The Oxford Illustrated History of the British Monarchy* (1989).

[15] *Ibid.,* p. 432.

[16] *Ibid.,* p. 548.

[17] Linda Colley, "Political Royal Coaster: Not So Happily Ever After," *The Guardian,* Jan. 10, 1995, p. T6.

[18] Quoted in Cannon and Griffiths, *op. cit.,* p. 597.

[19] *Ibid.,* p. 582.

[20] Robert Lacey, *Majesty: Elizabeth II and the House of Windsor* (1976), p. 295.

[21] For background, see Jonathan Dimbleby, *The Prince of Wales: A Biography* (1994). For more critical treatments, see Holden, *The Tarnished Crown, op. cit.,* pp. 220-256, and Wilson, *op. cit.,* passim.

[22] Dimbleby, *op. cit.,* p. 260.

[23] This account is drawn from *The New York Times,* July 30, 1981, p. A1.

[24] See Daniel Pearl, "Believe It or Not, Tabloids Were Right About Charles and Di," *The Wall Street Journal,* Jan. 29, 1996, p. A1.

[25] For a detailed chronology, see Holden, *op. cit.,* pp. 331-336.

[26] See Morton, *Diana: Her New Life,* pp. 45-46; Dimbleby, *op. cit.,* p. 483n.

[27] Morton, *op. cit.,* pp. 73-74.

[28] Philip Hall, *Royal Fortune: Tax, Money and the Monarchy* (1992). See also Holden, *op. cit.,* pp. 130-135.

[29] Holden, *op. cit.,* p. 14.

[30] Wilson, *op. cit.,* p. 150.

[31] Dimbleby, *op. cit.,* p. 560.

[32] Anna Pasternak, *Princess in Love* (1994).

[33] Quoted in *The Guardian,* Dec. 21, 1995, p. 1.

[34] See Tony Blair, "Power to the People Must Be Our Aim," *The Independent,* Feb. 7, 1996, p. 15.

[35] *The Times* (of London), Feb. 29, 1996, p. 3.

[36] Roberts, *op. cit.* Britain's other longest reigning monarchs are George III (59 years), Henry III (56 years) and Edward III (50 years).

[37] Hennessy, *op. cit.,* p. 71.

[38] Bogdanor, *op. cit.,* p. 309.

Bibliography

Selected Sources Used

Books

Barnett, Anthony, ed., *The Power and the Throne,* Vintage, 1994.
The book consists of essays or responses from more than 30 participants in the 1993 conference on the British monarchy cosponsored by the reform group Charter 88 and *The Times* of London.

Bogdanor, Vernon, *The Monarchy and the Constitution,* Oxford University Press, 1995.
Bogdanor, a professor of government at Oxford University, constructs a forceful historical and political argument that a constitutional monarchy promotes national unity and governmental legitimacy. The book includes several brief appendixes and a five-page bibliography.

Bradford, Sarah, *Elizabeth: A Biography of Her Majesty the Queen,* Farrar, Straus & Giroux, 1996.
Bradford, author of an earlier biography of Queen Elizabeth's father, King George VI, provides a thorough account of her life and reign and the lives and difficulties of other members of the royal family. The book is to be published in the United States in April. For earlier biographies, see Robert Lacey, *Majesty: Elizabeth II and the House of Windsor* (Harcourt Brace & Jovanovich, 1977) and Douglas Keay, *Elizabeth II: Portrait of a Monarch* (Ebury Press, 1991).

Cannon, John, and Ralph Griffiths, *The Oxford Illustrated History of the British Monarchy,* Oxford University Press, 1989.
This authoritative, richly illustrated history traces the British monarchy from the fifth century through the mid-1980s. The book includes summary biographies of all British kings and queens since the ninth century, detailed genealogical and chronological charts and a 14-page bibliography.

Dimbleby, Jonathan, *The Prince of Wales: A Biography,* William Morrow, 1994.
Dimbleby, a television journalist, had what was described as "unprecedented access" to Prince Charles in writing this authorized biography. The book includes an eight-page appendix updating "the achievements of the various organizations and projects with which the Prince of Wales is associated." There is also a three-page bibliography.

Hennessy, Peter, *The Hidden Wiring: Unearthing the British Constitution,* Victor Gollancz, 1995.
Hennessy, a professor of contemporary history at Queen Mary and Westfield College, University of London, examines the workings of the various components of the British government, including the monarchy.

Holden, Anthony, *The Tarnished Crown: Diana and the House of Windsor,* Random House, 1993.
Holden, an author and longtime royal watcher, details the problems of Prince Charles' and Lady Diana's marriage along with a critical examination of the monarchy itself. The book includes a schedule of crown estate properties and a four-page bibliography and detailed source notes. Holden also wrote two earlier biographies: *Charles, Prince of Wales* (1979) and *King Charles III* (U.S. title, 1988).

Morton, Andrew, *Diana: Her True Story,* Simon & Schuster, 1992; *Diana: Her New Life,* Simon & Schuster, 1994.
Morton, who covered the royal family for the *Daily Star,* had the cooperation of Lady Diana's family and friends — and, some surmised, the princess herself — in writing the candid, sympathetic portrait of her life and marriage to Prince Charles in his first book. His second book depicts Diana's life since their separation.

Wilson, A.N., *The Rise and Fall of the House of Windsor,* W.W. Norton, 1993.
Wilson, a novelist and biographer, mixes historical and contemporary material in a sometimes serious, sometimes wry survey of selected themes, including the monarchy's relations with the press, its role in the Church of England and its constitutional powers.

Articles

"The New Republic," *The Guardian*, Jan. 7-10, 1995.
This four-part series, comprising dozens of articles by staff correspondents and contributors from various walks of life, explored in detail questions that would be posed by Britain's transformation from a monarchy to a republic. The newspaper noted in an introduction that it "has always been agnostic about the monarchy, and remains so."

Reports and Studies

Buckingham Palace, *Royal Finances,* 1993.
This 28-page booklet summarizes public expenditures for the royal family and the queen's personal wealth and income, which it says "have often been greatly exaggerated."

Foreign and Commonwealth Office, *Britain's Monarchy: A Factual Guide,* 1993.
This 52-page booklet includes summary biographies of the members of the royal family, sections on the powers and function of the monarch, a listing of royal palaces and residencies and a short list of books for further reading.

The Next Step

Additional information from UMI's Newspaper & Periodical Abstracts database

British Royal Family

"A dreadful year for the royal family," ***U.S. News & World Report,*** **Dec. 25, 1995, p. 74.**
The British monarchy will survive in 1996, but there will be no letup in the internal bickering inside the House of Windsor.

Lejeune, Anthony, "Royal rumpus," ***National Review,*** **Dec. 25, 1995, pp. 25-26.**
Princess Diana's tell-all appearance on the BBC program "Panorama" raised her stature among Britons, but some felt it gave the royal family a collective black eye. While that may be too much to draw from the interview, polls showing support for Diana running as high as 85 percent should worry the Windsors.

MacLeod, Alexander, "Rift Threatens Monarchy, Prompts Calls for Reform," ***The Christian Science Monitor,*** **Dec. 18, 1992, p. 8.**
The current crisis in the royal family has many Britons calling for the monarchy to be scaled down or replaced with a republic. In addition, there are calls for a privacy law to shield citizens and the royal family from media intrusion.

Preston, Peter, "Who's for Christmas at Sandringham?" ***The Guardian,*** **Dec. 22, 1995, p. 13.**
Preston discusses the probable divorce of Prince Charles and Lady Diana and its effect on the British monarchy.

Robinson, Eugene, "Britain's Teflon Monarchy Finds Life a Bit Sticky," ***The Washington Post,*** **Sept. 13, 1992, p. A1.**
As Queen Elizabeth II celebrates 40 years on the throne, what once might have been called Britain's Teflon monarchy is finding that serious debate has arisen over issues the royal family would prefer to avoid. The scandals, failures and antics of the queen's grown children are discussed.

"The besmirched house of Windsor," ***San Francisco Chronicle,*** **Oct. 20, 1994, p. A22.**
An editorial laments the taint on the British monarchy from biographies and news stories and royal family members themselves.

"The undermining of Charles," ***The Economist,*** **Nov. 25, 1995, p. 54**
Princess Diana's depiction of Prince Charles in the BBC "Panorama" interview does nothing to inspire confidence in his ability to rule as king.

Wallace, Bruce, and Judith Timson, "The princess rattles the royals," ***Maclean's,*** **Dec. 4, 1995, pp. 64-67.**
During a televised interview, Lady Diana talked of her unhappy marriage, her affair with a calvary officer and the fact that she will not leave the monarchy quietly. She also referred to her husband, Prince Charles, and his friends and staff as the enemy.

Wood, Sue Ann, "Bet on the monarchy," ***St. Louis Post-Dispatch,*** **Feb. 5, 1995, p. D11.**
Two historians believe that the British monarchy will survive Prince Charles' love affair with Camilla Parker-Bowles but contend that she would never be accepted as queen.

Future of the British Monarchy

Boseley, Sarah, "Cutting the cloth," ***The Guardian,*** **Jan. 9, 1995, p. 10.**
As part of a special report on the future of Britain's monarchy, Sarah Boseley discusses how the end of the royal family's reign would affect the Church of England, noting the belief of many clerics and academics that such a change would mean the end of the established church.

Cassidy, Suzanne, "The British novelist who turned a class system upside down," ***The New York Times*****, Dec. 25, 1993, p. A13.**
Sue Townsend, the author of the novel *The Queen and I,* is profiled. The success of the novel, which imagines nothing less than the overthrow of the British monarchy and the banishment of the royal family to a public housing project, is a measure of just how much attitudes toward the once-sacrosanct royal family have changed in Great Britain.

Crick, Bernard, "The Fading Magic of Majesty," ***The Guardian,*** **Feb. 6, 1992, p. 21.**
Upon the occasion of the 40th anniversary of Queen Elizabeth II's ascension to the throne, Bernard Crick argues that the cult of monarchy produces good subjects rather than real citizens.

Greenslade, Roy, "Sad days ahead for snappers," ***The Guardian,*** **Jan. 9, 1995, p. 10.**
As part of a special report on the future of the British monarchy, Roy Greenslade examines how the passing of the royal family from power would affect tabloid newspapers in the United Kingdom.

Hennessy, Peter, "The throne behind the power," ***The Economist,*** **Dec. 24, 1994, pp. 77-79.**
Journalist and banker Walter Bagehot's claim that the United Kingdom is actually a republic in disguise is

refuted. The British monarchy has a central political role, especially when governments lose support and change.

Knight, Robin, "Prince not-so charming," *U.S. News & World Report,* Jan. 30, 1995, p. 18.
Many Britons continue to call for an end to the monarchy. The monarchy costs taxpayers $87 million per year to support, and many feel it has been damaged beyond repair by Prince Charles' admission of his relationship with Camilla Parker-Bowles.

Newman, Peter C., "The time has come to declare a republic," *Maclean's,* Dec. 11, 1995, p. 42.
Newman bases the survival of Canada as a country on whether it declares itself a republic and ditches the British monarchy. Canadian faith in the British monarchy and the effect a Canadian republic would have on Quebec's status are discussed.

Spillius, Alex, "The tourist trap," *The Guardian,* Jan. 9, 1995, p. 11.
As part of a special report on the future of Britain's monarchy, Alex Spillius details how an end to the monarchy could affect the tourism industry and highlights the popularity of tourist sites connected with the royal family.

Taylor, Antony, "Republican ruminations from down under," *History Today,* November 1995, pp. 6-9.
Due to the recent scandals surrounding the royal family of England, public opinion regarding the place of the family in government has been monitored. The history of English and Australian opposition to the British monarchy and their current opinions are examined.

Weale, Sally, "The true cost of patrons," *The Guardian,* Jan. 9, 1995, p. 10.
As part of a special report on the future of the British monarchy, Sally Weale discusses how charities could be affected by the royal family's passage from power and examines how royal patronage helps charities with fundraising.

Constitutional Issues

Hattersley, Roy, "About time we grew up," *The Guardian,* Jan. 5, 1996, p. 13
Hattersley says the British monarchy has made itself open to ridicule, but that only underscores the need for constitutional intervention.

"Reclaiming Britain's constitution," *The Economist,* Oct. 14, 1995, p. 18.
An editorial notes that power in the United Kingdom is far too concentrated and needs to be changed. Traditional modes of thought will need to be put aside if Britain's constitution is to be reformed.

Wintour, Patrick, "Labor voice breaks silence on monarchy," *The Guardian,* Jan. 19, 1993, p. 7.
On Jan. 18, 1993, Labor officials called for royalty reforms that would scale back the British monarchy's constitutional authority and ceremonial splendor, bringing it more into line with the Dutch and Scandinavian monarchies.

Queen Elizabeth II

MacAskill, Ewen, "A 'Horrible' Year, Queen Says," *The Washington Post,* Nov. 25, 1992, p. A11.
Queen Elizabeth II responded to criticism of her troubled monarchy and described the past year of 1992 as "horrible" in a frank and personal speech at a lunch given by the lord mayor of London to mark her 40th anniversary on the throne.

Phillips, Melanie, "Royal Unhappy Families," *The Guardian,* March 29, 1992, p. 6
Phillips describes how the recent formal separation of the Duke and Duchess of York has put further strain on Britain's monarchy and has in some ways damaged the institution's mystique. She argues that only Queen Elizabeth and the queen mother actually represent stability and loyalty to duty.

Wilson, Edgar, "The might of Her Majesty," *The Guardian,* Jan. 9, 1995, p. 5.
As part of a special report on the future of Britain's monarchy, Edgar Wilson details the powers held by Queen Elizabeth II within and over the government.

Monarchies in Other Countries

Bahgat, Gawdat, "The changing economic and political environment in the Gulf monarchies," *Journal of Social, Political and Economic Studies,* fall 1995, pp. 271-288.
The economic and political environments in the gulf in the mid-1990s look different from what they were a decade or two ago.

Browning, Daniel R., "Mideast Monarchies Fear Saddam's Goals," *St. Louis Post-Dispatch,* Sept. 7, 1990, D1.
The Middle East monarchies fear Saddam Hussein, because he is a threat to the national borders.

Mousavizadeh, Nader, "Copenhagen diarist: The royal we," *The New Republic,* Jan. 29, 1996, p. 42.
Mousavizadeh discusses the important cultural ritual Danes observe, that of the queen of Denmark's New Year's address. The Danish royal family has earned the allegiance of the Danish people by its impeccable behavior.

Back Issues

Great Research on Current Issues Starts Right Here...Recent topics covered by The CQ Researcher are listed below. Before May 1991, reports were published under the name of Editorial Research Reports.

AUGUST 1994
Genetically Engineered Foods
Electing Minorities
Prozac Controversy
College Sports

SEPTEMBER 1994
Home Schooling
Welfare Experiments
Courts and the Media
Regulating Tobacco

OCTOBER 1994
Historic Preservation
Religion and Politics
Arts Funding
Economic Sanctions

NOVEMBER 1994
Sex on Campus
Blood Supply Safety
Testing Term Limits
Religion in America

DECEMBER 1994
Farm Policy
Arms Sales
Earthquake Research
The Future of Television

Back issues are available for $5.00 (subscribers) or $8.00 (non-subscribers). Quantity discounts apply to orders over ten. To order, call Congressional Quarterly Customer Service at (202) 887-8621.

Binders are available for $18.00. To order call 1-800-638-1710. Please refer to stock number 648.

JANUARY 1995
Treating Addiction
Child Custody and Support
Parents and Schools
Non-Proliferation Treaty at 25

FEBRUARY 1995
Cracking Down on Immigration
The Business of Sports
Reinventing Government
Housing Discrimination

MARCH 1995
Death Penalty Debate
Primary Care
Democracy in Africa
Environmental Movement at 25

APRIL 1995
Abortion Clinic Protests
Dieting and Health
Combating AIDS
Rethinking Affirmative Action

MAY 1995
Assisted Suicide Controversy
Overhauling Social Security
Learning to Read
Mandatory Sentencing

JUNE 1995
Combating Infectious Disease
Property Rights
Repetitive Stress Injuries
Regulating the Internet

JULY 1995
War Crimes
Highway Safety
Combating Terrorism
Preventing Teen Drug Use

AUGUST 1995
Job Stress
Organ Transplants
United Nations at 50
Advances in Cancer Research

SEPTEMBER 1995
Catholic Church in the U.S.
Northern Ireland Cease-Fire
High School Sports
Teaching History

OCTOBER 1995
Quebec's Future
Revitalizing the Cities
Networking the Classroom
Indoor Air Pollution

NOVEMBER 1995
The Working Poor
The Jury System
Sex, Violence and the Media
Police Misconduct

DECEMBER 1995
Teens and Tobacco
Gene Therapy's Future
Global Water Shortages
Third-Party Prospects

JANUARY 1996
Emergency Medicine
Punishing Sex Offenders
Bilingual Education
Helping the Homeless

FEBRUARY 1996
Reforming the CIA
Campaign Finance Reform
Academic Politics
Getting Into College

Future Topics

- ***Preventing Juvenile Crime***
- ***Tax Reform***
- ***Managed Care***

THE CQ Researcher

PUBLISHED BY CONGRESSIONAL QUARTERLY INC.

Preventing Juvenile Crime

Is tougher punishment or prevention the answer?

A dramatic rise in violent youth crimes prompted Congress to include tougher penalties in the 1994 crime bill, as well as funds for intervention programs. States and cities, too, have reacted to violent youth crime with a mixture of get-tough and prevention measures, such as curfews, school uniforms and laws making parents responsible for their children's misbehavior. Now, an expected increase in the under-18 population threatens to produce another rise in youth crime. Prevention advocates insist that the most cost-effective way to defuse the coming "crime bomb" is early intervention programs for at-risk kids and their parents. But Congress has withheld funding for the intervention programs, a move endorsed by those who say tough punishments are the answer.

INSIDE THIS ISSUE

March 15, 1996 • Volume 6, No. 10 • Pages 217-240

Formerly Editorial Research Reports

PREVENTING JUVENILE CRIME

COVER: © 1993 ALON REININGER, CONTACT PRESS IMAGES, PICTURE NETWORK INTERNATIONAL, LTD.

March 15, 1996
Volume 6, No. 10

EDITOR
Sandra Stencel

MANAGING EDITOR
Thomas J. Colin

ASSOCIATE EDITORS
Sarah M. Magner
Richard L. Worsnop

STAFF WRITERS
Charles S. Clark
Mary H. Cooper
Craig Donegan
Kenneth Jost

EDITORIAL ASSISTANT
Tonya Harris

PUBLISHED BY
Congressional Quarterly Inc.

CHAIRMAN
Andrew Barnes

VICE CHAIRMAN
Andrew P. Corty

EDITOR AND PUBLISHER
Neil Skene

EXECUTIVE EDITOR
Robert W. Merry

ASSOCIATE PUBLISHER
Edward S. Hauck

The CQ Researcher (ISSN 1056-2036). Formerly Editorial Research Reports. Published weekly (48 times per year, not printed March 1, May 31, Aug. 30, Nov. 29, 1996) by Congressional Quarterly Inc., 1414 22nd St., N.W., Washington, D.C. 20037. Annual subscription rate is $319. Additional rates furnished upon request. Second-class postage paid at Washington, D.C. POSTMASTER: Send address changes to *The CQ Researcher,* 1414 22nd St., N.W., Washington, D.C. 20037.

Preventing Juvenile Crime

By Craig Donegan

The Issues

Yes, 16-year-old Tiana Hutchins acknowledges, she and her girlfriend were breaking the 11 p.m. weekday curfew for teenagers in Washington, D.C. But they were just walking and talking in the neighborhood, she says.

"We were only two blocks from my house when a police car pulled up," she recalls. "He said, 'Where ya'll going? Ya'll ain't supposed to be out this time of night. I can lock you up!' " The next time, the officer warned, he'd take them in.

The incident so upset Tiana, a high school junior, that she agreed to be the lead plaintiff in an American Civil Liberties Union (ACLU) suit challenging the city's year-old curfew.*

Tiana offers her own solution to violent youth crime. "Forget the curfews," she says. "Tighten up on the bad kids. Show them they can't be arrested one morning and out on the street the next day. Get on the parents to make their kids come to school. Have after-school recreational programs and community-service projects. Put more security in the schools."

Tiana's wide-ranging prescription embraces elements of the two basic approaches being advocated to reduce juvenile crime in America: prevention and punishment.

Prevention advocates insist that the only way to stop juvenile crime is to attack it before it starts, through early intervention in the lives of at-risk children. They call for prenatal care and parenting classes for young mothers as well as full use of social services such as Medicaid, Head Start and Aid to Families

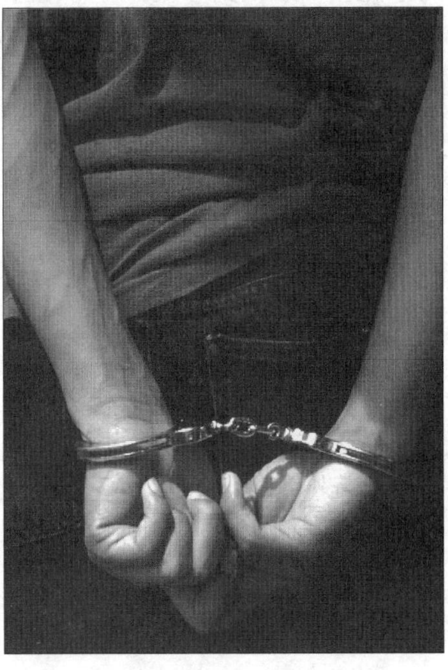

With Dependent Children (AFDC).

After at-risk children reach school age, prevention advocates say, education must play a key role in shaping youngsters' lives by offering in-school programs that teach conflict resolution, social skills and how to resist gangs and drugs. Violence-prevention curricula "must be a long-term and consistent" part of education, the Rev. Jesse Jackson and other civil rights leaders, educators and policy-makers said at a national conference on youth violence. [1]

"We don't have to raise children to be violent or criminal because this is a preventable problem," says Deborah Prothrow-Stith, assistant dean of government and community programs at the Harvard University School of Public Health. "If we admit this as a society, then we will become very creative about preventive strategies."

Moreover, says Marcia Chaiken, a respected social-policy researcher in Alexandria, Va., "prevention is more cost-effective than punishment. We have strong evidence from research that for the vast majority of at-risk children, approaches such as teaching parents good parenting skills combined with early education and youth development can prevent later delinquency."

Law-and-order advocates say that preventing youth crime hinges on harsher punishment, such as trying juveniles as adults and locking them up longer. [2] Today, the political mood leans toward punishment. Sen. John Ashcroft, R-Mo., who called for tougher sanctions in his Violent and Hardcore Juvenile Offender Reform Act of 1995, reflects that mood. "A small and increasingly violent segment of the teenage population roams free, committing violent and serious offenses without being held accountable for their actions," Ashcroft told colleagues last August in proposing the legislation.

The push for harsher punishments has been influenced by the dramatic rise in violent crimes committed by youths — including murder, forcible rape, robbery and aggravated assault. According to the Justice Department, the arrest rate for children ages 10 to 17 who committed violent crimes doubled from 1983 to 1992 — and could double again by 2010. [3]

Get-tough advocates say youth-crime could get even worse because of the expected increase in the under-18 population from 69 million Americans in 1995 to 74 million in 2010. "Americans are sitting on a demographic time bomb," writes John J. DiIulio Jr., director of the Brookings Institution's Center for Public Management. "The large population of 7-to-10-year-old boys growing up fatherless, Godless and jobless — and surrounded by deviant, delinquent and criminal adults — will give rise to a new and more vicious group of predatory street criminals than the nation has ever known." [4]

To stop the impending flood of "superpredators," DiIulio would protect schools with metal detectors, guards and other security measures; keep violent repeat offenders in jail or

---

* Seventy-seven percent of Washington-area youths — including 67 percent of youths in the District of Columbia — favor the city's curfew, according to an August 1995 *Washington Post* survey.

The Role of Juveniles in Violent Crime

Juveniles under age 18 were responsible for 13 percent of all violent crimes in 1992, including nearly 10 percent of the murders, according to FBI clearance data.

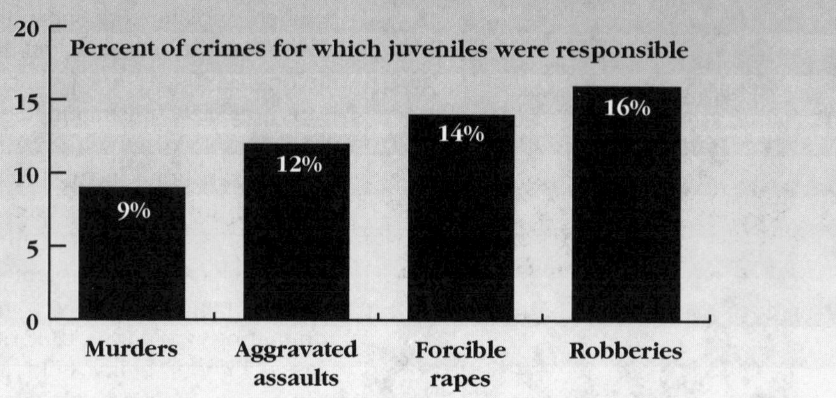

Source: "Juvenile Offenders and Victims: A Focus on Violence," Statistics Summary, Office of Juvenile Justice and Delinquency Prevention, U.S. Department of Justice, May 1995.

detention for longer periods; and target government crime-prevention resources to cities that really need them.

Cities and states have reacted to youth crime with a mix of get-tough and prevention measures, among them curfews, laws holding parents accountable for their children's delinquent behavior and requiring school uniforms.

A 1995 survey by the National Conference of Mayors shows that the number of youth curfews has increased by 45 percent since 1990. Of the 387 cities that responded to the survey, at least 270 have curfews. [5] Curfew supporters cite its success in New Orleans, where a dusk-to-dawn curfew for youths under 17 reportedly drove down crime 27 percent during restricted hours.

Yet some critics of curfews say that street-smart delinquents can lie their way around curfew requirements. Because most curfews have exceptions, including school-sponsored activities and evening jobs, "There are all sorts of things you can say to legally prohibit a police officer from taking you into custody," says Barry Krisberg, executive director of the National Council on Crime and Delinquency. "The only kids who get caught are the poor schnooks who don't know what they're doing." Other curfew critics, including the ACLU, question their constitutionality.

For their part, schools are using metal detectors to keep out guns and knives, video cameras to record violent confrontations and spot trespassers and uniformed police to keep the peace. A growing number of schools are requiring students to wear uniforms to eliminate clothing that signifies gang membership — or can be mistaken for gang "colors." The idea is to eradicate distinctions between kids in gangs and those who are not, and to lessen the visible disparities between children of affluence and those from poorer families.

President Clinton reiterated his support for uniforms on Feb. 24 and announced that the Education Department will distribute manuals to the nation's 16,000 school districts on how to implement a voluntary school-uniform policy. "If it means that the schoolrooms will be more orderly . . . and that our young people will learn to evaluate themselves by what they are on the inside instead of what they're wearing on the outside, then our public schools should be able to require their students to wear school uniforms," Clinton said, echoing sentiments he expressed in his Jan. 23 State of the Union address.

Two days after the president's remarks, 70 percent of the secondary school principals polled said uniforms could cut down violence. [6]

In addition to supporting curfews and uniforms, a number of state legislatures have increased criminal penalties for violent crimes by youths. In fact, from 1992 to 1994, 27 states passed laws to make it easier to prosecute children as adults, according to a recent National Governors' Association (NGA) report. [7]

Many states also have approved community-based prevention programs, such as employment training, mentoring and after-school recreational and academic programs. But lawmakers' support for such programs has usually hinged on passage of tougher penalties for violent juvenile offenders, according to the NGA report. "Almost only when coupled with more punitive initiatives do the preventive measures get approved," says co-author David E. Brown, an NGA senior policy analyst.

Similar restrictions have tied up federal prevention programs initiated under the 1994 omnibus crime bill. The $30 billion initiative promised, among other things, $8.8 billion for 100,000 more police officers and $6.9 billion for community-based crime prevention programs. [8] But local law-and-order advocates want the money for the extra police shifted into law enforcement bloc grants, which would give localities more flexibility in how they spend the money. Local jurisdictions also want prevention funds tied to promises from the states to build more prisons.

Clinton has vetoed efforts to substitute bloc grants for the 100,000 new officers. He also has condemned Congress for abandoning the Ounce of Prevention Council and other crime prevention efforts in its 1996 appropriations bill for the Department of Justice and other agencies. Created by the 1994 crime bill, the Ounce of Prevention program provides grants for after-school and summer youth programs (including tutoring and recreation), employment skills and job placement. The council was to coordinate prevention programs and help local areas improve crime-prevention policies.

Whatever Congress finally provides for prevention programs, it seems certain that the hard line on juvenile crime will continue. For example, Sen. Ashcroft wants the funds provided by the Juvenile Justice and Delinquency Prevention Act of 1974 to hinge upon states prosecuting certain violent juvenile offenders age 14 and up as adults.

If prevention efforts give way to more emphasis on punishment, warns Peter W. Greenwood, executive director of the Criminal Justice Program at the Rand Corporation, then DiIulio's time-bomb nightmare could come true. Treating juvenile criminals as adults, he says, is how "we'll get our superpredators: They'll come out of our adult institutions."

As educators, lawmakers and law enforcement experts grapple with the problem of juvenile crime and violence, these are some of the questions being asked:

Do curfews prevent juvenile crime?

A majority of Americans consider curfews as legitimate tools for keeping young people out of harm's way and reducing crime. (*See poll, p. 231.*) And cities that use curfews are high on them, too. According to a 1995 U.S. Conference of Mayors survey, 56 percent of the cities with curfews rated their curfews as somewhat or very effective while only 14 percent considered them not effective.

Treating juvenile criminals as adults is how "we'll get our superpredators: They'll come out of our adult institutions."

— Peter W. Greenwood
executive director,
Criminal Justice Program,
Rand Corporation

The Washington Metropolitan Police Department reports that felony arrests in the city during curfew hours declined 34 percent from July 16-Sept. 30, 1995, compared with the same period for 1994.

"Everybody claims they work," Krisberg says, "but I'd love to see some research studies." Most juvenile crimes, he notes, occur between 3 p.m. and 6 p.m. Nevertheless, he says, a well-enforced curfew might limit certain youth crimes, such as auto theft.

After reviewing the literature on curfews, Greenwood says he still does not know if they prevent crime. "I've never seen any systematic evidence to show they work," he says.

"I find it very hard to believe that a curfew could have any significant effect on teenagers who are selling drugs, stealing cars or carrying a gun," says Arthur Spitzer, legal director of the ACLU in Washington, D.C. "The very thought that they would be deterred by a $500 fine against their parents is laughable when these kids are facing up to 10 years in the pokey. A kid won't look at the Rolex he's just stolen and say, 'Oh, I've got to get home. It's 11 o'clock.' "

When it comes to protecting innocent people, Spitzer says, a curfew "is not the way we do that in this country. We don't say to all women you must be home at 10 p.m. so you won't be raped. People make these decisions for themselves, and parents can do so for their own kids, but the City Council can't control 50,000 kids."

Some critics say curfews are not always enforced even-handedly, which leads to public cynicism and undermines any effectiveness they may have. "Curfew laws tend to be applied in racially disparate ways," Krisberg says, with youths in middle-class or affluent white neighborhoods virtually immune from curfew enforcement.

Many cities report that curfews work best when parent participation is strong — whether voluntary or forced (through fines and mandatory counseling). But that's still not enough, says Edwin Delattre, dean of Boston University's School of Education and

Attitudes Toward Juvenile Crime

Most Americans think rehabilitation programs for juvenile offenders have been unsuccessful. Yet more than 40 percent of Americans think the government should spend its crime-fighting money on prevention.

How successful are programs that emphasize rehabilitation rather than punishment in controlling juvenile crime?

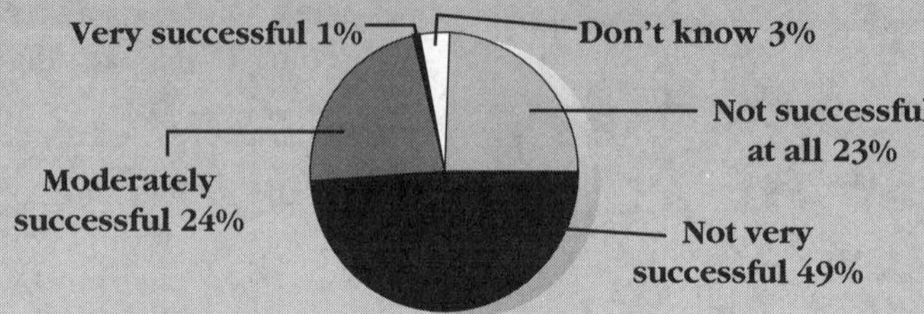

How should the government fight crime, if it could only spend money in only one of the following areas?

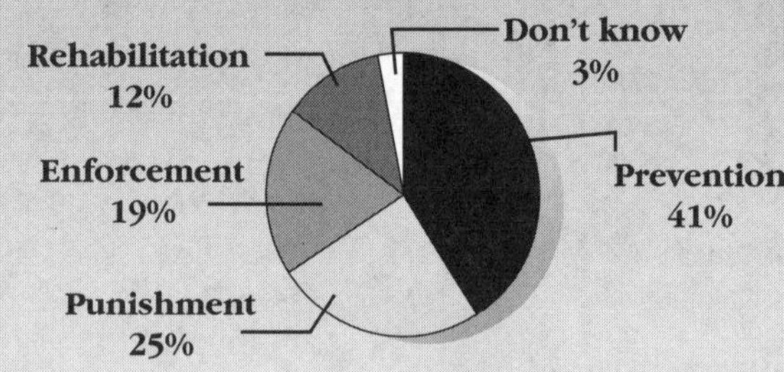

Which are the most effective ways to reduce crime?

	Percent who responded
Requiring mandatory life sentences for 3-time felons	36%
Youth crime prevention programs	35%
Expanding the death penalty	30%
Adding 100,000 more cops	22%
Trying some 13- and 14-year-olds as adults	19%
Banning assault weapons	15%
Drug treatment programs for criminals	13%
More money for state prisons	7%
Don't know	2%

Note: Percentages total more than 100 percent because each respondent was allowed two responses.

Sources: Gallup/CNN/ USA Today *poll, September 1994 (top); Wirthlin Group, September 1994 (middle);* Los Angeles Times, *April 1994 (bottom)*

an adjunct scholar at the conservative American Enterprise Institute. Successful curfews require broad, active community support, he says.

"Without adequate [staff] resources for police to enforce them, curfews are largely useless," Delattre says. They will be enforced sporadically, he says, and cities will divert resources once meant for curfews into police activities that satisfy political needs or get more media coverage. "That makes a mockery of the curfew and breeds public cynicism toward law and the police," Delattre says.

Moreover, he adds, curfews that work have communities that recognize youth crime as everybody's problem — not just a problem for those who live in high-risk neighborhoods. (*See story, p. 228.*)

Does punishing parents for their children's delinquent behavior prevent juvenile crime?

There is growing support for the theory that getting parents more involved in their children's lives is crucial to stemming youth crime. Indeed, some hard-liners say that punishing parents for their children's crimes is the place to start.

Paul J. McNulty, president of the First Freedom Coalition, a Washington anti-crime group, wants relatives to be required to sign agreements in which they promise to keep juvenile offenders on the straight and narrow. "Family members and friends would sign a contract with the court agreeing to forfeit particular assets if a juvenile offender fails to comply with the court's requirements," McNulty writes. "All who sign the bond would then have financial incentive to supervise the juvenile offender closely to ensure compliance." [9]

In several cities with curfews, including Washington, parents whose children violate the curfew can be charged with a misdemeanor, fined up to $500, required to attend parenting classes and assigned to community-service work.

In San Antonio, Texas, first-time curfew violators receive warning tickets. Second offenses require parents to meet with social workers and a third violation results in formal charges that can mean a $500 fine for the parents.

Police in Huntington Beach, Calif., charge parents $36 per hour to "babysit" for curfew violators held in custody. In Paterson, N.J., the parents of children who skip school must attend school with their kids. In Oregon, parents of children under 15 who commit crimes can be fined up to $1,000, made to pay $2,500 in restitution and required to attend parenting classes.

The Oregon law appears to be working, supporters say. Mayor Ken Hector of Silverton reports that after an initial flurry of arrests, the number of parents summoned to court quickly dropped to zero. Silverton educators have reported more parents getting involved in school activities. And enrollments in parenting classes have increased. [10]

"Our goal should not be to incarcerate kids but to use the authority of the law to get parents to fulfill their responsibilities, even if that means a judge ordering a parent to participate in counseling," says Howard Davidson, director of the American Bar Association's Center on Children and the Law. "When kids get arrested for shoplifting, or are truant from school, the focus should be on bringing in the parents, not punishing the kids."

But Douglas Bandow, a senior fellow at the libertarian Cato Institute, says that "We should never lose sight of the fact that crime is an individual responsibility" and that juvenile offenders must ultimately account for their actions. Moreover, he says, punishing parents is likely to affect juvenile crime only where it is least needed — in cities, towns or neighborhoods that already have cohesive community and family structures.

Rand's Greenwood says that police and city officials offer anecdotal evidence that holding parents accountable works, but "I can't find any studies that tell me yea or nay."

It may be a good idea in principle, adds Krisberg, but in practice it could make careless parents resentful and even more likely to abandon their children. "If somebody calls up and says, 'I've got your kid here, and when you show up you're going to get a $350 ticket,' plenty of people are going to say, 'Keep him,' " he says.

Poverty also complicates the picture, Krisberg says. "If the parents are poor — if dad's not working and mom's got a minimum-wage job — then what does parental responsibility amount to?"

In such cases, says Davidson, communities should provide evening counseling sessions to help troubled parents regain control of their delinquent children. Child care also should be available, he says. "The question is one of priorities," Davidson says. "Do we really care about getting parents involved when kids seem to be out of control? And I don't just mean the mothers. I mean the fathers, too."

Most parents want to do the right things for their children, says University of Minnesota law Professor Barry Feld. "To the extent that they don't," he says, "it's because they are too trapped by circumstances."

Krisberg and his colleagues found that programs that teach parents how to discipline and care for the health of their children can reduce anti-social behavior in kids. When combined with school-based programs that teach at-risk children how to follow rules, control anger and communicate effectively, parent training can also prevent juvenile delinquency and violence. [11]

"Rather than simply use a punitive approach, the courts can use their power to make parents attend proceedings with their children and to tell them, 'This is your responsibility, and we're going to see if we can't help you meet it,' " says Harvard's Prothrow-Stith.

The Metropolitan Police Boys and Girls Clubs

Hundreds of at-risk youngsters from Washington, D.C., spend a week each summer at Camp Brown, an early-intervention program of The Metropolitan Police Boys and Girls Clubs.

Are school programs on violence reduction, conflict resolution and peer mediation effective?

Supporters call programs to reduce violent and criminal behavior among schoolchildren the "fourth R" of American education.

Anti-violence and mediation courses have proliferated since the late 1980s, when Prothrow-Stith introduced her "Violence Prevention Curriculum for Adolescents." Instruction in violence prevention often revolves around videotapes depicting staged violent situations and methods for avoiding fights and resolving disputes non-violently.

Conflict-resolution programs also have grown in popularity, with more than 5,000 programs operating in elementary and secondary schools throughout the United States, says Judy Filner, program director for the National Association for Mediation in Education. While violence prevention focuses on teaching children to con-

Continued on p. 225

A Uniform Solution to School Violence

Until recently, only kids at prep schools or parochial academies wore uniforms. Then discipline in public schools disintegrated, and students starting attacking their classmates over designer jackets and fancy footwear. In desperation, public schools around the country turned to uniforms. Many school officials now say they are magic.

In the lower grades, dress codes and uniforms help to control classroom behavior and keep children focused on learning, says Naomi Gittins, a staff attorney at the National School Boards Association (NSBA). "But junior and senior high schools use them to keep kids from fighting over the latest fashions and to eliminate clothing and symbols that gangs use," she says.

A number of states allow school districts to require uniforms, including California, Georgia, Florida, Louisiana, Maryland, New York and Virginia. And several big cities require them, including Dade County (Miami), Fla., Seattle, Wash., and Washington, D.C.

Uniforms have won strong support from President Clinton, Attorney General Janet Reno and even Republican lawmakers. On Feb. 24, during his weekly radio address, Clinton announced that the Education Department will distribute manuals to the nation's 16,000 school districts on how to implement policies on school uniforms.

Long Beach Unified School District

Behavior problems dropped after Long Beach, Calif., introduced mandatory school uniforms in 1994.

Long Beach, Calif., launched the nation's first districtwide experiment with uniforms in 1994. The policy, which required the approval of two-thirds of local parents, currently applies only to elementary and middle schools. Within a year of its implementation, school-based crime and violence plummeted in Long Beach. Assault and battery cases declined 34 percent, fighting 51 percent, drug cases 69 percent and sex offenses 74 percent.[1]

Moreover, attendance rates and test scores are up in Long Beach, overall crime in the district has plunged 36 percent and suspensions are down 32 percent.

Whittier Elementary, in an impoverished Long Beach neighborhood, began requiring uniforms in 1991 as part of a pilot project. Today, the truancy rate is less than 4 percent, the lowest in the district.

Despite broad public support for regulating school attire, critics have warned that such policies might run afoul of the Constitution. To avoid constitutional quagmires, and to comply with state law, Long Beach allows parents to opt out of uniforms for their children. But the American Civil Liberties Union (ACLU) of California and the local Legal Aid Foundation have sued nonetheless, contending on behalf of parents that school officials discriminated against students who chose not to comply.[2]

"In some cases, we found that children were being given detention, academically penalized, forced to wear gym clothes to class and removed from lunch to endure lectures by uniformed school officials long after their parents had filled out exemption notices," write ACLU representatives Alan L. Friel and Ramona Ripston.[3] Uniform policies also have drawn criticism from anti-poverty advocates because some school districts have not made funds available for poor children to purchase uniforms.

The Supreme Court has yet to rule on the constitutionality of school uniforms. But a federal court last year upheld a New Mexico school that blocked a student's baggy pants. The student contended the First Amendment protected his attire because it expressed his black identity. But a Federal District Court judge held it would be unreasonable to expect most people to understand the cultural significance of baggy pants without someone explaining it to them. For dress to qualify as speech, says the NSBA's Gittins, it has to convey a specific message that just about anyone can understand.

The "Manual on School Uniforms" developed by the Education and Justice Departments includes exceptions for students who wear yarmulkes or head scarves for religious observances and for those who wear "expressive items" such as political buttons.[4]

The legal wrangling over uniforms perplexes first lady Hillary Rodham Clinton, whom the president credits with convincing him to support school uniforms. "I find it hard to understand why energy is being spent litigating that could be used to raise money for uniforms or to tackle some other school problem," she writes in her best-selling book *It Takes A Village.* If dress codes or school uniforms can reduce "friction caused by brand-name consumerism and gang identification," then schools should use them, she says.

But supporters and critics alike warn that uniforms are not panaceas. They stress that uniforms only reflect a school's larger commitment to stamping out disruptive behavior. Without that commitment, they say, uniforms will have only a limited effect.

---

[1] Kathryn Wexler, "Sizing Up a Uniform Answer to Address Problems at School," *The Washington Post,* Nov. 8, 1995, p. A3.

[2] See Sheila Muto, "Student Uniforms Pay Off, One School District Says," *The New York Times,* Sept. 20, 1995, p. B11.

[3] Alan L. Friel and Ramona Ripston, "The Administration's Uninformed Approach to School Uniforms," *The Washington Post,* Feb. 20, 1996.

[4] Alison Mitchell, "President Acts on School Attire," *The New York Times,* Feb. 25, 1996, p. A1.

Continued from p. 223

trol their own behavior, conflict resolution emphasizes interpersonal skills that students must have to manage potentially explosive situations from beginning to end.

In peer mediation, the most popular mediation program, students are used to defuse conflicts between other students. "The students are not policemen," Filner says. "It's just a small number of kids who learn mediation skills and then intervene to help resolve conflicts between other students, when everyone agrees."

Classroom programs in conflict resolution, which can last from six weeks to an entire semester, are also growing in popularity. Iowa, Illinois and Ohio have statewide programs in conflict resolution, and Texas has adopted legislation that endorses conflict-resolution courses for all the state's public schools, Filner says.

Until recently, however, there was no hard evidence that such programs work. Now, says Prothrow-Stith, two new studies suggest that conflict resolution and violence-prevention curricula do make a difference. One of the studies reports that suspension rates dropped by up to 70 percent in two schools that introduced her violence-prevention curriculum, she says.[12]

For violence- and conflict-resolution courses to work, she adds, they must acknowledge that Americans live in a social and cultural context that encourages fighting. They have to recognize that the country recently had "a kick-butt, make-my-day president" and that it is inundated by Power Rangers on television and in movies telling kids that violence is the way to solve conflict. A successful program also recognizes the reality that in some families, parents tell their children, "You go back outside and you beat him up, or I'm going to beat you."

"It's important to accept that anger is normal, but to know there are many ways to respond to it and that fighting is the response where you often lose more than you gain," she says.

To drive home the point, Prothrow-Stith includes the teenage version of cost-benefit analysis in her program, asking kids to think about what they gain and what they lose if they resort to violence. "Conflict-resolution works," she says, "but it is a very small piece of a larger prevention pie — it's probably not going to help the kid who's holding up a McDonalds."

"Conflict resolution works, but it is a very small piece of a larger prevention pie — it's probably not going to help the kid who's holding up a McDonald's."

— Deborah Prothrow-Stith
Assistant Dean of Government and Community Programs, Harvard University School of Public Health

In their review of mediation-program evaluations, however, Krisberg and his colleagues report they found no scientific evidence that such programs work. In fact, anti-social and delinquent behavior reportedly increased in some peer-counseling approaches, in which students were led in group settings to give mutual support for socially acceptable behavior.[13]

"I'm not surprised at the results," says Krisberg. "Most of these programs were not designed with kids in mind but were basically designed by and for adults."

While stressing that the findings on peer mediation are piecemeal, Krisberg relegates the talk-it-through approach to "the warm and fuzzy" category. Young people are very good at talking about the dangers of drugs and violence, he says, but the kids he has talked with tell him their peers are not good at mediating conflicts. "They feel that peer mediation tells them the adults can't help them," he says. "They want the teachers to step in."

Yet Prothrow-Stith says students are better than adults at knowing where, and when, trouble is brewing. Because of that, they can be very useful to one another, and to their teachers, in stopping fights before they get started. "Too often, the teachers find out about these conflicts after the shouting starts or a crowd is gathering," she says. "It is more difficult to prevent something worse at that stage."

Schools with large numbers of immigrants, particularly from non-Western cultures, present mediation programs with the biggest challenge. "Their cultural styles don't necessarily lend themselves to middle-class, white chit-chat, which is what some of these programs are about," says Krisberg.

Then there is the problem of actually getting students to the sessions. "You set up a 10-session curriculum, and the kids may attend three or four,"

Greenwood says. To make matters worse, "You might not get the truly at-risk kids in the programs to start with."

But Prothrow-Stith doesn't think instruction should be limited only to at-risk students. "It's for everybody," she says, "because if we were all better at handling conflict and anger, then America would be a less violent place." ■

BACKGROUND

Early Efforts

Juvenile delinquency is hardly a child of the 20th century. Parent-beating was apparently common enough in fifth-century Greece that the practice was outlawed. In ancient Rome, fathers had the legal right to put disobedient children to death, although there is no record that anyone ever did. The Emperor Nero once belonged to a gang of well-born youths whose members robbed and raped largely at will.

Juvenile delinquency in ancient Greece and Rome was essentially viewed as a family matter. Moreover, if a child broke the law, it was the head of the household, not the delinquent, who had to face the judge and take responsibility for the crime. [14]

It was not until the industrial age, and the rise of urban centers crowded with wage laborers and tenements, that juvenile delinquency made the leap from family problem to social dilemma.

As New York City's population rose from 15,000 in 1755 to 120,000 by 1820, youth gangs became the scourge of the streets. In response, the New York House of Refuge was established in 1825, not just to reform juvenile criminals but to prevent juvenile crime. Children sent to the facility learned the discipline of work while receiving heavy doses of moral instruction. Many were put on trains and shipped out West to work on farms. [15]

Shipping problems elsewhere soon was regarded as morally and strategically unacceptable. In addition, the advent of the Progressive movement at the end of the 19th century prompted middle-class reformers to create juvenile courts to separate children from the adult justice system.

The first U.S. juvenile court, established in Chicago in 1899, was built upon the idea of rehabilitation. "The original idea behind juvenile courts was that adolescents were more malleable than adults," says Feld at the University of Minnesota. It took a long time, he notes, but "increasingly, we are coming to recognize that, even by the mid-teens, some of these kids have suffered enormous damage. We know now that the ability to intervene effectively after the fact is extremely limited and very expensive. So the focus has shifted to preventing the damage at a much earlier point in time."

Prevention had become a national concern by 1935, when the Social Security Act funded services for children at risk of becoming delinquents.

Local efforts to help kids stay out of trouble accelerated as well. In the 1930s, a New York City policeman, Lt. Ed W. Flynn, started what later became the Police Athletic League (PAL), which offered an alternative to gangs and criminal activity. By 1995, more than 3 million kids were participating in PAL recreational and educational chapters nationwide.

In 1953, the first Boys and Girls Clubs were set up in public housing. By 1994, there were more than 250 chapters.

Changes in popular culture also affected Americans' views on juvenile crime prevention. Concern about movies, comic books and music that seemed to glorify violence and delinquency prompted the Senate to create the Subcommittee to Investigate Juvenile Delinquency in 1953. Two years later, its chairman, Sen. Estes Kefauver, D-Tenn., led an aggressive investigation into, among other things, the relationship between youth violence and the media.

Ultimately, Kefauver did not blame delinquency or violence on a single cause. "I feel strongly that juvenile delinquency essentially stems from the moral breakdown in the home and community and, in many cases, parental apathy," he wrote. "I think of delinquency as the scum that rises to the top from the imperfections within our society. As the imperfections are cleared, delinquency will decrease." [16]

Get-Tough Initiatives

Not long after Kefauver's work, John F. Kennedy established the President's Committee on Juvenile Delinquency and Youth Crime. It spearheaded passage of the 1961 Juvenile Delinquency and Youth Offenses Control Act, which allocated funds for research and demonstration projects aimed at controlling juvenile crime. Seven years later, the Juvenile Delinquency Prevention and Control Act of 1968 encouraged the development of community-based anti-delinquency programs.

Support for the juvenile justice system and prevention programs reached a new level in 1974 with the Juvenile Justice and Delinquency Prevention Act. The act established the Office of Juvenile Justice and Delinquency Prevention to help the states fund comprehensive rehabilitation plans to deal with record juvenile crime rates.

Meanwhile, advocates of tougher punishments not only questioned the effectiveness of rehabilitation but also "relegated to the margins of public discourse the idea that social programs might help prevent crime." [17]

The resulting get-tough movement began even before the Carter administration poured $25 million into 100 cities through its Delinquency Preven-

Continued on p. 228

Chronology

19th Century

Courts and charities grapple with growing juvenile crime as urban poverty becomes a problem.

1825
New York House of Refuge founded to reform juvenile delinquents.

1899
The first juvenile court in America is established in Chicago on the premise that delinquents can be rehabilitated.

1920s-1950s

Congress joins in the fight against juvenile crime.

1925
The Standard Juvenile Court Act recommends handling juveniles accused of serious crimes outside the adult-justice system.

1936
New York City police Lt. Ed W. Flynn organizes the Police Athletic League.

1953
Senate Subcommittee to Investigate Juvenile Delinquency recommends greater federal aid to the states for delinquency prevention and treatment.

1960s-1970s

Support grows for anti-crime programs that stress prevention rather than punishment.

1961
President John F. Kennedy signs the Juvenile Delinquency and Youth Offenses Control Act authorizing $30 million over three years to fund prevention programs and research.

1968
Juvenile Delinquency Prevention and Control Act emphasizes integrating approaches, including community-based programs.

1971
Omnibus Crime Control Act broadens the role of the federal Law Enforcement Assistance Administration to include funds for community-based prevention efforts.

1972
Congress creates the Office of Youth Development and Delinquency Prevention in the Department of Health, Education and Welfare.

1974
The Juvenile Justice and Delinquency Prevention Act is hailed as the nation's first major commitment to prevention. The act sets up an office to oversee grants and provide technical assistance to anti-crime programs.

1980s-1990s

Rising youth crime turns the nation's political mood to law and order; many cities and schools use curfews and uniforms to deter crime and violence.

1984
President Ronald Reagan moves to defund the Juvenile Justice and Delinquency Prevention Act, but Congress continues funding.

1992
President George Bush initiates Weed and Seed pilot projects in high-crime areas; Children At Risk program is launched.

1993
A federal appeals court rules that the youth curfew in Dallas, Texas, is constitutional.

1994
Virginia becomes the first state to ban possession of a handgun or assault weapon by a juvenile; Long Beach, Calif., becomes the nation's first school district to require uniforms.

Sept. 13, 1994
President Clinton signs $30 billion crime bill restoring prevention to a prominent role in curbing juvenile crime.

1995
Republican majorities in Congress block funding for 1994 prevention programs.

Dec. 19, 1995
President Clinton vetoes fiscal 1996 appropriations bill for the Departments of Commerce, Justice and State because it "unwisely abandons crime prevention efforts."

Jan. 23, 1996
In his State of the Union address, Clinton calls for school uniforms.

Feb. 1, 1996
Gov. George Allen, R-Va., announces a compromise juvenile justice reform plan that makes it easier for the state to treat young violent offenders as adults.

March 11, 1996
Legislature approves funding for most of Allen's proposal.

'Kids Will Do Whatever You Tolerate' . . .

Soon after Reuben Greenberg checked into his hotel in Charleston, S.C., the doorman gave him a warning. "I was going to walk off my supper," Greenberg recalls, "but he told me not to go more than three blocks away because it was a bad area. And that was one of the nice hotels."

The incident seemed significant to Greenberg, who was in town to interview for the job of police chief, and he brought it up when he met with city officials the next day. If hotel employees knew crime was bad enough in Charleston to warn patrons, then the police also must know, he said. Why hadn't they done something about it?

Their answer was to hire Greenberg. That was in 1982.

By 1994, Greenberg says, the city's burglary rate was lower than at any time in 32 years. In addition, the auto-theft rate has plummeted, drive-by shootings have become a thing of the past, gang graffiti has disappeared, school violence is limited to scuffles between kids and the city's public housing projects are as safe as any neighborhood in town.

Charleston Police Department

Police Chief Reuben Greenberg, Charleston, S.C.

"Kids will do whatever you tolerate," says Greenberg, who has earned a national reputation for not tolerating crime. Indeed, Greenberg's success brought attention in 1993 from a committee seeking a new police commissioner for New York City's mayor-elect, Rudolph Giuliani. The chief told them he was happy in Charleston.

If Greenberg has a guiding credo, it's "The quicker kids learn there are limits, the better off everyone is."

"We don't have graffiti because we eradicate it," Greenberg says. All graffiti reported by 10 a.m. is gone by 5 p.m. the same day, painted over by jail prisoners and police officers assigned to light work because of injuries.

And the eradication goes beyond public property. The city puts out fires and picks up garbage on private property, Greenberg reasons, so he removes graffiti from private property, too.

That's one reason Charleston no longer has a serious gang problem. "The presence of graffiti means it's their turf," Greenberg says. "The absence of graffiti means it's ours."

It took more than removing graffiti, however, to shut down the gangs. A decade ago, well before California's experiments with injunctions against gang activity (*see p. 232*), Greenberg implemented a similar policy to prevent a tough Jamaican "posse" from getting a foothold in Charleston.

When the gangsters showed up in town, Greenberg chipped away at them — mainly with the traffic division. "We'd nail them for everything we could — rolling past

Continued from p. 226

tion Through Youth Development program. Some observers think the program gave law-and-order advocates more ammunition while inadvertently pointing the way toward more effective prevention.

"The issues that plagued that program are still present today — targeting and dosage," says Krisberg. The program was based on the premise that spreading services around to all kids would reduce crime. "But that doesn't work because even in high-crime areas only about 10 percent of the kids become seriously involved in crime," says Krisberg. "So even if you target the highest crime areas, it's like finding a needle in a haystack."

Moreover, he says, "Most programs tend to be short-term, so there's just not enough medicine to cure the problem."

Rand's Greenwood also notes that some prevention advocates during the 1960s and '70s were so eager to prove that prevention works that they dealt primarily with low-risk youth or focused only on the most promising subjects. [18]

With many criminologists becoming increasingly skeptical about the ability of rehabilitation and prevention to stop criminal behavior, President Ronald Reagan declared that the two great liberal fallacies were the beliefs that reducing poverty would by itself reduce crime and that "there is nothing permanent or absolute about man's nature." [19]

Yet it was Reagan's own surgeon general, C. Everett Koop, who in 1985 organized a national workshop on violence and public health. That set the stage for officials to view juvenile delinquency as a public health problem — not unlike tuberculosis or polio — curable with the right combination of treatments. [20]

Reaction to Violence

By the end of the 1980s, gang violence, drug trafficking and violent crimes committed by armed youths

. . . and Charleston's Police Chief Doesn't Tolerate Much

stop signs, burned-out lights over their license plates, jay walking, throwing down cigarette butts."

Whenever police arrested a gang member, they would fingerprint him, run background checks and take photographs for their files. "People thought we were crazy for citing drug dealers for littering," Greenberg says, "but since they never paid their citations, after about six weeks we'd have warrants on them so we could arrest them pretty much at will."

That allowed police to search gang members' vehicles, and, if they found drugs or guns, confiscate their cars. "We literally ate them alive with minor violations," Greenberg says.

Even hooky players were not exempt from strict enforcement of the law. Because skipping school and juvenile crime frequently go hand-in-hand, Greenberg says, he used the state's truancy law to keep kids off the streets and out of the malls during school hours. Over the past three years, police department truancy officers have picked up 5,000 kids and returned them to school or, if they were suspended or expelled, to their homes.

"You don't have to catch them doing anything," Greenberg says. "All you have to do is look at your watch and your calender, and if they're not in school when they're supposed to be, you pick them up."

To keep convicted burglars, robbers and rapists off the street as long as possible, Greenberg opposes every parole request for anyone the department originally arrested. During 1994 and 1995, not a single potential parolee got out of prison early.

Greenberg even developed a novel way to deal with guns. Because kids carry "heat" mainly for prestige, Greenberg developed Operation Gun Stoppers to give gun-toting a bad reputation. Unlike gun buy-back programs that use tax dollars to purchase weapons — even ones that have been rusting in attics for years — Greenberg designed a program to take the panache out of carrying firearms.

Under the program, if a tip leads to the confiscation of an illegal gun, the tipster gets $100 within hours. "We changed the situation from one where kids were showing off their guns to one where they're afraid for anyone to know they even have a gun," Greenberg says.

Charleston's version of a curfew is Operation Midnight, which Greenberg began four years ago. Parents who participate in the program sign permission slips allowing police to bring their children home if they are out past midnight. Civil libertarians have not objected to the program, says Greenberg, because it is parent-based. "It's been very, very effective," he says. "We haven't had a single kid shot, shot at or stabbed since we started that program."

Greenberg's task has been eased by the city's tough-minded public housing policy, which denies leases to people convicted of serious crimes within the past 10 years, and sues to evict troublemakers. Only 50 tenants have lost their leases during the past decade for engaging in criminal activity, but the threat of eviction has had a broader impact, Greenberg says.

"People learned they couldn't live in ways that threatened their neighbors' safety and quality of life and be subsidized by the taxpayers while they did it," he says. "So they stopped committing crimes." As a result, there have been only two homicides in the past seven years in Charleston public housing, where 8,000 people live.

And, Greenberg adds, "Not a single kid [in the city] has been killed by another kid in six years. And that's in a town with a minority population of 41 percent."

prompted some beleaguered cities to enforce youth curfews for the first time in years. In Detroit, for example, the strictest restrictions in the country required kids under 16 to be indoors by 8 p.m. on week nights. To keep guns and knives off campus, some schools installed metal detectors and required students to use see-through backpacks.

Courts and prisons could barely keep up with the unprecedented level of violent crimes committed by youths. By 1991, there were 100,000 juveniles in American correctional institutions — twice the number incarcerated in 1965, when there were 6.5 million more U.S. youngsters under 18. The situation prompted the House Select Committee on Children, Youth and Families to declare youth crime a "national emergency." [21]

To meet the rising gang and youth violence, President George Bush in 1992 launched the "Weed and Seed" program, combining deterrence and prevention. Under the program, police, corrections officials, educators, social-service providers and community organizations joined together to remove criminals from the streets and foster community development in crime-ridden areas. They set up after-school and late-night athletics and recreational programs and harnessed local youngsters into removing graffiti and cleaning up neighborhood litter.

In 1994, with juvenile crime prevention efforts moving toward more punishment and deterrence, Sen. Joseph R. Biden Jr., D-Del., then chairman of the Senate Judiciary Committee, held hearings to lay the groundwork for a new crime bill that would renew the national commitment to prevention.

Prevention forces — having watched the states increase penalties for juvenile crimes and begin treating violent juvenile offenders as adults — sometimes seemed on the defensive. "Crime prevention is not some mush-headed liberal concoction," Sen. Christopher J. Dodd, D-Conn., told the committee in April. "It is not an excuse to throw more money at yet another social problem. It is not an attempt to take the teeth out of the crime bill."

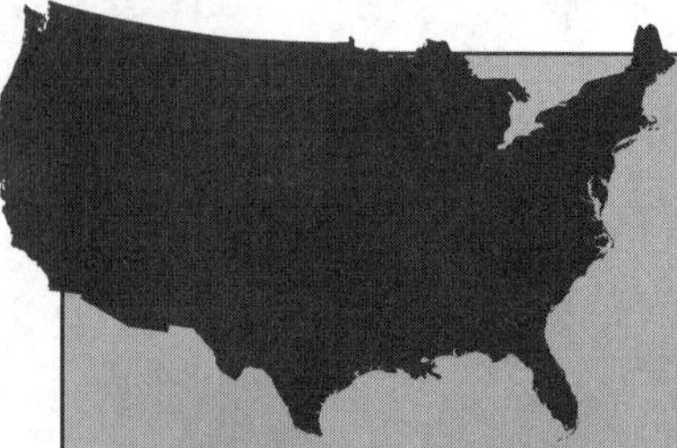

States That Initiated School-Based Anti-Violence Programs, 1992-94

Thirty-five states and Puerto Rico responded to rising youth violence by setting up school-based programs in the early 1990s. Conflict resolution, peer mediation and services for at-risk children were the most popular approaches.

State	Created gun-free school zones	Eased restrictions on suspension, transfer or expulsion of violent students	Established alternative schools for violent or disruptive students	Promoted measures to improve school security	Implemented conflict-resolution or peer-mediation curricula or programs	Targeted at-risk children and youth for special services
Alaska	✔					
Arizona	✔			✔		✔
California	✔	✔	✔	✔	✔	✔
Colorado	✔	✔				
Connecticut					✔	
Delaware		✔	✔	✔	✔	
Florida	✔	✔	✔	✔	✔	✔
Georgia	✔		✔	✔		✔
Hawaii			✔		✔	✔
Illinois	✔		✔	✔	✔	
Indiana				✔		✔
Iowa	✔			✔	✔	✔
Kansas		✔				
Kentucky		✔		✔		
Louisiana	✔		✔	✔	✔	✔
Maryland			✔			
Massachusetts		✔			✔	✔
Michigan	✔	✔				✔
Mississippi	✔		✔	✔	✔	✔
Minnesota	✔		✔	✔	✔	✔
Nebraska			✔		✔	
Nevada	✔					
New Hampshire	✔	✔				
New Jersey		✔	✔	✔	✔	✔
North Carolina	✔	✔	✔	✔	✔	✔
Ohio				✔	✔	✔
Oklahoma	✔	✔	✔	✔	✔	✔
Pennsylvania				✔	✔	✔
Puerto Rico	✔			✔	✔	✔
Rhode Island	✔	✔				
Tennessee						✔
Utah			✔	✔	✔	✔
Virginia	✔	✔	✔	✔	✔	✔
Washington	✔		✔	✔	✔	✔
West Virginia					✔	✔
Wyoming	✔	✔	✔			
Total	**21**	**16**	**18**	**21**	**22**	**22**

Note: States not listed either don't have programs or initiated programs earlier.

Source: National Governors' Association survey, February 1995

The editorial page of *The Wall Street Journal,* along with other conservative voices, was not convinced, calling the proposed bill a "$33 billion monstrosity." Putting 100,000 more police officers on the nation's streets and funding prevention programs such as midnight basketball amounted to "needless spending and phony anti-crime measures," the paper said. [22]

The bill that finally passed included $8.8 billion for hiring police, $7.9 billion for prison construction and almost $7 billion for community-based crime prevention programs. [23] Funding, however, has been severely affected by the impasse over the budget. Funding for the police officers was cut 25 percent, and virtually all the funds for the new prevention programs were eliminated. ■

CURRENT SITUATION

States Get Tough

Elected city officials consider youth crime the most virulent force eating away at America's quality of life, according to a recent National League of Cities survey. The officials ranked gangs second, violent crime fourth and school violence seventh. [24]

Although crime in general is down among all age groups, and violent crime has decreased among adults, violent juvenile crime has continued to increase dramatically, according to the Department of Justice. From 1989 to 1992, arrests for violent juvenile crimes increased by 38 percent. The 1992 arrest rate was far higher than any year since the mid-1960s, when authorities began to collect comparable statistics.

If the rate for violent juvenile crimes continues to increase at the 1983-1992 rate, by the year 2010 juvenile arrests for murder will have risen by 145 percent since 1992. [25]

Virginia is among the states handing out harsher punishments to juveniles. On March 11, the Virginia General Assembly approved Republican Gov. George F. Allen's compromise proposal to try youths age 14 and over as adults for most violent crimes, to keep violent youths in jail after age 21 and to transfer some violent offenders from juvenile detention facilities. In addition, lawmakers opened juvenile hearings to the public and gave authorities unfettered access to young criminals' records.

While Allen emphasized punishment and deterrence, he also included prevention initiatives such as boot camps, a wilderness work program and alternative schools. In return for supporting the governor's tough-on-crime package, however, Democrats' insisted on additional funding for other prevention and rehabilitation programs, including expanded counseling. [26]

Other states are getting tougher, too. From 1992 to 1994, 27 states made it easier to prosecute juveniles as adults, and 28 changed their rules on the confidentiality of juvenile records, according to the NGA. [27]

Intervention Programs

Like Virginia, many of the states' strategies also included prevention programs. From 1992 to 1994, 21 states created gun-free school zones, 16 made it easier to suspend or expel violent students, 18 established alternative schools for such students, 21 beefed up school security, 22 established conflict-resolution or peer-mediation programs and 22 targeted special services for at-risk youth. (*See table, p. 230.*)

In Colorado, Florida, Illinois, Iowa and Minnesota, legislators passed omnibus juvenile justice packages that included early-intervention programs for children in families and neighborhoods most likely to produce criminal behavior. Working with local communities that have special needs, these states are enrolling at-risk children in community-service projects, mentoring partnerships, structured and supervised youth programs during non-school hours and social- and job-skills training.

Many cities, meanwhile, are seeking their own solutions. In Columbus, Ohio, Mayor Gregory S. Lashutka says the youth curfew is working — and a vital part of the city's response to crime. "The sun goes down and crime increases," says Lashutka, president of the National League of Cities.

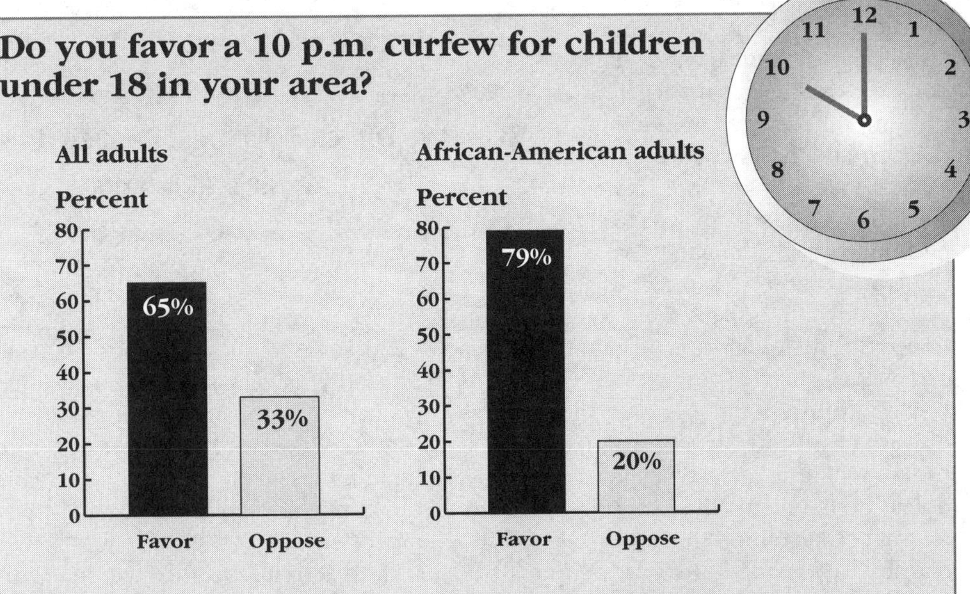

Note: Totals do not add up to 100 percent because "not sure" responses are not included.

Sources: Time/*CNN/Yankelovich Partners, January 1994 (left) and February 1994*

"That's the way it has been since the beginning of time, and that's a rational reason for a curfew."

Columbus also actively enforces its truancy law, and the schools use the "World of Difference" conflict-resolution curriculum, which includes materials the children must discuss with their parents.

Another popular approach to preventing youth crime, particularly on the West Coast, is the "gang injunction." Both supporters and detractors call the injunctions legalized harassment because they allow police officers to stop and question known gang members, even when they are engaging in otherwise legal behavior. In Norwalk, Calif., police have virtually put the Orange Street Locos out of business by forbidding members to make gang hand signals, wear baggy pants, carry bottles or baseball bats, sit in the park or wear large belt buckles. [28]

"The ACLU loves to go after the injunctions," says the Rand Corporation's Greenwood. "But the neighbors who complain about gang activity seem to report decreases in [gang] activity."

Comprehensive community policing also has gained popularity because of its crime-prevention potential. Done correctly, proponents say, community policing puts officers in substations all over town and trains them to listen to people and to help with solutions to community-safety issues. [29]

Despite the popularity of community policing and reports that it improves relations between citizens and police departments, obstacles remain to successful implementation. "In middle-class neighborhoods people are used to it, but to people in inner cities the idea is new" and often viewed initially with suspicion, says the Urban Institute's Roth.

Some observers even say that community policing can undermine grassroots anti-crime efforts either because citizens are suspicious of police motives or because they fear law enforcement's harsh style. That's why police must warn community leaders in advance when they're ready to implement community policing, Greenwood says.

"Midnight basketball is a very strategically targeted program that doesn't cost much and does a lot."

— Barry Krisberg
Executive Director, National Council on Crime and Delinquency

More broadly, says Donald J. Borut, executive director of the National League of Cities, different segments of local communities must become less suspicious of one another and learn to cooperate. "Our surveys show a loss of trust and connection between people," Borut says. "And that lack of trust leads to suspicion and a hardening of differences so that people don't listen to each other."

Boston University's Delattre endorses the need for communitywide cooperation. He notes that Abilene, Texas, reduced the city's gang population from 650 to 75 between 1988 and 1993, essentially by tackling youth crime as a communitywide responsibility. The city built boys and girls clubs next to elementary schools in high-crime areas, then let the schools use them as gyms during the day and the community use them after school and at night for recreation and midnight basketball. Reported crimes in those areas soon dropped 46 percent.

Local business leaders restored a run-down hotel in a dying section of town and used it as a catalyst for renovating the entire area and driving out criminals. Schools remove graffiti as soon as it goes up, and police do not tolerate prostitution, which is a proven lure for illicit drugs.

The city also demolishes gang and drug hang-outs. Police concentrate their patrols in areas with the most drive-by shootings. As a result, gangs that deal in drugs have been forced to look elsewhere for business and young recruits.

"Nothing of this magnitude can be accomplished in a city that views youth violence and gang predation as police problems or problems of a specific area or group of residents," Delattre writes. [30]

Krisberg is especially high on midnight basketball — "a very strategically targeted program that doesn't cost much and does a lot." Nevertheless, he says, Congress has been more willing to put money into boys and girls clubs that don't handle many high-risk kids and are not likely to do as much to prevent juvenile crime. "The crime bill proposed $40 million

Continued on p. 234

At Issue:

Are youth curfew laws constitutional?

UNITED STATES COURT OF APPEALS FOR THE FIFTH CIRCUIT
FROM DECISION IN *QUTB V. STRAUSS*, NOV. 19, 1993

yes

The minor plaintiffs [in this case] have argued that the curfew ordinance [adopted by the Dallas City Council in 1991] impinges upon their "fundamental right" to move about freely in public. . . .

The city's stated interest in enacting the ordinance is to reduce juvenile crime and victimization, while promoting juvenile safety and well-being. . . . In this case, the plaintiffs concede and the district court held that the state's interest in this case is compelling. Given the fact that the state's interest is elevated by the minority status of the affected persons, we have no difficulty agreeing with the parties and with the district court.

In the light of the state's compelling interest in increasing juvenile safety and decreasing juvenile crime, we must now determine whether the curfew ordinance is narrowly tailored to achieve that interest. . . . To be narrowly tailored, there must be a nexus between the stated government interest and the classification created by the ordinance. . . .

Although the city was unable to provide precise data concerning the number of juveniles who commit crimes during the curfew hours, or the number of juvenile victims of crimes committed during the curfew, the city nonetheless provided sufficient data to demonstrate that the classification created by the ordinance "fits" the state's compelling interest. . . .

Furthermore, we are convinced that this curfew ordinance also employs the least restrictive means of accomplishing its goals. The ordinance contains various "defenses" that allow affected minors to remain in public areas during curfew hours. . . .

It is true, of course, that the curfew ordinance would restrict some late-night activities of juveniles; if indeed it did not, then there would be no purpose in enacting it. But when balanced with the compelling interest sought to be addressed — protecting juveniles and preventing juvenile crime — the impositions are minor. . . . [N]one of the activities . . . are restricted if the juvenile is accompanied by a parent or a guardian. Even if the child is unaccompanied by a parent or a guardian, we can presume that most events such as a "midnight basketball league" or a church youth group outing ordinarily would be organized, sponsored or supervised by an adult or an organization, and these are exceptions to the curfew. Although it is true that in some situations unaccompanied juveniles may be forced to attend early evening features of a movie or leave a play or concert before its conclusion, this imposition is ameliorated by several of the ordinance's defenses so that the juvenile is not deprived of actually attending such cultural and entertainment opportunities. . . . Thus . . . any burden this ordinance places upon minors' constitutional rights will be minimal.

KARL A. RACINE
Staff Attorney, Public Defender Service for the District of Columbia

FROM TESTIMONY BEFORE D.C. CITY COUNCIL JUDICIARY COMMITTEE, JUNE 9, 1994. D.C. PASSED A JUVENILE CURFEW LAW IN 1995; IT WENT INTO EFFECT ON SEPT. 20, 1995.

no

Of course it is appropriate to set curfews for children. Still, the curfews should be enforced by parents and not by fines and police officers. It is one thing to strengthen parental responsibility; it is quite another to shift responsibility from the parents to the government. . . .

In holding an earlier juvenile curfew statute unconstitutional, the United States District Court for the District of Columbia said . . . "The act subjects the District's juveniles to virtual house arrest at night without differentiating either among those juveniles likely to embroil themselves in mischief, or among the juveniles whose activities most likely to produce harm. The act is a bull in a china shop of constitutional values.". . .

The current bill differs from the legislation struck down in some respects, but it still interferes with constitutionally protected activity. . . . Despite the exception for juveniles "exercising First Amendment rights. . .," the curfew statute is clearly not intended to allow juveniles to attend late night movies, plays or concerts, or to enjoy late night basketball games unless it is an "official" game sponsored by a governmental, civic or religious organization. . . .

We are also concerned about the discretion over enforcement the bill gives to police officers. It will be virtually impossible to tell whether a particular statutory "defense" applies to a particular juvenile. For example, how can a police officer know whether the young person at the wheel is "involved in interstate travel," or just going home late from the home of a friend? How can a police officer know whether the young man with the basketball in his arm is returning from an "official" game or from the informal pick-up game that has been going on at a school playground for years. How can a police officer know whether the young girl talking to friends is discussing politics . . . or just talking about boys, or an incident at school, or problem with her family? This means that even if an encounter with a police officer does not lead to an arrest and a night at the police station, many completely innocent juveniles will be required to identify themselves and explain their presence. . . .

Something must be done to curb the violence in our city. But this curfew legislation is not the answer. Our young people must have the space and freedom to star gaze or to talk about nothing. And young people whose parents cannot drive them to late movies in Bethesda or Northern Virginia, who do not have big backyards or basketball courts in their driveways, should be entitled to the same freedom as anyone else.

FOR MORE INFORMATION

Coalition for Juvenile Justice, 1211 Connecticut Ave. N.W., Suite 414, Washington, D.C. 20036; (202) 467-0864. Represents state juvenile justice advisory groups in promoting improvement of the juvenile justice system and preventing delinquency.

National Council on Crime and Delinquency, 685 Market St., Suite 620, San Francisco, Calif., 94105; (415) 896-6223. The council works with state governments and legislatures and the Department of Justice to reduce crime and delinquency. It seeks to make the juvenile justice system more "humane, effective, fair and economically sound."

National Governors' Association, 444 North Capitol St. N.W., Suite 267, Washington, D.C. 20001-1512; (202) 624-5300. The NGA makes policy recommendations to Congress and the president in a variety of areas, including criminal justice and public safety.

National League of Cities, 1301 Pennsylvania Ave. N.W., Washington, D.C. 20004-1763; (202) 626-3000. Provides city leaders with training and technical assistance and helps local governments implement federal programs that affect them.

Office of Juvenile Justice and Delinquency Prevention, Justice Department, 633 Indiana Ave. N.W., Suite 742, Washington, D.C. 20531; (202) 307-5911. Administers most federal programs related to prevention and treatment of juvenile delinquency, coordinates youth programs sponsored by various federal agencies and operates the Juvenile Justice Clearinghouse.

Continued from p. 232

for boys clubs and only peanuts for midnight basketball," he says.

Federal funding for midnight basketball programs became one of the most hotly contested issues during debate on the 1994 crime bill. McNulty of the First Freedom Coalition called it one of Clinton's "so-called 'crime-prevention' programs," reminiscent of failed Great Society initiatives.[31]

In McNulty's no-nonsense view, preventing juvenile crime takes making juveniles accountable when they break the law (including truancy laws); assessing more substantial penalties for violent crimes; and punishing juveniles each time they commit a crime.

"Older siblings are telling [the youngsters] that the current system is a joke," he writes. "The kindergarten boys of today will be tomorrow's violent thugs unless America gets serious about punishing juvenile criminals."[32]

Importance of Family

According to a recent Urban Institute report, however, the key to preventing juvenile crime is not tough law enforcement but "family factors."[33]

"Although social behavior is learned by youth through a variety of sources, including peers, school, the family and the neighborhood, it is the family that is the single most important influence on youth socialization," the authors write. They also cite the influence of "parental involvement and the amount of time spent with children, strong moral values, good communication and emotional closeness."

The most vital and cost-effective programs for parents of young, at-risk children are those that teach parenting skills and help the parents become economically independent, says social-policy researcher Chaiken.[34]

Early-education programs combined with home visits have been especially effective, she says. "They teach young parents how to carry out what were once considered natural activities with their children," she says. "But we now have grandmothers at 33 who have never learned to be parents, and now their children don't even know how to play with the children that *they* have."

What won't help such parents and children, she says, are programs that only provide a single service or activity. "You hate to say that any one program is bad, because in combination a lot can be accomplished," Chaiken says. "But it's very expensive to try to tackle children's needs activity by activity."

The biggest failures, however, are programs overseen by well-meaning individuals or organizations without deep and direct experience in child welfare, she says. "Those are the programs that are feeding the backlash in Congress against funding prevention programs." ■

OUTLOOK

The Medical Model

In an effort to bolster support for successful prevention programs, Sens. William S. Cohen, R-Maine, and Herb Kohl, D-Wis., introduced legislation last summer to mandate rigorous evaluations before juvenile-crime prevention programs can qualify for congressional support. "The problem with [the 1994] crime bill," Cohen said, "was that it became a vehicle for an assortment of unproven social programs . . . giving rise to the charge the bill was laden with pork and the programs were nothing more than social experimentation."

Cohen and Kohl's Juvenile Crime Prevention and Reform Act is designed to eliminate programs that do not work and to preserve and fund those that do.

Described by one Capitol Hill observer as a stop-gap measure, the legislation is among several in Congress designed to reshape the nation's juvenile justice system. "Our proposal takes a sensible middle ground," Kohl said in July. "While preserving essential prevention programs, the bill also consolidates and eliminates others and requires all prevention programs to prove themselves."

The act would eliminate 12 crime-prevention programs, including most of those created by the 1994 crime bill. It would mandate outside evaluations and proof of effectiveness before giving money to programs seeking federal funds. In addition, it would consolidate programs to eliminate redundancy.

At the same time, Congress is moving to give anti-crime funds to states through bloc grants, to encourage more locally conceived initiatives, including construction of more prisons.

As that happens, says Rand's Greenwood, more money will go to traditional anti-crime programs that criminal justice agencies and law enforcement prosecutors support. "They're better organized to get it," he says. "So my guess is that less of it would go for prevention and more will go into mandatory-sentencing laws."

Regardless of how the money gets to the states and the cities, Krisberg says, deciding how it is spent must be based on clearly defined targets and outcomes. Communities need to be systematic in preventing juvenile crime, he says, basing their decisions on hard data and a clear understanding of what needs fixing and which tools work best.

"If the biggest problem is drug dealing, then peer mediation is not going to solve that," says Krisberg. "You've got to bring in the cops."

But how does society prevent at-risk kids — who live in poverty, surrounded by violence, and have criminal role models and easy access to guns and drugs — from committing their first crime?

Some say America must adopt a medical, or public health, model for dealing with delinquency, violence and juvenile crime. Former Surgeon General Joycelyn Elders urged the American Medical Association's 1994 Conference on Family Violence to think of violence as "something that can be prevented and cured . . . something abnormal that can be changed, rather than a part of the human condition — in essence, to think of violence as a public health problem." [35]

Although Boston University's Delattre agrees there is merit in viewing juvenile crime as a public health concern, he warns against thinking that "violence is an actual health problem, because that leads to thinking that violence is an illness or affliction for which people are not responsible."

Harvard's Prothrow-Stith says that taking a public health approach can help to make children more responsible, and therefore more accountable, to themselves and society — but waiting until a child already has entered the juvenile justice system is too late.

From a public health perspective, she says, incarceration is to juvenile crime what surgery or chemotherapy is to lung cancer. Surgery doesn't decrease the rate of lung cancer, she says, and incarceration doesn't prevent crime. "Of course, I'm not anti-incarceration anymore than I am anti-chemotherapy," Prothrow-Stith says. "They are both necessary responses."

Still, she says, the only way to reduce lung cancer or violent and criminal behavior among juveniles is through prevention. And just as national public-health campaigns have changed the image of smoking from one of glamour to one of disease, she says, it can help change the image of violence from one of heroics to one of futility and degradation. "Kids must know that violence has consequences," she says.

The public health approach is not limited to prenatal care, parent training, after-school programs, traditional social services and family support such as Medicaid and AFDC. It includes teaching people how to resolve conflicts non-violently. It also means convincing the entertainment and news media not to glorify violence or to mislead the public into thinking their cities and towns are more violent and dangerous than they really are, Prothrow-Stith says.

Last year, however, when then-Rep. Ron Wyden, D-Ore.,* introduced his Consequences in Sentencing for Young Offenders Act, he blamed the medical model for creating a public backlash against the juvenile justice system. "The understandable anger Americans direct at the juvenile justice system stems from the fact that the medical model has often ended up putting our communities at serious risk from young offenders," Wyden said.

Wyden complained that only 50 percent of all juvenile cases go to court, and that most of the youths who actually stand before a judge receive probation. (The other 50 percent of juvenile cases are referred to the social services system.) In Portland, he said, less than half of the juvenile offenders actually served their court-ordered sentences, such as participating in counselling programs, providing community service or restitution or taking part in a Big Brother/Big Sister program.

In view of that record, Wyden said, "any new philosophy of juvenile justice should place . . . the highest priority [on] community safety," to prevent offenders from committing more crimes. [36]

Others say the real challenge to juvenile crime is balancing community-safety needs against the needs of at-risk and delinquent children, which translates into trying to get public health and law-and-order factions to cooperate. Public health people tend to see police as totally consumed with punishment and not at all interested in preventing violence, says the Urban Institute's Roth. Police, on the other hand, view public health advocates as oblivious to the issue of individual responsibility.

---

* Wyden was elected in January to replace former Sen. Bob Packwood, R-Ore., who resigned.

"There is real tension and competition between the two," Roth says. "Even when they agree, they get mad at each other."

That won't change any time soon, Greenwood adds. "The guy with the badge, and the woman with the master's degree in public health, represent two different cultures," he says. "Getting them to work together is a long, drawn-out process." ■

Notes

[1] Quoted in "Violence-Prevention Curricula: What Works Best?" *Education Week,* Nov. 9, 1994, p. 1. For background, see "Violence in the Schools," *The CQ Researcher,* Sept. 11, 1992, pp. 785-808, and "Youth Gangs," *The CQ Researcher,* Oct. 11, 1991, pp. 753-776.

[2] For background, see "Juvenile Justice," *The CQ Researcher,* Feb. 25, 1994, pp. 169-192.

[3] U.S. Justice Department, Office of Juvenile Justice and Delinquency Prevention, *Juvenile Offenders and Victims: A National Report,* 1995, p. 1.

[4] John J. DiIulio Jr., "Tougher Law Enforcement is Driving Down Urban Crime," *Policy Review,* fall 1995, pp. 12. *Policy Review* is published by The Heritage Foundation.

[5] John Pionke, "Conference Survey Finds Cities Moving to Youth Curfews," *U.S. Mayor,* Dec. 11, 1995, pp. 18-19.

[6] *USA Today,* Feb. 27, 1996, p. 1A. Clinton spoke Feb. 24, during his regular weekly radio address.

[7] Ginger Romero, with David E. Brown, *State Progress in Addressing Youth Violence* (1995), p. 14.

[8] See *1994 CQ Almanac,* pp. 273-294.

[9] Paul J. McNulty, "Natural Born Killers: Preventing the Coming Explosion of Teenage Crime," *Policy Review,* winter 1995, p. 84.

[10] "Help Stop Kid Crime," *USA Today,* Nov. 15, 1995, p. 12A.

[11] James C. Howell, ed., *Guide for Implementing the Comprehensive Strategy for Serious, Violent, and Chronic Juvenile Offenders,* Office of Juvenile Justice and Delinquency Prevention, U.S. Department of Justice, June 1995, pp. 84-86.

[12] Alice Hausman, "The Effects of Violence Prevention Education on Student Behavior," *The Journal of Adolescent Health* (forthcoming). Hausman is a professor of health at Temple University, Philadelphia, Pa.

[13] Howell, *op. cit.,* p. 79.

[14] Robert Garland, "Juvenile Delinquency in the Graeco-Roman World," *History Today,* October 1991, pp. 12-19.

[15] Thomas J. Bernard, *The Cycle of Juvenile Justice* (1992), pp. 62-67.

[16] Quoted in James Gilbert, *A Cycle of Outrage: America's Reaction to the Juvenile Delinquent in the 1950s* (1986), pp. 153-54.

[17] The National Coalition of State Juvenile Justice Advisory Groups, "Looking Back to the Future," *The Sixth Report to the President, the Congress and the Administrator of the Office of Juvenile Justice and Delinquency Prevention,* December 1990, p. 10.

[18] Peter W. Greenwood, "Juvenile Crime and Juvenile Justice," in James Q. Wilson and Joan Petersilia, eds., *Crime,* (1994), p. 112.

[19] Quoted in Wendy Kaminer, "Federal Offense: Politics of Crime Control," *The Atlantic,* June 1994, p. 102.

[20] Jo Ann Tooley, "Tackling Violence," *U.S. News & World Report,* March 21, 1994, pp. 96-97.

[21] Steve Manning, "A National Emergency," *Scholastic Update,* April 5, 1991, pp. 2-3.

[22] *The Wall Street Journal,* Aug. 10, 1994, p. A8.

[23] *CQ Weekly Report,* Jan. 21, 1995, p. 211.

[24] Herbert D. Green, *The State of America's Cities: The Twelfth Annual Opinion Survey of Municipal Elected Officials,* National League of Cities, January 1996.

[25] *Juvenile Offenders and Victims: A Focus on Violence, Office of Juvenile Justice and Delinquency Prevention,* U.S. Department of Justice, May 1995, p. 111.

[26] Peter Baker, "Va. Assembly Passes Crime, Budget Bills," *The Washington Post,* March 12, 1996, p. A1.

[27] Romero, *op. cit.*

[28] See *The New York Times,* June 11, 1995, p. 1A.

[29] For background, see "Police Corruption," *The CQ Researcher,* Nov. 24, 1995, pp. 1041-1064, and "Community Policing," *The CQ Researcher,* Feb. 5, 1993, pp. 97-120.

[30] Edwin J. Delattre, *Character and Cops: Ethics in Policing* (2d edition, 1994), p. 257.

[31] McNulty, *op. cit.,* p. 84.

[32] *Ibid.*

[33] Adele Harrell and William Adams, "Reducing Family Risk of Drug Use and Delinquency: Preliminary Findings from the Evaluation of the Children at Risk [CAR] Program," The Urban Institute, unpublished paper presented at the 47th Annual Meeting of the American Society of Criminology, Boston, Mass., Nov. 17, 1995. CAR targets high-risk children through local programs that utilize caseworkers, special family and education services, after-school and summer activities and mentoring.

[34] See Peter W. Greenwood, Karyn E. Model and C. Peter Rydell, "The Cost-Effectiveness of Early Intervention as a Strategy for Reducing Violent Crime," The Rand Corporation, prepared for the University of California, Berkeley, September 1995.

[35] Elders' speech was delivered March 13, 1994, and excerpted in *Focus,* published by the Joint Center for Political and Economic Studies, April 1994, p. 7.

[36] Statement in House of Representatives, Jan. 24, 1995.

Bibliography

Selected Sources Used

Books

Bernard, Thomas J., *The Cycle of Juvenile Justice,* Oxford University Press, 1992.
Bernard's succinct history of juvenile justice in the United States provides an overview of the various approaches tried over the years to stem juvenile crime.

Gilbert, James, *A Cycle of Outrage: America's Reaction to the Juvenile Delinquent in the 1950s,* Oxford University Press, 1986.
Gilbert looks at movies, comic books and Congress in this exploration into the causes and consequences of juvenile delinquency during a decade remembered less for wild hoodlums than for orderly neighborhoods.

Articles

DiIulio, John J. Jr., "Tougher Law Enforcement is Driving Down Urban Crime," *Policy Review,* fall 1995, p. 12.
DiIulio predicts the rise of a new crop of young criminals and calls for tough anti-crime measures and crime-prevention programs targeted at communities that really need them.

Greenberg, Reuben, et al, "What Can Be Done About the Scourge of Violence Among Juveniles? The Experts on Different Fronts of the Battlefield Discuss Strategies," *The New York Times,* Dec. 30, 1994, p. 24A.
Greenberg, the police chief in Charleston, S.C., and other experts offer their suggestions for reducing juvenile violence and crime.

Greenwood, Peter W., "Juvenile Crime and Juvenile Justice," in *Crime,* James Q. Wilson and Joan Petersilia, eds., 1994, pp. 91-117.
An excellent overview and assessment of juvenile crime trends and initiatives to reform the juvenile justice system.

McNulty, Paul J., "Natural Born Killers? Preventing the Coming Explosion of Teenage Crime," *Policy Review,* winter 1995, p. 84.
McNulty's prescription for averting a juvenile crime boom — predicted early next century because of a bulge in the teen population — is to hold lawbreakers accountable for their actions, assess appropriate penalties for violent crimes and enforce sanctions for every crime.

Sautter, Craig R., "Standing Up To Violence," *Phi Beta Kappan,* January 1995.
Sautter describes recent trends in curbing violence at schools — from locker searches to conflict-resolution curricula.

Reports and Studies

Majority Staff report to the Senate Committee on the Judiciary, *Catalogue of Hope: Crime Prevention Programs for At-Risk Children,* April 1994.
Prepared for the committee's hearings on the 1994 crime bill, this report discusses the causes of juvenile delinquency and includes a list of prevention programs.

Greenwood, Peter W., Karyn E. Model and C. Peter Rydell, *The Cost Effectiveness of Early Intervention as a Strategy for Reducing Violent Crime,* Rand Corp., September 1995.
The authors compare early intervention programs with California's mandatory-sentencing law and conclude that prevention is cheaper and more effective than punishment in curbing juvenile crime.

Green, Herbert L., *The State of America's Cities: The Twelfth Annual Opinion Survey of Municipal Elected Officials,* January 1996.
Green summarizes an October 1995 National League of Cities survey that reveals youth crime as municipal officials' No. 1 concern.

U.S. Department of Justice, Office of Juvenile Justice and Delinquency Prevention, *Guide for Implementing the Comprehensive Strategy for Serious, Violent, and Chronic Juvenile Offenders,* June 1995.
The best, single source available on how well prevention and rehabilitation programs work for at-risk children and violent juvenile offenders.

Jones, Michael A., and Barry Krisberg, *Images and Reality: Juvenile Crime, Youth Violence and Public Policy,* National Council on Crime and Delinquency, June 1994.
Jones, an NCCD researcher, and Krisberg, NCCD president, argue that the juvenile justice system has become increasingly punitive and costly because policy-makers are swayed by the public's emotional response to juvenile crime. They recommend integrated prevention and rehabilitation programs.

Snyder, Howard N., and Melissa Sickmund, *Juvenile Offenders and Victims: A National Report,* 1995.
Published by the Office of Juvenile Justice and Delinquency Prevention, this is widely considered the most comprehensive statistical overview of juvenile crime. A narrative provides background, context and explanations for the data.

The Next Step

Additional information from UMI's Newspaper & Periodical Abstracts database

Conflict Resolution

Allen, Eddie B. Jr., "NAACP program trains youth in how to Take Back Our Cities," *Detroit News,* May 19, 1994, p. S10.
Allen Martin worked as violence-prevention coordinator for Save Our Sons and Daughters before beginning an aggressive campaign against self-destruction through the Take Back Our Cities program, which was started in 1992 by the NAACP. TBOC focuses on youth conflict resolution, gang mediation and entrepreneurial training.

Arnold, David, "Parents urged to help prevent youth violence," *Boston Globe,* March 15, 1994, p. 20.
Rodney Dailey, founder of the youth advocacy program Gang Peace, called on the parents of Boston teenagers to play greater roles in teaching children peaceful conflict resolution.

Black, Chris, "Summer youth program is set," *Boston Globe,* April 21, 1994, p. 29.
In an effort to keep a lid on teenage violence during the summer, Mayor Menino is instituting a "Street Smarts" program that would revive the gun buy-back program, expand "Peace League" basketball games and train Boston workers in conflict resolution.

Zuniga, Jo Ann, "Professor blames adults for celebrating violence," *Houston Chronicle,* Oct. 14, 1994, p. A27.
Deborah Prothrow-Stith, a Harvard University professor, returned to Jack Yates High School in Houston, where she graduated in 1971, and talked to students about violence, saying that most children have few skills in conflict resolution besides fighting because adults have few skills to deal with it.

Curfews

Baca, Stacey, "Bedrock of youth violence: Damaged children," *Denver Post,* Sept. 6, 1994, p. A9.
A chronological account of the arrest of a 13-year-old Denver youth for violating the city's 1994 curfew law is presented. The boy's plight illustrates the conflicting views over the curfew program and his own personal story of parental neglect and substance abuse.

McCarthy, Peggy, "Gang violence forces Hartford curfew," *Boston Globe,* Sept. 19, 1993, p. A3.
Hartford, Conn., city officials approved the extension of a 9 p.m. youth curfew, hoping to prevent young people from becoming victims or perpetrators of gang violence.

Rendon, Ruth, "Pasadena considers a youth curfew to curb violence," *Houston Chronicle,* Aug. 15, 1993, p. C5.
Pasadena, Texas, is following in Houston's footsteps as it attempts to implement a youth curfew.

Weizel, Richard, "Street violence and teen-age curfews," *The New York Times,* June 19, 1994, p. CN1.
Late-night violence involving teenagers has become such a problem in Connecticut that a number of cities have ordered youth curfews. Around the state, the concept is supported by many politicians and most of the business community, but opposed by some law enforcement officials and by the teenagers themselves.

"Youth curfew is step in the right direction," *Atlanta Journal,* Oct. 4, 1994, p. A18.
An editorial urges the Fulton County, Ga., Board of Commissioners to support a proposal that the county adopt a youth curfew, since youth violence is on a pernicious upswing. The bill would require that youths 17 and younger be a home by 11 p.m. on weeknights and midnight on weekends.

Brimberg, Judith, "Two-way fight on violence pushed," *Denver Post,* March 5, 1994, p. B4.
Addressing a conference on violent youth crime in Colorado on March 4, 1994, U.S. Attorney General Janet Reno prescribed strong doses of punishment and prevention to control youth violence.

Punishing Juvenile Offenders

Anderson, Ed, "Youth Gangs Targeted," *Times-Picayune,* March 7, 1990, p. B12.
A bill calling for the death penalty for anyone convicted a second time of selling drugs to children under 12 will be introduced in the Louisiana Legislature to battle an increase in youth gang violence.

Goodman, Ellen, "A youth's plight in Singapore brings out the violence in us," *Boston Globe,* April 14, 1994, p. 15.
Goodman comments that public opinion in the U.S. seems to be on Singapore's side in the caning of Michael Fay, an 18-year-old American convicted of vandalism there.

Gottlieb, Alan, "Youth violence experts debate what to do next," *Denver Post,* Sept. 11, 1993, p. A15.
On Sept. 10, 1993, seven experts in law enforcement and inner-city youth gathered in the studios of KRMA-TV to discuss youth violence, but failed to break new ground on

the issue. They agreed that increased Colorado state spending on punishment for violent youthful offenders needs to be balanced with more prevention programs.

School Uniforms

Fears, Darryl, "Tennessee Could Require School Uniforms," *Atlanta Constitution,* Dec. 17, 1992, p. A3.
The Black Caucus in Tennessee's state Legislature is expected to propose a law demanding all schools to draw up some type of voluntary uniform dress code in an effort to stop violence in schools over clothes that are either gang-related or expensive status symbols.

"Are school uniforms a good idea?" *Current Events,* Sept. 18, 1995, p. 3.
The debate over whether school uniforms are a good idea is addressed. Some schools have noticed a downward trend in violence since uniform standards were implemented, but others claim it takes away students' individuality.

Siegel, Loren, "No to school uniforms," *USA Today,* Jan. 17, 1994, p. A8.
Siegel says the increasingly popular idea of mandatory school uniforms will not reduce the violence that plagues schools and violates a student's right to freedom of expression.

Youth Crime and Violence

Boseley, Sarah, "Parents who spare rod can beat child violence," *Guardian,* Oct. 26, 1995, p. 10.
According to a report by the Gulbenkian Foundation, which will be released in November 1995, parents have the power to prevent children from turning to violence by keeping aggression, including corporal punishment, out of the home.

Bracey, Gerald W., "Curing teen violence," *Phi Delta Kappan,* October 1995, pp. 185-186.
Whatever the situation overall, for teens in poverty settings violence is an all-too-common experience. Bracey offers some suggestions for stopping teen violence.

Jones, Alexander R., "Rights groups, churches join to end violence," *Chicago Defender,* May 14, 1994, p. 6.
The national Let's Stop Kids Killing Kids coalition has just completed a week-long series of activities throughout the country designed to reduce the senseless violence which is killing and seriously injuring an increasing number of African-American youth in U.S. cities. The diverse 84-member coalition, which includes such organizations as the NAACP, the Children's Defense Fund and the National Council of Churches, generated a myriad of events that got both adults and youth talking about the problem.

Jourdan, Jeanne, "A community's answer to teen violence," *Children Today,* 1994, pp. 20-24.
The "This Is My Neighborhood—No Shooting Allowed" program started in South Bend, Ind., is described. The program aims to change teens' attitudes about gun violence.

Lewis, Anne C., "Youth crime," *Education Digest,* September 1995, pp. 71-72.
The U.S. House has been debating crime prevention legislation and seems more concerned with punishment over prevention as a means of reducing criminal behavior in youth. Many insist that this is the wrong approach to dealing with the problem.

"12 points for breaking the cycle of violence," *Education Digest,* April 1995, pp. 9-11.
Twelve strategies for addressing the causes of youth violence while dealing with the growing problems at hand are presented. While these strategies are not new, they are newsworthy.

Rodriguez, Michael A., and Claire D. Brindis, "Violence and Latino Youth: Prevention and methodological issues," *Public Health Reports,* May 1995, pp. 260-267.
A study presents an overview of the scope of homicide and intentional injuries in Latino communities and discusses the implications of ethnic-specific factors for violence prevention and research efforts.

Sautter, R. Craig, "Standing up to violence," *Phi Delta Kappan,* January 1995, pp. K1-K12.
Many inner-city youth go to more funerals than movies. The psychological impact of violence in schools on children in the U.S. is discussed, including the example of the November 1993 murder of a 15-year-old girl at Sullivan High School in Chicago .

"Standing up against violence," *Times-Picayune,* July 2, 1994, p. B6.
An editorial comments on the Housing Authority of New Orleans' weeklong "Stop the Violence" tour, an effort to place some of the responsibility for ending the plague of killing and maiming on the shoulders of those most often affected by it: the young, the poor and people living in public housing.

Taylor, Jerry, "Classroom lessons aim to stop violence," *Boston Globe,* May 15, 1994, p. NW1.
The anti-violence message promoted by Joey Fournier Services Inc. is featured. The organization produced a violence-prevention curriculum, Second Step, offered to 5,200 Massachusetts schoolchildren.

Wallach, Lorraine B., "Breaking the cycle of violence," *Children Today,* 1994, pp. 26-31.
Children suffer the consequences of witnessing violence as well as of experiencing it directly. The effect of violence on a child's development and ways that child-welfare professionals can break the cycle of violence are discussed.

Back Issues

Great Research on Current Issues Starts Right Here...Recent topics covered by The CQ Researcher are listed below. Before May 1991, reports were published under the name of Editorial Research Reports.

SEPTEMBER 1994
Home Schooling
Welfare Experiments
Courts and the Media
Regulating Tobacco

OCTOBER 1994
Historic Preservation
Religion and Politics
Arts Funding
Economic Sanctions

NOVEMBER 1994
Sex on Campus
Blood Supply Safety
Testing Term Limits
Religion in America

DECEMBER 1994
Farm Policy
Arms Sales
Earthquake Research
The Future of Television

JANUARY 1995
Treating Addiction
Child Custody and Support
Parents and Schools
Non-Proliferation Treaty at 25

Back issues are available for $5.00 (subscribers) or $8.00 (non-subscribers). Quantity discounts apply to orders over ten. To order, call Congressional Quarterly Customer Service at (202) 887-8621.

Binders are available for $18.00. To order call 1-800-638-1710. Please refer to stock number 648.

FEBRUARY 1995
Cracking Down on Immigration
The Business of Sports
Reinventing Government
Housing Discrimination

MARCH 1995
Death Penalty Debate
Primary Care
Democracy in Africa
Environmental Movement at 25

APRIL 1995
Abortion Clinic Protests
Dieting and Health
Combating AIDS
Rethinking Affirmative Action

MAY 1995
Assisted Suicide Controversy
Overhauling Social Security
Learning to Read
Mandatory Sentencing

JUNE 1995
Combating Infectious Disease
Property Rights
Repetitive Stress Injuries
Regulating the Internet

JULY 1995
War Crimes
Highway Safety
Combating Terrorism
Preventing Teen Drug Use

AUGUST 1995
Job Stress
Organ Transplants
United Nations at 50
Advances in Cancer Research

SEPTEMBER 1995
Catholic Church in the U.S.
Northern Ireland Cease-Fire
High School Sports
Teaching History

OCTOBER 1995
Quebec's Future
Revitalizing the Cities
Networking the Classroom
Indoor Air Pollution

NOVEMBER 1995
The Working Poor
The Jury System
Sex, Violence and the Media
Police Misconduct

DECEMBER 1995
Teens and Tobacco
Gene Therapy's Future
Global Water Shortages
Third-Party Prospects

JANUARY 1996
Emergency Medicine
Punishing Sex Offenders
Bilingual Education
Helping the Homeless

FEBRUARY 1996
Reforming the CIA
Campaign Finance Reform
Academic Politics
Getting Into College

MARCH 1996
The British Monarchy

Future Topics

- ***Tax Reform***
- ***Managed Care***
- ***Interest in the Paranormal***

THE CQ Researcher

PUBLISHED BY CONGRESSIONAL QUARTERLY INC.

Tax Reform

Will Congress tackle major changes in 1997?

Publisher Steve Forbes made tax reform a key campaign issue before he quit the race for the Republican presidential nomination. Forbes proposed replacing the federal income tax system with a single-rate "flat tax." Forbes and other flat-tax advocates say an across-the-board tax would eliminate tax loopholes, stimulate the economy and take the frustration out of filing returns. Other reform advocates have called for a national sales tax or a European-style value-added tax. Although Congress and the White House have been bickering over less ambitious changes to the tax code, it is becoming increasingly likely that tax reform will be on the agenda in 1997, regardless of who wins the presidential election.

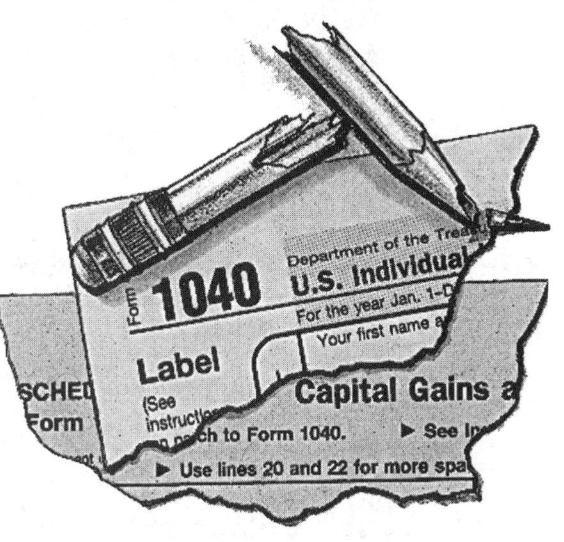

INSIDE THIS ISSUE

CQ | March 22, 1996 • Volume 6, No. 11 • Pages 241-264

Formerly Editorial Research Reports

COVER: BARBARA SASSA-DANIELS

March 22, 1996
Volume 6, No. 11

Bibliographic records and abstracts included in The Next Step section of this publication are from UMI's Newspaper and Periodical Abstracts database, and are used with permission.

The CQ Researcher (ISSN 1056-2036). Formerly Editorial Research Reports. Published weekly (48 times per year, not printed March 1, May 31, Aug. 30, Nov. 29) by Congressional Quarterly Inc., 1414 22nd St., N.W., Washington, D.C. 20037. Annual subscription rate for libraries, businesses and government is $319. Additional rates furnished upon request. Second-class postage paid at Washington, D.C. POSTMASTER: Send address changes to The CQ Researcher, 1414 22nd St., N.W., Washington, D.C. 20037.

Tax Reform

BY MARY H. COOPER

THE ISSUES

His quixotic quest for the Republican presidential nomination soared for a brief moment, then crashed to Earth. But before Malcolm S. "Steve" Forbes Jr. quit the race March 14, his call for a flat tax clearly struck a chord with voters.

The multimillionaire publisher of *Forbes* magazine emerged from obscurity with little to bolster his chances beyond his crusade to replace the ponderous federal income tax system with a 17 percent flat tax. His willingness to spend some $30 million of his own money on an aggressive media campaign was also a factor.

Forbes' tax plan is simplicity itself. It would end taxation of all investment income, including interest from savings accounts, stock dividends, pension distributions and inherited income. It would exempt low-income individuals from taxation, and it would terminate all deductions, among them those for mortgage interest and charitable contributions.

Forbes even promised beleaguered taxpayers — who currently spend more than a half-trillion dollars a year for professional tax help — that filing would be so easy they could use a postcard. [1] No more complicated tax returns. Goodbye to the huge and ever-changing tax code.

As Forbes soared in the early polls, his competitors jumped on the tax-reform bandwagon. (*See story, p. 252.*) Commentator Patrick J. Buchanan proposed a 25 percent flat tax. Former Tennessee Gov. Lamar Alexander, before dropping out of the race, supported a two-rate flat tax. Sen. Phil Gramm, R-Texas, suggested a 16 percent flat tax before withdrawing his candidacy. Sen. Richard G. Lugar, R-Ind., also an early drop-out, proposed replacing the income tax with a national sales tax. (*See "At Issue," p. 257.*) And Senate Majority Leader Bob Dole, R-Kan., now in a commanding lead for the nomination, called for a "simpler, flatter tax," though he did not endorse a flat tax.

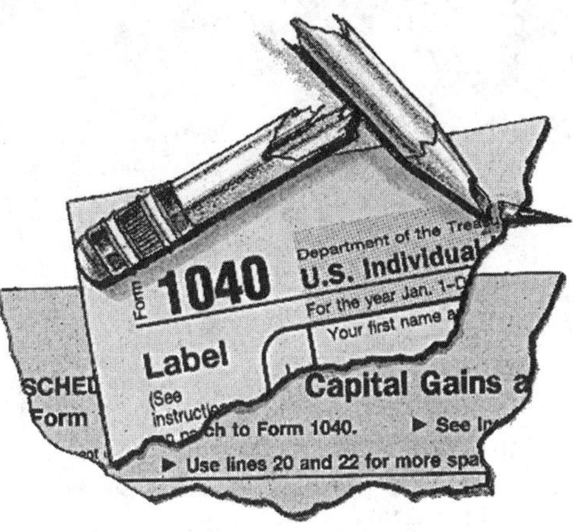

Other flat-tax proposals have been advanced by lawmakers on both sides of the aisle. The plan submitted by House Majority Leader Dick Armey, R-Texas, and Sen. Richard C. Shelby, R-Ala. is now the leading and most-detailed plan being discussed. Other versions of the flat tax came from Sen. Arlen Specter, R-Pa., and House Minority Leader Richard A. Gephardt, D-Mo. Sam Nunn, D-Ga., and Pete V. Domenici, R-N.M., would combine a flat tax on individuals with a version of the sales tax, called a value-added tax (VAT), on businesses. (*See story, p. 248.*) Reps. Dan Schaefer, R-Colo., and W.J. "Billy" Tauzin, R-La., would replace the income tax with a state-administered national sales tax.

Forbes based his plan on legislation first put forward in mid-1994 by Armey and later revised by Armey and Shelby. Many Democrats see the various flat-tax proposals as budget-breaking boondoggles favoring the wealthy at the expense of the middle class. And the Treasury Department in December said the Armey-Shelby plan would cost the federal government some $138 billion a year in lost revenue.

Even some Republicans have criticized flat taxes as simplistic. Dole himself has dismissed the Armey-Shelby plan as "snake oil"; Alexander repeatedly called Forbes' plan "a truly nutty idea."

But the flat tax isn't "nutty" to its enthusiastic supporters, including a handful of Nobel laureates in economics. "Far from being a nutty idea," said Milton Friedman, a winner of the 1976 prize, "the flat tax has a long pedigree — back to tithing for the church." Gary S. Becker, winner of the 1992 prize, said that "A flat tax that eliminates most deductions would be far more efficient and equitable than the present tax system." [2]

Still more support for a flat tax of some sort came on Jan. 17 from a commission headed by Forbes supporter and former Housing and Urban Development Secretary Jack Kemp. While the National Commission on Economic Growth and Tax Reform, set up last year by Dole and House Speaker Newt Gingrich, R-Ga., did not endorse a specific flat tax rate, Kemp said it could be set at about 19 percent. [3]

Opinion polls reflect taxpayers' dissatisfaction with the current system. Taxes ranked just behind the economy and jobs among the leading concerns of voters polled during the Feb. 20 New Hampshire Republican primary. But polls also show considerable ambivalence over plans to overhaul the system. Voters polled during the Feb. 12 Iowa caucus were about evenly split over their support for a flat tax and a graduated tax system, the kind now in place. [4]

Forty-eight percent of the respondents to yet another survey favored switching from the current tax system to a flat tax, while 42 percent opposed a change. But the same respondents solidly opposed a 17 percent flat tax if it meant losing the tax

The More Americans Know About the Flat Tax, the Less They Like It

Fewer than half of those responding to a recent Time/CNN *poll supported the principle of a flat tax, and most wanted to retain tax deductions for home mortgages, charitable contributions and state and local taxes.*

Do you favor . . .	Favor	Oppose	Not Sure
Changing the federal income tax system to a flat-tax system?	48%	42%	10%
A system that taxed all but low-income Americans at a flat rate of 17%?	41	48	11
A system that taxed all but low-income Americans at a flat rate of 23%?	17	74	9
A flat-tax system that taxed wages and salaries, but not profits from the sale of stocks, bonds and real estate?	34	57	9
A flat-tax system that eliminated all tax deductions for home mortgages?	29	60	11
A flat-tax system that eliminated all tax deductions for charitable contributions?	31	64	5
A flat-tax system that eliminated all tax deductions for state and local taxes, including property taxes?	35	55	10
A flat-tax system that increased the size of the federal budget deficit?	11	82	7

Source: Telephone poll of 800 adults taken on Jan. 17-18, 1996, for Time/CNN *by Yankelovich Partners Inc.*

deduction for charitable contributions and mortgage interest payments or increasing the federal budget deficit.[5] (*See poll, p. 244.*)

Many economists caution voters to closely study the major flat-tax proposals before agreeing to junk the current system, however onerous it may seem. Taxpayers should be especially wary, critics of the flat tax say, of claims based on the "supply-side" theory that cutting taxes will unleash so much economic activity that federal tax revenues will actually increase over current levels.

William Gale, a tax specialist at the Brookings Institution, dismisses as "silly" Kemp's claim that a flat tax would lead to a doubling of U.S. economic growth. Such a boost in output, Gale says, is "outside the range of U.S. experience. It's even bigger than the growth rate that we had when we had no income tax."[6]

The sheer complexity of tax law stands as a major obstacle to garnering public support for reform. While flat-tax advocates tout the simplicity of their proposals, meaningfully informing the public about tax law in an election campaign poses problems. "This is not something that lends itself to a sound bite," says Art Godi, president of the National Association of Realtors (NAR) and a vocal critic of eliminating the mortgage deduction. "You can have a simple tax code that ruins the country."

The ultimate litmus test — how a change in the tax code would affect the economy — defies easy prediction. Even critics of so-called double taxation (*see below*) under the current system, which the flat tax would correct, urge caution.

"Eliminating the double taxation of investment income is something you can take to the bank," says Arthur Hall, a senior economist at the Tax Foundation. But what the impact of that would be on taxpayers and the economy as a whole is unclear, he says.

For its part, the Clinton administration has remained virtually mum on the issue. The president gave only passing comment on taxation in general in his State of the Union message. Clinton has even refrained from endorsing a tax-reform proposal made by a member of his own Cabinet. In February, Labor Secretary Robert B. Reich suggested reducing or eliminating the corporate income tax for companies that provide their employees with benefits such as health-care coverage, pensions, job training and profit-sharing.[7]

Some experts oppose trying to replace the current tax system. "The perfect tax system will elude us," writes former IRS Commissioner Sheldon S. Cohen, who notes that Americans are already the least taxed citizens of any industrialized country. "We have a system that works. With a little discipline, Congress could simplify it, reduce deductions and credits and make it better."[8]

But in this election year, the buzzword is reform. While the candidates differ over how to approach tax reform, all are on record as favoring a simpler and fairer system, including Clinton.

As the countdown to the November election begins, these are some of the issues that will shape the tax-reform debate in the coming months:

Would a flat tax be a fairer way to raise revenue than the current, five-rate system?

The current tax system operates on the progressivity principle: Those earning more pay more. In human terms, the premise is that the lower a person's income, the greater portion of that income is needed to buy essential goods; conversely, wealthier Americans have more disposable income left over after expenses and should shoulder a heavier tax burden. Under the current progressive system, there are five tax rates ranging from 15 percent to 39.6 percent. The largest group of taxpayers are in the 15 percent bracket; taxpayers earning above $250,000 pay at the highest rate.

But progressivity has come under increasing criticism from economists who say the wealthy are unfairly penalized. The single-rate flat tax is fairer than the current system, proponents say, because it treats all taxpayers equally.

"Fairness, of course, is in the eyes of the beholder," says Hall at the Tax Foundation, "and my definition of fairness is proportionality," or taxing everyone at the same rate. Because the Forbes plan exempts low-income Americans from taxation, it does not completely eliminate progressivity. "But it's not nearly as progressive as the current system," Hall says. "So in my opinion, the flat tax is fairer."

Proponents of the flat tax also claim it would eliminate loopholes that favor constituencies with enough clout to convince lawmakers to enact them. "A single tax rate on all income (or consumption) above an exemption would restore the tax system to its proper purpose," said Nobel laureate Friedman, now an economist at the Hoover Institution. "It would make it difficult, if not impossible, to manipulate the tax code to favor, or punish, special interests."[9]

Reuters

Publisher Steve Forbes' flat-tax proposal made tax reform a major issue in the race for the Republican presidential nomination.

A third reason the flat tax is fairer, proponents say, is that it taxes income only once, eliminating double taxation. Under the current system, income may be taxed at each of the various stages it is received. Business profits, for example, are taxed at the corporate level as business income and then again at the individual level as dividend income on an investor's personal income tax return.

"The flat tax is fair in that it eliminates double, triple and quadruple taxation," says Rebecca Schaefer, director of tax studies for Citizens for a Sound Economy, an advocacy group that promotes lower taxes and deregulation. "It doesn't matter who earns what money or where it comes from. It's all going to be taxed at 17 percent under the flat tax, and that's it. The IRS is only going to get one bite."

But while eliminating multiple taxation of certain types of income may seem fair in theory, it hands a tax windfall to one class of taxpayers — investors in stocks and bonds. Investments are concentrated in the hands of wealthier Americans, many of whom live off their dividend and interest income alone. Letting them off the hook for taxes on their profits while shifting the entire tax burden to wage earners offends many Americans' sense of fairness.

"I think the core of the case against the flat tax is one of fairness," said Deputy Treasury Secretary Lawrence H. Summers. "Consider two individuals — a man who has been lucky enough to inherit $10 million, which is held in a stock that pays [dividends of] $500,000 each year, and his chef, [who earns] $50,000. . . . I ask you, which one should pay more in taxes each year? The flat tax provides a clear answer to that question — the chef pays taxes. The multimillionaire does not. That just makes the broad point that flat-tax proposals, if they are to balance the budget, will inevitably mean a substantial increase in the taxes on middle-income Americans and a substantial reduction in the taxes on the Americans with the highest income."[10]

Flat-tax supporters concede that they face an uphill battle on the fairness issue. "This is a perception prob-

To Figure Your Tax, Just Fill Out a Postcard

Proponents of the Armey-Shelby flat tax say taxpayers could calculate their taxes on postcard-sized returns, without the need for any additional forms or tables. Businesses would use similar forms.

Form 1 ARMEY-SHELBY FLAT TAX FORM 1998

Your first name and initial	Last name	Your social security number
Present home address		Spouse's social security number
City, Town or Post Office Box, State and ZIP code	Your occupation	
	Spouse's occupation	

	Line	Amount
1. Wages, Salary, and Pensions	1	
2. Personal Allowance		
a. $22,700 for married filing jointly	2(a)	
b. $11,350 for single	2(b)	
c. $14,850 for single head of household	2(c)	
3. Number of dependents, not including spouse	3	
4. Personal allowances for dependents(line 3 multiplied by $5300)	4	
5. Total personal allowances (line 2 plus line 4)	5	
6. Taxable wages (line 1 less line 5, if positive, otherwise zero)	6	
7. Tax (17% of line 6)	7	
8. Tax already paid	8	
9. Tax due (line 7 less line 8, if positive)	9	
10. Refund due (line 8 less line 7, if positive)	10	

Source: The Freedom and Fairness Restoration Act, Summary, July 1995

lem for the flat tax," Hall says. "Unfortunately for the flat-tax proponents, the most esoteric feature of tax analysis is this notion of who bears the burden of business taxes."

To illustrate his view of the current tax system's unfairness to stockholders, Hall points to the tax profile of a typical corporate executive, who owns a big chunk of company stock. "So if the company is paying corporate income taxes, he in effect is paying taxes twice" — once at the corporate level and again at the personal income level, on his dividends. "If you believe that double taxation is unfair, then removing one layer of the tax can't be unfair by definition."

Some experts say a pure flat tax — with no breaks for any special income group — could be made fairer by restoring some of the features of the current tax code. "I don't think that the pure flat tax is as fair as the current system," says Gale of the Brookings Institution. "One of the main reasons is that the pure flat tax eliminates the earned-income tax credit," a refund of up to $3,370 for low-income wage earners. "There's nothing in the flat tax that requires you to do that."

To restore fairness at the high end of the income spectrum, Gale suggests restoring the estate tax on inherited property and setting a second, higher tax rate for the wealthiest Americans. "I'm not out to soak the rich, but we do need to raise revenue from somewhere, and if it's not being raised from the wealthy, it's got to be raised from some other groups."

Should the deduction for mortgage interest payments be abolished?

Under the current tax code, taxpayers can reduce their tax bite by lowering the amount of their earnings that the IRS taxes. They can reduce their taxable income by deducting certain payments they made during the tax year, including interest on home mortgages and charitable contributions. For example, a homeowner who earned $40,000 a year but donated $1,000 to charity and paid $4,000 in mortgage interest payments would pay tax on only $35,000.

These tax breaks mean a lot to consumers, and to the federal government, which must look elsewhere for funds to recoup the lost revenue. The mortgage interest deduction, part of the tax code since its introduction in 1913, saves homeowners $59 billion in taxes annually.

Eliminating the mortgage deduction would raise the 1996 taxes of about 28 million homeowners by an average of about $2,100 and increase tax revenues by an estimated total of $313 billion between 1996 and 2000. Eliminating the charitable contributions deduction would increase tax payments of about 30 million households by an average of nearly $600 per return and increase tax revenues by about $78 billion over the same period. [11]

Flat-tax proposals reduce or eliminate these deductions as a way to increase tax revenues and thus allow for an overall lower tax rate. Most reform proposals, including Dole's ambiguous call for a "flatter" tax, would retain the most popular deductions, but the Armey-Shelby and Forbes plans do away with them all.

Eliminating the home mortgage deduction is only fair, says Schaefer of Citizens for a Sound Economy. She estimates that 78 percent of taxpayers earning more than $100,000 take the mortgage deduction, while only 6 percent of all households earning between $10,000 and $20,000 take the deduction. "Under the current system, we are giving tax breaks to 25 percent of the population under the mortgage interest deductions," she says. "Why is it fair for them to get a tax break and for me, a renter, or our grandparents, who have paid off their mortgages, to have to pay the higher tax rate?"

The home construction and real estate industries decry plans to eliminate mortgage deductions. By removing a major incentive to buy rather than rent, they say, the flat tax would devastate the housing market. According to a study commissioned by the 740,00-member National Association of Realtors, ending the deduction would lower home prices by 15 percent in the first two years, an average loss of about $26,000 for each homeowner household. [12] "That's a total of $1.7 trillion, the equivalent of about a seventh of the gross domestic product," says NAR President Godi, a Realtor in Stockton, Calif.

Godi says that highly leveraged homeowners — those who make 10-20 percent down payments on the purchase price and take out loans for the rest — are especially vulnerable. "If all of a sudden you lose 15 percent of your home's value, your equity is gone," Godi says. "So there would be a significant number of homeowners who would owe more than their house is worth."

The hardest hit group, he says, would be middle-class homeowners. "A lot of people have their life savings in their homes. That's probably the biggest investment that most people make, and it's probably where most of their assets are, and therefore their savings."

Some economists say this scenario is overblown for the very reason that most homeowners have such a small financial stake in their homes. "Most homes are only owned for seven years on average," says Hall of the Tax Foundation. "Because of the short duration, most people are highly leveraged in their homes, which means that the value of their home equity is a tiny portion of the total value of the home."

In what Hall calls a fairly typical example, he cites the home buyer who puts down 10 percent on a $100,000 house, or $10,000. "Suppose the house's value drops by 9 percent [following elimination of the mortgage interest deduction]," Hall says. "That's not really huge money. It's not like losing 9 percent of value of the whole home."

Hall says eliminating the mortgage deduction may be even less catastrophic when seen in the context of the flat tax's other likely effects. "In a flat-tax world, the likelihood is that financial assets in general — bonds and stocks — would increase in value a good bit," Hall says. That's because the flat tax encourages savings and investments by excluding interest and dividend income altogether. "Because homeowners tend to have higher incomes, the people who really have a vested interest in the home mortgage

How Families Would Fare Under the Flat Tax

*The flat tax proposed in July 1995 by Rep. Dick Armey, R-Texas, and Sen. Richard C. Shelby, R. Ala., has become the model for several subsequent flat-tax plans, including one promoted by Malcolm S. "Steve" Forbes Jr. Armey-Shelby includes a 17 percent flat tax * for all but low-income taxpayers, a standard $21,400 deduction for joint filers and a $5,000 deduction for each dependent. The actual tax bill paid by couples earning under $25,000 would be more under the flat tax than under the current tax system, while couples earning more than $75,000 would pay less. However, since businesses could not deduct expenses such as employee health insurance under Armey-Shelby, they would likely pass on those costs to taxpayers as lower wages or higher prices. Even when those business costs are factored into the calculations, couples with lower earnings still fare worse under the flat tax, while wealthier families come out ahead.*

	Current Income Tax		**Armey-Shelby Flat Tax 17%**	
Adjusted Gross Income	**Average Family's Tax Bill**	**Average Tax Burden with Businesses' Costs Included**	**Average Family's Tax Bill**	**Average Tax Burden With Businesses' Costs Included**
Under $25,000	$87	$582	$293	$793
$25,000 under $50,000	3,488	4,618	2,940	4,083
$50,000 under $75,000	6,865	8,902	6,879	8,940
$75,000 under $100,000	11,735	15,651	10,624	14,585
$100,000 under $200,000	19,400	29,789	15,469	25,978
$200,000 or more	118,658	197,576	47,492	127,323

* *The 17 percent rate would take effect after a two-year phase-in rate of 20 percent.*

Source: Tax Foundation, Aug. 2, 1995

Will America Follow Europe Into the VAT?

VATs are popular throughout Europe, but they have nothing to do with making wine — or beer for that matter. A VAT, or value-added tax, is a levy on goods and services at each stage of the production process.

The United States is one of the few industrial countries that has yet to adopt a VAT, and it is the only one with neither a VAT nor a national sales tax. More than 50 countries have adopted the VAT in place of income taxes, including all the countries of Europe except Iceland, plus Canada and Japan. [1]

Replacing the income tax with a VAT would mean a period of disruption for consumers and businesses alike, and whether it is worth the effort is debatable. Critics and supporters alike point to the VAT's track record in Europe, which has the longest experience with the tax.

"The VAT has the virtue of eliminating the headache of an income tax for everyone," Senate Finance Committee Chairman William V. Roth Jr. said earlier this year. "But, as our European trading partners who use the VAT tell us, it is no panacea." [2]

First introduced in France in 1954, the VAT was adopted in Denmark, the Netherlands and West Germany in the 1960s. By 1973, various forms of the VAT had taken hold in the United Kingdom, Italy, Belgium, Ireland and Luxembourg. A major impetus behind the VAT's broad reach in Europe was the desire to integrate the European Community (now the European Union). A common tax system was seen as the key to facilitating the free movement of goods and services across Europe's many national borders.

Before the VAT, each country in Europe taxed goods and services in a variety of ways. On top of that, import and export duties in each country also varied widely. This highly individualistic system persisted over the years because member states were reluctant to relinquish sovereignty in fiscal and trade matters.

Passage of the 1986 Single European Act, removing barriers to trade within the then 12-member federation, overcame much of this resistance. By next year, the 15 current union members will be required to eliminate any remaining sales taxes and replace them with a communitywide VAT.

Under the new VAT system, businesses will pay taxes on the full value of their sales and then claim a credit for the taxes they have already paid on raw materials and other goods purchased. In addition, all taxes previously collected at national borders are to be abolished. [3]

As in Europe, the VAT would offer disadvantages as well as benefits to Americans. Unlike the current U.S. tax system, which taxes the income of both individuals and businesses, a VAT would be paid by businesses alone. The VAT offers the advantage of making it harder to evade taxation because a paper trail of invoices follows everything that is sold. The VAT also would relieve individual taxpayers of the task of filing income tax forms each April.

For Americans, the downside of a VAT is that businesses could be expected to pass on at least part of the tax burden to consumers. Indeed, a major objection to the VAT is its regressivity. Because it taxes consumption, it falls more heavily on the shoulders of the poor, who must spend more of their income for essential goods than the better-off.

Europeans have tried to solve this problem by setting the VAT at different rates for different goods, typically exempting food, housing and medical care from taxation. This enables governments to encourage sales of certain goods as well as reduce the burden of taxation on the poor. [4] It also adds to the tax system's complexity, a negative aspect of VATs.

Adopting a VAT in the United States, as proposed by Sen. Sam Nunn, D-Ga., and Sen. Pete V. Domenici, R-N.M., would entail a far more wrenching change for Americans than it has in Europe. The problem is that income taxes alone have long accounted for the bulk of government revenues in this country, while most European countries traditionally have relied on a mix of income and sales taxes.

The Nunn-Domenici proposal, dubbed USA Tax, combines a flat tax on individuals' incomes with a VAT on business. (*See story, p. 252.*) Combining a VAT with the income tax would mean less of a change for individual taxpayers. But such a hybrid system would be costlier than simply replacing one system with the other.

Because it combines features of two popular taxation approaches — the VAT and flat tax — USA Tax could find widespread support. But skeptics note it's the worst of both worlds: Two tax systems instead of one.

---

1 See Congressional Budget Office, *Reducing the Deficit: Spending and Revenue Options*, February 1995.

2 Roth spoke Jan. 31, 1996, at the first of a series of Finance Committee hearings to be held this year on tax reform.

3 See Gary Clyde Hufbauer, *Fundamental Tax Reform and Border Tax Adjustments Institute for International Economics*, 1996, pp. 39-42.

4 See Congressional Budget Office, *Effects of Adopting a Value-Added Tax*, February 1992.

deduction are likely to be the same people who have a fairly large holding of stocks and bonds. So if you get a small drop in the equity value of your home, but you get a fairly large increase in the value of your stocks and bonds, are you better or worse off? It's either going to be a wash, or people are going to benefit slightly."

Forbes claims that his deduction-free flat tax would actually boost home values along with the rest of the economy. "Even critics acknowledge that the interest rates would go down," he said Jan. 21 on ABC-TV's "This Week With David Brinkley." "So your mortgage is cheaper, you have more money in your pocket. In the real world, that will help housing, not hurt it."

Supporters of the mortgage interest deduction insist that its elimination would cause harmful effects that would ripple through the economy. In addition to the housing and real estate industries, Godi says, mortgage lenders left holding the bag from bad loans would suffer losses when they are forced to sell foreclosed properties at depressed prices. Entities that are funded from property tax revenues also would suffer. "Property taxes are based on value, and if they lose 15 percent of the tax base, that's going to have a heck of an impact on local governments and on schools," Godi says.

Critics of the pure flat tax also defend the mortgage interest deduction as a positive tool for promoting social stability. "People who own real property are better citizens," Godi says. "Pick any neighborhood and look at the care homeowners take vs. where it's all rentals. People who own their own homes support their schools and they take better care of their property. Property ownership is valuable in our society, and it's still the great American dream."

Would a national sales tax or a value-added tax (VAT) be a better alternative to the current tax code than a flat tax?

Spurred by Forbes' early success in the presidential campaign, the flat tax has dominated the recent debate over tax reform. But other alternatives to the current system have garnered support among economists and policymakers, notably a national sales tax and a VAT. (*See story, p. 252.*)

Sen. Lugar offered a detailed plan to abolish the IRS and replace the income tax with a 17 percent national sales tax that would be collected by the states. "Replacing the income tax with a national sales tax would cause savings and investment to skyrocket," Lugar argued. "The result would be sustained economic growth." [13]

To supporters of the flat tax, the main virtue of most VAT and sales-tax proposals is their use of only one tax rate. "They're all better than the current system," says Schaefer of Citizens for a Sound Economy. Like the pure flat tax, she says, "they all get you to a single rate."

Another major virtue of the VAT and sales-tax plans is their simplicity, at least for individuals. In contrast to the flat tax — even the postcard variety — the sales tax and VAT would relieve individuals from the annual agony of filing tax returns of any kind.

Another major virtue of the VAT and sales-tax plans is their simplicity, at least for individuals. In contrast to the flat tax — even the postcard variety — the sales tax and VAT would relieve individuals from the annual agony of filing tax returns of any kind. A national sales tax would simply be added to the prices consumers pay for goods and services they purchase at the retail level, just as some states and localities impose sales taxes today.

A VAT would be even less intrusive to individuals. Businesses would pay a tax based on the difference between their gross revenue and expenses, or net profit. Individuals would feel the effect of a VAT, of course, but indirectly, through higher prices for the things they buy.

While simplifying life for ordinary wage earners, the VAT and sales-tax plans would complicate things for businesses, however, because they would introduce a new set of requirements after abolishing the system now in place. "The flat tax would certainly be the simplest system that we would likely move to," says Hall. "The sales tax would be somewhat simpler once in place, but there's a lot more complexity in getting from here to there with the sales tax."

One of the main objections to the sales tax is the difficulty of enforcing it, especially in the growing service sector of the economy. "Say it costs me $10 to get a suit dry-cleaned, and we had a 20 percent national sales tax," Schaefer says. "The total cost to me would be $12. But the cleaner can always charge me $11 and not record the sale. This way, I pay less than the $12 official price, and he makes more than the $10 he would have made, minus the $2 that would have gone to the government. We both have an incentive to hide the purchase altogether."

To make up for such revenue losses, Schaefer says, the government would have to raise the sales-tax rate, thus providing an even greater incentive to businesses and consumers to evade the tax, creating a snowball effect of rising rates and falling compliance. [14]

Gale of the Brookings Institution agrees with this criticism. "Sure, a sales tax would get the IRS off people's backs," he says, "but they wouldn't pay any taxes because the rates you'd need in a sales tax are very difficult to enforce in order to raise enough revenue. There's a link between enforcement and simplicity. We want to make the tax system simpler at the same time that we continue to enforce it. We do have to raise revenue."

In view of the administrative and compliance problems, Gale prefers the flat tax, then the VAT, over the sales tax among these reform proposals. "Many European countries tried to do sales taxes, and they all found them impossible to enforce," he says. "So they all went to value-added taxes."

A value-added tax, Gale explains, would be easier to enforce than a sales tax because it offers a built-in incentive for businesses to comply, since all parties to a transaction can deduct their expenses. "[B]ecause the purchaser reports the transaction to the authorities in order to claim the deduction," Gale writes, "the seller — who pays tax on the sales — is more likely to report as well," because the seller wants to deduct his costs also. [15]

Many economists reject sales taxes because of their lack of progressivity. The lower a person's income, the greater portion of that income must be spent on essential purchases, such as food and housing, and the less is available for saving and investment. The current income tax helps redistribute income by taxing interest and dividends and by imposing higher tax rates on higher-income individuals.

"All these single-rate plans face a similar problem," Hall says. "If you eliminate the double taxation of investment income at graduated rates, there's no getting around having a major shift downward or flattening out of the income distribution. If the public really does care about progressivity, then these plans are going to collapse."

Nunn and Domenici attempt to overcome the regressive nature of sales taxes by combining a simplified version of the current income tax with a VAT. Their "consumed income tax," dubbed the USA Tax, would enable individual tax filers to deduct all savings from their taxable income. For businesses, Nunn-Domenici would replace the existing corporate income tax with a VAT, enabling businesses to deduct all capital investments.

Other plans try to remedy the sales tax's regressive character with means-tested rebates or credits. The National Retail Sales Tax, proposed March 7 by Schaefer and Tauzin, would offer a credit against a worker's Social Security payroll taxes. (Tax reform proposals do not affect payroll taxes, including Social Security and Medicare taxes.) The credit would be set so that workers whose wages are below the poverty level would pay no taxes.

"The National Retail Sales Tax exemplifies simplicity, especially when compared to either the present system or a flat tax," the lawmakers proclaimed. "Without income tax withholding, taxpayers take home every penny they earn. The government only gets its cut when the consumer chooses to consume. Americans will finally have control over how much they pay in taxes and when." [16] ■

BACKGROUND

Never-ending Reforms

Resistance to the British king's authority to tax the Colonies sparked the American Revolution — and the Founding Fathers' determination that history would not repeat itself.

To avoid "taxation without representation" in the future, the Constitution placed the power to tax in the hands of the legislative branch. But because lawmakers are sensitive to the needs of their constituents, the tax code has become riddled with loopholes that often benefit the most powerful interest groups.

Since the federal government began collecting income taxes in 1913, there have been numerous efforts to remedy perceived flaws in the system. Most of these reforms had limited impact, because powerful lobbies often convinced lawmakers to carve out new tax breaks.

High income tax rates and the public's resulting low compliance prompted President John F. Kennedy to launch one of the most sweeping attempts to reform the tax code. "It is a paradoxical truth that tax rates are too high today and tax revenues are too low, and the soundest way to raise the revenues in the long run is to cut the rates now," Kennedy said in 1962. "The purpose of cutting taxes now is not to incur a budget deficit, but to achieve the more prosperous, expanding economy which can bring a budget surplus." [17]

By 1966, three years after the top individual tax rate was cut from a stratospheric 91 percent to 70 percent, tax revenues had grown by 16 percent, as a result of greater compliance as well as economic growth. The impact of Kennedy's reform effort was diluted, however, as lawmakers subsequently carved out new loopholes in the tax code. Presidents Lyndon B. Johnson and Jimmy Carter both failed to win passage of sweeping loophole-closing reforms. [18]

The Reagan Revolution

The focus of tax reform shifted in the 1980s, as efforts to end tax breaks for special interests gave way to a campaign to reduce tax rates. President Ronald Reagan's promise to "get the government off our backs" by cutting taxes and abolishing regulations on industry dovetailed with the "supply-side" economic theory espoused by some Republican lawmakers, notably Kemp, then a New York congressman, and Sen. William V. Roth Jr. of Delaware.

Supply-siders argued that lowering taxes would spur investments in the private sector and produce new wealth, ultimately yielding higher tax

Continued on p. 253

Chronology

1910s-1960s

The federal income tax, introduced in 1913, undergoes numerous changes.

1962
President John F. Kennedy launches a tax-reform plan that lowers the top tax rate from 91 percent to 70 percent in an effort to improve compliance with the tax code. Tax revenues increase by 16 percent over the next three years.

1980s ***Fueled by a citizen tax revolt, reform efforts focus on cutting rates and eliminating loopholes in the income tax.***

1981
The Economic Recovery Tax Act (ERTA) gives tax breaks to businesses, cuts taxes for individuals by 30 percent over three years and lowers the tax on capital gains. Stanford University economists Robert Hall and Alvin Rabushka propose the first "flat tax," aimed at spurring investment and simplifying tax filing for individuals.

1982
As a severe recession cuts into tax revenues, moderate Republicans led by Sen. Bob Dole, R-Kan., sponsor the Tax Equity and Fiscal Responsibility Act (TEFRA), which reverses some of the 1981 tax breaks. Versions of the flat tax are endorsed by former California Gov. Jerry Brown in his unsuccessful bid for the Democratic Party's nomination for the presidency, as well as then-Rep. Leon E. Panetta, D-Calif.

1986
The Tax Reform Act, one of the most radical overhauls of the tax code, introduces a three-bracket tax with a top rate of 28 percent and broadens the tax base by eliminating loopholes.

1990s ***As tax rates rise once again, pressure builds to replace the income tax with a simpler flat tax or a tax on consumption.***

1993
In an effort to reduce the budget deficit, Congress passes a Clinton administration measure that increases the top tax rate from 31 percent to 39.6 percent.

1994
After winning a majority of seats in Congress for the first time in 40 years, Republican lawmakers focus on cutting federal spending in an effort to balance the budget. House Majority Leader Dick Armey, R-Texas, introduces a version of the flat tax.

July 1995
Armey reintroduces the flat tax with Sen. Richard C. Shelby, R-Ala. The Freedom and Fairness Restoration Act includes a 17 percent rate on wages, pension distributions and business income.

Dec. 20, 1995
The Treasury Department issues a critical analysis of the Armey-Shelby flat tax, claiming it would cost the government $138 billion a year in lost revenue.

Jan. 17, 1996
The National Commission on Economic Growth and Tax Reform, chaired by former Housing and Urban Development Secretary Jack Kemp, recommends replacing the income tax with a flat tax that keeps most popular deductions. The commission defers a decision on the actual rate to congressional study.

Jan. 31, 1996
The Senate Finance Committee launches a series of hearings to be held throughout the year on tax-reform proposals expected to come up for congressional action in 1997.

Feb. 6, 1996
As an incentive to improve working conditions, Labor Secretary Robert B. Reich proposes giving tax breaks to corporations that offer health insurance, training and other benefits to their employees. Key administration officials criticize the proposal, which is later translated into legislation by Senate Minority Leader Tom Daschle, D-S.D., and Sen. Jeff Bingaman, D-N.M.

March 7, 1996
Reps. Dan Schaefer, R-Colo., and W.J. "Billy" Tauzin, R-La., propose replacing the income tax with a national retail sales tax.

March 14, 1996
Publisher Malcolm S. "Steve" Forbes Jr. pulls out of the race for the GOP presidential nomination, having made tax reform a key campaign issue.

March 19, 1996
President Clinton's budget plan for fiscal 1997 calls for increased capital gains taxes instead of lower rates, as Republicans wanted.

Comparing the Major Tax-Reform Proposals

Here are the main details of 13 major tax-reform proposals being discussed this year:

Hall-Rabushka flat tax: Known as the "bible" of flat-tax plans, this approach was first described in the 1980s by Robert Hall and Alvin Rabushka of Stanford University's Hoover Institution. It sets a single, 19 percent tax on all personal and business income. Individuals pay tax only on income from wages and pension distributions over a personal exemption ($25,500 for a married couple with two children) and can take no deductions. Businesses pay tax on revenues minus costs (including wages and pension contributions).

Armey-Shelby flat tax: The Freedom and Fairness Restoration Act was introduced last year by House Majority Leader Dick Armey, R-Texas, and Sen. Richard C. Shelby, R-Ala., based on a proposal introduced originally by Armey in 1994. Armey-Shelby calls for a 17 percent tax for all taxpayers except the poor on wage income and pension distributions, which goes into effect after a 20 percent tax rate for two years. There is no tax on investment income, capital gains or inheritances. Personal exemptions for a married couple with two children are initially $31,400, later $33,300. All individual and corporate deductions, including mortgage interest, charitable donations and state and local taxes, are eliminated. Businesses also pay the 17 percent rate, with no deductions for non-pension fringe benefits, such as health insurance. Supporters claim Armey-Shelby tax returns could be filed on a postcard.

Dole on tax reform: Senate Majority Leader Bob Dole, R-Kan., the GOP presidential front-runner, has not advanced a specific reform plan beyond calling for a "flatter, simpler" tax to be developed following further study by congressional committees. He favors retaining mortgage interest and charity deductions.

Forbes flat tax: Publisher Malcolm S. "Steve" Forbes Jr. hung his short-lived run for the Republican presidential nomination on a flat tax similar to Armey-Shelby, with a 17 percent rate on individual wage income minus a personal allowance ($36,000 for a married couple with two children). Forbes' version had no tax on investment income, capital gains or inheritances, and no deductions. Businesses pay the same 17 percent rate. Postcard-sized tax return.

Kemp Commission flat tax: The commission did not recommend a specific rate, but Chairman Jack Kemp has suggested 19 percent, but not more than 20 percent. Eliminates tax on capital gains, dividends and inheritances; retains mortgage interest and charitable donation deductions. Requires two-thirds "supermajority" to raise taxes.

Gramm flat tax: Before Sen. Phil Gramm, R-Texas, dropped out of the race for the GOP presidential nomination in early March, he called for a 16 percent rate and $32,000 exemption for married couples with two children. Unlike Armey-Shelby and Forbes, Gramm would continue to tax investment income and capital gains for individuals and would keep mortgage interest and charity deductions; requires supermajority to raise taxes and a balanced budget within four years.

Buchanan flat tax: Political commentator and Republican presidential hopeful Patrick J. Buchanan calls for a 15 percent tax on all personal income, including wages, salaries, dividends, interest and capital gains. Married couples with two children get $25,000 personal exemptions. Deductions retained only for mortgage interest and charitable contributions; exempts taxes on inheritances under $5 million. Businesses pay a flat 17 percent rate.

Alexander tax reform: Before former Tennessee Gov. Lamar Alexander dropped out of the Republican presidential race, he championed a two-rate system with lower taxes on income, capital gains and inheritances, higher exemptions for working families. Limits most deductions but keeps those for mortgage interest payments and charitable contributions.

Specter flat tax: Sen. Arlen Specter, R-Pa., suggests a 20 percent flat rate on personal and business income except capital gains, dividends and interest. Smaller personal exemptions than other plans; keeps limited deductions for mortgage interest and charity.

Gephardt 10 percent tax plan: House Minority Leader Richard A. Gephardt, D-Mo., would levy a 10 percent tax on all but the wealthiest 25 percent of Americans, who would pay a graduated tax of up to 34 percent on earned and unearned income, including capital gains; eliminates deductions and loopholes except the mortgage interest deduction.

Nunn-Domenici Unlimited Savings Allowance (USA) tax: This unusual bipartisan plan, introduced in 1995 by Sens. Sam Nunn, D-Ga., and Pete V. Domenici, R-N.M., features a graduated-rate tax of 8 percent to 40 percent on individuals' earned income. It replaces the business income tax with a single-rate 11 percent value-added tax (VAT) on business income. A VAT, which has some bipartisan approach, is applied to business gross receipts minus gross costs, or the amount that reflects the valued that is added to goods and services at each stage of production. The USA tax includes credit for payroll taxes paid by workers and employers and keeps deductions for mortgage interest and charitable contributions.

Lugar national sales tax: Sen. Richard G. Lugar, R-Ind., who dropped out of the GOP presidential race in early March, would abolish the Internal Revenue Service (IRS) and replace the income tax with a 17 percent, state-run tax on goods and services at the point of final sale to consumers.

Schaefer-Tauzin national retail sales tax: Introduced in early March by Reps. Dan Schaefer, R-Colo., and W.J. "Billy" Tauzin, R-La., it replaces the IRS and income tax with a state-administered tax at point of sale on all goods and services, estimated at 13 percent, to maintain current revenues. The rate could rise if rebates were needed to ease the burden on working poor. Would provide a used-property tax credit for sellers of used cars, houses and other goods.

Continued from p. 250

revenues than those generated under the higher tax rates. Lower tax rates would generate so much new revenue, they predicted, that the federal budget deficit — which stood at around $60 billion when Reagan became president in 1981 — would be wiped out.

Reflecting the supply-side view of fiscal policy, the Kemp-Roth tax reform bill included a 30 percent tax cut for individuals, spread over three years. At the same time, Reagan called for generous tax breaks for businesses. The reform measure that incorporated all these changes, the 1981 Economic Recovery Tax Act (ERTA), also lowered the top rate on capital gains — profits on the sale of investments — from 28 percent to 20 percent.

No sooner were the tax cuts introduced than the U.S. economy slid into a recession. Tax revenues plummeted at the same time that spending for federal programs was rising, largely due to expansion of the military budget. As the budget deficit grew, Dole and other moderate Republicans called for a reversal of some of the 1981 tax cuts, resulting in the 1982 Tax Equity and Fiscal Responsibility Act (TEFRA).

Flat-Tax Fever

The 1980s differed from previous periods because of the growing public dissatisfaction with the tax system, at both the local and federal levels. Agitation began in California in the late 1970s with a citizens' tax revolt that led to passage of Proposition 13, which froze state property taxes.

At the federal level, support for tax simplification, lower rates and elimination of preferences favoring special interests gained momentum across the political spectrum. In 1981, economists Robert Hall and Alvin Rabushka of the Hoover Institution proposed the original "flat tax," hoping to spur savings and investment and simplify tax filing for individuals.

The following year, former California Gov. Jerry Brown advanced a flat tax as a boon to lower- and middle-income workers in his unsuccessful bid for the Democratic presidential nomination. Also in 1982, Rep. Leon E. Panetta, D-Calif., now President Clinton's chief of staff, introduced the Income Tax Simplification Act, which would have established a 19 percent flat tax with almost no deductions, credits or exclusions.

Tax Reform Falters

Although these early flat-tax plans never became law, Congress eventually passed a radical overhaul of the tax code. The 1986 Tax Reform Act reduced the number of tax brackets to three, lowering the top rate from 50 percent to 28 percent. The law also eliminated many of the loopholes that had enabled wealthy individuals and large companies to escape taxation, and it created the alternative minimum tax, which is levied on individual and corporate income that escapes taxation through remaining loopholes.

The supply-siders' expectation that the lower tax rates would end the federal budget deficit failed to materialize, however, as spending for the military and other federal programs far outstripped the gains achieved in tax revenues. By the end of the 1980s, the deficit exceeded $200 billion.

Like earlier reforms, the 1986 act was short-lived. Once again, lawmakers opened new loopholes, shrinking the tax base. Then they raised tax rates to make up for the lost revenues, putting the top rate at 31 percent.

Resistance to tax increases under both the Bush and Clinton administrations contributed to today's renewed call for fundamental tax reform. Most recently, in 1993, Clinton called for, and Congress passed, an increase in the 31 percent top income tax rate to 36 percent for couples with taxable incomes of $140,000-$250,000 and to 39.6 percent for those with more than $250,000.

As *The Wall Street Journal* saw the situation, lawmakers got credit from the public for closing loopholes in 1986, then broke the faith soon afterward by raising rates. "In the 1986 act, the politicians pocketed the loophole-closing and then welshed on their side of the bargain," said an editorial supporting the flat tax. "The 28 percent . . . rate has soared to now more than 39 percent. . . . In only a few years, the politicians got . . . rates back to prohibitive levels." [19] ■

CURRENT SITUATION

'They're Just Tinkering'

Until Steve Forbes sparked national interest in his flat tax, fundamental tax reform was not a dominant issue in the recent political debate. In 1994, after winning a majority of the seats in Congress for the first time in 40 years, Republican lawmakers, guided by their "Contract With America," concentrated on balancing the federal budget, cutting taxes and reforming the welfare system.

But Clinton repeatedly thwarted their plans. On Dec. 6, 1995, he vetoed a sweeping congressional budget proposal designed to eliminate the deficit in seven years while cutting taxes by $245 billion. The GOP proposal also would have given families a $500 tax credit for each dependent child and reduced the tax on capital gains.

On Jan. 6, Clinton countered the Republicans' plan with a proposed tax cut of as little as $27 billion over seven years, a lower tax credit for families with children and a more limited cut in the capital gains tax. Paring the budget more than that, the president

Why Call It a Consumption Tax?

The whole point of tax reform is to make things simpler, but some of the terms the experts throw around are mind-bogglingly complex. For example, most advocates of tax reform say it's better to tax *consumption* rather than *income* because it encourages Americans to save more. But income and consumption mean different things to the experts than to average taxpayers.

To the average taxpayer, income tax, of course, is what is paid each year based on your earnings and other income. On the other hand, a consumption tax would be viewed by most Americans simply as what you'd pay at the cash register on items purchased — a simple sales tax.

But Rebecca Schaefer, director of tax studies at Citizens for a Sound Economy explains that the experts have a special definition for consumption based on the formula: *Income=Savings+Consumption.* The formula is based on the assumption that "there are only two things you can do with your income," she explains. "You can save it by investing it in bank accounts or securities, or you can consume it by making purchases."

Thus, a flat tax is considered a "consumption" tax because only the "consumption" part of a person's income is taxed; income from savings and other investments is not taxed. For example, if a person earns $50,000 per year in salary and $1,000 annually in bank interest, the $50,000 would be taxed at the flat-tax rate, but the interest income would not be taxed.

The theory is that the wage earner would be encouraged to save as much of the $50,000 as possible, because the interest on the money he saves would not be taxed in the future.

said, would cut into basic welfare programs such as Medicaid.

The impasse over the budget has twice led to government shutdowns, on Nov. 14 and again on Dec. 16, because many agencies had been left unfunded for the 1996 fiscal year, which began last Oct. 1. Although temporary spending measures enabled most agencies to resume work, the struggle continues between lawmakers and the White House over spending levels and tax changes. [20]

In any case, the tax changes included in the congressional and White House budget proposals do not amount to true tax reform, in the view of most economists. "They're just tinkering," says Hall of the Tax Foundation. "The only real sustainable change — assuming we ever get to a tax-reform model — is the indexing* of capital gains. If that becomes law, it will become institutionalized for the betterment of everybody." This, analysts say, would encourage investors to buy and sell securities and other assets more readily, freeing up capital and stimulating economic growth. [21]

* Indexing, or adjusting, capital gains to account for inflation would reduce the taxable portion of profits made from the sale of assets.

Godi of the NAR agrees that the budget proposals' capital gains provisions would help the economy. "That's one change that wouldn't hurt anything and that would more than pay for itself," he says. "Across the country, people are holding back on selling and making investments because the capital gains tax is too high."

Another change contained in budget legislation would end the tax on inheritances. "The estate tax is completely onerous," says Schaefer of Citizens for a Sound Economy. "It punishes success and primarily hurts farmers and small-business owners. I'm not trying to play class warfare, but the people who are very wealthy can afford the tax. They may be upset and frustrated, but it's the families that actually have to sell their businesses in order to pay the tax that are really hurt."

Schaefer also supports the Republicans' proposal to add a $500-per-child tax credit to the existing code. "We want to give people as much of a foothold in the system as we can," she says. "The $500 child tax credit helps out a lot of low- and middle-income families."

Brookings tax specialist Gale agrees that the budget legislation falls short of meaningful tax reform, but suggests other changes. "If I were going to tinker with the income tax, I would prefer to close up loopholes in deductions, rather than expand them. What they're doing is more targeted investment and savings incentives. The allure for these is great, but in my personal opinion, we've tried that, and it hasn't worked."

Democrats Enter Fray

As tax reform emerged early this year as a key issue among Republican contenders for their party's nomination, Democrats remained largely on the sidelines of the debate. In his State of the Union address, Clinton limited his comments on taxes to a defense of the earned-income tax credit and support for a new tax credit for working families with children.

"In 1993, Congress cut the taxes of 15 million hard-pressed working families to make sure that no parents who worked full-time would have to raise their children in poverty, and to encourage people to move from welfare to work," Clinton said. "This expanded earned-income tax credit is now worth about $1,800 a year to a family of four living on $20,000. The budget bill I vetoed would have reversed this achievement and raised taxes on nearly 8 million of these people. We should not do that."

For the most part, the administration has limited its participation in the heated campaign debate over tax reform to occasional criticism. "Beyond the budget debate this year, there will be a great deal of discussion of the future of our tax system," Deputy Treasury Secretary Summers said in January. "I think it's fair to say that no one is entirely satisfied with the current tax system. It is too complicated. It is too burdensome. In many ways, it is not fair. But . . . the flat tax is a bad idea whose time should never come." [22]

The Treasury Department had earlier released a scathing repudiation of the economic projections contained in Rep. Armey's flat-tax proposal, the most detailed of all the flat-tax proposals that have been advanced. Re-introduced last July by Armey and Shelby as the Freedom and Fairness Restoration Act, it includes a flat 17 percent rate on wages, pension distributions and business income, with only the standard deductions for filers and their dependents.

"As was true of the original Armey proposal," Treasury concluded, "the new proposal would lose substantial revenues and would increase average tax burdens for families with incomes under $200,000 while cutting average tax burdens substantially for families with incomes of $200,000 or more." [23]

Democrats jumped into the tax-reform debate on Feb. 6, offering an alternative to the Republican flat-tax initiatives. In a speech at the George Washington University School of Business, Reich proposed tax breaks for corporations that invest in their workers' well-being, the aim being the creation of a "new era of corporate citizenship." In contrast to the Republican-dominated discussion of tax measures that critics say most clearly benefit the wealthy, Reich targeted his proposal to benefit rank-and-file American workers. He said their job security had been severely eroded in a recent wave of corporate downsizings and benefit cutbacks, even as corporate profits have soared.

"If we want companies to do things which do not necessarily improve the returns to shareholders but which are beneficial for the economy and society as a whole — such as upgrading the general skills of employees, providing them with decent pension and health-care protections, sharing more of the profits with them and, when laying them off, retraining them and placing them in new jobs — we have to give business an economic reason to do so," Reich said.

Although Clinton has not endorsed Reich's proposal, the Democratic leadership in Congress moved quickly to translate it into a legislative measure. On Feb. 28, a group led by Senate Minority Leader Tom Daschle, D-S.D., and Sen. Jeff Bingaman, D-N.M., introduced legislation specifying the actions companies must take to be considered eligible for the tax break. These include providing health-care and pension benefits, spending 2 percent of payroll on employee training and paying the highest-paid employee no more than 50 times the earnings of the lowest-paid employee. At the same time, the measure would incorporate a VAT into the corporate income tax to raise more revenue.

But two top administration officials, National Economic Council Chairman Laura D'Andrea Tyson and Treasury Secretary Robert E. Rubin, reportedly "object to the strident tone of Reich's rhetoric and his policy suggestions." According to *The Washington Post,* "Tyson and Rubin think the idea of offering tax breaks for 'good companies' is unworkable." [24]

The Kemp Commission

The January release of the Kemp Commission's recommendations kept the main focus of the tax-reform debate on some version of the flat tax. Although it offered few details, the commission endorsed a flat tax that would include deductions for individuals for investment income and mortgage interest payments and deductions for businesses for workers' payroll taxes and business investments in buildings and equipment. The commission also endorsed eliminating the estate tax on inherited wealth and requiring a two-thirds majority vote in Congress to increase the tax rate.

"We believe the current tax code cannot be revised, should not be reinvented and must not be retained," the 14-member panel declared. "Therefore, the commission is unanimous: It is time to throw out the 7-million-word mess of tax laws and regulations and begin anew." [25]

While the commission shied away from endorsing a specific plan, it offered what Kemp called "a road map" to overhauling the income tax code using a flat tax. "We believe with all our hearts," he said, "that if the rate were low and single, with full deductibility of the payroll tax and a large exemption for the poor and low-income Americans, it would create a doubling of the rate of growth of the U.S. economy."

However, the commission raised questions about the political viability of several key elements of most flat-tax proposals. And the commission warned about the risks of eliminating deductions, including those for mortgage interest and charitable deductions, even though some tax experts say it is necessary to eliminate all preferences to get the lowest possible flat-tax rate.

Democrats rejected the Kemp Commission's proposals, as well as the Forbes and Armey-Shelby plans. "They want to give even more huge tax breaks to the wealthy — blowing what some believe is a $300 billion hole in the budget — without telling us how they'd pay for it," Gephardt said at a news conference the same day the commission released its report. ■

OUTLOOK

Talk But No Action?

Republican lawmakers welcomed the Kemp Commission report, launching a series of hearings to examine most of the tax-reform proposals. "In the months ahead, the [Senate] Finance Committee will examine many reform proposals, from flat to VAT, and I mean many," Chairman Roth said at the first hearing, on Jan. 31. "To follow the media these days, it would appear that there is only one proposal — the flat tax. But that is only one of several that we will carefully explore." House Ways and Means Committee Chairman Bill Archer, R-Texas, also has launched a series of hearings on tax reform, including his own sales tax proposal.

Forbes' primary victories in Delaware and Arizona kept the spotlight on tax reform through February. But Dole's subsequent dominance of the Republican race has marked a potential shift in the political debate away from tax reform. Dole, who has all but nailed down the Republican nomination, has refrained from endorsing any plan to radically change the tax code, emphasizing instead the need to balance the budget.

But Rep. Armey insists the flat tax is far from dead, despite the lack of support from Dole. "The flat tax came out of this primary experience where exit polls show that 55 percent of the voters in the Republican Party want it on the platform against 35 percent that don't want it on the platform," he said March 17 on NBC-TV's "Meet the Press." "The fact of the matter is the flat tax has grown stronger the more the nation's heard about it."

Schaefer of Citizens for a Sound Economy agrees that the flat tax seems likely to remain the main focus of the ongoing debate over tax reform. "Dole can't hide behind the fact that he co-chaired the Kemp Commission," says Schaefer, who supports the Armey-Shelby plan. "The flat tax will stay in the national spotlight."

Even though Lugar withdrew from the race, Schaefer predicts that his national sales tax plan will be scrutinized more fully in coming months. "I hear a lot of questions about the sales tax from the grass roots," she says. "They want to know if they should be for it because it sounds good — and it is a lot better than the current system."

But Congress' scrutiny of various tax-reform proposals is not likely to translate into action before the presidential election. At most, some modest changes in existing law, such as a reduction in the capital gains tax, may emerge in a budget agreement — if such an agreement can be reached at all amid the current standoff between Congress and the White House.

Clinton's fiscal 1997 budget plan, introduced March 19, gave little hope for an early agreement with lawmakers. For the most part, the plan merely provides details of proposals that Clinton has previously made and Republican leaders have rejected. The new plan would balance the budget by 2002, cut taxes for middle-income earners and close loopholes. Instead of reducing capital gains taxes as Republicans want, the president would tighten the rules in ways that would raise some taxes on profits from stock sales.

But in 1997, tax reform seems likely to emerge as a priority, no matter who wins the November election. Even lukewarm advocates of a radical overhaul, like Dole, predict that taxes will top the national agenda next year. "There is no doubt that tax reform will be one of the major priorities of the next Congress and the next president," he said in releasing the Kemp Commission's recommendations. "My hope is that the principles in this report . . . will form the basis for future congressional hearings

Continued on p. 258

Scott J. Ferrell/CQ Weekly Report

Chairman Jack Kemp of the National Commission on Economic Growth and Tax Reform tosses tax forms into a trash can Jan. 17 after releasing the commission's recommendation to replace the tax system with a flat tax. Senate Majority Leader Bob Dole and House Speaker Newt Gingrich, behind Kemp, established the 14-member panel last May.

At Issue:

Should the U.S. replace the income tax system with a national sales tax?

yes

SEN. RICHARD G. LUGAR, R-IND.
FROM STATEMENT IN RESPONSE TO KEMP COMMISSION RECOMMENDATIONS, JAN. 17, 1996.

Economists agree on few things, but the vast majority agree that we will not grow if we do not save more and invest more. The savings rate in the United States is the lowest of any major industrialized nation. A large share of the blame for this condition rests with our income tax system, which penalizes savings and entrepreneurship.

Tinkering with the income tax system is not the answer. Last year's reforms are reversed the following year. This year's complexity is made more complex next year. All the while, no significant improvement is achieved in the U.S. savings rate, and Americans struggle on with a needlessly complex and intrusive system.

Only replacing the income tax will bring dramatic improvement. Replacing the income tax with a national sales tax would cause savings and investment to skyrocket. The result would be strong sustained growth.

A national sales tax (NST) on goods and services would replace the federal personal and corporate income taxes. The capital gains tax and the estate tax would be eliminated as well.

Economists who have studied the national sales tax estimate that an NST rate of about 17 percent would replace the revenue generated by our current income tax system. The rate would be somewhat higher or lower depending on exemptions, although exemptions should be minimized. . . .

The national sales tax would allow for the dismantling of the current IRS and the intrusive, inefficient and costly enforcement of the current tax code. Estimates of uncollected income tax range as high as $150 billion per year.

Businesses and individuals devote billions of man-hours each year to comply with the tax code. Under an NST, that time could be spent more productively on other activities.

The simplicity of the NST and the absence of an IRS would have the effect of discouraging frequent tinkering with the tax code, which complicates business activities, leads to loopholes for special interests and creates uncertainties for many Americans. Thirty-one major tax reforms have been enacted in the last 41 years. . . .

Although a flat tax would be a step in the right direction, an NST is preferable because the flat tax would retain many of the complexities of the current income tax system. The IRS income tax collection apparatus would continue to exist. Furthermore, the flat tax retains the corporate tax and the complexities involved in its calculation. Also, tinkering with the flat tax would be a constant temptation. Many would seek to amend the tax code to promote special interests or social agendas. The history of revisions to the 1986 Tax Reform Act demonstrates that the government will always be tempted to amend the income tax code.

no

REP. DICK ARMEY, R-TEXAS
FROM THE HERITAGE FOUNDATION'S *POLICY REVIEW*, SUMMER 1995.

The case for a sales tax begins with one highly appealing applause line. It will allow us, supporters argue, to eliminate the income tax altogether. . . . Even if that goal were politically feasible — and I don't think it is — the exchange would come at a high price. We would give up the income tax for a more intrusive and pervasive tax system.

The reason is simple. If the government sets out to collect a new tax at the cash register, it will soon have no choice but to extend that tax beyond the retailer to every level of production, as it desperately tries to stop inevitable and massive tax evasion. Any sales tax will become a complex, pervasive, multi-rate, value-added tax. . . .

A national sales tax may well exempt many basic necessities from tax — beginning with food and clothing. This would lead to bitter disputes over the difference between food and candy, between real clothes and costume accessories. . . .

Worse, the federal sales tax and the dozens of different state sales taxes — aside from having different tax rates — would likely exempt different items. That means a small businessperson would need to look up the correct state sales-tax rate, apply the federal rate, subtract only the federal rate from items federal-only exempted. Then he would need to do separate calculations for each of the states in which he does business. . . . The likely consequence would be a slowdown in business activity — and a loss of jobs and dropping wages for millions of American workers.

Some sales-tax advocates argue that the sales tax would allow us to eliminate the IRS together. . . . The states, they say, could collect the new federal sales tax through their existing sales-tax systems. . . .

One immediate problem, however, is that five states do not have a sales tax and would not take kindly to enforcing one for Washington. Even those that do would consider the costs of collecting a huge federal sales tax (the main source of federal revenue) an unbearable federal mandate. . . .

But the point is purely academic. For reasons dating back to the unhappy years of the Articles of Confederation, the federal government will never rely on state governments for its prime source of revenue. It will not happen. . . .

We must not lose sight of the commendable motives behind the sales tax. Its supporters want a tax code that does not interfere with economic decision-making, minimizes the paperwork burdens on the taxpayers, limits the size of the federal government, avoids excessive taxes on savings and investment and is straightforward and fair. For all the above reasons, however, the sales tax is not likely to achieve those goals. The flat tax, however, will do so.

FOR MORE INFORMATION

Citizens for a Sound Economy, 1250 H St. N.W., Suite 700, Washington, D.C. 20005; (202) 783-3870. This grass-roots organization supports the flat tax as part of its quest for lower taxes and fewer regulations.

Citizens for Tax Justice, 1311 L St. N.W., Suite 400, Washington, D.C. 20005; (202) 626-3780. This group supports progressive taxation and opposes the flat tax as beneficial primarily to the wealthy.

Tax Foundation, 1250 H St. N.W., Suite 750, Washington, D.C. 20005; (202) 783-2760. This research organization is studying the fiscal impact of the various tax-reform proposals now under consideration.

Office of Tax Analysis, Department of the Treasury, 1500 Pennsylvania Ave. N.W., Washington, D.C. 20020; (202) 622-2920. Treasury's tax analysts say the flat tax would hurt middle-income Americans.

Continued from p. 256

and debate, and ultimately for tax-reform legislation."

Given earlier efforts, however, radical plans to alter the tax code will run into stiff opposition from interest groups that stand to lose valuable preferences. For this reason, few analysts expect any of the plans now on the table to become law without considerable modification.

"There's a big desire to move away from the income tax and toward the flat tax," says Gale of the Brookings Institution. "But ripping out the code and starting over may be too radical a solution. I think ultimately what they'll do is take the existing system, with all the built-in knowledge that we have about it, and try to move it in the direction of the flat tax, without necessarily going all the way." ■

Notes

[1] See James Flanigan, "Let's Be Careful What We Wish for in Tax Changes," *Los Angeles Times* (Washington edition), Jan. 29, 1996.

[2] Both were quoted in "The Flat Tax: 'Nutty' It's Not," *The Wall Street Journal,* Feb. 22, 1996.

[3] See the National Commission on Economic Growth and Tax Reform, *Unleashing America's Potential: A Pro-Growth, Pro-Family Tax System for the 21st Century,* January 1996.

[4] The New Hampshire and Iowa polls were conducted by Voter News Service of New York, an association of ABC News, The Associated Press, CBS News, CNN and NBC News.

[5] See Dan Goodgame, "Is This Tax Flat Unfair?" *Time,* Jan. 29, 1996, p. 30.

[6] The Commerce Department reported Feb. 23 that U.S. economic growth plummeted in 1995 to 1.4 percent, down from 3.4 percent in 1994.

[7] Reich laid out his proposal in a Feb. 6 speech at the George Washington University School of Business.

[8] Sheldon S. Cohen, "Taming the Tax Code," *The Washington Post,* Aug. 27, 1995.

[9] Quoted in *The Wall Street Journal, op. cit.*

[10] Summers addressed the New York Bar Association on Jan. 23, 1996.

[11] See Congressional Budget Office, *Reducing the Deficit: Spending and Revenue Options,* February 1995.

[12] See Roger E. Brinner, Mark Lasky and David Wyss, *Residential Real Estate Impacts of Flat Tax Legislation,* DRI/McGraw-Hill, May 1995, and David Wyss and Cynthia Latta, *The Impact of the Flat Tax on Mortgage Foreclosures and Losses,* DRI/McGraw-Hill, January 1996.

[13] Statement released Jan. 17, 1996.

[14] For background, see "Underground Economy," *The CQ Researcher,* March 4, 1994, pp. 193-216.

[15] William G. Gale, "Building a Better Tax System," *The Brookings Review,* fall 1995, p. 20.

[16] From a Feb. 15, 1996, press release distributed by Schaefer and Tauzin.

[17] From a Dec. 14, 1962, speech before the Economic Club of New York. Quoted by Jack Kemp in *Unleashing America's Potential, op. cit.,* p. 3.

[18] See Jeffrey H. Birnbaum and Alan S. Murray, *Showdown at Gucci Gulch* (1987), p. 14.

[19] "The Flat Tax: Why Not?" *The Wall Street Journal,* Jan. 30, 1996.

[20] See Ann Devroy and Eric Pianin, "GOP Weighs in on Ounce of Prevention," *The Washington Post,* March 14, 1996.

[21] For background, see Congressional Budget Office, "Indexing Capital Gains," August 1990.

[22] Summers addressed the New York Bar Association Jan. 23, 1996.

[23] Department of the Treasury, Office of Tax Analysis, *An Analysis of the New Armey-Shelby Flat Tax Proposal,* Dec, 20, 1995, p. 1.

[24] "Reich's 'Responsibility' Issue Irritates Colleagues," *The Washington Post,* March 8, 1996, p. F1.

[25] National Commission on Economic Growth and Tax Reform, *op. cit.,* p. 7.

Bibliography

Selected Sources Used

Books

Birnbaum, Jeffrey H., and Alan S. Murray, *Showdown at Gucci Gulch: Lawmakers, Lobbyists, and the Unlikely Triumph of Tax Reform*, Random House, 1987.
Two *Wall Street Journal* reporters recount the political maneuvering that led to passage of the 1986 Tax Reform Act, the most sweeping overhaul of the income tax.

Boskin, Michael J., ed., *Frontiers of Tax Reform*, Hoover Institution Press, 1966.
Tax experts review most of the tax-reform proposals now under consideration, including the flat tax, value-added tax (VAT), retail sales tax and other versions of the consumption tax.

Articles

Alterman, Eric, "Deflating the Flat Tax," *The Nation*, Jan. 22, 1996, pp. 5-7.
This editorial calls the flat tax "a hoax" that would enable rich CEOs to get away with paying no taxes at all by claiming all their earnings in the form of stock options, which would not be taxed under the flat tax.

Ebrahim, M., and A. Benes, "A Flat-Tax Future?" *The Public Interest*, December 1995, pp. 1+.
This article, appearing in a newsletter published by the Center for Public Integrity, a nonpartisan research organization, warns of the potential inequities posed by a flat tax that exempts investment income. Low- to middle-income wage earners, the authors write, may end up paying more in taxes than multimillionaire investors.

Gale, William G., "Building a Better Tax System: Can a Consumption Tax Deliver the Goods?" *The Brookings Review*, fall 1995, pp. 18-23.
The author, a tax analyst at the Brookings Institution, examines the main tax-reform proposals and concludes that they may be fairer, simpler and more efficient than the current system. But he warns of the risks inherent in replacing the income tax with any of these untested alternatives.

Lacayo, Richard, "Tax Cuts: Who Will Get the Breaks?" *Time*, Jan. 8, 1996, pp. 30-34.
The long-stalled budget negotiations between Congress and the White House include several tax changes, chiefly a $500-per-child credit for families, a cut in the capital-gains tax and several breaks for certain industries.

Reports and Studies

Department of the Treasury, Office of Tax Analysis, *An Analysis of the New Armey-Shelby Flat Tax Proposal*, Dec. 20, 1995.
The Treasury Department concludes that the Armey-Shelby flat tax would increase the tax burden for families with incomes under $200,000 while benefiting those with higher incomes. It also estimates that the change would cause a $138 billion shortfall in annual tax revenues at 1996 income levels.

Joint Economic Committee, *The Flat Tax: Vital for America's Future*, July 1995.
Chaired by Sen. Connie Mack, R-Fla., the committee calls for adoption of the flat tax, modeled after the original version described by Stanford University economists Robert Hall and Alvin Rabushka.

National Commission on Economic Growth and Tax Reform, *Unleashing America's Potential*, January 1996.
The 14-member commission, chaired by Jack Kemp, a former Housing and Urban Development secretary and Republican congressman from New York, recommends replacing the current income tax with a single-rate flat tax with few deductions and no tax on investment income. Although the study includes few details, Kemp has recommended a rate of 19 percent.

Schaefer, Rebecca S., "How the Flat Tax Ends Double Taxation," *Issue Analysis*, Citizens for a Sound Economy Foundation, Feb. 12, 1996.
The current system taxes business income twice, writes Schaefer — once as business income and again as investment income. By ending this double taxation, she claims, the flat tax would boost personal income and encourage investment.

Stephen Moore, *The Economic and Civil Liberties Case for a National Sales Tax*, Hoover Institution, May 11, 1995.
Moore, an economist with the CATO Institute, supports replacing the income tax with a national sales levied only on consumption, arguing that "it would no longer be the government's business how much money a person makes."

The Next Step

Additional information from UMI's Newspaper & Periodical Abstracts database

Charitable Contributions

"Flat tax imperils nonprofits' services," ***Denver Post,*** **Jan. 22, 1996, p. B7.**

An editorial discusses the proposed flat tax endorsed by GOP presidential hopeful Steve Forbes and says the proposal carries a provision that taxpayers would no long be able to write off charitable contributions at a time when charities are expected to help shoulder the burden of caring for the poor.

Hazard, Anne, "Charities prepare for threat to gifts," ***The New York Times,*** **Sept. 17, 1995, p. WC1.**

The preparations many Westchester County, N.Y., charities are making to deal with a possible congressional repeal of the tax deduction for charitable contributions are discussed. If the deduction was ended, the decline in contributions to charities could be substantial.

Lynch, Michael F., "Charitable contributions," ***Journal of Accountancy,*** **November 1995, p. 32.**

A taxpayer who receives membership benefits in return for payment to a qualifying organization may not claim a charitable deduction for more than the excess of the contribution over fair market value of the membership benefits. However, the IRS has just released proposed regulations that allow taxpayers and donee organizations to disregard certain membership benefits.

Newberry, Jon, "Making family gifts, donations pay," ***ABA Journal,*** **December 1995, p. 7.**

Making charitable deductions through a qualified investment fund or foundation gives donors many opportunities that they would not have otherwise. Newberry also discusses the benefits of making tax-free gifts to children or grandchildren.

Purdum, Todd S., "Clintons earn less but donate more," ***The New York Times,*** **April 15, 1995, p. A8.**

President Clinton and his wife, Hillary, claimed $30,125 in charitable contributions, or 11 percent of their adjusted gross income of $263,900, with most of it, their aides said, given to churches they attend. By contrast, Vice President Al Gore and his wife, Tipper, claimed no itemized deductions on their adjusted gross income of $411,713. The reason, an aide said, was that all the itemized deductions, including charitable contributions, amounted to less than the $6,350 standard deduction available.

Rowland, Mary, "When charity outgrows the home," ***The New York Times,*** **Feb. 5, 1995, p. 15.**

The tax regulations governing charitable contributions are examined. Gifts to individuals are never eligible for tax deductions as charitable contributions, nor are time, services or material donated to individuals. To provide a charitable tax deduction, the money must be donated to an organization recognized as a charity under 501(c)(3) of the revenue code.

Flat Tax

"An 'untested' flat tax?" ***The Wall Street Journal,*** **Feb. 9, 1996, p. A14.**

An editorial disagrees that presidential candidate Steve Forbes' flat-tax proposal is an "untested idea." The editorial points to Hong Kong as an example of a "virtual flat-tax system" that has been the "single biggest factor in the colony's record as the world's most consistently expanding economy for more than three decades."

Andress, Lauri, "Flat tax a feel-good, quick fix that would solve nothing," ***Houston Chronicle,*** **Feb. 4, 1996, p. C4.**

Lauri Andress discusses the flat tax proposal, saying that it is ultimately not fair, perpetuates a new, unvirtuous need for quick fixes and will not contribute to addressing the real concerns that people in the U.S. have.

Brinkley, David, "The long road to tax reform," ***The Wall Street Journal,*** **Sept. 18, 1995, p. A18.**

Brinkley says that after he has consulted, read or talked with one Washington tax authority after another, he has found only one idea for tax reform that comes anywhere close to genuinely wide acceptance by the taxpayers, and that is the flat tax, which imposes the same rate to all regardless of personal wealth or lack of it.

Calmes, Jackie, "Administration advisers say flat tax isn't the solution to a better system," ***The Wall Street Journal,*** **Feb. 15, 1996, A30.**

The Council of Economic Advisers, in its own annual economic report issued on Feb. 14, 1996, went beyond President Clinton's own recent criticisms of a flat tax, saying that such a plan could open up an "enormous potential loophole" for some businesses and would devalue housing, tax-exempt bonds and existing business plants and equipment.

Dowd, Ann Reilly, "Why a true flat tax could flatten you," ***Money,*** **January 1996, pp. 84-85.**

Middle-class taxpayers could face a 10 percent tax hike, plus the loss of some very popular shelters, if a flat-tax proposal is accepted in Congress. Presidential candidate Steve Forbes would win big under his own 17 percent flat-tax plan.

Eisner, Robert, "Talk of flat-tax plans overlooks bur-

dens placed on consumers," ***The Los Angeles Times,*** **Feb. 4, 1996, p. D2.**
Robert Eisner criticizes proposals for a flat tax, saying it would result in a tax decrease for those in the highest income levels and an increase for others, and since it would raise taxes on businesses, it would ultimately hurt consumers.

Friedman, Milton, "A 1962 flat-tax proposal revisited," ***The Wall Street Journal,*** **Feb. 9, 1996, p. A 14.**
Milton Friedman presents his revised proposal for a flat tax, which appeared in his 1962 book *Capitalism and Freedom*.

"Good, better, best in tax reform," ***Chicago Tribune,*** **Jan. 21, 1996, p. 18.**
An editorial briefly examines the flat-tax proposal by the so-called Kemp Commission, saying its general principles are fine but could have vastly different interpretations, and suggests that Sen. Bob Dole's, R-Kan., desire for merely a "flatter, simpler" tax system is probably best.

Lambro, Donald, "Flat tax would benefit America's middle class," ***Atlanta Journal,*** **Feb. 20, 1996, p.A8.**
Donald Lambro supports the flat rate income tax reform promoted by Republican presidential candidate Steve Forbes, adding that rather than attacking the proposal the other GOP candidates should be promoting it.

Ornstein, Norman, "Flat tax: Two hidden pitfalls," ***USA Today,*** **Feb. 19, 1996, p. A11.**
Norman Ornstein takes a look at the substantive and philosophical problems posed by a flat tax, specifically in the areas of federalism and social policy.

Pepper, Jon, "Former Fed governor likes flat tax's incentives, simplicity," ***Detroit News,*** **Feb. 1, 1996, p. B3.**
Jon Pepper interviews former Federal Reserve Board governor Martha Seger of Birmingham, Mich., regarding her views on the flat tax and the prospect for further declines in mortgage rates in 1996.

"Tax reform that's flat-out wrong," ***St. Louis Post-Dispatch,*** **July 14, 1995, p. B6.**
An editorial comments on the flat-tax proposals, opining that this type of tax is unfair and will not work in the U.S.

"The flat tax: 'Nutty' it's not," ***The Wall Street Journal,*** **Feb. 22, 1996, p. A14.**
Twelve notable economists respond to presidential candidate Steve Forbes' proposed flat tax, which has been characterized as "nutty."

Vedder, Richard, "On tax reform, learn from the states," ***The Wall Street Journal,*** **Nov. 14, 1995, p. A14.**
Vedder notes the favorable economic consequences experienced by states that have lowered their overall tax burden, asserting that the same advantages could be reaped by the federal government through a national flat tax.

Willette, Anne, and Beth Belton, "GOP advances argument for tax reform," ***USA Today,*** **Jan. 18, 1996, p. B1.**
With tax reform looming as a key issue among GOP presidential candidates, support for a flat tax is building. Ramifications of a flat tax on the corporate and personal financial landscapes are considered.

Mortgage Interest Deduction

Byars, Carlos, "Politicians pitch tax reform plans to home builders," ***Houston Chronicle,*** **Jan. 28, 1996, p. A2.**
A group of about 1,000 board members of the National Association of Home Builders heard pitches for tax reform from Sen. Arlen Specter, R-Pa., and Rep. Bill Archer, R-Texas. Specter has introduced a bill that calls for a flat tax of 20 percent and limited deductions for interest on home mortgages.

Curran, Karen, "Facing the flat tax," ***Boston Globe,*** **Feb. 18, 1996, p. A1.**
The National Association of Realtors released a study projecting that enactment of a flat tax would lop 15 percent off home values within two years, due largely to the elimination of the home mortgage interest deduction.

"Flattened taxpayers," ***USA Today,*** **Jan. 17, 1996, p. A10.**
An editorial explains that a real flat tax means abolishment of the home mortgage interest deduction, a staple of the middle class, resulting in upscale housing values dropping, as well as voiding business' stored-up tax benefits and eliminating deductions for charitable contributions.

Georges, Christopher, "Gingrich characterizes as nonsense parts of Forbes's flat-tax proposal," ***The Wall Street Journal,*** **Feb. 9, 1996, p. A16.**
House Speaker Newt Gingrich attacked Republican presidential candidate Steve Forbes' flat-tax proposal, calling parts of it "nonsense." Gingrich said he objected in particular to a provision that would eliminate taxes on interest income while continuing to tax earned income, as well as the elimination of mortgage interest and charitable giving deductions.

Haggerty, Maryann, "A battle over mortgage interest deduction," ***The Washington Post,*** **Feb. 17, 1996, p. E1.**
Builders, real estate agents and others are gearing up to protect the mortgage interest deduction from flat-tax reformers in the 1996 presidential election year.

Harper, Lucinda, "Gephardt outlines tax-reform plan cutting deductibles," ***The Wall Street Journal,*** **July 7, 1995, p. A2.**
Minority Leader Richard A. Gephardt, D-Mo., outlined a

House Democratic tax-reform proposal that would slash corporate write-offs, cut taxes for small businesses and set a 10 percent rate for most Americans, with nothing deductible but the mortgage interest payment.

Kass, Benny L., "Ending mortgage interest deduction poses a nightmare for homeownership dreams," *The Washington Post,* March 11, 1995, p. E4.
In the last of a series of articles on taxation and home ownership, Benny L. Kass discusses the deductions for mortgage interest and real estate tax payments and the fact that Congress may cut the maximum loan size for which interest could be deducted.

Klott, Gary, "Mortgage interest deduction remains unscathed," *Atlanta Constitution,* Feb. 27, 1995, p. E8.
It is good news for homeowners who just purchased a home that Congress tiptoed around deductions for mortgage interest and property taxes that have made homeownership such a treasured tax shelter. However, some who refinanced their mortgages will face a larger tax bill because there's less to write off.

"The mortgage interest deduction," *The Washington Post,* Feb. 24, 1996, p. A14.
An editorial comments on the flat-tax proposal that would eliminate the mortgage interest deduction.

Ratner, Juliana, "Targeting of mortgage interest deduction raises realtors' ire," *American Banker,* March 17, 1995, p. 10.
The National Association of Realtors is speaking out against the possible elimination of the mortgage interest tax deduction by Congress, which is seeking the elimination to recover lost revenue if the capital gains tax is reduced. Where the group once saw an ally, it is now loudly leery of the Republican-led Congress.

Sherman, Mark, "Flat tax finds favor in Georgia," *Atlanta Constitution,* Feb. 12, 1996, p. A1.
Nearly half of Georgia voters favor replacing the federal income tax with a flat tax, even if it means eliminating the home-mortgage interest deduction, according to a Georgia State University poll. Other poll findings are discussed.

National Sales Tax

Feldstein, Martin, and Kathleen Feldstein, "Building blocks of tax reform," *Boston Globe,* July 25, 1995, p. 36.
Martin and Kathleen Feldstein comment on the alternative plans emerging in the tax-reform debate.

Johnston, David Cay, "A Fed governor sees danger in shift to a national sales tax," *The New York Times,* Sept. 7, 1995, p. D2.
Lawrence B. Lindsey, an FRB governor, said on Sept. 6, 1996, that switching from the income tax to a national sales or value-added tax would probably plunge the economy into a steep recession. The comment was a setback to the retail sales tax championed by Sen. Richard G. Lugar, R-Ind..

Wartzman, Rick, and Jeffery H. Birnbaum, "Value-added tax is mulled in White House," *The Wall Street Journal,* Feb. 22, 1993, p. A2.
Although the prospect of a national sales tax was once considered political suicide, President Clinton and his top aides are mulling over the concept. The White House said the likelihood of such a tax being introduced anytime soon is remote; however, a value-added tax could be a possibility in the future.

Tax Reform

Barlow, Jim, "Tax reform may be catching on," *Houston Chronicle,* April 16, 1995, p. E1.
Jim Barlow comments on proposals to reform the U.S. tax system.

Epstein, Gene, "Economic beat: Congress is dancing the tax-reform tango; What two proposals might mean for investors," *Barron's,* Dec. 25, 1995, p. 35.
Epstein examines the different effects that two tax-reform proposals before Congress in late 1995 would have on investors. Epstein describes how the plan by Rep. Dick Armey, R-Texas, and Sen. Richard C. Shelby, R-Ala., to replace the current tax code with a flat tax would exempt interest, dividends and capital gains from taxation, while a proposal by Sen. Sam Nunn, D-Ga., and Sen. Pete Domenici, R-N.M., would transform the income tax into a consumption levy, and would also allow savings to be deducted from income.

Gephardt, Richard A., "Any tax reform has to pass the fairness test, too," *Houston Chronicle,* July 14, 1995, p. A31.
Rep. Richard A. Gephardt, D-Mo., offers an explanation of a tax plan he introduced in the House during the week of July 3, 1995. Gephardt says that under his plan "while everyone would lose small deductions, everyone would gain much more from a less complex and, for most, less expensive income tax."

Harney, Kenneth R., "Congress tries to speed along tax reform package for homeowners," *The Washington Post,* Feb. 10, 1996, p. F1.
Harney comments that a package of tax reforms designed to help homeowners is alive, if not completely well, in Congress.

Lambro, Donald, "Republicans can recapture the presidency if they push Jack Kemp's tax reform plan," *Atlanta Journal,* Jan. 22, 1996, p. A11.

Lambro praises the tax-reform plan proposed by Jack Kemp, which offers a single, low rate and a generous personal exemption, including a deduction of Social Security payroll taxes from taxable income, and adds that Republicans have a good chance of recapturing the presidency if they push the plan.

Petruno, Tom, "Tax reform noise begins to pressure muni bond yields," *The Los Angeles Times,* May 3, 1995, p. D3.
Tom Petruno says the threat of federal tax reform is beginning to worry some municipal bond investors. Petruno examines what tax reform would do to the municipal bond industry.

"Put tax reform at top of presidential agenda," *Atlanta Journal,* Sept. 27, 1995, p. A10.
An editorial opines that tax reform should top the leading 1996 presidential candidates' agendas.

Royko, Mike, "First tax reform also would clean up cultural pollution," *Chicago Tribune,* Jan. 23, 1996, p. 3.
Royko's proposal for tax reform includes the economic philosophy that all tax rates should be tied directly to whether an individual is a real pain in the butt to society or a reasonably useful creature.

Secter, Bob, "Tax reform falling flat in Senate race," *Chicago Tribune,* Jan. 31, 1996, p. C2.
Tax reform may dominate the next Congress. But of the major rivals for the seat being vacated by Sen. Paul Simon, D-Ill., only state Rep. Al Salvi embraces the notion of a one-size-fits-all tax rate.

Snow, Tony, "Tax reform: Tomorrow never comes," *Detroit News,* June 12, 1995, p. A9.
Tony Snow advocates tax reform which, along with regulation reform, would give the economy a much needed jolt and prove that the GOP has more than slashing on its mind.

"Tax reform should be major campaign issue," *Atlanta Journal,* Jan. 17, 1996, p. A10.
An editorial discusses the need for tax reform and says all the major candidates in the 1996 presidential race should state where they stand on tax reform and have a healthy debate on replacing the current code with a tax system that makes sense.

Wessel, David, "Rubin questions the economic impact of capital-gains tax cut, tax reform," *The Wall Street Journal,* March 3, 1995, p. A2.
Treasury Secretary Robert Rubin said that he doubts the economic efficiency of cutting the tax on capital gains or refashioning the U.S. tax code to encourage savings.

Wessel, David, "The outlook: Clinton faces pressure on tax-reform issue," *The Wall Street Journal,* Aug. 28, 1995, p. A1.
Pressure is mounting on President Clinton to do more than criticize Republican tax proposals by coming up with an initiative of his own. One option the administration is examining is to streamline the current income tax so that most people don't have to fill out a federal tax form.

Value-Added Tax

Chandler, Clay, "Clinton may jump into tax reform fray," *The Washington Post,* Aug. 2, 1995, p. F1.
President Clinton has been paying close attention to a plan by Rep. Sam M. Gibbons concerning a value-added tax.

Freedman, Eric, "State's value-added tax 'mixed blessing'," *Detroit News,* April 22, 1993, p. B3.
Patrick Anderson of the Mackinac Center for Public Policy says the Clinton administration should learn a lesson from Michigan and drop the idea of a federal VAT to pay for a national health insurance program. Michigan's version of VAT, the single business tax, has been hard for businesses to understand.

Freese, Duane, "Value-Added Tax," *USA Today,* Oct. 22, 1992, A15.
The value-added tax, similar to a sales tax, is explained, and how it affects differing incomes is shown.

Ratajczak, Donald, "Let's take a bold step: Use a value-added tax to replace corporate levy," *Atlanta Journal Constitution,* May 9, 1993, p. F7.
Ratajczak suggests that the VAT be used to eliminate the corporate income tax, which he says would reduce the distortions that U.S. tax codes create.

Thurow, Lester C., "Answer: A value-added tax," *The New York Times,* June 8, 1993, p. A25.
Thurow says that although no interest group wants taxes, most would go along with the value-added tax as the most equitable form of taxation.

"Value-added tax rises to 20.6 percent in France," *The New York Times,* Aug. 3, 1995, p. D7.
The value-added tax on nearly everything except food rose in France the week of July 30, 1995, giving consumers one of the highest sales taxes in Europe. The increase in the value-added tax, to 20.6 percent from 18.6 percent, will be used to finance President Jacques Chirac's anti-unemployment drive.

Weidenbaum, Murray, "Value-added tax has too many demerits," *St. Louis Post-Dispatch,* May 2, 1993, p. B3.
Weidenbaum contends that the value-added tax proposed by some lawmakers would be inflationary, regressive and burdensome.

Back Issues

Great Research on Current Issues Starts Right Here...Recent topics covered by The CQ Researcher are listed below. Before May 1991, reports were published under the name of Editorial Research Reports.

SEPTEMBER 1994
Home Schooling
Welfare Experiments
Courts and the Media
Regulating Tobacco

OCTOBER 1994
Historic Preservation
Religion and Politics
Arts Funding
Economic Sanctions

NOVEMBER 1994
Sex on Campus
Blood Supply Safety
Testing Term Limits
Religion in America

DECEMBER 1994
Farm Policy
Arms Sales
Earthquake Research
The Future of Television

JANUARY 1995
Treating Addiction
Child Custody and Support
Parents and Schools
Non-Proliferation Treaty at 25

Back issues are available for $5.00 (subscribers) or $8.00 (non-subscribers). Quantity discounts apply to orders over ten. To order, call Congressional Quarterly Customer Service at (202) 887-8621.

Binders are available for $18.00. To order call 1-800-638-1710. Please refer to stock number 648.

FEBRUARY 1995
Cracking Down on Immigration
The Business of Sports
Reinventing Government
Housing Discrimination

MARCH 1995
Death Penalty Debate
Primary Care
Democracy in Africa
Environmental Movement at 25

APRIL 1995
Abortion Clinic Protests
Dieting and Health
Combating AIDS
Rethinking Affirmative Action

MAY 1995
Assisted Suicide Controversy
Overhauling Social Security
Learning to Read
Mandatory Sentencing

JUNE 1995
Combating Infectious Disease
Property Rights
Repetitive Stress Injuries
Regulating the Internet

JULY 1995
War Crimes
Highway Safety
Combating Terrorism
Preventing Teen Drug Use

AUGUST 1995
Job Stress
Organ Transplants
United Nations at 50
Advances in Cancer Research

SEPTEMBER 1995
Catholic Church in the U.S.
Northern Ireland Cease-Fire
High School Sports
Teaching History

OCTOBER 1995
Quebec's Future
Revitalizing the Cities
Networking the Classroom
Indoor Air Pollution

NOVEMBER 1995
The Working Poor
The Jury System
Sex, Violence and the Media
Police Misconduct

DECEMBER 1995
Teens and Tobacco
Gene Therapy's Future
Global Water Shortages
Third-Party Prospects

JANUARY 1996
Emergency Medicine
Punishing Sex Offenders
Bilingual Education
Helping the Homeless

FEBRUARY 1996
Reforming the CIA
Campaign Finance Reform
Academic Politics
College Admissions

MARCH 1996
The British Monarchy
Preventing Juvenile Crime

Future Topics

- ***Pursuing the Paranormal***
- ***Centennial Olympic Games***
- ***Managed Care***

THE CQ Researcher

PUBLISHED BY CONGRESSIONAL QUARTERLY INC.

Pursuing the Paranormal

What's behind the new interest in the unexplained?

In this supposed age of reason, public officials and scientists find themselves facing a new wave of interest in unexplained phenomena. UFO sightings, testimony about alien abductions and government agencies that dabble in telepathy have produced a steady stream of headlines. Moreover, decades-old rumors about the coverup of a 1947 flying saucer crash in New Mexico have regained currency with the release of two new government reports. And tabloid newspapers, movies and television shows are attracting record audiences with paranormal claims that often blur the line between fact and fiction. A counterattack has been organized by skeptics and debunkers. They worry that credulous people are losing respect for science, and that the rising interest in UFOs coincides with high levels of mistrust in government.

INSIDE THIS ISSUE

CQ March 29, 1996 • Volume 6, No. 12 • Pages 265-288

Formerly Editorial Research Reports

PURSUING THE PARANORMAL

COVER: BARBARA SASSA-DANIELS

THE *CQ Researcher*

March 29, 1996
Volume 6, No. 12

EDITOR
Sandra Stencel

MANAGING EDITOR
Thomas J. Colin

ASSOCIATE EDITORS
Sarah M. Magner
Richard L. Worsnop

STAFF WRITERS
Charles S. Clark
Mary H. Cooper
Craig Donegan
Kenneth Jost

EDITORIAL ASSISTANT
Tonya Harris

PUBLISHED BY
Congressional Quarterly Inc.

CHAIRMAN
Andrew Barnes

VICE CHAIRMAN
Andrew P. Corty

EDITOR AND PUBLISHER
Neil Skene

EXECUTIVE EDITOR
Robert W. Merry

ASSOCIATE PUBLISHER
Edward S. Hauck

The CQ Researcher (ISSN 1056-2036). Formerly Editorial Research Reports. Published weekly (48 times per year, not printed March 1, May 31, Aug. 30, Nov. 29) by Congressional Quarterly Inc., 1414 22nd St., N.W., Washington, D.C. 20037. Annual subscription rate for libraries, businesses and government is $319. Additional rates furnished upon request. Second-class postage paid at Washington, D.C. POSTMASTER: Send address changes to The CQ Researcher, 1414 22nd St., N.W., Washington, D.C. 20037.

Pursuing the Paranormal

By Charles S. Clark

The Issues

Forty years after seeing his first UFO, Ray Stanford still gets goosebumps telling the story: On the night of Oct. 21, 1956, he and three other teenagers in his flying saucer club were out in the salt flats near Brownsville, Texas. Suddenly, a few hundred yards away, they saw an "oblate spheroid" about 40 feet in diameter, glowing with a pulsing, electric-blue light that lit the ground.

The strange craft swooped closer — neither casting a shadow nor reflecting moonlight — and emitted an eerie hum that terrified coyotes and waterfowl. An electrostatic charge made the boys' hair stand on end; they were unable to move. The saucer landed. Then, after a few minutes, it shot straight up into the stratosphere, leaving a column of charged air and some crushed vegetation.

The experience altered Stanford's life. As an award-winning high school science student, he had been offered a scholarship to study rocket engineering at the University of Texas. Instead, he took an adult-education course in advanced physics and launched a life-long search for alien propulsion techniques far more efficient than rockets.

Stanford eventually founded Project Starlight International, with funding from friends and a nonprofit corporation. In its heyday in Austin in the 1970s, Starlight boasted a staff of five, including engineers and physicists who took measurements of questionable phenomena using special instruments. Their hope was to blow the scientific world wide open by proving the existence of extraterrestrial spacecraft.

"The UFO research establishment hates me because I did what they should have done," Stanford says. "They focused on tales told in the night. But I don't care how much credibility you have, human perception cannot do the job that electronic and optical equipment can do."

Today, Project Starlight has fallen on hard times. It now consists of Stanford alone and a few pieces of equipment in a spare bedroom in his modest house in College Park, Md. When he gets a chance, Stanford makes recordings of the piercing sound of magnetic waves he says are from UFOs — potential proof, he says, that aliens have mastered a unified theory of gravitational and magnetic waves that has eluded human thinkers since Einstein.

Stanford's work is familiar to Philip J. Klass, an editor at *Aviation Week & Space Technology* who has been debunking UFOs for 30 years. The two maintain cordial relations and share information on the occasional UFO hoax. "There is no credible evidence for the existence of UFOs," Klass says. "And at this point in my life, unless one landed in my front yard or on the rooftop of CNN, I would remain very skeptical. There would have to be impressive and simple evidence."

UFO enthusiasts had their eyes on Washington last summer when the General Accounting Office (GAO) released a report requested by Rep. Steven H. Schiff, R-N.M., seeking to answer a 50-year-old question: Is the government sitting on documents proving that a flying saucer crashed near Roswell, N.M.? The Air Force beat the GAO to the punch by releasing a phone-book-sized report with its own version of what happened. (*See "At Issue," p. 281.*)

In recent years, the estimated 19 million Americans who say they have seen a UFO have been upstaged by the 4 million people who claim, according to a 1991 Roper poll, that they were abducted by alien spacecraft. Accounts of being taken aboard, forced to undergo intimate physical examinations and even made to mate with extraterrestrials made a believer of John E. Mack, a Pulitzer Prize-winning psychiatrist whose enthusiasm sparked an alarmed review of his status on the faculty of Harvard University Medical School.

"Most of the specific information that the abductees provided about the means of transport to and from the spaceships, the descriptions of the insides of the ships themselves and the procedures carried out by the aliens during the abductions had never been written about or shown in the media," Mack wrote in his widely noted 1994 book, *Abductions: Human Encounters with Aliens*. "Furthermore, these individuals were from many parts of the country and had not communicated with each other. They seemed in other respects quite sane, had come forth reluctantly, fearing the discrediting of their stories or outright ridicule." [1]

The modern debate over UFOs began raging in 1947, just after the frightening arrival of the Atomic Age. But surprisingly in the 1990s, UFOs remain a strong presence on the cultural radar screen, along with other

Many Americans Believe in Angels, Miracles and Flying Saucers

More than 70 percent of Americans believe in miracles and angels, and half think it is likely that flying saucers are real, according to recent polls.

Do you believe:	**Yes**	**Not Sure**	**No**
1. In miracles?	79%	9%	12%
2. In angels?	72	13	15
3. That people can hear from or communicate mentally with someone who has died?	28	21	51
4. In reincarnation — that is, the rebirth of the soul in a new body after death?	27	20	53
5. In astrology?	23	16	61

	Very likely	**Somewhat Likely**	**Unlikely**	**Not Sure**
6. That flying saucers are real?	19%	30.7%	43.1%	7.3%

Note: Percentages do not add up to 100 due to rounding.

Sources: CNN USA Today*/Gallup Poll, based on nationwide random telephone survey of 1,016 adults over age 18, conducted Dec. 16-18, 1994 (questions 1-5); Scripps Howard News Service/Ohio University poll, based on nationwide random telephone survey of 1,006 people, June 1995 (question 6).*

paranormal claims — such as psychic powers, communications from ghosts and "near-death experiences."

People who claim psychic powers — and whose cable TV ads offer pay-by-the-minute services — even offer hope to police departments desperate for clues in missing-persons cases. And last November, the public learned that beginning in the early 1970s the CIA and the Pentagon had ventured into the world of the paranormal. The military and intelligence agencies had spent $20 million on Operation Stargate, a series of "remote-viewing" experiments in which psychics attempted to visualize key enemy secrets, such as whether the Soviets had developed a new submarine or whether North Korea had dug underground tunnels.

The Internet and entertainment media offer persuasive indications that Americans are hot for the paranormal. The Net is abuzz with discussion groups reachable at the address alt.alien.visitors. Sci-fi dramas and programs reenacting the unexplained seem to dominate TV and movies. (*See story, p. 278.*) Thirty-six percent of Americans believe in ghosts, according to a 1994 Louis Harris and Associates Poll, while Gallup research reports that 8 million Americans have had a near-death experience, typically characterized by visions of being in a long, brightly lighted tunnel.

At the National Aeronautics and Space Administration (NASA), more than half of public inquiries concern UFOs, says Elsie Weigel, public information manager. Recently, "we counted 53 out of the past 139 letters forwarded to us from the White House that dealt with UFOs, and it's more if you count questions coming by phone and the Internet," she says.

Observers have noted that rising interest in UFOs coincides with high levels of mistrust in government. Stuart Vyse, a professor of psychology at

Connecticut College, is preparing a survey on the two trends. "People have become so jaded and negative about government that they are willing to accept a government-conspiracy theory," he says, "which makes it easier to accept the idea of UFOs landing on Earth. Otherwise, these people reason, how would the landings go undetected?"

Conspiracy theories have long been part of the "paranormal worldview," says Paul Kurtz, chairman of the Committee for the Scientific Investigation of Claims of the Paranormal (CSICOP) and a professor of philosophy emeritus at the State University of New York at Buffalo. "Like right-wingers who fear the Trilateral Commission or the New World Order, there are people who take things that can't be explained and give them occult or mystical or spiritual overtones," Kurtz says.

Now in its 20th year, CSICOP conducts probes and publishes aggressive exposés of hoaxers and credulous people whom it believes are falling victim to a weakening of respect for science. Several outright hoaxes have been documented, among them the huge, mysterious saucer-shaped imprints found in grain fields mostly in England throughout the 1980s. Many people thought the "crop circles" were messages from alien visitors. The theory collapsed in 1991 when two British pranksters confessed to using boards to flatten the grain. [2]

In the late 1980s, purported White House documents from 1952 were made public supposedly proving that outgoing President Harry S Truman and incoming President Dwight D. Eisenhower were receiving briefings on the military's handling of 1947 UFO incidents. Klass and other skeptics used handwriting analysis and won agreement from many UFO believers that the documents were forgeries. [3]

It is clear, however, that scolding lectures from skeptics often bounce right off many who are powerfully attracted to their beliefs. "The fascination with extraterrestrials," writes *Time* magazine essayist Lance Morrow, "may reflect an exhaustion of the secrets and novelties of Earth and of earthly behavior, which, on the whole, we have come to think, is nothing to write home about. We know one another too well." [4]

The future of society's handling of the paranormal may hinge on the following questions:

Is the government covering up information on UFOs?

Veterans of the UFO debates generally fall into one of two camps, depending on their view of what took place in 1947 near Roswell Army Air Field in New Mexico. The believers' camp is certain that two flying saucers collided July 7 during a thunderstorm. They believe that a local rancher alerted personnel from the air base, who recovered unearthly debris from the crash site, including the bodies of four aliens. The base, home to the 509th Bomber Group (which had dropped atom bombs on Japan), was then the only military unit with access to atomic secrets.

Base press officer Walter Haut (who now works at a UFO museum in Roswell), put out a statement that "a flying disc" had been found. After a flurry of news reports to that effect, and after the area was closed to the public, the commander of the Eighth Air Force issued a statement explaining that what was found was a weather balloon.

It wasn't until the late 1970s that new witnesses came forward and alleged that the aliens and otherworldly debris had been transferred to Ohio's Wright-Patterson Air Force Base for secret study. One witness was Roswell mortician Glenn Dennis, who said base officials asked him for hermetically sealed caskets. At the base hospital, he said he saw strange metallic wreckage with hieroglyphic-like markings before being hustled away and threatened into silence by military police.

A nurse friend (who Dennis said later disappeared without a trace) told him she helped two doctors examine the damaged, putrid bodies of three creatures. They were "three-and-a-half to four feet tall, with disproportionately large heads. . . . The eyes were deeply set; the skulls were flexible; the nose was concave, with two orifices; the mouth was a fine slit, and the doctors said there was heavy cartilage instead of teeth. The ears were only small orifices with flaps. They had no hair, and the skin was black." [5]

Thus began the alleged coverup of what believers would call the most amazing scientific event ever. The secret supposedly would be kept by an elite group at the Pentagon, the CIA, the National Security Council and later NASA, who would pass the conspiracy down to succeeding generations.

The coverup was used again in 1952, according to assertions recently disseminated over the Internet, when sailors aboard the *USS Franklin D. Roosevelt* photographed a UFO hovering in the sky. Another coverup allegedly occurred in 1965, when a wave of flashing UFOs swarmed military facilities in California near Edwards Air Force Base. (Tapes of "panicked" radio traffic from the event can be purchased from UFO groups for $14.95.)

In the late 1980s, coverup believers say astronauts aboard the space shuttle told ground controllers they had encountered strange visitors. And during the latter part of the Reagan administration, yet another coverup occurred when the Pentagon launched a top-secret "working group" to study reports of alien spacecraft, according to former *New York Times* reporter Howard Blum, who wrote a controversial book on the 40-year cover-up conspiracy. [6]

Belief in such government subterfuge is broad. A July 1995 poll by the Scripps-Howard News Service and Ohio University found that 50 percent of Americans think flying saucers are real

Continued on p. 271

Debunkers Zero in on Fox's 'Alien Autopsy' Film

Fans of UFOs loved the bizarre "documentary" shown last summer on Fox Television, "Alien Autopsy: Fact or Fiction?" But critics saw it simply as a hokey and cynical hoax.

Shown two weeks in a row in the United States as well as in several European countries, the "newly surfaced footage" of the purported autopsy of an alien added a new wrinkle to the debate over whether the U.S. government covered up an alleged 1947 UFO crash in Roswell, N.M.

The 17 minutes of seemingly old black and white film is of murky origins. The footage reportedly was presented to Fox by Ray Santilli, a London-based film distributor. The film is said to have sat for nearly 40 years in the home of the original cameraman, an unidentified member of the Army Air Force who supposedly was brought from Fort Worth, Texas, to Roswell to capture the historic first examination of an extraterrestrial.

Santilli says he spent two years seeking to authenticate the film. When asked in the Fox documentary how the alleged cameraman was permitted to keep a unique government film, he explained how the man "set aside certain canisters of film which needed special treatment in processing."

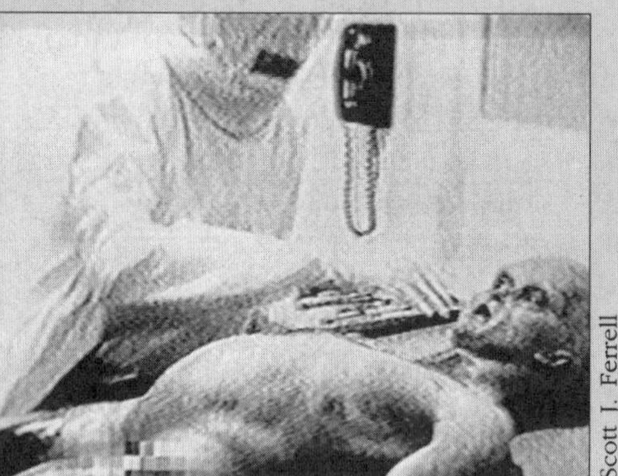

Scott J. Ferrell

The controversial star of Fox's "Alien Autopsy."

The film was produced by Robert Kiviat, who also does Fox's supernatural "Encounters" show. It is edited to introduce the alien's body only gradually, superimposing quick shots of it on the faces of an array of UFO investigators who offer contradictory conjectures about the footage's authenticity.

"The following program deals with controversial subjects," runs the opening disclaimer. "The theories, opinions and beliefs expressed are not the only possible interpretation. Viewers are invited to make a judgment based on all available information."

The ambiguity is furthered by the show's host, "Star Trek" actor Jonathan Frakes, who more recently began hosting a show called "The Paranormal Borderline." "Although we remain skeptical," he opines, "some experts believe what they saw was authentic proof of an alien life form."

Critics — from all sides of the UFO question — tore into the film. The Committee for Scientific Investigation of Claims of the Paranormal (CSICOP) devoted several pages of *Skeptical Inquirer* magazine to debunking the film. A Houston pathologist consulted by CSICOP noted that the operation was performed without a "body block" ordinarily used to prop up the body's trunk for examination and the head for brain removal. And the person performing the "autopsy" "used scissors like a tailor, not like a pathologist or surgeon," the pathologist said.

C. Eugene Emery Jr., a science writer for the *Providence Journal-Bulletin*, asked why there are only two people in the room. "How many people would turn down the chance to watch the historic autopsy of a creature from another world?" he asks. He also found the pathology work slipshod. "The origin and insertion of individual muscles would have been documented. Samples would have been taken, weighed, recorded and photographed." [1]

"The organs pour out with no connective tissue," griped a Wisconsin astronomer in a letter to *Skeptical Inquirer* magazine. Nowhere in the room does the viewer see sophisticated instruments. No X-rays are taken. "The insides of the mouth were never checked," he notes. The continuously moving camera operates in a style more characteristic of today's infomercials. [2]

UFO skeptic Philip J. Klass noted in his *Skeptics UFO Newsletter* that neither of the pathologists consults with one another or appears puzzled by the alien's strange organs. He raises questions about the reluctance of the film's distributor to permit expert lab analysis of the original film in its entirety, rather than the mere two-inch sample Santilli has offered. And most concretely, he offers research, originally prompted by an observation from a former AT&T executive, that the scuffed-up wall phone with coiled cord shown in the film (*see photo, above*) would have been an unusual and brand-new luxury in 1947. [3]

The Washington, D.C.-area Fund for UFO Research issued a statement saying further discussion of the film was a waste of time until there are more answers from producers. "The string of sausages that are supposed to be intestines are totally hokey," says Chairman Richard Hall. What's more, the emergence of the film last August, at precisely the time when the General Accounting Office was taking the Roswell incident seriously, Hall says, may be a sign that the whole documentary is government disinformation.

"Television executives have a responsibility not to confuse programs designed for entertainment with news documentaries," said Paul Kurtz, chairman of CSICOP.

At Fox, however, officials announced that they were pleased with "Alien Autopsy's" 8.1 late-summer rating — 14 percent of the national TV audience.

[1] *Skeptical Inquirer,* November-December 1995, p. 17.

[2] *Skeptical Inquirer,* March-April, p. 57.

[3] *Skeptics UFO Newsletter,* September 1995, November 1995, January 1996.

Continued from p. 269

and that the government is hiding the truth about them. And it was years of pressure from the public that prompted the Air Force and GAO to produce their recent reports on the Roswell incident.

What really happened at Roswell, according to the Air Force, was recovery of debris from a top-secret radar balloon designed to measure atomic testing by the Soviet Union. Personnel at Roswell knew nothing about it because it had blown across the Sacramento Mountains from top-secret military testing facilities in Alamogordo, where tight security procedures prevented further explanation. (The radar balloon project was declassified in the 1970s.)

What makes a coverup unlikely, the Air Force adds, is that the top base commanders, by prearranged schedules, were elsewhere on the fateful day. They did not return quickly, nor did they relay any amazing news to Washington. "If some event happened that was one of the 'watershed happenings' in human history, the U.S. military certainly reacted in an unconcerned and cavalier manner," the Air Force report noted. "In an actual case, the military would have had to order thousands of soldiers and airmen, not only at Roswell but throughout the U.S., to act nonchalantly, pretend to conduct and report business as usual, and generate absolutely no paperwork of a suspicious nature." [7]

The GAO report offered both camps some ammunition. It noted that the government's own UFO investigation, which lasted from 1948-69, did not even mention a crash at Roswell in 1947. But, the GAO added, "In our search for records concerning the Roswell crash, we learned that some government records covering [air base] activities had been destroyed. The debate on what crashed at Roswell," it concluded tantalizingly, "continues." [8]

Richard Hall, chairman of the Washington, D.C.-area Fund for UFO Research, which is preparing a new report on the government's handling of UFOs, was encouraged by the GAO's intimations. The Air Force report, by contrast, "is a terrible example of overkill that is padded with irrelevant material," he says. It is designed to discourage people from plowing through its hundreds of pages to corroborate its thesis, Hall adds. "The radar balloons it speaks of were launched long after the dates in question. We consider the Roswell thing wide open, and we have hard-core evidence from witnesses whom we videotaped. Something extraordinary crashed there. We're going to keep our eye on the ball."

Fund for UFO Research Inc.

The UFO in this May 11, 1950, photo from McMinnville, Ore., exceeded 30 meters in diameter, according to Bruce Maccabee of the Fund for UFO Research. No evidence could be found suggesting the use of a model suspended from power lines, Maccabee said.

CSICOP's Kurtz, whose committee has examined government files and found no sign of a coverup, asks what the motive possibly would be. "Why would all the governments on the planet Earth try to withhold from citizens what would be the most important discovery of our lifetime?" he asks.

The motive, counters Hall, must be seen in the context of the Cold War. "If a UFO crashes in Roswell, the chain of command is going to ask what it all means, and they're going to try to reproduce the vehicle's power system" before our enemies do. Second, Hall says, the fear of the aliens' possible agenda would cause confusion about how best to release news of the discovery. "It could cause panic or upset whole economies," Hall says. Finally, we must remember that "the incident was handled by military, not scientific, officials, which means they may have felt the public couldn't deal with it."

Such views are seconded by Larry W. Bryant, administrator of the Alexandria, Va., group Citizens Against UFO Secrecy, which files court cases and Freedom of Information Act requests to try to expose the government's "cosmic Watergate." The alien technology would be very valuable to military planners and logistics operators, he says, but the reasons for secrecy are as much political as military.

"My theory is that the coverup has taken on a life of its own, and that no one has the authority to let it out," he says. "There are perhaps 300 officials who handle the hard-core evidence,

For 'News' of the Bizarre or Just a Good Laugh . . .

"African Tribe Came From Mars," blares the Feb. 20 issue of the Florida-based *Weekly World News*. "Murdered Girl's Ghost Led Family to Her Buried Body," replies its Montreal-based competitor, *The Sun*.

For fans of the paranormal, supermarket tabloids are an unending source of material. Long familiar as the carnival barkers of the journalism world, the "tabs" enjoy a symbiotic relationship with enthusiasts of the unexplained — the publications get a wealth of material while the folks who make strange claims get to see their stories in print — and read by millions.

The papers flaunt a visual flair for the bizarre, as in *The Sun's* recent photo of the half-human, half-beast "leopard man." And they play well on fears of government secrecy, as in the *News'* recent scoop: "Reagan Built Star Wars Shield as Defense Against UFO Attacks!"

Though many readers accept the tabloids as cheap and harmless fun, skeptics of the paranormal worry that a gullible public is being exploited. "A lot of people take it for gospel even though the editors sit around roaring with laughter," says Leon Jaroff, a science writer for *Time* who is on the board of *Skeptical Inquirer* magazine. "Some of the stories stem from something real, but others are made up out of whole cloth, as when the *Weekly World News* a few years ago reported that a Russian cosmonaut aboard 'Soyez' was raped by an alien."

Tabloid sensationalism also gives heartburn to researchers who take the paranormal seriously. Kenneth Ring is a University of Connecticut psychologist who is studying a possible connection between alien-abduction claims and near-death experiences (NDEs). "After the publication of my first book on NDEs, *Life at Death*, my own work was the source of sensational (and misleading) tabloid headlines such as 'NEW AMAZING PROOF OF LIFE AFTER DEATH!' " he writes. "I would have to endure the reproachful and sometimes withering gaze of my department head as well as the good-natured, but often pointed, ribbing of my colleagues." [1]

Defenders of the tabloids point to at least one of the supermarket sisters, *The National Enquirer*, that has broken real stories in pages that nowadays are packed not with spacecraft kidnappings but with large-type exposés on the private lives of celebrities. In 1977, for example, the *Enquirer* beat *The Washington Post* and the Sunday supplement *Parade* in reporting a mass sighting of UFOs at missile sites and nuclear facilities. [2]

And as a sop to respectability, *The Sun* publishes a tiny disclaimer near its masthead, declaring that "*Sun* stories seek to entertain and are about the fantastic, bizarre and paranormal. Articles are written by and obtained from the *Sun* staff, the world press, free-lance correspondents and the general public. The reader should suspend belief for the sake of enjoyment."

Sal Ivone, managing editor of the *Weekly World News*, is happy to explain how his paper approaches tales of the bizarre. "If people make an outlandish claim, we would

and there's turnover. Many have probably realized over the past 15 years that the way to handle the situation is through leaks. Roswell won't be put to rest by a report that reflects human, preconceived notions," he says of the Air Force document. "That report has logical flaws since mobile radar balloons don't carry alien bodies."

Skeptics, however, have much more to say about Roswell. Klass, who is writing a book on the subject, notes that several key witnesses to the recovery of crash debris died before there were widespread reports of unearthly remains. A key officer who was there denies any coverup.

But the politics of the issue makes it hard for authorities to put the rumors to rest categorically. "If members of Congress say there's no coverup, they make enemies," Klass says. "And if the Air Force announces that a UFO is hoax, they get criticized, so they simply say there's not enough information."

Klass has written extensively about the belief in a decades-long conspiracy to keep wraps on UFOs. In the late 1970s, for example, when the government declassified 3,000 pages on UFOs from the Pentagon, FBI, CIA and National Security Agency, officials announced that they would continue to keep 192 pages secret. UFO conspiracy theorists, of course, went haywire. But is it plausible, Klass asked, that over three decades, a coverup of the biggest secret in history would generate only six pages a year from these agencies? [9]

Klass is equally dismissive of Blum's assertion about a Pentagon UFO "working group." In a review of Blum's book, he counted 25 factual errors in a single

. . . Supermarket Tabloids Satisfy Every Taste

tend to print it rather than throw it away," he says. "Our criteria are different. We're not bound by the same constraints as *The Washington Post.* We want to take our readers for a roller-coaster ride. To ask what happens if . . . to breathe as much as possible into a story."

Ivone notes that each of the well-known supermarket tabloid staples — UFOs, Big Foot, the Kennedy assassination conspiracy theories — has its own constituency. "These people love to be paid attention to, and don't like to be made fun of."

What the readers share is a demand for simplicity. The mainstream press might run a story on Bosnia that "would take 50 sidebars to bring the reader up to speed," Ivone says. "In a tabloid, all you need to understand the story is in the story."

As for sources, Ivone says generally, it is somebody's claim that forms the germ of a story. "But we exaggerate and put it in 270-point type where others use 14-point type. We're screaming our lungs out all the time, but that doesn't mean our stories aren't valid. Do we make things up? No. Do we exaggerate almost beyond recognition? Yes. But as my editor often says, 'I'm not going to question myself out of a great story.' We aim for entertaining reading, but that doesn't mean it's a serious story that will help you understand last night's Republican debate or how to find a better school for your kids. It will, however, go far as a way to make your buddies fall off their barstool laughing, or as a way to pass the time while folding clothes in the laundromat."

The tabloid practice of reporting uncorroborated claims is precisely what is avoided by the journalistic establishment. John Noble Wilford, science correspondent for *The New York Times,* says that if he were to receive a call from someone claiming to have seen a flying saucer, he would not drop everything to write a story. "I wouldn't want to encourage them since there are other people they can call such as the local sheriff or the Air Force. We don't have the resources to sort it out. We don't run such stories, even when they come over the wires, unless there is something unusual, such as a mass hysteria, that's bizarre enough to put on the record."

The Times does write about the paranormal, Wilford says, if there is some aspect that hasn't been covered that makes an editor take a new look. "If someone we consider reputable has taken something on as a cause, and is doing actual research, and has some reason to," it gets covered.

Media expert Everette Dennis, a vice president of the Freedom Forum in Arlington, Va., believes the paranormal is actually underreported in the mainstream press, leaving the tabloids and tabloid TV as the principal outlets. "There are people working in that area and talking about it. It's like aspects of religion in that it can be examined seriously without being endorsed," he says.

Larry W. Bryant, a retired Army technical editor, belongs to Operation Right-to-Know, a grass-roots group that has picketed *The Washington Post* to demand more coverage of UFOs. Bryant says the mainstream press is finally beginning to ask the right questions. "In the 1950s and '60s, the press was hoodwinked, but now they realize that where there's smoke, there will be fire," he says, citing recent broadcasts on UFOs by "Nightline" and "A Current Affair."

Such shows are "tapping a thirst for knowledge about a real mystery, even if the producers are trying to make a living and provide entertainment," Bryant says. But tabloids such as the *Weekly World News* have been "a hindrance" to the UFO movement, he says. "People with education, however, can see this, and they know it's just entertainment. The tabloids are simply part of UFO politics. They're always going to be there."

---

1 Kenneth Ring, *The Omega Project: Near-Death Experiences, UFO Encounters, and Mind at Large* (1992), p. 8.

2 Philip J. Klass, *UFOs: The Public Deceived* (1983), p. 90.

chapter, including Blum's description of a 2,500-foot elevator shaft at a secret base in Colorado; Klass says the shaft doesn't exist. [10] Even UFO believers called the book inaccurate and overly romantic. Celebrated *New York Times* investigative reporter Seymour Hersh, whom Blum says urged him to tackle his groundbreaking project, distances himself from the book, saying its "interpretations are from Blum's own mind."

As for the government agencies themselves, the denials are routine and longstanding. "During several space missions, NASA astronauts have reported phenomena not immediately explainable," says a space agency statement. "However, in every instance NASA determined that the observations could not be termed 'abnormal' in the space environment."

The CIA, though highly interested in UFOs in the early 1950s, has not gotten many questions in a long time, says spokesman David Christian. "We're not in the business of evaluating UFO sightings, though we have been asked to participate sometimes in review of data."

At the Defense Department, public affairs officer Maj. Tom LaRock says he is "not aware of any panel here in the building" dealing with UFOs. An Air Force boilerplate statement goes further: "Given the current environment of steadily decreasing defense budgets, it is unlikely the Air Force would become involved in such a costly project in the foreseeable future."

Barry Bitzer, press secretary for Rep. Schiff, explains that Schiff requested the GAO report on Roswell after pressure from citizens and after he "got the runaround from Pentagon, which simply told him to go to the National

Archives. The intention was to make the issue open and accessible, and we are satisfied that the GAO did what it could under the restraints of time," Bitzer says. "The original Air Force answer about a weather balloon didn't wash because you don't seal off an area for a weather balloon. When government is unnecessarily secretive, it fosters this kind of conspiracy theory. Now people can draw their own conclusions."

Is respect for the scientific method in danger?

"You're more alive after death than at any time since you were last born," writes P.M.H. Atwater, describing her three experiences of nearly dying and then returning to life. The sensation is different "because you no longer wear a dense body to filter and amplify the various sensations you had once regarded as the only valid indicators of what constitutes life." [11]

The writer's reliance on personal testimony, bathed in warm, spiritual language devoid of skeptical tones, is common to many who embrace the paranormal. The style permeates the alien-abduction claims discussed by Mack, who writes: "As we suspend the notion of our preeminent and dominating intelligence, we might open to a universe filled with life forms different from ourselves to whom we might be connected in ways we do not yet understand." [12]

To skeptics, such approaches are a worrisome trend. And the skeptics are getting organized. Last June, the New York Academy of Sciences assembled 200 scientists, physicians, philosophers and educators to its "Flight from Science and Reason" conference.

CSICOP's Kurtz, who addressed the gathering, asks with frustration, "How is the ordinary person to distinguish reality from fiction? If someone says he saw a poltergeist or a spaceship in his backyard, he never hears any criticism. There's a Hallelujah chorus around near-death experiences. The claims are not corroborated or tested. It's very troubling. If a patient tells you he's Bismarck or Napoleon, you'd say he's delusional. But John Mack is taking the reports from patients as true."

Kurtz worries that people concentrate on supposed "creatures who are more intelligent and technologically advanced than us and wonder whether they are benevolent or malevolent. The creatures are said to deliver some profound messages, such as 'Be peaceful' or 'Save the environment.' It's really a post-modern symbol of divine revelation. And because of the will to believe, people get angry when we skeptics come in."

R. Michael Jenkins

Sen. Claiborne Pell, D-R.I., is a well-known paranormal enthusiast.

Carl Sagan, the famed Cornell University astronomer, blasts the current fascination with the paranormal in his new book, *The Demon-Haunted World.* "Superstition and pseudoscience keep getting in the way" of scientific truth, he writes, "distracting us, providing easy answers, dodging skeptical inquiry, casually pressing our awe buttons and cheapening the experience, making us routine and comfortable practitioners as well as victims of credulity." [13]

Part of the skeptics' complaint is that the books, articles and television programs that meet their standards enjoy nowhere near the drawing power of those that circulate strange claims. Leon Jaroff, a long-time *Time* magazine writer who wrote the 'Skeptical Eye' column for *Discover* magazine, complains that on *Time's* new Internet venture, the most popular category of highlights from the magazine is not national news or the arts but a feature called "alien ruins on the moon."

"Most people are so desperate to believe that they lose all sense of rationality or objectivity," he says. "I say, why not look at the magic around you, look what you can do with your computer, look at the search for new planets. But it's not enough. People have got to have their neighbors being kidnapped and sexually examined by aliens."

One reason that many people reject science, writes mathematician John Allen Paulos, is that "New Age" beliefs in astrology, biorhythms or Tarot cards comfort them by offering "personally customized pronouncements." [14] Such people shy away from cold and impersonal scientific questions — How long? How fast? Which is more likely?

Psychology Professor Vyse points out that science does offer explanations for most strange phenomena. People who recount near-death experiences, for example, seem to have already known about such common details as the "tunnel of light. So, not surprisingly, they report what they're supposed to report," he says. "There's also the possibility that a physiological process could stimulate such experiences, such as neurological damage."

Paranormal enthusiasts, however, often reject the traditional church, science and medical establishments, preferring to revel in "the culture of the moment," Vyse says. "There is an excitement to being the individual who has sighted something unique and special. It is similar to religion. I used to think that education levels mattered when it came to such behavior. But now I see that certain people are simply brought up in social groups where it is accepted. Superstitions are common among college students, for instance. Harvard students still rub the foot of the statue of John Harvard on the day of an exam."

Many observers note that education can only go so far. Gerald Weissmann, a doctor at New York University Medical Center, told the June conference to consider Russia and France. "Both countries educate their young people in science far better than we do. But the belief in magic and the supernatural is certainly more widespread in France and Russia than it is in the United States." [15]

What's more, among explorers of the paranormal, there has long been frustration with scientists who come across as arrogant. As far back as 1961, a Brookings Institution report on the possibility of other life in outer space contained the following comment: "It has been speculated that of all groups, scientists and engineers might be the most devastated by the discovery of relatively superior creatures, since these professions are most clearly associated with the mastery of nature, rather than with the understanding and expression of man." [16]

Laurence W. Frederick, an astronomer at the University of Virginia who helps run the Society for Scientific Exploration, a paranormal investigative group, says: "There are dogmatists on one side, mostly scientists, who won't even think about the possibility that something about the paranormal might be real. But I point to the many times scientists have overlooked things that later became dogma. Stones coming out of the sky were long said by scientists to be the result of lightning hitting rocks. But in 1804, they were identified as meteors after chemical analysis showed they were extraterrestrial."

Frederick says he knows scientists at universities who believe in reincarnation and in the Loch Ness monster. But his group's only requirement is that researchers keep an open mind. "People who present evidence to us know that they have to make a good case. Sometimes we say these things are crazy, other times we say they make a little sense. But the skeptical approach taken by CSICOP is too one-sided," he adds. If something from the paranormal is eventually proved, "They will look bad."

Many UFO researchers distinguish between mere claims and scientific empiricism. As the Chicago-based J. Allen Hynek Center for UFO Research notes in a pamphlet, "the majority of sightings generally prove to be a misinterpretation of natural phenomena — meteors, planets, stars, odd clouds — or manmade objects, such as airplanes, balloons or satellites. Smaller number of reports cannot be investigated properly for various reasons — lack of pertinent details, for example, or inaccessibility of witnesses. However, in any given number of UFO reports, about 5 percent to 10 percent are truly puzzling. . . . These cases are considered true UFO reports."

Hall of the Fund for UFO Research, who earned a philosophy degree studying the scientific method, says he is "involved in gathering data and not pushing a theory. There are lots out there that need study, but it's not being recognized as a genuine problem, partly because CSICOP debunks it," he says. He recommends more research into data from radar sightings of UFOs; more studies on the effects of electromagnetism on cars, trucks, airplanes, animals and humans (a common detail reported in UFO sightings); and more analysis of films and photos of UFOs.

Such research, not surprisingly, does not seem pressing to skeptic Klass. "One of the important fingerprints in deciding whether something is proto-science or pseudo-science," he says, "is that the passage of time provides more evidence either to enhance or discredit a theory. Today we don't know one iota more about UFOs than we knew 40 years ago." ■

BACKGROUND

Appetite for the Eerie

Sightings of objects in the sky go back to biblical times, to the Books of Ezekiel and Exodus. That the concept has carried through the centuries is evidenced by Christian paintings of the Middle Ages, which portray prophets ascending to heaven in what at least in one case looks like an egg-shaped metallic vehicle. [17]

But the modern clash between the public's appetite for the eerie and the hard-won authority of science has its roots in the 19th century. It was in 1848 in upstate New York that two young girls who were said to communicate with the dead helped to launch the wave of spiritualism that swept the country. Hundreds visited Katie and Margaret Fox in their parlor to hear spooky, rapping noises in the dark. Believers included Abraham Lincoln, Susan B. Anthony, Horace Greeley, P.T. Barnum and Frederick Douglass. Eventually, the writer and psychologist William James became president of a group called the American Psychical Society, while the Society for Psychical Research arose in London.

Nathaniel P. Tallmadge, D-N.Y., a U.S. senator and later governor of the

Wisconsin territory in the 1840s, led a drive that gathered 15,000 names on a petition to push Congress to fund a scientific study of the powers of so-called mediums. Congress declined, however, and Katie and Margaret were eventually exposed as phonies. They had made the rapping sounds by cracking their toe joints. [18]

Americans' interest in the fantastic offered an enthusiastic reception to a 1882 book by former Rep. Ignatius Donnelly, R-Minn., boosting belief in the lost island of Atlantis. And several years before the Wright brothers took flight — when lighter-than-air craft were quaintly called "air ships" — sightings were reported across 19 states during a six-month period. In 1897, a "cigar-shaped object 300 feet long made of panels of glass" was reported by a Kansas farmer who, with his son, swore that "six of the strangest beings I ever saw" extended a red cable down from their vehicle and grabbed up one of his cows. [19]

One of the first people to suggest that UFOs were alien visitors was New Yorker Charles Hoy Fort. In 1919, after years of study at the New York Public Library and the British Museum, he published his *Book of the Damned* (recently republished) that encouraged study of paranormal phenomena. "Fort was skeptical about scientific explanations, observing how scientists argued according to their beliefs, rather than the rules of evidence, and that inconvenient data was ignored," says the London-based *Fortean Times,* which carries on Fort's tradition today, along with the Arlington, Va.-based International Fortean Organization.

It was in the 1920s that a psychologist named J.B. Rhine took up a post at Duke University, creating the first academic program in "parapsychology." He would become famous for coining the term "extrasensory perception" (ESP) and for experiments in which blindfolded subjects reportedly identified playing cards as many as 25 times in a row.

The Age of UFOs

The public had had two years to adjust to the existence of weapons of mass destruction when the era of UFOs dawned. The term "flying saucer" entered the national lexicon in 1947 — two years after atomic bombs had been dropped on Hiroshima and Nagasaki. Pilot Kenneth Arnold reported seeing UFOs travelling 1,000 mph above Mt. Rainier, Wash. They resembled "a saucer skipping over water," he noted in the inaugural issue of *Fate* magazine, still published in St. Paul, Minn.

Though some 853 UFO sightings were recorded in 1947, a Gallup Poll showed that only 1 percent of Americans felt flying saucers made an important news story that year (23 percent cited instead the high cost of living). By 1950, however, 47 percent believed in UFOs, nearly the same percentage as today.

The government, deep into the Cold War in the 1950s and operating on a war footing for the Korean conflict, denied public charges that it was hiding UFO evidence. In fact, the Air Force in 1948 had launched Project Grudge, a highly classified group headed by California Institute of Technology physicist H.P. Robertson, to study the phenomenon. In 1952 — the year of a record 1,501 UFO sightings — the inquiry (by then renamed Blue Book) reported to U.S. intelligence and military authorities that it had no evidence that UFOs were extraterrestrial. As sightings continued over the next dozen years, Congress consulted occasionally with the Air Force concerning UFOs, and private citizens formed their own investigative groups.

UFOs on Capitol Hill

In March 1966, Michigan congressman (and future president) Gerald R. Ford wrote to Armed Services Committee Chairman Mendel Rivers, D-S.C.: "In the firm belief that the American public deserves a better explanation than that thus far given by the Air Force, I strongly recommend that there be a committee investigation of the UFO phenomena." [20]

The following week, Rivers' committee took testimony from Air Force Secretary Harold Brown and Air Force consultant J. Allen Hynek, an astronomer then at Ohio State University. Brown said he knew of no one with scientific or executive standing in the Air Force who thought that UFOs were extraterrestrial. But Hynek said he knew of 20 UFO cases that needed further study and recommended creation of a civilian panel. One committee member, Rep. Felix Hebert, D-La., asked Hynek whether he'd conferred with Ray Walston, the actor then playing a Martian on a popular TV show.

Two years later, however, the topic was accorded more respectful treatment at a symposium on UFOs sponsored by the House Science and Astronautics Committee. This time no one from the Air Force appeared. Hynek testified as a private citizen, and pro-UFO meteorologist James E. McDonald was brought in with five other experts who called for more research on the topic.

McDonald said he took very seriously the possibility that UFOs are extraterrestrial and warned that witnesses were reluctant to come forward for fear of ridicule. University of Illinois sociologist Robert Hall, brother of Richard Hall, testified that while some UFOs may result from "hysterical contagion," there were hard-core cases that didn't lend themselves to that interpretation. Written testimony presented to the committee speculated on a link between UFO sightings and ESP. Even astronomer Sagan, though the only witness expressing skepticism toward flying saucers, recommended that the government fund research into life elsewhere in the universe. [21]

Continued on p. 278

Chronology

1940s Dawn of nuclear age coincides with first mass UFO sightings.

1947
Private pilot Kenneth Arnold sparks fascination with UFOs by reporting "flying saucer" above Mt. Rainier, Wash.; flying saucer allegedly crashes in Roswell, N.M.

1948
Air Force begins Project Grudge probe, later Project Blue Book.

1950s Hollywood picks up flying saucer theme; private UFO groups organize.

1951
Moviegoers flock to "The Thing."

1952-53
Classified government probe known as the Robertson Panel reports no evidence of UFOs.

1956
National Investigations Committee on Aerial Phenomena, a private group, is formed to counter government secrecy.

1960s First public government hearings and studies on UFOs.

1962
J.B. Rhine of Duke University establishes parapsychology research center.

1966
Air Force tells House Armed Services Committee there's no evidence for UFOs.

1968
House panel hears six UFO enthusiasts recommend government research.

1969
Condon Report from University of Colorado recommends no further study of UFOs; Air Force terminates Project Blue Book; Mutual UFO Network (MUFON) formed.

1970s Human-potential movement creates interest in paranormal; CIA starts psychic research.

1973
Two men in Pascagoula, Miss., claim abduction aboard spacecraft, fueling wave of sightings; astronomer J. Allen Hynek starts Center for UFO Studies.

1976
Air Force declassifies and transfers Project Blue Book files to National Archives.

1977
National Aeronautics and Space Administration declines White House suggestion to probe UFOs; First International Congress on UFOs held in Acapulco, Mexico.

1978
CIA releases UFO papers; United Nations considers UFO research.

1980s New Age Movement flourishes.

1980
U.S. District Court and Supreme Court decline to force declassification of UFO-related documents; story of 1947 UFO crash is resuscitated by book *The Roswell Incident.*

1987
National Research Council says there is no evidence for psychic powers; books *Intruders* and *Communion* popularize interest in alien abductions.

1988
Sen. Claiborne Pell, D-R.I., introduces bill to fund parapsychology experiments.

1990s Federal government issues reports on paranormal issues.

1991
Operation Right to Know urges end to UFO secrecy.

January 1994
Rep. Steven H. Schiff, R-N.M., asks General Accounting Office to probe alleged government coverup at Roswell air base; Air Force report says crash near Roswell was radar balloon.

July 28, 1995
GAO says there are no hidden documents about Roswell, but that questions remain.

Aug. 3, 1995
Harvard Medical School psychiatrist John E. Mack warned about his work on alien abductions.

Sept. 29, 1995
American Institutes for Research says there is no scientific evidence for "remote viewing."

January 1996
Congress, Pentagon and CIA halt funding for psychic research.

Most Viewers Tune to Sci-Fi for Thrills . . .

Truth may be stranger than fiction, but fiction draws the crowds. Fans of the paranormal have been flocking to sci-fi films and television shows in the 1990s.

Among TV's hottest hits is the Fox Network's "The X-Files," which recounts the spine-chilling adventures of two young FBI agents investigating an array of top-secret, weird doings from alien abductions to ghosts. A Golden Globe award winner in its third season, "X-Files" reaches an estimated 30 million viewers every Friday and, like the venerable "Star Trek," has spawned its own conventions, trading cards, comic books and Internet discussion groups.

Current TV listings are also sprinkled with a dozen drama, comedy, talk or "reality-based" shows such as "Unsolved Mysteries" and "Sightings." Among feature films, Steven Spielberg's "E.T.: The Extraterrestrial," released in 1982 and now a popular video, continues to top the list of top-grossing films of all time, according to the Motion Picture Association of America. "Independence Day," a major release scheduled for July, deals with an alien invasion.

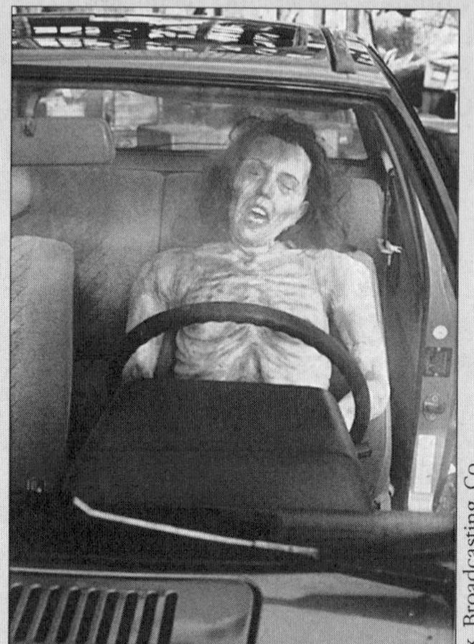

Fox Broadcasting Co.

Odd doings on "The X-Files" attract 30 million viewers every Friday.

The explosion of the strange in popular fare is worrisome to some in the community of skeptics. "With TV now in every home, people are engulfed and overwhelmed by it," says Paul Kurtz, chairman of the Buffalo-N.Y.-based Committee for the Scientific Investigation of Claims of the Paranormal (CSICOP). "It's big business, and it's part of our culture, but the fiction presented as truth bothers us. 'The X-Files,' for example, dramatizes things so that viewers think they're true."

Indeed, the show's chief conceit — that agents Mulder and Scully are handling the investigations that the government considers too hot to make public — is often taken literally. "I'm sure that the government is not too happy about 'The X-Files' because it reveals some things," a postal employee from Brooklyn told *TV Guide.* [1]

The entertainment value of aliens goes back at least to British author H.G. Wells' 1897 novel about a Martian invasion of Earth, *War of the Worlds.* When adopted for radio by Orson Welles in 1938, the show caused unprecedented panic among thousands of believing listeners. Beginning in the 1950s, Hollywood films such as "It Came From Outer Space" and "Mars Needs Women" popularized the notion of earthly landings by aliens intent on breeding with humans. Details suspiciously similar to those in sci-fi classics such as

Continued from p. 276

The symposium's chairman, Rep. J. Edward Roush, D-Ind., said that while the panel would take no stand on UFOs, "Events of the last half-century certainly verify the American philosopher John Dewey's conclusion that 'every great advance in science has issued from a new audacity of the imagination.' " (Roush was defeated for re-election in 1968 and went on to join a UFO group.)

Sightings in the 1970s

By the end of the 1960s, the Air Force had decided to get out of UFO investigations. It shut down Project Blue Book at Wright-Patterson Air Force Base, reporting that it had studied 12,618 sightings, and that only 701 remained "unidentified." The Air Force decision was based on the so-called Condon Report, after University of Colorado physicist Edward U. Condon. The report, "Scientific Study of Unidentified Flying Objects," concluded that further government study of UFOs was unlikely to advance science.

Although the report, released as a commercial paperback, hedged its bets by recommending that private groups continue the search, UFO enthusiasts protested loudly, calling it a political document unrepresentative of advanced science and even a CIA plot. "Had I known of the extent of the emotional commitment of the UFO believers and the extremes of conduct to which their faith can lead them," Condon wrote, "I certainly would never have undertaken the study." [22]

The 1970s were still young when UFO sightings began grabbing headlines anew. Dramatic testimony, such as the claim by two Mississippi fishermen that they had been taken aboard a spacecraft, prompted astronomer Hynek, then at Northwestern University, to switch to the pro-UFO camp and start his Center for UFO Studies. (It was Hynek who formulated the hierarchy of UFO encounters popularized by Steven Spielberg's 1977 movie "Close Encoun-

. . . But Some Take Shows Literally

the 1953 "Invaders from Mars" have cropped up in eyewitness accounts of UFOs, notably a famous 1961 sighting in Portsmouth, N.H. [2]

Producers of sci-fi are keenly aware of the cultural and political climate in which they're marketing. "In the 1950s, there was this incredible paranoia about Russia, with Americans building bomb shelters and kids ducking under desks at school," says Richard B. Lewis, president of Trilogy Entertainment Group, which recently produced a TV remake of the '60s sci-fi classic "The Outer Limits." The original "Outer Limits" and other such shows "drew from this fear of the unknown and found a way then to tell parables about the government and to represent evil as this alien, two-headed monster," Lewis says. "The fear has increased two-thousandfold now, but it's less the Red Scare than a fear of terrorists from within — AIDS, the Eboli virus, nuclear waste, things that we ourselves have created."

Adding to the unease, Lewis says, is the coming of the millennium, which "has people terrified of what's beyond that — it's a psychic waterfall. The same thing happened in the last century, when there was a rise in religious zealotry, a fear of the end, wild partying and people spending their life savings."

Lewis' company is preparing another fantasy show in April called "Poltergeist" — about an elite, ancient society that exists in secret. It will be optimistic, he says. "It will focus on the golden rule — do unto others as you'd have them do unto you — and will reassure people that bad things won't happen if you live a life of moderation."

Steven Spielberg's "E.T." is the top money-making film in history.

"The X-Files," by contrast, implies a means to "empower people in a way that is not realistic and is more than they're entitled to be," Lewis says. In fomenting mistrust of government, "It preys on a huge part of the population" that is tempted to put a gun on their trucks and blow up buildings. "That's lazy intellectually and emotionally. You can't let yourself use government as a cop-out for why you can't get things done."

Chris Carter, the show's creator, sees nothing in "The X-Files" that should encourage militia-type violence. "We're not suggesting revolution but a questioning of government," he says. "Just open the newspaper, and every week there's a story about some kind of government coverup," he adds, citing recent revelations from the Energy Department about decades-old radiation experiments on unwitting citizens.

As for his show's impact, Carter says: "There's already a pervasive attitude out there, a philosophical bent that government is not always acting in your best interest."

[1] *TV Guide*, Jan. 20, 1996, p. 33.

[2] Kenneth Ring, *The Omega Project: Near-Death Experiences, UFO Encounters and Mind at Large* (1992), p. 211.

ters of the Third Kind.")

Rumors of a government coverup persisted, and more amateur investigators took to the field with ever more complicated theories. On Indian reservations near Yakima, Wash., forest-fire lookouts began reporting orange-red balls and "deep rumbling noises." After years of investigation, researcher Greg Long of Philomath, Ore., wrote: "I toss out this idea as a wild idea — the orange spheres are an intelligence, capable of knowing the work of UFO researchers and of appearing in faulted, earthquake-prone areas during periods of tectonic strain buildup and release, as a red herring, while other UFOs carry out their operations." [23]

In 1977, Jimmy Carter assumed the presidency and followed through on a subject that had interested him since 1969, when he had seen and reported a UFO. (One investigator concluded that what Carter saw was the planet Venus.) Carter asked NASA Administrator Robert A. Frosch to consider conducting new research on UFOs. The NASA chief respectfully declined, citing "an absence of tangible or physical evidence available for thorough laboratory analysis." [24]

By this time, the UFO issue was of international concern. In 1977, Sir Eric Gairy, prime minister of Grenada, addressed the United Nations about his own sighting. And in 1990, Belgium became first government to openly investigate UFOs after a series of sightings. ■

CURRENT SITUATION

Remote Viewing

Last November, many Americans were startled to read that the government was discontinuing a program that most never even knew about. Intermittently since the early 1970s, the CIA and the Defense Department had spent some $20 million on research into a paranormal technique called "remote viewing." The program at Fort Meade, Md., and the Stanford Research Institute in Palo Alto, Calif., was designed to test whether people with the supposed paranormal power known as *psi* could provide otherwise unobtainable military data.

For years, the government kept several "psychics" on the payroll who were available for use by federal agencies. One of them, a former Army intelligence officer named Joe McMoneagle, won a decoration for pinpointing the location of a new Soviet submarine. He now offers his services as a psychic in Nellysford, Va., charging clients $1,500 a day. [25]

The Pentagon's decision to halt the remote-viewing program came after a consulting firm evaluated all recent research into psychic phenomena. The evaluation focused on experiments such as those in which subjects stared at *National Geographic* magazine photographs and attempted to send mental pictures of what they were looking at to psychics at other locations, who would then attempt to draw the same pictures. University of Oregon psychologist Ray Hyman was more skeptical than his co-evaluator Jessica Utts, a statistician at the University of California at Davis.

"Parapsychology, unlike the other sciences, has a shifting data base," Hyman wrote in rejecting remote viewing. "Experimental data that one generation puts forth as rock-solid evidence for psi is discarded by later generations in favor of new data."

Replied Utts: "I have never seen a skeptic attempt to perform an experiment with enough trials to even come close to insuring success." The consulting firm's conclusion, however, was that "evidence for the operational value of remote viewing is not available." [26]

For years, support for the remote-viewing project had come from Rep. Charlie Rose, D-N.C., and Sen. Claiborne Pell, D-R.I., a well-known paranormal enthusiast. [27] Pell sits on the boards of paranormal research groups — and has debated the merits of psychic phenomena with magician James "The Amazing" Randi, who now devotes his time to debunking psychics as charlatans. "I have long been interested in psychic phenomena, including the area of 'remote viewing,' as legitimate areas for scientific inquiry and possible practical applications," Pell said recently. "If the CIA is not interested, that's their business. I am convinced, however, that we should continue to research these and other areas that have the potential of improving the human condition."

Police and Psychics

Increasingly in recent years, news media accounts of crime investigations have noted that police have consulted "psychics." Frustrated officers in Montgomery County, Md., in 1992 followed leads provided by psychics to try to find the body of Laura Houghteling, a 23-year-old woman later found to have been murdered. And the family of Polly Klaas, the young girl kidnapped and murdered in Petaluma, Calif., in 1993, accepted help from psychics during a manhunt. Her grieving father, however, later denounced them as "predators." [28]

More recently, CSICOP members joined with station WCAU-TV in Philadelphia to unmask people who offer psychic services to crime victims. They concocted a story about a missing girl and then released the "details" of her life. A hundred people claiming to be psychics called the father with "insights" into her condition and whereabouts, but none figured out that she wasn't really missing. [29]

"Some police departments turn to psychics as facilitators when they run out of clues, or to show families that all possible leads are being followed," says Hubert Williams, president of the Police Foundation. "It's controversial in the law enforcement community. Some say it is not sufficiently scientific; others say they are getting good results."

Maggie Blackman, director of public relations at the Institute for Parapsychology, in Durham, N.C., says that many police departments use psychics but don't make the practice public, vaguely crediting any information they receive from psychics to "a source." "Some information [they receive] helps a case, and some doesn't," she says. "*Psi* scientists believe everyone is born with some *psi,* just as we can all draw and sing," Blackman explains. "But are we all artists and singers? Real psychics can't turn *psi* on and off like a faucet. They can have a bad day and bomb in the laboratory."

The institute, the off-campus successor to the original Rhine project at Duke, continues research into telepathy, clairvoyance and psychokinesis. Recent media exposés of phony psychics who work through 900 phone numbers and bilk people of their life savings are helping preserve her group's scientific dignity, Blackman says. "We're looking at what situations are conducive to having *psi* happen — your mood, the weather, the geomagnetic field. We'll never figure it out completely, but we can figure to what extent it's applicable."

The True Believers

When the Air Force receives calls about UFOs, it refers them to the many private interest groups listed in Gale's *Encyclopedia of Associations.* Recently three of the biggest UFO groups formed a partnership to foster more cooperation, with one-shot funding from Las Vegas developer Robert T. Bigelow. The Fund for UFO Research has raised more than $500,000 and awarded 30 research grants. The Seguin, Texas-based Mutual UFO Network holds conferences and coordinates an

Continued on p. 282

At Issue:

Has the U.S. Air Force dispelled longstanding claims of a government coverup of a UFO incident in Roswell, N.M., in 1947?

yes

U.S. AIR FORCE
FROM "THE ROSWELL REPORT: FACT VS. FICTION IN THE NEW MEXICO DESERT," 1995.

The overall thrust of [many recent] articles, books and shows is that the "Roswell Incident" was actually the crash of a craft from another world, the U.S. government recovered it and has been "covering up" this fact from the American public since 1947, using a combination of disinformation, ridicule and threats of bodily harm to do so. Generally, the U.S. Air Force bears the brunt of these accusations. . . .

Recent Air Force research did not locate or develop any information that the "Roswell Incident" was a UFO event. All available official materials . . . indicate that the most likely source of the wreckage recovered from the Brazel Ranch was from one of the Project Mogul balloon "trains" [designed to attempt to monitor Soviet nuclear tests]. Although that project was Top Secret at the time, there was also no specific indication found to indicate an official preplanned cover story was in place to explain an event such as that which ultimately happened. It appears that the identification of the wreckage as being part of a weather balloon device, as reported in the newspapers at the time, was based on the fact that there was no physical difference . . . between Mogul balloons and normal weather balloons. . . . Likewise, there was no indication in official records from the period that there was heightened military operational or security activity which should have been generated if this was, in fact, the first recovery of materials and/or persons from another world. The postwar U.S. military (or today's for that matter) did not have the capability to rapidly identify, recover, coordinate, cover up and quickly minimize public scrutiny of such an event. The claim that they did so without leaving even a little bit of a suspicious paper trail for 47 years is incredible.

[Our report makes little mention] about the recovery of the so-called "alien bodies." This is for several reasons: First, the recovered wreckage was from a Project Mogul balloon. There were no "alien" passengers therein. Secondly, the pro-UFO groups who espouse the alien bodies theories cannot even agree among themselves as to what, how many and where such bodies were supposedly recovered. Additionally, some of these claims have been shown to be hoaxes, even by other UFO researchers. Thirdly, when such claims are made, they are often attributed to people using pseudonyms or who otherwise do not want to be publicly identified. . . . [M]any of the persons making the biggest claims of "alien bodies" make their living from the "Roswell Incident." While having a commercial interest in something does not automatically make it suspect, it does raise interesting questions related to authenticity.

no

DON BERLINER
The Fund for UFO Research

FROM "A REBUTTAL OF THE AIR FORCE PROJECT MOGUL EXPLANATION FOR THE 1947 ROSWELL, N.M., UFO CRASH," NOVEMBER 1995.

In 1978, private UFO investigators began locating and interviewing the few surviving first-hand witnesses to the 1947 events. This resulted in several books claiming that the wreckage was of an alien spacecraft, and that it was accompanied by the bodies of several small aliens. By this time, however, the U.S. Air Force was insisting that nothing at all had happened in the Roswell vicinity that could possibly be connected with any such claims. . . .

In March 1993, Rep. Steven Schiff, R-N.M., responded to constituents' requests and asked the secretary of Defense what crashed on the sheep ranch in 1947. He received no useful information, and in February 1994, turned the matter over to the General Accounting Office for investigation. . . .

In July, 1995, the GAO issued its final report. . . . It stated that it could find no new documents relevant to the Roswell crash, but determined that several years (including 1947) of out-going message traffic from Roswell [Army Air Forces] had been destroyed against regulations. Also missing were records of the 1395th Military Police Company, which would have guarded the crash site and sensitive areas at the air base. Moreover, it could find no trace of who authorized the destruction of records, or why it had been done. The GAO report concluded: "The debate over what crashed at Roswell continues.". . .

The U.S. Air Force, in its 1995 report, says the debris was probably from Mogul test flight No. 4, which consisted of about 30 neoprene balloons and perhaps several radar reflectors. . . . Even if the neoprene balloons had survived long exposure to the sun . . . there is no way they could have covered the wide area [witnesses] described. All the Mogul balloons were filled with helium, an inert gas which cannot explode and scatter pieces over many acres. Balloons descend because they have sprung leaks which allow their lifting gas to escape. They land in one piece. . . .

If what was found at the sheep ranch was merely a lot of unclassified balloon materials, why was the ranch cordoned off from not only local residents, but the sheriff's men as well? What did the U.S. Army feel had to be kept far from the sight of everyone but its own people? In the case of Mogul test balloons that landed elsewhere, there is no evidence that extreme security measures were considered necessary. . . .

[W]hy did the Air Force go to all the trouble of creating this huge report, since it includes absolutely no evidence that a Project Mogul balloon landed on the Foster Ranch?

Continued from p. 280

amateur radio network. The Center for UFO Studies in Chicago takes telephoned reports of sightings and investigates those that look promising.

In Yucca Valley, Calif., Gabriel Green, the longtime head of the Amalgamated Flying Saucer Clubs of America and a former U.S. presidential candidate, recently sent out word in his newsletter that UFOs and government coverups will dominate this year's national elections. Moreover, he said that the Japanese government is threatening to release extensive UFO files if the U.S. government doesn't release its own.

Ed Komarek, co-founder of the Gaithersburg, Md., UFO group Operation Right to Know, is running for Congress. "The coverup of the reality of advanced space-faring civilizations coming to us from space by world governments is contributing to the stagnation and devolution of world societies," his campaign literature warns.

In the scientific realm, the Enterprise Mission, an investigative group in Weehawken, N.J., continues publishing and lecturing on an alleged NASA coverup of photographic evidence purportedly showing artificial structures on the moon. Believers say the huge, glass structures display advanced architectural techniques from a long-lost civilization. The group (formerly the Mars Mission) contends that films and photographs taken by Apollo astronauts are mysteriously missing from NASA's public offerings.

Other active paranormal groups include the Ancient Astronaut Society, of Highland Park, Ill., which claims members in 93 countries. It leads its members on expeditions to explore land formations and mysterious sculptures thought to be the work of aliens. The International Association for Near-Death Studies in East Windsor Hill, Conn., promotes research and publishes journals. And the Annapolis, Md.-based American Association of Electronic Voice Phenomena, with 250 members in 39 states, circulates cassette tape recordings of what it says are the voices of ghosts.

Interest in the paranormal continues as a boost for tourism. The UFO museum in Roswell offers a bronze medallion commemorating the 1947 "incident" to donors of $25. And 85 miles north of Las Vegas, the state of Nevada last winter spent $3,300 putting up signs proclaiming the "extraterrestrial highway." The region has a reputation for mystery because it is home to Area 51, a top-secret Defense Department facility thought to test special aircraft. Tiny Gulf Breeze, Fla., meanwhile, enjoys a reputation among cognoscenti as the "UFO capital of the United States."

But the skeptics are gearing up to respond to the continued activism. To mark its 20th anniversary, CSICOP is planning nothing less than "The First World Skeptics Congress," to be held in June in Buffalo, N.Y. The three-day conference, titled "Science in the Age of (Mis)Information," will feature numerous writers and scientists of note, including writer and zoologist Stephen Jay Gould of Harvard, who will deliver the keynote address. ■

OUTLOOK

One Iota of Evidence?

People who claim to have been abducted by aliens are not mentally ill, according to a team of psychologists at Carlton University in Ottawa, Canada, who conducted a battery of tests on such subjects in 1993. "They tend to be white-collar, relatively well-educated representatives of the middle class," they reported. However, the study also noted that 80 percent of the alleged abductions took place at night, 60 percent of them while the subject was asleep. [30]

Some scholars, among them University of Connecticut psychologist Kenneth Ring, suggest that UFO and near-death phenomena may represent something beyond the either-or choices of literal truth and pure fiction. "Perhaps there is, after all, a third realm of the imagination in its own right," he writes, "not as something unreal, but as something objectively self-existent, the cumulative product of imaginative thought itself." [31]

But CSICOP's Kurtz points out that most academic experts are skeptical of colleagues who get involved in the paranormal. "Hynek was virtually the only astronomer defending close encounters," he says, "yet a small fringe can get all the attention."

Many scholars are reluctant to criticize their peers, notes Terence J. Sandbek, a Sacramento, Calif., psychologist. "They feel uncomfortable in the public limelight; they don't want to be seen as a negative person; still others see the whole issue as so silly as to not deserve a response." [32]

Skeptic Klass, who has collected many times on his longstanding bet that no one can present proof of UFOs, is a familiar fixture at UFO conferences. He is treated amicably, even though the Mutual UFO Network sells dartboards bearing his likeness.

"The vast majority of UFO believers are not in it for the money — they fund many of their own investigations," he says. "But notice that none of these people who claim to have been abducted by UFOs has produced one iota of new scientific evidence. You might expect if these aliens are so wise, they would quickly give us a cure for AIDS or point to a place in the sky where we might discover a new planet."

Hall of the Fund for UFO Research finds Klass "intellectually dishonest. When you pin him down on one point, he makes a joke and won't debate."

Members of CSICOP do worry that their skepticism may come across as harsh. "We must be fair-minded and objective," says Kurtz. "But at some point, we become exasperated, and we have to debunk to keep alive an appreciation for the reflective mind."

The United States is "the most advanced technological culture in the world," he adds. "A failure to appreciate the scientific method will undermine our power in the world, our responsibility and our future."

Meanwhile, Stanford keeps up his searching, sometimes using computer-enhanced images of UFOs captured on film. One photo that he says he took at an altitude of 39,000 feet — while on a Braniff Airlines flight in 1977 — shows beams of plasma (hot ionized gas) emanating from a UFO. This is another sign, he says, of an alien technology that permits a craft to move at extraordinary speed.

"Whichever nation gets the secret to this could rule the world," Stanford says. "As a youth, I was naive in thinking that I could simply prove this with instruments," and then the U.S. government would reveal its secrets. "But now I see that the government has its hands on an incredibly complex problem, a legitimate intelligence issue. It has to protect potential breakthroughs from being leaked to our enemies." ■

FOR MORE INFORMATION

Committee for Scientific Investigation of Claims of the Paranormal, 3965 Rensch Rd., Amherst, N.Y. 14228; (716) 636-1425. Founded in 1976, this group of academics, researchers and journalists monitors claims it sees as unscientific in such areas as UFOs, psychic phenomena, astrology and creationism. It publishes *Skeptical Inquirer* magazine and many books, taking an aggressively debunking approach.

Fortean Times: The Journal of Strange Phenomena, c/o Fenner Reed & Jackson Inc., P.O. Box 754, Manhasset, N.Y. 11030; (212) 649-4484. This British monthly magazine devoted to an entertaining but realistic approach to paranormal phenomena is available through an American distributor. It is named for an early American paranormal researcher, Charles Fort.

Fund for UFO Research, P.O. Box 277, Mt. Rainier, Md. 20712; (703) 684-6032. Founded in 1979 by physicist Bruce Maccabee and others, this group provides financial support for scientific research and public education regarding unidentified flying objects.

Institute for Parapsychology, 402 North Buchanan Blvd., Durham, N.C. 27701; (919) 688-8241. Founded in 1962 by Duke University psychology Professor J.B. Rhine, the institute conducts research into extrasensory perception, psychokinesis and clairvoyance. It publishes a journal, serves as a public information resource and offers graduate-level studies.

J. Allen Hynek Center for UFO Studies, 2457 West Peterson Ave., Chicago, Ill. 60659; (312) 271-3611. Founded in 1973 by an astronomer and longtime consultant to the Air Force on UFOs, the center fields calls about UFO sightings and conducts investigations. It also publishes papers on UFO research.

Notes

[1] John E. Mack, M.D., *Abductions: Human Encounters with Aliens* (1994), p. 1.

[2] *Skeptical Inquirer,* May 1995, p. 41, published by the Committee for the Scientific Investigation of Claims of the Paranormal (CSICOP).

[3] Timothy Good, *Alien Contact: Top Secret UFO Files Revealed* (1993), p. 123.

[4] *Time,* Feb. 5, 1996, p. 51.

[5] Karl T. Pflock, " 'Project Snafu' and the Real Secret of Roswell," Fund for UFO Research, Issue paper No. 1, p. 59, 1994.

[6] Howard Blum, *Out There: The Government's Secret Quest for Extraterrestrials* (1990), p. 40.

[7] Headquarters United States Air Force, *The Roswell Report: Fact Versus Fiction in the New Mexico Desert,* 1995, p. 3.

[8] General Accounting Office, *Government Records: Results of a Search for Records Concerning the 1947 Crash Near Roswell, N.M.,* July 1995.

[9] Philip J. Klass, *UFOs: The Public Deceived* (1983), p. 50.

[10] Philip J. Klass, "Did the U.S. government set up a top secret UFO Working Group?" Book review of *Out There: The Government's Secret Quest for Extraterrestrials,* in *Scientific American,* February 1991, p. 140.

[11] P.M.H. Atwater, *Beyond the Light: What Isn't Being Said About Near-Death Experience* (1994), p. 182.

[12] Mack, *op. cit.,* p. 422.

[13] Carl Sagan, *The Demon-Haunted World: Science As a Candle in the Dark* (1996), as excerpted in *Skeptical Inquirer,* March-April 1996, p. 28.

[14] Quoted in Terence J. Sandbek, "Hungry People Who Buy Imaginary Food with Real Money: Psychology, Mysticism, Superstition and the Paranormal," paper at the American Psychological Association convention, Aug. 17, 1991.

[15] Quoted in Malcolm W. Browne, "Scientists Deplore Flight From Reason," *The New York Times,* June 6, 1995, p. C1.

[16] Quoted in Michael Zimmerman, "Why Establishment Leaders Resist the Very Idea of Superior Non-Human Intelligence," Fund for UFO Research, Issue Paper No. 1. The Brookings Institution report, "Proposed Studies on the Implications of Peaceful Space Activities for Human Affairs," was prepared for the National Aeronautics and Space Administration and distributed by the House Committee on Science and Astronautics, April 18, 1961.

[17] Editors of Time-Life Books, *The UFO Phenomenon* (1987), p. 17.

[18] From the PBS documentary "Telegrams from the Dead," *The American Experience,* broadcast Oct. 19, 1994.

[19] Marcia S. Smith, "The UFO Enigma," Congressional Research Service, June 20, 1983, p. 47.

[20] Timothy Good, *Above Top Secret* (1988), p. 260.

[21] Symposium on Unidentified Flying Objects: Hearings before the House Committee on Science and Astronautics, July 29, 1968.

[22] Cited in Smith, *op. cit.,* p. 75.

[23] *MUFON UFO Journal,* June 1990, p. 6.

[24] Quoted in C.B. Scott Jones, "Myth, Reality and Misinformation About Government Secrecy," Issue Paper No. 1, Fund for UFO Research, 1994. p. 1.

[25] *The Washington Post,* Nov. 30, 1995.

[26] Quoted in Michael D. Mumford, Andrew M. Rose and David A. Goslin, "An Evaluation of Remote Viewing: Research and Applications," American Institutes for Research, Sept. 29, 1995.

[27] Quoted in Martin Gardner, "The Senator from Outer Space," *Skeptical Inquirer,* March-April 1996, p. 12.

[28] Quoted in *The Washington Post,* March 10, 1994.

[29] *Skeptical Inquirer,* November-December 1995, p. 6.

[30] The Associated Press, Nov. 1, 1993.

[31] Kenneth Ring, *The Omega Project: Near-Death Experiences, UFO Encounters and Mind at Large* (1992), p. 218.

[32] Sandbek, *op. cit.*

Bibliography

Selected Sources Used

Books

Atwater, P.M.H., *Beyond the Light: What Isn't Being Said About Near-Death Experience,* Birch Lane Press, 1994.

A writer from Charlottesville, Va., who has undergone three brushes with death examines the experiences of hundreds who describe the "tunnel of light" and the joy — or sometimes terror — of near-death.

Blum, Howard, *Out There: The Government's Secret Quest for Extraterrestrials,* Simon and Schuster, 1990.

A former *New York Times* reporter recounts his findings about an alleged top-secret "working group" within the Pentagon that has been exploring the possibility that aliens have visited the Earth.

Editors of Time-Life Books, *The UFO Phenomenon*, Time-Life, 1987

As part of its Mysteries of the Unknown series, the popular publisher examines the history and worldwide impact of unidentified flying objects since ancient times.

Good, Timothy, *Above Top Secret: The Worldwide UFO Cover-Up,* William Morrow, 1988

A noted UFO researcher examines government handling of alleged sightings of alien spacecraft throughout the world.

Good, Timothy, *Alien Contact: Top-Secret UFO Files Revealed,* William Morrow, 1993.

A noted UFO researcher follows up an earlier work with reports on the government's handling of UFOs, alleged alien technology and strange happenings such as the systematic mutilation of farm animals.

Klass, Philip J., *UFOs: The Public Deceived*, Prometheus Books, 1980.

A writer for *Aviation Week & Space Technology* and longtime UFO debunker examines the claims, evidence, government policies and media coverage surrounding UFOs following World War II.

Lyons, Arthur, and Marcello Truzzi, *The Blue Sense: Psychic Detectives and Crime,* Mysterious Books, 1991.

The Center for Scientific Anomalies Research traces the history of efforts at practical uses for psychic powers from writer Arthur Conan Doyle in 19th-century London to the current use of psychics by police crime-solvers.

Mack, John E. M.D., *Abduction: Human Encounters with Aliens,* Charles Scribners' Sons, 1994.

A well-known psychiatrist at the Harvard University Medical School describes his experiences in treating dozens of patients who claim "missing time" and memories of being forced aboard a spacecraft for examination and breeding experiments.

Ring, Kenneth, Ph.D., *The Omega Project: Near-Death Experiences, UFO Encounters, and Mind at Large,* William Morrow, 1992.

A University of Connecticut psychology professor reports on his surveys seeking similarities among people who say they've encountered aliens and those who had close brushes with death.

Sagan, Carl, *The Demon-Haunted World: Science as a Candle in the Dark,* Random House, 1996.

The famous Cornell University astronomer decries the diminishing respect for the "beauty, power and majesty" of science, arguing that "superstition and pseudo-science keep getting in the way."

Stanford, Ray, *Socorro 'Saucer' in a Pentagon Pantry,* Blueapple Books, 1976.

A UFO researcher examines an alleged UFO encounter in 1964 in Socorro, N.M., and the supposed role of the U.S. intelligence community in keeping it secret.

Reports and Studies

American Institutes for Research, *An Evaluation of Remote Viewing: Research and Applications,* Sept. 29, 1995.

At the request of the CIA, a Washington consulting firm evaluates recent research to determine whether "psychics" have the ability to visualize objects and data outside their field of vision.

General Accounting Office, *Government Records: Results of a Search for Records Concerning the 1947 Crash Near Roswell, N.M.,* July 1995.

The GAO's report of the incident offered some ammunition for UFO believers, noting that some government records covering Roswell air base activities had been destroyed.

Smith, Marcia S., *The UFO Enigma,* Congressional Research Service, 1983.

A science policy analyst working for Congress compiled this detailed account of the government's handling of UFOs over 40 years.

U.S. Air Force, *The Roswell Report: Fact versus Fiction in the New Mexico Desert,* 1995.

Issued before the GAO's report, the Air Force review reports that a flying saucer didn't crash in New Mexico in 1947, attributing the secrecy to a radar balloon used to monitor Soviet atomic tests.

The Next Step

Additional information from UMI's Newspaper & Periodical Abstracts database

Alien Abduction

Carroll, Jerry, "Extraterrestrials and me," ***San Francisco Chronicle,*** **May 29, 1994, p. W3.**
Carroll comments on claims of abductions of human beings by extraterrestrial life.

McLaughlin, Paul, "E.T.: The extraterrestrial therapist," ***Saturday Night,*** **June 1995, pp. 44-52.**
Dr. David Gotlib treats those who believe they have been abducted by space aliens. He does not think they are crazy. He doesn't believe that aliens are literally visiting Earth, but something is happening.

McWhirter, Nickie, "Extraterrestrials become more than academic concern," ***Detroit News & Free Press,*** **Aug. 8, 1995, p. E7.**
Nickie McWhirter comments on Harvard Medical School professor and psychiatrist John Mack's startling conclusion that people who believe they have been taken aboard space ships have indeed experienced an alien abduction. His findings are found in his book *Abduction: Human Encounters with Aliens.*

Patterson, Randall, "Eyewitness accounts carry little weight with skeptics," ***The Houston Post,*** **June 21, 1993, p. B2.**
The Houston Association for Scientific Thinking is briefly discussed. The group's 25 members are skeptical about the claims of alien abductions.

Patterson, Randall, "I was abducted by . . . Aliens," ***The Houston Post,*** **June 21, 1993, p. B1.**
The efforts of Derrel Sims and the Houston UFO Network (HUFON) to gather evidence that supports the existence of aliens and alien abductions are discussed.

Sagan, Carl, "What's really going on?" ***The Washington Post,*** **March 7, 1993, p. W4.**
Sagan examines the bizarre reports of alien abductions and sexual experiments performed on the abductees. He questions whether people are really undergoing a massive but generally overlooked invasion by alien sexual abusers or whether they are experiencing some internal mental state, such as a hallucinatory experience, they do not understand.

Vick, Karl, "UFO abduction tales not quite so alien," ***The Washington Post,*** **May 9, 1995, p. A1.**
The growing acceptance of stories of alien abduction in U.S. society is examined.

Belief in the Paranormal

Berger, Arthur S., "Quoth the raven: Bereavement and the paranormal," ***Omega: Journal of Death & Dying,*** **1995, pp. 1-10.**
The relevance to bereavement of paranormal experiences and of the belief in a life after death is examined. Data from physical research that can be used to validate the experiences and belief and to help the bereaved restructure their lives are discussed.

Dumas, Lynne, "Heaven sent," ***Woman's Day,*** **Nov. 21, 1995, pp. 59-62.**
Spiritual phenomena have become a growth industry. Reasons why Americans seem to suddenly be opening their minds to believing in such occurrences are discussed.

Gallup, George Jr., and Frank Newport, "Normal and Paranormal," ***St. Louis Post-Dispatch,*** **Aug. 5, 1990, C1.**
In the first of a series of reports, what Americans believe about the paranormal is revealed through a Gallup Mirror of America survey.

Irwin, Harvey J., "Childhood trauma and the origins of paranormal belief: A constructive replication," ***Psychological Reports,*** **February 1994, pp. 107-111.**
A study found that adults who were children of alcoholics have stronger beliefs in witchcraft, superstitions and precognition.

Lawrence, Tony R., and Jerome J. Tobacyk, "How many factors of paranormal belief are there? A critique of the Paranormal Belief Scale," ***Journal of Parapsychology,*** **March 1995, pp. 3-46.**
An investigation was conducted to assess critically the Paranormal Belief Scale (PBS) developed by Tobacyk and Milford (1983). Lawrence argues that a new PBS and a more appropriate definition of paranormal are required, and Tobacyk responds.

Lester, David, and Kristin Monaghan, "Belief in paranormal phenomena and personality," ***Perceptual & Motor Skills,*** **August 1995, p. 114.**
Lester and Monaghan found that neither extraversion nor neuroticism was related to belief in paranormal phenomena in a sample of 66 middle-school pupils.

MacDonald, William L., "The effects of religiosity and structural strain on reported paranormal experiences," ***Journal for the Scientific Study of Religion,*** **September 1995, pp. 366-376.**
MacDonald tests whether or not religious orientation, religious behavior and structural strain predict the odds of

reporting telepathic and clairvoyant experiences. He concludes that sociocultural forces do affect the reporting of paranormal experiences.

Sagan, Carl, "The variety of supernatural experience," *Natural History,* February 1996, p. 16.
The belief in extraterrestrial beings visiting Earth and abducting humans is not too different from the belief in fairies, as similar accounts show. Humankind often shows an enthusiasm for its dreams, especially in popular culture.

Wiseman, Richard, Matthew Smith and Jeff Wiseman, "Eyewitness testimony and the paranormal," *Skeptical Inquirer,* November 1995, pp. 29-32.
Experiments have shown that witnesses of paranormal phenomena are influenced by their beliefs and expectations. The unreliability of eyewitness testimony is discussed.

New York Academy of Sciences Conference

Baum, Rudy, "Attacks on science require measured, reasoned response," *Chemical & Engineering News,* June 26, 1995, p. 34.
The New York Academy of Sciences recently held a conference entitled "The Flight from Science and Reason" to discuss recent attacks against science by radical environmentalists and religious fundamentalists.

Creque, Stuart, "We're not scientific heretics," *The Wall Street Journal,* July 31, 1995, p. A15.
Creque responds to the July 10, 1995, Christina Hoff Sommers article "The Flight from Science and Reason," defending the belief in things other than what can be measured by science.

Rios, Etienne, "The flight from science and reason: New York Academy of Sciences Conference airs issues," *Skeptical Inquirer,* November 1995, pp. 42-44.
Highlights of a meeting of the New York Academy of Sciences are discussed. The conference, titled "Flight from Science and Reason," focuses on the increasing anti-rational and anti-scientific rhetoric in academia.

Poplular Culture and the Paranormal

Carman, John, "Believe this, UFOs land at Nova," *San Francisco Chronicle,* Feb. 27, 1996, p. E1.
Carman reviews an episode of the PBS "Nova" series titled "Kidnapped by UFOs."

Emery, C. Eugene Jr., "Paranormal and paranoia intermingle on Fox TV's X-Files," *Skeptical Inquirer,* March 1995, pp. 18-19.
Some elements of the television program "The X-Files" may be of interest to the people who truly want to uncover the secrets of UFOs, psychic phenomena and things that go bump in the night. The program's merit is discussed.

Evans, E. S., "Paranormal tales on TV shows fail scientific scrutiny," *St. Louis Journalism Review,* July 1995, p. 78.
Daytime talk shows reflect the results of uncritical thinking, Evans writes, and science tends to get swept under the rug when they cover paranormal topics. Episodes of "Sally Jessy Raphael," "Oprah" and "Maury Povich" are discussed.

Headlam, Bruce, "Closing the X files," *Saturday Night,* December 1995, pp. 101-104.
The popularity of "The X-Files" TV program was unsuspected, but it rode on its suggestive power and enduring mysteries. The failure of the show and its cancellation was the solving of the mysteries that kept viewers so intrigued.

Kennedy, J.E., "Methods for investigating goal-oriented psi," *Journal of Parapsychology,* March 1995, p. 47-62.
Experimental research in parapsychology may be of little value if *psi* is goal-oriented and the sources of *psi* focus on certain types of goals, Kennedy writes. The concept of efficient goal-oriented *psi* operating in a hierarchy of goals suggests that the elusive, capricious nature of *psi* may sometimes reflect psi efficiently achieving goals relatively high on the hierarchy.

Roach, Mary, "A postcard from the twilight zone," *Health* (San Francisco), July 1995, pp. 42-48.
Roach describes participating in an experiment involving ganzfeld, a form of telepathy in which one person attempts to mentally transmit an image to another person.

Psychics

O'Brien, John, "When all else fails, cops turn to psychics," *Chicago Tribune,* Aug. 27, 1995, p. SW2.
In an age of computers and other advanced crime-fighting technology, it seems unlikely that police would think of consulting psychics, spiritual healers or astrologers for answers, but some do. Several cases in which psychics have allegedly helped solve a case in the Chicago area are examined.

Thurtell, Joel, "Psychics No Substitute for Clues," *Detroit News & Free Press,* June 13, 1992, p. B12.
Michigan police are wary of using psychics in criminal investigations, but at times find their insights helpful.

Truzzi, Marcello, and Robert A. Baker, "Reflections on *The Blue Sense* and its critics," *Journal of Parapsychology,* June 1995, pp. 99-130.
Truzzi examines critics' reactions to his book *The Blue Sense: Psychic Detectives and Crime* and their confusion of the term "blue sense." Baker does not agree with Truzzi's belief that the case for some sort of paranormal detective ability on the part of some psychics is worth considering. Truzzi responds.

Waller, Douglas, "The vision thing," ***Time,*** **Dec. 11, 1995, p. 48.**

A secret program of the Pentagon spent $20 million in the past 10 years to employ psychics in pursuit of the unknown. The ultra-secret Defense Intelligence Agency hoped it might get a real advantage in the world of military intelligence from the paranormal, but the CIA has determined the program was a waste of money and moved to shut it down.

UFOs and Extraterrestrials

Anderson, Jon, and Stacey Singer, "UFO enthusiasts say it's time to face facts: We aren't alone," ***Chicago Tribune,*** **Oct. 7, 1995, p. 1.**

The Chicago celebration of National UFO Awareness Week has spawned both believers and skeptics to debate the possibility of life-forms somewhere else besides planet Earth. The convention is examined.

Daly, Christopher B., "Harvard clears best-selling UFO author," ***The Washington Post,*** **Aug. 4, 1995, p. A20.**

After more than a year of closed-door hearings, Harvard officials disclosed they will not discipline psychiatrist John Mack, who has gained notoriety for taking seriously people who say they have been abducted by space aliens.

Greenwood, Tom, "Cornfield could be site of UFO visit or husky hoax," ***Detroit News,*** **Oct. 16, 1995, p. A1.**

Farmers near Filion, north of Bad Ax in Michigan's Thumb, are scratching their heads over what some believe might have been a visit by a UFO to a cornfield. Scores of visitors have been drawn to the field on Thomas Road to gape at a strange design cut into the rows of dry, rustling corn.

Hall, Carla, "For UFO buffs, the truth is out there on Highway 375," ***Los Angeles Times,*** **Dec. 25, 1995, p. A1.**

A Nevada state assemblyman and some locals want Nevada State Highway 375 designated the "Alien and Extraterrestrial Highway" because the desolate Nevada desert is famous for UFO sightings. Tours of the area that focus on UFO phenomena are discussed.

Kittredge, Clare, "UFOs have been flying around here for years," ***Boston Globe,*** **Feb. 4, 1996, p. 39.**

In an interview, Betty Hill, who was one of the first people to claim to have been abducted by aliens when she and her husband came forward in 1961, discusses UFOs and her own book, *A Common Sense Approach to UFOs.*

Puckett, Patti, "UFO conference simply out of this world," ***Atlanta Constitution,*** **Oct. 16, 1995, p. B2.**

The 32nd annual National UFO Conference drew more than 300 people to the Castlegate Hotel and Conference Center in Atlanta, including those who say they have had contact with extraterrestrials.

UFO Incident at Roswell, N.M.

Cauchon, Dennis, "1947 UFO finally identified," ***USA Today,*** **Sept. 9, 1994, p. A1.**

The Air Force, after 47 years of silence, finally admitted in September 1994 that it was responsible for the famous "flying saucer" of Roswell, N.M. Behind the mystery was wreckage found in a rancher's field in 1947.

Hannah, James, "Talk still flies of UFO coverup," ***Denver Post,*** **April 10, 1994, p. C5**

Walter Haut, a former public relations officer at the Army air field in Roswell, N.M., said in April 1994 that he believes the Army is covering up a UFO crash landing on July 2, 1947. In late 1993, Rep. Steve Schiff, R-N.M., asked the Pentagon for its records on the crash after New Mexicans pressed him for an explanation.

Pressley, Sue Anne, "UFO, or not, crash site's become a starship enterprise," ***The Washington Post,*** **Feb. 18, 1996, A13.**

The mystery of what happened in 1947 in Roswell, N.M., a military town and site of a possible UFO crash, is examined.

Sobel, Dava, "The truth about Roswell," ***Omni,*** **fall 1995, pp. 90-99.**

Rep. Stephen H. Schiff, R-N.M., has asked the GAO to investigate the alleged crash of an alien spacecraft near Roswell, N.M., and the alleged government coverup of the event. Though the government continues to deny the incident ever occurred, and the GAO says it is not investigating it, many eyewitnesses insist that the military is covering up what really happened.

Walker, Martin, "Space oddity," ***The Guardian,*** **July 25, 1995, p. 2.**

Walker discusses the mystery surrounding the crash of a strange aerial craft near Roswell Army Air Field in New Mexico on July 4, 1947, and details how the crash, thought by many to be that of a UFO, has brought about fresh controversy due to the film of an alleged autopsy conducted on supposed alien beings that has been brought to light.

"The X-Files"

Carman, John, " 'X-Files' from far-outer space," ***San Francisco Chronicle,*** **Sept. 10, 1993, p. C6.**

John Carman reviews the TV program "The X-Files," a Fox series about FBI agents who work on cases involving the supernatural and paranormal.

Headlam, Bruce, "Closing the X-Files," ***Saturday Night,*** **December 1995, pp. 101-104.**

The popularity of "The X-Files" TV program was unsuspected, but it rode on its suggestive power and enduring mysteries. The failure of the show and its cancellation was the solving of the mysteries that kept viewers so intrigued.

Back Issues

Great Research on Current Issues Starts Right Here...Recent topics covered by The CQ Researcher are listed below. Before May 1991, reports were published under the name of Editorial Research Reports.

SEPTEMBER 1994
Home Schooling
Welfare Experiments
Courts and the Media
Regulating Tobacco

OCTOBER 1994
Historic Preservation
Religion and Politics
Arts Funding
Economic Sanctions

NOVEMBER 1994
Sex on Campus
Blood Supply Safety
Testing Term Limits
Religion in America

DECEMBER 1994
Farm Policy
Arms Sales
Earthquake Research
The Future of Television

JANUARY 1995
Treating Addiction
Child Custody and Support
Parents and Schools
Non-Proliferation Treaty at 25

FEBRUARY 1995
Cracking Down on Immigration
The Business of Sports
Reinventing Government
Housing Discrimination

MARCH 1995
Death Penalty Debate
Primary Care
Democracy in Africa
Environmental Movement at 25

APRIL 1995
Abortion Clinic Protests
Dieting and Health
Combating AIDS
Rethinking Affirmative Action

MAY 1995
Assisted Suicide Controversy
Overhauling Social Security
Learning to Read
Mandatory Sentencing

JUNE 1995
Combating Infectious Disease
Property Rights
Repetitive Stress Injuries
Regulating the Internet

JULY 1995
War Crimes
Highway Safety
Combating Terrorism
Preventing Teen Drug Use

AUGUST 1995
Job Stress
Organ Transplants
United Nations at 50
Advances in Cancer Research

SEPTEMBER 1995
Catholic Church in the U.S.
Northern Ireland Cease-Fire
High School Sports
Teaching History

OCTOBER 1995
Quebec's Future
Revitalizing the Cities
Networking the Classroom
Indoor Air Pollution

NOVEMBER 1995
The Working Poor
The Jury System
Sex, Violence and the Media
Police Misconduct

DECEMBER 1995
Teens and Tobacco
Gene Therapy's Future
Global Water Shortages
Third-Party Prospects

JANUARY 1996
Emergency Medicine
Punishing Sex Offenders
Bilingual Education
Helping the Homeless

FEBRUARY 1996
Reforming the CIA
Campaign Finance Reform
Academic Politics
College Admissions

MARCH 1996
Preventing Youth Violence
The British Monarchy
Tax Reform

Back issues are available for $5.00 (subscribers) or $8.00 (non-subscribers). Quantity discounts apply to orders over ten. To order, call Congressional Quarterly Customer Service at (202) 887-8621.

Binders are available for $18.00. To order call 1-800-638-1710. Please refer to stock number 648.

Future Topics

- ***Centennial Olympic Games***
- ***Managed Care***
- ***Protecting Endangered Species***

THE CQ Researcher®

PUBLISHED BY CONGRESSIONAL QUARTERLY INC.

Centennial Olympic Games

Have the Games gotten too commercialized?

The 1996 summer Olympics, due to begin in Atlanta in July, will be the biggest and costliest ever. Nearly 11,000 athletes from 197 countries will compete in the $1.6 billion extravaganza. Organizers expect an astounding global TV audience of 3.5 billion people — more than half the Earth's population. And they anticipate none of the political boycotts that have marred the Games in recent years. But two perennial concerns remain: Many critics decry the drumbeat of commercialization surrounding the Games, and others worry about the use by some athletes of performance-enhancing drugs. For now, though, the mood is decidedly upbeat as the nation awaits the April 27 start in Los Angeles of the coast-to-coast, 15,000-mile Olympic torch relay.

INSIDE THIS ISSUE

CQ April 5, 1996 • Volume 6, No. 13 • Pages 289-312

Formerly Editorial Research Reports

CENTENNIAL OLYMPIC GAMES

THE ISSUES

BACKGROUND

CURRENT SITUATION

OUTLOOK

SIDEBARS AND GRAPHICS

FOR FURTHER RESEARCH

COVER: SWIMMERS IN THE 100-METER FREESTYLE VIE FOR SPOTS ON THE U.S. TEAM AT THE OLYMPIC SWIM TRIALS MARCH 8 IN INDIANAPOLIS, IND. (REUTERS/GARY HERSHORN)

April 5, 1996
Volume 6, No. 13

The CQ Researcher (ISSN 1056-2036). Formerly Editorial Research Reports. Published weekly (48 times per year, not printed March 1, May 31, Aug. 30, Nov. 29) by Congressional Quarterly Inc., 1414 22nd St., N.W., Washington, D.C. 20037. Annual subscription rate for libraries, businesses and government is $319. Additional rates furnished upon request. Second-class postage paid at Washington, D.C. POSTMASTER: Send address changes to The CQ Researcher, 1414 22nd St., N.W., Washington, D.C. 20037.

Centennial Olympic Games

BY RICHARD L. WORSNOP

THE ISSUES

The millions of Americans who get swept up in this year's summer Olympics in Atlanta, Ga., won't be alone. An astounding 3.5 billion TV viewers — more than half the world's population — are expected to tune in during the 16 days of competition. Two million more will be on hand as spectators. The biggest-ever Olympic extravaganza will begin July 19, when nearly 11,000 athletes from 197 countries march into the new Olympic Stadium.

For William Porter "Billy" Payne, however, the 1996 Atlanta Olympics began nine years ago — as a naive dream. Payne, an Atlanta attorney, was returning home from church on Feb. 7, 1987, when he was struck by what he termed "an idea founded in goodness" — bringing the 1996 Olympics to his hometown. [1]

Although Atlanta Mayor Andrew Young quickly pledged his support, few observers expected the venture to succeed. Because 1996 marked the 100th anniversary of the modern Olympics, conventional wisdom held that the centennial event would surely be awarded to Athens, Greece, site of the 1896 Games. Atlanta, moreover, was just one of 14 U.S. cities seeking the honor. [2]

But Payne, president of the Atlanta Committee for the Olympic Games (ACOG), and his supporters confounded the skeptics. In April 1988, the U.S. Olympic Committee chose Atlanta as the country's official candidate for the '96 Games, citing the city's existing sports facilities, hotel capacity and transportation system, not to mention its boosters' organizing abilities.

Two and a half years later, on its fifth ballot, the International Olympic Committee (IOC) voted for Atlanta over Athens, 51 to 35.

Though the Games weren't to start

for nearly six years, time was tight. More than $1.5 billion had to be raised — five times more than the cost of the 1984 Los Angeles Games — largely because of all the new construction needed. But construction didn't begin on the main Olympic Stadium until November 1993. [3] Work started even later on the facilities for archery and cycling, aquatics, field hockey, rowing and kayaking, shooting and tennis. In addition, in outlying areas impacted by the massive project, Olympic organizers had to make promised improvements to housing and neighborhood facilities.

With the Olympics still three months distant, Olympic fever — and grumbling over traffic congestion, high-priced tickets and scarce housing — has yet to spread much beyond Atlanta. But if history is any guide, the rest of the nation will begin catching the fever on April 27, when the Coca-Cola-sponsored 84-day, 15,000 mile Olympic torch relay begins in Los Angeles. (*See map, p. 300.*)

As the relay sparks interest in the Games, the inevitable complaints about rampant and unseemly commercialization of international sports will be heard, along with concerns about athletes' growing use of performance-enhancing drugs.

Indeed, critics are calling this year's Games the Coca-Cola Olympics. Coke, an Olympic sponsor since 1928, has launched a half-billion-dollar advertising blitz around the Games. (Pepsi is spending $375 million in a counter campaign.) In addition to Coke, nine other "worldwide sponsors" paid the IOC about $40 million each for global marketing rights and exclusive use of the Olympic rings. Eighteen domestic "sponsors" and 10 "partners" reportedly paid ACOG more than $10 million each for similar rights in the United States. In addition, at least 125 other companies signed up for product licenses for lesser amounts.

And to the amusement of some, and the dismay of others, "Wheel of Fortune" and "Jeopardy" bought the right to boast that they are the official game shows of the 26th Olympiad.

"Of course," noted humor columnist Dave Barry, "the Olympics are not just about big corporations paying ridiculous sums of money to be official sponsors. The Olympics are also about ordinary sports fans — people like you — paying ridiculous sums of money for lodging. I saw a classified advertisement . . . in which somebody was offering to rent a four-bedroom, two-bath home during the Olympics for $10,000, which doesn't sound too unreasonable until you notice that the home is located in central Alabama." [4]

Besides complaints about commercialization of the Games, concerns about drug abuse also are likely to receive a fresh airing at Atlanta. "Too many records have been pushed to heights that lie beyond the reach of normally functioning men or women," said gold medalist Olga Connolly. "The young talent who hopes to challenge such records is forced to fall into chemical step." [5]

How the Summer Games Have Grown

This year's Olympics feature more countries than ever before, reflecting the breakup of the Soviet Union into several independent nations and the absence of boycotts. For the first time, more than one-third of all the competitors will be women.

Year	Host City	Number of Nations	Number of Sports	Male Athletes	Female Athletes	Total Number of Athletes
1896	Athens, Greece	13	9	311	0	311
1900	Paris, France	22	17	1,319	11	1,330
1904	St. Louis, Mo.	12	14	681	6	687
1908	London, England	22	21	1,999	36	2,035
1912	Stockholm, Sweden	27	13	2,490	57	2,547
1916	Cancelled due to World War I					
1920	Antwerp, Belgium	27	21	2,543	64	2,607
1924	Paris, France	45	17	2,956	136	3,092
1928	Amsterdam, Holland	46	14	2,724	290	3,014
1932	Los Angeles, Calif.	37	14	1,281	127	1,408
1936	Berlin, Germany	49	19	3,738	328	4,066
1940	Cancelled due to World War II					
1944	Cancelled due to World War II					
1948	London, England	59	17	3,714	385	4,099
1952	Helsinki, Finland	69	17	4,407	518	4,925
1956	Melbourne, Australia	67	16	2,958	384	3,342
	Stockholm, Sweden (equestrian)	29	1	145	13	158
1960	Rome, Italy	84	17	4,738	610	5,348
1964	Tokyo, Japan	94	19	4,457	683	5,140
1968	Mexico City, Mexico	113	18	4,750	781	5,531
1972	Munich, Germany	122	21	6,659	1,171	7,830
1976	Montreal, Canada	92	21	4,915	1,274	6,189
1980	Moscow, USSR	81	21	4,320	1,192	5,512
1984	Los Angeles, Calif.	140	21	5,458	1,620	7,078
1988	Seoul, Korea	160	23	6,983	2,438	9,421
1992	Barcelona, Spain	171	25	7,555	3,008	10,563
1996	Atlanta, Georgia	197	26	6,582	3,779	10,788*

* *Total includes 427 men and women competing as equals in yachting and equestrian events.*

Source: United States Olympic Committee

Refinement of drug-detection policies and technology is believed to have marginally reduced the abuse of certain performance-enhancing drugs. However, few experts feel the practice can be totally eliminated, since several commonly used drugs remain difficult or impossible to detect by current means.

The drug abuse issue is linked in some ways to the debates on commercialism and professionalism of the Olympics and other international sports events. Because appearance fees and prize money typically are performance-related, the argument goes, some athletes worry that abstinence will soon render them uncompetitive at the elite level of their sport, and thus they will miss out on commercial endorsements and other money-making opportunities. Drug-testing results from previous Olympics suggest the lure of drugs is especially strong in track and field, swimming, wrestling and weightlifting.

On the positive side, the political and ideological disputes that have roiled most summer Olympic Games since World War II are not expected to be a major distraction at Atlanta. The breakup of the former Soviet Union has eased tensions between Western nations and those of the old communist bloc. Toppling of the Berlin Wall and reunification of democratic West Germany and communist East Germany, for instance, ended one of the bitterest rivalries in sports.

Still, the current threat of terrorism — and searing memories of the massacre of Israeli athletes in Munich in 1972 — ensure that security will be an overriding concern this summer.

For Payne, however, the event has no downside. At various times, he has called it "the most important event in the history of Atlanta," "the best Olympic Games of all times," "the most important peacetime event of the 20th century" [6] and even "the greatest peacetime event in history." [7]

As Atlanta's moment in the global spotlight approaches, these are some of the questions being asked about the Olympics:

Have the Olympic Games become too big and too commercialized?

Commercial involvement in the Olympics dates from the first Games of the modern era, in Athens. Eastman Kodak Co. advertised in the book of official Olympic results, thus becoming the modern Games' pioneer sponsor. And Kodak displayed its logo throughout the city during the competition.

Kodak's presence will be felt in Atlanta. At its sprawling imaging center, the company expects to process more than 175,000 rolls of film shot by the 900-plus professional photographers accredited to the Games. The center will be equipped to convert photographs into a digital format transmittable by phone or high-speed data line to points around the globe. At the closing ceremony, every athlete will receive a disposable Kodak camera to create a visual memento of the spectacle. Moreover, Kodak already has signed on as the first international sponsor of the 1998 winter Olympics in Nagano, Japan.

Atlanta-based Coke is pulling out all the stops. Besides sponsoring the torch relay, Coca-Cola is building a $20 million theme park in downtown Atlanta where visitors can compete electronically against Olympic champions.

"Coca-Cola is the biggest junk-food maker in the whole world," complains Michael F. Jacobson, co-founder of the Center for the Study of Commercialism. "It's amusing to see Coke associate its name with a competition of athletes in the peak of condition who presumably didn't get there by drinking Coca-Cola." [8]

Another major Olympic sponsor this year, Reebok International Ltd., inadvertently triggered a marketing mini-crisis at the 1992 summer Games in Barcelona. The company had contracted to supply U.S. team members with outfits to be worn at medal-presentation ceremonies. But pro basketball stars on the U.S. national team spurned the Reebok outfits because they were under contract to rival sportswear manufacturers. In the end, a compromise saved the day: Superstars Michael Jordan, Charles Barkley and Magic Johnson draped U.S. flags over their shoulders to conceal the Reebok logo.

U.S. Modern Pentathlon

Pentathletes Scott Christie (right) and James Gregory compete for slots on the U.S. Olympic team at the recent Kodak International Cup competition. The pentathlon includes shooting, fencing, riding, swimming and a 4,000-meter run.

In any case, Reebok plans a more ambitious marketing push this year. "We had a couple of hundred athletes competing in our shoes at Barcelona, but we didn't have any major national Olympic committee or sports federation sponsorships," says public relations director Dave Fogelson. In Atlanta, by contrast, 3,200 athletes — about one-third of all competitors — will wear Reebok apparel. The company negotiated sponsorships with seven national Olympic committees and less comprehensive agreements with smaller countries in Africa, the Caribbean and Latin America. * "We'll also be outfitting 1,400 trainers and coaches," says Fogelson.

McDonald's, which will operate six fast-food restaurants at the Olympic Village, may be the most controversial sponsor of all. Many elite athletes, accustomed to a training diet low in fat and high in complex carbohydrates, say they will shun the burgers and fries that are McDonald's stock in trade. But the company also plans to offer more nutritious fare, including carrot sticks, fresh fruit, yogurt and bottled water.

Hucksterism at the Olympics has long been a subject of unfriendly comment. "The commercialism of the Games has gone beyond shameless to preposterous," *New York Times* television critic John J. O'Connor noted about the 1992 winter Olympics at Albertville, France. He cited athletes "who serve as mov-

---

* Reebok is outfitting teams from Brazil, Ireland, Jamaica, New Zealand, Poland, Russia and South Africa. The U.S. team will wear uniforms from Champion Products Inc.

Events for Every Fans' Fancy

Athletes will compete in 26 sports at the summer Games, including three new events: women's softball, mountain biking and beach volleyball.

Reuters

Aquatics
- Diving
- Swimming
- Synchronized Swimming
- Water Polo

Archery
Badminton
Baseball
Basketball
Boxing
Canoe/Kayak
- Slalom
- Sprint

Cycling
- Mountain Bike
- Road
- Track

Robert Harrison

USA Gymnastics

Equestrian
Fencing
Football (Soccer)
Gymnastics
- Artistic
- Rhythmic

Handball
Hockey
Judo
Modern Pentathlon
Rowing
Shooting
Softball
Table Tennis
Tennis
Track and Field

© C.H. Halporn

U.S. Sailing

Volleyball
- Beach
- Indoor

Weightlifting
Wrestling
Yachting

Source: Atlanta Committee for the Olympic Games

ing billboards, brand names emblazoned on their shorts, helmets, equipment and even, for tight close-ups, goggles." [9]

Similarly, *Washington Post* columnist Jonathan Yardley argued that the flap over medal-presentation outfits at Barcelona missed the point. No one, said Yardley, "questioned the propriety of auctioning off the name and colors of the United States in exchange for advertising space." [10]

Robert A. Baade, an authority on the economics of sports at Lake Forest (Ill.) College, also feels that commercialism has gone too far — not only at the Olympic Games but at the U.S. college and professional levels as well. "When you allow these events to become too commercial, you sully them," he says. "You alienate people, making them cynical about sports in the same way they become cynical about politics."

But Lisa Delpy, a professor of sport management and marketing at George Washington University, argues that complaints about Olympic commercialism are overstated. For one thing, she notes that no commercial signage is permitted inside Olympic sporting arenas. "But if you recall the 1994 World Cup, there was signage ringing the field at every stadium, plus commercial messages superimposed on the TV screen while play was in progress."

Most people who watch the Olympics at home aren't bothered by the frequent commercial breaks, says Delpy. She takes the position that complaints about overcommercialization are more likely to come from sports fans who travel to Atlanta and find they "can't get tickets or hotel rooms because they've all been reserved for corporate sponsors."

The firms that support the Olympics acknowledge they are heavily commercialized, but they note that that's the only reasonable and practical alternative to government financing of the Games. In addition, says Mike May, communications director for the Sporting Goods Manufacturers Association (SGMA) in North Palm Beach, Fla., "The Games would not be covered extensively on television these days if it weren't for the commercial support."

Many Olympic events "are held at times that are good for television, so people at home can watch," notes May. "And of course, that's good for advertisers, too." In his opinion, commercial involvement in the Games has opened the Olympics to more sports and more participants, a development that constitutes "a positive that far outweighs the negative of commercial intrusion."

Fogelson of Reebok makes the further point that effective marketing of sporting goods requires, first and foremost, "an on-field presence, meaning athletes competing in your products." Without that presence, "no amount of advertising is going to establish your brand as a performance brand."

By the same token, "If you simply rely upon the on-field presence and don't reinforce it with a marketing and communications program, many people won't notice what the athletes are wearing."

For the sporting goods industry as a whole, the stakes are extremely high. According to SGMA projections, the Olympics will spark an overall $500 million increase in U.S. sales of sporting goods, much of which will carry over into future years. "The Olympic Games definitely represent the pinnacle," says May. "They're the Mount Everest of sports-marketing opportunities."

Can the Olympic Games be kept free of nationalistic and political pressures?

When the Olympics were revived a century ago, supporters considered them "a forum for the youth of the world to unite in peaceful competition through sport," Olympic historian Richard Espy observed. The purpose was not to encourage competition between countries but "to provide a setting where countries could meet peacefully — at worst, a surrogate battlefield without the bloodshed. The individuals, the athletes, the youth of the world were to provide the central purpose of the Games." [11]

USA Volleyball

Lori Endicott sets up a "spike" for Bev Oden. The highly rated U.S. women's volleyball team is thought to have a good shot at a gold medal in Atlanta.

However, Olympic reality was to fall well short of the founders' ideals. Instead of helping to soothe national rivalries, the Olympics often seemed to aggravate them, notably during the Cold War era (*see p. 301*). But some of the major disputes of that period — those involving the two Chinas, the two Germanys and South Africa — have since been largely resolved. The question now is whether the IOC can do more to make individual athletes the focal point of the Games and to erect safeguards against a resurgence of virulent nationalism.

John A. Lucas, a professor of sport history at Pennsylvania State University, would revamp the Olympic medal-presentation ceremonies as a first step toward denationalizing the Games. Medals are awarded shortly after the championship of each event is decided. The top three finishers receive their medals as their countries' flags are hoisted and the gold medalist's national anthem is played.

"This happens many times in a single day, and 200 or so times during the course of an Olympics," says Lucas, who has attended 11 Olympics over the years. "I don't like it, because an athlete from a small country such as Namibia hardly ever gets to mount the victory stand. It's almost always someone from the United States, Russia, Germany or one of the other great international sports powers."

Lucas would scrap the individual medal ceremonies in favor of a consolidated version that would be held once daily. "All of that day's champions would gather together as the Olympic hymn was played," he suggests. "The names of the athletes and their countries would appear on a screen for all the world to see. It would be a glorification of the individual — or, more important, a glorification of the whole human race."

U.S. Athletes Bring Home the Gold

Americans have earned nearly 2,000 medals since the first Olympic Games, including more than 775 first-place medals.

Year	Gold	Silver	Bronze	Total
1896	11	7	1	19
1900	21	16	16	53
1904	80	85	81	246
1908	23	12	13	48
1912	25	18	19	62
1920	41	27	27	95
1924	45	27	27	99
1928	22	18	16	56
1932	41	32	30	103
1936	24	20	12	56
1948	38	27	19	84
1952	40	19	17	76
1956	32	25	17	74
1960	34	21	16	71
1964	36	26	28	90
1968	45	28	34	107
1972	33	31	30	94
1976	34	35	25	94
1980	0	0	0	0
1984	83	61	30	174
1988	36	31	27	94
1992	37	34	37	108
Totals	**781**	**600**	**522**	**1,903**

Note: Along with several other nations, the U.S. did not participate in the 1980 Moscow Games to protest the Soviet Union's invasion of Afghanistan.

Source: United States Olympic Committee

As Lucas ruefully acknowledges, he has been "castigated for suggesting such an 'unpatriotic' solution'" to downplaying ultranationalism. Ironically, the most resistance comes from underdeveloped countries. "On the very rare occasions when such countries come up with a winner," Lucas says, "they want that young man or young woman standing on the top level of the victory stand, savoring the adulation of thousands of spectators and millions of TV viewers."

Olympic chauvinism was very much the rule in the United States before World War I, Lucas notes. Back then, Americans "wanted their athletes to bask in the glory of victory and stand shoulder to shoulder with their competitors from Britain, France and Germany, the leading world powers of the time."

Selecting a permanent site for the Olympics also would cool nationalistic fervor, Lucas believes. He would place the Games in a valley in central Switzerland, "with snow-capped mountains just a short distance away." Not only would a permanent site evoke the ancient Games, which were always held near the Greek city of Olympia, it would also save billions of dollars in future Olympic construction costs.

In 1981, Lucas presented the IOC with a 44-page proposal for a fixed-site Olympics. Committee members rejected the proposal 88-0. "Again, the most vociferous opposition came from underdeveloped countries that have never held the Olympics," he says. At least one member accused him of racism, saying his plan "would deny Africa, Central America and South America the opportunity of ever hosting the Olympics."

Baade agrees that the Olympics should be staged at a permanent site. However, he favors a site in Greece — "one that honored the classical tradition" of the Games. But since the Olympics have become "too much of a money thing," he doubts that they will return for good to the land of their origin. "As long as there's that potential for commercial benefit among a few powerful people, you'll continue to see the Games moved around."

Can the use of banned drugs by athletes be curtailed?

Experience suggests that at least one drug scandal will surface in Atlanta. Perhaps the most notorious incident to date involved Canadian sprinter Ben Johnson, who won the 100-meter dash in 1988 in Seoul, setting a new world record. However, a urinalysis showed Johnson had taken steroids before the race, and he lost his gold medal and his world record.

"You have to realize the money that's at stake," says Charles E. Yesalis III, a professor of health and human development at Pennsylvania State University. "I think Johnson lost $18 million in endorsement fees."

Several more recent steroid cases have involved world-class swimmers. Since 1990, 19 Chinese swimmers have tested positive for steroids in international competition, including seven at the 1994 Asian Games. Last August, moreover, U.S. swimmer Jessica Foschi failed a steroid test and was banned from competition for two years by the U.S. Swimming Federation. In February, however, the federation reduced Foschi's punishment to probation, allowing her to compete for a spot on the 1996 team.

Steroids are a family of synthetic hormones formulated to mimic the naturally occurring male sex hormone testosterone. They help the user build up muscle tissue, thus increasing body

Anyone for Ballroom Dancing?

It's enough to make a sports fan cry. Moves are afoot to qualify ballroom dancing, also known as "dance sport," as an official Olympic event. Well, why not? supporters ask. Ice dancing, which became an official winter Olympics sport in 1976, now rivals traditional figure skating in popularity among U.S. television viewers.

Other new sports haven't fared quite as well. Rhythmic gymnastics and synchronized swimming, added to the summer Games in 1984 to provide more opportunities for women athletes, command less support. Rhythmic gymnasts perform elaborately choreographed routines on a floor mat with the aid of such props as flags, hoops and ribbons. Critics concede that the athletes are skilled and the routines fun to watch, but they question whether the event qualifies more as show biz than sport.

Similar reservations are voiced about synchronized swimming, in which teams of eight swimmers go through a set of choreographed maneuvers, ideally in perfect unison, above and below the surface. Viewers of a certain age encountering synchronized swimming for the first time are likely to be reminded of MGM musicals of the 1940s and '50s starring Esther Williams.

Opinions about the intrinsic worth of a given Olympic sport vary widely from country to country. For instance, many Americans no doubt view table tennis as nothing more than a game played for fun at summer camp or in the family rec room. In China, on the other hand, Ping Pong is virtually the national sport. Beach volleyball, a newcomer on the Atlanta program, is well-established in California and certain other coastal areas, but it presumably has minimal appeal in landlocked or Northern European countries.

In any case, adding a new event to the Olympic program never has been easy, and it is about to become even less so. Under current standards, a men's sport proposed for inclusion in the summer Olympics must be played in at least 50 countries on at least three continents. For women's summer sports, the threshold is 35 countries on three continents. For both men's and women's winter Olympic sports, it is 25 countries on three continents.

Starting with the year 2000 Olympics in Sydney, Australia, a men's sport must be played in 75 countries on four continents to merit consideration by the International Olympic Committee (IOC). For women, the standard is at least 40 countries on three continents.

Even when a sport does pass IOC muster, it usually must undergo a lengthy probation period before joining the official program. But given the Games' already crowded menu, adding new sports usually can occur only if other sports are dropped.

As IOC President Juan Antonio Samaranch often says, "The bus is full; some will have to get off before someone else gets on." [1]

Two new events will be medal sports in Sydney: triathlon and taekwondo.

But it may be a while before ballroom dancing and 18 other "sports" that have been officially "recognized" by the IOC — including korfball, roller skating and water skiing — make the grade.

---

[1] Quoted in "Neglected Sports Strive to Join Olympics," *The Wall Street Journal*, Feb. 14, 1996, p. B1.

---

mass and strength. As an added benefit, the drugs help muscles recover more rapidly from fatigue or injury. Side effects include liver cancer, heart disease and testicular atrophy in men and masculinization in women. [12]

Steroids usually are taken in cycles lasting six to eight weeks, interspersed with rest periods ranging from weeks to months. To minimize side effects, athletes typically start steroid training at a low dosage and gradually build toward a peak intake. The dosage then is lowered in stages. Consequently, an athlete can schedule steroid-taking in such a way as to minimize the chance of failing a drug test at a major international competition like the Olympics.

Experts can only guess at the extent of illegal drug use by Olympic and international athletes. From the start of Olympic drug testing in 1968 through the 1992 Olympics, a total of 46 athletes have tested positive for drug use and have been disqualified. But most experts say this is only the tip of the iceberg. "From a scientific standpoint, there are two reasons why we don't know the extent of athletes' drug use," says Yesalis. "First, tests are easily circumvented. So you can't use the number of positives or negatives as an accurate indicator of use. Secondly, in trying to do systematic, scholarly surveys of athletes, I've noticed that athletes in the last five years have been increasingly hesitant to answer surveys accurately, even if they're anonymous.

"I hate to be skeptical," Yesalis continues, "but I really have a feeling that every once in a while, especially before major events, the IOC or USOC releases stories to say, 'Oh yeah, we've got the [doping] problem solved.' Every year I hear these claims. But I don't see any change in the use of drugs."

Yesalis believes testing has curtailed certain kinds of drug use in international sports competition. "Testing likely has lowered the dose of steroids taken, though not the number of steroid takers," he says. "That's good news, and I'm pleased about that. But many of us who were optimistic in the late 1980s that something could be done have changed our minds. Now my view is that none of us will see the day of drug-free sport. The science of the users has continuously bested the science of the testers."

Medical personnel at Olympic doping-control facilities "will get some improvement on the detection window, or detection limit" in testing for steroids, says David Black, a forensic pathologist in Nashville, Tenn. "If it's an oil-based, injectable steroid that was taken as far back as six to nine months before testing, we can still detect its presence," he says. "Oral steroids taken by athletes closer to the time of competition are flushed from the body more rapidly. Because of that, the current detection window for orals is only about 21 days."

Black says the use of a high-resolution mass spectrometer will bring some improvement in detection of oral steroid use at the Atlanta Games. But he cautions against expecting a major breakthrough. "They may get an extra week of detectability," he says. "Existing mass spectrometers are very elegant, very definitive tools. Giving them a high-resolution capability advances the technology just one step further."

Yesalis, moreover, notes that advances in steroid detection carry a downside risk. "One could argue that they have driven athletes to more dangerous drugs, such as human growth hormone [HGH] and erythropoietin [EPO]. And we still don't know precisely what long-term abuse of those drugs does to an athlete's health."

HGH is a genetically engineered equivalent of a substance produced naturally by the pituitary gland. Athletes take it in the belief that it will help augment strength and lean-muscle mass much as steroids do. In addition, anecdotal evidence indicates that athletes take HGH to prevent the breakdown of muscle tissue after steroids are discontinued, and to strengthen tendons and ligaments against possible ruptures or tears caused by added muscle. A further attraction is that no reliable test has yet been devised for detecting synthetic HGH.

Yesalis regards EPO as perhaps the most dangerous drug now being used by athletes. It, too, is a synthetic copy of a natural human hormone that stimulates the production of red blood cells from bone marrow.

Athletes in endurance events were quick to recognize EPO as a potentially powerful performance aid. By adding more red cells to the bloodstream, EPO increases the blood's oxygen-carrying capacity. The added capacity, in turn, translates into greater reserves of aerobic power for marathoners, cross-country skiers and long-distance bicycle racers. Like HGH, EPO is undetectable by available testing techniques.

Other drugs compound the challenge of testing and analyzing illegal drugs. Craig Kammerer, a research scientist for Bristol-Myers Squibb Co., notes that synthetic human choriotic gonadotropin (HCG) blocks the testicular atrophy caused by steroids and also stimulates the body to produce hormones that can enhance athletic performance.

"You usually can't find HCG in males," says Kammerer. "However, you may find quite a bit of it if certain malignancies are present. So if you do detect a significant amount of HCG in a male athlete, what do you do? Is he going to claim he's got some sort of undetected cancer, or has he been abusing the drug? You don't know."

HCG does occur naturally in females, "although usually at very low levels," Kammerer adds. "But when a woman becomes pregnant, her body produces astronomical amounts of it. That happens just one to three weeks after conception. Therefore, a female athlete who tests positive for HCG could claim she is in an early stage of pregnancy. There are lots of issues involving natural hormones besides confirming their presence in the body with a mass spectrometer."

Some sports officials argue that year-round, unannounced testing would help curb drug abuse. Gold medalist Connolly disagrees. The idea assumes that athletes the world over "will gleefully cast away their rights to privacy and advise the officials of their whereabouts in order to be available for surprise testing," she wrote. It further assumes that "every time an athlete sees a doctor, he or she will bring along a list of banned substances so that one of them is not accidentally prescribed." Testing, in Connolly's view, "deals with the symptoms rather than the problems. As long as the quest for victory is the primary goal, athletes will continue to augment natural strength, speed and endurance." [13] ■

BACKGROUND

Modern Revival

Many sports enthusiasts regard the Games as the greatest and oldest show on Earth. But the modern Olympics are barely adolescents compared with the original Olympics, which were held in ancient Greece every four years for 12 centuries, starting in 776 B.C. Initially, the competition was limited to foot races; the pentathlon, boxing and equestrian events were added later.

Unlike the modern Games, the Olympics of yore had a distinctively religious flavor. "Olympic athletes were motivated more by religious rapture than by secular or material motives," Lucas wrote. "Love of their city-states, a lifelong narcissistic emphasis on developing a beautiful . . . body and a lust for money all motivated the best athletes, but less powerfully than did their consecration to the . . . national religion." [14]

After the Romans conquered Greece in the second century B.C., the

Continued on p. 300

Chronology

Ancient Times

The original Olympic Games, spanning a period of more than 1,000 years, have religious as well as athletic significance.

776 B.C.
The first recorded Olympic Games are held in the valley of Olympia in northeastern Greece.

394 A.D.
The Roman Emperor Theodosius, a Christian opposed to all pagan spectacles, formally abolishes the Olympics.

1890s-1930s

Baron Pierre de Coubertin of France revives the Games.

1896
The first modern Olympic Games are held in Athens.

1904
The first Olympic Games in the U.S. are held in St. Louis, Mo.

1924
The first winter Olympic Games are held at Chamonix, France.

1936
Led by sprinter-broad jumper Jesse Owens, black U.S. track stars excel at the summer Games in Berlin, enraging German Chancellor Adolf Hitler.

1940s-1960s

Growing steadily bigger in the postwar period, the Games also become a focal point of Cold War tensions between the U.S. and Soviet Union.

1948
After a 12-year hiatus caused by World War II, London hosts the summer Olympics.

1964
NBC's coverage of the Tokyo Games' opening ceremony is the first live Olympic telecast.

1968
African-American sprinters Tommie Smith and John Carlos raise black-gloved fists in a black-power salute as the "Star-Spangled Banner" is played during a medal-award ceremony at the Mexico City Games.

1970s-1980s

Political and ideological disputes over the Olympics prompt some observers to wonder if the Games will long survive.

May 1970
The International Olympic Committee expels South Africa from membership because of the country's apartheid laws.

1972
Palestinian terrorists kill 11 Israeli athletes at the Munich Olympics. Nonetheless, International Olympic Committee President Avery Brundage declares that "The Games must go on."

1976
The Montreal Olympics are plagued by massive cost overruns.

1980
Western nations boycott the Moscow Olympics to protest the Soviet Union's invasion of Afghanistan.

1984
Communist-bloc nations boycott the privately financed Los Angeles Olympics, which records a surplus of over $200 million.

Oct. 14, 1986
The IOC votes to stagger the schedules of the winter and summer Olympics. After the 1992 winter Games in Albertville, France, the next winter competition is staged in 1994 in Lillehammer, Norway.

1990s

The last summer Olympics of the 20th century shapes up as the biggest and costliest to date, with more nations and athletes participating than ever before.

July 9, 1991
The International Olympic Committee's executive board readmits South Africa to the Olympic movement after a 21-year absence.

1992
"Dream Team I," a U.S. squad composed of National Basketball Association stars, wins a gold medal at Barcelona.

April 27, 1996
The Olympic torch relay begins in Los Angeles.

July 19-Aug. 4, 1996
The summer Olympic Games are held in Atlanta.

Aug. 16-25, 1996
The Paralympic Games, in which physically disabled athletes compete, are held in Atlanta.

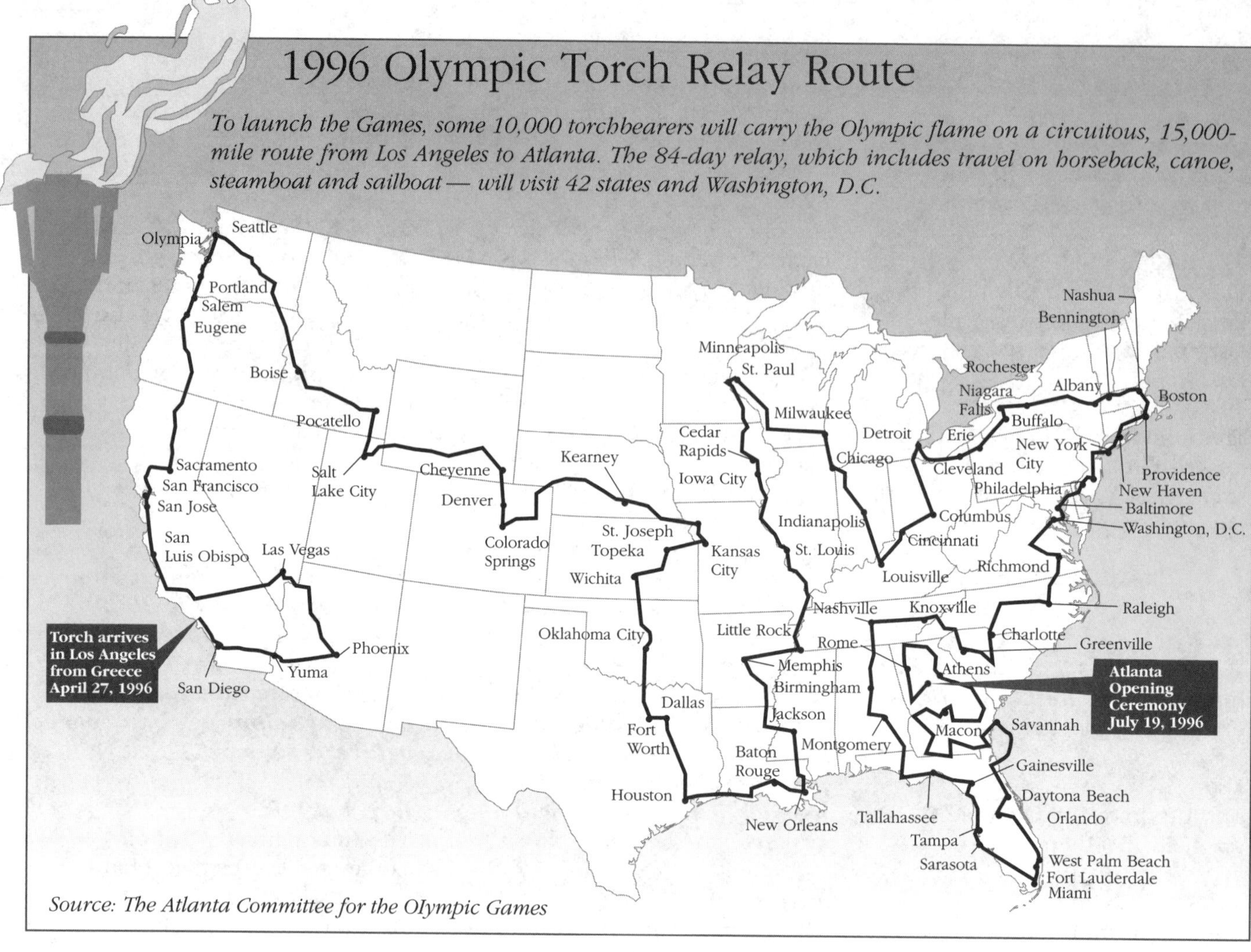

1996 Olympic Torch Relay Route

To launch the Games, some 10,000 torchbearers will carry the Olympic flame on a circuitous, 15,000-mile route from Los Angeles to Atlanta. The 84-day relay, which includes travel on horseback, canoe, steamboat and sailboat — will visit 42 states and Washington, D.C.

Source: The Atlanta Committee for the Olympic Games

Continued from p. 298

Games lost much of their luster. They reached their nadir in 66 A.D., when the Emperor Nero, accompanied by a retinue of 5,000, entered several equestrian events and won them all — besting opponents who feared the tyrant's wrath in defeat.

The Emperor Theodosius I, a Christian intent on eradicating pagan spectacles, formally abolished the Olympics in 393 A.D. Around the same time, a marauding band of Goths ravaged the sacred shrine of Olympia, where the quadrennial Games had always taken place.

Rebirth of the Olympic spirit in the 19th century owed much to the physical rebirth of Olympia itself. By 1881, after many years of digging, French and German archaeologists had largely uncovered the city's ruins. Stirred by the discovery, the Greek government sought to revive the Games on a national scale. Contests were staged in Athens in 1859 and 1870, but they failed to excite popular interest.

It remained for an idealistic Frenchman, Baron Pierre de Coubertin, to bring the idea to fruition. Disturbed by creeping commercialism in international sports, Coubertin yearned for a festival in which amateur athletes from around the world would compete. He arranged a world athletic congress in Paris in 1894 and managed to persuade a majority of delegates to revive the Olympics.

Fittingly, Athens was chosen to host the first Games of the modern era. They attracted 311 participants (230 of them Greeks) from 13 countries competing in 43 events in nine sports. A hastily assembled U.S. team of 13 — 10 track and field athletes, two revolver marksmen and a swimmer — won 11 championships, more than any other country. Local pride was salvaged, however, when a diminutive Greek shepherd, Spiridon Loues, won the final event — a foot race of nearly 25 miles from Marathon to Athens.*

The survival of the revived Olympics was not assured until 1912, when

* Along the same route nearly 2,400 years earlier, the Greek soldier Pheidippedes had carried on dying lips the news of the Athenian victory over invading Persians. The 1896 road race was not a revival of an ancient Olympic event but an added feature.

the Games were held in Stockholm. Twenty-eight countries entered 2,500 athletes, including 47 women, and daily attendance ranged between 20,000 and 30,000. Jim Thorpe, a Native American student at the Carlisle Indian School in Pennsylvania, won the decathlon and the pentathlon. A year later, however, the International Olympic Committee (IOC), having learned that Thorpe had once played minor-league baseball for $2 a game, declared him a professional, stripped him of his medals and erased his name from official Olympic history.*

Initially, the revived Olympics were held in the summer. Thus the improbable spectacle of figure skating at the 1908 Games in London and ice hockey at the 1920 Games in Antwerp, Belgium. But proposals to stage a separate winter Olympics were resisted by the Scandinavian countries, which wanted to protect their national winter sports festivals. Nonetheless, the IOC voted in 1922 to stage "International Sports Week" during the winter of 1924 in Chamonix, France. The event was so successful that it was retroactively named the First Winter Olympic Games. And since athletes from Scandinavia won 28 of the 43 medals awarded at Chamonix, regional objections to quadrennial winter Games quickly vanished.

In the annals of Olympic competition, no performance outshines Jesse Owens' feats at the 1936 summer Games in Berlin. Owens was one of 10 African-Americans on the 66-man U.S. track and field squad. These 10 men outscored every national team (including their 56 white teammates) in track and field events, winning a combined eight gold, three silver and two bronze medals. Owens himself collected four golds, putting the lie to German Chancellor Adolf Hitler's claims of Aryan athletic superiority.

The outbreak of World War II in 1939 led to cancellation of the 1940 and 1944 Games. Olympic competition resumed in 1948, first at the winter Games in St. Moritz, Switzerland, and later that year in London. Although the Soviet Union had been admitted to the IOC in 1947, it chose not to compete the following year. However, Moscow sent observers to the London Games. In 1952, the Soviets still spurned the winter Olympics at Oslo but turned out in force for the summer Games at Helsinki.

* Bowing to pressure from the U.S. Olympic Committee and Thorpe's children, the IOC posthumously restored Thorpe's two gold medals in 1982.

Cold War Era

It soon became apparent that Kremlin officials viewed the Olympics as a battleground in the escalating Cold War between the communist and Western blocs. Runners carrying the Olympic torch to Finland were denied permission to cross Soviet territory. Moreover, a separate Olympic Village, ringed by barbed wire, housed the Soviet team as well as the teams of Eastern European communist countries. The tense us-vs.-them atmosphere sparked a dispute over which superpower had "won" the 1952 summer Games. Though the U.S. medal count of 76 clearly exceeded the Soviets' 68, Moscow claimed victory on the basis of an unofficial team scoring system that differed from the West's.

Avery Brundage of the United States, the IOC president-elect, was dismayed at the blatant jostling for national advantage. Noting that the Olympic movement recognized only the winners of separate events, he declared: "If this becomes a contest between two great nations, the spirit of the Olympic Games will be destroyed." [15]

Brundage's warning did nothing to halt the political in-fighting. In large part, the trend reflected geographic and ideological divisions created by World War II. Postwar Olympic-representation disputes often focused on three pairs of countries, each formerly united under a single government and flag: East Germany and West Germany; North Korea and South Korea; and the People's Republic of China and Taiwan. Since then, only the two Germanys have been reunified.

Controversies at the 1968 summer Olympics in Mexico City stemmed from other causes. Shortly before the Games opened, for example, 15 Mexican students demonstrating against the government were killed in clashes with army troops. And at one of the medal-presentation ceremonies, African-American sprinters John Carlos and Tommie Smith raised gloved fists in a black-power salute when "The Star-Spangled Banner" was played.

The 1972 summer Olympics at Munich were the first to experience international terrorism. Seventeen persons, including 11 members of the Israeli team, were shot to death after Palestinian terrorists broke into the Israeli dormitory in the Olympic Village on Sept. 5. In response, the IOC suspended the Games for a day to hold a memorial service for the victims. But Brundage turned aside suggestions that he cancel the Olympics. "The Games must go on," he said at the service, "and we must continue our efforts to keep them clean, pure and honest and try to extend the sportsmanship of the athletic field into other areas." [16]

Nonetheless, sportsmanship came under severe strain at the 1976 Montreal summer Olympics. Eight days before the opening ceremony, Tanzania announced it would not attend the Games because New Zealand had sent its rugby team to South Africa. The IOC had revoked South Africa's membership six years earlier because of the country's apartheid policies. Thirty-one additional nations subsequently withdrew from the Games in sympathy with Tanzania. (The U.S. was not among them). Taiwan also declined to take part in the Montreal Olympics after Canada refused to allow it to compete as the Republic of China.

The Stakes Keep Rising for TV Coverage

Coverage of the Olympics has come a long way since CBS paid less than a half-million dollars for the 1960 TV rights. This year, NBC is spending nearly a half-billion dollars. For the 2004, 2006 and 2008 games, the network will spend $2.3 billion. Local organizers get 60 percent of TV revenues and 40 percent goes to the Internaitonal Olympic Committee, national Olympic committees and international sports federations.

Winter Games TV Coverage

Year	Location	Network	Amount Paid (in millions)
1960	Squaw Valley, Calif.	CBS	$.05
1964	Innsbruck, Austria	ABC	$.597
1968	Grenoble, France	ABC	$2.5
1972	Sapporo, Japan	NBC	$6.4
1976	Innsbruck, Austria	ABC	$10
1980	Lake Placid, N.Y.	ABC	$15.5
1984	Sarajevo, Yugoslavia	ABC	$91.5
1988	Calgary, Canada	ABC	$309
1992	Albertville, France	CBS	$243
1994	Lillehammer, Norway	CBS	$300
1998	Nagano, Japan	CBS	$375
2002	Salt Lake City, Utah	NBC	$545
2006	To be decided	NBC	$613

Summer Games TV Coverage

Year	Location	Network	Amount Paid (in millions)
1960	Rome, Italy	CBS	$.394
1964	Tokyo, Japan	NBC	$1.5
1968	Mexico City, Mexico	ABC	$4.5
1972	Munich, West Germany	ABC	$7.5
1976	Montreal, Canada	ABC	$25
1980	Moscow, Soviet Union	NBC	$87
1984	Los Angeles, Calif.	ABC	$225
1988	Seoul, Korea	NBC	$300
1992	Barcelona, Spain	NBC	$401
1996	Atlanta, Georgia	NBC	$456
2000	Sydney, Australia	NBC	$705
2004	To be decided	NBC	$793
2008	To be decided	NBC	$894

Source: U.S. Olympic Committee

To compound Canada's woes, the Montreal Games ran a massive deficit, much of it attributable to construction cost overruns on the Olympic Stadium, which was still uncompleted when the Games took place.

The no-show count at the 1980 summer Olympics in Moscow was even greater than at Montreal. Some 65 nations stayed away, mostly to protest the Soviet invasion of Afghanistan in December 1979. The boycott halved the number of athletes who were to compete and reduced tourist traffic by two-thirds.

After the turmoil of Montreal and Moscow, hopes for the 1984 summer Olympics in Los Angeles did not run high. In fact, the city's only rival as host had been Tehran, Iran, which withdrew its bid because of domestic unrest. Moreover, many observers expected the Soviets to organize a boycott of the Los Angeles Games in retaliation for the 1980 Western boycott.

That indeed happened, though only 15 nations joined the Soviet-led pull-out. Other anticipated problems, including traffic jams and throat-stinging smog, failed to materialize. Paid attendance at the Games came to 5.5 million, an Olympic record.

Still, IOC and USOC officials were stunned when Peter V. Uebberoth, president of the Los Angeles Olympic Organizing Committee (LAOOC), announced that the Games had produced a surplus of about $225 million. Besides ticket revenue of more than $100 million, income had come from broadcast rights ($225 million from ABC-TV) and corporate sponsorships ($140 million from numerous companies).

A major reason why the 1984 Games finished solidly in the black is that organizers made extensive use of existing sports facilities in the area, including the Los Angeles Coliseum (also the centerpiece of the 1932 Olympics), the Rose Bowl, the Forum, Pauley Pavilion, the Anaheim Convention Center and Long Beach Arena. Most athletes stayed in dormitories at the University of Southern California and UCLA. And labor costs were kept down by 50,000 volunteers.

Even before the '84 Games highlighted the potential of private funding, IOC officials recognized that the sale of U.S. TV rights was vital to the continued success of the Olympic movement. It was not always so. When CBS obtained rights to the 1960 Olympics, the network paid only $50,000 for the winter Games in Squaw Valley, Calif., and $394,000 for the summer Games in Rome. At that time, it must be remembered, global communications satellites did not exist. As a result,

U.S. television coverage of the 1960 summer Games in Rome consisted of film flown across the Atlantic Ocean. The first live telecast in the U.S. of a summer Olympic event was NBC's coverage of the 1964 Tokyo Games' opening ceremony.

Big-Money Era

Though bidding for Olympic broadcast rights has risen almost without interruption since the beginning, the sums involved took a quantum jump in the early 1980s. Rights to the winter Games sold for $15.5 million in 1980; four years later, they fetched $91.5 million. Similarly, the 1980 Moscow summer Games went for $87 million, while the 1984 Los Angeles Games commanded $225 million.

Around this time, IOC officials grew concerned that the movement was becoming overly dependent on television. To build a supplementary revenue stream, ISL, a German-Japanese firm, was hired to handle Olympic marketing in 1988. [17] ISL devised a plan by which only one company in each of 44 distinct product categories could purchase the exclusive right to feature Olympic symbols — notably the five interlocking rings — in advertising and promotional campaigns. This was the basic approach that the LAOOC had employed in 1984.

Today, revenues for ACOG's $1.61 billion budget are more balanced than was LAOOC's 1984 budget. ACOG expects to collect $559.5 million (34.8 percent of its total income) from broadcast rights, $505.7 million (31.4 percent) from U.S. and foreign commercial sponsorships and $422 million (26.2 percent) from ticket sales. [18]

As the Olympic movement gained a more secure financial footing, thanks in large part to private enterprise, it moved away from the principle of amateurism espoused by Coubertin. Indeed, the two trends were related. "The Games had become . . . a huge business because sport had become a huge business," wrote Espy. "The profits were available for everyone — the state, industry, the competitor, the sport federations, the media and the IOC. Amateurism, as the IOC defined it, no longer existed, nor was it practical or even desirable." [19]

But Brundage, who headed the IOC from 1952 to 1972, would not tolerate even a hint of professionalism. For example, 10 skiers who had each accepted $50 a day for coaching at a California ski camp were barred by Brundage from the 1972 Games at Sapporo, Japan. Six Alpine skiing countries threatened to boycott the Games if any skiers were disqualified. In the end, only Austrian skiing star Karl Schranz was kept out of Sapporo.

After Brundage left the IOC later that year, the internal debate over professionalism resumed. It was not until the 1980s, however, that the IOC opened the door to at least some participation by professional athletes. In 1981, it voted to give the 26 international federations that govern Olympic sports freedom to formulate their own eligibility rules, subject to IOC approval.

The U.S. Olympic Committee, still adhering to Brundage's view, opposed "Open Olympic Games" in which professional athletes could compete in all sports. "We do not endorse open Games or a wholesale change in all sports-eligibility rules that would ruin grass-roots encouragement of athletes," USOC President Robert H. Helmick said in 1986. "The Olympic Games should remain a goal for all athletes, and not degenerate into simply another forum for professional sports." [20] On the other hand, Helmick said the committee would support a compromise in which a pro athlete in one sport could compete as an amateur in another sport.

On April 8, 1989, the Fédération Internationale de Basketball, the sport's world governing body, voted 56-13 to permit stars of the U.S. National Basketball Association (NBA) and other pro leagues to play in amateur tournaments, including the Olympics. Even though it stood to be the main beneficiary, the United States voted against the proposal.

In any case, the basketball federation's 1989 decision had the effect of virtually guaranteeing a basketball gold medal for the United States at the 1992 summer Games in Barcelona. That's because the U.S. squad, popularly known as "Dream Team I," consisted mainly of NBA stars, including Larry Bird, Michael Jordan, Charles Barkley and Magic Johnson. The Dream Team crushed all its opponents, helping to erase memories of the 1988 summer Games at Seoul, where the U.S. team finished third.

Some international sports federations impose age requirements on Olympic athletes, usually for safety and health reasons. Bobsledders, divers and gymnasts must be at least 14, for example, while weightlifters and wrestlers must be at least 17. Under the rules of the Fédération Internationale de Football Association, only players under 23 may play Olympic soccer. The aim is not so much to protect the players as to safeguard the status of the World Cup, which many sports fans outside the United States regard as superior to the Olympics. The top players on foreign pro soccer teams, which supply the bulk of World Cup talent, are in their mid-20s or older.

In another significant policy decision, the IOC had voted in 1986 to stagger the schedules of the winter and summer Games. After the 1992 winter Olympics in Albertville, the next winter competition was staged in 1994 in Lillehammer, Norway. The next winter Games are to be held in 1998 in Nagano, Japan, and every four years after that at sites still to be chosen.

As the cost of staging the Olympics climbs, the number of qualified host cities shrinks. "So large are the Games that in practice only the richest of candidate cities, or those under the control of effective authoritarian governments, are plausible candidates to host them," Christopher R. Hill wrote. "Furthermore, the increasing number of journalists covering them, not to mention the proliferating Olympic family, means that accommodation for ordinary members of the public who would like to attend the Games becomes increasingly difficult to find." [21] ■

CURRENT SITUATION

Hot Times in Atlanta

Though ACOG officials have tried to anticipate every contingency, one key factor — weather — lies beyond their control. The average high temperature in Atlanta during the Olympics is projected at 87.3 degrees, as against the average high of 84.7 degrees recorded at the Barcelona Games four years ago. Atlanta, however, experiences much higher midsummer humidity than Barcelona, pushing the "discomfort index" to levels that many foreign athletes may find stressful.

Concern centers on distance running events, especially the grueling, 26-mile marathon.* The race had been scheduled to begin at 6:30 p.m. on Aug. 4, so that it would end inside the Olympic Stadium just before the closing ceremonies. But health concerns prompted a change to 7 a.m.

"There is no questioning the wisdom of the IAAF's decision to shift the start of the men's marathon from 6:30 p.m. to 7 a.m. on the final day of the Games," said *Sports Illustrated.* "No one should run a marathon in the late-day heat of Atlanta in August. The IAAF's move is a rare and welcome instance in which athletes' welfare has been given precedence over the needs of television." [22]

As the magazine also noted, the "tradition" of staging the marathon as the final Olympic event dates only from the 1984 Los Angeles Games. At that time, commentators warned that a combination of summer heat and Southern California smog could prove disastrous. But the worries turned out to be unfounded.

The 1994 World Cup soccer tournament in the United States suggested that well-conditioned athletes are better able to cope with extreme weather conditions than they are given credit for. Despite blistering temperatures at several stadiums, especially those in Dallas and Orlando, the Games were hard fought and the players seemingly unaffected by the heat.

Nonetheless, ACOG officials are not just crossing their fingers and hoping for the best. For instance, they note that half of all Olympic events will take place in air-conditioned facilities. And all rooms in the Olympic Village will be air-conditioned — an Olympic first.

The medal-presentation outfits that Reebok is producing also incorporate design features to minimize the heat. Jackets and pants will have vents as well as a poly-mesh lining that keeps moisture away from the body. The ensemble also will include mesh-lined shorts.

Meanwhile, many Olympians from overseas already have first-hand knowledge of the challenging climatic conditions awaiting them in Atlanta. All the teams from 23 foreign countries as well as 70 foreign teams in individual sports have taken part in a pre-Games acclimation program at various sites in Georgia and six other Southern states.

Combating Counterfeiters and Ticket Scalpers

As the Games draw closer, much of ACOG's energy goes into combating producers of bogus Olympic merchandise and persons asking exorbitant prices for tickets. On Feb. 6, for example, ACOG and USOC filed suit in U.S. District Court in Atlanta against five companies under the 1978 Amateur Sports Act, which extends "super-trademark" protection to merchandise bearing Olympic Games emblems or language. The committees acted after investigators spotted counterfeit Olympic items at an industry trade show.

"The financial support for the 1996 Olympic Games and the U.S. Olympic team comes almost totally from private sources — from sponsorship, broadcast fees, licensing programs and from individual Americans," said William McCahan, chief marketing officer for Atlanta Centennial Olympic Products, a joint marketing venture of ACOG and USOC. "It's critical to protect these sources of funding from infringements by companies who have contributed nothing." [23]

ACOG also has sent "cease and desist" notices to ticket brokers or agents who have offered Olympic tickets for sale at prices up to five times face value. Tickets to the most popular events, including the opening and closing ceremonies, gymnastics, swimming and diving, sold out long ago. Official prices range from a mere $7 for baseball to $212 for gymnastics and $265 for the final basketball game.

"[T]here are a total of 11 million event tickets for the Games," spoofs Barry, "and although most of these are snatched directly off the printing press by Olympic officials, corporate sponsors, heads of state, local politicians, the media, celebrities, organized crime and rich people in general, that still leaves, for distribution to the general public, a number (3) of prime tickets to the quarter-finals of the cross-country badminton event." [24]

Continued on p. 307

* The marathon has been 26 miles, 385 yards, since the 1908 Olympics in London. Originally, British officials had laid out a 26-mile course, but they tacked on the additional yardage so that the race would start at Windsor Castle and end in front of King Edward VII's box at the Olympic Stadium.

At Issue:

Should professional athletes be allowed to participate in the Olympic games?

yes

EDITORIAL
FROM *THE NEW YORK TIMES,* JULY 8, 1992

Some purists see nothing but runaway nationalism and crass commercialism in the star-studded basketball team that [represented] America at the [1992] Olympics in Barcelona. Once again, they say, the U.S. acts the bully, dispatching professionals — the cream of the National Basketball Association — to bring back the gold that has eluded recent amateur squads.

But why not basketball's best? Isn't that what the Olympic games aspire to measure?

Once upon a time the Olympics were dedicated to the ideal of amateur sport, back when the modern Games began in 1896. Amateurs were purer, more committed to sport itself, than were the pros who played for pay. Besides, there wasn't much professional sport in those days.

The line between amateur and professional was clearer then, but has long since frayed. For decades the Olympic authorities welcomed state-sponsored athletes from then-communist nations, and didn't blink when they took home most of the medals. Even purist America has compromised in recent years, maintaining fictional allegiance to amateurism while tolerating commercial subsidies and cash prizes.

While it is not certain that the U.S. basketball "Dream Team" will demolish the best anyone else has to offer, it's highly probable. They overwhelmed six Western Hemisphere teams in last week's Tournament of the Americas by an average margin of 51.5 points.

The sight of them mowing down the rest of the world might even be considered dull. Until you watch them. They dazzle with their style and skill, so awesome that even their victims didn't seem to mind. The victims knew they'd been tested by the best and, good sports to the end, happily lined up for pictures with the victors to prove it to the folks back home. If the Dream Team does win, American fans can be good sports too, by holding their gloating in check.

Despite all the hullabaloo about Magic Johnson, Michael Jordan, Larry Bird et al., the Olympics isn't just basketball. The dream of purely amateur Olympics may be dead, but the idea of athletes challenged to do their best is very much alive.

no

WILLIAM C. RHODEN
Sports reporter, *The New York Times*

FROM *THE NEW YORK TIMES,* AUG. 9, 1992

Long after the record setters and medal winners are forgotten, the XXV Olympiad will best be remembered as the one where National Basketball Association players made their Olympic debut — and ushered a new era of commercialism into the games.

As predicted, the professionals made a shambles of the competition, winning their first seven games by an average margin of 57 points, and seemed assured of reclaiming the gold medal that got away in 1988 when the Americans settled for a bronze.

But the same level of play that let the Dream Team wreak that overwhelming revenge stirred a controversy that won't end with the closing ceremonies: Do such ultra-professionals belong in the games?

And, as the trappings of professionalism — the big money, the expensive tastes, the ticklish contracts with sponsors — made it stingingly clear that the ultra-professionals were set apart from the rest of the American Olympic team, one high-ranking official wondered aloud last week: Were they even worth the trouble?

From the beginning of the games, other athletes complained that the whole United States basketball team and the wealthier tennis and track and field stars were staying in luxurious apartments or $900-a-night hotels while most other athletes lived in cramped Olympic Village quarters. . . .

Michael Jordan, the marquee player for the Dream Team, had warned officials months ago that using college players would be less complicated. For one thing, he pointed out, professionals have contract stipulations that compete with the deals the Olympic committees have cut with their sponsors.

Indeed, the basketball team's closest match of the entire tournament was with the U.S. Olympic Committee over commercial endorsements.

The team's plans to appear on the victory stand . . . were nearly thrown into disarray because several players have contracts with sportswear makers that obligate them not to wear clothes made by competitors. . . .

Ultimately, a compromise was reached: The players were given the option of using the flap of the warm-up jacket to cover the Reebok logo. . . .

In the past, iron-fisted Olympic officials were able to intimidate athletes into compliance by threatening to cut off the sponsorship money they could funnel to them.

But this time, Olympic officials have found themselves in the position of some professional team owners — sacrificing a measure of control in exchange for the dollars that high-profile athletes bring in.

Games for Disabled Athletes on the Rise

On the evening of Sunday, Aug. 4, the Olympic flame will be extinguished at Atlanta's Olympic Stadium, ending the centennial summer games. Within days, however, a new set of athletes will converge on the city for another major international sports event — the Paralympic Games, a quadrennial competition for the physically disabled. This year's Paralympics is expected to draw 3,500 athletes from 115 countries — two more athletes than competed in the summer Olympics held at Mexico City in 1968.

At Atlanta, paralympians will compete in 19 sports, 15 of which are Olympic sports. But since the athletes suffer from a wide array of physical limitations, all events are categorized by the nature and degree of disability, so that there might be 15 different versions of the 100-meter dash. In each paralympic sport, different rules apply to amputees, the blind, cerebral-palsy sufferers, dwarfs, paraplegics, quadriplegics and competitors with other kinds of handicaps.

If there is one thing paralympic athletes want even more than victory, it is respect as athletes. They shudder at the thought of eliciting pity or, worse, winning plaudits for "courage." They ask to be judged as other athletes are — by their performance in competition against their peers.

Respect for paralympian achievements has grown as performance levels have risen. For example, the record for the mile in wheelchair racing fell from 4:59.7 in 1979 — just under five minutes — to 3:30.2 in 1995. Much of the improvement was attributable to the development of lightweight, three-wheeled chairs designed expressly for racing. Advances in prosthetic limb design have enhanced performances in other paralympic events.

Significantly, the Paralymic Games' growing visibility has opened the way to commercial sponsorship of the kind — though not the dollar amount — seen at the regular summer and winter Olympics. In June 1993, for instance, the Atlanta Committee for the Olympic Games agreed to become the first sponsor of the upcoming Paralympic Games. Since then, the Atlanta Paralympic Organizing Committee has signed sponsorship deals with such major companies as Coca-Cola, Home Depot and IBM.

The Paralympic Games' rise to prominence calls to mind the emergence of the Special Olympics nearly 30 years ago. Planned and funded by the Kennedy Foundation, the first International Special Olympics Games were held in July 1968 at Chicago's Soldier Field. More than 1,000 athletes from the United States and Canada competed in track and field, floor hockey and aquatics.

The Special Olympics are open to mentally retarded children and adults at least 8 years old. As the competition's motto suggests, victory is not the overriding goal: "Let me win. But if I cannot win, let me be brave in the attempt."

French athletes participated in the second Special Olympics, staged in Chicago in 1970, giving the movement an international flavor. Seven years later, the first Special Olympics devoted exclusively to winter sports took place in Steamboat Springs, Colo. Some 500 athletes competed in skiing and skating. Special Olympics summer and winter games now are held every two years on a staggered schedule, as are the regular Olympics, but in odd-numbered rather than even-numbered years.

Charles Palmer

More than 7,000 athletes with mental retardation participated in the ninth Special Olympics World Summer Games in New Haven, Conn.

Another key development came in 1990, when the Soviet Union joined the Special Olympics. Last summer's Special Olympics World Games were the biggest to date, as more than 7,000 athletes from 143 countries competed in New Haven, Conn.

The U.S. Transplant Games, dating from 1988, are open to anyone who has undergone life-saving organ replacement surgery — defined as kidney, liver, heart, lung, pancreas and bone-marrow transplants. The summer transplant games are held biennially in even-numbered years, and the winter transplant games biennially in odd-numbered years. Some 1,100 transplant athletes took part in the 1994 summer games. Like this summer's Olympics and Paralympics, the 1994 transplant games were staged in Atlanta. [1]

For all athletes with disabilities, the words of Baron Pierre de Coubertin — founder of the modern Olympics — no doubt ring true: "The prime essential is not so much to have conquered as to have performed honorably and well."

But many disabled athletes also "hope that what they do will be revealed as sport: the kind of rigorous and cutthroat activity that fans pay to watch, that kids want to try." [2]

They are people like Shawn Brown, an athlete with one leg who set an unofficial world record in the discus last June at the National Wheelchair and Amputee Championships in Boston. He would only talk to the press on one condition. "Is this going to be a sports story?" he would ask. "I don't do human interest."

[1] For background, see "Organ Transplants," *The CQ Researcher*, Aug. 11, 1995, pp. 705-728.

[2] Richard Hoffer, "Ready, Willing and Able," *Sports Illustrated*, March 14, 1995.

Continued from p. 304

Rooms in hotels, motels and bed-and-breakfast facilities are limited by Georgia law to charging $100 a night or 5.7 percent more than their 1994 rates, whichever is greater, during the Olympics. But many families in the Atlanta area — no one knows precisely how many — hope to rent their homes to Olympic visitors at premium rates.

Sports economics expert Baade believes free-market forces may dash those hopes. "I know lots of homeowners are getting together to rent their homes, and some are even offering maid service and trips to and from the airport," he says. "But if everybody does that, there'll be a housing surplus. Some people may not be able to rent their places at all."

Economic Impact

In Baade's opinion, moreover, not enough attention has been paid to the economic downside of the Atlanta Olympics. "As we saw in Los Angeles in '84, a lot of locals just decide they're going to desert the community for the duration of the Olympics. So, much of the economic activity that's associated with those people is temporarily lost. And what you hear from some restaurant owners, interestingly enough, is that their business goes down during a major sporting event, not up, because their regulars don't want to contend with all the traffic and the other hassles."

In general, though, Baade feels the Olympics will bring lasting economic benefits to Atlanta. "When you consider the cost of the Olympic infrastructure, you're talking about an amazingly expensive show to put on," he says. "On the other hand, you are bringing in a lot of people from outside the area. There are commercial prospects of all sorts [tied to the Olympics] that are unequaled by just about anything else in the world of sports."

Still, much will depend on how Atlanta manages its Olympic infrastructure facilities in future years. "This is an area that requires great managerial acumen," says Baade. "It's not for the amateur planner." One difficulty is that the new facilities will necessarily compete with existing venues for sports and entertainment events, possibly limiting the rents that any one facility can charge.

Baade acknowledges that Atlanta has anticipated some of these problems. Atlanta-Fulton County Stadium, home of the defending World Series champion Atlanta Braves, will be torn down after the 1996 baseball season. In 1997, the team will move into the Olympic Stadium, which will have been downsized and reconfigured.

This shows, Baade says, that the 1996 Games can have "a positive and sustainable impact," given intelligent planning during the post-Olympic period. "And the prospects for that, I think, are quite good." ■

OUTLOOK

Bright Prospects

If the past is indeed prologue to the future, the prospects for the Olympics are bright. Consider only the matter of U.S. network television rights. The amount paid for rights to the winter Olympics rose from $50,000 for the 1960 Games at Squaw Valley to $300 million for the 1994 Lillehammer Games. For the summer Olympics, the amount soared from $390,000 for the 1960 Games at Rome to $456 million for Atlanta.

Further escalation of TV fees is assured. Last August, NBC locked up rights to the year 2000 summer Games in Sydney, Australia, and the 2002 winter Games in Salt Lake City for a total of $1.25 billion. Just four months later the network upped its commitment, paying $2.3 billion for rights to televise the 2004 and 2008 summer Games and the 2006 winter Games. The sites of the latter three Olympics have yet to be determined, and it is highly unlikely that any of them will be held in the United States.

According to May of the SGMA, NBC's coup reflects the enhanced appeal of the Olympics since the Games shifted to a staggered schedule in 1994. "Now that we have Games every two years, major sponsors like American Express, Coca-Cola and Kodak don't have to be zapped to the max every four years," he says. "The two-year cycle helps even out the expense situation [for advertisers]. It's also a plus in terms of TV viewership and marketing opportunities. The Games are strong, they get stronger every two years, and there's no sign they're losing their appeal."

Similarly, says Lucas, "My guess is that they reasoned, 'Strike now while the iron is hot.' The amounts NBC bid may seem exorbitant now, but they could look like a bargain by the turn of the century."

Baade disagrees. "These things are loss leaders for the networks," he says. "But who knows what it does for their business overall? I'm pretty skeptical that it makes sense for networks to bid that amount of money for the Olympics in the expectation that they'll make up for it with other programming. I don't think that usually happens. But obviously, the NBC gurus think this is good business."

Delpy of George Washington shares Baade's cautious analysis, but her main concern is that the new two-year cycle may overexpose the Olympics. "The Games could become so commonplace that people will lose interest in them," she says. "After all, how many times can a person become teary-eyed about the Olympics?"

FOR MORE INFORMATION

Atlanta Committee for the Olympic Games, 250 Williams St., Suite 6000, P.O. Box 1996, Atlanta, Ga. 30301-1996; (404) 224-5444. ACOG is staging the Olympic Games in coordination with the International Olympic Committee, the U.S. Olympic Committee, the Atlanta city government and the Metropolitan Atlanta Olympic Games Authority.

Atlanta Paralympics Organizing Committee, One Atlantic Center, Suite 2500, 1201 West Peachtree St. NE, Atlanta, Ga. 30303; (404) 588-1996. APOC is the private, nonprofit group running the Olympic-style international competition for disabled athletes that will be held in Atlanta following the 1996 summer Olympics.

Sporting Goods Manufacturers Association, 200 Castlewood Dr., North Palm Beach, Fla. 33408-5696; (407) 842-4100. The association, which represents makers of sports equipment and apparel, expects the Olympics to give the industry a $500 million sales increase.

U.S. Olympic Committee, One Olympic Plaza, Colorado Springs, Colo. 80909-5760; (719) 632-5551. USOC is a federation of sports-governing bodies that helps select, finance and outfit American athletes competing in the Olympics and the Pan American Games.

Delpy also feels that creeping professionalism could yield a similar effect. "Lots of times it's the human-interest story about an underdog winner that makes people sit up and take notice. Where's the human-interest story in the Dream Team?"

Some sports commentators argue that the Olympic movement would benefit from judicious trimming of the number of sports it sanctions. Lucas, for instance, would do away with yachting, "an event antithetical to the democratic principles of the Olympics; only extraordinarily wealthy countries can afford to enter the yachting competition." He would also drop the modern pentathlon* because of its "militaristic nature" and rhythmic gymnastics and synchronized swimming because they are "too exotic."

These are far from the only candidates for a hypothetical Olympic kill list. Some purists would banish all team sports, such as basketball and hockey, on the grounds that they help incite nationalistic passions. Others would axe sports in which subjective judging determines the order of finish (such as figure skating and diving) or in which drug abuse is a major problem (weightlifting, distance running). The difficulty is that if all flawed sports were excluded, few would remain.

In any case, critics and supporters agree that the Games will go on into the foreseeable future. Hill deplores the Olympic movement's "overweening sense of its own importance," adding that "the whole thing has gotten out of hand." At the same time, though, he believes it is likely that "self-interest, diplomatic skill, wealth and ideals will continue to hold the movement together."[25]

In the opinion of ACOG's Payne, the Games' future rests on firmer ground. "I have this belief that the Olympics is a movement that is founded in goodness, and it's the goodness that will make it achievable," he said. "I keep saying, 'Let's get it right this time. Let's show the power and hope of people coming together in a celebration of humanity.' "[26] ■

* The modern pentathlon includes a 300-meter freestyle swim, a 4,000-meter cross-country run, a 600-meter, 20-jump equestrian steeplechase, fencing and target shooting.

Notes

[1] Donald Katz, "Atlanta Brave," *Sports Illustrated,* Jan. 8, 1996, p. 74.

[2] Also bidding to host the 1996 Games were Belgrade, Yugoslavia, Manchester, England, Melbourne, Australia, and Toronto, Canada.

[3] The cost of the project is $209 million, including construction of the stadium, conversion to a baseball stadium after the Olympics, destruction of the old stadium and debt service.

[4] Dave Barry, *Washington Post Magazine,* February 18, 1996.

[5] Olga Connolly, "A Call for Returning to the Olympic Ideal," *Los Angeles Times,* Jan. 31, 1989. Connolly won her gold medal on the 1956 Czechoslovakian team. After becoming an American citizen, she competed on four U.S. teams.

[6] Quoted by Randy Harvey, "Atlanta's Ringleader," *Los Angeles Times* (Washington edition), Feb. 21, 1996, p. A9.

[7] Quoted by Allen R. Myerson, "Marathon Man of the Atlanta Games," *The New York Times,* Feb. 25, 1996, p. F1.

[8] *The New York Times,* March 28, 1996, p. D1.

[9] John J. O'Connor, "The Games Are Brought to You By . . . ," *The New York Times,* Feb. 13, 1992, p. B20.

[10] Jonathan Yardley, "How Much Is That Sunset Out the Window?" *The Washington Post,* Aug. 10, 1992, p. B2.

[11] Richard Espy, *The Politics of the Olympic Games* (1979), p. 163.

[12] For background, see "Athletes and Drugs," *The CQ Researcher,* July 26, 1991, pp. 513-536.

[13] Connolly, *op. cit.*

[14] John A. Lucas, *Future of the Olympic Games* (1992), p. 2.

[15] Brundage made the comment at an IOC meeting in Helsinki on July 28, 1952, when the IOC rejected a Soviet scoring proposal for future Olympics.

[16] Quoted by Allen Guttmann, *The Games Must Go On: Avery Brundage and the Olympic Movement* (1984), p. 354.

[17] ISL was 51 percent owned by Horst Dassler, the chairman of Adidas, the German producer of sports apparel and footwear, and 49 percent owned by Dentsu, a Japanese advertising agency.

[18] The remaining $122.8 million (7.6 percent) is projected to come from merchandising and miscellaneous sources.

[19] Espy, *op. cit.,* p. 136.

[20] Statement issued by USOC in Colorado Springs, March 18, 1986.

[21] Christopher R. Hill, *Olympic Politics* (1992), p. 241.

[22] "Scorecard," *Sports Illustrated,* April 1, 1996, p. 15.

[23] ACOG news release, Feb. 7, 1996.

[24] Barry, *op. cit.*

[25] Hill, *op. cit.,* pp. 249-250.

[26] Quoted by Katz, *op. cit.,* p. 92.

Bibliography

Selected Sources Used

Books

Bueno, Ana, *Special Olympics: The First 25 Years,* Foghorn Press, 1994.

Bueno covers the origins and highlights of the famed athletic festival for mentally retarded athletes, an event long associated with the Kennedy family and former Olympic gold medalist Rafer Johnson.

Espy, Richard, *The Politics of the Olympic Games,* University of California Press, 1979.

Espy discusses the public controversies that often plague the Olympics as well as the behind-the-scenes infighting that usually precedes and follows them.

Guttmann, Allen, *The Games Must Go On: Avery Brundage and the Olympic Movement,* Columbia University Press, 1984.

Brundage was one of the pivotal figures of the Olympic movement. A member of the U.S. team at the 1912 summer Olympics in Stockholm, he later served as president of the U.S. Olympic Committee and, for 20 years, as president of the International Olympic Committee. Throughout his long career, Brundage was noted for his unyielding opposition to professionalism in the Games.

Henry, Bill, and Patricia Henry Yeomans, *An Approved History of the Olympic Games,* The Southern California Committee for the Olympic Games, 1984.

The authors supply the background and results of all summer and winter Olympic Games held between 1896 and 1980.

Hill, Christopher R., *Olympic Politics,* Manchester University Press, 1992.

Despite efforts to make the Olympics a showcase for individual athletic excellence, nationalism and politics constantly intrude. Hill reviews the many incidents that made the Olympics as much an occasion of ill will as of goodwill.

Lucas, John A., *Future of the Olympic Games,* Human Kinetics Books, 1992

Lucas, a Pennsylvania State University professor of sport science, traces the development of the modern Olympic Games and suggests ways to strengthen them in the future. For instance, he favors selection of permanent sites for both the summer and winter Games.

Articles

Hoffer, Richard, "Ready, Willing and Able," *Sports Illustrated,* Aug. 14, 1995.

Hoffer writes of the physically disabled athletes who will be participating at the 1996 Paralympics — an Olympic-styled competition designed expressly for them — that will get under way in Atlanta shortly after the regular summer Olympics end.

Katz, Donald, "Atlanta Brave," *Sports Illustrated,* Jan. 8, 1996.

Katz profiles Billy Payne, the Atlanta real-estate lawyer who is credited with almost singlehandedly bringing the 1996 summer Olympic Games to the Georgia capital.

Solomon, Owen S., "The Politicization of Amateur Athletics: South Africa and the American Athlete's Legal Dilemma of Participation," *Loyola of Los Angeles International and Comparative Law Journal,* October 1992.

Solomon traces the developments that led to South Africa's expulsion from the Olympic movement because of its racial policies and then to its reinstatement after those policies were repudiated.

Reports and Studies

Atlanta Committee for the Olympic Games, *Press Guide: 1996 Olympics,* 1996.

Although aimed at the news media, this guide (also available on the Internet: http//www.atlanta.olympic.org) contains maps, profiles of Olympic officials and athletes and much more of interest to ordinary sports fans.

United States Olympic Committee, *Inside the U.S. Olympic Movement,* 1994.

This useful booklet provides answers to commonly asked questions about the Olympics. It also includes tables showing the number of athletes and countries participating in every Olympics since 1896, as well as the distribution of gold, silver and bronze medals. The long list of addresses, phone numbers and FAX numbers of sports federations and other groups associated with the Olympics is a welcome time-saver.

The Next Step

Additional information from UMI's Newspaper & Periodical Abstracts database

Advertising

Bounds, Wendy, "Advertising: Fuji move may miff Kodak at Olympics," *The Wall Street Journal,* Oct. 31, 1995, p. B9.

Eastman Kodak, which reportedly paid $40 million to be the sole imaging sponsor of the 1996, summer Olympic Games in Atlanta, is miffed with archrival Fuji Photo Film, which is co-sponsor of an exhibit called Images of Excellence, an elaborate display that honors 100 years of track and field. Kodak is concerned that people will think that another film company is an Olympic sponsor.

Dodge, John, "IBM has quite a bit riding on Olympics," *Atlanta Journal Constitution,* Feb. 25, 1996, p. H3.

IBM, buoyed by record profits, a soaring stock price and a work force lighter by 200,000 employees, is shelling out $40 million in cash, services and computers to manage the 1996 Olympic Games in Atlanta. The scale of the endeavor, the first by a single computer company, is breathtaking.

Frank, Robert, "Advertising: Coca-Cola ads star Olympic fans," *The Wall Street Journal,* March 6, 1996, p. B1.

Executives at Coca-Cola Co. are aiming to squeeze more sales out of its 68-year link with the Olympic Games. One big part of the strategy is a raft of new ads unveiled on March 5, 1996, by Coca-Cola's marketing chief, Sergio Zyman. The new slogan: "It's for the fans."

Meece, Mickey, "MasterCard ATM unit and American Express making presence known at Olympic Games," *American Banker,* Feb. 22, 1994, p. 22.

Despite Visa international's exclusive industry sponsorship for the Olympic Games, MasterCard International's ATM affiliate, Cirrus System Inc., and American Express Travel Related Services Co. have been publicizing their presence in Lillehammer, Norway.

Wells, Melanie, and David Lieberman, "Ad spending to vault on Olympics," *USA Today,* Dec. 5, 1995, p. B3.

The 1996 summer Olympics and political elections are expected to help boost advertising spending in the U.S. 7.8 percent to $174.1 billion, according to Robert Coen, the McCann-Erickson Worldwide senior vice president and director of forecasting. However, not everyone shares Coen's optimism.

Amateurism

Brennan, Christine, "Samaranch to Work Toward Adding Baseball, Soccer, Cycling Pros," *The Washington Post,* Aug. 11, 1992, p. C7.

IOC President Juan Antonio Samaranch defended the presence of professional athletes in the Olympic Games and said he will work with the federations of baseball, soccer and cycling to encourage pros from those sports to enter the Olympics as well.

Janofsky, Michael, "Rare Air and New Rules for Olympics," *The New York Times,* July 19, 1992, p. S1.

The new era in Olympic Games that begins with the 1992 summer Games in Barcelona is discussed. Gone are the notions of purity, integrity and amateurism, replaced by money.

Powers, John, "Times Changed for Olympics," *Boston Globe,* Dec. 24, 1989, p. 52.

Powers claims that the Olympics finally entered the 20th century during the 1980s by admitting that amateurism is a thing of the past.

Tyrrell, R. Emmett Jr., "Tuning Out the Olympics," *The Washington Times,* Aug. 2, 1992, p. B4.

Tyrrell states that the Olympics are fast becoming corrupted by evil, commenting that modern Olympic Games were founded on the ideal of amateurism, not professionalism. He adds that the top Olympic athletes are making tens of thousands of dollars for doing what earlier athletes did for fun.

Vincent, Charlie, "Dream Team's Foes Savor Thrill of Defeat," *Detroit News & Free Press,* July 4, 1992, p. B1.

Vincent comments that he does not like the idea of NBA players in the Olympics because it makes a mockery of competition and underscores the disappearance of amateurism in the games; however, he admits that the members of the teams that face the U.S. National Basketball Team do not care whether they win or lose as long as they can be near their heroes.

Atlanta Summer Games

Baxter, Tom, "Sobering problems await Atlanta officials after Olympics honeymoon," *Atlanta Constitution,* Feb. 1, 1996, p. B5.

Baxter comments on the politics of environmental policy in Georgia, House Speaker Newt Gingrich's, R-Ga., view on the subject and the polluted wastewater that Atlanta will have to face in the wake of the 1996 summer Olympics.

Kim, Lillian Lee, "Olympic Games duty to neighbors debated," *Atlanta Constitution,* July 29, 1994, p. F6.

Neighborhood leaders demanded greater financial support for poor communities while Olympic officials warned that the Games cannot solve the city's problems, during a lively debate among black leaders and citizens.

Ruffenach, Glenn, "Olympic Games ticket sales exceed organizers' plans," *The Wall Street Journal*, Sept. 19, 1995, p. B6.
Organizers of the 1996 summer Olympics in Atlanta said they sold more than 2.7 million tickets in the first round of sales, a figure that exceeded their own expectations and bodes well for Atlanta's tight budget.

Stacey, Julie, "USA snapshots: Volunteers working at Olympic Games," *USA Today*, May 9, 1994, p. C1.
Based upon statistics from the Atlanta Committee for the Olympic Games, there were 28,742 volunteers involved in the Los Angeles summer Games, 27,221 in the Seoul, South Korea Games, 30,000 in the Barcelona Games and a projected 40,000 for the Atlanta Games.

Williams, Dick, "Games create Olympic-size bickering," *Atlanta Journal Constitution*, April 9, 1994, p. A18.
Williams contends that the bickering over various aspects of the 1996 Olympic Games in Atlanta is getting in the way of the planning that is necessary for hosting the international event. Williams argues that debating "airy social abstractions" has no place in planning for the Games.

Broadcast Rights

Lazarus, George, "Advertisers cheer NBC's long-term Olympics deal," *Chicago Tribune*, Dec. 14, 1995, p. 2.
Lazarus comments on a variety of marketing news, including the positive response among advertisers to NBC's long-term Olympics deal for broadcast rights to five consecutive Olympic Games, beginning in the year 2000.

Martzke, Rudy, "Making of Olympic deal," *USA Today*, Aug. 8, 1995, p. C3.
The $1.27 billion deal NBC Sports President Dick Ebersol made for the 2000 Summer Olympics in Sydney, Australia and the 2002 winter Games in Salt Lake City is discussed. A list of money spent by NBC, ABC and CBS for broadcast rights to the Olympic Games is given.

Scott, Jeffry, "The Olympics' big winner," *Atlanta Constitution*, Feb. 16, 1996, C4.
NBC Sports President Dick Ebersol is on top of the world as the mastermind of two of the biggest TV deals ever, paying $3.5 billion for the U.S. broadcast rights to five of the next six Olympics. The 1998 Winter Games in Nagano, Japan will be on CBS. Ebersol is profiled on his winning drive.

Commercialization

Grimes, Charlotte, "Reality eludes my Olympics," *St. Louis Post-Dispatch*, Feb. 10, 1994, p. A6.
Grimes laments the commercialization of the Olympic games and discusses her own romanticized memories of Olympic games past.

Rodda, John, "Storm Breaks over the Five-Ring Circus," *Guardian*, April 25, 1992, p. 13.
The conclusions of "The Lords of the Rings," a book about the commercialization of the Olympics, are discussed. The book reserves its harshest criticisms for the ethics of IOC President Juan Antonio Samaranch and International Amateur Athletic Federation President Primo Nebiolo.

Saporta, Maria, "Sponsorships Widen Range of Olympics, Young Says," *Atlanta Constitution*, Aug. 4, 1992, p. B7.
Saporta says that former Atlanta Mayor Andrew Young believes corporate sponsorships of athletes have helped make the Olympics accessible to a broad range of people and that commercialization of the 1996 Atlanta Games is not bad.

Drug Use and Testing Among Athletes

Fish, Mike, "USATF favors no notice for drug testing," *Atlanta Constitution*, March 7, 1995, p. D7.
The executive committee of USA Track and Field approved the concept of testing without advance notice during meetings March 5, 1995 in Atlanta. By the 1996 Olympics, American track and field athletes likely will be subject to unannounced, out-of-competition drug testing.

Rosen, Karen, "Chinese truce sought amid drug allegations," *Atlanta Constitution*, April 10, 1995, p. D2.
USOC officials are trying to soothe Chinese hurt feelings as well as sign an agreement to keep an eye on the country's training and drug-testing procedures. Not only did the Pan Pacific charter nations vote to ban the Chinese from their swimming meet in the Olympic pool in Atlanta in August 1995, but U.S., Australian and Canadian coaching groups requested that China be banned from the Olympics .

Rosen, Karen, "USOC admits anti-doping efforts are behind schedule," *Atlanta Journal Constitution*, April 9, 1995, p. F2.
Since 1992, the USOC has conducted 1,400 out-of-competition drug tests and turned up only one positive and one no-show. USOC officials and some top steroid experts said doping is the biggest problem faced by the organization approaching the 1996 Atlanta Olympics, and one they haven't dealt with well.

Political and National Pressures

Harvey, Randy, "Olympics' Anthem of Politics," *Los Angeles Times*, Feb. 1, 1992, p. A1.
Since 1968, the Olympics have become increasingly politicized. Issues confronting Olympic officials in 1992 include the admission of professional athletes into some competitions and what to call teams representing the former Soviet republics.

Back Issues

Great Research on Current Issues Starts Right Here...Recent topics covered by The CQ Researcher are listed below. Before May 1991, reports were published under the name of Editorial Research Reports.

SEPTEMBER 1994
Home Schooling
Welfare Experiments
Courts and the Media
Regulating Tobacco

OCTOBER 1994
Historic Preservation
Religion and Politics
Arts Funding
Economic Sanctions

NOVEMBER 1994
Sex on Campus
Blood Supply Safety
Testing Term Limits
Religion in America

DECEMBER 1994
Farm Policy
Arms Sales
Earthquake Research
The Future of Television

JANUARY 1995
Treating Addiction
Child Custody and Support
Parents and Schools
Non-Proliferation Treaty at 25

Back issues are available for $5.00 (subscribers) or $8.00 (non-subscribers). Quantity discounts apply to orders over ten. To order, call Congressional Quarterly Customer Service at (202) 887-8621.

Binders are available for $18.00. To order call 1-800-638-1710. Please refer to stock number 648.

FEBRUARY 1995
Cracking Down on Immigration
The Business of Sports
Reinventing Government
Housing Discrimination

MARCH 1995
Death Penalty Debate
Primary Care
Democracy in Africa
Environmental Movement at 25

APRIL 1995
Abortion Clinic Protests
Dieting and Health
Combating AIDS
Rethinking Affirmative Action

MAY 1995
Assisted Suicide Controversy
Overhauling Social Security
Learning to Read
Mandatory Sentencing

JUNE 1995
Combating Infectious Disease
Property Rights
Repetitive Stress Injuries
Regulating the Internet

JULY 1995
War Crimes
Highway Safety
Combating Terrorism
Preventing Teen Drug Use

AUGUST 1995
Job Stress
Organ Transplants
United Nations at 50
Advances in Cancer Research

SEPTEMBER 1995
Catholic Church in the U.S.
Northern Ireland Cease-Fire
High School Sports
Teaching History

OCTOBER 1995
Quebec's Future
Revitalizing the Cities
Networking the Classroom
Indoor Air Pollution

NOVEMBER 1995
The Working Poor
The Jury System
Sex, Violence and the Media
Police Misconduct

DECEMBER 1995
Teens and Tobacco
Gene Therapy's Future
Global Water Shortages
Third-Party Prospects

JANUARY 1996
Emergency Medicine
Punishing Sex Offenders
Bilingual Education
Helping the Homeless

FEBRUARY 1996
Reforming the CIA
Campaign Finance Reform
Academic Politics
Getting Into College

MARCH 1996
The British Monarchy
Preventing Juvenile Crime
Tax Reform
Pursuing the Paranormal

Future Topics

- ***Managed Care***
- ***Protecting Endangered Species***
- ***Changing Military Culture***

THE CQ Researcher

PUBLISHED BY CONGRESSIONAL QUARTERLY INC.

Managed Care

Do health-care firms sacrifice quality to cut costs?

More than 50 million workers — 70 percent of the nation's eligible employees — now have health coverage through managed care. The rapid rise of managed-care firms reflects employers' efforts to reduce their expenses for workers' health benefits. But consumer groups worry that concern about costs will drive medical decisions in huge for-profit firms. And physicians' groups see the focus on cost as antithetical to professional ethics. The managed-care industry asserts that health care will improve under its cost-conscious custody. Health-care firms say they have a financial stake in intervening early and making sure patients get better, not sicker. But seriously ill patients, who are the most expensive gambles for cost-conscious plans, will lose out in the process, some experts predict.

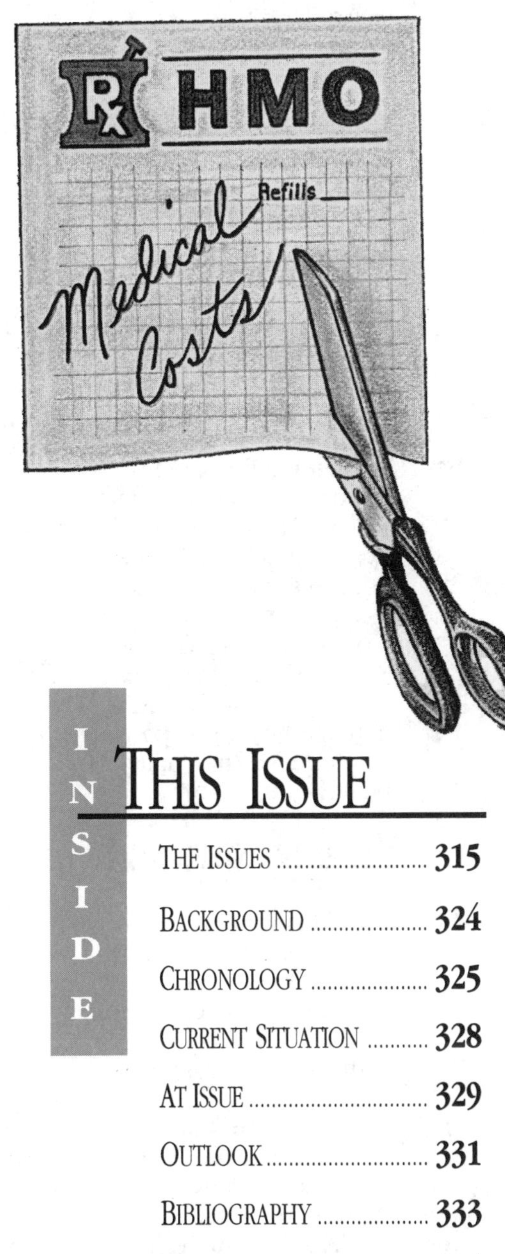

INSIDE THIS ISSUE

CQ April 12, 1996 • Volume 6, No. 14 • Pages 313-336

Formerly Editorial Research Reports

MANAGED CARE

THE ISSUES

BACKGROUND

CURRENT SITUATION

OUTLOOK

SIDEBARS AND GRAPHICS

FOR FURTHER RESEARCH

COVER: BARBARA SASSA-DANIELS

April 12, 1996
Volume 6, No. 14

EDITOR Sandra Stencel

MANAGING EDITOR Thomas J. Colin

ASSOCIATE EDITORS Sarah M. Magner, Richard L. Worsnop

STAFF WRITERS Charles S. Clark, Mary H. Cooper, Craig Donegan, Kenneth Jost

EDITORIAL ASSISTANT Tonya Harris

PUBLISHED BY Congressional Quarterly Inc.

CHAIRMAN Andrew Barnes

VICE CHAIRMAN Andrew P. Corty

EDITOR AND PUBLISHER Neil Skene

EXECUTIVE EDITOR Robert W. Merry

ASSOCIATE PUBLISHER Edward S. Hauck

Bibliographic records and abstracts included in The Next Step section of this publication are from UMI's Newspaper and Periodical Abstracts database, and are used with permission.

The CQ Researcher (ISSN 1056-2036). Formerly Editorial Research Reports. Published weekly (48 times per year, not printed March 1, May 31, Aug. 30, Nov. 29) by Congressional Quarterly Inc., 1414 22nd St., N.W., Washington, D.C. 20037. Annual subscription rate for libraries, businesses and government is $319. Additional rates furnished upon request. Second-class postage paid at Washington, D.C. POSTMASTER: Send address changes to The CQ Researcher, 1414 22nd St., N.W., Washington, D.C. 20037.

Managed Care

BY SARAH GLAZER

THE ISSUES

When doctors discovered Nelene Fox's breast cancer in 1991, the 38-year-old California school teacher and mother of three children thought her best hope for survival was a bone marrow transplant. But Health Net, her health maintenance organization (HMO), labeled the procedure experimental and refused to pay for one.*

Fox and her husband couldn't afford the $200,000 operation, but over the next few months she worked tirelessly with friends and family to raise the money through bake sales and other fund-raising events. Fox died in early 1993, nine months after undergoing the operation.

Fox's family sued Health Net and in December 1993 won an $89-million judgment — the largest ever made against an insurance company for denying health benefits. (Health Net appealed the jury's award but settled the case while on appeal for an undisclosed amount.)

The Nelene Fox case and others since have resounded throughout the medical world, raising fundamental questions about managed care's drive to curb expenses and the possible effects on health-care quality. Health Net said its decisions were based on medical factors, but the Fox family produced evidence that the HMO's managers received bonuses for keeping treatment expenses low. [1]

The same month that Health Net turned Fox down, $4.8 million was sitting in the HMO's transplant fund. "If the money isn't used, Health Net keeps it" and improves its profitability, says Fox's brother, attorney Mark Hiepler, who handled the family's lawsuit.

To many observers, however, performing the transplant against uncertain odds of success represented all that was wrong with the old-style, "unmanaged" system of medical insurance. Cost was rarely a consideration in its medical decisions — even if the procedure was likely to be ineffective.

"A lot of people said there was no reason to put [Fox] through the agony of prolonging death," says Donald W. Parsons, associate medical director for government relations at Kaiser Permanente Medical Groups in Washington. After all, Parsons says, Fox died within months of the operation, suggesting she was not an ideal candidate.

Hiepler vehemently disagrees that the operation merely prolonged his sister's suffering. "She had eight months [after the operation] when she was back to being a normal person," he says. "When you look at the human factors, there's a child who will remember her Mom, because she was almost 4 $^1/_2$ when her Mom died. . . . We played softball together on Thanksgiving, only a month after she had been in the hospital."

The question of whether Fox's treatment was appropriate or not may never be fully resolved, since the success of bone marrow transplants depends on each individual's case. Nor is there likely to be a ready answer to the question of how much society should spend for expensive treatments when there is little hope.

The underlying principle of managed care is to keep the entire community healthy by providing preventive care, such as immunizations and mammograms, at little or no cost. In exchange for lower premiums, copayments and deductibles, the consumer agrees to see a limited group of physicians selected by the plan. The plan keeps costs down by limiting the consumer's access to expensive specialists and procedures.

Hiepler says the trade-off is a bad one for the consumer. "The HMOs have seduced the public into not wanting to pay for anything — a tetanus shot, a breast exam, a physical — $60 procedures that any of us could afford. On the other hand, they have all kinds of structural impediments to deny us something else that maybe none of us can afford."

"Health plans have no interest in spending more money because they let someone get good and sick," retorts Susan Pisano, director of communications at the American Association of Health Plans (AAHP). "They have every reason to intervene early and make sure patients don't get sicker." Pisano says malpractice lawsuits are no more common in managed care than under traditional insurance plans.

The negative publicity over the Fox suit prompted Health Net and other HMOs to authorize bone marrow transplants more freely, Hiepler says. Since his sister's litigation, Hiepler has handled 127 similar cases, and in all but two cases the HMOs involved agreed to pay without going to court.

---

* The HMO covered bone marrow transplants but excluded "experimental" procedures. The plan said Fox's cancer was so far advanced that the procedure would be considered experimental in her case.

Rise in Managed Care Reflects Major Shift

The number of workers in managed-care health plans has risen steadily in recent years, reflecting a major shift away from traditional indemnity plans. In 1995, workers in managed care outnumbered those in traditional plans by more than two to one.

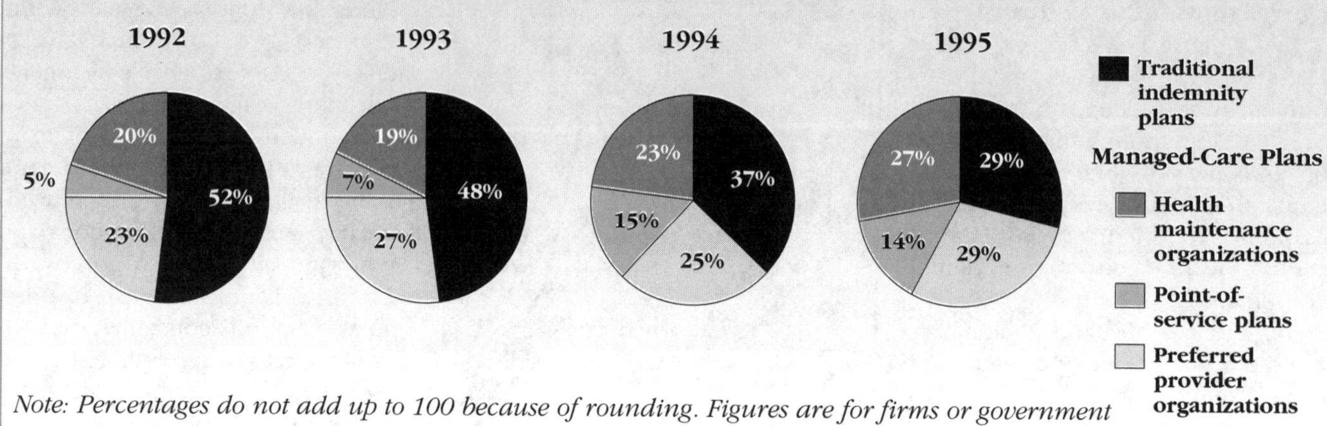

Note: Percentages do not add up to 100 because of rounding. Figures are for firms or government agencies with 10 or more employees.

Source: Foster Higgins National Survey of Employer-sponsored Health Plans, 1996.

Hiepler sees the new willingness to pay as a positive outcome of the Fox suit. But Parsons takes another view. "Most HMOs, because of the Nelene Fox case, are probably allowing more people to [have] bone marrow transplants than need them."

As the nation shifts to managed care and changes its focus from high-tech care for the very sick to keeping the overall population healthy, controversies like the Fox case are inevitable, some experts say.

"For some individuals, their quality of care will suffer even if for the population covered you can show that the quality of care has increased," predicts William S. Custer, an economist specializing in health care at Georgia State University. "I think some of these complaints are coming because we're trying to cut costs," he adds. "That means hard choices are being made, and some people are falling on the wrong side of those hard choices."

Questions over how well managed care actually works have taken on new urgency because managed care has swept the nation so rapidly. More than 50 million people, or 70 percent of the eligible employees, belong to some kind of managed-care plan, according to a major 1995 survey.* By comparison, fewer than half the eligible workers belonged in 1992.

The impetus behind the managed-care revolution has been employers trying to reduce their expenses for workers' health benefits. After years of increases as high as 18 percent, employers' per capita health costs dropped in 1994, and only rose about 2 percent in 1995. But as managed care has spread, it has run into resentment from doctors who see it as antithetical to professional ethics.

In a recent article in *The New England Journal of Medicine,* two Harvard doctors warned of economic threats from HMOs. Doctors who contract with HMOs may find that the fixed fee they receive for each patient, known as "capitation," just covers their costs, they said. To make a reasonable income, the authors said physicians must earn bonuses for keeping down hospitalizations, referrals to specialists and other costs. [2]

"Patients count on their doctor to tell them what they need. When the doctor is thinking, 'I will have to close my doors if I give too much care,' we will have a real quality problem," says co-author Steffie Woolhandler.

Woolhandler and David U. Himmelstein criticized a so-called "gag" clause in their contracts with the managed-care company U.S. Healthcare. They said it prohibits doctors in the plan from talking to patients about the plan's financial incentives to limit care or about treatments the plan won't cover.

A few days after Himmelstein criticized the policy on the "Donahue" show last November, U.S. Healthcare terminated his contract. In February, following a burst of publicity, the company changed its mind. That same month, U.S. Healthcare decided to allow its physicians to tell patients how the company reimburses doctors, though not

* The survey by Foster Higgins, an employee-benefits consulting firm, covered firms with 10 or more employees.

the specific rates paid.[3]

The AAHP contends Himmelstein and other doctors misunderstood their contracts' provisions. "Physicians are encouraged to discuss health treatment options whether they're covered or not," Pisano says. "What physicians are asked not to do is bring into the examining room their complaints about the plan or about their payment."

Organizations representing consumers and the chronically ill have joined with the American Medical Association (AMA) and physician specialty groups to fight for legislation they say would provide more accountability from HMOs and greater patient protections. In January, Massachusetts passed legislation forbidding HMOs from imposing "gag rules."

Citizen Action, a 3-million-member consumer group, has been lobbying in state legislatures for laws that would require plans to disclose how they pay their doctors; give patients the right to choose specialists outside the plan; and provide appeals for patients who get turned down for expensive treatments.

"When you have huge, for-profit managed-care companies that are concerned about making money, I don't know how anyone could think they would put the needs of patients ahead of making money," says Cathy Hurwit, Citizen Action's legislative director. "In many cases, it's not the consumer buying the plan — it's the employer. The employer is concerned about costs rather than quality."

Defenders of HMOs see patient-doctor forays into state legislatures as attempts to kill a new way of practicing medicine that eliminates overtreatment. They say their enemies are old-style fee-for-service doctors — including many specialists — who view HMOs as threats to their income. Under fee-for-service plans, the traditional system of billing, doctors charge an additional fee for each procedure or test.

To counter anti-managed-care sentiments, the AAHP recently launched a nationwide media campaign. "I believe the vested interests of the old fee-for-service [plans] have been successful in selling the public a bill of goods," says John Ludden, senior vice president of medical affairs for Harvard Pilgrim Healthcare, a managed-care plan, and an AAHP board member. "Every specialist knows there are too many specialists now, and there will be many more in the future. The trough will not be as full, and more bodies will be seeking to feed at the trough."

"Most HMOs, because of the Nelene Fox case, are probably allowing more people to [have] bone marrow transplants than need them."

— Donald W. Parsons
Associate medical director
Kaiser Permanente Medical Groups

As managed-care firms struggle with cost and quality issues, these are some of the questions legislatures, consumers and the medical community are asking:

Will the trend toward managed care hurt the quality of health care?

Studies comparing managed care to traditional fee-for-service find the quality of care about equal. A 1994 review of 16 studies generally found better or equal results for HMO patients suffering from a wide range of diseases, including congestive heart failure, colorectal cancer and diabetes. These studies based their conclusions on clinical results such as how many patients died or how far a patient's cancer had advanced before it was discovered.[4]

Consumer-satisfaction surveys tell a slightly more complicated story, the same review found. HMO patients are less likely to be satisfied with the care they're getting but happier with the costs than those in fee-for-service. In short, says review co-author Harold S. Luft, a professor of health economics at the University of California, San Francisco, consumers are willing to trade some quality in service for lower costs.

But critics of managed care say the published studies tend to be based on the best of managed care — old-style HMOs like Kaiser Permanente with salaried, dedicated staffs. The fastest-growing kind of managed care today is represented by looser networks of doctors under contract with health plans to care for their enrollees. (*See glossary, p. 320.*)

Doctors in these plans usually care for the plan's patients for fixed or discounted fees. Consequently, critics say, doctors in these networks are more likely to be influenced by financial incentives to deny care.

"HMOs are a minority of managed

HMO Costs Fell in 1995 for First Time

The average cost of HMO health-care coverage in the U.S. dropped nearly 4 percent from 1994 to 1995 — the first decline in 10 years. The average cost of traditional fee-for-service (indemnity) plans rose during the same period. The drop in HMO fees reflected lower costs for smaller employers.*

Medical Plan Costs

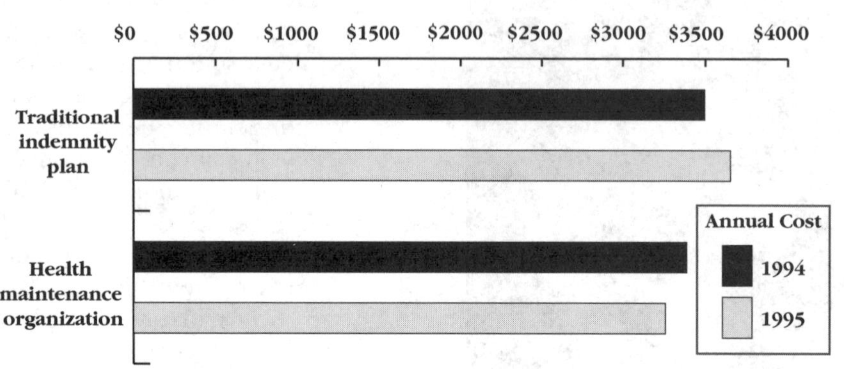

Note: The survey covered active employees in firms or government agencies with 10 or more employees.

** The drop was the first in the 10-year history of the Foster-Higgins survey.*

Source: Foster Higgins National Survey of Employer-sponsored Health Plans, 1996.

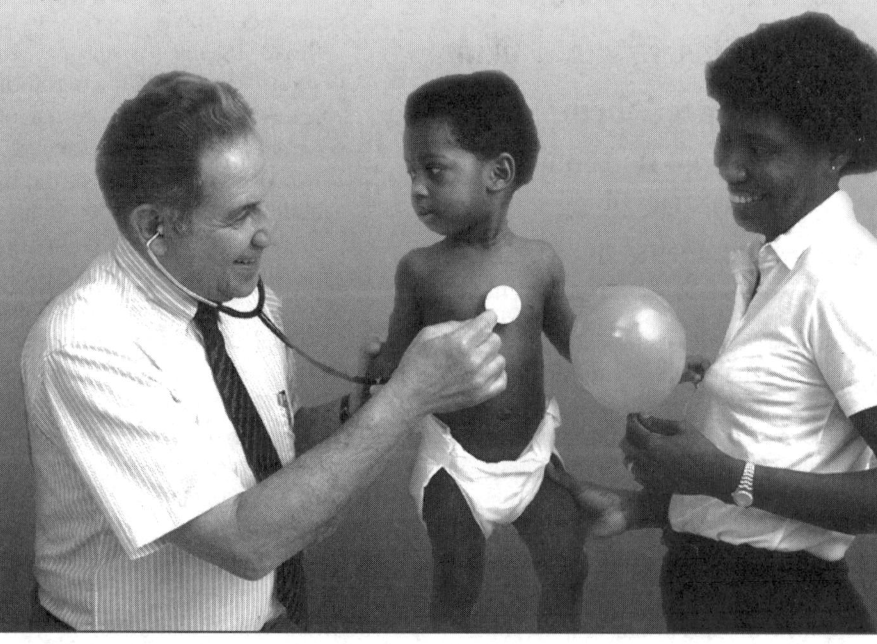

care; they're the best kind of care," says Barbara Starfield, a professor of health policy and pediatrics at Johns Hopkins University. "Now they're mixed up with all the rest, which are far inferior. What's more, they're being used to represent managed care, when managed care is something else."

Starfield says it's hard to study the impact of newer financial incentives on patients because consumers usually don't know if their doctor has a contract that encourages limitations on hospitalization or referrals. Generally, information in such contracts is confidential, and doctors are prohibited from sharing the information with patients. Further complicating matters, most doctors are affiliated with a variety of plans with different arrangements, some managed care and some not.

"This managed care thing is a big, black box, and that's to the advantage of managed care," says Starfield. "They can say anything they want about it."

Most experts agree there is a huge range in quality in managed care. "Managed care means something different in every region of the country," says Kevin Schulman, a professor in the clinical economics research unit at Georgetown University Medical Center.

In cities where managed care is a relatively new phenomenon, health companies are fighting for a share of the work-force market by offering the lowest possible premiums to employers rather than superior service, Schulman says. By contrast, where managed care has become established, plans tend to compete more on quality than cost, he finds. Those markets "can't cut doctors' payments anymore and all of a sudden have to deliver value," Schulman says.

Yet quality has suddenly become a hot issue for managed care. Much of it has been stimulated by recent horror stories in which patients charge fatal lack of treatment by HMOs. In September, the *New York Post* led off a front-page series with screaming headlines about a baby who died from a defective heart. The mother said she was convinced the problem would have been detected had the HMO allowed her an extra day in the hospital. [5]

In January, *Time* magazine's cover pictured a gagged doctor. The story questioned whether patients in managed care "can still trust their doctors." [6]

But many health-care experts say the anecdotes that reporters cite do not represent the experiences most people will have with managed care. "You see the demonizing of managed care in the press," says Helen H. Mills, president of the Mills Group, an employee-benefits consulting firm in Fairfax, Va. "They're featuring cases that test the outer limits of how plans balance economics and ethics."

Yet on balance, managed-care plans have the potential to raise the quality of medical care, Mills suggests, especially in small towns where doctors practice without monitoring from outside experts. Managed-care plans train administrative "cost cops" to insist that their doctors follow research-backed medical guidelines before approving a medical procedure. "By having this bureaucracy looking over the shoulder of doctors, forcing their continuing education, the bureaucracy is tracking the outcomes of procedures," she says. "That's not all bad."

Helen Darling, manager of health-care programs for Xerox Corp., says managed care generally delivers better value for the money. A traditional fee-for-service plan provided to the family of an average Xerox employee costs $12,000 a year, as opposed to $6,000 for an HMO, and the HMO plan is 17 percent richer in benefits, Darling says. Xerox has led the field in demanding high quality in its plans. "Our philosophy is good managed care is better care overall," Darling says. Traditional plans have become so expensive for employers, she adds, that "unmanaged fee-for-service is not going to exist in two to three years."

It's not always clear whether the widely publicized misjudgments made by managed-care doctors to limit care are due to the system of care itself or are medical mistakes of the kind that happen in fee-for-service as well. But critics say they presage new problems in the rapidly changing health-care market.

One of the long-heralded advantages of managed care has been its ability to offer one-stop shopping with a team of doctors from diverse fields working together on a patient's problems.

"HMOs can provide an integrated version of care for people with very complex illnesses," says Ludden, contrasting it to the "splintered, I-can-get-my-own-specialist" approach under fee-for service. He points to Harvard Pilgrim Healthcare's 20-year-old program for children with Down's Syndrome, which coordinates care by pediatricians, cardiologists and neurologists, as "an example of where HMOs function extraordinarily well."

But critics charge that newer-style plans lack that coordination because they tend to be loose networks of doctors in private practice who don't necessarily know one another. Often, they are in the same plan merely by virtue of their agreement to take the plan's patients for a fixed or discounted fee. Primary-care physicians in managed care reported that they referred patients more often to a specialist unknown to them and that they spoke personally with the specialist less often than doctors in fee for service, one study found.[7]

Delays in referrals to the right specialist can have serious consequences for people with complicated illnesses. Managed care relies on a generalist, such as a family physician or general practitioner, to act as the "gatekeeper" in deciding whether a patient gets referred to a specialist.[8]

"You've got to be sure the gatekeeper has enough knowledge and will refer quickly when needed," says Martha Keys, vice president of the National Multiple Sclerosis Society. When multiple sclerosis (MS) patients go into worsened conditions known as "exacerbations," a delay in getting the right treatment can sometimes mean the difference between paralysis or preventing it, experts at the society say.

Lisa Baynes, 39, an MS patient in Mission Viejo, Calif., battled with her HMO for a year before getting permission to see an MS specialist. Her medical group, an independent practice association (IPA) that contracted with CIGNA HealthCare of Southern California, required her to consult instead with three neurologists in the group. But Baynes maintains that none of the doctors were familiar with her side effects from a new MS drug.

CIGNA finally agreed to let Baynes see the outside specialist after she contacted the California Department of Corporations, which regulates HMOs. In a written statement, CIGNA said Baynes "was at all times under the care of highly qualified physicians who had access to" the specialist in question through consultations.

Research shows that it's important for patients to have a long-term relationship with their primary doctor. "Managed care right away interferes with that," Starfield says, "because managed care is under the control of employers generally and subject to change every year."

Every time the employer changes plan offerings, critics say, the list of doctors covered by the plan is also likely to change. This lack of continuity can also interfere with managed care's basic philosophy, which encourages physicians to deliver preventive care.

In dentistry, a branch of medicine that particularly stresses preventive care, some dentists say managed care's philosophy doesn't work in the real world because employers have ultimate control over the choice of doctors.

"The concept of HMOs makes sense," says Henry Hermann, a dentist in Falls Church, Va. "If someone pays me a set fee to take care of this patient for the next 15 to 20 years, I would give them the best care and wouldn't want complications."

But he adds, "In reality, I know I won't have that patient for 15 to 20 years" because employees' plan offerings change so often. "In the short-term, the incentive is to do least." Hermann no longer takes managed-care patients, he says, because the fees barely cover his costs and be-

A Managed-Care Glossary

Fee-for-Service: The traditional way of paying for medical services. Doctors in private practice charge a fee for each service provided, and the patient's insurer pays all or part of that fee.

Capitation: An arrangement in which managed-care plans pay a fixed-fee to physicians for each plan member they care for. Doctors receive the fixed amount per month, regardless of how much or how little care the plan member receives.

Health Maintenance Organization (HMO): An organization that provides health care in return for pre-set monthly payments. Most HMOs provide care through a network of doctors and hospitals that their members must use in order to be covered.

Independent Practice Association (IPA): A managed-care plan in which individual physicians, typically practicing out of their private offices as part of a medical group, contract with a health plan for a fee or fixed amount per patient.

Preferred Provider Organization (PPO): A managed-care plan in which a network of doctors and hospitals provides care at a lower cost than through traditional insurance. The choice is usually wider than under HMOs.

Point-of-Service (POS): A form of HMO, sometimes called a "freedom" plan, which allows members to choose services from providers outside the HMO's network as long as the consumer is willing to pay more — typically a higher deductible and a percentage of the cost of care.

Primary Care Physician: HMOs and managed-care plans usually require members to choose a physician devoted to general medical care — sometimes known as a "gatekeeper" — who provides routine care and authorizes care by specialists.

cause he can't count on managed-care patients to stay with his practice.

But others find managed care a vast improvement over the old method of picking a doctor, which relied on the anecdotes of friends and neighbors. Managed-care companies and the large employers that hire them are more likely to investigate doctors' credentials before accepting them into their plan, they say.

"Before, my employees had a telephone book," says benefits consultant Mills. "Now they have a directory of hospitals and physicians who have been pretty carefully screened."

Are managed-care plans great for healthy people but bad for sick people?

Critics say managed-care plans have healthier populations than a traditional health insurance plan, such as Blue Cross, because they market to people who have few health worries and like the idea of low premiums and free visits.

In "cherry picking," as such targeting is known, an HMO might seek out a computer company that employs healthy men in their 30s and offer a lower premium than the competing Blue Cross plan. In the elderly market served by Medicare, a company might advertise informational meetings at Pizza Hut, thus attracting elderly people vigorous enough to drive there. Critics who think HMOs cherry pick say they purposely shun sick people because they're expensive to care for.

"My summary of the evidence would be if you're a basically healthy person, care is probably fine in an HMO," Woolhandler says. "The sicker and more vulnerable you are the more likely quality problems are to surface. Pap smears and cholesterol tests are cheap. If they can keep you enrolled with that, they're delighted to have you. It's chronically sick people they don't want, and the data suggest they do a lousy job" with them.

Woolhandler cites studies showing that HMO treatment results are worse for vulnerable groups, such as the elderly and the poor. [9]

In the authoritative Rand Health Insurance Experiment conducted in the 1970s, patients were randomly assigned to an HMO or fee-for-service plan. On balance, patients fared about equally. But low-income, medically high-risk patients had a greater chance of dying in an HMO's care. [10]

One explanation for the disparity is that high-risk people may be daunted by an HMO's bureaucracy. "If you have to wait 20 minutes on a phone line, it may deter a person using a pay phone who has two children pulling on her skirt," says Woolhandler. "Or you may have to go to a specialist who may not be near your neighborhood."

Bolstering Woolhandler's case is a government-funded study that found Medicare patients who enrolled in HMOs in 1990 were more likely to be healthy than those in traditional fee-for-service plans. However, since that study there has been a dramatic increase in Medicare HMO enrollment, which rose by almost 1 million people from 1990 to 1994. [11] Today's HMOs may have a more representative cross-section of the elderly population, suggests Teresa Fama, deputy director of the Robert Wood Johnson Foundation's National Program Office for Chronic Care Initiatives in HMOs.

In fact, studies have been equally divided on the question of whether HMOs cherry pick. A recent study by Fama of consumers under age 65 with private insurance found equal numbers of chronically ill patients in HMOs and traditional plans. [12]

Fama thinks it may be harder for HMOs to pick and choose among employees these days as they penetrate an increasing share of the market. "They can't go to an employer and say we only want people who run three miles a day," she says. "They have to take the whole group."

The question of how well HMOs care for the chronically ill is hotly contested. Organizations representing chronically ill patients with diseases like MS, asthma and arthritis charge that their members are more likely to have trouble seeing specialists familiar with their diseases. Many of these groups have joined with physician specialists in the Patient Access to Specialty Care Coalition to demand that patients be allowed to see a specialist of their choosing outside an HMO's network.

According to a recent survey by the Harvard School of Public Health, sick managed-care enrollees report more problems getting in to see a specialist than their fee-for-service counterparts. Managed-care patients reported longer average waits to see a specialist (17 days vs. 12 days). They were also more likely to report incorrect care by their general physician (12 percent vs. 5 percent) and by a specialist they saw (10 percent vs. 3 percent).[13]

But when researchers have looked at how chronically ill patients fair from a health standpoint, managed care and fee-for-service have an equal track record, according to Fama. Alan L. Hillman, director of the Center for Health Policy at the University of Pennsylvania, goes even further. "In the few clinical situations that have been studied, managed care comes out better," he says.

It's true HMOs rely more heavily on generalists than specialists, says Fama, but that may constitute an improvement. A recent study found that diabetes and hypertension patients fared equally well in managed care and fee-for-service, even though managed-care patients got more of their treatment from a generalist.[14]

By relying heavily on a primary-care physician as an overall health-care coordinator, HMOs may give more comprehensive care to someone with a disease that crosses several specialties.

"My summary of the evidence would be if you're a basically healthy person, care is probably fine in an HMO. The sicker and more vulnerable you are the more likely quality problems are to surface."

— Steffie Woolhandler
Associate professor of medicine
Harvard Medical School

"Someone who has diabetes doesn't only have diabetes; he has other problems," says Fama, noting that diabetics are prone to kidney and heart trouble as well. "One of the dangers of relying too much on specialists is a lot of other things get neglected."

Are HMOs reducing costs by cutting fat or by cutting necessary medical services?

Numerous studies have shown that compared with traditional insurance plans, HMOs admit fewer patients to the hospital, get them out sooner and use fewer expensive procedures and tests.[15]

The result, many analysts say, has been to drive down the cost of health-insurance premiums. For the first time in 10 years, the average cost of HMO coverage declined last year (by 3.8 percent) while fee-for-service premiums continued to rise.[16]

But while health economists hail the cutback in services as an advance, patients and critics of managed care have raised alarums about whether it constitutes inferior care.

The trend toward reduced hospital stays should be "welcomed by the public as an advance in patient care," wrote Gifford Boyce-Smith, medical director of CIGNA HealthCare of Northern California, in a recent op-ed article.[17] High-technology medical innovations and more preventive care permit HMOs like CIGNA to send patients home sooner because they get better faster, according to Boyce-Smith.

Ten years ago, for example, gallbladder surgery required hospitalization for at least a week. Today, patients can be home in a day or two following laparoscopic surgery, which permits doctors to make a much smaller incision, operating with the aid of a tiny TV camera.

In addition, hospitals can be an unhealthful place to recuperate. Five out of every 100 hospitalized people pick up an infection in the hospital, noted Boyce-Smith.

But people who work in hospitals say they often feel uncomfortable with the pressure put on them to discharge patients as quickly as possible. Managed-care plans increasingly demand that medical procedures once done in the hospital be done in a less expensive setting like home, or that the patient return for outpatient visits.

While the insurer may be right about the specific procedure, it often means the nurse and the doctor don't get the opportunity to help the patient resolve other medical and psychological issues, says Kathleen Mitchell, director of medical nursing at Georgetown University Medical Center. She's especially concerned about the trend of releasing new mothers and their babies after just one day.

"We've had plenty of patients here who felt unready to go home within that 24-hour [maternity stay] but left because that's what their insurer mandated," Mitchell says. "Nursing staff have agonized that the individual would not have gotten information about breast feeding, skin care for the baby, diet, etc."

There's no research evidence that shortened hospital stays are worse for the health of mothers and newborns. In fact, says Kaiser's Parsons, when women were staying in the hospital routinely for five days, "We had women getting blood clots and urinary infections. We discovered less is better."

"It may not show up in a mortality statistic," Woolhandler concedes, "but when the patient is at home vomiting, in pain or unable to get to the toilet, it's a real quality of life issue."

Past studies have shown that as HMOs like Kaiser decreased hospital days, they substituted increased outpatient care. But judging from a recent study, some California doctors' groups that contract with HMOs to take over patients' medical care for a fixed fee are cutting back on both kinds of care. [18]

"One explanation is they're not giving enough care," says Woolhandler, who acknowledges they could also have a healthier-than-average group of patients.

A new study co-authored by Woolhandler shows managed care has boosted the number of people hired to push paper while reducing the number who directly care for patients. The paper-pushing comes as no surprise to doctors, who complain bitterly about the forms they have to fill out for managed-care firms. Some hospitals, like Georgetown, even have personnel devoted to dealing with managed-care staffers who question medical expenses.

From 1968 to 1993, administrative staff grew from 18 percent to 27 percent of the overall health-care work force. During the same period, doctors and nurses shrank from 51 percent of the work force to 43 percent. [19]

"The switch to [for-profit] managed care is substituting a lot of administrative work for hands-on care," says Woolhandler. "We're seeing patients receive less nursing care from physicians and others."

But advocates for corporate managed care say a certain amount of bureaucracy is necessary to reap the reduced costs and procedures for which managed care has been praised. In fact, according to Rand economist Glenn Melnick, having administrators occupy 27 percent of the work force "might be the right mix for consumers, in terms of creating administrative efficiency." [20]

Hurwit of Citizen Action points to a California Medical Association survey showing that some managed-care plans take more than 25 cents of each premium dollar for administration and profit. [21] "There are a lot of plans that are ripping consumers off," she says. "Before you start limiting consumer choice and cutting back on benefits, let's talk about getting rid of the fat and getting more of those dollars back to medical care." Citizen Action supports legislation to require HMOs to spend at least 85 percent of the premium dollar on medical care.

When California consumers discovered that Northern California Kaiser was cutting back on annual, routine Pap smears to detect cervical cancer in women, there was an outcry. Some press reports suggested Kaiser was streamlining under pressure to be cost-competitive with other managed-care plans. "It is very sad to see that Kaiser, which has been setting the standard in our state — and probably the nation — is taking these measures," said Jeanne Finberg of Consumers Union. [22]

But Kaiser said it was simply following the advice of the American College of Obstetricians and Gynecologists. Its revised guidelines say that a woman whose Pap smear is normal for three years does not benefit by having smears more frequently than every two to three years.

Southern California Kaiser, which adopted the guidelines first, used the money it had saved from cutting back on the exams to reach women in the plan who might never have gotten Pap smears before, particularly lower income, less-educated women. "The survival rate from cervical cancer is better because we're reaching more women," Parsons reports. Many plans send Pap smear reminders to members on their birthdays.

The controversy illustrates the inherent conflict in managed care between doing what's best for the community as a whole and doing what's best for the individual, says Georgia State economist Custer. "I guarantee you there's going to be a cancer undiscovered that would have been discovered had you done it every year," he says. "It's clearly a bad health result. But isn't society better off spending the money elsewhere?"

Will new financial incentives hurt the quality of medical care?

Under the fee-for-service system, doctors have an incentive to provide more procedures because they get paid for each one, economists have long argued.

Managed-care advocates point to a recent example reported in *The Wall Street Journal:* a rash of unneeded skull surgeries performed on babies misdiagnosed with a rare brain condition. A few babies died during the surgery, and some were permanently disabled.[23]

"If I go to a surgeon who wants to do an operation on a baby with a funny head, he gets an $8,000 fee," says Parsons, a surgeon. "Let me go to a managed-care surgeon without a financial stake."

In the 1980s, Dartmouth College epidemiologist John E. Wennberg found that doctors in Boston were much more likely to hospitalize patients for common conditions like pneumonia than were doctors in New Haven, Conn., who treated these conditions outside the hospital. It turned out that Boston had many more hospital beds per capita than New Haven.

Most economists thought the findings indicated that medical decisions were often driven by economics. Physicians would come up with additional tests and procedures to fill empty hospital beds and sparsely filled waiting rooms — and to pad their incomes.

The studies also helped to explain why the United States spent more of its national income on health care than other industrialized nations but had citizens who were no healthier. To employers suffering under the burden of skyrocketing health premiums, the studies seemed to point the way to cuts that could reduce costs — by cutting out unnecessary services — without hurting people's health.

In a new report published by the American Hospital Association, Wennberg again concluded that the supply of physicians and hospital beds has driven demand for hospital care. The report also found that rates for common medical procedures, such as mastectomies, can vary as much as 33-fold from one community to another.[24]

At a press conference releasing the report, Wennberg called it "dangerous" to permit such wide variations in medical practice when "there is no evidence . . . that more expenditure leads to better health."[25]

"There have always been financial incentives in medicine," says Hillman. "It's just the incentives in the past have been perverse because they reward doctors and hospitals for doing more. In the more-you-do-the-more-you-get-paid situation, that's a very important contributor to way too many surgical interventions for things like hysterectomies and Caesarean sections."

Ventura County Star/Helena Pacquarella

Attorney Mark Hiepler (left, holding 5-year-old Justin Ching), won a $3 million malpractice settlement for Dave Ching (right), in the 1994 death of his wife, Joyce. She had complained to doctors at her California HMO of rectal bleeding, but it took 11 weeks before they sent her to a specialist, who diagnosed her with colon cancer immediately. She died 20 months later.

Managed care has tried to modify and more recently to reverse these incentives. Under the early models, such as the one still employed by Kaiser, physicians are paid a salary, presumably removing the financial impetus to pile on additionally billed tests and procedures. Kaiser doctors also receive a bonus at the end of the year if the plan as a whole reduced expensive procedures and tests.

But newer types of incentives employed by managed-care firms have drawn fire. Under the capitation system, doctors earn a fixed monthly fee for each patient they sign up to care for no matter how much or how little care they give that patient.

In November 1995, California attorney Hiepler won a $3 million jury verdict against two doctors in a case where he essentially put the capitation system on trial. The doctors were paid a fixed monthly fee per patient and were responsible for the first $5,000 of care on each patient, including referrals, tests and some hospitalization.

The case concerned a 34-year-old woman who died of colon cancer in April 1994. Joyce Ching had visited the doctors at her plan complaining of rectal bleeding and pelvic pain. But it took 11 weeks and repeated requests before the doctors sent her to a specialist, who diagnosed her cancer immediately. By that time, the chances of curing her cancer had dwindled. She died 20 months later.

In the Ching case, Hiepler blames the form of payment. "There's an incentive not to treat, never to send to the emergency room; it comes out of the doctor's budget," Hiepler says. "The doctor makes more money if he doesn't see you, doesn't treat you, doesn't refer you."

Woolhandler and Himmelstein contended that the base capitation payment they receive from their HMO barely covers office overhead. They charged that physicians must earn their income from a collection of bonuses and penalties that essentially reward them for limiting care and punish them for exceeding certain targets for controlling hospital use and medical procedures.

For example, for each dollar of doctor-recommended emergency-room care, the plan penalizes the doctor up to 50 cents. A physician with 1,500 of the plan's patients might take home more than $150,000 from bonuses and incentives — or nearly nothing. [26]

"If your hospital days and patient tests are too high, you'll go out of business," says Woolhandler. "If you have a lot of sick patients, it's impossible to meet the targets."

Large managed-care companies, including U.S. Healthcare, say their financial incentives also reward high-quality care, based on patient-satisfaction ratings and monitoring of patient's health results. A doctor who has a much lower-than-usual rate of referrals may also be subject to review and possible penalties in some plans.

Hillman, who has conducted numerous studies of such incentives, thinks they can improve the quality of health care. "Financial incentives improve quality of care by reminding the physician to think twice about invading a patient's body," he says. "In the gray situations, I'd rather have the doctor say, 'I'm not going to chop your leg off right now. Let's see how oral antibiotics work, and then we'll make a decision.' "

But some doctors feel the pendulum has swung too far in the direction of reduced care under managed care's regime. Daniel P. Sulmasy, a general internist and associate director of the Center for Clinical Bioethics at Georgetown, argues that under capitation, he not only gets penalized for ordering "inappropriate" medical tests but also for tests that are necessary.

"It used to be that to change medical practice, you had to prove it was medically safe," Sulmasy fumes. "Managed care says, 'Prove to me that it's unsafe.' The burden is now on society to prove that the cut in care won't hurt someone."

Financial arrangements with doctors, such as capitation and bonuses, are usually considered proprietary by managed-care companies. The AMA has joined with patient groups to argue that these arrangements should be made public.

Even some advocates of managed care argue that the patient should know what deal the doctor has cut with the HMO. "As a patient, I have every right to know the strength of the incentives that a doctor has who has my life in his hands," says Uwe Reinhardt, a professor of political economy at Princeton University.

Representatives of managed-care firms say this kind of information is already often available from state agencies. Laws to require additional disclosure would constitute government "micromanaging," says Karen Ignagni, president of the AAHP. "We don't think government should be writing contracts between doctor and patient," she says. But consumers point out that even if some information is on file at state agencies, it is not easily accessible to them.

Some doctors interpret their HMO contracts to say doctors can't tell patients about treatments or doctors that may not be covered by the plan (*see p. 328*).

In January, the AMA's Council on Ethical and Judicial Affairs passed a resolution declaring such "gag" clauses an unethical interference in the physician-patient relationship and calling for legislation to prohibit them. The AMA urged physicians to continue providing patients with information regarding treatment alternatives "regardless of the provisions or limitations of the plan." [27]

HMOs say the clauses are aimed primarily at preserving the confidentiality of business arrangements. But the AMA points to cases that raise troubling questions about the influence of financial incentives and gag clauses.

Harry and Katherine Christie's 9-year-old daughter, Carley, was diagnosed with Wilms Tumor, a rare kidney cancer. Their plan did not advise them of National Cancer Institute guidelines providing that only surgeons with previous Wilms Tumor experience should perform surgery for Wilms. Instead the plan referred the Christies to general surgeons participating in the plan, none with Wilms Tumor experience.

The plan refused to pay for Carley's surgery by a Wilms specialist the family found at Stanford, prompting the California Department of Corporations to fine the HMO $500,000.

"People need to know what the plan covers before they get sick," says Nancy Dickey, a family physician in College Station, Texas, who chairs the AMA Board of Trustees. "We're not asking that we legislate out incentives. Patients should know what the incentives are so they can decide whether they're comfortable or not with them."

The National Committee for Quality Assurance (NCQA), which accredits managed-care organizations, says it has only found one contract that explicitly prevents doctors from discussing treatments not covered by the plan. But NCQA President Margaret E. O'Kane says a more common clause — in perhaps a quarter of accredited plans — prohibits physicians from discussing the plan's method of paying. "We think that's a problem," said O'Kane. "We think we will make some policy about this." ■

BACKGROUND

Birth of Managed Care

The idea of managed care has been around at least since the 1920s, but it was not until the 1980s that the idea caught on among employers as a way to control spiraling health costs.

Continued on p. 327

Chronology

1920s to 1940s

Health reformers promote prepaid group-health plans, which provide preventive health care for a pre-set monthly fee through salaried physicians. Urged by the medical profession, states bar group plans.

1929
The first cooperative health plan is established in Elk City, Okla., by local doctor Michael Shadid.

1934
In a veiled statement of opposition to prepaid plans, the American Medical Association (AMA) decrees that patients should have free choice of physicians, and there should be no restrictions on treatment.

1942
Industrialist Henry J. Kaiser sets up two prepaid health plans on the West Coast, known as Permanente Foundations, forerunners of one of the largest health maintenance organizations (HMOs) in the nation.

1970s

In an effort to control skyrocketing hospital costs, the federal government encourages HMOs — health plans that will "maintain health" rather than profit from sickness.

1973
President Richard Nixon signs the Health Maintenance Organization Act requiring businesses with more than 25 employees to offer at least one HMO as an alternative to conventional insurance.

1980s

Managed care delivers medical services to patients at a lower cost than traditional medicine without hurting patient health, studies find. In the late 1980s, inflation in health-premium costs explodes, increasing employers' interest in managed care.

1981
Political economist Harold Luft publishes study finding patients in HMOs are hospitalized less but more likely to see a physician and get preventive care than those with conventional health insurance.

1982
Under President Ronald Reagan, Medicare patients for the first time are offered the option of signing up for an HMO.

1988
Employers' health benefit costs rise 18.6 percent.

1990s

Employers' health benefit costs drop for the first time in recent history as managed care sweeps the insurance market. But consumers question whether quality is being sacrificed.

1993
Managed-care plans cover a majority of covered employees for the first time in history, according to benefits consultant Foster Higgins.

December 1993
Family of breast cancer victim Nelene Fox wins $89 million verdict against her HMO for denying Fox a bone marrow transplant. (The amount is reduced in a subsequent, undisclosed settlement.)

1994
Cost of health benefits falls for the first time in recent history.

Nov. 28, 1995
Harvard doctor David U. Himmelstein, appearing on the "Donahue" TV show, attacks an HMO he works for, U.S. Healthcare, for rewarding doctors who deny care.

Dec. 1, 1995
U.S. Healthcare terminates its contract with Himmelstein.

Jan. 19, 1996
Massachusetts enacts nation's first ban on "gag" clauses in contracts between HMOs and doctors, such as the one criticized by Himmelstein.

Jan. 30, 1996
Survey by Foster Higgins finds health benefit costs rose only 2.1 percent in 1995, suggesting health costs are finally leveling out.

February 1996
U.S. Healthcare rehires Himmelstein and modifies its "gag" rule, allowing doctors to tell patients about the incentives they receive from the HMO.

Feb. 27, 1996
Bipartisan bill is introduced in Congress barring HMO gag rules.

April 1, 1996
Aetna Life & Casualty Co. announces it will acquire U.S. Healthcare to create the nation's largest managed-care firm, serving 23 million people.

Why Demetrios Dekazos Lost Faith in HMOs

Avoid a health maintenance organization as if your life depended on it, advises Demetrios Dekazos. For proof, he points to what happened to his wife.

It was on a Friday in September 1991, when Senate aide Vicky G. Collins, 32, suddenly collapsed over her computer on Capitol Hill. Dekazos, then her fiancé, rushed over from his office in the Senate parking facility, where he is a manager.

A Senate nurse examined Collins and suggested she go straight to the hospital. But her HMO would not authorize emergency room treatment. [1]

The HMO doctor who examined Collins in his office that Friday told her she had a pinched nerve. He gave her some anti-inflammatories and sent her home to rest for a couple of days.

Over the weekend, Collins' symptoms worsened, according to her Arlington, Va., attorney, Mark D. Cummings. Collins was dizzy and having difficulty walking. The numbness she had felt on one side of her face on Friday was spreading to her limbs. At certain times she didn't recognize Dekazos.

Alarmed, Dekazos called the HMO again on Sunday. The person he finally reached told him to call back on Monday and make an appointment during the workweek. Finally, in desperation, he called 911 and had Vicky taken to a nearby hospital.

Demetrios Dekazos and Vicky Collins, before her stroke.

That Sunday, within a few hours of arriving at the hospital, Collins went into a coma. The emergency room doctor informed Dekazos that a massive stroke had completely blocked the artery to her brain stem.

Today, Collins suffers from "locked-in" syndrome. She can understand everything that occurs around her but cannot speak. Her brain receives signals but cannot send signals back down to her limbs to move them. At first, her eyes remained locked open, and she was unable to move. Now she can move her head and arms a bit but cannot grasp a pencil for writing. She is confined to a wheelchair.

As her husband recites the alphabet, Collins communicates by blinking or nodding at the letters that spell what she wishes to say. She also has a special computer, equipped with a camera, which allows her to "type" by resting her eyes on letters of a keyboard displayed on her video screen.

Had Collins been given a blood thinner or undergone vascular surgery on Friday or Saturday, the severity of the stroke could have been diminished, according to expert witnesses Cummings says he contacted. But by the time Collins arrived at the hospital, it was too late, he says.

"She was robbed of time," says Cummings. "One of the problems with HMOs is doctors have 10-minute windows to see patients," he says of her initial examination by the HMO's doctor. "If you're healthy, it's fine, but if you have an emergency situation you need more than a lick and a promise."

"It points out problems in how managed-care companies try to approach these problems," says Michael T. Rapp, chairman of the Emergency Medicine Department at Arlington Hospital, where Collins was taken. "They first will try to evaluate something over the phone instead of letting patients use their own best judgment as to whether they need to seek emergency care."

Collins sued the HMO. Under the conditions of a settlement reached last year, Collins and her lawyer cannot reveal the HMO or the amount of the settlement. However, Collins was adamant that she be allowed to "tell her story to make sure other people did not fall into this trap," Dekazos says.

In fact, she wants to testify in favor of legislation proposed by Rep. Benjamin L. Cardin, D-Md., requiring insurance companies to pay for emergency care even if the patient's symptoms later proved groundless. The managed-care industry generally opposes such requirements.

If Collins had received emergency care early in the weekend, her husband is convinced, she would not have suffered such a severe stroke. But how could he have known that at the time? he asks. "Vicky was not the expert, I'm not the expert," Dekazos says. "We are not here to play the medical role. That's what you hire the insurance company and the doctor to do."

He believes that HMOs are preoccupied with the bottom line and that "managed money care" is driving their medical decisions. "HMOs know we all want to save some money, so they pick up the cost of your eyeglasses and other small things in life, and it makes us feel so warm all over. But when you have your cardiac arrest, your cancer, your stroke, which are costly items, you want good, prompt medical treatment — you don't want to sit there and fight for your medical treatment."

---

[1] HMOs developed pre-authorization policies because people were running to emergency rooms for non-emergencies and racking up huge bills. Many HMOs still require pre-authorization. For background, see "Emergency Medicine," *The CQ Researcher*, Jan. 5, 1996, pp. 1-24.

Continued from p. 324

Beginning in the 1920s, socially conscious health reformers promoted prepaid group-health plans, in which a modest annual fee would cover each family's preventive and sick care. Growing out of the rural, populist movement, the first cooperative health plan was established in 1929 in Elk City, Okla., by a local doctor. The early cooperatives emphasized group practice, preventive medicine and consumer participation.

A number of other such cooperatives sprouted in the 1930s and '40s but didn't take hold. "The medical profession was unremittingly hostile," sociologist Paul Starr observed, and "succeeded in convincing most states to pass restrictive laws that effectively barred consumer-controlled plans from operating." [28] As late as the 1970s, more than 30 states had such restrictions.

During World War II, health insurance emerged as an employee health benefit. Such benefits were exempted from wage controls and provided a way for employers to attract workers in a tight labor market. After World War II, the number of Americans with some form of health insurance increased dramatically through the 1980s.

But the insurers acted as "shills for doctors and hospitals," agreeing to pay whatever fee was charged until the 1980s, wrote former Health, Education and Welfare Secretary Joseph A. Califano Jr. Nonprofit Blue Cross and Blue Shield organizations and commercial insurers pushed up premiums "with abandon," he noted, to pass on increased charges from doctors. [29]

Also in the 1960s, unions made health benefits a key demand in collective-bargaining negotiations. Many experts believed that because so many workers could visit the doctor without ever seeing a bill, they helped drive up demand for health services and, ultimately, health spending.

Rising Health Costs

In the 1970s, skyrocketing hospital costs caught the attention of government. Two Republican presidents embraced HMOs as a way to control costs. In 1973, Richard Nixon signed the Health Maintenance Organization Act, requiring businesses with more than 25 employees to offer at least one HMO as an alternative to conventional insurance. Ronald Reagan gave Medicare patients the option of signing up for an HMO in 1982.

In the late 1970s, managed-care organizations composed of loose networks of doctors began to proliferate.

By the early 1980s, research was starting to show that managed care could reduce health costs without hurting patients. In perhaps the most scientific study comparing HMOs to fee-for-service, the Rand Corporation's Health Insurance Experiment in Seattle, conducted from 1976 to 1980, found cost savings of 28 percent in prepaid practices without hurting overall patient health. [30] But some vulnerable groups, such as the poor, fared less well (*see p. 320*).

U.S. health costs continued to surge at alarming rates through the 1980s, however. On average, premiums rose about 15 percent annually during the early 1980s and in 1988 rose more than 18 percent. In fact, Americans spent more per capita on health than other industrialized countries but had higher rates of infant mortality and lower life expectancy.

During the 1980s, HMOs proliferated in a cutthroat environment. To attract and keep members, HMOs were forced to hold down fees at the same time they were facing increasing costs. Some went bankrupt. By 1986, 75 percent of HMOs faced business losses. [31]

Traditional insurance plans started to feel the competitive pressure to cut costs, too. By 1990, 95 percent of employees in traditional fee-for-service plans were subject to some kind of "utilization review," where insurers scrutinized doctors' procedures and fees, up from 41 percent in 1987. [32]

Yet managed-care fees continued to rise in the late 1980s, though less than fee-for-service costs, raising questions among experts as to whether they were cutting back sufficiently on unnecessary, expensive procedures. Studies by Dartmouth's Wennberg and others suggested that still more could be cut. These studies showed widely varying rates of surgical procedures throughout the U.S. for the same condition without necessarily benefiting the patients.

In the 1990s, managed care turned the corner. According to a survey by Foster Higgins, it went from insuring a minority of covered workers in 1992 to almost three-quarters in 1995. After years of steady increases, the cost of employee health-care benefits actually fell in 1994 for the first time.

Consumers' Concerns

But as managed care was being hailed for cutting costs, some consumers expressed concern that it was cutting muscle instead of fat. "HMOs are totally and purely a question of economics and how much money you can make," former Sen. Howard Metzenbaum, D-Ohio, chairman of the Consumer Federation of America, said last year. [33]

The rapid rise over the past 15 years of for-profit managed-care companies worries consumer advocates like Metzenbaum. In the earliest days of managed care, virtually all enrollments were in not-for-profit organizations like Kaiser Permanente. As of January 1995, for-profit companies accounted for 58 percent of HMO members, compared with only 12 percent in 1981. [34]

Once, most of those consumers

would have been covered by for-profit traditional insurance plans, says Mark D. Smith, executive vice president of the Kaiser Family Foundation. Furthermore, distinctions between for-profits and not-for-profits tend to blur in the medical world. Research finds little difference in the performance of for-profit and not-for-profit hospitals, for example, Smith notes. Profit margins among for-profit and nonprofit HMOs are also similar, according to Stephen Wiggins, CEO of Oxford Health Plans, a for-profit company.

A recent investigation by *The New York Times* found that the Health Insurance Plan of Greater New York (HIP), a not-for-profit HMO, has a far worse record than two for-profit competitors in the state when it comes to delays in paying its members' medical bills. But the investigation also pointed out serious deficiencies in the regulation of HMOs, regardless of whether they are for-profit. For example, there is no New York state law requiring prompt payment from HMOs. In contrast, regular insurers must pay claims or offer an explanation for a delay in 15 days or face penalties.[35]

Yet another development worrying consumers has been a trend toward mergers of HMOs, hospitals and insurance companies, threatening a managed-care monopoly. In the latest such merger, Aetna Life & Casualty Co., a traditional insurance company, announced plans this month to buy U.S. Healthcare Inc., a for-profit managed-care company. The merger would create the nation's biggest medical company. Most observers expect the new company to shift its emphasis from traditional health insurance to managed care. Patients who have resisted joining managed-care plans so far will be under increased pressure to do so, observed Consumers Union executive Gene Kimmelman, because "very soon there may be very little else that you can get."[36]

Challenging the domination of these giant companies is a new hybrid — doctors who band together to offer managed-care plans, cutting out the managed-care company as middleman. The Federal Trade Commission plans to issue regulations this summer relaxing its antitrust rules to make it easier for doctors to create such ventures.[37] Such operations might reduce pressure on doctors to satisfy the profit needs of giant companies, but some consumer advocates and regulators fear it will simply shift the cost-cutting pressures to doctors themselves, who lack sufficient capital to take on the risk of paying for extremely sick patients. ■

CURRENT SITUATION

Pro-Consumer Initiatives

Patient groups, medical specialists and the AMA have joined forces to push for legislation to protect patients in managed care. So far, they have had the most impact in state legislatures.

A number of "patient protection acts" generally would require plans to disclose to patients any financial arrangements with doctors that might limit their treatment and to provide grievance procedures for patients denied treatment. Some of the legislation also would permit consumers to see a specialist outside their plan's network for an additional charge, an option known as "point of service." More than half of the states are expected to consider versions of this legislation this year.

Last year, over 25 states considered such legislation and seven states — Arizona, California, Maryland, Oregon, Mississippi, Minnesota and Virginia — passed some version of it, according to the AMA. In Texas, Republican Gov. George W. Bush vetoed a patient-protection bill but ordered regulations covering some of its key provisions.

This year, as part of a package of six bills, the AMA is lobbying for a ban to abolish "gag clauses" in managed-care contracts. Such clauses prohibit doctors from discussing with patients treatments that may not be covered by the plan, the AMA says.

On Jan. 19, 1996, Massachusetts became the first state to prohibit gag clauses. Last year, Maryland went further than most other states in prohibiting insurers outright from paying physicians bonuses that "deter the delivery of medically appropriate care to an enrollee."

The managed-care industry has charged that most of this legislation is really "doctor protection" aimed at destroying managed care. Most patients-rights bills would "eviscerate the choice that is made available to consumers and prevent them from taking advantage of the cost savings in managed-care plans," says Richard Coorsh, a spokesman for the Health Insurance Association of America.

Requiring managed-care plans to let consumers see a doctor outside the plan, Coorsh says, would raise everyone's premiums, because plans would lose a prime tool for controlling costs — limiting the panel of doctors to those who agree to deliver medical care at a discount.

Because of a preemption clause in federal law, most of this state legislation won't affect a growing segment of health plans known as self-insured plans. Most large corporations self-insure by setting aside their own reserves of money to cover employee health benefits and paying insurers only to administer and screen claims. Self-insured plans are exempt from state legislation under the federal Employee Retirement Income Security Act. However, since many self-insured employers contract with big insurance companies, those health plans might extend state-mandated consumer protections to their self-insured members as well, Hurwit suggests.

Some patient activists have urged a

Continued on p. 330

At Issue:

Should Congress enact legislation barring restrictions on communications between doctors and patients?

yes

REP. GREG GANSKE, R-IOWA
FROM STATEMENT ISSUED FEB. 26, 1996

There is nothing more central to the doctor-patient relationship than trust. Patients and their families rely on doctors to fully inform them about the course of a disease and the various ways it can be treated. They deserve to know the risks and benefits and costs and chances of success of the treatments that will be inflicted on their own bodies or their loved ones. And they don't want information withheld because an HMO won't allow it.

Unfortunately, that essential doctor-patient trust is being undermined by some health plans that attempt to limit the content of discussions between patients and providers. Physicians are increasingly signing contracts with insurance companies that contain restrictive clauses preventing the physician from using sound medical judgment and undermin[ing] the essential notion of informed consent.

Sometimes, these contacts explicitly seek to limit the information a doctor can provide to a patient. The contract between providers and the Ohio Permanente Medical Group, for example, contains the following prohibition: "Do not discuss proposed treatment with Kaiser Permanente members prior to receiving authorization."

How can we expect patients to make informed decisions about their own health if doctors can only inform them of options that the plan is willing to pay for?

Other examples are more subtle. Some plans place a "general disparagement" clause in their contracts. One ChoiceCare plan included the following clause in [its] contracts: "Physician shall take no action nor make any communication which undermines or could undermine the confidence of enrollees, potential enrollees, their employees, plan sponsors or the public in ChoiceCare or in the quality of care which ChoiceCare enrollees receive."

The danger of this clause is just as significant as the example from the Ohio Permanente Medical Group. Patients rely on their physician to tell them which doctors or hospitals are better than others. But in plans with general disparagement clauses, a doctor could not tell a patient that seven of the last 11 patients he referred to the plan's heart surgeon have died! That is precisely the sort of information doctors should give to patients and is precisely the kind of communication that "general disparagement" clauses prevent. . . .

Whether explicit in a contract or communicated to doctors orally, [restrictions on communications between doctors and patients] deny patients access to critical information and make a farce out of the notion of informed consent.

While I understand the importance of the free market, Congress must protect patients who are unaware that some doctors are no longer able to communicate their best judgment.

no

AMERICAN ASSOCIATION OF HEALTH PLANS
FROM STATEMENT ISSUED MARCH 12, 1996

AAHP is committed to unrestricted communication between physicians and their patients about diagnosis, treatment and other information affecting the patients' care. We do not believe [however] that regulating the terms of contractual arrangements between providers and health plans is the way to ensure that patients receive the information they need about their care, nor is it the way to ensure that their physicians are acting in their best interests in the provision of care. . . .

Open communication between physicians and patients about health status, treatment, coverage, benefits and health-plan practices is strongly supported by network-based health plans. Due to the emphasis on prevention and early treatment that is fundamental to organized systems of care, physician efforts to ensure the full participation of patients in decisions affecting their care are encouraged, and it is in the plan's and the physician's interest, as well as the patient's, for patients to be directly involved in their care and to be well-informed.

Proposed legislation, the goal of which is to prohibit contract clauses that restrict physician-patient communication, has been drafted too broadly and would restrict contractual provisions that govern the physician-health plan business relationship.

For example, anti-disparagement clauses are not intended to restrict physician-patient communication but to require that physicians discuss criticisms of the health plan with the organization, the party in a position to address their problems, rather than with the members. It is inappropriate to bring these issues into the examining room where the focus should be only on the patient's care.

Similarly, contractual provisions that are designed to protect proprietary information are commonplace in many professional and business agreements. Respect for the confidentiality of proprietary information is a generally accepted standard of professional conduct.

While information concerning the types of compensation arrangements between managed-care organizations and physicians generally would not be proprietary, the specific amounts and terms of a particular compensation arrangement generally would be proprietary from the perspective of both the plan and the physician. This is particularly true when physicians may have contracts with several plans, and all parties are likely to value confidentiality concerning the nature and amount of the compensation.

Creation of statutory rules governing health plan-physician contract provisions is not the best way to foster unrestricted physician-patient communication about patient care.

Why Christine Blodgett Loves Her HMO

Every year, Christine Blodgett got a mammogram from her fee-for-service physician. And every year, for four years, he told the Huntington Beach, Calif., nurse that a spot on the mammogram needed watching, but was nothing to worry about.

Not until Blodgett switched to a health maintenance organization (HMO) in 1993 did she discover that the spot was breast cancer.

To Blodgett, her HMO's speed, efficiency and concern saved her life — in marked contrast to her experience with the private doctor. As soon as she signed up, the HMO required her to get a new mammogram. A week later, Blodgett was informed that her mammogram warranted follow-up. That same day, Blodgett's HMO doctor referred her to a surgeon, whose biopsy revealed the cancer.

Christine Blodgett

"I had been living with it undetected for four or five years," says Blodgett, 53. She had switched her insurance to PacifiCare of California, a for-profit HMO in Cypress, Calif., when she went to work for the company as a case manager. She underwent a mastectomy and describes her HMO doctors as "wonderful."

Currently employed as a project manager for PacifiCare, Blodgett isn't sure why her original doctor didn't detect her breast cancer. But she's convinced her cancer would have been discovered earlier if she had been in an HMO.

"In managed care, the doctors stand to win financially if they treat you in a timely manner and completely," says Blodgett, crediting the HMO's system of "capitation" payments to the doctors who handle its patients. Under capitation, the doctors are paid a fixed monthly fee per patient no matter how much or how little care they provide.

"Had they not treated me, and instead watched and waited another year and another year," says Blodgett, "I would have gotten to the point where it had spread and perhaps I would have needed a bone marrow transplant" — a risky operation that can cost up to $200,000. Blodgett says she never paid more than a $5 copayment in the course of her treatment.

By contrast, she says, her previous doctor, who billed separately for each service, had little financial incentive to provide preventive services. "They want you when you're sick," Blodgett says of traditional health insurance. "Managed care is interested in keeping you well."

Blodgett is keenly aware of several lawsuits against HMOs that refused to pay for bone marrow transplants for women with breast cancer (*see p. 315*). She objects to giving people expensive treatments when there's only a small chance of survival.

"If I knew that my chances of having the bone marrow transplant work were slim, I'd go out and get my life in order and enjoy my kids. I don't think I'd like to spend my last days being so sick," Blodgett says. "I think we all have the responsibility to handle our resources appropriately. You wouldn't write a big check for a car you know is a lemon."

Continued from p. 328

shift in focus to the federal level to overcome the weakness of state law. On Feb. 27, Reps. Greg Ganske, R-Iowa, and Edward J. Markey, D-Mass., introduced a bill to prohibit gag clauses. (*See "At Issue," p. 329.*)

Patient advocates acknowledge they have little hope of seeing action on their initiatives in this Congress. However, there could be congressional action on a related matter — managed care's limits on maternity stays in hospitals.

Sen. Bill Bradley, D-N.J., is expected to offer a floor amendment allowing new mothers to remain in the hospital for at least 48 hours after a normal birth and 96 hours after a Caesarean section. Bradley says some insurers routinely move new mothers out of the hospital in 12 hours. [38]

Four states enacted mandated maternity stays in 1995: Maryland, Massachusetts, New Jersey and North Carolina. Maternity-stay bills have been filed in at least 33 states this year.

Focus on Quality

Quality has become the buzz word in managed care in the past year, driven largely by interest from large employers. Now that managed-care plans are controlling costs, plans will have to start competing on how good a job they do, some employers say. But they face a dearth of information.

"We still don't know if the current health-care system is producing better quality" than the old fee-for-service system, says David Lansky, president of the Foundation for Accountability in Portland, Ore., which represents some of the nation's largest private employers, including American Express and AT&T. Last summer, the group said it would develop a framework for measuring how well health plans treat their patients. The group also will gather data on the results of medical treatment for major illnesses. [39]

Currently, the closest thing to a Good Housekeeping Seal of Approval is accreditation by the NCQA, which investigates the credentials of each plan's physicians and whether the plan's medical guidelines track current medical knowledge. About 14 percent of the plans it reviews are rejected outright. But most employers are not using NCQA accreditation to decide which plans to sign up, surveys suggest. [40]

That may be because NCQA has so far investigated only about half the managed-care companies eligible for accreditation. Or it may be that price is still the most important element for market success. "Let's be perfectly frank. We still are driven predominantly by the cost," says Mary Jane England, president of the Washington Business Group on Health, a nonprofit organization whose membership includes the nation's major employers. "When the cost is the same, the tie-breaker would be quality."

Several large employers under NCQA's lead have been collecting more detailed information on plans. The Health Plan Employer Data and Information Set can tell an employer what percent of a plan's enrollees have received immunizations and mammography screenings, for example.

Critics say this scorecard measures the area in which managed care already does well — prevention. It doesn't tell the consumer whether the plan will do a good job of taking care of a serious illness like cancer.

NCQA President O'Kane responds: "It's much easier to calculate how well a plan did in giving women mammograms, because you can calculate how many women should have mammograms," she says. "If you're looking at how effectively they treat heart disease, it's hard to know who in the population is at risk."

According to NCQA, a report card on performance is years away. Eventually managed care, with its large companies and ability to collect massive amounts of data, should do a better job of rating quality than the old system, advocates say. The old system never attempted to measure quality systematically, they assert, although the threat of malpractice litigation, as today, acted like a superego over doctors' performance.

"Managed care properly done in an accountable health plan . . . that can keep track of the health care given to an entire population just has to be better," says economist Reinhardt. ■

FOR MORE INFORMATION

American Association of Health Plans, 1129 20th St. N.W., Suite 600, Washington, D.C. 20036-3403; (202) 778-3200. The AAHP, recently formed by the merger of Group Health Association and the American Managed Care and Review Association, represents 1,000 managed-care plans nationwide.

American Medical Association, 515 North State St., Chicago, Ill. 60610-4378; (312) 464-5000. This mainstream doctors' organization supports "patient protection" controls on managed-care plans, including the right of doctors to tell patients about treatments not covered by their plan.

Citizen Action, 1730 Rhode Island Ave. N.W., Suite 403 A, Washington, D.C. 20036; (202) 775-1580. This consumer group lobbies for regulation of managed-care plans and has produced a "Managed Care Consumers' Bill of Rights."

National Committee for Quality Assurance, 2000 L St. N.W., Suite 500, Washington, D.C. 20036; (202) 955-3500. The NCQA is the major accrediting body for managed-care plans. It is developing a "report card" for consumers on the quality of health plans.

OUTLOOK

A Price to Pay?

Managed-care companies are like bounty hunters, Reinhardt likes to say, searching for waste in the health-care system with a double-barrelled shotgun.

But there's a price to be paid for a leaner, meaner system. In the days when doctors could charge whatever they liked, they padded the bill and could take care of the uninsured poor by shifting the cost to paying customers.

"In this new world, where the bounty hunters say, 'We are not paying,' doctors and hospitals sooner or later will not have the cushion to treat the uninsured," Reinhardt says. "Those people are the innocent bystanders who will get hurt by all this."

Another casualty of the bounty hunters, some experts believe, will be medical research at teaching hospitals, which has traditionally been subsidized by patient bills.

"The growth of managed-health care is threatening the survival of our academic medical centers," Steven A. Schroeder, president of the Robert Wood Johnson Foundation, warned last year. Managed-care companies, with whom teaching hospitals are now competing for patients, don't have to pay for research and education, he pointed out. [41]

But America's role in pioneering medical technology for the rest of the world ended up being costly,

Reinhardt says. "The average middle-class American is unhappy because his take-home pay is not going up. It all went into health care," he says, noting that health benefits in the 1980s ate up compensation that could have gone into wage increases.

Most experts think managed care is here to stay because the economic pressures on employers became too great. The shift to managed care is, Kaiser's Smith says, "a historically settled question."

Indeed, Aetna's plan to acquire U.S. Healthcare underscores the rise of HMOs and other managed-care plans and the decline of traditional health insurance.

But once managed care has cut out the easy things — unnecessary procedures like Caesareans for example — it will be faced with difficult trade-offs like denying a bone marrow transplant to a dying woman.

"Controversies like this are going to be with us for a long time as we transition from this pay-for-everything system," economist Custer predicts. A treatment like a bone marrow transplant "may not be effective, but it may also be some cancer victim's last hope," he says. "If someone's going to constrain costs, they're also going to have to say no." ■

Sarah Glazer is a Washington writer who specializes in health and social-policy issues.

Notes

[1] See Michael A. Hiltzik et al, "A Mixed Diagnosis for HMOs," *Los Angeles Times,* Aug. 27, 1995, p. A1.

[2] Steffie Woolhandler and David U. Himmelstein, "Extreme Risk — The New Corporate Proposition for Physicians," *The New England Journal of Medicine,* Dec. 21, 1995, pp. 1706-1707.

[3] "USHC Drops 'Gag Order' from Physician Contract," *Managed Healthcare Market Report,* Feb. 15, 1996.

[4] Robert H. Miller and Harold S. Luft, " Managed-Care Plan Performance Since 1980: A Literature Analysis," *Journal of the American Medical Association,* May 18, 1994, pp. 1512-1519.

[5] William Sherman, "What They Didn't Know About HMOs May Have Killed This Baby," *New York Post,* Sept. 18, 1995.

[6] Erik Larson, "The Soul of an HMO," *Time,* Jan. 22, 1996, pp. 44-52.

[7] Cited in John M. Eisenberg, "Economics," *Journal of the American Medical Association,* June 7, 1995, pp. 1670-1.

[8] For background, see "Primary Care," *The CQ Researcher,* March 17, 1995, pp. 217-240.

[9] Cited in Steffie Woolhandler and David U. Himmelstein, *Profits from Pain: The Case for Single Payer Reform; The National Health Program Chartbook and Slideshow* (1996), Center for National Health Program Studies, Harvard Medical School.

[10] Joseph P. Newhouse et al., *Free for All? Lessons From the RAND Health Insurance Experiment* (1993).

[11] Teresa Fama et al.,"Do HMOs Care for the Chronically Ill?" *Health Watch,* spring 1995, pp. 234-243.

[12] *Ibid.* The study was based on national data from 1992.

[13] "Harvard Study Says Ill and Disabled Have Problems with Managed Care," *Medicine and Health,* July 3, 1995, p. 3.

[14] Sheldon Greenfield, "Outcomes of Patients with Hypertension and Non-insulin-dependent Diabetes Mellitus Treated by Different Systems and Specialties," *Journal of the American Medical Association,* Nov. 8, 1995, pp. 1436-1444.

[15] Miller and Luft, *op. cit.,* p. 1512.

[16] Foster Higgins press release, "Health Benefit Costs Rose 2.1 percent in 1995," Jan. 30, 1996.

[17] Gifford Boyce-Smith, "Getting out of the Hospital," *Los Angeles Daily News,* Oct. 3, 1995.

[18] J.C. Robinson et al., "The Growth of Medical Groups Paid through Capitation in California," *The New England Journal of Medicine,* Dec. 21, 1995, pp. 1684-1687.

[19] David U. Himmelstein et al., "Who Administers? Who Cares? Medical Administrative and Clinical Employment in the United States and Canada," *American Journal of Public Health,* February 1996, pp. 172-178.

[20] David Segal, "Managed Care Generates a Paperwork Explosion," *The Washington Post, Feb. 15, 1996,* p. D1.

[21] California Medical Association, *Knox-Keene Health Plan Expenditures Summary, 1994-5,* February 1996.

[22] Quoted in Sabin Russell, "Kaiser Trims Care for Well Women," *San Francisco Chronicle,* Nov. 2, 1995, p. A1. For background, see "Women's Health Issues," *The CQ Researcher,* May 13, 1994, pp. 409-432.

[23] Bob Ortega, "Some Physicians do Unnecessary Surgery on Heads of Infants," *The Wall Street Journal,* Feb. 23, 1996, p. A1.

[24] John E. Wennberg, *The Dartmouth Atlas of Health Care,* American Hospital Association, Jan. 11, 1996.

[25] American Hospital Association press release, "New Report Questions Geographic Disparity in U.S. Surgery Rates, Numbers of Doctors, Hospitals," Jan. 29, 1996.

[26] Woolhandler and Himmelstein, *op. cit.,* p. 1706.

[27] AMA press release, "AMA Calls on Managed Care Providers to Cancel Gag Clauses and Submit Contracts for Ethical Review," Jan. 23, 1996.

[28] Paul Starr, *The Social Transformation of American Medicine* (1982), p. 302.

[29] Joseph A. Califano Jr., *Radical Surgery* (1994), p. 42.

[30] Cited in Paul Starr, *The Logic of Health Care Reform* (1992), p. 38.

[31] See "The Failure to Contain Medical Costs," *Editorial Research Reports,* Oct. 14, 1988, pp. 510-523.

[32] Paul Fronstin, "The Effectiveness of Health Care Cost Management Strategies: A Review of the Evidence," Employee Benefit Research Institute Issue Brief, October 1994, p. 6.

[33] "Marcus Welby Goes to Wall Street," Henry J. Kaiser Foundation Symposium, Dec. 13, 1995 (videotape).

[34] News release, Henry J. Kaiser Family Foundation, "Mixed Message from the Public on For-Profit Health Care," Dec. 13, 1995.

[35] Esther B. Fein and Elisabeth Rosenthal, "Delays by HMOs Leaving Patients Haunted by Bills," *The New York Times,* April 1, 1996, p. A1.

[36] Ron Winslow and Leslie Scism, "Aetna Agrees to Acquire U.S. Healthcare," *The Wall Street Journal,* April 2, 1996, pp. A2, A6.

[37] Robert Pear, "Doctors May Get Leeway to Rival Large Companies," *The New York Times,* April 8, 1996, p. A1.

[38] Steve Langdon, "Push for Insurance Changes Moving to Front Burner," *Congressional Quarterly Weekly Report,* March 9, 1996, p. 620. The amendment is expected to be offered to a bill introduced by Sen. Nancy Landon Kassebaum, R-Kan., and Edward M. Kennedy, D-Mass., requiring group-health insurance plans to cover all employees regardless of their medical history.

[39] Holcomb B. Noble, "Quality is Focus for Health Plans," *The New York Times,* Aug. 3, 1995, p. 7.

[40] See David Segal, "HMOs: How Much, Not How Well," *The Washington Post,* Jan. 9, 1996, p. F1.

[41] Steven A.Schroeder, "Point of View; Facing the Grizzly: Can Academic Medicine Beat the Competition?" *The Chronicle of Higher Education,* Nov. 10, 1995, p. A52.

Bibliography

Selected Sources Used

Books

Califano, Joseph A., *Radical Surgery,* Times Books, 1994.
Califano, who served as secretary of Health, Education and Welfare under President Jimmy Carter, takes a thoughtful look at how managed care is changing the human side of medicine.

Starr, Paul, *The Social Transformation of American Medicine,* Basic Books, 1982.
This Pulitzer Prize-winning history traces the rise of group-health practices and their battles with organized medicine to survive.

Starr, Paul, *The Logic of Health Care Reform,* Whittle Direct Books, 1992.
Though written as a brief for health reform under Clinton, this short book presents a good summary of the major problems and arguments that led to the rise of managed care.

Articles

Brink, Susan, "How Your HMO Could Hurt You," *U.S. News & World Report,* Jan. 15, 1996, pp. 62-64.
Brink examines managed care's financial incentives to reduce procedures and referrals and the effect on medical care.

Fein, Esther B., and Elisabeth Rosenthal, "Delays by H.M.O. Leaving Patients Haunted by Bills," *The New York Times,* April 1, 1996, p. A1.
New York's biggest HMO holds back money for huge medical bills, forcing its patients to fight off collection agencies, this *Times* investigation finds in an article pointing up the lack of regulation governing managed care companies.

Freudenheim, Milt, "Managed Care Empires in the Making," *The New York Times*, April 2, 1996, p. D1.
The trend toward consolidation of managed-care companies, of which the Aetna-U.S. Healthcare merger is the latest, is portrayed as a way to negotiate lower prices with medical suppliers and woo employers with low-cost health benefits.

Hiltzik, Michael A., and David R. Olmos, "Do HMOs Ration Their Health Care?" *Los Angeles Times,* Aug. 27, 1995, p. A1.
This is the first of a five-part series probing HMOs. The series concluded that HMOs "withhold some services from sicker patients solely because of high cost."

Larson, Erik, "The Soul of an HMO," *Time,* Jan. 22, 1996, pp. 45-52.
This is a detailed look at the case of Christy deMeurers and the charge that her HMO pressured doctors to deny her a bone marrow transplant because of the expense.

"Managing to Care," *The Economist,* Sept. 23, 1995, pp. 70-75.
This article looks at the threat to medical research as managed care forces teaching hospitals to tighten their belts.

Segal, David, "HMOs: How Much, Not How Well," *The Washington Post,* Jan. 19, 1996, p. F1.
Segal concludes that the rating accorded to an HMO through accreditation is not yet having a major influence on how employers pick plans.

Reports and Studies

Employee Benefit Research Institute, Issue Brief: The Effectiveness of Health Care Cost Management Strategies: A Review of the Evidence, October 1994.
Managed care does reduce costs, this review of recent studies concludes. Included is a useful history of health-care cost inflation.

Employee Benefit Research Institute, Issue Brief: Measuring the Quality of Health Care, March 1995.
While "great strides" have been made in measuring the quality of managed-care plans, this review of recent efforts says, most employers are not paying attention to quality ratings in deciding which plan to purchase.

Foster Higgins, National Survey of Employer-Sponsored Health Plans, 1995.
Foster Higgins, a benefits consultant, reports on the growing trend among employers to adopt managed-care plans in their benefit packages.

Wennberg, John E. et al., *The Dartmouth Atlas of Health Care,* Jan. 11, 1996, American Hospital Association.
Ten years after an earlier study that helped prod the move to managed care, Wennberg again finds that physicians in some areas of the country are far more likely to perform expensive surgery than in other areas, but with no better results.

The Next Step

Additional information from UMI's Newspaper & Periodical Abstracts database

Managed Care — Cost and Quality

Bass, Alison, "Focusing on managed care," *Boston Globe,* Dec. 21, 1995, p. 32.
More than half of the nation's managed-care plans tie the income of physicians to the amount of care they provide, paying bonuses for keeping costs down or penalizing them if they spend more than a set amount on patient care, according to a study commissioned by Congress.

Brussee, Frederic C., "Managed care means shared responsibility," *St. Louis Post-Dispatch,* Jan. 29, 1996, p. B7.
Brussee asserts that managed care is about people working together to provide more affordable access to ever higher quality health care.

DeBakey, Michael E., and William G. Anlyan, "Managed care puts us all at risk," *Houston Chronicle,* June 18, 1995, p. C1.
Anlyan and DeBakey comment that HMOs force physicians to put the cost of medical care ahead of the patient's well-being.

Etzioni, Amitai, "One fuming physician: Want a lesson in managed care? Take my wife's practice — Please," *The Washington Post,* Sept. 17, 1995, p. C3.
Etzioni criticizes the trend toward using HMOs, commenting that HMOs are incompatible with a free, consumer-driven society.

Foreman, Judy, "Managed-care cost-cutting may imperil teaching hospitals," *Boston Globe,* Nov. 17, 1994, p. 26.
With no national health-care reform, the 120 top academic medical centers in the nation face an increasingly perilous future because of cost-cutting pressure from managed-care plans, according to reports in *The New England Journal of Medicine.*

Gabuzda, Thomas G., "The ethical conflict in managed care," *The Wall Street Journal,* Oct. 3, 1994, p. A21.
Gabuzda responds to the Sept. 6, 1994, Page 1 article on the positive and negative aspects of HMOs in general and U.S. Healthcare Inc. in particular. Gabuzda says that not all HMO activities are bad, nor should there be the elimination of the concept of health insurance, but there is a need to develop a health-care system that unequivocally puts the patient first.

Knight, Al, "What happens if managers mismanage Managed Care?" *Denver Post,* Oct. 22, 1995, p. D1.
Knight comments on the disadvantages of HMOs.

Knog, Dolores, "Managed care," *Boston Globe,* March 20, 1995, p. 25.
Knog discusses the growing concern that HMOs, pressured by competition and demands to keep costs down, may sometimes deny procedures or referrals simply to save money, which has resulted in litigation, is discussed.

Knox, Richard A., "Health costs rise despite managed care, study finds," *Boston Globe,* Oct. 7, 1993, p. 1.
A new federal analysis of Massachusetts health spending finds that states where "managed care" has made the most inroads have experienced nearly the same rates of medical inflation as the nation as a whole.

Lipson, Benjamin, "Managed-care plans often ignore home care services for seniors," *Boston Globe,* June 8, 1995, p. 44.
Lipson assesses how effective managed-care health plans are for seniors who need home health care.

Miller, Andy, "Managed care's effect on mentally ill uncertain," *Atlanta Journal Constitution,* Nov. 12, 1995, p. R1.
In an interview, Rosalynn Carter, who is hosting a symposium at the Carter Center on managed care and mental health, discusses managed care, HMOs and other topics relating to the care of the mentally ill.

Olmos, David R., "Some doctors head to Idaho to escape managed care," *Los Angeles Times,* Aug. 29, 1995, p. A11.
About a dozen California doctors have relocated to Idaho, at least in part to escape practices that were crumbling under bombardment by HMOs. There are no HMOs in the Orofino area of Idaho, although several big employers are making noise about bringing them there.

Paris, Steven, and Richard Vernick, "Good managed care means good health care," *Boston Globe,* Nov. 21, 1995, p. 13.
Vernick and Paris, both primary-care physicians who have been treating patients under managed-care arrangements, comment that the case against managed care rests on a central fallacy: that under managed care doctors have a financial incentive to undertreat their patients.

Parsons, Christi, "Lawmakers vow to take on managed care," *Chicago Tribune,* Jan. 8, 1996, C2.
A group of women in the Illinois General Assembly has promised to explain managed care in a comprehensive proposal to regulate matters from emergency room coverage to hospital stays for mothers and their newborns. Because

state and federal proposals to regulate HMOs pit the powerful political forces of business and physicians against each other, any changes in the law face a difficult road.

Salerno, Steve, "Pricing health care: High price of managed care," *The Wall Street Journal*, Jan. 18, 1994, p. A16.
Salerno says a close look at the Kaiser Permanente Foundation Health Plan, which covers a sixth of the nation's 40 million HMO subscribers, raises concerns about the medical and ethical underpinnings of managed care, a cornerstone of the Clinton health plan and several reform alternatives.

Stein, Charles, "Doctors learn about managed care," *Boston Globe,* Aug. 23, 1995, p. 85.
Harris Berman, the president of Tufts Associated Health Plan, a major health maintenance organization based in Waltham, Mass., said the health plan would put up $1.8 million to create the Tufts Managed Care Institute, a nonprofit center that will train medical students and doctors in the ways of managed care.

Stocker, Michael A, "The ticket to better managed care," *The New York Times,* Oct. 28, 1995, p. A21.
Stocker discusses steps that must be taken to improve the services of HMOs under a managed-care system in New York.

Wood, Charles T., "Managed care is not health care," *Boston Globe,* Sept. 5, 1995, p. 15.
Wood comments on the "managed-care juggernaut" and how it rewards physicians for not giving services as health-care expenses increase to a crisis point.

Managed Care and States

Abramowitz, Michael, and Amy Goldstein, "Md. hopes to curb Medicaid with managed care," *The Washington Post,* June 2, 1995, p. C1.
With the specter of federal cutbacks looming over health funding for the poor, Maryland officials began work on a plan to shave the escalating costs of the state Medicaid program by requiring recipients to enroll in HMOs and other prepaid managed-care health plans.

Havemann, Judith, "HMOs, doctors battle in state legislatures over managed care limits," *The Washington Post,* Aug. 22, 1995, p. A4.
The economic shootout between doctors and insurance companies in state legislatures over managed-care limits is discussed.

Paik, Felicia, "HMO competition heats up as states pick managed care to save on Medicaid," *The Wall Street Journal*, June 13, 1994, p. B5.
As states continue to search for ways to slash budgets, local governments are turning to HMOs to manage the care of Medicaid recipients and, in turn, costs.

Winslow, Ron, "Medical upheaval: Welfare recipients are a hot commodity in managed care now," *The Wall Street Journal*, April 12, 1995, p. A1.
Long outcasts of the nation's health-care system, welfare recipients have become a hot commodity as state governments, battered by soaring Medicaid budgets, rush to move the recipients into managed-care programs where HMOs see those eligible for Medicaid as a major source for enrollment growth — and of profits.

Medicaid/Medicare and Managed Care

Abramowitz, Michael, "Glendening opts for HMOs: Medicaid plan puts patients in managed care," *The Washington Post,* Jan. 12, 1996, B1.
Most Medicaid recipients in Maryland would be required to enroll in managed-care organizations that tightly control expenses, under an overhaul of the state's health insurance program for the poor and disabled announced by the administration of Gov. Parris N. Glendening.

Fisher, Ian, "New York acts to curb fraud in managed care for the poor," *The New York Times,* June 24, 1995, p. A1.
Due to a sharp rise in complaints about fraudulent sales tactics, New York state and New York City officials announced on June 23, 1995, that in the city, they would no longer allow HMOs to enroll new members directly — a practice several other states have banned because of the potential for abuse. Officials are seeking a degree of objectivity by training city workers who will sit down with Medicaid recipients and enroll them.

"Managed care at regional hospital," *St. Louis Post-Dispatch,* Sept. 4, 1995, p. C6.
An editorial comments that with the launch of the state-administered managed-care program, Missouri began a promising new chapter in medical treatment for the poor and needy in the St. Louis area, under which Medicaid recipients will receive their health care through HMOs.

"Managed care can help curb Medicare costs," *USA Today,* Feb. 8, 1995, p. A10.
An editorial points to the advantages of the managed -care HMO option for older Americans eligible for Medicare, and says that in the absence of national health reform, managed care is the future of health care for all Americans; it may be the answer to holding down health-care costs.

McIlrath, Sharon, "Democrats' bill offers Medicare managed care safeguards," *American Medical News,* June 12, 1995, p. 6.
A group of key Democrats has countered the GOP bill to control Medicare costs through managed care with legislation intended to assure that quality of care is not lost in the process.

Back Issues

Great Research on Current Issues Starts Right Here...Recent topics covered by The CQ Researcher are listed below. Before May 1991, reports were published under the name of Editorial Research Reports.

OCTOBER 1994
Historic Preservation
Religion and Politics
Arts Funding
Economic Sanctions

NOVEMBER 1994
Sex on Campus
Blood Supply Safety
Testing Term Limits
Religion in America

DECEMBER 1994
Farm Policy
Arms Sales
Earthquake Research
The Future of Television

JANUARY 1995
Treating Addiction
Child Custody and Support
Parents and Schools
Non-Proliferation Treaty at 25

FEBRUARY 1995
Cracking Down on Immigration
The Business of Sports
Reinventing Government
Housing Discrimination

Back issues are available for $5.00 (subscribers) or $8.00 (non-subscribers). Quantity discounts apply to orders over ten. To order, call Congressional Quarterly Customer Service at (202) 887-8621.

Binders are available for $18.00. To order call 1-800-638-1710. Please refer to stock number 648.

MARCH 1995
Death Penalty Debate
Primary Care
Democracy in Africa
Environmental Movement at 25

APRIL 1995
Abortion Clinic Protests
Dieting and Health
Combating AIDS
Rethinking Affirmative Action

MAY 1995
Assisted Suicide Controversy
Overhauling Social Security
Learning to Read
Mandatory Sentencing

JUNE 1995
Combating Infectious Disease
Property Rights
Repetitive Stress Injuries
Regulating the Internet

JULY 1995
War Crimes
Highway Safety
Combating Terrorism
Preventing Teen Drug Use

AUGUST 1995
Job Stress
Organ Transplants
United Nations at 50
Advances in Cancer Research

SEPTEMBER 1995
Catholic Church in the U.S.
Northern Ireland Cease-Fire
High School Sports
Teaching History

OCTOBER 1995
Quebec's Future
Revitalizing the Cities
Networking the Classroom
Indoor Air Pollution

NOVEMBER 1995
The Working Poor
The Jury System
Sex, Violence and the Media
Police Misconduct

DECEMBER 1995
Teens and Tobacco
Gene Therapy's Future
Global Water Shortages
Third-Party Prospects

JANUARY 1996
Emergency Medicine
Punishing Sex Offenders
Bilingual Education
Helping the Homeless

FEBRUARY 1996
Reforming the CIA
Campaign Finance Reform
Academic Politics
Getting Into College

MARCH 1996
Preventing Youth Violence
The British Monarchy
Tax Reform
Pursuing the Paranormal

APRIL 1996
Centennial Olympic Games

Future Topics

- ***Protecting Endangered Species***
- ***Changing Military Culture***
- ***Russia's Political Future***

THE CQ Researcher

PUBLISHED BY CONGRESSIONAL QUARTERLY INC.

Protecting Endangered Species

Does the law work? Is it too costly?

The Endangered Species Act is credited by its supporters with helping to protect hundreds of rare plant and animal species from possible extinction. But critics say the 1973 law has not met its goals. Moreover, they charge it has infringed on property rights, stymied development and forced the elimination of thousands of jobs. The Clinton administration has been changing policies to try to make the law work better and reduce its impact on private landowners. Some House Republicans want to go further and free private landowners from most of its restrictions, but that legislation has stalled. Now environmentalists are pointing to major habitat protection plans in Texas and Southern California as proof that biological diversity and economic development need not be in conflict.

INSIDE THIS ISSUE

CQ April 19, 1996 • Volume 6, No. 15 • Pages 337-360

Formerly Editorial Research Reports

Protecting Endangered Species

The Issues

Background

Current Situation

Outlook

Sidebars and Graphics

For Further Research

Cover: Fish and Wildlife Service Biologist Joe Fontaine With a Gray Wolf Pup From the First Litter Born To Wolves Reintroduced Into Yellowstone National Park In January 1995. (U.S. Fish and Wildlife Service)

The CQ Researcher

April 19, 1996
Volume 6, No. 15

Editor
Sandra Stencel

Managing Editor
Thomas J. Colin

Associate Editors
Sarah M. Magner
Richard L. Worsnop

Staff Writers
Charles S. Clark
Mary H. Cooper
Craig Donegan
Kenneth Jost

Editorial Assistant
Tonya Harris

Published By
Congressional Quarterly Inc.

Chairman
Andrew Barnes

Vice Chairman
Andrew P. Corty

Editor and Publisher
Neil Skene

Executive Editor
Robert W. Merry

Associate Publisher
Edward S. Hauck

The CQ Researcher (ISSN 1056-2036). Formerly Editorial Research Reports. Published weekly (48 times per year, not printed March 1, May 31, Aug. 30, Nov. 29) by Congressional Quarterly Inc., 1414 22nd St., N.W., Washington, D.C. 20037. Annual subscription rate for libraries, businesses and government is $319. Additional rates furnished upon request. Second-class postage paid at Washington, D.C. POSTMASTER: Send address changes to The CQ Researcher, 1414 22nd St., N.W., Washington, D.C. 20037.

Protecting Endangered Species

BY KENNETH JOST

THE ISSUES

The golden-cheeked warbler spends most of the year in South America, but in spring the migratory songbird heads for the canyonlands west of Austin, Texas, to breed in the juniper trees.

Unfortunately for developers in the area, the warbler has a perch on the government's list of threatened and endangered species.

But folks in Austin wanted to avoid the kind of confrontation that the federal Endangered Species Act has provoked elsewhere over the Northern spotted owl, the snail darter and other pesky, protected critters.

Since 1988, conservation groups, developers and government officials have been working on ways to protect the warbler without stopping economic development. The fruits of those labors are expected to blossom early next month when the Interior Department approves a plan to set aside 60,000 acres in Austin and surrounding Travis County for the warbler in separate federal and local reserves. The plan, called the Balcones Canyonlands Conservation Plan or BCCP, at the same time establishes procedures for freeing more than 140,000 acres of warbler habitat for development.

The plan still has its critics, including some environmentalists and property rights advocates. [1] But it generally enjoys broad support from interest groups that, in other areas of the country, are at loggerheads over endangered species issues.

"Essentially, all the mainstream environmental organizations, the business community, the elected governmental leaders and the voters who have approved bond funding for land acquisition all believe in this project as a community-based conservation initiative," says Jim Fries, a Nature Conservancy official who played a pivotal role in negotiating the plan.

"We think it's a very positive step forward," says Amy McElhenney, executive director of the Real Estate Council of Austin, contending that the warbler's designation as endangered in 1990 halted development in the region.

McElhenney largely credits Interior Secretary Bruce Babbitt with the plan — to the point of inviting him to speak at a council luncheon on May 2 marking its official approval. And Babbitt cites the BCCP as a prime example of ways to defuse Endangered Species Act battles.

"People said, 'Here's a conflict to end all conflicts,' " Babbitt says. "Texas senators were all going crazy, giving speeches, pouring gasoline on conflicts. Now, I'm going to be a guest at a banquet to celebrate the completion of a plan that the Texas senators used for two years as case No. 1 of why the act doesn't work."

Since taking office in 1993, Babbitt has made a mission out of simultaneously preserving and moderating the Endangered Species Act. The landmark 1973 law sharply limits public or private projects that might threaten the survival of rare animal or plant species. Supporters say it has helped protect hundreds of species. Critics question the law's accomplishments but say in any event that the act has imposed substantial costs, on ordinary landowners as well as developers. [2]

"Species protection can be achieved more efficiently and at less cost to landowners than the law currently provides," says W. Henson Moore, co-chairman of the Endangered Species Coordinating Council, a timber industry-led coalition that supports sweeping changes in the law.

Opposition to the law has simmered since the late 1970s, when a newly discovered species of fish, the snail darter, temporarily blocked completion of the Tennessee Valley Authority's (TVA) Tellico Dam. Opposition grew in the 1980s as the number of protected species grew and the law's strictures came to be felt by a wide range of property owners, including farmers, ranchers, timberland owners and developers.

With the Republican takeover of Congress after the 1994 elections, the act itself seemed endangered. Congress voted in March 1995 to impose a moratorium on listing any more new species. And in October, the House Resources Committee approved a broad rewrite of the act lifting its mandatory provisions for private landowners and creating new hurdles for the government in listing species or implementing protection and recovery plans.

Despite those controversies, Babbitt and other supporters of the law say the American public still supports the goal of protecting endangered species. "There is overwhelming public support for the Endangered Species Act, has been for the last 20 years, and continues, undiluted," Babbitt says.

Critics, however, say the law sets an impossible goal of stopping the inevitable process of extinction and then

Status of Listed Species

Of the 955 species in the U.S. listed as endangered or threatened, more than 40 percent are stable or improving and more than a third are declining in number.

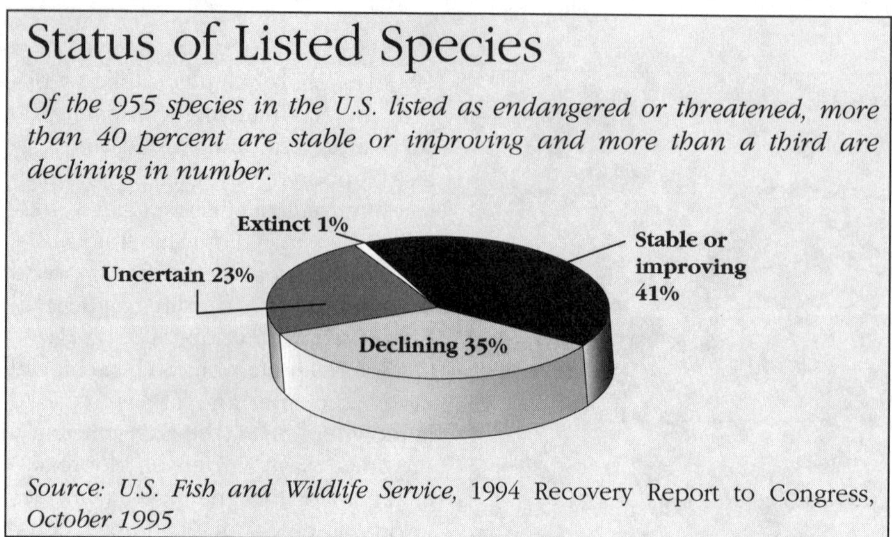

Source: U.S. Fish and Wildlife Service, 1994 Recovery Report to Congress, *October 1995*

imposes huge costs in the process. "Regardless of how much money there is for the Endangered Species Act, you still can't save everything," says R.J. Smith, senior environmental scholar with the Competitive Enterprise Institute, a free-market-oriented think tank. "There's not enough money."

Smith and other critics also insist that the law creates disincentives for landowners to protect plant and animal life by severely restricting the use of their land whenever endangered species are found. "Landowners are not afraid of wildlife on their land," Smith says. "Landowners are afraid of feds on their land."

The debate over the law comes as many biologists are warning that plants and animals are becoming extinct at an unprecedented rate. (*See story, p. 342.*) But scientists acknowledge the difficulty of selling the public on the importance of "biological diversity" when economic interests are at stake.

"You can make a first-class argument for why we ought to be concerned about preserving biodiversity," says Peter Raven, director of the Missouri Botanical Gardens in St. Louis, a leading plant conservation facility. "But when you get it down to the particulars and someone's own ox is being gored, then you have more trouble with it."

The policy modifications adopted by the Clinton administration in the past three years have been aimed at easing some of the criticisms of the law. In particular, Babbitt has moved to make greater use of so-called habitat conservation plans. These agreements — like the one set for adoption in Austin and another giant plan being negotiated in Southern California — allow landowners to use land designated as critical habitat for endangered or threatened species if they take other steps to mitigate the impact of their activities, such as setting aside other land (*see p. 354*).

Critics of the law grudgingly acknowledge Babbitt's changes, but they say more changes are needed. Meanwhile, the effort to rewrite the law has stalled in Congress. House Speaker Newt Gingrich, R-Ga., refuses to schedule the committee-approved bill for a floor vote, and moderate Republicans have drafted an alternative that makes less drastic revisions in the act.

Babbitt himself says Congress does not have to reauthorize the law even though it lapsed three years ago and has been kept alive by year-to-year funding measures. "I think codifying the changes into the law is a good idea," Babbitt says, referring to his administrative changes, "but not at the expense of doing bad things."

As the debates about the Endangered Species Act continue in Washington and beyond, here are some of the questions being asked:

Is protecting endangered species worth the cost?

When Congress passed the Endangered Species Act in 1973, it declared that endangered wildlife and plants are of "esthetic, ecological, educational, historical, recreational and scientific value." Supporters of the law continue to stress the value of individual species. But critics complain that the benefits of protecting species are outweighed by the costs in actual spending, economic disruption and political discontent.

Biologists write broadly about the benefits of biodiversity in both concrete and less tangible ways. "Biological diversity is the key to the maintenance of the world as we know it," Edward O. Wilson, the celebrated Harvard entomologist, writes in his influential 1993 book *The Diversity of Life.* [3]

In a new book, *The Value of Life,* Stephen Kellert of Yale University identifies nine "values" served by biodiversity. Kellert begins with the "utilitarian" value of plants and animals for food, clothing, medicine and more. He then proceeds through less tangible benefits, such as the joy of exploring nature ("naturalistic") and the pleasure of the physical splendor of nature ("aesthetic"). [4]

The interest groups that work the endangered species issue in Washington concentrate on the most concrete of these benefits. They have recently emphasized the importance of rare plant species as a source of medicines. The most famous example is the rosy periwinkle of Madagascar, which produces two alkaloids used in manufacturing drugs to treat Hodgkin's disease and acute lymphocytic leukemia. [5]

"Endangered species help save lives," says environmental consultant Randall Snodgrass, a former wildlife director for the National Audubon Society. "So if for no other reason than the health of humankind, protecting endangered species is important."

Critics of the law minimize the importance of rare species in new medicines. "Don't expect to find a cure for cancer from some endangered species," says Michael L. Plummer, co-author with science journalist Charles C. Mann of *Noah's Choice,* a critical look at the Endangered Species Act. [6]

Still, most critics of the act do not challenge the value of biodiversity but rather the priority that the law gives to the goal. "Grand statements about biodiversity being of utmost importance are true but trivial," says Plummer, who is a fellow at the Discovery Institute, a conservative, Seattle-based environmental think tank. "They don't help you set a strong, balanced policy toward protecting biodiversity."

In actual spending, the cost of the endangered species program is relatively small — about $79.3 million last year for the Fish and Wildlife Service (FWS) and $7.9 million for the smaller, and less controversial program, in the Commerce Department's National Marine Fisheries Service. Snodgrass notes that before the Clinton administration increased the FWS budget, it was spending about $40 million a year — around the cost of building a single mile of interstate highway. "With the millions and millions of dollars we spend on highways," Snodgrass says, "we can afford to do what is necessary to protect the habitat of threatened and endangered species."

But the critics say the act is causing huge economic dislocations, particularly the restrictions on timber harvesting in the Northwest. They say the restrictions, designed to protect the spotted owl, have cost thousands of jobs, higher housing prices and social dislocations in logging communities. "This decimated public timber harvesting in the Northwest," says Robert Nelson, a professor of public policy at the University of Maryland, College Park, and a senior fellow at the Competitive Enterprise Institute.

Some supporters of the law concede that the timber restrictions have hurt employment. But in December, 60 economists in the region said the industry faced a sharp downturn for other reasons, especially the reduction in old-growth forests due to earlier overharvesting. [7]

"The downsizing would have been required regardless of the spotted owl," says Thomas Power, chairman of the economics department at the University of Montana, Bozeman, and principal author of the report. "The role that Endangered Species Act actions solely by themselves have played has been quite modest."

As for broader effects, even critics like Nelson concede that the evidence is slim. "You can't pin the loss of jobs on the Endangered Species Act in other situations," he says. But Plummer still insists that the law has been disruptive. "If the purpose of the law were solely to put a monkey wrench in economic activities that threaten species," he says, "it's done that."

In the most thorough research on the question, however, Stephen Meyer, director of the Massachusetts Institute of Technology's Project on environmental studies, found no evidence of harmful economic effects. [8] Meyer's studies compared individual states'

U.S. Lists 955 Species as Endangered or Threatened

The Fish and Wildlife Service currently lists nearly 1,000 plant and animal species in the United States as endangered or threatened. Recovery plans have been approved for 520 species.*

Group	Number of Endangered Species	Number Threatened Species	Total Number of Species	Recovery Plans
Mammals	55	9	63*	40
Birds	74	16	88*	73
Reptiles	14	19	33	31
Amphibians	7	5	11*	11
Fishes	65	40	105	72
Snails	15	7	22	13
Clams	51	6	57	42
Crustaceans	14	3	17	4
Insects	20	9	29	20
Arachnids	5	0	5	4
Animal subtotal	320	114	430*	310
Flowering plants	405	90	495	197
Conifers	2	0	2	1
Ferns and others	26	2	28	12
Plant subtotal	433	92	525	210
Grand total	**753**	**206**	**955***	**520****

* *Separate populations of the gray wolf, piping plover, roseate tern and green sea turtle are listed as both endangered and threatened and are tallied twice.*

** *There are 419 individual recovery plans. Some plans cover more than one species, and a few species have separate plans covering different parts of their ranges.*

Source: U.S. Fish and Wildlife Service, Feb. 29, 1996

Scientists Link Rising Extinction Rate ...

Visitors strolling through the popular National Aquarium in Baltimore suddenly are greeted by a stark reality check: "Without firing a shot, we may kill one-fifth of all species on this planet in the next 20 years." The extinction warning, posted prominently in one of the exhibit areas, comes from Russell Train, chairman of the World Wildlife Fund, former head of the Environmental Protection Agency and one of the country's leading environmental advocates.

Warnings of an accelerating extinction crisis began in the 1970s and have grown steadily more insistent among environmentalists. Others have dismissed the warnings as too alarmist. But over the past decade, the warnings have moved from provocative hypotheses to conventional wisdom among scientists, even some who had previously criticized the studies that supported the dire predictions.

Daniel Simberloff, a professor of biology at Florida State University and an early critic of some extinction studies, today agrees that the world is going through "a dramatic event in history. I'd call it a crisis." A National Academy of Sciences report on the Endangered Species Act published last May agreed that human activities have brought on "a major episode of biological extinction" comparable to the extinction event 65 million years ago that wiped out dinosaurs. [1]

"If one cites an extinction rate, it's often hard to prove a hard number of species," Simberloff acknowledges. "Some of the [earlier] estimates were taken out of thin air," he continues, "but that's not true any more."

In their 1995 book *Noah's Choice*, Charles Mann and Mark Plummer trace the studies from the 1960s through the '80s that underlie the current warnings about accelerating extinctions. Harvard Professor Edward O. Wilson and Simberloff, then a graduate student at Harvard, designed some of the early studies, which literally involved wiping out all the plant and animal life on tiny islands off the Florida coast and watching to see whether species would regenerate. [2]

In fact, six- and eight-legged creatures returned to the islets — "survivors of heroic voyages," as Mann and Plummer put it. And over time, the number of species increased. By comparing islands of different size, Wilson and Simberloff took the experiments to prove an earlier hypothesis by an amateur English biologist, Frank Preston, that the number of species in small to mid-sized habitats increases sharply as the size of the area increases.

Conversely, sharp reductions in habitat size below a certain level would mean drastic reductions in the number of species that could survive. The shape of the so-called "species-area curve" varies from species to species and, in any event, cannot be plotted with the same kind of precision seen in the physical sciences. But most biologists agree that as humanity takes more habitat for itself, the number of plant and wildlife species being lost will increase sharply.

The precise number of extinctions occurring today is unknowable, scientists say. Mann and Plummer note that the projections from scientists and advocates have ranged widely — from one extinction an hour to several hundred a day or more. [3] Critics — such as Julian Simon, an outspoken economist at the University of Maryland, or journalists Gregg

economic performance with the number of endangered species in each state and found no effect on overall economic growth, agricultural production or construction activity. "If [the critics'] rhetoric is even partially true, then one should be able to look at the economies of the state and see some effects," Meyer explains. "There are no such impacts."

As for the impact on government projects, the Interior Department says the law has blocked only a very few. Out of 186,000 federal actions* reviewed between fiscal 1987 and fiscal 1995, only 600 were found to pose a danger to a species, and only 100 were actually blocked, the department's most recent data show. All but 13 of those involved timber sales in the Pacific Northwest, the department says.

Still, critics insist that the law has hurt individual landowners, creating political discontent and undermining support for the legitimate goal of protecting endangered species. "You're creating a class of incredibly pissed off people all across the country," says Smith at the Competitive Enterprise Institute.

Supporters concede the need to deal with the opposition to the law, but they also believe the public will back it when it's properly understood. "We have to try to address effectively the concerns of the populace," says Michael Clegg, chairman of a National Academy of Sciences (NAS) panel that issued a largely favorable assessment of the law last May. "We also have to make sure we're doing a good job of educating the people about the consequences of the loss of biological diversity."

Has the Endangered Species Act helped protect threatened animals and plants?

Two decades after its enactment, supporters and opponents differ sharply on how well, if at all, the act has protected the diversity of the nation's plant and animal life.

Supporters say the law has made a good start by halting the decline of many rare species. But they acknowledge that it has fallen short of broader goals. "It has been effective in preventing extinctions and saving species," says John Kostyack, general counsel of the National Wildlife Fed-

*Federal actions include anything funded by the federal government, such as a dam or a Federal Highway Administration-financed highway, or requiring a federal permit, such as draining a wetland or logging on U.S. Forest Service land.

. . . to Habitat Loss, Non-Native Species

Easterbrook and Stephen Budiansky — have accused the scientists of statistical manipulations for political purposes.

In his recent book, *Nature's Keepers,* Budiansky, a senior writer at *U.S. News & World Report,* mocks an extinction estimate Wilson has given: 50,000 a year. "The fact that the actual observed rate of extinction is not 50,000 a year but *one* species a year thus comes as a surprise to many," Budiansky writes. He also notes that Vernon Heywood and Simon Stuart, two scientists affiliated with the International Union for the Conservation of Nature, concluded in a 1992 article that there was "little evidence" to support the high rates of extinction projected by other scientists. But he did not note the pair's final comment predicting "much higher rates of extinction in the future." [4]

Stuart Pimm, an ecologist at the University of Tennessee, disagrees. He says that out of 10,000 known species of birds, about 100 have become extinct in the past century — which he says is 100 times the "background extinction rate" that he calculated from fossil records. Since birds are less vulnerable to extinction than other species, Pimm adds, the overall extinction rate for all species today is more than 100 times the historical background rate.

The causes of the increased rate of extinction — human activities — are less subject to uncertainty or debate. Habitat destruction and overexploitation are the most obvious threats to biodiversity. But scientists say a less obvious cause — the introduction of non-native species — may now constitute the greatest danger after habitat loss.

As one example, Wilson notes that the introduction of perch in Africa's Lake Victoria for sport fishing has led to the disappearance of many native fish. Pimm says that the inadvertent introduction of a non-native snake onto Guam after World War II has completely destroyed the island's bird population.

Despite their warnings, scientists say steps can be taken to slow the extinction rate. In its report, the NAS panel reaffirmed support for the Endangered Species Act and called for earlier legal intervention to protect threatened species. And most scientists reject the view of some critics that endangered-species policies should be prioritized to reflect the fact that it is impossible to save all species.

"We have to have priorities," says Simberloff, "but I don't know if the right way to assign priorities is to decide what species we should save and what species we shouldn't. I'm sure we'll lose species, but I'm not sure there's anything like a hopeless case."

[1] National Research Council, *Science and the Endangered Species Act,* 1995. See *The New York Times,* May 24, 1995, p. B12.

[2] See Charles C. Mann and Mark L. Plummer, *Noah's Choice: The Future of Endangered Species,* 1995, pp. 53-81. See also Edward O. Wilson, *The Diversity of Life,* 1992, pp. 223-225.

[3] See Mann and Plummer, *op. cit.*, pp. 64, 257 (note). See also Charles C. Mann, "Extinction: Are Ecologists Crying Wolf," *Science,* Aug. 16, 1991, pp. 736-738.

[4] Stephen Budiansky, *Nature's Keepers: The New Science of Nature Management* (1995), pp. 164-168, and n. 9. See Vernon Heywood and Simon Stuart, "Species Extinction in Tropical Forests," in T.C. Whitmore and J.A. Sayer [eds.], *Tropical Deforestation and Species Extinction* (1992), pp. 91-117.

eration (NWF). "It has not been effective in recovering species and in getting to the point that they no longer need the [act]."

Critics of the law, on the other hand, give the law little credit. "The Endangered Species Act has failed to help the overwhelming majority of species under its care" to be able to survive without legal protection, Plummer and Mann write. "The best that can be said," they add, "is that in many cases it has apparently slowed the fall to extinction." [9]

In its most recent report to Congress, the Interior Department has put a positive spin on the accomplishments under the law. [10] Of the more than 950 species that have been listed between 1968 and 1995, the department said, only seven, or 1 percent, have gone extinct — "perhaps the biggest success story of the Act." *

The statistics also show that the population of 41 percent of the listed species is either stable or improving. (*See graph, p. 340.*) As for individual success stories, the department highlights the delisting of the American alligator, the downlisting of the bald eagle from endangered to threatened and the increasing population of the whooping crane, peregrine falcon and black-footed ferret, among others.

Critics of the law counter by noting that only 21 U.S. species have been taken off the list — including the seven that went extinct, nine that were listed erroneously and only five domestic species that have actually been "recovered." Of those recoveries, Mann and Plummer say, only the alligator's is attributable to the Endangered Species Act. The brown pelican recovered because of the ban on DDT, they say, while three birds on the Western Pacific island of Palau probably had reached a viable population before they were listed. [11]

Similarly, Mann and Plummer minimize the law's importance in upgrading the status of species under the law. They say that from 1973 to 1993, the department upgraded only 11 species from endangered to threatened. And again they attribute most of the progress to factors other than the act — such as the ban on DDT, which helped the eagle and peregrine falcon to improve. They say that only in two cases — the Utah prairie dog and the Aleutian Canada goose — do recovery efforts under the act deserve credit for helping

*The species that have gone extinct include four fish (Tecopa pupfish, longjaw cisco, blue pike, amistad gambusia), two birds (Santa Barbara song sparrow, dusky seaside sparrow) and Sampson's pearly mussel.

Man and Nature, Conflict and Co-existence

1945
Effort launched to save the whooping crane.

March 11, 1967
More than 60 plant and animal species are listed as endangered under a predecessor to Endangered Species Act. List includes bald eagle, grizzly bear, gray wolf, Florida panther, California condor and Hawaiian goose, Hawaii's state bird.

1970
Red cockaded woodpecker, found in timber-rich southeastern forests, is listed as endangered.

June 1989
Fish and Wildlife Service starts process of listing Northern spotted owl as threatened species

1987
American alligator is removed from "threatened" list.

June 15, 1978
"Snail darter" case blocks completion of Tellico Dam; Congress later approves exemption for the project.

June 27, 1978
Fish and Wildlife Service says Dickey-Lincoln Dam in Maine must be modified to avoid destruction of the Furbish lousewort, a kind of snapdragon.

February 1994
Fish and Wildlife Service designates 6.4 million acres of land in California and two other states as critical habitat for the desert tortoise.

June 1994
Fish and Wildlife Service upgrades bald eagle from "endangered" to "threatened" and removes California gray whale from endangered list.

January 1995
Wolves are reintroduced to Yellowstone National Park.

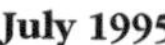

July 1995
National Marine and Fisheries Service lists coho salmon as threatened species along much of the West Coast.

February 1996
California condors are reintroduced to Grand Canyon

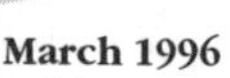

March 1996
California voters reject initiative to legalize "trophy hunting" of cougars. Four other states will vote in November on cougar protection measures.

Graphic by Sarah M. Magner.

the species' population improve.

Supporters of the law say the critics' analysis sets an unrealistic standard. "Those who criticize it on an effectiveness ground are being a bit premature and raising a standard that is unreasonable in the context of the demography of biological populations, particularly long-lived ones," says Clegg. In its report, the NAS panel said that without the law, there was "a strong, but hard-to-prove, possibility" that many species "would be closer to extinction than they are today." [12]

Beyond the statistical debate, critics insist that the law creates what they call "perverse incentives" for private landowners to make their property less attractive to endangered species so as to avoid coming under the act's regulatory powers. "Landowners all over the South are cutting their trees as fast as they can because they know what happens if you're a good steward of the land," says Smith. "If you let pine trees grow, you get red-cockaded woodpeckers on your land, and you're shut down."

Interestingly, Michael Bean, the Environmental Defense Fund's (EDF) director of wildlife policy and perhaps the environmental movement's most influential wildlife expert, agrees with Smith's criticism. "What is clear to me," he told an FWS training seminar in 1994, "is that on private lands at least, we don't have very much to show for our efforts other than a lot of political headaches." [13]

The Clinton administration's moves to revise enforcement policies by emphasizing larger-area habitat conservation plans and limiting the impact of the law on most homeowners also appear to accept part of the critics' arguments. But supporters of the law insist that legislative proposals to eliminate the mandatory provisions of the law for private landowners go too far. "Private landowners who acquire land that has threatened or endangered species have a responsibility to everyone because wildlife belongs to everyone," says Snodgrass.

Should Congress make major changes in the Endangered Species Act?

The Endangered Species Act has faced strong opposition in Congress every time it has come up from renewal since the snail darter controversy in 1978. Today, with a Republican-controlled Congress, the law faces the strongest-ever pressure for changes that would increase the government's burdens in protecting species and soften the regulations on private landowners. But moderate Republicans, with surprising assistance from House Speaker Gingrich, are pushing a less sweeping rewrite.

Critics say there is a broad consensus on the need for changing the law. "Everyone agrees that there has to be reform," says John Doggett, director of government relations for the American Farm Bureau Federation. "Everyone agrees that there have to be more incentives. Everyone agrees there have to be new ways of protecting species."

Some supporters of the law do, in fact, agree on the need for policy reforms. In testimony to the Senate Environment Committee's wildlife subcommittee last summer, the EDF's Bean urged several provisions giving landowners incentives to protect endangered species, including tax breaks for setting aside "conservation easements."

The tax proposals were among a package of changes endorsed in July by an array of advocates and experts from government, business and industry and conservation groups assembled by the Keystone Center, a Colorado-based environmental mediation organization. [14] "Some of the participants in that dialogue thought that in the area of endangered species, trying to create incentives and remove disincentives was a winner for all sides," explains Senior Vice President Michael Lesnick.

Other supporters of the law, however, stress other areas for improvements. The wildlife federation's Kostyack, for example, says recovery plans "now are often vague and useless. They need to be specific documents that lay out specific actions. They need to bring in the various federal agencies as early as possible, and to bring in state and local people much more than they do."

In testimony before congressional committees, Secretary Babbitt has both called for and taken credit for changes in enforcing the act. Appearing before the Senate's Wildlife subcommittee in March 1995, he said the administration had already acted to minimize the impact of the act on private landowners and to give "a greater role" to state, tribal and local governments in carrying it out. But Babbitt said then — and continues to say — that he needs no new legislation to carry out the changes.

"We don't need more legislation," Babbitt says. "We need to make this act work, to take it off the shelf, dust it off, breathe some life into it, get out on the landscape and talk to people, get them around the table, and say, 'OK, let's look at everyone's objectives.' "

Critics of the law, however, want more far-reaching changes. The bill approved by the House Resources Committee in October would require landowners' agreement before designating private property as protected habitat and compensate owners for regulatory restrictions on use of their property. The bill would also limit the obligation of federal agencies to consult with the FWS on projects that might affect threatened or endangered species; impose new procedural requirements on listing of species; and require consultation with states on listing decisions and recovery plans.

The bill, approved Oct. 12 on a 27-17 vote, is cosponsored by two Republican lawmakers who have been sharply critical of the act: Alaska's Don Young, chairman of the House Resources Committee, and California's Richard W. Pombo, who headed the committee's endangered species task force. The task force conducted hearings in Washington and around the country marked by sharp attacks on the law from farmers, ranchers, developers and other property owners.

Supporters say the bill reaffirms the goal of protecting endangered species, but uses balanced methods that protect the rights of property owners and workers. Opponents, including conservation groups, environmentally minded lawmakers in both parties and the administration, say the measure would effectively gut the law. "It weakens or abandons the most important provisions of the law," FWS Director Mollie Beattie said on the eve of the House committee markup. [15]

Clinton indicated earlier that he

would veto the bill if it reached his desk. But now the bill appears to be headed nowhere. Environmental lobbyists say that Gingrich has refused to bring the bill to the House floor for a vote. Meanwhile, a group of moderate Republicans, headed by New York's James H. Saxton, are working on a more moderate reauthorization measure.

Saxton's bill aims at simplifying the development of habitat compensation plans and enhancing states' role in administering the law. Saxton says he consulted with two timber companies, Georgia Pacific and Plumb Creek, as well as the EDF and three other environmental groups.

Lobbyists on both sides of the issue found fault with the compromise as its outlines were becoming known. Jack Mingus, director of communications for the National Endangered Species Act Reform Coalition, a coalition of farmers and other agricultural interests, calls the measure "ESA reform lite." But Heather Weiner, a lobbyist for Defenders of Wildlife, says the measure could substantially weaken enforcement of the law if the final version gives states veto power over species listings or recovery plans.

The debate, in any event, may be moot. Observers increasingly doubt that a reauthorization will be brought to the House floor this session, given the crowded legislative calendar and GOP leaders' wariness of a floor fight on an environmental issue. "It's most likely that it will stall again," says Kostyack. "It's an old truism that it's easier to stall something than it is to successfully enact legislation." ■

BACKGROUND

Early Extinctions

No one knows how many species have existed since life began on Earth some 3.8 billion years ago. But the 10 million to 100 million species that are believed to exist today represent a tiny fraction — fewer than 1 percent — of all the different species of animals, plants, protozoa, fungi, viruses and bacteria that have ever lived on this planet. The rest have become extinct, the vast majority through natural causes but many of them in recent centuries because of human impacts. [16]

Through examination of fossil records, scientists have identified five major extinction periods during prehistoric geological eras. The most severe of these extinction catastrophes occurred about 250 million years ago and wiped out an estimated 60 percent of all living species. The most recent, which took place about 65 million years ago, claimed about 11 percent of all species: 15 percent of marine species and about 6 percent of all continental organisms — including the greatest of land creatures, the dinosaur. [17]

Scientists debate competing hypotheses of the causes of these extinctions — mainly volcanic eruptions or impact from comets or massive meteorites. Wilson suggests a combination of factors. Whatever the causes, life on Earth rebounded after each catastrophe. But Wilson stresses that it took "tens of millions of years" each time for life on Earth to recover.

The evolution of the species homo sapiens created a new factor in the process of extinction. Anthropogenic extinctions — those caused by man — can be found from the last Ice Age, 11,000 years ago, to the present. And the rate at which species are falling victim to humankind is rapidly increasing, according to most biologists in the field. Even Mann and Plummer acknowledge alarm at man's impact on biodiversity. "In fact," they write, "there is a cataclysm: us." [18]

North and South America suffered some of the greatest man-made blows. Mann and Plummer draw a picture of a "fantastic continent-sized bestuary" populated, before the arrival of man, by camels, rhinoceroses, cheetahs, lions, and even elephants along with "beavers the size of bears," "bisons with horns six feet across" and "a four-foot turtle that weighed a ton." These animals fell easy victim to the so-called "paleo Indians" who crossed the Bering Sea land bridge 12,000 years ago. Within the space of 200 or at most 2,000 years, "species vanished by the score." [19]

Similar man-made extinctions occurred in the Pacific islands, the Earth's last habitable areas, reached by man about 1,000 to 4,000 years ago. Stuart Pimm, a biologist at the University of Tennessee, calculates that Polynesians exterminated more than 2,000 species of birds, some 15 percent of the world's total. [20] Wilson estimates that the Polynesians wiped out at least half of the "endemic" species — species found only in the given area. With little arable soil, the Polynesians turned to birds or other wildlife for food and moved on when the population was gone. "The voyagers ate their way through the Polynesian fauna," Wilson sadly concludes. [21]

European explorers and settlers continued the course of species destruction. About one-third of Hawaii's native bird species have disappeared since Captain Cook's visit in 1778, according to Wilson. British settlers accelerated the native Maoris' deforestation of New Zealand, with devastating effects on birds and the island's lush plant life.

The creation and expansion of the United States from its original Atlantic colonies wreaked similar devastation on North American wildlife through overhunting and destruction of habitat. Wolves were virtually eliminated from New England by 1800 and from the West by the early 1900s. The Atlantic gray whale became extinct in 1750. The list of other mammals that became extinct by 1900 or so includes the Eastern elk (1880), Southern California kit fox (1903), sea mink (1903), giant deer mouse (1870) and the Gulf island and Louisiana voles (1898, 1905). [22]

Continued on p. 348

Chronology

Prehistory

Fossil records indicate many waves of extinctions, including at least five major episodes, before human history.

Before 1900

Plant and animal life in North America suffers from migration of peoples from Asia, conquest by Europeans and westward U.S. expansion.

1900-1960

Congress passes several wildlife conservation laws and international wildlife protection treaties.

1900
Lacey Act prohibits interstate commerce of animals killed in violation of state game laws.

1914
Passenger pigeon becomes extinct with the death of "Martha" in the Cincinnati Zoo.

1918
Migratory Bird Treaty Act prohibits the taking of certain birds protected by U.S.-Canadian agreement reached in 1916.

1929
Migratory Bird Conservation Act provides acquisition authority for wildlife refuges and sanctuaries.

1940
Bald Eagle Protection Act is passed.

1945
U.S. and Canada join with Audubon Society to save whooping crane.

1960s ***Congress passes two species-protection laws that are precursors of the Endangered Species Act.***

1966
Endangered Species Preservation Act orders conservation of selected species and acquisition of land for habitat protection.

1969
Endangered Species Conservation Act authorizes secretary of Interior to prohibit importation of threatened species.

1970s ***Congress passes Endangered Species Act, called by many the world's toughest environmental law.***

1972
Marine Mammal Protection Act is passed.

March 3, 1973
Convention on International Trade in Endangered Species of Wild Fauna and Flora is signed.

Dec. 28, 1973
Endangered Species Protection Act (ESA) is signed by President Richard M. Nixon after overwhelming approval by Congress.

June 17, 1978
Supreme Court upholds use of ESA to block Tellico Dam (*TVA v. Hill*). Congress later in year permits federal action that could result in extinction of species if benefits outweigh costs.

1980s ***Expanding use of ESA on private property provokes opposition. Scientists warn of increasing extinction rates.***

1982
Congress amends ESA to permit "incidental takings" if property owners develop "habitat conservation plans."

1988
Congress reauthorizes ESA after delay caused by opponents of plan to reintroduce wolves and grizzly bears into Yellowstone park.

March 1989
To protect spotted owls, federal judge in Washington state issues first of several rulings to block some harvesting of "old-growth forest."

1990s ***Government officials and environmentalists seek to blunt continuing criticism of ESA with new recovery and preservation programs.***

Feb. 16, 1993
Interior Secretary Bruce Babbitt vows to avoid economic conflicts over endangered species by taking early steps to protect whole ecosystems.

June 29, 1995
Supreme Court upholds broad use of ESA to protect plant and animal life on private property (*Babbitt v. Sweet Home Chapter*).

Oct. 12, 1995
House Resources Committee OKs bill to give landowners veto power over ESA enforcement on private property, but bill is not brought to floor.

Threats to Tigers and Other Rare Species . . .

Save the tiger! Save the rain forests! Save the whales! The urgent appeals sounded by environmental groups in the United States dramatize the fragile status of some species around the world. They also point to the major threats to the planet's biological diversity — and the often failing efforts to counteract them.

Siberian and Bengal tigers face extinction because of loss of habitat in populous countries like China and India and because of illegal hunting to feed the lucrative market for tiger parts used for medicines in some Asian countries.

Rain forests are being cleared in many countries to make way for settlement and agricultural and industrial development. Some of the species-rich ecosystems are also dying from atmospheric pollution.

As for whales, eight species are listed as endangered, the result of commercial overharvesting in the past and gaps in enforcing an international moratorium agreed to by most of the world's nations.

Over the past 25 years, conservation groups in the United States and around the world have helped win international agreement on a number of international, regional and bilateral treaties to protect threatened animal and plant species. They have also helped raise public awareness of the issue. A Gallup Poll of about 30,000 people in 24 countries in 1992 found that most people — 57 percent in developing countries and 51 percent in industrialized countries — viewed the loss of animal and plant species as a "very serious" problem. [1]

But advocates and experts say the treaties, targeted conservation projects and public-education efforts have had only limited effects in easing the danger of extinctions. "We've got our finger in the dike," says Ginette Himley, director of international wildlife policy for the World Wildlife Fund.

Endangered species protection efforts around the world face the same types of difficulties they face in the United States: reconciling conservation with established economic activities and new development and overcoming ingrained customs about use of plant and wildlife. But none of the international treaties has the broad coverage or strict prohibitions of the federal Endangered Species Act.

The principal international treaty is the Convention on International Trade in Endangered Species, a U.S.-led agreement reached in 1973 and now signed by 135 countries. The treaty — known as CITES — essentially bans international trade in some 700 species that are threatened with extinction. It imposes limits on trade in a larger number of species — about 2,500 — that could become threatened without controls. [2]

Conservation groups credit CITES with such accomplishments as helping to increase the population of the endangered African elephant by controlling the trade in ivory. But it has proven less successful in ending the trade in two other critically endangered species — the black rhinoceros and the Siberian tiger. Rhinoceros horns and various tiger parts are widely used as traditional medicines in several Asian countries, including China, Japan and Korea. [3]

The widespread public belief in the medications — despite the lack of scientific evidence for their efficacy — creates a lucrative market that enforcement efforts have been unable to control, according to a U.S. expert. "How do you persuade 1 billion Chinese to take aspirin instead of rhinoceros horns?" John Copeland Nagle, an associate professor at Seton Hall University law school, in South Orange, N.J., remarked at a March conference on international biodiversity issues in Washington.

The United States in 1994 imposed sanctions on Taiwan for failing to control trade in tiger parts. The penalties were lifted a year later after Taiwan moved to tighten enforcement. But the U.S. has not acted against China, which Nagle says is the world's largest exporter of endangered species and

Continued from p. 346

Most prominent of the vanished species perhaps is the passenger pigeon, once North America's most common bird. The species vanished with the death of a pigeon named "Martha" in the Cincinnati Zoo on Sept. 1, 1914.

The Conservation Ethic

The American pioneer spirit that cleared the prairie of native grasses, slaughtered the buffalo nearly to extinction and reduced or eliminated hosts of other species of animals and plants gave way with the closing of the frontier to a growing conservation ethic. The increased concern about the country's natural heritage resulted in a steady stream of federal conservation efforts, including laws aimed at protecting wildlife beginning in 1900 and culminating 73 years later in the Endangered Species Act. [23]

The first of these federal laws, the Lacey Act, prohibited interstate commerce in any birds or animals killed in violation of state law. It also marked an initial step toward federal wildlife management by authorizing the secretary of Agriculture to adopt measures necessary for the "preservation" and "restoration" of game birds and other wild birds. The House report accompanying the bill noted that in many states native birds had been "well-nigh exterminated."

Birds continued to be a principal focus of the federal government's next wildlife protection moves. In 1916, the United States negotiated with Great Britain, on behalf of Canada, a treaty to protect migratory birds. The law, still on the books, was challenged by states as an infringement of their

. . . Often Overwhelm Best Efforts of Conservationists

one of the largest users.

Chinese officials claim to be trying to prevent illegal poaching of tigers: Some poachers have even been executed. But Nagle and Hemley both say that enforcement is difficult. "You're never going to have sustained enforcement in China on this subject," says Hemley. "It's just far too big and far too chaotic, and endangered species is way down on the list of priorities."

Even with stronger enforcement, however, conservation experts stress that CITES deals only with trade, not with any of the other dangers for plant and animal species. "Within the context of international trade, CITES has had some major effects," says Amie Brautigam, a Washington-based program officer with the International Union for Conservation of Nature (IUCN). "But CITES can address only one of the many impacts on species."

The most important gap in international treaties, advocates and experts agree, is protection for habitat. "We don't really have a major global treaty addressing habitat conservation," Brautigam says.

Hemley says the problems of protecting habitat differ from continent to continent. In Africa, poverty is so deep and human needs so great that protecting wildlife ranks far below agricultural needs on governmental priorities. In Asia, population pressures pose the most serious threat to habitat. In Europe, additional development is the greatest problem.

Some steps are being taken to protect habitat. Some Asian countries are setting aside land for nature reserves. The European Union adopted a habitats directive in 1992 calling on member nations to identify and protect threatened types of habitat. But money for land acquisition is hard to come by. And in Europe, most of the countries missed the June deadline for identifying sites to be protected. [4]

Wildlife protection efforts are also facing a new, direct challenge from the sustainable-use movement. The advocates of this growing school of thought argue that wildlife can best be protected by permitting some economic use rather than banning it altogether. "If there is no incentive to preserve wildlife among people who are starving, then you're not going to have wildlife," says Leslie King, a professor at the University of Northern British Columbia Law School.

King, who has worked in several African countries, says that Zimbabwe has adopted this philosophy by shifting wildlife management to local villages and allowing them to keep any money that is made from eco-tourism, including controlled big-game hunting. The result, she says, has been to more than double the elephant population in the country — from 35,000 in 1970 to 77,000 today.

Whaling advocates also call for "sustainable harvesting" of whales and note that some species — notably, the minke whale, found in Southern Hemisphere oceans — have substantial populations. But supporters of the moratorium on whaling, adopted by the International Convention on Whaling in 1984, argue that without controls, whaling countries will rapidly deplete species that are not now endangered.

Overall, Hemley says, the international conservation efforts have yielded "a lot of successes," but conservation groups need to work harder and smarter in the future. "We have to keep up political pressure on these things," she says. "We also have to be more strategic in our investments. And we have to work harder on public awareness."

[1] Quoted in *Science*, July 21, 1995, p. 356.

[2] See Ginette Hemley [ed.], *International Wildlife Trade: A CITES Sourcebook*, 1994, p. 1.

[3] See *The New York Times*, Sept. 5, 1995, p. A1; *The Washington Post*, Nov. 29, 1994, p. A1.

[4] See *Science*, July 21, 1995, pp. 320-322.

control over wildlife policy. But the Supreme Court upheld the act in 1920 as a proper exercise of the federal government's treaty-making power.

Two decades later, concern about the dwindling population of the national symbol led Congress to pass the Bald Eagle Protection Act. The 1940 act is still on the books and has been strengthened several times. In 1972, for example, Congress responded to reports of deaths of bald eagles from eating a poison used in the West for coyote control by prohibiting unintentional killings if they resulted from actions done "in wanton disregard" of the consequences.

Meanwhile, the government began establishing the national wildlife refuge system. The first refuges were established by presidential proclamation: Alaska's Afognak Island, reserved by President Benjamin Harrison in 1892, and Florida's Pelican Island refuge, established by President Theodore Roosevelt in 1903. Congress formally authorized the creation of wildlife refuges in 1906; it gave additional authority for acquisition of refuges for migratory birds in 1929.

Despite the protection laws, extinctions continued to be recorded. The California grizzly bear disappeared in 1925. Eight different species of wolves vanished from the Southeast, West and Alaska between 1925 and 1970. Two species of trout became extinct in Colorado (1910) and New Hampshire (1930s). Hawaii continued to lose native bird species. Among insects and other invertebrates, the list of extinctions included at least nine butterflies, two dozen moths and 18 different species of bees. [24]

Most of these extinctions occurred with little if any public notice. But beginning in the 1940s, the American public directly confronted the threatened extinction of one species: the whooping crane.[25] The population of this majestic bird, more than 4 feet tall with a 7-foot wingspan, had once dwindled to only 21 individuals, mainly because of destruction of marshy habitat along its migratory path between Canada and the Gulf of Mexico. U.S. and Canadian wildlife officials began working with the Audubon Society in 1945 on a full-scale campaign to save the whooping crane. One wildlife refuge for cranes had already been created in Nebraska in 1937; two more followed in Canada and Texas. Scientists conducted more research on the birds, while the Audubon Society drummed up public interest.

Within the federal government, the whooping crane's most influential champion was an FWS biologist named Ray Erickson. As Mann and Plummer relate, Erickson lobbied at the start of the John F. Kennedy administration to set up breeding pens for the birds to expand their population. He also helped win funds for the establishment of the first endangered-wildlife research program. And he helped assemble a committee of biologists to compile the nation's first list of threatened animals: 36 birds, 15 mammals, six fish and five reptiles and amphibians.

These efforts laid the groundwork for the Endangered Species Preservation Act of 1966, the first law aimed at protecting all threatened species of animals. The act established, within the conservation-minded Interior Department, a formal program of listing endangered species and authorized the government to use up to $5 million a year to acquire land for habitat. But as Bean notes, the law did not prohibit the taking of any endangered species or bar interstate commerce in endangered animals.[26]

Three years later, Congress acted to close a different gap left by the 1966 law: its failure to protect foreign threatened species. The Endangered Species Conservation Act authorized the secretary of the Interior to promulgate a list of fish or wildlife threatened with worldwide extinction and to prohibit their importation into the United States. It also called for the United States to convene an international conference to seek worldwide cooperation in protecting threatened wildlife. The conference took place in Washington in 1973, which was to become the watershed year in federal protection efforts.

Endangered Species Act

In an environmental message to Congress on Feb. 8, 1972, President Richard M. Nixon declared that existing federal wildlife law "simply does not provide the kind of management tools needed to act early enough to save a vanishing species." As Bean notes, Congress had already accepted that principle in passing the Marine Mammal Protection Act. Nixon's message recommended a comprehensive bill prohibiting the taking of any endangered species and requiring federal agencies to promote conservation of endangered species.[27]

The law that Nixon signed Dec. 28, 1973, has been called the ultimate environmental statute. It formalized the procedures established under the 1966 act for listing endangered or threatened species and added a requirement to designate "critical habitat" for a species' survival. Federal agencies were required to ensure that their actions not jeopardize the continued existence of a listed species or adversely modify its critical habitat. And the act banned the "taking" of any endangered species, a ban later extended to cover threatened species and to apply to actions adversely affecting habitat for an endangered or threatened species.

Initially, the FWS enforced the new law cautiously. The head of the agency, Lynn Greenwalt, now an NWF official, recognized that Congress had passed a broader, more powerful law than most legislators imagined. He asked for more money for staff and for land acquisition, but moved slowly to list new species. The service waited for a year before listing its first new species: three types of kangaroo, all native to Australia. Only in 1975 did it propose listing new domestic species, and only one of the new listings — the bayou darter, endemic to Mississippi — posed an immediate conflict with a federal project. The soil conservation project was modified to solve the problem.[28]

A lawsuit brought by a Tennessee law school student against a nearly completed TVA dam dramatized the impact of the legal mandate to protect endangered species.[29] Hiram G. Hill Jr., was a student at the University of Tennessee Law School when he learned of a new species of fish — the snail darter — discovered to be inhabiting a branch of the Tennessee River where the TVA was building the $110 million Tellico Dam. Hill filed an administrative action to force Fish and Wildlife to list the species as endangered and the river — the snail darter's only known location — as its "critical habitat." In early 1976, TVA went ahead with plans to complete the dam, and Hill filed suit.

The idea that a tiny fish of no evident value could halt an all-but-finished dam struck many people as preposterous, but in 1978 the Supreme Court ruled that the law required exactly that result. In a 6-3 decision — *TVA v. Hill* — the court held that the Endangered Species Act required federal agencies to take steps "to halt and reverse the trend toward species extinction, whatever the cost."

On Capitol Hill, lawmakers immediately sought to reverse the ruling by exempting the dam from the strictures of the Endangered Species Act. The law that emerged later that year, however, provided a broader remedy: an interdepartmental committee of federal officials was created with the power to grant such an exemption if a federal project's benefits outweighed the costs in endangered species terms. Ironically, the committee — dubbed the "God Squad" — thwarted the dam's proponents in its first action by ruling that the project's recreational benefits were in fact outweighed by its costs. Frustrated lawmakers then returned to the issue with an appropriations rider to a 1980 water projects bill that required completion of the dam.

TVA opened the floodgates on Nov. 29, 1979. And, in a postscript emphasized by critics of the Endangered Species Act, the University of Tennessee biologist who discovered the snail darter found a new population of the fish about a year later. By 1984, the fish's status had been upgraded from "endangered" to "threatened."

The act had engendered similar controversies involving dams in Nebraska and Maine. Nebraska's Grayrocks Dam and Reservoir won an exemption from the "God Squad" despite adverse impact on whooping-crane habitat. Fish and Wildlife recommended modifications for the Dickey-Lincoln dam in northern Maine to protect the endangered Furbish lousewort, a species of snapdragon. Later, the Maine dam was scrapped, for budgetary reasons.

The act suffered further after the change in administrations following the 1980 presidential election. The Reagan administration took more than a year to list two new species while the backlog of candidates grew to more than 100. Under Interior Secretary James Watt, the administration also said it would include cost-benefit considerations in its listing decisions — a stance that environmentalists said was in direct conflict with the law.

The law still enjoyed support on Capitol Hill, however, as lawmakers began work on reauthorizing the act in 1982. The three-year extension made relatively few changes, but some were significant. In response to the administration's footdragging, Congress set deadlines of one year for agency action on designating critical habitat or adding or removing a species from the endangered list.

But Congress also relaxed the law somewhat for private landowners and developers. The threat of criminal penalties or project shutdown for an "incidental take" of a species was lifted if the property owner filed a "habitat conservation plan" with Interior that outlined steps to mitigate the damage to the species.

Diversity of Protests

Over the next decade, the Endangered Species Act drew an increasing number of protests from property owners of all sorts. The critics claimed the law was infringing traditional property rights, hampering development and curtailing important economic sectors at a cost of lost jobs and higher prices. Defenders of the law insisted that critics were exaggerating the disruptions and costs while ignoring the many benefits — economic, environmental and esthetic, to name a few — of protecting the nation's biological heritage.

The law continued to complicate the planning and construction of government projects. Mann and Plummer open their book, for example, with the story of a state highway in Oklahoma that was rerouted, after a four-year delay, to protect a newly discovered endangered beetle. But the law suffered most in the realm of public opinion because of its increasingly frequent effect on private property owners.

The law's impact on private property stemmed from its prohibition against "taking" a species and a broad construction of that term. Within the act, "take" was defined as "to harass, harm, pursue, hunt, shoot, wound, kill, trap, capture, or collect" any species. The regulation further defined "harm" to include "any significant habitat modification or degradation where it actually kills or injures wildlife."

On the strength of that definition, the FWS ruled the law could prevent farmers from farming, developers from developing or loggers from logging on any land that was "critical habitat" for endangered or threatened species. However, developers who wanted to build a factory on San Bruno Mountain, just outside San Francisco, persuaded Congress to pass a 1982 amendment to the law. The new provision allowed "incidental takes" of a species — in this case an endangered butterfly — if a habitat conservation plan had been approved by the FWS.

Other property owners, however, did not work their way out of endangered species problems so readily. In California, farmers complained about restrictions aimed at protecting the desert kangaroo rat. In the Southeast, the red-cockaded woodpecker slowed timber harvesting in pine forests. In New York, protection of the Karner blue butterfly required complicated plans to set aside land for the species. These and a host of other examples gave critics ample ammunition to attack the Endangered Species Act as costly, disruptive and, ultimately, foolhardy.

Meanwhile, the federal government found itself in a bitter controversy with timber interests in the Pacific Northwest over the spotted owl.[30] The owl's dwindling population had been giving conservationists concern since the 1970s. Biologists said the owl needed "old-growth" trees for nesting and a large area of undisturbed land for habitat — 1,000 acres per nesting pair, according to a 1984 study. The FWS and major environmental groups hesitated to list the owl as endangered, fearing another public relations fiasco like the snail darter episode.

But a small, Massachusetts-based environmental group sued the agency to force it to list the owl. Then, a bevy of environmental organizations sued to block timber harvesting on private lands or in national forests. According to Alston Chase's critical account, *In a Dark Wood,* timber sales from national forests in 1993 were one-tenth what they were in 1989, before the first injunction had been issued.

Support From Supreme Court, Academy of Sciences

Timber interests scrambled to fight the restrictions on logging in the Pacific Northwest and on the mainly private-owned forests in the Southeast. They lobbied Congress to pass an appropriations rider limiting courts' authority to restrict logging, but the provision was ruled unconstitutional. Meanwhile, they also challenged the regulation that applied the Endangered Species Act to actions that reduced habitat on private land. But the Supreme Court upheld the regulation late last June, saying it was a reasonable construction of the statute (*Babbitt v. Sweet Home Chapter of Communities for a Great Oregon*). [31]

The high court ruling came one month after a broader victory for supporters of the Endangered Species Act: the favorable assessment of the law by the National Academy of Sciences panel. "In general, our committee finds that there has been a good match between science and the ESA," Chairman Clegg wrote. The report echoed the warnings from supporters of the law about the high rate of extinctions and joined in emphasizing the importance of protecting habitat, on public or private lands. "Habitat protection," the report concluded, "is a prerequisite for conservation of biological diversity." [32]

The scientists' conclusions carried little weight on Capitol Hill. The Republican takeover of Congress had given control of the House Resources Committee to a strong critic of the Endangered Species Act, Alaska's Young, who in turn created a special task force on the issue dominated by unsympathetic Southern and Western lawmakers. Young joined with the head of the task force, California's Pombo, in pushing through the committee their bill to rewrite the act to free private landowners from the law and add new regulatory hurdles for the government in listing species or implementing recovery plans.

Gingrich's ambivalence about the reform effort surprised some critics of the law. But *Audubon* magazine noted in January that Gingrich has "a child-like fascination" with animals and had talked over endangered species issues earlier with Harvard's Wilson and Terry Maple, the director of Zoo Atlanta and a personal friend. Gingrich ordered Young to work out a compromise with the moderate GOP lawmakers, the magazine said. [33] By April, moderates were close to a compromise, but Young and Pombo were giving no public signs of moving in their direction. ■

CURRENT SITUATION

Roads to Recovery

The California condor once flew all along the mountain ranges of the Pacific Coast. But the huge carrion feeder all but disappeared from the wild by the 1970s because of hunting and, more significantly, because of reduced food supply due to depletion of wildlife.

In the last few years, however, FWS biologists have established a colony of 13 condors in California's Santa Barbara County. And in late February, biologists released nine more California condors outside the Grand Canyon National Park in Arizona in an effort to establish a second colony in the wild. [34]

While endangered-species controversies usually focus on listing species or the impact on government projects or private property owners, recovery plans are the law's ultimate goal. Recovery plans, required for each species under the 1978 revision of the act, chart the steps needed to increase the population of a threatened or endangered species to a point where it no longer needs protection to survive.

The FWS has recently been touting progress in recovery plans — from the re-introduction of gray wolves in Yellowstone park early last year to the move last summer to remove the peregrine falcon from the endangered list. [35] But for supporters of the Endangered Species Act, the recovery plan process has been a major area of disappointment and controversy.

Conservation-minded critics say the service has been both too slow and too timid in developing recovery plans for many of the more than 900 listed species. In 1993, researchers at the University of Idaho, Moscow, wrote that, "Recovery plans have often been set that risk extinction rather than ensure survival." [36]

The FWS itself acknowledges a substantial backlog in writing recovery plans. In its latest report, published in February, the service said that of 955 species listed, recovery plans had been approved for only 520 species. Fish and Wildlife officials have blamed the backlog on fiscal and manpower constraints and inadequate scientific information; they promise to eliminate the backlog by the end of fiscal 1997. [37]

With or without complete recovery plans, Fish and Wildlife is now emphasizing, under Babbitt's lead, a new "multi-species" approach designed to increase the efficiency of the recovery process. This approach focuses less on saving individual species and more on saving whole "ecosystems" that provide habitat for several species. In addition to making better use of scarce resources, the policy aims at reducing conflicts with property owners through the use of habitat conservation plans

Continued on p. 354

At Issue:

Should the Endangered Species Act be re-enacted without major changes?

RODGER SCHLICKEISEN
President, Defenders of Wildlife

WRITTEN FOR *THE CQ RESEARCHER*

yes

Picture an America without its greatest national symbol, the bald eagle. But for the Endangered Species Act (ESA), it would have been extinct. Instead, eagles, gray whales, sea otters, brown pelicans and many other species are recovering. These are just a few of the success stories made possible by the ESA, one of America's greatest environmental achievements.

The ESA also has been successful in accommodating both development and conservation. More than 99 percent of proposed development projects reviewed for possible impact on wildlife have been allowed to proceed. In 1995, the National Academy of Sciences and the U.S. Supreme Court concluded that the ESA is sound. The assault on the ESA by "wise-use" extremists and industries is fueled by politics and anecdotes, not facts.

The timber industry, home of the "Endangered Species Coordinating Council," paints a conflict between spotted owls and jobs. However, a new study by a team of 60 economists in the Pacific Northwest concluded that, "Environmental protection has helped create and maintain economic health." It added, "The loss of jobs in natural resources . . . industries has not been primarily due to environmental restrictions."

By protecting critical owl habitat, we also protect a diversity of wildlife and economic interests. By contrast, logging this habitat jeopardizes commercial and recreational fisheries, already reeling from the loss of salmon.

Industry lobbyists drafted legislation introduced by Sen. Slade Gorton, R-Wash., and later reflected in even worse bills from Sen. Dirk Kempthorne, R-Idaho, and Reps. Don Young, R-Alaska, and Dick Pombo, R-Calif. These bills virtually dismantle the ESA. A group of distinguished scientists characterized the Young-Pombo bill as "so riddled with scientific errors and misstatements as to be indefensible."

Is the ESA perfect? No. But most of the problem lies not with the law but with its implementation and sparse funding. Perhaps most critically, the ESA could use more incentives to encourage conservation by private landowners.

Sometimes it is hard to remember that before the politics of polarization became epidemic, the ESA enjoyed overwhelming support from both political parties. President Richard Nixon set the bipartisan tone when he signed the original legislation in 1973. Wildlife, he noted, is "a many-faceted treasure, of value to scholars, scientists and nature lovers alike, and it forms a vital part of the heritage we all share as Americans." Hopefully, as the political opportunism underlying the current hysterical attacks on the ESA are exposed, we will once again find common purpose in protecting that heritage for future generations.

W. HENSON MOORE
Co-chairman, Endangered Species Coordinating Council

WRITTEN FOR *THE CQ RESEARCHER*

no

Congress has the obligation to correct any statute that produces harmful, unintended consequences. That is reason for Congress to fix the Endangered Species Act (ESA). But a more basic reason for reform exists: Twenty-three years with the ESA has shown what works and does not work for endangered species. The law should be changed accordingly.

Changed — not scrapped. No responsible party argues for "gutting" the ESA. However, responsible parties correctly argue that species protection can be achieved more efficiently and at less cost to landowners than the law currently provides.

One lesson we have learned with the ESA is that its characteristic approach to compelling landowner compliance is self-defeating. Threatening landowners with criminal prosecution for failing to provide habitat is almost calculated to harm protection efforts. By using the "stick" instead of the "carrot," the U.S. Fish and Wildlife Service (FWS) simply discourages landowners from protecting listed species or providing needed habitat.

In fact, current enforcement efforts virtually guarantee the opposite. Throughout the country, landowners have been prevented from clearing brush from fences, building vacation or retirement homes or harvesting their trees. All of this occurs in the name of "species recovery." Saddling landowners with the high costs of developing and implementing habitat conservation plans is more likely to force ranchers, woodland owners, builders and others to eliminate habitat altogether or face the dismaying prospect of losing valuable use of their property while paying for species recovery.

This is fine if the objective is to frustrate landowners. But it is not fine if the objective is to protect endangered species, which requires the willing cooperation of landowners. For example, about 57 percent of the nation's forest lands, home to many species of birds, animals and plants, is in the hands of about 10 million family woodland owners, most holding less than 50 acres. Doesn't it make more sense to encourage these woodland owners to identify and conserve habitat rather than put their property's value at risk for doing so?

Secretary of the Interior Bruce Babbitt admits the problem, but ignores the solution. He has applied a number of creative Band-aids to ESA controversies. But Band-aids are not enough to protect landowners from costly, arbitrary enforcement. The law can be changed to improve the consultation process between landowners and the FWS, to ensure that recovery plans are less cumbersome and costly, and to enhance the role of local authorities in devising and implementing such plans.

It's time to end the rhetoric that has arbitrarily divided Americans into two camps. Let's come together where social and economic needs can be balanced with the goal of species conservation.

'Our Natural and Spiritual Heritage' Is 'Worth Protecting'

The following excerpts are from an interview with Secretary of the Interior Bruce Babbitt, who spoke with staff writer Kenneth Jost on April 5, 1996, in the secretary's office:

Q: Why is it important to protect endangered species?

People give you many responses, but there seems to be a common strain that I hear from the American people: that this is God's creation, and we have an obligation to take care of it. There are many, many more what I would call utilitarian responses, but my experience is that underlying all them is a much more general, powerful, widespread belief that we have an obligation to take care of creation.

Q: Can we afford to try to protect all endangered species?

There is plenty of space in our communities to have robust development, to create jobs. In the long run, protection of the habitat actually increases the economic alternatives for creation of jobs. It's not an I-win-at-your-expense scenario. Everybody wins.

Q: Why did you change enforcement policies after you entered office?

The Endangered Species Act had been administered in a very passive, hands-off, resigned way which abdicated our responsibility to make it work, which allowed these issues to escalate into conflict, drift into litigation. It was all unnecessary. The act itself had lots more possibilities. What it really needed was to have some life and imagination.

Q: Aren't we losing species today and going to continue losing species at an accelerated rate?

What the scientists are saying is that if current trends continue, we're going to have a lot of problems. You can conclude from that two things. One, just forget about it. That's what the people who want to abolish the act are saying: This stuff just isn't worth protecting. I politely and vigorously disagree. It is worth protecting. It is part of our natural and spiritual heritage. And we can do it. And I believe the American people want it done.

Continued from p. 352

that can ease the restrictions on private activities.

The number of such plans approved by Fish and Wildlife has jumped dramatically during the Clinton administration. Only 14 such plans were approved from 1983 through 1992, according to an FWS fact-sheet. The Clinton administration signed off on almost double that number — 27 — in its first two years in office; and it approved 90 plans last year.

The Balcones Canyonlands Conservation Plan, set to be approved on May 2, typifies the new approach. It sets aside large blocks of biologically valuable habitat while also freeing more than twice as much land for development. Besides the golden-cheeked warbler, the plan will also protect a second endangered migratory bird — the black-capped vireo — and a half-dozen endangered insects and spiders.

A similar but more ambitious habitat conservation plan is now being negotiated in Southern California in a process involving federal, state and local officials; environmental organizations; and developers and other property owners.[38] The so-called Natural Communities Conservation Planning (NCCP) marked an important milestone this month when Orange County officials gave their final approval to setting aside a 39,000-acre reserve in the county's central and coastal region. Michael O'Connell, director of the NCCP for the Nature Conservancy, says the San Diego City Council will begin on April 23 to consider a plan for a 150,000-acre reserve, while Orange County officials will turn next to plans for a 40,000-acre reserve in the southern part of the county.

As in Texas, the Southern California plan was launched to protect an endangered bird: the California gnatcatcher. But the plan now aims at preserving a delicate desert ecosystem that is home to dozens of rare bird, animal, insect and plant species. The negotiations have been complex and difficult, but conservation groups have won agreements to limit development on some land while developers are looking ahead to the promise of being freed from Endangered Species Act restrictions elsewhere. For his part, Babbitt is bullish about the prospects for a final agreement. "It's moving along in a remarkable way," he says.

Foes Dig In

Babbitt's efforts to defuse the controversies over the Endangered Species Act have failed to win over the strongest critics of the law. When the House Resources Committee met last month to hear from property owners critical of the law, chairman Young called outright for its repeal.

"The biggest mistake I made was in not repealing this bill," Young declared. "And I voted for the damn thing."

Witnesses at the March 20 hearing included an Austin retiree, Margaret Rector, who owns a 15-acre tract outside the city. She told the panel she cannot sell the property because of what she called "the bird situation." A second witness, Cindy Domenigoni of Riverside County, Calif., blamed the act for the loss of her home during the

October 1993 brushfire. Domenigoni claimed that the fire would not have spread to her home if she had been allowed to plow under flammable vegetation from land that had been declared protected habitat for the endangered desert kangaroo rat.

Both stories have been widely published thanks to a vigorous media campaign by critics, including the property rights-oriented Grassroots ESA Coalition, which hosted a news conference for Rector, Domenigoni and others before the committee hearing. But independent inquiries cast doubt on both tales. The General Accounting Office (GAO) published a report in July 1994 that found no basis for blaming the loss of Domenigoni's home or other houses on the restrictions on plowing. [39] And *The Dallas Morning News* reported on the day of the committee hearing that a local developer, Darwin Macon, had offered to buy Rector's property for at least $300,000. [40]

Young told both witnesses, however, that their testimony indicated the real threat to the Endangered Species Act comes from overenforcement by an "overbearing" agency. "No act will survive if it doesn't have the support of the people," Young said. "And now people are fed up."

Babbitt insists that the public still supports the act and that the Capitol Hill debate about the law is fueled by "ideologues and radicals who are out to destroy" it. "This has turned into an abstract theological debate," Babbitt says. "The debate about legislation has no relation to reality at all." ■

OUTLOOK

'No Guarantees'

At the Eastern Neck Island National Wildlife Refuge on Maryland's Chesapeake Bay, biologists are trying to update their count of the endangered Delmarva fox squirrel. About twice the size of the common gray squirrel, the once common Delmarva is found only in several counties in the so-called Delmarva (Delaware, Maryland, Virginia) peninsula.

But the creature proved elusive on a blustery day in mid-March, and a visiting reporter had to be content with viewing the mounted specimen at refuge headquarters.

Refuge Manager Martin Kaehny was apologetic but philosophical. "That's the thing about wildlife," Kaehny said. "There are no guarantees."

So it is with the Endangered Species Act, supporters say. They recognize that it cannot alone guarantee the survival of the hundreds of animal and plant species now classified as endangered or threatened or the larger number labeled "of potential concern." The law is only a last-gasp rescue tool. It does not reverse the underlying threats to biological diversity: human population increases, overexploitation, loss of habitat, pollution and so forth.

"The driving issue is the rate of population increase and the way in which we consume resources to sustain the human population," says Clegg at the University of California. "There is no question that the conflicts associated with sustaining that kind of population will have an impact on the environment and the biological resources that we consider important."

A few critics of the law deny its underlying premise that plant and animal species are worthy of protection at all. "There are a lot of people [in the property-rights movement] who don't really care about wildlife," says Smith of the Competitive Enterprise Institute. Others — like Smith himself — say the goal is worthwhile, but the costs have become too great. "They're saying wildlife is getting in the way of my children," Smith says, "and when I have to choose between wildlife and children, I pick my children."

Supporters of the law insist the conflict between protecting endangered species and preserving jobs and development is exaggerated. But they have failed to win over the critics, who have succeeded in sowing a widespread public perception that the law has gone too far. The result in Congress is a stalemate between lawmakers who seek sweeping changes in the act and others who want to keep it as is or, at least, preserve its essential features.

Whatever happens to reauthorization legislation, the stalemate appears to doom any expansion of federal protection for endangered species in the near future. Congress voted to cut proposed FWS funding for endangered species by one-fourth last fall. President Clinton vetoed the bill, but the budget cut remained in interim funding bills negotiated by Republican leaders and the White House. And supporters of the law failed last month to lift the moratorium on new listings of endangered or threatened species that Congress voted a year ago.

The Senate on March 13 voted 49-51 against a parliamentary move aimed at repealing the moratorium. Instead, it adopted a provision aimed at allowing some "emergency" listings of species. That provision still has to be reconciled with a House-passed bill that retains the existing ban on any new listings.

Critics of the law hailed the Senate vote. The Endangered Species Coordinating Council said the vote would help ensure "a thorough review [of the law] before expending coverage . . . to hundreds of . . . species." But Babbitt opposes the moratorium, saying that it "is significantly impairing our ability to manage the act."

Despite the controversies, Babbitt still seems optimistic about the law's future. He talks with animation about the listed species that "might be extinct today" if not for the Endangered Species Act. Yes, he acknowledges,

FOR MORE INFORMATION

Competitive Enterprise Institute, 1001 Connecticut Ave. N.W., Suite 1250, Washington, D.C. 20036; (202) 331-1010. This free market-oriented think tank has been a leading critic of endangered species policies.

Defenders of Wildlife, 1101 14th St. N.W., Washington, D.C. 20005; (202) 682-9400. Defenders is one of many wildlife and conservation groups lobbying against so-called reform of the Endangered Species Act.

Endangered Species Coordinating Council, 1111 19th St. N.W., Suite 800, Washington, D.C. 20036; (202) 453-2700. This timber industry-led coalition has been a major lobbying force behind rewriting the Endangered Species Act.

Environmental Defense Fund, 1875 Connecticut Ave. N.W., 10th floor, Washington, D.C. 20009; (202) 387-3500. The EDF has been playing an influential role in seeking a compromise on endangered species legislation.

National Wildlife Federation, 1400 16th St. N.W., Washington, D.C. 20036; (202) 797-6800. The education-oriented NWF is among the conservation groups opposing efforts to rewrite the Endangered Species Act.

Nature Conservancy, 1815 Lynn St., Alexandria, Va. 22209; (703) 841-5300. The Nature Conservancy helped negotiate the habitat conservation plans in Austin, Texas, and Southern California, and has also been involved in forging a compromise on rewriting the Endangered Species Act.

some scientists are predicting that the rate of extinctions will increase. But he does not share their pessimism.

"I'm not as gloomy as a lot of scientists," Babbitt says, "because I have an essentially positive view of our ability to make this act work and to find a balance on the landscape, once people are engaged with this and work toward the possibilities." ■

Notes

[1] For background, see "Property Rights," *The CQ Researcher,* June 16, 1995, pp. 513-536.

[2] For background, see "Endangered Species," *The CQ Researcher,* June 21, 1991, pp. 393-420, and "Environmental Movement at 25," *The CQ Researcher,* March 31, 1995, pp. 283-306.

[3] Edward O. Wilson, *The Diversity of Life* (1993), p. 4.

[4] Stephen Kellert, *The Value of Life: Biological Diversity and Human Society* (1996), pp. 9-34.

[5] Wilson, *op. cit.,* pp. 283-287.

[6] Charles C. Mann and Mark L. Plummer, *Noah's Choice: The Future of Endangered Species* (1995).

[7] Thomas M. Power, ed., *Economic Well-Being and Environmental Protection in the Pacific Northwest,* December 1995, p. 12. For background, see "Saving the Forests," *The CQ Researcher,* Sept. 20, 1991, pp. 681-704; "Jobs vs. Environment," *The CQ Researcher,* May 15, 1992, pp. 409-432; and "Public Land Policy," *The CQ Researcher,* June 17, 1994, pp. 542-565.

[8] Stephen M. Meyer, "Endangered Species Listings and State Economic Performance," Massachusetts Institute of Technology Project on Environmental Politics and Policy, March 1995.

[9] Mann and Plummer, *op. cit.,* pp. 245-247.

[10] U.S. Department of the Interior, Fish and Wildlife Service, "Recovery Program: Endangered and Threatened Species — 1994," October 1995.

[11] Mann and Plummer, *loc. cit.*

[12] National Research Council, *op. cit.,* pp. 194-195.

[13] The Competitive Enterprise Institute provided a transcript of the closed Nov. 3, 1994, session.

[14] Keystone Center, "The Keystone Dialogue on Incentives for Private Landowners to Protect Endangered Species," July 25, 1995.

[15] See *Congressional Quarterly Weekly Report,* Oct. 14, 1995, pp. 3136-3137.

[16] For background on extinctions, see Wilson, *op. cit.,* pp. 24-32, 183-211; Mann and Plummer, *op. cit.,* pp. 28-52.

[17] See M.J. Benton, "Diversification and Extinction in the History of Life," *Science,* Vol. 268, April 7, 1995, pp. 52-58.

[18] Mann and Plummer, *op. cit.,* p. 14.

[19] *Ibid.,* pp. 46-47.

[20] Stuart L. Pimm et al., "The Future of Biodiversity," *Science,* July 21, 1995, pp. 347-350.

[21] Wilson, *op. cit.,* pp. 244-245.

[22] See Charles Bergman, *Wild Echoes: Encounters With the Most Endangered Animals in North America* (1990), pp. 249-265.

[23] Legislative summaries are drawn in part from Michael J. Bean, *The Evolution of National Wildlife Law* (1983). For a summary of federal wildlife legislation, see National Research Council, *op. cit.,* pp. 18-21.

[24] See Bergman, *loc. cit.*

[25] See Mann and Plummer, *op. cit.,* pp. 115-119, 149-153.

[26] Bean, *op. cit.,* p. 321.

[27] For legislative history, see Bean, *op. cit.,* 329-331; Mann and Plummer, *op. cit.,* pp. 155-160; *CQ Almanac,* 1973, pp. 670-673.

[28] Mann and Plummer, *op. cit.,* pp. 161-164.

[29] See *Ibid.,* pp. 164-175.

[30] For background, see Rocky Barker, *Saving All the Parts: Reconciling Economics and the Endangered Species Act* (1993), pp. 109-117; Alston Chase, *In a Dark Wood: The Fight Over Forests and the Rising Tyranny of Ecology* (1995), pp. 131-140, 244-256, 372-375; *Time,* June 25, 1990, p. 56.

[31] See Kenneth Jost, *The Supreme Court Yearbook, 1994-1995,* pp. 60-63.

[32] See *The Washington Post,* May 25, 1995, p. A3.

[33] Weston Kosova, "Ways to Skin the Act," *Audubon,* January/February 1996, pp. 43-45.

[34] See *Los Angeles Times,* Nov. 20, 1995, p. A3. For background on the California condor, see Peter Matthiessen, *Wildlife in America* (1987), pp. 261-265.

[35] See *The Washington Post,* Jan. 13, 1996, p. A3 (gray wolves); July 1, 1995, p. A1 (peregrine falcon).

[36] Timothy W. Tear et al., "Status and Prospects for Success of the Endangered Species Act: A Look at Recovery Plans," *Science,* Nov. 12, 1993, pp. 976-977.

[37] Department of the Interior, *op. cit.,* p. 12. The General Accounting Office also noted the backlog of undone recovery plans in a 1992 report. See General Accounting Office, "Endangered Species Act: Types and Numbers of Implementing Actions," May 1992, pp. 33-36.

[38] See *The New York Times,* Feb. 27, 1996, p. C1.

[39] U.S. General Accounting Office, "Endangered Species Act: Impact of Species Protection Efforts on the 1993 California Fire," July 8, 1994.

[40] *The Dallas Morning News,* March 20, 1996, p. 1A.

Bibliography

Selected Sources Used

Books

Bean, Michael J., *The Evolution of National Wildlife Law,* Praeger, 1983 [revised and expanded edition].

Bean, director of wildlife policy for the Environmental Defense Fund, traces the development of U.S. wildlife law from its roots in Roman and English law through the enactment and first decade of the Endangered Species Act. The book includes tables of court cases, federal statutes, international agreements and secondary sources.

Bergman, Charles, *Wild Echoes: Encounters With the Most Endangered Animals in North America,* McGraw-Hill, 1990.

Bergman, an English professor at Pacific Lutheran University and author of articles in several naturalist magazines, describes his encounters with such endangered animals as the gray wolf, the dusky seaside sparrow, the Florida panther and the manatee. The book includes a partial listing of extinctions in the United States since 1750.

Kellert, Stephen R., *The Value of Life: Biological Diversity and Human Society,* Island Press, 1996.

Kellert, a professor at Yale's School of Forestry and Environmental Studies, identifies nine basic values that underlie humanity's interest in preserving biodiversity.

Mann, Charles C., and Mark L. Plummer, *Noah's Choice: The Future of Endangered Species,* Knopf, 1995.

In a critical overview of legal efforts to protect endangered species, the authors acknowledge the importance of biodiversity but argue that it is impossible to protect all forms of plant and animal life. Mann is a contributing editor for *Science* and *The Atlantic Monthly;* Plummer is a senior fellow at the Discovery Institute in Seattle.

Matthiessen, Peter, *Wildlife in America*, Viking, 1987 [rev. ed.].

Matthiessen, a naturalist-explorer and novelist, wrote the first edition of this history of American wildlife in 1959. The updated edition includes a list of rare, declining and extinct species; a chronology of wildlife legislation from 1616 through the 1980s; detailed reference notes; and a six-page bibliography.

Simon, Noel, in association with the World Conservation Monitoring Centre, *Nature in Danger: Threatened Habitats and Species,* Oxford, 1996.

This well-illustrated volume gives a broad survey of ecologically threatened areas, organized by type of habitat, with a description of the flora and fauna of each location and suggestions on ways to counter ecological damage. Simon is former deputy director of the National Park of Kenya.

Wilson, Edward O., *The Diversity of Life*, Harvard University Press, 1992.

Wilson, an entomologist at Harvard University, provides a scientific overview of the origins and importance of "biological diversity" and a literate and impassioned plea to protect it from human activity. The book includes detailed source notes and a useful 17-page glossary.

Reports and Studies

Fitzgerald, Sarah, *International Wildlife Trade: Whose Business Is It?* World Wildlife Fund, 1989.

This book-length report explores a variety of issues surrounding international trade in wildlife and wildlife products, calling for stronger controls on poaching and smuggling as well as new ways to manage wildlife trade to enhance the environment and ensure species' long-term survival.

Lambert, Thomas, and Robert J. Smith, "The Endangered Species Act: Time for a Change," Center for the Study of American Business, Washington University, March 1994.

The authors of this 64-page monograph strongly argue that the Endangered Species Act has failed to accomplish its goals and should be changed to include cost-benefit analyses and use positive instead of negative incentives.

National Research Council, *Science and the Endangered Species Act,* May 1995.

This book-length report by a committee of 17 experts generally defends the scientific basis of the Endangered Species Act and calls for strengthening the law's protection of plant and wildlife habitat. The text of the Endangered Species Act is included as an appendix.

U.S. Department of the Interior, Fish and Wildlife Service, "Recovery Program: Endangered and Threatened Species — 1994," October 1995.

This illustrated 64-page report includes a narrative overview of the endangered species program along with a table showing the status of each of the species listed as endangered or threatened.

U.S. Department of the Interior, National Biological Service, *Our Living Resources: A Report to the Nation on the Distribution, Abundance, and Health of U.S. Plants, Animals, and Ecosystems,* 1995.

This book-length report by the Interior Department's newly created biological science arm provides an overview and detailed statistics on the health of plant and animal life in the U.S.

The Next Step

Additional information from UMI's Newspaper & Periodical Abstracts database

Endangered Species Act

Bonnicksen, Thomas M., "Protect endangered species with law that's fair," *Houston Chronicle,* Dec. 4, 1995, p. A19.
Bonnicksen asserts that as Congress takes up reauthorization of the Endangered Species Act, it needs to consider a new approach to maintain sensitive areas that protects job and property rights.

Cushman, John H. Jr., "House G.O.P. leaders propose to ease Endangered Species Act," *The New York Times,* Sept. 8, 1995, p. A20.
House Republican leaders proposed to scale back the Endangered Species Act by making it voluntary, not mandatory, for private landowners to conserve the habitat of creatures threatened with extinction. The bill would also require the government to compensate landowners if their efforts resulted in any significant reduction in land values.

Dawson, Bill, "State politics over Endangered Species Act gets more tangled," *Houston Chronicle,* June 3, 1995, p. A35.
Texas' already-tangled politics over endangered species got a little more complicated at a gathering arranged by prominent Houston conservation leader Terry Hershey. Hershey said she held the meeting so she and other conservationists could hear state wildlife officials describe proposals for revising the federal Endangered Species Act.

McClure, James A., "Fine-tune Endangered Species Act," *Detroit News & Free Press,* Aug. 1, 1995, p. A6.
In a letter to the editor, James A. McClure of the National Endangered Species Act Reform Coalition offer solutions to major problems with the Endangered Species Act.

Puga, Ana, "Two justices clash on endangered species," *Boston Globe,* April 18, 1995, p. 10.
Supreme Court Justices Antonin Scalia and Stephen G. Breyer clashed over how far the government can go to protect rare wildlife on private property.

Ridenour, David A., "To save wildlife, scrap the Endangered Species Act," *The Wall Street Journal,* July 18, 1995, p. A18.
Ridenour, vice president of the conservative National Center for Public Policy Research, says that Congress is now in the process of revising the Endangered Species Act, but in order to devise a species plan that will work lawmakers must first admit that the ESA has failed.

Salem, D. Jamila, "Stronger endangered species law urged," *The Los Angeles Times,* Feb. 1, 1996, p. A12.
Joining with environmentalists in an unusual political alliance, a coalition of evangelical Christians on Jan. 31, 1996, launched a campaign to keep Republicans in Congress from weakening the Endangered Species Act.

Steinfels, Peter, "Evangelical group defends laws protecting endangered species as a modern Noah's ark," *The New York Times,* Jan. 31, 1996, A12.
The Evangelical Environmental Network is announcing a nationwide drive to defend the Endangered Species Act against efforts in Congress to weaken it. The group calls the law "the Noah's ark of our day."

Stevens, William K., "Science Times: Future of Endangered Species Act in doubt as law is debated," *The New York Times,* May 16, 1995, p. C4.
The Endangered Species Act, hailed by its supporters as the strongest conservation law in the world, has come under heavy criticism in Congress, and its future is in doubt.

Watkins, T. H., "What's wrong with the Endangered Species Act? Not much-and here's why:" *Audubon,* January 1996, pp. 36-41.
Watkins, editor of *Wilderness* magazine, argues that few laws have come under such systematic and inflamed attack as the Endangered Species Act of 1973.

"A win for endangered species," *Chicago Tribune,* July 10, 1995, p. 10.
An editorial praises the U.S. Supreme Court's decision to uphold the full scope of the Endangered Species Act, and argues against proposed legislation in Congress that would effectively dismantle the law.

Habitat Conservation Plans

Boucher, Norman, "Species of the sprawl," *Wilderness,* summer 1995, pp. 10-24.
An unlikely alliance of planners, biologists, bureaucrats and developers struggles to maintain a fragile compromise between the protocols of habitat conservation and the etiology of growth on California's southern shore.

Mann, Charles C., "Filling in Florida's gaps: Species protection done right?" *Science,* July 21, 1995, pp. 318-320.
The effort to save the Pinhook Swamp and turn it into a 250,000-hectare wilderness reserve has been partially

accomplished, with 50 percent of the swamp purchased.

Stevens, William K., "Salvation at Hand for a California Landscape," *The New York Times,* Feb. 27, 1996, p. C1.
An ambitious effort to reconcile urban development with protecting the remaining wild landscape between Los Angeles and Mexico is approaching a make-or-break point. The Natural Communities Conservation Planning (NCCP) is nearing agreement on establishing nature preserves in Orange and San Diego counties to protect dozens of plant and animal species while freeing other land for development.

International Issues

Farley, Dixie, "Smuggled frog legs destroyed," *FDA Consumer,* December 1995, pp. 31-32.
U.S. Customs Service agents examining three import shipments from Bangladesh labeled as shrimp found the cartons contained frog legs instead. These frog legs were later identified as being from the endangered species *Rana tigerina* and were seized and destroyed.

Heimert, Andrew J., "How the elephant lost his tusks," *Yale Law Journal,* April 1995.
Two alternative strategies that African nations have used to halt the decline of elephant populations are examined. It is argued that the current international ban on ivory trade harms the conservation program in which some animals are culled in order to provide sufficient habitat and protection for the remaining ones.

"Illegal hunting: Kill the butterfly," *The Economist,* April 8, 1995, pp. 28-29.
The international poaching business continues to flourish, bringing in almost $3 billion in 1995. The U.S. National Park Service believes about 100 species have been poached in the United States' 367 parks.

White, Don, "DNA testing exposes whale trade," *Earth Island Journal,* summer 1995, pp. 6-7.
EarthTrust used DNA sampling techniques to uncover Japanese duplicity in the illegal global trade in whale meat. Japan keeps two sets of books on the number and kinds of whales it has hunted, White writes.

Wildlife Issues

Bass, Rick, "The woodland caribou: They're still out there," *Audubon,* May 1995, pp. 76-84.
Woodland caribou once covered the northern Rocky Mountain region in substantial numbers. Today, the few remaining woodland caribou in the Lower 48 are holding on for dear life.

Bestul, Scott, "Wolves fight the odds in Wisconsin," *E: The Environmental Magazine,* March 1995, pp. 16-17.
Adrian Wydeven is a timber wolf biologist for Wisconsin's Department of Natural Resources, and he and his colleagues trap, radio collar and monitor wolves in remote areas of northwestern Wisconsin. The wolf population is discussed.

Snow, Wayne, "Meeting to focus on agency's decision to protect mollusks as endangered species," *Atlanta Constitution,* Jan. 5, 1995, p. X2.
The U.S. Fish and Wildlife Service was to conduct an informational meeting to explain its decision to seek endangered species status for eight species of freshwater mollusks. That decision had been roundly criticized by developers in Georgia, Florida and Alabama.

Plant Life

Bronaugh, Whit, Emily Knack and Rick Crouse, "Champions on the brink," *American Forests,* winter 1996, pp. 16-19.
Four trees are officially endangered, while others face a doubtful future. Efforts to save these four tree varieties are described.

Recovery Plans

Askins, Renee, "Releasing wolves from symbolism," *Harper's,* April 1995, pp. 15-17.
The reintroduction of wolves to Yellowstone National Park and the central Idaho wilderness is discussed during testimony at a House Committee on Resources. Askins works for the Wolf Fund, an organization that is working for the return of wolves to Yellowstone.

Richardson, Valerie, "Decrying wolves," *National Review,* March 20, 1995, pp. 28-30.
Despite the destruction that wolves cause to Western ranchers, the U.S. Fish and Wildlife Service is going ahead with its wolf-reintroduction program in Idaho and Yellowstone National Park.

Science and Research

Murphy, Dennis D., "An overview of the National Academy of Sciences report: Science and the Endangered Species Act," *Endangered Species UPDATE,* September 1995, pp. 8-10.
Murphy, a biologist at Stanford University and member of a National Academy of Sciences panel that reviewed the implementation of the Endangered Species Act, discusses the panel's report.

Pennisi, Elizabeth, "Report backs Endangered Species Act," *Science,* May 26, 1995, p. 1124.
The National Academy of Sciences has come out in support of the Endangered Species Act. The group says the law's approach to protecting endangered species is scientifically sound.

Back Issues

Great Research on Current Issues Starts Right Here...Recent topics covered by The CQ Researcher are listed below. Before May 1991, reports were published under the name of Editorial Research Reports.

OCTOBER 1994
Historic Preservation
Religion and Politics
Arts Funding
Economic Sanctions

NOVEMBER 1994
Sex on Campus
Blood Supply Safety
Testing Term Limits
Religion in America

DECEMBER 1994
Farm Policy
Arms Sales
Earthquake Research
The Future of Television

JANUARY 1995
Treating Addiction
Child Custody and Support
Parents and Schools
Non-Proliferation Treaty at 25

FEBRUARY 1995
Cracking Down on Immigration
The Business of Sports
Reinventing Government
Housing Discrimination

MARCH 1995
Death Penalty Debate
Primary Care
Democracy in Africa
Environmental Movement at 25

APRIL 1995
Abortion Clinic Protests
Dieting and Health
Combating AIDS
Rethinking Affirmative Action

MAY 1995
Assisted Suicide Controversy
Overhauling Social Security
Learning to Read
Mandatory Sentencing

JUNE 1995
Combating Infectious Disease
Property Rights
Repetitive Stress Injuries
Regulating the Internet

JULY 1995
War Crimes
Highway Safety
Combating Terrorism
Preventing Teen Drug Use

AUGUST 1995
Job Stress
Organ Transplants
United Nations at 50
Advances in Cancer Research

SEPTEMBER 1995
Catholic Church in the U.S.
Northern Ireland Cease-Fire
High School Sports
Teaching History

OCTOBER 1995
Quebec's Future
Revitalizing the Cities
Networking the Classroom
Indoor Air Pollution

NOVEMBER 1995
The Working Poor
The Jury System
Sex, Violence and the Media
Police Misconduct

DECEMBER 1995
Teens and Tobacco
Gene Therapy's Future
Global Water Shortages
Third-Party Prospects

JANUARY 1996
Emergency Medicine
Punishing Sex Offenders
Bilingual Education
Helping the Homeless

FEBRUARY 1996
Reforming the CIA
Campaign Finance Reform
Academic Politics
Getting Into College

MARCH 1996
The British Monarchy
Preventing Juvenile Crime
Tax Reform
Pursuing the Paranormal

APRIL 1996
Centennial Olympic Games
Managed Care

Back issues are available for $5.00 (subscribers) or $8.00 (non-subscribers). Quantity discounts apply to orders over ten. To order, call Congressional Quarterly Customer Service at (202) 887-8621.

Binders are available for $18.00. To order call 1-800-638-1710. Please refer to stock number 648.

Future Topics

- ***Changing Military Culture***
- ***Russia's Political Future***
- ***Marriage and Divorce***

THE CQ Researcher

PUBLISHED BY CONGRESSIONAL QUARTERLY INC.

New Military Culture

Do women, blacks and homosexuals get fair treatment?

In the last quarter-century, the number of African-Americans and women in the armed forces has skyrocketed. There are more black officers than ever; women now hold scores of military jobs once reserved for men; and President Clinton's "Don't Ask, Don't Tell" policy has given homosexuals official sanction to serve in the military. The changes have subjected the military to what have been called the most significant cultural shocks since President Harry Truman desegregated the military in 1948. The role changes have been accompanied by reports of extremist activity on military bases, a surge in sexual harassment cases and a fierce battle over the right of homosexuals to serve. Some observers are asking whether the military is dealing fairly with minorities, women and gays.

INSIDE THIS ISSUE

April 26, 1996 • Volume 6, No. 16 • Pages 361-384

Formerly Editorial Research Reports

New Military Culture

April 26, 1996
Volume 6, No. 16

Editor
Sandra Stencel

Managing Editor
Thomas J. Colin

Associate Editors
Sarah M. Magner
Richard L. Worsnop

Staff Writers
Charles S. Clark
Mary H. Cooper
Craig Donegan
Kenneth Jost

Editorial Assistant
Tonya Harris

Published By
Congressional Quarterly Inc.

Chairman
Andrew Barnes

Vice Chairman
Andrew P. Corty

Editor and Publisher
Neil Skene

Executive Editor
Robert W. Merry

Associate Publisher
Edward S. Hauck

The CQ Researcher (ISSN 1056-2036). Formerly Editorial Research Reports. Published weekly (48 times per year, not printed March 1, May 31, Aug. 30, Nov. 29) by Congressional Quarterly Inc., 1414 22nd St., N.W., Washington, D.C. 20037. Annual subscription rate for libraries, businesses and government is $319. Additional rates furnished upon request. Second-class postage paid at Washington, D.C. POSTMASTER: Send address changes to The CQ Researcher, 1414 22nd St., N.W., Washington, D.C. 20037.

Cover: Members of the U.S. Navy Honor Guard at a Pentagon ceremony. (Department of Defense/Helene C. Stikkel)

New Military Culture

BY CRAIG DONEGAN

THE ISSUES

Jim Burmeister seemed to blame blacks for his disappointments. His upcoming murder trial may reveal what motivated him. This much police know: His dream of becoming a paratrooper with the famed 82nd Airborne Division at Fort Bragg quickly faded. Grounded by an injury, ridiculed by other recruits, Burmeister drifted into a small group of racist, neo-Nazi skinheads at the huge base in Fayetteville, N.C. [1]

Group members tacked up swastikas in their barracks rooms and sewed Nazi symbols on their civilian jackets. At least one sported a spiderweb tattoo, supposedly showing he had killed an African-American or a homosexual.

Last Dec. 6, according to authorities, Burmeister announced it was time to earn a spiderweb of his own. Shortly after midnight, cruising on an unpaved Fayetteville street, Burmeister and two buddies spotted a hapless African-American couple out for a stroll. After passing Jackie Burden, 27, and Michael James, 36, the trio turned around and cruised by again. Burmeister and Pvt. Malcolm Wright got out of the car, police say.

Then, Burmeister allegedly shot James twice at point-blank range. Burden ran, but Burmeister shot her in the back and then three times in the head. Within 24 hours, the three soldiers had been arrested and charged with murder.

The shootings raised an obvious question about the extent of extremism in the armed forces. But there was a deeper question: Is the extremism somehow related to the sweeping changes that have transformed the military in recent times?

In the last quarter-century, the number of African-Americans and women in the armed forces has skyrocketed. Indeed, there are more black officers than ever; women now hold scores of military jobs once reserved for men; and President Clinton's "Don't Ask, Don't Tell" policy has given homosexuals official sanction to serve in the armed forces. [2]

Some observers say the changes have subjected the armed forces to the most significant cultural shocks since President Harry S Truman ordered the armed forces to desegregate in 1948. And they are asking whether the military is up to the task of dealing fairly with minorities, women and homosexuals.

In response to the Fayetteville murders, Secretary of the Army Togo D. West Jr. ordered an investigation into possible extremist activities on Army bases around the world. West reported on March 21 that the task force had surveyed 28 representative bases and found minimal extremist activity. Moreover, the task force reported, most soldiers think extremism is incompatible with military service and that it lowers morale and should not be permitted.

"Targeting of active-duty Army soldiers [by extremist organizations] is simply not happening in any significant way," West said. Other observers agree that there are few extremists in the ranks.

"I don't think it's any worse in the military than with any other group in society," says Joe T. Roy, director of the Militia Task Force for the Southern Poverty Law Center in Montgomery, Ala. "The issue is, what will be the military's response to this problem."

West has ordered the Army to clarify and strengthen rules that govern participation in extremist organizations. * He also has said the Army will revise regulations to make it easier for officers to keep tabs on off-duty soldiers.

"[Most soldiers] are clear on the undesirability of extremism," West said, "but they're not so clear . . . on the Army's attitude about it."

To prevent extremists from joining the military, West said the Army will explore possible screening procedures. We need to "better inform ourselves as to whether we're bringing in an extremist — whether there is something we should know that we should be screening out," he said.

The North Carolina chapter of the National Association for the Advancement of Colored People (NAACP), which conducted its own probe of North Carolina military bases in the wake of the shootings, welcomed West's response. **

"We were comforted that we did not find successful organizing activity by racists on bases, but we got a very strong sense that they would like to," says chapter President Kelly Alexander.

Since the murders, Fort Bragg officials have counseled, disciplined or denied re-enlistment to at least 22

* The Army prohibits "active" participation in extremist organizations, such as fundraising, recruiting and training. "Passive" participation is permitted, such as receiving literature and wearing symbols of organizations.

** The Army initially blocked the NAACP from questioning soldiers at Fort Bragg, but Secretary West helped arrange a meeting with soldiers in late March.

Attitudes About Gays and Women

Asked of enlisted personnel:
Should the ban on homosexuals in the armed forces be lifted?

	Approve	Don't know	Disapprove
Servicemen	16%	8%	76%
Servicewomen	35%	10%	55%

Asked of the general public:
How do you feel about admitting homosexuals into the military?

Admit those who do NOT disclose their sexuality?

Admit those who DO disclose their homosexuality?

Asked of the general public:
Women should be assigned military combat roles just like men.

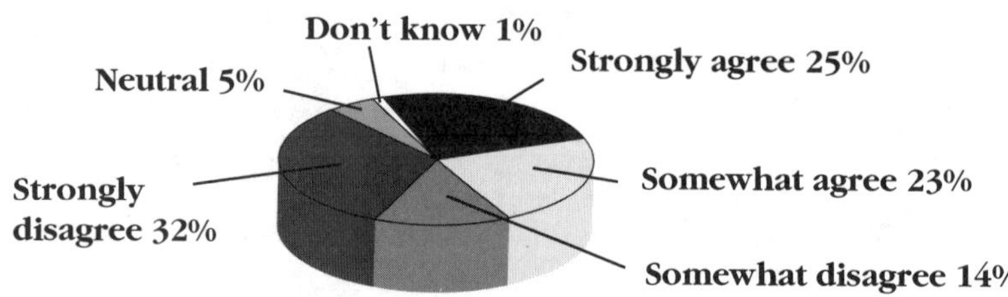

Sources: Los Angeles Times *Survey, February 1993, in* Gays and Lesbians in the Military, *1994 (top); ABC News Poll, May 25, 1993 (center); Family Research Council, September 1993 (bottom)*

skinheads, according to the Army. But to some observers, the presence of even a few extremists in the Army is disturbing for an institution that began integrating a half-century ago.

That legacy began in the early 1940s, when civil rights leaders demanded an end to segregated Army units. As the Army took its first halting steps toward becoming colorblind, other reformers began seeking equality for women and homosexuals.

Military sociologist Charles Moskos of Northwestern University contends that the need for military effectiveness, not social reform, has created equal opportunities for African-Americans in the armed forces. "Overlooking this fact," he writes, "political leaders and scholars have come to think of the military as a social laboratory, in which charged debates over gender roles and homosexuality and national service can not only be addressed but possibly resolved." [3]

In today's military, says Carolyn V. Prevatte, executive director of the Defense Advisory Committee on Women in the Services (DACOWITS), women face many of the same obstacles that blacks confronted during the 1970s, when racial disturbances broke out throughout the armed services. At that time, the military had been racially integrated for nearly 25 years. Today, the integration of women into the military is just reaching its 25th anniversary.

In some ways, however, women have yet to attain the acceptance blacks had a quarter-century ago. It is still acceptable in some military quarters for men to openly question whether women should even be allowed in the armed forces, Prevatte says. "This kind of thing affects the work environment," she adds. "It makes women feel that their male coworkers don't want them there. We have to get beyond that."

Some observers had expected the Persian Gulf War with Iraq to get women over that hurdle, especially after the

Department of Defense (DOD) concluded that "Women performed admirably and without substantial friction or special consideration." [4]

But women are still struggling, says Juanita Firestone, a sociologist at the University of Texas, San Antonio. "Letting women fly or be on ships was only a small step toward equality," she says. "But a lot of negative discussion followed those changes, particularly about women who were said to have gotten pregnant to avoid the war." Until women are welcomed in all military jobs, including ground combat, she says, they will remain second-class citizens in a male-dominated military culture. (*See polls, p. 364.*)

But according to Moskos, "most enlisted women don't want to go into combat." In the all-volunteer military, in fact, few recruits seek combat roles. Women, in particular, join for the education and job-training benefits, the travel or "to avoid marrying a jerk," Moskos says. Most of them have strong ties to America's blue-collar culture. "They're coming out of more traditionalist roles," Moskos says, "and they don't follow the feminist agenda."

But that does not mean they accept sexual harassment, says Firestone. They take harassment seriously because it is one of the clearest symbols of women's inequality in the military. (*See story, p. 370.*)

If sexual harassment bothers military women, it is a nightmare for homosexuals, says Michelle M. Benecke, co-director of the Servicemembers Legal Defense Network (SLDN). This is particularly true, she says, because of how the services enforce the Clinton administration's policy toward homosexuals in the military. Put into effect in 1994, "Don't Ask, Don't Tell" allows homosexuals to serve if they keep their sexual orientation private. * But Benecke says the military routinely undermines the policy. According to SLDN, the three services investigated and discharged 21 percent more homosexuals in 1995 than in 1994, many of whom were women. (*See chart, p. 367.*)

"The DOD's own figures show that 21 percent of those discharged under the gay policy are women although they make up only 13 percent of the active forces," says SLDN Co-Director C. Dixon Osburn. "Lesbian baiting is used as a tool to harass women and to root them out of the service," Benecke adds.

"I would say that's intolerable if that's the case," says John Luddy, an aide to Sen. James M. Inhofe, R-Okla., who serves on the Armed Services Committee staff. "Still, we should not force an unnatural situation by putting 18- and 19-year-old women or openly gay soldiers together with heterosexual men in forward, austere environments."

Some observers say, however, that the military could better use the time and money it spends dogging homosexuals to ferret out extremists. "The military has overreacted to the one while not reacting strongly enough to the other," says Lawrence Korb, a senior fellow at the Brookings Institution and former assistant secretary of Defense in the Reagan administration. "We've spent $20 million investigating gays, even calling up mothers and fathers to ask about their children's sexuality. We should be more worried about the signs of fascism, of soldiers with swastikas in their barracks."

As the armed forces struggle with the changing military culture, these are some of the questions being asked:

Are race relations in the military deteriorating?

During the Vietnam War, military race relations were severely strained. Many observers blamed the problem on draft deferments that enabled many middle-class and affluent whites to avoid the service. As a result, the Army had a disproportionate number of poor and minority personnel, and the high casualty rates among blacks during the early years of the war created an explosive situation. [5]

In the late 1970s, after the war ended, the all-volunteer military came into its own, and race relations began a decade of improvement, prompted in part by a new Army initiative on sensitivity training.

"Some of the most recent research data seem to show that race relations have improved," says Mary Katzenstein, an associate professor of government and women's studies at Cornell University. "But it worries me when I hear scholars praise the military for being out in front of all other institutions in trying to eliminate racism, because that invites the military to be too complacent. A lot of observers would agree that there still is a very long way to go."

The NAACP's Alexander shares her concern. "Assumptions about a high degree of conviviality among the races in the military are not warranted when you do a close investigation," he says. During the relatively placid 1980s, he explains, military and civilian leaders were lulled into a false belief that race relations in the military were stable. As a result, little attention was paid to what was going on among the troops. It took the Fayetteville shootings to focus attention on the problems.

Part of the problem, Alexander says, was a poor system for reporting trouble. Even when soldiers reported problems, he says, they often got inadequate responses. "During our investigation, we found that commanders on one base solved the problem of racist graffiti in a bathroom stall by removing the partitions that separate the toilets," he says. "That's treating the symptom. It does nothing to change the graffiti writer's opinions."

The general increase in racial and economic anxiety in civilian life is partly to blame for the tension in the military, Katzenstein says. And continued personnel cutbacks in the armed forces will only lead to more job competition, and more tension, she adds.

"The percentage of racist individu-

* The official name of the policy is "Don't Ask, Don't Tell, Don't Pursue, Don't Harass."

Women and Blacks in the Military, 1973-1996

The percentage of black officers in the armed forces increased from about 1 percent in 1973 to more than 7 percent in 1996; the percentage of women officers tripled. Among enlisted personnel, the number of blacks and women nearly quadrupled. The sharp increases from 1978 to 1983 reflected the new focus on recruiting women and greater interest among blacks in the military as a career.

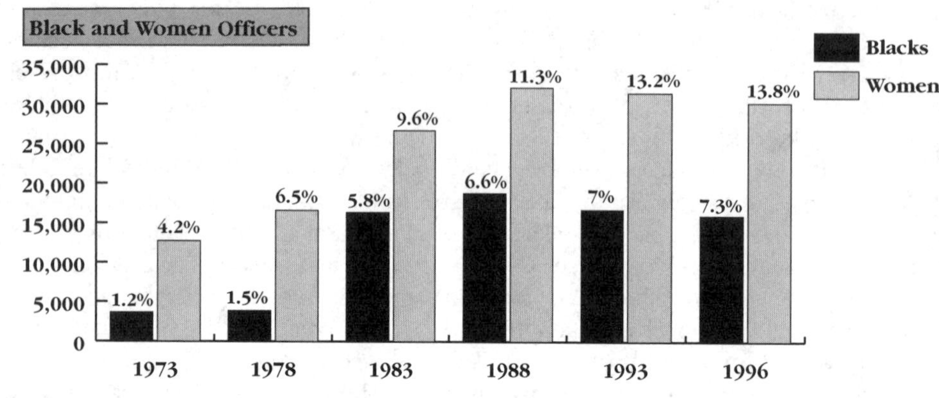

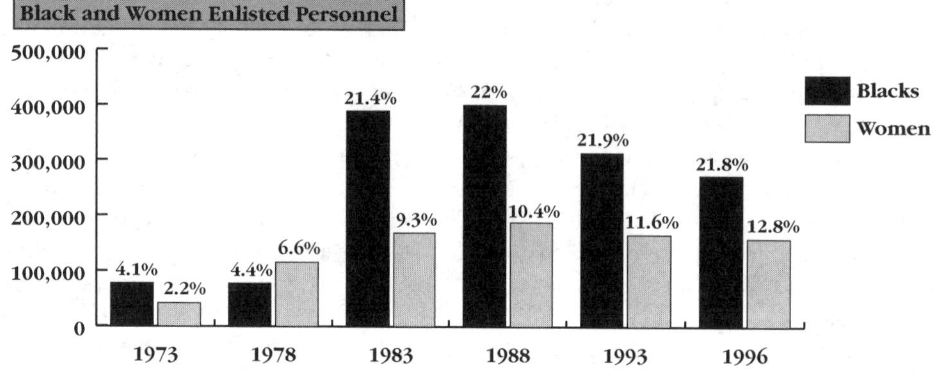

Note: The relative heights of individual bars cannot be compared for different years because the total number of personnel in the armed forces on which the percentages are based varies from year to year.

Source: Department of Defense, Defense Manpower Data Center, Jan. 31, 1996

als in the military has probably been enhanced by a more frustrated ilk of youth enlisting these days," says the poverty law center's Roy. "But overall, the military is no different in this than any other segment of society."

David Segal, a sociologist at the University of Maryland, College Park, argues that the military remains a step ahead of civilian society in matters of race. "There are more opportunities for African-Americans in the military — especially women — than in the civilian economy," he says.

Most women in the middle and higher ranks among non-commissioned officers are black, he says. As a result, the military has remained a magnet for minorities in general, but minority women in particular. "They're seeing the military as a more colorblind and more gender-blind employer than most others that are available to them," he says.

Katzenstein disagrees. "If you look at the data about fairness and promotions, and when you realize how under-represented women of color are in the military academies," she says, "you see there is a lot of unhappiness among African-Americans."

Overall, however, the opportunities for minorities to excel are greater in the military than anywhere else, Moskos says. He notes that recruits compete on a level playing field during basic training; that a white officer's advancement can be stopped dead by any display of racism that shows up on evaluation reports; and that the race-relations courses required by the armed forces seem to reduce racist behavior.

"Obviously, a level playing field is not enough," says Moskos. "You have to bring people up to standards, which the Army does with its U.S. Military Academy Prep School. It's like a 13th year of high school that brings students up to speed in math, reading and English. Blacks who enroll in it do better than the overall white population when they attend West Point."

Rather than setting minority-recruitment quotas, the military uses the Academy Prep School to increase the overall size and quality of its minority recruiting pool, which in turn enables it to recruit more qualified blacks. This approach is seen as limiting the kind of racial tension that quotas have caused in civilian society.

"I think a military that has some racists in it, but is filled with black leaders, is far preferable to a politically correct college campus where any kind of racist expression is prohibited, but where there are no black leaders," Moskos says. "The Army is the only place in American society where white men are routinely bossed around by blacks. Six percent of its generals and 35 percent of its first sergeants are black."

Should the government retain its "Don't Ask, Don't Tell" policy?

Launched in 1994, "Don't Ask, Don't

Tell" was a compromise between President Clinton and military and political leaders who opposed his promise to lift the ban on homosexuals in the military. The policy promises not to ask soldiers about their sexual orientation, not to investigate them for homosexuality without credible cause and to let gays and lesbians serve unless they openly reveal their homosexuality.

Opponents of homosexuals serving in the military say they disrupt discipline, lower morale and unit cohesion and threaten combat readiness. Supporters say they have served honorably in the military over the years and that the opposition is rooted in bigotry. Moreover, they argue, the military should reflect the civilian population, which includes gays.

"'Don't Ask, Don't Tell' is the worst of all possible worlds," says Brookings' Korb. "It says we're making the ban on gay soldiers less stringent when we have not. Under the current policy, they're just as hard on homosexuals as they were under the old."

Robert L. Maginnis, a senior policy analyst at The Family Research Council, argues that the new policy unwisely has neutered the military's traditional anti-gay rules while contradicting the law, which cleared Congress Nov. 17, 1993. "The Clinton policy is an accommodation policy," Maginnis says. "The law is an exclusion law. So what you have is an end-run by the Clinton administration around Congress. And right now Congress lacks the will to make the White House enforce the law."

As far as Cornell's Katzenstein is concerned, "It would be best for the military to drop the ban altogether." Adjusting to the change would require some effort, she says, because young men are typically very nervous about their sexuality. To deal with that, the military should establish and enforce strict rules governing sexual conduct, as it has tried to do with heterosexual relations."

"If the military can't tell its uniformed servicemen how to behave, then the military has a problem," Katzenstein adds.

The real problem, says Luddy, a former Marine rifle platoon leader, is that "Don't Ask, Don't Tell" undermines the military's credibility on the issue of sexuality. "To have a policy that says 'Don't Ask, Don't Tell,' is saying that homosexuality is incompatible with military service, but we're going to officially, passively, accept it," he says. "That contributes to the corruption of a certain morality — the integrity of the service."

"There are very sound reasons for not allowing homosexuality in the military," he adds, "and we ought to just say that." Most important among them, Luddy says, is that "distractions in combat — sexual or otherwise — get people killed."

SLDN's Osburn agrees that "Don't Ask, Don't Tell" sends mixed signals, and says he would like to see the ban abolished. It "has made things as bad or worse than prior policy," he says. "Many of our clients say they feel trapped. They feel they were lied to."

Nevertheless, says Osburn, axing the policy would be a mistake because the only alternative available today is a return to exclusion. "Congress will not change anytime soon," he says, "so this issue will have to wend its way through the federal courts and be settled on constitutional grounds."

Have women achieved greater equality in the military?

Beginning in the early 1970s, the military started taking many more women into the services. But does creating more positions necessarily mean

Personnel Discharged Under 'Gay' Policy

The number of men and women in the military who were discharged as homosexuals dropped from 1990 through 1994, when the "Don't Ask, Don't Tell" policy went into effect. In 1995, the number of discharges rose 21 percent, reflecting what critics of the policy said was intensified persecution of gays despite the new policy.

Year	Air Force	Army	Navy	Marine Corps	Total
1990	141	220	519	61	941
1991	151	206	545	47	949
1992	111	138	401	58	708
1993	152	156	334	40	682
1994	180	136	245	36	597
1995	234	182	260	46	722
Total	969	1,038	2,304	288	4,599

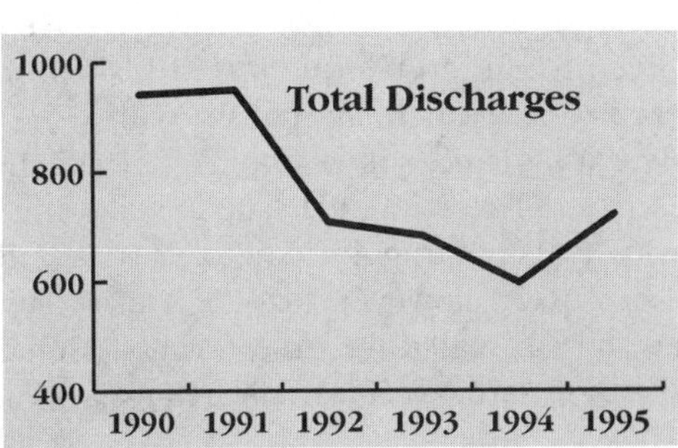

Source: "Conduct Unbecoming: The Second Annual Report on 'Don't Ask, Don't Tell, Don't Pursue' Violations," Servicemembers Legal Defense Network, Feb. 27, 1996

greater equality? That depends, observers say, on the meaning of "equality."

"If you measure equality in terms of the opportunity to get killed, then women are not yet equal," says Luddy, "but they are promoted at equal or faster rates than men."

"Compared with where we started, it's almost like night and day," says Georgia Sadler, director of the Women in the Military Project at the Women's Research and Educational Institute (WREI). "Until the 1970s, the roles women played remained very limited and stagnant. But with the all-volunteer Army and the Navy reforms begun by Adm. [Elmo] Zumwalt, things really began to change."

Since then, women secured some combat support roles that put them on the front lines. Almost every job in every branch of the service is open to women. * On March 22, Sgt. Heather Lynn Johnson became the first woman to serve as an honor guard at the Tomb of the Unknowns in Arlington National Cemetery.

During the last week of March, President Clinton nominated career Marine Carol A. Mutter to become a lieutenant general, making her the highest-ranking woman in the military. **

"In terms of promotions and policies, we've made tremendous strides," says DACOWITS' Prevatte. "But when you layer that over the culture and see the slow rate of change in behavior toward women in the workplace, you realize that attitudes have not kept pace with policy."

Despite greater equality, adds Katzenstein, women still put up with daily taunts and jokes about their presence. "The women I talk to tell me it's a daily struggle," she says.

Korb notes, however, that 25 years after Truman signed the desegregation order for the armed forces, military race relations were still terrible. Since real advances for women's equality did not begin until the 1970s, it's not surprising there's still resistance, he says. "All in all," he says, "women are pretty early on the integration curve."

Where the curve goes now depends partly on politics, says Martin Binkin, a senior fellow at the Brookings Institution. "Lyndon Johnson was the last Democratic president to have the military's support," he says. "Since then, each branch of the service has tended to apply new ground rules stipulated by Democratic administrations, but then they hope for a Republican president to reverse things."

The biggest expansion of women in the military came during Jimmy Carter's presidency, and when Ronald Reagan took office there was a lot of talk about having gone too fast, Binkin says. Reagan was a Republican but he didn't reverse Carter's advances, Binkin says, in part because Secretary of Defense Caspar W. Weinberger's wife had served in the military.

Today, Binkin says, "There's still a lot of resentment toward women" in the military.

As SLDN's Benecke explains, when formal barriers against women fall, informal ones rise up to take their place. Informal barriers, like sexual harassment and lesbian baiting, she says, have become very common, particularly since the 1991 Tailhook scandal. (*See story, p. 370.*) "There's been a real backlash," she says, "and it's especially true in the Navy where women pilots are concerned. There, the backlash is worse than ever because male pilots blame women for the fallout from Tailhook."

Because attitudes are so hard to alter, says sociologist Firestone, policy changes must force the issue of equality. And that means opening all combat positions to women. Until that happens, she says, women will not be treated equally with men.

Moskos says, however, that combat roles for women will always be limited by their physical size. Consequently, advances they make in combat will come where technology is more important than physical strength, much like the high-tech jobs women won aboard combat aircraft and ships. ■

BACKGROUND

Rise of Minorities

Since President Richard M. Nixon abolished the draft in 1973 and created an all-voluntary military, the culture of the armed forces has changed dramatically. Once a bastion of white males, today's military looks more like American society than ever before. [6]

A fundamental reason for the change was the need to attract high-quality recruits. The "new" military offered better pay, more private living quarters and greater education benefits while paying more attention to individual rights and equal opportunity.

The military also has tried to shed its negative Vietnam-era image, telling potential recruits in slick TV ads to "Be all you can be" and that "The Army wants to join you."

But critics say this message implies that the military is there to serve the soldiers when it ought to be the other way around. Too many concessions to individualism, they say, damage discipline and hurt the armed forces' ability to carry out its primary mission — to defend the United States from its enemies.

Minorities in the military have flourished in the volunteer era. More than their white counterparts, African-Americans, in particular, see the educational and career opportunities offered by the military as a way to get ahead. Predictably, larger percentages of blacks than whites re-enlist.

Blacks also find the Army alluring

Continued on p. 370

---

*Artillery, ground combat and submarines are still off-limits to women.

** Mutter will be the corps' deputy chief of staff for manpower and reserve affairs.

Chronology

1778-1919

Blacks play increasingly active roles in military while homosexuals face tighter restrictions.

March 11, 1778
The Army discharges an American soldier for homosexuality for the first time.

1861-1865
During Civil War, Union Army uses black soldiers when white recruits become scarce.

1916
The Articles of War make assault with intent to commit sodomy a felony.

1919
Race riots erupt across the country after 360,000 black soldiers return from World War I demanding more civil rights.

1940s

Women and blacks break down barriers in wartime.

1940-1941
During peacetime mobilization for World War II, the armed forces exclude women and blacks in the Marines and Army Air Corps.

World War II
Women serve in the Women's Airforce Service Pilots (WASPs), the Women's Army Corps (WACs) and other all-female units.

1943
Marine Corps enlists blacks for first time; homosexuals are banned from all services.

1947
Black leaders create the Committee Against Jim Crow in Military Service and Training.

1948
President Harry S. Truman desegregates armed forces.

1970s

During Vietnam War, restrictions slacken on homosexuals due to manpower needs; racial conflict, including riots, erupts among U.S. soldiers and sailors.

1972
First women enter Reserve Officer Training Corps (ROTC) on college campuses.

1973
Armed forces become all-volunteer; percentage of female and African-American enlistees climbs dramatically.

1976
First female cadets enter service academies.

1978
First women assigned to noncombatant ships.

1990s

Women, blacks and homosexuals continue to play greater role in military.

1990-1991
Operations Desert Shield and Desert Storm deploy 41,000 women.

1992
Blacks account for 30 percent of Army enlisted personnel, including more than one-third of senior non-commissioned officers and 12 percent of the officers; Presidential candidate Bill Clinton promises to lift the ban on gays.

April 28, 1993
Secretary of Defense Les Aspin announces women no longer will be excluded from combat aircraft or ships.

Nov. 30, 1993
President Clinton signs "Don't Ask, Don't Tell" policy into law.

Jan. 13, 1994
Aspin abolishes "at risk" rule barring women from serving in units likely to see combat.

Dec. 15, 1995
Secretary of the Army Togo D. West Jr. orders an investigation of extremist groups in the military.

Feb. 27, 1996
Servicemembers Legal Defense Network reports that discharges of gays hit a four-year high in 1995.

March 22, 1996
Sgt. Heather Lynn Johnson becomes first female honor guard for the Tomb of the Unknowns in Arlington National Cemetery.

April 5, 1996
Fourth U.S. Court of Appeals rules "Don't Ask, Don't Tell" policy is constitutional; issue appears headed to Supreme Court.

Women Who Resist Sexual Harassment ...

For Pfc. Shannon Emery, being assigned to a military police battalion in South Korea in 1994 seemed the perfect beginning of a wonderful career. Soon, however, sexual harassment surfaced. Some soldiers had warned her that if she didn't submit to their sexual advances, they would falsely report her as a lesbian — an accusation that could spark an investigation and end her Army career.

In September, Emery told her mother several soldiers in her barracks had nearly raped her: "Mom, they had me pinned against the wall. . . . If [the corporal] hadn't pulled them off me, I would have been raped right there or worse." [1]

When Emery reported her attackers, they made good on the threat to say she was a lesbian. That's when the witch hunt began, says attorney Michelle M. Benecke, co-director of the Servicemembers Legal Defense Network.

Emery's commander dismissed her charge of assault and pursued the counter-charge of lesbianism instead. Investigators then tried to get her to accuse other female soldiers of being lesbians, promising her lenient treatment in return. When a judge, citing lack of evidence, threw out court-martial charges against her, Emery's commanding officer tried to have her discharged.

Today, Emery is stationed in the United States and has been cleared of all charges by the Army inspector general; her former commanding officer has been disciplined.

"It may be hard to believe, but we count this a success story," says Benecke. "Despite what her family had to go through, and despite the difficulty of getting senior leaders to step in and stop what was a clear injustice and a witch hunt, the Army ultimately did the right thing."

Under existing anti-harassment guidelines, what happened to Emery was not supposed to happen to anyone. But Benecke says that the 200,000 women in uniform today are caught in the same double-bind that keeps victims from filing sexual harassment complaints because they're afraid they'll be called a lesbian, or labeled a troublemaker.

"This is a critical situation for military women, because the majority of them have suffered sexual harassment, or they have perceived harassment," says Juanita M. Firestone, a sociology professor at the University of Texas, San Antonio.

Firestone and co-researcher Richard J. Harris analyzed a 1988 Department of Defense (DOD) survey of men and women in the military and found that 51.8 percent of the men and 74.6 percent of the women reported either experiencing or knowing of sexual harassment. [2] Among the women surveyed, 70.1 percent had experienced "sexual talk or behavior at work [that] created an offensive, hostile or intimidating environment." Among the men, 36.9 percent gave the same answer.

Firestone and Harris also concluded that in work situations where it is understood that sexual harassment is wrong and will not be tolerated, 98 percent of those surveyed said no individual harassment occurred. In a "hostile" environment, 80 percent of the respondents said individual harassment happened as well. [3]

These findings led then Defense Secretary Dick Cheney to issue a July 1991 memorandum that included a seven-point action program to eradicate sexual harassment in the military.

Some members of the military, including many admirals, apparently did not heed Cheney's memo. Three months after his directive, the Tailhook Association of Navy and Marine Aviators met at a Las Vegas hotel for its 35th annual meeting — which one writer described as the most embarrassing event in naval history since Pearl Harbor.

A DOD inspector general's report later concluded that 83 women and seven men had been assaulted in a hotel hallway during Tailhook and that 117 officers had been involved in "one or more incidents of indecent assault, indecent exposure, conduct unbecoming an officer, or failure to act in a proper leadership capacity." [4] Tailhook also sparked an internal Navy investigation that found 42 percent of enlisted women and 26 percent of women officers had been harassed while on duty during the preceding year. [5]

Ultimately, at least 80 officers, including 30 admirals, were disciplined. Admiral Frank B. Kelso II, chief of naval operations, was forced into early retirement, and many others lost their chances for future promotions, although none of the 140 cases investigated brought convictions.

Some critics say that the punishments for Tailhook did not go far enough. Others argue that the episode prompted too-harsh punishments for subsequent missteps by otherwise worthy officers. They cite the case of Adm. Richard Macke, a former commander of U.S. Pacific forces, who was forced to retire after quipping that the three servicemen accused of raping a 12-year-old schoolgirl in Okinawa should have hired a prostitute instead.

Since Tailhook, every branch of the service, particularly the Navy, has acted to halt sexual harassment. These measures, which range from enacting stricter regulations to holding more thorough sensitivity training, grew out of 1994 House Armed Services Committee hearings on sexual harassment and the DOD inspector general's report.

Continued from p. 368

because it is among the most colorblind institutions in American society. [7]

From the early 1970s to the early '90s, the percentage of African-Americans in the military increased from 10 percent to 20 percent. In the Army, their numbers grew from 14 percent to 30 percent, peaking in 1979 at 37 percent. In fact, during the 1970s, 25 percent of all 18-year-old black men joined the armed forces. [8]

Historically, military service has been a way for immigrants and minorities to achieve standing as citizens worthy of equal rights in America. In the Colonial and revolutionary periods, slaves and freedmen used military service when

. . . Prompt New Training and Tough Punishments

Witnesses at the 1994 hearings described how the military failed to handle their complaints. For example, Navy Reserve Lt. Darlene S. Simmons reported receiving unwanted cards, letters and repeated comments from her administrative officer, including the remark, "That uniform does not show your body in a just light." Yet when she gave one of the incriminating letters to her executive officer, he destroyed it and tried to convince her to back down, she said.[6]

"I was continuously confronted by the [executive officer] to withdraw my complaints," said Simmons.

When Simmons failed to get action through the chain of command, she contacted Sen. John B. Breaux, D-La. And that, she said, led the executive officer to order her to have a psychiatric evaluation, which included holding her in a psychiatric unit for a weekend.

Eventually, after she complained through a DOD harassment hotline, the Navy inspector general ordered an inquiry, which substantiated her charges. Yet there was no formal independent investigation and it took a year, instead of the allotted 30 days, for the DOD to complete its report, she told the committee.

"Before this sexual harassment, I was a successful attorney with an impeccable reputation, and now I am regarded as a troublemaker with no future in the Navy," she said.

Since then, the Defense Equal Opportunity Council's Task Force on Discrimination and Sexual Harassment has identified several principles that effective equal-opportunity programs must have:

- Commanders must be committed to equal opportunity and held fully accountable for handling complaints.
- Policies must be clear and unequivocal.
- Definitions of harassment and discrimination must be unambiguous.
- Military personnel should receive periodic equal opportunity and human relations training.
- Complaint procedures must be fair, open, accessible, prompt and thorough while prohibiting reprisals.

"Enlisted men in the privacy of their own groups must also take steps," says military sociologist Charles Moskos of Northwestern University. "If some guy is acting in a boorish way toward women, then they have to tell him, 'Knock it off.' "

If that is to happen, says Firestone, the military must get better at changing attitudes enlistees bring with them from civilian culture. "The idea is to teach people that sexual harassment is an inappropriate type of behavior," she says. "But the training is not working because instructors do not take it seriously. It's still common for trainers to have the attitude that women who complain about certain types of harassment just don't have a sense of humor."

A model program to end harassment would demand that people "at every level of command, straight through the enlisted corps, take a firm stand against sexual harassment and set the example," she says.

Carolyn Prevatte, executive director of the Defense Advisory Committee on Women in the Services (DACOWITS), says the military is moving in the right direction. "We have good policies in place, and many leaders are committed to doing the right thing," she says. "Now we need to get a handle on what are appropriate sanctions."

That's important, says Moskos, because although harassment victims say they want the culprit to stop, they usually don't want to destroy that person's career. As things stand, punishment often means all or nothing.

Some service members complain that working in a "zero tolerance" atmosphere, where even the smallest infraction can derail a person's career, has created anger and resentment that could have been avoided. They say that the Navy, burned by Tailhook, has already fostered a backlash among men — and some women — who believe sanctions have gone too far.

"By overreacting [to sexual harassment] the Navy creates the appearance of a double standard, and that compounds the problem," adds Moskos.

Prevatte insists there must be a better balance. "As things stand now," she says, "a person must ask, 'Should I throw the book at someone and ruin their career, or should I do nothing' " and let a wrong go unpunished?

---

[1] Shannon's experiences were described in a statement by her mother, Mrs. Debbie Emery, released at a Feb. 27, 1996, press conference held by the Servicemembers Legal Defense Network.

[2] The 1988 survey will be updated this year.

[3] Juanita M. Firestone and Richard J. Harris, "Sexual Harassment in the U.S. Military: Individualized and Environmental Contexts," *Armed Forces & Society*, fall 1994, pp. 25-43.

[4] "Defense Equal Opportunity Council Report of the Task Force on Discrimination and Sexual Harassment," Vol. II, Department of Defense, May 1995, p. 28.

[5] *Ibid.*, p. 20.

[6] Testimony before the House Armed Services Committee hearing on "Sexual Harassment in the Armed Services," March 9, 1994.

---

they could "to lift themselves from low social status by distinguished action."[9]

Years later, during World War I, the celebrated black leader W.E.B. DuBois declared hopefully, "If the black man could fight to defeat the Kaiser, he could later present a bill for payment due to a grateful white America."

As in civilian society, however, blacks in the military worked apart from whites and were generally confined to the least strategic roles. At least 80 percent of blacks who served in World War I were assigned to non-combat jobs.

It was not until 1940 that Congress passed legislation outlawing discrimination in drafting recruits "on account of race or color." That same year,

President Franklin D. Roosevelt announced that blacks would be allowed to attend officer candidate schools.

Discrimination continued, however. When Truman finally moved to desegregate the armed forces in 1948, Army Chief of Staff Gen. Omar N. Bradley objected. Two years later, the Army's "Utilization of Negro Manpower" study concluded that lifting the official 10 percent limit on blacks would hurt morale and overall fighting ability.

Racial Tensions

In 1954, the Pentagon announced that the last of the segregated units in the military had been eliminated. But the draft and war in Vietnam converged with the civil rights movement during the 1960s, once again to highlight integration's shortcomings in the armed forces. "Race and war came together to create an image of white people using black people to kill yellow people," says Segal.

Pentagon statistics showed that blacks were more likely than whites to be drafted, sent to Vietnam and killed or wounded. From 1961 to 1966, blacks ages 19-21 made up 11 percent of the American population but accounted for 20 percent of all combat fatalities. In response, the Pentagon cut frontline participation by blacks.

Still, racial tension stayed high. In 1968, racial fighting broke out among prisoners at a stockade in Vietnam. Racial clashes occurred at several Marine installations in 1969 and on board naval vessels in the 1970s. In May 1971, four days of racial fighting broke out at Travis Air Force Base in California. [10]

Once the draft was abolished and the war had ended, however, race relations entered a relatively calm period. The Army in particular was emphatic about equal opportunities for minorities, but it avoided quotas. Instead, it practiced a rigid policy of no discrimination; a soldier using racial epithets, for instance, could be charged with incitement to riot.

At the same time, the Army improved its courses in racial-sensitivity training, shifting to an approach that emphasized problem-solving rather than accusation. It adopted higher standards for recruits and saw the number of black non-commissioned officers climb to 85,000.

The Army's Basic Skills Education Program, begun in 1976, helped recruits with an aptitude for leadership, but low academic test scores, get up to speed. The program has enabled many black recruits to compete successfully for skilled jobs. [11]

But when President George Bush announced he would send troops to the Persian Gulf in 1990, racial tensions increased again. There were predictions of thousands of U.S. casualties, and fears that "economic conscription" had lured job-hunting blacks into the military and now was going to have them killed in combat.

When Gen. Colin L. Powell, the black chairman of the Joint Chiefs of Staff, was asked if the situation warranted action, he replied, "Black fighting men and women, particularly in an all-volunteer force, would be offended to think that when duty called, they would be excluded on the basis of color." [12]

Powell told Rep. Julian C. Dixon, D-Calif, "When we come before Congress saying we have to cut the forces, you complain that we're reducing opportunities for blacks. Now you're saying [we're giving them] opportunities to get killed. But as soon as this crisis passes, you'll be back, worried about our cutting the force and closing off one of the best career fields for African-Americans." [13]

With an African-American reigning as the nation's top soldier, the Gulf war triumphantly over and the military's popularity restored to pre-Vietnam War levels, it appeared to many observers in the early 1990s that decent race relations in the military had been restored.

Women Get Their Shot

Women did not make significant gains in the military until the 1970s. Before then, they served only in times of dire national need. During World War II, women's non-combat support units included Women Accepted for Volunteer Emergency Service (WAVES), the Women's Airforce Service Pilots (WASPs) and the Women's Army Corps (WACs).

Barriers against women in all branches of service began to fall in 1973, when the military became all-volunteer. Recruiters made unprecedented efforts to enlist women to make up for shortages caused by a decline in male enlistees. As a result, the proportion of women in the military has climbed from 1.9 percent in 1972 to nearly 12 percent today.

"It's been a rapid, but evolutionary process," says Prevatte. "In 1971, promotion restrictions [against women] fell, and every year since then something else has been resolved to promote integration of women into the armed forces."

In 1973, aviation slots in the Navy opened to women. The Air Force followed suit in 1976. In 1978, the Navy put the first women on non-combatant ships. Yet that same year, when President Jimmy Carter reinstated draft registration for 18-year-olds, women were excluded.

The United States came close to drafting women at the end of World War II, says Segal, but that was because of a nursing shortage. "If we ever draft women, the major justification will be a severe shortage of men or a really massive threat," he says.

Nonetheless, the changes continued. The percentage of women assigned to traditionally female health-care and clerical jobs fell from 90 percent in 1970 to less than 50 percent in 1993. The most dramatic changes in women's status occurred after the Gulf war.

More than 7 percent of the 540,000 Americans who served in Operations

Desert Storm and Desert Shield were women, including six who were killed, 21 wounded and two captured. Fourteen female Marines received the Combat Action Ribbon for returning fire against Iraqi troops. It was the first time in U.S. military history that most of the women deployed had not been nurses.

"During the Gulf war, the United States crossed the Rubicon on the issue of women in the military, and there is no turning back," writes retired Col. Harry G. Summers. "[T]heir battlefield performance during the war confirmed their fitness to serve." [14]

Following the war, opportunities for women increased dramatically. Secretary of Defense Les Aspin announced on April 28, 1993, that women no longer would be excluded from combat aircraft or ships. Congress followed Aspin's lead in November, repealing a law that banned women on combat vessels. [15] Then, on Jan. 13, 1994, Aspin abolished the "at risk" rule, which had kept women from serving in units likely to see combat.

By the time Aspin, Congress and the White House were finished, more than 99 percent of Navy jobs were open to women, including an increase in the number of male/female flying squadrons from 42 to 200.

On Oct. 6, 1994, Assistant Secretary of Defense Edwin Dorn told Congress that over the previous 1 $^{1}/_{2}$ years the Defense Department had opened 260,000 positions formerly closed to women. This meant that 80 percent of all military jobs, and more than 90 percent of all career fields, had been opened to the most qualified individuals, men or women.

Such changes, said Dorn, were needed to enhance military readiness and to "remove unnecessary impediments to the recruitment, training and use of people." Units whose primary mission was ground combat, however, remained off-limits to women, as did submarine duty and artillery.

On the other hand, said Dorn, since the 1987 military drawdown began, the number of female officers and senior enlisted women had actually increased. [16]

Attitudes About Gays

In 1778, following a general court-martial, Lt. Gotthold Frederick Enslin became the first American ever dismissed from the military for homosexuality.

The armed forces waited until World War I, however, to codify punishment for homosexual soldiers. According to the Articles of War of 1916, assault with intent to commit sodomy became a felony. In 1919, the act of sodomy itself was classified as a felony.

After a purge of homosexuals at the Naval Training Station in Newport, R.I., however, a U.S. Senate subcommittee concluded in 1920 that the courts-martial for sodomy had been unfair. Treat them like patients, not like convicts, one lawmaker said.

Nevertheless, until World War II homosexuality in the military was considered a criminal act. But during the war, psychiatric explanations for homosexuality became popular, and gays were sent to hospitals for treatment rather than to prison.

A 1942 regulation instructed military psychiatrists that "persons habitually or occasionally engaged in homosexual or other perverse sexual practices" were "unsuitable for military service." Yet even after all branches of the military banned homosexuals in 1943, wartime manpower needs made it necessary to ignore the restrictions.

Throughout the 1950s and '60s, personnel who engaged in homosexual activity could be given less-than-honorable discharges. During the late 1970s, President Carter's administration declared "homosexuality is incompatible with military service" — a phrase that President Reagan incorporated into a 1981 presidential directive.

In 1982, new DOD guidelines made stated sexual orientation, not just overt homosexual behavior, the defining measure for homosexuality.

A decade later, the Democratic Party's presidential candidate, Bill Clinton, pledged to lift the ban on gays in the military. After the election, Clinton's attempt to keep his promise generated enormous opposition and led to a compromise on July 19, 1993.

The compromise, better known as "Don't Ask, Don't Tell," maintained the bans on homosexual conduct and openly professing one's homosexuality. But in implementing the policy, the White House declared that the military would not ask potential recruits or military personnel if they were gay. It also permitted investigations of service members only if there was credible evidence that they were homosexual.

The president's policy remains controversial, primarily for two reasons. Some critics say the policy overturns a 1993 federal law upholding the old standard that homosexuality is incompatible with military service. By ignoring the issue, the Clinton policy essentially condones homosexuals in the military, critics say.

Others say the policy has failed, not because the military ignores it but because officials purposely subvert it by digging into soldiers' backgrounds, questioning family, friends, doctors and priests, on the basis of unsubstantiated rumors that they are gay. ■

CURRENT SITUATION

Hate Groups

The presence of extremist groups on U.S. military bases is not a new phenomenon, nor is it a surprise to police and military authorities.

At Camp Pendleton, the big Marine base in Southern California, officials uncovered an active Ku Klux Klan chapter in 1976. In 1985, the White Patriot Party of North Carolina was discovered recruiting Marines and other members of the armed forces. Six years later, two Fort Bragg Green Berets were convicted of stockpiling weapons for an eventual race war. In 1992, the Army's Criminal Investigation Command reported several contacts between servicemen and skinhead or neo-Nazi groups. [17]

Then, in December 1995, came the murder of the black couple in Fayetteville, N.C. The murders occurred just months after a congressional task force on racial discrimination in the military reported hate group activity on several bases in the United States and Europe. [18]

To many observers, the senseless shootings, allegedly involving soldiers from Fort Bragg, were yet another indicator that extremist groups target the military as a source of recruits. "White supremacy is only one layer in these multilayered movements," says Roy of the Southern Poverty Law Center. "Anti-government terrorism is their main agenda."

Following the murders, the Pentagon ordered all U.S. military bases to require eight hours of racial-sensitivity training and to crack down on all signs of extremist activity. Army Secretary West also ordered a task force to probe possible extremist activity at 28 Army bases around the world. The task force found that only 1 percent of the 7,638 soldiers interviewed had direct knowledge of extremist activities, and West concluded that there is minimal extremism in the Army.

However, a parallel survey conducted by the task force, in which personnel were permitted to respond anonymously, showed a far higher level of extremism. Of the 17,080 soldiers who responded, 3.5 percent — about 600 service members — said they had been approached by extremist recruiters since joining the Army. Another 7.1 percent said they knew at least one other soldier involved in such activity.

The task force also noted that some commanders said that extremist recruiters — from neo-Nazis to anti-government, patriotic militias — have focused particularly on Army Special Forces units, such as the Green Berets. West said the Army will look into those concerns.

According to Moskos and other observers, the organization and makeup of today's military makes monitoring extremist activities more difficult than before. For example, to make the Army more attractive to new recruits, the Army has given soldiers more privacy in their living quarters than they had in traditional barracks. "You have a paradox," Moskos says. "Civil libertarians have pushed for more individual rights and less monitoring of enlistees on and off base. The more privacy you have, the more untoward behavior you get."

Moreover, the task force found that the proportion of minority soldiers entering combat and Special Forces units has plummeted in recent years, making the Army's most elite fighting units disproportionately white.

The North Carolina NAACP reached many of the same conclusions in its report on interviews with soldiers, base commanders and local civilians throughout North Carolina. "There are plenty of extremist groups that would like to systematically organize interlinking cadres on these bases, but I don't think that's happened," says Alexander. Nevertheless, he notes "a curious tolerance of this kind of abhorrent behavior at the lowest levels — mainly among the sergeants and the lieutenants."

NAACP investigators found local bars where skinheads mix with soldiers, and Ku Klux Klan symbols are openly displayed. Marines at Camp Lejeune reported seeing racist and anti-semitic graffiti on the base, as well as Nazi flags and a hangman's noose.

"Until recently, there was a billboard on Bragg Boulevard that invited people to contact the racist National Alliance," adds Tod Ensign, president of Citizen Soldier, a New York-based soldier's rights group.

Alexander says on-base racism has increased in recent years for two fundamental reasons. First, the relatively harmonious race relations in the services during the 1980s gave military leaders false confidence that they had solved the race issue. Second, with job opportunities in the private sector stagnant or shrinking, and with military budget cuts reducing active-duty personnel from 2.1 million in the 1980s to 1.5 million today, there is more competition than ever for slots in the armed forces.

"Volunteer recruits want jobs and job security, so it's easy to start scapegoating when it looks like somebody else is getting all the goodies," says Alexander. "With the Army population about 30 percent minority, it's not hard to see why you've got to keep teaching tolerance."

'Don't Ask, Don't Tell'

In a study of the "Don't Ask, Don't Tell" policy released in February, the SLDN reported that the military had discharged 722 service members for homosexuality in fiscal 1995 — an increase of 21 percent over 1994. During that period, SLDN says the policy was violated at least 363 times. [19]

Each service is different in how it enforces the policy, says SLDN's Dixon, but all of them have destroyed the soldiers' "zone of privacy" that the policy promised to protect.

Under the policy, declared homosexuals are excluded from military service based on the assumption that once they announce their sexual orientation, homosexual behavior may follow. And that behavior, critics say, destroys the morale and fighting ability of troops who must trust one another absolutely to be effective. If, for example, an officer plays favorites because of sexual attraction toward certain soldiers, then trust breaks down and endangers the unit, says Luddy.

"The clearest and strongest reason for the [policy]," Luddy writes, "is to remove the influence of sexuality — not heterosexuality, not homosexuality, just sexuality, period — from an environment where the stakes are literally life and death." [20]

Some argue, however, that the issue is not sexuality but human rights. To them, there is no difference between African-American soldiers who began winning equal treatment nearly 50 years ago and homosexual soldiers today.

Supporters of the policy, however, say that Gen. Powell has laid that argument to rest. Powell, who initially opposed "Don't Ask, Don't Tell," argues that skin color and sexual orientation are completely different. "Skin color is a benign, non-behavioral characteristic," he writes. "Sexual orientation is perhaps the most profound of human behavioral characteristics. Comparison of the two is a convenient but invalid argument." [21]

"Racial integration increased military efficiency," adds Moskos. "The acceptance of declared homosexuals will likely have the opposite effect, at least for a time." [22]

Still, SLDN's Benecke argues that banning or restricting homosexuals is unreasonable. There are 18 people serving openly as homosexuals in the military today, she says. And many have received superior performance evaluations. "If logic prevailed, we wouldn't have two classes of soldier," she says. "But logic and the facts have never been the basis for these policies."

Dealing With AIDS and HIV

Opponents of a new policy to remove personnel infected with HIV, the virus that causes AIDS, say there is no logic to that policy either. (*See "At Issue," p. 377.*) The new policy, sponsored by Rep. Robert K. Dornan, R-Calif., calls for removal of the military's 1,049 HIV-positive service members by Dec. 31, 1996. * (In 1986, all soldiers infected with HIV were banned from combat duty because of potential dangers associated with contaminated blood.)

On March 19, the Senate voted to repeal the new HIV law, but the House refused to follow. If Congress does not reverse itself, President Clinton predicts that the courts will declare the law unconstitutional. To help minimize the policy's chances for survival, Clinton ordered the Justice Department not to defend it in court.

Opponents of the new HIV policy argue that the real motive behind it has nothing to do with military readiness. "The proponents of this measure believe that people living with HIV/AIDS do not deserve the same consideration and compassion afforded those with other medical conditions," Rep. Gerry E. Studds, D-Mass., told fellow House members. "This provision is really a proxy by which they hope to bring about the discharge of HIV-positive service members who happen to be gay."

Benecke says, however, that about 60 percent of the affected service members seeking help from the SLDN are married women with children and were "infected by their husbands or boyfriends."

Whatever the case, Dornan argues that dismissing HIV-positive personnel is justified because they are "by definition unable to carry out duties for which they were trained. Like Magic [Johnson], these personnel are ill and disabled . . . notwithstanding that they can still physically function."

The New Republic magazine condemned the policy, comparing the rights of HIV-infected personnel in the military with those of HIV-positive people in civilian life. "Firing an HIV-positive employee in the private sector for no good reason is illegal thanks to the Americans with Disabilities Act," said a recent editorial. [23]

* Dornan attached the HIV provision to the National Defense Authorization Act for Fiscal Year 1996, which President Clinton signed Feb. 10, 1996.

Women in Combat

Despite high praise for women soldiers from the press and Pentagon during the Gulf war, soldiers in the field tell a somewhat different story. Some 45 percent of the service members who served in mixed-gender units said "sexual activity had a negative impact" on morale. More than half of those surveyed rated women's performance as fair or poor, compared with only 3 percent for men's performance. [24]

Regardless of such criticism, Congress lifted the ban on women in combat planes after the sacrifices female soldiers made during the Gulf war.

Women in the Army, however, are less enthusiastic about the opportunity for combat. In a 1992 survey, women in the military agreed they should have the choice to serve in combat. But when asked if they would volunteer themselves, only 4 percent of enlisted women and 11 percent of female officers said yes. [25]

Opponents of women in combat say that, as with homosexuals, mixing the sexes inevitably brings sexual tension that undermines good order and combat readiness. For proof, they point to the *USS Eisenhower*, the first combat vessel integrated by sex. After a six-month tour in the Mediterranean in 1994, the ship returned with at least 13 percent of the 415 women on board pregnant. [26]

"You put men and women together on a ship and sex happens," says Maginnis of the Family Research Council. "Commanders of dual-gender crews will tell you nightmarish stories — pregnancies, sexual favors and fraternization between senior non-commissioned officers and young females. But if they go public and say women are part of a morale-busting problem, they get charged with sexual harassment."

Sadler, of the Women's Research and Educational Institute, disagrees. "The women I spoke with from the *Eisenhower* said the greatest problem they had serving on a dual-gender crew was the 500 visits they got from the media," she said.

Maginnis points to another issue affecting women in the military: physical strength and combat readiness. "Combat is not any less physical today than it was 50 years ago," he says. "This is not a push-button military except in a very few places." Particularly in emergency situations, he says, men must take up the slack for women who cannot handle physically demanding tasks, including emergency procedures to save a ship that's been hit and is taking on water.

But according to Prevatte of DACOWITS, any ship's commanding officer will say that damage control is done by teamwork. "This muscle thing is not the issue some people make it out to be," she says. "You can always find one person who, regardless of sex, cannot open a jammed hatch."

Sadler adds that despite claims that women are unable to pull their share of the physical load on ships, they have done fine so far. "It's been a long time since Adm. Zumwalt began changes in command assignments for women," she says. "The Navy had support ships that couldn't be fully manned, so they put women on them. And now, more than 20 years later, the ships haven't sunk and everything seems to be working just fine."

Ships may not have sunk, but on Oct. 25, 1994, Navy Lt. Kara S. Hultgreen died while landing her F-14A Tomcat fighter on a carrier off the California coast. The incident sparked a bitter public debate over whether Hultgreen had been held to the same qualifying standards as male pilots. *Newsweek* magazine declared the accusation a "posthumous slur, cruel by any standard, [that] enrages feminists and fair-minded men as well." [27]

Yet Maginnis reports that the Navy's own Mishap Investigation Report described "repeated instances of pilot error," noting that "Hultgreen's flight-control mistakes were the most critical factors [in the accident]."

Cornell's Katzenstein questions the sincerity of people who use Hultgreen's death to suggest that the military promotes incompetent pilots. "It's remarkable when you look at the number of military aviation accidents in the last 12 months involving men, and you realize no one is claiming they were incompetent," she says. "The military is very concerned about the safety of its people. You don't see them taking unusual risks in training and promoting women." ■

OUTLOOK

Easing Tensions

In its report on extremism, the Army's task force recommended that the Army clarify the distinctions between passive and active participation in extremist organizations. Soldiers and their commanders, it said, should understand which behaviors will be accepted and which ones require counseling or punishment.

The task force also recommended that the Army look closely at extremists' ties to civilian military employees and members of the Army Reserve; make certain that soldiers can file complaints of racial discrimination without fear of retaliation; and offer human-relations training at all stages of a service member's career.

Beyond that, the North Carolina NAACP urged all branches of the military to prohibit racist materials on all bases and the use of racial slurs by military personnel. Each military base should conduct surveys, group discussions and hold meetings periodically to gauge racial tensions between soldiers, the NAACP said. And local NAACP branches should sponsor periodic meetings that include representatives from military bases and the surrounding communities.

"The traditional role of the NAACP has been to analyze, propose solutions and then work with folks to implement those solutions," says Alexander. "But what's been achieved in the past is only a benchmark that has to be readjusted."

Making those adjustments, and easing racial tensions in the military, will not be easy, says Brookings' Korb. "There is great concern among some of my African-American colleagues that budget cuts and force reductions will disproportionately hurt blacks," he says.

Others warn that too much emphasis on sensitivity training could backfire. For one thing, says Luddy, most members of the military already reject racism. For another, diversity training works against military training by emphasizing how different people are, he says. Supporters of sensitivity training "presume that skin color is the defining difference between people," he says. "By definition that's racist, and it goes against everything in military culture which is designed to break that down."

Gay Policy to Go on Trial

In its recent report, the SLDN asked the Pentagon to clarify what constitutes a violation of existing rules on homosexuals. It also asks the Air Force, Navy and DOD to rescind memoranda that SLDN says "gut the intent" of "Don't Ask, Don't Tell" and to appoint a senior DOD official to guarantee legal rights for all service members investigated under the policy.

"If the Pentagon is serious about ending abuses," says Osburn, "it's got to set the example and take action from the top down. Everyone is sensitive to

Continued on p. 378

At Issue:

Should individuals with HIV be discharged from the military?

yes

REP. ROBERT K. DORNAN, R-CALIF.
FROM A STATEMENT ISSUED FEB. 14, 1996

There are approximately 1,049 HIV/AIDS-infected military personnel on active duty today. . . . Not one of the world's 191 nations will let an HIV/AIDS-infected soldier serve on their soil. These personnel are excluded from the routine, revolving, universal deployment that defines military service. In fact, HIV/AIDS-infected military personnel are disallowed from doing anything that defines military life.

Prior to Bill Clinton taking command and downsizing our military by 700,000 servicemen and women, these . . . 1,000 or so persons were reluctantly absorbed by commanders who were doing their best to avoid the wild public relations battle that we see occurring now. But Clinton's downsizing created a new problem. To wit, bringing HIV/AIDS-infected personnel back to the states to serve in a "non-military" job with no heavy lifting meant either the demoralizing and immediate redeployment of another soldier, perhaps one who had just returned home, or a career-ending blow to a fully deployable serviceman or woman forced out of the military.

Far from being punitive or malicious, the Dornan provision, [which mandates the separation and discharge of all individuals who are infected with HIV/AIDS] is motivated by military reality. HIV/AIDS-infected personnel cannot do anything that you see in those gung-ho military television commercials about "aim high," "see the world" or "be all that you can be." In military terms, these personnel are noncombat assignable. If you can't be utilized, then why serve?

The Magic Johnson analogy is specious, especially in light of heavyweight boxer Tommy Morrision. The NBA is not the military. Unlike Magic, HIV/AIDS-infected military personnel are by definition unable to carry out duties for which they were trained. Like Magic, these personnel are ill and disabled, again by definition notwithstanding that they can still physically function. Even without [my] provision, if Magic was in the service playing basketball, he would only be allowed to play "home games." Not nearly the monetary incentive for the NBA to take such a risk!

HIV is one of various illnesses that classify personnel as non-deployable. Asthma, cancer, diabetes and heart disease are a few others. The military considers HIV as different than other illnesses because HIV is the only one that is irreversible and untreatable. If you become infected, sooner or later, you will die an HIV-related death. The same is not true of the others, which are treated on a case by case basis. . . .

HIV/AIDS-infected military personnel are different by the very nature of their irreversible terminal disease, and need to be treated differently.

no

AIDS ACTION COUNCIL
FROM FACT SHEET ISSUED FEB. 22, 1996

Service members become non-worldwide deployable due to a number of medical reasons, such as diabetes, asthma, heart disease, cancer and pregnancy. They still perform very significant duties but are restricted in overseas travel to remain close to adequate medical services. The secretary of the respective service determines when it is necessary to release a soldier from the military when personnel can no longer perform their duties. This policy is similar for all service members, regardless of their health status. It is inappropriate to single out HIV-positive individuals for premature separation from the armed services, and in so doing treat these individuals differently than the military treats other healthy, productive members with chronic illnesses. . . .

Benefits that would have to be paid to the discharged service members would be considerable, in addition to the loss of currently productive service members with HIV. The service members that are currently non-worldwide deployable provide valuable benefits to the military and would be difficult to replace without large additional costs.

Individuals with HIV need more than just medical benefits. They need to be able to earn a living for housing and food, rather than be forced to draw on public assistance programs. Keeping personnel with HIV, who are able to work, in the military is much more cost-effective.

Previous DOD policy was initiated and supported by both Reagan and Bush DOD officials. Current military policy has been in place since the Reagan administration and received the support of senior military officials. The policy is the product of serious analysis and deliberation by the Pentagon of the impact of HIV-positive individuals on military readiness. The Clinton administration has only moved to continue these policies, demonstrating bipartisan support for this approach.

The presence of HIV-infected service members in the military does not adversely affect its combat readiness or efficiency. These troops are still physically healthy and are valuable to the armed services. The training and experience of these service members positively adds to the military and should not be taken away as long as they can still perform their duties. These duties must be performed, and service members with experience in both overseas and domestic operations would be more qualified to handle a wider variety of duties.

The military has a proud tradition of taking care of its own. Military personnel who contract HIV during their military service have a right to experience the same supportive treatment extended to other military personnel who contract illnesses or disabilities during their military service.

Military Families Now Get More Attention . . .

To Gen. Carl E. Mundy Jr., commandant of the Marine Corps, there was a simple solution to the corps' growing divorce rate. In August 1993, he ordered married recruits barred from enlistment as of 1995. The directive was not well-received.

"Mundy's order lasted about two hours," says Georgia Sadler, director of the Women in the Military Project at the Women's Research and Educational Institute (WREI). "People no longer say, 'If the service wanted you to have a wife, they would have issued you one.' There is much more of a family orientation in the services today than 20 years ago."

"The military has undergone many changes since it became an all-volunteer force," says Carolyn H. Becraft, deputy assistant secretary of Defense for personnel support, family and education. "It has gone from a largely unmarried force under conscription to a predominately married force today. At least 90 percent of the career force is married. Most recruits are single when they enlist, but within four years after joining, 40 percent of them are married."

In the all-volunteer force, many enlistees come in a little older than they did during the draft. Almost all have high school degrees. And a larger number than before have college degrees, says Sylvia Kidd, director of government relations for the National Military Family Association. "After they get in, they're ready to marry and start families," she says.

According to Becraft, more than 60 percent of military spouses have jobs. They work either in the civil service or in private businesses located in communities that surround the bases. During the draft era, by comparison, the percentage of working spouses was only about 35 percent, she says, so issues such as child care were not as pressing as they are today.

In response to the new phenomenon of working parents, the military has established child-care programs in 300 locations around the world. These programs are a boon not only to married parents with children but also to single parents, most of whom are men, Becraft says.

As the availability of child care has increased, says Kidd, so has the quality. "Today, we have the top child-care centers in the United States, and they all include developmental programs for the kids."

Originally, child care in the military was designed to take care of children when officers wives had social obligations during the day, says Mady Segal, a sociologist at the University of Maryland, College Park. "Now they're much more educationally focused — but they're never able to meet the demand for their services."

The move toward better child care actually began before the end of the draft, Segal says. As military technology and weaponry became more sophisticated and required more specialized and better-trained personnel, the armed forces realized the importance of keeping talented people satisfied so they would re-enlist. "Of course, the longer you retain people the more likely they are to get married, which makes the need for more family services pretty obvious," she says.

Better family services also influence how married soldiers function in the field. "Soldiers deployed far from home, but who know their families are well cared for, will focus better on the mission," Becraft says. "We know that these things improve personal and military readiness by providing a kind of stability and helping families manage their lives."

Nonetheless, sociologist Juanita M. Firestone of the University of Texas, San Antonio, says family is the No. 1 reason people get out of the military. And with the cost of recruitment and training, it would be very inefficient for the military not to do something about that.

Defense Secretary William J. Perry has placed great emphasis on providing service members with reasonable lifestyles, Becraft says. The Army, for instance, has spent a lot of time and money upgrading base housing, much of which was built in the 1950s and '60s.

Another important change, says Kidd, is the inclusion of military families in discussions about quality-of-life issues.

Continued from p. 376

official directives because they want to advance their careers. There's no better way to send a signal that witch hunts must end than to make clear that witch hunters will be punished."

Elsewhere, the issue will play out in the courts. On March 30, 1995, District Judge Eugene H. Nickerson of New York declared "Don't Ask, Don't Tell" unconstitutional, calling it "Orwellian" and "inherently deceptive. To presume from a person's [sexual] status that he or she will commit undesirable acts is an extreme measure," he said. "Hitler taught the world what could happen when the government began to target people not for what they had done, but because of their status." [28]

The case, *Able, et al. v. U.S.*, is one of two that could make it to the Supreme Court this summer. It involves six self-proclaimed homosexuals who allege that the military's gay policy violates their First and Fifth Amendment rights.

The second case, *Thomasson v. Perry,* began when Navy Lt. Paul G. Thomasson petitioned the U.S. Court for the Eastern District of New York to declare the military's homosexual ban unconstitutional. Thomasson was discharged from the Navy after he declared he was gay in a March 2, 1994, letter to his boss at the Bureau of Naval Personnel in Arlington, Va.

"If one of these two cases goes to the Supreme Court this summer, we expect a 5-4 decision in favor of the ban," says Maginnis.

Osburn agrees the decision will be

. . . But Top Priority Still Goes to 'Readiness'

"In the past, someone else was always telling us what we needed," says Kidd, whose husband retired recently after 32 years in the Army. "Before the all-volunteer force, you didn't have much choice. But then they realized they had to do something to get people to re-enlist and stay in."

Another difference, says Becraft, is the 291 family centers the military has on bases worldwide. The centers offer services including employment assistance, personal financial management and outreach and crisis intervention. They also offer family advocacy to deal with spousal and child abuse.

In addition, each service has developed more direct family interaction with the military command. "This is very important during deployments," says Becraft. Family-support groups made up of spouses left behind meet with one another and the unit commander. Together, they share information about what's happening in the field and with their own lives at home.

Family centers also have programs to help families arrange for powers of attorney, wills, banking needs and so on, which makes it easier for spouses left behind to assume full responsibility for their affairs after the unit leaves.

To be really helpful, program leaders have to realize that reuniting the family at the end of a long separation is a more difficult process than the separation itself. "A lot of family members have an idealized image that everything will be wonderful when they reunite," she says, "but they find the adjustments much harder to make than they expected."

But those aren't the only adjustments military families need help with. Until recently, she says, the Army re-stationed people about every two to three years. It's not unheard of for a career officer to have moved 18 times in 20 years. As the military continues to cut personnel, and competition for the best jobs and promotions increases, matters will only get worse. "That puts a terrific strain on the family, especially the kids," Segal says.

She suggests giving officers better opportunities to keep their families in one place longer without damaging their careers. For working spouses whose jobs end with each move, the armed forces offer a spouse-preference program to help place them in civil service jobs when they are re-stationed. The Army Family Team Building Program is designed to boost self-sufficiency in military spouses. And Family Action Plans holds regular meetings to discuss problems in military life. Those that require more than local solutions eventually make their way to the DOD's regular Family Action Plan meeting in Washington, D.C., for discussion and then action by the senior leadership.

With all the attention the military has given to families, couples in which both spouses are enlisted still find it difficult to follow careers and stay close to each other. "The military has gotten much better in dealing with spouses, provided they're not both military spouses," says Firestone. "But they really would rather not deal with dual military couples."

Firestone says disincentives to dual military marriages are built into the system, one of which is difficulty getting assigned to the same post. "Couples assigned 100 miles apart are considered to be working in the same duty station," she says.

For those on career ladders, doing a remote tour of duty is essential to rising through the ranks, she says, and that raises the difficult issue of which spouse should take the best assignment. "The military," Firestone says, "does nothing to resolve those issues." Nor do such couples get special consideration during deployments, even if they have children. Every service member who has children must make arrangements for someone to take care of their children. The only accommodation, she says, is for a woman with an infant.

Still Becraft says, representatives from all over the world come to America to see how the U.S. armed forces deliver family services.

In the end, she says, the family policies are driven by one key factor.

"Everything we do," she says, "is linked to readiness."

close. "The court will be divided, but I hope the justices will look beneath the surface and deal with the facts," he says. "Having homosexuals in the military does not damage cohesion and morale, but having a policy that causes people constantly to look over their shoulders and engage in speculation about people's sexuality does."

Leadership Called Key to Equality

In a May 1995 report on discrimination and sexual harassment, the Defense Equal Opportunity Council observed that leadership is the key to ending injustice in the military. The report recommended holding senior officials accountable for ensuring equal opportunities for everyone under their commands. It also recommended that:

- the DOD require equal opportunity and training programs for all commanders and civilian managers;
- the chain of command always be followed in resolving complaints;
- all key terms in harassment and discrimination policies be clarified; and
- grievance procedures be made easily available. [29]

"Leadership is the key to equality," says SLDN's Benecke. "Whether at the level of a platoon or an entire branch of the service, until senior leaders themselves treat women as valued members of their teams, their subordinates will not either."

Cornell's Katzenstein adds that education and attitudes, not rules and regulations, are the big issues for women's equality today. "Tailhook made it clear that problems persist even though anti-

FOR MORE INFORMATION

National Association for the Advancement of Colored People, 1025 Vermont Ave. N.W., Suite 1120, Washington, D.C. 20005; (202) 638-2269. The NAACP works for equal opportunities for minorities in all areas of American life, including the military.

Women's Research and Education Institute, 1700 18th St. N.W., Washington, D.C. 20009; (202) 328-7070. Provides information and conducts research and policy analysis for members of Congress and other policymakers who support equity for women.

Family Research Council, 700 13th St. N.W., Suite 500, Washington, D.C. 20005; (202) 393-2100. Analyzes issues affecting families and seeks to ensure that family interests are considered in the formulation of public policy.

Servicemembers Legal Defense Network, P.O. Box 53013, Washington, D.C. 20009; (202) 328-3244. Offers legal representation to armed forces members disciplined under the "Don't Ask, Don't Tell" and HIV policies.

harassment policies are in place," she says. "What the military needs to address are cultural attitudes that are amenable to education. To create genuine cultural change, you have to change attitudes."

Changing attitudes through leadership and education are crucial, agrees DACOWITS' Prevatte, but getting enough women into the right assignments is equally important. "For example, until we get a critical mass of women on board Navy ships, their presence will not be fully accepted as normal or routine. To accomplish that, on a ship with 1,000 crew members, from 15-20 percent needs to be women," she says.

Regardless of official policies, says Segal, the percentage of women in the military may rise on its own. "The military has been very selective in the women brought in," he says. "As it downsizes on the basis of merit, women should be the last to go."

Some observers already predict that women will make up 25 percent of the armed forces by the early 2000s. Yet that growth will likely occur just in the Navy and Air Force, says Brookings' Binkin, because combat requirements for the Army and Marines will limit the number of slots women can fill.

Firestone speculates that further change in combat roles will be a long time in coming. "The masculine military myth holds that men must be able to prove themselves and that the presence of women removes the mystique that surrounds the rite of passage by combat," she says. "That's a very strong part of our process of socialization and culturalization, and it's not likely to change any time soon." ■

Notes

[1] Information on the Burmeister case is from Daniel Voll, "A Few Good Nazis," *Esquire,* April 1996, pp. 102-112, and "The Secretary of the Army's Task Force on Extremist Activities: Defending American Values," March 21, 1996, pp. 31-33. For background, see "Hate Crimes," *The CQ Researcher,* Jan. 8, 1993, pp. 1-24.

[2] For background, see "Women in the Military," *The CQ Researcher,* Sept. 25, 1992, pp. 833-856.

[3] Charles Moskos, "Mandating Inclusion: The Military as a Social Lab," *Current,* July/August 1993, p. 24.

[4] Quoted in Col. Harry G. Summers Jr., Ret., *The New World Strategy: A Military Policy for America's Future* (1995), p. 128. For background, see "Calculating the Costs of the Gulf War," *Editorial Research Reports,* March 15, 1991, pp. 145-156.

[5] Martin Binkin, *Who Will Fight the Next War: The Changing Face of the American Military* (1993), p. 221.

[6] For background, see "Should the U.S. Reinstate the Draft?" *Editorial Research Reports,* Jan. 11, 1991, pp. 17-30.

[7] David R. Segal and Naomi Verdugo, "Demographic Trends and Personnel Polices as Determinants of the Racial Composition of the Volunteer Army," *Armed Forces & Society,* summer 1994, pp. 619-32.

[8] Binkin, *op. cit.,* pp. 1, 73.

[9] *Ibid.,* p. 62.

[10] *Ibid.,* p. 70.

[11] Charles Moskos, "The Army's Racial Success Story: How Do They Do It?" *The New Republic,* Aug. 5, 1991, p. 16.

[12] Colin Powell with Joseph E. Persico, *My American Journey* (1995), p. XX.

[13] *Ibid.,* p. 501.

[14] Summers, *op. cit.,* p. 127.

[15] "Combat Roles for Women a Step Closer," *1993 CQ Almanac,* p. 463.

[16] Testimony before House Armed Services Subcommittee on Military Forces and Personnel, Oct. 6, 1994.

[17] Tod Ensign, "The Militia-Military Connection," *Covert Action Quarterly,* summer 1995, pp. 13-16.

[18] Rep. Ronald V. Dellums, D-Calif., chairman of the House National Security Committee during the 103rd Congress, had initiated the task force. In a Dec. 13, 1995, letter to Rep. Floyd D. Spence, R- S.C., the new committee chairman, Dellums called for hearings on racism in the military and noted that the task force had found "subtle forms of racism, mostly in the area of career advancement and more overt forms of racism, both continue to exist in the military." The task force report was titled "An Assessment of Racial Discrimination in the Military: A Global Perspective."

[19] "Conduct Unbecoming: The Second Annual Report on 'Don't Ask, Don't Tell, Don't Pursue' Violations," Servicemembers Legal Defense Network, 1996.

[20] John Luddy, "Make War, Not Love: The Pentagon's Gay Ban Is Wise and Just," *Policy Review,* spring 1993, pp. 68-71.

[21] Powell, *op. cit.,* p. 547.

[22] Moskos, "Mandating Inclusion," *op. cit.,* p. 26.

[23] Editorial, "Crossing the Line," *The New Republic,* Feb. 19, 1996, p. 9.

[24] Moskos, "Mandating Inclusion," *op. cit.,* p. 24.

[25] The survey is referred to in Moskos, "Mandating Inclusion," *loc. cit.*

[26] Lt. Col. Robert L. Maginnis, Ret., "Feminism Sinks Navy Readiness," *Insight,* Dec. 3, 1995, published by The Family Research Council.

[27] Tom Morganthau, et al., "The Military Fights the Gender Wars," *Newsweek,* Nov. 14, 1994, p. 37.

[28] Pat Towell, "Military Personnel: Federal Judge Strikes Down 'Don't Ask Don't Tell' Defense," *CQ Weekly Report,* April 1, 1995, p. 957.

[29] Defense Equal Opportunity Council, "Report of the Task Force on Discrimination and Sexual Harassment," May 1995.

Bibliography

Selected Sources Used

Books

Binkin, Martin, *Who Will Fight the Next War: The Changing Face of the American Military,* Brookings Institution, 1993.
Binkin, a senior fellow at Brookings, provides historical background on the roles that women, blacks and the reserves have played in wartime. He also discusses the military's evolving culture and how it is changing the strategic vision and fighting capacity of America's armed forces.

Holm, Jeanne, *Women in the Military: An Unfinished Revolution,* revised edition, Presidio, 1992.
From the Revolution through the Gulf war, this is a good history of the roles women have played in military life.

Naltz, Bernard C., *Strength for the Fight: A History of Black Americans in the Military,* Free Press, 1986.
Although dated, this is an excellent treatment of the black military experience, including the race troubles during the Vietnam War.

Scott, Wilbur J., and Sandra Carson Stanley, eds., *Gays and Lesbians in the Military: Issues, Concerns, and Contrasts,* Aldine De Gruyter, 1994.
This excellent collection of brief studies on homosexuals in the military includes essays on policies in foreign countries as well as the U.S.

Shilts, Randy, *Conduct Unbecoming: Gays & Lesbians in the U.S. Military,* revised and updated, Fawcett Columbine, 1994.
The late author of *The Boys in the Band* offers a brief history of the treatment of homosexuals in the military and dozens of individual case histories since 1954.

Articles

Firestone, Juanita M., and Richard J. Harris, "Sexual Harassment in the U.S. Military: Individualized and Environmental Contexts," *Armed Forces & Society*, fall 1994, pp. 25-43.
Using a 1988 Department of Defense survey on sex roles in the military, the authors conclude that sexual harassment is pervasive.

Luddy, John, "Make War, Not Love: The Pentagon's Gay Ban Is Wise and Just," *Policy Review,* spring 1993, pp. 68-71.
Luddy argues that sexuality, not just homosexuality, is disruptive in a military setting and that attempts to compare black and gay rights are invalid because skin color, unlike homosexuality, is a non-behavioral trait.

Moskos, Charles, "Mandating Inclusion: The Military as a Social Lab," *Current,* July-August 1993, pp. 20-26.
Moskos contrasts the success of racial integration in the military with the challenge of integrating homosexuals and suggests that the military increasingly has become a laboratory for social reform.

Segal, David R., and Naomi Verdugo, "Demographic Trends and Personnel Policies as Determinants of the Racial Composition of the Volunteer Army," *Armed Forces & Society,* September 1994, pp. 619-32.
The authors discuss how and why official policies, more than broad economic forces in the civilian economy, have determined the racial composition of the Army during the all-volunteer era that began in 1973.

Reports and Studies

Department of Defense, *Defense Equal Opportunity Council Report of the Task Force on Discrimination and Sexual Harassment,* Vol. I and II, May 1995.
This servicewide survey of rules and practices governing sexual harassment and discrimination includes descriptions of policies and procedures, recommendations for changes and a lengthy chronology of laws and regulations.

Osburn, C. Dixon, and Michelle M. Benecke, *Conduct Unbecoming: The Second Annual Report on "Don't Ask, Don't Tell, Don't Pursue" Violations,* March 1, 1995-Feb. 27, 1996, Servicemembers Legal Defense Network, March 27, 1996.
The authors find that since Don't Ask, Don't Tell was implemented in 1994, military discharges for homosexuality have increased dramatically, and investigations of alleged homosexuals have become more, not less, aggressive.

***Presidential Commission on the Assignment of Women in the Armed Forces: Report to the President,* Nov. 12, 1992.**
Ordered following the Persian Gulf War, this report summarizes women's status in the military including combat roles, pregnancy and deployment policies and differences in physical strength and abilities between male and female recruits.

Department of the Army, *The Secretary of the Army's Task Force on Extremist Activities: Defending American Values,* March 21, 1996.
The task force concludes that while there is little extremist activity on the 28 U.S. Army bases it investigated, some special forces commanders are concerned that recruiting activity by extremist groups has picked up around their bases. Report includes recommendations and policies on extremist activity in the various services an.

The Next Step

Additional information from UMI's Newspaper & Periodical Abstracts database

African-Americans in the Military

"Blacks found less likely than whites to be promoted in military," *The New York Times,* Nov. 22, 1995, p. A20.

A study of the military conducted by the GAO has found that blacks are less likely to be promoted than their white counterparts, but it stopped short of attributing the difference to racism. The report, released on Nov. 20, 1995, recommended that the Pentagon improve its equal opportunity monitoring.

Robinson, Regina, "Blanton blazed trail in military," *Chicago Defender,* June 10, 1995, p. 38.

Lewis Blanton's experience as a black in the U.S. Navy during World War II is recounted.

Williams, Armstrong, "Blacks in the military," *Afro-American,* Feb. 11, 1995, p. A5.

Williams notes famous blacks in military service, opining that their participation has been a major catalyst in advancing black Americans' drive toward equality.

"World-wide: A military commission," *The Wall Street Journal,* July 25, 1995, p. A1.

President Clinton awarded a military commission posthumously to one of the first blacks ever to attend West Point, more than a century after Johnson Chestnut Whittaker was expelled following a racist attack. When no one confessed to attacking Whittaker, the school concluded he faked the attack.

AIDS Policy and the Military

Gray, Jerry, "Senate votes to prevent ouster of HIV patients in military," *The New York Times,* March 20, 1996, p. D22.

The Senate voted without debate on March 19, 1996, to overturn a month-old law that requires the mandatory discharge of members of the armed forces who test positive for HIV, the virus that causes AIDS. Sen. Bob Dole, R-Kan., the majority leader, agreed to the move after Sens. William S. Cohen, R-Maine, and Edward M. Kennedy, D-Mass., told Dole they had lined up 56 votes to overturn the law. A similar vote in the House would be needed to overturn the provision, however.

Knutson, Lawrence L., "Clinton vows to fight military discharges over AIDS," *Boston Globe,* Feb. 10, 1996, p. 3.

President Clinton promised to fight in Congress and the courts against a new requirement to discharge military personnel with the AIDS virus. But aides said the administration would still enforce the provision.

Priest, Dana, "White House to challenge ban on HIV in military," *The Washington Post,* Jan. 27, 1996, p. A11.

The Clinton administration said it would try to repeal a defense bill provision requiring discharge of service members who have HIV and added it is also considering a legal challenge to the measure.

Gays in the Military

Black, Chris, "Gays in military find backlash," *Boston Globe,* Feb. 5, 1995, p. 1.

The backlash against gays and lesbians in the U.S. armed forces following President Clinton's imposition of the policy popularly referred to as "Don't ask, don't tell, don't pursue," is examined, including the view that the practices of military commanders, who surveys show overwhelmingly oppose homosexuals in their ranks, have contributed to and encouraged an environment of hostility toward them.

Jaschik, Scott, "Bowdoin College drops ban on military recruiters in response to a congressman's legislative campaign," *The Chronicle of Higher Education,* March 3, 1995, p. A25.

Bowdoin College has scrapped a policy it adopted in 1990 that barred on-campus recruiting by employers, including the U.S. military, that discriminate on the basis of sexual orientation. The move came after a legislative campaign by Rep. Gerald B.H. Solomon, R-N.Y.

Jones, Franklin D., and Ronald J. Koshes, "Homosexuality and the military," *American Journal of Psychiatry,* January 1995, pp. 16-21.

The history of the exclusionary policy on homosexuals serving in the armed forces in the U.S. is examined. Evidence indicates that homosexuals in the military pose no documented threat to national security and show no signs of poor work performance.

"The military and gays: Still asking," *Harper's,* June 1995, pp. 18-20.

An excerpt from a report on the military's policy on homosexuality notes that although the armed forces were supposed to incorporate a "Don't ask, don't tell, don't pursue" policy, many have continued to interrogate and harass those suspected of being homosexuals.

Tailhook Incident

Cohen, Richard, "Keelhauling Commander Stumpf: Not all the victims of Tailhook were women," *The Washington Post,* Jan. 12, 1996, p. A15.

Cohen discusses the case of Navy Cmdr. Robert E.

Stumpf, whose promotion to captain was denied because of his involvement in the 1991 Tailhook Convention scandal, although he was cleared of any misdoings.

"Tailhook figure files suit over Navy promotion," *The Washington Post,* March 19, 1996, p. B8.
Cmdr. Robert E. Stumpf, who was cleared of wrongdoing in the Tailhook scandal, has accused Navy Secretary John H. Dalton of improperly blocking his promotion to captain.

Women and the Military

Bass, Frank, "Military says women need care for post-traumatic stress disorder," *The Houston Post,* Jan. 26, 1995, p. A25.
Joan Furey, director of the women veterans program office for the U.S. Department of Veterans Affairs, said that female military personnel are facing more cases of post-traumatic stress disorder due to sexual assaults.

Boxer, Barbara, "Chavez should apologize to military women," *USA Today,* March 8, 1995, p. A8.
In a letter to the editor, Sen. Barbara Boxer, D-Calif., comments on Linda Chavez's Feb. 1, 1995, *USA Today* column, "Woes mount for 2-sex military," saying that Chavez's comments were insulting not only to the family of Lt. Kara Hultgreen but to the entire naval community.

Chavez, Linda, "Woes mount for 2-sex military," *USA Today,* Feb. 1, 1995, p. A11.
Chavez says an investigation should be mounted into women in the military, saying that neither men nor women are satisfied with working or sleeping arrangements.

DeCew, Judith Wagner, "The combat exclusion and the role of women in the military," *Hypatia,* winter 1995, pp. 56-73.
The lifting of the ban on women in combat to gain equal opportunity for women has implications for treatment of military women in the areas of sexual harassment and abuse. The feminist debate on women and the military is discussed.

Graham, Bradley, "Military short of victory in war on bias," *The Washington Post,* April 29, 1995, p. A1.
Several dozen newly promoted rear admirals who were asked to assess the "overall equal opportunity climate" in the armed forces rated it better than good. By contrast, African-American women in the military who were asked the same question scored the climate below average. What military personnel think the services have done in their 47-year effort at integration depends on a service member's rank, sex and skin color.

Herbert, Melissa S., "Feminism, militarism, and attitudes toward the role of women in the military," *Feminist Issues,* fall 1994, pp. 25-48.
Attitudes toward the role of women in the military require the reconciliation of two often conflicting beliefs: those toward the roles and rights of women and those toward the military. The relationships between positive attitudes toward women's roles in society and positive attitudes toward feminism are explored.

"History of black women in the military," *Afro-American,* Feb. 11, 1995, p. B7.
The contributions of black women in U.S. military service are discussed, including a list of prominent black women in various wars.

Kilian, Michael, "U.S. military takes aim at harassment," *Chicago Tribune,* May 13, 1995, p. 3.
U.S. military commanders would be held directly responsible for sexual harassment in their jurisdiction under a proposed 48-point Defense Department reform plan. The plan follows an investigation ordered by Defense Secretary William Perry into harassment and racial and gender discrimination in the armed services.

Kilian, Michael, "Women pilots face military resistance," *Chicago Tribune,* Nov. 14, 1995, p. 1.
When women pilots were first allowed into combat roles in 1993, Maj. Jacquelyn Parker, a 15-year-veteran Air Force test pilot, became the nation's third female fighter jock and the first one in the Air National Guard. But elation turned to disappointment when the male pilots in her Syracuse, N.Y.-based National Guard sqaudron decided she "would not fit in," a revealing example of renewed resistance the nation's female military pilots are confronting.

Landay, Jonathan S., "Harassment still dogs the Navy in post-Tailhook era," *The Christian Science Monitor,* Nov. 20, 1995, p. 1.
The continuing incidences of sexual harassment allegations against U.S. Navy personnel, following the Tailhook scandal, are noted. Analysts believe that the fact that there were no courts-martial for those involved led to the continuing male-dominated climate.

Rimer, Sara, "Women are no big deal at an old military college," *The New York Times,* Sept. 6, 1995, p. A16.
Norwich University in Northfield, Vt., the U.S.'s oldest private military college, admitted its first eight women in 1974, two years after it merged with Vermont College, a non-military institution. The 1995 freshmen military class has 245 men and a record 65 women, and cadets view women at the school as "no big deal." The attitudes toward female cadets are discussed and compared to the problems faced by Shannon Faulkner at the Citadel.

Voisin, Ailene, "Women at military schools," *Atlanta Journal Constitution,* Oct. 15, 1995, p. F4.
Profiles of five women who endured harassment, jokes and insults from male cadets as part of the first West Point class to include women are presented.

Back Issues

Great Research on Current Issues Starts Right Here...Recent topics covered by The CQ Researcher are listed below. Before May 1991, reports were published under the name of Editorial Research Reports.

OCTOBER 1994
Historic Preservation
Religion and Politics
Arts Funding
Economic Sanctions

NOVEMBER 1994
Sex on Campus
Blood Supply Safety
Testing Term Limits
Religion in America

DECEMBER 1994
Farm Policy
Arms Sales
Earthquake Research
The Future of Television

JANUARY 1995
Treating Addiction
Child Custody and Support
Parents and Schools
Non-Proliferation Treaty at 25

FEBRUARY 1995
Cracking Down on Immigration
The Business of Sports
Reinventing Government
Housing Discrimination

Back issues are available for $5.00 (subscribers) or $8.00 (non-subscribers). Quantity discounts apply to orders over ten. To order, call Congressional Quarterly Customer Service at (202) 887-8621.

Binders are available for $18.00. To order call 1-800-638-1710. Please refer to stock number 648.

MARCH 1995
Death Penalty Debate
Primary Care
Democracy in Africa
Environmental Movement at 25

APRIL 1995
Abortion Clinic Protests
Dieting and Health
Combating AIDS
Rethinking Affirmative Action

MAY 1995
Assisted Suicide Controversy
Overhauling Social Security
Learning to Read
Mandatory Sentencing

JUNE 1995
Combating Infectious Disease
Property Rights
Repetitive Stress Injuries
Regulating the Internet

JULY 1995
War Crimes
Highway Safety
Combating Terrorism
Preventing Teen Drug Use

AUGUST 1995
Job Stress
Organ Transplants
United Nations at 50
Advances in Cancer Research

SEPTEMBER 1995
Catholic Church in the U.S.
Northern Ireland Cease-Fire
High School Sports
Teaching History

OCTOBER 1995
Quebec's Future
Revitalizing the Cities
Networking the Classroom
Indoor Air Pollution

NOVEMBER 1995
The Working Poor
The Jury System
Sex, Violence and the Media
Police Misconduct

DECEMBER 1995
Teens and Tobacco
Gene Therapy's Future
Global Water Shortages
Third-Party Prospects

JANUARY 1996
Emergency Medicine
Punishing Sex Offenders
Bilingual Education
Helping the Homeless

FEBRUARY 1996
Reforming the CIA
Campaign Finance Reform
Academic Politics
Getting Into College

MARCH 1996
The British Monarchy
Preventing Juvenile Crime
Tax Reform
Pursuing the Paranormal

APRIL 1996
Centennial Olympic Games
Managed Care
Protecting Endangered Species

Future Topics

- ***Russia's Political Future***
- ***Marriage and Divorce***
- ***Year-Round Schools***

THE CQ Researcher

PUBLISHED BY CONGRESSIONAL QUARTERLY INC.

Russia's Political Future

Will voters turn the clock back in June?

Russia's upcoming presidential election, on June 16, will largely be a referendum on President Boris N. Yeltsin's program of economic and political reforms. In the five years since the Soviet Union collapsed, the bumpy transition from a state-controlled to a market economy has benefited relatively few Russians, leaving the vast majority of the population either no better off or even less prosperous than they were under communism. Yeltsin's main challenger, Communist Party leader Gennadi A. Zyuganov, is appealing to the nostalgia and resentment of Russia's weary electorate by promising to restore the Soviet empire — and communism — as well as to reimpose state control over large industries. Yeltsin, meanwhile, has been backtracking on his reform program, casting doubts on his commitment to democratic change.

INSIDE THIS ISSUE

CQ May 3, 1996 • Volume 6, No. 17 • Pages 385-408

Formerly Editorial Research Reports

Russia's Political Future

The Issues

Background

Current Situation

Outlook

Sidebars and Graphics

For Further Research

COVER: RUSSIAN FEDERATION PRESIDENT BORIS N. YELTSIN ANNOUNCES THAT RUSSIAN FORCES WILL STOP THEIR MILITARY OFFENSIVE IN CHECHNYA DURING A PRE-RECORDED TV APPEARANCE IN MOSCOW, MARCH 31, 1996. (REUTERS/ DIMA SOKOLOV)

THE *CQ Researcher*

May 3, 1996
Volume 6, No. 17

The CQ Researcher (ISSN 1056-2036). Formerly Editorial Research Reports. Published weekly (48 times per year, not printed March 1, May 31, Aug. 30, Nov. 29) by Congressional Quarterly Inc., 1414 22nd St., N.W., Washington, D.C. 20037. Annual subscription rate for libraries, businesses and government is $319. Additional rates furnished upon request. Second-class postage paid at Washington, D.C. POSTMASTER: Send address changes to The CQ Researcher, 1414 22nd St., N.W., Washington, D.C. 20037.

Russia's Political Future

By Mary H. Cooper

The Issues

Less than five years ago, Russian President Boris N. Yeltsin climbed atop an army tank in front of Moscow's besieged Parliament building and faced down a coup. Yeltsin's defiance made him a national hero overnight. But today, the once high-flying Russian president is fighting for his political future.

The chaotic scene on Aug. 19, 1991, was straight out of David and Goliath. Yeltsin, bullhorn in hand, captured the imagination of the world as he angrily denounced the attempted coup by hardline communists against Soviet President Mikhail S. Gorbachev. By year's end, the embattled Gorbachev was gone, the Soviet Union disbanded, the Communist Party routed.

Yeltsin immediately set his newly independent country on the road to sweeping reforms. Russians gained a constitution, a freely elected parliament and unimagined new political freedoms. And, aided by the United States and other Western countries, Yeltsin began to dismantle the state-run economy.

But the man who helped launch the second Russian Revolution may soon follow Gorbachev into political oblivion. In Russia's first presidential election since the Soviet Union's demise, scheduled for June 16, Yeltsin faces an uphill battle to hold onto his office. To add insult to injury, his main opponent is Gennadi A. Zyuganov, leader of the Communist Party that Yeltsin appeared to have consigned to history.

Yeltsin's popularity freefall stems in part from his poor health and other personal problems. His abuse of alcohol has been so serious that he sometimes has been intoxicated at public appearances — or failed to appear at all. Even more disquieting is a chronic heart problem that has put him in the hospital twice since last July.

But poor health may be the least of Yeltsin's problems with the electorate. He has incurred widespread wrath by his brutal repression of the 16-month rebellion in the breakaway province of Chechnya, in southern Russia. Since Dec. 11, 1994, Russian troops have bombarded villages and towns, killing more than 30,000 people, mostly civilians. Some 3,000 Russian soldiers have died in the conflict.

Yeltsin has acknowledged that he cannot win the election if the conflict continues. After ordering a brutal but unsuccessful offensive in late March, Yeltsin on March 31 announced a unilateral cease-fire and offered to negotiate virtual autonomy for Chechnya. [1] But the fighting still continues, and the April 21 death of rebel leader Dzhokhar Dudayev during a Russian rocket attack may further undermine Yeltsin's electoral prospects. [2]

A more fundamental complaint against Yeltsin is the failure of his reform program to improve living standards for ordinary Russians. "We may think democracy and free markets are wonderful things that bring us all kinds of benefits," says Russia expert Paul Goble, assistant director for broadcasting at Radio Free Europe. "But it's different if you're sitting in Moscow, watching your economy collapse by 50 percent in the last five years and watching Russia go from being a superpower to being treated like an increasingly marginal country."

It's not that the reforms haven't helped Russia's economy. Removing price controls on consumer goods, privatizing state industries and reducing government expenditures are beginning to have a positive impact. Inflation, which soared after price controls were lifted in 1992, has fallen to more bearable levels. Many Russians now have a financial stake in the plants and shops where they work. And consumer goods, once so scarce in cities that people waited hours in line for a loaf of bread, are abundant.

"Today there are no queues, and there are no shortages of consumer goods," says Vladimir N. Sterlikov, deputy chairman of the Russian Bank for Reconstruction and Development in Moscow. "Even the problem of food supplies has been solved. Despite the fact that most of it comes from abroad, it's available."

But the reforms have also brought wrenching changes. For 75 years, the Soviet state had guaranteed the basics Russians needed to survive — a place to live, adequate food, employment, an orderly society. Unfortunately for Yeltsin, some free-market reforms have destroyed those guarantees for a majority of voters while offering little in exchange.

The breakdown of communist authority left a void that was quickly filled by crime syndicates. Privatization has forced inefficient enterprises to "downsize" — a new concept for Russians — or to shut down entirely. As a result, many Russians are unemployed for the first time — and there is no safety net to save them from poverty.

The changes also have left many Russians resentful of the Yeltsin

Will Boundaries Change After the Presidential Election?

If Communist Party leader Gennadi A. Zyuganov defeats Russian President Boris N. Yeltsin June 16, Russia could attempt to assert its power over the other 14 autonomous republics of the former Soviet Union. The party has said that the Russian Federation's well-being is tied to the Soviet empire's restoration.

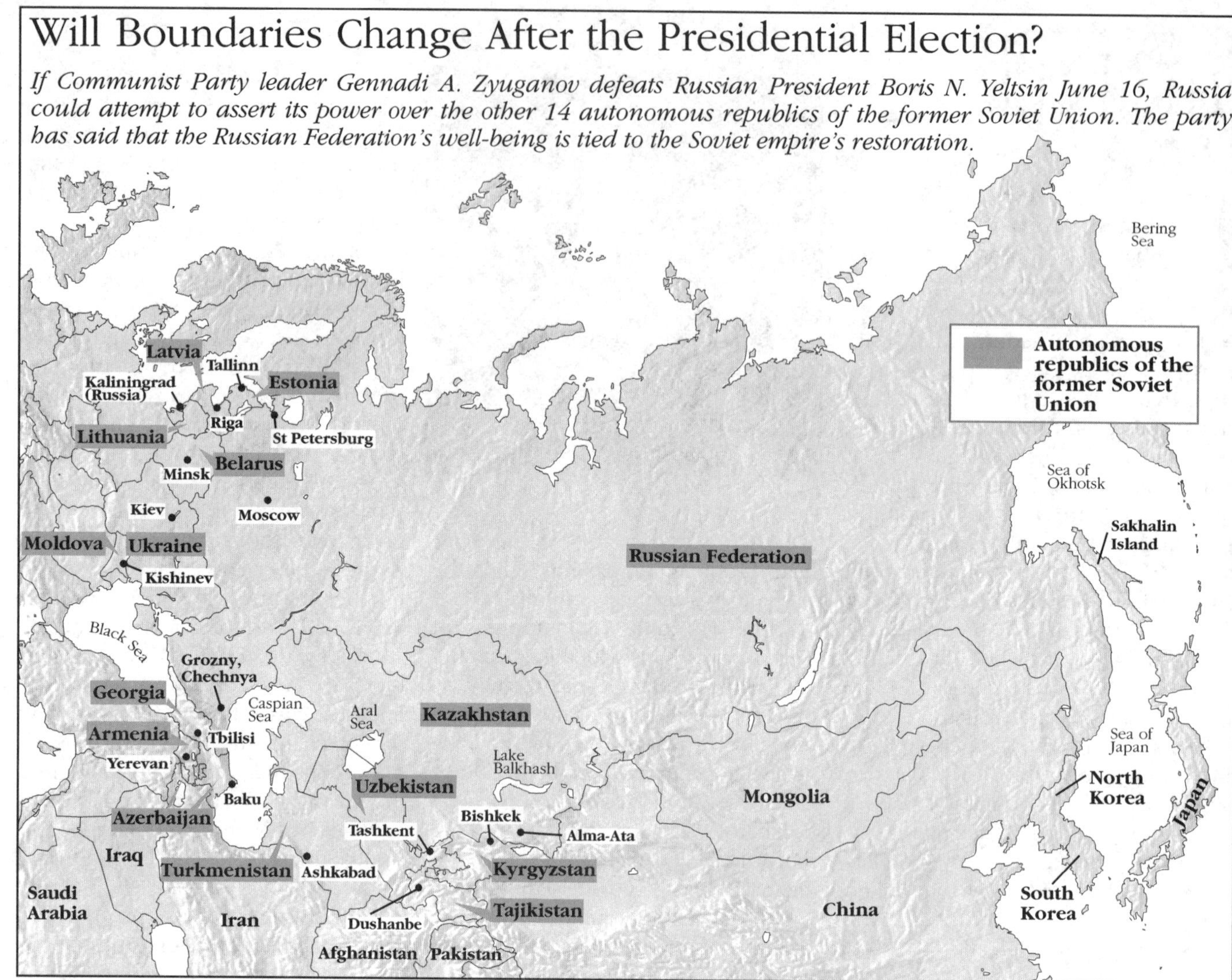

government's acquiescence to the United States and other Western providers of aid and loans. (*See story, p. 396.*) These donors insist that officials must accelerate the pace of reform to qualify for direct government aid as well as loans from the International Monetary Fund (IMF). Some Russians even see the reform program as a U.S.-engineered plot to destroy Russia, or at least to weaken it to the point where it can no longer challenge the United States' role as the world's sole superpower. [3]

"In the ideology of Zyuganov and the Communist Party, there's a tremendous need to reassert Russia's power presence," says David Remnick, a longtime Moscow observer and author of the Pulitzer Prize-winning account of the Soviet Union's demise, *Lenin's Tomb*. "The notion of one superpower, a unipolar world or a new global order — all those thing make these people hysterical."

Voters' discontent with the pace of reform is defining the issues of the upcoming elections. "The dynamics of Russian domestic politics is absolutely clear," says a high-level Russian official, who asked that his name not be used. "We are faced with a classical political dilemma: Either it is going to be democracy and free markets, or it's going to be a state-controlled economy and totalitarian regime like it used to be in the Soviet Union before 1985, when Gorbachev came to power."

Russian voters registered their discontent with the reforms during last December's parliamentary elections, when they handed a resounding victory to the Communist Party. By racking up 22 percent of the vote, the communists became the party with the most seats in the Duma, or lower house. The ultranationalist Liberal Democratic Party, led by Vladimir Zhirinovsky, captured 11 percent of the vote, leaving advocates of reform outnumbered by the extreme right- and left-wing parties. Although the parliament has far less power than the president in Russia's presidential republic, the vote stunned Yeltsin and his supporters.

After the vote, Yeltsin had just six months before the June presidential election, and he set about restoring public confidence in his leadership. He has reversed course on several key aspects of his policy, including the economic reform program. He fired Anatoly Chubais, who headed the program, and other key personnel in an evident show of understanding voters' frustration. Following charges of corruption in the sale of state-owned industries, the privatization program has ground almost to a halt. [4]

In an apparent attempt to undercut the communists' promise to restore Russia's world prominence, Yeltsin is walking a thin line, talking tough at home while trying not to alienate his supporters in the West, chiefly Germany and the United States. In April, after the Duma passed a nonbinding resolution rejecting the 1991 treaty that dissolved the Soviet Union, Yeltsin signed a pact establishing closer economic and political relations with Belarus. He also offered similar ties to the other 13 former Soviet republics. [5]

And in a move apparently aimed at quieting charges that he is too accommodating to Washington, Yeltsin loudly proclaimed a ban on U.S. chicken; he later allowed the sales to continue, but with higher tariffs.

Sensitive to charges of interference in Russia's domestic politics, the Clinton administration has refrained from expressing direct support for Yeltsin. But there is no doubt about its belief that a Yeltsin win is vital for U.S. interests. Among Yeltsin's challengers, Zyuganov and Zhirinovsky both decry Russia's opening to the West and promise to assume a more aggressive foreign policy. Secretary of State Warren Christopher, on a visit to Ukraine in March, denounced a communist proposal to restore the Soviet Union as "disturbing" and "highly irresponsible."

As recently as March, Yeltsin's prospects looked slim indeed, with the Communist Party seemingly poised to regain the Kremlin leadership. Since then, however, Yeltsin's chances have improved — not least because he has quashed media coverage of his opponents' campaigns — and some observers now predict that he will win.

Reuters

Russian Federation President Boris N. Yeltsin addresses a joint session of Congress, June 17, 1992.

If no candidate receives more than 50 percent of the vote, the first- and second-place winners will compete in a run-off election, probably in July. * In recent weeks, Zhirinovsky has fallen to a distant fourth place in the polls behind third-place Grigory Yavlinsky, a liberal economist who backs economic reforms. That leaves Zyuganov as the main challenger to Yeltsin, whose 14-15 percent approval rating in mid-March put him in second place behind Zyuganov, who enjoyed a 19-25 percent rating. [6]

But an upset victory is not out of the question, says Duke University political scientist Jerry Hough, a longtime Kremlin watcher. Hough, who recently conducted an opinion poll in Russia, says that the outcome may depend on Yeltsin's ability to pick up additional support by May.[7] If he doesn't, Hough says voters who fear a return to repressive Soviet-style rule under Zyuganov may shift their support from Yeltsin to Aleksandr Lebed. The retired general fashions himself after former Chilean strongman Augusto Pinochet, a ruthless dictator who launched reforms that bolstered the economy. If Lebed beats Yeltsin and makes it into the second round, Hough says, "he would be a formidable candidate against Zyuganov."

Hough also points to a more ominous outcome of a flagging Yeltsin campaign. "Someone could simply remove Yeltsin from the scene in May," he says. "That would make [Prime Minister] Viktor Chernomyrdin president, which would postpone the election three to four months and give him time to become a stronger candidate."

Yeltsin is reportedly so determined to hold onto the presidency that he has stopped drinking. "Yeltsin is physically fit, he's lost 24 pounds, and he

* Although more than 20 people expressed interest in running for president, only 11 candidates, including former President Mikhail S. Gorbachev, garnered the 1 million signatures required by April 16 to place their names on the ballot. Six people who were not permitted to put their names on the ballot have filed appeals.

plays tennis for two hours straight," the Russian official says. "He is very focused and has said very clearly he is not going to give the country back to the communists, that he started this to win."

But given the trends in Russia over recent months, a Yeltsin victory would be no guarantee that Russia will remain on its current path to capitalism — or even that such a course is in the country's long-term interest.

As the presidential campaign enters its final six weeks, these are some of the issues Russian voters — and the world community — are considering:

Should the United States more openly support Yeltsin as the candidate of reform?

From the moment Gorbachev began to loosen the central government's grip over the Soviet Union and its flagging economy, the United States has supported reforms in Russia and the former Soviet republics. That policy has translated into the warmest relations with Kremlin leaders since the outbreak of the Cold War in 1945.

The unifying theme of both the Bush and Clinton administrations' policies toward Moscow has been to do everything possible to support the reform process, lest Russia fall back into the hands of anti-Western communists who would reignite a costly, dangerous cold war. President George Bush enthusiastically encouraged Gorbachev's limited political and economic reforms until the Soviet leader's ouster in 1991. Similarly, the Clinton administration has backed increased assistance to Russia and signed a broad range of economic, military and political agreements reached by Vice President Al Gore and Prime Minister Chernomyrdin.

Despite its support of Yeltsin's reforms, the Clinton administration has avoided endorsing Yeltsin in the upcoming presidential election; Clinton also has taken pains to avoid criticizing Yeltsin. As recently as April 2, Clinton stated that as a matter of policy the United States should not "take any position on the elections in another country." [8] Getting overly involved in Russia's election could raise objections of meddling in Russia's internal affairs and possibly tip the scales in favor of Yeltsin's chief opponent, Communist Party leader Zyuganov.

In the late 1980s, the Reagan and Bush administrations strongly endorsed Gorbachev because of his reforms, only to see his presidency go down in flames. "There's a tendency to personalize politics in Russia, and I think that's a mistake," says Remnick. "It would be absurd for the United States to go too far in trying to push their obvious preference for Yeltsin because it might have a counterproductive effect."

Reuters

Communist Party leader Gennadi A. Zyuganov and former Russian Vice President Aleksandr Rutskoi, leader of the nationalist Derzhava ("Great Power") movement (at rear).

Meanwhile, the administration has supported Yeltsin indirectly, notably by using its international clout to speed the IMF's recent approval of a $10.2 billion loan eagerly sought by Yeltsin. The administration also has warned loudly against Yeltsin's communist opponent. During a recent trip to Eastern Europe, for example, Secretary of State Christopher denounced the recent vote by the communist-dominated Duma to reverse the Soviet Union's dissolution.

Some critics say the United States' enthusiasm for Russia's economic and political openings to the West has blinded it to the weaknesses of the Kremlin's leaders. The most glaring blind spot, many critics say, has been the administration's near silence over Yeltsin's decision to quash the Chechen insurrection in December 1994. The 16-month siege has cost the lives of some 30,000 people, mostly civilians, as government forces have brutally attacked apparently unarmed villages in an unsuccessful strategy to beat the rebels into submission.

"The Clinton administration has been so mild-mannered about Chechnya it is just inexcusable," says Marshall I. Goldman, associate director of Harvard University's Davis Center for Russian Studies. "We wouldn't let the Chinese get away with anything like that. We're applying a double standard."

An even more serious mistake, some analysts say, has been the administration's assumption that Yeltsin's reform program is good for stability in Russia and thus for U.S.-Russian relations. "Where I fault Clinton, and consistently, is the [economic reform] policy that he not only has accepted from Yeltsin but that he's pushed on Yeltsin," says Hough, who calls the program too drastic.

Through its influence on the IMF, Hough says, the U.S. has imposed stringent conditions on Russia for receiving its loans, such as removing tariffs, privatizing industry and effecting other sweeping changes, among them creating a stable currency and a reliable legal system. In short, Hough says, the Clinton administration is asking Russia to do the impossible: "Here you've got a president who knows he can't end the deficit in the United States in one year, who knows that you can't just cut Medicare to hell, and yet he's asking Yeltsin to go into the election with a policy 10 times more radical than anything that even Newt Gingrich would even think of."

Whatever their assessment of the Clinton administration's overall policy toward Russia, most analysts agree that it must refrain from openly endorsing any candidate in the Russian election. "They have no choice," says Goldman. "Whatever they do is going to be wrong. There are a lot of mistakes in the way it's been handled, but there is no way of emerging from this without some difficulty. They're damned if they do and they're damned if they don't."

Further complicating the administration's stance is the looming U.S. presidential election, which will pit Clinton against Senate Majority Leader Bob Dole, R-Kan. "On the one hand, Clinton can't pull the rug out from

Progress in Moving Toward a Market Economy

Most former Soviet republics and Soviet bloc members lagged behind Russia in creating market economies, as of 1994. In only a few cases did the private sector economy account for more than 50 percent of the gross domestic product (GDP). However, several republics have made progress in privatizing small firms, achieving market pricing and developing trade.*

Progress toward a market economy is rated on a 1-4 scale, where 1 represents "little progress" and 4 represents a "market economy."

	Private sector share of GDP, 1994 (percent)	Privatization: Large firms	Privatization: Small firms	Prices, competition	Trade, foreign exchange	Role of banks
Albania	50	1	3	3	4	2
Armenia	40	1	3	3	2	1
Azerbaijan	20	1	1	3	1	1
Belarus	15	2	2	2	1	1
Bulgaria	40	2	2	3	4	2
Croatia	40	3	4	3	4	3
Czech Republic	65	4	4	3	4	3
Estonia	55	3	4	3	4	3
Georgia	20	1	2	2	1	1
Hungary	55	3	4	3	4	3
Kazakhstan	20	2	2	2	2	1
Kyrgyz Republic	30	3	4	3	3	2
Latvia	55	2	3	3	4	3
Lithuania	50	3	4	3	4	2
Macedonia, former Republic of Yugoslavia	35	2	4	3	4	2
Moldova	20	2	2	3	2	2
Poland	55	3	4	3	4	3
Romania	35	2	3	3	4	2
Russian Federation	50	3	3	3	3	2
Slovak Republic	55	3	4	3	4	3
Slovenia	30	2	4	3	4	3
Tajikistan	15	2	2	3	1	1
Turkmenistan	15	1	1	2	1	1
Ukraine	30	1	2	2	1	1
Uzbekistan	20	2	3	3	2	1

* *Since the above data were collected, the most-privatized economies had 5-10 percent increases in the private sector share of the GDP, according to the World Bank. Its "World Development Report" is due to be released June 27, 1996. Less significant gains were experienced by republics with less private sector development.*

Source: European Bank for Reconstruction and Development, in Finance & Development, *September 1995* under Yeltsin and then have the Republicans say it was Clinton who elected the communists," Hough says. "But if he paints the communists as the end of the world and they win, then they'll say Clinton's the one who lost Russia.

"So he's got the problem of wanting to convey to the American public that if Yeltsin is defeated, that doesn't mean you have to elect Bob Dole. He's in a delicate balancing act where essentially he's got to have a positive posture toward Yeltsin."

Would a communist president of Russia rekindle the Cold War?

The emergence of Communist Party leader Zyuganov as the current frontrunner in the presidential race has raised fears of a return to the Cold War. This prospect alarms not only Washington and its NATO allies but also the former Soviet bloc countries of Eastern Europe that have embraced the West over the past five years.

The Duma's non-binding vote to nullify the Soviet Union's dissolution reflected the Communist Party's view that Russia's well-being is tied to the restoration of its former empire. The party also has called for the "voluntary" reconstitution of the Soviet Union.

On the economic front, the party has denounced Yeltsin's reform program, which it blames for the economic hardship experienced by a large segment of the population. Zyuganov has promised to renationalize the oil industry and other essential industries and halt the current privatization program.

Part of Zyuganov's message may be mere electioneering. Despite the rhetoric about restoring the Soviet Union, says the high Russian official, the party today is far less dogmatic than its Soviet predecessor. "They've changed a lot," he says. "They're typical classical social democrats."

If the official is right, a Russian communist president could be expected to support a non-confrontational policy with its neighbors. But to win the election, the official says, Zyuganov is relying heavily on older Russians.

"Their electorate is made up of senior citizens who have lived their whole lives under communism, and they want to go back for two reasons," he says. "Mentally, they are still in their young years, and economically, they are the most deprived part of the population. For that reason, Zyuganov cannot claim to be a typical, European-style social democrat who wants a mix of economic capitalism and a socialist approach to social issues. If he comes out and says he's a social democrat, he will immediately lose 50 percent of his electorate."

Reuters

A Russian armored personnel carrier passes a ravaged apartment building in Grozny, Chechnya. Since Dec. 10, 1994, Russian bombs have killed more than 30,000 people, mostly civilians, in the breakaway province in southern Russia.

Many Western analysts, including critics of Yeltsin, say that a communist victory would spell trouble. "A Zyuganov presidency would be a disaster on almost every account imaginable," Remnick says. "Economically, the threat of inflation is huge if they begin subsidizing large industries that are dying with state funds."

Moreover, Remnick says, the Communist Party is not picking up where it left off in 1991. "This is not the new thinking of Mikhail Gorbachev. This is a kind of national Bolshevism infused with a very heavy dosage of resentment about what's happened and an extraordinary determination to reassert Russia as a world power."

Of course, Russia has lost much of its military clout since 1991. It has dismantled part of its nuclear arsenal — with U.S. assistance — and its military is in disarray. "Despite all its nuclear weapons and its huge territory, Russia is quite weak compared to what our image of it was some years ago," Remnick says. "Militarily, it can't seem to win a war in Chechnya, even though it's managed to kill a lot of people."

Despite this weakness, in Remnick's view Russia has enough military clout to cause considerable trouble. "A lot of what Zyuganov says is quite confrontational," he says. "I think that we can expect a great deal more difficulty from Russia than we've been used to since 1991."

Others dispute Russia's ability to pose much of a threat, even under a more militant president. "Russia today is not what the Soviet Union was," says Goble. "That doesn't mean Zyuganov doesn't want to take everything back to where it was; it means he can't. Russia controls 150 million people today, not 300 million as before. The Russian army is much worse off than it was five years ago. It's not so much that democratization and reforms have gone too far, but that the process of decay has gone too far."

A more confrontational Russia under a communist president may have more domestic political implications for the United States than real strategic threat. "We've lived with the Cold War, and we can live with it now," Goldman says. "But it's going to be a big foreign policy debacle for Clinton. It's going to vindicate people like Sen. Jesse Helms [R-N.C.] who have said all along the reforms in Russia were not real. And it's going to lead to a return to spending for Star Wars, the B-2 bomber, nuclear submarines — all things that really haven't helped us that much."

Is Russia likely to pursue free-market and democratic reforms in a second Yeltsin term?

Yeltsin rose to power with the promise of improving living standards for ordinary Russians by bringing Russia into the community of free-trading nations. Over the past five years, he has overseen a radical dismantling of the immense state-controlled economy and embarked on a program to establish an entirely new economic system fashioned on the Western, capitalistic model. Political reforms have ended state control over much of the media and spawned an array of political parties that span the ideological spectrum. The Cold War has receded into distant memory as Russia's relations with the United States and the rest of the non-communist world have greatly improved.

Despite numerous setbacks, Yeltsin spent the first four years of his presidency as a staunch champion of reform. Since the Communist Party's advances in the December 1995 parliamentary election, however, Yeltsin appears to have had second thoughts. The communists and their supporters won close to a majority of the seats in the Duma with their call to reverse many of Yeltsin's reforms and return to the domestic stability and international prestige of the Soviet Union before its collapse.

Yeltsin responded to the communists' upset victory by following much of their platform. He fired officials in charge of economic reforms and called a virtual halt to privatization efforts. He assumed a less accommodating stance toward the United States by replacing his Western-leaning foreign minister, Andrei V. Kozyrev, with Yevgeny M. Primakov, a former head of foreign intelligence.

In another slap at the United States, Yeltsin banned American chicken imports, then allowed the sales to go ahead, but with high tariffs to protect Russian producers. Yeltsin also forged closer ties with neighboring Belarus, moving Russia one step closer to a reassertion of Russian dominance over the former Soviet republics now loosely associated in the Commonwealth of Independent States (CIS).

Some analysts say that if he is re-elected, Yeltsin will likely continue to reverse or slow his reform program. "I don't think Yeltsin is committed to reform," says Goldman. "Yeltsin is committed to power, either democratic or economic." If the voters demand a halt to the reforms, Goldman adds, that is what they would get in a second Yeltsin term.

Radio Free Europe's Goble, who finds it "impossible to believe that Yeltsin won't be re-elected," predicts sharp reversals after the election. "He's going to go back on a whole bunch of things," Goble says. "You're not going to see as much privatization, you're not going to see as much agreement with the West and you're going to see an increasing effort by the Russians to form alliances with pariah states — Iran, Libya, Iraq — against the West. You're going to see a tightening up of the Russian position right across the board."

In a second term, Goble says, Yeltsin's instinct would be to respond to the sentiment of the voters the communists appealed to in December. "Russia is a great power that feels wounded and aggrieved and that wants to strike out," Goble says. "It can do a lot of this rhetorically. Whether it can do some of the practical things is another matter."

Other analysts agree that the pace of reform will slow in a second Yeltsin term, but in ways that more accurately reflect the legitimate needs of Russian society. "With Yeltsin, a lot of the reform program has been one step forward, two steps back, to use the old Leninist formula," says Remnick. "What you're seeing now is a regrouping and posturing on the right, not only for short-term election purposes but also for very real political reasons."

In Remnick's view, Yeltsin's move to slow, if not reverse, the reform process was inevitable. "The notion that a Western liberal democracy was going to prevail in 15 minutes in Russia was preposterous," he says. "It's just an unrealistic scenario and, in a way, an unfair scenario. Who voted for a Western liberal democracy anyway?" ■

BACKGROUND

Yeltsin's Rise

The sweeping reforms that have stunned Russia have their roots in policies introduced by the last Soviet president, Gorbachev. Upon taking power in 1985, Gorbachev ushered in a series of political reforms, known as glasnost ("openness"), that granted freedoms of speech and political association unprecedented in the Soviet Union's seven decades. Gorbachev also introduced economic reforms, known as perestroika ("restructuring"), that permitted limited rights to private enterprise.

Yeltsin, who had risen through the Communist Party ranks in his home region of Sverdlovsk, clashed with Gorbachev over what he called the slow pace of democratic reforms and was ousted from the ruling Politburo in 1987. Over Gorbachev's strong opposition, Yeltsin won election to the Russian parliament in 1990 and quit the Communist Party.

In 1991, Yeltsin was elected Russia's president and emerged as a popular hero in the failed August coup by hard-liners against Gorbachev. But the central government's authority had been irreparably weakened. In December, Gorbachev resigned and the Soviet Union collapsed, leaving Yeltsin in control of the Russian Federation, by far the largest and most powerful of the former Soviet republics.

By the late 1980s, the Soviet economy had fallen so far behind other major world economies that Gorbachev's reform efforts were unable to prevent the country's collapse.

Even before the Soviet Union ceased to exist, Yeltsin announced plans for a vast economic reform program in Russia. Drawn up by Deputy Premier and Economics Minister Yegor Gaidar, a 35-year-old economist with no government experience, the program began Jan. 2, 1992, with the removal of price controls on most goods. Price controls later were loosened on essentials, such as energy and basic foods. The lifting of price controls set off a period of hyperinflation that caused widespread hardship among Russian workers, long accustomed to scarce but affordable consumer goods. Reformers defended the "shock therapy" as a necessary step to Russia joining the international trading system.

Privatization Begins

At the same time, the Yeltsin-Gaidar reform program began privatizing state property. Small businesses were sold either at auction or through buyouts by employees, who were issued vouchers to purchase shares in their enterprises. By July 1994, when the voucher program ended, more than 100,000 small businesses, as well as more than 15,000 medium and large firms, had shifted to private ownership. By the end of 1994, more than 70 percent of Russian industry — including half the work force and two-thirds of the country's production capacity — had been privatized. [9]

"The typical Russian Ivan curses the economists and all their reforms because the factory where he works has been shut down for the third month in a row. . . . Meanwhile his downstairs neighbor, a petty swindler and operator, has been made the chairman of a voucher privatization fund and not only has an apartment in Moscow but one in Paris as well. Ivan hasn't gotten a damn thing from this privatization stuff."

While privatization shifted ownership, it left unchanged many of the inefficiencies that had developed over the decades of state control. Newly privatized businesses that had the same managers and workers as before often were unable to compete on the open market with more efficient firms. As factories closed or laid off workers, unemployment soared, in some parts of the country exceeding 30 percent. [10]

Like inflation, layoffs were an unfamiliar hardship for most workers in the state-controlled Soviet economy.

In a reshuffling of his cabinet at the end of 1992 Yeltsin ousted Gaidar, by then prime minister. The move was one of a series of abrupt shifts in direction that have typified Yeltsin's first term. To succeed Gaidar, Yeltsin installed industrialist Chernomyrdin, who continued the reform program, but at a slower pace. The next major step was reducing the government subsidies that had propped up enterprises during the Soviet era. Although necessary to achieve a free market and curb inflation, the subsidy cuts left many businesses in debt and unable to pay their workers for months at a time.

"The typical Russian Ivan curses the economists and all their reforms," writes Russian journalist Galina Dutkina, "because the factory where he works has been shut down for the third month in a row due to non-payment of accounts between various enterprises, which means of course that he isn't being paid; because Ivan's wife has been fired as part of staff cuts, and no one will give her a job because she's too near pension age; because his student daughter is given a stipend that is only enough to buy a bottle of vodka. . . . Meanwhile his downstairs neighbor, a petty swindler and operator, has been made the chairman of a voucher privatization fund and not only has an apartment in Moscow but one in Paris as well.

Continued on p. 396

Chronology

1980s *A failing economy paves the way for the Soviet Union's decline and eventual demise.*

March 10, 1985
Mikhail S. Gorbachev takes power in the Soviet Union. He later relaxes some of the state's control over political expression and tries to revive the economy through limited market reforms.

—— • ——

1990s *Russia and the other states of the former Soviet Union embark on the transition from state control over their economies to free markets.*

1990
Boris N. Yeltsin, ousted from the Politburo in 1987 after criticizing the slow pace of Gorbachev's reforms, wins election to the new Russian parliament and quits the Communist Party.

1991
Congress passes the Nunn-Lugar Cooperative Threat Reduction Act to speed the collection and dismantling of nuclear weapons in the former Soviet Union. Rebel leaders in Chechnya, a province in southern Russia, declare independence.

Aug. 19, 1991
Yeltsin, the newly elected president of Russia, leads the opposition to an unsuccessful coup attempt against Gorbachev by hard-line communists.

November 1991
Economist Anatoly Chubais becomes head of Russia's state privatization committee, which will undertake the biggest transfer of property to private hands in history.

Dec. 25, 1991
Gorbachev resigns and the Soviet Union is dissolved.

Jan. 2, 1992
Under the direction of Deputy Premier Yegor Gaidar, Yeltsin launches his economic reform program. Price controls for most goods are lifted, causing rampant inflation but an increase in the availability of food and other consumer goods.

1992
Gaidar is replaced by industrialist Victor Chernomyrdin, who slows the pace of reform.

October 1993
Yeltsin orders an artillery attack on the White House, site of the Congress of People's Deputies, after members of the Soviet-era legislature refuse to obey his order to leave. He earlier had disbanded the legislature in response to its vote to end economic reforms.

December 1993
In a referendum, Russian voters adopt a constitution granting the president broad powers and creating a new parliament, the Federal Assembly. Ultranationalist Vladimir Zhirinovsky and other anti-reform legislators are elected in the first parliamentary elections.

Dec. 11, 1994
Russian troops launch their attack against the separatist rebels in Chechnya.

Dec. 17, 1995
Frustrated by economic hardship and Russia's weakened international image, voters hand the reconstituted Russian Communist Party a landslide victory in elections for the Duma, the lower house of parliament. Yeltsin responds by forcing the resignations of Chubais and other reformist officials and reversing course on several reform measures.

Jan. 26, 1996
The Senate approves the Strategic Arms Reduction Treaty (START II) cutting the number of long-range nuclear weapons deployed by the United States and Russia to no more than 3,500 weapons each.

March 31, 1996
After 16 months of fighting against Chechnyan rebels that has left more than 30,000 people dead, Yeltsin declares a unilateral cease-fire and offers to negotiate an agreement providing autonomy for the breakaway province.

April 2, 1996
Belarus and Russia sign agreement for closer economic and political ties.

April 21, 1996
President Clinton meets Yeltsin for a summit in Moscow to discuss arms control and other bilateral issues.

June 16, 1996
Presidential elections are scheduled to be held in Russia. If no candidate wins a majority of the votes, the top two contenders will compete in a runoff election, expected to be held in July.

U.S. Invests Its Aid in Trade

After the Soviet Union collapsed in December 1991, the United States began providing assistance to speed Russia's transition to a free-market economy. The theory was that the free exchange of goods through international trade creates common interests and diminishes the risk of hostility. [1]

In 1992 and every year thereafter, the United States has granted Russia most-favored-nation (MFN) trade status, imposing the same preferential tariffs on imports from Russia that it imposes on goods from its closest allies. [2]

Much of the U.S. aid is provided indirectly, through loans, loan guarantees and insurance to private U.S. investors. The main conduit of this assistance is the U.S. Export-Import Bank, which by March 1995 had provided some $2 billion in loans to spur U.S. investment in Russia. A major target of the bank's activity has been Russia's vast energy sector, including a $10 billion, multi-nation effort to develop offshore oil and gas deposits near Sakhalin Island on Russia's Pacific coast.

The Overseas Private Investment Corporation (OPIC), another federal agency, has helped finance and insure some 60 U.S. ventures in Russia, while the U.S. Trade and Development Agency spent $15 million last year alone to help U.S. firms locate investment opportunities in Russia.

The United States also has provided direct assistance to Russia in the form of grants — much of it for food — totalling some $3.4 billion through fiscal 1996, which ends Sept. 30. Citing criticism of the Yeltsin government's military action in Chechnya and its plan to support Iran's nuclear program, lawmakers reduced President Clinton's fiscal 1997 request of $788 million for aid to the former Soviet Union. The law, signed Feb. 12, 1996, would provide $641 million for all the countries of the former Soviet Union, down 25 percent from the previous year's appropriation.

Following lawmakers' criticism that aid to the former Soviet Union had been disproportionately generous to Russia in the past, the bill earmarked $225 million for Ukraine, $85 million for Armenia and $30 million for Georgia. So many conditions were placed on the aid that Russia could see less than $200 million of the total.

A separate defense appropriations bill, signed Nov. 30, 1995, would provide $300 million to dismantle nuclear armaments in fiscal 1997 in all countries of the former Soviet Union, $71 million less than Clinton had requested.

---

[1] Data in this section are based on Steven J. Woehrel, "Russia," *CRS Issue Brief*, Congressional Research Service, March 25, 1996, pp. 13-15.

[2] Under the Jackson-Vanik amendment to the 1974 trade act, MFN status is denied to Russia unless the president certifies it allows free emigration of Jews; such certifications have been made on an annual basis since 1992.

Continued from p. 394

Ivan hasn't gotten a damn thing from this privatization stuff." [11]

As a result of the discontent, Yeltsin faced a showdown in July 1993 with the Soviet-era legislature, the Congress of People's Deputies, when delegates voted to reverse many of the economic reform measures. Yeltsin responded in September by dissolving the legislature, but many delegates refused to leave, even after Yeltsin ordered an artillery attack against the White House, Russia's parliament building.

In a referendum held that December, Russian voters adopted a new constitution, which granted the president broad authority and established a new legislature, the Federal Assembly, comprised of an upper house, the Federation Council, and a lower house, the State Duma. The same month, voters registered their opposition to Yeltsin by electing anti-reform legislators, including ultranationalist Zhirinovsky, to the Federal Assembly.

Propping Up Russia

A major impetus to Russia's sweeping program of economic reforms has been the IMF, which provided $6.8 billion in low-interest loans to Russia in 1995 and recently approved an additional $10.2 billion credit package. To ensure that its loans will be repaid, the IMF requires recipient countries to strengthen their economies by adopting the kinds of reforms that Yeltsin has imposed in Russia, for example privatizing state-owned enterprises and eliminating price supports and subsidies.

The most recent IMF loan agreement appeared to be jeopardized in early 1996, when Yeltsin, responding to popular resentment of the reforms, forced Deputy Premier Chubais and other officials responsible for the reform program to resign. Yeltsin's sudden undercutting of reform was seen as an attempt to regain popular support from the communists, who had scored a major victory in December's parliamentary elections on an anti-reform platform.

Ever since Yeltsin launched his economic reforms in January 1992, he has received direct financial support from Western Europe, especially Germany, as well as the United States. U.S. assistance to Russia has come in several forms. (*See table, p. 397.*)

One approach has been the extension of low-interest loans by the U.S. Export-Import Bank to Russian enterprises that buy parts from American exporters. One such loan that recently received preliminary approval would provide $1 billion to help Aeroflot-

Russian International Airline buy U.S. Pratt & Whitney engines for a new line of Russian aircraft. Critics of this form of assistance say it actually delays privatization by propping up large enterprises still under Russian state control. [12]

The United States also provides direct assistance to Russia in the form of grants. A primary motivation of this type of assistance has been to reduce the threat of nuclear proliferation. With the fall of the Soviet Union and the subsequent disarray in the military, American lawmakers feared that Russia's nuclear arsenals were vulnerable to theft and that the lethal bomb-making materials would find their way into the hands of terrorists or countries eager to develop nuclear weapons.

In 1991, Congress passed legislation sponsored by Sens. Sam Nunn, D-Ga., and Richard G. Lugar, R-Ind., funding the dismantlement of Russia's nuclear weapons and the purchase of bomb-grade materials for permanent disposal in the United States. The law also helped convert Russia's vast military-industrial complex to civilian use. In addition, the Clinton administration has agreed with Russia and six other former Soviet republics to help improve security measures at their nuclear material storage sites. [13]

Other U.S. programs designed to encourage the reform process in Russia entail less direct funding but attempt to foster mutual understanding and cooperation in a wide variety of fields. Under American leadership, NATO's Partnership for Peace program sponsors joint military exercises with Russia and other former Soviet-bloc countries.

Other joint projects include the collaboration of NASA and Russian scientists aboard the Mir space station; NASA's research collaboration in a pilot project to develop a supersonic passenger plane; the sharing of spy technology to detect toxic-waste sites; and a joint naval oceanographic project slated for later this year. Many of these programs have come out of the agreements forged by Vice President Gore and Chernomyrdin in the course of six meetings, the most recent in January. ■

U.S. Aid to the Former Soviet Union

The United States has given more than $7 billion in business loans or credits to the former Soviet Union since its breakup. Most aid went to Russia, reflecting its importance to U.S. interests. Roughly $7.7 billion in grants wwent for disarmament, food and private-sector development. The drop in credits after 1994 reflects Russia's reluctance to take on more debt; the drop in grants since 1994 reflects declining congressional support for aid to Russia.

Fiscal Year	Total Credits (in millions)	Total Grants (in millions)
1992	2,662	906
1993	1,363	1,636
1994	1,638	2,792
1995	1,337	1,351
1996	106*	1,026
Total	**7,106**	**7,711**

* *The total for 1996 will rise as data from the Export-Import Bank and Overseas Private Investment Corp. become available.*

Source: Congressional Research Service, April 30, 1996

CURRENT SITUATION

Communists' Resurgence

The last two years have seen a steady erosion of public support for Yeltsin's policies, which caused widespread unemployment and economic hardship for a broad segment of the population. His standing eroded still more following his decision in December 1994 to send in troops to quell a rebellion in Chechnya. A heart condition that hospitalized Yeltsin twice in 1995, the lingering Chechnya conflict and the lack of evidence that the reform program was paying off for most Russians culminated in the December 1995 parliamentary victory for the Communist Party.

"The major source of support for the communists in December and for Zyuganov today is the dissatisfaction of the bulk of the population with the mid-term results of the economic reforms in Russia," says the Russian official speaking off the record. "Some people, mainly private sector workers, are satisfied with the situation because they are living much better

Continued on p. 399

Communist Party Rises Anew in Eastern Europe

Many Western observers hailed the collapse of the Soviet Union in 1991 as a victory for capitalism and democracy. In short order, it was thought, the peoples of the former Soviet Union would embrace economic reforms in pursuit of their version of the American dream.

The first few years of the post-Cold War era lent credence to the notion that communism, at least under its Soviet guise, was dead. Led by the Baltic states of Estonia, Latvia and Lithuania, former Soviet bloc republics from Eastern Europe established their independence from Moscow and threw out their communist leaders. These largely bloodless revolutions paved the way for parliamentary democracies and a transition to free markets.

Russia, by far the biggest and most powerful country to emerge from the breakup, moved toward democracy under President Boris N. Yeltsin, putting in place a new constitution, freely elected parliament and widespread personal freedoms. Russia enthusiastically embraced capitalism, freeing prices, privatizing industries and opening its vast economy to outside investment and trade.

But after only a few years, economic reforms seem to have brought more hardships than visible benefits in much of the former Soviet Union. The price of freedom has meant unprecedented rates of unemployment, severe poverty and a loss of social services once dependably provided under communist rule. The resulting problems unleashed a wave of nostalgia for the prestige and stability Russia enjoyed before 1991.

Thus it came as little surprise when the Russian Communist Party won more than 20 percent of the votes in last December's parliamentary elections. Now party leader Gennadi A. Zyuganov is the frontrunner in this year's presidential election campaign, set for June 16.

But Zyuganov is hardly the only communist politician making a comeback in the former Soviet bloc. Former Warsaw Pact countries of Eastern Europe, some of which began the transition to free markets long before 1991, also are seeing a resurgence of support for communist leadership.

Last November, Polish President Lech Walesa, the legendary head of the Solidarity movement that challenged the Communist regime in the 1980s, was defeated in his re-election bid by a former sports minister in that regime. Voters elected as their new president Aleksander Kwasniewski, who now heads the Democratic Left Alliance, which holds 37 percent of the seats in the Sejm, Poland's parliament. Hungary's prime minister, Gyula Horn, is a former Communist whose current party, the non-Marxist Hungarian Socialist Party, holds a majority of the seats in the National Assembly.

In Romania, where the most violent repudiation of the Communist order occurred in December 1989, President Nicolae Ceausescu was overthrown and executed. The current president also is a former Communist official. President Ion Iliescu, whose government also is heavily staffed by Ceausescu-era officials, has served two terms and is expected to run for re-election again this year with little effective opposition. The repressive policies of Vladimir Meciar, a former communist official and now prime minister of Slovakia, a sovereign country since the 1993 breakup of Czechoslovakia, are reminiscent of the hardline tactics used to quash the 1968 Czech revolt against Soviet domination.

Indeed, the only countries of the former Soviet bloc that have not elected former communists to high office are Albania, the Czech Republic and — alone among the 15 countries that once were part of the Soviet Union itself — Armenia. [1] The Czech Republic — the other new country that emerged from the 1993 split — even bars most former party members and collaborators in the old regime from holding political office. Memories of the regime's brutal suppression of a 1968 student demonstration in Prague run so strong that communist candidates stand little chance of gaining seats in next month's parliamentary elections. [2]

Differences among former Soviet bloc nations' attitudes toward communist politicians are less stark than may appear, however. The Italian Communist Party — Western Europe's largest — changed its name to the Democratic Party of the Left and softened its agenda after the Soviet collapse. Similarly, many of Eastern Europe's political leaders with roots in the region's communist past now favor democratic and economic reforms.

Far from providing evidence that Eastern Europeans reject democracy and capitalism, the election of former communist apparatchiks to political office may pave the way for a more gradual transition to the Western model than Yeltsin's shock-therapy approach.

"If you look at Poland and Hungary, the communists who have now won political office are essentially left-wing social democrats," says Jerry Hough, a political scientist at Duke University. "It's been a very useful stage in moving those countries in a Western direction. Zyuganov also could play that role."

Unlike Zyuganov and his supporters in Russia, however, most of Eastern Europe's political leaders, communist or otherwise, show little nostalgia for the past. Many of the Soviet Union's former military allies now are clamoring for membership in the 15-member European Union and the 16-member North Atlantic Treaty Organization (NATO).

In fact, NATO is expected to accept the Czech Republic, Hungary and Poland as members some time in the near future — over Russia's vehement opposition. (*See "At Issue," p. 401.*)

---

[1] "They're Ready to Be Red Again," *Time*, Jan. 8, 1996, p. 21. The Commonwealth of Independent States, the loose alliance that succeeded the Soviet Union, includes all the former Soviet republics except Estonia, Latvia and Lithuania.

[2] See Christine Spolar, "Region's Communist Revival Finding No Echo in Prague," *The Washington Post*, April 16, 1996.

Continued from p. 397
than they used to under the communist regime. But those in the state sector are still teetering on the brink of poverty, with a standard of living similar to that of the very, very low middle class in the United States."

According to supporters of Yeltsin's program, the election is falling at an unfortunate stage of the reform process, with the pain of dismantling state controls far outweighing the visible benefits. "When Margaret Thatcher started her reforms in Great Britain in 1979, it took five years for the richest part of her electorate to get the dividends and almost 10 years of strict monetary policy for the results to reach the common people," says Sterlikov of the bank for reconstruction.

He likens the transition to a free-market economy to a ride up the elevator in a high-rise building. "Keep in mind that Mrs. Thatcher was starting on the 30th floor of the building, while we started five years ago in the underground parking garage and wasted the first three years in non-constructive discussion about which way to go with reforms. So no one in Russia, unfortunately, can speak today about any visible results for the common citizen."

In the Dec. 17 election of the Duma, the common citizens spoke out. With a heavy 65 percent turnout, they handed over 22 percent of the votes to communists, more than twice the 10 percent result of the pro-Yeltsin party, Our Home Is Russia. The misnamed Liberal Democrats, led by ultranationalist Zhirinovsky, saw their share of the vote plummet from 23 percent in the 1993 parliamentary election to just 11 percent. The leading opposition party that supports reforms, Yabloko, led by presidential candidate Yavlinsky, came in a distant fourth, with 7 percent of the vote.

The vote gave 157 of the 450 seats in the Duma to communist deputies. But the support of two small parties of the left, the Agrarian Party and Power to the People, brings the communist voting bloc close to a majority, with a total of 186 seats, more by far than any other coalition in the legislature. No matter who emerges from the June ballot as Russia's next president, the legislature is in a position to support the Communist Party agenda for the next four years.

Yeltsin Backtracks

Just what the December election will mean for Yeltsin's chances for re-election this June is far from clear. Most analysts point to opinion polls placing Zyuganov ahead of Yeltsin as an indication of what to expect. But the Russian official speaking off the record cautions that people vote differently in parliamentary and presidential elections.

"I think the December results have been misinterpreted," he says. "In parliamentary elections, like your congressional elections, people tend to think in more economic ways. They want to get something out of this reform for themselves, and that's why they considered the election in December a good chance to express their protest against what they see as the unfairness of the reforms. But when it comes down to a question of principle, of where are we going to go, back to communism or move along the road to a better life, they are going to be thinking totally differently from how they did in December."

Yeltsin himself appears to be taking the Duma vote seriously. No sooner did he return to work Dec. 29 from his most recent hospitalization than he began shifting his policies, at times appearing to adopt the communist agenda. In January he replaced Foreign Minister Kozyrev with Primakov. By forging closer ties with neighboring Belarus, he moved in the direction of extending Russia's influence over its neighbors, a leading communist imperative.

In March, in an apparent bid to outflank growing communist support in the vast rural areas of Russia, he issued a decree permitting people to buy and sell land, a long-awaited first step toward land reform. [14] He also moved to shore up Russian industry and agriculture by adopting higher tariffs on a broad array of imported goods following a threat to ban U.S. chicken imports. [15]

At the same time, Yeltsin symbolically repudiated one of his most controversial reforms by sacking Chubais, architect of the privatization program and turning it over to Vladimir Kadannikov, who has close ties to state-owned enterprises. Under his direction, the program, plagued with reports of corruption, has virtually ground to a halt.

"You can see in the Yeltsin government a reflection of the resentment of reform policies," says Remnick. "It's natural that things have turned that way, because the pendulum probably had swung too far."

One of the few policy issues on which Yeltsin and the communists agree is their adamant opposition to plans by the U.S.-led NATO alliance to expand into Central Europe by admitting three former Soviet allies — Poland, Hungary and the Czech Republic. Although he agreed to contribute 1,500 Russian troops to the NATO mission overseeing the military settlement in Bosnia, Yeltsin and Zyuganov see NATO's planned expansion as a threat to Russia. (*See "At Issue," p. 401.*)

The Problem With Chechnya

Where Yeltsin has failed to reverse his unpopular policies is in Chechnya. Yeltsin himself has acknowledged that his chances at re-election depend on resolving the issue. "If we do not withdraw the troops, there is no way I can become president," he said in February. "The people will not elect me." [16]

On March 31 he declared a unilateral cease-fire and offered to negotiate the terms of an agreement to give Chechnya greater autonomy than any state in the Russian Federation. But the cease-fire has never taken hold, Russian troops continue to fire on villages in the region and rebel leader Dudayev was killed in a rocket attack barely three weeks later.

Even if Chechnya does not block Yeltsin's re-election, his handling of the autonomy effort there may haunt future Russian leaders for some time. "I think Yeltsin has made one of the grand mistakes of his life," says Radio Free Europe's Goble. "He's now said to the Chechens, 'You can have everything but independence, and you will be the most autonomous place in the whole country.' Well, there are many other places in Russia that would like autonomy, including the neighboring republic of Dagestan, the Tatars in the middle Volga, Russians in the Far East — even St. Petersburg. Once you've given it to one, why shouldn't you give it to all? From a Russian perspective, why should Chechnya have rights that St. Petersburg doesn't have? This will have enormous consequences."

Crucial Election Nears

By April 5, when Yeltsin formally entered the presidential race with a campaign appearance in southern Russia, his policy shifts had begun to pay off. Although he still trailed Zyuganov, Yeltsin had narrowed the margin by half since January to just 7 percentage points, according to one poll, and was continuing to gain ground. The poll also showed that if voters had to choose only between Yeltsin and Zyuganov, which will occur if they finish first and second in the June 16 election but neither wins more than half the votes, they would enter the July runoff in a dead heat. [17]

Yeltsin is benefiting from a virtual boycott of Zyuganov's campaign by the Russian media. Fearful of losing the press freedoms they have enjoyed since 1991 if the communists win, both state and independent television and print journalists are focusing their campaign coverage almost exclusively on Yeltsin while ignoring Zyuganov and downplaying the other probable candidates.

The selective coverage also is a result of Yeltsin's policy of riding roughshod over press freedoms. Earlier this year, he fired a TV station director he accused of devoting excessive coverage to the hostilities in Chechnya. "Television and the other media have been totally controlled," says Duke University's Hough. "Even if Zyuganov were for a free press, he would launch a major purge of the media if he's elected. Actually, they would need a major purge in order to make the media neutral."

Hough is one of the few observers who give someone other than Yeltsin and Zyuganov a shot at the presidency. If Yeltsin appears destined to lose by the end of May, Hough says his supporters may shift their votes to another candidate who can beat Zyuganov and prevent the return of communists, who could be expected to retaliate against people who have profited from the reforms.

"You have to remember what's going on in Russia today," he says. "The degree of corruption you find in places like South Korea is nothing in comparison. There are a lot of people who have the potential of going to jail, and they're really quite desperate."

In Hough's view, that upset candidate could well be retired Gen. Lebed, who promises to pursue less ambitious economic reforms while cracking down on crime and asserting a stronger role for Russia in the CIS and beyond. In addition to Lebed, other plausible alternatives to Yeltsin and Zyuganov include Yavlinsky, a supporter of liberal economic reforms who has stayed out of Yeltsin's government, and Svyatoslav Fyodorov, an entrepreneurial Moscow eye surgeon best known for his assembly-line surgical technique for curing nearsightedness.

Alternatively, two of the minor candidates could throw their support behind the other one to create a "third force" strong enough to make it to the second round. All three leading alternative candidates — Lebed, Yavlinksy and Fyodorov — are members of the Duma and support gradual economic reform. Under the third-force scenario, an alternative candidate could garner enough support from disgruntled but anti-communist voters to defeat Yeltsin in the first round and then take out Zyuganov in the second round. So far, however, there is little sign of popular support for such a third-force candidate. [18] ■

OUTLOOK

A Precarious Path

Judging by the campaign rhetoric emanating from Russia, the post-Cold War honeymoon between Russia and the West may be over. The prospect of a communist victory in Russia has raised alarms from the West and, perhaps more justifiably, from its neighbors in Eastern Europe.

Although little is known about Zyuganov's personal views of economic reform and Russia's rightful place in the world, the Communist Party openly advocates a return to some of the policies that undermined the Soviet Union five years ago. "If Zyuganov wins, externally he's going to make Russia a strong military, economic and political power," Harvard's Goldman predicts. "Internally, the people around Zyuganov are talking about bringing back the whole system of central planning."

But many Kremlin-watchers caution that Russia is headed in a different direction no matter who wins the presi-

Continued on p. 402

At Issue:

Would expanding NATO to include central and East European countries threaten Russia?

yes

KARL-HEINZ KAMP
Head of the Foreign Security Policy Section, Department of Political Research, Konrad-Adenauer-Stifung, a public policy institute in Germany

FROM "THE FOLLY OF RAPID NATO EXPANSION," *FOREIGN POLICY*, SPRING 1995.

What would be the Russian response to a hasty expansion of NATO, which would move it closer to Russia's borders? Although Moscow is troubled by political turmoil and economic chaos, it is still a nuclear superpower and the key player within the former Soviet Union. . . .

Not long ago, many in the West, particularly in the United States, argued in favor of a "strategic partnership" between Russia and the West. That concept, however, assumes a compatibility of interests between Russia and the West — an assumption that seemed realistic in light of sweeping Russian acquiescence in Western wishes in the early 1990s.

Today, even the architects of the "strategic partnership" admit that the honeymoon in Russia's relations with the West is over. Recent Russian complaints about Western military actions in Somalia and against the Serbs and Moscow's increasing efforts to reassert its influence over the former republics of the Soviet Union have revealed that Russia's own delineations of its national security will not necessarily be in harmony with the West's preferences. Nationalism with significant anti-Western components has reemerged as a defining factor in Russian foreign relations. In this context, some Russians are suspicious that Western governments hope to fragment the Russian Federation and thus will try to tip the geopolitical balance permanently in the West's favor.

These tendencies do not at all mean that a return to the old patterns of East-West conflict is inevitable. But avoiding a return will require a careful Western strategy of managing the difficult and sometime prickly relationship with Russia. In particular, it is important to take special precautions to avoid a Russian perception of Western encirclement, since it would inevitably weaken democratic forces in Moscow in favor of nationalists around the country. The reform process itself might then be seriously endangered. Russia must not be isolated unless it isolates itself by returning to the aggressive or imperialist tendencies of the past. Expanding NATO now would necessarily fuel Moscow's fears of Western attempts to fill the power vacuum in Eastern Europe at the expense of Russia. Explaining to a humiliated Russian military establishment that an extension of NATO for the sake of stabilizing Russia's western periphery would be a net gain for them, not another defeat, would probably exceed the ingenuity of even the most eloquent NATO expansionists.

no

SECRETARY OF DEFENSE WILLIAM J. PERRY
FROM REMARKS DELIVERED AT THE NATIONAL PRESS CLUB, FEB. 28, 1996.

I believe that the creation of the Partnership for Peace has been one of the most significant events of the post-Cold War era. By forging networks of people and institutions, working together to preserve freedom, promote democracy and build free markets, the Partnership for Peace today is a catalyst for transforming Central and Eastern Europe, much as the Marshall Plan transformed Eastern Europe in the 1940s and the '50s. It is the passage that this half of Europe did not take in 1947. It is the door that we never opened at that time.

To lock in these gains of reform, NATO must ensure that the ties it is creating in the Partnership continue to deepen and that NATO proceeds with a gradual and deliberate process of outreach and enlargement to the east.

NATO enlargement is inevitable, and if NATO enlargement is a carrot encouraging reforms, then NATO cannot keep that carrot out of reach forever. And even as some countries join NATO, it will be important to keep the door open for others down the road. NATO must make sure that the Partnership for Peace continues to provide a place for all in the security architecture of Europe so that we keep the door open to Marshall's Europe even for those nations that do not aspire to become NATO members.

For Marshall's vision to be truly fulfilled, one of the nations that must walk through this door is Russia. Russia has been a key player in Europe's security for over 300 years. It will remain a key player for better or for worse. Our job is to make it for better. . . .

It is fair to say that most members of Russia's political establishment do not welcome or even accept NATO's plans for enlargement.

When I was in Russia last summer, I had a number of conversations with Russian government leaders and Duma members about the future of European security. . . . [I told them that] NATO, far from being a threat to Russia, actually contributes to the national security of Russia as well as to the security of its own members. . . .

I have to tell you, I did not persuade my Russian colleagues with my arguments. But I do believe that as Russia deepens its involvement with NATO, it will come to believe in the truth of my conclusion. . . .

Russia is already developing a cooperative relationship with NATO, and is beginning to play a leading role in the Partnership for Peace. Through that real-world exposure, Russia will come to understand that NATO enlargement means enlarging a zone of security and stability that is very much in Russia's interest, not a threat to Russia.

For More Information

Carnegie Endowment for International Peace, 2400 N St. N.W., Washington, D.C. 20037; (202) 862-7997. This research organization, which focuses on international affairs and U.S. foreign policy, has offices in Moscow and closely monitors events in the former Soviet Union.

Embassy of Russia, 2650 Wisconsin Ave. N.W., Washington, D.C. 20007; (202) 298-5700. The embassy is a source of Russian election data, economic statistics and political analysis.

U.S. Information Agency, 301 4th St. S.W., Suite 868, Washington, D.C. 20547; (202) 619-4563. The agency administers USIA programs in central Europe and the former Soviet Union in support of U.S. policies and manages educational and cultural exchange programs in the region.

U.S. State Department, Independent States and Commonwealth Affairs, Main State Building, Room 4223, Washington, D.C. 20520; (202) 647-6729. This office handles relations with the countries of the former Soviet Union, except the Baltic states.

Continued from p. 400

dency. Even if Yeltsin wins, they say, he is unlikely to pursue free-market reforms at the same pace he has.

Goble blames much of the disarray in Russia's move toward free markets on overzealous Western donors, including the United States. "You and I may think democracy and free markets are the best thing since sliced bread," he says. "But we're talking about a country that has lost half its population [with the Soviet Union's demise], where lawlessness is at an all-time high and where there is intolerable income differentiation. The tragedy is that we in the West have proclaimed Russia a democracy and worried only about making the economic transition. As a very wise Russian has said, what we have seen in Russia is a democratic revolution without democrats."

Popular nostalgia for Russia's international strength as leader of the Soviet Union also makes it unlikely that the next president will be as accommodating to the United States and other Western interests. It is not only the communists who are pushing for tighter Russian control over the republics of the former Soviet Union. "So is Yeltsin," Goble says. "The whole country wants it. The difference between the liberals and the reactionaries is not all that great on the issue of having the place reunified. It's just a question of how they want to do it. I don't think Russia can pull off reunification, but I think it's going to try, and that is going to be a disaster."

But most analysts agree that Russia has embarked on a path that, however precarious, is unlikely to lead back to its Stalinist past. "I think Russia is in for a long period of development, in which they sort these things out, not only in practical terms but in theoretical terms," says Remnick. A Zyuganov victory would not necessarily halt that process, in his view, but it would delay it. "It's going to take a long time," Remnick says. "And if the communists win, it will take an even longer time, because I don't think the communists can last very long."

The Russian government official also predicts that his country is in for a long process of development. "The Russians have to ask themselves what they want to get out of this first national election, communism or free markets," he says. "We're not speaking about democracy, which is a bad word now in Russia. A better life or life as we used to know it — that's the dilemma in their minds. They still hope for a better life because Russians are very patient." ■

Notes

[1] See Lee Hockstader, "Fighting Eases in Chechnya," *The Washington Post,* April 2, 1996.

[2] Steve Liesman, "Chechen Leader's Death Could Hurt Yeltsin's Prospects," *The Wall Street Journal,* April 25, 1996.

[3] For background, see "Aid to Russia," *The CQ Researcher,* March 12, 1993, pp. 217-240.

[4] See David Hoffman, "Pre-Election Pause in Privatization," *The Washington Post,* March 30, 1996.

[5] For background, see "Soviet Republics Rebel," *The CQ Researcher,* July 12, 1991, pp. 465-488.

[6] See David Hoffman, "Poll Shows Yeltsin Gaining," *The Washington Post,* March 21, 1996.

[7] See Jerry Hough, "Why Ivan Mistrusts Us," *The Washington Post,* Feb. 11, 1996.

[8] See Ann Devroy, "U.S. Plans to Stay Out of Presidential Race in Russia, Clinton Says," *The Washington Post,* April 3, 1996.

[9] Steven J. Woehrel, "Russia," *Issue Brief,* Congressional Research Service, March 25, 1996, p. 7.

[10] *Ibid.*

[11] Galina Dutkina, *Moscow Days* (1996), pp. 22-23.

[12] See David J. Kramer and Heidi Kroll, "The Ex-Im Bank's Russian Disaster," *The Wall Street Journal,* March 21, 1996.

[13] See R. Jeffrey Smith, "Nuclear Theft Potential Worries U.S.," *The Washington Post,* Feb. 29, 1996. For background, see "Nuclear Arms Cleanup," *The CQ Researcher,* June 24, 1994, pp. 553-576.

[14] See Michael Specter, "With Land Sale Edict, Yeltsin Opens Way to Longed-for Era," *The New York Times,* March 17, 1996.

[15] See Neela Banerjee, "Yeltsin Seeks Textile Tariff Boost as Protectionism Grows in Russia," *The Wall Street Journal,* March 6, 1996.

[16] See Richard Boudreaux, "Yeltsin Admits Reelection Depends on Chechnya," *Los Angeles Times* (Washington edition), Feb. 9, 1996.

[17] The poll was taken by a Russian polling organization, the All-Russian Center for Public Opinion Research. See Lee Hockstader, "Yeltsin's Rough Campaign Trail Paved with Promises," *The Washington Post,* April 6, 1996.

[18] See Claudia Rosett, "'Third Force' Stumbles in Russian Race," *The Wall Street Journal,* April 1, 1996.

Bibliography

Selected Sources Used

Books

Dutkina, Galina, *Moscow Days: Life and Hard Times in the New Russia,* Kodansha International, 1996.
A Russian journalist documents the day-to-day hardships imposed on a large number of her countrymen as a result of what she says is a grossly mishandled reform program.

Remnick, David, *Lenin's Tomb: The Last Days of the Soviet Empire,* Random House, 1993.
This Pulitzer Prize-winning account of the last days of the Soviet Union describes the transition from Mikhail Gorbachev's decline to the early days of Boris Yeltsin's Russia.

Thomas, Bill, and Charles Sutherland, *Red Tape: Adventure Capitalism in the New Russia,* Dutton, 1992.
This lively account of Russia's emerging marketplace describes the myriad obstacles uninitiated foreign investors may encounter when they try to do business in Russia.

Yeltsin, Boris, *The Struggle for Russia,* Times Books, 1994.
Russia's first freely elected president provides his own account of the Soviet Union's collapse and his first two years in office.

Yergin, Daniel, and Thane Gustafson, *Russia 2010 and What It Means for the World,* Random House, 1993.
The authors use the confusing reality of today's Russia to construct four scenarios for the country's future development, ranging from integration with the West to a return to the authoritarian model of the past.

Articles

Goble, Paul A., "Ten Issues in Search of a Policy: America's Failed Approach to the Post-Soviet States," *Current History,* October 1993, pp. 305-308.
Both the Bush and Clinton administrations have failed to appreciate the extent of change occurring in the former Soviet Union, Goble writes. As a result, the United States has adopted a "*People* magazine approach" that focuses more on political leaders than the fundamental transformation taking place in the region.

Kozyrev, Andrei, "Partnership of Cold Peace?" *Foreign Policy,* summer 1995, pp. 3-14.
Kozyrev, until recently Russia's foreign minister, explains the Yeltsin government's opposition to the U.S.-led push for NATO's enlargement to include Eastern European countries, but not Russia. NATO's dealing with any member of the former Soviet bloc, Kozyrev writes, should include Russia as well.

Matlock, Jack F. Jr., "The Russian Prospect," *The New York Review of Books,* Feb. 29, 1996, pp. 43-46.
The author, U.S. ambassador to the Soviet Union from 1987 to 1991, downplays the threat posed by the possibility of a communist or ultranationalist victory in Russia's election. Given the changes of the past five years, he writes, no Russian president could restore the Communist system or Russia's global reach.

Remnick, David, "Gorbachev's Last Hurrah," *The New Yorker,* March 11, 1996, pp. 68-83.
Since his ouster in late 1991, former Soviet leader Mikhail Gorbachev has kept a low profile in Russia. Now he is challenging Yeltsin for the presidency, but he is far behind his competitors in the polls.

Voigt, Karsten, "NATO Enlargement: Sustaining the Momentum," *NATO Review,* March 1996, pp. 15-19.
The president of NATO's interparliamentary forum, the North Atlantic Assembly, strongly endorses the alliance's plans to extend membership to countries of Eastern Europe, despite Russian opposition.

Reports and Studies

Tarnoff, Curt, "The Former Soviet Union and U.S. Foreign Assistance," *CRS Issue Brief*, Congressional Research Service, March 21, 1996.
More than 20 U.S. federal agencies have been involved in providing assistance to the former Soviet Union since it broke up into 15 separate countries in December 1991.

Woehrel, Steven J., "Russia," *CRS Issue Brief,* Congressional Research Service, March 25, 1996.
This report prepared by the Library of Congress' research arm summarizes the political forces competing in Russia's upcoming presidential election. It also provides an overview of economic reforms and other campaign issues.

The Next Step

Additional information from UMI's Newspaper & Periodical Abstracts database

Eastern Europe and Communism

Amsden, Alice H., "Eastern Europe: Putting some government back in manufacturing," *Technology Review,* July 1995, pp. 56-61.

While leaders of the formerly communist nations of Eastern Europe are striving to embrace capitalism, they are failing to provide firms with the help they need to participate in the global economy. The failures of manufacturing in the countries of Eastern Europe are investigated.

"Eastern Europe's hungry children," *The Economist,* Dec. 16, 1995, p. 50.

In Russia, pensioners by the millions will vote for the Communist Party on Dec. 17, giving credence to the idea that the old have suffered most from market reform in Eastern Europe. The children have actually been the ones to suffer the most.

Frankland, Erich G., "Green revolutions?: The role of green parties in Eastern Europe's transition," *East European Quarterly,* fall 1995, pp. 315-345.

The universal emergence of "green" parties and movements in the former communist countries of Eastern Europe is discussed. The impact of green parties on the content and direction of transitions away from communism is examined.

Jakubowicz, Karol, "Media within and without the state: Press freedom in Eastern Europe," *Journal of Communication,* autumn 1995, p. 125-139.

History is repeating itself in the sense that central and Eastern European countries are the scene of the gradual disentanglement of the media from structures of the state, a process that took place a long time ago in other countries. The old broadcasting systems that had been controlled by the Communist Party are being renationalized and turned into government agencies in some cases.

Murphy, Dean E., "Ex-communist waits in wings of Poland's political stage," *Los Angeles Times,* Feb. 18, 1995, p. A2.

Although former Communist Party official Jozef Oleksy has agreed to become Poland's next prime minister, he may never get the job. In February 1995, Oleksy faces what many consider to be an impossible task of making peace between his left-wing coalition government and President Lech Walesa.

"Poland: Walesa by a neck?" *The Economist,* Nov. 11, 1995, pp. 47-48.

Polish President Lech Walesa looks set to clinch the presidency in the election run-off Nov. 19, 1995. Aleksandr Kwasniewski won the first round last week, but Walesa hopes to gain anti-communist votes.

Szulc, Tad, "Unpleasant truths about Eastern Europe," *Foreign Policy,* spring 1996, pp. 52-65.

The West is having to face some unpleasant questions about the meaning of democracy and its future in Eastern Europe and Russia six years after the collapse of communist systems there. The U.S. and its Western partners are also wondering how they should adjust their attitudes and policies to the new realities in that part of Europe.

Wandycz, Katarzyna, "Alice in Poland," *Forbes,* Oct. 23, 1995, pp. 242-248.

While Polish capitalists are forging ahead, Polish politics is mired in the past. Ex-communist politico Alexander Kwasniewski is running well ahead in the November 1995 presidential election race.

Zubek, Voytek, "The phoenix out of the ashes: The rise to power of Poland's post-communist SdRP," *Communist & Post-Communist Studies,* September 1995, pp. 275-306.

The 1989 political transition in Poland swept away the country's communist party, but out of the rubble emerged the Social-Democracy of the Polish Republic. The evolution of this new party from its political marginality in 1990 to its electoral triumph and return to power in 1993 is traced.

NATO

Albright, Joseph, "No growth for NATO in 1996, Russia told," *Atlanta Journal Constitution,* Feb. 11, 1996, p. A6.

U.S. Secretary of State Warren Christopher eased Russia's horror about the eastward expansion of NATO on Feb. 10, 1996, by privately assuring Russian Foreign Minister Yevgeny Primakov that it won't happen this year. The new chief Russian diplomat responded by soft-pedaling Russia's rhetoric on NATO and by promising to delay trade with Iraq.

"Enlarging NATO offers world peace, prosperity," *USA Today,* April 16, 1996, p. A10.

An editorial argues that an expanded NATO would spur democracy, provide stability and open more trade doors and contends that if central and Eastern European nations prove a commitment to democracy, they deserve an opportunity to guarantee it by joining NATO.

Filipov, David, "NATO arms may stir Russian use of

force," *Boston Globe,* Feb. 16, 1996, p. 2.
A senior aide to President Boris N. Yeltsin, in impromptu and sometimes angry remarks to journalists, warned that Moscow would use force to stop any NATO deployment of nuclear weapons in Eastern Europe.

Hockstader, Lee, "Russian warns of attack if NATO expands east," *The Washington Post,* Feb. 16, 1996, p. A29.
Viktor Mikhailov, Russia's atomic energy minister, said that if NATO expands into Eastern Europe and deploys tactical nuclear weapons there, Moscow should respond by destroying the sites where they are based.

Ingwerson, Marshall, "Mistrust of NATO unites wary Russia," *The Christian Science Monitor,* March 25, 1996, p. 1.
The Western desire to expand NATO to encompass the former Soviet bloc nations of Eastern Europe has affected Russian domestic politics, as the country prepares for its upcoming presidential election. The possibility of NATO expansion has intensified anti-Western feelings among Russians, who view the West with a volatile mixture of eager aspiration and deep distrust, and could boost the electoral fortunes of the Communist Party, which is strongly nationalistic.

Moffett, George, "U.S. sticks to NATO expansion, while trying to mollify Russia," *The Christian Science Monitor,* March 22, 1996, p. 4.
A speech by U.S. Secretary of State Warren Christopher on March 20, 1996, delivered before foreign ministers from a dozen central and Eastern European nations, underscored the Clinton administration's determination to stick to its plans to "enlarge" NATO to ensure the states of central and East Europe are permanently ensconced in the Western orbit. In pursuing such plans, the Clinton administration has gone to great lengths to assure Russia that NATO enlargement is not designed to isolate Russia, but rather integrate a post-Cold War Europe.

Traynor, Ian, "Kohl calms Yeltsin's fear of Nato expansion," *The Guardian,* Feb. 20, 1996, p. 9.
German Chancellor Helmut Kohl retreated from NATO's expansion into former communist central Europe, going some way to appease fierce Russian objections to the proposed enlargement.

Traynor, Ian, "West alarmed as Russia hardens stance on NATO," *The Guardian,* Feb. 5, 1996, p. 8.
Russia's hardening resistance to the expansion of NATO dominated the military science conference in Munich, Germany, in early February 1996, which was attended by senior NATO officials, U.S. and European politicians and military experts.

"Yeltsin and Kohl discuss investment and NATO," *The New York Times,* Feb. 20, 1996, p. A6.
Russian President Boris N. Yeltsin met on Feb. 19, 1996, with Chancellor Helmut Kohl of Germany for talks on Yeltsin's efforts to win re-election, the decline of German business interests in Russia and the expansion of NATO.

Presidential Elections

Erlanger, Steven, "Russia's next vote," *Nation,* Jan. 8, 1996, pp. 4-6.
Although Russia has gotten through its December 1995 parliamentary elections, the real test of its commitment to democracy will be the presidential elections in June 1996. Erlanger examines the possible effect that these elections will have on political life in Russia.

"Russia, bumbling through," *World Press Review,* October 1995, pp. 14-15.
The degree to which Russia will continue to evolve will depend on who gets elected president in 1996. An overview of Russia's progress and a discussion of its possible future are presented.

"Russia and Chechnya: Yeltsin's Vietnam?" *The Economist,* Feb. 10, 1996, pp. 51-52.
A swift resolution to the conflict in Chechnya, Russia, could do wonders for Russian President Boris Yeltsin's chances of re-election in June 1996. Yeltsin cannot let the conflict drift violently on if he seeks re-election.

"Russia: The feministki are coming," *The Economist,* Aug. 12, 1995, pp. 44-46.
Women's groups in Russia are cropping up everywhere. Women's groups are concerned with self defense, politics and theater. A female presidential candidate may be forthcoming in elections expected in June 1996.

"Russia: He who hesitates," *The Economist,* Jan. 27, 1996, pp. 43-44.
Russian President Boris Yeltsin says he will formally announce his decision whether to run for re-election by mid-February 1996. Yeltsin is setting up a "presidential election headquarters." The president's campaign-to-come is discussed.

"Russia takes a harder line on the West," *U.S. News & World Report,* Dec. 25, 1995, p. 74.
The probable results of the Russian presidential elections in 1996 and their resulting scenarios are discussed. In Russia's history, there has been only one transfer of power by democratic means, and the chances of a second such transfer occurring in 1996 are a long shot.

"Russia: Will he, won't he?" *The Economist,* Aug. 19, 1995, pp. 44-46.
Russian President Yeltsin probably won't run for re-election in 1996. His health is being questioned, and Prime Minister Viktor Chernomyrdin has been allowed to gain the political spotlight.

"Russia's awful choice," *The Economist,* March 16, 1996, pp. 18-20.
All of the candidates for the Russian presidential election in June 1996 have dire shortcomings. President Boris Yeltsin appears to be the least awful candidate among the hopefuls.

"$10.2 Billion Loan To Russia Approved," *The New York Times,* March 27, 1996, p. A10.
The IMF said on March 26, 1996, that it had approved a $10.2 billion loan for Russia. The move is expected to be helpful to President Boris N. Yeltsin in the presidential election in June. The three-year loan is the fund's second biggest, after a $17.8 billion credit granted to Mexico in 1995.

Russian Communist Party

Banerjee, Neela, "Communist leaders indicate their win won't mean an end to reform in Russia," *The Wall Street Journal,* Dec. 21, 1995, p. A8.
As the continuing vote count from Russia's Dec. 17, 1995, elections showed the Communist Party consolidating control over parliament, the party's leadership put forth an agenda that appears to tamper little with Russia's market reforms.

Filipov, David, "Russia leader backs reforms," *Boston Globe,* Dec. 20, 1995, p. 10.
Russia's victorious Communist Party added to its gains in the newly elected lower house of parliament, but Prime Minister Viktor Chernomyrdin rejected calls for major revisions to his government's reforms.

LeVine, Steve, "Strength of hard-liners in Russia worries ex-Soviet republics," *The New York Times,* Dec. 11, 1995, p. A6.
The former Soviet republic of Kazakstan tallied parliamentary election returns on Dec. 10, 1995, but officials could be forgiven if they were distracted by chest-beating in neighboring Russia, where elections take place on Dec. 17. On Dec. 9, as Kazakstan voted to fill its 67-member parliament, the Russian Communist Party leader, Gennadi Zyuganov, vowed in Moscow to hold a referendum on whether to resurrect the Soviet Union, drawing concerns from government officials and Western diplomats about how the anti-reform trend in Russia will affect the region.

Specter, Michael, "Communists gain in the second tier of Russia's vote," *The New York Times,* Dec. 20, 1995, p. A1.
The figures from individual parliamentary races in Russia started to pour in on Dec. 19, 1995, and the results seemed to indicate that Communists will control virtually a third of Russia's new Parliament, far more seats than even they had hoped for.

"The center appears to hold in Russia," *Los Angeles Times,* Dec. 19, 1995, p. B8.
An editorial examines the gains made by the Communist Party of Russia and the nationalist party of Vladimir Zhirinovsky in Dec. 17, 1995, parliamentary elections in Russia, stating that the growth of the political opposition is undeniable.

"Communist named head of Russia's parliament," *Boston Globe,* Jan. 18, 1996, p. 18.
Russia's new parliament elected Gennadi Seleznev, a Communist Party member, as speaker in a move that is likely to intensify confrontation with President Boris Yeltsin's government.

Cooperman, Alan, and Sander Theones, "Here's Russia's new face of communism," *U.S. News & World Report,* Dec. 18, 1995, pp. 50-54.
Many Russians are considering voting for the communists because they believe that the communists have turned moderate and flexible under the leadership of Gennadi Zyuganov. Most Russians do not want a return to totalitarianism, but they are nostalgic for the cradle-to-grave Soviet welfare system, which they think that the Communist Party will try to bring back.

Ford, Peter, and Marshall Ingwerson, "Russia's reds and right set the pace for presidential bid," *Christian Science Monitor,* Dec. 19, 1995, p. 1.
Russian voters have dealt President Boris Yeltsin a sharp blow but not derailed their country's fitful democratic and economic reform. The Dec. 17, 1995, elections to the Duma gave Yeltsin's fiercest critics, Communist leader Gennadi Zyuganov and radical nationalist Vladimir Zhirinovsky, an impressive victory.

Hoffman, David, "Russia's Communists: How far can they go?" *The Washington Post,* Feb. 26, 1996, p. A12.
Beyond the campaign rhetoric lies the question of just what the Russian Communist Party really stands for and to what extent it could, or would, seek to put Russia on a different path. Propelled by a wave of public disenchantment with reform, it has become the new parliament's largest faction.

Ingwerson, Marshall, "Long arm of Russia reaches out, but nation battles to hang together," *The Christian Science Monitor,* March 20, 1996, p. 1.
Five years after it crumbled from its own weight, the U.S.S.R. is stirring again, and the Russian Communist Party, which now controls parliament and runs well ahead in presidential polls, has made restoration of the Soviet Union a top political priority during the run-up to the June presidential election. However, few of the former Soviet republics are inclined to rejoin Moscow's political orbit.

U.S. Policy and Russia

Banerjee, Neela, "U.S. firms hold their breath in Russia," *The Wall Street Journal,* Feb. 21, 1996, p. A10.

U.S. and other foreign firms in Russia believe that the communists, if elected to the presidency in June 1996, will be unable to deliver on their more reactionary campaign promises, such as renationalization of privatized companies, because it would create internal chaos. The views of some U.S. companies operating in Russia, such as Dresser Industries Inc. and Cargill Enterprises Inc., of the impact of a win by Gennadi Zyuganov of the Communist Party are examined.

Bradley, Bill, "Eurasia letter: A misguided Russia policy," *Foreign Policy,* winter 1995, pp. 80-97.
Many of the factors that are shaping Russia, such as the end of the Cold War, globalization and the information revolution, are also shaping the rest of the world. Bradley proposes six principles to help guide U.S. foreign policy regarding Russia.

Mandelbaum, Michael, "Our outdated Russia policy," *Time,* Feb. 5, 1996, p. 39.
It is time for a change in the United States' foreign policy toward Russia. The consistency of U.S. policy has become foolish and harmful to the national interests of the U.S., *Time* says.

Boris N. Yeltsin

"Belarus and Russia: Trick or treaty?" *The Economist,* March 30, 1996, pp. 49-51.
Russian President Boris N. Yeltsin boosted his re-election chances in June 1996 when he agreed to sign a bilateral treaty promising economic convergence with Belarus. The agreement will help his chances in beating communist rival Gennadi A. Zyuganov at the polls.

Cooperman, Alan, "Yeltsin is down, but Russia isn't out," *U.S. News & World Report,* July 31, 1995, p. 37.
Amid political and economic improvement, Russian president Boris Yeltsin's illness has fueled Kremlin infighting. The Russian political system as a whole, however, is gaining stability.

Hoffman, David, "Russia will not leave the road of reform," *The Washington Post,* Dec. 21, 1995, p. A1.
President Boris Yeltsin vowed that Russia "will not leave the road of reform," despite major gains made by the Communist Party in parliamentary elections.

"Russia after Chechnya," *The Economist,* Feb. 25, 1995, pp. 49-50.
Although Boris Yeltsin announced that Russia would hold its parliamentary and presidential elections on schedule, the war in Chechnya, Russia, has driven a wedge between Yeltsin and the democrats. Russia's fragmented politics are examined.

Williams, Carol J., "Russia redirects foreign policy sights eastward," *Los Angeles Times,* March 25, 1996, p. A1.
The swing from West to East in Russia's foreign policy priorities has enabled President Boris Yeltsin to remove just about every contentious international issue from the resurgent Communist Party's campaign agenda. Yeltsin's popularity has swelled with the foreign policy change.

Williams, Carol J., "To backers' cheers, Yeltsin vows to keep Russia steady," *Los Angeles Times,* April 7, 1996, p. A1.
Proclaiming peace in Chechnya and prosperity just around the corner, Russian President Boris Yeltsin unveiled a re-election strategy on April 6, 1996, in an address to cheering supporters at the Russian equivalent of a party convention.

Vladimir Zhirinovsky

Nolan, Bruce, "Duke's trip to Russia debated," *Times-Picayune,* Sept. 28, 1995, p. B1.
Former Louisiana state Rep. David Duke flew to Moscow and met with Russian ultranationalist Vladimir Zhirinovsky to talk about the release of detained Louisiana missionary Charles Songe, a development Songe's supporters greeted with a mixture of cautious hope and skepticism.

Rosett, Claudia and John Bussey, "Russia's Bad Vlad knocks West to win votes," *The Wall Street Journal,* Feb. 13, 1996, p. A11.
Vladimir Zhirinovsky, who came in third in Russia's last presidential election, is running again on a campaign that vilifies America as the source of his country's troubles. Ultranationalist in his views, Zhirinovsky is no longer the comic relief in Russian politics. His Liberal Democratic Party won 11 percent of the vote in December 1995, parliamentary elections, second only to the Communists. Zhirinovsky's bid for the presidency is examined.

Gennadi Zyuganov

Korotchenko, Igor, "Gennadi Zyuganov nominated as a candidate for president of Russia," *Current Digest of the Post-Soviet Press,* Feb. 7, 1996, p. 17.
Zyuganov was nominated as a candidate for the presidency of Russia. Zyuganov is the leader of the Russian Federation Communist Party.

Zyuganov, Gennadi A. "New Communist Party key to Russia's rebirth?" *Houston Chronicle,* Feb. 13, 1996, p. A25.
Zyuganov maintains that a new Communist Party is the key to Russia's rebirth as a mighty state. Zyuganov considers the disruption of military and strategic parity caused by the collapse of the former Soviet Union dangerously destabilizing.

Back Issues

Great Research on Current Issues Starts Right Here...Recent topics covered by The CQ Researcher are listed below. Before May 1991, reports were published under the name of Editorial Research Reports.

OCTOBER 1994
Historic Preservation
Religion and Politics
Arts Funding
Economic Sanctions

NOVEMBER 1994
Sex on Campus
Blood Supply Safety
Testing Term Limits
Religion in America

DECEMBER 1994
Farm Policy
Arms Sales
Earthquake Research
The Future of Television

JANUARY 1995
Treating Addiction
Child Custody and Support
Parents and Schools
Non-Proliferation Treaty at 25

FEBRUARY 1995
Cracking Down on Immigration
The Business of Sports
Reinventing Government
Housing Discrimination

Back issues are available for $5.00 (subscribers) or $8.00 (non-subscribers). Quantity discounts apply to orders over ten. To order, call Congressional Quarterly Customer Service at (202) 887-8621.

Binders are available for $18.00. To order call 1-800-638-1710. Please refer to stock number 648.

MARCH 1995
Death Penalty Debate
Primary Care
Democracy in Africa
Environmental Movement at 25

APRIL 1995
Abortion Clinic Protests
Dieting and Health
Combating AIDS
Rethinking Affirmative Action

MAY 1995
Assisted Suicide Controversy
Overhauling Social Security
Learning to Read
Mandatory Sentencing

JUNE 1995
Combating Infectious Disease
Property Rights
Repetitive Stress Injuries
Regulating the Internet

JULY 1995
War Crimes
Highway Safety
Combating Terrorism
Preventing Teen Drug Use

AUGUST 1995
Job Stress
Organ Transplants
United Nations at 50
Advances in Cancer Research

SEPTEMBER 1995
Catholic Church in the U.S.
Northern Ireland Cease-Fire
High School Sports
Teaching History

OCTOBER 1995
Quebec's Future
Revitalizing the Cities
Networking the Classroom
Indoor Air Pollution

NOVEMBER 1995
The Working Poor
The Jury System
Sex, Violence and the Media
Police Misconduct

DECEMBER 1995
Teens and Tobacco
Gene Therapy's Future
Global Water Shortages
Third-Party Prospects

JANUARY 1996
Emergency Medicine
Punishing Sex Offenders
Bilingual Education
Helping the Homeless

FEBRUARY 1996
Reforming the CIA
Campaign Finance Reform
Academic Politics
Getting Into College

MARCH 1996
The British Monarchy
Preventing Juvenile Crime
Tax Reform
Pursuing the Paranormal

APRIL 1996
Centennial Olympic Games
Managed Care
Protecting Endangered Species
New Military Culture

Future Topics

- ***Marriage and Divorce***
- ***Year-Round Schools***
- ***U.S., China and Taiwan***

THE CQ Researcher

PUBLISHED BY CONGRESSIONAL QUARTERLY INC.

Marriage and Divorce

Is it time to crack down on easy divorces?

The ongoing debate over "family values" entered a new phase this past year as activists launched a renewed push to toughen divorce laws and promote stable marriages. They blame the nation's no-fault divorce laws for the excessive U.S. divorce rate and for the resulting calamitous increase in children from single-parent homes who are growing up poor, depressed and struggling in school. The activists also point the finger at therapists and clergy for failing to press the importance of marriage in an increasingly individualistic society. Opponents counter that adding legal complications to the divorce process will only make divorces more expensive and more painful. They argue that couples need to learn better skills in handling both marriage and divorce.

INSIDE THIS ISSUE

CQ May 10, 1996 • Volume 6, No. 18 • Pages 409-432

Formerly Editorial Research Reports

MARRIAGE AND DIVORCE

COVER: NEWLYWEDS TONYA AND MARK HARRIS OF SUBURBAN MARYLAND CHOSE A TRADITIONAL CEREMONY. (BOB ROBINSON)

May 10, 1996
Volume 6, No. 18

Bibliographic records and abstracts included in The Next Step section of this publication are from UMI's Newspaper and Periodical Abstracts database, and are used with permission.

The CQ Researcher (ISSN 1056-2036). Formerly Editorial Research Reports. Published weekly (48 times per year, not printed March 1, May 31, Aug. 30, Nov. 29) by Congressional Quarterly Inc., 1414 22nd St., N.W., Washington, D.C. 20037. Annual subscription rate for libraries, businesses and government is $319. Additional rates furnished upon request. Second-class postage paid at Washington, D.C. POSTMASTER: Send address changes to The CQ Researcher, 1414 22nd St., N.W., Washington, D.C. 20037.

Marriage and Divorce

By Charles S. Clark

The Issues

Together again, Mark and Betty Squier look back on that black day in 1986 when he announced that he had met with a divorce lawyer. Married 19 years and the parents of five children, the police officer and homemaker from Fraser, Mich., faced a crisis that neither had been brought up to expect. As she would learn later, he was having an affair.

"Mark couldn't bring himself to tell the children he was leaving," Betty says. "They had been suffering emotionally, and their school work had declined. Finally, I got fed up with the lies, and I needed support, so I took the older ones out and told them of the affair." It was an act that Mark would dub the "lynching."

As it turned out, however, there was a two-week wait while Mark's lawyer prepared divorce papers. Betty took the opportunity, first, to sign on with a temporary agency to update her job skills, and second, to beg Mark to reconsider.

Through the marriage ministry program at the Squiers' Roman Catholic church, Betty learned of a weekend program for troubled couples called Retrouvaille. (Founded in Quebec, Canada, in 1977, the program's name is French for "rediscovery.")

"Retrouvaille saved our marriage," Betty says, but it didn't happen overnight. It took two to three years to rebuild the relationship, a time in which the "other woman" tried repeatedly to rekindle her affair with Mark.

The Squiers had to rethink how each of them spends time. They had to regain the other's trust concerning money. ("When you have an affair, you're diverting money from your family," Mark says.) They had to renegotiate their sexual relationship. ("I had to get rid of the recordings playing in my mind about whom I was being compared with," Betty says.) Finally, they had to reestablish emotional, intellectual and spiritual intimacy.

The Squiers' success prompted their church to recruit them as a mentor couple for Retrouvaille, which claims an 85 percent success rate with 50,000 couples worldwide. [1]

Recently, the Squiers have become active supporters of efforts to toughen Michigan's no-fault divorce law. The quarter-century-old law allows a couple to divorce without citing who is at fault. Opponents say that makes getting a divorce too easy.

"You can't create a new law that will prevent bad things from happening," Mark says. But the proposed changes "would afford the people who've been affected by bad conduct a chance to seek justice. There were six people whose lives would have been ruined by my actions."

If the "fault" concept had been in effect during the Squiers' crisis, Mark adds, "We would have been forced to say, 'Hey, time out, let's reexamine why this is happening,' and Betty would have been able to declare that I was at fault. We would have been required to get some counseling. And if I had left her, I would have taken less than half of our property since I'd have been the one who broke the marriage vows."

Michigan is the leader among some 40 states that are considering legislation to repeal or adjust their laws allowing no-fault divorce, according to the National Conference of State Legislatures. Activists on the issue are disturbed by the U.S. divorce rate — the world's highest. Some 1.2 million divorces were granted in 1994, according to the National Center for Health Statistics. That translates to virtually one of every two marriages, a rate more than twice that of other industrial countries. (*See table, p. 413.*)

Of particular concern is the damage suffered by the children of divorce. Sixty-five percent of the divorces in 1994 involved couples with minor children, and experts link divorce to social problems spawned by poverty, fatherlessness and maladjusted youth. Children of divorce on average suffer a household income drop of 30 percent. They also are two-to-three times more likely to drop out of school and have out-of-wedlock births than children from intact families and are more likely to get divorced themselves, says Rutgers University sociologist David Popenoe. [2]

"At no time in history, with the possible exception of Imperial Rome, has the institution of marriage been more problematic than it is today," a demographer contends in a 1995 report published by the Council on Families in America. "In a high-divorce society, not only are more unhappy marriages likely to end in divorce, but in addition more marriages are likely to become unhappy." [3]

Indeed, recent headlines have brought bad news for marriage: two divorces in the British royal family, the heart-wrenching split-up of Nelson and Winnie Mandela and an eighth failed

Divorce Rates in the U.S.: One Nation Indivisible?

Divorce rates are generally lower in the Northeast and Midwest and higher in the West and Southeast. The nation's overall divorce rate per 1,000 population was 4.6 in 1994, down from 4.8 in 1992. Massachusetts had the lowest rate (2.4), and Nevada the highest (9.0).

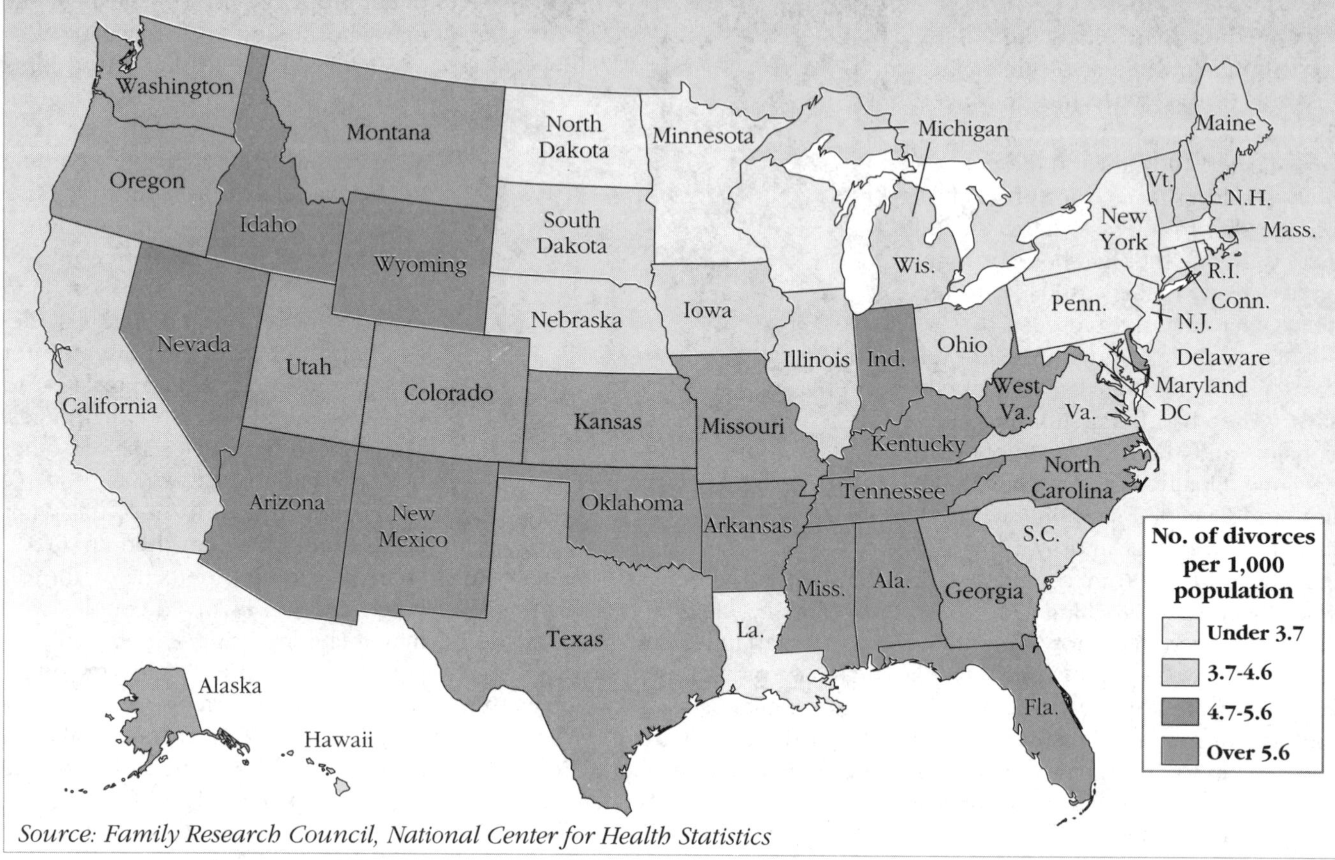

Source: Family Research Council, National Center for Health Statistics

marriage for actress Elizabeth Taylor. The frequency of divorce may be giving couples pause about marriage. The Census Bureau weighed in with news of America's continuing tendency to delay marriage: The estimated median age for a first marriage in 1994 was the highest ever recorded, 26.7 years for men and 24.5 for women. [4] (The age has been rising steadily for both sexes since 1960.)

And what are modern couples doing for romance while they dodge marriage and concentrate on, say, their careers? In 1990, 50 percent of couples lived together before marriage, compared with only 8 percent in the late 1960s, according to a recent study. What's more, those couples who co-habitate — and individuals who have more than one sex partner before they marry — are less likely to be faithful to their eventual partners than those who marry right away. [5]

It would be wrong, however, to ascribe today's marriage woes solely to a decline in sexual fidelity. The evolution of traditional gender roles at home and in the workplace, as well as the economic need for both partners to work, are also factors.

"The lack of clarity in men and women's roles opens opportunities for growth, but it also increases the chance of conflict," write marriage therapists Barry Dym and Michael L. Glenn. "Partners need to negotiate everything, from how to structure child care to how and when to make love. . . . In times of rapid social change, people move back and forth between old and new, between hope and fear, between a sense of expansiveness and the need to contract into old or defensive places." [6]

Others point out that the United States also enjoys the highest rate of marriage in the industrial world — a sign of faith, they say, in the future of the institution. (*See table, p. 413.*) Moreover, the divorce rate, 4.6 per thousand people in 1994, is actually down from 4.8 in 1992, according to the Center for Health Statistics.

"The divorce rate has actually plateaued in the past 17 years," says Larry Bumpass, a sociologist at the University of Wisconsin. "The current high levels are part of a long-term trend line that goes back 100 years. Nothing that was done in last several decades caused it. The implementation of no-fault divorce laws [in the

1970s] was clearly an adjustment by the legal process to a social change that had been under way."

The current attack on no-fault divorce "is just another election-year effort to bash the non-traditional family," says Constance Ahrons, a University of Southern California sociologist and author of the 1994 how-to book *The Good Divorce.* "In these conservative times, divorce is the national scapegoat," Ahrons adds. "It is much easier to attack divorce than to deal with the economy or the public school system or homelessness."

Though many critics of divorce are indeed conservative, both President Clinton and his wife Hillary have blamed divorce for the hurt it causes to children. In her best-selling book *It Takes a Village,* Mrs. Clinton lamented the silence over divorce, and in her syndicated newspaper column she asserted recently that "divorce has become too easy because of our permissive laws and attitudes." [7]

Divorce is also a tricky issue for conservatives because so many prominent Republican leaders — among them Sens. Bob Dole and Phil Gramm, Rep. Newt Gingrich and California Gov. Pete Wilson — are themselves divorced. This leads proponents of family values to point out that divorce is a very general problem that, unlike, say, teen pregnancy, hits home in the middle-class and among opinion-makers. "I don't think it's a Republican issue, which is why I like it," says William R. Mattox Jr., vice president of the conservative Family Research Council. "It doesn't offer either party a chance to one-up the other."

Still, there are complaints that efforts to boost marriage and cast shame on divorce make life unpleasant for people who divorce or never marry. "It's exhausting to be in the company of married people, with children or no," writer Alison Rose notes in a recent essay on sexual freedom and singles. "It forces me into a state of emergency alert, in which I have to rescue myself from interrogation and possible disgrace." [8]

The purpose of changing divorce laws to promote marriage is not simply to shame people, says David Blankenhorn, president of the New York City-based Institute for American Values and author of the 1995 book *Fatherless America: Confronting Our Most Urgent Social Problem.* "It is to create a certain fairness that corresponds to our intuitive sense of right and wrong. It is to communicate general attitudes that we take seriously, such as the idea that society cares whether a marriage lasts."

The public appears concerned about the high divorce rate while favoring the freedom to seek a divorce. A May 1995 CBS News-*New York Times* poll showed that 78 percent viewed divorce as a major cause of a "decline in personal values among the American people." But two-thirds

U.S. Leads in Tying — and Untying — the Knot

Marriage and divorce rates in the U.S. are roughly twice as high as those in other industrialized nations, according to the most recent available data.

Marriages per 1,000 population, ages 15-64

Country	1960	1970	1980	1990	1992
United States	14	17	16	15	14
Canada	12	14	12	10	NA
France	11	12	10	8	7
Germany*	14	12	9	9	8
Italy	12	11	9	8	8
Japan	15	14	10	8	NA
Sweden	10	8	7	7	6
United Kingdom	12	14	12	10	NA

Divorces per 1,000 married women

Country	1960	1970	1980	1990	1992
United States	9	15	23	21	21
Canada	2	6	10	11	11
France	3	3	6	8	NA
Germany*	4	5	6	8	7
Italy	NA	1	1	2	2
Japan	4	4	5	5	NA
Sweden	5	7	11	12	12
United Kingdom	2	5	12	13	12

* *Data for 1960 to 1990 refer to western Germany*

Source: "Population Bulletin," Population Reference Bureau Inc., March 1996; U.S. Census Bureau

Is It Fair to Penalize Married Couples ...

Fall in love, pop the question, tie the knot, pay more taxes.

A higher tax bill is indeed Uncle Sam's wedding gift to many married couples who file joint returns, a policy increasingly being challenged by boosters of family-friendly public policy.

The issue is the so-called marriage penalty, a quirk in the tax code that causes the average married couple to pay an estimated $1,720 more in federal taxes annually than they would if each of them had filed individually.

The penalty is caused by the differing tax rates, or brackets, created by the nation's progressive tax system. Take, for example, a typical couple in which the man and woman each earns $25,000. According to the Congressional Budget Office (CBO), they would each owe $2,790 if filing separately. Filing a joint return, however, does not merely double that total to $5,580. Instead, filing jointly forces them to take a standard personal deduction that is less than that granted to single filers. The lower deduction forces some of the couple's earnings into a higher tax bracket. Hence the couple must pay a total of $5,767.50, creating, in their case, a marriage penalty of $187.50. (Among high-income couples, the marriage penalty can top $9,000.)

To those intent on promoting stable marriages, ending the marriage penalty is important not as a financial incentive for conjugal commitment but as a symbol of what society values. "Only a small number of people would actually make a tax calculation in deciding to marry," says William R. Mattox Jr., vice president of the Family Research Council. "But that shouldn't be our primary concern. The more important question is whether the tax code treats married people fairly."

Mindful of this, the Republican-controlled House in spring 1995 fulfilled part of its "Contract With America" by passing a package of tax and spending cuts called the "American Dream Restoration Act." It included a provision easing the marriage penalty at a cost of $8.2 billion to the Treasury over five years. A version passed by the Senate switched the fix from a tax credit good to all who are hit with the penalty to an increase in the standard deduction good only to non-itemizers, or those making less than about $70,000. That version won in conference and was sent to the White House last November as part of the mammoth 1995 Balanced Budget Act. President Clinton vetoed that bill, and the marriage penalty proposal has not been raised since.

Defenders of the current tax code, noting that the marriage penalty brings in some $39 billion in revenue, say it is important to understand how the penalty came to be. It was back in 1948 that Congress revised the tax code to begin taxing married couples as families rather than individuals. The new policy allowed husbands and wives to evenly split their combined income for tax purposes, no matter how much each partner actually earned. If a husband earned, say, $30,000 and the wife earned $10,000, they would each be considered to have earned $20,000. This lowered the tax liability of many married couples, particularly those with a stay-at-home wife.

By the late 1960s, however, single taxpayers, many of them gay, were complaining that their taxes were higher, proportionately, than those of married partners because wives, in effect, were being used as a tax shelter. Congress responded with the 1969 Tax Reform Act, which, among other things, capped a single person's liability at 120 percent of that of a married couple with a comparable income. The act's adjustments in the standard personal deduction created the so-called marriage penalty.

In 1981, when President Ronald Reagan pushed through his major tax cuts, he eased the penalty by allowing married

---

of those responding to a March 1996 ABC News poll said divorce is the best option if a couple can't get along, even if they have children.

What observers from all political camps are beginning to agree on is that more marriages can succeed if the partners work at learning essential skills — either from therapists, clergy or other couples.

"In the past 20 years, there's been an explosion of knowledge about marriage," says Philadelphia-area marriage therapist Rita M. DeMaria. "In 1965, when the marriage counseling specialty was just beginning, a man and woman wouldn't go to see one person together. Each went to their own therapist, and the therapists never talked to each other. Now the research is clear that the chances of divorce are much less if they go to joint counseling."

Can marriage be strengthened by changing laws, changing therapists or changing procedures? As the debate rages on, here are some of the issues being discussed:

Should no-fault divorce laws be repealed?

"If society has to support casualties of divorce, then we need to know that these casualties were unavoidable," Mark Squiers says in explaining his support for divorce reforms in Michigan. "No-fault has created a huge population of divorced women with children. If freedom means non-accountability for [a father's] behavior, then the law should restrict it."

Much of the impetus for no-fault reform comes from a recent University of Oklahoma study, which showed that only three years after the advent of no-fault in the early 1970s, the divorce rate jumped in 44 of the 50 states.[9] After Michigan enacted no-fault in 1972, for example, its divorce rate climbed from 6.7 per 1,000 population in 1970 to 9.7 in 1980.

But analysts such as Wisconsin's

. . . Because of a Quirk in the Tax Code?

couples a 10 percent deduction for the spouse who earns the least (capped at $3,000). That relief, however, ended with the 1986 Tax Reform Act, which lowered tax rates and narrowed the number of tax brackets for most Americans to three.

"The '86 bill had to raise some revenue to be revenue-neutral, so there was a feeling that if we could cut rates from 50 percent down to 28 [for most filers], there would be less concern about the marriage penalty because it affected fewer people," says Mike Schuyler, a senior economist at the Institute for Research on the Economics of Taxation. "The marriage penalty used to be more extreme than it is now. But given our progressive tax system based on one's ability to pay, it's built in that there will always be some sort of penalty."

Robert S. McIntyre, executive director of Citizens for Tax Justice, defends the penalty by noting that its origin as a bonus for singles makes it comparable to the exemption the tax code gives to blind people. "People don't view *that* as a penalty against people who can see," he says, adding that neither the tax break for blind people nor the break for singles "amounts to a hill of beans. A cheap solution to the marriage penalty would be for the government to raise taxes on singles, but this would make the singles angry," McIntyre says. "The expensive way is for the government to give a tax break to the rest of the world," which is closer to what the Republicans are trying.

Defenders also point out that the tax code's structuring of standard personal deductions produces a "marriage bonus" for as many as are hit with the penalty. "Out of 49 million joint returns expected to be filed in 1996, 23 million are projected to have a penalty, 24 million to have a bonus and 2 million to have no change in tax," says a March 1995 CBO memo prepared for the House Ways and Means Committee. The average bonus is about $1,400, with most bonuses going to couples in which one spouse significantly out-earns the other.

Putting aside the conflict between the government's revenue needs and natural hostility toward taxes, there is the question of the impact that easing the marriage penalty would actually exert on decisions to marry. Two recent articles in the *National Tax Journal* reach slightly different conclusions. Both acknowledge that the rates at which Americans marry are affected by economic factors such as women's wages, education levels and taxes, but both assert that the impact of changes in the marriage penalty would be small. The marriage tax would have to fall by 20 percent to generate an increase in the marriage rate of 1 percent, analysts James Alm and Leslie A. Wittington conclude. [1]

David L. Sjoquist and Mary Beth Walker found that the impact would be virtually nil on long-term marriage rates, but they found past changes in tax law had some effect on the timing of marriages, such as postponements from November to January. [2] "For many couples, simply inviting a few less guests to the wedding reception would offset the cost of a higher marriage tax," they wrote.

Dan Mitchell, a senior fellow in tax policy at the Heritage Foundation, acknowledges that the marriage penalty is not the most damaging part of the tax code and that eliminating it is not as important to conservative activists as, say, fixing welfare. "On the other hand," he says, "it does seem counterintuitive to punish people for marrying. Some moral suasion from the government might be an effective tool."

---

[1] James Alm and Leslie A. Wittington, "Does the Income Tax Affect Marital Decisions?" *National Tax Journal*, December 1995, p. 565.

[2] David L. Sjoquist and Mary Beth Walker, "The Marriage Tax and the Rate and Timing of Marriage," *National Tax Journal*, December 1995, p. 547.

Bumpass point out that these hikes leveled off in the 1980s and '90s, and may simply have reflected a bulge of coming divorces that had long been "in the pipeline."

What is being proposed in Michigan is a 13-bill package that would restore the old requirement of proving fault in cases where only one spouse is seeking the divorce. "Faults" would include desertion, drug or alcohol abuse, physical or mental abuse, infidelity or a prison sentence of three or more years. The legislation would also require divorcing couples with minor children to undergo "divorce education" in an effort to ensure equitable property distribution and child custody arrangements. No-fault divorces would still be available to couples who mutually seek to end their marriages.

Limiting the restrictions to those seeking a unilateral divorce, analysts on both sides agree, probably would affect only a third of divorcing couples. A poll published in February by the Family Research Council showed that 55 percent of Americans favor making divorce harder when one partner wants to stay together.

"We don't want to keep people in a marriage that neither wants," says Mattox. "But we do want to encourage them to go the extra mile to try to preserve it. Post-divorce data show that people have this mistaken notion they're gaining freedom. But what they actually take on is a whole new set of problems, and many think that maybe they abandoned the marriage too quickly."

Currently, Mattox adds, "too many people feel that a bad marriage is like milk — once sour, it can never be made good and it smells up the refrigerator if you leave it there. But every relationship has its high and low points. The thing that distinguishes people in 50-year-old marriages isn't that they're scot-free of problems, but they've confronted those difficulties and persevered when others gave up."

How Americans Feel About Divorce

Do you agree that children suffer when their parents divorce?

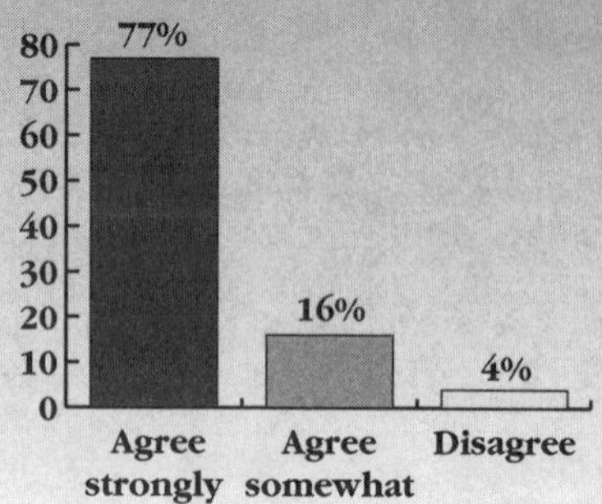

When there are children in the family, parents should stay together even if they don't get along.

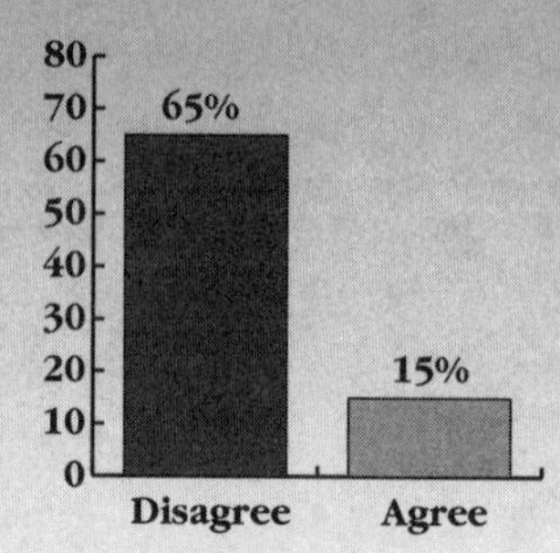

Even when there are no children, a married couple should stay together even if they don't get along.

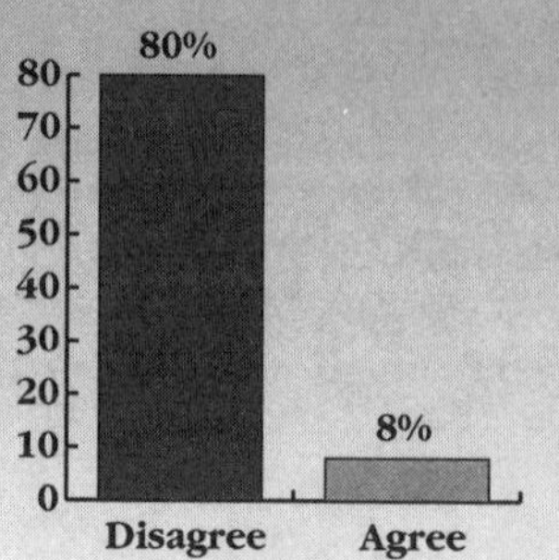

Note: Totals do not add up to 100 percent because some people didn't answer.

Sources: The American Enterprise, *July/August 1995; Family Research Council, September 1993 (left); National Opinion Research Center, January-May 1994*

Michael J. McManus, a columnist on religion and ethics and author of the book *Marriage Savers,* says that while there were abuses in the old fault-based divorce system, no-fault overreached and made it so "you can divorce someone easier than you can fire a secretary. Marriage is a civil contract in law that brings rights and responsibilities," he adds. "We can't make you love someone, but if the law closes the door so that if you run off with Suzy, you don't get all those assets, then you find ways to adapt. It's like attending a university that you find is a bit harder than expected. You study like heck rather than take a slow boat to China."

McManus says that no-fault promised to bring less litigation and controversy than fault-based divorce, "but the results were just the opposite. Lawyers are making lots of money — it's just that the fights are over custody and money."

Those who defend no-fault "conjure up an image of people who are miserable in marriage," says Blankenhorn. "But if both parties want out, they can go, and there is not much the state can do except encourage a waiting period or counseling." But protecting the rights of the one party who wants to stay in a marriage, he says, can have a major impact on social health.

"Show me a significant institution in society, a contract in the marketplace or whatever, that is not affected by the law around it," he says. "If people who get married know that it is a legally serious commitment, that it is different from living together simply 'until one of us doesn't want to,' then they won't enter this very fragile relationship with a bet-hedging approach that withholds full commitment."

Blankenhorn's ideas are hardly new, says Lynne Z. Gold-Bikin, an attorney in Norristown, Pa., and former chairman of the American Bar Association's section on family law. "No-fault legislation merely recognized what was going on in society, that people were living in limbo with someone else and wanted to [divorce and] remarry before they died," she points out. "You don't restabilize a family by making divorce tougher. If one party wants out, there's nothing that will keep them in. They used to go to Nevada, or Mexico. It's like abortion, they would find a way. Some women are desperately lonely and are married to a guy who won't sleep with them because he's too busy with business, so she goes out and has an affair. Now who's at fault?"

What's more, Gold-Biken adds, "people who are already fighting won't be kept together for the sake of children. It's the parents who end up hurting the kids, not the law. The kids will get pulled back and forth as the parents make them spies, threaten to withhold checks, don't show up at the kids' basketball games or parade different girlfriends and boyfriends in front of them. Despite what people say, divorce is not easy. Ending no-fault would simply add another layer to the procedure."

Others point out that restoring fault also will add new expense to getting a divorce, possibly making it out of reach for some, particularly poor women. "No one has looked at what this will cost," says Ahrons. "The courts are already backlogged and underfunded. It will take a lot of monitoring."

The National Organization for Women (NOW), while taking no official position on ending no-fault, points out that women stand to get hurt more than men by no-fault divorces, simply because they are more likely to be economically dependent homemakers rather than breadwinners. But NOW Executive Vice President Kim Gandy, an attorney, warns that, "Forcing people to stay in a bad marriage is a silly, unreasonable way to handle marital difficulties. It's folly to use the law to deal with individual weaknesses. A person whose marriage is in trouble because that person is selfish isn't going to take a sudden turn for the better because some law makes it more difficult to get a divorce."

Sociologist Bumpass points out that in an era that accepts cohabitation, two-thirds of the people who seek a divorce have already left their marriage partner and are living with someone else. "Marriage essentially ends when people stop living together, and divorce is the legal settlement," he says. "Making it harder won't have any effect at all. And since children usually go with mother, it means women would be forced to take legal action that may simply delay the time at which men will be obligated to pay support."

Others warn of additional unintended consequences of ending no-fault. Michael Bowers, executive director of the American Association for Marriage and Family Therapy, says requiring a "show of fault could inhibit people who are seeking therapeutic care for fear that the fact of a therapy session or something said within a session will later be used in court." Bowers also worries that ending no-fault would destroy the budding field of divorce mediation by attorneys or therapists: "Under a fault system, what is there to mediate?"

Children, Bowers adds, will suffer from more protracted divorces. "Research does show that divorce harms children, but the harm is from the conflicted relationship, not from the legal action." As for the assertion that divorce is approached too casually, Bowers says, "My experience as a clinician tells me that divorce is always perceived as a last resort."

Is bad therapy to blame for the high divorce rate?

In a commentary entitled "Where marriage is a scary word," *U.S. News & World Report* columnist John Leo recently attacked the Association for Marriage and Family Therapy. At the group's annual conferences, the word "marriage" appears only rarely in the workshop titles, reflecting, Leo says, the reluctance of today's marriage counselors to "bolster, promote or even talk" much about marriage. [10]

Individual therapists are accused of far worse. A psychologist for a health maintenance organization was recently described as giving a virtual blessing — after only one counseling session — to a man who wanted to leave his wife so he could date around. "The therapist said if I want to be single, I should just be single," the man told his stunned wife. "He says that my reasons have nothing to do with you, so we don't need counseling." [11]

Therapists, "in many ways, betrayed their tradition in the 1970s and '80s," says the Institute for American Values' Blankenhorn. "They became hostile to their job as custodian of the marital institution. The question, 'Can this marriage be saved?' was ridiculed, though this is starting to change. Yes, they're right that [whether to preserve a marriage] is a judgment. And there may be alcohol, drugs, violence or sexual abuse. But they've taken that hard complex truth and changed it to an excuse for us grownups to do whatever we want to do."

As with any profession, "therapists carry their personal values into what they do," says sociologist Ahrons. "And they are split on the issue the same as all of us. The debate is whether their role is to save marriages or help people sort out their relationships, whatever they want to do. A good therapist would work with that ambivalence, and help the person work on saving the marriage if that's what they want to do."

Therapist DeMaria agrees that some of her peers are too lenient in dealing with clients' key decisions. "I take strong stands. If a person is having an affair, I point out that it's detrimental to family life, and it's not a good parental role model. I say, yes, an affair can be more fun than being married, but if you're having one, you aren't putting your energy into your marriage."

Bowers of the therapists' association rebuts the *U.S. News* column by arguing that his colleagues are interested less in generalizations about marriage than in learning ways to help couples with specific problems. As for advocacy, "Any therapists worth their salt will help a client think through the implications of an action," he says. "But we have to distinguish between individual and conjoint therapy. Therapists are not advocates in the way attorneys are. When an individual seeks help, then our client is an individual. But when it's a couple or a family, then the client is the whole unit. Hence there are theoretical and substantive differences in the way we approach problems."

Others point out that simply extolling the virtues of preserving marriage is not always helpful to individuals seeking help. "Most research indicates that being married is usually associated with better adjustment and fewer health problems than being divorced or single," two psychologists recently wrote. "However, helping couples divorce is a legitimate part of marital therapy, and the therapy may help the adults have a better post-divorce adjustment." [12]

The two psychologists readily acknowledge, however, that marriage counseling is an inexact science. "The long-term effectiveness of marital therapy is not a glowing success story," they write, "but findings do suggest that such therapies are promising in promoting marital stability."

Should premarital counseling be made mandatory?

Michigan's proposed divorce reforms include a provision requiring engaged couples to take part in a premarital educational program or pay a higher fee for their marriage license. Columnist McManus has been urging clergy around the country to sign pledges saying that they will not marry couples who decline to undergo premarital counseling.

Among therapists and clergy, it has become common to ask betrothed couples to fill out a lengthy personal questionnaire. A popular version, "PREPARE/ENRICH," uses the responses to place couples into four categories of relationships: Vitalized, Harmonious, Traditional and Conflicted. "Conflicted" couples are most likely to fail at marriage; indeed, an estimated 10 percent of couples who complete the questionnaire end up postponing or canceling their engagement. [13]

McManus contends that church-based premarital counseling can head off years of ineffective and expensive marriage therapy. "Three quarters of people get married in churches, but most churches are blessing machines and wedding factories," he says. "They have no clue to saving marriages." Premarital counseling, he says, could impress upon young couples "how in Scripture, as in St. Paul's letter to the Corinthians, love is always defined as a decision, not as a feeling. It's like patience; it takes will."

Attorney Gold-Biken agrees that "churches and synagogues have abdicated their responsibility. They care more about how many people are attending [services] and how their flowers look than about teaching people about marriage. In our society, you can get a marriage license in three days, but to get a drivers' license, you have to take a course."

Joe Leonard, director of family ministries and human sexuality at the National Council of Churches, says it is wrong to blame pastors for high divorce rates. "Divorce is driven by profound social and economic forces in addition to people's spiritual and psychological needs," he says. "Women are no longer willing to put up with abuse, either physical or emotional, and they now have better economic opportunities."

"Exhorting couples and requiring clergy to sign pledges is healing a wound only lightly," he adds. "I don't think there's a clergy person who doesn't believe it's important to take premarital couples seriously. But the research data is ambiguous."

Leonard cites David Mace, a professor of human relations at Drew University who founded the Protestant marriage enrichment movement, who said premarital counseling is a waste of time because "the couple is too starry-eyed." Leonard believes intervention with troubled couples is more effective, using congregation-based communication and skill-building. The Quakers, for example, conduct "clearness meetings" in which members of the congregation ask a troubled couple probing questions.

Rabbi A. James Rudin, interreligious affairs director at the American Jewish Committee in New York City, notes that Judaism differs from many Christian denominations in that it has always accepted divorce. "We have a saying that a marriage is not a prison, and divorce is not a crime. Our approach is very practical, though spiritually based. We say that when love is there, oceans cannot separate a couple and they can sleep together on the head of a pin. But if a marriage is bad, then no bed is big enough for them."

"We have no zest for divorce, and there is a sadness to it," Rudin adds. "And I have no problem with people getting as much counseling as they can get. But I'm a little uneasy about laying on another layer of bureaucracy or regulations. Some of those calling for required counseling are most adamant about individual rights and getting the government out of our lives. There is a thin line between affirming positive family values and adding stigma to those who become divorced." ■

BACKGROUND

Is Marriage Universal?

Boosters of stable marriage emphasize that marriage as a civilizing force dates back thousands of years. They point to biblical injunctions against divorce, notably the New Testament verse in *Mark 10:6-9* that warns: "But from the beginning of the creation God made them male and female. For this cause shall a man leave his father and mother, and cleave to his wife; and they twain shall be one flesh: so then they are no more twain, but one flesh. What therefore God hath joined together, let not man put asunder."

But others point to the variety in human relations that can be found in the historical record. The Greek philosopher Plato, in *The Republic,* envisioned his Guardian elite as men without families who would be paired with healthy women for breeding purposes. "These women shall all be common to all these men, and none shall cohabit with any privately, and . . . the children shall be common, and . . . no parent shall know its own offspring nor any child its parent."

There is also a clear record of tolerance of divorce in ancient cultures. The Arab world, for example, gave rise to the Muslim ritual that permits a man to divorce his wife by declaring: "I divorce thee, I divorce thee, I divorce thee." Certainly a passion for the right to divorce was partly behind the Protestant Reformation and British King Henry VIII's break with Catholicism.

In recent decades, revisionists have questioned established beliefs in the longevity and integrity of the nuclear

Continued on p. 422

Chronology

1880s *Divorce rate in U.S. hits a historic high.*

1880
Commerce Department in first such count reports one in 16 marriages fails; National Divorce Reform League is founded soon afterward.

1888
Supreme Court comments in *Maynard v. Hill* that marriage is more than a mere contract.

1940s-1960s *Mainstream attitude that divorce is "shameful" changes as sexual revolution brings divorce into the open; Nevada becomes known as state with most lenient divorce laws.*

1948
Congress introduces income splitting on joint tax returns.

1968
Catholic Church introduces Marriage Encounters counseling program.

1969
Gov. Ronald Reagan, R-Calif., signs nation's first no-fault divorce law. Congress responds to complaints by unmarried taxpayers and creates "marriage penalty."

1970s *Women's movement gathers momentum; divorce rates hit record high.*

1971
Iowa becomes second state with no-fault divorce; others soon follow.

1977
Newly elected Democratic President Jimmy Carter asks Congress to curb the tax advantage of "living in sin."

1980s *Family values debate gathers steam, fueled by the religious right; divorce rate plateaus.*

1981
President Reagan provides partial relief to marriage penalty.

1984
PAIRS counseling program established in Falls Church, Va.

1985
Stanford University sociologist Lenore Weitzman contends in *The Divorce Revolution* that no-fault divorce penalizes women.

1986
Congress passes tax reform that cancels relief from tax code's marriage penalty.

1989
San Francisco psychologist Judith Wallerstein argues in *Second Chances* that impact of divorce on kids is worse than previously thought.

1990s *Family values advocates, mostly conservative, target no-fault divorce.*

May 19, 1992
Vice President Dan Quayle criticizes decision by TV character Murphy Brown to become a single mother.

1993
Hawaii Supreme Court says gay marriages would be legal unless lower court can show compelling state interest in banning it.

Sept. 16, 1994
Former Education Secretary William Bennett tells Christian Coalition that divorce has been more damaging than gay rights movement.

Jan. 24, 1995
President Clinton's State of the Union address introduces a couple whose ministry works with couples seeking to preserve marriage.

Nov. 24, 1995
Referendum in Ireland lifts constitutional ban on divorce.

December 1995
President Clinton vetoes the Balanced Budget Act containing relief for the marriage penalty.

Feb. 12, 1996
Religious and conservative groups rally against same-sex marriage proposals to force the issue at Iowa Republican presidential caucuses.

Feb. 14, 1996
Michigan state Rep. Jessie Dalman introduces marriage and divorce law reforms, sparking debate on no-fault.

March 26, 1996
New York Appeals Court loosens restrictions on divorced parents moving out of state with children; California Supreme Court issues a similar ruling in mid-April.

Summer 1996
Hawaii Supreme Court to rule in gay marriage case.

National Campaign for Same-Sex Marriage . . .

Tracey Bennett, who runs a bed and breakfast in Honolulu, recently bought her wedding dress. Her partner, a professional golfer, is planning to buy one, too.

The decision by the two women is well-timed: Hawaii may soon become the first state to legalize marriage between people of the same sex. Bennett, 49, has been working as a lobbyist for the Hawaii Equal Rights Marriage Project.

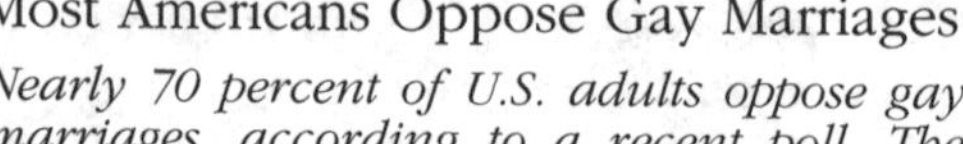

Most Americans Oppose Gay Marriages

Nearly 70 percent of U.S. adults oppose gay marriages, according to a recent poll. The least opposition comes from those who are young, female or better educated.

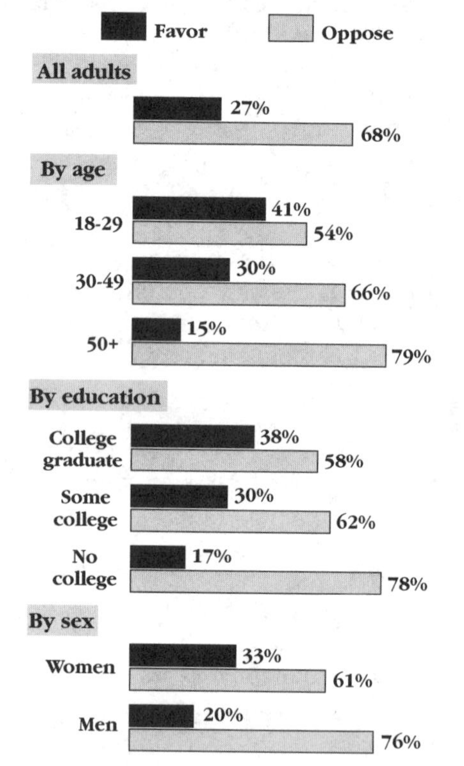

Source: USA Today/CNN/Gallup Poll of 1,006 adults conducted March 15-17, 1996

If a coming court ruling approves the concept, it "would mean sweeping benefits for gay and lesbian citizens of Hawaii," she says. "We want equal protection, not second-class citizenship. The definition of family needs to be expanded. Historically, it has changed over the years from the time when men used to capture wives or buy them, when men owned women and could legally beat them." Today's family, she adds, is in serious trouble because of drugs, violence, sexual abuse, illiteracy, homelessness and a lack of jobs. "Gays are not a problem for the family," she says. "We are loving people who want to be in the family of families."

Hawaii's movement for same-sex marriages has sparked opposition both religious and political. The Rev. Marc Alexander, executive director of the Hawaii Catholic Conference, says: "We're sensitive to gays, and the diocese has supported a bill against workplace discrimination. But we can't have this redefinition of marriage," he says. "We've seen one social experiment after another deteriorate family and marriage. Marriage is a special relationship that deserves to be supported, benefited and endorsed. As we often say, marriage is a relationship, but not every relationship is a marriage. This is not a religious argument," he adds. "It's about what's good for the human community."

Robert H. Knight, director of cultural studies at the Family Research Council in Washington, D.C., goes further. "It is not the duty of the state to facilitate unhealthy and immoral behavior," he says. "Same-sex marriage is a dire threat to legal order, to freedom of religion and speech. It will be the dominant issue of this election year."

Same-sex unions have been on the margins of the American agenda at least as far back as the 1950s, when the subject was debated in gay publications that had far less visibility than they do today. It arose more publicly at a 1970 meeting of the American Bar Association, when White House press spokesman Ron Ziegler declared, in response to a question, that President Richard M. Nixon opposed homosexual marriage. [1]

By the 1980s, some U.S. clergy were presiding over gay "marriages," and companies (now numbering at least 200) had begun offering benefits to same-sex partners of employees. In the mid-1990s, two books gave prominence to the issue. In *Same-Sex Unions in Premodern Europe*, the late John Boswell, a Yale University historian, suggested that ancient marriage ceremonies provide evidence that Greeks and medieval Christians celebrated same-sex relationships. In *Virtually Normal*, Editor Andrew Sullivan of *The New Republic* argues for acceptance of gay marriages — even those that aren't strictly monogamous. He calls them "a variation that does not eclipse the theme." [2]

In Hawaii, same-sex marriage hit the headlines in late 1990, when three gay couples were denied marriage licenses. They hired a lawyer, and their case, *Baehr v. Lewin,* went all the way to Hawaii's Supreme Court. Overturning a lower court ruling, Hawaii's top court in 1993 said that under the equal protection clause of the state's constitution, any law based on distinctions between the sexes was subject to strict judicial scrutiny. It said the lower court must show that the state has a compelling interest in banning same sex marriage.

Hawaii's Legislature — in tune with the 71 percent of state voters who say they oppose same-sex marriage — then passed legislation reinforcing traditional marriage. The governor, however, appointed a commission to examine the issue, and in 1995 it voted 5-2 in favor of same-sex unions. Hawaii's Supreme Court will rehear the case this summer.

Same-sex marriage would award gays an array of new legal and economic rights, among them joint parental custody, insurance and health benefits, joint tax returns, alimony and child support, inheritance of property, hospital visitation rights, a spouse's Social Security and retirement benefits, family leave, confidentiality of conversations and the right to decide what to do with a partner's body after death. [3]

Opponents of same-sex marriage in Hawaii worry that

. . . Draws Political and Religious Opposition

gays will flock to Hawaii the way divorcing couples once targeted Nevada. Perhaps a greater concern is that the 49 other states might be required to follow Hawaii's cue. That's because of the Constitution's clause stating that "full faith and credit shall be given to the public acts, records and judicial proceedings of every other state."

"The gay community is after bigger game than just Hawaii," says Walter Berns, adjunct scholar in legal studies at the American Enterprise Institute. "They want to change the 'bourgeois' culture to undermine the traditional idea of the family" articulated two centuries ago by French writers Jean-Jacques Rousseau and Alexis de Toqueville "as a sound basis for healthy civil society."

Conservative activists are organizing around such a threat. In Des Moines, Iowa, the Christian Coalition joined with local churches and seven other national groups at a rally in February denouncing same-sex marriage, forcing candidates in the Republican presidential caucus to weigh in. Kansas Sen. Bob Dole, the presumptive GOP candidate, sent a letter of support declaring that today's social ills are "directly linked to collapse of [the] two-income family." [4]

President Clinton "has taken no position on specific legislation, but does not support same-sex marriages," says Kathy McKiernan, a White House press spokeswoman.

Gay groups, for their part, have organized a Freedom to Marry Coalition. The National Gay and Lesbian Task Force Policy Institute has produced a manual called "To Have To Hold: Organizing for Our Right to Marry." These activists liken the debate to the fights over interracial marriage that flared in the 1960s. "Get ready for the greatest gay rights debate in history," wrote a commentator in the gay magazine *The Advocate.* [5]

In San Francisco in March, Mayor Willie Brown officiated at a "domestic partnership ceremony" for 200 gay couples, "leading the way," he said, "for the rest of the nation." The same month, the Central Conference of American Rabbis announced its acceptance of same-sex marriage.

At the state level, legislation to ban gay marriage has recently passed in six states — Utah, South Dakota, Arizona, Georgia, Kansas and Idaho — according to the Human Rights Campaign. Some 32 other states have considered bans, among them California, Alaska and New Hampshire. Courts have rejected gay marriage in Kentucky, Minnesota, Pennsylvania, Washington and the District of Columbia. The only case of approval was in Boulder, Colo., which granted a same-sex marriage license in 1975. It was overturned by a federal court in 1982. [6]

Gays were encouraged when the 11th Circuit Court of Appeals ruled in December ruled that a gay Atlanta woman was unfairly denied a new job in the Georgia attorney general's office after her prospective boss learned that she was soon to be married by a rabbi to another woman.

And gays are winning some support among conservatives. "Isn't it wrong for the same right-wing activists who have decried gay promiscuity to now deny gay love and commitment?" asks conservative writer Bruce Bawer. He pooh-poohs what he sees as the right's fear that a few gay marriages would somehow use up all the marriage licenses available to heterosexuals. [7]

The Rev. Alexander counters that even if gay marriages involved only 1 percent of the population, they would still have adverse effects "as a counter-model and symbol. Marriage is the best environment for children," he says, "We can't make people have children and be good parents, but we can help make conditions that make it possible. Marriage also helps men and women bring to the other what each lacks, so they humanize and civilize each other. Doesn't society have a right to set standards?"

The number who would apply for gay marriage doesn't matter, agrees the Family Research Council's Knight. "What is significant is that the law itself would no longer recognize marriage as the societal, economic, spiritual and legal union of one man and one woman. Once you destroy that definition, the sky is the limit. There would be no logic for the state to deny marriage to three to four people or to a father and daughter who was of age. If marriage is merely based on feelings and not gender or sanguinity, you underwrite a counterfeit and undermine the real article."

Same-sex marriage would have tremendous adverse effects on education, adoption and business decisions, Knight adds. "A tiny radical group is trying to seize the law for their own purposes." Homosexuality is a "misguided attempt to restore an incomplete gender identity," he says. Instead of marrying, they should seek help from organizations that can help them go straight.

Gay lobbyist Bennett says she is not surprised at the resistance, which she says is based on fear and the right wing's need to raise money. "Politicians need a bad guy since the communists aren't around anymore," she says. "Schools need to teach tolerance and respect for diversity, but that doesn't mean everyone has to adopt the other lifestyles.

"Marriage to us would be a celebration of a commitment between two people. Like straight people, we're optimistic that this is the person we want to spend the rest of our lives with.

"With the divorce statistics so horrifying, we think we can triumph. The state has an interest in fortifying stable relationships whether straight or gay. As partners, we can care for each other, emotionally, physically and financially. I didn't choose to be gay," she concludes. "It chose me."

---

[1] Peter M. Nardi, "Saying 'I Do' to Broadening the Debate," *Los Angeles Times* (Washington edition), Feb. 5, 1996.

[2] Critics point out that Sullivan's proposal for gay marriages is untested in any society. See James Q. Wilson, "Against Homosexual Marriage," *Commentary,* March 1996, p. 34.

[3] *USA Today,* Jan. 2, 1996.

[4] *The Washington Blade,* Feb. 16, 1996.

[5] *Lambda Report on Homosexuality,* January 1996.

[6] Family Research Council, "Gay 'Marriage': Hawaii's Assault on Matrimony," *Family Policy,* February 1996.

[7] *The New York Times,* March 8, 1996.

Continued from p. 418

family, calling it a modern phenomenon and stressing the brutal history of marriages filled with male dominance and loveless, arranged matches.

A critique of the revisionists, however, by British journalist Ferdinand Mount reveals many examples of "traditional" marriages from medieval history, including expressions of genuine romance between peasants. In short, he writes, the instinctive family as we know it has endured despite obstacles presented by governments, churches, economics and social mores. [14]

Looking at evolutionary evidence going back 3.5 million years, Rutgers University anthropologist Helen Fisher argues that both marriage and divorce have been part of a repeating cycle. "Young and childless couples tended to form pair-bonds, desert each other and bond again," she writes. "Couples with one or two children tended to remain together at least long enough to raise their young through infancy, then they 'divorced'; then they picked new mates." [15]

The desire for marriage and divorce "has been around since forever," notes Bowers of the therapists' association. "There was probably always as much marital trouble as we see today, but life expectancy was less, so the problem was often taken care of by widow- or widowerhood."

Divorce in America

The first divorce in the New World was recorded by the Puritans in Massachusetts in 1639. On grounds of bigamy, a Mrs. James Luxford was awarded all the couple's property. Her husband was fined, put in the stock and then exiled to England. [16]

Colonial records throughout the 17th and 18th centuries revealed scandals prompted by fornication and interracial adultery. In the 1770s, political pamphleteer Tom Paine, who was separated from his English wife, argued outspokenly for divorce law reform as editor of *The Philadelphia Magazine*.

The current charge that rising divorce is a product of selfishness has clear antecedents going back to 1852, when famed newspaper editor Horace Greeley used his *New York Tribune* to sound off against the droves of couples traveling for out-of-state divorces in "free-lovers' " paradises such as Indiana. "This is preeminently an age of individualism," he wrote. "The right of every man to do pretty nearly as he pleases is gaining ground daily." [17]

Marriage reigned when Constance Batt and Thomas McDonnell of Buffalo, N.Y., tied the knot in the 1950s.

Early feminists from the 19th century, such as Elizabeth Cady Stanton, foreshadowed their modern counterparts by crusading for the right to divorce. "An unfortunate or ill-assorted marriage is ever a calamity, but not ever, perhaps never, a crime," she wrote. [18] By 1880, one in 16 U.S. marriages was ending in divorce, already the highest rate in the world. This led to formation of the National Divorce Reform League, which pressed for a constitutional amendment to make state divorce laws uniform.

It was in 1888 that the Supreme Court, in *Maynard v. Hill,* was moved to describe the besieged institution of marriage as "creating the most important relation in life, as having more to do with the morals and civilization than any other institution." [19] In 1906, Pennsylvania Gov. Samuel W. Pennypacker organized a conference in Washington on uniform divorce legislation. It collapsed over such issues as the proper grounds for divorce and whether women delegates should be admitted to the meetings.

America's current notions of marriage and divorce probably have their roots in the Roaring '20s, when women won the vote, began entering the work force and started to acknowledge sexual desires that for centuries had been largely kept private. Following an eye-opening study by sex researcher Gilbert Hamilton asserting that as many as a quarter of Americans had committed adultery, psychologist John Watson in 1927 predicted the end of marriage within a half-century.

The adultery estimates would rise to half of all men and a quarter of the women in the famous sex studies by Alfred C. Kinsey in the late 1940s and early '50s. (The adultery count today is 25 percent for men and 15 percent for women, according to a 1994 University of Chicago survey. [20])

Still, divorce for most of the century was frowned upon. A sociology textbook in the 1940s flatly stated that "Divorce is the public acknowledgment of failure." [21] The exceptions were the serial-divorce lifestyles embraced by entertainment-world celebrities such as Mickey Rooney and band leader Artie Shaw.

Attitudes about divorce began to change in the 1960s with the oft-heralded "sexual revolution" and the awakening of suburban housewives to the women's movement. To help preserve marriage, the Catholic Church in 1968 started its Marriage Encounters program, which would counsel 500,000 couples within a decade and led to the Retrouvaille program. The period also saw the founding of the American Association for Marriage Counseling, a precursor of today's American Association for Marriage and Family Therapy.

During this period, however, there was a feeling that the religion-based approach was not taking advantage of new behavioral methods. "Unfortunately, unlike its psychologically based counterparts, Marriage Encounter weekends were traditionally limited to sharing thoughts and feelings regarding self, the couple and the couple and God," a therapist at a 1971 conference said. "No psychological theories, research or real skills-training were presented." [22]

"In the '60s, there was lots of stigma about divorce, divorces were fewer in number and no one wanted to be around them," recalls Ahrons. "You had to say something pretty nasty about your spouse to get a divorce, which would escalate an incompatibility into a public issue in which someone had to be right and the other wrong."

As it has on so many cultural trends, California led the way toward enacting no-fault. A 1966 Governor's Commission on the Family reported that divorcing couples cooperated more if the divorce was premised on the less severe charges of mental cruelty rather than adultery. In 1969, Gov. Ronald Reagan, himself a divorcé, signed the Family Law Act. It replaced California's previous seven grounds for divorce with two: "irremediable breakdown of a marriage and incurable insanity." The Golden State was quickly followed by Iowa, and soon no-fault was largely the law of the land.

New Freedoms?

As the laws changed, so did churches. In 1973, the Episcopal Church updated its policy so that a marriage no longer had to be annulled for a specific reason before the church would remarry a parishioner. The Catholic Church still rejected divorce, but did little lobbying in state capitals against the changes.

What also changed during this period were Americans' living patterns. Since 1970, the number of couples cohabiting has tripled. From 1970 to 1994, the number of never-married persons doubled from 21.4 million to 44.2 million. The number of divorced Americans quadrupled from 4.3 million to 17.4 million, with most divorces occurring after 11 years of marriage, at an average age of 35 for men and 33 for women. [23]

The modern view of marriage was further refined as advice books celebrated new varieties of relationships. One talked up the virtues of the childless marriage for couples seeking more time for careers and each other. "The pace of life is slower with just two people," said a female gift-shop manager. "We sit down and enjoy the fireplace together. I don't have to be upstairs bathing a child or worrying about planning nutritious home meals every night. I can just say, 'Hey, I'm beat,' and he'll say, 'Let's go out and have some spareribs.' " [24]

Also complicating the picture was the advent of commuter marriage, practiced by an estimated 700,000 Americans in 1982, mainly affluent, dual-career couples seeking "flexibility, common interests, interdependence and a desire for self-actualization." Such arrangements, with the partners living in different cities, are likely to have a fidelity rate only half that of normal marriages, a business professor says. But veterans say the time spent together is more precious. [25]

Finally, as the gay liberation movement brought homosexual practices out of the closet, books on gay relationships put a special slant on the fidelity issue. (*See story, p. 420.*) "Gay couples who make clear, open-sexuality agreements are not likely to be 'broken up' by third parties," advises therapist Tina Tessina. "What can destroy such relationships are poorly made agreements, which are prone to misunderstanding and resentment." [26]

Second Thoughts

One of the first significant challenges to the era of no-fault divorce came not from the religious right, but from feminists. In 1985, Stanford University sociologist Lenore Weitzman's book *The Divorce Revolution* concluded that women were being ill-served under no-fault as measured by their property settlements, alimony and child support payments in California over a 10-year period. [27] She found that women suffered an economic decline of 73 percent after divorce, versus a 42 percent decline for men.

The disparity left feminists with mixed feelings. On one hand, they were concerned about the impoverishment of women. But divorce also represented a new freedom. The rise in divorce, says NOW's Gandy, was a product not so much of women's sexual assertiveness or any kind of anti-marriage ideology, but of their new economic independence. "As employment opportunities became more available to women, large numbers of them left unhappy marriages," she says. "I'm all for duty and sacrifice, but it has to be a two-way street."

In 1989, the divorce debate was rocked by psychologist Judith S. Wallerstein's study tracking the children of 60 divorced couples. Only 34 percent of the kids were doing well, she reported, while the others were depressed, not performing in school and blaming themselves for their parents' split. "We were stunned," she wrote. "We found family after family still in crisis, their wounds wide open." [28]

Though many accepted Wallerstein's call for a new look at the impact of divorce, defenders of divorce challenged the findings. Is the glass half-full or half-empty? Ahrons asked in her own book, *The Good Divorce*. "What gets overlooked," she wrote "is that at the 10-year follow-up, almost half (45 percent) of the children did *not* experience any long-term psychological damage."

Ahrons argued that society should concentrate less on characterizing divorced families as failures and focus on teaching stepfamilies to cope. "These families want to know — and deserve to know — how to function in the best possible ways available to them, how to minimize the stress, and most of all, how to feel normal," she writes. [29] ■

Reuters/Jeff Vinnick

Hawaii's Supreme Court will decide in July whether Joe Melillo and Pat Lagon and other gay couples can legally marry.

CURRENT SITUATION

Michigan's Lead

In March, Michigan's package of divorce law reforms moved from a House subcommittee to the Committee on Judiciary and Civil Rights, with action by the full House likely this session. Its chief sponsor, Republican Rep. Jessie Dalman, hopes that the Senate will act on the legislation and that Republican Gov. John Engler will sign it before the session ends in June.

"No-fault divorce supposedly did away with acrimony in dissolving marriages," Dalman says. "Instead, the animosity has shifted to children, and it is they who suffer the most painful consequences. Children should not be the weapons in a battle for control."

One of Dalman's critics, Michael Robinson, a Birmingham, Mich., lawyer who formerly chaired the family law section of the Michigan Bar, told lawmakers in March that "the abolition of fault divorces in 1972 was no more than a recognition that you can't legislate morality and friendship. People were saying and doing almost anything to get around the law. It created needless hostility, collusion and perjury when dealing with the concept of fault. In the end, individuals who wanted a divorce ultimately found a way to obtain that divorce."

Watching from Washington, Clinton's former domestic policy assistant William A. Galston, now a professor of public affairs at the University of Maryland, recently proposed a compromise. He suggested a two-tier system, one applying current law for couples who have no children, and a new one that eliminates the unilateral, no-fault option for couples with dependent kids. "In the end, it comes down to a moral question," Galston writes. "Is our society willing to put the well-being of children first, even when it may conflict with adult desires and restrain our passion for autonomy?" [30]

The Michigan effort has spawned similar legislative action in many states, among them Georgia, Idaho, Illinois, Minnesota, Pennsylvania, Washington and Virginia. Many of these states are also joining Michigan in moving to require "divorce education" programs, in which splitting couples are required to attend classes on such topics as how children react to divorce and how to settle disputes amicably. In some localities, however, there is movement in the opposite direction. In Alexandria, Va., for example, circuit judges have recently streamlined the divorce process so that a couple can split up in a matter of two weeks instead of months. [31]

Counseling Creativity

Author McManus has reached 43 cities in his campaign to get clergy not to marry couples without premarital counseling. In Austin, Texas, some 250 pastors from two dozen denominations signed pledges, McManus

Continued on p. 426

At Issue:

Should divorce laws be changed to make marriages more difficult to dissolve?

yes

COUNCIL ON FAMILIES IN AMERICA
The council is sponsored by the Institute for American Values

FROM "MARRIAGE IN AMERICA: A REPORT TO THE NATION," MARCH 1995.

America's divorce revolution has failed. The evidence of failure is overwhelming. The divorce revolution — by which we mean the steady displacement of a marriage culture by a culture of divorce and unwed parenthood — has created terrible hardships for children. It has generated poverty within families. It has burdened us with unsupportable social costs. It has failed to deliver on its promise of greater adult happiness and better relationships between men and women.

We do not offer this assessment lightly. We recognize that these failures have been unanticipated and unintended. The divorce revolution set out to achieve some worthy social goals: to foster greater equality between men and women; to improve the family lives of women; and to expand individual happiness and choice. . . .

Yet the divorce revolution has not brought us closer to these goals but has cast us at greater distance from them. Relationships between men and women are not getting better; by many measures, they are getting worse. They are becoming more difficult, fragile and unhappy. Too many women are experiencing chronic economic insecurity. Too many men are isolated and estranged from their children. Too many people are lonely and unconnected. Too many children are angry, sad and neglected. . . .

By insisting that today's negative trends for children cannot be reversed without strengthening marriage, we realize that many people will regard us as nostalgic and as hopelessly unrealistic. It is now a common view, especially among family scholars and other opinion leaders, that indeed it would be nice if everyone had a strong marriage, but that will never happen. The forces of modernism run against marital permanence; a free society cannot legislate matters of the heart; and in any event, expressive individualism and self-fulfillment are the regnant values of our age that have liberated millions of adults. . . .

The tide against marriage does seem strong, and neither we nor anyone else can accurately predict the future. But nevertheless, and paradoxical though it may sound, we wish to assert that we, not our critics, are the realists. We are the ones, we submit, taking a tough-minded look at social realities. Our proposal is to arrest the downward spiral for children by reinvigorating marriage. This proposal stands a reasonable chance of reversing the current deterioration of child well-being in our society. The laissez-faire acceptance of the decline of marriage is premature and unwarranted. No consistent, widespread effort has been undertaken to try to reverse this trend. Until such an effort is made, it is irresponsible to say that nothing can be done.

no

GLENDA RILEY
Professor of American History, Ball State University

FROM DIVORCE: AN AMERICAN TRADITION (OXFORD UNIVERSITY PRESS, 1991).

Too many people chose a life partner under some form of duress: youth, romantic illusions, lack of self-awareness, a tendency to present only one's best side during courtship, sexual attraction, parental and societal pressures, a need for psychological or financial support, a desire to have children, a fear of being alone and advancing age, among others. Most of these pressures to marry are understandable, while others are healthy desires. But pressures to marry must be balanced by an understanding of oneself, one's potential mate and the nature of marriage. When these factors go unbalanced, the result is too often an unsatisfying or destructive marriage — a mismatch.

Divorce releases people from a lifetime of living with unsound judgments regarding their potential mates. In addition, it removes others from debilitating situations that develop after marriage. . . .

My support of divorce is not meant to suggest that we abandon our ideal of marriage as a lifetime commitment. It simply asks that we recognize that many couples are unable to sustain such a commitment. Divorce allows these couples to dissolve dysfunctional unions. After divorcing, they have the opportunity to reassess themselves and perhaps form functional, satisfying marriages with other mates.

Agreed, some people may exploit lenient divorce laws by divorcing their spouses heedlessly and impetuously. But the historical record indicates that people forced to stay in failed marriages against their will usually sabotage their relationships, either consciously or unconsciously. Adultery, abuse and desertion are frequent occurrences among such couples. In addition, other distraught spouses find illicit ways around restrictive divorce laws. They falsify grounds for annulments or perhaps leave the United States to obtain a divorce elsewhere. When people remain in difficult marriages or circumvent the law, it often costs them, their spouses, children, relatives, friends and employers, as well as society, dearly. . . .

I maintain that we need to reshape the institution of divorce with an eye to the people involved rather than according to our own attitudes toward divorce. History demonstrates that people will divorce. Given this reality, it serves everyone's best interests — even those people who oppose divorce — if the divorce process helps divorcing men and women become healthy, effective individuals. . . .

If we draw upon history to see that conflict over divorce in the past has led to problem-laden divorce, we can create more effective divorce in the future. We can continue to see lifetime marriage as a worthy ideal, while providing salutary divorce for those who are unable to achieve the ideal.

says. In Modesto, Calif., where 95 clergy have signed over the past decade, the number of divorces dropped from 1,983 in 1986 to 1,606 in 1995 despite a population increase.

For veteran couples, McManus favors a counseling regime that is similar to the 12-step program in Alcoholics Anonymous. "You make it a weekend assignment for a couple to write to each other," he says. "You think more deeply when you write, and because it's not customary to write to your spouse, you say things that you haven't said." Eventually, the couple communicates on practical issues such as, "If he picks up his clothes and watches less football, she'll be more amorous at night," McManus says. "The spiral that goes down can be reversed, and when one person changes, it encourages changes in the other. They can come back exalted and back in love."

McManus's approach does favor religion. He cites figures from the National Institute of Child Development showing that only 7 percent of couples who go to church at least once a month divorce within five years, compared with 17 percent who attend once a year or less.

"People in religion do have more stable lives because they have external as well as internal supports," says Bowers of the therapists' association. But he is less enthusiastic about requiring premarital counseling from clergy. "Most people who come in for it have some faith commitment already; others are more likely to game the system because they're more interested in where the flowers and candles are going to go. Most successful counseling occurs six months after the wedding, when the shine is off. That's when a couple needs the skills."

One successful program that attempts to teach such skills is PAIRS (Practical Application of Intimate Relationship Skills). Intended as education rather than therapy — an important distinction for many couples — it is a semester-long, 120-hour course founded in 1984 by Falls Church, Va., family therapist Lori Gordon. It has spread to 26 states in 13 countries, and a version of it organized by Gold-Biken is being used to teach high school students about marriage in some 50 schools.

"We teach people communication skills to resolve conflicts so they won't be caught in volatile fighting cycles," says PAIRS practitioner DeMaria. "We say people won't be in love everyday, but they have to love each other every day. We tell them that sex and physical affection are very important. If they neglect holding hands and hugs, then the desire to be together lessens, and there's no sexual excitement." ■

OUTLOOK

Realism vs. Idealism

I didn't have any failed marriages," said anthropologist Margaret Mead. "I've been married three times, and each marriage was successful."

It's a favorite quote of sociologist Ahrons, whose work easing the trauma of divorce has produced a typology of divorced couples: 17 percent are "perfect pals" (remained best friends after divorce); 33 percent are "cooperative colleagues" (couples who coped with their anger in productive ways); 25 percent are "angry associates" (couples who could not confine their anger to marital differences); and 25 percent are "fiery foes" (taunting each other for years or not speaking at all). [32]

To many, divorce is a fact of life that ought to be institutionalized. "Divorce is the only major family event for which there is little or no recognition," writes marriage counselor Stephanie Marston. "When a baby is born, a great fuss is made. Marriage, graduation, adoption, important homecomings — all inspire celebration. But when you divorce, you are left alone." [33]

The notion of "the good divorce" appalls author Blankenhorn, who believes that steps such as changing no-fault divorce laws are needed to send more messages to improve marriages. "It's hard to have less behavior that's bad if we don't view it as bad," he says. "It doesn't mean that all divorces are bad, and in our freedom-oriented society we'll always have a high rate. But do we have to have the highest in the world?"

Divorce critics such as Mattox note that the generation raised in the 70s — America's first to grow up under no-fault — has shown more signs of uneasiness about divorce. The May 1995 CBS News-*New York Times* poll showed that Americans ages 18-29 were more likely than other groups to oppose divorce as a solution "when a marriage isn't working out."

Ahrons agrees that the '70s generation "has had the experience to know divorce is a possibility, but rather than say marriage is not a long-term commitment, they say they don't plan to get divorces. We're still a marrying society, but we have serial marriages, and the majority who get divorced look back after five years and say that though it was painful, it was good."

Bowers points out that over the long-term, 90 percent of Americans marry, and that the generations react in cycles. It was the baby-boomers who said, "I don't want to live in a dead relationship. That's what my parents did."

The New Shame?

To some, the new crackdown on divorce is an effort to control people by reintroducing the concept of shame. Such a strategy can't work, according to Bumpass, because society has moved into an era in which there is an "enormous separation between sex and marriage. Much of the stigma attached to unwed childbearing, cohabitation and divorce was rooted in their implication that the people involved were sexually active yet unmarried. Society at large, and in particular, today's young, have come to accept that unmarried people have sex. With people delaying marriage while they get their educations etc., it's a fantasy to think that they will be abstinent."

Blankenhorn counters that "yes, if we only tell people they must eat their peas for the sake of society, then reform will fail. But we should say, yes, we do believe you should eat your peas, that marriage is a social good that is good for kids but also is a very important pathway to happiness. The goal is not to force miserable people to stay together, but to achieve some balance between the self and our relationship with community. Is the role of experts to tell us there is nothing we can do about that? I guess that's one point of view."

Gold-Biken says there's plenty that can be done in the form of teaching children the value of marriage. "TV teaches that all problems can be solved in 30 minutes," she says. "But this Cinderella story of everyone living happily ever after — it's not the end of the story." ■

FOR MORE INFORMATION

American Association for Marriage and Family Therapy, 1133 15th St. N.W., Suite 300, Washington, D.C. 20005; (202) 452-0109. This group of therapists promotes professional standards through training programs and by providing the public with educational material and referral services.

Family Research Council, 700 13th St. N.W., Suite 500, Washington, D.C. 20005; (202) 393-2100. This think tank and advocacy group run by former Reagan administration domestic policy adviser Gary Bauer publishes research and commentary on such issues as divorce, same-sex marriage and the effects of poverty on children.

Institute for American Values, 1841 Broadway, Suite 211, New York, N.Y. 10023; (212) 246-3942. Founded in 1987, this private, nonprofit group researches and publishes commentary on issues of family well-being and civil society, seeking to "bridge the gap between scholarship and policy-making."

Marriage Savers, 9500 Michael's Court, Bethesda, Md. 20817; (301) 469-5870. Founded by syndicated religion and ethics columnist Michael J. McManus, this resource center offers literature and videos on preserving marriages, and organizes clergy to commit to requiring premarital counseling of couples they plan to marry.

The PAIRS Foundation Ltd., 3705 South George Mason Dr., Suite C8S, Falls Church, Va. 22041; 1-800-477-2477. Founded in 1984 by therapist Lori Gordon, PAIRS (Practical Application of Intimate Relationship Skills) is an intensive, 120-hour course designed to teach couples skills in preventing marital breakdown.

Notes

[1] Retrouvaille can be contacted at (800) 470-2230.

[2] Quoted in "No-Fault Divorce Law Is Assailed in Michigan, And Debate Heats Up," *The Wall Street Journal*, Jan. 5, 1996, p. A1. For background, see "Child Custody and Support," *The CQ Researcher*, Jan. 13, 1995. pp. 25-48, and "Children and Divorce," *The CQ Researcher*, June 7, 1991, pp. 349-368.

[3] Council on Families in America, "Marriage in America: A Report to the Nation," March 1995.

[4] U.S. Census Bureau, "Marital Status and Living Arrangements: March 1994," February 1996. For background on the British royal family, see "The British Monarchy," *The CQ Researcher*, March 8, 1996, pp. 193-216.

[5] Renata Forste and Koray Tanfer, "Sexual Exclusivity Among Dating, Cohabitating and Married Women," *Journal of Marriage and Family*, February 1996, p. 33.

[6] Barry Dym and Michael L. Glenn. *Couples: Exploring and Understanding the Cycles of Intimate Relationships* (1993), p. 11.

[7] *New York Daily News*, Jan. 28, 1996.

[8] Alison Rose, "How I Became a Single Woman," *The New Yorker*, April 8, 1996, p. 82.

[9] *The Wall Street Journal*, Jan. 5, 1996. Also see Paul A. Nakonezny, Robert D. Shull and Joseph Lee Rodgers, "The Effect of No-Fault Divorce Law on the Divorce Rate in the 50 States and its Relation to Income, Education and Religiosity," *Journal of Marriage and the Family*, May 1995, pp. 477-488.

[10] *U.S. News & World Report*, Feb. 5, 1996, p. 22.

[11] Quoted in Joanne H. Meehl, "Managed Marriage," *The Washington Post*, March 26, 1996.

[12] James H. Bray and Ernest N. Jouriles, "Treatment of Marital Conflict and Prevention of Divorce," *Journal of Marital and Family Therapy*, Vol. 21, No. 4, October 1995, p. 461.

[13] "Predicting Marital Success for Premarital Couple Types Based on PREPARE," *Journal of Marital and Family Therapy*, January 1996, p. 103.

[14] Ferdinand Mount, *The Subversive Family: An Alternative History of Love and Marriage*, 1992.

[15] Helen Fisher, *Anatomy of Love* (1992), p. 187.

[16] Glenda Riley, *Divorce: An American Tradition* (1991), p. 12.

[17] *Ibid.*, p. 62.

[18] *Ibid.*, p. 73.

[19] The Supreme Court ruled in *Maynard v. Hill* that legislation annuling a man's first marriage was invalid, and that his first wife's children by him were entitled to part of his land.

[20] "Sex in America: Contented But Surprisingly Chaste," *The Washington Post*, Oct. 11, 1994. See *The Social Organization of Sexuality: Sexual Practices in the United States* (1994).

[21] Barbara DaFoe Whitehead, "Dan Quayle Was Right," *The Atlantic Monthly*, April 1993, p. 47.

[22] Quoted in Joan Rachel Goldberg, "The Business of Preventing and Treating Troubled Marriages," *Family Therapy News*, October 1993.

[23] Lis Harris, *Rules of Engagement* (1995), p. 220, and Census Bureau, *op. cit.*

[24] Quoted in Diana Burgwyn, *Marriage Without Children: Men and Women Tell What It is Like to be Childless By Choice or Chance* (1981), p. 123.

[25] See Fairlee E. Winfield, *Commuter Marriage: Living Together, Apart* (1985), p. 174.

[26] Tina Tessina, *Gay Relationships for Men and Women: How to Find Them, How to Improve Them, How to Make Them Last* (1989), p. 119. For background, see "Domestic Partners," *The CQ Researcher*, Sept. 4, 1992, pp. 791-714.

[27] *The Chronicle of Higher Education*, April 19, 1996, p. A12. Richard R. Peterson, a scholar at the Social Science Research Council, said Weitzman had miscalculated and that women only experienced a 27 percent decline and men a 10 percent improvement. Weitzman concurs with the new figures.

[28] See Judith S. Wallerstein, *Second Chances: Men, Women and Children a Decade After Divorce* (1989).

[29] Constance Ahrons, *The Good Divorce: Keeping Your Family Together When Your Marriage Comes Apart* (1994), pp. xv, 15.

[30] Op-ed column in *The New York Times*, Dec. 27, 1995.

[31] *The Washington Post*, Dec. 3, 1995.

[32] Ahrons, *op. cit.*, p. 6.

[33] Stephanie Marston, *The Divorced Parent: Success Strategies for Raising Your Children After Separation* (1994), p. 322.

Bibliography

Selected Sources Used

Books

Ahrons, Constance, *The Good Divorce: Keeping Your Family Together When Your Marriage Comes Apart,* HarperCollins, 1994.

In this how-to book, a University of Southern California sociologist takes issue with assertions that divorce should again be made shameful and that children of divorce are doomed to unhappy lives.

Dym, Barry, and Glenn, Michael, *Couples: Exploring and Understanding the Cycles of Intimate Relationships,* HarperCollins, 1993.

Two Cambridge, Mass., therapists outline the basic stages that most marriages go through, from expansion and promise, to contraction and betrayal, to resolution. They offer advice on how couples can change.

Fisher, Helen, *Anatomy of Love: A Natural History of Mating, Marriage, and Why We Stray,* Fawcett Columbine, 1992.

A Rutgers University anthropologist examines current research on how modern sexual behavior is likely to have developed through evolution. She concludes that serial monogamy is the historical norm.

Griswold, Robert L., *Fatherhood in America: A History,* Basic Books, 1993.

A University of Oklahoma history professor surveys the changes in paternal roles from early 19th-century breadwinners to the modern men's movement workshops on masculinity.

Harris, Lis, *Rules of Engagement: Four Couples and American Marriage Today,* Simon and Schuster, 1995.

A *New Yorker* writer weaves a narrative of changes in American society with profiles of couples from varying backgrounds that examine how modern partners work out conflicts.

Marston, Stephanie, *The Divorced Parent: Success Strategies for Raising Your Children After Separation,* William Morrow, 1994.

A Santa Fe, N.M., marriage and child counselor lays out ways for adults and children to navigate "the voyage into uncharted waters" that comes with divorce. She offers tips for children on how to avoid blaming themselves.

McManus, Michael J., *Marriage Savers: Helping Your Friends and Family Avoid Divorce,* Zondervan, 1995 edition.

A Bethesda, Md., religion columnist offers detailed advice on how engaged couples and experienced marriage partners can make it through rough periods. He favors reform of no-fault divorce laws and mandatory premarital counseling by clergy.

Mount, Ferdinand, *The Subversive Family: An Alternative History of Love and Marriage,* The Free Press, 1992.

A British newspaper editor surveys the history of marriage, arguing against much of the recent revisionist scholarship in favor of the view that the nuclear family built on true love has indeed been common to most societies.

Riley, Glenda, *Divorce: An American Tradition,* Oxford University Press, 1991.

A Ball State University history professor traces the long history of divorce in America, going back to the Puritans in the 1630s. She argues that people should stop arguing whether divorce is good or bad and simply work to make it equitable.

Tessina, Tina, *Gay Relationships For Men and Women: How to Find Them, How to Improve Them, How to Make Them Last,* Jeremy P. Tarcher, 1989.

A Long Beach, Calif., therapist specializing in "alternative and creative relationships" offers insights into the dynamics of gay relationships as well as advice on communication.

Wallerstein, Judith, and Sandra Blakeslee, *The Good Marriage: How and Why Love Lasts,* Houghton Mifflin, 1995.

San Francisco psychologists examine how 50 couples have coped with marital discord, arguing that "it is absurd to suggest that the need for enduring love and intimacy in marriage is passé."

Reports and Studies

Council on Families in America, *Marriage in America,* March 1995.

A group of academics and writers supported by a New York-based foundation compiled this critique of America's "high-divorce" society, offering proposals to promote stable marriage through changes in divorce law, taxation and values.

The American Enterprise Institute for Public Policy Research, *The American Enterprise,* May-June 1996.

A special issue of this conservative bimonthly contains more than a dozen articles on marriage, divorce and the family.

The Next Step

Additional information from UMI's Newspaper & Periodical Abstracts database

Divorce and Children

Chavez, Linda, "Children do suffer most from a divorce," *USA Today,* Jan. 24, 1996, p. A11.
Chavez says that divorces involving children are more than personal tragedies; they are a social problem with significant societal costs. Children of divorce are more likely to be truant, to do poorly in school and to get in trouble with the law, Chavez notes.

Dolan, Maura, "Justices ease relocation of children in divorce cases," *Los Angeles Times,* April 16, 1996, p. A1.
The California Supreme Court, decreeing a major shift in family law, ruled on April 15, 1996, that a divorced parent who has child custody can move to a new city or state even if the other parent objects.

Fox, Greer Litton, and Robert F. Kelly, "Determinants of child custody arrangements at divorce," *Journal of Marriage & the Family,* August 1995, pp. 693-708.
The likelihood that mothers vs. fathers would receive sole physical custody in final divorce judgments was assessed. If a mother has a higher educational level and a father has a higher income, the odds that the father will get custody are reduced.

Greene, Donna, "Sparing children the crossfire of divorce," *The New York Times,* Aug. 20, 1995, p. WC3.
Judge Adrienne Hofmann Scancarelli of Westchester County, N.Y., Family Court is interviewed about Parent Education and Custody Effectiveness, or Peace, a program intended to teach parents who are separating or divorcing to settle their differences in ways that will not hurt their children.

Morrison, Donna Ruane, and Andrew J. Cherlin, "The divorce process and young children's well-being: A prospective analysis," *Journal of Marriage & the Family,* August 1995, pp. 800-812.
The consequences of marital disruption for children's behavior problems and academic achievement were examined. The effect of disruption on boys' behavior problems may be partially attributed to downward mobility following the disruption.

O'Meara, Kevin, and Bill Jackson, "Divorce law reforms would aid children," *Detroit News,* Feb. 23, 1996, p. A8.
In a letter to the editor, Kevin O'Meara and Bill Jackson of Voices for Children Michigan say a *Detroit News* editorial on divorce reform legislation was incomplete and misleading, and that the *News* ignores the needs of children.

Pfeiffer, Sacha, "Pilot divorce courses aim to help children," *Boston Globe,* Aug. 6, 1995, p. SW1.
A pilot program lauded by supporters as providing much-needed education and criticized by opponents as infringing on personal freedom aims to aid couples and children during the divorce process. The program, an amendment to a child-support enforcement law passed in Massachusetts in 1994, requires all parents with minor children filing for divorce in Norfolk County, to complete a course before their case is heard by a judge.

Shirk, Martha, "Legislative committee to hold hearing on children, divorce," *St. Louis Post-Dispatch,* Sept. 24, 1995, p. D7.
An interim Missouri legislative committee is tackling one of the toughest problems the judicial system faces Today: how to help divorcing parents decide custody for their children in an equitable, humane way. The nine-member committee will hold a hearing on custody, visitation and child support issues on Sept. 25, 1995.

Smith, Lynn, "Children shouldn't be weapons in divorce war," *Los Angeles Times,* Oct. 18, 1995, p. E3.
Smith discusses the psychological toll on children who are the objects of bitter custody disputes, and suggests that parents who are divorcing seek mediation on custody issues.

Divorce Mediation

Emery, Robert E., "Divorce mediation: Negotiating agreements and renegotiating relationships," *Family Relations,* October 1995, pp. 377-383.
Emery offers an overview of divorce mediation and includes a discussion of the reasons for the rapid development of this innovative practice and a summary of distinctions between mediation and other areas of legal and psychological practice. He also assesses research findings and considers some of the key controversies in the field.

Marlow, Lenard, and Grier Raggio, "Mediation in divorce prevents bloody fights," *National Law Journal,* April 8, 1996, pp. A17-A18.
No-fault divorce and mediation are helping families minimize the damage of a breakup, and these useful tools should not become political footballs. The functions of divorce mediation in the legal system are discussed.

Gay Marriages

Dietz, Chris, "Can gay marriages harm families? Representative Whyman overreacts," *Detroit News & Free Press,* March 23, 1996, p. A10.
In a letter to the editor, Chris Dietz of Log Cabin

Republicans of Southeast Michigan says that with all of the real issues the Michigan Legislature has to worry about, it is disappointing that all state Rep. Deborah Whyman can think about is something that might not even happen, marriages between gay and lesbian couples.

Innes, David C., "A Christian view on gay marriages," *San Francisco Chronicle,* April 8, 1996, A19.
Inness, a Baptist minister in San Francisco, comments on the Christian view of gay marriages, and notes a mass gay "marriage" ceremony held in San Francisco in March 1996.

"Judicial fiat and gay marriage," *Detroit News,* March 26, 1996, p. A6.
An editorial says there are compelling reasons for Michigan to stake out its own position on outlawing gay marriages now rather than submit to the judicial fiat of Hawaii's court.

Nickel, Jeff, "Should government OK gay marriage?" *Detroit News,* March 28, 1996, p. A12.
In a letter to the editor, Jeff Nickel of Forum on the Right to Marriage in Boston expresses hope that the explosion of media coverage of the marriage issue will pave the way for the long-overdue legal recognition of gay and lesbian relationships.

Nolan, Bruce, "Allow same-sex marriage, rabbis say," *Times-Picayune,* March 30, 1996, p. A16.
With the concurrence of rabbis from three New Orleans synagogues, the Central Conference of American Rabbis, the largest association of Jewish rabbis in the U.S., in late March 1996 endorsed the idea of same-sex civil marriages and opposed state attempts to make them illegal.

Price, Deb, "Forward-thinking woman set the stage for gay marriage — 21 years ago," *Detroit News,* March 29, 1996, p. B1.
Price comments on Boulder County, Colo., Clerk Clela Rorex's willingness to give marriage licenses to six same-sex couples in 1975. Her gutsy decision prompted recall threats, hate mail and ridicule.

Snow, Tony, "Gay union not marriage," *USA Today,* April 1, 1996, A15.
Tony Snow discusses the effect of the ratification of a law in Hawaii that would recognize marriage between gay couples, saying the decision could become the law of the land because the full faith and credit clause of the U.S. Constitution orders all jurisdictions to honor judicial decisions of states.

"Vatican Denounces Gay-Marriage Idea," *The New York Times,* March 29, 1996, p. B2.
The Vatican has appealed to voters not to support politicians who endorse same-sex marriages. Gino Concetti, a moral theologian, wrote in the Vatican's official newspaper on March 27, 1996, that homosexual marriage would "undermine the foundation of the family model upon which human civilization was built."

Marriage tax penalty

Kirwan, Roberta, "Why seniors don't marry," *Money,* July 1995, p. 100.
Senior citizens sometimes choose to cohabit over marriage because of the tax penalty and Social Security. A married couple filing jointly can have only $32,000 in income before their benefits are subject to tax, while two singles living together can each earn $25,000 before being taxed.

Marshall, Jonathan, "Will you form a stable economic unit with me?" *San Francisco Chronicle,* Jan. 16, 1995, p. B3.
Marshall comments on the tax penalty imposed on two-income couples if they decide to marry, and notes the GOP "Contract With America" wants to change that through its proposed "American Dream Restoration Act."

Mintz, Bill, "Is true love too costly?" *Houston Chronicle,* Jan. 18, 1995, p. B1.
U.S. Rep. Bill Archer, R-Texas, the new chairman of the House Ways and Means Committee, wants to eliminate the tax penalty for being married. The GOP think that this is so important that they have put fixing it in the "Contract with America," their 10-point plan of action for the first 100 days of Congress.

Ravo, Nick, "Marriage penalty likely to decline, if not disappear," *The New York Times,* Feb. 26, 1995, p. 19.
Few inequalities in the federal tax code strike as many people as the marriage-tax penalty, which may be reduced in 1995 if Republicans in Congress have their way. As part of its "Contract With America," the Republican majority in the House has promised to introduce legislation within the first 100 days of the current session to repeal the marriage-tax penalty, but complete elimination of the penalty is unlikely.

Marriage Therapy

Larson, Jeffrey H., Thomas B. Holman, David M. Klein and Dean M. Busby, et. al. "A review of comprehensive questionnaires used in premarital education and counseling," *Family Relations,* July 1995, pp. 245-252.
Five comprehensive premarital assessment questionnaires that can be used in high school, university and church or secular settings by family life educators and premarital counselors are described and evaluated.

O'Donohue, William, and Julie L. Crouch, "Marital therapy and gender-linked factors in communication," *Journal of Marital & Family Therapy,* January 1996, pp. 87-101.
O'Donohue and Crouch raise the question of whether communication training programs in marital therapy have been sufficiently sensitive to the complexities of gender in communication.

No-Fault Divorce

Bauer, Gary L., "End no-fault divorce," *USA Today*, Dec. 29, 1995, p. A10.
Gary L. Bauer of the Family Research Council argues that reform of the nation's divorce laws is a matter of simple justice and advocates banning no-fault divorce, saying they cause further injury to the grieved spouse who is fighting to keep the marriage intact.

"Divorce law," *Detroit News & Free Press*, Jan. 13, 1996, p. A8.
A *Detroit Free Press* editorial argues against Michigan legislation to change the no-fault divorce law, saying lawmakers would do better to address the broader economic and social inequities that continue to hurt children and families more than divorce does.

Milbank, Dana, "Blame game: No-fault divorce law is assailed in Michigan, and debate heats up," *The Wall Street Journal*, Jan. 5, 1996, p. A1.
Saying that no-fault divorce legislation "has weakened the fabric of the family and devalued marriage," Rep. Jessie Dalman of Michigan's legislature has introduced a bill that would, in effect, repeal the state's 1972 no-fault divorce law. The debate over no-fault divorce laws, which some say have led to more divorces, is examined.

Peterson, Karen S., "Saying 'no' to the notion of no-fault divorce," *USA Today*, Jan. 25, 1996, p. D1.
Several states are attempting to change their laws to disallow no-fault divorce for the sake of children, who are highly affected during a divorce. Opponents of the measures say they would add to the pain of divorce, and make it hard for abused women to leave their husbands.

Bell, Dawson, and Jacquelynn Boyle, "Blame is cast at no-fault divorce," *Detroit News & Free Press*, Feb. 4, 1995, p. A3.
Michigan Family Forum Executive Director Randall Hekman said Michigan's two-decade-long experiment with no-fault divorce has been no good for women, children or society and should be scrapped.

Cole, Kenneth, "Bills would make divorce harder," *Detroit News*, Feb. 13, 1996, p. D1.
A 13-bill package that would gut Michigan's no-fault divorce laws in cases where one spouse opposes the separation, sponsored largely by state Rep. Jessie Dalman, is set for introduction on Feb. 14, 1996, in the state House.

Gallagher, Maggie, "Why make divorce easy?" *The New York Times*, Feb. 20, 1996, p. A19.
Gallagher examines the debate over no-fault divorce laws and concludes that imposing a five-to-seven-year waiting period for contested no-fault divorces could raise the number of marriages that ultimately succeed. Gallagher argues that making divorce more difficult would give weight to the original contract and put the law on the side of those who want to wait, think and reconsider.

Ilka, Douglas, "Proposed changes in divorce law upset some," *Detroit News*, March 8, 1996, p. C5.
Proposed legislation to dismantle Michigan's "no-fault" divorce laws is under heavy attack by Oakland Family Services, a nonprofit, private human service agency. The group contends the proposal bills will push parents further apart and harm children.

Johnson, Dirk, "Attacking no-fault notion, conservatives try to put blame back in divorce," *The New York Times*, Feb. 12, 1996, p. A10.
In several states, conservatives are moving against "no-fault "divorces as a way of strengthening families. Critics, however, say the attempts would not save marriages, but rather would worsen hostilities in a fault-based divorce proceeding, with more pain for children.

Puente, Maria, "Lawmakers counsel against divorce," *USA Today*, Feb. 21, 1996, p. A6.
The burgeoning movement to repeal no-fault divorce laws has spawned a campaign to encourage, or even compel, premarital counseling as a way to reduce America's sky-high divorce rate. Encouraged by church leaders, conservative politicians and studies of the negative effects of divorce, lawmakers are looking at ways to promote happy marriages, or stop bad ones from ever getting started.

Vobejda, Barbara, "Critics, seeking change, fault to no-fault divorce laws for high rates," *The Washington Post*, March 7, 1996, p. A3.
Alarm over high divorce rates is propelling efforts to tighten the laws again. Determined to discourage divorce, legislators in several states have suggested "cooling-off" periods and mandatory counseling and are trying to restrict no-fault divorce.

Willats, Brian, "Finding fault in state divorce law," *Detroit News*, March 26, 1996, p. A6.
In a letter to the editor, Brian Willats of the Michigan Family Forum says Michigan's no-fault divorce law has failed miserably on its promised benefits, while also removing any substance to the marriage commitment. He adds that moving to a mutual-consent divorce system, as proposed by the Legislature, would change that.

Young, Cathy, "The faults of ending no-fault divorce," *Detroit News*, March 19, 1996, P. A7.
Young criticizes Michigan state Rep. Jesse Dalman's legislative proposal to restore fault-based divorce in the state, saying among other things that in today's world, tougher divorce laws may simply deter many couples from marrying.

Back Issues

Great Research on Current Issues Starts Right Here...Recent topics covered by The CQ Researcher are listed below. Before May 1991, reports were published under the name of Editorial Research Reports.

NOVEMBER 1994
Sex on Campus
Blood Supply Safety
Testing Term Limits
Religion in America

DECEMBER 1994
Farm Policy
Arms Sales
Earthquake Research
The Future of Television

JANUARY 1995
Treating Addiction
Child Custody and Support
Parents and Schools
Non-Proliferation Treaty at 25

FEBRUARY 1995
Cracking Down on Immigration
The Business of Sports
Reinventing Government
Housing Discrimination

MARCH 1995
Death Penalty Debate
Primary Care
Democracy in Africa
Environmental Movement at 25

APRIL 1995
Abortion Clinic Protests
Dieting and Health
Combating AIDS
Rethinking Affirmative Action

MAY 1995
Assisted Suicide Controversy
Overhauling Social Security
Learning to Read
Mandatory Sentencing

JUNE 1995
Combating Infectious Disease
Property Rights
Repetitive Stress Injuries
Regulating the Internet

JULY 1995
War Crimes
Highway Safety
Combating Terrorism
Preventing Teen Drug Use

AUGUST 1995
Job Stress
Organ Transplants
United Nations at 50
Advances in Cancer Research

SEPTEMBER 1995
Catholic Church in the U.S.
Northern Ireland Cease-Fire
High School Sports
Teaching History

OCTOBER 1995
Quebec's Future
Revitalizing the Cities
Networking the Classroom
Indoor Air Pollution

NOVEMBER 1995
The Working Poor
The Jury System
Sex, Violence and the Media
Police Misconduct

DECEMBER 1995
Teens and Tobacco
Gene Therapy's Future
Global Water Shortages
Third-Party Prospects

JANUARY 1996
Emergency Medicine
Punishing Sex Offenders
Bilingual Education
Helping the Homeless

FEBRUARY 1996
Reforming the CIA
Campaign Finance Reform
Academic Politics
Getting Into College

MARCH 1996
The British Monarchy
Preventing Juvenile Crime
Tax Reform
Pursuing the Paranormal

APRIL 1996
Centennial Olympic Games
Managed Care
Protecting Endangered Species
New Military Culture

MAY 1996
Russia's Political Future

Back issues are available for $5.00 (subscribers) or $8.00 (non-subscribers). Quantity discounts apply to orders over ten. To order, call Congressional Quarterly Customer Service at (202) 887-8621.

Binders are available for $18.00. To order call 1-800-638-1710. Please refer to stock number 648.

Future Topics

- ***Year-Round Schools***
- ***U.S., China and Taiwan***
- ***Rethinking NAFTA***

THE CQ Researcher

PUBLISHED BY CONGRESSIONAL QUARTERLY INC.

Year-Round Schools

Do they improve academic performance?

For most of the nation's 44 million schoolchildren, summer vacations begin in June. However, more than 1.7 million students will remain in classes a few weeks longer and get a shorter vacation break. They attend schools with "year-round education" (YRE) programs designed to improve academic achievement and/or ease overcrowding. YRE programs rearrange the school schedule into several instructional time blocks separated by shorter and more frequent vacation breaks. In most YRE schedules, the number of days in the school year remains the same as in traditional calendars. Supporters claim, among other things, that YRE reduces learning loss during the usual 10-12 week summer hiatus. Opponents say that time off is itself part of the learning and maturing process, and that YRE disrupts family activities.

INSIDE THIS ISSUE

CQ May 17, 1996 • Volume 6, No. 19 • Pages 433-456

Formerly Editorial Research Reports

YEAR-ROUND SCHOOLS

COVER: STUDENTS AT PARK VIEW ELEMENTARY SCHOOL IN MOORESVILLE, N.C. — ONE OF THE FIRST SCHOOLS IN THE STATE TO OFFER AN OPTIONAL YEAR-ROUND EDUCATION PROGRAM.

May 17, 1996
Volume 6, No. 19

EDITOR
Sandra Stencel

MANAGING EDITOR
Thomas J. Colin

ASSOCIATE EDITORS
Sarah M. Magner
Richard L. Worsnop

STAFF WRITERS
Charles S. Clark
Mary H. Cooper
Kenneth Jost

EDITORIAL ASSISTANT
Tonya Harris

PUBLISHED BY
Congressional Quarterly Inc.

CHAIRMAN
Andrew Barnes

VICE CHAIRMAN
Andrew P. Corty

EDITOR AND PUBLISHER
Neil Skene

EXECUTIVE EDITOR
Robert W. Merry

The CQ Researcher (ISSN 1056-2036). Formerly Editorial Research Reports. Published weekly (48 times per year, not printed March 1, May 31, Aug. 30, Nov. 29) by Congressional Quarterly Inc., 1414 22nd St., N.W., Washington, D.C. 20037. Annual subscription rate for libraries, businesses and government is $319. Additional rates furnished upon request. Second-class postage paid at Washington, D.C. POSTMASTER: Send address changes to The CQ Researcher, 1414 22nd St., N.W., Washington, D.C. 20037.

Year-Round Schools

By Richard L. Worsnop

The Issues

As June edges closer, the countdown to summer vacation begins for millions of schoolchildren across the nation. For a small but growing number, however, vacations will start later and end sooner. They attend schools that have scrapped the familiar September-to-June schedule in favor of "year-round education" (YRE).

Despite the off-putting name, YRE does not actually require pupils to attend school all year. It is, rather, a catch-all term for programs that rearrange the traditional school calendar into several instructional time blocks, separated by shorter and more frequent vacation breaks. In most YRE arrangements, the number of days in the school year is the same as in the September-to-June model.

Year-round schooling is attracting interest at a time of mounting dissatisfaction with the state of U.S. elementary and secondary education. Studies have repeatedly shown that American high school students score well below students from other advanced countries in core academic subjects such as mathematics and history. These countries typically require longer instructional days — and more of them — than most American schools, where the eight-hour-per-day, 180-day-a-year model is standard. (*See story, p. 440.*)

To many U.S. fans of YRE, the arithmetic is as easy as two and two: To make U.S. students more competitive, school officials must lengthen the school year.

Nonetheless, "America's attachment to the 180-day school year is still strong," observed Michael J. Barrett, a Massachusetts attorney who often writes on public policy issues. "In a world already reeling from future shock, the notion of extending the year seems punitive, an assault on the idea of summer itself. It raises the specter of joyless cramming. It implies that American parents have somehow failed their children." [1]

That negative attitude is shared by many parents and educators and helps to explain why YRE now occupies only a tiny niche in American primary and secondary education. According to the National Association for Year-Round Education (NAYRE), 2,368 public schools in 37 states currently operate on some sort of year-round schedule. More than 1.7 million students were enrolled in such schools in the 1995-96 academic year, up from 350,000 students a decade ago. By comparison, more than 42 million students attend some 83,000 public schools nationwide that follow the traditional school calendar, according to the National Center for Education Statistics.

Year-round schools tend to be clustered in certain regions and states. Charles Ballinger, NAYRE's executive director, notes that "83 percent of our year-round schools currently are west of the Mississippi," whereas Eastern schools have been "far more resistant to change."

In fact, 76 percent of the YRE schools are concentrated in just three states — California, Florida and Texas. That's hardly surprising, since all three have experienced robust population growth in recent decades, which has caused severe school overcrowding.

Under such trying circumstances, financially squeezed school boards find one form of year-round education — the so-called "multi-track" schedule — almost irresistibly appealing. A multi-track schedule makes fuller use of existing facilities, thus eliminating or postponing the need to build additional classrooms.

The word "track," in the world of YRE, does not connote the separation of students into groups ranked by academic ability — a once popular practice that has fallen out of favor. [2] Rather, a track refers to one or more equally sized groups of students attending the same school on staggered schedules. (*See glossary, p. 438.*) At any given time, one of the groups is "off-track" — that is, on vacation — while the others are attending class regularly. The net effect of such arrangements is to substantially increase the number of students the school can accommodate.

"Implementing a four-track, year-round calendar extends the capacity of a school by 33 percent," according to NAYRE. "[A] school with [a normal] capacity of 750 students can accommodate 1,000 students, as only three tracks of [250] students [each] would be in school at the same time. There would always be one track on vacation every day of the school year. At no time will there ever be more than 750 students on campus." [3]

By the same token, a three-track program allows a school to enroll up to 50 percent more students than its designed capacity, while a five-track schedule permits a 25 percent enroll-

States with Year-Round Public Schools

Thirty-seven states (shaded blue) had at least one public school with year-round education (YRE) during the 1995-96 school year. The four states with the most year-round schools — California, Texas, Florida and North Carolina — had high population growth and a corresponding need to make maximum use of existing school facilities. Year-round schools usually offer the same amount of instruction as schools on a nine-month calendar — 180 days — though a few YRE schools add school days to the calendar.*

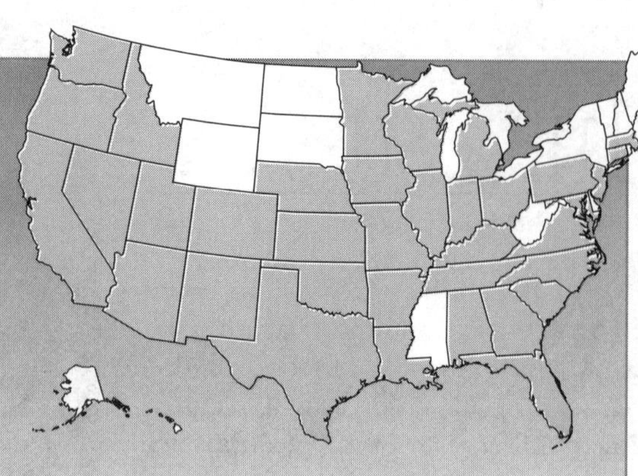

Number of year-round public schools in each state

State	Schools	State	Schools	State	Schools	State	Schools	State	Schools
Alabama	44	Hawaii	15	Maryland	1	New Jersey	2	South Carolina	8
Arizona	69	Idaho	3	Massachusetts	2	New Mexico	9	Tennessee	2
Arkansas	2	Illinois	20	Michigan	19	North Carolina	93	Texas	352
California	1,284	Indiana	6	Minnesota	6	Ohio	10	Utah	85
Colorado	44	Iowa	4	Missouri	8	Oklahoma	2	Virginia	1
Connecticut	1	Kansas	3	Nebraska	1	Oregon	13	Washington	17
Florida	168	Kentucky	12	Nevada	53	Pennsylvania	2	Wisconsin	2
Georgia	1	Louisiana	4						

* *Schools with YRE are defined as those with modified calendars and eight weeks or less of summer vacation.*

Source: National Association for Year-Round Education, May 1996

ment increase.

"Every multi-track calendar, like most everything else in life, has its pluses and minuses," says Ballinger. "Each community has to choose which calendar makes sense for it."

Multi-tracking generally is the preferred year-round option at the elementary and middle-school levels, where the object is to relieve overcrowding. Elementary schools have few extracurricular activities, which tend to be disrupted by multi-tracking. High schools, in contrast, tend to favor single-track schedules that apply to the entire student body and are designed to improve academic performance. A typical single-track program divides the school year into four nine-week terms (45 school days), separated by four three-week vacations or "intersessions."

YRE advocates contend that shorter, more frequent vacations help minimize the learning loss that often occurs during the 10-week summer break served up by a traditional school calendar. YRE critics question whether any such improvement actually occurs.

Single- and multi-track programs are by no means the only YRE choices available to a community. A few schools have expanded the academic year to 240 instructional days — about the same number as in German and Japanese schools. That's seven days shy of 247 days, which is the maximum number of school days a school could use, not counting weekends and holidays, if it wanted to make the calendar as long as possible.

Another YRE possibility is the double-session (sometimes called two-track) approach, in which students attend school in two shifts, each somewhat shorter than a traditional school day. Doubling up in this fashion typically entails lengthening the school year to approximately 225 days to meet minimum state requirements for total instruction time. Parents and students generally dislike double-session schooling, since the first shift has to arrive at school very early in the morning, while the second one must remain until early evening.

In recent years, the debate over year-round education has broadened to embrace more fundamental questions about the use of educational time. Block scheduling, long utilized in higher education, varies the length of class periods to accommodate the particular needs of the subject being taught. For instance, some science classes might be twice the usual length so that students can test the knowledge gained from a lecture in a laboratory session held immediately afterward.

"Students don't have to stop and start so often," says John Lammel, director of high school services at the National Association of Secondary School Principals (NASSP). "Reducing the number of classes per school day saves time."

Indeed, a widely noted report issued in 1994 by the congressionally appointed National Education Commission on Time and Learning stressed the need for more imaginative ways of scheduling and presenting material (*see p. 448*). "We should not forget that students are like adults in many ways," the panel asserted. "Some are able to focus intensely on demanding materials for long periods; others need more frequent breaks. Many students, like many adults, learn best by reading; some learn best by listening; others, by doing, or even by talking amongst themselves. Offering more frequent breaks, providing more opportunities for hands-on learning, encouraging group work — these techniques and others can parole some of the students who today feel most confined by the school's rigid time demands." [4]

Since there is wide agreement that a well-educated populace is the key to assuring a prosperous future, debate on year-round schooling and related issues seems likely to continue. These are some of the key issues being discussed:

Does year-round schooling improve academic performance?

The acid test for year-round schooling, supporters and opponents agree, is whether it raises the academic achievement of students exposed to it. (*See "At Issue," p. 449.*) Many would agree with public policy expert Barrett that "additional time by itself does not guarantee successful learning." [5]

In Barrett's opinion, "More is not necessarily better, because other factors come into play, ranging from the quality of the teacher to the quality of the textbooks to the health of the student. Second, time is a commodity that comes in different sizes. The length of the school year, the length of the school week, the length of the school day, the number of minutes diverted to 'classroom management' and lost to instruction, the number of minutes allocated to a particular subject, the amount of homework, the rate of pupil attendance and absenteeism — these blocks of time interrelate, and the importance of any one of them cannot be analyzed without considering its impact on the others." [6]

"There are educational pressures to change the structure of the school year. As we build up documentation showing that there is such a thing as summer learning loss, and that a way exists to curb that loss, the onus will be on schools and educators to take corrective action."

— Charles Ballinger, executive director, National Association for Year-Round Education

Notwithstanding these complexities, opinion on the academic effectiveness of year-round education tends to be sharply divided. Enriqueta Chavez, a counselor at Eastlake High School in San Diego, has sent three of her children through area YRE schools and is enthusiastic about the results. "Attendance has increased in most of the schools on year-round schedules," she reports, "and test scores have improved, too."

The intersession vacation periods benefit both students and teachers, adds Chavez. "During those three-week breaks, students have a choice. They can continue coming to school on a half-day basis, pick up a class for credit or attend some enrichment courses." She estimates that "close to half of the students come back to class during the intersessions."

Similarly, if teachers "want to work and make a little extra money during the intersessions, they can. If they don't want to, they can go on vacation. And we have found that three or four weeks is just about long enough for a break. By then, the kids are pretty bored and really want to come back to school."

Norman R. Brekke, former superintendent of the Oxnard (Calif.) Elementary School District, also strongly supports YRE. [7] Oxnard schools covering grades K-8 switched from a traditional to a year-round schedule in 1976 and are still on it. After the shift, "Our state test scores clearly indicated progress in academic achievement," says Brekke. "We exceeded the statewide average in test-score improvement."

Brekke acknowledges that "Oxnard was never, overall, at the statewide average," and still is not. That's because the local population "was heavily minority, with limited facility in English." Nonetheless, "the amount of test-score growth from one year to the next was greater in Oxnard than

A Year-Round Education Glossary

Core academic curriculum: Defined by the National Education Commission on Time and Learning as the subjects that all students should take during the academic day — English and language arts, mathematics, science, civics, geography, history, the arts and foreign languages.

Extended year: A type of year-round education (YRE) that actually lengthens the school year substantially, up to 240 days of instruction compared with the standard 180 days. Only a handful of U.S. schools have initiated the extended year.

Intersession: Designated days students or teachers are not in school.

Juku: A private Japanese tutorial school that supplements regular school programs, offering remedial and enrichment programs to prepare students for university exams.

Multi-track year-round education: A type of YRE that divides students in one school into three, four or five same-size groups, each with different class and vacation schedules. Groups attend on staggered schedules, so that one group is always on vacation. Multi-tracking is designed primarily to relieve overcrowding and make better use of facilities.

Single-track year-round education: A type of YRE in which all students attend school on the same schedule of instructional sessions and vacations; designed to improve educational performance.

Track: A group of students attending the same school on the same schedule.

Year-round education: A concept that reorganizes the school year to provide more continuous learning by breaking up the long summer vacation into shorter, more frequent vacations. It does not eliminate the summer vacation, but reduces it. The total amount of vacation ordinarily remains the same as in traditional schedules.

Sources: National Association for Year-Round Education, National Education Commission on Time and Learning

in similar schools elsewhere in California. And when our local newspapers pointed that out, support for the year-round program rose."

Critics of YRE challenge claims that it improves the educational performance of students and teachers. Heather Tepe, a homemaker in Columbia, Md., who helped defeat a proposed year-round education program for Howard County schools, contends that a traditional schedule gives children the freedom they need "to explore other opportunities and other interests."

In her opinion, kids already "are spending so much time in scheduled activities — whether it's in day care, after-school programs, or school itself — that they're stressed out and over-regimented. They need some down time — time to be kids."

Don Patterson, a member of the Albuquerque, N.M., school board, takes the position that YRE is one of "a lot of gimmicks in education that are reintroduced every 20 or 25 years." He likens the process to "infatuation with change for change's sake" or "reinvention of the flat tire."

In Albuquerque, says Patterson, "we had more absenteeism among kids on year-round schedules than among kids on traditional schedules. Also, the grade-repetition rate among kids on year-round schedules was twice that of kids on traditional schedules. I think that came about because year-round use of school buildings leaves no opportunity to operate summer remediation programs."

Patterson also scoffs at claims that intersession breaks create openings for enrichment courses. "When you have a multi-track schedule, you have no space for enrichment programs," he says. "Overcrowding is why a school goes to multi-track in the first place."

In addition, argues Patterson, YRE erodes the morale of teachers and school administrators. Public education "is taxing, it's hard work," he says. "The traditional summer vacation is like when an actor goes on hiatus between roles. It gives the individual time to recharge internal batteries. The short breaks under a year-round schedule never quite do that."

Perhaps the most contentious YRE issue of all is the so-called "summer effect," or the partial learning loss that many students experience during a traditional summer vacation. YRE enthusiasts contend that shorter, more frequent breaks help students retain more of what they have learned. But many educators either disagree or say that such claims are unproven and possibly unprovable.

A forthcoming review of 39 studies on the effect of a traditional summer vacation on achievement test scores found that scores did in fact generally decline. "The effect of summer break was more detrimental for math than for reading and most detrimental for math computation and spelling," the researchers concluded. "Also, middle-class students appeared to gain on grade level equivalent reading tests over summer while lower-class students lost on them." Middle-class students, the researchers suggested, may have had more opportunities to hone their academic skills during the long summer break than did lower-class students. [8]

Sandy Hawkins of Sandy, Utah, a past president of NAYRE, has two children who performed equally well in a YRE elementary school and a traditional-calendar secondary school. But she knows of parents in her area who had to hire tutors for their children at the beginning of each new traditional school year. These parents were delighted to find that tutoring wasn't needed under a year-round schedule, "because the children weren't away from the learning environment as long."

Patterson, on the other hand, feels it's "ridiculous" to assert that shorter vacations enhance knowledge retention. "The argument I use," he says, "is that if I know your name, and I remember it tomorrow, then I'm going to remember your name for a month or two. You know, long-term. Short-term memory loss is very acute. Studies show that the only discernible summer loss occurs in the first two or three weeks. So by introducing all these multiple breaks, all you're doing is maximizing forgetting."

Multiple breaks can be detrimental in other ways as well, Patterson believes. As a scheduled school break approaches, students "lose focus in anticipation of having time off from school. Then, when they return to class, they need additional time to reacclimate themselves to the learning environment. Consequently, short breaks probably do more harm than good."

Traditional summer-school programs, operated for students who need to make up credits lost through absence or failure, obviously do not lend themselves well to a year-round schedule, critics say. YRE supporters say students in need of remediation can receive help during the short intersession breaks. But since all classrooms are in use at all times under many YRE programs, administrators would have to lease outside space, incurring additional costs for the school district. [9]

"It could be true" that a year-round schedule enhances knowledge retention, says Barbara Heyns, a sociology professor at New York University, but "there's no good evidence" to support that conclusion. "When people test kids, they aren't sure whether they are assessing retention or learning," she says. "Generally, it's a bit of both. The problem is that the tests are not set up to evaluate time periods — what kids learn in a specific unit of time. Teachers tend to have very fixed opinions about this, but I really don't see much supporting evidence."

"The traditional summer vacation is like when an actor goes on hiatus between roles. It gives the individual time to recharge internal batteries. The short breaks under a year-round schedule never quite do that."
— Don Patterson, a member of the Albuquerque, N.M., school board

Heyns' views accord with one of the conclusions of a 1990 survey of year-round schooling by Phi Delta Kappa, the honorary education fraternity. "Despite the claims that long summer vacations lead to lessened achievement, year-round schools are not associated with great leaps in academic achievement," the group reported. "Standardized testing shows that year-round programs have little impact on scores one way or another. If a district is looking to show major increases in standardized tests, year-round schools are not the answer." [10]

For homemaker Tepe, the knowledge-retention debate focuses on the wrong issue. "If children are losing what they have learned over 10 weeks or three weeks," she says, "it indicates to me that the material wasn't taught correctly in the first place."

Is year-round education more cost-effective than the traditional model?

For many school administrators, the most persuasive argument in favor of YRE is that it offers a cost-effective way of relieving classroom overcrowding. Instead of renting commercial space or portable classrooms — or constructing new schools — administrators can enlarge the capacity of existing facilities by converting them to year-round operation.

"All new buildings cost money to build, of course, but they also cost money to operate and maintain each year they are in use," Ballinger wrote. "A secondary school costing $20 million to build will require at least another $20 million to service the bond debt, to repair and maintain and to operate over a period of 30 years. That total of $40 million or more — for one new building —

Foreign Students Rack Up Classroom Hours

Everyone knows about the yawning trade gap between the United States and Japan. Less familiar, perhaps, though just as troubling to many observers, is the classroom achievement gap between the countries.

Some educators attribute the gap to the traditional 180-day U.S. school year, which is relatively short by world standards. In Japan and Germany, for instance, the school year runs about 240 days.

Other educators say the main problem is that U.S. students don't spend enough classroom time on such core academic subjects as science and mathematics. To bring American students up to international speed, reformers are urging greater emphasis on the core curriculum, a longer school year or both.

In a widely noted April 1994 report, the congressionally appointed National Education Commission on Time and Learning estimated that French, German and Japanese students received more than twice as much core academic instruction as Americans. But that didn't mean the overseas students were shunning extracurricular activities, the panel added.

"Up to 50 percent of German students, even in farming areas, remain at the school after the academic day to participate in clubs, sports and additional classes of one kind or another," the panel stated. "In Japan, students clean their school when the academic day ends and then enter activity periods." [1]

Greater exposure to the core curriculum was not the only advantage enjoyed by German and Japanese students. In both countries, out-of-school learning reinforces classroom instruction. As the commission noted, "Large numbers of Japanese students . . . attend *jukus* — private, tutorial services that enrich instruction, provide remedial help and prepare students for university examinations." [2]

In the commission's view, the disparate educational practices of Germany, Japan and the United States reflect fundamental differences in educational outlook. "In Germany and Japan, learning matters," it concluded. "Performance, not seat time, is what counts. Students understand that what they learn in school will make a real difference to their chances in life. In the United States, paper credentials count." [3]

Some educators complain that international comparisons of test scores can be misleading. One frequently made point, observed Massachusetts attorney Michael J. Barrett, who writes about public policy issues, is that "secondary education in the United States is universal . . . while systems elsewhere are closed or elite, with a consequent creaming effect that inflates test scores." [4]

In any case, there are signs that the core-curriculum achievement gap between U.S. and foreign students is narrowing, though on a spotty basis. A recent report by the National Science Foundation (NSF) stated that elementary schools have beefed up math and science instruction since 1977 and that more high school students are enrolled in advanced science courses. [5]

Scores on the National Assessment of Educational Progress test, most recently administered in 1992, disclosed sharp variations in academic achievement. For instance, math scores for 13-year-olds in the top-performing states — Iowa, North Dakota and Minnesota — ranked with comparable scores from Taiwan, South Korea and the former Soviet Union — the best-performing of the 14 nations covered in the survey. [6]

On the other hand, test scores from Alabama, Louisiana, Mississippi and the District of Columbia ranked with those from Jordan, the lowest-rated foreign nation tested. The results underscored once again the local character of U.S. primary and secondary education, with test scores often reflecting regional differences in family income and public-school funding.

"In the international arena," the NSF summed up, "U.S. elementary school students compare favorably on science tests with students from other countries, but U.S. middle school students have some of the lowest mathematics scores in the world. . . . These trends in student achievement remain unexplained." [7]

---

[1] National Education Commission on Time and Learning, *Prisoners of Time*, April 1994, p. 25.

[2] *Ibid.*

[3] *Ibid.*, p. 26.

[4] Michael J. Barrett, "The Case for More School Days," *The Atlantic Monthly*, November 1990, p. 84.

[5] National Science Foundation, *Indicators of Science and Mathematics Education 1995*, January 1996.

[6] The 14 foreign countries, listed in descending order of mathematics proficiency, were Taiwan, Korea, Soviet Union, Switzerland, Hungary, France, Israel, Italy, Canada, Ireland, Scotland, Slovenia, Spain, Jordan. For background, see "Education Standards," *The CQ Researcher*, March 11, 1994, pp. 217-240.

[7] National Science Foundation, *op. cit.*, p. 29.

is forever lost to the more important instructional considerations of materials and supplies, field trips, instructional aides and adequate salaries for the professionals involved in the education of the nation's young." [11]

Opponents say YRE's purported economies often fall short of expectations. Experience shows, they say, that staff and operating costs inevitably rise after an existing school switches from a traditional to a year-round schedule. Indeed, they argue, these expenses may be so great as to eat up much of the money saved by not building a new school.

The unexpectedly high cost of air conditioning is a typical example. Because installing a central cooling system is so costly, year-round education usually is limited to schools that already have such equipment. But heat waves like the ones that seared much of the country last summer can send school energy bills soaring well beyond budgeted levels. At the same time, opponents say, stressful weather conditions make learning more difficult for many students.

A year-round schedule also can pose problems for school custodians accustomed to doing major maintenance and repair jobs during the summer. The Oxnard Elementary School District's solution was to contract out most big maintenance projects and transportation services. Painting, plumbing and electrical contractors worked during off-hours and on weekends, thus saving much of the money that would have gone toward medical benefits, worker compensation and overtime pay if additional school staff had been hired. Switching from in-house to contract services provided "significant savings" to the Oxnard district, Brekke said. [12]

Some experts argue that a longer school year helps deter juvenile crime, thus benefiting the entire community. "Although juvenile crimes occur throughout each calendar year, the school vacation periods and the peak periods of juvenile delinquency are closely related," veteran educator Mossie J. Richmond Jr. noted in an early report on YRE. Police records show, he noted, that the number of juvenile offenses abruptly falls after school holiday periods. Nonetheless, "the length of our school year continues to stand as a monument to a bygone agrarian life and as an opportunity for increased juvenile crime in America." [13]

Richard Johnson, assistant superintendent of schools in Loudoun County, Va., outside Washington, says the cost-effectiveness of multi-track YRE vanishes if track sizes become imbalanced. "It's a numbers game," he says. "If you've got four tracks, say, and you don't maintain equal numbers of students on each, then you lose the gains you were looking for by going multi-track. In other words, you can't have 100 students on one track, 300 on the second one, 250 on the third and 200 on the fourth. They have got to be roughly equal in size."

Although tracks are equal size at the start, says Johnson, disparities are bound to develop as students move into and out of the district. "If those calendars get out of balance, then your ability to administer that program gets out of balance also," he says. "In some cases, you end up spending more money for teachers when you don't need them. In other cases, you don't have enough teachers on staff to handle a heavy influx of students."

A bigger problem, in Johnson's view, concerns "specialty classes" at both ends of the education spectrum, such as advanced-placement courses in mathematics and special-education classes for emotionally disturbed or learning-impaired youngsters. The difficulty here is that "you generally don't have many sections of those classes, because not every student takes them," Johnson says. This could cause scheduling and teacher-hiring headaches, since there may be too many specialty-class students to accommodate on a single track, but not enough to divide between two or more tracks.

Scheduling problems arose in the 1970s in suburban Prince William County, Va., where Johnson formerly was a division superintendent of schools. In 1980, as a result, 24,100 students on year-round schedules in the fast-growing eastern part of the county were put back on a traditional schedule.

"We found we were spending more money operationally than anybody had ever anticipated," Johnson says. "We were hiring people to cover problems we could not solve admin-

Students Abroad Get More Instruction

High school students in France, Germany and Japan receive more than twice as much core academic instruction as American students, according to a recent study.*

Total estimated core academic hours required in the final 4 years of secondary school

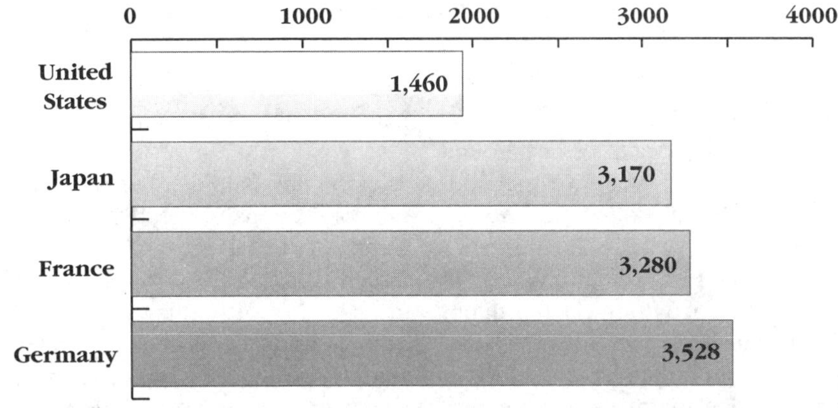

* *The estimate for Germany is based on the coursework requirements in Berlin.*

Note: Core academic subjects are native language and literature, mathematics, science, history, geography, the arts and second and third languages.

Source: Prisoners of Time, *National Education Commission on Time and Learning, April 1994*

Students at Park View Elementary School in Mooresville, N.C., work in the outdoor learning lab and study insects on the nature trail. The Mooresville School District has been offering an optional year-round education program since 1990. Students in the program attend school on a repeating 45-15 day calendar of nine weeks in school and three weeks out. Required attendance is 180 days. The program is available to students in grades K-8. In 1994-95, more than 1,150 students — 48 percent of the district's K-8 population — chose the alternative calendar.

istratively. That goes counter to everything that proponents of year-round schooling will tell you. We tried our level best to make it work, and we couldn't do it."

From Ballinger's perspective, equalizing the size of YRE tracks is a minor irritant at best. "Generally, new arrivals in a community are assigned a track for balancing purposes," he says. "And we have found that most parents, once they settle into a track, tend to stick with it." He adds that most multi-track schools maintain waiting lists for parents seeking to switch schedules, "but there just aren't that many requests for a change."

The sharply differing analyses of Johnson and Ballinger bear out one of the conclusions of the 1990 Phi Delta Kappa YRE survey: "Owing to the individualized quality of various programs, the difficulty in matching schools and districts for comparative studies, the differences between year-round and traditional-calendar schools in the same district, individual biases and excessive levels of enthusiasm or pessimism, much of what is reported about year-round schools is inconclusive or contradictory." [14]

As for YRE's economic impact, the study declared: "Cost savings which result from the avoidance of new construction are reduced by higher operating and maintenance costs. In growing districts, savings may be entirely offset if inevitably necessary new construction is completed above original estimates, due to inflation or other increases. A district should not consider implementing year-round school simply to save money." [15]

Does year-round schooling disrupt family leisure patterns and extracurricular activities?

Year-round education turns off many parents and schoolchildren because it eliminates the traditional 10-week summer vacation. "They see summer as special," writes Barrett, "as a time for young people to be with their families, to do something that helps them grow — even if it is only attending summer camp — or to earn some money." [16]

Indeed, many families argue that the long summer break is an integral part of the learning process, enabling children to acquire guidance and skills that schools are ill-equipped to impart. "Time goes by so quickly," says Tepe, "and there's so much that children have to learn. Values, for instance; things like that are better taught by families themselves."

Last summer, Tepe recalls, her children "took part in karate camp, nature camp, swim team, family outings and backyard carnivals. I know it's difficult to pinpoint or measure what children learn from activities like those, but I regard them as being just as important as the more organized, formal type of learning in a classroom."

Tepe's comments are comforting to leisure industries that heavily depend on spending for summer vacation activities. The American Camping Association (ACA), for example, favors year-round education ("a lifelong process which cannot be confined to four walls") but opposes year-round schools because of their truncated summer break.* In a 1991 resolution, the ACA Board of Directors said "organized camping is a vital component in the development and education of the whole child" and voiced support for "the extension of organized camping experiences to all children."

Ballinger says NAYRE has "no problem" with the camping industry's position. "We take issue with the ACA, not in its basic philosophy, but rather in the reality of life — which is, that no more than 15 percent of American students go to summer camp. Thus, the question for those of us in public education is, what do we do with the other 85 percent? Public policy is always made for the benefit of the largest number of people, not for the exceptions."

The traditional school calendar gives children the freedom they need "to explore other opportunities and other interests. . . . Kids already are spending so much time in scheduled activities . . . that they're stressed out and over-regimented. They need some down time — time to be kids."

— Heather Tepe, a housewife in Columbia, Md., who helped defeat a proposed year-round education program for Howard County Schools

Heyns, however, questions the educational value of most summer camps. "All camps would like to be endorsed as educationally valuable," she says. "But you can't really evaluate them in terms of what their purposes are and/or what kids gain from them. They're set up for very different purposes than traditional summer-school programs."

Many parents of children in year-round schools say the more frequent vacation breaks increase family leisure options. Hawkins acknowledges that she was initially wary of the YRE schedule, wondering, "How am I going to manage this? What will we do without that long summer vacation?" But then, she says, "You come to realize that there are lots of places you can go and things you can do — especially in the fall and spring, but also in the winter. We have winter sports here in Utah, so my kids took skiing and ice-skating lessons when they were off-track in cold-weather months. You can never do stuff like that during the summer."

Indeed, some observers argue that the leisure industry would benefit if school vacations were distributed more evenly throughout the year. With traditional scheduling, Richmond wrote, energy consumption soars and the quality of services suffers because of "the need to push equipment beyond the normal capacity during peak tourist seasons," which generally coincide with the traditional school schedule. "Extending the length of the school year or year-round education . . . would level out substantially this undesirable tendency in tourism and travel," especially in summer. [17]

Critics of YRE at the high school level contend it disrupts the continu-

* The International Association of Amusement Parks and Attractions also opposes the shorter summer vacations typical of year-round schooling.

ity of extracurricular activities because all the students are not there at the same time; ultimately, they say, YRE frays school spirit. One study found that "performing arts programs suffer [under YRE] and there is an increasing cost to maintain rehearsals on a year-round basis." Band, chorus, drama and student government were reported to be "particularly hard hit," while support for after-school programs in general was "very weak during the summer months." [18]

Interscholastic sports, on the other hand, tend to adapt relatively well to a year-round schedule. In the San Diego area, says Chavez, "Heavy workouts in football, cross-country and water polo usually begin in September, and that's when we're off on our first break. Our kids begin their school year in July and get to know their teachers and what's expected of them. Then, when the fall sports season begins two months later, they have already settled comfortably into their academic routine. The same thing happens in the spring. Soccer, baseball, volleyball and track seasons generally begin in March. And we're on break that month also." ■

BACKGROUND

Early Interest Fades

In Colonial times, year-round schooling was a familiar concept to at least some American children. In 1645, for instance, the town records of Dorchester, Mass., indicate that the schoolmaster began teaching at 7 a.m. and dismissed the students at 5 p.m. from January through July. For the remaining five months of the year, he started classes at 8 a.m. and ended at 4 p.m. [19] Not until the 1800s, however, did school attendance become mandatory in Massachusetts and other parts of the country.

A different schooling pattern emerged in rural areas, where schools were open for two relatively short periods each year: a winter term for older children, who usually were taught by men, and a summer term for young children, usually taught by women. Many contemporary observers assume that the system was guided by the needs of a rural economy, the older children being out of school when their labor was needed on the farm.

Barrett, however, dismisses the idea that the agricultural cycle shaped the academic calendar. "The historical record gives evidence that the period of mandatory school attendance increased steadily over time as it was shaped by two broad influences: on the one hand, the always growing demand for an educated work force, and on the other, the instinct to spare children from formal schooling during the hottest months of the year, regardless of whether they had any role to play in farming." [20]

By contrast, virtually year-round operation often was the rule in city schools during the 18th and 19th centuries. In the 1840s, for instance, public schools in Baltimore, Buffalo, Cincinnati, Detroit, New York, Philadelphia and Washington stayed open at least 11 months a year, and the school day ran from six to seven hours.

But the school year was gradually shortened. By 1890, 20 to 60 days had been lopped off in those cities; by 1900, the 180-day school year, extending over a nine-month period of five-day weeks, had become firmly established across the nation.

The trend did not meet with universal applause. In his annual report for 1894, U.S. Commissioner of Education William T. Harris lamented a "distinct loss this year, the average number of days of school having been reduced from 193.5 to 191." He added: "The boy of today must attend school 11.1 years in order to receive as much instruction, quantitatively, as the boy of 50 years ago received in eight years. . . . It is scarcely necessary to look further than this for the explanation for the greater amount of work accomplished . . . in the German and French [schools] than in the American schools." [21]

In 1898 Irwin Shepard, president of Minnesota's Winona Normal School (forerunner of Winona State University), became the first U.S. educator to propose a year-round, four-term school year. Shepard split the year into four three-month periods, corresponding roughly to the four seasons. His proposal was, in effect, an early version of today's multi-track school calendar. The four-quarter plan was first implemented in Bluffton, Ind., in 1904; it was dropped 11 years later.

Under the four-quarter format, students generally may choose, "or be assigned to, any combination of three of the four quarters," Ballinger and his colleagues wrote. "They may attend the fourth quarter on a voluntary basis, either on or off campus. The curriculum is organized so that each quarter is a separate entity. A course begins and ends with each 12-week period. For example, social studies and English programs may offer a series of separate but related courses. Subject areas requiring sequential treatment such as mathematics will be offered in each of the four quarters to complete a year of work." [22]

During the 1920s, more than a dozen school systems operated on a year-round basis, but by 1930 the number had dwindled to six. One of the complaints about such schools was that students who attended them were too young on graduation from high school to go to college or to find permanent work. By 1950, Richmond reported, "only Chattanooga, Tenn., was on the four-quarter plan." [23]

Continued on p. 447

Chronology

17th Century

In some American schools during the Colonial era, education is virtually all-day-long and year-round.

1645
In Dorchester, Mass., the schoolmaster starts teaching at 7 a.m. and sends his pupils home at 5 p.m. from January to June. From July through December, he teaches from 8 a.m. to 4 p.m.

1890s-1900s

As the average school year approaches its current length of about 180 days, the first proposals for year-round education (YRE) are voiced.

1894
U.S. Commissioner of Education William T. Harris, lamenting a reduction in the average length of the school year, declares that, "The boy of today must attend school 11.1 years in order to receive as much instruction, quantitatively, as the boy of 50 years ago received in eight years."

1898
Minnesota educator Irwin Shepard proposes that schools operate continuously throughout the year on a four-quarter schedule.

1904
Bluffton, Ind., becomes the first American community to adopt a four-quarter school calendar, an early variant of the year-round model. The town returns to a traditional school schedule in 1915.

1930s-1950s

Year-round schooling falls out of fashion under the twin pressures of the Great Depression and World War II.

1949
Lexington, Ky., institutes a year-round school schedule but abandons it 10 years later because of financial difficulties.

1954
Los Angeles concludes that an all-year school calendar would cost too much, entail too many administrative problems and fail to win popular support.

1957
Atlanta school officials decide it would cost more to convert the school system to a four-quarter calendar than to build new schools.

1960s-1970s

California emerges as a pacesetter in year-round education movement.

1968
Hayward, Calif., introduces the first contemporary single-track, YRE calendar in the nation at Park Elementary School. The program is still in place.

1969
The Francis Howell School District in St. Charles, Mo., implements the country's first multi-track YRE schedule.

1971
La Mesa-Spring Valley and Chula Vista school districts, both in San Diego County, launch California's first multi-track programs.

1990s

Year-round education records gains and setbacks.

June 7, 1993
Los Angeles discontinues the year-round schedule at more than 540 schools.

April 1994
The National Education Commission on Time and Learning issues its *Prisoners of Time* report, which warns: "We have been asking the impossible of our students — that they learn as much as their foreign peers while spending only half as much time in academic subjects."

September 1994
A follow-up report by the National Education Commission shows the many options available to school administrators wishing to make more productive use of classroom time.

February 1996
The National Association for Year-Round Education reports that more than 1.7 million students attended year-round schools in 1995-96. The National Association of Secondary School Principals urges that U.S. schools "operate on a 12-month basis to provide more time for professional staff development, collegial planning and the added instruction needed to promote better student learning."

April 25, 1996
A National Science Foundation report points to significant though geographically uneven progress in U.S. mathematics and science education, all the way from elementary school to the graduate school level.

Colleges Took Early Lead in Year-Round Education

Year-round education today is associated mainly with primary and secondary schools. For many years, though, colleges and universities were the trailblazers in academic scheduling.

Harvard, for example, operated from 1638 until 1801 — more than 150 years — on a year-long calendar of four terms of unequal length. In 1801, Harvard shifted to a three-term, year-round plan, which was used by many other colleges in the 19th century. By 1900, however, Harvard and most institutions of higher learning had changed over to the semester system, which divided the academic year into two periods of 17-18 weeks each, including holidays, with long summer vacations.

World War I and World War II both prompted colleges to extend the school year to make maximum use of educational facilities. But most of the institutions that had lengthened their schedules reverted to their traditional calendars after peace returned.

The postwar movement for year-round academic programming at the college level began in 1959 with the trimester system at the University of Pittsburgh. Pittsburgh divided the academic year into three trimesters of approximately 14 or 15 weeks each. The third trimester was an integral part of the basic academic calendar, offering a full program of courses and the same opportunity to earn credits toward a degree. [1]

Two years later, in 1961, Antioch College, in Yellow Springs, Ohio, put its distinctive work-study program on a four-quarters basis. Students alternated between studying on campus one quarter and working the next quarter, in the United States or abroad. Antioch was unusual, moreover, in requiring its students to attend all four sessions and in not scheduling a four-week vacation at the end of summer. [2]

Today, reports Charles Ballinger, executive director of the National Association for Year-Round Education, "There are still a number of schools that do year-round education at the higher level. Many colleges have a quarter system, for example, with some quarters more heavily attended than others. Ohio State, where I attended graduate school for both my master's and doctorate, has operated on a quarter system for at least three or four decades." Ballinger says he enrolled in all four quarters at Ohio State, reasoning that the two-to-three-week breaks separating them were sufficient for "a little R&R."

Colleges that operate on the semester system don't take full advantage of their resources, says Ballinger, adding that he "just can't see billions of dollars worth of buildings being largely empty during the summer. That's a terrible, terrible use of public resources."

Converting to a year-round academic calendar would help many colleges use their facilities in a more productive way, Ballinger argues. He acknowledges that some educators "will object that, 'Well, a lot of our students have summer jobs.' My response to that is, 'They can hold jobs throughout the year. They're adults; other adults work throughout the year.'"

Moreover, he says, "there is a strong rationale for bringing in freshmen during the summer season and acclimating them to college life without the presence of upperclassmen." In sum, Ballinger says, "I take the same position with respect to higher education that I do with K-12 schools. That is, we need to assure that education does, in fact, become a lifelong process and not perpetuate this ancient idea that summers are not for learning."

Colleges use their facilities as best they can, responds Roger M. Swanson, associate executive director of the American Association of Collegiate Registrars and Admissions Officers, which publishes an annual academic calendar survey. "Most campuses will run as many summer-session classes as they can," he says. "Increasingly, too, campuses are aggressively marketing their space to businesses for summer conferences. These are one-time programs that may last just half a day or as long as a week. With extended conferences, the college can also rent out its residence halls. The basic aim is to bring in more revenue during the summer."

Today, about 60 percent of the 3,798 U.S. colleges and universities surveyed recently operated on a semester plan, including both the traditional September-June calendar and the currently more popular "early semester" format, which runs from August-May. The roughly 40 percent of schools remaining operated on year-round academic calendars. Twenty percent of those followed a quarter calendar, 2 percent were on a trimester calendar, 7 percent followed the so-called 4-1-4 schedule and 11 percent were classified in miscellaneous YRE categories. [3]

Under 4-1-4, students attend classes from September through December; then comes a one-month January term that can be used for either vacation or additional instruction, followed by a second four-month academic term. During the June-August period, 4-1-4 students again have the option of classes or vacation.

Orville C. Walz, who has been conducting the annual calendar surveys since 1978, thinks he sees a modest trend building for the future. "I don't think we'll ever see all schools operating on the same calendar," says Walz, president of Concordia College in Seward, Neb., "but I think more of them will switch to early semester."

---

[1] The University of Pittsburgh's College of Arts and Sciences currently operates on a modified trimester calendar, with the summer session shorter than the other two. Students can attend classes year-round, if they choose, or take the summer off.

[2] Starting this fall, Antioch will switch to a year-round trimester calendar. As before, students will alternate work and study periods. A student who obtains a degree over four years will have completed six work trimesters and six study trimesters.

[3] American Association of Collegiate Registrars and Admissions Officers, "Annual Academic Calendar Changes Study," Aug. 16, 1995. The study covered the 1995-96 academic year. Totals do not add to 100 percent because some schools were in miscellaneous calendar categories.

Continued from p. 444

Postwar Interest

The end of World War II sparked a revival of interest in year-round schools but yielded little positive action. Communities that looked into the question differed on whether proposed plans would result in savings or entail added costs.

In 1952, the Fairfield (Conn.) Citizens School Study Council reported that a proposed $5 million school building program would cost taxpayers $368,750 a year for interest, amortization and maintenance, but that it would cost only $81,900 a year to air-condition existing schools and operate them on a four-quarter plan. Atlanta, on the other hand, concluded in 1957 that it would cost more to operate a four-quarter system with existing facilities than to build new schools.

Los Angeles also had decided, in 1954, that an all-year school plan would be too costly, involve too many administrative problems and fail to meet with public approval. The Florida State Department of Education rejected a year-round school proposal in 1956 for the same reasons. And the school board of Montgomery County, Md., near Washington, turned down a four-quarter plan in 1961.

After World War II, Lexington, Ky., was one of the few communities actually to institute a year-round schedule for its public schools, but financial difficulties ended the program after 10 years. Although more than one-third of the city's students attended classes in some summers, the plan never was fully embraced by the community.

Although the year-long academic calendar made little headway in American school systems in the 1950s and '60s, traditional summer schools were enlarged, prompting a spurt in attendance.

Summer schools had been started in the 19th century, when shortening of the school year increased delinquency problems among city children. To combat the problem, civic and charitable groups began to sponsor what were called "vacation schools" for youngsters from poor families. Such schools stressed character building and manual training.

"We have found three or four weeks is just about long enough for a break. By then, the kids are pretty bored and really want to come back."

— Enriqueta Chavez, counselor, Eastlake High School, San Diego, Calif.

These private ventures were gradually taken over by the public school systems. In Providence, R.I., the school superintendent reported in 1870 that school-sponsored vacation sessions proved "a great blessing to the city" because the children had been "saved from the dangers and temptations of the streets" and had received "useful instruction."

The Board of Education of Newark, N.J., established a summer school in 1885 for slow learners who needed to make up classwork. As more vacation schools came under the control of school boards, they tended more and more to offer standard courses, thus giving slow pupils a chance to catch up and bright students a chance to move ahead.

Indeed, some educators of the period concluded that growth of summer schools and enlargement of their curriculums would lead eventually to year-round operation of public schools. In 1962, Robert F. Williams, a Virginia educator, noted the robust growth of summer schools in the state and predicted: "As the world's knowledge increases and it becomes more and more imperative that we utilize to the fullest possible extent the time and talents of both children and teachers, not to mention making the fullest possible use of an enormously expensive educational plant, we will move forward toward a longer school year." [24]

California Leads Way

However, movement toward that goal has been slower and more fitful than Williams probably imagined. It was not until 1968 that Hayward, Calif., introduced a single-track YRE schedule at Park Elementary School. Park thus became the first YRE school of the modern era. Still in operation, Park reigns as the nation's oldest year-round program.

Another YRE milestone came in 1969, when Francis Howell School District in St. Charles, Mo., implemented the nation's first multiple-track year-round program. It was initially dubbed a 9-3 calendar, because students attended school for nine consecutive weeks (not counting weekends and holidays), then had three weeks off and then started the cycle again. Today the program is known as a 45-15 calendar, for the number of school and vacation days in the cycle.

California's first two multi-track YRE schools began operating in 1971 in the Chula Vista District (grades K-6) and La Mesa-Spring Valley District (grades K-8), both in San Diego County. More significantly, the schools served as models for similar schools in 13 other California districts that adopted YRE schedules by 1974. Today, more than half of all schools in the country operating year-round are in the Golden State.

California's embrace of YRE has been less than wholehearted, however. In June 1993, the Los Angeles Unified School District Board of Education voted to return 542 of its schools from a single-track year-round schedule back to the traditional September-June calendar. The board acted after parents, teachers and administrators turned thumbs down on YRE.*

"The vote was a surprise to me," said school board member Mark Slavkin. "It counters the myth that only a handful hated the new [year-round] calendar, that the opposition was an elitist thing." [25]

Parents had opposed the single-track calendar since its inception. They complained that the eight-week winter break interrupted learning momentum, disrupted family summer plans and created child-care problems. Many also complained about sweltering, unair-conditioned classrooms in summer.

For strictly personal reasons, returning to the traditional calendar dismayed some students. Reseda High School student Payan Khalepari said his family had planned a ski trip during the long winter intersession, a time when most adults worked. "Now, we can't book reservations because we'd have to go the two weeks everyone else goes," he said, "and they are all booked." [26] ■

* One school among the 543 Los Angeles schools that voted on year-round education opted to retain YRE. Schools on a multi-track YRE schedule did not vote; serving about 40 percent of the city's approximately 640,000 students, they are multi-track to ease severe overcrowding.

CURRENT SITUATION

'Prisoners of Time'

The largely unvarying schedule of the U.S. school day and school year perplexes and dismays many educators. Although American public schools are governed largely by local boards of education with broad scheduling freedom, the 51-minute class period, 180-day school year and 10-week summer vacation have been standard across the country for generations.

"That there should be an identifiable American school year at all is remarkable in itself," wrote Barrett. "The federal system in the United States is supposed to encourage variety. . . . But no single state with a choosy citizenry has undertaken to remold its schools to meet changing social and economic needs. Instead, conformity rules with an iron hand." [27]

However, three recent reports suggest that the iron hand may be relaxing its grip. *Prisoners of Time,* issued in April 1994 by the National Education Commission on Time and Learning, declared that "Time is the missing element in our great national debate about learning and the need for higher standards for all students." The report added, "Our schools and the people involved with them — students, teachers, administrators, parents and staff — are prisoners of time, captives of the school clock and calendar."

"We have been asking the impossible of students — that they learn as much as their foreign peers while spending only half as much time in core academic subjects," the report continued. "The [education] reform movement of the last decade is destined to founder unless it is harnessed to more time for learning." [28]

Many of the commission's comments were aimed at the scheduling and crediting of classroom instruction: "No matter how complex or simple the school subject — literature, shop, physics, gym or algebra — the schedule assigns each an impartial national average of 51 minutes per class period, no matter how well or poorly students comprehend the material." The panel also found fault with secondary school graduation requirements, which "are universally based on seat time [or] 'Carnegie units,' a standard of measurement representing one credit for completion of a one-year course meeting daily." [29]

Moreover, the commission found, U.S. secondary schools devoted far less time to core academic subjects than did comparable schools in Germany and Japan. An analysis of time requirements for core subjects* in 41 states and the District of Columbia yielded "startling" results: "on average, students can receive a high school diploma — often sufficient in itself for university entrance — if they devote only 41 percent of their school time to core academic work." [30]

To rectify these and other shortcomings of U.S. secondary education, the panel urged more creative use of the time available for instruction. "Block scheduling — the use of two or more periods for extended exploration of complex topics or for science laboratories — should become more

Continued on p. 450

* The commission defined core subjects as English and language arts, mathematics, science, civics, history, geography, the arts and foreign languages.

At Issue:

Does year-round education improve academic performance?

yes

CHARLES BALLINGER
Executive Director, National Association for Year-Round Education

FROM "RETHINKING THE SCHOOL CALENDAR," *EDUCATIONAL LEADERSHIP*, FEBRUARY 1988.

The September-June school calendar has outlived its usefulness. Originally it had a strong purpose: to enhance the prevailing agricultural economy of the late 19th and early 20th centuries. It was not designed to enhance instruction then, and it does not do so now. . . .

Children learn continually; that thesis underlies a school's formal curriculum, which is usually sequential in nature or tied to the learner's earlier experiences. The customary long summer vacation disrupts the continuity of instruction that curriculum planners desire. Further, the extensive reviews most teachers conduct in September and October limit the number of days available for introduction of new material and subsequent mastery of that material.

Accumulated over a period of 12 years, review time takes its toll on the subsequent achievement of most students. A less interrupted flow of instruction throughout the year will certainly enhance the education of the most able students, who learn continuously, whether in or out of school. Likewise, average students are also ill-served by the traditional calendar because the long review early in the school year is largely wasted time for them. Interestingly, the least able students are not well served by the traditional school calendar either. A summer away from school disrupts the learning pattern required by slower students, who learn best from a continuous cycle of teaching, practice, reteaching and practice. . . .

Besides instructional considerations, contemporary social factors demand a rethinking of the traditional school calendar. An increasing number of students come from homes where English is not the primary language. Formal language instruction, which is best offered on a continuous basis, is disrupted by a long break. For most students, the language of the summer is going to be the language of the community, whether it is English or not. . . .

Another troubling social factor is the number of students with little to do during the summer months. Of what value to society is a situation in which urban and suburban teenagers are free to roam neighborhood streets, unsupervised, unemployed and unoccupied, for up to three months? . . .

If year-round education were the traditional school calendar and had been so for 100 years or more, and if someone came along to suggest a "new" calendar wherein school students were to be educated for only nine months each year . . . would the American public allow, or even consider, such a calendar?

no

TIME TO LEARN
Coalition based in Charlotte, N.C., that supports the traditional school calendar

FROM "YEAR-ROUND SCHOOLS MAY NOT BE THE ANSWER," JANUARY 1995.

Changing the days that students attend school does not address what many believe are the real problems in education, which include lack of parent involvement, curriculum that needs restructuring, teacher continued education and effectiveness of teaching methods.

Proponents claim that with the shorter, more frequent breaks of a year-round calendar, students retain more of what they've learned. But psychologists believe this is an unproven and illogical claim. Randall Engle, the Georgia Tech psychology department chair specializing in human memory, says children forget most of what they learn in the first three weeks after a lesson. Therefore, shorter, more frequent breaks would give children more opportunities to forget and increase the need for review. . . .

Few comprehensive studies are available to prove the effectiveness of year-round schools. Educators caution that research supporting year-round schools is scant and unscientific. From the country's 2,000+ year-round schools, a National Association for Year-Round Education researcher could find only 13 comprehensive studies on the issue. Ten of those studies show year-round students performing better; only seven show significant improvement. Tom Payne, a year-round consultant for the California Department of Education, says each study is flawed in some way, using improper methodology or lacking control groups and breadth. . . .

School districts often consider implementing year-round schools to solve an overcrowding problem. In some cases, year-round schools have provided temporary relief. However, several districts report year-round schools did not accomplish this goal or were merely a band-aid solution to a long-term problem. If overcrowding is a long-term concern, new construction is inevitable and postponing construction merely increases future construction costs. . . .

Although some parents and teachers find the year-round schedule more convenient, many who experience year-round schools — students, teachers, parents and administrators — express frustration and dissatisfaction. . . .

Before experimenting with the school calendar, it is important to learn all sides of the issue. It is questionable whether year-round programs enhance learning and save money. It is not questionable that quality education is essential to the well-being of our children, state and nation — or that improving educational standards is a commendable, constant goal. But year-round education is not an effective approach.

Students at Park View Elementary School in Mooresville, N.C., study different stages in the lifecycle of tadpoles in Julie Morrow's 4th-grade class. Park View was one of the first schools in the state to offer a voluntary year-round education program. Enrichment and remediation classes are offered during the 15-day intersessions. "These thematic sessions, coupled with on-site child care programs, address the needs of working parents throughout the year," school officials report.

common," it declared. "Providing a more flexible school day could also permit American schools to follow international practice — between classes students remain in the room and teachers come to them." [31]

However, the commission deliberately refrained from recommending a fixed number of hours per school day or days per year. That's because "No single configuration will satisfy every need," it stated. "Districts of any size, with a sense of vision, boldness and entrepreneurship can experiment with block scheduling, team teaching, longer days and years and extending time with new distance-learning technologies." [32]

In a follow-up report issued in September 1994, the commission published brief case histories of selected elementary, middle and high schools with flexible scheduling formats. At top-rated Thomas Jefferson High School for Science and Technology in Alexandria, Va., for example, each school day is lengthened by one period, during which students are required to take part in a student activity or related coursework such as tutoring, laboratories or guidance sessions. "Daily schedules are also flexible enough to let classes meet for extended times as required. This [blocking] arrangement also provides flexibility for professional development time for teachers." [33]

At Davis Elementary School in Gresham, Ore., math instruction is provided before and after school, during the noon hour and recess and during the summer. "Test results between the fall of 1990 and the fall of 1991 indicated that Davis' third-, fourth- and fifth-graders' math skills increased at a rate about 50 percent higher than other students in the system," the commission noted. [34]

Principals' Group Endorses Commission Report

A recent report by the National Association of Secondary School Principals (NASSP) endorsed many of the National Education Commission's proposals. "Scheduling and the length of both the school day and the school year . . . can serve as allies in creating a more intimate environment," the NASSP asserted. It added that "Lengthening the day or the year can also allow for staggered schedules so that the school accommodates smaller numbers of students at any one time." [35]

Flexible instruction schedules, "especially in conjunction with a 12-month school year, can facilitate enrichment, make it easier to offer tutoring and provide time for students to work on projects — alone, in groups and in collaboration with teachers," the report argued. "Time will be available for students who lag to catch up and for the ablest students to delve deeper into their studies." [36]

In addition, the report called attention to instructional options outside the school setting. "For years," it stated, "high schools have made minimal use of programs that reach beyond the four walls of the classroom: work-study, independent learning, distance learning, apprenticeships, mentorships, internships, job shadowing, independent study, field trips, travel, courses at college, student-conducted research."

As the National Education Commission observed in its September follow-up report, many schools across the country already have revamped their instructional schedules. At San Diego's Eastlake High, reports counselor Chavez, students have a "full menu" of classes with all their teachers on Mondays, Wednesdays and Fridays. "But on Tuesdays and Thursdays, they only meet with three teachers, for two hours each. This gives them time to listen to a lecture and then do a lab experiment or write a report all at once, rather than having to wait until the next day to do part of it."

Nationwide, says NASSP's Lammel, "about 40 percent of high schools are now considering or implementing block scheduling of classes. That compares with just 25 percent a year or so ago."

A key advantage of the longer class period under block scheduling, notes Lammel, comes from eliminating the time spent walking from classroom to classroom between periods of traditional length. Moreover, he says, "We're beginning to see test results suggesting that block scheduling improves educational achievement. I'm certain it's going to continue to expand." ■

OUTLOOK

'Inertia of Tradition'

Eventually, the debate on year-round education centers on a single question: "If this is such a great idea, why aren't more schools doing it?" Critics make much of the fact that only a tiny fraction of all U.S. pupils attend year-round schools, most of which are concentrated in rapidly growing states vulnerable to classroom overcrowding. This shows, the critics argue, that year-round education has little inherent appeal.

"The most difficult part of implementing a year-round program is breaking . . . the inertia of tradition — getting used to something new."

— Norman R. Brekke, former superintendent of the Oxnard, (Calif.) Elementary School District

Supporters of YRE retort that the statistics cited by critics must be viewed in historical context. Since the modern movement is barely more than 25 years old, they say, the current extent of year-round schooling — 2,368 year-round public schools in 37 states — is respectable, if unspectacular.

NAYRE's Ballinger foresees continued growth of year-round education over the foreseeable future. "Year-round will become more prevalent, for several reasons," he says. "First, the American lifestyle is changing. Summer isn't the only vacation season. Families pack up the kids and head for Orlando every month of the year. They just pull the kids out of school and go.

"Second, there are educational pressures to change the structure of the school year. As we build up documentation showing that there is such a thing as summer learning loss, and that a way exists to curb that loss, the onus will be on schools and educators to take corrective action. I think the public will demand that.

"And finally, there are societal changes as well. People are questioning the wisdom of that long summer vacation. Social workers and law-enforcement officials don't like the idea of kids having very little to do for up to three months — there's too much chance for them to get into trouble."

Maryland homemaker Tepe vehemently disagrees, arguing that the traditional summer school vacation has proved its worth again and again. Paraphrasing the oft-quoted passage from Ecclesiastes, she says: "There is a time for school, and there is a time for there not to be school. In other words, there are sound reasons for some of these traditions. And in this case the main one is, kids need time to be with their families."

Albuquerque's Patterson shares Tepe's view. "I think the National Association for Year-Round Education is pretty well burned out," he says.

FOR MORE INFORMATION

AMERICAN CAMPING ASSOCIATION, 5000 State Rd., 67 N., Martinsville, Ind. 46151-7902; (317) 342-8456. ACA, whose members do the bulk of their business during the traditional summer vacation period, opposes year-round schooling programs.

NATIONAL ASSOCIATION OF SECONDARY SCHOOL PRINCIPALS, 1904 Association Dr., Reston, Va. 22091; (703) 456-5432. NASSP supports more flexible and innovative scheduling of classroom time to improve high school students' achievement.

NATIONAL ASSOCIATION FOR YEAR-ROUND EDUCATION, P.O. Box 711386, San Diego, Calif. 92171-1386; (619) 276-5296. NAYRE fosters the study of year-round schooling as a way to improve primary and secondary education programs.

TIME TO LEARN, P.O. Box 12525, Charlotte, N.C. 28220; (704) 525-7151. Time to Learn, partially funded by the International Association of Amusement Parks and Attractions, lobbies against the adoption of year-round schooling calendars.

"They're going to be around a while longer, but they have very little credence. They're pushing an education gimmick that has failed. Kids need to have unstructured time [in the summer] to develop properly. Unstructured play is probably the most useful socialization tool that we have."

Heyns of New York University says it's difficult to assess the future of year-round education, since "Schooling in the U.S. is, of course, a local initiative. Therefore, it's impossible to say something about every program in every district. The number and diversity of programs that exist is extraordinary. So one would not want to judge what is happening, and with what kinds of effects. There has never been such an evaluation, and it's hard to imagine that one could be done. But in general, I think year-round schooling's time may have come."

Brekke, the former Oxnard, Calif., superintendent, agrees. "The most difficult part of implementing a year-round program is breaking what I call the inertia of tradition — getting used to something new," he says. "In Oxnard, we found that that transition period was relatively short. After the first year, people recognized that the sun continued to rise in the East, and the solar system hadn't ground to a halt. Though there were a lot of fears initially that year-round education would undermine family traditions, people found it did not. In fact, they found it enhanced the quality of family life."

In its 20 years of existence, Brekke says, Oxnard's year-round schooling program has become institutionalized — a gradual process he feels could be duplicated in other communities. Year-round "clearly is a permanent fixture of Oxnard's educational environment," he says. "I think there would be great anguish today among parents, school staff and the community as a whole if there was a serious attempt to return to the old schedule. That's because year-round education has become, in Oxnard at least, the traditional school calendar." ■

Notes

[1] Michael J. Barrett, "The Case for More School Days," *The Atlantic Monthly,* November 1990, p. 79. A former Massachusetts state senator, Barrett ran unsuccessfully for the state's Democratic gubernatorial nomination in 1994.

[2] For background, see "Why Schools Still Have Tracking," *Editorial Research Reports,* Dec. 28, 1990, pp. 745-760.

[3] National Association for Year-Round Education, "Year-Round Education Fact Sheet," February 1996, p. 2.

[4] National Education Commission on Time and Learning, *Prisoners of Time,* April 1994, p. 31. The commission released a follow-up report in September 1994.

[5] Barrett, *op. cit.,* p. 99.

[6] *Ibid.*

[7] Brekke, who headed the Oxnard district for 20 years, retired in 1994 and now lives in Silverton, Ore.

[8] Harris Cooper, et al., "The Effects of Summer Vacation on Achievement Test Scores: A Narrative and Meta-Analytic Review," paper submitted to *Review of Educational Research.* Cooper is a psychology professor at the University of Missouri, Columbia.

[9] Duane Stiff, "Year-Round School: Some Constraints to Consider," *Thrust for Educational Leadership,* October 1986, p. 14, published by the Association of California School Administrators, in Sacramento.

[10] Center for Evaluation, Development and Research, Phi Delta Kappa, *Year-Round Schools: Do They Make a Difference?* May 1990, p. 243, a collection of scholarly articles and studies from various sources on year-round education.

[11] Charles Ballinger, "Rethinking the School Calendar," *Educational Leadership,* February 1988, p. 61.

[12] Quoted in Joe Agron, "Stretching the School Calendar," *American School & University,* September 1993, p. 30.

[13] Mossie J. Richmond Jr., *Issues in Year-Round Education* (1977), p. 58.

[14] Center for Evaluation, Development and Research, *op. cit.,* p. 243.

[15] *Ibid.*

[16] Barrett, *op. cit.,* p. 89.

[17] Richmond, *op. cit.,* pp. 75-76.

[18] David J. Mussatti, "Year-Round High School Programs," paper presented at the annual meeting of the National Council on Year-Round Education, April 2-4, 1981.

[19] Richmond, *op. cit.,* p. 44.

[20] Barrett, *op. cit.,* p. 91.

[21] National Education Commission on Time and Learning, *op. cit.,* p. 10.

[22] Charles Ballinger, Norman Kirschenbaum and Rita Pokol Poinbeauf, "The Year-Round School: Where Learning Never Stops," in Center for Evaluation, Development and Research, Phi Delta Kappa, *op. cit.,* p. 25.

[23] Richmond, *op. cit.,* p. 29.

[24] Robert F. Williams, "The Year-Round School Is Here," *Virginia Journal of Education,* December 1962, p. 8.

[25] Quoted in the *Los Angeles Times,* June 3, 1993.

[26] Quoted in the *Los Angeles Times,* May 29, 1993.

[27] Barrett, *op. cit.,* p. 81.

[28] National Education Commission, *op. cit.,* p. 4.

[29] *Ibid.,* p. 7.

[30] *Ibid.,* p. 23.

[31] *Ibid.,* p. 31.

[32] *Ibid.,* p. 38.

[33] *Ibid.,* p. 51.

[34] *Ibid.,* p. 25.

[35] National Association of Secondary School Principals, *Breaking Ranks: Changing an American Institution,* February 1996, p. 46.

[36] *Ibid.,* p. 48.

Bibliography

Selected Sources Used

Books

Fisher, Charles W., and David C. Berliner, eds., *Perspectives on Instructional Time,* Longman Inc., 1985.
The contributors to this anthology examine the relationship between instructional time and learning from a variety of angles. Editors Fisher and Berliner sum things up in the final chapter by attempting to answer such questions as, "Is Research on Instructional Time Trivial?" "Can We Use the Results of Research on Instructional Time to Improve Schools?" and "How Does Research on Instructional Time Have Implications for Educational Research in General?"

Richmond, Mossie J. Jr., *Issues in Year-Round Education,* The Christopher Publishing House, 1977.
Richmond describes operational options for implementing a year-round schooling program, and describes how the concept affects such things as juvenile crime and the economy. He concludes that generalizations about year-round education are bound to be unsatisfactory, since individual programs are shaped by local circumstances and thus resist comparisons.

Williams, Scott, *Year-Round Schools: Do They Make a Difference?* Phi Delta Kappa, Center on Evaluation, Development and Research, 1990.
This collection of articles and professional papers examines several aspects of year-round education grouped under five broad headings: year-round education defined; the potential of year-round education; drawbacks, constraints and caveats; evaluation; and interpretation. Each section is preceded by an overview, and the book ends with a summary and conclusions.

Articles

Agron, Joe, "Stretching the School Calendar," *American School & University,* September 1993.
After setting forth the pluses and minuses of year-round schooling, Agron concludes: "Switching to a year-round schedule doesn't have to break the educational bank. Teacher salaries, transportation and building upgrades account for some of the more costly increases. The largest expense, however, is for air conditioning."

Barrett, Michael J., "The Case for More School Days," *The Atlantic Monthly,* November 1990.
Citing studies showing that U.S. high school students lag well behind their peers in other industrialized countries in test scores on core academic subjects, Barrett argues for a substantially longer academic year.

Canady, Robert Lynn, and Michael D. Rettig, "Unlocking the Lockstep High School Schedule," *Phi Delta Kappan,* December 1993.
The authors note that secondary-school educators increasingly are viewing the academic schedule "not simply as [a] barrier blocking the path to school improvement, but as an untapped resource that can be drawn on to solve problems and implement needed programs." Among the innovations under study, they report, are scheduling three classes a semester instead of the traditional five to seven, and scheduling full-day academic programs one day and vocational programs the next.

Daniels, Alex, "Schools That (Almost) Never Close," *Governing,* June 1995.
"Beyond questions of cost-effectiveness," writes Daniels, ". . . there is a lot of sentiment among educators that year-round schools, whether multi-tracked or not, can be educationally beneficial."

Reports and Studies

General Subcommittee on Education, U.S. House Committee on Education and Labor, *Year-Round Schools* (published proceedings of hearing held April 24, 1972).
Though these hearings took place nearly a quarter-century ago, many of the issues discussed by witnesses are strikingly similar to those advanced today by supporters and opponents of year-round schooling.

National Association of Secondary School Principals, *Scheduling the Secondary School,* 1983.
"A secondary school cannot function without competent scheduling," this study asserts. "The curriculum is activated through scheduling; students proceed through the program of studies as a result of scheduling; teachers are assigned to students through scheduling. In short, scheduling sets the stage for learning."

National Association of Secondary School Principals, *Breaking Ranks: Changing an American Institution,* 1996.
Chapter 5 of this study on what the U.S. high school of the 21st century might be like deals with "Organization and Time — Restructuring Space and Time for a More Flexible Education." Among other things, it supports proposals to lengthen the school year and vary the length of individual class periods, depending on the nature of the subject being taught.

National Education Commission on Time and Learning, *Prisoners of Time,* April 1994 and September 1994 (two related reports).
The first of these identically titled reports by a congressionally appointed blue-ribbon panel argues that more classroom time should be devoted to core academic subjects. It also supports calls for a longer school year. The second report consists largely of short case studies of schools around that country that have redesigned their calendars in innovative ways.

The Next Step

Additional information from UMI's Newspaper & Periodical Abstracts database

Advantages of Year-Round Schooling

Ballinger, Charles, "Prisoners no more," ***Educational Leadership,*** **November 1995, pp. 28-31.**
Many schools are choosing the year-round calendar over the traditional nine-month calendar as a way of eliminating the significant learning loss that occurs during the summer vacation. The benefits of the year-round calendar and advice on establishing a year-round calendar are discussed.

Cauvin, Henri E., "Holy Angels pupils, teachers say all-year classes heavenly," ***Chicago Tribune,*** **July 27, 1994, p. C1.**
In Chicago's Oakland neighborhood, where almost three out of four people live in poverty and violent crime is an hourly occurrence, Holy Angels Elementary School provides the safety and structure its pupils need to make the most of their education, so most don't mind taking a mere three weeks of summer vacation. That's the longest break of the year at the school, which has a school year almost 40 days longer than the Chicago public schools' calendar.

Haynes, V. Dion and Jacquelyn Heard, "Learning gets no vacation," ***Chicago Tribune,*** **June 18, 1995, p. C2.**
Though the idea is wrought with problems and some parents are against it, many educators say a year-round school calendar could help Chicago students raise their lagging achievement test scores, keep them off the streets during the summer, when juvenile crime increases, and even address classroom overcrowding.

Warrick-Harris, Elaine, "Year-round school: The best thing since sliced bread," ***Childhood Education,*** **1995, pp. 282-287.**
The growing trend toward holding school sessions year-round is discussed. The benefits of year-round school are presented, and the implementation of year-round school at Balfour Elementary in Asheboro, N.C., is described.

Disadvantages of Year-Round Schooling

Puente, Teresa, "City taking a closer look at year-round schooling," ***Chicago Tribune,*** **May 14, 1995, p. C2.**
Year-round schools can help solve severe overcrowding at some Chicago public schools, but not all parents and educators are sold on the concept. There are already about 20 year-round schools in Illinois, and 12 are Chicago public schools.

Rubin, Dorothy, "A disaster for families," ***USA Today,*** **July 19, 1995, p. A10.**
Rubin says that year-round school as a cure for overcrowding and tight budgets isn't as cost effective or as efficient as supporters claim, and that many proponents are downplaying the psychological impact on families and students.

"Sentenced to School," ***The Washington Times,*** **Dec. 3, 1990, p. G2.**
An editorial comments that there's no reason to think that simply keeping some students in school all year long, as some school districts are trying to do, teaches them any more then they learn now.

Overcrowding and Year-Round Schooling

Arnold, Michael S., "Year-round schools shelved by committee," ***Times-Picayune,*** **March 15, 1995, p. AT1.**
Faced with overwhelming public opposition, a St. Tammany Parish, La., school board task force has decided to shelve the idea of year-round education, sending administrators back to square one in their efforts to relieve overcrowding.

Hill, James, "Year-round school soon a Lake reality," ***Chicago Tribune,*** **Jan. 21, 1996, p. L1.**
Mundelein Elementary District 75, looking to ease overcrowding, will reopen Lincoln School in the fall of 1996 as the Lincoln Magnet School, with an innovative year-round program, while Woodland Elementary District 50 in Gages Lake has proposed a year-round school program as a realistic way of looking at the future of education in Lake County, IL.

King, Ronette, "All-Year School Favored to Battle Overcrowding," ***Times-Picayune,*** **May 16, 1992, p. B1.**
If most Mandeville, La., parents had their way, they would rather send their kids to school all year then send them in the evenings or at the crack of dawn as a way to alleviate the problem of overcrowding in the five area schools.

Lueck, Thomas J., "Year-round classes to begin in summer," ***The New York Times,*** **Jan. 31, 1995, p. B1.**
In an attempt to ease what officials call a crisis in New York City school overcrowding, Schools Chancellor Ramon C. Cortines said on Jan. 30, 1995, that he plans to move even faster than his advisers recommend on an experiment in year-round schooling. At least two schools, and probably more, will be placed on year-round schedules in the summer of 1995, he said.

Newman, Maria, "New York schools consider year-round classes," ***The New York Times,*** **Jan. 20, 1995, p. B1.**
Officials are so concerned about the rapid growth in the number of New York City students and about the city's inability to build more classroom space as it is consumed by its own budget crisis, that a commission will recommend that the public school system begin a pilot test of a year-round school calendar in September 1995 in two yet-to-be-named high schools.

Oulton, Stacie, "Year-round classes shelved," ***Denver***

Post, Jan. 9, 1996, p. B2.
The Adams County, Colo., School District 12 board opted on Jan. 8, 1996, to build more elementary schools instead of using multitrack year-round schedules to solve expected overcrowding.

Shear, Michael D., "Prince William to study year-round schools," *The Washington Post,* Nov. 3, 1994, p. C2.
Faced with severe crowding and no money to build new schools, the Prince William County, Va., School Board directed school administrators to study the possibility of conducting classes year-round with students on staggered schedules.

Summer Learning Loss

"Longer, rounder school year needed," *Atlanta Journal Constitution,* Sept. 4, 1993, p. A18.
An editorial comments that children need to go to school all year long, saying that the extended summer vacation interferes with students' learning. Although some Atlanta-area schools are looking toward the future in proposing year-round education, many parents are banding together to resist reform.

Mydans, Seth, "In an Assault on Tradition, More Schools Last All Year," *The New York Times,* Aug. 18, 1991, p. 1.
The trend at U.S. schools toward employing year-round schedules that do away with the traditional summer vacation is discussed. Educators say that taking shorter but more frequent breaks allows students to retain more knowledge, requiring less time for review and more time for new material. Some see the revised scheduling as a step toward lengthening the school year, which could make the U.S. educational system competitive with those of Europe and Japan.

State and Local Considerations

Bingham, Janet, "All-year classes growing," *Denver Post,* April 7, 1993, p. B1.
On April 6, 1993, the Aurora, Colo., school board voted 5-0 to move about a third of its elementary and middle school students to year-round schedules by the summer of 1994. Under the system, students attend school nine weeks, then are off for three.

Dickerson, Ann, "Cure for summertime blues?" *Atlanta Constitution,* April 25, 1996, p. D1.
Bob Heaberlin, principal at Newnan Crossing Elementary School in Coweta County, Ga., says a year-round calendar is what his school needs to rise from the bottom of the academic barrel.

Henry, Tamara, "L.A. scales back year-round schools," *USA Today,* June 15, 1993, D8.
The innovative idea to keep children in school all year with only brief vacations is alive and well, although 543 Los Angeles schools have voted to return to the traditional September-to-June calendar.

Kass, John and Dion V. Haynes, "All-year school gets resounding vote from Daley," *Chicago Tribune,* June 15, 1995, p. 1.
Mayor Richard Daley opened the door on a possible year-round calendar for all Chicago public schoolchildren , saying kids should be working on improving failing reading scores rather than being on the streets, running into danger.

Nabonne, Rhonda, "Costs Force Change in All- Year Schools," *Times-Picayune,* May 11, 1992, p. A1.
School officials at Johnson C. Lockett Elementary School in New Orleans said the extended school year has improved student discipline, attendance and performance, but funding problems will probably prevent the program from being a permanent arrangement.

Opheim, Cynthia, Kristine Hopkins Mohajer, Kristine and Robert W. Jr. Read, "Evaluating year-round schools in Texas," *Education,* fall 1995, pp. 115-120.
The attitudes of both year-round and traditional elementary school principals in Texas were examined on the issues of professional staffing and development, administrative issues, student achievement, parental and community concerns and cost factors. Both year-round and traditional elementary school principals have positive experiences and/or perceptions of year -round education.

Sanchez, Felix, "All-year plan forces Cy-Fair election," *The Houston Post,* Jan. 10, 1994, p. A13.
What began as a response to booming enrollment in the Cypress-Fairbanks Independent School District in Harris County, Texas, has evolved into a fiery debate over the relationship between schools and families and an election on Jan. 15, 1994, that could attract statewide notice. At the center of the controversy is a year-round school concept that proponents contend will utilize existing facilities and district funds better but opponents believe will disrupt families and be of no educational benefit.

Shear, Michael D., "Year-round classes lauded: Report arrives as Board is pushing bond, tax," *The Washington Post,* June 15, 1995, p. VAP1.
The Prince William County, Va., School Board is considering a year-round school calendar as it pushes a $75 million bond referendum and 4 percent meals tax for new schools and maintenance.

Weizel, Richard, "Schools stay open after classes end," *Boston Globe,* Sept. 4, 1994, p. A43.
Since its inception in 1987, the School of the 21st Century program now operates in 13 states, financed with a combination of federal and state grants and sliding scale fees. The schools provide year-round services, the first in Massachusetts opened in Ayer in August 1994.

White, Betsy, "All-year schooling dealt blow," *Atlanta Constitution,* Dec. 1, 1993, p. A1.
Year-round schooling, hyped by business and education leaders as a way to propel education into the 21st century, suffered its worst defeat yet in Georgia when Carrollton parents rejected the idea. Fifty-two percent of parents in the college town voted against redistributing the traditional 12-week summer vacation throughout the school year.

Back Issues

Great Research on Current Issues Starts Right Here...Recent topics covered by The CQ Researcher are listed below. Before May 1991, reports were published under the name of Editorial Research Reports.

NOVEMBER 1994
Sex on Campus
Blood Supply Safety
Testing Term Limits
Religion in America

DECEMBER 1994
Farm Policy
Arms Sales
Earthquake Research
The Future of Television

JANUARY 1995
Treating Addiction
Child Custody and Support
Parents and Schools
Non-Proliferation Treaty at 25

FEBRUARY 1995
Cracking Down on Immigration
The Business of Sports
Reinventing Government
Housing Discrimination

MARCH 1995
Death Penalty Debate
Primary Care
Democracy in Africa
Environmental Movement at 25

APRIL 1995
Abortion Clinic Protests
Dieting and Health
Combating AIDS
Rethinking Affirmative Action

MAY 1995
Assisted Suicide Controversy
Overhauling Social Security
Learning to Read
Mandatory Sentencing

JUNE 1995
Combating Infectious Disease
Property Rights
Repetitive Stress Injuries
Regulating the Internet

JULY 1995
War Crimes
Highway Safety
Combating Terrorism
Preventing Teen Drug Use

AUGUST 1995
Job Stress
Organ Transplants
United Nations at 50
Advances in Cancer Research

SEPTEMBER 1995
Catholic Church in the U.S.
Northern Ireland Cease-Fire
High School Sports
Teaching History

OCTOBER 1995
Quebec's Future
Revitalizing the Cities
Networking the Classroom
Indoor Air Pollution

NOVEMBER 1995
The Working Poor
The Jury System
Sex, Violence and the Media
Police Misconduct

DECEMBER 1995
Teens and Tobacco
Gene Therapy's Future
Global Water Shortages
Third-Party Prospects

JANUARY 1996
Emergency Medicine
Punishing Sex Offenders
Bilingual Education
Helping the Homeless

FEBRUARY 1996
Reforming the CIA
Campaign Finance Reform
Academic Politics
Getting Into College

MARCH 1996
The British Monarchy
Preventing Juvenile Crime
Tax Reform
Pursuing the Paranormal

APRIL 1996
Centennial Olympic Games
Managed Care
Protecting Endangered Species
New Military Culture

MAY 1996
Russia's Political Future
Marriage and Divorce

Back issues are available for $5.00 (subscribers) or $8.00 (non-subscribers). Quantity discounts apply to orders over ten. To order, call Congressional Quarterly Customer Service at (202) 887-8621.

Binders are available for $18.00. To order call 1-800-638-1710. Please refer to stock number 648.

Future Topics

- ***U.S., China and Taiwan***
- ***Rethinking NAFTA***
- ***First Ladies***

THE CQ Researcher

PUBLISHED BY CONGRESSIONAL QUARTERLY INC.

Taiwan, China and the U.S.

How will Taipei-Beijing relations affect the U.S.?

Taiwan has just held its first popular election for president since the Nationalists fled to the island 47 years ago after China's civil war. As he was sworn in May 20, President Lee Teng-hui voiced pride in Taiwan's democratic reforms but also offered to visit Beijing for the first summit between leaders of the self-styled Republic of China on Taiwan and the People's Republic of China. Since Lee's election in March, however, Chinese leaders have repeated their opposition to independence for Taiwan and have rebuffed overtures at resuming talks on closer relations. For the United States, Taiwan's surging economic self-confidence and China's increasing assertiveness pose difficult policy choices with significant implications for peace, stability and trade in the Asia-Pacific region.

INSIDE THIS ISSUE

CQ May 24, 1996 • Volume 6, No. 20 • Pages 457-480

Formerly Editorial Research Reports

TAIWAN, CHINA AND THE U.S.

THE ISSUES

BACKGROUND

CURRENT SITUATION

OUTLOOK

SIDEBARS AND GRAPHICS

FOR FURTHER RESEARCH

COVER: LEE TENG-HUI IS SWORN IN AS PRESIDENT OF THE REPUBLIC OF CHINA (TAIWAN) ON MAY 20, 1996. (REUTERS)

THE *CQ Researcher*

May 24, 1996
Volume 6, No. 20

Bibliographic records and abstracts included in The Next Step section of this publication are from UMI's Newspaper and Periodical Abstracts database, and are used with permission.

The CQ Researcher (ISSN 1056-2036). Formerly Editorial Research Reports. Published weekly (48 times per year, not printed March 1, May 31, Aug. 30, Nov. 29) by Congressional Quarterly Inc., 1414 22nd St., N.W., Washington, D.C. 20037. Annual subscription rate for libraries, businesses and government is $319. Additional rates furnished upon request. Second-class postage paid at Washington, D.C. POSTMASTER: Send address changes to The CQ Researcher, 1414 22nd St., N.W., Washington, D.C. 20037.

Taiwan, China and the U.S.

BY KENNETH JOST

THE ISSUES

Just two months ago, China and Taiwan were nose to nose in a tense pushing and shoving match. China was holding war games in the Taiwan Strait, and Taiwan's President Lee Teng-hui was defiantly insisting that the island's first-ever direct election for president would go forward despite the barely veiled threat. But as Lee took the oath of office on May 20, he offered an olive branch of sorts to the world's most populous nation: a suggested first summit meeting between leaders of the People's Republic of China and the so-called Republic of China on Taiwan. *

"In the future, at the call of my country and with the support of my people, I would like to embark upon a journey of peace to mainland China taking with me the consensus and will of [the] 21.3 million people [of Taiwan]," Lee said. [1]

"I am also ready to meet with the top leadership of the Chinese Communists," Lee continued, "for a direct exchange of views in order to open up a new era of communication and cooperation between the two sides and ensure peace, stability and prosperity in the Asia-Pacific region."

Lee made no explicit reference, however, to the terms for such a meeting. And he coupled the gesture with a swaggering assertion of Taiwanese superiority over China, which regards the island as a renegade province and had viewed the presidential election as a possible prelude to a declaration of independence by Taiwan.

Lee promised in his speech that Taiwan would not seek independence. But he also bragged that Taiwan has been able simultaneously to preserve "traditional culture" and interact with "Western democracy and science and modern business culture." As a result, he said, Taiwan has achieved "a much higher level of education and development than in other parts of China." Taiwan, he concluded, is ready "to take upon itself the responsibility for nurturing a new Chinese culture."

Lee's inauguration capped a tumultuous year in the history of Taiwan and its relations with its giant mainland neighbor. Lee provoked Chinese leaders with a precedent-setting visit last June to the United States, traveling to his alma mater, Cornell University, in a trip officially labeled non-official. China protested to the United States for granting Lee a visa and later, as Taiwan's election approached, began a series of military exercises overtly aimed at cautioning Taiwanese voters against any moves toward independence.

For its part, the Clinton administration sought to walk a tightrope between supporting Taiwanese democracy without altering its official "one-China" policy of recognizing Beijing as the legitimate government of all of China. As China conducted its missile exercises on Taiwan's doorstep, President Clinton sent naval war groups into the Taiwan Strait, a move aimed at emphasizing the U.S. insistence that the Taiwan-China dispute must be settled peacefully, not by military force.

Lee's inauguration marks the culmination of a decade-long reform process. Larry Diamond, a Stanford University professor and expert on democracy in developing countries, calls Taiwan's experience "one of the most important instances of democratization" in recent years. But it also represents a potential watershed in Taiwan's relations with the mainland, one that could further delay or even prevent the reunification that Taipei and Beijing both say they support.

For the United States, Taiwan's election heartens advocates of democracy. "Taiwan is important because it is an important cog in this whole conflict between democracy and authoritarianism," says James Lilley, a fellow at the American Enterprise Institute and former diplomat in Taipei and Beijing. "You have a country of 20 million people that is prosperous and practicing democracy at the same time."

Taiwan's surging self-confidence raises fears, however, of increased tensions between the United States and an increasingly assertive China. "The question is how do you integrate this new power, China, as smoothly as possible into the international community," says James Shinn, senior fellow for Asia at the Council on Foreign Relations. "Taiwan is just one of the volatile issues that has to be managed."

The people of Taiwan themselves voice justifiable pride in their conversion from a single-party police state to a vibrant and free-wheeling democracy. "Taiwan's democratic development has made tremendous progress and has now entered the phase of democratic consolidation," Hung-mao Tien, president of the Institute for National Policy Research in Taiwan, told a Washington

* This report will refer to the People's Republic of China (PRC) as China and denote the Republic of China as Taiwan.

Taiwan: 'Terraced Bay' Off China's Coast

The island of Taiwan — the name combines two Chinese words for "terraced bay" — lies about 100 miles east of the south-central coast of China. About 230 miles long and 85 miles wide at the center, the island itself has a total area of 13,814 square miles — roughly that of Massachusetts, Connecticut and Rhode Island combined. The self-styled Republic of China on Taiwan also claims jurisdiction over the Pescadore Islands, several islands off Taiwan's eastern coast and the Offshore Islands — the so-called Quemoy and Matsu groups.

Source: John F. Copper, Taiwan: Nation-State or Province *[2d ed.], 1996.*

forum co-sponsored by the institute and the U.S. National Endowment for Democracy on April 16.

But Hung, a sometime adviser to President Lee, acknowledges that the transformation is not complete. Despite a decade of multiparty elections, Hung told the conference, Taiwan still has "a dominant-party system with the Kuomintang [KMT] still in charge."

Some U.S. human rights experts are more pointed in criticizing the KMT, also known as the Nationalist Party. They note, for example, that it controls the island's three television networks and a conglomeration of business enterprises valued at between $13 billion and $19 billion. [2] "The KMT still has a dominant grip on the political situation," says Charles Grawbow, an expert on Asia at Freedom House, a New York-based human rights group. "It still is not a fully competitive playing field."

Taiwan's growing international stature, meanwhile, is not only a painful reminder to China of its continuing division nearly 50 years after its civil war but also a challenge to its claim that Taiwan is only a renegade province. "Taiwan, whether a country or not, is a reality," Arthur Waldron, a professor at the Naval War College in Newport, R.I., told a Freedom House forum on March 25, two days after the Taiwan election. "And it's a reality that the whole world, and particularly China, is going to have to deal with."

Taiwan's turn to democracy has come at a time of political and ideological flux on the mainland. Chinese leader Deng Xiaoping, now 92 and reportedly near death, initiated political and economic reforms in the 1980s that displaced traditional communism as the country's established ideology. "Communism is shrinking very dramatically," says Lilley. "What do they do? They turn to nationalism."

Through its recent military exercises, China apparently intended to intimidate Taiwanese voters and to caution the rest of the world against interfering in what it considers a purely domestic issue. On one level, Lee's victory and the 76.9 percent voter turnout suggest that the show of bluster failed. But it did highlight the dilemma Taiwan's leaders face in pushing self-determination without provoking a military response from the mainland.

The United States, which counts Taiwan as an ally despite withdrawing diplomatic recognition 17 years ago, has tried to resolve that dilemma by cautioning Taipei against independence and Beijing against military force. "We have hoped and worked for restraint on both sides," Winston Lord, assistant secretary of State for Asian affairs, told the Freedom House forum.

That policy of restraint survived the difficult testing period created by the Taiwanese election and China's show of military might. Now, U.S. policymakers say they hope that Taipei and Beijing both can put their differences behind them and resume work on establishing ties.

As Taipei, Beijing and Washington consider their next political moves, these are among the questions being considered:

Should Taiwan push for greater international recognition?

Despite its moves toward democracy at home, Taiwan only enjoys second-class international status. China has blocked Taiwan from participating in most international organizations since Taipei's expulsion from the United Nations in 1971. In recent years, however, President Lee has worked to raise Taiwan's international profile. And Taiwan's supporters say it is entitled to an equal position among the nations of the world.

"There is no doubt that the Republic of China should be recognized as a state and represented in all major international organizations," says Hungdah Chiu, director of the East Asian Legal Studies Program at the University of Maryland Law School in Baltimore.

Hungdah, a Taiwanese who has lived in the United States for 20 years, notes that Taipei now has diplomatic recognition from many countries. Officially, 31 mostly small countries recognize the Taiwan government, according to the Taipei Economic and Cultural Representative Office (TECRO) in Washington. In addition, Hungdah says 14 other countries have allowed Taiwan to establish commercial outposts under the Republic of China name.

The United States and most other countries, however, follow the so-called "one-China" policy, under which only Beijing is officially recognized. The U.S. and Taiwan conduct relations through ostensibly private organizations: TECRO for Taiwan and for the United States the Taiwan-based American Institute. The Clinton administration decided in 1994 to continue adhering to the one-China policy, first enunciated in 1972.

The mainland government has watched Taiwan's diplomatic offensives with growing concern — climaxed by its sharp protest of the U.S. decision to permit Lee to visit Cornell last summer. Today, many China experts warn that future U.S. support for raising Taiwan's international profile would further strain U.S. relations with China. "You can't subordinate everything to Taiwan," says Shinn at the Council on Foreign Relations.

The issue of U.S. support for Taiwan's diplomatic offensive split an independent, 30-member task force that the council created last year to review U.S. relations with Taipei. The task force's report, published in November, called for blocking visits to the United States by Taiwanese officials "in the current tense environment" and controlling such trips in the future.

But, more favorably for Taiwan, the report called for the United States to support Taiwan's membership in those international organizations — including the International Monetary Fund (IMF), the World Bank and many specialized United Nations agencies — that do not require statehood for admission. [3]

Some task force members dissented from each of those positions. Three of the members urged stronger support for Taiwan, including granting Taipei officials visas to visit the United States. But five other task force members, led by A. Doak Barnett, one of the country's leading China experts, warned against U.S. support for Taiwan's admission to U.N. agencies at the present time. [4]

Barnett, professor emeritus at the Johns Hopkins University School of Advanced International Studies in Washington, wrote that U.S. sponsorship for Taiwan's membership in U.N. agencies "would not only evoke a strongly negative [Chinese] response but also would create a major new obstacle to the task of repairing U.S.-China relations." (*See "At Issue," p. 473.*)

Taiwan itself asserts a more ambitious goal: admission to the United Nations itself. "The Republic of China on Taiwan is fully justified and qualified to participate in the United Nations," its ministry of foreign affairs

Comparing China and Taiwan

	China	Taiwan
Area	3.7 million sq. miles [excl. Taiwan]	13,969 sq. miles
Population	1.2 billion	21.5 million
Population density	326/sq. mile	1,539/sq. mile
Population growth rate	1.0 %	1.0 %
Life expectancy	67, male; 69, female	72, male; 79, female
Literacy	78%	94%
Leaders	Jiang Zemin, president and general secretary of Chinese Communist Party	Lee Teng-hui, president
Political system	Communist people's republic, established Oct. 1, 1949; president elected by National People's Congress, which is indirectly elected	Transitional democracy; president popularly elected; National Assembly and Legislative Yuan, both popularly elected
Political parties	Chinese Communist Party; at least nine minor parties permitted but expected "to work under the leadership of the Communist Party"	Kuomintang is dominant party; major opposition: Democratic Progressive Party (pro-independence); New Party (reformist; seeks reconciliation with China)
Mass media	All news media under government control	Three television stations run by ruling Kuomintang party; 34 radio stations (12 state-run, 22 private); 311 newspapers, many state- or party-run
Active troop strength	2.9 million (est.)	425,000
Gross National Product	$2.6 trillion	$224 billion [gross domestic product]
Per Capita Gross National Product	$2,200	$10,600
Total Exports	$84.5 billion (1992)	$85.0 billion (1993)
Total Imports	$80.6 billion (1992)	$77.1 billion (1993)
Exports to U.S.	$38.8 billion (1994)	$26.7 billion (1994)
Imports from U.S.	$9.3 billion (1994)	$17.1 billion (1994)

Sources: World Almanac and Book of Facts, *1996;* Political Handbook of the World, *1995-1996*

contends.[5] China has succeeded in blocking any consideration of Taiwan's membership, however, even after Taipei last year offered the U.N. $1 billion in aid if it were admitted.

Some U.S. experts support Taiwan's bid for U.N. membership. "Taiwan belongs in the United Nations," says June Teufel Dreyer, director of East Asian programs at the University of Miami. "It's a travesty of the spirit of the United Nations that Taiwan is not a member."

But others, including Jeane J. Kirkpatrick, who served as U.S. ambassador to the United Nations under President Ronald Reagan, say the United States should leave the issue to be resolved by China and Taiwan. "I don't think there is anything we can do to significantly affect the outcome, we or anybody else," Kirkpatrick says.

The Beijing government in the past few years has accepted Taipei's participation in two important regional economic forums: the Asian Development Bank and the Asian-Pacific Export Council. Beijing also did not block Taiwan's participation in the Asian Games in 1994. Taiwan supporters look on these examples as hopeful signs that China might agree to Taipei's participation in other international bodies if the issue is handled delicately.

"We should be saying to China that in those situations where national sovereignty is not an issue, we will support Taiwan's participation because it's in all our interests," says Nancy Bernkopf Tucker, a professor of history at Georgetown University and author of a well-regarded history of U.S. relations with Taiwan. "It's in China's interest as well."

Should the U.S. increase pressure on China over Taiwan and other issues?

President Clinton was widely praised for his handling of China's aggressive military maneuvers in the months before Taiwan's presidential election. But foreign policy advocates and experts representing a wide range of views sharply criticize the administration's overall policy toward China as weak and indecisive.

"It would make life a lot easier if they had a consistent strategy for dealing with China," says the Council on Foreign Relations' Shinn, a Republican who worked in the State Department during the Jimmy Carter administration. "One would be hard-pressed to find an excess of consistency."

The critiques of Clinton's policies, however, come from different directions. Taiwan supporters want the United States to be firmer in backing Taipei. Other advocates and experts, however, say the administration needs to give top priority to repairing relations with Beijing, which have been strained over a range of issues besides Taiwan, including human rights, copyright piracy, nuclear proliferation and China's territorial claims in the South China Sea. [6]

On Taiwan, the Clinton administration contends that it has stuck to the policy first enunciated by President Richard M. Nixon of "acknowledging" that Beijing and Taipei both regard Taiwan as part of a unified China. "We remain committed to the one-China policy," says Assistant Secretary of State Lord.

Taiwan supporters say that policy — reflected in the Shanghai Communique issued after Nixon's 1972 trip to China — should be changed to reflect the changes on the island. "Taiwan no longer claims to be the government of China," Harvey Feldman, a former State Department official in Taiwan, remarked at the April conference. "It claims to be in control of the territory of Taiwan and the other islands. The policy of February 1972 no longer corresponds to reality."

Most China experts, however, including some strong supporters of Taiwan, say the United States should continue to warn Taipei away from any moves toward formal independence. "You've got to protect prosperity and democracy in Taiwan, but you've got to do it without threatening sovereignty and unity," says Lilley, who headed the U.S. mission in Taiwan in the 1980s and served as U.S. ambassador to China during the Bush administration.

"If China really believed that Taiwan was going to declare independence, I think China would attack it," says Tucker. "And I don't think that the United States wants to go to war with China. That's not in anybody's interest."

Many observers simultaneously praised the administration's decision to send U.S. warships into the Taiwan Strait in response to the Chinese military exercises while also criticizing the administration for a vacillating policy toward China up to that time. "They had to do it to re-establish credibility," Shinn remarks.

In the critics' view, Clinton invited the strained relations with China first by taking a hard line toward Beijing during his 1992 campaign and then in 1994 by "delinking" China's trading status from its controversial handling of human rights issues. These critics say the administration has continued to be weak on other issues with China — for example, the evidence that China has allowed the shipment of nuclear weapons technology to Pakistan in violation of the Nuclear Proliferation Treaty.

Lord acknowledged the criticism of administration policy in his March 25 remarks. "I would not claim that our policy has been perfectly steady toward China," Lord said. "I would claim that we would still be having problems even if it had been."

Some advocates and experts say the administration should adopt a more confrontational policy toward China. "It's got to be a combination of very heavy diplomatic pressure and very heavy public pressure," says Grawbow of Freedom House.

"Beijing is testing our willpower," says John Copper, a professor of international studies at Rhodes College in Memphis, Tenn., and author of several books on Taiwan and China. "Asians, China in particular, view American foreign policy as not making much sense, certainly not reflecting any strength of resolve or purpose."

But other experts, like Shinn, warn that a hard-line stance may only aggravate the current tensions between Washington and Beijing. "We have a real risk, 20 percent to 50 percent, of sliding into another belligerent relationship, a fundamentally adversarial relationship, with the PRC, which, far from helping solve these problems, is going to make them intractable," Shinn says.

The experts are virtually unanimous, however, in predicting a period of instability in U.S.-China relations until Beijing resolves its own political difficulties. (*See story, p. 464.*)

"The mainland is going to need some time to work out the succession crisis," says Dreyer. "This is not a popular leadership they have. I really see Beijing's ability to do anything weakening over the next decade."

Will Taiwan and China move closer together or farther apart?

For most of the past 50 years, China and Taiwan have glowered at each other from opposite sides of the Taiwan Strait, refusing any official contact and threatening each other with rhetoric or, on a few occasions, military might. Yet in the past decade, Beijing and Taipei have moved, tentatively, to relax the restrictions that separate their peoples and their economies.

The tensions of the past year put a pause to that process. Now, observers are watching to see whether the two Chinas can again come closer together.

All observers agree that formal unification is impossible any time in the foreseeable future. And one adviser to President Lee cautioned last month against expecting any dramatic breakthroughs in the next few years either. "No matter what you do," said Hung Mao-tien of the Institute for National Policy Research on Taiwan, "it's not going to be enough unless you totally subjugate yourself to the PRC, which Taiwan is unwilling to do."

Still, most observers expect — and hope — that Beijing and Taipei will continue forging closer economic ties. Cash-rich Taiwan has become the second-largest investor in cash-poor China, with more than $20 billion invested, most of it in the southern provinces. "China and Taiwan have linked up considerably in terms of investment by Taiwan in China and

The Biggest Riddle for China-Watchers ...

Deng Xiaoping became China's leader after the death of the revolutionary leader Mao Tse-tung in 1976 and guided China through more than a decade of economic and political liberalization. Now the 92-year-old Deng is reportedly near death. But who will rule China next — and what policy will be followed — puzzles policy-makers and experts in the United States as well as in Taiwan and Hong Kong.

China-watchers in the United States are divided into two basic camps. The optimists see a continuing commitment among China's third- and fourth-generation leaders to broader free-market economic policies and predict a resulting move toward democratization. The pessimists acknowledge the economic liberalization but see no increase in political freedom. Instead, they see a clique of mediocre and insecure leaders in Beijing turning to nationalism and political repression to stay in power.

Both descriptions are, to some extent, accurate, according to Arthur Waldron, a China expert at the U.S. Naval War College. "China is really moving in two directions," Waldron says. "If you look at the society, the overwhelming trend is still toward society becoming more and more independent. But if you look at the central government, you find an attempt to renew authoritarianism, a reassertion of the idea that you can have a society that is modern economically but is still a one-party dictatorship."

Deng himself came to power after a bitter struggle with Mao's nominal successor, Hua Guofeng, and other "radicals" who favored a continuation of communist economic policies. Today, China's rapid economic growth under the evolving free-market policies has left committed communists on the sidelines, according to William H. Overholt, managing director in charge of Asian research for Bankers Trust Co. "All tendencies are toward market prices, development of capital markets, increased competition, an open economy and reorganization of state enterprises," Overholt writes in the current issue of *Foreign Affairs.* [1]

But human rights advocates say these economic freedoms are still limited and in any event have not yet led to political freedoms. "Only a minority of Chinese have been able to take advantage of the market economy to the degree that they're no longer dependent on the state," says Charles Grawbow, an Asia expert at Freedom House, a New York-based human rights organization. "And we see no improvement in political liberalization."

China-watchers generally agree that Deng remains an important figure, even in his frail state, because of the emphasis in the Chinese system on personal loyalty to leaders. But with Deng out of public view, the government has been in the hands of three aging leaders: Jiang Zemin, president and general secretary of the Communist Party; Premier Li Peng; and Vice Premier Zhu Rongji. Overholt dismisses all three as narrow technocrats, and both he and Waldron predict that no single leader will emerge after Deng's death. "The society is so complex that the strong-man system doesn't work any more," says Waldron.

Waldron also sees signs of political liberalization in the recent efforts by the National People's Congress to assert independent legislative power and by the spread of local elections in Chinese towns and villages. He says leaders in Beijing will ultimately realize they have no choice but to accept democratization. "If they want stability," Waldron says, "they're going to have to try democracy and let the people in."

Hong Kong has the most immediate stake in the political succession in Beijing. Overholt believes that Beijing has a solid consensus on preserving Hong Kong's economic system after the British colony reverts to Chinese control next July. (*See story, p. 468.*) But other China experts, citing the turbulence in Hong Kong over the past two months, are

in terms of trade," says Copper at Rhodes College.

The two governments continue to avoid all official contacts, however. Taiwan insists that Beijing must renounce the use of military force against Taiwan before any official talks can be held. Beijing has refused to do so. When PRC President Jiang Zemin proposed a cross-strait summit in January 1995, he went so far as to say that Chinese should not fight fellow Chinese. But Jiang reserved the right to use force against "foreign forces attempting to interfere in China's reunification and seek the independence of Taiwan." [7]

Despite the ban on official talks, Taipei and Beijing each have created semiofficial organizations to work on improving relations: the Straits Exchange Foundation in Taiwan and the Association for Relations Across the Taiwan Strait in China. Cheng-yi Lin, a scholar at the Academica Sinica in Taipei, noted in a paper presented at the Washington conference last month that the two organizations had conducted seven rounds of negotiations between April 1993 and June 1995 and concluded agreements on three topics: delivery of registered mail, verification of official documents and the establishment of a regular channel of communication between the two organizations. But Beijing called off scheduled talks between the two organizations last summer to protest President Lee's visit to the United States and rebuffed Taipei's overture last month to resume the contacts.

U.S. experts generally say that the United States should avoid any direct role in encouraging cross-strait negotiations but continue trying to pro-

. . . Is What Will Happen After Deng's Death

less optimistic.

"I think things will continue to go badly," says Nancy Bernkopf Tucker, a professor of history at Georgetown University. "Despite China's best intentions, it will find that what is necessary to keep Hong Kong running on the basis that it runs now is so far from the Chinese experience that they will have enormous difficulty preserving Hong Kong's laissez-faire system."

Taiwan's interest in the transition in Beijing is also keen but less immediate. Some observers believe China's saber rattling before Taiwan's presidential election in March stemmed in part from the uncertain political situation in Beijing. "Jiang is a weak leader," says June Teufel Dreyer, a professor of political science at the University of Miami. "He is being pressured by his rivals to take a strong stand."

For its part, Taipei still wants China to formally renounce the use of force against Taiwan before moving on to other issues. Some observers say the growing nationalism in Beijing precludes any shift in policy toward Taiwan even after the succession issue is resolved. But Waldron is more optimistic. "If you have democratization within the PRC [People's Republic of China], that's very, very good for Taiwan," he concludes. "A democratic or liberalized China would be able to make an offer that Taiwan could accept."

As for the United States, the uncertain succession in Beijing is only one factor, and perhaps a minor one, behind the current chill in relations with China. James Lilley, the Bush administration's ambassador to Beijing and now a fellow at the American Enterprise Institute in Washington, says China responded to the collapse of the Soviet Union by refocusing its energies on economic growth and on assertive diplomacy in Asia — both of which produced sharpened conflicts with the United States.

"They're economically very strong, and they're sitting on a volcano of activity," Lilley says. And, he adds, "they view the United States as the only power that stands in [their] way."

In Washington, meanwhile, political conditions are operating to stiffen U.S. policy toward China. Pressure from Congress forced the Clinton administration to allow Taiwan's president, Lee Teng-hui, to visit the U.S. last summer despite China's protests. The administration also had an eye on Capitol Hill in the last month as it shaped its response to two other high-profile issues: China's export of restricted nuclear technology to Pakistan and its illegal copying of U.S. videos and computer software (*see p. 474*).

Dramatizing the issue, Senate Majority Leader Bob Dole, R-Kan., the presumptive Republican candidate for president, faulted President Clinton in a major foreign policy speech on May 9 for vacillating on China. Even so, Dole lined up behind the administration's expected stand in favor of extending most-favored-nation (MFN) trading status for China.[2]

With the presidential campaign season about to begin in earnest, any relaxation of U.S. policy toward China seems unlikely for the time being. As for China, observers are divided and uncertain about the future. "There are some positive trends, but also some trends toward increasingly virulent nationalism," Michel Oksenberg, a professor at Stanford University and former National Security Council staffer, told a conference in Washington last month. China, he concluded, "is a huge set of unknowns."[3]

[1] William H. Overholt, "China after Deng," *Foreign Affairs*, May/June 1996, p. 66.

[2] "Dole and Clinton See Eye to Eye on Favored Trade with Beijing," *CQ Weekly Report*, May 11, 1996, p. 1316. Dole announced May 15 he was quitting the Senate to concentrate on his presidential campaign against Clinton.

[3] The conference, "Presidential Elections and Democratic Consolidation in Taiwan," was sponsored by the Taiwan-based Institute for National Policy Research and the National Endowment for Democracy.

mote dialogue by urging restraint on both sides. "Our most important role is to say, 'you guys keep it peaceful,' " says Lilley. "At the same time, we say self-determination in Taiwan has its limits."

Taiwan's presidential election confirms that its people are divided on how far to go with self-determination. A significant minority — indicated by the 15 percent who cast votes for the Democratic Progressive Party (DPP) — remain committed to independence even in the face of the Chinese military exercises.

"The presidential election is the beginning of one China, one Taiwan," Huang-hsiung Huang, a former DPP member of the Legislative Yuan and now a visiting scholar at Harvard University, remarked at the Washington conference. Taiwan, he said, "should be seen as a new country, different from the one that existed before the election."

Another minority — 25 percent according to one recent poll — still looks to reunification with the mainland. "There are some people who are genuinely committed to reunification, provided there was a different political structure in Beijing," says Elizabeth Economy, project director for the Council on Foreign Relations task force on Taiwan.

Economy says that the Taiwan government reflects the same divisions on independence. And Dreyer at the University of Miami says Lee himself has given mixed signals on the question. "President Lee wants to fairly represent all these views," Dreyer says, "and the only way it is possible to do so is to be ambiguous."

Just when Taiwan was celebrating

its presidential election, however, Beijing acted to raise doubts about the possibility of improved cross-strait relations with its firm putdown of democratic structures in Hong Kong. The British colony is scheduled to revert to Chinese control next year. (*See story, p. 468.*)

"Things have not gone smoothly over Hong Kong," says Georgetown's Tucker. "Taiwan is watching that closely. If things go badly, it will confirm feelings in Taiwan that reunification is not a good idea."

"Taiwan has become a real democracy, China has not," concludes Copper. "It's way behind in political modernization, and the gap is maybe getting bigger than smaller. The best thing is to maintain the status quo rather than fight it." ■

BACKGROUND

A Distant History

Taiwan lies only 100 miles off the coast of China, but it has been separated from the mainland — politically and culturally as well as physically — for much of their history. [8] The island was only loosely integrated with the mainland during the 212 years (1683-1895) when it was an official part of China. It was then occupied by Japan for 50 years before China's civil war created the current division.

The geological and ethnic origins of Taiwan are disputed, but prevailing views also attest to distinct histories. While some geologists believe Taiwan was once part of the Asian mainland, most today believe the island is of volcanic origin, akin to the island chain extending from the Alaskan Aleutians to Japan and the Philippines. Ethnically, Taiwan's aboriginal population is believed to have come from Southeast Asia rather than from China and to be related to the present-day Malay people.

The Chinese explored Taiwan as early as 239 A.D. and began to emigrate there as early as the seventh century. But historian Copper, in his book *Taiwan: Nation-State or Province,* says the evidence fails to show a clear intention in China to permanently settle or rule Taiwan during this period. Only after being caught up briefly in the colonial conflicts between European powers did China unambiguously lay claim to rule over Taiwan.

Portuguese sailors in 1517 were the first Europeans to sight the island, which they named Ilha Formosa ("beautiful island"). Spanish forces briefly held parts of the island, but they were defeated by the Dutch in 1642. Taiwan then became a Dutch colonial enterprise for two decades. But in 1661 Cheng Ch'eng-kung, son of a pirate who had operated from Taiwan, attacked the Dutch and forced them to concede defeat two years later. Cheng and his son ruled for the next two decades, but internal dissension opened the way for a successful invasion by China's Manchu dynasty in 1683.

Peking (now Beijing) ruled Taiwan for the next two centuries, treating the island as a frontier area. It prohibited emigration and sent inefficient and corrupt leaders to put down local uprisings. As of the mid-19th century, the island's population was only half Chinese, and Chinese control was only nominal, Copper writes. But rebellions in southern China in the 1880s led Peking to appreciate Taiwan's strategic value and to upgrade its status to a separate province in 1886.

Less than a decade later, however, China was forced to surrender Taiwan to Japan after its defeat in the Sino-Japanese War. Copper describes Japan's five decades as "beneficial and progressive on the one hand, and discriminatory and predatory on the other." [9] Japan strengthened the legal and political systems to ensure control and helped build an economic infrastructure and improve the island's agriculture. But it also took most of Taiwan's exports for itself and gave little regard to Taiwanese customs or feelings. Schools, for example, taught Japanese rather than native Taiwanese or Chinese dialects.

China's Civil War

China began the 20th century as a weak and divided country. The Chinese Revolution, led by Sun Yat-sen, overthrew the hapless Ch'ing dynasty in 1911 and created a republic. But divisions surfaced quickly. By the late 1920s, the revolutionary movement split into the Kuomintang (or Nationalist Party), led after Sun's death in 1925 by Chiang Kai-shek, and the Chinese Communist Party (CCP), led by Mao Tse-tung.

The Kuomintang (KMT) ostensibly supported a parliamentary system of government, but the party operated under a Leninist-style centralized structure. [10] After Sun's death, Chiang led the National Revolutionary Army from its base in the south northward, defeating military warlords as he sought to unify the country. But the split with the Communists opened wide in 1927. The Nationalists expelled the Communists from the KMT, who proceeded to organize the peasantry in central and western China as they conducted an orderly trek — the "Long March" — into the country's interior.

Even as Japan turned its expansionist eye toward China, the country's split remained. Japan occupied Manchuria in 1931 to thwart Chinese unification and then launched all-out war in 1937. The Communists called for a united front against Japan, but Chiang continued the anti-Communist campaign. As Britain, France and then the United States were drawn into the Pacific War, Chiang was made an ally

Continued on p. 468

Chronology

1500-1899

Taiwan is visited by Portuguese explorers and colonized by the Dutch before coming under Chinese rule for more than two centuries.

1517
Portuguese vessels sight Ilha Formosa ("beautiful island").

1622-1661
Taiwan is under Dutch rule.

1683-1895
Taiwan is ruled by China and in 1886 is made a province.

1895
China cedes Taiwan to Japan after its defeat in Sino-Japanese War.

• • •

1900-1949

Taiwan is ruled by Japan until end of World War II and then becomes a refuge for the Nationalists defeated in the Chinese civil war.

1911
Chinese revolution topples Ch'ing Dynasty and establishes Republic of China.

1931-1945
Nationalist (Kuomintang) government and Communist rebels vie for support and position while resisting Japan; Allies promise Chiang Kai-shek return of all Japanese-occupied areas, including Taiwan, after war.

Oct. 25, 1945
Taiwan officially reverts to China.

1946-1949
Chinese civil war ends in victory for Communists; Chiang Kai-shek flees with supporters to Taiwan.

1950-1969

Beijing and Taipei each claims to be legitimate government of China. United States backs Nationalists despite growing support for mainland government among other countries.

1954
United States signs mutual defense treaty with Taiwan.

• • •

1970s

Beijing is admitted to United Nations; U.S. downgrades relations with Taiwan.

Oct. 25, 1971
U.N. General Assembly votes 76-35 to admit the People's Republic of China and expel Taiwan.

April 5, 1975
Chiang Kai-shek dies. He is succeeded three years later by his son, Chiang Ching-kuo.

Dec. 15, 1978
United States announces it will recognize China and withdraw diplomatic recognition from Taiwan, effective Jan. 1, 1979.

March 29, 1979
Congress completes action on Taiwan Relations Act, establishing unofficial relations with Taiwan.

• • •

1980s

Taiwan adopts democratic reforms and becomes economic powerhouse.

1986
Taiwan holds first two-party election ever in Chinese nation when newly formed Democratic Progressive Party (DPP) formally competes with Nationalist Party.

July 14, 1987
President Chiang Ching-kuo lifts martial law on Taiwan.

Jan. 13, 1988
Vice President Lee Teng-hui succeeds to presidency after death of Chiang.

• • •

1990s

Taiwan continues democratic reforms. China founders as aging leadership faces uncertain succession.

Dec. 21, 1991
First full election for National Assembly in Taiwan: Kuomintang (KMT) receives 71 percent of vote.

Dec. 19, 1992
First direct election of Legislative Yuan in Taiwan: KMT receives 53 percent of vote.

Dec. 2, 1995
KMT wins narrow majority (85 of 164 seats) in Legislative Yuan; pro-independence DPP wins 50 seats.

January-March 1996
China conducts military exercises in Taiwan Strait before presidential election.

March 23, 1996
Lee Teng-hui wins first popular election for president of Taiwan; China ends military exercises the next day.

May 20, 1996
Lee says in his inaugural speech he is willing to visit mainland China.

Hong Kong's Democracy May Be Short-Lived . . .

Martin Lee has seen Hong Kong's future, and it is not pretty. The leader of Hong Kong's pro-democracy Democratic Party thinks the British colony faces a bleak political outlook after it reverts to Chinese rule July 1, 1997. "China can control the executive, the legislature and the judiciary," Lee told a sympathetic crowd at a Washington reception last month. "The rule of law will not survive."

Lee's remarks, to an April 18 gathering sponsored by the New York-based human rights group Freedom House, came after a turbulent few weeks in the prosperous enclave of British rule on China's southern coast. The tension began after China sent worrisome signals about its commitment to limited autonomy for Hong Kong after the transfer of sovereignty. That prompted Hong Kongers to jam the British consulate to obtain special visas that will allow free travel after Chinese rule begins.

Meanwhile, Lee and other Hong Kong democrats stepped up their international efforts to pressure China to honor the treaty it signed with Britain in 1984. The treaty calls for Britain to return Hong Kong to China at the end of the 99-year "lease" the two countries signed in 1898. China, in turn, promises to preserve Hong Kong's economic, social and legal institutions for 50 years afterward — or until 2047.

In a jarring juxtaposition, the peril for Hong Kong's young democracy became clear on March 24, just one day after voters in Taiwan participated in their first direct presidential election. As the Taiwanese celebrated their ripening democracy, a provisional council appointed by Beijing reaffirmed China's plan to abolish Hong Kong's popularly elected legislature as soon as China takes over next year.

China had previously stated its intention to replace the legislature — which Britain created only in 1991 — with an appointed body. As the hand-picked transition group prepared to vote, Chinese Foreign Minister Qian Qichen personally urged it to reject an elected legislature. "To mechanically ape the Western democratic model," Qian said, "does not accord with Hong Kong's actual condition or accommodate the interests of all social strata." Afterward, Beijing drove home its point by barring the lone dissenter from the council's decision from further participation in the transition. [1]

In his April remarks, party Chairman Lee, who is also a member of the legislature, cited China's plan to abolish the body as the latest in a list of "terrible things" that Beijing has done in preparing for the transition. Previously, China proposed in October to downgrade Hong Kong's Bill of Rights, enacted in 1991. The plan calls for the Basic Law, the legal outline Britain and China agreed to in 1984, to take precedence over any conflicting provisions in the rights charter.

Legal experts were already concerned about the plan for a new Supreme Court that China negotiated with Britain in 1995. The agreement calls for the court to begin operation in 1997, instead of earlier, and bars the tribunal from exercising jurisdiction over "acts of state such as defense and foreign affairs" — a rubric that can readily embrace cases against political dissidents. [2]

For Britain, the lowering of the Union Jack ends a 150-year rule that began with the wresting of the island of Hong Kong from China in 1842. [3] The colony grew to its present size by the addition of China's Kowloon peninsula in 1860 and with the addition of the so-called New Territories on the mainland under terms of the 1898 lease.

Initially, the British government had little interest in the barren island. But it quickly became a valuable trade center for Britain and, beginning around the turn of the century, for the United States as well. For China, the colony was a constant reminder of its 19th-century humiliations by foreigners, but a low political priority as the country suffered through the ordeals of revolution, Japanese occupation and civil war.

During World War II, the United States gently urged Britain to relinquish Hong Kong along with its other imperial holdings, but London ignored the proddings. Later, the U.S. came to see the advantages of British-ruled Hong Kong, both as a commercial and financial center and as a political and diplomatic listening post. In the 1980s, however, Britain recognized that it had to negotiate with China over the colony's future.

As Georgetown University historian Nancy Bernkopf Tucker writes, Britain quickly discovered that China had no inclination to permit continued British rule but wanted only to negotiate the terms of British withdrawal. The Sino-British Joint Declaration of 1984 fixed the date for the reversion — July 1, 1997 — and provided that China would

Continued from p. 466

and partner, at American insistence. President Franklin D. Roosevelt and British Prime Minister Winston Churchill met Chiang at the Cairo Conference in November 1943 and vowed to support the return of all Japanese-held territories to China, including Taiwan and the Pescadores, a group of islands in the Taiwan Strait.

In August 1945, the Communists took advantage of the war's end to move into Manchuria, where the Soviet Union helped them acquire most of the light weaponry abandoned by the Japanese. Peace negotiations between the Communists and Nationalists produced an agreement in October to move toward a multiparty assembly to draft a new constitution. President Harry S Truman dispatched Gen. George C. Marshall to try to forge a coalition government and prod Chiang to make needed reforms. But the U.S. efforts failed, on both counts. By early 1947, the Communists had made military gains that foretold their

... After China Takes Over Next Year

govern Hong Kong as a "special administrative region" with a "high degree of autonomy" for 50 years thereafter. [4]

The prospect of Chinese rule caused little concern in Hong Kong at a time of political and economic liberalization in China. But the Tiananmen massacre in Beijing on June 4, 1989, led to popular pressure to install some democratic and legal structures before 1997. Britain moved slowly at first, but in 1992 a new governor, Chris Patten, arrived from London. Patten set in motion the process that culminated Sept. 17, 1995, in legislative elections, the colony's most open election ever.

The balloting produced a victory for Lee's Democratic Party, which gained 20 seats and could count on at least another six to eight votes from pro-democracy allies. The two pro-Beijing parties held fewer seats: 16 for the Democratic Alliance for the Betterment of Hong Kong, which portrayed itself as best able to work with the Chinese government, and 10 seats for the business-oriented Liberal Party. [5]

For its part, China has viewed Hong Kong's eleventh-hour democratization as a change in the terms of its 1984 agreement with Britain. It has largely ignored the Hong Kong legislature and instead relied on a hand-picked advisory body made up mostly of business leaders who are viewed by Hong Kong democrats as too eager to please the future rulers in Beijing.

With the 1997 deadline nearing, the British government sent conflicting signals about its future role in Hong Kong. In January, Foreign Secretary Malcolm Rifkind visited Hong Kong to warn that Britain would have little power to influence events. But less than two months later, Prime Minister John Major flew in to say that Britain would continue to take an active interest in China's compliance with the 1984 treaty. "If there were any suggestion of a breach of the Joint Declaration, we would have a duty to pursue every legal and other avenue available to us," Major said. [6]

Realistically, however, Britain will have only limited ability to guard Hong Kong's interests after 1997. And foreign-policy experts agree that the United States is in an even weaker position. "The United States cannot do very much because it is a British-Chinese agreement," Tucker says.

Still, some advocates and experts believe that the U.S. can protect Hong Kong's interests by helping pro-democracy leaders such as Lee get international attention. "If we can give these people more stature and more exposure, I think the Chinese will think hard before they crack down on them," says Charles Grawbow, an Asia expert at Freedom House.

More concretely, economic considerations may help Hong Kong preserve its promised measure of autonomy after China takes over next July. China already benefits from Hong Kong financially. In recent years, Hong Kong has been the source of more than half the direct foreign investment in China, and Hong Kong firms provide jobs for about 3 million workers in bordering Guangdong province. [7] Hong Kong-watchers hope, with varying degrees of optimism, that those economic benefits will temper any moves by Beijing to clamp down after it reclaims the enclave next year.

For the moment, however, the mood on Hong Kong is less than hopeful. One poll last year showed that 70 percent of the colony's residents favor independence or continued British rule rather than rule by China. A poll in January showed that 43 percent of young people ages 15 to 24 would rather emigrate than stay behind in 1977. [8] Many people are leaving — about 1,000 daily as of February, according to one report. [9] And for those who cannot leave, the feeling, according to Lee, is one of "helplessness."

"They can't go away, so what do they do?" Lee asks rhetorically. "They won't dare express support for us. But when there are elections, they will express support provided the vote is secret."

---

[1] See *The Economist,* March 30, 1996, p. 38; *The Wall Street Journal,* March 25, 1996, p. A10, and March 26, 1996, p. A18.

[2] See *The Los Angeles Daily Journal,* Feb. 20, 1996, p. A1; *Far Eastern Economic Review,* Nov. 16, 1995, p. 36, and *The Washington Post,* July 1, 1995, p. A21.

[3] For background, see Nancy Bernkopf Tucker, *Taiwan, Hong Kong and the United States, 1945-1992: Uncertain Friendships* (1994), pp. 197-223; and Frank Welsh, *A History of Hong Kong* (1993).

[4] Tucker, *op. cit.,* pp. 218-219.

[5] See *Far Eastern Economic Review,* Sept. 28, 1995, p. 16; *The Economist,* Sept. 29, 1995, p. 12 (editorial), pp. 29-32 (news story).

[6] See *The Washington Post,* Jan. 13, 1996 (Rifkind's visit); *The New York Times,* March 5, 1996, p. A3 (Major's visit).

[7] *USA Today,* Feb. 20, 1996, p. 5B.

[8] *McLean's,* Feb. 5, 1996, p. 26.

[9] *USA Today, loc. cit.*

coming victory over the Nationalists.

Taiwan itself celebrated its return to China after the war's end with ambivalence. A significant minority on the island favored independence. Over the next two years, the Nationalist government gave the Taiwanese further cause for apprehension. The government "systematically looted the island" of $1 billion worth of property, historian Tucker writes. Then, on Feb. 28, 1947, the Nationalists brutally put down a wave of protests that were touched off by a minor incident, the arrest of a woman for unauthorized sale of cigarettes. "[E]xecutions and terror eliminated thousands of opponents of Nationalist rule," Tucker writes. [11]

In 1949, the Nationalists' final year on the mainland, Chiang proved militarily inept and politically insensitive. By mid-year, Chiang had begun to withdraw troops to Taiwan — the first wave of an eventual immigration of 1.5 million mainlanders to the island. Chiang also carted off money and property, including a vast collection of art from the imperial eras. By fall, the Nationalists' collapse was complete. On Oct. 1, 1949, Mao stood at Tiananmen Square in Peking and proclaimed the People's Republic of China. He declared it "the day China stood up."

The Two Chinas

Chiang Kai-shek insisted that his regime on Taiwan was the legal government of all of China. Initially, the Truman administration had no inclination to support him. But Truman was forced into backing Chiang by the Korean War and the Chinese Communists' decision to enter the war on North Korea's side. For the next two decades, the United States gave Chiang political, diplomatic, military and economic support that angered the mainland government but enabled Taiwan to survive, strengthen and prosper.

The United States gained from the relationship a valuable military outpost — "an unsinkable aircraft carrier," as Gen. Douglas MacArthur famously described Taiwan — and, later, an important trading partner.

But Taiwan gained much more, thanks to Chiang's deft manipulation of anti-Communist sentiment in the United States and his brazen diplomatic shakedowns of successive U.S. presidents. The Eisenhower administration agreed to a mutual defense treaty with Taiwan in 1954 in exchange, Tucker says, for Chiang's agreeing not to veto the Korean ceasefire resolution in the United Nations Security Council. A decade later, President John F. Kennedy persuaded Chiang not to block Outer Mongolia's admission to the United Nations by promising that the U.S. would veto U.N. membership for mainland China.

Chiang continued through the 1960s to insist on U.S. support — to the point several times of seeking permission and support of an invasion of the mainland. But U.S. policy was slowly changing. Assistant Secretary of State Roger Hilsman broached the idea of a two-China policy in December 1963. More ominous for Taiwan was an article in *Foreign Affairs* in 1967 written by a leading Republican of unquestioned anti-Communist credentials, Richard M. Nixon. The United States, Nixon wrote, "simply cannot afford to leave China forever outside the family of nations." [12]

International support for the U.S. policy of isolating China was also eroding. The United States had fended off the PRC's membership in the U.N. by having the issue declared "an important question" requiring a two-thirds vote in the General Assembly. In 1965, the U.S. had prevailed on that procedural issue only by virtue of a tie vote. Six years later, however, the General Assembly rejected the "important question" resolution on a 55-59 vote with 15 abstentions. With the die cast, the member nations on Oct. 25, 1971, voted 76-35 to admit the People's Republic of China as "the only lawful representative of China" and expel "the representatives of Chiang Kai-shek."

By this time Nixon, now president, was already conducting secret diplomacy with China through his national security adviser, Henry A. Kissinger. The overtures culminated in Nixon's trip to China in February 1972. In the joint communique ending the trip, issued in Shanghai on Feb. 27, the United States crafted a diplomatic sleight-of-hand on Taiwan. "The United States acknowledges," the oblique communique stated, "that all Chinese on either side of the Taiwan Strait maintain there is but one China and that Taiwan is part of China." The U.S. called for the issue to be settled peacefully between Taiwan and China, but it also pledged to gradually reduce U.S. military forces and installations on the island. [13]

Nixon's moves to "normalize" relations with China fell victim to the Watergate scandals that drove him from office in 1974. His Republican successor, Gerald Ford, hesitated to work for improved relations with China for fear of offending the GOP's conservative wing. But in 1978, President Jimmy Carter dropped the other shoe: In a joint communique, he announced on Dec. 15 that the United States would recognize the PRC, effective Jan. 1, 1979. As for Taiwan, the U.S. would sever its diplomatic relations, end the defense treaty and remove all military installations from the island. [14]

The reaction on Taiwan was one of shock and betrayal. Those feelings were only partly assuaged by the enactment the next spring of the Taiwan Relations Act. The new law, initially proposed by Carter and somewhat strengthened in Congress, provided for the United States and Taiwan to continue relations through unofficial, private organizations and to maintain all trade, transportation and cultural links. U.S. arms sales were also to continue. The act also stated that the U.S. would regard an attack on Taiwan as "a matter of grave concern." [15]

The United States continued to distance itself from Taiwan through the 1980s, despite Taipei's expectations of better relations with a conservative Republican administration. President Ronald Reagan in 1982 yielded to pressure from China to block the sale of sophisticated FX fighters to Taiwan and then in August to limit future U.S. arms sales based on 1979 levels. Although Reagan actually managed to increase sales by using a statistical adjustment, the agreement put the stamp of a conservative president on the new premise of U.S.-China policy: preserving good relations with China even at the expense of what the Republican platform of 1980 had described as "our longtime friend and ally, Taiwan."

Economic Miracles

Despite its diplomatic isolation, Taiwan by the 1980s was a muscular presence in Asia and the world.

It had considerable military might, though its security continued to depend on the United States' presumed protection. In addition, Taiwan boasted a remarkable prosperity that belied its lack of natural resources or other inherent economic advantages.

Initially, Taiwan's build-up could be attributed to U.S. aid, in massive amounts. Economic assistance from 1950 to 1965 averaged $100 million a year — more per capita than for any other country, according to Tucker. President Lyndon B. Johnson ended the economic assistance in 1965 to show Congress that foreign aid could be terminated when the recipient country no longer needed it. Military aid during the same period totaled $2.5 billion.

In addition, Taiwan leveraged the U.S. aid brilliantly, through economic policies that successively modernized the country's agricultural system and then created and expanded a solid industrial base. Historian Copper says Taiwan has achieved double-digit economic growth in more years over the past three decades than any other country — and without much inflation or income inequality besides. [16] By the 1980s, Taiwan was being commonly and aptly described as an "economic miracle."

Agricultural output grew beginning in the early 1950s thanks to Chiang's land reform policies, which increased the percentage of owner-farmers from about 30 percent in 1948 to 60 percent in 1953. Chiang had been tied to landlords on the mainland. But with no obligations to Taiwan's landholders he felt free to implement policies requiring them to sell property to farmers in exchange for bonds in government corporations. Under the new ownership patterns, production increased an average of 5.6 percent per year from 1953 to 1970. And, as Copper notes, through taxation and savings farmers provided most of the capital for industrialization as well as a market for the developing industrial base.

Industrialization came next, beginning in the late 1950s. In addition to U.S. aid, Copper credits the growth in industrial production over the next three decades to several other factors, including rising industrial employment and labor productivity; substantial local savings (the world's highest savings rate, 40 percent, as of 1987; around 20 percent today); foreign investment; a solid economic infrastructure; and "astute planning" by government and business communities. [17]

The government policies combined privatization of ownership with a clear strategy to increase industrial production for export. The government had taken over many of the manufacturing enterprises left by the Japanese, but the private sector began advancing in the 1960s. By 1984, nearly 90 percent of industrial production was in the hands of the private sector, Copper writes. At the same time, the government favored export-producing industries by reducing tariffs and easing taxes and regulations on the import of raw materials. The result: Exports rose nearly 20 percent a year during the first half of the 1960s.

Taiwan's prosperity stood in stark contrast to economic conditions on the mainland. As Copper notes, Taiwan's per capita income was the same as China's not too long ago, but is now 20 times that on the mainland. China's dismal performance up to the 1980s can be attributed to economic ideology as well as the political unrest of the Great Proletarian Cultural Revolution of the 1960s. But under Deng, China in the 1980s began to restructure its economy, permitting private ownership and adopting other free-market policies.

The result has been a second Chinese economic miracle. China has averaged 9 percent economic growth since 1980 — and more than 10 percent over the past three years — and is moving to become the world's largest economy. For Taiwan and the United States, China's economic growth presented new opportunities for investment and trade, but it also posed heightened risks in the event of a diplomatic or military confrontation.

Unfolding Democracy

Taiwan is now being credited with a second miracle on top of its economic success: a transformation over the past decade from a single-party dictatorship to a fledgling democracy. The process has unfolded slowly — moved along by generational changes, economic affluence and the increasing proportion of native-born Taiwanese among the island's population.

Despite his role as U.S. ally in the Cold War, Chiang Kai-shek saw no reason to follow democratic policies on Taiwan. He held total power until the last years of his life, presiding over a regime that permitted no opposition parties and sent dissidents to jail or exile. Two of the current leaders of the DPP — unsuccessful presidential candidate Peng Ming-min and party Chairman Shih Ming-teh — were both given long prison sentences in the 1960s for advocating democracy and independence. Historian Tucker notes another example of political suppression. In 1967, the writer Bo Yang drew an 18-year prison sentence for an anti-government cartoon depicting Popeye as a tyrannical ruler of a small island country. [18]

The Kuomintang began to loosen its grip beginning in 1972, with Chiang's appointment of his son, Chiang Ching-kuo, as premier. CCK, as he was fondly known, instigated steps against official corruption and freed some political prisoners, including Bo Yang, who was pardoned in 1977, two years after the elder Chiang's death. CCK succeeded to the presidency in 1978. Two years later, in 1980, in what is now regarded as a pivotal event, he reverted to his father's authoritarian pattern, crushing an anti-government demonstration in the southern port city of Kaohsiung and ordering the leaders jailed. But, as a leading government official remarked recently, Chiang began to realize after the crackdown that those policies were "not tenable." [19]

Over the next eight years, Chiang moved more decisively toward democracy. As one important step, in 1984 he picked the native-born Lee, a popular figure as mayor of Taipei and then governor of Taiwan province, as his vice president. Chiang, who suffered from diabetes and other health problems, also announced that no one in his family would hold political power after his death.

In 1986, the government tacitly allowed the newly formed Democratic Progressive Party (DPP) to campaign openly in balloting for the Legislative Yuan even though the party was technically illegal. Chiang also announced that the government planned to lift martial law; he then carried out his promise in July 1987 — six months before his death on Jan. 13, 1988.

Lee Takes Over

Lee, promptly sworn in as Taiwan's new president, promised to finish Chiang's "mission," including "the great task" of reuniting Taiwan with mainland China. But Lee faced more immediate political problems at home: the declining popularity of the Kuomintang and the growing calls for greater political liberalization. Over the next four years, he committed the government more and more to democratization as a means of bolstering the KMT's political fortunes as well as his own.

The KMT had been moving since the 1970s to widen its political base by recruiting rural Taiwanese members to add to its traditional cadre of mainlanders. Its strength depended in part on a system of corruption, including vote-buying and favoritism from state-owned enterprises, but a string of well-publicized scandals in the 1980s embarrassed the party and fueled anti-KMT movements. In addition, the KMT's leadership was visibly aging, especially in the two legislative bodies — the National Assembly and the Legislative Yuan — where members chosen before 1949 had been allowed to maintain their seats pending the hoped for return to the mainland.

The discontent fed pro-democracy demonstrations by students and others in Taiwan through the late 1980s. Lee personally met with demonstrators in March 1990 and promised to work for reforms. Over the next four years, Lee pushed the sometimes reluctant Kuomintang to constitutional amendments to require the resignation of all aging parliamentarians, to shorten the term of the president and members of the National Assembly and, in 1994, to provide for direct election of the president.

As the reforms progressed, the Nationalists saw their dominant position reduced. The KMT had won 71 percent of the vote in the first full elections for the National Assembly in 1991. One year later, in the first direct election of the Legislative Yuan, the party won only 53 percent of the vote, with the opposition DPP winning 31 percent. In the next parliamentary election, in December 1995, the KMT won the narrowest of majorities — 85 of 164 seats — with only a plurality, 46 percent, of the popular vote. The pro-independence DPP captured 54 seats; and the newly formed New Party, led by defectors from the KMT, won 21 seats on a platform of domestic reform and reconciliation with the mainland.

Lee's convincing 54 percent victory in the presidential election four months later climaxed a tense year-long period that began with the preparations for his visit to the U.S. China protested the visit with harsh rhetoric and military exercises that began shortly after the visit in June and continued, off and on, through the presidential election campaign. Most observers believe the exercises may have helped Lee gain votes from the DPP. Its candidate, Peng Ming-min, won 21 percent of the vote — well below the DPP's showing of 34 percent in the parliamentary balloting. The New Party's candidate, Lin Yang-kang, won 15 percent of the vote; independent Chen Li-an gathered 10 percent.

Lee hailed his victory as a triumph for democracy. "On March 23, 1996, the door to democracy was swung open in the Republic of China on Taiwan," he said from a stage outside his headquarters on election night. The next week, *The Economist* captured the same thought with an unstated comparison to Mao's famous proclamation 47 years earlier. The headline on the magazine's story read simply: "The day Taiwan stood up." [20] ■

CURRENT SITUATION

Crossing the Strait

During the presidential campaign, Lee answered questions about his future travel plans by saying that people might be surprised where he would go first if elected. The comment was taken to indicate an interest in making a precedent-setting visit to the mainland to meet directly with Beijing's leaders.

But after the election, Lee played down the prospect of any quick breakthrough in cross-strait relations. In an interview with the Japanese newspaper *Sankei Shimbun* in mid-April, Lee said he wanted to reach an accord with Beijing but doubted that the Chinese leaders were ready for any fresh moves in that direction. [21]

Continued on p. 474

At Issue:

Should the U.S. support Taiwan's membership in international organizations?

COUNCIL ON FOREIGN RELATIONS

FROM "MANAGING THE TAIWAN ISSUE," REPORT OF INDEPENDENT TASK FORCE, NOVEMBER 1995.

YES

While the [People's Republic of China] occupies a central position in U.S. calculations of its interest in the Asia-Pacific region, Washington also should enhance the scope of its bilateral relationship with Taiwan and Taiwan's standing in the international arena . . . .

Following on measures to re-establish U.S.-PRC working relations, and in the context of a reiterated "one-China" policy, the United States should support Taiwan's membership in certain international organizations that do not require statehood. . . . We should assure the PRC that we continue to regard such membership as fully consistent with U.S. refusal to recognize a unilateral declaration of independence by Taiwan. Also, any such memberships should be pursuant to formulas that are consistent with both the absence of recognition of statehood as well as U.S. support of continued PRC-Taiwan interactions and unification negotiations.

The United States previously sponsored Taiwan's accession to the Asian Development Bank, and it can benefit substantially from Taiwan's participation and economic lending power in agencies such as the International Monetary Fund and World Bank. There are other organizations linked to the United Nations that do not require being a "state member" of the General Assembly, including the World Health Assembly, the United Nations Development Program and the Food and Agriculture Organization. . . .

A. DOAK BARNETT

Professor emeritus, Johns Hopkins University

FROM "POINTS OF DISSENT, " REPORT OF INDEPENDENT TASK FORCE, COUNCIL ON FOREGN RELATIONS, NOVEMBER 1995.

NO

The reality we now face is that it is the recent deterioration and current crisis in U.S.-PRC relations, rather than any problems in relations between the United States and Taiwan, that endanger important long-term U.S. interests and, whether we like it or not, higher priority must therefore be given to actions that can halt this deterioration than to actions that are motivated by a desire to respond to Taiwan's desires, even though they are understandable, not just for preservation of its present situation but for an enhanced international status. . . .

I agree that some sort of membership for Taiwan in most U.N.-related economic organizations would certainly be highly desirable from the point of view of the United States as well as Taiwan, and this may eventually be possible. However, it is strongly opposed at present by China, because it is seen as weakening China's claim to sovereignty over Taiwan, and in the current U.S.-China crisis situation, U.S. sponsorship of such membership would not only evoke a strongly negative PRC response but also would create a major new obstacle to the task of repairing U.S.-China relations.

Should Taiwanese leaders be allowed to visit the U.S.?

YES

In the current tense environment of U.S.-PRC relations, it is not desirable to approve visits to the United States by senior Taiwan officials until we have at least taken further steps to attempt to rebuild our relationship with the PRC and had the opportunity to explain comprehensively to the PRC our policies concerning Taiwan. Thereafter, we should allow visits by Taiwan representatives, either to conduct business or for personal reasons, as long as the nature and timing of such visits remain within the discretion of the administration and it is articulated clearly that such visits imply neither recognition nor de jure sovereignty. . . .

Given the scope and depth of our trade, military, cultural, and unofficial political relations with Taiwan, and certainly in light of the recent resounding congressional support for President Lee's visit, the continuation of our past restriction on unofficial visits by Taiwan leaders would appear unrealistic and politically untenable, as well as undignified for the United States and insulting to Taiwan.

NO

Because the present crisis in U.S.-China relations was precipitated by President Lee's visit to the United States, if the United States wishes to halt the deterioration of relations with the PRC, it must accept considerably greater limits than we would like on visits both by senior Taiwanese leaders to the United States and by senior American leaders and officials to Taiwan. . . .

[P]eace and stability in the East Asia-Pacific region requires peace and stability in the Taiwan area. This is not something the United States itself can achieve; it can only be achieved by an eventual modus vivendi negotiated between China and Taiwan. . . .

If Taiwan-related issues further undermine U.S.-PRC relations, the danger is that trends could lead to a new cold war in East Asia, which would not only damage many important U.S. national interests, but could destabilize the region, and at worst could substantially increase regional tensions and the risks of military conflicts that could involve the United States.

Continued from p. 472

Some U.S. observers hoped Lee would use his election to try to achieve such a breakthrough. In an op-ed article published a week after the Taiwan election, Ralph Cossa, executive director of the Pacific Forum CSIS, a Honolulu-based research institute, called on Lee to make an unconditional offer to meet with China's Jiang. "A genuine overture by Mr. Lee toward Beijing," Cossa wrote, "creates a win-win situation for Taiwan and the mainland, one which Mr. Jiang may find too tempting to reject." [22]

But other observers agreed with Lee's early assessment that it was premature to be looking for a new opening toward Beijing. "A summit is such a complicated thing," says historian Tucker, "that it's not going to happen quickly."

China itself had stirred hopes for a possible summit the day after the Taiwan election with a statement issued by the Foreign Ministry in Beijing calling for a meeting between Lee and Jiang. "The door is open," a ministry spokesman said. But the suggestion died after a cross-strait exchange of unacceptable conditions. Taiwan's Premier Lien Chan insisted that Beijing must first renounce the use of force, while the ministry spokesman said Taiwan must stop seeking a higher international profile. [23]

Nonetheless, China-watchers on both sides of the Pacific say that with the election over, the stage is set for both Taipei and Beijing to resume talks. Lilley of the American Enterprise Institute (AEI) notes that both China and Taiwan stand to profit from resuming the process of improving economic ties that went on from the mid-1980s until the past year. "They were making money, both sides, with each other," he says.

Lee himself noted the economic incentives for improving relations with Beijing in his immediate post-election comments. "We will seek further development in our mainland relations," Lee told cheering crowds on March 24. "I know you want stability, and you want to make money." [24]

What Will Happen in Beijing?

The major unknown in the equation, however, is Beijing, where the government appears to be in a state of suspended animation — its nominal leader, Deng, apparently near death, and no clear successor in sight. Many observers say the military has gained influence during the extended transition — citing the saber rattling in the Taiwan Strait as proof. "The military has more authority, and the military has never liked Taiwan," says Copper. "That probably explains the missile tests and the other problems."

Other observers, however, see evidence to suggest that Beijing may adopt a more favorable attitude toward Taiwan, if not now, then sometime in the future. "China is changing economically and politically," says Marc Plattner, co-director of the National Endowment for Democracy's International Forum for Democratic Studies. "Taiwan has to look toward some kind of change in Beijing, and that kind of change is likely."

One issue that would be high on the agenda for any talks between Taipei and Beijing would be the question of permitting direct air, shipping and mail links between the island and the mainland. Currently, trade and transportation links are channeled indirectly through Hong Kong. But, as Michel Oksenberg, a China expert at Stanford University, notes, Hong Kong's scheduled reversion to China in July 1997 will force Taipei and Beijing to come up with some new trade and transportation procedures by that time, if not sooner.

Beijing, however, has a more ambitious goal for any cross-strait negotiations: reunification. China has offered Taiwan an arrangement similar to the "one country, two systems" approach it has promised for Hong Kong. Under the plan, Taiwan would continue to have its own government and maintain a capitalist economy. The plan would also afford greater autonomy than envisioned for Hong Kong by allowing Taiwan to maintain its own army.

But U.S. observers say that Taiwan is unlikely to agree to such formal reunification, at least not in the near future. "For understandable reasons, no one on Taiwan trusts China," says former Rep. Stephen J. Solarz, D-N.Y., who headed the House Foreign Affairs subcommittee on Asia for several years and is now a lobbyist in Washington. "Any ultimate resolution of the problem is going to require trust."

Whatever stance Beijing and Taipei take on cross-strait relations, American observers say the United States should stay out of the middle. "At this point in time, the U.S. needs to step back and let Beijing and Taipei get their talks back on track," says Economy of the Council on Foreign Relations. "This is a time when Lee and Jiang and the other people involved need to cool down and start talking."

Clinton's Dilemma

The Clinton administration joined in celebrating Taiwan's election with a March 24 statement from the White House congratulating "the people of Taiwan" for having made "great strides in the past several years toward democracy." The statement continued, "We hope to see tensions in the Taiwan Strait greatly reduced in the days to come."

President Clinton was basking in the credit he received for strengthening Taiwan's resolve by sending naval forces into the Taiwan Strait before the election. But the administration found itself immediately beset by a backlog of disputes with an ever more truculent Chinese government and confronted with sharply conflicting advice from U.S. foreign policy experts and advocates about the best posture to adopt toward Beijing.

The disagreements with China ranged from nuclear proliferation and weapons testing to software piracy and other trade disputes. Meanwhile, the administration was also preparing for a fight in Congress over renewing normal trading privileges for China. President Clinton announced on May 20 that he would renew most-favored nation (MFN) status, subject to disapproval by Congress. Most observers expect Congress to go along, but only after a politically divisive debate led by critics of China in both parties.

China-watchers generally agree that the administration needs to give more attention to its relations with Beijing. "Secretary [of State Warren] Christopher makes 18 trips to Syria and one trip to China, which was badly handled and poorly timed," historian Tucker remarks. "Our policy has been very reactive, with very little sense of where we want to go."

"We've been pushing in different directions," adds Stanley Roth, director of the research and studies program at the U.S. Institute for Peace. "We've had this hodgepodge of signals that China finds puzzling and less than reassuring."

Clinton's critics say the president himself bears the blame for the administration's mixed signals on China policy. Candidate Clinton blasted President George Bush for being soft on China, but as president he acted in 1994 to separate human rights issues from trade policy.

In announcing the decision to delink human rights, Clinton attached a list of other steps to promote human rights in China. Critics say Clinton never followed through and that Beijing viewed the episode as a sign of U.S. weakness. "The human rights situation deteriorated after the delinkage," says Copper. "China thumbed their nose at us right after that, and they have been ever since."

The administration drew more criticism this month, but from opposite perspectives, for its handling of two thorny disputes with China: China's shipment of weapons-grade enriched uranium to Pakistan and the widespread copying of U.S. video and computer software in China.

The administration said May 10 that it would not impose sanctions over the nuclear materials after China gave an oral assurance that it would not allow such transfers in the future. Five days later, however, the administration escalated the copyright piracy dispute by announcing plans for sanctions in the form of higher tariffs on a range of Chinese-manufactured consumer products, including clothing and electronic equipment.

Some critics complained the administration had caved in to China on the nuclear proliferation dispute. But retailers and some business leaders reacted to the threatened trade sanctions by warning that the U.S. could end up being hurt by an all-out trade war with China.

Meanwhile, both the U.S. and China were moving to shore up their diplomatic positions. Clinton traveled to South Korea and Japan for a three-day visit in mid-April highlighted by the renewal of the U.S.-Japan military alliance. For its part, China moved to play the "Russia card" by hosting Russian President Boris Yeltsin for an April 25 summit in Shanghai, where he and Chinese President Jiang signed several agreements as part of what both countries described as a "strategic partnership." In addition, Jiang made a goodwill visit to six African countries in May, aimed at countering Taiwan's success in winning diplomatic recognition from several African countries in recent years.

Despite the welter of pressures and uncertainties, the administration continues to insist that U.S. policy toward both China and Taiwan has produced positive results. Speaking at the March 25 forum, Assistant Secretary of State Lord said the policy — "through several administrations" — had "helped to provide an atmosphere where on the one hand we've been able to pursue relations with Beijing while on the other hand Taiwan has had its security taken care of in a de facto way. It has had an economic miracle and now it has a democratic miracle. So something must be going right." ■

FOR MORE INFORMATION

Center for Taiwan International Relations, 110 Maryland Ave., N.E., Suite 206, Washington, D.C. 20002; (202) 543-6287. This organization of Taiwanese-Americans advocates greater international recognition for Taiwan.

Council on Foreign Relations, 58 East 68th St., New York, N.Y. 10021; (212) 734-0400. The council, which also maintains a Washington office, has recently published reports on U.S. relations with Taiwan and China.

Embassy of the People's Republic of China, 2300 Connecticut Ave., N.W., Washington, D.C. 20008; (202) 328-2500. The embassy represents the People's Republic of China in the U.S.

Freedom House, 120 Wall St., New York, N.Y. 10005; (212) 514-8040. The human rights group recently sponsored a forum on U.S.-Taiwan relations.

Taipei Economic and Cultural Representative Office, 4201 Wisconsin Ave., N.W., Washington, D.C. 20016; (202) 895-1800. This is Taiwan's office for unofficial relations with the United States.

OUTLOOK

Studies in Ambiguity

Winston Lord had a momentary lapse March 25 as he congratulated Taiwan on its first- ever popular election for president. "It's a little awkward for a U.S. official to be analyzing another country's election," he said, then quickly corrected his phrasing, "and in this case not a country. I want to be careful with my nomenclature — another election, another election." Thus, the island's legal status was left officially ambiguous, at least in the eyes of the United States.

Ambiguity rules on Taiwan as well. Some advocates of independence say there is no need to make a declaration on the subject: Taiwan already is independent, they say. Other people on the island say they want to rejoin the mainland, but not if it means a change in government or the economy. For most people on Taiwan, however, the status quo — ambiguous and uncertain though it may be — appears to be the best available option, at least for the time being.

China also cloaks its policy toward Taiwan with ambiguity. It rails against foreign interference and fires missiles into the Taiwan Strait as the renegade province prepares for election. But even as the missiles are firing, a top state economist tells a visiting U.S. columnist, Thomas Friedman of *The New York Times,* that China cannot afford to attack Taiwan. "It would stop investment in China, stop growth, stop our last chance to catch up with the rest of the world," Friedman quoted the economist, whom he did not identify, as saying. [25]

China's crisis of self-confidence forms a pervasive backdrop to the tensions with Taiwan and the United States over the past year. The world's most populous country wants to be viewed as a superpower, but is treated as something less than that. Meanwhile, Taiwan is celebrated around the world for its miraculous economic and political turnaround.

A more self-confident China might ease the tensions with Taiwan, according to Roth of the U.S. Institute for Peace — for example, by dropping its opposition to Taiwan's membership in the IMF or World Bank or agreeing to some form of dual representation in the United Nations. But a China that feels underrespected by the rest of the world cannot give way on those issues.

China's leadership crisis also works against any moderation toward Taiwan. "If you want to be the future leader of China," Lord remarked at the March 25 forum, "you can't afford to be too flexible."

China's decision to escalate its dispute with Taiwan gave the Clinton administration an opportunity to correct what some critics had viewed as ambiguity in its own commitment to Asia. "The United States has not paid enough attention to Asia," Tucker says. "Our inattention allowed the crisis to become worse than it might have been. The administration finally did wake up to this being a much more serious problem than they anticipated."

Observers expect the tensions with China to continue. "You're going to have lots of friction," says the AEI's Lilley. "This is China." Even without the Taiwan issue, the United States and China have a range of disagreements that would be difficult to resolve given the best of intentions. And China's hardline toward Hong Kong in the past few months threatens to exacerbate tensions, even if the United States can do little to influence events there.

Taiwan's advancing democracy may add to those tensions by offering a contrast to the authoritarian policies now being followed in Beijing. In interviews before his inauguration, Lee described his mainland counterpart, Jiang, as "quite reasonable" compared with other Chinese leaders and voiced optimism about negotiations if Jiang survives the post-Deng succession. [26] But in his inaugural speech May 20, Lee also made clear that Taiwan plans to stand up to, and for, China.

"The Chinese who were regarded as dictatorial, feudalistic, penurious and backward by Western countries one century ago have by now created in the Taiwan area a new land of democracy, wealth and progress," Lee said. "We believe that whatever is achieved by the Chinese in Taiwan can also be achieved by the Chinese in mainland China." ■

Notes

[1] The account of Lee's inauguration speech is taken from *The New York Times,* May 20, 1996, p. A3, and *The Washington Post,* May 20, 1996, p. A14.

[2] Julian Baum, "The Money Machine," *Far Eastern Economic Review,* Aug. 11, 1994, p. 62.

[3] Council on Foreign Relations, "Managing the Taiwan Issue: Key Is Better U.S. Relations with China — Report of an Independent Task Force," November 1995, pp. 27-29.

[4] See *ibid.,* pp. 32-39.

[5] Republic of China, Ministry of Foreign Affairs, "The Case for Participation of the Republic of China in the United Nations," August 1995.

[6] For background, see "U.S.-China Trade," *The CQ Researcher,* April 15, 1994, pp. 313-336; "U.S. Policy in Asia," *The CQ Researcher,* Nov. 27, 1992, pp. 1025-1048; and "New Era in Asia," *The CQ Researcher,* Feb. 14, 1992, pp. 121-144.

[7] Quoted in Cheng-yi Lin, "Taiwan's Presidential Election and Cross-Strait Relations," paper presented at conference in Washington, D.C., sponsored by Institute for National Policy Research and National Endowment for Democracy, "Presidential Elections and Democratic Consolidation in Taiwan," April 16, 1996.

[8] Early history is drawn from John F. Copper, *Taiwan: Nation-State or Province* (2d. ed., 1996), pp. 1-4, 21-29.

[9] *Ibid.,* pp. 29-32.

[10] Historical discussion from the 1920s on is drawn in part from Nancy Bernkopf Tucker, *Taiwan, Hong Kong, and the United States, 1945-1992: Uncertain Friendships* (1994).

[11] *Ibid.,* p. 28.

[12] Richard M. Nixon, "Asia After Viet Nam," *Foreign Affairs,* October 1967, p. 46, cited in Tucker, *op. cit.,* p. 102.

[13] For the text of the 1972 communique, see Harry Harding, *A Fragile Relationship* (1992), pp. 373-377.

[14] For the text of the joint U.S.-Chinese communique, see Council on Foreign Relations, *op. cit.,* pp. 46-47.

[15] See *1979 Congressional Quarterly Almanac,* pp. 99-117.

[16] Copper, *op. cit.,* p. 139.

[17] *Ibid.,* pp. 121-124.

[18] Tucker, *op. cit.,* p. 117.

[19] Quoted in *The Washington Post,* March 22, 1996, p. A28. The official quoted was Chen Pi-chao, national security adviser to President Lee.

[20] *The Economist,* March 30, 1996, p. 37.

[21] *Sankei Shimbun,* April 17, 1996, p. 1. The interview was briefly referenced in an April 17 dispatch by Reuters from Tokyo.

[22] *The International Herald Tribune,* April 1, 1996.

[23] See *The New York Times,* March 25, 1996, p. A1; March 27, 1996, p. A13. The spokesman was Shen Guo-fang.

[24] Quoted in *USA Today,* March 25, 1996, p. 1A.

[25] *The New York Times,* March 10, 1996, p. E15.

[26] See *Newsweek,* May 20, 1996, p. 38.

Bibliography

Selected Sources Used

Books

Copper, John F., *Taiwan: Nation-State or Province* (2d. ed.), Westview Press, 1996.
Copper, a professor of international studies at Rhodes College in Memphis, Tenn., gives a compact overview of Taiwan's history, society, political and economic systems and foreign and military policies through 1995.

Harding, Harry, *A Fragile Relationship: The United States and China since 1972*, Brookings Institution, 1992.
Harding, formerly a fellow at the Brookings Institution and dean of the Elliott School of International Affairs at George Washington University, provides a thorough overview of U.S-China relations since 1972, including extensive discussion of Taiwan. The book includes detailed source notes and 10 pages of appendices. Harding's other books include *China's Second Revolution: Reform after Mao* (Brookings Institution, 1987).

Mosher, Steven [ed.], *The United States and the Republic of China,* Transaction Publishers, 1992.
The book includes three pairs of articles by six contributors on Taiwan's international status and its economic and strategic relationships with the United States. Mosher was formerly director of the Asian Studies Center at Claremont Institute in Claremont, Calif.

Tucker, Nancy Bernkopf, *Taiwan, Hong Kong, and the United States, 1945-1992: Uncertain Friendships,* Twayne Publishers, 1994.
Tucker, a professor at Georgetown University, provides a thorough and balanced overview of U.S. relations with Taiwan from the 1930s through the early 1990s as well as one chapter discussing U.S. relations with Hong Kong. The book includes an 11-page chronology and a nine-page bibliographic essay.

Shinn, James [ed.], *Weaving the Net: Conditional Engagement with China,* Council on Foreign Relations, 1996.
Shinn, senior fellow for Asia at the Council on Foreign Relations, argues for a policy of conditional engagement aimed at integrating China into the world economy and reducing the risks posed by its rapid military expansion. Six contributors evaluate the policy from specific perspectives.

Welsh, Frank, *A History of Hong Kong,* Harper/Collins, 1993.
Welsh, a British author, details the history of Hong Kong from its "accidental" acquisition by Britain in 1830 through the preparations for its reversion to China in 1997. The book includes a 16-page bibliography.

Wu, Hsin-Hsing, *Bridging the Strait: Taiwan, China, and the Prospects for Reunification,* Oxford University Press, 1994.
Hsin, a Taiwanese scholar, examines the history of relations between the People's Republic of China and the Republic of China and the prospects, admittedly unlikely, for reunification. The book includes a 15-page bibliography of English- and Chinese-language books, articles and newspapers.

Articles

"Special Report: China," *Newsweek,* April 1, 1996, pp. 26-52.
The comprehensive series of articles examines U.S. relations with China and political, legal and cultural developments within China.

Reports and Studies

Chiu, Hungdah, *Chinese Yearbook of International Law and Affairs: Vol. 13* (1994-1995), Chinese Society of International Law/Chinese (Taiwan) Branch of the International Law Association, 1995.
President Lee Teng-hui's speech at Cornell University last summer is reprinted at the opening of the volume, which also includes the proceedings of the Asian-Pacific regional conference of the International Law Association and other scholarly legal articles. The appendixes include listings of bilateral agreements that Taiwan has entered into and countries that officially recognize Taiwan or maintain unofficial relations with it.

Council on Foreign Relations, *Managing the Taiwan Issue: Key Is Better U.S. Relations with China — Report of an Independent Task Force,* 1995.
This 66-page report by a 30-member task force calls for the United States to "strongly caution" Taiwan against a declaration of independence, but also to support Taiwan's membership in some United Nations-related economic organizations. The appendixes include the texts of the Shanghai Communique (1972), the U.S.-China Normalization Agreement (1978), the Taiwan Relations Act (1979) and the U.S.-China agreement on U.S. arms sales to Taiwan (1982).

The Next Step

Additional information from UMI's Newspaper & Periodical Abstracts database

China: Political Developments

Brauchli, Marcus W., "With China's economy cooling, Beijing renews rhetoric on regaining Taiwan," *The Wall Street Journal,* Feb. 3, 1995, p. A8.

With China's inflation-wracked economy slowing after three years of double-digit growth and the country's patriarch, Deng Xiaoping, believed to be in poor health, the government of President Jiang Zemin is aiming to bolster its credibility by making overtures to Taiwan, a move that attempts to attach Jiang's name to one of his government's pillars of legitimacy, nationalism.

Goldstein, Steven M.,"China in transition: The political foundations of incremental reform," *China Quarterly,* December 1995, p. 44.

Goldstein explores the political dimensions of China's transition from a planned economy to a market economy, focusing on the emergence of the "non-state" sector, an essential element in the "gradualist" reform strategy.

Wei Jingsheng, "Bullying won't cow Taiwan," *Denver Post,* March 17, 1996, p. D2.

An excerpt is presented from Chinese dissident Wei Jingsheng's Sept. 30, 1984, memo on Taiwan, regarding China's policy toward Taiwan.

Whiting, Allen S., "Chinese nationalism and foreign policy after Deng," *China Quarterly,* June 1995, pp. 295-316.

The role of nationalism in China is examined. Causal factors that pertain to monitoring the prospective role of assertive or aggressive nationalism in post-Deng China are highlighted.

Hong Kong

Lau, Siu-kai, and Hsin-chi Kuan, "The attentive spectators: Political participation of the Hong Kong Chinese," *Journal of Northeast Asian Studies,* spring 1995, pp. 3-24.

A study delineated the pattern of political participation of the Hong Kong Chinese. Data found that though the overall level of participation remains low, political activism has nonetheless increased since the early 1980s.

Richburg, Keith B., "Hong Kong youth becoming politicized as their first chance to vote nears," *The Washington Post,* Sept. 16, 1995, p. A25.

The politicization of young voters in Hong Kong as the Sept. 17, 1995, elections draw near is analyzed.

Steinberger, Michael, "Hong Kong politician has made himself useful to Beijing," *San Francisco Chronicle,* March 14, 1996, p. A10.

With time running short before the British colony of Hong Kong is returned to China in 1997, influential Hong Kong politicians, including Lo Tak-Shing, are scurrying to reposition themselves for a new and highly uncertain era. Lo has emerged in early 1996 as a leading contender to become the first chief executive of Hong Kong's post-1997 government. The growing ties between Lo and China are discussed.

Tse, Patricia Wen-Sei, "The impact of 1997 on political apathy in Hong Kong," *Political Quarterly,* April 1995, pp. 210-220.

Political apathy on the part of the Hong Kong Chinese from the 1960s through the 90s is discussed. The transfer of sovereignty to China in 1997 may have contradictory effects on political participation.

"Undermining Hong Kong," *The Economist,* March 30, 1996, p. 38.

China's Preparatory Committee, which oversees the transition of Hong Kong from the UK to China, voted on March 24, 1996, to abolish Hong Kong's Legislative Council. An appointed "provisional" legislature will replace the council.

Wilkins, Karin Gwinn, "Gender, news media exposure and political cynicism: Public opinion of Hong Kong's future transition," *International Journal of Public Opinion Research,* fall 1995, pp. 253-269.

The relationship between gender and political cynicism regarding Hong Kong's future transition to Chinese rule was examined. The study found that women are less likely to have faith in the political future of Hong Kong than men.

Jiang Zemin

Higgins, Andrew, "Beijing divided on Taiwan strategy," *Guardian,* Feb. 8, 1996, p. 12.

Chinese President Jiang Zemin and his generals were seriously at odds over what to do about Taiwan, according to a report in Hong Kong on Feb. 7, 1996. A split would be a serious blow to President Jiang, who will need the army's backing to stay in power after the death of Deng Xiaoping.

Zuckerman, Mortimer B., Susan V. Lawrence and Emily MacFarquhar, "The problem is political will," *U.S. News & World Report,* Oct. 23, 1995, p. 72.

In an interview, China's President Jiang Zemin discusses his upcoming visit to the U.S., China's policy toward Taiwan, his leadership, and Deng Xiaoping.

Lee Teng-hui

Brauchli, Marcus W. and Leslie Chang, "Taiwan's president reaches out to China," *The Wall Street Journal*, March 25, 1996, p. A10.
Hoping to turn his March 23, 1996, election victory into bargaining clout with China, President Lee Teng-hui of Taiwan plans to seek talks with the Chinese government aimed at lowering tensions and forging economic links.

"People in the news: President Lee Teng-hui," *News for You*, June 28, 1995, p. 2.
Taiwan's President Lee Teng-hui visited the U.S. this month to attend a reunion at Cornell University in New York, his alma mater. Lee's trip angered China, which declared Chinese-U.S. relations will suffer as a result.

Taiwan: Political Developments

Brauchli, Marcus W. and Leslie Chang, "Taiwan unveils stimulus plan for its economy," *The Wall Street Journal*, Feb. 13, 1996, p. A10.
The Taiwanese government unveiled a sweeping, $8.6 billion fortification package for its economy, aimed primarily at shoring up a stock market whipsawed by warlike rhetoric and military moves by China. The measures got a cool reception from stock-market analysts but were the first clear sign that Taiwan will put its considerable economic muscle to work to protect its economy.

Ku, Samuel C. Y., "The political economy of Taiwan's relations with Southeast Asia: The Southward policy," *Contemporary Southeast Asia*, December 1995, pp. 282-297.
Taiwan's "Southward policy" is aimed at strengthening the country's economic relations with Southeast Asian countries. The government would like to expand economic linkages in exchange for Taiwan's political participation in regional organizations and activities.

"Taiwan's day in the sun," *The Wall Street Journal*, March 25, 1996, p. A14.
An editorial characterizes the election in Taiwan, won by President Lee Teng-hui, as "the culmination of an extraordinary story of human perseverance and political maturation." The editorial asserts that Taiwan is on the right path to democracy and criticizes the "ambiguity" of the U.S.'s policy toward Taiwan and China.

"The power of democracy in Taiwan," *Chicago Tribune*, March 26, 1996, p. 14.
An editorial discusses the failure of China's intimidation tactics, which contributed to the election of Lee Teng-hui as president of Taiwan, and concludes it is time for China to pursue foreign policy goals through diplomacy rather than by military intimidation.

U.S. Policy and China

Atlas, Terry, and William Neikirk, "U.S., China quietly worked to defuse Taiwan crisis," *Chicago Tribune*, March 31, 1996, p. 1.
For months, the U.S. and China have held a series of confidential talks seeking to anticipate the approaching sources of tension regarding Taiwan and to prevent the U.S.-Sino relationship from careening completely off-track. However, President Clinton is concerned China may still respond in a negative way to Taiwan.

"Gambling over Taiwan with wild cards," *San Francisco Chronicle*, March 13, 1996, p. A16.
An editorial urges the Clinton administration to halt its saber rattling toward China over Taiwan in mid-March 1996, and contends that the government should emphasize that the U.S. would react to a forceful reunification attempt by all means short of war, including an end to China's most-favored-nation status.

Halloran, Richard, "Clinton faces huge risks if China attacks Taiwan," *Houston Chronicle*, March 24, 1996, p. A31.
For President Clinton, the billowing conflict with China over the fate of Taiwan has become a far more demanding foreign policy issue than any he has encountered before, with the outcome to determine U.S. security posture in Asia and to affect the security of every Asian nation for decades.

U.S. Policy and Taiwan

Farley, Maggie, "U.S. carrier off Taiwan trails analysts' worries in its wake," *Los Angeles Times*, March 19, 1996, p. A8.
The deployment of the aircraft carrier *U.S.S. Independence* to the area near Taiwan to monitor Chinese war games being performed near the island is discussed. Analysts believe that by doing so, the U.S. has chosen Taiwan's side in the island's long-running conflict with mainland China.

"Taiwan and the U.S. Navy," *Detroit News*, March 26, 1996, p. A6.
An editorial says that America needs to keep a close sense of its own interests in what is likely to remain a volatile situation between China and Taiwan.

"What Taiwan needs more," *The Wall Street Journal*, March 29, 1996, p. A10.
An editorial says that in the wake of recent Chinese military threats and the 1996 presidential election in Taiwan, the latter needs the U.S. to show support while remaining within the confines of its "one-China" policy.

Back Issues

Great Research on Current Issues Starts Right Here...Recent topics covered by The CQ Researcher are listed below. Before May 1991, reports were published under the name of Editorial Research Reports.

NOVEMBER 1994
Sex on Campus
Blood Supply Safety
Testing Term Limits
Religion in America

DECEMBER 1994
Farm Policy
Arms Sales
Earthquake Research
The Future of Television

JANUARY 1995
Treating Addiction
Child Custody and Support
Parents and Schools
Non-Proliferation Treaty at 25

FEBRUARY 1995
Cracking Down on Immigration
The Business of Sports
Reinventing Government
Housing Discrimination

MARCH 1995
Death Penalty Debate
Primary Care
Democracy in Africa
Environmental Movement at 25

Back issues are available for $5.00 (subscribers) or $8.00 (non-subscribers). Quantity discounts apply to orders over ten. To order, call Congressional Quarterly Customer Service at (202) 887-8621.

Binders are available for $18.00. To order call 1-800-638-1710. Please refer to stock number 648.

APRIL 1995
Abortion Clinic Protests
Dieting and Health
Combating AIDS
Rethinking Affirmative Action

MAY 1995
Assisted Suicide Controversy
Overhauling Social Security
Learning to Read
Mandatory Sentencing

JUNE 1995
Combating Infectious Disease
Property Rights
Repetitive Stress Injuries
Regulating the Internet

JULY 1995
War Crimes
Highway Safety
Combating Terrorism
Preventing Teen Drug Use

AUGUST 1995
Job Stress
Organ Transplants
United Nations at 50
Advances in Cancer Research

SEPTEMBER 1995
Catholic Church in the U.S.
Northern Ireland Cease-Fire
High School Sports
Teaching History

OCTOBER 1995
Quebec's Future
Revitalizing the Cities
Networking the Classroom
Indoor Air Pollution

NOVEMBER 1995
The Working Poor
The Jury System
Sex, Violence and the Media
Police Misconduct

DECEMBER 1995
Teens and Tobacco
Gene Therapy's Future
Global Water Shortages
Third-Party Prospects

JANUARY 1996
Emergency Medicine
Punishing Sex Offenders
Bilingual Education
Helping the Homeless

FEBRUARY 1996
Reforming the CIA
Campaign Finance Reform
Academic Politics
Getting Into College

MARCH 1996
The British Monarchy
Preventing Juvenile Crime
Tax Reform
Pursuing the Paranormal

APRIL 1996
Centennial Olympic Games
Managed Care
Protecting Endangered Species
New Military Culture

MAY 1996
Russia's Political Future
Marriage and Divorce
Year-Round Schools

Future Topics

- ***Rethinking NAFTA***
- ***First Ladies***
- ***Teaching Values***

THE CQ Researcher

PUBLISHED BY CONGRESSIONAL QUARTERLY INC.

Rethinking NAFTA

Does the trade pact help or hurt U.S. workers?

The North American Free Trade Agreement (NAFTA) is no longer a decisive issue in the 1996 presidential campaign. But Pat Buchanan's protectionist rhetoric struck a chord with voters worried about job security and stagnant wages. Critics of the free-trade agreement between the United States, Canada and Mexico say it has encouraged U.S. manufacturers to move their operations south of the border to take advantage of Mexico's low wages, flooded the market with defective goods and aggravated environmental problems in the Southwest. Supporters say NAFTA has helped U.S. workers by creating new high-skill, high-wage jobs. The debate may determine the outcome of ongoing negotiations to expand NAFTA to include the rest of the Western Hemisphere by 2005.

INSIDE THIS ISSUE

CQ June 7, 1996 • Volume 6, No. 21 • Pages 481-504

Formerly Editorial Research Reports

RETHINKING NAFTA

COVER: ANTI-NAFTA RALLY AT THE CAPITOL NOV. 15, 1993 (R. MICHAEL JENKINS)

THE *CQ Researcher*

June 7, 1996
Volume 6, No. 21

The CQ Researcher (ISSN 1056-2036). Formerly Editorial Research Reports. Published weekly (48 times per year, not printed March 1, May 31, Aug. 30, Nov. 29) by Congressional Quarterly Inc., 1414 22nd St., N.W., Washington, D.C. 20037. Annual subscription rate for libraries, businesses and government is $319. Additional rates furnished upon request. Second-class postage paid at Washington, D.C. POSTMASTER: Send address changes to The CQ Researcher, 1414 22nd St., N.W., Washington, D.C. 20037.

Rethinking NAFTA

BY MARY H. COOPER

THE ISSUES

Does the North American Free Trade Agreement help or hurt U.S. workers? It depends on who you ask.

Many employees at Whirlpool Corp.'s Evansville, Ind., plant believe NAFTA is costing U.S. workers their jobs. Three months ago, Whirlpool announced it was shutting down the production of small refrigerators in Evansville at the end of May and moving the operation to a joint venture in Mexico. About 260 of the plant's 3,860 workers will lose their jobs. [1]

Company spokeswoman Deborah Castrale says the layoffs have nothing to do with NAFTA. "The joint venture has existed since at least 1985," she says. "It can absorb the production and also improve its productivity."

But Charles Stephens insists that "NAFTA had a big role in [Whirlpool's] decision." Stephens is president of Local 808 of the International Union of Electrical Workers, which represents all the hourly employees at the Evansville plant. "Without [NAFTA] I don't think Whirlpool would have sent our jobs down there," he says. "Whirlpool can go from paying us $13 an hour to paying workers in Mexico 75 cents an hour. Like other corporations, they're acting absolutely un-American."

Employees at American Gentor Corp. in Tulsa, Okla., have a very different view of NAFTA. The company has hired more than 300 new workers in recent years to help keep up with the demand for its energy-related industrial equipment.

"Right now Mexico is our largest market," says spokesman Loring Bugbee. The company manufactures mobile co-generation systems — basically power plants on wheels. "Sales to Mexico dropped last year with the [December 1994] devaluation of the peso,"

Bugbee says, "but they're picking up again now, as are sales to Canada."

That's just what NAFTA supporters hoped would happen to American exports. The agreement, which took effect Jan. 1, 1994, will eliminate all tariffs and most other trade barriers among the United States, Canada and Mexico over 15 years, allowing goods produced anywhere in North America to move freely across a continent with 380 million people and a combined economic output of nearly $8 trillion. [2]

NAFTA grew out of a 1988 free-trade agreement between the United States and Canada, two of the world's most advanced industrial nations. Bringing Mexico in on the deal was controversial from the start. Unlike its partners, Mexico is a developing country, with widespread poverty, low wages and limited control over worker safety, product quality and environmental protection.

Nevertheless, free traders predicted that Mexico's thirst for American technical and industrial products would spawn new industries in the United States and boost employment in high-wage enterprises like American Gentor in Tulsa. NAFTA's critics, on the other hand, forecast a future of factory closures and job losses, as U.S. manufacturers fled south in search of cheap labor.

The debate reached an emotional climax during the 1992 presidential campaign. Independent candidate Ross Perot repeatedly warned voters that NAFTA's approval would be followed by a "big sucking sound," as American jobs were swept into Mexico's low-wage economy. President George Bush made NAFTA's passage a cornerstone of his re-election bid. Candidate Bill Clinton endorsed NAFTA during the final weeks of the campaign, but said he would seek tougher protections for U.S. workers and the environment. A year later, President Clinton would place his prestige on the line in persuading a bitterly divided Congress to pass legislation implementing the trade agreement, which had been signed by President Bush on Dec. 17, 1992 (*see p. 492*).

The NAFTA issue cropped up again during this year's presidential campaign. Conservative commentator Patrick J. Buchanan rode the anti-NAFTA bandwagon to victory in the New Hampshire primary and several early state caucuses. "There are losers in these trade deals," Buchanan said at a Feb. 28 campaign stop at a closed textile plant in Clearwater, S.C. "The vast majority of middle Americans are seeing their standard of living going down. . . . Someone has to speak up." [3]

Advocates of free trade say Buchanan's analysis of NAFTA's impact is simplistic. Gary Clyde Hufbauer, a trade expert at the Institute for International Economics dismisses as "complete hogwash" Buchanan's oft-repeated claim that the U.S. lost 300,000 jobs last year because of NAFTA.

According to one commonly used rule of thumb, 15,000 jobs are lost for every $1 billion increase in the trade deficit. Last year, the U.S. had a $15 billion trade

Trade in the Western Hemisphere

Negotiations are now under way to expand NAFTA to include all the countries of Central and South America except Cuba in a "Free Trade Area of the Americas" by the year 2005. Nearly 40 percent of U.S. exports, valued at $223 billion, already are shipped to countries in the Western Hemisphere. By comparison, only $180 billion of U.S. goods are sold in Japan and other countries of the Pacific Rim; $124 billion in U.S. exports go to the 15-member European Union.

Source: U.S. Department of Commerce

deficit with Mexico (*see below*).

"Even if you say that 225,000 people were impacted since NAFTA took effect, what is lost in the debate are all the trade relationships we have with other countries," Hufbauer says. "All that gets forgotten when you just look at one country. I've come to the conclusion that because all these qualifications get lost in the debate, it's better not to talk about the job impact at all."

Indeed, trade statistics paint a far more complex picture than NAFTA critics portray. In 1994, the first year NAFTA went into effect, exports and imports boomed. U.S. exports to Mexico — America's third largest trading partner after Canada and Japan — rose by 22 percent that year, to $50.8 billion, while imports from Mexico rose more than 23 percent, to $49.5 billion, resulting in a small trade surplus for the United States.

Problems arose in late 1994, however, when the Mexican government was forced to devalue its currency, the peso. The crisis occurred when foreign investors began to withdraw their funds. The investors were concerned about increasing political violence in Mexico and the government's heavy reliance on foreign loans. With the support of the Republican leadership in Congress, President Clinton extended a $20 billion credit line to Mexico as part of a $49 billion international bailout.

Despite the financial rescue, the peso devaluation skewed trade flows between the two countries. Facing a depressed economy and high unemployment, Mexican consumers were not able to buy as many imported goods, and U.S. exports to Mexico plummeted. U.S. consumers, on the other hand, benefited from the falling prices of Mexican imports, and exports to the U.S. shot up. By the end of 1995, the $1.3 billion trade surplus the United States enjoyed with Mexico in 1994 had turned into a $15.4 billion deficit.

The growing trade deficit helped fuel anti-NAFTA fever in the U.S., including attacks on the Clinton administration for bailing out Mexico. "Guess who's on the hook now for the $50 billion [bailout]?" Buchanan asked an enthusiastic crowd in Memphis, Tenn., last March. "The American people and the American nation. . . . Next time they default, they'll just slide that right on over the national debt of the United States. That's how you bankrupt a great country like America, my friends." [4]

The Clinton administration sees the peso crisis in an entirely different light. "From our point of view, if anything the balance of payments crisis in Mexico has really proved the worth of NAFTA," says a U.S. trade official who asked not to be identified because he is involved in ongoing negotiations. "Part of the U.S. motivation in NAFTA all along was to support the process of economic reform in Mexico. With a healthy Mexican economy, we would have less undocumented immigration and we would have a more profitable country to trade with."

Other advocates of free trade say that NAFTA simply doesn't have the potential to dramatically affect the U.S. economy one way or the other. "We have to remember that the whole Mexican economy is very small compared with the U.S. economy," says Clyde V. Prestowitz Jr., head of the Economic Strategy Institute and a trade official during the Reagan administration. "So the impact of NAFTA on the United States was always going to be relatively small, just because of the fact that the two economies are so very much different in scale."

Almost lost in the NAFTA debate is the third party to the agreement, Canada. The U.S. and Canada enjoy the world's largest two-way trading relationship, totaling some $1 billion a day. The United States actually has a bigger trade deficit with its neighbor to the north — $18 billion last year — than with Mexico. And NAFTA has not resolved longstanding trade disputes with Canada, notably American allegations that Canada unfairly subsidizes its softwood, dairy and wheat industries. [5]

But it's the fear of jobs moving to Mexico that energizes anti-NAFTA forces. "There is much more attention given to Mexico [than to Canada] because that's where we perceive a lot more companies are moving their operations," says Mark Anderson, director of trade affairs for the AFL-CIO.

The controversy over NAFTA has made strange political bedfellows, uniting labor leaders like Anderson and consumer advocate Ralph Nader with conservative politicians like Buchanan and Perot. But, Anderson emphasizes, opposition to NAFTA is one of the few things they have in common.

"If I listen to Pat Buchanan for five minutes, the first three minutes he spends plagiarizing me," Anderson says. "Then the next two minutes are filled with this awful nativist, isolationist approach, which isn't us at all. Our opponents want to paint us with the same brush as Buchanan and Perot," he continues, "but we're interested in a more positive engagement with a focus on worker rights and labor standards, something that's not high on Mr. Buchanan's list of priorities."

Now that Bob Dole, the outgoing Senate Majority Leader and a NAFTA supporter, has secured the Republican presidential nomination, the trade pact is unlikely to be a major issue in the presidential campaign. (*See story, p. 494.*) But the issue won't go away. Negotiations are now under way to expand NAFTA to include the countries of Central and South America in a "Free Trade Area of the Americas" that would cover the entire Western Hemisphere except Cuba by 2005.

"How much they get done in the next presidential term is the big question," says Hufbauer. "In 1997, the most I see happening is Chile [joining NAFTA] and maybe in 1998 the Caribbean countries may come into the free-trade area. But I don't see the Free Trade Area of the Americas coming into place in a big way for several years."

As the negotiations proceed, these are some of the issues that will come under scrutiny:

Has the United States lost jobs as a result of NAFTA?

During the debates over NAFTA in 1992 and '93, free-trade advocates convinced a skeptical Congress that removing trade barriers with Mexico would spur demand for superior U.S. technology and equipment south of the border. This, they said, would revitalize flagging U.S. industries and create new high-skill, high-wage jobs.

In one widely publicized analysis at the time, Hufbauer of the Institute for International Economics predicted that NAFTA would result in a net gain of some 170,000 jobs in the United States by 1995. [6] Hufbauer came up with that figure using the standard formula of the time, which estimated that every billion dollars worth of net exports creates 19,000 new jobs in the U.S. economy. (The number of jobs affected by trade is now often estimated to be around 15,000.)

Hufbauer's prediction fell flat with the peso's devaluation in late 1994. Mexican demand for American products plummeted, and the U.S. trade surplus with Mexico turned into a $15.4 billion deficit.

As the trade deficit grew, NAFTA's critics flipped the old exports-into-jobs formula to make the case that NAFTA was responsible for the loss of U.S. jobs. "[N]ot only did NAFTA fail to create U.S. jobs, it lost them," Sen. Byron L. Dorgan, D-N.D., wrote recently. "Increased trade deficits with our NAFTA trading partners (Mexico and Canada) have so far

Balance of Trade

The small trade surplus the United States enjoyed with Mexico in the early 1990s had turned into a $15.4 billion deficit by the end of 1995. The U.S. had an even larger trade deficit with its neighbor to the north last year. The U.S. trade deficit with Canada has tripled in the past four years.

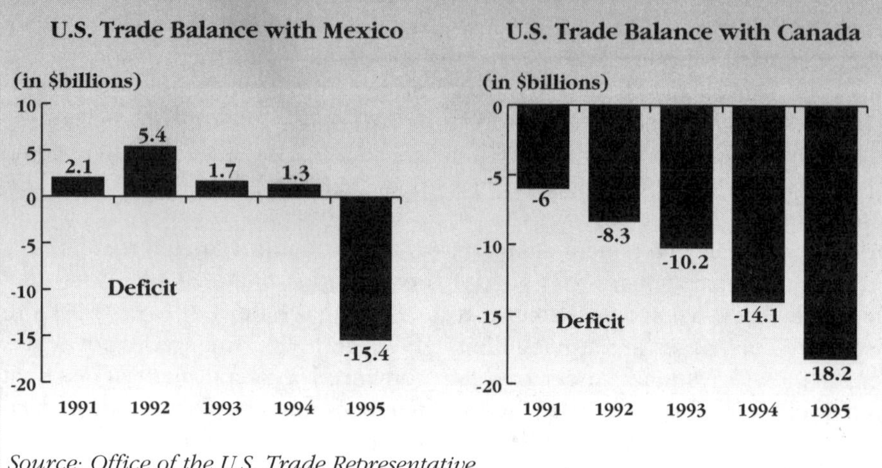

Source: Office of the U.S. Trade Representative

cost the United States 377,000 jobs — approximately the number of new U.S. jobs its backers promised NAFTA would create." [7]

The notion that imports or trade deficits cost jobs is "ridiculous," says the U.S. trade official. "Some imports do not displace jobs, including the petroleum we import from Mexico," he says. " The reason the U.S. trade deficit has gotten bigger in the last three years is because the United States has been growing faster than anybody else and adding jobs faster than anybody else. We added 1.75 million jobs in 1995, we've added 8.4 million jobs in the last three years into the first couple of months of 1996. I just don't know what the evidence is of U.S. job losses."

Hufbauer also believes NAFTA's impact on U.S. employment has been slight. "When we published the [170,000 job-gain estimate] in 1993, we thought the whole purpose of the calculation was to show how small this number was in terms of the overall U.S. job market," he says. "Instead, it got touted in the NAFTA debate as a very large number. But in an economy such as ours, which has 120 million jobs with a job turnover in any given year of 2 million people, this really is statistically not large; in fact, it's very small."

Hufbauer points to the relatively small number of people who have received benefits from a special fund established to help American workers who lose their jobs as a result of NAFTA.* This, he says, is proof that free trade with Mexico has been far less harmful than even he had predicted.

"If you take the total number of people who have been certified for NAFTA benefits — and there are about 50,000 since the agreement went into effect — it's much more favorable than we expected," Hufbauer says. "For any one person who's lost his job, of course, that's a big number. But in the overall U.S. economy, it's quite small."

The U.S. trade official predicts that NAFTA, by stimulating Mexico's export industries, will reduce the number of illegal immigrants coming to the United States. "It's not the attraction of high incomes in the U.S. that brings undocumented workers from Mexico," he says. "It's the absolute lack of any opportunity at home. The policies in Mexico that expand job opportunities for Mexicans to earn a decent wage are also the best policies for reducing undocumented immigration into the United States."

Such arguments do not persuade labor representatives, who blame American corporate executives for U.S. job losses. "If we were trading Corona Beer for Ben & Jerry's Ice Cream, NAFTA would probably be a good deal, but that's not what this is about," says Anderson of the AFL-CIO. "It's more about General Motors trading with General Motors, or AT&T trading with AT&T. It's about American companies moving parts and assembly production from the United States to Mexico."

In Anderson's view, NAFTA merely legitimizes the practice of outsourcing production to the *maquiladora* factories that have been allowed to operate just across the border for the past 30 years. Under the *maquiladora* program, duty-free imports of components are allowed into Mexico, where they are assembled into finished products and exported. If exported to the United States, which the vast majority are, these products are assessed for duty only on the value added in Mexico. [8]

Anderson estimates that top wages in auto assembly plants in Mexico are around $1.25 an hour, compared with around $17 an hour in a union plant in the United States. "GM does not set up a parts production facility in Matamoros, Mexico, because the weather is pleasant," he says. "They

*The NAFTA implementation bill approved by Congress in November 1993 established a temporary program to provide income payments and retraining to workers who lost their jobs as a result of NAFTA. Workers were to be eligible for benefits if a significant number in a company or a division of a company were laid off or threatened with layoffs due to imports from Mexico or Canada. The secretary of Labor was required to make a preliminary determination of eligibility within 30 days of receiving a petition from a group of workers. See *1993 CQ Almanac*, p. 175.

set it up for one reason and one reason alone, and that is their ability to take advantage of the poverty of the Mexican worker."

Are consumers better off as a result of NAFTA?

In theory, consumers in countries that lower tariffs benefit as long as the reductions are passed on to them in the form of lower retail prices. Under those conditions, an imported doll that sells for $10 when a 10 percent tariff is in place would sell for just $9 if the tariff were removed.

In the case of NAFTA, however, American consumers probably have noticed little benefit from tariff reductions. One reason, says the U.S. trade official, is that "Even before NAFTA, we had very few barriers against Mexican imports. Our base average tariffs on imports from Mexico [at the time] was 4 percent."

U.S. participation in the World Trade Organization (WTO) further diluted NAFTA's benefits to American consumers. Created Jan. 1, 1995, as a result of the seven-year Uruguay Round of international trade negotiations, the WTO required the United States to immediately cut its tariffs on Mexican imports by a third. "So we're talking about a 2.5 percent tariff, which will be gradually reduced to zero over roughly eight years," the trade official says. "In effect, we had very little protection to give up."

NAFTA advocates insist that Mexico's inclusion in the free-trade area has helped American consumers, especially at the grocery checkout counter. "Probably more Mexican products are in our market now, and that certainly gives consumers wider choice," says Doreen L. Brown, president of Consumers for World Trade, a pro-trade consumer advocacy group. "The competition in citrus fruits and vegetables that are out of season in the United States helps keep prices down and food quality up. It also allows American consumers to have access to food products year round instead of just seasonal food products."

American consumers also are finding that Mexican-made toys and textiles have become more plentiful and less expensive, Brown says. "Although Mexican toys were coming in duty-free even before NAFTA, probably more toys are coming in now," she says. "In this case, it's the quantity that's keeping prices down. For the same reason, some textiles also are more reasonable."

Most analysts agree that Mexican consumers had much more to gain from NAFTA than American consumers. "Mexico had 10 percent tariffs, as well as significant non-tariff [trade] barriers," the U.S. official says. "They were in many ways a much more closed market than the United States." The peso's sudden devaluation in December 1994, however, quashed NAFTA's benefits to Mexican consumers by making U.S. goods more expensive at the same time they were facing a severe economic crisis at home.

Still, Brown says Mexican consumers are better off with NAFTA than they would have been without it. "When NAFTA came into being, they were able to reap some benefits right away," she says. "You could also argue that even with their economic crisis, they are better off with the competition of American goods, which has to a degree kept consumer prices low. Mexicans' inability to purchase would be even worse without NAFTA."

By depressing the prices of Mexican-made goods, Mexico's balance-of-payments crisis may have done more to help American consumers than NAFTA itself, says Prestowitz of the Economic Strategy Institute. "Because of the collapse of the Mexican peso, our imports from Mexico have risen dramatically," he says. But American consumers may not be seeing the benefits in their wallets, Prestowitz adds.

Automobiles, for example, top the list of Mexican imports. (*See chart, p. 488.*) These imports were worth nearly $6 billion last year. But Mexican-made cars are much less noticeable to U.S. consumers than the Japanese Toyotas and Hondas that flooded the U.S. market in the late 1970s. For one thing, the cars bear familiar U.S. nameplates.

"Cars are the biggest category [of imports] because Ford Motor Co., in particular, is importing cars from its big plant in Hermosillo," Prestowitz says. Another reason U.S. consumers may not notice the presence of Mexican-made cars is that they account for a very small segment of the U.S. auto market. "Cars are big-ticket items," Prestowitz says. "You don't have to import a lot of cars to get the value up pretty high."

Most other auto-related imports from Mexico are invisible to the buyer. "Much of what we import from Mexico is not something that goes directly to the consumer, but rather intermediary products like auto engines and wire harnesses, the assemblies that contain all the switches and electronic components in a car's dashboard," Prestowitz says. For these reasons, he concludes, "It's very hard to measure the impact of NAFTA on consumers in this country."

Labor representatives look at the paucity of evidence of consumer benefits as proof that corporate interests have pocketed the gains. "Probably what has happened is that the companies that produce in a lower-cost setting — and that's largely in Mexico, but in some respects it's also Canada — are taking those lower costs in the form of higher profits and higher executive salaries," says Anderson of the AFL-CIO. "They buy a new executive jet or put gold-plated faucets in the executive washroom."

"One of the biggest trading relationships with both Canada and Mexico, and one that's grown a lot with Mexico, is the trade in autos and auto parts," he continues. "Just ask yourself this ques-

North American Trade: The Top Imports and Exports

Automobiles and auto parts and accessories dominated U.S. trade with Canada and Mexico in 1995, topping the lists of leading imports and exports.

Top 10 U.S. Imports from Canada

	$Billions
Cars and other passenger vehicles	$24.9
Paper and paperboard	$8.0
Motor vehicles for transporting goods and special purpose vehicles	$6.6
Motor vehicle parts and accessories	$6.5
Crude oil from petroleum or bituminous minerals	$6.1
Simply worked wood and wooden railway sleepers	$5.2
Aluminum	$3.4
Natural gas	$3.2
Pulp and waste paper	$3.2
Parts for office machines and automatic data processing machines	$3.0

Top 10 U.S. Imports from Mexico

	$Billions
Cars and other passenger vehicles	$5.8
Crude oil from petroleum or bituminous minerals	$5.4
Equipment for distributing electricity	$3.3
Telecommunications equipment	$2.6
Television receivers	$2.5
Motor vehicle parts and accessories	$2.4
Internal combustion piston engines and parts	$1.9
Electrical apparatus for switching or protecting electrical circuits	$1.8
Motor vehicles for transporting goods and special purpose vehicles	$1.7
Electrical machinery and equipment	$1.5

Top 10 U.S. Exports to Canada

	$Billions
Motor vehicle parts and accessories	$13.4
Cars and other passenger vehicles	$7.6
Thermionic, cold cathode and photocathode valves	$5.6
Internal combustion piston engines and parts	$4.6
Automatic data processing machines and units	$4.5
Motor vehicles for transporting goods and special purpose vehicles	$3.0
Electrical machinery and apparatus	$2.3
Measuring/checking/analysing and control intruments and apparatus	$2.3
Telecommunications equipment	$2.3
Electrical apparatus for switching or protecting electrical circuits	$2.3

Top 10 U.S. Exports to Mexico

	$Billions
Motor vehicle parts and accessories	$3.4
Thermionic, cold cathode and photocathode valves	$2.6
Electrical apparatus for switching and protecting electrical circuits	$2.0
Electrical machinery and equipment	$1.5
Equipment for distributing electricity	$1.4
Telecommunications equipment	$1.4
Manufactures of base metals	$1.2
Articles of plastic	$1.1
Internal combustion piston engines and parts	$0.97
Parts for office machines and automatic data processing machines	$0.84

Source: Commerce Department

tion. Has anybody seen the price of cars go down lately?"

Should the United States renegotiate the terms of NAFTA?

Anti-NAFTA politicians such as Pat Buchanan say the only way to repair the damage done by the agreement is to scrap it altogether and refrain from helping Mexico overcome any future financial difficulties it may encounter on the path to industrialization. "When I get [to the White House], there will be no more NAFTA," Buchanan promised at a March 5 rally in Buffalo, N.Y. "And there will be no more $50 billion bailouts of socialist regimes anywhere on Earth."

Buchanan is not the only politician or aspirant to public office to sound the retreat on free-trade agreements. "We must disenthrall ourselves from the idea that 'protectionism' is evil," Sen. Ernest F. Hollings, D-S.C., the ranking minority member of the Senate Commerce Committee, said earlier this year. In Hollings' view, tariffs are a valuable tool for protecting U.S. jobs. "The fundamental duty of government is to protect," he wrote. [9]

But the political momentum in Washington appears to be heading in the opposite direction. Rather than withdrawing from NAFTA or renegotiating its terms, the Clinton administration is backing an effort to expand the agreement to include Chile, arguably South America's healthiest economy (*see p. 498*). Talks also are under way with the other governments of Central and South America to create a Free Trade Agreement of the Americas, encompassing the entire Western Hemisphere except Cuba by 2005.

While free-trade critics argue their case in the name of protecting American jobs, supporters of extending NAFTA do so in the name of improving the U.S. job market. "Enlargement [of NAFTA] has never been about increasing [the number of] jobs," says Hufbauer. "It's about better jobs. The difference may be subtle, but we know that export jobs pay better."

Hufbauer estimates that firms producing goods primarily for export pay wages that are roughly 15 percent higher than those paid by companies that focus on the domestic market. "Almost by definition, those firms are going to be growing because exports have been growing by about 15 percent a year, whereas the domestic market has been growing at about 6 percent a year," he says. "So it's the 'better jobs' argument, not the 'more jobs' argument, that is a valid reason [for Americans] to support an expansion of NAFTA."

NAFTA FINALLY PAYS OFF

The "RALL" cartoon by Ted Rall is reprinted by permission of Chronicle Features, San Francisco, Calif.

Labor representatives do not rule out new trade agreements but say they must wait until after NAFTA is renegotiated to better protect workers' rights here and abroad. "I don't see any great groundswell to scrap NAFTA," says Anderson. "And even if it were scrapped, that wouldn't change the real fundamentals of our relationship with Mexico."

A better solution, Anderson says, would be to tighten the terms of two side agreements, or amendments, to NAFTA that the Clinton administration negotiated with Mexico in 1993 (*see p. 493*). "We want very hard-and-fast protections for workers' rights and labor standards, as well as stronger measures on environmental protection, beyond what exists in the side agreements," Anderson says.

Prestowitz warns advocates of NAFTA's expansion to be cautious. "It's very early to judge whether NAFTA will work or not," he says. "For that reason it's hard to say that you should scrap it, but it's equally hard to support rushing headlong into expanding it."

The main reason for exercising caution, Prestowitz says, lies in the political uncertainties inherent in dealing with any foreign government. "When NAFTA was being negotiated there was the prevalent view in the United States that [then-President Carlos] Salinas [de Gortari] and his technocrats were straight, honest, hard-working reformers who were bringing Mexico in the direction of open markets and liberal democracy and that NAFTA would be not only a means of stimulating trade and economic growth, but also a means of encouraging liberalization and political reform in Mexico and cementing a better long-term relationship between the United States and Mexico. It's obvious in retrospect that some of those assumptions were wrong and that the political situation in Mexico was much more corrupt and much more opaque than we thought."

Indeed, the victor in Mexico's August 1994 presidential elections was Ernesto Zedillo, who campaigned on a platform of political and economic reform. [10]

In negotiating NAFTA's expansion, Prestowitz suggests, the United States should follow the example of the European Union, which insisted that Greece, Portugal and Spain adopt democratic systems of government before joining the economic area in the 1970s. "With Mexico, we did it the other way around," he says. "As we look down the road, I think we ought to learn from the European example and recognize the importance of the political situation in other countries and attempt to deal with it in any negotiations that we have."

Some lawmakers say NAFTA's track record is so bad that plans to expand it should be abandoned unless the agreement is drastically modified. Citing the U.S. trade deficits with Canada and Mexico, Rep. Marcy Kaptur, D-Ohio, told a House subcommittee that the agreement has destroyed jobs and depressed wages in the United States and made it easier for drugs and illegal immigrants to flow across borders.

"NAFTA has proven in its initial two years to be an economic disaster for the U.S., Mexico and Canada," she said. "In a very real sense, NAFTA has also become a national security threat. Therefore, to the question, 'Should NAFTA be expanded to Chile and other Latin American countries?' my answer is an emphatic no. NAFTA should be taken back to the drawing board to be fixed before the expansion of NAFTA is contemplated." [11]

One of the most outspoken congressional critics of NAFTA is Rep. Peter A. DeFazio, D-Ore. He told a House subcommittee last year that he adamantly opposes expansion. (*See "At Issue," p. 497.*) "The Roman statesman Cicero once said, 'Any man can make mistakes, but only an idiot persists in his error,'" DeFazio said. "NAFTA has been worse than a mistake; it has been a dismal failure by any and every measure. To even begin to consider repeating this failure by expanding this turkey is nothing short of idiocy." [12] ■

BACKGROUND

Free Trade Takes Hold

Free trade is a relatively recent goal of U.S. foreign policy. For the first two centuries of its history, in fact, the U.S. government shielded its developing industries from European competition with a high wall of protective tariffs. It was not until after Congress passed the 1930 Tariff Act — better known as the Smoot-Hawley Act — that questions were raised about the viability of "protectionism' as a policy option. [13]

Passed in the wake of the 1929 stock market crash that unleashed the Great Depression, Smoot-Hawley increased tariffs on more than 20,000 imports. Its backers were trying to shore up the country's failing industries and slow the rapidly growing unemployment rate. But the Depression quickly spread to America's European trading partners, which retaliated against the U.S. tariffs with tariff increases of their own. As world trade ground nearly to a halt, the industrial nations realized that the tariff war was merely aggravating an already desperate economic situation. They officially declared a tariff truce in 1933.

Another turnabout in American trade policy was inaugurated with the Reciprocal Trade Agreements Act of 1934. That law authorized the president to negotiate and implement tariff-reducing trade agreements with other countries, subject to congressional review every three years. By 1945, the U.S. had signed 32 agreements with 27 countries, thereby reducing tariffs on more than half of its imports.

After World War II, the United States took the lead in trying to establish a broader approach to tariff reduction and trade liberalization. It was largely due to American initiative that 23 countries signed the General Agreement on Tariffs and Trade (GATT) in 1947.

Before the oil shocks of the mid-1970s, postwar international trade had grown about 7 percent a year, thanks in part to the removal of barriers under the various GATT negotiations. The undisputed winner in this situation was the United States, which claimed in the economic boom years of the 1950s and '60s about one-fourth of the world market in manufactured goods, and 95 percent of all domestic sales of automobiles, steel and consumer electronics in 1960.

Growing competition from Japanese and European industries in the 1970s gave rise to periodic outbursts of protectionist sentiment in the U.S., but for most of the decade, tariff reduction had widespread bipartisan support.

The Trade Act of 1974 gave the president additional authority to negotiate the reduction of non-tariff trade barriers, such as product standards that American goods could not meet. The 1974 law also barred amendments to trade pacts submitted by the president, putting them on a "fast track" to congressional action within 90 days.

By 1975, U.S. tariffs had fallen from 32 percent to 8 percent, while tariffs in the industrial countries as a whole fell to an average of 11 percent. As tariffs became less of an issue, U.S. trade laws increasingly focused on non-tariff barriers such as unfair product standards, subsidies and import licensing procedures.

These issues were embodied in the 1988 Omnibus Trade and Competitiveness Act, the most sweeping overhaul of U.S. trade law since Smoot-Hawley. The law extended fast-track authority to cover the Uruguay Round of GATT negotiations; beefed up Section 301 of the Trade Act of 1974, which was aimed at unjustifiable and unreasonable foreign trade practices; and transferred power to investigate and retaliate against unfair trade practices from the president to the U.S. trade representative.

Canadian Trade Pact

In 1985, the Reagan administration signed an unprecedented free-trade agreement with Israel. For the first time, the U.S. agreed to remove all tariffs on trade with another country.

Three years later, the U.S. signed a similar agreement with its leading trading partner, Canada. The 1988 U.S.-Canada Free Trade Agreement (FTA), which took effect Jan. 1, 1989, called for the gradual elimination of all tariffs between the two countries over 10 years. The pact also established a binational commission to adjudicate trade disputes between the two countries.

The U.S.-Canadian agreement might have had more of an effect on both sides of the border if the two countries had not excluded certain important areas from the agreement and put off dealing with others. The agreement, for example, while including services under its provisions, exempted certain critical sectors, including transportation, telecommunications, medical and legal services and "cultural industries" such as film, television and publishing. Each country also retained the ability to impose anti-dumping sanctions against goods exported at below-market prices. [14]

Despite its shortcomings, the FTA greatly increased the flow of trade across the U.S.-Canadian border. Despite slow economic growth in Canada in the early 1990s, U.S. exports to Canada had grown by 50 percent by 1994. Most tariffs had been eliminated by then, years ahead of

Continued on p. 492

Chronology

1930s ***The United States and other major trading countries erect steep tariff barriers to protect their domestic industries during the Great Depression.***

1930
Congress passes the Tariff Act, better known as the Smoot-Hawley Act, raising tariffs on more than 20,000 imports. America's major trading partners retaliate with tariffs of the own.

1933
Following a debilitating trade war, the U.S. and its trading partners agree to reduce many tariffs.

1934
Congress passes the Reciprocal Trade Agreements Act, which authorizes the president to negotiate and implement tariff-reducing agreements with other countries, subject to periodic congressional review.

—— • ——

1970s ***International trade accounts for a growing share of U.S. economic growth; opposition to protectionist trade policies mounts.***

1974
Congress passes the Trade Act, which introduces a "fast-track" legislative procedure that bars lawmakers from amending trade agreements and requires them to act on them within 90 days.

—— • ——

1980s ***The rapid expansion of world trade spurs agreements to remove trade barriers.***

1985
President Ronald Reagan signs a free-trade agreement with Israel.

1988
The Omnibus Trade and Competitiveness Act extends fast-track authority to the Uruguay Round — negotiations on world trade carried out under the General Agreement on Tariffs and Trade (GATT).

Jan. 1, 1989
The 1988 U.S.-Canadian Free Trade Agreement (FTA) takes effect. It calls for the gradual elimination of tariffs between the two countries by 1999.

—— • ——

1990s ***Regional trade blocs expand.***

1992
The North American Free Trade Agreement (NAFTA) becomes an issue in the presidential election campaign. Ross Perot warns Americans that NAFTA would encourage U.S. businesses to shift production to Mexico and cause widespread unemployment in the United States.

Aug. 12, 1992
President George Bush announces that Mexico, Canada and the U.S. have reached preliminary agreement on the details of the trade pact.

Oct. 7, 1992
Negotiators from the U.S., Mexico and Canada initial a final text of NAFTA at a ceremony in San Antonio, Texas.

Dec. 17, 1992
President Bush, Mexican President Carlos Salinas de Gortari and Canadian Prime Minister Brian Mulroney sign the NAFTA agreement at separate ceremonies in the three countries. Bush leaves the job of getting the agreement through Congress to his successor, Bill Clinton.

November 1993
After months of acrimonious debate, Congress passes a measure to approve and implement NAFTA. President Clinton signs the measure on Dec. 8.

Jan. 1, 1994
NAFTA takes effect.

December 1994
Representatives of 34 countries of the Western Hemisphere meet in Miami for the Summit of the Americas and agree to create a Free Trade Area of the Americas by 2005.

Jan. 1, 1995
After seven years of negotiations in GATT's Uruguay Round, the World Trade Organization is set up to oversee international trade and implement trade agreements.

1995
Following a devaluation of the Mexican peso, the United States agrees to help stabilize the currency with a $20 billion credit line. Mexico's ability to import U.S. goods falls. The $1.3 billion trade surplus the U.S. had with Mexico in 1994 turns into a $15.4 billion deficit.

January and February 1996
NAFTA becomes an issue in the presidential election campaign. Patrick J. Buchanan tells voters that NAFTA is to blame for job losses in the U.S. and promises to scrap the agreement if he is elected president. NAFTA wanes as political issue as Buchanan's campaign falters.

Continued from p. 490

schedule. From Jan. 1, 1992, to Dec. 31, 1995, total U.S.-Canadian imports and exports grew from $188 billion to more than $271 billion.

Many Canadians feared that a free-trade agreement with the United States would amount to economic suicide. Canada's tariffs at the time were about twice as high as those in the U.S., averaging 9-10 percent compared with 4-5 percent in the U.S. Canadians worried that removing the tariffs would leave their country's industries vulnerable to larger U.S. competitors. Outweighing those fears, however, was the promise that Canadian exporters would gain access to a market 10 times the size of their domestic market.

That bet appears to have paid off. Between Jan. 1, 1992, and Dec. 31, 1993, Canada's exports to the United States grew by 37 percent. Canadian exports to the rest of the world grew by just 6 percent over this two-year period. [15] Canadian exports to the U.S. grew by 16 percent in 1994 and 12 percent in 1995.

NAFTA Negotiations

In early 1990, Mexican President Carlos Salinas de Gortari broached the idea of a U.S. Mexican free-trade agreement with President Bush. Bush's initial response was cool. But he changed his mind, partly because of pressure from his home state of Texas, where the idea was popular. [16] In September, he notified Congress that the administration would begin negotiations with Mexico. On Feb. 5, 1991, he announced that Canada would join in.

In Congress, the idea met with little immediate opposition. In fact, Congress had inserted authority for the president to negotiate with Mexico into the omnibus trade bill enacted in 1988. Opposition gradually mounted, however, particularly from organized labor, which feared it would mean the loss of U.S. jobs, and from environmentalists, who feared that Mexico's pollution problems would spread to the U.S. [17]

Reuters

Former Presidents Gerald R. Ford, Jimmy Carter and George Bush joined President Clinton at the signing ceremony for NAFTA's side agreements on Sept. 14, 1993.

After several months of acrimonious debate, Congress voted in May 1991 to authorize fast-track negotiations between the U.S. and Mexico. This gave the administration the authority to negotiate a trade pact on the understanding that Congress would have 90 days to act once an agreement was submitted and that the final document would be voted up or down without amendments.

On Aug. 12, 1992, President Bush announced that Mexico, Canada and the U.S. had reached preliminary agreement on the details of the trade pact. Two months later, negotiators from the three countries initialed a final text of the agreement at a ceremony in San Antonio, Texas. On Dec. 17, President Bush, President Salinas and Canadian Prime Minister Brian Mulroney signed the agreement at separate ceremonies in the three countries. Bush left the job of getting the agreement through Congress to his successor, Bill Clinton.

Clinton had endorsed the pact during the campaign, but he also vowed to negotiate side agreements to ensure enforcement of labor and environmental laws. The three countries finally agreed to sign supplemental accords covering these areas, but they failed to satisfy NAFTA's critics, including many Democratic members of Congress. By the time Clinton was ready to seek congressional approval, the pact seemed doomed. Populist politicians as diverse as Ross Perot and Jesse Jackson were stumping the country, warning voters that NAFTA threatened the security of U.S. workers and their families.

In the end, the prize was too good to vote down. The measure putting NAFTA into effect passed the House on Nov. 17, 1993, by a comfortable 234-200 vote. Three days later, it cleared the Senate on a vote of 61-38. President Clinton signed the measure on Dec. 8.

NAFTA's Provisions

The tripartite trade agreement provided for eliminating all tariffs between the U.S., Canada and Mexico and for dropping most other trade barriers. Some of the tariffs were to be eliminated immediately, but most were to be phased out gradually over 10 years. Other tariffs would be eliminated in five years and a few in 15 years. [18]

The pact barred governments from imposing special requirements on foreign investors, such as requiring a U.S. company located in Mexico to buy from a local parts supplier or make a product that had a certain amount of Mexican content. Existing restrictions of this sort were to be phased out.

NAFTA did not specifically bar nationalization of a business or an investment in Mexico, but it set guidelines, such as requiring immediate compensation at fair market value. And unlike the U.S.-Canadian agreement, NAFTA allowed foreign investors targeted for government takeover to seek monetary damages through binding international arbitration rather than through the host country's court system. This was an important victory for U.S. businesses, which had concerns about corruption in the Mexican court system.

NAFTA included rules designed to prevent countries outside the pact from using a NAFTA country as a so-called export platform from which products could be assembled and sold in North America, taking advantage of the open market. In general, goods assembled from parts or components from outside the NAFTA region would qualify for low tariff treatment only if the end product was different enough to require a change in tariff classification. That meant, for example, that wood molding manufactured in North America from imported Indonesian logs would be deemed a North American product and thus could be moved duty-free among NAFTA countries.

Automobiles, footwear and chemicals were subject to even stricter rules. Parts or components going into these products had to have at least half and in some cases more than 60 percent North American content in order to move duty-free in the NAFTA region.

Foreign companies operating subsidiaries in North America were to receive the benefits of the agreement. For example, U.S. subsidiaries of Japanese automakers could transport their vehicles duty-free as long as they were in compliance with the regional content requirements.

One of the more noteworthy concessions obtained by the United States was Mexico's commitment to open its market for services. That included areas such as banking, telecommunications, transportation and government procurement. To prevent piracy of intellectual property, NAFTA required each country to provide effective protection for copyrights, patents, trademarks and similar items.

NAFTA also includes a means for settling trade disputes among the three parties. In general, the process closely followed that established by the U.S.-Canadian Free Trade Agreement. The measure also required the administration to seek elimination of subsidies provided to foreign industries in future trade negotiations.

The U.S., Canada and Mexico signed two side agreements to the accord to broaden protections in the areas of workers' rights and environmental cleanup and enforcement. The side accords established a Commission for Environmental Cooperation and a Commission for Labor Cooperation, on which each country was to be represented, to be responsible for monitoring compliance with labor and environmental laws. They also could appoint special panels to investigate complaints and recommend fines or sanctions if a country refused to enforce its own laws.

But fines or sanctions could be imposed only if a long process of consultation failed to resolve the dispute. Moreover, the panels would have no power to compel a government to pay fines, although they could authorize the other two countries to raise tariffs against the third country's goods. Fines would be levied against the government — not against businesses or individuals.

The agreements also specified that no fines could be imposed if a government failed to enforce its environmental or labor laws because of a decision to expend its resources on other priorities.

NAFTA Takes Effect

When NAFTA took effect on Jan. 1, 1994, tariffs on half of all U.S. exports to Mexico were eliminated. This included such valuable items as semiconductors, computers and machine tools. By Jan. 1, 1996, the average tariff on U.S. exports to Mexico had fallen from 10 percent to 4.9 percent, while the average U.S. tariff on Mexican imports had fallen from 4 percent to 2.3 percent. To compensate for lower tariffs on U.S. imports, Mexico raised tariffs on goods from other countries, giving American exporters an added boost in the Mexican market. [19]

Many observers believe NAFTA helped maintain stable trade relations in North America during last year's financial crisis in Mexico. During a similar crisis in 1982, the Mexican government imposed 100 percent tariffs on many imports in an effort to shore up Mexican industries. U.S. exports to Mexico dropped by 50 percent that year, and it took six years for them to return to their pre-crisis levels. Because Mexico was required by NAFTA to keep tariffs low, the fallout from the recent peso devaluation did far less damage to American exporters.

Although U.S. exports to Mexico fell last year, they still were 11 percent higher than they were in 1993, the year before NAFTA took effect. Although Mexico raised duties on 4,500 products last year, NAFTA goods were exempted, and the tariffs hit Mexico's other trading partners, including Japan and the members of the European Union.

Summit of the Americas

In December 1994, representatives of 34 Western Hemisphere countries met in Miami for the so-called Summit of the Americas, where they adopted a U.S. proposal to extend the free-trade area and create a Free Trade Area of the Americas (FTAA) by 2005. Formal talks to set up the free-trade area got under way with ministerial

NAFTA Is No Longer a Major Issue in Campaign '96 . . .

Earlier this year, it looked like the North American Free Trade Agreement (NAFTA) would be a decisive issue in the presidential election campaign. The anti-NAFTA and protectionist rhetoric of Patrick J. Buchanan struck a chord with voters worried about job security and stagnant wages.

Following Buchanan's early successes at the polls, other Republican candidates, including outgoing Senate Majority Leader Bob Dole, R-Kan., began soft-pedaling their free-trade positions. In December 1995, before the primary season got under way, the Clinton administration announced it was delaying implementation of a controversial NAFTA provision that would have given Mexican trucks greater access to U.S. highways (*see p. 495*).

As Buchanan's campaign faltered, NAFTA moved off the political radar screen. But other trade issues have taken its place.

It's not that the leading candidates disagree on the overall goals of U.S. trade policy. Dole and President Clinton have both spoken out in favor of lower tariffs, fewer subsidies to protect domestic industries and less government interference in commerce in general.

"Our own nation has the greatest potential to benefit from the emerging economy," Clinton said in an address outlining his trade priorities shortly after taking office. "But to do so, we have to confront the obstacles that stand in our way. Many of our trading partners cling to unfair practices. Protectionist voices here at home and abroad call for new barriers. Indifferent policies have left too many of our workers and communities exposed to the harsh winds of trade without letting them share in the sheltering prosperity trade has also brought." [1]

Clinton outlined five steps he said were necessary to encourage international trade: balancing the federal budget, enforcing trade laws and agreements, coordinating economic policies among America's trading partners, increasing trade with developing countries and supporting democracy abroad. All are longstanding objectives of the Republican Party as well.

But some of Clinton's specific actions on trade issues have been criticized by Dole and other free-trade Republicans. During an April 17-18 trip to Tokyo, for example, the president refrained from publicly chastising Japanese Prime Minister Ryutaro Hashimoto for his country's longstanding practice of shutting U.S. goods and services out of Asia's leading market. Clinton instead focused on a new security agreement that would maintain a significant U.S. presence in the region.

Dole seized on the issue to criticize Clinton for what he calls a weak stance on trade. "While President Clinton deserves credit for renewing and strengthening [U.S.-Japan security] ties on his recent trip, the administration's amateurish and ineffective posturing on trade disputes has strained those ties and necessitated the president's recent attempt at damage control," Dole said in a major foreign policy speech in Washington on May 9.

Dole blamed Clinton's "uncoordinated and contradictory tactics" for last year's $60 billion trade deficit with Japan. "If our trade disputes are not resolved, American public support of the U.S.-Japan security relationship will inevitably decline, to the detriment of both countries," he said.

The presumptive Republican candidate also took Clinton

meetings last June in Denver and in March 1996 in Cartagena, Colombia.

Even before NAFTA took effect, support was growing for extending the free-trade area to all of Central and South America. Nearly 40 percent of U.S. exports, valued at $223 billion, already are shipped to countries in the Western Hemisphere. By comparison, only $180 billion of U.S. goods are sold in Japan and the other countries of the Pacific Rim; $124 billion in U.S. exports go to the 15-member European Union.

Many Central and South American countries still have high tariffs. Eliminating them would likely increase U.S. exports to the region. An expanded free-trade area also would provide a strong boost to economic development in the region, as member countries would gain greater access to consumer markets throughout the Western Hemisphere, including the world's largest, the United States. ■

CURRENT SITUATION

Backpedaling on NAFTA?

As the Republican primaries and caucuses got under way early this year, it looked like NAFTA would be a defining issue in the presidential campaign. Pat Buchanan set the tone, attacking the trade agreement at every opportunity.

"That trade surplus, they told us that would really grow, but we don't have a trade surplus with Mexico anymore," Buchanan told his audience in Memphis, Tenn. "We had a trade deficit last year of $15 billion. That equals 300,000 lost American jobs from NAFTA last year alone."

As Buchanan's political fortunes waned, NAFTA seemed to disappear from the campaign debate. Bob Dole, the likely Republican nominee, has long supported the agreement. "I think trade will have some role in the cam-

. . . But Other Trade Issues Are Taking Its Place

to task over his policy toward China. Citing the $34 billion U.S. trade deficit with China, Dole called for stronger enforcement of trade agreements with the world's fastest-growing economy. "China must live up to the trade agreements it has freely entered into, whether on intellectual property or on textiles and apparel, because China has not to date," he said. "And we should move to a targeted proportional response, including proposing an immediate list of sanctions under U.S. trade law." [2]

The day after Dole's address, however, the Clinton administration announced that it was not penalizing China for its widely reported sale of nuclear-weapons equipment to Pakistan, which would be a violation of the 1970 Nuclear Non-Proliferation Treaty. A State Department spokesman said the administration decided not to impose economic sanctions because Chinese leaders promised not to provide such equipment to developing countries in the future.

The administration adopted a tougher stance in a dispute with China over copyright protection. For years, Washington has been trying to get Beijing to halt the widespread piracy of American software, compact discs and other intellectual property, which is costing U.S. businesses an estimated $2 billion a year. On May 15, acting U.S. Trade Representative Charlene Barshefsky threatened to impose retaliatory sanctions on $3 billion worth of silk clothing and other Chinese imports. Beijing immediately threatened to raise tariffs on U.S. automobiles and other American exports and to bar new U.S. business ventures in China. [3]

The copyright dispute did not keep the administration from going ahead with plans to extend China's favorable trading status. In announcing his decision to renew China's most-favored-nation (MFN) trading privileges, Clinton said the action was not intended to reward China. "MFN renewal is not a referendum on all China's policies," the president said May 20. "It is a vote for America's interests."

This is one issue on which Dole and Clinton agree. [4] In his May 9 foreign policy address, Dole offered the administration a pledge of support. "We should extend MFN to China, not because it is in our economic interest but because it is in our national interest," Dole said.

Dole's support could influence the MFN renewal debate in Congress, which promises to be more contentious than usual. [5] Dole puts much of the blame for rising congressional opposition on the president himself. Clinton has "failed to articulate a coherent policy toward China and how MFN extension fits in with that policy," Dole said in a statement issued May 20.

Without backing away from his support for MFN renewal, Dole said the president's "history of zigzags on China has put extension of MFN in serious doubt this year." [6]

---

[1] Clinton spoke at American University in Washington, D.C., on Feb. 26, 1993.

[2] Dole spoke at the Center for Strategic and International Studies.

[3] See Paul Blustein and Steven Mufson, "U.S., China Raise Stakes in Dispute Over Trade," *The Washington Post,* May 16, 1996, and Carroll J. Doherty, "Clinton Seeks to Extend China's Trade Status," *CQ Weekly Report,* May 18, 1996, p. 1398.

[4] See Carroll J. Doherty, "Dole and Clinton See Eye-to-Eye on Favored Trade with Beijing," *CQ Weekly Report,* May 11, 1996, p. 1316.

[5] See Carroll J. Doherty, "Focus of China Trade Debate Shifts to Capitol Hill," *CQ Weekly Report,* May 25, 1996, p. 1475.

[6] Cited in the *Los Angeles Times* (Washington edition), May 21, 1996, p. A3.

---

paign, but probably not a decisive one," says Prestowitz at the Economic Strategy Institute. "Dole has been sharply critical of Clinton's trade policies with Japan. On NAFTA, however, there's not a great deal of difference between the two." (*See story, p. 494.*)

In fact, Dole recently voiced grudging support for the Clinton administration on this particular issue. "There have been times when I supported Clinton, whether it was GATT or NAFTA or Bosnia, because I thought it was the right thing to do," Dole said in an April 19 address to the American Society of Newspaper Editors. "It may not have been the politic thing to do, but in my view it was the right thing to do."

Buchanan's anti-NAFTA rhetoric clearly struck a chord with the electorate, however, and both Dole and Clinton have tried to address the concerns of Americans who fear that free trade threatens their job security.

Although Dole generally supports the idea of expanding NAFTA to include the rest of the Western Hemisphere, he has said it should happen more slowly than the 2005 deadline agreed to at the Summit of the Americas. Dole has called for a "cooling-off period" before any new free-trade agreements are signed. "It only makes good common sense to step back a little and assess the results," he said last November on the Senate floor. [20]

In recent months, the Clinton administration has backpedaled on several NAFTA provisions. On Dec. 18, Transportation Secretary Federico Peña announced that the U.S. and Mexico would delay implementation of a provision that would grant trucks from Mexico unlimited access to U.S. highways in California, New Mexico, Arizona and Texas. (Currently, the U.S. and Mexico restrict trucks from each other's countries to travel within a 20-mile "commercial zone" on either side of the border.) U.S. officials requested the delay after NAFTA critics voiced concerns that Mexican trucks fell short of U.S. safety and environmental standards.

The American Trucking Association, which supports open borders, criticized the administration for caving in to special interests. But the decision was applauded by the International Brotherhood of Teamsters labor union, which was worried that U.S. trucking companies might be tempted to move their operations into Mexico's low-wage economy, eliminating jobs in the U.S. [21]

In early 1996, the Clinton administration bowed to anti-NAFTA forces in Florida, another pivotal state in this fall's election. Florida tomato growers had long complained that Mexican growers were pushing them out of the winter tomato market. Their complaints intensified last year when the peso's devaluation enabled Mexican exporters to sell winter tomatoes in the U.S. even more cheaply.

Former U.S. Trade Representative Mickey Kantor supported a measure sponsored by Sen. Bob Graham, D-Fla., that would have limited imports of certain agricultural products — including tomatoes — that are imported in large enough quantities to cause "serious injury" to domestic producers. [22] The Senate unanimously approved the measure on Jan. 26, but a similar bill introduced in the House by Rep. Porter J. Goss, R-Fla., has failed to advance beyond the Ways and Means Committee.

Free-trade advocates are dismayed by the administration's faltering support of NAFTA. "The president should offer reassurance, in both word and deed, that NAFTA is here to stay in full," Nora Lustig, an analyst at the Brookings Institution and an authority on Mexico, wrote recently. "The recent decision to postpone the licensing of Mexican trucks to operate in U.S. soil and the row over Mexican tomatoes are not good omens. . . . [T]he United States should treat Mexico as a partner — not as a defeated enemy — in managing the recurrent problems in the bilateral relationship — migration, narcotics trafficking, border pollution — as well as new ones arising from the implementation of NAFTA. Unfortunately, electoral politics are pulling U.S. policy toward Mexico in the opposite direction." [23]

Protectionist sentiment in the United States poses a threat to the 16-month-old government of President Zedillo, who has introduced reforms aimed at eliminating political corruption and privatizing the country's remaining state-owned industries. Despite the $20 billion U.S. credit package, Mexico remains financially vulnerable and could be hurt if international investors perceive that NAFTA is in trouble.

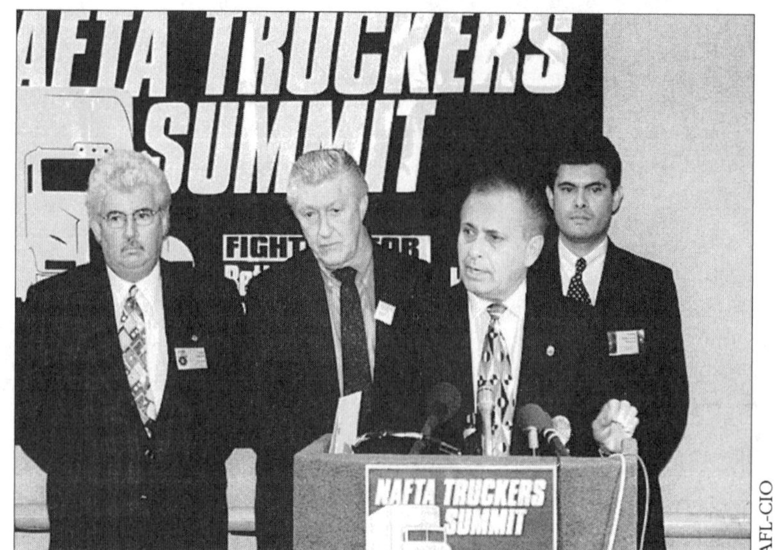

AFL-CIO

Teamsters President Ron Carey is joined by representatives of independent and union trucking groups from the U.S., Canada and Mexico at a March 13 truckers summit. The groups pledged to continue their efforts to prevent implementation of NAFTA's cross-border trucking provisions, which they say would hurt jobs, highway safety and the environment.

"For most Mexicans, Buchanan and his culture warriors are the personification of evil, confirming their worst suspicions about the gringo mentality," Wayne A. Cornelius, a professor of U.S.-Mexican relations at the University of California at San Diego, wrote recently. "Mexicans feel insulted by the candidate's frequent assertions that Mexicans are pouring across the border to 'go on welfare and commit crimes.' " [24]

Mexicans are used to being attacked during U.S. election years, Cornelius writes. "But Buchanan's candidacy has injected Mexico into presidential politics in a more damaging way, by forcing the major parties to harden their positions on issues of vital importance to the Mexicans." [25]

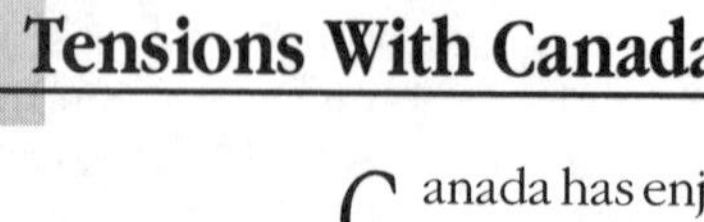

Tensions With Canada

Canada has enjoyed an export boom in recent years, in part because of its seven-year-old free-trade agreement with the United States. Exports now account for 33 percent of Canada's gross domestic product, making it the most trade-dependent of the seven leading industrial nations. [26] Canada's stake in liberalized trade is so strong that it has commenced negotiations on its own to remove tariffs on commerce with Chile and other Central and South American countries.

But NAFTA has not eliminated some of the leading sources of tension between Ottawa and Washington. These include Canadian exports of dairy products, woolen suits and steel, and U.S. exports of television programs, movies and other "cultural" products.

Canada only recently agreed to settle a longstanding quarrel over softwood lumber exports to the United States. The U.S. lumber industry had claimed the imports were subsidized. The five-year settlement, announced April 2,

Continued on p. 498

At Issue:

Should the North American Free Trade Agreement (NAFTA) be expanded to cover the entire Western Hemisphere?

yes

IRA S. SHAPIRO

Senior trade negotiator for Japan and Canada, Office of the U.S. Trade Representative

FROM TESTIMONY BEFORE SUBCOMMITTEES OF THE HOUSE INTERNATIONAL RELATIONS COMMITTEE, OCT. 25, 1995.

Just as the United States has a strong interest in a healthy and growing trade relationship with Mexico, the United States has a strong economic interest in moving forward now with an ambitious and timely trade-agreement agenda in the Western Hemisphere. Chile's accession to NAFTA is an essential component of a two-part strategy to shape and pursue this hemispheric agenda. . . .

For many years the United States had a very limited trade relationship with Latin America. . . . Now that has dramatically changed. A market-based economic policy transformation, coupled with a renewed commitment to democracy, has turned a region with little promise into a region that inspires.

Officials from the World Bank, for example, recently issued a report indicating that growth in Latin America could accelerate to more than 6 percent per year over the next few years, thus providing even more new opportunities for our exporters. Latin America is already the second fastest-growing region in the world. U.S. exports to Latin America already approximate our exports to Western Europe, and if current trends continue they will exceed those to Western Europe and Japan combined by the year 2010. . . .

No other country in Latin America has a better record of economic accomplishment in the last 10 years than Chile. . . . U.S. exports to Chile quadrupled during 1985-94, growing from $682 million to $2.8 billion. . . . Virtually every state in the United States dramatically increased its exports to Chile from 1987 to 1994, with 42 states more than doubling their exports to Chile during the same period. . . . Last year, the United States ran a trade surplus with Chile of nearly $1 billion. . . .

The negotiation of Chile's accession to NAFTA will remove significant remaining barriers that impede U.S. exports to Chile and thus further increase the potential for export gains. NAFTA and its related agreements cover a broad spectrum of disciplines. Chile's adherence to these rules will help to upgrade trade and regulatory practices and policies in Chile that will ensure a continually growing and mutually productive trade relationship. Chile's adherence to the NAFTA disciplines will also encourage in the most concrete way movement by other important trading partners in the region toward disciplines that benefit U.S. traders, workers, investors and service providers.

no

REP. PETER A. DEFAZIO, D-ORE.

FROM TESTIMONY BEFORE THE TRADE SUBCOMMITTEE OF THE HOUSE WAYS AND MEANS COMMITTEE, JUNE 21, 1995.

The Roman statesman Cicero once said, "Any man can make mistakes, but only an idiot persists in his error." NAFTA has been worse than a mistake; it has been a dismal failure by any and every measure. To even begin to consider repeating this failure by expanding this turkey is nothing short of idiocy. . . .

NAFTA's record shows that the agreement has been an abysmal failure. NAFTA promised job growth, with some claiming that NAFTA would create 100,000 jobs in its first year. In fact, NAFTA has been a job loser. A recent analysis by the University of Maryland shows that 16,873 jobs were eliminated in 1994 as a result of increased trade with Mexico and that with the sharp decline in the peso, at least 219,000 more US jobs could be eliminated in 1995. . . .

NAFTA was enacted on the premise that in order for the U.S. to compete, we must do like the Europeans and form larger markets for our products. If the president and the Congress are insistent about expanding NAFTA, at least let's do it the same way the Europeans expanded the European Community (EC).

The EC did not spring up during one year or one decade, but was put together deliberately over 40 years. And it wasn't until recent times that many nations — namely Greece, Portugal and Spain — were included. Why? Because until recently they were dictatorships, countries without democracy, with lower standards for workplace health and safety, less stringent environmental laws and a poorer standard of living than the rest of Europe.

The European countries said "We don't want to enter into free-trade agreements with you because all of our businesses will move to your countries." Europe required them to become democratic. They required them to adopt worker health, safety and environmental laws. They helped foster democratic leadership and institutions.

We cannot afford to rush into a new agreement without looking carefully at the full impacts, not only in this country, but in Chile. What would the effects be on Chile's forests, which are being consumed at an enormous rate? Or on their agricultural practices, in which agricultural chemicals that were banned for sale in this country are exported to Chile for use on their crops, only to be imported back here? Or what about human rights, where a brutal dictator, Augusto Pinochet, remains commander-in-chief of the Army, and has the ability to shield his secret police thugs from the "justice" system? These questions must be addressed before expanding this treaty.

FOR MORE INFORMATION

AFL-CIO, Task Force on Trade, 815 16th St. N.W., Washington, D.C. 20006, (202) 637-5000. The federation of U.S. labor unions supports trade agreements that protect the interests of American workers. It favors the negotiation of tougher labor terms within NAFTA to protect U.S. jobs and wages.

ECONOMIC STRATEGY INSTITUTE, 1100 Connecticut Ave. N.W., Suite 1300, Washington, D.C. 20036, (202) 289-1288. This private, nonpartisan organization analyses domestic and international economic policies. It urges caution on the question of expanding NAFTA membership to other countries of the Hemisphere.

INSTITUTE FOR INTERNATIONAL ECONOMICS, 11 Dupont Circle N.W., Washington, D.C. 20036, (202) 328-9000. This private, nonprofit research organization analyzes trade and other aspects of international economic policy. It supports the expansion of free trade.

U.S. TRADE REPRESENTATIVE, 600 17th St. N.W., #209, Washington, D.C. 20506, (202) 395-3230. This Executive Branch office advises the president on trade matters and acts as his chief negotiator of trade agreements.

Continued from p. 496

calls for Canada to levy a tax on softwood exports over an established ceiling. In exchange, the U.S. has promised not to erect barriers to lumber imports.

Canada has joined other U.S. trading partners in condemning a recently enacted law sponsored by Sen. Jesse Helms, R-N.C., and Rep. Dan Burton, R-Ind., that would impose sanctions against foreign companies that acquire or otherwise "traffic" in Cuban properties that have been confiscated from U.S. citizens. Congress passed the bill in early March, in response to Cuba's downing of two American civilian planes on Feb. 24.

"[I]f indeed Canadians are denied an opportunity to enter the United States on lawful business arrangements, I think that could well be a violation of NAFTA," said Canadian International Trade Minister Art Eggleton. "I have no quarrel with their attempts to deal with the situation with Cuba. It's pulling Canada and other countries into it that I think creates this problem." [27]

A more recent tiff over publishers' rights erupted in April, when amendments to Canada's Copyright Act barred foreign companies from distributing books in Canada and denied American performers royalties collected from songs played on Canadian radio and television. Canadian officials are awaiting a response from acting U.S. Trade Representative Charlene Barshefsky.* "I don't think they have a basis for objection," Eggleton said. "It's nothing that's going to be of harm to them." [28] His office is expected to call for a special NAFTA panel to arbitrate the dispute. ■

OUTLOOK

Chile's Accession

Even before NAFTA took effect, many free-trade advocates were looking beyond Mexico to Chile, arguably Latin America's biggest success story. Rocked by political and economic turmoil in the 1970s, the Andean country has undergone a transformation unequaled in the region. Chile now boasts annual economic growth of 4 percent, unemployment of less than 5 percent, a 10 percent inflation rate and annual trade volume of more than $20 billion. [29]

America's NAFTA partners are eager to include Chile in NAFTA as a first step toward broadening the pact into the Free Trade Area of the Americas by 2005. Both Canada and Mexico have negotiated bilateral trade deals with Chile without the United States. The main stumbling block to Chile's accession to NAFTA is congressional opposition to granting the president fast-track authority to negotiate new trade agreements. That authority expired in 1994.

Without fast-track authority, which requires Congress to act on negotiated trade pacts within 90 days without adding amendments, the president has limited credibility at the negotiating table. Although most Republican lawmakers are strong free-trade advocates, they are holding out on granting Clinton sweeping authority to negotiate trade agreements because they oppose his goal of including provisions to protect workers' rights and the environment, as he did with NAFTA.

A Republican-backed bill to extend the president's negotiating authority excluded these subjects from the agenda of any future trade negotiations. The 1995 Trade Agreements Authority Act, introduced Sept. 21, 1995, by Rep. Bill Archer, R-Texas, was approved by the House Ways and Means Committee but then stalled because of strong opposition from the administration and congressional Democrats.

Labor leaders want to make sure that any talks to expand NAFTA address the question of better protections for workers' rights and the environment. "We support negotiations with Chile because we'd like to see improvements in NAFTA," says Anderson of the AFL-CIO. "We also support fast-track negotiating authority, as long as it main-

* Barshefsky was Deputy Trade Representative when she was appointed to the position April 12, 1996, to replace Mickey Kantor, who was nominated as Commerce secretary following the death of Ronald H. Brown on April 3, 1996.

tains workers' rights and the environment as negotiating objectives. The [NAFTA] side agreements were a good first effort because they mark the first time that workers' rights are associated in any way with a trade agreement. That being said, however, more needs to be done. We need to at least have the same kinds of protections for workers that are available for the owners of intellectual property."

But the stalemate over fast-track authority seems likely to continue until after this fall's elections. That means little progress in Chile's admission to NAFTA and little movement toward the 2005 deadline for the Free Trade Area of the Americas.

"Because it's going to be hard to get fast-track legislation through Congress, it will be hard to have Chile formally accede to NAFTA," says Prestowitz. "The idea of a Free Trade Area of the Americas also has been slowly percolating. But in the present climate that's going to be hard going."

Many analysts are optimistic about the long-term prospects for NAFTA's enlargement to all of Central and South America. There has been remarkable progress toward stable democratic governments and economic growth throughout the region, which had long been plagued by civil wars and brutal dictatorships. Peace talks are now under way to end Guatemala's 35-year-old civil war, and in April the democratic government of Paraguay decisively defeated an attempted military coup with the diplomatic intervention of the Organization of American States.

In the long run, these developments may outweigh remaining domestic opposition to the Free Trade Area of the Americas.

"The more thoughtful opponents recognize that Latin America is not a big commercial threat to the United States," says trade expert Hufbauer. "Most of them know that all of our trade with the rest of Latin America is about equal to our trade with Mexico and that we have a trade surplus with South and Central America."

"What's really at stake for them [in NAFTA's expansion]," Hufbauer continues, "is that it would make it more difficult [for opponents of free trade] to backpedal or put restrictions on FTAA or any other trade agreements." ■

Notes

[1] For background, see David Kameras, "Trade and Credibility Gaps Widening," *AFL-CIO News,* April 22, 1996.

[2] United States Trade Representative, *1996 Trade Policy Agenda and 1995 Annual Report of the President of the United States on the Trade Agreements Program,* April 1996, p. 75.

[3] See Alissa J. Rubin, "Buchanan's Protectionism Slows Trade Agenda," *CQ Weekly Report,* March 2, 1996, p. 532.

[4] Buchanan spoke March 8, 1996, at a campaign rally in Memphis.

[5] For background, see "North America Trade Pact: A Good Idea?" *Editorial Research Reports,* Dec. 8, 1989, pp. 681-696.

[6] Gary Clyde Hufbauer and Jeffrey J. Schott, *NAFTA: An Assessment, Institute for International Economics,* 1993, p. 14.

[7] Byron Dorgan, "Net Loss With NAFTA," *The Washington Post,* April 12, 1996.

[8] For background, see *Editorial Research Reports, op. cit.,* pp. 687, 691.

[9] Ernest F. Hollings, "Protectionist and Proud of It," *The Washington Post,* March 17, 1996.

[10] Salinas was not a candidate in 1994. For background, see "Mexico's Emergence," *The CQ Researcher,* July 19, 1991, pp. 489-512.

[11] Testimony before the Subcommittee on International Economic Policy and Trade and the Western Hemispheres Subcommittee of the House International Relations Committee, Oct. 25, 1995.

[12] Testimony before the Trade Subcommittee of the House Ways and Means Committee, June 21, 1995.

[13] The measure was sponsored by Sen. Reed Smoot, R-Utah, and Rep. Willis C. Hawley, R-Ore. Material in this section is based in part on Sondra J. Nixon, "Protectionism's Rise and Fall in Congress Since the 1930s," *Congressional Quarterly Weekly Report,* March 2, 1996, pp. 534-535.

[14] For background, see *Editorial Research Reports, op. cit,* pp. 683-685.

[15] See Early Fry, "In Spite of Trade Frictions, NAFTA's Been a Success," *The Financial Post,* March 23, 1996.

[16] Some of the information in this section is from the *1992 CQ Almanac,* pp. 154-156, and the *1993 CQ Almanac,* pp. 171-181.

[17] For background on Mexico's environmental problems, see *The CQ Researcher, op. cit.,* p. 503.

[18] Provisions described in this section are from the *1993 CQ Almanac,* pp. 180-181.

[19] United States Trade Representative, *op. cit.,* p. 75.

[20] See David LaGesse, "Silence on NAFTA Could Prove Fleeting," *Dallas Morning News,* April 6, 1996.

[21] See Helene Cooper, "Ban on Mexican Trucks in U.S. Interior Shows Rise of Protectionism," *The Wall Street Journal,* Feb. 5, 1996.

[22] See "Rotten Tomatoes," *The Economist,* Feb. 10, 1996, pp. 74-75.

[23] Nora Lustig, "Mexico: The Slippery Road to Stability," *The Brookings Review,* spring 1996, p. 9.

[24] Wayne A. Cornelius, "Buchanan Strikes Fear in Hearts of Mexicans," *Los Angeles Times* (Washington edition), March 17, 1996.

[25] *Ibid.*

[26] "Canada Leads G7 in Exports," *Globe and Mail,* April 22, 1996.

[27] Eggleton spoke with reporters March 4, 1996, during a meeting in Washington, D.C., with U.S. Trade Representative Mickey Kantor. For background, see *CQ Weekly Report,* March 9, 1996, pp. 632-633.

[28] Quoted in the *Financial Post,* April 29, 1996.

[29] International Monetary Fund, *Annual Report 1995,* p. 76.

Bibliography

Selected Sources Used

Books

Orme, William A. Jr., *Continental Shift: Free Trade & the New North America,* The Washington Post Co., 1993.

This "briefing book" by a *Washington Post* economics reporter reviews the issues in the NAFTA debate, including the pact's likely impact on jobs, the environment and investments among the three member countries.

Articles

De Long, Bradford, Christopher De Long and Sherman Robinson, "The Case for Mexico's Rescue," *Foreign Affairs,* May/June 1996, pp. 8-14.

The authors — a former Clinton administration Treasury official, a New York lawyer and a former member of the President's Council of Economic Advisers — argue that NAFTA's impact on American jobs and economic growth will never be significant. They also maintain that last year's financial rescue of Mexico was a positive move that will foster political stability south of the border.

Levinson, Marc, "Mickey Kantor's Cant," *Foreign Affairs,* March/April 1996, pp. 2-7.

An economics writer for *Newsweek* takes the former U.S. trade representative to task for focusing excessively on U.S. exports as the key to economic health. Kantor's heavy-handed stance toward Mexico, Levinson writes, ignored NAFTA's overriding goal of strengthening political stability and economic reform in Mexico.

Lustig, Nora, "Mexico: The Slippery Road to Stability," *The Brookings Review,* spring 1996, pp. 4-9.

Political instability makes it harder for the new Mexican government to recover from the financial crisis that began in December 1994, writes a Brookings Institution senior fellow, because foreign investors may pull their funds out of the country at a moment's notice.

Morici, Peter, "Export Our Way to Prosperity," *Foreign Policy,* winter 1995-96, pp. 3-17.

Exports are increasingly essential to America's economic prosperity, writes a professor of international business at the University of Maryland, and regional trade blocs such as NAFTA are a useful means of opening new markets.

Shiells, Clinton, "Regional Trade Blocs: Trade Creating or Diverting?" *Finance & Development,* March 1995, pp. 30-32.

The growth of regional trade blocs has been a mixed blessing for global trade, according to a trade economist at the International Monetary Fund.

Reports and Studies

AFL-CIO Task Force on Trade, *NAFTAmath — Two Years Later,* Discussion Paper, April 1996.

NAFTA has worsened conditions for workers in all three countries covered by the trade agreement, the labor confederation concludes, and workers in the United States have suffered the most. More than 52,000 U.S. workers have applied for special assistance under a program targeted at workers who lose their jobs as a direct result of NAFTA, the group notes.

Council of Economic Advisers, *Job Creation and Employment Opportunities: The United States Labor Market, 1993-1996,* April 23, 1996.

Although it does not address NAFTA's impact on employment, this report prepared by President Clinton's economic advisers paints a picture of rising job opportunities, especially in high-skilled, high-wage sectors.

Hufbauer, Gary Clyde, and Jeffrey J. Schott, *NAFTA: An Assessment,* revised edition, Institute for International Economics, October 1993.

The authors, economists at the Institute for International Economics, analyze NAFTA's impact on jobs, trade and investments in all three countries covered by the agreement. They reject contentions that NAFTA causes widespread unemployment.

United States Trade Representative, *1996 Trade Policy Agenda and 1995 Annual Report of the President of the United States on the Trade Agreements Program,* 1996.

The annual report of the Office of the U.S. Trade Representative reviews all the trade agreements currently in force as well as provisions of U.S. laws governing international trade, including anti-dumping actions and trade-adjustment assistance for displaced workers.

The Next Step

Additional information from UMI's Newspaper & Periodical Abstracts database

The Environment and NAFTA

Bacon, David, "After NAFTA," *Environmental Action*, fall 1995, pp. 33-36.
Worsening border pollution and mounting job losses appear to be the legacy of NAFTA's first 600 days. Pollution problems are worse in Mexico than the U.S., and Mexico's financial crisis has not helped matters.

Fox, Annette Baker, "Environment and trade: The NAFTA case," *Political Science Quarterly*, spring 1995, pp. 49-68.
Until the recent passage of NAFTA, the U.S. and Canada had conspicuously avoided linking environmental and trade issues in international agreements. Fox examines the changes in policy that brought about the inclusion of environmental provisions in NAFTA.

Wheat, Andrew, "NAFTA's environmental side show," *Multinational Monitor*, January 1996, pp. 35-38.
The environmental side agreement that President Clinton negotiated to fix NAFTA's environmental deficiencies appears to be falling short of the mark. The reasons behind the measure's failure are discussed.

NAFTA and Canada

"Happy ever NAFTA?" *The Economist*, Dec. 10, 1994, pp. 23-24.
NAFTA's influence is hard to disentangle from that of other economic policies. America's trade with Mexico and Canada has expanded at about twice the rate of trade with non-NAFTA countries in the first nine months of 1994 compared with the same period in 1993.

Magner, Mike, "Michigan worries as tensions over trade, other tiffs rise among United States and Canada," *Detroit News & Free Press*, April 7, 1996, p. B5.
Magner says the relationship between the U.S. and Canada is tense eight years after the countries exchanged vows of free trade, and talk of a border tax in the U.S. Congress will make things worse.

Symonds, William C., "Meanwhile, to the North, NAFTA is a smash," *Business Week*, Feb. 27, 1995, p. 66.
Trade between the U.S. and Canada is exploding as a result of NAFTA. Both countries are racing to complete a far-reaching "open-skies" aviation agreement.

NAFTA Expansion

"Ahead: A southbound NAFTA," *U.S. News & World Report*, Dec. 19, 1994, p. 10.
Leaders of the Western Hemisphere's 34 democracies agreed last week that the year 2005 is the deadline for negotiating a free-trade zone from Alaska to the tip of Argentina.

Clinton, Bill, Jean Chretien, Eduardo Frei and Ponce de Leon Zedillo, "Chile welcomed to NAFTA partnership," *U.S. Department of State Dispatch*, May 1995, p. 30.
Chile will be entering formal negotiations to accede to NAFTA. Chile is an ideal partner due to its high economic growth, low inflation and commitment to the labor and environmental standards that are embedded in NAFTA.

Waitzkin, Howard, "Next in line for NAFTA? Images from Chile," *Monthly Review*, March 1995, pp. 17-27.
The legacy of dictatorship and economic and military scandals in Chile are examined. There is considerable talk in Chile about joining NAFTA.

Watson, Alexander F., "The NAFTA experience: Chile and the future of hemispheric trade," *U.S. Department of State Dispatch*, Oct. 30, 1995, pp. 803-804.
The importance of Latin American trade to the U.S. economy and America's desire to strengthen economic ties throughout the Western Hemisphere are discussed. The U.S. is presently considering adding Chile as the next NAFTA member.

NAFTA and Mexico

Espana, Juan R., "The Mexican peso crisis: Impact on NAFTA and emerging markets," *Business Economics*, July 1995, pp. 45-49.
The 1994 financial crisis in Mexico has led to a pessimistic reassessment of the risk-return trade-off of portfolio foreign investment in developing economies, causing a temporary halt to capital flows to those countries. The effects of the crisis on NAFTA and future trade agreements are discussed.

Heredia, Carlos A., "NAFTA and democratization in Mexico," *Journal of International Affairs*, summer 1994, pp. 13-38.
NAFTA has led to increased scrutiny of Mexico and the emergence of a supranational grassroots movement. Both developments have furthered the democratization process in Mexico. Heredia describes how Mexican civil actors view the link between NAFTA and the fight to establish a democratic process in Mexico.

Hosmer, LaRue Tone and Scott E. Masten, "Ethics vs. economics: The issue of free trade with Mexico," *Journal of Business Ethics,* April 1995, pp. 287-298.

The issue of free trade with Mexico and other low wage rate countries from the ethical and economic perspectives is examined. The two disciplines differ on their priorities and analytical methods, not on their objectives.

Kelley, Kevin J., "Good NAFTA?" *Utne Reader,* January 1996, pp. 20-22.

Many liberals oppose NAFTA on parochial, even myopic, grounds. Contrary to their opinions, NAFTA appears to be helping the Mexican economy and democratization process.

McDonald, Greg, "Clinton, Zedillo meet, reaffirm ties, NAFTA," *Houston Chronicle,* Oct. 11, 1995, p. A17.

President Clinton and Mexican President Zedillo reaffirmed their nations' strong ties as Zedillo visited Washington D.C., offering a spirited defense of NAFTA and the controversial U.S. decision in 1994 to help ease the Mexican currency crisis.

Poole, Dennis L., "NAFTA, American health, and Mexican health: They tie together," *Health & Social Work,* February 1996, pp. 3-7.

Poole explains how NAFTA will have major health and social consequences for people living in the U.S. and Mexico. Health social workers have a unique opportunity to develop innovative solutions to border health problems.

NAFTA as a Political Issue

Blustein, Paul, "U.S. seeks compromise on NAFTA truck rules," *The Washington Post,* Dec. 18, 1995, p. A13.

Clinton administration officials, responding to safety and environmental concerns, negotiated with Mexican officials on whether to delay the implementation of a free-trade provision that would allow Mexican trucks unlimited travel in U.S. border states.

Chapman, Stephen, "Buchanan and Perot: At odds with NAFTA and, if you think about it, reality," *Chicago Tribune,* March 10, 1996, p. 21.

Chapman examines NAFTA's effect on both Ross Perot and Republican presidential candidate Pat Buchanan, saying the free trade agreement is to them a betrayal along the lines of Benedict Arnold's and suggesting that both men aren't dealing with reality very well.

Clinton, Bill and Pat Buchanan,"Is NAFTA good for the U.S.?" *Scholastic Update,* Nov. 17, 1995, p. 15.

NAFTA took effect on Jan. 1, 1994, wiping out most trade barriers between the U.S., Canada and Mexico. President Bill Clinton offers his views in support of NAFTA, and Pat Buchanan, a Republican candidate for president, explains why he is opposed to NAFTA.

Davis, Diane E., "New-Age politics drives NAFTA," *Forum for Applied Research & Public Policy,* summer 1995, pp. 43-49.

Davis examines the different historical perspectives from which the U.S. and Mexico approached NAFTA. Both President Clinton and President Salinas sought to move their parties away from working-class-oriented political positions.

Kraul, Chris, "Mexico trucking delay signals shift in NAFTA support," *Los Angeles Times,* Dec. 23, 1995, p. D1.

President Clinton's December 1995 decision to delay the free movement of trucks between Mexico and the U.S. is discussed. Although the decision was billed as a temporary safety measure, some believe it was intended mainly to win election-year support from critics of NAFTA.

LaFranchi, Howard, "NAFTA buffeted by U.S. politics," *The Christian Science Monitor,* Jan. 19, 1996, p. 6.

NAFTA's progress, which was supposed to involve the inclusion of Chile as the pact's fourth member, has been slowed in 1996, due to the American presidential election. Foreign trade is developing as a major issue in the campaign, and several Republican candidates are sounding less than harmonious on the issue of free trade. President Clinton is caught between his support of free trade and polls showing American voters becoming increasingly concerned about the effects of foreign trade on jobs and income.

"NAFTA politics," *Houston Chronicle,* Dec. 28, 1995, p. A30.

An editorial asserts that President Clinton is blatantly massaging some of the key elements of NAFTA in an effort to avoid losing votes in Texas and other border states in the 1996, presidential election.

Sanger, David E., "Dilemma for Clinton on NAFTA truck rule," *The New York Times,* Dec. 17, 1995, p. 36.

Facing a Dec. 18, 1995, deadline, Clinton administration and Mexican officials talked intensively on Dec. 16 about how they might back away from an important provision of the NAFTA that would let trucks from Mexico travel freely in American border states starting the week of Dec. 24.

Willing, Richard, "NAFTA-bashing may hurt Buchanan in heart of Dixie," *Detroit News & Free Press,* Feb. 25, 1996, p. C1.

The southern states' reliance on international trade is among a number of factors that may thwart Pat Buchanan's bid for the 1996 GOP presidential nomination as he campaigns in the south on an anti-NAFTA platform.

NAFTA'S Impact

"Alabama trade mission to Mexico finds opportunities in this big emerging market," *Business America,* January 1995, pp. 8-9.

An Alabama delegation to Mexico brought back 15 agent/

distributorship agreements and $1.5 million in first-year sales. Factors that make Mexico an ideal partner to trade with are examined.

Anderson, Sarah and John Cavanagh, "NAFTA's unhappy anniversary," *The New York Times,* Feb. 7, 1995, p. A25.
Economists Sarah Anderson and John Cavanagh dispute the Clinton administration's claim that NAFTA has created 100,000 U.S. jobs in its first year and present statistics showing that, in fact, there has been a net loss of 10,000 U.S. jobs. Anderson and Cavanagh suggest that the Mexican peso crisis might offer the U.S. an opportunity to add strong enforcement mechanisms to NAFTA to hold companies accountable for the abuse of workers' rights and environmental standards.

Bernal, Richard L., "The Americas: A Jamaican's case for trade parity with NAFTA," *The Wall Street Journal,* March 22, 1996, p. A13.
Bernal says that recent changes in U.S. trade law, including NAFTA and GATT, have put the long-term viability of the U.S.-Caribbean trade relationship in jeopardy.

Burke, Melvin, Kraig A. Schwartz and William G. Steele, "NAFTA numbers don't add up," *Humanist,* March 1995, p. 36.
Although NAFTA was enacted a year ago, there has been very little discussion about its economic effects. NAFTA has not performed very well during the past year.

Cooper, Helene and Bruce Ingersoll,"Playing catch-up: With little evidence, Florida growers blame tomato woes on NAFTA," *The Wall Street Journal,* April 3, 1996, p. A1.
Florida tomato growers are decrying a surge of Mexican tomatoes, which they say threatens to drive Florida growers out of business. However, Florida growers these days lay the blame on NAFTA, exploiting the anti-NAFTA backlash in this election year. The Clinton administration is heeding the plea for special protection and U.S. Trade Representative Mickey Kantor has endorsed legislation sponsored by the Florida delegation that would make it easier to slap tariffs on Mexican tomatoes.

Dorgan, Byron, "Net loss with NAFTA," *The Washington Post,* April 12, 1996, p. A25.
Sen. Byron Dorgan takes exception to a James Glassman column about NAFTA's success in the March 26 *Washington Post,* asserting that the biggest myth of all about NAFTA is that it is a good deal for the U.S.

Friedman, Thomas L., "Politics In the Age Of NAFTA," *The New York Times,* April 7, 1996, p. 11.
Friedman says that people everywhere are struggling to find a balance between NAFTA and neighborhood — between their desire to preserve a sense of national identity and control over their own lives in a world where they can only survive economically if they link up to distant global institutions and markets that don't reflect any identity. Friedman comments on Michael Sandel's book *Democracy's Disconent,* which argues that modern democracies will not be able to sustain themselves unless they can find ways of contending with the global economy, while also giving expression to their people's distinctive identities.

"Give NAFTA some time," *The Christian Science Monitor,* Oct. 11, 1995, p. 20.
An editorial discusses the October 1995 meeting between President Clinton and Mexican President Ernesto Zedillo, and examines the presidents' expectations concerning the economic effects of NAFTA.

Jackson, Sally A., "NAFTA and Illinois," *Chicago Tribune,* May 3, 1996, p. 22.
In a letter to the editor, Illinois State Chamber of Commerce CEO and President Sally A. Jackson comments on an April 15, 1996, *Tribune* article "Opponents say NAFTA is raw deal for workers," saying that NAFTA has helped Illinois in several ways.

Longworth, R. C., "Opponents say NAFTA is raw deal for workers," *Chicago Tribune,* April 15, 1996, p. 1.
NAFTA has failed to deliver on its promise to make life better for workers in Illinois or in the rest of the three countries united by the trade pact, a coalition of anti-NAFTA organizations charged on April 15, 1996, in a report issued by the Illinois Fair Trade campaign.

McClenahen, John S., "NAFTA after two years," *Industry Week,* Jan. 8, 1996, pp. 21-24.
Two-year-old NAFTA has yet to live up to promises put forth by both President Bush and President Clinton. Canada, Mexico and the U.S. are more focused in 1996 on their domestic political and economic concerns than on free trade.

"NAFTA-effects," *Boston Globe,* April 22, 1996, p. 10.
An editorial comments on the ongoing trade disputes among the U.S., Mexico and Canada, problems which NAFTA was supposed to eliminate.

Quinn, Matthew C., "Women make Mexico trade trip," *Atlanta Constitution,* May 7, 1996, p. F2.
Carolyn Stradley, CEO of C&S Paving Inc. of Marietta, Ga., was one of a 14-member delegation to Mexico City and Monterrey in April 1996 that was part of the Clinton administration's efforts to promote new trade opportunities under NAFTA. Other international business topics are also noted.

Back Issues

Great Research on Current Issues Starts Right Here...Recent topics covered by The CQ Researcher are listed below. Before May 1991, reports were published under the name of Editorial Research Reports.

NOVEMBER 1994
Sex on Campus
Blood Supply Safety
Testing Term Limits
Religion in America

DECEMBER 1994
Farm Policy
Arms Sales
Earthquake Research
The Future of Television

JANUARY 1995
Treating Addiction
Child Custody and Support
Parents and Schools
Non-Proliferation Treaty at 25

FEBRUARY 1995
Cracking Down on Immigration
The Business of Sports
Reinventing Government
Housing Discrimination

MARCH 1995
Death Penalty Debate
Primary Care
Democracy in Africa
Environmental Movement at 25

Back issues are available for $5.00 (subscribers) or $8.00 (non-subscribers). Quantity discounts apply to orders over ten. To order, call Congressional Quarterly Customer Service at (202) 887-8621.

Binders are available for $18.00. To order call 1-800-638-1710. Please refer to stock number 648.

APRIL 1995
Abortion Clinic Protests
Dieting and Health
Combating AIDS
Rethinking Affirmative Action

MAY 1995
Assisted Suicide Controversy
Overhauling Social Security
Learning to Read
Mandatory Sentencing

JUNE 1995
Combating Infectious Disease
Property Rights
Repetitive Stress Injuries
Regulating the Internet

JULY 1995
War Crimes
Highway Safety
Combating Terrorism
Preventing Teen Drug Use

AUGUST 1995
Job Stress
Organ Transplants
United Nations at 50
Advances in Cancer Research

SEPTEMBER 1995
Catholic Church in the U.S.
Northern Ireland Cease-Fire
High School Sports
Teaching History

OCTOBER 1995
Quebec's Future
Revitalizing the Cities
Networking the Classroom
Indoor Air Pollution

NOVEMBER 1995
The Working Poor
The Jury System
Sex, Violence and the Media
Police Misconduct

DECEMBER 1995
Teens and Tobacco
Gene Therapy's Future
Global Water Shortages
Third-Party Prospects

JANUARY 1996
Emergency Medicine
Punishing Sex Offenders
Bilingual Education
Helping the Homeless

FEBRUARY 1996
Reforming the CIA
Campaign Finance Reform
Academic Politics
Getting Into College

MARCH 1996
The British Monarchy
Preventing Juvenile Crime
Tax Reform
Pursuing the Paranormal

APRIL 1996
Centennial Olympic Games
Managed Care
Protecting Endangered Species
New Military Culture

MAY 1996
Russia's Political Future
Marriage and Divorce
Year-Round Schools
Taiwan, China and the U.S.

Future Topics

- ***First Ladies***
- ***Teaching Values***
- ***Labor Movement's Future***

THE CQ Researcher

PUBLISHED BY CONGRESSIONAL QUARTERLY INC.

First Ladies

What is the proper role for the president's spouse?

The travails of Hillary Rodham Clinton — criticism of her activism as well as questions about her credibility in the Whitewater and "Travelgate" affairs — have reminded Americans that the proper role for a first lady remains an unsolved national puzzle. Historians note that resentment of the political influence often exerted by this unelected leader goes back to the dawn of the republic. Yet the 20th-century rise of the career woman has highlighted a built-in tension between the traditional duties of the White House hostess and the modern role for an independent woman. The 1996 presidential race, in which both prospective first ladies — Mrs. Clinton and Elizabeth Dole — are accomplished professionals, marks a turning point in this historic debate.

INSIDE THIS ISSUE

CQ | June 14, 1996 • Volume 6, No. 22 • Pages 505-528

Formerly Editorial Research Reports

FIRST LADIES

COVER: HILLARY RODHAM CLINTON DONATES HER INAUGURAL GOWN TO THE FIRST LADIES COLLECTION AT THE SMITHSONIAN'S NATIONAL MUSEUM OF AMERICAN HISTORY, MARCH 6, 1995. (REUTERS)

June 14, 1996
Volume 6, No. 22

EDITOR
Sandra Stencel

MANAGING EDITOR
Thomas J. Colin

ASSOCIATE EDITORS
Sarah M. Magner
Richard L. Worsnop

STAFF WRITERS
Charles S. Clark
Mary H. Cooper
Kenneth Jost

EDITORIAL ASSISTANT
Tonya Harris

PUBLISHED BY
Congressional Quarterly Inc.

CHAIRMAN
Andrew Barnes

VICE CHAIRMAN
Andrew P. Corty

EDITOR AND PUBLISHER
Neil Skene

EXECUTIVE EDITOR
Robert W. Merry

The CQ Researcher (ISSN 1056-2036). Formerly Editorial Research Reports. Published weekly (48 times per year, not printed March 1, May 31, Aug. 30, Nov. 29) by Congressional Quarterly Inc., 1414 22nd St., N.W., Washington, D.C. 20037. Annual subscription rate for libraries, businesses and government is $319. Additional rates furnished upon request. Second-class postage paid at Washington, D.C. POSTMASTER: Send address changes to The CQ Researcher, 1414 22nd St., N.W., Washington, D.C. 20037.

First Ladies

By Charles S. Clark

The Issues

The first lady "is not doing the president any good," warned a prominent Washington editor. "She is becoming altogether too active in public affairs, and I think she is harmful rather than helpful."

Another critic of Hillary Clinton's health-care plan? More gender politics in the 1990s? Quite plausibly, except the year was 1934, and the first lady Eleanor Roosevelt. [1]

Throughout American history, a range of first ladies have charmed the nation with style, raised the spirits of troubled chief executives or kept to themselves demurely behind the scenes. They have helped push through legislation, represented the nation overseas and nudged the president toward key decisions. They also have inflamed political opponents, divided public attitudes and grated against Washington power brokers. But at no time during the history of White House life has the first lady been as powerful, politically visible and excoriated as Hillary Rodham Clinton is today.

A corporate lawyer and her family's chief breadwinner before Bill Clinton won the presidency, Mrs. Clinton is the first in what many predict will be a succession of presidential spouses with their own career identities. Indeed, Bill Clinton was proud of his accomplished wife, and they campaigned together under the slogan "Buy one, get one free." In 1993, she set a precedent when she was placed in charge of the president's key domestic-policy priority, health-care reform.

On top of the debate generated by Mrs. Clinton's (ultimately unsuccessful) health-care role, she has struggled in the eye of a storm of ethical controversies — from the probe into the Arkansas land deal known as Whitewater, to

the sudden firing of the White House travel office staff in 1993, to her own highly profitable earnings in cattle futures in the 1980s. In January, she became the only first lady in history ever to be subpoenaed. *

The issues that have embroiled Mrs. Clinton in controversy have a common thread: They all reflect a woman who is an independent decision-maker. And the fact that a president's wife would become a lightning rod for ethics charges and broadsides from the president's political opponents brings the institution of first lady into new territory in which few holds are barred.

"Like horse-racing, Hillary-hating has become one of those national pastimes which unite the elite and the lumpen," Harvard University English Professor Henry Louis Gates Jr. recently wrote. [2]

* Mrs. Clinton testified before a federal grand jury in Washington, D.C., concerning the disappearance and sudden recovery of her law firm's billing records as well as other matters related to the Whitewater land deal.

Early on, the Clintons' ascent to national prominence brought snide comments about rule by "Clinton and Clinton," or "Billary." An image of a domineering Mrs. Clinton elbowing her husband aside became a staple among editorial cartoonists. And the ribbing continues. A tabulation of jokes from late-night talk shows in January and February showed that while Bill Clinton was the butt of 57 jokes, Hillary, the butt of 47, was a close second. [3]

Millions of Americans, of course, still admire Mrs. Clinton as a model of female achievement and view her travails as politically inspired. Still, the political rhetoric and the ethics issues have handed her record-setting negative ratings.

In *Los Angeles Times* public opinion polls, Mrs. Clinton's unfavorable rating shot up from 25 percent in January 1994 to 35 percent in January 1995 to 44 percent this April. A Gallup Poll in January put her negatives at 54 percent, twice that of another controversial first lady, Nancy Reagan. In an NBC News-*Wall Street Journal* poll in March, 43 percent said that Mrs. Clinton has too much influence over the president, while only 30 percent said she had the right amount. More recently, a June CBS-*New York Times* poll showed Mrs. Clinton's popularity had improved slightly in the past two months.

When it comes to career women, Elizabeth Dole, wife of presumptive Republican presidential candidate Bob Dole, could be Hillary Clinton's twin. Dole, as her golden résumé documents, is a trailblazing Harvard Law School graduate (Mrs. Clinton went to Yale) and the only woman to have held two separate Cabinet posts (Transportation and Labor). Mrs. Dole went on leave from her job as president of the American Red Cross to campaign for her husband but has said that she would return to the organization if he is elected.

First Ladies Are Traveling More Often . . .

Even when the first lady journeys overseas, there are domestic repercussions. After Hillary Clinton spent five days in Latin America last fall, reporters noted that she had reverted to "softer," more traditional first lady activities, such as visiting schools and watching performances by native dancers. "After being hammered for her role in health-care reform and Whitewater," *Newsweek* commented, "Hillary Rodham Clinton finally appears to have found her niche — as roving ambassador." [1]

But to many observers both at home and abroad, trips by Mrs. Clinton and other contemporary counterparts such as Nancy Reagan and Rosalynn Carter increasingly are having substantive — even historical — impact. During her trip to Latin America, Mrs. Clinton lunched with Nicaraguan President Violetta Chamarro, met with 16 spouses of Latin American leaders in Paraguay and announced a new U.S. contribution of $8 million to the international effort to combat measles. State Department officials said that Mrs. Clinton helped make a strong case against the Republican Congress' plans to cut foreign aid to the region.

"This first lady has had a huge impact," says Charlotte Feldman-Jacobs, a senior communications specialist at the Washington-based International Center for Research on Women. "Generally, any first lady's travels have impact. But traditionally, other first ladies concentrated on women's reproductive issues such as family planning. Not to take away from those issues, but Mrs. Clinton has branched out to 'productive' issues such as economic participation. In India and Bangladesh, she spoke of the importance of getting bank loans to women. In Chile and Pakistan, she spoke of educating girls and women. And in Bosnia, she focused world attention on violence against women and rape as an instrument of war."

Hillary Rodham Clinton addresses the U.N. Summit for Social Development in Copenhagen, Denmark, on March 7, 1995.

Most important, says Feldman-Jacobs, is the effect on women "from rural villages, who are willing to walk for 10-12 hours just to hear her speak."

Such activism would be out of place in many other countries. During Mrs. Clinton's April visit to Japan, for example, it was noted that Japanese first lady Kumiko Hashimoto not only walked several paces behind her husband in public but also had commented, "I don't interfere with my husband's business, not with my mouth, hands or legs." [2]

In many parts of the world, "the political woman's role is still that of social smoother — being gracious, beautiful and decorative, making the social arrangements and making everyone comfortable," says Deborah Tannen, a professor of linguistics at Georgetown University who has written widely on gender roles. "There are plenty of women leaders, but there is a paradox. Less-developed countries have put women in power [such as Indira Ghandi in India and Benazir Bhutto in Pakistan], yet these are countries in which status and hierarchy are extremely significant. When a high level is reached by a woman in these countries, that fact overshadows the fact that she is female. By contrast, the United States is a more egalitarian society, so the fact that someone is female overshadows the position she achieves."

The international influence of U.S. first ladies goes back at least to the century's first decade, when President William H. Taft on a visit to Mexico remarked to Mexican dictator Porfirio Diaz on the importance of their wives' public roles. [3]

The first important solo trip overseas by a first lady was made by Eleanor Roosevelt during World War II, notes Carl Sferrazza Anthony, a historian of first ladies. During her Red Cross-sponsored 1943 visit with troops on the Pacific island of Guadalcanal, "She played the mother role for the

Observers say Mrs. Dole's conservative credentials — and her easygoing manner — may make her more palatable to traditionalists than her feminist counterpart. Mrs. Dole was always "very ambitious," says historian Doris Kearns Goodwin, author of *No Ordinary Time,* the 1994 best-seller about Franklin and Eleanor Roosevelt. "But there was a softness to her ambitious edge, so that she was talking about guys, about other things besides her career desires, and I think somehow she's managed, throughout her life, to camouflage those career ambitions so that people don't feel threatened by her." [4]

The result in this election year will be "a good deal of contrasting between the two," says Stephen Hess, a senior fellow at the Brookings Institution. "How often do you find two spouses of contenders with such established public histories?"

. . . And Making Marks Both Here and Abroad

homesick boys, who approved of her as their mom even though her style differed from their view of what the American woman should be," Anthony writes.

Important benefits were also gained from travels by Jacqueline Kennedy, Anthony adds. Though Mrs. Kennedy may be remembered mainly for a pleasure trip to exotic India, she helped her husband at arms control talks in Vienna, Austria, by sharing her impressions of Soviet negotiators.

Pat Nixon, too, was considered a prolific traveler and effective ambassador, though she and her husband did not always display perfect teamwork. Mrs. Nixon visited some 54 countries with her husband during his political career. President Richard M. Nixon once said in a filmed interview that other first ladies should emulate his wife's style of traveling by "visiting hospitals and showing concern for people." Yet when Mrs. Nixon returned from what the press had hailed as a triumphant visit to Africa as "personal representative of the president," she found the president and his top aides nearly oblivious to her achievement.[4]

Rosalynn Carter pioneered a role for the first lady as high-level diplomat. Her 1977 trip to seven Latin American countries to explain U.S. trade, arms sales and foreign policy was intricately planned by President Jimmy Carter and his secretary of State, national security adviser and vice president. Polls showed that 70 percent of the public approved of Mrs. Carter's trip, and she briefed the Senate Foreign Relations Committee upon her return. But press commentators questioned whether she could be held accountable for her diplomacy. Meg Greenfield, editorial page editor of *The Washington Post*, derided her as "Mrs. President."[5]

An unusual clash of "dueling first ladies" made headlines in 1985, when Nancy Reagan met her Soviet counterpart Raisa Gorbachev during an arms control summit in Geneva, Switzerland. As they jockeyed with each other for the media spotlight, Mrs. Reagan was put off, she later complained, that Mrs. Gorbachev lectured her on the merits of communism rather than discussing children and charities. "There isn't even a Russian word for first lady," she wrote in her memoirs.[6]

Mrs. Reagan's efforts, however, were as effective as any of her peers in raising the visibility of women in foreign political cultures, notes Norman J. Ornstein, a senior fellow at the American Enterprise Institute. "It was about then that Raisa Gorbachev began to be seen in public, and when she came to Washington, she said, 'I'm not going to just do the tourist thing.'" Such changes in first lady status could be seen more recently, Ornstein adds, in the fact that the widow of slain Israeli Prime Minister Yitzhak Rabin in the past year has met with key world leaders.

Perhaps the most dramatic trip by a first lady occurred in September 1995, when Hillary Clinton addressed the United Nations fourth international conference on women, in Beijing. Because of longstanding U.S. disputes with China over human rights and trade policy, the Clinton administration was warned by congressional leaders such as Sen. Richard G. Lugar, R-Ind., that it should send a professional diplomat on this sensitive mission. Undeterred, Mrs. Clinton took to the podium in China and declared, "It is time for us to say here in Beijing, and the world to hear, that it is no longer acceptable to discuss women's rights as separate from human rights," including the right of people to assemble, organize and debate openly.[7]

Mrs. Clinton's rhetoric and frankness on such issues as female genital mutilation impressed Republicans and the U.S. foreign policy establishment, as well as Democrats and feminists. To Ann Lewis, now deputy manager of the Clinton-Gore campaign, it was a "speech heard round the world."

"I don't think this ground-breaking expansion of the first lady's role will be turned back in the future," says Feldman-Jacobs. "In the United States, we don't have cultural taboos against the first lady speaking out on issues of importance to women, but in some other countries, one has to work within the taboos."

---

[1] "Periscope," *Newsweek*, Oct. 9, 1995, p. 6.

[2] Quoted in *The Washington Post*, April 15, 1996.

[3] Carl Sferrazza Anthony, *First Ladies* (1990), p. 318.

[4] Margaret Truman, *First Ladies* (1995), p. 199.

[5] Quoted in Betty Boyd Caroli, *First Ladies* (1987), p. 266.

[6] Quoted in Germaine Greer, "Abolish Her," *The New Republic*, June 26, 1995, p. 20.

[7] Quoted in *The New York Times*, Sept. 6, 1995.

More than in the past, the first lady question could actually affect the election, notes Larry Sabato, a professor of government at the University of Virginia. "The conventional wisdom is that vice presidential candidates make only a 1-2 percent difference in the vote, and that the first lady makes even less," Sabato says. "But I don't know, given the controversial nature of Hillary Clinton, it could be a larger percentage. They're a package. It's hard to evaluate him without her."

Norman J. Ornstein, a senior fellow at the American Enterprise Institute, forecasts that Hillary Clinton will be "a public issue in the sense that reporters will cover her and people at the office water cooler will talk about her. But it will have no effect on voters. In 1992, there were no votes against Bill Clinton on account of Hillary, though perhaps she hurt his 1993-94 approval ratings," he says.

The role of first lady "is the world's second-toughest job," in the phrase of presidential daughter and author Margaret Truman. The first lady clearly plays an essential role in fulfilling the aspect of the presidency that has been called "a focus of feelings." The public reacted unfavorably, for example, to Mary Todd Lincoln, who spent days in hysterics after her husband was shot, in dramatic contrast with the courage shown later in similar circumstances by Lucretia Garfield, Jacqueline Kennedy and Nancy Reagan. Less dramatically, the warm and talkative nature of Grace Coolidge was a much-needed contrast to the withdrawn style of Calvin "Silent Cal" Coolidge.

Regardless of her individual personality, "the first lady contributes to the nation as the most nationally visible woman in politics, even though she holds no specific elected position," says Edie Mayo, curator of the first ladies collection and women's history at the Smithsonian Institution's National Museum of American History. "But particularly in the latter 20th century, her role has also been to extend the visibility and legitimacy of public roles for women."

The first lady really fulfills two roles, says Carl Sferrazza Anthony, an author who specializes in first lady history. "For most of the public, those who can't comprehend the depth and level of policy minutiae, it's easier to focus on her role as a symbol. But it's in the more politically visible role that the first lady has problems finding her place."

The uniqueness of Mrs. Clinton's experiences should not, historians caution, obscure the fact that nearly all first ladies struggled with their role. (*See story, pp. 516-517.*) Indeed, soon after Franklin D. Roosevelt won the presidency in 1932, Eleanor, the mother of five children, was busy editing a children's magazine and appearing on radio with corporate sponsors. The *Hartford Courant* warned her in an editorial that "being the first lady of the land is a full-time job in itself and that the dignity of the president and the country cannot but suffer when his name is used for commercial purposes." [5]

Lt. Joe Roberts

Eleanor Roosevelt and Madam Chiang Kai-Shek on the lawn of the White House in February 1943.

As the role played by the first lady continues its inevitable evolution, these are some of the questions being asked:

Should the first lady be active in policy-making?

"Elizabeth won't be in charge of health care, don't worry about that," candidate Bob Dole is fond of telling crowds in an effort to contrast his governing approach to that of the Clintons. But many observers, noting Mrs. Dole's vast experience running government agencies, ask, Why wouldn't she?

"He talks as if Elizabeth is retarded," sneered *Newsday* columnist Robert Reno. "Unless she behaves like an insipid, unopinionated cow, we persist in characterizing the president's wife as a meddler, dragon lady and ambitious harridan." [6]

The issue of formal assignments for a presidential spouse — unelected, immune from firing — has been thrown into relief by the current Hillary-Elizabeth matchup. But in truth, it has simmered for decades behind the scenes.

The closest parallel to Hillary Clinton's work on health care was Eleanor Roosevelt's World War II designation as assistant director of the Office of Civilian Defense. Though her tenure was productive and gave her a sense of accomplishment that eased tensions in her marriage, she clashed over priorities with New York Mayor Fiorello LaGuardia, and Congress and the press blasted her for turning the office into "a personal parking lot for the pets and protégés of Mrs. Roosevelt." [7]

Like Mrs. Clinton, Mrs. Roosevelt was also famous for her independent advocacy of issues her husband may or may not have embraced. (In one famous display of discord, FDR publicly lambasted members of the communist-influenced American Youth Congress after Eleanor had welcomed them to the White House.) As Goodwin points out, the Roosevelts had an agreement in which Eleanor could advocate whatever she pleased, and Franklin would paper over it by saying, "That is my wife, I can't do anything about her." Overall, she served as a "a voice for those people outside pushing against the system, rather than being a designated inside player," Goodwin says.[8]

Actually, Anthony says, one can sift through the legacies of the first ladies and find "that most influenced policy or legislation or lent their insights or knowledge for what in modern times would be called PR — how the president presented himself, spoke or campaigned." Mamie Eisenhower vetted her husband's campaign speeches, he notes, and encouraged him to send federal troops to desegregate schools in Little Rock, Ark. Eliza Johnson clipped news items about her husband Andrew's impeachment to help him keep abreast of the proceedings. And Ida McKinley, a believer in Christian missionaries, persuaded her husband that the United States should hold on to the Philippine Islands in defiance of the recommendation by his appointed commission.

Others point out that publicity-shy Bess Truman urged her husband to fire the leftist Henry Wallace as Commerce secretary,[9] and that Nancy Reagan, sometimes derided as the "associate president," played a central role in the 1987 firing of White House Chief of Staff Donald T. Regan.

Mrs. Reagan's behind-closed-doors technique was described by former White House Press Secretary Marlin Fitzwater, who was stunned on his first day on the job to get a call from the first lady confirming her feelings about Regan. Mrs. Reagan "had decided that Regan should have somehow prevented [the] Iran-contra [scandal]. She resented his occasional upstaging of the president, and perhaps she even resented his closeness to the president," Fitzwater wrote.

"Here's how it works," Fitzwater continued. "Mrs. Reagan tells Paul Laxalt, the president's oldest friend, that Regan is hurting Ronnie and has to go. Laxalt calls Stu Spencer, the California political consultant who has advised all the Reagan campaigns, and says Regan has to go. Spencer tells Lou Cannon of *The Washington Post*, his old friend from many California campaigns, and says Regan has to go. Cannon writes that close Reagan friends and associates feel Regan has to go."[10]

Sheila Tate, former press secretary for Nancy Reagan and now president of the consulting firm Powell Tate, said that "Mrs. Reagan merely joined a chorus of critics of Regan that included practically every editorial writer in the country. Nancy had more influence with her husband than most first ladies, but she was not in charge." Unlike Hillary Clinton's role in health-care reform, Mrs. Reagan "didn't determine policy in secret meetings with handpicked players trying to manage one-seventh of the economy," Tate adds.

Tate hopes Bob Dole will continue his campaign line about his wife not running health care. "Hillary's not elected, that's the distinction," she says. "It has nothing to do with gender. Women cry wolf and damage themselves when they point to gender in circumstances that don't apply. The American electorate has a long tradition of holding officials accountable. That's the mistake Bill Clinton made."

Many political observers agree. The substantive issues pursued by previous first ladies — Nancy Reagan's anti-drug campaign, Lady Bird Johnson's highway beautification program, Betty Ford's efforts against breast cancer — "were still all-American projects that remained a reflection of the traditional husband-wife role," notes Ornstein. "Never put someone in a truly powerful position whom you can't fire."

New York Times columnist A.M. Rosenthal recently called the decision to give health-care reform to Mrs. Clinton "an evasion of federal anti-nepotism law, a distortion of the constitutional duties and rights of the presidency ... and an insult to every woman who did not get her job through a marriage ring."[11]

The outcome of the health-care reform effort, says Sabato at the University of Virginia, "showed that you don't appoint someone people can't say no to, whom no one else can contradict. It is clear from recent books that staff people bit their tongues. It's dangerous to get the first spouse too heavily in policy because they have more influence than anyone else, even though it's private."

Conservative activist Floyd Brown, president of the Fairfax, Va.,-based Citizens United and a publisher of material criticizing the Clintons, says both the health-care episode and the firing of the travel office staff showed that "this first lady has abused power and is out of control. She's unelected, yet she took a specific action to have her cronies hired, and clearly lied about it. First ladies have been criticized for a long time," he adds, "but she's gone out of her way to exercise power more than her predecessors. Policy-makers must be able to take criticism."

But the Smithsonian's Mayo, no stranger to divisive first ladies, argues that if Hillary Clinton "had positioned herself as the latest in a long line of activist first ladies, she would not have been perceived as a radical departure."

And others point out that key White House players from Roosevelt's Harry Hopkins to John F. Kennedy's brother Robert successfully took on policy roles despite their intimacy with the chief executive. "The question is to what degree does it fall within the White House organizational structure," says Shirley Anne Warshaw, a Gettysburg College political scientist specializing in the modern presidency. "Hillary Clinton and [health-reform strategist] Ira Magaziner were above the structure. Usually, you would have decision memos on which senior staff each put in their two cents as to whether a bill is likely to be successful politically or legislatively. Had Hillary operated within the domestic-policy structure, her plan would have been subjected to more discussion and would have moved further ahead."

But, Warshaw adds, Mrs. Clinton's health-care woes were a product less of her mere participation than of the difficulty of health-care policy itself. "If it had been children's rights or the environment or the war on poverty, it would have been consistent with a Democratic administration," she says. "But health care was terribly unpopular and came back to haunt her. I admire her for tackling it, but where were her smarts?"

Finally, one can argue with the assumption that the first lady "can't be fired." White House watchers took note in October 1994 when Chief of Staff Leon E. Panetta announced that future health-care reform efforts would be spearheaded by White House advisers Robert E. Rubin and Carol Rasco. "Since then, Mrs. Clinton has never been given anything that overt and visible," notes Anthony. "Her current work on children's issues comes directly from her 20 years with the Children's Defense Fund. She tried health reform, and she moved on."

Is sexism behind the resistance to politically active first ladies?

From the distance provided by a trip overseas, Hillary Clinton reflected last fall on the "double bind" faced by modern first ladies.

"There is something about this role that has such a complex psychological component" that it provokes criticism, she said after her trip to Latin America. "Part of this is deflected criticism of the husband and part is a 'feeling of unaccountable power.' The criticism is clearly meant to try to demean and divide men and women. You know, 'Know your place, know where you are supposed to be,' that is something I wish we could overcome. I mean, judge people on their merits. You don't like my health-care plan, criticize my health plan. But don't turn it into some huge attack on the role." [12]

Many feminists and first lady watchers believe this criticism is prompted less by Mrs. Clinton's performance than by old-fashioned sexism. They see it when maverick author Camille Paglia describes Mrs. Clinton as "Ice queen, drag queen: the Great White Feminist Hope," or when the *National Review* refers to her as "that smiling barracuda." [13] They see it in the rash of sexual jokes and rumors that have floated around Mrs. Clinton: that Mrs. Clinton is a lesbian; that she threw a lamp at Bill; or that, as feminist writer Katha Pollitt scoffed in an essay on first lady bashing, "She's got Bill in some incredible sexual stranglehold." [14] And they see sexism in author Texe Marrs' provocatively titled 1993 paperback *Big Sister is Watching You: Hillary Clinton and the White House Feminists Who Now Control America — And Tell the President What to Do.*

NATIONAL URBAN LEAGUE

The White House

Rosalynn Carter was the first president's wife to attend Cabinet meetings.

Many see a predictable pattern in the attacks but acknowledge a variety of motives. In a widely noted op-ed piece headlined "Stop Pillorying Hillary," feminist Betty Friedan linked the criticism to sexism against prominent women, economic interests going after Bill Clinton's health-care plan through Hillary and "female journalists proving they're not feminists by getting Hillary as meanly as the men." [15]

Lynn Cutler, a longtime Democratic activist who coordinates an ongoing public relations defense of Mrs. Clinton, says "the right-wing extremists hate her because of what she is, while the sexists hate her because she's strong and fighting for change. It's the fighting for change that gets them. As she is struggling to balance roles, many women identify with her and take it very personally when she's attacked."

Sexism, of course, is hardly new. Eleanor Roosevelt once commented that "beneath the veneer of courtesy and outward show of consideration universally accorded women, there is a widespread male hostility — age-old perhaps — against sharing with them any actual control." [16]

Though women have clearly gained power since Mrs. Roosevelt spoke in the 1930s, today's society is still adjusting. One reason for the backlash against Mrs. Clinton, says the Smithsonian's Mayo, "is that the first lady mirrors the role of women in society, and there is still so much conflict over balancing the roles of career and homemaker. Women today still do not have political parity with men," she adds. "First ladies still reflect society's concepts about family, motherhood and femininity. This view is important to the older generation, which is more likely than the younger one to see a conflict between motherhood and career."

Women, more than men, are judged by their style, even their manner of speaking. "Expectations for how a woman should speak are at odds with expectations for how a person with authority should speak," says Deborah Tannen, a Georgetown University linguistics professor who has written widely on gender roles. "If we speak as women are expected to, we aren't taken seriously, and if we speak with authority — as a lawyer is trained to speak — we're seen as not feminine and too aggressive. You can't win."

There are plenty of modern women, however, who reject the sexism theory. They argue that public reaction depends on the first lady herself. "Hillary Clinton is opinionated in a way that allows no room for dissension or discussion — it's off-putting," says Mrs. Reagan's former aide Tate. "She and Mrs. Dole have mirror-image educations, but Dole has a better sense of who she is. She's less strident. She's gracious and courteous, but she's confident in what she's talking about, which is less threatening."

Mrs. Dole, to be sure, takes pride in her own pathbreaking climb in a man's world. In the autobiography she and her husband wrote, she recalled her law school days, when "Harvard's sexual caste system was crumbling. Take it from an old hand at leaping walls." [17]

The general acceptance of Mrs. Dole proves that the resistance to Mrs. Clinton "is not a gender issue," Tate continues. "If a woman were running for president and her husband behaved like Mrs. Clinton did in the first Clinton administration, he would have been jumped on, too. Mrs. Clinton was actually given a lot of leeway at first."

Peggy Noonan, a former speechwriter for Presidents Reagan and Bush, also says the sexism theory no longer applies. For Mrs. Clinton "to suggest that her problems stem from the fact that many Americans just can't stand a strong woman is infuriating to people, because she's hiding behind the charges of 'you are a sexist' and they think she is trying to divert attention from the real problem, which is who she is and what she's doing." [18]

Anti-Clinton activist Brown says many women are turned off by Hillary Clinton, noting that Bill Clinton has higher approval ratings among women than his wife does. "Most women are traditionalists, and even though many work and expect to be treated equally, they don't want to throw away the institution of marriage and motherhood," Brown says. "Hillary Clinton's problem with the electorate is that she wants power but no criticism. She can't be both the savvy tough politician/trial lawyer and also play the helpless maiden in distress."

Brookings' Hess agrees that Mrs. Clinton's "in-your-face attitude" would be out of character for Mrs. Dole. He points to Clinton's "irritated and flip remarks, such as, 'What do you want me to do, bake cookies?' There are also some very interesting inconsistencies in her handling of things like Whitewater," he says. "The question is, is she fair game? They can't have it two ways. If they campaign on a co-presidency, they open themselves up."

Sabato says the first spouse is in a "no-win situation unless you force her to sit on her hands." But Mrs. Clinton's troubles are a combination of sexism, the health-care failure, Whitewater and Travelgate, he says. "They feed on each other and reinforce the view that she's domineering."

To Margaret Truman, who has observed many first ladies firsthand, the notion of the president's spouse becoming a crusading policy leader is futile. "Becoming first lady does not, after all, endow a woman with magical qualities, enabling her to deal expertly with any and every problem that floats into the modern White House," she writes. "While I am heartily in favor of women achieving maximum opportunities and power, I doubt that the first lady is the ideal symbolic vehicle for this ascent." [19]

Anthony points out that a first lady's identity as a person is often unrelated to her image in the cultural consciousness. "She's a symbol like Paul Bunyan or the Statue of Liberty," he says, "and that either works in her favor or against her, depending on what the country is going through." Eleanor Roosevelt was criticized for being active in policy in the traumatic era of change during the New Deal and Great Depression. Yet later on, "during World War II, her politically overt efforts found support and were championed."

Today, things are as paradoxical as they've always been, Anthony concludes. "I would like to say the role of women in America has evolved," he says, "and that there is more public or press acceptance of a politically visible first lady, but I don't believe it has."

Mrs. Clinton, meanwhile, has taken a bow toward emphasizing the traditional first lady's role. "My first responsibility . . . is to do whatever my husband would want me to do that he thinks would be helpful to him," she told *U.S. News & World Report* last year. "It may be something of great moment, but more likely it's just to kick back, have a conversation or even play a game of cards and just listen to him ruminate." [20] ■

BACKGROUND

An Ill-Defined Role

The tiny sorority of women who have become first lady achieved it largely by accident, by virtue of a personal relationship that in most cases began decades before their husbands set sights on the White House. Yet there were reasons why men of presidential timber were attracted to certain women. As historian Beverly Boyd Caroli writes, "Most of the men who later achieved the country's highest office married up into socially or economically superior strata of American society, while the women married into more adventure, travel or risk than they had found in their parents' home." [21]

Ignored in the Constitution and denied a slot on the federal payroll, the first lady didn't even have a title until the mid-19th century. Contemporaries of the first president's wife, Martha Washington, fumbled with and discarded such monikers as "Lady Washington," "Presidentress," "Mrs. President" and "Marquise."

The first known public use of the term was in 1849, when President Zachary Taylor delivered a eulogy at the funeral of Washington fixture and former first lady Dolley Madison, calling her "truly our first lady for half a century." The term was first popularized by society columnists, beginning in the Grant and Hayes administrations of the 1870s, though during the Civil War the wife of Jefferson Davis was referred to as "first lady of the Confederacy." [22]

The title was not anchored in *Webster's* dictionary until 1934, and as recently as 1961 Jacqueline Kennedy disdained it, saying it made her sound like a "saddle horse." A search for alternatives by White House adviser Arthur Schlesinger Jr. came up dry. [23]

Successful Teamwork

Precedent for the role of beloved, yet junior partner to the president was set by Martha Washington, who was accorded a 13-gun salute when she arrived in New York City shortly after her husband's first inauguration. Wary of Jeffersonian critics who frowned on trappings of European-style royalty, she spoke only once in public, though she substituted for her husband at a widely noted New York church service.

Library of Congress

Grace Coolidge with her pet raccoon Rebecca.

Early in the country's history, it became clear that men who aspire to the presidency must satisfy voter demand for a model of family life. In 1823, a Tennessee legislative clerk named James K. Polk asked Gen. Andrew Jackson how he could rise in politics. "Stop this philandering," Jackson replied. "They tell me you are a gay Lothario; you must settle down as a sober married man." Jackson recommended a lass named Sarah Childress, who would "give him no trouble." That future first lady agreed to marry Polk, but only if he first ran for the legislature. [24]

Public demand for a first lady was evident in the campaign of 1848, when Zachary Taylor, a Whig and a hero from the Mexican War, was attacked by opposition Democrats because his sickly wife Margaret, whom they derided as "poor white of the wilds," eschewed social life. [25]

It seems inevitable that at least a few men who ascended to the presidency would fulfill the adage that "behind every successful man, there's a woman." Helen "Nellie" Taft was known to be blunt about having pushed her husband to the highest office when all he wanted to be was a U.S. Supreme Court justice. And Florence Harding, who said, "I have only one hobby — my husband," was thought to have been the brains behind her husband's positions as small-town newspaper publisher, senator and president.

"She wasn't criticized, but there were jokes about 'The president and Mr. Harding,'" says Anthony, who is working on her biography. During the 1920 "front-porch" campaign, she expressed sophisticated views in favor of women's suffrage and against President Woodrow Wilson's proposed League of Nations, but "she also knew to bake waffles for a *New York Times* reporter," Anthony says.

To be the president's wife was an ambition that often required sacrifice. Abigail Adams once returned the visits of 60 callers over three or four afternoons. Pat Nixon financed Richard M. Nixon's first congressional campaign with money she had been saving for a down payment on a house. [26] And Eleanor Roosevelt took public-speaking lessons and grew accustomed to

Continued on p. 518

Chronology

1700-1800s
Role of first lady evolves gradually.

1789
Martha Washington avoids queenly airs in establishing role of first lady; franking privileges given to first lady.

1809
Dolley Madison persuades Congress to appropriate $5,000 to renovate White House.

1849
First recorded use of term "first lady," in eulogy for Mrs. Madison.

1869
Publication of Laura Langord Holloway's history, *Ladies of the White House.*

1881
Congress extends pension and expanded franking privileges to presidential widows.

1889
During centennial of George Washington's inauguration, Martha Washington becomes only first lady to appear on U.S. currency; the celebration in New York City features first ladies Caroline Harrison, Julia Grant, Mary Arthur McElroy and Frances Cleveland.

1900s-1950s
First lady hires White House staff members, gets more involved in outside activities.

1900
Edith Roosevelt becomes first first lady to hire a staff member.

1909
Helen Taft is first first lady to ride with her husband in inaugural parade.

1932
First lady Lou Hoover organizes series of half-hour radio talks for Girl Scouts featuring Frances Cleveland Preston, Edith Roosevelt, Nellie Taft and Grace Coolidge.

1933
Eleanor Roosevelt becomes first first lady to hold her own press conferences.

1943
Mrs. Roosevelt becomes first first lady to visit troops overseas, traveling to Guadalcanal for Red Cross.

1946
Rep. James G. Fulton, R-Pa., proposes giving president's wife annual salary of $10,000; idea is abandoned as unlawful.

1945-53
Bess Truman's East Wing office staff grows to five.

1960s-70s *First lady's staff grows to 16, plus others on loan and full-time press secretary.*

1961
Inauguration of John F. Kennedy prompts largest gathering ever of past, present and future first ladies: Edith Wilson, Eleanor Roosevelt, Bess Truman, Mamie Eisenhower, Jacqueline Kennedy, Lady Bird Johnson, Pat Nixon and Betty Ford.

1977
Rosalynn Carter's request for more staff is denied by her husband, President Jimmy Carter.

1978
Mrs. Carter becomes first first lady to attend Cabinet meetings.

1980s *First lady's staff hits 26.*

1982
Betty Ford, Rosalynn Carter and Nancy Reagan attend funeral of Bess Truman.

1985
Nancy Reagan hosts foreign first ladies at drug abuse conference.

1990s *Size of first lady's White House staff settles at 16.*

1993
Hillary Rodham Clinton, in unprecedented move, directs administration's health-care reform effort.

1994
Mrs. Clinton hosts Latin American first ladies at Summit of the Americas in Florida.

Oct. 29, 1995
Elizabeth Dole announces she will stay as president of the Red Cross if her husband, Bob Dole, is elected president.

Jan. 26, 1996
Mrs. Clinton, first presidential wife to be subpoenaed, testifies before Whitewater grand jury.

The Select Club of American Women. . .

The White House lives of 50 women who have been cast in the role of first lady reflect the sweep of American history and the evolving role of women in the United States. Most first ladies were wives, and most were married for decades before attaining the Executive Mansion. Presidents who were bachelors or widowers, or whose wives preferred private life, appointed relatives to serve as their official hostesses.

Martha Dandridge Custis Washington (1731-1802); wife of George Washington; served 1789-1797; prosperous Virginia widow who had to invent role of president's wife without airs of royalty.

Abigail Smith Adams (1744-1818); wife of John Adams; served 1797-1801; daughter of noted Massachusetts family who became known for her letters expressing political opinions and early feminism; exhorted husband to "Remember the ladies."

Martha Jefferson "Patsy" Randolph (1772-1836); daughter of Thomas Jefferson; served 1801-1809; because Jefferson's wife Martha had died in 1782, Patsy and future first lady Dolley Madison shared the duties of White House hostess; Patsy and her husband Thomas Mann Randolph Jr. later lived with her father at Monticello.

Dolley Payne Todd Madison (1768-1849); wife of James Madison; served 1809-1817; famous during War of 1812 for rescuing White House portrait of George Washington; eulogized on her death by President Zachary Taylor as "truly our first lady for half a century."

Elizabeth Kortright Monroe (1768-1830); wife of James Monroe; served 1817-1825; born to a prominent New York family, she went to Paris when Monroe was U.S. ambassador and rescued Madame Lafayette from prison; in White House, she declined to make social calls.

Louisa Catherine Johnson Adams (1775-1852); English wife of John Quincy Adams; served 1825-1829; only foreign-born first lady; suffered poor health as first lady and stayed aloof from politics.

Emily Rachel Donelson (1808-1836); niece of Andrew Jackson; served 1829-1837 after Jackson's wife Rachel died in 1828, just months before his inauguration; Emily quarreled with Andrew Jackson when he disapproved of her joining Cabinet women in snubbing Peggy Eaton, wife of the secretary of War, because of alleged promiscuity; died of tuberculosis just months before Jackson's term ended; his daughter-in-law, **Sarah Yorke Jackson,** served final months.

Angelica Singleton Van Buren (1817-1878); daughter-in-law of Martin Van Buren; served 1837-1841; because the president's wife Hannah had died in 1819, he gave hostess role to Angelica, daughter of a rich South Carolina planter.

Anna Tuthill Symmes Harrison (1775-1864); wife of William Henry Harrison; served briefly because Harrison died a month after being inaugurated in March 1841, before she moved to Washington; only first lady to be grandmother to a president (Benjamin Harrison).

Letitia Christian Tyler (1790-1842); first wife of John Tyler; served 1841-1842; sickly after bearing nine children, she stayed largely in White House quarters before dying of a stroke 18 months into Tyler's term; hostess duties handled by Tyler daughter-in-law **Priscilla Cooper Tyler.** Tyler then married **Julia Gardiner Tyler** (1820-1889); served 1844-1845; 30 years younger than the president and called "The Rose of Long Island," she began tradition of band playing "Hail to the Chief."

Sarah Childress Polk (1803-1891); wife of James K. Polk; served 1845-1849; active as president's secretary, she banned anti-slavery politicians from White House; dancing at parties also banned; during Civil War, her Tennessee home remained neutral for visiting dignitaries.

Margaret Mackall Smith Taylor (1788-1852); wife of Zachary Taylor; lived in White House 1849-1850; raised on the frontier, she declined duties of first lady; president's daughter **Mary Elizabeth "Betty" Taylor Bliss** (1824-1909) took over until the president's sudden death after sitting in the sun at cornerstone ceremony for the Washington Monument.

Abigail Powers Fillmore (1798-1853); wife of Millard Fillmore; served 1850-1853; first working woman to become first lady; created White House library; because she didn't relish hostessing, her daughter **Mary Abigail Fillmore** (1832-1854) substituted; a former school teacher who spoke five languages, Mary died at 22, nearly two years after her father's presidency ended.

Jane Means Appleton Pierce (1806-1863); wife of Franklin Pierce; served 1853-1857; grief-stricken at the death of son Benny in railroad accident, she shunned White House social life; relied on friend **Abby Kent Means** as hostess for first two years of husband's term.

Harriet Lane (1830-1903); niece of James Buchanan; served 1857-1861; already had served bachelor uncle when he was ambassador to England; well-educated when she moved to White House at 26, she was known for fashion sense and gay parties (the song "Listen to the Mockingbird" was written for her); art collection donated to the federal government.

Mary Todd Lincoln (1818-1882); wife of Abraham Lincoln; served 1861-1865; well-born Kentucky woman was criticized for lavish spending on clothing during Civil War; retreated from public after her husband's assassination and suffered mental problems following death of son.

Eliza McCardle Johnson (1810-1876); wife of Andrew Johnson; served 1865-1869; steadied husband during impeachment trial; because of her tuberculosis, she appointed daughter, **Martha Johnson Patterson** (1828-1901) as hostess; Martha redecorated White House and grazed cows on lawn.

Julia Boggs Dent Grant (1826-1902); wife of Ulysses S. Grant; served 1869-1877; entertained lavishly at White House with 29-course meals; first of first ladies to write memoirs.

Lucy Ware Webb Hayes (1831-1889); wife of Rutherford B. Hayes; served 1877-1881; first college graduate among

. . .Who Played the Role of First Lady

first ladies; called "Lemonade Lucy" by reporters because she and husband banned alcohol.

Lucretia Rudolph Garfield (1832-1918); wife of James A. Garfield; served 1881; studious daughter of Hiram College founder, was planning redecoration of White House when she contracted malaria; husband en route to visit her when assassinated in 1881; she presided over funeral.

Mary Arthur McElroy (1842-1917); sister of Chester Alan Arthur; served 1881-85 because Arthur's wife Ellen had died of pneumonia in January 1880; president refused Mary protocol rank equal to first lady.

Frances Folsom Cleveland (1864-1947); wife of Grover Cleveland; served 1886-89, and again 1893-1897; before bachelor Cleveland married 21-year-old Frances, he gave social duties to his sister **Rose Cleveland** (1846-1918), a scholar and lecturer in literature and languages; Frances Cleveland, youngest first lady, was the first to be married in White House; gave birth to baby Ruth, namesake to candy bar.

Caroline Lavinia Scott Harrison (1832-1892); wife of Benjamin Harrison; served 1889-1892; known as White House's "best housekeeper"; planned major renovations but Congress wouldn't fund them; started White House china collection; sickly, she died two weeks before husband's defeat for second term.

Ida Saxton McKinley (1847-1907); wife of William McKinley; served 1897-1901; invalid who suffered from epilepsy; when he was fatally shot in 1901, his final words asked about her.

Edith Kermit Carow Roosevelt (1861-1948); wife of Theodore Roosevelt; served 1901-1909; upgraded White House security and separated family quarters from work; started gallery of first lady portraits.

Helen "Nellie" Herron Taft (1861-1943); wife of William H. Taft; served 1909-1913; first president's wife to ride with husband in inaugural parade; canceled traditional Cabinet wives lunch to focus more on presidential politics; responsible for planting Tidal Basin's Japanese cherry trees.

Ellen Louise Axson Wilson (1860-1914); first wife of Woodrow Wilson; served 1913-1914; backed legislation to rehabilitate District of Columbia slums; died of Bright's disease; **Edith Bolling Galt Wilson** (1872-1961); Wilson's second wife; served 1915-1921; with husband ill and bedridden for 17 months, she monitored paper flow, exerted considerable influence.

Florence Kling Harding (1860-1924); wife of Warren Harding; served 1921-1923; called "the Dutchess" by Harding; played crucial role in propelling him from small-town newspaper publisher to national candidate. After his sudden death, she burned papers of scandal-plagued administration.

Grace Anna Goodhue Coolidge (1879-1957); wife of Calvin Coolidge; served 1923-1929; first president's wife to attend co-ed college; stayed out of politics; called herself "the national hugger" because frequently photographed meeting children; suffered death of son during White House tenure.

Lou Henry Hoover (1874-1944); wife of Herbert Hoover; served 1929-1933; expert in mining; first first lady to speak on radio; active in Red Cross and other philanthropies.

Anna Eleanor Roosevelt Roosevelt (1884-1962); wife of Franklin D. Roosevelt; served 1933-1945; regarded as first independent first lady, she had her own newspaper column and daily press conferences; traveled alone on behalf of president.

Elizabeth Virginia Wallace "Bess" Truman (1885-1982); wife of Harry S Truman; served 1945-1953; called "the Boss" by husband, who consulted her regularly; avoided reporters and public speaking.

Marie Geneva "Mamie" Doud Eisenhower (1896-1979); wife of Dwight D. Eisenhower; served 1953-1961; last first lady born in 19th century; famous for decorating in pink; suffered from weak heart.

Jacqueline Lee Bouvier Kennedy (1929-1994); wife of John F. Kennedy; served 1961-1963; among youngest first ladies; redecorated White House and started guidebook. Noted for courage after husband's assassination.

Claudia Alta "Lady Bird" Taylor Johnson (1912-); wife of Lyndon B. Johnson; served 1963-1969; active on the campaign trail; advocated highway-beautification legislation.

Patricia Ryan Nixon (1912-1993); wife of Richard M. Nixon; served 1969-1974; traveled widely with husband; brought antiques and portraits back to White House; made it accessible to the disabled.

Elizabeth "Betty" Bloomer Warren Ford (1918-); wife of Gerald R. Ford, served 1974-1977; backed the unsuccessful Equal Rights Amendment; broke taboos by announcing her treatments for chemical dependency and breast cancer.

Rosalynn Smith Carter (1927-); wife of Jimmy Carter; served 1977-1981; husband's campaign partner; first president's wife to attend Cabinet meetings; chief issues were mental health and child immunization; published autobiography in 1984.

Nancy Davis Reagan (1921-); wife of Ronald Reagan; served 1981-1989; as film actress appeared alongside future husband in "Hellcats of the Navy"; as first lady, presided over selection of new White House china, regularly consulted astrologer; launched campaign against drug abuse; published memoirs in 1989.

Barbara Pierce Bush (1925-) wife of George Bush; served 1989-1993; as first lady promoted child and adult literary and wrote best-selling book in voice of family dog, "Millie"; published memoirs in 1994.

Hillary Rodham Clinton (1947-), wife of Bill Clinton; served 1993 to present; Yale University Law School graduate who worked as corporate attorney; broke precedent by heading president's most important domestic initiative, the unsuccessful effort to reform health-care system; best-selling book, *It Takes a Village*, published in 1995.

Continued from p. 514

frequent travel once her husband had contracted polio.

On the campaign trail, Mamie Eisenhower, who could be even more partisan than her husband, was said to be worth "50 electoral votes" due to her smile and pleasant figure. [27] Lyndon B. Johnson's wife was such a key campaigner that she stumped the South in her own train, the Lady Bird Special.

The only men to successfully run for president as bachelors (several widowers have done it) were James Buchanan and Grover Cleveland (during his first campaign). Though 19th-century politicians enjoyed more privacy than today's do, Buchanan's lifestyle prompted opponents to mock his "feminine traits" and *The New York Times* to snarl that other famous bachelors included Judas Iscariot. [28]

Today's public would have a problem electing a bachelor, says the Smithsonian's Mayo. Though former Gov. Edmund G. "Jerry" Brown Jr., D-Calif., and consumer activist Ralph Nader are two who have run, "there needs to be a perception of stability and family that is normal and responsible," she says. "No matter how we rationalize it, the president's family does present an image of the value system for the country."

Inability to capitalize on the image of a stable home and hearth can ruin a presidential campaign. In 1988, for example, Democratic nominee Michael S. Dukakis was roundly criticized when he failed to make an emotional defense of his wife when he was asked a tricky hypothetical question about capital punishment during a nationally televised debate: "If Kitty Dukakis were raped and murdered, would you favor an irrevocable death penalty for the killer?"

The Down Side

The vague and shifting role of first lady watched so avidly by the public was described aptly by Grace Coolidge: "This was I and yet not I — This was the wife of the president of the United States, and she took precedence over me; my personal likes and dislikes must be subordinated to the consideration of those things which were required of her." [29]

Lyndon Baines Johnson Library

"Lady Bird" Johnson advocated highway-beautification legislation.

To many, such a role was tough to swallow. Life as the president's mate was described by Martha Washington as "more like a state prisoner than anything else." The nonstop entertaining of congressional wives made Louisa Johnson Adams feel like a "bird in a cage." Margaret Taylor called her husband's nomination "a plot to deprive her of his society and shorten his life." To Eleanor Roosevelt, the job was "the only case of involuntary servitude in the USA." To Betty Ford, it was "a 24-hour-a-day volunteer job."

A number of first ladies during the "log cabin" era of the early 19th century felt wracked by social insecurity as they were judged through the poised lorgnettes of Washington's "cave dwellers," as its high-society crowd was known.

And many resented the pressure to be a role model. "As the first lady of the United States, you from your official position must take a greater interest in the development of women's industries than any lady in the land," Lucy Hayes was admonished as the country awaited her leadership as "the new woman." Yet Hayes stayed behind the scenes, declining to attend women's conferences or to press for women's right to vote. [30]

And perhaps most difficult, several first ladies endured their famous husbands' infidelities while in the White House, notably Florence Harding, Eleanor Roosevelt and Jacqueline Kennedy. [31]

Going Their Own Way

For reasons both personal and societal, many first ladies have charted a course that veered from that of being their husband's helpmate. Abigail Adams, who admired early feminist writers such as Mary Wollstonecraft, wrote in one of her many surviving letters that, "I will never consent to have our sex considered in an inferior point of light." (Adams was also the first president's wife to leak news to the press, using inside information from her son, an ambassador and future president, to influence debate on politics in Europe.)

Sarah Polk displayed an independent streak when her husband's opponents in the 1844 election threatened to back Sen. Henry Clay of Kentucky because his wife was a good housekeeper and could make fine butter. "If I get to the White House, I expect to live on $25,000 a year, and I will neither keep house nor make butter," she said. [32]

Mary Todd Lincoln, who often badgered her husband on behalf of favor seekers, raised eyebrows in March 1865 when she berated the president during a victory ceremony at a Richmond battlefield. She was angry at being seated in the rear.

Julia Grant reveled so much in the role of first lady that she weepingly implored her reluctant husband to seek an unprecedented third term. "I do not want to be here another four years," said President Grant. "I don't think I could stand it. Don't bother [me] about it, I beg of you." [33]

In perhaps the most remarked-upon episode, Edith Wilson, the second wife of President Wilson, became the talk of the town in 1919 after her husband had a stroke and was bedridden for 17 months. At the doctors' request, she insisted, Mrs. Wilson took over control of paper flow to her husband, learned the secret military codes and routed many documents to various departments. Her actions provoked such comments as "petticoat government" and "secret president." A Republican senator called her project "a regency not contemplated in the Constitution."

More recently, Betty Ford upset her husband during the 1976 campaign when she admitted on CBS' "60 Minutes" that her son had tried marijuana and that she would not be surprised if told that her daughter was having premarital sex. "You just cost me 10 million votes," Gerald R. Ford told her, only half-jokingly.

The risks of being on the public stage, however, seem worth the benefits in the view of most modern first ladies. "They'll listen to the first lady, though they don't always react the way you want them to," noted Rosalynn Carter. "If you really care about something," said Nancy Reagan, "the first lady position gives you a platform you'll never have again, so you'd be foolish not to use it." [34] ■

CURRENT SITUATION

Making Wives an Issue

This year's primary season opened with a flock of first lady hopefuls — Elizabeth Dole, Wendy Gramm, Honey Alexander, Joan Specter — all career women. As the Republican field narrowed to Mrs. Dole, strategists began speculating over whether she would raise or lower the prominence of the first lady issue in the election.

Ann Lewis, deputy manager of the Clinton-Gore campaign, says she doesn't expect it to be central, "but the Republicans can't resist attacking Mrs. Clinton, even though they know at some rational level it can go too far and do them damage. President Clinton is doing better now, so they are raising the level of invective, and she's a target. That's why there's a gender gap."

Lewis says the criticism of Mrs. Clinton reflects the GOP's 1992 national convention, in which speakers went after Mrs. Clinton in ways many now feel were strident. "Hillary has compared marriage and the family as institutions to slavery and life on an Indian reservation," unsuccessful candidate Patrick J. Buchanan told the convention. "Well, speak for yourself, Hillary."

Officials at the Dole campaign, meanwhile, slyly refer to Elizabeth Dole as their "secret weapon" while apparently being careful to include Hillary Clinton's picture in advertisements attacking the president. [35] "Mrs. Dole is by far one of the campaign's most treasured assets," says deputy press secretary Christine Martin. "Her warmth and conviction cannot be matched on the campaign trail. The strength of her affection and belief in husband Bob Dole can be heard in her every word."

"Mrs. Dole's active role will mitigate against the GOP taking too many shots at Hillary," says Gettysburg College's Warshaw. "The fact is, we're a society in which women work. Mrs. Clinton is a corporate lawyer. The question is not whether she'll work, but what should she do. The White House staff is there to make the tea sandwiches."

"If Hillary is unpopular, Mrs. Dole's softness will be an advantage for Dole," says Sabato. "But he has to be careful; many think his wife is a much stronger candidate."

Ornstein says the first lady issue is "tricky to exploit because you risk a backlash in sympathy from feminists and others saying don't gang up on the first lady just because you don't want to gang up on the president. Hillary is the champion of a lot of the Democratic base, and the GOP doesn't want that base to turn out in massive numbers unless they have a more compensating advantage on the other side, perhaps Whitewater."

Any Republican attacks "would have to be subliminal, by indirection," says Hess. "The chances of them backfiring are too great. There will be some sniping at the Floyd Brown level. But Hillary's ratings may rise. Historically, the president and first lady go up and down in tandem. His [ratings] going up could bring hers up."

Brown's Citizens United is as active as ever, its February newsletter taunting, "Will Hillary Ever Testify? Or Stop Lying?" A steady stream of attacks on Mrs. Clinton have been sent out on TV and radio by political commentator Rush Limbaugh. In February, he broadcast an off-color joke combining Mrs. Clinton's ethics troubles with an old expression about under-age sex. "Imagine Hillary Clinton, still jailbait at age 46," he said.[36]

Brown, for his part, says, "There are always risks in politics, but if you look at the poor approval ratings for Hillary, the risk-reward ratio [in attacking] is pretty good. Mrs. Clinton is already an issue with conservatives. We won't back off just because it's an election year."

Republican adviser Tate emphasizes that "Mrs. Clinton is not running. All mistakes she has made on health care, etc. redound to the president. The focus should be on him, but if she makes a major mistake, we would jump on it."

Surveys show the public somewhat split on the candidates' wives. In a March *USA Today*-CNN-Gallup poll, Mrs. Clinton's favorable-unfavorable ratings were at 47 percent-48 percent. Mrs. Dole's favorables topped out at 46 percent, but her unfavorables were only 16 percent.

Defending Hillary

Several organizations have lent their energies to defending the embattled Hillary Clinton. Protest marches have been spearheaded by the National Organization for Women, the Hollywood Political Women's Committee and the Democratic National Committee, many participants wearing buttons reading, "Stop Pillorying Hillary."

In April, Emily's List, a Democratic women's fund-raising group, feted Mrs. Clinton at a banquet "pep rally" for 1,000 supporters at which speakers ridiculed Senate Whitewater committee Chairman Alphonse M. D'Amato, R-N.Y., and Whitewater prosecutor Kenneth W. Starr. "When you've got no vision of how to make the world a better place for yourself or your children, then you go negative," Mrs. Clinton said. "Let's not let them get away with anything in the next seven months."[37]

Also active is the Back to Business Committee, a group of prominent feminists and Democrats run from the offices of The Kamber Group, a Washington public relations firm. The committee was set up in spring 1994, when it raised $50,000 and took out a full-page ad in *The New York Times*. "In the last month, we have witnessed a rising level of attacks on Hillary Clinton, a rise both in volume and in their personal nature," said the text signed by politicos and celebrities such as Joanne Woodward, Tony Randall and Franklin D. Roosevelt III. It compared the attacks to the hits against Eleanor Roosevelt, "who stood for things this nation desperately needed to address in the 1930s. . . . We are proud of Hillary Rodham Clinton."

Historically, says Back to Business Committee leader Cutler, "this [committee] is probably a first. Eleanor saw attacks just as vitriolic but had no organized defense. The Right has already gone too far, but is prepared to go further. They are playing with fire. For the last year, the Clintons have turned over every scrap of paper [on Whitewater and Travelgate], yet literally hundreds of subpoenas hit the White House every day. There is no criminal intent in her behavior. And Mrs. Clinton has said she should have handled things differently. Her idea of [maintaining] a zone of privacy is different now."

Furthermore, Cutler says, criticisms of the Clintons for being "greedy" back in the 1980s "drive me nuts. Here's a young couple on the path to public service, and it's clear he won't make any money. She makes an investment because she's pregnant or wants to be pregnant, for Chelsea's college fund. Why is that greedy and for other people it's a shrewd investment? They accuse us of hypocrisy but none of us liberals ever said we didn't want a few bucks in the bank, or we don't want our children to have the best education. That's different from buying up companies to absorb them and fire the entire work force."

Since her retreat from health care, Hillary Clinton has written a best-selling book, *It Takes a Village* (with proceeds to charity), launched a newspaper column (like Eleanor Roosevelt) and, according to press reports, still sends a representative to important White House meetings, even if she doesn't attend herself. She and her husband have also responded to criticisms about being unwilling to admit error. "Look, health care is the toughest, meanest issue in the world," Bill Clinton said. The administration made mistakes, "But I don't think these had anything to do with her being involved in it. They were my mistakes, and I was responsible for it."[38]

Mrs. Clinton, in a May 28 interview with PBS anchorman Jim Lehrer, said that in the future she would "not take on a high-visibility national issue with a great big target on my face."

Dole at the Red Cross

Elizabeth Dole has not escaped the scrutiny that comes to modern candidates' wives, particularly those with a long professional record. Last January, *The New Yorker* magazine raised questions about her investments in Kansas and her former business manager who was convicted of tax fraud.[39] In February, she rushed a check for $75,000 to the Red Cross, saying an accounting error had caused her to

Continued on p. 522

At Issue:

Is the role of first lady outmoded?

GERMAINE GREER
Feminist and author

FROM "ABOLISH HER: THE FEMINIST CASE AGAINST FIRST LADIES," THE NEW REPUBLIC, JUNE 25, 1995.

yes

Though feminism is often said to have changed the world, it is still true at the end of the millennium that the surest strategy for a woman who is seriously interested in executive political power is to marry a man who either is or is going to be the president of the United States. . . .

The elevation of a democratically elected leader's unelected consort makes a mockery of the democratic process itself but, as long as the media are the real arbiters of leader selection, neither politician nor party will dare to buck the trend. . . .

The phenomenon was created by the American newspapers that reported the first public appearances of George Washington's almost-60-year-old wife, Martha, in 1789. . . . Because few women appeared in print, the fuss made over Martha Washington . . . catapulted her to a position of enormous influence. People began to care what she thought about things, but the contradiction that has tormented all first ladies already afflicted her. The more people cared what she thought, the more careful she had to be about keeping her thoughts to herself and saying nothing that might complicate her husband's affairs. Then, as now, the president's wife was expected to play the role of virtuoso housekeeper, to run the residence and to entertain visiting dignitaries. . . .

All the contradictions in the historic role of the first lady meet in the embattled figure of Hillary Clinton. . . . For the president to bring his wife out of seclusion may seem like progress, but to dub her first lady at the same time and to display her in every conceivable medium as such is as retrograde to the cause of human equality as the tendency to turn elected office into hereditary rulership. In a democratic world, mere relationship to an elected officeholder should simply never be a route to power. The courtesies extended to male politicians' wives in the West should never be justified in the name of equality because the duties expected of politicians' wives are demeaning and dishonorable. . . .

It can no longer be acceptable that a person should achieve high visibility, influence and even a degree of executive power simply because she shares a bed . . . with a head of state. In this, at least, the communists were surely right. The old Soviet practice of allowing a politician's wife her privacy and the continued exercise of her profession is a more hopeful precedent than the one set by Nancy Reagan. With any luck, in the 21st century . . . [n]o woman anywhere will be expected to relinquish her privacy and her own work, to diet and dress up and give interviews every day simply because she has married a man who has a prospect of success in politics.

ZOFIA SMARDZ
A former correspondent for Newsweek

FROM "IT DOESN'T TAKE A VILLAGE IDIOT," THE WOMEN'S QUARTERLY, SPRING 1996.

no

Hillary Clinton's misfired efforts to expand the first lady's role into the policy-making arena have been followed by Elizabeth Dole's landmark announcement that she would keep her job as president of the American Red Cross if her husband managed to win the White House. . . . Both seem to be saying that being a first lady is not worth a smart woman's time or talent. And that, ultimately, is a snub not only to all the first ladies who have gone before, but to the American public itself.

Viewed from the car pool lane, after all, the first ladyship looks like a dream job, the best job for a woman in all America, barring the day when a woman becomes the chief executive herself. It's a position of unique privilege, prominence and, yes, power to which only a handful of women ever have the opportunity to accede.

For all the difficulties attendant upon it — the fishbowl existence, the fierce media spotlight, the roller-coaster ride of public praise and criticism — the role offers rewards unattainable to most American women. It's hard to imagine how any job, however demanding or important, could compete with hosting state leaders from Japan, Israel or Russia, or representing the United States abroad, or bringing one's personal influence to bear on a campaign for children's welfare, or against illiteracy or drugs, or any number of other worthy causes. It's hard to see how any one job could be more important than serving one's country, even in the part of second fiddle. (The first lady also gets to be mistress of the White house, a fantasy for which I for one would willingly give up a few years of privacy.). . . .

A woman like Elizabeth Dole, who has been a Washington supercrat for most of her career, is hardly at a stage of life where proving herself professionally is a major goal, or where taking off four to eight years would be detrimental to her future career pursuits (as if having been first lady could ever be detrimental to any woman's future career pursuits).

Mrs. Dole's promise to maintain an outside profession only promotes the view that the East Wing and its offices should serve as another platform for asserting a feminist vision of women's role in society. And it has the ring of a politically correct appeal to baby boomer careerism unashamed to place the pursuit of personal satisfaction ahead of less lucrative public concerns. At a time when the whole country could use another look at the old-fashioned notion of personal sacrifice for the general and future good, who better than the first lady to illuminate it for us?

Elizabeth Dole surveys damage from the 1993 Midwest floods with a Red Cross disaster supervisor.

Continued from p. 520

donate less than she had pledged. And this month, *The New York Times* examined in depth how Mrs. Dole uses her powerful political connections to benefit the Red Cross. [40]

But nothing has caused more of a stir than her announcement, made last fall but reemphasized recently, that if her husband becomes president, she will perform first lady duties while returning to run the Red Cross. Critics ranging from campaign finance analysts to conservative anti-feminist Phyllis Schlafly raised concerns about time constraints and conflicts of interest.

There is a fear that in soliciting corporate donations for the Red Cross, Mrs. Dole would be manipulated by companies seeking to influence the president. "The Red Cross is not General Motors — it intersects regularly with the federal government, in international policy, in blood supply issues and as a leader of nonprofits and in health care," says Ornstein. "No one is more venerated than the Red Cross, but she's CEO of a billion-dollar corporation, while being first lady is full-time job."

Brown of Citizens United counters that having Mrs. Dole at the Red Cross would mean "she will be meddling less in policy than Hillary because she won't have an office in the White House west wing."

Red Cross spokesman Roy Clason points out that Mrs. Dole's plans are welcomed by the organization's Board of Governors, many of whom are Clinton appointees.

Mrs. Dole herself said that she and her husband always "compartmentalize" their careers. "Bob has been handling every issue known to man as majority leader," she said. "There has been absolutely not one bit of conflict and concern." [41]

Mrs. Dole also plans to continue working with at-risk youth and promoting volunteerism and philanthropic giving. "She will have the time and can do whatever she wants," says first lady authority Anthony. "Think about the public face and image of the Red Cross. It's not different from being first lady. When she opens a blood bank and they take her picture, it's still first-lady stuff. But if she reported to a law firm every day, the public wouldn't stand for it. It's not whether she takes a job but the type of job that's the issue."

Mayo says Mrs. Dole's decision is an "innovative way to grapple with the problem. She profits from the perception that she is a conservative, just like Nixon the red-baiter" was able to pull off his trip to China, Mayo says. "Imagine if a Democrat like Hillary had said 'to hell with being first lady, I want a career.' It would generate greater controversy."

Would the president's wife be able to fulfill her responsibilities as first lady if she had an outside job? According to a January CBS News-*New York Times* poll, 50 percent of Americans say yes (including more Democrats than Republicans), compared with 52 percent in 1992. ■

OUTLOOK

To the Nation's Heart

In the future, the president's spouse is likely to hold a job, says Hess. "The spouse could be a teacher of law in Washington, or something else that couldn't possibly cast aspersions on the office. But it has to be carefully considered by the family. The presidency comes to few people, and one must be willing to subordinate their career. It's not a blow to feminist ideology," he adds. "I assume Dennis Thatcher [husband of the former British prime minister] made a decision to suspend his career because his wife's job was important."

Tate disputes the notion that the country has entered a new era. "Each first lady has to redefine the role for herself," she says. "Since Eleanor Roosevelt, the public has come to expect only that she use this exalted position to do some good for someone or some cause."

And will the first lady always be expected to gaze adoringly up at her husband, in a style made famous by Nancy Reagan? "The first lady is the kinder, gentler side of a presidency," says Mayo. "She's still in a mediation role between the male power structure and those without access to power."

Tannen argues that Hillary Clinton has "this adoring gaze, too, but people filter this through their expectations, with the image of her as career woman. They forget that Mrs. Clinton is the one with a child, not Mrs. Dole."

Anthony says some of Mrs. Clinton's difficulties come from her being too honest about the kind of political roles she and her husband have sought for her. "The press needs a good cop and bad cop, to categorize people to make a colorful story and good headlines," he says. "She becomes a 'bitch' from the mere fact that she will discuss policy. She could go to a tea at the Daughters of the American Revolution and recite word for word a White House statement on say, the gas tax, and she would be criticized as too 'in your face.' Nancy Reagan was used the same way by liberals and the press during the recession when she acquired the new White House China," he adds. "It's a caricature, but it persists as a legend."

In the final analysis, says Margaret Truman, no matter what role she plays or how the press labels her, "a first lady speaks to the nation's heart. A president has to do that too, but he represents other things — power, pride, policy — that can easily interfere with the unqualified caring the heart evokes. Simply by being there, creating, as Martha Washington did, the tone, the emotional aura of a president's administration, the first lady reminds us that American politics has been different from the start. It has always recognized the need to win hearts as well as minds." [42]

More changes are underway in this most fluid of American institutions. As Barbara Bush once put it when she spoke to a Wellesley College graduation: "Who knows, maybe someone who's here today will follow in my footsteps and preside over the White House as the president's spouse. I wish HIM well." [43] ■

FOR MORE INFORMATION

White House Historical Association, 740 Jackson Pl., N.W., Washington, D.C. 20503; (202) 737-8292. Publishes a wide variety of books on the White House, the presidents and first ladies. Other sources of information include the Library of Congress and several presidential libraries.

Smithsonian Institution, National Museum of American History, Publications Office, MRC646, 14th and Constitution Ave. N.W., Washington, D.C. 20560. Publishes *First Ladies: Political Role and Public Image* and other related books.

Notes

1 Margaret Truman, *First Ladies: An Intimate Group Portrait of White House Wives* (1995), p. 63. Mrs. Roosevelt's critic was newsletter editor Willard Kiplinger of the Kiplinger Washington Letter.

2 Henry Louis Gates Jr., "Hating Hillary," *The New Yorker,* Feb. 26/March 4, 1996, p. 119.

3 Reported by the Center for Media and Public Affairs, a Washington, D.C., research and educational organization that studies media coverage of social and political issues.

4 Interviewed on National Public Radio, "All Things Considered," April 17, 1996.

5 Carl Sferrazza Anthony, *First Ladies* (1990), p. 453.

6 *Newsday,* March 30, 1996.

7 Doris Kearns Goodwin, *No Ordinary Time* (1994), p. 324.

8 Quoted in *The Washington Post,* Nov. 24, 1994.

9 Truman, *op. cit.,* p. 82.

10 Marlin Fitzwater, *Call the Briefing!: Reagan and Bush, Sam and Helen: A Decade With Presidents and the Press* (1995), p. 169.

11 *The New York Times,* Feb. 13, 1996.

12 Quoted in *The Washington Post,* Oct. 18, 1995.

13 Camille Paglia, "Ice Queen, Drag Queen: A psychological portrait of Hillary," *The New Republic,* March 4, 1996, p. 23. Florence King, "The Great Girl," *National Review,* May 11, 1992, p. 64.

14 Katha Pollitt, "The Male Media's Hillary Problem," *The Nation,* May 17, 1993, p. 657.

15 *Los Angeles Times,* April 26, 1994.

16 Blanche Wiesen Cook, *Eleanor Roosevelt: Volume One, 1884-1933* (1992), p. 368.

17 Bob and Elizabeth Dole, with Richard Norton Smith, *The Doles: Unlimited Partners* (1988), p. 78.

18 Quoted in Gates, *op. cit.,* p. 119.

19 Truman, *op. cit.,* p. 154.

20 *U.S. News & World Report,* Feb. 27, 1995, p. 35.

21 Beverly Boyd Caroli, *First Ladies* (1987), p. 186.

22 *Ibid.,* p. xv.

23 Diana Dixon Healy, *America's First Ladies: Private Lives of the Presidential Wives* (1988), p. xii.

24 Paul F. Boller Jr., *Presidential Wives: An Anecdotal History* (1988), p. 91.

25 Healy, *op. cit.,* p. 61.

26 Anthony, *op. cit.,* p. 538.

27 Truman, *op. cit.,* p. 214.

28 Caroli, *op. cit.,* p. 309.

29 *Ibid,* p. 171.

30 Boller, *op. cit.,* p. 151.

31 For background, see "Politics and Privacy," *The CQ Researcher,* April 17, 1992, pp. 337-360.

32 Caroli, *op. cit.,* p. 62.

33 Truman, *op. cit.,* p. 212.

34 Quoted in television news footage included in the Smithsonian First Ladies exhibit.

35 Quoted in *The New York Times,* Jan. 16, 1996.

36 Reported by the Langhorne, Pa.-based *Rush Watch Weekly,* March 18, 1996. See "Talk Show Democracy," *The CQ Researcher,* April 29, 1994, pp. 361-384.

37 Quoted in *The New York Times,* April 27, 1996.

38 Quoted in *The Washington Post,* Feb, 9, 1996.

39 Jane Mayer, "Blind Trust," *The New Yorker,* Jan. 22, 1996, p. 62.

40 Douglas Frantz, "Elizabeth Dole: Her Power as Leader of Red Cross," *The New York Times,* May 31, 1996, p. A1.

41 Quoted in *USA Today,* May 5, 1996.

42 Truman, *op. cit.,* p. 354.

43 *Boston Globe,* June 2, 1990.

Bibliography

Selected Sources Used

Books

Anthony, Carl Sferrazza, *First Ladies: The Saga of the President's Wives and Their Power, 1789-1961,* William Morrow, 1990 (Vol. 1), 1991 (Vol. 2).
An author noted for his specialization in first ladies offers detailed portraits of their lives and times. Vol. 1 stops at Mamie Eisenhower; Vol. 2 covers Jacqueline Kennedy through Barbara Bush.

Boller, Paul F. Jr., *Presidential Wives: An Anecdotal History,* Oxford University Press, 1988.
A professor of history emeritus at Texas Christian University produced this collection of detailed anecdotes about first ladies through Nancy Reagan.

Caroli, Betty Boyd, *First Ladies*, Oxford University Press, 1987.
A historian and college teacher offers portraits of the lives and times of first ladies through Nancy Reagan, adding her own commentary on political marriage and first ladies' relations with the media.

Diller, Daniel C., and Stephen L. Robertson, *The Presidents, First Ladies and Vice Presidents: White House Biographies, 1789-1989,* Congressional Quarterly, 1989.
These fact-oriented sketches of White House occupants (including substitute first ladies) also analyze the evolution of the role of first lady.

Gould, Lewis L., *Lady Bird Johnson and the Environment*, University of Kansas Press, 1988.
A historian at the University of Texas, Austin, who specializes in first ladies produced this detailed study of the politics, policies and long-term impact of the Johnson administration's highway-beautification legislation.

Grimes, Ann, *Running Mates: The Making of a First Lady, A Penetrating Look at Private Women in the Public Eye,* William Morrow, 1990.
A Washington-based reporter examines the 1988 presidential race from the point of view of candidates' wives Barbara Bush and Kitty Dukakis.

Healy, Diana Dixon, *America's First Ladies: Private Lives of the Presidential Wives,* Atheneum, 1988.
A writer specializing in political history compiled these profiles of every first lady through Nancy Reagan, highlighting each profile with a nickname or emblematic quote.

Klapthor, Margaret Brown, *The First Ladies,* White House Historical Association in cooperation with the National Geographic Society, 1995.
This set of profiles written by a former curator of the political division of the Smithsonian's National Museum of American History has been updated regularly since it was first published in 1975.

Mayo, Edith P., and Denise D. Meringolo, *First Ladies: Political Role and Public Image*, Smithsonian Institution, 1994.
A curator and former research assistant at the National Museum of American History assembled this collection of anecdotes, portraits, artifacts and candid shots of first ladies in the White House and on the campaign trail.

Mayo, Edith P. (ed.), *The Smithsonian Book of the First Ladies: Their Lives Times and Issues,* Henry Holt, 1996.
This assemblage of material from the National Museum of American History offers biographies and a discussion of changing women's roles in U.S. history; introduction by Hillary Rodham Clinton.

Truman, Margaret, *First Ladies: An Intimate Group Portrait of White House Wives,* Random House, 1995.
The daughter of Bess and Harry Truman offers observations and anecdotes about selected first ladies, including her own thoughts on the impact and limitations of the job.

The Next Step

Additional information from UMI's Newspaper & Periodical Abstracts database

Elizabeth Dole

Beck, Joan, "Redefining the role of first lady: Elizabeth Dole will push envelope further," ***Chicago Tribune,*** **Jan. 18, 1996, p. 19.**

Beck comments on Elizabeth Dole, wife of Republican presidential candidate Bob Dole. She notes that Dole is a highly competent woman with professional credentials easily a match for Hillary Rodham Clinton's and says she is a lot more savvy about politics. Beck looks at what Americans really want in their first lady.

Seelye, Katharine Q., "Mrs. Dole to resume career even if she is the first lady," ***The New York Times,*** **Jan. 16, 1996, p. A1.**

Elizabeth Dole says that she plans to return to her post as president of the Red Cross upon the election of her husband, Sen. Bob Dole, R-Kan., as president. As she campaigns for her husband, Elizabeth Dole seems to be also campaigning for herself — and for her desire to upend the more than 200-year-old expectation that the first lady will stay home. If she has her way, Dole would be the first first lady to work full time at her own career outside the White House.

Szegedy-Maszak, Marianne, "Ladies-in-waiting," ***Harper's Bazaar,*** **March 1996, pp. 351-352.**

Hillary Clinton has redefined the role of first lady, and the wives of the men running for president in 1996 are playing major roles in their campaigns. Elizabeth Dole, Wendy Gramm, and Honey Alexander and their work on their Republican husbands' campaigns are discussed.

Thomas, Helen, "A first lady's work is never done," ***Chicago Defender,*** **Nov. 6, 1995, p. 12.**

Thomas comments on the job of first lady, noting Elizabeth Dole's indication that she would keep her job as head of the Red Cross if her husband is elected president.

First Ladies and Their Issues

"Asides: Just say welcome back," ***The Wall Street Journal,*** **March 13, 1995, p. A14.**

A brief editorial endorses the need to return to the "Just Say No" antidrug campaign of former first lady Nancy Reagan, saying that it is "time to reprise Mrs. Reagan's powerful message for a new generation of young people."

Sallee, Rad, "Former first lady promotes literacy," ***Houston Chronicle,*** **March 15, 1995, p. A22.**

In a call to promote literacy, former first lady Barbara Bush told a gathering of Houston Club women that parents must take time to read with their children.

Hillary Rodham Clinton

Barta, Carolyn, "Would-be first ladies no Hillary wannabes," ***Atlanta Journal Constitution,*** **Feb. 25, 1996, p. D1.**

Barta opines that Hillary Rodham Clinton has redefined the role of first lady, opening new doors to potential presidential spouses; however, one should not look for any of the GOP candidates' wives to emulate her style. As they campaign, in separate appearances or simply standing by their men, the message of the GOP women seems to be: "I'm not Hillary."

Benedetto, Richard, "First lady's role takes traditional, political turn," ***USA Today,*** **Oct. 16, 1995, p. A6.**

Benedetto analyzes the transformations Hillary Rodham Clinton has undergone during President Clinton's term of office, noting the traditional roles she currently embraces.

Chapman, Stephen, "Redefining the role of first lady: A sexist backlash against Hillary?" ***Chicago Tribune,*** **Jan. 18, 1996, p. 19**

Chapman comments on first lady Hillary Rodham Clinton's admirers, who are mad because they see her decline in public approval as a sexist backlash against a woman whose only sin is being too strong and too powerful. He says Clinton's fans shouldn't blame sexism for her troubles, but rather should blame her for them.

Cytrynbaum, Pamela, "First lady pushes her U.N. stands," ***Chicago Tribune,*** **Sept. 18, 1995, p C2.**

In her first public appearance since her highly publicized role at the U.N.'s women's conference in Beijing, first lady Hillary Rodham Clinton told an audience of 2,000 at the 30th annual dinner of the Chicago Region of the American Committee for the Weizmann Institute of Science that ensuring that women and girls worldwide have access to health care, education and safety should concern everyone.

Devroy, Ann, "First lady defends role she calls a partnership," ***The Washington Post,*** **Oct. 18, 1995, p. A1.**

First lady Hillary Rodham Clinton, in a rare discussion of her rocky tenure and her working relationship with her husband, said she should be judged on her performance and not on her "partnership" with President Clinton, which "is threatening" to some Americans.

Goodman, Walter, "First lady as star of the TV talk-show circuit," ***The New York Times,*** **Jan. 18, 1996, p. C19.**

Goodman discusses first lady Hillary Rodham Clinton's appearances on several "not-quite-news shows" to publicize her book about raising children. Goodman also discusses the "ongoing mini-series" starring the first lady, provided by the Senate Whitewater committee, with Sen. Alfonse D'Amato, R-N.Y., "at his most hilarious in the role of impartial arbiter."

"Hillary Clinton: The first lady does not need a personality change," ***Detroit News & Free Press,*** **Jan. 14, 1995, p. A6.**
An editorial insists that first lady Hillary Rodham Clinton doesn't need to change her image to present herself as kinder and gentler, saying the failure of the Clinton administration's health-care plan was one of process and presentation.

Holmes, Cecile S., "First lady urges fellow Methodists to be living witness for children," ***Houston Chronicle,*** **April 25, 1996, p. A11.**
In a stirring address April 24, 1996, to United Methodists in Denver, first lady Hillary Rodham Clinton recalled her Methodist roots and urged fellow believers to be a living witness to and for children.

Malone, Julia, "No new Hillary, first lady says," ***Atlanta Journal Constitution,*** **Feb. 18, 1995, p. A7.**
First lady Hillary Rodham Clinton contends that reports that she is seeking to develop a "softer" and more traditional image may be exaggerated and that she is still working on issues that have always been important to her, including health care and welfare reform.

Moore, Molly, "First lady takes a traditional role," ***The Washington Post,*** **April 1, 1995, p. A1.**
The traditional role that first lady Hillary Clinton has taken during her five-nation tour of South Asia is discussed.

Purdum, Todd S., "First lady emphasizes human issues," ***The New York Times,*** **March 20, 1995, p. A13.**
First lady Hillary Rodham Clinton pledged on March 19, 1995, to work on "the human issues" at home and abroad, said Republican spending cuts would finance tax breaks for "very rich people" and played down her role in her husband's decision to provide tax relief for the middle class. Clinton took call-in questions from viewers in the hourlong session on CNN's "Late Edition," and touched on topics ranging from affirmative action to welfare reform to the 1996 elections.

Purdum, Todd S., "The first lady's newest role: Newspaper columnist," ***The New York Times,*** **July 24, 1995, p. A10.**
First lady Hillary Rodham Clinton made her debut as a newspaper columnist on July 23, 1995, with her syndicated weekly column "Talking It Over," which will appear in more than 100 magazines and newspapers worldwide. In her first column, she recalls a recent effort to blend into the crowd at a Washington, D.C., art museum.

Whitewater, "Travelgate" and Hillary Clinton

Baum, Geraldine, "First lady assails Whitewater critics," ***Los Angeles Times,*** **Jan. 13, 1996, p. A1.**
First lady Hillary Rodham Clinton on Jan. 12, 1996, gave her most detailed explanation in more than a year of her role in the Whitewater land deal and accused Republicans of mounting a dishonest, politically motivated investigation.

"Book excerpts say first lady active in Whitewater deal," ***Los Angeles Times,*** **March 10, 1996, p. A16.**
According to excerpts from the book *Blood Sport: The President and His Adversaries* by James B. Stewart, first lady Hillary Clinton played an active role in the Whitewater investment, seeing it as a source of funds for her daughter's education even as her husband was agreeing to get out of it.

Carvajal, Doreen, "First lady is treated with care by audience," ***The New York Times,*** **Jan. 20, 1996, p. A10.**
First lady Hillary Rodham Clinton's Jan. 19, 1996, appearance on the CBS TV program "This Morning" is discussed. Clinton blamed election politics for the continuing scrutiny of her role in the Whitewater and White House travel office affairs and said she hoped those issues would not overwhelm the release of her book, *It Takes a Village and Other Lessons Children Teach Us*. Audience members were allowed to ask questions, and many declared their support for her.

Fritz, Sara, "Papers bolster link between first lady, travel scandal," ***Los Angeles Times,*** **Jan. 11, 1996, p. A10.**
Newly revealed confidential documents came to light on Jan. 10, 1996, supporting allegations that first lady Hillary Clinton, despite her denials, played a central role in the White House travel office scandal.

"Hearings approach harassment of first lady, Clinton aide says," ***The New York Times,*** **Jan. 22, 1996, p. A12.**
President Clinton's chief of staff, Leon E. Panetta, said on Jan. 21, 1996, that a Republican congressional inquiry into Hillary Rodham Clinton's role in the Whitewater affair was getting dangerously close to political harassment. On the NBC TV program "Meet the Press," Panetta said that the Republicans are "getting dangerously close to crossing" the "fine line between what is a legitimate continuing inquiry into a situation and what becomes political harassment."

Jackson, Robert L., "2 Arkansans defend first lady's role in deal linked to Whitewater," ***Los Angeles Times,*** **Feb. 15, 1996, p. A17.**
Two Arkansans involved in a questionable land transaction linked to the Whitewater case defend first lady Hillary Rodham Clinton against suggestions that she knew the 1985 deal was fraudulent.

Kranish, Michael, "Scandal question puts first lady on defensive," ***Boston Globe,*** **Jan. 7, 1996, p. 1.**
The article examines questions surrounding the possibility that first lady Hillary Rodham Clinton was involved in a coverup with regard to whether she ordered the firings of workers in the White House travel office, as well as her role in the Whitewater case.

McManus, Doyle, "First lady labeled a liar; Clinton raises verbal fist," *Los Angeles Times,* Jan. 10, 1996, p. A1.

President Clinton on Jan. 9, 1996, responded to an article by *New York Times* columnist William Safire calling first lady Hillary Clinton "a congenital liar" by expressing a desire to punch Safire. Safire was referring to Hillary Clinton's role in the Whitewater case.

Mitchell, Alison, "Issue-oriented first lady is the issue," *The New York Times,* Jan. 7, 1996, p. 17.

First lady Hillary Clinton was supposed to be taking advantage of a media blitz arranged by her publisher to sell her new book. Instead, a newly discovered White House memorandum and copies of billing records from her Arkansas law firm have once again raised questions about her role in the 1993 travel office scandal and the Whitewater scandal.

Page, Susan, "First lady may offer to testify," *USA Today,* Jan. 16, 1996, p. A1.

First lady Hillary Rodham Clinton said she'll do "whatever it takes" to settle controversy over her role in the Whitewater affair, perhaps volunteering to testify before Congress, adding "I think it would be like going to have your teeth drilled."

Pollock, Ellen Joan, "Whitewater hearings to question role of first lady following Foster suicide," *The Wall Street Journal,* July 17, 1995, p. B3.

Republicans on the special Senate committee holding hearings on the Whitewater case are expected to raise many questions about first lady Hillary Rodham Clinton's role in the days following the suicide of Deputy White House Counsel Vincent Foster. Clinton directed her chief of staff, Maggie Williams, to safeguard a Whitewater file found in Foster's office.

Purdum, Todd S., "With resolve, first lady lays out defense," *The New York Times,* Jan. 17, 1996, p. A12.

First lady Hillary Rodham Clinton has popped up all over the news this week, once again rebutting, dismissing, explaining and defending her role in the Whitewater and White House travel office affairs.

"Some questions for a beleaguered first lady," *Atlanta Journal,* Jan. 22, 1996, p. A10.

An editorial says Hillary Clinton should take the initiative and voluntarily testify before the Senate committee investigating Whitewater and lists some of the questions she should answer, adding that it would behoove her to find a public arena to offer her own personal view of the proper role of an independent professional woman cast in the role of first lady.

Role of the First Lady

Auster, Bruce B., "Defining the first lady's difficult role," *U.S. News & World Report,* Feb. 5, 1996, p. 33.

All first ladies suffer in public esteem when the power they wield is glimpsed by voters. First lady Hillary Clinton is as much like Nancy Reagan as she is like Eleanor Roosevelt.

Carter, Jimmy, "A first lady finds her own way," *Atlanta Journal Constitution,* Jan. 25, 1996, p. A13.

Carter examines the role of a first lady in the White House, explaining how she can be a major influence in shaping political strategy and saying how past first ladies who were strong of character each rendered great service to America.

Cooper, Matthew, "The missing issues: first ladies: speak up," *Washington Monthly,* January 1996, pp. 36-37.

All Americans would benefit from knowing more about first ladies before they take office. All of the wives of the major candidates in the 1996 presidential campaign would have huge impacts on their husbands' presidencies.

Gould, Lewis, "There's history to role of first lady," *Quill,* March 1996, p. 29.

The public controversy over Hillary Rodham Clinton arises from her own actions. However, the terms of the controversy derive from the historical experiences of other first ladies as political and media celebrities.

Creager, Ellen, "First lady scholar says Clinton is trapped," *Detroit News & Free Press,* Jan. 15, 1995, p. J1.

Attempts by Hillary Rodham Clinton to make the nation like her have been unsuccessful; many believe the first lady's role should remain ceremonial. Lewis Gould, a first lady scholar at the University of Texas at Austin, discusses Clinton's role.

Estrich, Susan, "The next first lady," *Glamour,* August 1995, pp. 236-237.

Win or lose in 1996, Hillary Clinton has changed the role of the first lady forever. Although the Republican presidential candidates stress that their wives aren't involved in politics, Mrs. Clinton has shown that first ladies can be.

Fields, Suzanne, "First lady's role: Be seen, but not heard, on policy issues," *Insight on the News,* April 24, 1995, p. 40.

Hillary Rodham Clinton has reacted acutely to the changing requirements of a first lady. The power of a first lady depends on the power of her husband, and Hillary Clinton has almost shed the arrogance of divisive politics.

Shepard, Scott, "Beyond first lady," *Atlanta Journal Constitution,* March 19, 1995, p. A11.

The days when the role of presidential candidate's spouse was limited to homemaker and mother are fading fast. Of all the wives of the current candidates for the 1996 GOP presidential nomination, only Indiana Senator Richard Lugar's wife, Charlene, would come close to what is generally perceived as a traditional political spouse, a full-time mother active in charities rather than the pursuit of a career.

Back Issues

Great Research on Current Issues Starts Right Here...Recent topics covered by The CQ Researcher are listed below. Before May 1991, reports were published under the name of Editorial Research Reports.

DECEMBER 1994
Farm Policy
Arms Sales
Earthquake Research
The Future of Television

JANUARY 1995
Treating Addiction
Child Custody and Support
Parents and Schools
Non-Proliferation Treaty at 25

FEBRUARY 1995
Cracking Down on Immigration
The Business of Sports
Reinventing Government
Housing Discrimination

MARCH 1995
Death Penalty Debate
Primary Care
Democracy in Africa
Environmental Movement at 25

APRIL 1995
Abortion Clinic Protests
Dieting and Health
Combating AIDS
Rethinking Affirmative Action

Back issues are available for $5.00 (subscribers) or $8.00 (non-subscribers). Quantity discounts apply to orders over ten. To order, call Congressional Quarterly Customer Service at (202) 887-8621.

Binders are available for $18.00. To order call 1-800-638-1710. Please refer to stock number 648.

MAY 1995
Assisted Suicide Controversy
Overhauling Social Security
Learning to Read
Mandatory Sentencing

JUNE 1995
Combating Infectious Disease
Property Rights
Repetitive Stress Injuries
Regulating the Internet

JULY 1995
War Crimes
Highway Safety
Combating Terrorism
Preventing Teen Drug Use

AUGUST 1995
Job Stress
Organ Transplants
United Nations at 50
Advances in Cancer Research

SEPTEMBER 1995
Catholic Church in the U.S.
Northern Ireland Cease-Fire
High School Sports
Teaching History

OCTOBER 1995
Quebec's Future
Revitalizing the Cities
Networking the Classroom
Indoor Air Pollution

NOVEMBER 1995
The Working Poor
The Jury System
Sex, Violence and the Media
Police Misconduct

DECEMBER 1995
Teens and Tobacco
Gene Therapy's Future
Global Water Shortages
Third-Party Prospects

JANUARY 1996
Emergency Medicine
Punishing Sex Offenders
Bilingual Education
Helping the Homeless

FEBRUARY 1996
Reforming the CIA
Campaign Finance Reform
Academic Politics
Getting Into College

MARCH 1996
The British Monarchy
Preventing Juvenile Crime
Tax Reform
Pursuing the Paranormal

APRIL 1996
Centennial Olympic Games
Managed Care
Protecting Endangered Species
New Military Culture

MAY 1996
Russia's Political Future
Marriage and Divorce
Year-Round Schools
Taiwan, China and the U.S.

JUNE 1996
Rethinking NAFTA

Future Topics

- ***Teaching Values***
- ***Labor Movement's Future***
- ***Repressed Memory Syndrome***

THE CQ Researcher

PUBLISHED BY CONGRESSIONAL QUARTERLY INC.

Teaching Values

Do school-based programs violate parents' beliefs?

Thousands of schools in more than a dozen states are participating in a new movement to teach values in schools. Leaders of the "character education" movement point to moral decline among America's youth — evidenced by rising rates of teen pregnancy and youth crime — as the main reason schools should teach values. The programs, which vary greatly depending on the school, have provoked relatively little controversy locally. However, both conservative Christians and civil libertarians see the potential for schools to impose ideologies contrary to parents' values. Leading character-education advocates contend that schools can teach such basic values as respect and responsibility without wading into controversial areas like abortion, sex education and homosexuality.

INSIDE THIS ISSUE

CQ June 21, 1996 • Volume 6, No. 23 • Pages 529-552

Formerly Editorial Research Reports

COVER: STUDENTS FROM JEFFERSON JUNIOR HIGH SCHOOL IN WASHINGTON, D.C. (THOMAS J. COLIN)

June 21, 1996
Volume 6, No. 23

The CQ Researcher (ISSN 1056-2036). Formerly Editorial Research Reports. Published weekly (48 times per year, not printed March 1, May 31, Aug. 30, Nov. 29) by Congressional Quarterly Inc., 1414 22nd St., N.W., Washington, D.C. 20037. Annual subscription rate for libraries, businesses and government is $319. Additional rates furnished upon request. Second-class postage paid at Washington, D.C. POSTMASTER: Send address changes to The CQ Researcher, 1414 22nd St., N.W., Washington, D.C. 20037.

Teaching Values

By Sarah Glazer

The Issues

As 8:30 a.m. approaches, the boys and girls outside Jefferson Junior High School form separate lines at the door. They wait quietly, neat and tidy in their private school-style uniforms. At a signal from Vera White, their imposing principal, they file inside. She has a cheery "Good morning" for every child, and a personal word for many: Why were you absent yesterday? I see you're playing baseball! Why didn't you take your test yesterday? White misses nothing. Baseball caps are whisked off at her glance. Shirttail hanging out? Please go outside and tuck it in.

It's easy to see why the immaculate inner-city Washington, D.C., public school is often favorably compared with parochial schools, with their higher level of discipline.

Part of the secret of Jefferson's success is its broad character-education program. Seventh-graders take courtesy classes. Before assemblies, students are reminded about proper audience deportment. Once a week, homerooms discuss the school's values of courtesy, caring, respect and responsibility.

"I'm so proud of you this morning," math teacher Anthony Antoniswami tells his homeroom students, who have been silently doing homework. As he turns things over to the class president for a brief meeting, Antoniswami exhorts, "Let's respect our leaders. That's character."

Since White beefed up the school's character-education program in 1992, pregnancies have plummeted from 12-15 a year to one this year; thefts and fighting have dropped, too. The gains are impressive for the predominantly African-American school, where 70 percent of the students come from single-parent families. Jefferson's

ninth-graders score above grade level in reading, science and math on national standardized tests. The school boasts the best junior high attendance record in Washington.

Jefferson is among thousands of U.S. schools that have instituted character education in recent years. At inner-city schools, the aim is to reverse the worst signs of social decay, such as rising violence and pregnancy, and to give children the social survival skills they need to make it in mainstream society.

White, now going on 17 years as principal, introduced character education at Jefferson years ago. But in 1992, after some of her students appeared in TV news footage of a rock-throwing melee, she turned up the heat. "If I didn't do anything else," she says, "I would let them know that they have some dignity."

At the end of every day, Jefferson students file past White with their "objectives notebook" open to that night's homework assignments. Through that ritual, White says, "We demonstrate every day that we care enough to help our children accomplish the goals they want in life."

Caring reflects the essence of White's approach. "If I had a choice between a knowledge-based teacher and one who cared about children, I would choose the caring teacher," she says. "I could retrain a teacher who really cares for children, but I can't retrain a teacher who doesn't care; that ruins a child's life."

Many suburban schools, though faced with less extreme social problems than inner-city schools, also have initiated character education, mainly to combat declining decorum and rising cheating and disrespect toward teachers.

Across the Potomac River and a world away from Jefferson Junior High, prestigious Thomas Jefferson High School for Science and Technology, in Alexandria, Va., also saw a need for character education following a controversial student prank six years ago. Two seniors cropped photos of two male faculty members to suggest homosexual activity and printed the altered picture on T-shirts they planned to sell to other students.

The students were suspended. But teachers were outraged when several students circulated a petition arguing that the pranksters' freedom of speech had been denied, and said that the feelings of the defamed faculty members were irrelevant.

"At that point we realized that the words 'right' and 'wrong' had years ago been stripped from our school vocabulary," two Jefferson High teachers wrote. "High schools in our experience had been values neutral for so long that our ability to engage students in conversations about moral issues had become rusty." [1]

The character-education movement has won endorsements from political leaders as ideologically different as President Clinton and former Education Secretary William J. Bennett, author of the *Book of Virtues* and the

Students' Ethics

The Josephson Institute of Ethics conducts surveys to gather information on the behavioral ethics of young people. Here are some of the findings from its "1996 Report Card on American Integrity."

Did you cheat on an exam or quiz during the previous 12 months?

	At least once	More than once
High school	65%	47%
College	33%	21%

Have you stolen something from a parent or relative in the previous 12 months?

	At least once	More than once
High School	29%	17%
College	13%	6%

Did you take something from a store without paying for it in the previous 12 months?

	At least once	More than once
High school	39%	26%
College	17%	9%

Do you agree that "If necessary to get or keep a job, I would lie?"

	Agreed	Disagreed
High school	41%	59%
College	24%	76%

Source: "1996 Report Card on American Integrity," Joseph & Edna Josephson Institute of Ethics, 1996. Nearly 12,000 Americans over age 12 were surveyed.

recent *Book of Virtues for Young People*. This month, Sens. Nancy Landon Kassebaum, R-Kan., and Bill Bradley, D-N.J., joined the White House in co-hosting the third conference on character building organized by the Communitarian Network. (*See story, p. 534.*)

So far, character-education programs have provoked relatively little controversy. About one in five schools uses character education, according to the Character Education Partnership in Alexandria, Va., a consortium of educational groups. The programs range from an occasional assembly to full-blown curricula.

By sticking to values that everyone agrees upon, like respect and honesty, character-education advocates say they can avoid controversy. But the first question skeptics raise is, "Whose values?"

More than 90 percent of the public favors public school teaching of such specific values as respect for others and hard work, according to a 1994 poll. But when pollsters asked about character education in general, 39 percent of the respondents thought that teaching values and ethical behavior should be left to parents and churches. [2]

On both the left and the right, there is concern that character education could touch on issues that bitterly divide Americans. "We believe teaching civility is a great virtue, but if included in that is, 'You must accept homosexuality as a valid alternative lifestyle,' then it's problematic," says Perry Glanzer, education policy analyst at Focus on the Family, a conservative Christian group in Colorado Springs, Colo.

Despite the potential for such conflict, Glanzer says, "We support the teaching of character in grades K-12. There are strengths and weaknesses. We see the strengths as a grass-roots response to moral decline."

At the other end of the political spectrum, the American Civil Liberties Union (ACLU) worries that character education could pose constitutional problems, though the organization cannot cite any instances of violations. "It really depends on whether you're talking about a thinly veiled way of getting religious, ethical and moral issues into the classroom that are not seen by the entire population as American civic values, or you're talking about good citizenship, fairness, tolerance — those sorts of things," says Loren Siegel, the ACLU's director of public education.

"I would be very surprised if there weren't problems," Siegel adds. "Not everyone believes a fetus is a human being or that children should always be obedient and never question authority."

"It's impossible to run a values-free school," responds A. John Martin, executive director of the Character Education Partnership. "Wouldn't these groups prefer we develop respect, rather than disrespect?" Martin is convinced the movement can dodge controversy by avoiding three lightning-rod issues: abortion, gay rights and sex education. Yet some observers believe that discussions about character inevitably will touch on stormy issues, such as tolerance for behaviors that some people consider immoral.

The current character-education movement is a self-conscious reaction against the last great wave of values education — so-called "values clarification" — which first became popular in the 1970s (*see p. 540*). The approach encouraged students to "clarify" their values in class discussions. But teachers were not supposed to offer a judgment as to whether Johnny's values were right or wrong.

"[I]t took the shallow moral relativism loose in the land and brought it into the schools," Thomas Lickona, a professor of education at the State University of New York in Cortland, wrote in *Educating for Character,* a widely read 1991 manual of the character-education movement. [3] Values clarification is "at odds with the basic premise of character education, which is that there are objective standards," Lickona says today. "One can tell the difference between right and wrong and teach it to young people."

Values clarification made generations of teachers afraid to take strong stands on basic issues of right and wrong, critics like Lickona charge. As Martin puts it, "Kids felt there was no ethical anchor there."

Values clarification developed such a bad reputation that today's movement strives to avoid the word "values"— with its connotation of mere personal preference — by discussing "character," presumably a less divisive term.

One of the political strengths of character education is the fact that it differs enormously in style and substance from school to school. But that diversity is also a weakness, because parents don't immediately know what type of character-education program a school may have. Does it fit easily into a school's atmosphere and curriculum, or does it impose an artificial layer of autocracy, with stern slogans tacked up around the school?

Most supporters of character education say it should remain diverse, representing the consensus views of individual communities.

"Character education does not lend itself to didactic instruction," says Chester E. Finn Jr., a senior fellow at the conservative Hudson Institute and a supporter of the movement. "You learn it by example, by discussion." Consciously introducing character education as formal education carries the risk that it will be "fake, insincere, not very effective," says Finn, a former assistant secretary of Education in the Reagan administration.

As schools like Jefferson Junior High make apparent, character education "depends upon the quality, outlook and commitment of the teachers and administration," says Jay Winsten, associate dean at the Harvard University School of Public Health. He points out that White and her staff are routinely at school until 10 p.m. to meet with parents. "From what I've seen," he says, "Jefferson is pretty darn impressive."

Both detractors and supporters agree that at its best, character education embodies what good teachers have always tried to do: exemplify good character by their example and their choice of great literature.

In fact, Finn says, "It's a pity" that schools have to consciously decide to include character education. "If we had a properly conceived school curriculum, we wouldn't need a dietary supplement called character," he says. "It would be built into what kids read and into classroom discourse."

As parents, educators and policymakers debate values education, these are some of the questions being addressed:

Should schools teach values?

"The truth is, a school couldn't run a class for five minutes without some kind of moral values," Lickona says. "You need rules against fighting and cheating on tests." So unavoidable is the transmittal of values, in Lickona's view, that the relevant issue is not "Should schools teach values?" but "Which values will they teach?" and "How well will they teach them?" [4]

Inevitably, teachers and principals convey values simply by how they behave and what they say in class. "What you don't teach is just as important as what you teach," maintains teacher Patricia Giegerich, who has spearheaded a new character-education effort at Annandale (Va.) High School. "And if you ignore values or ethical issues as something you can't talk about, you're teaching nonetheless. You're saying they're not important."

What's driving the current campaign to make character education as much a part of schooling as English or math? In Lickona's words, it's a widely perceived "societywide moral decline."

In his book, Lickona cites the rising rates of youth murder and vandalism and surveys showing that half of all Americans ages 9-21 have shoplifted. Lickona's litany of social ills includes disrespect for teachers, cruelty toward fellow students, bigotry, bad language and self-destructive behavior like drug use and sexual precocity. [5]

In large part, Lickona blames the moral decline on the breakdown of the traditional family unit. He says children are no longer being socialized at home, where increasingly there is a single or divorced parent, and there is less time for the children. "Parents have not taught kids the most basic things about interacting with other people," Lickona says, "like taking turns, asking questions politely, saying please and thank you and obeying an adult."

Teachers report seeing seeds of the problem as early as pre-school. Starting in the 1970s, the prevailing educational view was that building self-esteem was the foundation for every child's success. Kindergarten teachers often had their students put together "All About Me" books that stressed what kids liked about themselves. "Now kindergarten teachers say kids are so self-centered that they need to do an 'All About You' book," Lickona reports.

At the same time, advocates point to the negative forces filling the character-education vacuum, including television and video game role models that Lickona says encourage kids to be "selfish, dishonest, sexually

Task Force Enters Sex Education Debate . . .

First lady Hillary Rodham Clinton delayed her speech until 5 p.m. so that she could spend the afternoon with her daughter Chelsea. Harvard government Professor Michael J. Sandel missed the first day of the conference so that he could coach his 10-year-old son's Little League baseball game.

These last-minute schedule changes did not seem to bother the more than 300 educators, academics and parent activists from around the country who attended the character building conference co-hosted by the White House and Sens. Nancy Landon Kassebaum, R-Kan., and Bill Bradley, D-N.J., on June 6-8 in Washington, D.C.

George Washington University sociologist Amitai Etzioni, master of ceremonies for the event, mentioned these commitments as examples of the character education movement's philosophy — that children need to be taught good character through their parents' and teachers' behavior.

"Children are born without values; they're not naturally benign," he told the participants. "I have five wonderful sons. They were not born wonderful. A lot of effort went into that."

This is the third conference on character building organized by the Communitarian Network, a nonpartisan, nationwide coalition founded by Etzioni in 1993 to foster socially responsible communities. (The 1994 and 1995 conferences also were hosted by the White House.)

In addition to serving as master of ceremonies, Etzioni chaired a task force on sex education. His task force recommended that schools abandon what it called "value-free" sex education focusing on the biology of sex but also avoid moralistic programs that urge "abstinence only." Instead, the task force favored a middle ground sometimes dubbed "abstinence plus." The approach urges students to postpone sexual activity until they are mature enough to handle the consequences — including pregnancy and the risk of sexually transmitted diseases — but also provides them with information on how to use contraceptives if they do start.

The moral component of sex education is essential, Etzioni said. "We don't think sex education should take place as if it's dental hygiene."

Asked by one conference participant "whose values" would be promoted in such a curriculum, Etzioni suggested that schools focus on disturbing behaviors all parents want to prevent rather than on lists of virtues, like virginity before marriage. There is likely to be little disagreement among parents when they are asked, "Do you believe 12-year-old children should have sex? Do you believe children should have children?" Etzioni said.

An argument often raised against teaching contraception is that it will entice students into sexual activity. But the "enticement factor is so huge to begin with" in television, movies and other media, Etzioni observed, that "adding to it is almost impossible." On the other side of the moral balance, he said, are the "many lives we lose" through AIDS and teen pregnancies "when people don't have the information on how to conduct themselves."

In a paper prepared for the conference, the task force stated that sex education programs "should stress that bringing children into the world is a moral act, one that entails a set of personal and social responsibilities." The task force rejected the liberal Swedish-style approach to sex education, saying "Statements such as 'sexuality is natural and [a] healthy part of living' . . . are open to gross

---

promiscuous and violent."

"A lot of high school students think about their rights without the corollary responsibility," Giegerich says, citing a growing tendency for students to talk back to teachers and use foul language. "We're talking about not doing homework, not getting to class on time, not being honest about attendance, not respecting other people's property."

Michael Josephson, founder of the Josephson Institute of Ethics in Marina del Rey, Calif., blames the disturbing trend on America's slide into a "no-consequences society." While nearly two-thirds of the high school students polled for the institute's annual "Report Card on American Integrity" admitted to cheating in the previous year, school records indicate that only a handful are being disciplined.[6] (*See table, p. 532.*)

It's not that young people don't know that cheating violates ethical behavior, Josephson observes. "But to an increasing degree," he says, "people are thinking they're not bound by it." Adults who lie about a child's age to get a cheaper movie ticket or who use radar detectors "have generated cynicism" among youth, he says.

But not everyone sees society going downhill. "I happen to believe that we are more moral [today] than we used to be," says ACLU Executive Director Ira Glasser. "We have far less racial prejudice and gender discrimination and intolerance for gays and discrimination against the disabled than we had when I was growing up."

To say that America is in moral decay "is an outrageous denial of the largest moral advance this or any other nation has ever experienced in so short a time," Glasser says. He stresses that the civil rights advances since the 1960s did not come about because of character education courses. Quite the contrary. "During all those years of segregation, subjugation and state-sanctioned terror," he argues, "children prayed in school and were taught virtues of politeness, civility, respect and the like."

In the new fashion for extolling virtue in political speeches, some observ-

. . . at White House Character Education Conference

misinterpretation when given to children."

The recommendations on sex education were endorsed by task force members as politically divergent as conservative Neil Gilbert, professor of social welfare at the University of California-Berkeley, and liberal economist Isabel Sawhill, a senior fellow at the Urban Institute in Washington, D.C., who served in the Clinton administration from 1993 to 1995. Researchers have found that the "Not yet" approach advocated by the task force is effective in reducing the percentage of students who begin having sex and in increasing birth control among those who start sexual intercourse. [1]

The character building conferences are part of a larger effort by the Communitarian Network to inject the teaching of values into all aspects of school life, including sports. The first lady strongly endorsed the movement in her remarks. Schools "must be part of a conscious effort to shape the values we expect our children to live by," Mrs. Clinton said. Noting that President Clinton had addressed last year's conference, she added, "My husband saw character education as part of a larger community vision of what our country can be."

But even character education enthusiasts see problems when it comes to specific recommendations, like those on sex education. "I think it will raise a lot of questions," said Teri J. Traaen, human resources director of the Paradise Unified School District in Phoenix, Ariz. "Some of our single parents would say, 'I never was married and that doesn't mean our family is not OK.' Others may say, 'I don't want you talking to my child about contraceptives.' The flash point will be religious differences."

Dean L. Ryerson, superintendent of the Wisconsin Rapids Public Schools, raised similar concerns. "We have a strong Roman Catholic community. [The approach to sex education advocated by the task force] would just blow us out of the water," he said. "We teach it in a very non-directional way. This is how babies are made. This is the science."

At the same time, Ryerson also said he would like to introduce more explicit discussions of good character into his school system. "I'm concerned about the amount of cheating, the casualness, the lack of self-discipline among students," he said. But, he added, teachers already feel overloaded with a host of social agendas from combating drugs to sex education. "We're just committed to death."

Picking up on that theme, an English teacher from St. Paul, Minn., asked Mrs. Clinton, "What do you say to administrators who say the real business of education is academic instruction and anything else is soft — or fluff?"

Mrs. Clinton responded like a true adherent of today's character-education movement: "It's almost impossible for me to imagine standing in front of a class of 25 to 30 kids — teaching any class — where there wasn't a chance, an opportunity nearly every day to say or do something about values and about character. Even if it's 'Jack, your being late today disadvantages everyone else.' "

Mrs. Clinton said that while many teachers are concerned about the deteriorating quality of life in schools, they also are understandably skeptical about character education, wondering if it is just the latest educational fad. "When it comes to a formal character-education curriculum," Mrs. Clinton said, "it is going to take some proof-is-in-the pudding experience for a lot of people to think it's real."

[1] See "Preventing Teen Pregnancy," *CQ Researcher*, May 14, 1993, pp. 409-431.

ers perceive a politically motivated return to the Victorian inclination to blame poverty on a lack of moral rectitude.

"[A]lmost all of the virtue books emanate from the right," satirist Joe Queenan complains in a recent article on the Bennett-led boom in values publishing. Moreover, he notes, "almost all preach the same message: The liberal welfare state has created a huge underclass of urban psychopaths who are ruining life for decent people like us with their drugs, rap and guns." [7]

Yet the message has also struck home with middle-class baby-boomers, as indicated by the popularity of parenting books like William Kilpatrick's *Why Johnny Can't Tell Right from Wrong and What We Can Do About It.*

Student misbehavior was on the minds of teachers and parents from the private Sheridan School in Washington, D.C., who attended a week-long seminar on character education conducted by Lickona last summer. The Sheridan contingent traveled to Cortland to learn how to counter rowdiness in class, disrespect toward teachers and talking out of turn. They were surrounded by public school teachers discussing far more extreme social problems, like students bringing weapons to school.

"We found ourselves feeling a little silly sitting next to people talking about teen pregnancies," headmaster Hugh Riddleberger recalls.

Yet even at Sheridan, where children are overwhelmingly from well-off, professional families, Riddleberger has become increasingly concerned with students' moral sense. "I saw that kids were taking less and less responsibility for their behavior," he says, "blaming others and making excuses" when teachers reprimanded them. "I saw the teachers hardening their responses by thinking of longer lists of rules."

Families are spending less time with children, surveys show. As a result, Riddleberger says, parents are missing opportunities to deal with moral issues as they come up — recognizing a child's act of honesty explicitly and saying, "That was a decent thing to do."

What Would You Do?

The Josephson Institute of Ethics presented students and adults with situations that called for morally challenging decisions for its "1996 Report Card on American Integrity." A majority of the high school students surveyed said they would lie or cheat to save money or get a better job.

Dilemma	Percent who said they would or probably would: High school	College	Adult (not in school)
You apply for a job you wanted very much. You're sure you can do it well, but unless you make some untrue statement, the job will go to someone else. Would you "enhance" your resume?	54%	43%	14%
Your 12-year-old could get into a much better school if you lived in your sister's school district. Your sister is willing to let you use her address when you enroll your child. Would you do it?	81%	75%	32%
An application for health insurance asks whether you have had previous injuries. If you admit previous injuries, premiums would go up at least $50 a month. Would you hide the fact of your previous injuries?	59%	47%	20%
You hosted a dinner party at a restaurant. When the bill comes there is a $60 error in your favor. A friend suggests you say nothing about the mistake but leave a large tip. Would you do it?	57%	51%	17%
Your 13-year-old looks 11. You could save $14 at an amusement park if you say he is under 13. Would you do it?	81%	71%	37%
You badly need a loan which you will get only if you understate what you owe. Would you do it?	52%	39%	19%
After a collision, the auto body repairman offers to fix other damages not caused by the collision in an insurance claim. Would you do it?	68%	67%	47%

Source: "1996 Report Card on American Integrity," Joseph & Edna Josephson Institute of Ethics, 1996. Nearly 12,000 Americans over age 12 were surveyed.

"If you're not hanging around and waiting for a kid to drop a comment, you'll miss it," he says. "If it's left to a Spanish-speaking housekeeper, you're definitely going to miss it."

Since attending Lickona's seminar, Riddleberger has instituted class meetings, at which children are asked to come up with solutions to problems such as teasing. (*See story, p. 542.*) He also has begun delivering homilies on honesty and other virtues at weekly assemblies.

Can schools teach values that are acceptable to both liberals and conservatives?

Some conservatives as well as liberals fear that character education will impose a political agenda on children that runs counter to their parents' views.

While people of different political persuasions might agree on a list of common values, "you and I might define citizenship or justice differently," says Janet Parshall, a conservative syndicated radio talk show host.

Parshall cites a California grade school where the children pledged allegiance to a "mother Earth" flag to honor the environment. "What if I happen to find that against my value system because in my home we tell them ... father God is the one who is preeminent?" Parshall asks.

She envisions a values war erupting in the classroom if a child is taught at home that homosexuality is wrong but learns in school that justice requires recognizing every kind of family equally, including lesbian marriages, as depicted in the children's book, *Heather Has Two Mommies*. In that case, Parshall says, the school's message is that " 'Your set of values, son, daughter, is up for review.' I think that flies in the face of the definition of public education and sends the message home that, 'Parent, you haven't done a good job.' "

Conservative Christian groups also question whether values can be discussed without discussing their genesis — in the case of Christians, the New Testament. "If you're going to teach the need to be self-controlled or honest, the kids will ask for justification," Glanzer says. "Will the appeals [for good behavior] mainly be based on pragmatic reasons?" If so, many Christians will find that unacceptable, he says, because "We believe the greatest motivation for goodness is belief in a transcendent and loving God."

Character-education proponents see little danger of wading into controversial political or religious areas. "In 98 percent of the cases, it won't be a matter of conflict whether you should be polite or not shove the kid at the water fountain," Lickona says. If school districts avoid such divisive issues as abortion, gay rights and sex education, some character-education advocates are convinced the movement can avoid value wars.

But Parshall is skeptical: "If you cut all of that out, basically what you're left with is good manners — which has been around since the inception of public schools."

Denis Doyle, senior fellow in education at the conservative Heritage Foundation and an advocate of character education, argues that manners and values are linked inseparably. [8] "Good manners are a lower-order form of character development," says Doyle, co-author of the 1991 book *Winning the Brain Race*. "It's the Aristotelian notion that a man becomes virtuous by behaving virtuously. Good manners are good training to become a person of character."

Because of volatile issues like homosexuality, schools must tread a delicate line between blandness and controversy when introducing character education. On the one hand, gay-rights activists see dangers in the movement's determination to avoid controversial issues. "I think the silence adds to and creates this atmosphere of neglect, harassment and non-support," says Jenie Hall, executive director of the American Friends Service Committee's Bridges Project in Philadelphia, which works with gay teenagers facing harrassment in school.

On the other hand, if schools confront controversial issues in class, "All it takes is one or two parents concerned about something, and the whole program can be blown out of the water," says James S. Leming, an expert on evaluating values-education programs who teaches at Southern Illinois University (SIU) in Carbondale. "The upshot is you ignore controversy and take these things to an inane, innocuous level."

Recently, a national parental-rights movement backed by conservative Republicans and Christian groups has put its weight behind the primacy of the home in teaching values. The movement has focused mainly on school sex education and condom distribution programs. Proposed parental-rights amendments to state constitutions have been introduced in 28 states. The model language for the bills, proposed by the pro-family group Of the People, holds that, "The right of parents to direct the upbringing and education of their children shall not be infringed." [9]

Supporters of the amendment say they are trying to give parents the right to remove their children from school events they find objectionable. The Supreme Court this year refused to hear appeals of three cases that typify the problems advocates say their amendment would address. In one case, parents sued the school district in Chelmsford, Mass., over a mandatory AIDs-awareness assembly that featured sexually explicit language. [10]

Critics of the proposed amendment, including the ACLU, say it would give parents veto power over curriculum and counseling programs. They point to the proposal as one more sign of the conflict that character education might spur between liberals and conservatives.

But leaders of the parental-rights movement say their proposed amendment does not target character education. "I'm certainly in favor of teaching character," says Jeffrey Bell, Of the People's chairman. "Most people in the parental-rights movement would say the educational elites are moving away from teaching traditional values."

Pointing to controversies over sex education, condom distribution and other such issues, civil libertarians wonder if character education will become a stalking horse for the religious right. "There are some aspects of this return [to character education] that are a cover for religious dogma," says Stephen B. Pershing, legal director of the Virginia ACLU. Noting that religious conservatives are in the majority on some Virginia school boards, he comments, "It's unlikely that tolerance will ever make it into the values curriculums of those school districts."

The Supreme Court has ruled that schools must provide "opt-out" provisions for students whose parents have religious objections to classroom material. [11] But Pershing emphasizes that the court opinions have been based narrowly on religious dissent. "One of my concerns is that an individual family with a philosophical difference of opinion will be shut out of constitutional, legal recourse," he says.

Professor Amitai Etzioni of George

Washington University stresses that his vision of character education puts little emphasis on classroom content, which he agrees might incur a parent's wrath and the desire to keep the child out in the hallway. "I'm in favor of opt-out," says Etzioni, who advocates character education in his 1993 book, *The Spirit of Community*. "If classes preach something that deeply offends parents' values, they should opt out."

But when it comes to a schoolwide ambiance of civility, "You can't opt out of civil corridors," says Etzioni, who is also director of the Communitarian Network, which organized the recent White House character conference. [12] "I'm looking at character education as a set of experiences. No one should opt out of it."

Rather than merely teaching a list of virtues, Etzioni advocates fostering two basic psychological capabilities necessary for good character: control of impulses and empathy.

Yet for teachers, character instruction is "a field full of land mines," Leming cautions, even if they avoid obvious religious or political controversies. In one school, he recalls, "I saw teachers asking kids examples of being responsible. One kid said, 'My parents told me to clean up my room. I shoved everything under my bed, and that was cool.' Does the teacher point out to the kid what's wrong? Are you humiliating the kid? Quickly, this becomes difficult to teach."

Does character education make a difference in behavior?

Only one comprehensive, long-term study of character education has been completed. [13] From 1982 through 1989, the nonprofit Developmental Studies Center in Oakland, Calif., tested its Child Development Project in San Ramon, a middle-class suburban school district. The project sought to strengthen children's tendencies to be caring and responsible by creating "caring communities" within the school. Children participated in the program from kindergarten through sixth grade, and then researchers tracked their progress in seventh and eighth grade.

The program teaches reading through literature rather than textbooks. It fosters a collaborative approach to learning and a warm, friendly classroom. A Buddies Program pairs older and younger students for reading and other activities. At family film nights, parents and children discuss a movie with a socially meaningful message.

"We demonstrate every day that we care enough to help our children accomplish the goals they want in life."

— Vera White, Principal
Jefferson Junior High School
Washington, D.C.

When three local schools that used the program were compared with three schools that did not, participants were found to be more cooperative and friendly in class. They were committed not only to letting everyone voice their own opinions but also to asserting their own views, however unpopular. The children were evaluated by outside observers who did not know which of the six classrooms participated in the program.

Through the fifth grade, the researchers found no differences in the two groups' scores on standardized tests. Since San Ramon students generally score at around the 90th percentile, there is little room for improvement, the researchers observed. But starting in sixth grade, when tests required the children in the experimental group to read a short story or poem and write their own interpretation, they outscored their peers in the control group.

Eric Schaps, president of the Developmental Studies Center, which conducted the study, speculates that the higher scores were due to the program's early emphasis on literature, which "shows what it means to be a caring person, as opposed to textbooks, which are drier."

In a summary of their findings, the researchers elaborated: "[W]e think that [the project's] major impacts on achievement will ultimately be seen with measures that reflect deeper comprehension and critical thinking — because of the program's emphasis on explanation, reflection, intrinsic motivation and engagement with meaningful literature." [14]

Upon entering middle school, students from the experimental program displayed more self-esteem than their peers, participated more in extracurricular activities and continued to have superior skills at resolving conflicts, the researchers found. There was no difference between the grades of students from the experimental program and those of other district students by the time they reached middle school.

But among the students who had participated in the project, better grades were received by those students whose elementary school teachers had done a superior job of carrying out the project's principles in the classroom.

In many ways, the experiment integrated two basic principles of progressive private schooling — making school interesting and friendly — with the traditional one-room schoolhouse, where children of different ages interact. For example, the Buddies Program and the use of literature to teach reading have long been staples at Sheridan and many other private schools.

"I worry about the preachy kind of character education," Schaps says. "If taught in an impersonal, punitive environment, it's not going to take. A humane, caring, stimulating school is as important as the teaching of character."

"I think this is the best example of a carefully researched program we have in the field," Leming of SIU comments. But, he adds, the greater harmoniousness found in classrooms with character education is not the goal behind the current movement. "Every one of the books on character education points to declines in society: increased drug use, promiscuity, violence, teen suicide," he observes. "Can a teacher in the classroom have an effect on those things?"

Leming is doubtful because he sees the family as the primary socializing institution. "Realistically, the children most at risk come from home environments almost beyond our understanding," he says. "If 95 percent of kids were raised in loving, caring, two-parent homes, we would not have a character-education movement."

The Child Development Project was also tested in Hayward, a poorer, more ethnically diverse school district than San Ramon. Implementation of the program was spottier in Hayward, partly because of budget problems and high teacher turnover. While Hayward pupils in the experimental program showed improved classroom behavior, the program did not affect their social development, such as concern for others and democratic values, as much as in San Ramon, researchers found. [15]

Beyond painstakingly designed studies like the Child Development Project, character education is hard to evaluate, Leming notes, because the movement embraces such a wide variety of programs. In addition, many schools already have several add-on programs aimed at preventing drug use, violence and other deviant behaviors. [16] So it's hard to know which program to credit for success.

For example, character-education advocates point to Jefferson Junior High's decline in pregnancies as a sign of success. But Principal White is quick to note that Jefferson also runs a special program for girls, Best Friends, that advocates abstinence until after high school graduation. The school also features lunchtime rap sessions held by the school nurse to steer adolescents away from early sexual activity.

Henry A. Huffman, director of the Character Education Institute at California University of Pennsylvania, has noted another difficulty in measuring how character education affects children: "[T]he real tests of character occur when no one is watching. Will a student return the extra change that a clerk mistakenly gave him?" [17]

Nevertheless, occasional success stories give the movement reason to hope. In 1989, when Principal Rudy Bernardo arrived at Allen Classical/Traditional Academy in Dayton, Ohio, an inner-city public elementary school, students were usually lined up outside his office each morning waiting to be disciplined for fighting, cursing or bringing drugs to school. By the end of the year, he had suspended 150 of the 543 students. The school rated 28th out of 33 elementary schools in the district on standardized tests.

After a year of soul-searching seminars with his faculty, Bernardo instituted a character-education program. Each week, teachers weave one of 18 character traits throughout their class discussions. * Then, at an assembly, the "Word of the Week" is driven home through skits or speeches. When "honesty" is highlighted, for example, a problem in math class involving making change might include an ethical component: Should Johnny return the extra change to the store owner who made a mistake in his favor? In addition, academy students must perform community service, and those whose parents don't attend orientation sessions can be dismissed from the school.

Today Allen ranks No. 1 in achievement scores among the districts's 33 elementary schools. Suspensions have declined to just eight last year, and 87 percent of students turn in their homework, up from 10 percent before character education was instituted.

Perhaps the most marked change involves the faculty. Before, Bernardo says, the teachers were so worn-down that they typically reacted to their students' failings by criticizing them. A new recipe for mixing kindness with values changed that. "If we do not see the good in the student, if we focus on the bad behavior, then the student will always feel that he is a bad student," Bernardo says. "That will be instilled in his mind and heart, and the chance of his changing will be lost."

Character-education advocates point to schools like Allen Academy and Jefferson Junior High as proof that character education works. But one could argue that they merely demonstrate an obvious but often overlooked truth: that the best education involves both nurturing teachers and excitement about learning.

---

* The 18 traits are respect, kindness, patience, cheerfulness, self-control, punctuality, courtesy, sportsmanship, tolerance, loyalty, responsibility, thrift, helpfulness, cleanliness, courtesy, self-reliance, citizenship and honesty.

Character education may simply be a new name for an old-fashioned concept — good education. "In effect," Etzioni says, "all the schools you consider good schools are good because they have it." ■

BACKGROUND

Timeless Teachings

Since the time of Plato, philosophers have defined moral education as a primary aspect of schooling. The concept was taken up by some of America's Founding Fathers. Thomas Jefferson's Bill for the More General Diffusion of Knowledge argued for an educational system that would educate citizens at an early age in democratic virtues like respect for the rights of the individual. [18]

Later presidents embraced the sentiment, as in Theodore Roosevelt's famous line: "To educate a man in mind and not morals is to educate a menace to society." [19]

Colonial schools were originally established to teach reading so children could study the Bible and better understand religious principles. This tradition continued into the early 20th century. By 1919, *McGuffey's Readers,* which were full of biblical stories and other moral lessons, were the nation's most widely used schoolbooks.

The prevailing approach was didactic, with teachers imparting moral wisdom to their students. But John Dewey and other educational innovators favored a "progressive" approach, which actively involved children in moral decision-making.

Some of today's champions of character education blame progressive education for moral decay in America's schools. But, says the Heritage Foundation's Doyle, "Dewey was not against rigor; he was reacting to an arch Edwardian sensibility — narrow and frequently unpleasant and dreadful for children."

'Values Clarification'

In the 1960s, moral instruction of the traditional, didactic type began to disappear from American public schools. After the Supreme Court held that school prayer and devotional Bible reading violated the Constitution, many teachers mistakenly believed that the court had prohibited moral education, according to B. Edward McClellan, a professor of education at Indiana University and author of the 1992 book *Schools and the Shaping of Character.* [20]

During this period, cultural "relativism" took hold with a new generation of young people, popularized by the expression "Do your own thing" and the indignant objection, "That's a value judgment!"

"Values clarification," a new approach to character education, reflected that relativism. "Clarification" made its debut in 1966 with the book *Values and Teaching* by New York University education Professor Louis Raths. He advised teachers to help children clarify their values by acting as moderators of discussions, rather than as moralizers.

The approach took off with the 1972 publication of a values-clarification handbook. [21] More than 600,000 copies were sold, placing it in practically every school in the country. The teacher, the authors explained, was to be presented as "just another person with values (and often with values confusion) of his own." [22]

In one typical handbook exercise, the teacher asks students to raise their hands in answer to the question, "How many of you think there are times when cheating is justified?" In practice, writes Lickona, "teachers often weren't sure what to do after students had clarified their values." [23]

"It was a very optimistic view that, given enough discussion, students would come to realize on their own why cheating was not a good way to go," handbook co-author Howard Kirschenbaum says today.

The values-clarification approach and a competing approach developed by Harvard psychologist Lawrence Kohlberg often posed dilemmas pitting one moral value against another. Michael Bocian, a staffer at the Communitarian Network who organized the recent White House conference on character building, cites the "Alligator Island" dilemma. In this classic classroom exercise, the only way students can reach a loved one stranded on a desert island is to pay an armed boatman $1,000. But the students don't have the money. The lesson is, apparently, that stealing the boat is justified for the greater good of helping someone they care about.

In a critique of values clarification, Bocian wrote: "In the 'Alligator Island' example, the students had to decide between respect for other people's property and care for a loved one. But in the vast majority of human experiences, respecting other people's property is unquestionably the right thing to do." [24]

The philosophical roots of values clarification lay in the "Human Potential" movement, started in the 1960s and '70s by two prominent American psychologists, Carl Rogers and Abraham Maslow. They believed that human beings were basically good and needed to have their true selves liberated. "The basic nature of the human being, when functioning freely, is constructive and trustworthy," Rogers said. [25]

Encounter groups and experiments in group dynamics at the Esalen Institute in California were among the most

Continued on p. 542

Chronology

1700s-1800s

Moral education with strong Christian overtones is an integral part of American public schooling.

1836
First publication of *McGuffey's Readers*, emphasizing patriotism, parental respect and adherence to Christianity.

1900s

"Progressive" educator John Dewey challenges the use of moral tales to teach character.

1918
A National Education Association report, *Cardinal Principles of Secondary Education*, endorses "progressive" principle of learning by doing rather than memorizing moral lessons.

1960s

American society increasingly views ethics as a matter of personal choice, and moral instruction wanes in public schools.

1962
Supreme Court rules in *Engel v. Vitale* that daily prayer in New York State public schools violates constitutional separation between church and state. Many teachers respond by avoiding discussions of morals.

1966
"Values clarification" debuts as a teaching method with the publication of *Values and Teaching* by New York University Professor Louis Raths. He urges teachers to help students "clarify" their values without being judgmental.

1970s-1980s

Initial popularity of "values clarification" fades amid growing youth violence, prompting several public school systems to begin teaching positive values.

1972
Values Clarification, a handbook for teachers, sells more than 600,000 copies.

September 1975
Alan L. Lockwood of the University of Wisconsin writes in *Teachers College Record* that "values clarification embodies ethical relativism as its moral point of view."

1977
Warsaw, Ind., drops values clarification in schools and burns the textbook.

1978
Lawrence Kohlberg endorses the presentation of moral dilemmas to students as a teaching method in *Essays on Moral Development, Vol. 1: The Philosophy of Moral Development.*

1982
In Baltimore, Md., a countywide values-education program is based on 24 common moral values from the Constitution and the Bill of Rights.

1982
Supreme Court declares, in *Board of Education, Island Trees Union Free School District, No. 26 v. Pico*, that "local school boards must be permitted to establish and apply their curriculum in such a way as to transmit community values."

1990s

Educators organize to promote character education in American schools and gain a presidential endorsement.

July 1992
Josephson Institute of Ethics convenes educators to draft a statement endorsing character education. "Aspen Declaration" becomes the basis of the Character Counts! Coalition.

Feb. 5, 1993
Educational organizations form Character Education Partnership to promote character education.

1994
Congress authorizes funds to encourage the development of character education under the Elementary and Secondary Education Act.

July 1994
White House hosts the first of three conferences on character building organized by the Communitarian Network.

Nov. 1, 1995
An Alabama law requiring at least 10 minutes a day of values education takes effect.

Jan. 23, 1996
President Clinton endorses character education in his State of the Union address.

June 6-8, 1996
White House co-hosts the third conference on character building.

Giving Lessons in Character . . .

Fifth-grade teacher Kathleen Higley keeps a folder at her desk where her students can place notes about their personal crises. Usually they're along the lines of "Someone called me a wimp."

Mrs. Higley often takes these notes as her cue to call class meetings, where students discuss moral issues like teasing and cruelty. The meetings are a new wrinkle at the private K-8 Sheridan School, in Washington, D.C., which is experimenting with teaching values.

Headmaster Hugh Riddleberger got the idea from a workshop last summer held by Thomas Lickona, an education professor at the State University of New York in Cortland and a leader in the movement to introduce "character education" into schools. Riddleberger says his interest in character education grew out of the increasing tendency of Sheridan students to make excuses for their misbehavior — whether it involved doing a sloppy job on homework, making demeaning remarks about a friend or calling answers out of turn. The class meetings, he says, are designed to teach the children to take greater responsibility for their actions.

Kathleen Higley's fifth-grade class

One morning recently, Mrs. Higley decided to convene a class meeting after one of her students — we'll call her "Anna" — came to her in tears. The problem had started a few days before when a science teacher asked the students to list occupations that required electricity. As a joke, Anna passed a note to a girlfriend: "Does a hooker need electricity?" The friend passed the message on, and soon it had made the rounds of the class. Like the children's party game "telephone," the message changed into a hurtful rumor — "Anna wants to be a hooker" — as it went from student to student. Anna found herself being teased by other children. One boy told Anna another boy in the class would pay her for her services.

Anna responded by criticizing another girl she believed responsible for spreading the hurtful message. The girls in the class began to divide into camps behind the two girls.

Mrs. Higley assembles the fifth-grade girls in the library and explains the problem. "Can you see how it went from a joke to meanness to outright sexual harassment?" she asks.

Each girl insists she is not to blame. "I only told three people," the girl whom Anna has accused says indignantly.

Mrs. Higley makes it clear she is not looking for people to blame. In keeping with the character-education philosophy, she tries to place responsibility for recognizing the problem — and solving it — on the students. "This has happened," she says. "It's reached the boys, and now they're saying very

Continued from p. 540

famous offshoots of this movement. In many ways, writes Kilpatrick, the movement inherited the doctrine of "natural goodness" propounded by 18th-century philosopher Jean Jacques Rousseau. In *Emile,* Rousseau developed the idea that children are naturally good if not corrupted by society.

Kirschenbaum, an adjunct professor of education at the State University of New York in Brockport, now says the movement made a "mistake" in advocating, exclusively, that students should determine their own values.

"I'm sorry to say we denigrated the direct teaching of traditional civic values," he says. "We took it for granted and assumed it happened. History clearly shows that was a very bad assumption," he adds, citing the same litany of social ills that concern character-education proponents: youth violence, teen pregnancy and rising levels of cheating. Learning values "doesn't just happen unless society consciously works at teaching those values," he says.

Kirschenbaum and his colleagues feared direct indoctrination because they equated it with the propagandistic campaigns of pre-World II fascism. Looking back at the Nazi period, they believed the greatest good came from individuals who had resisted the cultures that perpetuated atrocities. Values clarification "came as a desire to help people stand up for their own values even against peer and society pressure," Kirschenbaum says.

The same concern about state-imposed values is occasionally voiced today. Responding to a generally positive *New York Times Magazine* article on character education, one skeptical reader wrote, "Do you suppose that if [Nazi] Germany had had character education . . . it would have

. . . One Teacher's Experience

inappropriate things to Anna. How can we make it better?"

Several girls pick up on the sexual-harassment theme, saying the boys in the class have started to make embarrassing comments to them about women's bodies. "When someone says a rude joke to me," advises Mrs. Higley, "I say, 'I don't find it very funny.' "

The emotional breaking point comes when Anna tearfully faces her rival. "You made me feel really bad yesterday," she says. "People came up and started teasing me."

The other girls are anxious to see the two contenders make peace. At Mrs. Higley's urging, the two girls hug, followed by a spontaneous group hug.

But when Mrs. Higley brings the boys into the meeting, they become indignant at the charge of "sexual harassment" and demand a meeting of their own. In the boys' meeting, most of them complain that the girls frequently taunt them but never seem to get into trouble. "We have feelings, too," says one boy. But, he adds, "We're not supposed to cry."

Mrs. Higley's meetings point up the difficult task teachers face when it comes to labeling behavior and deciding what moral lesson to draw from a troubling incident.

Though character-education proponents insist they can teach morals in schools without bumping up against controversy, experts asked about this case gave differing advice. Kevin Ryan, director of the Center for the Advancement of Ethics and Character at Boston University, sees Mrs. Higley's use of the term "sexual harassment" as unnecessarily political. "Why didn't she just call it unkindness?" he asks. [1]

Lickona says he would have discussed sexual harassment under the larger umbrella of disrespect. "I think there's a consensus that sexual harassment is wrong and that schools ought to prevent it," he adds. Both Ryan and Lickona agree that any real-life problem is more complicated than it may appear at first.

Mrs. Higley's view is pragmatic. Afterward, she expresses confidence that the meetings achieved their primary goal — killing the rumor and ending the teasing. The class meeting, rather than preaching to the children, "gives them ownership" of the problem, she says. "I'm no psychologist, but it's like group therapy — or a family meeting."

"I like the class meetings," says Kathi Sullivan, former president of the Sheridan Parents Association. "I think it sets up a forum where kids are comfortable discussing things they're not normally comfortable discussing." Sullivan hopes the children will apply the conflict-resolution skills they have learned from class meetings to settling their tiffs on the playground.

As for changes in the school, Sullivan says, "One thing I've noticed this year is kids now hold doors open for me." She attributes that to a week that the school devoted to teaching courtesy.

In addition, fewer children are being sent out into the hall this year for misbehaving in class, teachers have told Sullivan. She believes that's due to a new rule the students helped develop: Do nothing in the classroom to prevent others from learning. "I think the teachers have better control over the classroom," she says. "Part of it is by getting the kids to buy into this rule. When the kids are acting up, the teachers say, 'Are you making this a classroom where everyone can learn?' "

Headmaster Riddleberger favors class meetings for teaching values because they deal with real-life problems. And with students ages 12 to 14, "You won't get far by preaching to them about honesty," he says. "It's only our actions that speak to them."

[1] For background on sexual harassment in schools, see "Education and Gender," *The CQ Researcher*, June 3, 1994, pp. 494-495.

encouraged children to fight Nazism or to support it?" [26]

Results Questioned

Though enormously popular in the 1970s, values clarification dropped off the radar screen of public schools in the 1980s. "As the political climate changed, parents would go to school boards and say, 'You mean my kids can go through values clarification and still believe in cheating and lying?'" recalls Leming. "School boards dropped it like a hot potato."

In addition, researchers were finding, for the most part, that values clarification wasn't having the hoped-for effect on students. After reviewing nearly 100 studies, Leming found fewer than 20 percent that produced the desired outcomes, such as clearer student thinking about their values or lower rates of youth crimes. "In the overwhelming number of cases, there was no change in any of those things," Leming says.

Though values clarification waned as a formal approach, it left an enduring impression on teachers. Kirschenbaum agrees with critics that "it made teachers more timid" about telling students directly that certain values were wrong. Kevin Ryan, a professor of education and director of the Center for the Advancement of Ethics and Character at Boston University, says schools of education still give teachers the message that when it comes to moral education, "They should stay away from it and stick to the information-dispensing role."

Partly, this grew out of a psychological stress on the importance of self-esteem. "There was a great deal of fear that any criticism would damage a child's self-esteem," says Lickona. "So in discussion, a teacher would never want a child to think their judgment about something was wrong."

Today, Kirschenbaum says he finds himself directly inculcating values in his young daughter, contrary to his old approach. Just as a conservative is often described as a liberal who has been mugged, he says, "A character educator is a values clarifier who's had children."

What should a parent say to a child who remarks, for example, that radar detectors are a good way to avoid speeding tickets? "In the old days," Kirschenbaum says, "we would have confined our remarks to, 'Do you think the world would be a better place if everyone did that?' " Today, he says, as a parent, "I would feel comfortable adding my own opinion: 'I don't think the world would be a good place.' " ■

CURRENT SITUATION

Methods Debated

At least a dozen states have recently incorporated character education into their school curricula, either through legislative mandates, regulation or pilot projects, according to the Character Education Partnership. In the most explicit mandate to date, Alabama passed legislation requiring 10 minutes of each school day to be dedicated to teaching character.

Many other states have had moral-education mandates in their curricula for decades, legacies of an earlier era, but have not implemented them, according to Martin of the Character Education Partnership.

In his Jan. 23 State of the Union address, President Clinton said, "I challenge all our schools to teach character education, to teach good values and good citizenship." Under the Elementary and Secondary Education Act of 1994, $1 million a year was authorized for grants to states to develop character-education curricula and pay for teacher training. Last year, state education departments in California, Iowa, New Mexico and Utah received grants.

While some schools have introduced separate ethics classes, most proponents of values education say character should be taught through behavior and literature. Teachers are urged to seize opportunities to point out moral lessons as they arise in classroom crises or in the material they are teaching.

Early this year, Boston University's Ryan issued a manifesto, signed by more than 30 other educators, criticizing some existing approaches to character education and defining how it should be taught. "The public support character education has won is threatened [by] several skimpy or mislabeled programs being marketed as character education," Ryan charged in a statement. [27]

Ryan has also singled out the Josephson Institute's popular "Character Counts" program for criticism. Five hundred communities have adopted its principles, according to the institute, including school districts in Toledo, Ohio, Albuquerque, N.M., and Dallas, Texas. Last month, the institute released a 60-minute children's videotape about values, starring 30 popular TV characters from Barney the dinosaur to dashing Tom Selleck.

The character-education movement is being trivialized, Ryan says, by the production of coffee cups, pens and T-shirts with the "Character Counts" slogan. "I think that characterizes their approach," he says. "It's in no way a return to teaching about virtue and helping children acquire virtue."

In its videotape and educational materials, "Character Counts" stresses six "pillars of character": trustworthiness, respect, responsibility, fairness, caring and citizenship.

Ryan has no problem with the list — in fact he helped develop it. But Ryan and others active in the movement are concerned that proliferating character-education programs will not move beyond preaching and posters. Ryan, for example, stresses the importance of high-quality teacher-training seminars, such as those conducted at Boston University, where teachers discuss works by great philosophers like Aristotle.

"My fear is schools will adopt programs under the delusion they represent a quick fix to social problems they've identified," says Huffman, another signer of the manifesto. When Huffman consults with school boards interested in adopting character education, he tells them not to get involved unless they are prepared to carry out the values they espouse in every aspect of the school's management. That includes being respectful to employees across the bargaining table and training janitors to be kind to a crying child they encounter in a hallway.

Huffman also advocates that community meetings be held with parents and residents to come up with the consensus values the community will stress. "One of the challenges of character education is to get everyone to become morally reflective," Huffman says.

But Josephson, a former law professor, argues that it's "an academics' myth that if you have a debate you will get everyone to agree. If you believe that, you have to do it every year, every moment you change the city council or the school board."

Josephson says the intention behind the six pillars of character was to develop a list of widely accepted ethical values that would attract the backing of a broad political spectrum. This would "provide the political permission to unleash the talents of teachers," he says.

The program has won the endorsement of conservatives like former

Continued on p. 546

At Issue:

Should schools teach moral values?

THOMAS LICKONA
Professor of Education, State University of New York, Cortland, and author of Educating for Character.

FROM "THE RETURN OF CHARACTER EDUCATION," EDUCATIONAL LEADERSHIP, NOVEMBER 1993.

yes

In the 1990s, we are seeing the beginnings of a new character-education movement, one which restores "good character" to its historical place as the central desirable outcome of the school's moral enterprise. No one knows yet how broad or deep this movement is. . . . But something significant is afoot. . . .

In the face of a deteriorating social fabric, what must character education do to develop good character in the young? First, it must have an adequate theory of what good character is, one which gives schools a clear idea of their goals. Character must be broadly conceived to encompass the cognitive, affective and behavioral aspects of morality. Good character consists of knowing the good, desiring the good and doing the good. Schools must help children understand the core values, adopt or commit to them and then act upon them in their own lives.

The cognitive side of character includes at least six specific moral qualities: awareness of the moral dimensions of the situation at hand, knowing moral values and what they require of us in concrete cases, perspective-taking, moral reasoning, thoughtful decision-making and moral self-knowledge. . . . People can be very smart about matters of right and wrong, however, and still choose the wrong. Moral education that is merely intellectual misses the crucial emotional side of character, which serves as the bridge between judgment and action. . . .

At times, we know what we should do, feel strongly that we should do it, yet still fail to translate moral judgment and feeling into effective moral behavior. Moral action, the third part of character, draws upon three additional moral qualities: competence (skills such as listening, communicating and cooperating), will (which mobilizes our judgment and energy) and moral habit (a reliable inner disposition to respond to situations in a morally good way).

Once we have a comprehensive concept of character, we need a comprehensive approach to developing it. This approach tells schools to look at themselves through a moral lens and consider how virtually everything that goes on there affects the values and character of students. Then, plan how to use all phases of classroom and school life as deliberate tools of character development. . . .

As we close out our turbulent century and ready our schools for the next, educating for character is a moral imperative if we care about the future of our society and our children.

DAVID R. CARLIN JR.
Associate professor of Social Sciences, Rhode Island Community College, Warwick, Rhode Island

FROM "TEACHING VALUES IN SCHOOL," *COMMONWEAL*, FEB. 9, 1996.

no

There is much talk nowadays about the need for public schools to teach moral values. In a society that, for 30 years, has been drifting downriver toward the Niagara of moral anarchy, there is no doubt about it: Somebody needs to teach moral values to the young. But can the public schools do it? I doubt it.

Leaving aside a number of other difficulties, let's focus on the vexed question of *whose* values will be taught. Will the schools teach liberal or conservative values? Values of self-expression or self-control? Values rooted in religion or in secularism? Values of individual autonomy or of community?

Now there happens to be a standard way of trying to meet this difficulty. It is argued (by Bill Bennett, for one) that, no matter what our moral disagreements, all Americans share many important values. . . .

Everyone agrees that fairness, honesty, courage and respect for others are good qualities, while unfairness, dishonesty, cowardice and disrespect are bad. . . . So let schools teach a broad range of noncontroversial values while maintaining a prudent silence about the narrow range of controversial questions.

Note well, we are told, that this sensible policy does not mean that children will learn nothing about controversial matters. Far from it. Parents, churches and other non-school agencies of socialization will be quite free to give instruction on such issues. . . . As an abstract proposal, this seems reasonable. But as usual, the devil is in the details. . . .

[C]onsider fairness. We all believe in fairness as an abstract principle, but what does it mean in practice? What does it mean, for instance, when applied to divorce? Or when applied to social policy questions, like affirmative action, food stamps, Medicare? Or when applied to abortion and euthanasia?. . .

Maybe the schools will respond to this dilemma by saying: "Our fairness curriculum will teach kids not to cut in line and not to steal one another's pencils; but we'll take no stands on divisive questions like divorce, social policy, abortion and euthanasia." But this is tantamount to teaching that fairness applies to small matters only, not to big matters. Once again, what's the point?. . . .

Schools can be effective moral teachers when they represent communities that are morally homogeneous. The trouble is, American society is no longer a morally homogeneous community.

FOR MORE INFORMATION

American Civil Liberties Union, 132 West 43rd St., New York, N.Y. 10038; (212) 944-9800. The ACLU has not taken an official position on character education in schools, but some of its affiliates express concern that the movement could provide an entrée for the religious right into schools.

Character Education Partnership, 809 Franklin St., Alexandria, Va. 22314-4105; (703) 739-9515. This consortium of national education associations promotes character education in the nation's schools and provides information on school programs.

Josephson Institute of Ethics, 4640 Admiralty Way, Suite 1000, Marina del Rey, Calif. 90292-6610; (310) 306-1868. This nonprofit group established the Character Counts! Coalition, a popular program promoting character education in schools and community groups.

Focus on the Family, 8605 Explorer Dr., Colorado Springs, Colo. 80920; (719) 531-3400. This Christian group dedicated to "the preservation of the home" produces moral-education materials for schools and endorses a conservative Christian perspective on character education.

Continued from p. 544

Education Secretary Bennett and liberals like Marian Wright Edelman, who heads the Children's Defense Fund. Josephson has also attracted a bipartisan coalition of 10 members of Congress who support Character Counts, led by Sens. Pete V. Domenici, R-N.M., and Sam Nunn, D-Ga. "That political success is what has made it so popular," Josephson says.

In addition to the cups and T-shirts that "celebrate" character, the program provides serious curriculum material and teacher-training seminars, Josephson adds. "We bring in three to four trainers and train 35 people for 3 1/2 days." The program typically costs $20,000 to $30,000 for a community, and about 20 percent of the attendees receive scholarships from the institute.

Responding to his critics, Josephson says: "Why did [Dallas and Toledo] decide this was a significant program? Here are people who decided that they wanted to do this for their entire school systems. None of the other programs can show this broad-based support." ■

OUTLOOK

Potential Pitfalls

The debate over how character and values should be taught is sure to continue. Some of the more sophisticated observers of the movement are wary of a return to the dull moralizing of the 19th century. In a review of Bennett's *The Book of Virtues for Young People,* children's author Katherine Paterson noted that much of its poetry is "primly Victorian." She questioned whether teaching virtues is simply a matter of "getting rules down."

"We all know," Paterson wrote, "how literature has made us grow in understanding and compassion, but the learning was our own choice — not something imposed by someone else, but something we gained by entering emotionally, intellectually and spiritually into the heart of a great writer. Shouldn't we trust our children to do the same?" [28]

Meanwhile, the ACLU and conservative Christian groups are taking a wait-and-see attitude toward character education. Olivia Turner, executive director of the Alabama ACLU, views Alabama's 10-minute-a-day character-education mandate as a legislative capitulation to the religious right. While she knows of no instances in which religion is being taught under the mandate, she notes that Christian groups have offered religious textbooks to impoverished school districts. The mandate "creates a window of opportunity for the religious right," she says.

Glanzer of Focus on the Family commends the character-education movement for its grass-roots orientation and emphasis on seeking a consensus of parents' common values. "It has not been a top-down movement, for the most part," he says.

Neither the right nor the left can cite objectionable programs in character education today. But both sides frequently bring up sex education and parental rights as potential pitfalls. Community-service requirements, a component of some character-education programs, also have come under fire from parents. In Mamaroneck, N.Y., the parents of Daniel Immediato sued Rye Neck High School, arguing that its community-service requirement would "destroy any moral value in serving others" because of its involuntary nature. [29]

On Jan. 2, 1996, the 2nd U.S. Circuit Court of Appeals upheld Mamaroneck's community-service requirement; the Immediato family has appealed to the Supreme Court. [30]

Some observers believe the character-education movement will succeed as long as it sticks to an individual school-by-school approach and does not evolve into mandates. At the federal and state level, they note, efforts to establish mandatory educational standards have become mired in controversy over graduation requirements that students meet character-related objectives, such as working cooperatively with people of diverse lifestyles or obeying authority. [31]

"A lot of parents think schools should stick to teaching knowledge, not get into behavioral aspects of kids," Finn says. "It's a lot more palatable to have school 'A' say we'll teach virtues the Bennett way, school 'B' say we'll teach it the Ten Commandments way and school 'C' say we'll teach tolerance and equality."

Martin of the character-education movement is quick to declare that, "We're not necessarily wanting state mandates. Often, when a mandate comes down there's resistance to what people think is going on in schools."

To the extent that parents like what they see of the character-education movement, they will vote with their feet. Jefferson Junior High and Allen Academy boast long waiting lists. But both schools are doing so much besides character education — from providing mentors to improving academics — that it may be hard to write a formula easily followed for success. ■

Sarah Glazer is a freelance writer in Washington, D.C., who specializes in health and social-policy issues.

Notes

[1] Carolyn Gecan and Bernadette Mulholland-Glaze, "The Teacher's Place in the Formation of Students' Character," *Journal of Education,* Vol. 175, No. 2, 1993, p. 46.

[2] Gallup/Phi Delta Kappa poll cited in *Character Education in U.S. Schools: The New Consensus,* Character Education Partnership, February 1996, p. 21.

[3] Thomas Lickona, *Educating for Character* (1992 ed.), p. 11.

[4] *Ibid.*, p. 21.

[5] *Ibid.*, pp. 13-19.

[6] Joseph & Edna Josephson Institute of Ethics, "1996 Report Card on American Integrity," 1996.

[7] Joe Queenan, "Good as Gold," *George,* April/May 1996, p. 108.

[8] See David T. Kearns and Denis Doyle, *Winning the Brain Race* (1991).

[9] See Peter Applebome, "Array of Opponents Battle Over 'Parental Rights' Bills," *The New York Times,* May 1, 1996, p. A1.

[10] *Ibid.*

[11] The Supreme Court's *Wisconsin v. Yoder* (1972) ruling created an exception to a state compulsory school-attendance law. Several Amish families had argued that requiring their children to attend high school violated their religious beliefs. See "Parents and Schools," *The CQ Researcher,* Jan. 20, 1995, pp. 49-72.

[12] The Communitarian Network is a nonpartisan, nationwide coalition devoted to fostering socially responsible communities.

[13] Developmental Studies Center, *The Child Development Project: Summary of Findings in Two Initial Districts and the First Phase of an Expansion to Six Additional Districts Nationally,* August 1994.

[14] *Ibid.*, p. 20.

[15] *Ibid.*, p. 31.

[16] For background, see "Preventing Juvenile Crime," *The CQ Researcher,* March 15, 1996, pp. 217-240.

[17] Henry A. Huffman, "The Unavoidable Mission of Character Education," *The School Administrator,* September 1995, p. 14.

[18] Cited in William J. Bennett, "Parents, Schools and Values," *Network News & Views,* January/February 1996, p. 59, and Lickona, *op. cit.*, p. 6. *Network News & Views* is published by the Education Excellence Network, a project of the Hudson Institute

[19] Quoted in Boston University press release accompanying *Character Education Manifesto,* April 3, 1996.

[20] The Supreme Court's series of rulings on school prayer and Bible reading began with its 1962 decision in *Engel v. Vitale,* declaring the daily prayer in New York State public schools a violation of the constitutional separation between church and state. See "Religion in Schools," *The CQ Researcher,* Feb. 18, 1994, pp. 145-168.

[21] Sidney Simon, Leland W. Howe and Howard Kirschenbaum, *Values Clarification: A Handbook of Practical Strategies for Teachers and Students* (1972).

[22] Cited in Stephen Bates, "A Textbook of Virtues," *The New York Times,* Education Life section, Jan. 8, 1995, p. 18.

[23] Lickona, *op. cit.*, p. 11.

[24] Michael Bocian, "A Communitarian Approach to Character Education," *Basic Education,* March 1996, p. 8.

[25] Cited in Kilpatrick, *op. cit.*, p. 105.

[26] Letter from Marc Desmond, "Letters" column, *New York Times Magazine,* May 21, 1995, in response to Roger Rosenblatt, "Teaching Johnny to Be Good," *The New York Times Magazine,* April 30, 1995.

[27] Boston University press release accompanying *Character Education Manifesto,* April 3, 1996.

[28] Katherine Paterson, "Family Values," *The New York Times Book Review,* Oct. 15, 1995, p. 32.

[29] See Chester E. Finn Jr. and Gregg Vanourek, "Charity Begins at School," *Commentary,* October 1995.

[30] The Institute for Justice, a libertarian group in Washington, D.C., filed the Immediato family's appeal.

[31] See "Education Standards," *The CQ Researcher,* March 11, 1994, pp. 217-240.

Bibliography

Selected Sources Used

Books

Etzioni, Amitai, *The Spirit of Community,* Crown Publishers, 1993.
George Washington University Professor Etzioni, founder of the Communitarian Network, describes his vision of moral education. Distancing himself from an "authoritarian" approach to discipline, he advocates helping students to develop psychological "muscles" like self-discipline, then imparting values through positive experiences at the school.

Fine, Melinda, *Habits of Mind: Struggling over Values in America's Classrooms,* Jossey-Bass, 1995.
Fine describes "Facing History and Ourselves," a middle school curriculum on the Holocaust that draws moral lessons on tolerance and racism. Fine, a supporter of the program, chronicles attacks by conservatives on the program and gives a historical overview of conservative-liberal struggles over values education in public schools.

Kilpatrick, William K., *Why Johnny Can't Tell Right from Wrong and What We Can Do About It,* Touchstone, 1993.
Boston College Professor Kilpatrick decries American education's values-neutral turn in an extended attack on the moral relativism of the 1960s and its philosophical roots. His conservative viewpoint comes through in his passing criticisms of progressive educator John Dewey and Mark Twain's *Tom Sawyer* as contributors to the moral decline of American children.

Lickona, Thomas, *Educating for Character,* Bantam Books, 1992.
Lickona, a professor of education at the State University of New York in Cortland, is a widely recognized authority in the character-education movement. In this book, orginally published in 1991, he describes how character education works, with numerous anecdotes from schools.

Articles

Bates, Stephen, "Morality 101," *The New York Times,* Education Life, Jan. 4, 1995, p. 16.
This is an excellent summary of the current debate over teaching values in American public schools.

Etzioni, Amitai, "Who's to Say What's Right or Wrong?" *Washington Post Education Review,* April 2, 1995.
In a review of *Habits of Mind,* Etzioni says the conservative criticism of the Holocaust curriculum "Facing History and Ourselves" is fair: It depicts America as a society with no core values other than procedural ones. But he maintains it is possible to teach values without pressing either leftist or right-wing opinions.

Gecan, Carolyn, and Bernadette Mulholland-Glaze, "The Teacher's Place in the Formation of Students' Character," *Journal of Education,* Vol. 175, No. 2, 1993, pp. 45-58.
In a special issue of this Boston University journal devoted to ethics in education, two teachers describe how they helped start a character education program at Thomas Jefferson High School for Science and Technology in Alexandria, Va.

Henry, Tamara, "Growing Debate Centers on Who Teaches Values," *USA Today,* March 20, 1996, p. 1.
The parental-rights movement, led by parents who object to the values taught by schools in sex education, condom distribution and community service programs, indicates potential controversies that could plague the character-education movement.

Lawton, Millicent, "Values Education: A Moral Obligation or Dilemma?" *Education Week,* May 17, 1995, p. 1.
Lawton describes the national movement among schools to introduce character education and some of the criticisms that have been raised.

Ryan, Kevin, "Character and Coffee Mugs," *Education Week,* May 17, 1995, p. 48.
Boston University education Professor Kevin Ryan, a proponent of character education, expresses concern that the movement is becoming a "cluttered bandwagon," emphasizing slogans more than substance.

Rosenblatt, Roger, "Teaching Johnny to be Good," *The New York Times Magazine,* April 30, 1995, p. 36.
Rosenblatt profiles character-education proponent Thomas Lickona and examines his ideas in the context of the current movement to teach values in schools.

Reports and Studies

Character Education Partnership, *Character Education in U.S. Schools: The New Consensus,* February 1996.
This is a useful report on developments from 1993 to 1995 in government and schools in support of character education. The partnership is a coalition of education groups that promotes character education.

Joseph & Edna Josephson Institute of Ethics, "1996 Report Card on American Integrity," 1996.
This annual survey shows high rates of lying and cheating among high school and college students and is often cited by advocates of character education.

The Next Step

Additional information from UMI's Newspaper & Periodical Abstracts database

Value and Character Education in Schools

Bates, Stephen, "A textbook of virtues," *The New York Times,* Jan. 8, 1995, p. A16.
Henry Huffman, the assistant superintendent of schools in Mount Lebanon, Pa., is the moving force behind the district's efforts to teach children about courage and other moral values. Huffman says the question is not whether the schools should engage in character education but how they should do it. The way that Huffman introduced character education to the Mount Lebanon schools is described.

Booth, Michael, "Religion part of every class in curriculum," *Denver Post,* Oct. 1, 1995, p. A14.
The principal of St. Thomas More school in Denver says "A Catholic education is not different because they have a religion class every day. It's different because everything we say and do is permeated by Christian values." Education in Denver's Catholic schools is discussed.

Cesarone, Bernard, "Character education," *Childhood Education,* fall 1995, pp. 53-54.
A summary of ERIC documents and journal articles that discuss character education.

Cottom, Carolyn, "A bold experiment in teaching values," *Educational Leadership,* May 1996, pp. 54-58.
A religiously diverse school, the City Montessori School in Lucknow, India, has proven that teachers can instill both personal and social virtues and a desire to excel, and that academic excellence flows from character development.

Governali, Joseph F., "Health education and character education," *Journal of School Health,* November 1995, pp. 394-396.
The article discusses the historical context within which to view character education, the current state of character education and the need to stimulate health education interest in this area. Although differences exist, consensus exists over many core values that need to be taught.

Healy, Melissa, "Concerned parents push character movement," *Los Angeles Times,* May 28, 1996, p. A1.
As part of an occasional series on America's search for common values, the article examines the burgeoning "character education" movement, which aims to teach children in public schools right from wrong and to internalize the core values of the community.

Little, Joan, "Character education gets attention at conference," *St. Louis Post-Dispatch,* July 2, 1995, p. B7.
At a teachers' conference in St. Louis, attention was given to a new course of study, that of character education. The article describes how the program is designed to help children.

Stafford, Tim, "Helping Johnny be good," *Christianity Today,* Sept. 11, 1995, pp. 34-39.
The pros and cons of "character education" in the public schools are discussed. A substantial group within public education says that teaching values is important.

Tice, Terrence N., "Morality and spirituality," *Education Digest,* May 1996, pp. 43-45.
Several resources concerning moral education and spirituality are discussed. They represent a burgeoning interest in what is going on in "values or character education."

Tomaselli, Joseph M. and Joseph P. Golden, "Character development in education: The ABCD's of valuing," *NASSP Bulletin,* April 1996, pp. 66-73.
Tomaselli and Golden discuss the role that character development and values play in educating America's children, whether these values can be integrated into the standing curriculum without overloading the system, and if understanding their own values will help students make better personal, academic and life decisions.

Weiner, Susan, "Values are learned by example," *Christian Science Monitor,* May 18, 1995, p. 20.
Weiner speculates on the success of character education and concludes that teachers and parents already teach values by example.

Reasons for Moral Education

Bennett, William J., "The national prospect: A symposium," *Commentary,* November 1995, pp. 23-29.
Bennett discusses how moral decline is undermining America's traditional confidence about itself, its mission and its place in the world.

Clinton, William J., "The president's radio address," *Weekly Compilation of Presidential Documents,* March 4, 1996, pp. 366-368.
In his weekly radio address, President Clinton discusses breaking the hold of gangs and violence in American

schools and what must be done to create an atmosphere in American schools that promtes discipline, order and learning.

Herbert, Wray, "The moral child," ***U.S. News & World Report,*** **June 3, 1996, pp. 52-59.**
There has been much debate over how to raise decent children when the traditional ties to church, school and community have been badly frayed. Information about the efforts of Americans to regain the ability to raise their kids is presented.

Howard, John A., "Troubled America," ***Vital Speeches of the Day,*** **March 15, 1996, pp. 340-343.**
The virtuous norms of Christendom were abandoned long ago, which has led the U.S. into a deplorable state, Howard argues. He calls the United States a land without wisdom.

Weinberger, Caspar W., "One way to fix our schools," ***Forbes,*** **May 6, 1996, p. 33.**
Advances have been made toward reinstating character education in the U.S. school system. Restoring values and character to curricula should improve student behavior and reduce crime in schools.

School Programs

Amoroso, Victor, "For kids' sake, let's teach values," ***Vocational Education Journal,*** **September 1995, p. 62.**
Amoroso offers some reasons why vocational education may be the place for teaching values and ethics instruction. Vocational educational teachers can show students the pragmatism of treating people fairly and honestly.

Bacon-Blood, Littice, "Education with character: Teacher's pets give core lessons," ***Times-Picayune,*** **Dec. 11, 1995, p. B1.**
John Q. Adams Middle School teacher JoAnn Vincent used pets to drive home the point of respecting life and being responsible, a core element of the character and values education curriculum pushed by the Jefferson Parish, La., school system.

Cumming, Doug, "Building character," ***Atlanta Constitution,*** **March 20, 1996, p. B1.**
The "word of the week" program at West Point Elementary takes 10 minutes every morning and covers 34 positive traits such as punctuality and cleanliness in a year's time. It has transformed the troubled Troup County school into Georgia's showcase for a movement called character education.

Griffin-Nolan, Ed, "Students are hungry for values," ***National Catholic Reporter,*** **Oct. 6, 1995, p. 15.**
LeMoyne College's Values Program, which is designed to promote discussion of values on campus, is discussed. The LeMoyne effort is part of a serious effort by Catholic colleges to reexamine how values are connected with the overall academic effort on campus.

Jones, Arthur, "Inner-city peer counselors foster values," ***National Catholic Reporter,*** **Dec. 22, 1995, p. 6.**
Franklin Middle School in Long Beach, Calif., has implemented a program of leadership among students who are chosen to act as peer counselors to help out in student-conflict management. More and more schools are using programs like Community of Caring to promote "values" education, just as Franklin Middle School has done.

Logan, Claudia, "Character education by the book," ***Instructor,*** **July 1995, pp. 74-79.**
Jean Johnson and Penny Levy describe how they harnassed the power of literature to help students explore universal values. In an interview, Eleanor Childs, founder of the Heartwood Institute, tells why she started the institute and how she responds to people who feel character education does not belong in school.

Mecca, Marilyn E., "Classrooms where children learn to care," ***Childhood Education,*** **winter 1995, pp. 72-74.**
The whole language philosophy and its contributions to children's literacy developments are discussed. Although the literacy strengths of the approach are well documented, the approach also helps improve the moral climate of the classroom.

Swanson, Richard L., "Research foundations of moral and ethical education," ***Education,*** **winter 1995, pp. 296-301.**
Educators have focused on the approach of Lawrence Kohlberg, the Moral Calculus approach. However, as educators plan and design curriculum and instruction, they need to carefully consider the research that includes the content and motivational mechanisms discussed by the internalization and social-learning approaches as well.

Zuniga, Jo Ann, "Paige praises HISD morality lessons," ***Houston Chronicle,*** **May 26, 1995, p. A35.**
Leaders of an ongoing program teaching ethics and morality to Houston students, the largest character-education program in the country, met with its group of foundation and corporate sponsors on May 25, 1995. Houston Independent School District Superintendent Rod Paige praised the program, which emphasizes self-esteem and self-discipline.

"20 years of moral education," ***Boston Globe*****, April 22, 1996, p. 10.**
An editorial commends the success of the Facing History and Ourselves educational organization, a national program based in Boston, which links the monumental human capacity for evil with the importance of moral, individual choices.

Encouraging Community Service

Bringle, Robert B. and Julie A. Hatcher, "Implementing service learning in higher education," *Journal of Higher Education,* March 1996, pp. 221-239.
The implementation of service learning in universities is discussed by delineating a set of activities for four constituencies — institution, faculty, students and community. Service learning offers a unique opportunity to engage students in community service, to expand their educational agenda and to build reciprocal partnerships within the community.

Finn, Chester E. Jr. and Gregg Vanourek, "Charity begins at school," *Commentary,* October 1995, pp. 46-48.
With the federal government's connivance, American schoolchildren are being required to "volunteer" their services, the authors argue. This is most troubling because now the nation's schools are diverting time, energy and money to nonacademic matters while the performance of students continues to decline.

Kahne, Joseph and Joel Westheimer, "In the service of what? The politics of service learning," *Phi Delta Kappan,* May 1996, pp. 592-599.
Legislators and educators have both noted that service learning can improve the community and invigorate the classroom by providing rich educational experiences for students at all levels of schooling. The moral, political and intellectual aspects of service learning are noted, and the challenge for practitioners and advocates are outlined.

Morton, Keith and Marie Troppe, "From the margin to the mainstream: Campus compact's project on integrating service with academic study," *Journal of Business Ethics,* January 1996, pp. 21-32.
An introduction to service learning and a brief review of the research on the effects of service learning on academic and values development are offered. The findings are based on a three-year, national project supported by the Ford Foundation and an anonymous donor, and two service-learning case studies.

Miscellaneous

Brandt, Ron, "On finding common ground with religious conservatives: A conversation with Charles Haynes," *Educational Leadership,* April 1996, pp. 72-75.
In an interview, Charles Haynes discusses traditionalist parents' opposition to school programs and their suspicions of educators. Haynes believes that religion should be properly represented in school curriculums.

Clinton, William J., "Memorandum on the school uniforms manual," *Weekly Compilation of Presidential Documents,* March 4, 1996, pp. 368-369.
In a memorandum, President Clinton discusses the need for school uniforms as a means to improve school safety and discipline. School uniforms, however, are just one of the many initiatives undertaken by schools and parents to better school discipline and safety.

Grant, Ruth W., "The ethics of talk: Classroom conversation and democratic politics," *Teachers College Record,* spring 1996, pp. 470-482.
Grant explores the impact of classroom dialogue on the development in students of the ethical characteristics necessary for a deliberative democracy.

Guerra, Daniel S., "Integrate violence prevention into schools," *Education Digest,* February 1996, pp. 8-12.
Guerra, a school social worker at Snyder Academy, Jersey City [N.J.] Public Schools, and school psychologist Sally Juliano developed a multiphased program, emphasizing prevention and education, to prevent students from becoming violent and to afford all students a safe environment in which to learn. Guerra discusses two tools—mediation and grief counseling.

Marks, John, "The American uncivil wars," *U.S. News & World Report,* April 22, 1996, pp. 66-72.
Crude, rude and obnoxious behavior has replaced good manners in the United States. This behavior is hurting America's culture and its politics.

Marshak, David, "Re-humanizing our children," *Education Digest,* December 1995, pp. 7-11.
In the 1960s high-school consolidation became a nationwide movement. As a result, these increasingly large high schools promoted the growth of a youth culture, marked by a profound alienation from adult society. Ways that teachers can restore young people to a meaningful place in the adult culture are outlined.

Back Issues

Great Research on Current Issues Starts Right Here...Recent topics covered by The CQ Researcher are listed below. Before May 1991, reports were published under the name of Editorial Research Reports.

DECEMBER 1994
Farm Policy
Arms Sales
Earthquake Research
The Future of Television

JANUARY 1995
Treating Addiction
Child Custody and Support
Parents and Schools
Non-Proliferation Treaty at 25

FEBRUARY 1995
Cracking Down on Immigration
The Business of Sports
Reinventing Government
Housing Discrimination

MARCH 1995
Death Penalty Debate
Primary Care
Democracy in Africa
Environmental Movement at 25

APRIL 1995
Abortion Clinic Protests
Dieting and Health
Combating AIDS
Rethinking Affirmative Action

Back issues are available for $5.00 (subscribers) or $8.00 (non-subscribers). Quantity discounts apply to orders over ten. To order, call Congressional Quarterly Customer Service at (202) 887-8621.

Binders are available for $18.00. To order call 1-800-638-1710. Please refer to stock number 648.

MAY 1995
Assisted Suicide Controversy
Overhauling Social Security
Learning to Read
Mandatory Sentencing

JUNE 1995
Combating Infectious Disease
Property Rights
Repetitive Stress Injuries
Regulating the Internet

JULY 1995
War Crimes
Highway Safety
Combating Terrorism
Preventing Teen Drug Use

AUGUST 1995
Job Stress
Organ Transplants
United Nations at 50
Advances in Cancer Research

SEPTEMBER 1995
Catholic Church in the U.S.
Northern Ireland Cease-Fire
High School Sports
Teaching History

OCTOBER 1995
Quebec's Future
Revitalizing the Cities
Networking the Classroom
Indoor Air Pollution

NOVEMBER 1995
The Working Poor
The Jury System
Sex, Violence and the Media
Police Misconduct

DECEMBER 1995
Teens and Tobacco
Gene Therapy's Future
Global Water Shortages
Third-Party Prospects

JANUARY 1996
Emergency Medicine
Punishing Sex Offenders
Bilingual Education
Helping the Homeless

FEBRUARY 1996
Reforming the CIA
Campaign Finance Reform
Academic Politics
Getting Into College

MARCH 1996
The British Monarchy
Preventing Juvenile Crime
Tax Reform
Pursuing the Paranormal

APRIL 1996
Centennial Olympic Games
Managed Care
Protecting Endangered Species
New Military Culture

MAY 1996
Russia's Political Future
Marriage and Divorce
Year-Round Schools
Taiwan, China and the U.S.

JUNE 1996
Rethinking NAFTA
First Ladies

Future Topics

- ***Labor Movement's Future***
- ***Repressed Memory Syndrome***
- ***Native Americans at a Crossroads***

THE
CQ Researcher
PUBLISHED BY CONGRESSIONAL QUARTERLY INC.

Labor Movement's Future

Can unions regain some of their lost power?

The labor movement has been losing members over the past two decades — and political and economic clout as well. Now, the new president of the AFL-CIO is vowing to reinvigorate the labor federation. John J. Sweeney promises to organize more workers, increase union activism and spend up to $35 million to mobilize pro-labor voters for the November elections. Business groups and other labor critics maintain that unions are no longer needed to protect workers' rights. And Republicans charge that the planned media campaign violates federal campaign disclosure laws. Despite the criticisms, Sweeney insists that his new policies are laying the groundwork for a much stronger labor movement in the future.

INSIDE THIS ISSUE

CQ June 28, 1996 • Volume 6, No. 24 • Pages 553-576

Formerly Editorial Research Reports

Labor Movement's Future

The Issues

Background

Current Situation

Outlook

Sidebars and Graphics

For Further Research

COVER: TERRY WYS OF EAST PEORIA, ILL., AND OTHER STRIKING UNITED AUTO WORKERS SHOUT PROTESTS AT PEOPLE ENTERING THE CATERPILLAR INC. PLANT IN MOSSVILLE, ILL., ON APRIL 9, 1992. (AFL-CIO NEWS)

THE CQ Researcher

June 28, 1996
Volume 6, No. 24

The CQ Researcher (ISSN 1056-2036). Formerly Editorial Research Reports. Published weekly (48 times per year, not printed March 1, May 31, Aug. 30, Nov. 29) by Congressional Quarterly Inc., 1414 22nd St., N.W., Washington, D.C. 20037. Annual subscription rate for libraries, businesses and government is $319. Additional rates furnished upon request. Second-class postage paid at Washington, D.C. POSTMASTER: Send address changes to The CQ Researcher, 1414 22nd St., N.W., Washington, D.C. 20037.

Labor Movement's Future

BY KENNETH JOST

THE ISSUES

It's "Justice for Janitors Day" in Washington, and about 250 people have gathered in the city's business district to show their solidarity with the hard-working men and women who clean up after the lawyers, lobbyists and office workers call it a day.

"We're here to demand that all janitors in D.C. get better benefits, health insurance and respect on the job," says Maria Naranjo, an organizer for Local 82 of the Service Employees International Union (SEIU), which arranged the June 12 rally.

The crowd — a mix of union members and activists, students and a few middle-aged professionals — listens to speeches and chants labor slogans. Then, armed with placards, bullhorns and noisemakers, they slowly march around the block.

The hour-long rally, one of a series of demonstrations the SEIU local has staged over the past year to highlight the janitors' cause, is only a pale imitation of the great labor rallies of the past. But it exemplifies the labor movement's recent efforts to reawaken worker militancy and win public support. Through such efforts, labor leaders hope to regain some of the economic and political clout the movement has lost in the past three decades.

No union has done more to take its cause to the workplace and to the streets in recent years than the SEIU, whose 1.1 million members include janitorial, maintenance and clerical workers. Last October, SEIU President John J. Sweeney took his activist philosophy to a new position: the presidency of the giant AFL-CIO, the 13.1 million-member umbrella organization for 78 individual unions.

Sweeney, 62, climbed to the U.S. labor movement's top post after waging a two-year campaign that forced

the federation's longtime president, Lane Kirkland, to retire last August. Then, in the labor federation's first contested election for president since 1895,[1] Sweeney defeated Kirkland's handpicked successor, Acting President Thomas R. Donahue (*see p. 565*).

"It was time for a reinvigoration of the labor movement," Sweeney says during an interview in his eighth-floor office in the AFL-CIO's headquarters across Lafayette Square from the White House. "When I campaigned for the presidency of the AFL-CIO, I used the line frequently that it wasn't really about who headed the AFL-CIO. It was about where the AFL-CIO was headed."

For the past 25 years, the AFL-CIO, which represents about 80 percent of the country's estimated 16.4 million union members, has been headed down, not up. Union membership has been declining both in absolute terms and as a percentage of the total work force. In the late 1940s and early '50s, about a third of the nation's work force belonged to unions. Today, unions represent only 15 percent of the total work force — and just 10 percent of workers in the private sector. (*See graph, p. 556.*)

The labor movement's decline stems in part from changes in the U.S. economy. "Manufacturing jobs were being replaced by service sector jobs," explains Peter Seybold, director of the division of labor studies at Indiana University in Bloomington. "This hurt the labor movement in the area where it was strongest."

Labor's decline would have been even sharper except for unions' steady growth among government workers. Unions represented about 903,000 public employees in 1960; the number more than doubled, to 2.2 million, in 1962 — the year the National Education Association was reclassified as a union. Membership in public-employee unions has continued to grow almost every year since then. Today, nearly 7 million government workers belong to unions; they account for more than 42 percent of all union members in the country.

Outside the public sector, however, organized labor was doing little to reverse its declining membership. The AFL-CIO devoted little attention to organizing and failed to come up with strategies to counter the increased resistance to its agenda in the workplace and in the political arena. "For a long time, labor was headed by people who didn't realize the seriousness of the problem that we faced," says Thomas Geoghegan, a Chicago labor law attorney and author.

Meanwhile, labor has all but lost its most potent weapon of years past: the strike. The number of strikes last year — 385 — was the lowest in 50 years, according to the Federal Mediation and Conciliation Service, an independent agency that tries to help resolve labor-management disputes. The number of major work stoppages — those involving more than 1,000 workers — also was at a 50-year low: 31. (*See*

Union Membership in Decline

The percentage of U.S. workers belonging to unions has been steadily declining for the past 25 years. In the late 1940s and early '50s, about a third of the nation's work force belonged to unions. Today, unions represent only 15 percent of the total work force — just 10 percent of workers in the private sector. Labor organizers have had more success in the public sector; nearly 38 percent of government employees are union members.

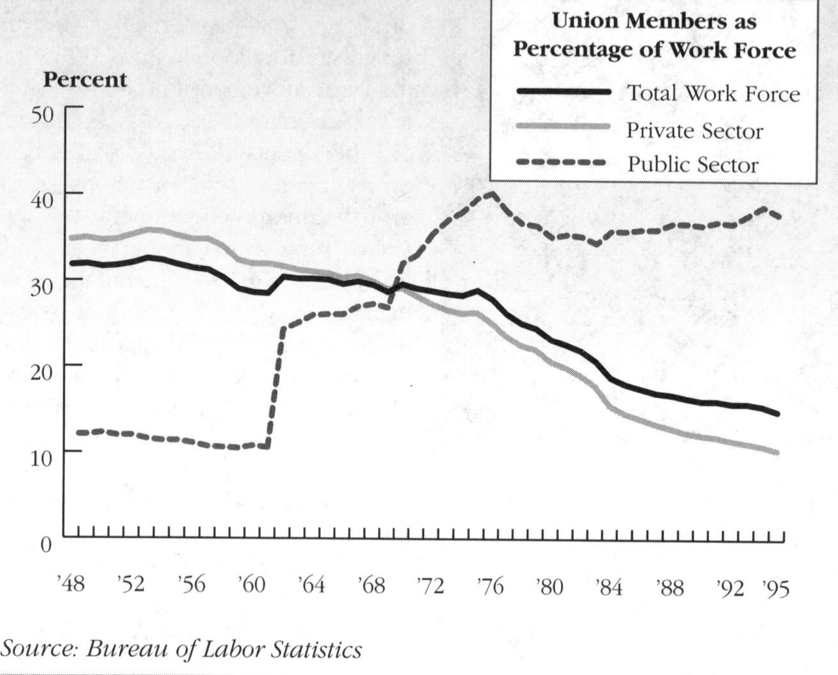

Source: Bureau of Labor Statistics

graphs, p. 570.)

"The big, classic industrywide strike is almost a thing of the past," says Raymond Hilgert, a professor of management and industrial relations at Washington University in St. Louis. "Employers are generally able to keep the production and services going. A strike only works if you can seriously hamper a company's ability to produce."

Sweeney's election, however, has brought new vigor to the labor movement. He has gone out on the hustings himself, telling audiences in city after city that American workers "need a raise." He has pushed through the AFL-CIO's Executive Council plans for a $20 million organizing campaign and a $35 million media campaign aimed at electing pro-labor candidates to Congress in November. And, in imitation of the civil rights movement of the 1960s, he is recruiting students to work with local unions around the country on organizing and other campaigns this summer. (*See story, p. 567.*)

Despite the flurry of activity, labor's opponents and critics are skeptical that Sweeney and his leadership team can reverse labor's decline. "The underlying economic forces, the market forces, that have been responsible for the decline in the first place are not going away," says Leo Troy, a professor of economics at Rutgers University in Newark, N.J., and a vocal labor critic. "In fact, they're getting stronger."

"The lines of communication between workers and management have opened up dramatically over the past decade," says Diane Generous, director of employee relations for the National Association of Manufacturers (NAM). "Employees have not been convinced that they need to have an organized union representative between them and their employer, and they certainly don't need to pay dues to have a representative between them and their employer."

As for labor's political campaign, Generous calls it "a blatant attempt to buy the 1996 election."

Business lobbyists and Republican strategists complain that the television commercials already aired as part of the campaign misrepresent the record of the GOP-controlled Congress. They also point out that labor has continued to line up closely with the Democratic Party even though nearly 40 percent of union members voted for Republican congressional candidates in the 1994 elections. (*See chart, p. 560.*)

But Sweeney makes no apology for attacking congressional Republicans. "The mistake that the Gingrich crowd made," he says, referring to House Speaker Newt Gingrich, R-Ga., "was in going after issues that were very important to a majority of the American people." He vows to mobilize at least 100 activists in each congressional district in November to elect candidates — regardless of party, he insists — "who want to address the issues of working people."

As the labor movement seeks to rebuild — and its critics and opponents move to counter its efforts — here are some of the issues being debated:

Are unions necessary in today's workplace?

Unions emerged at the time of the Industrial Revolution and advanced with the growth of mass production as a means of giving workers a collective voice in fighting for better wages and working conditions. But today's workplace is vastly different, with old-style assembly lines yielding to more flexible work arrangements, and manufacturing giving way to service sector jobs. Under these circumstances, some observers contend that unions are no longer needed to protect workers' rights.

"As companies delegate more decision-making authority to employees, as front-line management is reduced, you have a situation where the old adversarial relationship tends to loosen up," says Jeffrey C. McGuiness, president of the Labor Policy Association, which follows federal labor policy issues for about 230 major U.S. corporations. "You don't have a shop steward fighting with a supervisor over what the employees are going to do."

Supporters of organized labor, however, insist that unions are as essential today as they ever have been. "I am really irritated at this idea that when you give somebody a computer at their desk and they write reports rather than make widgets, that there's no longer a conflict between them and their employer," says Nelson Lichtenstein, a professor of history at the University of Virginia in Charlottesville. "The white-collar class has come to realize this in the recent [wave of] downsizing. This whole conception of a post-industrial computerized world, that this eliminates the basis for [worker-management] conflict, is just ridiculous."

Some critics of organized labor maintain that the array of federal civil rights and workplace laws now in place give workers adequate legal protection without unions. "Federal labor law is so comprehensive that unions are no longer necessary," says McGuiness. "A worker who feels he is being mistreated can get far more through a plaintiff's lawyer than through a union."

But Geoghegan vehemently disagrees. "What unions primarily do is to go in and ask the boss to raise wage levels so that workers aren't being screwed — screwed out of productivity gains, screwed out of a decent wage," the Chicago attorney says. "There's nobody but the union to go in and ask the boss for a raise."

Supporters and critics of unions generally agree on one point: Unions do help raise the wages of organized workers. "The main effect [unions] have is to raise the wages of members in comparison with similarly skilled workers in non-union companies," says Gary Burtless, a senior fellow in economic studies at the Brookings Institution in Washington.

According to Burtless, the "union wage premium" varies from industry to industry. He says unionized workers are likely to get a bigger wage boost in non-competitive industries — local telephone companies, for example — than in competitive ones — such as apparel manufacturing. The effect also varies between different groups of employees. Unions typically narrow workplace wage disparities, Burtless says, so lower-paid workers with less education are likely to receive greater benefit from unionization than are higher-paid workers with college or advanced degrees.

Barry Hirsch, a professor of economics at Florida State University in Tallahassee and author of several critical studies on the economic effects of unions, says it is an "undisputed" fact that unions raise wages and improve benefits for their members. He agrees with Burtless that the size of the effect varies from industry to industry, but says a ballpark range would be 10-20 percent.

Economists are more divided over the effects of the higher union pay scales. "Unions do tend to raise wages, but they do so at the expense of employment," says Rutgers' Troy. "They cost jobs of union workers when they push wages up. Moreover, and more importantly, the expense of higher union wages has come at the expense of non-union workers."

Troy concedes that unions have given workers a mechanism for dealing with workplace grievances, but he says some unions have gone too far in regulating job assignments, working conditions and the like. And he insists that unions are not needed to ensure that workers get a fair wage.

"Workers are trained and educated by their employers in order to make them efficient, productive workers," Troy says. "Intelligent employers do not tend to underpay their human capital. That would be foolish."

But Seybold argues that unions are still needed to give workers leverage to gain better pay and to ensure fairness in the workplace. "Without a union, management can basically do whatever it wants," Seybold says. "It's a sort of one-party dictatorship."

Charles B. Craver, a professor at George Washington University Law School in Washington, argues that further weakening of the labor movement will aggravate the problems of stagnant wages and income inequality. "Real wages for most workers have decreased over the past 25 years," he says, "while compensation for major CEOs has grown from 40 times worker earnings in 1960 to more than 200 times worker earnings today."

"If unions continue to languish," Craver continues, "non-union companies that provide generous employment benefits to avoid unionization will no longer feel the need to do so. And that will further erode American employment standards."

Are unions hampering productivity and competitiveness?

Some critics of the labor movement argue that unions make it more difficult for the United States to compete in a global economy. These critics blame unions for high wage levels that supposedly force U.S. companies to export jobs abroad and rigid rules that prevent employers from implementing needed changes in the workplace.

Some economists agree with this critique. Unions "make the [U.S.] economy less competitive in the world economy," says Troy at Rutgers. "In

New AFL-CIO President Says "the Labor Movement . . . Has to Change"

John J. Sweeney was elected president of the AFL-CIO on Oct. 25, 1995. Sweeney, 62, who had been president of the Service Employees International Union (SEIU) since 1980, was known for his aggressive and successful efforts to boost membership in that organization. CQ Researcher *staff writer Kenneth Jost interviewed Sweeney at the federation's headquarters in Washington on June 5:*

Why do American workers, in the words of your campaign slogan, "need a new voice"?

We recognized that our numbers were continuing to decline, and our political strength seemed to be weakening. . . . Just as we reached out during the campaign . . . we have continued the same kind of momentum within the labor movement as well as outside the labor movement, reaching out to allies, using some of the strategies and tactics of the civil rights movement, in terms of reinvigorating our movement and building support for an agenda that addresses [the issues] workers are concerned about.

John J. Sweeney

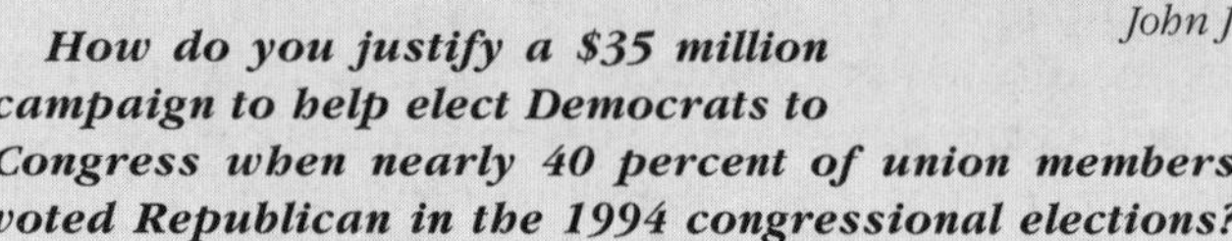

How do you justify a $35 million campaign to help elect Democrats to Congress when nearly 40 percent of union members voted Republican in the 1994 congressional elections?

None of that money is going to candidates. None of that money is going to any political party. All of that money is [going] to educate and mobilize our membership. . . . We will hopefully be mobilizing workers to support candidates regardless of what party they're in who want to address the issues of working people.

How will you overcome the obstacles to new union organizing?

The work that we're doing on organizing and political organizing really complement each other. And in both areas of focus, it's as much for the long term as it is for the short term. . . . My hope is that we will be able to turn the trend around in terms of declining membership and get on a positive track of continuous organizing programs with all the affiliates in the AFL-CIO, in all of the industries and in all of the regions.

Has the strike weapon been rendered obsolete by economic trends?

No. We've had some successful strikes as well as some very difficult strikes. . . . I think that we should be doing more while negotiations are going on as well as after the contract expires and before a strike is decided upon. We should be making better use of our pension resources . . . tying those investments in campaigns against major employers where it is required to achieve a fair contract.

You were described at the time of your election as a "militant." Are you?

If representing workers aggressively is the definition of a militant, I'll be happy to have that label. But I firmly believe that the labor movement has to recognize that it, too, has to change and build a stronger labor movement if we're going to have higher wages and represent a greater percentage of the work force.

terms of the trade deficit, American goods are too expensive because of unions . . . so people buy abroad rather than domestically."

Other economists, however, minimize the importance of the U.S. wage structure in the migration of jobs abroad. Paula Voos, a professor of economics at the University of Wisconsin in Milwaukee and co-editor of the book *Unions and Economic Competitiveness,* [2] says that the U.S. trade deficit has persisted even though U.S. unit labor costs — a measure that combines hourly compensation and productivity — have been declining relative to America's major trading competitors.

In any event, Voos says, it would be "a mistake" for the United States to try to keep wages low to compete globally. "America does better when we have a high standard of living," she explains. "The challenge is to be competitive with a high standard of living, and that's a high productivity or high performance approach."

Voos explains that a union can be "a plus" for a company because it gives workers a sense of involvement. "In those situations where the companies know they cannot escape the union," she says, "American employers have often worked with the unions to implement changes with very strong results for quality and productivity."

Hirsch is more skeptical about such claims, but he agrees that the evidence does not show an overall negative effect on productivity. "Unions appear on average to have very little effect on productivity," he says. "They have positive effects in some work environments, negative in others."

Whatever the academic studies show, employers' groups insist that unions are making it harder to adopt more flexible production techniques and more flexible work schedules. Major business groups are particularly critical of labor's opposition to so-called employer-employee "teams," worker-management groups created by some companies to address questions of productivity, quality control and safety.

The National Labor Relations Board (NLRB) has interpreted the statutory ban on "company-dominated" unions to prohibit such groups if they discuss wages, work rules or the like. Business groups are urging Congress to amend the law. "If John Sweeney truly wants to represent today's work force," says R. Bruce Josten, a senior vice president of the U.S. Chamber of Commerce, "he ought to be an advocate of employee involvement teams, at any workplace, whether it's unionized or non-union."

Republicans wanted to add the team provision to a labor-backed bill that would increase the minimum wage, but Democrats blocked the move (*see p. 570*). The Clinton administration had opposed the provision, and Labor Secretary Robert B. Reich said he would recommend the president veto the measure if it reached his desk.

Labor leaders and their supporters say the workplace teams do not give workers any real power because the employee members are handpicked by management. A recent AFL-CIO newsletter said employer-employee teams are "a smokescreen for union busting."[3]

But even labor's supporters admit that the sharp decline in union membership in recent decades has greatly diminished the economic impact of unions. "The union movement represents 10 percent of the private work force," says Lichtenstein. "It's so small that [for it] to have an impact across the whole economy [would be] a Herculean task."

Are unions out of touch with their members' political views?

The labor movement has aligned itself closely with the Democratic Party ever since it shed its political neutrality by endorsing President Franklin D. Roosevelt's re-election in 1936.

Republicans insist that labor leaders are out of touch with the growing Republican leanings of rank-and-file union members. As evidence, they point to a survey showing that 39 percent of union members voted for Republican congressional candidates in the 1994 elections. The same survey — the National Election Survey conducted by the University of Michigan's Center for Political Studies — shows that Republican presidential candidates have captured at least 40 percent of the votes from union households in seven out of the past 11 presidential elections. (*See chart, p. 560.*)

Against that background, GOP officials and strategists, along with business groups and other labor critics, complain that the AFL-CIO leadership is misrepresenting union members by planning a $35 million campaign to help elect Democrats to Congress in November. The campaign is being financed by a $1.50 per month assessment on union members. They are "being made to pay compulsory dues to defeat the very people they voted for without them having a voice in it at all," says Mary Crawford, press secretary for the Republican National Committee.

Sweeney acknowledges that the number of union members who voted Republican in 1994 was "disappointing." But he says the GOP voters were not endorsing the agenda Republicans have pushed in Congress.

"Those members who supported the [Republicans in 1994] voted out of their own anxiety, their own concerns, their problems with the establishment, their feeling that Washington wasn't addressing their issues," Sweeney says. "They didn't vote to see Social Security attacked, or Medicare and Medicaid or educational programs."

Sweeney also notes that the federation's media campaign is ostensibly independent of the Democratic Party. So far, however, the advertising has been targeted at House Republicans who have opposed labor on key issues, such as increasing the minimum wage. Business lobbyists say the campaign is clearly aimed at helping Democrats in November. "They have undertaken a very comprehensive effort aimed at returning the Congress to a Democratic majority," says McGuiness of the Labor Policy Association.

Labor union political action committees (PACs) are important contributors to the Democratic Party. Labor PACs spent $42.5 million on the 1994 elections, about 95 percent of which went to Democrats, according to the Center for Responsive Politics, a campaign finance watchdog group. Labor officials are quick to point out, however, that business PACs spent more than three times as much — $130.4 million — in the 1994 congressional races.

The AFL-CIO's planned $35 million campaign translates into nearly $500,000 for each of the 75 targeted GOP House seats — slightly more than the average cost of a House campaign in 1994, $440,000. Democratic campaign operatives say the money may help, but they also stress that the federation's campaign is independent of the party.

"Any money spent on getting Democrats elected is helpful to the Democratic Party," says Amy Weiss Tobe, the Democratic National Committee's press secretary. "But we have no control over how the money is spent, where the money is spent or when the money is spent."

Republicans contend that many union members do not support the AFL-CIO's planned campaign. They cite a survey, conducted by Republican pollster Frank

The Union Vote

The labor movement has aligned itself closely with the Democratic Party since the 1930s. Republicans insist that labor leaders are out of touch with the growing Republican leanings of rank-and-file union members. As evidence, they point to a survey showing that 39 percent of union members voted for Republican congressional candidates in the 1994 elections. The same survey — conducted by the University of Michigan's Center for Political Studies — shows that Republican presidential candidates have captured at least 40 percent of the votes from union households in seven out of the past 11 presidential elections.

Union Households Voting Republican for President

Year	Candidates	Percentage
1952	Eisenhower vs. Stevenson	44%
1956	Eisenhower vs. Stevenson	57%
1960	Kennedy vs. Nixon	36%
1964	Johnson vs. Goldwater	17%
1968	Nixon vs. Humphrey	44%
1972	Nixon vs. McGovern	57%
1976	Carter vs. Ford	36%
1980	Reagan vs. Carter	45%
1984	Reagan vs. Mondale	43%
1988	Bush vs. Dukakis	41%
1992	Clinton vs. Bush	32%

Union Households Voting Republican for Congress

Year	Percentage	Year	Percentage
1952	39%	1974	29%
1954	NA	1976	28%
1956	38%	1978	30%
1958	22%	1980	35%
1960	31%	1982	30%
1962	NA	1984	38%
1964	20%	1986	36%
1966	32%	1988	32%
1968	42%	1990	28%
1970	37%	1992	34%
1972	38%	1994	39%

Source: National Election Survey, University of Michigan's Center for Political Studies

Luntz in April, that found most union members did not know about the campaign and that, after it was explained, about 62 percent of those questioned said they opposed it. But the question was provocatively worded: Respondents were told the campaign would be financed by "mandatory monthly dues" and most of the money would be spent on "negative political advertising." [4]

In any event, labor officials and Democratic spokespersons note that, under a 1988 Supreme Court ruling, in *Beck v. Communication Workers of America,* union members are entitled to withhold the portion of their dues that goes to political activities. Few union members take advantage of the option, however. Labor supporters say that indicates union members are satisfied with labor's political orientation. Critics say the reason is that most union members — 78 percent, according to Luntz's poll — are unaware of their right to refuse to pay for political activities.

Some observers question the wisdom of labor's strategy of lining up so closely with the Democratic Party. After President Clinton and many congressional Democrats bucked labor in supporting the North American Free Trade Agreement (NAFTA) three years ago, some in the labor movement called for withholding support from Democrats who voted for the treaty (*see p. 566*). More recently, some moderate Republicans have said labor's alliance with the Democrats jeopardizes support on their issues from within the GOP.

Most observers, however, expect no change in organized labor's support for the Democratic Party in the near future. "Labor realizes it will get virtually none of its agenda from the Republicans, whereas Democrats will deliver at least some things if they are in charge," says Larry J. Sabato, a professor of government at the University of Virginia. "You can make the argument that labor ought to be supporting at least some moderate Republicans. But the other argument is strong — that labor's best interests are served by partisan choice, meaning Democrats." ■

BACKGROUND

Solidarity and Strife

The modern labor movement began to emerge with the Industrial Revolution that took place in the United States after the Civil War.[5] After a failed attempt in the 1860s, leaders of local craft unions began to work during the depression of the 1870s to create a national labor federation. The result was the formation in 1881 of the Federation of Organized Trades and Labor Unions of the United States and Canada. Five years later, the organization reconstituted itself as the American Federation of Labor (AFL) and elected as its first president, Samuel Gompers, who was to serve as its leader (with a one-year interruption) until his death in 1924.

Unions attempted to organize workers in the face of armed resistance from industry and government. Businesses hired private security guards — the famous Pinkertons — to harass and intimidate union organizers. Companies also had the benefit of court rulings that treated unions as unlawful monopolies and strikes as criminal conspiracies. Police were used to break up picketing and demonstrations and arrest strikers. Even after unions helped win passage of pro-labor statutes, courts sometimes invalidated the laws on the ground that they interfered with property rights and freedom of contract.

The public viewed unions with suspicion and hostility during much of their early history. While labor's legislative agenda won support from the populist and progressive movements of the late 19th and early 20th centuries, protests and strikes raised fears of violence and coercion among the general public. The fear was fed by a few dramatic incidents of violence, such as the 1886 bombing during a union protest in Chicago's Haymarket Square that killed seven persons, including several police officers.

Many Americans also viewed the labor movement as radical, run by anarchists or socialists and dedicated to the destruction of the free enterprise system. Even though radical elements — like the International Workers of the World, the so-called Wobblies — never dominated the labor movement, the public's fear grew during and after World War I, contributing to a "red scare" that swept up some labor leaders along with other dissidents.

The labor movement nevertheless made progress in the early 20th century with passage of wage and hours legislation in many states and a federal law, the Clayton Act, aimed at protecting unions from antitrust doctrine. But by the time of the Great Depression, most workers still had no federally protected right to join unions or bargain collectively over wages and conditions of employment.[6]

President Franklin D. Roosevelt moved to establish those rights in his first major economic recovery legislation: the National Industrial Recovery Act, which required industry codes of "fair competition" to include organizing and bargaining rights for workers. But the U.S. Supreme Court struck down the law in 1935.

Roosevelt responded by seeking a broader law: the National Labor Relations Act, also called the Wagner Act after its chief sponsor, Sen. Robert Wagner, D-N.Y. The act guaranteed workers the right to join unions, prohibited employers from interfering with unions and required employers to bargain in "good faith" with unions certified by a majority of their employees. Employers expected the Supreme Court to strike that law down, too, but the justices upheld it in 1937.

The National Labor Relations Act remains a major guarantee of union rights, but later measures weakened labor's powers. The Taft-Hartley Act, enacted in 1947 by a Republican-controlled Congress over President Harry S Truman's veto, prohibited so-called secondary boycotts, a means of pressuring an employer by targeting its suppliers or customers. The law also permitted states to prohibit "union shops" — workplaces where an employee was required to join a union after being hired — and established a procedure for a mandatory "cooling-off period" in strikes declared by the president to be a "national emergency."

A decade later, Congress responded to dramatic exposés of corruption and racketeering in some unions by passing the Landrum-Griffin Act. The law sought to prevent misuse of union funds or powers and also further limited some union tactics in contract disputes.

Era of Labor Peace

Despite Congress' moves to curb union power, the 1950s marked the beginning of a quarter-century of prosperity and relative labor peace that union leaders today regard as the golden era of labor-management relations. AFL-CIO President Sweeney harks to the era in his speeches as a time when workers "shared in the gains of a growing economy" thanks to "a strong labor movement and the understandings it achieved with business and government."

The labor movement owed its strength in part to the consolidation of its two major wings into the AFL-CIO in 1955. The Congress of Industrial Organizations had split from the AFL in the 1930s in a walkout led by, among others, John L. Lewis and Philip Murray. Lewis and Murray wanted to organize the growing number of factory workers, but failed in 1934 and again in 1935 to prevail on the issue at AFL conventions. In frustration, they created the CIO in 1935 as a committee within the AFL and three years later seceded altogether.

The two labor federations coexisted, alternating between cooperation and rivalry, for the next 15 years. Then in November 1952 — within the space of 12 days — the presidents of both federations, the AFL's William Green and the CIO's Murray, died. The new leaders — the AFL's George Meany and the CIO's Walter Reuther — resolved to end the dispute. The two federations agreed on a "no-raiding" pact in June 1954 and then agreed to reunify in February 1955. The consolidation was formally completed in December — creating a unified labor federation with more than 15 million members.

Over the next two decades, the AFL-CIO's member unions often fared well at the bargaining table, but collectively the labor movement began to falter. AFL-CIO membership peaked at 15.5 million a year after its formation, followed by a steady attrition. Total union membership also peaked in absolute terms and as a percentage of the work force. Some of the reasons are now familiar: the shift from blue-collar to white-collar jobs and the migration of jobs from the industrialized Northeast and Midwest to traditionally non-union states in the Southeast and Southwest.

In addition, the AFL-CIO did not give organizing a high priority. Meany, who served as the AFL-CIO's president from its creation until 1979, even said he was not interested in "organizing groups of people who do not want to be organized." [7]

Politically, labor also compiled a mixed record of successes and failures. The AFL-CIO had become a major constituency of the Democratic Party, providing money through its Committee on Political Education (COPE) and manpower through its local unions. The alignment with the Democrats dated from the New Deal and became closer over time, although labor groups occasionally supported or adopted neutrality toward moderate Republicans. Labor's support contributed to the Democrats' 40-year domination of Congress that began in 1954 and continued uninterrupted until 1994, except for the loss of the Senate from 1980 to 1986.

Labor's political strategy paid off with the passage of such worker protection measures as the Occupational Safety and Health Act in 1970 and the Employee Retirement Income Security Act in 1974. But it failed repeatedly in one of its major legislative goals: the repeal of the Taft-Hartley provision, Section 14(b), that authorized states to prohibit union shops. These so-called right-to-work laws have been enacted in some 21 states — mostly in the South and West — and they serve as a barrier to union organizing. Congress, despite hefty Democratic majorities, has never approved a 14(b) repeal measure.

After eight years of Republican presidents, organized labor in 1977 greeted the new Democratic president, Jimmy Carter, with renewed optimism about its political prospects. High on its legislative agenda was a somewhat modest reform of the National Labor Relations Act that would have given union organizers limited access to workplaces during organizing drives and strengthened remedies for unfair labor practices by employers.

According to law Professor Craver, labor leaders were "shocked" by the "vehement opposition" to the measure from business groups. [8] The opposition fueled a Senate filibuster that led to the bill's demise. The episode demonstrated that energized business opposition could derail labor's agenda, even on relatively low-profile issues. The same scenario was to be repeated often during the rest of the 1970s and through the Reagan and Bush administrations in the 1980s and early '90s.

The Era of Decline

Ronald Reagan, a former president of the Screen Actors Guild and the only former union member to serve in the White House, won the presidency in 1980 in part by peeling away about 45 percent of union voters from the Democratic ticket. But his election ushered in an era of conservative leadership in Washington that brought labor's influence to the lowest point since the New Deal and left unions with little help in meeting fortified opposition from employers.

Reagan set the tone for the next 12 years in August 1981 with an unexpectedly severe response to a walkout by a government employees' union, the Professional Air Traffic Controllers' Organization (PATCO). Public employee strikes had bedeviled state and local governments over the past two decades, and officials in a few cases had gone to court to order the striking workers back to work. But Reagan went further. After declaring the strike illegal, Reagan fired the strikers, announced they would not be rehired and initiated steps to decertify the union. Ominously for labor, the public overwhelmingly supported Reagan's tough actions. [9]

The PATCO episode had its greatest impact in the private sector. "A kind of green light was signaled to employers that it was now OK to go after labor unions," says Seybold of Indiana University. In the past, companies had rarely hired permanent replacement workers in response to a strike. But over the next few years, several major companies, including Greyhound, Phelps Dodge and Eastern Airlines, followed Reagan's example in hiring permanent replacements during work stoppages. [10]

The tactic had a chilling effect on strikes. Strike activity had gone up and down with the business cycle since World War II, but the number of major strikes — those involving 1,000 or more workers — had fallen below 200 per year only twice before 1980, according to the Bureau of Labor Statistics. In the first full year after the

Continued on p. 564

Chronology

Before 1900

The modern labor movement is born during the post-Civil War industrial revolution in the United States.

1886
American Federation of Labor (AFL) is formed by number of craft unions, succeeding the earlier Federation of Organized Trade and Labor Unions (1881); Samuel Gompers is elected president; he serves in that office, with a one-year interruption, until 1924.

1890s
Management puts down strikes by workers at Homestead Steel (1892) and Pullman railway car company (1894), with help from states and the federal government and support of public alarmed by industrial strife.

1900-1949

Labor and management continue industrial warfare. New Deal legislation establishes workers' rights to unionize.

1935
National Labor Relations Act establishes federal right for workers to organize and bargain collectively and prohibits "unfair labor practices" by employers.

1938
Congress of Industrial Organizations (CIO) formally splits from AFL three years after it began as dissident internal group aimed at organizing factory workers and raising labor's political profile.

1947
Taft-Hartley Act, enacted by Congress over President Harry S Truman's veto, establishes pro-management provisions regarding union organizing and authorizes procedure for "cooling-off period" in national strikes.

1950-1979

Labor and management ease relations with mutual acceptance. AFL-CIO is formed and aligns itself closely with Democratic Party.

December 1955
AFL-CIO is formed, with about 15.5 million members.

1959
Landrum-Griffin Act, passed after McClellan Committee exposes racketeering and corruption in some unions, guarantees internal rights for union members.

1977
Failure of labor law reform bill in Congress dramatizes unions' declining political power.

1980s

Unions lose economic and political power during Republican administrations, with declining membership, deregulation at home and increased competition abroad.

1981
President Ronald Reagan fires striking air traffic controllers and decertifies their union.

1982
Number of work stoppages involving more than 1,000 workers falls below 100. By 1995, number had fallen to 31.

1990s

Labor movement seeks to reverse decline in power. New AFL-CIO leadership mounts new organizing and political drives.

November 1993
Congress overrides opposition from organized labor to approve North American Free Trade Agreement (NAFTA).

Nov. 8, 1994
Republicans capture control of both houses of Congress for the first time since 1954.

Oct. 25, 1995
John J. Sweeney is elected president of the AFL-CIO after he and other dissident union leaders force Lane Kirkland to bow out of re-election bid.

Dec. 3, 1995
United Auto Workers (UAW) calls off protracted strike against Caterpillar, Inc., with no contract; company won't promise to rehire strikers.

March 21, 1996
UAW ends strike against General Motors plants in Dayton, Ohio, with both sides claiming victory.

March 25, 1996
AFL-CIO Executive Committee endorses President Clinton for re-election and authorizes dues assessment to help build $35 million political fund to target House Republicans.

May 23, 1996
House votes to increase minimum wage.

National Labor Relations Board . . .

When the Amalgamated Clothing and Textile Workers union started an organizing drive at the Wilen Manufacturing Co., the company pulled out all the stops to fight it. First, the Atlanta mop-maker gave its 250 employees an across-the-board wage increase, then it threatened union supporters with reprisals. When the union won a certification election in 1994, the company followed through with its threats, vowing never to sign a contract with the union, unilaterally imposing new workplace rules and discharging 13 workers for union activity.

The workers' plight was brought to the attention of the National Labor Relations Board (NLRB), the federal agency charged with enforcing federal labor law. The agency went to federal court and asked for an immediate injunction to reinstate the fired workers and undo the new work rules. Faced with the court action, the company settled the dispute by agreeing to take back some of the employees and to give backpay to those who agreed to waive reinstatement.

William B. Gould IV

The agency's action exemplifies a deliberate policy change under its current chairman, William B. Gould IV, to try to move more quickly to remedy labor law violations. Since Gould took office in March 1994, the board has filed a record number of so-called 10(j) actions — named after the applicable section in the National Labor Relations Act — asking for immediate court orders to halt unfair labor practices.

"That's the heart of the statute," Gould says. "Justice delayed is justice denied. That goes for both union and employer. The passage of time frequently makes impossible or unlikely the fashioning of effective remedies.

"In the case of dismissed workers, they may not be able to be found two or three years later. Backpay is not adequate compensation under those circumstances. Similarly with respect to violent union strikes, there cannot be remedies unless relief is sought here and now."

The agency authorized 83 injunction requests in 1994 and 104 in 1996 — compared with only 26 in 1992, the last year of the Bush administration. The agency's success rate in court is also up: it prevailed in 82 percent of the injunction cases taken to court in 1994 and 91 percent in 1995. The compilation does not reflect the nature of the cases, but labor experts say most injunctions are sought on behalf of workers who have been illegally disciplined or fired, often during union organizing drives.

Gould, a well-respected law professor at Stanford University with strong pro-labor views, was named to the board by President Clinton. He was confirmed by the Senate in 1994 only after giving repeated assurances that he would be impartial in enforcing the law.

The five-member board was created by the 1935 National Labor Relations Act, which guaranteed private non-agricultural workers the right to organize and bargain collectively. The board's major responsibilities include supervising union certification elections and investigating and adjudicating charges of "unfair labor practices" by

Continued from p. 562

PATCO episode, however, the number fell below 100. The number has continued to fall ever since, reaching a record low of 31 in 1995.

Meanwhile, unions met increasingly stiff opposition in organizing drives. As one indication, the number of retaliatory discharges — dismissals of employees to discourage union support — continued to increase. The NLRB had ordered reinstatement of 3,779 individuals because of anti-union discrimination in 1970. The number reached 10,000 by 1980 and continued to rise to 10,905 in 1985, even though the number of union representation elections had declined by half, from about 7,200 to 3,600. [11] By one count, unlawful terminations occurred in one of every three NLRB elections in the late 1980s, affecting one of every 36 pro-union voters. [12]

In addition to the firings, companies employed a variety of increasingly sophisticated tactics in battling union organizing drives. The tactics were shaped and refined by a growing number of labor relations lawyers and consultants — around 700, according to one count [13] — that specialized in anti-union campaigns. With their guidance, employers countered union organizing campaigns with leaflets, letters, private meetings with supervisors, promises of improvements and veiled threats of plant closings or relocations.

Kate Bronfenbrenner, director of labor education research at Cornell University's School of Industrial and Labor Relations, found that 75 percent of employers engaged in these kinds of "aggressive tactics" during organizing drives. The tactics appeared to have had the desired effect. Bronfenbrenner found that when such tactics were used, union victory rates were 10-20 percent lower than in cases where they

. . . Its Aggressive Policies Get Mixed Reviews

employers or employees.

The NLRB has been in constant controversy since the 1980s when President Reagan named several strong labor critics to the board, including its chairman, Donald Dotson. Reversing several NLRB precedents, the Dotson board somewhat narrowed the scope of collective bargaining and gave employers more leeway in union organizing drives. "It was particularly bad for labor during President Reagan's first term," says Charles B. Craver, a law professor at George Washington University. [1]

Dotson was not reappointed when his term expired in 1987, and Craver and others say the board shifted back toward the center during Reagan's second term and the Bush administration. But labor lawyers still felt the board was tilted against them and anticipated more sympathetic appointees with a Democrat in the White House.

The board currently has three members with pro-labor backgrounds: Gould; Margaret A. Browning, a Philadelphia labor lawyer; and Sarah M. Fox, a former Senate Labor Committee staffer. The fourth member, Charles I. Cohen, was a management lawyer in Washington. One seat is vacant. [2]

Business lawyers give the board's new policies mixed reviews. Francis T. Coleman, a Washington lawyer representing management, says the board is "openly sympathetic" to labor. "The Clinton board makes the Reagan board look like pikers when it comes to partisanship," he says. But Edward B. Miller, a management attorney in Chicago who served as NLRB chairman in the early 1970s, writes in a recent article that the board "has not swung as far to the left as the business community might have anticipated." [3]

Labor lawyers and supporters deny that the board is biased toward unions and argue that it needs to do more to create a level playing field between employers and employees. "Despite the outcry from management, the current board is not that liberal," Craver says. He credits the board with increasing the number of injunction actions, but says the power is used in "only a minuscule percentage" of the cases. "It's still a greatly underused remedy," he says.

Gould also denies that the board is biased in favor of unions. "There's not a tilt toward unions," he says. "There's a tilt toward the intentions of the framers of the statute when they enacted it. There's an attempt to be fair to both parties." In listing his accomplishments, he cites administrative changes that have reduced the backlog of cases he inherited — reforms that he says have won approval from labor and management lawyers alike.

Still, Gould's views on legislative issues are clearly pro-union. He opposes a business-backed bill to broaden employer-employee work teams, saying it would promote "sham unions." But he favors changes that unions would welcome — for example, increasing penalties for "egregious misconduct" by employers and barring employers from permanently replacing striking workers.

Gould also looks with favor on the changes going on at the AFL-CIO. He had lunch with the federation's new president, John J. Sweeney, earlier this year and came away "impressed" with him and his leadership team. "I think that they have expressed a commitment to re-energize and revive the labor movement," Gould says. "The country is the better for that."

---

[1] For opposing assessments, see Thomas F. Phalen Jr., "The Destabilization of Federal Labor Policy Under the Reagan Board," *The Labor Lawyer,* winter 1986, pp. 1-31; Fred W. Batten, "Recent Decisions of the Reagan Board: A Management Perspective," *ibid.*, pp. 33-47.

[2] For background, see *The New York Times*, June 2, 1996, p. A32.

[3] Edward B. Miller, "What Has the Gould Board Been Doing," *Labor Law Journal*, February 1996, pp. 75-76.

were not utilized. [14]

Broader economic trends were also tilting against unions. Within the United States, employment continued to shift from unionized areas to non-union regions. The number of manufacturing jobs in the U.S. dropped as firms shifted production to other countries to take advantage of lower wage scales. Moreover, unions had no broad strategy for winning the support of the ever increasing number of clerical, white-collar and semi-professional workers in the labor force. No wonder then that by the 1990s, many labor experts — sympathizers and critics alike — were openly questioning whether unions could survive.

A Try for Resurgence

When the AFL-CIO's Executive Committee met in February 1995, federation President Lane Kirkland opened by bluntly confronting critics of his leadership. "What's the beef?" Kirkland was quoted as saying. His critics — including his eventual successor, Sweeney — were just as blunt in their response: After 16 years in his post, they told him, it was time for Kirkland to retire. [15]

Kirkland assumed the AFL-CIO presidency on Nov. 19, 1979, as George Meany's handpicked successor and presided over the federation during the period of labor's precipitous decline. Even acknowledging the adverse political and economic conditions, Kirkland had to bear part of the blame for labor's sagging fortunes. He concentrated, his critics pointed out later, more on media visibility and international issues than on the nuts-and-bolts of organization, workplace disputes and politics.

Sweeney had begun talking with other critics of Kirkland's leadership as early as 1993, according to an account of the internal coup he gave *The New York Times*. He directly broached the question of retirement to Kirkland in a meeting at the AFL-CIO headquarters in August 1994. Kirkland rebuffed the suggestion. Four months later, *The Washington Post* published the first major media account of the internal dispute, using anonymous criticisms later acknowledged to have been from Sweeney and his main collaborator, Gerald McEntee, president of the American Federation of State, County and Municipal Employees (AFSCME). [16]

The internal dispute came at a time when the labor movement was continuing to struggle in both the political and economic arenas. With a Democrat in the White House, organized labor had made some progress in 1993 and 1994. President Clinton had pushed through the labor-backed Family and Medical Leave Act early in his administration. He had also appointed a friend of labor, Stanford law Professor William B. Gould IV, to be chairman of the National Labor Relations Board, an agency that labor said had tilted toward business during the Reagan and Bush administrations. (*See story, p. 564.*)

But labor had also suffered some defeats. At Clinton's urging, the Democratic-controlled Congress in November 1993 approved the North America Free Trade Agreement (NAFTA), despite labor's warnings that it would cost domestic jobs. [17] A year later, Congress again rebuffed labor on a free trade issue when it refused to block U.S. participation in the World Trade Organization as provided in the General Agreement on Trade and Tariffs (GATT).

By that time, labor had suffered a more ominous defeat: the Republican victory in the November 1994 congressional elections. The new Republican majority came to Washington with a platform of reducing labor-backed workplace regulations and controlling labor-backed social welfare programs. "When Republicans poured into Congress," Craver remarks, "there was a sense that [unions] were really dead."

Meanwhile, labor was faring badly in workplace disputes as well. Unions could claim some successes in organizing drives, especially among government workers, and some strikes. But most strikes seemed to end in defeat or at best standoffs.

One major defeat came in December 1995 when the United Auto Workers (UAW)* was forced to capitulate after an 18-month work stoppage against Caterpillar, the agricultural machinery manufacturer. Caterpillar had rejected the union's pay demands and, once the strike began, adopted a strategy of continuing production with managerial and temporary workers. While the UAW was spending $30 million in strike benefits, the company's sales and profits actually rose. In December 1995, the union ordered the strikers back to work, even though 80 percent of the workers had voted to reject Caterpillar's last contract offer. [18]

Sweeney and his supporters saw a change of leadership at the AFL-CIO as essential to lift labor out of its political and economic slump. They urged Kirkland to step aside in favor of his lieutenant, Thomas Donahue, the federation's secretary-treasurer. Kirkland initially refused, and Donahue similarly refused to run against him. By May, however, Kirkland realized he faced an impossible situation and decided to announce his retirement, along with his endorsement of Donahue to succeed him. But events were now out of his control. Sweeney decided to seek the presidency himself, forming a politically appealing ticket with two other union leaders: Richard Trumka, president of the United Mine Workers, running for secretary-treasurer; and Linda Chavez-Thompson, an AFSCME vice president, listed for a new position of executive vice president.

In waging his campaign against Donahue — who became acting president on Aug. 1 — Sweeney promised to revitalize the AFL-CIO through the same kind of confrontational tactics that he had used as president of the Service Employees International Union. When the two men made their final campaign appearances to AFL-CIO delegates in New York on Oct. 24, Donahue criticized the SEIU's militancy, citing as an example the union's rush-hour blockade of a bridge connecting Washington, D.C., and the Virginia suburbs the previous month to dramatize its "Justice for Janitors" campaign.

Sweeney did not flinch. "I believe in building bridges whenever the shelling lets up long enough for us to put up steel and pour concrete," he told the delegates. "But I believe in blocking bridges whenever these employers and those communities turn a deaf ear to the working families that we represent." [19]

The next day, Sweeney won the votes of delegates representing 56 percent of the federation's members. He marked his victory with the same fired-up rhetoric he had used to capture the presidency. "We're going to do whatever it takes, work as hard as it takes and stick with it as long as it takes, to help American workers win the right to speak for themselves in strong unions," he told the delegates. [20] ■

* The UAW's full name is International Union, United Automobile, Aerospace and Agricultural Implement Workers of America.

CURRENT SITUATION

'Union Summer'

Organized labor marked this Memorial Day weekend with more

'Union Summer': A New Generation of Activists?

Dominic Perry grew up in a union household. His father, a member of the International Association of Machinists, earned $13 an hour running the presses at a large commercial printing house in Louisville, Ky. Then, in 1992, the company closed and moved its operations to a non-union plant in Oklahoma. Perry's father got a new job, at a non-union company, paying half as much.

But Perry says his father was no blind follower of the union. "I grew up hearing both sides," Perry says. "He'd complain that the union was used to protect slackers or that the union would demand that more people be kept on the job than it needed."

Today, Perry, 27, is a graduate student in economics and sociology at the University of Maryland in College Park, just outside Washington. And he is working this summer as one of 1,000 people, most of them students, recruited by the AFL-CIO to work around the country as union organizers and activists. [1]

"Union Summer" is a project of the labor federation's new president, John J. Sweeney, who likens it to the student-dominated summertime campaigns of the civil rights movement in the 1960s. "It's an effort to reach out to young people and give them a little bit of taste of the history of the union movement," Sweeney explains.

Perry was one of about 35 "Union Summer" recruits assigned to work with the "Justice for Janitors" campaign being conducted by Local 82 of the Service Employees International Union in Washington. Many were from union families like him. But others came from white-collar or professional backgrounds, with no natural sympathy for working-class issues.

The activists' schedule was rigorous: 70-hour weeks devoted to nuts-and-bolts work ranging from picketing and mobilizing workers to painting signs and hanging banners. The long hours did not sap the group's enthusiasm, however. When union organizer Maria Naranjo asked for volunteers to get up at 6 a.m. the next day to hang banners on local bridges, more than a dozen people raised their hands.

The recruits received a $200 per week stipend and lived in a dormitory at Catholic University in northeast Washington. The group was evenly divided between men and women and was ethnically diverse, with a significant number of Hispanics — useful in talking with the predominantly Hispanic janitorial workers.

Labor supporters have greeted Sweeney's idea with enthusiasm. "On one level, it's symbolic," says Nelson Lichtenstein, a professor of history at the University of Virginia in Charlottesville, "but it's powerfully symbolic. It's saying the old methods don't work: we're calling in a new generation."

But the labor movement's critics are less impressed. "This is not how the CIO recruited their organizers in the 1930s," says Leo Troy, a professor of economics at Rutgers University in Newark, N.J. "John L. Lewis very knowingly and willingly hired Communists to go have their heads beat in. These students are not going to do that."

Richard Bensinger, who is overseeing the program as the AFL-CIO's new director of organizing, dismisses the criticism. "Every social movement on Earth that has been successful has been led by and heavily involved with students," Bensinger says. "This is really a wonderful program to show young people how they make a difference in doing social justice work and reaching out to us, and we reach out to them to show them something about the labor movement."

The students themselves cite other benefits, including the close fellowship with a diverse group of like-minded people. Whatever their motivations, Sweeney's hope of instilling pro-union sympathies appears to be paying off.

"People came for a lot of reasons," says Lisa Davis, a student at Russell Sage University in New York, "but now that they're here, they're really committed."

[1] For background, see the *Los Angeles Times*, May 2, 1996, p. B1; *The New York Times*, March 11, 1996, p. B1.

than patriotic celebrations and family picnics. Labor unions and their supporters took advantage of two high-visibility gatherings — the Indianapolis 500 automobile race and Yale University's commencement — to try to rally public support for workers in two protracted labor-management disputes.

At Yale, the Rev. Jesse Jackson led a demonstration in support of the Connecticut university's clerical and maintenance workers, who are in stalled negotiations over their efforts to limit Yale's right to contract out jobs now performed by union members.

"This is not just a New Haven or Yale fight any more," Jackson told a crowd of several hundred union members gathered on the city green. "There is a movement being reborn today. It'll be felt behind those walls, behind the White House gates and on Capitol Hill." [21]

On the same day in Indianapolis, members of the United Steelworkers demonstrated to pressure the Bridgestone/Firestone Co. to rehire workers who were replaced during a 22-month strike that ended in defeat in May. The workers called for a boycott of Firestone tires even as the company was using the race to try to lift its sagging tire sales.

"The company's plowing $20 million dollars into this campaign to try and get their name back in the public for a promotion," said Roger Gates, president of the Steelworkers' Local 713. "So we're going to get their name in the public for the way they treat the American workers."

The two holiday-weekend rallies

exemplify the way the labor movement is trying to get its message across to Americans accustomed to giving unions little thought and little support. But at a time of growing anxiety among workers, blue-collar and white-collar alike, labor leaders hope to find a new reservoir of support for working-class militancy.

Labor's supporters and critics both agree that unions face an uphill struggle in organizing new members, because of opposition from employers as well as skepticism and fear among many workers.

"Getting people to join a union is a hard sell," says Hilgert of Washington University. "White-collar people still have that image that unions just aren't for them. And aside from that, there's just that basic fear that if they join a union, the company will shut it down."

Employer opposition is a critical factor to unions' decreasing success rate in representation elections, pro-labor observers contend. Cornell's Bronfenbrenner found that during 1991 and 1992, unions won 85 percent of representation elections among government workers — where employers usually mount little if any opposition — compared with only 48 percent of the elections at private companies. [22]

But Bronfenbrenner says unions can still win organizing drives if they commit enough resources and take the campaign directly to the workers. "It means a rank-and-file intensive strategy focusing on personal contact," she explains. "It's one-on-one contact and small group meetings, not standing outside the gates and handing out leaflets."

Some labor supporters say that Congress should revise federal labor law to give unions a level playing field with employers in organizing campaigns. A worker-management commission created by the Clinton administration recommended some steps along those lines. The commission, headed by John T. Dunlop, an economics professor at Harvard who served as secretary of Labor under President Gerald R. Ford, called for speeding up union representation elections by delaying hearings on disputed legal issues until after the balloting. In addition, the 11-member commission, which business groups said was stacked in favor of labor, called for quicker action to reinstate workers illegally fired during organizing campaigns. [23]

Congress is unlikely to act on these suggestions any time soon, however. This may not discourage union activists. "We haven't really seen a substantial increase [in organizing activity], but we feel something is coming," says McGuiness of the Labor Policy Association.

McGuiness and other business lobbyists voice concern about the unions' use of so-called corporate campaigns, like the steelworkers' campaign against Firestone, which use boycotts, demonstrations or other protests to pressure companies on labor issues. "In a corporate campaign situation, the union tells the company either you recognize us or we'll put you out of business," McGuiness says. "The focus of these campaigns is to drive the stock way down and cause the corporation real financial harm."

Bronfenbrenner insists the unions are merely responding to the increasingly confrontational tactics employers have adopted. "American employers have right now an arsenal of tactics: they can shut plants down, they can fire [workers], they can threaten," she says. "There's no question that American employers are very scared about the new tactics because those tactics are very effective."

For his part, Sweeney says the AFL-CIO will continue to back corporate campaigns in some disputes, but only after more cooperative efforts fail. "My first goal is to build bridges, not to block them," Sweeney says. "I think we want to take the highest road, but we have to have cooperation from our employers as well."

Political Battles

Judging from the Republican Party's reactions, the AFL-CIO hit a nerve with its plans for a $35 million political offensive to mobilize workers in the November congressional elections. Republicans from GOP national Chairman Haley Barbour on down have wasted no time in denouncing unnamed labor leaders as "union bosses," accusing the federation of violating federal campaign disclosure laws and criticizing television ads targeted at GOP House members as misleading.

"The union bosses don't want a balanced budget," Barbour told a meeting of Republican state party chairmen in Washington on May 31. "They have a vested interest in more government," he continued. "They're going to spend hundreds of millions of dollars trying to buy back Democratic control of Congress and trying to keep Bill Clinton in the White House." [24]

AFL-CIO officials promptly disputed Barbour's claim that the federation had spent $40 million on advertising in 1995, insisting the true figure was no more than $5 million. "They're flat-out lying," Political Director Steven Rosenthal told *The New York Times*. "It just feels like $40 million to them." [25]

The barbed exchange typified the GOP response to the AFL-CIO's new burst of political activism. The weekend after the federation's Executive Council approved the $35 million spending plan, Barbour denigrated the program by noting that government employees now constitute 42 percent of all union members. [26] A few days later, a *Wall Street Journal* editorial elaborated on the theme by noting a recent poll that found Republicans outnumbering Democrats — 48 percent to 40 percent — among private-sector union members. [27]

The National Republican Congressional Committee took a more con-

Continued on p. 570

At Issue:

Will private sector unions begin to grow again?

Charles B. Craver
Professor of law, George Washington University

WRITTEN FOR *THE CQ RESEARCHER*, JUNE 1996.

yes

The proportion of private sector workers in labor unions has declined significantly over the past 40 years, resulting in stagnant wages and reduced job security. Today, for the first time in at least a decade, the labor movement seems intent on stemming the hemorrhaging.

The decline of the labor movement has resulted from demographic, industrial and global changes beyond the control of domestic unions. In an effort to become more competitive, organized companies have aggressively sought to rid themselves of their unions and non-union firms have fought to remain unorganized. While many workers would like a collective voice to influence corporate decisions that affect their employment situations, most are reluctant to organize in the face of open employer hostility.

Employees today are the only significant group who have no collective voice to advance their interests. But workers are beginning to recognize that they lack the individual capacity to influence firm decisions and that their corporate managers are not concerned about their employment interests.

The increasing discontent among workers parallels the circumstances that gave rise to the union movement more than a century ago. And as their positions become more routinized and less secure, workers in such industries as banking, insurance, computers and retail may begin to recognize the benefits they can receive through unionization.

Over the past several decades, the labor movement has been a discouraged institution. But the new AFL-CIO leadership is changing this picture. Some unions have already developed innovative organizing campaigns designed to appeal to women and minority workers. Corporate campaigns are being used to organize service firms — for example, the "Justice for Janitors" movement. The new leadership is also moving to get workers mobilized politically so as to advance labor's interests in the legislative arena and at the polls.

It is time to acknowledge that the individuals who contribute their working lives to the success of their employers deserve a collective say in how those firms operate. At the present time, labor unions provide the only vehicle to accomplish this objective.

When labor-management relationships are based on mutual respect and cooperation — as, for example, between the Saturn Corporation and the United Auto Workers — employees, managers, shareholders and consumers benefit. But if businesses continue to oppose unionization and treat employees like disposable machinery, our long-term outlook will be bleak.

Leo Troy
Professor of economics, Rutgers University

WRITTEN FOR *THE CQ RESEARCHER*, JUNE 1996.

no

Private sector unionism — what I call "Old Unionism" — will continue to decline into the next century. By the beginning of the 21st century, unions will represent only 7 percent of the private work force — the same level that existed at the beginning of this century and below the current level of about 10 percent of private workers.

The forces responsible for the dwindling of private unionism are competition and economic change. Increased competition, domestic and international, has eroded private unionism in the United States and in all other G-7 nations as well — Japan, the United Kingdom, France, Italy, Canada and probably Germany. In the United States, only public sector unions — what I call "New Unionism" — have been growing over the past 30 years, and I anticipate that their growth also has topped out.

Competitive forces have effectively "repealed" the National Labor Relations Act, the country's basic labor law. Market forces have separated the Old Unionism from its industrial base and the rising service industries. Even if the Clinton administration's plan to amend the act with pro-labor provisions in 1993-94 had succeeded, these would not have revitalized the Old Unionism. The same competitive forces not only continue to operate, but have become stronger.

Employer opposition is blamed by union supporters for the decline of unions, but it is only a marginal factor. More important is opposition from employees. Polls over the last decade show that most unorganized workers do not want to be represented by unions. In addition, unions lose about half of the representation elections — even though they target companies that they believe will be receptive to organizing campaigns.

The AFL-CIO now has new leadership claiming new ideas. However, just as demand and supply frustrated the previous leadership's efforts to reverse labor's fortunes, so will they frustrate the new leadership's plans.

What does this assessment imply for private unionism's role in the economy and polity? Pockets of collective bargaining will remain in manufacturing, construction and transportation. Overall, however, private unionism is entering the "twilight zone."

Nevertheless, unions will continue to have a powerful impact on politics. Unions have billions of dollars in income and assets and are willing to commit resources to pro-labor candidates. So, despite their greatly reduced economic influence, unions will still have formidable political power into the next century.

Strike Out

The number of strikes last year — 385 — was the lowest in 50 years. The number of major work stoppages — those involving more than 1,000 workers — also was at a 50-year low: 31.

Sources: Federal Mediation and Conciliation Service (total number of strikes); Bureau of Labor Statistics (major work stoppages)

crete step, initiating legal action against the AFL-CIO. In a complaint filed with the Federal Election Commission (FEC) in February, the GOP group claimed that the federation violated federal election law with television ads in December that criticized some 40 GOP House members for voting for the Republican-backed budget plan. The ads amounted to direct campaign spending, which unions are prohibited from doing except through political action committees, the complaint charged. The planned 1996 campaign is a "clear violation" of the law, the GOP group added.

Rosenthal and other federation officials, however, insist that the media campaigns are legal because they are "issue-oriented" advertising rather than election spending. Legal precedent appears to support the labor group's position. Federal courts have treated commercials as issue advocacy outside the scope of campaign finance laws unless they explicitly endorse or call for the defeat of a specific candidate — which the AFL-CIO ads do not do. [28]

Republican operatives and business groups also denounce the labor ads as misleading, most specifically for claiming that the GOP-backed budget proposals would "cut" Medicare spending. "They have run ads on Medicare that are flat out factually incorrect in an attempt to scare people," says RNC press secretary Crawford. But labor leaders and Democratic lawmakers have insisted throughout the Medicare debate that the GOP proposals amount to cuts because they would reduce spending below the levels that would result without changes in the program.

Republicans also winced as the AFL-CIO began a second round of TV spots in March and April targeting some 20 GOP House members who had voted to block a vote on the labor-backed bill to increase the minimum wage. The ads depicted corporate profits rising sharply while the minimum wage has remained unchanged and contrasted the lawmaker's vote on the issue with votes to "cut Medicare and college loans" in order to give a "big tax break to the rich."

The ads had some immediate impact, as *Wall Street Journal* columnist Gerald Seib noted. "Within three weeks," Seib wrote in May, "14 of the Republicans who originally voted to block a minimum wage broke party ranks" to co-sponsor a minimum wage proposal. [29] More Republicans deserted the party position as the month continued. When the proposal finally reached the House floor, it passed by an overwhelming vote of 281-144 — with 93 Republicans among those voting for it. [30]

House passage of the minimum wage bill was a significant labor victory, but the measure still faces opposition from GOP conservatives in the Senate. For business groups, the vote was another indication that the GOP-controlled Congress has failed to deliver much relief on labor-management issues.

Business lobbyists had hoped that with a Republican majority, Congress would approve a number of proposals that they had pushed unsuccessfully in years past, including the "Team Act" (*see p. 559*) and a repeal of the Davis-Bacon Act, which requires employers to pay "prevailing wages" on federal construction projects. But none of the business-backed proposals has been approved, and none appears likely to be passed in the remaining months of the 104th Congress. [31]

Meanwhile, AFL-CIO leaders are gearing up for the fall elections. Rosenthal says labor PACs will continue to contribute to candidates even while the federation carries out its issues campaign. "We're doing what we have to do to mobilize our membership," he says.

Opposing party spokespersons have differing assessments of the likely impact of the labor campaign. "I think that in the long run it doesn't pass the credibility test," says the RNC's Crawford. "So in the long run it will fail."

But DNC press secretary Tobe thinks the spending will help her party. "No one can say for sure until the polls are closed on Nov. 5," she says. "But the more people out there are talking about issues that Americans care about, the better it is for the Democratic Party come November." ■

OUTLOOK

The 'New' Unionism

When United Auto Workers (UAW) President Stephen Yokich showed up for an initial bargaining session with Ford Motor Co. on June 10, he and his aide carried "Louisville Slugger" baseball bats — sent by the Louisville local to help the leaders "go to bat" for union workers. Ford officials, tipped off about the props, also brought bats with them to show they could "play ball" with the union. [32]

The staging could have evoked memories of the rough days of the 1930s, when Ford hired security guards armed with bats to beat up labor organizers, including the leader of the incipient UAW, Walter Reuther. But today, the bats were carried in good spirits, and UAW and Ford officials went out of their way afterward to minimize the likelihood of a strike when the union's contract with the Big 3 automakers — General Motors, Ford and Chrysler — expires in October.

The jocular exchange indicates that some U.S. industries still accept unions as part of the reality of labor-management relations. But many other industries — the poultry industry is one prominent example — are fighting tooth-and-nail to stay non-unionized. And even in unionized industries, companies such as GM are trying to trim labor costs by, among other things, "outsourcing" — buying parts from non-union plants instead of manufacturing them in-house. [33]

Against this background, the AFL-CIO's new aggressiveness represents an attempt simultaneously to mobilize workers and to confront business. On one day, President Sweeney can be found marching arm-in-arm with union members — as he did in November to support the International Association of Machinists' ultimately successful strike against the Boeing Company, the Seattle-based aircraft manufacturer. On another, he can be found confronting American business in its own quarters, as he did at a June 6 rally on Wall Street where he denounced "corporate America" for "putting profits before people."

Business leaders insist that Sweeney misreads the mood of American workers. "To most of America, employees and employers, having aggressive conflict and militancy in the workplace would be the antithesis of what we need to have a productive workplace," says Josten at the U.S. Chamber of Commerce.

Workers themselves apparently want more involvement in workplace decisions but have mixed views about how to achieve it, according to a detailed research survey conducted in late 1994 and early 1995 by two leading labor experts, Harvard's Richard Freeman and the University of Wisconsin's Joel Rogers. [34]

The researchers found that 63 percent of employees say they want to have more influence in workplace decisions. About 40 percent say they would vote union in an election — less than a majority, but nearly three times as high as the actual proportion of union members in the U.S. work force today. And a significant bloc of those who say they would vote against a union — about 12 percent — say they would change their vote if they thought management was not opposed to the move.

Some labor experts have called for new ways to achieve employee involvement, but the talk has resulted in relatively little change. In his 1988 book *The New Unionism,* Charles Heckscher, a professor at Rutgers University in New Brunswick, N.J., called for a new "associational unionism" that would give workers a collective voice in workplace issues but under more flexible arrangements than the current two-way labor-management negotiations. Heckscher worked with the Communications Workers of America (CWA) in drawing up the proposal, and the union put the idea into effect in 1992 by agreeing with AT&T to form joint labor-management councils to plan future workplace changes. [35]

But relations soured after AT&T announced job cuts totaling 40,000 earlier this year and refused to allow CWA members to transfer to its non-union unit, AT&T Wireless. "It's a schizophrenic relationship," says CWA spokesman Jeffrey Miller. "We're prepared to work cooperatively where it works. And where we don't see cooperation, we're prepared to fight them."

Troy, the most prominent academic critic of unions, predicts that private-

FOR MORE INFORMATION

AFL-CIO, 815 16th St., N.W., Washington, D.C. 20006; (202) 637-5000. The federation's 78 member unions represent 13.1 million U.S. workers.

Economic Policy Institute, 1600 L St., N.W., suite 1200, Washington, D.C. 20036; (202) 775-8810. The institute analyzes a variety of economic issues, including income distribution and competitiveness.

Labor Policy Association, 1015 15th St., N.W., Washington, D.C. 20005; (202) 789-8670. The association follows labor issues for about 230 major U.S. companies.

National Association of Manufacturers, 1331 Pennsylvania Ave., N.W., Washington, D.C. 20004; (202) 637-3127. NAM is an important business lobby for manufacturers in Washington.

U.S. Chamber of Commerce, 1615 H St., N.W., Washington, D.C. 20062; (202) 463-5300. The chamber is a major business lobbying group in Washington.

sector unionism will continue to diminish — to 7 percent of the private work force by the year 2000. He contends that the only "new" unionism is in the public sector, but even there he says the growth of the past three decades has now topped out. In fact, the number of government workers represented by unions fell slightly in 1995 — to 6.9 million, from 7.1 million in 1994.

For his part, Sweeney avoids making specific predictions about the labor federation's push to organize new workers. "I'm not going to say we're going to double our membership in the next two years," he says. But he feels confident that union rolls will begin to grow again — and labor's voice will grow as well.

"You will see a stronger voice for our membership," Sweeney says. "We will be continuously motivating grassroots activists in our unions around the issues that are of concern to workers. I think all of this will help improve the perceptions of the labor movement both with our own members and with the public." ■

Notes

[1] Samuel Gompers was defeated for president of the AFL in 1894 by a Socialist-backed candidate, John McBride. Gompers regained the post by defeating McBride the following year. Until last year, there were no contested elections since the AFL and CIO merged in 1955.

[2] Lawrence Mishel and Paula B. Voos, eds., *Unions and Economic Competitiveness* (1992).

[3] *AFL-CIO News,* May 20, 1996, p. 3. For background, see *Congressional Quarterly Weekly Report,* May 11, 1996, p. 1278.

[4] The telephone survey of 1,000 persons was conducted April 23-28, 1996, by the Luntz Research Companies for Americans for a Balanced Budget.

[5] Historical background is drawn in part from Charles B. Craver, *Can Unions Survive? The Rejuvenation of the American Labor Movement* (1993), pp. 10-33. Also see Foster Rhea Dulles and Melvyn Dubofsky, *Labor in America: A History* (4th ed., 1984).

[6] The Railway Labor Act of 1926 established the right to organize for railway workers; it also established a mechanism for forcing strikers back to work and using mediation to resolve contract disputes. The act is still in effect; it was expanded in 1936 to cover airlines.

[7] Quoted in Craver, *op. cit.,* p. 3. The remark is from 1963; Craver says Meany "frequently" voiced similar views.

[8] *Ibid.,* p. 32.

[9] Dulles and Dubofsky, *op. cit.,* pp. 395-396.

[10] See *The New York Times,* Jan. 29, 1996, p. A1.

[11] Craver, *op. cit.,* pp. 48-49.

[12] Robert LaLonde and Bernard Meltzer, "Hard Times for Unions: Another Look at the Significance of Employer Illegalities," *University of Chicago Law Review,* Vol. 58, 1991, p. 994, Table 7, cited in Craver, *loc. cit.*

[13] Martin Jay Levitt, *Confessions of a Union Buster* (1993), p. 5.

[14] Kate Bronfenbrenner, "Employer Behavior in Certification Elections and First Contract Campaigns: Implications for Labor Law Reform," in Sheldon Friedman et al., eds., *Restoring the Promise of American Labor Law* (1994).

[15] Peter T. Kilborn, "Bringing Down Labor's Leader," *The New York Times,* Sept. 4, 1995. Other details of events leading up to Kirkland's retirement also are drawn from this article.

[16] See *The Washington Post,* Jan. 28, 1995, p. A1.

[17] For background, see "Rethinking NAFTA," *The CQ Researcher,* June 7, 1996, pp. 481-504.

[18] See *The New York Times,* Dec. 5, 1995, p. A18.

[19] Quoted in *The New York Times,* Oct. 26, 1995, p. D25.

[20] Quoted in *The Washington Post,* Oct. 29, 1995, p. A1.

[21] Quoted in *The New York Times,* May 28, 1996, p. B2.

[22] Kate Bronfenbrenner and Tom Juravich, "The Impact of Employer Opposition on Union Certification Win Rates: A Private/Public Sector Comparison," *Economic Policy Institute,* February 1995, p 4.

[23] Commission on the Future of Worker-Management Relations, "Report and Recommendations," December 1994, pp. 18-21.

[24] Quoted in *The New York Times,* June 1, 1996, p. 9.

[25] *Ibid.*

[26] NBC, "Meet the Press," March 31, 1996.

[27] *The Wall Street Journal,* April 3, 1996, p. A14.

[28] See *Congressional Quarterly Weekly Report,* April 13, 1996, pp. 996-997.

[29] *The Wall Street Journal,* May 3, 1996, May 2, 1996, p. A16.

[30] *Congressional Quarterly Weekly Report,* May 25, 1996, p. 1461.

[31] See *The Washington Post,* Feb. 11, 1996, p. H1.

[32] See *The New York Times,* June 11, 1996, p. D2.

[33] See *The New York Times,* April 11, 1996, p. D1.

[34] Richard B. Freeman and Joel Rogers, "Worker Representation and Participation Survey," Princeton Survey Research Associates, Dec. 5, 1994, and June 6, 1995. The project included a national telephone survey of about 2,000 persons in September-October 1994 and a follow-up survey of about 800 of the participants in December 1994-January 1995.

[35] See Aaron Bernstein, "Why America Needs Unions — But Not the Kind It Has Now," *Business Week,* May 23, 1994, p. 52.

Bibliography

Selected Sources Used

Books

American Social History Project, City University of New York, *Who Built America? Working People and the Nation's Economy, Politics, Culture and Society. Vol. 1: From Conquest and Colonization through Reconstruction and the Great Uprising of 1877,* Pantheon, 1989; *Vol. 2: From the Gilded Age to the Present,* Pantheon, 1992.

This comprehensive, illustrated history, prepared by a battery of distinguished labor historians, moves from the Colonial era and early beginnings of workers' associations through the birth of the modern labor movement in the late 1800s and its development as a political and economic force in the 20th century. Each volume contains detailed chapter-by-chapter source notes.

Craver, Charles B., *Can Unions Survive? The Rejuvenation of the American Labor Movement,* New York University Press, 1993.

Craver, a professor at George Washington University Law School, briefly traces the history of the labor movement through its recent declines and then sets out steps needed for its rejuvenation, including organizing non-union workers and revising federal labor law. The book includes detailed source notes, a three-page table of labor law cases and a 13-page bibliography.

Dulles, Foster Rhea, and Melvyn Dubofsky, *Labor in America: A History* [5th ed.], Harlan Davidson, 1993.

This one-volume survey traces the history of labor from Colonial America through the early 1990s. Dulles wrote the first three editions of the book; Dubofsky, a professor at the State University of New York in Binghamton, wrote updated material for the fourth and fifth editions.

Heckscher, Charles, *The New Unionism: Employee Involvement in the Changing Corporation,* Basic Books, 1988.

Heckscher, a professor at Rutgers University, argues in favor of replacing industrial unionism with what he calls "associational unionism," which he describes as "more appropriate to rapid economic change, flexible systems of management and shifting employee loyalties." The book includes detailed source notes and a 10-page bibliography.

Geoghegan, Thomas, *Which Side Are You On? Trying to Be for Labor When It's Flat on Its Back,* Farrar, Straus & Giroux, 1991.

Geoghegan, a Chicago labor law attorney, writes an impassioned, personal critique of the labor movement, which he depicts as moribund and ineffectual. He places blame for its failures variously on union officials, corporations and federal labor policy-makers in Congress, the executive branch and the National Labor Relations Board.

Mishel, Lawrence, and Paula B. Voos, eds., *Unions and Economic Competitiveness,* M.E. Sharpe, 1992.

The book includes eight research essays analyzing such issues as the effects of unions on economic performance, technological change and labor-management collaboration. Mishel is research director of the Economic Policy Institute, a liberal-oriented think tank in Washington; Voos is a professor of economics and industrial relations at the University of Wisconsin. The book includes a 28-page bibliography.

Troy, Leo, *The New Unionism in the New Society: Public Sector Unions in the Redistributive State,* George Mason University Press, 1994.

Troy, a professor of economics at Rutgers University in Newark, N.J., critically examines the steady growth since the 1960s of public sector unions — what he calls "the new unionism." The book includes eight pages of references.

Articles

Bernstein, Aaron, "Why America Needs Unions — But Not the Kind It Has Now," *Business Week,* May 23, 1994, pp. 70-82.

Bernstein surveys the reasons for the labor movement's decline, then argues unions can revitalize themselves by adopting a less adversarial attitude toward management.

Greenwald, Juliana, and Robert Marshall Wells, "At Odds With Some Workers, AFL-CIO Takes Aim at GOP," *Congressional Quarterly Weekly Report,* April 13, 1996, pp. 993-998.

The article describes and analyzes the AFL-CIO's $35 million plan to mobilize workers for the November congressional elections.

Worsham, James, "Labor Comes Alive," *Nation's Business,* February 1996, pp. 16-24.

The article gives a balanced account of the AFL-CIO's efforts to rejuvenate itself after the election of John J. Sweeney as its new president.

Reports and Studies

Commission on the Future of Worker-Management Relations, *Report and Recommendations,* December 1994.

This 11-member commission, created by the Clinton administration and headed by John Dunlop, the Harvard professor and former Labor secretary, called for steps to help unions during organizing campaigns but also urged clearer legal standards to permit management-backed "employee teams." The 70-page report details the recommendations and includes the names of the commissioners and witnesses who testified at four national hearings from July through September 1994.

The Next Step

Additional information from UMI's Newspaper & Periodical Abstracts database

AFL-CIO

Bole, William, "Putting move back into labor movement," ***National Catholic Reporter,*** **Jan. 12, 1996, p. 3.**
Many union officials and even union outsiders believe that if labor movements want to maintain any kind of effectiveness, they will have to become more feisty and less bureaucratic. The election of John J. Sweeney to head of the AFL-CIO and the reaction the election caused among other union members are discussed.

Kaplan, Bill, "Real democracy will put muscle back into labor movement," ***Christian Science Monitor,*** **June 15, 1995, p. 19.**
Bill Kaplan applauds the June 1995 withdrawal of Lane Kirkland from the race for AFL-CIO president, and notes that Kirkland's 16-year tenure as head of the group has not stopped the sharp decline in labor union power and workers' security in the U.S.

Rose, Robert L., "AFL-CIO's power struggle reflects frustration with labor movement," ***The Wall Street Journal,*** **May 15, 1995, p. A2.**
The failure of organized labor to make significant political progress and an escalating power struggle led to a split in the ranks of the AFL-CIO over who should lead labor into the next century. Lane Kirkland, the organization's 73-year-old president, refused to step down from the post he has held for 16 years, prompting 11 unions to say they would find someone to oppose him.

Election of John Sweeney

Franklin, Stephen, "On the record: John Sweeney," ***Chicago Tribune,*** **May 5, 1996, p. 3.**
In an interview, AFL-CIO President John Sweeney discusses his job and the direction that labor unions are going.

Greenwald, John, "The battle to revive the unions," ***Time,*** **Oct. 30, 1995, pp. 64-66.**
John Sweeney and Thomas Donahue are battling for the presidency of the AFL-CIO. No matter who wins the race, reviving the labor movement will take a heroic effort.

"John Sweeney's disruption," ***The Economist,*** **March 16, 1996, p. 36.**
While Pat Buchanan now pushes the problems of the working class for the Republican Party, AFL-CIO President John Sweeney will soon be the Democratic leader talking about economic security. Sweeney may prove much harder to control than Buchanan is.

Kilborn, Peter T., "Militant is elected head of A.F.L.-C.I.O., signaling sharp turn for labor movement," ***The New York Times,*** **Oct. 26, 1995, p. D25.**
With the election of John J. Sweeney on Oct. 25, 1995, as the new president of the AFL-CIO, the American labor movement took a sharp turn toward militancy, rebuilding union membership, moving women and minorities into the policy-making ranks and tackling a hostile Congress.

Rose, Robert L., "John Sweeney plots a revolution at AFL-CIO," ***The Wall Street Journal,*** **June 14, 1995, p. B1.**
John Sweeney, the president of the Service Employees International Union, is expected to win a two-year term to succeed the retiring Lane Kirkland as president of the AFL-CIO. Sweeney's election would signal a revolution at the top of organized labor.

Seligman, Daniel, "The Kennedy-Goldberg labor movement," ***Fortune,*** **Dec. 11, 1995, pp. 236-237.**
The biggest question concerning unions is whether John J. Sweeney, the militant new head of the AFL-CIO, will transform the labor movement and get workers moving in a giant wave of activism.

Historical Perspective

Bahr, Morton, "In '95, the labor movement is more relevant than ever," ***Christian Science Monitor,*** **Aug. 25, 1995, p. 19.**
Communications Workers of America President Morton Bahr discusses the importance of labor unions in America's past, and claims that labor unions are more relevant in the 1990s than ever before.

Ballam, Deborah A., "The law as a constitutive force for change, part II: The impact of the National Labor Relations Act on the U.S. labor movement," ***American Business Law Journal,*** **1995, pp. 447-479.**
The impact of the National Labor Relations Act on the U.S. labor movement is examined within the context of the 20th century. The labor movement's successes in effecting broad reform efforts may be the key to the NLRA's viability.

Scharnau, Ralph, "The labor movement in Iowa," ***Journal of the West,*** **April 1996, pp. 19-28.**
The labor movement in Iowa in the first decade of the 20th century saw dramatic changes marked by an emerging militancy that included a surge in trade unionism, radical politics and other factors usually associated with more urbanized and industrialized states.

International Labor Movements

Adler, Glenn and Eddie Webster, "Challenging transition theory: The labor movement, radical reform and

transition to democracy in South Africa," ***Politics & Society,*** **March 1995, pp. 75-106.**
The emergence of the democratic trade union movement in South Africa and the central role that labor has played in shaping the transition process in South Africa are discussed. The case of South Africa has significant implications for debates about transitions to democracy.

Gurdon, Meghan Cox, "Labor party chief walks a fine line with Britain's unions," ***San Francisco Chronicle,*** **Sept. 16, 1995, p. A8.**
Britain's Labor Party appears to have shed its image as the tool of militant unions in 1995. The party and its leader Tony Blair, who is said to have been much influenced by American politics, are examined.

"Trade unions: Adapt or die," ***The Economist,*** **July 1, 1995, p. 54-56.**
The changing work force worldwide is presenting both opportunities and difficulties for labor unions. Wider changes in the workplace and society have hurt union membership rolls.

"Unions for the poor," ***The Economist,*** **July 1, 1995, p.56.**
Labor unions have not been successful in developing countries because governments see unions as an opposition base that could cause trouble. African and Arabian governments are openly hostile to independent unions.

Labor Movement's Resurgence

Dine, Philip, "Labor movement has made some meaningful strides in the last year," ***St. Louis Post-Dispatch,*** **Sept. 1, 1995, p. E1.**
Dine comments that much has changed in the organized labor movement, enough so that labor may be positioning itself to play a larger role in the last half of the century's last decade. He also states that observers eventually may be able to spend their time evaluating labor's actions rather than analyzing its well-being.

Fraser, Steve and Nelson Lichtenstein, "New life for the labor movement," ***The Washington Post,*** **Dec. 31, 1995, p. C1.**
Fraser and Lichtenstein assert that the rebirth of a dynamic labor movement would be the most heartening development in U.S. political life since the heyday of the civil rights movement.

Medearis, John, "Labor movement finds new home — Universities," ***Los Angeles Times,*** **April 21, 1996, p. M3.**
Medearis discusses the new activism spreading across U.S. college campuses to demand the right to bargain collectively with administrations and to support labor rights.

Reilly, Sean, "The case for unions," ***Washington Monthly,*** **July 1995, p. 26-31.**
Corporate attempts to redistribute the wealth of companies away from the workers to management have been dramatically increasing lately, making unions more important than ever. A strong labor movement could be the last chance for a better life for American workers.

Political Activies and Impact

Kilborn, Peter T., "Labor Movement Endorses the President," ***The New York Times,*** **March 26, 1996, p. B9.**
Setting aside its anger over President Clinton's trade policy, the U.S. labor movement on March 25, 1996, endorsed him for re-election. Just two of the 78 unions in the AFL-CIO dissented, saying they wanted more time to consider their action.

Leiter, Lisa, "Unions hope to cashier the GOP," ***Insight on the News,*** **May 6, 1996, pp. 8-10.**
The AFL-CIO has committed $35 million to defeat Republican lawmakers, especially freshmen, and return Congress to liberal Democrats.

Morain, Dan, "Unions plan ambitious political campaign in state," ***Los Angeles Times,*** **May 20, 1996, p. A1.**
With union ranks depleted and labor protections under attack in the GOP-controlled California Assembly, state labor leaders are preparing to wage what they say will be their most aggressive political effort in years. Union leaders are denouncing GOP proposals to cut wages for construction workers.

Rosenblatt, Robert A., "After years in hibernation, resurgent labor movement has GOP worried," ***Los Angeles Times,*** **May 18, 1996, p. A23.**
The 13-million-member AFL-CIO has reemerged in 1996 as a potentially powerful political force, winning new respect and even fear among its foes in Congress and the business world. GOP leaders fear a labor movement on the offensive politically.

Women and Minorities in Unions

McCabe, Kathy, "Trumka says revival of labor movement hinges on diversity," ***Boston Globe,*** **Jan. 23, 1996, p. 34.**
Richard L. Trumka, secretary/treasurer of the AFL-CIO, said the union must diversify its ranks with more women and minorities and build coalitions with political and community groups to revitalize the American labor movement.

"Trends in U.S. labor movement," ***Futurist,*** **January 1996, p. 44.**
The U.S. labor movement is becoming more activist, driven by such trends as the increasingly important roles of women and minorities.

Unions and Strikes

Tyson, James L., "As strikes lose potency, unions turn to tactics outside the workplace," ***Christian Science Monitor,*** **Feb. 16, 1996, p. 1.**
With the number of strikes at a 50-year low, unions are using so-called corporate campaigns to try to pressure companies over wages, benefits and other issues.

Back Issues

Great Research on Current Issues Starts Right Here...Recent topics covered by The CQ Researcher are listed below. Before May 1991, reports were published under the name of Editorial Research Reports.

DECEMBER 1994
Farm Policy
Arms Sales
Earthquake Research
The Future of Television

JANUARY 1995
Treating Addiction
Child Custody and Support
Parents and Schools
Non-Proliferation Treaty at 25

FEBRUARY 1995
Cracking Down on Immigration
The Business of Sports
Reinventing Government
Housing Discrimination

MARCH 1995
Death Penalty Debate
Primary Care
Democracy in Africa
Environmental Movement at 25

APRIL 1995
Abortion Clinic Protests
Dieting and Health
Combating AIDS
Rethinking Affirmative Action

Back issues are available for $5.00 (subscribers) or $8.00 (non-subscribers). Quantity discounts apply to orders over ten. To order, call Congressional Quarterly Customer Service at (202) 887-8621.

Binders are available for $18.00. To order call 1-800-638-1710. Please refer to stock number 648.

MAY 1995
Assisted Suicide Controversy
Overhauling Social Security
Learning to Read
Mandatory Sentencing

JUNE 1995
Combating Infectious Disease
Property Rights
Repetitive Stress Injuries
Regulating the Internet

JULY 1995
War Crimes
Highway Safety
Combating Terrorism
Preventing Teen Drug Use

AUGUST 1995
Job Stress
Organ Transplants
United Nations at 50
Advances in Cancer Research

SEPTEMBER 1995
Catholic Church in the U.S.
Northern Ireland Cease-Fire
High School Sports
Teaching History

OCTOBER 1995
Quebec's Future
Revitalizing the Cities
Networking the Classroom
Indoor Air Pollution

NOVEMBER 1995
The Working Poor
The Jury System
Sex, Violence and the Media
Police Misconduct

DECEMBER 1995
Teens and Tobacco
Gene Therapy's Future
Global Water Shortages
Third-Party Prospects

JANUARY 1996
Emergency Medicine
Punishing Sex Offenders
Bilingual Education
Helping the Homeless

FEBRUARY 1996
Reforming the CIA
Campaign Finance Reform
Academic Politics
Getting Into College

MARCH 1996
The British Monarchy
Preventing Juvenile Crime
Tax Reform
Pursuing the Paranormal

APRIL 1996
Centennial Olympic Games
Managed Care
Protecting Endangered Species
New Military Culture

MAY 1996
Russia's Political Future
Marriage and Divorce
Year-Round Schools
Taiwan, China and the U.S.

JUNE 1996
Rethinking NAFTA
First Ladies
Teaching Values

Future Topics

- ***Repressed Memory Syndrome***
- ***Native Americans at a Crossroads***
- ***Sexual Harassment Update***

THE CQ Researcher®

PUBLISHED BY CONGRESSIONAL QUARTERLY INC.

Recovered-Memory Debate

Can painful memories be repressed and later recalled?

Some mental health experts claim that memories of personal childhood trauma, often sexual abuse by a family member, may be totally repressed. Years later, they say, the memories may surface, typically during psychotherapy. Such cases have drawn heavy media coverage in recent years — and have generated widespread controversy among legal and mental health professionals. Some experts cite studies supporting the thesis that the mind can bury painful memories. Others contend the studies are inconclusive and that ill-trained psychotherapists plant false memories in their patients. To add to the controversy, some recovered memories include lurid details about alien abductions or satanic rituals. But all parties to the debate agree on one thing: Child sex abuse is a serious problem requiring urgent attention.

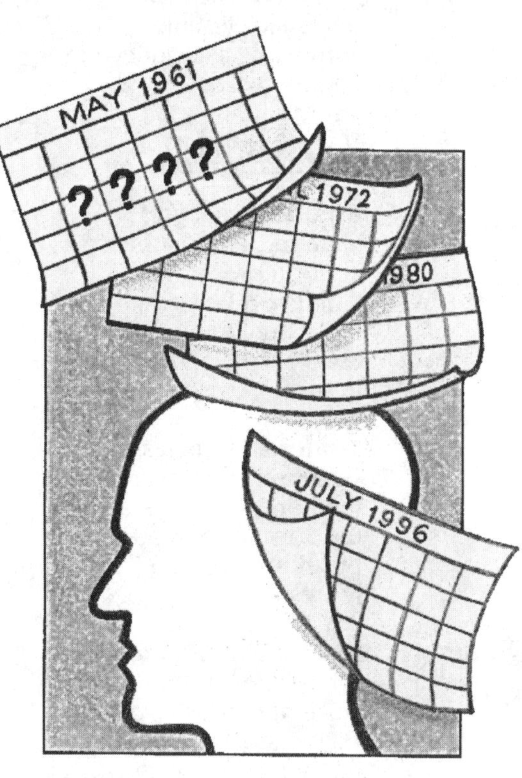

INSIDE THIS ISSUE

CQ July 5, 1996 • Volume 6, No. 25 • Pages 577-600

Formerly Editorial Research Reports

Recovered-Memory Debate

COVER: BARBARA SASSA-DANIELS

July 5, 1996
Volume 6, No. 25

The CQ Researcher (ISSN 1056-2036). Formerly Editorial Research Reports. Published weekly (48 times per year, not printed March 1, May 31, Aug. 30, Nov. 29) by Congressional Quarterly Inc., 1414 22nd St., N.W., Washington, D.C. 20037. Annual subscription rate for libraries, businesses and government is $319. Additional rates furnished upon request. Periodicals postage paid at Washington, D.C. POSTMASTER: Send address changes to The CQ Researcher, 1414 22nd St., N.W., Washington, D.C. 20037.

Recovered-Memory Debate

BY RICHARD L. WORSNOP

THE ISSUES

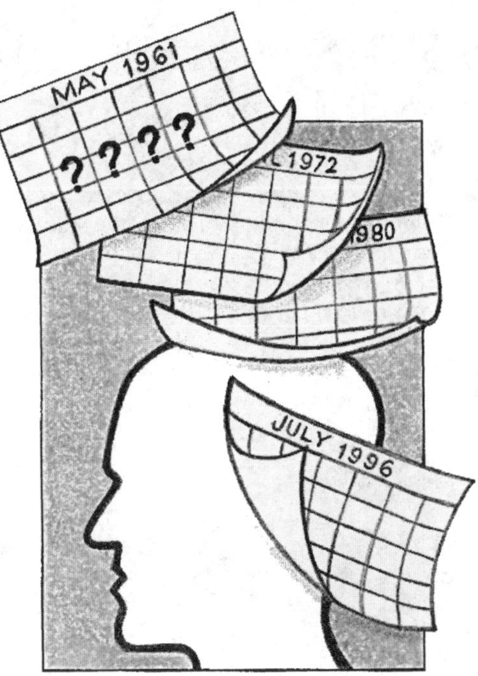

It was a balmy, California day in 1989, and Eileen Franklin, 29, was relaxing at home with her 6-year-old daughter, Jessica. As sunlight and shadow dappled Jessica's face, Franklin was stirred by feelings of maternal warmth and contentment — and something else.

Suddenly, Franklin later testified, a horrifying memory flashed into her mind. She found herself recalling — for the first time — an event that she now says occurred almost 20 years earlier. Franklin saw herself as a 9-year-old, watching as a man killed her closest friend, 8-year-old Susan Nason, with a large rock. The murderer, Franklin later told police investigators and a jury, was her father.

In 1990, George Thomas Franklin was convicted of the child's murder, largely on the basis of his daughter's "recovered" memory of the slaying. It is believed to be the first criminal conviction based on such evidence in a U.S. court.

Franklin's conviction was overturned last year, and he was ordered to be retried. But on July 2 prosecutors announced they would not retry him (*see p. 590*). Although the Franklin case is over, the fierce debate it ignited — among mental health professionals, lawyers, jurists and the lay public — seems likely to rage for years.

The controversy centers on two questions: Can the mind repress all recollection of a traumatic childhood event? And second, if that memory somehow surfaces in adulthood, should it be considered valid or suspect? Some experts argue that repressed memories do not occur; others support the concept as well as the possibility of recovering such memories in therapy. Still other professionals say some memories may be false and others true.

Most recovered-memory cases involve recollections of alleged childhood sexual abuse by one or more members of the immediate family. Typically, an adult woman undergoing psychotherapy recalls being raped or fondled at an early age by her father. Some adult men have recalled similar abuse, often at the hands of clergymen. [1]

The list of purported victims of child sexual abuse includes several public figures. In 1991, for example, Marilyn Van Derbur, Miss America of 1958, disclosed her recovered memories of sexual abuse by her father. That same year, comedienne Roseanne Barr told a group of incest survivors in Denver, Colo., that she had remembered, some 30 years later, being molested by her parents.*

In some cases, the recovered memories of childhood trauma include lurid details about ritual abuse by satanic cults, prior lives or abduction by aliens from outer space. [2] (*See story, p. 594.*) Members of the Philadelphia-based False Memory Syndrome Foundation (FMSF) and other skeptics say such outlandish claims reinforce doubts about the validity of recovered memory in general. But many therapists view them as bizarre metaphors for more mundane abuse that actually occurred early in life.

All parties to the recovered-memory debate agree that child sex abuse is a serious problem requiring urgent attention. A widely cited study by psychiatrists Judith Lewis Herman and Emily Schatzow noted that various surveys have concluded "that for girls, the risk of a sexual assault prior to adolescence is approximately one in 4, and for boys, one in 10." [3]

The number of civil and criminal cases involving alleged or actual childhood sexual abuse has exploded in recent years, largely due to the relaxation of state statutes of limitations governing prosecution of such offenses (*see p. 590*). Washington was the first state to take such action, in 1989; today, half the states permit adults who say they were victims of childhood sexual abuse to bring legal action against alleged perpetrators.

Though sexual abuse of children is a profoundly repellent crime, victims are by no means assured of prevailing in court on the basis of recovered memories. According to an informal tally by the FMSF, two-thirds of the civil suits reported to the group "are dropped, dismissed or concluded in favor of the accused." And in 1994, only one in 12 criminal cases reported to the foundation resulted in a conviction. [4]

FMSF was founded to combat the wave of accusations and lawsuits brought by purported victims of child sex abuse. Family members claiming to be falsely accused form the core of

---

* Other celebrities claiming to be victims of childhood sexual abuse include Patti Davis, daughter of former President Ronald Reagan, singer La Toya Jackson, actress Suzanne Somers and magazine editor Frances Lear.

Patient's False Memories of Sexual Abuse . . .

On Jan. 24, 1996, a jury in Ramsey County, Minn., awarded $2.5 million to Elizabeth J. Carlson, 42, a resident of the St. Paul suburb of Oakdale. Carlson had sued her psychiatrist, Diane Humenansky, for malpractice, claiming she became suicidal after Humenansky prompted her to have false memories of childhood sexual abuse. Six months earlier, a different Ramsey County jury awarded more than $2.6 million to Vynette Hamanne, another former Humenansky patient who had sued on similar grounds. On March 17, 1995, the Minnesota Board of Medical Practice ordered Dr. Humenansky to undergo a physical and mental evaluation or have her license suspended. She underwent the examination and is still licensed. Carlson, who has two children and is separated from her husband, spoke with Associate Editor Richard L. Worsnop.

"My ordeal started with an emergency visit to the hospital in October 1989. I was in a depression-crisis situation, and things were pretty much out of control. At first, I was assigned to a male psychiatrist who specialized in electroshock therapy, which I didn't want to do. Also, I thought I might feel more comfortable with a female therapist. That's how I came to see Dr. Humenansky.

Dr. Humenansky wanted to use what she called 'safe-place imagery.' The idea was to guide me to a site within myself where I would feel secure. She had me close my eyes and imagine that I was walking down flights of stairs. I didn't realize until much later that I was actually undergoing hypnosis.

At the bottom of the stairs I found myself in a cavelike room with people wearing black-hooded robes and holding daggers. I also saw a woman on an altar giving birth to a baby, and the afterbirth being cut up and eaten. It was gory and horrible.

But these mental images did not form spontaneously, Carlson says.

Dr. Humenansky had told me, 'Look for a cold, dark place.' And that's what I saw in my mind: a rocky, cavelike area. Then she said, 'You are a child in there, aren't you?' I nodded yes. 'How old are you?' 'About 4 or 5.' 'Who else is there?' 'I see some other children.' 'Now look around the room. Do you see an altar?' Well, it's so weird, this image of an altar just popped into my head. She then told me to look for people wearing black, hooded robes. And boom, just like that, the image appeared in my head. My eyes were closed all this time. She also told me to look for the daggers, the candles, the baby.

I fought against her leading questions and suggestions many times. But she always seemed to have a pat explanation handy. 'You're in denial, and that's normal,' she would say. 'This is very common, but it's a secret women don't talk about — that's why you've never heard about this.' Another thing she said was, 'Your mind works like a video recorder; your memories are all back there, and I can help you access them.' And I didn't know any better.

I was in therapy for over two years with her. I look back on it now as nothing more than being in a religious cult, sort of like Jim Jones' Peoples Temple. For instance, she told me that the Catholic Church was based on voodoo, and that that's why my parents were satanists. The pope, she said, was the highest-ranking black priest of all.

All this time, she had me read a lot of books that dealt with incest, multiple-personality disorders and satanic ritual abuse. I think if I had stayed in therapy much longer, we probably would have got into the alien-abduction thing, and who knows what else.

the 5,000-member foundation, which was established in 1992 (*see p. 589*). FMSF reserves its greatest scorn for therapists it says are ill-trained and plant false notions of childhood sexual abuse in their patients.

Like most other issues involving recovered memory, the size and influence of this "school" of psychotherapy is hotly disputed. Richard Ofshe, a sociologist at the University of California at Berkeley and a leading critic of the recovered-memory movement, views the therapy as a "politically correct" mania sweeping the nation. "Responding to the competition for clients and the demands of students for trendy treatment methodologies, clinical psychology programs in universities . . . are moving away from tradition and are rapidly embracing recovered-memory theory," he writes. [5]

Practitioners of recovered-memory therapy have become so sensitive to criticism, says Elizabeth F. Loftus, a psychology professor at the University of Washington, that they tend to deny their involvement. "If you ask people if they do recovered-memory therapy, they'll say, 'No, I don't.' But if you ask them about the components of what they do, they admit to all kinds of things — to suspecting abuse when the client has not disclosed it; to sharing their suspicions with the client, who has no memories of abuse; to using techniques to try to dig out allegedly buried trauma memories. You've got to ask the question the right way if you want them to admit to what they're actually doing."

To law Professor Alan Scheflin of California's Santa Clara University, recovered-memory therapy is "not a recognized school of therapy and not an epidemic; it's just the bad practice of a very small group of therapists." Scheflin, who has a master's degree in counseling psychology, adds, "There are no conferences on recovered memory. What you have is a bunch of people reading a lay literature and following agendas of their own. You'll find that in any profession."

... Linked to Psychotherapist's Leading Questions

Videotapes she lent me had to do with multiple-personality disorder, how repressed memory works, those kinds of things. One of them was done just like a documentary, and it talked about the Catholic Church being a voodoo religion. To me, that raised serious questions about the whole course of my therapy. I mean, I was raised as a Catholic, and so were my parents, grandparents and great-grandparents. How in the world, I thought ... they can't all be into this!

Later, Carlson says she was persuaded that she was suffering from multiple-personality disorder, also called dissociative-identity disorder (DID).

Dr. Humenansky told me, 'I want you to try this on for size, like a coat, and see how it fits.' That was her metaphor for [DID]. So if I was feeling depressed and spending more time in bed than usual, the person who was doing that actually was one of my 'alter' personalities. Or if I was giggling and playing games on the floor with my kids, that wasn't really me, either. It was one of my 'childlike' alters.

At other times, I would feel old and exhausted. I wouldn't get dressed, walked around the house all day in nightgowns and went for a week or more without showering. That behavior, I was told, represented the 'old lady' in me.

Sometimes I'd pray a lot, and that was supposed to be characteristic of the nuns in me. I had alters called Sister Mary Margaret and Sister Theresa.

I had been molested as a child, and the abuse occurred more than once. I never forgot, but [as an adult] I chose not to think about it because I was trying to get on with my life. Occasionally, though, I'd feel uncomfortable with my husband. Maybe it was because the problems we were having in our relationship reminded me of those childhood incidents, making physical intimacy with him difficult for me.

But when I told Dr. Humenansky about all this, she said, 'Those are only the incidents you remember. Your alter personalities hold all the memories of the abuse that you don't recall.'

Eventually, Carlson and several other women in a therapy group organized by Dr. Humenansky decided to meet without her — though they continued to consult with her individually.

Two to three months after we began meeting on our own, one of the women said, 'You know, all of us had an alter named Nikki.' Actually, I didn't have one, and I had felt left out, so I made one up. But the important thing about that is, it got us talking and comparing notes about other parallels in our experiences with Dr. Humenansky. What we found was that many of our recovered memories were remarkably alike.

Now, how could that be? How could we all have alters with the same or similar names and the same or similar personality traits? Maybe it was because we had all read the books and watched the videos that Dr. Humenansky had lent us. Anyway, our structure of shared belief began to crumble. And I think that was because Dr. Humenansky was no longer there to keep it all cemented together."

Looking back, Carlson offers the following advice for persons experiencing emotional problems like those she confronted.

I do believe there are times when people should seek professional help, especially if they lack support from family members, friends or their church. I also feel that certain kinds of medication can help them deal with their mental or emotional difficulties. But to those people who consult a therapist who *tells* them they have hidden memories, I would say this: Do not walk to the door — get up and run out of there as fast as you can.”

But Scheflin and other professionals do not dismiss recovered memory itself. "Every memory is a recovered memory," he says. "That's what it means to be a memory. When some people talk about recovered memory, they intend it as a pejorative term. But all it really means is repetition. To be a memory, you've got to recover it from somewhere."

The American Psychological Association (APA) also supports the notion of recovered memory: "Remembering is facilitated by retrieval clues, reading something in the newspaper, for example, or by re-experiencing an effect similar to the original memory. Research has also shown that memory seems to be stronger and less subject to alteration for events ... that have strong emotional impact." [6]

Moreover, the APA says, "denials by alleged perpetrators should ... not be taken as evidence that the client is experiencing other than an accurate recollection. Indeed, known perpetrators of child sexual abuse can also deny and lie about their behavior, even in the presence of physical evidence that incontrovertibly links them to the abuse." [7]

As professionals debate the existence of recovered memory and the techniques being used to recover them, these are some of the questions being asked:

Are "recovered memories" of childhood trauma reliable?

The sharpest disagreement over recovered-memory theory concerns the accuracy of long-repressed recollections of childhood trauma. Recovered-memory therapists contend that these painful thoughts emerge from the patient's unconscious mind in a virtually pristine state.

In contrast, skeptics argue that memory is elusive and infinitely changeable, because the mind commingles truth and fantasy. "Think of your mind as a bowl filled with clear water," writes Loftus. "Now imagine each memory as a teaspoon of milk stirred into the water. Each adult mind holds thousands of these murky memories. . . . Who among us would dare to disentangle the water from the milk?" [8]

The FMSF makes the same point with a different metaphor: "Memory does not work like a video tape recorder. There is just no button or pill that anyone can take to guarantee historically accurate memories. Memory is constructive. People take bits and fragments and reconstruct a narrative that makes sense to them in the here and now. There is a lot of filling in the blanks. Those blanks get filled in with new information that mixes with the old information, and it becomes impossible to separate. There is just no way to tell the truth or falsity of a memory except by external corroboration." [9]

In their landmark 1987 study, Herman and Schatzow reported that nearly three-fourths of 53 women undergoing individual and group therapy for childhood sexual abuse were able to substantiate the accuracy of their memories. "Twenty-one women (40 percent) obtained corroborating evidence either from the perpetrator himself, from other family members or from physical evidence such as diaries or photographs. Another 18 women (34 percent) discovered that another child, usually a sibling, had been abused by the same perpetrator. An additional five women (9 percent) reported statements from other family members indicating a strong likelihood that they had also been abused, but did not confirm their suspicions by direct questioning." [10]

Ofshe has raised strong reservations about the Herman-Schatzow study, noting that only 28 percent of the 53 women suffered from "severe memory deficits" while the remaining 72 percent had had either full or partial recall of childhood abuse before entering therapy. In other words, most of the women had not, strictly speaking, recovered memories that had been completely lost.

Moreover, Ofshe asks, referring to the 39 women who said they had corroborated their memories of childhood abuse, "Why did Herman and Schatzow not view any of this physical evidence for themselves or double-check the stories by speaking directly to the source of the confirmation?" [11]

"When some people talk about recovered memory, they intend it as a pejorative term. But all it really means is repetition. To be a memory, you've got to recover it from somewhere."

—Alan Scheflin, Professor of Law Santa Clara University

Mental health professionals acknowledge that they must approach the child-abuse memory issue gingerly. "A therapist can overresonate, become [a victim's] advocate and thus accept and champion false memories and false beliefs," wrote psychoanalyst John G. Watkins, a professor emeritus at the University of Montana. "The therapist, with 'one foot' resonating within the patient's internal milieu, must be certain that the 'other foot' is firmly planted in reality if the patient is to be helped to cross that gulf and emerge as a mature and reality-oriented individual. It is precisely the failure of some practitioners to maintain this balance that has lent weight to the accusations that they uncritically accept and promote 'false memories.' " [12]

Watkins conceded that therapists, "who are very aware of the prevalence and perniciousness of child abuse, may at times 'push' their clients to recall such incidents. To the extent to which they do, they are not practicing sound therapeutic techniques." But while "some parents may be falsely accused, it is not in the interest of society that therapists be discouraged from helping suffering patients who recall memories of abuse during their treatment. The actual number of falsely accused parents is likely to be far fewer than the number of abused children." [13]

Keith Russell Ablow, a psychiatrist at Boston Regional Medical Center and a syndicated columnist, doesn't think broad generalizations can be made about whether recovered memories "are reliable or suspect. But I, as a clinician, have never seen anyone who remembers something all of a sudden for which there is absolutely no basis."

Ablow feels that "people are fairly critical of their childhood memories [and] the toughest editors of their own recollections." For instance, he cites a woman patient who told him about a childhood memory of her father entering her bedroom when she was unclothed. The recollection didn't bother the patient years later, she told Ablow, because he "was probably just in there getting something out of the closet."

Many recovered memories of childhood sex abuse seem almost cinematic. "With time and retelling, these visions tend to become highly detailed, in vivid color and crystal clear," noted Ofshe. "Details may include what people were wearing, what someone smelled like and specific dialogue. [Recovered-memory] therapists take such vividness and detail as proof of the accuracy of the memory when it actually implies the opposite," they say, because memory gaps are filled in with details from various sources. [14]

Lawyer Sherry A. Quirk, president of the Washington-based National Alliance for Abuse Awareness, defends the accuracy of recovered memories. When a traumatic memory is recovered "through a flashback or whatever, it comes back in an extremely visceral, sensory way," she writes. "The person feels as if she's back in the place where the event occurred. In that sense, the memory is very much a re-creation, a remembering of what happened long ago." [15]

To law Professor Scheflin, "Memory is tremendously accurate, even in children, for what's called 'gist' — but not for peripheral details."

The phenomenon known as "flashbulb memory" describes the recollections people have of such shared tragedies as the assassination of President John F. Kennedy and the "Challenger" explosion. "Generally, these events are not personally traumatic," says Scheflin. "It's not as if you've been mugged or raped. But if you're an adult, you're absolutely certain you remember where you were and what you were doing at the time."

However, he adds, research indicates that individual flashbulb memories "are often wrong about where you were when the event occurred, how you learned about it and who you spoke with — but never wrong about the nature of the event itself. Of course, a lot of people will remember even the peripheral details very well."

Leading mental-health organizations approach recovered-memory issues with caution, finding merit in at least some of the arguments advanced by both sides. For example, the American Psychiatric Association said recently that some of the coping mechanisms used by sexually abused children "result in a lack of conscious awareness of the abuse for varying periods of time. Conscious thoughts and feelings stemming from the abuse may emerge at a later date." At the same time, the association noted, "repeated questioning" by a therapist "may lead individuals to report 'memories' of events that never occurred." To complicate matters further, "It is not known how to distinguish, with complete accuracy, memories based on true events from those derived from other sources." [16]

Above all, the association said, "Psychiatrists should maintain an empathic, non-judgmental, neutral stance toward reported memories of sexual abuse." That's because "A strong prior belief by the psychiatrist that sexual abuse, or other factors, are or are not the cause of the patient's problems is likely to interfere with appropriate assessment and treatment. Many individuals who have experienced sexual abuse have a history of not being believed by their parents or others in whom they have put their trust. Expression of disbelief is likely to cause the patient further pain and decrease his/her willingness to seek needed psychiatric treatment." [17]

Earlier this year, an American Psychological Association task force concluded that, "Most people who were sexually abused as children remember all or part of what happened to them." However, "It is possible for memories of abuse that have been forgotten for a long time to be remembered," and "also possible to construct convincing pseudomemories for events that never occurred." [18]

In contrast, the American Medical Association (AMA) seems openly dubious of the claims advanced in support of recovered memory. "[A]s the issue of repressed memories has

Doonesbury Flashbacks

BY GARRY TRUDEAU

The Mystery of Split Personality

Once it was known as "split personality." Then "multiple-personality disorder" became the term of choice for the idea that a person can have more than one personality. And now dissociative-identity disorder (DID) is the name assigned to the condition in the fourth and latest edition of the *Diagnostic and Statistical Manual of Mental Disorders,* or DSM-IV, the bible of the mental health field.

Over the years, two films based on actual multiple-personality cases have won critical and popular praise. Joanne Woodward took home the 1957 Academy Award for best actress for her performance in "The Three Faces of Eve," about a woman with three contrasting personalities and three separate lives. In 1976, Sally Field played the title role in "Sybil," a made-for-TV movie about a young woman whose traumatic childhood experiences caused her to develop 17 separate identities. (Woodward played Sybil's psychiatrist.)

In fact, experts on DID say, some sufferers develop 100 personalities or more. DID theory holds that multiple personality formation is a defensive mechanism designed to protect the primary identity from knowledge of past traumatic events, notably childhood sexual abuse, with each secondary personality safeguarding a particular memory.

The process is called "dissociation," a psychological term that is sometimes confused with the "repression" of painful childhood memories. Many critics of recovered-memory theory question whether either mechanism exists.

Dissociative-identity disorder "reflects a failure to integrate various aspects of identity, memory and consciousness," according to DSM-IV. "Each personality state may be experienced as if it had a distinct personal history, self-image and identity, including a separate name. Usually there is a primary identity that carries the individual's name and is passive, dependent, guilty and depressed. The alternate identities frequently have different names and characteristics that contrast with the primary identity (e.g., are hostile, controlling and self-destructive)." [1]

The manual also notes that, "Alternative identities . . . may deny knowledge of one another, be critical of one another or appear to be in open conflict. Occasionally, one or more powerful identities allocate time to the others. Aggressive or hostile identities may at times interrupt activities or place the others in uncomfortable situations." [2]

"Individuals with dissociative-identity disorder frequently report having experienced severe physical and sexual abuse, especially during childhood," according to DSM-IV. But Paul R. McHugh, director of the Johns Hopkins University department of psychiatry and behavioral sciences, questions the validity of such reports.

"These patients have not come to treatment reporting a sexual assault in childhood," McHugh wrote. "Only after therapy has promoted [DID] behavior is the possibility that they were sexually abused as children suggested to them. From recollections of the mists of childhood, a vague sense of vulnerability may slowly emerge, facilitated and encouraged by the treating group."

According to McHugh, the long-forgotten abuse "is finally 'remembered' after months of 'uncovering' therapy, during which long conversations by the therapist with 'alter' personalities take place. Any other actual proof of the assault is thought unnecessary." [3]

Psychiatrist Christine A. Courtois acknowledges that "many mental health professionals are extremely skeptical" about DID and believe it is "fabricated by the individual as a means of gaining attention and approval" or "created by naive or suggestive therapists."

But Courtois, director of clinical training for the post-traumatic and dissociative-disorders program at the Psychiatric Clinic of Washington, contends that the condition does exist. Moreover, she says, therapy "can lead to a dramatic lessening and an ultimate resolution of very severe symptoms. Treatment usually takes several years and has a fairly good prognosis." [4]

[1] American Psychiatric Association, *Diagnostic and Statistical Manual of Mental Disorders,* fourth edition (1994), p. 484.

[2] *Loc. cit.*

[3] Paul R. McHugh, "Psychiatric Misadventures," *The American Scholar,* autumn 1992, p. 506.

[4] Christine A. Courtois, "The Therapist's View: How 'Multiple Personalities' Are Born," *The Washington Post,* Aug. 6, 1995, p. C4.

grown, there have been reports of therapists advising patients that their symptoms are indicative — not merely suggestive — of having been abused, even when the patient denies having been abused," the AMA's Council on Scientific Affairs stated in 1994. Official AMA policy on the issue declares "the technique of memory enhancement in the area of childhood sexual abuse to be fraught with problems of potential misapplication."

Should "hypnotically refreshed" testimony be admissible as evidence in court?

Buried memories of childhood sex abuse often are "retrieved" through hypnosis. From its earliest days, however, hypnotism has been regarded with some skepticism in medical and legal circles. Opponents argue that hypnotized patients become unduly receptive to suggestion and thus may be made to "remember" events that never happened.

The AMA cautions: "With witnesses and victims, the use of hypnosis should be limited to the investigative process," and new information should be independently corroborated. "[W]hile the information may be accurate," the AMA notes, "it may also include confabulations [filling memory gaps with fantasy] and pseudomemories." [19]

Pamela Freyd, executive director of the FMSF, also questions other memory-enhancing exercises, such as guided imagery and relaxation techniques. "These things can put people into an almost trancelike state without their being totally aware of it," she says. "They become more suggestible. They stop doing their usual critical analysis of what's going on around them, and simply go with the flow."

The status of "hypnotically refreshed" recollection in criminal and civil trials is still unsettled. The first court decision on the issue was handed down by the California Supreme Court in 1897. Ruling in *People v. Ebanks,* the court refused to admit the testimony of a hypnotist who planned to relate statements made by the defendant while hypnotized.

The legal status of hypnosis remained essentially unchanged until 1968, when the Maryland Special Court of Appeals ruled in *Harding v. State* that hypnotically refreshed testimony was admissible. The case centered on the victim of a shooting and alleged rape who was hypnotized several weeks afterward in an effort to sharpen her recollection of the incident. The court said it had "no difficulty" accepting the woman's testimony, even though it may have been a blend of originally remembered and hypnotically refreshed recollection: "The fact that she had told different stories or had achieved her present knowledge after being hypnotized concerns the questions of the weight of the evidence which the trier of fact [the judge or the jury] . . . must decide."

Courts in other states, however, have remained wary of hypnosis. In *State v. Mack,* for instance, the Minnesota Supreme Court in 1980 refused to admit hypnotically refreshed testimony because "no expert can determine whether memory retrieved by hypnosis . . . is truth, falsehood or confabulation." Courts in several other states — including Maryland in 1983 — subsequently adopted the Minnesota position that hypnotically induced testimony was inadmissible.*

Memory-enhancing exercises, such as guided imagery and relaxation techniques, "can put people into an almost trancelike state without their being totally aware of it."

—Pamela Freyd, Executive Director False Memory Syndrome Foundation

Scheflin, a leading expert on hypnosis and the law, attributes the shift toward inadmissibility to the influence of researchers who argued in the 1970s that hypnosis not only had a confabulation effect but also a "concreting" effect — that is, memories recovered in hypnosis tend to become hard and unyielding. The impression grew, he says, that "people become unduly suggestible in hypnosis and therefore their memories are always contaminated." Moreover, the idea that hypnosis "will increase the amount of memories that you recover, but it can't separate truth from falsity" gained increasing acceptance. "The courts bought all of these arguments, and they still do," says Scheflin. "But almost every one of those arguments was made in the absence of supporting scientific studies."

The U.S. Supreme Court addressed hypnotically refreshed testimony in 1987 in *Rock v. Arkansas.* The case involved the manslaughter conviction of Vickie Lorene Rock, who had fatally shot her husband during an argument. Following her lawyer's advice, she underwent hypnosis to refresh her memory of the slaying. The prosecutor moved to exclude Rock's testimony, citing Arkansas' inadmissibility rule. The trial judge agreed, restricting the defendant's testimony to notes taken by the hypnotist before the first hypnosis session. Rock appealed her conviction on the ground that the limit placed on what she could say under oath violated her constitutional right, under the Sixth and 14th Amendments.

In its decision, the Supreme Court declared that a defendant's right to testify outweighed the state's interest in excluding possibly unreliable evidence. However, the court did not completely overturn the Arkansas rule. Instead, it ruled that, when the admissibility of hypnotically refreshed testimony is at issue, the trial court must apply a case-by-case test balancing a criminal defendant's right to testify against the state's interest in excluding unreliable testimony.

Thus, says Scheflin, *Rock* "dealt

* Some states will admit hypnotically refreshed testimony provided the hypnotist followed certain procedural guidelines before and during hypnosis.

with a very small question — as to whether a state could automatically exclude a criminal defendant's hypnotically refreshed recollection. And it said no, the state can't do that. But the state could still have an evidentiary hearing, which *Rock* requires, find the hypnosis unreliable and exclude it on that basis. So *Rock* didn't say that a defendant can always introduce hypnotically refreshed recollection, only that a state can't automatically . . . exclude it."

Quirk of the Alliance for Abuse Awareness feels that such rules on hypnotically refreshed testimony are difficult to support "because the reaction to hypnosis is extremely individual. Questions involving a person's memory — whether it's hypnotically refreshed or whatever — will vary depending on circumstances."

To put the *Rock* decision in perspective, Scheflin points out that "the amount of hypnosis done with criminal defendants is quite small. And in any event, there's reason to believe that a defendant's hypnotic statements that exonerate are not often believed by juries. Juries are very, very skeptical of that kind of evidence."

Hypnosis is "not like radar, where the jury will assume that the machine is infallible," he adds. "This is social science, where juries know there's a lot of slippage. In fact, the only study that I'm aware of on this point showed that juries were not only skeptical of hypnotically refreshed recollection introduced by prosecutors but also tended to discount the testimony of non-hypnotized witnesses who said the same thing."

At the same time, Scheflin says it's wrong "to say that memory is contaminated inevitably by hypnosis. Memory is fallible; that's the problem. Hypnosis can make it worse. But hypnosis can also be used effectively and neutrally in the recovery of memories that are historically accurate. And so the problem isn't with hypnosis, but how it's used." ■

BACKGROUND

Freud's Legacy

Child sex abuse was recognized as a serious social problem long before psychologists gained insight into the emotional damage it inflicted on its victims. Between 1730 and 1790, for example, 25 percent of the capital rape prosecutions at the Old Bailey, London's main criminal court, involved victims under 10 years old. And in France between 1858 and 1869, three-quarters of all accused rapists were charged with assaulting children. [20]

The first serious studies of sexual abuse and its aftereffects were conducted in the late 19th century by the French neurologist Jean-Martin Charcot and his students, notably Pierre Janet and Sigmund Freud. Their findings emerged from research into the nature of hysteria, a psychoneurosis marked by emotional excess or unmanageable fear.

"At that time," the American Psychological Association task force noted, "hysteria was viewed by the medical/neurological community as a highly problematic condition affecting mostly women and characterized by multiple and chronic physical complaints (that often defied medical diagnosis) in addition to numerous psychological symptoms." [21]

Working independently, Freud and Janet concluded that the physical symptoms of hysteria were psychological rather than products of bodily illness. Hysteria, in their view, was a condition of altered consciousness deployed as a defense mechanism against psychological trauma. Janet called the condition dissociation — the splitting off of a group of mental processes from the main body of consciousness for defensive purposes. Today, dissociation is often linked with multiple-personality disorder. (*See story, p. 584.*)

In 1896, Freud's research on hysteria took a fateful turn. "The ultimate cause of hysteria is always the seduction of a child by an adult," he wrote in *The Etiology of Hysteria*. "The actual event always occurs before the age of puberty, though the outbreak of the neurosis occurs after puberty. The symptoms of hysteria can only be understood if they are traced back to experiences which have a traumatic effect."

Before long, however, Freud abandoned his theory about the cause of hysteria. The reports of abuse that surface in therapy, he subsequently proposed, represent unfulfilled fantasies and wishes, not descriptions of actual events. These fantasies, Freud wrote in *The Interpretation of Dreams* (1899), often originate in a child's desire for sexual involvement with the parent of the opposite sex and in the concomitant sense of rivalry with the parent of the same sex. Although most children pass safely through this "Oedipus complex" period, Freud wrote, the presence of trauma (typically sexual) can trigger an "infantile neurosis" that may lead to similar reactions in adult life. In his view, an individual buries childhood sexual fantasies through repression — the expulsion from consciousness of painful or disagreeable ideas, memories, feelings or impulses.

Freud's repression model held sway in psychoanalytic psychology until the 1950s, when the issue of child sexual abuse again came to the fore. The landmark studies of human sexual behavior by Alfred C. Kinsey and his colleagues provided the first solid documentation of such abuse. However, the Kinsey team suggested in *Sexual Behavior in the Human Female* (1953) that "adult-child sexual contact" was potentially within the realm of normal childhood experience "and was therefore not particularly damaging." [22]

Continued on p. 588

Chronology

1890s *As the 19th century draws to a close, issues concerning child sexual abuse and memory claim increasing attention by the medical and legal professions.*

1896
In *The Etiology of Hysteria,* Sigmund Freud asserts that, "The ultimate cause of hysteria is always the seduction of a child by an adult." Three years later, in *The Interpretation of Dreams,* Freud abandons this hypothesis in favor of the "Oedipus Complex" — the sexual feelings that a child develops toward the parent of the opposite sex and that may lead to personality disorder in adulthood.

1897
Declaring that "the law of the United States does not recognize hypnotism," the California Supreme Court, in *People v. Ebanks,* refuses to admit testimony by a hypnotist detailing statements made by the defendant while in a hypnotic state.

1980s *Cases in which adults accuse their parents or other relatives of childhood sex abuse raise concern.*

June 1987
Ruling in *Rock v. Arkansas,* the U.S. Supreme Court strikes down an Arkansas law barring the use of hypnotically refreshed testimony because it infringes on the constitutional right of defendants to testify on their own behalf.

1988
The Courage to Heal, a controversial "survivor's manual" for adult victims of childhood sexual abuse, is published. One frequently cited passage advises, "If you don't remember your abuse, you are not alone. Many women don't have memories, and some never get memories."

1989
Washington becomes the first state to extend its statute of limitations for child-abuse cases.

1990s *As persons accused of child sexual abuse mount a counterattack on recovered memory, it becomes clear that the mental health and legal professions are divided on the question.*

1990
George Thomas Franklin is convicted of murdering Susan Nason, 8, in 1969. The verdict follows testimony by the defendant's adult daughter, Eileen, that she had a sudden recovered memory of seeing him abuse her childhood friend and kill her.

May 1992
The False Memory Syndrome Foundation is founded in Philadelphia by adults accused by family members of sexually abusing them during childhood.

December 1993
In a statement on recovered memories of child abuse, the American Psychiatric Association notes, "We are especially concerned that the public confusion and dismay over this issue and the possibility of false accusations not discredit the reports of patients who have indeed been traumatized by actual previous abuse."

May 13, 1994
A Napa County (Calif.) Superior Court jury awards $500,000 in damages to Gary Ramona, a former winery executive who accused two psychotherapists of implanting false memories of childhood sexual abuse in the mind of his adult daughter.

June 1994
The American Medical Association declares that it "considers recovered memories of childhood sexual abuse to be of uncertain authenticity, which should be subject to external verification."

October 1994
The National Center on Child Abuse and Neglect reports that "purported evidence for claims of ritualistic abuse, especially in cases involving alleged adult survivors of satanic cult activity, is questionable."

April 4, 1995
A U.S. District Court judge in San Francisco overturns George Franklin's 1990 conviction.

Feb. 14, 1996
The American Psychological Association warns that, "Controversies regarding adult recollections should not be allowed to obscure the fact that child sexual abuse is a complex and pervasive problem in America that has historically gone unacknowledged." But the panel adds that it is "possible to construct convincing pseudomemories for events that never occurred."

July 2, 1996
Prosecutors announce they will not retry George Franklin for the murder of his daughter's childhood friend.

Modern Theories

The 1960s ushered in the contemporary period of formal child-abuse studies. Initially, physical abuse occupied center stage, thanks largely to "The Battered Child Syndrome," an influential 1962 study. [23] Moreover, the reemergence of feminism around the same time prompted research into other forms of domestic violence, notably wife-beating.

Questions were being raised, meanwhile, about Freud's reasons for discarding the seduction theory in favor of the Oedipus complex. For instance, psychoanalyst Jeffrey M. Masson wrote in a much-noted 1984 book, *The Assault on Truth,* that Freud only retracted the seduction theory because his colleagues and the public at large recoiled from the idea that child sexual abuse was as prevalent as the theory implied. [24]

Today, the conviction that Freud was right the first time is a guiding precept of the recovered-memory movement. "Freud was simply unwilling to believe that so many fathers — possibly including his own — could abuse their children," wrote Ellen Bass and Laura Davis in *The Courage to Heal,* a "survivor's manual" for adult victims of childhood sexual abuse. "Freud's new theory was obviously more palatable to society and to the patriarchal profession in which he worked. . . . [H]e substituted Oedipal theory, thus turning the reality of abuse into a child's fantasy." [25]

Bass, a creative-writing teacher, and Davis, a member of one of her workshops, published their book in 1988. Since then, it has become one of the most widely read — and most controversial — works on recovered-memory therapy. Critics of the movement are quick to pounce on the book's sweeping statements, of which there are many. "If you don't remember your abuse, you are not alone," the authors assure their readers. "Many women don't have memories, and some never get memories. This doesn't mean they weren't abused." [26] On the other hand, "If you think you were abused and your life shows the symptoms, then you were." [27] They also are firm believers in the mind's repression process: "Forgetting is one of the most common and effective ways children deal with sexual abuse." [28]

Psychologist Loftus questions whether a person "can massively banish from conscious awareness a stream of horrific traumas and brutalization" and then recall the abuse later.

—Elizabeth F. Loftus
Professor of Psychology
University of Washington

Bass and Davis also offer tips to psychotherapists. "Recognize the symptoms of early sexual abuse," they advise. "If sexual abuse isn't the presenting problem but your client has eating disorders, an addiction to drugs or alcohol, suicidal feelings or sexual problems, these may be symptoms of sexual abuse." [29]

Most psychologists and psychiatrists reject the notion that any symptom or set of symptoms automatically affirms that a patient suffered childhood sexual abuse. Indeed, notes Scheflin, *The Courage to Heal* "was not written by licensed healers. And most licensed healers have not read it and do not follow it." He suspects that its actual target audience is "people who are non-licensed therapists."

Concept of Repression Challenged

According to Ofshe, the chief failing of Bass and Davis and other recovered-memory proponents is their insistence on "the validity of the concept of repression, the central mechanism of the theory." From Ofshe's perspective, "If repression is a valid concept, clients could be recovering long-hidden memories of abuse. If invalid, repression is nothing more than a pseudo-scientific smoke screen for treatment techniques that create false memories." [30]

Paul R. McHugh, director of the Department of Psychiatry and Behavioral Sciences at Johns Hopkins University, also is skeptical of claims that children repress memories of traumatic events. "In fact, severe traumas are not blocked out by children but remembered all too well," McHugh wrote. "They are amplified in consciousness, remaining like grief to be reborn and re-emphasized on anniversaries and in settings that can simulate the environments where they occurred." [31]

Harvard's Herman says the main virtue of her 1987 study with Schatzow is that it was the first one of its kind. Now, however, she regards it as "kind of obsolete . . . not nearly as sophisticated" as more recent studies. But she adds that the 1987 findings "have been borne out by everything that's been published since."

"I don't think people who are serious about the science are quibbling about the fact that some traumatized people have amnesia and delayed recall," she says. "The interesting questions now are, 'How come some people have it, but others don't? What brings the memories back? What's the psychophysiology of it, the biology of it?' From my perspective, those are the interesting scientific questions. But they're not very sexy from a controversy point of view."

A study by University of New Hampshire psychologist Linda M. Williams, published last October in the *Journal of Traumatic Stress,* reached conclusions similar to Herman and Schatzow's. Williams focused on 129 women in the same community who had documented histories of childhood sexual abuse dating from the early 1970s. Nearly two-thirds of the victims remembered the incidents 17 years later, though 16 percent of them had gone through periods in which they had no recollection of being abused.

Williams found that "The women who had recovered memories and those who had always remembered had the same number of discrepancies when their accounts of the abuse were compared to the reports from the early 1970s." To underscore the significance of this finding, Williams noted: "Because the abuse was documented in hospital and research records, this is the first study to provide evidence that some adults recall actual events which occurred in childhood. These findings also are not limited to a clinical sample of women in treatment for child sex abuse." In other words, not all the women were undergoing group therapy as were the 53 women in the Herman-Schatzow study.[32]

Loftus feels that the concept of repression — or, as some experts prefer to call it, amnesia or just plain forgetting — must be carefully defined before assessing its validity. "If you define it to mean, 'Something awful happens to you that you don't think about for a long time, and then something reminds you of it,' well, of course that kind of situation exists." But she questions whether a person "can massively banish from conscious awareness a stream of horrific traumas and brutalization" and then recall the abuse later.

Rise of FMS Foundation

The founding of the False Memory Syndrome Foundation in early 1992 heightened the longstanding controversy over repression. A series of columns that had appeared in the *Philadelphia Inquirer* starting in November 1991 provided the impetus. In them, columnist Darrell Sifford questioned "therapists who assume that their adult female patients may have been sexually abused as children." In many cases, he concluded, the abuse "apparently never happened."[33]

Although many *Inquirer* readers accused Sifford of casting doubt on the prevalence of child sexual abuse, he won plaudits from parents and family members claiming to have been falsely accused of such offenses. Scores of those families, plus professionals affiliated with the University of Pennsylvania and Johns Hopkins, were charter members of the FMSF.

Executive Director Freyd has firsthand knowledge of how allegations of child sex abuse can tear a family apart. In 1990, her daughter Jennifer, then a 33-year-old psychology professor at the University of Oregon, entered psychotherapy. Shortly afterward, she accused her father of sexually abusing her between the ages of 3 and 16. She also claimed that her mother had allowed the abuse to occur. Jennifer's charges led her and a younger sister to a complete break with their parents.

Doonesbury Flashbacks

BY GARRY TRUDEAU

The FMSF has attracted a broad following among persons accused of child sexual abuse, but it also has been dismissed by many mental-health professionals. "They're disrespectful," says David Spiegel, a psychiatry professor at Stanford University. "I think they're out to discredit the psychiatric profession."

Scheflin credits the FMSF for finding "legitimate fault in the way some people were doing therapy. But I think they overplayed their hand by taking an adversarial and hostile stance from the outset. If they had approached [mental health] organizations and said, 'Listen, we have unearthed a problem here, and something needs to be done about it,' all this would have been over by now. People would have moved together to correct the problem."

Instead, says Scheflin, "The false-memory people were immediately overtaken by the more extremist elements on their scientific [advisory] board. This led to such things as Ofshe's statement that robust repression never exists, which is not true."

Legal Climate Evolving

Court decisions and statutes, meanwhile, are constantly evolving, reflecting the intense disagreements over recovered memory. Starting with Washington in 1989, half the states have extended the statute of limitations in child sex-abuse cases. New Jersey's law, signed earlier this year, abolishes the statute of limitations for criminal sexual assault. Previously, homicide and manslaughter were the only two crimes for which the prosecution window never closed in the Garden State. The new law also provides that, in cases involving sexual-assault claimants under age 18, prosecutors may file charges before the victim's 23rd birthday "or within two years of the discovery of the offense by the victim, whichever is later." [34]

Many legal experts, though by no means all, expect the new state laws to trigger a wave of childhood sexual-abuse litigation by adult victims. Similarly, some commentators wondered whether the Supreme Court's 1987 ruling in *Rock v. Arkansas* would spark efforts to introduce hypnotically refreshed recollections into evidence in civil as well as criminal cases (*see p. 585*).

"We're now starting to get an answer to that question," reports Scheflin, "and it seems that the state will usually apply the same rule in civil cases that it applies in criminal cases. Of the 700 or 800 hypnosis cases that have been decided, only about 20 have dealt with civil litigation. The law in that area has focused almost entirely on the criminal scenario."

No recovered-memory case to date has received heavier media coverage than the 1990 murder conviction of retired California firefighter Franklin.

His daughter, Eileen, testified that she was in her father's van when he picked up her friend Susan near their homes. Then, she said, he drove to an isolated spot, molested Susan in the back of the van and smashed her skull with a rock. Eileen Franklin told the court her father threatened to kill her if she ever revealed what she had witnessed.

Until 1989, Eileen Franklin testified, she had lost all memory of the tragedy. Deputy District Attorney Elaine Tipton credited the "compelling nature of the evidence" that corroborated her testimony for sealing the guilty verdict. One key detail was Eileen Franklin's description of a ring that Susan had been wearing on the day of the murder.

Bill Hensel, who had been the lead detective in the case, later said that after Franklin's arrest he should have interviewed all the children in the neighborhood. If he had, he told a reporter, young Eileen might have told him what she knew. But now that Franklin had been apprehended, Hensel added, the case "will go to sleep. . . . There will be rest." [35] ■

CURRENT SITUATION

Key Legal Cases

Detective Hensel's confident forecast failed the test of time. In April 1995, Judge Lowell Jensen of U.S. District Court in San Francisco overturned Franklin's conviction on grounds unrelated to the recovered-memory issue. Jensen ruled that the prosecution had been improperly permitted to introduce evidence of a pretrial conversation in jail between Franklin and his daughter. At that time, she urged her father to "tell the truth" about the murder, and he made no reply. Jensen held that the prosecution should not have been allowed to argue that Franklin's silence was tantamount to an admission of guilt.

Jensen also ruled that the trial judge had erred in blocking Franklin's lawyers from introducing evidence showing that details of the murder related by his daughter under oath had been reported in the news media, including information about the ring Susan Nason was wearing when she was killed.

Franklin's retrial in San Mateo County Superior Court was to begin in September, but on July 2 prosecutors decided to drop the charges. Prosecutors said they still consider Franklin guilty. In fact, says Quirk of the National Alliance of Abuse Awareness, the state was expected to introduce evidence it was barred from presenting at the first trial: the extensive collection of child pornography and child paraphernalia that the defendant had in his possession when he was arrested.

But prosecutors said the disclosure that Franklin's daughter had been hypnotized by therapists before she testified in the first trial probably ruled out her testimony again, making a conviction problematical. The state Supreme Court has ruled that a previously hypnotized witness cannot testify because the reliability of hypnotically induced memory is questionable, and effective cross-examination is difficult. Prosecutors also said that new evidence showed that Franklin could not have committed a second murder his daughter said she also remembered him committing when she was 15.

Jury Awards $500,000 to Accused Father

A civil suit involving traumatic memories recovered during therapy drew almost as much media attention as the Franklin case. Gary Ramona, a 50-year-old former California winery executive, sought $8 million in damages from psychotherapists who he claimed had wrongly convinced his daughter, Holly, 23, that he had sexually abused her in childhood. A Napa County Superior Court jury agreed, 10-2, awarding him $500,000 on May 13, 1994.

During the two-month-long trial, Ramona said Marche Isabella, a licensed counselor, had told his daughter that the eating disorder bulimia, for which she had initially sought therapy, was usually triggered by incest or other sexual abuse. Ramona also charged that psychiatrist Richard Rose had questioned Holly after administering sodium amytal, a drug once regarded as a "truth serum" but now generally discredited by the medical profession as a therapeutic tool.

"The jury saw what I've always known," Ramona said after the trial, "that Holly's supposed memories are the result of the defendants' drugs and quackery, not anything I did." Psychology Professor Loftus said the verdict "demonstrates that juries are willing to listen to the evidence and come to the conclusion that therapists should be held accountable for engaging in risky and dangerous practices." [36]

But Scheflin said that if the verdict "had been appealed, it would have been reversed" because "the judge made several reversible errors."

There was no appeal, Scheflin says, because "the award was so low. It would have cost probably twice as much to appeal and get reversal. The insurance company no doubt reasoned, 'Hell, we're getting off cheap here. We would have had to pay more [than $500,000] through a settlement.'"

"The basic issue is that the patient must decide if [she is] willing to [risk] a form of treatment that everyone agrees is very controversial" when "safe and effective" alternatives are available.

—R. Christopher Barden lawyer and psychologist

In some cases, patients themselves have sued their therapists for malpractice. Last year, for instance, a jury in Ramsey County, Minn., awarded almost $2.7 million to Vynnette Hamanne and her husband after a six-week trial. It was the largest award yet made in such a case. Hamanne had accused her psychiatrist, Diane Bay Humenansky, of implanting false memories of childhood sexual abuse during therapy that sometimes included hypnosis or questioning under the influence of sodium amytal. The alleged molesters included Hamanne's parents, grandmother, uncles, neighbors and others. (*See story, p. 580.*)

R. Christopher Barden, the Minneapolis attorney and psychologist who represented Hamanne, claimed that Humenansky had failed to obtain the patient's informed consent before beginning an experimental mode of treatment. "The basic issue," he said, "is that the patient must decide if [she is] willing to [risk] a form of treatment that everyone agrees is very controversial" when "safe and effective" alternatives are available. "That's the bottom-line legal issue that everyone continues to miss." [37]

Courts Accept and Reject Recovered-Memory Testimony

Recent court rulings on the validity of recovered memories, however, display no consistent pattern. In May 1995, for example, Presiding Justice William J. Groff of Hillsborough County (N.H.) Superior Court held in two related assault cases that "the testimony of the victims as to their memory of the assaults shall not be admitted at trial because the phenomenon of memory repression, and the process of therapy used in these cases to recover the memories, have not gained general acceptance in the field of psychology, and are not scientifically reliable." [38]

Six months later, however, Justice Linda S. Dalianis of the same court ruled that the recovered memories at issue in another case were admissible as evidence. "Because the alleged victim's memories were recovered spontaneously rather than through any scientific process enabling her to retrieve the alleged memories, and because no evidence has been presented casting doubt upon the reliability of allegedly recovered memories in particular, any challenge to the victim's testimony shall go to its weight rather than to its admissibility." [39]

In yet another recent case, Judge Edward F. Harrington of U.S. District Court in Boston ruled May 8 that a plaintiff's repressed-memory evidence of sexual abuse that occurred more than 50 years ago could be admitted as evidence because "dissociative amnesia," the technical term for repressed memory, is listed in the current edition of the American Psychiatric Association's authoritative *Diagnostic and Statistical Manual of Mental Disorders.*

"[I]t is not the role of the court to rule on the credibility of this plaintiff's memories," Harrington ruled, "but rather on the validity of the theory itself." Moreover, it would be "folly" for the law "to reject a diagnostic category accepted by those who practice the art and science of psychiatry. . . . Rules of law are not petrified in the past but flow with the current of expanding knowledge." [40]

OUTLOOK

Few New Cases?

With opinion on the recovered-memory issue fractured so badly, it's hardly surprising that the two sides also differ on how the controversy will play itself out. In psychiatrist Ablow's opinion, "Truth prevails in the end. And since I don't feel that people fabricate trauma, the vast majority of these cases will prove to have some merit. There is no such thing as false-memory syndrome, in my opinion. And eventually, people will realize that."

Similarly, Scheflin believes the false-memory movement "will pass into history, as all things do. How soon or how far down the road that will be, is hard to tell. But I would say it is clear that the current scientific literature [on repressed memory] is disproving the hypotheses of the False Memory Syndrome Foundation's scientific board. I also believe that when the literature is evaluated in the future by people who are removed from the debate, the false-memory side will be shown to have been advocating pseudoscience."

> **"There is a developing awareness, among people who believe they have been sexually abused, that litigation is a very difficult course to follow."**
>
> ***—Sherry A. Quirk, President, National Alliance for Abuse Awareness***

At the same time, Scheflin is "hopeful" that "people who do what they call recovered-memory therapy will stop doing it. But precisely what it is they should stop doing is a matter of debate that I don't think is going to be resolved quickly."

In Ofshe's view, the shift to managed health care will result in less insurance coverage for recovered-memory therapy — indeed, for psychotherapy in general. "The whole [psychotherapy] industry has ridden the coattails of medicine by presenting itself as a health issue," he says. "By doing that, it has worked itself into a position of being funded by health-care insurance. This is what has fueled the tremendous expansion in the number of practitioners who are hanging out shingles and billing insurance companies for their services."

Attorney Barden feels that the best way to resolve the debate on recovered-memory therapy and other contentious issues in psychology and psychiatry is to improve the performance of clinicians. "The majority of mental-health professionals fail to learn the risks and benefits of the treatments they use," he contends. "They do an inadequate job of reading professional journals in their own field to learn about what alternative therapies are available for the conditions they're treating."

To correct the shortcomings he perceives, Barden has written model legislation called the Truth and Responsibility in Mental-Health Practices Act. A version of the bill passed this year by the Indiana legislature requires providers of mental-health-care services to obtain written consent from each patient in advance of treatment. The law also states that the consent "must include a statement that the patient is consenting only to those mental health services that the . . . provider is qualified to provide."

The model statute would also require "some documentation of [a mental-health treatment's] safety and effectiveness before public money is used to pay for it, and [require] that mental-health practitioners tell the truth when they testify in court about limitations" on their therapeutic methods. "It's a very non-controversial bill," Barden says, but many mental health professionals would take issue with that.

In any case, Barden is confident that more states will enact his bill, because "it gives a tremendous incentive to the

Continued on p. 594

At Issue:

Should child abuse be prosecuted decades after an alleged incident occurred?

PAULA L. BOLAND AND SHERRY A. QUIRK
Boland is a member of the California Legislature; Quirk is a Washington. D.C., lawyer and president of the National Alliance for Abuse Awareness

FROM *ABA JOURNAL*, SEPTEMBER 1994

yes

An estimated one in three to four females and one in six to eight males are sexually assaulted before they are 18 years old, according to some studies. Yet prosecuting these cases has until now been difficult, if not impossible.

In recent years, a number of states have passed laws that have extended, in some cases indefinitely, the statute of limitations for bringing charges against alleged perpetrators of sexual abuse. Some, however, argue that a short period of limitations would better protect the accused from having to face charges brought years later, possibly based on lost or unreliable evidence.

Individuals accused of sexual abuse who deny their guilt, and the "experts" hired for defense, claim that memories of sexual abuse are implanted by therapists and that they ultimately destroy families.

Recent professional research has revealed that many victims suffer amnesia of childhood sexual abuse, often into their adult years. Another study indicated that in cases of documented childhood sexual abuse, nearly half of the adult victims have no recall of the crime for some period of their lives.

Why do victims withhold information and fail to report these crimes to the proper authorities? Many children are frightened of their victimizers, and most are unaware that a crime has occurred at all. A study into causes of why victims did not disclose abuse revealed a multitude of reasons, such as fear of the perpetrator, fear of being blamed themselves and fear of the potential of breaking up the family unit.

As the rate of sexual abuse cases rises, we must take necessary steps to ensure protection of victims' rights. California has recently enacted legislation to reform the statute of limitations laws for child sexual abuse cases. Incidents of sexual abuse committed against children can now be prosecuted years later if clear and corroborating evidence is presented. Repressed memory is not a fantasy of the victim, but rather a vivid memory of a criminal action that should not go unpunished.

No persuasive argument exists for closing courts to adult survivors or in protecting pedophiles who clearly rape and molest more than one child in a short period of time. Actually, adult survivors are at a much better place to name their perpetrators and seek justice than are child victims. Our children are our most vulnerable segment of society, and the failure to address crimes against them is unconscionable.

ELIZABETH F. LOFTUS
***Professor of Psychology, University of Washington, and co-author,* The Myth of Repressed Memory**

FROM *ABA JOURNAL*, SEPTEMBER 1994

no

We live in a strange and precarious time that resembles at its heart the hysteria and superstitious fervor of the witch trials of the 16th and 17th centuries. Men and women are being accused, tried and convicted with no proof or evidence of guilt other than the word of the accuser.

Even when accusations involve numerous perpetrators, and inflict grievous wounds, the alleged victim's testimony is enough to make believers of some therapists, judges and juries. Individuals are being imprisoned on the "evidence" provided by memories that come back in dreams and flashbacks — memories that did not exist until a person sought therapy and was asked, "Were you ever sexually abused as a child?"

And thus begins the process of excavating the "repressed" memories through invasive therapeutic techniques such as age regression, guided visualization, trance writing, dream work, body work and hypnosis. Sadly, once the "memories" take hold, the clients are often encouraged to rip their families apart, engage in confrontations, or use the legal system to create untold misery for people around them.

What decades of memory research have shown, however, is that the techniques in question can seriously contaminate memories, and even create false memories in vulnerable minds. This growing body of psychological science shows that suggestions can become incorporated into a person's memory, along with dreams, imagination, fears and desires, and can alter that memory.

Suggestion is insidious — no one knows the extent to which it operates beneath the cover of authentic therapy. This is why the American Medical Association recently issued a policy statement saying "the use of recovered memories is fraught with problems of potential misapplication."

What should the legal system do when claims are based on "de-repressed memories" decades after some alleged acts? In some rare cases, the legal system might want to allow victims to use the justice system to bring their suits, regardless of the limits placed upon their actions by traditional statutes of limitations. But the cases should not go forward without full recognition of the rights of the mothers, fathers, teachers, neighbors and others who are being accused.

Given the outrage against defendants produced by even a hint of accusation involving child sexual abuse, I urge caution, at least until the whole subject of repressed memories and their authenticity receives better scientific support.

Evaluating Claims of Satanic Abuse

As readers of supermarket tabloids know all too well, accounts of satanic ritual abuse often accompany recovered memories of sexual molestation in childhood. "Hundreds of patients in therapy have related the same incredible stories of being born into multigenerational satanic cults, being abused and tortured at an early age, forced to partake in violent sexual rituals with black-hooded figures gathered around an altar, sacrificing animals and babies to Satan," author Eleanor Goldstein wrote in her 1994 book, *Confabulations: Creating False Memories, Destroying Families.* "The victims claim they were brainwashed and prevented from telling anyone because of terrible threats."

Many commentators have likened the flood of satanic-abuse claims to the witchcraft mania that swept Salem, Mass., in 1692. It began that spring, when a group of young women and girls who had been listening to the lurid tales of the local minister's elderly slave showed signs of hysteria. Before long, the "afflicted children" began to accuse various people in the community of bewitching them. They fell down in fits supposedly caused by the alleged witches, who were also accused of pinching them and sticking pins into them.

The community doctor could find no physical explanation for the childrens' condition, so the Rev. Samuel Parris summoned other ministers to confer on the matter. At length, local people became convinced that the children had fallen victim to the machinations of the devil. A special court to try the alleged witches was appointed by the governor, and between May and September several hundred persons were arrested. Nineteen of the accused were hanged (no accused witch was ever burned in Salem).

The frenzy lifted as swiftly as it had arrived. By early 1693, all those arrested had been released from confinement with or without trial, and the episode ended.

Are today's claims of ritual satanic abuse a replay of the mass hysteria that gripped Salem three centuries ago? A report issued in October 1994 by the National Center on Child Abuse and Neglect, an agency of the U.S. Department of Health and Human Services, could easily lead one to think so. Based on reports from across the nation by mental-health professionals, social workers, law-enforcement personnel and social service agencies, the survey covered 12,264 accusations of ritual abuse. [1]

The survey didn't find a single case with clear, corroborating evidence for the most common charge, that a "well-organized, intergenerational satanic cult" existed that "sexually molested and tortured children in their homes or schools for years and committed a series of murders," said Gail S. Goodman, the University of California-Davis psychologist who directed the study. [2]

But the very absence of corroboration for satanic abuse claims could create problems, the study suggested, noting that scientists and courts now "question the credibility of child and adult witnesses who make such allegations." Consequently, "there is increasing risk that actual victims of abuse, especially sexual abuse, will not be believed." [3]

Keith Russell Ablow, a psychiatrist at the Boston Regional Medical Center, cautions that reports of satanic abuse or alien abduction should be neither taken at face value nor dismissed out of hand.

"I view those reports as metaphors," he says. "I think that's the only way you can approach them. I would say to a patient making such a claim, 'It's within the realm of possibility, I suppose, that you were abducted by aliens. But I wonder if we can also entertain the possibility that you may have felt that way because you were with people who didn't respond to you as a human being, or who treated you as if you were part of a laboratory experiment.' I wouldn't tell the patient that in so many words, necessarily, but I'd try to have an alternative scenario emerge from our discussions."

---

[1] Gail S. Goodman, et al., "Characteristics and Sources of Allegations of Ritualistic Child Abuse" (final report to the National Center on Child Abuse and Neglect), October 1994.

[2] Quoted in *The New York Times*, Oct. 31, 1994, p. A13.

[3] Goodman, *op. cit.*, p. 3.

Continued from p. 592

mental health industry to improve the way it selects and uses new treatments. By focusing on science and empirical research, psychology and psychiatry and social-work treatments will begin to improve at a much more rapid pace." At present, he says, "outmoded treatments and psychological tests linger for decades, because the legal system and the health-care funding system are not enforcing the rules requiring the use of . . . treatments proven safe and effective by documented scientific research."

Despite all the interest in recovered memory, and despite changes in the statute of limitations, attorney Quirk foresees little change in the number of future cases. Extending the statute of limitations for such cases, she argues, "removes only one impediment to bringing this kind of lawsuit. It's still very difficult to prove to the satisfaction of a judge or a jury that sexual abuse occurred many years ago.

"Even today, many Americans find it hard to believe that these offenses occur. We see that attitude reflected not just in the decisions of judges and juries but in the reactions of lawyers asked to take on such a case.

"And really, it doesn't matter if the person has always remembered being sexually abused as a child or if she recovers memories of the abuse years later. It is almost out of the question that that person will go to court based solely on their own testimony and without corroboration — especially if the defendant is someone who looks very respectable."

Ultimately, Quirk adds, "There is a developing awareness, among people who believe they have been sexually abused, that litigation is a very difficult course to follow. It's not necessarily a healing experience, or a vindication, or a validation, as much as it is a wrenching ordeal.

"That realization, I think, will chill many people from going to court — maybe even in instances where they have excellent proof that they were abused. Litigation is something to be approached with great caution." ■

FOR MORE INFORMATION

American Psychiatric Association, 1400 K St. N.W., Washington, D.C. 20005; (202) 682-6083. The association promotes the availability of high-quality psychiatric care, provides the public with information and publishes the authoritative reference work *Diagnostic and Statistical Manual of Mental Disorders*.

American Psychological Association, 750 First St. N.E., Washington, D.C. 20002-4242; (202) 336-5500. The association works toward improving the qualifications, training programs and competence of psychologists. It also monitors federal legislation on mental health issues.

False Memory Syndrome Foundation, 3401 Market St., Suite 130, Philadelphia, Pa. 19104; (215) 387-1865. The foundation seeks to help persons accused by family members of childhood sexual abuse on the basis of long-repressed memories that allegedly surfaced during psychotherapy.

National Alliance for Abuse Awareness, P.O. Box 27958, Washington, D.C. 20038-7958; (202) 667-1160. The alliance "seeks to improve the quality of life for children and adult survivors of incest and sexual abuse, physical abuse and emotional abuse."

Notes

[1] For background, see "Child Sexual Abuse," *The CQ Researcher,* Jan. 15, 1993, pp. 25-48.

[2] See "Pursuing the Paranormal," *The CQ Researcher,* March 29, 1996, pp. 265-288.

[3] Judith Lewis Herman and Emily Schatzow, "Recovery and Verification of Memories of Childhood Sexual Trauma," *Journal of Psychoanalytic Psychology,* Vol. 4, No. 1, 1987, pp. 1-2.

[4] False Memory Syndrome Foundation, "Frequently Asked Questions," September 1995, p. 10. Almost 90 percent of the child-abuse suits reported to the group are civil suits.

[5] Richard Ofshe and Ethan Watters, "Making Monsters," *Society,* March/April 1993, pp. 15-16. *Society* is a social science and public policy journal published by Rutgers University.

[6] American Psychological Association, "Questions and Answers About Memories of Childhood Abuse," August 1995.

[7] American Psychological Association, "Working Group on Investigation of Memories of Childhood Abuse: Final Report," Feb. 14, 1996, p. 6.

[8] Elizabeth Loftus and Katherine Ketcham, *The Myth of Repressed Memory* (1994), pp. 2-3.

[9] False Memory Syndrome Foundation, *op. cit.,* p. 15.

[10] Herman and Schatzow, *op. cit.,* pp. 10-11.

[11] Richard Ofshe and Ethan Watters, *Making Monsters: False Memories, Psychotherapy, and Sexual Hysteria* (1994), p. 312.

[12] John G. Watkins, "Dealing With the Problem of 'False Memory' in Clinic and Court," *The Journal of Psychiatry and Law,* fall 1993, pp. 305-306.

[13] *Ibid.,* pp. 301-302.

[14] Ofshe and Watters, *Society, op. cit.,* p. 11.

[15] Paula L. Boland and Sherry A. Quirk, "Repressed Memories," *ABA Journal,* September 1994, p. 42.

[16] American Psychiatric Association, policy statement, "Memories of Sexual Abuse," April 1994, pp. 1-2.

[17] *Ibid.,* p. 3.

[18] American Psychological Association, "Working Group," *op. cit.,* p. 1.

[19] American Medical Association, "Council on Scientific Affairs, Report K," 1984.

[20] One Voice: the National Alliance for Abuse Awareness, "Awareness of Child Sex Abuse: A Brief Time Line," April 5, 1996.

[21] American Psychological Association, "Working Group," *op. cit.,* p. 18.

[22] *Ibid.,* p. 20.

[23] Henry C. Kempe, et al., "The Battered Child Syndrome," *Journal of the American Medical Association,* Vol. 181, No. 1, 1962, pp. 17-24.

[24] Ofshe and Watters, *Making Monsters, op. cit.,* p. 291.

[25] Ellen Bass and Laura Davis, *The Courage to Heal* (1988), p. 347.

[26] *Ibid.,* p. 81.

[27] *Ibid.,* p. 22.

[28] *Ibid.,* p. 42.

[29] *Ibid.,* p. 349.

[30] Ofshe and Watters, *Society, op. cit.* p. 5.

[31] Paul R. McHugh, "Psychiatric Misadventures," *The American Scholar,* autumn 1992, p. 508.

[32] Linda M. Williams, "Recovered Memories of Abuse in Women With Documented Child Sexual Victimization Histories," *Journal of Traumatic Stress* (special issue: "Research on Traumatic Memory"), October 1995, p. 670.

[33] Darrell Sifford, "When Tales of Sex Abuse Aren't True," *Philadelphia Inquirer,* Jan. 5, 1992.

[34] False Memory Syndrome Foundation, "FMS Foundation Newsletter," May 1996, p. 3.

[35] Quoted in *Los Angeles Times,* Dec. 1, 1990, p. A38.

[36] Quoted in Mark Hansen, "More False Memory Suits Likely," *ABA Journal,* August 1994, p. 36.

[37] Quoted in Michael Jonathan Grinfeld, "Psychiatrist Stung by Huge Damage Award in Repressed-Memory Case," *Psychiatric Times,* October 1995, p. 1.

[38] From Judge Groff's ruling in *New Hampshire v. Hungerford* and *New Hampshire v. Morahan,* May 23, 1995.

[39] *New Hampshire v. Walters,* Nov. 21, 1995.

[40] *Shahzade v. Gregory,* May 8, 1996.

Bibliography

Selected Sources Used

Books

Bass, Ellen, and Laura Davis, *The Courage to Heal*, Harper & Row, 1988

Bass, a creative-writing teacher, and Davis, a participant in one of Bass' workshops, authored one of the central — and most controversial — texts of the recovered-memory movement. "The human mind has tremendous powers of repression," they write.

Goldstein, Eleanor, with Kevin Farmer, *Confabulations: Creating False Memories, Destroying Families*, Upton Books, 1994.

Psychotherapists, says Goldstein, "must develop a code of ethics which recognizes that accused parents have rights, that repressed memories are not always valid, and that books, tapes and seminars that are programmed for specific objectives are improper tools for psychotherapy."

Loftus, Elizabeth, and Katherine Ketcham, *The Myth of Repressed Memory*, St. Martin's Press, 1994.

Loftus, a University of Washington psychologist and member of the False Memory Syndrome Foundation's scientific and professional advisory board, stresses the fragility and changeability of one's recollections of the past.

Ofshe, Richard, and Ethan Watters, *Making Monsters: False Memory, Psychotherapy and Sexual Hysteria*, Charles Scribner's Sons, 1994.

Recovered-memory therapy, the authors write, "illustrates how easily the 'science' of psychotherapy changes to confirm our society's current phobias and beliefs."

Articles

Gill, Charles D. Jr., "The Admissibility of Hypnotically Refreshed Testimony: *Rock v. Arkansas*," *Boston College Law Review*, March 1989.

Gill comments on the implications of a June 1987 U.S. Supreme Court decision that struck down an Arkansas rule excluding a criminal defendant's hypnotically refreshed testimony as unconstitutional.

Herman, Judith Lewis, and Emily Schatzow, "Recovery and Verification of Memories of Childhood Sexual Trauma," *Journal of Psychoanalytic Psychology*, Vol. 4, No. 1, 1987.

This study, often cited over the past decade to support the validity of recovered memories, reports that three-fourths of 53 women patients who underwent individual and group therapy for childhood sex abuse "were able to validate their memories by obtaining corroborating evidence from other sources."

Pope, Harrison G. Jr., and James I. Hudson, "Can Memories of Childhood Sexual Abuse Be Repressed?" *Psychological Medicine*, Vol. 25, 1995, pp. 121-126.

Pope and Hudson, psychiatrists at Harvard Medical School, conclude that "present clinical evidence is insufficient to permit the conclusion that individuals can suppress memories of childhood sexual abuse."

Watkins, John G., "Dealing With the Problem of 'False Memory' in Clinic and Court," *The Journal of Psychiatry and Law*, fall 1993.

Watkins, a past president of the Society for Clinical and Experimental Hypnosis, reviews the main points at issue in the "false memory" debate and concludes, "The challenge now to researchers is to find ways of distinguishing verifiable from fantasized or contaminated memories."

Williams, Linda M., "Recovered Memories of Abuse in Women With Documented Child Sexual Victimization Histories," *Journal of Traumatic Stress*, October 1995.

Williams reports the results of interviews with 80 women conducted 17 years after they had experienced childhood sexual abuse. "Because the abuse was documented in hospital and research records, this is the first study to provide evidence that some adults who claim to have recovered memories of child sexual abuse recall actual events which occurred in childhood."

Reports and Studies

American Psychological Association, *Working Group on Investigation of Memories of Childhood Abuse: Final Report*, Feb. 14, 1996.

A collection of articles expressing different points of view on recovered memory. "When clients report . . . memories of previous unrecollected trauma," the introduction says, "therapists should take a number of steps to avoid imposing a particular version of reality on these experiences and to reduce risks of the creation of pseudomemories."

Goodman, Gail S., et al., *Characteristics and Sources of Allegations of Ritualistic Child Abuse* (final report to the National Center on Child Abuse and Neglect), 1994.

Goodman, a psychologist at the University of California-Davis, and her fellow researchers find scant corroboration for reports that American children are subjected to "satanic or ritualistic abuse." As a result, they voice concern that "actual victims of abuse, especially sexual abuse, will not be believed."

The Next Step

Additional information from UMI's Newspaper & Periodical Abstracts database

False Memory Syndrome

Berger, Louis S., "Cultural psychopathology and the "false memory syndrome" debates: A view from psychoanalysis," *American Journal of Psychotherapy,* spring 1996, pp. 167-177.
The typical "false memory syndrome" debates assume that clinicians must establish whether a recovered memory of abuse is objectively true. Berger criticizes that assumption from three psychoanalytic perspectives and proposes that it reflects a pervasive underlying societal psychopathology.

Boakes, Janet, "False memory syndrome," *Lancet,* Oct. 21, 1995, p. 982.
False memory syndrome threatens to undermine the credibility of the psychotherapy profession. This syndrome describes the "recovery" of vivid memories of events that did not take place.

Brashler, Bill, "A daughter calls, a family is still divided," *Chicago Tribune,* Feb. 26, 1995, p. 13.
Kristin Vance, who accused her parents, Ralph and Joanne Vance, of sexually abusing her when she was a toddler, reestablished contact with her parents after three and one-half years, though she hasn't recanted her memories. Ralph Vance, who was featured in the *Tribune's* Feb. 27, 1994, magazine, is working on a book and is involved in the False Memory Syndrome Foundation, a national organization of those who have been similarly accused.

Lattin, Don, "Careful guide in dispute on false memory," *San Francisco Chronicle,* Aug. 14, 1995, p. A2.
The American Psychological Association, attempting to calm the controversy over child sexual abuse, psychotherapy and human memory, has issued a cautious set of guidelines for families wondering how to investigate claims of childhood mistreatment remembered later in life.

"You must remember this," *Guardian,* June 29, 1995, p. 15.
The correspondence of several Britons to the Guardian, in which they discuss their experiences with childhood sexual abuse and the possibility of False Memory Syndrome, is detailed.

Psychotherapy and Memory

Levin, Kenneth, "Unconscious fantasy in psychotherapy," *American Journal of Psychotherapy,* spring 1996, pp. 137-153.
In recent years, writers representing virtually all schools of psychoanalysis have given unconscious fantasy a more prominent place in their theories of psychodynamics and psychotherapy. Levin discusses some of the reasons for this and reviews the perspectives offered in these reconsiderations of unconscious fantasy.

Martinez-Taboas, Alfonso, "Repressed memories: Some clinical data contributing toward its elucidation," *American Journal of Psychotherapy,* spring 1996, pp. 217-230.
Two well-documented cases of patients with the diagnosis of dissociative identity disorder (DID) that presented unique opportunities to verify by independent means some abusive experiences suffered in childhood are presented.

Neimark, Jill, "The diva of disclosure," *Psychology Today,* January 1996, pp. 48-52.
Psychologist Elizabeth Loftus is profiled. Loftus is an expert on the malleability of memory, but her work has made her a villain to some, especially as it relates to child abuse.

Parks, Evan D., and Richard Balon, "Autobiographical memory for childhood events: Patterns of recall in psychiatric patients with a history of alleged trauma," *Psychiatry,* August 1995, pp. 199-208.
Parks and Balon investigated the relationship between early trauma and memory for childhood events in adult psychiatric patients. The findings suggest that patients with an alleged history of trauma have a measurably different pattern of recall of early events than patient and non-patient comparison groups.

Poole, Debra A., Amina Memon, Stephen D. Lindsay and Ray Bull, "Psychotherapy and the recovery of memories of childhood sexual abuse: U.S. and British practitioners' opinions, practices, and experiences," *Journal of Consulting & Clinical Psychology,* June 1995, pp. 426-437.
Licensed U.S. doctoral-level psychotherapists randomly sampled from the National Register of Health Service Providers to Psychology and British psychologists sampled from the Register of Chartered Clinical Psychologists were surveyed regarding clients' memories of childhood sexual abuse.

Shapiro, David, "Character and psychotherapy," *American Journal of Psychotherapy,* winter 1996, pp. 3-13.
Psychoanalytic theory of psychopathology began as a theory of particular pathogenic agents in the form of repressed memories or drive-generated fantasies. It has developed in the direction of a theory of the mind's

organization—that is, a theory of character pathology.

Recovered/Repressed Memories

Bower, Bruce, "Trauma survey delves into delayed recall," *Science News,* Aug. 26, 1995, p. 135.

Research into the delayed recall of traumatic events by the sexes is examined. A recent survey found that a substantial minority of both sexes who had survived a range of severe traumas reported having had episodes of partial or complete memory loss due to their experiences.

Genoni, Tom Jr., "The AMA issues policy on recovered memories," *Skeptical Inquirer,* January 1995, p. 6.

The American Medical Association (AMA) has issued a statement about its policy concerning recovered memories. The AMA deems that the technique of "memory enhancement" in the area of childhood sexual abuse is potentially very dangerous.

Haaken, Janice, "The debate over recovered memory of sexual abuse: A feminist-psychoanalytic perspective," *Psychiatry,* May 1995, pp. 189-198.

A feminist-psychoanalytic analysis of the debate over the veracity of memories of sexual abuse recovered in treatment is offered. The jettisoning of the idea of fantasy in much of the clinical literature on sexual abuse has contributed to a deification of memory and a sacrifice of complexity in the clinical elaboration of women's abuse experiences.

Hayes, Monica L., "The necessity of memory experts for the defense in prosecutions for child sexual abuse based upon repressed memories," *American Criminal Law Review,* fall 1994, pp. 69-85.

Many states have adopted statutes that have opened the door to prosecution of alleged sexual abusers based on repressed memories of childhood sexual abuse recovered many years after the incident. Hayes argues that defendants charged with this crime, based on repressed memories, must be provided with certain procedural safeguards.

Neimark, Jill, "It's magical. It's malleable. It's ... memory," *Psychology Today,* January 1995, pp. 44-49.

Research psychologist Elizabeth Loftus experienced firsthand the myths of repressed memory. The creative blending and reblending of experience and emotion creates memories that provide a sense of self.

Pendergrast, Mark, "Remembering the past: A new chapter in the old story of women and oppression," *Omni,* February 1995, p. 6.

Although there exists no evidence that supports the theory that humans can completely forget years of abuse, many women are being coerced by psychiatrists by recovered-memory therapy (RMT) to create imagined abuse. The dangers that RMT poses to the feminist movement are discussed.

Pope, Harrison G. Jr., and James I. Hudson, "Recovered memory therapy for eating disorders: Implications of the Ramona verdict," *International Journal of Eating Disorders,* March 1996, pp. 139-145.

Recovered-memory therapy for eating disorders and other psychiatric conditions seeks to help the patient recover repressed memories of childhood sexual abuse and other traumatic experiences. However, this method was questioned in the recent Ramona case, where a father successfully sued two therapists and a hospital for allegedly implanting false memories of childhood sexual abuse in his bulimic daughter.

Robbins, Susan P., "Wading through the muddy waters of recovered memory," *Families in Society: The Journal of Contemporary Human Services,* October 1995, pp. 478-489.

Robbins reviews the professional debate about recovered memories of childhood sexual abuse and addresses conceptual errors, unwarranted assumptions and factual inaccuracies in Benatar's essay "Running Away from Sexual Abuse: Denial Revisited" in the May 1995 *Families in Society.*

Shaeffer, Robert, "Recovered memories cross the oceans," *Skeptical Inquirer,* July 1995, pp. 10-11.

The American practice of "recovering memories" of unspeakable abuse is in vogue in a number of other countries. Some incidents of ritual abuse and Satanism that have been reported in the U.K., Canada and the U.S. are discussed.

Young, Allan, "Suffering and the origins of traumatic memory," *Daedalus,* winter 1996, pp. 245-260.

Traumatic memory is a variety of memory that began to be investigated in the late 19th century. Young discusses the history of embodied traumatic memory.

Repressed Memory Syndrome and Litigation

Bowman, Cynthia Grant, and Elizabeth Mertz, "A dangerous direction: Legal intervention in sexual abuse survivor therapy," *Harvard Law Review,* January 1996, pp. 549-639.

Bowman and Mertz question recent popular and academic commentary that disputes the validity of all delayed-recall memories of childhood sexual abuse. They examine one court's decision to allow a father, accused by his daughter of childhood sexual abuse, to recover malpractice damages from his daughter's therapist in connection with therapy during which the daughter recovered memories of the abuse.

Freedman, Eric, "Fate of women's sex abuse charges rests with high court," *Detroit News,* Jan. 11, 1995, p. B4.

The Michigan Supreme Court will consider whether to let Marlene Lemmerman and Gale Williford pursue civil suits stemming from decades-old allegations. The validity and reliability of "repressed memories " of childhood sexual abuse is a question confronting courts countrywide.

Gorman, Christine, "Memory on trial," ***Time,*** **April 17, 1995, pp. 54-55.**

In a closely watched case, Judge William J. Groff will rule on the credibility of witnesses who repress and then remember incidents of rape, incest and murder. In recent years, thousands of Americans, with the help of psychotherapy, have recalled bad memories of crimes.

"Judge overturns conviction based on recovered memories," ***Skeptical Inquirer,*** **September 1995, p. 8.**

U.S. District Judge Lowell Jensen overturned the conviction of George Franklin, a man whose daughter testified that she now remembers him killing her playmate 20 years ago. Franklin was the subject of the first criminal prosecution based on "recovered-memory" testimony.

Milne, John, "Judge bars repressed-memory testimony in sex-abuse cases," ***Boston Globe,*** **May 26, 1995, p. 27.**

New Hampshire Judge William J. Groff has barred testimony from victims in sexual abuse cases who believe they have recovered long-lost memories through psychotherapy .

Pankratz, Howard, "Defense: Memories not false," ***Denver Post,*** **Oct. 17, 1995, p. B1.**

Therapist Beverly Nussbaumer never planted false memories of childhood sexual abuse in the mind of patient Jane Brennan, a defense attorney told a Denver jury on Oct. 16, 1995. Rather, Brennan told Nussbaumer that her father sexually abused her. Brennan is suing Nussbaumer for planting false memories of sexual abuse.

Rakowsky, Judy, "Memory expert supports woman," ***Boston Globe,*** **April 10, 1996, p.26.**

An expert on memory and trauma told a federal judge April 9, 1996 that Ann Shahzade, 68, of Falmouth, Mass., suffers from repressed memory brought on by childhood sexual abuse. Shahzade has sued her older cousin, George Gregory, for molesting her over 50 years ago.

Tatone, Kathy A., "Sexual abuse litigation: Opportunities and obstacles," ***Trial,*** **February 1995, pp. 66-71.**

Sexual abuse cases present a formidable mix of legal and psychological issues. Statutes of limitations, doubts about recovered memories and limits on insurance coverage present challenges for lawyers representing clients devastated by childhood sexual abuse.

Weidlich, Thom, "Repressed memories: Unreliable?" ***National Law Journal,*** **June 12, 1995, p. A7.**

Judges in four cases — two civil, two criminal — have ruled that testimony based on so-called repressed memories cannot be admitted in evidence because scientists say there is no evidence that such recollections are reliable.

Wexler, David B., "Therapeutic jurisprudence in clinical practice," ***American Journal of Psychiatry,*** **April 1996, pp. 453-455.**

Therapeutic jurisprudence is the study of the role of law as a therapeutic agent. Paul Appelbaum and Rose Zoltek-Jick engaged in therapeutic jurisprudence in their analysis of the *Ramona v. Ramona* case, in which a California trial court allowed a father to sue his daughter's therapists for damage caused him by their negligently implanting or reinforcing false memories regarding childhood sexual abuse by him.

Sexual Abuse

Beckett, Katherine, "Culture and the politics of signification: The case of child sexual abuse," ***Social Problems,*** **February 1996, pp. 57-76**

An analysis demonstrates that the framing of one "valence" issue — child sexual abuse — in media discourse has undergone significant transformation. The ability of social actors to contest the construction of this issue highlights the complex and contradictory nature of culture.

Benatar, May, "Running away from sexual abuse: Denial revisited," ***Families in Society: The Journal of Contemporary Human Services,*** **May 1995, pp. 315-320.**

After a period of increased professional and public awareness of how pervasive the sexual maltreatment of children is in society, it now appears that the hard-won insights into this major public health issue are in danger of being forgotten. Social, legal, political and psychological pressures are undermining all that has been learned about the etiology and sequelae of this devastating societal problem.

Bower, Bruce, "Child sex abuse leaves mark on brain," ***Science News,*** **June 3, 1995, p. 340.**

Two recent independent studies that found that severe, uninterrupted sexual abuse in childhood underlies damage to the hippocampus, which helps orchestrate memory, are discussed. Scientists are still trying to determine the point at which this neural loss takes place.

Bullough, Vern L., "Catholic priests and adult-child sexual interaction," ***Free Inquiry,*** **summer 1995, pp. 9-10.**

Until recently, the Catholic Church tried to cover up cases in which priests had sexual interaction with children. A priest's isolation from society is one of the main causes of the problem.

Monahan, Matthew G., "View from a pew," ***America,*** **March 2, 1996, p. 7.**

Monahan discusses three cases of alleged sexual abuse by Catholic priests. He disagrees with the Roman Catholic Church's policy of silence on the issue and claims it hurts the church's credibility.

Stein, Harry, "Our times: Do TV reports on sexual abuse reflect progress?" ***TV Guide,*** **April 8, 1995, p. 53.**

Stein discusses "Divided Memories," a "Frontline" two-parter on the current vogue in "repressed memories" in childhood sexual abuse, and a "20/20" story on the outbreak of molestation charges lodged against school teachers. He wonders whether the growing panic and suspicion surrounding child molestation really constitutes progress.

Back Issues

Great Research on Current Issues Starts Right Here...Recent topics covered by The CQ Researcher are listed below. Before May 1991, reports were published under the name of Editorial Research Reports.

DECEMBER 1994
Farm Policy
Arms Sales
Earthquake Research
The Future of Television

JANUARY 1995
Treating Addiction
Child Custody and Support
Parents and Schools
Non-Proliferation Treaty at 25

FEBRUARY 1995
Cracking Down on Immigration
The Business of Sports
Reinventing Government
Housing Discrimination

MARCH 1995
Death Penalty Debate
Primary Care
Democracy in Africa
Environmental Movement at 25

APRIL 1995
Abortion Clinic Protests
Dieting and Health
Combating AIDS
Rethinking Affirmative Action

MAY 1995
Assisted Suicide Controversy
Overhauling Social Security
Learning to Read
Mandatory Sentencing

JUNE 1995
Combating Infectious Disease
Property Rights
Repetitive Stress Injuries
Regulating the Internet

JULY 1995
War Crimes
Highway Safety
Combating Terrorism
Preventing Teen Drug Use

AUGUST 1995
Job Stress
Organ Transplants
United Nations at 50
Advances in Cancer Research

SEPTEMBER 1995
Catholic Church in the U.S.
Northern Ireland Cease-Fire
High School Sports
Teaching History

OCTOBER 1995
Quebec's Future
Revitalizing the Cities
Networking the Classroom
Indoor Air Pollution

NOVEMBER 1995
The Working Poor
The Jury System
Sex, Violence and the Media
Police Misconduct

DECEMBER 1995
Teens and Tobacco
Gene Therapy's Future
Global Water Shortages
Third-Party Prospects

JANUARY 1996
Emergency Medicine
Punishing Sex Offenders
Bilingual Education
Helping the Homeless

FEBRUARY 1996
Reforming the CIA
Campaign Finance Reform
Academic Politics
Getting Into College

MARCH 1996
The British Monarchy
Preventing Juvenile Crime
Tax Reform
Pursuing the Paranormal

APRIL 1996
Centennial Olympic Games
Managed Care
Protecting Endangered Species
New Military Culture

MAY 1996
Russia's Political Future
Marriage and Divorce
Year-Round Schools
Taiwan, China and the U.S.

JUNE 1996
Rethinking NAFTA
First Ladies
Teaching Values
Labor Movement's Future

Back issues are available for $5.00 (subscribers) or $8.00 (non-subscribers). Quantity discounts apply to orders over ten. To order, call Congressional Quarterly Customer Service at (202) 887-8621.

Binders are available for $18.00. To order call 1-800-638-1710. Please refer to stock number 648.

Future Topics

- ***Native Americans at a Crossroads***
- ***Sexual Harassment Update***
- ***Animal Rights Debate***

THE CQ Researcher

PUBLISHED BY CONGRESSIONAL QUARTERLY INC.

Native Americans' Future

Do U.S. policies block opportunities for progress?

American Indians have the highest unemployment, poverty and disease rates of any ethnic group in the country. Yet Indian leaders say Americans are indifferent to their plight, as reflected in recent funding cuts for Indian programs. Congressional budget-cutters argue that Indians should share the burden of balancing the federal budget, but Indian advocates say aid programs for Indians are cited — and protected — in scores of treaties between tribes and the federal government. Many tribes see the key to their survival in economic development fueled by revenues from gambling. But Indian advocates say that mounting efforts to curtail their casino operations and other moves toward self-determination are only the latest in a long history of violations of Indian sovereignty guaranteed in the Constitution.

INSIDE THIS ISSUE

CQ July 12, 1996 • Volume 6, No. 26 • Pages 601-624

Formerly Editorial Research Reports

NATIVE AMERICANS' FUTURE

COVER: BARBARA SASSA-DANIELS

July 12, 1996
Volume 6, No. 26

EDITOR
Sandra Stencel

MANAGING EDITOR
Thomas J. Colin

ASSOCIATE EDITORS
Sarah M. Magner
Richard L. Worsnop

STAFF WRITERS
Charles S. Clark
Mary H. Cooper
Kenneth Jost

EDITORIAL ASSISTANT
Tonya Harris

PUBLISHED BY
Congressional Quarterly Inc.

CHAIRMAN
Andrew Barnes

VICE CHAIRMAN
Andrew P. Corty

EDITOR AND PUBLISHER
Neil Skene

EXECUTIVE EDITOR
Robert W. Merry

The CQ Researcher (ISSN 1056-2036). Formerly Editorial Research Reports. Published weekly (48 times per year, not printed March 1, May 31, Aug. 30, Nov. 29) by Congressional Quarterly Inc., 1414 22nd St., N.W., Washington, D.C. 20037. Annual subscription rate for libraries, businesses and government is $319. Additional rates furnished upon request. Periodicals postage paid at Washington, D.C. POSTMASTER: Send address changes to The CQ Researcher, 1414 22nd St., N.W., Washington, D.C. 20037.

Native Americans' Future

BY MARY H. COOPER

THE ISSUES

To the somber thump of a cottonwood drum, eight young men and women filed into the dusty schoolyard. The men's bodies were striped with paint, red ocher symbolizing the blood of the Earth, white to ward off evil spirits. The men wore headdresses with majestic rams' horns, the women colorful dresses. Facing North, South East and West, they began dancing to the rasp of gourd rattles and the drum's slow cadence.

For centuries, the Havasupai Indians of northwest Arizona have performed the ram dance to conduct the spirits of their dead relatives to the next world. But today the sacred ceremony has become more than just a funeral rite. It is a vital teaching tool in the 650-member tribe's fight for cultural survival. On a recent afternoon, the dancers performed for a hushed audience of children and elders alike. Afterwards, everyone, including a non-Indian visitor, joined hands in a circle dance for peace.

"We use any occasion we can to dance before our tribe because our customs and language will die with us if we don't teach them to the next generation," says Matthew Putesoy, a dancer and member of the tribal council. "People from other tribes are surprised when they hear our kids speak because their kids speak English only. Our young people all speak Havasupai."

The Havasupais' concerns are shared by American Indians across the country. "I wasn't raised on the 'rez,' so I don't speak the language except for a few words," says Sen. Ben Nighthorse Campbell, R-Colo., a Northern Cheyenne and the only Native American in Congress. "But most tribes are trying to record their songs or dances and compiling dictionaries to preserve their languages."

To many observers, economic survival is an even more pressing concern for the country's 2.1 million Indians. They not only have the highest unemployment and poverty rates of any group in the United States but also the nation's worst disease rate. (*See story, p. 608.*)

But Americans seem indifferent to their plight, Indian leaders say, pointing to recent cuts in funding for the Bureau of Indian Affairs (BIA), which operates most housing, education and welfare programs on reservations. Even with the nation's Indian population growing at some 4 percent annually in recent years, Congress cut funding for Indian programs by $160 million in fiscal 1996, down 9 percent from BIA's $1.7 billion 1995 budget. And while President Clinton proposed restoring the 1995 spending levels for fiscal 1997, House and Senate budget committees have recommended even deeper cuts for BIA — as much as $193 million below the 1995 level. These cuts follow a 20-year decline in funding for Indian affairs. [1]

"American Indians have always been underfunded and shortchanged," says Ada E. Deer, a member of Wisconsin's Menominee tribe, who as assistant Interior secretary for Indian affairs heads the BIA. "This country was built on the land and the resources that were ceded to the government by the tribes. If the tribes had been allowed to develop in a more just way, we would not have some of the problems we have. But Congress doesn't understand or acknowledge the obligation of this country to the native peoples. This country can send a man to the moon, and we're talking about spending billions of dollars for space programs. We should be able to invest a few billion more in Indian tribes to address this historic injustice."

Congressional budget-cutters say Indians should share the burden of balancing the federal budget. For example, in addition to funding the BIA, the Interior appropriations bill now before Congress also funds a number of major, non-Indian programs, including the National Park Service, the Forest Service and many museums and cultural institutions. "It's probably safe to say that all of these groups are going to be treated fairly equally, because no one can get an increase over 1996 without someone else getting a decrease," says Sen. Slade Gorton, R-Wash., chairman of the Senate Interior Appropriations Subcommittee and an outspoken advocate of cutbacks in Indian programs. "And I don't propose to close national parks or the Smithsonian." [2]

Indian advocates say their programs are legally protected because they are cited in scores of treaties between various tribes and the U.S. government. Though Congress granted Indians U.S. citizenship in 1924, they also are considered members of sovereign nations. "Indians are not a minority group," says Gwen Carr, a Cayuga who chairs the National Urban Indian Policy Coalition, a Chicago organization that represents Indians who live off reservations. "Indians are a distinct political entity, the only group of

"If We Could Develop Our Land . . .

It's an eight-mile hike down Havasu Canyon to the village of Supai, Ariz. The narrow switchback down the canyon wall eases into a winding, rocky descent among towering ocher cliffs toward the Colorado River. Pack horses carrying mail and supplies share the trail.

The clear blue waters of Havasu Creek mark the town limits. A narrow footbridge leads to the main street, a dusty road bordered by a 600-year-old irrigation ditch funneling precious water from the creek to the fields. A sign warns riders not to gallop in town. The road leads past the office where tourists pay their visitation fees, an elementary school and the administrative office of the Havasupai Tribe's seven-member council.

With no access to motor vehicles, Supai is the most remote village in the lower 48 states. While its location clearly distinguishes the 650-member Havasupai tribe from the other 551 federally recognized tribes in the United States, the problems the council members addressed recently could be heard almost anywhere in Indian country.

The Havasupai tribal council grapples with issues faced by many tribes.

Mary H. Cooper

"The Havasupai people have been living here a long time," says Tribal Chairman Wayne Sinyella. "We've also been struggling a long time." Known as the Guardians of the Grand Canyon, the Havasupai once occupied hundreds of square miles of territory extending from the Grand Canyon southward about 80 miles, as far as present-day Flagstaff. But like other tribes across the country, the Havasupai lost most of their homeland to settlers and cattle ranchers after the mid-1800s. They suffered a major blow to their heritage after Teddy Roosevelt, awed by the Grand Canyon, declared the area a national park in 1903 and had the Indians driven out of the Colorado River basin — the Havasupai into adjacent Havasu Canyon. "The Forest Service bulldozed our homes, filled our wells and chased us out," Sinyella says. "Finally, this is where we ended up."

Supai village once served as a summer refuge where the tribe grew corn, melon, beans and other crops. These they stored for use during the winter months, when they moved to the plateau above to hunt. The tribe's seasonal migrations ended, Sinyella says, "when the government insisted on our kids going to school." After a nine-year struggle to regain part of their aboriginal homeland, the Havasupais received 124,000 acres under the 1974 Grand Canyon Enlargement Act. "This was a fraction of what we claimed to be our aboriginal territory," Sinyella says.

Deprived of most of their winter hunting and gathering lands, they also suffered a radical change to their traditional way of life. Today only a few families live on the plateau, where the tribe grazes its horses and cows. Tribal members occasionally travel there to gather pine nuts and medicinal herbs or to hunt deer and rabbits. But most of the tribe now live permanently in Supai, close to the school and clinic as well as the small tourist hotel and rustic cafe.

Apart from territorial restrictions, the tribe's biggest concern, as it is throughout most of Indian country, is the impact of federal budget cuts on Indian programs. The 1975 Indian Self-Determination and Education Assistance Act (Public Law 93-638), dubbed "638," turned the administration of federal education, health, housing, law enforcement and other Indian programs over to the tribes that choose to manage them. The Havasupai run all the federal programs they participate in, except for law enforcement, which the Bureau of Indian Affairs (BIA) administers.

While 638 was welcomed by tribes as a means of achieving some independence from Washington, it was accompanied by progressive cuts in funding for Indian programs. The

people [in the U.S.] who have two governments. There are treaties that were made between American Indians and the federal government, so there is a government-to-government relationship, just like the one between the United States and Italy or any other foreign country."

Gorton dismisses the notion that tribal sovereignty makes Indians immune to budget cuts. "These are peculiar treaties because they are clearly the law of the land, but they can also be abolished by Congress at will," he says. "It's not like a treaty with Russia or Great Britain, where it's between two equal sovereigns." Such views have made Gorton a leading champion of non-Indian property owners, who challenge tribal claims to water and hunting and fishing rights that conflict with their own property rights.

Tribes across the country feel their very survival is threatened by what they see as an increasingly hostile attitude toward Indians by a government that seems to have forgotten its

. . . We Could Become More Self-Sufficient"

Havasupai receive $168,000 a year to run all their programs, or about $255 for each member of the tribe. (The tribe says the state of Arizona's total contribution is $4,000 a year.) "Allocations from BIA are very low," Sinyella says. "Congress approves dollars to the central office of BIA, but by the time every dollar comes down through the area offices to the tribes, we get only a few cents. We need more dollars to operate social services, senior citizens' program, education and housing. The list goes on and on."

Federal funds are crucial to the Havasupai because tourism is their only other source of income. Each year, about 25,000 visitors hike, ride horses or fly in by helicopter to see the spectacular waterfalls below Supai that have earned the tribe its designation as the "people of the blue-green water." The tribe was concerned that its fragile desert habitat was being harmed by the flow of tourists. But that concern has been replaced by a new worry: A devastating flood in 1991 and two later floods have all but destroyed the fragile falls, threatening the tribe's sole independent income base.

Mary H. Cooper

An 8-mile path down Havasu Canyon leads to the Havasupais' remote village in northwestern Arizona.

Desperate for an alternative, the tribal council tried to set up a casino in Williams, population 2,500 and 100 miles away — the closest town. "The plan was to set aside eight to 10 acres of city property," Sinyella explains. "The tribe would then go to the federal government to have the land converted to a reservation and later apply to the governor to negotiate a gaming compact." Negotiations were progressing with the town government, but Arizona Gov. Fife Symington rejected the proposal, refusing to discuss it with the tribe, and the deal fell through early this year.

Now the tribe is seeking to have restrictions lifted on its use of reservation lands on the plateau, the only part of the reservation that is accessible by car. "We want Congress to change restrictions that say we can't harvest timber or mine or even issue public hunting permits on our land," Sinyella says. "We'd also like to build up on top, maybe a motel, a restaurant, an RV park and a gas station. Our people need jobs, and these things could help meet the essential needs of our community. If we could develop and improve our land, we could become more self-sufficient instead of depending only on the BIA year after year."

The Havasupai Tribe's isolation is not all bad, tribal members concede. For one thing, young people have been largely spared exposure to urban gangs that have plagued other reservations. For another, it has been easier for tribal elders to pass on their language and culture to the next generation. Like other Indian children of his generation, Sinyella was taken from his family at an early age to attend school far from home, speak English and renounce his traditions. Sinyella and other Havasupai children were sent to school at Fort Apache, hundreds of miles away. "We were there for nine months a year for six years," he says. "Our parents became strangers to us. When we weren't speaking English, we spoke Apache. I didn't want this to happen to my kids."

Today children attend an elementary school in Supai, and all of them speak Havasupai. After the eighth grade, however, they must go on to high school in Kingman or Flagstaff, where most live with relatives. Far from home, as many as two-thirds drop out before obtaining a diploma. Despite the lack of employment opportunities in Supai, young people tend to return to the reservation to live. "Most young people come back to the reservation after school," Sinyella says. "Very few stay out for more than a year."

debt to the country's "first people." Some tribes see economic development — fueled by revenues from gambling operations — as the key to their survival. Since the 1988 Indian Gaming Regulatory Act (IGRA) allowed the nation's 552 tribes to set up casinos and other gambling operations on their reservations, 220 Indian casinos have cropped up in 26 states.

Indeed, gambling is by far the most lucrative industry in Indian country, and a few Indian casinos have been spectacularly successful. The Foxwoods Casino Resort in Ledyard, Conn., operated by the tiny Mashantucket Pequot Tribe, amassed profits of $319 million last year. [3] But Indian gaming has come under increasing attack in states that oppose gambling on moral grounds or already have non-Indian casino operations that don't want competition from the Indians.

Some Indians see the opposition to Native American gaming as yet another expression of racism by a society that can't come to grips with its bloody past. "It's very, very difficult for people to deal with successful Indians," says Marjorie Mitchell Bear Don't Walk, a Flathead and director of the Indian Health Board, a clinic in Billings, Mont. "Has Congress reacted to Donald Trump in the same way? I don't think so. We're being punished if we're successful in the free-market system."

Opponents of Indian gambling won an important victory March 27, when the U.S. Supreme Court ruled that Florida's Seminoles could not force the state to allow them to launch casino operations. While the ruling did not jeopardize existing Indian gaming operations in other states, it effectively placed a moratorium on new ones in states that oppose Indian gambling.

Most tribes, however, probably could not profit from gambling even if they could open casinos. Reservations typically are located in isolated areas far from the large population centers that gaming enterprises need to flourish. Some tribes rely entirely on tourism: The Havasupai run a small hotel to house visitors who hike, ride or helicopter into the canyon to visit the spectacular waterfalls along Havasu Creek. Other tribes, such as the Oneidas of Wisconsin and the Mississippi Band of Choctaw Indians, are entering the mainstream economy by setting up factories on their reservations that employ both Indians and non-Indians.

"Native American people want to be contributors to this society just as much as anyone else," says Oneida Chairman Deborah Doxtator. "We don't want a handout. But we also need to be given the means to bring ourselves up by our bootstraps. We're willing and able, but we've not always had the opportunities in front of us in a viable way."

As Indians look for ways to prosper in the American economy while protecting their unique heritage, these are some of the issues they face:

Do Indian tribes depend too heavily on aid from the federal government?

Many tribes on remote reservations with no tourist attractions or other economic enterprises depend almost entirely on government assistance to run their schools, health clinics, tribal governments and other institutions. These reservations are often the most severely afflicted with unemployment, alcoholism, crime and a pervasive sense of hopelessness.

"The single group of people who have had the most systematic and longest-lasting welfare system are at the same time the group of people who are most despairing, most out of the mainstream, generally speaking have low educational attainments and a very high percentage of unemployment."

—Sen. Slade Gorton, R-Wash.

Some critics of federal Indian policy say it's to blame for the desperate living conditions in many Indian communities. One thing is certain: No other issue sparks such heated exchanges between Indian advocates and their opponents.

"The single group of people who have had the most systematic and longest-lasting welfare system are at the same time the group of people who are most despairing, most out of the mainstream, generally speaking have low educational attainments and a very high percentage of unemployment," says Sen. Gorton. "So that association is absolutely clear. When you're deprived of the ability to make your own decisions, you're not very likely to do the kinds of things that are necessary to improve your condition. The fact that the system has gone on longer and is more pervasive [among Indians] than any place else and that its failure has been overwhelming simply can't be argued by anyone."

"It's not dependency that has fomented those things," counters Carr of the Urban Indian Policy Coalition. "It's genocide." Carr agrees with Gorton that the government is to blame for the misery in Indian country. But where the senator sees paternalistic welfare handouts as the culprit, she blames a long history of betrayals. "Picture the Jewish people being in concentration camps for the past 200 years, and ask them if that's about the welfare state," Carr says. "I don't think so. It's much deeper and much uglier than that."

But even on reservations where residents depend almost entirely on government programs, the recent federal budget cutbacks are being seen as a boost for Indian self-reliance. "Some

Indian people are looking at the cutbacks as a blessing in disguise," says Tom Arviso Jr., managing editor of *Navajo Times* in Window Rock, Ariz. "They say we've become too complacent, that we're too dependent on the government and that now we need to get off our butts and start working and taking care of things on our own."

The Navajos are the second-largest tribe in the country, counting some 300,000 members, about 250,000 of whom live on the vast reservation overlapping parts of Arizona, New Mexico and Utah. The Navajos have few prosperous enterprises. Like the Hopi, whose reservation lies inside Navajo lands, the Navajos have rejected gaming on moral grounds. They are hoping instead to enhance their small tourist industry by building hotels and restaurants to draw more visitors to the reservation's natural and archaeological treasures, such as Canyon de Chelly, Chaco Canyon and Monument Valley.

Like other rural tribes, the Navajos also view the revival of their traditional livelihood as a way out of their current problems. "We need to go back to farming and livestock and stop depending so much on buying food at the supermarket and using the microwave," says Arviso. "We need to start growing our own traditional foods again, like corn, melons and squash, and taking care of our water and livestock so we can fend for ourselves like we used to. We've gotten too far away from that kind of lifestyle."

While self-sufficiency remains a widely accepted goal, Indian advocates point to significant obstacles. Few people realize, for example, that the federal government holds reservation lands in trust for the tribes. Since they don't own the land and thus can't use it for collateral for loans, tribes often cannot obtain credit as easily as non-Indians to start up their own businesses.

"Indian people generally have said that they would welcome the same opportunities that anybody else has to develop factories or to build jobs, and if they did they probably wouldn't need so much government help," says Sen. Campbell. "The fact of the matter is, they can't do it. If you're in an Indian tribe and you want to build a factory on the reservation, you can't get the investment capital to do it because you have nothing you can put up for collateral."

Given such obstacles, Campbell and other advocates remind budget-cutters of the events that placed Indians in their current desperate straits. "If you gave back all the lands that were taken by force or subterfuge from Indian people long ago, they would be very happy to give up any government subsidies or programs," Campbell says. "In lieu of that, Indians feel they have a special right to earn whatever they can through 20th-century America's normal system of business. But at the same time, the government has a trust responsibility to them."

Oneida Bingo and Casino

The casino opened by Wisconsin's Oneida tribe in 1991 has provided revenue for investments in a hotel, convenience stores and a printing plant.

Is gambling the Indians' best hope for economic development?

Since Congress passed the Indian Gaming Regulatory Act in 1988, gambling has become an important source of revenue for many tribes. Operations ranging from one-room bingo halls to glitzy casinos generated $3.4 billion in gross earnings for tribes in 1994. [4]

Supporters of Indian gaming say it is by far Native Americans' most promising avenue to prosperity. "Gaming has had the broadest impact on economic development for the tribes and has produced the greatest amount of revenue on a broad basis for the tribes that are engaged in it," says Tom Acevedo, a member of the Confederated Salish and Kootenai Tribes in Montana and executive director of the National Indian Gaming Commission.

The IGRA requires tribes to invest their gaming profits in tribal services. After meeting its obligations under the act, the Foxwoods casino in Connecticut distributes $200,000 annually to each of the tribe's 200 adult members. [5]

But opponents of gambling point to the phenomenal success of Foxwoods and other casinos as proof that gambling is socially destructive. They cite nationwide data showing that about a quarter of casino and state lottery prof-

Health and Social Problems Plague Native Americans

If health statistics provide a reliable barometer of a group's well-being, Indians are at the very bottom of the ladder in American society. No group fares worse than Indians on a number of health indicators, according to the federal Indian Health Service, which serves recognized tribes and Alaska Natives.

The death rate among Indians from alcoholism is four and a half times that of the total U.S. population; from tuberculosis, three and a half times higher; from accidents and from diabetes mellitus, about one and a half times higher. Suicide and homicide also claim a disproportionately high number of Indians. [1]

Ever since Europeans first introduced whiskey to the New World, alcoholism has exacted a huge toll among Indians. Although the death rate among Indians from alcoholism has fallen by half since the early 1980s, it continues to plague Indian communities, even on reservations where tribal councils have banned alcohol altogether. Some scientists have suggested that a genetic anomaly explains Indians' susceptibility to alcoholism, a theory that may soon be tested by genetic mapping. [2]

But many Indians reject this theory and attribute alcoholism and most other health and social problems among Indians to their mistreatment by U.S. society. "Because there is institutional racism against Indians in this country, we have needed to comfort ourselves with food, alcohol and drugs," says Marjorie Mitchell Bear Don't Walk, executive director of the Indian Health Board of Billings, Mont. "If you are constantly told that you are no good, how can you be good? If you put other people down, you teach them not to be self-sufficient, you teach them that they are not capable of taking care of themselves. And yet the very people who do that don't want to support Indians by paying taxes to fund Indian programs."

Bear Don't Walk's outpatient clinic is one of 34 urban facilities established under the 1976 Indian Health Improvement Act to provide health care to non-reservation Indians or those who do not qualify for federal Indian programs because their tribal affiliations are not recognized by the government. Not being officially considered a Native American is blamed for contributing to alcoholism among Indians wherever they live. "My dad was a full-blood Little Shell Chippewa who was born and died without ever being a legal Indian in the eyes of the United States government," she says. "How do you think he felt about himself? My dad was stabbed to death when he was drunk."

Alcoholics don't always die of liver disease, but often succumb to suicide and accidents. "My experience of being around alcoholics my whole life and directing this facility for 10 years is that alcoholics who survive alcoholism will become diabetics," says Bear Don't Walk. Obesity, another persistent health problem among Indians, also is a contributing factor in diabetes. "My grandparents probably never ate more than 5 percent of what we eat today," says Bear Don't Walk. "The natural foods that they ate and the exercise they got are extremely different from what is socially acceptable for our way of life today."

Indian women, Bear Don't Walk says, die from alcoholism at 10 times the rate of non-Indian women, of diabetes at triple the rate and of cervical cancer at twice the rate of non-Indian women. "We have more than a 50 percent chance of having gall bladder problems and diabetes," she says. "Indian women are now drinking at the same rate as Indian men, and some studies show that of childbearing-age women, one in four is giving birth to children with fetal alcohol syndrome or other effects of the mother's alcohol abuse."

Poverty contributes not only to disease but also to social problems within the Indian community. Per capita income in 1989 among Indians was $8,284, compared with $14,420 for the total U.S. population, the Census Bureau reported in its 1990 survey. Nearly a third of Indians live in poverty, more than twice the overall U.S. poverty rate. And unemployment on some reservations exceeds 50 percent, especially those far from towns and job opportunities.

But proximity to urban centers is a mixed blessing for many reservations. Like young people in poverty-stricken inner cities across the country, Indian youth are falling prey to gang violence. "We've got stabbings, shootings, beatings and deaths every weekend, and most of them go unreported," says Tom Arviso Jr., managing editor of *Navajo Times* in Window Rock, Ariz. Although alcohol is banned on the Navajo reservation, he says, "Most of the time alcohol and drugs are involved."

Most of the gang activities are introduced by Indians or non-Indians from major cities such as Albuquerque or even from smaller towns, such as Gallup, N.M., and Flagstaff, Ariz., that lie just outside the vast reservation's borders. "The reason gangs take hold is that there's not a whole lot for our young people to do," Arviso says. "Without jobs, young people wander because they have too much idle time. It's really scary because we've all been touched in one way or another by the gang violence. Loved ones are killed needlessly, and our young people are killing themselves for no reason. It's hurting us and our culture."

---

[1] Indian Health Service, *Trends in Indian Health — 1995*, p. 5.

[2] See Rick Weiss, "Discovery May Be Brewing in Search for Genetic Link to Alcoholism," *The Washington Post*, July 1, 1996.

its come from just 5 percent of all players, evidence that gambling is addictive. [6] "There's very little socially redeeming about gambling," says Sen. Gorton. "The social pathology — the family breakup, the welfare created by widespread organized gambling — is an extremely serious problem. I'm relatively indifferent as to who gets the profits from it, so my concentration isn't on Indian gambling, though at the present time most of the expansion is through Indian tribes."

Some Indian tribes have resisted the economic lure of gambling for some of the same reasons cited by non-Indian critics. "There are a lot of tribes who have done quite well using Indian gaming to better themselves, but here on the Navajo reservation we turned it down," says Arviso. "Just last week our council voted for the second time against legalizing gaming. We feel there are better ways to generate revenue.

"Gaming just creates more problems," Arviso adds. "Alcoholism and drug abuse would go up, and people would be [throwing away] their money. The general belief is that it would be a large negative."

In comparison with Las Vegas or Atlantic City, Indian gambling is a small-stakes industry. Indian casinos raked in less than 10 percent of the $40 billion in U.S. gambling revenues in 1994. Like their non-Indian counterparts, most highly profitable Indian gaming operations are near population centers. "But those in the Midwest or the West — where the populations are small — are doing very modestly," says Acevedo. "So while gaming is a plus for them, it clearly isn't answering all their needs."

Some tribes that have prospered from gaming are investing their profits in new enterprises. Wisconsin's Oneidas, whose reservation encompasses part of Green Bay, found themselves in the same financial bind as other tribes. "We have properties, but they're in trust status with the government," says tribal Chairman Doxtator. "So they cannot be encumbered for bonding or financing purposes."

But the Oneidas, blessed by their urban location, have been able to develop a wide variety of new businesses using the revenues earned from a bingo hall that opened in 1976 and, since 1991, a casino. "Gaming has taken away a lot of the development barriers that we've run into over the years," Doxtator says. "It's a very quick source of revenue that has given us the leverage to do things that we could not do before." The tribe now runs a 301-room Radisson Hotel at the local airport, a chain of convenience stores and a small printing plant.

The Wisconsin Oneidas have been so successful that they are currently negotiating to buy some of the tribe's aboriginal lands near another Oneida reservation in New York state. The tribe also is branching out into off-reservation ventures. The Wisconsin Oneidas now own a one-third interest in a local bank, making them the first tribe with a federally chartered financial institution. In mid-June, the tribe broke ground on a new $6.9 million plant on the reservation that will produce computer chips for automatic car-door openers, medical devices and other electronic equipment. The joint venture between Oneida Nation Electronics and Plexus Corp., a high-technology firm based in Neenah, Wis., will employ almost 400 Indians and non-Indians from the Green Bay area.

A few tribes have managed to establish a foothold in their local economies without the benefit of gaming revenues. With little to offer but their members' labor, the Mississippi Band of Choctaws attracted a General Motors electronics assembly plant to their reservation outside Philadelphia, Miss. (The tribe later set up a riverboat gambling operation as well). The Salish and Kootenai Tribes co-manage a privately owned hydroelectric dam that has generated revenues enabling the tribes to invest in other businesses on and off their Montana reservation. But these are the exceptions. "Each of these enterprises has worked for those individual tribes," says Acevedo, "but they don't have the same general impact that gaming has had for all the tribes that are engaged in it."

"This country was built on the land and the resources that were ceded to the government by the tribes. . . . But Congress doesn't understand or acknowledge the obligation of this country to the native peoples."

—Ada E. Deer, Assistant Interior Secretary for Indian Affairs

Are Indians today victims of widespread discrimination?

Few Americans would challenge the

notion that Indians have long been victimized. From the time Columbus landed in the New World, whites seeking gold, farmland or simply a new homeland established their claims at the expense of the continent's original inhabitants. Even after the United States was founded, official policy continued to discriminate against Indians, who reluctantly ceded their ancestral lands before the inexorable push westward. Decimated by new diseases, vanquished during decades of Indian Wars, deprived of their traditional hunting way of life and confined to infertile reservation lands, Indians died by the hundreds of thousands in the first two centuries of U.S. history.

Many American Indians say the victimization continues unabated. Less apparent than the outright massacres of the past, critics say, the federal government's Indian policy today is still based on a form of racism that relegates Indians to the bottom rungs of the country's social and economic ladder. "The history of Indian-American governmental relations is full of betrayal, bloodshed and tears," says Carr of the Urban Indian Policy Coalition. "The Indian people represent collectively this country's shame. The entire BIA is dedicated to having Indians not be successful. So they keep them in a corner, out of sight, to manage them."

BIA head Deer says the Clinton administration is trying to change things. "Government policy is moving away from paternalism toward self-determination and self-governance," Deer says. But she agrees that racism still permeates American views of Indians. "There's always been an underlying racism in this society," she says. "This was the attitude from day one. Many tribes met the settlers with peace and friendship, but this was not reciprocated. The country still does not want to recognize our history, and we need to."

Racism directed against Indians continues to crop up in the society at large. "The Freemen that just left Jordan ranch [in Montana] in mid-June refer to Indians as prairie niggers, and this attitude is not limited to extremists," says Marjorie Bear Don't Walk. "People in Billings call the local K-Mart the Crow-Mart as a putdown because there are a lot of [Crow] Indians there. As a people, we have suffered racism since Columbus landed. The laws of this country are founded on racist attitudes from Europe. Racism today is a fact of life for us."

Bear Don't Walk says racism toward Indians is far more prevalent in the West, but others disagree. "You should go up to Connecticut" if you want to see racism, says Herb Becker, director of the Justice Department's Office of Tribal Justice. "It's not necessarily region-peculiar anymore."

Becker sees anti-Indian racism in the Northeast springing directly from the phenomenal success of the Mashantuckets' casino. "I'm a firm believer that non-Indians just can't stand to see Indians prosper." He says recent actions in his home state of New Mexico back up his claim. In compliance with the 1988 gaming act, Republican Gov. Gary E. Johnson signed compacts with a number of tribes allowing them to open casinos. But last summer the state Supreme Court ruled the agreements were invalid because they had not been ratified by the Legislature. When some tribal leaders refused to close their casinos, claiming that Indian gaming falls under federal jurisdiction, the state court ruled that no one in New Mexico could operate casino-type gaming.

"The Supreme Court ruled that gaming as a matter of public policy is illegal," says Becker. "But this was a blatant lie. In New Mexico you've got horse racing, you've got parimutuel betting, you've got every fraternal organization with slot machines and card rooms. They said that just so they could try to shut off tribal gaming." Becker concludes that racism is at the heart of the decision. "You still have racism in the South, of course, but it's no longer institutional," he says. "That has been replaced by institutional racism against Indians in the West and other places where tribes are successful." *

Critics of Indian gaming adamantly deny that racism colors their views. "Racism doesn't have anything to do with it," says Sen. Gorton. "It has to do with the feeling that gambling itself is highly socially undesirable." The senator backs a bill now before Congress that would establish a special commission to study the impact of gambling, including state lotteries and both Indian and non-Indian casinos, on players' behavior, on local crime patterns and on local and state economies. ■

BACKGROUND

Early Treaties

In the four centuries since Columbus' "discovery" of the Western Hemisphere in 1492, the indigenous peoples of what became the United States were nearly wiped out through war, starvation, disease and U.S. policies that many call genocidal. [7]

Today, federal relations with Indian tribes are based on treaties that were drawn up by the British during Colonial times and later by the U.S. government. [8] During the Colonial period, as European settlers competed for lands, they negotiated at least 175 treaties with tribes and tribal alliances, such as the powerful Iroquois confederacy in the North and the Creek confederacy in the South.

Under Article II of the U.S. Constitution, treaties must be ratified by a

Continued on p. 612

* New Mexico's Indian gaming operations are running pending the outcome of a court challenge to the shutdown.

Chronology

1800s

Settlers, ranchers and prospectors push westward, forcing Indians to abandon much of their aboriginal territory.

Aug. 13, 1868
The last Senate-ratified Indian treaty is signed, with the Nez Perce Tribe of Idaho, bringing the number of ratified Indian treaties to 370. Three years later, Congress abolishes the ratifying process as a means of dealing with tribes.

1887
The General Allotment Act forces Indians to accept non-Indian ownership of reservation lands under a system that permits the federal government to purchase and resell reservation parcels not claimed by Indians under the law's terms.

1900-1950s

Goals of federal Indian policy shift between forced assimilation and exclusion of Indians.

1905
U.S. Supreme Court upholds Indian treaty rights in *United States v. Winans.*

1924
Indians are granted U.S. citizenship.

1934
The Indian Reorganization Act ends the allotment policy and provides funding for economic development on reservations.

1945
Over the next 15 years, some 12,000 Indians are "terminated," as the federal government rescinds official recognition of their tribes and removes 2.5 million acres of Indian land from protected status.

1960s-1980s

Self-determination becomes the watchword of federal Indian policy.

July 7, 1970
President Richard M. Nixon denounces termination policies and promises federal assistance to help Indians achieve greater autonomy.

1973
Two Indians die and an FBI agent is wounded during a shootout between federal agents and followers of the militant American Indian Movement (AIM) who had occupied the village of Wounded Knee on the Pine Ridge Reservation in South Dakota.

1975
The Indian Self-Determination and Education Assistance Act enables tribes to elect to administer federal education, health and other Indian programs. In *Antoine v. Washington* the U.S. Supreme Court rules that treaty rights hold for U.S.-tribal agreements signed after formal treaty-making ended.

1978
The Indian Child Welfare Act allows tribes to have limited authority to prevent adoption of Indian children by non-Indians.

1988
The Indian Gaming Regulatory Act (IGRA) allows tribes to negotiate compacts with their state governors to operate casinos. The same year House Concurrent Resolution 331 reaffirms "the constitutionally recognized government-to-government relationship with Indian tribes."

1990s

Indian rights are challenged by cuts in the funding of federal Indian programs and efforts to curtail Indian gaming.

April 29, 1994
President Clinton holds an unprecedented White House conference with more than 300 tribal leaders to hear their grievances.

1995
Amid growing resistance to Indian gaming, the New Mexico Supreme Court rules that existing gaming compacts are illegal and orders the casinos shut down. In December, Sen. John McCain, R-Ariz., introduces a bill that would shift authority away from BIA headquarters in Washington to area offices to give tribes greater influence over BIA decisions.

March 27, 1996
The U.S. Supreme Court challenges the IGRA by ruling in *Seminole Tribe of Florida v. Florida* that the tribe cannot force the state government to negotiate an agreement allowing it to open casino operations in Florida.

Not All Native Americans Are Indians

The term Native American is widely used today to describe the tribal peoples, or Indians, who were the original inhabitants of what is now the United States. But they are not the country's only Native Americans.

The aboriginal people of Alaska are Native Americans, too. They include three distinct groups: Indians, Aleuts and Eskimos. Like the ancestors of the Indians who populate the rest of North and South America, the ancestors of Alaska's Indians are believed to have migrated from Asia between 20,000 and 35,000 years ago, crossing the "land bridge" then connecting Siberia and Alaska (now the Bering Strait). Like Indians in the lower 48 states, Alaska's Athabaskan and coastal Indians live in tribes and speak languages that are distinct from the other Alaskan aboriginal peoples.[1]

The Aleuts crossed the land bridge later, though still in prehistoric times, and traditionally inhabited western Alaska and the Aleutian Islands. As many as 80 percent of the Aleuts died from disease and violence after coming in contact with Russian fur traders in the mid-1700s. Alaska's Eskimos, or Inuit, arrived still later and settled along the coasts and riversides as far north as the Arctic Ocean. Like the Aleuts, Eskimos traditionally lived in family units, or clans.

All three groups of Alaska's Native Americans have fared better than their counterparts in the lower 48 states. Under the 1971 Alaska Native Claims Settlement Act, these groups received collectively $1 billion in cash and 44 million acres of land rich in natural resources. They established regional corporations, in which all Native Alaskans are entitled to shares, to develop timber and oil industries and fisheries in Alaska, and to invest outside Alaska.[2]

Native Hawaiians comprise another distinct group of Native Americans, a title many disdain because of their turbulent relations with the United States. Descendants of Polynesians who sailed thousands of miles to settle in the Pacific island chain between 1,000 and 1,500 years ago, Native Hawaiians first came into contact with Europeans in 1778, when Captain James Cook landed. Some 90 percent of the island's 300,000 inhabitants soon died from diseases they contracted from the newcomers.

Hawaii was a sovereign country with a constitutional monarchy until a coup backed by American businessmen in 1893 overthrew the government. It became a U.S. territory in 1900. In 1959, Hawaii became the 50th state. Despite numerous laws aimed at improving their lot, many Native Hawaiians continue to live in severely impoverished conditions.

[1] See Jack Utter, *American Indians* (1993), pp. 14-17.

[2] See "From Fur-Trading to Portfolios," *The Economist*, May 25, 1996, p. 31.

Continued from p. 610

two-thirds majority of the Senate. Article VI further states that treaties are binding on the states and others as "the supreme law of the land." U.S. treaties with Indian tribes, many of which predated the Constitution itself, were subsequently considered to be Article II treaties. As such, they had the same legal force as treaties with other countries, and were filed with the State Department.

But after the War of 1812 assured American sovereignty, Indian tribes lost their value as military assets, and treaty-making slowed. The last Senate-ratified Indian treaty was signed Aug. 13, 1868, with the Nez Perce tribe of Idaho, bringing the number of ratified Indian treaties to 370. At the same time, resentment toward the treaty-making process was building in the House of Representatives, which was responsible for funding the Indian programs emanating from treaties approved by the Senate.

In 1871, Congress abolished the constitutional treaty-making process with Indians. The law expressly refrained, however, from challenging the legal status of existing Indian treaties: ". . . [N]othing herein contained shall be construed to invalidate or impair the obligation of any treaty heretofore lawfully made and ratified with any such Indian nation or tribe."[9]

When Native Americans speak of treaty rights, they often take pains to note that they are not referring to rights that were given to them by the federal government, but rather to rights they retained for themselves in exchange for land they handed over to the United States. The U.S. Supreme Court upheld this interpretation in 1905 in *United States v. Winans,* noting that "the treaty was not a grant of rights to the Indians, but a grant of rights from them."[10] By the same token, Indian reservations are by law not a kind of ghetto to which tribal members are to be confined, but rather a small portion of a treaty-making tribe's ancestral homeland that it "reserved" for its exclusive domain.

Because westward expansion continued well into the 20th century, Indian tribes were forced to continue negotiating reductions in their land holdings with the federal government long after formal treaty-making ended in 1871. Subsequent Indian pacts, called "agreements," were subject to approval by both houses of Congress and generally were attached as riders to appropriations bills covering funding for Indian programs. Almost 100 such agreements were ratified by Congress. The last Indian land agreement, with the Wiminuche Band of Southern Ute Indians in Colorado, was approved in 1913.

After 1913, all future agreements between the federal government and Indian tribes were treated by Congress as any other initiative in the legislative process. But in its 1975 ruling in *Antoine v. Washington,* the Supreme Court declared that traditional treaty rights pertain to Indian agreements concluded after 1871 as well. "Once ratified by Act of Congress, the provisions of the agreements become law, and like treaties, the supreme law of the land." [11]

Indians Pushed Out

As a matter of political reality, however, Indian treaty rights were largely forgotten whenever they blocked other national policy goals. Since the early 1800s, Indians have been at the mercy of the policy pendulum: Successive generations of lawmakers have tried to solve the "Indian problem" by conflicting programs aimed either at segregating Indians or assimilating them into the larger society.

Beginning in the early 1800s, waves of settlers moved westward into Indian country. To make way for them, tribes were forceably relocated from 1817 until the mid-1880s. The first to go during this so-called "removal era" were virtually all the Eastern tribes, including the Delaware, Seminole and Cherokee, who were pushed west of the Mississippi and forced to relocate in Oklahoma, then considered to be of no interest to white settlers. By the 1880s, more than 40 tribes were in Oklahoma.

Even as it was relocating Indians far from white society, however, Congress in 1819 began appropriating money for a "Civilization Fund" run by missionaries. Its aim: to convert Indians to Christianity.

After the United States extended its territory to the Pacific Ocean under the 1848 Treaty of Guadalupe Hidalgo, westward expansion moved still deeper into Indian country, triggering the Indian wars of 1860-1880. Treaties were made and broken as successive waves of ranchers, prospectors and other newcomers took over Indian lands.

Forced Assimilation

During the last half of the century, efforts to assimilate Indians gave rise to Indian boarding schools, where children were forced to live away from their families, speak English and adopt American dress and customs.

Further changes in Indian life were carried out under the 1887 General Allotment Act, which ended Indians' communal ownership of reservation lands. The act forced Indians to adopt the European model of land ownership, allotting 160 acres to every reservation family head. The parcels were not actually owned, however, but were to be held in trust by the federal government.

In addition, the act permitted surplus lands within reservations to be sold by the government to non-Indians, with the proceeds to be used for the tribes' benefit. As a result of the allotment policy, which continued into the 1930s, more than half the people living within the boundaries of many reservations today are non-Indians.

Indians were granted U.S. citizenship in 1924. But the policy of forced assimilation proved a dismal failure for most Indians. Confined to marginal lands, deprived of the buffalo that had been slaughtered by non-Indians during the westward expansion, Indians were beset by poverty, alcoholism and disease. The federal government finally acknowledged the failure of forced assimilation in 1928.

Allotment Policy Ends, Termination Begins

In another policy about-face, the 1934 Indian Reorganization Act ended allotment, provided funding for economic development on reservations and restored some degree of tribal self-governance. Concluding that the federal government had failed as an effective administrator of Indian affairs, Congress also that year gave the states a greater role in administering some Indian programs.

Barely a decade later, however, federal Indian policy again shifted, this time ushering in the so-called termination period of 1945-1960. Tribes occupying valuable lands, such as the Klamath who lived in Washington's timber forests and the Agua Caliente of Palm Springs, Calif., were among more than 100 tribes that were "terminated." In other words, they were deemed no longer qualified to own reservation land or receive benefits reserved for Indians.

In addition to making valuable land available to non-Indians, termination reduced the federal government's welfare burden and enabled it to physically relocate Indians to cities where they were expected to blend into the dominant society. By 1962, some 12,000 Indian people had lost official recognition, while some 2.5 million acres of Indian land were removed from protected status. [12]

Self-Determination

Termination gave way to self-determination as a major goal of Indian policy after 1960. Presidents John F. Kennedy (1961-63) and Lyndon B. Johnson (1963-69) called for investments in economic development on reservations. The 1968 Indian Civil Rights Act further prohibited states from assuming jurisdiction over Indian lands without obtaining tribal consent.

President Richard M. Nixon (1969-74) went further than any of his predecessors in denouncing termination and in supporting Indian autonomy while continuing federal assistance programs. "Self-determination among the Indian people can and must be encouraged," Nixon proclaimed July 7, 1970. "This, then, must be the goal of any new national policy toward the Indian people." [13] With presidential support, Congress passed a number of laws in the 1970s to strengthen Indian self-determination.

Key legislation of this period included the 1975 Indian Self-Determination and Education Assistance Act (Public Law 93-

638), which Indians often refer to as 638. By funneling federal monies directly to tribes through contracts and grants, 638 encourages tribal councils to assume control over school, health, housing, law enforcement and other programs formerly administered by federal agencies. In this way, the federal government grants tribes some autonomy in much the same way as it does other localities.

The self-determination movement continued through the 1970s and '80s, with several Supreme Court decisions strengthening Indian sovereignty. The movement reached a climax in 1973 when a group of Indians led by Russell Means of the militant American Indian Movement (AIM) occupied the village of Wounded Knee, S.D., on the Pine Ridge Reservation. Two Indians died and an FBI agent was critically wounded in the shootout with federal agents ending the 71-day siege. AIM, which had been founded to help Indians who had been displaced to cities, lost much of its support among Indians after Wounded Knee.

Though President Ronald Reagan (1981-89) reaffirmed his support for Indian self-determination and economic development, budget cuts during his administrations reduced federal spending for Indian programs. Still, Indian tribes obtained a congressional statement of support for their unique status in U.S. society. A House resolution adopted Oct. 4, 1988, reaffirmed "the constitutionally recognized government-to-government relationship with Indian tribes which has been the cornerstone of the nation's official Indian policy." It also acknowledged the government's "need to exercise the utmost good faith in upholding its treaties with the various tribes."

Indian Gaming

In 1988, the same year that the House reaffirmed tribal rights, Congress also passed legislation defining conditions under which Indians could engage in gambling operations. Gambling not only became the most promising source of revenue for many tribes but also "by far the most politically charged economic issue in Indian country during this final decade of the 20th century," according to Professor Jack Utter of the Center for Indian Bilingual Teacher Training at Prescott (Ariz.) College.[14]

"If you gave back all the lands that were taken by force or subterfuge from Indian people long ago, they would be very happy to give up any government subsidies or programs. In lieu of that, Indians feel they have a special right to earn whatever they can through 20th-century America's normal system of business."

— Sen. Ben Nighthorse Campbell, R-Colo.

Although many tribes traditionally engaged in various forms of gambling, it was not until 1979, when the Seminoles opened a commercial bingo operation, that any tribe operated profitable gambling halls. Consistent with its support of Indian self-determination, the Reagan administration endorsed Indian gaming. As many tribes across the country followed the Seminoles' lead, however, conflicts erupted among state, federal and tribal governments over jurisdiction over the new gambling operations.

The issue was at the center of a landmark dispute between California and the Cabazon Band of Cahuilla Mission Indians, who ran a gambling operation on their reservation 20 miles east of Palm Springs. A federal court ruled in *California v. Cabazon* — and the U.S. Supreme Court affirmed — that tribes could legally engage in forms of gambling that were not expressly prohibited by the state in which the tribe is located.

The Supreme Court further held that because all state gaming regulations fall under civil law — under which Indian tribes cannot be held accountable — states are required under federal law to enter into negotiations with tribes to establish mutually acceptable regulations of Indian gaming operations. The states can only refuse to negotiate compacts for types of gambling that they expressly prohibit under criminal law.

To establish a regulatory framework for Indian gaming, Congress passed the 1988 Indian Gaming Regulatory Act. The law defines three classes of

Indian gambling. Class I, including traditional Indian games, are under the exclusive jurisdiction of tribes. Class II games, comprising bingo, lotto, pull tabs and some card games, are allowed on Indian lands if they are conducted in a state that allows them for any other group. Only two states, Hawaii and Utah, prohibit all gambling. The tribes share regulatory jurisdiction over Class II gaming with the National Indian Gaming Commission, created under IGRA.

Class III gaming includes all other forms of gambling, primarily the games found in casinos, such as slot machines, roulette, blackjack and any electromechanical versions of games such as video poker and video bingo. Horse and dog racing also fall into this category. A tribe can offer Class III gaming only after it has negotiated a compact with the state stipulating the size and type of gaming facilities. Because of resistance to Indian gambling either from the non-Indian gambling industry or citizens who oppose gambling on moral grounds, some state governments have refused to negotiate compacts for Class III gaming. In several cases, as a result, tribes have sued their states for failing to negotiate with them in "good faith," as the law requires. ■

CURRENT SITUATION

Clinton's Policy

Continuing a policy outlined by President George Bush (1989-93), President Clinton early in his term championed tribal sovereignty and Indian self-determination. He appointed Deer, a Menominee, to head the BIA. "President Clinton said he wanted a government that looked like America," says Deer. "So here I am, the first woman to serve in this position. And I'm not doing things in the way they've been done in the past."

On April 29, 1994, Clinton and his top officials listened to the concerns of more than 300 tribal leaders invited to air their grievances at an unprecedented White House conference on Indian issues. Following the meeting, Clinton ordered the heads of 15 federal departments and agencies to consult directly with tribes when dealing with Indian issues "in order to ensure that the rights of sovereign tribal governments are fully respected." [15]

"This is the first time that any administration has taken the time and energy to put together a procedures document for each one of its resource agencies that deals with Indian tribes," says Jim Pace, a spokesman for the Interior Department's Office of American Indian Trust. The office was set up in 1991 by the Bush administration as a separate entity from BIA to strengthen the federal government's trust responsibility toward Indian tribes. "The procedures are dynamic," Pace says, "in that the agencies can change them as they need to, to make sure they're meeting the needs of the tribes."

The policy of tribal self-determination also is changing the way tribes receive federal support. Deer says that about 55 tribes to date have chosen to take advantage of this new approach by signing self-governance compacts with the federal government that enable them to receive federal monies in block grants, which they then spend according to their particular needs. "In the past, a lot of control and decision-making were exerted by the federal government," she says. "But now there is much more flexibil-

Fydel A. Jones

Ceremonial dancers from Arizona's Havasupai tribe performed this year at the SuperBowl and the Arizona Indian Festival, both in Phoenix.

ity. Government policy is moving toward self-determination."

The Clinton administration also has tried to increase funding for Indian programs. "This administration has submitted the largest budget request for the BIA ever, and that was the $1.9 billion budget request for fiscal 1997," says Deer. "This reflects the sensitivity of the administration in trying to meet the longstanding needs in Indian country. Also under this administration, 12 new tribes have been recognized."

The administration is not without critics among Indians, however. Urban Indian activist Carr faults the president for failing to defend Indian programs from the budget ax. "I think he's a decent man who's in a lousy job and has to make incredibly unpleasant decisions," she says. "Because American Indians are a segment of the population that is not a huge voting bloc, we are at the mercy of the whims of someone else's conscience. The monies that they cut from the budget are not going to balance the budget. What they're going to do is create starvation, disease and despair in people who have had more than a bellyfull of all those things."

Program Cuts

The administration's advocacy of Indian rights lost momentum after Republicans won control of both houses of Congress in the November 1994 elections. As balancing the budget became the overriding priority for Congress, spending for Indian programs fell dramatically. The fiscal 1996 budget for BIA programs totaled $1.6 billion, a decrease of $160 million from the year before.

Budget cutbacks are taking a heavy toll on the tribes. A 4 percent annual increase in the school-age population on reservations, for example, means that education programs can't keep up with the need. "The per student allocation of the bureau is about $3,000, which is about half that of the public schools," says Deer, who notes that Indian child welfare protection services, law enforcement and family services are among the programs that have suffered as a result of budget cuts. "Cutting these funds is like blaming the victim. It gets really tedious. As President Nixon stated back in 1970, by any socioeconomic indicator, Indians and Alaska Natives are at the bottom of the ladder. The funding that has been approved will not enable the tribes to get over this. I don't even know if it will maintain the status quo."

Although the Clinton administration requested $1.8 billion in BIA funding for fiscal 1997, there is little support in Congress to boost spending for Indian programs. Despite charges from the White House that the fiscal 1997 appropriations bill for the Interior Department would violate Indian rights by eliminating services promised in treaties, the House on June 20 passed a $12.3 billion spending bill that includes $239 million less than Clinton requested for BIA.

There is little indication that the Senate will augment the bureau's budget. "Basically, we'll have a freeze," says Sen. Gorton, who chairs the Appropriations Subcommittee overseeing Interior Department funding. "We'll have the same amount of money for 1997 as for 1996 for the Interior Department, and out of that total I've got to fund almost all of the Indian programs, as well as national parks and monuments, the Bureau of Land Management, the National Forest Service, energy conservation and all of our cultural institutions."

The conflict over funding Indian programs is pitting a Republican-dominated Congress against a Democratic White House. But Indian policy is not a strictly partisan issue. The most vocal advocates on both sides of the debate over Indian rights in Congress — Arizona Sen. John McCain, an Indian supporter, and opponent Gorton — are both Republicans. And the lone Indian member of Congress, Campbell of Colorado, was elected in 1992 as a Democrat but switched to the Republican Party in March 1995 because he supported the GOP call for a constitutional amendment to balance the budget.

Lawmakers on both sides of the budget debate agree on the need to restructure the oft-criticized BIA. Citing a General Accounting Office finding released May 3 that government auditors were unable to account for an astounding $2.4 billion held in trust accounts for Indian tribes, McCain charged the agency at a recent hearing with "theft from the Indian people. I'm afraid the BIA's approach has been as bad as the land-grabbing policies of the past by which United States agencies separated Indians from their lands. This time-weary way of handling Indian assets has got to stop." [16]

In December, McCain introduced a bill that would shift authority away from BIA headquarters in Washington to area offices in order to give tribes greater influence over bureau operations.

Tribal Sovereignty

At the same time that Indian tribes are suffering program cutbacks at the hands of Congress, they are facing a mounting challenge from states over the extent of tribal sovereignty.

The U.S. Supreme Court handed a number of states a key victory in their quest to limit the ability of tribes to start gaming operations. On March 27, the court ruled in *Seminole Tribe of Florida v. Florida* that states cannot be sued in federal court for refusing to engage in good-faith negotiations with Indian tribes over opening casinos. The 5-4 ruling challenges the 1988 IGRA, which granted tribes the right to sue recalcitrant states over this issue.

The *Seminole* decision does not

Continued on p. 618

At Issue:

Should Congress make it easier for non-Indians to adopt Indian children?

yes

Rep. Gerald B.H. Solomon, R-N.Y.
From testimony before the Senate Indian Affairs Committee, June 26, 1996

As some of our sociologists and social workers negatively portray adoption and adoptive families, it is up to those of us who work with personal experience of adoption to relay its importance to the formation of our children and the strengthening of the family. . . .

It is up to those of us who have been adopted not only to share our stories with others but to speak out in favor of the adoption decision. My support has grown out of my fundamental view that every human life is precious and that every person deserves the right to life and a happy home.

I, myself, was blessed to be adopted by a generous stepfather and raised in a loving family. For these reasons, I wholeheartedly supported recent adoption legislation in the House, HR 3286. This bill makes adoption an option for families of all income levels by offering a $5,000 tax credit while also streamlining the process for interracial cases. This groundbreaking legislation will decrease the backlog of children in foster care and help find caring homes for all children. This legislation is extremely important in reforming adoption regulations. In the limited legislative schedule we have remaining, we must finish work on this bill to allow for the soonest relief for American families.

I am here today to also offer my full support for reform of the Indian Child Welfare Act to add to this adoption legislation. The Indian Child Welfare Act was passed in 1978 in response to a terrible problem within the Indian community; the high numbers of Indian children being placed in foster care and the breakup of many Indian families because of the unwarranted removal of their children by non-tribal public and private agencies. . . .

The problem that the act was created to correct, namely the inordinate number of Indian children in foster care, has actually risen since its enactment because of the increased authority the act can give an Indian tribe.

There have been cases of parents being blocked from adopting children because the Indian Child Welfare Act allows retroactive registration even after the biological parents have given up all legal rights to the child. . . .

This legislation is extremely important to the families of this country, Indian and non-Indian. Adoption plays a vital role in strengthening the family unit and protecting the values of this great nation. We must remember that the best interests of the children must be paramount in all child custody proceeding. Congress must work diligently to remove barriers to adoption and provide a sense of security to adoptive parents and children that their adoptions will be permanent.

no

Sen. Daniel K. Inouye, D-Hawaii
From testimony before the Senate Indian Affairs Committee, June 26, 1996

The removal of Indian children from their families and tribal communities has deep roots in this country. From the very beginning of our history as a nation, deliberate efforts by Europeans to "civilize" and "Christianize" the inhabitants of this country were directed at Indian children. . . .

These attitudes have also served to promote the removal of Indian children from their homes and place them in adoptive homes. . . . The adoption of Indian children became popular at a time when there was a decline in healthy, white children available for adoption by childless couples. Religious groups also encouraged their members to become foster or adoptive parents to Indian children. The Latter-day Saints placement program removed as many as 2,000 Hopi and Navajo children every year from their reservations, placing them in Mormon homes throughout the country.

In the early 1970s, the erosion of Indian family life received extensive publicity. Surveys conducted in 1969 and 1974 by the Association on American Indian Affairs disclosed the shocking disparity in placement rates for Indian and non-Indian children. These surveys revealed that over 25-35 percent of all Indian children were separated from their families and placed in foster homes, adoptive homes or institutions. . . .

The Indian Child Welfare Act was a reform measure enacted by the Congress in 1978 to combat "the wholesale separation of Indian children from their families" and tribal communities. With the passage of the act, federal law required that preference by given to Indian families, and Indian foster care and group homes in the placement of Indian children by state and private social service agencies. The act authorized an Indian tribe to intervene on behalf of a child in court proceedings that involve child custody matters and the placement of Indian children. . . .

Despite its shortcomings, the Indian Child Welfare Act serves as a ray of hope and promise to Indian people striving to retain their heritage and pride in a pluralistic society. The law was enacted by Congress to secure a long-overdue protection for Indian children. Tribal leaders have been resisting the removal of their children for over two and a half centuries. For each time an Indian child is taken from their ranks, their very existence as a culturally distinct people is diminished, and this nation's first Americans are threatened to the point of extinction.

I believe that it is time that Washington hears from Indian country on this matter that is of such critical importance to their efforts to preserve Indian families. After all, it is their children that will be affected by any amendments to the act.

FOR MORE INFORMATION

BUREAU OF INDIAN AFFAIRS, Interior Department, Main Interior Bldg., 18th and C Sts. N.W., Washington, D.C. 20240; (202) 208-3711. The main agency involved in federal Indian policy administers programs benefiting federally recognized tribes, mostly on reservations.

NATIONAL CONGRESS OF AMERICAN INDIANS, 900 Pennsylvania Ave. S.E., Washington, D.C. 20003; (202) 466-7767. The largest advocacy group representing Indians monitors legislation and regulations and provides information on member tribes.

NATIONAL INDIAN GAMING COMMISSION, 1441 L St. N.W., 9th floor, Washington, D.C. 20005; (202) 632-7003. Created under the 1988 Indian Gaming Regulatory Act, the commission oversees the management of casino gambling operations run by Indian tribes.

NATIONAL URBAN INDIAN POLICY COALITION, 4753 N. Broadway, Suite 1126, Chicago, Ill. 60640; (312) 784-0808. The coalition represents the interests of non-reservation Indians, who comprise more than half the Indian population and who do not qualify for most government support programs.

jeopardize existing gaming compacts, but it does call into question tribes' ability to open new casinos as the law allows. "The question is, in the long run, when some of these compacts have to be renewed, whether *Seminole* will impact them," says gaming commission Director Acevedo. "For those tribes that have not compacted with states, the ruling in effect acts almost like a moratorium on new gaming operations."

Because the 1988 law allows tribes to turn to the Interior Department for help when they run into obstacles with states over gaming, the Supreme Court ruling effectively left the issue in the hands of Interior Secretary Bruce Babbitt. But hostility to Indian gaming runs high in states that could prove influential in the November presidential election, such as Florida and California. For this reason, observers agree that it is highly unlikely that Babbitt will force the issue until after the election.

Meanwhile, states'-rights advocates welcomed the Supreme Court ruling. "I think it is entirely wrong to tell a state, whether it's Washington or Florida, that it cannot control the gambling within its boundaries," says Gorton. "I'm opposed to the expansion of Indian gambling because I'm opposed to the expansion of all gambling unless it's the decision of the people of an entire state that they want to go ahead with the activity. Under those circumstances, obviously I approve of the Supreme Court decision."

Gorton is at the center of another challenge to Indian rights in his home state of Washington, where the Lummi tribe is contesting the rights of non-Indian homeowners on their reservation to have unlimited access to reservation water. As a result of the allotment policies that enabled non-Indians to purchase reservation land, about half the residents of the Lummi Reservation are non-Indian homeowners. When the tribe dug a large well close to these private properties, the homeowners complained that the Lummis were threatening their water supply.

The homeowners cannot sue the tribe, however, because it is protected by the Indians' longstanding right to sovereign immunity. "It is the feeling of the non-Indians that what the Indians want to do is to make their property close to worthless, buy it at distressed prices and drive them off the reservation," says Gorton, who advocates abolishing Indian rights to sovereign immunity. "I believe that Indian self-determination and sovereignty are totally appropriate to the extent that they apply to the affairs of the members of the tribe," he says. "I do not believe that they should grant them special rights against their non-Indian neighbors, who can't vote in their elections and who aren't members of their tribe."

States won another concession June 20, when the House granted them more power to collect taxes on all Indian-run businesses. Under current law, tribes may buy land outside reservations and place it in trust with the government, thus shielding any businesses opened there from retail sales taxes. The new measure, an amendment to the $12.3 billion Interior appropriations bill for fiscal 1997, would require tribes to agree with states on tax collection before the land could be placed in trust. [17] The measure has long been sought by states such as New York, where Republican Gov. George E. Pataki plans to begin this summer taxing sales at gas stations and convenience stores run by the Senecas and other tribes. [18]

Another challenge to Indian sovereignty now before Congress would restrict the authority of tribes to intervene in the adoption of Indian children by non-Indians. (*See "At Issue," p. 617.*) A measure passed May 10 by the House to provide a tax credit of up to $5,000 to defray adoption expenses would also prohibit officials from making race the determining factor in adoption decisions. This would overturn a provision of the Indian Child Welfare Act, enacted in 1978 to halt longstanding adoption practices that handed as many as a third of Indian children over to non-Indian parents. [19]

Calling the measure "well-intended but misguided," McCain promised to try to keep the restriction on tribal authority out of the adoption measure when it goes to the Senate floor. "Nothing is as precious as our children," he said. "This is as true for Indians as for non-Indians." [20] ■

OUTLOOK

Taking Control

Many experts on Indian policy see the assault on tribal sovereignty by Congress and the states as a threat to Indians' ability to survive. Joseph Kalt, director of Harvard University's Project on American Indian Economic Development, believes that sovereignty is the key to economic development on reservations. "Our research says quite clearly that the successful tribes, which have broken their institutional dependency on the federal government, have done it in a two-step process of first asserting and taking control of their own sovereignty, and second, backing that up by building their own institutions of government," Kalt says.

Kalt compares Indian lands to Eastern Europe. "The countries like Hungary and the Czech Republic, which got out early from under the Soviet umbrella and are succeeding now, were able to establish the rule of law," Kalt says. "The story is the same in Indian country, where we keep finding that sovereignty precedes economic development."

To thwart current moves to erode tribal sovereignty, many Indian advocates are calling for greater participation by tribal members in local and national politics. "There should be more Indians here, or none at all," says Sen. Campbell. "One [Native American in Congress] is the wrong number; I can't do enough because I don't have the resources. There are 1.3 million enrolled Indians in this country, and anthropologists say there may be as many as 15 million Americans who have Indian ancestry that are not on a [tribal] roll. I can't very well say I speak for all Indians because they're not alike."

Campbell may have company after this fall's elections. At least three Indians are running on the Democratic ticket for the House — Bill Yellowtail, a Crow from Montana, Joe Bowen, an Upper Skagit from Washington state, and Georgianna Lincoln, an Athabaskan from Alaska.

Meanwhile, younger Indian leaders are gaining experience in tribal government with an eye toward higher office. "This is definitely the way we are going to have to go," says the Oneidas' Doxtator, who at 35 is thought to be the youngest female tribal leader in the country. "I'm not at the point of entering national politics just yet, but I do have that as a goal down the road for myself. That's the way we're going to be able to help America know and understand what our issues are on a political level." ■

Notes

[1] See "How to Succeed, How to Fail," *The Economist,* April 6, 1996, pp. 25-31.

[2] For a critical view of Gorton's record on Indian affairs, see Paul Shukovsky, "Sincerely Yours," *Common Cause Magazine,* fall 1995, pp. 22-23.

[3] See Howard Rudnitsky, "Big Chief Kerzner," *Forbes,* April 22, 1996, pp. 176-180.

[4] From testimony by Associate Deputy Attorney General Seth P. Waxman at hearings before the Senate Indian Affairs Committee held May 9, 1996.

[5] See Bruce Upbin, "Indian Chief," *Forbes,* May 20, 1996, pp. 179-180.

[6] See Blaine Harden, "Gambling Study Clears Senate Hurdle," *The Washington Post,* May 11, 1996. See also "Gambling Boom," *The CQ Researcher,* March 18, 1994, pp. 241-264.

[7] For background, see "Native Americans," *The CQ Researcher,* May 8, 1992, pp. 385-408.

[8] Unless otherwise specified, material in this section is based on Jack Utter, *American Indians* (1993).

[9] *Ibid.,* p. 46.

[10] *Ibid.,* p. 50.

[11] *Ibid.,* p. 54.

[12] *Ibid.,* p. 256.

[13] *Ibid.,* p. 257.

[14] *Ibid.,* p. 134.

[15] The White House, "Memorandum for the Heads of Executive Departments and Agencies," April 29, 1994.

[16] McCain, chairman of the Senate Indian Affairs Committee, spoke June 11, 1996, at the committee's hearing on Indian trust fund management.

[17] See Allan Freedman, "House Passes Interior Bill, But Difficulty Lies Ahead," *Congressional Quarterly Weekly Report,* June 22, 1996, pp. 1748-1749.

[18] See Raymond Hernandez, "Reservations May Be Taxed on Some Sales Outside Tribes," *The New York Times,* May 5, 1996.

[19] See Lori Nitschke, "Panel Votes to Delete Limits on Tribal Role in Adoptions," *Congressional Quarterly Weekly Report,* June 22, 1996, p. 1767. See "Adopting Native American Children," in "Adoption," *The CQ Researcher,* Nov. 26, 1993, pp. 1033-1056.

[20] Utter, *op. cit.,* pp. 258-259.

Bibliography

Selected Sources Used

Books

Bordewich, Fergus M., *Killing the White Man's Indian: Reinventing Native Americans at the End of the Twentieth Century*, Doubleday, 1996.

The author, who spent much of his childhood on Indian reservations, challenges white society's myths about Indians as mindless victims or inhuman savages to examine their place in modern U.S. society.

Gattuso, John, ed., *Insight Guides: Native America*, Houghton Mifflin, 1994.

Introduced by an insightful overview of American Indian history, this tour guide of Indian country describes the culture and history of individual tribes of North America.

Matthiessen, Peter, *Indian Country*, Penguin, 1979.

A noted naturalist and author cites 10 tragic episodes of encroachment by whites on Indian lands that reflect mainstream society's threat to Indian culture.

Utter, Jack, *American Indians: Answers to Today's Questions*, National Woodlands Publishing Co., 1993.

A professor at the Center for Indian Bilingual Teacher Training at Prescott (Ariz.) College offers an excellent review of legal, cultural and social issues facing Indians today.

Articles

"The Native — and Not So Native — American Way," *The New York Times Magazine,* Feb. 27, 1994, pp. 45-52.

Two articles point out differing approaches to economic development. In "The Apaches," Eric Eckholm describes a tribe that is trying to survive by combining traditional enterprises with assembly shops. In "The Pequots," Francis X. Clines shows how a small Eastern tribe has struck it rich with casinos.

Reno, Janet, "A Federal Commitment to Tribal Justice Systems," *Judicature*, November-December 1995, pp. 113-117.

The U.S. attorney general reviews the history of U.S.-Indian relations in the area of law enforcement and the courts in an issue of the magazine dedicated entirely to the Indian tribal court system.

Shukovsky, Paul, "Sincerely Yours," *Common Cause Magazine*, fall, 1995, pp. 22-23.

With his campaigns to defend non-Indian property rights and reduce funding for many Indian programs, Sen. Slade Gorton, R-Wash., has earned a reputation as the one of the most ardent critics of Indian sovereignty in Congress.

Van Biema, David, "Bury My Heart in Committee, " *Time*, Sept. 18, 1995, pp. 48-51.

Many of the country's poorest Indians, such as the Pine Ridge Oglala Sioux, live on remote reservations with few employment opportunities. They faced even greater destitution last fall as Congress cut funding for Indian programs.

Reports and Studies

Cornell, Stephen, and Joseph P. Kalt, *Reloading the Dice: Improving the Chances for Economic Development on American Indian Reservations,* Harvard Project on American Indian Economic Development, March 1992.

The authors examine the myriad obstacles to economic development in Indian country and conclude that success depends on three factors: sovereignty, effective governing institutions and a realistic economic plan that harnesses each tribe's particular assets.

Indian Health Service, U.S. Department of Health and Human Services, *Trends in Indian Health 1995.*

The Indian Health Service, set up in 1954 to provide health care to members of recognized tribes, publishes statistics that provide a barometer of health in Indian country. Indians are far more likely to suffer from alcoholism, diabetes and a number of other diseases than other Americans.

National Indian Gaming Association, *A Historical Review of Gaming in the United States,* April 1994.

An advocacy group presents an overview of both Indian and non-Indian gambling in the United States and assess the impact of Indian gaming on the industry as a whole.

Walke, Roger, *Indian Issues in the Second Session of the 104th Congress*, Congressional Research Service, Feb. 23, 1996.

The author, an analyst at the Library of Congress' research branch, found that more than 340 bills introduced during the current session of Congress have provisions that would affect Indian tribes.

The Next Step

Additional information from UMI's Newspaper & Periodical Abstracts database

American Indian Civil Rights Movement

Ayers, Jane, "Leonard Peltier should be freed," *San Francisco Chronicle,* June 5, 1996, p. 21.
Ayers examines the case of Leonard Peltier, a member of the American Indian Movement who has been listed for the 20th year in a row on Amnesty International's list of "prisoners of conscience." She concludes by calling for the Clinton administration to free Peltier.

Barnes, Dave, "Protest turns to prayer as street is renamed," *Chicago Tribune,* Aug. 4, 1995, p. 1.
Forty representatives from the Chicago and Joliet, Ill., chapters of the American Indian Movement traveled to Prairie Grove, Ill., to lend their support to local efforts to change the name of Squaw Creek Rd. because it was viewed as offensive.

Boaz, Amy, "Becoming part of what is known: The autobiography of Russell Means," *Library Journal,* Oct. 15, 1995, p. 68.
Russell Means' forthcoming autobiography, *Where White Men Fear To Tread,* illuminates a sensational life. Means has been a leader of the American Indian Movement since the early 1970s.

Glier, Ray, and Chuck Murr, "AIM secures permits, plans Series protests," *USA Today,* Oct. 19, 1995, p. 3.
At the 1995 World Series games between the Cleveland Indians and Atlanta Braves in Atlanta-Fulton County stadium, American Indian protesters will rally against both clubs. In order to protest outside Jacobs Field in Cleveland, the American Indian Movement had to go to federal court to secure permits.

"Indian trial documents open to public," *Denver Post,* Oct. 10, 1995, p. 4.
For the first time, FBI reports and tape-recordings from the trials of Leonard Peltier and Dennis Banks and materials documenting the work of Indian activists in the emerging American Indian Movement in the 1970s and 1980s have been donated to the University of New Mexico and will be available to the public.

McKay, David, "UP Indians hole up in protest," *Detroit News & Free Press,* Aug. 24, 1995, p. B4.
About 20 members of the Keweenaw Bay Indian Community in the western Upper Peninsula of Michigan continued their occupation on Aug. 23, 1995, of a tribal center in a dispute over their loss of voting rights. The tribal chairman, however, said the protesters were making a grab for shares in the tribe's casino gambling profits.

Bureau of Indian Affairs

Anderson, Terry L., "How the government keeps Indians in poverty," *The Wall Street Journal,* Nov. 22, 1995, p. 10.
Anderson discusses the causes of "the appalling economic conditions" on Indian reservations in the U.S. and places part of the blame on BIA trusteeship of Indian land, which he says imposes layers of bureaucracy and legal constraints on Indian land-use decisions. Anderson urges Congress and federal bureaucrats to give Native Americans "the freedom they deserve"and loosen the grip of the BIA.

"Cuts in Indian budget would hamstring tribes," *Denver Post,* Aug. 10, 1995, p. 10
An editorial comments on the proposed deep cuts in the Bureau of Indian Affairs budget by the GOP-controlled Congress in 1995, arguing that the cuts are so deep that tribal governments may cease to exist.

"How to succeed, how to fail," *The Economist,* April 6, 1996, p. 25-31.
The difference between success and failure for Indian tribes lies in keeping the Bureau of Indian affairs at arm's length. A tribal government that fosters initiative and insulates the tribe from petty politics also helps.

"Indian Bureau sees 'devastation' in its budget," *The New York Times,* Sept. 10, 1995, p. 29.
The Bureau of Indian Affairs says that layoffs it plans because of cuts in its budget expected to be approved by Congress will gut its administrative staff and "wreak devastation" on tribes. The bureau plans to eliminate at least 3,000 full-time and part-time positions, about a fourth of its work force, on the assumption that Congress will go ahead with a 15 percent budget cut approved by the Senate in August 1995.

McAllister, Bill, "BIA plans to cut at least 2,600 from work force," *The Washington Post,* Sept. 7, 1995, p. 1.
The Bureau of Indian Affairs plans to lay off between 2,600 and 4,000 of its 12,000 workers, the most severe personnel cuts any federal agency has undertaken in the round of budget reductions in 1995.

Miniclier, Kit, "Budget ax due to chop up to 3,000 jobs at BIA," *Denver Post,* Sept. 9, 1995, p. B1.

Anticipating a major hit from a budget-cutting Congress, the BIA is preparing in September 1995, to fire about a quarter of its work force. The agency says such cutbacks could reduce funding for individual tribal services by one-third.

Gambling and Gaming

Chappell, Kevin, "Black Indians hit the jackpot in casino bonanza," *Ebony,* June 1995, pp. 46-50.
The members of the Connecticut Mashantucket Pequot Indian tribe — half of whom are black — have hit the jackpot with their multimillion-dollar Foxwoods Resort Casino. Their operation, which boasts 15 restaurants and two luxury hotels, is grossing $2.5 million a day, which could make them $1 billion by year's end.

Dao, James, "Indians offer part of profit from casino," *The New York Times,* March 2, 1995, p. B6.
As they unveiled a plan to build a casino in the Catskill Mountains of Sullivan County, N.Y., leaders of the Oneida Indian Nation said on March 1, 1995, that they would discuss giving the state a share of their profits in exchange for Gov. George E. Pataki's approval. Pataki, who wields virtual veto power over such proposals, has said he opposes the plan, and his aides again reiterated his opposition.

"Harrah's pact with Indians," *The Wall Street Journal,* June 13, 1996, p. A10.
Harrah's Entertainment Inc. said it reached an agreement with the Prairie Band of Potawatomi Indians for a $37 million casino project near Topeka, Kan. The transaction is subject to approval by the National Indian Gaming Commission.

"Highly effective Indians," *The Economist,* April 6, 1996, p. 26.
The Oneida tribe of Wisconsin has spent the money it has made from its 2,000-slot-machine complex outside Green Bay on economic development and projects to improve the general quality of life. The tribe now has money to spend reviving its dying language.

Sileo, Chi Chi, "Indians and states up ante in high-stakes legislation," *Insight on the News,* Sept. 18, 1995, pp. 16-17.
American Indians say gambling revenue has made tribes self-sufficient and claim it provides income for education and business ventures. But most observers say that these establishments will not continue to offer as much revenue as they do now.

Orwall, Bruce, "High stakes casino game: Mirage vs. Indians," *The Wall Street Journal,* Sept. 21, 1995, p. B1.
The battle between the Mashantucket Pequot Indians of eastern Connecticut and Mirage Resorts Inc. for the rights to develop a seaside property in Bridgeport into a gambling resort is discussed. The Indians own the Foxwoods Resort Casino in Ledyard, which has enjoyed a state-sanctioned monopoly on casino gambling, but when it became clear that legal gambling was likely to hit Bridgeport, the Pequots entered the fray.

Williams, Mike, "Indians lose court fight on casinos," *Atlanta Constitution,* March 28, 1996, p. 1.
Indian tribes hoping to bring gambling casinos to their reservations suffered a setback on March 27, 1996, when the U.S. Supreme Court sided 5-4 with Florida in a dispute with Seminole Indians. Ruling in the case brought by the Seminoles, the high court said Congress cannot force states into federal court to settle disputes over allowing casino gambling on reservations.

Indian Health Issues

Cheadle, Allen, David Pearson, Edward Wagner and Bruce Psaty, et. al., "A community-based approach to preventing alcohol use among adolescents on an American Indian reservation," *Public Health Reports,* July 1995, pp. 439-447.
The effectiveness of a five-year community-based health promotion program to reduce the rate of substance use, particularly alcohol, by adolescents on a Plains State American Indian reservation is examined. The results showed that the use of both alcohol and marijuana declined substantially among American Indian adolescents living on the reservation.

Hagaman, Dianne, "On a mission," *News Photographer,* April 1996, p. 4-8.
Photojournalist Hagaman describes her investigation of alcoholism among Native Americans in Seattle. She quickly realized the people whose stories most interested her weren't necessarily on the street.

Kimball, Ernest H., Howard I. Goldberg and Mark W. Oberle, "The prevalence of selected risk factors for chronic disease among American Indians in Washington State," *Public Health Reports,* May 1996, pp. 264-271.
The health status of American Indians continues to lag behind that of other Americans. Tobacco use, alcohol consumption and weight are discussed.

Peterson, Dan E., Patrick L. Remington, Marie A. Kuykendall and Marty S. Kanarek et. al., "Behavioral risk factors of Chippewa Indians living on Wisconsin reservations," *Public Health Reports,* November 1994, pp. 820-823.
A survey was conducted to determine the prevalence of behavioral risk factors among members of the Chippewa tribe living on reservations in Wisconsin. Chippewa adults seem to have higher prevalences of several chronic disease and injury risk factors.

Indian Schools

"Neglected Indian schools," *Christian Science Moni-*

***tor,* Sept. 19, 1995, p. 20.**
An editorial discusses the need for funding for schools on America's Indian reservations, and criticizes congressional cuts in what the Bureau of Indian Affairs spends on school repair and construction.

Ratelle, Louise, "Gains for Indians and Inuit," *Chronicle of Higher Education,* Jan. 20, 1995, p. A45-A46.
An increase in the number of Indians and Inuit enrolling in Canada's postsecondary schools is due in part to the growth in academic programs designed specifically for Canada's aboriginal peoples.

"Schools on reservations crumbling for lack of repair money," *The New York Times,* Sept. 3, 1995, p. 17.
The horrible condition of schools on American Indian reservations is examined. Tribal school leaders say the schools are crumbling because of budget cuts, inefficiency and neglect by the federal Bureau of Indian Affairs and Congress.

Snyder, Jim, "Michigan plan to end scholarship program for American Indians infuriates beneficiaries," *Chronicle of Higher Education,* March 24, 1995, p. A32.
A proposal made by Gov. John Engler of Michigan to eliminate full scholarships for American Indians who attend public colleges in his state has infuriated Indian students. The controversy is discussed.

Stecker, Naseem, "Indians will protest plan to scrap tuition program," *Detroit News,* Feb. 20, 1995, p. A7.
Native Americans angered by Michigan Gov. John Engler's 1996 budget proposal to eliminate the state's tuition waiver program plan to protest March 8, 1995, in Lansing. Engler has said profits that Indians receive from casino gambling have eliminated the need for the $3.3 million program.

Waldmeir, Pete, "American Indians have two words for Engler's stance on native tuition: Buffalo chips," *Detroit News,* Nov. 22, 1995, p. D3.
Pete Waldmeir says Michigan's Native Americans are angered over Gov. John Engler's vow to terminate the Indian Tuition Waiver Program while the Indian-run gaming casinos contribute more than $18 million a year to the state treasury, and while Engler has raided some $55 million from the Indian casino-financed Michigan Strategic Fund for multimillionaire Mike Ilitch's new Detroit ballpark.

Native American History

Edmunds, R. David, "Native Americans, new voices: American Indian history," *American Historical Review,* June 1995, pp. 717-740.
There was a general belief in the late 19th century that Native Americans, as a separate and unique ethnic minority group, would essentially disappear, and the "American Historical Review" reflected this perspective. Since the 1960s, there has been an explosion of interest in Native American history.

Emspak, Jesse, "Repatriation battles," *Progressive,* July 1995, pp. 14-15.
Under the Native American Graves and Repatriation Act of 1990, museums must catalog and return human remains and sacred objects at the request of Native American tribes.

"The Indians lose again," *The Economist,* Jan. 28, 1995, pp. 81-82.
A new museum is being set up at the Smithsonian Institution to exhibit aspects of American Indian culture. The museum seems designed to improve Indian self-esteem rather than for historical accuracy.

Rankin, Charles E., "Savage journalists and civilized Indians: A different view," *Journalism History,* Autumn 1995, pp. 102-111.
To the minds of a number of historians, western correspondents have become symbols for hostile attitudes toward Native Americans. Such correspondents were somehow immune to viewing native peoples humanely, and they needlessly exacerbated tensions between the races.

Poverty

Freemantle, Tony, "A state of emergency for Indians," *Houston Chronicle,* Jan. 4, 1996, p. A2.
For about 10,000 American Indians living in reservations in South Dakota, North Dakota and Nebraska, one of the nation's poorest regions, the political standoff in Washington D.C., over the federal budget has reached crisis proportions.

Harlan, Bill, "Impoverished Sioux tribe may face fund cuts," *Los Angeles Times,* Sept. 27, 1995, p. A5.
The Republican-controlled Congress has proposed cutting the Bureau of Indian Affairs budget by $180 million as part of the push to slash the federal deficit. House lawmakers are also considering a tax on Native American casinos. The proposed cuts are galling to the Oglala Sioux of South Dakota.

Walsh, Catherine, "Perspectives," *America,* Oct. 14, 1995, p. 8.
Explicit guarantees for Native Americans' well-being are being violated. Congress is proposing deep cuts for Native American programs in the 1996, Interior appropriations bill.

Back Issues

Great Research on Current Issues Starts Right Here...Recent topics covered by The CQ Researcher are listed below. Before May 1991, reports were published under the name of Editorial Research Reports.

JANUARY 1995
Treating Addiction
Child Custody and Support
Parents and Schools
Non-Proliferation Treaty at 25

FEBRUARY 1995
Cracking Down on Immigration
The Business of Sports
Reinventing Government
Housing Discrimination

MARCH 1995
Death Penalty Debate
Primary Care
Democracy in Africa
Environmental Movement at 25

APRIL 1995
Abortion Clinic Protests
Dieting and Health
Combating AIDS
Rethinking Affirmative Action

MAY 1995
Assisted Suicide Controversy
Overhauling Social Security
Learning to Read
Mandatory Sentencing

JUNE 1995
Combating Infectious Disease
Property Rights
Repetitive Stress Injuries
Regulating the Internet

JULY 1995
War Crimes
Highway Safety
Combating Terrorism
Preventing Teen Drug Use

AUGUST 1995
Job Stress
Organ Transplants
United Nations at 50
Advances in Cancer Research

SEPTEMBER 1995
Catholic Church in the U.S.
Northern Ireland Cease-Fire
High School Sports
Teaching History

OCTOBER 1995
Quebec's Future
Revitalizing the Cities
Networking the Classroom
Indoor Air Pollution

NOVEMBER 1995
The Working Poor
The Jury System
Sex, Violence and the Media
Police Misconduct

DECEMBER 1995
Teens and Tobacco
Gene Therapy's Future
Global Water Shortages
Third-Party Prospects

JANUARY 1996
Emergency Medicine
Punishing Sex Offenders
Bilingual Education
Helping the Homeless

FEBRUARY 1996
Reforming the CIA
Campaign Finance Reform
Academic Politics
Getting Into College

MARCH 1996
The British Monarchy
Preventing Juvenile Crime
Tax Reform
Pursuing the Paranormal

APRIL 1996
Centennial Olympic Games
Managed Care
Protecting Endangered Species
New Military Culture

MAY 1996
Russia's Political Future
Marriage and Divorce
Year-Round Schools
Taiwan, China and the U.S.

JUNE 1996
Rethinking NAFTA
First Ladies
Teaching Values
Labor Movement's Future

JULY 1996
Recovered-Memory Debate

Back issues are available for $5.00 (subscribers) or $8.00 (non-subscribers). Quantity discounts apply to orders over ten. To order, call Congressional Quarterly Customer Service at (202) 887-8621.

Binders are available for $18.00. To order call 1-800-638-1710. Please refer to stock number 648.

Future Topics

- ***Sexual Harassment Update***
- ***Public Education Under Attack***
- ***Animal Rights Debate***

THE CQ Researcher

PUBLISHED BY CONGRESSIONAL QUARTERLY INC.

Crackdown on Sexual Harassment

Is the nation overreacting to the problem?

The nation's sensitivity to sexual harassment has changed profoundly since October 1991, when Anita Hill's harassment charges against Supreme Court nominee Clarence Thomas riveted Americans to their TV sets. Sexual harassment claims filed with the federal government have increased dramatically, as have damages paid to successful plaintiffs. Some critics sympathetic to business say the nation has overreacted. They attack several recent multimillion-dollar jury awards as excessive punishments for what they claim is nothing more than crude sexual joking at work. Women's-rights activists respond that sexual harassment is often emotionally devastating, and that only a tiny proportion of the women who have been harassed ever file formal complaints, though harassment is a widespread problem in the workplace.

INSIDE THIS ISSUE

CQ July 19, 1996 • Volume 6, No. 27 • Pages 625-648

Formerly Editorial Research Reports

CRACKDOWN ON SEXUAL HARASSMENT

COVER: WOMEN AGAINST SEXUAL HARASSMENT MARCH IN PROTEST JUNE 27 AT A NEVADA MITSUBISHI DEALERSHIP. IN APRIL, THE EQUAL EMPLOYMENT OPPORTUNITY COMMISSION FILED SUIT AGAINST MITSUBISHI MOTOR MANUFACTURING OF AMERICA INC. ALLEGING RAMPANT HARASSMENT AT ITS PLANT IN NORMAL, ILL. (JOHN GURZINSKI)

THE CQ Researcher

July 19, 1996
Volume 6, No. 27

The CQ Researcher (ISSN 1056-2036). Formerly Editorial Research Reports. Published weekly (48 times per year, not printed March 1, May 31, Aug. 30, Nov. 29) by Congressional Quarterly Inc., 1414 22nd St., N.W., Washington, D.C. 20037. Annual subscription rate for libraries, businesses and government is $319. Additional rates furnished upon request. Periodicals postage paid at Washington, D.C. POSTMASTER: Send address changes to The CQ Researcher, 1414 22nd St., N.W., Washington, D.C. 20037.

Crackdown on Sexual Harassment

By Sarah Glazer

The Issues

Peggy Kimzey, a Wal-Mart shipping clerk in Warsaw, Mo., was bending over a package when she heard the store manager and another male employee snickering behind her. Kimzey stood up and asked what they were doing. "Well," the manager smirked, "I just found someplace to put my screwdriver." When Kimzey asked him to stop the crude remarks, he replied, "You don't know, you might like it."

That may have been the most offensive comment directed at Kimzey during her four years at Wal-Mart, but it was far from all she endured, according to her attorneys. Toward the end of her employment, Kimzey says, female employees were subjected almost daily to kicks and degrading remarks.

Kimzey quit her job in April 1993 and a year later sued Wal-Mart for sexual harassment, claiming that the company never responded to her complaints about harassment. In June 1995, a jury ordered the huge retailer to pay her more than $50 million — the largest damage award ever in a sexual harassment case. [1]

Some observers see the jury's award as an example of the sexual harassment litigation wave run amok. *Forbes* magazine recently cited the case as an example of lawyers going after companies "with the deepest pockets" for trivial slights. [2]

"We have denied that much of the [alleged] activity occurred, and what activity occurred [Kimzey] didn't complain about," says Wal-Mart spokeswoman Betsy Reithmeyer. The company's position is that Kimzey "wasn't offended by it because she didn't complain about it," Reithmeyer adds.

The case is currently under a two-pronged appeal. Wal-Mart is challenging the verdict itself, and Kimzey is appealing the judge's decision to reduce the $50 million award for punitive damages to $5 million. "Fifty million sounds like a lot," says Carla Holste, one of Kimzey's lawyers, "but when compared with Wal-Mart's $32 billion in assets, even they admit it's not enough to bankrupt them. I think the jury felt like $50 million is enough to deter [Wal-Mart] from doing it again. Five million is nothing; they'll make it up in a day."

The Kimzey case is a reminder that sexual harassment cases are rarely simple. As Americans learned during the October 1991 Supreme Court confirmation hearings for Clarence Thomas, every story has two sides, and it is often difficult to discern the truth (*see p. 638*).

In the five years since University of Oklahoma law Professor Anita Hill charged Thomas with sexual harassment, men and women alike have become much more aware of the issue.

The Thomas hearings gave Americans a "crash course" in sexual harassment, says Helen Norton, director of equal opportunity programs at the Women's Legal Defense Fund. Although many Americans didn't believe Hill, Norton says the hearings opened women's eyes. "Women saw there was a legal name for what they had experienced — and it was illegal," she says. "It emboldened them to come forward."

Since the hearings, sexual harassment complaints filed with the federal Equal Employment Opportunity Commission (EEOC) have more than doubled, and monetary awards have more than tripled. (*See graphs, p. 630.*) "A lot of us forget how recently sexual harassment has been accepted as a violation of the law," says EEOC Legal Counsel Ellen Vargyas. "It's been only 10 years since it was accepted as a viable legal theory" by the Supreme Court (*see p. 633*).

Yet new cases continue to touch raw nerves, years after some experts had predicted that sexual harassment would die away with the growing acceptance of women in the workplace. On April 9, the EEOC sued Mitsubishi Motor Manufacturing of America Inc. in what could become the largest sexual harassment suit ever prosecuted.

The class-action suit alleges that sexual harassment has been rampant at the Japanese automaker's Normal, Ill., plant since at least 1990. The agency says that if it wins, the victims could number in the hundreds, the damages in the tens of millions.

The alleged harassment ranged from sexual graffiti to making women's acquiescence in sexual relationships a condition of their employment. Women complainants have said that male workers circulated photographs of sex parties with naked women, drew obscene pictures on the assembly line and grabbed women's breasts and genitals.

Mitsubishi's initial defiance surprised the business community. *The Wall Street Journal* called the company's denial of all charges and hardball tactics a "risky" strategy. [3] On April 11, shortly after the

Sexual Harassment in the Workplace

Nearly 75 percent of the mid-sized and large firms surveyed recently reported sexual harassment claims last year, compared with just over 50 percent in 1991. Most of the complaints were against co-workers rather than superiors.*

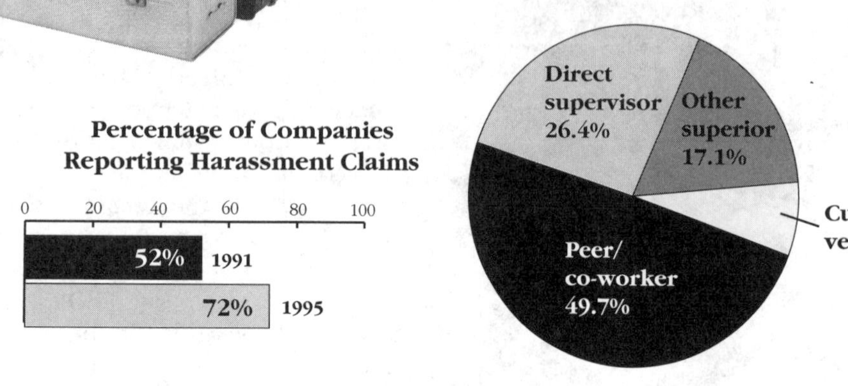

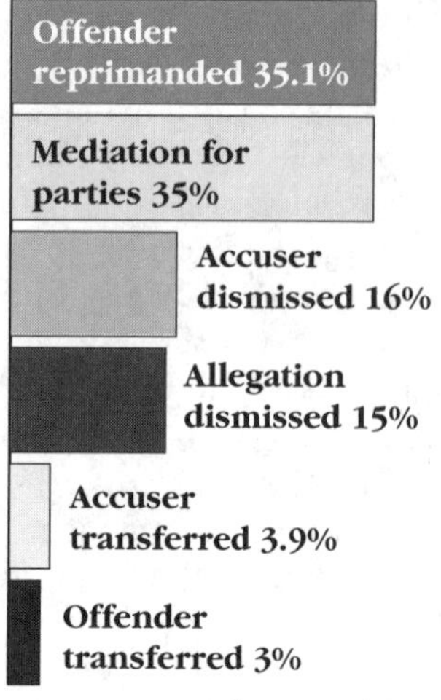

Percentages do not add to 100 percent.

* *Of the 456 firms surveyed, 325 reported a total of 1,376 harassment claims since 1991.*

Source: American Management Association, June 4-6, 1996

suit was filed, Mitsubishi sponsored an all-expenses-paid trip for employees and their families to protest the suit in front of the EEOC's Chicago offices. Afterwards, a female worker who had complained of sexual harassment said she received an anonymous death threat — a scrawled note in her locker with the words, "Die Bitch! You'll be Sorry." [4]

The business community has rarely reacted to sexual harassment charges with "the kind of in-your-face challenge to the EEOC" that Mitsubishi initially exhibited, says Peter Eide, manager of labor relations at the U.S. Chamber of Commerce. Mitsubishi's conciliatory step in May, when it hired former Labor Secretary Lynn Martin to review the company's policies and practices, was "more indicative of what companies are doing," Eide says. "Most employers, I think, understand the need to take complaints seriously."

By comparison, the Swedish pharmaceutical company Astra USA Inc. responded swiftly when it was thrown on the defensive. (*See story, p. 631.*) On April 29, just days before *Business Week* published the results of a six-month investigation reporting wide-ranging sexual harassment, the company quickly suspended its U.S. chief executive and two top lieutenants. [5]

Women's-rights groups credit passage of the sweeping Civil Rights Act of 1991 for the increase in sexual harassment litigation. By giving women alleging sexual harassment the right to jury trials and the right to sue for compensatory and punitive damages, the act led to much larger monetary awards. [6] Previously, the law only allowed women to win reinstatement in their old job and back pay.

But some critics believe the nation overreacted in its determination to respond to sexual harassment complaints. The Independent Women's Forum was founded in 1992 by a group of politically conservative women, some of whom had been active in Thomas' defense. "We don't deny sexual harassment exists," says Anita Blair, executive vice president and general counsel of the Arlington, Va.-based organization, "but we do not think it should be trivialized. Unfortunately, a lot of times real, serious harassment is overlooked in favor of things that are really more a case of people not getting along together in the workplace."

In the same vein, *Forbes* assailed the trend toward million-dollar sexual harassment suits as Washington's attempt "to stamp out sex in the workplace." The magazine calculated that the EEOC's suit against Mitsubishi could result in damages of up to $210 million — if every female employee receives the maximum $300,000 allowed under the 1991 civil rights law. "[D]oes the punishment truly fit the crime? Do we really want lawyers and bureaucrats dictating personal behavior?" the authors asked. [7]

Lawsuits, usually long and costly, can become Pyrrhic victories even if they're successful. Alice W. Ballard, an employment-rights lawyer in Philadelphia, warns clients to be prepared to lose their jobs if they sue. "It's likely you'll get fired or life will get so unpleasant you will have to leave," she says.

Most women don't face the kind of

A Tale of Harassment — and Vindication

"The things that were said to me and done to me were unprintable," says Barbara Martin, "so when people read the newspaper, they think [what happened] is nothing."

In 1988, Martin became the first woman to work as a plant operator at the Youngstown, Ohio, wastewater treatment plant. A year later she sued the city for sexual harassment.

This is what really happened, she says: At one point, a co-worker pinned her up against the wall and pressed his body into hers. Another time, her supervisor told her, "I don't [have oral sex] with women because they smell like dead fish."

Press reports cleaned up such incidents, simply describing them as innocent sexual "innuendo," she says. Yet to Martin, the continual comments by her boss about her body in front of co-workers, his attempt to kiss her in a locked car and his threats to drill a peep-hole into the woman's shower room felt more sinister.

"It is such a horrible feeling," she says of the harassment from her boss and several other employees. "They make it so you're not a human being."

After Martin complained to the city, she says she received death threats over the phone and was assigned to risky jobs. Martin quit in January 1989 and filed suit against the city for sexual harassment. She lost in 1990, but the 6th U.S. Circuit Court of Appeals reversed the lower court's jury verdict, declaring that Martin had been sexually harassed and retaliated against by her employer for complaining. The city appealed, but in 1992 the U.S. Supreme Court upheld the appeals court decision. Martin settled out of court in 1994.[1]

Martin is ambivalent about whether the whole process was worth it. "I lost my job, I lost my career," she says. "It took me six years, to the point where it destroyed my marriage and my family." Martin, 39, a mother of two, says she doesn't remember Christmases or birthdays since so many family occasions were marred with death threats and other retaliatory acts — like the smashing of her car windshield.

"The only reason I started the lawsuit was to try to get back my dignity," Martin says. Today, when she see anti-sexual harassment posters hanging in city offices, she views them as "plaques" commemorating her fight. She says women hired after her appear to be treated much better. But she's not sure she would go through with it again, knowing what she knows now. "If faced with the same situation," Martin says, "I would decide to leave [the job] or put up with it, because trying to stop it is so hard."

[1] The 1992 Supreme Court decision was *Youngstown, Ohio, v. Martin.*

---

retaliation reported at Mitsubishi. "The more common thing is the person just loses position," Ballard says. "They don't get anything important to do; they're put in an uncomfortable workspace; they're left out of meetings; their messages get lost; there's more and more petty harassment."

Employers trying to avoid costly lawsuits tend to invest in employee training, consultants and strongly worded policies. But conservatives charge that these efforts mainly create unnecessary paranoia and tension between men and women. "Men are retreating to the safety of their offices, avoiding private contact with female co-workers and carefully censoring their speech," two management professors wrote last year in the conservative *National Review.*[8]

"Every insult, joke and dirty picture shouldn't be a federal case," agrees Ellen Frankel Paul, professor of political science at Bowling Green State University in Ohio and a longstanding critic of current trends in sexual harassment law. Her advice to women is to "cool it" before reacting to unpleasant incidents or remarks. These days, she complains, things have gotten so bad that men have to think twice about everything. "Should I be saying, 'You look nice today?' If someone is upset, do you put your arm around them and say, 'Is something wrong?' Everything is under a fine microscope, which I don't think is good for men and women."

But San Francisco psychiatrist Peter Rutter, author of the 1996 book *Sex, Power and Boundaries: Understanding and Preventing Sexual Harassment,* sees the new tension as an inevitable consequence of changes in what is socially acceptable. "Society has taken a stand" against sexual harassment, he says, "that creates a new standard for people to meet in daily life." This stage may be awkward, he adds, but it can also be educational.

Indeed, although women are still more likely than men to see certain kinds of workplace behavior as sexual harassment, surveys show the differences in perception between the sexes are narrowing. But differences still remain. (*See chart, p. 632.*)

"It's very clear that men have been raised to think they should push against boundaries at least until they've been told 'No' — then maybe a little bit after they've been told 'No,' " Rutter says.

As Americans grapple with changing attitudes about sexual harassment, these are among the questions being asked:

Are the penalties for sexual harassment excessive?

In one of the nation's first sexual harassment cases, an Environmental Protection Agency employee alleged in 1974 that her job was abolished after she refused to sleep with the

Harassment Cases and Awards on the Rise

The number of sexual harassment cases filed with the Equal Employment Opportunity Commission more than doubled from 1990 to 1995, and damages paid to plaintiffs more than tripled, rising from $7.1 million to $24.3 million. The rising caseload has been linked to increased awareness of the issue following Anita Hill's charges against Clarence Thomas in 1991 during his confirmation hearings for the Supreme Court.

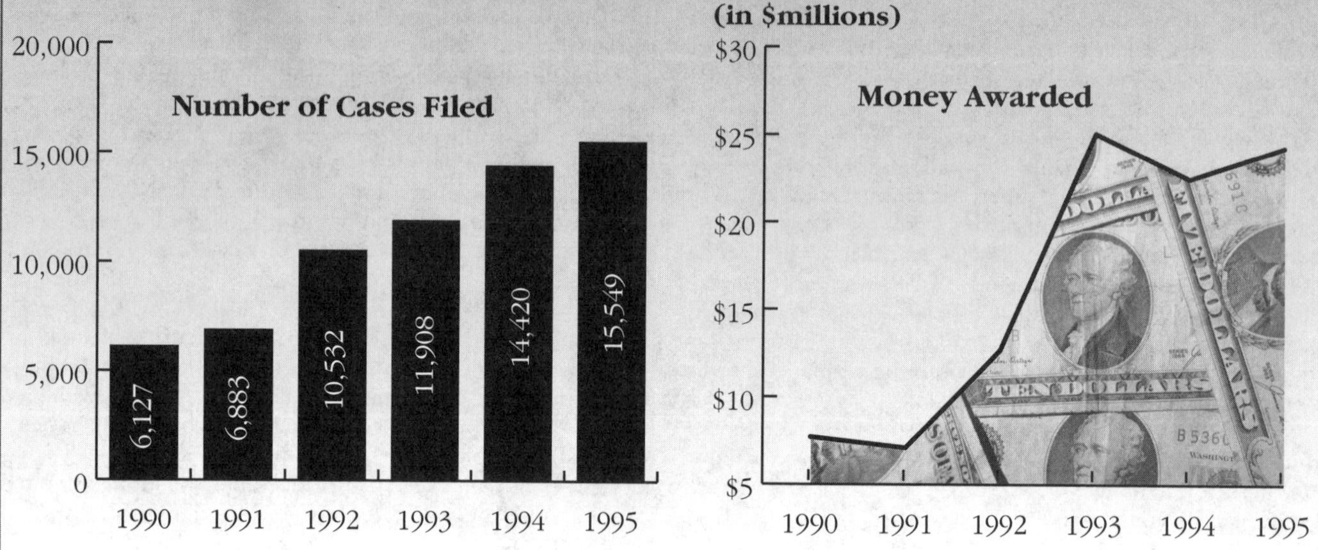

Note: The totals include data from local Fair Employment Practices Agencies (FEPAs), which are state and local agencies that process employment discrimination charges for the EEOC.

Source: Equal Employment Opportunity Commission, Oct. 27, 1995

boss. She charged it was a case of discrimination based on her sex. A federal district court dismissed the case because, it said, the discrimination was based not on the fact that the plaintiff was a woman but that she refused to have sex with her supervisor.

Three years later, the decision was reversed on appeal, and the woman was awarded $18,000 in back pay. The U.S. Court of Appeals for the District of Columbia ruled, in *Barnes v. Costle,* that sexual harassment is a form of discrimination in employment, which is illegal under Title VII of the 1964 Civil Rights Act. [9] It was the first federal court to do so.

Women's rights activists often cite the *Barnes* case in spotlighting past deficiencies in the old legal system, when sexual harassment was not yet widely recognized as a form of discrimination. Even once it was recognized, women still could not receive much in damages.

"A lot of harassment victims were just made miserable — they couldn't leave their job because they needed to pay the rent," says Norton at the Women's Legal Defense Fund. "You saw cases where the woman proved the case but because she hadn't lost her job, the judge said, 'There's no remedy for you' and ordered her to pay her employer's court costs."

The 1991 Civil Rights Act gave women the right not only to collect "compensatory damages" for the abuse they suffered but also "punitive damages" aimed at punishing the employer. President George Bush, who had opposed an earlier version of the bill, agreed to a compromise that limited the damages an employee could recover to $300,000, depending on the number of employees in the company. The bill also permitted sexual harassment cases to go before juries, a provision opposed by business lobbyists because juries tend to be more sympathetic than judges to plaintiffs.

In the bill's wake, some critics say, juries are awarding verdicts far out of proportion to the offense. The most heavily publicized verdicts far exceed the $300,000 federal cap because lawyers often invoke state employment-discrimination laws that allow higher money damages or they bring additional legal actions for personal injuries — known as torts — on such grounds as intentional infliction of emotional distress.*

* About half the states allow plaintiffs to recover greater money damages than permitted under the 1991 Civil Rights Act. In the other states, plaintiffs can receive more damages under federal law than under state law.

Drug Firm's Actions Earn Good and Bad Marks

The pharmaceutical company Astra USA Inc. has received kudos in the press for its swift response to allegations of sexual harassment.[1] But it is also embroiled in a legal fight with the Equal Employment Opportunity Commission. The EEOC says Astra scared employees away from cooperating with the agency's investigation of sexual harassment charges at the company.

On June 26, the Westborough, Mass.-based subsidiary of the Swedish firm Astra AB, announced it was firing CEO and President Lars Bildman for "inappropriate behavior" at company functions and misuse of funds. Astra had suspended Bildman in April, pending an investigation, after receiving an inquiry from a *Business Week* reporter outlining charges of sexual harassment at the company focusing on Bildman (*see p. 628*).[2]

Former Astra President Lars Bildman

Experts say that Astra's initial response to the charges outlined by *Business Week* could serve as a model for other companies that are serious about fighting sexual harassment. Astra USA, which reported $330 million in revenues last year, retained an outside law firm to conduct an independent investigation of the charges, instituted a toll-free, confidential hotline for employees to call about problems and began planning to offer sexual harassment prevention training to all employees in the fall, according to Astra spokesman Ben Kincannon.

Kincannon declined to comment on the specific allegations in *Business Week's* May 13 article, which described widespread fondling of women sales trainees at company functions and executives soliciting them for sexual favors. However, officials of the Swedish parent company described themselves as "shocked" by the revelations and said that Bildman hid his behavior from the company.[3] In a press statement announcing Bildman's firing, the company said it "has been actively cooperating with the EEOC" and will cooperate "fully" with other government agencies.

However, according to the EEOC, several Astra employees, in settling with Astra, signed agreements promising not to file sexual harassment claims with the EEOC or assist the agency in investigating cases.

"They [Astra] are paying these people not to help us, so we can't do our investigation," says EEOC attorney Elizabeth Grossman. The settlement agreements at issue provided amounts ranging from $20,000 to $100,000. The EEOC is investigating three separate charges alleging sexual harassment at Astra.

On June 27, a federal judge issued a temporary injunction against Astra USA, saying the company may not enforce the provisions of the settlement agreements in which employees promise not to assist the EEOC or file charges. U.S. District Judge Nathaniel M. Gorton said that EEOC's unsuccessful attempts to interview such witnesses in the case demonstrate the "chilling" effect of the settlement agreements.

The firm succeeded in obtaining a temporary stay of the injunction from the 1st U.S. Circuit Court of Appeals until Aug. 1, when the court is to hear oral arguments on the appeal. One of the issues the court has directed the parties to address is whether the EEOC made full use of its subpoena powers to compel the women who settled with Astra to cooperate in its investigation.

"Our position is we have written letters to every employee and their attorney saying, 'Feel free to cooperate fully with the EEOC in their investigation, and the company would not consider this a violation of any terms of the settlement agreement,'" says Kincannon. As to whether employees should be allowed to file charges with the EEOC, Kincannon says the company's position is that "by reaching an out-of-court settlement, they have waived the right to file additional charges."

But Judge Gorton noted in his June ruling that such an agreement could deprive the EEOC of valuable information: "[I]t is clear that the filing of a charge often helps identify individuals — other than the charging party — who have suffered discrimination."

[1] For background, see Mark Maremount, "Day of Reckoning at Astra," *Business Week*, July 8, 1996, p. 36.

[2] Two other executives were suspended with Bildman at the time. The company also announced June 26 it had fired one of the executives, and the other had resigned.

[3] Statement by Carl-Gustav Johannsson, executive vice president, Astra AB, June 26, 1996.

Writing in the quarterly journal of the Independent Women's Forum, California business analyst Elizabeth Larson recently compared Barnes' $18,000 award in 1977 to the $50 million Wal-Mart was ordered to pay Kimzey. "How did the courts come to regard a tasteless remark as nearly three thousand times more serious than a woman losing her job for refusing sex with her boss?" Larson asked.[10] The answer, she suggested, lies in a legal system that "has gone from punishing behavior that is objectively wrong to that which is subjec-

How Men and Women View Harassment

Women workers in the federal government generally are more likely than men to see "uninvited" behavior as sexual harassment, but the gap has been closing. Women are much more likely than men, however, to view sexual teasing and remarks as harassment. Both men and women more often view uninvited behavior from a supervisor as harassment compared with similar behavior from a co-worker.

Type of Uninvited Behavior By a Supervisor	Percentage Who Consider It Harassment: Women			Men		
	1980	1987	1994	1980	1987	1994
Pressure for sexual favors	91	99	99	84	95	97
Sexual teasing, jokes, remarks	62	72	83	53	58	73

Type of Uninvited Behavior By a Co-worker	Percentage Who Consider It Harassment: Women			Men		
	1980	1987	1994	1980	1987	1994
Pressure for sexual favors	81	98	98	65	90	93
Sexual teasing, jokes, remarks	54	64	77	42	47	64

Source: "Sexual Harassment in the Federal Workplace: Trends, Progress, Continuing Challenges," U.S. Merit Systems Protection Board, October 1995

tively offensive."

Forbes, too, singled out the Wal-Mart award as a case of money-hungry lawyers suing wealthy companies for trivial slights. "Consider the plight of Wal-Mart with 630,000 employees and sales last year of $94 billion," the article said. "Since punitive damages are allowed in sexual harassment cases, companies with the deepest pockets are hit hardest." [11]

"The punitive damages are based on an amount that is supposed to deter the company from doing that again," counters Kenneth Kowalski, who teaches employment law at Cleveland State University's Marshall College of Law. "To have a big company like Wal-Mart sit up and take notice, it's going to take a lot of money. Ten thousand dollars is nothing to Wal-Mart."

The perception that big awards go to women overreacting to trivial remarks or crude jokes is inaccurate, women's-rights groups maintain. According to the federal government's most recent survey, only 6 percent of those who experience sexual harassment take formal action. [12] That suggests that only the most egregious behavior leads to lawsuits, the groups contend.

"It's inaccurate to say companies pay millions of dollars because someone told an off-color joke," says Ellen Bravo, executive director of 9 to 5, the National Association of Working Women, based in Milwaukee, Wis. [13] "No one has ever called our hotline to say, 'My manager calls me Honey or says I looked nice today.' People call to say, 'So and so is groping me, came to my hotel room with only a shirt on, insists on telling me about sexual exploits, raped me.' They are unable to make it stop even though they've tried."

Some conservative critics charge that employers get hit with lawsuits no matter how they handle harassment complaints. Employers who act promptly — as the EEOC urges — and fire the alleged harasser may get hit with countersuits on such grounds as defamation or unjust dismissal. On the other hand, if the company does a thorough investigation, more harassment may occur in the meantime, worsening the employer's position if the complaining employee later sues.

"It's this type of Catch-22 situation that I think is going to be a big problem as these lawsuits proliferate," says Timothy Lynch, assistant director of the Center for Constitutional Studies at the libertarian Cato Institute.

Indeed, some critics say, it's not the size of jury awards that is the problem with sexual harassment cases but rather the prospect of paying lawyers' fees to fight or settle a suit.

"We all know there are way too many lawyers, and there's harassment value in a bad case," says Michael Weiss, an adjunct professor at the University of Houston School of Law. "There's a lot of frivolous threats brought and money paid by companies" in settlements that amount to blackmail, he says. "You say to the company, 'I'm going to sue and it will cost you $8,000 [in legal fees to fight it]. Pay us $8,000' " to settle.

Weiss recently co-authored a paper for the Cato Institute criticizing trends in sexual harassment law. It charges that "feminist pressure has . . . resulted in increasingly loose and subjective definitions of harassment." [14]

The paper was issued on the 10th anniversary of the landmark 1986 Supreme Court Case recognizing sexual harassment, *Meritor Savings Bank v. Vinson*. The paper attacked the ruling, which held that a "hostile environment" constitutes sexual harassment. Previously, courts had recognized the kind of sexual harassment known as "quid pro quo" — unwelcome sexual advances or requests for sexual favors made as a condition of an individual's employment.

"Hostile environment" sexual harassment is defined by the EEOC as unwelcome sexual advances, requests for sexual favors and other verbal or physical conduct of a sexual nature. To be considered harassment, the conduct must unreasonably interfere with an individual's work performance or create an intimidating, hostile or offensive working environment.

But the Cato Institute paper contends that *Meritor* "replaced an objective legal standard with a subjective one in which the victim, rather than a specific law, defines the offense." [15]

As an example, Weiss points to the 1991 ruling in *Robinson v. Jacksonville Shipyards,* which held — for the first time — that pornography at the workplace constituted sexual harassment. District Court Judge Howell Melton of the Middle District of Florida ruled that the workplace posting of pictures of nude and partially nude women "is and encourages sexually harassing conduct."

Lois Robinson, a welder who brought the suit, charged that the pinups and calendars of nude women were displayed, sometimes by managers, throughout the workplace. In addition, Robinson said demeaning comments were regularly heard in the shipyard, and women were often called "Honey" and "Momma."

Robinson had complained that she found the behavior harassing, but other women at the yard said they did not. Based on the judge's reasoning in that case, the Cato Institute critique said, "it is difficult to imagine how any behavior with sexual overtones could escape classification as harassment defined by the reaction of the most sensitive woman, even if she is the only one who takes offense." [16]

Weiss contrasts the legal standard for sexual harassment to that for emotional distress and suffering, which requires evidence that the plaintiff suffers medically recognized symptoms.

But sexual harassment "is not about psychological injury; it's about economic injury," argues Sara Mandelbaum, a staff attorney with the Women's Rights Project at the American Civil Liberties Union. "This is not about women having to come to court and prove with doctors' notes that their feelings were hurt. This really goes much more to women's economic equality."

In the most recent Supreme Court decision on sexual harassment, *Harris v. Forklift Systems Inc.,* the court held in 1993 that a woman did not have to show she had suffered a psychological injury for a work environment to be considered hostile.

Harris laid out a two-pronged test requiring the complaint to satisfy both objective and subjective standards. The objective standard required proof that the workplace was permeated with discriminatory behavior severe enough for a reasonable person to find it to be a hostile and abusive environment. Under the subjective standard, the plaintiff had to actually perceive the environment as hostile or abusive.

Sexual harassment law, the Supreme Court said in *Harris,* "comes into play before the harassing conduct leads to a nervous breakdown." Some observers were disappointed that the court did not define more precisely what constitutes a hostile environment. As if anticipating the disappointment, the court said, "this is not and by its nature cannot be, a mathematically precise test." [17]

Are companies doing enough to prevent sexual harassment?

Most large companies now have policies against sexual harassment, and a growing number train employees in an effort to head it off. According to a June survey by the American Management Association (AMA), 89 percent of the 456 mid-size and large companies polled have formal policies or procedures for dealing with sexual harassment and 65 percent provide training. [18] Nonetheless, women's-rights groups note, many smaller firms don't have training programs or written policies.

The growth in training has tracked the rise in companies that have experienced allegations of sexual harassment. Between 1991 and 1996, the percentage of companies that reported at least one claim grew from 52 percent to 72 percent, according to the AMA. In 1991, only 40 percent of the firms surveyed offered training on the issue.

Eric Rolfe Greenberg, director of management studies for the association, says "companies tend to be reactive rather than proactive. They wait for a second claim [before they] develop a policy." But he also notes that companies that already had training programs were less likely to see claims

'The More He Was Nasty . . .

Jonneigh Adrion was sure she was being mistreated by her boss at Del Laboratories Inc., but the young secretary didn't think it was sexual harassment.

Last year, however, Adrion was among 15 women who collected nearly $1.2 million from the Farmingdale, N.Y., cosmetics and pharmaceutical company. It was the largest sexual harassment settlement ever negotiated by the federal Equal Employment Opportunity Commission (EEOC).

On one occasion, Adrion says, Dan K. Wassong, Del's chief stockholder and its CEO and chairman, slapped Adrion's buttocks as she was leaning over a filing cabinet. On another, she says, he grabbed her breasts. When Adrion told him to stop, he just smiled.

Frequently, Adrion says, Wassong told her she would prosper with the company if she would perform oral sex on him, as he claimed other secretaries had done.

"The atmosphere was filled with tension," Adrion remembers. No one wanted to answer the phone if Wassong called or talk to him when he came to the office because he would release a barrage of epithets. "He was abusive to everybody," Adrion says, but "he was a lot different with women. Everything was of a sexual nature, very degrading to women."

Adrion, who joined the company in 1989, at age 21, took a position as Wassong's executive secretary in 1991, hoping it would help her advance. That's when the harassment started, she says. Over the next 15 months Adrion trained nine women to work directly under Wassong. But his behavior was so abusive, she says, that "it was rare anyone stayed more than two weeks." Some employees went to lunch their first day and never came back. Finally in 1992, fed up with the treatment, Adrion quit.

After she left, she contacted numerous government agencies to complain but kept running into dead ends. In August, she contacted the Long Island chapter of 9 to 5, National Association of Working Women, a women's advocacy group, which led her to the EEOC.

When 9 to 5 told Adrion she had been sexually harassed, Adrion said it was the first time anyone had used that term. "I thought he [Wassong] had to say, 'Have sex or you'll be fired.' I was dumbfounded when I got the sheet from the EEOC defining what sexual harassment was." Until then, she had assumed she would be filing assault charges against Wassong.

During the time Adrion worked at Del Labs, she says she had contacted two male lawyers, both of whom told her she would have little chance in court against a man of Wassong's prominence. One attorney told her to leave scratch marks on Wassong the next time he attacked her; the other suggested she hire a temporary secretary to divert his attention.

Adrion also complained to the company's personnel director, who she says was "petrified" of Wassong. "Why all of a sudden is this bothering you? You know what he's like," she recalls the director responding. He tried to convince her that Wassong could advance her career if she stayed on.

Larry Pincus, a spokesman for the EEOC's New York office, says of the case, "The issue is where do you go when it's the boss? Do you sit there and tough it out or do you challenge it?"

The EEOC located 45 women with similar tales, says Elizabeth Grossman, the EEOC trial attorney in the case. [1] They said that Wassong asked several women for oral sex, conducted business with his pants zipper open, urinated with his bathroom door open and assailed his employees daily with sexual remarks and insults.

Under the terms of the EEOC settlement, Del admitted no wrongdoing. But in addition to paying damages, the company agreed to develop a training program to prevent sexual harassment, including an individual program for Wassong, then age 65. Del also agreed to let employees report future sexual harassment incidents to an outside company, which would be responsible for investigating the complaints. [2]

"Del absolutely denies the allegations," says Del public relations counsel Howard J. Rubenstein. "The settlement was done to avoid costly litigation and also in an effort to avert continuing negative publicity for the firm. Dan Wassong runs an effective and honorable company, and the company has put this behind them. The company has instituted very

develop into lawsuits. Eight percent of companies with training were sued as opposed to 12 percent of those with no training.

"If a company puts in a training program," Greenberg says, "it may find an increase in reported incidents because of heightened awareness among victims of what constitutes sexual harassment and of the company's policy saying it's not acceptable. The good news is [complaints are] less likely to rise to the level of a legal claim."

For the most part, employers are not bucking the trend toward taking sexual harassment seriously, business groups say. "No business benefits from sexual harassment," says Eide at the Chamber of Commerce. "It decreases productivity. Most enlightened employers don't want it." The key to avoiding expensive lawsuits, Eide says, is a preventive approach: having a written policy against sexual harassment and well-publicized procedures for investigating complaints.

Women's-rights activists say that while more companies have policies against sexual harassment than five years ago, problems remain, such as retaliation against women who complain, supervisors who tolerate harassment and lack of neutral investigations. The death threats that were reported in the Mitsubishi case are a

. . . the More I Tried to Please Him'

extensive sensitivity-training programs."

Adrion addresses women's groups about sexual harassment and grants interviews, but she still doesn't like speaking about her experiences. "It brings back a rush of memories," she says. "I'm ashamed and embarrassed that I put up with what I did. I blamed myself for a long time."

Adrion says she thought if she could prove herself to Wassong with her work, he would become less abusive. "I kept hoping he would come around. The more he was nasty, the more I tried to please him."

Melissa Josephs, a policy associate at Women Employed, a Chicago-based group devoted to advancing women in the workplace, says trying to tolerate an abusive boss is a common reaction among women who call in complaining of sexual harassment. Most women don't want to file complaints, even within their company, she says. "They always say, 'I just want it to go away. I still want to do my job.' "

But Josephs says women make a mistake thinking that if they ignore the behavior it will disappear. "If someone wants power and makes a person feel subservient and incapable of doing a job, why would he stop? He's getting what he wants," she says.

Grossman observes that as majority stockholder of Del, Wassong had vast power. And the fact that he "had his own staff of several women, which was physically isolated from the rest of the office, provided him the opportunity to abuse the women in a very powerful way," she adds. "When the harasser *is* the company, there's nowhere for them to go."

After Adrion filed her claim with the EEOC, she says she often felt like dropping the draining three-year challenge. It took the EEOC 13 months to find that there was "probable cause" in the case, another nine months before the agency filed suit and a year after that to settle the case. The delay was partly due to the fact that the EEOC was investigating two other women's charges against Del during that period, Grossman says. Adrion's case was settled before trial.

One of Adrion's fears was that Del would try to discredit her as an incompetent employee — a typical tactic in such cases, according to Grossman. In the course of the investigation, Adrion was told by the EEOC that the company's lawyer had charged she had been late on three occasions. "I would come back and explain, 'I worked till midnight.' " Today, Adrion says, "I would never go through that process if I didn't have to. It's very invasive."

In the year before the settlement, several prominent women who were friends of Wassong cast doubt on the charges, saying they had never seen him behave crudely toward a woman. Helen Gurley Brown, then editor of *Cosmopolitan* magazine, said the women at Del Labs were overreacting to passes by men. "What's the big whoop-de-do?" she told *Newsweek*. "It's part of being an attractive woman." [3]

A year later, at the time of settlement, Brown agreed that "these things did happen." But she said she did not think the charges merited filing a suit or the payment of large damages. She advised that women simply leave such bosses. [4]

"It's easy to say that," says Adrion, "but when I left Mr. Wassong, the economy was very depressed." Adrion could not use Del or Wassong as a reference, and it took her more than a year to find another job.

As for Brown and others who say that sexual harassment awards are excessive, Adrion answers, "It wasn't about getting money or going to court and winning. The only thing that drove me is I didn't want him to do it to anyone else. I didn't want him to make anyone feel the way I did when I left — helpless."

In the future, she says, "I think someone will be a little bit more inclined to report [such abuse] if they're in that situation."

---

[1] The EEOC's suit named only 15 claimants because the statute of limitations had run out for the other women, whose grievances dated back as far as 1965.

[2] Jay Mathews, "Firm Reaches Record Harassment Settlement," *The Washington Post*, Aug. 4, 1995, p. B1.

[3] Quoted in Jolie Solomon and Susan Miller, " 'Hero' or 'Harasser'?" *Newsweek*, Sept. 12, 1994, pp. 48-50.

[4] Quoted in Mathews, *op. cit.*

grim reminder that harassment victims face a "double whammy," Norton says. "When [women] complain about it, they face retaliation, additional harassment or they're fired." Moreover, a woman who files a complaint with the EEOC can wait months or more for a resolution.

Predictably, there has been enormous growth in consultants offering sexual-harassment training. The growth has been fueled in part by new state laws, such as California's requirement that employers take reasonable steps to prevent sexual harassment and Maine's that employers provide sexual-harassment seminars for new employees.

But some critics say all this activity actually fuels claims rather than prevents them. "Employers may think they are hiring consultants to protect them from lawsuits," Larson wrote, "but what is actually being taught is a very different lesson: A wink or a leer can be money in the bank." [19]

Management Professor Anthony Townsend of the University of Nevada, Las Vegas, criticizes training videos used by corporations for generally portraying men as harassers and women as victims. The message, he says, is "Men are bad." It "doesn't leave open to men the possibility that they may be victims, too. And that possibility is very real as more and more women are put in charge of men." (*See "At Issue," p. 641.*)

In fact, a backlash has been quietly developing, not just in the pages of conservative journals but also among a growing number of men who say they were unfairly accused of sexual harassment and who counter-sue.

John Kirsch was publisher of the *South Florida Business Journal* in 1992 when, he said, he told Advertising Director Karen Van Der Eems that she would either have to quit or be demoted because of poor sales. As a "face-saving" way to explain the demotion, Kirsch said he suggested that Van Der Eems say she wanted to devote more time to her marriage. In response, Van Der Eems sent Kirsch a memo implying, he recalls, that her marriage "was something I couldn't emotionally stand and I was firing her because of that." The next week Kirsch was fired.

Kirsch sued for defamation. His lawyer argued that Kirsch had been forced to defame himself by admitting in job interviews that he had been fired for sexual harassment. Kirsch says the company never investigated the charges. He also says that contrary to the memo's implication, he never had a romantic relationship with Van Der Eems.

In an out-of-court settlement in 1993, the newspaper's parent company, American City Business Journals, paid Kirsch $40,000. Kirsch says he also received a letter from Van Der Eeems saying he had not sexually harassed her.

"The reality today is that the easiest person to get rid of, the person that will cost you the least to fire, is a middle-aged white male," Kirsch says. Kirsch's lawyer, Donna M. Ballman of North Miami Beach, says, "The company thought it's easier to fire someone than do the right thing by both parties." Ballman says the case shows that companies should do thorough investigations when charges arise.

Critics of current trends in sexual harassment law say cases like Kirsch's stand as warnings that the rights of innocent men could be trampled in the stampede by employers eager to show they are doing something about sexual harassment. Under federal guidelines, the main way employers can avoid liability after being sued for sexual harassment is by showing they took prompt action to remedy the situation.

"There's a possibility of sexual harassment [charges being used] in organizational or political power struggles," says Harsh K. Luthar, assistant professor of management at Bryant College in Smithfield, R.I. "If it's decided a manager has to be gotten rid of, it's a nice pretext to hide behind." In a recent article, Luthar calls for more research on the extent of "baseless accusations of sexual harassment made against males." [20]

About 19 percent of male federal workers surveyed in 1994 reported experiencing sexually harassing behaviors during the preceding two years, up from 14 percent in 1987. [21]

Townsend cites a lawsuit filed by an air traffic controller against the Federal Aviation Administration in connection with a sexual harassment training workshop. Controller Douglas Hartman charged he was forced to walk through a crowd of female co-workers who grabbed his body and commented derisively on his attributes in an exercise aimed at making men sensitive to the harassment experienced by women in control towers. [22]

"What men and women have to look out for is real discrimination," Townsend says. "I think [corporate training] has gone overboard with political correctness. There isn't a direct relationship between someone having a foul mouth in the office and someone not getting a job." Adds political science Professor Paul, also a critic of such training, "It's made people second-guess their behavior."

Barbara Spyridon Pope, a Bethesda, Md., training consultant, says she hears men say "they are afraid to have normal work relations. They're afraid that someone may sue them when they do performance appraisals."

Using professional actors in skits and simulated game shows, Spyridon demonstrates that the difference between friendliness and harassment can be as subtle as the length of a touch or a look. "Two seconds is OK; 10 seconds is too long," Pope says. "When you see it, you know exactly."

Ironically, when employees watching the training sessions are asked to say when the lingering touch or look becomes sexual harassment, men tend to call it harassment before the women do,

Reuters/Scott Olson

Auto workers from the Mitsubishi plant in Normal, Ill., along with relatives and friends, protest at the Chicago office of the Equal Employment Opportunity Commission April 22. The protest was held to show support for Mitsubishi after the company became the target of a sexual harassment probe.

she says. "Some of that comes from paranoia about where the boundaries are."

Some consultants acknowledge the criticisms of training programs that badmouth men. "With high-quality training, that's the last thing you do, because that is divisive," says Susan L. Webb, president of Pacific Resource Development Group in Seattle, Wash.

Alan McEvoy, a professor of sociology at Wittenburg University in Springfield, Ohio, compares the nervousness around sexual harassment to the heightened awareness of child abuse in recent years and the overreaction of teachers who avoid any physical intimacy with children. "One of the prices we pay for heightened awareness is paranoia and fear," McEvoy says. "But by the same token, I don't know that we have an alternative. The alternative of ignoring it and pretending it doesn't exist and allowing it to persist is worse."

Do men and women see harassment differently?

Though women are more likely than men to define certain behaviors as harassment, they have more areas of agreement than disagreement, surveys show. The most recent surveys show that if the majority of women think something is harassment, the majority of men tend to agree, though by a smaller margin.

Men and women are most likely to agree when it comes to the starkest kind of harassment, such as pressure for sexual favors from a supervisor, says John Pryor, a professor of psychology at Illinois State University in Normal, Ill. "Where you see the larger differences are in the more gray areas," Pryor says, such as sexual joking among co-workers. It is these grayer areas, which come under the umbrella of "hostile environment" harassment, that are the most common form of sexual harassment, according to the American Psychological Association. [23]

Over time, the gap in perception between men and women has been closing, says Barbara A. Gutek, a psychologist at the University of Arizona. In her oft-cited 1980-81 study of 1,200 working men and women in Los Angeles, Gutek researched the reactions of men and women to a sexual proposition from a co-worker. Sixty-seven percent of the men but only 17 percent of the women said they would be flattered by a proposition. [24]

In a more recent unpublished survey of faculty, staff and students at the University of Arizona, "Fewer men say they would be flattered by such overtures," Gutek says. Why the change? "I think it was an issue men hadn't thought about very much [in 1980]," she says. "The sensitization to sexual harassment in the workplace [has made them aware] there can be strings attached."

When federal workers were surveyed in 1987, less than half the men considered a co-worker's sexual teasing, jokes or remarks to be sexual harassment while 64 percent of the women did. When the survey was repeated in 1994, the percentage of men who considered such remarks harassment had risen to 64 percent; among women, the proportion had risen to 77 percent. [25]

The differing perceptions among men and women of what constitutes sexual harassment can put employers in a difficult position. "What you're often faced with as a practical matter is two people, one of whom says an event occurred and another who denies it," says Eide. "The employer is judge and jury as to whether a situation occurred. We're no better than anyone else at [determining] what happened. If you discharge the alleged harasser, you're subject to a suit for defamation or wrongful dismissal."

Differing perceptions have been at the heart of an ongoing legal controversy over how to define sexual harassment. Is a harassment claim valid if a "reasonable person" views a situation as sexual harassment — the traditional legal standard for establishing an injury in tort law? Or should sexual harassment be defined from a woman's point of view?

In 1991, the 9th U.S. Circuit Court of Appeals ruled in *Ellison v. Brady* that courts should consider the victim's perspective — that of the "reasonable woman" — in deciding if an incident constitutes sexual harassment.

The case involved Kerry Ellison, an Internal Revenue Service agent in California, who charged that a co-worker persisted in pressuring her for dates and sending her "love letters," which she found frightening.

"Women who are victims of mild forms of sexual harassment may understandably worry whether a harasser's conduct is merely a prelude to violent sexual assault," the court said. "Men, who are rarely victims of sexual assault, may view sexual conduct in a vacuum without a full appreciation of the social setting of the underlying threat of violence a woman may perceive." [26]

The court stated that examining the case from the "reasonable person" perspective would risk "reinforcing the prevailing level of discrimination" merely because certain kinds of discriminatory behavior were common.

Since *Ellison,* courts have been split as to whether to apply the reasonable person or reasonable woman standard. In its most recent pronouncement on sexual harassment, *Harris v. Forklift,* the Supreme Court used the reasonable person standard. The court made no mention of the reasonable woman approach, as some observers had hoped it would do in order to resolve the split.

Nevertheless, some plaintiffs' lawyers try to persuade judges to instruct juries to apply the reasonable woman test, believing it will make the jury more sympathetic to a victim. Courts are increasingly open to this kind of test, according to the Women's Legal Defense Fund.

Psychiatrist Rutter, who has testified as a plaintiff's expert witness in favor of the reasonable woman perspective, argues that men and women have been raised to view sexual behavior differently. "The psychological experience of women has a particular cast to it that is different from men," he says. "We hope eventually that won't matter before the law — when we have 50-50 equal rights everywhere."

But the reasonable woman test infuriates some conservatives. When the 9th Circuit "uncritically embraced the neo-feminist notion that men and women do not and perhaps cannot see the same events similarly," the Cato Institute critique argued, it had the effect of "gutting the concept of neutrality under the law." [27]

The 9th Circuit based its decision in part on research like Gutek's showing that men and women define sexual harassment differently. But today Gutek expresses doubts about the reasonable woman standard. "Using the reasonable woman standard has made it more difficult for the woman," Gutek says. "The obvious reaction is to say, 'She's this hyper-reactive woman.' The company marches in other women who see the situation differently, and now the courts are supposed to say who's reasonable."

Some men argue that as females gain more power, males are being discriminated against, too. Townsend questions surveys showing that 40-60 percent of working women have been sexually harassed but less than 20 percent of men. "If men were subjected to the same kind of cultural exposure to this notion," he says, "I think we would see very similar numbers for men."

Townsend still remembers the female teacher in graduate school who called him a "typical anal-retentive male." He said the comment made him worry she would mark his papers down.

When Townsend asks students how many have heard a female faculty member make disparaging jokes about men, about 60 percent of the males raise their hands. But only a handful say they've suffered sexual harassment.

"Men really are experiencing this stuff; it's just that they're not sensitized to potential damage on their education and careers," Townsend says. "Men like to think, 'I can overcome this problem.' But women are tough, and if they have power they have to be stopped from [harassing people] just like men.' " ■

Background

The Thomas Brouhaha

The uproar over the 1991 Senate hearings to confirm Clarence Thomas for the Supreme Court woke the country up to the issue of sexual harassment. But it's still not clear whether the watershed event made most people more or less sympathetic to charges like Anita Hill's. [28]

In the most recent polls, the public remains sharply divided on who, in effect, was telling the truth. As Sen. Herb Kohl, D-Wis., said at the time, "You clearly have to say one of them is lying. That's pretty stark." [29]

Hill, who had worked for Thomas at the Education Department and the EEOC, testified that Thomas had asked her out socially early on, that she had declined and that he had conducted sexually oriented conversations of an embarrassing nature — mostly when they were alone in his office. Thomas categorically denied that he had ever harassed Hill or tried to date her.

By the close of the hearings, polls showed that the majority of Americans — men, women, blacks and whites — believed Thomas. A year later, sentiment had shifted. Polls taken in October 1992 showed Hill's credibility rating 4-10 percentage points ahead of Thomas'. [30]

Americans' attitudes about Hill's testimony changed in the same way they changed about AIDS when people they knew started getting sick, says Bravo of 9 to 5. "Many people during that year found someone who had an experience with sexual harassment," she says. "It became credible to them." In the month after the hearings, 9 to 5 says it received calls from about 2,000 women, some of whom had suffered indignities decades before.

Skeptics attributed the shift in attitudes to "pro-Anita Hill effusions from white media feminists" and "elite opinion." [31] Indeed, from the beginning there was a stark class difference in how women viewed Hill: 31 percent of college-educated women opposed Thomas' confirmation compared with 19 percent of non-graduates. [32]

Hill was still ahead, but by a smaller margin, when *Newsweek* polled Americans in November 1994. Forty percent thought Thomas had sexually harassed Hill, 34 percent did not and 26 percent weren't sure. Respondents were split 40 percent to 40 percent on whether the Senate should have confirmed Thomas. [33]

Rise in Complaints

But the hearings had far-reaching implications beyond the question of whom Americans believed. The year after the hearing, a record number of women were elected to Congress. Several women candidates said they were inspired by Hill's testimony and their dissatisfaction with the Senate's handling of the hearings.

Also in the wake of the hearings, President Bush signed the Civil Rights Act of 1991, which gave plaintiffs in sexual harassment suits the right to a jury trial and the right to seek compensatory and punitive damages. Noting that Bush had vetoed a previous version of the bill, Bravo says that pas-

Continued on p. 640

Chronology

1960s *Women enter work force in record numbers. The women's movement emerges.*

July 2, 1964
President Lyndon B. Johnson signs the Civil Rights Act prohibiting employment discrimination and creating the Equal Opportunity Employment Commission (EEOC) to investigate complaints.

1970s *Sexual harassment cases begin showing up in court. Women's groups and academics formalize the concept of sexual harassment*

November 1976
Redbook magazine publishes the results of the first major survey on sexual harassment in the workplace.

1977
In *Barnes v. Costle*, the U.S. Court of Appeals in Washington, D.C., rules that sexual harassment constitutes sex discrimination under Title VII of the 1964 Civil Rights Act. It is the first such ruling by a federal court.

1980s *U.S. Supreme Court issues its first major ruling on sexual harassment.*

Nov. 10, 1980
EEOC publishes guidelines defining sexual harassment.

June 19, 1986
In *Meritor Savings Bank v. Vinson*, the Supreme Court rules that sexual harassment in the workplace is sex discrimination when it creates an offensive or hostile working environment.

1990s *Feminists win major victories in the courts.*

Jan. 18, 1991
In *Robinson v. Jacksonville Shipyards*, a federal district court in Florida rules that nude pinups in the workplace constitute illegal sexual harassment.

Jan. 23, 1991
In *Ellison v. Brady*, the 9th U.S. Circuit Court of Appeals recognizes the "reasonable woman" doctrine in considering what constitutes sexual harassment. The case involved an Internal Revenue Service agent who said that she was frightened by a co-worker's "love letters" and pressure for dates.

October 1991
University of Oklahoma law Professor Anita Hill accuses Supreme Court nominee Clarence Thomas of sexual harassment in televised nomination hearings.

Nov. 21, 1991
In the politically charged wake of the Thomas hearings, President George Bush signs the Civil Rights Act of 1991, giving plaintiffs in sexual harassment cases the right to jury trials and the right to seek compensatory and punitive damages.

Nov. 10, 1993
In *Harris v. Forklift Systems,* the Supreme Court says plaintiffs do not have to prove psychological trauma or reduced productivity on the job to establish sexual harassment in a hostile environment.

September 1995
Sen. Bob Packwood, R-Ore., resigns after 27 years in the Senate in the face of sexual harassment charges.

April 9, 1996
EEOC announces it is filing what could be the largest sexual harassment suit ever against Mitsubishi Motor Manufacturing of America Inc.

April 29, 1996
Astra USA Inc., a pharmaceutical firm, suspends its president a few days before *Business Week* publishes results of a six-month investigation into sexual harassment at the Massachusetts company.

June 22, 1996
Mitsubishi asks a federal judge to dismiss the class-action suit filed by the EEOC.

June 26, 1996
Astra fires its president and another executive.

June 27, 1996
A federal judge issues a temporary injunction against Astra USA stopping the company from enforcing settlement agreements in which employees promise not to file EEOC claims or assist the EEOC in its investigation.

July 10, 1996
First U.S. Circuit Court of Appeals grants temporary stay of the Astra injunction until Aug. 1.

Continued from p. 638

sage of the law was a "victory directly tied to the Hill-Thomas hearings."

The new law permitted plaintiffs to seek substantial damages for the first time. By 1994, the median jury award for sexual harassment was $104,750, according to Jury Verdict Research Inc. in Horsham, Pa. From 1990 to 1995, EEOC complaints more than doubled, rising from 6,127 to 15,549, and damages more than tripled, rising from $7.1 million to $24.3 million.

While complaints have been rising, the amount of sexual harassment reported in surveys remains relatively unchanged, suggesting that sexual harassment has not been increasing but that people are more likely to report it. In 1994, for example, 44 percent of female federal workers reported they had experienced unwanted sexual attention during the preceding two years, compared with 42 percent in 1987.*

In about 30 percent of its cases, the EEOC finds "no reasonable cause" for the complaint. Attorney Vargyas says that the complainant may have been mistreated, but the situation doesn't necessarily meet the legal standards for harassment. "It's rare the person comes to us with facts tied up in a neat ribbon with the legal theory attached," she says.

As for the suggestion that people are filing trivial claims just to get the money, Vargyas comments: "This notion is preposterous and just plain wrong. We have plaintiffs who have come forward and their reward is death threats. People who come forward are gutsy and the tip of the iceberg."

According to EEOC statistics, less than 20 percent of cases result in some kind of outcome, such as a monetary award, favorable to the complainant.

Supreme Court Sends Message

In its 1993 *Harris v. Forklift* decision, the Supreme Court said women did not have to prove psychological trauma or lowered productivity to win a sexual harassment suit.

For more than two years, Teresa Harris, the manager of a Nashville, Tenn., truck-leasing firm, said she was subjected to repeated sexual comments from the company's president. Once, he asked Harris in front of other employees whether she had obtained a particular account by having sex with the client. [34]

In essence, the *Harris* decision reaffirmed the standard developed by the EEOC in 1980 and reaffirmed by the Supreme Court in 1986 — that the harassment must be pervasive enough to affect a person's working conditions. As Justice Ruth Bader Ginsburg said in a concurring opinion, it's enough to show that the behavior makes it more difficult to do the job.

"It reaffirmed the status quo, but it was a strong message from the Supreme Court," Norton says.

Packwood Case

Last year, sexual harassment once again became a subject of nationwide public fascination with the release of the diaries of then-Sen. Bob Packwood, R-Ore., in which he boasted of "the 22 staff members I've made love to and probably 75 others I've had a passionate relationship with." [35]

The Senate Ethics Committee unanimously voted to oust Packwood, but last September, after three years of news stories and investigations, he resigned the office he had held for 27 years.

Anita Hill took the occasion to argue that proving sexual harassment remains extraordinarily difficult for the ordinary person."[I]f even an easy case requires 33 months of political pressure and 10,000 pages of testimony to be resolved," she wrote, "the average complainant has little hope for a swift and certain resolution."

Hill noted that harassment cases are typically dismissed as nothing more than a mere flirtation, or the complaint of a spurned lover or disgruntled employee. But she pointed out that "the vast majority of cases are far murkier and more complex than what brought down Packwood." [36] ■

CURRENT SITUATION

New EEOC Policy

The EEOC, long criticized for its slowness in investigating claims, changed its policy in 1994 to focus on cases with significant legal issues.

Formerly, the agency had pledged to fully investigate every charge and seek relief for the complainant in all the cases it found substantiated. But, Vargyas says, "Full investigation was always a fiction. We just couldn't do it." The EEOC's jurisdiction had widened over the years, and the number of complaints kept rising, but the agency's funding and staff did not keep pace, she says.

Today, "We're looking for cases that are going to give a bang for the buck — a case where many people are involved, and it can move the law forward," Vargyas says, pointing to the agency's suit against Mitsubishi.

The EEOC has trimmed its infamous backlog in the past year. At the end of June, it stood at 90,166 cases — down 16 percent from 108,000 at the same time last year. However, Vargyas notes, it still takes "much too long" — 371 days — to resolve the average case.

The EEOC's new policy of turning away run-of-the-mill cases may not be an unvarnished success to the ordinary

Continued on p. 642

---

* Between 40-60 percent of working women report that they have experienced sexually harassing behavior, according to the American Psychological Association.

At Issue:

Is sexual harassment a problem for men as well as women?

yes

HARSH LUTHAR AND ANTHONY TOWNSEND
Luthar is an assistant professor of management at Bryant College in Rhode Island; Townsend is an assistant professor of management at the University of Nevada, Las Vegas

FROM "MAN HANDLING," *NATIONAL REVIEW*, FEB. 6, 1995.

Though a popular success, [the movie] "Disclosure" was derided by feminists who considered its premise — sexual harassment of a man by a woman — silly at best, dangerous at worst. After all, everyone knows sexual harassment is something a man does to a woman. That assumption is reflected in the Equal Employment Opportunity Commission's guidelines on sexual harassment, where the harasser is always a "he" and the victim a "she." You have to refer to a footnote to verify that the law, in theory, protects men as well as women.

Most of the published research on sexual harassment agrees: Women are victims; men are harassers. In surveys, some 40 percent of women report being harassed at work, compared to a negligible proportion of men. When men do report harassment, their harassers are often other men.

But these indicators may not give us an accurate picture of what is going on. To begin with, the leading sexual-harassment researchers are feminist ideologues who are mainly concerned with finding evidence of patriarchal oppression. They design their studies accordingly: Most of the research does not even include male subjects.

More to the point, most men would not recognize sexual harassment if it hit them in the face. Ask a number of men if they have been harassed, and nine out of 10 will say, "No, but I'd like to be." Men generally do not consider teasing, sexual jokes and lewd innuendoes from female co-workers harassment; they are not upset by the kinds of comments and incidents that have brought female plaintiffs millions of dollars in awards for "hostile environment" claims. . . .

To get beyond this barrier, male subjects in harassment surveys should be asked not whether they have been sexually harassed but whether certain kinds of behavior have occurred. When we ask male undergraduates if they have ever been sexually harassed by a female instructor, almost all of them say no. But when we ask if they have experienced specific types of treatment in a female instructor's classroom, such as derogatory or off-color comments about men, some 60 percent of them report such incidents.

As for "sleep with me or else" harassment — the kind dramatized in "Disclosure" — we are starting to see court cases indicating that some men (and women) have been pressured into sex by a predatory female boss. There is every reason to believe that more such cases will appear as more women assume positions of power.

no

SHELLY M. MANDELL
Los Angeles attorney

FROM A COLUMN IN THE *LOS ANGELES TIMES*, DEC. 20, 1994.

Since reading *Disclosure* by Michael Crichton, I've withheld judgment pending the film's release. . . . [Having seen the film] I am now more concerned than I thought I would ever be.

My qualifications to pass judgment on this film?. . .

First, I am a women who has actively participated in the American work force for 30 years. I experienced sexual harassment when it didn't have a name. Ask a woman in the *real* work force, and she will tell you [about] . . . the vile comments, the slaps on the butt and the quid "I can help you sweetheart if you're nice to me" pro quo.

Traversing the Rubicon, I became a feminist and assisted the National Organization for Women in the creation of laws deterring abusive work force behavior toward women, gays and minorities. The law has since grown teeth, setting forth specific damage provisions aimed at perpetrators of harassment. Legislation was needed then; continuing enforcement is needed now.

Lastly, as an attorney in Los Angeles, I have encountered hundreds of victims seeking legal assistance for abuse at work, in schools, in residences and from husbands. Ninety-eight percent of these victims are women forced by social and economic realities to endure unlawful behavior in the name of "two kids and a missing father." Glamorous?

Unfortunately, for all of us, Hollywood cheated. The film-going public and the countless employees in the garment industry, law enforcement, security and other fields were not considered as Crichton offered his twisted message.

Reality was quickly pedaled away by the Stairmaster in the "perpetrator's" design command post. With macabre humor, a major social issue of our times is submerged in a gender-ironic confrontation between two people.

Forgotten is that the issue of sexual harassment is not about gender or sexual orientation. It's about people fostering integrity among themselves at home, at work and in the classroom.

The film is an inaccurate diagnosis of a rampant social disease. Of course, sexual harassment is not about sex: It's about the misuse of power. The film, however, was about sex and personal agendas.

Sexual harassment is about people forgetting other people are human and not only a vice president, secretary, student or wife. It's about people's fear of a lack of control over their own lives.

To suggest otherwise discloses nothing of value to society. In fact, it does just the opposite.

Does the First Amendment Protect Workplace Smut?

Lois Robinson, a welder at a Jacksonville, Fla., shipyard, was offended by what she saw and heard at work, and when her complaints were ridiculed, she filed a sexual harassment suit.

Robinson's suit prompted U.S. District Judge Howell Melton to prohibit pornography from being brought into the shipyard and to order sexual harassment training for the shipyard's employees. [1]

Such legal decisions, conservative critics warn, are undercutting workers' First Amendment rights to free speech in the workplace. "We're talking about rules against calling women 'Honey,' says Michael Weiss, adjunct professor of law at the University of Houston School of Law. "This is southern Florida; this is a restriction on everyday speech. We're talking about rules against pinups in lockers. People think they have a right to have these materials in private areas of the workplace. You spend more time in the workplace than at home."

Martha Davis, legal director of the NOW Legal Defense and Education Fund, which represented Robinson, argues that Melton's decision reflected the totality of circumstances, not isolated issues of *Playboy*. "That was a workplace where there were pervasive pornographic images of women in a workplace dominated by men, where women were trying to break into traditional male-dominated employment." says Davis. "The targeting of women with pornographic images and the pervasive presence of them was used as a way of trying to keep women out of the work force and making them uncomfortable there. That case didn't have to do with someone calling someone honey."

As for whether Robinson was alone in her objections, Davis concedes, "There were women who said they didn't care. But the point is that what the court has to look at is whether the plaintiff is reasonable in her feeling that this is a sexually hostile environment."

The question of whether workplace restrictions on pornography violate workers' free speech rights "is an issue that the Supreme Court has yet to address squarely," says Davis. In December 1995, the court declined to hear a case that might have clarified the issue. The appeal came from a state office worker in Massachusetts who claimed free speech protections for pasting photographs of the head of a female union office candidate on magazine centerfolds of nude women.

The Massachusetts Supreme Judicial Court had rejected the argument by worker David M. Heller that his public attacks on co-worker Sylvia Bowman were fair because she was a candidate for the union president's job. In June 1995, the Massachusetts high court overturned a lower state court's sexual harassment judgment in her favor but upheld the charge that involved infliction of emotional distress.

"The excuse was that [the centerfold] was put up during a union election," says Davis. "The lower court ruled that was outweighed by the fact it was a workplace. It did not give rise to strong First Amendment interests."

The question of workers' rights to pornography in the workplace has taken on a modern tinge recently in connection with the availability of pornography over the Internet. *The New York Times* recently reported that an increasing number of companies are taking steps to keep employees away from sex sites on the Worldwide Web, blocking them with software originally designed to restrict children's access.

Compaq Computer recently dismissed 20 workers singled out for heavy use of sex sites on the Web. No suits are known to have been filed against corporations by workers claiming that they were offended after seeing such images on another worker's screen. Nonetheless, sexual harassment consultants advise employers to prohibit viewing sexually explicit material on computers, the *Times* reported.

"An employee shouldn't have to give up his or her First Amendment rights when they enter the workplace," objected David Banisar, a lawyer and policy analyst at the Electronic Privacy Information Center, a public interest group. [2]

"There are a lot of Bill of Rights freedoms we give up at work," says Ellen Bravo, president of 9 to 5, the National Association of Working Women. "I don't have the right to bring arms to work, or to tell the boss to go to hell. The company can tell you to wear certain clothes, tell you how to behave, say certain phrases when you answer the phone. The idea that it's inappropriate to have boundaries on what people can say at work is pretty amazing."

[1] The case, *Robinson v. Jacksonville Shipyards,* was settled for an undisclosed amount last year.

[2] Quoted in Trip Gabriel, "New Issue at Work: On-Line Sex Sites," *The New York Times,* June 27, 1996, p. C1.

Continued from p. 640

complainant. Many women who file a claim, particularly those who can't afford to hire a lawyer, count on the EEOC to investigate and resolve their claim. Now they are more likely to receive a "right-to-sue" letter, which lets them take their case to court themselves but requires them to pay their own legal fees.

Mitsubishi Sued

The Mitsubishi case is a reminder that sexual harassment happens in blue-collar settings and among co-workers as well as in white-collar offices where the top executive is a lecherous tyrant. Many theories have tried to account for why it allegedly happened on such a large scale at Mitsubishi and seemed to be so ingrained in the company culture.

Psychologist Pryor points to Mitsubishi's single-minded focus on its production targets, perhaps at the expense of the quality of life in the plant. He also thinks that exposing American managers to Japanese customs during visits to Japan may have contributed to the atmosphere at the Illinois plant. In what one worker called "a rite of passage" for American managers visiting Japan, they were taken by their Japanese hosts to bars where sex acts were performed on stage. [37]

Pryor's research indicates that men who engage in the most obvious forms of sexual harassment tend to "think about sexuality as related to feelings of wanting to dominate people." But he says the social atmosphere also plays a big part among men who don't fit that profile.

"People will do what they can get away with," Pryor says. "Mitsubishi is a situation where one has to assume there was some toleration of this behavior on the part of management for it to be as pervasive as it's alleged to be."

Some articles have described how male workers didn't speak out against what they saw because they feared ostracism or physical threats. [38] "That's the old male culture," psychiatrist Rutter says. "We could call it the locker room culture; it has a bit of the mob mentality. When they get going, egging one another on, it's hard for one person to oppose it without risking danger to himself."

The Mitsubishi allegations support survey findings that most sexual harassment occurs among co-workers. In its recent survey of businesses, the American Management Association found that about half the cases of sexual harassment involved the victims' peers or co-workers. (*See graph, p. 628.*) Only 26 percent involved the victims' direct supervisors. [39]

FOR MORE INFORMATION

9 to 5, National Association of Working Women, 238 West Wisconsin Ave. Suite 700, Milwaukee, Wis. 53203-2308; (414) 274-0925. This national grass-roots membership organization for working women conducts training on sexual harassment awareness and maintains a hotline (800 522-0925) to help callers with sexual harassment problems.

American Psychological Association, 750 First St. N.E., Washington, D.C. 2002-4242; (202) 336-5500. This professional association has issued a brochure summarizing psychological research on sexual harassment and presents research in the field at its national conferences.

Equal Employment Opportunity Commission, 1801 L St. N.W., Washington, D.C. 20507: (800) 669-EEOC. This is the federal agency charged with enforcing the federal laws governing sexual harassment and investigating individual sexual harassment claims.

Independent Women's Forum, 2111 Wilson Blvd, Suite 550, Arlington, Va. 22201-3057; (703) 243-8989. Women sympathetic to Supreme Court Justice Clarence Thomas formed the forum in the wake of his nomination hearings to present a more skeptical side of the sexual harassment debate. It publishes *The Women's Quarterly*, a forum on women's issues.

New Legal Trends

Law journals have started taking note of countersuits by people accused of harassment. In a dramatic verdict last December, a Philadelphia jury awarded $10 million to a former private school English teacher who sued for defamation after several male students accused him of molestation. As rumors began swirling, the teacher, Wendell Chestnut, resigned under duress. The jury found that the school defamed Chestnut by allowing the rumors to flourish and never investigating the charges. [40]

Hope A. Comisky, a Philadelphia attorney who represents employers in sexual-harassment cases, calls the Chestnut verdict "a real wake-up call" for corporate employers. The lesson, she says, is to conduct an investigation, and "you better keep it confidential."

So far, alleged harassers have been "largely unsuccessful" in cases against their accusers or employers, according to Alba Conte, a consultant in Portland, Ore. [41] Many states hold to the "employment-at-will" doctrine, which allows employers to fire a worker without cause unless the employee has an employment contract specifically limiting the terms of employment and termination. Defamation cases are also difficult to prove, Conte points out, because the key issues are whether the defamatory information is true and whether the person spreading the information did so with malice. It's particularly hard to show malice if the employer who disciplines an employee believes he committed the harassment, Conte says.

Even if an employer defeats a countersuit, however, "it costs a whole lot of money to defend it," Comisky says. "It takes people out of the workplace to go to trials, testify, take depositions; it's very unproductive time." ■

OUTLOOK

More Legal Battles?

Sexual harassment emerged as an outgrowth of a revolutionary change in America's work force: women flooding into previously off-limits areas of employment in record numbers.

For women's-rights activists, sexual harassment litigation is an important avenue for ending discrimination against women as they make new forays into employment. Critics see the court suits as an overreaction to some natural resentment among men.

Battles are likely to continue in the courts over whether sexual harassment restrictions violate First Amendment rights (*see p. 642*). Some legal experts predict that employers will also try to contest the extent to which federal law makes them liable for harassing behavior by their employees. Sexual harassment cases by men remain rare, but some believe they will grow as women gain more power in the workplace.

Ideological arguments over the value of policies against sexual harassment are sure to continue. But even if they have doubts, many mainstream employers have decided to adopt anti-harassment strategies to deflect litigation.

Myron D. Rumeld, a New York attorney who represents employers, agrees with conservative critics who are concerned about the larger judgments now allowed. "The marginal cases are more likely to settle for a higher sum," he says, "and more marginal cases are likely to be taken by lawyers."

But Rumeld also sees a positive side to the new climate. "I'd like to believe the most profound trend is employers being increasingly sensitive to these issues and dealing with them up front before they mushroom into litigation." ■

Sarah Glazer is a New York-based freelance writer who specializes in health and social-policy issues.

Notes

[1] See "Wal-Mart Ex-worker awarded $50 million in sex-harassment suit," *The Wall Street Journal,* June 30, 1995. The case was *Kimzey v. Wal-Mart Stores Inc.*, U.S. District Court, Western District of Missouri.

[2] Alexander Alger and William G. Flanagan, "Sexual Politics," *Forbes,* May 6, 1996, pp. 106-110.

[3] Rochelle Sharpe, "A Mitsubishi U.S. Unit is Taking a Hard Line in Harassment Battle," *The Wall Street Journal,* April 22, 1996, p. A1.

[4] Kirstin Downey Grimsley and Warren Brown, "Woman Alleging Harassment at Mitsubishi Plant Receives Death Threat," *The Washington Post,* April 26, 1996, p. A19. Also see Kirstin Downey Grimsley, Frank Swoboda and Warren Brown, "Fear on the Line at Mitsubishi," *The Washington Post,* April 29, 1996, p. A1.

[5] See Mark Maremont, "Abuse of Power: The Astonishing Tale of Sexual Harassment at Astra USA," *Business Week,* May 13, 1996, pp. 86-96, and Michael Meyer, "School for Scandal," *Newsweek,* May 20, 1996, p. 44.

[6] The landmark act allowed limited money damages for victims of harassment and other intentional discrimination based on sex, religion or disability. In addition, the act countered nine Supreme Court decisions that made it harder for workers to bring and win job discrimination lawsuits. See *1991 CQ Almanac,* pp. 251-261.

[7] Alger and Flanagan, *op. cit.*, pp. 106-110.

[8] Harsh K. Luthar and Anthony Townsend, "Man Handling," *National Review,* Feb. 6, 1995, pp. 58-59. Luthar and Townsend are assistant professors of management at, respectively, Bryant College in Smithfield, R.I., and the University of Nevada, Las Vegas.

[9] The appeals court's decision in *Barnes v. Train* was reported as *Barnes v. Costle* (1977) to reflect the new EPA administrator, Douglas Costle.

[10] Elizabeth Larson, "Shrinking Violets at the Office," *The Women's Quarterly,* spring 1996, p. 8.

[11] Alger and Flanagan, *op. cit.*, pp. 106-110.

[12] U.S Merit Systems Protection Board, *Sexual Harassment in the Federal Workplace* (1995), p. viii.

[13] 9 to 5 is a nonprofit membership organization for office workers. Its toll-free, confidential telephone hotline (800 522-0925) provides information and referrals on dealing with workplace problems.

[14] Michael Weiss and Cathy Young, "Feminist Jurisprudence: Equal Rights or Neo-Paternalism?" *Policy Analysis,* June 19, 1996, p. 1. Young is an associate policy analyst at the institute.

[15] Cato Institute press release, "10th anniversary of Vinson case no cause for celebration," June 19, 1996.

[16] Weiss and Young, *op. cit.*, p. 10.

[17] Quoted in Peter Rutter, *Sex, Power and Boundaries* (1996), pp. 229-231.

[18] Kirstin Downey Grimsley, "Co-workers Cited in Most Sexual Harassment Cases," *The Washington Post,* June 14, 1996, p. D1.

[19] Larson, *op. cit.*, p. 8.

[20] Harsh K. Luthar, "The Neglect of Critical Issues in the Sexual Harassment Discussion: Implications for Organizational and Public Policies," *Journal of Individual Employment Rights,* Vol. 4, No. 4, 1995-96, pp. 261-276.

[21] U.S. Merit Systems Protection Board, *op. cit.*, p. 13.

[22] See Maria Puente, "Reverse Tailhook," *USA Today,* Sept. 22, 1994.

[23] American Psychological Association, *Sexual Harassment: Myths and Realities* (undated pamphlet).

[24] Barbara A. Gutek, *Sex and the Workplace: The Impact of Sexual Behavior and Harassment on Women, Men and Organizations* (1985), p. 60.

[25] U.S. Merit Systems Protection Board, *op. cit.* p. 7.

[26] Quoted in Rutter, *op. cit.*, pp. 216-217.

[27] Weiss et al., *op. cit.*, p. 9.

[28] For a pre-1991 history of the subject, see "Sexual Harassment," *The CQ Researcher,* Aug. 9, 1991, pp. 537-560.

[29] See Rhodes Cook, "Hill vs. Thomas," *Congressional Quarterly Weekly Report,* Dec. 9, 1995, p. 3719.

[30] Ellen Frankel Paul, "Sexual Harassment: A Defining Moment and its Repercussions," in David A. Rochefort and Roger W. Cobb, eds., *The Politics of Problem Definition: Shaping the Policy Agenda* (1994), p. 77.

[31] *Ibid.*, p. 77.

[32] Eloise Salholz et al., "Dividing Lines," *Newsweek,* Oct. 28, 1991, p. 25.

[33] Lincoln Caplan, "Who Lied?" *Newsweek,* Nov. 14, 1994, commenting on *Strange Justice,* a book by *Wall Street Journal* reporters Jane Mayer and Jill Abramson, who argued that Hill told the truth.

[34] Linda Greenhouse, "Court, 9-0, Makes Sex Harassment Easier to Prove," *The New York Times,* Nov. 10, 1993, p. A1.

[35] Quoted in Evan Thomas and Thomas Rosenstiel, "Decline and Fall," *Newsweek,* Sept. 18, 1995, p. 32.

[36] Anita F. Hill, "Hill: 'The Dismal Reality Remains,'" *Newsweek,* Sept. 18, 1995, p. 34.

[37] Kirstin Downey Grimsley, "Why Men Stay Silent," *The Washington Post,* May 26, 1996, p. H1.

[38] *Ibid.*

[39] Grimsley, "Co-workers Cited in Most Sexual Harassment Cases," *op. cit.*, p. D1.

[40] See Suzanne Sataline, "$10 Million Awarded to Ex-Teacher," *Philadelphia Inquirer,* Dec. 9, 1995, p. A1. The judge asked the parties in the case to submit the case to mediation, which could affect the verdict itself as well as the amount of damages, according to Chestnut's attorney, Richard E. Stabinski.

[41] Alba Conte, "When the tables are turned; Courts consider suits by alleged sexual harassers," *Trial,* March 1996, p. 30, published by Association of Trial Lawyers of America.

Bibliography

Selected Sources Used

Books

Bravo, Ellen, and Ellen Cassedy, *The 9 to 5 Guide to Combating Sexual Harassment,* John Wiley and Sons, 1992.
The authors, director and co-founder, respectively, of 9 to 5, National Association of Working Women, put together one of the first guides for employees and employers in the wake of the Hill-Thomas hearings.

Petrocelli, William, and Barbara Kate Repa, *Sexual Harassment on the Job*, Nolo Press, 1995.
This easy-to-read reference on sexual harassment law is aimed primarily at workers who want to file a sexual harassment claim.

Rutter, Peter, *Sex, Power and Boundaries: Understanding and Preventing Sexual Harassment*, Bantam Books, 1996.
Rutter, a San Francisco psychiatrist, discusses cases in which men accused of sexual harassment and women who were victims of it are struggling to deal with new social boundaries.

Celia Morris, *Bearing Witness: Sexual Harassment and Beyond — Everywoman's Story,* Little, Brown, 1994.
This collection of stories of sexual harassment, based on interviews, is told by women in their own words.

Articles

Alger, Alexandra, and William G. Flanagan, "Sexual Politics," *Forbes*, May 6, 1996, p. 106.
The authors attack sexual harassment litigation for penalizing business unfairly for trivial affronts.

Annin, Peter, et al., "School for Scandal," *Newsweek,* May 20, 1996, p. 44.
Two employers' different responses to sexual harassment claims are discussed — Mitsubishi's defiant stance and Astra USA's prompt suspension of its chief executive.

Burns, Sarah E., "Issues in Workplace Sexual Harassment Law and Related Social Science Research," *Journal of Social Issues*, spring 1995, pp. 193-207.
Burns, associate professor of clinical law at New York University School of Law, discusses the social science underpinnings for such legal debates as the "reasonable woman" standard. She notes that the research on which court rulings have been based continue to be debated among social scientists. The article is part of a special issue on sexual harassment and gender stereotyping.

Grimsley, Kirstin Downey, et al., "Fear on the Line at Mitsubishi," *The Washington Post,* April 29, 1996, p. A1.
Based on numerous interviews with female workers at Mitsubishi, this article describes the type of sexual harassment and retaliation that led to the Equal Employment Opportunity Commission suit against the company.

Grimsley, Kirstin Downey, "Why Men Stay Silent," *The Washington Post,* May 26, 1996, p. H1.
In interviews, male Mitsubishi workers explain why they did not stand up for female co-workers who were being harassed — even when they thought it was wrong.

Kruger, Pamela, *Working Woman,* June 1995, pp. 32-77.
This article discusses what employers can do to protect themselves from sexual harassment suits and countersuits.

Maremont, Mark, "Abuse of Power," *Business Week,* May 13, 1996, pp. 86-98.
After a six-month investigation, *Business Week* finds a dozen cases of women who were fondled or solicited for sexual favors by top executives of Astra USA Inc., a pharmaceutical company. The article discusses the lasting psychological problems some of the women suffered as well as the lack of neutral investigations inside the company.

Reports and Studies

Cato Institute, "Feminist Jurisprudence,: Equal Rights or Neo-Paternalism?" *Policy Analysis*, June 19, 1996.
In this paper issued by the libertarian Cato Institute, the authors charge "feminist pressure has . . . resulted in increasingly loose and subjective definitions of harassment" in landmark court cases.

U.S. Merit Systems Protection Board, *Sexual Harassment in the Federal Workplace*, October 1995.
This is the third and most recent survey of federal workers' experience with sexual harassment. It contains data on men and women's differing definitions of sexual harassment and how those have changed since earlier surveys in 1980 and 1987.

Women Employed Institute, *Sexual Harassment: The problem that isn't going away,* 1994.
This Chicago-based organization interviewed 47 women who called their hotline with complaints of sexual harassment. Half of the women were fired or quit their jobs as a result of the harassment.

The Next Step

Additional information from UMI's Newspaper & Periodical Abstracts database

Corporate Response to Sexual Harassment

Crain, Karen A., and Kenneth A. Heischmidt, "Implementing business ethics: Sexual harassment," *Journal of Business Ethics,* April 1995, pp. 299-308.

The importance of developing personnel policies that detail and prohibit sexual harassment in the workplace is addressed. Companies must understand that sexual harassment is both an illegal and unethical practice.

Huebner, Janice Anderson, "How to avoid sexual harassment traps," *HR Focus,* March 1995, pp. 15-16.

Human resource managers should educate line managers on the issues surrounding sexual harassment and instruct them on traps that have caught even the most conscientious managers.

Irvin, A. McArthur, "Firms need written policy covering sexual harassment," *Atlanta Journal Constitution,* Jan. 22, 1995, p. D3.

A. McArthur Irvin discusses the explosion in the number of sexual harassment claims that employers are being faced with, suggesting that employers publish a written policy inviting employees to report sexual harassment and offering advice to minimize the risk of harassment claims.

Laabs, Jennifer J., "HR puts its questions on the line: Sexual harassment," *Personnel Journal,* February 1995, pp. 36-45.

Because companies such as Avon, Corning and MGM haven't been afraid to ask tough questions about sexual harassment, they've found solutions that work. Common human resource questions about sexual harassment in the workplace and the importance of having clear policies to limit corporate liability are examined.

Nobile, Robert J., "Sexual harassment: Do you know how to respond?" *HR Focus,* January 1996, pp. 13-14.

Jury awards in sexual harassment cases show that people have a very low tolerance for this form of discrimination. A comprehensive policy against sexual harassment and a sound internal procedure to ensure complaints of such harassment are investigated properly will help protect companies against large jury awards.

Tyson, Ann Scott, "U.S. companies move to curb sexual harassment on job," *Christian Science Monitor,* May 30, 1996, p. 1.

As sexual harassment emerges as one of the most sensitive workplace issues of the 1990s, a growing number of companies are quietly working to check the problem before it gets beyond the office suite or factory floor and into the courts. Dozens of firms are holding training seminars, quizzing employees about sexual harassment policies and appointing special in-house representatives to field complaints.

Equal Employment Opportunity Commission

Kilborn, Peter T., "A sexual harassment case draws swift action from an agency," *The New York Times,* Jan. 10, 1995, p. A16.

The case of Jacqueline M. Lia and Amy M. Beichler, two women who accused a fellow worker, Lance Carson, of sexual harassment and found speedy relief from the EEOC, is examined as an example of an instance in which the agency, frequently accused of being agonizingly slow, acted swiftly.

Swanson, K.C., "How the EEOC is trying to right itself," *National Journal,* May 18, 1996, pp. 1104-1105.

The Equal Employment Opportunity Commission, one of Washington's favorite punching bags, is shedding its image as an ineffectual meddler and occasionally punching back. Gilbert F. Casellas, the agency's head, is credited with the turnaround.

Federal Legislation

Johnson, Stephen, "Federal laws cited in lawsuit," *Houston Chronicle,* Jan. 16, 1996, p. A14.

The federal Equal Employment Opportunity Act allows two female Texas Ranger investigators to sue the laenforcement agency for sexual harassment despite the 11th Amendment that prohibits states from being sued in federal court, according to a plaintiffs attorney.

Sixel, L M., "Wrongs without remedy," *Houston Chronicle,* Sept. 17, 1995, p. D1.

The loophole in federal laws that makes it difficult for employees to make a stand in court when they are the victims of same-sex discrimination is examined.

Penalties for Sexual Harassment

Bailey, Eric, "Conroy helped aide sidestep penalty, lawyers claim," *Los Angeles Times,* Oct. 26, 1995, p. A3.

Attorneys for Robyn Boyd, who is suing California Assemblyman Mickey Conroy and staff member Pete Conaty for sexual harassment, have complained about the punishment doled out by the Assembly in 1994. Conaty was suspended for a week without pay, but Conroy paid the staffer's salary with campaign funds.

Brelis, Matthew, "Southborough faults its police, winces at harassment penalty," *Boston Globe,* Sept. 6, 1995, p. 26.

Public outrage greeted the disclosure that police officers in Southborough, Mass., sexually harassed and demeaned a female dispatcher to such an extent that the state would levy a $250,000 penalty against the town via the Massachusetts Commission Against Discrimination.

Jacobs, Margaret A, "Del Laboratories agrees to record sum for settling sexual-harassment lawsuit," *The Wall Street Journal,* Aug. 4, 1995, p. B7.

Del Laboratories Inc. agreed to the largest settlement ever of a sexual-harassment lawsuit by the EEOC. Under the agreement, approved on Aug. 3, 1995, Del will pay $1.2 million to 15 women who claim that they were harassed by Dan K. Wassong, CEO, president and chairman of the Farmingdale, N.Y., cosmetics company. Del denied any wrongdoing.

Keating, Stephen, "Bellco credit union settles sexual harassment lawsuit," ***Denver Post,*** **Oct. 17, 1995, p. C2.**
Fourteen women have settled a year-old discrimination and sexual harassment lawsuit against Bellco First Federal Credit Union, based in Greenwood Village, Colo.

Mathis, Nancy, "Senate panel votes to kick Packwood out," ***Houston Chronicle,*** **Sept. 7, 1995, p. A1.**
The Senate Ethics Committee voted unanimously to recommend Bob Packwood be expelled from the Senate on charges of sexual and official misconduct, the harshest penalty that can be levied and one not invoked since the Civil War.

Shuman, Mark, "City penalty given to cop to be appealed," ***Chicago Tribune,*** **Sept. 19, 1995, p. C8.**
Des Plaines, Ill., Mayor Ted Sherwood said that city attorneys will file a court appeal because the Fire and Police Commission did not fire a police officer accused of sexual harassment and disobeying an order from the police chief. Sherwood called Officer Clifford L. Cadle's punishment excessively light.

Walt, Kathy, "Sexual harassment suit against judge is settled," ***Houston Chronicle,*** **Sept. 23, 1995, p. A1.**
The state of Texas has agreed to pay $10,000 to Velika Johnson of Houston, who claimed Court of Criminal Appeals Judge Morris Overstreet fired her because she rebuffed his sexual advances.

Sexual Harassment in the Military

Colvin, Leonard E., "Navy petty officer guilty in sexual harassment of junior sailor on airplane," ***Journal & Guide,*** **March 13, 1996, p. 1.**
Navy Petty Officer Angela Shanks, who was at the center of a Navy sexual harassment case in the fall of 1995, says she has been receiving threatening phone calls and has been the object of reprisals from male supervisors.

Schmitt, Eric, "Court-martial clears Navy captain of sexual harassment," ***The New York Times,*** **Oct. 20, 1995, p. A28.**
Capt. Everett L. Greene, the former top equal-opportunity officer for the Navy who was picked to be an admiral and led his service's effort to fight sexual harassment after the Tailhook scandal, was acquitted on Oct. 19, 1995, of sexually harassing a woman who had worked for him. Greene is the highest-ranking naval officer to be court-martialed since WWII.

Sexual Harassment in Schools

Bryant, Anne, "Sexual harassment in school takes its toll," ***USA Today,*** **March 1995, pp. 40-41.**
The 1993 report "Hostile Hallways: The AAUW Survey of Sexual Harassment in America's Schools" helped raise awareness of the problems of sexual harassment students face in U.S. schools. Findings of this research are discussed.

Evans, Sherrell, "Schools get tough on sexual harassment," ***Atlanta Journal Constitution,*** **Dec. 17, 1995, p. G8.**
A pending lawsuit against the Monroe County, Ga., school district about student-on-student contact and a 1988 Gwinnett County case are prompting changes in the sexual harassment policies of a number of metro Atlanta school systems.

McCarthy, Rebecca, "UGA professor accused of sexual harassment," ***Atlanta Constitution,*** **Feb. 13, 1996, p. C3.**
University of Georgia officials are investigating Herman van Halbeek, a tenured chemistry professor who is accused of sexually harassing eight students and staff members.

Sexual Harassment in the Workplace

Flatow, Gail, " Sexual harassment in Indiana daily newspapers," ***Newspaper Research Journal,*** **Summer 1994, pp. 32-45.**
In a survey, 68 percent of women in newsrooms reported sexual harassment. Verbal harassment was by far the most common problem.

Losey, Michael R, "Sexual harassment: A growing workplace dilemma," ***USA Today*****, March 1995, pp. 38-39.**
Increasing awareness of what constitutes sexual harassment has led to increased confusion about what it means in the workplace. Employers need to develop clearer guidelines for handling complaints and settling disputes before they result in litigation.

Neuborne, Ellen, "Workplace sexual harassment knows no rank," ***USA Today,*** **May 7, 1996, p. B6.**
Several executives at Astra USA, the U.S. division of the Swedish drugmaker, have had disciplinary action taken against them over charges of sexual harassment.

"Philip Morris unit faces sexual-harassment suit," ***The Wall Street Journal,*** **May 31, 1996, p. D7.**
Philip Morris USA faces a sexual-harassment lawsuit alleging that women at a cigarette plant in Louisville, Ky., were pressured to trade sex for promotions and favorable job assignments. The suit was filed by five women on May 28, 1996, in Jefferson Circuit Court.

"Suit accuses Mitsubishi of sexual harassment," ***Detroit News,*** **April 10, 1996, p. A1.**
In one of the biggest sexual harassment cases ever brought by the EEOC, authorities on April 9, 1996, accused a Japanese automaker of allowing sexual harassment on an "outrageous scale" at an Illinois plant. The lawsuit contends as many as 700 women were subjected to groping and sexual remarks by male co-workers and supervisers, creating a "hostile and abusive work environment" that went unchecked for years at the Mitsubishi Motor Manufacturing of American Inc. plant.

Back Issues

Great Research on Current Issues Starts Right Here...Recent topics covered by The CQ Researcher are listed below. Before May 1991, reports were published under the name of Editorial Research Reports.

JANUARY 1995
Treating Addiction
Child Custody and Support
Parents and Schools
Non-Proliferation Treaty at 25

FEBRUARY 1995
Cracking Down on Immigration
The Business of Sports
Reinventing Government
Housing Discrimination

MARCH 1995
Death Penalty Debate
Primary Care
Democracy in Africa
Environmental Movement at 25

APRIL 1995
Abortion Clinic Protests
Dieting and Health
Combating AIDS
Rethinking Affirmative Action

MAY 1995
Assisted Suicide Controversy
Overhauling Social Security
Learning to Read
Mandatory Sentencing

JUNE 1995
Combating Infectious Disease
Property Rights
Repetitive Stress Injuries
Regulating the Internet

JULY 1995
War Crimes
Highway Safety
Combating Terrorism
Preventing Teen Drug Use

AUGUST 1995
Job Stress
Organ Transplants
United Nations at 50
Advances in Cancer Research

SEPTEMBER 1995
Catholic Church in the U.S.
Northern Ireland Cease-Fire
High School Sports
Teaching History

OCTOBER 1995
Quebec's Future
Revitalizing the Cities
Networking the Classroom
Indoor Air Pollution

NOVEMBER 1995
The Working Poor
The Jury System
Sex, Violence and the Media
Police Misconduct

DECEMBER 1995
Teens and Tobacco
Gene Therapy's Future
Global Water Shortages
Third-Party Prospects

JANUARY 1996
Emergency Medicine
Punishing Sex Offenders
Bilingual Education
Helping the Homeless

FEBRUARY 1996
Reforming the CIA
Campaign Finance Reform
Academic Politics
Getting Into College

MARCH 1996
The British Monarchy
Preventing Juvenile Crime
Tax Reform
Pursuing the Paranormal

APRIL 1996
Centennial Olympic Games
Managed Care
Protecting Endangered Species
New Military Culture

MAY 1996
Russia's Political Future
Marriage and Divorce
Year-Round Schools
Taiwan, China and the U.S.

JUNE 1996
Rethinking NAFTA
First Ladies
Teaching Values
Labor Movement's Future

JULY 1996
Recovered-Memory Syndrome
Native Americans' Future

Back issues are available for $5.00 (subscribers) or $8.00 (non-subscribers). Quantity discounts apply to orders over ten. To order, call Congressional Quarterly Customer Service at (202) 887-8621.

Binders are available for $18.00. To order call 1-800-638-1710. Please refer to stock number 648.

Future Topics

- ***Public Education Under Attack***
- ***Animal Rights Debate***
- ***Privatizing Government Services***

THE CQ Researcher

PUBLISHED BY CONGRESSIONAL QUARTERLY INC.

Attack on Public Schools

Has the education "crisis" been overstated?

Headlines raise what seem to be unceasing alarms about plummeting test scores, illiterate high school graduates and wasted tax dollars. In the 13 years since the federal *A Nation at Risk* report warned of rising school mediocrity, parents and educators have seized on a rash of reforms and alternatives ranging from national standards and private management to school choice, charter schools and home schooling. But a growing number of scholars and public school advocates recently have questioned whether the "crisis" really exists. They complain that data pointing to failing schools often has been distorted by critics, some of whom seek to build taxpayer support for private schools. Such charges, the critics counter, represent the education establishment in a state of denial.

INSIDE THIS ISSUE

CQ July 26, 1996 • Volume 6, No. 28 • Pages 649-672

Formerly Editorial Research Reports

Attack On Public Schools

The Issues

Background

Current Situation

Outlook

Sidebars and Graphics

For Further Research

COVER: ILLUSTRATION BY SARAH M. MAGNER

July 26, 1996
Volume 6, No. 28

EDITOR
Sandra Stencel

MANAGING EDITOR
Thomas J. Colin

ASSOCIATE EDITORS
Sarah M. Magner
Richard L. Worsnop

STAFF WRITERS
Charles S. Clark
Mary H. Cooper
Kenneth Jost

EDITORIAL ASSISTANT
Tonya Harris

PUBLISHED BY
Congressional Quarterly Inc.

CHAIRMAN
Andrew Barnes

VICE CHAIRMAN
Andrew P. Corty

EDITOR AND PUBLISHER
Neil Skene

EXECUTIVE EDITOR
Robert W. Merry

The CQ Researcher (ISSN 1056-2036). Formerly Editorial Research Reports. Published weekly (48 times per year, not printed March 1, May 31, Aug. 30, Nov. 29) by Congressional Quarterly Inc., 1414 22nd St., N.W., Washington, D.C. 20037. Annual subscription rate for libraries, businesses and government is $319. Additional rates furnished upon request. Periodicals postage paid at Washington, D.C. POSTMASTER: Send address changes to The CQ Researcher, 1414 22nd St., N.W., Washington, D.C. 20037.

Attack on Public Schools

BY CHARLES S. CLARK

THE ISSUES

Last February, a hard-driving real estate agent in Northern Virginia placed a provocative advertisement in a local newspaper. "Mt. Vernon Schools Have Got You Down?" the ad asked. "Move!"

The agent received close to 100 calls, but instead of hearing from potential clients he found himself hounded by a succession of teachers, parents and school officials. Most were furious at his slur on the schools in Mount Vernon, an area of affluent Fairfax County with many recent immigrants, but others congratulated him for raising the issue of the schools' questionable reputation.

The upshot, according to School Superintendent Robert "Bud" Spillane, was a healthy community debate. "People got interested, and there was lots of publicity," he says. "People were asking, 'What do you mean schools are bad? Look at their achievements. Is it because there are more black, brown and immigrant students?' There was a backlash that was very positive." And, Spillane adds, "The real estate agent apologized, and since then he's almost been doing community penance by spending his time in schools."

The reputation of a school system is precious to a community, often exerting a make-or-break impact on property values as well as the area's overall economic and demographic character. But describing a community solely on the basis of its racial makeup is a violation of federal fair housing laws — and a reason why Realtors are supposed to follow careful procedures when they introduce prospective homebuyers to a school system's pros and cons.

What agents *are* supposed to tell concerned clients, says Fred Underwood, staff vice president for equal opportunity at the National Association of Realtors, is something like this: " 'There are many qualities that make a school good, and while I can't answer your question specifically, I can help you find the information.'

"There are differences in what people consider good," Underwood continues. "People have different levels of education and culture, and some might value math and science while others value athletics or art. Schools are beginning to give out their test scores and college placement levels. So we advise people to set up an appointment at school district headquarters."

This eye-of-the-beholder aspect to school quality is a big reason for many of the controversies that swirl around public education. And what has become clear is that when it comes to talk of schools, many Americans today are inclined to assume the worst.

American schools are operating in an "age of dissatisfaction," as many in education have called it. A Gallup Poll conducted for CNN and *USA Today* earlier this year asked Americans to list the nation's most pressing problems; "quality of education in public schools" was ranked first, over crime, the economy and health care.

Hardly a week goes by without newspaper reports of illiterate high school graduates, "plummeting" test scores or guns being found in student lockers. The view that public schools are "failing" has become routine rhetoric among politicians. A new book by former Vice President Dan Quayle criticizes "mediocre" public schools that fail to teach proper values. [1] Ominous-sounding titles have become familiar on the publishing landscape — Myron Lieberman's *Public Education: An Autopsy* (1993), and Charles J. Sykes' *Dumbing Down Our Kids: Why America's Children Feel Good About Themselves But Can't Read, Write or Add* (1996), to name just two.

It has been 13 years since the federal government's famous *A Nation at Risk* report warned that "for the first time in the history of our country, the educational skills of one generation will not surpass, will not equal, will not even approach those of their parents." [2]

Since then, center stage has been held by an unceasing wave of reforms and alternatives — national standards, school choice, charter schools, privatization, home schooling — all in one way or another signaling a thumbs-down evaluation of public schools. [3]

Private school enrollment, meantime, has increased by 9.3 percent in the past decade, according to the National Association of Independent Schools (NAIS).

More recently, however, a less gloomy view of public schools has bubbled to the surface. The optimism was stoked last year by a widely noted book, The *Manufactured Crisis: Myths, Fraud and the Attack on America's Public Schools.* Psychology professors David C. Berliner and Bruce J. Biddle assert that an honest look at test scores nationally and internationally shows that U.S. schools are as good or even better than they were a

Rating Local Public Schools

When asked to grade their local schools on a scale of A to F, more than twice as many people give them A's or B's as give them D's or F's. Local school ratings generally have remained stable over the years, although many education critics say the nation's schools are getting worse.

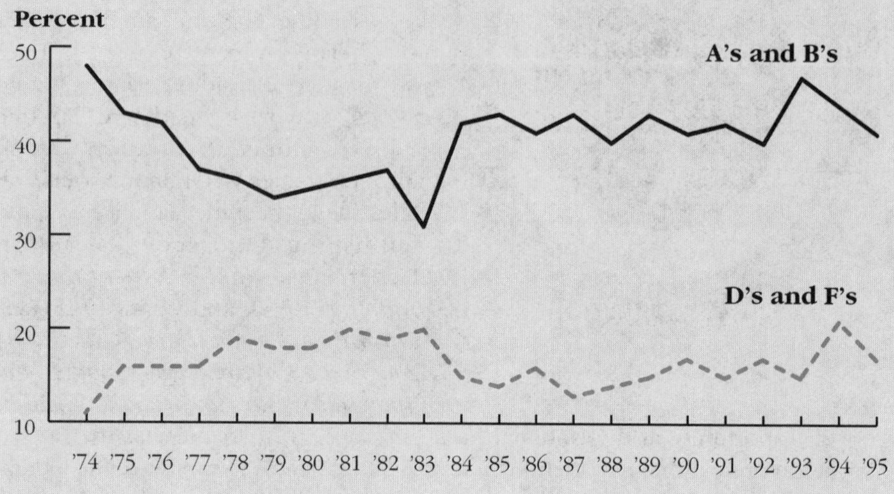

Source: "The 27th Annual Phi Delta Kappa/Gallup Poll of the Public's Attitudes Toward the Public Schools," Phi Delta Kappan, *September 1995*

few decades ago. What's more, the authors allege that much of the criticism is a political ploy by conservatives to discredit public schools so they can cut school funding and win tax breaks for families that want to send their children to private and religious schools.

"This book was written in outrage," Berliner and Biddle note. "Throughout much of recent history, our federal government seemed to be willing to promote the interests of public education. . . . Events in the last decade have challenged these beliefs. In 1983, the Reagan White House began making sweeping claims attacking the conduct and achievements of America's public schools — claims that were contradicted by evidence we knew about. . . . As time passed, even leading members of the education community. . . . began to state these lies as facts." [4]

Berliner and Biddle's upbeat brief has been balm on the wounds of battered education professionals. "I've been seeing more school administrators turning inward and pulling away from this constant barrage of criticisms and pressure and media exposure of public schools," says Arnold F. Fege, director of governmental affairs for the National PTA. "The academic establishment has just awakened to the fact that misperceptions have to be countered."

It is tricky to speak of quality in the nation's public schools when vast differences separate decaying inner-city schools from wealthy suburban ones, and when two public schools, in some cases only blocks apart, can enjoy strikingly different degrees of parental support. What's more, surveys show that Americans think much more highly of their local school than the abstract notion of U.S. schools in general. Surveys also show a disconnect between educators, parents, community leaders and the public, with educators more inclined to rate schools more favorably.

Those who would spread a good word about schools face a forbidding national climate. Economic anxieties about disappearing or shifting jobs have today's parents spooked. Many members of the media-spotlighted baby-boom generation are scrambling to outfit their kids with every advantage — private tutors, college admissions counselors and extracurricular strategies that start in kindergarten.

"In one of history's more astonishing transformations," complains *Washington Post* book critic and columnist Jonathan Yardley, today's parents "metamorphosed overnight from dewy-eyed partisans of Flower Power into flinty-eyed goose-steppers of dress for success." [5]

Such parents are often willing to shell out as much as $15,000 a year for private schools — even when the local public schools are well-regarded. "Everyone knows people in their 40s and 50s who have lost a job and have no ability to teach themselves a new body of knowledge," said Bruce Johnson, a computer programmer and parent in Tolland, Conn. "Twenty years ago, a public education was sufficient to be successful. That's no longer the case." [6]

Such attitudes are reinforced by a political climate in which many established public institutions are held in poor regard. Note the recent proposals, for example, to privatize Medicare or Social Security. [7]

"There's a troubling trend that seeks personal solutions over solutions for the needs of the entire community," says Kelly Butler, executive director of Parents for Public Schools, a Jackson, Miss.-based advocacy group that seeks to lure middle-class parents back to racially integrated public schools. "Wealthy parents have the financial privilege of removing themselves from the public system at the expense of others. But it doesn't solve the problem of educating the citizenry."

Finally, those who hope for a resurgence of confidence in public schools must confront an army of longtime critics who will demand substantive reforms before they offer their seal of approval. Chester E. Finn Jr., a Bush administration Education official who is now a senior fellow at the Hudson Institute, says the upbeat message of books such as *The Manufactured Crisis* is "part of a tradition of denial in which a broad swath, but by no means all, in the field of education engage in defensiveness and blame-shifting."

So far, there is little sign of a new consensus on public school performance. As wave after wave of reforms has crested, "School-reform discussions became politically polarized and loaded with code words," write John Katzman and Steven Hodas, founders of The Princeton Review, a firm that prepares college-bound students to take national academic tests. "Asserting the importance of traditional academic standards and values was associated with a reactionary political agenda, while political progressives were stereotyped as favoring a mushy-headed disregard for measurable achievement." [8]

As educators and citizens try to gauge the status of America's public schools, these are some of the questions they are asking:

Has the quality of public schools declined?

From 1950 to 1989, "we probably experienced the worst educational decline in our history," former Education Secretary William J. Bennett wrote several years ago. "Between 1963 and 1980, for example, combined average Scholastic Aptitude Test (SAT) scores — scores which test students' verbal and math abilities — fell 90 points, from 980 to 890." [9]

Indictments of this kind touched off the debate over *The Manufactured Crisis,* a debate that necessarily hinges on test scores, international comparisons and glasses half-full or half-empty.

In rebutting reports of falling scores, Berliner and Biddle embrace a widely held view that the SAT is not a good measure of public school progress. That's because, they say, it is a predictor of college success that is designed for a primarily white, male, affluent test pool. They also note that the proportion of students who take the SAT varies widely from state to state — from as few as 10 percent in Alabama, Arkansas or Iowa to more than 70 percent in Connecticut, New Jersey and Rhode Island. Furthermore, they write, "large shifts in scale scores represent only small shifts in the number of SAT test questions answered correctly." They maintain that Bennett's 90-point drop was caused by mistakes on only six to nine questions. [10]

Others point out that the biggest decline in SAT scores, from the early 1960s to the early '70s, has since been restored and even improved upon. "I don't accept that there's a decline," wrote Gerald W. Bracey, an Alexandria, Va.-based consultant who prepares an annual report on public schools. "The proportion who top 650 in math, for example, is at an all-time high." [11]

Michael A. Resnick, senior associate executive director of the National School Boards Association, is one of many educators who are impressed with Berliner and Biddle's analysis of the factors affecting test trends. "The SAT was never designed as a measure of achievement since it is not designed around the curriculum," he says. "More kids are now taking it, and the ones being added are not from the top of the

SAT Scores Fuel Both Sides of Debate

SAT scores fell from the 1960s through the '70s, then began gradually rising (graph at left). Education critics dismiss the gains as minor. Defenders of U.S. education performance say the improvements reflect meaningful progress, including improvements in minorities' scores (graph at right).

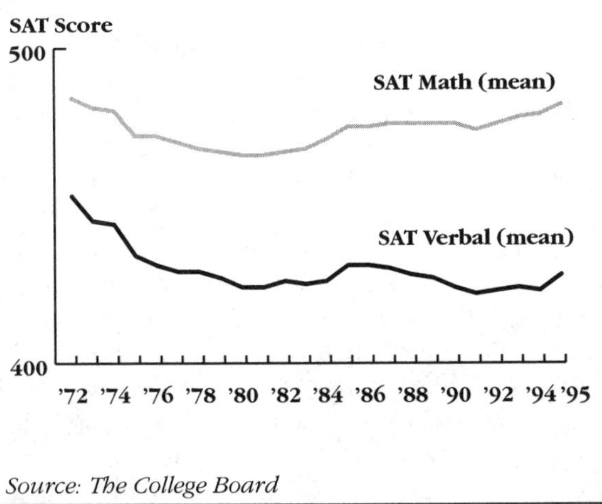

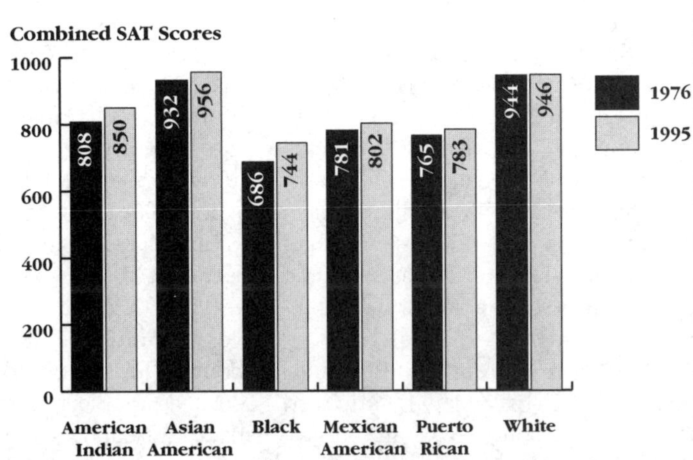

Source: The College Board

Science and Math Scores Rose

From 1982 to 1992, scores in science and math on national achievement tests rose among fourth-, eighth- and 12th-graders (top). Scores in reading and writing showed some improvement in 1992.

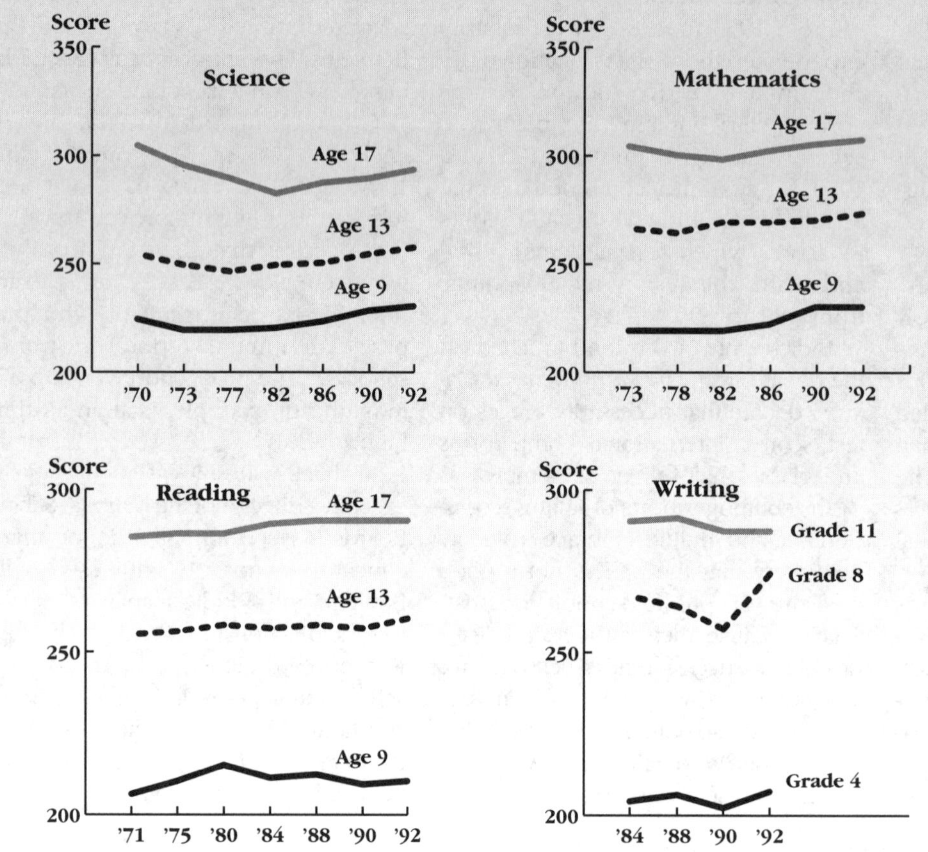

Note: Scores for 1992 are the most recent available.

Source: "National Assessment of Educational Progress: 1992 Trends in Academic Progress," National Center for Educational Statistics, July 1994

class. Given that, I'm surprised scores haven't dropped even more."

What many consider the more scientific representation of school achievement is the National Assessment of Education Process (NAEP), the so-called "nation's report card" administered regularly by the Education Department to a national cross section of fourth-, eighth- and 12th-graders.

The most current NAEP results, released in July 1994, showed progress, tempered by some disappointments. "In mathematics and science there have been substantial gains made since around 1980," said Mark D. Musick, chairman of the National Assessment Governing Board, which administers the NAEP. "Reform efforts of the 1980s may be paying off."

But in reading and writing, there has been little change over the past decade. Reading "achievement among 9-year-olds has dropped since the 1980s, although it leveled off from 1990 to 1992," Musick said. Blacks and Hispanics have made substantial gains over the past two decades, but both groups remain far behind whites, and progress in closing these gaps seems to have stalled since the mid-1980s.

Albert Beaton, former director of data analysis for the NAEP and now a professor of education at Boston College, says that over time, the NAEP "shows very little change in the ability of students, and scores have moved up a little and down a little. The question is, what exactly is a crisis? If the issue is, are the kids going to hell in a handbasket, there's more data to say it isn't so than to say it is."

Still, such mixed reports arm the critics of public education, among them the American Legislative Exchange Council, a conservative, state-level advocacy group. Its education "report card," released in May, relied on NAEP and other data to conclude: "[T]he single, largest government enterprise in America, our public schools, [is] still in neutral while most everything else is in high gear. This year's study (covering 1994-1995) is summed up in one word: stagnation."

Indeed, the absence of dramatic progress prompts many critics to argue that schools need to raise their standards. Diane Ravitch, a senior research fellow at New York University and a former Bush administration Education official, has assembled what is considered one of the best compilations of data on the problems of public schools. She says she can't take Berliner and Biddle's research seriously. "It's a selective rather than an honest dealing with the data," she says. "It doesn't give both the good news and bad news."

In a 1995 book, Ravitch acknowledges clear improvement in the NAEP from 1970 to 1992, but she points out that "NAEP scores reflect what students know, not what they should know." Proof that schools can do better lies in the fact that "the changes observed during the past generation indicate that student achievement goes up and down in response to expectations and standards." [12]

Ravitch gives her blessing to the gloomy international comparisons made by Harold W. Stevenson, a research psychologist at the University of Michigan who studied student scores in the United States, Taiwan and Japan in the early 1980s. "American students performed best in reading in first grade, but Asian students caught up by fifth grade," says her summary. "In mathematics, the differences among the first-graders in different nations were small. By fifth grade, however, American students were far behind students from Japan and Taiwan. [13]

More recently, a discouraging survey by *U.S. News & World Report* found that 76 percent of U.S. high school seniors spend less than five hours per week on homework, compared with only 35 percent in Japan. In Spain, the survey found, 90 percent of high school students study a foreign language, compared with only 43 percent of American students. [14]

Bracey, however, lampoons Stevenson and other critics for worshiping foreign education cultures that he believes stunt students' social and psychological development. Koreans study up to 80 hours a week, and their parents spend 20-30 percent of their income on private tutoring, Bracey says. Educators should not try to "convince American students that if they sleep four hours a night, they will get into college, but if they sleep five hours a night, they won't," he says.

Berliner and Biddle also poke holes in the veneer of foreign superiority. They recite an alarming list of familiar school horror stories — murder, gang extortion, shoplifting, high school prostitution, suicide, assault — all reported in Japan. [15]

More recently, public school boosters point to the "encouraging picture" painted in a new international study of reading scores by the National Center for Education Statistics. It found that American fourth-graders outperformed their peers from 25 other advanced countries. The U.S. was bested only by Finland. The study also reported that 60 percent of U.S. students meet or beat the average of students in member countries of the Organization for Economic Cooperation and Development, even America's most disadvantaged. The only group below average were black fourth- and ninth-graders, particularly those whose parents did not complete high school. [16]

Still, Thomas Toch, a senior editor for *U.S. News* who covers education, warns that much of the international data is "unreliable because the tested groups vary widely," he says. "What's more, Berliner and Biddle distort them," he adds. In truth, American schools continue to fail to educate vast numbers of students, he says. "The number of Americans who take advanced-placement courses is about 7 percent, of whom 4 percent pass. But in countries like Israel, Sweden, Japan or Germany, a third to half take advanced placement, and 25 percent pass."

Overall, Toch says, "U.S. schools are better than they've ever been, and are educating more kids to a higher level, but they're still not very good. Conservatives are wrong to say there used to be a golden age of schools, because back in 1900, 95 percent of kids were excluded, and in 1950, nearly half of students dropped out. But the civil rights movement redefined the schools' mission, and in the 1980s the excellence movement launched by *A Nation at Risk* sought to redefine schools. Today our schools' gains are exclusively at the low end of the scale, where the easy questions are. Students are not yet demonstrating higher-level thinking."

Laurence Steinberg, a Temple University professor of psychology and author of the new book *Beyond the Classroom*, argues that student achievement is low and will remain low as long as American culture encourages a "disengagement" from academics. "The crisis is not manufactured," he says. "Every time someone tries to draw attention to the failure of schools, someone comes up with a different denial theory. [Berliner and Biddle] can argue that there's been an expanding pool of test takers, but studies by the Rand Corp. and the Congressional Budget Office show that scores have declined among white middle-class students as well.

"The decline in SATs is real, and there's been no progress in the past 20 years despite the billions of dollars we've spent. I don't think we ought to be complacent or sanguine when we can read about freshmen entering California State University who need remedial reading. We have coddled our students into ignorance. That's why they're so bored and disengaged."

That dim view is shared by many in the business community, which has been active in pushing school reform. "I'm not going to argue whether the glass is half-full or half-empty, and there is surely lots of good going on that deserves credit," says Milton Goldberg, vice president of the National Alliance of Business and a longtime educator. "But the reality is that too many students are graduating without the schooling that's necessary. Others are not graduating, and this can drain our nation's economy of its productivity."

The Clinton administration, while acknowledging a long road ahead, seeks to accentuate public schools' momentum. "The small gains never make much headlines, but we've had small gain after small gain in the last 15 years," says Marshall S. Smith, undersecretary of Education. "We have the lowest dropout rate ever, the highest college attendance level ever and

The Growing Movement Toward Charter Schools

Of all the education reforms proposed in the past dozen years, charter schools have gathered the most steam, with backing from conservative critics, President Clinton and even some members of the teachers' unions.

Charter schools are small, publicly funded academies that can be launched by any group of parents or teachers. Freed from most state regulations and bureaucracy, they typically are given five years to make a go of it. Twenty states have passed charter legislation, and some 250 schools are in operation nationwide, with 400 planned for next year. A charter school in Somerville, Mass., for example, focuses on English and math. One in Boulder, Colo., specializes in at-risk students.

"What distinguishes charter schools is not the originality of their educational vision but their uncommon commitment to it," write three proponents at the Hudson Institute. "Only teachers who share a school's particular approach are hired . . . and only parents who want that approach enroll their children." [1]

A charter school's freedom from such constraints as local salary scales and collective-bargaining agreements has led to some discomfort among unions. "Charter schools are a mix, from the good to the ugly," says Bella Rosenberg, assistant to the president of the American Federation of Teachers. "Some are clearly efforts at establishing a private school in a public system. In a way, that's giving up on having the public school system that every industrial nation has." The National Education Association, meanwhile, has launched some charter schools of its own.

Charter schools also have drawn criticism from Americans United for Separation of Church and State, which argues that in states such as Colorado and Michigan, some charter schools appear to be teaching Christianity or New Age religion.

Opposition is also heard from public school advocacy groups. Mary Ann Hardenbergh, president of Citizens for Public Schools, in Cambridge, Mass., says that in Massachusetts, "We recognize that politically we have to support some innovation, but we are distressed by the guise under which it comes. Charters cost more per pupil, and they're taking money from our cities and towns. It's destructive to public education to imply that the public itself is not as supportive of public schools as it should be."

Scott Hamilton, undersecretary of Education for charter-schools in Massachusetts, says that under the state's charter school legislation, "money follows the child." In other words, when a student switches to a charter school, the per-pupil funding his old school received is deducted from its funding and given to the charter school. But charter schools actually get more than allocated under the per-pupil funding, Hamilton notes. That's because an amount equal to the child's share of the money spent for his old school's upkeep also goes to the charter school.

However, the state legislature has been reimbursing communities, particularly disadvantaged ones, for losses of aid due to charter school enrollment. As a result, Hamilton says, "charters cost Massachusetts taxpayers $30 million a year." Eventually, he expects the reimbursements to be phased out.

---

[1] Chester E. Finn Jr., Louann A. Bierlein and Bruno V. Manno, "Finding the Right Fit: America's Charter Schools Get Started," *Brookings Review*, summer 1996, p. 18.

three to four times more students in advanced placement. That's happened all over the country, even with poverty and increased immigration."

But others warn against listening to the "Don't worry, be happy crowd," as Jeanne Allen, president of the Center for Education Reform, describes Berliner, Biddle and others. "You can cook the numbers any way you want, but they say there's no problem when every month we're overloaded with news reports and complaints from parents that rigor and standards are not what they used to be."

Recent nationwide polls, however, show some improvements in the schools' public standing. In the annual Gallup Poll for the Phi Delta Kappa education fraternity, 41 percent gave public schools a grade of A or B last year, compared with only 20 percent in 1981.

A less rosy picture emerged in a *U.S. News* poll in March; 62 percent of the respondents said the quality of U.S. education in general is poor, while three-fourths want academic standards raised.

"Citizens are not yet ready to abandon the public system, but unless schools begin to deliver on what the public considers to be the essential elements of education, support for public schools is in jeopardy," warns Deborah Wadsworth, executive director of Public Agenda, a New York group that measures public opinion on education and other issues.

Nearly half of those responding to a poll conducted by Wadsworth's group in May 1995 said that it was possible to get a diploma from their own local high school without possessing even the most minimal attributes of education — writing and reading English and basic arithmetic. [17] The poll also uncovered "a surprising degree of disdain toward highly educated people and some sense of antagonism toward an educational cultural elite," Wadsworth says. "Too much learning is suspect [and] no match for the concept of being well-rounded."

Are attacks on public schools politically motivated?

"The manufactured crisis" in education, according to Berliner and Biddle, is rooted in demographic changes that, beginning in the 1950s and '60s, threatened traditionalists with experimental education and a growing presence of minorities in schools. By the late 1970s, numerous conservative groups had organized to counter what they believed to be a decline in discipline and the dominance of politically liberal "educrats." Yet as far as the public was concerned, the authors continue, "the manufactured crisis began on April 26, 1983 — the date when, amid much fanfare, the Reagan White House released its critical report on the status of American schools, *A Nation at Risk*.[18]

Though the report was prepared by an outside panel of top educators and business leaders, its release by the Reagan administration led Berliner and Biddle to view it as the "blossoming of conservative ideologies."

Consultant Bracey calls the report a "xenophobic screed" that scapegoats educators and raises undue alarm at the fact that U.S. trade rivals still recovering from World War II had made great leaps in education. Bracey says he doesn't view the attacks on schools "as a conspiracy as much as collusion. Clearly, some persons are pushing the notion of a crisis in order to win [approval for] vouchers, privatization or charter schools, just as the Reagan people were trying for prayer in schools, tuition tax credits and the abolition of the Education Department."

Evidence for this view of the "crisis" can be found in the memoirs of the late Terrel H. Bell, the Reagan Education secretary who presided over preparation of *A Nation at Risk*. In the following passage, Bell describes the hours before release of the report, when he had been told the president was pleased with the draft, and a nearby room was packed with waiting reporters, TV cameras and education leaders:

"During these preparations, I wondered about the reticence of the ultraconservatives who had been so persistently my nemesis over the months. Where were they? Were they not aware of what was about to happen? Had they given up? Late on the day before the April 26 release date, I received evidence that they were still alive and feisty. I had a call from my usual informant in [Chief of Staff James A. Baker's] camp. 'Doctor Bell,' she began, 'I hate to tell you this, but I just saw a draft of the president's remarks for tomorrow. It misses the point of your report. In fact, it ignores the report.'

"What do you mean?" I asked. "How could it ignore the report? The purpose of the meeting is for its release."

" 'Well, it doesn't exactly ignore the report, but it spends a lot of time on school prayer, tuition tax credits, the value of private schools and the evils of the [National Education Association].'

"We'll get that changed," I said.

" 'I doubt it. These remarks were put in there at the insistence of [counselor to the president] Ed Meese.'

"I was stunned.

" 'A group went to see Ed. They were led by your "friend" [Meese aide] Ken Cribb,' she said sardonically. 'Ken's the one who hit Ed hard on this. He argued that you can't have the president speaking on education before an audience of this size and not hit tuition tax credits and school prayer.' "

"I'll call Jim Baker in the morning," I said.

" 'I doubt he'll' want to fight Ed on this. It's not that big a deal.' "[19]

As was widely reported, and as Bell had been warned, the president mixed his comments on the report with items from his separate agenda. *A Nation at Risk* was such a hit that Reagan political strategists began using its call for higher-education standards as an issue for the 1984 campaign. This new enthusiasm helped Bell and others block efforts to abolish the Education Department, but critics noted that the report's recommendations for increased education funding were ignored, and that spending eventually would be cut by 25 percent.[20]

To Charles Willie, a faculty member in the graduate school of education at Harvard University, the spending cuts were no coincidence. He began noticing in the *Statistical Abstract of the United States* that expenditures on education at the local level had begun falling in the early 1980s. "I don't often use single-factor explanations, but I can't help conjecture that local spending on schools was a victim of the bashing of public education by educators," he says. "The scare tactics of *A Nation at Risk* were not justified by the data. The report's recommendations all dealt with teacher certification and salary scales and [poor performance by] students, but they mentioned nothing about requirements to educate the handicapped and women, or the innovations from desegregation, or Head Start."

To many active in school issues in the mid-1990s, *A Nation at Risk* left a legacy beyond the "excellence movement" and school reform. "We've tracked the religious right during the 1980s," says Mary Ann Hardenbergh, president of the Cambridge, Mass.-based group Citizens for Public Schools. "Their goal is to switch public education to a private voucher system. Their handouts recommend that activists focus on one hot issue in public schools, and they make sure everything they say is negative."

The Hudson Institute's Finn, a founder of the "excellence movement," dismisses the "manufactured crisis" theory. What Berliner and Biddle are doing is "like the fire-fighting technique in which, if you can't control one fire, you start a backfire and work on that one," he says. "They bring an additional political twist to the discussion, but it's a bum rap. They basically argue that things are swell or can be made swell if only government would spend more money, and that it's all a right-wing plot to do in the public schools. For this, they're getting a degree of celebrity."

Finn also disputes the charge that

Is the Democratic Dream of the 'Common' School . . .

Horace Mann was asking a lot when he laid the foundation for America's public schools. The pioneering 19th-century educator exhorted the "professional men of Massachusetts" to put their children in his new "common schools" so that the sons and daughters of lawyers and doctors would mix with the children of farmers and bricklayers. Otherwise, he warned, "children of the less-favored classes" will be degraded by "the consciousness that they are attending a school unworthy of the patronage of those whom they have been led to regard as the better part of the community." [1]

In the 1990s, many argue, Mann's democratic vision lies in tatters. An April cover story in *Time* magazine — headlined "Back to Segregation" — contended that court rulings and segregated housing patterns have effectively ended the country's five-decade experiment in school integration. [2]

And parents who during the 1960s civil rights struggles might have embraced the common school as a cause now watch their modern-day counterparts take a consumer approach to schooling their kids, shopping carefully for academic excellence and safety from crime.

"We raised our children during desegregation and never questioned the public schools," says Mary Ann Hardenbergh, president of Citizens for Public Schools, in Cambridge, Mass. But when her son's family recently moved to a mixed-income area of Northern Virginia, they rejected the local schools because they were "fearful of influences of those other kids," she said.

Many observers speak of a public that is disconnected from public schools. "The situation resembles the sad case of a 20-year marriage in which the husband no longer sees his wife as his soul mate but thinks of her as his housekeeper," writes David Mathews, former Health, Education and Welfare secretary. "And the wife no longer sees the husband as the man of her dreams but merely as the breadwinner. Though still married, they are ready to live apart." [3]

It must also be noted that for most of this century, the notion of the public school as a melting pot has largely been workable only when students have the option of being "tracked" according to perceived abilities. Take away the special "honors" or accelerated courses, and many families threaten to quit the common school.

Such was the situation at a high school in Ithaca, N.Y., last year, when administrators became concerned that "honors" students bound for top colleges — many of them children of Cornell University faculty — were spending days isolated from the less academically oriented students.

Research in recent years has pointed steadily, though not conclusively, to the verdict shared by many educators that tracking, without fostering gains among students overall, merely "amplifies inequity," in the phrase of David N. Perkins, a professor at Harvard University's Graduate School of Education." [4]

In January 1995, Ithaca High School announced that its science teachers were planning to merge honors classes with those known in New York state as "regents" classes. Groups of parents erupted in protest. "It's a shameful way to treat bright students," said Cornell chemistry Professor John McMurry. "They won't be prepared to take chemistry at Cornell." [5]

Yet, a year later, according to Ithaca High Principal Kathryn Hellweg, the merged science curriculum is "extremely successful, and is being evaluated over the long term by a school-community team that includes many researchers from Cornell." The so-called heterogeneous grouping policy was put in place incrementally, she says, and has made science instruction more dynamic and hands-on. "There are still some individuals who are skeptical, but most vocal opponents now say publicly it's been an incredibly good experience."

Even so, the politics of the episode were straining enough to prompt Hellweg to leave Ithaca to take a principal's job in Richmond, Ind., this September. "There's an attitude of intellectual elitism in this country, so it's impossible to create a school that meets the needs of all children," she says. Many parents, sometimes with support from school boards, say, "I want the best for my young person, and I don't care what happens to the other kids. It creates a community of haves and have-nots, and many kids with potential are not having their needs met."

It is one thing to bemoan inequity, however, and another

the Reagan administration's secret motive was to introduce private-school vouchers. "Reagan never did all that much about vouchers," he says, "and the federal government is a weak form of leverage to bring that about."

Goldberg of the National Alliance of Business, who directed the commission that produced *A Nation at Risk,* says Berliner and Biddle are "off-base." They "offer an 'X-Files' view of American life that suggests that parts of a report that they disagree with must be a conspiracy," he says. Parents are nervous about schools not because of criticism but because they legitimately recognize that education and technology needs have expanded so rapidly that their children might not be able to keep up, he says. "The school reform movement does not discredit public schools," he adds. "One of its purposes is to open the door to a variety of options, so students know what's going on in the world of business."

As for the political manipulations of *A Nation at Risk,* Goldberg says, "When you issue a report, you can't prevent individuals and groups from

. . . Being Abandoned in the Nervous 1990s?

to design a public school that transcends it. "No one believes any child should spend all day with kids exactly like them," says Mary Hynes, a school board member in Arlington, Va. "But some parents, judging by the appearance of the kids or the type of work being assigned, may conclude that their expectations for a class are not being met. They deserve some recourse to an education with more rigor." The strategies used for slower learners often involve time-consuming drilling and practice, she adds, which means that some students will be treated differently. "I don't see a way around some form of tracking, with regular opportunities for regrouping."

Gerald W. Bracey, an Alexandria, Va., consultant who writes frequently on public schools, sees some swings of the pendulum on the subject of tracking. "It started in the 1920s, when the creators of racist IQ tests felt it would be inhumane to put children of new immigrants in the same room with the higher-level kids because it would damage their self-esteem. In the 1980s and '90s, things have swung the other way. People chant the mantra that all children can learn. But it's not going to work out that way."

That may be because parents are too anxiety-ridden over their children's prospects for getting good jobs. For economic as well as academic reasons, "they are applying increased pressure on kids not just to get into any college, but to get in a pedigreed school like Brown, Stanford or Amherst," Bracey adds.

Chester E. Finn Jr., a Bush administration Education official now at the Hudson Institute, notes that "it has been a very long time since the public school was a common school that cut across socioeconomic lines. Our most segregated schools are in the affluent suburbs, and the sons of Beverly Hills gardeners will meet the daughters of Beverly Hills psychiatrists only if they can afford to live in Beverly Hills," he says. "The history of compulsory busing shows that you will drive people away if they think the situations are unsafe or unwholesome. Much of it is white flight, but minorities who have entered the middle class do exactly the same thing."

Historian Diane Ravitch, a Bush administration official who is now a senior research fellow at New York University, points out that the feasibility of a common school depends greatly on the region of the country. "The Horace Mann concept was good for small New England villages, but it has nothing to do with New York City," she says. "What is our goal here? The children are more important than some concept."

Others argue that educational research points the way to progress toward the common school goal. Marshall S. Smith, undersecretary of Education for the Clinton administration, says: "We now know more than ever before about whether kids from low socioeconomic backgrounds can learn. We have a curriculum far more challenging than before. Instead of having a watered-down curriculum for the inner city that differs from that in the suburbs, let's give everyone a challenging curriculum." And even though the most segregated suburbs are a far cry from Thomas Dewey's "crucible of democracy," Smith adds, there are many schools throughout the nation that serve all sorts of kids, kids who speak 30 different languages. I think the common school has a great future."

Sociologist Charles Willie, a colleague of Perkins at Harvard, goes further. "If the common school is a thing of the past, then this democracy is teetering on exploding," he says. "No group is self-sufficient, though unfortunately, affluent people think they're self-sufficient."

Willie says his belief that poor blacks and wealthier whites both benefit if they have classes together has been put into practice successfully in the Boston area. Under this system, low- and middle-class students have equal access to a range of schools within zones designed with "racial fairness guidelines," and 90 percent of families get their first or second choice of school, he says. "You have to do desegregation, school choice and school improvement simultaneously."

[1] Charles Leslie Glenn Jr., *The Myth of the Common School* (1987), p. 219.

[2] *Time,* April 29, 1996, p. 39.

[3] David Mathews, *Is There a Public for Public Schools?* (1996), p. 24.

[4] Quoted in *The Washington Post,* Education Review, Oct. 31, 1993. See also Jay Mathews, "To Track or Not to Track," *The Washington Post,* Education Review, April 7, 1996.

[5] *The New York Times,* June 4, 1995.

using it for their own purposes."

Equally skeptical about the manufacturing of a crisis is former Bush administration official Ravitch. "No one will believe Berliner and Biddle except the people who run schools who like that message and pay their speaking fees," she says. "The business community is who sees the need for remedial reading for employees. They're not involved in an ideological argument. They are dealing with the real world."

Ravitch takes some lumps from Berliner and Biddle, partly because she played a role in the decision not to publish a 1990 government report that offered a positive assessment of America's schools. The so-called Sandia report, named for the Energy Department national laboratory that was asked to evaluate the schools, provides Berliner and Biddle with much of their good-news data and evidence of an anti-schools political bias. The two psychology professors complain that the Bush administration, allegedly stumped by the report's favorable verdict, subjected it to "unprecedented reviews" and found "trivial flaws." [21]

Ravitch counters that Sandia "was a very bad report. It said there was no SAT decline, and when confronted with the fact that the decline started in 1963-64, the authors merely said that this earlier period didn't interest them," she says. What's more, the Energy Department product "was reviewed by relevant professionals at the National Center for Education Statistics and the National Science Foundation, and even the Democratic leadership of the Senate Budget Committee. They asked for revisions because the report omitted important information. But instead of responding to the peer review, the Sandia people simply said, 'We're being repressed.' No one has the guaranteed right to have a report published by the government," Ravitch says. (The report was eventually published in the *Journal of Educational Research.*)

Resnick of the School Boards Association says politicization of school progress reports is ongoing. "The people who believe schools are not doing their jobs pass information around the Heritage Foundation and the American Legislative Exchange Council, and political types buy into it. Some represent a broader philosophy that wants to privatize government generally, and for them, what greater symbol to voters could there be than schools?"

"We all want to see schools improve," Resnick continues, "but our concern is that if we start from the premise that schools are failing, that will lead to a different set of policy prescriptions than if we say here's what is working." Citing a falling drop-out rate, Resnick argues that, "We're keeping them in school, but some are still moaning that those students are not top caliber. Look, our commitment to universal education is expensive."

The National PTA's Fege says educators sometimes feel they can't win. "When the economy is bad, schools are blamed, and when the economy is good, schools are still blamed," he says. "Certain people do have a hidden agenda to keep the public schools stirred up. The concept of public schools is anathema to them, and they may want more individualistic learning. Often only a small percentage of the community can dictate a policy because most people don't know about it or don't care."

Kathleen Lyons, a spokeswoman for the National Education Association, the nation's largest teachers' union, says Berliner and Biddle "did a good job of showing that problems with public schools are overstated for political gain. Since *A Nation at Risk,* we've been dealing with public education as a political issue more than ever before," she says. As an example, she cites anti-tax groups. "If the purpose isn't to cut education spending, why are anti-tax groups supporting all these reforms? It's a self-serving way to argue the tax-cuts agenda."

"Large parts of the school establishment would rather get a blank check with no questions asked," counters Pete Sepp, vice president for communications at the National Taxpayers Union. "It's also difficult to gauge schools when there are no national standards and few local ones, and teachers' unions resist them."

School-reform advocates also say that stating a problem in strong terms is often the only way to win media attention. "If we conclude that a problem is very serious, we might in good faith and conscience go for a dramatic solution," says Finn. "It's like when a slum has gone down too far to rehabilitate, you bring in the bulldozers."

"This country is crisis-oriented," says Allen at the Center for Education Reform. "If that means spending more money, then fine, or decentralize, or whatever it takes. It transcends ideology. But the [establishment] doesn't want change. They want to convince us that everything is A-OK. They want change only within the system — fixing toilets and adding some professional courses for teachers or some curriculum changes. The system has to be fundamentally altered."

Others argue for a middle ground. "Berliner and Biddle provided the jolt that moves the discussion toward a more realistic picture of what's happening," says Fege at the National PTA. "You don't have to agree with *The Manufactured Crisis,* but it has created a new civic discussion over the perception of schools." Some say schools are rotten, he says, while the apologists in schools say there's no problem. "We need something in between." ■

BACKGROUND

'Asinine System'?

Historians of education are fond of recounting how fears that the next generation is hell-bound in a handbasket go back at least to Socrates. The philosopher is quoted in *The Republic* bemoaning the chances for a young man of ancient Greece to grow intellectually amid "these evil surroundings."

In the United States, a writer for *Ladies Home Journal* in 1912 sounds eerily like a modern Jeremiah: "Imagine a more grossly stupid, a more genuinely asinine system tenaciously persisted in to the fearful detriment of over 17 million children and at a cost to you of over $403 million each year — a system that not only is absolutely ineffective in its results, but also actually harmful in that it throws every year 93 out of every 100 children into the world of action absolutely unfitted for even the simplest tasks in life?" [22]

Apocalyptic rhetoric seemed to accompany every bid for reform in education, including the establishment of kindergartens, junior highs, voca-

Continued on p. 664

Chronology

1950s School desegregation and overseas competition cause first stirrings of modern school reforms.

1954
Supreme Court in *Brown v. Board of Education* outlaws school segregation.

1955
Rudolph Flesch's *Why Johnny Can't Read* blasts schools for abandoning phonics instruction.

1958
National Defense Education Act boosts spending on public schools in reaction to Soviet Union's success with Sputnik satellite.

1960s Federal government aids poor school districts. Experiments in educational freedom launched.

1965
Elementary and Secondary Education Act provides federal aid to disadvantaged schools.

1966
University of Chicago sociologist James S. Coleman issues famous report saying schools have less impact on students than family.

1970s Declining test scores prompt education critics and conservative political activists to organize.

1972
Experimental federally sponsored school voucher program launched in Alum Rock, Calif.

1975
Scholastic Aptitude tests show decline over previous decade.

1980s New high-tech job market and fears of overseas competition prompt worries about school quality and launching of "excellence movement" and school reforms.

April 26, 1983
A Nation at Risk report warns of a "rising tide of mediocrity" in U.S. schools.

1987
Chester E. Finn Jr. and Diane Ravitch publish *What Students Should Know*. West Virginia physician John James Cannell releases report on test scores for all 50 states showing that none reports itself below average. University of Chicago sociologist Coleman and Northern Illinois University researcher Thomas Hoffer publish *Public and Private High Schools* saying private schools, particularly parochial ones, perform better.

1989
Governors gather in Charlottesville, Va., to launch America 2000 plan for national education standards.

1990s Movement for world-class education standards organizes; political attacks on public schools put educators on defensive.

1990
Brookings Institution publishes John E. Chubb and Terry M. Moe's influential *Politics, Markets and America's Schools*, arguing for school choice; National Center for Education and the Economy's *America's Choice: High Skills or Low Wages!* sounds alarm for school-work mismatch. Wisconsin Legislature passes voucher legislation; pilot program set up in Milwaukee.

1993
Education Department study says "half of adults in U.S. can't read or handle arithmetic." California voters reject Proposition 174 school voucher ballot initiative. Organization for Economic Cooperation and Development releases international study in December showing U.S. world standing in education is improving.

1994
Congress passes Goals 2000 legislation launching standards movement; scores on "nation's report card" show strongest gains in U.S. math and science performance.

1995
Publication of David C. Berliner and Bruce J. Biddle's controversial *The Manufactured Crisis: Myths, Fraud and the Attack on America's Public Schools*.

Feb. 27, 1996
Senate Democrats defeat Republican proposal offering vouchers to low-income District of Columbia students to help pay for private schools.

March 26, 1996
Governors gather in Palisades, N.Y., to review progress on education standards and reform.

March 29, 1996
Wisconsin Supreme Court deadlocks 3-3 on whether Milwaukee can expand school voucher program to re-ligious schools, a victory for opponents.

Friends and Foes of Vouchers Envision . . .

It began as an academic pipedream to bring free-market principles to public schools. It was revived as a way for private and parochial school parents to win a tax break. Nowadays it is offered as the salvation of the urban poor.

The idea is school vouchers, taxpayer-provided stipends that families unhappy with their public school can apply toward tuition at any private school that will accept them. To enthusiasts, such as Stanford University political scientist Terry M. Moe, vouchers "can bring about the dramatic improvement [in education] Americans yearn for." [1] To critics, such as Education Secretary Richard W. Riley, vouchers represent "a retreat from public education, a way to divert public tax dollars." [2]

The yawning gap between those views mirrors the ongoing dispute over whether America's public schools are truly failing or actually improving.

Vouchers are often discussed under the rubric of "school choice," a broader category that also encompasses magnet schools and other versions of choice within public schools. Though voucher proposals differ in detail, the purest versions are the most controversial because they would permit tax dollars to go to religious schools and would be available to the wealthy as well as the poor. President Clinton opposes vouchers and favors public school choice.

The roots of vouchers go back to a 1955 essay by free-market economist Milton Friedman, who thought public schools needed competition as an incentive to improve. His idea was picked up by Marquette University political scientist Virgil C. Blum, who in 1957 helped to launch Citizens for Educational Freedom, which continues to push vouchers. [3]

In 1966, an article in *The Public Interest* by Harvard University sociologist Christopher Jencks supported vouchers and asked, "Is the Public School Obsolete?" Within a few years, his writings prompted the federal Office of Economic Opportunity to offer a $14 million federal grant to test the voucher concept in a few cities.

From 1972-1976, a voucher system limited to public elementary and junior high students was tested in Alum Rock, Calif., a suburb of San Jose, with lukewarm results. [4] Denis P. Doyle, who ran the program and is now a visiting fellow at the conservative Heritage Foundation, says, "It got a bad rap because it was not a startling success, but it succeeded within its own terms in the form of greater mobility, creation of a gifted program and equal numbers of black, Hispanic and white students participating."

In the early 1980s, the Reagan administration promoted the concept in the form of "tuition tax credits" for families with children at private and parochial schools. In 1990, the Brookings Institution published a book by Moe and another leading advocate of school choice, John E. Chubb, that called for a radical restructuring of American education. Under their plan, private schools, including religious schools, would compete for students with public schools in a free market. [5]

The school choice idea also was befriended by Polly Williams, an African-American state representative in Wisconsin who had worked with civil rights leader Jesse Jackson. She argued that black parents were tired of having their children bused to outlying schools and called for drastic action to restore neighborhood schools. In May 1990, the state Legislature passed her bill setting up a pilot program providing vouchers of $2,500 annually for 1 percent of the public school families in Milwaukee.

Since then, a program has been launched in the troubled school system of Cleveland, and others are under consideration in the legislatures of nearly half the states. A federal version, called the Low Income School Choice Demonstration Act, was introduced last year by Sens. Daniel R. Coats, R-Ind., and Joseph I. Lieberman, D-Conn. It would have allocated $30 million to set up 10-20 demonstration projects.

In recent months, however, the voucher movement has hit snags. In Cleveland, the program was blocked in court. In Wisconsin, an effort to expand the Milwaukee program from just over a thousand students to nearly 15,000 was blocked by a deadlocked state Supreme Court, citing constitutional concerns about religious schools.

In Washington, the Republican-controlled Congress tried to attach a $42 million five-year voucher experiment to the appropriations bill for the District of Columbia. It was defeated in February by Democrats led by Massachusetts Sen. Edward M. Kennedy, after strong lobbying by the National Education Association (NEA) and other groups.

"This is a very, very wealthy man denying the poorest kids in our society an opportunity to get a good education," argued Rep. James T. Walsh, R-N.Y. "Our goal is to support public schools, not abandon them," replied Kennedy. "Private schools can decide whether to accept a child or not. The real choice is given to the private schools, not parents or students." [6]

Many observers blamed the defeat on the jobs-conscious NEA, though the teachers' union was quick to point out that philosophical opposition came from 100 groups, among them the National PTA, the NAACP, the Association of School Administrators and the American Civil Liberties Union.

Surveys show the public divided on vouchers. In a September 1995 Gallup Poll, 65 percent of respondents opposed allowing students to attend a private school at public expense, compared with 33 percent in favor. But a survey released this spring by the Joint Center for Political and Economic Studies found that African-Americans were less satisfied with public schools than Americans as a whole, with 61 percent favoring vouchers. Over the past 30 years, at least 19 states have offered ballot initiatives on public aid to private schools. All were rejected, except for a textbook loan program in South Dakota.

Jeanne Allen, president of the Center for Education Reform, says opposition comes not only from the public school establishment but also from conservative, middle-class

. . . Salvation for Poor and Tax Breaks for Rich

parents who either resent "special treatment" for low-income families or who don't see the need because their own schools are working fine. Indeed, a report from the Family Research Council criticizes vouchers targeted at low-income families for giving recipients a disincentive to climb out of poverty. It cites polls showing some "class resentment over policies that tax Reagan voters to bestow benefits on Clinton backers." [7]

But in the current climate, only proposals targeted at low-income families seem to have a chance. "It's the parents of children in the inner city where you see the most supporters," Allen says. "How can we tell 2,000 low-income kids in Cleveland they can't go to another school? They've been trying to make those schools work for these children's entire lifetime."

Chester E. Finn Jr., of the Hudson Institute, agrees that "across-the-board vouchers with no grandfathering and no income test would simply mean a tax windfall for those already in private schools."

Another obstacle is the question of public funds for religious schools. Voucher supporters point out that minorities do very well in parochial schools. The National Catholic Education Association argues that the First Amendment permits such funding and that "any campaign to improve American schools must include a commitment to educational choice." Its efforts are opposed on constitutional grounds by Americans United for Separation of Church and State.

"Vouchers can be structured in a way the public finds acceptable, whether that means accepting any and all comers" or means-testing, says Tim Sullivan, a spokesman for the Center for Education Reform. "If a school is ill-equipped, dangerous, has no textbooks and no good teachers, what's a parent to do? It's like their house is on fire, and they're being told they have to wait and do what's best for everyone. Parents shouldn't be forced to sacrifice the well-being of their children on a promise that things might get better in the future."

Public school boosters, however, see a serious threat. "Vouchers are based on the theory that if you throw the thing out that's broken, what will emerge is better," says Kelly Butler, executive director of the Jackson, Miss.-based Parents for Public Schools. "Instead, they will polarize society, so that schools will work for some but not others."

Bella Rosenberg, assistant to the president of the American Federation of Teachers, sees the voucher movement causing "the balkanization of America. Do we want to support a non-system of schools segregated by race, religion, sect and taste, with everybody consorting only with like-minded people?" she asks.

Private school officials are torn over vouchers. Peter D. Relic, president of the National Association of Independent Schools, sees serious logistical problems. In Washington, D.C., for example, most of the private schools have waiting lists, leaving the only open spaces in the Catholic schools, whose tuition rates are about equal to the bill's cap of $3,000 per child.

"School choice is a good idea," Relic says, "but it shouldn't hurt existing public schools. If we generally believe in educational improvement, then a reform should also include an additional appropriation for the bad school that everyone's leaving." [8] Relic agrees, however, with voucher advocates' projections that new private schools will probably crop up, in spite of likely resistance to new regulations that might come with public funding.

Still others point to new costs of sending kids to schools outside the neighborhood, such as transportation, which can weigh heavily on low-income families. [9]

Politically, the voucher movement appears alive and well — pending results of the 1996 elections. The California legislature is considering a voucher plan targeted at low-income students. A similar initiative was defeated in 1993. In Congress, Reps. J.C. Watts, R-Okla., and James M. Talent, R-Mo., have introduced new federal legislation. [10] Doyle has been pressing Congress to make a voucher program for low-income children out of the 30-year-old Title I program of federal aid to disadvantaged school districts. [11]

Another voucher supporter is Republican presidential candidate Bob Dole. In remarks July 17 during a campaign swing through the Midwest, Dole proposed helping students to attend any private or parochial school that would accept them. Using rhetoric long familiar in the education debate, Dole blasted school performance, contending that "the scores keep falling" and "the dropout rate deeps rising." [12]

---

[1] Writing in *The Washington Post*, Education Review, Oct. 31, 1993, p. 5.

[2] Annual state of education address, delivered Feb. 28, 1996, at a high school in St. Louis, Mo.

[3] See Martin Morse Wooster, *Angry Classrooms, Vacant Minds: What's Happening in Our High Schools?* (1994), p. 147.

[4] See "School Choice," *The CQ Researcher*, May 10, 1991, 253-276.

[5] John E. Chubb and Terry M. Moe, *Politics, Markets and America's Schools* (1990).

[6] Quoted in *The Washington Post*, Feb. 28, 1996.

[7] Family Research Council, "With Liberty and Justice for All: Redefining the Educational Choice Debate," *Family Policy*, April 1996.

[8] For background, see Caroline Minter Hoxby, "The Effects of Private School Vouchers," in Helen F. Ladd (ed.), *Holding Schools Accountable* (1995), p. 180.

[9] See Henry M. Levin and Cyrus Driver, "Estimating the Cost of an Educational Voucher System," paper for American Educational Finance Association, May 18, 1994.

[10] *Church and State*, June 1996, p. 15.

[11] Denis P. Doyle, "Why Vouchers Are Needed for Poor Children," Special report to the House Appropriations Committee, May 10, 1996.

[12] "Dole Attacks Clinton on Education Issues," *The New York Times*, July 18, 1996, p. D22.

Continued from p. 660

tional schools and even the original common school. As one observer has noted, Horace Mann, the father of the public school, attracted such attention in the 19th century largely because "he managed to present the situation of education as simultaneously triumphant and imperiled." [23]

The clash between the doomsayers and the deep-dyed defenders of public education has its own rich tradition. It was characterized archly by critic Arthur Bestor, who compared the early 1950s education establishment to the bizarre world of Alice in Wonderland: "The logic is that of 'Looking-Glass Land,' where, the Red Queen explained to Alice, 'it takes all the running you can do to keep in the same place.' In every other area of American life, progress is measured in terms of defects overcome. Only the professional educationists take pride in the fact that, though they run several times as hard, they can always be found by their critics in pretty much the same spot." [24]

Lost Golden Age?

More harmonious times in school history can be found. In the early years of public education, "People built the schools, controlled them through local trustees — not county school boards — and selected and housed their teachers," former Health, Education and Welfare Secretary David Mathews recently wrote. "The community wasn't just involved in the school, the two were inseparable." [25] In a 1940 Gallup Poll, 85 percent agreed that young people were getting a better education than their parents had received.

In Finn's view, the decline of the nation's schools coincided with a series of worrisome events in the early 1970s that shook America's confidence. "Vietnam, Watergate, oil embargoes, energy shortages, economic stagnation, the decline of smokestack industries, the surging success of Asian and European rivals, domestic problems of crime, violence and drug addiction — these and other symptoms were associated with what President Jimmy Carter termed our national 'malaise.' " [26]

Mary Hynes, a school board member in Arlington, Va., says that one reason today's parents are so nervous about schools is that "they look back and feel they missed out on something. When they went to school in the 1960s and '70s, college professors were concerned about young men getting drafted, so they inflated grades to keep kids from dropping out. This filtered down to the high school level. Students demanded more choice and fewer requirements. Everything had to be 'relevant.' The rigor was gone."

But others caution against romanticizing the qualities of the schools of the past. Researcher Dale Whittington tracked down some test questions administered to students in 1915, many of them the same basic history and geography questions that modern students are scorned for flubbing. In this exercise, today's students scored better than their ancestors on a third of the questions, performed at the same level on a third and performed worse on a third. [27]

To the news media, the contrast of a gauzy view of a bygone era with the anxious present is the formula for a ready-made story. Just such a story was provided recently by a widely circulated "survey" purportedly ranking what educators said were the major school problems in the 1940s vs. those of today. For the 1940s, petty issues such as "talking, chewing gum, making noise, running in the halls, getting out of place in line" were cited. In contemporary schools, the survey lists "drug abuse, alcohol abuse, pregnancy, suicide, rape, robbery and assault."

The "survey" has been widely cited — by such prominent conservative critics as former Education Secretary Bennett and radio host Rush Limbaugh as well as by *The Wall Street Journal*, CBS News and even *The CQ Researcher*. There was only one problem with the survey: It was a fake. Two years ago, a Yale University professor traced it to T. Cullen Davis, a Fort Worth, Texas, man who said he had composed it in the early 1980s. "How did I know what the offenses in the schools were in 1940? I was there," he said. "How do I know what they are now? I read it in the papers." [28] ■

CURRENT SITUATION

PR Campaigns

With the controversy over education showing no signs of a letup, schools around the nation are not sitting by passively while their reputations become political footballs. Many have launched public relations efforts to get out the news about good test scores, new programs and other attributes, using brochures and newsletters.

In Prince George's County, Md., where the school board chairman has complained about negative approval ratings and an exodus of disgruntled families, a four-person PR department polishes the school system's reputation at a cost of $450,000 a year. "We have a rotten image, and it's not deserved," she said. [29]

At Marlborough High School in Bayfield, Mass., an English teacher is paid $1,300 to organize students to write articles for the local paper and to appear on a local cable sports show. [30]

Finn says that typically, "Parents are not as well-informed about schools as they might be, and to some extent, they haven't wanted to be. Schools have engaged in a conspiracy to keep consum-

Continued on p. 666

At Issue:

Is the reported decline in public education quality largely a myth?

yes

DAVID C. BERLINER AND BRUCE J. BIDDLE
Berliner is a professor of psychology, education and curriculum instruction at Arizona State University; Biddle is a professor of psychology and sociology at the University of Missouri

FROM *THE MANUFACTURED CRISIS: MYTHS FRAUD AND THE ATTACK ON AMERICA'S PUBLIC SCHOOLS* (1995)

In recent years leaders in industry [and government have] claimed in documents and public statements that American education was in deep trouble, that as a result our country was falling behind foreign competitors, and that these various charges were all confirmed by "evidence."

To the best of our knowledge, no campaign of this sort had ever before appeared in American history. Never before had an American government been so critical of the public schools, and never had so many false claims been made about education in the name of "evidence." We shall refer to this campaign of criticism as the Manufactured Crisis.

The Manufactured Crisis was not an accidental event. Rather, it appeared within a specific historical context and was led by identifiable critics whose political goals could be furthered by scapegoating educators. . . . Moreover, it was tied to misguided schemes for "reforming" education — schemes that would, if adopted, seriously damage American schools.

Unfortunately, the Manufactured Crisis has had a good deal of influence — thus, too many well-meaning, bright and knowledgeable Americans have come to believe some of its major myths, and this has generated serious mischief. Damaging programs for educational reform have been adopted, a great deal of money has been wasted, effective school programs have been harmed and morale has declined among educators.

But myths need not remain unchallenged; in fact, they become shaky when they are exposed to the light of reason and evidence. When one actually looks at the evidence, one discovers that most of the claims of the Manufactured Crisis are, indeed, myths, half-truths and sometimes outright lies. . . .

[S]upport for the myth of achievement decline has always been weak. Indeed, the two of us know of only one test, the SAT, that ever suggested such a decline — and, as readers know by now, the SAT is a voluntary test and each year is taken by differing types of students, which means that its aggregate results are not valid for judging the performance of American schools. . . .

The myth that American schools fail badly by comparison with schools in other industrialized countries is also not supported by the evidence. Instead, when we analyze that evidence responsibly and think carefully about its implications, we discover that American schools stack up very well.

no

LAWRENCE C. STEDMAN
Professor of education, State University of New York at Binghamton

FROM *EDUCATION POLICY ANALYSIS ARCHIVES*, VOL. 4, NO. 1, JAN. 23, 1996.

I am sympathetic to the concerns [of Berliner and Biddle], but as a scholar who specializes in this material, I find their analysis deeply flawed and misleading. They mischaracterize the test score decline data, mishandle the international findings and fail to acknowledge students' continuing low levels of academic achievement. . . .

Although Berliner and Biddle are generally right that achievement has been stable, they ignored important contradictory evidence and the 1970s decline. They claimed "only 'one' test, the SAT" ever suggested a decline. This is remarkable.

High school students' NAEP civics scores, for example, dropped substantially between 1969 and 1976 and have been slipping ever since. Their science scores also fell during the 1970s and have only partly rebounded. . . .

They attributed the SAT decline to demographic changes in test takers, yet never reviewed the evidence which shows this explains much, but not all, of the decline. They used "average" SAT scores to claim minority gains, but this masked minority verbal declines in the late 1970s and late 1980s. . . .

Given changing school populations and societal conditions, generally stable scores are still a remarkable accomplishment for U.S. schools. This is an important message that the public needs to hear. Nevertheless, the reality is more complicated than they suggested. Although school critics often exaggerated the extent and ramifications of the declines, many did occur. Berliner and Biddle should have admitted that, on several indicators, our students are not performing as well as they once did.

U.S. performance in the international arena is not as dismal as school critics have asserted, but it certainly is not as glowing as Berliner and Biddle claim. Our students have done well in reading and elementary school science, middling to poor in geography and secondary school science and last or near-last in mathematics. . . .

In the 1980s, school critics often exaggerated the size and extent of the test score decline. In spite of enormous changes in society and school populations U.S. achievement has been remarkably stable for many decades. But it remains inadequate and at low levels. Ignoring this evidence or arguing it is a right-wing fabrication hampers much-needed school reform. The crisis is real; what is actually being manufactured here is a new mythology about U.S. student achievement.

Does Spending by States Affect Test Results?

None of the top 10 states in per-pupil spending are among the top 10 in performance on the ACT or SAT tests, according to the American Legislative Exchange Council. That indicates that money alone won't solve educational problems, the conservative group contends. But opponents counter that children from poorer states can't be expected to compete with more affluent areas, and that performance is affected by how the money is spent.

Top-Performing States

Iowa
Montana
Minnesota
Nebraska
New Hampshire
North Dakota
Oregon
Utah
Wisconsin
Wyoming

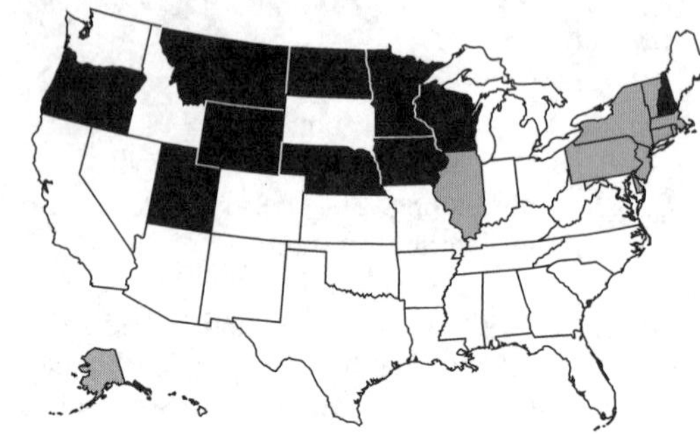

Top-Spending States

Alaska
New Jersey
New York
Connecticut
Pennsylvania
Rhode Island
Vermont
Delaware
Massachusetts
Illinois

Source: "Report Card on American Education, 1995," American Legislative Exchange Council, May 1996

Continued from p. 664

ers in the dark. It's tough to get solid performance data, there's no external audit, only press releases from those who administer the tests. What parents learn is spun by administrators."

Parents and prospective homebuyers can get objective data on local schools from such firms as National School Reporting Services Inc., in Stamford, Conn., and School Match, in Westerville, Ohio. School Match offers profiles of any accredited public or private school or district for $49, as well as counseling by a staff of experts. The profiles supply audited data. "Research on school data, test results and financial and demographic information is complicated and requires significant skill on the part of the researcher," the firm says. "Typically, self-reported school data is unreliable."

While such services are useful, says Massachusetts Education Secretary Michael J. Sentance, particularly in the real estate industry, they do "not acknowledge fast enough when people are doing the right thing and trying to change the school. Schools turn around in a short period of time." [31]

Teacher Morale

What some see as the unending blast of criticism at public schools has taken a toll on teachers and administrators.

"Morale is very bad among teachers," says Bella Rosenberg, assistant to the president of the American Federation of Teachers. "The prime reason is the horrific problems of educating the disadvantaged, as well as parental indifference. Teachers feel beaten down, and are asked to do more with less for out-of-school problems like AIDS, divorce, death counseling, obesity, self-esteem. People want these problems solved by schools, so there's less time for academics, yet they're still held accountable" for the students' educational progress.

When it comes to education, says the NEA's Lyons, "it is barbecue season, and teachers are finding out they're the main dish. Everyone thinks they know something about education, and they all say, 'Back when I was in school...' and they take you apart. I tell our teachers to talk up their successes and to ask critics where they get their information. Polls show that the average American with kids in school is positive, yet so much of the press coverage is from cities where schools are needy and crumbling. I say go in and spend some time, then if you still want to bash schools, you will have some reasons for it."

Researcher Ravitch replies that "some teachers might resent all the criticism, but you don't employ censorship and pretend all is fine so that no one's feelings will get hurt. Schools as public institutions are finite, so there's got to be some way to influence them socially and politically. Culture, by contrast, is not finite, and no one knows how to shape it." ■

OUTLOOK

Turning Point?

Good news *does* get reported. "Great schools are not always suburban, free-spending or white," says *Money* magazine in a recent upbeat evaluation of 100 public school districts. [32]

More broadly, the National Education Goals Panel, established by the nation's governors in 1990, recently reported that it sees progress in reducing the number of threats and injuries in schools; increasing the number of preschoolers being read to; and increasing the number of women getting math and science degrees. The goals panel found no changes, however, in the high school completion rate; the gap in preschool participation between rich and poor; minority college enrollment; and student alcohol use. It found worsening effects in drug use, threats and injuries to teachers and classroom disruptions. [33]

It is for such reasons that the exodus of those who would abandon failing public schools continues apace. Lewis J. Perelman, an Alexandria, Va., consultant and the author of a recent critique of American education, *School's Out,* proposes replacing public education with what he calls a "microvoucher program." The program would be means-tested, "like the food-stamp program, but use electronic card accounts similar to a bank ATM or credit card," he said. "Families could use their micro-vouchers to purchase a broad spectrum of knowledge- and skill-building products and services in the highly competitive and exploding Knowledge Age marketplace." [34]

Rosenberg of the AFT says the country is "at a turning point for its schools that is a mirror image of the larger society and politics. We must decide whether to come together around common-sense notions or break apart," she says. "There's a terrible anti-institutional mood of retreating into one's self. There's no trust in leaders, no public responsibility. You're on your own."

Fege also thinks the country is at a "critical juncture. It's almost to the point where those who believe in public schools are the radicals," he says.

Ravitch disagrees. "People make choices in life about where to live and work, and it doesn't balkanize America," she says. "Let's be pragmatic. You can't tell kids they have to stay in the worst school in town because of what Horace Mann once said."

Finn says the concept of universal public education "has to be defined differently to be something other than government agencies staffed by government employees."

Doubtless, the fur will to continue to fly in the debate. Noting that *The Manufactured Crisis* recently was chosen outstanding book of the year by the American Education Research Association, co-author Biddle says his critics "have good reasons for saying our book is no good: That's because we're saying that they are liars. To say the only reason we did the book is to make money on the lecture circuit is to say that worrying about the truth of the matter is not important." And to label him and his co-author as members of the "don't worry, be happy," crowd misses the fact that their book offers their own detailed prescriptions for school reform, Biddle says.

But Goldberg of the business alli-

U.S. Ranks High in Global Study

American fourth-graders ranked second and ninth-graders ranked ninth in a 32-nation study of reading comprehension conducted in 1992.

4th-Grade Reading

Country	Score
Finland	569
United States	547
Sweden	539
France	531
Italy	529
New Zealand	528
Norway	524
Iceland	518
Hong Kong	517
Singapore	515
Switzerland	511
Ireland	509
Belgium (French)	507
Greece	504
Spain	504
Germany (West)	503
Canada (British Columbia)	500
Germany (East)	499
Hungary	499
Slovenia	498
Netherlands	485
Cyprus	481
Portugal	478
Denmark	475
Trinidad/Tobago	451
Indonesia	394
Venezuela	383

Note: Although 32 countries participated in the study as a whole, not all provided usable data.

9th-Grade Reading

Country	Score
Finland	560
France	549
Sweden	546
New Zealand	545
Hungary	536
Iceland	536
Switzerland	536
Hong Kong	535
United States	535
Singapore	534
Slovenia	532
Germany (East)	526
Denmark	525
Portugal	523
Canada (British Columbia)	522
Germany (West)	522
Norway	516
Italy	515
Netherlands	514
Ireland	511
Greece	509
Cyprus	497
Spain	490
Belgium (French)	481
Trinidad/Tobago	479
Thailand*	477
Philippines	430
Venezuela	417
Nigeria*	401
Zimbabwe*	372
Botswana	330

* *Sampling response rate of schools below 80%.*

Source: "Reading Literacy in the United States: Findings From the IEA Reading Literacy Study," U.S. Department of Education, 1996, from "How in the World Do Students Read?" International Association for the Evaluation of Education Achievement, 1992.

FOR MORE INFORMATION

Center for Education Reform, 1001 Connecticut Ave. N.W., Suite 204, Washington, D.C. 20036; (202) 822-9000. This clearinghouse for reforms, research and action in public education tracks legislation, local action and publications relating to charter schools, vouchers, standards and testing.

National Congress of Parents and Teachers, 2000 L St. N.W., Suite 600, Washington, D.C. 20036; (202) 331-1380. The National PTA, headquartered in Chicago, has a Washington office that tracks legislation and monitors national policy issues affecting public schools.

Parents for Public Schools, P.O. Box 12807, Jackson, Miss. 39236; (601) 982-1222. Founded in 1989, this group of parents is committed to ending de facto segregation in public schools. It promotes the value of public schools, raises money and organizes volunteer workers to improve facilities. It has spread to 41 cities.

Public Agenda, 6 East 39th St., New York, N.Y. 10016; (212) 686-6610. Founded by former Secretary of State Cyrus Vance and pollster Daniel Yankelovich, this group conducts opinion research and stages forums to explore citizen attitudes on public policy issues, particularly public education.

ance favors a different emphasis: "Unless we're honest about the improvements that are needed, we will continue missing the boat. It's not a matter of bashing schools but of recognizing the successes and taking advantage of them. It's providing support and rewards for those doing a good job, and supporting those individuals and groups who need it."

Public schools can benefit from techniques pioneered by private schools, such as smaller classes, more parental involvement and use of brain research that can benefit low-achieving or disabled children, says Peter D. Relic, president of the National Association of Independent Schools.

In fact, Relic says, "People working in independent schools are committed to the idea that the foundation of American education is public schools. Forty-five million out of 50 million students in the U.S. are in public schools. We can't have healthy independent schools with weak public schools. None of us would survive."

And will the confidence of all those nervous parents ever be restored? "When parents have only one child, it's do-or-die for that child," says school board member Hynes. "But if they have more kids, they see that each child may experience the same system differently. The parent community has gotten into demanding accountability without taking the time to understand the circumstances. They see the SAT as a measure of high school, when we have no control over who takes it, how long they've been in the system and what resources they've had."

The issue should be what have the schools given in "added value," Hynes says. "Parents must understand that public schools can't make everything perfect for everyone. Are any of our lives perfect?" ■

Notes

[1] Dan Quayle, *The American Family: Discovering the Values that Make Us Strong* (1996). For background, see "Teaching Values," *The CQ Researcher*, June 21, 1996, pp. 529-552.

[2] Quoted in David Tyack and Larry Cuban, *Tinkering Toward Utopia: A Century of Public School Reform* (1995), p. 14.

[3] For background, see the following *CQ Researcher* reports: "School Choice," May 10, 1991, pp. 253-276; "Education Standards," March 11, 1994, pp. 481-504; "Private Management of Public Schools," March 25, 1994, pp. 265-288; "Home Schooling," Sept. 9, 1994, pp. 769-793; and "Parents and Schools," Jan. 20, 1995, pp. 66-89.

[4] David C. Berliner and Bruce J. Biddle, *The Manufactured Crisis: Myths, Fraud and the Attack on America's Public Schools* (1995), p. xi.

[5] *The Washington Post,* May 13, 1996.

[6] Quoted in *The Wall Street Journal,* March 1, 1996.

[7] For background, see "Overhauling Social Security," *The CQ Researcher,* May 12, 1995, pp. 417-440.

[8] John Katzman and Steven Hodas, *Class Action: How to Create Accountability, Innovation, and Excellence in American Schools* (1995), p. 50.

[9] William J. Bennett, *The Devaluing of America* (1992), p. 55. The SAT is now known as the Scholastic Assessment Test.

[10] Berliner and Biddle, *op. cit.,* pp. 17-24.

[11] Gerald W. Bracey, "The Third Bracey Report on The Condition of Public Education," *Phi Delta Kappan,* October 1993, p. 104.

[12] Diane Ravitch, *National Standards in American Education: A Citizen's Guide* (1995), pp. 75, 97.

[13] *Ibid.,* p. 108.

[14] *U.S. News & World Report,* April 1, 1996, p. 52.

[15] Berliner and Biddle, *op. cit.,* p. 12.

[16] U.S. Education Department, Office of Educational Research and Improvement, "Reading Literacy in the United States," June 1996.

[17] Jean Johnson, "Assignment Incomplete: The Unfinished Business of Education Reform," October 1995, written for the New York research group Public Agenda.

[18] Berliner and Biddle, *op. cit.,* p. 139.

[19] Terrel H. Bell, *The Thirteenth Man: A Reagan Cabinet Memoir* (1988), p. 128.

[20] Katzman and Hodas, *op. cit.,* p. 33.

[21] Berliner and Biddle, *op. cit.,* p. 167.

[22] Quoted in Berliner and Biddle, *op. cit.,* p. 145.

[23] Charles Leslie Glenn Jr, *The Myth of the Common School* (1988), p. 170.

[24] Quoted in Ravitch, *op. cit.,* p. 63.

[25] David Math, *Is There a Public for Public Schools?* (1996), p. 14.

[26] Chester E. Finn Jr., *We Must Take Charge: Our Schools and Our Future* (1991), p. 10.

[27] Cited in Cynthia L. Patrick and Robert C. Calfee, "A Textbook Case of Hype," *The Washington Post,* April 7, 1996.

[28] Barry O'Neill, "Anatomy of a Hoax," *The New York Times Magazine,* March 6, 1994, p. 46.

[29] Quoted in *The Washington Post,* May 26, 1996.

[30] *The Boston Globe,* June 9, 1996.

[31] Quoted in *The Boston Globe,* April 21, 1996.

[32] *Money,* January 1996, p. 110.

[33] *The Washington Post,* March 26, 1996.

[34] *Philadelphia Inquirer,* June 4, 1995.

Bibliography

Selected Sources Used

Books

Berliner, David C., and Biddle, Bruce J., *The Manufactured Crisis: Myths, Fraud, and the Attack on America's Public Schools,* Addison-Wesley, 1995.

Two professors at Arizona State University and the University of Missouri produce a compendium of data backing up their scathing attack on ideological efforts to discredit public schools.

Bracey, Gerald W., *Final Exam: A Study of the Perpetual Scrutiny of American Education,* Technos Press, 1995.

An Alexandria, Va.-based consultant and author of an annual report on the condition of public education reviews the history and politics of school reform, arguing that many of the criticisms are overstated.

Finn, Chester E. Jr., *We Must Take Charge: Our Schools and Our Future*, The Free Press, 1991.

A former Bush administration education official now with the Hudson Institute outlines the history and purpose of "the excellence movement" launched in U.S. education in the early 1980s with the report *A Nation at Risk.*

Glenn, Charles Leslie Jr., *The Myth of the Common School*, University of Massachusetts Press, 1988.

A former state official who is an evangelical Christian examines the history of Horace Mann's pioneering of the "common school," arguing that its history and its present often clash with religious-minded citizens.

Katzman John, and Hodas, Steven, *Class Action: How to Create Accountability, Innovation, and Excellence in American Schools*, Villard Books, 1995.

Two founders of The Princeton Review, an academic-testing preparation service, outline their take on the problems of American public education, offering solutions such as public release of standardized data and multiple national curricula.

Mathews, David, *Is There a Public for Public Schools?* Kettering Foundation Press, 1996.

A former Health, Education and Welfare secretary who is now a foundation president argues that public schools have become disconnected from the public they used to serve and that a return to community involvement is essential for democracy.

Must, Art Jr., *Why We Still Need Public Schools: Church/State Relations and Visions of Democracy,* Prometheus Books, 1992.

The executive director of the National Coalition for Public Education and Religious Liberty edited these essays criticizing proposals to spend public money for private and religious schools.

Ravitch, Diane, *National Standards in American Education: A Citizen's Guide,* Brookings Institution, 1995.

A New York University researcher who served as a Bush administration Education official outlines the case for establishing national standards in American education, including a weighing of the evidence that schools are in trouble.

Steinberg, Laurence, with Brown, B. Bradford, and Dornbusch, Sanford M., *Beyond the Classroom: Why School Reform has Failed and What Parents Need to Do,* Simon and Schuster, 1996.

A Temple University professor of psychology and specialist in how adolescents learn argues that American culture has caused students to become disengaged from academic achievement, and that schools will not improve until society itself changes.

Tyack, David, and Cuban, Larry, *Tinkering Toward Utopia: A Century of Public School Reform,* Harvard University Press, 1995.

Two historians of public education won a Harvard University education award for this commentary arguing that school criticisms and attempted reforms come in cycles and that raising expectations too high can turn the public cynical.

Wooster, Martin Morse, *Angry Classrooms, Vacant Minds: What's Happened to Our High Schools?,* Pacific Research Institute for Public Policy, 1993.

A conservative journalist who has written for *Wilson Quarterly* and *American Enterprise* magazine examines the history of changes in education, arguing that "our high schools are in crisis." The article includes an examination of decentralization, site-based management and school choice.

The Next Step

Additional information from UMI's Newspaper & Periodical Abstracts database

Charter Schools

"Advancement for charter schools," ***Boston Globe,*** **April 19, 1996, p. 18.**
An editorial asserts that charter schools are not the panacea for public education as some believe but that well-managed, strategically placed charter schools can be an important prod for stalled school systems.

Cohen, Muriel, "Charter schools 1 and growing," ***Boston Globe,*** **June 16, 1996, p. 35.**
The popularity and growth of charter schools in Massachusetts are gauged.

Martinez, Michael, "Parents find hope in charter schools," ***Chicago Tribune,*** **March 10, 1996, p. C1.**
State legislation that allows the creation of 15 charter schools in Chicago could be the ticket to decreasing the school dropout rate, according to Englewood, Ill., school council member Ted Thomas.

McWhirter, Nickie, "Idea of public schools under siege," ***Detroit News & Free Press,*** **Jan. 13, 1996, p. C6.**
Nickie McWhirter sounds a cautionary note regarding the creation and operation of charter schools in Michigan, indicating that the entire concept of "public education" is under quiet, but desperate siege.

Waldmeir, Pete, "Battle over charter schools is far from over, but appeals court has rebuffed Engler for now," ***Detroit News,*** **April 5, 1996, p. C3.**
Pete Waldmeir comments on a Michigan Appeals Court decision to refuse to approve a law which would free up $11 million in state aid for a home-based charter school.

Defense of Public Schools

Hornbeck, Mark, "Public school students hold their own in state MEAP tests," ***Detroit News,*** **Feb. 22, 1996, p. A1.**
The scores of Michigan public school students on statewide math and reading tests held up well against those of private and charter school students. The news was welcomed by public educators.

Martin, Albert, "How public school rescued my child," ***The Wall Street Journal,*** **Sept. 7, 1995, p. A15.**
Albert Martin responds to the Aug. 23, 1995, article "Dates to Remember," saying that many children need "special services," and the public school system delivers these services very well.

Shuster, Beth, "Parents taking a second look at public schools," ***Los Angeles Times,*** **Dec. 31, 1994, p. B1.**
A group of parents and principals throughout the Los Angeles Unified School District are trying to draw families back to public education. Such efforts mirror those of parent recruiters for public education throughout the country.

Dissatisfaction With Public Schools

Gallagher, Maggie, "The real crisis in public schools," ***Atlanta Constitution,*** **March 29, 1996, p. A19.**
Maggie Gallagher comments on the second National Education Summit at which some of the top U.S. executives and governors gathered, saying the needs of businesses are not being met by workers hired from a public school system in which educators resist reform standards.

Heiderson, Mazin A., "How the public schools failed a union parent," ***Detroit News & Free Press,*** **June 9, 1996, p. B7.**
Mazin A. Heiderson comments on the East Lansing, Mich., school system's failure to provide quality education to his daughter, forcing him to send her to a Catholic school.

Raspberry, William, "Loss of public commitment is what troubles public schools," ***Detroit News,*** **June 3, 1996, p. A7.**
William Raspberry comments on former Secretary of Health, Education and Welfare David Mathews' proposal that the problem with public schools lies more in the public than with the schools. Raspberry says that schools are dreadful because teachers are ill-trained or afraid to exert discipline or because schools are cheerless, underfunded and unsafe.

Shockley, Shelley M., "The trouble with Cleveland Public Schools," ***Call & Post,*** **March 21, 1996, p. A5.**
Shelley M. Shockley discusses why she thinks the Cleveland public schools and every other deteriorating public school system in the state should be closed.

"Study finds public schools are low on productivity," ***The Wall Street Journal,*** **Aug. 30, 1995, p. A4.**
A study by the Consortium on Productivity concluded that America's public schools have too many administrators, spend too little money on research on better practices and lack financial incentives to improve productivity.

Funding Public Schools Through Private Financing

Baldauf, Scott, "Towns tap private pockets to fill empty public-school wallets," ***The Christian Science Monitor,***

Oct. 4, 1995, p. 4.

In the last article of a series on urban education, the growing number of schools which are relying on private sector finances is examined. The Newton School Foundation, which provides funds for schools in Newton, Mass., is featured.

Mathews, Jay, "More public schools using private dollars," *The Washington Post,* Aug. 28, 1995, p. A1.

Wealthy communities throughout the U.S. with celebrated public high schools are setting up private foundations to make up the difference between the public money available to them and what they think their children need and deserve.

Public schools vs. private schools

"Don't abandon public schools; fix them," *St. Louis Post-Dispatch,* Nov. 9, 1995, p. B6.

An editorial comments that the Senate and the White House should not go along with a plan passed by the House for providing families with tax money they can use to abandon public education and send their children to private school, but should come up with ways to fix the public school systems.

Kaufman, Jonathan, "Grade inflation: Suburban parents shun many public schools, even the good ones," *The Wall Street Journal,* March 1, 1996, p. A1.

Twenty years ago, a public-school education was sufficient to be successful, but in today's society, in which many parents fear for their own job security, a growing number of middle- and upper-middle-class parents are abandoning public schools in an effort to give their children the best education possible.

McCabe, Coco, "Private schools are thriving; public schools aren't fretting," *Boston Globe,* Dec. 10, 1995, p. N1.

Increased enrollment in private schools in suburban areas north of Boston is examined.

Shenk, Joshua Wolf, "The public schools' last hurrah?," *Washington Monthly,* March 1996, pp. 8-17.

Without quick and decisive change, U.S. public schools could deteriorate to the point that they are beyond saving. It is no accident that America's elite almost uniformly choose private schools for their children.

"Split is found on alternatives to public schools," *The New York Times,* Oct. 11, 1995, p. B7.

Many Americans think private schools are better than public schools at keeping order and pushing high academic standards, according to a poll, which also found that most adults still believe the public schools can be fixed.

Woodhead, David, "Private education is not worth it, claims a new study," *The Guardian,* Dec. 19, 1995, p. 14.

According to an analysis of the National Child Development Study by Sussex University Professor Peter Saunders, one's class destination owes more to one's ability and innovation than class background.

School Choice and Vouchers

"California chief proposes school-choice plan," *The New York Times,* Jan. 10, 1996, p. A13.

Republican California Gov. Pete Wilson has proposed a limited voucher system in which the state would pay a large part of the costs for students from the state's worst schools to attend the public, private or religious school of their choice.

Grillo, Margra L., "Should state families have more public school choices? No," *Detroit News & Free Press,* Dec. 3, 1995, p. A15.

Michigan Association of School Boards President Margra L. Grillo details why she is against SB 639, which would allow students to attend any public school in Michigan.

Lewis, Anne C., "Public schools, choice, and reform," *Phi Delta Kappan,* December 1995, pp. 267-268.

Congressional proposals for voucher programs have been renewed. The debate is no longer about whether or not to have charter schools, but about how autonomous they should be.

Schneider, Howard, and Rene Sanchez, "For vouchers, a key test," *The Washington Post,* Dec. 20, 1995, p. D1.

Although all its key financial questions are resolved and local officials anxiously are waiting for final congressional approval of a spending plan, Washington, D.C.'s., annual appropriations bill has become the vehicle for what national education groups view as a pivotal debate over "school choice."

Stearns, Kathryn, "School choice: Survival of the fittest," *The Washington Post,* Nov. 24, 1995, p. A29.

Kathryn Stearns, a senior fellow for the Carnegie Foundation for the Advancement of Teaching, discusses the issue of school choice, noting that it has become a kind of liberation movement and that proponents should study how it has been working for 10 years in England.

Walters, Laurel Shaper, "School choice moves ahead despite lack of public funds," *The Christian Science Monitor,* June 5, 1996, p. 3.

In cities across the nation, private corporations, foundations and citizens are jumping in to help poor families foot the bill to send their children to private schools. The giving is an attempt to advance the school choice movement, which advocates giving families public money (in the form of vouchers) and allowing students to attend the private or public school of their choice.

Back Issues

Great Research on Current Issues Starts Right Here...Recent topics covered by The CQ Researcher are listed below. Before May 1991, reports were published under the name of Editorial Research Reports.

JANUARY 1995
Treating Addiction
Child Custody and Support
Parents and Schools
Non-Proliferation Treaty at 25

FEBRUARY 1995
Cracking Down on Immigration
The Business of Sports
Reinventing Government
Housing Discrimination

MARCH 1995
Death Penalty Debate
Primary Care
Democracy in Africa
Environmental Movement at 25

APRIL 1995
Abortion Clinic Protests
Dieting and Health
Combating AIDS
Rethinking Affirmative Action

MAY 1995
Assisted Suicide Controversy
Overhauling Social Security
Learning to Read
Mandatory Sentencing

Back issues are available for $5.00 (subscribers) or $8.00 (non-subscribers). Quantity discounts apply to orders over ten. To order, call Congressional Quarterly Customer Service at (202) 887-8621.

Binders are available for $18.00. To order call 1-800-638-1710. Please refer to stock number 648.

JUNE 1995
Combating Infectious Disease
Property Rights
Repetitive Stress Injuries
Regulating the Internet

JULY 1995
War Crimes
Highway Safety
Combating Terrorism
Preventing Teen Drug Use

AUGUST 1995
Job Stress
Organ Transplants
United Nations at 50
Advances in Cancer Research

SEPTEMBER 1995
Catholic Church in the U.S.
Northern Ireland Cease-Fire
High School Sports
Teaching History

OCTOBER 1995
Quebec's Future
Revitalizing the Cities
Networking the Classroom
Indoor Air Pollution

NOVEMBER 1995
The Working Poor
The Jury System
Sex, Violence and the Media
Police Misconduct

DECEMBER 1995
Teens and Tobacco
Gene Therapy's Future
Global Water Shortages
Third-Party Prospects

JANUARY 1996
Emergency Medicine
Punishing Sex Offenders
Bilingual Education
Helping the Homeless

FEBRUARY 1996
Reforming the CIA
Campaign Finance Reform
Academic Politics
Getting Into College

MARCH 1996
The British Monarchy
Preventing Juvenile Crime
Tax Reform
Pursuing the Paranormal

APRIL 1996
Centennial Olympic Games
Managed Care
Protecting Endangered Species
New Military Culture

MAY 1996
Russia's Political Future
Marriage and Divorce
Year-Round Schools
Taiwan, China and the U.S.

JUNE 1996
Rethinking NAFTA
First Ladies
Teaching Values
Labor Movement's Future

JULY 1996
Recovered-Memory Syndrome
Native Americans' Future
Crackdown on Sexual Harassment

Future Topics

- ***Animal Rights Debate***
- ***Privatizing Government Services***
- ***Child Labor and Sweatshops***

THE CQ Researcher

PUBLISHED BY CONGRESSIONAL QUARTERLY INC.

Fighting Over Animal Rights

Has public support for the movement peaked?

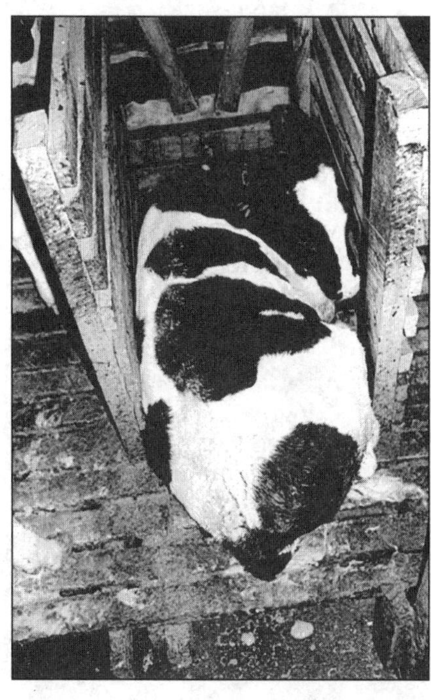

These are heady days for animal rights activists. From its humble beginnings just over 20 years ago, the movement has grown tremendously, both in size and importance. Public opinion polls show broad support for parts of the animal rights agenda, including the movement's campaigns against wearing fur, eating veal or using animals to test cosmetics and other consumer products. But while many Americans sympathize with the animal rights movement, most people still eat at least some meat and most believe in the necessity of using animals for biomedical research. The movement's successes also have prompted medical researchers, AIDS activists, farmers and others to devote more time and resources to countering animal rights activists.

INSIDE THIS ISSUE

CQ August 2, 1996 • Volume 6, No. 29 • Pages 673-696

Formerly Editorial Research Reports

FIGHTING OVER ANIMAL RIGHTS

COVER: VEAL CALVES SPEND THEIR LIVES IN SMALL STALLS TO PREVENT THEM FROM MOVING AND BUILDING MUSCLE THAT WOULD TOUGHEN THEIR PRIZED TENDER MEAT. (THE HUMANE FARMING ASSOCIATION)

THE *CQ Researcher*

August 2, 1996
Volume 6, No. 29

Bibliographic records and abstracts included in The Next Step section of this publication are from UMI's Newspaper and Periodical Abstracts database, and are used with permission.

The CQ Researcher (ISSN 1056-2036). Formerly Editorial Research Reports. Published weekly (48 times per year, not printed March 1, May 31, Aug. 30, Nov. 29) by Congressional Quarterly Inc., 1414 22nd St., N.W., Washington, D.C. 20037. Annual subscription rate for libraries, businesses and government is $319. Additional rates furnished upon request. Periodicals postage paid at Washington, D.C. POSTMASTER: Send address changes to The CQ Researcher, 1414 22nd St., N.W., Washington, D.C. 20037.

Fighting Over Animal Rights

BY DAVID MASCI

THE ISSUES

Inside a small, dark room, six long-tail macaques dart back and forth in their cages. One monkey, a bold fellow named Socrates, bares his teeth at a first-time visitor, as if to challenge his presence.

On many levels, life is quite good for Socrates and the other primates at Rockefeller University, a biomedical research institution in New York City. Their quarters are spotlessly clean, and they have ample food and water. Someone from the university checks on the monkeys each day, affording them regular social contact. And although their individual cages are small — roughly two feet wide by three feet high and deep — the macaques all have poles and rubber swings to simulate their arboreal life in the jungle.

"These animals are better kept than most humans," says Karen Sokol, a veterinarian at the university, where scientists use animals in a variety of experiments; the macaques, for example, are helping to test a new male contraceptive.

Still, confinement to a small cage over a long period of time can create problems. "These are intelligent animals, so they probably suffer from depression," Sokol says. As a result, some of the macaques have engaged in acts of self-mutilation or developed "compulsive disorders, where they pick at something repeatedly until it bleeds," she says. To alleviate these problems, the macaques are given Prozac, an antidepressant used by millions of people around the world.[1] The drug has helped some of them to stop their self-destructive behavior.

Situations like this trouble Sokol. She knows that no matter how humanely she and her colleagues treat the animals under their care, some will suffer, if not physically then

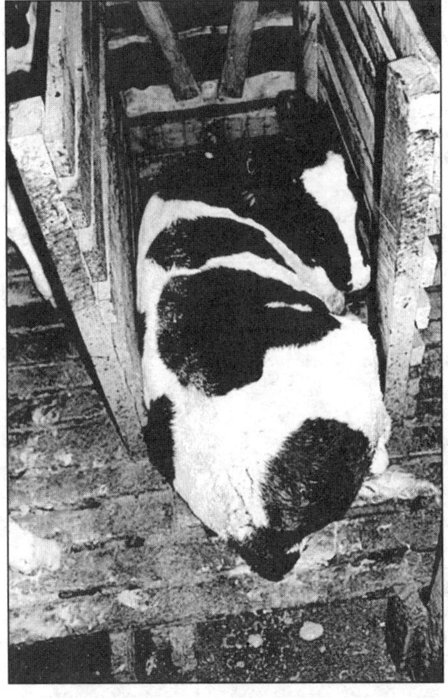

emotionally, from their captivity. "It is difficult for me to be at an animal facility because I have a genuine love for them," she says.

Still, Sokol believes in her work. Some of the research currently being conducted at Rockefeller could lead to advances in the fight against heart ailments, Parkinson's disease, tuberculosis and other afflictions. "We're trying to make animal life, human life and plant life better, and unfortunately [animal-based research] is all we have now," Sokol says.

But this opinion is not shared by everyone. A small, but growing minority of Americans believe that using animals to meet even the most pressing human needs is cruel and unnecessary. "On a moral level it's all unacceptable because you can't justify gain based on exploitation," says Ingrid Newkirk, co-founder of People for the Ethical Treatment of Animals (PETA).

PETA and a number of other groups form the core of what has become known as the animal rights movement, which aims to transform the relationship between people and animals. Animal rights activists have worked tirelessly to raise public consciousness, using everything from local grass-roots efforts to sophisticated national media campaigns to bring their views before the public.

So far, their efforts have been paying dividends. From its humble beginnings just over 20 years ago, the movement has grown tremendously, both in size and importance. No longer considered part of "the lunatic fringe," animal activism is rapidly entering the American mainstream. Polling data show that at least on some issues, animal rights activists have substantial support among the general population.

According to a poll commissioned by The Associated Press in November 1995, two-thirds of all Americans believe that animals have just as much right to live without suffering as humans do. Two-thirds of the respondents oppose the use of animals in cosmetics testing, while 59 percent say it is "always wrong" to kill another creature for its fur. (*See poll, p. 676.*)

Organizations like PETA have shown great skill at generating publicity, whether demonstrating against animal testing at companies like Gillette or enlisting celebrities to speak out against wearing fur. But while the movement may be media savvy, it is ultimately succeeding because of what its supporters say is moral outrage at man's inhumanity toward other creatures. Animals have the right to live free of human exploitation, says Newkirk. "Basically, don't eat animals, don't wear them and don't use them for experiments or entertainment."

This creed commits Newkirk and other animal rights supporters to a war on many fronts, from laboratories and farms to zoos and circuses. And while animal activists have chalked up some victories, most notably against the use of fur and the consumption of veal, the problems that

How the Public Views Animal Rights

Do you think laws protecting animals from inhumane treatment are adequate?

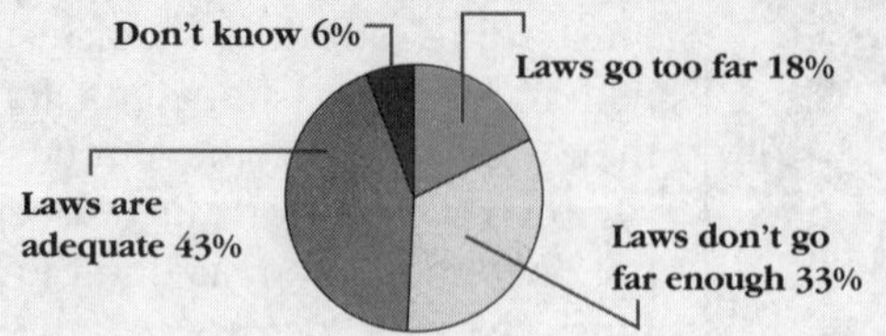

Some people say an animal's right to live free of suffering is just as important as a person's right to live free of suffering. Do you agree?

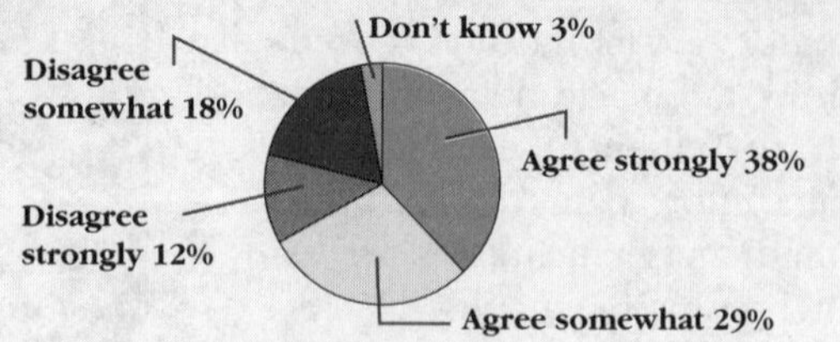

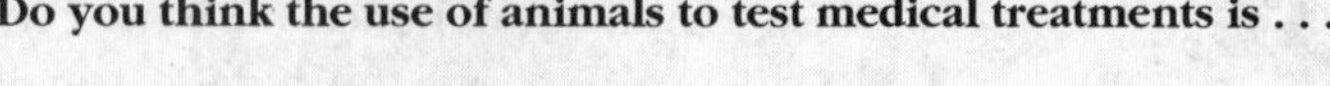

Do you think the use of animals to test medical treatments is . . . .

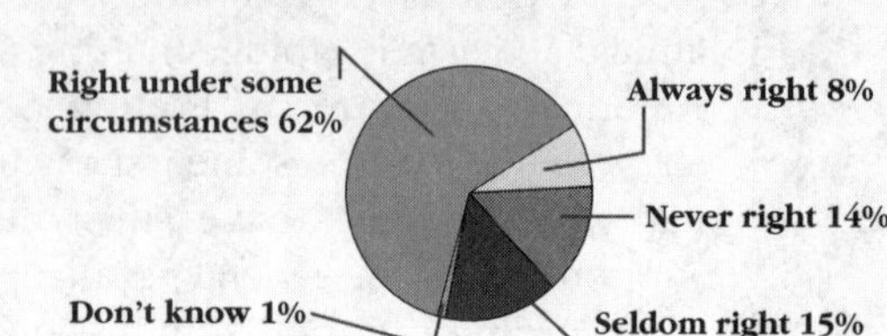

Do you think the use of animals to test cosmetics is . . .

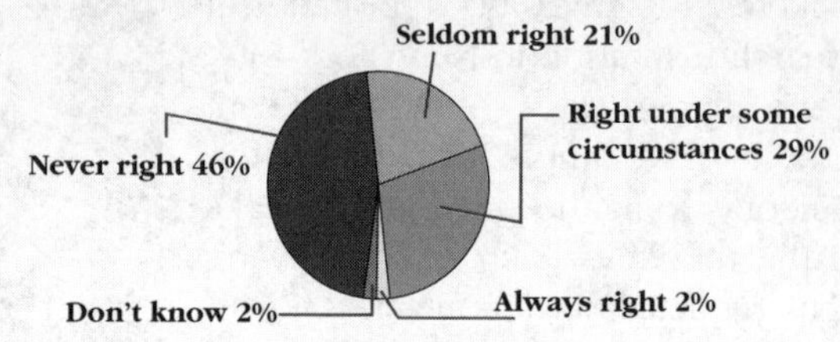

Do you think there are circumstances where it's acceptable to use an animal for its fur?

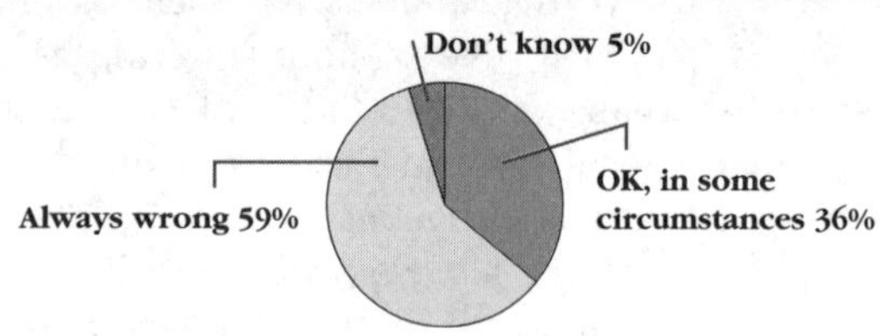

Do you think there are circumstances where it's acceptable to hunt an animal for sport?

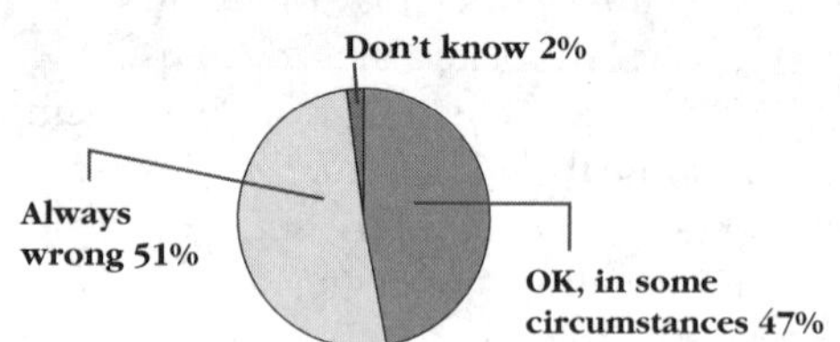

How often do you eat meat, poultry or fish?

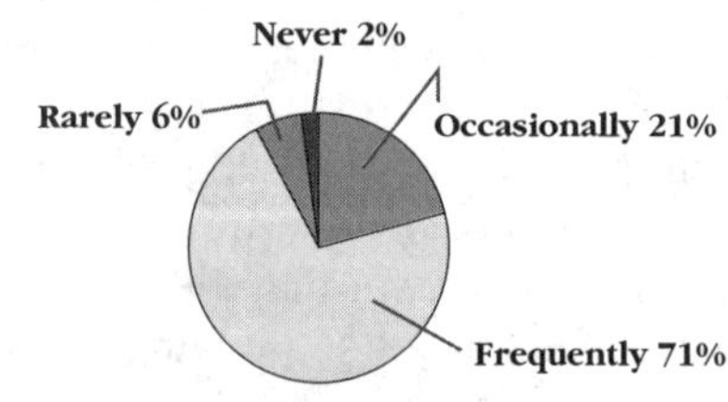

Source: National telephone poll of 1,004 adults taken for The Associated Press on Nov. 10-14, 1995, by ICR Survey Research Group of Media, Pa., part of AUS Consultants. Results have a margin of sampling error of 3 percentage points, plus or minus.

they are fighting against persist.

They point out that more than 7 billion farm animals are slaughtered each year for food and other products. Typically raised on large mechanized farms, these cows, pigs, chickens and other creatures lead cramped, stressed lives that do not allow them to fulfill any of their behavioral prerogatives, activists say.

Another area of concern for the movement are laboratories like the ones at Rockefeller University, where, animal rights groups say, tens of millions of rats, cats, dogs, primates and other animals are in effect tortured to test the safety of new consumer products or determine the efficacy of new drugs. Some animal activists are particularly incensed by the use of animals in biomedical research, arguing that it is unnecessary and even detrimental to the advancement of science because alternatives like cell cultures or computer models can produce the same or even better results.

But the claims of animal rights groups do not go unchallenged. For instance, farmers say that new farming techniques have made meat and other animal products more affordable for consumers. If forced to return to traditional farming, they argue, meat would become too expensive for most people. In addition, they say, raising animals in an indoor and controlled environment is infinitely more humane than older farming methods, which left animals exposed to disease, the elements and predators.

Researchers are also fighting efforts to keep animals out of laboratories, arguing that alternatives are no substitute when it comes to testing the efficacy of a new drug or the possible toxicity of a new cosmetic. Alternatives like cell cultures or computer models do not provide a complete picture of how something will react in a real living body, scientists say. Moreover, they point to statistics showing that laboratory animals are not maltreated and are only subjected to pain in the rarest of cases.

These arguments are still persuasive with most Americans, who accept that animals are necessary for food and scientific research. Some segments of the public may now have second thoughts about wearing fur, eating veal or using rabbits to test cosmetics, but the argument against animal exploitation is a much harder sell when it entails giving up meat altogether or the next advance in the war against cancer, AIDS or other life-threatening diseases. Indeed, 98 percent of those responding to the AP poll still eat at least some meat, and two-thirds support the use of animals in biomedical research under some circumstances.

But even though a solid majority of Americans favor the continued use of animals for a variety of purposes, many industries and organizations have started treating the animal rights movement as a serious threat. Groups representing agriculture, medical research and other interests are becoming increasingly active in their efforts to counter the movement's influence.

This was in evidence recently when animal rights activists came to Washington for a week of events capped by a June 23 "March for Animals" in front of the U.S. Capitol. Ten years ago, "World Animal Awareness Week," as it was called, would have been largely ignored by the movement's traditional foes. But this year, opposing groups ranging from the National Pork Producers Council to the National Association for Biomedical Research (NABR) hosted their own well-organized counter-events.

Some of the most visible events were organized by a coalition of the nation's major AIDS organizations, who say animal research is crucial to finding a cure for AIDS. "We had to make sure our side of the story was told," says Michael Shriver, director of public policy for the National Association of People with AIDS.

In the past, AIDS activists have been reluctant to speak out against the animal rights movement, fearing that they would alienate some of their supporters in Hollywood, many of whom also favor animal rights. But that reluctance has faded in light of recent medical advances in the war against AIDS, all of which involved animal-based research. [2]

Sally Morrison, vice president of the American Foundation for AIDS Research, says discussions about organizing a counteroffensive "became more intense" last December after PETA and other animal rights groups criticized an experimental AIDS treatment that involved transplanting bone marrow from a baboon into an AIDS patient. (*See story, p. 684.*)

"They were too aggressive about that," Morrison says, referring to the animal rights community's attacks.

Throughout World Animal Awareness Week, AIDS activists were a constant presence, not only holding competing press conferences and demonstrations but at times directly confronting animal rights activists. "We had to stand up against the whole rhetorical diatribe [against animal testing] that was coming from animal rights groups," says Shriver.

Supporters of animal rights remain optimistic that the public will support their goals as people learn more about what happens on farms or in laboratories. "The more people learn what's done to animals the more they will be against it," says Suzanne E. Roy, project director at the group In Defense of Animals.

What is done to animals and why is, of course, the crux of the debate. Here are some of the questions being asked about this emotional issue:

The Foundation for Biomedical Research distributes posters defending the use of animals in laboratory research.

Animals Used in Biomedical Research

Species Used

The overwhelming majority of laboratory animals are rats and mice bred for this purpose by licensed suppliers.

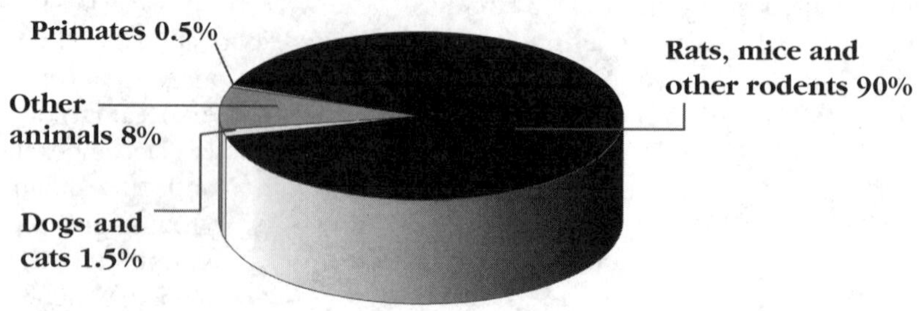

Number of Animals Used

More than 1.6 million animals other than rats or mice were used by registered research facilities in 1994, according to the U.S. Department of Agriculture (USDA).

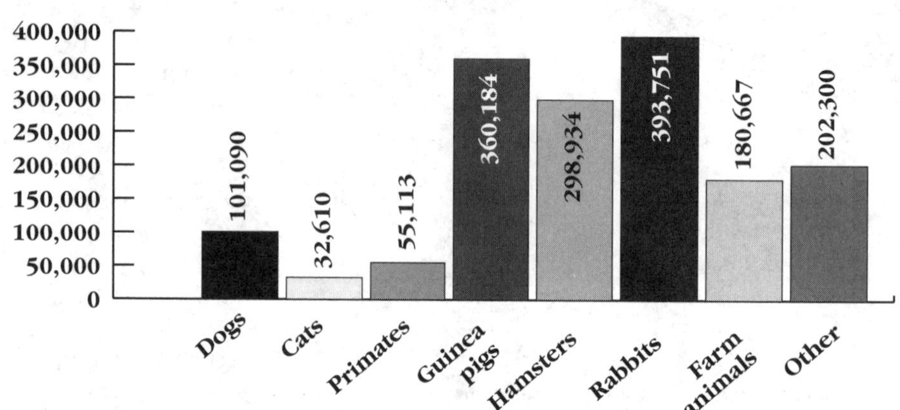

Experiments Involving Pain

Most research was not painful to the animals involved, the USDA reports. However, USDA data on lab animals excludes experiments involving rats and mice, which are not covered by the Animal Welfare Act.

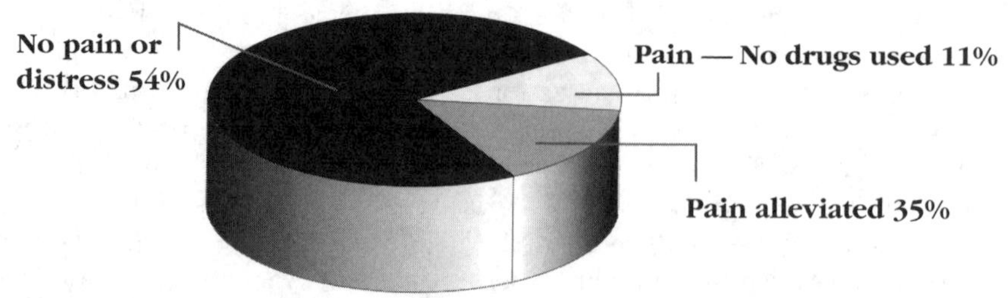

Sources: Foundation for Biomedical Research, "Figures on Animal Research," Sept. 11, 1995, and Animal Reseach and Human Health, *1992; U.S. Department of Agriculture,* Animal Welfare Enforcement, Fiscal Year 1994.

Are there adequate alternatives to animal experimentation for developing and testing drugs and consumer products?

In recent decades, researchers have developed and made greater use of alternatives to animal testing to accomplish their research goals. For instance, scientists have been able to grow human cell or tissue cultures in the laboratory to test drug safety and efficacy. Researchers also are increasingly using computer models and epidemiological data as alternatives to animal testing.

As a result, the number of animals used in laboratory research in the United States has dropped, although just how low it has fallen depends on who is providing the statistics. According to a 1994 report issued by the Center for Animals and Public Policy at Tufts University, the use of animals in research declined by about 50 percent from 1968 to 1992. [3] Some private firms, like drug maker Hoffmann LaRoche, say that they have reduced their use of animals by 90 percent in recent decades. [4]

The trend toward using fewer animals is continuing. The Environmental Protection Agency (EPA) announced on April 15 that, in the future, it would rely less on animal testing when determining which chemicals and pollutants cause cancer. Instead, the agency said, it will use "new techniques of microbiology." Previously, the EPA tried to determine whether a substance would cause tumors in humans by giving large doses of it to animals. [5]

Still, the number of animals used in laboratory testing remains substantial, with estimates ranging anywhere from 10 million to over 100 million per year.

Some researchers say that while alternatives to animal testing are increasingly important, these methods will never totally replace animal models because they can only be used in certain limited circumstances. Indeed, says Louis Sibal, director of the Office of Laboratory Animal Research at the National Institutes of Health (NIH), many scientists use the word "adjunct" instead of "alternative" because they see non-animal experiments largely as a complement to animal-based research.

Researchers who defend animal-based models say that they are the only way to see how a substance will react in an entire body system. They argue that alternatives or adjuncts are usually only useful in determining how something will affect a specific part of the body. For example, exposing human liver cells grown in vitro or in the laboratory to a specific chemical can tell a scientist how that chemical will affect the liver. But the test cannot show researchers how that chemical was changed when it was digested and absorbed by the body before reaching the liver. It also cannot demonstrate how that chemical might be affected by body temperature, blood pressure and other factors. Finally, researchers say, the in vitro test would not paint a complete picture of the chemical's impact on the body after leaving the liver.

"There are so many things going on in the body that to take one facet of that and try to say, 'now that's done it' is just too great a leap of faith," says Fred Oehme, a toxicologist at Kansas State University. Oehme predicts that every major medical advance in the foreseeable future will entail the use of animals.

AIDS activists have stepped up their efforts to publicize medical advances linked to animal research. "Every drug presently employed to treat HIV-infection and the opportunistic infections that kill most people with HIV were developed using animals," according to a coalition of 34 AIDS advocacy groups. In addition, the coalition says, "many other compounds, which seemed extremely promising in computer models and in vitro, were proved in animal models to be extremely toxic." [6]

But others, including some doctors, say that alternatives should supplant animal-based research, and not just because using other creatures in laboratory research is cruel. Ron Alison, a New York oncologist, says there are profound differences between humans and other creatures, starting at the molecular level, and this makes animal experiments inherently flawed. "Drugs work differently within the human species," he says, referring to differences in age and gender. "Yet, biomedical researchers believe that they can extrapolate from a mouse."

Neal D. Barnard, president of the Physicians Committee for Responsible Medicine, expresses similar reservations about animal-based research. "It's like seeing if a part might work in your Ford by first putting it in a Sherman tank," he says. "Animals are a whole system," Barnard admits, "but they are always the wrong system." Furthermore, he says, animals in laboratories are so stressed due to cramped conditions and fear that their immune functions and hormone levels are not normal. This further complicates researchers' efforts to extrapolate test results to humans, he says.

Barnard and Alison maintain that animal tests often give researchers data that is totally incorrect. For instance, FIU, a drug intended to treat hepatitis, was found to be non-toxic in numerous animal tests. But, Alison says, "it was 50-80 percent lethal in humans."

Barnard says examples like FIU are more common than most people think. He points to a 1990 General Accounting Office report that found that 102 of 198 drugs released between 1976 and 1985 (51.5 percent) were ultimately determined to be more dangerous than pre-market tests had indicated. [7]

Barnard, Alison and others also argue that by using non-animal alternatives scientists would generally get better results, and get them more quickly. "The non-animal models are more sophisticated in many areas than the animal models," Alison says. For instance, laboratory methods allow scientists to test something on tens of thousands of cells, giving them greater statistical power when testing for rarely occurring side effects in a substance. In addition, Alison says, while "animal research always takes years, with in vitro you can get results in an hour."

Do animals have rights?

"When it comes to hunger, thirst or suffering, a rat is a pig is a dog is a boy," says PETA's Newkirk. She and many other animal rights activists believe that on a fundamental level, humans and animals are the same and deserve the same basic rights. They argue that animals, like humans, have the right to life, liberty and the fulfillment of their behavioral prerogatives, which is the same as the pursuit of happiness if you are a dog or a chimpanzee. Consequently, PETA and similar groups say, humans do not have the right to exploit animals whether it be for food and clothing or biomedical research. "It's all immoral," Newkirk says.

This argument has been developed over the centuries by English philosopher Jeremy Bentham and others (*see p. 682*). Its greatest proponent today is probably Peter Singer, whose 1975 book *Animal Liberation* is considered by many to be the bible of the animal rights movement.

Singer argues that the capacity to feel pain is what links the rights of animals to those of humans, since both share an interest in avoiding suffering. We know animals feel pain, he writes, because, like humans, they writhe and scream when in pain and generally try to avoid its recurrence. That's why kicking a cat and kicking a rock are morally different acts, he says. "Nothing we could do to [the rock] could possibly make any difference to its welfare," he writes. [8]

Singer also argues that inflicting pain on animals simply because they

Dogs in the Dock: Protecting Animal Rights in Court

Prisoner 914095 waited on death row in New Jersey's Bergen County jail while his lawyer worked furiously to have his sentence overturned. The case had taken years to wend its way through the state's court system. Now the prisoner's attorney was making a final appeal to the New Jersey Supreme Court. Friends and family knew that if the tribunal rejected the defense argument, state officials would likely be given the go ahead to carry out the sentence: death by lethal injection.

Meanwhile, calls of support for the condemned were coming in from all over the world. French actress Brigitte Bardot wrote a letter to then Gov. James J. Florio asking him to pardon the prisoner. Public demonstrations against the conviction and sentence were taking place as far away as Kenya. All of this activity was attracting the attention of *The New York Times*, *The Washington Post* and other newspapers.

It is not unheard of for people on death row to receive support from celebrities and others. Still, this case was special. First, the condemned was not a person, but a dog named Taro, whom the state had ordered euthanized after finding that he had bitten a 10-year-old girl. More important, Taro's case was taken on by attorneys working in a new and nebulous realm of public advocacy known as animal rights law.

Using the courts to work on behalf of animals is not easy. Unlike other forms of public interest law, there are no clear constitutional or statutory markers, like the 14th Amendment or the Clean Water Act, to guide judges and attorneys. "We try to argue that the law, at least on some level, recognizes that animals have some sort of rights," says Gary Francione, founder and co-director of the Animal Rights Law Center at Rutgers University.

Often, animal rights lawyers try to reinterpret existing animal welfare laws. In Taro's case, lead attorney Isabelle Strauss of East Orange, N.J., argued that the state's vicious-dog statute, under which the 2-year-old Akita was impounded, was flawed because it did not account for normal canine behavior. She also offered evidence to suggest that Taro, a dog with no history of violent behavior toward humans, had been provoked by the little girl.

Sometimes animal rights lawyers base their arguments on laws that were written without animals in mind. For instance, Francione has used the First Amendment to successfully argue that students have the right to refuse to dissect or vivisect animals. In several cases, attorneys have filed suits against policemen for shooting people's pets, arguing that this deprived the individuals of their property without due process of law.

Strategies like these have given lawyers some latitude in making their case for animal rights in the courts. But, Francione says, as long as animals continue to be considered property in the eyes of the law, he and other lawyers will never be able to make more than incremental improvements in the lives of other creatures.

Still, animal rights law is slowly becoming more established. "It's definitely an area of the law that's growing . . . and is more recognized now than it was 10 years ago," says Strauss. Indeed, the Animal Legal Defense Fund (ALDF), a San Rafael, Calif., group that litigates on animal issues, maintains a compendium of animal rights cases and attorneys. A growing number of law firms are now accepting animal rights cases as part of their pro bono or charity work. In addition, there are now a number of animal rights law journals as well as textbooks on the subject, including Francione's *Animals, Property and the Law*.

Moreover, a number of schools, including the Pace University School of Law in New York and the Detroit College of Law, offer animal rights law courses. And there is the animal rights law clinic, run by Francione and his wife, attorney Anna Carlton, at Rutgers. Law students at Rutgers can earn six credits by taking an animal rights law class taught by Francione and working on animal rights cases at the clinic. [1]

Still, animal rights is not likely to become a major source of public interest litigation any time soon. For one thing, animal rights law is not regarded by most lawyers and judges as a valid legal discipline. According to Francione, Strauss and others, most people in the legal profession are skeptical, dismissive or downright hostile to the field.

Another important, if more mundane, problem is money. Many animal rights cases pay little or nothing, making it difficult for lawyers to do this type of work unless they are paid by a university or other nonprofit organization. Strauss, for example, at one time worked almost exclusively on animal cases. Although Taro's owners and other clients paid for her services, "it simply was not lucrative enough," says Strauss, who is no longer a practicing attorney.

Still, she can take some satisfaction in the final resolution of her star client's case. Although the courts never reversed the order to euthanize Taro, New Jersey's Republican Gov. Christine Todd Whitman pardoned him on Jan. 28, 1994. [2] The dog is now living in New York state.

[1] See *The Wall Street Journal*, Jan. 6, 1994, p. A13.

[2] *The New York Times*, Jan. 29, 1994, p. A1.

are of a different species is no more justified than hurting people because they are of a different race or sex. He characterizes the abuse of animals in medical and cosmetics testing and on farms as a form of unethical, institutionalized discrimination that he calls "speciesism."

Another leading thinker in the animal rights camp, philosopher Tom Regan, approaches the issue from a slightly different perspective. In his

1983 book, *The Case for Animal Rights,* Regan argues that mammals and many other animals have a sense of themselves and their desires. Or, to put it another way, their lives have value to them. Regan maintains that all animals with what he terms "inherent value," including humans, have the same basic moral rights, most notably protection from intentional harm. [9]

Some groups associated with the animal rights movement share some but not all of the philosophical views of Regan, Singer, Newkirk and other activists. "Basically, animals have the right to be free of exploitation and pain," says Clare Haggarty, communications director for the National Anti-Vivisection Society, which opposes the use of animals in scientific experiments but not for food.

At the other end of the philosophical spectrum are those, like some farmers and biomedical researchers, who say that it is absurd to even ask if animals have rights. "Humans have the responsibility to care for them properly," says NIH's Sibal. But, he and others argue, humans have always used animals to better their lives, an arrangement that was, is and always will be part of the natural order.

Between these two positions lies the majority of Americans. They eat and wear animal products and support the use of animals in medical research, so long as it is done in a humane manner. At the same time, polls show that a large number of people are in sympathy with at least part of the animal rights agenda.

Andrew Rowan, director of the Center for Animals and Public Policy at Tufts University, says this ambiguity reflects the fact that most people have not considered the moral or social implications of using animals. For many, their opinion on whether animals have rights rests somewhere between what is convenient and what sounds good.

Rowan does not take the position that people should not use animals for their own ends. "But, if we're going to kill animals," he adds, "we should see that there is a moral cost to it."

PETA has enlisted Cindy Crawford and other models for a provocative advertising campaign against wearing fur.

Is large-scale or factory farming inhumane? Would ending the practice turn meat, poultry and other animal products into luxury items?

Large-scale and mechanized farming methods first came into practice in the early 20th century. At the time, almost half of all Americans still lived and worked in rural areas. Animals were raised outside on small, low-tech farms.

But America's transformation from a rural to an urban society was already well under way by the early 1900s. And as the century progressed, the exodus from the farm to the factory increased. World wars, the consumer culture and a population boom further accelerated this trend. Today, only 2 percent of all people in the United States are employed in agriculture.

Factory farming, as it is called by its critics, was developed so that a shrinking number of farmers could provide for an ever-growing urban population. The idea behind these new methods was to reduce the amount of space and labor needed to raise animals in order to lower costs and boost productivity.

As in many other sectors of society, increased productivity on the farm has been achieved through a greater reliance on technology. Today, most farm animals are raised in mammoth buildings, where every aspect of their environment, from climate to diet, is regulated. Gone are the days when a farmer threw his chickens a few handfuls of feed as they scrambled around the barnyard. Animals on modern farms are kept on a scientifically controlled diet, which often includes antibiotics to control disease and hormones to encourage productivity or speed growth.

These methods have proved very successful. Farmers have kept up with the demands of a growing urban population and even lowered the cost of many animal products for consumers. For instance, the price of broiler chickens has dropped an average of 3 percent a year for the last 20 years. The cost of beef, pork, milk and eggs has also dropped during this period. [10]

But the new methods of raising animals have come under intense criticism from animal rights activists and others who say that factory farming brings untold misery to billions of animals each year. Veal calves, for instance, spend their lives in small stalls in order to prevent them from moving and building muscle that would toughen their prized tender meat. Egg-laying hens are stuffed into small cages in groups of four or five. Pregnant sows are kept in metal cages just large enough to accommodate their bodies, leaving almost no room to move.

Animal rights activists say that creatures living in such close quarters and confinement are subject to a great deal of stress. As a result, they say, these animals are highly susceptible to infections and other diseases that frequently sweep through a farm. Bradley Miller, director of The Humane Farming Association, a San Francisco, Calif., group that opposes modern farming methods, says animals are given antibiotics and hormones to enable them to survive and grow in spite of these unnatural and horrendous conditions. "They would be dropping like flies without these drugs," he says.

Yet farm industry groups say that modern methods are humane because it is in a farmer's interest to raise healthy and contented animals. "They will respond to stress, bad feed and overcrowding by being less productive," says Al Tank, vice president of the National Pork Producers Council, which represents the nation's hog farmers. If an animal is not happy, he says, it won't produce as many eggs or offspring or grow as big as the farmer wants.

Tank also questions the obsession with returning to traditional farming methods. Due to exposure to the elements, many more animals die on traditional farms than on modern enclosed facilities, he says. "How humane is that?" he asks.

If factory farming were banned, Tank and others say, only upper-income consumers would be able to afford meat and other animal products on a regular basis. And for the poor, these goods would be largely out of reach. As proof, they point to some European countries, where regulations require farmers to give animals more space and greater freedom of movement. As a result, they say, animal products are more expensive for European consumers.

Critics of modern farming disagree. Yes, they admit, ending factory farming would result in price increases for many animal products, especially chicken and eggs. But it would not put these goods out of people's reach. Miller at the Humane Farming Association says the difference in price between factory and non-factory farmed meat, poultry and other products would be similar to the difference between non-organic and organic vegetables.

Opponents also say that raising the price of animal products may be profoundly beneficial to society if it ultimately reduces the consumption of meat. Alex Hershaft, president of the Farm Animal Reform Movement (FARM), which opposes the use of animals for food, predicts that the rate of heart disease, cancer and other serious illnesses would drop if animal products were removed from the American diet.

But Rowan at Tufts University disagrees. "The problem is that we consume too many calories in general," he says, adding that meat can be part of a healthy diet so long as one's overall caloric intake is not too high. [11] ■

BACKGROUND

Animals' Role in Society

The controlled use of animals by humans began thousands of years before recorded history with the domestication of dogs, cattle and other creatures. Their use in medicine also has a long history. In the second century A.D., the Greek physician Galen used animals to show that arteries carried blood not air, as was generally believed at the time.

Eight hundred years later, the Italians began dissecting animals at the new medical schools that had been established at Salerno and elsewhere. By the 17th century, scientists were using animals to make important anatomical discoveries, like the role of nerves in the body and the processes used by the stomach to digest food.

In 1796, physician Edward Jenner developed a vaccine for smallpox by giving his patients cow pox, a harmless disease caused by exposure to cows. Jenner's discovery was followed by a parade of medical advances derived from animal-based research, from Frederick Banting's use of dogs in the development of insulin to the role of rats in Jonas Salk's discovery of a vaccine for polio. [12]

Yet while Salk and even Galen were making their discoveries, people also were thinking about the role of animals in human society. Many early cultures viewed animals as resources to be used for the benefit of humanity. In the Old Testament, for instance, it is made clear that God has given man "dominion" over the animals (*Genesis 1:28*). And during biblical times, ancient Hebrews sacrificed tens of thousands of animals each year in the name of God.

Christian doctrine, which has its roots in the Old Testament, teaches that humans are the only creatures that God has chosen to endow with a soul. Still, the Judeo-Christian tradition also teaches that animals are part of God's creation and, as such, are deserving of humane treatment. [13]

The other great pillars of Western thought, the cultures of Greece and Rome, also grant animals little in the way of rights. For instance, Aristotle said that man, as the only rational creature on the planet, should have dominion over all other animals and be free to use them as he liked. This arrangement, Aristotle said, was part of the natural order.

Rene Descartes, a 17th-century French philosopher, echoed this idea when he argued that animals were

Continued on p. 685

Chronology

1800s *The first animal welfare groups are founded in England and the United States.*

1822
The British Parliament passes the first law aimed at preventing cruelty to animals.

1824
The Society for the Prevention of Cruelty to Animals (SPCA) is formed in England; Henry Bergh forms the American SPCA in 1866.

1870
The anti-vivisectionist movement starts in England. It is followed in 1883 by the founding of the American Anti-vivisection Society.

1960s *Congress enacts the Animal Welfare Act of 1966, the first and only federal law regulating the treatment of animals; the law is amended in 1970, 1976 and 1985.*

1970s *Beginning of the present-day animal rights movement.*

1975
Australian philosopher Peter Singer publishes *Animal Liberation: A New Ethics for Our Treatment of Animals.* The book inspires early leaders of the animal rights movement.

December 1977
American Museum of Natural History in New York terminates a 20-year series of cat experiments after a group of activists led by Henry Spira campaigns for 18 months to close it down on humanitarian grounds.

1980s *Animal rights movement adopts new activist strategy.*

July 21, 1980
People for the Ethical Treatment of Animals (PETA) is incorporated.

December 1980
Revlon Inc. agrees to contribute $250,000 a year for three years for university research on alternatives to the Draize test, which is widely used on rabbits to ensure the safety of cosmetics. Revlon's action follows a two-year campaign by Spira and other animal rights activists.

Sept. 11, 1981
Police in Montgomery County, Md., raid a laboratory in Silver Spring, seizing 17 monkeys used in research. This is the first time police have raided a research laboratory due to allegations of animal cruelty. One of the owners is convicted of animal abuse, but the conviction is later overturned by an appeals court.

April 2, 1989
Members of the underground Animal Liberation Front break into a laboratory at the University of Arizona in Tucson, setting free more than 1,200 frogs, mice, rabbits and pigs. The group also sets fires in the laboratories and an administration building.

1990s *The animal rights movement continues to grow, as does opposition to it within the scientific and agricultural communities.*

June 7, 1991
Secretary of Health and Human Services Louis W. Sullivan calls animal rights activists who raid research laboratories "terrorists."

December 1995
AIDS patient Jeff Getty receives a baboon bone marrow transplant in an effort to revive his flagging immune system. The procedure sets off a storm of protest from animal rights activists and some within the scientific community.

June 18-24, 1996
Thousands of animal rights advocates converge on Washington D.C. for "World Animal Awareness Week," a series of events capped by a march at the Capitol. These activities prompt AIDS advocates and others who oppose the animal rights movement to organize press conferences, demonstrations and other events to counter the animal rights activists.

New Science of Xenotransplantation Sparks Fierce Debate

Last December, doctors at San Francisco General Hospital transplanted bone marrow from a baboon into the body of Jeff Getty, a 38-year-old man with AIDS. Baboons are resistant to HIV, the virus that causes AIDS, and scientists had hoped that the transplanted marrow would help to restore Getty's ravaged immune system. [1]

This well-publicized and controversial experiment is only the latest in a series of recent attempts at xenotransplantation, which involves transferring tissue from one species to another. Animal rights groups and some scientists say that transplanting animal tissue or parts into a human being is immoral and dangerous. But many scientists believe that xenotransplantation could be the key to mitigating or even eliminating a host of medical ills.

Already, some patients with Parkinson's disease have received injections of pig brain cells that stimulate the production of the brain chemical dopamine. In the near future, scientists hope to use genetically engineered pig livers and other organs as a temporary means of saving people who are waiting for a suitable human donor (*see below*).

The search for transplantable animal organs is driven by a severe and chronic shortage of human organs. [2] According to the United Network for Organ Sharing (UNOS), in Richmond, Va., more than 45,000 people were on waiting lists for organs in 1995. However, only 19,136 organ transplants were performed last year, leaving thousands of people — eight per day, UNOS estimates — to die while waiting for a donor.

"We are clearly not meeting the need for organs," says Joel Newman, a spokesman for UNOS. The organ shortage problem is likely to get worse, Newman adds, since the waiting lists have been growing at least twice as fast as the transplant list. Newman cautions that for now, the xenotransplantation of organs is likely to remain experimental. Still, he says, "in combination with other medical and surgical advances, xenotransplantation could be a viable alternative in the long term."

But while xenotransplantation may seem like a future wellspring of medical miracles, it has more than its share of critics. Animal rights activists are appalled at the notion that pigs, baboons and other creatures will be "harvested" for organs and other tissue. "These animals are not ours to cut open and use as spare parts," says Lisa Lange, director of public relations at People for the Ethical Treatment of Animals (PETA). [3]

PETA and other animal rights groups say that the solution to the organ shortage is to increase access to human organs. A first step, they say, would be for the United States to adopt a presumed-consent law, whereby everyone is presumed to be an organ donor unless they specifically declare otherwise. Currently, organs can only be taken from a body after consent has been given.

Opponents also argue that receiving tissue from animals could expose the patient and possibly the entire human population to a dangerous virus. For instance, many scientists believe that the virus that causes AIDS was spread to humans through contact with African monkeys. Xenotransplantation, they say, would make similar tragedies much more likely.

"When a virus crosses the species barrier, it can mutate and change, presenting all kinds of problems," says Neil D. Barnard, president of the Physicians Committee for Responsible Medicine, a group that opposes the use of animals in medical research. "The species barrier is there for a reason," he adds.

An Institute of Medicine panel recently concluded that "the potential for transmission of infectious agents . . . from animals to human transplant recipients is real." However, the panel concluded that given the shortage of human donors, "the potential benefits of xenotransplants are great enough to justify the risks." [4]

Many opponents of xenotransplantation doubt that the human body will ever accept animal organs and tissue, since the immune system tries to destroy any foreign entity. "When you do a human-to-human transplant, even with relatives, you have a huge rejection problem," Barnard says.

Since 1984, when a surgeon at Loma Linda University Medical Center in California transplanted a baboon heart into the body of an infant known as Baby Fae, every one of the more than 30 patients who have received an animal organ has died soon after surgery. Drugs given to these patients to suppress their immune systems did little to stop the rejection process.

Still, xenotransplantation advocates say, the future is brighter than the past would indicate. Scientists are using genetic engineering to create animal organs that will not be rejected by the human immune system. For example, scientists at Duke University and Nextran, a Princeton, N.J., biotechnology firm, have been injecting human genes into pig embryos to create a pig whose organs will have enough human chemical characteristics to fool the immune system and thwart rejection. [5]

Pigs are becoming particularly popular with xenotransplant researchers because they are easy to breed and their organs are roughly human-sized. In addition, pigs "are more acceptable [than baboons or other primates] because they are already slaughtered every day for meat," says Louis Sibal, director of the Office of Laboratory Animal Research at the National Institutes of Health.

But while the use of pigs for xenotransplantation may generate little public outcry, animal rights activists plan to fight any attempt to use animals for tissue or organ transplants, regardless of species. "Scientists think that if they use so-called lower species — whatever that means — then it's OK," says PETA co-founder Ingrid Newkirk. "Well, it's bloody not OK."

---

[1] See *The New York Times*, Dec. 18, 1995, p. A15.

[2] For background, see "Organ Transplants," *The CQ Researcher*, Aug. 11, 1995, pp. 705-728.

[3] Quoted in *The Washington Post Health Section*, Jan. 15, 1996, p. 11.

[4] See *Science*, July 19, 1996, pp. 305-306.

[5] See *The Washington Post*, *op. cit.*

Continued from p. 682
completely different from humans because they did not have a soul. Thus, he said, it was not immoral to use and even abuse them to benefit mankind. [14]

But this concept of total sovereignty over other creatures did not go unchallenged. British philosopher Jeremy Bentham (1748-1832) chose to look at the issue from a different angle. He contended: "The question is not, Can they reason? nor Can they talk? but Can they suffer?" [15]

Bentham's question was given greater weight by Charles Darwin, whose theory of natural selection transformed man's view of himself. In *On the Origin of Species* (1859) and *The Descent of Man* (1871), Darwin argued that one animal could evolve into a different creature and that human beings had their origins in the animal world. This belief, which had gained wide acceptance by the early 20th century, shattered the biblical view of man's unique and special place in the universe. Human beings were closer to the natural world than earlier believed, leaving some to ask whether man had underestimated the power of animals to feel.

This belief was underscored a century later when Jane Goodall, Dian Fossey and other researchers showed that chimpanzees, apes and other primates had the capacity for many of the same emotions, like love, jealousy and hate, previously thought to be the sole province of humans. "Some of the emotional states of chimpanzees are so obviously similar to ours that even an inexperienced observer can understand what is going on," Goodall wrote recently. [16]

Turning Thought into Action

By the early 19th century, a movement dedicated to the humane treatment of animals began to coalesce in England. In 1822, Parliament passed the first law aimed at preventing the mistreatment of animals. Two years later, the Society for the Prevention of Cruelty to Animals was founded in London.

In the United States, the American Society for the Prevention of Cruelty to Animals (ASPCA) was established in 1866. Its founder, Henry Bergh, was moved to action after watching someone beat a horse mercilessly. [17] The ASPCA was followed by other anti-cruelty groups, such as the National Anti-Vivisection Society in 1929, the Humane Society in 1954 and the Fund for Animals in 1967.

Meanwhile, most states were enacting laws with the aim of protecting animals from abusive treatment. As a result, in most jurisdictions today, a conviction on a cruelty to animals charge can result in a fine and even jail time.

On the federal level, a number of statutes were enacted to encourage the humane treatment of farm animals. The most important of these laws was the Humane Methods of Slaughter Act of 1958, which required companies that sell meat to the federal government to stun the animals before they were put to death. [18]

Animal Welfare Act

In 1965, Rep. Joseph Y. Resnick, R-N.Y., called an animal dealer in his district to inquire about Pepper, a missing Dalmatian which at one time had been held on the dealer's property. Resnick was so incensed by the dealer's lack of concern for the missing pet that he introduced a bill in Congress to regulate the trafficking of dogs and cats for research. [19]

Resnick's bill was the basis for the Laboratory Animal Welfare Act of 1966. The law set basic standards for the care and handling of dogs, cats, monkeys and some rodents used in research. It also required the licensing of animal dealers. The act was amended in 1970 and 1976 to set standards for animals in zoos and circuses. In addition, new requirements were established for the transportation and handling of non-farm animals. [20]

Following a highly publicized scandal involving experiments on baboons at the University of Pennsylvania (*see p. 687*), Congress in 1985 once again amended the act to include a number of far-reaching provisions. Researchers were now required to give animals drugs to prevent pain and suffering, unless measuring pain was the purpose of the experiment. Each research facility had to establish an animal care and use committee to approve and monitor each experiment involving living creatures. In addition, laboratories were subjected to surprise inspections by the Department of Agriculture and required to keep meticulous records of their animal experiments. [21]

Birth of Rights Movement

Until the 1970s, what is thought of today as the animal rights movement did not exist in the United States. In England, a number of rights groups, most notably Hunt Saboteurs and Animal Liberation Front, had formed in the 1960s and early '70s. But in the United States, there were only long-established and respected animal welfare groups, like the ASPCA, which worked to prevent cruelty to other creatures but did not question the premise that animals can and should be used for the benefit of humanity.

That all changed in 1975, with the publication of Singer's book, *Animal Liberation: A New Ethics for Our Treatment of Animals*. Singer, an Australian philosopher, argued that discrimination based on difference of species (or "speciesism" as he called it) was as immoral as racism or sexism.

Singer's book provided the intellectual spark that lit the animal rights flame in the United States. The year following its publication, Henry Spira, a New York City high school teacher, began a campaign that would raise the animal rights banner and provide the movement with its first victory.

Spira, who had heard Singer lecture, was looking to expose "a single significant injustice" in order to put those who used animals for research on the defensive. His search led him to the American Museum of Natural History, where scientists were conducting an experiment to study feline sexual behavior. The experiment, which was funded by NIH, involved, among other things, blinding and deafening the cats.

Spira first tried to negotiate with museum officials. But when they refused to consider his demands or even talk to him, he and other activists began a very public and media savvy campaign against the institution. After 18 months of bad publicity, including a continuous demonstration in front of the museum, the NIH withdrew funding and the experiment ended. [22]

For the first time in the United States, an experiment involving the use of animals had been shut down because of public pressure. More important, the protest against the museum had galvanized like-minded people to come together to fight what they saw as an injustice. The animal rights movement was still small, but it had already shown that it could be a force for change.

In the years following their Museum of Natural History victory, Spira and his fellow activists worked on other high-profile issues. In 1979, they succeeded in convincing the New York Legislature to repeal a law that had allowed researchers to seize unwanted animals in the pound. During the 1980s, Spira convinced many of the nation's largest cosmetics firms, including Revlon, Avon and Fabergé, to stop using animals to test the safety of their products.

Peta and the Silver Spring Monkeys

In 1980, People for the Ethical Treatment of Animals was founded by Alex Pacheco and Ingrid Newkirk. Like Spira, they had been profoundly influenced by Singer's book and had worked during the 1970s on animal issues.

By forming PETA, Pacheco and Newkirk sought to bring a greater sense of structure and focus to what had so far been a diffuse movement. The organization began with little fanfare or money. But that all changed in 1981, when the group created a furor by exposing some of the practices used in a primate experiment at the Institute for Behavioral Research in Silver Spring, Md.

Pacheco had begun volunteering at the institute in May with the intention of gaining firsthand knowledge of the workings of a research laboratory. But instead of a clean, well-run lab, Pacheco said he found a filthy facility housing 17 monkeys that were malnourished, diseased and otherwise neglected. The animals were also being subjected to surgery under unsanitary conditions, he said. Referring to the operating room, Pacheco wrote that "rat droppings and urine covered everything, and live and dead cockroaches were in the drawers, on the floor and around the scrub sink." [23]

After documenting the situation at the facility, Pacheco went to the police, who raided the lab and arrested its owner, Edward Taub, charging him with cruelty to animals. Taub was convicted on six of 17 counts of animal cruelty. Those convictions later were overturned by an appeals court, but the "Silver Spring Monkey Case" transformed PETA almost overnight into the nation's most visible animal rights group.

Over the next 15 years, the organization would use similar undercover investigations to keep animal issues and PETA in the news. The group is also an acknowledged master of using public demonstrations to great effect. In 1994, for instance, three PETA members dressed in rabbit suits chained themselves to a flagpole in front of Gillette headquarters in Boston, Mass., to protest the company's use of animals in product testing. The stunt was a publicity coup for the group and an embarrassment to the company.

In recent years, PETA has often relied on celebrities, like singer k.d. lang and model Cindy Crawford, to keep its name and causes in the news. For instance, PETA has used Crawford and other famous models in a provocative and well-publicized campaign against wearing fur. Tactics like this have made the group into the 800-pound gorilla of the animal rights movement, with 500,000 members and a paid staff of about 90.

Animal Liberation Front and Other Groups

While PETA may be the most visible animal rights group, it is by no means alone. In addition to animal welfare organizations such as the ASPCA, there are dozens of "rights" groups that, like PETA, are pursuing a more far-reaching agenda. Some, like the Farm Animal Reform Movement, focus primarily on one issue, in this case ending the use of animals for food. Others, like In Defense of Animals, work in a variety of areas, from laboratory testing to hunting

One animal rights group that is unique in its tactics if not its outlook is the Animal Liberation Front (ALF), a secretive and amorphous organization first established in Britain that takes direct and illegal action against those it believes are exploiting animals.

Since its emergence in the United States in the late 1970s, ALF has claimed responsibility for destroying or damaging more than 100 animal labs and farms around the nation. In some cases, the damage has run into the millions of dollars. In addition, ALF has removed thousands of creatures from these facilities in order to set them free or place them in less harmful environments. At one University of California laboratory in Riverside, the group "liberated" more than 1,000 animals in 1985. [24]

Unlike PETA and other animal protection groups, ALF has no visible structure or organization. There is no central office, in-house publication or spokesperson. Instead, ALF is more of a loose collection of like-minded people who see a need for action.

The group's image within the animal rights movement is mixed. A number of organizations tacitly support at least some of ALF's activities, arguing that the group unearths scandalous behavior at laboratories and farms that would otherwise go unnoticed. PETA has even acted on ALF's behalf to publicize findings from laboratory raids that show animal mistreatment.

Yet others in the movement fear that ALF's actions, while well motivated, will lead to a backlash against animal rights cause. The group's activities, they argue, have given the biomedical research and farming communities ammunition in their efforts to paint the animal rights movement as a dangerous, fringe element in society. ■

CURRENT SITUATION

Biomedical Research

In September 1984, the Animal Liberation Front released videotapes that shocked the nation. The tapes, which the group had stolen from the Head Injury Clinic at the University of Pennsylvania, showed baboons being knocked repeatedly on their heads without first being properly anesthetized. Other scenes recorded the primates coming out of anesthesia before doctors had finished operating on their brains. These and other grisly scenes were part of a government-funded experiment to study head injuries of the type received in automobile and sporting accidents.[25]

In the months following the release of the tapes, millions of Americans saw excerpts of the baboon experiments on television. Soon, members of Congress were calling for something to be done, not only at the University of Pennsylvania but at every laboratory in the country, to ensure that animals were humanely treated.

"This was a wake up call to the research community . . . to clean up their act," says Rowan at Tufts University, adding that the incident led many scientists to pay more attention to how they use and treat animals in their care. The outcry over the baboon experiments also prompted Congress in 1985 to significantly strengthen the safeguards and oversight provisions of the Animal Welfare Act (*see p. 685*).

As a result, Rowan says, creatures used in laboratories are now generally treated humanely. NABR's Trull agrees. "As long as humans are involved there are going to be flaws, but the system is better than it's ever been," she says.

Scientists who use animals say that before they can begin their work, they must jump through a significant number of hoops designed to ensure that animals are not misused. For example, each institution is required by the Animal Welfare Act to have an animal care and use committee to approve and oversee each experiment. The committee reviews all requests for animal use to make sure that the researchers actually need to use living subjects and that they have adequately planned for their care and feeding. The same factors are considered by government agencies when they review grant requests for research involving animals.

Under the law, the committee must contain at least one member from the local community and one veterinarian. "This ensures that it is not a rubber stamp," says Trull.

Laboratories are also subject to surprise inspections by the Department of Agriculture to make sure that the facility is abiding by the Animal Welfare Act. This, researchers say, keeps them in a state of constant vigilance.

But animal rights activists dismiss these protections as cosmetic. They point to a 1992 report by the Department of Agriculture's inspector general stating that almost half of the animal care committees "were not adequately fulfilling their responsibilities under the act."

In addition, they claim that the so-called outside members on most of these committees are completely in league with the research establishment. "These are not people with the local humane society, let alone animal rights activists," says PETA's Newkirk. "If they take their jobs seriously," she adds, "they're made to feel small and are forced off" the committee. As for the veterinarians, Newkirk says, "They are on the payroll of that institution and are not going to buck the system."

Animal rights activists point out that the Animal Welfare Act does not cover rats and mice used in biomedical research, even though they are used in roughly 90 percent of the experiments. (*See chart, p. 678.*) They also say that the Department of Agriculture does not have the resources to adequately monitor experiments. According to Cathy Liss, executive director of the Animal Welfare Institute in Washington, inspectors rarely visit laboratories more than once a year. "They should be visiting labs three to four times per year," she says.

But researchers say that outside of their public image or their legal obligations, scientists are self-motivated to keep their animals well treated. "The animals need to be healthy and happy — and by happy I mean not psychologically stressed — in order for the experimental data not to be skewed," Trull says.

Moreover, says Oehme at Kansas State, researchers, like other human beings, are compassionate people who do not want to cause other creatures unnecessary pain. "I want to feel good when I go home at night," he says.

But Barnard at the Physicians Committee for Responsible Medicine is skeptical of such sentiments. "If you look at someone who is forced to do something cruel everyday, they kind of glaze over," he says. "The idea that their hearts are bleeding every day that they experiment on animals is ridiculous."

And regardless of the scientists' motivations, Barnard adds, "there isn't such a thing as a humane experiment."

New Guidelines

In addition to the Animal Welfare Act, many laboratories also follow the standards laid out in the "Guide for the Care and Use of Laboratory Animals," which was first published by NIH in 1963.

The guide contains detailed instructions, based on the Animal Welfare Act and other sources, for the day-to-day care and treatment of animals. While its use is only required in experiments that receive some or all of their funding from the U.S. Public Health Service, it is widely accepted by many researchers to be the standard reference on the treatment of laboratory animals. [26]

Many animal rights activists have long viewed the guide as a welcome but inadequate tool for protecting animals in the lab. "Historically, the guide had not had any teeth," says Roy at In Defense of Animals. But the concerns of Roy and others over the guide's efficacy were further raised when, in May, a substantial revision of the document — the first since 1985 — was released.

Prior to the revision, the guide was fairly specific, setting minimum requirements for cage size, room temperature and ventilation, feeding and other factors in animal care. The new document allows more flexibility, suggesting broader standards as opposed to specific requirements. This approach is intended to give researchers more discretion in deciding how to meet the specific needs of the animals in each experiment. [27]

Scientists laud this new approach saying that it will allow researchers to focus on making the animals content rather than ensuring that their cages meet some arbitrary size requirement. "These are the first guidelines that make the welfare of the animal the priority," says NIH's Sibal.

For example, while the new guide sets ventilation levels for rooms where animals are kept, it also encourages scientists to adjust these requirements when warranted. So, ventilation may be reduced if the room is housing only a few animals without violating the guidelines. [28]

But some animal rights activists do not trust scientists to know what is best for the animals. "I'd say that [the guide] has been weakened because it leaves everything up to the research institution," Roy says. "We see over and over that institutional self-policing does not work." At least the older guidelines offered animals some basic minimum guarantees of care, she says.

But scientists maintain that the new system gives researchers not only more latitude, but more responsibility for the welfare of the animals. "It's a whole lot easier to check off on a list whether a cage is the right size, or if the wall is tall enough, or if the temperature is just so," says J. Derrell Clark, a professor of microbiology at the University of Georgia's College of Veterinary Medicine. "We are trying to bring more focus to the animals." [29]

Products Testing

Fewer than 1 percent of all the animals used in laboratory research are devoted to testing cosmetics and consumer products. Still, the issue has become a mainstay for animal rights activists, who have succeeded in arousing a large amount of public support for abolishing the practice.

As a result, a substantial number of big consumer products companies, including Avon, Estee Lauder and Revlon, have stopped using animals to test the safety of their new products. Others, like Gillette and Proctor and Gamble, have significantly reduced their reliance on animal testing. "We have reduced animal testing by 70 percent over the last 10 to 15 years," says Michael Petrina, vice president for legislative affairs at the Cosmetic, Toiletry and Fragrance Association, an industry group.

There are a number of factors behind the success of the animal rights movement in curtailing animal testing in the consumer products industry. First, unlike the lifesaving drugs that may come from animal-based biomedical research, the release of a new shade of lipstick or an improved bathroom cleaner is not seen by the public as a necessity.

In addition, some of the experiments used to test consumer products sound particularly unappealing. For example, the Draize test, in which a substance is inserted under the eyelid of a rabbit, has been used by animal rights groups to arouse public anger against companies that test on animals. Another test, known as the Lethal Dose 50 (LD 50) involves giving 100 animals increasingly large doses of a harmful substance until 50 or half of the subjects die.

Opponents of animal testing for product safety say that the fact that a large number of companies have been able to give up the practice is proof that it is unnecessary. "Everything has been tested on animals at one time or another," says Haggarty at the National Anti-Vivisection Society. She argues that with data from previous animal tests as well as non-animal alternatives, companies should be able to safely bring new products to market without bringing further harm to animals.

Haggarty and others say that the Food and Drug Administration (FDA)

Continued on p. 690

At Issue:

Are animal dissection and vivisection still necessary as teaching tools?

yes

Thomas R. Lord
Professor of biology, Indiana University of Pennsylvania

FROM "THE IMPORTANCE OF ANIMAL DISSECTION," *THE JOURNAL OF COLLEGE SCIENCE TEACHING,* MAY 1990.

Recently, a surprisingly large number of articles has appeared in magazines and journals on the use of live and preserved animals in studies in the life sciences. The authors of the articles contend that a large quantity of animals, from frogs to cats, is being needlessly destroyed for classroom experimentation and dissection. These articles question whether the amount of knowledge gained by the student through such activity can justify the sacrifice of the living creatures. The authors contend that the rights of the animals are violated by such activities.

Many of the writers argue further that modern-day computer graphics in the biological sciences have become so advanced that animal dissections in the high school and college classrooms can no longer be justified. . . .

We have come to a time where teachers who value the learning potentials of specimen dissection must respond to the charges. While no responsible biologist would recommend the wanton destruction of animal life, the majority would not want to eliminate the dissection phase of their laboratory courses. In a survey I took on animal dissection laboratories, most of the life-science instructors polled felt that the hands-on exploration of a specimen was not only an important phase of learning biology but also was absolutely necessary for its understanding. . . .

Furthermore, I have yet to read a legitimate, statistically valid study that supports the contention that computer graphics can provide the same level of conceptual learning as the experimental laboratory. How can it? Students in the experimental laboratory are involved not only in theoretical learning but in manipulative-skill learning. They handle the structure, feel its weight, probe its consistency and explore its composition. Students in a dissection lab can wonder about a structure's unity and marvel at a structure's complexity in a way not possible for a student behind a computer. Experimentation allows a student to be truly involved in his or her learning. . . .

The removal of specimen dissection from the life-science curriculum will only cause biology students to slide farther behind their colleagues in other countries. If we truly want to give our students the best biology we can, we must continue to allow them to explore the anatomy and physiology of animal specimens through dissection.

* The journal is published by the National Science Teachers Association in Arlington, Va.

no

Pat Graham
Dissection Hotline director, National Anti-Vivisection Society

FROM "NAVS BULLETIN," APRIL 1995.

The pro-dissection forces do not want to examine the issue on an intellectual, results-oriented basis. They are working to protect their economic interests, not scientific progress. It is to their advantage to keep the debate emotionally oriented, so that the status quo remains and the cash flow continues. The burden is on those of us who oppose dissection to illustrate that alternative methods in no way lessen academic standards. . . .

One of the main arguments made by those educators still clinging to dissection is the need for "hands on" experience. If anyone required hands on experience, it would be medical students. Yet a brochure from The Physicians Committee for Responsible Medicine states, "According to a 1988 survey published in the *Journal of Medical Education,* of all U.S. medical schools, only three did not allow students an option not to participate" in animal labs. Medical schools apparently realize that for manual and surgical skills, operating room experience is far more appropriate than animal labs.

Dissection alternatives are also environmentally benign. No carcinogenic chemicals, such as formaldehyde, are required. Wildlife populations, such as leopard frogs, are not decimated, and ecosystems are not thrown out of balance.

Alternatives are also cost-effective. Though the initial purchase cost may exceed the price of one year's dissection specimens, alternatives can be reused almost indefinitely. According to one biological supply catalog, a dozen bullfrog specimens average $90. In a small school using only four dozen specimens per year (a total of 96 biology students), this would cost $360 per year — exceeding $1,000 in just three years. There are numerous permanent models and/or computer programs which can be purchased for less than $1,000.

Another issue which needs to be addressed is the psychology of dissection. Are we teaching students respect for life or human control over it? Using animals for classroom experiments teaches that human interests, even curiosity, take precedence over the life of non-human animals. This lesson can cause quite a psychological dilemma for some students, many of whom have a natural affinity for animals. The ritual desensitization of this affinity through dissection can leave a young person confused about values, not to mention turned off to science in general.

Alternatives to dissection and vivisection are the tools that will allow young people to learn without compromising their values, to obtain an education with their interest in science intact. This is a goal worth fighting for.

Where Laboratory Animals Come From . . .

Every year, tens of millions of animals are used for research and product testing at private and public facilities around the country. Needless to say, this work has created an enormous demand for laboratory animals. But where do the mice, dogs and other creatures needed by scientists come from?

Like every other question in the animal rights debate, there is more than one answer. Almost everyone agrees that the majority of laboratory animals are either raised by the research institutions themselves or are purchased from biological suppliers that breed them exclusively for experimental use. Others are taken from animal shelters or are captured in the wild. Some are even stolen from pet owners, although the extent of this problem is sharply debated.

Rats and mice make up the vast majority of animals used in laboratory research, in part because they are easier and cheaper to breed and maintain than other creatures. All of these rodents are what is known as "purpose bred" — raised in strictly controlled environments by institutions or biological supply companies. Purpose or controlled breeding allows scientists to eliminate many variables, such as disease, that might be present in an animal captured from the outside. This is important because one diseased rat or mouse could start an epidemic at a laboratory, wiping out many or all of an institution's animals.

Many purpose-bred animals have very sophisticated pedigrees. For example, some mice have been genetically engineered to have weak or non-existent immune systems, allowing researchers to mimic a condition common in people who have AIDS or certain forms of cancer. "These are not your average field mice," says Frankie Trull, president of the National Association for Biomedical Research (NABR).

The price of laboratory animals can vary significantly. According to Karen Sokol, a veterinarian at Rockefeller University in New York City, a mouse purchased from a biological supplier can cost anywhere from $2.50 to more than $50, depending on what, if any, special alterations have been made to the animal. Larger animals are naturally more expensive. A purpose-bred dog usually costs about $600, according to Louis Sibal, director of the Office of Laboratory Animal Research at the National Institutes of Health (NIH). Dogs with special genetic alterations can cost as much as $1,700, he says.

Supplying laboratory animals and the cages and other equipment used to maintain them is a big business, generating hundreds of millions of dollars in revenue each year. Companies that raise animals themselves are designated Class A dealers under the Animal Welfare Act, which regulates the breeding and sale of animals for research and other uses (*see p. 685*). Many Class A dealers are relatively small companies that breed one or two types of animals, often rats or mice. A few, like Charles River Laboratories of Wilmington, Mass., are large corporations, raising and supplying a variety of animals on a large scale.

Some research animals are captured in the wild. Many monkeys, for example, come directly from the jungles of Asia and South America. Not chimpanzees, however, which were last imported from Africa in 1975. The following year,

Continued from p. 688

doesn't automatically require animal testing in order to approve a new cosmetic. But, they say, companies are scared of lawsuits and see animal testing as a powerful evidentiary tool against those who question their product's safety in court.

But many consumer products companies maintain that animal tests are necessary to ensure a product's safety. "We are under a legal obligation to demonstrate the safety of our products," Petrina says. "In order to meet that obligation, we sometimes have to do animal testing."

Petrina says that while the FDA does not automatically require animal tests when approving a cosmetic, "they have said that there are numerous occasions when . . . animal testing can be necessary for approval."

NIH's Sibal insists that the FDA generally will not approve a new product that contains substances that are either untested or are mixed a new way, unless animal trials have been performed first. "If you don't present animal data," he says, "you don't get approval."

Supporters of animal testing also argue that it is done humanely and is not overused. "The Draize [test] has been modified . . . and in most cases doesn't cause pain," Petrina says. In addition, he claims, researchers now have other methods of discovering whether a substance is acidic or otherwise harmful. Hence, animals are not needed to test those chemicals that are likely to cause the most harm and pain. "You don't have to use [Draino] on an animal to know it's harmful," he says. ■

OUTLOOK

Change of Focus?

"The animal rights movement is at a crossroads," says Tufts University's Rowan, adding that PETA and other groups are moving from a position outside the mainstream to a point where they are being taken seriously by the public at large.

While Rowan's contention is disputed by few, there is little agreement as to where the movement should or will go from here.

Rowan argues that animal rights groups need to stop trying to "grab

. . . And the Truth About Cats and Dogs

researchers agreed to stop taking human beings' closest cousin from the jungle due to concerns over dwindling chimp populations in the wild.

In the 1980s, scientists became concerned that there might not be enough chimpanzees available for AIDS research. This prompted the NIH in 1986 to begin funding the breeding of chimpanzees for laboratory use. Today, there are roughly 1,500 chimps living in American research institutions.[1]

Animal rights activists decry the entire biological supply industry, whether it's providing chimps or mice. But they are especially disturbed by what they say is an alarmingly high incidence of pet theft.

According to Judith Reitman, author of *Stolen for Profit: The True Story Behind the Disappearance of Millions of America's Beloved Pets*, up to 2 million dogs and cats are illegally taken from families each year. Many of these animals end up in research institutions, Reitman says.

The conduits between a person's backyard and the laboratory, she says, are unscrupulous Class B dealers, who are licensed under the Animal Welfare Act to supply what are known as "random source" animals. These animals, usually dogs and cats, are often not raised specifically for laboratory use and are bought from animal shelters and other sources by Class B dealers, who then sell them to institutions.

Researchers and others say that while there are some unscrupulous Class B dealers who are willing to acquire animals illegally, most are playing by the rules. "We call municipal police departments to ask if they have a problem with stolen animals and they always say no," says NABR's Trull.

U.S. Department of Agriculture (USDA) statistics for 1994 show that 101,090 dogs and 32,610 cats were used in registered research facilities in the United States.[2] About half of the dogs and cats come from random sources, most from Class B dealers, according to the association for biomedical research.[3]

The notion that many animals used in laboratories are stolen from people's homes is simply a ploy on the part of animal rights activists to scare pet owners into opposing animal-based research, says Sibal at NIH. "It's a myth that's been perpetuated for years . . . to make researchers look like cruel inhumane people who torture pets."

But, Reitman counters, "it's not about animal rights, it's about the law." She says most Class B dealers are not able to account for the origins of the animals they sell, as is required under the Animal Welfare Act. This is because up to 90 percent of their animals are stolen, she says. These practices continue because the USDA, which is responsible for enforcing the act, does not have the resources or desire to adequately police Class B dealers, Reitman adds.

"This issue should be embraced by the general public because it involves their pets," she says.

[1] "Chimpanzees in Research: Ethics, Exploitation and Ongoing Tragedy," *NAVS Bulletin*, spring, 1996, pp. 10-15. The bulletin is published by the National Anti-Vivisection Society.

[2] United States Department of Agriculture, *Animal Welfare Enforcement, Fiscal Year 1993*, Appendix, Table 2.

[3] Foundation for Biomedical Research, "Figures on Animal Research," Sept. 11, 1995.

headlines" because that will only alienate people. "When you live by media novelty . . . after a while, in order to maintain that novelty you go over the boundaries of good taste and lose support," he says.

Rowan says the animal rights movement needs to become less confrontational and more like the environmental movement: a well-established and trusted voice on the issues. "Twenty years ago the environmental movement was like the animal rights movement now," he says. "But today, everyone has a Sierra Club calendar on their desk." To accomplish this, Rowan says, the animal rights movement will need leaders who are willing to negotiate and even compromise in order to make a difference.

But others do not think abandoning confrontational tactics is going to make the movement more effective. "There is a need for groups like PETA that will push the envelope," says Roy, adding that the animal rights movement in Britain has become a powerful force in that society without abandoning confrontational tactics.

Opponents of the animal rights movement say that the same thing will not happen in the United States. According to representatives in the farming and medical research communities, animal rights will remain a fringe movement because its leaders will not be able to move beyond their extremist position prohibiting the use of animals under any circumstances. "I think that they are starting to lose ground because they are pushing too far," says NABR's Trull, adding that this "all or nothing" strategy has saddled the movement with new and vocal opponents, like AIDS activists.

In addition, Trull says, the public's support for the use of animals in biomedical research is unlikely to change since most people are close to at least one person who has or has had a life-threatening disease. "By trying to portray themselves as being on a higher moral plane than the rest of us, [animal rights activists] are going down a dangerous path when you consider the suffering caused by disease and the desire by everyone to do something about it," she says.

But while not abandoning confrontational tactics, animal rights groups will likely devote more time and resources in the future to public education and awareness. According to PETA's

FOR MORE INFORMATION

People for the Ethical Treatment of Animals, 501 Front St., Norfolk, Va. 23570; (757) 622-7382. Founded in 1980, PETA now has about 500,000 members and is the best-known animal rights group in the nation. It provides information on laboratory research animals, cosmetics testing, factory farming, vegetarianism and other animal rights issues.

National Association for Biomedical Research, 818 Connecticut Ave., N.W., Suite 303, Washington, D.C. 20006; (202) 857-0540. NABR supports the humane use of animals in medical research, education and product safety testing. Its members include scientific and medical professional societies, academic institutions and research-oriented corporations.

Animal Welfare Institute, P.O. Box 3650, Washington, D.C. 20007, (202) 337-2332. This educational group opposes cruel treatment of animals used in research. It seeks to curtail animal experimentation and favors research methods that rely on non-animal subjects whenever possible.

National Association of People with AIDS, 1413 K St., N.W., Washington, D.C. 20005; (202) 789-2222. This is one of many AIDS organizations that oppose efforts to curtail animal-based research.

Newkirk, the movement must convince more people to stop eating meat and wearing fur and to boycott products that are tested on animals. Newkirk and others see children as an integral part of this strategy, since they, unlike adults, have fewer preconceived notions about the role of animals in society. "They're the ones who are going to drag the rest of us along," she says. As a result, many groups like PETA are presenting programs in schools to get their point across.

Gary Francione, co-director of the Animal Rights Law Center at Rutgers University, agrees that education is crucially important for the future of the movement. "As long as the majority of people use animal products, no one is going to be interested in the issue of animal rights," he says. Francione thinks the movement should focus its energies on removing meat from the American diet. "When people begin to regard meat in the same way they regard cigarettes today . . . then things will begin to change," he says.

Parallels with the struggle against slavery and with the civil rights and women's rights movements are not lost on animal activists. And, as with the earlier crusades, advocates for animal rights feel that the momentum is with them and that their day of deliverance will eventually come.

"It's simply a question of breaking down barriers of prejudice," Newkirk says, adding that "there are prejudices that cannot be justified and have to be eliminated no matter how inconvenient." It is this kind of zeal that is likely to give the animal rights movement both its handicap and its edge in the years to come. ■

David Masci is a freelance writer in Washington, D.C.

Notes

[1] For background, see "Prozac Controversy," *The CQ Researcher,* Aug. 19, 1994, pp. 721-744.

[2] For background, see "Combating AIDS," *The CQ Researcher,* April 21, 1995, pp. 345-368.

[3] *The New York Times,* March 3, 1994, p. A18.

[4] *The Economist,* April 22, 1995, p. 83.

[5] *The New York Times,* April 16, 1996, p. A1.

[6] "On the Use of Laboratory Animals in HIV/AIDS Research and Treatment," June 17, 1996.

[7] U.S. General Accounting Office, *FDA Drug Review: Post Approval Risks 1976-1985,* April 1990.

[8] Peter Singer, *Animal Liberation* (1975), p. 8.

[9] Tom Regan, *The Case for Animal Rights* (1983), pp. 235-280.

[10] *The Wall Street Journal,* June 14, 1993, p. A14.

[11] For background, see "Dieting and Health," *The CQ Researcher,* April 14, 1995, pp. 321-344.

[12] Marna Owen, *Animal Rights: Yes or No?* (1993) p. 38.

[13] *Ibid.,* p. 15.

[14] Charles Patterson, *Animal Rights* (1993), p. 8.

[15] Owen, *op. cit.,* p. 17.

[16] Jane Goodall, *Through a Window: My Thirty Years with the Chimpanzees of Gombe* (1990), p. 16.

[17] Patterson, *op. cit.,* pp. 8-10.

[18] Owen, *op. cit.,* pp. 29-31.

[19] Lawrence and Susan Finsen, *The Animal Rights Movement in America* (1994), pp. 56-57.

[20] Clifford J. Sherry, *Animal Rights* (1994), pp. 73-74.

[21] Owen, *op. cit.,* p. 32.

[22] Finsen, *op. cit.,* pp. 58-62.

[23] Quoted in *ibid.,* pp. 62-67.

[24] *Ibid.,* p. 104.

[25] *Ibid.,* pp. 67-71.

[26] Sherry, *op cit.,* pp. 155-156.

[27] See *The Chronicle of Higher Education,* April 19, 1996, p. A38.

[28] *Ibid.*

[29] Quoted in *ibid.*

Bibliography

Selected Sources Used

Books

Owen, Marna, *Animal Rights: Yes or No?*, Lerner Publications Company, 1993.
Owen provides a broad overview of the animal rights debate, carefully detailing the arguments for and against the use of animals, be it for food, entertainment or medical research. The author also reviews the history of man's long relationship with other creatures, including attempts by philosophers and others to discern a proper role for animals in society.

Sherry, Clifford, *Animal Rights: A Reference Book*, ABC-CLIO, 1994.
Sherry's book is a nuts and bolts reference guide to the animal rights movement. He presents profiles of animal rights organizations and key players in the movement as well as explanations of relevant state and federal statutes. The book also provides a detailed analysis of the world of animal-based research, from an explanation of types of experiments conducted to an overview of all animal welfare laws and guidelines.

Singer, Peter, *Animal Liberation: A New Ethics for Our Treatment of Animals*, New York Review of Books, 1975.
Singer, a professor of philosophy and director of the Centre for Human Bioethics at Monash University in Australia, is widely credited with providing the philosophical basis for the modern-day animal rights movement. He characterizes what he sees as the abuse of animals in medical and cosmetics testing and on factory farms as a form of unethical, institutionalized discrimination that he calls "speciesism."

Finsen, Lawrence and Susan, *The Animal Rights Movement in America: From Compassion to Respect*, Twayne Publishers, 1994.
The Finsens have produced a thorough history of the animal rights movement, from early anti-cruelty societies to the dozens of groups that have sprung up in the last few decades. The book also gives clear and detailed analysis of the philosophical underpinnings of the movement.

Articles

Ichinose, Lester Y., "Xenotransplantation: Mix-and-match animal experimentation raises ethical concerns; may open gateway for dangerous new infections," *National Anti-Vivisection Society Bulletin*, spring 1996.
Ichinose argues that xenotransplantation, the transferring of tissue or organs from animals to humans, is dangerous to patients and society at large. He points out that transplanting animal organs into humans has so far met with no success. In addition, he says, xenotransplantation greatly increases the danger that humans could become exposed to new and deadly virus.

"Message in a Bottle," *The Economist*, April 22, 1995.
This article details the latest alternatives to laboratory animal testing, from computer modeling to cell cultures. It argues that recent progress in developing these testing alternatives has and will continue to reduce the scientific community's reliance on live subjects for biomedical and other research.

McMillen, Liz, "The Meaning of Animals," *The Chronicle of Higher Education*, April 21, 1995.
McMillen examines the latest thinking on the relationship between humans and animals. Scientists do not agree where to fix the boundary separating humans from other creatures. Still many researchers say that the more we learn about animals, the more we realize that they are psychologically complex creatures.

Weiss, Rick, "Cause Celebre Conflict: It's AIDS Research vs. Animal Rights," *The Washington Post*, June 15, 1996.
Weiss examines the growing opposition to the animal rights movement on the part of AIDS activists. Groups like ACT-UP and the AIDS Action Council have joined with more traditional foes of the animal rights movement, like biomedical researchers, to fight attempts to take animals out of the laboratory.

Wright, Robert, "Are Animals People, Too?" *The New Republic*, March 12, 1990.
Wright examines the moral and philosophical arguments of the animal rights movement and concludes that they have much merit. Still, Wright argues that human rights is more important than animal rights, if for no other reason than pragmatism. Thus, he concludes, using animals for necessities like food or medical research can be justified.

Reports and Studies

U.S. Department of Agriculture, Animal and Plant Health Inspection Service, *Animal Welfare Enforcement, Fiscal Year 1994*, 1994.
The report includes figures on the number of animals (other than rats and mice) that were used by registered facilities for research purposes in fiscal 1994 (Oct. 1, 1993, to Sept. 30, 1994).

The Next Step

Additional information from UMI's Newspaper & Periodical Abstracts database

Animals and Biomedical Research

DeBakey, Michael E., "Animal rights agenda destructive to research," *The Wall Street Journal,* Oct. 19, 1995, p. A23.

DeBakey, in a letter to the editor, responds to a Sept. 21, 1995, article, saying that increasing regulations and red tape are hindering medical research using animals.

Henrich, Gus, "Animal rights agenda destructive to research," *The Wall Street Journal,* Oct. 19, 1995, p. A23.

Henrich, in a letter to the editor, says that animal rights groups have failed to acknowledge that researchers have changed their experiments recently to "minimize pain and suffering" of their animal subjects.

Herreid, Clyde F., "Case study teaching in science: A dilemma case on animal rights," *Journal of College Science Teaching,* May 1996, pp. 413-418.

With varying degrees of success, students have challenged the traditional use of animals in the classroom. The relationship between animals rights and biology labs is discussed.

Szymczyk, Jessica, "Animals, vegetables and minerals," *Newsweek,* Aug. 14, 1995, p. 10.

Szymczyk, a vegetarian and animal lover, discusses why she works at a biomedical research lab that uses animals in its experiments. The work done in the lab benefits everyone, including animals, she writes.

Animals as Food

Dillingham, Maud, "From great spirit to great steak?" *E: The Environmental Magazine,* January 1996, pp. 44-45.

Buffalo ranches are springing up in the Midwest as ranchers raise the bison for their meat. Some believe that buffalo ranching will exploit the animal, but others believe that it is better to raise buffaloes on their indigenous terrain than cattle.

"New animal rights cause urges, 'free the lobsters'," *The New York Times,* Dec. 31, 1995, p. 25.

The movement in the U.S. to stop a practice that some see as animal cruelty — boiling lobsters alive — is discussed. Animal rights activists have resorted to buying live lobsters at grocery stores and setting them free in the ocean.

Anti-fur Campaign

Martindale, Mike, "2 animal rights activists arrested during anti-fur demonstration," *Detroit News,* Dec. 27, 1994, p. B1.

Two animal rights activists who said they belong to PETA were arrested after handcuffing themselves to the front door of Ceresnie and Offen Furs, a Birmingham, Mich., store that sells furs.

Quick, Harriet, "But Britain is a fur-free zone," *The Guardian,* Jan. 13, 1995, p. 7.

Quick notes that while fur is making a comeback elsewhere, in England wearing fur is still taboo.

Reina, Laura, "Newspapers reject PETA ad," *Editor & Publisher,* Jan. 20, 1996, pp. 20-21.

The New York Times, Boston Globe, and *Los Angeles Times* rejected PETA's holiday version of its long-running "Rather Go Naked than Wear Fur" ad campaign. *Penthouse* magazine picked up the ad and ran it on its Web site.

Factory Farming

Brown, Paul, "Food poisoning linked to farms," *The Guardian,* Jan. 6, 1996, p. 7.

Research indicates that prolonged hot weather combined with factory farming and production-line slaughtering to produce a dramatic rise in food poisoning cases across the United Kingdom during the summer of 1995.

Mason, Jim, "Fowling the waters," *E: The Environmental Magazine,* September 1995, p. 33.

The move from natural and pasture-based farms to so-called factory farms has created a manure problem that can wreak havoc in the local environment. The environmental problems of factory farming are investigated.

Schildgen, Bob, "Murphy's laws," *Sierra,* May 1996, pp. 29-30.

High-tech "confinement facilities" for hogs are dumping liquified manure into lagoons, some of which have broken down and caused considerable water pollution. In North Carolina, these facilities are not subject to local zoning rules. Farmers and environmentalists are fighting to pass legislation to force these facilities to treat their sewage.

Taylor, Diane and Simon Hattenstone, "Fat of the land?" *The Guardian,* Jan. 20, 1995, p. 2.

Factory farming is discussed in terms of what the animals live through before going to slaughter and how the final product affects humans.

Organ Transplants

Bishop, Jerry E., "Organ transplants may lead to spread of animal viruses," *The Wall Street Journal,* Nov. 30, 1995, p. B3.

Researchers working toward transplanting animal tissues to humans will need to guard against an animal virus getting loose and causing an epidemic among humans, federal scientists warned. Concern about an unpredictable human epidemic being set off by animal-tissue transplants was expressed in an article in the *New England Journal of Medicine,* published the week of Nov. 26, 1995.

Dillner, Luisa, "Pig organs approved for human transplants," *British Medical Journal,* March 16, 1996, p. 657.
The Nuffield Council on Bioethics last week approved the use of pig organs for transplantation into humans. The council warned, however, that problems with rejection and the risks of transferring infectious diseases between species have not been adequately dealt with.

Hilts, Philip J., "Success in tests of pigs' hearts in baboons," *The New York Times,* May 1, 1995, p. A13.
Researchers at Duke University have taken a significant step toward transplanting the organs of other animals in humans by successfully implanting genetically altered pig hearts into baboons. The leader of the transplant team said the partial-transplant study, reported in the journal *Nature Medicine* on April 30, 1995, is a first step toward pig-to-human organ transplants.

Animal Rights Organizations

Adams, Lorraine, "What is PETA's beef?" *The Washington Post,* May 28, 1995, p. F1.
The organization People for the Ethical Treatment of Animals and its role in the animal rights movement are discussed.

Blankenau, Gail Shaffer, "Children and the animal rights agenda," *Field & Stream,* August 1995, pp. 56-58.
Animal rights groups like PETA are targeting children by distributing literature and videos to schools. Blankenau discusses how schools, films and television help disseminate animal rights "propaganda."

Freedland, Jonathan, "Animal rights activists scale new depths of compassion," *The Guardian,* Oct. 12, 1995, p. 15.
Pisces, Britain's leading fish rights movement, has dispatched a top official to the Washington, D.C., headquarters of PETA to talk strategy. The two movements are planning a transatlantic campaign to outlaw commercial fishing.

Nethaway, Roland, "In attacking the sacred art of fishing, animal rights activists have gone too far," *Atlanta Journal,* Oct. 16, 1995, p. 11.
Nethaway explores the ever-spiraling excessive lengths to which animal rights activists like PETA are going, saying that they have finally stepped over the line in wanting a ban on fishing.

Roberts, Rich, "PETA feels their pain," *Los Angeles Times,* Nov. 22, 1995, p. C4.
The organization People for the Ethical Treatment of Animals is campaigning to stop sport fishing. The group claims that the fish feel pain and should be accorded the same protection from suffering that animals deserve. The reaction of fishing enthusiasts to the campaign is noted.

Shioya, Tara, "Vancouver closing its zoo — Animal rights activists win," *San Francisco Chronicle,* Feb. 15, 1996, p. A10.
The closing of the Stanley Park Zoo in Vancouver, British Columbia, is discussed. Only one aged polar bear inhabits the once popular 21-acre zoo, which was forced to close after Vancouver residents voted in 1993 to close it. Stanley Park conservationists joined animal rights activists in the "anti-zoo" campaign, angry at the city's plans to redo the facility.

Smith, Gita M., "Animal rights groups aim anti-cruelty message at the South," *Atlanta Journal & Constitution,* March 2, 1996, p. D9.
The efforts of the animal rights groups in the South are discussed.

Weiss, Joanna, "Animal rights group pushes abuse cases," *Times-Picayune,* Jan. 19, 1995, p. BB1.
Members of Plaquemines Parish's new Louisiana Animal Protection Society, formed in the fall of 1994, are investigating animal abuse cases.

Public Attitudes Toward Animal Rights

Foster, David, "Animal rights activists getting message across," *Chicago Tribune,* Jan. 25, 1996, p. 8.
The radical actions of animal rights crusaders appear to be working; an AP poll found wide support for the tenets of the animal rights movement among mainstream Americans. More Americans say they rarely or never eat meat, and fewer animals are used in scientific research.

Herzog, Harold A, Jr., "Has public interest in animal rights peaked?" *American Psychologist,* November 1995, pp. 945-947.
Herzog examines public interest in the animal rights movement. There are signs that suggest that interest in animal protectionism has peaked.

Paris, Susan E., "Animal rights activists take things to extremes," *Atlanta Journal,* Dec. 12, 1995, p. A23.
In a letter to the editor, Paris of Americans for Medical Progress Educational Foundation argues that PETA's "bizarre pronouncements" about animals being equal to humans do not reflect how most Americans feel toward animals.

Sissons, Michael, "The wrongs of animal rights," *Spectator,* Sept. 2, 1995, pp. 17-20
Sissons explains why the animal rights movement in the United Kingdom will ultimately collapse under the weight of its own contradictions. Public opinion will eventually find the animal rights movement irritating and ridiculous, he says.

Back Issues

Great Research on Current Issues Starts Right Here...Recent topics covered by The CQ Researcher are listed below. Before May 1991, reports were published under the name of Editorial Research Reports.

JANUARY 1995
Treating Addiction
Child Custody and Support
Parents and Schools
Non-Proliferation Treaty at 25

FEBRUARY 1995
Cracking Down on Immigration
The Business of Sports
Reinventing Government
Housing Discrimination

MARCH 1995
Death Penalty Debate
Primary Care
Democracy in Africa
Environmental Movement at 25

APRIL 1995
Abortion Clinic Protests
Dieting and Health
Combating AIDS
Rethinking Affirmative Action

MAY 1995
Assisted Suicide Controversy
Overhauling Social Security
Learning to Read
Mandatory Sentencing

Back issues are available for $5.00 (subscribers) or $8.00 (non-subscribers). Quantity discounts apply to orders over ten. To order, call Congressional Quarterly Customer Service at (202) 887-8621.

Binders are available for $18.00. To order call 1-800-638-1710. Please refer to stock number 648.

JUNE 1995
Combating Infectious Disease
Property Rights
Repetitive Stress Injuries
Regulating the Internet

JULY 1995
War Crimes
Highway Safety
Combating Terrorism
Preventing Teen Drug Use

AUGUST 1995
Job Stress
Organ Transplants
United Nations at 50
Advances in Cancer Research

SEPTEMBER 1995
Catholic Church in the U.S.
Northern Ireland Cease-Fire
High School Sports
Teaching History

OCTOBER 1995
Quebec's Future
Revitalizing the Cities
Networking the Classroom
Indoor Air Pollution

NOVEMBER 1995
The Working Poor
The Jury System
Sex, Violence and the Media
Police Misconduct

DECEMBER 1995
Teens and Tobacco
Gene Therapy's Future
Global Water Shortages
Third-Party Prospects

JANUARY 1996
Emergency Medicine
Punishing Sex Offenders
Bilingual Education
Helping the Homeless

FEBRUARY 1996
Reforming the CIA
Campaign Finance Reform
Academic Politics
Getting Into College

MARCH 1996
The British Monarchy
Preventing Juvenile Crime
Tax Reform
Pursuing the Paranormal

APRIL 1996
Centennial Olympic Games
Managed Care
Protecting Endangered Species
New Military Culture

MAY 1996
Russia's Political Future
Marriage and Divorce
Year-Round Schools
Taiwan, China and the U.S.

JUNE 1996
Rethinking NAFTA
First Ladies
Teaching Values
Labor Movement's Future

JULY 1996
Recovered-Memory Debate
Native Americans' Future
Crackdown on Sexual Harassment
Attack on Public Schools

Future Topics

- ***Privatizing Government Services***
- ***Child Labor and Sweatshops***
- ***Cleaning Up Hazardous Wastes***

THE CQ Researcher

PUBLISHED BY CONGRESSIONAL QUARTERLY INC.

Privatizing Government Services

Can for-profit businesses do a better job?

Many Americans — average citizens and policy experts alike — think government would cost less and run more smoothly if private-sector businesses operated troublesome government programs. In recent years, privatization efforts in many cities, notably Indianapolis and Phoenix, have lent support to the idea. Advocates of "contracting out" argue that government functions more efficiently when it is exposed to the competitive pressures faced daily by the business world. However, public-employee unions generally oppose the idea, claiming that privatizers cut costs by trimming workers' pay. So far, privatization in the U.S. has occurred mainly at the state and local levels. Now, though, policy-makers are considering privatizing two of the largest federal programs of all — Social Security and the Postal Service.

INSIDE THIS ISSUE

CQ August 9, 1996 • Volume 6, No. 30 • Pages 697-720

Formerly Editorial Research Reports

PRIVATIZING GOVERNMENT SERVICES

COVER: BARBARA SASSA-DANIELS

August 9, 1996
Volume 6, No. 30

EDITOR
Sandra Stencel

MANAGING EDITOR
Thomas J. Colin

ASSOCIATE EDITORS
Sarah M. Magner
Richard L. Worsnop

STAFF WRITERS
Charles S. Clark
Mary H. Cooper
Kenneth Jost

EDITORIAL ASSISTANT
Tonya Harris

PUBLISHED BY
Congressional Quarterly Inc.

CHAIRMAN
Andrew Barnes

VICE CHAIRMAN
Andrew P. Corty

EDITOR AND PUBLISHER
Neil Skene

EXECUTIVE EDITOR
Robert W. Merry

The CQ Researcher (ISSN 1056-2036). Formerly Editorial Research Reports. Published weekly (48 times per year, not printed March 1, May 31, Aug. 30, Nov. 29) by Congressional Quarterly Inc., 1414 22nd St., N.W., Washington, D.C. 20037. Annual subscription rate for libraries, businesses and government is $319. Additional rates furnished upon request. Periodicals postage paid at Washington, D.C. POSTMASTER: Send address changes to The CQ Researcher, 1414 22nd St., N.W., Washington, D.C. 20037.

Privatizing Government Services

By Richard L. Worsnop

The Issues

Shortly after Stephen Goldsmith became mayor of Indianapolis in 1992, he fired many of the city's middle-managers. But trimming the municipal payroll wasn't his main purpose, he says. Nor was he planning to contract out city services to private-sector firms. "My goal," he told local business executives at the time, "is to produce the most efficient service at the lowest cost, maybe by government, maybe by some of you in the room." [1]

Goldsmith is widely credited with making good on his promise. Over the past four years, he has shaved the city's operating budget by $26 million while still investing more money in public safety and infrastructure improvements than any other Indianapolis mayor.*

As things turned out, many of the cost savings and service improvements did come from privatization. At the same time, city government departments are encouraged to bid for the contracts themselves. In 1995, for example, Indianapolis city workers bested three national firms to win a three-year, $16-million maintenance contract for city vehicles. The winning bid featured "a combination of reductions in management costs, greater worker productivity, a reduced work force and age-and-benefit concessions," noted the Reason Foundation, a leading advocate of privatization. [2]

According to Deputy Mayor Charles "Skip" Stitt, Indianapolis officials prefer to call their approach competition rather than privatization. "We allow, encourage and facilitate city employees to compete against private vendors for the right to do work that has historically been done by cities," he says. "We're always going to try to provide better service at lower cost, with competition as our chief tool."

Stitt acknowledges that privatization carries with it "an enormous amount of baggage — some good, some very bad." In fact, he says, "moving from a traditional public-sector monopoly to a private-sector monopoly is only going to be marginally more efficient at best. When we examined our goals, we realized we wanted continual competition — much like any private business experiences every day. We do some privatization, yes, but it's not our main objective."

Indianapolis' approach to privatization is one of many variations in use throughout the country at the local, state and federal levels. In the most common form, known as contracting out, the government hires a private supplier to provide a specific service, such as processing Medicaid claims or operating publicly owned recreational facilities. Other forms of privatization involve selling public assets, such as dams, schools and hospitals, to private purchasers; lease-back arrangements, under which private parties buy or build public facilities that are then leased to government agencies; and vouchers, which consumers may use like cash for food, housing, education and other needs.

Sales of public assets to private interests have been relatively infrequent in the United States, at least at the federal level. In contrast to many other nations, the United States has no tradition of government ownership of the economy — railroads, airlines, telecommunications, mining, the steel industry and so on. (*See story, p. 708.*)

The fundamental structure of the federal government also accounts for the relative lack of action, suggests Reason Foundation President Robert W. Poole Jr. "We don't have a parliamentary system with strict party discipline, as in Britain," he says, "where [Prime Minister] Margaret Thatcher was able to push her ambitious privatization program through in the 1980s over Labor Party objections."

"It's not that we don't have things to privatize" at the federal level, Poole adds, among them the often-criticized air traffic control system. And though efforts to privatize federal prisons and big power-generating networks like the Tennessee Valley Authority have faltered in recent years, the battle surely isn't over. For instance, a new company comprised of several hundred employees from the Office of Personnel Management was awarded a contract this spring to conduct background investigations on prospective federal employees and officials (*see p. 714*).

In addition, a House subcommittee recently completed hearings on a bill that could allow privatization of the U.S. Postal Service. And Congress this year may pass legislation allowing private-sector companies to pay royalties to use national park sites for advertising or movies. Bill sponsors cite the parks' $4 billion backlog of maintenance and repair needs and

---

* The current Indianapolis operating budget is $439 million; it will be $438 million in 1997.

Collective Bargaining Barred for Many Public Employees

State and local public employees in more than half the states (white and gray areas) have limited or no rights to union representation and collective bargaining. Union officials argue that without the right to bargain, workers fear losing their jobs to the lowest bidder and thus don't perform at peak efficiency.

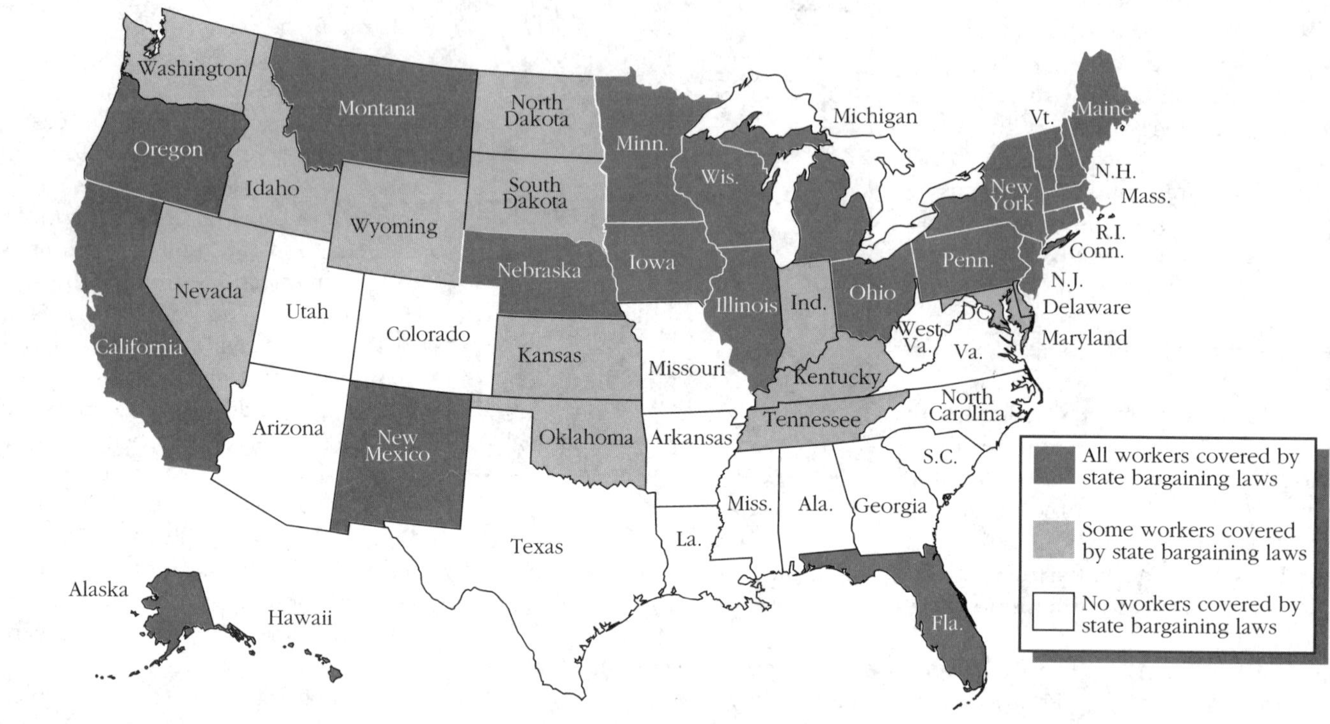

Source: "Working Together for Public Service: Report of the U.S. Secretary of Labor's Task Force on Excellence in State and Local Government Through Labor-Management Cooperation," U.S. Department of Labor, May 1996

estimate the measure could generate $100 million annually. There even has been talk, by President Clinton and others, about a "test" of partial privatization of the Social Security system to help bolster its shaky finances. [3] (*See story, p. 704.*)

For the most part, though, state and local governments have been the nation's privatization leaders over the past decade or so. "Nearly 40 percent of cities [surveyed] told us they had entered into new contracts to provide municipal services in the past year," said Donald J. Borut, executive director of the National League of Cities. [4]

And the trend continues. Late last year, privately financed toll roads — the first in the U.S. in a century — opened in Northern Virginia and Los Angeles. In April, moreover, Gov. Pete Wilson, R-Calif., issued a report arguing that privatization could help California cope with its "limited resources." Wilson proposed to "eliminate the obsolete, consolidate the overlapping, sell the surplus, privatize the independent and turn over to local government or nonprofits those tasks that don't require state-level intervention, along with the resources to fund them." [5]

But even though Republicans control the state Assembly, Wilson "faces formidable barriers to privatization," the Reason Foundation noted. "California's constitution and personnel code severely limit contracting out in most instances, and pro-privatization reforms are unlikely to make their way out of the Democrat-controlled Senate." [6]

Foreign governments have far outstripped the United States in privatizing infrastructure projects, which are viewed in this country as primarily the responsibility of states and localities. Overall, Poole told lawmakers in February, "some 980 specific [privatization] projects [worth] almost $700 billion are in some stage of active consideration by governments in 95 countries. Unfortunately, only a handful of these projects — and only a small fraction of this massive investment — is taking place in the United States. While the World Bank and [the Agency for International Development] are telling governments worldwide why they should privatize major infrastructure, the United States itself relies primarily on government finance, ownership and operation for airports, highways, seaports, water supply and waste-disposal facilities." [7]

Poole and other privatization advocates contend that private operation of government services, if properly planned, almost invariably brings significant cost savings and service improvements. Skeptics, notably officials of public-employee unions, challenge those claims. "Many . . . would have us believe that government usually fails and that the answer is not to try to correct its failings but to turn to the private sector," Al Bilik, president of the Public Employee Department of the AFL-CIO, told a House subcommittee last year.

"But when looking for ways to improve government, we cannot afford to forget our history," Bilik continued. "We must remember the countless scandals and stories of fraud, political corruption and unreliable services that flooded newspapers in the early decades of this century, inspiring the public to insist that government hire workers directly to collect garbage, maintain roads and infrastructure, police our neighborhoods, treat the ill and teach our children. We must remember how private-sector promoters reaped hundreds of millions of dollars at the taxpayers' expense from Sam Pierce's ill-advised privatization schemes at the U.S. Department of Housing and Urban Development just five years ago." [8]

As the privatization debate continues, these are some of the questions being asked:

Does privatization cut costs and improve service?

Poole contends there is "a very powerful case that private ownership of major infrastructure will generally lead to greater efficiency, wiser investment decisions and greater customer friendliness. Those types of infrastructure where the United States has relied primarily on the private sector — electricity and telecommunications — are the world standard in their field. But the same cannot be said about the quality of our airports, our highways, our seaports, our water supply, or our waste-disposal facilities," which are not privatized. [9]

Professor Charles W. Thomas, director of the Private Corrections Project at the University of Florida, makes a similar claim on behalf of privately operated prisons. (*See story, p. 710.*) Contracting out the construction of a correctional facility, Thomas told a House subcommittee last year, can save 15-25 percent on site acquisition and preparation, architectural design and furnishings and equipment. Another plus, he said, is that "contracting out allows government to decrease the total number of public employees, or at least to decrease the rate of growth in the number of public employees." [10]

"No earnest, hard-working employee whose position has been eliminated but wants to keep working for the city" would be denied a job.

—Mayor Stephen Goldsmith
Indianapolis, Ind.

Critics often seize on such remarks to support their claim that privatization's cost savings and productivity gains come at the expense of workers. H. George Frederickson, a professor of public administration at the University of Kansas, says, "Every detailed assessment of privatization that I've seen concludes that, where money is saved, it is ordinarily not saved as a consequence of efficiencies and better management [but] through lower wages. Either that, or by decertifying unions, not having unions, or moving to part-time or flextime. To put it crudely, these economies come out of the hides of the workers." [11]

Frederickson also believes that support for privately operated prisons will quickly fade after the first major riot. "If that happens, then somebody's going to say, 'Hey, who's responsible here?' It's a little like the ValuJet crash. Who was responsible for that? Was it Sabre, which was on contract to ValuJet to do plane maintenance? Was it ValuJet itself? Or was it the Federal Aviation Administration?"

Louis G. Albano, president of the New York City Civil Service Technical Guild, disputes the notion that free-market competition can revitalize government services.* "Competition for government contracts exists more in theory than in practice," he testified in 1995. "When competitive bids are opened to the private sector, frequently only one or two companies make a bid. In a typical year, New York City awards more than $1 billion in contracts to companies that were sole bidders. And even when com-

* The guild is a local affiliate of the 1.3-million-member American Federation of State, County and Municipal Employees, the nation's largest union of government workers.

Federal Enterprises Offer Tempting Targets

The sale of federal enterprises ranging from the Tennessee Valley Authority to the Corporation for Public Broadcasting would yield more than $75 billion, according to the Reason Foundation, which promotes privatization.

Federal Enterprise	Estimated Revenue If Sold ($Billions)	Estimated Annual Savings ($Billions)
Tennessee Valley Authority	12.0	?
5 Power Marketing Administrations (PMAs)*	14.0	2.0
Dams	20.0	?
General Services Administration, Veterans Administration and Department of Defense energy facility	10.0	?
U.S. Postal Service	8.1	--
Air Traffic Control System	--	1.8
Global Positioning System**	7.0	
National Weather Service	2.5	0.4
U.S. Geological Service	0.5	0.6
4 NASA Aeronautics Labs	1.5	0.3
Amtrak	--	1.0
Corporation for Public Broadcasting	0.3	0.3
Totals	**76.9**	**6.2**

* *PMAs generate and distribute electricity. The 5 PMAs are the Bonneville PMA, Western Area PMA, Southwest and Southeast PMAs and the Alaska PMA, which was privatized this year.*

* *The global positioning system is an Air Force satellite-tracking system.*

Source: "Privatization 1996: A Comprehensive Report on Privatization of Government Assets, Enterprises and Public Services," The Reason Foundation, 1996

petitive bidding takes place at the time a contract is first awarded, it rarely occurs at renewal time."

Albano went on to assert that, "Private contractors must find a way to sustain their profit margin, and that often comes at the expense of quality. These companies either hire low-wage, temporary and often unqualified workers or slash costs on the services they provide." [12]

Bilik of the AFL-CIO raised a related point before the same panel. "[I]n both the public and private sector," he said, "when employees . . . do not have the security of a collective-bargaining agreement, when they are under constant threat that their jobs could be given away at any point to the lowest bidder, when employers do not invest in training or skills development, you will find little commitment to excellence. A high-skill, high-performance workplace is not built on contingent, part-time workers earning poverty-level wages. Excellence depends on committed, career public employees." [13]

Indianapolis officials respond that public employees need not feel threatened when municipal services are subjected to competition from private vendors. No rank-and-file city workers have lost their jobs since Mayor Goldsmith's initial purge of middle management. Indeed, Goldsmith pledged that "no earnest, hard-working employee whose position has been eliminated but wants to keep working for the city" would be denied a job. [14]

Training programs aimed at creating a skilled, flexible work force enable Indianapolis workers to shift jobs within the city government. Even so, some employees remained skeptical. "When management of the waste-water treatment program was privatized, some layoffs were expected," a recent Labor Department task force report noted. "However, this was avoided by a combination of efforts developed with the new contractor and in a 'safety net' provision negotiated into the city's collective-bargaining contract" with the American Federation of State, County and Municipal Employees (AFSCME). These provisions, the report stated, "contribute to employment security in a way that provides cooperation toward service efficiency." [15]

Goldsmith, as always, attributes Indianapolis' privatization successes to the competitive process itself. In "every one of our competitions, the quality of the service has gone up, not down, as we have competed out and lowered the cost," he said last fall. "We have not yet had a competition where the quality did anything other than go up. . . . And the reason quality goes up is because these competitions force a focus on the customer." [16]

Nonetheless, some privatization tools, such as vouchers, are seen as double-edged. "While vouchers can increase efficiency, they do nothing to control overall expenditure levels," wrote William D. Eggers, director of the Reason Foundation's Privatization Center. "Vouchers in and of themselves have no rationing mechanism. . . . In fact, [when] the quality of government-financed services [is improved], vouchers will likely increase demand for the service. The result: Reductions in unit costs generated by competition may be overwhelmed by rising program caseloads." [17]

Most privatization advocates concede that government should never relinquish control of some core functions. "Services can be contracted out or turned over to the private sector," said the authors of the 1992 best-seller *Reinventing Government*. "But governance cannot. We can privatize discrete steering functions, but not the overall process of governance. If we did, we would have no mechanism by which to make collective decisions, no way to set the rules of the marketplace, no means to enforce rules of behavior."[18]

According to Stitt, such limits are guiding principles of privatization in Indianapolis. "Police officers on the beat and fire department workers who actually fight fires are not subject to competition," he says. "Nor are the folks who make zoning and land-use decisions. We don't believe it is appropriate, in any circumstance, to contract out policy-making, rule-making or contract-management responsibility. Regardless of whether it is a private or a public entity delivering the service, the city is responsible for ensuring that it is delivered. And that responsibility never goes away."

Should the U.S. Postal Service be privatized?

Privatization backers point to many federal programs that they claim would benefit from outside competition, including the National Weather Service, Amtrak, government-owned hydroelectric dams and the air traffic control system. But to many true believers, the most tempting target of all is the U.S. Postal Service (USPS), which employs more workers than any other civilian unit of the federal government.*

The chief reason for privatizing USPS, the Reason Foundation argues, "is not to raise money but to improve the organization's ability to survive. The USPS has already lost large market segments in the area of packages and express delivery to more efficient private-sector competitors. It continues to internally cross-subsidize its weaker operations with its monopoly [on first- and third-class mail delivery]. This monopoly status amounts to a pair of 'golden handcuffs.' Until USPS gives up its statutory monopoly, it will not be free to compete."[19]

Giving private delivery firms access to mail boxes would "lead to a glut of unwanted materials and destroy the security and sanctity of the mail."

—Moe Biller, President American Postal Workers Union

But the powerful labor unions that represent USPS employees are sure to resist any moves to repeal the statutes mandating the postal monopoly on first- and third-class mail. They recall what happened after the USPS monopoly on express mail was lifted in 1979. Federal Express, Purolator Courier and other private carriers quickly seized the lion's share of the overnight-delivery market.

"Once monopoly status was removed from express service, we saw the private postal sector blossom, to the great benefit of the public," says David F. Linowes, chairman of the President's Commission on Privatization during the Reagan administration. "The Postal Service had to cut its own express mail rates to stay competitive," he adds. "But USPS should be exposed to more outside competition. If it turns out that industry cannot compete effectively, OK, so be it, and let USPS continue to provide the service."

Linowes, a professor of public policy at the University of Illinois in Urbana-Champaign, says he is "not arguing for a massive turnover of USPS to private enterprise." But he contends that the postmaster general wouldn't dare introduce a delivery service as innovative as Federal Express "because he wouldn't have the authority to take a dramatic step like that. We're living in a technological age where you have to be able to make dynamic decisions expeditiously, and government — even a quasi-government entity like the Postal Service — just isn't geared for that type of response."

A bill introduced June 25 by Rep. John M. McHugh, R-N.Y., chairman of the House Postal Service Subcommittee, would take USPS a few steps further down the road to privatization. Among other provisions, the measure would:

- Create a new system for setting the price of stamps and other services;
- Allow the postal service to negotiate volume discounts with bulk mailers, such as L.L. Bean, J.C. Penney and even the federal government itself;
- Authorize an experiment allowing private delivery companies to use the mail boxes now reserved for the U.S. mail;
- Use antitrust laws to open the USPS to outside competition; and,
- Limit the Postal Service monopoly

* With more than 845,000 workers, the USPS has moved ahead of the Defense Department's civilian work force as the government's biggest employer of non-military workers.

Fixing the Social Security System

For the U.S. Social Security system, the day of reckoning will arrive in 2013. That is when experts say the federal pension system will begin going broke, to put it bluntly. In financial terms, the year marks the point when outlays for retirees' pensions will exceed the retirement system's income from payroll tax revenues and taxes on Social Security benefits.

To postpone what some worried observers are calling doomsday for the retirement system, economists have proposed a number of reforms, including proposals to partially privatize the system.[1]

In fact, an upcoming report by the Social Security advisory council will recommend the need for changes to the system, changes that Democrats and Republicans alike acknowledge are necessary. President Clinton jumped into the fray at the end of July, suggesting that a "test" of changes in the system might be possible, though he said he favored studying the issue closely "before we made a big sweeping decision."[2] Meanwhile, a Cato Institute study released July 23 said low-wage workers would be among those who would gain the most from privatization of Social Security.[3]

One of the most widely discussed privatization "solutions" calls for investing some of the billions of dollars in Social Security Trust Funds in corporate stocks and bonds. Historically, private-sector equities have provided substantially higher rates of return than Treasury bonds, in which Social Security revenues are currently invested. The system would still run out of money eventually, but it would remain solvent longer.

Under one privatization scenario, the government would make private-sector investment decisions for each taxpayer. Alternatively, taxpayers themselves would place a percentage of their payroll contributions in tax-deferred savings accounts of their choice, much as millions now do under 401(k) plans at their workplace.

The individual investment approach already has earned high marks in Chile. Starting in 1981, the Chilean government required workers to place 10 percent of their earnings in a government-regulated retirement account. Retirement benefits ultimately would depend on the returns from those accounts, with a minimum benefit guaranteed by the government. In addition, Chilean workers are required to pay an additional 3 percent of wages for commercial life and disability insurance.

So far, the benefit-to-contribution ratio of Chile's privatized system is substantially higher than yields from the old, publicly managed system.

Still, some experts caution that privatizing the U.S. Social Security system would entail drawbacks that could offset the advantages. Lawrence J. White, an economics professor at the New York University School of Business, recently warned that "any diversion of the . . . Trust Funds' assets or future surpluses into equity investments would increase the federal government's [overall] deficit on the remainder of its operations," since Social Security funds in hand are used in budget calculations. "In turn, this would mean that the government would have to borrow more money from the general public by selling bonds; raise taxes; and/or reduce other expenditures by a commensurate amount."[4]

White also suggested that letting the Social Security Administration (SSA) decide where to invest trust fund money would have political repercussions. "For example, a decision to restrict the SSA's investments to equity shares in the [Standard & Poor's] 500 is a policy that favors large companies over small ones and equity security investments over all others," he asserted. "Is this politically appropriate? An improved risk-return position can be achieved by having the SSA devote 20-30 percent of its equity portfolio to foreign companies. Is this politically appropriate?"[5]

Adopting the Chilean model also would pose problems, according to John B. Shoven, a Stanford University economics professor. To begin with, he noted recently, "Chileans had a much, much more favorable set of initial conditions for change than we do. We have 3.2 workers [contributing funds] for every retiree; they had 9. They have an extremely young society, and . . . it's easier to change the retirement system when you don't have many retired people or people nearing retirement."

Chile also benefited from having a large budget surplus, which enabled the government to pay for the existing retirement system's liabilities out of general revenues. "Obviously, we can't do that here," wrote Shoven. "We do not have a large federal government surplus. Finally, Chile had a strong dictatorship, which . . . may have some disadvantages, but it certainly makes a radical change simpler to implement."[6]

[1] For background, see "Overhauling Social Security," *The CQ Researcher*, May 12, 1995, pp. 417-440.

[2] "Social Security: A private matter?" *U.S. News & World Report*, July 29, p. 53.

[3] Cato Institute, "Privatizing Social Security: A Big Boost for the Poor," July 26, 1996.

[4] Lawrence J. White, "Investing the Assets of the Social Security Trust Funds in Equity Securities: An Analysis," *Investment Company Institute Perspective*, May 1996, p. 2. (The institute is the mutual fund industry's trade association.)

[5] *Ibid.*, p. 15.

[6] John B. Shoven, "The Coming Crisis in Social Security," *Investment Company Institute Perspective*, April 1996, p. 13.

on letter mail to items bearing postage of $2 or less.

Postal union leaders lost little time voicing their displeasure with the bill. In a letter to McHugh dated June 27, President Moe Biller of the American Postal Workers Union complained that giving private delivery firms access to mail boxes would "lead to a glut of unwanted materials and destroy the security and sanctity of the mail." He also said it would "open the door to privatization of the Postal Service — a concept to which we are adamantly opposed."

The proposed $2 ceiling on letter-mail delivery was blasted as a betrayal of the American principle of "universal postal services at reasonable and uniform prices. Over time, Biller predicted, "this $2 cap would allow private carriers to skim away more and more profitable, easy-to-serve areas of letter delivery and leave unprofitable areas for the Postal Service. . . .This is another unacceptable step toward privatization of letter-mail service."

Kenneth Vlietstra, executive director of the National Association of Postmasters of the United States, shares Biller's misgivings about partially lifting the USPS monopoly on letter mail. "Ever since the Continental Congress founded our postal system, the aim was to provide essentially the same service to all Americans no matter where they lived — whether in metropolitan or rural communities. In my opinion, the only way we can continue to provide that total, universal service at reasonable cost is through retention of the statutes that give the Postal Service the exclusive right to handle certain classes of mail."

Like Biller, Vlietstra also believes that private delivery companies would shed unprofitable routes. "United Parcel Service [UPS] used to go to Alaska," he notes. "And then, a couple of years ago, they pulled out, because it just wasn't profitable for them. UPS likes to say, 'We go everywhere.' But the truth is, they don't."

In sharp contrast to Biller and Vlietstra, Poole contends the McHugh bill doesn't go nearly far enough toward privatizing USPS. McHugh's proposals "probably are worthwhile tinkerings" with the existing system, he says, but "we need competition across the board to spur the kind of accountability, innovation and cost reduction that postal customers deserve. And we're not going to get that without real deregulation of the whole postal field."

In Poole's view, the Postal Service "has to become a private enterprise to compete effectively" in the open market. After cutting its ties to the government, USPS could "go to the capital markets for the money it needs to modernize in a major way."

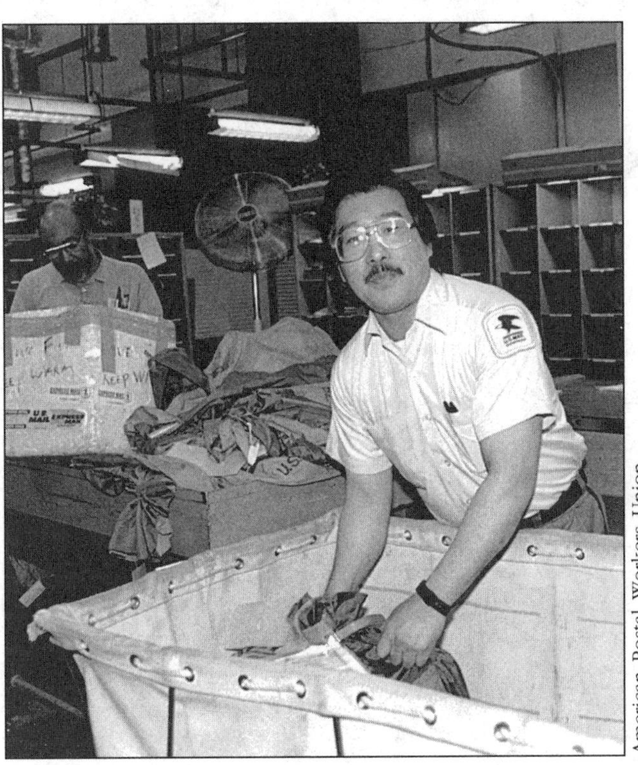

American Postal Workers Union

With more than 845,000 employees, the U.S. Postal Service is the nation's largest civilian employer.

Above all, Poole says the Postal Service "needs total freedom to revamp its work force. That means doing away with the Civil Service protection that stands in the way of deciding which people do which jobs, and so on. You've got to take a radical approach to achieve true reform. Other countries are doing that, and the McHugh bill doesn't come close."

Is labor-management acrimony over privatization easing?

In areas where public-employee unions are strong, efforts to privatize government services typically run into fierce opposition. However, the Labor Department's task force report suggested that confrontation increasingly may be yielding to cooperation. [20]

In the public workplace of the future, the report stated, traditional approaches to service delivery, workplace communication and collective bargaining "will not be sufficient." Recognizing this, "many state and local governments" have started "depending upon the participation of employees."

Workplace cooperation, the task force added, "requires that the confrontational rhetoric be lowered and that elected officials, union leaders and workers focus on their common tasks." This approach, in turn, can be "a doorway to reducing confrontation in collective bargaining relationships that have had a history of conflict." [21]

The task force cited numerous examples of labor-management cooperation in the delivery of government services. In Peoria, Ill., for example, health-care costs were climbing 9-14 percent a year at a time when municipal revenues were falling. To control costs, the city and the unions agreed in 1993 to take health care off the bargaining table and entrust it to a joint labor-management panel. The next year, health-care costs for city workers were $1.2 million less than the projected amount of $6 million. As a further "bonus," no health-care decisions in Peoria have gone to arbitration since the joint panel was formed. [22]

In Phoenix, Ariz., long at the forefront of local privatization efforts, labor-management détente brought similar results nearly 20 years ago. The opportunity arose in 1978, when a new fire chief and new president of the firefighters local took office and resolved to end almost 40 years of labor-management strife. "They initiated annual planning retreats, during which labor and management jointly develop annual plans for addressing problems and seeking improvement," the task force noted. "Arbitration has not been used in Phoenix for 10 years." [23]

Poole is among the privatization experts who question whether a broad nationwide trend can be extrapolated from these and other examples scattered through the task force report. "That's the public-employee union party line," says Poole. "But, 'Where's the beef?' I'm a skeptic waiting to be persuaded by the evidence."

Donald F. Kettl, a political science professor at the University of Wisconsin in Madison, believes that worker fear colors the privatization decisions made in both government and private industry. "There is more cooperation today, for sure, than there had been in the past on many fronts," he says. "But on the other hand, tensions are rising in the private sector because of management pressure to contract out and outsource work. And in the public sector, you'll find a mood bordering on panic at the prospect of contracting out more government work to private companies. It's fair to say that government employees are deeply worried about the threat that privatization poses for their job security."

Meanwhile, where privatization has bolstered efficiency, both labor and management often claim the credit. Stitt, for example, believes that the cooperation model touted in the task force report clearly applies to Indianapolis.

"We started out really at odds with our AFSCME union" when Goldsmith became mayor, he says. "Part of the problem was that we weren't communicating as well as we needed to. Another part concerned focus. When we made it clear that our goals were to lower the cost of government services while improving their quality, the local union leadership came to us and said, 'We believe we've got a vital role to play in that effort. And assuming there's a level playing field, we're interested in competing head-to-head for these services that you're thinking about moving into the private sector.' That was a key turning point. From that point on, we worked much more collaboratively than we did initially."

Stitt cites a recent example of such collaboration to illustrate his point. "When we solicited proposals for the operation of our sewer-collection system, our union partnered with a private vendor in going after the contract. When you contrast that with where we were four years ago, it's safe to say we've come a long way. That is, we and they together have come a long way."

The AFL-CIO's Bilik, who served on the Labor Department task force, views the Indianapolis experience from a rather different perspective. When Goldsmith became mayor, Bilik says, he soon realized he couldn't fulfill his pledge to privatize many of the non-uniformed services of the city government.

"So he cast about for a fallback position and said, 'I'm going to try to get our city employees to compete against private contractors, and see who can do the job most effectively. And we'll give it to whoever submits the best offer.'

"Once he started to do that, he forced the employees into a bidding process," Bilik continues. "But it has since become clear that the city workers do the best job. They do it much more cheaply, and more effectively, than any private contractor can. Even before Goldsmith became mayor, the union in fleet maintenance and the department director got together and started to work cooperatively without any threat of privatization. And they did a tremendous job."

That should have surprised no one, says Bilik, because "Working people, by and large, want to do a good job; they don't have to be threatened or whacked into submission. All they need is some recognition, appreciation and involvement. And they want to be asked what they think.

"To me, that's the essence of the whole thing. We encourage the leaders of all our unions to recommend to their members, and to the managers with whom they deal, that there be free and open entry into cooperative relations, with all issues discussed and with full effort made to improve the quality of service. That's our position as a labor organization, and it's shared by the leaders of all our unions." ■

BACKGROUND

Progressives' Reforms

Public-private partnerships have existed in the United States since the early days of the Republic. "It simply made no sense for the government to produce all of its own goods and services when private suppliers stood ready to do business with the government," Kettl wrote.

The suppliers ranged from naval "privateers" — non-governmental agents who took in customs duties at sea for a commission — to the original Secret Service, which was operated by the Pinkerton detective agency. Almost until 1900, the federal government jailed federal prisoners through contracts with state and local governments, which often allowed private companies to use the prisoners' labor. [24]

At the turn of the century, the Progressive Movement spurred demands for government action to check

Continued on p. 708

Chronology

1900s-1910s

Progressive reformers seek to impose government controls on railroads and corporations.

1903, 1906
The Elkins and Hepburn acts ban free passes and rebates on railroads and strengthen the authority of the Interstate Commerce Commission.

February 1918
The U.S. Railroad Administration begins operating the nation's railroads. Private control returns two years later.

—— • ——

1920s-1930s

In the heady economic climate after World War I, government regulation of private enterprise loses support. During the Depression, President Franklin D. Roosevelt revives the old Progressive program of the New Deal to spark the ailing economy.

—— • ——

1950s

Business finds a friendlier climate in Washington during the post-war Eisenhower administration.

1955
A Bureau of the Budget directive states, "The federal government will not start or carry on any commercial activity to provide a service or product for its own use if such product or service can be procured from private enterprise through ordinary business channels."

1960s

Privatization is suggested for the Tennessee Valley Authority (TVA), one of the proudest achievements of the New Deal.

1963
Sen. Barry Goldwater of Arizona, the 1964 Republican presidential nominee, proposes that the federally owned TVA be sold to private interests.

—— • ——

1980s

President Ronald Reagan and British Prime Minister Margaret Thatcher promote privatization.

1981
Congress privatizes the National Consumer Cooperative Bank.

November 1984
The British government sells its 50.2 percent stake in British Telecommunications Pc (British Telecom) for $4.8 billion.

1986
By prohibiting the use of tax-exempt financing, accelerated depreciation and investment tax credits for environmental infrastructure projects, the Tax Reform Act makes water and wastewater-treatment facilities less attractive as candidates for full private ownership.

March 26, 1987
Conrail, the federally owned freight carrier, is sold to the public for $1.65 billion.

1987
The British government sells the former British Airports Authority for $2.5 billion. BAA's properties included the three main London airports and four airports in Scotland.

—— • ——

1990s

State and local governments turn increasingly to privatization to trim costs and improve services.

Dec. 18, 1991
President Bush signs the Intermodal Surface Transportation Efficiency Act, permitting states to impose tolls on non-Interstate highways, bridges and tunnels, or even sell them to private enterprises.

1991
Gov. William F. Weld, R-Mass., voices interest in selling the Massachusetts Turnpike.

February 1992
Gov. Mario M. Cuomo, D-N.Y., says he will entertain offers from private interests wishing to buy the New York State Thruway.

April 30, 1992
Bush signs an executive order aimed at helping state and local governments sell or lease to private interests such publicly owned "infrastructure assets" as roads, bridges and airports.

September 1995
A 14-mile toll road links Dulles International Airport and Leesburg, Va. It is the first private toll road to be built in the United States in a century. Three months later, a private toll highway opens in suburban Los Angeles.

June 25, 1996
The Postal Reform Act of 1996 would allow the Postal Service to negotiate volume discounts with bulk mailers and to give private delivery companies access to residential mailboxes.

The Growing Global Privatization Club

The global privatization club keeps growing. In a July 11 address at the New York Stock Exchange, Israeli Prime Minister Benjamin Netanyahu invited U.S. business to invest in his country. "I'm committed to privatize just about all of the government firms and many of the government services," he said, "and we are eagerly seeking out experiences from other countries."

There are plenty of examples to choose from. Britain led the way toward privatization in the 1980s, as Prime Minister Margaret Thatcher sold off numerous government-owned enterprises to private business. Today, Latin America and the formerly communist countries of Eastern Europe are the pacesetters.

If experience elsewhere is any guide, Israelis probably will have mixed feelings about privatization. "Russians are unhappy about the spectacle of the state transferring potentially fabulous assets on the cheap to a coterie of rapacious insiders," *The Economist* noted last winter. "And Britons appear to be less cross about privatization in principle than about a handful of not obviously deserving utility bosses turning themselves into millionaires on the way" from public to private ownership.[1]

Nowhere, perhaps, has the privatization process been more difficult than in Eastern Europe. According to United Nations information officer Christopher McIntosh, the obstacles "include lack of a free-market culture; confusion over who owns the enterprises and how much they are worth; poor physical infrastructure, which discourages foreign investment; the absence of a legal framework governing the conduct of business; and shortage of investment capital."[2]

In such a climate, problems are almost sure to arise. For example, noted McIntosh, "when a government sells a viable enterprise, the profits go to investors, who tend to be wealthier than the average taxpayer. Thus, income disparities are increased. Other consequences can include higher prices for basic goods and services, large-scale layoffs, loss of national assets to foreign buyers and the possible closure of vital industries."

Nonetheless, privatization continues to advance throughout the region, including Russia. By July 1, 1994, when the first phase of Russia's privatization program ended, two-thirds of the nation's industry was in private hands, and 40 million Russians owned shares in privatized companies. Today, more than 75 percent of the country's work force is employed in the private sector. In addition, the Federal Property Fund, one of Russia's main privatization agencies, announced in June that it would sell stakes this year in six oil firms and the nation's biggest power producer. Boris Yeltsin's July 3 election to a second term as Russia's president signaled that his free-market reform program likely would remain on course.

Similar reforms are making inroads in Latin America. Last year, for example, the Brazilian Congress voted to end the government monopolies of telecommunications, oil refining and exploration, mining and coastal shipping. The purpose was to attract urgently needed foreign investment. Neighboring Argentina, meanwhile, reinvigorated its energy industry by auctioning off individual state-owned units to private investors, including North Carolina's Duke Power Co. and Louisiana's Entergy Corp. The privatization program brought improved service, sharply lower prices and escalating demand for electricity.

Mexico already has undergone widespread privatization, but there is resistance to privatizing one of the country's most sacred cows. In February, Mexican Energy Minister Jesus Reyes Heroles said he did not favor privatizing Petroleos Mexicanos (Pemex), the state oil monopoly. Three foreign energy companies had proposed a natural-gas development project in which they would share in the profits but not ownership of the gas reserves. Such an arrangement, they argued, would be permissible under the Mexican constitution.

Reyes disagreed. "Let's not lose time trying to come up with schemes to go around the law," he said. "We want to say loud and clear: 'Here is the line. It won't move.' "[3]

Meanwhile, Canada this summer will join 16 other countries that have privatized air traffic control systems, according to the Reason Foundation, which supports privatization. "They've shifted it out of being a government department, funded by taxes, and made it a stand-alone corporation funded by user fees," says foundation President Robert W. Poole Jr. "A new user-owned corporation, owned by the various segments of aviation, will buy the Canadian system from the government for $2 billion."

---

[1] "Selling the State, Contd.," *The Economist*, Dec. 9, 1995, p. 14.

[2] Christopher McIntosh, "To Market, to Market," *The Futurist*, January-February 1994, p. 24.

[3] Quoted in *The Wall Street Journal*, Feb. 20, 1996, p. A14.

Continued from p. 706

the social upheaval caused by industrialization after the Civil War. During the 1890s, for example, reform mayors such as Hazen Pingree in Detroit, James Phelan in San Francisco and Samuel Jones in Toledo, Ohio, were elected on platforms pledging municipal ownership of public utilities.

Urban reformers often were thwarted, however, because state legislatures, largely controlled by railroads and big corporations, blocked municipal agitation for greater control over their own local affairs. Consequently, progressives shifted their attention to gubernatorial politics. Their most noteworthy success was the election of Robert M. La Follette, who served as governor of Wisconsin from 1901 to 1906.

Among his achievements, La Follette won from the Legislature a state banking-control measure and an anti-lobbying law aimed at big corporations. Furthermore, corporate taxes were raised, a railroad commission was formed to set rates and a conservation commission was established. Similar laws and policies came into force in other states where progressives attained positions of power.

As progressives gained strength at the state level, they began to seek comparable influence in national politics. Some headway was made against the great corporate trusts during Theodore Roosevelt's presidency, when Congress approved two important laws regulating the railroads. (*See "Chronology," p. 707.*) Meanwhile, a series of exposés by muckraking journalists led to the passage of federal laws such as the Pure Food and Drug Act and the Meat Inspection Act (both 1906), which sought to combat abuses in the food industry.

William Howard Taft, who succeeded Roosevelt as president, staunchly opposed progressivism. But Woodrow Wilson, who followed Taft, endorsed many progressive measures, among them the Federal Reserve Act (1913), which reformed the currency system; the Clayton [Antitrust] Act (1914) and the Federal Trade Commission Act (also 1914), which extended government regulation of big business; and the Keating-Owen Act (1916), restricting child labor.

Railroad Experiment

With one notable exception, U.S. entry into World War I effectively ended the short but intense period of progressive reform in the United States. As a war-emergency measure, railroads were placed under the control of the United States Railroad Administration (USRA), headed by Treasury Secretary William G. McAdoo. President Wilson had taken possession of the railroads on Dec. 26, 1917, using a provision of the Army Appropriations Act of 1916. In doing so, he sought to achieve enough railroad efficiency to meet wartime transportation demands. Government operation of the railroads began in February 1918.

Under the new Federal Control Act of 1918, the president could guarantee the carriers annual compensation not to exceed the average of their net operating incomes in the three previous years. No carrier was to pay dividends in excess of its regular rate during the test period. The president was empowered to fix passenger fares and freight rates, subject to modification by the Interstate Commerce Commission (ICC), and to require carriers to make additions and improvements to their equipment.

In one sense, the experiment proved successful: The entire rail system became far more efficient than at any time previously. Accumulation of traffic at terminals had reached a peak in May 1917, when there was a nationwide "shortage" of 164,000 freight cars. At war's end in November 1918, the shortage had been virtually eliminated, despite an enormous surge of freight traffic in the intervening period. The reduction, however, was effected in part through such costly expedients as moving empty boxcars to areas where they were needed, sometimes across the country.

Walker D. Hines, who succeeded McAdoo as director general of USRA in January 1919, computed the average annual cost of operating the railroads under federal control at $4.4 billion, or 83 percent more than the average annual operating cost of $2.4 billion during the three-year period before the war. Hines pointed out, however, that the rise in operating costs was not out of line with increases in costs in private industry during the war. Moreover, he noted that the system of wartime government control did not have the advantage of permanency, which facilitates long-range planning.

While public opinion favored private ownership of the railroads after the war, organized labor and various farm organizations began campaigning for continued public operation. A proposal advanced in February 1919 by Glenn E. Plumb, counsel of the Associated Railway Employees of America, called for operation of the carriers by a National Railways Operating Corporation, managed by a board representing rail employees, rail management and the public. The federal government was to buy the railroad properties and lease them to the corporation, while the ICC was to retain power to regulate rates. A bill embodying the so-called Plumb Plan was introduced in the House in August 1919, but it never came to a vote. Six months later, in February 1920, the nation's railroads returned to private operation.

Policy Seesaw

In fact, the 1920s saw the resurgence of big business and conservative Republicanism on a major scale. In the heady postwar economic climate, government regulation of private enterprise no longer commanded broad popular support. The Progressive Party's last hurrah at the national level came in 1924, when La Follette ran as its presidential candidate and was able to carry only his home state of Wisconsin.

However, popular opinion shifted once more as the Great Depression worsened in the early 1930s. Hoping to spark the ailing economy, President Franklin D. Roosevelt revived and expanded the old progressive program under the banner of the New Deal. Legislative and policy proposals issued by the White House during the "Hundred Days" after FDR's inauguration left no doubt that the federal

The Big Business of Private Prisons

As recently as the early 1980s, "not a single privatized jail or prison [existed] either within or beyond the boundaries of the United States," writes Charles W. Thomas, director of the University of Florida Private Corrections Project. [1] What a difference a decade makes. At the end of 1995, 104 privately run adult correctional facilities with a combined rated capacity of 63,595 inmates were operating in this country.

Today, private firms manage correctional facilities in 18 states, the District of Columbia and Puerto Rico. [2] Overseas, private correctional facilities are operated in Australia and Britain. But the story doesn't end there. Last year, 10 states arranged to house some of their prison inmates in privatized facilities in other states. [3]

Prison privatization disturbs some policy-makers, who cite the potential for abuse of inmates when operators implement cost-trimming measures. History provides some justification for worry, Thomas told a House Judiciary subcommittee last year. He noted that Alabama and Florida "were involved in convict lease arrangements with private firms" until the 1920s. These deals "yielded significant financial benefits to both the firms and the coffers of the jurisdictions." [4]

Thomas went on to note that courts long maintained an arm's-length posture with respect to prison management. An 1891 Virginia Supreme Court decision, *Ruffin v. Commonwealth*, summed up the prevailing attitude for decades afterward: "[A prisoner] has, as a consequence of his crime, not only forfeited his liberty, but all his personal rights except those which the law in its humanity accord him. He is, for the time being, the slave of the state."

The situation today is quite different, Thomas testified: "[Correctional] facility contracts — whether by statute, contractual provisions or a combination of the two — prohibit private corrections management firms from deriving financial benefits either by charging prisoners a fee for the services they receive or by exploiting the labor of prisoners for their own [personal] benefit. In and of itself, this change in the relationships [that] contracts establish between government, private management firms and prisoners reduces the probability of many of the abuses that characterized private involvement in corrections previously."

From 1991 through 1995, the rated capacity of all privately operated adult correctional facilities grew at an average rate of 35.11 percent a year, according to Thomas. Recognizing that, "Nothing can continue to compound out at an annual average rate of growth of 35 percent," Thomas calculated that the rate would drop by 3 percent a year starting in 1996, eventually plateauing at 19 percent. Thomas projects a total inmate population of 236,036 in 2001.

At the start of 1995, 19 firms operated U.S. prisons; 17 remained at year's end. The two dominant companies are Corrections Corp. of America (CCA) and Wackenhut Corrections Corp., which together account for about 75 percent of the market.

Though Thomas feels that additional companies will enter the private corrections field, he senses a trend toward further consolidation. "The competitive and economic advantages of size are too consequential. Thus, the real question is not whether there will be more consolidation. Instead, it would appear to be a matter of who will merge with or acquire whom." [5]

---

[1] Charles W. Thomas and Dianne Bolinger (project assistant), *Private Adult Correctional Facility Census*, ninth edition, March 15, 1996, p. i.

[2] The 18 states with privatized prisons are Arkansas, California, Colorado, Florida, Kansas, Kentucky, Louisiana, Mississippi, Nevada, New Mexico, Oklahoma, Pennsylvania, Rhode Island, Tennessee, Texas, Utah, Virginia and West Virginia. Georgia is scheduled to join the list later this year.

[3] The 10 states that send inmates to prisons in other states are Alaska, Colorado, Hawaii, Missouri, New Mexico, North Carolina, Oklahoma, Oregon, Utah and Virginia.

[4] Testimony before House Judiciary Subcommittee on Crime, June 8, 1995.

[5] Thomas and Bolinger, *op. cit.*, p. v.

government intended to play a pivotal role in guiding the nation's economy. Congress and the Supreme Court generally went along, though often with great reluctance.

World War II sent progressivism into hibernation yet again. And with the 1952 election of Dwight D. Eisenhower — the first Republican to occupy the White House in 20 years — opposition to government interference in the economy began to mount. In 1955, the Bureau of the Budget (now the Office of Management and Budget, or OMB) issued a policy directive discouraging federal agencies from producing any "product or service [that] can be procured from private enterprise through ordinary business channels."

That policy has remained in force ever since. However, conservatives complain that it is honored more in the breach than in the observance. Joseph R. Wright Jr., former deputy director of the OMB, noted that a revised version issued in 1960 allowed for exceptions in cases where "procurement from commercial sources involved higher costs." [25]

As conservatives began to displace moderates as the Republican Party's dominant force during the 1960s, calls for privatization of government programs became more insistent. Sen. Barry Goldwater of Arizona, who was to be the 1964 GOP presidential nominee, made waves when he suggested in an Oct. 28, 1963, letter to Rep. Richard Fulton, D-Tenn., that the Tennessee Valley Authority (TVA) be sold to private interests. Goldwater argued that the massive public power network "would be better operated and . . . of more benefit for more people if it were part of private industry." He added that "it would be a benefit and a great boon to Tennessee to have TVA placed on the tax rolls."

Goldwater's proposal would raise no eyebrows today. In 1963, however, it came under fire even from Southern Republicans, who recognized that TVA was politically sacrosanct in the region it supplied with low-cost electricity and recreational waterways. Nonetheless, Goldwater would not yield. In a February 1964 news release, he said he meant only to turn "a federal white elephant into a more productive and useful part of our economy — without in any ways penalizing the people of the Tennessee Valley or taking anything away from them."

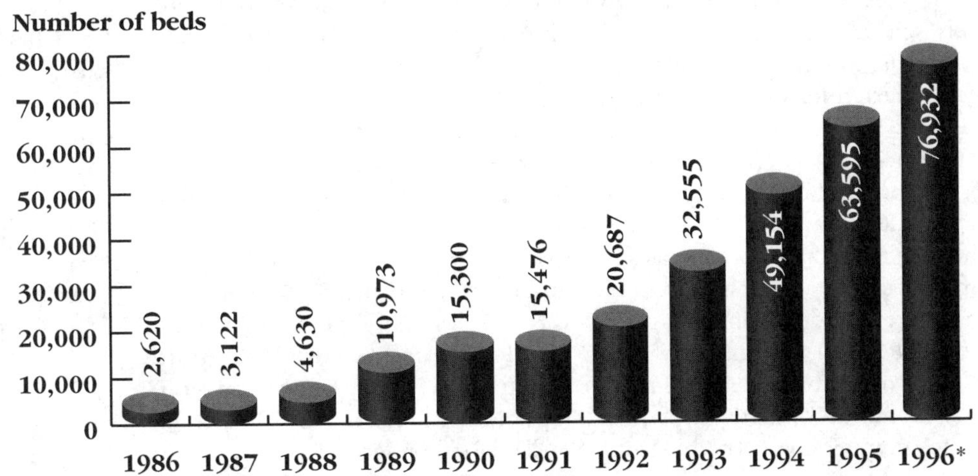

Because he lost the 1964 election to incumbent President Lyndon B. Johnson, Goldwater never got the chance to put his ideas about privatization into practice. Indeed, the term had yet to emerge. Peter F. Drucker, the celebrated business writer and consultant, is credited with originating the term in his 1969 book *The Age of Discontinuity*. The fledgling concept got an additional boost when Anthony H. Pascal, a Rand Corp. analyst, examined the private delivery of public services in a much-noted study published three years later. [26]

Reagan's Impact

By the time Ronald Reagan became president in 1981, privatization had become a prime domestic goal of the Republican Party. A 1988 OMB report summed up the general philosophy: "Competition is the driving force behind quality and economy of operations in the private sector. Private-sector managers are continually challenged by competitors who may force them out of business if they do not operate in the most efficient manner. This constant competitive pressure forces managers to be innovative and flexible as they promote performance-based management to serve their customers."

On the other hand, the report said, "Government managers, in normal operations, do not encounter the same pressures for efficiency that private sector managers do. . . .Competition with the private sector can highlight these inefficiencies and consequently help identify the changes necessary either to streamline the government operation or to determine whether the private sector can more efficiently perform the service." [27]

One of the Reagan administration's first efforts to privatize government assets involved the sale of millions of acres of federally owned land, mostly in Western states. "I want to open as much land as I can," Interior Secretary James G. Watt said. "The basic difference between this administration and the liberals is that we are market-oriented. We are trying to bring our abundant acres into the market so that the market will decide the value." [28]

The land-sale proposal was hailed by private industries that stood to benefit from it and by economic analysts who shared the administration's view that private enterprise can manage a large-scale land program more competently than government. However, the plan alienated many ranchers, who dreaded losing access to land they had long used for grazing. And real estate speculators and state land managers feared that massive sales of public land would depress property prices throughout the region for years to come.

When the dust settled, the opponents of land sales had carried the day. In July 1983, Watt withdrew lands controlled by the Interior Department from the sale program. Department officials said he had come to regard the plan as a political liability to Reagan, particularly in the West. Outrage over an insensitive joke Watt had told led to his resignation in October, and little more was heard of the land-sale program.

The Reagan administration was still committed to privatization, however. The issue returned to center stage in January 1984 with the final report of the President's Private Sector Survey on Cost Control, popularly known as the Grace commission.* The blue-ribbon panel cited numerous "random examples of bureaucratic absurdity" and predicted the federal government would post annual deficits of $1 trillion or more by the end of the century unless spending was brought under control. The antidote to such a financial debacle, the commission said, was the adoption of private-sector management practices.

The Grace commission's chief privatization proposal concerned the government's policy of selling federally subsidized electricity to customers in the Northwest at one-third the private-market rate. If the federal power were sold at market prices, the panel stated, revenues over three years would increase $4.5 billion.

The administration, meanwhile, was pursuing other privatization opportunities. In 1981, Reagan signed legislation directing the Treasury to dispose of its stock in the National Consumer Cooperative Bank by the end of the year. The bank was left to function as a private entity without further government assistance.

Then, in 1987, during the second Reagan administration, the government sold its 85 percent stake in Conrail, the federally owned freight carrier, for $1.65 billion — a deal that Transportation Secretary Elizabeth H. Dole called "the largest privatization in U.S. history." She predicted it would "break ground for more privatizations to come."

Report of the Commission on Privatization

Later that year, Reagan directed his newly appointed President's Commission on Privatization to evaluate past and current privatization ventures by U.S. and foreign governments and to develop a framework for future privatization efforts. The commission's report, released March 18, 1988, went well beyond previous Reagan attempts to trim the size of the federal government and sell off many of its assets.

In presenting the report, Linowes of the University of Illinois, the commission's chairman, described federal agencies as "muscle-bound to the point of paralysis when it comes to considering more effective alternatives." Government, he added, "should not be in the business of business."

The panel's 78 recommendations included:

- Repealing the statutes that give the Postal Service a monopoly on delivering letter mail;
- Selling Amtrak, the government-owned passenger rail network;
- Selling the federal government's $250 billion portfolio of housing, business, agricultural and educational loans;
- Converting airport traffic-control to private operation, with the federal government continuing "to regulate the national airspace" and to remain responsible for air safety; and
- Converting U.S. military commissaries and federal, state and local correctional facilities to private management.

"Our report," Linowes said, "is not about money, budgets or political ideologies. It is about programs and services and restoring to the American people their basic rights and obligations upon which our nation has been built." [29]

The report was issued at the start of the 1988 presidential campaign season, and there was no time to implement it before Reagan left office the following January. But privatization remained a key White House concern under George Bush, Reagan's successor.

Bush Carries On

In December 1991, for example, Bush signed into law the Intermodal Surface Transportation Efficiency Act (ISTEA), which reversed 70 years of federal opposition to toll roads. The law permits federal highway funds to be funneled into a variety of user-fee projects, including construction of new toll highways, bridges and tunnels and rebuilding of existing toll facilities. (*See "At Issue," p. 713.*)

Such projects may be privately owned under ISTEA, provided the state transportation agency has a contractual relationship with the private operator. The law also permits the federal matching share to run as high as 80 percent.

ISTEA's supporters predicted it would help states deal more effectively with the mounting problem of "crumbling infrastructure." Instead of scrambling for more tax revenue to finance bridge and road repairs, state governments could turn the job over to private enterprise and also realize a one-time windfall.

President Bush gave further encouragement to the privatization movement in an executive order issued April 30, 1992. Its aim was to help cities and states privatize "infrastructure assets" ranging from roads, power plants and rail systems to airports, housing, schools and hospitals.

The order greatly eased a financial regulation that had blocked many state

Continued on p. 714

* The commission was chaired by J. Peter Grace, chairman of W.R. Grace & Co.

At Issue:

Is privatization the best way to solve the nation's highway congestion problems?

Peter Samuel
Author of 1995 Cato Institute policy paper, "Highway Aggravation: The Case for Privatizing the Highways"

FROM *INSIGHT ON THE NEWS,* OCT. 9, 1995.

yes

Our cities are choking on traffic, and the gas-tax system of paying for highways has to go. . . .

The Federal Highway Administration estimates that the United States is spending $32 billion a year on roads overall but needs to spend $46 billion to maintain current conditions and $14 billion a year on top of that to overcome current deficiencies during the next 20 years. That kind of money isn't going to be generated from increased taxes because the American people won't stand for it. We need a radical reform of the way we run and fund our highways. . . .

Financing highway use by means of a federal gas tax is a crude, one-size-fits-all straitjacket. It charges automobile drivers far too much for the use of uncongested highways and far too little for the use of scarce rush-hour congested highway space in the big cities. The diesel-fuel tax on trucks needs overhauling as well: It bears no relation to the damage that trucks do to highway pavement and provides no incentive to truckers to configure their vehicles (with lighter loads or more axles) so as to minimize pavement damage. Tolls that could be varied by level of congestion, time of day and truck-axle weight would be a far more sensitive pricing instrument than fuel taxes, since they would reflect more closely the cost imposed by the user's use of the highway. . . .

The beauty of the market mechanism of tolls over the crude gas/diesel tax and hand-down system we currently suffer is that it provides the right incentives to the various participants. A state highway authority relying on increased gas taxes for its activities has an incentive to make life miserable for motorists, since frustrated drivers in stop-and-go traffic are most likely to support the state agency's higher funding. So, the state highway superintendent on that repaving job may ponder: Why rush to remove those cones closing off two out of three lanes well before the evening rush hour begins? By contrast, a for-profit toll company will lose its customers to "free" roads or competing toll facilities whenever it doesn't provide free-flowing conditions. . . .

And with time-variable tolls in rush hours (congestion pricing) there will be an incentive to a proportion of motorists to rearrange their trips out of the rush-hour highway lanes (rescheduling them, carpooling, taking transit or rearranging where they live, work, shop or visit), lessening the tendency for the facility to become overloaded and reducing the highway expansion required.

William D. Fay
President, Highway Users Federation for Safety and Mobility

FROM INSIGHT ON THE NEWS, OCT. 9, 1995.

no

Peter Samuel argues that, because traffic congestion is so annoying, roads should be sold off piecemeal to the highest (private) bidder, who would charge drivers for use. Because new technologies would make paying the tolls almost effortless, Samuel implies, no one would mind the charges. Congestion would end because drivers magically would find new routes to the workplace or be able to change their work schedules so that no one else would be on the road at the same time.

Someone should tell the Cato analysts that when formulating highway policy they should stand upwind from the gas fumes. Our roads do have problems, but congestion — while bad — isn't the worst of them. Our nation's highway system is the economic envy of the world. But it's falling apart. . . .

When Americans are asked to name programs in which government should be involved, they invariably name highways. When asked which roads are the best, they point to the federally funded interstates. They also believe the federal gas tax is justified if it goes toward road and bridge improvements. With so many other less popular candidates for privatization, why change the one that people applaud?

The Highway Users Federation supports a dialogue on federal vs. state roles, innovative financing and privatization. While there is a real need for more private capital in road construction, operation and maintenance, a federal highway program remains essential to meeting America's interstate commerce and national defense needs. There are better solutions to the problems threatening our nation's highways, including full funding of highway programs and more public-private partnerships. . . .

The Cato Institute's remedy to charge on a sliding scale according to road congestion adds up to a new tax on drivers. Instead of pushing people off the road and onto welfare, why not encourage companies to develop telecommuting programs, flextime and compressed workweeks?

If roads were owned by companies instead of government, the theory goes, private operators would rush to fix every pothole to keep customers. In exchange for their vigilance, drivers would pay happily to drive on these roads. Private investors are building roads for public use today in a few densely populated urban areas. These projects, if successful, will provide much-needed congestion relief, profiting both the investors and commuters.

But privately owned highways are not, and never will be, a substitute for the most successful transportation-development project history: the federal highway program. Among the most fundamental responsibilities of the federal government today is providing the financial wherewithal to maintain a coast-to-coast and border-to-border network of highways.

Continued from p. 712

and local privatization initiatives. It required states or cities that sold facilities built with federal aid to repay the amount originally contributed to the project by Washington.

Bush allowed state and local governments selling infrastructure assets to recoup their project costs first. If any money remained, the federal government would then get its share. Any remaining funds would be kept by the seller. Taxpayers "still come out ahead" under the Bush executive order, Poole declared. "The facilities will remain in use by the public, so the [federal] grants will have accomplished their intended purpose. And the privatized facilities will begin paying federal corporate income taxes." [30] ■

CURRENT SITUATION

Overcoming Obstacles

Four years later, it appears that the Bush executive order did little to bring about the sale or leasing of publicly owned infrastructure properties. According to the National Center for Public-Private Partnerships, the repayment requirement and difficulties in valuing such facilities have "virtually precluded efforts" to dispose of public assets. [31] To break the impasse, the center has urged that the power to sell government enterprises be codified in legislation and that the repayment provision be abolished.

Reimbursement provisions are by no means the sole obstacles to privatization at the federal level. For example, three Agriculture Department agencies — the Farmers Home Administration, the Agricultural Stabilization and Conservation Service and the Soil Conservation Service — must maintain minimum employment levels. This limits opportunities to save money by contracting out work to private companies.

Similarly, the Defense Department is barred from contracting out security and firefighting services, and the executive branch is prohibited from using appropriated funds to pay commercial firms to produce government publications. The publications ban is designed to protect the turf of the Government Printing Office (GPO), the congressional agency that publishes the *Congressional Record* and numerous federal reports, catalogs and documents. However, on occasion GPO itself invites bids from commercial suppliers on a wide variety of printing and binding services.

Despite all the roadblocks, privatization of federal programs creeps forward. On July 6, for example, the Office of Personnel Management (OPM) allowed employees in its Office of Investigations Service to form a profit-oriented private company to conduct background and security checks on federal job applicants. The new company, called U.S. Investigations Services Inc., was sold to the employees under an employee stock ownership plan (ESOP), a device that originated in the private sector. OPM Director James B. King called the initiative a "unique" arrangement "that no one else has done" in the federal government. [32]

Similarly, Poole told lawmakers last year, giving postal workers partial ownership of a privatized Postal Service would be the best way to reassure postal workers and their unions that privatization "is truly in their interest. Turning workers and managers into shareholders is one of the best-known ways to change the corporate culture of a bureaucratic enterprise, giving every individual a tangible stake in its success as a profitable private enterprise." He added, "Privatizing USPS could involve the creation of the world's largest employee stock ownership plan." [33]

However, privatization advocates doubt that Congress will approve so sweeping a change in the foreseeable future. Poole himself concedes he is frustrated by the lack of progress toward privatizing federal power generating and distribution systems. "It's fine that the Alaska PMA [power marketing administration], which is tiny, was privatized this year," he says, "but what about TVA [and] the other major enterprises owned and operated by the federal government that make it the largest single provider of electricity in the United States?

"Everybody else is getting out of electricity. It's being privatized in Italy, Germany, Britain, Argentina, Brazil and Australia, among other countries. Why isn't this happening in the United States? It's very bizarre that the issue is not even seriously on the national policy agenda."

The University of Florida's Thomas, likewise, is disappointed that privatization of federal prisons seems to be on indefinite hold. He says he was "surprised" by the Justice Department's recent announcement that the Bureau of Prisons (BOP) "is not going to privatize one or more of its facilities, as Clinton proposed in his fiscal 1996 budget message. The president recommended the privatization of four BOP facilities then being built, plus a majority of all future pretrial-detainee and low- and minimum-security facilities."

But when the proposal came before the House Appropriations Committee, Thomas notes, "the Republican-dominated panel said, in effect, 'This may be a little too much, too soon.' So the committee targeted a 2,000-bed facility under construction in Taft, Calif., and said, 'Let's use that as a pilot project.' And then the BOP decided it didn't want to go along with the idea."

Local-Level Progress

Why does the federal government continue to drag its feet on privatization, while many state and local governments eagerly embrace it? Linowes believes it's a question of perspective. "Generally, in all matters of this type, local administrators can function much more expeditiously than national administrators," he says. "They have freedom to experiment more. And they can see for themselves any improvements in areas such as garbage collection and water supply."

Another advantage, Linowes says, is that "the risks aren't as great in local government, and unions usually aren't as strong. On the national level, though, unions can be a major impediment to change." By the same token, state legislatures "are much more responsive to new ideas" than Congress is. "They're more receptive to requests by private industry to take over a government function, and they can get in and out of a privatization deal much more rapidly than federal officials can."

In Kettl's view, state and local governments are more comfortable with privatization than the federal government is because they were the first to feel acute fiscal stress. He notes that seven years separate Proposition 13, the tax-limitation initiative that California voters approved in 1978, and Gramm-Rudman, the mandatory deficit-reduction legislation that Congress passed in 1985.

As a result, state and local governments "got on the privatization bandwagon earlier," Kettl says. The jump-start, he says, nurtured a new kind of leadership at the state and local level — "mayors and governors who staked their reputations on trying much more aggressively than their predecessors did to improve government's performance."

Finally, says Kettl, "state and local governments simply provide more direct services than the national government. Most of what the national government does is write checks and manage contracts. If you're already contracting out a lot, as the federal government is, it's hard to contract out even more. The national government, in fact, has contracted out and relied on privatization strategies far more extensively than its critics realize." ■

OUTLOOK

More Opportunities?

Kettl anticipates no turning back from privatization gains made to date. "I expect privatization to continue at all levels of government," he says, "because the experience of cities such as Indianapolis and Phoenix shows not only a potential for saving money and improving services but also an opportunity to build political capital. Again and again, we've seen state and local officials squeeze political juice out of this."

At the national level, Kettl believes the country is "only at the first stage of a lengthy debate over what the federal government should do and how it should do it. [Vice President] Al Gore's National Performance Review and [House Speaker] Newt Gingrich's "Contract With America" were just the opening salvos of that battle."

Linowes also sees privatization gaining ground, "because it has proved its effectiveness. There will be slip-ups here and there. But by and large, government institutions will have to develop a sense of entrepreneurship if they want to continue functioning effectively."

At the same time, Linowes believes, private industry will continue to try to outperform government. "That will produce a healthy, marketplace situation in which the party that delivers the products or services more effectively — be it public or private — wins out in the long run. Only after we abandon the myth that government *must* provide certain services will government be able to meet the needs of the people more effectively than private industry can."

The University of Kansas' Frederickson also envisions further privatizing of government programs, but he is not enthusiastic at the prospect. What bothers him is that privatization's failures, notably in elementary and secondary education, often are blamed on unions. "People aren't willing to say, 'Hey, isn't it possible that privatization wasn't a good idea to start with?'

"The real issue, in my opinion, is how much people are willing to pay for quality services. I'll readily grant that abuses occur in government; and some terrible things go on in the public sector. But I'm pretty sure they won't be solved by privatization."

In Deputy Mayor Stitt's opinion, the ongoing fiscal squeeze and limited opportunities to engage in deficit spending assure that state and local governments will continue to embrace privatization. "In Indianapolis, we're entering our eighth consecutive year of a property-tax freeze," he says. "Even so, our citizens are still demanding that we do a better job. We hope to rise and meet that challenge."

Even in communities skeptical of the contracting-out process, Stitt believes, "people will find it tougher and tougher to get by without capturing the savings that privatization brings. I have heard mayors and staff people from around the country say, 'We really ought to focus on these issues now, before we get into a situation where we have to lay off lots of city workers.' "

Indianapolis' privatization experience, says Stitt, is notable for "the scope, the intensity and the pace at which we've pursued competition as a core strategy. It's not that we were a city in trouble to begin with. In fact, there was

FOR MORE INFORMATION

Investment Company Institute, 1401 H St. N.W., 12th floor, Washington, D.C. 20005-2148; (202) 326-5800. ICI, the mutual fund industry's trade association, frowns on the diversion of Social Security Trust Fund revenue to equity mutual funds.

Reason Foundation, 3415 S. Sepulveda Blvd., Suite 400, Los Angeles, Calif. 90034; (310) 391-2245. The foundation promotes privatization of government programs in the United States and overseas and publishes books and journals on the issue.

Private Corrections Project, Center for Studies in Criminology and Law, University of Florida, Gainesville, Fla. 32611-5950; (904) 392-1025. The corrections project tracks developments at the state and local levels.

Public Employee Department, AFL-CIO, 815 16th St. N.W., Washington, D.C. 20006; (202) 393-2820. The department represents unions of public workers at all levels of government.

a good deal of opposition initially from folks who said, 'We're not a city in crisis. Why should we do this?'

"But the mayor encouraged us not to look two or four years down the road, but 20 years. As we did that, we saw potential trends that concerned us, such as slowing or even diminishing population growth, disparities in income between suburban and urban residents and continuing flight of wealth and economic opportunity from the community.

"So, we asked ourselves, 'How can we create wealth in our community, rather than redistributing it?' And privatization, or whatever you want to call it, was one of the strategies we chose."

But to New York City union President Albano, better management, not privatization, is the answer to increased efficiency. "Our most successful companies treat their frontline workers as assets, not expendable parts," he told lawmakers last year. "These companies have transformed themselves by replacing the hierarchical workplace of old with one that respects workers' knowledge and experience. . . . If we were to begin with this assumption, I believe we would be asking ourselves a different question today. Not how do we find ways to privatize more public services, but rather what is the mission of government and what kind of work force is necessary to carry out that mission.

"[I]n the case of our own experiences with engineering and architectural services in New York City . . . we would save money and improve the quality of service . . . if more of this work were done in-house." [34] ■

Notes

[1] Address to Indianapolis Chamber of Commerce, Indiana Convention Center, Jan. 30, 1992.

[2] Reason Foundation, "Privatization 1996: A Comprehensive Report on Privatization of Government Assets, Enterprises, and Public Services," 1996, p. 7.

[3] See "Social Security: A private matter?" *U.S. News & World Report,* July 29, 1996, p. 53.

[4] Quoted in Reason Foundation, *op. cit.,* p. 1.

[5] Gov. Pete Wilson, "Competitive Government: A Plan for Less Bureaucracy, More Results," April 1996, p. 14.

[6] Quoted in Reason Foundation, *op. cit.,* p. 6.

[7] Testimony before the Joint Economic Committee, Feb. 5, 1996.

[8] Testimony before House Government Reform and Oversight Subcommittee on Government Management, Information and Technology, March 14, 1995.

[9] Testimony before the Joint Economic Committee, Feb. 5, 1996.

[10] Testimony before House Judiciary Subcommittee on Crime, June 8, 1995.

[11] For background, see "Labor Movement's Future," *The CQ Researcher,* June 28, 1996, pp. 553-576.

[12] Testimony before House Government Reform and Oversight Subcommittee on Government Management, Information and Technology, March 14, 1995.

[13] *Loc. cit.*

[14] Quoted in U.S. Labor Department, "Working Together: Report of the U.S. Secretary of Labor's Task Force on Excellence in State and Local Government Through Labor-Management Cooperation," May 1996, p. 37.

[15] *Loc. cit.*

[16] Stephen Goldsmith, "The Politics of Privatization," in "Privatization 1996," *op. cit.,* p. 12. (Excerpted from remarks at the Reason Foundation's 21st Century Government conference, September 1995.)

[17] Quoted in Reason Foundation, *op. cit.,* p. 25.

[18] David Osborne and Ted Gaebler, *Reinventing Government: How the Entrepreneurial Spirit Is Transforming the Public Sector* (1992), p. 45.

[19] Reason Foundation, *op. cit.,* p. 3.

[20] The 14-member task force was headed by Mayor Jerry Abramson of Louisville, Ky., and former Gov. James J. Florio, D-N.J., and also included labor and management representatives and academics.

[21] U.S. Labor Department, *op. cit.,* p. 3.

[22] *Ibid.,* p. 4.

[23] *Ibid.,* p. 5.

[24] Donald F. Kettl, *Sharing Power: Public Governance and Private Markets* (1993), p. 7. For additional historical background, see "Privatization," *The CQ Researcher,* Nov. 13, 1992, pp. 985-1008.

[25] Joseph R. Wright Jr., "Let's Get the Feds to Use the Private Sector," *The Privatization Review,* winter 1987, p. 28.

[26] Anthony H. Pascal, "Clients, Consumers and Citizens: Market Mechanisms for the Delivery of Public Services," paper presented at the Conference on Centrally Planned Social Change, Quail's Roost, N.C., April 1972.

[27] Office of Management and Budget, "Enhancing Governmental Productivity Through Competition: A New Way of Doing Business Within the Government to Provide Quality Government at Least Cost," August 1988, p. 1.

[28] Quoted in *The New York Times,* July 3, 1982.

[29] Press release accompanying report of the President's Commission on Privatization, March 18, 1988.

[30] Robert W. Poole Jr., "Invest in Infrastructure — Privatize," *The Wall Street Journal,* May 5, 1992.

[31] Statement submitted to House Government Reform and Oversight Subcommittee on Government Management, Information and Technology, March 14, 1995.

[32] Quoted in *The Washington Post,* April 14, 1996, p. A4.

[33] Testimony before House Budget Committee, March 1, 1995.

[34] Testimony before House Government Reform and Oversight Subcommittee on Government Management, Information and Technology, March 14, 1995.

Bibliography

Selected Sources Used

Books

Kettl, Donald F., *Sharing Power: Public Governance and Private Markets,* The Brookings Institution, 1993.
Shifting from public to private operation does not automatically make a government program less expensive and more efficient, writes Kettl, a political science professor at the University of Wisconsin. "Market competition substitutes one set of problems, revolving around conflicts of interest and monitoring, for the manifest problems of direct government administration. The problems associated with the market must be managed, not chanted away with the competition mantra."

Osborne, David, and Ted Gaebler, *Reinventing Government: How the Entrepreneurial Spirit Is Transforming the Public Sector*, Addison-Wesley, 1992.
"Privatization is one arrow in government's quiver," argue Osborne and Gaebler. "But just as obviously, privatization is not the solution. Those who advocate it on ideological grounds — because they believe business is always superior to government — are selling the American people snake oil."

Articles

McIntosh, Christopher, "To Market to Market: Navigating the Road to Privatization," *The Futurist*, January-February 1994.
This survey of privatization efforts in foreign countries concludes that "Legal and physical infrastructures tend to be more conducive to privatization in the developed market economies than in the developing countries or in the transitional economies. Nevertheless, some very poor countries have had successes in their privatization programs."

Pulley, John, "U.S. Air Force Inc.: The Privatization of Newark AFB, Ohio," *Federal Times*, July 8, 1996.
Pulley describes the hard choices facing longtime employees of Ohio's Newark Air Force Base, which has been bought by Rockwell International Corp. and is scheduled this fall to become a private operation called Rockwell Guidance Repair Center.

Shenk, Joshua Wolf, "The Perils of Privatization," *The Washington Monthly*, May 1995.
Many of the complaints about inefficient, unresponsive government stem from shoddy contracting practices, writes Shenk. "Without clear guidelines, good information on what [private] contractors are doing and the ability to fire them when they screw up, government often ends up spending much more than it would cost to do the work with its own employees."

Reports and Studies

Investment Company Institute, *Investing the Assets of the Social Security Trust Funds in Equity Securities: An Analysis,* May 1996.
This study by the ICI, which represents publicly traded investment funds, examines proposals to head off a Social Security funding crisis by investing part of the money in the Trust Funds in U.S. corporate stocks and bonds. It concludes that such a course would entail more risk and, possibly, less return than proponents believe.

Reason Foundation, *Privatization 1996*, 1996.
In its 10th annual report on privatization, the Reason Foundation, a leading advocate of privatization, reviews notable 1995 developments at the local, state and federal levels as well as in foreign countries.

U.S. Department of Labor, *Working Together for Public Service: The Secretary of Labor's Task Force on Excellence in State and Local Government Through Labor-Management Cooperation,* May 1996.
The task force argues that "cooperative workplace partnerships" between management and labor hold the key to service improvement in the future. "A focus on service with employee participation can also be a doorway to reducing confrontation in collective bargaining relationships that have had a history of conflict," the task force notes.

House Government Reform and Oversight Subcommittee on Government Management, Information and Technology, *Hearing on The Federal Role in Privatization* (published proceedings of hearings on March 14, 1995).
Proponents and critics of privatization air their views on what the federal government should and should not do to clear the path for private operation of government programs.

Thomas, Charles W., and Dianne Bolinger, *Private Adult Correctional Facility Census,* Ninth edition, March 15, 1996.
Thomas, director of the University of Florida's Private Corrections Project, reviews 1995 developments in prison privatization, a movement that dates only from the early 1980s.

House Committee on the Budget, *Privatization*, (published proceedings of hearings on Feb. 28 and March 1, 1995).
Privatization supporters, including Rep. Scott L. Klug, R-Wis., University of Illinois Professor David F. Linowes and Reason Foundation President Robert W. Poole Jr. explain why government, private enterprise and taxpayers all would benefit if more public programs were privately operated.

The Next Step

Additional information from UMI's Newspaper & Periodical Abstracts database

International Privatization Efforts

Barrie, Chris, "Government attacked for privatization 'failure'," *The Guardian*, Aug. 9, 1995, p. 14.
On Aug. 8, 1995, the UK government was warned that its privatization of the gas, water, telecommunications and electricity industries had failed in promoting competition and giving customers a wider choice of supplier.

Bokhari, Farhan, "Pakistani government rings up investors for phone privatization," *The Christian Science Monitor*, Nov. 29, 1995, p. 9.
The 1995 privatization of parts of the Pakistan Telecommunications Corp is discussed. The response to the offer of shares in PTC may determine the response by investors to other privatization plans.

Castaneda, Jorge G., "A cooling trend settles on government 'fire sales'," *Los Angeles Times*, April 12, 1996, p. B9.
Castaneda discusses backlash against privatization in Latin America, noting that mass demonstrations in La Paz, Bolivia, in March 1996, indefinitely delayed the privatization of Bolivia's oil industry. Castaneda says there are lessons to be learned and errors not to repeat in the privatizations.

Curtin, Matthew, "South Africa's privatization gets going as government guidelines are unveiled," *The Wall Street Journal*, Sept. 5, 1995, p. A9.
South Africa's long-awaited and still politically sensitive privatization program is off the ground with the release of government guidelines, an essential first step in a process that promises rich rewards for President Nelson Mandela's administration and foreign investors.

Foot, Paul, "Government in the golden age of avarice," *The Guardian*, Aug. 28, 1995, p. 11.
Foot comments on British political issues from late August 1995 and criticizes the takeover of the private electricity monopoly in southwest Britain by an American company. Foot says that this scandal will be repeated as foreign companies take advantage of the low prices at which public utilities were privatized.

"Manitoba government plans privatization of telephone system," *The Wall Street Journal*, May 3, 1996, p. A2.
The Manitoba, Canada, government said it intends to privatize the government-owned Manitoba Telephone System, which operates the province's telephone network. Winnipeg said it would introduce legislation to authorize an initial public offering of the utility's stock.

Surovtsev, Dmitry, "Gazprom follows unique course to privatization," *Oil & Gas Journal*, March 25, 1996, pp. 62-65.
Gazprom, Russia's officially sanctioned gas monopoly, faces a number of challenges on the road to privatization, including financing a major pipeline and collecting on debts. Gazprom's privatization plan is examined.

Privatization at the Federal Level

Carney, Dan, "Gingrich proposals lessen government role in space," *The Houston Post*, March 4, 1995, p. A14.
House Speaker Newt Gingrich, R-Ga., said he favored privatizing NASA's space shuttle program and would push for passage of legislation by the end of the year setting up a tax-free zone for any product manufactured in space.

Dickinson, Rachel, "The rush to sell off government," *American Demographics*, February 1996, p. 41.
In recent years, the trend to put many government services into private hands has grown rapidly in recent years. Efforts to downsize government are discussed.

Fitzgerald, Mark, "Should government information be privatized?" *Editor & Publisher*, Nov. 11, 1995, pp. 30-31.
First Amendment activists are sounding the alarm that ordinary citizens are losing access to public information as private-sector firms gain greater control of government records. However, the private-sector firms say their role is as important as the press' in preserving liberty.

"Government phasing in direct loans; Congress to take Sallie Mae private," *Chicago Tribune*, June 8, 1995, p. 3.
A House panel approved legislation to convert the federally chartered Student Loan Marketing Association into a private company. The bill has the backing of the leadership in both houses of Congress.

Lesher, Richard L., "Privatization is the key," *Chicago Defender*, Aug. 7, 1995, p. 12.
Lesher suggests that instead of abolishing several government agencies and public assistance programs outright, Congress should cut them loose to see if they can make it on their own as competitive providers in the free-enterprise marketplace.

Lochhead, Carolyn, "A radical plan to shrink government," *San Francisco Chronicle*, April 18, 1995, p. A3.
On April 17, 1995, the Heritage Foundation unveiled a plan that would balance the budget by the year 2000 through the wholesale elimination of federal agencies, mass privatization and a major governmental reorganization.

"Private Eyes and Government Files," *The New York*

Times, **July 6, 1996, p. A18.**
An editorial criticizes the Clinton administration's plan to turn over to private business 40 percent of its employee security checking, asserting that the potential for misuse of privileged information is too great.

Wolf, Richard, "Making government someone else's business," ***USA Today,*** **June 22, 1995, p. A6.**
As part of its drive to balance the federal budget, the House will vote on contracting out services at the U.S. Capitol, everything from raising the flags to cutting hair in the barbershop. That measure, part of a $1.7 billion spending bill for Congress, is a small but symbolic part of the federal goverment's drive to privatize. Arguments pro and con on privatization are presented.

Privatization vs. Public Sector

Chen, David W., "Privatization: Leaner government, or just another fad?" ***The New York Times,*** **May 28, 1995, p. 6.**
In an interview conducted by conference call, Lewis M. Eisenberg and Marc Holzer discuss the issue of privatization of government services. Holzer, the director of the National Center for Public Productivity and a Rutgers University professor, says the public sector should be made more competitive, whereas Eisenberg, the chairman of the New Jersey Advisory Council on Privatization, endorses the plans of Gov. Christine Todd Whitman, R-N.J., to privatize services.

Frederickson, George H., "When it's better to be a customer of government," ***Governing,*** **April 1996, p. 10.**
Frederickson uses the example of electrical utilities to demonstrate how governments can often be more effective than businesses in terms of customer service. The lessons learned from electric utilities suggest that privatization plans may be unwarranted.

Goodman, John C., "Welfare privatization," ***The Wall Street Journal,*** **May 28, 1996, p. A18.**
Goodman says that after more than 30 years of the War on Poverty, the federal government has proved it does a poor job of dispensing welfare. Goodman calls for the privatization of welfare.

"In an era of shrinking government, is privatization the American way?" ***Civil Engineering,*** **October 1995, pp. 22-24.**
Many people are beginning to feel that privatization is the way to save the U.S. This falls in line with federal budget cuts and the return of power to the states and localities.

Linowes, David, "The rationale for privatization," ***Vital Speeches of the Day,*** **Nov. 15, 1995, pp. 86-88.**
Privatization is a recognition that government in any guise cannot be all things to all people. The proper division of responsibility between business and government when resolving the question of privatization is discussed.

Mollins, Carl and John DeMont, "Prisons for profit," ***Maclean's,*** **June 5, 1995, pp. 34-36.**
The latest trends in penal treatment in the U.S. include privatized prisons and hard time. Some of these companies are showing spectacular financial success. Many feel that New Brunswick may become the first Canadian province to allow privately run prisons.

State and Local Initiatives

Baker, Peter, "Face of Va. government changes little," ***The Washington Post,*** **July 19, 1995, p. B1.**
Even as Gov. George Allen, R-Va., pursues his crusade to restructure state government, his initiatives to turn over a variety of functions to private business are creating more opportunities for insiders to profit from their connections, which raises a series of ethics questions.

Behr, Peter, "Solving the privatization puzzle: In anti-tax atmosphere, District considers plan to contract out services," ***The Washington Post,*** **February 13, 1995, p. 1.**
The efforts of the Washington, D.C., city government to join a rapidly growing parade of cities and states that are turning major government services over to private contractors who promise to save taxpayers money by doing the work more cheaply are described.

Connors, Thom, and Dick Shaff, "Three cities reduce government subsidy of public assistance facilities," ***Nation's Cities Weekly,*** **Aug. 14, 1995, pp. 9-10.**
Some government officials have streamlined their operations and are offering better services as a result of privatizing public assembly facilities. Officials in Denver, Colo., Mobile, Ala., and Long Beach, Calif., privatized public assembly facilities and have had great success with their efforts.

Goodale, Gloria, "Orange County's new rallying cry: Slice government thinner," ***The Christian Science Monitor,*** **Feb. 27, 1995, p. 3.**
Orange County, Calif., residents are using the continuing county government crisis to redefine government by downsizing and restructuring county administration and management, privatizing some services and selling government assets. The county announced a $1.7 billion loss from risky investments in Dec. 1994.

Greene, Donna, "Board fails to block O'Rourke's main privatization plans," ***The New York Times,*** **Jan. 7, 1996, p. WC1.**
With the ink barely dry on the $948.8 million 1996 Westchester County, N.Y., budget and fresh from victories for privatization, County Executive Andrew P. O'Rourke is forecasting that other forced savings are in store for the county.

Kim, Lillian Lee, "Privatization catching on in government," ***Atlanta Constitution,*** **June 1, 1995, p. XJ1.**
Keeping pace with the metrowide trend toward privatizing government services, Gwinnett County, Ga., hires outside firms to handle some large projects, and the Republican administration hopes to pare down operations even further.

Back Issues

Great Research on Current Issues Starts Right Here...Recent topics covered by The CQ Researcher are listed below. Before May 1991, reports were published under the name of Editorial Research Reports.

FEBRUARY 1995
Cracking Down on Immigration
The Business of Sports
Reinventing Government
Housing Discrimination

MARCH 1995
Death Penalty Debate
Primary Care
Democracy in Africa
Environmental Movement at 25

APRIL 1995
Abortion Clinic Protests
Dieting and Health
Combating AIDS
Rethinking Affirmative Action

MAY 1995
Assisted Suicide Controversy
Overhauling Social Security
Learning to Read
Mandatory Sentencing

JUNE 1995
Combating Infectious Disease
Property Rights
Repetitive Stress Injuries
Regulating the Internet

JULY 1995
War Crimes
Highway Safety
Combating Terrorism
Preventing Teen Drug Use

AUGUST 1995
Job Stress
Organ Transplants
United Nations at 50
Advances in Cancer Research

SEPTEMBER 1995
Catholic Church in the U.S.
Northern Ireland Cease-Fire
High School Sports
Teaching History

OCTOBER 1995
Quebec's Future
Revitalizing the Cities
Networking the Classroom
Indoor Air Pollution

NOVEMBER 1995
The Working Poor
The Jury System
Sex, Violence and the Media
Police Misconduct

DECEMBER 1995
Teens and Tobacco
Gene Therapy's Future
Global Water Shortages
Third-Party Prospects

JANUARY 1996
Emergency Medicine
Punishing Sex Offenders
Bilingual Education
Helping the Homeless

FEBRUARY 1996
Reforming the CIA
Campaign Finance Reform
Academic Politics
Getting Into College

MARCH 1996
The British Monarchy
Preventing Juvenile Crime
Tax Reform
Pursuing the Paranormal

APRIL 1996
Centennial Olympic Games
Managed Care
Protecting Endangered Species
New Military Culture

MAY 1996
Russia's Political Future
Marriage and Divorce
Year-Round Schools
Taiwan, China and the U.S.

JUNE 1996
Rethinking NAFTA
First Ladies
Teaching Values
Labor Movement's Future

JULY 1996
Recovered-Memory Debate
Native Americans' Future
Crackdown on Sexual Harassment
Attack on Public Schools

AUGUST 1996
Fighting Over Animal Rights

Back issues are available for $5.00 (subscribers) or $8.00 (non-subscribers). Quantity discounts apply to orders over ten. To order, call Congressional Quarterly Customer Service at (202) 887-8621.

Binders are available for $18.00. To order call 1-800-638-1710. Please refer to stock number 648.

Future Topics

- ***Child Labor and Sweatshops***
- ***Cleaning Up Hazardous Wastes***
- ***Gambling***

THE CQ Researcher

PUBLISHED BY CONGRESSIONAL QUARTERLY INC.

Child Labor and Sweatshops

Do U.S. consumers abet worker exploitation?

American shoppers may not know it, but many of the name-brand products they purchase — from clothing to carpets to sports equipment — were made under appalling circumstances. Grim reports of worker exploitation contain images straight out of a Charles Dickens novel: children kidnapped and sold into prostitution, or toiling at age four in hazardous worksites alongside adults struggling for subsistence-level wages. Though the bulk of the abuse takes place in Third World countries, Americans were stunned by the recent discovery of virtual slave-labor conditions in garment sweatshops in California and New York City. Now a growing movement of U.S. and international officials, union and business leaders, human rights activists and celebrities has mobilized to challenge these deep-rooted practices.

INSIDE THIS ISSUE

CQ August 16, 1996 • Volume 6, No. 31 • Pages 721-744

Formerly Editorial Research Reports

CHILD LABOR AND SWEATSHOPS

THE ISSUES

BACKGROUND

CURRENT SITUATION

OUTLOOK

SIDEBARS AND GRAPHICS

FOR FURTHER RESEARCH

COVER: A YOUNG GIRL IS AMONG THE SCRAP PICKERS IN A PHILIPPINES GARBAGE DUMP. (INTERNATIONAL LABOUR OFFICE/J. MAILLARD)

August 16, 1996
Volume 6, No. 31

EDITOR
Sandra Stencel

MANAGING EDITOR
Thomas J. Colin

ASSOCIATE EDITORS
Sarah M. Magner
Richard L. Worsnop

STAFF WRITERS
Charles S. Clark
Mary H. Cooper
Kenneth Jost

EDITORIAL ASSISTANT
Tonya Harris

PUBLISHED BY
Congressional Quarterly Inc.

CHAIRMAN
Andrew Barnes

VICE CHAIRMAN
Andrew P. Corty

EDITOR AND PUBLISHER
Neil Skene

EXECUTIVE EDITOR
Robert W. Merry

The CQ Researcher (ISSN 1056-2036). Formerly Editorial Research Reports. Published weekly (48 times per year, not printed March 1, May 31, Aug. 30, Nov. 29) by Congressional Quarterly Inc., 1414 22nd St., N.W., Washington, D.C. 20037. Annual subscription rate for libraries, businesses and government is $319. Additional rates furnished upon request. Periodicals postage paid at Washington, D.C. POSTMASTER: Send address changes to The CQ Researcher, 1414 22nd St., N.W., Washington, D.C. 20037.

Child Labor and Sweatshops

BY CHARLES S. CLARK

THE ISSUES

Women who shop at upscale clothing stores have a connection with Nancy Peñaloza. She makes the clothes they wear to work. For the past nine years, the thirtyish seamstress has been sewing business suits that retail for $120 and up. Her cut: $6 per outfit. She is able to feed her family by putting in at least 56 hours a week, usually taking home $207. Unlike the women who wear her suits, Peñaloza gets no vacation or holidays off. And her employer does not pay her Social Security taxes.

"The shop is hot in the summer and cold in winter, and the boss is angry and screams," she says in halting English. "I cannot ask him questions because I am scared he will hit me. There is one bathroom for 100 people. If I were to ask for overtime pay, I would be fired."

Peñaloza's bleak account may conjure images of a Third World sweatshop, but as she revealed recently, she works in New York's famous garment district. She went public with her story in July, appearing at the behest of the Labor Department before a conference of apparel industry executives, human rights activists and Labor officials, including Secretary Robert B. Reich.

Sweatshops and child labor — supposedly eradicated in the U.S. early in the century — have re-emerged dramatically on the global landscape, just as the century is wrapping up.

In the past year, several events have propelled the issue onto American consumers' radar screens. In August 1995, law enforcement officers freed 72 illegal Thai immigrants who were being held behind barbed-wire in a compound in El Monte, Calif., near Los Angeles. They had been working as virtual slaves in an around-the-

clock garment factory. During the trial of the owners, the workers said they had been paid 69 cents an hour to fill the racks of such American stores as Montgomery Ward's and Sears. [1]

In Canada last year, a 12-year-old boy drew world attention to the tragedy of child labor. Craig Kielburger, of Thornhill, Ont., founded the group Free the Children after hearing about the assassination of a Pakistani boy his own age who had been agitating against child labor. Craig gathered thousands of signatures calling for an import ban on products made with child labor and presented the petition to Canadian Prime Minister Jean Chretien. [2]

In May, TV talk-show host Kathie Lee Gifford found herself being vilified after a human rights activist charged that her Wal-Mart fashion line was being produced with child and sweatshop labor. (*See story, pp. 726.*) But Gifford surprised her critics. Newly sensitized to the problem of child labor, she re-emerged as an activist and weathered the unflattering publicity. "I want to leave this planet a very different place for my children," she told a congressional panel in July. "Why should other children be denied childhood — the basic right to bounce a ball, to play with jacks, to be safe? Why should my child be born to privilege and others to suffering?" [3]

Around the world, there are at least 73 million child laborers* ages 10-14, according to the United Nations' International Labour Organization (ILO) in Geneva, Switzerland. The ILO puts the figure for working children of all ages at up to 200 million, noting that 25 percent of all the children in Africa are working. In Asia the figure is 18 percent, in Latin America, 7 percent.

Most labor abuses take place in industries producing everyday products such as clothing, toys, sneakers, carpets and sports equipment. But some of the worst cruelties are found in areas where household slave labor is common, such as the Sudan, and in the underground world of forced child prostitution, which is rampant in Thailand and the Philippines. [4]

The dangers of child labor are not always apparent to the employers and parents who encourage it. "Pound for pound, children breathe more air, eat more food and drink more water than adults," says Philip J. Landrigan, a pediatrician at New York City's Mount Sinai Medical Center. "So if there are chemical contaminants in the workplace, children will be exposed to more of them. Children are also less biologically mature and less physically strong, which makes them more susceptible to injury. They're more likely to trip or get caught in machinery, and their bodies have more trouble breaking down chemical toxins and excreting them. Finally, children may be

---

* Millions of children work as bonded laborers, defined by the ILO as forced labor in payment for the debts of the child's parents or work offered under a false pretext from which children are not allowed to leave. Bonded child labor also includes children who are kidnapped and exported as prostitutes or camel riders, "recruited" for work on plantations and those maimed by criminal gangs and forced into beggary or other rackets.

said to 'have a longer shelf-life,' which means that after exposure to, say, dangerous benzine or asbestos, they have more years ahead of them in which to develop diseases."

Experts say the child labor problem has worsened in recent years with the consolidation of the U.S. retail industry into a few huge conglomerates. These giants seek competitive advantages by "outsourcing," or subcontracting, to low-paying suppliers around the world. In 1987 the 20 biggest U.S. apparel companies accounted for 33 percent of domestic sales, according to the Census Bureau. By 1992, the share of the 20 largest had climbed to 41 percent of sales. Wal-Mart, K Mart and J.C. Penney, to name a few, have emerged as global empires that farm out thousands of manufacturing contracts.

The impact worldwide has been "growing insecurity and a downward spiral in labor standards," according to Neil Kearney, president of the International Textile, Garment and Leather Workers Union. "El Salvador, for example, has gained 50,000 jobs in the last 10 years, and its exports have jumped 4,000 percent. But its real wages have been halved. Its women can't afford to buy the clothes they make, and people who protest are subject to rape and murder."

Within the United States, analysts note, the garment industry's threats to send work overseas have brought down wages while easing the way for sweatshop operators to take advantage of frightened illegal immigrants desperate for work. A 1994 study by the General Accounting Office found that 2,000 of the 6,000 garment shops in New York City could be called sweatshops, and 4,500 out of 5,000 in Los Angeles. "You can have a sweatshop even if it's air-conditioned," says Jay Mazur, president of the Union of Needletrades, Industrial and Textile Employees (UNITE). "They violate wage and hour laws, pay no taxes, use child labor and require homework. In this New World Order of the global village, the laws haven't followed the changes."

International Labour Organization

Young agricultural workers are still a common sight in parts of India.

Many companies agree that there is a problem, and in response many have created codes of conduct and supplier-monitoring programs. But others — including several California retailers who supposedly sold garments made in the El Monte sweatshop — say the abuses are not their fault because they have no control over their subcontractors. Overseas, they point out, suppliers must operate within the local cultures, economies and laws, where the American notion that children belong in school is often dismissed as quaint.

"In some Latin American and African countries, a child's right to schooling is related to birth order," notes an ILO study. "Older siblings receive preference for schooling, and parents are reported to be making large financial investments in older children in the expectation that they will . . . help finance the education of younger brothers and sisters" who are currently working. [5]

Finally, businesses point out that boycotts of sweatshop operators either by consumers or company managers can backfire. When the Pakistani carpet industry lost $10 million in orders recently because of a government crackdown on violators the buyers simply went to neighboring India or Nepal, where child labor is also common. [6]

Changing the apparel industry will be difficult "because it's competitive, and people want a good price," says Jonathan Mudd, public policy manager for the Gap clothing chain, considered a leader in opposing worker exploitation. "But sweatshops and child labor are very topical now. People are talking about it in the carpool, not just in some ninth-floor office. A company can no longer ignore its social responsibility."

American consumers appear to be warming to such responsibility. A convincing 84 percent of adults surveyed recently would be willing to pay an extra $1 on a $20 garment if it were guaranteed not to have been made with sweatshop or child labor. And 66 percent said they would be more likely to patronize stores that cooperate with law enforcement to prevent sweatshops. [7]

But in today's global economy, it is difficult to make comforting distincions between products fashioned according to America's usual standards of fair treatment and those turned out in the developing world, where child labor and sweatshops are built into local economies. Nor is it possible to know which American-made products reflect such standards.

"Forced labor is illegal in most parts of the world, and yet it is on the increase in Asia, Africa and Latin America because children are profitable and easily exploitable," says Rep. James P. Moran, D-Va., who closely follows the issue. "We as consumers are at fault. We want cheap handmade products without asking whose hands were on them."

As lawmakers and social activists work to curb labor exploitation, these are among the questions being asked:

Are governments doing enough to curb the use of sweatshops and child labor?

About 35 million soccer balls, or 80 percent of the world's annual supply, are produced in Pakistan. Last spring, members of Congress and the press alleged that children stitch as many as one-fourth of Pakistan's soccer balls, working 8-12 hours a day for as little as six cents an hour. Many of the children are bonded servants.

Pakistani employers scramble to hide children whenever human rights activists arrive to inspect conditions. Western journalists attempting to investigate have been threatened and assaulted. [8]

Like most countries, Pakistan has child-labor laws on the books, notably the 1991 Employment of Children Act. Pakistan's 1973 Constitution prohibits child labor, and the nation has ratified the 1989 United Nations Convention on the Rights of the Child. (Pakistan, however, is not among the 49 nations that have ratified the ILO's 1973 convention requiring a minimum working age of 15.)

As is often the case in the Third World, there is a yawning gap in Pakistan between law and reality. "The complicity of the state in the bonded labor system is explicitly illustrated by the fact that employers of bonded laborers are rarely arrested, prosecuted or punished for holding workers in bondage," says a Human Rights Watch study of Pakistan. "Furthermore, employers usually escape punishment for illegal confinement, rape or physical abuse of bonded laborers, all of which are clearly prohibited under the Pakistan Penal Code." [9]

In July, Pakistani Labor Minister Ghulam Akbar Lasi announced that he had ordered local authorities to raid factories employing children. "They will conduct surprise visits to those areas where soccer balls are being made," he said. "If they find children working over there, they will arrest the contractors and report to me in a month," he said. The government says that, already, from January 1995 to March 1996, it has conducted 7,003 raids and prosecuted 2,538 employers, levying $1,428 fines and/or two to five years in prison.

Other Third World governments have made headlines by taking action. In India last year, then Prime Minister P.V. Narishma announced a plan to relieve 2 million children from work duties by the year 2000. Essentially, parents would receive monthly stipends and food rations in return for enrolling their children in school.

Meanwhile, many Indian industries, including hand-made carpet manufacturing, still use child labor, says newspaper reporter K. Arora, of *United News of India*. "Banning it is not practical because the carpets are made in rural villages, not in [more easily watched] cities," he says. "Today there is more awareness of child labor, and women's non-governmental organizations have protested it. But often the guy who writes about it or discusses it at the office water cooler is himself using it at home."

Uneven enforcement of the law in India has even drawn international lending institutions into the debate. Francoise Remington, founder of Forgotten Children in Arlington, Va., says the World Bank is financing major coal mining and dam construction projects in India that employ young children. She told a House subcommittee in July that since 1988 she has visited numerous factories in India and estimates there are 55 million Indian workers ages 6-14. [10]

Human rights advocates want the United States and European nations to ban all imports made by bonded labor. They demand that international lenders only aid businesses that comply with fair labor standards and that governments work out procedures for on-site inspections. They also want industrialized countries to suspend tariff benefits for offending countries. "Ultimately," writes consumer advocate Ralph Nader, "standing up to the cruelty of child labor will require the United States to challenge or quit the anti-democratic, anti-child" World Trade Organization (WTO). [11]

But to some observers, such aggressive actions run the risk of appearing to interfere in the affairs of sovereign nations. John Donaldson, external affairs officer of the World Bank, says: "We do not condone anything illegal in countries in which we have projects, and I am not aware of anything illegal. We do take reports seriously and investigate them, but if someone under 18 is working in a non-hazardous job that is legal in his country, then there is not much we can do. The World Bank works on alleviating poverty and promoting education, which help more than anything mandated to end child labor."

In fact, developing countries charge that industrialized countries use child labor and other similar issues as an excuse for protectionist efforts to shield domestic industries against cheap imports. At a June ILO conference in Washington in which child labor topped the agenda, representatives of Bangladesh, Indonesia, Pakistan and the Philippines objected to proposed solutions that were not

Celebrity Endorsers Get Shaken Up . . .

When the talk-show star met the lawmakers, the atmosphere was electric. Kathie Lee Gifford, on a break from television's "Live With Regis and Kathie Lee," arrived on Capitol Hill July 15 amid a sea of cameras and jutting microphones. The celebrity-turned-human-rights activist was showered with praise.

"You are an ambassador to the world's exploited workers," Rep. Christopher H. Smith, R-N.J., told her at a hearing of the House Subcommittee on International Operations and Human Rights. "We welcome you as our comrade in arms," said Rep. Tom Lantos, D-Calif. "It is lonely in the human rights arena. There are very few touchdowns and many fumbles."

Only a few short months before, Gifford had been the activists' favorite punching bag. The apolitical entertainer had been blindsided in late April by the charge that her women's clothing line, marketed through Wal-Mart Stores Inc., had been produced by sweatshop labor in Honduras, and, it was later revealed, in New York City. The accusations were lodged at a congressional hearing by Charles Kernaghan, executive director of the National Labor Committee, a human rights group.

Scott Ferrell

Talk-show star Kathie Lee Gifford testifies at congressional hearing.

Gifford's first reaction had been to lash out emotionally. "I truly resent this man impugning my integrity," she said tearfully on her morning show. "You can say I'm ugly, you can say I'm not talented, but when you say I don't care about children, that I will exploit them for some sort of monetary gain, for once, mister, you better answer your phone, because my attorney is calling you today. How dare you!" [1]

Ten days earlier, an emotional Gifford had told 20,000 shareholders at Wal-Mart's annual meeting about the "viciousness" of the news media that were blowing the matter out of proportion. She had considered discontinuing her clothing line, but changed her mind after phone calls from Labor Secretary Robert B. Reich, New York Gov. George Pataki and Jay Mazur, president of the Union of Needletrades, Industrial and Textile Employees (UNITE). In a private meeting with Kernaghan, she was introduced to Wendy Diaz, a 15-year-old Honduran who toiled on Kathie Lee-endorsed garments, earning $22 for a 60-hour week.

Soon after the revelations, Gifford's husband Frank, a television sportscaster and former football star, paid a visit to Seo Fashions in Manhattan's garment district, where he passed out packets of $300 in cash toward the $48,000 in back pay due the workers.

"The allegation from [Kernaghan] hit me like a truck," Gifford told the July hearing. "Our first instinct was to run, but Frank did not want a spin control or damage-control thing, but the right thing. We were a national model for what's wrong in the system. We now have to be national model for what's right."

Gifford's transformation prompted her to meet with Wal-Mart to rethink strategy. An investigation revealed that unexpectedly high demand for her clothing had prompted a Wal-Mart supplier to subcontract to an unregulated New York sweatshop. Gifford was reminded that her contract had required the retailer to specify which suppliers were being used. She soon set up her own watchdog organization to monitor the situation, and has been meeting regularly with government, industry and human rights officials.

Since her activism blossomed, Gifford's critics have become her strongest boosters. Rep. James P. Moran, D-Va., told her that activists in Congress had not known that as much as 20 percent of the multimillion-dollar profits from Gifford's four-year-old clothing line were already benefiting homes for children victimized by AIDS and crack cocaine.

"We thought you had lent your name for selfish profits," he told her. "We didn't realize at the time that your motivation shouldn't be questioned. But now your leadership will change the lives of millions in ways you couldn't have imagined. It would have taken much longer without someone of your sensitivity, visibility and communicative skills. God works in strange ways."

As an anti-sweatshop crusader, Gifford stands in marked contrast to several other celebrities whose names have been dragged into the human rights debate. Actress Jaclyn Smith, who has a successful clothing line with K Mart, has declined

---

"trade-neutral."

Many Western business groups agreed, speaking of a "need to respect local culture and customs." Abraham Katz, president of the New York City-based United States Council for International Business, warned that "no one-solution-fits-all-problems approach can deal constructively with this complex issue. The organized employers community believes that this issue is best tackled through cooperation, example and sympathetic assistance on the ground rather than politically motivated coercion on the part of wealthy

. . . by Controversy Over Sweatshops and Child Labor

comment on the issue. And the seemingly indifferent attitude of basketball megastar Michael Jordan, who has a lucrative contract to advertise Nike sneakers made by low-wage Indonesian workers, has disappointed some fans. It's up to Nike to "do what they can to make sure everything is correctly done," Jordan told The Associated Press in June. "I don't know the complete situation. Why should I? I'm trying to do my job. Hopefully, Nike will do the right thing." [2]

Kevin Sweeney, a vice president at Patagonia, a Ventura, Calif., clothing maker, says that "Jordan made a big mistake in saying that [fighting worker exploitation] is not what he does. Nike does a lot of good things, and I have been a Jordan fan. But he gets $20 million from Nike. You've got to do something for your money. I have no interest in him now."

Other celebrity endorsers have been sensitive to the sweatshop issue for years, but behind the scenes. Supermodel Cheryl Tiegs has had her own women's sportswear line since 1980. "By being in the spotlight, by my appearing on the cover of *Sports Illustrated*, I accept a certain moral responsibility," she told a conference on sweatshops organized by the Labor Department in July.

Tiegs explained how she did background checks on all suppliers and won approval rights to ascertain that all goods were fairly and properly made. She said she had ended up putting about 120 days a year into the effort instead of the 20 days she had originally planned. She cautions that celebrities must depend on trust and can't be responsible for every phase of the manufacturing and marketing process. "I do design and photography, but not the shipping or display," Tiegs says. Still, "My celebrity status depends on my good name, and it's the public that casts the final vote."

Another longtime celebrity activist is exercise guru Richard Simmons. For 12 years he has marketed a clothing line for overweight women that is sold in 4,000 stores. "I've never had a child make a piece of clothing, and I do go to the factories," Simmons says. "Few of us would take this on as a career, but it has affected me emotionally, even if some in the [entertainment] business don't want me to be active. My advice to celebrities is to *mean it*. Don't just make cute celebrity visits."

Back in 1980, Tiegs says, it was easier for a celebrity to insist on control over the terms of a clothing-endorsement contract. But because of consolidation in the retail industry that has put small operators out of business, she says, "Today, they will tell you, 'Sorry, honey, there are other celebrities waiting in line.' "

Gifford says she is disappointed that other celebrities have failed to respond to her entreaties to get involved. "They take the attitude that the issue will go away if they ignore it," she told the Labor Department gathering. "But in the future, many celebrities will be careful about what they endorse and will get involved in the process."

"I was probably the right person to pick on," Gifford says, describing herself as the granddaughter of Russian Jewish immigrants raised to believe that "if you are privileged, you don't have the right to horde it all. You should share it." In 30 years of endorsing products — her first was for Kraft Foods at age 17, when she won a Junior Miss contest — Gifford says the issue of sweatshops and child labor had never arisen. Now, she says, she has come to realize that "my own pain seemed selfish and insignificant. Now my anger has a focus. Even if we have to downsize growth, I would be willing to pay to stop an obscene practice by people who are more like a cockroach than a human being."

Not all observers give Gifford rave reviews. "People are turned off by Kathie Lee becoming an activist because she's been so whiny in her approach," says Duncan Muir, a spokesman for J.C. Penny Co. "Everyday people are wondering what she is doing getting involved in things like that."

Robert Hall, vice president and international trade counsel for the National Retail Federation, says that activist groups are targeting celebrities in order to build support for unionizing foreign factories. The issue "never made it into *People* magazine until they went after Kathie Lee," he says. [3]

Does Gifford's husband think the producers of her TV show are pleased with her activism?. "I don't see how they would not be pleased," he says. "And if not, it doesn't matter."

Gifford herself now flicks off critics' barbs with her usual exuberance. "I didn't want accolades for what we're doing, but I didn't feel we deserved to be criticized," she says. "Now I know I'm not the victim. I go home at night to a lovely home, a loving husband and healthy kids. I'm hooked on the feeling that one person can make a difference."

---

[1] Cited in transcript from ABC News "Nightline," June 19, 1996.

[2] See Bob Herbert, "Nike's Pyramid Scheme," *The New York Times*, June 10, 1996.

[3] Quoted in *USA Today*, June 6, 1996.

importing countries. . . . There are cases in which contracting companies, under the threat of action in importing countries, emptied their factories of children, who were put on the street with no recourse but to engage in prostitution, begging or at best work in far-less-favorable conditions." [12]

Labor Secretary Reich agrees that trade restraints risk making things worse for exploited workers and children. "The World Trade Organization and other nations are not with us on this," he says. "Our power to get the facts out is limited overseas," he adds,

Firms That Pledge 'No Sweat'

The Labor Department's list of "Fashion Trendsetters" recognizes firms that support the department's "No Sweat" campaign to eradicate sweatshops in the U.S. and ensure that stores don't carry products made by suppliers that exploit workers.

Abercrombie & Fitch	Galyans Trading	Mast Industries
Baby Superstore	GapKids	NFL Properties
Banana Republic	Gerber Childrenswear	Nicole Miller
Bath & Body Works	Guess Inc.	Nordstrom
Bergner's	Henri Bendel	Old Navy Clothing Store
Boston Stores	Jessica McClintock	Patagonia
Brylane	Lands End	Penhaligon's
Cacique	Lane Bryant	Structure
Carson Pirie Scott	Lerner New York	Superior Surgical Mfg.
Dana Buchman	Levi Strauss	The Limited
Elisabeth	Limited Too	The Gap
Express	Liz Claiborne	Victoria's Secret

Note: Any companies interested in joining the list may contact the Department of Labor.

Source: Department of Labor, March 25, 1996

which is one reason he has been concentrating his department's efforts on U.S. companies. "If we have embarrassed some members of industry, I'm sorry, but it may be necessary."

For three years now, Reich has presided over a "No Sweat" campaign within the United States. The crackdown involves surprise inspections (Reich himself has popped in on New York City sweatshops), fining companies and conducting hearings and conferences with businesses and non-governmental organizations to search for voluntary solutions. The conferences typically focus on enhancing enforcement and education efforts.

Thus far, Reich's campaign has persuaded nearly 50 U.S. firms to monitor subcontractors to prevent labor abuses and 20 major importers to consider tougher codes of conduct. The department publishes a list of "Trendsetters" — companies that are making progress on curbing sweatshops and child labor — ranging from Abercrombie & Fitch to Victoria's Secret. The campaign has distributed 50 million information sheets dubbed "Clues for Consumers," and Reich is exploring a campaign to put "No Sweat" labels on international products.

Activists against labor abuse say Reich is doing yeoman's work. "Before the Department of Labor stepped in, this wasn't even recognized as an international problem," says UNITE's Mazur.

The Trendsetters list, which requires continuing efforts by companies for inclusion, has raised awareness in the industry, says the Gap's Mudd. "But the list could be a lot longer. Many of the smaller companies that are making progress are not getting recognized in the press in the way the Gap and Wal-Mart are."

Duncan Muir, a spokesman for Dallas-based J.C. Penney, complains that his firm did not make the list. "We encourage monitors, but we only require it if a supplier has previously violated the law," he says. "We have 6,600 suppliers in 80 countries, so it would be burdensome."

Peter J. Eide, manager of labor law policy at the U.S. Chamber of Commerce, questions the whole premise of Reich's campaign. "He has the Fair Labor Standards Act, so let him enforce it instead of talking about boycotts and shame," he says. "Now we've got the government saying which is a good company and which is a bad one. It's wholly inappropriate."

An opinion poll released in June by the International Mass Retail Association showed that 46 percent of Americans think that the U.S. and foreign governments have the main responsibility to police exploitive labor practices abroad, while only 29 percent said manufacturers are responsible, and 18 percent put the onus on retailers.

But companies that want the Labor Department to beef up its enforcement "have not been heard calling for increased funding for inspections," says Alan Howard, assistant to the president of UNITE. "That subjects the companies to fairly credible accusations of hypocrisy."

Is business doing enough to curb sweatshops and child labor?

As Reich is wont to point out, the Labor Department employs only 800 inspectors to monitor compliance with wage and hour laws at 6.5 million U.S. worksites employing 110 million workers. If sweatshops and child labor are to be policed, he says, industry's active cooperation is essential.

Since the sweatshop issue has become front-page news — particularly after the Kathie Lee affair — many large retailers such as Wal-Mart and K Mart have announced new codes of conduct for subcontractors, beefed-up internal monitoring and plans to sever ties with suppliers who violate the rules.

The National Retail Federation, the largest industry group, last November established an "honor roll" of businesses that sign its new statement of principles, which has attracted 200 companies. The federation has developed a "supplier non-compliance form" intended for use by the Labor Department to notify retailers of subcontractors who abuse the law.

The Sporting Goods Manufacturers Association lept into action following the soccer ball controversy. "The U.S. soccer industry has taken unprecedented steps to address the issue of child labor in a conscientious and responsible manner," Thomas J. Cove, the group's vice president, told the Labor Department in June. "Representatives of several companies traveled to [Pakistan] accompanied by industry critics who assisted in their inquiry. At the same time, the industry . . . established a task force on global manufacturing practices to organize research and develop recommendations for joint action."

Despite such industry action, Cove argues that the news media has sensationalized some of the problems. He points to two surveys by human rights groups within Pakistan that found that the vast majority of soccer balls are stitched by workers over age 14. What's more, over half of the working children who reportedly do stitch an estimated 10-25 percent of Pakistan's soccer balls perform the work in their own homes. "The soccer industry does not seek out child labor or compensate child stitchers differently than their adult counterparts," he said.

Others point to a more tepid performance by corporate America. "Companies differ in their degree of seriousness," says Pharis Harvey, executive director of the International Labor Rights Fund in Washington. "Over the past several months, more companies have realized that this is not an issue they can shrug off by saying, 'We have thousands of suppliers and don't know who they are, so we're not responsible.' This was their common reaction two years ago. Now, those with a great deal of equity value in their corporate name are the first to take steps because their products are traceable back to a company in the way that, say, Liz Claiborne is linked to Liz Claiborne Inc."

International Labour Organization

Young girls in Morocco work at a rug loom.

Two of the pioneers in corporate activism against sweatshops are Guess jeans and Levi Strauss. At Guess, says former General Counsel Stan Levy, quality-control inspectors are trained in the nuances of labor law so that compliance monitoring is "integrated into the production process every step of the way."

Levi Strauss, credited with inaugurating the first such integrated approach in 1991, has set an example for the industry by dropping suppliers in Myanmar, China and the Pacific island of Saipan who had violated labor laws. "It's innately how we do things, part of how we measure performance," says Senior Vice President John Ermatinger. "It's not as an add-on or a burden." Levi Strauss has also simplified monitoring by reducing its number of suppliers.

According to Howard of UNITE, the company that has come farthest is the Gap. "They're in a class by themselves, not because they've accomplished so much, but because they've really gone out there in setting up the first truly independent monitoring operation," he says.

Last December, following charges that its clothing suppliers in El Salvador ran sweatshops, GAP representatives met with three American activist groups: the National Labor Committee, Business for Social Responsibility and the Interfaith Center for Corporate Responsibility. They announced formation of the Independent Monitoring Group of El Salvador, which by March had reached agreement with Salvadoran managers, workers and union leaders to strive toward a "humane, productive, successful business." As a pilot program, the Gap hired two full-time compliance officers to enforce its newly updated Code of Vendor Conduct, which specifies worldwide safety and sanitation standards, as well as limits on management prerogatives, in factories and worker dormitories.

Mudd views many other corporate codes as too subject to interpretation, resulting in confusion as workers look for their rights and responsibilities while managers strive to satisfy their clients. "Ours is a living document," he says. While he is hopeful about the monitoring experiment, the fact that the Gap pays the compliance officers invites skepticism about their independence, he says. "They are open to claims of being co-opted, but they have to get their money from somewhere. Hopefully, they should be like the Maytag repairman — not very busy but ready to swing into action."

One of the least responsive companies, according to Howard, is Walt Disney, which markets children's clothing bearing images from hit movies such as "The Hunchback of Notre Dame" and "The Lion King." But the billion-dollar-a-year business depends, Disney's critics allege, on workers in Haiti who make 28 cents an hour.

The National Labor Committee, the union group that confronted Kathie Lee Gifford, has produced a muckraking video called "Mickey Mouse Goes to Haiti." To the familiar Disney tune "Hi ho, hi ho, it's off to work we go," the video reveals shocking footage of shantytowns where Haiti's garment workers toil. The workers reportedly earn five cents for every $11.99 children's outfit they produce. "They treat us badly, like we are dirt, like we were dumb, with no respect," a worker says. "You can't even speak to the bosses. If you try, they fire you. The supervisors are always screaming at us to work faster. The pressure to make the quota is great."

Thomas Deegan, Disney's vice president for corporate communications, says that Disney subcontractors "follow all applicable employment and environmental laws." He says the company inspects factories with which it has direct supplier contracts, and that "inspections to guarantee product quality have been augmented with additional checks into workplace safety and legal compliance."

In checking out the charges, Disney says it consulted the U.S. ambassador to Haiti, Washington human rights monitors, two Disney licensees in Haiti and a business group. The company also sent a representative to Haiti. "Having thoroughly investigated these matters, we have been able to find no evidence of minimum wage, child labor or other violations in the manufacture of Disney merchandise," Deegan says. "We believe that our licensees are managing their manufacturing operations in a reasonable manner."

Howard argues that "obeying the laws is just the beginning of a corporation's responsibility. In a world from which they earn enormous profits, they have a responsibility to put resources back in," he says.

The owners of the factories used by Disney point out that they're running a business, not a charity. "All we have to sell is our cheap labor," said one. "Our workers are weak and anemic and produce only 60 percent of what workers sew in the U.S.," said another. [13]

Also in the human rights hot seat has been the highly successful Nike athletic shoe company. It is regularly attacked as an exploiter of Asian labor by Jeffrey Ballinger, who runs the organization Press for Change, and by *New York Times* columnist Bob Herbert. In June Herbert slam-dunked Nike founder Philip H. Knight for paying workers in Indonesia about $2.20 a day while his own stock in Nike is worth $4.5 billion. "More than a third of Nike's products are manufactured in Indonesia, a human rights backwater where the minimum wage was deliberately set below the subsistence level in order to attract foreign investment," Herbert writes. "What's next, employees who'll work for a bowl of gruel?" [14]

Nike spokeswoman Donna Gibbs argues that the average wage of a Nike worker in Indonesia is double the local minimum wage, that the company offers them free meals and health care, and that the company has monitors in 25 countries. "Could there be abuses? There could be," she says. "It's better to have companies like Nike with a brand image at stake operating in these countries to assure that abuses don't occur." [15]

Overall, says Robert Dunn, president of Business for Social Responsibility, "the good news is that over the last few years there has been a concentrated effort by business leaders to get their arms around the problem. They're still experimenting, but companies are making a clear commitment. They are aligning themselves with partners who recognize the problem throughout their supply chain. It's an enormous and complex problem that has raged for centuries in some countries. They are looking to find collective solutions and stop pointing fingers." ■

BACKGROUND

England's Grim Legacy

The term "sweatshop" stems from the word sweating, originally used in late-19th-century America to describe "a subcontracting system in which the middlemen earned their profit from the margin between the amount they received for a contract and the amount they paid workers," according to UNITE. "This margin was said to be 'sweated' from the workers because they received minimal wages for excessive hours worked under unsanitary conditions." [16]

Child labor, however, has been an issue since the Industrial Revolution began in England in the late 18th century. The brilliant increases in productivity permitted by newfangled machinery came at a ghastly social price: Increasingly monotonous tasks, such as manipulating a shuttle back and forth through a textile loom, seemed "designed with the express

Continued on p. 732

Chronology

1800s ***Industrial Revolution makes child labor and sweatshops commonplace.***

1833
English law bans children from working in textile mills.

1842
Massachusetts law caps factory workday at 10 hours for children 12 and under.

1870
U.S. Census counts 250,000 children ages 10-15 in non-farm work.

1899
Founding of National Consumers League.

1900s ***Number of child workers in U.S. rises to 2 million.***

1911
Triangle Shirtwaist Factory fire kills 146 garment workers in New York City, sparking reforms.

1916
Congress bans interstate commerce in products made by children under 16 in mines and under 14 in factories.

1918
Supreme Court overturns child labor law as unconstitutional.

1919
International Labour Organization (ILO) founded, passes first convention against child labor.

1920s-1930s

Congress initiates action on wage and hour violations.

1924
Congress passes constitutional amendment banning child labor, but states fail to ratify it.

1938
Congress passes Fair Labor Standards Act (FLSA) regulating worker hours and pay.

1960s-1970s

Plight of farmworkers wins federal attention.

1960
Edward R. Murrow's TV documentary on migrant workers, "Harvest of Shame," shocks nation.

1973
International agreement sets minimum working age at 15.

1974
Amendments to FLSA restrict children working in agriculture to those 12 and older.

1980s-1990s

Third World countries begin working to curb child labor as labor exploitation issue gains renewed visibility in U.S.

1989
United Nations adopts Convention on the Rights of the Child.

1990
Congress gives Labor Department authority to raise penalties on child labor.

1991
ILO launches International Program for the Elimination of Child Labor.

June 1994
International Confederation of Free Trade Unions launches campaign to end child labor.

April 16, 1995
Iqbal Masih, a 12-year-old activist against child labor, is assassinated in Lahore, Pakistan.

July 4, 1995
Bangladesh Garment Manufacturers sign agreement against child labor with UNICEF and ILO.

Aug. 2, 1995
Government raid on locked compound in El Monte, Calif., frees 72 Thai immigrants working in slave-labor garment factory.

Dec. 15, 1995
The Gap becomes first employer to have independent monitoring of plants in Central America.

April 29, 1996
The head of the National Labor Committee tells congressional hearing that TV star Kathie Lee Gifford's Wal-Mart clothing line is made in sweatshops.

June 4-20, 1996
ILO and its employer members meet in Geneva to adopt resolution against child labor.

July 15, 1996
Gifford testifies at congressional hearing on sweatshops.

Aug. 2, 1996
President Clinton hosts meeting of Gifford and apparel industry executives to consider new steps against sweatshops.

Many Children Still Work on U.S. Farms

Businesses accused of using child labor often put the blame on their ever-shifting army of subcontractors, over whom they say they exert little control. In no American industry is this more evident than agriculture.

Children working on the nation's farms and orchards were scarcely affected by passage of the 1938 Fair Labor Standards Act, which focused on industries using interstate commerce. It was only as recently as 1974 that Congress specifically restricted child farmworkers, barring children under 12 from working on any farm except family farms. (Children from 12 to 14 could work on non-family farms, but only outside school hours and if their parents were also working there. [1])

Today, an estimated 300,000 to 800,000 children perform farm labor in the United States, according to the Farmworker Justice Fund, a legal advocacy group. Most children work under the auspices of freelance crew leaders signed up by the growers. Many of these crew leaders are "fly-by-night operators," says Shelley Davis, co-director of the Justice Fund, "but it is to the growers' economic advantage to have the crew leaders be the employers."

The problem, she says, is that farmworkers make too little money. (Since 1985, farmworkers' wages have fallen 53 percent, adjusted for inflation, her group reports.) "For a family to survive, the children must work. A family of four people working for piecemeal pay can produce more than one minimum-wage earner. But the wages of the full family are listed under just the father's name in the records, so it is hard to document," Davis says.

Because there's no minimum wage for the children, it's a bonus to the growers. "When we find that crew leaders are not fulfilling the wage, hour and safety laws, the growers say, 'Go sue them.' But they know the crew leader has no assets. They know it's a sham," Davis says.

Sharon Hughes, executive vice president of the National Council of Agricultural Employers, says: "Child labor was big in the past, but children are not in the field now because they must have their parents' consent." Typically, she says, "both parents in a family are picking in the fields and have no day care. So the real problem is keeping the kids off the fields, because if they're adding to the parents' [produce] bins, the farmers have to pay them. That's why many growers are promoting use of the Head Start program for kids."

As for the stories of unscrupulous crew leaders, Hughes says, "There are problems with some farm labor contractors, and the states and the Labor Department have tried to crack down. The good ones get their eyes blackened by a few bad actors." Growers are not able to recruit workers without the crew leaders because the migrant-worker stream doesn't come very far North on its own, she says. Government procedures require contractors to be registered. Those who don't comply with the wage laws have their licenses revoked, and a list of non-complying contractors is being distributed, though it is not always up-to-date.

Finally, Hughes says, the reason the Farmworkers Justice Fund wants to hold growers legally responsible for crew leaders' violations is that the growers have "deep pockets."

[1] Michael A. Pignatella, "The Recurring Nightmare of Child Labor Abuse and Solutions for the 1990s," *Boston College Third World Law Journal*, winter 1995.

Continued from p. 730

purpose of laying the world's work upon the child's shoulders," as one historian wrote. [17]

Children as young as four were routinely assigned work that took advantage of their small bodies, from sweeping chimneys to hauling coal out of mineshafts. At the legendary Wedgewood pottery factory in England, one observer in the early 1800s was startled to behold some pillars of clay that, upon closer inspection, turned out to be young workers: "I saw little children, three-parts naked, tottering under the weight of wet clay, some of it on their heads, and some on their shoulders, and little girls with large masses of wet, cold and dripping clay pressing on their abdomens. Moreover, the unhappy children were exposed to the most sudden transitions of heat and cold, for, after carrying their burdens of wet clay, they had to endure the heat of the kiln, and to enter places where the heat was so intense that I was myself able to remain for no more than two or three minutes." [18]

The heartbreaking sights prompted wide social protest that found expression in popular fiction and poetry. In the 1840s, British poet Elizabeth Barrett Browning's "The Cry of the Children" captured the pathos: "They look up with their pale and sunken faces, and their look is dread to see. . . . 'How long,' they say, 'how long, O Cruel nation, will you stand to move the world on a child's heart?' "

Novelist Charles Dickens, who dwelt on the child labor issue time and again in such works as *Hard Times* and *David Copperfield,* also blasted the practice in policy commentaries: "If the state would begin its work and duty at the beginning," he wrote in *The Short Timers,* a collection of essays, "and would with the strong hand take those children out of the streets, while they are yet children, and wisely train them, it would make them a part of England's glory, not its shame — of England's strength, not its weakness — would raise good soldiers and sailors, and good citizens, and many great men, out of the seeds of its criminal population."

In 1836, Parliament outlawed child

workers in textile mills and required government inspections, though it would be decades before abuses actually waned.

Abuse American-Style

In the early economy of the United States, child labor was considered acceptable by such notables as Treasury Secretary Alexander Hamilton. He believed that "children are rendered more useful by manufacturing establishments than they otherwise would be."

The centrality of children in industry was dramatized by a strike in 1828 in the bustling New Jersey milltown of Paterson. Young workers walked off the job to protest management's shift of the dinner hour from noon to 1 p.m. "The children would not stand for it," an observer reported, "for fear if they assented to this, the next thing would be to deprive them of eating at all." [19]

At a Rhode Island cotton mill, young workers in 1835 were putting in 14-hour shifts for seven cents per day. As one worker later recalled: "A mother with several children suggested to the proprietor that the pay seemed small. The proprietor replied, 'You get enough to keep the wolf from the door.' He then remarked, 'You get enough clothes to wear, don't you?' To which she answered, 'Barely enough to cover our nakedness.' 'Well,' said the proprietor, 'We want the rest.' " [20]

Reforms in the USA

The struggle for wage and hour restrictions gathered force in the late 19th century, after thousands of immigrants from Ireland and Southern Europe had brought more exploitable labor to the American work force. Desperately poor parents commonly lied about their children's ages to win them paying jobs.

Union pioneer Samuel Gompers in 1888 told workers: "Some of you may be tempted to send your children out to work. That may seem a very grateful addition to the income. But don't you know that the child is employed because its labor can be had cheaper than that of a man? He becomes a competitor of his father. And if the father is not discharged, some other child's father often is. In this competition, the rates of labor are often so reduced that the combined wages of the father and child are less than the father's wages alone before." [21]

International Labour Organization/J. Maillard

Young boys carry bricks at a brick-making operation in Colombia.

Social workers, such as those at Chicago's famed Hull House, attracted widespread press coverage as they exposed exploitive workplace conditions in Illinois and brought members of Congress to plants to see for themselves. Florence Kelley, a Marxist who would later become president of the New York City-based National Consumers' League, engaged in what she called a "systematic endeavor to clear out [Chicago's] sweating dens."

In a letter to socialist theorist Friedrich Engels, Kelley wrote: "The factory inspector of today, like the militiaman, is the child of the struggle of labor against capital. The factory inspector enforces the law for the worker against the capitalist, the militiaman shoots down the worker by command of the capitalist." [22]

By 1892, reformist efforts in Illinois had succeeded in getting the legislature to limit female workers to eight hours a day and require physicians' certificates for workers ages 14-16. Under the new law, some 13 factory owners were prosecuted before the Manufacturers Protective Association took its case to the state Supreme Court. The law was struck down, the judges ruling that interfering with the manufacturers' right to contract for female labor was unconstitutional.

It was in the 1890s that the National Consumers League* began circulating lists of stores using products made under "just conditions." These were defined as a 10-hour day, 45 minutes for lunch, paid vacation and paid overtime. Only eight of some 1,400 locations surveyed, however, made the cut. The league also began encouraging the placement of labels in garments testifying that they were made without workplace abuse, a practice later superseded by "the union label."

---

* The league's motto was: "To live means to buy, to buy means to have power, to have power means to have duties."

In the Debate Over Reforming OSHA . . .

Republicans took control of Congress last year with anti-regulatory guns ablazing. Their celebrated "Contract With America" vowed to defang federal regulations believed to be oppressive to businesses, notably the costly and paperwork-demanding regulations of the Occupational Safety and Health Administration (OSHA).

The subsequent struggle over reforming OSHA has raised issues very similar to the debate on sweatshops, namely: Can management be trusted to protect workers, or is outside enforcement needed?

Since its founding in 1970, OSHA has been viewed as a guardian angel by trade unions and "a four-letter word" by many in business. Its efforts to prevent worker exposure to such evils as unsafe machinery, chemical toxins and noise pollution are regarded by backers as a proven necessity. Just look at the 6,588 deaths and 6.8 million workplace injuries reported to the Labor Department for 1994, they say — an accident rate that costs the economy $115.9 billion in a single year, according to the National Safety Council.

But such protections come at a price. In his widely noted book *The Death of Common Sense,* attorney Philip K. Howard excoriated OSHA's 4,000 often complex regulations. One classifies ordinary sand as a poison because it contains silica, he scoffs. "Keeping up with OSHA's forms . . . takes 54 million hours per year," he writes. "At $20 per hour, that's about $1 billion to catalog the dangers of Windex and Joy." [1]

During the 1970s, OSHA critics circulated a parody poster entitled a "A Cowboy Under OSHA." It featured a drawing of an old cowpoke on horseback with absurdly precise size specifications marked on his saddle, spurs, rope and reins.

In the early 1990s, when the Democrats controlled Congress, proposals for OSHA reform were common from such pro-labor stalwarts as Sen. Edward M. Kennedy, D-Mass., and now-retired Rep. William D. Ford, D-Mich. The reformers would have boosted OSHA fines, empowered the agency to shut down businesses that are habitual violators and set up mandatory labor-management workplace safety committees for all but the smallest employers.

OSHA at this time was seen by many union and human rights activists as too weak to protect workers who speak out about abuses at their worksites. The Washington-based Government Accountability Project revealed that weakness, it says, when it investigated conditions at several factories in North Carolina on the second anniversary of the 1992 fire that killed 25 and injured 56 in a seldom-inspected poultry plant in Hamlet, N.C. It found that "plant floors are covered with grease, water and ice. The drains are cleared only when inspectors visit." [2]

Reform proposals for OSHA were opposed as overly broad and pro-union by such groups as the National Federation of Independent Business.

In 1995, newly empowered Republicans moved in the opposite direction. Legislation offered by Rep. Cass Ballenger, R-N.C., along with a companion bill by Sen. Judd Gregg, R-N.H., would have changed OSHA from an enforcement agency to more of an educational agency. It would have required OSHA to give companies a warning before issuing a citation (except in cases of imminent danger) and required workers to report hazardous conditions to their bosses before contacting the federal agency.

An end to OSHA's image as an out-of-touch squad of bureaucrats who play "gotcha" with businesses was a key goal of large lobby groups such as the U.S. Chamber of Commerce. "The majority of OSHA violations are paperwork violations," notes Peter J. Eide, manager of labor law policy at the chamber. "But it goes much deeper than that. Not even labor lawyers can understand OSHA's compliance regulations. And someone at each company has to find the

In 1903, the celebrated labor activist known as Mother Jones led a "March of the Mill Children" up and down the East Coast, attracting help from social workers and some famous, wealthy wives whose conversions to social activism presaged Kathie Lee Gifford's experience. Sweatshop conditions of the period would also give rise to the Amalgamated Clothing and Textile Workers Union and the International Ladies' Garment Workers' Union, which merged in 1995 to form UNITE.

Tragic Fire Spawns Legislation

What truly caught the nation's attention, however, was the tragic fire in 1911 in New York City's Triangle Shirtwaist Factory. It killed 146 garment workers, most of them young Jewish immigrants. The following year, presidential candidate Theodore Roosevelt called for the abolition of child labor and other Progressive Era labor law reforms. Though nearly all states had nominal minimum working-age laws, most were honored in the breach, and plant owners were constantly seeking opportunities to move to lower-wage locations, particularly in the South.

In 1916, Congress passed the Keating-Owen Child Labor Act banning interstate commerce in products made in factories by children under age 14 or mined by those under 16. President Woodrow Wilson initially opposed the legislation, but he rallied behind it to avoid losing votes to pro-Roosevelt Republicans. The law was overturned by the Supreme Court in 1918 (*Hammer v. Dagenhart*). The court said that if the law were upheld, "all freedom of commerce will be at an end and the power of the states over local matters may be eliminated, and thus our system of government practically destroyed."

A constitutional amendment banning child labor was passed by Con-

. . . Anti-Sweatshop Campaign May Play a Role

regulations, find the time to read them, see what they say and then implement them. No one has that time."

Prospects for the Ballenger approach faded last fall, all parties agree, when President Clinton vetoed Republican budgets, marking a political and ideological turning point. Whether the Republican setback is long- or short-lived will be determined by this fall's elections.

Last spring, Ballenger offered a scaled-back version of reform that would basically codify the Clinton administration's own proposals to streamline OSHA, based on Vice President Al Gore's National Performance Review, better known as the "Reinventing Government" project. (Neither OSHA nor anyone in the administration, however, was consulted.) Ballenger's legislation would reduce OSHA penalties, require a cost-benefit analysis before setting new regulations and abolish citations for paperwork violations.

On April 17, Ballenger's bill cleared his Education and Economic Opportunities Subcommittee on Workforce Protection by a party-line vote. Opponents exploded.[3] OSHA spokeswoman Cheryl Byrne said the bill would turn OSHA inspectors into "toothless tigers." Twelve days later, the AFL-CIO organized a nationwide "Memorial Day" to mark OSHA's 25th anniversary, blast Republican efforts to curb the agency and remember workers who suffered or died in industrial accidents. The Ballenger bill is not considered likely to pass this Congress.

Meanwhile, on July 11, Republican OSHA critics suffered a defeat when the House, by a 216-205 vote, rejected their long-sought provision prohibiting OSHA from promulgating standards or guidance on the growing problem of repetitive-stress injury among workers.[4]

And the next day, OSHA weighed in on an issue that teamed it up with the Labor Department's Wage and Hour Division, which is mounting a campaign against sweatshop labor. OSHA proposed a $3.6 million fine against one of the nation's largest egg producers, Decoster Egg Farms, in Turner, Maine. It cited the company because "workers toiled 10-15 hours a day, with no equipment to protect them from disease, picking up dead chickens with their bare hands and handling manure potentially infected with the Salmonella virus." The Wage and Hour Division hit the company for back pay owed workers due to violations of the Fair Labor Standards Act.

Labor Secretary Robert B. Reich is confident his recent publicity coups in drawing bipartisan attention to sweatshops may spill over into the OSHA debate. "Mounting public concern over sweatshops strengthens the argument that we need to reverse the steady depletion of funding for protecting workers," he says. OSHA's budget wasn't cut as deeply this year as he had feared, he adds, and his department has requested an increase for next year.

But Ballenger says there is little spillover between the sweatshop/child labor issue and OSHA reform. "With sweatshops, the laws and regulations are already on the books, and it's a matter of targeting government resources, something the government isn't always very good at," he says. The Labor Department, "even if it gets no more money, could have more impact on sweatshops by cooperating with the Immigration and Naturalization Service to block illegal immigration."

---

[1] Philip K. Howard, *The Death of Common Sense* (1994), p. 93.

[2] Government Accountability Project, "Labor Notes," February 1994, p. 11.

[3] See *CQ Weekly Report*, April 20, 1996, p. 1052.

[4] See "Repetitive Stress Injuries," *The CQ Researcher*, June 23, 1996, pp. 537-560.

gress in 1924, but it failed to win ratification by the states. By the 1930s, the Census Bureau was estimating the number of underage workers at 2.5 million. Abuses were particularly common in non-union, Southern lumber mills and oyster and canning operations. The abuses led in 1938 to passage of the Fair Labor Standards Act, which for the first time created federal restrictions on child labor and unreasonable wages and hours.

In promoting the act, President Franklin D. Roosevelt asked, "What does the country ultimately gain if we encourage businessmen to enlarge the capacity of American industry to produce, unless we see that the income of our working population actually expands to create markets to absorb that increased production?"[23] The National Association of Manufacturers called the act "a step in the direction of communism, bolshevism, facism and Nazism."

The Modern Revival

In the 1980s, with the world economy increasingly interlinked, sweatshops and child labor regained high visibility. Abuses in the Third World were becoming commonplace. In Brazil, alarming reports told of possibly 2 million children under 14 living on the streets, working on farms and plantations, cutting sugar cane or picking oranges. In the Philippines, a spotlight was shined on the so-called Muro-ami fishing operations off the island of Palawan, where boats with as many as 300-500 children would go to sea for 10 months at a stretch.

"The divers . . . undertake the most hazardous tasks performed in the whole operation, diving to a depth of

100 feet to attach the nets to coral reefs," said an ILO study. "The lowest rank in the Muro-ami hierarchy is occupied by the swimmers, whose main function is to drive the fish toward the net. . . . Although most functions are open to all ages, children and youngsters between the ages of 12 and 14 form the bulk of the swimmers and divers." [24]

In India in 1989, a human rights activist named Kailash Satyarthi founded the South Asian Coalition on Child Servitude. After being approached by numerous parents of children trapped in bonded labor, he began pressuring authorities, leading protest caravans and conducting raids at work sites. Eventually, he helped liberate 40,000 workers, among them 28,000 children, and last year he received the Robert F. Kennedy Freedom Award.

In the United States, physician Landrigan in the late 1980s was introduced to two Hispanic children from the Bronx who had been working in butcher shops carrying sides of beef. Each had slipped and fallen into a whirring bandsaw, requiring amputations. "I asked a fellow doctor, does this mean that child labor is making a comeback?" he recalls. Soon they were running seminars on the subject for the American Academy of Pediatrics.

In 1990, the Labor Department, having seen its budget for wage and hour inspections cut steadily, launched a three-day surprise sweep of worksites. Operation Watch uncovered 7,000 children working, mostly in garment factories, fast-food businesses, grocery stores, hotels and farms. (*See story, p. 732.*)

That same year, Rep. Tom Lantos, D-Calif., chaired a series of hearings on youth labor at his Government Operations Employment and Housing Subcommittee, confronting operators of fast-food and door-to-door sales companies with evidence that they had been exposing teens as young as 14 to abuses such as late-night hours. ■

CURRENT SITUATION

Bipartisan Legislation

The currency of the child labor and sweatshop issue has prompted several bills introduced late in the election-year session of the 104th Congress. Sen. Tom Harkin, D-Iowa, and Rep. Barney Frank, D-Mass., have reintroduced legislation Harkin first took up in 1992 that would ban imports of goods produced by children under 15, while punishing violators with fines and prison terms of up to a year. "We have import bans that protect animals, ivory and prisoners, but we fall silent on children," says Harkin.

The Child Labor Coalition supports use of the "Rugmark" label on carpets from South Asian factories that have been inspected for child labor abuses.

Rep. Christopher H. Smith, R-N.J., has introduced a bill that would also ban imported products made by children. It would prohibit foreign aid, other than humanitarian aid, to countries that don't enforce child labor laws; restrict loans to those countries from bilateral and multilateral lending agencies such as the World Bank; and boost the U.S. contribution to ILO's International Program on the Elimination of Child Labor. Smith notes that the U.S. share to that five-year-old Geneva-based effort has totaled just $3.6 million (compared with Germany's $50 million) and that the current Congress recently reduced the U.S. contribution. "All of us need to put our money where our mouth is," he says.

Rep. William L. Clay, D-Mo., would go further. He plans to introduce the Stop Sweatshops Act of 1996, which would amend the Fair Labor Standards Act to make U.S. manufacturers and contractors jointly liable for violations. (A similar bill passed the California legislature in 1994, but Republican Gov. Pete Wilson vetoed it.)

Robert Hall, vice president of the National Retail Federation, says his group supports increased money for the ILO program but is concerned about Congress' efforts to redefine child labor. "Some may require other countries to have higher standards than those within the U.S.," he says, adding that he may also have problems with efforts by unions and human rights groups to require a role by independent, non-governmental groups in factory monitoring. "Because of the media and celebrity attention to this issue, things have become polarized," he says. "The increased attention has made minor differences seem more significant."

Though most in Congress emphasize that efforts against sweatshops enjoy bipartisan support, Democrats seem most eager to lead the charge. In their "Families First Agenda," released in June to give November voters a taste of what they would do if they retake Congress, Democrats included a plank to ban foreign products from the United States that are made with child labor.

Demand for Labels

Rep. George Miller, D-Calif., who has been vocal on child labor, is

Continued on p. 738

At Issue:

Should the United States crack down on companies doing business with overseas sweatshops?

yes

CHARLES KERNAGHAN
Executive director, National Labor Committee

FROM TESTIMONY BEFORE HOUSE INTERNATIONAL OPERATIONS AND HUMAN RIGHTS SUBCOMMITTEE, JUNE 11, 1996.

Approximately one-half of all the apparel purchased in the United States last year, over $190 billion worth, was composed of imports made offshore. In Central America and the Caribbean alone, there are 500,000 mostly young women producing apparel exclusively for sale in the United States. . . .

Honduras has 65,000 to 70,000 *maquiladora* workers or assembly workers [who manufacture apparel and other labor-intensive goods, mostly for the U.S.]. We estimate that about 13 percent of those workers are between 12 and 15 years of age. . . . But it's not, by any means, just Honduras. And there's no reason to target any [single] country. . . . There are minors in El Salvador working. There are minors in Guatemala working. There are children working in Bangladesh and India and Pakistan. . . .

[T]he retailers and multinationals search the world, searching for misery because, they'll tell you themselves, that where there's the greatest unemployment, you're always going to find the lowest wages.

And so the Wal-Marts and the K Marts and the Nikes and the mass industries, they trot the world looking for the lowest wages, whether that's in Honduras at 31 cents an hour or Nicaragua, 24 cents an hour. Whether that's El Salvador at 56 cents an hour. Whether that's Sri Lanka at 18 cents a hour, or Vietnam at 11 cents an hour or China at 11 cents.

They have these Third World countries competing against each other. Who will accept the lowest wages? Who will have the lowest wages, the most miserable working conditions?. . .

It's a system that now is coming back to the United States again. Everybody is beginning to recognize it. The growth of the sweatshops offshore comes back to the United States. We see it in New York and Los Angeles and Boston. We see the retailers telling U.S. manufacturers that they have to meet the same prices that they're paying offshore in these Third World countries — one of the reasons we lost 99,000 apparel jobs last year. . . .

If retailers and manufacturers begin to pay a living wage in these countries, sweatshops would be a thing of the past, and so would child labor, because they could hire their parents . . . and the kids could go back to school where they belong. It's nonsense to think that companies have to hire children.

no

LUCY MARTINEZ-MONT
Professor of economics, Francisco Marroquin University, Guatemala City, Guatemala

WRITTEN FOR *THE CQ RESEARCHER*, AUGUST 1996.

In the early-1990s, it seemed that Guatemala had found the road to development. By 1993, 400 new factories, many owned and operated by Koreans, were manufacturing brand-name apparel for some 50 U.S. companies. Today, only 220 factories remain. Close to 30,000 women and teenagers, who were making between 40 cents and 80 cents an hour in the clothing factories, are unemployed or were forced to settle for much lower wages.

Some countries find it harder than others to attract private capital. Guatemala, for instance, has a tradition of political unrest, corrupt governments, unstable tax laws and deplorable communications (only three telephone lines per 100 inhabitants). We have little to offer other than cheap labor, and cheap labor is precisely what attracts Korean entrepreneurs to Guatemala. . . .

It is easy to understand why nice people in rich countries are aghast at the working conditions in Central American factories. It is true that thousands of children work nights, that workers are locked in until production quotas are fulfilled, that wages are obscenely low and that, in extreme cases, women and children are beaten up by their supervisors. But it also true that there are no slaves in Central America. People choose to work in the *maquilla* industry of their own free will, because those are the best jobs available to them. Given that unemployment compensation is unheard of in Central America, a lousy job is always better than no job at all. . . .

So, from the Guatemalan standpoint, the public enemy is not the foreigner who invests in our country. He may be greedy and cruel, working conditions in his shop may be harsh, but we know that the workers will walk away as soon as a better job becomes available to them. He has no way of forcing them to stay against their will.

The public enemy is that other foreigner, the individual with labor union and human rights connections, whose mission in Guatemala is to alienate private capital. The decline in output and jobs in the clothing industry witnesses to his success. The outcry against exploitation and child labor in the U.S. creates the illusion that he is fighting for a noble cause. The poor people of Guatemala, those who had found hope for a better future in the clothing industry of the early-1990s, know very well that he has shattered their dreams.

Continued from p. 736

encouraging voluntary use of a label to be sewn in retail garments reading "No Sweat: Product Not Made with Child or Exploited Labor." Such a label has been advocated for decades by the National Consumers League and just this month was endorsed by President Clinton.

"The key to labeling is providing the information that consumers want," says league President Linda Golodner. "Names of individual sweatshops mean nothing; consumers want the names of retailers and manufacturers. They want uncomplicated, easy lists, and they won't have confidence in the label unless there is regular review, monitoring and a resolution procedure."

For the past year, the league-led Child Labor Coalition has been working to publicize the "Rugmark" label that is beginning to appear on hand-knotted carpets. Originated by Indian activist Satyarthi, the label appears on carpets from South Asian factories that have been inspected for child labor abuses. A comparable label is expected soon on a portion of the retail trade in soccer balls.

One problem with such labels, say retailers, is the expense. Charles Castro, vice president of C.I. Castro & Co., a high-end children's clothier in San Antonio, says his company would want a well-designed label, not some cheap stamp, so that it would add prestige to the product.

A stronger concern is how to determine eligibility for labels. "If it contributes to better conditions, then we're interested," says the Gap's Mudd. "But how do you come up with tenets that lead to labeling. Independent monitors? It has to do more than sound great."

Maria Echaveste, administrator of the Labor Department's Wage and Hour Division, supports such labels but points to a need for constant verification. "Obviously, in an industry where contractors break the laws at levels of 55 percent not paying overtime and 43 percent not paying minimum wage, they would very likely break the law on labeling," she says.

International Labour Organization/J. Maillard

A young girl sells her wares in an open-air market in Lomé, Togo.

Pressure on Retailers

The Labor Department in May released a report finding 222 labor law violations nationwide in garment and sweatshops after 472 investigations. It said it recovered $1.3 million in back wages for 3,603 workers and levied $265,000 in fines affecting 237 contractors and 200 manufacturers. [25]

UNITE is circulating a wallet-size "consumer's card" for shoppers who want to avoid clothes made by exploited workers. It suggests the following questions: "Does your store have a code of conduct for all factories that make the clothes you sell? Does it forbid child labor and protect human rights? Does it specify living wages? Is the code of conduct posted in every factory? Is there an independent monitoring agency to make sure that everybody lives up to the code?"

Sweatshop Watch, a nonprofit San Francisco group, has been asking companies such as Montgomery Ward, Sears, Federated Department Stores (R.H. Macy & Co., Bloomingdales), Nordstrom and Neiman Marcus to meet with activists and to adopt a code of conduct. Only two firms agreed to meet, the group says, and both refused the activists' demands.

Such efforts, including mass mailings encouraged by the Child Labor Coalition, do not have much effect on retailers, says J.C. Penney spokesman Muir. He says the facts alleged about exploitation are often wrong, repetitive or out-of-date based on the company's own investigations.

Companies do respond, however, to bad publicity. Laurence Jarvik, a fellow with the Capital Research Center and a longtime critic of public broadcasting, appeared before a congressional appropriations subcommittee in March and attacked the Children's Television Workshop (CTW), creators of "Sesame Street." Jarvik said its spinoff toys had been manufactured by "sweatshop" labor in China, a longtime human rights violator where toy workers earn less than $1 an hour.

Janice Hearty, CTW public affairs manager, says her bosses quickly sent the panel a letter explaining that "we work with the Toy Manufacturers Association, which includes the major companies like Hasbro, Tyco, Fisher-Price, and has a code of conduct and ethics attached to all its supplier contracts. We're careful who we sign with, and we conduct on-site factory inspections. It's not that we're set on doing business in China, but that China is where lots of toys are made." [26] ■

OUTLOOK

Underlying Problems

If sweatshops and child labor are to vanish from the Earth, a multi-pronged effort will be needed to tackle some sizable related problems — illegal immigration, intemperate corporate profit-seeking and inadequate schooling for the developing world's women and children.

Within the United States, notes Secretary Reich, "sweatshops are a magnet for illegal immigrants because unscrupulous employers know that they are willing to take a risk and not complain about work conditions." Yet efforts to cooperate with the Immigration and Naturalization Service in enforcing the law are hampered by the fact that Labor's inspectors "rely on these workers for information on the shops, so if we notify the [Immigration and Naturalization Service], they won't talk to us," Reich says.

Julie Su, who heads the team of attorneys representing the 72 Thai workers enslaved in California, says the immigration laws are confusing to foreigners. "These people were tricked," she says. "They were told they could come to America and make a living and feed their family, but these gangsters took advantage of their being destitute and desperate."

Su believes the solution is to hold U.S. retailers liable for the clothes they sell that were made by undocumented workers, which is the basis on which she is pressing a civil suit against several companies. "I'm tired of the lip service by companies that have been fighting tooth and nail to evade any responsibility by pointing fingers at workers, subcontractors or the government," she says. "Undocumented workers are still protected by labor law. The owners want it both ways. They say illegal immigration is bad, but it still creates profits."

Another unresolved issue is who should perform and finance the monitoring of U.S. and foreign factories. Inspecting and monitoring are difficult, says Labor's Echaveste, because "it is hard to get the workers to tell you what's going on. It's surprising how many workers 'just started work today,' or have 'no idea' what they're being paid."

UNITE's Mazur favors employer consortiums that pay for monitoring by unions and human rights groups. "You can't have the fox guarding the henhouse," he says. "Ultimately the solution is unionization."

But such talk makes business groups nervous. "Unions provide another set of eyes and ears, but there are many places where there is no tradition of unionization," says Dunn of Business for Social Responsibility.

Others say the responsibility lies with governments. Monitoring is viable only for a few companies, says Robin Lanier, vice president for international trade and environment with the International Mass Retail Association. "Retailers who are vertically integrated and therefore produce their own goods can probably set up useful monitoring operations," she told the July Labor Department hearing. But other companies that simply sell what others manufacture may have thousands of factories to monitor, she notes. It is the governments that "can enter factories unannounced and make spot inspections."

Bud Konheim, CEO of Nicole Miller, an upscale clothier in New York, says that companies themselves are in a position to know the true price of production, so they can tell when they lose a bidded contract to a competitor who relies on sweatshops. "Let every company rat on everyone else," he suggests.

"National legislation and international conventions banning child labor have symbolic value as an expression of society's desire to eradicate this practice," says a World Bank study. "But they cannot deliver results unless accompanied by measures to shift the balance of incentives away from child labor and toward education." [27]

The problem, notes the ILO, is that the children who are working — in some countries more than 25 percent of the youth — are often ignored when school budgets are set. And as concerned as American retail companies might be about education levels in countries where they do business, their priority social concerns, says the Gap's Mudd, must be in their primary areas of business, such as New York and San Francisco.

But child labor activists argue that there are feasible solutions. In Egypt, for example, the World Bank reports that a mere 10 percent hike in mothers' wages produced a 15 percent decline in labor among children ages 12 to 14, and a 27 percent decline in work among those 6 to 11. [28] Union President Kearney points out that children who stitch mocassins in Pakistan are paid 10 cents to produce a pair of shoes that, after passing through further production, transport, subcontractor and wholesaler stages, sells for $120 in Italy. "You could double that wage without hurting the business," he says.

The outcome will depend on whether businesses continue to change voluntarily, as many already are. "We

FOR MORE INFORMATION

International Labour Office, Washington Branch, Suite 801, 1828 L St. N.W., Washington, D.C. 20036; (202) 653-7652. Headquartered in Geneva, this United Nations agency sets and monitors world labor standards.

International Mass Retail Association, 1700 N. Moore St., Suite 2250, Arlington, Va. 22209; (703) 841-2300. The association monitors legislative issues on behalf of the fastest-growing segment of the retail industry, including discount department stores, warehouse clubs and suppliers.

National Child Labor Committee, 1501 Broadway, Suite 1111, New York, N.Y. 10036; (212) 840-1801. Founded in 1904, this group of social activists and business leaders advocates improved education and working conditions for youth and migrant workers.

National Consumers League, 1701 K St. N.W., Suite 1200, Washington, D.C. 20006; (202) 835-3323. Founded in 1899 to tap consumer power in improving work conditions, the league currently coordinates the Child Labor Coalition along with religious groups, labor unions and public interest organizations.

UNITE, 1710 Broadway, New York, N.Y. 10019; (212) 332-9365. The Union of Needletrades, Industrial and Textile Employees was formed in 1995 by the merger of the Amalgamated Clothing and Textile Workers and International Ladies' Garment Workers' unions.

National Retail Federation, Liberty Place, 325 7th St. N.W., Suite 1000, Washington, D.C. 20004; (202) 783-3971. "The world's largest retail trade association" represents major department stores as well as independent and specialty stores in monitoring legislative and regulatory issues.

need an increased sense of urgency," says Lee Scott, executive vice president of Wal-Mart. "We will take a strong stand and put the full weight of Wal-Mart stores behind our dealings with vendors. We won't be humiliated in front of our customers. This black eye belongs to us as a nation."

And should the government crack down, is there a risk of economic disruption — inflation, new unemployment or a trade war? "Our object is not to close down and eliminate jobs, but to improve conditions," says Reich. "We would like to exhaust all multilateral treaties and conventions first because the opinions of mankind speaking together are more eloquent. Our nation has problems itself, so who are we to cast the first stone?"

The question today, Reich adds, is: "Will we still be troubled by all this two weeks from now, or six months from now? It is the responsibility of all of us to keep this issue alive." ■

Notes

[1] Seven members of the Thai family that ran the El Monte sweatshop pleaded guilty to involuntary slavery charges and were sentenced to prison terms ranging from two to seven years. In addition, U.S. District Judge Audrey B. Collins ordered the family to pay $4.5 million to the workers, one of whom was kept imprisoned for seven years.

[2] *Maclean's,* Dec. 11, 1995, p. 29. Craig Kielburger was inspired by the death of Iqbal Masih, a former child laborer who had received the 1994 Reebok Youth in Action award for his efforts against child labor.

[3] Testimony before House International Relations Subcommittee on International Operations and Human Rights, July 15, 1996.

[4] For background, see "Prostitution," *The CQ Researcher,* June 11, 1993, pp. 505-528.

[5] Assefa Bequele and Jo Boyden, eds., *Combating Child Labor* (1988), p. 7.

[6] *The Economist,* June 3, 1995, p. 58.

[7] The November 1995 survey was conducted by the Center for Ethical Concerns and the Department of Fashion Design and Merchandising at Marymount University in Arlington, Va.

[8] Sydney Schanberg, *Life,* June 1, 1996, p. 38.

[9] Human Rights Watch/Asia, "Contemporary Forms of Slavery in Pakistan," July 1995, p. 68.

[10] Testimony before Subcommittee on International Operations and Human Rights, July 15, 1996.

[11] Guest editorial in *USA Today,* June 21, 1996. For more on the WTO, see "Rethinking NAFTA," *The CQ Researcher,* June 7, 1996, pp. 481-504.

[12] Testimony at International Labour Organization hearing at the Labor Department, June 28, 1996.

[13] Quoted in Barry Berak, "Stitching Together a Crusade," *Los Angeles Times,* July 25, 1996.

[14] *The New York Times,* June 10, 1996.

[15] Quoted in *USA Today,* June 6, 1996.

[16] UNITE and the National Consumers League, "Stop Sweatshops: A Partnership for Responsibility," 1995.

[17] Milton Meltzer, *Cheap Raw Material: How Our Youngest Workers Are Exploited and Abused* (1994), p. 26.

[18] *Ibid.,* p. 29.

[19] David R. Roediger and Philip S. Foner, *Our Own Time: A History of American Labor and the Working Day* (1989), p. 11.

[20] Meltzer, *op. cit.,* p. 36.

[21] *Loc. cit.*

[22] Roediger and Foner, *op. cit.,* p. 169.

[23] *Ibid.,* p. 254.

[24] Quoted in Victoria Rialp, *Children and Hazardous Work in the Philippines* (1993), p. 7.

[25] Labor Department, Wage and Hour Division, "Garment Enforcement Report: October 1995-March 1996."

[26] For background, see "U.S.-China Trade," *The CQ Researcher,* June 15, 1994, pp. 313-336.

[27] World Bank, "World Development Report 1995: Workers in an Integrating World," June 29, 1995, p. 72.

[28] World Bank, *op. cit.*

Bibliography

Selected Sources Used

Books

Bequele, Assefa, and Jo Boyden, eds., *Combating Child Labour,* International Labour Office, 1988.

These case studies examining work conditions in the Philippines, Brazil, Peru, Egypt and India shed light on the complexities of moving traditional societies away from dependence on child labor.

Bequele, A., and W.E. Myers, *First Things First in Child Labour: Eliminating Work Detrimental to Children*, International Labour Office, 1995.

This overview of the practice of exploiting children as laborers discusses legal, economic and cultural reasons why existing laws are not effective in curbing abuses.

Howard, Philip K., *The Death of Common Sense: How Law is Suffocating America,* Random House, 1994.

A New York attorney active in zoning issues produced this scathing look at what he sees as irrational excesses of legal and bureaucratic requirements by Congress, courts and such agencies as the Occupational Safety and Health Administration.

Meltzer, Milton, *Cheap Raw Material: How Our Youngest Workers Are Exploited and Abused,* Viking, 1994.

An author of more than 80 books details the use of child labor from the days of slavery in ancient Rome and the excesses of the Industrial Revolution to the U.S. reforms of the early 20th century and the present-day campaign against exploitation.

Roediger, David R., and Philip S. Foner, *Our Own Time: A History of American Labor and the Working Day,* Greenwood Press, 1989.

Two academic historians discuss the issues, individuals and organizations that shaped America's ongoing struggle over wages, hours and working conditions.

Articles

Pignatella, Michael A., "The Recurring Nightmare of Child Labor Abuse and Solutions for the 1990s," *Boston College Third World Law Journal*, winter 1995.

An attorney examines the history and current effectiveness of the Fair Labor Standards Act in preventing abuses in child labor in the United States.

Reports and Studies

Human Rights Watch, *Children of Sudan: Slaves, Street Children and Child Soldiers*, 1995.

The Africa division of this international human rights monitoring group documents the buying and selling of children in a Civil War-torn east African nation.

International Labour Office, *Child Labour: What is to be Done,* June 12, 1996.

This report from an international meeting of unions, employers and non-governmental bodies lays out the current scope of the child labor problem in the developing world.

U.S. Labor Department, *By the Sweat and Toil of Children,* Vols. I & II., 1994, 1995.

These twin volumes from the Bureau of International Labor Affairs document the problem of child labor, first in mined and manufactured imports and second in agricultural imports and the use of forced or bonded labor overseas.

U.S. Labor Department, *Forced Labor: The Prostitution of Children,* 1996.

These proceedings from a September 1995 symposium document and analyze the growing practice in many Third World countries of conscripting children in the sex trade patronized primarily by international businessmen.

U.S. Labor Department, *No Sweat: Garment Enforcement Report,* October 1995-March 1996.

This compilation by the Wage and Hour Division of the Labor Department itemizes the number of inspections, fines and back-wage collections achieved by the federal government in its campaign against U.S. sweatshops.

World Bank, *World Development Report 1995: Workers in an Integrating World*, June 29, 1995.

This economic and social analysis of the current world economy contains a section on child labor, arguing that general economic development and compulsory schooling are more promising solutions than consumer boycotts.

The Next Step

Additional information from UMI's Newspaper & Periodical Abstracts database

Child Labor

Chapman, Stephen, "How to end child labor in the Third World," ***Chicago Tribune,*** **June 13, 1996, p. 31.**
Chapman says that if Nike closed its factories in Indonesia or the U.S. government banned the Indonesian-made shoes or consumers boycotted them, thousands of poor Indonesian children and adults who work long hours for little money would have no work at all.

Chimhete, Caiphas, "Child labor rampant in southern Africa," ***Amsterdam News,*** **Jan. 6, 1996, p. 2.**
Child labor continues to increase in southern Africa, despite a growing commitment by government, non-governmental organizations and individuals to curb it. Reasons for this growth and the problems for children created by it are discussed.

Guest, Iain, "Child labor — A shadow over the Atlanta Games," ***The Christian Science Monitor,*** **July 15, 1996, p. 18.**
Guest discusses the impact of child-labor abuses on clothing and sports-equipment manufacturers on the 1996 Olympic Games in Atlanta. Guest says "child labor exposes the seamy side of free trade and unfettered capitalism. In an age of unprecedented deregulation, this makes it one of the most explosive items on the international agenda."

Harkin, Sen. Tom, "Put an end to the exploitation of child labor," ***USA Today,*** **January 1996, pp. 73-75.**
The U.S. fails to protect children from exploitive and abusive labor by continuing to allow the importation of goods made through the exploitation of children, writes Sen. Harkin, D-Iowa. The problem of child labor is discussed.

Harvey, Pharis J., "Where children work: Child servitude in the global economy." ***Christian Century,*** **April 5, 1995, pp. 362-365.**
The prevalence of child servitude in India and around the world is discussed, as are efforts to draw attention to the problem and end it. Most solutions to the problem will have to be generated on the national and local level.

Leipziger, Deborah, and Pia Sabharwal, "Companies that play hide and seek with child labor," ***Business & Society Review,*** **1996, pp. 11-13**
Child labor is increasing as the economy becomes more global and is also becoming a significant problem in many industrialized countries. The Council on Economic Priorities has launched a study of the records of U.S. companies with regard to the employment of child labor by contractors in Asia and Latin America.

Prince, Cathryn J., "Ending child labor: Tall task for nations," ***The Christian Science Monitor,*** **June 19, 1996, p. 8.**
The International Labour Organization (ILO), a U.N. agency, held its annual labor conference in Geneva between June 4-20, 1996. The ILO focused on the issue of child labor at the conference, and hopes by 1999 to develop a convention banning the most severe forms of child labor, including forced or slave labor, prostitution and labor in mines and glassworks.

"Report cites forced child labor in Asia," ***USA Today,*** **Sept. 19, 1995, p. B4.**
More than 100 million Asian children, some as young as four, are forced to work in appalling conditions to make consumer products for Western nations, according to the Anti-Slavery Society, an Australian group.

Schanberg, Sydney H., "Six cents an hour," ***Life,*** **June 1996, pp. 38-48.**
Pakistan's still-feudal society supports a large child labor market. There are industries where legions of small children toil for 60 cents a day to make products for exports to the U.S. and other developed countries.

Silvers, Jonathan, "Child labor in Pakistan," ***Atlantic Monthly,*** **February 1996, pp. 79-92.**
Despite new laws limiting child labor and indentured servitude, about 11 million children ages 4-14 work in Pakistan's factories and fields. Their working conditions are often brutal and squalid.

Wildavsky, Ben, "A noble cause, unintended harm?" ***National Journal,*** **Nov. 18, 1995, p. 2897.**
Opposition by the International Labour Organization (ILO) to a bill sponsored by Sen. Tom Harkin, D-Iowa, that would ban imports of goods produced by children under the age of 15 is discussed. Claiming the high moral ground in the debate will probably do little to help the situation.

Celebrity Endorsements

Jones, Del, "Critics tie sweatshop sneakers to 'Air' Jordan," ***USA Today,*** **June 6, 1996, p. B1.**
Just in time for the 1996 NBA finals, labor activists say Michael Jordan's line of Nike athletic shoes are made by Indonesian children in sweatshops. It is unknown whether Jordan is aware of the complaints.

Solomon, Norman, "The company behind Kathie Lee," ***Atlanta Constitution,*** **June 5, 1996, p. A15.**
Solomon discusses the child labor scandal surrounding the making of Kathie Lee Gifford's line of clothing for Wal-Mart, saying Walt Disney Co., which owns the "Live With Regis & Kathie Lee" show, should also be called upon to

end its dealings with cheap, overseas labor. Solomon says Disney's Pocahontas and Lion King clothing for kids are made by poor women in Haiti.

Thomas, Karen, "Kathie Lee goes to Washington," *USA Today,* July 15, 1996, p. D1.
Kathie Lee Gifford, who will testify July 15, 1996, on Capitol Hill about the sweatshop problem and attend a garment industry summit on July 16, says the worst of her clothing-line scandal is over, but she's angrier than before.

Carpet and Rug Industries

"Child labor," *Maclean's,* June 19, 1995, p. 43.
The alleged death threats made against India's chief opponent of child labor, Kailash Satyarthi, are discussed. Satyarthi was arrested in early June 1995 and accused of defrauding a local carpet manufacturer, which claims it lost a contract as a result of Satyarthi's participation in a documentary depicting child slavery in India's carpet industry.

"Child labor critic is slain in Pakistan," *The New York Times,* April 19, 1995, p. A16.
Iqbal Masih, a 12-year-old boy who won international acclaim for highlighting the horrors of child labor in Pakistan, was shot and killed on April 16, 1995, as he and two friends rode their bicycles in their village. Iqbal had received several death threats from people in the carpet industry.

Erlich, Reese, "India battles illegal child labor," *The Christian Science Monitor,* Nov. 8, 1995, p. 9.
The Indian government has begun a crackdown on the use of child labor in the carpet-weaving industry. Critics are skeptical that the plan, which is financed by a small tax on exporter sales, will succeed. Because consumers in Germany and the U.S. are increasingly concerned about the child-labor issue, the success or failure of the program could help determine the future of the industry.

Foreign Governments' Response

Bermudez, Roberto Flores, "Latin America isn't in favor of child labor," *The Wall Street Journal,* Aug. 16, 1995, p. A11.
Bermudez, ambassador to the U.S. from Honduras, responds to the July 3, 1995, article "Broken Rules." Bermudez says no Central American country is trying to develop its economy through the use of child labor.

Mulet, Edmond, "Latin America isn't in favor of child labor," *The Wall Street Journal,* Aug. 16, 1995, p. A11.
Mulet, ambassador to the U.S. from Guatemala, responds to the July 3, 1995, article "Broken Rules." Mulet says Guatemala and the nations throughout the region are concerned about labor issues, including child labor.

Tefft, Sheila, "In China's rush to riches, it tries to curb child labor," *The Christian Science Monitor,* Jan. 31, 1995, p. 1.
China has launched an initiative against the recruitment and employment of children under 16, under a new labor law effective on Jan. 1, 1995. The hiring and abduction of children to work small jobs, sell, beg or be forced into prostitution in Chinese cities is reportedly on the rise in the booming economy.

Sweatshops

Epstein, Jack, "Dickens revisited in Brazil sweatshops," *The Christian Science Monitor,* Aug. 24, 1995, p. 1.
The use of underage workers for the shoe industry in Franca, Brazil, is discussed. The city and its 388 shoe factories have captured headlines in 1995 as the "child-labor capital of Brazil." A 1994 study found that 73 percent of 1,561 Franca children ages 7 to 13 said they made shoes in poor working conditions for little pay.

"Honduran girl testifies of sweatshop abuse," *San Francisco Chronicle,* May 30, 1996, P. A5.
Surrounded by congressmen, labor advocates and human rights workers, Wendy Diaz, a 15-year-old Honduran girl, on May 29, 1996, appealed to celebrity Kathie Lee Gifford to help end the abuse of children in sweatshops that make garments bearing Gifford's name.

Yeh, Emerald, and Christine McMurry, "Sweatshop bargains: A shopper's dilemma," *San Francisco Chronicle,* July 14, 1996, p. S5.
Yeh and McMurry discuss the consumer's dilemma with shopping. They question how consumers can be certain that the clothing they buy isn't stained with sweatshop labor and wonder whether they would be willing to pay more for apparel if it helps wipe out sweatshops. Yeh and McMurry note that 60 percent of the clothing sold in America is made elsewhere, but sweatshops also exist in the U.S.

U.S. Department of Labor

Chandler, Susan, and Wendy Zellner, "Prime Time for Sweatshops," *Business Week,* June 17, 1996, p. 44.
Labor Secretary Robert B. Reich's campaign against sweatshops is rolling following a scandal surrounding perky TV celebrity Kathie Lee Gifford. Wal-Mart, K Mart and other retailers are being asked to avoid using child labor.

"8 firms hit with labor fines," *Denver Post,* Jan. 26, 1996, p. B6.
The U.S. Department of Labor has fined eight Colorado employers more than $164,000 for violations of child-labor laws uncovered during a one-week enforcement sweep during the summer of 1995. Four of the eight were amusement parks.

Shepardson, David, "Inspectors fight to curtail unfair fruits of child labor," *Detroit News,* April 25, 1996, p. D1.
An estimated 270,000 Michigan teenagers, ages 14-19, held jobs in 1995, up 3 percent from 1994, Labor Department figures show. There has been a concurrent increase in citations for violations of child labor laws.

Back Issues

Great Research on Current Issues Starts Right Here...Recent topics covered by The CQ Researcher are listed below. Before May 1991, reports were published under the name of Editorial Research Reports.

FEBRUARY 1995
Cracking Down on Immigration
The Business of Sports
Reinventing Government
Housing Discrimination

MARCH 1995
Death Penalty Debate
Primary Care
Democracy in Africa
Environmental Movement at 25

APRIL 1995
Abortion Clinic Protests
Dieting and Health
Combating AIDS
Rethinking Affirmative Action

MAY 1995
Assisted Suicide Controversy
Overhauling Social Security
Learning to Read
Mandatory Sentencing

JUNE 1995
Combating Infectious Disease
Property Rights
Repetitive Stress Injuries
Regulating the Internet

JULY 1995
War Crimes
Highway Safety
Combating Terrorism
Preventing Teen Drug Use

AUGUST 1995
Job Stress
Organ Transplants
United Nations at 50
Advances in Cancer Research

SEPTEMBER 1995
Catholic Church in the U.S.
Northern Ireland Cease-Fire
High School Sports
Teaching History

OCTOBER 1995
Quebec's Future
Revitalizing the Cities
Networking the Classroom
Indoor Air Pollution

NOVEMBER 1995
The Working Poor
The Jury System
Sex, Violence and the Media
Police Misconduct

DECEMBER 1995
Teens and Tobacco
Gene Therapy's Future
Global Water Shortages
Third-Party Prospects

JANUARY 1996
Emergency Medicine
Punishing Sex Offenders
Bilingual Education
Helping the Homeless

FEBRUARY 1996
Reforming the CIA
Campaign Finance Reform
Academic Politics
Getting Into College

MARCH 1996
The British Monarchy
Preventing Juvenile Crime
Tax Reform
Pursuing the Paranormal

APRIL 1996
Centennial Olympic Games
Managed Care
Protecting Endangered Species
New Military Culture

MAY 1996
Russia's Political Future
Marriage and Divorce
Year-Round Schools
Taiwan, China and the U.S.

JUNE 1996
Rethinking NAFTA
First Ladies
Teaching Values
Labor Movement's Future

JULY 1996
Recovered-Memory Debate
Native Americans' Future
Crackdown on Sexual Harassment
Attack on Public Schools

AUGUST 1996
Fighting Over Animal Rights
Privatizing Government Services

Back issues are available for $5.00 (subscribers) or $8.00 (non-subscribers). Quantity discounts apply to orders over ten. To order, call Congressional Quarterly Customer Service at (202) 887-8621.

Binders are available for $18.00. To order call 1-800-638-1710. Please refer to stock number 648.

Future Topics

- ***Cleaning Up Hazardous Wastes***
- ***Gambling***
- ***The States and Federalism***

THE CQ Researcher

PUBLISHED BY CONGRESSIONAL QUARTERLY INC.

Cleaning Up Hazardous Wastes

Will Congress improve the "superfund" law?

Concern about pollution from toxic-waste dumps — dramatized by New York's Love Canal — prompted Congress to pass a tough cleanup law in 1980. Known as "superfund," it quickly became a lightning rod for criticism of federal environmental regulations. Industries and individuals held responsible for toxic-waste sites say the law has driven many innocent parties into bankruptcy while delaying cleanups with expensive litigation. Advocacy groups representing communities near toxic dumps say proposed Republican reforms would enrich corporate profits while ignoring citizens needing protection. The Clinton administration has suggested several reforms to make superfund fairer and more efficient without abandoning the law's "polluter pays" principle: Polluters must clean up the hazardous sites they created.

INSIDE THIS ISSUE

CQ August 23, 1996 • Volume 6, No. 32 • Pages 745-768

Formerly Editorial Research Reports

CLEANING UP HAZARDOUS WASTES

COVER AND PAGE 747: HAZARDOUS-WASTE DISPOSAL EXPERTS FROM THE ENVIRONMENTAL PROTECTION AGENCY TAKE SAMPLES FOR TESTING FROM A TOXIC-WASTE SITE. (ENVIRONMENTAL PROTECTION AGENCY)

August 23, 1996
Volume 6, No. 32

The CQ Researcher (ISSN 1056-2036). Formerly Editorial Research Reports. Published weekly (48 times per year, not printed March 1, May 31, Aug. 30, Nov. 29) by Congressional Quarterly Inc., 1414 22nd St., N.W., Washington, D.C. 20037. Annual subscription rate for libraries, businesses and government is $319. Additional rates furnished upon request. Periodicals postage paid at Washington, D.C. POSTMASTER: Send address changes to The CQ Researcher, 1414 22nd St., N.W., Washington, D.C. 20037.

Cleaning Up Hazardous Wastes

BY MARY H. COOPER

THE ISSUES

Nestled high in the Sawatch Range of central Colorado, Leadville glories in its colorful past. Every summer during the Boom Days festival, residents parade through town as gun-toting lawmen, grizzled prospectors and ladies of the night.

It all began in 1875, when a gold miner named Chicken Bill stumbled onto one of the world's richest veins of silver. Within two years, the silver rush had turned the remote mining camp into the state's second-largest town, teeming with assorted scoundrels and would-be mining magnates.

Before the Great Silver Crash of 1893 ended the boom, many Leadville locals had indeed made fortunes in silver — among them storekeeper Horace Tabor and his mistress Baby Doe. Even after the big lodes petered out, mining of gold, silver and, more recently, molybdenum, continued to feed Leadville well into the 1980s.

So when the Environmental Protection Agency (EPA) identified much of Leadville as a hazardous-waste dump in 1983, townspeople reacted with predictable outrage.

In fact, they even hung a picture of the EPA project manager from a noose looped over a mock hanging tree, recalls Mary Hagan, an EPA community-relations specialist. "This was a mining town for 100 years," she says. "You can imagine how they reacted when we came in and told them that what had provided the sustenance for themselves and their families is bad. The Leadville site was nothing but trouble, terrible trouble."

Trouble is what many critics say the nation's hazardous-waste cleanup program has been from the start. Launched in 1980 by the Comprehensive Environmental Response, Compensation and Liability Act (CERCLA), it was

based on the fundamental principle that polluters should pay for cleaning up the hazardous wastes they create. In Leadville, that meant getting rid of the lead-laced mine tailings and smelter waste on which the city was built.

The law authorized the EPA to identify the nation's most seriously contaminated sites and force the polluters to clean them. The law also established a "superfund" to pay for emergency cleanups and cleanups where the responsible party was unknown or unwilling or unable to pay. It is financed by taxes on petroleum products and the raw materials used to make chemicals, as well as a general environmental tax on corporate earnings.

Superfund, as the ambitious EPA program quickly became known, was Congress' response to the outcry that went up in 1977 over Love Canal. The Niagara Falls, N.Y., subdivision, it was discovered that year, had been built atop a highly toxic chemical dump. As residents — many of them sickened from toxic exposure — abandoned their homes, public officials discovered that the company responsible for the contamination was no longer in business, and that existing law provided no means to clean it up.

But Leadville is a far cry from Love Canal, residents of the rugged mining town insist. "The [scientific] model the EPA used to predict the effects of lead contamination was based on some really off-the-wall assumptions by wannabe, do-gooder scientists who couldn't get jobs in real industry," protests David Dunn, a metallurgical engineer and mining consultant who has lived in Leadville for 34 years. One assumption, he says, would have required people to eat locally caught fish at every meal for a year. "If a person catches two or three fish a year around here, they're generally considered pretty lucky because our streams are few, small and — for more than half the year — covered with ice."

Because lead is especially toxic to children, it can no longer be used in most paints, gasoline and other consumer products. [1] But Dunn says the EPA's estimates of lead uptake by Leadville children were also overstated. "A kid would have had to eat a pound of dirt a day to pick up the amount of lead that they estimated," he says.

Dunn and other critics of superfund clean-up efforts at Western mining sites also insist that the lead found in the region's tailings and smelter waste is not readily absorbed by the body. "The lead here is present in the form of galena, which is lead sulfide, a very chemical-resistant mineral that decomposes very, very slowly and is almost totally insoluble in common acids," Dunn says. "But the EPA made no differentiation among lead sources."

Bad science is only one of the charges critics level at the superfund program. Even more controversial is the way it assigns liability for cleanup to anyone who once contributed to contamination — even if the contribution was minimal

Midwest and Coastal States Have Most Hazardous-Waste Sites

Since the country's hazardous-waste-disposal program was launched in 1980, 1,387 seriously polluted dump sites have been identified by the Environmental Protection Agency. The total includes 362 sites where the construction needed to clean up the site has been completed. States with the most sites (dark shading) have substantial industrial development. New Jersey (116 sites) and Pennsylvania (111 sites) lead the nation in sites.

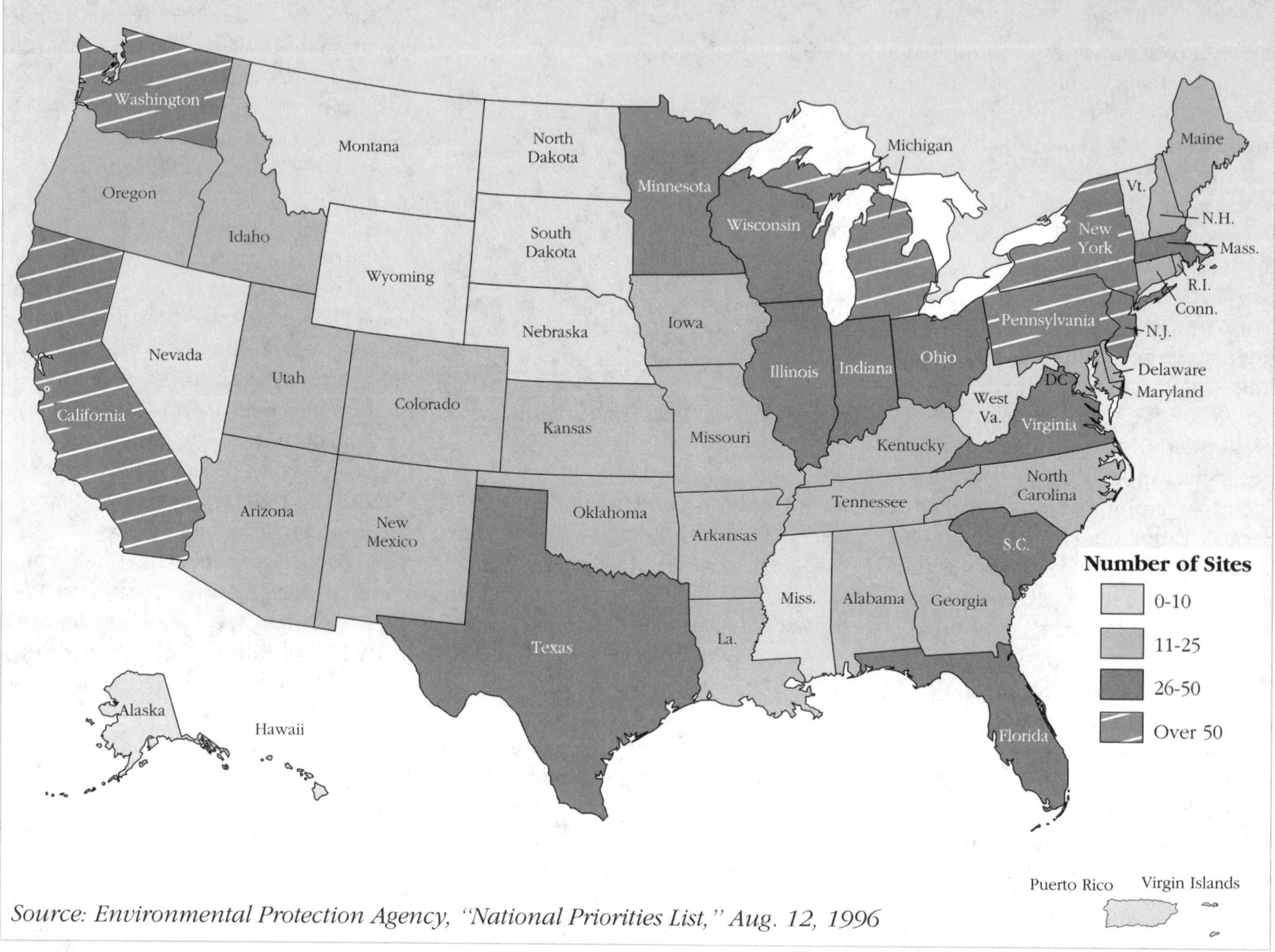

Source: Environmental Protection Agency, "National Priorities List," Aug. 12, 1996

and the polluter broke no law by depositing waste at the site.

Not surprisingly, lengthy litigation has plagued the program from the start, often delaying needed remediation for several years. Since the superfund program was launched 16 years ago, a total of 1,387 sites have been placed on the EPA's "national priorities list" of seriously contaminated sites. At 362 of those sites, private contractors working under EPA direction have completed the construction necessary for cleaning up the contamination caused by chemical dumps, mines and abandoned industrial plants.

"Reforming superfund is not a luxury, it is a necessity," Rep. Blanche Lambert Lincoln, D-Ark., testified at one of several congressional hearings held earlier this year on proposals to rewrite the law. "The program has not worked as intended. Small businesses and charitable organizations such as the Girl Scouts have been hauled into court; large corporations who have contributed only a small amount of hazardous waste have been liable for the lion's share of the cleanup because of their deep pockets; banks have been held liable only because they have mortgages on the land; and municipalities have been forced into hiring lawyers where their limited resources could be better used to upgrade essential citizen services." [2]

Many Republican lawmakers concur with Lincoln on superfund. "Of all the items that remain on the Senate agenda for 1996, there is probably no issue that is more complicated, more explosive and more important than reform of superfund," said Sen. Rick Santorum, R-Pa. "To let this situation drag on another year or two . . . while politicians squabble is unconscionable." [3]

Criticism of the superfund program runs so deep that it has been threatened with extinction every five years, when the law has come up for reauthorization. Last Dec. 31, after Congress was unable to agree on reforms, superfund's taxing authority was allowed to expire for the first time. Lawmakers recently gave up trying to reauthorize the program with broad reforms this year as well. The program is able to continue operating only because it has collected enough funds to keep it going through fiscal year 2000 (*see p. 758*).

"There is room for improvement," concedes Timothy Fields Jr., deputy assistant administrator for EPA's solid waste and emergency response office, which runs the superfund program. "That is one thing that we and Congress agree on. There is a need to fix the law in order for us to have the kind of program we all want to have."

Noting that one in four Americans lives near a toxic waste site, Fields says, "America cannot survive without a cleanup program. The problems of Love Canal and hundreds of other toxic waste dumps in this country demand that we have a program, and that program will be needed for some time into the future."

Fields also notes that superfund has become far more effective and fairer in the past three years as a result of Clinton administration reforms that have speeded up cleanups, in part by letting marginal polluters off the hook. Another Clinton reform encourages the use of less heavily polluted sites, known as "brownfields," for commercial and industrial development by protecting potential buyers from future liability suits. Such developments provide job opportunities to area residents, supporters say, offering hope for reviving some of the country's poorest inner-city neighborhoods. (*See story, p. 752.*)

Mary H. Cooper

Mounds of lead-laced mine tailings in and around Leadville, Colo., led to its designation as a superfund site.

Despite such reforms, superfund still has its critics — including some residents who complain that the agency should use even tougher standards of cleanliness. "Unfortunately, when we go into some communities, we've become the enemy, more so than the people who caused the contamination," Fields says. "But we've got to uphold the law, and we've got to make sure that we're protecting people, even when people want us to go away."

When lawmakers take up superfund's reauthorization again, these are some of the questions they will be asking:

Is superfund a failure?

The chemical, oil and mining industries say the superfund program has been an abject failure, primarily because it has delayed the cleanup of dumps that pose serious health hazards. These delays are caused mainly by lengthy and expensive lawsuits to determine who will pay the cleanup costs. This process, critics say, only enriches technical consultants hired to evaluate the contamination and lawyers who profit from the often drawn-out litigation process.

"Every month that continues to go by without reauthorization means more delays in cleanups, more litigation resulting from an inequitable liability scheme, more controversy between the public and EPA and more wasteful spending by both the government and the private sector," said J. Lawrence Wilson, chairman of the Chemical Manufacturers Association, whose members have been heavily assessed for superfund cleanups. "With current superfund spending estimated at $10 million per day, each month that goes by means another $300 million poured into a program that everyone now agrees is badly broken." [4]

Some of superfund's most vocal critics are marginal polluters who have been dragged into the liability process by major polluters trying to spread their cleanup costs. Barbara Williams, owner of the Sunnyray Restaurant in Gettysburg, Pa., told her story to lawmakers. "My being brought into this suit defies common sense," she said. "I have recycled for years. I have used the trash hauler that was approved and permitted by my borough government. I am told that my trash was then dumped into the Keystone landfill, a site permitted by the Commonwealth of Pennsylvania. I would appreciate someone explaining how I have become liable even after I obeyed all state and local regulations. What was I supposed to do with the food scraps? What have I disposed of that isn't found in every household?" [5]

Williams' experience with superfund's liability system underscores what critics say is the law's main flaw. The EPA initially sued to force Keystone Sanitation Co. and eight other polluters to pay for cleaning up the landfill. They in turn sued some 180 small businesses as third-party defendants because their wastes had ended up in the Keystone dump. The third-party defendants then sued about 550 additional small businesses, municipalities and school districts, including Williams' restaurant.

"I am a fourth-party defendant in this case," Williams said. "I have been sued by my friends and neighbors. Why did they do this? Because the only options they were given by their attorneys was to either pay the exorbitant amount of money that the first and second parties had sued for, or to sue others in order to lessen the amount they would be forced to pay for settlement."

Some community activists condemn superfund for different reasons. Florence T. Robinson, representing the North Baton Rouge [Louisiana] Environmental Association, said the law has left millions of low-income Americans exposed to toxic wastes. "Government has failed these citizens, who through no fault of their own have been horribly exposed," she said, citing the program's inadequate treatment of people living near two superfund sites in Pensacola, Fla. "These citizens, and millions like them, need not to be just relocated, but given medical assistance. . . . The location of many waste sites is in low-income areas where people have no insurance, or very limited insurance. Because they are low-income . . . they do not go to the doctor for regular checkups and treatment. Consequently, by the time they realize they are sick, too often their illness has progressed beyond the easily treatable stage." [6]

Environmental Protection Agency

Drums filled with toxic chemicals are routinely disposed of illegally by "midnight dumpers" in vacant lots, swamps and even tractor trailers abandoned along highways.

Other community activists defend superfund. "You've got to understand that superfund addresses the worst sites in our society," says Charles Lee, director of environmental justice for the United Church of Christ's Commission for Racial Justice in New York City. "To call superfund a failure is an oversimplification. Superfund isn't that old in terms of the age of these problems. To say the program is a failure is like saying we can solve racism in 20 years. How do you expect to solve something that's embedded in our society for so long in just 20 years?"

Clinton administration officials involved in superfund operations acknowledge the program's shortcomings but largely blame them on the reluctance of the Reagan administration's openly anti-environmental appointees to enforce the law. Reagan's first EPA administrator, Anne M. Burford, was a vocal critic of her own agency's mandate to protect the environment to the law's full extent and was forced to resign in 1983. [7]

"The superfund got off to a rocky start in the early 1980s with the leadership we had at the time," says Fields of the EPA. "However, over the last several years superfund has made tremendous strides. It's a very different program now than it was during the early days."

Since 1993, when President Clinton appointed Carol M. Browner, formerly Florida's top environmental regulator, to head the EPA, the superfund program has accelerated its operations. Over the past three years, Fields says, construction has been completed at nearly 200 superfund sites — more than the number that were completed in the 12 years before the Clinton administration came into office. The EPA also has conducted on average 300 emergency responses a year to thwart existing or threatened releases of toxic wastes around the country.

Even though Congress has yet to modify the law, the EPA has been able to act unilaterally, through administrative reforms, to make superfund fairer and more efficient, defenders say. One such reform goes to the heart of Barbara Williams' complaint. It permits the agency to free parties that contributed only marginally to site contamination — so-called de minimis parties — from the program's far-reaching liability net. This change not only enables the agency to concentrate on the heavier polluters but also reduces the volume of litigation to be waded through before cleanups can actually proceed.

Although Browner strongly supports sweeping legislative reforms to make the program more effective, she says the recent administrative changes have greatly improved superfund. "We believe that many of these initiatives have provided measurable benefits to superfund stakeholders, to public health and the environment," Browner told lawmakers. "We anticipate that these investments in long-term performance improvement will continue to produce significant resource savings, more cleanups and more effective public participation." [8]

Should polluters have to pay for cleaning up sites they contaminated before superfund went into effect?

One of the basic principles embodied in superfund law is the notion that polluters should pay for the contamination they cause. While the Clinton administration supports broad changes in the law, it stands firmly behind the "polluter pays" principle.

"We don't believe that the American people should pay for the contamination caused by major contributors of environmental contamination," Fields says. "We believe strongly that the polluter should pay the cost of cleanups, and that's one thing that we have not compromised on in the superfund debate."

But critics of the law say it is unfair to penalize individuals and companies that contributed to pollution before Dec. 11, 1980, when the law went into effect. Many superfund sites, such as a mine at Smuggler Mountain in Aspen, Colo., and a coal-tar dump in Saratoga Springs, N.Y., were abandoned a century or more ago.

"Under superfund . . . liability it is not necessary to prove that those found liable for cleanup costs did anything wrong, or were substantially responsible for the hazards present at a site," said Robert E. Vagley, president of the American Insurance Association (AIA).

"We anticipate that these investments in long-term performance improvement will continue to produce significant resource savings, more cleanups and more effective public participation."

—Carol M. Browner
Administrator
Environmental Protection Agency

"Fault or wrongdoing are irrelevant under this liability scheme. While this [sweeping] scope of liability might increase the chance that the government will recover its costs, it is inconsistent with the notion of corrective justice which purportedly underlies the 'polluter pays' principle." [9]

In addition to being unfair, critics say the law's insistence that all polluters be held responsible for past contamination — no matter how little they may have contributed or how long ago — explains why the program has so often been mired in litigation.

"The superfund liability system wastes more resources, in the form of time and money, than any other single element of the superfund program," Vagley said. "The superfund's retroactive, strict, joint and several liability system, in effect, gives practically unlimited access to private funding sources, with virtually no accountability. Thus, cleanup decisions have been made under a federal structure that often has little concern for cost, little concern for economic and social disruption and little concern for the litigation which necessarily results."

But administration officials say polluters bear a special responsibility for cleaning up contaminated sites, even though they may have broken no laws when they dumped toxic wastes into the environment. "They are the ones who spent 50 years or more dumping contaminated materials into the groundwater, into the soil," Fields says. "Those fuel companies, those chemical companies, those major industries that caused environmental harm to their fellow citizens need to pay the price of environmental cleanup because they are the ones that profited from the products that they produced."

Even the harshest critics of superfund's retroactive liability provision acknowledge that it cannot be done away with entirely, because current taxpayers can't be expected to shoulder all the costs involved in cleaning the country's most polluted sites. "The AIA, together with the entire insurance industry, has long supported the full repeal of retroactive liability," Vagley said. "Neverthe-

Environmental Justice Movement Focuses on Minorities

When the environmental movement began in the 1970s, it reflected the priorities of its prosperous, mostly white leadership. Since the mid-1980s, however, minorities have assumed an increasingly prominent role. A growing environmental justice movement is calling for special efforts to clean up minority communities, claiming that inner-city black and Hispanic residents, as well as American Indians on remote reservations, are more likely to be exposed to toxic wastes and other pollutants.

The movement's approach toward environmental problems differs from that of the superfund program, which identifies specific waste sites and cleans them up. "We look at the hazards in a community as a whole, rather than each being site-specific," says Charles Lee, director of the United Church of Christ's Commission for Racial Justice, who has advised the Environmental Protection Agency (EPA) on environmental justice issues. "If you were to take a bunch of sites, all of which may comply with standards, it doesn't mean that cumulatively there is no risk in that community. Moreover, there may be other sites that are completely undocumented."

Lee says the high incidence of asthma in many minority communities underscores the importance of emphasizing the multiple aspects of environmental problems. "Asthma is a controllable disease that is caused by several different sources and is exacerbated by many others," Lee says. "The incidence is so high in minority communities because of greater exposure to allergens, greater susceptibility to those allergens because of inferior living conditions and the inability to address it because many residents lack adequate health care."

On Feb. 11, 1994, President Clinton lent support to the environmental justice movement by issuing an executive order requiring that all federal agencies include the achievement of environmental equity among their goals. The same year, the EPA created an Office of Environmental Justice and set up the National Environmental Justice Advisory Council to study the impact of environmental policies on different income and racial groups. The council also will provide grants to help communities around the country identify and address local environmental problems.

Some activists say the environmental justice movement is getting a vital boost from efforts to encourage redevelopment of contaminated industrial wastelands in cities across the country. These "brownfields" usually are empty lots that once contained factories, oil-tank farms or smelters. Because the level of contamination is too high to permit redevelopment but too low to merit priority treatment under the federal superfund program, brownfields often are left to languish as urban eyesores. Potential buyers are frightened away by fears that they will be held liable for past pollution in future lawsuits, while others give up because bankers and insurers refuse to provide financing and liability coverage for such risky investments.

The Clinton administration has taken steps to encourage urban redevelopment by introducing a two-year "brownfields initiative" aimed at luring businesses to locate in these lightly polluted areas. The program, announced last year by EPA Administrator Carol Browner, provides federal grants of $200,000 to industrial developers of polluted sites. The agency has launched about 60 brownfields pilot projects around the country, many of them former superfund sites that have been partially cleaned up and removed from the program.

This year, Clinton expanded the initiative by proposing to grant tax breaks to companies that buy brownfield sites, clean them up and build new businesses on them. Under the proposal, included in the president's fiscal 1997 budget, businesses could deduct the full cost of cleaning up brownfield sites. The administration estimated that the deduction would cost about $2 billion over seven years but that it would more than pay for itself by generating an estimated $10 billion in investments that would in turn yield tax revenues. [1]

According to the EPA, there may be up to a half-million brownfield sites around the country, including about 27,000 that may qualify for the tax deduction. But some analysts say that many of these sites are ill-suited for redevelopment because the costs of cleaning them up would far outweigh the tax deduction, placing the sites out of reach for all but the largest companies. Many of the sites are not in suitable locations for businesses, are too small or present other obstacles to redevelopment. [2]

Yet environmental justice activists insist that the brownfields initiative offers a vital ray of hope, especially to inner-city minority neighborhoods that have few job opportunities for area residents. "The heart of the issue is to bring back to life communities which are distressed," Lee says. "There is no point to brownfields if it's not going to be part of an overall strategy toward revitalization of the area as a whole."

---

[1] See Alissa J. Rubin, "Clinton's 'Brownfields' Tax Break," *Congressional Quarterly Weekly Report*, March 23, 1996, p. 757.

[2] See John Carey, "Urban Fields of Dreams," *Business Week*, May 27, 1996, pp. 80-86.

less, we recognize that full repeal cannot be achieved: There is simply not enough revenue produced by the superfund corporate taxes to pay for the necessary cleanup."

Are minority communities more heavily exposed to hazardous wastes than the rest of American society?

When the environmental movement was launched in the 1970s, it had few vocal supporters in the black, Hispanic or American Indian communities. At the time, minority spokesmen focused their attention on civil rights issues while leaders of the clean air and water movement were for the most part university-educated and white.

In recent years, however, minority communities have turned their attention increasingly to environmental issues. Because many black and Hispanic communities, in particular, are located in or near heavily industrialized urban areas, they are more exposed to pollution than non-industrial suburbs. With the passage of superfund and other laws dealing with remediation of toxic wastes, concern mounted in minority communities about the health effects these sites might have on their constituents. These concerns have given rise to a growing environmental justice movement across the country.

"The best way to describe many of these so-called other-side-of-the-track communities is oversaturation with multiple sources of environmental contaminants, as well as a host of other negatives, including noise, infrastructure decay and other social ills," says Charles Lee, director of environmental justice for the United Church of Christ's Commission for Racial Justice. Lee co-authored with former NAACP President Benjamin F. Chavis Jr. a landmark 1987 study linking hazardous waste sites with minority communities. [10] "There is definitely a significant difference between white and non-white communities," Lee adds.

The 1987 study, "Toxic Wastes and Race in the United States," found that the percentage of non-white residents in communities with operating commercial hazardous-waste facilities or large landfills was more than three times the percentage in communities with no waste facilities. Overall, the authors concluded, three out of five blacks and Hispanics lived in communities with toxic-waste sites, including "15 million blacks, 8 million Hispanics, 2 million Asians and Pacific Islanders and 700,000 American Indians." [11]

Critics say this view is oversimplified, that by their very nature, hazardous wastes threaten human health far beyond the immediate neighborhoods where they are found. "Since toxic air emissions, pesticide runoffs and groundwater contamination cannot neatly select their victims by race or income, the inequities visited upon minorities afflict a great many others as well," writes Christopher H. Foreman Jr., a senior fellow at the Brookings Institution. "Indeed, the range of arguably significant environmental equity comparisons is so broad that some doubtless cut the other way: Many Native Americans, for example, breathe cleaner air than urban Yuppies and live further from hazardous waste than New Jersey's white ethnics." [12]

Indian advocates reject this reasoning out of hand. "For people such as we, whose identity is defined in terms of how we live in a particular place, hazardous-substance contamination is a particularly deadly threat — to our culture as well as our lives," said Michael J. Farrow, a spokesman for the Umatilla tribe of northeastern Oregon.

The tribe's 160,000-acre reservation lies near the Hanford Nuclear Reservation, home to four superfund waste sites containing chemical and nuclear wastes that Farrow says have already contaminated 120 square miles of groundwater and threaten to poison the Columbia River. Trains carrying hazardous substances from Hanford cross reservation lands daily. "A derailment of one of these trains could easily precipitate a hazardous-substance release that would render our river unusable, our reservation unlivable," Farrow said. "Where would we go then? There are no other Umatilla Indian reservations available for our use." [13]

The Clinton administration has embraced the notion of environmental justice, but applies it to all disadvantaged Americans, not only members of minority communities. In an executive order issued early in 1994, the president directed all federal agencies, including the EPA, to implement programs to make sure that low-income as well as minority communities are not disproportionately harmed by environ-

Environmental Protection Agency

During the first 12 years of the superfund program, $13.3 billion was spent to clean up contaminated sites.

mental pollution. "Environmental justice is a very important priority for EPA," says Fields, "especially for those of us who are involved in managing the cleanup programs." ■

Background

Love Canal

When the first Earth Day celebration launched the U.S. environmental movement in 1970, hazardous wastes were not at the top of the agenda. [14] Early environmental concerns focused on air and water pollution and the harmful effects of pesticide use — the more visible byproducts of two centuries of unprecedented industrialization and agricultural growth. Landmark environmental legislation of the 1970s — the 1970 Clean Air Act and the 1972 Clean Water Act — reflected those concerns.

The discovery in 1977 that an entire subdivision in upper New York state lay atop a long-forgotten, toxic-chemicals dump abruptly expanded the environmental agenda. As residents of the Niagara Falls community of Love Canal evacuated their homes to escape the poisons that had leaked into their lawns from underground chemical drums, Americans across the country had a startling realization: The adverse legacy of modern industrial development also posed an invisible threat to their health as well as to the environment as a whole.

Prompted by Love Canal, state and federal agencies discovered other hazardous-waste dumps in virtually every state. The EPA estimated that in 1980 alone 126 billion pounds of hazardous waste would be produced, only a tenth of which would be disposed of safely.

So-called "midnight dumpers," operating without permits, routinely disposed of toxic chemicals in vacant lots, swamps and ditches and even tractor trailers filled with drums of chemicals and abandoned along highways. EPA officials estimated that nationwide there were as many as 50,000 sites, perhaps 2,000 of which might be extremely dangerous. Up to 800 of these most-dangerous sites were believed to be either abandoned or owned by operators who could not afford to clean them up.

Rise of Superfund

Existing laws offered little guidance for the cleanup of toxic wastes and the restoration of contaminated land. The Clean Water Act provided $35 million to clean up spills of oil and 297 toxic chemicals, but only into water. By contrast, EPA estimated that it would cost up to $44 billion to clean up hazardous-waste dumps on land.

The 1976 Resource Conservation and Recovery Act (RCRA) authorized EPA to require the cleanup of abandoned waste sites that posed "imminent and substantial" hazards to public health. However, because the law required the agency to go through time-consuming legal proceedings to demonstrate the existence of the hazards, emergency responses to threats were virtually precluded. RCRA also fell short by failing to provide funding for cleaning up abandoned sites, such as Love Canal, where the owners were either unknown or could not afford to clean them up.

Love Canal's devastating impact shocked the country and spurred Congress to draft the first national policy for dealing with toxic wastes. The 1980 Comprehensive Environmental Response, Compensation and Liability Act — better known by its acronym, CERCLA — outlined procedures for identifying and cleaning up contaminated sites.

CERCLA authorized the EPA to force individuals thought to have contributed to the contamination, known as "potential responsible parties," to pay the often astronomical expense of removing hazardous wastes and restoring sites to acceptable levels of cleanliness. The law also authorized the agency to undertake cleanups itself and then collect, or try to collect, the cleanup costs from the responsible parties.

Trust Fund Established

Many toxic sites, however, are abandoned mines or waste dumps of long-defunct industries for which no responsible parties can be identified. To pay for cleaning up such sites, lawmakers took the unprecedented step of establishing a federal trust fund financed primarily from fees levied on the chemical and oil industries — the main contributors of hazardous wastes.

Initial funding of the Hazardous Substance Response Trust Fund — known as superfund — amounted to $1.6 billion. The monies were to pay 90 percent of cleanup costs (the remainder to be paid by the states where the sites are located); the cost of health studies and diagnostic examinations related to health problems caused by contamination; and up to $50 million to restore waterways and other natural resources destroyed by contamination. Lawmakers drew the line at proposals to cover the costs of treating and compensating victims of hazardous-waste dumps because of cost considerations.

CERCLA broadly defines hazardous wastes covered under the law, as well as the conditions for their containment and removal. It defines hazardous waste as any toxic substance except most products of petroleum, natural gas and synthetic fuels, which are covered under the Clean Water and Clean Air acts. The law further authorizes the president to designate as hazardous any other substances

Continued on p. 756

Chronology

1970s *After decades of rapid industrialization, long-abandoned toxic-waste dumps are found to leach hazardous materials that threaten public health.*

April 22, 1970
The first Earth Day celebration launches the U.S. environmental movement. Later that year, President Richard M. Nixon creates the Environmental Protection Agency (EPA) to administer environmental laws.

1972
Congress passes the Clean Water Act, prohibiting the discharge of pollutants into navigable waters.

1976
The Resource Conservation and Recovery Act authorizes the EPA to regulate the disposal and treatment of municipalities' solid and hazardous wastes. The law does not, however, address problems associated with emergency cleanups.

1977
Following reports of mysterious illnesses among the residents of Love Canal, it is discovered that the Niagara Falls, N.Y., community was built atop a hazardous waste dump. Residents are later forced to abandon their homes.

1980s *Hostility toward environmental regulations builds with the mounting legal costs associated with the new superfund law.*

Dec. 11, 1980
The Comprehensive Environmental Response, Compensation and Liability Act (CERCLA) goes into effect. The law creates a federal "superfund" to cover the costs of cleaning up hazardous-waste sites where parties responsible for contamination cannot be made to pay for the cleanup.

1983
Anne M. Burford, President Ronald Reagan's first chief of the Environmental Protection Agency (EPA) and a vocal critic of superfund, is forced to resign after refusing to release to Congress documents detailing her management of the program.

1986
Amid growing criticism of the program's high legal costs, Congress passes the Superfund Amendments and Reauthorization Act (SARA). The new law adds an environmental income tax to increase revenues for the trust fund, formerly financed by the chemical and oil industries alone.

1990s *Superfund reauthorization stalls amid disagreement on ways to reform the program.*

1991
The annual appropriation for superfund grows from about $320 million during the first five years of the program to about $1.5 billion.

1993
President Clinton appoints Carol M. Browner, formerly Florida's top environmental regulator, to head the EPA.

Feb. 11, 1994
Clinton supports the growing environmental justice movement by issuing an executive order that directs all federal agencies, including the EPA, to implement programs to make sure that low-income and minority communities are not disproportionately harmed by environmental pollution.

1995
With superfund's taxing authority due to expire Dec. 31, Republican lawmakers introduce proposals to reauthorize the program with broad reforms aimed at exempting certain polluters from liability for cleanups. Clinton administration officials oppose the proposals for weakening the "polluter pays" principle embodied in the 1980 law.

March 12, 1996
Clinton proposes a $2 billion tax cut for companies that clean up lightly polluted waste sites and then build plants on them. The "brownfields" tax initiative is aimed at speeding cleanup and providing new job opportunities in inner cities, where many waste sites are located.

June 4, 1996
EPA chief Browner issues administrative reforms to speed the pace of cleanups at superfund sites, such as relieving some small businesses and local governments from financial liability for remediation.

July 1996
Lawmakers announce they have failed to reach agreement on superfund reform legislation for the current session.

Notorious Mining Operation in Colorado . . .

If the number of hazardous-waste sites on the Environmental Protection Agency (EPA) National Priorities List is any indication, Colorado is a relatively clean state. With 19 superfund sites, the Rocky Mountain state ranks far behind such industrial hubs as New Jersey — which tops the toxic-site list at 116. *(See map, p. 748.)*

One thing that sets Colorado apart is the relatively high number of mines and smelters among its superfund sites. While the chemical and oil industries are the leading sources of toxic wastes nationwide, mining accounts for seven of Colorado's most dangerous sites. Mining for hardrock minerals — mainly gold, silver, lead and molybdenum — was the state's leading industry from the early gold rush of the mid-1800s well into this century. Most of the mines were abandoned long ago, but their legacy continues to be felt as lead-laced mine tailings and other pollutants leach into streams and rivers.

But Colorado's notorious Summitville Mine is in a class by itself, EPA officials say. In 1986, the long-abandoned mine, high in the San Juan range in southern Colorado, was reopened by the Summitville Consolidated Mining Co., a subsidiary of Galactic Resources Ltd., a Canadian firm. Robert Friedland, the company's CEO, had hoped to strike it rich by using a new technique to coax gold from the rock. But he overestimated Summitville's gold resources and underestimated the technical problems that would be caused by the severe weather at the 11,000-foot-high site. After extracting 294,000 ounces of gold from 10 million tons of ore scraped off the mountainside, Galactic notified state regulators in December 1992 that it was abandoning the site in two weeks, declared bankruptcy and left the country.

Mary H. Cooper

The EPA expects to spend $140 million cleaning up pollution caused by the Summitville gold mine in southern Colorado.

When Colorado environmental officials reached the abandoned mine, they realized they had an impending disaster on their hands. Galactic had used a technique known as heap leach mining, in which cyanide is sprayed over huge mounds of ore to leach out the gold. The cyanide is collected in holding ponds for reuse. At Summitville, however, heavy snows and frigid temperatures had caused a crack to develop in the liner used to seal the collecting pond. Records show that Galactic's managers knew of the leak even before the mine's formal opening but continued operations without closing it. The cyanide leak, combined with acidic runoff from the mine, had killed all the fish in a long stretch of the Alamosa River. "When we took over the site in 1992, there was no aquatic life whatsoever between the site and the Terrace Reservoir 25 miles downstream," says Victor Ketellapper, EPA's project manager at Summitville. "Not even little bugs. It was all just dead."

More ominously, the regulators discovered that holding ponds containing 150 million gallons of cyanide-laced water were close to overflowing. With the annual snow melt and spring runoff only a few months away, the ponds could overflow and contaminate the crops and livestock of the San Luis Valley east of Summitville. The officials appealed for help to the EPA, which launched an emergency response and later added the mine to the superfund list.

Since 1992, EPA contractors have worked year-round to contain Summitville's pollutants. The fish have not returned to the two polluted rivers, and the impact of acid runoff on the farmlands downstream has to be determined. "We still haven't yet achieved our goals, though every year it gets better," Ketellapper says. "It took a long time to get bad, and it's going to take a long time to turn around. At a lot of other mining sites where we've done this kind of work, it's taken eight to 10 years before the water quality gets to the point where fish can survive." The agency has spent more than $100 million on Summitville Mine — including some $50,000 a day to keep a water-treatment plant running to reduce the flow of toxins into the rivers — and expects to spend up to $140 million before completing the cleanup in 1999.

Meanwhile, officials say Friedland has eluded attempts to make him pay for the Summitville disaster. His role in the

Continued from p. 754

that may pose significant threats to public health, welfare and the environment.

CERCLA apples to dumps — wherever they may occur — affecting the air, land, surface water, groundwater or public water supplies. Superfund specifically applies to any toxic "release" into the environment that poses a real or potential threat to the public, with a few notable exceptions covered under other laws: releases in the workplace; releases of nuclear materials or byproducts; normal field applications of fertilizers; and engine exhaust.

. . . Challenges EPA Technology and Funding

company and other business ventures became clearer after the Canadian press succeeded in getting a temporary gag order on the story lifted. According to *The Denver Post,* Friedland was originally from Massachusetts and was sentenced to two years in federal prison for trafficking in $120,000 worth of LSD in the early 1970s. He had the conviction erased from the court records, according to the *Post's* account of Canadian press reports, before obtaining Canadian citizenship in 1986. Once in Canada, Friedland became a major figure on the Vancouver Stock Exchange, known as the "scam capital" for its high-risk mining ventures.[1]

In a letter to the editor of *The New York Times,* Friedland denied all responsibility for the Summitville disaster, pointing out that he resigned as CEO and a director of Galactic Resources on Nov. 2, 1990, before EPA declared the mine a superfund site.[2] Friedland failed to mention, however, that his resignation came on the same day the EPA issued an ultimatum to Colorado regulators that the agency would take over the mine if they failed to fine Summitville operators for water-quality violations. Meanwhile, Friedland has launched new mines in Guyana, Venezuela and other countries and now resides in Singapore.

Mary H. Cooper

Pollution at the Smeltertown superfund site near Salida, Colo., was caused by lead, arsenic and creosote from early smelter and wood-treating operations.

There is little chance that the operators of Summitville will end up paying much of the cost of removing the pollution they left behind. In May, Summitville Consolidated pleaded guilty to 40 counts of violating the Clean Water Act and other laws and agreed to pay fines of $20 million. But because the company has less than $1 million in remaining assets, it is unlikely to meet its obligation. Last November, a federal grand jury in Denver indicted the company and two of its managers — but not Friedland — for criminal violations including lying to federal regulators.[3] The EPA, meanwhile, is preparing a civil suit against Friedland to try to recover some of the costs of cleaning up Summitville.

Often when the EPA comes to town over a superfund site, townspeople rise up in opposition. That's what happened when the EPA designated a site in Leadville (*see p. 747*). But with all the headaches the Summitville Mine has caused the surrounding community, the greetings extended to the EPA when it arrived in town were relatively warm. For one thing, restricting mine operations did not create economic hardships for area residents. For another, the mine posed a very real threat to the area's overall economy.

"These are farmers, and their water supply comes entirely from the mountains around Summitville," says Mary Hagan, a community-involvement representative at EPA's Denver office, "so water contamination is a very serious issue for them."

When Republican Gov. Roy Romer met with more than 100 area farmers and ranchers in the elementary school gym in Capulin, some 30 miles down the mountain from Summitville, reactions to EPA's intervention were mostly positive. Worries that publicity surrounding the cleanup might produce a food scare harmful to area beef and produce growers proved unfounded.

Most of the negative response to the Summitville disaster was directed at the mine operators, not the EPA. "Our salaries have been frozen since 1993 because $800,000 in tax revenues expected to be generated by the mine didn't materialize," complains a Rio Grande County employee who asked not to be identified. "But that was the fault of the mine company, not the EPA." Hagan says the community's reaction has made the agency's job easier. "Of course, nobody welcomes EPA," she says, "but they were glad for the work that was done."

[1] See Mark Obmascik, "Canada Lifts Gag," *The Denver Post,* Sept. 22, 1993.

[2] Friedland's letter in *The New York Times* appeared Aug. 21, 1994.

[3] See Mark Heinzl and Bob Ortega, "The Business of Law — Legal Beat: Galactic's Colorado Mining Unit and Two Managers Are Indicted," *The Wall Street Journal,* Nov. 6, 1995.

Who Should Pay?

Because of the high costs involved, the debate over who should pay for cleaning up the country's toxic waste has raged from the outset of superfund's legislative history.

The chemical industry has argued that all Americans have profited from the improper disposal of wastes, which translates into cheaper consumer products. For this reason, they say, taxpayers should pay for cleaning up the mess. The industry also argues that the law's across-the-board taxes unfairly penalize firms that dispose of their wastes safely, forcing them to pay for the improper practices of other firms.

Environmentalists have consistently argued that polluters should bear the brunt of cleanup costs because they have profited most directly from the cheap disposal of hazardous wastes.

The "polluter pays" principle has continued to be the most controversial element of the superfund debate. Rejecting the chemical industry's arguments, CERCLA establishes a liability scheme that holds anyone who produces or handles hazardous wastes "strictly, jointly and severally" liable for cleanup and damages they cause.

Under common law, strict liability means that anyone who produces or handles hazardous wastes — whether carefully or negligently — can be held responsible for damages they cause. That would have enabled victims or the EPA to sue for damages or cleanup costs from companies without first proving they were negligent in disposing of their wastes.

The Justice Department endorsed strict liability for superfund as a way to make it easier for the government to recover the costs of cleanups. But lawmakers rejected this argument. CERCLA softened this aspect of corporate liability by providing that a company would not be held liable if it could prove it was careful in packaging, labeling and handling the substance, and if it had tried to ensure that the transporter would properly dispose of the waste.

Joint and several liability means that anyone along the hazardous-waste chain — from the factory owner to the dump owner — can be held equally responsible for cleanup or damages resulting from a spill or a leak. Under this legal doctrine, it doesn't matter who is negligent or who is more responsible for a spill or a leak. Once the victims or the government are reimbursed, the companies involved can sue each other and leave it to the courts to sort out the relative degrees of negligence.

The joint-and-several provision allows EPA to quickly recover the costs of cleanups to reimburse the superfund. Industry representatives argued that they should not be held responsible for wastes once they left their factories, that they should not be held responsible for the negligence of waste haulers or operators of waste dumps.

Superfund law, like the Clean Water Act, holds anyone who releases hazardous substances without permits responsible for up to $50 million in cleanup costs and damage to natural resources.

Correcting a potentially grave shortcoming in prior law, CERCLA outlines specific conditions for the EPA to intervene in emergency threats posed by toxic wastes. It authorizes the president to order a company to remove or control hazardous substances that threaten public health or the environment. It also authorizes the president to order emergency action in the event toxic pollutants are released or likely to be released. The government response can include cleanup and the provision of alternative water supplies and housing to affected populations.

Finally, the superfund law imposes penalties for mishandling hazardous wastes. Operators of facilities where hazardous substances are stored or disposed of must notify the appropriate government agency of the type of substances involved, the facility's location and the likelihood of discharges. Failure to do so can result in a fine of up to $10,000, imprisonment for up to a year, or both. Failure to immediately notify the appropriate federal agency of a hazardous substance release can also result in a $10,000 fine. Tampering with records documenting hazardous-waste inventories or storage can result in a $20,000 fine and imprisonment.

"No one could disagree that the Congress should enact superfund reform this year. No one is happy with the status quo — not industry, not environmentalists, not insurers, not state and local governments, not even the EPA and other federal agencies."

— Sen. John H. Chafee, R-R.I., Chairman, Environment and Public Works Committee

Superfund Reforms

While early critics decried the anticipated costs imposed by superfund, even the EPA's original cost estimates quickly proved far too conservative. The initial list of several hundred sites soon grew into well over a thousand. Superfund appropriations increased accordingly, rising from about $320 million a year during the first five years of the program to about $1.5 billion a year since 1991. [15]

Congress broadly amended CERCLA when it first came up for reauthorization. The 1986 Superfund Amendments and Reauthorization Act (SARA) added an environmental income tax on firms outside the chemical and petroleum industries, to increase revenues for the trust fund. The new tax, of 0.12 percent on every corporation's taxable income over $2 million, accounts for about a third of superfund expenditures to clean up contaminated sites. The oil industry pays just over 40 percent of the total, and the chemical industry accounts for the remainder. [16]

The 1986 amendments also offered incentives for polluters to quickly settle with the government on cleanup costs as a means of speeding up remediation and reducing legal costs. In an effort to make superfund fairer, SARA also allowed EPA to release from liability so-called de minimis parties, polluters that contributed only small amounts of toxic waste to a site.

But superfund's woes did not end with passage of SARA. Not only did the program prove to be far larger than anticipated, but the government ended up footing the bill for cleanups to a much greater extent than lawmakers had expected. During the first 12 years of the program, $13.3 billion was spent to clean up superfund sites. But polluters only paid $6.3 billion, slightly less than half the cost. [17]

Even more controversial than superfund's cost has been the volume of lawsuits the program has sparked. Because the law allows the EPA to force a single polluter to pay all the costs of cleaning up a site, potential responsible parties identified by the EPA have turned to the courts to decide who must foot the bill.

As polluters draw in municipal waste haulers and insurance companies in an attempt to spread the costs, litigation often drags on for a decade or more before the cleanup process even begins. A 1994 study by the RAND Corp., a think tank in Santa Monica, Calif., found that more than a third of the money that had been spent to clean up superfund sites through 1991 had gone toward legal fees. [18]

Like the original 1980 superfund law, the 1986 amendments were due to expire after five years. Because of the high cost and steady stream of litigation generated by the program, however, lawmakers feared that the law would not be reauthorized when it was due to come up for consideration in 1991. So in 1990, Congress extended superfund's taxing and funding authority as part of the 1990 Omnibus Budget Reconciliation Act. That authority expired Dec. 31, 1995, setting the stage for this year's push to reauthorize the superfund law with substantial reforms. ■

CURRENT SITUATION

Stalemate in Congress

Even as a presidential candidate in 1992, Gov. Bill Clinton, D-Ark., called for overhauling the superfund program as a centerpiece of his environmental agenda. His legislative proposal, presented in early 1994, called for creating an arbitration process to end the lengthy litigation that had held up toxic-waste cleanups since the program's inception. To further discourage suits, Clinton also proposed extending liability for cleanups from single parties to all companies found to have polluted a superfund site.

The president also called for setting aside about $300 million a year to pay for cleaning up "orphan" sites, such as abandoned mines, that were polluted by defunct or insolvent companies. Noting that some 73 million people lived near toxic-waste sites, Clinton said the proposal also would have given affected communities a greater say in deciding how cleanups would be conducted.

A particularly controversial provision of Clinton's proposal would have set different remediation standards for superfund sites according to their anticipated future use. A site targeted for road construction or industrial development, for example, would not have to meet the same rigorous standards of cleanliness required for a site zoned for future housing. Environmentalists opposed the concept, which businesses and insurers supported, saying it let polluters off the hook.

Although the administration proposal won support from Republicans and Democrats in the 103rd Congress, lawmakers failed to bridge their differences over its details before adjournment.

The Republican-controlled 104th Congress took up the superfund program with some urgency in 1995 because the taxing authority required to fund it was due to expire at the end of the year. But this time, proposals more closely reflected the business interests represented by the new congressional majority, and again there was a stalemate.

Lawmakers expressed hope during this spring's debate that Congress would finally reauthorize superfund and correct what they viewed as major flaws in the law. "No one could disagree that the Congress should enact superfund reform this year," said Sen. John H. Chafee, R-R.I., chairman of the Environment and Public Works Committee, which held hearings on the law. "No one is happy with the status quo — not industry, not environmentalists, not insurers, not state and local governments, not even the EPA and other federal agencies."

The superfund reform proposal considered by Chafee's committee was introduced Sept. 29, 1995, by Sen. Robert C. Smith, R-N.H. A key provision of Smith's Accelerated Cleanup and Environmental Restoration Act would have weakened the law's retroactive liability provision by excusing polluters from paying cleanup costs if they had contributed relatively small amounts of toxic waste to a superfund site before 1980. Bigger polluters, however, including waste haulers, would not be exempted from liability, even if they contributed to the contamination before the law took effect.

A new allocation system would decide how cleanup costs would be spread among major polluters. In an attempt to end the lengthy legal battles associated with superfund cleanup, Smith's proposal required the trust fund — not the actual polluters — to foot the bill. Similar legislation was introduced in the House Oct. 18, 1995, by Rep. Michael G. Oxley, R-Ohio.

The chemical and oil industries, as well as insurance companies, supported most of the reform proposals' provisions. Oil interests, for example, which contribute the largest percentage of revenues to the cleanup trust fund, welcomed language in Smith's proposal that would require the EPA to loosen its cleanliness standards by considering costs when deciding how to clean up a given site and by basing such decisions on the expected future use of the land. Similar in some respects to Clinton's brownfields initiative, the Republican proposal goes further by eliminating superfund's liability provisions at sites that have satisfied the cleanup standards set by states where they are located.

"[American Petroleum Institute] members have long advocated remediation standards that are site-specific and risk-based," said Barbara J. Price, chairman of the institute's general committee on health, environment and safety. "The remediation process should provide protection of human health and the environment through methods that are practical and achievable in a cost-effective fashion." [19]

The Clinton administration and many environmentalists rejected the Republican reform proposals, contending they undermined the superfund law's "polluter pays" principle. "We believe strongly that the major companies who generated contamination, even though they may not have been violating any regulation or law at the time, are the ones who should be held primarily responsible for cleaning up their contamination," says Fields of the EPA. "That is a major issue that we have not been able to reach closure on with the Congress."

EPA Administrator Browner Implements Reforms

Even as lawmakers and administration officials continued to debate superfund reauthorization proposals, the Clinton administration introduced changes to the program by adopting several so-called administrative reforms, which do not require congressional approval. On June 4, EPA Administrator Browner implemented four reforms that she said reflected the administration's commitment to making cleanup of waste sites "faster, fairer and more efficient."

In an effort to smooth relations with communities where cleanups are occurring, Browner appointed an ombudsman to each of the 10 EPA regions. To expedite cleanups in cases where a polluter's insolvency had stalled remediation work, the agency set aside $50 million. To spur faster settlement among polluters, EPA will set up interest-bearing accounts whose earnings will help cover cleanup costs at specific sites. Finally, Browner announced that more small businesses and municipalities, many of which could not afford to clean up sites they helped pollute, would be taken off the list of responsible parties.

"These steps demonstrate the Clinton administration's commitment to cleaning up toxic-waste sites and protecting the health of one in four Americans who live near them," Browner said. "With these reforms, we are following through on our efforts to fundamentally improve the superfund program by limiting the costly role of lawyers and increasing community participation." [20]

In the end, lawmakers and the administration could not overcome their differences over superfund's retroactive liability provision in time for Congress to act on reform legislation this year. "When the Democrats had the presidency and controlled both chambers of Congress . . . they weren't able to get a [reform] bill passed," Chafee said. "Obviously, when you have a Congress controlled by one party and the White House in another, it's even more difficult." [21] ■

OUTLOOK

Reforms in '97?

The current legislative impasse over superfund does not immediately doom the program. Although superfund's taxing authority expired Dec. 31, 1995, the Congressional Budget Office estimates that the $3 billion the fund has already collected in environmental tax revenues will sustain the program through fiscal 2000. [22]

How reform efforts fare next year will, of course, largely depend on the results of the November elections. Although there is strong bipartisan support for making the cleanup program fairer, less costly and more efficient, both political parties are counting on victories in both the presidential and congressional elections to help lift the legislative impasse that blocked superfund reauthorization this year.

Clinton administration officials see reason for hope that the recent softening of the Republican majority's opposition

Continued on p. 762

At Issue:

Should Congress repeal a superfund provision that can hold a company responsible for cleanup of hazardous waste dumped legally before superfund was enacted in 1980?

yes

JOHN F. SPISAK
President and CEO, Terranext Inc., Lakewood, Colo.

FROM TESTIMONY BEFORE SENATE COMMITTEE ON ENVIRONMENT AND PUBLIC WORKS, APRIL 23, 1996.

When superfund was enacted at the end of 1980, it was a well-intentioned program targeted at cleaning up the nation's worst hazardous-waste sites. Business taxes financed the administration of the program, and a "polluter pays" system was instituted to get so-called "responsible parties" to pay for the cleanups. The cornerstone of this system, site-specific, strict, joint and several, retroactive liability enabled EPA to pull in any and all parties with any connection to a waste site and require them to pay an unlimited amount.

While in theory this system may have made sense when Congress created superfund, it is clear after nearly 16 years that this theory does not work in the real world. Today's program pulls in tens of thousands of parties who followed local and state laws on waste disposal, drains parties' management and financial resources, spends years on negotiations and litigation and wastes billions of dollars each year. More importantly, this system has not cleaned up the bulk of superfund's sites.

Today's superfund program is crippled by a liability system that has negative consequences for those entangled in litigation for years and for the thousands of communities that await cleanup actions. Fundamentally, retroactive liability is not really about making "polluters pay" at all. The "polluter pays" concept is and always has been a myth. The criminal "midnight dumpers" are long gone and are not pursued. In reality, people who had little, if any, responsibility for polluting activity have been ensnared in the web of retroactive liability because they can be connected minimally to a waste site (as opposed to having actually caused the site's pollution), and because they are "deep pockets." In the process, firms that over the last 100 years were producing goods and providing services for consumers in accord with the generally accepted manufacturing processes and disposal practices at the time are now stigmatized as "bad actors."....

The objective of superfund reform should be to eliminate today's leading superfund activity: years of shoveling mounds of paper at EPA's bureaucracy and in law firm conference rooms and courthouses as thousands of parties fight over money — who did what, who should pay and how much for cleanup. Instead, superfund needs to focus on cleanup — removing real health risks at toxic waste sites.

no

CAROL M. BROWNER
Administrator, Environmental Protection Agency

FROM TESTIMONY BEFORE SENATE COMMITTEE ON ENVIRONMENT AND PUBLIC WORKS, APRIL 23, 1996.

The administration cannot support the sweeping liability exemptions and other liability relief included in the bill [under consideration]. S 1285 rejects the "polluter pays" principle and essentially removes the great bulk of retroactive liability [by requiring] the Trust Fund to pay for the cleanup of all waste disposed of prior to December 1980 at any site where generators disposed of waste before that date. . . .

[The bill] will remove the burden of cleanups from those responsible for the contamination to federal and state governments. The approach is unaffordable and would prove to be a windfall for great numbers of polluters, who would no longer be responsible for their past activities. . . .

The administration firmly believes that any liability reform must retain the "polluter pays" principle. . . . This does not preclude, however, granting relief when the polluters are unable to bear the financial burdens associated with their superfund liability. The administration believes that such relief can be provided, but maintains that those polluters capable of paying should be responsible for remediation. This belief is consistent with the principle of creating a faster, fairer and more efficient superfund, with less litigation.

In a recent counterproposal to [the bill's] liability scheme, the administration, together with Sens. Max Baucus, D-Mont., and Frank R. Lautenberg, R-N.J., proposed numerous liability reforms that would address the concerns of those parties unable to pay for cleanup. Where S 1285 is unaffordable and broadly exempts polluters from their cleanup responsibilities and overly burdens smaller parties, the administration's proposal carefully addresses many of the unintended consequences of [the 1980 Comprehensive Environmental Response, Compensation and Liability Act's] liability scheme. Among other things, the proposal provides a way to get the smallest parties out of the process early, exempts most small businesses, exempts some municipalities and allows others to sharply limit their aggregate response costs and expedited settlements for many other small contributors of waste.

We believe this proposal strikes the proper balance among responsibility, fairness and efficiency, and is affordable under the current budget constraints. EPA's entire superfund budget for FY 1995 was $1.4 billion. With dozens of superfund sites awaiting construction funding to complete cleanup, now is not the time to force the government to grant liability repeal to polluters at the expense of cleanup dollars. As a result, we strongly urge serious consideration of the administration's counterproposal.

FOR MORE INFORMATION

Chemical Manufacturers Association, 1300 Wilson Blvd., Arlington, Va. 22209; (703) 741-5000. The CMA provides members with technical research and legal affairs counseling and monitors legislation and regulations regarding environmental safety and health and other issues.

Environmental Protection Agency, Solid Waste and Emergency Response, 401 M St. S.W., Suite 5101, SE 360, Washington, D.C. 20460; (202) 260-4610. The EPA office that administers and enforces the superfund act also manages the handling, cleanup and disposal of hazardous wastes.

Natural Resources Defense Council, 1350 New York Ave. N.W., Suite 300, Washington, D.C. 20005-4709; (202) 783-7800. The NRDC is an environmental group staffed by lawyers and scientists who conduct litigation and research on toxic wastes and other environmental hazards.

Communities at Risk Network, 421 Springfield Rd., Baton Rouge, La. 70807; (504) 775-0341. The network represents communities threatened by toxic-waste dumps.

Resources for the Future, 1616 P St. N.W., Washington, D.C. 20006; (202) 328-5000. This group conducts research and provides information on environmental issues including hazard wastes.

U.S. Public Interest Research Group, 218 D St. S.E., Washington, D.C. 20003; (202) 546-9707. USPIRG is a national organization that coordinates grass-roots efforts to advance environmental laws.

Continued from p. 760

to environmental legislation bodes well for superfund's eventual reauthorization. "It seems that some of the mood of Congress may have changed in the last several months," Fields says, pointing to passage of the Safe Drinking Water Act and other environmental bills. "That gives us some hope that we can work together and agree on some compromise around comprehensive superfund reform."

Meanwhile, some of superfund's most vocal critics hope that Congress eventually will pass legislation that goes after big polluters quickly and enables the EPA to actually get to work remediating contaminated sites.

As a start, says Leadville metallurgist Dunn, the FBI or the state police should take over enforcement efforts from the overextended EPA and let the environmental agency do what it does best — clean up the environment.

"The filthy water that might come out of mines in this area goes right down the Arkansas River into Bill Clinton's home state," he says. "I'd like to see the monies that go into superfund turned into diesel fuel for bulldozers and water-treatment plants. It seems to me that those funds should actually go toward the remediation process instead of lining the pockets of lawyers." ■

Notes

[1] For background, see "Lead Poisoning," *The CQ Researcher,* June 19, 1992, pp. 525-548.

[2] Testimony before House Government Reform and Oversight Subcommittee on National Economic Growth, Natural Resources and Regulatory Affairs, May 8, 1996.

[3] *Ibid.*

[4] Wilson is chairman and CEO of Rohm and Haas Co., Philadelphia, Pa. He testified April 23, 1996, before the Senate Environment and Public Works Committee.

[5] Testimony before the Senate Environment and Public Works Committee, April 24, 1996.

[6] Testimony at House Superfund hearing, May 8, 1996.

[7] For background on Superfund's early record, see "Living With Hazardous Wastes," *Editorial Research Reports,* July 29, 1988, pp. 377-389.

[8] Testimony before Senate Environment and Public Works Committee, April 23, 1996.

[9] Testimony at Senate Environment and Public Works Committee hearing, April 24, 1996.

[10] Benjamin F. Chavis Jr. and Charles Lee, " Toxic Wastes and Race in the United States," Commission for Racial Justice, United Church of Christ, 1987.

[11] *Ibid.,* p. 13.

[12] Christopher H. Foreman Jr., "A Winning Hand? The Uncertain Future of Environmental Justice," *The Brookings Review,* spring 1996, p. 24.

[13] Testimony at Senate Environment and Public Works Committee, April 24, 1996.

[14] For background on the origins of the environmental movement, see "Environmental Movement at 25," *The CQ Researcher,* March 31, 1995, pp. 273-296. Unless otherwise noted, information in this section is based on Congressional Quarterly, *1980 CQ Almanac,* pp. 584-593.

[15] See Congressional Quarterly, *1995 CQ Almanac,* pp. 5-11 to 5-13.

[16] See Katherine N. Probst et al, "Footing the Bill for Superfund Cleanups: Who Pays and How?" The Brookings Institution and Resources for the Future, 1995, p. 56.

[17] *1995 CQ Almanac, op. cit.*

[18] RAND Corp., "Fixing Superfund: The Impact of the Proposed Superfund Reform Act of 1994 on Transition Costs," July 28, 1994.

[19] Testimony at Senate Environment and Public Works Committee hearing, April 23, 1996. Price is vice president for health, environment and safety at Phillips Petroleum Co.

[20] EPA press release, June 4, 1996.

[21] Quoted by Allan Freedman, "With Bipartisan Deal Elusive, Superfund Effort Dies," *Congressional Quarterly Weekly Report,* July 20, 1996, p. 2044.

[22] *Loc. cit.*

Bibliography

Selected Sources Used

Books

Probst, Katherine N., Don Fullerton, Robert E. Litan and Paul R. Portney, *Footing the Bill for Superfund Cleanups: Who Pays and How?,* The Brookings Institution and Resources for the Future, 1995.

As Congress debated proposals to reform the 1980 superfund law, the authors analyzed several alternative sources of funding for the federal program. Disagreement over this issue blocked passage of superfund's reauthorization in 1995 and 1996.

Articles

Boerner, Christopher, and Thomas Lambert, "Environmental Justice," *The Public Interest*, winter 1995, pp. 61-82.

The authors criticize research that lends credence to claims of environmental racism — that minority communities are more exposed to environmental toxins than white communities. They further discuss flaws in proposals aimed at eliminating supposed environmental racism.

Carey, John, "Urban Fields of Dreams," *Business Week*, May 27, 1996, pp. 80-86.

Federal, state and private initiatives are turning "brownfields," marginally contaminated toxic sites, into construction sites for new industrial enterprises, offering job opportunities to inner-city residents.

Foreman, Christopher H., Jr., "A Winning Hand? The Uncertain Future of Environmental Justice," *The Brookings Review*, spring 1996, pp. 22-25.

A movement that calls for special efforts to thwart the impact of environmental pollution on minority communities faces problems, the author writes, stemming from inconclusive evidence that non-white Americans are disproportionately harmed by pollutants.

Kusek, Kristyn, "Pollution & Prejudice," *Government Executive*, October 1994, pp. 36-41.

President Clinton issued an executive order in February 1994 requiring all Cabinet-level agencies to advance the cause of environmental justice by trying to eliminate the disproportionate level of pollutants in non-white communities. The order prompted a debate over policy options as well as the very existence of environmental racism.

Reports and Studies

African American Environmentalist Association, National Association of Neighborhoods and National Wildlife Federation, *Our Unfair Share: A Survey of Pollution Sources in Our Nation's Capital*, June 1994.

This study found that the cleanest neighborhood in Washington, D.C., is the predominantly white Ward 3, while the most polluted areas are found in the overwhelmingly black neighborhoods of the city's Northeast and Southeast quadrants.

Dixon, Lloyd S., *Fixing Superfund: The Effect of the Proposed Superfund Reform Act of 1994 on Transaction Costs,* RAND, 1994.

This report from the California think tank addresses the main criticism of the superfund law — that too much money is spent on litigation among parties potentially responsible for cleaning up contaminated sites, holding up the work of remediation.

Chavis, Benjamin F., Jr., and Charles Lee, *Toxic Wastes and Race in the United States: A National Report on the Racial and Socio-Economic Characteristics of Communities with Hazardous Waste Sites*, Commission for Racial Justice, United Church of Christ, 1987.

A five-year study of environmental conditions in minority communities found that commercial toxic-waste sites are far more likely to be located in black, Hispanic, Indian or Asian/Pacific Islander communities than in predominantly white areas.

Congressional Budget Office, *The Total Costs of Cleaning up Nonfederal Superfund Sites*, January 1994.

The Library of Congress' research arm estimates that the superfund program will spend about $75 billion to clean up a total of 4,500 private sites. About a quarter of that amount will go toward litigation and settlement of liability suits.

National Environmental Justice Advisory Council, *Environmental Justice, Urban Revitalization, and Brownfields: The Search for Authentic Signs of Hope*, 1996.

Initiatives to encourage the redevelopment of polluted sites known as brownfields can help revitalize neglected urban neighborhoods by offering job opportunities to area residents.

The Next Step

Additional information from UMI's Newspaper & Periodical Abstracts database

Environmental Justice

Brown, Alice L., "Environmental justice: New civil rights frontier," *Trial,* July 1993, pp. 48-53.

Poor, minority communities bear a disproportionate share of environmental hazards. Lawyers fighting "environmental racism" have used environmental, public health and civil rights to force governments to clean up polluted areas.

Dinkins, Carol E., "Impact of the environmental justice movement on American industry and local government," *Administrative Law Review,* summer 1995, pp. 337-353.

Environmental justice, or environmental equity, is an idea that received its first expression about 12 years ago, when residents in a poor, African-American North Carolina county banded together with civil rights and political leaders to protest a proposed landfill. A brief consideration of this movement, government actions and their impact on business and industry is offered.

Foreman, Christopher H. Jr., "A winning hand?: The uncertain future of environmental justice," *Brookings Review,* spring 1996, pp. 22-25.

Many obstacles stand in the way of a thoughtfully reformed regime of environmental policy. Problems within the environmental justice movement and an examination of current federal environmental justice policy are addressed.

Hartley, Troy W., "Environmental justice: An environmental civil rights value acceptable to all world views," *Environmental Ethics,* fall 1995, pp. 277-289.

Minority communities are often disproportionately subjected to a higher level of environmental risk than other segments of society. Concern over this unequal environmental risk has led to a grass-roots civil rights campaign called the environmental justice movement.

Jackson, Bernice Powell, "An environmental justice story," *Michigan Chronicle,* June 19, 1996, p. A7.

Jackson comments on environmental racism, relating the story of an effort on the part of African-American citizens in Pensacola, Fla., to have toxic wastes, left by companies that abandoned plants in their neighborhoods, removed.

Mitchell, Carolyn M., "Environmental racism: Race as a primary factor in the selection of hazardous waste sites," *National Black Law Journal,* Winter 1993, pp. 176-188.

Mitchell suggests that the remedies for environmental racism are akin to the grass-roots community participation of the civil rights movement of the 1960s and the judicial activism of the Warren Court.

Oakes, John Michael, Douglas L. Anderton and Andy B. Anderson, "A longitudinal analysis of environmental equity in communities with hazardous waste facilities," *Social Science Research,* June 1996, pp. 125-148.

Early "environmental equity" studies claimed hazardous- waste facilities were disproportionately located in minority and disadvantaged communities, but recent research has challenged such claims. Findings from the first national tract-level longitudinal study of such communities are presented.

Rosen, Sanford Jay, and Tim Nolan, "Seeking environmental justice for minorities and poor people," *Trial,* December 1994, pp. 50-55.

Toxic wastes are more likely to end up in low-income and minority communities, whose residents carry little political weight and a grave burden—fighting to stay alive and well.

Sefa-Boakye, Kofi, "A test for environmental justice," *Los Angeles Times,* Aug. 21, 1995, p. B5.

Sefa-Boakye states that the Alameda Corridor project to link downtown Los Angeles to the ports of Los Angeles and Long Beach would cripple the economies of the region's minority communities by disrupting and replacing commercial establishments with industrial concerns.

Smith, Michael A., "Environmental justice needed for Anacostia," *Afro-American,* April 1, 1995, p. A5.

Smith comments on environmental justice, which calls attention to the unfairness to the poor and/or people of color as it relates to their environment, noting the pollution in the Anacostia River, which runs along the predominately African-American Washington, D.C., community of River Terrace.

Swanson, Sandra, "Can we balance the scale of environmental justice?" *Safety & Health,* Oct. 1995, pp. 76-80.

It appears that low-income communities and minority groups are exposed to a disproportionate amount of environmental hazards. Grass-roots groups are working for environmental justice and better working conditions for minorities. Risk mapping is being used in the California electroplating industry to prevent accidents among the minorities who work in this field.

Taylor, Dorceta E., "Primer — Environmental justice: The birth of a movement," *Dollars & Sense,* March

1996, pp. 22-23.
Many poor and working class people make their homes in areas near landfills, factories emitting toxic fumes, and other environmental hazards. These people are forming environmental justice groups that focus on occupational safety, toxic contamination and the siting of noxious and hazardous facilities.

Environmental Protection Agency (EPA)

Allen, Scott, "EPA to fund hazardous waste cleanup of shut-down electroplating company," ***Boston Globe,*** **April 12, 1995, p. 31.**
The U.S. Environmental Protection Agency has agreed to pay for the cleanup of a Roxbury, Mass., electroplating plant that was shut down for illegal hazardous-waste handling, ending months of neighbors' concerns about the site.

"Concentration of hazardous waste to determine listing," ***Environmental Science & Technology,*** **January 1996, p. 11.**
Under a proposed EPA rule, industry will be able to avoid stringent treatment and disposal requirements for any waste that contains hazardous chemicals by keeping the concentrations of hazardous chemicals in their waste streams below defined levels.

Meiners, Roger, and Bruce Yandle, "Get the government out of environmental control," ***USA Today,*** **May 1996, pp. 70-73.**
The environment is more effectively protected by individuals seeking to preserve their rights than by standards that are determined by legislators and regulators, the authors write.

"New hazardous waste baselines proposed," ***Environmental Science & Technology,*** **August 1995, pp. 348A-349A.**
The EPA is working to develop new baseline concentrations for almost 400 hazardous materials listed under the Resource Conservation and Recovery Act.

Hazardous-Waste Reduction

Anders, Jason, "Bill would regulate hazardous waste wells," ***Detroit News,*** **Feb. 29, 1996, p. D3.**
Plans to operate a hazardous-waste injection well in Romulus, Mich., have prompted state Sen. Loren Bennett and state Rep. George Pitoniak to draft legislation to make it more difficult for such disposal facilities to operate in the state.

"Audit faults DEQ on hazardous waste cleanups," ***Times-Picayune,*** **Nov. 15, 1995, p. B3.**
The Louisiana Department of Environmental Quality, the state agency that regulates hazardous-waste firms, does not adequately enforce regulations, leaving taxpayers to pick up the tab for millions of dollars in cleanup costs for abandoned sites, a state audit report said.

Cascio, Stefanie, "Hazardous waste site cleans up reputation," ***Chicago Tribune,*** **Feb. 27, 1996, p. 4.**
Environmental officials hope they can give a three-acre parcel near Marengo, Ill., which was once a dumping ground for hazardous waste, a clean bill of health in spring 1996. Commonwealth Edison Co has paid $240,000 for the cleanup.

"City develops new collection model for household hazardous waste," ***Biocycle: Journal of Waste Recycling,*** **February 1996, p. 20.**
In Keene, N.H., the Northeast Resource Recovery Association offered residents eight collections of household hazardous waste (HHW) and increased HHW removal by 800 percent, yet reduced costs to one-third of previous program costs.

Farrell, Molly, "Roving for household hazardous waste," ***Biocycle: Journal of Waste Recycling,*** **July 1995, pp. 40-43.**
The Chittenden Solid Waste District in Chittenden County, Vt., created a comprehensive collection system for household hazardous waste that compares favorably to the costs of other programs. The county's mobile logistics unit is described.

Grady, William, "Hazardous waste effort picks up," ***Chicago Tribune,*** **June 20, 1996, p. D6.**
DuPage County, Ill., will launch its community household hazardous-waste disposal program in July. The program is part of a new effort by the county's Solid Waste Department to provide DuPage residents with more convenient opportunities to dispose of leftover paint, pesticides, batteries and other household hazardous wastes.

Grady, William, "State derails hazardous-waste plan," ***Chicago Tribune,*** **Jan. 12, 1996, p. D4.**
DuPage County, Ill., officials are scrambling to repair the damage done to their ambitious plans for a recycling program by the state, which will now put the targeted money toward cleanup of abandoned commercial and industrial facilities.

Gray, Chris, "Fire uncovers hazardous waste," ***Times-Picayune,*** **Nov. 21, 1995, p. B2.**
An overnight fire in an abandoned building owned by the New Orleans Aviation Board turned up at least 15 drums of waste, some containing hazardous antifreeze.

Ilka, Douglas, "City plans to collect all hazardous waste on May 4," ***Detroit News,*** **April 9, 1996, p. D4.**
Rochester, Mich., officials have declared May 4, 1996, "Household Hazardous Waste Collection Day" and plan to spend as much as $30,000 to help residents dispose of dangerous waste products, such as cleaners, paints, auto products and pesticides.

Mason, Julie, "Plans for hazardous waste storage may not quell Pleasantville concerns," ***Houston Chronicle,*** **Dec. 19, 1995, p. A23.**

Proposed new city regulations for storing hazardous materials developed in response to the warehouse fires in the summer of 1995 in Pleasantville, Texas, may not go far enough to satisfy residents' safety concerns.

Matier, Phillip, and Andrew Ross, "Snafu stalls hazardous waste drop-off center in Oakland," *San Francisco Chronicle*, June 5, 1996, p. A17.

Matier and Ross note that Alameda County's $4.2 million drop-off center for hazardous wastes has been sitting idle for the past seven months because no one can pull together the paperwork needed for a state operating permit.

Rankin, Bill, "3 charged in hazardous waste export conspiracy," *Atlanta Constitution*, April 18, 1996, p. E3.

Fulton County, Ga., library employee Michael N. Nweke and alleged accomplices Stephen O. Nwosu and Tony Obiora were indicted on April 17, 1996, for an alleged scheme to transport hazardous waste to Nigeria from the port of Brunswick. Nweke and Nwosu are in custody, while Obiora is a fugitive believed to be living in Nigeria. The men were charged with wire fraud and conspiracy to commit money laundering and illegally transport hazardous waste.

Sutin, Phil, "Reservation needed for last pickup of hazardous waste," *St. Louis Post-Dispatch*, May 11, 1995, p. W1.

St. Louis residents on June 10, 1995, will have their last chance of the year to get rid of their household hazardous waste safely. The refuse division is taking reservations from people wanting to dispose of this material.

Tedford, Deborah, "Man gets 8 months in prison for dumping hazardous waste," *Houston Chronicle*, April 5, 1996, p. A30.

Clarence Holcomb was sentenced to eight months in federal prison April 4, 1996, for dumping thousands of pounds of hazardous waste in an inner-city neighborhood in Houston.

Health Risks

Abatemarco, Diane J., Cristine D. Delnevo, Audrey R. Gotsch, Mitchel Rosen, and Louise B. Weidner, "Medical surveillance practices of blue collar and white collar hazardous waste workers," *Journal of Occupational & Environmental Medicine*, May 1995, pp. 578-582.

The possible differences in medical surveillance practices among blue and white collar workers were examined. Blue collar trainees are more likely to be injured and less likely to be enrolled in medical surveillance programs.

Jacobs, Margaret A., "Desert battle: Secret air base broke hazardous-waste act, workers' suit alleges," *The Wall Street Journal*, Feb. 8, 1996, p. A1.

A citizens' lawsuit is being waged against the Department of Defense by four former civilian workers at a top-secret Air Force base and the widows of two former workers. They contend that the base violated federal hazardous-waste law by repeatedly burning ordinary chemicals and highly toxic classified materials in open pits at the base, which is located 125 miles northwest of Las Vegas and is commonly called Area 51. The workers say their exposure to toxic fumes in the 1980s caused health problems.

Prophet, Erin L., "Hazardous-waste workers: How much medical monitoring is enough?" *Safety & Health*, February 1995, pp. 64-67.

OSHA's guidelines for medical monitoring of hazardous-waste workers are discussed. Companies are paying more attention to areas like heat stress and trauma, and OSHA has plans to issue more specific guidelines.

Superfund

Allen, Scott, "EPA drops 273 N.E. sites from superfund list," *Boston Globe*, Jan. 30, 1996, p. 18.

The EPA has dropped 273 New England sites from the superfund hazardous-waste cleanup program, part of a campaign to reduce the stigma attached to land that one day could be redeveloped.

Barlow, Jim, "Emotion led to superfund mess," *Houston Chronicle*, June 20, 1996, p. C1.

Barlow discusses superfund legislation, including two pending bills in Congress that would partially eliminate retroactive liability on superfund sites — one in the House for any pollution deposited before 1980, the other in the Senate with a 1987 date.

Bartels, Paul, "Superfund reaches settlement with 2 firms for $20 million," *Times-Picayune*, June 22, 1996, p. B3.

The federal superfund is expected to receive $20 million plus interest from Kerr-McGee Corp. and Kerr-McGee Chemical Corp., two of the current defendants in the lawsuit filed to recover the $100 million-plus spent cleaning up the contaminated creosote plant site along Bayou Bonfouca in Slidell, La.

Braile, Robert, "Congress, EPA debate changing superfund," *Boston Globe*, March 31, 1996, p. NH1.

The debate between Congress and the EPA over how to solve the problems of the superfund, the multibillion dollar program to clean up hazardous waste sites in America, is examined, focusing on the 17 waste sites in New Hampshire.

Cushman, John H. Jr., "Superfund finds itself in deeper mess," *Houston Chronicle*, Jan. 15, 1996, p. A1.

The superfund, the long-troubled 15-year-old program to clean up the U.S.' most seriously polluted toxic-waste sites, is now in nearly complete disarray, a victim of political indecision and fiscal gridlock.

Derderian, Joseph P., "Approve superfund reforms now," *Detroit News*, March 27, 1996, p. A8.

In a letter to the editor, Derderian of Means Industries

Inc. in Saginaw, Mich., says he hopes Congress will get its reform of the superfund program right in 1996, adding that without reform money will continue to be wasted, and cleanup sites will remain untouched.

"Dump superfund," ***Detroit News,*** **June 26, 1996, p. A8.**
An editorial anticipates the end of the superfund environmental cleanup law enacted by Congress in 1980, concluding that it would be no loss because there is every reason to believe states would better manage local clean-ups than the EPA.

"EPA plans to provide $50 million payment for superfund cleanup," ***The Wall Street Journal,*** **June 5, 1996, p. A16.**
The EPA said it will provide $50 million to relieve hazardous-waste cleanup costs for businesses under its superfund program. The one-time expenditure was announced along with several other administrative changes intended to ease pressures on the program while Congress and the Clinton administration wrangle over how to rewrite the superfund law.

Knickerbocker, Brad, "Legal costs, budget cuts bedevil superfund," ***The Christian Science Monitor,*** **March 5, 1996, p. 11.**
The U.S. law that created "superfund" to clean up toxic-waste sites is facing reform in Congress. An accompanying map and table show the top 10 superfund states in the U.S. and the superfund priority sites for the 50 states.

Mahoney, Richard J., "Revising the superfund: This time let's get it right," ***USA Today,*** **January 1996, pp. 70-72.**
Because the current law is poorly crafted and counterproductive, most parties accused of degrading the environment would rather litigate and delay than clean up the sites involved. The necessary revisions of the superfund law are discussed.

Noah, Timothy, "Superfund plan is revised by GOP for Senate action," ***The Wall Street Journal,*** **March 25, 1996, p. A9.**
Senate Republicans unveiled a revised version of their superfund bill that grants greater relief from cleanup liability to polluting companies. Under the Senate bill, proposed by Sens. Bob Smith, R-N.H., and John Chafee, R-R.I., all so-called multiparty sites would be exempt from cleanup liability if the dumping took place before the original superfund bill became law in late 1980.

"Stringfellow superfund proposal," ***The Wall Street Journal,*** **May 13, 1996, p. B2.**
The EPA and other government authorities proposed a $4.8 million settlement with about 100 individuals and businesses to resolve their liabilities related to the Stringfellow superfund site in Glen Avon, Calif.

Treatment Techniques and Technologies

Adler, Tina, "Botanical cleanup crews," ***Science News,*** **July 20, 1996, pp. 42-43.**
Adler reports on the use of phytoremediation — the use of plants to absorb pollutants from air, water and soil. In one such project, a floating garden of sunflowers absorbs radionuclides from a small pond on the Chernobyl, Ukraine, site.

Ashley, Steven, "Instantly detecting hazardous waste," ***Mechanical Engineering,*** **February 1996, p. 14.**
A new hazardous-waste detector designed to monitor, in real time and with high sensitivity, toxic metals in the off-gas emissions of incinerators and plasma furnaces has been developed by engineers at the Massachusetts Institute of Technology's Plasma Fusion Center.

"Clean up at munitions sites," ***Biocycle: Journal of Waste Recycling,*** **March 1996, pp. 49-50.**
Military bases in Oregon and Washington cut costs to treat hazardous wastes by using windrow composting instead of incineration. The Umatilla Army Depot in Hermiston, Ore., has the largest ongoing project using composting to treat explosives.

Conner, Jesse R., "Stabilizing hazardous waste," ***CHEMTECH,*** **December 1993, pp. 35-44.**
Information about the process of stabilizing metal-bearing hazardous wastes is presented. Factors such as pH control and additives that can be used to immobilize the toxic materials are discussed.

"Live organisms turn hazardous waste into useful materials," ***Resource,*** **March 1995, p. 8.**
Researchers have developed a strategy for eliminating hazardous waste that also produces feedstock materials for manufacturing useful end-products. The dual process exemplifies a new kind of chemical synthesis and production process that is both economically viable and environmentally safe.

Novak, Anne M., "Central and Eastern Europe: U.S. exports of environmental technologies are fueled by new market economies," ***Business America,*** **April 1996, pp. 50-52.**
Central Europe and Eastern Europe's new market economies are fueling U.S. exports of environmental technologies. The U.S. industry has a good reputation for expertise and quality in this European region.

Scales, Ann, "New technology will be used to clean up N.H. superfund site," ***Boston Globe,*** **January 25, 1996, p. 52.**
New technology will be used to clean a toxic waste site in the southeastern New Hampshire city of Somersworth, that, if successful, could lower costs and accelerate efforts at other superfund sites.

Valenti, Michael, "Ironing out industrial wastes," ***Mechanical Engineering,*** **March 1996, pp. 106-110.**
Engineers are using molten iron and other metals to make hazardous wastes reusable instead of sending them to an incinerator or landfill. The catalytic extraction process stabilizes and reduces low-level radioactive wastes.

Back Issues

Great Research on Current Issues Starts Right Here. . .Recent topics covered by The CQ Researcher are listed below. Before May 1991, reports were published under the name of Editorial Research Reports.

FEBRUARY 1995
Cracking Down on Immigration
The Business of Sports
Reinventing Government
Housing Discrimination

MARCH 1995
Death Penalty Debate
Primary Care
Democracy in Africa
Environmental Movement at 25

APRIL 1995
Abortion Clinic Protests
Dieting and Health
Combating AIDS
Rethinking Affirmative Action

MAY 1995
Assisted Suicide Controversy
Overhauling Social Security
Learning to Read
Mandatory Sentencing

JUNE 1995
Combating Infectious Disease
Property Rights
Repetitive Stress Injuries
Regulating the Internet

JULY 1995
War Crimes
Highway Safety
Combating Terrorism
Preventing Teen Drug Use

AUGUST 1995
Job Stress
Organ Transplants
United Nations at 50
Advances in Cancer Research

SEPTEMBER 1995
Catholic Church in the U.S.
Northern Ireland Cease-Fire
High School Sports
Teaching History

OCTOBER 1995
Quebec's Future
Revitalizing the Cities
Networking the Classroom
Indoor Air Pollution

NOVEMBER 1995
The Working Poor
The Jury System
Sex, Violence and the Media
Police Misconduct

DECEMBER 1995
Teens and Tobacco
Gene Therapy's Future
Global Water Shortages
Third-Party Prospects

JANUARY 1996
Emergency Medicine
Punishing Sex Offenders
Bilingual Education
Helping the Homeless

FEBRUARY 1996
Reforming the CIA
Campaign Finance Reform
Academic Politics
Getting Into College

MARCH 1996
The British Monarchy
Preventing Juvenile Crime
Tax Reform
Pursuing the Paranormal

APRIL 1996
Centennial Olympic Games
Managed Care
Protecting Endangered Species
New Military Culture

MAY 1996
Russia's Political Future
Marriage and Divorce
Year-Round Schools
Taiwan, China and the U.S.

JUNE 1996
Rethinking NAFTA
First Ladies
Teaching Values
Labor Movement's Future

JULY 1996
Recovered-Memory Debate
Native Americans' Future
Crackdown on Sexual Harassment
Attack on Public Schools

AUGUST 1996
Fighting Over Animal Rights
Privatizing Government Services
Child Labor and Sweatshops

Future Topics

- ***Gambling***
- ***The States and Federalism***
- ***Civic Journalism***

THE CQ Researcher

PUBLISHED BY CONGRESSIONAL QUARTERLY INC.

Gambling Under Attack

How serious is the current backlash?

Americans love to moralize about gambling — almost as much as they love to gamble. Last year, the U.S. gaming industry posted record revenues of more than $44 billion. At the same time, though, more than 30 statewide efforts to legalize various forms of gambling were being rejected, often by whopping margins. Opponents contend the setbacks reflect a growing nationwide backlash against legalized gambling. But gaming analysts see exciting growth possibilities ahead, including airliner-based gambling and at-home wagering via telephone, interactive television or the Internet. Meanwhile, a recently approved federal gaming study will attempt to paint a clearer picture of the industry's impact on U.S. society — and the role gaming may play in the future.

INSIDE THIS ISSUE

CQ Sept. 6, 1996 • Volume 6, No. 33 • Pages 769-792

Formerly Editorial Research Reports

GAMBLING UNDER ATTACK

COVER: RIVERBOAT GAMBLING HAS PROVED WILDLY POPULAR WITH CONSUMERS.
(PHOTO: © DONN YOUNG/BOYD GAMING CORPORATION)

Sept. 6, 1996
Volume 6, No. 33

Bibliographic records and abstracts included in The Next Step section of this publication are from UMI's Newspaper and Periodical Abstracts database, and are used with permission.

The CQ Researcher (ISSN 1056-2036). Formerly Editorial Research Reports. Published weekly (48 times per year, not printed March 1, May 31, Aug. 30, Nov. 29) by Congressional Quarterly Inc., 1414 22nd St., N.W., Washington, D.C. 20037. Annual subscription rate for libraries, businesses and government is $319. Additional rates furnished upon request. Periodicals postage paid at Washington, D.C. POSTMASTER: Send address changes to The CQ Researcher, 1414 22nd St., N.W., Washington, D.C. 20037.

Gambling Under Attack

BY RICHARD L. WORSNOP

THE ISSUES

Is the gambling industry's hot streak finally cooling off?

Not from where Bradford Williams sits at his favorite blackjack table in Las Vegas. A retired newspaper publisher who lives in Florida, Williams has been taking extended gambling/golf jaunts to the Nevada gambling mecca for years, and he sees no letup in the city's explosive growth. This year alone, Las Vegas expects to increase its 93,997 hotel rooms by 10 percent, at a cost of more than $1.7 billion. [1]

Even so, Williams says, demand continues to outstrip supply in Las Vegas. As a result, room and meal prices are going up, and fewer discounted or free goods and services are being offered. Moreover, while families still are courted, many casino-hotels are returning to the racy adult-oriented floor shows of yore.

At the same time, Williams reports, the city's continuing boom is spawning a local backlash. "A lot of residents are upset about what's happening to the city because of all the new casinos," he says. "They resent having to pay higher taxes for roads and other amenities."

Elsewhere, opposition to new gambling operations has been more pronounced, particularly where cities and states have tried to legalize casinos. One reason for the opposition, according to gambling industry analyst Eugene Martin Christiansen, is that "gambling remains deeply troubling to many ordinary Americans." Moreover, he writes, "against the benefits of jobs and tax receipts must be set the costs of compulsive gambling, and the community dislocation that is the price of any substantial economic development." [2]

Growing awareness of such drawbacks has led to the failure of more than 30 statewide legislative and ballot proposals to legalize or expand gambling in 25 states since mid-1994, when the National Coalition Against Legalized Gambling (NCALG) was founded. Pro-gambling forces won in just two states. NCALG claims credit for the string of defeats, though gaming industry officials disagree.

In any case, the industry established its own advocacy group, the American Gaming Association (AGA), in June 1995. One of AGA's first publications, "Gaming Industry Myths and Facts," challenged critics' claims, such as "the social costs of gaming far exceed the economic benefits" and "pathological gamblers are the main sources of revenues for casinos."

More recently, AGA and NCALG locked horns over proposed congressional legislation to establish a blue-ribbon panel to study the impact of gambling on American society. The bill that eventually passed, signed into law by President Clinton Aug. 3, calls for the appointment of a nine-member study commission by early October. Its final report is due within two years (*see p. 781*).

"After two decades of explosive growth, it's time to look at the ledger to see what government-backed gambling is doing to our society," Sen. Paul Simon, D-Ill., said during debate on the measure. [3] Sen. Richard G. Lugar, R-Ind., said the commission's report would give state and local officials "objective, unbiased information they can use to make their own informed decisions about gambling."

Some of those decisions are sure to involve casino gambling on Indian tribal lands, a powerful engine of gaming industry growth over the past eight years. However, a Supreme Court decision handed down in March not only cast doubt on further expansion of Indian gaming but also raised the possibility that existing operations could be forced to close when their licenses expire.

Nonetheless, many industry experts remain upbeat about the gaming industry's long-range prospects. They point to the possibilities in such untapped venues as international flights and at-home wagering by phone, computer or interactive cable television. Some analysts believe at-home gambling alone could generate as much as $10 billion a year. Gambling opponents view such prospects with dread, claiming that they will further swell the ranks of compulsive gamblers.

At any rate, it seems too early to say whether the gambling industry's recent run of bad luck at the state level represents the start of a trend or a mere speed bump on the road to continuing growth.

As industry opponents and proponents debate the impact of gambling on U.S. society, these are some of the questions being asked:

Is there a nationwide backlash against gambling?

Recent events leave no doubt about the intensity of the anti-gambling backlash, according to Bernard P. Horn,

Riverboats, Cruises Led Industry's Growth

Record revenue increases from riverboats and cruises-to-nowhere led the U.S. gaming industry to 11.4 percent growth from 1994 to 1995. Casinos and lotteries were the biggest overall contributors to the industry's $44.4 billion in gross gaming revenues, or the amount won from bettors.

	1995 Gross Revenues (in $millions)	Increase/decrease in Gross Revenues From 1994
Parimutuels		
HORSES		
On-Track	$954.4	-$200.83 (-17.4%)
ITW*	1,085.6	212.92 (24.4%)
OTB (off-track betting)	1,034.6	121.44 (13.3%)
Total	3,074.6	133.52 (4.5%)
GREYHOUNDS		
On-Track	444.8	-65.01 (-12.8%)
ITW*	136.2	33.35 (32.4%)
OTB	26.7	5.04 (23.2%)
Total	607.8	-26.62 (-4.2%)
Jai Alai	64.2	-6.00 (-8.5%)
Total Parimutuels	3,746.6	101.0 (2.8%)
Lotteries		
Video Lotteries	618.1	157.11 (34.1%)
Traditional Games	14,618.1	952.62 (7.0%)
Total Lotteries	15,236.2	1109.73 (7.9%)
Casinos		
Nevada/NJ Slot Machines	7,092.3	487.26 (7.4%)
Nevada/NJ Table Games	3,856.6	287.47 (8.1%)
Deepwater Cruise Ships	228.8	-12.04 (-5.0%)
Cruises-to-nowhere	180.0	60.0 (50.0%)
Riverboats	4,652.0	1,392.76 (42.7%)
Other Land-Based Casinos	440.3	69.07 (18.6%)
Other Commercial Gambling	159.1	36.83 (30.1%)
Non-Casino Devices	1,405.7	321.82 (29.7%)
Total Casinos	18,014.7	2,641.76 (17.2%)
Legal Bookmaking		
Sports Books	79.4	-43.09 (-35.2%)
Horse Books	22.2	-14.62 (-39.7%)
Total Bookmaking	101.6	-57.71 (-36.2%)
Card Rooms	762.7	36.47 (5.0%)
Charitable Bingo	980.8	-7.81 (-0.8%)
Charitable Games	1,505.0	113.69 (8.2%)
Indian Reservations		
Class II	483.3	34.1 (7.6%)
Class III	3,555.9	588.59 (19.8%)
Total Indian Reservations	4,039.2	622.69 (18.2%)
GRAND TOTAL	**$44,386.8**	**$4,559.82 (11.4%)**

* *In ITW, or intertrack wagering, bettors at a race track during the off-season can bet on live races at other tracks, watching on closed-circuit television.*

Source: International Gaming & Wagering Business, *August 1996; Christiansen/Cummings Associates Inc.*

NCALG's political director. Since mid-1994, he notes, there have been 35 ballot or legislative proposals to legalize gaming at the state level. The score to date: opponents 33, supporters 2.

"People turned against gambling because they woke up to its dangers," Horn says. "Before 1994, they had been taken by surprise. No organized effort to halt the spread of legalized gambling existed back then, and not much research was available, either."

Studies had been done about the Nevada gaming industry, he says, but they were "completely inapplicable" to other states, especially those with no prior exposure to legalized gambling. What was needed was accumulated evidence of gambling's social impact. It wasn't until 1993 or 1994 that reliable data became available "indicating what was likely to happen if gambling was introduced into an Iowa or an Illinois." Horn says many of the studies concluded that casino-style gaming encouraged street crime and exploited compulsive gamblers, helping to reshape public opinion.

Shannon Bybee, director of the International Gaming Institute at the University of Nevada-Las Vegas, agrees that the gambling backlash is for real. "Anytime something gains visibility, it becomes much more of a target," he says. "Many people don't like casino gambling, but they didn't get upset about it as long as it was confined to Nevada and New Jersey. But when it began spreading to other states, they did get upset. It was a natural reaction to the gambling industry's success and expansion."

Bybee says today's anti-gambling movement is fueled in part by Nimby ("Not in my back yard!") sentiment. "There's always some of that, even in Las Vegas," he says. "But in addition, gambling is an activity that generates, and always has generated, opposition by some people on moral or social grounds."

Many observers have noted that opposition to gambling spans the political spectrum, uniting liberals and members of the Christian Coalition. William Safire, the conservative *New York Times* columnist, is perhaps the best-known opponent to gambling. "Gambling is a $40-billion-a-year-industry that is inherently immoral, corrupting public officials, enriching criminals, addicting and impoverishing the young and vulnerable," he wrote last year. "But the gambling racket — whether in state-licensed casinos, state-sponsored lotteries or on glitzy reservations of phony Indian tribes — has been promoted by public officials as a great way of painlessly raising revenues, with state voters acting as suckers. As a result, officially endorsed and government-advertised gambling now has Americans by the throat." [4]

William R. Eadington, director of the Institute for the Study of Gambling at the University of Nevada-Reno, contends that the gambling industry's fortunes rise when the economy slumps and recede when the economy surges. That explains why the industry is "in a fairly quiet period now," he says. By the same token, gambling's boom period coincided with the 1989-91 recession and the slow job recovery that followed. During that period, Eadington says, "There was a very strong impetus at the state level to introduce casinos for economic-development or job-creation purposes."

Today, with the economy and the anti-gambling movement both flexing muscle, the impulse to establish gambling in new areas has weakened. Correspondingly, existing gambling states — notably Nevada, New Jersey and Mississippi — have become increasingly attractive to gaming companies wishing to expand.

"In Las Vegas right now, $8 billion worth of capital projects are under construction or on the drawing board," notes Eadington. "That includes 35,000 new hotel rooms, which amounts to a 30-40 percent increase in capacity. That's pretty amazing all by itself."

Meanwhile, he says, "Atlantic City is going through its first boomlet in 10 years. That reflects the fact that New York and Pennsylvania are not going to have major casinos for at least the next few years. Consequently, investors are taking a closer look at the market potential of existing gambling jurisdictions."

The gambling backlash, then, seems largely confined to states without casino-style gaming. Horn acknowledges that, "It's very difficult to prohibit gambling once it is introduced, because the state government becomes literally addicted to the revenue it generates. That's why we concentrate on keeping gambling from spreading any further."

New revenues from gaming have certainly been welcome in Central City, one of three historic Colorado mining towns where casinos were legalized in 1990. Central City now has 11 casinos and a general-fund budget of $4 million, up from $350,000 just before legalization. The police force has grown from two to 10 officers.

According to City Manager Jim Drinkhouse, gambling has had a positive impact overall. "The goal of Central City and its elected officials was to become a viable community, with gaming as just another industry — like agriculture or a computer company, for instance." That objective has been met, he says, and street crime has not been a problem.

Gambling revenue has enabled Central City to lay plans for a 305-unit residential development outside the gaming area. "We hope to persuade some of the casino employees to become permanent residents of our town instead of commuters from Denver," Drinkhouse says.

According to gambling authority William N. Thompson, a professor of public administration at the University of Nevada-Las Vegas, resistance to gambling appears to be growing because "the political proponents of gambling have hit all the states" most receptive to gaming and now are dealing with the entrenched opposition. The industry now "has 10 gaming states," observes Thompson. "How many do they need? And why mess around with a jurisdiction that figures to be hostile?"

Such hostility could make for a close vote in Ohio, where a riverboat-gaming proposal will be on the ballot in November. Thompson expects the measure to be defeated. "But if riverboats win," he says, "it won't be by 60 percent to 40 percent; it'll be more like 52-48. So when the lawmakers develop the enabling legislation, they're not going to say, 'How can we help you?' They'll say, 'Okay, now, we're going to control you.' And it's probably not going to be friendly control; it's going to be adversarial control."

Like Eadington, Thompson notes that the industry's expansion plans are limited to just a handful of existing casino states. What the companies are looking for is not just a friendly political climate, he says, but a friendly tax structure. "The tax rate is 6.25 percent in Nevada, 8 percent in New Jersey. But New Jersey also levies a corporate income tax on gambling companies, while Nevada doesn't. So Nevada has by far the most favorable tax situation possible. South Dakota comes next, with something like an 8 percent gaming tax and no corporate income tax. The other gambling jurisdictions don't come close."

Does gambling benefit the economy?

Opponents of gambling claim that consumer spending on gambling is a zero-sum game. "The casinos produce no wealth (except for the owners, of course)," contributing editor Marc Cooper asserted in *The Nation*. "No goods are manufactured or exchanged. Almost every dollar lost in the casino is 'cannibalized,' sucked out of the community and not spent somewhere else or, God forbid, socked away in a savings account." [5]

Christiansen views such thinking as

Gambling Plays Key Role in Leisure Economy

Of the nearly half-trillion dollars spent by leisure-loving consumers in the U.S. in 1995, 10 percent was spent on gambling — more than the total spent on theme parks, video games, cruise ships, live entertainment, spectator sports and films.

(in $billions)

Video, audio and computer	$76.6
Other recreation	$69.2
Publications	$46.5
Gambling gross revenues	$44.4
Durable toys and goods	$43.8
Non-durable toys and goods	$42.7
Commercial amusements	$32.8
Leisure hotels	$18.6
Flowers and plants	$14.2
Recorded music	$12.2
Non-sport live entertainment	$9.0
Theme parks	$7.0
Video games	$7.0
Cruise ships	$6.7
Film box office	$5.5
Spectator sports	$5.3

Total $441.5 Billion

Sources: A.D. Murphy, The Hollywood Reporter, International Association of Amusement Parks and Attractions, Recording Industry Association of America; Christiansen/Cummings Associates Inc.

deeply flawed. Consumer outlays on commercial games, he argues, "pay the wages and salaries of the hundreds of thousands of [gaming industry] employees, provide a return on the equity component of the tens of billions of dollars invested in casinos and racetracks and companies that vend computerized wagering systems, service the debt component of these investments, support the stock prices of the hundred or so publicly owned companies involved with gambling, and in sum, are the motivating force of an economic engine that is most visible in Nevada but that less visibly drives an annually growing portion of the American leisure economy." [6]

Similarly, AGA predicts that "the gambling-entertainment industry will make direct capital investments in excess of $3 billion for new construction projects across the country" in 1996. "This growth," the association adds, "will generate new jobs, local infrastructure improvements and increased business opportunities." [7]

Horn, on the other hand, contends that, "When people spend $100 on a slot machine instead of a local restaurant, the local restaurant obviously loses $100. Overall, in the local economy as a whole, just as much money is lost by local businesses as is gained by the casino. And the result is that just as many people lose their jobs outside the casino as gain jobs inside the casino."

In such cases, Horn says, gambling "is quite literally a zero-sum game, because nothing is being created. The only way an area can benefit from gambling is to develop a tourism industry that brings in out-of-state visitors."

Thompson agrees. After studying riverboat casino gaming in Illinois, he found that 62 percent of all money wagered came from people "who lived within 20 miles of the casinos. There's no way a community can live with that formula." Thompson recalls that a mayor in one of the riverboat gambling communities told him, "We built a million-dollar firehouse with our gambling proceeds." Thompson's reply: "Well, of course you did. But you took the money out of your local economy to do it."

Bybee says it's misleading to compare spending on gambling to spending on consumer goods like clothing and food. Gambling "doesn't produce a product; it produces an experience," he says. "It's part of the economic engine that zips money through the economy, turning it over and over again. The same dollars get counted many times as they're transferred from one person or activity to another. Wagering is only one stage of the process. When a casino patron places a bet, that money helps the casino pay its employees and buy products and services to keep its business going."

In short, Bybee says, gambling is no more of a zero-sum game than traditional industries. Increasingly, he says, private enterprise "isn't concerned with products, as such; it's looking to provide information and experience — entertainment experience."

There's no question, Eadington says, that "If you introduce casinos into a region, you're bound to take some business away from existing discretionary-income activities, such as restaurants, bars and bowling alleys."

However, he argues, "We work on the assumption that in free-enterprise economies consumers have the right to spend their money where they choose. You may regard some of those choices as regrettable, but they certainly don't call for public-policy decisions."

"On the other hand," Eadington adds, "if you view gambling as a vice that, overall, creates no net value for the people who consume it, then you end up balancing the economic gains — such as job creation — against the social costs — such as compulsive gambling. That's where the zero-sum debate usually begins."

Do compulsive gamblers provide most casino revenues?

When the House Judiciary Committee held hearings last fall on whether to establish a federal commission to study gambling, University of Illinois economist Earl L. Grinols offered controversial testimony. Compulsive gamblers, he asserted, account for the bulk of casino revenues.

One of Las Vegas' new "spectacle properties," the Treasure Island hotel-casino lures crowds with a mock sea battle every 90 minutes.

"Evidence from pathological gamblers about how much they lose in casinos, combined with data about average casino gross revenues per adult from those living near casinos, suggests that the casino industry relies surprisingly heavily on the losses of problem and pathological gamblers," Grinols told the panel. [8]

A recent study co-authored by Grinols defines pathological gamblers as those who lose an average of $4,013 a year on betting, and problem gamblers as those who lose an average of $669 a year. The two groups represent just 4.11 percent of the gambling-age population but accounted for 52 percent of total U.S. casino gross revenues, according to the study. [9]

Grinols' thesis has not gone unchallenged. Eadington says that his statistics are nothing more than "back-of-the-envelope" calculations.

Several years ago, Eadington noted in a study of problem gambling that "Even if there were a common understanding of what constituted a pathological gambler, there is still no clear litmus test, no on-the-spot equivalent of a blood-alcohol reading, that would allow for the unambiguous classification of a pathological gambler. It is largely an invisible problem, with symptoms quite hard to distinguish from non-pathological gamblers." [10]

Williams agrees that it's not easy to spot a compulsive casino bettor, though he has come to know at least one over the years: "He owes the IRS; everything he owns is attached; he has no money in the bank; he's rooming with somebody else, because he can't afford a place of his own. He used to have a wife, but he doesn't now."

"It's a typical story," Williams adds, "except it doesn't end with him in the gutter. Maybe it's the same as with alcoholics — most don't drink themselves to death, or even into the hospital, but there's no mistaking what their problem is."

Williams describes himself as a "smart recreational gambler" who has visited many of the city's casinos. He tends to favor single-deck blackjack, and would view a $200 loss after a day

Helping Compulsive Gamblers Break the Habit

It may come as a surprise, says New Jersey gambling-industry consultant Arnold Wexler, but about 25 percent of compulsive gamblers are women, based on calls to gambling hotlines. "That's way up from 10 years ago," says Wexler, a former problem gambler himself, "when the number of women was 3-5 percent."

Typically, Wexler says, compulsive gamblers have more than $40,000 of gambling debt by the time they get into treatment. Many are pushed to seek psychiatric help — usually at the urging of a family member or friend — before reaching bankruptcy.

Compulsive gamblers "are definitely a growing population," says Keith P. Arnold, marketing director at Sierra Tucson, a private psychiatric hospital in Arizona that treats addiction and other mental and behavioral disorders. "With the ease of getting into gambling, more people than ever before are being exposed to it," Arnold says. "And inevitably, that includes people with addictive personalities."

Cyndi Collier, a compulsive-gambling counselor at Sierra Tucson's 325-acre campus in the foothills of the Santa Catalina Mountains, says the first step in treatment involves breaking down the patient's system of denial that a problem exists. "I try to get them to look at what lies underneath the denial, because if you don't confront that, there's a very high risk of relapse."

Sierra Tucson

Sierra Tucson psychiatric hospital in Arizona treats compulsive gamblers.

The treatment format extends also to family members. "We're dealing not just with the gambler's feelings of guilt and shame, but with the family members' anger," Collier says. "Their lives usually are pretty messed up because of all the betting losses."

Compulsive-gambling treatment at Sierra Tucson typically lasts 24 to 30 days, says Collier, followed by "structured aftercare — that's where the recovery actually takes place." Patients are encouraged to join Gamblers Anonymous, which adheres to a 12-step program modeled on Alcoholics Anonymous.

In addition, patients are asked to keep in touch with counselors after they leave Sierra Tucson. "Some do, some don't," she reports. "And sometimes they can't be reached at the phone number they give us. You've got to remember that compulsive gamblers are hustlers, always on the go. That behavior doesn't just go away after 24 to 28 days of treatment."

David Osinga, who also treats gamblers at the hospital, says compulsive gambling "is not necessarily just about the guy who goes to the racetrack or the casino. We also see a tremendous number of people who have a problem with sports betting — and that usually starts in high school. In addition, we treat people whose problems stem from speculative investments. As far as I'm concerned, anyone involved in speculative investments or venture capital is essentially a socially sanctioned gambler."

If he had to compare compulsive gambling with other addictive disorders, Osinga says "it might match up most closely with sexual addiction — compulsive sexual behavior." That's because both are associated with feelings of euphoria. Moreover, "sex and money and power are sort of three and the same in our culture."

Can compulsive gamblers be cured? "I wouldn't base success on complete abstinence," Osinga says. "Clearly, I wouldn't recommend that anyone who's a compulsive gambler go out and wager again. However, just because they have a relapse doesn't mean they're the same as they were before treatment. They may have reorganized their life, and are functioning much more appropriately than before they came to us.

"In fact, that very improvement may be one of the things that contributes to the relapse. They may be doing so well that they think they can get away with gambling this time."

Although Sierra Tucson has no ties to casinos at present, Arnold believes "that will happen in the future." First, though, "Casino operators need to develop a social conscience about people who get into trouble with gambling. I can't believe they want people to destroy their lives over an addiction. What they *do* want is the recreational gambler whose goal is to have fun."

of wagering as excessive.

"I never win big," Williams says. "Sometimes I make a fair amount of money, because luck just stays with me. But once I have a couple of losses after a string of wins, I get up from the table and call it a day."

The odds always favor the casino (or lottery operator), as Williams well knows. Consequently, he keeps a running account of his winnings and losses during his annual jaunts to Las

Vegas, where he gambles perhaps two or three hours a day, four or five days a week. "Over the last 11 weeks," he said recently, "I've lost $961." ■

BACKGROUND

A Nation of Gamblers

American ambivalence about gambling dates from the early Colonial period, when Puritan attitudes held sway. In March 1630, within a decade of the arrival of the *Mayflower,* Boston enacted the first law in the colonies against games of chance. "All persons whatsoever that have cards, dice, or tables in their houses, shall make away with them . . . under pain of punishment," it was ordered.

But gambling proved hard to suppress. In fact, all 13 original Colonies established lotteries to raise revenue. The proceeds helped establish some of the nation's leading private colleges — among them Dartmouth, Harvard, Princeton and Yale.

The Continental Congress even approved a lottery to help finance the Revolutionary War, but the scheme was abandoned when officials realized that most people supporting the war could not afford to gamble and that wealthy Tories had no desire to aid the American Revolution. The last attempt by Congress to establish a national lottery came in 1823. Profits were earmarked for beautifying the city of Washington. Promoters sold thousands of tickets, held a drawing, announced the winners — and then vanished with the money.

Nonetheless, licensed and unlicensed lotteries spread rapidly in the young country. Corruption soon followed. "Illegal lotteries flourished, the proprietors often disappearing between the drawings," attorney Rufus King wrote in *Gambling and Organized Crime.* "Nearly every large community had its much-publicized bankruptcies, embezzlements and suicides attributable to profligate spending on lottery tickets." [11] By 1830, lotteries were collecting an estimated $60 million a year, or five times more than the federal budget.

In 1832, Massachusetts and Pennsylvania became the first states to outlaw all lottery games. Other states did the same. Then, in the 1890s, a series of scandals involving the Louisiana state lottery prompted Congress to bar printed lottery material from the mails. The Federal Lottery Act of 1895 extended the ban to all forms of interstate commerce.

Casino-style gambling also thrived in the United States for much of the 19th century. Games of chance from abroad entered the country at New Orleans, where the first establishments devoted exclusively to gambling opened, at about the time of the Louisiana Purchase in 1803. From New Orleans, card sharps moved northward along the Atlantic coast, up the Mississippi and Ohio rivers to Chicago and westward as new territories gained enough settlers to support gambling operations.

Vigilantes drove gamblers from Natchez, Miss., Memphis, Tenn., and other river towns in 1835. But river gaming rebounded in the early 1840s and reached its peak the following decade, when some 2,000 professional gamblers worked the boats plying the Mississippi River between New Orleans and St. Louis.

In Nevada, the only state with a long tradition of legalized gambling, wide-open gambling flourished until early in this century, when reformers succeeded in outlawing gaming. The law, however, was little enforced.

Las Vegas Arrives

In 1931, to build tourism in the midst of the Depression, Nevada legalized most forms of gambling. That same year, Massachusetts decriminalized bingo. And in 1933, Michigan, New Hampshire and Ohio legalized parimutuel betting.

Meanwhile, legalized gambling was being touted as a way to combat organized crime. In a 1935 report to Illinois Gov. Henry M. Horner, University of Chicago sociologist Ernest W. Burgess wrote that partial legalization of gambling not only was discriminatory and hypocritical but also advantageous to criminals. [12] Full legalization, Burgess argued, would not only end the hypocrisy but also allow gambling to be regulated, dry up a major source of underworld income and provide the state with a lucrative new revenue source.

Shortly after World War II, however, mobsters erected elaborate casinos in Nevada and undercut Burgess' argument. The first, the Flamingo, was built by Benjamin "Bugsy" Siegel in 1946. Other racketeer-controlled casinos opened soon afterward. Televised hearings held in 1951 by the Senate Special Committee to Investigate Organized Crime alerted the public to mob involvement in gambling throughout the country.

The arrival in Las Vegas of industrialist Howard Hughes in 1966 "was a watershed event in the transition of the Nevada gaming industry to respectability," wrote sociologist John Dombrink and the University of Nevada's Thompson. Signalling his confidence in the city's future, the reclusive billionaire bought three casinos. The Nevada Legislature then passed the Corporate Gaming Act, which further exposed casinos to public scrutiny by allowing casino ownership by publicly held corporations. [13]

"Within six years," they continue, "Hilton, Hyatt and Metro-Goldwyn-Mayer invested in Nevada and upgraded the image of the mob-controlled city." Today, says Thompson, casino owners "want the state government to make sure the industry stays clean. They don't want owners who cheat players or do other sleazy things that soil the town's image. Gaming is honest here; there's no question in my mind about that."

Gambling Explosion

State lotteries, long in disrepute, led the way in making gambling respectable in the postwar era. In 1964, the century's first statewide lottery, in New Hampshire, bore scant resemblance to today's games. Initially, the New Hampshire lottery was based on just two horse races a year — a concept borrowed from the Irish Sweepstakes. Revenue fell considerably short of projections.

It remained for New Jersey to launch the first financially successful modern lottery in 1971. Cheaper and faster action made the difference. Besides offering 50-cent tickets and weekly drawings, New Jersey returned 45 cents of every dollar wagered as prize money, as against 35 cents in New Hampshire and 30 cents in New York. In its first six months, the New Jersey lottery netted $30 million.

Three additional lottery innovations followed, further boosting the game's appeal. First came "instant-winner" games, in which players bought tickets with the potentially winning numbers or symbols hidden beneath an opaque film, which they scratched off. The second innovation was an on-line daily "numbers" game — similar to the illegal version popular in many inner-cities — in which players tried to guess the three-digit number that would be selected at random.

The third and most important new lottery game was "lotto," featuring dauntingly long odds and mind-boggling jackpots. The key to lotto's popularity is that the jackpot is rolled over each time it isn't won. Thus, when there are no winning tickets for several consecutive drawings, multimillion-dollar prizes and "lotto fever" result.

Casino Fever

Since the late 1970s, casinos have supplanted lotteries as legalized gambling's main source of gross revenue. The shift began in 1976, when New Jersey became the second state to legalize casino gambling. In contrast to Nevada, New Jersey restricted casinos to a single location — the rundown beach resort of Atlantic City. State officials hoped that casinos would help revitalize the community.

But Atlantic City continued to decline. Some observers said overzealous state regulation of the casinos made casino operators feel unwelcome and unwilling to take part in community-improvement projects. Others cited Atlantic City's gambling clientele — largely day-trippers from the New York-Washington corridor who arrived and left by bus without setting foot outside the casino sector. Now, though, there are signs that Atlantic City's long-awaited redevelopment may finally be at hand. (*See story, p. 782.*)

In the meantime, casino-style gambling has spread to many other parts of the country. The Supreme Court's 1987 ruling in *California v. Cabazon Band of Mission Indians* facilitated the expansion. Although the court held that state laws prohibiting a particular form of gambling applied to Indian tribes in the state, the court also held that if a state permitted a form of gaming, tribes could operate such games.

The Indian Gaming Regulatory Act (IGRA), signed in 1988 by President Ronald Reagan, laid out a framework for implementing the *Cabazon* decision. IGRA defined three classes of gambling:

• Class I, consisting of traditional ceremonial gaming or social games for prizes of limited value, was placed under the tribes' exclusive control.

• Class II, comprising bingo, lotto and certain card games, would be overseen by a 15-member National Indian Gaming Commission appointed by the president and confirmed by the Senate;

• Class III activities, including casino gambling, slot machines, horse and dog racing and jai alai, were prohibited unless they were legal in the state and the state and tribe entered into a "compact." Under the law, states that offered one form of Class III gaming, such as a lottery, had to negotiate with tribes that wanted to set up casinos.

Meanwhile, non-Indian casino gaming was expanding into several states in the West, Midwest and South. In 1989, for example, South Dakota legalized limited-stakes gambling in the historic mining town of Deadwood — where legendary gambler and Indian scout Wild Bill Hickok was shot dead while playing poker. The following year, Colorado voters approved a constitutional amendment to allow small-stakes gambling in three historic mining towns: Black Hawk, Central City and Cripple Creek. And in 1991, riverboat-based casino gambling was permitted on the Iowa side of the Mississippi River. Five additional states have since legalized riverboat casinos: Illinois, Indiana, Louisiana, Mississippi and Missouri.

Waterborne gaming also is prospering on cruise ships and smaller passenger vessels offering "cruises to nowhere" — actually, round trips to international waters, where gambling is legal. Until four years ago, however, federal law barred American-flag vessels from offering gaming. To sidestep the ban, gaming operators used foreign-flag ships. Then, in 1992, President George Bush signed the U.S. Flag Cruise Ship Competitiveness Act, which permitted gaming on U.S. vessels.

Other legislation signed by Bush in 1992 earned praise from professional sports leagues as well as anti-gambling forces. Sports gambling generates big bucks, but most of the action is illegal, largely because the leagues fiercely oppose efforts to legalize wagering on games. The bill signed by Bush barred additional states from sponsoring sports lotteries based on

Continued on p. 780

Chronology

1600s-1700s

Americans' ambivalent feelings about gambling surface early in the Colonial era.

1630
Boston enacts the first American law against games of chance, directing that "All persons . . . that have cards, dice, or tables in their houses, shall make away with them . . . under pain of punishment."

1737
Massachusetts legislators amend the anti-gambling law to read: "All lawful games and exercises should not be otherwise used than as innocent and moderate recreations, and not as trades or callings, to gain a living or make unlawful advantage thereby."

19th Century

As America expands westward, so does gambling.

July 1835
Five gamblers are lynched by vigilantes in Natchez, Miss.

August 1876
Wild Bill Hickok is fatally shot while playing poker in Deadwood, S.D.

1930s-1940s

The Great Depression makes gambling more attractive as a public revenue source.

1931
Nevada legalizes most forms of gambling to spur tourism.

1933
Michigan, New Hampshire and Ohio legalize parimutuel betting.

1946
Mobster Bugsy Siegel opens the Flamingo hotel and casino.

1960s-1970s

The modern lottery-casino era dawns.

1964
New Hampshire becomes the first state in more than 70 years to sponsor a lottery.

1976
New Jersey becomes the second state to legalize casino gambling, but only in Atlantic City.

1980s

Indian tribes become a major presence in U.S. gambling.

Feb. 25, 1987
U.S. Supreme Court allows Native Americans to operate gaming facilities if gambling is legal elsewhere in the state.

1988
President Ronald Reagan signs a bill establishing standards for three classes of gambling controlled by Native Americans.

1990s

Legalized gambling keeps rolling despite setbacks at the state level.

November 1990
Colorado voters approve casino-style gambling for three historic Rocky Mountain mining towns.

1991
Riverboat gambling returns to the Iowa side of the Mississippi River.

November 1991
Massachusetts becomes the first state to allow residents to play the lottery by phone.

October 1992
President George Bush signs legislation outlawing lotteries based on team sports.

May 1994
The National Coalition Against Legalized Gambling is formed. It soon claims credit for the defeat of numerous state efforts to legalize gambling.

June 1995
The American Gaming Association, an industry trade group, is established.

1995
U.S. gross gambling revenues rise in 1995 by 11 percent, to a record $44.4 billion.

Aug. 3, 1996
President Clinton signs legislation establishing a commission to examine the impact of legalized gambling on American society.

Sept. 21, 1996
Louisiana voters will decide the fate of a proposed constitutional amendment allowing each of the state's parishes to determine whether to keep or abolish existing casinos and slots.

Nov. 5, 1996
Louisiana parishes hold local-option elections on gambling.

Will Gambling Survive in New Orleans?

Few U.S. cities would seem to offer more fertile opportunities for casino gambling than New Orleans. Besides boasting a long and colorful gaming history, the Mississippi River port is a major tourist and convention destination year-round. Yet legalized gambling is on the verge of collapse in New Orleans, and possibly elsewhere in Louisiana as well.

Louisiana became the third state to legalize casino gambling in 1992, narrowly approving legislation allowing riverboat casinos as well as a mammoth land-based facility in downtown New Orleans. This was to be Harrah's New Orleans Casino, occupying a prime downtown site within easy walking distance of the popular French Quarter and the Louisiana Superdome. Gambling's prospects in the Big Easy looked rosy indeed.

However, things began to unravel in spring 1995. In May, the Flamingo riverboat casino at the foot of Canal Street laid off part of its work force; two nearby gambling boats shut down completely the following month. Then, in August, Harrah's Jazz Co. dismissed 460 of the nearly 3,000 workers at its temporary gambling hall in the old Municipal Auditorium. Moreover, the company closed off 14,000 of the casino's 76,000 square feet of gambling space and pulled the plug on 700 of the 2,800 slot machines. Harrah's officials said the cutbacks were necessitated by revenues for May 1-July 30 that fell 60 percent short of projections.

But worse news was yet to come. On Nov. 22, Thanksgiving Eve, Harrah's closed the temporary casino, halted construction on the larger "permanent" facility and filed for protection under Chapter 11 of the federal bankruptcy laws. C.B. Forgotston, a local business lobbyist and outspoken casino critic, described Harrah's actions as "a catastrophe brought on by greed and corruption." He added, "This is the Chernobyl of the gambling industry — a complete meltdown." [1]

Even before Harrah's threw in the towel, it was clear that disenchantment with legalized gambling was on the rise. In August 1995, the FBI said it was conducting a major probe of Louisiana's truck stop video poker parlors. The FBI alleges that in wiretaps it made public, owners of the parlors bribed powerful state lawmakers to kill a voter referendum on banning poker machines. Earlier in 1995, 18 men, most with ties to the Genovese and Gambino crime families in New York and the Marcello crime family in New Orleans, were convicted of secretly trying to operate a video poker company in New Orleans. [2] In the Nov. 18 election runoff, Louisiana voters had turned several pro-casino legislators out of office. For governor, they elected Murphy J. "Mike" Foster, a Republican who had run on an anti-gambling platform. [3]

Making good on a campaign promise, Foster called a special session of the Legislature this April to consider a proposed constitutional amendment barring the expansion of legalized gambling without prior voter consent. The amendment, which the lawmakers approved, will be on the statewide ballot Sept. 21. Local-option elections on whether to keep or drop legalized gambling will follow on Nov. 5.

"Most people say Orleans Parish will give gambling another chance," says William N. Thompson, a professor of public administration at the University of Nevada-Las Vegas and a leading expert on gambling. However, he adds, "People resent the fact that Harrah's sought bankruptcy protection at a time when the company was very prosperous nationwide; they feel Harrah's didn't follow through on their commitments. Company officials now say they will make a decision about Harrah's New Orleans future after the November elections.

So, Thompson says it's possible that people in New Orleans will troop to the polls in November and say, in effect, "Hell, no! We've had enough of casinos!"

Most Louisiana parishes with riverboat gambling will vote to retain it, Thompson believes, "because they don't want to go through the messy process of closing down a business. If they tried to do that, the gaming companies would file lawsuits along the lines of, 'You gave me a license, and now you're shutting me down.' The only way you could avoid a nasty court fight, I think, would be to negotiate a 10-year phaseout, or something like that."

[1] Quoted in *The Washington Post*, Dec. 3, 1995, p. A3.

[2] *The New York Times*, Dec. 3, 1995, p. A3.

[3] Foster defeated Rep. Cleo Fields, D-La. Former Democratic Gov. Edwin W. Edwards did not seek re-election. Foster's grandfather, who passed on his name to his grandson, was governor from 1892 to 1900 and was instrumental in closing down the state's corrupt lottery.

Continued from p. 778

college and professional basketball, football and baseball. The measure did not outlaw wagering on horse and dog racing, or on the state-run numbers games that are the most common form of lottery. And it allowed Delaware, Montana, Nevada and Oregon to continue their existing casino or sports-based lottery operations.

Opposition Builds

Opponents of legalized gambling point to 1994 as the year when legal and popular opinion began to shift in their favor. In a major decision on two Indian-gaming cases, the 11th U.S. Circuit Court of Appeals in Jacksonville, Fla., ruled that tribes could not sue states over gambling because "the states retain their sovereign immunity" from suits under the 11th Amendment. [14]

At the same time, however, the court noted that IGRA expressly allowed tribes that were blocked from negotiating gaming compacts by a state claim of sovereign immunity to appeal to the secretary of the Interior: "The secretary then may prescribe regulations governing Class III gaming on the tribe's lands," the court ruled. But some observers said that getting such permission would not be easy.

Founding of the National Coalition Against Legalized Gambling was another key 1994 development. Led by Tom Grey, a United Methodist minister, the coalition set out to defeat 10 statewide ballot proposals aimed at legalizing various forms of gambling. Proposals lost at the ballot box in Colorado, Florida, Minnesota, Oklahoma, Rhode Island and Wyoming and were invalidated by the courts in Arkansas and New Mexico. Pro-gambling forces prevailed only in Missouri and South Dakota, where, NCALG noted, "voters agreed by narrow margins to reinstall slot machines that had previously been operating and then removed by court order." [15]

Florida voters handed the gambling industry its worst defeat of 1994, rejecting by a vote of 62 percent to 38 percent a plan permitting 47 casinos to be opened in the state.

Gambling proponents endured another string of setbacks in 1995, including the two-to-one rejection of a ballot proposal to allow Native Americans in Washington state to operate casinos. On the legislative front, bills to legalize riverboat casinos failed in Texas, West Virginia and four East Coast states: Virginia, Maryland, Pennsylvania and Connecticut. [16] The East Coast outcomes reassured operators of Atlantic City casinos, which draw many customers from the region.

Gambling Industry Fights Back

The launching of the American Gaming Association in June 1995 provided a clear sign of gambling's emergence as a national issue — and industry's concern. Significantly, the AGA described its members as part of the "gaming-entertainment" industry, not the "gambling" industry. "Gaming-entertainment communities are becoming full-scale destination resorts with many amenities to offer, including Broadway-type shows, golf, theme parks and sports and health facilities," the AGA said. [17]

Almost immediately, however, AGA found itself in a tug-of-war over proposals to conduct a national study of gambling and related issues. "The industry did not object to a study," the AGA said in June, "but the original legislation blatantly represented only the views of the anti-gaming moralists who introduced it." [18]

Former Republican National Committee Chairman Frank J. Fahrenkopf Jr., the AGA's president and CEO, elaborated on this theme in testimony before the House Judiciary Committee in September 1995. "While [a commission] sounds good at first blush, the real intent of the proponents . . . is the complete abolition, on moral grounds, of the gaming-entertainment industry," he said. He also argued that "the federal government clearly does not have jurisdiction over gaming in the states" and that there was "no demonstrated need" for a national study of the industry. [19]

NCALG's Grey, testifying before the same panel, asserted that the political tide had turned against legalized gambling "not simply because all of the major conservative Christian groups oppose the expansion of gambling, although they do. It is not simply because mainline churches — liberal, conservative and moderate — are almost universally opposed to more gambling, although they are. Resistance to government-sponsored gambling is growing because voters from every walk of life recognize that legalized gambling is . . . poor public policy."

Grey added that he was "astonished" by AGA's opposition to a national study of the industry. "If they believe that the spread of gambling enhances our national economy, then what is it about an objective study that makes them afraid?" ■

CURRENT SITUATION

Gambling Study

Industry opposition to the gambling study softened somewhat as the legislation authorizing the study wound its way through Congress. From the start, AGA said it objected mainly to a provision giving the study commission wide-ranging subpoena powers. In a compromise that helped assure the bill's passage, subpoena authority was limited to records and documents controlled by casino operators. Language permitting the commission to subpoena witnesses was dropped.

"Granting this commission subpoena power is unwarranted and is an intrusion into an industry that is more closely regulated than the overwhelming majority of U.S. businesses," Fahrenkopf complained in a statement issued May 10, before the compromise was reached. But he voiced satisfaction with the final version of the bill after the House cleared it for President Clinton's signature on July 22: "With the adoption of the significant structural changes proposed by the Senate, including less intrusive subpoena powers, the legislation provides the commission [with] the tools necessary to conduct a fair and balanced study of the gaming industry, while recognizing the privacy rights of our customers and the privileged business information of our companies."

Signed by Clinton on Aug. 3, the law authorized the establishment of a

Casino Operators Are Betting on Atlantic City

Twenty years after New Jersey voters approved casino gambling in Atlantic City, the down-at-the-heels seaside resort seems poised at last to reap the promised benefits. The city's 13 casinos reported combined gross revenues of $3.7 billion in 1995, slightly more than the $3.6 billion taken in by casinos on the Las Vegas Strip. [1] Moreover, a mammoth convention center is under construction, and the city also boasts a new airport and new middle-income housing.

Most important of all, perhaps, the state's Republican governor, Christine Todd Whitman, unveiled plans in July for a transportation program that should spur further economic growth. It calls for upgrading two existing highways and several feeder roads to improve access to the casinos clustered along the Boardwalk. In addition, a new highway-tunnel will lead to an undeveloped landfill that is slated to become another major gambling district.

The chief beneficiary of the highway-tunnel project figures to be Stephen A. Wynn, the dynamic chairman, president and chief executive officer of Mirage Resorts Inc., one of the largest U.S. gaming companies. Wynn wants to build a $500 million hotel-casino on the landfill, about a mile from the Boardwalk casinos.

Wynn has locked horns over the project with New York developer Donald J. Trump, head of Trump Hotels & Casino Resorts Inc., the city's main casino operator with three casinos — the Castle, Plaza and Taj Mahal. Trump tried to block the highway-tunnel, claiming it would "wipe out a neighborhood" and be "an environmental disaster." [2] Whitman's announcement effectively overruled Trump's objections.

Las Vegas-based Wynn is no stranger to Atlantic City. As head of Golden Nugget Inc., Mirage's former corporate name, he operated the Golden Nugget casino there in the 1970s and '80s. However, he sold the property in 1987 to Bally Manufacturing Corp., assailing New Jersey gambling regulators for overzealousness and vowing never to return.

Gaming industry officials now say a friendlier regulatory climate helped persuade Wynn to change his mind. In 1993, for example, Atlantic City casinos received permission to operate around the clock; before then, they had to observe a 20-hour-a-day weekend limit. Rules changes that took effect last year lifted the old three-casino-per-owner limit and allowed casinos to introduce new games.

Atlantic City has benefited also from its relative lack of competition. Proposals to legalize casino-style gambling in neighboring jurisdictions, including New York, Pennsylvania, Maryland, the District of Columbia and Virginia, have gone nowhere so far. That has left Atlantic City and the huge Foxwoods casino operated by the Mashantucket Pequot Indians in Ledyard, Conn., as the two prime gambling destinations in the eastern United States.

But Atlantic City needs more than additional casinos and a new convention center to shed its dowdy image, argues gaming-industry analyst Eugene Martin Christiansen. Wynn "is an enormously gifted creator of entertainment, right up there with Walt [Disney], and one of the great businessmen of this or any other time," Christiansen recently wrote. "But he's not a miracle worker, and casinos, as Atlantic City ought to understand by now, are not some kind of magic bullet for America's social ills." [3]

What the community needs above all, in Christiansen's view, are non-gaming attractions such as upscale shops and restaurants, parks and trees, golf courses and tennis courts. "Entertainment is a new entitlement, an absolute consumer demand," Christiansen said. "To prosper in the resort business, Atlantic City has to be fun."

[1] See Eugene Martin Christiansen, "The United States Gross National Wager," *International Gaming & Wagering Business,* August 1996. In Nevada as a whole, casinos recorded gross revenues of $7.2 billion in 1995.

[2] Quoted in *The Wall Street Journal,* March 8, 1996, p. A1.

[3] Christiansen, *op. cit.,* pp. 72-73.

nine-member commission to report within two years on the economic impact gambling has on families and businesses in areas where it is legal. The commission also is expected to examine such issues as links between gambling and crime; gambling establishments operated by Indian tribes; the impact of political contributions on the spread of legalized gambling; the demographics of gamblers; and gambling on the Internet.

The legislation calls for the president, the Speaker of the House and the Senate majority leader each to appoint three commission members by early October. Jockeying for commission seats has been intense, with pro- and anti-gambling forces both voicing concern that a stacked panel will favor the "wrong" side. It has been noted, for example, that Speaker Newt Gingrich, R-Ga., urged in April that the commission be denied subpoena power; that Majority Leader Trent Lott, R-Miss., represents a major gambling state; and that Clinton has received campaign contributions from the gaming industry (as have Gingrich and Lott).

Regardless of who finally sits on the commission, Thompson doesn't believe it will accomplish much. "Everything is just going to be studied and buried — studied to death," he says. "The basic questions can be approached directly, but I don't think the commission will do that. The essential question is economic: Does gambling help or hurt an area?

"The commission should also delve into compulsive gambling and crime," Thompson says, "because there is an economic component of both. But it should leave morality out; I don't think the moral question is worthy of discussion."

Horn views the commission's prospects more optimistically. "If members use their subpoena power shrewdly, they can obtain an enormous amount of information from the gambling companies. That's because the companies spend millions on research. I feel sure that casino operators know a lot about who gambles at their establishments — what the customers' incomes are, say, and what percentage of them are unable to control their wagering. If the commission obtained that research through subpoena, it would learn an awful lot about gambling that's not publicly known right now."

Industry Growth

A great deal is known, however, about the industry's finances. Much of the data comes from the annual surveys prepared by Christiansen, who for comparison purposes denotes the U.S. gaming industry as a giant, fictional company, U.S. Gambling Inc. (USGI). He then determines where USGI would rank on *Forbes* magazine's annual list of the 500 biggest U.S. corporations in terms of sales — the equivalent of gross revenue in gambling.

In 1995, USGI, at $44.4 billion, would have finished 11th, between Philip Morris Cos. Inc. ($53.1 billion) and E.I. du Pont de Nemours & Co. ($36.5 billion). That was USGI's highest position since Christiansen began making the comparisons in 1982, and an 11 percent increase in gross revenues over 1994. (*See table, p. 772.*)

In 1995, casinos and lotteries accounted for almost 83 percent of all U.S. gross gambling revenues, continuing a long-term pattern. For the second straight year, the casino share of the total increased slightly, while the lottery share fell slightly. However, Christiansen noted that the increase in non-Indian casino revenue in 1995 fell short of the 1994 increase in both numerical and percentage terms. "The absence of new markets, the fact that no new entertainment megastores opened in Las Vegas and soft results in deep-water cruise ship gaming were the principal reasons for the slowdown," he wrote. [20]

Christiansen was "impressed" by the lotteries' performance in 1995, despite their modest loss of overall gambling market share. "Conventional wisdom was that once most people had access to lottery games, growth would stop. That hasn't happened. . . . The industry is maintaining double-digit wagering gains despite the spread of casinos and the absence of new markets." [21]

At the same time, wagering on horse and dog racing and jai alai continued to languish. "Twenty-five years ago, racing dominated U.S. gambling," Christiansen observed. "In that far-off time, parimutuels were the largest game in town, with a 28 percent share of the national market. In 1995, they held just 8.4 percent." [22]

The underlying reason for the parimutuel industry's slide, in Christiansen's view, is its longstanding failure to persuade the younger generation of gamblers that racing is relevant to their lives. "A visual comparison of the smiling crowds flooding into Orlando and Las Vegas with the annually decreasing trickle of aging, cigarette-smoking fans into thinly populated racetrack grandstands says more about what has happened to the industry than any amount of statistical description." [23]

Bucking the nationwide trend, Delaware's three racetracks have posted healthy revenue gains this year. They did so largely by installing hundreds of slot machines. In the first six months of slot play at Delaware Park in Wilmington and Dover Downs, bettors dropped more than $895 million into the machines, greatly exceeding projections. [24]

Delaware's slot boom sent tremors through racetrack circles in neighboring Maryland. Track operators there began clamoring for permission to introduce slots of their own. Gov. Parris N. Glendening, a longtime opponent of casino gambling, indicated at one point that he might support slots at Maryland tracks if the state industry truly were imperiled. But on Aug. 12, he declared: "No bill that authorizes slots will pass my desk. I am locking the door and throwing away the key." [25]

Recent Reverses

Glendening's rebuff was just one of many suffered by state gaming interests across the country in 1996. On June 11, for example, North Dakota voters defeated a proposed constitutional amendment, 69 percent to 31 percent, that would have legalized slots in bars, restaurants and hotels. Meanwhile, at least 12 other state legislatures rejected bills to legalize various forms of gambling this year.*

Further reverses for gambling could be on the horizon in Louisiana. During a special session of the Legislature called earlier this year by Republican Gov. Murphy J. "Mike" Foster, lawmakers approved a proposed constitutional amendment preventing any new form of gambling from being placed in a parish against the voters' will. [26] Statewide balloting on the amendment will take place Sept. 21. Local-option elections on gambling are to follow Nov. 5. The proposed constitutional change was inspired in part by voters' disgust with last year's gambling debacle in New Orleans,

* Legislation to legalize gambling was rejected in 1996 by legislatures in Alabama, Hawaii, Illinois, Kansas, Maryland, Nebraska, New Hampshire, New Mexico, Vermont, Virginia, West Virginia and Wisconsin.

which saw Harrah's Jazz Co. bail out of almost all its existing and planned casino operations. (*See story, p. 780.*)

Indian Casinos Affected

No segment of the U.S. gaming industry took a bigger hit in recent years than Indian casino gambling. The Supreme Court delivered the blow in its March 27, 1996 decision in *Seminole Tribe of Florida v. Florida,* holding that the 1988 Indian Gaming Regulatory Act (IGRA) violated the sovereignty rights granted to states under the 11th Amendment. The challenged portion of the act permitted Indian tribes to file suit in federal court against states that failed to negotiate "in good faith" with tribes seeking to operate casinos on tribal lands.

The Seminole tribe had filed such a suit after negotiations with Florida officials on setting up a casino on tribal property broke down in 1991. Frustrated by the state's unwillingness to bargain, the tribe invoked its right under IGRA to sue. But a U.S. appeals court ruled in 1994 that the suit was barred by the 11th Amendment, which protects states from being sued in federal courts. The March Supreme Court ruling affirmed the lower-court opinion.

Though the *Seminole* decision does not disturb existing tribal gambling operations, it raises questions about tribes' ability to open new casinos and renew gaming compacts. A decisive test could come in Wisconsin, where compacts are due to start expiring in 1998.

In Christiansen's opinion, Indian gaming has a future, even after *Seminole.* [27] In his industry report last year, he wrote: "We live in an age of minority politics. Native Americans are a minority. Not only that, Native Americans are, by any standard, a minority this country has abused." Consequently, he does "not expect Congress to stand idly by and acquiesce in the judicial slaughter" of the gambling industry, much as the government allowed the buffalo to be killed in the 19th century. [28]

Compulsive Gambling

Seminole was widely seen as a victory not just for state governments but for the non-Indian segment of the casino industry. But the ruling by no means left the industry problem-free. Above all, it still faces criticism for contributing to the spread of compulsive gambling. The issue is expected to be one of the main concerns of the national study commission.

Faced with rising public awareness of the problem, the AGA in February announced the formation of the National Center for Responsible Gaming at the University of Missouri-Kansas City. Among other activities, the center will conduct studies into the prevalence of problem gambling, aid in the development of treatment programs and try to devise early-intervention and prevention strategies.

"The American Gaming Association has met with prominent leaders in the field who tell us that the vast majority of Americans are social gamblers who can participate in a gaming activity without harmful effects," the AGA's Fahrenkopf says. "Prevalence studies conducted in 14 states show that the percent of those with a problem ranges from 1.7 percent in Iowa to 6.3 percent in Connecticut. Our view is that one problem gambler is one too many. We need to learn more about the issue of problem gambling and its effects on gamblers, their families and society. Through the creation of the center, we will be better equipped to identify a problem gambler and address the issue on an educated, well-informed level." [29]

Arnold Wexler, a recovered compulsive gambler who with his wife Sheila counsels problem gamblers and serves as a consultant for the gambling industry, reports that many individual gambling companies and casinos are addressing the problem on their own. At a May training session for employees of the Casino Rouge in Baton Rouge, La., for example, the Wexlers helped casino employees identify compulsive gamblers by their appearance and behavior. "We also had casino employees tell us that they themselves had a gambling problem," Arnold Wexler says.

Why are the casinos booking these training sessions? "Some of them, I'm sure, are doing it because they want to look socially OK and show that they have a compulsive-gambling policy," he says. "And some of them are doing it because they sincerely believe that it should be done."

Cyndi Collier, a state-certified counselor in compulsive gambling at Sierra Tucson Inc., a psychiatric hospital in Tucson, Ariz., questions the gaming industry's motives. "I would say that's something that sounds pretty good on the surface but doesn't carry any weight at all," she says. "It's just talk. There are several things that [the gaming industry] could do, such as return money to problem gamblers, or develop programs for them and their family members. But I don't see any of that yet."

Thompson also is skeptical. He notes that Harrah's spent about $146,000 last year "telling people about how bad a problem compulsive gambling is, and training their workers to spot it. Well, this is nice, but the tragedy is that Harrah's is spending more on this than any other gaming company. I commend Harrah's because it's a start, but they're the biggest player in dealing with compulsive gambling, and $146,000 is just a pittance." ■

OUTLOOK

The Sky's the Limit

The U.S. gambling industry's recent past makes it hard to divine its

Continued on p. 786

At Issue:

Does gambling lead to increased crime?

L. Scott Harshbarger
Attorney General of Massachusetts

FROM TESTIMONY BEFORE THE HOUSE JUDICIARY COMMITTEE, SEPT. 29, 1995.

yes

Almost every attorney general who has faced the issue of casino gambling in their state has cautioned me that there are a range of public safety, regulatory and social issues that are never addressed before the introduction of gambling. . . .

One of the most noted consequences of casino gambling has been the marked rise in street crime. Across this nation, police departments in cities that have casino gambling have recorded surges in arrests due to casino-related crime. In many cases, towns that had a decreasing crime rate or a low crime rate have seen a sharp and steady growth of crime once gambling has taken root.

The most storied downturn is, without a doubt, Atlantic City. Atlantic City's crime rate had been on the decline before casinos came to New Jersey. However, between 1977-1990 there was a 230 percent increase in crime in Atlantic City. . . . Other states that have legalized land-based casino gambling — including Colorado, South Dakota and Connecticut — have similar stories. . . .

[O]rganized crime is a second danger that accompanies casino gambling. While proponents might argue that organized crime's connection with casinos stopped with Bugsy Siegel in Las Vegas, the facts do not bear that out. In 1994 in Louisiana, 17 individuals associated with the Marcello, Genovese and Gambino crime families were indicted for RICO violations for profit skimming through video poker machines that had recently been legalized. . . .

The easy response to these problems is that by increasing the amount of police officers or allocating more money for law enforcement agencies, the crime problems can be averted. To local officials prone to give into this quick-fix solution, I would point to the example of Atlantic City: Recognizing the dramatic increase in crime, Atlantic City increased [its] officers-to-inhabitant ratio twofold and [its] budget threefold. Nevertheless, since these increases, the crime rate has nearly tripled.

Outside of having to make increased outlays for the operation of local law enforcement agencies, cities and towns will have to absorb other law enforcement expenditures such as the cost for prosecution and incarceration. . . . Gambling comes with high administrative and regulatory costs as well. The state of New Jersey expends $57 million a year just to regulate casino activity. They have 300 state troopers and over 30 assistant attorneys general working solely on casino investigations.

The question for elected officials and policy-makers is whether the supposed benefits have taken into account all of these costs.

Jeremy D. Margolis
Former assistant U.S. attorney and former director, Illinois State Police

FROM TESTIMONY BEFORE THE HOUSE JUDICIARY COMMITTEE, SEPT. 29, 1995.

no

People often ask whether the presence of gaming in their community would cause an increase in street crime. The facts are these: Las Vegas, Nevada, the city that is synonymous with casinos, is among the safest cities in America. . . .

Those who cite crime as a reason to oppose legalized gaming tend to ignore the Las Vegas example and instead tend to focus on a misleading interpretation of crime statistics in America's other major gaming venue, Atlantic City. . . . Those who raise the specter of an Atlantic City teeming with crime bred by casinos serving as a blueprint for a crime wave in any community that legalizes gaming obviously misunderstand (or intentionally misconstrue) the statistical realities in Atlantic City. . . .

The most exhaustive research on post-casino crime in Atlantic City was conducted by the noted criminologist and sociologist Jay Albanese. . . . Albanese examined the increase in Atlantic City's crime rates between 1978-1982 but measured them against the increases that occurred during the same time period throughout the entire state of New Jersey. He also examined the crime rates in light of the dramatic changes in Atlantic City's average daily population. . . . He found that the individual risk of victimization in Atlantic City was actually less than it had been before the advent of casinos, and that crime rate for people actually present was less than it had been before visitors tripled the city's average daily population.

In Illinois and in other jurisdictions that have implemented riverboat casino gaming, detractors have relied heavily on the theory and "research" of an admittedly anti-casino economics professor in New Orleans. The professor's uncommissioned work . . . included as a major tenet the discovery of a "casino factor" that could mathematically predict the amount of crime that would be caused by the operation of a single casino in New Orleans. The professor claimed that his formula could be applied to predict the amount of crime that would result from casino gaming in any city in America.

The casino-factor theory . . . . does not take into account the vast disparity in the specific crime factors that are present in different cities. It does not address the question of what the likely impact on crime rates would be if an impoverished community like Atlantic City had its average daily population tripled by tourists, no matter how they spent their time and money upon arrival. It considers statistically insignificant the impact of police initiatives and performance and totally ignores what is perhaps the most important variable of all — the basic nature and decency of a people in a community.

FOR MORE INFORMATION

American Gaming Association, 555 13th St. N.W., Washington, D.C. 20004; (202) 637-6500. Founded in June 1995, AGA acts as an information clearinghouse and advocate for the gaming-entertainment industry.

Arnold and Sheila Wexler Associates, 1101A Beach Ave., Bradley Beach, N.J. 07720; (908) 774-0019. The Wexlers counsel compulsive gamblers and conduct training sessions for casino employees on how to spot compulsive gamblers and deal with their own gambling problems.

National Coalition Against Legalized Gambling, 110 Maryland Ave. N.E., Washington, D.C. 20002; (202) 546-2254. NCALG claims major credit for the defeat of state gaming proposals since the group's founding in mid-1994.

North American Association of State and Provincial Lotteries, 1700 E. 13th St., Suite 4PE, Cleveland, Ohio 44114; (216) 241-2310. The association serves as an information clearinghouse and helps jurisdictions to establish new lottery operations.

Continued from p. 784

future. On the one hand, the industry continued to post double-digit revenue gains in 1995. However, statewide gaming initiatives failed completely in 1995 and so far this year. Can legalized gambling continue to grow within its existing market? Or will that market shrink in the face of increasingly hostile public opinion?

Christiansen hesitates to make a firm prediction. "The strong [1995] performance of casinos was expected," he wrote. "Despite the absence of new markets, riverboats and their land-based competitors are still in the process of soaking up unsatisfied latent demand for blackjack and slot machines. Someday, perhaps in 1996 or 1997, this process will work itself out and supply and demand for casino games will come into balance, as it has in older casino markets." [30]

Pooh-poohing the arguments of anti-gambling groups could be costly to the industry, Christiansen warns. "Investors should never forget that casinos and lotteries and race tracks and bingo halls conduct business at the sufferance of the state, meaning as long, and only as long, as people approve of them. All of the . . . hard-to-quantify [negative] consequences of supplying demand for commercial games are thus very important." [31]

Wexler, no friend of legalized gambling, nonetheless feels that the industry has ample opportunity for future expansion. "We're probably nearing the end of what I call the second stage of legalized gambling in this country," he says. "The third stage will feature electronic games, which kids already are familiar with. I also think states will start running lotteries three times a day — breakfast, lunch and dinner lotteries, if you will. We're still at the tip of the gambling iceberg in America."

Some gambling analysts believe in-flight gambling holds great potential. "There was gaming on airplanes many years ago, using old-fashioned slot machines," notes Bybee. "Airline gambling of the future will be done through the video screens that are used to show movies, games and other forms of entertainment on long-haul flights. How big it will grow, I don't know. But my feeling is that an opportunity to gamble in some fashion on international flights will open up within the next year or two."

At present, however, gambling in the skies is limited to foreign carriers. In 1994, Congress approved legislation barring gambling on international flights. Opponents of in-flight gaming say it is not clear who would regulate the activity and whether bettors would be allowed to wager unlimited amounts on credit.

Failure to address these issues could prove disastrous to individual bettors, Wexler says, citing this hypothetical worst-case scenario: "A vacationing family gets on an in-flight gambling plane headed for Orlando. By the time they arrive, dad has maxed out the credit line on his Visa card. As a result, they can't check into their hotel, let alone spend any time at Disney World. So, what do they do then — turn around and go home?"

Christiansen speculates that changes in federal policy on airline gaming will come, if at all, only after the gambling study commission completes its work. "Congress might defer action on in-flight gambling to the study commission's final report and recommendations, on the principle that the essence of political wisdom is passing the buck. In that eventuality, the airline industry will take its place in the long line of witnesses that will be queuing up to testify before the commission." [32]

In-home gambling, via the telephone, the Internet or interactive cable television, already exists to some extent. For instance, parimutuel horse-race wagering by phone has been available in Connecticut and New York since the 1970s. But Bybee believes home-based gaming on a nationwide scale is "much further off" than in-flight gaming. "Technologically, it's not a problem. Rather, it's a question of protecting the nation's youth — keeping young people from getting caught up in gambling. I don't see that market developing very quickly."

As industry executives review their marketing options, they also are hoping to head off any future attempts to levy a federal tax on gambling revenues. The Clinton administration last year proposed a 4 percent federal gaming tax, but dropped the idea after 31 governors objected. A House Ways and Means Committee attempt to tax

Indian gaming proceeds also got nowhere. But this doesn't mean that the gaming industry can let down its guard, warned Jana McKeag, vice president for government relations at Inland Casino Corp. and a member of the Cherokee Nation of Oklahoma. "Both of these proposals have set a precedent that will likely be revisited in the years to come." [33]

In the meantime, Eadington foresees "increasing acceptance of gambling as a commodity by society at large, in spite of the backlash from what I consider a small but vocal minority." If that happens, he says, "it's going to be difficult to prevent new gaming technology from being introduced. Governments have put themselves in a hypocritical position by marketing lotteries while saying, in effect, 'This is a heinous activity, but it's not heinous for us. We can use it to raise revenue instead of raising taxes.' I think that attitude has undermined the public's willingness to accept government claims that gambling is bad for you."

Nonetheless, Eadington expects gambling opponents to press ahead with their crusade. "The Christian Coalition fears that once gambling comes into the home, it will destroy millions of lives. But I suspect the reality is not going to be that dire. I view problem gambling in much the same light as problem drinking — it's always going to be there, and it's always going to generate terribly sad and regrettable stories. There will be societal efforts to mitigate [problem gambling]. But you can't make the problems disappear, and prohibition generally doesn't work."

Christiansen's vision of the U.S. gaming world of tomorrow assumes further refinement of "a new leisure product: Gaming packaged in state-of-the-art entertainment." [34] Even now, he has noted, "Orlando West" (Las Vegas) has much in common with "Orlando East" (the Florida home of Disney World). For instance, both resorts offer family theme parks, water rides and fantasy architecture evoking distant lands and historical periods.

The key difference, of course, is that Orlando West also offers gambling, while Orlando East doesn't. But even that distinction may fade over time. That's because, Christiansen wrote, "the world changes every day, even in magic kingdoms. . . .[B]y century's end we will see Hollywood entertainment companies enter gaming, by merging with, or acquiring outright, one of the casino companies that helped build Orlando West." [35] ■

Notes

[1] See Eugene Martin Christiansen, "The United States Gross National Wager," *International Gaming & Wagering Business,* August 1996, p. 70.

[2] *Ibid.,* p. 60.

[3] For background, see "Gambling Boom," *The CQ Researcher,* March 18, 1994, pp. 241-264.

[4] "New Evil Empire," *The New York Times,* Sept. 28, 1995, p. A27.

[5] Marc Cooper, "America's House of Cards," *The Nation,* Feb. 19, 1996, p. 16.

[6] Christiansen, *op. cit.,* p. 67.

[7] American Gaming Association, "Gaming Industry Myths and Facts," 1995, p. 2.

[8] U.S. House Judiciary Committee, National Gambling Impact and Policy Commission Act (published proceedings of hearing held Sept. 29, 1995).

[9] E.L. Grinols and J.D. Omorov, "Development or Dreamfield Delusions?: Assessing Casino Gambling's Costs and Benefits," University of Illinois, September 1995, p. 5.

[10] William R. Eadington, "Problem Gambling and Public Policy: Alternatives in Dealing With Problem Gamblers and Commercial Gamblers," in Howard Schaeffer, *Compulsive Gambling* (1989), p. 177.

[11] Rufus King, *Gambling and Organized Crime* (1969), p. 74. In 1951, King served as counsel to the Senate Special Committee to Investigate Organized Crime.

[12] Ernest W. Burgess, "The Next Step in the War on Crime — Legalize Gambling: A Report to Gov. Henry M. Horner," 1935.

[13] John Dombrink and William N. Thompson, *The Last Resort: Success and Failure in Campaigns for Casinos* (1990), p. 22. Dombrink is an associate professor in the School of Social Ecology, University of California-Irvine.

[14] The cases were *Seminole Tribe of Florida v. Florida* and *Poarch Creek Indians v. Alabama.*

[15] "Legalized Gambling on a Losing Streak," National Coalition Against Legalized Gambling, 1996.

[16] The Connecticut legislature's anti-casino vote was limited to Bridgeport.

[17] American Gaming Association, "About the AGA," 1995.

[18] American Gaming Association, "AGA Marks First Anniversary," June 1996, p. 5.

[19] Testimony before House Judiciary Committee, Sept. 29, 1995, on the proposed National Gambling Impact and Policy Commission Act.

[20] Christiansen, *op. cit.,* p. 69

[21] *Ibid.,* p. 77.

[22] *Ibid.,* p. 80.

[23] *Loc. cit.*

[24] The 1994 Delaware Horse Racing Redevelopment Act allowed the state's three racetracks to operate slot machines.

[25] Quoted in *The Washington Post,* Aug. 13, 1996, p. A1.

[26] The Legislature rejected a similar local-option measure in August 1995.

[27] Christiansen, *op. cit.,* p. 89.

[28] Eugene Martin Christiansen and Will E. Cummings, "The United States Gross National Wager," *International Gaming & Wagering Business,* Aug. 1, 1995, p. 64. For additional information on Indian gaming, see "Native Americans' Future," *The CQ Researcher,* July 12, 1996, pp. 601-624.

[29] Quoted in AGA news release, Feb. 21, 1996.

[30] Christiansen, *op. cit.,* p. 58.

[31] *Ibid.,* p. 60.

[32] *Ibid.,* p. 68.

[33] Jana McKeag, "Gaming Tax Still Has Momentum," *International Gaming & Wagering Business,* August 1996, p. 111.

[34] Christiansen and Cummings, *op. cit.,* p. 40.

[35] *Ibid.,* p. 42.

Bibliography

Selected Sources Used

Books

Dombrink, John, and William N. Thompson, *The Last Resort: Success and Failure in Campaigns for Casinos,* University of Nevada Press, 1990.

The authors provide an overview of efforts to legalize casinos in the past two decades. As they completed their book, they write, they came across a 1955 *Life* magazine article that featured glitzy Las Vegas hotels and asked, "Has Las Vegas expanded to its limits?" The question is still being asked, but these authors offer no predictions.

Ginsburg, Daniel E., *The Fix Is In: A History of Baseball Gambling and Game-Fixing Scandals,* McFarland, 1995.

Ginsburg examines infamous baseball gambling scandals such as those involving the 1919 Chicago "Black Sox," Detroit Tigers pitcher Denny McLain and Cincinnati Reds infielder Pete Rose, as well some scandals that are largely forgotten.

McGowan, Richard, *State Lotteries and Legalized Gambling,* Praeger, 1994.

McGowan traces the development of lotteries since Revolutionary times and examines strategies for conducting and even privatizing state-run lotteries.

Spanier, David, *Inside the Gambler's Mind,* University of Nevada Press, 1994.

Spanier, who has written several books and articles about gambling, declares in his preface: "Gambling is good for you. That's my thesis, and I don't feel I need to apologize for saying it straight out." The book is part of a series on gambling published by the university.

Articles

Christiansen, Eugene Martin, and Will E. Cummings, "The Gross Annual Wager of the United States," *International Gaming & Wagering Business,* Aug. 1, 1995.

Entertainment industry analysts Christiansen and Cummings review developments in U.S. legalized gambling in 1994 and speculate on what the future may hold.

Christiansen, Eugene Martin, "The Gross Annual Wager of the United States," *International Gaming & Wagering Business,* August 1996.

Christiansen surveys gambling's robust growth in 1995, but cautions that some belt-tightening may be in store.

Cooper, Marc, "America's House of Cards," *The Nation,* Feb. 19, 1996.

The subtitle of Cooper's article — "How the Casino Economy Robs the Working Poor" — sums up its thesis. "Gambling in today's United States — repackaged, sanitized, video-ized, down-marketed and ubiquitous — is not an issue of temperance or free choice but rather one of social class and public economic policy," he argues.

Kaye, Melissa Weinstein, "Smooth Sailing Is Expected for Gambling Commission," *CQ Weekly Report,* July 20, 1996.

Kaye supplies background on the bill (passed shortly after this article appeared) to create a blue-ribbon federal panel to examine the impact of legalized gaming on American society.

Labich, Kenneth, "Gambling's Kings: On a Roll and Raising Their Bets," *Fortune,* July 22, 1996.

Labich tells the story of the competition between gambling moguls Steve Wynn and Donald Trump to be the top dog in Atlantic City casinos.

Perlman, Ellen, "The Gambling Glut," *Governing,* May 1996.

Perlman zeroes in on the increasing visibility of the anti-gambling movement. "States are finding that each new game impacts existing ones," she writes. "There's only so much gambling money to go around."

Shapiro, Joseph P., "America's Gambling Fever," *U.S. News & World Report,* Jan. 15, 1996.

Like Perlman, Shapiro finds considerable merit in the arguments of those who oppose legalized gambling. Casinos, he writes, "mostly shift jobs and money around communities."

Reports and Studies

U.S. House Judiciary Committee, National Gambling Impact and Policy Commission Act (published proceedings of hearing held Sept. 29, 1995).

Supporters and opponents of gambling air their views on a bill to establish a federal commission that would examine legalized gaming's impact on American society.

Grinols, Earl L., and J.D. Omorov, *Development or Dreamfield Delusions?: Assessing Casino Gambling's Costs and Benefits,* University of Illinois, September 1995.

In an oft-cited study, economists Grinols and Omorov write that expansion of legalized gambling "would be more costly to the nation than an additional Hurricane Andrew every year in perpetuity ($32 billion, the costliest natural disaster in American history), or it would be the equivalent of an additional 1990-91 recession roughly every decade."

The Next Step

Additional information from UMI's Newspaper & Periodical Abstracts database

Backlash Against Gambling

Hornblower, Margot, "No dice: The backlash against gambling," *Time,* April 1, 1996, pp. 28-33.
Cash-strapped towns only recently embraced casinos as their economic salvation, but they were soon accompanied by economic dislocation and broken lives. Gaming initiatives nationwide are now meeting resistance.

Marks, Alexandra, "Gambling surges, and backlash grows," *The Christian Science Monitor,* June 3, 1996, p. 1.
As gambling's popularity has grown in the U.S. so has the backlash against it. Communities across the U.S. are staging quiet, fierce battles over whether to continue gambling's spread or stop it. Even Las Vegas, a longtime mecca of legalized gambling, is feeling the impact and retooling its image to attract families.

Shapiro, Joseph P., "America's gambling fever," *U.S. News & World Report,* Jan. 15, 1996, pp. 52-61.
The gambling industry is coming under fire from those who fear it won't help communities and families in the long run. Tom Grey, a United Methodist minister, is leading a nationwide campaign to stop the spread of casinos.

Wartzman, Rick, "Bayou backlash: Gambling is proving to be a poor wager for state of Louisiana," *The Wall Street Journal,* Sept. 11, 1995, p. A1.
Complaints about legalized gambling are emerging among large segments of Louisiana's generally easy-going populace. Mom-and-Pop commercial enterprises are feeling the dollar drain, job creation has fallen fall short of promises and political cronyism and corruption is rampant.

Wilcox, Melynda Dovel, "Gambling: More states are folding," *Kiplinger's Personal Finance Magazine,* July 1996, p. 14.
Twenty-two of the 24 states that have taken up the issue of legalized gambling in the past two years have gone against it. Casinos take away money from local businesses such as theaters and restaurants and cost the state money when gamblers file bankruptcy or commit fraud, Wilcox writes.

Wilkie, Curtis, "Rocky start causes La. to reconsider gambling," *Boston Globe,* April 8, 1996, p. 1.
Following political scandals and the financial failure of several casinos, Louisiana is wrestling with the first serious effort by a state to roll back legalized gambling since the industry branched out from Nevada two decades earlier.

Compulsive Gambling

Adelman, Ken, "The human cost of gambling outweighs state profits," *San Francisco Chronicle,* July 14, 1996, p. C13.
Adelman comments on the wasted life of his cousin Alby, a compulsive gambler who spent more than half of his life in prison and suggests that lost in the policy debate over state-sponsored gambling — via lotteries, casinos, horse races — is the personal dimension. Adelman suggests that government focus on the human toll gambling takes and on tales of wasted lives.

Haberman, Clyde, "Video gambling aids education. Ask the losers," *The New York Times,* Dec. 3, 1995, p. 49.
Haberman discusses the added temptation that compulsive gamblers must face because of the explosion of government-supported betting across the U.S., such as Quick Draw, the casino-style game that New York introduced in September 1995.

Herard, Vladimire, "African Americans hardest hit by compulsive gambling," *Chicago Defender,* Jan. 8, 1996, p. 1.
Extensive studies from the Texas Anti-compulsive Gambling Council report that African American gamblers are most disproportionately impacted by gambling addiction.

Lakshmanan, Indira A R., "A woman's life lost to gambling," *Boston Globe,* March 9, 1996, p. 13.
Penniless and apparently hopeless, Laura Fitzgerald Grauer, 38, of Stamford, Conn., drowned herself in the Thames River the week of March 4, 1996, after maxing out her credit cards gambling at the Foxwoods Resort Casino. Her suicide has led to calls from groups that counsel compulsive gamblers for stronger measures to help hardcore gamblers overcome their addiction.

Miller, Julie, "Legalization, record revenues and gambling as a serious illness," *The New York Times,* Sept. 17, 1995, p. CN1.
As gaming gains greater social acceptance, compulsive gambling has become a public health problem, according to a survey by the Southeastern Connecticut Problem Gambling Task Force. Although gaming generates nearly $300 million yearly in state revenue, Connecticut provides only $170,000 a year to support one treatment program. Compulsive gambling is examined, and Connecticut's response to the problem is discussed.

"Miss. on lookout for gambling woes," *Times-Picayune,* March 3, 1996, p. B4.
The Mississippi Council on Problem Gambling, chosen to address compulsive gambling, was told by Joanna Franklin, vice president of the National Council on Problem Gambling, that the problem shows up in 2 percent to 7 percent of the adult population.

Reinholz, Mary, "Women recovering from compulsive gambling, step by step," *The New York Times,* Nov. 26, 1995, p. LI34.
The help that Long Island, N.Y., Gamblers Anonymous has been able to give to women addicted to gambling is discussed.

Crime and Gambling

Berenson, Alex, "Gambling-limits bill dies," *Denver Post,* April 26, 1996, p. D1.
Colorado legislation to raise gambling limits in the state's casinos failed on April 25, 1996, and the bill may not be back for awhile. Teller County Sheriff Guy Grace testified how calls for service have risen from 2,000 before gambling in 1990 to 9,000 in 1995, and his department has not been able to keep up with the increase.

"Gulf Coast: Gambling and crime," *Times-Picayune,* March 29, 1995, p. B6.
An editorial suggests that as Louisiana's legislators take up bills dealing with gambling regulation in the 1995 session, they would do well to consider the quality-of-life issue at the heart of the Gulf Coast's crime statistics.

Snyder, David, "Crime, social problems rise with gambling," *Times-Picayune,* March 26, 1995, p. A1.
Casinos have brought a lot of money to the Gulf Coast of Mississippi, but they've also fueled a crime wave and aggravated social problems, law officials and social service workers say.

Economic Impact of Gambling

Jackson, Bernice Powell, "Gambling on proverty (sic) in America," *Michigan Chronicle,* Feb. 7, 1996, p. A6.
Jackson expounds on her objections to the argument that bringing casinos to poor regions improves that region's quality of life for its citizens.

Jinkner-Lloyd, Amy, "Gambling on economic development," *American City & County,* July 1996, pp. 57-60.
While riverboats and casinos can stimulate a local economy, their reputation as a cure for poverty is exaggerated. Information about how several cities and counties have learned that gambling has not provided the economic cure that they were hoping for is presented.

Kilborn, Peter T., "Portrait from new era of nation's gambling," *The New York Times,* Feb. 28, 1996, p. A10.
With the growth of gambling across the U.S., casinos now employ tens of thousands of dealers. Legalized gambling has been the salvation of Joliet, Ill., which had been suffering from an unemployment rate that reached 27.6 percent for a month in 1983. Thanks largely to casinos, it is now about 5 percent. Casino workers earn an average of $24,000 a year and get health insurance. All this has made Joliet a place of relative prosperity.

Krampf, Leslie, "Colorado towns find gambling is a roll of the dice," *The Christian Science Monitor,* Sept. 14, 1995, p. 3.
The social cost inflicted on the city of Central City, Colo., by the advent of legalized gambling is discussed. Although the city has seen its coffers swell with proceeds from gambling, as well as rocketing employment, many local merchants were bankrupted by casinos. The town also suffered increased traffic due to the casinos.

Weeks, George, "Engler looks at gambling across U.S.," *Detroit News,* June 26, 1995, p. A1.
Michigan Gov. John Engler's administration examined statistics from 17 states not reviewed by the Blue Ribbon Commission on Michigan Gaming to determine whether to sanction casinos and found that casinos are big revenue producers for state and local governments, but they also mean more crime.

Gambling on the Internet

Lucas, Allison, "The high price of Internet gambling," *Sales & Marketing Management,* May 1996, p. 23.
Gambling on the Internet in the U.S. may or may not be against the law. Toronto-based Internet Casinos President Warren Eugene says that since there are no laws established, his company is not breaking any law.

Narvaes, Emily, "Gambling on Internet? Don't bet on it, yet," *Denver Post,* Aug. 1, 1996, p. A1.
CEEE Group Corp of Colorado announced July 30, 1996, that it would manage an on-line casino for the Aruba Palms Beach Resort and Casino on the island of Aruba near Venezuela. The legality of all this is subject to some debate, such as where cyber-gambling is allowed and who will regulate it.

Growth of Legalized Gambling

Ferguson, Hayes, "Mexico may bet on casino gambling," *Times-Picayune,* Oct. 30, 1995, p. A1.
Cash-starved Mexico is considering legalizing casino gambling, which may result in casinos along the U.S.-Mexican border, as well as in the popular resorts of Cancun and Acapulco. No legislation has been drafted, but debate on the issue, which was outlawed in the 1930s, has begun.

Fisher, Anne B., "Gambling in New York? Mr. Trump is horrified at the thought," *Fortune,* Oct. 2, 1995, p. 33.
New Jersey casino owner Donald Trump is outraged that in New York State the lottery commission is installing a casino-style keno setup in about 2,000 bars and other places to raise money for the state's education fund.

Halbfinger, David M., "Bill seeks to expand gambling," *Boston Globe,* April 25, 1996, p. 59.
Massachusetts state Sen. Michael W. Morrissey said he will introduce legislation calling for an expansion of gambling statewide.

Marks, Alexandra, "Shifting attitudes toward gambling," *The Christian Science Monitor,* June 3, 1996, p. 11.
Gambling and Americans' ambivalence toward it are woven into U.S. history. It boomed through the 1800s, died out in the 1890s, but rose again by the 1980s, with more than 30 states authorizing lotteries. In 1996, all but two states, Utah and Hawaii, allow some form of legalized gambling.

National Gambling Commission

Alpert, Bruce, "Senate OKs panel to study legal gambling's impact," *Times-Picayune,* July 18, 1996, p. A7.
The Senate voted July 17, 1996, to establish a commission to conduct a two-year study on the impact of legalized gambling. Other provisions of the bill are also noted.

"Gambling," *Houston Chronicle,* July 15, 1996, p. A16.
An editorial speaks in support of legislation that would establish a national commission to study the effects of gambling on the U.S. and its people.

"Gambling: A bad bet," *The Christian Science Monitor,* May 20, 1996, p. 20.
An editorial calls for the Senate to pass the bill to set up a national commission to study the effects of gambling in the U.S.

Volland, Victor, "Anti-gambling group calls for national commission," *St. Louis Post-Dispatch,* April 28, 1996, p. C2.
Leaders of the National Coalition Against Legalized Gambling, meeting in Missouri on April 28, 1996, said a proposed federal monitoring commission could help blunt the spread of gambling.

Wolf, Frank R., "A close look at gambling," *The Washington Post,* Oct. 3, 1995, p. A19.
Rep. Frank R. Wolf, R-Va., argues for his proposed legislation to establish a National Gambling Impact and Policy Commission, noting that the bill does not outlaw, regulate or tax gambling, but merely concludes that it is time to take a look at its effects on business, crime, local governments and families.

Native Americans and Gambling

"Another tribe has gambling plans," *Detroit News & Free Press,* April 1, 1995, p. A13.
The Little Traverse Bay Bands of Odawa Indians of northern Michigan said it plans to build a casino, most likely in Emmet County, within a year. Recognized by the federal government as a tribe in September 1994, the Little Traverse Bay Bands has enrolled 1,000 members in Charlevoix and Emmet counties.

Forstenzer, Martin, "Gambling on a roadside attraction," *Los Angeles Times,* Nov. 16, 1995, p. A3.
Hoping to draw local gamblers and lure tourists, the Bishop Paiute Tribe opened a temporary 24-hour casino outside of Bishop, Calif. Construction has begun on a three-story structure that will house the Paiute Palace Casino in November 1995.

Martin, Glen, "Billion-dollar jackpot: State tribes gambling on their future," *San Francisco Chronicle,* June 26, 1996, p. A1.
As part of a special series of occasional reports on legalized gambling in California, Martin examines the dispute between Native Americans leaders and the administration of Republican Gov. Pete Wilson over the use of electronic gambling machines on Indian reservations.

Riverboat Gambling

Kilborn, Peter T, "An Illinois city, once down and out, finds rebirth in riverboat gambling," *The New York Times,* March 9, 1996, p. A6.
The economic rebound being enjoyed by Joliet, Ill., due to its downtown riverboat gambling casino is discussed.

Mannies, Jo, "Two images of riverboat gambling have yet to come into clear focus," *St. Louis Post-Dispatch,* Sept. 13, 1995, p. B5.
Mannies discusses the debate over riverboat gambling in Missouri, where supporters say it will cure the cities' money woes, while critics claim that it is slowly spreading a cancer of costly social ills.

Orwall, Bruce, "States take 'River' out of riverboat gambling," *The Wall Street Journal,* Oct. 18, 1995, p. B1.
Four years after several Midwestern states began to allow casino gambling during riverboat cruises, some states are making one not-so-small adjustment to the rules: The boats no longer have to go anywhere, they may simply tie up at the dock and let the games begin.

"Riverboat's ultimatum on gambling," *San Francisco Chronicle,* July 9, 1996, p. A14.
The owners of the Petaluma Queen, California's first riverboat casino, say that if they don't win the battle over Petaluma's final gambling permit, they are leaving for more accommodating waters.

Toroian, Diane, "Way cleared to build largest complex for riverboat gambling," *St. Louis Post-Dispatch,* Sept. 25, 1995, p. N1.
The Maryland Heights, Mo., City Council has cleared the way for Harrah's Maryland Heights Corp to start work on its 460,000-square-foot riverboat gambling complex near Riverport on the Missouri River. It will be the nation's largest such complex.

Turner, Vernon Kitabu, "Portsmouth's bid for riverboat gambling," *Journal & Guide,* March 8, 1995, p. 1.
The controversial bid of Portsmouth, Va., for riverboat gambling is detailed.

Back Issues

Great Research on Current Issues Starts Right Here...Recent topics covered by The CQ Researcher are listed below. Before May 1991, reports were published under the name of Editorial Research Reports.

FEBRUARY 1995
Cracking Down on Immigration
The Business of Sports
Reinventing Government
Housing Discrimination

MARCH 1995
Death Penalty Debate
Primary Care
Democracy in Africa
Environmental Movement at 25

APRIL 1995
Abortion Clinic Protests
Dieting and Health
Combating AIDS
Rethinking Affirmative Action

MAY 1995
Assisted Suicide Controversy
Overhauling Social Security
Learning to Read
Mandatory Sentencing

JUNE 1995
Combating Infectious Disease
Property Rights
Repetitive Stress Injuries
Regulating the Internet

JULY 1995
War Crimes
Highway Safety
Combating Terrorism
Preventing Teen Drug Use

AUGUST 1995
Job Stress
Organ Transplants
United Nations at 50
Advances in Cancer Research

SEPTEMBER 1995
Catholic Church in the U.S.
Northern Ireland Cease-Fire
High School Sports
Teaching History

OCTOBER 1995
Quebec's Future
Revitalizing the Cities
Networking the Classroom
Indoor Air Pollution

NOVEMBER 1995
The Working Poor
The Jury System
Sex, Violence and the Media
Police Misconduct

DECEMBER 1995
Teens and Tobacco
Gene Therapy's Future
Global Water Shortages
Third-Party Prospects

JANUARY 1996
Emergency Medicine
Punishing Sex Offenders
Bilingual Education
Helping the Homeless

FEBRUARY 1996
Reforming the CIA
Campaign Finance Reform
Academic Politics
Getting Into College

MARCH 1996
The British Monarchy
Preventing Juvenile Crime
Tax Reform
Pursuing the Paranormal

APRIL 1996
Centennial Olympic Games
Managed Care
Protecting Endangered Species
New Military Culture

MAY 1996
Russia's Political Future
Marriage and Divorce
Year-Round Schools
Taiwan, China and the U.S.

JUNE 1996
Rethinking NAFTA
First Ladies
Teaching Values
Labor Movement's Future

JULY 1996
Recovered-Memory Debate
Native Americans' Future
Crackdown on Sexual Harassment
Attack on Public Schools

AUGUST 1996
Fighting Over Animal Rights
Privatizing Government Services
Child Labor and Sweatshops
Cleaning Up Hazardous Wastes

Future Topics

- ***The States and Federalism***
- ***Civic Journalism***
- ***Foreign Aid***

THE CQ Researcher

PUBLISHED BY CONGRESSIONAL QUARTERLY INC.

The States and Federalism

Should more power be shifted to the states?

The size and scope of the federal government has been a major issue throughout U.S. history. Now, after a century of steady growth, the federal government is being viewed by politicians in both parties and by many observers as too big and too powerful. Republicans took control of Congress in 1994 promising to shift power to the states. President Clinton supported some of their proposals, but opposed others. Meanwhile, the Supreme Court has tilted toward the states in some important federalism cases. Advocates of the so-called "devolution revolution" say state and local governments are more efficient and more politically accountable than the federal government. But supporters of an expansive federal role argue that many social and economic problems are best addressed at the national level.

INSIDE THIS ISSUE

CQ Sept. 13, 1996 • Volume 6, No. 34 • Pages 793-816

Formerly Editorial Research Reports

The States and Federalism

The Issues

Background

Current Situation

Outlook

Sidebars and Graphics

For Further Research

Cover: Barbara Sassa-Daniels

Sept. 13, 1996
Volume 6, No. 34

Editor
Sandra Stencel

Managing Editor
Thomas J. Colin

Associate Editors
Sarah M. Magner
Richard L. Worsnop

Staff Writers
Charles S. Clark
Mary H. Cooper
Kenneth Jost

Editorial Assistant
Tonya Harris

Published By
Congressional Quarterly Inc.

Chairman
Andrew Barnes

Vice Chairman
Andrew P. Corty

Editor and Publisher
Neil Skene

Executive Editor
Robert W. Merry

The CQ Researcher (ISSN 1056-2036). Formerly Editorial Research Reports. Published weekly (48 times per year, not printed March 1, May 31, Aug. 30, Nov. 29) by Congressional Quarterly Inc., 1414 22nd St., N.W., Washington, D.C. 20037. Annual subscription rate for libraries, businesses and government is $319. Additional rates furnished upon request. Periodicals postage paid at Washington, D.C. POSTMASTER: Send address changes to The CQ Researcher, 1414 22nd St., N.W., Washington, D.C. 20037.

The States and Federalism

BY KENNETH JOST

THE ISSUES

Out in western Montana, Ravalli County Sheriff Jay Printz oversees a rugged domain twice the size of Rhode Island. Three years ago, when the new "Brady bill" required his small office to run background checks on handgun buyers, the self-described "independent son of a gun" simply refused.

"I've got too much to do, and here they are telling me I have to do federal background checks," says Printz, who also serves as coroner. "I basically felt this was not my job."

In rural southeastern Arizona, Sheriff Richard Mack felt the same way. "I was elected by, for and of the people of Graham County to do their bidding," Mack says. "They're my boss, and the federal government has no right to divert my attention from Graham County matters to serve their agenda."

But gun-control advocate Sarah Brady, who worked for more than eight years on the bill, says the federal government had "a responsibility" to enact the law. "When states do not do their own work, there are certain issues that cross state lines," says Brady, whose husband, James, was seriously wounded in the 1981 assassination attempt on President Ronald Reagan. "Gun control is one of those issues."

"A patchwork of state laws and local laws never was effective in the past," Brady continues. "You need to have some broad general laws and then let the states pick up from there. You certainly have to have a standard from which the whole country operates."

Printz and Mack won rulings from federal judges in their states striking down the Brady bill as a violation of the 10th Amendment, which protects states' rights. But a federal appeals court panel voted 2-1 against the two lawmen last September, saying the law imposed only "minimal obligations" on local police.

Now the Supreme Court has agreed to hear Printz's and Mack's appeals. Conservative groups such as the National Rifle Association (NRA) have joined in urging the justices to invalidate the law, as have the National Conference of State Legislatures and other state-government organizations. The Clinton administration is vigorously defending the act, supported by groups such as Handgun Control, headed by Sarah Brady, which spearheaded the drive to enact the statute. [1]

For the high court, the Brady bill case will mark the third consecutive term that major states' rights disputes have been on the justices' calendar. Two earlier Supreme Court rulings, in 1995 and last March, set new limits on Congress' power and signaled a desire among the court's conservative majority to re-examine federalism, which had gotten little attention from the court in the past 60 years. * (*See story, p. 798.*)

The idea of shifting power from Washington to state and local jurisdictions has been taken up by the legislative and executive branches of the federal government, as well as the courts. In Congress, Republican leaders have repeatedly vowed to shrink the federal government. "We will continue in our drive to return power to our states and our people," then-Senate Majority Leader Bob Dole of Kansas, now the GOP presidential nominee, declared in his first speech in the new Congress on Jan. 4, 1995. [2]

President Clinton has also said that he wants to transfer more responsibilities to the states. "I believe we should ship decision-making responsibility and resources from bureaucracies in Washington to communities, to states and, where we can, directly to individuals," Clinton told the National Governors' Association on Jan. 31, 1995. [3]

In 1993, during his first year in office, Clinton sought to give states more discretion in managing federally financed programs, as part of his so-called "reinventing government" initiative. But the Republican victory in the 1994 congressional elections pushed state-federal relations to the top of Washington's agenda.

In their "Contract With America," House Republicans included one major federalism proposal — elimination of so-called "unfunded mandates," or provisions of federal law that raise costs for state or local governments without providing funds to offset them. More broadly, House Speaker Newt Gingrich of Georgia and other Republican leaders promised to "devolve" power in a host of areas from Washington to state and local governments or, eventually, into the private sector.

The Republicans delivered on their first promise, pushing through a bill to restrict unfunded mandates within the first three months of the new Congress. And this summer, they won passage of a much-debated welfare bill that gives states greater control over benefit programs.

---

* Federalism is a political system based on a national government and one or more levels of subnational governments, each with specified powers and responsibilities.

Confidence in Federal Government Is Low . . .

Public opinion polls and other surveys indicate Americans have far less confidence in the federal government than they used to — and more confidence in state and local governments (1). They also think the federal government delivers the fewest services for their tax money (2) and that the states should take over more of the responsibilities now handled by the national government (3). However, the public continues to support federal leadership in a number of critical fields, including economic policy, civil rights and the environment (4).

1. Confidence in governmental institutions

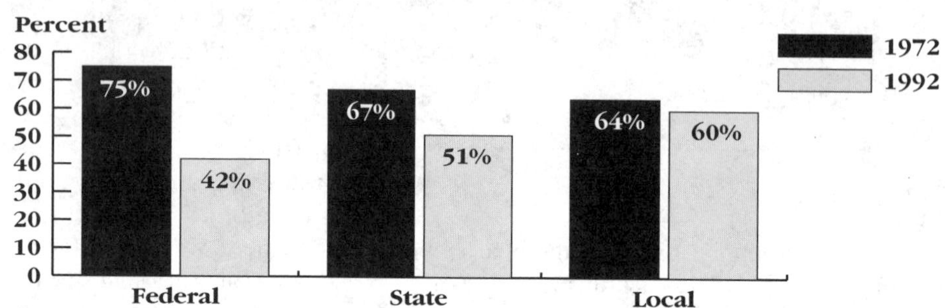

2. What level of government gives the *least* for your money?

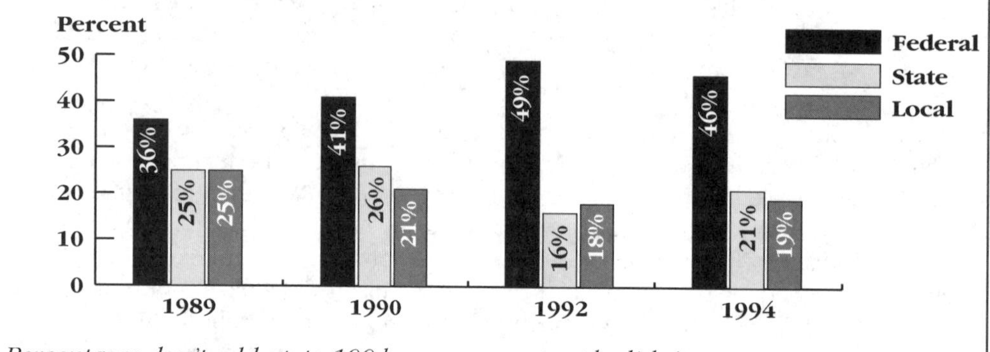

* *Percentages don't add up to 100 because some people didn't answer.*

Some experts view the Republicans' victory in the November 1994 elections as ushering in a long-term realignment in state and federal powers. "This is a power shift that is not likely to be reversed soon," Richard Nathan, director of the Rockefeller Institute of Government at the State University of New York in Albany, wrote early this year. Nathan, a sometime adviser to Dole, is credited with coining the phrase "devolution revolution." [4]

But other experts on federalism say Congress has accomplished less than GOP leaders promised. "There's only one item that directly helps state and local governments — the unfunded mandates bill," says David Walker, a professor of political science at the University of Connecticut and author of the recently published *The Rebirth of Federalism*.

Even some Republican supporters agree that the GOP-controlled Congress fell short of its far-reaching goals. "It has tried to affect [state-federal relations] a lot more than it has, but it has affected them a lot nonetheless," says Jeffrey A. Eisenach, president of the Progress & Freedom Foundation and an adviser to Gingrich.

Advocates of devolution say the movement reflects a belief that "one-size-fits-all" policies imposed from Washington are not the best way to deal with state and local problems. "Devolution allows the individual community to have the freedom to do it the way that best fits it," Eisenach says.

But critics warn that the reaction against the growth of the federal government in the past 60 years may be going too far. "There is a role for a strong national government," says Ronald Walters, a professor of government and African-American studies at the University of Maryland in College Park. "You can't go back to the 19th century. There are national standards that are important."

Such warnings reached a crescendo this summer as liberal interest groups and many Democratic lawmakers bitterly attacked the welfare overhaul measure as a retreat from a federally guaranteed safety net for the poor. But Clinton signed the measure Aug. 22, despite having vetoed two somewhat similar measures earlier. And at the national conventions in August, both parties embraced the goal of shifting power from Washington to state and local governments.

Federalism has been a dominant domestic issue throughout the country's history, and it promises to be an important issue in the upcoming presidential and congressional elections, as well as several legal cases facing the courts. In the months ahead, these will be some of the questions about federalism being debated:

Has the federal government taken on too much power from the states?

A century ago, the federal government had little impact on Americans' daily lives. Today, citizens come into contact with the federal government every day. The federal government provided land for the interstate highway system and operates the air traffic control network. It provides Social Security benefits for retirees and helps pay for medical care for the elderly and the indigent. It regulates the food we eat, the water we drink and the air we breathe. And it takes a chunk of withholding tax out of every paycheck.

Conservatives have maintained for at least the past three decades that Washington has grown too powerful at the expense of state and local governments. Barry Goldwater largely staked his Republican presidential campaign in 1964 on that proposition — and lost in a landslide. Since then, however, conservatives have grown more confident in attacking the size and scope of the federal government, and even many moderates and liberals have urged a shift in power from Washington to state capitals.

Conservatives' calls for reducing the federal government's power stem from a general opposition to taxes, spending, economic regulation and social programs — combined with a belief that state and local governments can better adapt policies to local conditions.

"We believe state and local government does a better job of understanding local communities," Gingrich told Republican governors last year, "than does some Washington bureaucrat in a high-rise office building, who has never been in the state, never visited the community and is making decisions based on paperwork done by another bureaucrat." [5]

Moderates and liberals have joined the call for scaling back the federal government, in part out of political necessity. But some also believe that the federal government grew too large for its own good and that state and local governments are more likely to provide services efficiently. That was the thesis of an influential 1992 book by Alice M. Rivlin, who recently became a member and vice chairman of the Board of Governors of the Federal Reserve System after serving as Clinton's budget director.

"The proliferation of federal programs, projects, offices and agencies in so many parts of the country made the federal government increasingly unmanageable," Rivlin wrote while a senior fellow at the Brookings Institution. "It resembled a giant conglomerate that has acquired too many different kinds of businesses and cannot coordinate its own activities or manage them all effectively from central headquarters." [6]

Even the supporters of devolution

Continued on p. 799

. . . But Public Still Sees Leadership Role

3. Should the states take over more responsibilities now performed by the federal government?

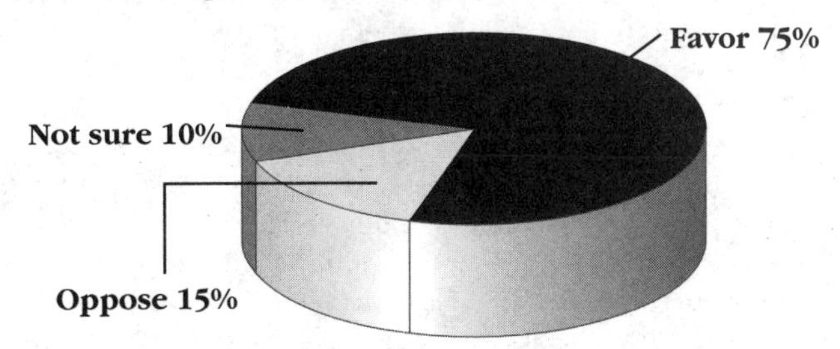

4. Who should be in charge?

Percent

	Federal	State
Improving education	22%	72%
Reducing crime	24%	68%
Job training	31%	55%
Reforming welfare	42%	46%
Improving health care	48%	41%
Protecting environment	50%	38%
Protecting civil rights	67%	26%
Strengthening economy	64%	24%

Sources: Timothy J. Conlan and James D. Riggle, "New Opportunities/Nagging Questions: The Politics of State Policymaking in the Nineties," Nov. 27, 1995 (1,4); "Changing Public Attitudes on Governments and Taxes," U.S. Advisory Commission on Intergovernmental Relations, 1994 (2); Yankelovich/Time/CNN, Jan. 25-26, 1995, Roper Center for Public Opinion Research (3).

Brady Bill Poses Latest Court Test on Federalism

After nearly 60 years of consistently backing expansion of federal powers, the Supreme Court finally is giving states' rights advocates good news: The justices are tilting toward the states in some disputes.

Within the past two years, the court — as final arbiter in power disputes between the states and federal government — twice has struck down provisions of federal laws on states' rights grounds. In *United States v. Lopez,* the court in 1995 ruled that Congress exceeded its power to regulate interstate commerce with a law making it a federal crime to possess a gun near a school. Then, this March, the court held in *Seminole Tribe of Florida v. Florida* that a federal law giving Indian tribes the right to sue states in federal court over gambling issues violated the 11th Amendment's restrictions on federal court jurisdiction over suits against state governments.

Court observers said the two decisions — both by 5-4 votes — signaled a new desire by conservative justices to re-examine the court's approach to federalism issues. "There is a very active interest by a majority of the court in rethinking the power relationship between Congress and the states," says Stephen Wermeil, a professor at Georgia State University in Atlanta who formerly covered the court for *The Wall Street Journal.*

Now, the court is poised to hear a new states' rights challenge to another federal law, the so-called Brady bill. The 1993 gun-control law established a five-day waiting period to buy a handgun and requires local law enforcement agencies to conduct background checks on prospective handgun purchasers during that period.

Even though law enforcement groups supported passage of the law, local sheriffs in several states challenged the background-check provision as an infringement of state sovereignty. They won several lower court rulings, but two of the three federal appeals courts to rule on the law so far have upheld it. In June, the high court agreed to hear an appeal by two sheriffs — Jay Printz of Ravalli County, Mont., and Richard Mack of Graham County, Ariz. — seeking to overturn the decision by the 9th U.S. Circuit Court of Appeals upholding the law (*Printz v. United States; Mack v. United States*).

The new interest in federalism comes after a period of nearly 60 years in which states' rights challenges rarely succeeded at the Supreme Court. President Franklin D. Roosevelt gave the court a solidly nationalist majority with a series of appointments of liberal justices beginning in 1937. Previously, a conservative majority on the court had used a narrow conception of federal power over interstate commerce to strike down some of Roosevelt's New Deal programs.

Since that time, the court has taken an increasingly broad view of Congress' power over interstate commerce. It has also upheld Congress's right to impose conditions on the states for receiving federal aid. In the most recent such case, the court in 1987 voted 7-2 to uphold a provision requiring states to establish a minimum drinking age of 21 in order to receive federal highway-assistance funds (*South Dakota v. Dole*).

The court did side with the states in a 5-4 decision in 1976 that Congress had no power to require state and local governments to comply with the wage and hour provisions of the federal Fair Labor Standards Act. But nine years later, the court reversed itself on the issue in another 5-4 decision, *Garcia v. San Antonio Metropolitan Transit Authority.* "States must find their protection from congressional regulation through the national political process, not through judicially defined spheres of unregulable state activity," Justice Harry A. Blackmun wrote in the 1985 decision.

The dissenters in the 1985 decision were led by then-Associate Justice William H. Rehnquist, a staunch defender of states' rights who a year later became chief justice. Ten years later, Rehnquist now leads a tenuous five-vote majority ready to side with states on some federalism issues.

The latest revival of federalism issues at the court began with a complex decision in 1992, *New York v. United States.* The 6-3 decision struck down a portion of a 1985 federal law dealing with radioactive wastes generated by nuclear power plants.

As part of a scheme to encourage states to establish sites for the disposal of radioactive wastes, the act required any states that did not establish such a site to take legal title to the material themselves and assume full legal responsibility for it. The court agreed with lawyers for the state of New York that that provision intruded on its sovereignty. "The federal government may not compel the states to enact or administer a federal regulatory program," Justice Sandra Day O'Connor wrote for the majority.

The 1992 decision will be the focus of the Brady bill cases, which the high court is likely to schedule for arguments in January. Stephen Halbrook, the Fairfax, Va., lawyer who will argue the case for the two sheriffs, says the case supports the challenge to the law.

"I think our prospects are very good at the Supreme Court based on the 1992 decision, which flatly holds that the Congress cannot require the states or local governments to administer a federal program," Halbrook says. "The courts that did uphold the Brady Act had to strain to interpret the word 'administer' to the point that it had no meaning."

But Dennis Henigan, general counsel of Handgun Control, the lobbying group that led the fight for enactment of the law, believes the act will be sustained. "The plaintiffs are arguing for an absolute prohibition on any kind of federal mandate to state or local officials," Henigan says. "Supreme Court precedent has never gone that far. We think that the 10th Amendment permits the federal government to enlist the help of state and local officials where the federal policy is made more effective through their participation."

Continued from p. 797
concede, however, that the federal government ballooned in part because state and local governments were unable or unwilling to deal with problems. States couldn't alleviate the effects of industrialism at the turn of the century or get the country out of the Great Depression in the 1930s. And later, many states were unwilling to deal with racial discrimination and poverty.

"Maybe there was an argument for [federal action] in the 1930s," says Eisenach. "Maybe there was an argument for that in the 1960s. On issues of poverty and race, there was much more diversity than there is today."

But some supporters of federal policies on social issues also concede that the federal government has lost public confidence by its seeming inability to solve the problems. "The social problems haven't gone away," says Larry Thompson, director of the Urban Institute's New Federalism Project. "There is a sense that the social programs that were operated with more prescription from Washington didn't work."

Still, some political scientists say the pressure for federal action will continue even while politicians of all stripes are calling for transferring power to the states. "People have this crazy idea that the water they drink should be safe, and the air they breathe shouldn't kill them,' says Donald Kettl, director of the LaFollette Institute of Government at the University of Wisconsin in Madison. "They want the government to solve these problems, and it's easier to get the federal government to try to solve them than to get 50 states and even more localities to solve them."

Do the states have a greater capacity to deliver services efficiently than the federal government?

Advocates of devolution want to shift power to the states in part because of what they depict as enormous waste and inefficiency in Washington. Some experts agree that states have an edge over the federal government in terms of efficiency. But others, including some who call for a larger role for the states, doubt that government programs are significantly more efficient in state capitals than in Washington.

"That kind of blanket generalization is meaningless at best or deceptive at worst," says Timothy Conlan, a professor of political science at George Mason University in Fairfax, Va., and author of the book *New Federalism*. "States are different. There's a lot of diversity. The programs that we're talking about often differ in a fundamental way." [7]

"Some states are probably superior in capacity to the national government," Kettl says. "Some are a long way away."

"They're roughly in the same ballpark," says David Osborne, co-author of *Reinventing Government,* the path-breaking book that outlined ways to deliver government services more efficiently. "There's a little less bureaucracy and red tape in state governments than in the federal government, but the feds are working very hard to reinvent government." [8]

The public views the federal government as less efficient than state or local governments, according to surveys taken by the Advisory Commission on Intergovernmental Relations since 1989. When Americans were asked which level of government delivers "the least for the money," the federal government was consistently the most frequent response. In the most recent survey, 46 percent of those responding gave the federal government the worst rating, compared with 21 percent for state governments and 19 percent for local governments. (*See chart, p. 796.*)

"IF YOU'LL PASS THE BRADY BI... I'LL SURE SIGN...

HANDGUN CONTROL

R. Michael Jenkins

Sarah and James Brady join Rep. Charles E. Schumer, D-N.Y. (left) at a press conference on Feb. 2, 1993, announcing the re-introduction of the "Brady bill" in Congress.

Clearly, state governments have made great strides in professionalizing in the past three to four decades. "Institutionally, states are more sophisticated" than they were before the 1950s, Conlan says. "They have stronger revenue systems and more professional bureaucracy."

In addition, Rivlin and another former Brookings scholar, Paul Peterson, contend that state and local governments are in a better position to manage what Peterson calls "developmental activities" — such as education, transportation and economic development.

"States are the most efficient on the productivity side," says Peterson, now a professor of government at Harvard University. "The United States has the

New Mandates Law May Have Little Effect

House Republicans made it a major goal of their "Contract With America." President Clinton heartily embraced it. And both parties took credit for it at their national conventions last month. But the new law aimed at preventing the federal government from imposing costly requirements on state and local governments may have little immediate effect, many experts say.

"It's an important statement," says Don Boyd, director of the Center for the Study of the States at the State University of New York in Albany, "but whether it has any real world impact is something we won't know for a while."

"A lot of it is psychological," says David Walker, a professor of political science at the University of Connecticut in Storrs. "It's not in any way drastic."

But proponents of the new law, which limits so-called unfunded federal mandates maintain that it already has had an important effect: increasing attention in Congress and in the federal agencies to the impact federal laws and regulations have on state and local governments.

"We set about trying to pass a bill that would begin the process of revolutionizing state-federal relations," says Scott DeFife, who works on federal budget issues at the National Conference of State Legislatures. "It has helped start the process. The bill has worked to help begin to balance state, federal and local relations."

The new law was among the first passed by the Republican-controlled Congress last year. When President Clinton signed the bill on March 22, 1995, he hailed it as a model of bipartisan cooperation. "This unfunded mandates law will be another model on how we have to continue to change the way Washington does business," Clinton said.

The new law is weaker, however, than its supporters' rhetoric suggests. Under the law, bills that impose unfunded costs of more than $50 million on state and local governments would be subject to a point of order, or challenge, in either the House or the Senate. But the procedural hurdle can be overcome by a simple majority vote.

Skeptics suggest the majority-override provision means lawmakers will have little difficulty ignoring the new law in the future. But DeFife says supporters deliberately rejected the idea of requiring a supermajority vote to impose new mandates on state and local governments.

"From a bipartisan standpoint, the idea is not to create more tools for gridlock," DeFife says. "The last thing we wanted to do was to create another mechanism where you could muck up the works."

The new law also exempts two major types of federal mandates: anti-discrimination laws and requirements states must meet in order to receive federal assistance. Bruce McDowell, director of governmental policy research at the Advisory Commission on Intergovernmental Relations, said when the bill was signed into law that two-thirds of the 27 unfunded mandates passed by Congress during the 1980s would have been in those two categories and thus exempt. [1]

The law also did not apply to any federal mandates already on the books. Instead, the law required the Intergovernmental Relations Commission, a bipartisan, 26-member body, to study how to reduce the impact of existing mandates.

After canvassing state and local government organizations, the commission's staff prepared a draft report this spring recommending more flexibility or increased funds to help state and local governments comply with a number of federal laws, including the Fair Labor Standards Act, Clean Air Act, clean water act and Endangered Species Act. [2] But the commission rejected the report in July by a 13-7 vote after administration officials lobbied against it. The commission will not have a chance to return to the issue; it is scheduled to go out of business at the end of this month, a victim of budget cutting.

Despite its limitations, DeFife says the unfunded mandates law is achieving its major objectives: providing Congress more information about the impact of proposed legislation on state and local governments and promoting consultation between lawmakers and state and local officials as legislation moves through Congress. He says the law "played a huge part" in shaping some of the provisions of the new welfare law.

"We have brought the parties together — the states and the federal government — before legislation gets voted on to fix unfunded mandates before they happen," he says. "From our standpoint, that says the bill is working because they're talking more about how to avoid legislation that would involve unfunded mandates."

---

[1] Quoted in *The Washington Post*, March 23, 1995, p. A10.

[2] U.S. Advisory Commission on Intergovernmental Relations, "The Role of Federal Mandates in Intergovernmental Relations" (draft report), July 9, 1996.

most elaborate industrial policy of any country in the world, but it's mostly at the state level. It would be much less efficient if it were controlled by the federal government." [9]

Some observers, however, note that several of the most frequently criticized areas of government policy are managed by state and local governments rather than by the federal government. "Criminal justice and elementary and secondary education are almost wholly state responsibilities," author Forrest Chisman wrote last year. "If the states are so good at solving difficult social problems, why have they failed to satisfy the public on issues of far more immediate importance to most people?" [10]

Business Week magazine noted some other failures of state governments in a cover story last year entitled "Power to the States." More than 20 states are under court order to reform their child welfare systems, the magazine noted. In addition, states have been strongly criticized for their handling of child support enforcement and their administration of federally financed job training programs. "[M]any local bodies can be as bureaucratic and inefficient as the feds — and often far more corrupt," the magazine concluded. [11]

Some devolution proponents minimize the importance of state and local government efficiency by stressing that their real goal is reducing the size of government at all levels. "The fact is that states aren't per se more efficient, less bureaucratic, more humane than the federal government," says Eisenach at the Progress & Freedom Foundation. "I see devolution as the first step toward trickle-down empowerment — getting [social welfare] back to individual charity."

To the University of Maryland's Walters, however, devolution "has very little to do with efficiency and more with ideology. That is where this impulse is coming from."

Are the states more politically accountable than the federal government?

Supporters of transferring power to the states say that besides being more efficient than the federal government, states are more politically accountable — and hence more responsive. Again, however, experts warn that state governments vary widely. In addition, even some advocates of enlarging state responsibilities criticize the decision to shift welfare programs to the states, fearing that they will have no incentive to provide adequate benefits for the needy.

Republicans have stressed the theme of Washington as a distant government, captive to lobbyists and special interests and unable to appreciate the problems of people "outside the Beltway." Writing shortly after the 1994 congressional elections, former Rep. Mickey Edwards, R-Okla., praised the Republican majority for promising to turn programs "back to those governments closest to the people — the state and municipal governments, where the mayors live across town, the council members may live next door and the legislators and governors live close enough to be pestered by concerned citizens." [12]

State and local governments are generally viewed as more politically responsible than they were for much of this century. The passing of big-city political machines, badly malapportioned state legislatures and blatant domination of state governments by business interests has made state and local governments more democratic than they were as recently as the 1950s and '60s.

Author Osborne also argues that the concentration of competing interest groups in Washington often makes it impossible to reshape programs. "The more politicized your environment is, the harder it is to reinvent," Osborne says. But some state capitals, especially in larger states, are equally politicized, he says. "If you're in Albany, you feel like you're in Washington. It's not much different."

For his part, Brookings' Peterson believes state and local governments are more accountable than the federal government in some areas, but not because of the political process. "People are much less likely to participate in politics at the state or local level," Peterson says. "There is less public interest, less press interest and fewer interest groups."

Instead, Peterson argues that market forces "discipline" decisions about public services more at the state or local level than at the federal level. "Local governments must be sensitive to market considerations when designing and administering roadways, sanitation systems, public safety services and educational programs," he writes. State and local governments get quicker feedback about the quality of their services, he says, and people who are dissatisfied can move to another city or another state where the services are better. [13]

But Peterson contends that those same conditions will encourage state and local governments to shortchange social welfare programs. "The better your program, the more you will attract poor people to your community and the more your higher-income people will move to other states," Peterson says. "States have an incentive to race to the bottom."

Supporters of the welfare overhaul bill have dismissed this argument, insisting that state and local governments will feel pressure to avoid severe hardships under the new system. "I certainly don't think individual states are going to base their policies on what is cheapest and meanest," says Gingrich adviser Eisenach. "That's a disservice to state governments, to state legislatures and to people who vote in the states."

But Thompson of the Urban Institute suggests the political pressure for taking care of the poor is less strong at the state or local level than in Washington. "The advocates for aid to low-income people have more influence at the national capital," Thompson says.

At the least, Thompson and other experts say, the welfare reforms will lead to wide variations in benefit programs among the states. "One of the difficult questions," adds Kettl, "is whether we as a country are prepared to accept the variations that are going to result." ■

BACKGROUND

Competing Visions

The new American nation created two federal systems of government within eight years of winning independence in the Revolutionary War. Both systems provided for a national government of limited, specified powers and state governments of general, unspecified powers.

The first of the two systems, established by the Articles of Confederation in 1781, ended in failure because the national government was too weak. It could not force states to accept treaties, prevent trade wars between the states, stop the states from printing money or indeed exercise any direct authority over the citizens of the respective states. By 1787, as the University of Connecticut's Walker writes, "nearly all of the nation's leading statesmen had come to recognize the defects in the design of the first constitution, and the drive for reform became irresistible." [14]

The new Constitution created a stronger chief executive — the president — and gave the national legislature — the Congress — a lengthy list of "enumerated powers." More important, it specifically prohibited the states from exercising some powers — including making treaties, printing money or laying duties on trade with other countries or other states. It also provided for direct popular election of the members of one of the chambers of the new Congress, the House of Representatives. Under the Articles of Confederation, members of Congress were chosen by the state legislatures; the Constitution used that method only for the new Senate.

Writing in the series of pro-ratification articles now known as *The Federalist Papers,* James Madison and Alexander Hamilton articulated differing visions of the new national government to be established under the Constitution. Hamilton wrote of a national government with sufficient power to deal with the widest "variety of national exigencies." Madison, by contrast, described the national government's powers as "few and limited." It was also Madison who sought to reassure liberty-loving Americans that the federal system would safeguard their rights in two ways. It created a national government with the power to protect local minorities from local majorities while at the same time it gave state governments sufficient power to resist coercion by the national government. [15]

Despite those reassurances, opponents of ratification wrung a concession from the Constitution's supporters: a promise to add a Bill of Rights after ratification. The 10 amendments, ratified in 1791, guaranteed a variety of individual freedoms against the feared risk of infringement by the new national government. It was held that the amendments did not apply to the states, although most states had similar rights protections in their own constitutions. In addition, the 10th Amendment reiterated the idea of a limited national government: "The powers not delegated to the United States by the Constitution, nor prohibited by it to the States, are reserved to the States respectively, or to the People."

The competing visions of the national government's powers formed the basis of the principal political disputes in the United States for the next 70 years. With an expansive view of the national government's powers, the Federalists established a national bank, enacted tariffs, began regulating commerce between the states and launched road- and canal-building projects. The Anti-Federalists — who took the name Democratic-Republicans and later simply Democrats — generally opposed these ventures. The Supreme Court, under the Federalist Chief Justice John Marshall, upheld the assertions of federal power. But Marshall's successor, Chief Justice Roger Taney, led a more states'-rights-minded court for the quarter-century before the Civil War.

Throughout this period, the dominant philosophy was one of "dual federalism." As the late political scientist Edward Corwin characterized this philosophy, the national government was viewed as having limited powers while the state governments were regarded as having equal or sovereign status within their own spheres. The relationship between the national and state governments was "one of tension rather than collaboration." [16]

The seeds of the Civil War were sown as early as the 1830s, when South Carolina's John Calhoun argued that states had the power to "nullify" an act of Congress. The immediate target of Calhoun's nullification theory were tariffs that favored Northern manufacturing at the expense of the agrarian South. But slavery proved to be the issue that eventually split the Union. The pro-slavery South felt threatened by abolitionist sentiment in the North, even though the national government never sought to eliminate slavery before the Civil War. The war ended with the Union triumphant, slavery abolished and the right of secession officially repudiated by the Supreme Court.

Era of Centralization

The national government grew steadily in the next hundred years. In the decades after the Civil War, it helped to usher in the American industrial revolution. Then at the turn of the century, and repeatedly during the 20th century, the federal government took on added powers in dealing with the social and economic problems caused by industrialization, urbanization and the continuing legacy of racial discrimination.

Republican administrations were the first to expand the powers of the national government, as political columnist E.J. Dionne Jr. of *The Washington Post* has recently pointed out. Republicans "built land-grant colleges and railroads, opened the Western

Continued on p. 804

Chronology

1781-1865

The United States establishes a federal system of government, with a national government of limited powers and states exercising all other governmental power. The Civil War ends with Union victory over secessionist states.

1865-1970

National government grows in size and power.

1933-1938
President Franklin D. Roosevelt wins congressional approval of "New Deal" measures expanding federal authority over the economy and establishing federal social insurance and relief programs.

1964-1968
President Lyndon B. Johnson pushes "Great Society" legislation through Congress, expanding federal role in social welfare programs, environmental protection and other areas.

1970s

The Nixon administration wins enactment of revenue sharing as part of its "New Federalism" program but also implements major expansions of federal regulatory power over state and local governments.

Oct. 20, 1972
President Richard M. Nixon signs into law "general revenue sharing," providing state and local governments more than $6 billion per year in unrestricted funds from federal revenues.

Oct. 30, 1972
Nixon signs bill federalizing existing programs of assistance for the aged, blind and disabled. Lawmakers rejected Nixon's proposal to replace family welfare programs with a guaranteed annual income.

1980s

The Reagan administration promises to reduce the federal government's size and powers. Budget deficits result in reduced aid to state and local governments.

1981
President Reagan wins approval of a federal income tax cut and budget that reduces federal aid to the states by 15 percent.

1985
With Reagan's support, Congress allows general revenue sharing to state and local governments to die.

1990s

Leaders in both major parties call for further power shifts to the states.

June 19, 1992
Supreme Court strikes down as an infringement of state sovereignty a federal law requiring states with no disposal site for radioactive waste from nuclear power plants to assume responsibility for the material themselves.

Sept. 7, 1993
President Clinton and Vice President Gore release "reinventing government" proposals giving states greater discretion over federally financed programs.

Nov. 5, 1994
Republicans win control of both houses of Congress for first time in 40 years after calling for more decisive steps to shift power to the states.

March 22, 1995
President Clinton signs bill, pushed by Republicans as top priority, establishing parliamentary hurdle for any new law imposing unfunded mandates on state or local governments.

April 26, 1995
Supreme Court strikes down federal law prohibiting possession of firearms near public schools (*United States v. Lopez*).

Jan. 23, 1996
President Clinton, in State of the Union address, declares "The era of big government is over."

March 27, 1996
Supreme Court rules in dispute over Indian gaming law that Congress cannot authorize private individuals to sue states in federal court except under civil rights laws (*Seminole Tribe of Florida v. Florida*).

Aug. 22, 1996
President Clinton signs welfare overhaul bill to change Aid to Families with Dependent Children from a federally guaranteed entitlement program to a block grant system giving states greater control over benefits and eligibility.

January 1997
Supreme Court is expected to hear cases testing the constitutionality of the Brady bill's requirement that local police conduct background checks of handgun purchasers (*Printz v. United States; Mack v. United States*).

Continued from p. 802

lands for settlement and set up a massive pension system for Civil War veterans," Dionne noted. Republican Congresses also pushed through the 13th, 14th and 15th Amendments — the so-called post-Civil War constitutional amendments — and later civil rights laws aimed at bringing the newly freed slaves into the economic and political mainstream. Republican administrations at the turn of the century made the first extensive use of federal antitrust laws, enacted the first pure food and drug laws and began creating national parks and forests. [17]

Some of the national government's activities proved more popular and more long-lived than others. The country celebrated the establishment of state universities and national parks and the building of the intercontinental railroad, for which the national government provided generous land grants. But Reconstruction was resented in the South and then allowed to lapse. And the Supreme Court invoked states' rights in 1876 to throw out a federal voting rights law benefiting blacks and again seven years later to invalidate the federal law prohibiting racial discrimination in public accommodations. A decade later, in 1895, the court also weakened the newly enacted Sherman Antitrust Act by holding, on states' rights grounds, that the statute did not apply to manufacturing.

The populists and progressives of the late 19th and early 20th centuries concentrated their campaigns for reforms first, and predominantly, not at the national government but at the states. The dislocating effects of the industrial revolution were felt first in localities rather than nationally. The reformers were also not strong enough initially to carry on a national reform campaign. As a result, some of the major features of the modern regulatory and welfare state — for example, wage-and-hour laws and aid to needy families — began not in Washington but in the states. It was during this period that the states first earned the label "laboratories of experimentation." [18]

Reformist sentiment subsided in the decade after World War I at both the national and state levels. But the Great Depression of the 1930s brought calls for bold action to lift the country out of an unprecedentedly severe economic downturn. Under President Franklin D. Roosevelt, the federal government took on many new powers. But, as Walker points out, many of the New Deal relief and assistance programs consisted of conditional grants to the states — including free school lunches, emergency relief work and unemployment compensation. Federal aid to the states increased from a paltry $193 million in 1933 to more than 15 times as much — around $2.9 billion — in 1939. [19]

The New Deal's philosophy came to be called "cooperative federalism," and the idea of cooperation was emphasized at the time. "Throughout the web of federal-state relationships," a political scientist wrote in 1938, "run the threads of an informal cooperative association which depends entirely on mutual understanding and is not a necessary result of law or administrative requirement on either the federal or the state side." [20] Years later, a prominent political scientist, Morton Grodzins, coined the phrase "marble-cake federalism" to describe the pattern of shared activities and services between the national, state and local governments. [21]

Over time, however, the federal government attached more and more conditions to grant programs. An advisory commission on intergovernmental relations in 1955 noted "increasing legislative attention to conditions, standards, sanctions and methods of supervision" as well as "the evolution of national administrative machinery and procedures." [22]

Federal state-aid programs increased during the two Democratic administrations in the 1960s in number, overall spending and complexity. The number of aid programs tripled from 132 in 1960 to 397 in 1967. Spending nearly tripled, rising from $7 billion in 1960 to $20.3 billion in 1969. President Lyndon B. Johnson called his approach "creative federalism" and continued to stress the need for intergovernmental cooperation.

But as Walker, a self-described centrist Democrat, concedes, the decade witnessed a major change in federal-state relations. With the passage of a variety of civil rights, environmental and consumer-protection laws, the "carrot of grant funds" was being replaced by "the stick of coercive grant conditions," Walker writes. [23]

New Federalisms

Since the 1960s, presidents from both parties adopted policies that they described as efforts to shift power from the federal government to the states. Through the 1970s, as George Mason's Conlan points out, the policies were aimed mainly at improving the management of government programs through block grants and decentralized decision-making. In the 1980s, the Reagan administration pursued a more ideological goal of reducing government functions at all levels.

President Richard M. Nixon came to the White House in 1969 pledged, as he put it in his first major domestic policy address, to reverse "the trend toward ever more centralization of government in Washington." Toward that end, he proposed some management changes aimed at improving consultation and coordination between federal, state and local agencies. He also called for increased use of block grants — an approach that had gained some ground in the Johnson administration — which provided aid to the states with fewer specific requirements than so-called categorical grants.

More important, Nixon proposed

— and eventually signed into law — a "revenue-sharing" plan that called for the federal government to turn over billions of dollars to state and local governments with no strings attached. The idea had been put forth as early as 1958 by a Republican congressman, Melvin R. Laird of Wisconsin, and later endorsed by a leading Johnson administration economic adviser, Walter Heller. Leading members of Congress of both parties — including House Ways and Means Committee Chairman Wilbur D. Mills, D-Ark. — opposed the idea. But vigorous lobbying by state and local governments finally overcame the opposition. As finally passed, the measure called for $6 billion in revenue sharing over a five-year period; Nixon signed the bill on Oct. 20, 1972. [24]

Despite his commitment to "New Federalism," Nixon also presided over what Conlan calls "the greatest expansion of federal regulation of state and local governments in American history." [25] The Clean Air Act required states to develop plans to meet national air quality standards. The National Health Planning and Resources Act required states to establish procedures for approving construction of new health-care facilities. A 1974 highway-funding amendment effectively required states to adopt the 55-mile-per-hour speed limit — repealed by the current Congress.

As Conlan notes, Nixon opposed some of the intrusions on state prerogatives — for example, the 1972 water pollution control law that Congress enacted over his veto. But most of the major changes, he says, had Nixon's full or partial backing.

Nixon also proposed the most sweeping plan ever to federalize the welfare system: a guaranteed minimum annual income. The plan failed, victim of opposition from Republicans and conservatives and suspicion from Democrats and liberals. Nonetheless, Nixon supported two other major changes in programs that amounted to what Conlan calls an implicit national welfare policy. First, he established the Supplemental Security Income program to provide a national income floor for elderly, blind and disabled Americans. Second, he presided over the expansion of the Food Stamp program from an optional scheme to distribute surplus commodities into a mandatory food-assistance program for poor people. The result was a sharp increase in federal spending on entitlement programs — from $24 billion, or about one-fourth of the federal budget, in 1969, to $54 billion, or nearly half, in 1974. [26]

President Jimmy Carter promised in his "New Partnership" plan in 1978 to simplify federal aid to state and local governments and improve federal-state-local relations. [27] But his most concrete accomplishment was simply to raise the status of the White House office of intergovernmental relations. Other management changes initiated in his first two years fell by the wayside in the second half of his administration, according to Walker. By the end of his term, however, budget constraints were beginning to emerge as a major force for reshaping federal-state relations.

The Reagan Era

Like Nixon, President Ronald Reagan took office in 1981 with a promise — as he put it in his first inaugural address — "to curb the size and influence of the federal establishment." [28] Unlike Nixon, Reagan was interested not simply in freeing state and local governments but in reducing government activity at all levels. Through a series of tax-cutting, budget-cutting and deregulatory initiatives, Reagan succeeded at some of his objectives and, more broadly, reshaped the nature of the debate over the role of the federal government.

Reagan's successes came foremost through fiscal policies. In his first year in office, he pushed through massive personal and business tax cuts. In addition, he won congressional approval for consolidation of 77 categorical, or separate, programs into nine new block grants, with budget authorizations cut by 15 percent. The moves set the stage for a substantial scaling back of aid to the states through the remainder of Reagan's eight years in office. Measured in constant dollars, aid to states fell by some 15 percent from 1981 to 1987. [29]

Reagan in 1981 also proposed reducing general revenue sharing by 12 percent. The proposal died in the face of concerted opposition from state and local governments. But Reagan returned with proposals to eliminate revenue sharing altogether. And by 1985 the growing federal budget deficit forced Congress to agree that Washington could no longer afford the program.

Budget cuts were also used to achieve deregulatory goals, as author and presidential scholar Garry Wills recently pointed out. Writing in *The New York Times Magazine,* Wills said that even though Reagan failed to deregulate a single industry or abolish any important governmental agency, he "accomplished his own purposes by a malign neglect of governmental machinery." Tight budgets left many agencies with no effective capacity to enforce federal laws and regulations. [30]

Many of Reagan's proposals to reduce the federal government's role were thwarted by Democrats, who controlled one or both houses of Congress throughout his presidency. But, as Conlan writes, the fiscal policies of 1981 created a "politics of deficits" that limited the opportunity for new initiatives during his two terms and the single term of his Republican successor, George Bush. And the same fiscal reality was to confront President Clinton when the Democrats reclaimed the White House in 1992.

'Devolution Revolution'

Clinton heartened observers of intergovernmental relations with some modest steps toward improving state-federal programs in his first two years in office. Then the 1994 elections put federalism issues at the top of Washington's agenda as the new Republican majority in Congress promised — in the phrase frequently used by House Budget Committee Chairman John R. Kasich, R-Ohio — to "return money, power and responsibility to the states."

After winning passage of a budget shaped around tax hikes and deficit reduction, Clinton was able in 1993 to provide small increases in some state aid programs. The "Reinventing Government" proposals contained in the National Performance Review issued by Clinton and Vice President Al Gore in September 1993 called for reducing the number of categorical grants and giving states more flexibility in administering programs. But Clinton also supported other proposals to strengthen the role of the national government. And — although states' rights was not the primary focus of the debate — he pushed hard for approval of the Brady bill, now being challenged on federalism grounds before the Supreme Court.

The new Congress turned immediately to federalism issues — or what some lawmakers called devolution of power from Washington to the states. Republicans in both houses introduced among their very first bills similar measures to restrict so-called unfunded mandates. The proposals had enjoyed bipartisan support in the previous Congress but had failed to win final approval. House Republicans included the proposal in their "Contract With America," and Clinton in his State of the Union address promised to work with lawmakers to approve a "reasonable" bill on the issue. Some Democrats in Congress tried to slow or soften the bill, but Republicans brooked no delays and few amendments. Both houses approved the final version of the bill in mid-March, and Clinton signed it into law a week later.[31]

As enacted, the measure provided that any future bill imposing unfunded costs of more than $50 million on state or local governments would be subject to a parliamentary challenge in either chamber. It also required the Congressional Budget Office to estimate the cost of new mandates on state and local governments and on private businesses. Republicans turned back Democratic-backed amendments in both chambers to exempt environmental or public health laws from the bills. Still, the bill did not apply to any federal mandate already on the books, and it exempted civil rights provisions. In addition, the law provided that the procedural hurdle it imposed could be overridden by a simple majority — a provision that some experts said would limit its future impact. (*See story, p. 800.*)

In contrast to the quick work on the unfunded mandates bill, the second centerpiece of Congress' efforts to shift power to the states — welfare reform — took more than 18 months to complete.[32] Both Clinton and congressional Republicans said they favored giving states greater flexibility in administering Aid to Families with Dependent Children (AFDC), the state-federal assistance program established in 1935. Twice, Republicans passed bills built around a central provision to change the existing AFDC entitlement — guaranteeing benefits to eligible individuals — to a block grant for states. But Clinton vetoed the measures, terming them too punitive.

Republicans tried again this summer. Clinton, who had promised in his 1992 campaign to "end welfare as we know it," said he would sign the measure even though he still objected to some of its features — such as limiting food stamps and restricting aid to legal immigrants. The House and the Senate completed action on July 31 and Aug. 1, just as Congress was about to take a month-long recess for the political party conventions.

Even though the welfare overhaul bill gives states greater control over awarding benefits, the measure also contains a new federal mandate as a central provision. The bill specifies a five-year lifetime limit for any individual to receive assistance. In addition, states are required by next year to have at least 25 percent of welfare recipients working at least 20 hours per week. The requirement increases to 50 percent of recipients working at least 30 hours per week in five years. States that do not meet the requirement would have their block grant reduced — initially, by 5 percent and eventually by up to 21 percent. Some experts and welfare officials have warned that states will find it difficult or impossible to meet the targets.[33]

As he signed the bill Aug. 22, Clinton emphasized that attention would now shift to how the states carried out the new law. "The governors asked for this responsibility," Clinton said. "Now they have to live up to it."

Congressional Republicans had other proposals aimed at reversing the trend toward centralization of power in Washington. One measure — the 10th Amendment Enforcement Act, sponsored by Sen. Ted Stevens, R-Alaska — would provide for new legislative procedures to assure a constitutional basis for legislation approved by Congress. It also seeks to limit the ability of federal agency regulations to pre-empt state laws or regulations. Stevens, chairman of the Governmental Affairs Committee, held hearings on the bill, but no markup had been scheduled as of Sept. 10.

The strong states' rights sentiment in Congress did not prevent lawmakers from expanding federal power in response to the highly publicized wave of church arsons in the past year. With bipartisan majorities, Congress approved legislation expanding federal jurisdiction over the arson or bombing of a place of worship. "On the one hand, you have Congress urging a restoration of the doctrine of enumerated powers as implicit in the 10th Amendment," says Roger Pilon, president of the libertarian Cato Institute. "On the other hand, you have Congress ignoring that doctrine when it comes to a piece of legislation before it."

Still, the new Republican majorities in Congress had clearly shifted the debate in Washington. Clinton himself recognized the change with a calculated applause line in his State of the Union address in January. "The era of big government is over," Clinton declared — drawing the heartiest applause from the Republican side of the aisle.

"There is now an acceptance of the idea that more and more things ought to be turned back to the states, that states ought to have more flexibility," says former Rep. Edwards. Even if Republicans fell short in concrete legislative accomplishments over the past two years, he says, "they did change what people expect of the states vs. the federal government." ■

CURRENT SITUATION

Federalism in the Courts

Christy Brzonkala was a newly arrived freshman at Virginia Polytechnic and State University on the night of Sept. 21, 1994, when two members of the school's football team called out to her and a friend from their dormitory room window and invited them up. Brzonkala claimed that after her friend left, the two men raped her. A university disciplinary committee initially found one of the two men, Antonio Morrison, guilty of sexual assault and suspended him for two semesters. But, after a second hearing, the offense was reduced to using abusive language, and Morrison was allowed to return to campus. *

Brzonkala, fearful of remaining at Virginia Tech, enrolled in another Virginia state school. But she also decided to take her accusation to a different forum: federal court. In December she sued Morrison and his teammate under the 1994 Violence Against Women Act, which permits women to bring damage suits for "crimes of violence motivated by gender."

In late July, however, a federal judge in Roanoke ruled the law unconstitutional; it was the most recent judicial ruling to limit Congress' power in areas traditionally left to the states. Judge Jackson Kiser said in *Brzonkala v. Virginia Polytechnic Institute and State University* that the law went beyond Congress' power to regulate interstate commerce. ** Upholding the law, Kiser said, "would have the practical result of excessively extending Congress' power and of inappropriately tipping the balance away from the states." [34]

Six weeks earlier, a federal judge in Connecticut reached an opposite conclusion about the law in a suit brought by a woman who sued her husband for an alleged 17-year history of abuse and violence. Judge Janet Bond Arterton said in *Jane Doe v. John Doe* that the evidence of widespread violence against women gave Congress a "rational basis . . . for concluding that gender-based violence . . . is a national problem with substantial impact on interstate commerce."

The conflicting rulings — both certain to be appealed — reflect the increased attention that federalism issues are being given in federal courts. States' rights challenges to federal statutes have increased since the Supreme Court's 1995 decision in *United States v. Lopez,* striking down a popular federal law that made it a crime to possess a gun near a school. By a 5-4 vote, the court said the Gun-Free School Zones Act could not be justified under Congress' power to regulate interstate commerce. [35]

Since that ruling, defendants have challenged several federal criminal laws on similar grounds, according to Barry Friedman, a professor at Vanderbilt Law School in Nashville, Tenn., who wrote a brief attacking the Gun-Free School Zones Act for state-government organizations in the *Lopez* case. The challenged statutes include a federal arson law, a recently enacted carjacking statute and an enhanced penalty provision for selling drugs on school grounds.

So far, however, states' rights advocates have no clear victories in these cases. Judges have narrowed the arson statute by requiring proof of some connection to interstate commerce, Friedman says, but the other laws have been upheld.

A number of challenges have also been filed against the 1992 Child Support Enforcement Act, which makes it a federal crime to "willfully" refuse to pay support to a child living in another state. So far, three federal district judges have ruled the law unconstitutional, while six have upheld the measure.

Last month, in the first appellate ruling on the law, the federal appeals court in New York also upheld the statute. "Nothing about the act threatens the existence or significance of the states or interferes with the exercise of their powers," the three-judge panel said. "On the contrary, the act aims to help the states in their efforts, often unsuccessful, to enforce their child support decrees." [36]

Supporters of the Violence Against

* Charges against the second student were dropped because of insufficient evidence. Morrison admitted having sexual relations with Brzonkala, but claimed she consented. Brzonkala has asked that she be identified in reports on the case.

** The "commerce clause" has been the principal constitutional provision used to expand federal laws and regulations during the 20th century.

Women Act say the law is justified because states have failed to solve the problem. "The existing legal remedies were not working to stop this problem," says Julie Goldscheid, a staff attorney with the National Organization for Women's Legal Defense Fund in New York, who argued for upholding the law in the Connecticut case.

But opponents insist that Congress had no authority for passing the measure. "Congress is limited by the Constitution and the enumerated powers," says Michael Rosman, associate general counsel for the Washington-based Center for Individual Rights, which represented Morrison in the Virginia Tech case.

Rosman says he is confident that appellate courts will uphold Kiser's decision to strike the law down. But Goldscheid disagrees. "I think Congress acted squarely within its authority," she says, "and I think the act should and will be upheld as constitutional."

Federalism in the States

The 1994 elections — which produced the first Republican-controlled Congress in 40 years — also gave the GOP a majority of state governorships for the first time since 1970. Republicans held 30 governorships, including eight out of the country's nine biggest states (all but Florida). They spoke boldly about restoring what they saw as a proper balance between the federal and state governments. And many Republicans also made plans to turn their states into laboratories for the same kind of conservative policies that GOP congressional leaders were pushing in Washington.

The Republican governors laid out a manifesto on federalism after a meeting in Williamsburg, Va., less than three weeks after the elections. The so-called Williamsburg Resolves called on Congress to complete action on the legislation to restrict unfunded federal mandates. The document also called for litigation to enforce the 10th Amendment in order to reverse what were called "usurpations by federal legislators and bureaucrats of powers not delegated to them under the Constitution." [37]

Meanwhile, Republican governors were leading the way in efforts to revamp the welfare system at the state level. Wisconsin's Tommy G. Thompson was capturing national attention by limiting benefits for recipients who bear children while on welfare and requiring able-bodied recipients to stay in school, get a job or face a cut in benefits. Other Republican governors — John Engler in Michigan, Jim Edgar in Illinois and George E. Pataki in New York — followed with similar plans. So did a leading Democratic governor, Evan Bayh of Indiana, who called his plan "the most aggressive and comprehensive" welfare reform in the country. [38]

Proponents of the plans said the states were following the tenets of federalism by developing experiments to find the best ways to reduce "welfare dependency." Some conceded the goal was also to reduce costs, although Thompson acknowledged that the job-training programs needed to put welfare recipients to work could actually increase costs.

Critics, however, said the plans were aimed less at innovating than at cutting benefits. "You don't see a lot of surprising things or new ideas," Michael Wiseman, a welfare expert at the University of Wisconsin, told *The Washington Post*. "What we see is variations on a basic theme." [39]

The Republican governors also shared a common goal in reducing state taxes and spending. New Jersey's Christine Todd Whitman provided a model: She had won a come-from-behind victory in 1993 by pledging to cut state taxes by 30 percent, and then battled skepticism and opposition to push the plan through the state's Legislature.

As Michael Barone, senior writer for *U.S. News & World Report,* pointed out, their fiscal policies distinguished the current crop of GOP governors from those of a generation ago. Republican governors of the 1960s and '70s, such as Nelson A. Rockefeller in New York or James R. Thompson in Illinois, were, according to Barone, "some of the biggest increasers of public spending of all time." But the governors of the 1990s, Barone said, "all want to trim back, cut, limit, hem in and discipline government." [40]

The tax-cutting mood led some critics to warn that the states would either be unwilling or unable to take on responsibilities being transferred out of Washington. "The argument that the states will do these things is troublesome," says Walters at the University of Maryland. "Some of these states are going to have great difficulty managing not only the programs but also the financial requirements."

"Reducing the federal government's role does not of itself get hard jobs done," says the University of Wisconsin's Kettl. "It doesn't solve the state capacity problem. It simply means that some other level of government has to try to solve the problem."

The federal government's own budgetary problems were adding to the pressure on the states. Despite a generally healthy fiscal climate, the states could be hurt by reductions in federal funds, which amount to more than 20 percent of total state and local outlays, according to the Advisory Commission on Intergovernmental Relations. [41] But most of the block grant proposals being debated in Congress called for reducing funding along with giving states greater discretion over spending.

The welfare bill exemplified some of the conflicting pressures. While giving states greater control over welfare policies, the measure also cut funding for food stamps and for aid to legal immigrants. Some observers

Continued on p. 810

At Issue:

Does the Brady bill violate states' rights?

COUNCIL OF STATE GOVERNMENTS AND NATIONAL CONFERENCE OF STATE LEGISLATURES
FROM BRIEF IN* PRINTZ V. UNITED STATES, *U.S. SUPREME COURT.

yes

The Brady Act impermissibly blurs the political accountability of Congress and of the states because responsibility for substantive handgun regulation policies is divorced from the duty to provide the administrative and financial resources required to enforce these policies. Although Congress established the substantive policy that handgun purchasers are subject to background checks, it compelled the states and local governments to provide the enforcement resources. There is no political check because Congress does not have to appropriate funds or allocate any administrative resources to enforce its policies. . . .

While Congress escapes political responsibility under Brady, state and local officials are held accountable for decisions made by the federal government. State and local legislatures, as well as CLEOs [chief law enforcement officers], are compelled under the Brady Act to allocate their limited administrative and financial resources to implement federal policies even though their constituents may "prefer their government to devote its attentions and resources to problems other than those deemed important by Congress.". . . . If there is no increase in their budgets, these state and local officials will have to decrease enforcement of state and local laws. . . .

In *New York v. United States,* [the Supreme Court in 1992] . . . concluded that the Constitution does not "permit Congress to employ state governments as regulatory agencies.". . . In providing for state enforcement of federal law, Congress authorized state officials to act, but, with only a few exceptions, it did not impose any duty on them to enforce federal laws. . . .

If federal regulations, like the Brady Act, are sufficiently important, Congress can establish an entirely federal program. . . . Congress could have assumed some of the costs of its regulatory program by authorizing and appropriating funds for grants to states and local governments that agreed to enforce federal handgun regulations by making background checks. . . . Congress could also have pre-empted state regulation of handgun transfers in states that do not have state laws meeting federal standards. . . . Finally, Congress could simply have delegated federal authority to enforce the Brady Act and relied on the voluntary cooperation of state and local CLEOs to conduct background checks of handgun purchasers. . . .

Unfortunately, Congress did not choose any of these constitutionally valid means of providing for state and local enforcement of federal handgun regulations. Instead, the Brady Act violates the constitutional principles of political accountability that are at the foundation of our federal system.

CENTER FOR HANDGUN CONTROL ET AL
FROM BRIEF IN* FRANK V. UNITED STATES, *2ND U.S. CIRCUIT COURT OF APPEALS.*

no

The enactment of legislation designed to prevent felons and other unauthorized persons from acquiring handguns falls well within the broad powers conferred under the Commerce and Necessary Proper Clauses [of the Constitution]. . . .

Given that Congress has ample power to regulate the sale of handguns, the sole question . . . is whether the *method* of regulation that Congress employed in the Brady Act threatens the "federal structure" established in the Constitution. . . .

The Supreme Court has sustained a broad array of other federal directives requiring that state or local officials "take or refrain from taking certain actions.". . . For a number of important reasons, the duties imposed on local law enforcement officials are less intrusive on state sovereignty than those upheld in . . . other cases. . . . Most significantly . . . the Brady Act does not set a political or legislative agenda for the states. Rather, the act merely requires that local officials perform certain ministerial duties. . . .

Similarly . . . this is not a case in which the federal government is avoiding political accountability by shifting to the states some function that the federal government might equally well perform. To the contrary, the Brady Act enlists the assistance of local officials because — at least in the near term — background checks are most effectively performed by local officials. . . .

The duties imposed on local law enforcement officials, furthermore, are not onerous. The act makes clear that local law enforcement personnel must make only "a reasonable effort" to determine whether the proposed transfer is lawful. . . . [T]he act affords local law enforcement officers the discretion to tailor background checks to local conditions and circumstances.

Finally, there is no reason to believe that any increased costs that the states may bear as an indirect result of the Brady Act even approach those imposed by the requirement, for example, that state courts adjudicate certain causes of action. The Brady Act, moreover, authorized the appropriation of $200 million to the states, among other things, to improve their computerized criminal history records, and Congress more recently authorized the appropriation of billions of dollars to the states for law enforcement. These appropriations plainly outweigh any cost that the Brady Act may impose on the parties.

In short, the obligations imposed on local officials under the Brady Act are not the sort of obligations that are likely to undermine the ability of the states to govern as distinct, sovereign entities. . . .

* Eight law enforcement organizations joined in the brief; Handgun Control has until Oct. 10 to file a comparable brief in the Supreme Court.

Continued from p. 808

forecast that states would face pressure to provide assistance out of their own budgets if hardships result. But one longtime observer of state government says most states are likely to meet their responsibilities.

"Can most states handle a welfare system as well as the federal government? Yes, I think they can — they're proving they can," says Alan Ehrenhalt, executive editor of *Governing* magazine, which covers state and local governments. "This is not the 1930s any more. The idea that the states are a primitive cold-hearted Uncle Scrooge and the federal government is Santa Claus doesn't really match reality." ■

Outlook

Federalism and Politics

In the political treatise he completed four years before his election as president, Woodrow Wilson described the relation of the states to the federal government as "the cardinal question of our constitutional system." The issue, Wilson wrote in 1908, "cannot . . . be settled by the opinion of any one generation, because . . . every successive stage of our political and economic development gives it a new aspect, makes it a new question." [42]

In the platforms they adopted last month at their national conventions, the Republican and Democratic parties both proposed shifting more responsibilities to state and local governments. The GOP charter promised to "restore the force of the 10th Amendment" and seek to enact other "structural reform that will permanently restore balance in our federal system." For their part, the Democrats repeated President Clinton's declaration that the "era of big government is over" and, without citing specifics, said the administration had worked to "shift problem-solving out of Washington and back to communities who understand their situations best." [43]

But the two presidential contenders struck different chords in their acceptance speeches. Labeling Democrats "the party of government," Republican nominee Dole stressed his call for a 15 percent federal income tax cut and listed virtually no new federal-level domestic policy initiatives. By contrast, President Clinton attacked congressional Republicans for trying to cut money for health care, education and the environment, saying Dole's tax-cut plan would require "huge cuts" in government services.

As the contrasting acceptance speeches indicated, the debate over federalism during the past two years has mixed attacks on the federal government with a broader push to reduce the size of government at all levels. "Much as I sympathize with both state and local governments," House Speaker Gingrich wrote in his political manifesto, *To Renew America*, "what we really want to do is to devolve power all the way out of government and back to American working families." [44]

The efforts to reduce the federal government's powers have fed on a sharp reduction in the public's confidence in Washington. "The federal government is unquestionably in the midst of a legitimacy crisis," says George Mason's Conlan. He notes that in the past 20 years, it has dropped from the highest public approval rating of any level of government to the lowest. "Every institution [in American society] has undergone an erosion of public trust," he says, "but at the government level, the feds had the deepest drop."

Yet polls also indicated that the public disapproved of some of the reductions in government programs that congressional Republicans pushed during the past two years. And when TWA Flight 800 crashed into the Atlantic Ocean off Long Island in late July, there were immediate calls for the federal government to take stronger steps to guarantee airline security.

As President Bush's budget director, Richard Darman, said recently, "All politicians for the last 15 years have favored cutting spending in the abstract, and almost all of them have favored keeping the spending going when they've gotten to the particulars," like the TWA crash. [45]

For the very reason that state and local governments are closer to their constituents, they are likely to feel pressure even more directly to provide public services than the federal government. And Don Boyd, director of the Rockefeller Institute's Center for the Study of the States, warns that the federal contribution to state and local budgets "will clearly decline" in the coming years.

"The current structure of the federal budget is simply unsustainable" because of the rising cost of Medicare and Social Security, Boyd says. "There will have to be cuts, and it's clear that they will have to include cuts in aid to states and localities."

The new welfare law will provide one initial test of the states' abilities to take on new responsibilities. Even some advocates of shifting power out of Washington acknowledge uncertainty about the outcome.

"Anybody who isn't a little bit nervous about this hasn't thought it through," says Wilfred McClay, an associate professor of history at Tulane University. "We could in certain states see a period of really pronounced social pathologies. A lot depends on the willingness of the states and localities to step up to the plate."

Some defenders of an expansive federal government warn that devolution will not automatically solve any of the country's social and economic problems. "Reducing the federal government's role does not of itself get hard jobs done," says Wisconsin's Kettl. "It simply means that some other level of government has to try to solve the problem."

But other observers say the changed attitude toward Washington may prove to be more lasting. "The view now is that state governments ought to be entrusted with more power to figure out how to design, manage and implement programs," says the Urban Institute's Thompson. "We're shifting to an environment where the notion has been rejected that folks in Washington know more about how to manage programs than the people in the states." ■

FOR MORE INFORMATION

National Conference of State Legislatures, 444 N. Capitol St., Suite 515, Washington, D.C. 20001; (202) 624-5400. The nonpartisan organization coordinates and represents state legislatures at the federal level.

National Governors' Association, 444 N. Capitol St., N.W., Suite 267, Washington, D.C. 20001; (202) 624-5300. The organization makes policy recommendations to Congress and the president on issues affecting the states.

Progress & Freedom Foundation, 1301 K St., N.W., Suite 650W; Washington, D.C. 20005; (202) 289-8928. The conservative research and educational organization has promoted the cause of "devolution."

The Urban Institute, 2100 M St., N.W., Washington, D.C. 20037; (202) 833-7200. The liberal-leaning research organization has evaluated the effects of federalism issues on social and economic policies.

Notes

[1] For background see "Gun Control," *The CQ Researcher,* June 10, 1994, pp. 505-528.

[2] See *The Washington Post, J*an. 5, 1995, p. A10.

[3] See "American Federalism Today," *Rockefeller Institute Bulletin,* 1996, p. 28. The institute is part of the State University of New York-Albany.

[4] Richard P. Nathan, "The Devolution Revolution: An Overview," *Rockefeller Institute Bulletin,* 1996, p. 5.

[5] Quoted in *Rockefeller Institute Bulletin,* p. 22.

[6] Alice M. Rivlin, *Reviving the American Dream: The Economy, the States, and the Federal Government* (1992), p. 9.

[7] See Timothy Conlan, *New Federalism: Intergovernmental Reform from Nixon to Reagan* (1988).

[8] See David Osborne and Ted Gabler, *Reinventing Government: How the Entrepreneurial Spirit Is Transforming the Public Sector* (1992).

[9] See Paul Peterson, *The Price of Federalism* (1995), pp. 18-20.

[10] Forrest P. Chisman, "Can the States Do Any Better?" *The Nation,* May 1, 1995, p. 600.

[11] "Power to the States," *Business Week,* Aug. 7, 1995, p. 50.

[12] Mickey Edwards, "Getting the Big Boys Off Our Backs," *Los Angeles Times,* Dec. 20, 1994, p. B7. Edwards retired from Congress in 1992; he now teaches at Harvard's John F. Kennedy School of Government.

[13] Peterson, *op. cit.,* p. 18.

[14] Walker, *op. cit.,* p. 46.

[15] See *ibid.,* pp. 57-60.

[16] Edward S. Corwin, "A Constitution of Powers and Modern Federalism," in Robert G. McCloskey, ed., *Essays in Constitutional Law* (1962), cited in Walker, *op. cit.,* p. 67.

[17] E.J. Dionne Jr., "Straying From Tradition," *The Washington Post,* Aug. 12, 1996, p. A13.

[18] See Walker, *op. cit.,* pp. 86-89.

[19] *Ibid.,* pp. 102-104.

[20] Jane Perry Clark, *The Rise of a New Federalism* (1938), p. 12.

[21] See Morton Grodkins, *The American System: A New View of Government in the United States,* edited by Daniel J. Elazar, 1966. Grodkins, a professor at the University of Chicago, died before finishing the book, which Elazar, a colleague at Temple University, completed.

[22] Cited in Walker, *op. cit.,* p. 106.

[23] *Ibid.,* p. 133.

[24] Cited in Conlan, *op. cit.,* p. 28.

[25] *Ibid.,* p. 84.

[26] *Ibid.,* pp. 81-84.

[27] See Walker, *op. cit.,* pp. 141-145; Conlan, *op. cit.,* pp. 95-97.

[28] Cited in Conlan, *op. cit.,* p. 97.

[29] See *ibid.,* p. 154.

[30] Garry Wills, "It's His Party," *The New York Times Magazine,* Aug. 11, 1996, pp. 52, 55. Wills attributed the point in part to Theodore Lowi, professor of government at Cornell University.

[31] See *1995 Congressional Quarterly Almanac,* pp. 3-15 to 3-19.

[32] See *Congressional Quarterly Weekly Report,* Aug. 3, 1996, pp. 2190-2196.

[33] See *The Wall Street Journal,* Aug. 5, 1996, p. A2.

[34] Judge Kiser had earlier dismissed Brzonkala's claim that the university discriminated against her on the basis of gender in the disciplinary process. For background, see "Sex on Campus," *The CQ Researcher,* Nov. 4, 1994, pp. 961-984, and "Violence Against Women," *The CQ Researcher,* Feb. 26, 1993, pp. 169-192.

[35] See *The Supreme Court Yearbook, 1994-1995* (1995), pp. 43-46.

[36] The case is *United States v. Sage,* 2nd U.S. Circuit Court of Appeals, Aug. 12, 1996.

[37] See excerpts in *Rockefeller Institute Bulletin, op. cit.,* pp. 17-20.

[38] See *The Washington Post,* March 10, 1995, p. A1. For background, see "Welfare Experiments," *The CQ Researcher,* Sept. 16, 1994, pp. 793-816.

[39] Quoted in *The Washington Post,* March 10, 1995.

[40] Michael Barone, "Statehouse Knights of the GOP," *The American Enterprise,* March/April 1995, pp. 35-36.

[41] Cited in *Rockefeller Institute Bulletin, op. cit.,* p. 7.

[42] Woodrow Wilson, *Constitutional Government in the United States* (1908), p. 173, cited in Clark, *op. cit.,* p. vii.

[43] See *Congressional Quarterly Weekly Report,* Aug. 17, 1996, p. 2321 (Republican platform); Aug. 17, 1996, Supp. pp. 40, 43 (Democratic platform).

[44] Newt Gingrich, *To Renew America* (1995), p. 105.

[45] Darman was interviewed on NBC-TV's "Meet the Press" by host Tim Russert, Sept. 8, 1996.

Bibliography

Selected Sources Used

Books

Conlan, Timothy, *New Federalism: Intergovernmental Reform from Nixon to Reagan*, Brookings Institution, 1988.
Conlan, a professor of public affairs at George Mason University, examines the Nixon administration's "managerial" approach to federalism issues and the Reagan administration's more ideological efforts to reduce the federal government's role. The book includes detailed source notes.

Grodzins, Morton (Daniel J. Elazar, ed.), *The American System: A New View of Government in the United States*, Rand McNally, 1966.
Grodzins, a political scientist at the University of Chicago, created the metaphor of a "marble cake" to describe the complex pattern of state-federal relations in modern times. This classic work was left unfinished at Grodzins' death; it was completed by Elazar, a colleague at Temple University.

Peterson, Paul E., *The Price of Federalism*, Brookings Institution, 1995.
Peterson, a professor of government at Harvard University, calls for shifting responsibility for "developmental" activities to state and local governments but criticizes proposals to give states responsibility for social welfare programs. The book includes detailed source notes and a 13-page bibliography.

Peterson, Paul E., Barry G. Rabe and Kenneth K. Wong, *When Federalism Works*, Brookings Institution, 1986.
The book provides an overview of federalism issues and an examination of a number of specific federal-state programs. Peterson was a senior fellow at the Brookings Institution at the time; Rabe was at the University of Michigan, Wong at the University of Oregon.

Rivlin, Alice M., *Reviving the American Dream: The Economy, the States, and the Federal Government*, Brookings Institution, 1992.
Rivlin argues in this influential book for reducing the federal government's role in "developmental" activities but retaining the federal responsibility for welfare and other "redistributive" functions. Rivlin served as head of the Congressional Budget Office and President Clinton's budget director before her current position as a member and vice chairman of the Federal Reserve System Board of Governors.

Walker, David B., *The Rebirth of Federalism: Slouching toward Washington*, Chatham House, 1995.
Walker, a professor of political science at the University of Connecticut and former staff member with the Advisory Commission on Intergovernmental Relations, traces the history of federalism from Colonial times through the first year of the current Republican-controlled Congress.

Articles

Barnes, James A., "How Much Government? Are We Ready for a Devolution," *The Public Perspective*, April/May 1995, p. 6.
The article in this publication of the Roper Center for Public Opinion Research provides an overview of the political and policy debates over shifting power from Washington to state governments. The journal also contains detailed polling data on public attitudes toward the federal, state and local governments.

Chisman, Forrest P., "Can the States Do Any Better," *The Nation*, May 1, 1995, pp. 600-602.
Policy analyst Chisman argues against giving states greater responsibility for social welfare programs.

McClay, Wilfred, "A More Perfect Union? Toward a New Federalism," *Commentary*, September 1995, pp. 28-33.
McClay, an associate professor of history at Tulane University, argues for shifting power to the states as a first step toward reducing the size of government at all levels.

Moore, W. John, "Pleading the 10th," *National Journal*, July 29, 1995, pp. 1940-1943.
The article explores efforts to use the 10th Amendment to limit the powers of the federal government.

"Power to the States," *Business Week*, Aug. 7, 1995, pp. 49-56.
The article gives a good overview of proposals to shift responsibility for welfare and other programs to the states, along with an analysis of the states' ability to take on the new powers.

Reports and Studies

"American Federalism Today," *Rockefeller Institute Bulletin*, 1996.
This report on federalism from the Rockefeller Institute of the State University of New York, includes statements on federalism from President Clinton, then-Senate Majority Leader Bob Dole, R-Kan., House Speaker Newt Gingrich, R-Ga., and others, as well as discussions of federal mandates and welfare and Medicaid reform.

Gold, Steven D., "Issues Raised by the New Federalism," *National Tax Journal*, June 1996, pp. 273-287.
Gold, a leading expert on intergovernmental relations who died in August, outlined some of the questions raised by the recent discussions of a "new federalism." Gold was co-director of a multiyear research project by the Washington-based Urban Institute, "Assessing the New Federalism." The project will continue under the direction of his colleague, Larry Thompson.

The Next Step

Additional information from UMI's Newspaper & Periodical Abstracts database

History of Federalism

Farber, Daniel A., "The Constitution's forgotten cover letter: An essay on the new federalism and the original understanding," *Michigan Law Review,* December 1995, pp. 615-650.
At the end of the summer of 1787, the Philadelphia Convention issued two documents. One was the Constitution, the other an official letter to Congress, signed by George Washington on behalf of the Convention. The letter is used to examine current assertions about the original understanding of federalism.

Jensen, Paul, and Peter Henle, "Not made-in-Washington: This time, the new federalism could actually work," *The Washington Post,* Jan. 1, 1995, p. C2.
Jensen and Henle assert that amid the new surge of voter revolt that features a healthy cynicism not only about government but also about any program made in Washington, D.C., it is not surprising that the Republicans have begun to raid the pantry of good old ideas regarding revenue sharing, block grants and federalism.

Rakove, Jack, "Does disdain of Washington signal return of 19th-century federalism?" *Los Angeles Times,* March 12, 1995, p. M2.
Rakove discusses the animus against national government and the revival of federalism in the U.S.

Walker, David B., "The advent of an ambiguous federalism and the emergence of new federalism III," *Public Administration Review,* May 1996, pp. 271-280.
American federalism has experienced continuing centralizing tendencies in the political, judicial and operational arenas since 1964. Walker analyzes the current deadlock between and among President Clinton, the House and Senate.

City Governments

Borut, Donald J., "Cities: Essential partners in federalism discussions," *Nation's Cities Weekly,* March 13, 1995, p. 2.
The debate in the House about the roles and responsibilities of government is discussed. Important questions about the basic responsibilities of all levels of government — federal, state, and local — are now on the table for discussion.

Pearson, Hugh, "Cities discover federalism," *The Wall Street Journal,* Dec. 8, 1995, p. A12.
Pearson comments on the reality that both Washington and state governments are decreasing their aid to cities in a new move toward federalism.

Congress and Federalism

"Federalism, too," *The Wall Street Journal,* Jan. 3, 1995, p. A8.
An editorial says the eyes of the nation will be on the new GOP Congress when it convenes on Jan. 4, 1995. The editorial comments on the goal of many of the new generation of Republicans to redistribute power and authority away from Washington back to the states.

"Forgotten federalism," *Houston Chronicle,* March 7, 1995, p. A16.
An editorial criticizes the GOP for saying that the "Contract With America" initiatives reduce Washington, D.C.'s power, asserting that they do the very opposite, and adds that federalism should lie at the heart of any conservative agenda.

Hohler, Bob, "GOP vows to shift power, not deficit, to states," *Boston Globe,* Jan. 7, 1995, p. 1.
Vowing to create a new federalism, Republican congressional leaders guaranteed GOP governors swift action to shift power to the states, without threatening their fiscal stability.

Hunt, Albert R., "Politics & people: Federalism debate is as much about power as about principle," *The Wall Street Journal,* Jan. 19, 1995, p. A19.
Hunt discusses the GOP's march to devolution, or transferring power from the federal government back to state and local governments. He says that federalism is neither as simple nor as tidy as its proponents would suggest, and adds that the debate is often more about power than principle.

Pagano, Michael A., and Ann O. M. Bowman, "The state of American federalism," *Publius,* Summer 1995, pp. 1-21.
The new Republican-controlled Congress is bent on devolving more authority to the states by reducing federal mandates. A look at the current state of federalism in Washington, D.C., is presented.

Perry, James M., "After years of trying, GOP is on the threshold of making history by scaling back federalism," *The Wall Street Journal,* Oct. 27, 1995, p. A16.
For years, Republican politicians have talked about cutting the size of the federal government. No one, though, has ever succeeded in doing very much to rein the budget in. Now, however, resurgent Republicans in the House are pushing for mammoth changes intended to shrink the size of the federal government and to pass on

to the states responsibility for many social programs.

Federal Mandates

Conlan, Timothy J., James D. Riggle and Donna E. Schwartz, "Deregulating federalism? The politics of mandate reform in the 104th Congress," *Publius,* Summer 1995, pp. 23-40.

Efforts to pass mandate reform in the 104th Congress are discussed. The Unfunded Mandates Reform Act of 1995 creates new procedures to restrict Congress from passing unfunded mandates onto the states.

Fletcher, Jeff, "Mandate madness unjustified, commission says," *Nation's Cities Weekly,* Jan. 22, 1996, p. 1-2.

According to a recent preliminary study of the Advisory Commission on Intergovernmental Relations, unfunded federal mandates are a symptom that something is seriously wrong with U.S. federalism.

Fort, Denise D., "The Unfunded Mandates Reform Act of 1995: Where will the new federalism take environmental policy?," *Natural Resources Journal,* Summer 1995, pp. 727-730.

On March 22, 1995 President Clinton signed into law the Unfunded Mandates Reform Act. The law will radically restructure the federal-state relationship in the area of environmental regulation. Fort examines the potential effects of the law.

Tolley, Michael C., and Bruce A., Wallin, "Coercive federalism and the search for constitutional limits," *Publius,* Fall 1995, pp. 73-90.

Tolley and Wallin explore several constitutional bases for questioning the federal government's use of unfunded mandates and other forms of coercive intergovernmental regulation.

Turner, John H., "Unfunded mandates — A view from the private sector," *Spectrum: The Journal of State Government,* Fall 1995, pp. 43-47.

"Unfunded" state and federal mandates are a concern of policy-makers at all levels. The impact of the Federal Unfunded Mandates Reform Act is discussed.

Federalism and Welfare Reform

"Federalism and welfare reform," *Detroit News & Free Press,* Dec. 11, 1994, p. A18.

An editorial discusses the Republican push in Congress for an overhaul of the welfare benefits delivery system, advocating the "pure federalism" approach in which federal taxes would be cut and the states allowed to construct their own welfare programs.

"Federalism and welfare reform," *Chicago Tribune,* Aug. 4, 1995, p. 16.

An editorial opines that as long as Washington is taxing to raise the money for welfare programs, it will have a say in how the cash is spent, adding that what should be important to lawmakers is how to make that relationship as comfortable as possible.

Shroder, Mark, "Games the states don't play: Welfare benefits and the theory of fiscal federalism," *Review of Economics & Statistics,* February 1995, pp. 183-191.

A study found no evidence supporting the widespread belief among economists that central-government redistribution is preferable to lower-level redistribution because the external effects of state welfare policies will lead to strategic underprovision of assistance.

Weeks, George, "Welfare chief gives powerful arguments for dispensing with government red tape," *Detroit News,* July 6, 1995, p. C4.

Weeks relates that Jerry Miller, Michigan Gov. John Engler's welfare director, has emerged as one of the field commanders in the battle for a New Federalism being pushed by Republican governors and those who now run Congress.

New Federalism

Dionne, E. J. Jr., "The new, new, new federalism," *The Washington Post,* March 7, 1995, p. A17.

Dionne comments on the limits of the new federalism that inspires many in the current Congress.

McClay, Wilfred M., "A more perfect union? Toward a new federalism," *Commentary,* September 1995, pp. 28-33.

An intellectual shift is taking shape in American politics that is likely to be deep and enduring. These changes, which may be leading to a new federalism, are discussed.

Reuben, Richard C., "The new federalism," *ABA Journal,* April 1995, pp. 6-81.

Limiting the reach of the federal government has always been a dream of conservatives, and now they are waging war on many fronts to make it a reality.

Stanfield, Rochelle L., "The new federalism," *National Journal,* Jan. 28, 1995, pp. 226-230.

New Federalism may be an idea whose time has come, but figuring out what it really means or would do is about as easy as nailing Jell-O to the wall.

Supreme Court and Federalism

"Federalism and guns in school," *The Washington Post,* April 28, 1995, p. A26.

An editorial comments on the Supreme Court's decision to strike down a 1990 federal statute that made it a crime to carry a firearm near a school. The case is important because of what it says about the "commerce clause" of the Constitution, which justifies federal action in areas that might otherwise be controlled by the states.

"Federalism's future," ***National Law Journal,*** **July 31, 1995, p. A20.**
An editorial notes that federalism's future has been defined by recent Supreme Court decisions. Questions of a fundamental nature concerning federalism are now being examined by the Supreme Court.

Greenhouse, Linda, "Justices step in as federalism's referee," ***The New York Times,*** **April 28, 1995, p. A1.**
The Supreme Court's stunning decision on April 26, 1995, that Congress lacked the authority to bar gun possession in or near schools was a forceful reminder not only of the court's raw power but also of its inevitable role in shaping the country's ongoing political dialogue.

"Lurching Toward States' Rights," ***The New York Times,*** **March 29, 1996, p. A20.**
An editorial criticizes the Supreme Court's decision to uphold a lower court ruling that the 11th Amendment barred the Seminole Indian tribe from suing the state of Florida in a dispute over gambling on Seminole land.

"Restoring federalism," ***Detroit News,*** **March 29, 1996, p. A8.**
An editorial comments that the U.S. Supreme Court, in a ruling involving Indian gambling casinos, took a big step toward reinvigorating the idea of federalism by breathing new life into the Constitution's 11th Amendment. The Supreme Court ruled that the 11th Amendment precluded the ability of the Indians to sue the state of Florida.

Transferring Power to the States

Babington, Charles, "Potholes on the road to a new federalism: Bugs plague effort to computerize states' collection of child support," ***The Washington Post,*** **Oct. 15, 1995, p. A2.**
The story of the federally mandated child support computerization effort, in which many states are suffering major cost overruns and many parents are not getting their payments, underscores the difficulties states face in adopting the technologies needed to run major social programs being shifted to them.

Balz, Dan, "Power is on states' agenda," ***The Washington Post,*** **Oct. 25, 1995, p. A17.**
A coalition of five organizations representing governors and state legislators who convened a three-day federalism summit agreed on a "states' agenda" designed to chip away at the power of the federal government and give states more power to challenge laws and regulations that impinge on their sovereignty.

Behn, Robert D., "The management of reinvented federalism," ***Governing,*** **February 1995, p. 54.**
The job of the federal government could be redefined now that the GOP has taken over Congress. The result could be a shift to the states and localities of more authority and responsibilities for managing the delivery of government services.

Edwards, Mickey, "Republicans to give local governments a powerful chance," ***Chicago Tribune,*** **Dec. 19, 1994, p. 21.**
Edwards opines that the Republicans who dominate state governments are determined to set their own agendas and will push hard for a return to federalism, the division of power between national government and the states, predicting that the new GOP Congress will be eager to go along in an effort to reduce the size of the federal government.

"Federalism 101," ***The Washington Post,*** **Dec. 27, 1995, p. A18.**
An editorial reflects on the GOP's stated goal of transferring power to the states through budget cuts, adding that a report on states' finances in the 1990s is a reminder that the GOP would be shifting a major burden, and it is not clear the states would have the resources to handle it.

"Federalism's shifting balance," ***The Christian Science Monitor,*** **Oct. 2, 1995, p. 20.**
An editorial examines the rationale behind converting Medicaid's federal entitlement status to one of block grants given to states, and argues that states may be able to prove themselves more efficient in the rationing of Medicaid than the federal government.

Karr, Albert R., "State officials ready to take control of more programs, but many see risks," ***The Wall Street Journal,*** **Oct. 23, 1995, p. C13.**
State officials say they're ready to take control of more government programs, but many see pitfalls in this new opportunity, according to executive committees of five national state-government groups that are holding an unprecedented meeting in Cincinnati on "federalism."

"More federalism proposals," ***The Christian Science Monitor,*** **Nov. 3, 1995, p. 20.**
In the last installment of a three-part series of editorials on federal-state relations, proposals to institute a mechanism that would allow states to propose constitutional amendments to the U.S. Congress and reforms to address conditions attached to federal spending grants, regulations and mandates are discussed.

Nathan, Richard P., "American federalism — A great experiment," ***Spectrum: The Journal of State Government,*** **Summer 1995, pp. 47-51.**
Nathan discusses federal grants to states and localities and the implications of the current American federalism. The actions taken by Congress in 1995 constitute a huge change in direction from previous federal aid policies.

Shafroth, Frank, "Federalism summit explores returning power to the states," ***Nation's Cities Weekly,*** **Nov. 6, 1995, p. 3.**
The nation's elected state officials will consider whether or not to give states greater power to challenge federal laws and regulations. Four options that would shift greater power to states from the federal government are discussed.

Back Issues

Great Research on Current Issues Starts Right Here...Recent topics covered by The CQ Researcher are listed below. Before May 1991, reports were published under the name of Editorial Research Reports.

MARCH 1995
Death Penalty Debate
Primary Care
Democracy in Africa
Environmental Movement at 25

APRIL 1995
Abortion Clinic Protests
Dieting and Health
Combating AIDS
Rethinking Affirmative Action

MAY 1995
Assisted Suicide Controversy
Overhauling Social Security
Learning to Read
Mandatory Sentencing

JUNE 1995
Combating Infectious Disease
Property Rights
Repetitive Stress Injuries
Regulating the Internet

JULY 1995
War Crimes
Highway Safety
Combating Terrorism
Preventing Teen Drug Use

AUGUST 1995
Job Stress
Organ Transplants
United Nations at 50
Advances in Cancer Research

SEPTEMBER 1995
Catholic Church in the U.S.
Northern Ireland Cease-Fire
High School Sports
Teaching History

OCTOBER 1995
Quebec's Future
Revitalizing the Cities
Networking the Classroom
Indoor Air Pollution

NOVEMBER 1995
The Working Poor
The Jury System
Sex, Violence and the Media
Police Misconduct

DECEMBER 1995
Teens and Tobacco
Gene Therapy's Future
Global Water Shortages
Third-Party Prospects

JANUARY 1996
Emergency Medicine
Punishing Sex Offenders
Bilingual Education
Helping the Homeless

FEBRUARY 1996
Reforming the CIA
Campaign Finance Reform
Academic Politics
Getting Into College

MARCH 1996
The British Monarchy
Preventing Juvenile Crime
Tax Reform
Pursuing the Paranormal

APRIL 1996
Centennial Olympic Games
Managed Care
Protecting Endangered Species
New Military Culture

MAY 1996
Russia's Political Future
Marriage and Divorce
Year-Round Schools
Taiwan, China and the U.S.

JUNE 1996
Rethinking NAFTA
First Ladies
Teaching Values
Labor Movement's Future

JULY 1996
Recovered-Memory Debate
Native Americans' Future
Crackdown on Sexual Harassment
Attack on Public Schools

AUGUST 1996
Fighting Over Animal Rights
Privatizing Government Services
Child Labor and Sweatshops
Cleaning Up Hazardous Wastes

SEPTEMBER 1996
Gambling Under Attack

Back issues are available for $5.00 (subscribers) or $8.00 (non-subscribers). Quantity discounts apply to orders over ten. To order, call Congressional Quarterly Customer Service at (202) 887-8621.

Binders are available for $18.00. To order call 1-800-638-1710. Please refer to stock number 648.

Future Topics

- ***Civic Journalism***
- ***Foreign Aid***
- ***The Business of Politics***

THE CQ Researcher

PUBLISHED BY CONGRESSIONAL QUARTERLY INC.

Civic Journalism

Can press reforms revitalize democracy?

The press is in trouble. Fewer people are reading newspapers or watching TV news, and many Americans say journalists make the nation's political problems worse, not better. But a reform movement is seeking to rebuild public trust for journalists and, in the process, revitalize American democracy. It aims to draw people back into public life and steer political discourse away from attack ads and sound bites toward a more constructive search for solutions to society's problems. Critics worry that this noble-sounding goal could undermine such journalistic ideals as detachment and objectivity. But this is a debate about more than journalism alone. Ultimately, proponents say, the relationship between citizens and their government — and the prospects for participatory democracy — are at stake.

INSIDE THIS ISSUE

CQ Sept. 20, 1996 • Volume 6, No. 35 • Pages 817-840

Formerly Editorial Research Reports

Civic Journalism

COVER: BARBARA SASSA-DANIELS

THE CQ Researcher

Sept. 20, 1996
Volume 6, No. 35

The CQ Researcher (ISSN 1056-2036). Formerly Editorial Research Reports. Published weekly (48 times per year, not printed March 1, May 31, Aug. 30, Nov. 29) by Congressional Quarterly Inc., 1414 22nd St., N.W., Washington, D.C. 20037. Annual subscription rate for libraries, businesses and government is $319. Additional rates furnished upon request. Periodicals postage paid at Washington, D.C. POSTMASTER: Send address changes to The CQ Researcher, 1414 22nd St., N.W., Washington, D.C. 20037.

Civic Journalism

By Chris Conte

The Issues

Two years ago, when the longtime school superintendent in Bradenton, Fla., announced he was retiring, the *Bradenton Herald* took a bold journalistic step: It launched a campaign to ensure that the public had a voice in selecting a successor.

First, the Herald dispatched two reporters into the community, sending them to church groups, PTA meetings, festivals and other public gatherings. After extended informal discussions with community members, the reporters concluded that the public wanted to break up the school system's old-boy network and bring in new blood. The paper then invited citizens to the Herald to discuss the issue further.

"Much to our surprise," recalls City Editor Neil Besougloff, "a lot of people came. And once the ball got rolling, they took over the discussion."

In no time at all, the school board decided to launch a national search, passing over an administrator recommended by the former superintendent. Moreover, it turned the citizens' group that was formed at the newspaper's offices into a review panel to help screen applicants. The newspaper, meanwhile, dispatched reporters to the hometowns of leading contenders, where they researched stories about the candidates based on interviews with what Besougloff describes as "regular people," not officials.

In the end, Besougloff says, "the citizens' advice made for a much more thoughtful search."

All over the country, journalists like those in Bradenton are shedding their traditional detachment for more active involvement in community affairs. Their activities — variously known as "public," "civic" or "community" journalism — seek to give the average citizen, not the expert or the political insider, the starring role in the drama of democracy.

Public journalists also seek to push decision-making power, wherever possible, out of government bureaucracies and corporate boardrooms and into communities and neighborhoods. In the process, they are raising profound questions about the role of the press, and, ultimately, the prospects for democracy in a time of rapid economic and technological change.

"We aim to put the 'participatory' back in 'participatory democracy,'" says Tom Warhover, regional editor for *The Virginian-Pilot* in Norfolk, Va., a leading practitioner of public journalism. (*See story, p. 822.*)

In Norfolk and elsewhere, public journalism has taken many forms:

- *The Virginian-Pilot* periodically convenes "community conversations" to plumb the views of citizens before deciding how to cover community issues, such as a proposal to build a regional transit system.
- *The Charlotte Observer* in North Carolina sent a public relations expert to organize community meetings and help leaders in inner-city neighborhoods draw up lists of their needs, which the newspaper then published alongside its more conventional reports on conditions in the troubled communities.
- In Florida, the *Tallahassee Democrat* and WCTV 6, the local CBS affiliate, organized a citizens' forum that met in the state House of Representatives to chart "The Public Agenda," and then helped citizens continue the discussion in their homes and over the city's public-access computer network.
- In Spokane, Wash., *The Spokesman-Review* eliminated most of its traditional, omniscient editorials. Now, two "interactive editors" spend most of their time helping community members write their own opinion columns. When the staff writers do prepare "editorials," they usually carry bylines and read more like one person's contribution to a conversation than the authoritative view of the newspaper itself.
- And in California, the *San Jose Mercury News* now runs letters from readers throughout the paper — in the sports pages, for instance — rather than just on the editorial page. By using more reader-generated material, the paper has freed the editors for new projects, such as a recent report exploring why schools don't seem to be preparing students adequately for jobs.

Laudable as such activities may sound, they've drawn criticism from many working journalists. Critics variously have branded public journalism a marketing gimmick and a presumptuous bid to control the public agenda. They warn that it could undermine the role of the press as an independent provider of the unvarnished truth, and weaken journalists' commitment to the traditional values of their trade.

"It is hard to hear those old bells ringing for objectivity, detachment, independence [and] the courage to print stories that are unpopular and for which there is no consensus," William F. Woo, former editor of the *St. Louis Post-Dispatch,* said in a 1995 speech on the new journalism. [1]

As the reformers see it, however, these are troubled times that call for a new approach. For journalists, the current problems come close to home: The audience for traditional news organizations may be slipping away. Analysts blame that partly on the changing lifestyles of Americans and the emergence of new information providers, such as cable television and computer-based communications.

But public disenchantment clearly is a factor, as well. According to the Yankelovich Monitor, a yearly tracking study, the portion of Americans expressing "a great deal of confidence" in television news reports dropped from 55 percent in 1988 to 23 percent in 1995, while those expressing confidence in newspapers fell from 51 percent to 21 percent and those expressing confidence in magazines declined from 38 percent to just 14 percent.

Things aren't going well for democracy either. Only 55 percent of eligible voters participated in the 1992 presidential election. Fewer than 40 percent bothered to vote in the congressional elections two years later — and that was the highest turnout in a decade for a non-presidential election.

"In recent years, a cynical culture of big money, attack ads, personal criticism and reluctance to engage the public on real issues has contributed to a turning away from politics by many citizens," says Edward M. Fouhy, head of the Pew Center for Civic Journalism in Washington.

In the absence of thorough public debate, government seems to lurch from one policy to another without resolving underlying problems — as demonstrated in 1994, when voters gave Republicans control of Congress for the first time in 40 years, only to turn on the new majority once the new lawmakers tried to enact their promised "Contract With America."

The Charlotte Observer

Volunteerism rose in Charlotte, N.C., after newspaper coverage focused on inner-city neighborhood needs. Here firefighter Steve Cambria takes 13-year-old Greg McCullough under his wing at the fire station in Seversville.

Public journalism advocates believe the troubles in the press and problems with democracy are directly linked. "Public journalism," writes Jay Rosen, an associate journalism professor at New York University and a leading proponent of the movement, "is a confrontation with a long-suppressed fact: The press is a participant in our national life. It suffers when the quality of public life erodes. And when the performance of the press deteriorates — as it has in recent years — then public life suffers as well." [2]

To address this situation, public journalists propose a multipart strategy. First, they seek to entice people to participate anew in public life. When Ohio's *Akron Beacon Journal* published a Pulitzer Prize-winning series on race relations in 1994, for instance, it included coupons that citizens could sign pledging to work to improve the situation. *The Herald-Dispatch* in Huntington, W. Va., went a step further. After convening a public meeting on economic development, the paper helped find volunteers to serve on six task forces that subsequently were formed to address specific issues such as education and training. Then its reporters helped the citizens' groups track down information on questions such as how other regions had handled specific economic problems.

Public journalists also believe it's their responsibility to foster healthy public discourse. In its "Minnesota Compact," for instance, the *Minneapolis Star-Tribune* called on candidates to participate in debates and refrain from negative advertising, the press to "emphasize substantive concerns of citizens" and "families and churches and labor groups and private clubs" to gather for one hour after every debate to discuss the issues. If dialogue isn't occurring naturally, public journalists say the press should jump-start it by calling town-hall meetings itself.

Finally, public journalists contend that the press should strive to ensure that public dialogue is rational, civil and focused on seeking solutions to society's problems. When *The Boston Globe* convened groups of citizens in Derry, N.H., last fall to discuss what issues they considered most important in the coming presidential campaign, reporters urged people not just to ask questions but also to propose what should be done. In 1993, when rowdies were taking over a neighborhood park, *The Charlotte Observer* invited readers to suggest how the problem could be resolved.

All these activities raise difficult ethical questions for journalists, who traditionally have defined their professional role as being strictly detached. "Should reporters be investigators of system failure or initiators of solutions?" asks Robert M. Steele, director of the ethics program for the Poynter Institute for Media Studies in St. Petersburg, Fla. "Should journalists be detached observers or activist participants? Should newspapers be independent watchdogs or conveners of public forums?"

But this is a debate ultimately about more than journalism. Public journalism is part of a much broader effort to revitalize civic life in America and to return decision-making power as much as possible to churches, schools, nonprofit groups and other non-governmental institutions. "This is a movement that seeks a new social compact," writes Nancy Kruh, a staff writer for *The Dallas Morning News*. "The public sector is rejected as an answer. So is the private sector. The two sectors combined aren't it either. The only thing that will work — so say the voices of this movement — is an equal and concerted effort from all three sectors of society: public, private and civic." [3]

So far, the debate over public journalism has been confined largely to journalism circles. But as journalists reexamine their own trade, they are asking difficult questions about the role of the public and the future of democracy as well. These are some of the questions on which the debate will hinge:

Have journalists lost touch with the American public?

"I think the media and politicians are connected. They are tied together by money and power, and they just don't know about people like me."

That's how "Kathy," a homemaker who participated in a New England focus group conducted for the Pew Center for Civic Journalism earlier this year, described the role the press plays in American democracy today. [4]

She's not alone. In its 1991 study *Citizens and Politics: A View from Main Street,* the Bethesda, Md.-based Harwood Group reported that Americans have grown increasingly frustrated with a political system that they believe has "pushed them out" and "left them little room to understand, engage and make a difference."

While people who participated in the study didn't blame the press exclusively, they did describe the media as driven by "sound bites and negativism." And they said the standard journalistic version of events "often does not resonate with citizens' concerns and the realities of life they experience and see around them." The study was commissioned by the Kettering Foundation in Dayton, Ohio, whose president, David Mathews, concluded from it that people have come to see the press as part of an elite "political class, the rulers of an oligarchy that has replaced democracy." [5]

A number of journalists and researchers concede that the charge is well-founded. "Who's kidding who?" asked Teresa Hanafin, city editor for *The Boston Globe*, at a 1995 forum. "It's reporters who have access to the governor, who go out and play golf with the mayor, have dinner or drinks with the political handlers, the movers and shakers in the community." [6] Alex Johnson, an editor at *The Washington Post,* put it more bluntly: "Bleached by snobbery and starched by intellectual insecurity, our collars are so white that they blind our insight. If you think that we in the big-city media are elitist, it's only because we are." [7]

One aspect of the elitism of the press, according to public journalism advocates, is its tendency to view public affairs from the perspective of insiders rather than everyday people — and therefore to treat readers as spectators rather than democracy's real decision-makers. For years, notes *Washington Post* political correspondent David Broder, political reporters writing about campaign advertisements "told our readers and viewers how shrewd these ad-makers were. We let the consultants explain the strategies that they were using to manipulate the voters' reactions." Adds Broder, "Frankly, it never occurred to us . . . that people might honestly feel a bit resentful about a collaboration between the press . . . and the media advisers to tell . . . the public how easily they, the voters, were being jerked around." [8]

Public journalism advocates say they aim to break the habit of emphasizing strategy — the "horse-race" aspect of politics — and instead make citizens once again the focal point of the news. *The Charlotte Observer* launched its coverage of the 1992 elections by polling 1,000 area residents about what issues most concerned them and then by persuading half of the respondents to join a "citizens' panel" to advise the paper through the campaign season. The resulting "citizens' agenda" formed the backbone of the paper's coverage of the campaigns. Reporters were assigned to write stories exploring the issues from the citizens' point of view. The paper regularly charted the candidates' positions on various agenda items.

On some occasions, members of the citizens' group were able to ask questions of candidates in public forums. Other times, reporters relayed their questions to the candidates. On three evenings, the Observer's partner in the project, WSOC-TV, broadcast conversations among the citizens on issues.

The result was a far different por-

Putting Public Journalism Into Practice . . .

City Council members in Norfolk, Va., were so angry at neighboring Virginia Beach last year that they took out a full-page newspaper ad. Their charge: Virginia Beach officials had put Norfolk in a tough spot by negotiating a regional water deal behind their backs.

The belligerent ad, pitting well-known community figures against each other, handed the local newspaper the kind of ready-made, sizzling story that news media have traditionally loved. But *The Virginian-Pilot* made an unusual decision: It buried the battle of the political heavies deep inside the paper, and instead focused on how civic groups in both cities wanted the politicians to set aside their differences so Virginia Beach could get the water it needed.

There were no journalism review articles about *The Virginian-Pilot's* decision, but it is easy to imagine what they might have said: Had the paper implicitly editorialized by giving prominent coverage to the views of minor players just because it agreed with them? Was the paper playing down an important political conflict in order to engage in some civic boosterism? Was it naively ignoring the real decision-makers?

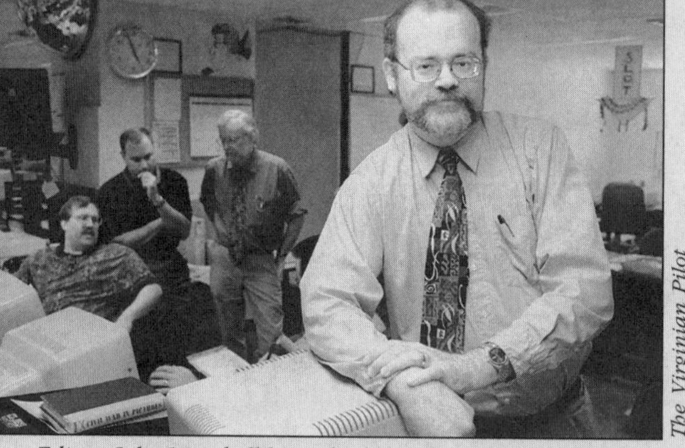

Editor Cole Campbell launched The Virginian-Pilot *into public journalism by reorganizing the paper's beat system.*

The Virginian Pilot

Editor Cole C. Campbell answers no to all these questions. "The citizens were being far more reflective than their leaders were," says Campbell, who is slated to become editor of the *St. Louis Post-Dispatch* in October. By addressing the issues reasonably and constructively, Campbell says, the civic leaders were helping citizens work through their views on the water controversy. And that, he adds, would contribute more to shaping public opinion — and hence, to resolving the water controversy — than the posturing and chest-beating of rival city council members.

At *The Virginian-Pilot*, the idea that everyday citizens are democracy's real decision-makers, and that public opinion often bubbles up rather than trickles down, is more than a catch phrase. It is a firm conviction that has helped build the newspaper's reputation as one of the nation's leading practitioners of civic, or public, journalism.

While civic journalism most often is associated with eye-catching "town hall meetings" and voluminous articles on weighty issues, the Norfolk paper has taken a much less flashy approach, quietly building into much of its daily reporting what Campbell describes as a "strong citizen orientation" that "engages people as political players, not consumers."

Many people say that's exactly what the public journalism movement needs. "The public isn't looking for newspapers to become a different kind of institution, or to be places where people can come together to solve problems," notes Richard Harwood, a Bethesda, Md., public affairs researcher and public journalism advocate. "They're looking for newspapers to produce better journalism — not to provide answers or solve their problems."

One of the Norfolk paper's main techniques for covering the community is to convene "community conversations" — not splashy televised events but quiet discussions in which a reporter gathers a cross-section of citizens to consider issues of common concern. According to reporter Karen Weintraub, these sessions can produce insights that might not emerge from one-on-one interviews: People often begin with one point of view but their attitudes change as they discuss issues with each other. Underlying values become clarified, and common ground often becomes much easier to find than appeared possible at the beginning of the discussion. In the process, she says, the citizens show themselves to be much more thoughtful than sound-bite news stories or simplistic public opinion polls suggest.

In one recent conversation about a proposal to build a regional light rail system, for instance, participants were almost universally against the idea at first. But about halfway through the discussion, they suddenly started sounding more favorable. "They all thought the traffic today was bearable, but that the city should be planning for the future," observes Weintraub. "When phrased as a long-term solution, all of a sudden, 13 of the 14 participants thought it was worth considering." When Weintraub and fellow reporter Debbie Messina wrote their story — a careful explanation of the transit issue and the

trayal of the election season than what the Observer had offered its readers just two years earlier. The Poynter Institute for Media Studies reported that the paper's coverage of issues jumped from 18 percent (of total campaign coverage) in 1988 to 32 percent in 1992, while reporting on campaign strategy fell from 21 percent to 11 percent. [9]

Not all public journalism projects involve direct citizen participation. In some cases, journalists go about their jobs in traditional ways, but they seek to address readers in a different manner, treating them as if they were real

. . . How *The Virginian-Pilot* Interprets Its Mission

practical issues surrounding it — they highlighted the distinction between short-term and long-term considerations.

The Virginian-Pilot began its transformation to public journalism several years ago, when Campbell reorganized the paper's beat system. Previously, reporters had been assigned to cover individual city halls or school boards in the paper's five-city circulation area, an arrangement that almost guaranteed that their stories would have a strong institutional slant. But Campbell formed them into interdisciplinary teams. Instead of having five city hall reporters, for instance, *The Virginian-Pilot* formed a single "public life" team. And instead of having separate police and court reporters, it created a "public safety" team.

Next, Campbell hired Harwood to train the "public life" team on "public listening," a technique for interacting with ordinary citizens in ways that prevent stereotyping them or oversimplifying their views. Harwood urges reporters to look for ambivalence, to stress the shades of public opinion rather than just the blacks and the whites, and to try to get beneath emotionally charged terms like "family values" to people's underlying values on such issues. He also says reporters should pay attention to areas of agreement, as well as conflict, and to listen closely for the connections people draw between seemingly disparate issues.

Later, Campbell invited New York University associate professor of journalism Jay Rosen, a leading advocate for public journalism and head of the Project on Public Life and the Press, to train a larger group.

The Virginian-Pilot may have an easier time looking at civic life because its five-city circulation area, known as Hampton Roads, has a strong tradition of civic involvement. Community conversations sometimes occur without *The Virginian-Pilot's* instigation. Recently, for instance, a housewife came to the paper and asked its help setting up neighborhood discussions about education; the paper agreed to help. In Portsmouth, a private, nonprofit corporation is helping a small, black neighborhood rehabilitate homes, and a cultural-diversity committee brought in consultants to help citizens meet in living rooms to consider race relations. And the city of Hampton has a Department of Neighborhood Services, which sponsors a free, 10-class "college" to train activists in community organizing, public speaking and building partnerships with private businesses.

The citizen orientation doesn't mean *The Virginian-Pilot* has turned its back on government, however. In a memo on how to cover the 1996 political campaigns, Regional Editor Tom Warhover said, "While I've emphasized the role of citizens in covering the elections, I don't want to suggest cutting out the political players. If we think of politicians as job candidates, then we must give them the space to describe their vision of the job and what they intend to do with it."

Indeed, government backing is crucial to the success of citizen initiatives, says Toni Whitt, a *Virginian-Pilot* reporter who described the phenomenon in a 1995 article. "Where the programs have succeeded, government has offered its support, encouraging and nurturing the groundswell," she wrote. "Where government erects roadblocks, public involvement almost always collapses, creating more citizen apathy and dissatisfaction." [1]

Warhover says the newspaper's goal is to help narrow the gulf between citizens and government: "We bring the politicians' questions to the people, and the people's questions to the politicians. We can do a lot to bridge the gap."

Weintraub engaged in some bridge building this spring, when she examined widespread anger among Virginia Beach voters at the city's leaders. The citizens, she wrote, accused their City Council of allowing runaway development that threatens the city's suburban ambiance. But the leaders felt falsely accused; they were powerless to prevent much of the growth that had occurred in recent years because it had been allowed by permits granted many years earlier. [2]

Less than two weeks later, Weintraub wrote that the Virginia Beach Planning Department was seeking public comment on possible revisions to its comprehensive plan. The paper could have given the announcement the perfunctory treatment newspapers frequently accord such notices, but instead it made a big deal of it. This was an opportunity, Weintraub told readers, to "change your city's future; to decide which empty lots become city parks and which turn into shopping centers; to suggest where new homes should be built or farmland preserved." [3]

Was she just setting up readers for another disappointment, asking them to buy into a process that might not make much difference and, in any event, wouldn't show results for years to come?

"It's a leap of faith," Weintraub concedes. "But what's the alternative?"

---

[1] "When Citizens Take Charge: We Have to Do It Ourselves," *The Virginian-Pilot*, Feb. 12, 1995.

[2] "Leadership and Listening," *The Virginian-Pilot*, April 22, 1996, p. A1.

[3] "Hungry for Change: Beach Planners Hope Fliers on Pizza Boxes Will Entice Ideas on How to Improve the City," *The Virginian-Pilot*, May 1, 1996, p. B1.

participants in political life, not observers on the sidelines.

When Virginia Sen. John W. Warner refused to endorse fellow Republican Oliver North in the 1994 race for the U.S. Senate, for instance, *The Virginian-Pilot* didn't dwell on the likely impact of the decision on Warner's or North's political future; rather, it invited readers to discuss when loyalty should give way to independence in politics. The goal of such coverage, explains Editor Cole C. Campbell, who is leaving to become editor of the *St. Louis Post-Dispatch* in October, is to "look at readers as actors — people who have a stake in the news, who want to see the possibilities beyond troubling developments, who want to participate in solving shared problems."

All these reforms imply a different role in politics not just for journalists but for citizens as well. In particular, they assume that citizens want to play a more active role in political affairs. The findings of the Harwood Group's study seem to confirm this belief, challenging the notion that Americans are apathetic. People "want to participate," the report says. "But they believe that there is no room for them in the political process they now know." [10]

Should journalists go beyond reporting the news and assume a more active role in their communities?

If public journalism were simply about paying more attention to citizens, it probably wouldn't have stirred much controversy. But it goes further. Public journalists believe they have a responsibility to make sure, as *Wichita Eagle* Editor Davis "Buzz" Merritt puts it, that "public life goes well."

If healthy public discourse isn't occurring naturally, public journalists say, the press should get it started. And if the political system is spinning its wheels, then the press should help steer it toward finding constructive solutions to society's problems. As advocates of public journalism see it, this is simply fulfilling the press's time-honored responsibility to promote democracy — albeit with a somewhat different emphasis than in the past.

"We have always assumed that democracy is what we have, and information is what we need," explains Rosen. "In fact, information is what we have, and democracy is what we need."

But some critics argue that convening public meetings comes uncomfortably close to making the news, rather than reporting it. "I don't think you can convene a meeting without having a voice in the agenda, guiding the conversation, potentially settling disputes or possibly setting agendas for next steps of action," says the Poynter Institute's Steele. The danger, he says, is that the press will slide from hosting a meeting to becoming identified with a particular agenda that comes out of it.

Doug Jones/The Portland Newspapers

Gov. Angus King, I-Maine, responds to questions during a citizens' forum at North Parish Congregational Church in Sanford.

Similarly, former *New York Times* Editor Max Frankel argues that focusing on solutions could diminish the role of the press as an unflinching critic holding a mirror up to society. "The emphasis on 'solutions' and 'connections' will inevitably distort the news agenda, devalue problems for which no easy remedy is apparent and end up compromising the paper's independence," he warns. "Reporters, editors and publishers have their hands full learning to tell it right. They should leave reforms to reformers." [11]

Underlying these criticisms is a concern that if the press abandons its detachment from society, it soon will slide down a slippery slope to partisan advocacy — and in the process, damage its credibility and usefulness to society. "Our central mission is to report the news, to set priorities, to analyze but not to shape or direct events or outcomes," writes Jane Eisner, editorial page editor at *The Philadelphia Inquirer*. "Subsume or diminish the central mission, and we become like any other player in society, like any other politician, interest group, do-gooder, thief." [12]

Woo, the former *St. Louis Post-Dispatch* editor, has a somewhat different concern. He worries that the press will sacrifice its role as community leader by convening its own citizens' groups. "Damn right that we should listen to the public," Woo says. "But should the consensus at the town meeting automatically become our agenda, not merely in editorial support but in the expenditure of resources that determine what other stories do not get covered? . . . I have yet to hear of a paper that said 'No' to what citizens wanted when the paper itself mobilized the people, of a paper that said to its community, 'Sorry, the agenda we helped create is not for us after all.' "

Arthur Charity, author of *Doing Public Journalism,* a self-described "primer and desktop reference" on the subject, insists that public journalism has an ethical rule "every bit as sharp as mainstream journalism's rule" — namely, that "journalism should advocate democracy without advocating particular solutions." [13]

When the *Tallahassee Democrat* called Florida citizens to its November 1994 forum to set the "public agenda," for instance, Publisher Carroll Dadisman told readers that neither the paper nor its television partner, WCTV6, had any agenda of its own. "'The Public Agenda' is just a forum, the blank sheet of paper," the publisher said. "You, the citizens of the community — all of you who get involved — will determine what issues, what solutions, what common goals will be written on that paper." [14]

Some members of the public have responded favorably to efforts by journalists to stimulate public discourse and civic engagement. About 300 people turned out for the first public agenda meeting in Tallahassee. In Madison, Wis., this year, an hour-long broadcast aired by WISC-TV, the CBS affiliate, and WHA-TV public television on how to deal with the problems surrounding suburban sprawl won higher Nielsen ratings during its time slot than "TV Nation" on Fox, "Family Matters" on ABC and "Unsolved Mysteries" on CBS.

When the *Maine Sunday Telegram* and *Portland Press Herald* supported the Maine Council of Churches' 1994 effort to stage small-scale meetings around the state to discuss education reform, some 700 people showed up; a second round of meetings attracted 500 more. And after the *Springfield News-Leader* in Missouri ran a month-long series examining issues such as juvenile crime, job training and homelessness and describing steps individuals could take to help, 7,000 people attended a "Good Community Fair" staged by service agencies and nonprofit organizations to sign up volunteers. The sponsors had expected just 200-300 people to attend.

Can journalists become involved in solving society's problems without compromising their role as government watchdogs?

Some of the most vehement criticisms of public journalism come from journalists who see it as a form of civic boosterism that compromises the ability of the press to keep guard against government misbehavior.

When James Fallows, the new editor of *U.S. News & World Report*, had some kind words about public journalism in his recent critique of the press, *Breaking the News*, he quickly drew the wrath of Howell Raines, editorial page editor of *The New York Times*, for being co-opted by officialdom. [15] Noting that Fallows had worked as a speechwriter for President Jimmy Carter, Raines complained that "journalists influenced by early political employment are more apt to judge journalism by whether it makes life easy for candidates and officeholders and promotes the formulation of sound public policy." This "deeply ahistoric view of American newspapering," Raines said, disregards an ethical tradition that "calls on reporters to forswear partisan advocacy, to be indifferent to the fortunes of individual candidates, to be agnostic as to public policy outcomes, to be dogged in the collection and delivery of information for its own sake." [16]

In a similar vein, Carl Sessions Stepp, an associate professor of journalism at the University of Maryland-College Park and a senior editor of the *American Journalism Review*, complains, "At its core, public journalism assumes that government is broken, and the press must fix it. But to do so will inevitably link press and government as collaborators in both the public arena and the public mind. At some point, press independence could be compromised." [17]

Public journalists say these arguments miss the point. They insist they aren't trying to fix or replace government, but to strengthen the public. Traditional journalism, argues Bill Theobald, a public life reporter for *The Indianapolis Star/News*, follows a "script" that goes: "identify problem, decry problem, demand what government is going to do to solve the problem." But "that lack of public involvement in solving problems and the handing off of responsibility to government is one of the issues public journalism attempts to address," he argues. [18]

Public journalism advocates aren't the only ones talking about putting decision-making power back in the hands of citizens. Numerous nonprofit organizations have rallied around the cause of civic engagement and neighborhood empowerment, and many local governments are encouraging the same thing. Scores of cities have created neighborhood boards to participate in planning and, in a number of cases, administer public funds. In Portland, Ore., for instance, citizen committees help prepare the city budget. And in Seattle, the city helps pay for community policing, anti-violence programs, arts projects, planning and other neighborhood improvement projects designed and run by citizens.

"Citizens must be engaged as problem solvers rather than passive recipients of services," explains Del Borgsdorf, assistant city manager in Charlotte, N.C. Government can't afford to do everything that communities need, he says. Moreover, problems such as crime or teen pregnancy defy top-down solutions, he notes. The answers to them appear, at least in part, to reside more in strengthening family and community ties, Borgsdorf says.

The Center for Living Democracy, based in Brattleboro, Vt., has launched the American News Service to keep track of the many citizens' initiatives. Founded by authors Frances Moore Lappé and Paul Martin Du Bois, the center operates on the premise that democracy is resurgent in almost all walks of American life, from the corporate world where a hierarchical form of organization is giving way to a more egalitarian, team-based structure, to self-starting projects in neighborhoods around the country.

"Despite all the bad news," the news service says, "something extraordinary is happening in America. . . . Millions are now learning that public life is not just for officials and experts, but part of a rewarding life for each of us." [19] ■

BACKGROUND

'Something Is Broken'

After the 1988 presidential campaign, the editor of *The Wichita Eagle* was fed up. In Buzz Merritt's opinion, serious discourse had been drowned out by sound bites on issues like the Pledge of Allegiance, photo opportunities involving Vice President George Bush's trip to a flag factory and Michael S. Dukakis' ride in a tank and negative advertisements such as the infamous Republican commercial accusing Dukakis of freeing rapist Willie Horton.

Shortly after the election, Merritt told readers that something had to change. "There was no discussion of issues in that campaign," he recalls. "Something is broken. Public life isn't going as well as it should, and journalists have some responsibility for it."

Merritt's views were reinforced by a report on the 1988 campaign by the Joan Shorenstein Barone Center on the Press, Politics and Public Policy at Harvard University. "If a single overriding theme emerges from this work," it said, "it is a concern that campaigns have become distant from the concerns of voters, that a 'disconnect' has developed between the electorate and their prospective leaders — and that journalism, rather than bridging the gap, has helped create and sustain it." The report faulted the press for taking an "insider" approach to campaign coverage, focusing on political strategy and advertising rather than substantive issues. [20]

News people like Merritt decided the solution was to turn press coverage away from the campaign and toward the election — that is, away from what the candidates, handlers and spin-meisters were doing and toward the choice voters would be making. So, even before the 1990 political campaign began, the Eagle polled citizens to learn what issues they wanted the candidates — and the press — to address. It subsequently published lengthy background articles on each issue, followed by weekly "Where They Stand" charts describing each candidate's position on the issues.

The idea of putting citizens first quickly caught on, as newspapers sought to dig still deeper into voters' expectations. In 1992, *The Charlotte Observer* initiated its "Your Vote in 1992" project fully 10 months before the election. Like the Eagle, the Observer used a poll to define issues citizens wanted discussed, but it also named a citizens' advisory panel to keep coverage focused on those issues.

By 1994, the idea of the citizens' agenda had evolved to the point that in some places it became completely independent from elective politics. *The Tallahassee Democrat* and WCTV6, for instance, launched their "public agenda" project a week after the November 1994 midterm elections. Though the project was initiated at two large public hearings, it quickly led to smaller, ongoing citizens' groups that tackle such matters as education, crime, race relations, growth and the environment, jobs and the economy and teenagers' issues. The groups are controlled by participants, with media representatives acting as observers and resource people but not controlling the agenda.

Understanding the Public

Public journalism gained momentum in the early 1990s, when a number of analysts and commentators had concluded that the low quality of public discourse was contributing to the seemingly fickle nature of public opinion.

For Mathews at the Kettering Foundation, the problem was best illustrated by Congress' dramatic flip-flop on catastrophic health insurance. Concerned about the financial impact that long-term illness can have for families, lawmakers in 1988 passed a catastrophic health insurance bill in just 18 months. But the public outcry against the new law prompted Congress to repeal it 17 months later. [21]

"The legislation itself became a catastrophe," noted Mathews. "Too little time had been allowed for the authentic formation of public opinion." [22]

About the same time, pollster Daniel Yankelovich was trying to make sense of the seemingly fickle nature of public opinion. He distinguished between "mass opinion," which sways back and forth from poll to poll, and more enduring and consistent attitudes, which he called "public judgment." People move from lightly held, inconsistent opinions to firmly held beliefs only when they get beyond "consciousness-raising," or information-gathering, to a more laborious process of "working through" the issue, he said.

But, according to Yankelovich, this second stage is often short-circuited for a variety of reasons: Experts often address problems on a different timetable than citizens, and they often use a different vocabulary; people generally aren't presented clear choices, and they rarely are challenged to weigh and balance different options; nor are they forced to consider the consequences of different decisions.

The press, according to Yankelovich, doesn't help. "The media-held model of public opinion is a two-step process: from consciousness raising directly to resolution," he wrote. "If the media were to involve themselves in the working-through stage of public opinion as skillfully as they now carry out

Continued on p. 828

Chronology

1980s-1990s

Public journalism gains support from private foundations eager to improve the quality of public discourse and civic life. By the mid-1990s, the movement has taken hold at hundreds of news organizations.

Nov. 13, 1988
Following the 1988 political campaigns, *Wichita Eagle* Editor Davis "Buzz" Merritt calls for a "total rearranging of the contract between the candidates and journalists." Merritt says the paper will focus on candidates' views on issues that concern citizens, rather than on campaign antics.

Jan. 3, 1990
Veteran *Washington Post* political reporter David Broder writes, "It is time for those of us in the world's freest press to become activists, not on behalf of a particular party or politicians, but on behalf of the process of self-government."

Feb. 8, 1990
Knight-Ridder Inc. Chairman James K. Batten says a readership survey shows that people with a real sense of "connection to the places they live are almost twice as likely to be regular readers of our newspapers" as people who lack such ties. "If we can help revitalize our communities by cracking through the apathy and indifference, we keep faith with the Founding Fathers and, at the same time, look after our own important interests."

Sept. 9, 1990
Wichita Eagle launches its coverage of the 1990 elections by declaring that its "election bias" is that "voters are entitled to have the candidates talk about the issues in depth." Citing poll results, the Eagle says it will track the candidates' views on 10 citizen concerns, including education, economic development, environment, crime and health care.

1991
Kettering Foundation releases Harwood Group's *Citizens and Politics: The View from Main Street,* which suggests that average Americans haven't dropped out of public life because they are apathetic, but rather because they feel they have been excluded from a meaningful role in politics.

January 1992
Charlotte Observer begins its election coverage more than 10 months before the elections, polling citizens on what they want candidates to discuss.

April 1993
Poynter Institute for Media Studies issues "Community Connectedness: Passwords for Public Journalism: How to Create Journalism that Listens to Citizens and Reinvigorates Public Life." Co-authored by New York University Associate Professor of Journalism Jay Rosen and Knight-Ridder's Batten, the paper represents the first documented use of the term "public journalism," according to the Project on Public Life and the Press.

June 1993
Kettering Foundation, New York University and American Press Institute establish Project on Public Life and the Press, with funding from the John S. and James L. Knight Foundation.

October 1994
Pew Charitable Trusts establishes the Pew Center for Civic Journalism in Washington. The center becomes a major source of funding, and publicity, for civic journalism projects.

January 1994
Pew-funded media partnerships, involving newspapers and broadcast outlets, are established in Boston, San Francisco, Dallas, Seattle and Wichita. Broader projects are launched in several other cities, including Tallahassee, Fla.

April 1994
Akron Beacon Journal wins a Pulitzer Prize for a series on race relations that solicits 22,000 pledges from citizens to work to improve the situation.

1995
James Fallows' scathing critique, *Breaking the News: How the Media Undermine American Democracy,* endorses public journalism.

May 1996
Pew center gives its first "Batten Awards for Excellence in Civic Journalism" to *The Charlotte Observer* for a 19-month series on crime in nine inner-city neighborhoods; *The Argus Leader* in Sioux Falls, S.D., for a year-long report on citizens' efforts to rebuild Tyndall, S.D.; and the *Kansas City Star* for a year-long exploration of the core values that drive society and how those values have been distorted.

In Wisconsin's Laboratory of Civic Journalism . . .

What do you get when you cross C-SPAN with the classic New England town meeting? Democracy, Wisconsin-style.

Since 1992, a multimedia partnership[1] has offered Wisconsinites the opportunity to watch — and participate in — an imaginative series of discussions about issues ranging from property taxes to teen violence. Sometimes, citizens talk amongst themselves. Other times they explore the issues with public officials. But in every case, the programs consciously seek to evoke the idea of participatory democracy. For example:

- In a June 1994 broadcast from a state Capitol hearing room, a panel of citizens sat in legislators' chairs listening to Republican Gov. Tommy G. Thompson and others, who were perched in witnesses' seats, present the pros and cons of a property-tax reform plan. (Thompson turned an audience that was evenly split into a 70 percent majority for his plan.)
- Another time, a circuit court judge presided over a mock trial in which a jury of eight Wisconsin citizens heard two congressmen, a state legislator and an economist argue three alternative health-reform plans. (The verdict: A Canadian-style, single-payer system would be best.)
- Once, a seven-member citizens' panel took over the state Supreme Court chambers to hear candidates for the court argue their "case" for election.
- In yet another session, citizens armed with a nine-page handbook and other handouts hammered out their own "people's" version of the state budget, and then had their efforts reviewed by members of the state Legislature's Joint Finance Committee.

"We the People"

Two Wisconsin Supreme Court candidates field questions at "We the People" citizens' forum.

Sponsors say the discussions seek not only to educate people but also to empower them. In one widely publicized forum, Dave Johnston, a citizen representative selected to question Gov. Thompson and his 1994 Democratic challenger, state Sen. Chuck Chvala, told the two candidates: "We haven't bought the answers on property tax that you've given us. And we would like a specific commitment from you tonight — both of you — that you would provide, in writing, in detail, your plan on how you are going to raise the revenues or cut the programs to meet the property tax cut. And we would like to see them at least two weeks — in writing — before the election." The candidates complied.[2]

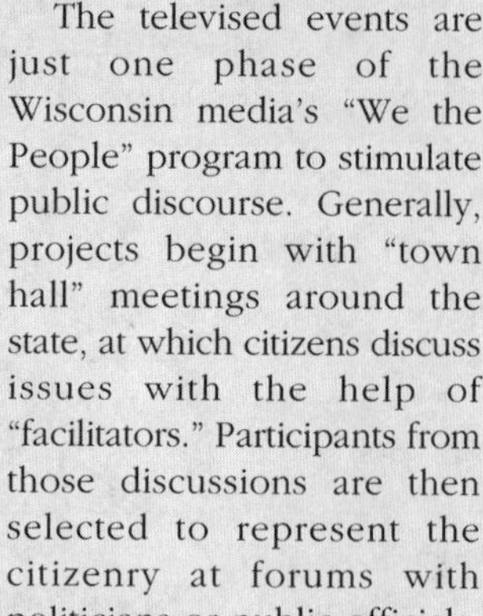

The televised events are just one phase of the Wisconsin media's "We the People" program to stimulate public discourse. Generally, projects begin with "town hall" meetings around the state, at which citizens discuss issues with the help of "facilitators." Participants from those discussions are then selected to represent the citizenry at forums with politicians or public officials.

"This process is designed not to give us [journalists] more power, but to make the people more powerful and to make the leaders more effective by making them more grounded in the people," says *Wisconsin State Journal* Editor Frank Denton.

But critics say such unbounded faith in public discourse is naive — or worse. "Many of the people who espouse civic journalism seem to have a view of the world drawn directly out of the professional classes in the Progressive Era," says Robert McChesney, a professor at the University of Wisconsin School of Journalism and Mass Communication. "There seems to be this belief that U.S. society is a meritocracy played out

Continued from p. 826

the consciousness-raising stage, the quality of public opinion in America would improve immediately."[23]

At the Kettering Foundation, Mathews hired The Harwood Group to take a closer look at how people "work through" complex issues. Harwood convened a series of focus groups, consulted experts and, in 1993, Kettering published the results. The report, *Meaningful Chaos: How People Form Relationships with Public Concerns,* suggested that political discussion occurs far differently among citizens than what passes for political discourse in the media.

In the press, Harwood argued, issues and concerns are addressed one at a time in a highly fragmented manner. But people more often look for connections, linking teen pregnancy, education and welfare, for instance. While the press tends to look to experts to catalyze debate, most citizens rely far more on family members, friends and neighbors. And while highly partisan people tend to dominate discourse in the press, citizens want more "room for ambivalence," more opportunities "to question, listen, learn, test ideas — to 'work through' their views."

According to Harwood, the press

. . . Participatory Democracy Comes to Life

on a level playing field, where political decisions are made according to rules laid down by the Marquis of Queensbury. The argument goes that if journalism works with individuals to enlighten them, then we will select the best policies and everyone will live happily ever after."

In fact, McChesney argues, society is characterized by extreme inequality in wealth and power — a problem that can only be addressed in the clash of organized political interests. "If one starts with this fiction that we all are in the same boat and all we need to do is talk about policy issues in a technocratic and preferably nonpartisan manner, then it seems that the resulting journalism will contribute as much to the problem as the solution."

John Nichols, a reporter for Madison's afternoon paper, *The Capital Times*, says civic journalism exercises in Madison stifle real political debate because activists often are excluded from participating. "Nothing is better for the power elites than to randomly select participants," Nichols says. If the forum sponsors really wanted to make politicians "quake in their boots," he argues, they'd choose as citizen representatives people with more experience and knowledge about issues.

Civic journalists make no bones about the desire to keep activists from dominating "We the People" sessions. Participants are recruited through newspaper advertisements that include clip-out coupons. But to ensure a diverse audience, the sponsors contact churches and community organizations. Sponsors say they seek to ensure that special interests don't stack the meetings; on at least one occasion, some people were asked to leave because they were recognized as representatives of special interests or candidates. [3]

As civic journalists see it, everyday citizens should control sessions in order to keep debate from becoming artificially polarized by interest groups. Most Americans could reach agreement on the issues that divide us, but are kept apart by organized interests, they argue, citing *Washington Post* columnist E.J. Dionne Jr.'s 1991 best-seller, *Why Americans Hate Politics*. "Liberalism and conservatism," Dionne said, "are framing issues as a series of false choices. Wracked by contradiction and responsive mainly to the needs of their various constituencies, liberalism and conservatism prevent the nation from settling the questions that most trouble it. On issue after issue, there is consensus on where the country should move or at least on what we should be arguing about; liberalism and conservatism make it impossible for that consensus to express itself." [4]

Nichols, meanwhile, brands the *Wisconsin State Journal* as elitist since it periodically convenes meetings of community leaders to discuss its investigations of community problems — in some cases even before the newspaper publishes its findings. "I can't think of anything that produces cynicism more than having newspaper editors and reporters sitting down with business and political leaders," Nichols contends.

But Madison Mayor Paul Soglin, for one, defends the practice. After the *Journal* ran "City of Hope," a series of articles on urban problems, businesses effectively assumed responsibility for financing a city program to provide "job coaches" for at-risk teenagers, and the "leadership group" agreed to develop "career ladders" to help people advance beyond low-paying jobs.

Soglin says he initially was concerned about the newspaper setting the agenda in the "leadership group" meetings; in fact, he pulled out of the City of Hope project until Denton persuaded him to rejoin. But now, the mayor says he is satisfied that the newspaper has limited its role to that of facilitator. And in one notable case, he chortles, civic journalism actually thwarted the newspaper's own political preferences: After the newspaper ran a series of articles and held town meetings on how to deal with suburban sprawl, voters elected a new slate of county supervisors who favored land-use controls, even though the newspaper had endorsed the pro-growth incumbents.

"I am convinced their land-use project changed the county board," Soglin says.

[1] The partners include the *Wisconsin State Journal*, Wisconsin Public Television, Wood Communications Group, WISC-TV3 (a CBS affiliate), and Wisconsin Public Radio.

[2] Pew Center for Civic Journalism and the Poynter Institute for Media Studies, "Civic Journalism: Six Case Studies," p. 12.

[3] *Ibid.*, p. 16.

[4] E. J. Dionne Jr., *Why Americans Hate Politics* (1991), p. 11.

should provide more of the "grays" of public debate rather than stressing just the "black and white" positions. And, he suggested, people need to be more than just passive recipients of information: "They want more room to engage in give-and-take discussions — in which they can listen to one another, ask questions, learn new insights, gain confidence in what they think and how they feel on a public concern." [24]

Economic Incentives

Newspapers have a special incentive to try public journalism: They have been losing readers and, with them, advertising. By the 1990s, the problem had become sufficiently serious that some analysts questioned whether newspapers could continue to claim to be a mass medium. "There is no question that if journalism were not in a crisis atmosphere, these ideas [public journalism] never would have been considered," says Lisa Austin, research director for the Project on Public Life and the Press at New York University. [25]

Daily newspaper circulation — 58.2 million in 1995 — has been edging downward since the mid 1960s — even though the population has climbed by more than a third. By 1995, 64.2 percent of Americans reported reading a daily newspaper, down from 77.6 percent in 1970. Particularly worrisome is the low rate of readership among younger people: While 75 percent of people over age 65 read a daily newspaper, just 55 percent of those between the ages of 25 and 34 do.[26]

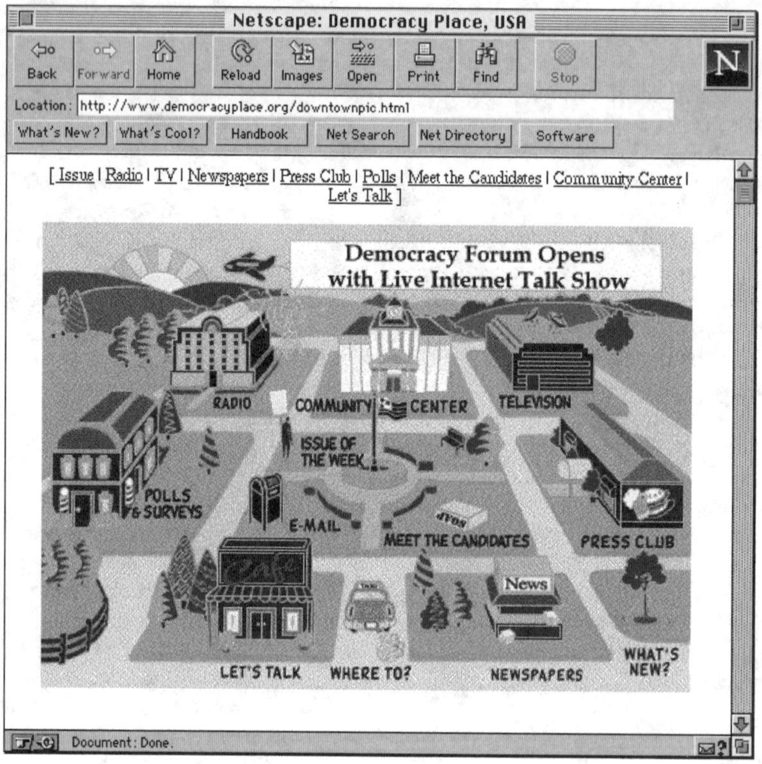

Newspapers have tried various strategies to win back readers, from introducing easier-to-read color graphics, briefs, indexes and no-jump stories to publishing special sections on topics ranging from auto news and education to fashion and entertainment. But the stagnation in readership has continued.

In the meantime, the transition of many newspapers from private to public ownership has increased pressures to achieve higher profits at the very time new communications technologies — talk radio, cable television and, more recently, on-line services — have given households more options for getting their news. "This is a moment of truth for the major journalism organizations," warns Ellen Hume, director of the Corporation for Public Broadcasting's Project Democracy. "They cannot rely any longer on their most precious assets: a monopoly on defining what's news, exclusive access to official sources and the public's trust."[27]

Civic Journalism On-line: Democracy Place USA, a Web site maintained by the Pew Charitable Trusts and the Pew Center for Civic Journalism, offers Internet users an electronic guide to the new journalism. It can be found at http:/www.democracyplace.org.

Knight-Ridder Swings into Action

Amid such uncertainty, some voices have been suggesting that the salvation of newspapers lies in strengthening communities. In 1991, Simmons Market Research Bureau told Knight-Ridder Inc., the nation's second largest newspaper chain, that there is a direct correlation between newspaper readership and civic engagement. Regular newspaper readers, the bureau said, participate in civic activities such as voting, volunteering or working for political candidates or parties far more frequently than occasional readers, and occasional readers participate more often than non-readers.

"To increase Knight-Ridder newspaper readership share, a 'community strategy' is needed — one that is designed to foster interest in and 'connectedness' to the community," the bureau's report concluded. "The most loyal newspaper readers are those who participate in the community."

James K. Batten, then-chairman and chief executive of Knight-Ridder, picked up the banner. In a lecture delivered at the University of Kansas in 1990, he said, "If we can help revitalize our communities by cracking through the apathy and indifference, we keep faith with the Founding Fathers and, at the same time, look after our own important interests."[28]

The corporate interest in public journalism has raised some suspicions among conventional journalists, who see it as just one in a series of superficial efforts to increase circulation. "Civic journalism is all about marketing," says John Nichols, a reporter for *The Capital Times,* an afternoon paper in Madison, Wis. "It's about selling newspapers and making newspapers popular with a feel-good philosophy that's unrelated to what journalism is about."

Advocates of public journalism say critics like Nichols are too sweeping in their criticism. "Sure, there are some who have latched onto this bandwagon," says Edward D. Miller, former editor and publisher of *The Morning Call* in Allentown, Pa., and an associate at the Poynter Institute. "They figure if you do a community forum or a citizens' panel and look like you're really listening to the voter, you'll get attention and drive up your ratings."

Miller says some consultant-driven features of television news, such as flashy polls, sound bites and "man-on-the-street" interviews, differ from genuine "community journalism," which relies on intensive polling, use of focus groups and other techniques designed to truly understand everyday people. "Don't think this is going to sell papers, don't think this is cheap and don't think you're going to see results in a year or two," Miller concludes. "This is a long-term change in the relationship between paper and readers."

"You're not going to see instant number takeoffs," agrees Austin. "This is long-term cultural change."

Reviving Civic Life

Public journalism is part of a broader movement to revive civic life generally. Although the movement isn't new, it gained momentum in the 1980s, as scholars increasingly noted a correlation between the extent of citizen participation in civic affairs and the stability of democratic government. Such observations were reinforced after the collapse of the Soviet Union, when societies in Eastern Europe were hampered in their attempts to adopt democratic government by their lack of vibrant civic sectors.

In a 20-year study of regional governments in Italy, Harvard political science Professor Robert D. Putnam noted that high rates of voter turnout, newspaper readership and even participation in choral societies and football clubs all seemed to be hallmarks of successful regions. Putnam said research in fields as varied as education, urban poverty, unemployment, crime, drug abuse, health and economic development consistently reached the same conclusion: Societies with a high level of civic engagement dealt more successfully with social problems than societies where people were less engaged.

There are various explanations for this pattern, according to Putnam. Civic engagement facilitates coordination and communication, fosters the emergence of leaders who can help generate collective action, reduces the incentives for people to act opportunistically and otherwise encourages people to take collective action, he said.

But, ominously, Putnam noted that civic engagement in the United States has fallen sharply over the last generation. Voter turnout has declined by about a quarter from its peak in the early 1960s, labor unions have shrunk, PTA membership is down drastically (from more than 12 million in 1964 to barely over 5 million in 1982 to about 7 million currently) and participation in civic and fraternal organizations has dropped. Even participation in bowling leagues has declined. While the number of bowlers increased by 10 percent between 1980 and 1993, Putnam said, people increasingly did it alone rather than in organized groups; bowling-league membership decreased 40 percent during the period. [29]

Even as Putnam wrote, however, efforts were under way in neighborhoods and communities to rebuild public life. They ranged from efforts to build community computer networks to the formation of countless ad hoc coalitions organized to address issues such as proposed developments or specific neighborhood problems like crime. Many involved "visioning," or attempts to involve large numbers of people in community planning; others sought to foster dialogue among small groups meeting in living rooms.

In 1994, the Rockefeller Foundation commissioned Washington-based Millennium Communications Group to take the pulse of the community revitalization movement. Its conclusion: There were "thousands" of local, citizen-led civic efforts in communities all around the country, "a rich and complex matrix of involvement."

The efforts cut across normal ideological lines but share several themes, according to the report's authors, Marcia Sharp and Ann Beaudry: "They involve coming together, or 'convening,' as a regular mode of operation. They involve learning as a regular part of the process through which opinions are formed, decisions are made, commitments are forged and tolerance is built. They reflect citizens who see the public domain as 'ours' and not 'theirs' — who feel responsible for and are empowered to make change." [30]

Although the revitalization movement remains decentralized, it has started to develop greater self-awareness. A number of organizations — the Civic Practices Network, the Center for Policy Alternatives and the Communitarian Network, to name a few — have all started serving as clearinghouses for local efforts. In 1994, the National Civic League announced formation of an Alliance for National Renewal linking many such efforts. It hailed "a growing, if unheralded, stirring of problem-solving energies at the grass-roots level that cover virtually every relevant topic." By 1996, the alliance had grown to include 139 members. [31]

Philanthropic Support

When Sharp and Beaudry wrote their report, very few of the people involved in civic renewal efforts were aware of the thousands of projects by like-minded people around the country. "We found the groups generally surprised to learn that all these other people — in their communities and in other communities across the country — were engaged in the same large process of revitalization, and shared their values and aspirations," they wrote. This was especially true, they added, of people involved in civic journalism. [32]

That was starting to change, however. In 1993, Batten at Knight-Ridder persuaded the John S. and James L. Knight Foundation to donate $513,000 to set up the Project on Public Life and the Press, building on work the Kettering Foundation already was doing with Rosen at New York University.

At the same time, the Pew Charitable Trusts, one of the nation's largest philanthropies, also began promoting public journalism. Once again, Batten played a pivotal role, this time by interesting Pew's president, Rebecca W. Rimel, in the new approach to journalism.

Under Rimel's leadership, Pew established the Center for Civic Journalism in Washington, which has financed more than 30 civic journalism projects, conducted seminars, administered a

$25,000 awards program named for Batten (who died in 1995) and — perhaps most important — has tirelessly publicized public journalism efforts around the country.

Pew also has contributed to the Radio-Television News Directors Foundation to support civic journalism efforts. It financed a "Voter Project" by public radio stations in 1994 and a "Citizen Election Project" in 1996, both designed to encourage citizen interest in elections. And when Times Mirror announced it was closing its Center for the People & the Press, Pew took over the respected polling project. In all, Pew has donated $9.3 million to civic journalism projects since 1993.

Pew has gone out of its way to demonstrate that it doesn't seek to compromise traditional journalistic ethics or independence. It named a respected journalist, Edward Fouhy, to run the Pew center. Fouhy previously was a Washington bureau chief for both CBS and ABC, and was Walter Cronkite's senior Washington producer. Similarly, former *Time* magazine Washington Bureau Chief Stan Cloud runs Pew's Citizen Election Project.

"We certainly don't presume to reform journalistic practices," says Rimel. "But we do hope the news media will embrace practices that re-engage the public in the democratic process." ■

CURRENT SITUATION

Measuring Results

By 1996, public journalism had taken root at literally hundreds of newspapers and other news media. The Project on Public Life and the Press has counted about 400 public journalism projects around the country over the last four years. As the movement has matured, its practitioners are starting to ask whether it is possible to demonstrate if the impact has been positive.

Public journalists set a different standard than conventional journalists in evaluating whether they are succeeding. It isn't enough, they say, just to report the news or enlighten the public. "The final word on a public journalist's news choices," writes Charity, "can never come from the publisher, colleagues or the Pulitzer Prize committee, but only from what happens or doesn't happen in the community as a whole." [33]

But measuring the results can be tricky. In Wichita, Merritt has tried to look at some variables. In 1990 and 1992, he says, the Eagle found that voter turnout was somewhat higher where the paper circulated, compared with other nearby areas. But Merritt pulled the plug on the research, in part because it was impossible to determine whether the increases will turn out to be lasting or whether they even resulted from changes in news coverage. "It is probably more costly to measure than it's worth," he says. "If people think we should do this because it's going to have an immediate effect, they're going to be disappointed. This is long-term stuff."

One of the most tantalizing developments in Wichita is a sharp increase in the number of active neighborhood associations. In 1992, there were just four, but that number has grown to about 40 in the last four years. That growth is being spurred by more than the newspaper, though. In 1993, then-Mayor Elma Broadfoot established an office in City Hall to encourage neighborhood activism and help associations form and go about their business.

The Eagle has played an important supporting role, though. Merritt says he considers the mayor's "Neighborhood Initiative" and the growth of neighborhood associations significant news. "We run lists of when they meet, stories on things they're discovering or breakthroughs they have made," he says. "We treat civic news as important news."

Ultimately, many public journalists argue, the measure of success for journalists is the extent to which communities develop "civic capital," or "social capital." Harvard political scientist Putnam defines social capital as "features of social organization such as networks, norms and social trust that facilitate coordination and cooperation for mutual benefit." [34] Neighborhood associations are one example.

The Charlotte Observer consciously was seeking to build civic capital in its 1994 project on inner-city neighborhoods. Alongside conventional feature stories describing life in the troubled areas, the paper published lists of what community leaders said the neighborhoods needed, and subsequently reported on volunteer efforts to meet those needs.

Lewis Friedland, an assistant professor of journalism at the University of Wisconsin, visited some of the neighborhoods two years after the project and reported a "tangible, measurable" increase in social capital. Volunteer efforts have increased, and the pace of housing rehabilitation has quickened, he said. The mayor quickly acceded to public demands to build a community center in one neighborhood, and the city heeded previously unmet calls to clear an overgrown lot where there had been a rape.

According to the Observer, 175 individuals, groups and businesses responded to the neighborhood's call for help after the 1994 news reports, including a woman who donated $2,000 to send 30 kids to summer camp and others who helped buy uniforms for a girls' drill team. The city is spending $3.5 million to install new sidewalks, curbs, storm drains and water lines. First Union Bank donated a double-wide trailer that serves as a temporary recreation center.

Continued on p. 834

At Issue:

Should journalists abandon their traditional detachment and become more actively involved in their communities?

yes

JAY ROSEN
Associate professor of journalism, New York University

FROM *GETTING THE CONNECTIONS RIGHT: PUBLIC JOURNALISM AND THE TROUBLES IN THE PRESS* (1996).

In 1970, *The New York Times* inaugurated its op-ed page. The idea was hardly new (it had been tried in the 1920s), but it was out of favor at nearly all newspapers. With the success of the Times' page, others soon followed suit — and today it is impossible to imagine political dialogue without the exchange of ideas on all the similar pages around the country.

More than an improved product, the result of the Times' experiment was a tangible improvement in public life. The op-ed page added something to our daily capacity to make sense of the world, creating a new and highly visible forum where, with the help of able writers, we can work out our responses to public events. This too was journalism, but of a type we rarely contemplate. It does not report on events, or tell entertaining tales. The "journalism" involved in creating and maintaining the op-ed page does something different: It clears a space where the public can do its work.

That we need more of this kind of journalism — the kind that invites people to become a public — is the premise behind a small reform movement that has risen from the ranks of the American press. It is called "public journalism," or at times "civic journalism," and its aim is to experiment with the power of the daily press, just as the Times did to such impressive effect in 1970.

Public journalism calls on the press to help revive civic life and improve public dialogue — and to fashion a coherent response to the deepening troubles in our civic climate, most of which implicate journalists. At a time of grave doubts about the future of the press and broad concern about the health of American democracy, those involved see this as the hour for creative experiment and piecemeal reform, for frank discussion about ultimate aims and possible ends, for innovations as bold and lasting as the arrival of the op-ed page. By changing what they do and how they approach their task, those experimenting with public journalism have rediscovered the power of the democratic ideal as an organizing principle for their work. Self-governance, public deliberation, participatory democracy — these familiar themes, if taken seriously, can recharge the batteries of the press and show the way to much-needed reforms. . . .

Public journalism is thus a confrontation with a long-suppressed fact: The press is a participant in our national life. It suffers when the quality of public life erodes. And when the performance of the press deteriorates — as it has in recent years — then public life suffers as well.

no

MICHAEL GARTNER
Chairman and editor,* The Daily Tribune, *Ames, Iowa

FROM "GIVE ME OLD-TIME JOURNALISM," *QUILL,* NOVEMBER/DECEMBER 1995.

I'm not sure what public journalism really is. . . . But, like Potter Stewart and pornography, I know public journalism when I see it. And I'm beginning to see it everywhere. And I think that's just awful.

News pages are supposed to explain the community, not convene it. News reporters are supposed to explore the issues, not solve them. Newspapers are supposed to expose the wrongs, not campaign against them. Reporters and city editors are not supposed to write legislation or lead campaigns or pass moral judgments. They're supposed to tell the truth. And God knows that's hard enough to do all by itself. . . .

I fear that the people who are touting [public journalism] believe that newspapers should be like a branch of government — holding hearings, like council members; or writing legislation, like Congress members; or leading campaigns, like political candidates; or nabbing crooks, like police officers. . . .

I firmly believe that the new journalism is bad journalism. It ultimately will cost a newspaper its most precious asset — its credibility. Don't get me wrong, I'm all for talking with readers, and listening to them. I'm all for reader advisory boards and for nights at the library explaining how you operate and listening to readers' concerns. I think we all should be more attentive and more polite, less defensive and less arrogant. But I also think we should be objective.

For newspapers are not supposed to take sides — even for motherhood or apple pie or the flag. Even, in the news pages, against a Unabomber or for racial peace. That's stuff for the editorial pages — where you are supposed to argue and lead and rant and rave and say what you think, not just what you know. . . .

In this cycle of tough times, publishers and editors seem to be diverting some of their scarce resources into this new journalism, into these projects with a cause, these stories with a view, these campaigns for a solution. And by doing that, they're cutting back on real news.

They're cutting back on readers' real needs — not the needs for solutions, the needs for facts. Readers need facts, facts about their towns, their schools, their taxes, their city councils, their zoning boards, their neighborhoods. And if you don't give them facts, they'll quit reading. . . .

If you want to change the world, become a teacher or a politician or a missionary or an editorial writer. If you want to explore the world, to explain the world, to expose the world, become a reporter. That's what the old journalism is.

Continued from p. 832

The Observer itself returned to one neighborhood, Seversville, this summer. It reported that the improvements have proven long-lasting. Overall, the Observer noted, crime in the neighborhood has dropped 24 percent in the last year. And, the paper noted, "Most of the neighborhood's drug peddlers are gone. So is the nightly gunfire." [35]

As in Wichita, the changes reflect more than just changes in news coverage. Assistant City Manager Borgsdorf says city government had been encouraging community-based problem-solving even before the Observer started focusing on neighborhoods. Under a 1993 reorganization plan, the city began seeking to help neighborhoods develop their own capacity to address problems, rather than just relying on government to take care of everything. The plan, known as City Within a City, "puts neighborhoods at the focal point of resource allocation and neighbors at the table when decisions are made." [36]

Toning Down Rhetoric

Public journalists insist that they seek long-term reform. But the movement is starting to adopt techniques and rhetoric that are less flashy than characterized its earlier days, and to emphasize ways in which they adhere to traditional journalism values.

"We are doing a lot of things people would call civic journalism, but increasingly I avoid the labels and go for the substance," says Sandra Rowe, editor of the *Portland Oregonian*. And author Fallows notes, "If we stop talking about the theory, and just concentrate on the projects done in the name of public journalism, the reality is that 99 percent of all journalists will agree on which are good and which are bad." [37]

Beyond the desire to cool down the debate's rhetoric, there are several other reasons why public journalists have drawn back a bit from some of the more unconventional techniques. For one thing, critics have noted that media events, whether done in the name of traditional or public journalism, aren't the same thing as genuine civic engagement.

In Charlotte, Borgsdorf notes, televised public meetings sometimes took on the tone of a "media inquisition," rather than of the more deliberative democracy civic journalists advocate. Some people who had never been active in public life previously grabbed the limelight and made unsubstantiated charges against the city government, he argues. In some cases, officials were stampeded into making decisions without the usual deliberation; the new community center, for instance, probably wasn't justified based on the underlying demographics and probably wasn't the community's biggest need, Borgsdorf says.

Moreover, while eager to encourage citizen activism, public journalists have grown wary of tactics that could undermine their nonpartisan stance. The *San Jose Mercury News,* for instance, found itself in an awkward position last year when it followed up an investigative series on special interest influence in the state Legislature by inviting readers who wanted to do something about the problem to contact it. About 200 citizens accepted the invitation. But when some started pushing the group to lobby for an initiative limiting campaign contributions, the paper got cold feet. It insisted that the group confine itself to nonpartisan activities — with the result that the fired-up citizens' group dropped its more ambitious plans and instead pushed the Legislature to sign a more generic statement of accountability.

"We were pushing the envelop" of what journalists should do, says Assistant Managing Editor Jonathan Krim. He says he wished in retrospect that the effort had focused more exclusively on public education.

In an attempt to give people an opportunity to discuss public issues on neutral territory, the Mercury News also sponsors National Issues Forums along with public libraries in its circulation areas. Editor Rob Elder says that invariably the sessions that involve just small groups are far more successful than large-scale ones. What goes on in discussions is "so personal and intense," he says. One session that attracted 200 participants was very disappointing because it was too unwieldy, Elder says.

Studying Civic Society

Most public journalists remain committed to the idea of covering civic society, rather than focusing, as journalists traditionally have, on political leaders and institutions. In fact, they are concentrating more on how the press can deepen its understanding of civic society.

At the invitation of *Wichita Eagle* Editor Merritt and with funding from the Pew center, The Harwood Group spent 18 months studying the structure of civic society in Wichita. It concluded that there are five different layers of civic life: "official" (or governmental); "quasi-official" (formal civic organizations); "third places" such as barber shops, churches, playgrounds, donut shops, bars, bookstores, cafes and recreation centers; "incidental" places like parks, where people meet more randomly; and "private" places. [38]

The Harwood Group found there are different kinds of social actors in Wichita besides the official leaders, whom the press traditionally has covered best, and the "civic leaders" who are starting to get more attention from public journalists. There also are "connectors," or people who move between organizations and civic conversations, who tend to interact with various organizations, institutions and people, and therefore spread ideas from place to place. And, Harwood said, there are "catalysts," to whom people look for community expertise, historical perspective and wisdom.

Finally, Harwood said, there are different kinds of neighborhoods, and each requires a different reportorial technique to understand. "Professionalized" neighborhoods generally are made up of career couples and their families and tend to have highly structured civic groups and public discussions. The press does a pretty good job of covering them, Harwood said, partly because many reporters live in such neighborhoods.

"Grapevine" neighborhoods, in which information spreads through an informal network of personal interactions and conversations, pose greater challenges to reporters, according to Harwood. Harwood says no one civic space or leader is likely to be able to give a reporter the whole story about what's going on in these neighborhoods, so journalists will have to develop a variety of "go to" places where they can get a sense for what's going on.

There also are "unorganized" neighborhoods, such as rapidly growing and economically diverse West Wichita. According to Harwood, these neighborhoods have few places for civic conversation and few links between different layers of civic life. Reporters will have to find neighborhood "catalysts" who can point them to public events such as Little League games or to "invisible places" like back yards and homes where people convene.

According to Merritt, the Eagle is just starting to think about how to apply Harwood's ideas. "We're struggling with how we do public journalism in our everyday reporting, because that's where we really can have an impact," he says. "But this is a long-term process. It's cultural, generational change." ■

FOR MORE INFORMATION

Pew Center for Civic Journalism, 1101 Connecticut Ave., N.W., Suite 420, Washington, D.C. 20005; (202) 331-3200; email: news@pccj.org. Worldwide Web site: www.pewcenter.org. Besides financing civic journalism projects, the center publishes case studies on civic journalism projects, sponsors symposiums and publishes "Civic Catalyst," a newsletter.

Project on Public Life and the Press, New York University Department of Journalism, 10 Washington Place, New York, N.Y. 10003; (212) 998-3793. Financed in part by the John S. and James L. Knight Foundation, the project publishes case studies and brief summaries of public journalism projects.

The Poynter Institute for Media Studies, 801 Third St. South, St. Petersburg, Fla. 33701; (813) 821-9494; Worldwide Web site: http://www.nando.net/prof/poynter/. Through research and education programs on topics ranging from copy-editing to the electronic media, the institute seeks to help journalists examine and improve their craft. The institute's home page provides a wealth of information on all aspects of journalism today.

Civic Practices Network, Center for Human Resources, Heller School for Advanced Studies in Social Welfare, Brandeis University, 60 Turner St., Waltham, Mass. 02154; (617) 736-4890; email: cpn@tiac.net. Worldwide Web site: http://www.cpn.org. This network of community organizers, journalists and civic activists provides training manuals, case studies and links to the main organizations involved in the civic revitalization movement.

OUTLOOK

Rebirth of Democracy

In a 1996 op-ed piece, *Virginian-Pilot* reporter Mike Knepler wrote nostalgically about an earlier time when America was more of a deliberative democracy than it has become.

"We don't have time to talk with each other like we once did," Knepler wrote. "We have fewer traditional places to informally meet and test ideas on each other, to mix opinions with banter and tell our stories. We're losing the ingredients for what politics once was about, people learning to reason together to solve common problems. . . . Can grass-roots Americans do anything about it? Perhaps the answers are in our traditions." [39]

Though nobody knows what lasting impact public journalism will have, some scholars believe journalism and democracy could evolve into something that more closely resembles the good old days described by public journalism advocates like Knepler. The key issue, they say, is whether the idea of the public as an entity with an identity all its own, distinct from special interests or isolated individuals, will re-emerge.

This notion of the public harkens back to the Colonial period of American history, according to James W. Carey, a leading journalism scholar. Then, he says, the public was seen as a "concrete social group who gathered in public houses to talk, read the news together, dispute the meaning of events and relate political impulses to political actions." But the public of Colonial days went into eclipse with the rise of the mass media and national society, Carey writes. "The public has been replaced," he says, "by the interest group as the object of analysis and key political actor, and the public has ceased to have a real existence." [40]

Now, argues Carey, a "fragmented and dispersed public" is starting to make a comeback. "There is a widespread demand," he says, "for less pro forma political representation, whether by the press or elected officials, and for more real participation."

Will it succeed? Carey, for one, is an optimist. "Modern journalism began around 1890 with the advent of a national system of communication and has had a pretty long run," he writes. "Its time now seems to be about up. Yet, there was democracy before modern journalism, and there will be democracy after it, despite difficult and dangerous transitions to be negotiated." ■

Chris Conte is a freelance writer in the Washington, D.C., area.

Notes

[1] William F. Woo, "As Old Gods Falter: Public Journalism and the Tradition of Detachment," Press Enterprise Lecture No. 30, University of California-Riverside, Feb. 13, 1995.

[2] Jay Rosen, *Getting the Connections Right: Public Journalism and the Troubles in the Press* (1996), p. 2.

[3] Nancy Kruh, "Public Journalism and Civic Renewal: A Reporter's View," *National Civic Review,* winter-spring 1996, p. 33.

[4] Quoted in Howard Kurtz, "When News Media Go to the Grass Roots, Candidates Often Don't Follow," *The Washington Post,* June 4, 1996, p. A6.

[5] The Harwood Group, *Citizens and Politics, A View from Main Street, 1991,* pp. 3-4; 22. Mathews' remarks are in the foreword to the study. For background, see "Political Scandals," *The CQ Researcher,* May 27, 1994, pp. 457-480; "Talk Show Democracy," *The CQ Researcher,* April 29, 1994, pp. 361-384, and "Politicians and Privacy," *The CQ Researcher,* April 17, 1992, pp. 337-360.

[6] Hanafin's comments are contained in a transcript of the James K. Batten Symposium on Civic Journalism and Award for Excellence in Civic Journalism, Sept. 13, 1995, p. 25.

[7] Alex Johnson, "Snob Journalists: The Ink-Stained Wretches of Yore are the Wretched Elites of Today," *The Washington Post,* June 23, 1996, p. C5.

[8] Broder's remarks are contained in a transcript of the James K. Batten Symposium on Civic Journalism and Award for Excellence in Civic Journalism, Sept. 13, 1995, p. 3.

[9] Cited in Rosen, *op. cit.,* p. 45.

[10] The Harwood Group, *op. cit.,* p. 4.

[11] Max Frankel, "Fix-It Journalism," *The New York Times Magazine,* May 21, 1995.

[12] Jane Eisner, "Should Journalists Abandon Their Detachment to Solve Problems?," *The Philadelphia Inquirer,* Oct. 16, 1994, p. E7.

[13] Arthur Charity, *Doing Public Journalism* (1995), p. 145-146.

[14] Quoted in Jan Schaffer and Edward D. Miller, eds., *Civic Journalism, Six Case Studies* (1995), p. 22.

[15] See James Fallows, *Breaking the News: How the Media Undermine American Democracy* (1996). When Fallows wrote the book, he was Washington editor of *The Atlantic Monthly.* He became editor of *U.S. News & World Report* in September 1996.

[16] Howell Raines, "The Fallows Fallacy; A Plan for Turning Reporters into Lackeys," *The New York Times,* Feb. 25, 1996, Section 4, p. 14.

[17] Carl Sessions Stepp, "Public Journalism: Balancing the Scales," *American Journalism Review,* May 1996, p. 40.

[18] Bill Theobald, letter to the editor, *American Journalism Review,* July/August 1996, p. 5.

[19] Lappe and Du Bois authored *The Quickening of America: Rebuilding Our Nation, Remaking Our Lives* (1994). The American News Service maintains an Internet Web site at http://www.americannews.com/. The quote is from the Web site.

[20] Marvin Kalb, "Restoring the Bond: Connecting Campaign Coverage to Voters," Joan Shorenstein Barone Center on the Press, Politics and Public Policy, 1992, p. 8.

[21] For background, see *1988 CQ Almanac,* pp. 281-292, and *1989 CQ Almanac,* pp. 149-156.

[22] Quoted in The Harwood Group, *Meaningful Chaos: How People Form Relationships with Public Concerns,* 1993, p. v. Mathews wrote the foreword to the book.

[23] Daniel Yankelovich, *Coming to Public Judgment: Making Democracy Work in a Complex World* (1991), p. 251.

[24] The Harwood Group, *Meaningful Chaos, op. cit.,* pp. 20-21.

[25] For background, see "Hard Times at the Nation's Newspapers," *Editorial Research Reports,* Aug. 24, 1990, pp. 477-492. Portions of the "Background" section and "Chronology" draw from information compiled by Austin and project Director Jay Rosen.

[26] Newspaper Association of America, "Facts About Newspapers," 1996.

[27] Ellen Hume, "Tabloids, Talk Radio and the Future of News," The Annenberg Washington Program in Communications Policy Studies of Northwestern University, 1995. Hume was a senior fellow of the Annenberg Washington program.

[28] Knight-Ridder papers include the *San Jose Mercury News, Tallahassee Democrat, Wichita Eagle, Akron Beacon Journal, Charlotte Observer* and *Philadelphia Inquirer.*

[29] Robert D. Putnam, "Bowling Alone: America's Declining Social Capital," *Journal of Democracy,* Vol. 6, No. 1, January 1995, pp. 65-78.

[30] Marsha Sharp and Ann Beaudry, *Communications as Engagement: A Communications Strategy for Revitalization* (1994).

[31] The Civic Practices Network's Internet address is http://www.cpn.org/cpn/cpn.html. The Web address for the Center for Policy Alternatives is http://www.cfpa.org/pub/cfpa/homepage.html. The Alliance for National Renewal can be reached at http://www.ncl.org/anr/index.html; the Communitarian Network at http://www.gwu.edu/~ccps/index.html.

[32] Sharp and Beaudry, *op. cit.*

[33] Charity, *op. cit.,* p. 50.

[34] Putnam, *op. cit.,* p. 67.

[35] Ames Alexander, "Residents Reclaiming Their Streets: Makes You Proud to Live Here," *The Charlotte Observer,* July 21, 1996, p. 1.

[36] Del Borgsdorf, "Charlotte's City Within A City: The Community Problem-Solving Approach," *National Civic Review,* summer-fall 1995, pp. 224.

[37] Keynote speech at James K. Batten Symposium and Award for Excellence in Civic Journalism, in Washington, D.C., May 14, 1996. Fallows' speech, "Journalism: From Citizens Up," was later published by the Pew Center for Civic Journalism.

[38] "Tapping Civic Life: How to Report First, and Best, What's Happening in Your Community," Pew Center for Civic Journalism, 1996, pp. 10, 17.

[39] Mike Knepler, "The Bygone Art of Talking Politics." This op-ed essay can be found on the Democracy Place USA Web site sponsored by Pew Charitable Trusts and Pew Center for Civic Journalism (1996). The Internet address is www.democracyplace.org/~democracy/knepler.html.

[40] James W. Carey, "The Mass Media and Democracy: Between the Modern and the Postmodern," *Journal of International Affairs,* summer 1993, pp. 1-21.

Bibliography

Selected Sources Used

Books

Dionne, E.J., *Why Americans Hate Politics,* Simon and Schuster, 1991.
Washington Post columnist Dionne examines the intellectual reasons for American political gridlock, arguing that on many of the seemingly intractable issues of the day, the public is far closer to agreement than the nation's political leaders, who continue to fight the ideological battles of the 1960s. Civic journalists have seized on Dionne's arguments to support their contention that the public should wrest control of political discourse away from polarizing elites.

Merritt, Davis, *Public Journalism and Public Life: Why Telling the News Is Not Enough,* Lawrence Erlbaum Associates, 1995.
This thoughtful and entertaining book by one of civic journalism's first advocates explains how a veteran newsman grew concerned that "public life is not going well," and concluded that the solution lies in abandoning detachment in favor of the stance of "fair-minded participant."

Charity, Arthur, *Doing Public Journalism,* Guilford Press, 1995.
A "primer and desktop reference" produced under the supervision of Jay Rosen's Project on Public Life and the Press at New York University, this book lacks the intellectual elegance of Rosen's work, but makes up for it by providing details of numerous public journalism experiments.

Rosen, Jay, *Getting the Connections Right,* Twentieth Century Fund Press, 1996.
This volume elegantly and concisely explains the ideas that lie behind the reform movement that Rosen, a passionate advocate of public journalism, has helped spawn.

Yankelovich, Daniel, *Coming to Public Judgment: Making Democracy Work in a Complex World,* Syracuse University Press, 1991.
A respected pollster examines the difference between ephemeral "mass opinion" and more enduring "public judgment." As president of the Public Agenda Foundation, Yankelovich believes that much of the apparently fickle nature of public opinion stems from a disconnect between experts and the public, and he has developed a methodology for helping the public work its way through to abiding positions on issues.

Articles

Carey, James W., "The Mass Media and Democracy: Between the Modern and the Postmodern," *Journal of International Affairs,* summer 1993, pp. 1-21.
Carey, often described as today's leading journalism scholar, offers a sweeping view of the evolving relationship between journalism and democracy, from Colonial times through the "modern" era of mass media and national society, to a just-emerging "post-modern" period that he predicts will have much in common with the days of the Founding Fathers.

"Rethinking Journalism: Rebuilding Civic Life," *National Civic Review,* Vol. 85, No. 1, winter-spring 1996.
The National Civic League devoted this entire issue to an examination of civic journalism. In a series of brief articles, some of the movement's leading theorists and practitioners describe their views and explore the relationship between journalism reform and the movement to revitalize civic life in America.

Putnam, Robert D., "Bowling Alone: America's Declining Social Capital," *Journal of Democracy*, Vol. 6, No. 1, January 1995.
Often cited by advocates of public journalism, this article describes the growing disengagement of Americans from all aspects of public life.

Steele, Robert M., *The Ethics of Civic Journalism: Independence as the Guide,* The Poynter Institute for Media Studies, 1995.
This essay takes a middle-of-the-road position in the philosophical combat between public journalists and more traditional journalism. In the process, Steele summarizes most of the arguments that have appeared in speeches and editorials on the new journalism.

Reports

Pew Center for Civic Journalism and Poynter Institute for Media Studies, *Civic Journalism: Six Case Studies*, July 1995.
This enthusiastic report describes collaborations involving newspapers and television and radio stations in six cities.

Harwood, Richard C., and the Harwood Group, *Tapping Civic Life: How to Report First, and Best, What's Happening in Your Community,* Pew Center for Civic Journalism, 1996.
The ubiquitous Harwood Group seeks in this report to push the boundaries of public journalism's effort to improve how reporters and editors can understand their communities. It contains interesting ideas but doesn't supply many illustrations about what the more scrupulous reporting it recommends might produce.

Harwood, Richard C., and the Harwood Group, *A Meaningful Chaos: How People Form Relationships with Public Concerns,* Kettering Foundation, 1993.
This seminal study in the literature on public journalism enumerates nine factors that contribute to the formation of "authentic" public opinion — that is, opinion that genuinely reflects people's enduring beliefs rather than their short-term manipulated views.

The Next Step

Additional information from UMI's Newspaper & Periodical Abstracts database

Civic Journalism and the Community

Beaudry, Ann E., "The civic role in public journalism," *National Civic Review,* winter 1996, pp. 26-28.

Community leaders, civic activists and public officials need to view civic journalism as a community team sport requiring their active participation. Civic sector/media partnerships for civic journalism are essential tools for achieving any type of community action.

Byrd, Joann, "Conversations with the community," *The Washington Post,* February 5, 1995, p. C6.

Byrd comments on the need for "civic" journalism, which takes into consideration the role citizens play in the world.

Charity, Arthur, " Public journalism for the people," *National Civic Review,* winter 1996, pp. 7-13.

Public journalism has the potential to be an extraordinary organizing force in American culture and is one of the greatest tools for increasing public participation. Charity examines the five basic tasks of public journalism .

Kruh, Nancy, "Public journalism and civic revival: A reporter's view," *National Civic Review,* winter 1996, pp. 32-34.

Rather than relying on experts or public officials to solve community problems, citizens are increasingly becoming involved in arriving at solutions themselves. Public journalism, an accompaniment to this trend of civic renewal, has the potential to open up an entirely new way of developing communities.

McCarthy, Abigail, "The media vs. the people," *Commonweal,* February 23, 1996, pp. 8-9.

The national media has virtually abandoned any responsibility for the well-being of community. To correct this, advocates of civic journalism say journalists should move beyond mere reporting to active concern for community.

Debating Civic Journalism: Pros and Cons

Corrigan, Don, "Public journalism: Does "public journalism" serve the public or the publishers," *St. Louis Journalism Review,* July 1995, p. 9.

Jay Rosen of New York University calls for journalists to take an active role in improving their community. Rosemary Armao of the Investigative Reporters and Editors says that public journalism is "lazy journalism," or merely public relations.

Fitzgerald, Mark, "Decrying public journalism," *Editor & Publisher,* Nov. 11, 1995, p. 20.

Publisher Michael Gartner recently told the Society of Professional Journalists conference that the practice of public journalism is a "menace," and he denounced the publication of the Unabomber manifesto. Gartner characterized the Unabomber decision as "public journalism run amok."

Merritt, Davis, "Missing the point," *American Journalism Review,* July 1996, pp. 29-31.

The heated debate over the role of public journalism has focused on the movement's tactics but ignored its underlying philosophy, which is primarily a commitment to fulfilling journalism's obligation to public life. A look behind the rancor is offered.

Rieder, Rem, "Public journalism: Stop the shooting," *American Journalism Review,* December 1995, p. 6.

After years of hotly contested debating over the role of public or community journalism, the protracted polarization seems to be easing. In an editorial, the significant areas of overlap between the two opposing sides of the debate are examined.

Shepard, Alicia C., "The pros and cons of civic journalism," *World & I,* January 1996, pp. 112-117.

The ways in which civic or public journalism can serve local communities are examined. These outlets can tailor their news coverage to community concerns.

Shine, Neal, "If we don't do it, who will?" *Detroit News & Free Press,* May 28, 1995, p. F3.

Shine responds to *New York Times Magazine* columnist Max Frankel's comments concerning "public journalism," saying Frankel makes it clear that he believes public journalism to be a well-meaning but misguided approach. Shine says public journalism concentrates on the quest for a better tomorrow.

Woo, William F., "Public journalism: Should the press be an observer or an actor in public affairs," *St. Louis Journalism Review,* July 1995, pp. 10-12.

In a speech given at the University of California in Riverside, Woo, editor of the *St. Louis Post-Dispatch,* discusses the public journalism movement. Some critics believe that detached journalism has led to the decrease in daily newspaper readers, and that public journalism would bring these readers back. Public journalism could cause reporters to forget their heritage, Woo says.

Politics and the Press

Garment, Suzanne, "Suicide of an admiral, exploitation in the press," *Los Angeles Times,* May 26, 1996, p. M2.

Garment discusses Adm. Jeremy M. Boorda's suicide in May 1996, stating that it brought political types face to face with human mysteries they prefer to ignore and illuminated some people's willingness to exploit human flaws and political cleavages.

Hertsgaard, Mark, "Washington's court press," *Nation*, June 10, 1996, p. 10.
Coverage of the Clinton presidency has been mixed for the same basic reasons that coverage of President Reagan was adulatory: Coverage of the White House tends to be only as adversarial as the opposition party is. Hertsgaard criticizes the U.S. news media.

Hunt, Albert R., "Politics & people: Phony debate on press bias obscures real issues," *The Wall Street Journal*, June 22, 1995, p. A17.
Hunt comments on the writings of media critic and conservative activist Brent Bozell, who says the real threat to Republicans in 1996, is not Bill Clinton or powerful constituencies like the elderly — it's the national media that out of desperation "have targeted the GOP."

Kurtz, Howard, "When news media go to grass roots, candidates often don't follow," *The Washington Post*, June 4, 1996, p. A6.
The dozens of grass-roots efforts in the 1996, campaign season orchestrated by newspapers and TV and radio stations are part of a growing movement called public journalism that is trying to foster unscripted encounters between the public and the politicians. Candidates have not embraced the movement.

Sperling, Godfrey, "Most politicians cause their own bad press coverage," *The Christian Science Monitor*, May 28, 1996, p. 19.
Sperling discusses criticism that Washington, D.C., journalists have a left-wing bias, arguing that while most tend to be liberals or moderates, they do not give their news accounts a liberal slant. Sperling says most print journalists that he knows are dedicated to "getting the story right."

Walsh, Kenneth T., "Folks America loves to hate," *U.S. News & World Report*, May 13, 1996, p. 3.
In his new book, *Feeding the Beast: The White House Versus the Press*, Walsh examines the adversarial relationship between the White House and the press. An excerpt from the book, in which Walsh argues American citizens are too often the losers of this battle, is presented.

Public/Civic Journalism in Action

Glaberson, William, "Press," *The New York Times*, February 27, 1995, p. D8.
Frank Denton, the editor of the *Wisconsin State Journal*, says he tries to meet the needs of readers who are sick of old-fashioned journalism, which simply points out problems, by offering what is called civic or public journalism. The widespread attention given to public journalism is examined.

Jurkowitz, Mark, "The media's best-kept secret," *Boston Globe*, May 27, 1996, p. 17.
Boston Globe ombudsman Jurkowitz discusses the Globe's efforts at a "public journalism" campaign in 1994, and an upcoming one covering the U.S. Senate race between Sen. John Kerry and Gov. William Weld in 1996.

Marks, Alexandra, "Three papers' projects in public journalism," *The Christian Science Monitor*, July 24, 1995, p. 12.
The efforts of three newspapers, *The Charlotte Observer* (N.C.), *The Spokane Spokesman-Review* (Wash.), and the *Oregonian*, to further "public journalism," which attempts to reconnect reporters and the communities which they serve, are discussed.

Peterson, Iver, "Civic-minded pursuits gain ground at newspapers," *The New York Times*, March 4, 1996, p. D5.
In 1996, the public, or civic, journalism movement marks roughly its fifth birthday. About 40 dailies in medium and large cities, up from perhaps a dozen two years earlier, are using public journalism techniques that blur the traditional distinction between reporting and editorializing. In the process, newsrooms become more directly involved in shaping local news, in the name of civic improvement.

Schorr, Daniel, "Publishing the Unabomber: Responsible or reckless? Printing was a tough but conscionable choice," *The Washington Post*, Sept. 24, 1995, p. C3.
Shorr, senior news analyst for National Public Radio, asserts that *The Washington Post* was right to publish the manuscript of the Unabomber because of the idea of "civic journalism" and notes similar cases in the past.

Public Cynicism and the Press

Glass, Andrew J., "The people vs. the press: Journalism gets dose of its own cynicism," *Atlanta Journal Constitution*, Oct. 1, 1995, p. B1.
Glass examines the public's perception of the press, in connection with a Times Mirror survey from 1995, "The People, The Press and Their Leaders." In the survey it was found that most people feel the press is too adversarial, but journalists disagree.

Hernandez, Debra Gersh, "Bewildered by the media," *Editor & Publisher*, Feb. 24, 1996, p. 11.
In the report "America's Struggle Within," the Pew Center for Civic Journalism details the public's belief that the news media have lost a sense of their mission in society. Focus groups have stated that too much of what the news media offer is dirt and gossip.

Tharp, Mike, "The media's new fix," *U.S. News & World Report*, March 18, 1996, pp. 72-74.
The mission and ethics of journalists are in turmoil due to the public's despair about the media. Analysts say that reporters are plagued with a deep cynicism about politicians, a predisposition to cover national issues as narratives of electioneering and conflict, egoism that makes reporters act as if they are the stars of the stories they cover and a tendency to cover politics in packs.

Back Issues

Great Research on Current Issues Starts Right Here...Recent topics covered by The CQ Researcher are listed below. Before May 1991, reports were published under the name of Editorial Research Reports.

MARCH 1995
Death Penalty Debate
Primary Care
Democracy in Africa
Environmental Movement at 25

APRIL 1995
Abortion Clinic Protests
Dieting and Health
Combating AIDS
Rethinking Affirmative Action

MAY 1995
Assisted Suicide Controversy
Overhauling Social Security
Learning to Read
Mandatory Sentencing

JUNE 1995
Combating Infectious Disease
Property Rights
Repetitive Stress Injuries
Regulating the Internet

JULY 1995
War Crimes
Highway Safety
Combating Terrorism
Preventing Teen Drug Use

AUGUST 1995
Job Stress
Organ Transplants
United Nations at 50
Advances in Cancer Research

SEPTEMBER 1995
Catholic Church in the U.S.
Northern Ireland Cease-Fire
High School Sports
Teaching History

OCTOBER 1995
Quebec's Future
Revitalizing the Cities
Networking the Classroom
Indoor Air Pollution

NOVEMBER 1995
The Working Poor
The Jury System
Sex, Violence and the Media
Police Misconduct

DECEMBER 1995
Teens and Tobacco
Gene Therapy's Future
Global Water Shortages
Third-Party Prospects

JANUARY 1996
Emergency Medicine
Punishing Sex Offenders
Bilingual Education
Helping the Homeless

FEBRUARY 1996
Reforming the CIA
Campaign Finance Reform
Academic Politics
Getting Into College

MARCH 1996
The British Monarchy
Preventing Juvenile Crime
Tax Reform
Pursuing the Paranormal

APRIL 1996
Centennial Olympic Games
Managed Care
Protecting Endangered Species
New Military Culture

MAY 1996
Russia's Political Future
Marriage and Divorce
Year-Round Schools
Taiwan, China and the U.S.

JUNE 1996
Rethinking NAFTA
First Ladies
Teaching Values
Labor Movement's Future

JULY 1996
Recovered-Memory Debate
Native Americans' Future
Crackdown on Sexual Harassment
Attack on Public Schools

AUGUST 1996
Fighting Over Animal Rights
Privatizing Government Services
Child Labor and Sweatshops
Cleaning Up Hazardous Wastes

SEPTEMBER 1996
Gambling Under Attack
The States and Federalism

Back issues are available for $5.00 (subscribers) or $8.00 (non-subscribers). Quantity discounts apply to orders over ten. To order, call Congressional Quarterly Customer Service at (202) 887-8621.

Binders are available for $18.00. To order call 1-800-638-1710. Please refer to stock number 648.

Future Topics

- ***Foreign Aid***
- ***The Business of Politics***
- ***Insurance Fraud***

PUBLISHED BY CONGRESSIONAL QUARTERLY INC.

Reassessing Foreign Aid

Should the U.S. keep cutting back on aid?

Foreign aid has been a key tool of American foreign policy ever since the Marshall Plan helped war-torn Europe rebuild after World War II. Multibillion-dollar aid programs helped win allies in the Cold War against the Soviet Union as well as trading partners for American industry. But in the post-Soviet era, critics say foreign aid's original rationale — countering the spread of communism — no longer exists. Moreover, they contend that U.S. economic assistance has failed dismally to boost developing countries and should be scaled back or eliminated. But supporters argue that programs to bolster free markets and improve education and health care guard against social ills that might lead to problems requiring far more costly U.S. military intervention.

INSIDE THIS ISSUE

CQ Sept. 27, 1996 • Volume 6, No. 36 • Pages 841-864

Formerly Editorial Research Reports

Reassessing Foreign Aid

The Issues

Background

Current Situation

Outlook

Sidebars and Graphics

For Further Research

Cover: Barbara Sassa-Daniels

Sept. 27, 1996
Volume 6, No. 36

Published By
Congressional Quarterly Inc.

The CQ Researcher (ISSN 1056-2036). Formerly Editorial Research Reports. Published weekly (48 times per year, not printed March 1, May 31, Aug. 30, Nov. 29) by Congressional Quarterly Inc., 1414 22nd St., N.W., Washington, D.C. 20037. Annual subscription rate for libraries, businesses and government is $319. Additional rates furnished upon request. Periodicals postage paid at Washington, D.C. POSTMASTER: Send address changes to The CQ Researcher, 1414 22nd St., N.W., Washington, D.C. 20037.

Reassessing Foreign Aid

BY MARY H. COOPER

THE ISSUES

When it comes to sending aid overseas, Americans consider themselves to be generous and compassionate — too generous, in fact. A majority of respondents to a recent national survey estimated that the U.S. spends 15 percent of the federal budget on foreign aid — and recommended slashing that amount to 5 percent.

But Americans' self-image is far from reality. Like an anorexic teenager who sees somebody overweight peering back at her in the mirror, the American people have an exaggerated perception of their generosity: The U.S. actually spends less than 1 percent of the federal budget on foreign aid. [1]

"When the American people consistently say we are spending too much money abroad, I think they are confusing in their own minds what we're spending on both international affairs and military security," says J. Brian Atwood, administrator of the U.S. Agency for International Development (AID), the government agency that directs the nation's foreign aid program. "That's a very high percentage of the national budget, up to 18 percent. But the fact is, foreign aid accounts for only about one-half of 1 percent of the budget." *

One reason for Americans' distorted perception of their government's largess is the country's once-undisputed leadership in foreign aid. After World War II, the United States poured billions of dollars into Western Europe through the Marshall Plan to help rebuild the continent's war-torn economies. The U.S. also took the lead in creating the United Nations, the World Bank and other multilateral institutions that today fund most international development programs. For most of the postwar era, the United States was the world's biggest contributor of overseas development assistance.

Today, the United States is far from the world's aid leader. (*See graphs, p. 844.*) The U.S. spent $7.3 billion on "official development assistance" in 1995, half of Japan's $14.5 billion expenditure, according to the 27-nation Organisation of Economic Cooperation and Development (OECD), based in Paris.

Moreover, when the U.S. foreign aid budget is expressed as a portion of the nation's overall wealth, it looks even smaller. Last year, the world's richest country spent just 0.1 percent of its gross national product (GNP) — one-tenth of 1 percent — on foreign assistance. (*See graph, p. 845.*) Denmark, by comparison, spent 1 percent of its GNP — 10 times that amount. [2]

"We've fallen in absolute levels of aid to number four, behind Germany, France and Japan," Atwood says. "We're dead last when it comes to the percentage of our gross national product spent on foreign aid. And that's not putting our best foot forward in terms of American interests."

Two factors explain why the United States has cut back its development assistance. First is the end of the Cold War. The demise of the Soviet Union in 1991 eliminated one of the primary goals of U.S. foreign aid — halting the spread of communism in the developing world. When the superpowers were vying for allies among poor countries of Africa, Asia and Latin America, the United States willingly provided food aid, health care and economic development assistance, the assumption being that if the U.S. didn't, the Soviets would. It is no coincidence that since the height of the Cold War in the mid-1980s, spending on international programs has been cut almost in half, when inflation is taken into account. [3] (*See graph, p. 846.*)

The second explanation for the decline in the foreign aid budget is the overriding desire of lawmakers to reduce government spending and balance the federal budget. Unlike spending for defense and such popular programs as Social Security and Medicare, foreign aid has little visible impact on Americans' retirement income or health care. For this reason, lawmakers have been able to pare the foreign aid budget with little opposition from the public.

"The biggest problem with foreign aid — and many politicians will even tell you this — is that there's no constituency there," says Rep. Tony P. Hall, D-Ohio, a former Peace Corps volunteer who chaired the Select Committee on Hunger from 1989 until 1994, when it was abolished, along with three other select panels, in an effort to trim House operating costs. "But if lawmakers looked below the surface, they'd see that as many as three out of 10 jobs in most districts are related to trade. And a lot of countries that we have helped over the years are now our trading partners. The fact is that for every dollar that we invest overseas in these kinds of programs, we get back about $2.57.

---

* The total includes overseas spending for the Defense, Commerce and State departments, Central Intelligence Agency and other international programs, as well as the Agency for International Development.

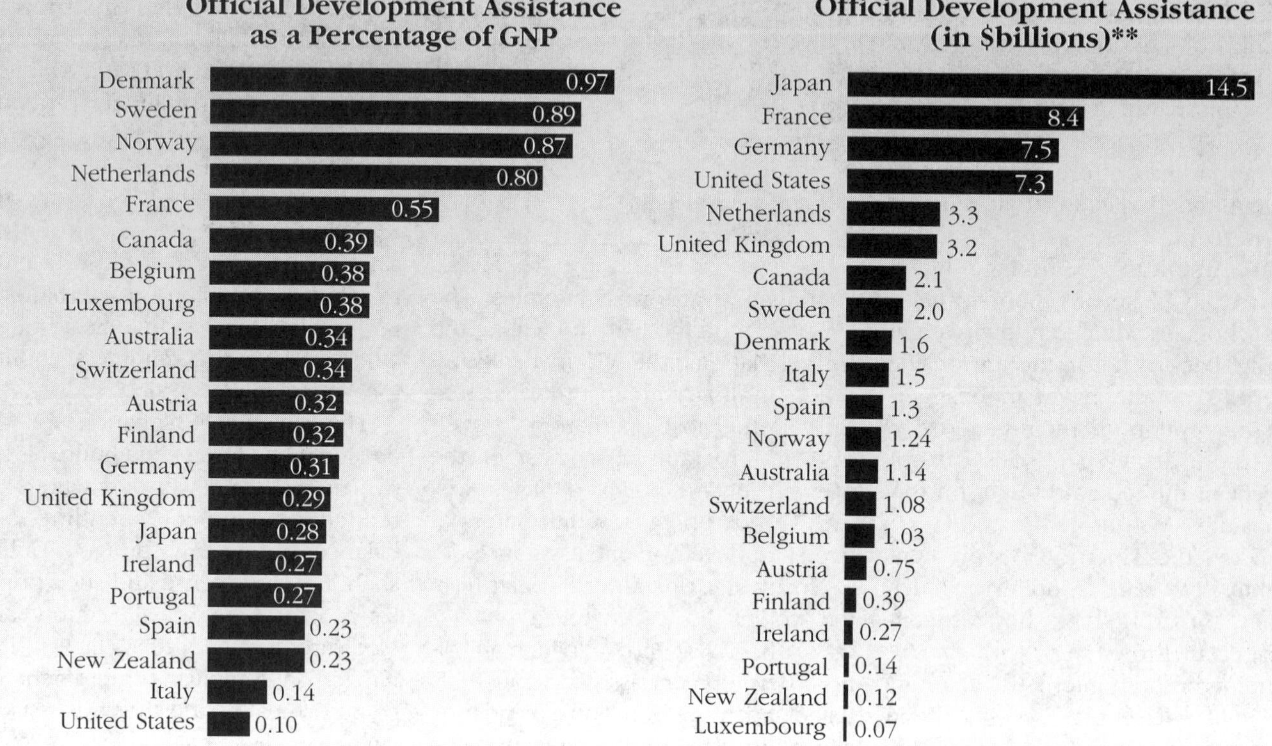

So foreign aid is a very good deal for the American people."

Hall and other supporters of foreign aid have found little support in the current Congress, where many Republican lawmakers say aid programs not only don't serve U.S. security interests in the post-Cold War era but also largely have failed to improve living conditions in recipient countries. In addition to calling for even deeper cuts in AID's budget, Senate Foreign Relations Committee Chairman Jesse Helms, R-N.C., introduced legislation last year that would eliminate the agency altogether and hand over responsibility for economic assistance and emergency food aid to the State Department.

"We've reached a place in our foreign policy that we need to concentrate on what's good for America and stop this business of handing out to governments all over the world money that they take and then vote against us in the United Nations," Helms said after introducing his proposal. "I have said for years and years that I don't like foreign aid. I don't like the concept of it. I think the Congress ought to act on individual cases, upon individual recommendations by the president and the secretary of State." [4]

While admitting that some former U.S. aid recipients, such as Zaire, have failed to improve living conditions for their citizens, proponents of a strong development assistance program credit AID with a 35-year record of major advances in the developing world, including:

• tens of millions of lives saved as a result of AID-developed and sponsored oral rehydration therapy;

• more than 50 million couples using family-planning methods provided by AID;

• more than 3.2 million people reached by HIV/AIDS prevention programs in 32 countries;

• millions of lives saved by preventing a major famine in southern Africa in 1992; and,

• crop research resulting in the development of drought-resistant grains that enabled farmers to feed a billion more people than they otherwise would have been able to feed over the past 20 years. [5]

AID supporters also say that many developing countries have been drawn along the road to democracy by AID, which provides about one-fifth of their revenues. "If you look at 1980, in our hemisphere there were only four democracies, and now all but one country — Cuba — has had at least one democratic election," says Julia Taft, president of InterAction, an umbrella group of some 150 private, voluntary organizations. "We didn't buy those democracies, but we helped them with development assistance programs. I find it very discouraging that after having made those investments over the years in holding up the values of democracy, the importance of open markets and of more equitable social programs, we are ready to say, 'Well, thank you very much, we're glad you've made all these changes, and now we're going to go on and just care about ourselves.' "

Critics dispute these glowing assessments of foreign aid so strongly that one wonders if they're talking about the same programs. "Development assistance has been a real failure," says Bryan Johnson, a policy analyst for international economic affairs at the Heritage Foundation, a conservative think tank. In a study of 77 countries that have received U.S. development assistance for at least 35 years, Johnson concluded that 39 were no better off, in terms of economic growth, than they were before they began receiving the aid. [6] "Of those 39 countries, fully half actually are worse off," Johnson says.

In this view, foreign aid impedes development by protecting corrupt or inept governments from the harsh realities of today's global economy, which rewards the most efficient, free-market systems. While aid supporters point to Taiwan and other former recipients of American development assistance as success stories, Johnson contends that their economies took off only after they were weaned from U.S. aid programs.

"In a country like Tanzania, where 50 percent of the government budget comes from foreign assistance, there are no incentives whatsoever to open their borders to international trade and investment, to establish a judicial system that protects contract rights or to privatize their banks," he says. "The government simply takes this money from outside sources and gives it to government-owned banks, which in turn give it to government-owned industries, which are losing money because they're inefficient. It's a cycle that just keeps going on, and we're partly responsible for it."

When the new 105th Congress begins grappling with foreign aid next year, these are some of the key questions that lawmakers will be asking:

Does foreign aid serve U.S. national interests?

No question elicits more diametrically opposed statements from the two sides of the foreign aid debate. Supporters say foreign aid is a vital com-

Foreign Aid Is Tiny Slice of U.S. Budget

*Less than 1 percent of the $1.5 trillion U.S. budget for fiscal 1996 is for foreign aid. **

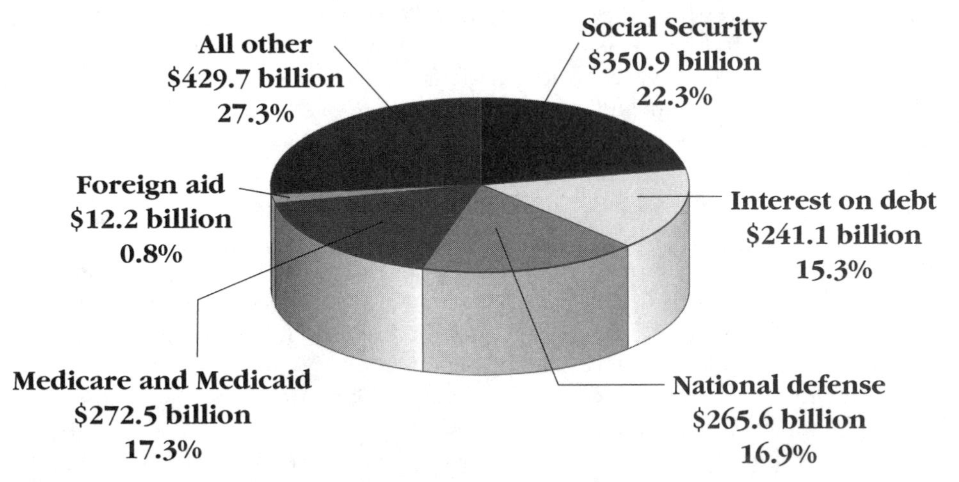

* *The foreign aid total includes funds for international development and humanitarian and security assistance, but not aid from the Justice, Commerce and State departments.*

Note: Total does not add to 100 percent due to rounding.

Source: U.S. Office of Management and Budget

Foreign Aid's Steady Decline

U.S. foreign aid has fallen steadily since the Marshall Plan helped rebuild Western Europe after World War II. In the 1960s and '70s, aid increased to the Middle East and Asia, while in the mid-eighties, increased military aid went to non-communist allies such as Pakistan. With the decline of the Soviet threat, aid levels fell again.

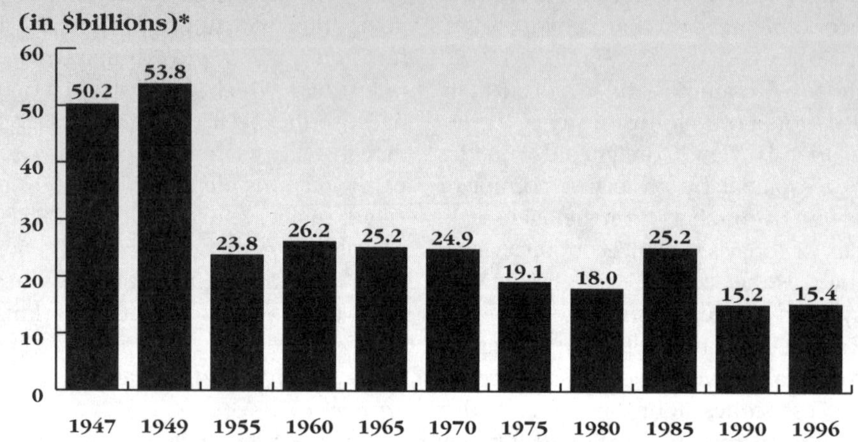

* *Amounts are adjusted for inflation in 1996 dollars.*

Note: Totals do not include international aid from the Defense Department.

Source: Congressional Research Service

ponent of U.S. foreign policy because it spreads American values of democracy and free markets in an increasingly volatile world. Democratically elected governments are less likely to engage in reckless aggression, this reasoning goes, while free markets make countries more dependent on the international trading system and thus more likely to seek cooperation, not conflict, with other countries.

The post-Cold War era poses new foreign aid opportunities as well as new threats to U.S. interests. Competition with the Soviet Union forced the United States to seek allies among autocratic regimes, simply to keep them from turning to the Soviet Union for assistance. Such aid was often guided by political as well as humanitarian motives, and frequently failed to spur moves toward democracy and free markets. With Cold War geostrategic interests no longer in play, supporters say, aid can focus more sharply on the business of economic development. At the same time, rising population growth, ethnic conflicts, environmental degradation and the emergence of new diseases such as the Ebola virus threaten stability in many of the world's poorest countries.

"The opportunity to develop the new markets of the next 10 to 30 years is greater now than ever before," says AID Administrator Atwood. "If we're going to see our own economy grow, it has to be through its access to the global economy. We need desperately to see the global economy grow overall in order to see the increase in exports for the United States economy. And if that global economy is disrupted through crises, disasters, refugee flows, food shortages, environmental disaster, new diseases — all of which contribute to what I call international chaos — we will not realize our potential in terms of opportunity, and we will see major expenses related to our having to deal with the chaos that will ensue."

But some critics see the Cold War's end as an opportunity to curtail or even cancel most types of foreign aid. During the years of U.S.-Soviet tension, they considered development assistance as an ineffective, albeit necessary, evil to win friends in the effort to counter Soviet expansion. But they say it has no place in today's foreign policy. "Militarily, I think you can make the argument that during the Cold War some of the money was probably useful in helping America maintain its interests abroad," Johnson of the Heritage Foundation says. "But there are a lot of cases where the United States gave foreign aid to countries that did not serve America's interests during the Cold War."

Johnson cites Somalia and Ethiopia, both of which received assistance, first from one superpower and then the other at different times during the Cold War. "We got no support from either one then or later, and the aid did nothing to help their economies."

The one thing that supporters and opponents of foreign aid come close to agreement on is the need to help certain allies cope with regional conflicts by offering security assistance, either through economic aid or low-interest loans to buy weapons. "There are programs which I think are useful," Johnson says, "and these are programs that enable America's military to train with foreign militaries and that provide some of the money that the U.S. spends to help countries like Israel purchase arms." Since they signed the 1979 Camp David peace accords, Israel and Egypt have received the bulk of U.S. foreign aid. (*See story, p. 848.*)

But Atwood acknowledges that while security assistance is an important component of foreign aid, development assistance is most critical because it can help avert the kinds of crises that the U.S. military has recently been called in to resolve. "The military is being used as the first re-

Major U.S. Foreign Aid Programs

The U.S. Agency for International Development (AID) has funneled more than $125 billion to more than 100 developing countries and emerging democracies through a broad array of programs since AID was established in 1961.[1] In addition to AID programs, foreign aid is also handled by several other government agencies. Among the main foreign aid programs are:

Bilateral Development Assistance: AID provides funds to recipient governments, private charities and its own field missions to operate programs to improve agriculture, education, family planning, environmental protection and private enterprise. These funds are targeted to programs that promote "sustainable development," or activities that do not deplete a country's natural resources. Logging on tree farms where harvested land is replanted is sustainable development; logging old-growth forests to make way for agricultural development is not. Development assistance also is required by law to stress programs that meet the basic needs of the poor. AID also provides bilateral economic assistance to countries of Eastern Europe and the former Soviet Union. Bilateral programs such as international narcotics control, anti-terrorism assistance and migration and refugee aid are administered by the State Department.

Multilateral Development Assistance: The United States contributes to regional multilateral development banks and the World Bank, whose International Development Association provides low-interest loans to developing countries. The U.S. also contributes to development agencies affiliated with the United Nations, such as the U.N. Development Program, the U.N. International Children's Emergency Fund (UNICEF) and the U.N. Environment Program (UNEP).

Food Aid: The Food for Peace program, or PL-480 program, was originally devised in the early 1950s as a way to promote U.S. farm exports. Today, only a quarter of the funds are used to promote farm exports; the rest support emergency and humanitarian feeding programs operated by private charities and multilateral organizations. Food aid is funded by the Department of Agriculture and administered through AID.

Security Assistance: Until recent years, military-related assistance comprised the bulk of U.S. foreign aid. The Economic Support Fund, administered by AID, provides funds to allies to advance U.S. economic and security interests. It also provides cash or funding for specific development projects. The Defense Department's Foreign Military Financing account provides grants and loans to enable governments to buy U.S. military equipment. Nearly all of AID's security assistance goes to Israel and Egypt, though a small portion — $60 million in 1996 — is spent to harmonize military equipment between NATO and the former Soviet allies of Eastern Europe. The Defense Department also pays for multilateral peacekeeping operations and administers the International Military Education and Training (IMET) program, which provides training for foreign military personnel. All members of the U.N. are assessed a proportion of the funds the organization spends each year for its operations. The United States has emerged as the U.N.'s leading debtor, with more than $1.2 billion in arrears out of the total $2 billion the United Nations was owed by its members in unpaid assessments at the end of 1995.

[1] Information in this section is based on Casimir A. Yost and Mary Locke, *U.S. Foreign Affairs Resources: Budget Cuts and Consequences* (1996), pp. 28-37.

sort, as opposed to the last resort," he says. "They're being put into places such as Rwanda to handle the refugee flow. They're being used even in places like Haiti, where if we had spent a lot more time on development, [the military] might not have been used. I think we are weakening our capacity to preserve our national security by cutting [foreign aid] to the extent we have."

Should the Agency for International Development be merged into the State Department?

Budget cuts are not the only tool lawmakers are using to reduce foreign aid. In 1995, Foreign Relations Committee Chairman Helms introduced legislation to abolish the Agency for International Development and two other foreign affairs agencies he said were no longer needed since the Cold War's end — the Arms Control and Disarmament Agency (ACDA) and the United States Information Agency (USIA). Helms called for the State Department to handle major programs of the former agencies that were necessary to preserve.

Democrats in Congress, backed by the Clinton administration, blocked Helms' reorganization plan, which was included in the State Department authorization bill. Helms, in turn, blocked Senate action on a number of ambassadorial nominations and arms control treaties. The reorganization measure was later modified to require the president to eliminate just one of the three agencies — and cut $1.7 billion from the other two over the next four years.

Clinton vetoed the measure on April 12, saying it "would undercut U.S. leadership abroad and damage our ability to assure the future security and prosperity of the American people. It would unacceptably restrict the president's ability to address the complex international challenges and opportunities of the post-Cold War era. It would also

Israel and Egypt Get Most Foreign Aid

When Israeli Prime Minister Menachem Begin and Egyptian President Anwar Sadat shook hands in the White House Rose Garden in 1979, they didn't just make peace between their two countries. They also received a commitment from President Jimmy Carter, who had helped broker the Camp David Accords, to provide massive amounts of U.S. military and economic aid to help them keep the peace in the Middle East.

As a result of that commitment, Israel and Egypt have received the lion's share of U.S. foreign aid ever since. Even as the foreign aid budget has declined by almost half since 1985, (when amounts are adjusted for inflation) spending for the two Camp David signatories has remained steady. In fact, their share of the U.S. foreign aid budget has grown from 30 percent in 1991 to nearly 40 percent today.

Israel, the leading recipient of American assistance, gets $3 billion a year, about half of which is military assistance provided by the Defense Department. The rest comes from the U.S. Agency for International Development (AID) and is used by Israel to pay off debts it has incurred over the years to buy weapons from the U.S. and other countries. Egypt receives $2.4 billion annually in U.S. aid, including $815 million from AID mainly in the form of development assistance.

Supporters of Israel say that maintaining the high level of U.S. aid to Israel and Egypt serves the interests of the United States as well as the Middle East peace process. "The Middle East continues to be a vital region for the United States' interests, and it is still the most volatile region in the world," says Brad Gordon, legislative director of the American Israel Public Affairs Committee (AIPAC), the main pro-Israel lobby in Washington. "The United States still spends some $100 billion a year for the defense of NATO. When you consider that we continue to have 100,000 American troops deployed in Europe but none in Israel and very few in the entire Middle East, aid to Israel continues to be a very cost-effective use of American resources in defense of our own national security."

Thanks to AIPAC and other groups supported by American Jews and others, aid to Israel enjoys far more visible domestic support than does aid to Egypt. But supporters of the high level of foreign aid to both countries point out that it has been a key weapon against the spread of Islamic fundamentalism in Egypt by helping moderate, pro-American governments increase food availability, reduce infant mortality and improve education. "If we hadn't made the contribution that we've made in Egypt, today it would look more like Iran or Iraq than it does," says AID Administrator J. Brian Atwood. "And while the Egyptian government still has a long way to go in terms of economic and political reform, we have served our purpose of defending the Camp David Accords and maintaining the peace."

Some foreign aid experts are concerned that U.S. foreign aid is excessively skewed in favor of the United States' chief allies in the Middle East. "Although [we] are very good friends, they also have a very powerful lobby — there's no question about that," says Rep. Tony P. Hall, D-Ohio, Congress' leading activist on the issue of hunger. "They are getting more and more of our foreign aid, to the point where the way we're going now they'll soon be getting two-thirds of the budget. If that happens and everything else has to suffer, then something's got to give. You just can't continue to make those kinds of appropriations to two countries."

Israeli Prime Minister Benjamin Netanyahu appeared to offer an unexpected remedy to the budgetary dilemma during a recent visit to the United States. "With America's help, Israel has grown to be a powerful, modern state," he said in an address to Congress July 10. "I believe that we can now say that Israel has reached childhood's end, that it has matured enough to begin approaching a state of self-reliance. . . . In the next four years we are going to begin the long-term process of gradually reducing the level of your generous economic assistance to Israel, and I am convinced that our economic policies will lay the foundation for total self-reliance and great economic strength."

Netanyahu's offer to end Israel's reliance on U.S. foreign aid drew so much attention that the second part of his statement went almost unnoticed. But some observers said that it was highly unlikely that Israel would begin that "long-term process" anytime soon.

In Atwood's view, the problem is not that Israel and Egypt are getting too much U.S. assistance, but that other deserving aid recipients are being squeezed out of the picture. "The question that ought to be asked, it seems to me, is why we are giving so little to Africa, as opposed to why we are giving so much to Israel and Egypt," he says. "The entire foreign affairs budget is being squeezed to the point where our interests are not being met overseas. We're cutting our contributions to the United Nations and the World Bank, and we're having to close down embassies. We are missing opportunities on a daily basis because we don't have the resources, and we don't have the people in place. And I think when you look at the world that is coming in the next 20 years, a world where there will be a lot more trade competition among our so-called allies, I think it's a major national security problem that we have reduced it to the level we have."

restrict presidential authority needed to conduct foreign affairs and to control state secrets, thereby raising serious constitutional concerns." [7]

The proposal to eliminate AID enjoys considerable support, at least among Republicans. "The proposal got mired down in Washington politics this time, but a lot of people thought it was a really good idea and say AID shouldn't exist any more," says Christopher J. Walker, a member of the

Senate Foreign Relations Committee majority staff. "Pending the outcome of the elections, I think that there will again be an effort to abolish the agency."

Some supporters of abolishing AID say Helms' proposal needs to be part of a broader effort to reform the entire foreign affairs bureaucracy. Contending that Helms' plan "at once went too far and not far enough," former Secretary of State Lawrence S. Eagleburger and Robert L. Barry, a former ambassador to Indonesia, have called for the State Department itself to be streamlined by eliminating many non-essential high-level positions before taking on the additional functions of three independent agencies. "Mergers that simply graft agencies onto State's existing structure set a bad precedent," they write. "The United States cannot overcome the challenges of the next century with an outmoded State Department and an obsolete mission." [8]

Foreign aid supporters fear that AID's mission could not survive a merger with the State Department because of basic differences between the two organizations. "Career Foreign Service officers are taught to be diplomats, reporters and analysts, and they're superb at presenting policy options," says Atwood, who came to AID from the State Department. "They're not operational in the same way that AID people are. They're also crisis managers at the State Department, whereas AID people think in longer time frames. If you were to put the AID budget into the State Department you would, especially in times of austere budgets, not have the resources available for long-term development. They would be used for crises. The secretary of State cannot really afford to do much other than worry about the crises that are on his desk at any given moment. There's not enough time in the day."

Some observers say the whole debate over AID's organizational future is misguided. "We ought to be having a different debate," says Taft of InterAction. "We've ended up dealing with an organizational issue, arranging the deck chairs on the *Titanic,* without stepping back and figuring out what is an appropriate role for the United States as the leading country in the world in reaching out to the developing countries. Before you discuss structure, you've got to figure out what you're doing."

© World Concern/Adam Buchanan

In Dhaka, Bangladesh, Halima Begum makes cane stools for sale at a local market. Her new business was started with a $250 loan from World Concern, a Seattle-based Christian relief organization funded by AID. In Bangladesh alone, similar loans have helped some 2 million women start businesses.

Should aid for economic development and emergency humanitarian needs be privatized?

While AID is responsible for coordinating the various aid programs funded by the government, much of the actual work is handled by private charities known as private, volunteer organizations (PVOs) or non-governmental organizations (NGOs). There are more than 400 such groups working hand in hand with AID, among them the American Red Cross and World Vision, which transport, store and hand out emergency food aid; teach new agricultural methods; or run family-planning clinics. [9]

Some experts contend that private charities play such a critical role in distributing U.S. humanitarian assistance that they overshadow AID's part in the process. "AID has in most cases become a pass-through agency," says Brad Gordon, a former staffer on both the House and Senate foreign affairs committees who spoke on background. "The people at AID simply take the money that they get and give it to the PVOs to do the work."

While some critics of the government's foreign aid programs stop short of advocating simply bypassing AID altogether, others say private charities can do the job of distributing emergency humanitarian assistance on their own. "Members of the American public give $15 billion a year to private charities to directly meet the humanitarian needs of poor people around the world," says Johnson. "This is how people are being fed, this is how babies are being immunized, this is how education and health care are being provided — not through AID."

Johnson also contends that private charities are less wasteful than AID in administering the distribution of humanitarian assistance. "Even private charities have come under some criticism for waste because they say that some 20 cents out of every dollars stays in the United States to administer the programs," he says. "But in the U.S. foreign aid program, 70-80 cents stays in the United States, which means that only 20-30 cents actually gets to people abroad. So from the humanitarian angle, foreign aid is a disaster."

Taft acknowledges the key role members of InterAction play, but she says PVOs can't entirely take the place of government in helping less-developed countries. "We don't do research, we don't find new gene pools for drought-resistant corn, we don't really engage in dialogue with governments about how they should change their tax systems to promote more private enterprise or to allow our companies to make investments in their countries," she says. "We don't do that sort of thing, and yet all of that is terribly important to be able to establish a more progressive environment in many of these countries."

Taft says that private charities receive about $4.7 billion in private donations for international programs and that the U.S. government provides them with about $1.6 billion in food and direct funding. "What this says to me is that there are large groups of people out there in the United States who care very much about the kinds of programs we support, and when we are able to get matching funds from AID for programs, that makes our money go even further. The problem is, we're only a little piece of AID funding. And there's not going to be a real change in poverty levels or policies in many of these countries if there's not also a corollary investment at the multilateral level or in the government-to-government programs. To me, it is anathema to say there is no need for foreign assistance and just let the NGOs do it. You cannot let these programs just be given to the private sector. There is a government interest here." ■

BACKGROUND

The Marshall Plan

Today's foreign aid program has its roots in efforts to restore the economies of Western Europe, and to contain Soviet expansion, in the aftermath of World War II. In 1947, the same year that George F. Kennan formulated the policy of "containment," aimed at halting expansion of the Soviet Union into Western Europe, former Gen. George C. Marshall called for a massive infusion of economic aid to help restore the continent's war-torn economies.

Marshall, who had been Army chief of staff during the war and later became President Harry S Truman's secretary of State, described this policy in a commencement speech at Harvard University on June 5, 1947. The real enemies of democracy, he said, were "hunger, poverty, desperation and chaos." By providing funds that the recipient countries could spend as they saw fit, Marshall said, the United States could restore "the confidence of the European people in the economic future of their own countries."

The Marshall Plan, as the aid program became known, was a brilliant success in strengthening U.S. ties with the recipient nations. At its peak in 1949, the United States provided more than $50 billion for the effort, which was administered by the 16-nation Committee for European Economic Cooperation to rebuild bombed out cities and factories and provide food. By the early 1950s, Western Europe had embarked on a protracted economic boom that today has placed Britain, Germany, France and Italy among the leading industrial nations.

The committee also provided a model for cooperation that helped launch the North Atlantic Treaty Organization (NATO) as well as the European Community. Vanquished Japan, which also received assistance under the Marshall Plan, went on to become the United States' leading ally in East Asia as well as its toughest trade competitor. Marshall received the 1953 Nobel Peace Prize for his farsighted plan.

'Bold New Program'

The Marshall Plan's phenomenal success provided the impetus for later efforts to use economic assistance to win allies when the Soviet Union shifted its efforts to win influence to Asia, Latin America and Africa. President Truman actually launched the effort in his 1949 inaugural address, when he declared that a new element of U.S. foreign policy was to be a "bold new program" to provide assistance to developing countries. But it was not until 1961 that President John F. Kennedy institutionalized the nation's foreign aid mission by establishing the Agency for International Development as a semiautonomous agency within the State Department. He also set up the Peace Corps to harness the skills of young American volunteers who wanted to help improve education, agriculture and health care in less-developed countries.

Foreign aid levels fell as Western Europe got back on its feet. During the 1960s and '70s, the focus of assistance shifted to U.S. allies in the Middle East and Asia, as well as to poor countries in sub-Saharan Africa and south Asia. It is in these areas that AID claims a broad range of accomplishments since it began operations 35 years ago. Financed

Continued on p. 852

Chronology

1940s-1950s

Foreign aid becomes a key tool of U.S. foreign policy in the wake of World War II.

June 5, 1947

In a commencement speech at Harvard University, former Army Chief of Staff George C. Marshall calls for a massive infusion of economic aid to help restore the war-torn economies of Western Europe.

January 1949

In his inauguration speech, President Harry S Truman introduces foreign aid as a component of U.S. foreign policy by announcing a "bold new program" to provide assistance to developing countries. Spending for the Marshall Plan peaks that year at more than $50 billion, paving the way for a protracted economic boom in the recipient countries of Europe and Japan.

1960s-1970s

Spending on foreign aid shifts from Western Europe to U.S. military allies in the Middle East and Asia and to poor countries in sub-Saharan Africa and south Asia.

1961

President John F. Kennedy institutionalizes the foreign aid mission by establishing the Agency for International Development (AID) as a semi-autonomous agency within the State Department.

1979

The United States promises to provide massive economic and military assistance to Israel and Egypt as part of the Camp David Accords ending hostilities between the two Middle Eastern countries.

1980s ***Criticism of AID mounts amid reports of mismanagement and misuse of foreign aid funds.***

1985

Reports of forced abortions in China lead President Ronald Reagan to suspend U.S. funding for the United Nations Fund for Population Activities (UNFPA). Spending on foreign aid begins a downward trend that will continue to the present.

1990s ***The end of the Cold War leads to cuts in foreign aid.***

Dec. 25, 1991

The Cold War ends when Mikhail S. Gorbachev gives up the presidency of the Soviet Union, effectively dispersing the United States' leading postwar adversary into 15 sovereign countries.

1992

President George Bush sends 22,000 U.S. troops to Somalia as part of a multinational team to help distribute food aid. Two years later, after the troops are drawn into the country's civil war, the mission ends in defeat.

1993

President Clinton takes office stressing the importance of overseas development assistance. As one of his first official acts, he restores funding for UNFPA and overturns restrictions on overseas family-planning programs imposed by Presidents Reagan and Bush. AID Administrator J. Brian Atwood launches reforms that are expected to reduce the agency's overseas missions by almost half by the year 2000.

1995

Senate Foreign Relations Committee Chairman Jesse Helms, R-N.C., introduces legislation to abolish AID and two other independent agencies — the Arms Control and Disarmament Agency (ACDA) and the United States Information Agency (USIA) — as part of his effort to reorganize the State Department and reduce spending on foreign aid.

1996

In an effort to restore Reagan-era restrictions on abortions, the House votes to include in the fiscal 1997 foreign operations appropriations a provision limiting funding of all overseas population programs. But the Senate version of the legislation would increase funding of AID's family-planning programs and contain no abortion restrictions, thus setting the stage for a showdown as the 104th Congress draws to a close.

AID Chief Credits Foreign Aid . . .

J. Brian Atwood, administrator of the U.S. Agency for International Development since 1993, talked about his efforts to reform the agency with staff writer Mary H. Cooper, at his office in Washington, Sept. 9, 1996.

What effect has U.S. foreign aid had on the developing world?

One wonders what the world would look like if we hadn't had foreign aid programs over the last 50 years. We've seen in that period the income of the world rise from $3.4 billion to something like $24 trillion today. We've seen a 50 percent reduction in infant mortality rates, which is a key indicator of development. We've seen a major increase in agricultural production spurred by the Green Revolution and by all the other investments we've made in research. We've seen a 20-year increase in the average age of individuals who live in the so-called developing world, from 42 to 62. We've seen a 75 percent increase in the amount of potable water that is now available to people. So you can imagine what the world would look like if that investment hadn't been made.

U.S. AID Administrator J. Brian Atwood

What have foreign aid programs done for the United States?

That investment has basically created consumers for American products as well as products from other parts of the industrial world. The markets that we are now enjoying, that are pulling American exports toward them, in Asia and Latin America in particular, are markets that were developed because of a concerted effort to invest in development in those countries, at first primarily by the United States and later by other countries that were encouraged by American leadership.

Doesn't foreign aid sometimes get in the way of development by enabling governments to avoid making the painful adjustment to a free-market system?

There is a very ideological point of view that poor countries would do fine if they just adopted the Adam Smith view of economics and got their political framework put right. The problem is that many extremely poor countries need to be given training in what economic framework they should be creating for themselves. More importantly, they don't have the finances to invest in human capacity — the health and education of their own people. So even if they had the framework right, there's no way they could translate it into development success. That is a lesson we've learned from countries like South Korea and Taiwan. They didn't have the resources for health and education either, and that was provided by external aid. Now they're tremendous markets for us, and they're stable international actors that help us maintain the global economy.

How has the Cold War's end affected the need for development assistance?

The opportunities for making progress in development in

Continued from p. 850

largely by AID's agricultural research program in India during the 1960s, scientists developed high-yielding varieties of grains that enabled India to boost food production by 20 percent. As the "Green Revolution" spread to other parts of south and east Asia, production of rice and other grains helped avert widespread famine that many experts had predicted would result from the rapid increase in population that occurred during the period.

Global Population Worries

The population rise was in large measure a result of significant improvements in health care that also was funded mainly by U.S. foreign aid. Programs to immunize children against infectious diseases, ensure access to clean water and improve health care have resulted in a 50 percent drop in infant and child mortality and a rise in the average lifespan from 42 to 62 years. The lives of more than 3 million children are saved each year as a result of AID-sponsored immunization programs. U.S. foreign aid also contributed to a global effort that wiped out smallpox, once among the developing world's deadliest scourges. Oral rehydration therapy, a simple and inexpensive treatment for diarrheal diseases that was developed in the early 1970s through an AID program in Bangladesh, is credited with saving tens of millions of lives around the world.

Despite the increase in food supplies brought by the Green Revolution, by the early 1970s concern was mounting over the impact of rapidly rising populations on the world's poorest countries. Even though more children could be expected to reach adulthood by the early 1970s, couples continued the traditional practice of having large families, especially in the

. . . With U.S. Jobs and Other Economic Benefits

the next 50 years are even greater today because we no longer face the same obstacles to development that we faced during the Cold War. That is, the ideological debates on what kind of an economic or political system you should have have been largely removed. It seems somewhat ironic that at the very moment when we're able to do real development work — as opposed to doing Cold War-related political work — with our development dollars, we are being cut to the point where we're becoming less and less effective. Whether we like it or not, the world is going to become more complicated, in part because it is going to add 2 billion more people over the next two decades. We have so much to gain and so much to lose that foreign aid is a vital investment in U.S. national security.

With no natural constituency among voters, how can you expect foreign aid to be spared the budget knife?

Certainly the phrase foreign aid doesn't have a popular ring to it, but I think foreign aid has a lot of different domestic constituencies. If you broke down our program into its parts, you would find in the contribution that we make on the environment that we have a very strong environmental constituency. We have a very strong constituency among Americans when you talk about the provision of family-planning services. We certainly have a broad, bipartisan constituency in favor of the notion that we have to be supporting new democracies around the world, to help them get on their feet and to learn the techniques of democracy. And we certainly have a strong constituency, made up of some of the largest businesses in this country, in support of economic development for the purpose of freeing markets. In just the last year, a coalition of over 1,000 businesses has called for the foreign aid budget to be increased to $18 billion a year, which is what they say in real terms we were providing in 1985. Since then, we've had about a 40 percent decrease. I think these constituencies have really come together because of the deep cuts that were taken in the fiscal 1996 budget.

How have your reforms changed the way AID does its work?

We've made major reforms within AID. The most significant change we've made is to re-engineer the way we design development projects. In the past, we basically imposed development on people rather than having them participate in the process itself. Now the AID missions are organized differently to emphasize participation. For example, if AID has a strategic objective in a particular country of working with the health ministry on improving immunizations for children, we create what we call a results package which [AID team members] review with the health ministry and with [non-governmental organizations] that are working in this field to determine whether our goals are realistic. Then they will negotiate and sign a contract to get the results that they want to achieve. That really gives people a stake in what we're trying to do. It's never been done that way before.

If President Clinton is re-elected to a second term, what plans do you have for AID over the next four years?

I would like to consolidate the reforms that have been put in place here, and I would like to see Congress and the administration begin incrementally to build back our capacity to do this work. If I could walk away from here seeing that happening, then I would have some confidence that maybe I had contributed something to the country, and I'd walk away a happy person.

poorest countries. Fearing that population growth threatened future food supplies as well as the environment, AID launched family-planning programs in many developing countries. Because educated and employed women tend to have fewer children, the agency also broadened education programs for women. In the 28 countries with the largest AID-sponsored programs, the average number of children per family has dropped from 6.1 in the mid-1960s to 4.2 today.

AID-sponsored economic development programs also have produced notable accomplishments by earlier recipients of U.S. assistance such as Taiwan and South Korea, which have "graduated" to become leading trading partners of the U.S. Of the top 50 importers of American agricultural products, according to AID, 43 are former recipients of U.S. grants and loans. The value of U.S. exports of food-processing and packaging machinery has increased almost sevenfold since the mid-1980s, as AID programs have fostered a better economic climate for new businesses in recipient countries.

Despite these and other success stories, the developing world faces threats that advocates of foreign aid say require still greater intervention by AID and other sources of development assistance. Even though population growth is expected to slow and eventually halt before the middle of the next century, at current rates the developing world's population will double in 34 years, placing greater strain on the Earth. *(See "At Issue," p. 857.)* Despite aggressive education programs, 100 million elementary school-age children around the world today will never attend school. And new diseases — notably HIV/AIDS and drug-resistant tuberculosis — are spreading at alarm-

Top Recipients of U.S. Foreign Aid, 1996

The largest share of Agency for International Development (AID) funds went to Israel and Egypt in 1996 to advance U.S. economic and security interests. Israel used the funds to pay off loans for military equipment. Other AID funds went to former Soviet republics, mainly as technical assistance designed to help them make the transition to free-market economies, and to sub-Saharan Africa, for development and humanitarian assistance.

	(in $millions)
Israel	$1,200
Egypt	815
Bosnia	248
Ukraine	225
Russia	144
South Africa	121
Armenia	85
Haiti	84
West Bank/Gaza	75
Indonesia	52
India	48.7
Philippines	47.5
Poland	46.0
Bangladesh	41.6
Ghana	38.8
Uganda	37.7
Mozambique	37.5
Ethiopia	32.8
Malawi	32.8
Mali	30.3

Food program in Mali

Fertilizer plant in India

Small farmers in Ethiopia

Note: Funds are distributed from three AID accounts: Development Assistance; Special Assistance Initiative/Newly Independent States and the Economic Support Fund. Haiti received both development and economic support funds.

Source: Agency for International Development

ing rates. AID estimates that 5,000 people become infected daily with the AIDS virus. An additional 7 million adults die each year of preventable or curable conditions, 2 million of tuberculosis alone. [10]

AID Under Attack

Despite the long list of its accomplishments, foreign aid came under growing criticism during the 1980s. Reassessment of AID's development assistance began with protests from anti-abortion advocates who opposed the use of American funds for family-planning programs that provided abortion services overseas. The United States had taken the lead in population programs, both through AID and through the United Nations Fund for Population Activities (UNFPA). Established in 1969, the fund received nearly a third of its budget from the U.S. government. [11] The UNFPA supported population programs throughout the developing world, including China, whose government had imposed a restrictive "one-child" policy in an effort to keep its fast-growing population from outpacing the country's ability to feed itself.

Media reports that the Chinese government was forcing women to undergo abortions to enforce the one-child policy, however, prompted an outcry among anti-abortion advocates in the United States. Although AID declared that neither it nor the UNFPA funded abortions or coercive family-planning practices, President Ronald Reagan ordered $10 million of the $46 million U.S. contribution to UNFPA withheld in 1985. For the next seven years, the Reagan and Bush administrations suspended all U.S. contributions to the population fund.

The controversy over population policy prompted a debate over the value of foreign aid in general. After the Cold War, criticism of AID's programs escalated further among those who all along had viewed foreign aid chiefly as a means of winning allies in the struggle to deter Soviet influence in the developing world. As long as the Soviet Union offered military and economic aid to leftist forces in the developing world, conservatives had supported AID's security and development assistance programs, even to authoritarian leaders such as Zaire's President Mobutu Sese Seko and Ferdinand E. Marcos of the Philippines, without scrutinizing how the funds were spent. In the 1990s, however, reports of fraudulent use of AID funds by corrupt governments helped fuel calls to reduce or eliminate most U.S. development assistance.

Calls to cut back on foreign aid escalated with the outbreak of regional conflicts and disasters that critics said illustrated the failure of development assistance. In 1992, the East African country of Somalia, which had received U.S. assistance during the Cold War, was torn by a civil war and resulting famine that by 1993 had left nearly a half-million people dead of starvation. President Bush ordered 22,000 U.S. troops to Somalia as part of a multinational team to help distribute food aid. That contingent was later reduced, and American forces came under U.N. command. In the confusion over military authority and the multinational force's political goals, the troops were drawn into the conflict. In March 1994, after 18 G.I.s were killed in the streets of Mogadishu, President Clinton withdrew all remaining U.S. forces.

The debacle in Somalia was followed a month later by the outbreak of a human-rights disaster in Rwanda, in central Africa, where the wholesale slaughter carried out by the rival Hutu and Tutsi factions left hundreds of thousands of people dead and millions facing starvation in refugee camps scattered in neighboring countries. While these and other regional conflicts underscored the volatility of the political realities of the post-Cold War era, critics of foreign aid also suggested that they testified to the failure of 35 years of development assistance through AID. ■

CARE

In Thailand, a CARE field officer demonstrates how to collect mulberry leaves used to feed silkworms raised by poor Thai farmers. It's one of thousands of programs throughout the developing world funded by U.S. foreign aid that stress conservation-based development.

CURRENT SITUATION

AID Reforms

The Cold War's end brought significant changes in the scope and goals of U.S. foreign aid. In 1991, even before the Soviet Union's collapse, Congress set aside nearly $400 million in AID funds to encourage the countries of Eastern Europe to adopt democratic, free-market policies. While funding was targeted at the United States' former Cold War adversaries, cuts in the overall foreign aid budget left many developing countries with less assistance than they had received earlier.

At the same time, AID came under unprecedented criticism for wasting funds and mismanaging programs that had been considered essential for geopolitical reasons during the Cold War. As concern over the economy and other domestic issues displaced foreign policy from the top of the political agenda, AID came under pressure to radically overhaul its operations.

President Clinton took office in 1993 stressing the importance of development assistance as an essential component of U.S. foreign policy. In one of his first acts in office, he overturned the Reagan and Bush administrations' family-planning restrictions and restored U.S. funding of the U.N. Population Fund. Clinton also promised to revamp the country's foreign aid structure and appointed Atwood to head up AID and undertake the reform effort.

Identified as one of the lead agencies targeted by Vice President Al Gore's program to "reinvent government," AID has defined the focus of its development strategy on four areas: economic growth, population and health-related programs, environmental protection and support of democratic institutions. Since 1994, Atwood has closed more than 20 overseas missions, with a total of 24 more scheduled for closure by Sept. 31, 1997. He has reduced AID's work force by nearly a third. The agency has invested some $50 million in a new computer system in an effort to streamline AID operations.

"All these changes will mean that from the start of the Clinton administration until the year 2000, USAID will have been radically transformed," Atwood testified at hearings earlier this year. "We started in 1993 with programs in over 120 countries, with over 70 missions. By the year 2000, USAID's programs will be targeted on approximately 75 countries, with no more than 30 sustainable development missions." [12]

Atwood gets mixed reviews for his efforts. "While Atwood has done an excellent job on all these gee-whiz terms that have come out in the Clinton administration about sustainable development and reinventing government, we haven't seen anything different about the way they are carrying out their programs in the field," says Walker of the Senate Foreign Relations Committee staff. "This is clearly a public relations, politically correct version of doing foreign aid. But the fact is, the people inside tell me this is new labels on old wine."

Not surprisingly, advocates of a strong foreign aid program offer a radically different assessment of Atwood's tenure. "Atwood has found himself pretty much alone over there trying to defend AID against a Congress that is pretty belligerent toward foreign aid," says Rep. Hall. "I think he's been wonderful, especially when you consider that he's fighting an uphill battle."

Speaking on behalf of private charities, about half of which work with AID in the field, Taft also gives Atwood high marks for his efforts. "I respect him for his articulateness and his ideas about where he wants the enterprise to go," she says. "But I think it's been more difficult than he expected, and there is a real lack of visible support from the administration for what he's doing."

Taft points to confusion over the agency's plan to funnel 40 percent of AID funds through non-governmental groups over the next five years. "There has been no real guidance or program to really make that happen, so some of the reform effort gets messed up in the translation from the commitment to how it really is implemented. We as a community often are quite frustrated that the words are not always translated into action in the field."

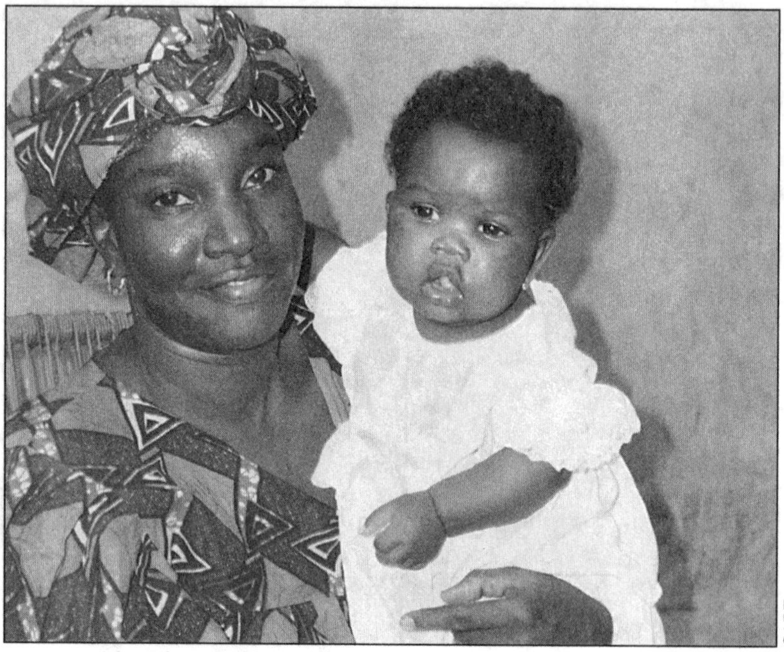

CARE

The infant daughter of farmer Foita Djiga of Mali was named their community's most beautiful baby at a contest sponsored by CARE to promote good health care. CARE, the world's largest private relief and development organization, is among 400 non-governmental organizations (NGOs) that receive Agency for International Development funds.

Action in Congress

Appropriations for foreign aid have been heading downward since the mid-1980s. Today, as Atwood focuses on streamlining AID's operations, Congress continues to tighten the agency's purse strings. While Congress appropriated $12.4 billion for the foreign aid budget in fiscal 1996, only $5.9 billion went to pay for AID-administered programs. Of that total, less than $1.7 billion was used to promote development assistance.

Cuts in the foreign aid budget mirror reductions in spending on international affairs overall. The $18.6 billion 1996 budget for international affairs is down almost $1 billion from last year. In inflation-adjusted dollars, that is the lowest amount the United States has spent on international activities over the past decade. [13]

Some observers charge that lawmakers, by continuing to cut foreign aid, have failed to fulfill their obligations. "Congressmen and senators may not remember it, but they wear two hats, and they need to care about something beyond their direct constituencies," Taft says. "They represent — at least to the rest of the world — the most important parliament in the world. Therefore they have a transcending responsibility to go beyond what their mail is back home and to do what George Marshall did, which was to consider our responsibilities beyond the United States."

In Taft's view, further cuts in foreign aid run counter to a long-standing American tradition of compassion. "There is so much for us as a country to be grateful for that it does seem to me very mean-spirited and shortsighted to assume that we who are so

Continued on p. 858

At Issue:

Should U.S. foreign aid programs place greater emphasis on curbing world population growth?

yes

Sen. Alan K. Simpson, R-Wyo., Chairman, Senate Finance Subcommittee On Social Security And Family Policy

From testimony at a hearing on international population growth, July 20, 1995.

Of all the challenges facing us in this country and around the world, none compares to that of increasing population growth. All of our efforts to protect the environment and to promote economic development around the world are compromised by the staggering rate of growth in our world's population. There are currently 5.7 billion people on the Earth. In 1950, there were only 2.5 billion. . . . Projections for 2015 range from 7.1 billion to 7.83 billion, and for 2050 from 7.9 billion to 11.9 billion. . . .

Despite some progress in reducing fertility rates, birthrates in developing countries are declining too slowly to prevent a cataclysmic near-tripling of the human race before stabilization can occur. The real issue here is that we spend an inordinate amount of time talking about things like methane gas in cows and how much propellant is contained in a shaving cream can and how they will destroy the Earth's atmosphere, while the real issue [is] how will we sustain a huge population of many billions of people without thoroughly trashing the environment?. . .

I have been here a long time, and every time we bring up the issue of stabilizing the Earth's population, somebody throws in the issue of abortion. That is not what this is all about!

Women in these countries are desperately seeking ways to take control of their reproductive lives and cannot do so because there is a severe lack of access to such high-quality, affordable services. Worldwide, estimates are that more than 350 million couples want to space or prevent another pregnancy but lack access to the full range of modern family planning methods. An estimated 120 million women would practice family planning if a modern method were available, affordable and acceptable to their partners, families and communities.

In addition, any comprehensive family planning initiative must include access to primary health care with an emphasis on child survival to reduce infant mortality. In many developing countries, parents have a perception that many of their children will not survive beyond their first birthdays. If these parents' fears are allayed, they will not feel much pressure to have more children than they actually desire. . . .

It is our aim to [make] global population stabilization . . . a vital part of U.S. foreign aid and development-assistance programs. We need to begin to make much-needed policy changes in international population stabilization, and the United States needs to take this lead to ensure that these new policy developments are recognized worldwide. This one is long overdue.

no

Sheldon Richman, Senior Editor, Cato Institute

From testimony at a hearing on international population growth, Senate Finance Subcommittee on Social Security and Family Policy, July 20, 1995.

How many people are too many? We know that 5.5 billion people walk the Earth today. But that number by itself says nothing. Maybe it is too few.

In arguing their case, the believers in overpopulation make vague, tautological references to a standard known as "carrying capacity," colorfully illustrated with stories about gazelle herds and bacteria (anything but human beings). When the verbiage is cleared away, what are adduced as the symptoms of overpopulation? Famine, deepening poverty, disease, environmental degradation and resource depletion. Yet on no count does the evidence support the anti-population lobby's case. . . .

The TV pictures of starving . . . Africans are heartbreaking, but they are not evidence of overpopulation. Since 1985, we have witnessed famine in Ethiopia, Sudan and Somalia. Those nations . . . are among the least densely populated areas on Earth. Although their populations are growing, the people there are not hungry because the world can't produce enough food. They are hungry because [of] civil war. . . .

In the 20th century, there has been no famine that has not been caused by civil war, irrational economic policies or political retribution. Not one. Moreover, the number of people affected by famine compared to that in the late 19th century has fallen — not just as a percentage of the world's population but in absolute numbers. . . .

[T]he population is not in need of stabilization by government intervention. As the world becomes richer and more Westernized, the fertility rate falls on its own. The growth in human numbers is accounted for by the plunging death rate — a universal sign of progress. There is no population problem to be solved. . . .

The record of government-to-government transfers is dismal for a simple reason. Providing cash to central governments puts off the day when those governments grasp the necessity of relinquishing power and letting the liberal market order — complete with women's rights — flourish. Foreign aid intensifies the politicization of society. When the state is the primary cash cow in society, people will expend effort to curry favor with rulers rather than set their minds to economically productive activities. . . .

Of course, most people wish to see economic progress in the developing world. But the truth is that U.S. government money cannot produce it. The only things that can are the diminution of government power in those countries, the rule of law and the expansion of the private, productive sector of society — in a word, capitalism.

FOR MORE INFORMATION

Foreign Agricultural Service, U.S. Department of Agriculture, 14th St. and Independence Ave. S.W., Suite 5065-S, Washington, D.C. 20250-1000; (202) 720-7115. Administers the U.S. foreign food aid program with the Agency for International Development.

InterAction, American Council for Voluntary International Action, 1717 Massachusetts Ave., N.W., Suite 801, Washington, D.C. 20036; (202) 667-8227. The 150 U.S. private, voluntary organizations in this membership association are engaged in international humanitarian efforts.

Organisation for Economic Cooperation and Development (OECD), 2001 L St. N.W., Suite 700, Washington, D.C. 20036; (202) 785-6323. This Paris-based membership organization of 27 nations serves as a forum for the world's leading industrial countries to coordinate economic policies.

United Nations Development Program (UNDP), One United Nations Plaza, New York, N.Y. 10017; (212) 906-5315. Funded by voluntary contributions from member nations, the program administers technical assistance programs provided through the United Nations.

U.S. Agency for International Development (AID), Main State Building, Room 5942, Washington, D.C. 20523; (202) 647-1850. AID is the lead government agency for coordinating and administering foreign aid programs. It provides developing countries and the countries of Eastern Europe with economic assistance and disaster relief.

Continued from p. 856

well-blessed can turn our back on the rest of the world," Taft says. "And I don't think the American people want it turned. I think what they want is to make sure that the investments we make are targeted and well-spent. That's valid, but spending less is not."

Judging by the foreign aid spending bill now before Congress, the majority of lawmakers reject Taft's argument. The $12.1 billion fiscal 1997 foreign operations appropriations bill — which includes funding for multilateral organizations, military aid, State Department operations, the Peace Corps and export assistance programs in addition to AID — calls for further reductions in spending for international affairs and ultimately grants about $800 million less that President Clinton had requested. The president had requested $6.1 billion for AID, about $100 million over the current level. The Senate approved a slight increase, but the House appropriated slightly less than the current budget.

Although they are not far apart on spending levels, lawmakers hit an impasse over abortion language contained in the House appropriations bill. In an effort to restore Reagan-era restrictions on abortions, House Republicans included a provision to limit funding of population programs to 65 percent of the fiscal 1995 level — $356 million. Overseas organizations that use their own funds to provide abortions would be eligible to receive only half of their fiscal 1995 funding. The Senate version, in contrast, would actually increase funding for family-planning programs to $410 million and impose no conditions related to abortion.

The Clinton administration supports the Senate bill, both for its recommended funding level and for the absence of abortion restrictions. "The House restrictions would severely undermine U.S. leadership in international population assistance efforts and would result in an increased incidence of unintended pregnancy, maternal and infant death and abortion," wrote Jacob J. Lew, acting director of the White House Office of Management and Budget. "The House bill, in effect, would impose limitations in law on international family planning assistance that were rejected by the administration when it overturned the so-called Mexico City policy. . . . Should the House language, or similar language, be included in the bill sent to the president, the president's senior advisers would recommend that he veto the bill." [14]

Private Charities Pitch in

Meanwhile, private charities and advocacy groups are stepping up their efforts to inform the public about the impact the cuts in foreign aid spending have had over the past decade. "In the past, we didn't have to do this, because members of Congress made our case for us," says Mike Kiernan, media director for InterAction. "But with the new Congress, all that radically changed. People need to know that there is a mix of different sectors, including conservative evangelical groups such as World Vision, that feel very strongly about the federal government playing a role in helping the world's poor. If you explain development assistance in ways that people can understand — feeding the hungry and trying to help people help themselves — Americans will basically resonate to that."

Other groups are emphasizing the economic payoff that foreign aid has at home. According to AIPAC, which has compiled lists of U.S. companies, universities and organizations that benefit from contracts related to foreign aid, 73 percent of all foreign aid dollars are spent in the United States. The Massachusetts economy, for example, benefitted from more than $430 million in foreign aid spending last year, while Florida received more than $34 million, according to USAID.

"I think there is a deep misunderstanding about where aid money goes," says Toby Dershowitz, director of media relations at AIPAC. "Many people, even a lot of members of Congress, do not know that most aid money is spent in this country." [15] ■

OUTLOOK

More Cuts?

Election-year politics may delay further serious discussion of foreign aid this year. Eager to return to their home districts in time to campaign for re-election this fall, lawmakers appear likely to include foreign operations in an omnibus spending bill, which would fund appropriations bills not completed by Congress by Oct. 1, the beginning of fiscal 1997.

The only way the foreign aid budget could emerge from Congress as a separate bill would be for a last-minute resolution of the longstanding disagreement over AID's population program. "It's not out of the question," says Charles O. Flickner, clerk of the House Appropriations Subcommittee on Foreign Operations, Export Financing and Related Programs. "But we'd have to have a settlement on population."

Even funding for foreign aid, which conferees agreed Sept. 17 to maintain at last year's level of $12.1 billion, remains a subject of debate. The conferees' proposal to arrive at that total by including a $140 million rescission from aid that has been appropriated but not yet spent prompted a veto threat from the State Department.[16] "The administration is protesting our rescission, so I don't think funding has been resolved," Flickner says. "We think it's resolved, but I don't think the Executive Branch thinks it's resolved."

For his part, Atwood fears that Congress will once again impede his agency's ability to carry out its mandate in the coming year. "The bill in conference now would basically give us what we had last year, which is a continuation of what I see as an almost $1 billion cut in foreign aid," he says. "It would mean that we're not able yet to recoup the losses we've already been dealt. It's very damaging in the long run."

Foreign aid advocates are looking to other donor nations to help persuade the American public to halt the erosion of AID funding, no matter who wins the presidential contest or which party wins a majority of the seats in Congress. In what appears to be a message to the U.S. government to resume its historic leadership role in providing development aid, the OECD's Development Assistance Committee has issued an appeal for all donor nations to strengthen their commitment to a coordinated and efficient aid program. "Those of us in the industrialized countries have a strong moral imperative to respond to the extreme poverty and human suffering that still afflict more than 1 billion people," the committee declared. "All people are made less secure by the poverty and misery that exist in the world. Development matters."[17]

If the U.S. fails to renew its commitment to foreign aid, Taft fears, other donors may well follow its lead. "The rest of the world now perceives that although we're still great militarily, we are losing our moral leadership," she says. "Unfortunately, because we have walked away from this commitment to development cooperation in the last several years, we are seeing other donors giving less because they want to be like the United States." ■

Notes

[1] Steven Kull, "Americans on Foreign Aid: A Study of American Public Attitudes," Program on International Policy Attitudes, March 1, 1995. Part of a series of polls conducted by the University of Maryland's Center for International and Security Studies and the Center for the Study of Policy Attitudes. For background, see "Foreign Policy and Public Opinion," *The CQ Researcher*, July 15, 1994, pp. 601-624.

[2] The OECD's Development Assistance Committee released its report on June 11, 1996.

[3] See Casimir A. Yost and Mary Locke, *U.S. Foreign Affairs Resources: Budget Cuts and Consequences*, Institute for the Study of Diplomacy, Georgetown University, 1996. For background, see "Democracy in Africa," *The CQ Researcher*, March 24, 1995, pp. 241-264; "Aid to Russia," *The CQ Researcher*, March 12, 1993, pp. 217-240; and "World Hunger," *The CQ Researcher*, Oct. 25, 1991, pp. 801-824.

[4] From an interview on John McLaughlin's "One on One," March 3, 1995.

[5] U.S. Agency for International Development, *Why Foreign Aid?* (undated).

[6] Thomas P. Sheehy and Bryan T. Johnson, "The 1996 Index of Economic Freedom," Heritage Foundation, November 1995.

[7] For background on the State Department reorganization measure, see Carrol J. Doherty, "Clinton, with Veto Pen Poised, Gets Agency-Cutback Bill," *Congressional Quarterly Weekly Report*, March 30, 1996, p. 895.

[8] Lawrence S. Eagleburger and Robert L. Barry, "Dollars and Sense Diplomacy: A Better Foreign Policy for Less Money," *Foreign Affairs*, July/August 1996, pp. 4, 8.

[9] For more information on the role of private charities in foreign aid, see U.S. General Accounting Office, "Foreign Assistance: Private Voluntary Organizations' Contributions and Limitations," December 1995.

[10] U.S. Agency for International Development, *op. cit.*

[11] See Shanti R. Conly, *Taking the Lead: The United Nations and Population Assistance*, Population Action International, Sept. 29, 1996.

[12] Atwood testified April 25, 1996, before the House International Relations Committee.

[13] Office of Management and Budget, *Budget of the United States Government: Analytical Perspectives*, 1996, pp. 69-70.

[14] From a letter to House Appropriations Committee Chairman Robert L. Livingston, R-La., Aug. 8, 1996.

[15] For background, see American Israel Public Affairs Committee, "Foreign Aid at Work in Massachusetts," April 1, 1993, and "Foreign Aid at Work in Florida," March 30, 1993.

[16] See Carroll J. Doherty, "Foreign Aid Bill May Stall Over Family Planning," *Congressional Quarterly Weekly Report*, Sept. 21, 1996, pp. 2679-2680.

[17] Development Assistance Committee, OECD, *Shaping the 21st Century: The Contribution of Development Cooperation*, May 1996, p. 1.

Bibliography

Selected Sources Used

Books

United Nations Development Program, *Human Development Report 1996,* Oxford University Press, 1996.
The U.N. agency reports that foreign aid has failed to stem the gap between rich and poor nations. Despite economic growth in 15 countries over the past 30 years, 89 countries that received aid — and their 1.6 billion inhabitants — are worse off today.

Articles

"Aid: Falling Fast," *The Economist,* June 22, 1996, pp. 43-44.
The United States has fallen far behind other donors in its foreign aid contributions, and the total amount industrial countries give to the developing world has dropped since 1992.

Campbell, Blair, "Race for Survival," *Government Executive,* March 1996, pp. 32-36.
Brian Atwood, administrator of the Agency for International Development since 1993, has introduced sweeping reforms to the agency. In light of efforts by Congress to eliminate AID, he believes the reforms are the key to the agency's survival.

Eagleburger, Lawrence S., and Robert L. Barry, "Dollars and Sense Diplomacy: A Better Foreign Policy for Less Money," *Foreign Affairs,* July/August 1996, pp. 2-8.
Before eliminating the Agency for International Development and merging its operations into the State Department, write a former secretary of State and a former ambassador, State itself should be reorganized and many high-level positions eliminated.

Kaplan, Robert, "Proportionalism," *The Atlantic Monthly,* August 1996, pp. 16-20.
A more common-sense approach to foreign aid, writes Kaplan, would emphasize programs with proven track records, such as population control, women's literacy and environmental programs, as well as better information-gathering to enable policy-makers to identify crises before they erupt and a strict limit on military intervention.

Rieff, David, "The Humanitarian Trap," *World Policy Journal,* winter 1995/96, pp. 1-11.
The author, a fellow at the World Policy Institute in New York City, argues that while the need for humanitarian assistance is likely to grow in coming years, current foreign aid policies can do little to improve the situation. He points to disasters in Somalia, Rwanda and Bosnia as evidence that neither government-to-government nor charity-run programs are up to the task.

Reports and Studies

Congressional Budget Office, *Enhancing U.S. Security Through Foreign Aid,* April 1994.
In the wake of the Cold War, according to this report by the nonpartisan office that provides fiscal analysis to Congress, some foreign aid programs are more useful than others. Cutting back on aid to Israel and Egypt and to 30 middle-income developing countries and limiting food aid to countries hit by disasters would save about $2 billion a year by 2000.

Conly, Shanti R., *Taking the Lead: The United Nations and Population Assistance,* Population Action International, Sept. 29, 1996.
As the world's leading agency involved in programs to curtail population growth, the U.N. Fund for Population Activities (UNFPA) supports family-planning programs in more than 100 countries. Conly reports that the agency requires more funding from donor countries, especially the United States, to continue its work.

Development Assistance Committee, Organization for Economic Cooperation and Development, *Shaping the 21st Century: The Contribution of Development Co-operation,* May 1996.
In this manifesto, the 21 industrialized countries that contribute aid to the developing world pledge to cooperate on programs likely to enhance trade relations with aid recipients.

Sachs, Jeffrey, and Andrew Warner, *Sources of Slow Growth in the African Economies,* Harvard Institute for International Development, February 1996.
Foreign aid, the authors argue, has helped stymie economic growth in most African countries by enabling governments to postpone needed free-market reforms.

U.S. General Accounting Office, *Foreign Assistance: Private Voluntary Organizations' Contributions and Limitations,* December 1995.
Private voluntary organizations (PVOs) play an essential role in delivering foreign aid by distributing food, caring for the sick and helping refugees around the world. But because they play little or no part in diplomacy, private charities cannot take the place of the U.S. government in providing foreign aid.

The Next Step

Additional information from UMI's Newspaper & Periodical Abstracts database

Agency for International Development (AID)

"AID chief denounces potential U.S. cuts in foreign aid," *Boston Globe,* Jan. 18, 1995, p. 11.
Brian Atwood, the head of the Agency for International Development, battling to preserve the government's foreign assistance program, accused critics of U.S. aid to poor countries of "moral indifference."

Greenhouse, Steven, "It's a hard job saving foreign aid (but the job is still there)," *The New York Times,* Feb. 19, 1995, p. 18.
Eager to chop foreign aid and to demolish what they view as an outdated, inefficient bastion of bureaucratic self-preservation, Republican leaders announced plans the week of Feb. 12, 1995, to push through legislation to scrap AID and merge it with the State Department. For J. Brian Atwood, who is the director of the agency, this new threat means remounting his lobbying campaign to ensure the survival of AID.

Lippman, Thomas W., "Foreign aid staff waits to see what to subtract," *The Washington Post,* Nov. 23, 1995, p. A21.
The staff of the AID will have to make cuts in spending for fiscal 1996, but no one knows how much needs to be cut. Under the interim measure passed by Congress, agencies whose annual appropriations bills have not been signed into law must operate at the lowest funding level set in other bills.

Moffett, George, "A flap over privatizing foreign aid," *The Christian Science Monitor,* Feb. 27, 1995, p. 4.
In February 1995, non-governmental agencies criticized a Senate Republican plan to abolish the U.S. Agency for International Development and privatize foreign aid. The agencies claim that NGOs cannot provide a substitute for government aid programs.

Powell, Margaret, "A U.S. foreign aid project that has a Hungarian accent," *The Christian Science Monitor,* Jan. 11, 1995, p. 18.
Powell discusses a four-year, $729,000 project helping Hungarian artisans, funded by the Agency for International Development, and details how the Connecticut organization Aid to Artisans has helped skilled, struggling workers in the folk-art crafts to blossom in a world market.

Aid to Africa

Lorch, Donatella, "Rwandan killings set back effort to provide foreign aid," *The New York Times,* April 26, 1995, p. A3.
U.N. and Western diplomats in Kigali, Rwanda, say that the killing of an estimated 2,000 ethnic Hutu by Rwandan government troops the week of April 17, 1995, is a major setback to efforts to bring international aid to the cash-strapped, desperately poor nation.

Matloff, Judith, "Tiny Eritrea says 'no thank you' to foreign aid that has strings," *The Christian Science Monitor,* April 8, 1996, p. 7.
The tiny nation of Eritrea is shattering the mold of how African nations develop. The country has emerged from 30 years of war with neighboring Ethiopia determined to rebuild with no dictates from Western foreign aid donors. Eritrea is determined to lift up its poor while courting private and foreign investment.

Raghavan, Sudarsan, "Foes of Kenya's Moi see opportunity in falloff of foreign aid," *Houston Chronicle,* Oct. 7, 1995, p. A31.
Unlike other African leaders, Kenyan President Daniel arap Moi may never get the chance to build a lavish monument in his tribal heartland. At a foreign donors' meeting in Juiy 1995, the World Bank declared an $83 million airport project in Kenya unnecessary and a barrier to further aid.

"U.S. should heed Diallo on foreign aid to Africa," *Chicago Defender,* May 14, 1996, p. 9.
An editorial urges the U.S., on the advice of U.N. official Djibril Diallo, to continue to pay its U.N. debt and continue to invest in the betterment of African nations.

Foreign Aid Reforms

Crossette, Barbara, "Gore says U.S. will shift more foreign aid to private groups," *The New York Times,* March 13, 1995, p. A7.
Vice President Al Gore, speaking on March 12, 1995, in Copenhagen at the close of the U.N. World Summit on Social Development, said that within five years the Clinton administration plans to channel nearly half its foreign aid through private organizations rather than governments. Gore said the U.S. will also increase support to projects that decentralize political power and give more authority to local communities in less developed countries.

Eberstadt, Nicholas, "Foreign aid is beyond repair," *The Wall Street Journal,* July 22, 1996, p. A14.
Eberstadt criticizes the U.S.' foreign aid policy, saying it is "indefensibly misguided and ineffective" and "should be scrapped entirely." Eberstadt offers suggestions on how to reform aid policies.

Kennedy, Paul, "Devote foreign aid to the important few," *Los Angeles Times,* February 18, 1996, p. M5.

Kennedy asserts that the U.S. should concentrate on improving foreign aid to a few "pivotal states," including Mexico, Brazil, Algeria, Egypt, Turkey and South Africa.

Perkins, Joseph, "Foreign aid worthy of $1 billion cut," *Atlanta Constitution,* May 17, 1995, p. A11.
Perkins supports the idea of cutting foreign aid to several countries he deems unworthy, offering reasons for the cuts and suggestions for better spending.

Selle, John R., "The politics of foreign aid," *World & I,* May 1995, pp. 64-69.
The U.S. foreign aid program, which Selle calls one of the most ineffectual of government expenditures, is perhaps the one program that Americans are willing to cut. Selle argues for a reform of the current program.

Public Opinion

Crossette, Barbara, "Foreign aid budget: Quick, how much? Wrong," *The New York Times,* February 27, 1995, p. A6.
As Congress moves to cut foreign aid, supporters of such assistance are getting evidence that Americans have little or no idea of how small the aid budget actually is. Although the U.S.'s foreign aid budget is about 1 percent of the federal budget, respondents to a January 1995, poll said they believed an "appropriate" expenditure for aid is about 5 percent.

"Foreign aid investments pay off in healthy kids," *Denver Post,* July 31, 1996, p. B6.
An editorial comments on the 1996 foreign aid appropriations measure, asserting that Congress is about to gut affordable but effective international programs that protect children and that, dollar for dollar, give the country the best return on its foreign aid.

Greenhouse, Steven, "Foreign aid: Under siege in the budget wars," *The New York Times,* April 30, 1995, p. 4.
In their search for budget cuts that will generate the least amount of protest, the new Republican majority in Congress has made foreign assistance a prime target. Americans typically overestimate the amount of the federal budget that goes toward foreign aid, and most feel the aid is ineffective.

Kempster, Norman, "Foreign aid outlays — A tiny bite," *Los Angeles Times,* May 30, 1995, p. A5.
Although public opinion polls have shown that Americans think their government spends as much as 25 percent of its budget on foreign aid, the total is actually less than 1 percent.

Sawyer, Jon, "Foreign aid is falling from favor," *St. Louis Post-Dispatch,* March 26, 1995, p. A6.
Foreign aid's fall into disfavor with the American public is examined.

Scowcroft, Brent, "Foreign aid has its uses," *The New York Times,* June 12, 1995, p. A15.
Scowcroft makes the case for foreign aid, saying that it is a fundamental instrument of foreign policy and that it is one of the three main ways in which the U.S. can exert influence abroad. He asserts that we must refocus our aid programs to make them directly relevant to our national interests.

Speth, James Gustave, "Foreign aid for the price of cat food," *The Washington Post,* Aug. 6, 1995, p. C6.
Speth, administrator of the U.N. development program, argues against the cutting of U.S. aid to poor countries, especially foreign aid that goes through the U.N., noting that such programs do not cost much for taxpayers.

"UNICEF shows the way on foreign aid," *San Francisco Chronicle,* June 12, 1996, p. A18.
An editorial says that an annual UNICEF report, released on June 11, 1996, demonstrates the importance of continued foreign aid and underscores the great benefits than even small contributions can bestow on needy countries.

Reducing Foreign Aid

"Foreign aid," *Houston Chronicle,* May 15, 1995, p. A18.
An editorial comments that Congress should not blindly slash the U.S.' foreign aid budget in an effort to reduce spending, because the result would be a profound reduction of the country's presence around the globe.

"Foreign aid is no luxury," *Chicago Tribune,* June 23, 1995, p. 20.
An editorial says it would be short-sighted and self-defeating not to promote safer, healthier, more equitable living standards globally through foreign aid spending, saying that while some cuts in such spending may be inevitable, the U.S. and other wealthy nations must continue to help so poor nations can become trading and investment partners rather than always in need of humanitarian or military intervention.

French, Howard W., "Donors of Foreign Aid Have Second Thoughts," *The New York Times,* April 7, 1996, p. 5.
The 1990s have proven a grim time for foreign aid as we know it—the grants and loans that are the traditional form of international development assistance. Everywhere these days, it seems, support for such aid is dwindling, and once-generous donors are focusing their energies inward. Alarmed by the downward spiral of their budgets, and chastened by the lack of results, many of the world's leading aid agencies have begun the most serious rethinking of their efforts since the boom days of the development aid business began in the 1960s.

Greenberger, Robert S., "As Congress sharpens knives to cut foreign aid, critics warn of damage to U.S. policy-making," *The Wall Street Journal,* May 18, 1995, p. A18.
Although foreign aid makes up only about 1 percent of overall federal spending, the Republican-controlled Con-

gress is rushing headlong toward dismantling what some Republicans contend are wasteful and failed foreign-assistance programs. Critics counter, however, that the result is likely to sharply limit the White House's ability to conduct foreign policy in a changed world.

Lippman, Thomas W., "Senate votes 10 percent cut in foreign aid," ***The Washington Post,*** **Sept. 23, 1995, p. A21.**
The 1996 foreign aid spending bill approved by the Senate, which will cut foreign aid spending in 1966 by $1.2 billion or 10 percent below current levels and give President Clinton 16 percent less than he sought, has been generally accepted by administration officials and supporters of foreign aid volunteer agencies.

'Making the most of less foreign aid," ***Chicago Tribune,*** **April 4, 1996, p. 26.**
An editorial examines the slashing that Congress is making in the foreign affairs department, saying how and where the U.S. spends its shrinking foreign-assistance dollars will have a profound bearing on the strength and reach of the nation's influence in the world.

Meisler, Stanley, "U.S. slips to 4th place in foreign aid donations," ***Los Angeles Times,*** **June 18, 1996, p. A4.**
The U.S., once the world's largest donor of foreign aid to poor nations, has slipped to fourth place, behind Japan, France and Germany, the OECD reported on June 17, 1996.

Mitchell, Jon, "Costa Rica Graduates from U.S. foreign aid," ***The Christian Science Monitor,*** **Aug. 28, 1996, p 9.**
After half a century and $2.7 billion in assistance, Costa Rica in July 1996, slipped quietly off the roster of nations receiving funds from AID. While some in the U.S. criticize foreign aid as a wasteful use of tax money, observers and residents of Costa Rica consider the program a huge success.

Moffett, George, "Skeptical Congress accelerates foreign-aid cuts," ***The Christian Science Monitor,*** **Nov. 30, 1995, p. 4.**
The efforts of the 104th Congress to cut foreign aid in late 1995, are noted. The foreign-aid bill approved by Congress appropriates $12.1 billion for the current fiscal year, some $2.7 billion less foreign aid than the amount requested by President Clinton. Post-WWII U.S. foreign aid policy is examined.

Wright, Robin, "Foreign aid hits lowest level in two decades," ***Los Angeles Times,*** **June 13, 1995, p. H1.**
In a time of mounting economic and humanitarian challenges, help in the 1990s for the world's poorest countries is steadily decreasing as rich nations follow the U.S.'s lead in cutting back on foreign aid. Half of the wealthiest nations cut their aid programs by more than a third between 1993 and 1994.

U.S. Benefits From Foreign Aid

"A net payback on U.S. foreign aid," ***Atlanta Constitution,*** **Jan. 20, 1995, p. A10.**
An editorial says the payback on U.S. foreign aid comes in the form of real money with international trade conducted between U.S. businesses and companies in the nations that the U.S. is helping, citing several examples based on research by Brian Atwood of AID.

Alpert, Bruce, "Foreign-aid cutbacks resisted," ***Times-Picayune,*** **Sept. 21, 1995, p. A9.**
As Congress considers GOP proposals to reduce foreign aid, State Department officials are fighting back with data they think will surprise people. Eighty percent of the foreign aid budget, for example, goes for consultants, manufacturers or universities in the U.S. In Louisiana, the Agency for International Development, the major dispenser of foreign aid, handed out $33.7 million in grants in 1994, the largest of which was $23 million to Tulane University.

"Foreign aid cuts draw blood at home," ***Los Angeles Times,*** **Oct. 30, 1995, p. B4.**
An editorial says Californians can expect to lose plenty of business and jobs if Congress, as expected, downgrades foreign aid as a component of government policy. The editorial says the foreign-aid bill as it stands in Oct. 1995, would mean that California could lose millions.

Greene, Marilyn, "Foreign aid, domestic concern," ***USA Today,*** **Oct. 18, 1995, p. A3.**
About 600 families in Dothan, Ala., rely on salaries from three plants that produce 510 million condoms annually for shipment to foreign nations.

"How foreign aid helps American interests," ***The Los Angeles Times,*** **May 24, 1995, p. B6.**
An editorial states that Congressional Republicans are in the process in May 1995, of decimating foreign aid, noting that Egypt and Israel would escape the proposed budget cuts. The editorial examines the need for the U.S. to assist less fortunate countries and says jobs for Americans are also at stake.

Lacey, Marc, "Foreign aid cuts could hit close to home," ***Los Angeles Times,*** **Oct. 23, 1995, p. B1.**
The U.S. AID doles out nearly 80 percent of its contracts and grants to U.S. firms, which in turn provide aid to recipient nations overseas. Cuts in foreign aid approved by Congress in 1995 could result in less business for U.S. firms, officials say.

Stewart, Jon, "Cost-effective foreign AID," ***San Francisco Chronicle,*** **Feb. 26, 1995, p. 6.**
Stewart comments that the Agency for International Development (AID) has been targeted in early 1995 by the Republican Congress for "reform," noting that a large amount of the funds for international development return to California to buy food, commodities, technology and services. Stewart debunks some myths about foreign aid.

Back Issues

Great Research on Current Issues Starts Right Here...Recent topics covered by The CQ Researcher are listed below. Before May 1991, reports were published under the name of Editorial Research Reports.

APRIL 1995
Abortion Clinic Protests
Dieting and Health
Combating AIDS
Rethinking Affirmative Action

MAY 1995
Assisted Suicide Controversy
Overhauling Social Security
Learning to Read
Mandatory Sentencing

JUNE 1995
Combating Infectious Disease
Property Rights
Repetitive Stress Injuries
Regulating the Internet

JULY 1995
War Crimes
Highway Safety
Combating Terrorism
Preventing Teen Drug Use

AUGUST 1995
Job Stress
Organ Transplants
United Nations at 50
Advances in Cancer Research

SEPTEMBER 1995
Catholic Church in the U.S.
Northern Ireland Cease-Fire
High School Sports
Teaching History

OCTOBER 1995
Quebec's Future
Revitalizing the Cities
Networking the Classroom
Indoor Air Pollution

NOVEMBER 1995
The Working Poor
The Jury System
Sex, Violence and the Media
Police Misconduct

DECEMBER 1995
Teens and Tobacco
Gene Therapy's Future
Global Water Shortages
Third-Party Prospects

JANUARY 1996
Emergency Medicine
Punishing Sex Offenders
Bilingual Education
Helping the Homeless

FEBRUARY 1996
Reforming the CIA
Campaign Finance Reform
Academic Politics
Getting Into College

MARCH 1996
The British Monarchy
Preventing Juvenile Crime
Tax Reform
Pursuing the Paranormal

APRIL 1996
Centennial Olympic Games
Managed Care
Protecting Endangered Species
New Military Culture

MAY 1996
Russia's Political Future
Marriage and Divorce
Year-Round Schools
Taiwan, China and the U.S.

JUNE 1996
Rethinking NAFTA
First Ladies
Teaching Values
Labor Movement's Future

JULY 1996
Recovered-Memory Debate
Native Americans' Future
Crackdown on Sexual Harassment
Attack on Public Schools

AUGUST 1996
Fighting Over Animal Rights
Privatizing Government Services
Child Labor and Sweatshops
Cleaning Up Hazardous Wastes

SEPTEMBER 1996
Gambling Under Attack
The States and Federalism
Civic Journalism

Future Topics

- ***The Business of Politics***
- ***Insurance Fraud***
- ***Rethinking School Integration***

THE CQ Researcher©

PUBLISHED BY CONGRESSIONAL QUARTERLY INC.

Political Consultants

Are advisers and handlers harming democracy?

That political animal known as the consultant has come a long way since the days when faceless advisers stood discreetly behind candidates and whispered folksy suggestions. Today, no campaign is fully written up without profiles of those media-savvy gurus who sometimes float above party loyalty. But consultants — who rose to influence along with television — get blamed for many of the political system's problems. Critics say the professionalization of politics encourages negative campaigning, escalates campaign costs, reduces debate on the issues to sound bites, corrupts the science of opinion polling and even reduces once-eager campaign volunteers to spectators. Consultants respond that responsibility for their decisions must be borne by the candidate, and that they are paid, first and foremost, to win.

INSIDE

THIS ISSUE

CQ Oct. 4, 1996 • Volume 6, No. 37 • Pages 865-888

Formerly Editorial Research Reports

Political Consultants

COVER: BARBARA SASSA-DANIELS

Oct. 4, 1996
Volume 6, No. 37

The CQ Researcher (ISSN 1056-2036). Formerly Editorial Research Reports. Published weekly (48 times per year, not printed March 1, May 31, Aug. 30, Nov. 29) by Congressional Quarterly Inc., 1414 22nd St., N.W., Washington, D.C. 20037. Annual subscription rate for libraries, businesses and government is $319. Additional rates furnished upon request. Periodicals postage paid at Washington, D.C. POSTMASTER: Send address changes to The CQ Researcher, 1414 22nd St., N.W., Washington, D.C. 20037.

Political Consultants

BY CHARLES S. CLARK

THE ISSUES

In the 1790s, politics gave America George Washington, John Adams and Thomas Jefferson. In the 1990s, politics has given the nation . . . Dick Morris? Ed Rollins? James Carville? It is only a slight exaggeration to say that political battles in the United States today are waged more by paid consultants than statesmen.

"The most influential private citizen in America," *Time* called Morris, President Clinton's politically ambidextrous chief adviser, in a Sept. 2 cover story. A week later, Morris again made the magazine's cover, this time after a scandal involving a prostitute forced him to resign. In the weeks thereafter, commentators handicapping the 1996 presidential election continued their debates over whether Morris, Rasputinlike, had been too influential in moving a liberal-leaning Clinton to the political center. [1]

In the rival campaign of Republican Bob Dole, the consultants made their presence felt beginning in July, after Dole ran into a rough patch after making some unscripted comments. Among them: revealing uncertainty about the dangers of tobacco, and spurning an invitation to address the NAACP.

"I've taken my vow of silence," the former Senate majority leader said with a grimace as he followed his handlers' command to avoid taking questions from reporters. Soon there were leaked reports that Republican strategists — even those on Dole's staff — were disappointed in the candidate's public speaking, and that feuding had erupted among the Dole team.

"It used to be that every campaign had one principal consultant the candidate would spend time with, whom he understood, who was on the same wavelength, who would govern the other consultants," says Doug Bailey, publisher of the on-line political news service "Hotline," who helped run the 1976 presidential campaign of Republican Gerald R. Ford. "Dole has got every consultant known to man tied in some way to his campaign, and it's not clear how it's set up. They may have conflicting views and egos, but no one person gets close to Dole. From time to time, someone appears to be in charge, then something happens and another one pops up. It looks like all of them will get their 15 minutes of fame."

In what might be called the "year of the consultant," the public recently got a glimpse of the darker side of politics with the tell-all memoir by former Republican strategist Rollins, *Bare Knuckles and Back Rooms: My Life in American Politics*. Rollins angered many in the political world by, among other things, heaping scorn on candidates whose campaigns he had mentored. He branded Ross Perot "an extremely dangerous demagogue . . . who would have been a disaster in the White House." He called California businessman Michael Huffington, who ran unsuccessfully for a Senate seat in 1994, and his wife Ariana, "two of the most unprincipled political creatures I'd ever encountered."

The impact of consultants on politics is evident in the frequent use by the press of lingo that began as insider-speak: "sound bites," "spin doctors," "theme of the day," "photo opportunity" and, most recently, "message modules." "Lots of the coverage of politics is like sports coverage," says Todd Gitlin, a professor of sociology at New York University. "It invites the reader to become a connoisseur of dugout maneuvers by the candidates and their handlers acting like coaches at a chalkboard. The readers become fans of the process by which their impressions are being managed; they become appreciators of their own bamboozlement."

Since its rise as a profession in the 1960s, political consulting has ballooned into a billion-dollar-a-year industry that services up to 50,000 national, state and local campaigns every year. Around the country, some 7,000 professional consultants market expertise in campaign management, polling, advertising, direct-mail and fund-raising, according to Ron Faucheux, editor and publisher of *Campaigns and Elections* magazine. (Counting part-timers, the number of consultants may be closer to 35,000, says Peter Levine, a University of Maryland research scholar.)

Of the nearly half-billion dollars spent on congressional elections in 1994, 46 percent went to consultants, according to Dwight Morris, a researcher on campaign spending in Springfield, Va.

"The most significant change in consultants is their indispensability," says Larry J. Sabato, a University of Virginia government professor. "Back in the 1950s, they were rare, except at the presidential level. Then in the '70s you got consultants for senators and governors, and in the '80s, consultants in House races. Now you have them for ballot referendums, and every race for state legislature and city council."

Campaign consultants have their own professional organization, and consulting has even become an academic discipline. At American University, the Campaign Management Institute offers a two-week program taught by strategists and professors imparting insight into scheduling, strategy, theme and message. George Washington University, also in Washington, offers advanced degrees at its Graduate School of Political Management.

The field has also spawned its own specialized products. "Get Ready Now for the Post-Election Gold Rush," says an ad in *Campaign and Elections* soliciting entries for a political consultants' directory. Washington-based Aristotle Industries sells "campaign manager software" as well as databases with "Enhanced Voter Lists," which help campaigns weed out inactive voters and identify "fat cat" donors.

With campaigns stretching ever-longer over the calendar, consultants have stepped in with more in-depth and detailed research. Some is aggressive, delving into opponents' credit histories, adoption records or sex lives, using information from ex-spouses and "moles" inside opposing campaigns. There are now more than 40 firms specializing in opposition research, and their number has grown by 200 percent in the 1990s, according to Sabato.[2]

Many observers say it is no coincidence that the consulting field has exploded in the same period the country has seen a loosening of party loyalty, an electorate made passive through television and a drastic decline in voter turnout. The percentage of eligible voters who participate fell steadily from 63 percent in 1960 to 50 percent in 1988, before upticking to 55 percent in 1992, according to the *Statistical Abstract of the United States*. Only 5 percent of adults are politically active, and the percentage of Americans who designate $3 on their tax returns for election financing was only 17 percent in 1992.[3]

Whether this alienation can be linked to the rise of consultants is an often-asked question. Critics decry the strategists' encouragement of candidates to speak in slogans and "sound bites," which have been reduced by TV news shows from an average of 43 seconds in 1960 to about eight seconds today, according to the Free TV for Straight Talk Coalition, a new group advocating free airtime for candidates. (*See "At Issue," p. 881.*)

Critics also note how campaigns now devote most of their budgets to 30-second TV spots. Spending on political TV ads has risen from $24.5 million in 1972 to $299.6 million in 1992, and is expected to hit a half-billion dollars this year, according to the National Association of Broadcasters. In 1992, candidates Clinton and George Bush spent 60 percent of their budgets on TV ads, providing a sizable commission from each spot for their consultants.

"Voters are fed up with TV politics," two former leaders of both major parties, Republican Frank J. Fahrenkopf Jr. and Democrat Charles T. Manatt, wrote this spring. "The media, too, are critical of the system they helped create. And we, as former chairmen of the Republican and Democratic parties, can attest that politicians themselves don't like the current situation."[4]

Reuters/Peter Morgan

Dick Morris and his wife, Ellen McGann, at their Connecticut home after he resigned as a campaign strategist for President Clinton following reports of his relationship with a prostitute.

Similarly, the proliferation of polls — from news media, private pollsters and advocacy sponsors — has saturated the electorate and opened new avenues for manipulation (*see p. 878*). "Back in 1952, there were 10 polls overall, and now you have 10 a week," says Sheldon R. Gawiser, president of the National Council on Public Polls. "In 1996, this adds to the despondency of the Republican camp because every day there's a new poll showing them 20 points down."

Consultants themselves, not surprisingly, see broader forces at work. Consultants are merely stepping into a gap, they argue, opened by the decline in party loyalty, the increase in party primaries, the rise of independent candidates and technological changes in communication.

"While it is true that more campaigns have switched from kitchen advisers to the professionally trained, consultants are also more visible today," says Victor Kamber, president of the Kamber Group, a public relations firm in Washington. "And one reason they are so much a part of the story now is that we live in an age of news." Decades ago, the TV news used to be a half-hour or an hour, counting national and local, but today there are two and three hours of time to fill with features, he notes.

Paul Taylor, a former *Washington Post* political reporter who quit this year to launch the Free TV for Straight Talk Coalition for the Pew Charitable Trusts, is reluctant to finger consultants or any other single group as culprits for the sorry state of debate. "All of the major actors in our grand pageant of democracy are bringing out the worst in each of us," he says. "It's a vicious cycle, made cynical by the way we do campaigns, which triggers a certain set of rewards and penalties. For consultants, all the rewards are in 30-second attack ads. More often than not, it works, and if I were in the consultants' shoes, I would want to win the election. That's the political marketplace."

As the role that consultants play is analyzed in the weeks leading up to and after the 1996 elections, these are some of the key questions that will be asked:

Are consultants harming the political process?

"We are the pre-selectors. We determine who shall run for office." So declared Patrick Caddell, famed as chief pollster for President Jimmy Carter, speaking of the new consultant kings in the early 1980s.[5] These unelected powerbrokers, however, are not always regarded as a blessing.

The University of Virginia's Sabato, author of *The Rise of Political Consultants* (1981), says the central problem is that consultants make candidates "too responsive to public opinion" rather than encouraging them to lead. "They rely on negative campaigning that drives down turnout, and they produce homogenized campaigns, like Holiday Inns and McDonald's, where a campaign in Idaho is like one in Pennsylvania, with the same consultant, the same slogans."

Consulting has become such a big business that the message sent to voters is that "a campaign is for the pros, and the rest of us are spectators," Sabato adds. What's more, "all the blue smoke and mirrors necessary to win a campaign are not necessarily the same as the tools needed to govern successfully."

Evidence that negative advertising diminishes turnout was supplied in a recent academic study of Senate races in 12 states during 1992. In states in which candidates ran basically positive campaigns, turnout was 57 percent; in states with a mixture of positive and negative campaigns, turnout dropped to 52.4 percent; and in states with basically negatively run races, turnout was only 49.7 percent.[6]

Consultants also have been shown to have used ads to surreptitiously manipulate reality. In 1992, independent right-wing activist Floyd Brown used doctored photos to make Clinton and liberal Sen. Edward M. Kennedy, D-Mass., appear to be raising their joined hands. That same year, consultants working for Republican presidential candidate Patrick J. Buchanan made ads with speeded-up or slowed footage of rival George Bush to make him look physically clumsy.[7]

Surprisingly, some political ads have become outrageous enough to draw the wrath of Madison Avenue. In a recent speech, Burt Manning, chairman of the American Association of Advertising Agencies, noted with alarm an opinion poll showing that the percentage of Americans who want more government regulation on truth in advertising had risen from 49 percent in 1993 to 63 percent in 1995. He called on political consultants to emulate commercial advertisers by setting up their own self-regulating process to monitor accuracy and fairness.[8]

Consultants also take raps from advocates of campaign finance reform, who see them as driving the cost of campaigns ever higher.[9] "Consultants certainly benefit from unrestricted spending," says Paul Hendrie, managing editor at the Center for Responsive Politics. "They push the prevalent theory that large blocks of TV ads" are the way to campaign, and in "states with major media markets, the high costs of campaigning will make candidates there less receptive to spending caps."

The increasing use of technology dangled in front of candidates by electronic-age consultants also gives pause. The Perception Analyzer, for example, an instrument sold for $9,000 by Columbia Information Systems in Portland, Ore., allows a candidate to deliver a speech and gauge the emotional reactions of a dozen average citizens in a focus group. If the listener likes a word or phrase, he turns a dial toward

'I Couldn't Work for Both Parties'. . .

In nearly 40 years as a political consultant, Matt Reese has watched the world of politics evolve from a system of party machines and smoke-filled rooms to today's array of superstar handlers armed with computer databases and instant polling. Reese first gained notice for delivering the state of West Virginia for John F. Kennedy's presidential campaign in 1960. Having perfected the "block captain" system of door-to-door voter contact, he went on to become director of operations for the Democratic National Committee (DNC) and to supervise President Lyndon B. Johnson's 1964 voter registration and get-out-the-vote drives. Since setting up Reese Communications in 1966, he has run some 500 campaigns, including those of Sen. Edward M. Kennedy, D-Mass., Sen. John Glenn, D-Ohio, and Sen. John D. "Jay" Rockefeller IV, D-W.Va. He has supplied public affairs counseling to numerous Fortune 500 companies and has directed political campaigns in the Philippines, Costa Rica and Venezuela. He is a past president of the American Association of Political Consultants. Reese spoke with CQ Researcher *staff writer Charles S. Clark on Aug. 20 at his home in McLean, Va.*

Political consultant Matt Reese

What do you think is the most important change in politics in the last 30 or 40 years?

Number one, the party has disappeared as the runner of campaigns. When I got started back in the 1950s, campaigns for governor, president or whatever were left to a county, ward or party precinct captain. That's all gone, probably even in Chicago. Although the party has important functions now, that is not one of them.

Then there's the incredible technology. I mean, I still think in terms of 3-by-5 cards, but I have learned to use the instant response of the computer and the variations it allows you. Certainly targeting/polling is so much more sophisticated than it was. We are now able to read down to the four-square-block area the demographics of what kind of folks live there, what kind of bathtubs they have, how many cars, how much education, how much money, what is their ethnic background — and we can poll them. We used to say things are good on the North Side and bad on the South Side, or that certain areas were 'golden precincts,' whatever that was, but the targeting can be so superb it's almost scary as to what you can do to communicate/manipulate.

Next is the means of communications. Not only television, but the Internet and cyber-whatever. Communication is instant and omnipresent. Finally, the negative attack has proved so successful. It's used not because politicians are any meaner than anyone else, but because the damn stuff works.

Will negative campaigns be used more in the future?

I think they will be used a little less, a little more skillfully, at any rate. No longer can we just call our opponents [bad names]. People today are so cynical, and, though the politicians have helped make them that way, they made the politicians the way they are, too. They won't elect them if they tell the damn truth. So they get a candidate of good quality like Bob Dole, who tells them pie-in-the-sky crazy stuff [about balancing the budget while cutting taxes].

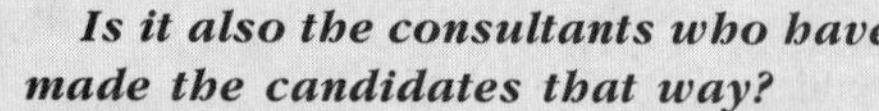

Is it also the consultants who have made the candidates that way?

Sure. We know the people better than the politicians do. We know what moves them better than the politicians do. We know how to deliver messages better than politicians do.

Is there any danger of the modern candidate being overshadowed by his handlers, particularly if the consultants talk to the press?

It has happened many times. The media talk about [longtime consultants] Bob Squire and Roger Ailes on Main Street at high noon ready to shoot it out. Who was the candidate? No one remembers, and neither Bob nor Roger will tell you. I love to see great stories about me in the press, but I didn't like it much when they said nasty things. And I got in trouble a time or two with my candidates. But look at [Bill Clinton's 1992 strategist] James Carville. He's made a million dollars talking to the press, hasn't he? Carville's a sweet, interesting guy, but knowing him when I knew him, you'd never think he'd be on an American Express ad. I get fund-raising mail *from him* for the president. It means he has a better name than [DNC chairmen] Don Fowler or Chris Dodd, or Jimmy Carter or half a dozen other people. So a lot of times the

the number 10; if he reacts negatively, he turns it toward zero.

"People may not like this," acknowledges Mark Mellman, a Democratic pollster. "There is a certain Orwellian potential. People think everything is being choreographed to how they respond. They're not wrong. But in a democracy, there's no inherent reason a politician has to say something in a way that turns people off." [10]

The methods of opinion polling increasingly are being slanted by slick pollsters to gain an advantage for a candidate or to provide backing for a

. . . Veteran Political Consultant Matt Reese Says

consultants are more interesting than the candidates. And a lot of consultants know how to work the press.

Have a lot of consultants gotten wealthy?

When I got into this in the mid-1960s, there were probably 25 consultants in the country. What we had to do was convince the campaign that they needed a consultant, and for 10 years I never went up against another consultant. Now there's thousands. Are all of them making lots of money? No. Are all of them good? No. It's like a sports team. There are some who are probably overpaid. It's hard to lose your reputation once you make it. You also have to work for a candidate everybody's heard of. [Former House Speaker Thomas P.] "Tip" O'Neill, [D-Mass.] and Ted Kennedy would have won had I never been born, but everybody's heard of them. You have to win, so part of that is picking your candidates. And occasionally you have to win campaigns that you weren't supposed to win.

What do you think of modern consultants, like [recently departed Clinton strategist] Dick Morris, who work for both parties?

I don't know how people trust you if you work for both parties. I couldn't do it. I didn't always get the one I wanted to work for, but I never worked for anybody I wouldn't vote for.

Are there candidates who wouldn't take your advice?

It happens all the time. Or they appear to take your advice and don't. I think my success in consulting was an ability to *oomph* them, as I call it. I could resell them, and you have to constantly. They're buying magic, and that's what I sold, but when you ain't got none, then it's hard and sticky work. So you have to resell the magic when they begin to not believe. One of the values of a consultant is he will intelligently, hopefully, describe a way to go. I would come in on a big, white horse with a stone tablet on my arm and say, 'God wrote this, and this is what you have to do.' Yeah, it's silly, but it worked for me.

The party conventions are becoming more and more controlled to avoid spontaneity. It this a big part of the consultant's job?

Who wants confrontations and fights in-house? You try to cover those up. You try to compromise, you try to say let's hold off. But anybody with any sense knew what was happening at [this year's] Republican convention. The 1968 Democratic convention was very interesting, wasn't it? Who won the election? The 1972 Democratic convention was very interesting. Who won the election? The 1992 Republican convention was very interesting. Who won the election?

Does the consulting community have any obligation to the public to offer substance in a campaign?

I get upset at the cynicism of the American voters, but I am also amazed at their duplicity. They want to believe there's someone who can cut taxes by 15 percent, increase defense including the 'Star Wars' thing, balance the budget and create a thriving economy. We all want that, so someone comes along and says, I'll do that for you. And if he says it nicely, they'll say OK. The political consultants' duty is to win. Now, most of us attempt to do it with honor. My problem always was when I make the case, which I always do in writing, I believe it, I convince myself. I think just like a lawyer when he does a brief. He's trying to tell everything that is good about his client and everything that is bad about his opponent, and doing it makes him *feel* it.

Is it true that many politicians who are good at campaigning are not good at governing?

That's a stereotype, like blacks have rhythm and fat men are jolly. I mean, if a person can't manage a campaign, how can he manage his state? It's a nasty business, like making sausage. Having to campaign changes people. Take John Kennedy. What was the first thing he did when he got to the White House? His executive order No. 1 was food stamps for people in Appalachia. Why, here's a Boston socialite many times a millionaire, but during the campaign he saw hungry kids for the first time in his life. So it helps a candidate for office to have to go through the line getting spanked with paddles.

Do handlers make voters feel like spectators rather than participants?

I don't think voters are aware or care that handlers are running political campaigns. I think they're interested for a few minutes in late October, and if you can get them, then all the stuff you do before is preparing yourself to get them then.

Is the name of the game to bamboozle voters?

Of course not. If you understand voters, after some experience with them you understand that they want simple answers to complex problems. All the simple problems have been solved. It's not that voters are dumb, it's just that they don't want to listen. My job is to convince, to persuade. The way you get people to do what you want them to do is through repetitive, persuasive contact. To simplify it to the 18 seconds that you have their attention, sometimes it becomes bamboozling. But bamboozling is what your opponent does. *You* are informing.

preconceived notion. "More pollsters today are advocates who don't have a professional reputation to maintain," says Gawiser. "Even if one is a Republican or Democrat, you still don't want to be known for cooking the stuff."

Gawiser and others cite conservative polling guru Frank Luntz, who gained fame for "test-driving" the legislative planks being considered for the House Republicans' "Contract with America" in 1994. Luntz announced at the time that each of the 10 items had about 70 percent popular support, but last November *The Miami Herald* revealed that Luntz had not actually polled on the contract's provisions, but had merely conducted focus groups, which primarily had been asked for their reaction to sugar-coated slogans. For example, "We should stop excessive legal claims, frivolous lawsuits and overzealous lawyers" was translated into a contract plank to limit the collection of punitive damages. [11]

Finally, there is the ever-present issue of consultants who shield their candidate from unscripted contact with the news media. Dan Balz, a *Washington Post* reporter covering the Dole campaign, speaks of "a continuing point of tension over the amount of time Dole is made accessible. Dole has held no press conferences with reporters since the Florida primary [in March]. There have been a few shouted questions, and there were some TV interviews following his [July] departure from the Senate, but they haven't allowed free-floating questions with follow-up."

Balz finds it astonishing that Dole hasn't appeared on NBC's "Meet the Press" since December 1995, when previously he had been the show's most frequent guest. "The handlers' view is that the candidate is better off not being subjected to press questions," Balz says. "But a guy running for president has an obligation to make himself available on a regular basis."

Dole deputy press Secretary Christina Martin counters that Dole has been very accessible, saying he is followed so closely "by a pool of reporters that he can't even drop off his laundry. Because of the number of reporters, we have to keep them on a separate platform so that Dole can reach his audience, but that doesn't curtail their ability to ask questions," she adds. "Any candidate will make an effort to stay on message. The idea is not to cut off access, but to respond on message."

Complaining of a lack of candidate spontaneity sounds good," says Kamber, but "Thomas Jefferson [may have] had a black mistress, and if his handlers had allowed it to become a major factor, would we now see him as the leading thinker that we do? A consultant looks to put the candidate's best foot forward. In any campaign, the press tries to ferret out news, while the candidate is packaged to make news less likely, and the opponents try to ferret out a weakness. They're all sort of adversaries, but no one point of view is right or wrong."

"I had star quality, and I had people interested in meeting me as much as meeting the candidate."

—Ed Rollins
Republican strategist

The suggestion that consultants are to blame for 30-second attack ads is rejected by consultant Bailey. "It's the fault of a lot of people," he says. "Consultants have contributed mightily to the mess politics is in, but on the other hand, we have dealt with the world as we found it. Prime-time TV is where the numbers [of viewers] are, and they want things in 30 seconds. Everything on TV is totally confrontational. If you want to produce a soft spot showing a candidate walking by the river, a couch potato will use his clicker at the sound of the first violin and go off to watch professional wrestling or exploding volcanoes."

A big change in the culture from 20 years ago, Bailey adds, is that there is less risk of turning people off by running negative ads; indeed, the failure to respond to an opponent's negative ad will accord it credibility. "It is much easier to run a negative ad to get the voter to go against your opponent than it is to run a positive ad and get the voter to vote for you," he says. "To persuade someone to vote for your candidate requires a complex combination of issues and personalities. But one 30-second spot can get a voter to vote against your opponent. You can do it with a silver bullet."

Commercial advertising's distaste for political ads is a "classic case of the pot calling the kettle black," says Tom Edmonds, a Republican media consultant and chairman of the American Association of Political Consultants. "They sell beer to teens, they say nicotine is not addictive. Look at the ads for MCI vs. AT&T and tell me that is not a negative ad. Political consultants control the 5 percent of the advertising that Madison Avenue doesn't control, and they want to clean that up."

"What's really going on is that they're upset because we work in the autumn when they have new products and model lines," Edmonds adds. "We get the lowest prices, and that throws a grenade into their marketing plans."

Edmonds also rejects the charge that consultants have homogenized political campaigns, pointing to a rising number of regional specialists.

Many consultants scoff at criticism that the professionalization of politics has discouraged volunteers. "TV is extraordinarily expensive and takes technological know-how," says Bailey.

"Mrs. Jones and her teenage kids can't go down to the congressman's corner headquarters and volunteer to make his TV spots."

Gary Nordlinger, a Democratic consultant who chairs the consultants' association ethics committee, sees modern candidates and their consultants as "small businesses. They run in primaries, and if they win, they have the franchise. This is good for democracy because it puts constituents ahead of the party. Candidates still find their own volunteers in interest groups such as the National Education Association or the Christian Coalition," he says. "Besides, in the old days, volunteers came with strings attached. The party machines had to give them a turkey, some coal, or some whiskey, and later, a patronage job. As disorganized as the system is now, it is cleaner than it was 20 years ago."

The consulting field does have some unethical and sleazy members, Nordlinger continues, just as the fields of law and public relations do. "The big difference in our industry is it's done out in public, with expense reports filed. Ethics issues are decisions for the candidates to make." Like lawyers advising a client, "Consultants simply say, if you do it this way, you have a better chance to win."

A point in the consultants' favor is that most candidates clearly value them. "I like having a manager who runs my campaigns, and if I don't have someone who is clearly in charge, I have problems," says 1988 Democratic presidential candidate Michael S. Dukakis, now teaching at Northeastern University. "You have to have someone for advice on things like media, and we had an in-house polling operation that was as accurate as any you could hire. I never felt hemmed in or frustrated by handlers."

On the contrary, Dukakis' chief regret about his unsuccessful campaign was the failure to respond to the Bush campaign's attacks on such unforeseen issues as prison furloughs. "That issue was as phony as a $3 bill, but obviously we did not handle it right because of our inexperience, which is partly my fault. The kind of research and information it takes to respond to tough attacks should have been done in advance, not just to counter them but to turn the opponent's attack into a character issue for him," Dukakis adds. "Clinton's people learned a lot from what we didn't do in 1988, and they did a nice job of blunting the Bush attacks in 1992."

Faucheux of *Campaigns and Elections* says the system's woes should be pinned not on consultants, or the press, or on interest groups, but on technology. "Technology is driving everything — the increased costs, the quickening pace, the need for real-time response," he says. In addition, opposing sides in a political battle increasingly are wont to hire consultants to one-up the other side. "There's a saying that every election has a campaign, but not every campaign has an election," he adds. "Ten years ago, issues such as gambling and the North American Free Trade Agreement would have been decided in back rooms and boardrooms. Now everything is done in public debate."

Do political consultants upstage the candidates?

"I had star quality, and I had people interested in meeting me as much as meeting the candidate," Republican strategist Rollins said in explaining why he boasted, untruthfully, he later said, of spending money to suppress black voter turnout in the 1993 New Jersey governor's race. [12]

Consultant Carville and his wife, Mary Matalin, a former political director to President Bush, made the point in their best-selling campaign memoir that media coverage of their Romeo-and-Juliet intraparty romance became a factor in the 1992 election. Matalin recalled resentfully that her political enemy/future husband used the news media to "look like a good guy, saying nice things about me, but it was really a backhanded way to keep the story alive and keep the [Bush] campaign off our game and off our message." [13]

More substantively, Stan Greenberg, the vaunted Clinton pollster/adviser who was paid $2.7 million over 14 months only to watch in dismay as Democrats lost Congress, became the center of post-mortem analysis of the 1994 elections. *Newsweek* writer Howard Fineman, when asked what Clinton should do to rebuild his political fortunes, zeroed in immediately on getting rid of Greenberg. [14]

Portrayals of consultants as the candidates' "puppetmasters" have become standard in modern campaign coverage. Part of the explanation, says Sabato, is that consultants have large egos and often harbor deep professional jealousies. "One reason they get to believe they're the important people is that part of their job is to keep the candidate on message, to prevent spontaneity," he says. "God forbid that we might find out what the candidate really thinks."

The brassiest of the handlers sometimes approach the press, on a not-for-attribution basis, to criticize their own candidate's performance. "Every campaign that doesn't go well has some staff members who will blame the candidate," says Balz. "They get frustrated, so they decide to openly to send a message to the candidate to pay more attention to skills."

The self-important tendencies of consultants are also dramatized in the fact that some have worked for candidates of different parties. Numerous big-name consultants — Rollins, Luntz and former Carter operative Hamilton Jordan — worked for Perot's presidential effort in 1992. And when Luntz left, disgusted (and unpaid), Democrats tried to recruit him.

The most notable example of switch-hitting consultants is Morris. Since working with Democrat Clinton when he was Arkansas governor in the 1980s, Morris has signed on with such prominent Republicans as Sens. Jesse Helms of North Carolina and Mississippi's Trent Lott and California Gov. Pete Wilson. Indeed, in 1991, Morris worked simultaneously for Mississippi Republican gubernatorial candidate Pete Johnson and Democratic Lt. Gov. Brad Dye. [15]

Morris' recent role in bringing Clinton back from threatened oblivion infuriated Republicans, who attacked him as a "Svengali," or "President Morris." "The Founding Fathers did not have Dick Morris as their consultant," sniffed New York's Republican Gov. George E. Pataki. [16]

Clinton insiders such as Chief of Staff Leon E. Panetta argue that Morris was merely one consultant among many, noting that the president's decision not to try and match Dole's proposed 15 percent tax cut evidenced his independence from Morris. Still, Clinton-Gore deputy campaign Manager Ann Lewis asked Morris to avoid talking to the press, because it suggested that it is not the president making the final decisions.

"I know Clinton, and he's the person in charge, not Morris or [Clinton's veteran media consultant Robert] Squier," Dukakis says. "There are few elected leaders who are smart enough to run their own operation, and [Vice President Al] Gore is no slouch, either."

Consultants who try to work both sides are likely to be distrusted by party loyalists reluctant to share sensitive information such as polling data and strategies. "Few kids grow up saying they want to be political consultants," Nordlinger says. "You fall into it, after starting as a staffer or partisan operative, so you already have an allegiance. It's a referral business, and you can't be meeting with progressives in one campaign and then go and tell all to another."

The industry does place some value on loyalty, notwithstanding the "tales out of school" from Rollins and the public carping from the Dole team. "Consultants who accept a candidate's money and then turn around and trash that candidate are nothing but trash themselves," Nordlinger says.

The charge that consultants eclipse their clients ignores the fact that many politicians are too stubborn to be led around by the nose, others say. "I can't imagine anyone handling [former Connecticut senator and governor] Lowell Weicker," says Kamber. "He's a bull in a China shop who listens to advice and then makes his own decision. Perot is another who is not handleable."

"The articles always say how powerful consultants are, but consultants will tell you that there are 20 candidates who don't listen for every one or two that do," Faucheux says. "And candidates don't have just one consultant. There's usually a group that is at odds with itself. The process is usually rancorous, with yelling and screaming from all sides."

And when it comes to dirty tricks, consultants say, the candidate can be more to blame than the handler. "All candidates at first say they want a clean, positive election," Nordlinger says. "But after the first rock flies, they say, 'Gary, give 'em all you've got,' and I have to restrain *them*. Candidates don't take orders from consultants. They can only get so far up the political food chain without having some sense of their own self and beliefs."

Republican adviser Edmonds says he can work with a candidate who rejects his advice, but it is harder. "I just worked with a Senate candidate who lost a primary because he was not willing to compromise his pro-choice position on abortion," Edmonds says. "I said, 'Fine, I respect that, and I'll have to find another way to help you win.' I probably could have gotten him elected [doing it my way], but like a lawyer who believes his client might be guilty, I had to try to get him off on a technicality."

Consultants also argue that blind loyalty to a politician might tie them too closely to that candidate's fate. Candidates often fire consultants when things go wrong, they point out. Dole, for example, after his unsuccessful presidential bid in 1988, rated Ronald Reagan's superstar pollster Richard Wirthlin as "Dr. Worthless."

Even so, the typical consultant's free-lance modus operandi — political participation while rarely taking responsibility for the post-election challenge of governing — leads many consultants to betray a subtle hubris. "When reporting to the president, you put on a happy face," writes former Clinton confidant Carville. "That's the politics of politics. Nobody wants to be the bearer of bad tidings. You've either got a happy face to cover your butt or a happy face because, in your presentation, you have just saved him from a near-death experience he never knew of in the first place." [17] ■

BACKGROUND

Plato Paves the Way

The first political consultants, the American Association of Political Consultants asserts, emerged in ancient Greece and Rome. They had names like Aristotle, Plato and Quintus Cicero, who wrote a "Handbook of Electioneering" for Romans in 63 BC. The more modern historical model for a political strategy paper was *The Prince,* written in 1532 by Italian philosopher Niccolo Machiavelli.

In the United States, political campaigns traditionally have been noteworthy for their domination by party machines and volunteers. When William Henry Harrison and John Tyler won the White House in 1840, their "Tippecanoe and Tyler Too" campaign

Continued on p. 876

Chronology

1930s-1940s

First professional consultants and pollsters set up shop.

1936
Famous readers' poll by *Literary Digest* errs in picking Republican Alf Landon to beat Democratic incumbent President Franklin D. Roosevelt, paving the way for pioneer pollster George Gallup.

1948
Republican presidential candidate Thomas Dewey and his team succumb to major error of overconfidence and lose election to incumbent Harry S Truman, putting egg on pollsters' faces, too.

1950s ***National parties still play key role in selecting presidential candidates at conventions.***

1952
Republican Dwight D. Eisenhower becomes the first presidential candidate to rely on television ads, defeating the less-telegenic Adlai Stevenson.

1960s ***With presidential primaries proliferating and television dominating campaigns, consultants working for candidates begin offering private services.***

1960
Time-Life journalist Theodore H. White publishes first insider look at campaign handlers in *The Making of the President 1960.* John F. Kennedy's campaign becomes first to use computers and first to bring a pollster into a candidate's inner circle.

1965
White's *The Making of the President 1964* is published.

1968
Divisive Democratic convention in Chicago prompts rules changes shifting influence from open conventions to primaries. Republican presidential candidate Richard M. Nixon becomes first to hire admen and PR men to fashion his new image.

1969
Publication of *The Making of the President 1968* and journalist Joe McGuiness' *The Selling of the President,* exposing Nixon consultants who sell candidates like soap; founding of American Association of Political Consultants and National Council of Public Polling.

1970s ***National party influence continues to deteriorate.***

1972
Publication of White's *The Making of the President 1972.* Robert Redford stars in "The Candidate," a film about an empty-suit politician created by handlers.

1976
"Washington outsider" candidate Jimmy Carter wins presidency, aided by media consultant Gerald Rafshoon and "theme" pollster Patrick Caddell.

1980s ***Campaigns become increasingly visual and emotional, while candidates are shielded from spontaneous dialogue.***

1984
Republican President Ronald Reagan runs evocative "Morning in America" TV ads, beating Democratic challenger Walter F. Mondale, whose ads adopt the more pragmatic "Teach Your Children" theme.

1988
Republican presidential candidate George Bush uses ads attacking Democrat Michael Dukakis for his prison furlough program and pollution in Boston Harbor. Independent production of influential anti-Dukakis ad featuring rapist Willie Horton stirs controversy.

1990s ***Consultants become celebrities.***

1993
"The War Room" documentary makes stars of Bill Clinton presidential campaign strategists James Carville and George Stephanopoulos.

February 1996
At Republican Iowa caucuses, presidential campaign managers admit they're using "push poll" phone campaigns that pose as opinion polls while spreading damaging information about opposing candidates.

Aug. 29, 1996
Top Clinton strategist Dick Morris resigns after tabloid reports he had affair with a prostitute and let her eavesdrop on calls to president.

Trade Secrets of Direct-Mail Campaigning . . .

"We were flying under their radar." That's how direct-mail wizard Richard A. Viguerie describes the surprise success Republicans had in derailing the Clinton administration's ill-fated health-reform plan in 1994.

"We [in the conservative movement] said that health care would be the biggest battle since the [1977] debate over the Panama Canal," he recalls, "and that if there were a new middle-class entitlement to health care, we wouldn't survive."

So Viguerie's Fairfax, Va.-based consulting firm blanketed right-leaning small donors across the nation with an estimated 18 million mailings featuring dire rhetoric about government-run health care. "The Left didn't see it coming, and the media wasted their time interviewing people like Sen. John Chafee" of Rhode Island, he says gleefully of the successful effort. For weeks, members of Congress were barraged with angry postcards, phone calls, personal visits, letters to the editor and calls to radio talk shows blasting the Clinton plan.

Viguerie rose to prominence as political mail czar for the early Ronald Reagan for president movement, but since then he has largely kept out of the limelight. However, his American Target Advertising Co. still cranks out 75 million pieces of mail each year for conservative clients.

"Most issues that can be worked with direct mail are populist, conservative issues such as taxes," he says. "Not a lot of mail goes out opposing Bob Dole's proposed 15 percent tax cut, or arguing for increased government regulation. About 80 percent focus on such populist issues as crime, school prayer, a balanced budget and drugs. The Left can't really raise money by mail."

Yet the Left, be it the Democrats, liberal advocacy groups or public interest nonprofits, is certainly doing its share to create a steady flow of work opportunities for a national industry of some 3,000 direct-mail specialists.

"Will Michigan 'Gingrichize' the Senate?" asks the cover of a recent mailout from the re-election campaign of Sen. Carl Levin, D-Mich., alluding to his opponent's putative similarities to the controversial House Speaker. "Your voice can make a big difference in breaking the National Rifle Association's choke hold on Congress," announces an appeal from Handgun Control Inc.

"Direct mail is a polarizing sort of activity," says Bill Brent, a direct-mail consultant in Arlington, Va., who has worked for numerous Democratic and independent candidates. "It's tough to get people moved or excited, so your client needs something to compare himself against, some kind of devil who is nationally known."

Favorite foils used in Demo-cratic mailings have included conservative Sen. Jesse Helms, R-N.C., Reagan's Interior Secre-tary James Watt and, particularly this year, House Speaker Newt Gingrich, R-Ga.

Conservatives like to stir up their true believers using references to liberal Sen. Edward M. Kennedy, D-Mass., and openly gay Rep. Barney Frank, D-Mass. Viguerie expects the next conservative foil to be AFL-CIO President John J. Sweeney.

Language is very important in direct-mail letters, whether it is for purposes of persuasion or fund-raising, Brent says. "You

was run by handlers, who relied on an army of free-whiskey-guzzling volunteers to pack their rallies. [18]

Credit for bringing Abraham Lincoln to the national stage in 1860 went to political clubs called the "Wide Awakes," who wore special caps and organized torchlight parades when Lincoln traveled to New England. "After the campaign opened," wrote one biographer, "there was scarcely a county or village in the North without its organized and drilled association of Wide Awakes, immensely captivating to the popular eye, and forming everywhere a vigilant corps to spread the fame of, and solicit votes for, the Republican presidential candidate." [19]

During the next century, the national parties gained supremacy, developing powerful machines in cities such as Chicago and Albany, N.Y. Only occasionally did ad hoc entrepreneurs become national players. In 1940, for example, the presidential candidacy of businessman Wendell Willkie was primarily the fruit of a draft movement set in motion by a petition circulated in *Fortune* magazine by a young New York lawyer. [20]

. . . 'Get People to Open the Envelope'

use short, punchy sentences and lots of I's and You's to keep it personal. You have to hook people in the first paragraph because much of direct mail is never read. The trick is getting them to open the envelope with clever teasers." Reliable fire-alarm words include "ultra-right" and "pro-union," he says.

Direct mail is also a tactile medium, which means that details down to the texture of the paper are important in "bonding with the recipient and creating a relationship that hopefully is symbiotic," Brent says. Much persuasion mail is "just preaching to the choir, but it still educates people on how they might think about an issue."

Increasingly, both Repub-licans and Democrats are using "involvement" tools such as surveys, which flatter the recipients by asking for their opinions, but which also ask for donations. Direct-mailers can also boost response to fund-raising appeals if they add personal touches such as postscripts to letters and use actual stamps instead of postage meters, Viguerie says.

One risk with direct mail is that after all the expense of renting a mailing list, writing, designing, printing and postage, a major event can unfold that renders the mailing obsolete. Brent cites the mailout for Democratic presidential candi-date Gary Hart just before he dropped out of the race in a 1987 sex scandal. There was also the National Republican Congressional Committee anti-tax mailout launched in 1990 on the day President George Bush broke his campaign pledge not to raise taxes.

Candidates, it seems, often feel their campaigns are not complete without a direct-mail component, even though they often don't work, Brent says. Because political campaigns frequently have cash-flow problems, direct-mail contractors often insist on payment in advance.

The invention of the direct-mail strategy, Viguerie says, came about when he was new to politics in the 1950s and '60s, and conservative strategists were frustrated that the "biased" news media were ignoring their issues. "We decided, rather than curse the darkness, that we would light a candle," he says. The first successful direct-mail race was the 1969 special election that brought conservative Rep. Phil Crane, R-Ill., to Washington. "We soon found, as *National Review* founder William Rusher put it, that like Hannibal, we had found a pass through the Alps," Viguerie says.

In the mid-'70s, Viguerie took on the National Right to Work Committee as a client and sent out some 4 million letters to generate opposition to a bill in Congress expanding picketing rights for labor unions. It brought more than 700,000 cards to Congress and, after candidate Reagan took up the cause, played a big role in pressuring President Gerald R. Ford to reverse an earlier position and veto the bill. By the time of Reagan's successful run for the White House in 1980, Viguerie says, it was clear that direct mail worked for non-elite candidates who attracted grass-roots donations of $10, $15 or $50. Except for television, it became the most important campaign tool, he says.

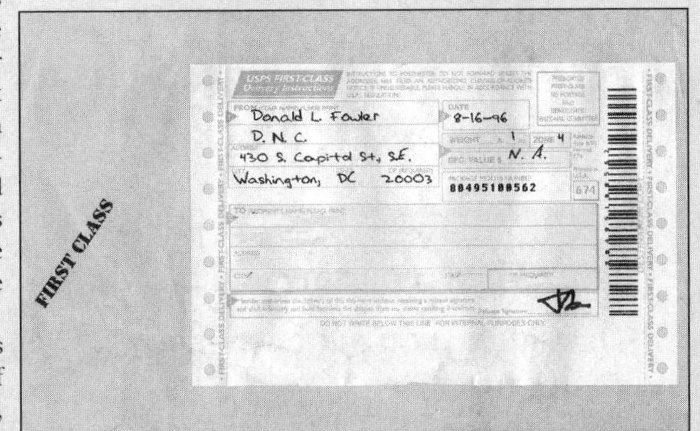

Some direct-mail campaign materials come disguised as priority mail to get voters to open them.

"Almost all my mail encourages people to do a number of things — to call, or write or vote, or pass the mailing on to their neighbors and send $10 to pay for it," he says. "It advertises a cause, a candidate and the need for money all in the same message."

The U.S. Postal Service estimates that the average household received 4.68 political mailings in 1994. Viguerie believes that Republicans, at least, will be sending out more mailings than ever. "People have been saying the market is saturated for 30 years," he says. "But direct-mail professionalism is increasing, and so is the practitioners' ability to identify people's interests so that they receive only the mail they really want."

Birth of an Industry

The first consulting business in the United States is thought to be the firm established in the 1930s in California by a husband-wife team of advertising professionals, Clem Whitaker and Leone Baxter. For two decades, their firm presided over some 75 major campaigns, among them state ballot referendums and the gubernatorial campaigns of Republican Earl Warren. [21]

In the late 1930s and '40s professional pollsters such as George Gallup and Elmo Roper set up shops as full-time analysts of electoral trends. Their elite fraternity was joined by regional pollsters such as Mervin Field in California, who began to meet annually at Gallup's New Jersey farm.

By the 1950s, the presidential campaigns of Dwight D. Eisenhower and Adlai E. Stevenson were employing advertising men and ghostwriters. But these early consultants toiled mostly outside the public eye.

It wasn't until the 1960s that the occasionally discomfiting "sausage-making" of a political campaign was unveiled to the public in all its moral complexity. *Time-Life* journalist Theodore H. White, in what became the quadrennial series *The Making of the President,* documented the 1960 presidential race between John F. Kennedy and Richard M. Nixon with more behind-the-scenes detail than ever before, such as Kennedy's voice lessons and Nixon's decision not to wear TV makeup during the first debates.

"Campaign scheduling is an art in itself," White wrote. "Each day, each minute of a candidate's time is counted, from the moment he launches his campaign until he goes to bed on election eve. To use that time most effectively, schedules have to be meshed and geared with political need, with the requirements of time and transportation, with the shepherding of a herd of newsmen and staffmen at the candidate's heels, with the feuds and sensitivities of all local political leaders.

"Advance men — the small teams of operatives who arrange tours for major candidates — are practitioners of one of the most complicated skills in American politics; a good advance man must combine in himself the qualities of a circus tout, a carnival organizer, an accomplished diplomat and a quartermaster general." [22]

End of Innocence

The 1968 election was a turning point for political consulting. Republican presidential candidate Nixon, seeking to reinvent his image as the exiled loser of the 1960 race, brought in a team of advisers — not from politics but from the news media and Madison Avenue. Luminaries such as CBS News executive Frank Shakespeare and TV producer Roger Ailes persuaded Nixon that television — far from being a cheap gimmick — was the key to winning elections. It was particularly effective if the candidate avoided handling substantive questions from the press or from audiences and took policy positions designed mostly to jar the opponent.

"When reporting to the president, you put on a happy face. That's the politics of politics. Nobody wants to be the bearer of bad tidings."

—James Carville
former Clinton strategist

What's more, this revolutionary advice was later captured by journalist Joe McGuiness in an eye-opening follow-up to White's books, *The Selling of the President 1968.*

"Politics has nothing to do with running for office," said a member of Nixon's advisory team. "When you run for office, there is a product, the candidate, and people who buy the product. It's a market, and you can get a list of all the customers, the registered voters. The dumbbells in politics don't understand this." [23]

Nixon's opponent, Vice President Hubert H. Humphrey, hired Springfield, Mass., consultant Joe Napolitan. He had helped JFK win key primaries in 1960 and had even helped elect Ferdinand E. Marcos president of the Philippines. A specialist in survey techniques, Napolitan made dramatic recommendations that Humphrey could not agree to, such as breaking with President Lyndon B. Johnson's efforts to continue the Vietnam war; and he pleaded unsuccessfully with Humphrey to debate Nixon on TV.

Following Nixon's narrow victory, the new political handlers — now subject to increased public scrutiny — were saddled with a negative image. It was Napolitan who spotted the need for a professional organization to counter the criticism and develop bipartisan industry guidelines. He teamed up with Republican strategists F. Clifton White and Stuart Spencer and several Democrats, among them consultants Robert Squier and Matt Reese and pollster Bill Hamilton, to form both the American Association of Political Consultants and the International Association of Political Consultants. "We're all good friends in this business," Napolitan said. "The guy you're fighting against today may be the guy you're working with tomorrow. And there are no real secrets in consulting, anyway." [24]

By the early 1970s, there were some 300 political consulting firms plying the trade. The motives for joining the field were explored by social scientist James Q. Wilson. In a survey of consultants, 76 percent said they got into consulting because "politics is where the action is," and 80 percent said they were attracted because "we make good money in political campaigns," but only 50 percent agreed with the statement, "We have a civic responsibility to use our skills for the public good." [25]

Decline in Substance?

The 1970s brought more personalities to prominence. Hal Evry, a Republican public relations man who also worked for presidential candidate George Wallace, gained a reputation as the "enfant terrible" of consulting for openly defending campaign gimmicks and unrestrained spending. "The more money a candidate spends, the more likely he is to win," he once said.[26]

Carter's campaigns were guided by two men who became household names: Media adviser Gerald Rafshoon (satirized by Garry Trudeau for manipulative "Rafshoonery" in the comic strip "Doonesbury") and pollster Caddell, a wunderkind since he polled for leaders of the Florida Legislature while a senior in high school in 1968. Caddell is credited with providing overarching themes for Carter (among them, a national "malaise"), and it was his polling that revealed during the 1980 campaign that attacks from the detail-oriented Carter against Reagan's perceived ignorance on the issues would backfire.

By this time, election postmortems commonly adopted the consultants' perspective, more often viewing the conduct of the campaign than its substance. "Carter's people just did not know how to run as incumbents," said Spencer. "There wasn't any consistency in their campaign. They played hatchet ball one week and high road the next."[27]

The Reagan camp's own superstar pollster, Wirthlin, gave consultancy the "hierarchical values map," which divided polling data on issues into color-coded charts. In 1984, his research showed that Democratic candidate Walter F. Mondale would win if the main issues of the campaign were the Equal Rights Amendment to the Constitution, abortion, poverty and fairness. Reagan would win if the top issues were working to build "a better America and preserve world peace" and "make U.S./World a better place for future generations."

"Wirthlin will not reveal what survey designs and statistics he used to create the model, implying that to do so would be to reveal some statistical invention that would help his competitors," writes historian David W. Moore. "Keeping the method secret can avoid embarrassing critiques, and perhaps the recognition that there is indeed much less than meets the eye."[28]

"Downplaying the conventions would take the soul out of politics — pretty soon there will be no people participating, and all politics will be conducted by mail or computer."

—Michael K. Deaver
former Reagan adviser

The Reagan strategists' reliance on emotional, visual advertising with lots of American flags flapping in the breeze gave rise to a famous episode in the continuing clash between political handlers and the press. In 1984, CBS News correspondent Lesley Stahl broadcast a hard-hitting report on alleged hypocrisy in the Reagan campaign. Her spot juxtaposed footage of a Reagan speech on mental disabilities given at a Special Olympics event with a voice-over pointing out that Reagan had cut funding for mental health. White House strategist Richard Darman subsequently called Stahl and praised her work. The puzzled newswoman replied: "Did you hear what I said? I killed you." "You television people still don't get it," Darman countered. "No one heard what you said. Don't you people realize that the picture is all that counts. A powerful picture drowns out the words."[29]

After losing the election, Mondale declared bitterly that "American politics is losing its substance. . . . It's losing the depth that tough problems require to be discussed, and more and more it is that 20-second [sound bite] snippet."[30]

In the 1988 campaign, strategists dealt with the "issues" by having their candidates visit flag factories or ride in an Army tank, or by raising racial fears by highlighting the case of Willie Horton, the furloughed black prisoner who raped a white woman. It was then that substance hit an all-time low, according to veteran journalist Marvin Kalb, director of the Joan Shorenstein Center on the Press, Politics and Public Policy at Harvard University.

"The press responded slowly to this evolving new fact of campaign life," Kalb says. "Teddy White, who had so much to do with creating this way of covering politics, had long ago said he'd made a terrible blunder. Reporters' approach of looking for small, behind-the-scenes issues about who's doing what to whom set up a sort of triangle with the candidate, the press and the handlers. The press and the handlers tended to see each other as more important than the candidate." ■

CURRENT SITUATION

Lock-Step Conventions

Nowhere was the modern political handler's handiwork more visible than at the 1996 national party conventions. With every speech and video carefully scripted — *Time* magazine referred to the Republican gathering in San Diego as "the Stepford convention" — the press corps whined in frustration at the absence of "news," such as intraparty conflict on sticky issues such as abortion or welfare reform. Citing poor ratings, the networks began floating the possibility that coverage of future conventions would be scaled back.

Such grousing is unfair, according to Michael K. Deaver, the former Reagan White House adviser who helped run this year's GOP convention. "A lot of the criticism of things like 60-second sound bites comes from the TV news people, as if the handlers created those. But it was the TV networks who came to us a year ago and said we could have one hour of prime time on Monday through Wednesday and two hours on Thursday. So we created the convention for the bottom line of commercial TV, knowing that we're competing with 50 other channels."

Deaver, now an executive at Edelman Public Relations Worldwide, also argues that the networks gave the Democratic convention in Chicago more airtime simply because the Democrats were "undisciplined and disorganized and went over their allotted time."

Downplaying the conventions "would take the soul out of politics — pretty soon there will be no people participating, and all politics will be conducted by mail or computer," Deaver complains. "Conventions are a get-together, a reward system for participating in democracy. There were ways this year to see the proceedings gavel to gavel, and I know a lot of people used their clicker to get rid of the commentary. As for the objection that there was no news, that's because the reporters didn't get off their duffs. I knew of at least 20 stories I was afraid some of them would find, but they didn't. The networks say they're in the news business and that we're in entertainment, but they haven't been in news for 20 years. If they were, why are they judged by their ratings?"

Straight Talk

To restore substance to political discourse, Deaver and many broadcasters and academics favor "straight talk," or comments from candidates on key issues unadorned by music, visuals or surrogates. In reaction to pressure from public broadcasting and the Free TV for Straight Talk Coalition, most networks are planning to provide time for straight talk this fall.

ABC plans a one-hour prime time special in the campaign's final week, while NBC and CBS plan to put candidates more regularly on existing news programs. PBS plans to help its 344 member stations allot several minutes every day at the same time to candidate talk. The Fox network, meanwhile, has been allotting 10 minutes to each candidate on a list of issues, plus an hour on election eve. [31]

Kalb says he likes this year's plan for quick but regular segments "in theory, but in practice it has the effect of minimizing opportunities for substance. You need to block out hours at a time," he says. "In a $1\,{}^{1}/_{2}$-to-2-minute statement, the handlers can still tell the politician how to perform." In 1991, the Shorenstein Center at Harvard proposed a straight-talk plan that would have offered 90 minutes to candidates every Sunday for nine weeks.

Consultant Bailey calls straight talk "an extremely important reform that could, along with the presidential debates, dominate the campaign." But it will only work, he says, if all the networks are willing to "roadblock," or carry the candidates' message at the same hour to prevent channel changing. "I'm all for one-hour talk shows," he adds, "but the viewers have to tune them in. You can still say a lot in two minutes, not by sneaking up on the viewer, but by providing an important message broadcast in a convenient way."

Consultant Edmonds says the straight-talk requirements are "as dangerous as suspending the Constitution. It amounts to playing God and standing between the elected officials and the voting public."

Spending Limits

Though straight talk can be a good way to open communications, it should not, says Faucheux, "be a substitute for paid ads, a Trojan Horse for campaign spending limits."

Political consultants have long held complicated views on efforts to curb the high cost of campaigns, Faucheux says. Many of them view regulations enacted in the early 1970s as unproductive, he notes, but they did not speak out against the current system because it lets them make plenty of money.

Consultants defend their freedom to spend a candidate's money in ways they think will win elections. They go to great lengths to market their expertise in the highly technical area of campaign finance disclosure law and ad buying. But they also own up to being one of the reasons that politicians constantly have to chase money.

"Too many consultants, both Democratic and Republican, hire inexperienced 'buyers' to spend millions of dollars," Jan Ziska Crawford,

Continued on p. 883

At Issue:

Do political consultants harm the electoral process?

YES

PETER LEVINE
Research scholar, Institute for Philosophy and Public Policy, University of Maryland

FROM *PHILOSOPHY & PUBLIC POLICY,* SUMMER/FALL 1994

In past generations, political party officials played a major role in electoral campaigns: They chose candidates, raised money and provided expertise, labor and voter lists. Today the parties play a diminished role, but political consultants often operate in their place. Consultants design and produce broadcast advertisements and mass mailings; they conduct fund-raisers and contact donors; they maintain lists of voters and contributors; they manage campaign logistics; and they write speeches and position papers. They are major repositories of political experience and employers of skilled labor. . . .

The profound influence of consultants invites us to ask whether we should blame them for the rise of certain kinds of campaign tactics that alienate American voters. Admittedly, few of the disturbing aspects of modern campaigns were invented by consultants. Personal attacks, lavishly funded advertising campaigns, the reliance on divisive "hot-button" issues and similar tactics were all present before the first consulting firm was founded in 1934. . . .

Nevertheless, it appears that consultants have reasons to favor and encourage certain unsavory tactics that are now endemic to the political system. In part, this is because for-profit political experts have their own interests, distinct from those of candidates, activists, parties and voters.

For example, many politicians are motivated by strongly held beliefs and policy commitments, and not only by the ambition to win elections. Though candidates often try to evade politically difficult questions, some will risk defeat rather than ignore or finesse the issues that prompted them to run in the first place. But the subculture of professional consultants is famous for a general lack of interest in ideology or the legislative process. . . .

The consultants' indifference to issues would not matter if candidates set the agenda. But in a recent survey of consultants, 44 percent agreed: "When it comes to setting issue priorities, candidates are neither very involved nor very influential." If candidates relinquish leadership in choosing issues, then consultants presumably fill that role. . . .

They will select a campaign theme on the basis of polls and focus groups, and then concentrate on wooing the swing vote through commercials and mass mailings. . . . Thus they are adept at using rhetorical formulas that discourage reflection and discussion, that freeze public opinion in place and that polarize and inflame voters.

NO

JOSEPH R. CERRELL
Past president, American Association of Political Consultants

WRITTEN FOR *THE CQ RESEARCHER,* SEPTEMBER 1996

'Tis the season. No, we're not talking about Christmas, Thanksgiving or New Year's Eve, but the 1996 campaign season. It's a time when visions of electoral victory, not sugarplums, dance in the heads of candidates and, yes, their political consultants. In the wake of Ed Rollins' book and the Dick Morris "affairs," the hue and cry has arisen, once again, about whether or not we need political consultants.

This plaintive wail, which is usually reserved for the domain of Beltway pundits and never-been-in-the-real-world academicians, once again misses the point. As a consultant who's been in the business since 1958 and who is most proud of my profession and track record, let me be the defender of the faith and make the case for our noble craft by offering these bordering-on-cliché:

Top 10 Reasons Why We Need Consultants

1) To protect candidates from themselves, most of the time.

2) To make campaigns infinitely more interesting, professional and organized.

3) To bring a picture of the real world to candidates.

4) To give Beltway pundits something to write and talk about.

5) To protect the campaign from the candidate's wife, partner and/or significant other.

6) To know the candidate better than the candidate does.

7) To contribute to the gross national product and keep lots of people gainfully employed, including ivory tower academics.

8) To have someone handy who has forgotten more about media, mail, fund-raising and strategy than most candidates will ever know.

9) To know how to spend campaign money better than anyone.

10) And because consultants can handle being fired, most of the time.

Finally, I thank all the candidates and causes who have hired me and my colleagues over the years, helped provide for our families and who have added to the democratic debate. And to those who continue to decry our business and call for curbs or even the elimination of our profession, I offer one parting shot: Just think how much you'd miss us if we were gone!

As Politics Go, So Go Campaign Buttons

Exactly 100 years ago, the modern political campaign button was born. Since backers of presidential candidate William McKinley wore his portrait on buttons promising a "full dinner bucket," these evocative autumn perennials have become more high-tech, more raunchy and, thanks in part to consultants, more removed from official campaigns.

"It used to be that the political parties bought up buttons and gave them away," says Nelson Whitman, president of Capitol Stamp and Coin Co., a Washington dealer in campaign buttons, past and present. "But the arrival of television advertising and computers has meant less money for buttons, so now the parties only give them out in return for donations."

John Cranford

Voters, however, continue to expect campaign buttons, just as they do bumper stickers and patriotic balloons. So an industry of private vendors has emerged to satisfy the demand — for the sacred *and* the profane.

A most jarring change in buttons of recent vintage, Whitman says, is that the most popular ones are negative or vulgar, such as "Neuter Newt," directed at controversial House Speaker Newt Gingrich, R-Ga., and not-so-subtle allusions to President Clinton's alleged sexual indiscretions.

"It was about three months after the inauguration that these anti-Clinton buttons began selling like crazy, probably due to scandals such as Travelgate and Whitewater," Whitman says. "They still sell well, and people put them on right in the store, while with the positive buttons they usually walk out with them in a bag."

This spring, however, Clinton's political fortunes improved, as measured both in opinion polls and in the market for political paraphernalia. Political Americana, with six outlets in the Washington area, had planned to open a new store carrying items targeted at both Democrats and Republicans. "But the popularity of the Clinton-Gore ticket is now much higher, so we ended up doing the store for Democrats only," says Director of Operations Linda Cobb. The majority of buttons are sold to individuals and collectors, though county parties occasionally place bulk orders.

Americans since George Washington's time have decorated their lapels with printed political statements. But in the early days, the items were made of cloth that often was homemade, and most commemorated sitting presidents or events such as the inauguration rather than political campaigns. The first buttons used as vote-chasing gimmicks appeared in 1840, when William Henry Harrison and John Tyler won the White House with the slogan "Tippecanoe and Tyler Too."

Harrison's buttons were coin-like tokens that could be worn in a buttonhole. By the 1860s, with the invention of photography, black-and-white portraits were added to these metalplate tokens, which were then called "ferrotypes." Within a few elections, photos were commonly being mounted on cardboard or paper that could be pinned to the wearer's clothing.

In 1893, the first patent was granted for a process that wrapped celluloid over a metal disc that was fastened using a pin on a separate metal ring. This was the campaign button as it is known today. In the 1920s, portrait reproduction was enhanced through the use of lithographs on the buttons. And most recently, this once-elementary concept has been embroidered to create buttons with pop-up or moving parts, blinking lights, holograms or even tape-recorded messages.

A Clearwater, Fla.-based organization called American Political Items Collectors publishes a newsletter and magazine and organizes trading conventions. Button cognescenti toss off such terms as "jugate," which is a button featuring the faces of two candidates, and "trigate," which shows three faces, often including a congressional candidate hoping for a coattail effect from the national ticket. Collectors also divide into purists, who insist on official campaign buttons only, and more broad-based collectors who accept "vendor" buttons because official ones are often colorless and ugly.

The most valuable button, said to be worth up to $50,000, dates from 1920 and features unsuccessful Democratic presidential candidate James M. Cox and his running mate, Franklin D. Roosevelt.[1]

The most common collectibles are "Nixon Now" buttons from the 1972 campaign, and a series of Wendell L. Willkie buttons created by the dozens of Willkie clubs that sprang up when the relatively unknown businessman challenged incumbent Roosevelt in the 1940 presidential campaign.

Campaign buttons reveal much about America's past, and not all of it is flattering. When New York Gov. Al Smith ran for president in 1928, anti-Catholic opponents put out an anti-Smith button that called for "A Christian in the White House." Opponents of Roosevelt's ground-breaking bid for a third presidential term produced buttons that read: "Washington Wouldn't. Lincoln Couldn't. Roosevelt Shouldn't."

What is clear is that the national political climate is often reflected in the political button industry. "As America's interest in politics declined after Watergate, so did the frenzy of collectors," writes button expert Mark Warda. "It did not pick up until 1992, when Americans were excited again by the prospect of a serious third party, and Democrats were excited by the first chance in years of regaining the White House."[2]

---

[1] Mark Warda, *100 Years of Political Campaign Collectibles* (1996), p. 8.

[2] *Ibid.*, p. 165.

Continued from p. 880

a board member of the American Association of Political Consultants, told Congress this year. "Strategic time-buying includes knowing the law and maximizing every dollar raised. Given that most consultants are paid on a percentage basis, there is no incentive to keep media expenditures down." [32]

Kamber points out that consultants could probably find loopholes in any new laws limiting advertising expenses. Makers of political spots, for example, currently charge the candidate a percentage of what they spend to buy airtime, but they don't charge for their creative or production costs. If new laws required networks to provide free airtime, the consultants would simply begin charging for creating and producing the candidates' ads, he says.

FOR MORE INFORMATION

American Association of Political Consultants, 900 Second St. N.E., Suite 217, Washington, D.C. 20002; (202) 371-9585. Founded in 1969, this bipartisan organization of nearly 1,000 professionals holds annual conferences and administers a code of ethics for association members, whom it refers to as "informal officers of the nation's democratic electoral system."

Campaign Management Institute, American University, 4400 Mass. Ave. N.W., Washington, D.C. 20016; (202) 885-6247. Founded in 1983, this academic training program offers courses in conducting local, state and federal election campaigns.

The Joan Shorenstein Center on the Press, Politics and Public Policy, John F. Kennedy School of Politics and Public Policy, 79 John F. Kennedy St., Cambridge, Mass. 02138; (617) 495-8269. The center conducts research and offers fellowships for the study of such issues as the media's role in the electoral process. It has been active in seeking to restructure political campaigns to provide more substantive debate.

National Council on Public Polls, Suite 300, 1375 Kings Highway East, Fairfield, Conn. 06430; (800) 239-0909. Founded in 1969, this group of polling organizations strives for high standards of professionalism while working for greater understanding of polls by the news media, politicians and the public.

Push Polls

The 1996 campaign has laid bare one of the dirty tricks of the consulting world, the practice of "push polling." In a February appearance on the "The Larry King Weekend" show, a group of Republican campaign managers in Des Moines for the Iowa caucuses acknowledged that some of their contractors had phoned households under the guise of conducting an opinion poll, and then planted negative information about an opposing candidate.

Push-polling traces its roots to Nixon's first run for Congress in the late 1940s, Nordlinger says, when Nixon campaign workers made anonymous calls telling voters that Nixon's opponents were Communists. In more recent times, it was used in the Florida gubernatorial race in 1994, to the embarrassment of successful candidate Lawton Chiles. What is different today, Nordlinger says, is technology that permits computers to dial thousands of households at a rapid pace, and then efficiently route only the consummated calls to a campaign employee ready to read from a script. Phone banks can now blitz entire areas at a third the cost of such operations just a few years ago.

The practice of asking the recipient of a call whether he would still vote for a candidate if he knew, for example, that he cheated on his taxes, is not easily detectable, unless a household that received such a call complains to the press. Push polling occurs because "politics frequently encourages a win-at-all-costs mentality," says Bailey. "What seems an easy moral dilemma from the outside doesn't seem wrong when you're in the midst of it, so you push ahead."

This spring, the National Council on Public Polls and the political consultants associations condemned "this abuse of legitimate public polling" as thinly disguised telemarketing. The Clinton campaign has pledged not to use the practice. The Dole campaign, which paid more than $1 million to New York City-based Campaign Tel Ltd. to do push polling during the primaries, declined to make such a promise. [33] ■

OUTLOOK

Ideals vs. Reality

The national consultants association has a code of professional ethics that requires members to vow that they "shall not indulge in any activity which would corrupt or degrade the practice of political campaigning."

But as they continue to gain prominence in politics — indeed, consulting American-style has become a lucrative export to such countries as England, France and the former Soviet Union — ideals do not always match reality. Dick Morris, following his recent fall from grace with former clients of both parties, has been rewarded by Random House with a seven-figure book contract. Others are building empires and reputations that will no doubt prompt awe in those who will someday need them — the politicians. (During non-election years, consultants increasingly are marketing services to private corporations dazzled by their political connections.)

Most have ready responses to charges that they have damaged political discourse with manipulative strategies and 30-second attack ads. Political ads, says Deaver, simply reflect the fact that most Americans get their political information from TV. "Television has dumbed down America in every aspect, not just politics. That's why the ads appeal to the lowest medium of interest and intellect."

Overall, says Faucheux, "voters don't care about consultants and frills; they assume every campaign has them. They are turned off by the candidates' hypocrisy, broken promises and partisanship."

Former candidate Dukakis recalls the time in 1988 when he gave a key environmental speech at Rutgers University only to see the evening news focus instead on the fact that one of his Secret Service cars got a flat tire. "You can't blame consultants — it's the craziness of an election, and the media's incessant search for the new and the visual."

"The whole process is intertwined," says Edmonds. "Perception and reality lines are blurred. Do we take a poll or a position first? It's a chicken or egg situation. Ultimately, it's up to the candidate to have core convictions. You can't blame the people around him." ■

Notes

[1] For background, see "Political Scandals," *The CQ Researcher,* May 27, 1994, pp. 457-480, and "Politicians and Privacy," *The CQ Researcher,* April 17, 1992, pp. 337-360.

[2] See Larry J. Sabato and Glenn R. Simpson, *Dirty Little Secrets: The Persistence of Corruption in American Politics* (1996), p. 155. Simpson is a reporter for *The Wall Street Journal.*

[3] See column by Richard Harwood, "All-Pro Politics," *The Washington Post,* March 23, 1996.

[4] Op-ed column in *The Wall Street Journal,* April 10, 1996.

[5] Roland Perry, *Hidden Power* (1984), p. 230.

[6] Stephen Ansolabehere and Shanto Iyengar, *Going Negative: How Attack Ads Shrink and Polarize the Electorate* (1995), p. 108.

[7] Darrell M. West, *Air Wars: Television Advertising in Election Campaigns, 1952-1992* (1994), p. 153.

[8] Speech at annual meeting of American Association of Advertising Agencies, April 26, 1996.

[9] For background, see "Campaign Finance Reform," *The CQ Researcher,* Feb. 9, 1996, pp. 121-144.

[10] Quoted in *The New York Times,* Aug. 26, 1996.

[11] *CQ Weekly Report,* Nov. 25, 1995, p. 3622.

[12] Quoted in *The Washington Post,* Dec. 5, 1993.

[13] Mary Matalin and James Carville, *All's Fair: Love, War, and Running for President* (1994), p. 283.

[14] Quoted in Eleanor Clift and Tom Brazaitis, *War Without Bloodshed* (1996), p. 35.

[15] See James A. Barnes, "In the Shadows," *National Journal,* July 20, 1996, p. 1568.

[16] Quoted in *The New York Times,* Aug. 14, 1996.

[17] Matalin and Carville, *op. cit.,* p. 439.

[18] Gil Troy, *See How They Ran* (1991), p. 30.

[19] Jane Dick, *Volunteers and the Making of Presidents* (1980), p. 8.

[20] *Ibid.,* p. 19.

[21] David Lee Rosenbloom, *The Election Men* (1973), p. 44.

[22] Theodore H. White, *The Making of the President 1960* (1961), p. 271.

[23] Quoted in Rosenbloom, *op. cit.,* p. 67.

[24] Quoted in David Chagall, *The New Kingmakers* (1981), p. 375.

[25] Rosenbloom, *op. cit.,* p. 95.

[26] Quoted in Chagall, *op. cit.,* p. 298.

[27] *Ibid.,* p. 294.

[28] David W. Moore, *The Super Pollsters: How They Measure and Manipulate Public Opinion in America* (1992), p. 219.

[29] Quoted in James Fallows, *Breaking the News: How the Media Undermine American Democracy* (1996), p. 62.

[30] Quoted in Troy, *op. cit.,* p. 252.

[31] *The Washington Post,* Aug. 22, 1996.

[32] Testimony before the Senate Rules and Administration Committee, May 15, 1996.

[33] *The Wall Street Journal,* March 12, 1996.

Bibliography

Selected Sources Used

Books

Bennett, W. Lance, *Governing Crisis: Media, Money and Marketing in American Elections,* St. Martin's Press, 1992.
A University of Washington political scientist with a speciality in journalism examines the consequences of the country's move into an era of campaign media sound bites and Madison Avenue politics.

Matalin, Mary, and James Carville, with Peter Knobler, *All's Fair: Love, War and Running for President,* Random House, 1994.
The celebrity political consultants who faced off against each other in the 1992 election, and later married, have produced an entertaining blow-by-blow account of life in the eye of the campaign storm.

Chagall, David, *The New Kingmakers,* Harcourt Brace Jovanovich, 1981.
A California-based writer conducted interviews with many of the big names who built the field of political consulting, among them Joe Napolitan, Hal Evry, Stuart Spencer and Matt Reese.

Clift, Eleanor, and Tom Brazaitis, *War Without Bloodshed: The Art of Politics,* Scribner, 1996.
A *Newsweek* contributing editor and the Cleveland *Plain Dealer* Washington bureau chief profile key actors in Washington's current political dramas, offering insights into the work of pollsters, lobbyists, members of Congress and congressional staff.

Dick, Jane, *Volunteers and the Making of Presidents,* Dodd, Mead, 1980.
This specialized history by a former U.S. adviser at the United Nations tracks the influence of volunteer groups in selecting political candidates before the decline of parties and the rise of political consultants.

Hernson, Paul S., *Congressional Elections: Campaigning at Home and in Washington,* Congressional Quarterly, 1995.
A University of Maryland political scientist produced this portrait of how modern congressional campaigns are run, with bountiful data on spending and fund-raising involving paid consultants.

Jamieson, Kathleen Hall, *Packaging the Presidency: A History and Criticism of Presidential Campaign Advertising,* 2nd Edition, Oxford University Press, 1992.
The dean of the Annenberg School of Communications at the University of Pennsylvania examines the use and abuse of political advertising from the early 1950s to the 1990s.

Moore, David W., *The Super Pollsters: How They Manipulate Public Opinion in America,* Four Walls Eight Windows, 1992.
A University of New Hampshire political scientist profiles several major pollsters, among them Lou Harris, Patrick Caddell and Mervin Field, examining such issues as how the wording of questions — the addition of the word "big" before the word "business" — for example, dramatically alters results.

Perry, Roland, *Hidden Power: The Programming of the President,* Beaufort Books, 1984.
Written from a European's perspective, this discussion of prominent political consultants features interviews and profiles of practitioners such as Jimmy Carter pollster Patrick Caddell and Ronald Reagan guru Richard W. Wirthlin.

Rosenbloom, David Lee, *The Election Men: Professional Campaign Managers and American Democracy,* Quadrangle Books, 1973.
A Hamilton College political scientist produced one of the earliest studies of the history, impact and future of political handlers, including a discussion of whether they are a threat to democracy.

Sabato, Larry J., and Glenn R. Simpson, *Dirty Little Secrets: The Persistence of Corruption in American Politics,* Times Books, 1996.
A University of Virginia government professor and a *Wall Street Journal* reporter team up to expose the less savory side of modern politics, including candidate use of such controversial tools as "push polling" and opposition research.

Troy, Gil, *See How They Ran: The Changing Role of the Presidential Candidate,* The Free Press, 1991.
A McGill University political scientist produced this historical survey of political candidates and their relation to the public, the media and their handlers. He tracks campaigning from the days when leaders felt they were too dignified to campaign to the modern era of 30-second TV ads.

The Next Step

Additional information from UMI's Newspaper & Periodical Abstracts database

Direct Mail

Teepen, Tom, "The politics of hysteria in your mail," *Atlanta Constitution,* May 16, 1995, p. A9.
Teepen comments on the hysterical prose being circulated in direct-mail fund-raising literature, suggesting that it is eclipsing the opportunity for discourse in which common ground among opposing interest groups might be found.

Weber, Tracy, "The Darth Vaders of direct mail," *Los Angeles Times,* March 3, 1996, p. A1.
William Butcher and Arnold Forde, two political consultants who call themselves the "Darth Vaders of Direct Mail," made a fortune mailing out political scare letters, reaping donations and renting out names of donors, all without running afoul of the law.

Negative Advertising

Budiansky, Stephen, "Tune in, turn off, drop out," *U.S. News & World Report,* Feb. 19, 1996, pp. 30-32.
A recent study has found that the damage done by negative campaigning is far graver than previously assumed. The real problem with negative advertising is that it suppresses voter turnout.

Elliott, Stuart, "Advertising agencies make a pitch to politicians and consultants, urging them to clean up their act," *The New York Times,* April 29, 1996, p. D27.
In an innovative initiative to reduce the personal attack and invective in political advertising, U.S. advertising agencies will urge broadcast and print media to assume watchdog duties during the 1996 election campaign season. The effort is motivated by growing fear among agency executives that the product advertising they create for the marketers is increasingly damaged by the growing public disdain for negative political advertising.

Goodman, Adam, "Producing TV: A survival guide," *Campaigns & Elections,* July 1995, pp. 22-24.
Seven "commandments" for creating, producing and using hard-hitting campaign ads are discussed. There is often a fine line between negative advertising and comparative advertising — what sets the two apart is tone.

Poor, Tim, "Digging up dirt gets nastier in American politics," *St. Louis Post-Dispatch,* June 30, 1996, p. A7.
The increasing use of negative advertising and personal attacks has provided an expanding market for knowledge about almost every aspect of a candidate's life. There are few limits now on what information is obtained — or how.

Sheckels, Theodore F. Jr., "Mikulski vs. Chavez for the Senate from Maryland in 1986 and the "rules" for attack politics," *Communication Quarterly,* summer 1994, pp. 311-326.
The status of rules governing attack politics is examined. The 1986 Maryland Senate race between Barbara Mikulski and Linda Chavez did not follow the normal course.

Skaperdas, Stergios and Bernard Grofman, "Modeling negative campaigning," *American Political Science Review,* March 1995, pp. 49-61.
Negative campaigning is an important aspect of campaign competition, but plays little or no role in existing models of campaigns. The incentives that affect the use of negative campaigning are modeled.

Political Consultants

Brack, Elliott, "Just a note about political consultants' tactics," *Atlanta Journal Constitution,* Aug. 4, 1996, p. XJ9.
Brack opines that there's nothing wrong with a spouse writing a support letter for her husband during an election campaign, but the sinister nature of such cookie-cutter letters is nothing more than another weapon in the arsenal of the political consultant.

Carlson, Tucker, "James Carville, populist plutocrat," *Weekly Standard,* March 18, 1996, pp. 20-24.
James Carville is famous today as the architect of the 1992 Clinton victory, and he has become a millionaire several times over. Carville and his career as a campaign adviser, author and plutocrat are discussed.

Grove, Lloyd, "Taken under advisement: Morris is just the latest political consultant to find the spotlight," *The Washington Post,* Aug. 31, 1996, p. D1.
After years of toiling in obscurity, political consultant Dick Morris is now in the media spotlight. Morris is only the latest example of the celebrification of political consultants.

Harwood, Richard, "Blood sport," *The Washington Post,* Nov. 15, 1995, p. A25.
Harwood comments on the role of political consultants in political campaigns.

Lannon, Linnea, "Politico Ed Rollins is part of the problem," *Detroit News & Free Press,* Aug. 18, 1996, p. E1.
Lannon comments on political strategist Ed Rollins' book "Bare Knuckles and Back Rooms," saying that because Rollins and other have so devalued American politics, elections are increasingly alienating voters, which means it's increasingly easy for political operatives like Rollins to

get someone elected.

Proffitt, Steve, "James Carville," *Los Angeles Times*, Aug. 25, 1996, p. M3.
In an interview, political writer James Carville discusses political conventions and campaigns in 1996, his belief in government and the failure of progressives to counter the rhetoric of the GOP right.

"Talk of the town: Dick Morris, Republican F.O.B.," *New Yorker*, April 24, 1995, pp. 35-36.
The relationship between Republican Dick Morris and President Clinton has caused quite a stir in Washington. Morris, who runs a one-man consulting firm out of his home, describes his relationship with the president as friendly rather than professional.

Toner, Robin, "Campaign consultants find benefits in budget impasse," *The New York Times*, Jan. 12, 1996, p. A1.
There was little mourning among political consultants when the budget talks were suspended the week of Jan. 7, 1996. The strategists were already planning congressional campaigns revolving around the great, unresolved differences between the two parties on balancing and reconfiguring the federal budget, and the lack of a deal just makes those differences sharper. Democrats are convinced that their party can prosper mightly if it presents itself as the last line of defense against Republican cuts in Medicare, education and environmental protection.

Turque, Bill, "The Carville industry," *Newsweek*, April 8, 1996, p. 32.
James Carville, political consultant for Bill Clinton in the 1992 elections, is profiled. With his Cajun-flavored populism, Carville has become the Democratic equivalent of Rush Limbaugh.

Warren, James, "Cult of political consultants thrives in moral vacuum," *Chicago Tribune*, Sept. 1, 1996, p. 2.
Warren discusses what he calls the cult of the consultant, a distinctly modern development whose existence thrives on self-promotion, and the media's frenzied coverage of it, spurred on in part by the personal downfall of Dick Morris, one of the group's more secretive members.

Waxman, Sharon, "Hollywood's power channelers — Some celebs have acquired the ultimate status symbol: Their own political consultants," *The Washington Post*, June 23, 1996, p. G2.
Hollywood may have hit on the ultimate status symbol as celebrities have begun acquiring their own personal political strategists.

Yoachum, Susan, "Dole campaign roasts Ed Rollins over ethnic slur," *San Francisco Chronicle*, May 20, 1995, p. A3.
On May 19, 1995, Sen. Bob Dole's presidential campaign denounced consultant Ed Rollins for making an ethnic slur against two Jewish congressmen at a roast for California Assembly Speaker Willie Brown. Rollins reportedly used the term "Hymie boys" to refer to the two congressmen.

Polls and Pollsters

Clymer, Adam, "Association of Political Handlers Attacks Ruse Polls as Unethical," *The New York Times*, June 27, 1996, p. A20.
The trade association of political managers, the American Association of Political Consultants, on June 26, 1996, denounced phony "push polls," in which campaigns hire companies to make thousands of calls spreading negative and sometimes false information about an opponent while posing as pollsters. Leading pollsters for both parties who are members of the organization said that consultants should quit any campaign that engages in the practice.

"Democracy, sans pollsters," *Boston Globe*, April 18, 1995, p. 14.
An editorial notes France's ban on the publication of poll results within one week of an election, and suggests the adoption of similar measures in the U.S.

Maloney, Carolyn B., and Thomas E. Petri, "Telephone smear artists," *The Washington Post*, July 17, 1996, p. A19.
Reps. Carolyn B. Maloney, D-N.Y., and Thomas E. Petri, R-Wis., applaud the American Association of Political Consultants for denouncing the use of anonymous and false phone bank attacks in political campaigns.

Holmes, Steven A., "Broad poll of the public on politics," *The New York Times*, Dec. 3, 1995, p. 31.
The National Issues Convention is in some respects little different from the thousands of polls on politics and national affairs that will be conducted for the 1996 presidential elections. However, this poll will measure the views of respondents before and after they have studied and discussed the issues, and hopefully quizzed the presidential candidates, including President Clinton. The pollsters will then determine if the views of the participants have changed.

Jacobs, Lawrence R., and Robert Y. Shapiro, "Presidential manipulation of polls and public opinion: The Nixon Administration and the pollsters," *Political Science Quarterly*, winter 1995, pp. 519-538.
The Nixon administration pursued public pollsters Louis Harris and the Gallup organization in order to manipulate poll results and public opinion.

Lessard, Suzannah, "The missing issues: Banish the pollsters," *Washington Monthly*, Jan. 1996, pp. 26-27.
The most serious problem in U.S. political life today is the colonization of the minds of leaders by opinion research. Unless politicians act out of deep convictions arrived at by independent thinking, none of the serious problems in the country will ever be solved.

Back Issues

Great Research on Current Issues Starts Right Here...Recent topics covered by The CQ Researcher are listed below. Before May 1991, reports were published under the name of Editorial Research Reports.

APRIL 1995
Abortion Clinic Protests
Dieting and Health
Combating AIDS
Rethinking Affirmative Action

MAY 1995
Assisted Suicide Controversy
Overhauling Social Security
Learning to Read
Mandatory Sentencing

JUNE 1995
Combating Infectious Disease
Property Rights
Repetitive Stress Injuries
Regulating the Internet

JULY 1995
War Crimes
Highway Safety
Combating Terrorism
Preventing Teen Drug Use

AUGUST 1995
Job Stress
Organ Transplants
United Nations at 50
Advances in Cancer Research

SEPTEMBER 1995
Catholic Church in the U.S.
Northern Ireland Cease-Fire
High School Sports
Teaching History

OCTOBER 1995
Quebec's Future
Revitalizing the Cities
Networking the Classroom
Indoor Air Pollution

NOVEMBER 1995
The Working Poor
The Jury System
Sex, Violence and the Media
Police Misconduct

DECEMBER 1995
Teens and Tobacco
Gene Therapy's Future
Global Water Shortages
Third-Party Prospects

JANUARY 1996
Emergency Medicine
Punishing Sex Offenders
Bilingual Education
Helping the Homeless

FEBRUARY 1996
Reforming the CIA
Campaign Finance Reform
Academic Politics
Getting Into College

MARCH 1996
The British Monarchy
Preventing Juvenile Crime
Tax Reform
Pursuing the Paranormal

APRIL 1996
Centennial Olympic Games
Managed Care
Protecting Endangered Species
New Military Culture

MAY 1996
Russia's Political Future
Marriage and Divorce
Year-Round Schools
Taiwan, China and the U.S.

JUNE 1996
Rethinking NAFTA
First Ladies
Teaching Values
Labor Movement's Future

JULY 1996
Recovered-Memory Debate
Native Americans' Future
Crackdown on Sexual Harassment
Attack on Public Schools

AUGUST 1996
Fighting Over Animal Rights
Privatizing Government Services
Child Labor and Sweatshops
Cleaning Up Hazardous Wastes

SEPTEMBER 1996
Gambling Under Attack
The States and Federalism
Civic Journalism
Reassessing Foreign Aid

Back issues are available for $5.00 (subscribers) or $8.00 (non-subscribers). Quantity discounts apply to orders over ten. To order, call Congressional Quarterly Customer Service at (202) 887-8621.

Binders are available for $18.00. To order call 1-800-638-1710. Please refer to stock number 648.

Future Topics

- ***Insurance Fraud***
- ***Rethinking School Integration***
- ***Parental Rights***

THE CQ Researcher

PUBLISHED BY CONGRESSIONAL QUARTERLY INC.

Insurance Fraud

Will a new crackdown reduce the losses?

A multibillion-dollar crime wave is sweeping the country, but the public doesn't seem to notice. Although elaborate scams occasionally grab headlines, insurance fraud remains a largely invisible and ordinary crime — homeowners padding claims for fire and storm damage; doctors overbilling for Medicare; insurance agents pocketing policyowners' premiums. Yet insurance fraud costs the U.S. economy an estimated $80 billion a year, making it the nation's second largest economic crime, after tax evasion. Insurance fraud flourishes in part because insurers often hesitate to challenge dubious claims, and police give top priority to violent crime. Now the insurance industry and government law enforcement agencies are cracking down on fraud — but how much success they will have remains to be seen.

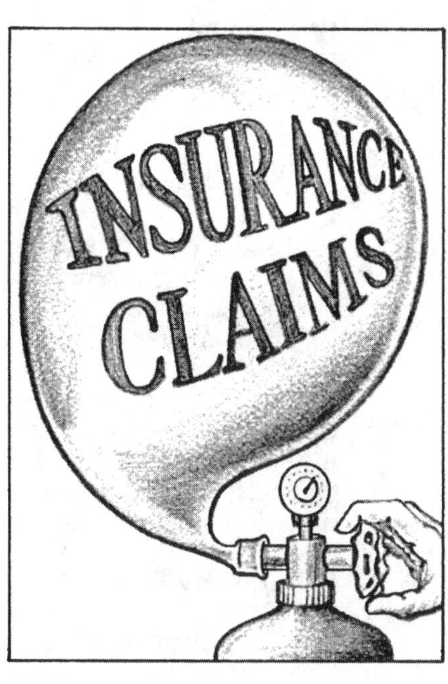

INSIDE THIS ISSUE

CQ Oct. 11, 1996 • Volume 6, No. 38 • Pages 889-912

Formerly Editorial Research Reports

INSURANCE FRAUD

THE ISSUES

BACKGROUND

CURRENT SITUATION

OUTLOOK

SIDEBARS AND GRAPHICS

FOR FURTHER RESEARCH

COVER: BARBARA SASSA-DANIELS

Oct. 11, 1996
Volume 6, No. 38

The CQ Researcher (ISSN 1056-2036). Formerly Editorial Research Reports. Published weekly (48 times per year, not printed March 1, May 31, Aug. 30, Nov. 29) by Congressional Quarterly Inc., 1414 22nd St., N.W., Washington, D.C. 20037. Annual subscription rate for libraries, businesses and government is $319. Additional rates furnished upon request. Periodicals postage paid at Washington, D.C. POSTMASTER: Send address changes to The CQ Researcher, 1414 22nd St., N.W., Washington, D.C. 20037.

Insurance Fraud

By Richard L. Worsnop

The Issues

There are con artists who devise scams so elaborate they leave investigators in awe. Then there is psychologist Carl H. Lichtman. He recently pleaded guilty to running a $3 million insurance scam — the largest ever uncovered in New Jersey. Lichtman billed insurance companies for hundreds of counseling sessions he never conducted, paying "patients" 25 percent of the reimbursements he received. He even paid $750 referral fees — using personal checks — for the names of others to enlist in the scheme.

"I've seen scams where they create dummy corporations to shuffle money around," says Lichtman's attorney, Brian Neary. "Lichtman left a paper trail that a seeing-eye dog could follow." [1]

Less preposterous, but equally unsuccessful, was the plot hatched by California brothers Neil and Stewart Woodman. They hired hitmen to kill their parents, hoping to use their mother's $500,000 insurance policy to rescue the failing plastics company their father had founded. Jurors in Los Angeles thought otherwise. This spring they sentenced 52-year-old Neil Woodman to 25 years to life for his role in the 1985 murders. [2]

But it is not outrageous and high-profile cases that have made insurance fraud the nation's second largest economic crime, after tax evasion. Industry and law enforcement experts say most frauds are far more ordinary, and invisible, such as:

- doctors billing Medicare for procedures they never performed or patients they never had;
- medical labs that bill for phantom tests;
- couples that work for different firms with different insurance companies and double-bill for health-care expenses;

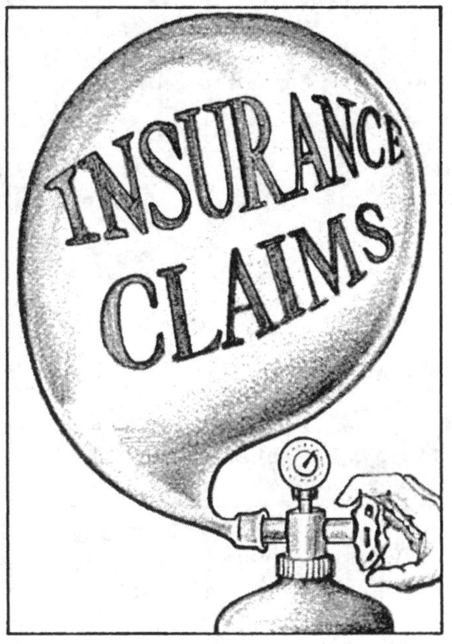

- home and car owners who pad their claims for fire, storm or auto damage to cover the policy's deductible; and,
- commuters who shave a few hundred miles off their annual mileage total to reduce their auto insurance bill.

In addition, there are swindlers who collect premiums for bogus insurance companies and agents for legitimate insurers who simply pocket policyholders' premiums, betting they won't file claims.

The list of possible scams is virtually infinite, and since most fraud escapes detection, its extent can only be estimated, industry and law enforcement experts say. Fraud cost the economy at least $80 billion in 1994, according to the Coalition Against Insurance Fraud (CAIF), a nationwide group of consumers, government agencies and insurers. * But the U.S. General Accounting Office (GAO) puts the total for health insurance fraud alone at about $100 billion annually, while the Insurance Information Institute says property/casualty insurance fraud runs $20 billion a year.

One thing is certain: Insurance fraud is so widespread that the chances of getting caught or punished are relatively low. "In most places, insurance fraud is an extremely low-risk behavior with an extremely high payoff," says Janet Bachman, vice president for claims administration at the American Insurance Association. "It requires almost no investment. So the payoff, once you succeed in your scheme, is almost pure profit, with almost no downside. And the deterrence is minuscule."

"There's a big tolerance factor" in insurance fraud, adds Dennis Jay, executive director of CAIF. "It's not a priority for law enforcement. There's lots of money in it, and chances are that not much is going to happen to you if you get caught. You couldn't build a better system to rip off." Indeed, 18 states and the District of Columbia don't have specific statutes making insurance fraud a felony. *(See table, p. 894.)*

Bachman also notes that "Insurance companies generally are not high in the public's esteem. To begin with, we sell a product that nobody wants to buy anyway. It seems that people sometimes apply a different moral code toward institutions they don't like."

Popular attitudes about insurers tend to track attitudes about federal tax collectors, Bachman says. "I'm not trying to draw a complete parallel between the insurance industry, which sells a voluntary product, and the Internal Revenue Service (IRS)," she says. "But I think it's fair to say that many people don't consider it deeply immoral to cheat on their taxes. Why? Because they don't like to pay taxes, and they don't like the IRS."

Opinion surveys tend to support Bachman's view. In a 1995 poll by the Insurance Research Council (IRC), for

---

* CAIF defines insurance fraud as "any deliberate deception perpetrated against or by an insurance company or agent for the purpose of unwarranted financial gain. It occurs during the process of buying, using, selling and underwriting insurance."

U.S. Insurance Fraud Estimated at $80 Billion

Two-thirds of the estimated $80 billion in fraudulent insurance claims filed in 1994 involved health care. Insurance fraud cost each U.S. family nearly $1,000 in additional costs, such as higher premiums.

Type of Insurance	Fraudulent Claims	Estimated Cost Per Family
■ Auto	$13.4 billion	$162
■ Homeowners	$2.0 billion	$24
■ Commercial	$11.0 billion	$133
■ Health	$53.6 billion	$648
Totals	**$80 billion**	**$967**

Source: Coalition Against Insurance Fraud, based on estimates and data from U.S. Census Bureau, National Insurance Crime Bureau, Health Insurance Association of America, U.S. Health Care Financing Administration, Insurance Information Institute

instance, 23 percent of those questioned condoned inflating insurance claims to recoup their premiums. [3] And 28 percent said it was OK to pad claims by the amount of the policy's deductible.

The IRC, which has tracked popular opinion on padding claims since 1981, said the 1995 survey ended a five-year decline in approval of the practice. Similarly, a survey conducted for the National Insurance Crime Bureau (NICB) in 1994 found that 23 percent of the respondents did not deem it a serious lapse to understate the number of miles driven annually in order to qualify for a lower auto-insurance premium.

The lax attitude reflects the general belief that "insurance carriers are making big profits" while not providing 'fair' coverage for premiums paid, according to surveys taken for the Insurance Information Institute. [4]

Insurance fraud also flourishes because rip-off artists know that insurance companies rarely challenge claims that fall below a confidential dollar threshold. "Professional criminals know what the thresholds are, and proceed accordingly," Jay says. "Companies that establish a threshold of $10,000, say, find themselves getting lots of claims for between $9,000 and $9,500."

"Workers' compensation fraud and health-insurance fraud probably are the most worrisome to the industry at present," says Janet S. Kloenhamer, vice president and claims counsel for Firemen's Fund Insurance Co. "Another category that's timely right now is claims fraud that arises from natural disasters," such as this summer's Hurricane Fran, which caused an estimated $1.5 billion in damage.

Why don't insurers take a harder line against questionable claims? "The question almost answers itself: The risks and high costs of litigation," associate editor Carolyn T. Geer wrote in *Forbes*. "An insurance company that disputes a claim and loses in court faces the danger of a multimillion-dollar verdict for the tort of bad-faith denial of an insurance claim." Moreover, she added, "Juries just don't like insurance companies — nor are [juries] wise enough to understand that when they gouge insurance companies they are only pushing up their own premiums." [5]

The claims-adjusting process also provides opportunities for fraud, Geer noted. "Most carriers pay little attention to claims under $50,000. And they're often forced to rely on independent contractors — salvors, accountants and the like — over whom they have little control, to size up claims on their behalf. Inevitably, some of these apples are rotten, as are some of the underwriters' own employees." [6]

Though insurance fraud will never be eradicated, fraud fighters are starting to chalk up some victories. Special investigation units (SIUs) set up by individual insurers over the past decade reportedly save up to $10 for every dollar spent on such efforts. And industrywide anti-fraud groups have been established as well.

Indeed, CAIF was founded only three years ago. "Insurance fraud was seen as a serious problem before then," Jay says, "but it wasn't until 1993 that all the parties were able to put aside their differences. There had been some anti-fraud involvement by the industry for years. Consumer groups started looking into it in the late 1980s, when a lot of insurer insolvencies occurred. But it took a long time for all the interests to agree it was time for a unified approach."

Legislative and law enforcement bodies also have launched anti-fraud actions, as have lawmakers on Capitol Hill. For instance, the omnibus crime bill approved by Congress in 1994 defined certain types of insurer fraud — fraud committed by an insurance agent or a company itself — as federal crimes. Moreover, the health insurance bill recently signed by President Clinton stiffens penalties for defrauding both private and public health-care programs. [7] And the FBI has become more deeply involved in fraud since launching a program to combat health-care fraud in 1992.

Most significant of all, perhaps, are developments in the states, which are largely responsible for regulating the U.S. insurance industry. More than half the states now operate insurance fraud bureaus and/or have enacted laws

Scams Often Target Immigrants

It's a problem that insurance officials don't like to discuss, but it's impossible to ignore. Much of the insurance fraud in the United States involving *organized* groups of criminals is committed by recent immigrants who target fellow immigrants with a limited command of English.

"Immigrant groups are disproportionately victims of insurance fraud — whether it's insurance agents who pocket their premium dollars, or crooks who form a bogus company that rarely pays claims," says Dennis Jay, executive director of the Coalition Against Insurance Fraud (CAIF). "That's what we saw after the 1992 riots in Los Angeles, when about 200 Korean business owners learned the hard way that the offshore companies they had bought insurance from were just shells."

It's not surprising that bogus insurers flourish among limited-English speakers, says Ken McEldowney, executive director of Consumer Action, an advocacy group primarily for limited-English speakers based in San Francisco. "They have the advantage of being able to speak the same tongue as their potential policyholders. Established insurance companies often don't have bilingual or multilingual agents. Also, insurance regulatory agencies may lack staff investigators or consumer advocates who speak the language of the immigrant community."

"A popular scam involving life insurance is the faking of deaths of foreign nationals, who purchase insurance in the United States, return to their home country and 'die' suddenly," wrote Philip E. Stano, senior counsel at the American Council of Life Insurance. "This scenario is often referred to as a 'white van' case, due to the numerous 'white vans' reported to have taken the lives of so many foreign nationals on back roads. Of course, these white vans mysteriously disappear after the accident and are never located." [1]

Recent immigrants are implicated in many fake-death cases, Jay says, because "It's often very easy to get a fake death certificate in your native country, as well as other 'proof' of death and burial. And the country is likely to be far away, making it very expensive for an insurance company to establish fraud. The life insurance industry has really been way behind the curve in rooting out this kind of scam."

Staged motor-vehicle accidents are also common among poor immigrants. In a typical incident, two or three cars will box in a late-model auto that likely has good insurance coverage. The driver of the lead car brakes suddenly, forcing the victim into a collision. Injury claims then are filed against the victim's insurer, alleging various internal injuries.

A variant of the staged-accident scam involves "ghostriders." In a sting operation lasting three years, the fraud division of New Jersey's insurance department staged more than a dozen fake bus accidents. The investigation led to the arrests of 107 people who jumped aboard after the accidents with the intent of collecting on a false-injury claim.

The crime rings specializing in staged auto and truck accidents "generally consist of three different levels," according to *Mother Jones* magazine. "At the top, there are the professionals — doctors or lawyers — who make the schemes profitable by diagnosing false injuries or filing fraudulent claims. Next are the 'cappers' or 'runners,' the middlemen who obtain the cars to crash, farm out the claims to the professionals at the top and recruit the bottom-rung participants — people desperate enough to be in a car when it actually wrecks. According to investigators, cappers usually hire within their own ethnic groups." [2]

Though better law enforcement is needed to reduce the incidence of insurance fraud, McEldowney says, improved educational efforts also would be useful. "All too often, limited-English immigrants lack access to information about insurance laws. The consequences can be seen in the workers' compensation area when job layoffs occur. Scam artists show up at the back door, recruiting folks to file fraudulent workers' comp claims. They probably score most heavily in workplaces where there's nothing posted about worker comp laws in languages other than English, and the scam artists speak the language spoken by the laid-off employees."

Ingrained attitudes shared by many poor immigrants may be harder to address effectively. According to Don Garrard, a Los Angeles lawyer who defends insurers against bogus claims, insurance fraud is rampant in the city because "there are a lot of people from poor backgrounds and from [countries] where corruption runs rampant, from the government on down. People don't see insurance fraud as corrupt. It's just another way to get money." [3]

---

[1] Philip E. Stano, "Recent Developments in Life and Health Insurance Fraud Legislation in the United States," June 1996, p. 4.

[2] Ashley Craddock and Mordecai Lawrence, "Swoop-and-Squats," *Mother Jones*, September-October 1993, p. 16.

[3] Quoted by Craddock and Lawrence, *Ibid.*, p. 20.

---

classifying insurance fraud as a felony. Twelve of the laws were approved in the past two years. (*See table, p. 894.*)

Meanwhile, the bogus claims being honored by insurance companies leave attorney Neary incredulous. "How the hell can insurance companies pay these kinds of claims?" he asks. "Don't they check? The insurance industry has a responsibility to its claimants, stockholders and the general public to watch their money. In a strange way, Lichtman may help the industry get its house in order by forcing it to pay attention to a serious problem."

As industry and law enforcement officials evaluate the many public and

Continued on p. 895

States Putting New Emphasis on Insurance Fraud

In the past three years, more than half the states have set up bureaus to investigate insurance fraud. More than three-fourths of the states now have specific statutes making insurance fraud a felony. Few states, however, require state licensing authorities to be notified when professionals are convicted of insurance fraud.

State	Fraud Classified as a Felony	Fraud Bureau Established	Licensing Board Notification Required
Alabama			
Alaska	■	■	
Arizona	■	■	
Arkansas		For workers' compensation	
California	■	■	■
Colorado	■		■
Connecticut	■	■	■
Delaware	■	■	
District of Columbia			
Florida	■	■	■
Georgia		■	
Hawaii			
Idaho	■	■	
Illinois	■		■
Indiana	■		
Iowa	■	Pending	
Kansas			
Kentucky	■	■	■
Louisiana		■	
Maine			
Maryland	■	■	■
Massachusetts	■	■	■
Michigan	■		■
Minnesota	■	For workers' compensation	■
Mississippi			
Missouri		■	
Montana		For workers' compensation	
Nebraska	■	■	
Nevada		■	
New Hampshire	■	■	
New Jersey	■	■	■
New Mexico	■		
New York	■	■	
North Carolina	■	■	
North Dakota			
Ohio	■	■	
Oklahoma		For workers' compensation	
Oregon			
Pennsylvania	■	■	■
Rhode Island	■		■
South Carolina	■	■	
South Dakota	■		
Tennessee	For workers' compensation	For workers' compensation	For workers' compensation
Texas	■	■	■
Utah	■	■	■
Vermont			
Virginia			
Washington	■		■
West Virginia			
Wisconsin	■		
Wyoming			

Source: Coalition Against Insurance Fraud, Aug. 2, 1996

private initiatives against insurance fraud, these are some of the questions being asked:

Are existing laws against insurance fraud adequately enforced?

Concerted action against insurance fraud got under way only recently, with the insurance industry itself leading the charge. Federal and state law enforcement agencies were slow to join the battle, since few laws directly addressing the problem existed before 1990. Not surprisingly, opinion is divided on whether investigators and prosecutors are making effective use of statutes now on the books.

AIA's Bachman feels law enforcement in the area is flagging. (*See "At Issue," p. 905.*) "The most obvious reason is that those responsible for enforcing criminal laws on insurance fraud generally lack the tools to do so," she says. "Law enforcement agencies — whether local, state or federal — already are stretched to the limit fighting crimes people worry about most, such as violent crime. Insurance fraud is such a frequent crime that it's unrealistic to expect truly aggressive enforcement of laws against it with the resources now available."

Stephen Perry, vice president for investigative services at the American International Group, a New York-based insurer, rates current law enforcement efforts as adequate and likely to improve in coming years. "Because of rising concern in the workplace about insurance fraud costs," he says, "I think all the states eventually will enact laws mandating investigations of suspect claims. New state laws are being put on the books all the time, and state-insurance fraud bureaus and other agencies are being established to enforce them."

Jay of the CAIF tends to see the cup as half-empty. "We've seen several states step up and make the commitment, both in enacting solid anti-fraud laws and in putting resources behind them," he says. "But it takes more than laws, and more than state fraud bureaus, to enforce them. The industry itself has to be able to detect claims fraud and then refer it to the authorities and help them gather evidence." But even then, he adds, "Sometimes results aren't forthcoming because we don't have prosecutors willing to take some of these cases. That's a real weak link."

Jay suspects that investigators and prosecutors shy away from insurance fraud because of their preference for cases with a higher profile. "Remember, a lot of law enforcement people are in elective positions," he says, "such as district attorneys and statewide prosecutors. Insurance-fraud cases usually don't attract much attention in the news media."

Moreover, Jay says, law enforcement officials are under "tremendous public pressure to prosecute violent crime, sex offenses and major property crime. And insurance fraud cases are tremendously complex, and thus very time-consuming. One prosecutor told me that he can dispose of five homicides in the time it takes him to do one insurance case. That's because uncovering fraud tends to be very paper-intensive."

Finally, Jay says convictions and meaningful sentences in insurance-fraud cases are by no means assured: "Prosecutors will say, 'Hey — even when I take it all the way, chances are they're going to get off with a light sentence. Prosecuting these cases isn't a deterrent, and the courts aren't cracking down on this type of crime, so why should I concentrate my resources on it?' "

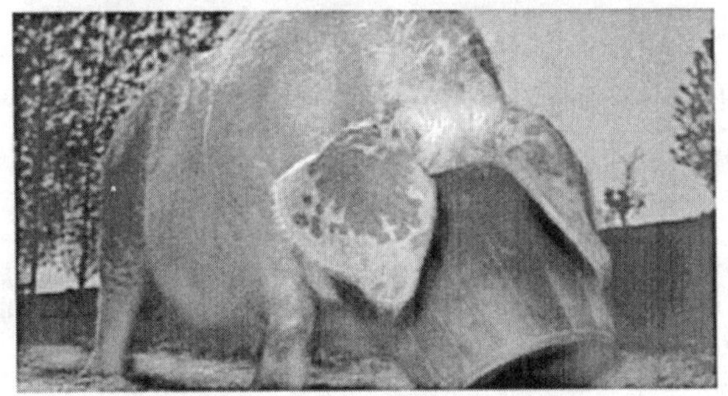

© 1996 John Wine Design, Washington, D.C.

Newspaper ads for the Coalition Against Insurance Fraud are designed to raise awareness of the huge monetary losses due to insurance scams and fraudulent claims.

Nonetheless, there are a few bright spots. Maryland, Jay notes, has two assistant attorneys general in its state fraud bureau. "That's all they do — prosecute insurance fraud," Jay says. "They're knowledgeable about it, and they bring dedication and willingness to the job. For that reason, their cases are taken seriously when they arrive in court. Judges respect their track record."

Florida provides a modest financial incentive to go after insurance fraud. Prosecutors there "can go to the state fraud bureau and receive up to $1,500 per case," Jay says. "That may not sound like much, but it can spell the difference

Is It Fraud, Or Isn't It?

When the owner of a failing business hires an arsonist to torch his building, it's fraud, plain and simple. But some practices of insurers and claimants fall into a gray area that resists pigeonholing.

For example, says Ken McEldowney, executive director of Consumer Action, a San Francisco consumer advocacy group, "What about an insurance agent who sells you a policy, stating that the premium is X, but later comes back and says the premium actually is Y? The difference may be just a few dollars. But the question is, did the agent act deceptively — or fraudulently? Where does one draw the line?"

Paul Cordish, counsel to the National Association of Public Insurance Adjusters (NAPIA), poses another hypothetical case. "Your house burns down, and your grandmother's photo is one of the things destroyed. You say on your insurance claim that the photo was worth $100, because it had great sentimental value to you. NAPIA wouldn't regard that as fraud. But the insurance company might. It might say the photo was worth 79 cents."

In the life insurance field, the practice known as "churning" has drawn mounting criticism in recent years. It occurs when an agent persuades a policyholder to transfer the cash value of an existing policy into a replacement policy, thus generating a new commission for the agent. "Typically, agents play this game by convincing customers that because of inflation, the existing policy's death benefit is no longer adequate, or that the insurer has recently introduced a new and improved policy that will build cash value better," according to *Money* magazine. [1]

Life insurance policyholders lose approximately $6 billion a year to churning and related practices, said a study last year by the Consumer Federation of America (CFA). "We're not criticizing most agents, but there are some who make money this way," said Stephen Brobeck, CFA's executive editor. "And most people out there are simply uninformed." [2]

Consumer groups also warn people to be wary of insurance policies touted as investments, retirement plans or savings vehicles for their children's college tuition. That marketing strategy is "perfectly legal," *Money* noted, "as long as customers are adequately informed that they are indeed buying insurance." Agents, he added, have a "tendency to gloss over potential pitfalls."

Still another questionable insurer practice centers on the discounts that insurers negotiate with hospitals and other health-care providers. In some cases, the insurer computes its share of a medical bill based on the discount formula but figures the insured person's share as a percentage of the full price.

"Say you have an insurance policy that requires you to pay 20 percent of your medical bills," *Kiplinger's Personal Finance Magazine* reported recently. "You have an operation, for which the bill shows a $1,000 charge, and you pay $200. Your insurer, however, has privately negotiated a deal with the hospital to reduce the charge to $800. The insurer then pays $600 — its discounted rate minus your $200. You've been sucker-punched into paying 25 percent of the bill," instead of just 20 percent. [3]

What's more, a time bomb could await policyholders caught in such a situation. As *Kiplinger's* noted, they run the risk of "maxing out on [their] coverage earlier than [they] should because [their] lifetime or annual cap is calculated on the 'retail' rather than the discounted cost" of the medical treatments they received.

[1] Walter E. Updegrave, "Don't Be Suckered Into the Life Insurance Mess," *Money*, January 1995, p. 114.

[2] Quoted in *Fraud Focus*, bimonthly newsletter of the Coalition Against Insurance Fraud, September-October 1995, p. 3.

[3] Jane Bennett Clark and John Parmelee, "Insurance Discounts You Should Get," *Kiplinger's Personal Finance Magazine*, April 1996, p. 108.

between taking on a case or ignoring it when other resources run thin."

At the federal level, Mark Bullock, chief of the FBI's economic crimes unit, says it's too early to assess the government's fight against insurance fraud. That's mainly because it was only two years ago that Congress defined insurance fraud as a federal crime. Since then, he notes, "There have been only one or two instances where that statute has been put to use (*see p. 902*). But as our investigators and Justice Department prosecutors become more familiar with the law, we expect the pace to accelerate."

Should doctors, lawyers and others convicted of insurance fraud lose their license to practice?

No one challenges the notion that career criminals guilty of insurance fraud should be severely punished. But opinion is divided on the appropriate penalties for convicted professionals — chiefly doctors and lawyers. For the most part, insurance officials say a conviction warrants virtually automatic revocation of a license to practice in the state where the offense occurred. But professional societies generally take the position that each case should be judged on its merits and that any mitigating circumstances should be taken into account.

"Basically, if a physician is convicted of insurance fraud and is an American Medical Association member, we revoke their membership," says an AMA official. "We're a membership organization, so we're separate from a licensing board, although we do try to inform them when we find out that an adverse action has been taken. Also, Medicare and Medicaid will exclude physicians who are convicted of insurance fraud, and licensing boards [also] may take action."

Ken McEldowney, executive director of Consumer Action, a San Francisco-based public interest group that often works with non-English-speaking immigrants, finds the current situation exasperating. A doctor or a lawyer "may face criminal action for insurance fraud, but nothing ever happens to their license," he says. "They just keep practicing. A policyholder who pads a claim will be slapped much harder than a professional who is convicted of a more serious offense." Too often, McEldowney complains, judges and juries swallow the argument that, 'If we suspend or revoke the license, there's no way this professional can make restitution.' "

Bachman endorses McEldowney's hard-line approach. "If you are licensed by the state in any capacity and are found guilty of a crime — particularly when that crime was committed under your licenseship — your license should be lifted. Not suspended — revoked." The same standard should apply to body-shop personnel, claims adjusters and other holders of state licensees, Bachman says.

"A lot of doctors will say allegations of insurance fraud arise from faulty paperwork by people who work for them," says Perry, the American International Group's investigative vice president,. "I'm willing to concede there may be instances of mistaken double-billing. But where there is clear-cut intent to defraud, people should lose their licenses."

But revocations are rare, according to Jay. "State laws on the subject either don't exist," he says, "or they're not enforced." The first time a doctor is convicted of insurance fraud in Florida, "it's basically a gimme — they'll let you go. In some other states, it's even worse. We've seen instances of people being convicted of insurance fraud five, six or seven times without suffering any disciplinary action."

Nina Bottcher, a spokesperson for Florida's Agency for Health Care Administration, says health-care fraud, including insurance fraud, has been treated "much more harshly" in Florida since the Board of Medicine decided in December that "it had had enough." Since then, Bottcher says, the board has routinely issued an emergency license-suspension order whenever it determined that a fraud charge was "legally sufficient." So far in 1996, 11 of 14 health-care fraud cases against Florida doctors (most involving insurance fraud) have resulted in license revocations.

First-time offenders can expect no breaks, Bottcher says. "Fraud is not open to interpretation. You did it or you didn't. You knew from the outset it was wrong. So why do you deserve a second chance?"

She adds that the board fully supports proposals that state licensing bodies be notified whenever one of their licensees is convicted of fraud. "We have asked other state agencies that might become involved in these cases to contact us early on, not after everything has been settled. And we, in turn, share information with them."

National Insurance Crime Bureau

Burn patterns on furniture help teach claims adjusters to recognize arson at Allstate's Tech-Cor auto research facility in Wheeling, Ill.

The legal profession takes a similar approach to dealing with attorneys convicted of "serious crime," defined by the American Bar Association (ABA) as any felony or lesser offense that "reflects adversely on the lawyer's honesty, trustworthiness or fitness." Fraud is among the specific offenses cited. Under the ABA model legislation rules, the court where the conviction occurs can place the lawyer on interim suspension until final disciplinary action by the state licensing board.

"Proof of guilt must be more convincing in a criminal case than in a disciplinary proceeding," the ABA model rules state. "Thus, the respondent found guilty under the higher standard in the criminal case should not be able to relitigate the issue of guilt in the course of a disciplinary proceeding with its relatively lower standard of crime." ■

BACKGROUND

Rise of Fraud

The use of insurance can be traced back to 2000 B.C. and the ancient Babylonians. Under so-called bottomry contracts, a form of marine insurance, creditors advanced money to merchants with the provision that the loan did not have to be repaid if the shipment was lost at sea. A surcharge was added to the usual rate of interest as a premium to the creditor, who assumed the risk of loss. At that time, Babylonia was a trading power whose caravans transported goods to and from all parts of the known world.

Historians date the use of life and health insurance to ancient Greece and Rome, but fire insurance didn't emerge until much later, gaining impetus from London's Great Fire of 1666. Many of the insurance companies that sprang up in Britain in the early 18th century were fraudulent, get-rich-quick schemes, concerned mainly with selling stock in the insurance company to unsuspecting private investors. [8]

The first U.S. insurance company was organized in Philadelphia in 1752 by Benjamin Franklin. Many insurance firms were established over the next 150 years, but the industry was in constant turmoil because of poor management, speculative investments and inadequate regulation. Thirty-three life insurance companies failed between 1870 and 1872, and another 48 between 1873 and 1877. Similarly, many property insurance companies went belly up after the Chicago fire of 1871 and the San Francisco earthquake and fire of 1906.

Nonetheless, the U.S. insurance industry continued to expand, largely free of stringent government oversight until well into this century. Remarkably, insurance fraud "received little public attention until the 1980s," the Insurance Information Institute has noted. In part, that was because law enforcement officials "had other priorities and were reluctant to provide the training needed to investigate and prosecute cases of insurance fraud." [9]

At the same time, individual companies hesitated to seize the initiative in attacking fraud. "[G]iven the fine line between investigating suspicious claims and harassing legitimate claimants, some insurers were afraid that a concerted effort to eradicate fraud might be perceived as an anti-consumer move," the institute observed. "In addition, the need to comply with the time requirements for paying claims imposed by fair-claim-practice regulations in many states make it difficult to adequately investigate suspicious claims." [10]

Early Anti-Fraud Actions

State governments also were slow to respond to insurance fraud. It was not until 1945, for example, that North Carolina became the first state to establish a statewide insurance fraud bureau. And more than 30 years had to pass before the next two states organized such agencies, Florida in 1976 and California in 1979.

In the mid-1980s, however, insurance companies recognized the need for more aggressive anti-fraud measures. They were prodded into action not only by a sharp rise in organized fraud schemes but also by the rising cost of insurance, especially auto and health policies. From this perspective, industry officials viewed anti-fraud programs as cost-containment tools.

Insurers found a ready ally in the consumer movement, which also was concerned about the escalating cost of insurance coverage. In addition, societies representing lawyers and health practitioners worried that their reputations were being tainted by organized insurance-fraud rings that recruited legal and medical professionals to help cloak the criminal intent of their schemes.

Problems With ERISA

In 1982, Congress inadvertently gave fraudulent insurance company operators an opening when they amended the Employee Retirement Income Security Act (ERISA). The 1974 law was designed to establish uniform federal regulation of private plans for employee pensions and benefits, including health insurance. To this end, it exempted certain benefit plans from state regulation. But the law was unclear on whether health insurance plans were covered by the exemption. Despite the uncertainty, many employers and labor unions set up self-funded health insurance plans, which, ostensibly, were not subject to state regulation.

The 1982 amendment to ERISA was designed to clarify state authority over employee benefit plans covering multiple employers — "multiple employer welfare arrangements" (MEWAs), as they were termed. MEWAs enable small companies to form purchasing coalitions that negotiate for employee health insurance and other benefits that the companies could not afford individually. The 1982 amendment specifically authorized states to regulate MEWAs.

But problems remained, as David J. Randall, deputy director of the Ohio Insurance Department, told a Senate committee last year. "Unfortunately, even after the 1982 amendments, the ERISA provisions relating to MEWAs are complex and confusing," he testified, "and this confusion encourages entrepreneurs to operate unauthorized, self-funded MEWAs under false claims of ERISA pre-emption [of state law]. These enterprises often are able to operate for significant periods without any supervision or oversight until financial troubles — for example, the failure to pay claims — cause participants to complain to state regulators." [11]

Operators of bogus MEWAs soon found that they could stay in business by masking their activities as benefit plans negotiated as part of a collective bargaining agreement or as employee-leasing firms,* both of which are exempt from state regulation. (ERISA also

Continued on p. 900

* Employee-leasing firms represent groups of small companies that can't afford to purchase group health coverage on an individual basis. Using "paper" transactions, member companies "fire" all their employees, who are then "hired" by the employee-leasing firm, which has promised to provide health coverage at lower cost than established insurers.

Chronology

1940s *Insurance companies and government regulators are slow to respond to fraud problems, though experts say insurance fraud in the United States probably emerged soon after the first policies were issued in the 18th century.*

1945
North Carolina becomes the first state to establish an insurance fraud bureau. The second such agency is not formed until 1976, in Florida.

1980s *Changes in the economy, immigration policy and insurance-industry awareness help make insurance fraud a hot-button issue.*

1982
An amendment to the 1974 Employee Retirement Income Security Act (ERISA) opens the door to increased health-insurance fraud by allowing non-traditional providers to offer coverage to small companies that might not be able to afford it.

1984
To coordinate anti-fraud efforts, special investigation units (SIUs) at individual insurance companies form the International Association of SIUS.

1985
Seven commercial health insurers, one state Blue Shield plan and several law enforcement officials form the National Health Care Anti-Fraud Association.

1986
The National Practitioner Data Bank (NPDB) is established under the federal Health Care Quality Improvement Act. The data bank contains the names of more than 80,000 health-care practitioners who have had malpractice payments made on their behalf by an insurer or have been disciplined after undergoing professional review.

1990s *State governments, which bear primary responsibility for regulating the insurance industry, intensify their efforts to fight fraud. Similar initiatives are launched by the federal government and the insurance industry itself.*

January 1992
The Insurance Crime Prevention Institute and the National Auto Theft Bureau merge to form the National Insurance Crime Bureau (NICB).

1992
The FBI launches a health-care fraud initiative that includes new training, new agents and task forces to address the problem.

1992
In the wake of widespread rioting and arson in Los Angeles, hundreds of merchants — many of them recent immigrants — find that their property insurance policies are bogus.

1993
Coalition Against Insurance Fraud (CAIF) is established by a group of insurance companies and consumer and law enforcement organizations.

1994
President Clinton signs the Violent Crime Control and Law Enforcement Act, which establishes federal penalties for certain types of insurance fraud — mainly offenses committed by industry insiders.

January 1995
"[P]atterns of fraud are so pervasive that systemic criminal activity is accepted as a way of 'doing business' in many segments of the health-care industry," an FBI report warns.

February 1995
Pennsylvania's Auto Theft Prevention Act and Insurance Fraud Prevention Act take effect, funded by levies on insurance companies.

March 2, 1995
CAIF adopts a broad model insurance fraud statute.

July 14, 1995
Prudential Insurance Co. of America, the nation's largest life insurer, agrees to pay $35.3 million in fines and to reimburse customers across the country after regulators accuse Prudential of sales abuses.

Jan. 18, 1996
George Lindemann Jr., son of a cellular telephone magnate and the operator of a Connecticut horse farm, is sentenced to 33 months in prison for his role in killing a show horse for $250,000 in insurance.

Aug. 21, 1996
President Clinton signs the Health Coverage Availability and Affordability Act, which stiffens penalties for defrauding government and private health-care programs. It also provides for the establishment of fraud-prevention programs.

Continued from p. 898

bars states from regulating the health insurance benefits provided by companies — large ones, for the most part — that self-insure.)

According to Robert Tillman, an assistant professor of sociology at St. Johns University in New York and an expert on white-collar crime, Congress amended ERISA with the best of intentions. "Starting in the 1970s," he notes, "the crunch on small businesses made it very difficult for them to get health insurance for their employees. At the same time, the traditional big health insurers were leaving the market because it wasn't profitable."

As Tillman sees it, the 1982 change was "a case of good intentions gone bad. My guess is that people in Congress were thinking, 'This is going to make health insurance more available.' They simply didn't foresee the opportunities for insurance fraud that crooks did." But, Tillman hastens to add, "Not all MEWAs are corrupt; in fact, quite a few of them are legitimate."

In any event, bogus MEWAs were quick to exploit the opening Congress unwittingly handed them. In the typical MEWA scam, "You rake in the premiums, pay off a few claims to keep the fraud rolling for a year or two, and then skip with a large amount of money — millions of dollars," Tillman says. "In the meantime, you've sent the funds you skimmed to some offshore haven or built a couple of mansions for yourself."

Industry Action

The collective cost of such fraud has been devastating. According to Leslie G. Aronovitz, associate director of the GAO, almost 400,000 persons were left with more than $123 million in unpaid claims by MEWAs between January 1988 and June 1991. Many others, he added, were left without health insurance. [12]

The insurance industry, meanwhile, has been taking steps of its own to combat fraud. The founding in 1984 of the International Association of Special Investigation Units (IASIU) reflected those efforts. Special investigation units (SIUs) are formed by individual insurers to detect and investigate suspicious claims. Results to date have been gratifying to the industry, with some companies reporting $10 in savings for every dollar spent to operate their SIU. The association draws its members from insurance carriers in the United States, Australia, Britain and Canada. [13]

The broad-based National Health Care Anti-Fraud Association (NHCAA), established in 1985, includes not only insurers but also the chief of the FBI's economic crimes unit, the U.S. Department of Health and Human Services' assistant inspector general for monetary civil penalties and the director of Florida's Medicaid fraud control unit, among others.

The organization's job was made easier by the Health Care Quality Improvement Act. The 1986 law created a National Practitioner Data Bank containing the names of more than 80,000 health-care providers who either have had malpractice awards paid on their behalf by an insurer or have been disciplined after undergoing professional review. "Hospitals are required to query the data bank whenever they're considering issuing credentials to a new practitioner," wrote Michael E. Diegel, CAIF's communications director. "They also must query every two years on all staff to uncover any actions that might have been taken, and may query more often if they desire." [14]

A similar database, designed to uncover auto insurance fraud, was established in 1992 by the Insurance Crime Prevention Institute and the National Auto Theft Bureau, which merged to form the National Insurance Crime Bureau (NICB). In 1993, the new organization's first full year of operation, its 200 agents investigated more than 43,000 questionable auto-insurance and theft claims.

NICB members have the use of "NICB Online," a computer database with information on a wide variety of vehicle and driver characteristics. The online tool enhances investigators' ability to develop leads by allowing them to access vehicle identification numbers, drivers' licenses, license plates, Social Security and tax numbers as well as previous claims information.

Insurance Fraud Bureau of Massachusetts

FBI Gets Involved

The FBI emerged as a major force in the fight against health-care insurance fraud the same year that NICB was formed. "[P]atterns of fraud are so pervasive that systemic criminal activity is accepted as a way of 'doing business' in many segments of the health care industry," the FBI declared in a 1995 report. [15]

The bureau's decision to get involved stemmed from a 1991 probe, code-named GOLDPILL, that uncovered widespread fraud by doctors, dentists, hospitals, ambulance services, medical-equipment suppliers, nursing homes and home-health agencies. Likening the health-care situation to the savings and loan crisis, the FBI concluded that "trust within the reimbursement system, lack of oversight and escalating costs between 1982 and 1990 . . . attracted thousands of criminals, con artists, corrupt business interests and seedy marketers to a profession dedicated to healing." [16]

To help clean up the health-care industry, the FBI in 1992 reassigned 50 agents from other programs to tackle the burgeoning medical fraud caseload. At the same time, the bureau established medical fraud squads in its Baltimore, Chicago, Detroit, Los Angeles, Miami, New York and Philadelphia field offices. Additional squads have since been formed in the Dallas, Houston, New Haven, and Washington, D.C., offices. Agents who specialize in medical fraud must become experts not only in criminal investigation techniques but also in diagnosis and treatment codes and reimbursement schedules used by insurers. The Washington and Miami offices now have two anti-fraud squads to handle the high volume of cases.

Health-care fraud involving Medicare and Medicaid is the No. 1 priority of the FBI's white-collar crime program, says economic crimes unit chief Bullock. "But we also investigate internal insurance scams, which are committed by insurance companies that are fraudulently capitalized," he adds. "The principals of such a company set up shop by obtaining fraudulent assets — often from a shell corporation based in the Caribbean. They use those worthless assets to capitalize a bogus insurance company. That's important, because your capital or your surplus determines how much insurance you can write. So the fictitious assets allow the phony insurers to write policies and collect premiums, which are pocketed."

According to Larry A. Potts, assistant director of the FBI's criminal investigative division, senior citizens' homes often are targeted by health-care scam artists. "Operators of rolling labs advertise free medical testing and screening and often 'screen' the patient for Medicare, Medicaid or private insurance coverage," Potts told a House Judiciary subcommittee in 1993. "Once they obtain the insurance information, they perform and bill for many unnecessary medical tests. It is common for these businessmen to perpetrate their frauds by paying kickbacks to senior citizens' home managers or bill for phony services." [17]

By working with insurers and other government agencies, the FBI unraveled many such schemes. For instance, the Justice and Health and Human Services departments joined the bureau in forming the Executive Level Health Care Fraud Policy Group to devise more effective ways of fighting medical fraud and removing bureaucratic barriers to enforcement efforts.

Many such barriers existed at the outset, primarily because existing federal statutes did not directly address health-care fraud. "Drug-tampering and adulteration laws did not adequately correlate to the criminal activity," the FBI report noted. "Tampering laws had penalties too harsh to fit the crime, and the penalties under the Food, Drug, and Cosmetic Act were too lenient. The criminal activity under inquiry fit somewhere in between." [18]

Congress Acts

Mail fraud statutes also proved unequal to the task of apprehending crooks who sold tainted prescription drugs paid for by Medicaid to pharmacists. The drug traffickers could evade arrest by shipping their packages via Federal Express or United Parcel Service (UPS). Because they did not use the U.S. Postal Service, they could not be prosecuted for mail fraud. And since the drugs were not controlled substances like heroin or cocaine, federal drug laws did not apply either.

Congress amended the mail-fraud statute to include commercial carriers like UPS as part of the omnibus crime bill enacted in 1994. In addition, penalties were established for fraud committed by insurance company employees. The measure made it a federal offense to defraud an insurer engaged in interstate commerce, such as by knowingly filing a false statement with an insurance regulator or by embezzling money from a company. Offenders were made liable for criminal penalties, including fines and jail terms of up to five years.

The 1994 law also barred anyone convicted of a federal crime involving dishonesty, such as insurance fraud, from working in the insurance business except with the written permission of a state insurance regulator. And it authorized the U.S. attorney general to impose civil fines of up to $50,000 for the insurance fraud violations. However, the law did not address fraud committed by claimants or beneficiaries of insurance policies.

Philip E. Stano, senior counsel for litigation at the American Council of Life Insurance (ACLI), has argued that the insurance fraud provisions of the 1994 law were based on a flawed premise — Congress' failure to respond in timely fashion to the savings and loan crisis of the late 1980s. "Congress erroneously believed that parallels could be drawn between the insurance

Rough Stuff on the Horse-Show Circuit

On the horse-show circuit, it's widely assumed, participants are rich enough not to fret about money. But even in this rarefied world, animals are killed so that their owners can collect tens or even hundreds of thousands of dollars in insurance benefits. "When these millionaires get tired of them," said convicted horse killer Tommy Burns, "they throw the horses away like broken toys." [1]

Burns and an accomplice were arrested near Gainesville, Fla., in February 1991 shortly after they broke the leg of a horse, Streetwise, and summoned a veterinarian. Told that the horse had broken the leg in a fall, the vet put the animal down. As Burns and his partner drove away, they were arrested by local law enforcement officers, who had been following them on a tip.

Burns soon found that the wealthy owners who had sought his services wanted nothing to do with him once he was behind bars. So he began naming names and details about his gruesome specialty. His fees ranged between $5,000 and $40,000 a horse, netting him some $150,000 over a period of nearly 10 years. Burns' stories led to the indictment in July 1994 of 23 owners, trainers, riders and veterinarians, most of whom pleaded guilty.

The biggest name among those cited in the indictment was George Lindemann Jr., the multimillionaire son of a cellular telephone magnate and one of the country's leading show-horse riders. He was accused of hiring Burns in 1990 to kill a show horse, Charisma, to collect $250,000 in insurance money.

Lindemann claimed he was the victim of an extortion attempt and that his horse had died of natural causes. As his defense, he further said that he was so wealthy that he didn't need the money. Lindemann filed a $100 million lawsuit against the American Horse Shows Association for trying to bar him from competition. Lindemann dragged the association through a series of injunction hearings and appeals that allowed him to continue competing on a limited basis. He even switched from Grand Prix jumping to dressage in an effort to secure a spot on the U.S. equestrian team at the 1996 Olympics.

However, Lindemann's fight for exoneration was unavailing. He was found guilty in September 1995 on three federal counts of wire fraud and was sentenced in January to nearly three years in prison. He was also ordered to pay a $500,000 fine, $250,000 in restitution to the insurance company he defrauded, plus the cost of his imprisonment. [2]

"We had never heard about this kind of insurance fraud before," says Dennis Jay, executive director of the Coalition Against Insurance Fraud (CAIF). "When we tried to get a sense of how widespread it was, more than a few people told us it was something that wasn't really talked about in horse-show circles. Apparently, some people thought it was an acceptable way to recoup some of the cost of maintaining a horse. I think silence had the effect of condoning the activity."

The insurance industry itself was not entirely blameless, in Jay's view. "According to what we were told, some companies that insured show horses suspected that claims fraud was occurring. But they chose not to do anything about it because they were still making a profit from that line of business."

[1] Quoted in *The New York Times*, Sept. 5, 1993, p. A1.

[2] Marion Hulick, a trainer at the Lindemann family's horse farm in Connecticut, was sentenced to 21 months in prison on the same charges, but was not fined.

industry's and the savings and loan industry's financial condition and the degree of criminality occurring within those industries," Stano wrote. [19]

Stano noted that ACLI favors amending the 1994 law to "clarify that employees not in positions of significant authority . . . would not be subject" to its harsher insurance-fraud penalties. "The prohibition against certain felons engaging in the business of insurance could be an effective weapon if prosecutors focus on 'company busters' attempting a subsequent scam. Further, insurance regulators should not succumb to political pressure to readmit habitual felons whose activities have been injurious to the insurance business." [20] ■

CURRENT SITUATION

Model Fraud Statutes

The first insurance-fraud indictment under the 1994 law was filed in September 1995, a year after President Clinton signed the measure. Paul R. Tubbs, a broker with Financial Guarantee Underwriters, was charged by the U.S. attorney's office in Houston with opening a bank account he controlled in the name of Financial Guarantee Inc., and depositing $129,000 in premium payments that policyholders had sent to his employer. The indictment also alleged mail fraud, stating that Tubbs had used Federal Express to carry out his scheme. [21]

The Tubbs case surfaced at a time of mounting activity against insurance fraud at both the state and federal levels. Some of the state initiatives were based on model anti-fraud statutes independently adopted in 1995 by CAIF and the National Association of Insurance Commissioners (NAIC).

CAIF's model, the more far-reaching of the two, addresses three types of fraud: claims fraud; fraud involving applications for insurance; and fraud committed by employees in the insurance industry, including agents, adjusters, brokers or persons claiming to be in the business of insurance.[22] CAIF defines insurance fraud as a specific crime and makes it a felony in most cases.

Under the CAIF model, a "fraudulent insurance act" is defined as an act "committed by anyone who, knowingly and with intent, defrauds another person for gain. Such acts include claims, application and insurer fraud. Convictions under this section of the statute must meet the "proof beyond a reasonable doubt" standard required to find a defendant guilty of criminal charges. An individual convicted of a fraudulent act would have to make monetary restitution for any financial loss connected with the offense.

The CAIF model defines an "unlawful insurance act" as one "committed by anyone who commits or allows to be committed an act "with an intent to induce reliance" on false information. Convictions under this section need only meet the lower civil standard of proof — that "a preponderance of the evidence" supports a finding of guilt. The model further provides that anyone defrauded by an unlawful insurance act can recover money lost as a result of the offense, plus legal fees not to exceed $5,000.

"This section expands the legal scope of insurance fraud into an entirely new arena," says CAIF. "Those who have shielded themselves from the actual act of fraud — signing a false claim form, for example — can be charged through this civil remedy. . . . This provision is designed to punish individuals who create a fraudulent scheme, such as a medical mill, but have underlings execute it."[23]

The NAIC model statute, adopted in September 1995, would create a fraud bureau within state insurance departments, require persons having "knowledge or reasonable belief" of insurance fraud to report it, and provide broad immunity for reporting suspected fraud. It would also expand insurance commissioners' authority by giving them the power to revoke the license of any state licensee convicted of insurance fraud and to bar persons convicted of felonies involving dishonesty or breach of trust from participating in the insurance business in that state.

NAIC's model contains fewer civil causes of action and remedies than does the CAIF version. "There's been a critical difference in our approach since day one," commented Frank Doolittle, head of the NAIC anti-fraud committee. "We're trying to produce a product that's congruent with the needs of all 50 states. It's more plain vanilla."

"The coalition's model requires a pretty well-defined fraud bureau," Doolittle added. "The NAIC model meets the needs of the state with a three-person fraud bureau. It's a good start. The NAIC model goes far enough, if you're a state that has nothing on the books and are trying to get off the ground."[24]

Stano pointed to another key difference between the CAIF and NAIC models. "The coalition's bill is far broader than the NAIC bill in that it requires the court or prosecutor to notify the appropriate [state] licensing authority of any practitioner (i.e., attorney, physician, building contractor, automotive repair shop licensee, etc.) convicted of insurance fraud. The NAIC has never asserted jurisdiction over non-insurance practitioners and declined to include such a section in its model bill."[25]

State Initiatives

Several states — notably Colorado, Minnesota and Tennessee * — approved insurance-fraud laws in 1996 based largely or in part on the CAIF model. Among other provisions, the Colorado bill requires that the appropriate state licensing authority be notified in cases of fraud-related criminal action or civil judgment against a licensed professional. State Rep. Dave Owen, one of the measure's sponsors, said it expands existing Colorado laws "to include all types of insurance fraud, whether committed by claimants or people in the insurance industry, and sets up a partnership of government, industry and consumers in the fight."[26]

The Minnesota law's definition of a fraudulent insurance act tracks the CAIF provision. It also establishes a strike force in the attorney general's office to be funded by voluntary contributions from insurance companies.

David Orbuch, Minnesota's assistant attorney general in charge of prosecuting insurance fraud, attributes the law's passage to two factors. "One, we had an insurance-fraud working group in Minnesota," he says, "made up of insurance industry officials, local prosecutors and representatives of other state agencies. There was growing belief within the group that prosecutors needed more tools to combat insurance fraud effectively.

"Two, we realized that many insurance frauds are not prosecuted because of the low monetary loss to the insured. Instead, prosecutors were concentrating on murders, rapes and other violent crimes. We felt that if we could turn the spotlight on insurance fraud, prosecutions would increase. We also believed consumers would get the message that law enforcement was concerned about this type of crime and would aggressively go after those who commit it."

In Minnesota, Orbuch says, "It's estimated that every family loses $1,000 a year, or pays an extra $1,000 in insurance premiums and other costs, because of insurance fraud." As people become more aware of these invisible out-of-pocket costs, "They're going to require their elected officials and urge their prosecutors to focus on these offenses."

At least 28 states now have anti-

---

* The Tennessee law covers only workers' compensation fraud.

fraud units in the state insurance department or attorney general's office, while about 20 states mandate the reporting of fraudulent acts. At least five states require insurers to establish SIUs or devise plans to combat fraud. Fraud warnings on claims forms and/or applications are mandatory in about 14 states.

In addition, some 38 states provide some form of immunity for the reporting of insurance fraud. In Nevada, for example, the reporting individual's identity and the nature of the information may be kept confidential by the insurance commissioner unless a court rules otherwise. Wisconsin offers immunity for defamation actions only. And Rhode Island provides "employment protection" to individuals reporting fraud, but not immunity from civil litigation. [27]

ERISA Bill Fizzles

The health insurance bill signed by President Clinton on Aug. 21 stiffened federal penalties for defrauding the government through federal health-care programs such as Medicare and Medicaid. In addition, the law would establish programs to monitor efficiency and prevent fraud.

On the other hand, the measure would soften some existing anti-fraud laws. Under certain parts of current law, for example, health providers can be prosecuted for negligence. The newly enacted law would weaken that legal standard so that they could be prosecuted only for acting with a "reckless disregard for the truth." [28]

A bill aimed at protecting workers whose health benefits are provided through self-funded company plans went nowhere in this session of Congress. ERISA currently exempts employers' self-funded health insurance plans from state regulation. According to Sen. James M. Jeffords, R-Vt., the exemption has left many participants "without certain basic insurance safeguards and has, in some instances, left employers and employees alike at the mercy of unscrupulous promoters of fraudulent insurance schemes." [29]

Legislation introduced by Jeffords in July 1995 sought to improve matters by making it clear that states have the authority to regulate self-insured health plans and to shut down fraudulent MEWAs. In addition, the Jeffords bill would have established health-plan purchasing coalitions under ERISA. The private, voluntary alliances would be composed of individuals and businesses who buy health insurance and negotiate with providers.

The Senate Labor and Human Resources Committee held a hearing on the Jeffords bill but there has been no further action in either house of Congress. Tillman of St. John's isn't surprised that the bill died. IBM and many other giant corporations want ERISA to remain just as it is, he says, and not simply because it bars states from regulating their self-insured health plans. He notes that an employer funding its own health insurance "doesn't have to maintain minimum capital assets, and it doesn't have to contribute to state guarantee funds. In short, it's more profitable to go the self-funding route. ERISA is good for the bottom line."

Big companies even tend to oppose amendments to ERISA that would target only fraudulent insurance schemes. "I'm not sure why," says Tillman. "It may be something like gun control, where the NRA [National Rifle Association] fights any modification of firearms laws because they think it will lead to further changes." ■

OUTLOOK

Fraud on 'Upswing'

Will the fight against insurance fraud succeed in the future? The answer, many experts say, lies in a recent report by Conning & Co., an investment and research firm based in Hartford, Conn. "Whether because of economic pressures, weakening social values, low risk of being caught or some combination of the three, insurance fraud is on the upswing," the report stated. "And even with increased insurer involvement, there is no evidence that the tide has turned. However, we see that a growing momentum to fight fraud may turn that tide sometime soon, perhaps by the turn of the century." [30]

But progress will only occur, experts say, when individuals become more aware of the impact insurance fraud has on their own pocketbooks. "Like a lot of white-collar crime, insurance fraud doesn't worry people very much because it's so complicated," Tillman says. "Eyes glaze over if you start talking about multiple-employer welfare arrangements. People can understand a guy taking his car out and torching it and then sending in a claim saying it was stolen. Or a doctor claiming he saw 100 patients when he actually saw five. But the great majority of insurance fraud cases are so convoluted, so messy, that people just lose interest."

Minnesota Assistant Attorney General Orbuch feels there will be increased attempts to defraud insurance companies "because it's the easy crime of the '90s. You don't need to go into the 7-Eleven with a gun and a mask and put your life at risk. You can commit fraud in the comfort of your own home by submitting bogus claims to your insurance company via computer.

Continued on p. 906

At Issue:

Are criminal sanctions more useful than civil remedies in dealing with insurance fraud?

EDWARD G. FELDMAN
Acting head deputy, Workers' Compensation Fraud Division, Los Angeles County District Attorney's Office

WRITTEN FOR *THE CQ RESEARCHER*, OCT. 8, 1996

yes

The essential contribution made by criminal sanctions to the fight against insurance fraud can be summed up in one word: deterrence.

Perpetrators of insurance fraud vary greatly in their sophistication and avarice. They range from individuals who exaggerate their losses after a minor fender-bender or homeowners claim to the corrupt health-care provider who routinely pads the bills to insurance carriers by including charges for services not actually performed. Insurance fraud perpetrators share one common characteristic: Their conduct is the product of a calculated decision. For them, the decision to cheat is not deterred by common ethical values. Instead, it must be deterred by their perceptions of the risks being caught.

The ability of any sanction to deter wrongful conduct can be measured by two factors: the likelihood of its being imposed and the magnitude of the sanction. If potential insurance fraud offenders believed that their detection was a near certainty, civil sanctions could be fully effective in preventing fraud. The anticipated loss of unlawful gains and the imposition of monetary sanctions would eliminate the profit potential that drives the fraud. Of course, only a modest percentage of frauds are actually detected, and fewer still are documented and proven to support an action for sanctions, civil or criminal. As a consequence, most offenders proceed in the comfort that the likelihood of being caught is acceptably small.

The advantage presented by a system of criminal sanctions is that the perceived risk of being detected is greatly magnified by the potential severity of the sanctions imposed. The prospect of months or years of imprisonment with murderers, robbers and street hoodlums can weigh heavily on potential offenders, even if the likelihood of detection is modest.

To be effective, the law enforcement presence must be credible and visible to potential offenders. It does not have to be comprehensive. A relatively small number of prosecutions resulting in heavy sentences against the most egregious offenders can have an enormous chilling effect on other potential offenders.

A five-year-old program to combat workers' compensation fraud in California represents a particularly effective example of establishing an effective criminal deterrent. The program, currently funded at $25 million annually, is responsible for saving several billion dollars a year by focusing law enforcement activity on the core of the fraudulent activity, large medical-fraud mills. A modest number of prosecutions of heavy offenders chased numerous others out of business.

JANET BACHMAN
Vice president for claims administration, American Insurance Association

WRITTEN FOR *THE CQ RESEARCHER*, OCT. 8, 1996

no

Criminal prosecution is clearly a valuable remedy in the effort to reduce insurance fraud. It is not, however, the most effective overall. Consider that insurance fraud has always been against the law. Every state has, at the least, a general fraud statute. Nonetheless, the fact the behavior is illegal has done little to keep fraud in check; to the contrary, fraud has grown significantly over the last decade.

Public treasuries cannot, and should not, pay to investigate and prosecute every case of insurance fraud. And as taxpayers, we can certainly not afford to incarcerate all these white-collar criminals. If we did, we would have to triple our prison space.

Fraud statutes frequently call for victim restitution. In reality, however, victims rarely are reimbursed for their losses, and criminals end up retaining their ill-gotten gains. Doctors, lawyers and other professionals who are convicted of insurance fraud rarely are required to forfeit the professional licenses that allowed them to perpetrate the fraud in the first place. Some even continue their activities from prison.

Criminal sanctions alone obviously do little to affect the behavior of career criminals. If our objective is to substantially reduce the financial costs of fraud, and this *is* the goal, then we literally cannot afford to rely on criminal sanctions alone or even in large measure.

What we badly need is civil laws aimed at reducing the opportunity and profit in this crime. But significant change will occur only when victims are empowered to act on their own behalf and in their own self-interest, without relying on public treasuries for enforcement.

One of the civil measures we advocate is statutory immunity for insurers to exchange information about fraud cases with each other, thereby enormously increasing the ability of an insurance company to detect fraud. We also favor allowing victims to regain their losses and expenses through the civil courts. And to stop professional criminals from continuing to defraud in perpetuity, we advocate the automatic revocation of any license upon criminal conviction.

We also acknowledge that at times, insurance companies are part of the problem. Some fail to police their own staffs and agents; some take an indifferent attitude toward the fraud that inflates their customers' premiums; and officials at a few companies loot the company from the inside. And so with equal conviction, we insist that all insurance companies, not just the most progressive, must assume an active, responsible and vigilant role.

FOR MORE INFORMATION

American Council of Life Insurance, 1001 Pennsylvania Ave. N.W., Washington, D.C. 20004-2599; (202) 624-2000. ACLI works to further the interests of the life insurance industry and to provide effective relations with government.

American Insurance Association, 1130 Connecticut Ave., N.W., Washington, D.C. 20036; (202) 828-7100. AIA works to further the interests of the property/casualty insurance industry.

Coalition Against Insurance Fraud, 1511 K St. N.W., Suite 622, Washington, D.C. 20005; (202) 393-7330. Founded in 1993, CAIF is an alliance of insurance companies and consumer and law enforcement groups.

Insurance Information Institute, 110 William St., New York, N.Y. 10038; (212) 669-9200. The institute, which represents property and casualty insurers, publishes "Insurance Facts," an annual compilation of insurance statistics.

National Health Care Anti-Fraud Association, 1255 23rd St., N.W., Washington, D.C. 20037; (202) 659-5955. Members, including health-insurance firms and regulatory and law enforcement agencies, work to identify and prosecute those who defraud health-care reimbursement systems.

National Insurance Crime Bureau, 10330 S. Roberts Rd., Suite 3A, Palos Hills, Ill. 60465; (708) 430-2430. The nonprofit NICB uses its extensive electronic database to combat insurance fraud and motor vehicle theft.

Continued from p. 904

For that reason, I think more people will attempt it. I'm encouraged that insurance companies are becoming more aggressive in the war against insurance fraud, and that they're trying to stem the tide through internal programs. But those are new programs, for the most part, and it's too early to tell how effective they will be."

Computers the Answer?

But while computers may facilitate insurance fraud attempts, they also can help turn the tables on would-be defrauders. "Computers can save an insurance company an enormous amount of money by detecting fraud at an early stage, before the claim has been paid," Orbuch notes. Indeed, many state and local governments already are using computer-based artificial intelligence programs to sort through Medicare, Medicaid and other insurance claims for fraud, according to *Governing* magazine.

Artificial intelligence can readily detect the "unbundling" of medical codes, a practice that enables unscrupulous doctors to collect higher Medicaid fees. Instead of "submitting one code for an appendectomy, with that procedure's established fee," wrote M. J. Richter, "the doctor will submit one code for an office visit, another code for a hospital stay, another for an anesthesiologist's treatment and a fourth for surgery. The resulting total amount is much higher than it would have been had the doctor used the single correct code." [31]

Computers also can sniff out fraudulent workers' compensation claims. Workers' compensation plans and company health plans are usually handled by two different insurance companies, with only one of them paying a given claim. "Sometimes, however, a doctor will deliberately submit a claim for the same patient to the other carrier and get paid twice," Richter writes. "The chances are pretty good that an artificial intelligence program will detect that doctor's interesting approach to professional compensation." [32]

CAIF's Jay agrees that artificial intelligence gives insurers a potent weapon against fraud, but he cautions that criminals can exploit the same technology. "Database systems allow an investigator to review a person's claims history, match up Social Security numbers with names and examine relationships between individual doctors and lawyers," he says. "Some of the artificial intelligence programs that are coming online now enable investigators to do in a few minutes what used to take them hundreds of hours."

At the same time, he says, "Some of the professional criminals specializing in insurance fraud have good counterintelligence — they understand the systems, the red flags and they change their modus operandi accordingly." For example, bogus insurance companies use computers "to falsify assets, if they're trying to set up a fake insurance company, or to hide premium dollars skimmed off the top."

But overall, Jay says, computer technology has "helped the insurance industry combat claims fraud more than it has helped the defrauders."

The FBI's Bullock predicts that law enforcement will make headway against insurance fraud in coming years, but he stresses the importance of cooperative efforts. "Progress isn't going to come about just because of our efforts, but through collaboration with inspectors general in the federal government, the National Association of Insurance Commissioners and the insurance companies themselves — they're in the front lines of this battle," he says. "They are in a position to identify these cases on a timely basis, which will allow us to investigate them more effectively. We have a long way to go, but, working as a team, we feel confident of gaining the upper hand over those responsible for insurance fraud."

Perry of the American International Group worries that the recently enacted federal welfare reform law could lead to increased insurance fraud. "People who have been defrauding the welfare system may now turn to insurance scams as an alternative," he says. "They would have to get a job before they could rip off the workers' compensation system," he says. "But they could still operate in the casualty/property area, where questionable 'slips and falls' claims are common."

Bachman of the American Insurance Association says that the state of the economy will do much to determine future levels of insurance fraud. "There has always been a connection, to some degree, between insurance fraud and general economic condition," she says. "If we enter a down cycle in a few years, accompanied by rising unemployment, the incidence of insurance fraud will shoot up — irrespective of anything else that might occur at the same time."

But if the economy remains healthy, Bachman sees insurance fraud declining. "That's because insurance companies are doing a much better job detecting fraud than they were even five years ago," she says. "Also, the industry is beginning to realize that its customers are potentially its most valuable partners in preventing and detecting fraud. That's a real break with the past. In dealing with anything, including fraud, insurance companies have had a tendency to think, 'Well, if I have a problem, it's up to me to solve it.' They failed to realize that their customers could help."

But customers can only do that, Bachman notes, if insurance fraud victims are empowered to seek civil remedies from those who cheat them. She points to the restitution and civil-remedy provisions of the CAIF model law, which she helped draft, as one approach to empowerment.

Fraud victims would have to take the initiative, she says, because "It's not a law that will automatically do anything. It just creates an opportunity for victims to recover the money they lost. If the victim does nothing, then the law will have no effect at all. Really, the victims must come forward and empower themselves.

"If they were to do that in sizable numbers in any state, I think you would see insurance fraud drop significantly within two years." ■

Notes

[1] Lichtman is scheduled to be sentenced Jan. 17, 1997, and faces up to 10 years in prison. He is cooperating with the state attorney general's ongoing investigation of others involved in his scam. Lichtman's license was suspended.

[2] Stewart Woodman was convicted in 1990 of first-degree murder and is serving a life sentence. He escaped a possible death sentence by testifying against his brother.

[3] See Insurance Information Institute, "Insurance Issues Update," July 1996, p. 4.

[4] Kathryn Baker and Herbert Edelhertz, "Fighting the Hidden Crime: A National Agenda to Combat Insurance Fraud," Battele Seattle Research Institute, March 1992, p. 8. The institute is a division of Battele Memorial Institute, an independent, nonprofit international research organization founded in 1929 with a staff of 7,500.

[5] Carolyn T. Geer, "Low-Risk Crime," *Forbes,* Sept. 27, 1993, p. 58.

[6] Carolyn T. Geer, "Inside Jobs," *Forbes,* May 23, 1994, p. 56.

[7] See Steve Langdon with Alissa J. Rubin, "Health Insurance Bill Fight Ends With Deal on Savings Accounts," *CQ Weekly Report,* Aug. 3, 1996, pp. 2198-2199.

[8] *Encyclopedia Brittanica,* Vol. 9 (1978), p. 657, *Encyclopedia Americana,* Vol. 15 (1984), pp. 236-237.

[9] Insurance Information Institute, *op. cit.,* p. 9.

[10] *Loc. cit.*

[11] Testimony before Senate Committee on Labor and Human Resources, July 25, 1995.

[12] Testimony before House Way and Means Subcommittee on Health, May 27, 1993.

[13] Richard J. Matysiak, "The Impact of Special Investigation Units on Insurance Fraud" (unpublished paper).

[14] Michael E. Diegel, "Banking On It," *Fraud Focus,* September-October 1995, p. 4.

[15] Federal Bureau of Investigation, "Health Care Fraud," January 1995, p. 2.

[16] *Ibid.,* p. 4.

[17] Testimony before House Judiciary Subcommittee on Crime and Criminal Justice, Feb. 4, 1993.

[18] *Ibid.,* p. 6.

[19] Philip E. Stano, "Recent Developments in Life and Health Insurance Fraud Legislation in the United States," paper presented to Colloquium of the International Association for Insurance Law, Prague, the Czech Republic, June 1996, p. 10.

[20] *Ibid.,* p. 17.

[21] "First Indictment Filed Under 1994 Federal Insurance Fraud Act," *Fraud Focus,* November-December 1995, p. 6.

[22] Coalition Against Insurance Fraud, "Model Insurance Fraud Act," September 1995, p. 1.

[23] *Ibid.,* p. 4.

[24] Quoted in *Fraud Focus,* September-October 1995, p. 1.

[25] Stano, *op. cit.,* p. 29.

[26] Quoted in *Fraud Focus,* May-June 1996, p. 1.

[27] Stano, *op. cit.,* pp. 19-23.

[28] Langdon and Rubin, *op. cit.*

[29] Remarks on Senate floor, July 21, 1995.

[30] Conning & Co., "Insurance Fraud: The Quiet Catastrophe," 1996, p. 5.

[31] M.J. Richter, "Smart Machines and the Fight Against Medical Fraud," *Governing,* April 1994, p. 84.

[32] *Loc. cit.*

Bibliography

Selected Sources Used

Articles

Craddock, Ashley, and Mordecai Lawrence, "Swoop-and-Squats," *Mother Jones,* September-October 1993.
The authors examine staged motor-vehicle accidents, many involving recent immigrants. "So long as there are criminals and a steady supply of people at the bottom of the American economy, any scheme that returns large profits, no matter how dangerous, will be hard to deter," they write.

Diegel, Michael E., "Philly Frustration," *Fraud Focus,* March-April 1996.
Diegel, communications director for the Coalition Against Insurance Fraud, describes Philadelphia's efforts to shed its longstanding reputation as the nation's insurance-fraud capital — in auto-insurance fraud, in particular.

Geer, Carolyn T., "Low-Risk Crime," *Forbes,* Sept. 27, 1993.
According to Geer, insurance fraud is attractive to criminals because it entails little risk: Below a certain dollar threshold, insurers will routinely pay claims rather than face the uncertainties and high costs of litigation.

Longo, Tracey, "There is No Free Insurance: Don't Get Taken to the Cleaners by Agents Pushing Replacement Policies," *Kiplinger's Personal Finance Magazine,* October 1995.
Longo explains how some unscrupulous insurance agents persuade customers to roll the cash value of an existing policy into a new one. This "churning" means higher premiums for the policyholder — and a hefty sales commission for the agent.

Richter, M.J., "Smart Machines and the Fight Against Medical Fraud," *Governing,* April 1994.
Richter shows how advances in computer technology are enabling insurance companies to successfully fight fraud.

Updegrave, Walter L., "Don't Be Suckered Into the Life Insurance Mess," *Money,* January 1995.
Updegrave flags deceptive insurance-industry sales practices, including agents' claims that policies are tantamount to investments.

Vladeck, Bruce C., "Medicare, Medicaid Fraud and Abuse," *The Journal of the American Medical Association,* March 8, 1995.
Vladeck recounts efforts by the federal Health Care Financing Administration to identify and combat Medicare and Medicaid fraud. "The overwhelming majority of physicians . . . are as trustworthy as they are committed to professional excellence," he writes. "But as in so many other areas of life, the few bad apples pose a risk of poisoning the whole barrel."

Reports and Studies

Baker, Kathryn, and Herbert Edelhertz, *Fighting the Hidden Crime: A National Agenda to Combat Insurance Fraud,* Battele Seattle Research Center, March 1992.
In a report commissioned by the Insurance Information Institute, the authors pinpoint the areas where insurance fraud fighters should focus their resources.

Federal Bureau of Investigation, *Health Care Fraud,* January 1995.
This report describes how the FBI investigates insurance health fraud and details the laws under which such cases are prosecuted. It also contains proposals for additional investigative resources and statutes.

Matysiak, Richard J., *The Impact of Special Investigation Units on Insurance Fraud,* January 1994 (unpublished paper).
Matysiak, senior fraud investigator for the Georgia insurance commissioner's office, provides a brief overview of special investigative units (SIUs), which many insurance companies have established to combat fraud.

Insurance Information Institute, *Insurance Issues Update,* July 1996.
This survey reviews the extent of fraud in the insurance industry as a whole as well as in specific insurance lines. It also explores possible reasons why many consumers don't consider filing fraudulent insurance claims as a major ethical or legal offense.

Stano, Phillip E., *Recent Developments in Life and Health Insurance Fraud Legislation in the United States,* American Council of Life Insurance, June 1996.
Stano, the council's senior counsel for litigation, examines the types of fraud occurring in all lines of insurance, analyzes the insurance provisions of the 1994 Violent Crime Control and Law Enforcement Act and summarizes recent state legislative and regulatory developments.

Subcommittee on Crime and Criminal Justice, U.S. House Judiciary Committee, *Health Care Fraud* (published proceedings of hearings held Feb. 4 and May 27, 1993).
Representatives of the insurance industry, consumer groups and law enforcement agencies present their views.

The Next Step

Additional information from UMI's Newspaper & Periodical Abstracts database

Arson

"Hinton convicted of torching house," ***Atlanta Constitution,*** **Jan. 18, 1996, p. D3.**
Colvin "Butch" Hinton III, who is the prime suspect in the disappearance of Emory University student Shannon Melendi, was found guilty of setting fire to his metro Atlanta home in order to defraud his insurance company.

Jimenez, Teresa, "Stable owner found guilty in arson fatal to 23 horses," ***Chicago Tribune,*** **May 4, 1996, p. 1L5.**
On May 3, 1996, after three hours of deliberations, a Lake County, Ill., jury found John Garvey guilty of hiring someone to set fire to his Prairie View stable so he could collect on an insurance policy. Garvey now faces a prison sentence of three to seven years. Twenty-three horses died in the fire.

O'Connor, Matt, "8 more charged in horse-insurance scam," ***Chicago Tribune,*** **March 1, 1996, p. C8.**
In a second round of indictments from a federal investigation of fraud in the equestrian industry, eight people were charged in connection with the killing of four show horses for thousands of dollars in insurance payouts. The latest charges bring to 36 the number of Chicago-area individuals who have been charged by state and federal authorities in the five-year, nationwide investigation.

"Restaurateur convicted in Va. arson scheme," ***The Washington Post,*** **June 15, 1995, p. D2.**
Abbas Sadegh, a former Alexandria, Va., restaurateur, was convicted of federal arson and mail fraud charges for burning down adjoining restaurants that he owned as part of an insurance fraud.

Costs of Insurance Fraud

"Business bulletin: Wiping out fraud," ***The Wall Street Journal,*** **Aug. 1, 1996, p. A1.**
According to research and investment firm Conning & Co., wiping out fraud could improve an insurer's average return on investment by as much as 18 percent. It adds that insurance fraud cost the insurance industry some $120 billion in 1995, up 33 percent from 1990.

Collins, Rachel M., "At least $42 million lost to auto insurance fraud," ***Boston Globe,*** **March 26, 1995, p. NH1.**
Insurance companies lost at least $42 million to automobile insurance fraud in New Hampshire in 1994. Although the state is fighting back with a new law enforcement unit, it could be years before the frequency rate and cost of fraud are reduced.

Galifianakis, Nick, and Cindy Hall, "USA snapshots: The cost of insurance fraud," ***USA Today,*** **Feb. 9, 1995, p. B1.**
According to the Coalition Against Insurance Fraud, each U.S. family pays $448 a year for health insurance fraud, $205 for commercial or business insurance fraud, $157 for auto insurance fraud and $23 for homeowners insurance fraud.

Insurance Fraud

Boling, Rick, "Is your insurer ripping you off?" ***Modern Maturity,*** **Jan. 1996, pp. 68-69.**
Large health insurance companies and managed-care facilities often negotiate volume discounts with hospitals and other health-care providers but fail to disclose discounts to policyholders. This problem and how consumers can protect themselves are discussed.

Cook, Rhonda, "44 arrested, 17 sought in alleged insurance fraud," ***Atlanta Constitution,*** **May 25, 1995, p. E5.**
Forty-four people were arrested in central Georgia May 24, 1995, as part of a nationwide crackdown on insurance fraud. Seventeen more suspects are being sought.

Donegan, Lawrence, "The fraud that failed," ***Guardian,*** **Dec. 20, 1995, p. 3.**
Lord Brocket filed a $4.5 million insurance claim after the disappearance of three vintage Ferraris and a Maserati from the UK's Brocket Hall in 1991. After detectives were alerted to a dispute over Lloyd's of London's refusal to pay out, they reopened the investigation into the theft, eventually charging Lord Brocket with conspiracy to defraud an insurance company.

Fields, Gary, "FBI sweep nabs 100 in auto scams," ***USA Today,*** **May 25, 1995, p. A1.**
The FBI arrested 126 people in a 31-state crackdown on criminal fraud schemes involving staged automobile accidents. The arrests are part of an 18-month investigation that FBI Director Louis Freeh says is the largest insurance fraud probe in bureau history.

"FBI raids suspects in fraud against car insurance firms," ***Boston Globe,*** **May 25, 1995, p. 7.**
FBI agents conducted arrest and search raids in 31 states in an investigation begun a year and a half earlier into syndicates that stage automobile accidents and defraud health insurers.

Johnson, Paul H., "Six arrested in connection with

auto insurance fraud ring," *Los Angeles Times,* April 17, 1996, p. B3.

California insurance investigators arrested an attorney, Noel Stephen Olshan, on April 16, 1996, on suspicion of masterminding a major auto insurance ring that bilked insurers out of $20 million in phony claims.

Marquis, Julie, "UC medical centers accused of fraudulent insurance claims," *Los Angeles Times,* Aug. 10, 1996, p. A21.

A whistleblower lawsuit by two former University of California employees alleges that the university's five medical centers billed the government for millions of dollars in fraudulent insurance claims.

Matthews, Neal, "Sinking boats for fraud & profit: The scams and schemes of insurance pirates," *Boating,* May 1995, pp. 156-163.

Between 10 percent and 25 percent of boat-related insurance claims are fraudulent, and many feel the actual number is much higher. Many feel that no one gets hurt as a result of such fraud.

McQuiston, John T., "Doctor and Wife Accused of Insurance Fraud on L.I. Home and Yacht," *The New York Times,* July 30, 1996, p. B1.

Arthur Graff and his wife, Marnette, were charged by Long Island, N.Y., authorities with insurance fraud on July 29, 1996. The authorities said they tried to collect almost $600,000 in connection with the sinking of their yacht, the *Night Nurse,* and the fire at their former waterfront home, Windemere Dunes. They have not been charged with setting the fire.

Mendel, Barbara Linkin, "15 people sentenced for roles in car accident insurance scam," *The Houston Post,* March 31, 1995, p. A28.

Fifteen of 100 people indicted in a multimillion-dollar insurance scam were sentenced on March 30, 1995. In January, Harris County, Texas, authorities announced the breakup of a major insurance fraud ring they said staged hundreds of car wrecks and fraudulently received millions of dollars in personal injury and damage claims.

Mulligan, Thomas S., "46 arrested in alleged insurance fraud ring," *Los Angeles Times,* June 6, 1995, p. D2.

In early June 1995, California and Los Angeles investigators cracked a major auto insurance fraud ring based in a Hollywood insurance agency where uninsured drivers who had car accidents could obtain backdated insurance policies.

Novak, Viveca, "FBI probe of auto insurance fraud nets more suspects," *The Wall Street Journal,* May 25, 1995, p. C20.

The FBI announced a broad, 31-state sweep of arrests, indictments and searches in its continuing probe of health-insurance-fraud schemes involving staged automobile accidents. More than 100 people were either named in indictments on May 24, 1995, or were the subject of criminal complaints.

Reuben, Richard C., "California scheming," *ABA Journal,* February 1996, p. 6.

Over 175 California lawyers are under investigation for a medical insurance scam in which attorneys allegedly took kickbacks from clients' medical providers. The scams appear to be the acts of individuals rather than a concerted effort, but the numbers involved are staggering.

Sanchez, Jesus, and Thomas S. Mulligan, "FBI cracks down on staged car accidents," *Los Angeles Times,* May 25, 1995, p. D1.

The FBI and other law enforcement agencies on May 24, 1995, arrested or issued indictments against 126 people nationwide as part of its biggest crackdown ever on staged automobile accidents — a fast-growing form of insurance fraud that has long flourished in Southern California.

Shioya, Tara, "Arrest at clinic part of insurance fraud probe," *San Francisco Chronicle,* Aug. 22, 1996, p. A18.

FBI and California insurance department agents on Aug. 21, 1996, arrested Joseph Wagoner, a doctor at Crocker Chiropractic Center in Daly City, who is one of 16 people believed to have defrauded auto insurance companies of millions of dollars through false accident claims.

Smith, Doug, and Thomas S. Mulligan, "7 charged in statewide insurance fraud probe," *Los Angeles Times,* Sept. 29, 1995, p. D1.

Federal prosecutors announced a statewide auto insurance fraud crackdown on Sept. 28, 1995, charging key figures in an alleged multimillion-dollar kickback scheme involving several legal offices and more than 100 chiropractors, about half of them in Los Angeles.

Teegardin, Carrie, and Martha Woodham, "Rider facing biggest obstacle: Federal charges in horse's death," *Atlanta Constitution,* Sept. 6, 1995, p. B6.

George Lindemann Jr. will go on trial in Chicago on federal charges that he had his horse Charisma killed in order to collect $250,000 in insurance money. Lindemann is among 23 pople indicted on federal charges in a horse industry insurance fraud investigation. The case has put the clubby, upper-crust horse world in the media spotlight.

"Top equestrian is convicted in horse insurance scheme," *The New York Times,* Sept. 22, 1995, p. A24.

George Lindemann Jr., a prominent equestrian who is the son of one of the richest men in America, was convicted of three counts of wire fraud on Sept. 21, 1995, in the climax of a four-year federal investigation into horse killing and insurance fraud.

"Two face fraud counts in fertility scandal," *Los Angeles Times,* June 28, 1996, p. A17.

Two of the three physicians accused of stealing eggs and implanting them in unsuspecting women at UC-Irvine's now-defunct fertility clinic were each indicted on June 27, 1996, on 30 counts of federal mail fraud for allegedly submitting false claims to insurance companies.

Wallace, Bill, "S.F. chiropractor to be charged in probe of insurance fraud ring," *San Francisco Chronicle,* March 13, 1996, p. A18.
Sergei Chidlowsky, a San Francisco chiropractor, surrendered to authorities on March 11, 1996. Chidlowsky will be arraigned during the week of March 17 on charges of filing false insurance claims, conspiracy, grand theft and receiving fees for accepting or referring clients involved in an insurance fraud ring.

Insurer Fraud

Mulligan, Thomas S., "Insurer to pay record settlement," *Los Angeles Times,* June 4, 1996, p. D3.
Allianz Life Insurance Co. of North America agreed to pay a record $5.1 million to settle charges that it misled consumers by selling them universal life insurance policies in the guise of retirement plans, the California Department of Insurance said on June 3, 1996.

Voelker, Bill, "Insurance execs get jail," *Times-Picayune,* Jan. 26, 1996, p. C1.
Michael J. Bowler was sentenced to six and a half years in prison, and Walter L. Sentenn Jr. was sentenced to three years and nine months, in an insurance fraud case involving Pelican State Mutual Insurance Co. They were ordered to pay $100,000 in restitution to Louisiana guarantors who covered $23 million in unpaid claims. They are accused of siphoning off insurance premium dollars for personal gain.

Special Investigation Units

Lippman, Helen, "New ways to fight fraud," *Business & Health,* August 1995, pp. 40-46.
Employers, insurers, and federal agencies are increasing their efforts to snare the crooks who bilk the health-care system of billions of dollars.

Mantius, Peter, "Oxendine cleans house in insurance fraud office," *Atlanta Journal Constitution,* May 7, 1995, p. G4.
Georgia Insurance Commissioner John Oxendine fired four fraud investigators from January-April 1995, saying the purge of his department's small anti-fraud section is part of his plan to crack down on fraud. The fired examiners warn that Oxendine is shifting the unit's focus from crime against consumers to crime against the insurance industry.

Staged auto accidents

Armstrong, Ken, "Complaint ties lawyer to insurance fraud plot," *Chicago Tribune,* July 20, 1996, p. 5.
The Attorney Registration and Disciplinary Commission has filed a disciplinary complaint alleging that Chicago personal-injury lawyer Brian David Alpert participated in a cash-for-crash scheme in which automobile collisions were staged to defraud insurance companies.

Bardwell, S K., "Accused insurance fraud kingpin jailed," *Houston Chronicle,* July 24, 1996, p. A18.
Tan Kien Tu, the accused kingpin of an insurance fraud ring, has been arrested and charged by Harris County, Texas, officials after more than two years of investigation and the indictment of more than 100 people.

Cox, Gail Diane, "Lawyer's role in accidents called murder," *National Law Journal,* Aug. 26, 1996, p. A10.
Los Angeles attorney Gary P. Miller has been charged with second-degree murder. Miller allegedly took on cases involving staged auto accidents on freeways and paid fees for referrals. In one case, a person was killed.

Eldridge, Earle, "States crack down on fake crash claims," *USA Today,* May 31, 1996, p. B1.
Prosecutors and insurance companies are targeting a growing number of doctors, lawyers and motorists who stage car accidents and exaggerate injuries to collect insurance money.

Hyman, Vicki, "Wrecks were faked in scam, police say," *Times-Picayune,* Aug. 28, 1996, p. A1.
Law enforcement agents on Aug. 27, 1996, said they had exposed a ring of at least 27 people who staged fake auto accidents that involved 70 victims in Jefferson and Orleans parishes in Louisiana. The insurance scam involved more than $1.5 million in fraudulent claims for vehicle damage and personal injuries.

"Man admits insurance fraud scheme," *Atlanta Journal Constitution,* Dec. 10, 1995, p. G12.
Michael Lawrence of Griffin, Ga., accused of staging car accidents, has been sentenced to 15 years in prison after pleading guilty to his part in an insurance fraud scheme.

Opatrny, Dennis J., "Car crash insurance fraud ring uncovered," *San Francisco Chronicle,* June 23, 1996, p. B1.
After a three-year probe, Solano County, Calif., officials in June 1996 have cracked a car crash insurance scam that collected as much as $1.5 million. Six people were arrested and charged with insurance fraud and conspiracy. State officials and local authorities have issued arrest warrants for 21 others, some of whom are believed to be hiding in Hawaii.

Streater, Scott, "60 arrested in massive wreck scam," *The Houston Post,* Jan. 20, 1995, p. A6.
Harris County, Texas, authorities announced on Jan. 19, 1995, the breakup of a major insurance fraud ring that they said staged hundreds of car wrecks and fraudulently received millions of dollars in personal injury and damage claims. One hundred persons were indicted and 60 have been arrested.

Back Issues

Great Research on Current Issues Starts Right Here...Recent topics covered by The CQ Researcher are listed below. Before May 1991, reports were published under the name of Editorial Research Reports.

APRIL 1995
Abortion Clinic Protests
Dieting and Health
Combating AIDS
Rethinking Affirmative Action

MAY 1995
Assisted Suicide Controversy
Overhauling Social Security
Learning to Read
Mandatory Sentencing

JUNE 1995
Combating Infectious Disease
Property Rights
Repetitive Stress Injuries
Regulating the Internet

JULY 1995
War Crimes
Highway Safety
Combating Terrorism
Preventing Teen Drug Use

AUGUST 1995
Job Stress
Organ Transplants
United Nations at 50
Advances in Cancer Research

Back issues are available for $5.00 (subscribers) or $8.00 (non-subscribers). Quantity discounts apply to orders over ten. To order, call Congressional Quarterly Customer Service at (202) 887-8621.

Binders are available for $18.00. To order call 1-800-638-1710. Please refer to stock number 648.

SEPTEMBER 1995
Catholic Church in the U.S.
Northern Ireland Cease-Fire
High School Sports
Teaching History

OCTOBER 1995
Quebec's Future
Revitalizing the Cities
Networking the Classroom
Indoor Air Pollution

NOVEMBER 1995
The Working Poor
The Jury System
Sex, Violence and the Media
Police Misconduct

DECEMBER 1995
Teens and Tobacco
Gene Therapy's Future
Global Water Shortages
Third-Party Prospects

JANUARY 1996
Emergency Medicine
Punishing Sex Offenders
Bilingual Education
Helping the Homeless

FEBRUARY 1996
Reforming the CIA
Campaign Finance Reform
Academic Politics
Getting Into College

MARCH 1996
The British Monarchy
Preventing Juvenile Crime
Tax Reform
Pursuing the Paranormal

APRIL 1996
Centennial Olympic Games
Managed Care
Protecting Endangered Species
New Military Culture

MAY 1996
Russia's Political Future
Marriage and Divorce
Year-Round Schools
Taiwan, China and the U.S.

JUNE 1996
Rethinking NAFTA
First Ladies
Teaching Values
Labor Movement's Future

JULY 1996
Recovered-Memory Debate
Native Americans' Future
Crackdown on Sexual Harassment
Attack on Public Schools

AUGUST 1996
Fighting Over Animal Rights
Privatizing Government Services
Child Labor and Sweatshops
Cleaning Up Hazardous Wastes

SEPTEMBER 1996
Gambling Under Attack
The States and Federalism
Civic Journalism
Reassessing Foreign Aid

OCTOBER 1996
Political Consultants

Future Topics

- ***Rethinking School Integration***
- ***Parental Rights***
- ***Global Warming***

THE CQ Researcher

PUBLISHED BY CONGRESSIONAL QUARTERLY INC.

Rethinking School Integration

Is the era of court-ordered desegregation over?

More than four decades after the U.S. Supreme Court outlawed racial segregation in public schools, most black and Latino youngsters still attend predominantly minority schools — and the number is increasing. Federal courts are making it easier for school districts to drop mandatory desegregation plans and be released from judicial supervision. Some black leaders are questioning the value of integration and joining other critics of court-ordered busing. Civil rights advocates say that the trend toward "resegregation" will hurt minorities' opportunities in school and afterward. But critics say that desegregation produces few educational gains for minorities, causes whites to flee inner-city schools and weakens popular support for public education.

INSIDE THIS ISSUE

CQ Oct. 18, 1996 • Volume 6, No. 39 • Pages 913-936

Formerly Editorial Research Reports

RETHINKING SCHOOL INTEGRATION

COVER: *NEA TODAY*/NATIONAL EDUCATION ASSOCIATION

Oct. 18, 1996
Volume 6, No. 39

EDITOR
Sandra Stencel

MANAGING EDITOR
Thomas J. Colin

ASSOCIATE EDITORS
Sarah M. Magner
Richard L. Worsnop

STAFF WRITERS
Charles S. Clark
Mary H. Cooper
Kenneth Jost

EDITORIAL ASSISTANT
Tonya Harris

PUBLISHED BY
Congressional Quarterly Inc.

CHAIRMAN
Andrew Barnes

VICE CHAIRMAN
Andrew P. Corty

EDITOR AND PUBLISHER
Neil Skene

EXECUTIVE EDITOR
Robert W. Merry

The CQ Researcher (ISSN 1056-2036). Formerly Editorial Research Reports. Published weekly (48 times per year, not printed March 1, May 31, Aug. 30, Nov. 29) by Congressional Quarterly Inc., 1414 22nd St., N.W., Washington, D.C. 20037. Annual subscription rate for libraries, businesses and government is $319. Additional rates furnished upon request. Periodicals postage paid at Washington, D.C. POSTMASTER: Send address changes to The CQ Researcher, 1414 22nd St., N.W., Washington, D.C. 20037.

Rethinking School Integration

BY KENNETH JOST

THE ISSUES

To understand the ups and downs of school segregation in America, it helps to know about Barrett Elementary School in Denver, Colo.

City officials built the tidy brick schoolhouse in 1960 for one reason: to give black children their own neighborhood school, and thus keep schools in the adjacent district predominantly white.

But for the past 20 years, thanks to court-ordered busing, whites have attended Barrett and blacks from the neighborhood have gone across town, to predominantly white Cory Elementary.

This September, however, was like old times: Barrett once again had only a scattering of Anglo students, and Cory had fewer blacks. The turnabout resulted from a federal judge's decision to end court-ordered busing and allow a return to neighborhood schools.

Ironically, the demise of busing in Denver was blessed by the black plaintiffs who first challenged Denver's segregated schools 25 years ago, as well as by the African-American head of the school board.

"With busing, our students were not achieving," says board President Aaron Gray, a minister. "The concern of the school district must be achievement, and that wasn't working out."

At both Barrett and Cory, meanwhile, the return to a neighborhood system has been greeted with mixed feelings.

"I appreciated all the years when we had more of a diverse student population," Barrett Principal Debbie Pugliano says, "because students do learn from each other — the way they're the same and the way they're different." Out of a total of 260 students, Barrett's Anglo enrollment has fallen from 14 percent last year to only 4 percent this year.

"We all felt some of the bitter-

sweet," says Cory Principal Pat Trujillo, whose school dropped from 45 percent minority enrollment last year to 17 percent today. "Quite frankly, I'm delighted that we were able to maintain some diversity," she adds.

Gray says minority families were among those who urged an end to busing. "What I was hearing from young black and Hispanic parents was that busing had served its purpose, and what they were concerned about now was equity," Gray says.

But the president of the local NAACP chapter has regrets. "We did not want [the end of busing], because that is what we fought so long and hard for," says Menola Upshaw, a former teacher in Denver. "In northeast Denver, the schools that were very segregated have gone back to that — 90 percent black. And we still say that separate cannot be equal."

With the end of busing for racial diversity, Denver joins numerous other cities that have been moving to dismantle mandatory school desegregation plans. Cleveland, for example, also opened the new school year freed of court-ordered desegregation. And Oklahoma City received judicial permission to drop its busing plan a few years ago.

Similar changes are under way in other cities, encouraged by a string of recent Supreme Court decisions urging federal judges to return schools to local control. Proponents of local control applaud the trend away from mandatory desegregation.

"The courts should not be in the business of permanently enforcing racial balance," says David Armor, a research professor at George Mason University in Fairfax, Va., and a longtime critic of busing. If a school district has eliminated racial segregation, Armor says, "the district should be allowed to show that and should be allowed to go back to total control of its policies."

Supporters of desegregation, however, say that the new trend amounts to "resegregation" — a return to a system of racially separate, and unequal, schools. (*See "At Issue," p. 929.*) They note that for the first time since the 1970s, African-American youngsters are becoming more racially segregated in schools, while segregation for Hispanic students is at an all-time high. (*See chart, p. 926.*)

"A lot of communities are going back to segregated schools," says Gary Orfield, a professor of education and social policy at Harvard University and principal author of the new book *Dismantling Desegregation*. "They're doing it with the expectation that we know how to make racially isolated schools equal and fair, and we do not." [1]

Several factors have spurred the move away from mandatory desegregation. Many federal judges, as well as the Supreme Court's conservative majority, are openly impatient with school desegregation cases — some in their third decade. And neither Congress nor the Justice Department

Northeast Has Most-Segregated Schools

Half the black students in the Northeast attended intensely segregated schools — with at least 90 percent minority enrollment — during the 1991-92 school year.

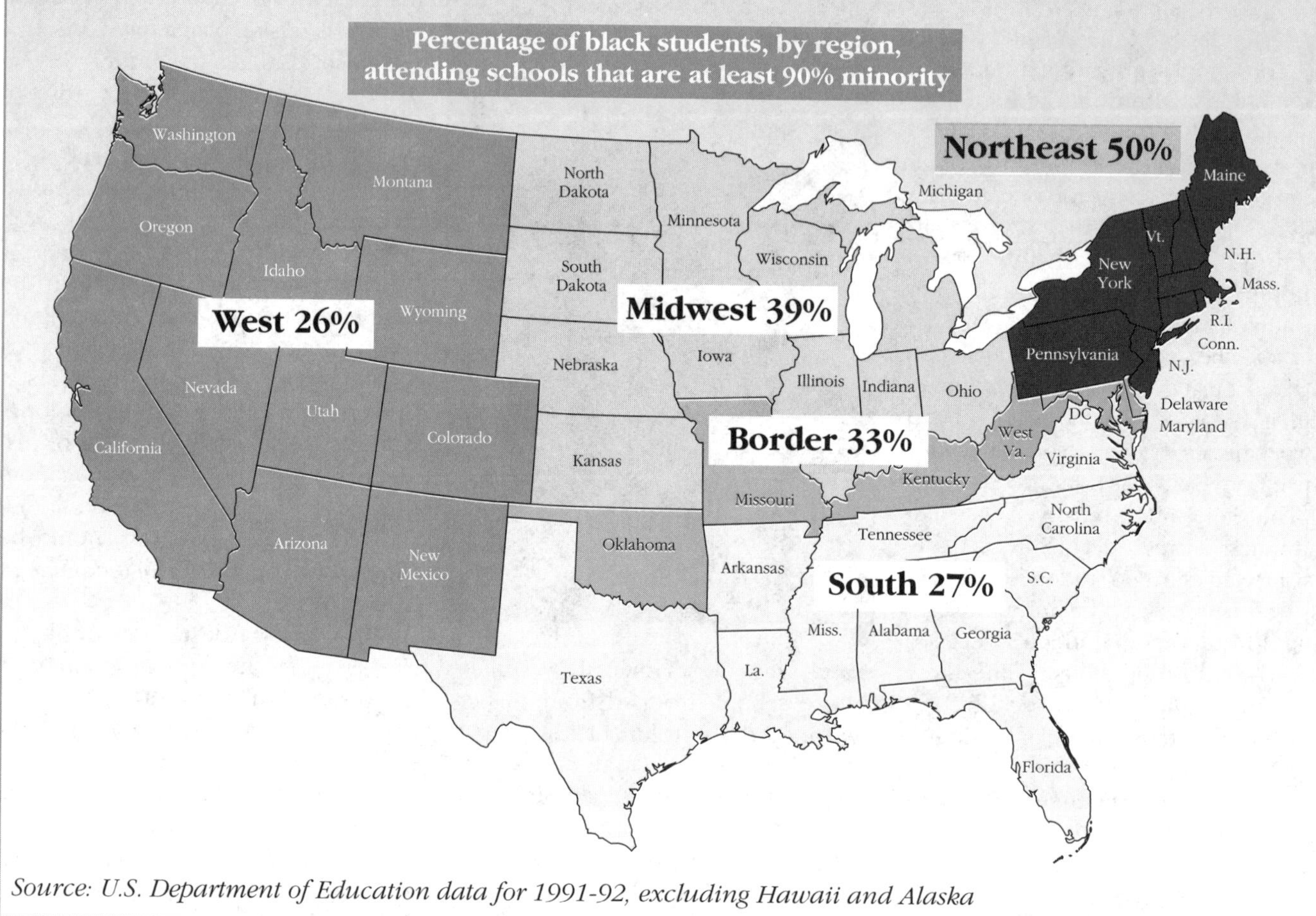

Source: U.S. Department of Education data for 1991-92, excluding Hawaii and Alaska

has given school desegregation much attention since the 1980s, except to try to limit the use of busing.

Moreover, many school officials, some education experts and a growing minority of black leaders and families question the value of desegregation altogether. From a variety of perspectives, these critics contend that desegregation has yielded few benefits for African-American or Hispanic youngsters. Among other things, they say it has contributed to "white flight" from public schools and decreasing support for public schools while diverting attention away from improving education quality for all children.

"Pretty much, the outcomes were negative," says Armor, who often testifies for school boards seeking to end court-ordered desegregation. "Busing caused substantial white flight, making racial isolation worse. We've never been able to document achievement increases [for minority students]. And certainly, the middle-class public has never embraced busing."

Supporters of desegregation, however, contend that the critics paint an unduly bleak picture of the changes in the nation's schools in the 42 years since the Supreme Court outlawed racial segregation in its historic *Brown v. Board of Education* decision. They say many school districts have succeeded in operating successful desegregation plans through such techniques as magnet schools with specialized curricula aimed at attracting a racially mixed student body. [2] They also insist that desegregated schools have helped raise educational achievement for minority youngsters and improved their chances for successful integration after school.

"Desegregation has not been as successful as we all hoped it would be," says Christopher Hansen, a senior attorney for the American Civil Liberties Union (ACLU) in New York who handles education-related litigation, "but there's more success out there than we give it credit for."

"It's impossible to make a blanket

statement that school desegregation was a failure or a success," agrees Dennis Parker, associate counsel of the NAACP Legal Defense and Educational Fund, which has spearheaded the school desegregation court fight for nearly 60 years. "A lot more people are going to integrated schools today than in the past, and there are a lot of school systems that have been very stably desegregated."

Still, the trend among federal courts and local school boards is away from mandatory desegregation plans. Some critics of those plans insist, however, that voluntary plans will actually produce more racial mixing in the schools than mandatory methods. "The key to integration is compromise," says Christine Rossell, a political science professor at Boston University. "Voluntary integration plans most of the time produce more integration than existed before."

Even as federal courts and school boards abandon mandatory desegregation, however, civil rights groups are moving into state courts to equalize educational opportunities for minority youngsters. In Connecticut, civil rights groups used the state constitution to win a pathbreaking ruling from the state Supreme Court in July. It required state officials to devise a plan for eliminating segregation from all the state's school districts (*see p. 928*).

The renewed attention to desegregation comes at a time of public concern about racial attitudes as well as educational quality. These are some of the questions being asked in the debate:

Is integration important for minority groups to succeed in school?

In outlawing school segregation in 1954, the Supreme Court declared that racially separate schools were "inherently unequal" because they generated a "feeling of inferiority" that had "a tendency to retard the educational and mental development of Negro children." Forty-two years later, integrationists continue to believe that minority youngsters fare badly in what are now often called "racially isolated" schools.

Nevertheless, the benefits of desegregation for minority youngsters are at best difficult to document. And many educators and policy-makers, as well as a growing minority of black parents and advocates, argue that other changes are more important than integration for improving the education of African-American youngsters.

Among social scientists, the effects of desegregation on educational achievement are the grist for a sharp, and statistically complex, academic debate. In a detailed account of the dispute, mandatory-desegregation critic Armor describes the research as "inconclusive." [3]

Armor and other critics, including Rossell, generally say the evidence for any educational gains for blacks from desegregation is either weak or nonexistent. "There's no evidence that integration has any positive effect on black children," Rossell says. "Certainly, there's no evidence that it has anything more than a trivial effect."

Supporters of desegregation, however, say the most detailed studies show a modest but significant gain for minority youngsters who attend desegregated schools. "Desegregation seems to raise test scores by about 30 points on the SAT [scholastic achievement test], which would close about one-third of the 100-point gap" between black and white students, says Robert Crain, a professor at Columbia University's Teachers College and a leading researcher on desegregation. "We've gotten that finding quite consistently."

Crain and other pro-integration researchers, such as Jomills Braddock at the University of Miami and James McPartland at Johns Hopkins University, also say that minority students who attend desegregated schools are more likely to live and work in integrated environments after school. "I've always said that test scores were the least interesting story," Crain says. "The more interesting question is what effect desegregation has on getting into college and getting a job."

Harvard's Orfield also emphasizes the effect of desegregation on students after schooling. "Desegregation is part of an effort to socialize all people in our society as we become a half-minority society by the middle of the next century," he says.

Some black educators and advocates, however, are now questioning the importance — or even the value — of "socialization" within predominantly white schools. These critics of integration, who constitute a small but seemingly growing minority among black Americans, include, as *The New York Times* reported a year ago, "such divergent figures as Louis Farrakhan, the head of the Denver school board and Justice Clarence Thomas." [4]

"I think desegregation is dead and should have died a long time ago, if the focus is on trying to have a physical mixing of the races," Edward J. Newsome, a black member of the Kansas City school board, told the *Times*. Kansas City schools have been given more than $1.4 billion over eight years under a court-ordered desegregation plan aimed at drawing white students from the suburbs to the predominantly black schools.

In Denver, school board president Gray bluntly challenges the assumption of the *Brown* decision. "A segregated school does not mean an inferior school," Gray says.

Other black educators say that predominantly black schools offer black youngsters advantages in developing self-esteem and racial pride. "The most critical task facing black America is the need to determine the reality of our collective circumstance within this society," says Pansye Atkinson, director of affirmative action programs at Frostburg State University in Frostburg, Md. Atkinson, author of a book that criticizes the rationale of the *Brown* decision, says that black students need to learn more about the history of blacks in America. [5]

"We need to learn about some of

Hispanic Americans: The 'Other' Minority

Latinos are the most segregated minority in America's public schools. Moreover, the percentage of Latinos attending predominantly minority schools has been steadily increasing in the 30 years since the government began keeping such figures. (*See chart, p. 926.*)

"We have very severe levels of school segregation," says Charles Kamasaki, a vice president for the National Council of La Raza, an Hispanic lobbying group. "The highest degree occurs in school districts and schools with the fewest resources. In our judgment, it undeniably has a negative effect on school achievement among Hispanic children."

Nearly three-fourths of Latino students attend schools with at least 50 percent minority enrollment, according to Department of Education figures for the 1991-92 school year, the most recent available. About one-third of Latinos attend schools where the minority enrollment is 90 percent or greater.

Despite the pervasive segregation, Latinos have been less active than African-Americans in bringing traditional school desegregation suits. Kamasaki notes that Latinos have sometimes been treated as a minority group in school desegregation cases but sometimes — most notably, in Texas — have been counted as whites for calculating racial balance. "When Dallas was ordered to desegregate, the kids who were bused into black schools were Latinos," Kamasaki says.

Latinos did play a lead role in bringing two of the earliest suits aimed at equalizing funding between school districts. In one of those cases, *San Antonio Independent School District v. Rodriguez,* the U.S. Supreme Court in 1973 refused to recognize education as a fundamental right under the U.S. Constitution. But three years later, the California Supreme Court ruled in *Serrano v. Priest* that education was a fundamental right under the state's constitution, and the state had to take steps to equalize state aid to local school districts.

School funding litigation has steadily increased in the two decades since then and remains active today, but Kamasaki says the results have been "equivocal." Meanwhile, Latino enrollment in public schools nationwide nearly doubled between 1972 and 1992.

Today, segregation is highest for Latino students in the Northeast, where nearly half — 46.2 percent — of Latinos attend schools with greater than 90 percent minority enrollment. Segregation for Latinos is also high in the West, especially in California and Texas. In each state, more than one-third of Latinos attend schools with 90 percent minority enrollment.[1]

In Connecticut, Latino families are among the plaintiffs in the class-action suit that resulted in a precedent-setting ruling in July requiring the state to produce a statewide desegregation plan. The suit was filed in Hartford, where Latinos now constitute a majority of public school enrollment.

Sandra Del Valle, an attorney with the Puerto Rican Legal Defense Fund who is working on the case, says the Puerto Rican plaintiffs in the case have interests similar to the African-American plaintiffs. "Everybody wants better schools," Del Valle says. "They're very close to West Hartford [a better-funded suburban district], and they see a qualitative difference in what their kids are getting."

A special state commission is now working to develop a desegregation plan to present to the Connecticut Legislature early next year. Del Valle says there will be some special issues for the Hispanic plaintiffs — chiefly, language. "They don't want to send their kids into hostile territory where no one speaks their language," she says.

For his part, Kamasaki says school segregation for African-Americans and Hispanics alike stems from the same problem: housing segregation.[2] "Both blacks and Hispanics experience very significant levels of housing discrimination and housing segregation," he says. To combat the problem, Kamasaki calls for increasing fair-housing litigation as well as expanding recent "housing mobility" programs aimed at helping minorities move into predominantly white areas.

Kamasaki also says that the Department of Education has an important role to play in monitoring local school districts to detect so-called "within-school segregation" — as when tracking practices result in isolating Hispanic or African-American students. "Most people agree that this can be just as pernicious and just as harmful as other forms of segregation," he says.

[1] Gary Orfield *et al.*, "The Growth of Segregation in American Schools: Changing Patterns of Separation and Poverty Since 1968," National School Boards Association, December 1993, pp. 9, 14.

[2] For background, see "Housing Discrimination," *The CQ Researcher*, Feb. 24, 1995, pp. 169-192.

those [slaves] who mutinied on those ships . . . so that we get a sense that we are a strong people and that we need to struggle against oppression," Atkinson says. Unlike some black nationalists, Atkinson says she still favors integration, but says black youngsters are "losing strengths because we're following the other culture."

Advocates of integration — both black and white — acknowledge this new sentiment by reshaping their own arguments in favor of racial mixing within the schools. "I'm not going to say that you can only learn in a completely desegregated world," says Parker at the NAACP Legal Defense Fund. "I think all students get a better education in a desegregated environment. We live in a society that is becoming increasingly multicultural, and being prepared to work in a desegregated environment is an educational advantage for all students."

Do mandatory desegregation plans cause "white flight" from public schools?

Critics of mandatory desegregation contend that court-ordered plans, especially those based on cross-neighborhood busing, have driven white students out of public schools and contributed to a general loss of support for public education. Advocates of desegregation insist that the declining white enrollment in inner-city public schools stems primarily from other factors, chiefly the rapid growth of predominantly white suburbs since the 1960s and the increased percentage of minorities in the U.S.

Again, the statistical debate among academic experts over "white flight" is both complex and heated. The argument flared first in a controversial 1975 study by James S. Coleman, a University of Chicago sociologist who contended in an influential study a decade earlier that blacks learn best in racially mixed schools. In the 1975 report, however, Coleman said that busing was causing a massive departure of whites from public schools. Coleman's report was so controversial that some advocates of desegregation sought, unsuccessfully, to expel him from the American Sociological Association.[6]

With another two decades of experience, critics of busing say it continues to cause white flight. "Fifty percent of the white students who are reassigned to those schools will not show up," says Rossell. She notes that Boston, where busing in the 1970s led to violent and protracted conflict, has shifted from a predominantly white student enrollment to 82 percent minority.

"If you care only about balanced racial distribution," Rossell adds, "the best plan is a mandatory reassignment. Of all the plans, it drives the most whites out of [public schools], but it evenly distributes [the ones who stay] very nicely."

Civil rights advocates concede that busing has contributed to white flight in some places. But they also blame other factors for the increasing percentage of minority students in inner-city schools, including changing birth rates and immigration. In addition, they say that white flight can be reduced with metropolitan-wide desegregation plans. "The most successful programs have been those that eliminated or stemmed white flight," says Hansen of the ACLU. "In Kansas City, the desegregation program has been quite successful in stemming white flight."

In Denver, however, school board President Gray blames white flight on busing and says the end of busing is bringing some white students back. "Already, we are seeing a return of Anglo kids to the school district, so obviously it played a part in the kids' thinking," he says.

Critics also say that desegregation plans have contributed to a general deterioration in public schools and erosion of popular support for public education. "It's a downhill spiral," says Joyce Haws, president of the Cleveland chapter of the National Association for Neighborhood Schools. "And that's what it's been in every city, which of course affects everybody, black and white."

But civil rights advocates say desegregation has benefited blacks and whites. "Integration has improved education throughout the country," says University of Connecticut law Professor John Brittain, the lead attorney in the Connecticut school desegregation case. "The South was no bastion of education before the *Brown* decision. Neither was South Boston before the desegregation suit there."

Can voluntary desegregation plans work?

The *Brown* decision set the stage for hundreds of school desegregation suits over the next four decades, first in the South and then throughout the country. No one knows today exactly how many such suits are still pending. The U.S. Justice Department reported a year ago that it was either a party or intervenor in 513 cases with pending court orders. Civil rights experts say there probably is an equal number of cases where the federal government is not involved.[7]

Even though many of those cases are dormant, civil rights advocates say litigation and judicial oversight continue to be essential in ensuring school desegregation. "In many places, if it weren't for court supervision, things would be just as they were 40-50 years ago," Parker says.

Critics contend, however, that desegregation suits have proven to be costly, inefficient and ultimately counterproductive. They say voluntary desegregation methods are more likely to increase racial mixing without reducing public support for the schools.

"The key to a good integration plan is satisfying white demands as well as black demands," Rossell says. "You ignore white demands at your peril. They'll just vote with their feet."

As Harvard's Orfield points out, however, desegregation plans today encompass a variety of voluntary features, such as magnet schools, as well as mandatory provisions like busing. In addition, some courts have used the power first recognized by the Supreme Court in 1977 to order extra funding for school districts to compensate for the effects of past racial segregation.

Critics of mandatory desegregation say school boards should be allowed to pursue voluntary steps rather than be forced to adopt busing or other compulsory pupil assignment systems. "The opportunity for integration should be encouraged, and incentives for integration should be established," says Armor. "With just those two things, you're going to get more integration than if you just go back to neighborhood schools and go back to business as usual."

Most advocates of integration also look favorably on magnet schools, but Orfield and his colleagues at Harvard's Project on School Desegregation question some of the broad claims made on their behalf. They point to problems in Prince George's County, Md. — the predominantly black suburban county outside Washington that is often held up as a showcase for magnet schools.

How Americans Feel About School Integration

Most Americans approve of school integration and say more should be done to promote it. Blacks and whites disagree, however, on how much integration has improved education quality for both races, though an increasing minority of whites see improvement. The poll was conducted on the 40th anniversary of the Brown v. Board of Education *ruling, which made segregation in all public schools illegal.*

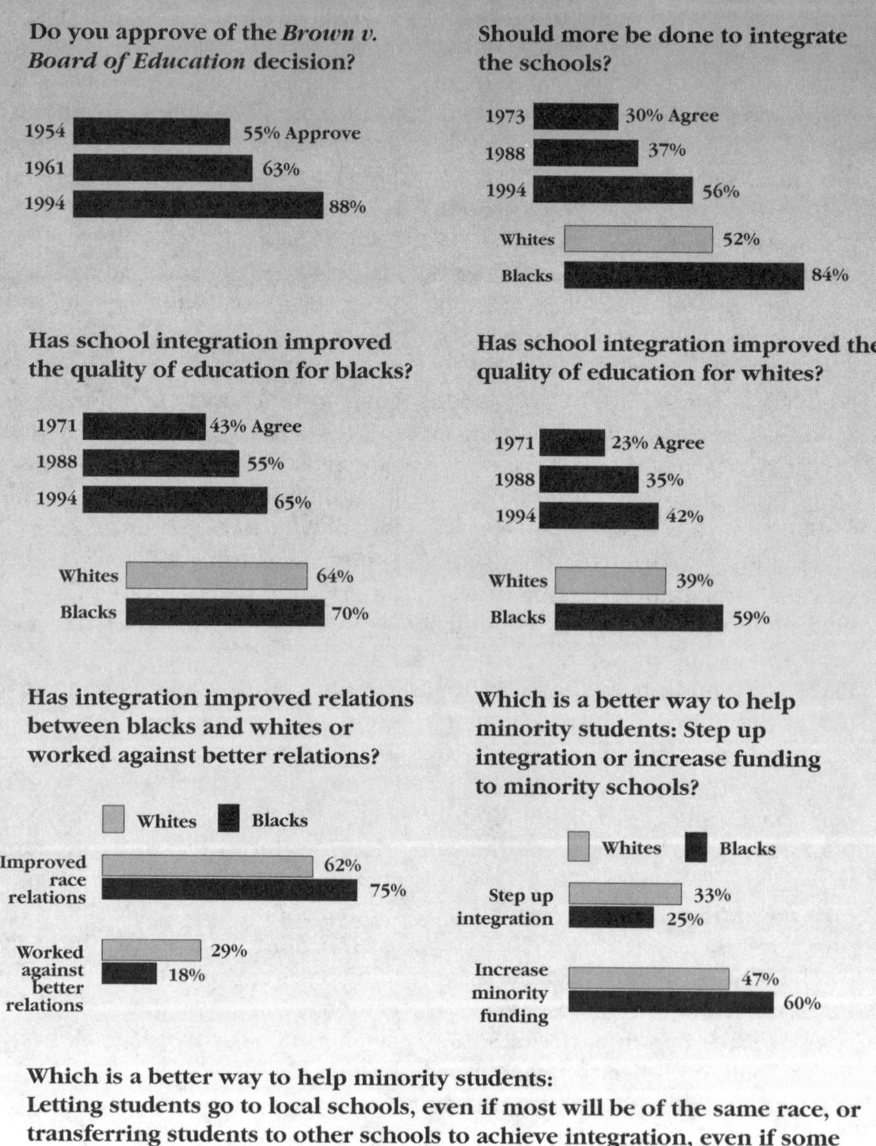

Which is a better way to help minority students: Letting students go to local schools, even if most will be of the same race, or transferring students to other schools to achieve integration, even if some have to travel out of their community?

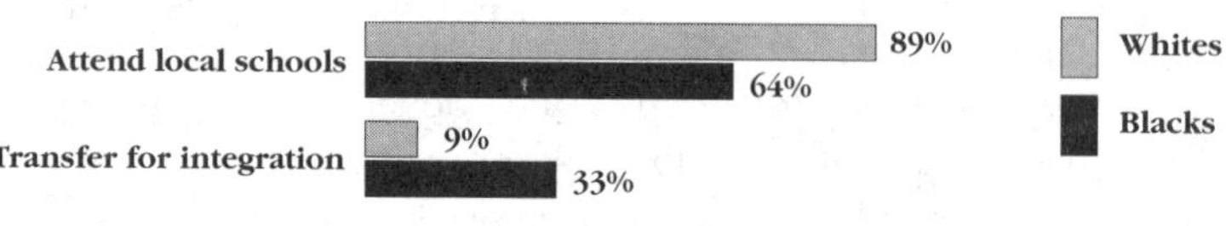

Source: USA Today*/CNN/Gallup Poll, conducted April 22-24, 1994*

They say county education officials exaggerated the academic gains for students enrolled in the special curricula. In addition, they say that even though magnet programs may have been racially balanced, many of them were housed in schools where the overall enrollment was still 90 percent black or higher. [8] (*See story, p. 924.*)

Orfield also questions the impact that compensatory funding can have in improving educational achievement at schools without effective desegregation. "You can pump a lot of money into these systems without getting actual results for the kid," Orfield says. "The most important influences [on achievement] are parents and other children, the level of competition within the school and the quality of the teachers. None of those things can be bought with money."

Some black leaders support school choice — plans that provide public funds to help parents pay for private or parochial schools — as a way to increase integration. [9] Armor agrees. "I like the choice movement, and I like plans that try to combine choice and desegregation," he says. "One of the best channels of integration in our society is to allow minority students to attend private schools of their choice."

For his part, Orfield says school choice "threatens to foster resegregation by both race and class," but also has "positive possibilities for cross-district desegregation" if minority families interested in schools outside their districts are given adequate information and support. But without "strong civil rights policies," Orfield writes, "choice plans can pay to transfer white students from integrated city schools to all-white suburbs." [10]

In the meantime, the sharpest debate is between those who favor court intervention and supervision in school desegregation cases and those who want courts to reduce their role and restore local control of schools. "The courts should recognize the practicality of the alternatives, that voluntary plans in the long term have been just as successful, or no more unsuccessful, than mandatory plans," Armor says.

But Parker says courts still have an essential role where school districts have failed to remove the effects of segregation. "These cases were meant to address serious constitutional violations," he says. "The age of the case is less important than whether those constitutional violations have been successfully addressed. If the school district hasn't taken care of the problem, then it doesn't matter whether the case is five years old or 50 years old." ■

BACKGROUND

The Road to Brown

Black and white youngsters attended separate schools from America's earliest days, by custom or law, in all parts of the country. Although racial segregation was never universal, it became more widespread and more formalized with the growth of public education in the late 19th and early 20th centuries. And legally mandated segregation survived, despite court challenges, until the Supreme Court's historic 1954 decision, *Brown v. Board of Education*.

The first of those challenges had come more than a century earlier — at a time when most blacks were slaves and their children were denied education altogether. In Massachusetts — seat of the anti-slavery movement — Boston assigned free black youngsters to racially segregated schools. The abolitionist lawyer Charles Sumner urged the state's highest court in 1845 to declare the policy a violation of the state's constitution, but the court unanimously rejected the plea. Six years later, however, the Massachusetts Legislature outlawed school segregation. [11]

The abolition of slavery after the Civil War resulted in a flurry of laws in the South and elsewhere consigning blacks to segregated schools. The number of legal challenges to segregation also grew. One historian counts more than 30 local court contests in the late 19th century and says more than half were successful. [12]

But the U.S. Supreme Court effectively closed the door to those challenges with a pair of decisions in the 1890s. In *Plessy v. Ferguson,* the court in 1896 upheld the legality of legally enforced racial segregation on interstate railroads. Three years later, the court in *Cumming v. Richmond County Board of Education* similarly spurned a challenge by black parents in Georgia protesting a local school board's decision to provide a high school for white youngsters but not for blacks.

The court's decisions paved the way for widespread segregation laws, but they also prompted the formation in 1909 of a national civil rights organization for African-Americans: the National Association for the Advancement of Colored People. By the 1930s, the NAACP began charting a legal attack on school segregation under the leadership of a young Howard University Law School graduate from Baltimore, Thurgood Marshall. At age 27, Marshall won his first rights victory with a ruling from Maryland's highest court in 1935 desegregating the University of Maryland's law school. In 1940, NAACP Chairman Walter White chose Marshall to head the newly formed Legal Defense and Educational Fund. [13]

Marshall plotted a two-stage attack on school segregation. He first wanted to challenge the doctrine of "separate but equal" in graduate education and, if successful, then tackle the more emotional issue of segregation in public schools. The first stage bore fruit in 1950, with two rulings barring segregation at state law schools in Missouri and Oklahoma. By that time, Marshall was also shepherding a number of cases challenging segregation in elementary and secondary schools through the federal courts. In each of the cases, NAACP lawyers developed evidence showing that the "separate but equal" schools provided for black youngsters were decidedly inferior to those for whites.

The Supreme Court agreed to hear five cases from Delaware, Kansas, South Carolina, Virginia and Washington, D.C. The cases were argued in December 1952. But the justices were badly divided, and in June 1953 requested a second round of arguments. In September, Chief Justice Fred Vinson died, and President Dwight D. Eisenhower appointed Earl Warren to the court as his successor. A progressive Republican from California, Warren was a gregarious and skillful politician who took the lead in forging a unanimous vote among the justices to strike down school segregation as a violation of the 14th Amendment's guarantee of equal protection under the law.

Warren's opinion in *Brown v. Board of Education of Topeka* was short — only 13 pages — and deliberately free of any accusatory language toward the South. But it was decisive in wiping away legally mandated segregation: "We conclude that in the field of public education the doctrine of 'separate but equal' has no place," Warren wrote. "Separate educational facilities are inherently unequal." [14]

'All Deliberate Speed'

Despite its seeming breadth, *Brown* did not order immediate desegregation anywhere. Instead, the court asked the lawyers in the case — including attorneys for the U.S. Justice Department, which supported the NAACP — for advice on how to implement the ruling. A year later, in the so-called *Brown II* decision, the court rejected Marshall's plea that desegregation begin at once. Instead, the court adopted the government's suggestion that school districts dismantle the separate school systems "with all deliberate speed." [15]

The court's gradualist approach was designed to deflect opposition, but — in hindsight — the strategy failed. Most prominent Southern politicians attacked the ruling, some counseling "massive resistance." NAACP lawyers had to go to court to make any progress toward desegregation at all. Federal judges — many with no sympathy for the court's ruling — willingly accepted school boards' arguments for delay and token compliance.

Some states enacted "pupil placement statutes" that allowed local boards to use flexible criteria for assigning students to schools so as to minimize any integration. Many school boards adopted "freedom of choice" school assignment plans that — predictably — resulted in virtually no crossover between black and white schools. In other places, school boards decided to desegregate very gradually — for example, one grade a year.

Even token desegregation brought protests, sometimes violent. In Little Rock, Ark., President Eisenhower was forced to call out the National Guard in September 1957 to protect four black youngsters being enrolled at the city's Central High School. Five years later, President John F. Kennedy used guardsmen to stem rioting at the University of Mississippi touched off by the court-ordered admission of its first black, James Meredith.

A full decade after the *Brown* decision, little integration had been achieved. Only 2 percent of Southern black children attended integrated schools as of 1964, Orfield notes, and Northern school segregation was essentially unchanged. [16]

In his book *From Brown to Bakke,* J. Harvie Wilkinson, a former Virginia newspaper editor and now a federal appeals court judge, places much of the blame for the slow pace of desegregation on the Supreme Court itself. Except for a strongly worded ruling in 1957 upholding desegregation in Little Rock, the court stayed out of school cases for eight years after *Brown II,* leaving federal judges with no guidance or instructions on what the ruling required. The court, Wilkinson writes, "neglected to insist on more than token progress, or to have done with naked stratagems for evasion and delay." [17]

The pace of desegregation picked up in the latter half of the 1960s. One important change was a provision of the Civil Rights Act of 1964 authorizing the Justice Department to initiate school desegregation suits; up until then, the NAACP had waged the legal battles essentially alone. In addition, the Department of Health, Education and Welfare (HEW) in 1966 set specific numerical desegregation goals for school systems to achieve. Failure to meet the goals could result in a cutoff of federal aid. In effect, as Wilkinson notes, school boards were now to be judged not by "paper plans" but "by the number of whites and blacks together in schools." [18]

The Supreme Court itself was finally moved to adopt a more insistent stance. In 1968, the court used a challenge to a freedom-of-choice plan adopted by rural New Kent County in Virginia to signal the end of token desegregation. School boards must dismantle segregated systems "root and branch," the court said — not only as to student enrollment but also as to facilities, staff, faculty, extracurricular activities and transportation. "The burden on a school board today," the court declared, "is to come forward with a plan that promises realistically to work, and promises realistically to work *now.*"

A year later, in a Mississippi case, the court underscored the point, saying that school boards must "now and hereafter operate only unitary schools." [19]

Battles Over Busing

The new emphasis on concrete evidence of racial mixing set the stage for the next phase of school desegregation: the battle over busing. Given the general pattern of residential segregation, busing students between racially identified neighborhoods was the most available technique for placing black and white students in the same schools. Although white parents often opposed what they called "forced busing," and Congress tried to block courts from ordering it, the Supreme Court upheld its use in certain situations.

The issue reached the court in 1970. Using a freedom-of-choice plan, Charlotte-Mecklenburg County, North Carolina, had achieved scant integration as of the late '60s. Armed with the new Supreme Court rulings, civil rights attorneys moved to require the school board to take more affirmative steps to end segregated schools.

Federal Judge James B. McMillan, who had criticized busing before taking the bench, ordered a desegregation plan that called for pairing and clustering previously one-race schools. [20] Blacks in lower elementary grades and junior and senior high schools were to be transported to suburban schools, while whites were to be brought to inner city schools for fifth and sixth grades. All told, about one-fourth of the system's 40,000 students were to be bused outside their neighborhoods.

McMillan's plan touched off a firestorm. On appeal, a divided federal appeals court ruled that McMillan had gone too far in requiring busing of elementary school pupils. Civil rights attorneys then took the case to the Su-

Continued on p. 924

Chronology

19th Century

Racial segregation in public schools becomes common practice and, despite some successful challenges, is upheld in the most prominent court decisions.

1899
Supreme Court allows county school board in Georgia to eliminate funds for black high school while paying for high school for whites.

1900-1950 ***The founding of the NAACP in 1909 marks the rise of the civil rights movement.***

1940
Thurgood Marshall is named head of the NAACP Legal Defense and Educational Fund.

1950
Supreme Court bars racial segregation in public graduate education (*Sweatt v. Painter; McLaurin v. Oklahoma State Regents*).

1951-1969

Supreme Court outlaws racial segregation in public schools. The decision provokes "massive resistance" in some Southern states but gradual moves toward desegregation elsewhere.

May 17, 1954
Supreme Court unanimously bars "separate but equal" doctrine in public elementary and secondary schools (*Brown v. Board of Education*). A year later, court says school districts must eliminate legal segregation "with all deliberate speed."

September 1957
President Dwight D. Eisenhower authorizes use of National Guard to enforce desegregation order at Central High School in Little Rock, Ark.

1964
Civil Rights Act of 1964 authorizes federal government to institute desegregation suits.

1968
Supreme Court says local school boards have an affirmative obligation to eliminate dual school systems "root and branch" as soon as possible (*Green v. New Kent County [Va.] Board of Education*).

1970s ***Supreme Court approves use of busing as a tool in desegregation, but limits federal courts' power to impose desegregation plans across school district lines.***

April 20, 1971
Supreme Court unanimously rules that federal courts may order busing of pupils as part of desegregation plan (*Swann v. Charlotte-Mecklenburg [N.C.] Public Schools*).

July 25, 1974
Supreme Court refuses to order consolidation of Detroit and suburban school districts to achieve desegregation (*Milliken v. Bradley*).

September 1974
Boston public schools open under court-ordered desegregation plan requiring busing; plan provokes boycotts, protests and scattered violence.

1980s ***Reagan and Bush administrations oppose use of busing in desegregation plans; courts shift away from busing in favor of other techniques to achieve desegregation.***

1981
Reagan administration eliminates earmarked assistance for school desegregation.

1990s ***Supreme Court eases way for federal courts to lift desegregation decrees.***

January 15, 1991
Supreme Court says school systems can be freed of busing plans if elements of past discrimination have been removed to all "practicable" extent (*Board of Education of Oklahoma City Public Schools v. Dowell*).

March 31, 1992
Supreme Court rules that school boards have no obligation to remedy racial disparities that arise after they have removed all vestiges of legal segregation (*Freeman v. Pitts*).

June 12, 1995
Supreme Court says federal judge went too far in ordering Kansas City school system to create "magnet schools" to attract white students from adjoining suburbs (*Missouri v. Jenkins*).

July 9, 1996
Connecticut Supreme Court says racial segregation in Hartford's public schools is unconstitutional, regardless of cause.

September 1996
Denver and Cleveland open school year with no court-ordered busing.

From Busing to Magnets to Money...

Busing and magnet schools failed to desegregate Prince George's County, Md. Now the sprawling school district wants to try something else: money.

School officials in the predominantly black suburban county outside Washington admit that the county's modest busing plan and its more ambitious magnet school program have failed to bring black and white students together. Now the school board wants a federal judge to allow a return to neighborhood schools. But not the old and substandard neighborhood schools.

The board also wants the judge to order the state and county to pay hundreds of millions of dollars for new school construction and operating expenses to improve educational quality.

"We've gone as far as we're going to be able to go to reach numerical desegregation," says Marcy Canavan, chairman of the school board. "So we're trying to move to a new step: Allow kids to return to neighborhood schools, which is overwhelmingly popular among white and black students.

"But we're focused on not moving any kids until we're sure that they're going to good schools that will improve their educational opportunities and educational performance," Canavan says.

To do that, Canavan says the school board plans to seek a federal court order requiring Prince George's County and the state of Maryland to pay for $180 million in new school construction over the next six years. In addition, the board will be asking for about $30 million per year in additional operating expenses, mainly to reduce classroom size to between 20 and 25 students per class.

Canavan says the new money is needed "with or without desegregation" because of the county's explosive growth. School enrollment has grown by 22,000 in the past 10 years, but only two new schools have been built. Currently, about 10,000 students are housed in modular or temporary classrooms instead of in regular school buildings.

The school system is currently under federal court order in a desegregation suit filed in 1970. Prince George's was then what its current black county executive, Wayne Curry, calls "a sleepy Southern hollow." The county was about three-fourths white, and its school system rigidly segregated. Since then, the county, and its school system, have been racially transformed. The current school enrollment is about 72 percent African-American, 19 percent white, 5 percent Hispanic and 4 percent Asian-American.

To desegregate the schools, a federal judge in 1973 ordered a plan requiring busing of students between predominantly black neighborhoods near Washington and the predominantly white neighborhoods in outlying areas. But as the county's black population grew and whites continued to move toward outlying areas, school officials found it impossible to keep enrollment within the racial balance guidelines set by the court.

A court-appointed panel of experts recommended a new plan in 1981 that called for even more extensive busing to offset the changing demographics, or what Canavan, who is white, today describes as "massive" busing. The proposal drew a firestorm of criticism and eventually was shelved in favor of a magnet school plan. The schools, featuring special curricula, were to be located in predominantly black neighborhoods with the hope of attracting white students to achieve a measure of racial balance.

Since the program was instituted in 1985, the number of magnet schools has grown to 53, featuring some 16 specialized curricula and enrolling some 20,000 students. The programs have been popular, but Alvin Thornton, a former school board

Continued from p. 922

preme Court. There, the Nixon administration joined with the school board in urging the justices to limit the use of busing. Initially, as Supreme Court scholar Bernard Schwartz recounts in his book on the case, the justices were divided. Chief Justice Warren E. Burger was inclined to overturn McMillan. But Burger shifted positions after two Republican-appointed justices — John Marshall Harlan and Potter Stewart — helped forge a strong majority for upholding McMillan's order. [21]

Burger authored the court's final, ultimately unanimous opinion in the case, *Swann v. Charlotte-Mecklenburg Board of Education*. Courts had "broad" authority to act if school boards failed to eliminate "all vestiges of state-imposed segregation," the 1971 ruling declared. Busing — "a normal and acceptable tool of educational policy" — was one permissible remedy for courts to use, the court said. But it also said that "objection" could be raised if the time or distance of travel was "so great as to either risk the health of children or significantly impinge on the educational process."

Decisions Outside the South

Two years later, in its first major desegregation case outside the South, the high court again sanctioned busing — this time in a city, Denver, that had never maintained a stated policy of segregation. Nonetheless, the justices agreed with the federal trial judge that the city had gerrymandered attendance zones and manipulated school construction to keep blacks and whites in separate schools. The ruling in *Keyes v. Denver School District No. 1* sent the case back to lower courts for additional findings, with a clear signal to approve citywide busing to remedy the past segregation.

The *Keyes* ruling prompted new desegregation suits in several Northern and Western cities. But a year

. . . a County's Struggle to Desegregate

member now working as a consultant in developing the new desegregation plan, says the magnets were "only 50 percent successful" in promoting racial balance.

The magnets' popularity complicated their effects on racial mixing. For one thing, in response to pressure from whites, some of the programs were placed in white neighborhoods. In addition, there is a huge waiting list of blacks — about 4,100 students as of last fall — who cannot get into magnet schools because slots have been reserved for whites.[1]

Black parents complained about the difficulty of getting into programs that had been established in the first place to benefit black students. In addition, black parents were also complaining about busing. Although only about 12,000 students are subject to busing for racial balance, about 90 percent of those affected are black.

The two lines of criticism converged this summer to produce a majority on the predominantly black school board in favor of going to court to try to ease the quotas at magnet schools, end racial balance busing and win release from court supervision altogether. U.S. District Judge Peter Messitte agreed in August to ease the magnet school quotas, but he put other issues on hold pending a full-scale re-examination of the status of desegregation in the county.

In a public briefing last month, Canavan acknowledged that the board's plan to abandon busing would put more black students in "schools that are now considered segregated." But she said educational quality would be improved if the new construction and operating funds are approved. The plan calls for construction of 12 new schools, renovation of 22 existing schools and reopening of four closed schools.

"The board is unwilling to return kids to schools where they will not thrive," Canavan told the Sept. 12 meeting. "It is incumbent on us to be sure that these children's educational opportunities increase rather than decrease because of an end to busing."

Few of the people at the meeting — most of them black — had anything good to say about busing. "What I could never understand was busing," one black woman said. "They were busing black children to a black school."

On the minds of most parents at the meeting were the problems common to school systems around the country: discipline, teacher quality and educational improvement. "What I want," one black father told the group, "is to be able to say that you can go into any school in Prince George's County and be able to compete with any school" in the predominantly white adjoining counties.

At the meeting, County Executive Curry pledged strong support for the board's plan despite the price tag. Curry endorsed the move to get out from under court supervision, but he added, "I relish the help of the court" in ordering the state to help pay for the new plan. A spokesman for Gov. Parris Glendening, a Democrat and former Prince George's County executive, attended the session but was noncommittal, saying only that the governor was "prepared to consider and approve a significant increase in construction funds."

For their parts, both Canavan and Thornton voiced optimism that the school board could win a court order requiring funding of the plan. "We would not have done this unless we thought we could win,"' Canavan says. "We think that when the facts are examined, the court will come to the same conclusion that the board did: that we can't do any more to desegregate under the original definition."

[1] *The Washington Post,* Oct. 30, 1995, p. A1.

later, the Supreme Court drew the line at ordering busing between city and suburban school districts. Two lower federal courts had cited evidence of intentional segregation in issuing orders requiring busing between Detroit's predominantly black schools and the overwhelmingly white schools in the surrounding suburbs. By a 5-4 vote, however, the justices overturned the ruling, saying there was no evidence that the suburban school districts had done anything intentional to further segregate the schools.

The 1974 ruling in *Milliken v. Bradley* weakened the ability of civil rights forces to desegregate in predominantly black inner cities — except in places like Charlotte with consolidated urban and suburban school districts. Still, federal judges continued to call for cross-neighborhood busing within cities, provoking resentment among white parents who saw no reason for their children to suffer for past segregation.

Violence in Boston

The resentment turned to anger — or worse — in many places. The most wrenching battle came in Boston. In September 1974, federal Judge W. Arthur Garrity required busing between black Roxbury and the predominantly Irish sections of South Boston. Violence erupted on the opening day of school: A bus carrying black students was stoned and some of the children injured by shattered glass. Turmoil continued for a decade, with protest marches, school boycotts, the election of an anti-busing school board and repeated efforts to overturn or limit Garrity's decrees.

The judge's order withstood the appeals. But, as historian Ronald Formisano writes in his book *Boston Against Busing,* the anti-busing forces never relented. The desegregation plan was also widely seen as causing — or at least accelerating — an exo-

Segregation Increasing for Blacks, Latinos

After dropping for many years, the proportion of black students in minority schools began rising in the late 1980s. The change, due in part to court decisions freeing school districts from mandatory desegregation, marks the first time since the 1954 Brown v. Board of Education *decision that resegregation of African-American students has occurred. Meanwhile, the trend toward greater racial isolation of Latino students has steadily increased.*

	Attending Predominantly Minority Schools		Attending 90-100% Minority Schools	
	Blacks	**Latinos**	**Blacks**	**Latinos**
1968-69	76.6%	54.8%	64.3%	23.1%
1972-73	63.6	56.6	38.7	23.3
1980-81	62.9	68.1	33.2	28.8
1986-87	63.3	71.5	32.5	32.2
1991-92	66.0	73.4	33.9	34.0

Source: Gary Orfield et al., "The Growth of Segregation in American Schools: Changing Patterns of Separation and Poverty Since 1968," National School Boards Association, December 1993, based on data from U.S. Department of Education Office of Civil Rights

dus of white students from Boston schools. Formisano concludes that by the time Garrity lifted major parts of his decree in 1987, Boston schools were "more highly segregated by race than before."[22]

Elsewhere, busing battles of the 1970s were less heated, but opposition was still strong. When a state judge ordered busing in Los Angeles in 1980, opponents mounted an initiative that resulted in a state constitutional amendment prohibiting state judges from requiring busing. But efforts to enact a federal constitutional amendment to limit busing failed in Congress.

Still, by the end of the decade the issue was fading. Supporters of desegregation insist that the calm reflected a gradual acceptance of busing as a necessary and useful tool for bringing the races together in public schools. Critics contend that opponents were simply thwarted from using the political process to prevent busing and that many parents circumvented busing by fleeing to the suburbs or enrolling their children in private schools.

'Resegregation'?

By the 1980s, many of the school systems that had been subject to desegregation orders for a decade or longer began pressing courts to lift the decrees. Many school officials argued that desegregation plans were producing few educational benefits while contributing to white flight from inner-city schools. Supporters of desegregation countered by arguing that lifting court decrees would merely lead to "resegregation" — a return to "racially identifiable" schools. But the Supreme Court gave the critics of mandatory desegregation crucial help with a series of rulings beginning in 1990 that made it easier for lower courts to return schools to the control of local officials.

The opposing camps both focus on Norfolk, Va., which won relief from court-ordered desegregation in 1986, as a prototype of the arguments for or against dismantling busing plans to return to neighborhood schools.[23] In seeking permission to end busing for elementary school children, the city's school board said the move would stem white flight and increase parental involvement in school activities. The Reagan administration filed a brief supporting the move. Supporters of mandatory desegregation argued that the desegregation plan was not the main cause of white students' exodus and that lifting the plan would mean a return to virtually all-black schools in many inner-city neighborhoods.

The federal courts that ended the desegregation plan based their rulings on evidence that white flight would end. Armor, who testified for the board in the case, says the ending of busing succeeded: White enrollment in Norfolk schools increased beginning from the initial proposal in 1982 through the late '80s. But Orfield says more recent data, through 1993, again show that white enrollment has fallen.

Orfield also says that despite overall gains in parental involvement, most of the 10 schools with the highest black enrollment — more than 90 percent — registered declines. And test scores for blacks in those schools have worsened, he says, while scores for blacks in more integrated schools have improved.

Tough Decisions in Oklahoma and Georgia

Norfolk was the first school district to win relief from desegregation orders after being declared a "unitary" system. Federal courts that confronted similar pleas later in the decade took a more skeptical attitude. In two of those cases, federal appeals courts in 1989 refused to lift desegregation decrees imposed on Oklahoma City and DeKalb County, outside Atlanta. Both school boards asked the Supreme Court to review the decisions, and the high court used the cases to signal its impatience with desegregation litigation and to set a lower standard for ending desegregation decrees.

In the first of the rulings, *Board of Education of Oklahoma City Schools v. Dowell,* the court in 1991 ruled, 5-3, that judges should dissolve desegregation decrees if school officials have eliminated the vestiges of legal segregation "as far as practicable." Evidence in the case showed that ending busing would result in 11 schools with 90 percent black enrollment, 22 schools with 90 percent white enrollment and 31 with racially mixed enrollment. But the high court majority said the school system could end the plan if it had complied in good faith with the decree and the schools' racial makeup resulted from residential segregation. Federal court supervision of local schools, the justices added, was intended only as "a temporary measure to remedy past discrimination."

A year later, in the DeKalb County case, the high court allowed lower courts to dissolve part of a school desegregation decree even if a school system had not complied with the entire order. The ruling, *Freeman v. Pitts,* allowed the suburban school district to end busing between the county's predominantly black southern half and its predominantly white northern half, even though it had not satisfied the court that it had ended discrimination in regard to faculty assignment and what the court termed "resource allocation."

The court again stressed the desirability of returning schools to local control, and it brushed aside concerns about "resegregation" of the schools. When resegregation resulted from residential patterns rather than state action, the court said, "it does not have constitutional implications."

The two Supreme Court rulings helped spur more school boards to consider going back to federal court to end desegregation decrees requiring cross-neighborhood busing. Other factors were also at work. Many urban districts were continuing to lose white enrollment, limiting the potential for racial mixing even with busing. Support for busing was also lagging among black parents and youngsters, many of whom saw few benefits to offset the transportation burdens that typically fell disproportionately on black students. And, although the social science data were hotly debated, an increasing number of school officials and other policy-makers were becoming convinced that desegregation had failed to help black youngsters and had helped shift attention away from the more important issue: educational quality.

Compensatory Funding

Federal courts had one limited tool in working toward that goal within desegregation cases. In 1977, the Supreme Court in the so-called *Milliken II* case had upheld the power of lower federal courts to order state and local governments to pay for compensatory education programs as one remedy for past segregation. For the *Milliken* case itself, the ruling resulted in a total of $238 million in compensatory payments from the state of Michigan to Detroit schools over a 12-year period.

Last year, however, the Supreme Court signaled federal judges that this desegregation remedy also could be carried too far. The ruling came in the Kansas City school desegregation case, where a federal judge had ordered Missouri to help pay for dramatic improvements in the schools to try to attract white students from outlying suburbs into the predominantly black inner-city schools.[24] Judge Russell Clark's ruling required a 30 percent pay increase for teachers and construction of magnet schools with state-of-the-art facilities and equipment.

The cost of the plan totaled $1.4 billion by 1995, with the state paying about half of the amount. Lawyers for the state asked the Supreme Court to overturn the decree, saying it went beyond correcting past discrimination. In a 5-4 decision in June 1995, *Missouri v. Jenkins,* the high court agreed. Chief Justice William H. Rehnquist said the judge's effort to create "desegregative attractiveness" to draw suburban students to Kansas City schools amounted to an impermissible "interdistrict remedy."

The court also noted once again its impatience with protracted desegregation cases. There appeared to be, Rehnquist wrote, "no limits to the duration of the District Court's involvement." In a dissenting opinion, however, Justice Ruth Bader Ginsburg wrote: "Given the deep, inglorious history of segregation in Missouri, to curtail desegregation at this time and in this manner is an action at once too swift and too soon." ■

CURRENT SITUATION

Bus Stops

For more than three decades, busing has been the most volatile flashpoint of the desegregation debate. To a considerable extent, the issue receded in the 1980s, as courts and school boards turned to other methods to achieve racial mixing. But the specter of cross-neighborhood busing can still stir anger among whites and, increasingly, resentment among blacks.

Now, advocates on both sides of the issue are ready to write the obituary on court-ordered busing. Clint Bolick, litigation director of the conservative Institute for Justice, predicts that busing for racial balance will disappear from big-city school districts within the decade. [25] "A dying form of desegregation" was NBC News' recent description of busing in a feature story on Denver's decision to return to neighborhood schools. [26]

Civil rights advocates continue to insist that busing is a legitimate tool — indeed, a respected tradition of American education — that has been seized upon by people who essentially oppose desegregation. They also contend that busing can be made to work as part of a successful — and politically viable — desegregation plan.

"The more choices parents have, the more likely they are to feel comfortable with the remedy," says the ACLU's Hansen. "If there's a terrific school for drama on the other side of town, busing suddenly becomes a good thing, not a bad thing."

Opponents, however, insist that busing has been a failure, both educationally and politically. "It was supposed to narrow the achievement gap between whites and blacks, and it hasn't done that," says William D'Onofrio, a Wilmington, Del., accountant and national president of the National Association for Neighborhood Schools. "It was supposed to bring the races closer together and, as many had predicted at the time, it served to exacerbate racial tensions."

In the past few years, black school board members and other black officials have also joined the chorus of critics. Denver board President Gray echoed criticisms that busing encouraged blacks as well as whites to pull their children from public schools. "I saw persons of color who did not want their children bused," he says, "and those kids were mostly in private or parochial schools."

Other black officials now oppose busing mainly because it failed to yield any gains for minority schoolchildren. In Prince George's County, Alvin Thornton, a former school board member now working as a consultant to draft a new desegregation plan for the predominantly black county, calls busing "a non-issue." He adds, "I don't see that as anything I should be spending my time on."

The abandonment of busing plans has also been encouraged by the recent Supreme Court decisions allowing lower courts to free previously segregated school districts from judicial supervision. Civil rights lawyers say lower courts are frequently receptive to school boards' pleas.

Despite the trend against busing and other mandatory desegregation plans, some courts are balking at ending judicial oversight. The federal appeals court in Atlanta refused in September to end the desegregation suit against Muskogee County, which includes Columbus, Ga. In addition, most school boards continue to operate some type of desegregation plan even after winning release from court supervision. In Wilmington-New Castle County, Del., for example, the school board has so far continued busing despite a court ruling ending the desegregation suit a few years ago.

Busing between inner-city and suburban schools is also continuing in the district that prompted the Supreme Court's first ruling on the issue 25 years ago: Charlotte-Mecklenburg County, N.C. In the late 1980s, the school system appeared to be moving away from busing under the leadership of Superintendent John Murphy, a critic of busing and advocate of magnet schools. But a heated school board election in 1995 produced a majority in favor of the existing policies, and Murphy resigned. [27]

Still, a black school board member in Charlotte says the issue is likely to resurface in the 1997 election, and the support for the existing busing plan is not assured. "Public policy right now is to support a desegregated public school system," says Arthur Griffin Jr. "But it's going to be difficult to maintain what we've had in the past. The segregated housing pattern is what's making it difficult. You've got a black Charlotte and a white Charlotte, and that's what makes it difficult to desegregate the schools without busing."

New Legal Avenues

With federal courts withdrawing from school desegregation issues, civil rights advocates are now turning to state courts to break down racial separation. State courts had proved receptive to suits aimed at equalizing funding between wealthy and poor school districts. [28] And civil rights lawyers found Hartford, Conn., an ideal place to try a new approach to court-ordered desegregation.

Hartford's school system is a stark example of the high concentration of poor, minority students in the country's major cities today. The district's enrollment is nearly 95 percent minority — chiefly, African-Americans and a rapidly growing number of Latinos. A majority of the children come from economically disadvantaged homes. By contrast, the 21 surrounding suburban school districts are predominantly white — only seven have greater than 10 percent minority enrollment.

Unlike many urban school districts, however, Hartford does not suffer funding inequities. In Connecticut, needy districts receive a larger share of state aid than well-to-do systems. As a result, Hartford actually spends more money per pupil than the state average and more than the average amount in its neighboring school districts. Nevertheless, Hartford's schoolchildren score significantly lower on standardized achievement tests than students

Continued on p. 930

At Issue:

Should the courts reduce their role in school desegregation?

yes

DAVID J. ARMOR
Research Professor, George Mason University

WRITTEN FOR *THE CQ RESEARCHER,* OCTOBER 1996.

As arbiters of the U.S. Constitution, the federal courts will always have a proper role in the area of school desegregation. Whenever a school system is charged with racial discrimination in violation of the 14th Amendment, the courts must decide the issue of liability. If a court finds liability, it must also fashion or approve an appropriate remedy. This is the area where the courts should modify or reduce their role.

First, courts have ordered mandatory busing plans that require students to be bused among schools in order to attain specific racial quotas. Not only are these plans disruptive and controversial, they also often cause white and middle-class flight, thereby leading to school resegregation over the long run.

Even where mandatory busing has not led to resegregation, it remains an unpopular and divisive issue. A recent Gallup poll shows that seven out of 10 white adults oppose busing for the use of racial balance, and even four out of 10 non-white parents oppose busing. This pattern of opposition remains unchanged more than 25 years after busing was introduced. Courts should be more amenable to voluntary desegregation plans, including magnet schools, which have proven to be just as effective as mandatory plans.

Second, the Supreme Court has made it clear that desegregation remedies are temporary measures. Once a school system has implemented a plan in good faith and ended the discrimination, the system should be declared "unitary" and dismissed from the court order. At that time, a district can return to neighborhood schools, even if that means increased racial imbalance.

Yet hundreds of school systems are still under court orders that are more than 20 years old. Many of these systems maintain mandatory busing plans for racial balance, where students are assigned to schools solely on the basis of their race. There is little justification for such remedies lasting longer than 13 years, the time it takes a kindergartner from the former segregated system to graduate from the desegregated system.

Unfortunately, many school boards no longer want to end these orders, either because they receive funds because of their desegregation plan or because they find it easier to hide behind a court order when they want to make unpopular decisions. It is also true that many lower courts themselves seem to treat these orders as opportunities for long-term school reform.

Whether or not the parties or the court find it advantageous to treat a court order as permanent, the courts should not be coopted into this political posture. They have a judicial responsibility to bring these matters to a conclusion and to dismiss all cases where school systems have reasonably fulfilled their remedial obligations.

no

GARY ORFIELD
Professor of Education and Social Policy at Harvard University

WRITTEN FOR *THE CQ RESEARCHER,* OCTOBER 1996.

Federal courts face complex responsibilities concerning school desegregation. A deeply divided Supreme Court has given highly ambiguous messages to the lower courts. It has left standing the basic requirements for desegregation, which have been in place since the early 1970s, but has also urged lower courts to end their orders soon after a reasonable period of full compliance. The Supreme Court's recent decisions authorizing a return to segregated schools and seriously limiting orders for special educational programs to make up for the history of inequality give federal trial judges broad discretion over the future of school segregation.

Once a judge dissolves an order, he returns all the key decisions to local politics. Some courts have approved this transfer of responsibility after very superficial examination of evidence from the school district on such important questions as whether attending better schools improves the education of minority students and whether segregated schools will be fair and equal. In our research across the country, we find that cities end up with profoundly unequal schools after the minority children lose their right to court protection.

Desegregation has clear educational benefits. Almost two-thirds of white and minority parents of bussed children report a "very satisfactory" experience. Huge public majorities say integrated schools are better, and most desegregation plans now include choice and educational reforms.

Courts should treat these cases with the greatest care since they will help shape the racial future of the community. Courts should be sure that they get reliable, non-biased information on the key issues. There is a very serious risk of unjust decisions since the school districts usually control data and can use tax money to spend many times more than civil rights groups to prepare evidence. Judges should appoint outside experts to answer some of the basic questions: Has everything feasible been done to meet the desegregation and equity obligations? Have the goals set out in the educational components of the desegregation plan been met? Did the school district make any siting, zoning or assignment decisions that made segregation worse? Were students resegregated at the classroom level? Are there feasible steps that can be taken to improve the outcomes that have not been considered? Have the key elements of the plan being put forward by the school district for the post-desegregation period actually succeeded in equalizing segregated schools in any city?

A century ago, after *Plessy v. Ferguson*, the white public assumed that the separate but equal policy under state and local control would be fair. It took 70 years to correct that error. We are in danger of repeating that failure today.

FOR MORE INFORMATION

NAACP Legal Defense and Educational Fund, 99 Hudson St., 16th floor, New York, N.Y. 10013; 212-219-1900. The civil rights litigation group, which is not connected with the NAACP, handles school desegregation suits and monitors enforcement of federal civil rights laws.

National Association for Neighborhood Schools, 2022 Wildwood Dr., Wilmington, Del. 19805; (302) 998-6646. This anti-busing organization claims to have active chapters in 30 states.

National Council of La Raza, 1111 19th St., N.W., Suite 1000, Washington, D.C. 20036; 202-785-1670. The national lobbying group works on educational issues affecting Hispanics.

National School Boards Association, 1680 Duke St., Alexandria, Va. 22314; 703-838-6722. The federation of local school boards has published several reports on school desegregation.

in the suburbs. In 1989, Hartford's schools were described by the state education commissioner as suffering from "triple segregation based on race, poverty and performance."

Supreme Court decisions effectively bar any legal remedy in federal courts for racial separation resulting from housing patterns, as in Hartford. But when civil rights lawyers looked to Connecticut's own constitution, they found a provision added in 1965 — at the peak of the civil rights movement — that explicitly prohibited "segregation or discrimination in the exercise or enjoyment" of any civil or political right.

Building on a previous Connecticut Supreme Court ruling that declared education a fundamental right, civil rights groups filed suit in state court in 1989 contending that Connecticut's entire system of school districts amounted to unconstitutional segregation. This summer, the Connecticut Supreme Court agreed. "We conclude," the court ruled July 9 in *Sheff v. O'Neill,* "that the existence of extreme racial and ethnic isolation in the public school system deprives schoolchildren of a substantially equal opportunity and requires the state to take further remedial measures."

The majority justices in the 4-3 decision made no statement about what remedies the state should adopt, saying the question should be left to the governor and the legislature. The three dissenting justices complained, however, that the ruling would require "a statewide system of transportation of schoolchildren . . . based solely on racial, ethnic and religious factors."

Republican Gov. John G. Rowland responded to the ruling by creating a commission of legislators, officials and citizens to make recommendations for legislative action next year. Rowland and some legislators said they would oppose any forced busing. So far, the plaintiffs in the case have refused to specify what steps the state should take. But lead attorney Brittain acknowledges that busing — "transportation" is his term — is likely to be part of a solution.

"Transportation will be involved, just like curriculum, just like building, just like staff," Brittain says. "Many students travel long distances to regional schools," he adds. "I don't think it's how the students travel to school. It's what's at the end of the [trip]."

The busing issue flared at the commission's Sept. 26 meeting when state Sen. John Kissell, a Republican representing suburban Enfield, unsuccessfully urged the panel to exclude any consideration of busing. "I don't want to walk out of here and have forced busing on our list," Kissell said. Other panel members said the group had to keep busing as an option despite political opposition. "I know it's a difficult issue, but race is a difficult issue," said Dudley Williams Jr., a black member of the group.[29]

For critics of mandatory desegregation, the Connecticut ruling represents an unwanted return to court-ordered plans that they said have brought few improvements but resulted in weakened support for schools. "We have a state court acting as though none of those things ever happened," says Armor of George Mason University. "It's almost as if the [Connecticut court] majority has ignored the history of the past 20 years."

But civil rights lawyers say the Connecticut suit may be the first of many such cases filed around the country. A similar suit was filed in Minnesota in September 1995, and attorneys in other states are also closely watching the case. "Plaintiffs' lawyers are going to continue to pursue alternative ways of exploring these issues in the courts," says Hansen. ■

OUTLOOK

Enduring Dilemma

Forty-two years after the Supreme Court outlawed school segregation, the case that gave the ruling its name is still in court. Linda Brown Thompson, whose father, the Rev. Oliver L. Brown, was the lead plaintiff in *Brown v. Board of Education,* joined a new group of plaintiffs in 1979. They are seeking federal court action to eliminate what they call continuing segregation in Topeka schools.

"It's disheartening that we are still fighting," Thompson, now 53, told *The New York Times* on the 40th anniversary of the Supreme Court decision. "But we are dealing with human beings. As long as we are, there will always be those who feel the races should be separate." [30]

Many other observers of today's debates on race and education share Thompson's disappointment that the battle against segregation has been so long and its results so ambiguous. But they differ sharply over why the dilemma persists, or how best to resolve it.

Civil rights advocates insist that desegregation has been incomplete and that racial mixing is necessary to ensure educational equity for minority youngsters. "No one knows how to make racially isolated schools equal," says Harvard's Orfield. "There are a lot of elements that make high-concentrated-poverty schools unequal, and in reality only minority students end up in those schools."

But critics of mandatory desegregation say the battle against segregation went astray when courts went beyond the removal of legally mandated racial barriers and began imposing specific "racial balance" in enrollments. "I don't like the preoccupation with balance and statistical quotas," Armor says. Despite Supreme Court rulings that racial balance is not required, Armor says some lower courts "continue to try to rewrite the Constitution, to try to find an excuse for maintaining racial balance forever." [31]

Despite the difficulties and disagreements, however, most Americans — blacks and whites — profess support for the principle of desegregation and for more steps to promote school integration. In a *USA Today*/CNN/Gallup poll taken on the 40th anniversary of *Brown*, 88 percent of Americans polled approved of the landmark ruling. In addition, 56 percent of those responding — including 52 percent of whites and 84 percent of blacks — wanted more done to integrate schools. [32]

But Rossell and others say that white Americans remain more committed to integration in theory than in practice. "Ninety-three percent of Americans support the principle of integrated schools," Rossell says. "But it's integrated schools with wonderful black children like the ones you see on TV coming in to their own neighborhoods."

Still, Rossell says the country should not give up the effort to bring students of different races together. "There's something wrong with a society where people of one color live in one area and go to school in one area and people of another color live in another area and go to school in another area," she says.

Similar sentiments come from those who differ with Rossell and other critics and argue for stronger steps to promote integration. "I don't think that we have yet found the way to live together in a completely peaceable and workable way," says Parker of the NAACP Legal Defense Fund. "But I do think we have to find that, in education, housing and a lot of other areas." ■

Notes

[1] Gary Orfield, Susan E. Eaton and the Harvard Project on School Desegregation, *Dismantling Desegregation: The Quiet Reversal of Brown v. Board of Education* (1996).

[2] For background, see "Magnet Schools," *Editorial Research Reports,* May 15, 1987, pp. 225-240.

[3] David Armor, *Forced Justice: School Desegregation and the Law* (1995), pp. 76-98.

[4] Steven A. Holmes, "Look Who's Saying Separate Is Equal," *The New York Times,* Oct. 1, 1995, p. E1.

[5] See Pansye Atkinson, *Brown vs. Topeka: Desegregation and Miseducation — An African American's View* (1993).

[6] Coleman died in March 1995. For a brief recapitulation of the debate, see *The New York Times,* March 28, 1995, p. B11.

[7] See *The New York Times,* Sept. 26, 1995, p. A1.

[8] See Orfield, *op. cit.,* pp. 265-289.

[9] For background, see "School Choice," *The CQ Researcher,* May 10, 1991, pp. 253-276, and "Attack on Public Schools," *The CQ Researcher,* July 26, 1996, pp. 662-663.

[10] Orfield, *op. cit.,* p. 355.

[11] See Richard Kluger, *Simple Justice: The History of Brown v. Board of Education and Black America's Struggle for Equality* (1975), pp. 92-94. Some other details in this section are also derived from Kluger.

[12] J. Morgan Kousser, "Dead End: The Development of Nineteenth-Century Litigation on Racial Discrimination in Schools," 1986.

[13] The fund was part of the NAACP until 1957, when it became a separate organization with no official ties to the NAACP.

[14] The Brown decision applied to the four state cases; a companion decision in the Washington case, *Bolling v. Sharpe,* held that the federal government was also barred from maintaining segregated schools under the Fifth Amendment's Due Process Clause.

[15] The next two sections are drawn from J. Harvie Wilkinson, *From Brown to Bakke: The Supreme Court and School Integration, 1954-1978* (1979).

[16] Orfield, *op. cit.,* pp. 7-8.

[17] Wilkinson, *op. cit.,* p. 126.

[18] *Ibid.,* p. 104.

[19] The cases are *Green v. New Kent County School Board* (1968) and *Alexander v. Holmes County* (1969).

[20] See Bernard Schwartz, *Swann's Way: The School Busing Case and the Supreme Court* (1986), p. 4.

[21] *Ibid.,* pp. 100-184.

[22] Ronald P. Formisano, *Boston Against Busing: Race, Class and Ethnicity in the 1960s and 1970s* (1991), p. 203.

[23] See Orfield, *op. cit.,* pp. 131-141, and Armor, *op. cit.,* pp. 51, 79-81.

[24] See *The Supreme Court Yearbook, 1994-1995* (1996), pp. 36-40.

[25] Quoted in *The New York Times,* Sept. 26, 1995, p. A1.

[26] NBC Nightly News, Sept. 4, 1996.

[27] Orfield, *op. cit.,* p. 206.

[28] For background, see "School Funding," *The CQ Researcher,* Aug. 27, 1993, pp. 745-768.

[29] Quoted in *The Hartford Courant,* Sept. 27, 1996, p. A1.

[30] Quoted in *The New York Times,* May 18, 1994, p. B7.

[31] For background, see "Racial Quotas," *The CQ Researcher,* May 17, 1991, pp. 277-290, and "Rethinking Affirmative Action," *The CQ Researcher,* April 28, 1995, pp. 369-392.

[32] *USA Today,* May 12, 1994, p. 8A.

Bibliography

Selected Sources Used

Books

Armor, David J., *Forced Justice: School Desegregation and the Law,* Oxford University Press, 1995.
Armor, a research professor at George Mason University, details social science findings to argue that mandatory desegregation plans have failed to produce racially mixed schools or increase black students' academic performance. The book includes detailed source notes, a table of cases and a seven-page bibliography.

Kluger, Richard, *Simple Justice: The History of Brown v. Board of Education and Black America's Struggle for Equality*, Knopf, 1975.
Kluger, the author of several nonfiction books, comprehensively traces the history of the separate school desegregation cases that culminated in the 1954 *Brown* decision. The book, exquisitely written, includes detailed source notes and a seven-page bibliography.

Orfield, Gary, Susan E. Eaton and the Harvard Project on School Desegregation, *Dismantling Desegregation: The Quiet Reversal of Brown v. Board of Education,* New Press, 1996.
Orfield and his colleagues argue that despite the benefits of desegregation for minority group students and society generally, school boards and courts are now permitting schools to be "resegregated." The book includes detailed source notes and a three-page listing of major school desegregation decisions.

Rossell, Christine, *The Carrot or the Stick for School Desegregation Policy: Magnet Schools or Forced Busing,* Temple University Press, 1990.
Rossell, a professor at Boston University, argues that voluntary techniques of desegregation, including the use of magnet schools, are more effective in promoting "interracial exposure" than mandatory methods. The book includes detailed source notes and a 14-page list of references.

Schwartz, Bernard, *Swann's Way: The School Busing Case and the Supreme Court,* Oxford University Press, 1986.
Schwartz, a longtime Supreme Court scholar now at the University of Tulsa law school, describes the history of the Charlotte-Mecklenburg, N.C., school desegregation case and even details the internal deliberations that resulted in the Supreme Court's 1971 decision upholding the use of busing as a tool in court-ordered desegregation. The book includes the text of the court's opinion as well as Chief Justice Warren E. Burger's initial draft of the ruling.

Wilkinson, J. Harvie III, *From Brown to Bakke: The Supreme Court and School Integration, 1954-1978,* Oxford University Press, 1979.
Wilkinson, a former Virginia newspaper editor and now a federal appeals court judge, provides a thoughtful account of the Supreme Court's school desegregation decisions and the controversy over the use of busing in the South and in other parts of the country. The book includes detailed source notes.

Articles

"*Brown* Plus Forty," *Teachers College Record,* summer 1995.
This special issue of the respected education journal includes articles and essays by 23 prominent experts evaluating the impact of the *Brown* decision.

"Have Schools Really Changed? Forty Years of Desegregation," *USA Today*, May 12, 1994, pp. 1A, 2A, 8A, 9A.
Several articles explore the impact of the *Brown* decision on the eve of its 40th anniversary.

Kunen, James S., "The End of Integration," *Time*, April 29, 1996, pp. 39-45.
The article examines the trend away from school desegregation in the courts and among educators and some African-American officials and families.

Reports and Studies

National School Boards Association, *Still Separate, Still Unequal? Desegregation in the '90s,* May 1995.
The report by the association's Council of Urban Boards of Education relates the results of a survey of urban school administrators on a variety of school desegregation issues.

Orfield, Gary et al., *The Growth of Segregation in American Schools: Changing Patterns of Separation and Poverty Since 1968*, National School Boards Association, December 1993.
This report by the Harvard Project on School Desegregation says that school segregation increased for African-American students from 1988 to 1991 and that segregation for Latino students continued to increase, reaching the highest level since such data were first collected in the 1960s.

The Next Step

Additional information from UMI's Newspaper & Periodical Abstracts database

Busing

Brenner, Elsa, "Rethinking school busing in Yonkers," *The New York Times,* Feb. 4, 1996, p. WC1.
Kenneth W. Jenkins was suspended from his post in the NAACP for suggesting that busing students across town in Yonkers, N.Y., to achieve racial balance may not be worth the trouble. A growing number of people share Jenkins' concern with busing and believe it has outlived its usefulness.

Gottlieb, Alan, "DPS board adopts new school boundaries," *Denver Post,* Feb. 21, 1996, p. A1.
The Denver Public Schools board of education on Feb. 20, 1996, adopted new school boundaries, putting an end to 21 years of busing for integration and returning the district to a system of neighborhood schools. Changes take effect in fall 1996, for elementary schools and in 1997 for middle and high schools.

Haynes, V. Dion, "Americans rethink desegregation," *Chicago Tribune,* Nov. 10, 1995, p. 1.
The history of busing and the effects of busing on the educational atmosphere of Evanston, Ill., Boston, Riverside, Calif., and Seattle are discussed.

Hillbery, Rhonda, "Black mayor urges end to busing for integration," *Los Angeles Times,* Jan. 9, 1996, p. A5.
Democrat Sharon Sayles Belton, the black mayor of Minneapolis, said that the city needed to rethink the $8 million it spends each year on school desegregation and whether the money should be redirected to student achievement.

McCabe, Michael, and John Wildermuth, "Federal judge agrees to end school busing in San Jose," *San Francisco Chronicle,* Sept. 11, 1996, p. A13.
A federal judge ruled in early September 1996 that the San Jose, (Calif.) Unified School District can stop busing as many as 6,700 students a day for racial balance. Instead, San Jose youngsters can attend their neighborhood schools next fall.

Neal, Terry M., and David Montgomery, "School board in P.G. seeks end to busing," *The Washington Post,* July 26, 1996, p. B1.
The Prince George's County, Md., school board announced July 25, 1996, that it would ask a federal judge to end more than two decades of busing for racial balance and instead force the county and the state of Maryland to pay for enhanced neighborhood schools.

Walters, Laurel Shaper, "School busing at end of line in Missouri," *The Christian Science Monitor,* March 4, 1996, p. 1.
Since voluntary busing began in St. Louis as part of a court-approved settlement in the early 1980s, the number of black students attending integrated schools has risen from 18 percent to 59 percent. But the state of Missouri is fighting to end the desegregation program. A federal court hearing on the matter is scheduled to take place in St. Louis on March 4, 1996, providing another opportunity to outline the endgame for desegregation efforts nationwide.

Current Desegregation Cases

Archer, Jeff, "Conn. Supreme Court orders desegregation for Hartford," *Education Week,* Aug. 7, 1996, p.6.
A divided Connecticut Supreme Court recently ordered state officials to begin the desegregation of the Hartford schools, where 95 percent of the city's 25,000 students are black or Hispanic. Details of *Sheff v. O'Neill* are discussed.

Colvin, Richard Lee, and Lucille Renwick, "Proposal would reallocate funds for desegregation," *Los Angeles Times,* June 1, 1996, p. B1.
Obscured by headlines promising a financial windfall for public schools in 1996 is a California budget proposal that would yank $118 million from the Los Angeles Unified School District and more than $100 million from other urban districts around the state.

Daley, Beth, "Cities wary as state mulls desegregation," *Boston Globe,* April 28, 1996, p. N1.
As state officials discuss dismantling the 1974 Massachusetts law governing desegregation of suburban public school systems, five cities north of Boston that have adopted desegregation plans are reviewing their programs to determine what would happen if the law is repealed.

"Desegregation case to cost school system half a million dollars," Times-Picayune, Aug. 26, 1996, p. B2.
The latest desegregation settlement will cost East Baton Rouge Parish, La., schools more than $483,000 in consulting and legal fees. The school system has been billed $483,626, about $103,700 more than the board budgeted for the fiscal year that ended June 30, 1996.

Frazier, Lisa, "School desegregation faces review in P.G.," *The Washington Post,* July 19, 1996, p. A1.
U.S. District Judge Peter J. Messitte has told Prince George's County, Md., school officials that he will conduct the first full-scale review of the school system's

desegregation efforts since the mid-1980s, a review that could determine the fate of mandatory busing, popular magnet school programs and a proposed neighborhood schools plan.

Freivogel, William H., "School desegregation dilemma," *St. Louis Post-Dispatch,* March 3, 1996, p. B1.
The status of the St. Louis school desegregation program is examined, as a federal court hearing begins to decide the future of the program.

Hanley, Robert, "18 Bergen Towns Propose Voluntary Racially Balanced School in Englewood," *The New York Times,* May 1, 1996, p. B2.
Eighteen towns caught up in the volatile issue of desegregating Dwight Morrow High School in Englewood, N.J., agreed on a plan on April 30, 1996, that would change the school into a racially balanced, specialized six-year academy offering two years of college courses.

Reid, Alexander, "Optimism, uncertainty over desegregation plan," *Boston Globe,* April 28, 1996, p. SW1.
In a step toward racially balancing the public schools, school administrators in Brockton, Mass., have mailed out school assignments to parents of hundreds of children who will be attending first grade in September 1996.

"School desegregation settlement is reached," *Times-Picayune,* Aug. 1, 1996, p. A4.
A decades-old desegregation lawsuit against the East Baton Rouge Parish, La., school system appeared at an end July 31, 1996, U.S. Attorney L. J. Hymel said. The new desegregation plan centers on "community-sensitive" school attendance zones that will end forced busing.

Effects of School Desegregation

Dawkins, Marvin P., and Henry Jomills Braddock, "The continuing significance of desegregation: School racial composition and African American inclusion in American society," *Journal of Negro Education,* summer 1994, pp. 394-405.
The impact of school desegregation on individuals and the broader society in the U.S. during the 40 years since the Supreme Court's ruling in *Brown v. Board of Education* is discussed. Findings of an examination of desegregation indicate long-term benefits in facilitating African-American inclusion in important areas of American life.

Dickerson, Jeff, "DeKalb's generation of desegregation a failure," *Atlanta Journal,* June 18, 1996, p. A8.
Dickerson examines how the DeKalb County, Ga., school system has been affected by 28 years of busing, minority-to-majority transfers and desegregation.

Rossell, Christine H., and David J. Armor, "The effectiveness of school desegregation plans," *American Politics Quarterly,* July 1996, pp. 267-302.
A study examined the effects of different types of desegregation plans on white flight, racial imbalance and interracial exposure from 1968 to 1991. The results show that voluntary plans result in lower levels of white flight and higher levels of change in interracial exposure than mandatory-reassignment or controlled-choice plans.

Smith, Bill, "The young faces of school desegregation," *St. Louis Post-Dispatch,* March 17, 1996, p. B1.
The lives of students who started fifth grade together at Barretts School in St. Louis in 1988 are examined, showing why the areawide school desegregation program is good for some but not for all.

History of Desegregation

Freeman, Gregory, "Painful memories of segregation motivate local man in school fight," *St. Louis Post-Dispatch,* March 19, 1996, p. B11.
Freeman comments on the activism of James A. DeClue, a doctor who has been working on desegregation in the St. Louis area since 1976.

Gottlieb, Alan, "Early days of integration painful ones for one student," *Denver Post,* Aug. 27, 1996, p. A10.
Sandra Coates is profiled with regard to her painful memories of being bused to the largely white Thomas Jefferson High School in Denver in 1969.

Hendrie, Caroline, "Court ends oversight of desegregation in Georgia district," *Education Week,* July 10, 1996, p. 9.
U.S. District Judge William C. O'Kelley recently declared an end to more than a quarter-century of court oversight of the DeKalb County. Ga., school district outside Atlanta. The county's past segregationist policies are discussed.

Reza, H. G., "Historic school bias lawsuit nearly forgotten," *Los Angeles Times,* Sept. 10, 1996, p. A3.
Gonzalo Mendez sued the Westminster, Calif., School District in 1945 after his children were not allowed to attend school with white children and were ordered to enroll in an all-Mexican American school. His suit set in motion the integration of schools in Orange County in 1946.

Magnet Schools

Baron, Kathryn, and Barbara Bailey Kelley, "Are magnet schools working?" *Parenting,* April 1996, p. 65.
Magnet schools, which aim to improve educational opportunities for children of all races, are designed to attract white children to predominantly minority neighborhoods by offering advanced courses and state-of-the-art technology. However, some suspect that magnets give admissions preference to white students.

Gottlieb, Alan, "Move upsets parents: DPS facing a tempest over magnet schools' fate," *Denver Post,* Nov. 16, 1995, p. A1.

Parents of children at three magnet elementary schools in northeast Denver are threatening to revolt over a school board decision the week of Nov. 6, 1995, to move the magnet programs to the southeast or kill them when desegregation busing in Denver public schools ends in fall 1996.

Henig, Jeffrey R., "Race and choice in Montgomery County, Maryland, magnet schools," *Teachers College Record,* summer 1995, pp. 729-734.

Analysis of the pattern of requests to transfer into elementary school magnet programs in Montgomery County, Md., suggests that the direction in which choice points may exacerbate, rather than ameliorate, racial segregation.

Markley, Melanie, "Magnet schools for Acres Home," *Houston Chronicle,* June 17, 1995, p. A29.

Three Acres Home schools in the Aldine, Texas, Independent School District will begin offering magnet programs in August 1995 as a result of a newly revised desegregation plan.

Montgomery, David, "NAACP attacks magnet school vote," *The Washington Post,* Aug. 1, 1996, p. MDP1.

The NAACP has agreed with the Prince George's County, Md., school board's move to abandon racial quotas in the magnet schools for the school year, but the group blasted the board for failing to recruit white children and for ignoring the terms of a federal desegregation order.

Pimentel, Benjamin, "San Mateo parents camp out to get kids in magnet schools," *San Francisco Chronicle,* April 20, 1995, p. A23.

Although registration for about 75 spots in San Mateo, Calif., City School District's two Montessori magnet schools opens on April 22, 1995, parents began camping outside district offices at least four days in advance to try to assure a spot for their children. The campout has become a yearly event.

Ramos, Dante, "Science school still has bugs," *Times-Picayune,* April 13, 1996, p. BR1.

The Garyville-Mount Airy Math and Science Magnet School was built under a federal court order to attract white students from around St. Bernard Parish, La., to an area with a large African-American population. The school has struggled with difficulties and criticism from parents and administrators.

Weaver, Jacqueline, "Magnet schools and programs expanding," *The New York Times,* Aug. 27, 1995, p. CN1.

Students in several Connecticut school systems will return to newly expanded regional magnet schools in Sept. 1995. Several other districts are planning regional magnet programs with themes that range from multiculturalism to Japanese as a second language.

White Flight

Bryant, Tim, "Judge is warned of white flight," *St. Louis Post-Dispatch,* March 6, 1996, p. A1.

Consultant Christine H. Rossell testified on March 5, 1996, that neighborhood schools and magnet schools could attract additional white city students to St. Louis Public Schools and that mandatory student assignments probably would cause more whites to leave the public schools. Rossell testified on behalf of the state of Missouri on its plan to phase out state spending for school desegregation in St. Louis.

Sutton, Bea, "Beyond busing: The myth of white flight," *Denver Post,* Sept. 27, 1995, p. B8.

Sutton accuses the Denver news media of exaggerating the "white flight" from Denver public schools to schools in the city's suburbs. Sutton claims that the white public-school population in the suburbs has increased at a much lower rate than students of color or the population as a whole.

Back Issues

Great Research on Current Issues Starts Right Here...Recent topics covered by The CQ Researcher are listed below. Before May 1991, reports were published under the name of Editorial Research Reports.

APRIL 1995
Abortion Clinic Protests
Dieting and Health
Combating AIDS
Rethinking Affirmative Action

MAY 1995
Assisted Suicide Controversy
Overhauling Social Security
Learning to Read
Mandatory Sentencing

JUNE 1995
Combating Infectious Disease
Property Rights
Repetitive Stress Injuries
Regulating the Internet

JULY 1995
War Crimes
Highway Safety
Combating Terrorism
Preventing Teen Drug Use

AUGUST 1995
Job Stress
Organ Transplants
United Nations at 50
Advances in Cancer Research

SEPTEMBER 1995
Catholic Church in the U.S.
Northern Ireland Cease-Fire
High School Sports
Teaching History

OCTOBER 1995
Quebec's Future
Revitalizing the Cities
Networking the Classroom
Indoor Air Pollution

NOVEMBER 1995
The Working Poor
The Jury System
Sex, Violence and the Media
Police Misconduct

DECEMBER 1995
Teens and Tobacco
Gene Therapy's Future
Global Water Shortages
Third-Party Prospects

JANUARY 1996
Emergency Medicine
Punishing Sex Offenders
Bilingual Education
Helping the Homeless

FEBRUARY 1996
Reforming the CIA
Campaign Finance Reform
Academic Politics
Getting Into College

MARCH 1996
The British Monarchy
Preventing Juvenile Crime
Tax Reform
Pursuing the Paranormal

APRIL 1996
Centennial Olympic Games
Managed Care
Protecting Endangered Species
New Military Culture

MAY 1996
Russia's Political Future
Marriage and Divorce
Year-Round Schools
Taiwan, China and the U.S.

JUNE 1996
Rethinking NAFTA
First Ladies
Teaching Values
Labor Movement's Future

JULY 1996
Recovered-Memory Debate
Native Americans' Future
Crackdown on Sexual Harassment
Attack on Public Schools

AUGUST 1996
Fighting Over Animal Rights
Privatizing Government Services
Child Labor and Sweatshops
Cleaning Up Hazardous Wastes

SEPTEMBER 1996
Gambling Under Attack
The States and Federalism
Civic Journalism
Reassessing Foreign Aid

OCTOBER 1996
Political Consultants
Insurance Fraud

Future Topics

- ***Parental Rights***
- ***Global Warming***
- ***Copyright Protection on the Internet***

THE CQ Researcher

PUBLISHED BY CONGRESSIONAL QUARTERLY INC.

Parental Rights

Are new laws needed to empower parents?

Conservative lawmakers and the Religious Right say liberal bureaucrats, courts and legislators have usurped parents' authority over their children. They have mounted an aggressive campaign to win new parental rights guarantees in state constitutions and federal law. On Nov. 5, Coloradans will vote on a constitutional amendment giving parents the "inalienable" right "to direct and control the upbringing, education, values and discipline of their children." Sponsors in 27 other states are pushing similar amendments, and parental rights legislation has been introduced in Congress. A broad coalition of opponents argues that parental rights laws are dangerous and unnecessary. Such laws would not only put children at new risk for abuse, they say, but also throw schools into gridlock and lead to costly lawsuits.

INSIDE THIS ISSUE

CQ Oct. 25, 1996 • Volume 6, No. 40 • Pages 937-960

Formerly Editorial Research Reports

THE ISSUES

BACKGROUND

CURRENT SITUATION

OUTLOOK

SIDEBARS AND GRAPHICS

FOR FURTHER RESEARCH

COVER: BARBARA SASSA-DANIELS

THE CQ Researcher

Oct. 25, 1996
Volume 6, No. 40

The CQ Researcher (ISSN 1056-2036). Formerly Editorial Research Reports. Published weekly (48 times per year, not printed March 1, May 31, Aug. 30, Nov. 29) by Congressional Quarterly Inc., 1414 22nd St., N.W., Washington, D.C. 20037. Annual subscription rate for libraries, businesses and government is $319. Additional rates furnished upon request. Periodicals postage paid at Washington, D.C. POSTMASTER: Send address changes to The CQ Researcher, 1414 22nd St., N.W., Washington, D.C. 20037.

Parental Rights

By Thomas J. Billitteri

The Issues

John Burrington of Colorado Springs has seen too much ugliness in his years as a pediatric surgeon. Children with bones fractured by angry parents. Children with welts from electric cords. Children who have been burned and scarred, and worse.

And now Burrington thinks he sees something every bit as abhorrent: a proposed amendment to the Colorado Constitution that would give parents the "inalienable" right "to direct and control the upbringing, education, values and discipline of their children." Indeed, Burrington worries that the amendment — to be decided by voters Nov. 5 — has the potential to shield child abusers.

On the surface, Colorado's "parental rights" initiative seems as uncontroversial an election-year issue as clean air and full employment. "To vote no is like voting no to mom, apple pie and the flag," Burrington acknowledges.

But Burrington thinks the proposal, by sanctioning parental discipline, would put children at greater risk for abuse and neglect. Moreover, he fears, it would encourage parents to sue teachers, principals or other government representatives over school curricula and many other decisions affecting their children that the parents didn't like.

"It's fairly difficult to prosecute child abuse cases now," Burrington says. If parents have an "inalienable" right to discipline their children, "then it will be almost impossible to prosecute child abuse short of mayhem or murder." The amendment, he says, "is absolutely criminal and will set things back 100 years."

Amendment supporters, including conservative lawmakers and the Chris-

tian Right, call such statements nonsense. The measure grants no new rights, they argue, but simply codifies existing ones that lower courts, bureaucracies, school boards and legislators have taken away. A short, clearly worded amendment would give parents a more streamlined and economical means than they have now to challenge government intrusion into family decisions — such as how a child learns about sex or whether a parent may spank a misbehaving child.

"Like many Coloradans, I'm concerned about what appears to be an assault on the American family," said Denver lawyer Mike Norton, a former U.S. attorney in the Reagan administration and a spokesman for the Coalition for Parental Responsibility, which is leading the initiative drive. "This would give parents a [legal] basis on which to argue that they are in the best position to control the upbringing of their children." [1]

Norton views as "outrageous" arguments that the measure would protect child abusers. "Everybody knows what discipline is and what child abuse is," he said. "Our parental rights amendment is not going to supersede the Criminal Code." [2]

As the first state to bring a parental rights amendment to a vote, Colorado is at the epicenter of an emerging nationwide movement. Proponents hope that codifying parental rights will help limit how far government can "intrude" on children's lives and parents' right to raise their children as they see fit. The outcome could have profound consequences for public education, family law and child protection — and any other area where government and the rights of children and parents intersect. [3]

Approval of Colorado's initiative could give momentum to nascent efforts in more than two dozen other states, and perhaps rekindle interest in parental rights in Congress, where two such bills were introduced in 1995. (*See map, p. 940.*)

"Once we win in Colorado in November, it will prove this is a successful concept," says Greg D. Erken, executive director of "Of the People," an Arlington, Va., group that has been pushing parental rights amendments nationwide since 1993. "We expect that a number of states in 1997 and 1998 will renew their efforts to adopt their own parental rights amendments."

Those backing parental rights measures include such conservative stalwarts as the Christian Coalition (which had a parental rights plank in its 1995 Contract With the American Family), the Traditional Values Coalition, the Home School Legal Defense Association and the Heritage Foundation.

Supporters claim that the Supreme Court long ago classified parental rights as "fundamental," thus giving them the same strict level of judicial protection as free speech and religion and racial equality. That hotly contested claim rests largely on a pair of high court rulings from the 1920s (*see p. 950*).

Status of Parental Rights Amendments in the States

Proposed parental rights amendments to state constitutions have been introduced or sponsored in more than half the states, according to Of the People. In Colorado, an amendment proposal is on the Nov. 5 ballot.

Amendment proposal on ballo

Passed legislative committee in 199

Passed legislative committee in 199

Amendment introduced or sponsored in legislature

Source: Of the People

Proponents of new parental rights laws say teachers, school boards, child-welfare agencies, lower courts, bureaucrats and professional "elites" such as psychologists, physicians and birth-control counselors have ignored the court's intentions and chopped away at parental authority.

"All of our institutions of authority in this country have been undermined, and in some cases been under frontal assault, for some time — schools, government, law enforcement, churches, families. . . . Parents are no different," says Rep. Steve Largent, R-Okla., who with Sen. Charles E. Grassley, R-Iowa, introduced the "Parental Rights and Responsibilities Act" in Congress last year (*see p. 943*). "We literally see hundreds, if not thousands, of cases across the country [in which] parents' ability to direct the upbringing of their children is undermined or usurped by a government agency."

Parental rights advocates point to a litany of perceived intrusions, especially in the schools, including birth-control counseling, condom distribution and lessons about homosexuality, as well as the abrupt separation of children from parents accused of abuse.[4]

"We really believe legislation is needed to address the growing attack against the parent-child relationship," says Andrea Sheldon, director of government affairs at the Traditional Values Coalition. "You can see that in so many different ways: When the federal government says, 'It doesn't matter what your parents say, we're going to give you money to go off and get an abortion, and your parents don't need to weigh in,' [and when] children are given questionnaires about their family, about their sexual activities, and parents don't know about it."

Psychologist James C. Dobson, a conservative radio broadcaster and founder of Colorado Springs-based Focus on the Family, sees the struggle for parental rights as a "contest between two world views. There are those of us who . . . believe that we should bring our children up to worship God and understand his principles . . . including the sanctity of life and premarital chastity [and] those on the other end of the continuum who hold to no eternal truths. . . .

"This contest . . . is [being] played out . . . throughout government, in the educational system and everywhere else decisions are being made for the culture. It is especially relevant to children because we all know children are the prize to the winner. You know, those who are able to tell children what is right and wrong, those who are able to write the curricula for kids, will necessarily determine the future of the culture because in just 20 years those youngsters will be adults and will be taking over. And so there is an intense struggle for the hearts and minds of kids. That's what's behind this invasion of parental rights." [5]

Dozens of professional organizations and liberal advocacy groups are fighting the parental-rights push. They include groups as diverse as The National PTA, the National Education Association (NEA), the American Civil Liberties Union, Planned Parenthood Federation of America, the American Academy of Pediatrics and the National Council of Churches of Christ. They argue that codifying parental rights into an "ambiguous" new law would have catastrophic consequences: gridlock in the public education system; greater incidence of child abuse and teen pregnancy; soaring government legal bills; and a virtual dismantling of child-protection safeguards.

"By giving parents a new cause of action to assert their views in court, this legislation would open to challenge virtually any governmental action or policy involving the health, safety and welfare of children," warned the Academy of Pediatrics. [6]

"None would [disagree] that active parental involvement in the care, upbringing and education of our children is the cornerstone of a strong, healthy society," Sammy J. Quintana, president of the National School Boards Association, told a Senate Judiciary subcommittee hearing last December on the proposed Parental Rights and Responsibilities Act. "[But] this bill is about making it more difficult for public schools to teach our children. It is about lining the pockets of lawyers and draining the scarce educational resources in our schools. It is about putting the health and safety of our children in jeopardy. It is about playing politics with our children." [7]

"The question is: Who is in charge of public education? It is the job of educators and schools to determine the curriculum that is going to best [produce] a learned citizen."

— Anne Bryant, executive director, National School Boards Association

Some opponents also charge that parental rights activists are engaged in a "stealth" effort to gain greater control of the public schools, erode the wall of separation between church and state and win approval for tax-paid vouchers to fund private or parochial schooling.

The strict legal test in the bills proposed in Congress requires government to show a "compelling interest" in any action it takes impinging on "parental rights." That troubles Rebecca Isaacs, director of public policy for People for the American Way, a seasoned liberal advocacy group that is heading up an opposition coalition.

"The law would let any parent sue over something that they believe in an extremely vague, broad way interferes with their right to bring up their child," Isaacs says. "You can't have any [law] with a lower threshold or broader right with a harder burden for government to meet. It's unprecedented."

Public support for codifying parental rights is, in some ways, difficult to predict. A *Rocky Mountain News* poll of registered Colorado voters in early September found a 76 percent approval rate for the state's constitutional amendment (72 percent of Democrats approved and 83 percent of Republicans). [8]

While foes of Colorado's parental rights amendment acknowledged the difficulty of making their case on such a complex and emotional issue, they predicted that much of the support would evaporate once voters learned the implications of the simply worded measure.

"My experience in focus groups is that as soon as you start talking about what this [Colorado measure] could mean, the support drops off very rap-

From Peyote to Religious Freedom . . .

It was an obscure religious practice involving the hallucinogenic drug peyote, but it touched off a national controversy that now involves parental rights.

In 1990, the U.S. Supreme Court affirmed Oregon's denial of unemployment benefits to two Native Americans dismissed from their jobs at a private drug rehabilitation center. The reason for their dismissal: ingesting peyote as part of tribal religious rituals.

The Native Americans claimed the First Amendment's guarantee of religious freedom made the state's action unconstitutional. But Oregon argued that they had been fired for "work-related misconduct" — and thus didn't deserve jobless benefits — because using peyote was a criminal offense under state law. [1]

Fearing the Smith decision could curtail religious freedoms far beyond peyote use, an unusually broad coalition of religious groups — from the liberal National Council of Churches of Christ to the National Association of Evangelicals — helped push a bill through Congress to preclude such rulings in the future. President Clinton signed the Religious Freedom Restoration Act (RFRA) in 1993. [2]

Now, some parental rights advocates are saying that the parental rights act proposed last year by Sen. Charles E. Grassley, R-Iowa, and Rep. Steve Largent, R-Okla., is the secular complement to RFRA, with both protecting fundamental rights guaranteed by the Constitution. [3]

A leading proponent of that view is Michael P. Farris, president of the Home School Legal Defense Association. Farris co-chaired the drafting committee on RFRA and was a chief architect of the Grassley-Largent legislation.

"Religious liberty was undermined by a single stroke of a Supreme Court guillotine" in the peyote case, Farris said in congressional testimony last year. "Parental liberty is dying from the cuts of a thousand switchblades." [4]

To Farris, the disconnect between parents' secular and religious rights became abundantly clear in a pair of home-schooling cases he brought before the Michigan Supreme Court in the early 1990s. [5]

In the cases, consolidated for oral arguments, two families contended that a Michigan law requiring all teachers to be certified was an unconstitutional infringement on their rights. One family, the DeJonges, wanted to home school for religious reasons. The other, the Bennetts, had non-religious reasons.

In the DeJonge case, the court "used the fundamental rights test and concluded that the [Michigan] statute was unconstitutional because it violated the principles of religious freedom when combined with parental rights," Farris told the congressional hearing.

In the Bennett case, Farris said he argued that the parents' rights "to direct the upbringing of their children was also a fundamental right." But the Bennetts lost.

The court, rendering both decisions on the same day in 1993, said in the Bennetts' case that "the fundamental rights analysis did not apply to a parental rights claim standing alone without a religious component," Farris testified.

And that brings Farris back to his RFRA argument. "The difficulty that parents face in court when they're trying to

idly. The devil is really in the details," says Michael Hudson, vice president of People for the American Way, a leading member of the Protect Our Children Coalition, which is opposing the Colorado initiative.

Outside Colorado, similar amendments have found sponsors in 27 state legislatures, to a large extent due to the efforts of the group Of the People, which has support from the American Legislative Exchange Council, a group of conservative state lawmakers.

Central to the debate over parental rights are several high-profile cases that proponents say reflect the growing usurpation of parental authority by government: Parents who say they were told it was "none of your business" after they objected to their teen daughters being taken by a school counselor to a clinic where birth-control materials were dispensed; students who say they were unable to "opt out" of sex-education courses; parents outraged by a school-sponsored physical exam that included genital inspections of sixth-grade girls.

Foes claim parental rights backers are exaggerating or altering details of cases, and in some instances using "bogus horror stories" to wage a disinformation campaign, according to Americans United for Separation of Church and State. [9]

Movement backers "specialize in lurid, tabloid-type anecdotes to try to show there is some broad, sweeping problem, rather than [a problem] that should be — and could be — taken care of in the local community," says Isaacs.

"In my experience, the Chicken Little, sky is falling phenomenon is occurring," says Gloria Feldt, president of Planned Parenthood. "I would not want to say no parent has ever been treated unfairly; the justice system is sometimes imperfect. But those of us who have been teachers and worked with youth and families in different situations tend to know that there is seldom a clear black and white" picture of what happens when children are involved.

But parental rights advocates counter that it is the liberals who are engaging in hyperbole, predicting dire consequences from parental rights measures in attempts to derail the movement. Not only are courts and

. . . to the Fight Over Parental Rights

litigate their cases is exactly the same" as that faced by claimants after the peyote case, he says. "Courts are using the wrong standards for evaluating their rights. Nobody denies parents have rights — the question is, what level: fundamental or non-fundamental?"

In the Smith decision, Farris says, "The Supreme Court decided religious freedom was not a fundamental right. In parental rights cases (without a religious dimension), a lot of appellate and lower courts in the federal and state system have decided parents' rights are not fundamental. RFRA gives all religious-based claims in public schools fundamental-rights status. So what's left to be established are secular-based claims."

And that is why those who argue that the parental rights movement is a stealth attempt to inject religion into the schools "can be proven almost silly in their arguments," Farris maintains.

"It's the secular parents who are the only ones who stand to win anything (from parental rights laws) in terms of their interaction with the public schools," he says. Religious parents, he adds, already have RFRA.

Opponents of the parental rights movement reject Farris' argument that a parental rights bill is the needed complement to RFRA. "It's a snow job," says Rebecca Isaacs, director of public policy at People for the American Way.

Isaacs and other critics say RFRA is unlike the Parental Rights and Responsibilities Act because RFRA provides a narrow remedy whereas the parental rights bill takes a broad-brush approach.

Under RFRA, they say, a person could be individually exempted from a law that substantially infringes on his religious freedom. Under the parental rights bill, an aggrieved party could suspend some government functions for all citizens.

Not only that, critics say, a parental rights measure would allow individual parents to manipulate local policy to reflect their personal religious beliefs. And unlike RFRA, where the individual has to prove the government took away his religious freedom, a parental rights measure would put an onerous burden of proof on government, critics say.

"Under parental rights legislation, all you have to show is that you're a parent and that you think some activity a local institution is doing interferes with your newly named fundamental rights," Isaacs says. "Then the government has to show a compelling interest for that activity and that it was accomplished by the least restrictive means."

For schools, child-abuse workers and health and safety agencies, she says, that burden of proof "is going to wreak havoc."

---

[1] Kermit L. Hall, ed., *The Oxford Companion to the Supreme Court* (1992), p. 725. The case is *Employment Division v. Smith.*

[2] See *1993 CQ Almanac,* p. 315.

[3] The bills died when the 104th Congress ended and must be reintroduced next year.

[4] Farris testified before the Senate Judiciary Subcommittee on Administrative Oversight and the Courts, Oct. 26, 1995.

[5] For background, see "Home Schooling," *The CQ Researcher,* Sept. 9, 1994, pp. 769-792.

bureaucracies usurping parental authority, parental rights advocates counter, but liberals are engaging in hysteria of their own.

"It's Chicken Little, the sky is falling," says Sheldon of the Traditional Values Coalition, echoing Feldt from across the ideological chasm. "It doesn't matter what the issue is."

But if parental rights pass, Sheldon adds, courts and bureaucracies will think twice about usurping parental authority, and school personnel and other government workers "will have to be more careful" about how they deal with students' rights. "They're not careful now — they don't have to be."

As the debate continues over parental rights, these are some of the questions being asked:

Is it necessary to codify parental rights into law?

A parental rights law or amendment is needed, advocates insist, because lower courts, school boards and legislators have chipped away at the rights established long ago by the Supreme Court.

While parental rights may still exist on paper, they say, the "little guy" can't afford to pursue them against powerful groups like the NEA and well-organized bureaucracies such as school boards and child protective services. Even members of the "humane professions" — educators, lawyers, doctors, social workers and school counselors — have usurped the role of parents, critics contend.

The answer, according to parental rights backers, is a variety of legal tacks that critics say would be destructive and unnecessary.

The Grassley-Largent parental rights bills that died in the 104th Congress could well resurface next year. They guaranteed parental rights in education, health decisions, discipline (including "reasonable corporal discipline") and religious instruction. The measures excluded abuse, neglect and custody disputes from their scope, and prevented parents from withholding medical treatment in cases involving serious harm.

The Colorado initiative, bearing the characteristic brevity of most constitutional amendments, contains no stated exclusions, and supporters say its reference to "discipline" is tied to existing state definitions. The Grassley version of the federal bill required a parent to try to settle a dispute out of court, but Colorado's measure has no such stipulation.

Many other proposed state constitutional amendments are even more broadly written. The key portion of the model language proposed by Of the People simply says: "The right of parents to direct the upbringing and education of their children shall not be infringed."

The federal bills sought to erect the highest legal hurdle for the "government" — be it a kindergarten teacher, child-welfare bureau or federal agency. To justify an action that impinged on parental rights, the government would have to demonstrate that the action was essential to "accomplish a compelling governmental interest" and that it used "the least restrictive means of accomplishing" that interest. Parents who believed their rights were trampled could sue in state or federal court.

In requiring the government to show "clear and convincing" evidence that an action was necessary, Grassley's proposed federal standard is even stricter than the "preponderance" of evidence standard called for in racial-discrimination cases. But critics of the bill say the cases cited by parental rights proponents do not warrant imposing draconian legal burdens on school boards and juvenile-welfare boards.

Proponents frequently point to the controversial 1995 case *Brown v. Hot, Sexy and Safer Productions Inc.*, in which parents in Massachusetts charged they were not given an opportunity to review or remove their children from a graphic high school "AIDS-awareness" assembly. According to the parents' suit, the program's speaker allegedly used profane language to describe body parts and excretory functions and advocated oral sex, masturbation, gay sexual activity and condom use.

The appeals court found no violation of family rights protections, adding fuel — and another oft-used anecdote — to the parental rights debate. "It is this type of unbending governmental abuse of authority in transgressing the fundamental right of the family that requires the 'compelling interest' standard to be applied in these situations," declared the American Center for Law and Justice, a Christian legal advocacy group in Virginia Beach, Va. [10]

"There's a clear move in this country to outlaw spanking. We want to say that parents always have a right to reasonable spanking."

—Michael P. Farris, president, Home School Legal Defense Association

Of the People founder Jeffrey Bell agrees. He says that the model state amendment proposed by Of the People is intentionally broad to spark a debate about parental rights and responsibilities. He says the group wants to leave the details of the amendment to be worked out at the community level — and, if need be, in the courts. "It doesn't argue each and every controversial educational practice," Bell told the Christian Coalition in September. "It gets it back to a sovereignty issue: populism vs. elitism. Who is in charge? Who should be in charge?"

Critics of the proposed parental rights legislation argue, however, that imposing a compelling-interest standard on government would lead to an explosion of destructive social consequences and the nullification of dozens of state laws that carefully balance parental rights and the needs of children.

"Communities would be paralyzed under the threat of lawsuits about virtually all the services and programs they provide," said People for the American Way. "Child protective services would be discouraged from investigating reports of abuse. . . . Basic health care in schools, such as hearing and vision testing and sports physicals, could be prohibited. Local decisions between parents and educators about curriculum content, textbook selection and student assessments could be overturned." [11]

"This bill does not 'codify' existing law," the NEA says. It "creates a *new* fundamental right and will have dire consequences for this country's public schools. [12]

Besides, the NEA and other opponents argue, parents already have a wide array of rights and options to fight what they consider unreasonable government interference. Pediatric surgeon Burrington notes, for example, that parents in Colorado can home-school their children. [13] "The problem is parental responsibility," he says. "You can't legislate responsibility."

Would a federal Parental Rights and Responsibilities Act or similar state laws produce educational gridlock?

Critics call parental rights legislation a train wreck waiting to happen. "The legislation is so broad that it could be read to give [parents] a veto over everything that's done in the school," said Gwen Gregory, deputy general counsel for the National School Boards Association. "Schools would come to a screeching halt." [14]

The 2.4-million-member NEA, the nation's largest teachers' union, claims the federal Parental Rights and Responsibilities Act would, among other things, force schools to provide a "designer" curriculum for each student, allow parents to sue a teacher for saying anything in class the parents don't like, give parents the right to opt their children out of required courses and allow parents to win suits challenging such policies as "no pass/no play" rules and teacher grading standards.

"This legislation is disruptive, intrusive, expensive and unnecessary, and will wreak havoc in the public schools," the NEA declared in a recent statement.

Many educators also claim that parental rights laws would destroy the traditional democratic underpinnings of the public school system, making litigation the preferred engine of change instead of traditional approaches such as school board elections, referendums and parent-teacher negotiations.

Shirley Igo, the National PTA's vice president for legislation, also worries that parental rights initiatives could chill parental involvement in the schools because volunteers would fear being dragged into court. "It would destroy the level of trust the PTA has been working to build over the past 100 years," Igo says.

With parental rights laws in place, control of curricula decisions, ancillary services such as drug and birth-control counseling, sex education and even choice of library books would be in the hands of a religious or ultra-conservative minority rather than professional educators, opponents say.

"The question is, who is in charge of public education?" says Anne Bryant, executive director of the school boards association. "It is the job of educators and schools to determine the curriculum that is going to best [produce] a learned citizen."

Critics say the proposed measures would also discourage school districts and public health agencies from making pregnancy and drug counseling available to teens, resulting in higher rates of illegitimacy, drug abuse and disease.

"A major concern," says Feldt of Planned Parenthood, is that parental rights measures would gut confidentiality laws that now protect teens seeking sensitive services such as prenatal care, birth control and treatment for sexually transmitted disease. "Obviously in the ideal world, teens would be communicating with parents about these issues," Feldt says. "We'd support programs to further that, but laws that are punitive in nature don't further that parent-child relationship. Not every family comes from the 'Ozzie and Harriet' mold."

Some also see a hidden agenda in the movement: supporting tax-paid vouchers for private religious schools. [15] "It's going to be an easy move from this to vouchers, because the schools won't be able to comply with all the requests for designer curriculum," Isaacs says.

But backers of parental rights dismiss warnings of dire consequences or nefarious motives, saying groups like the NEA are trying to protect their power base and advance an ultra-liberal agenda.

"There's nothing in this legislation," Grassley says of his bill, "that's going to change traditional control of education."

Adds Largent, "There is no coalition of moms and dads that has [a lobbying] office on K Street in Washington. The principal opponent to this bill is the education bureaucracy. It's understandable why. This is threatening their power because we're saying, 'Let's empower parents to become partners in education decisions.'"

Of the People founder Bell says the NEA and other parental rights foes "believe parents aren't competent to raise their child, but they don't talk about that." Instead, he says, they claim parental rights laws will lead to increased child abuse, designer curricula, even a ban of Shakespeare's Romeo and Juliet, which contains references to teen love and suicide, and Macbeth, with its themes of witchcraft and murder.

Such fears are off base, Bell told the Christian Coalition forum. Besides, he said, "I thought the school system had been doing a pretty good job already of taking Shakespeare out of [education]."

Would children be at greater risk for abuse and neglect from proposed parental rights laws?

Marilyn Van Derbur, Miss America in 1958, has said she was sexually abused by her father. Now she sees a similar threat to a new generation of youngsters — from the proposed federal parental-rights bill.

"Do not make it more difficult than it already is for child-protection services" to investigate abuse, she urged a House Judiciary subcommittee hearing last year. [16]

It's a plea being repeated by a battalion of child-welfare organizations, from the National Child Abuse Coalition to the National Safe Kids Campaign, chaired by former Surgeon General C. Everett Koop. They argue the measure would dismantle health and safety protections that courts, legislatures and other public bodies have carefully constructed over the decades. (*See "At Issue," p. 953.*)

"Proponents [of parental rights legislation] cite instances of children being summarily removed from the care of protective parents," says the Chicago-based American Professional Society on the Abuse of Children. "Cer-

Sex Education Fires Controversy . . .

In the battle over parental rights, no issue is more incendiary than sex education.

Conservative advocates of stronger parental rights believe public schools have gone too far in efforts to teach youngsters about the hazards of teen pregnancy, sexually transmitted disease and the availability and use of contraceptives. "Government officials have no right to form moral beliefs in children that contradict the beliefs of parents," declares the Heritage Foundation. Under parental rights laws, the group says, school officials would either refrain from teaching about issues like contraception and abortion, or parents would have the "clear right to opt out from the official imposition of 'values' hostile to their beliefs." [1]

But foes of new parental rights guarantees, such as proposed federal legislation, say too many parents are ignoring the harsh realities of life in the late 20th century. Competent sex education and confidential sex-related health services are among the most effective ways of stemming teen pregnancy rates and the spread of AIDS and other sexually transmitted diseases among young people, they argue.

"When I look at what this legislation is about," says Gloria Feldt, president of Planned Parenthood Federation of America, "it really seems to me an attempt to play on the fear parents have of being out of control of their kids. That's not an altogether unfounded fear, but not one that can really be solved by legislation of this nature."

Clearly, sexual mores and differing notions about sex education are driving forces of the parental rights movement. It was former New York City school chief Joseph A. Fernandez's ill-fated program to distribute condoms in the schools that helped launch the parental rights movement — and led to his firing in 1993. And cases such as *Brown v. Hot, Sexy and Safer Productions Inc.* — in which parents protested the sexual explicitness of an AIDS awareness assembly presented to Massachusetts high school students — gave the movement important momentum.

"It is not bad for a loving mother — whether secular or religious — to tell her 13-year-old daughter that she will not take her to a doctor for birth control pills," wrote Rep. Steve Largent, R-Okla. "It is bad to let an immature child or an uninformed government official veto a good parent's best judgment." [2]

Under parental rights bills proposed in Congress last year by Largent and Sen. Charles E. Grassley, R-Iowa, parents could oppose "government officials handing out condoms and prescribing contraceptives for their children," just as "religious parents" can object now under the Religious Freedom Restoration Act (RFRA), Largent wrote.[3] *(See story, p. 942.)*

"Under the Parental Rights and Responsibilities Act, laws which interfere with the rights of secular parents would be evaluated under the compelling interest standard," Largent wrote. "A law permitting all 13-year-old girls to consent to birth control pills would likely fail this test. It would unnecessarily interfere with the rights of responsible parents to make health-care decisions for their children." [4]

Grassley, Largent and other supporters of parental rights say that the Supreme Court has clearly classified parental rights as "fundamental," thus giving them the same strict

tainly, mistakes of overintervention occur." But "American children are killed and maimed every day by parents who have not been adequately restrained by the state." [17]

Opponents of parental rights laws are especially worried that health and abuse agencies would hesitate to report or treat cases for fear of being sued. Even if the government eventually could prove a compelling interest in a case and that its actions were the least restrictive, time-consuming legal proceedings could intensify the risk to the child, opponents argue.

"Communities would be virtually paralyzed in the child protection services they provide, including vital counseling services to troubled or despondent youth," the American Humane Association said. [18]

The Safe Kids campaign, in a June 4 letter to Sen. Orrin G. Hatch, R-Utah, chairman of the Judiciary Committee, said the federal bill would let parents sue "over virtually any public rule or law that affects children" — including bike helmet, smoke detector, child-safety seat and seat-belt laws.

The Academy of Pediatrics also noted the bill's corporal punishment provision. "It forces courts to decide whether child abuse applies and opens a wedge to challenge and relitigate issues of child maltreatment in a separate cause of action apart from the original case," the group said in a March statement.

In the Colorado amendment, there is no explicit exemption for abuse. Advocates say "discipline" is defined by existing state law. The amendment's broad language bothers Hudson of People for the American Way. "It will be a lawyer's field day to argue what those terms like discipline, values and education mean," he says.

"No parent has a right to abuse a child," the Heritage Foundation responds. "The truth is that this [federal] bill would reinforce the right of states to protect children from abuse." [19]

"This [bill] does not alter, amend or change any current child-protective service's ability to remove a child from a home" or report abuse or neglect, Largent says. Criticism from child-welfare advocates "is really a red-herring argument against parental rights."

Of the People's Erken echoes the point in reference to the Colorado

. . . Over Teaching 'Hostile' Values

level of judicial protection as free speech and racial equality. But, they say, school boards, teachers and professional "elites," to name a few, have ignored the court's intentions and assaulted parental authority.

Yet critics of the parental rights movement say curbs on education or availability of professional help could have devastating consequences. "Adolescents seeking family planning services, screening and treatment for sexually transmitted diseases, and prenatal care might have no other alternatives to school and public clinics," the American Public Health Association said. The proposed federal Parental Rights and Responsibilities Act "could result in poor health outcomes for adolescents including unintended pregnancy, sterility, HIV infection and unhealthy pregnancies." [5]

The Alan Guttmacher Institute, a reproductive-health policy organization in New York City, noted recently that many states have laws authorizing minors to consent to health care related to sexual activity. The group said, for example, that 23 states and the District of Columbia have laws authorizing minors to give consent for contraceptive services. Twenty-seven states and the District allow pregnant minors to obtain prenatal care and delivery services without parental consent or notification, and 49 states plus the District allow minors to consent to the diagnosis and treatment of sexually transmitted disease. [6]

Referring to Largent's parental rights legislation, the institute said, "Although the proposal seems eminently reasonable at first glance, in practice it would override longstanding efforts by both the states and Congress to reconcile the right of parents to guide and protect their minor children and minors' need and desire for confidentiality in certain situations." [7]

But the Family Research Council says the legislation is needed more than ever today because of changing policies in schools regarding sex education. "Public schools are . . . increasingly adopting policies whereby an entire class is subjected to mandatory psychological testing or explicit sex education [that] contradicts the values taught at home. Psychological testing of children is often performed under the guise of standardized tests which include intrusive questions about the child's emotional state and sexual experiences, the child's relationship with his or her parents, and values and habits within the home." [8]

---

[1] Heritage Foundation, "How Congress Can Protect the Rights of Parents to Raise Their Children," *Issue Bulletin No. 227*, July 23, 1996, p. 26.

[2] Rep. Steve Largent, "Questions and Answers About the Parental Rights and Responsibilities Act, p. 23.

[3] *Ibid.*

[4] *Ibid.*

[5] "Parental Rights and Responsibilities Act Fact Sheet," American Public Health Association.

[6] "Lawmakers Grapple with Parents' Role in Teen Access to Reproductive Health Care," *Issues in Brief*, November 1995, published by Alan Guttmacher Institute.

[7] *Ibid.*

[8] Cathleen A. Cleaver and Greg Erken, "Who Decides How Children Are Raised?" *Family Policy*, August 1996, published by Family Research Council. Cleaver is the council's director of legal studies; Erken is executive director of Of the People.

---

measure. "The rude misunderstanding is that we are legislating an absolute right for parents," he says. "If that were the case, sure, then there would be gridlock in the schools, and government would be prevented from acting to protect the children's welfare. However, parental rights are not absolute."

Erken and Bell say legal precedents clearly establish that a parent can't abuse a child and then claim "parental rights."

Michael P. Farris, president of the Home School Legal Defense Association, says that while "real abuse is exempted wholesale" from the federal bill he helped to shape, what opponents don't like is that "parents have a federally recognized right to spank their children. [That's] not real abuse."

"There's a clear move in this country to outlaw spanking," Farris says. "We want to say that parents always have a clear recognition that they have a right to reasonable spanking. We don't want our prisons any fuller than they are. We don't want our kids doing drug abuse. We want kids to obey the law. My belief is that children who are disciplined are better citizens."

Of course, many cases of alleged child abuse or neglect fall into gray areas that could become arenas of increased controversy under a parental rights measure. Consider, for example, parents who withhold or alter medical treatment and child-welfare workers who disagree.

That scenario occurred late last summer in Dallas after doctors told the parents of 10-year-old Rachel Stout that she could die unless her ulcerated colon was removed. The parents refused, child protective authorities stepped in and Rachel's father took her to Canada for treatment by a practitioner of holistic medicine. After a blood infection halted the alternative treatment, Rachel's parents consented in October to the surgery. [20]

Other conflicts arise over government efforts to stem child abuse and neglect. The Heritage Foundation cites a set of 1995 guidelines in Durham, N.C., for judging the presence of child abuse. "Though most of these 'Minimum Standards of Care' make sense," the foundation says, "a number of them indicate a dangerous overreach by bureaucrats." For example, a parent could be investigated for child abuse for confining a child to his room or for violating government standards "governing the supervision, nutrition, clothing, cleanliness and even the bedtime of children," the foundation says.[21]

Durham County Social Services Director Daniel Hudgins dismisses the foundation's characterization, noting the standards of care are guidelines and not regulations, and were developed by community representatives to help doctors, teachers and others better evaluate reports of potential abuse.

The idea was to help the community "screen out reports that didn't meet any level of maltreatment or abuse," Hudgins says. "Taken alone, none of those guidelines would result in any kind of action by the department against a parent. They were [developed] to improve the quality of what we do and reduce [government] intervention. As opposed to government coming up with standards, this was an attempt to involve the community."

Would parental rights laws lead to an explosion in costly litigation?

Supporters see parental rights laws reducing litigation by encouraging parents to become more involved in school and other community decisions, thereby stemming conflicts before they explode into expensive legal battles.

"It's going to end up in a lot less lawsuits," Grassley claims. "It's going to promote dialogue between educators and parents."

Furthermore, Grassley says, the 90-day "administrative remedy" procedure that he added to his bill was designed expressly to settle disputes between parents and bureaucrats before they get to court.

Besides, Farris points out, parents have long been able to sue in state or federal court if they feel their rights have been violated. And since 1993, they have been able to sue under the Religious Freedom Restoration Act. On Oct. 15, the Supreme Court agreed to rule on the constitutionality of the far-reaching law, which makes government infringement on religious practices more difficult.[22] *(See story, p. 942.)*

"Where's the avalanche of cases?" Farris asks.

Advocates also say that because those rights are not absolute — consider cases of abuse, for example — parents wouldn't be assured of winning every case under a parental rights law.

Noting that the high court has delineated rights for school boards as well as parents, the Heritage Foundation says, "If parents raised ridiculous claims under [a federal bill], their cases would be thrown out of court. . . . Frivolous litigation would be costly for parents and of no benefit to them."[23]

Opponents of the parental rights movement find little comfort in such assurances. They contend parental rights laws would benefit lawyers because parents would be able to sue at the drop of a hat, and the government would have to clear exceedingly high legal hurdles to win. Moreover, says the Academy of Pediatrics, suits involving parental rights laws "would decimate the resources of a community [earmarked to] safeguard children and support families, and put more children at risk of abuse and neglect."

"The bill allows parents to file an action in state or federal court, even if that parent is also arguing before another tribunal," Quintana of the school boards association testified last December. "A school district would be forced to fight on both fronts, doubling the costs." Not only that, Quintana said, the federal bill would award attorney's fees to the victor — discouraging mediation or mutual agreement.[24]

Isaacs of People for the American Way calls the 90-day administrative remedy in Grassley's bill "a joke," saying it is a pressure tactic rather than a means of conflict resolution. "Say [I'm a parent who claims] teaching evolution interferes with my right to raise my child as I see fit," she says. "So the administrative remedy kicks in. It means the school must stop teaching evolution to everybody during the period — or does it mean only my kid would be taken out of that class? It's completely unclear — it has to be litigated," she says. Or, she says, a parent could simply wait 90 days and then sue.

The NEA estimates the cost in the billions just to hire more teachers to meet the demands of the federal bill. "An enormous, unfunded federal mandate," the teachers' union called the Grassley-Largent proposal. "Depending on how widely parents exercise this new fundamental right . . . the costs to school districts of providing such 'designer' curricula will be exorbitant. If, for example, [a parental rights act] forces school districts to hire just *one* extra teacher for each school, the annual cost will be . . . $3,346,330,650."[25]

Parental rights advocates scoff at the NEA's resistance to the movement, saying the big union is running scared from demands for accountability while trying desperately to protect its power base in the public school system.

Besides, Grassley says, the NEA's unfunded-mandates argument doesn't hold water. "They've got to be joking," he says. "They opposed the unfunded mandates bill we got passed in 1995. They're talking out of both sides of their mouth." ■

BACKGROUND

A 'Fundamental' Right

The Founding Fathers didn't mention parental rights in the Constitution and Bill of Rights, but their silence on the matter is not surprising.

In early America, children had few if any rights. There was little question of parents' rights to freely direct their offspring.

Conservatives argue, nonetheless, that

Continued on p. 950

Chronology

1700s-1800s

Formation of the new nation's constitution sets the stage for battles over parental rights.

Dec. 15, 1791
The first 10 amendments to the Constitution take effect. They include the First Amendment, which guarantees religious freedom, and the 9th, which says listing of certain rights in the Constitution "shall not be construed to deny or disparage others retained by the people."

July 9, 1868
Ratification of the 14th Amendment, which says no state may deprive a person of "life, liberty, or property, without due process of law."

1900-1980

Parental rights become an issue in the courts and schools.

June 4, 1923
Supreme Court says a state law limiting the teaching of foreign languages in public schools violates the Constitution's "liberty" guarantee, which includes right "to marry, to establish a home and bring up children." (*Meyer v. Nebraska*).

June 1, 1925
Supreme Court says Oregon law requiring children to attend public school unreasonably interferes with parents' liberty to direct the education and upbringing of their children (*Pierce v. Society of Sisters*).

1960s ***A ban on school prayer signals courts' increasing involvement in issues of values, religion and family life.***

June 25, 1962
Supreme Court bars use of prayer written by New York state Board of Regents in public school classrooms (*Engel v. Vitale*).

May 15, 1967
Supreme Court expands juvenile rights (*In re Gault*).

1976
Supreme Court rejects Missouri law requiring parental consent for a minor to have an abortion (*Planned Parenthood of Central Missouri v. Danforth*).

1979
Supreme Court supports rights of parents to commit their children to mental institutions (*Parham v. J.R.*).

1980s ***Courts and policy-making bodies enhance the rights of children, opening the door for a parental rights movement among conservatives.***

Dec. 4, 1980
Washington state Supreme Court allows troubled teen to remain in alternative residential placement, saying interests of the state and child are sufficient to justify "relatively minor degree of intrusion" on parents' constitutional rights (*In re the Welfare of Sheila Marie Sumey*).

Nov. 20, 1989
U.N. Convention on the Rights of the Child unanimously approved by U.N. General Assembly.

1990s ***Parental rights activists push for changes in Congress and the states.***

1990
Supreme Court denies Native Americans unemployment compensation after they are fired for using the drug peyote in tribal religious rituals. The ruling leads to the Religious Freedom Restoration Act in 1993 (*Employment Division v. Smith*).

1992-1993
New York City diversity curriculum touches off grass-roots protest that helps inspire parental rights movement.

Dec. 30, 1993
New York appeals court finds New York City's condom distribution program unconstitutional without a parental opt-out provision (*Alfonso v. Fernandez*).

1993
Arlington, Va.-based Of the People begins promoting parental rights amendments to state constitutions.

May 17, 1995
Christian Coalition introduces its "Contract With the American Family," which calls for a parental rights act and rejection of the U.N. Convention on the Rights of the Child.

June 1995
Sen. Charles E. Grassley, R-Iowa, and Rep. Steve Largent, R- Okla., introduce parental rights bills.

Nov. 5, 1996
Ballot initiative for parental rights constitutional amendment set for vote in Colorado.

The Case of the Troubled Teenager

The Sheila Marie Sumey case offers a textbook example of how interpretations can vary in an emotional issue such as parental rights. Supporters of efforts to codify parental rights say the state of Washington trampled on the rights of Sheila Marie's parents. Opponents say the parents never lost their rights in the first place.

The basic facts are not in dispute: In 1978, Sheila Marie was a troubled 15-year-old. She flouted rules set by her parents, ran away from home and did not benefit from counseling. In June 1978, to prevent Sheila Marie from running away again, her mother called police and had her placed in a juvenile-care facility. The teenager later requested placement in an alternative residential facility; her request was granted, against the parents' wishes. The parents appealed, contending their parental rights had been violated.

In the indignant view of Rep. Steve Largent, R-Okla., who introduced parental rights legislation last year, "the Supreme Court of Washington ruled that it was not a violation of constitutional parents' rights to remove a child from the home because she objected to her parents' reasonable rules. The parents had grounded their eighth-grade daughter because she wanted to smoke marijuana and sleep with her boyfriend. The Supreme Court found that it was reasonably within the lower court's jurisdiction to remove the girl from her family home. No strict standards were applied. The parents' rights were completely terminated for simply grounding their daughter to stop her from using illegal drugs and engaging in illicit activity!" [1]

Michael P. Farris, president of the Home School Legal Defense Association, calls the ruling "perhaps the most infamous decision in the history of American parental rights." When the parents had trouble getting their daughter to obey their rules, they asked the state for help, he said in congressional testimony last year. "Rather than telling this girl she was required to follow her parents' instructions," Farris said, "the state of Washington took this girl from her parents." [2]

Foes of parental rights laws say that a close reading of the Washington Supreme Court opinion indicates Sheila Marie's parents' rights were never terminated. "That's totally false," says Rebecca Isaacs of People for the American Way. "The parents' rights were not terminated. It couldn't be more explicit."

Critics also note that the court granted the teenager's request to live in the second juvenile facility, where the parents had visiting rights, as a last resort, in view of the severely strained relations between the teenager and her parents. The foes also point out that it was not until Sheila Marie was permitted to be moved to the second facility that the parents sued, claiming violation of their constitutional rights.

While the state's Supreme Court did not find the parents unfit, it held in December 1980 that the "interests of [the] state and child supporting the alternative residential placement procedure were sufficient to justify [a] relatively minor degree of intrusion upon [the] parents' constitutional rights to [the] care, custody and companionship of the child."

As things turned out, parental rights activists say, Sheila Marie years later came to agree with her parents.

After the courts and welfare agency backed the girl, her "teenage and early adult years were extraordinary troubled," the Heritage Foundation wrote in a passage critical of the court's decision. "Now an adult and mother herself, she sees the wisdom of her parents' approach and says that she wishes the local and state authorities had backed them instead of her." [3]

[1] Rep. Steve Largent, "Why Do We Need the Parental Rights and Responsibilities Act?" position paper. The case is *In re the Welfare of Sheila Marie Sumey.*

[2] Testimony before Senate Judiciary Subcommittee on Administrative Oversight and the Courts, Dec. 5, 1995.

[3] Patrick F. Fagan and Wade F. Horn, "How Congress Can Protect the Rights of Parents to Raise Their Children," *Heritage Foundation Issue Bulletin No. 277*, July 23, 1996.

Continued from p. 948

the Ninth and 14th amendments to the Constitution leave no doubt that parental rights are on a par with freedom of speech, press and religion.

The Ninth Amendment, as interpreted by parental rights backers, means that a right doesn't have to be explicitly mentioned in the Constitution to merit judicial protection.

"This constitutional presumption in favor of the traditional rights of citizens was recognized and in place at the time of the adoption of the Bill of Rights," Farris wrote. "Parental rights have long been recognized as 'implicit in the concept of ordered liberty.' " [26]

Indeed, many conservatives reach back to English legal theorist Sir William Blackstone, who wrote in 1769 that parental power includes the "restraint and correction" of children. His ideas helped shape those of the Founders and live on today.

Key Cases From the 1920s

Besides the Ninth Amendment, movement backers rest their argument on the 14th Amendment's Due Process clause and its protection of "life, liberty, or property." The clause figures prominently in a number of cases cited by conservative activists, most notably a pair of decisions from the 1920s that are the legal pillars of today's parental rights movement.

In *Meyer v. Nebraska,* the Supreme Court in 1923 struck down a state law banning the teaching of foreign languages to elementary school pupils. Writing for the majority, Associate Justice James Clark McReynolds cited the Due Process guarantee of liberty, which includes, he wrote, the right of the individual "to marry, to establish a home and bring up children."

According to Rep. Largent, the court invalidated the foreign language ban because it "did not 'promote' education but rather 'arbitrarily and unreasonably' interfered with 'the natural duty of the parent to give his children education suitable to their station in life.' The court chastened the legislature for attempting 'materially to interfere . . . with the power of parents to control the education of their own.' "[27]

Two years later, in *Pierce v. Society of Sisters*, the court struck down an Oregon statute that required parents to send children ages 8-16 to public schools. Again citing the Due Process clause, McReynolds wrote that Oregon's initiative undermined the right of parents and guardians "to direct the education and upbringing of their children" — language adopted verbatim by today's parental rights advocates.

"The child is not the mere creature of the state; those who nurture him and direct his destiny have the right and high duty to recognize and prepare him for additional obligations," the court also said.

Though critics say the court never described parental rights as "fundamental" in the *Meyer* or *Pierce* decisions, advocates say the two cases — taken with other high court rulings in ensuing decades — clearly establish the constitutional supremacy of parents' rights.

Opponents view the *Meyer* and *Pierce* legacies quite differently than parental rights activists, arguing that the Supreme Court has never deemed parental rights "fundamental." And they say that courts traditionally have sought to balance parental rights with those of children and to allow the state to step in to protect children when a situation warrants it.

"The lower courts have not misconstrued the law, because the U.S. Supreme Court has *never* recognized parental rights as fundamental," The National PTA argues. "The lower courts have simply followed suit by refusing to apply a 'compelling state interest' test to parental rights claims."[28]

Isaacs of People for the American Way says conservatives are reading way too much into *Meyer* and *Pierce*. The court took "very specific [and] limited fact situations and . . . ruled against certain kinds of legislation as an infringement on parents rights," she says.

But, she emphasizes, the court's decisions were "not some wholesale, across-the-board" characterization of parental rights as fundamental, as many conservatives argue. "That view is a fantasy," she says.

U.N. Treaty

Conservatives are troubled by another legal issue: the United Nations Convention on the Rights of the Child, which President Clinton signed in 1995 and now awaits Senate action. The convention's 54 articles, which lay out a comprehensive charter of civil, social and economic rights for children, left conservatives worried about how the treaty would affect U.S. laws on abortion, capital punishment and other sensitive issues.

The treaty, already ratified by more than 175 nations, "would virtually undermine parents' rights as we know them in the United States," the Christian Coalition said in its Contract With the American Family. "Parents no longer would have the basic right to control what their children watch on television, whom they associate with and what church they attend."

The Heritage Foundation calls the treaty "incompatible with traditional Western conceptions of the liberty of parents and with the U.S. Supreme Court's settled view of parental rights as 'beyond debate.' Worse, the state is the only other entity whose rights are made clearly superior to the domestic life of the family as an institution."[29]

John C. Green, director of the Ray C. Bliss Institute of Applied Politics at the University of Akron and an expert on the Christian Right, says conservatives are hostile to the treaty partly because it contains "liberal values and liberal code words," such as "village." The word upset the Christian Right when first lady Hillary Rodham Clinton used it to describe community influence on family formation in her best-selling book *It Takes A Village*.

In addition, Green says Christian conservatives are "very suspicious of things international," such as talk of a "new world order," because their eschato-logical views — their ideas about the end of the world and the process of salvation — emphasize the threat of an Antichrist and a final battle between the forces of good and the evil rulers of the world. With the U.N. treaty, "You're reducing parental authority along with national sovereignty," Green says. "It's a double whammy."

The Rev. Jay Lintner, a policy official in Washington for the United Church of Christ, a liberal Protestant denomination, says those who back parental rights measures are trying to "absolutize the rights of parents" and give "no weight to the rights of the community or the rights of children."

Lintner calls the movement "a thinly disguised attack on the public school system," and adds: "While the radical Christian Right who is pushing this bill says parents' rights are not absolute, in fact, the way this is written would make it extremely difficult for many child welfare agencies to protect children." ■

CURRENT SITUATION

An Ironic Approach?

The parental rights movement may seem, at first glance, like it emerged from nowhere to take the ideological stage in America. But observers say it is of a piece with many other conservative and religious causes of the recent and distant past.

"Seeking to protect rights in law or in constitutions is a very American thing, and something that conservatives have always identified with," says Green at the University of Akron. "So in that sense, people are pushing these parental rights laws out of a conservative tradition that is many centuries old."

Still, Green and others see an incongruity in conservative advocates of limited government seeking a legal remedy that involves federal authority in local issues. "There's a powerful irony" in going to higher levels of government to deal with local affairs, says Green.

That's not the only unusual aspect of the parental rights movement, Green says. While seeking full "rights" for all Americans has traditionally been the province of liberals — rights for gays and people with disabilities, for example — conservatives have, in recent years, taken the same approach.

"The Christian Right has adopted the [approach] of liberalism," Green says, noting, for example, the quest for tax-funded vouchers for private school tuition. "That to me is just powerfully ironic."

Some politicians see an irony, too. Rep. Barney Frank, D-Mass., called the federal bill "the most direct assertion of federal superiority over the states I have ever seen." [30]

And David Blankenhorn, president of the Institute for American Values and an adviser to Of the People, has conceded being troubled by "the notion that we're to solve our problem by creating more rights," though he has endorsed the parental rights push. [31]

But proponents say they are not seeking a top-down solution to local issues. Grassley says he has sought a "floor, not a ceiling" for parental rights, with plenty of room left for states and localities to set higher boundaries. [32]

"The PRRA does not manufacture a single new federal program or create a need for new bureaucrats at any level of government," Largent wrote. [33] "Rather, it simply establishes the legal standard to be employed in judging cases where the right of parents comes in conflict with the decisions or policies of government officials."

"This is not a big-government issue," Farris argues. "It's about limiting the power of all governments."

Battles in the States

Limiting the power of government is indeed the key objective in Colorado and many other states where conservatives are fighting for stronger parental rights guarantees. In Colorado, advocates tried unsuccessfully to attach parental rights wording to the Colorado children's code.

Backers of the constitutional amendment drive subsequently gathered more than 83,000 signatures to put the measure on the ballot. As of late September, proponents had raised nearly $150,000 (including about $137,000 from Of the People). The opposing Protect Our Children Coalition had collected almost $65,000. [34]

Democratic Colorado Gov. Roy Romer has blasted the amendment, saying it is "absolutely unnecessary" because parents already can control the upbringing of their children. "It is a constitutional amendment proposed by a group on the far right of our culture," he told reporters. "I think its intent is to have the government have its hands off children almost totally, and I worry about this heavy-handed, generalized use in the constitution." [35]

In other states, meanwhile, the battle to pass amendments is just beginning. "We expect the momentum to continue" regardless of what happens in Colorado, says Of the People's Erken.

Already, a number of state Republican platforms reflect parental rights language, and in August such wording was inserted into the Republican national platform.

"Fourteen of the 22 [state] platforms reviewed by People for the American Way included so-called 'parental rights' language," the group said in August. [36]

There is other evidence of the movement's growth. In Kansas this year, the legislature passed legislation making it the "public policy" of the state "that parents shall retain the fundamental right to exercise primary control over the care and upbringing of their children" and "that children shall have the right to protection from abuse and neglect."

And Of the People said in late May that constitutional amendment proposals had found legislative sponsors in 28 states, including California, Florida, New York and Texas. Yet few of those measures have seen floor action, and even conservative supporters of parental rights have balked in some states at the notion of changing constitutional language.

Both Erken and Bell cite Michigan as fertile ground for the parental rights movement, and there's little wonder why. Parental rights language has already been added to Michigan's school code; the state has a conservative Republican governor, John Engler; and Elisabeth "Betsy" DeVos, Of the People's national co-chairman, chairs the Michigan Republican Party, serves as a Republican national committeewoman and is married to Dick DeVos, chief executive officer of the Amway Corp., a generous backer of conservative causes.

Yet the sponsor of Michigan's proposed parental rights amendment, state Sen. Joanne Emmons, R-Big Rapids, has shifted strategies. She says "concerns by friends on my side" caused her to "back off" and first pursue a legislative rather than a constitutional approach. Among other things, she says, there was the worry that the amendment "might be used in ways we

Continued on p. 954

At Issue:

Would the Parental Rights and Responsibilities Act undercut established legal protections for children?

yes

AMERICAN CIVIL LIBERTIES UNION
FROM A LETTER TO THEN SENATE MAJORITY LEADER BOB DOLE, JAN. 25, 1996.

As an organization that has consistently defended family integrity against unwarranted government intrusion, we are painfully aware of the need for vigilance in this sensitive area. However, although we agree with one of the major premises of this legislation — that the vital role that parents play in the raising of their children is of critical importance and must be respected — we have seen no evidence warranting this broadly written federal statute that undermines longstanding protections for children.

This legislation [would forbid] federal, state and local governments and their officials from "interfer[ing] with or usurp[ing] the right of a parent to direct the upbringing of the child of the parent." Parents would be able to assert this right in lawsuits in either federal or state courts. . . . A government or official may only prevail in such a suit by proving that the government actions were "essential to accomplish a compelling governmental interest," which is an extraordinarily high standard of proof.

This legislation will make it especially difficult for the government to assist children in situations in which their health is endangered because of their parents' actions or inaction. It prohibits a government official or agency from becoming involved in health-care decisions, no matter how injurious the parent's actions may be to the child, unless the very strict "compelling government interest" test is met. . . .

This bill could make it impossible for education professionals to design and implement public school curricula. [It] permits any parent of a public school student to file a lawsuit challenging almost any aspect of the school's curriculum or extracurricular activities. . . .

This bill will reduce protections for children who are physically disciplined by their parents. . . . The language explicitly condoning a parent's right to physically discipline a child is, to our knowledge, without precedent in federal law. . . .

This bill could put children who are victims or potential victims of child abuse and neglect at great risk. Currently child abuse and neglect cases are handled almost exclusively by our state courts. This bill, however, creates a two-tiered system where parents may ask a federal judge to second-guess the decision of a child welfare agency official in a lawsuit alleging that the agency's action "interferes" with the parents' rights.

This dual track will create unnecessary lawsuits, and will create expensive litigation costs for child welfare agencies forced to defend their actions in federal court. The existence of this new cause of action will also have a chilling effect on child protective service workers and government officials.

no

CATHLEEN A. CLEAVER, DIRECTOR OF LEGAL STUDIES, FAMILY RESEARCH COUNCIL, GREG D. ERKEN, EXECUTIVE DIRECTOR, OF THE PEOPLE
FROM "PARENTAL RIGHTS: WHO DECIDES HOW CHILDREN ARE RAISED?" *FAMILY POLICY*, AUGUST 1996.

Critics of both the federal parental rights bill and the state constitutional amendments typically claim that parental rights laws would make it tougher for the state to protect children from abuse and would give one parent the right to dictate school curriculum for everyone else's child, leading to education gridlock.

These and most other criticisms are grounded in the mistaken notion that these proposals would provide an absolute right for parents, which would override any state interest in the welfare and education of children. But . . . the well-established limits to parental rights under this doctrine would continue to apply.

For example, in *Prince v. Massachusetts* (1944), the high court made it clear that "neither the right of religion nor the rights of parents are beyond limitation." *Prince* identified numerous areas in which the state may set limits on parental rights, such as compulsory school attendance, mandatory vaccination policies and child labor laws. And in *Runyon v. McCrary* (1976), the Supreme Court held that parents "have no constitutional right to provide their children with education unfettered by reasonable government regulation." All constitutional rights have their limits, and parental rights are no exception.

The clash over parental rights proposals begs the fundamental question: Who decides what's in the best interests of children? Parents? Or the government? Are ordinary parents generally competent to raise their children or should parents defer to elite authorities backed by state power? . . .

If successful, the parental rights movement will provide parents with greater legal standing to ensure that government respects their rights through its policies, and when necessary, in the courts. But beyond this immediate, practical benefit, a national debate on parental rights also has great potential to foster more parental responsibility.

The key to encouraging greater parental responsibility is to explicitly recognize the link between rights and duties upon which this nation was founded, and to renew our optimism in the ability of the people to manage their own affairs, as citizens and as parents. Indeed, [as G.K. Chesterton observed in *Orthodoxy*], "the most terribly important things must be left to ordinary men themselves," including the right of parents to protect their children from harmful influences and to direct their children's upbringing. Recognizing the irreplaceable role of parents is essential to keeping the power of the state in check, revitalizing citizenship and ensuring that children receive the love, protection and guidance only a parent can provide.

FOR MORE INFORMATION

American Center for Law and Justice, 1000 Regent University Drive, Virginia Beach, Va. 23467; (804) 579-2489. Founded in 1990, ACLJ is dedicated to the promotion of pro-liberty, pro-life and pro-family causes. It engages in litigation, provides legal services and supports attorneys who are involved in defending religious and civil liberties.

Focus on the Family, 8605 Explorer Dr., Colorado Springs, Colo. 80920; (719) 531-3336. Founded in 1977, the nonprofit Christian organization works to preserve traditional values and the institution of the family.

National Child Abuse Coalition, 733 15th St. N.W. Suite 938, Washington, D.C. 20005; (202) 347-3666. The coalition contends that amendments and legislation aimed at codifying parental rights would put children at risk of abuse from abusive parents.

National Education Association, 1201 16th St. N.W. Washington, D.C. 20036-3290; (202) 822-7230. The NEA is the largest teachers' union and views laws designed to bolster parents' rights as potentially detrimental to school quality.

National School Boards Association, 1680 Duke St., Alexandria, Va. 22314-3493; (703) 838-6225. This federation of school board associations is interested in such issues as local governance and quality of education programs.

Of the People, 2111 Wilson Blvd., Suite 700, Arlington, Va. 22201; (703) 351-5051. Founded in 1993, this organization is a leader of the movement pushing state constitutional amendments on parental rights.

People for the American Way, 2000 M St., N.W., Suite 400, Washington, D.C. 20036; (202) 467-4999. This nonpartisan organization promotes protection of First Amendment rights. It is leading a coalition of groups opposed to parental rights laws.

Traditional Values Coalition, 139 C St. S.E., Washington, D.C. 20003; (202) 547-8570. The coalition is a legislative interest group that supports conservative Judeo-Christian values.

Continued from p. 952

could not anticipate by a judge, and then you have no legislative redress."

A constitutional amendment would be harder to fix if problems arose, Emmons acknowledges. "Once it goes into the constitution, it will have to have another vote of the people to change it."

In Illinois, state Sen. Patrick O'Malley, R-Palos Park, cosponsored a parental rights amendment with Rep. Al Salvi, now a Republican candidate for the U.S. Senate. "The intrusion of government into our personal lives is stifling our individual freedom and discouraging personal responsibility," O'Malley declared in April. "With this amendment, we reassert the importance of parental authority and responsibility as a means of balancing parental rights with other interests competing for the control of family life." [37]

O'Malley's proposed measure passed the Executive Committee of the Republican-controlled Senate, but it did not make it onto the Illinois ballot this fall. "The groups most interested in its passage felt on balance they needed to do more public education," O'Malley says. "We intend to go back at it in [January] and get it on the ballot at the next available date."

In Virginia, whose conservative leanings make it another bellwether in the parental rights movement, Republican Gov. George F. Allen supported an amendment that passed the Senate Privileges and Elections Committee 8-2 last February and moved to the Senate floor. But Democratic Lt. Gov. Donald S. Beyer Jr. voted against the bill, kicking the proposal back to committee.

Such setbacks don't seem to discourage the movement's chief backers. "The parental revolt a year from now is going to be much bigger than it is today," a confident Bell predicted at the Christian Coalition's September conference. ■

OUTLOOK

'Building Momentum'

Former pro football receiver Largent uses a sports metaphor to analyze the future of the parental rights movement. "This is a marathon," he says. "It's not a 100-yard dash."

That marathon won't be an easy one for parental rights backers to win in Congress, beginning with the November elections. Largent is up for reelection this year, and the loss of the Republican majority in either chamber could cripple the conservative parental rights cause.

Indeed, support for the measures falls largely along partisan lines. Of the 140 sponsors of Largent's bill, for example, all but about a dozen were Republicans. Largent concedes that if Republicans lose the House, his bill "will go nowhere." Nonetheless, Largent plans to reintroduce the measure in the 105th Congress, even if Republicans lose control of Congress in November.

Grassley seems less definite. "I would like to reintroduce" the bill in the next Congress, he says, "and at the same time I would like to garner more bipartisan support for the initiative in the Senate. Right now, our job is to continue building grass-roots support and educating the public about the goal of the legislation, in the face of disinformation from special interests in Washington, D.C."

Grassley's bill faced tough opposition from Democrats. The Senate Subcommittee on Administrative Oversight and the Courts, chaired by Grassley, voted in April to send the bill to the full Judiciary Committee after it had been through significant revision, including addition of the 90-day administrative process clause.

But heavy resistance came from Sen. Howell Heflin, D-Ala., a former school board president and ranking Democrat on the subcommittee. The bill, he said, "is premised on a false idea: that the rights of parents are being vastly undermined across the country." The measure would "open the floodgates of litigation," Heflin added, and "could impose chaos in matters relating to curriculum content, textbook selection, dress codes and home schooling, just to name a few." [38]

As for Largent's bill, which died in a House Judiciary subcommittee, legislative aide Paul Webster says subcommittee Chairman Charles T. Canady, R-Fla., had concerns about use of the legislation by a liberal judge. "I think his primary concern [was] that some federal court judge could begin decreeing all manner of family law that's not consistent" with the bill, Webster says. "[He] has a real concern that a very liberal federal judge could just say [children's] reproductive rights are outside the fundamental rights of parents [to oversee] and . . . in one judicial act" gut a significant portion of the bill's intent.

Of the People Chairman Bell said at the Christian Coalition meeting that Canady had bottled up the bill because he thought parental rights should be a state rather than federal issue. (Canady's press aide did not respond to phone calls.)

Even if parental rights legislation were to reach the marathon finish line, backers expect that it would be tripped at the end by a presidential veto, assuming Bill Clinton remains in the White House.

Still, Grassley is sanguine about the long-term prospects. "We're in the first step of promoting an important national debate," he says. "Our job is to continue building momentum."

Adds Sheldon of the Traditional Values Coalition: "Just because you introduce a bill doesn't mean you expect it to become law that year," she says. "A public-policy debate — that's what we want." ■

Thomas J. Billitteri is a freelance writer in the Washington, D.C., area.

Notes

[1] Quoted in *The Rocky Mountain News,* Sept. 22, 1996.

[2] Quoted in *The Denver Post,* Sept. 22, 1996.

[3] See "Parents Rights Amendment Foils Colorado Senate Race," *The Washington Post,* Oct. 20, 1996, p. A1. For background, see "Children's Legal Rights," *The CQ Researcher,* April 23, 1993, pp. 337-360.

[4] For background, see "Parents and Schools," *The CQ Researcher,* Jan. 20, 1995, pp. 49-72.

[5] Dobson's remarks were made during a discussion of parental rights on his syndicated show, "Focus on the Family Radio Hour," June 17-18, 1996.

[6] Letter to U.S. senators from Dr. Maurice E. Keenan, president of the American Academy of Pediatrics, March 19, 1996.

[7] Testimony before Senate Judiciary Subcommittee on Administrative Oversight and the Courts, Dec. 5, 1995.

[8] The poll of 482 voters was taken in conjunction with the Scripps-Howard News Service.

[9] See "The Parent Trap: Relying on Bogus Horror Stories And Mega-Bucks Backing, The 'Parental Rights' Movement Is Luring Americans Into An Attack On Public Schools And Church-State Separation," *Church & State,* June 1996, published by Americans United for Separation of Church and State.

[10] "Commentary on Protections Which Should Be Afforded Parental Rights and Responsibilities," position paper, The American Center for Law and Justice, undated, p. 10.

[11] From "Oppose H.R. 1946/S. 984: The 'Parental Rights And Responsibilities Act,'" People for the American Way, September 1996.

[12] "Statement of the National Education Association Regarding The Parental Rights and Responsibilities Act," February 1996, p. 2.

[13] For background, see "Home Schooling," *The CQ Researcher,* Sept. 9, 1994, pp. 769-792.

[14] Quoted in "Parental-Rights Advocates Push for Constitutional Amendment," *Insight on the News,* Sept. 9, 1996, p. 40.

[15] For background, see "School Choice," *The CQ Researcher,* May 10, 1991, pp. 253-276, and "Attack on Public Schools," *The CQ Researcher,* July 26, 1996, pp. 662-663.

[16] Quoted in *The Washington Times,* Oct. 27, 1995.

[17] Letter to U.S. senators, March 19, 1996.

[18] Letter to U.S. senators from Adele Douglass, director, Washington office, American Humane Association, March 19, 1996.

[19] Heritage Foundation, "How Congress Can Protect the Rights of Parents to Raise Their Children," *Issue Bulletin No. 227,* July 23, 1996, p. 23.

[20] For background, see *The New York Times,* Oct. 14, 1996.

[21] Heritage Foundation, *op. cit.,* pp. 13-14.

[22] See "High Court to Rule on Religion Law," *The Washington Post,* Oct. 16, 1996, p. A1.

[23] Heritage Foundation, *op. cit.,* p. 25.

[24] Testimony before Senate Judiciary Subcommittee on Administrative Oversight and the Courts, Dec. 5. 1995.

[25] National Education Association, *op. cit.*

[26] Michael P. Farris, "The Parental Rights and Responsibilities Act: Establishing a Standard of Liberty," National Center for Home Education Special Report, undated, p. 2.

[27] Steve Largent, "Questions and Answers About the Parental Rights and Responsibilities Act," undated, p. 1.

[28] "Oppose the Parental Rights and Responsibilities Act," position paper of The National PTA.

[29] Heritage Foundation, *op. cit.,* p. 19.

[30] Quoted in *The Washington Times,* Oct. 27, 1995.

[31] Quoted in "Parental-Rights Advocates Push for Constitutional Amendment," *op. cit.*

[32] Opening statement of Sen. Charles E. Grassley on the Parental Rights and Responsibilities Act of 1996, Senate Judiciary Subcommittee on Administrative Oversight and the Courts, April 17, 1996.

[33] Largent, *op. cit.,* p. 14.

[34] *The Denver Post,* Sept. 22, 1996.

[35] Quoted in *The Daily Camera,* Sept. 21, 1996.

[36] People for the American Way, "The Republicans and the Religious Right: A Study of 1996 State Republican Party Platforms," Aug. 2, 1996, p. 6.

[37] Press release, April 18, 1996.

[38] Quoted in *School Board News,* published by the National School Boards Association, April 30, 1996.

Bibliography

Selected Sources Used

Books

Bates, Stephen, *Battleground: One Mother's Crusade, the Religious Right, and the Struggle for Control of Our Classrooms,* Poseidon Press, 1993.
Bates, formerly a senior fellow at the Annenberg Washington Program of Northwestern University, chronicles the case of Vicki Frost, a Tennessee mother who sued school officials after she found such themes as evolution, feminism and telepathy in her children's schoolbooks. The high-profile case, dubbed "Scopes II" by journalists, pitted two powerful advocacy groups against each other: Concerned Women for America and People for the American Way.

Christian Coalition, *Contract With the American Family*, 1995.
This book lays out the political priorities of one of the nation's most powerful conservative religious organizations, including enactment of a parental-rights measure and defeat of the U.N. Convention on the Rights of the Child.

Hawes, Joseph M., *The Children's Rights Movement: A History of Advocacy and Protection,* Twayne Publishers, 1991.
Hawes, a professor of history at Memphis State University, provides a well-organized overview of children's rights from the establishment of child aid societies in the 1800s and the creation of broader government programs in the early 20th century to the maturing of the children's rights movement beginning in the 1960s. The book includes a useful chronology and a nine-page bibliographic essay.

Nelkin, Dorothy, *The Creation Controversy: Science or Scripture in the Schools*, Beacon Press, 1982.
Nelkin, a Cornell University professor, provides a broad overview of the evolution vs. creationism controversy in American schools.

Samuels, Sarah E., and Mark D. Smith, eds., *Condoms in the Schools*, Kaiser Family Foundation, 1993.
The authors provide a useful overview of a key point of contention in the parental rights debate: making condoms available to public school students. The book includes a survey of condom programs, the views of school officials and discussions of funding and policy options and legal issues.

Articles

Applebome, Peter, "Array of Opponents Battle Over 'Parental Rights' Bills," *The New York Times*, May 1, 1996.
This front-page overview of the parental rights movement surveys the issues and quotes the chief spokesmen on either side of the debate.

Glanzer, Perry L., "Parental Rights and Public Education," *Focus on the Family*, July 1996.
Glanzer is an education policy analyst at Focus on the Family, a conservative Christian organization in Colorado Springs, Colo. This 29-page booklet surveys "current rights and threats" to parental rights in education and securing parental rights through legislative reform, among other issues.

Green, John C., James L. Guth, Lyman A. Kellstedt and Corwin E. Smidt, "Evangelical Realignment: The Political Power of the Christian Right," *Christian Century,* July 5-12, 1995.
Green, director of the Ray C. Bliss Institute of Applied Politics at the University of Akron, and his colleagues provide a wide-ranging and incisive look at the Christian Right's influence in the 1994 Republican triumph in Congress and at evangelical politics at the dawn of a new millennium.

Grunes, Rodney A., "Creationism, the Courts and the First Amendment," *Journal of Church and State,* fall 1989.
Grunes, associate professor of political science at Centenary College, examines the political and legal contexts of the creationism controversy and analyzes Louisiana's 1981 "Balanced Treatment" Act mandating that creationism be given equal time whenever evolution was taught in the public schools.

O'Connor, Karen, and Gregg Ivers, "Education At Risk?: Creationism, Evolution and the Courts," *Political Science and Politics*, winter 1988.
O'Connor and Ivers, both of Emory University, give a useful history of the creationism controversy and address the impact of a series of "creationism-evolution" cases on the place of religion in the public schools.

Stepp, Laura Sessions, "Who's in Charge?: A Parents' Rights Movement Is Stirring Controversy," *The Washington Post*, July 15, 1996.
Reporter Stepp provides an overview of the emerging parental rights movement and quotes many of the principal players.

Reports and Studies

People for the American Way, *The Republicans and the Religious Right: A Study of 1996 State Republican Party Platforms*, Aug. 2, 1996.
The liberal advocacy group analyzes Republican platforms and various issues, including parental rights, concluding that the "Christian Coalition is well on its way to its stated goal of taking over the Republican Party."

The Next Step

Additional information from UMI's Newspaper & Periodical Abstracts database

Colorado's Parental Rights Amendment

Brown, Fred, "2 ballot-issue petitions filed," *Denver Post,* Aug. 6, 1996, p. A1.
Petitions for two ballot issues — a parental rights amendment and another changing the mission of the state land board — were turned over to the Colorado secretary of state's office on Aug. 5, 1996, in time to meet the deadline for citizen initiatives.

"Clarify parental rights," *Denver Post,* April 4, 1996, p. B6.
An editorial discusses a bill in the Colorado Legislature that defines what acceptable corporal punishment is, thereby acknowledging parents' right to spank their kids. The editorial makes it clear that parents can't abuse their children, and criticizes an amendment that clouds the meaning.

Culver, Virginia, "Clergy group denounces parental rights proposal," *Denver Post,* Sept. 26, 1996, p. B2.
The Denver Area Interfaith Clergy Conference on Sept. 25, 1996, denounced Amendment 17, a parental rights amendment that will be on the state's November general election ballot.

Johnston, Michelle Dally, "Parental rights stirs a tempest," *Denver Post,* Sept. 22, 1996, p. A1.
The question at the heart of the parental rights amendment is just how absolute are parents' rights to impose their will on their children. The three-line initiative on the Nov. 5, 1996, ballot asks Colorado voters to add to the state Constitution "the inalienable right" of parents to "direct, and control the upbringing, education, values and discipline of their children."

Knight, Al, "Huge forces collide on parents rights," *Denver Post,* June 12, 1996, p. B11.
Knight examines the proposed parental rights amendment to the Colorado Constitution.

Lamm, Dottie, "Our children are not our property," *Denver Post,* April 14, 1996, p. E3.
Lamm criticizes a Colorado House bill and a proposed amendment to the Colorado Constitution that would make parental rights "inalienable."

Mallory, Jim, "Groups join to defeat controversial proposal," *Denver Post,* Sept. 22, 1996, p. A18.
More than a dozen organizations in the Colorado Springs, Colo., area, representing diverse interests, have joined forces to help defeat the controversial parental rights initiative on the Nov. 5, 1996, ballot. Colorado is the first state to vote on a constitutional amendment on parental rights.

Court Cases

Flynn, George, "Judge rules ex-convict father should retain parental rights," *Houston Chronicle,* Nov. 29, 1995, p. A34.
Texas District Judge Bill Henderson ruled that ex-convict Brendon Lamar Baker should retain parental rights over two boys, even though a jury had awarded custody to the adoptive couple who have raised the boys for two years.

McClear, James A., "Mom loses parental rights after child is offered for sale," *Detroit News,* Dec. 19, 1994, p. B5.
Pamela D. Williamson, the mother of a 2-year-old girl who was offered for sale at an Independence Township, Mich., supermarket, has been stripped of her parental rights to the child. Williamson, described in court testimony as an alcoholic, pleaded no contest to a misdemeanor charge of child neglect.

Shnay, Jerry, "Judge dismisses father's civil suit for parental rights," *Chicago Tribune,* May 15, 1996, p. 7.
The legal conflict over Joliet, Ill., resident Darrin Affrunti's rights as an unwed father shifted to Cook County on May 14, 1996, after a Will County judge dismissed a civil suit challenging a state custody law. Affrunti is seeking custody of his child born to a Lockport woman who has given the baby up for adoption.

"Supreme Court rejects review of parental rights law," *Times-Picayune,* June 6, 1995, p. B3.
Acting in a Jefferson Parish, La., case, the U.S. Supreme Court on June 5, 1995, let stand a ruling that makes it just as hard for Louisiana officials to temporarily suspend an allegedly abusive parent's right to custody as it is to permanently sever a parent-child relationship.

Wildermuth, John, "Woman lose parental rights," *San Francisco Chronicle,* April 28, 1995, p. A27.
Charlene Dineen, a homeless woman who abandoned her 10-month-old baby on a foggy turnout on Skyline Boulevard in Pacifica, Calif., pleaded guilty to child endangerment on April 27, 1995, and was sentenced to a year in jail. Dineen also lost her parental right to her two children.

Parental Rights Movement

Allen, Mike, "Conservatives lobby for parental rights," *The New York Times,* Jan. 15, 1996, p. A10.
Christian conservatives in legislatures across the country have begun promoting a parental rights amendment, which supporters claim would keep governments from interfering in how parents educate and discipline children. Critics say the amendment would give small groups of parents veto power over the curriculums of public schools, promote litigation against school boards and hinder child-abuse investigations.

Applebome, Peter, "An Array of Opponents Do Battle Over Parental Rights Legislation," *The New York Times,* May 1, 1996, p. A1.
Congress and state legislatures are becoming battle-grounds over politically charged parental rights bills, hailed by conservatives as ways to protect parents' ability to raise their children and criticized by many education and health organizations as threats to children's safety and schools' ability to function.

"Black dads are now fighting back for their parental rights," *Los Angeles Sentinel,* Jan. 12, 1995, p. A3.
My Child Says Daddy, a group for fathers seeking custody of their children or the right to spend more time with them, is featured. The experiences of founder Reginald Brass that led him to start the organization, which meets Mondays in Los Angeles, are described.

Cole, John R., "The new "parental rights" crusade," *Humanist,* March 1996, p. 41.
A new crusade for parental rights is under way, but critics fear the power that legislation protecting parental rights could have. The Christian Coalition is one of the organizations spearheading this campaign.

Lawton, Kim A., "The right to parent: Should it be fundamental?" *Christianity Today,* April 29, 1996, p. 57.
A national parents' movement for recognition of a "fundamental right" to raise children without government intrusion is rapidly growing. The battle is being fought in courts and legislatures.

Gonnerman, Jennifer, "Do parents need special protection?" *Ms.,* September 1996, pp. 14-18.
A new battlefront is appearing as parental rights, which Republicans are using to regain control of the U.S.' political agenda through parents' deep-seated dissatisfaction with the public education system. This new movement is discussed.

Owen, Kelly, "Parents' group seeks law for more say at children's schools," *Los Angeles Times,* Feb. 7, 1995, p. A5.
The Virginia-based organization Of the People is pushing for adoption of a parental rights amendment to state constitutions to give parents more say in their children's education and more control over what they are doing while in school. The issue of parental rights is examined.

Tyson, Ann Scott, "Parental-rights revolt takes root across U.S.," *The Christian Science Monitor,* July 30, 1996, p. 1.
Across America, parents are joining a backlash by conservative and Religious Right groups against what they view as widespread government infringements on parental rights. The push to empower parents has provoked strong opposition from child advocates and educators, who say it comes at the expense of children and schools. An accompanying map shows states that have taken up parental rights amendments.

Impact of Parents' Rights on Public Schools

Burron, Arnold, "Parents' rights — society's imperatives: A balancing act," *Educational Leadership,* April 1996, pp. 80-82.
By articulating and responding to the principles that underlie parent vs. school rights controversies, public school officials can reduce conflict and even arrive at a consensus on some issues.

Chiusano, Michael, "Parents' rights," *National Review,* Sept. 30, 1996, pp. 55-57.
Across the country, bizarre and intrusive programs are part of everyday business in public schools, a world virtually at war with the everyday values of parents, Chiusano writes. The issue of parents' rights in schooling is going to be important in the political battles to come, he says.

Lameiras, Maria M., "Parental rights act under fire," *Atlanta Constitution,* Sept. 25, 1996, p. XJ1.
Some members of the Gwinnett County, Ga., Interfaith Alliance ecumenical group that gathered Sept. 24, 1996, to discuss a parental rights act pending in both the state legislature and Congress said they fear it could destroy the public school system.

Simpson, Michael D., "Get off," *NEA Today,* March 1996. p. 22.
The Parental Rights and Responsibilities Act of 1995 would give every parent the right to force the public schools to provide their children with a "customized" education, Simpson writes. The purpose and possible effects of this bill are discussed.

Pros and Cons of Parental Rights Initiatives

Dority, Barbara, "Parental rights" at the expense of children," *Humanist,* September 1996, pp. 37-38.

Dority criticizes the Parental Rights and Responsibilities Act of 1995. She considers the legislation another Republican offering to the Christian Coalition. Of particular concern is the legislation's impact on education.

Erken, Greg D., and Jack C. Westman, "Question: Does the U.S. need a parental-rights amendment?" *Insight on the News,* May 15, 1995, pp. 18-21.

Erken argues that constitutional remedies would protect schoolchildren from social engineering. Westman counters that it is better to mandate parental competency before children come along.

Gahr, Evan, "Parental-rights advocates push for constitutional amendment," *Insight on the News,* Sept. 9, 1996, p. 40.

Hoping to reclaim child-rearing authority from school officials and government bureaucrats, parental rights advocates are lobbying for federal legislation and a constitutional amendment. The pros and cons of a Parental Rights and Responsibility Act are discussed.

Margolis, Lewis H., and Neil J. Salkind, "Parents as advocates for their children," *Journal for a Just & Caring Education,* April 1996, pp. 103-120.

Children need their parents to act as individual advocates, particularly given the lack of institutions to promote children's well-being. The different roles that parents can play as advocates are reviewed.

"Parental Rights and Wrongs," *The New York Times,* May 5, 1996, p. 12.

An editorial warns that bills being pushed in Congress and in many state legislatures that advocate "parental rights" would disrupt school boards and child welfare agencies with lawsuits. The editorial argues that disputes between parents and child welfare and school authorities are best resolved at the local level.

"Parents already have rights," *St. Louis Post-Dispatch,* Jan. 23, 1996, p. B10.

An editorial comments on the parental rights amendment, the latest family values initiative by the Christian Right that opens the door for legal attacks on controversial textbooks, sex education and the teaching of evolution.

Statement of Ownership Management, Circulation

Act of Aug. 12, 1970: Section 3685, Title 39, United States Code

Title of Publication: The CQ Researcher. Date of filing: October 21, 1996. Frequency of issue: Weekly (Except for 3/1, 5/31, 8/30, 11/29/96). No. of issues published annually: 48. Annual subscription price for libraries, businesses and government: $319.00. Location of known office of publication: 1414 22nd Street, N.W., Washington, D.C. 20037-1097. Names and addresses of publisher, editor and managing editor: Publisher, Neil Skene, 1414 22nd Street, N.W., Washington, D.C. 20037-1097; Editor, Sandra Stencel, 1414 22nd Street, N.W., Washington, D.C. 20037-1097; Managing Editor, Thomas J. Colin, 1414 22nd Street, N.W., Washington, D.C. 20037-1097. Owner: Congressional Quarterly, 1414 22nd Street, N.W., Washington, D.C. 20037-1097. Known bondholders, mortgagees and other security holders owning or holding 1 percent or more of total amount of bonds, mortgages or other securities: none.

Extent and Nature of Circulation	Average Number of Copies Each Issue During Preceding 12 months	Actual Number of Copies of Single Issue Published Nearest to Filing Date
A. Total number of copies printed (*Net Press Run*)	6,568	5,872
B. Paid Circulation		
1. Sales through dealers and carriers, street vendors and counter sales	—	—
2. Mail subscriptions	4,986	4,874
C. Total paid and/or requested circulation	4,986	4,874
D. Free distribution by mail carrier or other means. Samples, Complimentary and other free copies	378	295
E. Total distribution (*Sum of C and D*)	5,364	5,169
F. Copies not distributed		
1. Office use, left over, unaccounted, spoiled after printing	1,204	703
2. Returns from news agents	—	—
G. Total (*Sum of E and F*) — should equal net press run shown in A)	6,568	5,872

Back Issues

Great Research on Current Issues Starts Right Here...Recent topics covered by The CQ Researcher are listed below. Before May 1991, reports were published under the name of Editorial Research Reports.

APRIL 1995
Abortion Clinic Protests
Dieting and Health
Combating AIDS
Rethinking Affirmative Action

MAY 1995
Assisted Suicide Controversy
Overhauling Social Security
Learning to Read
Mandatory Sentencing

JUNE 1995
Combating Infectious Disease
Property Rights
Repetitive Stress Injuries
Regulating the Internet

JULY 1995
War Crimes
Highway Safety
Combating Terrorism
Preventing Teen Drug Use

AUGUST 1995
Job Stress
Organ Transplants
United Nations at 50
Advances in Cancer Research

SEPTEMBER 1995
Catholic Church in the U.S.
Northern Ireland Cease-Fire
High School Sports
Teaching History

OCTOBER 1995
Quebec's Future
Revitalizing the Cities
Networking the Classroom
Indoor Air Pollution

NOVEMBER 1995
The Working Poor
The Jury System
Sex, Violence and the Media
Police Misconduct

DECEMBER 1995
Teens and Tobacco
Gene Therapy's Future
Global Water Shortages
Third-Party Prospects

JANUARY 1996
Emergency Medicine
Punishing Sex Offenders
Bilingual Education
Helping the Homeless

FEBRUARY 1996
Reforming the CIA
Campaign Finance Reform
Academic Politics
Getting Into College

MARCH 1996
The British Monarchy
Preventing Juvenile Crime
Tax Reform
Pursuing the Paranormal

APRIL 1996
Centennial Olympic Games
Managed Care
Protecting Endangered Species
New Military Culture

MAY 1996
Russia's Political Future
Marriage and Divorce
Year-Round Schools
Taiwan, China and the U.S.

JUNE 1996
Rethinking NAFTA
First Ladies
Teaching Values
Labor Movement's Future

JULY 1996
Recovered-Memory Debate
Native Americans' Future
Crackdown on Sexual Harassment
Attack on Public Schools

AUGUST 1996
Fighting Over Animal Rights
Privatizing Government Services
Child Labor and Sweatshops
Cleaning Up Hazardous Wastes

SEPTEMBER 1996
Gambling
The States and Federalism
Civic Journalism
Foreign Aid

OCTOBER 1996
The Business of Politics
Insurance Fraud
Rethinking School Integration

Back issues are available for $5.00 (subscribers) or $8.00 (non-subscribers). Quantity discounts apply to orders over ten. To order, call Congressional Quarterly Customer Service at (202) 887-8621.

Binders are available for $18.00. To order call 1-800-638-1710. Please refer to stock number 648.

Future Topics

- ***Global Warming***
- ***Copyright Protections on the Internet***
- ***Consumer Debt***

THE CQ Researcher

PUBLISHED BY CONGRESSIONAL QUARTERLY INC.

Global Warming Update

Are limits on greenhouse gas emissions needed?

This year marks the 100th anniversary of the discovery of the greenhouse effect by the Swedish chemist Svante Arrhenius. Thanks to sophisticated computers and satellites, scientists today know more about how burning fossil fuels and other industrial activities release carbon dioxide and other gases that trap solar heat in the Earth's atmosphere. Predictions about the increasing pace of global warming caused by human activity have so alarmed policy-makers that efforts are under way to draw up an international treaty — due to be signed in Kyoto, Japan, in 1997 — to curb greenhouse gas emissions. These efforts have sparked controversy in the United States, where some scientists and industry representatives dispute the accuracy of future warming predictions and oppose limits on energy consumption.

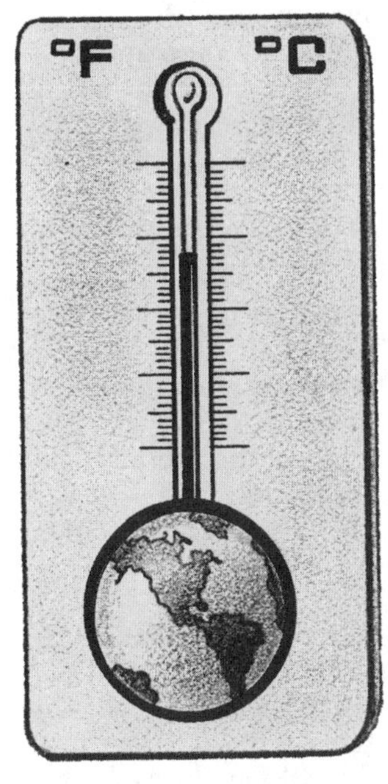

INSIDE THIS ISSUE

CQ Nov. 1, 1996 • Volume 6, No. 41 • Pages 961-984

Formerly Editorial Research Reports

Global Warming Update

COVER: BARBARA SASSA-DANIELS

THE CQ Researcher

Nov. 1, 1996
Volume 6, No. 41

EDITOR
Sandra Stencel

MANAGING EDITOR
Thomas J. Colin

ASSOCIATE EDITORS
Sarah M. Magner
Richard L. Worsnop

STAFF WRITERS
Charles S. Clark
Mary H. Cooper
Kenneth Jost

EDITORIAL ASSISTANT
Tonya Harris

PUBLISHED BY
Congressional Quarterly Inc.

CHAIRMAN
Andrew Barnes

VICE CHAIRMAN
Andrew P. Corty

EDITOR AND PUBLISHER
Neil Skene

EXECUTIVE EDITOR
Robert W. Merry

The CQ Researcher (ISSN 1056-2036). Formerly Editorial Research Reports. Published weekly (48 times per year, not printed March 1, May 31, Aug. 30, Nov. 29) by Congressional Quarterly Inc., 1414 22nd St., N.W., Washington, D.C. 20037. Annual subscription rate for libraries, businesses and government is $319. Additional rates furnished upon request. Periodicals postage paid at Washington, D.C. POSTMASTER: Send address changes to The CQ Researcher, 1414 22nd St., N.W., Washington, D.C. 20037.

Global Warming Update

By Mary H. Cooper

The Issues

Swedish chemist Svante Arrhenius was ahead of his time. So far ahead, in fact, that for almost a century scientists couldn't confirm his far-sighted theory.

Contemplating the intense industrial development swirling around him, Arrhenius theorized in 1896 that all the coal being burned was affecting Earth's temperature. The vast amounts of carbon dioxide and other gases being released as a result, he said, were trapping solar heat in the atmosphere, much as the glass roof and walls of a greenhouse trap heat. Arrhenius predicted that escalating industrialization would add still more gases to the atmosphere, causing global temperatures to rise several degrees.

In recent years, modern technology has proved that the Earth is indeed getting warmer, launching an intense global debate. Industrialized countries and environmentalists say it is time to limit emissions of so-called greenhouse gases; developing nations and industry groups want more latitude to grow.

According to widely accepted meteorological evidence, the average global temperature has risen about 1 degree Fahrenheit since the turn of the century. Scientists are now predicting an additional 2-7 degree rise in the 21st century if current trends continue unchecked.

A temperature rise of a few degrees may seem insignificant, considering that humans have thrived for millennia in inhospitable locales from the Arctic to the tropics. But even a small rise could wreak havoc throughout the world. Some scientists predict that melting polar ice could cause a three-foot rise in sea levels. That would inundate low-lying coastal areas, threatening entire countries, such as the Netherlands and Bangladesh. Small island nations such as the Maldives, Guam and Sri Lanka could be virtually wiped out.

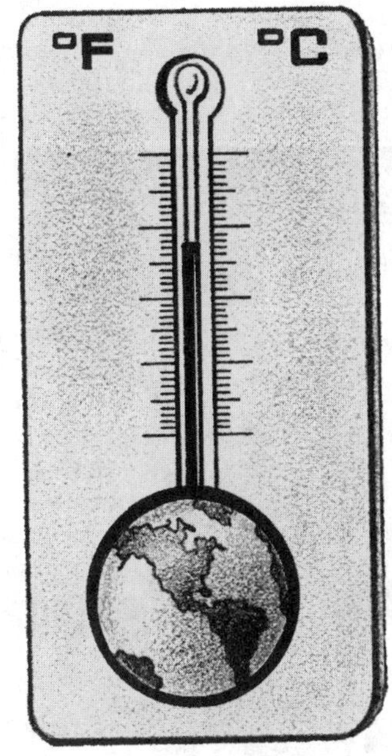

Warming also is expected to cause the spread of malaria, dengue fever and other deadly tropical diseases. As tropical regions expand in size, disease-carrying mosquitoes will be able to extend their range. Human suffering could be further compounded by starvation. Rising temperatures are expected to disrupt weather patterns all over the world, possibly bringing drought to vital food-producing regions, especially in sub-Saharan Africa, South Asia and tropical Latin America. Entire species of plants and animals could become extinct.

In the 1960s and early '70s, satellites and powerful supercomputers began providing additional support for Arrhenius' theory. In 1990, concerned world leaders called on scientists to help them understand the implications of global climate change and decide what to do about it. Last December, the United Nations' Intergovernmental Panel on Climate Change (IPCC), a worldwide network of 2,500 scientists, announced that the evidence of global warming was undeniable, albeit difficult to accurately quantify. "Nevertheless," the panel declared in its report, "the balance of evidence suggests that there is a discernible human influence on global climate." [1]

As the world's leading economy and biggest consumer of fossil fuel, the United States is also the biggest producer of greenhouse gases, accounting for more than one-fifth of all the CO_2 — some 4.9 billion metric tons. (*See graphs, p. 968.*) But because the U.S. economy depends so heavily on oil, coal and natural gas, political leaders have been reluctant to ask industry to curb greenhouse gas emissions without definitive proof of Arrhenius' theory.

The unequivocal IPCC declaration, however, prompted the Clinton administration to toughen U.S. environmental policy. In July, former Sen. Tim Wirth, D-Colo., now under secretary of State for global affairs, announced that the United States would seek to develop yet-to-be-determined targets and timetables for reducing gas emissions. Under the sponsorship of the United Nations, the United States and other nations have been working on a global climate-change treaty and are scheduled to sign the finished document in Kyoto, Japan, in December 1997 (*see p. 976*).

"We think that there are lots of possible impacts from changes to the climate system, many of which are undesirable," says Eileen B. Claussen, assistant secretary of State for oceans and international environmental and scientific affairs and a lead U.S. negotiator at the treaty talks. "The fact that there is now some clear evidence of human input into those changes suggests to us that we ought to be serious about how we respond."

Although the Clinton administration refrained from stipulating either precise limits on emissions or the deadlines for achieving them, the commitment to reach such goals has roiled an already heated international

How the Greenhouse Effect Warms Earth

Carbon dioxide and other greenhouse gases released into the Earth's atmosphere trap solar heat, warming Earth's surface and lower atmosphere.

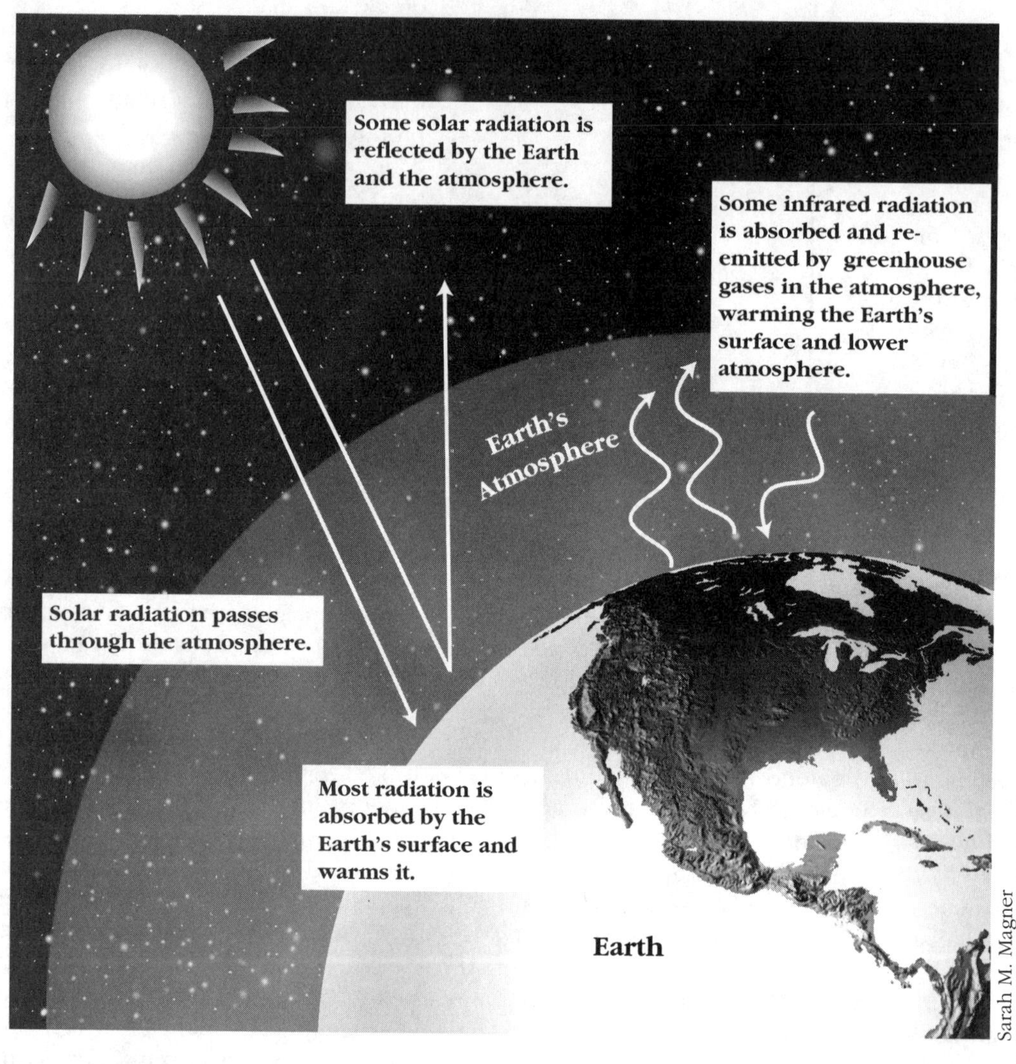

Sarah M. Magner

Source: National Aeronautics and Space Administration

debate. Environmentalists and scientists who support immediate curbs say they are crucial to preventing future disaster. But some industry spokesmen and scientists say the evidence does not warrant policies that they say will cause irreparable harm to the U.S. economy.

"We oppose legally binding targets and timetables, as well as mandatory command-and-control policies and measures," says John Novak, a spokesman for the Edison Electric Institute (EEI), which represents electric power companies and electric utility holding companies. Most of EEI's members burn coal and would come under any caps on fossil fuel use. "We believe that those types of policies will force premature emissions reductions that will be costly and are not warranted at this time," Novak says. "All the science shows that this is a long-term issue and that there is sufficient time to take action to mitigate climate change."

The Global Climate Change Coalition, another industry group, is leading the charge against mandatory limits on greenhouse gas emissions, predicting that they would ruin the economy. "We've got to be cautious because the stakes are so high," says Executive Director John B. Shlaes. "All the relevant economic analyses say that the United States is going to take a major hit on the economy if any of the [limits] that have been on the table are adopted."

A study commissioned by the coalition predicts that adoption of some proposals would cause a 3 percent fall in U.S. gross domestic product by 2010, resulting in a 23 percent drop in the growth rate of Americans' living standards. [2]

Some scientists also take issue with the need for immediate steps to cut greenhouse emissions. "There has been an intentional confusion between the concept of global warming and the magnitude of global warming," says Patrick J. Michaels, a climatologist at the University of Virginia. "A lot of people can correctly state that global warming is real, that the planet warmed in this century. But the argument then stops without going into the details. You have to ask the question, not whether the planet will warm, but how much, and how. How much do we want to spend to deal with a problem that we're not even so sure is a problem?"

Supporters of curbs dismiss such critics. "They are only a small handful of people," says Michael Oppenheimer, an atmospheric physicist at the Environmental Defense Fund in New York. "The consensus view on the nature of the problem has been established by the Intergovernmental Panel on Climate Change. It's fair to question their findings, but you have to ask what evidence the few critics are putting forward. Basically what they mostly do is pick at details without offering any new evidence. Their arguments have been considered and laid aside because they don't deliver anything new to the equation."

Even some U.S. industries that stand to suffer initially from caps on emissions view the stricter policy as both environmentally necessary and potentially beneficial economically, because it will encourage the development of new technology. "We believe that the science is compelling enough to urge action on the national and international level," says Michael L. Marvin, executive director of the Business Council for Sustainable Energy, whose members include electric utilities, natural gas companies and appliance manufacturers. "It's a two-sided coin, because the costs of inaction are of consequence as well. According to our estimate, with limited government intervention we can increase the number of jobs and decrease by about 12 percent the overall amount of carbon dioxide that goes into the atmosphere."

As negotiations on the global climate treaty proceed, the debate in the United States and other nations will continue to center on the following questions:

Have scientists conclusively proven that human activities cause global warming?

For most of this century, scientists lacked the technology to prove or disprove the existence of global warming. It is only with the development of highly precise satellite measuring equipment and supercomputers able to process vast quantities of weather data that scientists in recent years have established firm grounds for their climate assessments.

"A lot of people can correctly state that global warming is real, that the planet warmed in this century. But the argument then stops without going into the details. You have to ask the question, not whether the planet will warm, but how much, and how. How much do we want to spend to deal with a problem that we're not even so sure is a problem?"

— Patrick J. Michaels
climatologist, University of Virginia

As a result, certain findings are supported by virtually all climate scientists. "We know that greenhouse gases warm Earth because they are there naturally," Oppenheimer says. "We know that they trap heat — otherwise we wouldn't be here because the Earth would be 60 degrees colder. Nobody argues about all that. We also know that greenhouse gases are building up and that the buildup of gases will warm Earth further. Nobody argues with that either. The question is how much, how fast."

The consensus view expressed by the IPCC is that current rates of emissions will leave twice as much carbon dioxide in the atmosphere in the next several decades as there was before the Industrial Revolution. Such an increase, the panel predicts, would result in global temperatures up to 7 degrees Fahrenheit higher than today — and the fastest warming trend of the past 10,000 years.

But while climatologists agree that Earth's temperature is rising, some dispute the level of man's contribution to the rise. The main flaw in the science, they say, lies in the computer representations of global climate known as "general circulation models." *(See "At Issue," p. 977.)*

Sallie Baliunas, an astrophysicist at Harvard University, said that "only a small part of the 0.5 degree Celsius [about 1 degree F] rise in the past 100 years — no more than a few tenths of a degree — could have been caused by human-made greenhouse gases." That's because most of the warming occurred before 1940, while most of the 50 percent increase in gas emissions by industrial development and transportation came after 1940, she said. For this reason, Baliunas said, "the 0.5-1.5 degree C warming predicted by the computer simulations exaggerates the greenhouse effect produced by the equivalent 50 percent buildup of carbon dioxide."[3]

As the debate intensifies over what to do about global warming, questions about the reliability of scientific

Cars That 'Burn' Hydrogen . . .

The United States is currently the world's biggest emitter of carbon dioxide, the main greenhouse gas, and gasoline-powered vehicles account for nearly a third of the U.S. total. [1] If the United States is going to get serious about reducing greenhouse gas emissions, clearly something must be done about the kinds of cars Americans make and use.

Automakers are working on developing cleaner cars by searching for alternatives to the gasoline-powered internal-combustion engine. But their goal primarily has been to reduce smog-causing pollutants, rather than CO_2 and other greenhouse emissions.

Toward that end, the California Legislature in 1990 passed a law requiring automakers to include a "zero-emissions" vehicle among the models they sell in the state by model year 1998. Early this year, however, the state bowed to industry pressure and dropped the 1998 deadline. But by then automakers had already dusted off an old idea — a battery-powered electric car — which made its market debut this fall. [2]

General Motors' Saturn division has introduced the first commercially available electric passenger car — the EV1 (for Electric Vehicle 1) — in Southern California and Arizona, the only states where GM has set up service centers for the new model.

Reuters

Toyota says its new non-polluting car runs on electricity generated by a reaction between hydrogen and oxygen.

The car offers few real improvements over earlier electric prototypes, which were plagued by sluggish performance and the need for frequent and time-consuming battery recharging. The EV1 can go just 90 miles between recharging its lead-acid battery, which can take more than two hours. In any case, American consumers in recent years have been drawn more to high-performance, gas-guzzling sport utility vehicles and luxury cars than energy-efficient models. With its technical drawbacks and $35,000 sticker price, the EV1 is not likely to break any sales records.

Experts say that smog in Los Angeles and other cities would lift significantly if electric cars took hold. But while they can greatly reduce ground pollution by eliminating tailpipe emissions, electric cars are not entirely pollution-free. Many utility plants supplying the electricity they run on still burn coal, the dirtiest fossil fuel of all. And coal-fired utilities would still generate particulate matter and sulfates in an electric-car era.

For the same reason, electric cars would be of limited

data have at times led to charges impugning the integrity of the scientists themselves. Each side accuses the other of bending its findings to suit political and business interests.

Critics say the way the IPCC found "a discernible human influence on global climate" throws the finding itself into doubt. After the report was submitted to scientists for review and the peer-review process was completed, wording expressing uncertainties about the report's findings reportedly was altered. [4] The revised text was then published without again undergoing the full peer-review process. [5]

The University of Virginia's Michaels concedes that panel members did nothing technically wrong in changing the wording after the peer-review process was completed because their own rules permitted the change. "But the real question is, Was it the right thing to do?" he asks. "Was it right to insert a few sentences [about the human role in climate change] that the authors knew were political dynamite and then to disingenuously turn the other way and pretend they didn't realize that they would be used like this? That is hokum."

Supporters of the IPCC dismiss the criticism. "It's nonsense," Oppenheimer says. Claussen suggests that the issue has been blown out of proportion by people with an interest in subverting the treaty negotiations. "I think there are people — some, but not all, of the industry groups — who have tried to create a controversy," she says. "But I don't actually think there is much of a controversy."

Michaels himself has been charged with bias because the coal industry funds some of his research. "Where in the Constitution is it written that industry cannot ask a scientific research question, and that in asking the question it tarnishes the reputation of the person they asked it of?" he responds indignantly. Michaels also says that

. . . Would Reduce Greenhouse Emissions

use in reducing global warming unless non-fossil energy sources are used to produce the electricity needed to recharge their batteries. Carbon dioxide, the main greenhouse gas implicated in warming, is emitted by all fossil fuels, including the main current alternative to coal in U.S. power plants, natural gas. According to Mark Delucchi, a researcher at the Institute of Transportation Studies at the University of California, Davis, the reduction in greenhouse gases emitted from using an electric car vs. a gasoline-powered car amounts to less than 20 percent.

Other technologies may offer greater hope for reducing greenhouse gas emissions from cars. The most frequently cited alternative to conventional lead-acid batteries is the "hydrogen fuel cell," which produces electricity by "burning" hydrogen. Because the process takes place on board the vehicle, the fuel cell would eliminate one of the main drawbacks of the EV1, plugging it into a wall outlet for hours when its battery runs down. [3]

Fuel cells are the main focus of research supported by the Clinton administration's Partnership for a New Generation of Vehicles, a cooperative venture with the Big Three U.S. automakers. The program's goal is to triple fuel economy in passenger cars without sacrificing the performance, comfort and affordability available in today's gasoline-driven models, all by 2003.

The main drawback of fuel cells involves hydrogen storage. "Hydrogen in its natural state is a very diffuse gas, so to get it in a compact form that you can carry around with you on a vehicle requires compressing it or reacting it with something else," Delucchi says. "Systems exist to do this, but so far they are expensive, heavy and bulky."

Ultimately, the electric car's ability to reduce greenhouse gas emissions, whether it is run by a conventional battery or a fuel cell, depends on where the fuel comes from. "Even if you just limit the electric vehicle to California, you'll still have a fairly large reduction in greenhouse gases," Delucchi says, "because California's fuel mix includes a lot of natural gas and imported hydropower, a little nuclear power and not too much coal." But in places like the Midwest, where utilities depend heavily on burning coal to produce electricity, switching to battery-powered electric cars would have much less of an effect on greenhouse gas emissions.

The same caveat holds for fuel-cell electric vehicles. "Eventually we could obtain the hydrogen from electrolysis, or water-splitting," Delucchi explains. "But the question remains, Where do you get the electricity to split the water? It would be a pollution-free system only if the electricity comes from solar energy."

Ultimately, the usefulness of the next generation of electric cars in combating global warming — whether they run on batteries or hydrogen fuel cells — depends on the future development of alternative energy sources.

"If you charge the electric vehicle from places that use pretty much exclusively solar power," Delucchi says, "then you can pretty much eliminate emissions of greenhouse gases. The real attraction of electric vehicles is not so much what they can do now, but what they can do in the long run."

---

[1] Alliance to Save Energy, American Gas Association and Solar Energy Industries Association, *An Alternative Energy Future* (1992), p. B1.

[2] For background, see "Electric Cars, *The CQ Researcher*, July 9, 1993, pp. 577-600.

[3] See Daniel Sperling, "The Case for Electric Vehicles," *Scientific American*, November 1996, pp. 54-59.

industry accounts for only about 16 percent of his research funds, with the rest coming from government grants. "Does this make me 16 percent biased and 84 percent unbiased?" he asks.

Michaels says he received at most $210,000 from the coal industry last year for climate research, compared with the federal government's $2.1 billion budget for climate research over the same period. "If you are telling me that $2.1 billion is being derailed by $210,000, I think you might have an inaccurate perception of conspiracy," he says. "Someday that funding disparity is going to get out in public, and people are going to wonder where in the heck the $2.1 billion is going and what it's buying."

Would global warming cause irreparable harm to the environment or human health?

The IPCC report summarized the findings of recent scientific studies, listing several likely negative outcomes of global warming, including:

- Sea levels would rise on average 15-90 centimeters, or 6 inches to 3 feet, by 2100, because rising temperatures would cause some melting of glaciers and polar ice sheets, and water expands as it gets warmer. Seas would continue to rise at the same rate thereafter.
- The number of extremely hot days would increase, while extremely cold days would decrease.
- Weather patterns would change, bringing more floods or droughts to some areas.
- Rainfall would be more intense, though scientists could not say if tropical cyclones and other severe storms would change in location and intensity. [6]

Since the report came out, other media and scientific reports have predicted dire consequences from climate change in the absence of measures to curtail emissions of greenhouse gases. In January, for example, newspaper and magazine stories blamed climate

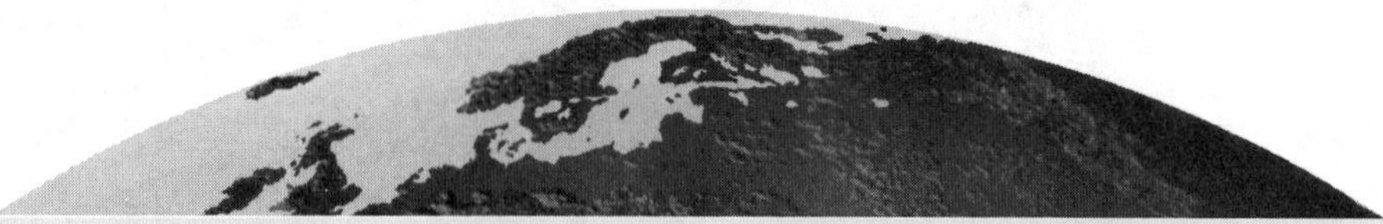

The 15 Countries With the Highest CO_2 Emissions

Highest Total CO_2 Emissions, 1992

Heavily industrialized countries, led by the U.S., are among the world's biggest emitters of industrial carbon dioxide. Rapidly industrializing China and India could account for more than half the developing world's CO_2 by 2010.*

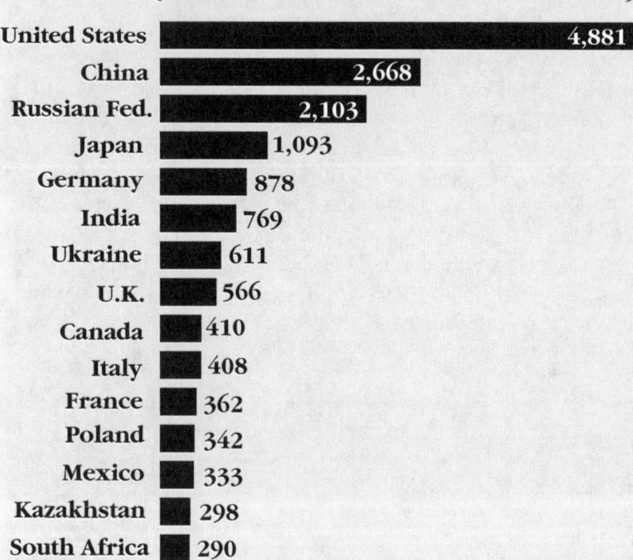

(million metric tons of carbon dioxide)

United States	4,881
China	2,668
Russian Fed.	2,103
Japan	1,093
Germany	878
India	769
Ukraine	611
U.K.	566
Canada	410
Italy	408
France	362
Poland	342
Mexico	333
Kazakhstan	298
South Africa	290

Highest Per Capita CO_2 Emissions, 1992

Wealthy, industrialized countries tend to release more industrial carbon dioxide per person than other countries. In largely undeveloped Kazakhstan, however, the high per capita rate is largely due to oil production.

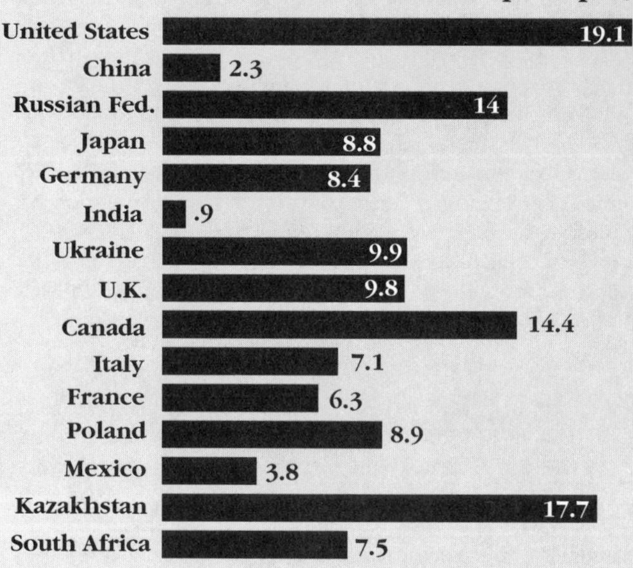

(metric tons of carbon dioxide per capita)

United States	19.1
China	2.3
Russian Fed.	14
Japan	8.8
Germany	8.4
India	.9
Ukraine	9.9
U.K.	9.8
Canada	14.4
Italy	7.1
France	6.3
Poland	8.9
Mexico	3.8
Kazakhstan	17.7
South Africa	7.5

Note: A metric ton equals 1,000 kilograms or 2,204.6 pounds.

* *Industrial carbon dioxide refers to any CO_2 produced by burning fossil fuel, including automobiles.*

Sources: World Resources 1996-97, *The World Resources Institute, 1996; based on data from Carbon Dioxide Information Analysis Center, Oak Ridge National Laboratory, September 1995; Population Action International.*

instability brought on by global warming for the blizzard that paralyzed the East Coast.[7]

Of all the predicted results of climate change, none is more certain to many scientists than rising sea levels. "I would consider it firm that the sea level will rise by a global average of a half-foot to three feet in the next century," Oppenheimer says. "To understand whether that's important or not, over the last 100 years sea level has risen about five inches, and we're already experiencing difficulties in managing that level of sea-level rise."

In the United States, he says, a three-foot rise "would extensively flood areas where a lot of people live, like southern Louisiana and parts of South Florida, and would require expensive infrastructure changes in places like Dallas, Texas, Charleston, S.C., and to some extent New York City."

While wealthy countries like the United States or even the low-lying Netherlands could probably manage such a threat, the same is not true for many threatened regions, such as the Maldives, the Ganges delta in Bangladesh and Egypt's Nile delta. "For many countries, managing three feet of sea level rise is not going to be possible," Oppenheimer says.

Even if warming does occur, critics respond, the sea-level predictions are exaggerated because temperatures in the polar regions would still remain below freezing. They also suggest that a slight warming would likely cause an increase in snowfall, binding up some of the projected melt in snowpack. [8] According to another report, however, a regional warming trend over the past 50 years already has caused ice shelves along the coast of Antarctica to collapse. [9]

Another widely cited threat to human life resulting from climate change is the spread of mosquito-borne infectious diseases, such as malaria and dengue fever, as the insects' tropical habitat expands northward. Concern mounted in the United States last year when a dengue outbreak spread to northern Mexico. [10]

But skeptics say that faulty climate models were used to predict an increase in the mosquitoes' habitat, and that technological advances such as air-conditioning and improved living conditions eradicated malaria from the United States in the past and can protect humans from these diseases in the future. [11] Similarly, a report predicting that algal blooms enhanced by warming waters would spread cholera was criticized as unfounded by the evidence. [12]

Other studies indicating irreversible damage to the environment as a result of climate change have emerged in recent months. One study, hailed as the first direct observation of global warming's biological impact, found that the range of Edith's checkerspot butterfly had shifted northward along the West Coast as the small insect died out in Mexico and spread into southern Canada at the same time that temperatures rose throughout the region. [13] Michaels refutes the finding, saying there has been no measurable warming in the region. [14]

Some critics of the global warming theory suggest that even if they are proved wrong over time and temperatures do rise, people will benefit from change. *World Climate Report* argues that warmer temperatures will open Siberia and northern Canada to agricultural production, increase global rainfall and reduce the hazards of winter driving. "If global warming occurs," the magazine says, "the many benefits will offset [the] drawbacks. People like warm climates. Heating bills are lower. Clothing costs are reduced. Transportation is less troubled. And death rates are lower." [15]

Agence France Presse

Scientists consider this iceberg, which recently broke away from Antarctica, as an important clue to the rate of global warming. Some experts predict that increasing global warming could melt polar ice and cause a three-foot rise in seas levels, flooding low-lying areas around the world.

Can an international treaty succeed in reducing global greenhouse emissions?

The major challenge to policymakers intent on thwarting global warming is the pervasive nature of greenhouse gases. Some of the gases, such as chlorofluorocarbons (CFCs), are man-made. They can be removed from the equation if people agree to stop producing them.

This is already happening in the case of CFCs, once widely used as propellants in aerosol containers, as refrigerants and as solvents in computer chip production. After it was found that CFCs were destroying the stratospheric ozone layer, allowing more of the sun's harmful ultraviolet radiation to reach the Earth, the world's CFC producers agreed, by signing the 1987 Montreal Protocol on Substances that Deplete the Ozone Layer, to phase out their production for most uses by January 1996. [16]

But man-made gases contribute only slightly to the greenhouse effect, so removing CFCs will do little to mitigate global warming. By far the biggest contributor is carbon dioxide, which people the world over release, chiefly by burning fossil fuels and cutting down the forests that remove the gas from the atmosphere. That makes carbon dioxide much harder to curtail than CFCs. "The economics underlying the Montreal Protocol are different than what underlies global warming," Oppen-heimer says, "just because carbon is so pervasive."

Industry critics adamantly oppose any treaty with binding targets and timetables. "All economic analysis that's been done so far says this will cost the United States up to 4 percent in lost gross domestic product (GDP) at the same time that lots of countries that will not be part of the treaty will be able to develop their fossil fuel sources unfettered," says John B. Shlaes, executive director of the Global Climate Coalition, the chief industry group opposed to the IPCC findings and the treaty process. "We've probably never been confronted by a treaty of this scope in United States history, perhaps outside of a major trade negotiation. There's also never been a treaty where governments are negotiating on behalf of firms and households. We're looking for a more rational, sensible and balanced approach to this issue."

Despite the challenge, supporters of curbs on greenhouse gases see the Montreal Protocol — the first global treaty dealing with climate — as reason for optimism. "We learned something from the Montreal Protocol process," says Claussen, who helped negotiate the treaty and directed the Environmental Protection Agency (EPA) program implementing it in the United States. "For one thing, the treaty is legally binding, and countries that agreed to phase out CFCs have done so. It also has in it a rational system for reconsideration of the targets, which was very helpful, both scientifically and in terms of the technology."

Supporters also embrace the Montreal Protocol as a model for its differentiation between developed and developing countries. Because industrial countries benefited from CFCs long before the rest of the world, developing countries argued that they should receive concessions for agreeing to forgo the chemical. They signed on to the treaty after they were given additional time to live up to its provisions. "I'm not sure if a time lag is the perfect example in this case," Claussen says. "But the developing countries have moved forward [in phasing out CFCs], so it's not as if they decided not to do anything just because they aren't required to until later."

Some critics say a treaty to curb greenhouse gases would be impossible to enforce. "Who's going to verify and monitor every power plant every minute, or every factory every minute?" Shlaes asks. "And yet that's what you've got to do to if you want to go to that kind of process."

But the kind of enforcement needed to monitor, say, an arms control agreement may not be necessary for a climate treaty. "There is no enforcement mechanism in the Montreal Protocol," says Claussen. "There is reporting and an implementation committee, which helps countries comply rather than punishing them for not complying."

Industry response to U.S. acid rain legislation provides another model treaty supporters say could be included to help countries comply with caps on greenhouse gas emissions. [17] After Title IV of the 1992 Clean Air Act required utilities and other industries to reduce their emissions of sulfur dioxide released by burning coal, many companies that exceeded their clean-air quotas sold their excess allowances to companies that failed to comply. A market in sulfur dioxide allowances emerged, which today is conducted on the Chicago Board of Trade along with markets for pork belly futures and other agricultural commodities.

"I think that, too, is a model because in the end that system gave us greater reductions in sulfur dioxide emissions than we expected, and at a much cheaper price," says Claussen, who also ran the acid rain compliance program at EPA. She concedes, however, that setting up an international market in carbon emissions poses a far more daunting challenge. "It wasn't easy to set up the system domestically, and it will be far harder to do it internationally," she says. "To make that kind of system work, you have to have something in place that assures you that the emissions that are being traded are real, which is much harder to do internationally."

Some industry representatives are more pessimistic. "The only way something like the sulfur dioxide market can work is if you have a cap on emissions," says Novak of the Edison Electric Institute, who opposes any mandatory limits or timetables on carbon emissions. "We can provide the emissions reductions to help mitigate climate change on a voluntary basis. We don't need mandatory targets and timetables that will force us to reduce in ways that would be more costly." ■

BACKGROUND

Proof at Last

Carbon dioxide, the predominant greenhouse gas, occurs naturally, as do other greenhouse gases such as methane, nitrous oxide and water vapor. Indeed, without them, Earth would be too cold to sustain life as we know it.

Over the millennia, greenhouse gases have become part of the complex exchange of elements that allows life to thrive. In one of these vital cycles, plants take up carbon dioxide through their leaves, use it in photosynthesis and then release oxygen, which animals require to live. Completing the cycle, the same carbon dioxide that animals exhale returns to the atmosphere to be taken up once again by plants, as well as by the oceans that cover most of the Earth's surface.

Until human populations soared and began burning fossil fuels, greenhouse gases remained in relative balance. The huge climate changes that produced periodic ice ages and heat waves were the result of natural variations caused by sudden fluctuations in the sun's emission of radiation, volcanic eruptions on Earth and other phenomena beyond man's control.

But the Industrial Revolution, which began in 19th-century Britain, ushered in a new age of rapid industrialization that greatly increased man's impact on the natural environment. By 1896, when Arrhenius postulated what became known as the green-

Continued on p. 972

Chronology

1800s ***Svante Arhennius, a Swedish chemist, postulates in 1896 that increasing amounts of carbon dioxide released into the atmosphere by coal-fired industries will cause global temperatures to rise.***

1950s-1960s

Scientists begin monitoring the atmosphere for carbon dioxide and temperature variations.

1958
Charles Keeling and other scientists from the Scripps Institute of Oceanography in La Jolla, Calif., begin monitoring carbon dioxide levels in Hawaii and other sites. Their work later shows a steady buildup of the gas.

1970s-1980s

Computer and satellite technologies permit more precise detection of greenhouse gas trends.

1974
Chemists Sherwood Roland and Mario Molina warn that emissions of chlorofluorocarbons (CFCs) and other man-made chemicals are destroying the layer of stratospheric ozone protecting Earth from the sun's harmful ultraviolet B radiation.

1985
A large ozone hole is discovered over Antarctica, confirming the ozone hole theory. Roland and Molina later receive the Nobel Prize in chemistry (1995).

1987
Some 150 countries, including the United States, sign the Montreal Protocol on Substances that Deplete the Ozone Layer, which restricts industrial use of CFCs.

June 23, 1988
James E. Hansen, a climate specialist at the Goddard Institute for Space Studies in New York City, tells a Senate committee that global warming is occurring. The U.N. General Assembly sets up the Intergovernmental Panel on Climate Change (IPCC), a global network of scientists to advise world leaders.

1990s ***The climate-change debate intensifies as world leaders narrow their differences over a global treaty to curb greenhouse gas emissions.***

1990
In its first report, the IPCC announces that greenhouse gases are building up at an unprecedented pace but refrains from recommending emission cuts under political pressure from the United States and other industrial countries dependent on fossil fuels.

May 9, 1992
The United States and about 130 other countries sign the U.N. Framework Convention on Climate Change, the first binding agreement dealing directly with climate change. Signatories agree to try to reduce their greenhouse gas emissions to 1990 levels by the year 2000.

June 1992
At the Earth Summit in Rio de Janeiro, Brazil, more countries sign the climate change convention, bringing the total to 165.

April 1993
President Clinton announces his Climate Change Action Plan, a set of voluntary programs aimed at meeting the framework target by enabling companies to join in partnerships with federal government agencies to improve energy use and cut greenhouse gas emissions.

March 1995
Framework signatories issue the Berlin Mandate calling for concrete plans to toughen the agreement by the end of 1997.

December 1995
The IPCC announces for the first time that the scientific evidence shows a "discernible human influence on global climate."

July 17, 1996
Under Secretary of State Tim Wirth announces that the United States has abandoned its call for voluntary steps to reduce greenhouse gas emissions and will press instead for legally binding targets and timetables in treaty negotiations in Kyoto, Japan.

December 1997
Negotiators from the United States and other nations are scheduled to produce a U.N.-sponsored climate-change treaty in Kyoto.

Continued from p. 970

house effect, the Industrial Revolution was at full throttle and much of Europe and the United States had switched from wood to coal to drive their economies. With the invention and mass production of automobiles, demand for gasoline and other petroleum derivatives to fuel an ever-growing technological revolution mushroomed, pouring more excess carbon dioxide into the atmosphere.

Arrhenius predicted that a doubling of carbon dioxide in the atmosphere would cause a rise in the Earth's surface temperature of four to six degrees Celsius (7.2 to 10.8 degrees Fahrenheit). But it would take almost a century to prove him right.

The first major effort to confirm the theory came in 1958, when Charles Keeling and other scientists at the Scripps Institute of Oceanography in La Jolla, Calif., began monitoring carbon dioxide levels in Hawaii's famed Mauna Loa volcano.

Using actual measurements of the increase in carbon dioxide levels to date, scientists began developing ways to predict how much greenhouse warming might occur in the future. Their efforts laid the groundwork for the so-called general circulation models in use today to predict future climate conditions. The first credible projections came in the mid-1960s, when Syukuro Manabe of Princeton University estimated that average global temperatures would rise by 2 degrees C in the 21st century if carbon dioxide levels doubled. In the 1970s, scientists were able to better establish the role of other greenhouse gases, including man-made chemicals such as CFCs.

Doubts Emerge, and Then New Evidence

The development of advanced computers and satellite technology enabled scientists to take ever more detailed measurements of greenhouse gas emissions. But their work also uncovered what critics said was a major discrepancy in the greenhouse theory. While the global temperature was found to have risen from around 1880 and 1940, it leveled off between 1940 and 1970. Scientists discovered that particulate matter cast aloft by volcanic eruptions and by coal burning itself could deflect sunlight back into space, perhaps countering the greenhouse effect. Some scientists began to predict instead a coming ice age.

By the late 1980s, however, the warming trend had reappeared, and there was a growing consensus within the scientific community that Arrhenius' prediction was indeed coming to pass. New evidence brought up in ice core samples from Antarctica and Greenland bolstered that view. By analyzing the gases trapped in ice for up to 20,000 years, scientists found that carbon dioxide levels had held relatively steady until the beginning of industrialization in about 1800, when they began to rise. Further evidence of global warming emerged as the carbon dioxide measurements from Mauna Loa and other stations confirmed a continuing buildup of the gas since 1958.

In 1988, concern over the threat of global warming was brought to the world's attention. On June 23, James E. Hansen of the Goddard Institute for Space Studies in New York testified before a Senate committee that the evidence was growing daily that global warming already was under way. The same month, participants at an international conference in Toronto, "The Changing Atmosphere: Implications for Global Security," warned that global warming posed a threat second only to nuclear war.

Action by U.S., U.N.

In 1988, the same year as Hansen's call to action to curb global warming, the U.N. General Assembly set up a special body — the Intergovernmental Panel on Climate Change — to advise world leaders on the nature of the problem. The panel, established as a partnership of the World Meteorological Organization and the U.N. Environment Programme, eventually would involve more than 2,500 scientists from more than 100 countries.

Reflecting the unprecedented complexity of climate change, the IPCC called on three working groups to address major areas involved in the issue: one to assess the scientific measurements and predictions; another to analyze the probable impacts of climate change on the environment, human health, society and the economy; and a final group to recommend policies to address the problem.

Most government leaders were reluctant to act on the early warnings. Reducing emissions of carbon dioxide and other greenhouse gases not only would mean burning less fossil fuel for industry and transportation but also curbing deforestation, a process that adds to the excess carbon dioxide by destroying trees, which absorb it. Carbon dioxide also is released when wood is burned. But such steps threatened to undermine economic growth and even destroy entire industries if undertaken too quickly. The world's oil, coal and natural gas industries alone are worth more than a trillion dollars, while many developing countries are undergoing rapid deforestation as a result of population growth, a trend that may take many decades to reverse. [18]

Although they were loath to take action, political leaders were coming under pressure from both sides either to curb emissions or resist such efforts, even before the IPCC released its first reports on climate change. In 1989, a Dutch government official, for example, warned the president of Brazil that if his government failed to curb deforestation of the Amazon basin, the Netherlands would cease to exist, as rising temperatures would melt polar ice caps and raise sea levels. At the same time, industry representatives in the United States called on the Bush administration to "hang tough on this one" and reject calls to curb emissions.[19]

For his part, President George Bush was quick to acknowledge the threat of climate change. He clearly stated at a February 1990 IPCC meeting in Washington that, "We all recognize that the atmosphere is changing in unexpected and unprecedented ways," and that "the future of the Earth must not be compromised."[20]

But Bush was reluctant to make policy changes without further evidence that global warming was occurring. When he called on other industrial countries to adopt a wait-and-see approach, he was met with strong criticism from many European allies who accused him of risking the global environment to protect U.S. industries — collectively the biggest emitters of greenhouse gases in the world. (*See graphs, p. 968.*)

The new U.N. panel's scientific working group concluded in its first report in 1990 that emissions of greenhouse gases were already heating up the planet at an unprecedented pace. They predicted that if current trends continued the average global temperature would rise one degree C — nearly two degrees Fahrenheit — within the next 30 years.

But the overall IPCC report issued that August containing the findings of all three working groups struck a more cautious note, clearly reflecting the controversial nature of the debate between scientists and industry interests. In contrast to the scientists' warning of global warming, the report referred only to "potential climate change" and refrained from calling for cuts or even a freeze in greenhouse emissions, steps the IPCC scientists had said were necessary to slow the warming trend.[21]

Climate Treaty Signed

On May 9, 1992, the United States and about 130 other countries signed the first binding agreements dealing directly with climate change — the United Nations Framework Convention on Climate Change. The pact, which was presented at the Earth Summit held the next month in Rio de Janeiro, Brazil, eventually was signed by 165 countries and the European Union.* The pact called for "stabilization of greenhouse gas concentrations at a level that would prevent dangerous anthropogenic [human] interference with the climate system."

Most industrial countries agreed to try to reduce their greenhouse gas emissions to 1990 levels by the year 2000. Developing countries were given extra time to meet the target and were asked to report on their energy use and emission levels and the steps they intended to take to reduce them. Because developing countries are expected to account for a growing portion of gas emissions as they industrialize, industrial countries promised to provide financing and technology to help them meet their targets.

"Continued use of non-binding targets that are not met makes a mockery of the treaty process. It leaves the impression that rhetoric is what counts rather than real emission reductions — an outcome that is both unacceptable and counterproductive."

— Tim Wirth, Under Secretary of State

As it became increasingly clear that few countries would meet their emissions targets, the framework signatories met in March 1995 in Berlin, Germany, to discuss ways to strengthen their commitment. In a decision called the Berlin Mandate, the parties agreed to come up with concrete plans to toughen the treaty by the end of 1997. Developing countries such as China, India and Brazil would be exempted from any new commitments, however.

The meeting revealed significant disagreements in how to make the treaty tougher. The European Union called for the adoption of a carbon tax, an energy tax based on the amount of carbon dioxide released by a given energy source. A group of 37 countries with the most to lose from rising sea levels — the Alliance of Small Island States (AOSIS) — urged the industrial countries to cut their emissions 20 percent below 1990 levels by 2005. The United States and other industrial countries rejected this goal as potentially ruinous to their fossil-fuel-driven economies.

One innovative scheme that emerged from the Berlin summit was an agreement to start a pilot program to encourage firms in industrial countries to set up renewable energy or reforestation projects in developing

* The 15 members of the European Union also signed the treaty individually.

How YOU Can Fight Global Warming

While the United States and other nations continue to negotiate a U.N. treaty to reduce emissions of greenhouse gases, there are many things that consumers can do on their own:

1. Drive less. Cars account for about one-third of all U.S. carbon dioxide emissions. Take public transportation, walk or bike when possible. If you have to use your car, consolidate errands into a single trip.

2. Buy a fuel-efficient model. Geo Prizm, Acura Integra, Ford Contour 4, Chrysler Concorde and Honda Odyssey/ Isuzu Oasis are among the most efficient vehicles in their classes, according to *Consumer Reports.* Popular sport-utility vehicles and pickup trucks generally consume more fuel than cars and minivans.

3. Buy energy-efficient appliances. Federal law requires manufacturers to place an Energy Guide label on most major appliances. Refrigerators, the biggest electricity consumers in most households, are now about 75 percent more efficient than those made in the 1970s.

4. Weatherize your home. Caulking, weatherstripping, insulation and replacement windows can stop leaks of heated or cooled air. Use heating and air-conditioning wisely to reduce fuel consumption.

5. Lighten up your roof. Air-conditioning use can be cut by one-fifth in hot climates by replacing a dark roof with a light-colored roof that reflects sunlight.

6. Plant trees. By absorbing carbon dioxide, trees reduce greenhouse gas emissions. Strategically planted deciduous trees can be used to shade houses in the summer while allowing sunlight to penetrate in the winter, reducing demand for both air-conditioning and heating. Evergreens also can be used as wind breaks, further reducing heating needs.

7. Replace conventional incandescent light bulbs. Compact fluorescents and Tungsten-halogen lamps cost more to buy, but save money over time in reduced electricity consumption.

8. Buy fewer things. About half the energy we consume goes into the myriad products and services we buy.

9. Speak up. Urge your political representatives to enact laws that save energy and combat greenhouse gas emissions.

Sources: Natural Resources Defense Council; "Turning up the Heat," *Consumer Reports*, September 1996, p. 43.

countries. This "joint implementation" plan came immediately under attack by developing countries and some industry representatives alike. Developing countries worried that industrial countries would try to get credit for such projects as a way to get out of their commitments to cut carbon emissions at home. Energy industries insisted that they would only go along with a stronger treaty if they were allowed to get credit for helping reduce emissions abroad.[22]

Meeting again in Rome last December, signatories to the framework convention endorsed the IPCC's finding of a "discernible human influence" on global climate change. Participants at both the Berlin and Rome conferences failed, however, to agree to legally binding targets and timetables for greenhouse gas emissions. ■

CURRENT SITUATION

Voluntary Programs

President Clinton has placed environmental protection near the top of his policy agenda from the start of his administration. Shortly after entering the White House in 1993, Clinton signaled his support for international environmental efforts by creating the position of under secretary for global affairs and naming Wirth, a longtime environmental advocate, to the post. He also named Claussen, a longtime environmental regulator, to assume the top State Department post dealing directly with climate change negotiations.

Until this year, the Clinton administration's stance focused on encouraging U.S. industry to voluntarily reduce their emissions of greenhouse gases. On Earth Day 1993, the president introduced the Climate Change Action Plan, a set of voluntary programs enabling companies to join partnerships with the Department of Energy, the Environmental Protection Agency and other federal agencies to help improve energy use and cut emissions at the same time. The plan's goal was to enable the United States to meet its commitment to reduce carbon emissions to 1990 levels by 2000 through voluntary incentives rather than mandatory regulations.

The EPA's Green Lights program, for example, encourages businesses to install energy-efficient lighting in stores and plants, saving 800,000 tons of greenhouse gases a year. Stated another way, energy saved through the program would light 3 million homes for a year. The Energy Department's Climate Wise program to publicly recognize companies' voluntary efforts to cut emissions and Motor Challenge program to improve industrial motors systems are expected to reduce carbon emissions by a total of nearly 10 million metric tons of carbon equivalent (MMTCE) by 2000. The EPA's Voluntary Aluminum Industry Partnership is expected to reduce emissions of purofluorocarbons, another greenhouse gas, by nearly 2 MMTCE by 2000.

"The beauty of the voluntary programs is that there is a presumption that the actions they encourage will actually be profitable," says Paul Stolpman, director of the EPA's Office of Atmospheric Programs, which runs the administration's voluntary emissions programs. "When people sign up for these programs they actually make money because they're saving so much energy. We're hopeful that voluntary efforts to reduce greenhouse gases in ways that are economically efficient will actually improve the state of the U.S. economy and lead to increased employment and output because our economy will be more efficient."

Perhaps more than any other sector, the electric utility industry has taken advantage of voluntary programs to reduce greenhouse emissions. Utilizing a provision of the 1992 Energy Policy Act, the industry has since 1993 worked with the Energy Department to cut emissions by encouraging consumers to cut their electricity use by purchasing more efficient lighting, appliances and building materials. Utilities have also switched from coal to less-polluting natural gas and improved the efficiency of coal-fired plants.

Deni McIntyre/Allstock/Picture Network International

A section of Amazon forest in Brazil is cleared by slash and burn. Many developing countries are undergoing rapid deforestation, increasing emissions of carbon dioxide and other greenhouse gases. Trees remove CO_2 from the air during photosynthesis; burning of brush and tree limbs releases large amounts of CO_2 into the atmosphere.

According to EEI's Novak, more than 600 electric utilities, accounting for 60 percent of the industry, are participating in the voluntary program, which he estimates will reduce emissions by 44 million metric tons of carbon by 2000. "We're encouraging our members to continue their efforts," Novak says. "And we're working with the administration to make sure that if there are targets or timetables after 2000, we will get credit" for the cuts already made. "If we're not going to get allowances, we may consider not doing them."

The administration's voluntary programs have been far less successful in reducing carbon dioxide emissions from cars, trucks and airplanes, the leading sources of greenhouse gas emissions in the United States. One voluntary program, the Partnership for a New Generation of Vehicles, is designed to encourage the auto industry to go beyond current research into electric battery-driven cars to develop an emission-free, efficient vehicle.[23] (*See story, p. 966.*) But results from this initiative will not come soon enough to meet the 2000 target.

Last year, the administration also called a meeting in Detroit — dubbed the "Car Talks" — aimed at improving fuel economy standards beyond existing corporate average fuel economy (CAFE) standards mandated by Congress in 1975. By 1985, domestic automakers had reached the fleetwide CAFE target of 27.5 miles per gallon, but lower gasoline prices and rising consumer demand for more powerful vehicles have stymied further improvements. After energy and auto industry representatives failed to resolve their differences over whether to tighten CAFE standards to raise the gasoline tax, the talks broke up without reaching a final agreement.

Clinton Gets Tougher

As it became clear that the voluntary programs would not enable the United States to meet its emissions goal by 2000, the administration toughened its policy. At the most recent meeting of the parties to the U.N.

climate change agreement, Under Secretary of State Wirth announced that the United States was abandoning its insistence on non-binding goals for emission cuts.

"Continued use of non-binding targets that are not met makes a mockery of the treaty process," Wirth said. "It leaves the impression that rhetoric is what counts rather than real emission reductions — an outcome that is both unacceptable and counterproductive." [24]

The administration emphasizes that it supports making the target and the timetable for emission reductions binding — not the measures used to meet them. This puts the United States at odds with the European Union and some developing countries that have proposed introducing a worldwide carbon tax to force compliance with the treaty's eventual targets.

"The Europeans' position going into the Geneva meeting was that they wanted binding policies and measures, like refrigerator efficiency standards and uniform taxes, and a non-binding target," Claussen says. "That gives you the ability to say you're doing great things, even though the target isn't real. We essentially reversed that by saying you have to achieve a certain level of emissions by a certain date." This more flexible approach would leave the matter of how to reach the goal up to the countries themselves.

The Clinton policy also rejects the island nations' timetable for a 20 percent cut in greenhouse gas emissions by 2005. "This is too much too fast," Claussen says. "In the United States, where we would have to have any treaty we negotiate ratified by the Senate and would probably need implementing legislation to do that, we couldn't even get off the ground for a couple of years."

With no treaty feasible before the December 1997 meeting in Kyoto, Claussen says, "We couldn't possibly do anything like that by 2005." ■

Tom Carroll/Phototake/Picture Network International

Heavy smog virtually obscures high-rise buildings in downtown Los Angeles, Calif. Auto exhausts are a major source of carbon dioxide, the predominant greenhouse gas.

OUTLOOK

Opposition to Treaty?

Most participants at the Framework Convention on Climate Change in Geneva agreed with the Clinton administration's new strategy. By the end of the meeting, all but 14 countries had endorsed the proposal to adopt binding targets and timetables — chiefly the 11 members of the Organization of Petroleum-Exporting Countries (OPEC) and Russia, which see a binding treaty as a threat to oil-dependent economies.

But opposition remains strong in the United States, where many industries that have supported the Clinton administration's voluntary programs to cut greenhouse gas emissions oppose binding targets and timetables. "This is a competitiveness issue," says Shlaes of the Global Climate Coalition. "The United States is 85 percent dependent on fossil fuel, so it is [vital] for our manufacturing. Meanwhile China, which is going to equal all the world's emissions today in the next 25 years, has no meaningful obligation to cut emissions."

Shlaes and other critics continue to downplay the urgency of taking steps to mitigate carbon emissions and call for more research before committing the United States to any binding treaty obligations. "There's time to get it right, both in terms of understanding how the science is working and also understanding what our economic options are," Shlaes says. "Rather than give us a balanced worldwide approach, this could end up hurting the United States because we haven't really done our homework."

Aside from declared opponents to a binding treaty, such as Shlaes' coalition, American businesses are by no means united in their views of U.S. policy on climate change. "This whole concept of the economy vs. the environment is a non-starter," says Marvin of the Business Council for Sustainable Energy. "We need to figure out how we can preserve our quality of

Continued on p. 978

At Issue:

Are computer models reliable tools for predicting climate trends?

MICHAEL C. MACCRACKEN
Director, Office of the U.S. Global Change Research Program

FROM TESTIMONY BEFORE HOUSE SCIENCE COMMITTEE, MARCH 6, 1996.

yes

For simple systems or single processes, conceptual models can be particularly useful. For systems as complex as the full Earth system, arguably the most complex of all research endeavors, a systematic means must be found for incorporating our understanding into a quantitative framework.

The approach that is used is to construct mathematical models that to the greatest extent possible rely on fundamental and immutable laws of nature. Reliance must be placed on various approximations because understanding will never be fully complete and computer size and resources are limited. Uncertainties will always exist — and there will always be questions — for not everything can be explained; but uncertainties are also the reason for an aggressive associated program of observations, analysis and process studies.

The mathematical climate models (variously called climate models, general circulation models or Earth system models, depending somewhat on their implementation) strive to include all that is understood about the climate system. Because there is no means to prove them right — only to see where they break down — the models are constantly being put through an increasingly grueling series of tests to see how well or poorly they match observations.

Models reproduce many aspects of the observed climate. That there are shortcomings, however, is to be expected — all modelers acknowledge them (just as all good observationalists acknowledge the shortcomings in their observations). The challenge is to identify why they are not precisely reproducing nature and how to make them better.

But at any given time, models are at the cutting edge of what we understand. They treat dozens of processes spread out over the globe and up through to atmosphere and down through the oceans, all the time requiring that everything be done consistently — no leaving out a process here and including it there, no assuming that changing one thing will not change something else and so on. While experiences from past climatic conditions can be a rich source of tests of models (hence we study paleoclimates), only models can provide quantitative projections of future conditions. . . .

While it might be tempting to wait until each process is understood before model calculations are attempted, making and analyzing such calculations is as much part of the research and learning process as are observational and process studies. All of these efforts must proceed in parallel.

ROBERT E. DAVIS
Associate professor, Department of Environmental Sciences, University of Virginia

FROM TESTIMONY BEFORE HOUSE SCIENCE COMMITTEE, MARCH 6, 1996.

no

Measurements of atmospheric circulation (a term that encompasses wind flow at and above the surface) have been taken over much of the Earth for 50 to 100 years or more. Circulation is a critical climate variable since it is closely linked to temperature, rainfall and other weather events. Models that generate daily weather forecasts are founded upon principles that describe changes in the atmosphere's circulation. Similarly, general circulation models (GCMs), like the ones used as the motivation for the Rio climate treaty, are based on fundamental circulation principles. . . .

The developers of GCMs frequently state that, although their forecasts are not suitable for analysis on smaller spatial scales (regions or sub-regions), the models properly describe the large-scale features of the atmosphere accurately. Thus, the model predictions for an atmosphere with double the preindustrial concentrations of greenhouse gases should be basically correct over large areas.

Although individual GCMs differ substantially in their regional forecasts, most are in agreement with respect to some larger-scale features that should be expected in an enhanced greenhouse atmosphere. Tropical temperatures are expected to increase only slightly relative to polar temperatures. Furthermore, this polar temperature increase is predicted to be concentrated largely in the winter. Thus the models predict a decrease (in comparison to current values) in the equator-to-pole temperature gradient. In response, the winter atmospheric circulation should become more summer-like, as represented by a weakening of the jet stream and a contraction of the circumpolar vortex.

Based on observations of the upper atmosphere taken since the late 1940s, the winter circumpolar vortex has actually exhibited a statistically significant expansion. . . . This response is the opposite of what would be expected from a greenhouse warming influence. Furthermore, these observed, large-scale changes are not depicted by GCMs. . . .

Models can serve a very useful scientific purpose, such as the proposition and testing of hypotheses. The use of GCMs to examine changes in greenhouse gas concentrations in the atmosphere is an appropriate and important scientific question. However, when the results of these experiments are used to influence public policy (both nationally and globally), then concerns about the various models' accuracy must be raised. The simple fact is that the current generation of GCMs are incapable of reproducing the historic climate of the Earth sufficiently at anything but the broadest time and space scales.

For More Information

Global Climate Coalition, 1331 Pennsylvania Ave. N.W., Suite 1500, North Tower, Washington, D.C. 20004; (202) 637-3158. The coalition is the main energy industry lobbying and public relations arm that opposes binding restrictions on greenhouse gas emissions.

Global Greenhouse Network, 1660 L St. N.W., Suite 216, Washington, D.C. 20036; (202) 466-2823. This coalition of legislators and public interest groups concerned with global warming promotes cuts in fossil fuel use.

Environmental Defense Fund, 257 Park Ave. South, New York, N.Y. 10010; (212) 505-2100. The EDF is a citizens' interest group that conducts research and provides information on global warming and other environmental issues.

Environmental Protection Agency, Atmospheric Programs, 401 M St. S.W., Washington, D.C. 20460; (202) 233-9140. This office of the EPA examines strategies to mitigate climate change.

Continued from p. 976

life and continue our economic growth in the most sustainable way possible. It's a simple question, and it deserves to be approached with the seriousness of the issue and not the hyperbolic response that we're seeing from all sides, frankly."

The tone of the debate will depend on the details that will emerge from negotiations leading up to the Kyoto meeting next December, when a treaty is scheduled to be finalized. The Clinton administration has carefully avoided all reference to specific targets and timetables, except to reject the island nations' proposal of a 20 percent reduction in emissions by 2005.

Claussen suggests that a "midterm" timetable for achieving emission targets might be between 2010 and 2020. "But we can't say exactly what the date will be and exactly what the target will be and how you define that target," she says. "All those things we are still looking at, and we think others are as well."

For supporters of a strong treaty to curb global warming, the main challenge will be to maintain the U.S. commitment to binding targets and timetables over the year remaining before the meeting in Kyoto next December. "The negotiations should produce something by the end of 1997," Oppenheimer says. "If they don't, I think credibility in the whole treaty process will disintegrate." ■

Notes

[1] Intergovernmental Panel on Climate Change, *Climate Change 1995: The Science of Climate Change* (1996), p. 5.

[2] See Peter B. Jaquette and Mary H. Novak, "Review of Recent Estimates of the Economic Impacts of Proposed Carbon Abatement Policies," WEFA Group, an economic forecasting company in Eddystone, Pa., October 1996, p. 3.

[3] Testimony before the Senate Energy and Natural Resources Committee, Sept. 17, 1996.

[4] IPCC, *op. cit.,* p. 439.

[5] For a critical view of the panel's procedures, see Frederick Seitz, "A Major Deception on 'Global Warming,'" *The Wall Street Journal,* June 12, 1996, p. A16.

[6] IPCC, *op. cit.,* pp. 6-7.

[7] See, for example, "The Hot Zone," *Newsweek,* Jan. 22, 1996.

[8] See Global Climate Coalition, "Science and Global Climate Change: What Do We Know? What Are the Uncertainties?" Backgrounder, undated.

[9] See D.G. Vaughan and C.S.M. Doake, "Recent Atmospheric Warming and Retreat of Ice Shelves on the Antarctic Peninsula," *Nature,* Jan. 25, 1996, pp. 328-330.

[10] For background, see "Combating Infectious Diseases," *The CQ Researcher,* June 9, 1995, pp. 489-512.

[11] See "Global Warming Pests and Pestilence," *World Climate Report,* Sept. 30, 1996, p. 3, a biweekly newsletter edited by the University of Virginia's Patrick J. Michaels and funded by the Western Fuels Association, which supplies fuel to electric utilities.

[12] See Jonathan A. Patz, Paul R. Epstein, Thomas A. Burke and John M. Balbus, "Global Climate Change and Emerging Infectious Diseases," *Journal of the American Medical Association (JAMA),* Jan. 17, 1996, pp. 217-223. See also letter to the editor by John S. Gray, Michael Depledge and Anthony Knap, "Global Climate Controversy," *JAMA,* Aug. 7, 1996, pp. 372-373.

[13] Camille Parmesan, "Climate and Species' Range," *Nature,* Aug. 29, 1996, pp. 765-766.

[14] "Chasing Butterflies," *World Climate Report,* Sept. 16, 1996, p. 2.

[15] Thomas Gale Moore, "Global Warming: Costs and Benefits," *World Climate Report,* Aug. 19, 1996, p. 2. Moore is an editor of the newsletter.

[16] See "Ozone Depletion," *The CQ Researcher,* April 3, 1992, pp. 289-312.

[17] For background, see "Environmental Movement at 25," *The CQ Researcher,* March 31, 1995, pp. 273-296.

[18] See Jeremy Leggett, ed., *Global Warming: The Greenpeace Report* (1990), p. 4. For background, see "Saving the Forests," *The CQ Researcher,* Sept. 20, 1991, pp. 681-704.

[19] Intergovernmental Panel on Climate Change, Report to IPCC from Working Group 1: Policymakers' Summary of the Scientific Assessment of Climate Change, June 1990, p. 4.

[20] *Ibid.,* pp. 4-5.

[21] *Ibid.,* p. 5.

[22] See "The Berlin Climate Summit," in *World Resources 1996-97* (1996), pp. 322-323.

[23] For background, see "Electric Cars," *The CQ Researcher,* July 9, 1993, pp. 577-600.

[24] Wirth spoke July 17, 1996, at the second conference of the parties to the Framework Convention on Climate Change, held in Geneva, Switzerland.

Bibliography

Selected Sources Used

Books

Gore, Sen. Al, *Earth in the Balance: Ecology and the Human Spirit,* Houghton Mifflin, 1992.

The vice president's manifesto outlines the principles behind much of the Clinton administration's environmental policy. Even a slight rise in global temperatures, he warns, "would have disruptive and potentially catastrophic effects on human civilization."

Intergovernmental Panel on Climate Change, *Climate Change 1995: The Science of Climate Change,* Cambridge University Press, 1996.

The United Nations panel of scientists examining global warming reports that human activities are having a "discernible" influence on global climate and recommends that policymakers take steps to curb emissions of greenhouse gases.

Singer, S. Fred, ed., *Global Climate Change: Human and Natural Influences,* Paragon House, 1989.

This collection of essays on the impact of industrial development on climate includes pieces by editor Singer, who opposes policies to curb greenhouse gas emissions before further scientific evidence proves that human activities are in fact warming the planet.

Articles

Dowie, Mark, "A Sky Full of Holes," *The Nation,* July 8, 1996, pp. 11-16.

Negotiators for a climate change treaty look for guidance to the 1987 Montreal Protocol, which phased out the production of chlorofluorocarbons (CFCs), man-made gases that destroy the stratospheric ozone layer. New evidence suggests the treaty may have been less effective in closing the ozone hole than was once believed.

Keller, Kenneth H., "Unpackaging the Environment," *World Policy Journal,* fall 1996, pp. 11-23.

Global warming should be treated as an urgent problem and economic solutions found to help slow the current rise in greenhouse gas emissions from developing countries, writes Keller, a senior fellow at the Council on Foreign Relations.

Linden, Eugene, "Global Fever," *Time,* July 8, 1996, pp. 56-57.

Recent scientific studies are raining concern that global warming may spread deadly infectious diseases such as cholera, dengue fever and hantavirus by extending the tropical conditions in which they thrive.

"Reading the Patterns," *The Economist,* April 1, 1995, pp. 65-67.

While evidence is mounting that greenhouse gases are affecting global climate, its implications are uncertain. Fossil fuel burning releases both carbon dioxide, which heats the atmosphere, and sulfates, which appear to cool it.

"Turning Up the Heat," *Consumer Reports,* September 1996, pp. 38-44.

This review of the debate over global warming takes up the implications of climate change projected by the U.N. Intergovernmental Panel on Climate Change and steps that can be taken to curb greenhouse gas emissions.

Reports and Studies

Alliance to Save Energy, American Gas Association and Solar Energy Industries Association, An Alternative Energy Future, April 1992.

By replacing mandatory regulations with incentives to develop new technologies, the authors report, governments can help industry curb carbon dioxide emissions associated with fossil fuel use.

George C. Marshall Institute, *Are Human Activities Causing Global Warming?* 1996.

A research group that questions the consensus view of global warming claims that recent weather patterns show no sign of adverse effects and that policy-makers have up to 30 years to further their research before the greenhouse gas buildup will have a significant influence on climate.

Macdonald, Norman J., and Joseph P. Sobel, *Changing Weather? Facts and Fallacies About Climate Change and Weather Extremes,* Accu-Weather Inc., undated.

This report, compiled in the last two years, concludes that it is still unclear whether global warming would result in more intense or more frequent violent weather such as tornadoes, hurricanes, floods and droughts.

Montgomery, W. David, *Toward an Economically Rational Response to the Berlin Mandate,* Charles River Associates, July 1995.

Prepared for the Global Climate Coalition, the main lobby opposed to mandatory reductions in greenhouse gas emissions, this report calls on political leaders to conduct further research on the economic impacts of such measures.

World Resources Institute, United Nations Environment Programme, United Nations Development Programme and World Bank, *World Resources 1996-97,* Oxford University Press, 1966.

This joint report on global environmental trends contains a chapter that summarizes recent findings on climate change and U.N. efforts to produce a treaty to mitigate it.

The Next Step

Additional information from UMI's Newspaper & Periodical Abstracts database

Global Climate Change

Changnon, Stanley A., "State roles in the global climate change issue," *Bulletin of the American Meteorological Society,* February 1995, pp. 227-233.
Events in 1988 helped focus the attention of several states on the global climate change issue. By 1994, 22 states had enacted laws or regulations and/or established research programs addressing climate change.

Cowen, Robert C., "Global warming is real many scientists agree," *The Christian Science Monitor,* Oct. 10, 1995, p. 14.
Scientists are increasingly convinced that global warming is a reality in late 1995. Subtle changes in weather patterns which conform to predictions of improved computer climate simulations suggest that man-made climate changes are upon us.

Dawson, Bill, "Experts debate global warming's effect on tropical storm climate," *Houston Chronicle,* Oct. 22, 1995, p. A21.
The possible connection between global warming and the formation of hurricanes is examined. As of Oct. 1995, 18 tropical storms have been formed, with 10 reaching hurricane force.

Gray, Gerry, "A second look at global climate change," *American Forests,* summer 1996, pp. 22-23.
Findings of a recent study on the adverse effects of global warming on the world's ecosystems are discussed. The potential impact of climate change is being taken more seriously by policymakers and citizens alike.

McMichael, A. J., "Global climate change and health," *Lancet,* Sept. 23, 1995, p. 835.
Participants at the conference on the potential health impacts of global climate change, held in Washington, D.C., September 11-12, 1995, directed a considerable amount of their attention to the two most predictable indirect health impacts — changes in vector organism habitat and parasite transmissibility and in regional productivity of agriculture and fisheries.

Rubin, Barry M., and Mark D. Hilton, "Identifying the local economic development impacts of global climate change," *Economic Development Quarterly,* August 1996, pp. 262-279.
The need to evaluate and plan for the region-specific economic development impacts of potential global climate change is receiving increasing attention. Rubin and Hilton present a method for estimating such consequences and the results of exploratory research that applies this method to determining the employment impacts in a recreationally based region.

Sawyer, Kathy, and Gary Lee, "Global warming forecast is for slower rate than previously feared," *The Washington Post,* Oct. 25, 1995, p. A3.
Sea levels will rise and average global temperature will increase over the next century, but not as fast and not as high as was feared earlier, according to new estimates from two scientific organizations that have led the way in warning about the effect of future climate change.

Stevens, William K., "Blame global warming for the blizzard," *The New York Times,* Jan. 14, 1996, p. 4.
While it seems a paradox, some experts cite evidence suggesting that climatic changes associated with global warming are actually creating more severe snowstorms.

Toner, Mike, "Butterfly exodus: Global warming may be pushing species northward," *Atlanta Constitution,* Aug. 29, 1996, p. A1.
The apparent flight from global warming of the small Edith's checkerspot butterfly is giving West Coast scientists their first look at the kind of biological havoc that climate change may one day create in the world's ecosystems.

Global Warming

Allen, Scott, "Global warming debate joined," *Boston Globe,* Nov. 17, 1995, p. 20.
A handful of scientists with connections to the oil and coal industry are giving the public the false impression that global warming is not a serious threat, environmentalists asserted, as three such skeptics testified on the issue before Congress.

Anderson, John, "Why global warming matters to the Texas Gulf Coast," *Houston Chronicle,* Aug. 18, 1996, p. C4.
Anderson discusses the consequences for future generations and the quality of life on Earth of global warming, as well as the effects that rising sea levels will have on the Gulf Coast of Texas.

Brown, Paul, "Global warming divide deepens," *Guardian,* July 17, 1996, p. 11.
A speaker at the climate convention in Geneva, Switzerland, urged journalists not to listen to individual scientists whose theories had not been tested and whose motives appeared dubious concerning global warming. Man is dangerously altering the Earth's climate, the journalists were warned.

Davis, Robert E., "Don't worry about global warming — end is not near," *Houston Chronicle,* Sept. 22, 1996, p. C4.

Davis asserts that because the belief in apocalyptic greenhouse-related warming persists — despite what he called an almost total lack of hard evidence — some politicians and international policy-makers are determined to legislate.

"Getting serious about global warming," *St. Louis Post-Dispatch,* Aug. 4, 1996, p. B2.

An editorial notes the Clinton administration's announcement that it will seek binding targets for curbing fossil fuel burning in an effort to retard global warming and suggests that targets need to be set and plans made for how the targets are to be enforced among nations.

Goering, Laurie, "Global warming may bring more epidemics," *Chicago Tribune,* Feb. 13, 1996, p. 4.

Public health officials warn that subtle warming of the Earth's climate during the next 50 years may nearly double the number of malaria deaths worldwide, prompt more frequent outbreaks of cholera and put the U.S. at risk of epidemics of encephalitis and other infectious diseases.

Hertsgaard, Mark, "Who's afraid of global warming? Surprise! It's big business that's worried now," *The Washington Post,* Jan. 21, 1996, p. C1.

Hertsgaard comments that while global warming does not exist according to the oil and coal lobbies, the global insurance and banking industries are now coming to believe that their self-interest is incompatible with humanity continuing to pump 6 billion tons of heat-trapping greenhouse gases into the atmosphere every year.

Lee, Gary, "U.S. urges binding accord on global warming," *The Washington Post,* July 18, 1996, p. A3.

The Clinton administration announced July 17, 1996, that it is seeking the adoption of a binding agreement requiring the world's industrial nations to reduce the levels of industrial emissions that are contributing to global warming.

Lempert, Robert, and Michael Schlesinger, "A global warming middle ground," *Los Angeles Times,* Nov. 16, 1995, p. B9.

Lempert and Schlesinger discuss the inability of humans to predict how the Earth's climate will change in the future. Lempert and Schlesinger advocate an adaptive strategy in which humans carefully monitor the environment for changes and develop environmentally benign technologies.

"More than hot air needed in resisting global warming," *Los Angeles Times,* July 22, 1996, p. B4.

An editorial criticizes the U.S. for not naming the air pollution targets it has committed to address in an effort to halt global warming.

"Pact on global warming a step in the right direction," *Denver Post,* Aug. 10, 1996, p. B7.

An editorial discusses the Clinton administration's urging of all nations to accept a binding agreement to slow global warming.

Perlman, David, "New support for theory of global warming," *San Francisco Chronicle,* Sept. 12, 1996, p. A2.

New evidence linking the recent warming of the Pacific Ocean's surface waters with records of melting glaciers high in the Andes shows that temperatures in the tropics are higher now than they have been for thousands of years. Scientists say the study adds fresh confirmation that global warming is real.

Perlman, Michael, "Face up to global warming troubles," *Houston Chronicle,* Jan. 7, 1996, p. C5.

Perlman comments that the world community is in denial about the threat of global warming, and must turn to face the problem.

Sinisi, J. Sebastian, "Global warming solutions simple, many experts say," *Denver Post,* March 24, 1996, p. A31.

The world doesn't need expensive, grandiose projects to combat global warming, but it does need simple measures to slow the encroaching environmental problems, scientists agree. Some plans to combat global warming are discussed.

Snow, Tony, "Global warming plague looming? Wrong," *USA Today,* Feb. 19, 1996, p. A11.

Snow takes issue with Vice President Al Gore's warning that global warming will set off a plague of infectious disease, arguing that he generated a false sense of urgency about a dubious public-health problem and proposed to solve things by increasing the government's power to micromanage the economy.

Spotts, Peter N., "New global warming report: Don't panic, but let's take action," *The Christian Science Monitor,* Dec. 18, 1995, p. 3.

Global warming is discussed, including conclusions from a U.N.-sponsored report which will guide policymakers who are setting targets for gas emissions in the next century.

Tyson, Ann Scott, "A Kansas detective is hot on the trail of global warming," *The Christian Science Monitor,* Sept. 25, 1996, p. 1.

The Atmospheric Radiation Measurement Program, aimed at providing the missing link in scientists' knowledge of global warming, employs a wide variety of people in

Hillsboro, Kan., to monitor conditions and launch weather balloons.

Greenhouse Effect

"Atlanta, Georgia: Recycling reduces greenhouse effect," *Biocycle: Journal of Waste Recycling,* March 1996, p. 22.

A study by the Institute for Local Self-Reliance for the Environmental Protection Agency's Region IV in Atlanta indicates that recycling of construction and demolition debris significantly reduces the emissions of carbon dioxide by saving energy.

Bishop, Jerry E., "Long-ignored cycle in climate suggests worse greenhouse effect than thought," *The Wall Street Journal,* April 11, 1995, p. B5.

David J. Thomson, a researcher for AT&T Bell Labs, found that a long-ignored cycle in the Earth's temperatures suggests that burning oil, natural gas and coal may be having a greater effect on the climate than previously thought.

Gribbin, John, and Mary Gribbin, "The greenhouse effect," *New Scientist,* July 6, 1996, pp. SS1-SS4.

While life on Earth depends on it, the greenhouse effect has also boosted global temperatures alarmingly, and vast climatic changes are predicted. The greenhouse effect is discussed.

Jones, Owen Bennett, "Insurance firms join alarm over global warming," *Guardian,* July 10, 1996, p. 13.

A group of 58 international insurance companies on July 9, 1996, called on governments of industrialized nations to achieve "early substantial reductions" in greenhouse gas emissions.

Miles, Henry, "Greenhouse effect," *Architectural Review,* May 1995, pp. 50-56.

An office and workshop complex in the small town of Ettlingen, Germany, perfectly illustrates the country's concern with the imaginative, beneficial use of ambient energy to improve the well-being of building inhabitants. The design of the structure is described.

Morgan, Dan, "Strengthened U.S. commitment lights a fire under global warming debate," *The Washington Post,* Sept. 13, 1996, p. A4.

A U.S. pledge to seek binding limits on releases of "greenhouse gases" after the year 2000 has produced an angry response from the domestic coal, oil and utility industries.

Nissani, Moti, "The greenhouse effect: An interdisciplinary perspective," *Population & Environment,* July 1996, pp. 459-489.

Claims that the greenhouse controversy is legitimate, that it involves hard choices, that it is value-laden, or that it cannot be resolved by disinterested analysis, are tragically mistaken, Nissani writes. Given the stakes of the greenhouse debate, concerned scholars and citizens ought to understand this issue.

Pittock, A. Barrie, "Climate change and world food supply," *Environment,* November 1995, pp. 25-30.

The security of the world's food supply is one of the key goals of reducing greenhouse gas emissions, but this is fraught with difficulties. Documents pertinent to this issue are reviewed and discussed.

Reiss, Bob, "Fran's early warning — The curfew life: A hint of what global warming has in store," *The Washington Post,* Sept. 22, 1996, p. C2.

Reiss describes life under curfew in Wrightsville Beach, N.C., following the disaster of Hurricane Fran and comments on the conclusion of a panel of prominent climatologists that the greenhouse effect is changing how people live.

"Sign of global warming cited," *Boston Globe,* Sept. 21, 1995, p. 16.

The U.S. is getting more rain in heavy downpours now than early in the century, a possible sign of global warming from greenhouse gases.

Stevens, William K., "Science Times: In rain and temperature data, new signs of global warming," *The New York Times,* Sept. 26, 1995, p. C4.

In a new study of weather trends in the U.S., China, Australia and the former USSR, scientists have turned up further evidence that some of the predicted effects of greenhouse gases on the world's climate are being felt.

Stocker, Carol, "The greenhouse effect," *Boston Globe,* Dec. 7, 1995, p. A1.

Stocker comments on Saugus, Mass., resident Nancy Potter's greenhouse, which was a sunroom in her home that she converted and she and her husband now call their retirement room.

Toner, Mike, "Past rapid shifts in climate cast new light on greenhouse effect," *Atlanta Journal Constitution,* Feb. 18, 1995, p. A6.

Dramatic swings in the world's climate can come and go with surprising swiftness, sometimes within the course of a single lifetime, according to evidence from the Greenland icecap and from the floor of the North Atlantic Ocean presented by researchers at the American Association for the Advancement of Science meeting in Atlanta.

Victor, David G., and Julian E. Salt, "From Rio to Berlin: Managing climate change," *Environment,* December 1994, pp. 6-15.

On March 28, 1995, the nations that have ratified the Framework Convention on Climate Change will meet in Berlin to resolve issues and establish procedures. The

FCCC is focusing on the targets and timetables for controlling emissions of greenhouse gases and technological and financial transfers. The preparations for the Berlin meeting are discussed.

Weiss, Rick, "The sun also braises: Renewable energy advocates offer invention that can harness and ease global warming," *The Washington Post,* Oct. 7, 1996, p. A3.
As advocates of solar cooking know, the greenhouse effect can be harnessed in a way that benefits the environment. All it takes is some cardboard, aluminum foil and a plastic bag.

Montreal Protocol

Smith, Gar, "Blowing holes in the Montreal Protocol," *Earth Island Journal,* fall 1995, p. 13.
According to an Ozone Action report entitled "Deadly Complacency," the Montreal Protocol has been rendered ineffective by waivers that extend the CFC-production rights of DuPont, LaRoche, Allied Signal and Elf Atochem.

Solomon, Susan, and John S. Daniel, "Impact of the Montreal protocol and its amendments on the rate of change of global radiative forcing," *Climatic Change,* January 1996, pp. 7-17.
Increases in chlorinated and brominated halocarbons are believed to be responsible for the depletion of stratospheric ozone. A study found that the increasing atmospheric concentrations of ozone-depleting halocarbons has led to a negative forcing of the climate system.

U.N. Intergovernmental Panel on Climate Change

Abbott, Alison, "Climate change panel to remain main source of advice," *Nature,* April 13, 1995, pp. 584-585.
The Intergovernmental Panel on Climate Change is to continue as the major scientific advisory body to governments that have signed the United Nations Climate Change Convention.

Cushman, John H. Jr., "Report Says Global Warming Poses Threat to Public Health," *The New York Times,* July 8, 1996, p. A2.
As international negotiations on global warming resume in July 1996, U.N. health and environmental agencies are warning of serious threats to public health if actions to reduce climate change come too slowly. In a report to be issued during the talks that resume on July 8, scientists from U.N. agencies warn that warming due to air pollution "could have a wide range of impacts on human health, most of which would be adverse."

"Heating up the climate change debate," *Environment,* January 1996, pp. 22-23.
The economic and social implications of climate change that were addressed at the U.N.'s Intergovernmental Panel on Climate Change's plenary session are discussed. Delegates' conclusion that the costs required to fight greenhouse gas emissions may exceed estimates of damage due to climate change was, in effect, canceled.

Masood, Ehsan, and Ayala Ochert, "U.N. climate change report turns up the heat," *Nature,* Nov. 9, 1995, p. 119.
Unless a dispute between the authors can be settled, a key chapter of the U.N. report on the economic dimensions of climate changes may be missing. The disputed chapter forms part of an overall study from the Intergovernmental Panel on Climate Change.

Mathews, Jessica, "Global warming: No longer in doubt," *The Washington Post,* Dec. 26, 1995, p. A23.
Mathews notes the Intergovernmental Panel on Climate Change's declaration that global warming was, indeed, underway.

"Report on global warming makes dire predictions," *The Wall Street Journal,* Oct. 25, 1995, p. B4.
A report issued on Oct. 24, 1995, from the Intragovernmental Panel on Climate Change foresees global warming bringing an increase in diseases, dramatic shifts in forests and consequences for industries from insurance to tourism.

Santer, Benjamin D., "Global warming critics, chill out," *The Wall Street Journal,* July 23, 1996, p. A23.
Santer responds to the July 11, 1996, Letters to the Editor "Coverup in the Greenhouse." Santer defends his role as lead author of a key chapter in a recent report by the Intergovernmental Panel on Climate Change.

"The long view on global warming," *Boston Globe,* July 30, 1996, p. A12.
An editorial comments on the early world health warning that scientists, environmentalists and some government officials sought to convey at the U.N. Intergovernmental Panel on Climate Change.

Back Issues

Great Research on Current Issues Starts Right Here...Recent topics covered by The CQ Researcher are listed below. Before May 1991, reports were published under the name of Editorial Research Reports.

APRIL 1995
Abortion Clinic Protests
Dieting and Health
Combating AIDS
Rethinking Affirmative Action

MAY 1995
Assisted Suicide Controversy
Overhauling Social Security
Learning to Read
Mandatory Sentencing

JUNE 1995
Combating Infectious Disease
Property Rights
Repetitive Stress Injuries
Regulating the Internet

JULY 1995
War Crimes
Highway Safety
Combating Terrorism
Preventing Teen Drug Use

AUGUST 1995
Job Stress
Organ Transplants
United Nations at 50
Advances in Cancer Research

SEPTEMBER 1995
Catholic Church in the U.S.
Northern Ireland Cease-Fire
High School Sports
Teaching History

OCTOBER 1995
Quebec's Future
Revitalizing the Cities
Networking the Classroom
Indoor Air Pollution

NOVEMBER 1995
The Working Poor
The Jury System
Sex, Violence and the Media
Police Misconduct

DECEMBER 1995
Teens and Tobacco
Gene Therapy's Future
Global Water Shortages
Third-Party Prospects

JANUARY 1996
Emergency Medicine
Punishing Sex Offenders
Bilingual Education
Helping the Homeless

FEBRUARY 1996
Reforming the CIA
Campaign Finance Reform
Academic Politics
Getting Into College

MARCH 1996
The British Monarchy
Preventing Juvenile Crime
Tax Reform
Pursuing the Paranormal

APRIL 1996
Centennial Olympic Games
Managed Care
Protecting Endangered Species
New Military Culture

MAY 1996
Russia's Political Future
Marriage and Divorce
Year-Round Schools
Taiwan, China and the U.S.

JUNE 1996
Rethinking NAFTA
First Ladies
Teaching Values
Labor Movement's Future

JULY 1996
Recovered-Memory Debate
Native Americans' Future
Crackdown on Sexual Harassment
Attack on Public Schools

AUGUST 1996
Fighting Over Animal Rights
Privatizing Government Services
Child Labor and Sweatshops
Cleaning Up Hazardous Wastes

SEPTEMBER 1996
Gambling Under Attack
The States and Federalism
Civic Journalism
Reassessing Foreign Aid

OCTOBER 1996
Political Consultants
Insurance Fraud
Rethinking School Integration
Parental Rights

Back issues are available for $5.00 (subscribers) or $8.00 (non-subscribers). Quantity discounts apply to orders over ten. To order, call Congressional Quarterly Customer Service at (202) 887-8621.

Binders are available for $18.00. To order call 1-800-638-1710. Please refer to stock number 648.

Future Topics

- ***Clashing Over Copyright***
- ***Consumer Debt***
- ***Running Washington, D.C.***

THE CQ Researcher

PUBLISHED BY CONGRESSIONAL QUARTERLY INC.

Clashing Over Copyright

Is intellectual property safe in the Internet Age?

The information superhighway has reached a crossroads. Internet enthusiasts accustomed to near-limitless freedoms are growing worried about government and industry attempts to introduce commerce into cyberspace. Film studios, record companies and book publishers are demanding greater legal protections for copyright holders. But Clinton administration and congressional proposals to thwart copyright infringements have met resistance from academics and librarians concerned about longtime protections for "fair use" in scholarship and journalism. Telecommunications companies and on-line service providers, meanwhile, are wary of being held liable for copyright violations committed by their users.

INSIDE THIS ISSUE

CQ Nov. 8, 1996 • Volume 6, No. 42 • Pages 985-1008

Formerly Editorial Research Reports

Clashing Over Copyright

COVER: BARBARA SASSA-DANIELS

THE CQ Researcher

Nov. 8, 1996
Volume 6, No. 42

Bibliographic records and abstracts included in The Next Step section of this publication are from UMI's Newspaper and Periodical Abstracts database, and are used with permission.

The CQ Researcher (ISSN 1056-2036). Formerly Editorial Research Reports. Published weekly (48 times per year, not printed March 1, May 31, Aug. 30, Nov. 29) by Congressional Quarterly Inc., 1414 22nd St., N.W., Washington, D.C. 20037. Annual subscription rate for libraries, businesses and government is $319. Additional rates furnished upon request. Periodicals postage paid at Washington, D.C. POSTMASTER: Send address changes to The CQ Researcher, 1414 22nd St., N.W., Washington, D.C. 20037.

Clashing Over Copyright

BY CHARLES S. CLARK

THE ISSUES

"Dilbert," Scott Adams' popular comic strip about workplace absurdities, can be browsed for free on the World Wide Web. The cartoonist's syndicate, United Media, presents the strips surrounded by paid advertisements that finance its Internet operation.

But Dan S. Wallach, a puckish Princeton University graduate student, decided last January that the Dilbert page layout was "really lame." "I thought I could do better," he explains. So he created his own "Dilbert Hack Page," pointing fans to a Web site where Adams' strip was displayed *without* the advertisements. "I was pretty sure I could avoid copyright problems by [electronically] linking directly to their images," Wallach says.

It didn't take long for United Media to hit him with a cease-and-desist letter. "United Media intellectual property cannot be used . . . without the express, written consent . . . ," went the familiar language.

Wallach posted word of the warning on the Internet. Soon he had received hundreds of comments via e-mail, most of them supportive. An Internet "user group" of lawyers began debating his situation on-line. One attorney in particular, Joseph Lester of Bloomington, Minn., had advised him that even though the World Wide Web gave him "implied license" to create his hack page, the right was probably revoked by the cease-and-desist letter. Lester called the case "a cutting-edge issue of law where there is no clear-cut answer." Eventually, Wallach reluctantly dismantled his Dilbert page.

The techno-revolution surrounding the Internet has brought countless benefits of instant, global and low-cost communication. But it has also brought multiple uncertainties — concerns over privacy, indecency, educational inequity and shifting job markets as well as the anxieties of coping with new gadgetry and vocabularies. [1]

Vexing as these issues are, none is as hazy and divisive as the age-old problem of copyright. It lies at the heart of the ambitious vision many hold for the Internet, now used by an estimated 35 million-48 million people with usage growing by as much as 70 percent a year. [2] One such vision is "the celestial jukebox," in the phrase popularized by Stanford University law Professor Paul Goldstein: "Whether it takes the form of a technology-packed satellite orbiting thousands of miles above the Earth or remains entirely Earth-bound, linked by cable, fiber optics and telephone wires, the celestial jukebox will give millions of people access to a vast range of films, sound recordings and printed material, awaiting only a subscriber's electronic command for it to pop up on his television or computer screen." [3]

The chief obstacle at present is the fact that on the Internet, everyone from the corporate CEO to the aspiring novelist to the schoolchild can be a global publisher. Most of these amateurs, of course, are untrained in the subtleties of copyright law, and lack access (or the desire to gain access) to the legal advice that is routinely available to traditional publishers. [4]

Indeed, "information wants to be free" has become a common slogan in the Internet's world community of "Netheads." On the question of copyright, many of them share the views of newsletter editor and futurist Esther Dyson, the chairwoman of the San Francisco-based Electronic Frontier Foundation, who recently predicted that writers in the future will have to get used to giving their work away and earning income through giving speeches.

"As the Web expands, the big effect will be that intellectual property is likely to lose a lot of its market value [because there] is much less cost associated with distribution of content," Dyson said recently. Yet "the idea of copyright will still be important," she hastened to add, "because it is the law and it is moral. . . . [And] even if I get no royalties, I want to make sure that my work isn't dumbed down and sold under someone else's name." [5]

To the large industry of what in the Internet age are called "content providers" — the film, television, recording, publishing and computer software industries — the opportunities offered by digital technology seem outweighed by the threat of piracy. Copyright holders in the past year lost $18 billion to $20 billion worldwide in stolen books, video games and tests, according to Kenneth Kay, executive director of the Creative Incentive Coalition, an industry alliance.

Book publisher E.P. Dutton last year had to crack down on an Iowa State University academic who thought it would be fun to upload the text and illustrations for the still-copyrighted children's classics featuring Winnie the Pooh. The Recording Industry Association of America this March had to sue the Send-a-Song Corp. of Vienna, Va., because it was offering customers

Estimated Trade Losses Due to Piracy

Pirated movies, software and other copyrighted materials worth more than $6 billion were sold in 1995 in the 32 countries being monitored by the International Intellectual Property Alliance for theft of U.S. intellectual property. More than half the losses were in China, Russia and Italy.

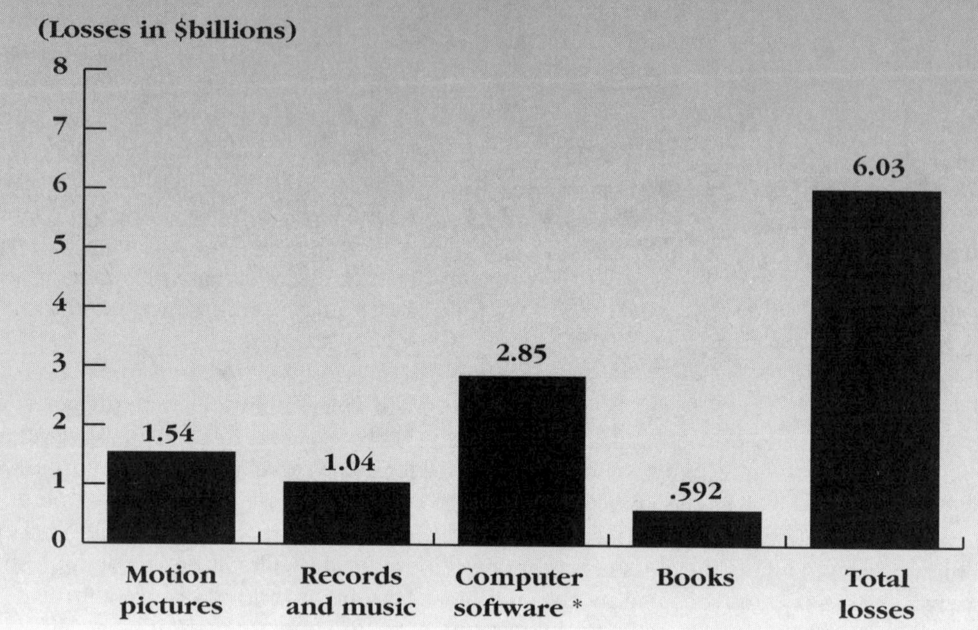

** Includes entertainment but not business software.*

Sources: Recording Industry Association of America; International Intellectual Property Alliance

an "aural greeting card," a computerized phone call that plays the song of the sender's choice without licensing from the copyright owners.

The ease with which computer software can be duplicated has raised alarms among creators. "It would be quite possible," writes attorney William J. Cook, "for a million-dollar computer program to be released on Monday, improperly obtained on Tuesday, uploaded to the Internet on Wednesday, become shareware by Thursday and worthless freeware by Friday." [6]

The film industry feels threatened by new machinery such as the pending digital video disk, which facilitates the transmission of pristine-quality movies. (*See story, p. 998.*) "Each time a new device transmits [the current hit movie] 'The First Wives Club,' that will be one less person who will pay to go to the theater," says Richard Taylor, director of public affairs at the Motion Picture Association of America (MPAA). "If you can't protect what you own, you don't really own anything."

In response to such concerns, the Clinton administration, following two years of public hearings, in September 1995, released a white paper calling for new protections to be added to the nation's copyright law, last revised substantively in 1976. The potential of the National Information Infrastructure, as the administration has dubbed the proposed information superhighway, "will not be realized if the education, information and entertainment products protected by intellectual property laws are not protected effectively," it said. "Creators and other owners of intellectual property rights will not be willing to put their interests at risk." [7] (*See "At Issue," p. 1001.*)

The paper's recommendations were introduced as legislation in the House in September 1995 by Carlos J. Moorhead, R-Calif., and Patricia Schroeder, D-Colo., and in the Senate by Orrin G. Hatch, R-Utah, and Patrick J. Leahy, D-Vt. The bills included proposals to codify court decisions concerning liability for copyright infringements, a ban on devices designed to circumvent copyright protection and a prohibition against tampering with copyright notices and other copyright information attached to electronic data. Most dramatically, observers noted, the legislation interpreted existing copyright law as defining the making of a single copy of an electronic file — such as downloading a copyrighted file simply to browse through it — a potential copyright infringement unless the user first pays a fee.

Critics pounced. A group of 100 law professors sent Congress and the administration a critique protesting the plan as "a radical measure which has negative implications for . . . public, journalistic and scholarly access to information, for free speech and for privacy."

"Why would the Clinton administration want to transform the emerging information superhighway into a publisher-dominated toll road?" asked Cornell Law School visiting Professor Pamela Samuelson. "The most plausible explanation is a simple one: campaign contributions." [8]

Though the legislation died in the

final days of the 104th Congress, it is likely to reappear next year, and the bulk of its provisions will be discussed at diplomatic talks in Geneva this December on an international copyright treaty for the digital age (*see p. 1002*).

Copyright law — called by one professor the area of the law "closest to theology" — has forever been an anguishing puzzle. "Even the most basic issue of copyright — the nature of copyright — remains a matter of dispute," writes former Rep. Robert W. Kastenmeier, D-Wis. "The question is whether copyright is a natural-law property right of authors or society's grant of a limited statutory monopoly." [9]

Since the dawn of the printing press, a nonstop succession of copyright controversies have played out, erupting in modern times over photocopying, the taping of TV shows, reselling of magazine articles (*see story, p. 998*) and even friends singing around the campfire. (*See story, p. 996.*)

Rival camps have formed. One group leans toward maximalist copyright protection to promote incentives for original creators. Another gives priority to looser enforcement that emphasizes the benefits of sharing the world's knowledge with society overall. The rise of media conglomerates in recent years has meant that some interests have a foot in both camps.

Given the complexity of the law, it is not surprising that "intellectual property law" has emerged as one of the nation's fastest-growing legal specialities. [10]

As government and industry "begin to lay down the rules of the road for the information superhighway," as Sen. Hatch puts it, Internet habitués may find their cyberspace "ground" shifting under them. "When computers are seized because they contain allegedly stolen intellectual property, or the security of anonymous 'remailers' is pierced by police," warns a writer for the hip magazine *Wired,* "the days of the Internet as a cozy, private, intellectual cocktail party are over." [11]

As industry representatives, librarians and lawmakers continue the copyright debate, here are some key questions being asked:

Will new proposals to protect copyright inhibit "fair use?"

Fair use has been a vital component of copyright law since 1976. Yet it now bids to be the undoing of any consensus on copyright in the digital age. The law's fair-use language sketches out the exceptions to strict copyright ownership, the implied permissions that allow libraries to lend books, journalists and scholars to quote from others' works, book reviewers to criticize authors' works and parodists to take off on an original's language or melody.

In determining that a use is fair, the following factors must be considered:

- the purpose and character of the use (whether it is commercial or nonprofit);
- the nature of the copyrighted materials (whether, say, they are for entertainment or social benefit);
- the amount of the total work used (quoting three lines may not seem like much, unless it's half an entire poem); and
- the effect of the use on the market (will it deprive the original author of sales?).

Since work on the Clinton white paper began, an informal group of some 50-70 librarians, educators, publishers and authors has been meeting periodically as the Conference on Fair Use (CONFU) trying to agree on guidelines for fair use in the 1990s. Under discussion are such issues as whether libraries can offer electronic interlibrary loans and make archival copies for preservation. Also being debated is whether universities can use an electronic version of the old practice of making customized collections of published works available "on reserve" for multiple students at the campus library. Equally at issue is whether universities can adapt published works to offer computerized long-distance learning without compensating publishers of the material.

In the more high-tech areas, the debate centers on whether permiting electronic links from one Web site to another is a fair use, and whether computer software designers can dismantle their competitors' products — a process called "decompiling" — in order to design new programs that build upon or improve it.

All such acts can be done technologically; the dispute centers on whether they should be done without paying a fee to avoid a lawsuit for copyright infringement. The white paper makes clear the Clinton position that most computer transactions require making a copy of someone else's copyrighted work, and that under existing law, this is a potential infringement.

"When a work is placed into a computer, whether on a disk, diskette, ROM [read-only memory] or other storage device or in RAM [random-access memory] for more than a very brief period, a copy is made," the white paper says, citing the legislative history of the 1976 copyright law revisions. "Whenever a digitized file is 'uploaded' from a user's computer to a bulletin board system or other server, a copy is made." The paper asserts that copyright owners have the right to control "abridgement, adaptation, translation, revision or other 'transformation' of their works." [12]

Such a view is one-sided in favor of the copyright holders, says James Boyle, a law professor at American University who recently authored *Shamans, Software and Spleens: Law and the Construction of the Information Society.* "It is true that we have to give creators an incentive, but the mistake of the white paper is to see the Internet as nothing but a giant copying machine for which they have to jack up the level of copyright protection. Yes, the Net makes copying easier, but it also makes distribution

What Is a Copyright?

Copyright grants authors control over their expression of ideas, leaving the ideas themselves as public property. Nowadays, copyright is automatic whether or not a work is registered with the Library of Congress' Copyright Office (though registration is recommended because it is required before legal action can commence). To be copyrighted, a work need not be unique or totally original.

This contrasts with a patent, the government-registered description of an invented product or process, which by definition must be unique, as proven by an extensive and costly search through previously registered patents. The public filing of detailed patents, believed to aid other inventors in building on them, stands in contrast to the practice of keeping trade secrets (such as the formula for Coca-Cola), which protect the owner's proprietary interests but discourage the shared knowledge that might help future inventors. A registered trademark, to round out the list, is a distinguishing word or device, the use of which is controlled by the owner.

and advertising easier. It is easier for them to think of uses that are potential infringements than it is to think of money-making uses."

The classic case is the VCR, he adds. Hollywood originally felt threatened by the prospect of home-taping and took legal action to try and block it, but now videos make up a vital part of studio revenues.

Rather than boosting fair use as a vital exercise of First Amendment freedoms that enrich society's cultures, the white paper, in Boyle's view, portrays acts such as quoting from others' works and browsing on the Internet as "mere holes in the copyright regime, when actually they are functional parts of it." Court decisions on fair use are actually a mixed picture, he adds, yet the white paper focuses on the restrictive decisions (such as the one case declaring a computer's RAM copy a copyright infringement), reducing the looser rulings to footnotes.

Congress deliberately made the fair-use language flexible to accommodate changing needs, according to Kenneth Crews, a professor of law and library sciences at the University of Indiana-Purdue University combined campus in Indianapolis. "But just as it is important to understand the rights of owners, it is important to understand the rights of fair use and the rights of the public as spelled out in the Constitution's language promoting the progress of useful arts and sciences."

Crews, who directs the Copyright Management Center, a policy group, has participated in the slow-going CONFU talks about fair use. He recently published proposed guidelines for handling the issue of professors making customized selections of publishers' copyrighted materials available for lending at college libraries. It suggests that electronic reserve copies be used only; they would be for educational use only; the copies would never include an entire issue of a journal; they would be kept on reserve for only a short period of time; the professor would get permission if the copies were reused in future semesters; and all reserve room copies would retain the formal copyright notice. [13]

"I took a middle-of-the-road position, and I've been hit by both sides," Crews says, citing academics who object to the single-semester limit and publishers who say the practice denies them a new sales opportunity. "We're proposing to make the copies available at one location, not mounting it on a Web site for the whole world." he says. "But just because you call something a new product and say that fees could be charged doesn't make it not a fair use."

In fact, Crews adds, fair use could play a big role in helping publishers decide whether there really is a new market for certain compilations. "If industry were ready to offer the items at reasonable prices," he says, "thousands of institutions would prefer buying them to copying them."

What academics call an electronic reserve room is more aptly called "an electronically facilitated course pack," argues Carol A. Risher, vice president for copyright and new technologies at the Association of American Publishers. "You have to get permission because this represents significant income to publishers," she says, citing court precedent. Publishers such as McGraw-Hill are already offering reserve-room-type products such as on-demand printing and customized collections of individual chapters of books, she says.

Many academic librarians, however, are rejecting the licensing terms publishers are offering with their electronic products as too restrictive and commercial for an educational setting. [14] And they're concerned that publishers' wishes to keep tabs on electronic projects, and to charge usage fees, may interfere with academic freedom. "We should not be looking over the shoulders of faculty and students in a way that would chill research and educational initiatives inappropriately," said John C. Vaughn, executive officer of the Association of American Universities. [15]

The digital revolution, says Risher, has prompted a change in the whole nature of publishing. "Business models are changing, and we're responding to the library and academic communities. The bottom line is that the digital world is different from the print world, and you can't input wholesale practices developed in a photocopying environment into an electronic environment. Publishers, after all, are in business to make materials available to the public," she adds. But groups such as on-line computer services and librarians want an exemption from the new proposals on copyright that would allow them to transmit electronically. "They want a law that gives them an absolute right to access any material, even though they don't have that right even now."

Bruce A. Lehman, the assistant Commerce secretary and commissioner of patents and trademarks, who oversaw the white paper, says that the notion that libraries should have an exemption from copyright for such things as interlibrary loans is unacceptable. "If publishers simply gave away their wares to libraries, they wouldn't be able to stay in business," he says. "What is really going on here is an undefined fear of inadequate resources. Libraries and educational institutions are being savaged by a right-wing political attack [in Congress] to take away their funding." The Clinton administration is "working overtime to get it back," he adds. But in the meantime, "the country can't afford to do without a vital and thriving information-creating sector."

Content providers are not reassured by the example of the VCR, dismissing the suggestion that the film industry's profitable adaptation to video technology could be applied to the digital revolution. "We benefited from the VCR, but the same flame also burned us," says Taylor of the MPAA. "We currently lose billions of dollars to piracy from analog video bootlegs, and digital will be an even larger flame." Taylor suggests picturing the Internet as "a shopping mall. The shopkeepers have no problem with you browsing, just like teasers on the Internet encourage looking around. But if customers could just walk in a store and take a whole item, the shops wouldn't tolerate it."

Even so, skeptics point out that many of the problems raised by technology can be solved by technology, too. Christine Owens, the Washington representative for Sun Microsystems Inc., in Mountain View, Calif., points to her company's "firewall" encryption products as examples of ways to safeguard electronic intellectual property without requiring major changes in copyright law.

Computer designers value what's called "interoperability," the design of new hardware and software in ways that permit them to link up with products already owned by consumers. This often requires aspiring inventors to make copies of a competitor's product, "much like you can buy a Chrysler Minivan and take it apart in your garage to see how it works," Owens says. The quirk with computers, however, is that such research requires duplicating the copyrighted software, which gives an opening to the copyright holder to cry infringement. "The reason we're successful as a high-tech and entertainment culture is that the country's [intellectual property] system is very dynamic," she says. "In Silicon Valley, intellectual property is protected, but not in ways that block research and information."

As for the World Wide Web users' conundrum over whether it is permissible to link to other people's Web sites, many Net users profess not to see why it's a problem. "Hyperlinks are a cornerstone of the operation of the Web," says Edward J. Black, president of the Computer & Communications Industry Association. "I refer people to, say, the Smithsonian [Web site] for information all the time."

Others say the solution may lie in the honor system. Risher points out that proper "netiquette" dictates that people first obtain permission before linking to other sites, in case the other site is overloaded with visitors.

Should on-line service providers be liable for their users' copyright infringements?

All players in the copyright debate took note in June when a district court panel in Pennsylvania issued a ruling that sent shock waves all over the Internet. The court struck down as unconstitutional key provisions of the Communications Decency Act, passed last year by Congress in an effort to prevent underage Internet users from being exposed to pornography and other "adult" material. [16]

Though the Justice Department quickly announced it was appealing the decision, a collective sigh of relief swept through the community of commercial on-line service providers and library system administrators. Many had been fearful that the law would have opened them up to prosecution for abuses committed by the users of their Internet services — in areas such as indecency, sexual harassment, hate crimes and copyright. (Some 11 states have passed similar laws.)

What is new about crime in the Internet age are the enforcement problems — whom to hold responsible for crimes on a global medium in which the service providers — much like the telephone companies — are for the most part unaware of the nature of the information speeding across their wires. Some drafts of the federal copyright legislation that bogged down this year called for a $1,000 fine on on-line service providers for unintentional violations and a $250,000 fine and up to three years in prison for willful violations. Also discussed were proposals for cooperative monitoring, in which the copyright holder would notify an on-line provider when a theft had taken place, and the provider would attempt to block access to the stolen material and remove it from the Internet. [17]

Some commercial on-line groups question the motives of those seeking

Writers Organize to Reap . . .

How convenient it is. Just sit at your keyboard, type in the subject of your computer search, sit back and watch as hundreds of articles from magazine and newspaper indexes are offered to your desktop printer.

But such convenience is seen by a growing number of writers as "information highway robbery." These authors want a piece of the action. Their efforts to organize and collect a share of this new industry's profits represent one of the many conundrums of the information revolution.

Over the past decade, electronic retrieval systems have swept the country's libraries, newsrooms and home computers. To stock them, publishers of magazines and newspaper op-ed pages have been selling secondary rights for their articles to electronic databases such as InfoTrac, Lexis-Nexis and the Magazine Index.

Much of the content in general-interest magazines and newspaper op-ed pages is written by non-staff free-lancers, who are paid a fixed sum on publication. The publishers argue that the purchased work is thereafter theirs to showcase as part of their publication — and to market and profit from as best they can.

"The arrangement between a publisher and a free-lancer is one of contract," says Ken Richieri, assistant general counsel at *The New York Times*. "It's a deal, whatever we agree on. It's like I can sell you a car for $3,000 or for $10,000. There is no right or wrong to it."

In 1993, however, a group of writers cried foul. The National Writers Union, since its founding in 1983, has assembled a roster of professionals obscure and famous that has included novelists Erica Jong, Dan Wakefield, Marilyn French and Isabel Allende, as well as journalists Jessica Mitford and Ben Bagdikian. From its offices in Oakland, Calif., and New York City, the group filed a lawsuit against the Times and six other publishers and database operators.

"We want the law changed," says Irvin Muchnick, the union's assistant director. "At issue is the meaning of the phrase 'North American print rights.' The publishers are grabbing rights and asking questions later. They want to turn creators into 'workers for hire,' so-called 'content providers,' which would not be good for the diversity of American culture. Their [contract] language claims second and third rights to every medium that might be invented into the future, which is like the claim-jumping that occurred during the Gold Rush of the Old West."

As the court case nears its resolution, Muchnick says publishers have been busy "changing contract language to spell all this out, which is an implied recognition that they're on the losing side." [1]

"Writers don't want to stifle spontaneity or block the democratization of digital media," Muchnick continues. "We're not trying to stop Joe Blow from transmitting a copy of an article to one or 10 or a hundred of his friends, which is a high-tech version of showing it around the water cooler. What we do want is to share in this emerging new industry. And they only way we can challenge the big publishers is through organizing."

The Times' Richieri says the lawsuit is actually narrow in scope, affecting only the question of whether a publisher, absent any agreement on other uses for a freelancer's piece, may sell the work on-line as part of that original collective work, a provision that is already part of the copyright statute.

"We don't have to get a writer's permission to include his piece in the Times on microfilm because that's a different version of the same work," he says. "But nor are we saying that we can use it any way we want, as in an anthology or a book. What is under challenge is the resale to a Nexis-type publisher."

Publishers also argue that paying customized royalties to

on-line liability. Owens of Sun Microsystems says that commercial companies are being targeted because they have greater financial resources. In fact, much of the Internet service is provided by universities and non-profit research communities, or small companies with maybe five employees, she says.

Liability concerns are particularly threatening to academic and public libraries, which are driven not only by the cost considerations of commercial providers, but also by their mission of serving the public. "Libraries are among the strongest advocates of good copyright law and are constantly informing users of the rules of the road," says Prudence S. Adler, assistant executive director of the Association of Research Libraries. "But with on-line provider liability, we could be forced to monitor our users, which violates user confidentiality and privacy. And on Web sites, we'd have to know hour by hour what has been posted, since by nature they are constantly being updated."

Indeed, Fred Heath, library director at Texas A&M University in College Station, says it would be nearly impossible for his staff of 200 to police the 111,000 electronic accounts offered to his student community. (Texas A&M is currently addressing issues of on-line indecency and copyright with a "complaint-driven" system of case-by-case investigation and mediation. It currently has 1,000 complaints pending.)

Complicating the equation, says Professor Boyle, is the fact that copyright law imposes "strict liability, meaning that ignorance that one is making an unauthorized copy is no excuse. The law, however, is not self-applying," he adds. The government

. . . a Piece of the Internet Action

free-lance writers is an administrative nightmare. "The Times in the past year may have had, say, 15 people reporting from Bosnia," Richieri says. "Seven of them may be on staff, and eight are free-lance. Some might have sent us items that are four sentences long. There's not going to be different rules for different types of articles. From the Times' point of view, it's important that we be able to treat any body of Times work as a discrete unit. So that we can use it, for example, on the Web with historical material on Bosnia."

As for authors' rights in the greater scheme of things, Richieri agrees that "yes, the next Thomas Wolfe may someday find that he sold his first novel too cheaply. But all but a tiny fraction of the short-term factual pieces we're talking about are not going to be valuable in five years. Most don't appreciate with age. We have to consider the likely needs of our readers."

The struggling band of writers does have some reason for hope. In a related case involving the publishing industry's Copyright Clearance Center, the 8th U.S. Circuit Court of Appeals in 1994 ruled that companies wishing to photocopy texts whose copyright is owned by others cannot cite the impracticality of contacting the owner if a structure has been set up to calculate and collect licensing fees.

The writers union has set up just such a structure, called the Publications Rights Clearinghouse. In March it won a key agreement with one of the largest on-line databases, UnCover Co., based in Denver and owned by Knight-Ridder Information Inc. UnCover controls electronic and photocopying rights to 17,000 popular magazines and journals. Under its agreement with the clearinghouse, customers who order a previously published article for $11.50 give 30 percent of it to the original author. Muchnick sees a possible alternative to such pay-per-use pricing in an annual flat fee, or "collective licensing."

Last March, *The Atlantic Monthly* settled a case brought by Rutgers University historian H. Bruce Franklin, author of a 1992 book on U.S. soldiers missing in action. Franklin had objected when the magazine made previously published excerpts from the book available on the Internet.

A competing writers organization, meanwhile, is also getting into the act. The Author's Registry, launched in May 1995 in New York City, announced in February "a historic breakthrough for writers." *Harpers' Magazine* had agreed to use the registry to award its writers a share of the profits from electronic resale by using the pricing and billing apparatus organized by the registry. The service is run by the Authors' Guild, the American Society of Journalists and Authors, the Association of Authors' Representatives and the Dramatists Guild.

Whether other publishers come on board will depend largely on the writers union's court case. "There's a whole range of publishers," says Author's Registry spokesman Terry King. "Some say we don't owe you authors anything. Others say, just help us do the bookkeeping, and there will be payouts."

This fall, a group of free-lance writers in Eugene, Ore., plans to create an Internet Web site called "Bylines," on which writers can showcase their work and collect pay-per-read fees from readers. Entrepreneur and University of Oregon writing Professor Jon Franklin says the site will offer long pieces not usually found in national magazines and will keep each piece available for years.

The Washington Post, meanwhile, made clear this year it would keep all proceeds from Internet use of its free-lancers' work, including that of popular and longtime lawn and gardening columnist Jack Eden. When Eden protested and the paper refused to budge, he promptly transferred his column to a competing suburban paper.

[1] The case, *Tasini et al v. The New York Times et al,* may be decided this fall in the 2nd District Court in New York.

---

and industry could decide that mere service providers, as is the case with photocopying shops, in general are not responsible for crimes committed without their knowledge by customers using their services.

Risher of the publishers' group disagrees. "There are levels of standards for liability," she says. Some providers, such as the telephone companies in their traditional mode, are just pipelines. But some modern-day telephone companies and other on-line information providers offer customers "forms of monitoring as well as chat rooms with moderators, menus and pointers * such as 'interesting things for your child.' "

"They can exercise varying degrees of control and knowledge of the materials moving through their pipelines." Risher continues. "It used to be that Xerox machines had to bear notices stating that it's a federal offense to copy U.S. currency, etc. But nowadays some providers don't seem willing to accept shared responsibility, even for voluntarily taking [objectionable] things off-line when they are brought to their attention. Many of them like to say, 'I'm just a common carrier,' but then they allow their on-line users to point to so-called neat stuff you can get for free because it's illegal."

Clinton official Lehman says: "It is not reasonable for these companies to have zero liability for what goes through their networks. We will continue to seek a balance between the legitimate interests of the business and user communities," he says. But much of the complaints about the threat of liability

* Pointers are optional electronic links from one Web site to another.

for on-line providers is really "just different interest groups jockeying for position." Telecommunications companies, for example, want to be considered as nothing more than "mere conduits" in order to "seek advantage in competition with content providers."

Larry Clinton, associate vice president of the U.S. Telephone Association, notes that while regional phone companies have substantial business interests in Internet access, "We also own substantial amounts of pretty valuable copyrights in software and directories, and we don't want them pirated." He is confident that a consensus will be achieved for a balanced approach that would exempt mere conduits, go after willful copyright infringers and create a "reasonable, practical law" under which on-line providers would cooperate in addressing a violation once they are given notice.

It can be done, but it won't be easy, says the computer association's Black. "There are all kinds of gradations as you travel down the path from being a mere conduit to being a willful and intentional copyright infringer." Some proposals for monitoring seem doable conceptually, he says, but there's a difference in the potential liability between a service that truly edits material and one that simply scans for a list of words. "Somebody who designs some software that simply identifies all restaurant reviews on the Web could be called an infringer by the original writer of a review," he notes. "The new copyright law has to be well-targeted to the problems and not so overly broad that it causes collateral impact. There needs to be the same balance that has produced the success of the current system."

This fall, the Software Publishers Association sent hundreds of on-line services a proposed "Code of Conduct." It asked them to sign it and agree to monitor their traffic and report any incidences of software piracy. Jill Lesser, an attorney with America Online, says the reaction from most on-line providers has been "fear." Only the small companies that can't afford lawyers are signing the code, she says. For America Online, taking such responsibilities would mean that it would have to monitor millions of customer e-mail accounts and cut off links with foreign Web sites.

"We could no longer be a viable commercial service," Lesser says. ■

BACKGROUND

Publisher vs. Author

Perhaps the earliest dispute over what today is called copyright unfolded in sixth-century Ireland. The man who would become known as Saint Columbia had handcopied a manuscript of the Latin Psalter from an original owned by one Finnian of Druim Finn. The owner objected, and the matter was brought before the king, who ruled in the owner's favor. "As the calf belongs to the cow, so the copy belongs to its book," his reasoning went. Saint Columbia reacted by waging war, eventually winning the right to keep his hard-earned copy. (It is on display today in Dublin. [18])

At the time Gutenberg invented the printing press in the 15th century, copyright was understood in a context radically different from that of modern times: It was less a right of an individual author to control his work than a right — bestowed by the government on a select few publishers — to produce copies of a work. Hence in England in 1476, William Caxton was granted an exclusive printing license for all the nation's books, and any produced by others would be burned. By 1557, that right was awarded to the Royal Stationer's Company, which published the only authorized editions of the Bible and *The ABC Book,* England's first children's school book. [19]

It was the goal of Britain's notorious Star Chamber judicial body to see that all books were free of heresy, both religious and political. In 1637, the Star Chamber decreed that "no person or persons whatsouer shall presume to print, or cause to bee printed, either in the parts beyond the Seas, or in this Realme, any seditious, scismaticall, or offensive Bookes or Pamphlets, to the scandall of Religion, or the Church, or the Government, or Governours of the Church or State." [20]

Such censorship later would be blasted by writers such as John Milton, author of *Areopagitica,* an argument defending freedom of the press, who nonetheless was sympathetic to the need for publishers to reap profits.

By the late 17th century, monopolistic licensing of printers was eased in England, paving the way for the world's first true copyright law, the Statute of Anne of 1711. It gave publishers and, as subcontractors, the authors, a 21-year term of copyright for their work. It marked the first time since the print revolution that the concept of the public domain was invoked. [21]

Efforts to assert the rights of authors were mostly drowned out by business interests. In a famous English court case from 1769, an attorney summarized a common argument: "What property can a man have in ideas? Whilst he keeps them to himself they are his own, when he publishes them they are his no longer. If I take water from the ocean, it is mine, if I pour it back it is mine no longer." [22]

The American Model

When English law was adopted by the newborn United States, the Founding Fathers emphasized the notion that society deserved the benefits of shared knowledge. Thomas Jefferson, a pro-

Continued on p. 996

Chronology

1700s-1800s

Since the nation's first days, copyright protection is held important.

August 1787
Constitution includes clause for copyright and inventors' patents, making U.S. the first nation with such constitutional protections.

May 1790
Congress enacts first copyright law, with extendable 14-year renewal period.

1831
First general revision of copyright law protects sheet music and extends first term, with option for another 14 years.

1870
Second general revision of copyright law protects works of art and creates Copyright Office in Capitol.

1887
Europeans create Berne copyright convention emphasizing authors' rights.

1897
Copyright Office moves to Library of Congress. Copyright law amended to protect against unauthorized public musical performance.

1900-1950s

World communications become increasingly interlinked.

1909
Third revision of copyright law extends second-term renewal term from 14 to 28 years.

1912
Copyright law amended to protect motion pictures.

1955
International copyright convention takes effect in U.S.

1960s-1980s

Photocopiers, office and personal computers and digital technologies raise new copyright issues.

1974
U.S. becomes party to 1971 revision of Universal Copyright Convention; President Gerald R. Ford creates commission to determine copyright policy on photocopying.

1976
Copyright law rewritten to include fair use provisions and updates for new technology.

1980
Copyright law amended to cover computer programs.

1981
Educators and Hollywood interests agree on guidelines for home taping of television shows for educational purposes.

March 1, 1989
U.S. adheres to international Berne Convention for Protection of Literary and Artistic Works.

1990s ***Electronic copyright disputes intensify.***

February 1993
Clinton administration Commerce Department forms information infrastructure task force.

1993
In *Playboy v. Frena*, a lower court rules that *Playboy* magazine can prevent its pictures from being uploaded on an unauthorized computer bulletin board service.

Sept. 5, 1995
Commerce Department task force releases white paper on intellectual property; legislation introduced in House and Senate based on recommendations.

November 1995
Senate and House Judiciary Committees hold joint hearings on copyright; President Clinton signs Digital Performance Right in Sound Recordings Act.

Feb. 7-9, 1996
Rep. Carlos J. Moorhead, R-Calif., holds House Judiciary Subcommittee hearings on implementing the Clinton administration's white paper.

June 12, 1996
In a victory for advocates of Internet freedom, a three-judge District Court panel blocks portions of the Communications Decency Act that threatened to criminalize on-line dissemination of indecent material.

Aug. 4, 1996
Church of Scientology settles out of court with Netcom On-Line Communications Services after electronic bulletin board subscriber put copyrighted church texts on the Internet.

December 1996
World Intellectual Property Organization is scheduled to hold a conference in Geneva to amend Berne Convention.

Girl Scouts Heading Off to Camp . . .

When Girl Scouts gather at campfires to sing such standbys as "Puff the Magic Dragon," copyright law is no doubt as far from their thoughts as "a land called Hanalee" is from reality. Yet last summer, these paragons of innocence were thrust unwittingly into a lobbying battle over rights of ownership and usage of the nation's popular songs.

"Guess who's charging the Girl Scouts for singing around a campfire?" screamed a newspaper advertisement taken out by the National Restaurant Association. "Girl Scouts Threatened by ASCAP? Absurd!" countered an ad from the American Society of Composers, Authors and Publishers.

On the surface, the issue appeared an almost surreal clash over propriety in the everyday act of companions joining in a favorite song. Underneath, it was only the most visible skirmish in an ongoing legal feud that puts millions of dollars at stake.

It began a couple of years ago when New York City-based ASCAP, an 82-year-old licensing body representing 68,000 songwriters and other music copyright holders, approached the American Camping Association, a Martinsville, Ind., group that represents 2,200 summer camps. Camps whose programs make use of copyrighted songs, ASCAP said, would henceforth have to pay an annual licensing fee to compensate the songs' creators.

The camp group checked with a lawyer, recalls Executive Vice President John Miller, and was stunned to learn that ASCAP was correct. Not a single one of the typical camp's traditional uses of songs — including singing round the campfire — appeared exempt from copyright protection. "ASCAP's people had a clear picture of what happens at camps from sending their own kids to camp, so this was not just an off-the-wall fishing expedition," Miller says.

ASCAP was clearly intending to require fees from both for-profit and nonprofit camps, as evidenced by their proposed fee differential, he adds, and the fact that the ACA represents numerous nonprofit camps such as those sponsored by 4H Clubs, the YMCA, the Boy Scouts and various religious denominations.

Last January, ASCAP reached agreement with the camping association to begin collecting the fees. Some 300 camps agreed to pay $257 annually for rights to ASCAP songs (a total of $90,000), while a smaller number of camps, those that meet only two weeks a year, agreed to pay $77 each.

ASCAP, meanwhile, was facing action on another front. For years, music licensing bodies — which in addition to ASCAP include New York City-based Broadcast Music Inc. (BMI) and the French-run corporation SESAC — have pressed for the right to collect licensing fees from restaurants, bars and other small businesses that play music on radios or televisions for their customers. ASCAP currently collects some $436 million a year in fees primarily from TV, cable and radio broadcasters, including an estimated $65 million from bars, skating rinks, restaurants and airlines. [1]

The National Restaurant Association, in alliance with 30 small-business groups that include health clubs, dentists, offices and racetracks, has been seeking to head off such fees by pushing "Fairness in Music Licensing" bills at the state and federal levels.

Now the law in 20 states, these bills establish "codes of conduct" that permit small businesses to use TV and radio as incidental entertainment for customers without fear of visits from traveling agents from the "music police," as the restaurant group calls ASCAP and the other licensing bodies. The bills require the licensing bodies to provide businesses with a list of songs they own (ASCAP alone controls 4 million songs), but would not relieve businesses of paying for rights to music from compact discs or for copyrighted music performed by live musicians.

Katy McGregor, the restaurant association's director of state relations, argues that "music that's being played on a small business' radio or TV has already been paid for, often multiple times." The proposals to begin charging, which her group calls "double dipping," show that "the system is broke and needs fixing." She says the restaurant owners hope for passage next year of some version of the federal bills banning such fees introduced in the 104th Congress by Rep. F. James Sensenbrenner Jr., R-Wis., and Sens. Larry E. Craig, R-Idaho, and Hank Brown, R-Colo.

ASCAP, of course, sees it differently. Marilyn Bergman, chairman of ASCAP's board, as well as the lyricist for such hits as "The Way We Were" and "You Don't Bring Me Flowers," argues that "restaurants pay for every other service: flowers on the tables, peanuts on the bar, all of which contribute to the atmosphere that makes people come, stay and order another drink. For songwriters, it's a separate stream of revenue that is very important." The wealthy superstar songwriters who are familiar to the public are only "a small tip of an iceberg," she says. "The number of songwriters who are lucky enough to support themselves

Continued from p. 994

lific writer and inventor who presided over the granting of America's first patents, argued that when someone took his idea, he himself was left intact, "as he who lights his taper at mine receives light without darkening me." [23]

But it was also clear that society's interests were best met by providing creators an incentive. At the Constitutional Convention in 1787, New Jersey delegate David Brearly introduced the concept expressed in Article 1, that Congress should have the power "to Promote the Progress of Science and the Useful Arts, by securing for limited Times to Authors and Inventors the

. . . Get Dragged Into a Copyright War

full time is only a handful."

ASCAP is fond of pointing out that its claim of fees for "incidental" music was supported as far back as 1917. In a Supreme Court case originally brought by ASCAP founder Victor Herbert against the Stanley Restaurant, Justice Oliver Wendell Holmes wrote: "It is true that music is not the sole object, but neither is the food, which probably could be got cheaper elsewhere. The object is a repast in surroundings that to people having limited powers of concentration or disliking rival noise give a luxurious pleasure not to be had from eating a silent meal." [2]

It was against the backdrop of this licensing dispute that the Girl Scouts got dragged into the fray. Nearly a year after the restaurant association began a public relations push for "fairness in music licensing" — and about five months after ASCAP negotiated fees with summer camps — *Bloomberg Business News* reported that Girl Scout camps were being charged for singing around the campfire. The restaurant association the same day began using the theme in a series of ads in such Washington publications as *Roll Call* and *The Hill,* just as Congress was taking up the music-licensing legislation.

The national press weighed in after a front-page feature appeared in *The Wall Street Journal* ridiculing the situation at a Lafayette, Calif., Girl Scout camp at which little girls were forced to learn to dance the "Macarena" without using any music. Counselors spoke of a fear of being sued for leading the campers in singing "Edelweiss," and "This Land Is Your Land." ASCAP's chief executive officer was quoted threatening camps with litigation if they don't pay fees. "When in doubt, don't sing," a counselor said. [3]

Barraged by queries, ASCAP took out its own ads to try to set the record straight. The group had never intended to sue the Girl Scouts, its ads said. A misunderstanding occurred when ASCAP began collecting licensing fees from camps and the camping association's lists were less than clear as to which of the affected camps were run by the Girl Scouts. ASCAP, in fact, has long been a supporter of scouting, as evidenced in the fact that ASCAP member Irving Berlin in 1940 donated all future royalties to his classic "God Bless America" to Boy Scout and Girl Scout councils in New York City.

ASCAP quickly refunded the fees it had collected from 16 Girl Scout camps.

ASCAP does have some flexibility in interpreting the law, says Bergman. "We would prefer a less strict, more generous interpretation because the more kids are exposed to educational music the better." What is unusual in this arrangement with the American Camping Association, she explains, "is that this is the first time a third party has been involved in fee collection."

Singing around the campfire without paying fees is definitely legal, ASCAP spokesmen say. What is not legal is hiring a hall, engaging a band and charging admission to hear copyrighted music if the promoter has not paid fees. "We look at each situation," says Bergman. "Some camps are clearly commercial."

All parties agree that the copyright law specifies that fees are chargeable only if songs are sung when "a substantial number of persons outside of a normal circle of a family and its social acquaintances [are] gathered."

The camping association's Miller acknowledges that there are legitimate rights of songwriters and composers who deserve to be compensated. But the rights to some songs require getting permission from more than one licensing body, and the licensing agreement has forced some camps to question whether they can afford it, he says. "We are trying to hold ASCAP's feet to the fire on giving children at camp access to all life's experiences, so they can appreciate music from a young age."

The issue is so messy that songwriters themselves can have mixed feelings. Cathy Fink, a folksinger in Silver Spring, Md., who records with partner Marcy Marxer, says: "I'm an ASCAP member, and their job is to protect songwriters. But there's something scary about this royalty structure. Unlike at a music club, there's no real commercial gain for the Girl Scouts. And sitting around the campfire and singing is already a dying art, which is why it has been my job to encourage it."

And what of the Girl Scouts themselves? Judy Welage, a spokesperson for the New York City-based Girl Scouts of the USA, says the whole flap "was blown way out of proportion. We are confident that ASCAP never intended to penalize us. We always cooperate with copyright laws on those rare occasions when we pay for a commercial event." On Sept. 5, the Girl Scouts released a statement declaring that, "this unfortunate situation is resolved."

[1] *The New York Times,* April 15, 1995.

[2] Quoted in commentary by Marilyn Bergman, *Billboard,* Oct. 21, 1995.

[3] Quoted in Lisa Bannon, "The Birds May Sing, But Campers Can't Unless They Pay Up," *The Wall Street Journal,* August 21, 1996.

Exclusive Right to their Respective Writings and Discoveries."

This language — which bore the influence of James Madison — established for all the 13 original states a principle that all but one (Delaware) had already adopted. This was due largely to Noah Webster, the famous dictionary creator, who beginning in 1783 had persuaded legislatures to pass a copyright law to protect his interest in sales of his classic spelling book *Grammatical Institute of the English Language.* (It later sold millions of copies.)

What was unique about this part of the U.S. Constitution, says Michael Novak, a scholar of social and politi-

Are Electronic 'License Plates' the Answer?

"The answer to the machine is the machine," says a European publishing executive wrestling with the issue of copyright protection. [1]

Digital technology — the conversion of all electronic data to 0 and 1 symbols for easy transmission — has facilitated the quick, inexpensive and high-quality reproductions that can be threatening to copyright owners.

Book and magazine publishers are wary of the electronic scanners used increasingly by libraries and home businesses to convert printed texts to computer files without laborious keyboarding. Such "optical character recognition" devices are becoming more compact and less expensive, and they can produce documents in color. Retailing for as low as $1,000 from such companies as Visioneer Inc. of Palo Alto, Calif., some 1.6 million of them were shipped in 1995, a fourth of them to private homes, according to InfoTrends Research Group. [2]

For libraries tackling large bibliographic projects that even include sound recordings, Minolta offers a $16,000 scanner that one reviewer says is "making it increasingly attractive for libraries to make their unique print resources available to a wider audience." [3]

The film and recording industries are watching carefully for the pending market debut of the digital videodisk, a storage device that holds 26 times as much data as current compact discs with quality twice as clear as current videocassette recorders. It would greatly improve the ease and quality with which movies and recordings could be transmitted over the Internet. Manufacturers and Hollywood lawyers reached an agreement on guidelines in October after the film industry demanded that anti-piracy devices be included on all digital videodisks and players, set to sell for $500-$1,000. [4]

In response to such inventions, the Association of American Publishers in September announced it was setting up a team to develop a kind of "electronic license plate" that would assign each publisher a digital number and permit it to count and subsequently bill the users of material for which the publisher owns the copyright. Such identifiers would also help users know immediately where to find the material they seek to purchase.

And recently, some long-awaited accounting tools for measuring borrowings and collecting fees over the Internet were made available by a Reston, Va.-based company called CyberCash. Its "Cybercoin" system allows users of the Netscape Internet browsing tool to be billed for downloaded electronic items costing as little as 25 cents. [5]

Copyright holders seeking protection are excited about a product being offered by IBM in cooperation with the Xerox Corp. The "cryptolope" is a program creating a sort of electronic envelope in which a document can be transmitted over the Internet, but which can be read only by someone equipped with a prearranged decoder key.

Protection for copyrighted visual images is available with "SiteShield," for sale for $499 by Maximized Software of Irvine, Calif. It permits vendors to allow potential on-line buyers to view low-resolution, approval copies of photos or works of arts, but intercepts the images if they are downloaded to unauthorized computers.

To combat plagiarism, a program called the Stanford Copy Analysis Mechanism (SCAM) is now electronically scanning Internet traffic seeking a list of key words that might indicate what the industry legalistically calls text infringements. [6]

---

[1] Quoted in *The Economist,* July 27, 1996. p. 59.

[2] Cited in *The Wall Street Journal,* May 20, 1996.

[3] See *American Libraries,* March 1996, p. 71.

[4] Philip E. Ross, "Cops versus Robbers in Cyberspace," *Forbes,* Sept. 9, 1996, p. 134. See also *Los Angeles Times,* June 3, 1996.

[5] See Michael Krantz, "Cyber Vending Machine," *Time,* Oct.7, 1996, p. 78.

[6] See *The Washington Post,* May 10, 1996.

cal studies at the American Enterprise Institute, was the clarity with which it specified copyright as a right for individuals, not a favor granted by the state. "Washington and Adams knew they would blaze a trail for other nations," he adds.

In 1790, Congress enacted the first U.S. copyright law, "an act for the encouragement of learning, by securing the copies of maps, charts and books, to authors and proprietors of such copies, during the times therein mentioned." (At the time this was 14 years.) The first U.S copyright was awarded to John Barry's *The Philadelphia Spelling Book,* which was registered in the U.S. District Court of Pennsylvania.

Six decades later, the "natural rights" implied in the Constitution's copyright clause would be celebrated by Abraham Lincoln, who himself had filed a patent (for a buoy vessel to aid ships in navigating shoals). In an 1859 speech in Jacksonville, Ill., Lincoln described the clause as adding "the fuel of interest to the fire of invention." [24]

19th-Century Adjustments

Over the following century, intellectual progress and case law would subject copyright law to continuing amendments. As distinctions arose between copying someone's work and making use of it, adjustments were made to extend copyright to music, in 1802, to engravings in 1831, to dramas in 1856 and to photographs in 1865.

What would become the fair use

concept was first discussed as "justifiable use," "fair abridgement" and "fair and reasonable criticism" in an 1843 Supreme Court case, *Folsom v. Marsh*. It involved a book called *Life of Washington in the Form of an Autobiography* for which the author, the Rev. Charles W. Upham, had taken 353 pages of his 866 pages from letters and documents contained in a 7,000-page *Writings of President Washington* edited by Jared Sparks. The court ruled in favor of Sparks.

Writing for the majority, Justice Joseph Story used pioneering words that would be cited when fair use was codified in law in 1976. Story, in his 1843 ruling, also noted the frustrating reality that copyright and patent disputes, more than any other type, are nearer "to what may be called the metaphysics of the law where the distinctions are, or at least may be very subtile [sic], and sometimes evanescent." [25]

Another vagary of the period was the fact that copyright law seemed to stop at the border, which made for frequent disputes over rights to foreign works. In 1853, a German won a U.S. court ruling allowing him to translate and publish *Uncle Tom's Cabin* without permission from the author, Harriet Beecher Stowe. This was around the time that British novelist Charles Dickens came to America to talk up reform of copyright law after finding that his own works were being freely pirated in American magazines.

Though Congress in 1870 amended the law to cover translations, the United States in the mid-1880s would decline to join the Berne Convention, the international copyright treaty negotiated in Paris. With participation by such prominent authors as Victor Hugo, Berne put much greater emphasis on "the natural rights of authors" than American thinking permitted.

What the 1870 law accomplished was creation of a system of registering copyrighted works with a newly created office in the Library of Congress. The system was the brainchild of Thorvald Solberg, the register of copyrights, who had more than one motive: The law's new requirement that copies of published works be sent to the Library of Congress became a source of free acquisitions for the nation's collection.

Impact of Technology

By the turn of the century, Thorvald was leading a charge for a new revision of copyright law. An 1897 amendment had recently permitted songwriters to collect fees for public performances of their music, and there was pressure for even further expansion of authors' benefits. (In a decision that today seems odd, the Supreme Court in 1908 rejected the infringement complaint of a composer who was seeking redress from a manufacturer of music rolls for player-pianos, who had transcribed and marketed his music without permission.)

President Theodore Roosevelt was also demanding action, making remarks in 1905 that were remarkably similar to rhetoric in today's debates: "Our copyright laws urgently need revision. They are imperfect in definition, confused and inconsistent in expression; they omit provision for many articles, which under modern reproductive processes, are entitled to protection; they impose hardships upon the copyright proprietor which are not essential to the fair practices of the public; they are difficult for the courts to interpret and impossible for the Copyright Office to administer to the public." [26]

The major revision in copyright law in 1909 made copyright more proprietary and less regulatory. It established the doctrine of work-for-hire, under which the copyright for work created by employees belongs to their employer. And it expanded the list of protected media to include statuettes, bookends, clocks, lamps and even salt and pepper shakers. "Compare these copyrightable works," write two historians, "with newspapers — for which one court in the 19th century had actually refused to recognize copyright protection on the grounds that they did not contribute to learning." [27]

The march of new technologies raised new copyright issues. In 1912, the newfangled "motion pictures" were included under copyright law, creating a plethora of issues of free speech that persist today. In the 1960s, a researcher preparing a book on film history would complain that his requests for permission to reproduce movie stills was met with a fee demand of $200 per shot, which would have added up to more than the author's entire profits for the book. [28] A researcher preparing a book on the 1963 assassination of President John F. Kennedy had to go to court against Time Inc., which claimed unsuccessfully that it controlled the still shots from the famous 8 mm. film of the killing, which *Life* magazine had purchased from amateur photographer Abraham Zapruder. [29]

A notable invention of the 1960s — the photocopying machine — raised multiple copyright challenges. In 1963, Baltimore medical publisher William Passano began a lawsuit to block the National Library of Medicine from photocopying thousands of pages from his journals to lend to patrons rather than buying extra copies from him. He said he was willing to spend $50 to collect $10 "on a matter of principle." [30] He lost his case, but not until 1973.

The following year President Gerald R. Ford appointed a National Commission on New Technological Uses of Copyrighted Works to prepare guidelines on photocopying policy. It devised the "rule of fives" compromise, requiring copiers to compensate a publisher if they made more than five copies per year within five years. Soon after that, the publishing industry organized the Copyright Clearance Center in Danvers, Mass., which collects royalties on behalf of publishers when someone requests permission to make significant numbers of photocopies. (In recent years, the service has gone on-line, and after years of struggling with poor enforcement and bookkeeping troubles, it is finally making a profit.)

Such long-simmering disputes were the reason the next revision of the copyright act was 20 years in the making. When Ford finally signed it in October 1976, it codified the principles of fair use; expanded copyrightable works to include pantomime and choreography; extended the copyright term to the author's life plus 50 years (non-renewable); and declared that displaying the copyright symbol was no longer required for a work to be protected.

As the Clinton white paper argues, the 1976 act was written with a '90s-style understanding that technological changes had "generated new industries and new methods for the reproduction and dissemination of copyrighted works, and the business relations between authors and users [had] evolved new patterns." It also specified some things that are not copyrightable: titles, names, short phrases, slogans, "utilitarian elements of industrial designs, familiar symbols and designs, simple geometrical shapes, mere variations in typographic ornamentation, letter or coloring; and common works considered public property, such as standard calendars, height and weight charts and tape measures and rulers." [31] ■

CURRENT SITUATION

Court Cases

The elusive nature of copyright continued to keep courts busy during the 1980s and into the '90s. Reclusive author J.D. Salinger in 1987 successfully blocked a biographer from publishing 44 of his personal letters, prompting Congress to pass an amendment saying that unpublished works can still be subjected to fair use.

In another case, the rights of parodists to fair use were bolstered in a 1994 case brought unsuccessfully by the Acuff-Rose Music Inc., owners of the copyright to Roy Orbison's '60s hit "Oh, Pretty Woman," against Luther Campbell, lead singer of the rap group 2 Live Crew, which had converted the lyrics into a raunchy parody.

But the majority of copyright headlines nowadays concern the Internet. Unauthorized Netheads have uploaded the text of Douglas Adams' popular 1980 book, *Hitchhiker's Guide to the Galaxy*. Elvis Presley fans have drawn the wrath of the King's estate for putting snippets of "Hound Dog" and "Blue Suede Shoes" on the Web. In June, ABC television closed down an area of its Tape Traders' Central site on America Online, which used the Net to promote sales of bootleg concert tapes. [32]

Last summer, the Church of Scientology settled out of court with Netcom On-Line Communications Services in a well-publicized case in which a former church member posted the Church's "sacred" (and copyrighted) texts on an electronic bulletin board, suggesting, at least, that on-line providers could be liable for infringements, even if they were unintentional. [33]

Legislative Solutions

The copyright legislation that died with the 104th Congress spawned several industry alliances. Pressing for a new crackdown on copyright violations was the raison d'être of the Creative Incentive Coalition, representing publishers, newspapers, motion picture studios, the recording industry, software companies and television studios, including IBM, Microsoft, Viacom and Time-Warner.

Seeking a more permissive, go-slow approach to revising the law is the Digital Future Coalition, comprised of such groups as the Association of Research Libraries, the American Council of Learned Societies, the National School Boards Association, the National Writers Union and the Consumer Federation of America. A third group, organized to resist copyright liability for on-line service providers, is the Ad Hoc Copyright Coalition, representing on-line service providers and national and regional telephone companies.

Representatives of all three groups gathered with members of Congress last winter under the auspices of Rep. Robert W. Goodlatte, R-Va., but consensus proved elusive.

Dealing With Pirates

At the meeting organized by Goodlatte, participants discussed the all-important question of on-line liability, as well as proposals in the Clinton administration's white paper to crack down on people who tamper with electronic copyright management data and ban "black box" equipment, or new programs designed to circumvent copyright protective devices.

Critics of the ban warn that such well-intended policies may stifle legitimate innovations. "We don't disagree that there are problems with piracy," says the computer association's Black. "But the provisions are too sweeping. Every computer is potentially an infringement device because every computer can be used for math calculation. A lock pick can be used as a burglar's tool, but that doesn't mean we want to prevent a legitimate locksmith or the police from using one. The focus needs to be on behavior and people, not tools."

Clinton official Lehman says the ban on black boxes is "nothing new, just a fundamental effort at protecting privacy. But within this culture of anarchy on the Internet, there are some

Continued on p. 1002

At Issue:

Do copyright holders need new protections in the digital era?

yes

THE CLINTON ADMINISTRATION
FROM "INTELLECTUAL PROPERTY AND THE NATIONAL INFORMATION INFRASTRUCTURE: THE REPORT OF THE WORKING GROUP ON INTELLECTUAL PROPERTY RIGHTS," SEPTEMBER 1995.

Some assert that copyright protection should be reduced in the National Information Infrastructure (NII) environment. The public wants information to be free and unencumbered on the NII, it is argued, and the law should reflect the public interest.

Without doubt, this is a valid concern. Information per se should not be protected by copyright law — nor is it. Facts and ideas from any work of authorship may be freely copied and distributed; the Copyright Act expressly excludes such information from the scope of the protection it accords.

The copyright law should also serve the public interest — and it does. While, at first blush, it may appear to be in the public interest to reduce the protection granted works and to allow unfettered use by the public, such an analysis is incomplete. Protection of works of authorship provides the stimulus for creativity, thus leading to the availability of works of literature, culture, art and entertainment that the public desires and that form the backbone of our economy and political discourse. . . .

Others assert that technological advances justify reduced protection. Since computer networks now make unauthorized reproduction, adaptation, distribution and other uses of protected works so incredibly easy, it is argued, the law should legitimize those uses or face widespread flouting. This argument is not valid. Technology makes many things possible. Computer networks can be and have been used [to commit acts] prohibited by law. Simply because a thing is possible does not mean that it should be condoned.

Finally, there are those who argue that intellectual property laws of any country are inapplicable to works . . . in "Cyberspace," a sovereignty unto itself that should be self-governed by its inhabitants, individuals who, it is suggested, will rely on their own ethics — or "netiquette" — to determine what uses of works, if any, are improper.

[T]his argument relies on the fantasy that users of the Internet, for instance, are somehow transported to "chat rooms" and other locations such as virtual libraries. While such conceptualization helps to put in material terms what is considered rather abstract, activity on the Internet takes place neither in outer space nor in parallel, virtual locations. Satellite, broadcast, fax and telephone transmissions have not been thought to be outside the jurisdiction of the nations from which or to which they are sent. . . . Further, such a legal free-for-all would transform the Global Information Infrastructure into a veritable copyright Dodge City. As enticing as this concept may seem to some users, it would hardly encourage creators to enter its confines.

no

JAMES BOYLE
Professor of law, American University
FROM *THE WASHINGTON TIMES*, NOV. 14, 1995.

What if the ground rules for the information society were written and no one paid any attention? What if they were bad? Given the current frenzy of articles about the information superhighway . . . this scenario is almost impossible to believe. But the ground rules have been written, almost no one noticed and they are bad. . . .

[In September 1995], the Clinton administration released its white paper on intellectual property on the Internet. . . .

The public could be forgiven for thinking that nothing significant was happening. The report itself says it is just a "minor readjustment" of the law. In fact, the white paper is an astoundingly radical measure which makes reading a document on the screen of your Web browser a copyright violation, cuts those who cannot afford to "license" information off from the information highway and dramatically restricts the "fair use" of copyrighted material. . . .

The promise of the information highway — universal access, rapid, free exchange of information, the promotion of technological innovation, free speech and personal privacy — would be replaced by its exact opposite. And all of this is being done in the name of "saving" the Internet, as if it weren't growing exponentially right now, largely because it isn't currently stunted by protectionist rules like these. . . .

[I]ntellectual property is unfamiliar territory for most people, and so it's easy for a smart lawyer to make arguments about "property rights" that sound reasonable when applied to something like owning your own sneakers, but which are ridiculous in the realm of copyright and patent.

Intellectual property rights are limited monopolies conferred in order to produce present and future public benefits. For the purposes of producing those benefits, the "limitations" on the right — like the fact that all of us are allowed to make "fair use" of copyrighted material for news reporting or educational purposes, or that programmers can "decompile" another company's computer program so as to produce better innovations themselves — are just as important as the grant of the right itself. It's the implicit quid pro quo of intellectual property; we will give you this extremely valuable legal monopoly, backed with state power and enforced through the courts (and by the FBI). In return, we will design the contours of your right so as to encourage a variety of socially valuable uses.

The white paper's strategy is to talk as though the rights of copyright holders were absolute and thus to squeeze most of the limitations on those rights out of existence. [The Clinton administration] wants to give copyright holders the "quid" while claiming that the "quo" is a tax, or a forced subsidy. Only the unfamiliarity of intellectual property conceals the ludicrousness of the argument.

Continued from p. 1000

people who don't like copyright. They're using this issue to reduce 200 years of evolving copyright law."

As for proposals to beef up protection of copyright notices, Crews of the University of Indiana points out that much of the information contained in copyright notices is inaccurate. People who don't own copyrights claim they do, he says, and notices such as the familiar "No part of this book may be reproduced" often violate fair use.

The Clinton white paper has reversed some long-held assumptions, he says. "We've gotten to the point where the assumption is that if there's no notice, we must assume something is copyrighted," he says.

The 104th Congress also considered legislation to extend all terms of copyright by 20 years. And the Senate Judiciary Committee held a hearing in September on a plan introduced by Sen. Hatch to create a new government corporation, the Intellectual Property Organization. Combining the Library of Congress' Copyright Office with the Commerce Department's Patent and Trademark Office, the new agency was intended to streamline bureaucracy and accelerate the patent application process. It, too, died with the 104th Congress, but not until the opposition weighed in against the provision to move the Copyright Office.

Librarian of Congress James Billington warned that his collection would be out the roughly 500,000 free books that come with copyright registrations yearly. And Register of Copyrights Marybeth Peters said the public would be deprived of her staff's perspective on balancing rights of copyright owners with the educational and cultural needs of society. [34]

World Conference

Although this year's copyright legislation stalled, the Clinton administration still plans to proceed with long-planned treaty negotiations in Geneva in December under the auspices of the World Intellectual Property Organization, which administers the Berne Protocol for 155 nations. [35]

Though the touchy issue of on-line service provider liability has been removed from the American agenda, most of the other unresolved issues will be acted upon in Geneva. American University's Boyle calls the move "an end run," an effort by the administration and many of the content-providing companies to grab overseas what they can't get domestically and then to use the international treaty as leverage in Congress. Sen. Hatch has written a letter to the Geneva negotiators asking them to avoid signing any treaty that implements the Clinton white paper precisely because it would threaten Senate ratification.

Lehman says the treaty will go forward as part of a "long-scheduled, transparent process" in which all interests will be consulted in the hope of arriving at "the best synthesis of overall U.S. interests." But he is puzzled by his critics' "bizarre notion" that international negotiations require that all domestic issues be unanimous, pointing to opposition from President Clinton's own party to the recently ratified GATT and NAFTA trade treaties.

"It would be disastrous if the U.S. abdicates leadership on the copyright treaty," Lehman says. "How would America Online and AT&T like it if the French telephone companies were setting the rules of the road for the information highway?" ■

OUTLOOK

Passage Next Year?

Wouldn't it be ironic if Washington, in its zeal to safeguard books from piracy, actually killed off the [Internet]?" That's the apocalyptic prospect raised by author and Internet enthusiast David H. Rothman, who has proposed that the federal government help libraries and the poor by financing a massive offering of books available electronically for free downloading. [36]

Indeed, those who envision a "celestial jukebox" look forward to a day of plenty, when most copyright disputes have become moot because piracy will no longer be worth the effort. "The capacity of the celestial jukebox to post a charge for access, and to shut off service if a subscriber does not pay his bills, should substantially reduce the specter of transaction costs," Goldstein writes. "As these costs dissolve, so, too, should the perceived need for safety valves such as fair use. Indeed, the economic logic of the celestial jukebox, when superimposed on the text of the Copyright Act, might produce a law that contains no exemptions from liability at all." [37]

Perhaps more realistically, a panel of Georgetown University Law Center experts in December 1995 proposed the establishment of "virtual magistrates," or on-line private arbitrators who would resolve disputes over intellectual property. [38]

It is hard to imagine the average citizen mastering many of the intricacies of copyright law. "Much of copyright is taken for granted," says Adler of the Association of Research Libraries, "browsing at bookstores and libraries, making a few photocopies, giving books to friends. Libraries make much of what we do invisible so you don't see the fees that a library is paying" to service scholars, education and life-long learning. That's why any digital-age revisions in the law should contain clear protections for fair use, she says. "Just because there is the ability to collect fees doesn't mean that libraries will have the financial resources to pay them."

Many observers say it is still possible for all parties to come out ahead in the digital age. "We think the electronic world has a bright future, and that the content providers will be winners with expanded opportunities," says Black of the computer association. "But they will have some increased risks, just as we will have increased risks, such as copyright infringement. We need a balance that works for everyone, and that lets everyone assume some risks."

Professor Boyle says there are both good and bad aspects to the Nethead's battle cry that "information wants to be free. If we take a tight approach, we will get less creativity." When the approach is looser, Boyle says, "we get more creativity. Look at the success of Silicon Valley in the 1960s, or take Elizabethan England, where all those playwrights were stealing each others' ideas. Right now the Internet is expanding, and there is no crisis. We shouldn't rush to change the law. We should let the dust settle."

Lehman maintains that there is no basis for the idea that the Internet is in danger of dying. "There are thousands of bytes moving every minute, and I'm not aware of anyone feeling chilled," he says. The disputatious 104th Congress was too distracted by politics to tackle copyright reform, he says. "A little more oomph and push, and our bill would have passed," he adds. "It will pass next year because neither users or access providers think the status quo is satisfactory. The competing interests all want some change." ■

FOR MORE INFORMATION

Association of American Publishers, 1718 Connecticut Ave. N.W., Suite 700, Washington, D.C. 20009; (202) 232-3335. The professional association for publishers of books, journals, tests and software tracks legislation and international agreements affecting such issues as copyright.

Association of Research Libraries, 21 Dupont Circle, N.W., Washington, D.C., 20036; (202) 296-2296. The membership group for university libraries in the United States and Canada is a leader in various alliances and advocacy efforts to shape proposed digital age revisions of copyright law.

Copyright Office, Library of Congress, Washington, D.C. 20559; (202) 707-3000; http://lcweb.loc.gov/copyright. The central registration point for all copyright holders is staffed with information specialists to answer questions and provide forms.

Creative Incentive Coalition, 1001 G St. N.W., Suite 900 East, Washington, D.C. 20001; (202) 393-1010; e-mail, cic@cic.org; Internet http://www.cic.org/ This alliance of publishers, software creators and television, film and record companies presses for a government crackdown on copyright infringements made easier by digital technology.

Digital Future Coalition, P.O. Box 7679, Washington, D.C. 20004; (202) 628-6048; http://www.dfc.org/dfc/ This alliance of libraries, scholars, educators and on-line civil liberties groups is resisting proposed major changes in copyright law that might restrict development of the Internet.

Notes

[1] For background, see "Regulating the Internet," *The CQ Researcher,* June 30, 1995, pp. 561-584.

[2] See *USA Today,* Oct. 9, 1996. Survey by Nielsen Media Research cited in *The Washington Post,* Aug. 14, 1996, p. F1.

[3] Paul Goldstein, *Copyright's Highway* (1994), p. 28.

[4] See Penny Pagano, "Intellectual Property Rights and the World Wide Web," advertising supplement in *American Journalism Review,* September 1996, p. 46.

[5] Quoted in Claudia Dreifus, "The Cyber-Maxims of Esther Dyson," *The New York Times Magazine,* July 7, 1996.

[6] Column in *Chicago Lawyer,* April 1996, p. 60.

[7] Commerce Department Information Infrastructure Task Force, "Intellectual Property and the National Information Infrastructure: The Report of the Working Group on Intellectual Property Rights," September 1995, p. 10.

[8] Pamela Samuelson, "The Copyright Grab," *Wired,* January 1996, p. 135.

[9] Introduction to L. Ray Patterson and Stanley W. Lindberg, *The Nature of Copyright: A Law of User's Rights* (1991), p. xi.

[10] See Saundra Torry, "Intellectual Property Specialists Flex Their Muscles," *The Washington Post,* July 1, 1996.

[11] Wendy M. Grossman, "alt.scientology. war," *Wired,* December 1995, p. 172.

[12] Commerce Department, *op. cit.,* p. 63.

[13] Kenneth D. Crews, "What Qualifies as Fair Use," *The Chronicle of Higher Education,* May 17, 1996. Section 2, p. B1.

[14] *The Chronicle of Higher Education,* July 5, 1996, p. A15.

[15] Quoted in *The Chronicle of Higher Education,* May 10, 1996, p. A29.

[16] For background, Michael Krantz, "Cyber Vending Machine," *Time,* June 24, 1996, p. 56.

[17] See *CQ Weekly Report,* June 22, 1996, p. 1752.

[18] See Ann Okerson, "Who Owns Intellectual Property," *Scientific American,* July 1996, p. 80.

[19] Patterson and Lindberg, *op. cit.,* p. 19.

[20] John Shelton Lawrence and Bernard Timberg (eds.), *Fair Use and Free Inquiry: Copyright Law and the New Media* (1980), p. 5.

[21] Patterson and Lindberg, *op. cit.,* p. 30.

[22] *Ibid.,* p. 39.

[23] Quoted in *The Economist,* July 27, 1996.

[24] Cited in speech by Michael Novak, "The Fire of Invention, the Fuel of Interest," American Enterprise Institute, Sept. 24, 1996.

[25] Cited in Patterson and Lindberg, *op. cit.,* p. 67. See also Lawrence and Timberg, *op. cit.,* p. 10.

[26] Lawrence and Timberg, *op. cit.,* p. 3.

[27] Patterson and Lindberg, *op. cit.,* p. 88.

[28] Lawrence and Timberg *op. cit.,* p. 77.

[29] William S. Strong, *The Copyright Book* (1993), p. 171.

[30] Goldstein, *op. cit.,* pp. 79, 143, 220.

[31] Commerce Department, *op. cit.,* pp. 13, 32.

[32] See *Rolling Stone,* Sept. 5, 1996, p. 25.

[33] Knight-Ridder news dispatch, Aug., 4, 1996.

[34] Testimony before the Senate Judiciary Committee, Sept. 18, 1996.

[35] For background on the Berne Convention, see "Artists' Rights and Copyrights," *Editorial Research Reports,* May 13, 1988, pp. 245-256, and "Software Piracy," *The CQ Researcher,* May 21, 1993, pp. 433-456.

[36] David H. Rothman, "Real Books on the Internet," *The Washington Post,* Aug. 21, 1996.

[37] Goldstein, *op. cit.,* p. 224.

[38] See *PCMagazine,* Dec. 5, 1995, p. 32.

Bibliography

Selected Sources Used

Books

Boyle, James, Shamans, *Software and Spleens: Law and the Construction of the Information Society,* Harvard University Press, 1996.

An American University law professor examines the myriad unresolved issues of contemporary intellectual property law, among them copyright, privacy, insider trading and genetic engineering.

Fishman, Stephen, *The Copyright Handbook: How to Protect and Use Written Works,* Nolo Press, 1994.

Written by an attorney and up-to-date for the electronic and multi-media age, this how-to guide offers concrete tips for those seeking to use copyright law for their own written works.

Fishman, Stephen, *Copyright Your Software,* Nolo Press, 1994.

An attorney offers sample documents and condensed explanations for how computer programmers and software creators can protect their original work.

Foster, Frank H., and Robert L. Shook, *Patents, Copyrights and Trademarks: The Total Guide to Protecting the Rights to Your Invention, Product or Trademark,* John Wiley & Sons, 1993.

This logically organized compendium offers quick summaries and lists that answer common questions about intellectual property, while including an entertaining sampling of related trivia.

Goldstein, Paul, *Copyright's Highway: From Gutenberg to the Celestial Jukebox,* Hill and Wang, 1994.

A copyright expert at Stanford University Law School reviews copyright's long and disputatious history, offering a vision of a technological "jukebox" from which modern consumers at their home computers will be able to order and pay for all manner of information, art and entertainment.

Lawrence, John Shelton, and Bernard Timberg (eds.), *Fair Use and Free Inquiry: Copyright Law and the New Media,* Ablex Publishing, 1980.

A textbook released before the personal computer revolution offers a useful history of copyright issues in law, education and culture during the first seven decades of the 20th century.

Patterson, L. Ray, and Stanley W. Lindberg, *The Nature of Copyright: A Law of Users' Rights,* University of Georgia Press, 1991.

Two University of Georgia law professors offer an authoritative overview of the history and application of copyright law, citing numerous instructive controversies leading up to the age of the Internet.

Strong, William S., *The Copyright Book: A Practical Guide,* Fourth Edition, MIT Press, 1993.

A Boston lawyer has updated this legal discussion of the requirements of worldwide copyright law, presenting material in a clear, question-and-answer format.

White, Herbert S., *At the Crossroads: Librarians on the Information Superhighway,* Libraries Unlimited, 1995.

A veteran professor of library and information science examines dilemmas common to libraries in the Internet Age, linking such issues as copyright and public access to information to larger social issues of the day.

Reports and Studies

Association of Research Libraries, *Copyright and the NII: Resources for the Library and Education Community,* May 1996.

The Washington headquarters for the nation's academic libraries compiled these documents analyzing current legislation and administration policy on digital copyright and the proposed National Information Infrastructure (NII).

Commerce Department, Information Infrastructure Task Force, *Intellectual Property and the National Information Infrastructure: The Report of the Working Group on Intellectual Property Rights,* September 1995.

The Clinton administration released this comprehensive discussion and set of recommendations on digital copyright following two and a half years of research, conferences and public hearings.

The Next Step

Additional information from UMI's Newspaper & Periodical Abstracts database

Book Reviews

Chartrand, Sabra, "Patents: Books provide lively insights," *The New York Times,* July 17, 1995, p. D2.
Chartrand reviews several books dealing with patents, including *The Patent Wars* by Fred Warshofsky, *Copyright's Highway: The Law and Lore of Copyright From Gutenberg to the Celestial Jukebox* by Paul Goldstein, and *Peculiar Patents,* compiled by Rick Feinberg.

Kirsch, Jonathan, "Lively excursion into the complexities of copyright law," *Los Angeles Times,* Jan. 4, 1995, p. E4.
Kirsch reviews *Copyright's Highway: The Law and Lore of Copyright From Gutenberg to the Celestial Jukebox* by Paul Goldstein.

Yardley, Jonathan, "Copyrights: A divided 'Highway'," *The Washington Post,* Jan. 11, 1995, p. C2.
Yardley reviews *Copyright's Highway: From Gutenberg to the Celestial Jukebox* by Paul Goldstein.

Copyright Protection and the Internet

Ardito, Stephanie C., "Electronic copyright: Under siege," *On-line,* September 1996, pp. 83-88.
In this age of electronic transmission, copyright is a contentious, ugly problem from which no one is immune. The issue is complicated by differing interpretations of what copying and downloading rights the Copyright Act of 1976 permits.

Belsie, Laurent, "Who pays for what on tomorrow's Internet?" *The Christian Science Monitor,* Oct. 25, 1995, p. 1.
Publishers, technologists and legal scholars are involved in a debate in 1995, over how to protect copyrights in cyberspace and the value of information in the coming information age. Many Internet experts argue that copying technology will soon overwhelm copyright laws that discourage copying, which would mean that creative artists, publishers and software developers would be in trouble.

Blumenstyk, Goldie, "Copyright Clearance Center offers services on the Internet," *The Chronicle of Higher Education,* April 21, 1995, pp. A32-A33.
The Copyright Clearance Center has unveiled an Internet service designed to simplify the process of getting permission to reprint copyrighted materials. This new service is discussed.

Browning, Graeme, "Copycats," *National Journal,* Jan. 6, 1996, pp. 23-26.
The Internet allows users to make endless copies of films, software, songs and texts. The owners of these works are monitoring the Internet and demanding that on-line users stop copying their materials. The result is a nasty battle over how far copyright law extends into cyberspace.

Browning, Graeme, "Tiffing over copyrights and wrongs," *National Journal,* April 6, 1996, pp. 772-773.
Talks taking place under the auspices of the House Judiciary Subcommittee on Courts and Intellectual Property involving copyrights on the Internet are discussed. The fuss is over on-line service provider liability.

Caruso, Denise, "Should an extension of current copyright law, tweaked a bit, govern the Internet?" *The New York Times,* July 15, 1996, p. D7.
Caruso discusses the newest Internet law making the rounds on Capitol Hill. The new legislation is an extension of current copyright law, updated to be applied to the Internet.

Chapman, Gary, "Copyright bill would infringe on the Internet's real promise," *Los Angeles Times,* May 20, 1996, p. D7.
Chapman discusses how the National Information Infrastructure Copyright Protection Act of 1995, will affect the Internet.

Coates, James, "On Internet, copyrights are easy prey for a thief's hungry mouse," *Chicago Tribune,* Jan. 21, 1996, p. 1.
Thousands of institutions are under siege as they grapple with ways to protect their intellectual property rights from thieves on the Internet, creating copyright chaos for the owners of music, films, books, newspapers, magazines, cartoons and other original material.

DeLoughry, Thomas J., "Copyright in cyberspace," *The Chronicle of Higher Education,* Sept. 15, 1995, pp. A22-A24.
The Clinton administration has proposed minor changes in the copyright law to placate those concerned about the hijacking of intellectual property on the information superhighway. The federal modifications are discussed.

Evans, Judith, "Copyright comes to the Internet," *The Washington Post,* May 10, 1996, p. F1.
In Falls Church, Va., more than 200 IBM employees have launched infoMarket, whose cryptolope technology is

leading to a new secured electronic commerce system that experts anticipate may boost what many consider the lack of published works available on the Internet.

Frazier, Kenneth, "Protecting copyright — and preserving fair use — in the electronic future," *The Chronicle of Higher Education,* June 30, 1995, p. A40.
The publishing and software industries, in their attempts to revise the U.S. Copyright Act, are seeking an absolute monopoly on the rights to digitize, store, and transmit copyrighted information. It is important to remember that the protection of intellectual-property rights does not require the destruction of the public's right to gain access to knowledge.

Gailey, Elizabeth Atwood, "Who owns digital rights? Examining the scope of copyright protection for electronically distributed works," *Communications & the Law,* March 1996, pp. 3-28.
New communications technology continues to pose problems for copyright law. The chief problem is ownership of electronic rights.

Harvey, James A., "Troublesome legal issues can snare Internet users," *Atlanta Journal Constitution,* Oct. 1, 1995, p. D3.
Harvey discusses issues of copyright infringement and trademarks and domain names that may be of interest to Georgia high-tech entrepreneurs promoting and selling their goods on the Internet.

Hernandez, Debra Gersh, "Congress considers updating copyright law to cover on-line information," *Editor & Publisher,* Nov. 25, 1995, pp. 31-39.
Congress is considering legislation to update copyright law in order to cover on-line information. The NII Copyright Protection Act of 1995, is aimed at protecting on-line intellectual property rights.

Jacobson, Robert L., "No copying," *The Chronicle of Higher Education,* March 10, 1995, pp. A17-A19.
The time of college students and faculty being able to routinely use electronic versions of copyrighted works without seeking permission or paying a fee is running out. Educators are concerned about big curbs on "fair use" of copyrighted works in the digital world.

Jentzsch, Herber C., "Internet needs standards," *USA Today,* Dec. 27, 1995, p. A10.
In a letter to the editor, Jentzsch of the Church of Scientology International opines that leaders of the online industry must develop standards of voluntary compliance to deal with copyright infringers in order to prevent excessive regulation of the Internet.

Kerber, Ross, "Vigilant copyright holders patrol the Internet," *The Wall Street Journal,* Dec. 13, 1995, p. B1.
With the spread of the Internet — and especially its World Wide Web segment, which includes audio and video — copyright holders are going after fans and other non-commercial users who reproduce copyrighted materials on their home pages. Never, they say, has there been a threat quite like the Internet.

Lewis, Peter H., "Posting matter from church on Internet is ruled illegal," *The New York Times,* Jan. 20, 1996, p. A37.
Judge Leonie M. Brinkema of the U.S. District Court in Alexandria, Va., ruled on Jan. 19, 1996, that Arnaldo P. Lerma violated the copyrights of the Church of Scientology by posting confidential church documents on the Internet, even though the material was obtained from public court records.

Millar, Stuart, "BBC cracks down on Internet webzines," *Guardian,* July 29, 1996, p. 4.
The BBC has become embroiled in the latest dispute over freedom of information on the Internet after launching a crackdown on the use of copyright material on unofficial sites set up by fans of its programs.

Muchnick, Irvin, "Protecting writers' rights on-line," *MacWorld,* July 1996, p. 236.
The National Writers Union has proposed a system called collective licensing to protect writers' rights on-line. The union's Publication Rights Clearinghouse is utilized to protect these rights.

"New threats of censorship of libraries and the Net loom in Congress," *Humanist,* July 1996, p. 41.
Two bills pending in Congress — HR 2441 and HR 989 — threaten to censor libraries and the Internet, according to the author. Changes need to be made in each of these bills to protect libraries and schools.

Ross, Philip E., "Cops versus robbers in cyberspace," *Forbes,* Sept. 9, 1996, pp. 134-139.
As ever more assets assume digital form, intellectual property thieves see a golden opportunity. Ross discusses how copyrights can be protected against piracy in the digital age.

Shiver, Jube Jr., "Lawmakers debate Internet copyright bill," *Los Angeles Times,* Feb. 8, 1996, p. D2.
Hollywood studios and software developers squared off against Internet traditionalists on Feb. 7, 1996, as a congressional panel began debate on a bill aimed at updating copyright laws to protect music recordings, software, movies and other creative works from piracy on the Internet.

Zaharoff, Howard G., "Showdown on the electronic frontier," *Writer's Digest,* June 1996, pp. 36-38.
As computer networks grow, so does the risk of one's writing being copied and distributed without permission or pay. Zaharoff offers suggestions on what to expect and

how to protect oneself and one's writing.

Music Industry Concerns

Levine, Robert, "ABC television boots concert-tape traders off its America On-line site," *Rolling Stone*, Sept. 5, 1996, p. 25.
In June, ABC television shut down an area on its America On-line site that promoted the exchange of illegal concert recordings of live concerts.

Newman, George, "Watermarks could thwart Internet piracy," *Billboard*, July 13, 1996, p. 8.
Newman says it is imperative that the copyright protection issue is addressed before free, CD-quality music starts being pirated on the Internet. Watermarks containing copyright information can be embedded in music that is distributed over the Internet.

Traiman, Steve, "Licensing, pub reps' on-line views," *Billboard*, June 29, 1996, p. 36.
The exponential growth of World Wide Web sites and music delivery on the Internet has made Web site copyright protection a vital concern among music licensing and publishing representatives. Various copyright views are presented.

Publishers' Concerns

Anthes, Gary H., "Cyber copyright issue sparks fierce debate," *Computerworld*, May 20, 1996, p. 28.
Legislation in the Senate that would protect publishers of software, books and other intellectual property from electronic piracy has sparked debate between owners of the copyrighted materials and on-line access providers.

Ardito, Stephanie C., "Publishers, authors, and copyright," *On-line*, September 1996, p. 86.
Most publishers are resistant to compensating authors for electronic versions of their works. Several recent developments regarding this issue, including *Publisher Weekly's* decision to pay authors back and future royalties and K-III Communications' new contracts demanding free, future electronic rights from its authors, are discussed.

Blumenstyk, Goldie, "Talks on 'fair use' of copyrighted materials make some progress," *The Chronicle of Higher Education*, Sept. 20, 1996, p. A32.
Publishers and educators have agreed on some points in their negotiations over what constitutes "fair use," but differences remain. Guidelines formulated by a group representing 100 publishing, library and academic organization on what constitutes fair use are discussed.

Carvajal, Doreen, "Book publishers worry about threat of Internet," *The New York Times*, March 18, 1996, p. A1.
Publishers contend that copyright infringement on the Internet is the most critical threat facing the industry. Worried publishing executives are pressing for new legislation that will tighten copyright restrictions on the Internet and impose penalties for violations of as much as $500,000 in fines and five-year jail sentences. The Senate Judiciary Committee in March 1996, will hold a hearing on the proposed legislation, focusing on the piracy of books on the Internet along with music, videos and software.

Longmuir, Jeanne E., and Daniel J. McMullen, "On-line content providers search for protections," *National Law Journal*, May 20, 1996, pp. C32-C34.
Without guarantees that rights can be protected, many content creators will remain reluctant to make material available on-line. To protect content in cyberspace, one must for now rely on a strategy combining self-help technology, such as encryption, and contractual provisions in enforceable license agreements.

Marks, Alexandra, "Photographers' battle over royalties could affect artists," *The Christian Science Monitor*, July 1, 1996, p. 3.
The dispute over who has the rights to profits from the reuse of free-lance work has erupted, thanks in part, to the Internet, where a photo or a story may sit on-line for weeks rather than be printed once in a daily paper. The outcome has profound implications for all involved in creative work, whether they're freelancers or full-time staff. Many publishers are now demanding all rights to freelance work, when once they were content with permission for a single use. Writers and photographers say the effort is designed to cut them out of profits to which they're entitled.

Penchina, Robert, "Venturing on-line: Protecting you and your product in cyberspace," *Editor & Publisher*, June 24, 1995, pp. 56-57.
The risks of copyright and contractual violations increase when information sources and publication mediums are electronic due to the accessibility of on-line services and the extraordinary research and dissemination opportunities they provide.

Back Issues

Great Research on Current Issues Starts Right Here...Recent topics covered by The CQ Researcher are listed below. Before May 1991, reports were published under the name of Editorial Research Reports.

MAY 1995
Assisted Suicide Controversy
Overhauling Social Security
Learning to Read
Mandatory Sentencing

JUNE 1995
Combating Infectious Disease
Property Rights
Repetitive Stress Injuries
Regulating the Internet

JULY 1995
War Crimes
Highway Safety
Combating Terrorism
Preventing Teen Drug Use

AUGUST 1995
Job Stress
Organ Transplants
United Nations at 50
Advances in Cancer Research

SEPTEMBER 1995
Catholic Church in the U.S.
Northern Ireland Cease-Fire
High School Sports
Teaching History

OCTOBER 1995
Quebec's Future
Revitalizing the Cities
Networking the Classroom
Indoor Air Pollution

NOVEMBER 1995
The Working Poor
The Jury System
Sex, Violence and the Media
Police Misconduct

DECEMBER 1995
Teens and Tobacco
Gene Therapy's Future
Global Water Shortages
Third-Party Prospects

JANUARY 1996
Emergency Medicine
Punishing Sex Offenders
Bilingual Education
Helping the Homeless

FEBRUARY 1996
Reforming the CIA
Campaign Finance Reform
Academic Politics
Getting Into College

MARCH 1996
The British Monarchy
Preventing Juvenile Crime
Tax Reform
Pursuing the Paranormal

APRIL 1996
Centennial Olympic Games
Managed Care
Protecting Endangered Species
New Military Culture

MAY 1996
Russia's Political Future
Marriage and Divorce
Year-Round Schools
Taiwan, China and the U.S.

JUNE 1996
Rethinking NAFTA
First Ladies
Teaching Values
Labor Movement's Future

JULY 1996
Recovered-Memory Debate
Native Americans' Future
Crackdown on Sexual Harassment
Attack on Public Schools

AUGUST 1996
Fighting Over Animal Rights
Privatizing Government Services
Child Labor and Sweatshops
Cleaning Up Hazardous Wastes

SEPTEMBER 1996
Gambling Under Attack
The States and Federalism
Civic Journalism
Reassessing Foreign Aid

OCTOBER 1996
Political Consultants
Insurance Fraud
Rethinking School Integration
Parental Rights

NOVEMBER 1996
Global Warming

Back issues are available for $5.00 (subscribers) or $8.00 (non-subscribers). Quantity discounts apply to orders over ten. To order, call Congressional Quarterly Customer Service at (202) 887-8621.

Binders are available for $18.00. To order call 1-800-638-1710. Please refer to stock number 648.

Future Topics

- ***Consumer Debt***
- ***Running Washington, D.C.***
- ***Welfare Reform***

THE CQ Researcher

PUBLISHED BY CONGRESSIONAL QUARTERLY INC.

Consumer Debt

Do Americans buy too much on credit?

In the weeks ahead, millions of consumers will use credit cards to charge their holiday gifts, possibly pushing consumer debt to unprecedented heights. The prospect of new debt levels disturbs some economists, who note that delinquent credit card accounts and personal bankruptcies already have reached historic highs. Others contend that personal indebtedness waxes and wanes over time, and that the cycle tends to be self-correcting. Some experts worry that in the years ahead, consumer debt will continue to rise as card issuers use sophisticated marketing techniques to put cards in the hands of students and consumers of limited means. They also predict that the increasing use of credit cards in such non-traditional venues as supermarkets and doctors' offices will further increase the debt load.

INSIDE THIS ISSUE

CQ Nov. 15, 1996 • Volume 6, No. 43 • Pages 1009-1032

Formerly Editorial Research Reports

Consumer Debt

The Issues

Background

Current Situation

Outlook

Sidebars and Graphics

For Further Research

COVER: BARBARA SASSA-DANIELS

Nov. 15, 1996
Volume 6, No. 43

Editor
Sandra Stencel

Managing Editor
Thomas J. Colin

Associate Editors
Sarah M. Magner
Richard L. Worsnop

Staff Writers
Charles S. Clark
Mary H. Cooper
Kenneth Jost

Editorial Assistant
Tonya Harris

Published By
Congressional Quarterly Inc.

Chairman
Andrew Barnes

Vice Chairman
Andrew P. Corty

Editor and Publisher
Neil Skene

Executive Editor
Robert W. Merry

Bibliographic records and abstracts included in The Next Step section of this publication are from UMI's Newspaper and Periodical Abstracts database, and are used with permission.

The CQ Researcher (ISSN 1056-2036). Formerly Editorial Research Reports. Published weekly (48 times per year, not printed March 1, May 31, Aug. 30, Nov. 29) by Congressional Quarterly Inc., 1414 22nd St., N.W., Washington, D.C. 20037. Annual subscription rate for libraries, businesses and government is $319. Additional rates furnished upon request. Periodicals postage paid at Washington, D.C. POSTMASTER: Send address changes to The CQ Researcher, 1414 22nd St., N.W., Washington, D.C. 20037.

Consumer Debt

BY RICHARD L. WORSNOP

THE ISSUES

Computer technician Dewey Paris of Pasadena, Texas, had six children, a failing marriage and $18,000 in bills to various credit card companies.

"A lot of people assume that money problems cause the tension in a marriage," he says. "But in our marriage, the tension accelerated our spending on credit. I wouldn't stand my ground on some financial issues, because I was trying not to rock the boat."

When the couple divorced in 1993, Paris, then 43, agreed to accept full responsibility for their debts. About six months later, a Houston consumer-credit counseling firm helped arrange a five-year program to help him wipe the slate clean. Paris has whittled his debt to just $6,000, and he plans to write his last check to the counseling firm sometime in 1998.

"At some point," Paris now says, "we have to make sacrifices to get in a better position financially. We can do that early on, by waiting until we have enough money for the things we want before actually buying them. Or, we can make much greater sacrifices later, after the credit damage has been done — which is what I'm in the process of doing now."

Millions of Americans have found themselves in the same leaky boat in recent years. For example, a survey issued Sept. 26 by Bankcard Holders of America, a nonprofit consumer advocacy group in McLean, Va., found that 53 percent of all credit card users questioned said they were in debt because of "overspending." Medical bills and college expenses each were cited by 11 percent of the respondents, while 9 percent blamed their indebtedness on a job layoff. Other reasons cited for outsized credit card balances included divorce costs, home-repair bills and travel or vacation outlays.

More worrisome to experts who track U.S. credit trends are the rises to record levels of two key indicators. In the second quarter of 1996, for example, the credit card delinquency rate climbed to 3.66 percent, the highest number recorded for accounts delinquent at least 30 days since the American Bankers Association began monitoring such data in 1974. [1]

In addition, personal bankruptcies are on track to surpass 1 million this year, for the first time ever. Indeed, some observers expect the total to approach 1.1 million. Job layoffs, medical calamities and other unforeseen emergencies account for much of the personal-bankruptcy total, as in past years. But ethicists as well as financial executives voice concern over a recent trend toward fraudulent bankruptcy filings by consumers seeking protection from their creditors without first passing through the delinquency phase. (*See story, p. 1022.*)

However, some experts feel that a more positive spin can be put on some of the supposedly alarming data. It is often remarked, for example, that the credit card delinquency rate is 3.66 percent, but that also means that more than 96 percent of credit card holders are current on their payments.

David Robertson, president of *The Nilson Report,* a credit card newsletter in Oxnard, Calif., argues that rising credit card indebtedness shows that consumers are simply taking advantage of opportunities to get cards.

"The opportunity for credit card issuers is terrific now," he says. "Sales volume generated on cards will continue to grow and grow, particularly because Americans have the opportunity to use the cards in non-traditional venues, such as supermarkets. Also, consumers are being rewarded for doing so. No one rewards them for writing a check, or for paying cash. But you can earn eight frequent-flyer miles if you buy something for $8 with a credit card at a convenience store."

In Robertson's view, "There has never been a better time to have a credit card than today. Rates and benefits have never been more competitive. Rewards have never been more lucrative. That's because the industry is dominated by very large players who realize they have to spend money to make money. They realize that the name of the game is building the size of their portfolios, because the average profitability per account will diminish as they continue to offer rewards and other bells and whistles to keep their customers happy."

Skeptics retort that competition for market share inevitably will mean extending credit to unwary consumers who may assume more debt than they are able to repay, as reflected in delinquency figures. Another concern is the spread of credit-identity fraud. (*See story, p. 1018.*) Moreover, consumer advocacy groups and credit industry officials worry that American consumers are prone to indebtedness because many of them are poorly informed, at best, about buying on credit. (*See story, p. 1020.*)

Bankcard Debt Is Rising

American consumers owed nearly a half-billion dollars on bank-issued Visa and Mastercards as of July 1996, according to the consumer advocacy group Bankcard Holders of America. The total is more than five times the amount owed in 1980. *

* *Includes Visa and Mastercard but not American Express and Discover*

Source: Bankcard Holders of America, Sept. 26, 1996

Few experts view the current level of consumer indebtedness as portending major trouble for the economy. But virtually all say that the situation bears close scrutiny. *

With the approach of the year-end holiday season, traditionally a peak period for credit purchases, here are some of the questions economists, consumer advocacy groups and others are asking about rising credit use:

Do record levels of credit card delinquencies and personal bankruptcies spell serious economic trouble for the nation?

According to James Medoff and Andrew Harless, the authors of a recent book on debt in America, mounting consumer indebtedness is troubling because it "is mirrored by a fall in consumer savings. This is a major development. Not only is the economy in general worse off for neglecting its savings, but the individual consumer also finds himself or herself between the proverbial rock and a hard place. . . . Without savings, Americans must find other ways to bridge the gap between income and expenses when the times get rough. Unfortunately, it appears that more borrowing is fast becoming the solution to this problem." [2]

Another worrisome side effect of mounting credit card debt, "especially at interest rates much higher than those applied to other types of debt, is the loss of regulatory control over credit," Medoff and Harless write. "Under current conditions, the Federal Reserve Board cannot effect any reliable changes in the amount or timing of debt increases or credit use. Therefore, a situation exists in which billions of dollars flow into and out of the marketplace without regulation, checks or balances. We can only imagine the long-term effects of this outlaw monetary system. But it is foolish to believe that it will have no effect on the typical American family." [3]

But James Chessen, chief economist for the American Bankers Association, says that increasing credit card delinquencies "pose no serious threat" to the U.S. banking system. Testifying before a House committee in September, he asserted: "Banks' exposure to losses per individual is very small, banks' loan portfolios are well-diversified and the industry has record high levels of capital and reserves. In fact, if the banking industry wrote off every dollar of every non-performing loan — both consumer and business loans — there would still be $23 billion in reserves left over, without even touching the $365 billion in bank capital." [4]

According to Chessen, much of the recent increase in consumer debt stems from "the rapid expansion in the number of places that accept credit cards as a means of payment." The list includes supermarkets, movie theaters and even doctors' offices, he noted, adding: "As consumers substitute credit cards for checks and cash, average balances tend to rise. But that does not necessarily mean that the capacity of individuals to meet their obligations has diminished." [5]

Warren G. Heller, research director for Veribanc Inc., a Wakefield, Mass., firm that evaluates the condition of banks and other financial institutions, also feels the current level of credit card delinquency is tolerable. That's because, he says, self-correcting mechanisms come into play when strains develop within the credit system.

"If the system is well set up, it has built-in feedbacks that counter adverse trends," Heller says. "Today's situation is a classic case of this. First, the delinquency trend developed. Then, as more and more people noticed it and discussed it, card issuers started tightening their credit standards. And very few of them have lost money on

* Household debt dropped sharply in September, according to the Federal Reserve, falling 2.7 percent to $1.17 trillion. It was the first drop in consumer installment debt, mostly credit cards and auto loans, in more than three years.

a net-income basis." In this connection, he notes that, "Losing money to card charge-offs is part and parcel of the business."

At the same time, Heller is disturbed by individual instances of "pernicious" credit card abuse. For example, he cites the college student who used her 20 or so credit cards to support herself as an undergraduate. "She managed to stay current on her debt by robbing Peter to pay Paul," he says. "But then, as she neared graduation, she went to the card issuer and said, in effect, 'Look: I'm over my head, and I can't take the hit that this will put on my credit record. My parents want to see me get out from under this, and they're willing to put up 25 cents on the dollar to accomplish that. If you're willing to accept the offer on condition my credit record stays clean, my Dad will write you a check.' "

The moral of the story, Heller says, is that "some cynical gaming" is going on among a minority of cardholders.

Larry Shimmerine, a consulting economist for MasterCard International, feels rising credit card delinquency rates reflect "a change in the way credit cards are used. For instance, many small-business people use their personal credit cards for business purposes rather than taking out more traditional types of loans. Then, when some of those businesses fail, their credit card debts are reported as delinquent.

"Ten years ago, the debts of a failed small business would have shown up as delinquencies or defaults on other kinds of loans. So to some extent, higher credit card delinquencies represent a shift from one form of borrowing to another. We really should be looking at all delinquencies [including home-equity and car loans], instead of looking at just one loan category [credit cards]. When you do that, delinquency levels appear quite low."

Ruth E. Susswein, executive director of Bankcard Holders of America, notes that credit card delinquencies are "at record levels, and that's disturbing. But at the same time, we have to keep in mind that 96 percent of cardholders are not delinquent." Personal bankruptcies, on the other hand, have reached "hazardous levels," she says.

> **"It's clear that issuers are responsible for marketing practices that encourage people to open new credit card accounts, incur more debt and make only minimal monthly payments to retire that debt. All these practices have contributed to the delinquency problems we now confront."**
>
> *— Ruth E. Susswein*
> *executive director*
> *Bankcard Holders of America*

Susswein's assessment is shared by newsletter publisher Robertson. "Particularly egregious is the rise in fraudulent bankruptcies," he says. These typically involve a middle-income consumer with a half-dozen or more credit cards but no history of delinquency. Then, to the consternation of creditors, the consumer suddenly files for bankruptcy.

"What we have in America today is a situation where, unfortunately, consumers feel that personal bankruptcy is part of their menu of financial services," Robertson says. "And we have attorneys who, for a relatively modest fee, will help a consumer file for personal bankruptcy. These attorneys are advertising more aggressively all the time, making personal bankruptcy and the ease with which a consumer can file for it more readily apparent to the average person."

Howard Hoemann, president of the International Credit Association, in St. Louis, Mo., also worries about the prospect of 1 million-plus personal bankruptcies. But fraudulent filings account for only a fraction of the total, he notes. Many are prompted by unexpected calamity, such as job loss or major medical bills not covered by insurance. "You also have people who have been living quite well and paying their bills on time, but who suddenly realize they're in over their head," adds Hoemann. "At that point, they turn to bankruptcy as the easiest way to climb out of debt. And then there are flagrant abusers of credit. People who file for personal bankruptcy fall into all of those pockets."

Hoemann is intrigued by data suggesting that the personal bankruptcy problem is "fairly evenly distributed throughout the country." In the past, the number of filings varied from region to region depending on economic conditions. Today, inexplicably, "There is no area of the country that has more bankruptcies proportionate to population than any other," he says.

Have credit card companies been overzealous in seeking new customers?

Experts disagree on the root cause of mounting consumer card delinquency rates. Some say charge-happy cardholders are the main culprits,

Profile of a 'Typical' Consumer in Debt

Consumers who seek help in managing their finances typically earn $24,000 a year and owe more than $19,000 to 11 creditors, according to the nonprofit National Foundation for Consumer Credit. Foundation members maintain nearly 1,200 offices throughout the U.S. and Canada, under the name Consumer Credit Counseling Service.

Age	35
Sex	
Male	50%
Female	50%
Marital Status	
Single	24%
Married	52%
Separated, Divorced or Widowed	24%
Number in the Family	3.1
Buying or Own Their Home	40%
Average Monthly Gross Income	$2,000
Average Total Debt (excluding mortgage)	$19,688
Average Number of Creditors	11
Primary Cause of Financial Problems:	
Over Obligation — poor money management	46%
Reduced income or unemployment	26%
Divorce or separation	11%
Medical	9%
Other	8%

Source: National Foundation for Consumer Credit

while others indict card issuers for marketing their products to young people without credit experience and to adults with checkered credit histories. A third school of thought holds that the problem is far too complex to be solved by finger-pointing alone.

In Susswein's view, responsibility for today's high delinquency levels "is certainly shared" by consumers and issuers. "No doubt about it, we each have to be responsible for the debts we incur," she says. "At the same time, it's clear that issuers are responsible for marketing practices that encourage people to open new credit card accounts, incur more debt and make only minimal monthly payments to retire that debt. All these practices have contributed to the delinquency problems we now confront."

Linda Sherry, editorial director for Consumer Action, an advocacy group in San Francisco, faults card issuers for targeting college students and so-called B and C credit risks — adults with mottled credit records. Beyond that, she is troubled that "easy credit is pushed on people across the board. For instance, every time you walk into a store, you're asked, 'Do you want a credit account opened right now, so you can get 10 percent off?' It's an enticement to take on more credit than you may require."

Sherry also looks askance at "the plethora of preapproved credit offers that arrive in the mail after people have been 'prescreened' by the credit card companies. Now, the person may have a wonderful credit history, but that doesn't mean he or she needs the temptation that additional credit represents."

Shimmerine, the MasterCard economist, notes that issuers "have tried to make credit cards more available to a wider share of the population." He regards that as "a very healthy development, because it helps bring people into the mainstream of the country's economic life.

"But let's face it — the issuers might have gone too far. Some people are getting cards who shouldn't have them. However, this is the exception, not the rule. And the issuing banks are now tightening their lending standards in an effort to limit their losses."

Nonetheless, Shimmerine expects credit card issuers to continue exploring, though "very judiciously," the B and C credit risk market. "To the extent that the loss rates there are acceptable, the issuers will expand their promotion efforts. If the losses get too high, they'll cut back. It's an ongoing experiment whose outcome is unclear."

Robertson also foresees additional efforts to market cards to subprime credit risks. "They might be issued debit cards, not credit cards," he says, adding that the hazards of exploring the subprime market have been overstated. "People who are less well-off get a bad rap. They are considered high credit risks because they often are the first ones laid off in a downturn. In fact, people who are lower middle class tend to be very good at paying their bills. They're not the ones who are running off to bankruptcy court. It's the middle class and upper-middle-class folks who are doing that."

Some of the sharpest criticism of credit card marketing practices concerns the college market.[6] Many consumer advocates argue that college students aren't mature enough to handle a credit card responsibly. Ken McEldowney, executive director of Consumer Action, told a congressional subcommittee two years ago that the credit card industry "must shoulder the blame for ... the aggressive ways in which it pushes credit card applications [on] students without balancing messages of easy credit with explanations of how to use credit wisely.... There is no justification for encouraging students to apply for and use credit lines that are beyond their ability to pay." [7]

Credit card industry representatives beg to differ. "College students may constitute a unique market, but they share many attributes with the credit card population as a whole," Paul Allen, senior vice president of Visa U.S.A. Inc., told the subcommittee. "They demand credit cards for the extraordinary utility and convenience they offer. They want credit cards for emergency uses in order to establish a credit history, and indeed to pay for books and tuition.... College students use credit cards mainly as a device to transact purchases, not to obtain an unsecured loan." (*See "At Issue," p. 1025.*)

Are Americans knowledgeable about handling credit?

Not surprisingly, credit card issuers and consumer advocates disagree on whether Americans are as savvy about the pitfalls of borrowing as they are about the benefits. Allen told the House subcommittee that Visa regards college students as adults, and treats them as such.

"Like the rest of us, college students need a credit card to make a purchase by mail, to order an airline ticket and to rent a car." Allen said. "...[C]ollege students are responsible consumers," he added. "They pay the balance in full one-half of the time, whereas the population at large carries a balance 60 percent of the time.... Losses per college account typically are much less than half of the average non-college account." [8]

McEldowney retorted that many of the people who seek help from Consumer Action "are besieged by credit debts and are confused about how to handle them." Most callers, he said, "do not understand how to determine the true cost of credit or how much they really owe." For instance, a frequent comment is that the credit card issuer "must be making a mistake: I make the minimum payment every month, but the balance I owe hardly goes down."

For McEldowney, the lesson is this: "If so many adults lack a basic understanding of how to use credit wisely, how can we expect their children to do any better? We do not believe college students are miraculously better at handling credit than their elders." [9]

Shimmerine rates the credit knowledgeability of U.S. consumers as "very high, in the sense that most people don't get themselves into deep trouble by overspending or overborrowing. It's true that credit cards may make it easier to overspend. Remember, though, that people also ran into serious debt problems before credit cards became widely available."

Michael E. Staten, director of Purdue University's Credit Research Center, believes consumers find it hard to comprehend, let alone adjust to, the rapidly evolving world of credit. "It's clear," he says, "that the sophistication of credit products over the last 10 years has increased faster than people's understanding of them, especially in terms of day-to-day budgeting. Today's financial instruments, whether they be credit cards or home-equity lines, are far more subject to abuse than they were a decade ago."

In Heller's opinion, Americans are more informed about credit than they used to be, but "a tremendous gap still exists between what they know and what they should know. A lot of people don't have a basic understanding of how interest works, so compound interest just eats them alive. Something like 80 percent of all cardholders use them as a credit mechanism rather than as a payment mechanism."

Tahira K. Hira, a professor of human development and family studies at Iowa State University, holds similar views. "The difference between the credit we had in the past and the credit that we have today is really the most crucial point," she says. "People today are less informed about the cost of using credit cards and not paying off balances in full each month."

Before the credit card era, Hira notes, most credit purchases involved installment loans, payable in fixed monthly amounts of principal and interest over a prearranged period.

"We now have about a million people a year filing for personal bankruptcy and another million or so going into credit counseling. These are not uneducated, poor people — they're average Americans, by and large."

— Tahira K. Hira
professor of human development and family studies
Iowa State University

The concept was easy to grasp, even by poorly educated consumers. But the open-ended credit available through credit cards has led even affluent consumers astray, Hira says.

"We now have about a million people a year filing for personal bankruptcy and another million or so going into credit counseling," Hira says. "These are not uneducated, poor people — they're average Americans, by and large. Research shows that most of them are educated, and that 90 percent are employed. In fact, data show that the proportion of people with serious credit problems who are in managerial and professional occupations is higher today than it was 15 years ago. So, the problem isn't lack of formal education; it's inadequate knowledge of a specific area of personal finance."

Consumers aren't the only ones in need of a brush-up course on credit, says Consumer Action's Sherry. Experience has convinced her that, "The people who man the customer-service lines at credit card banks and finance companies don't know very much, either." She recounts a recent visit to a Radio Shack store to pick up a copy of the disclosure form for the company's credit card. The clerk told her he had no such forms. "I said, 'Sorry, but by law you've got to have them.' So then he went to the manager, who told me the disclosure information was on the back of the credit card application, which I couldn't take out of the store. I said, 'I don't think that's correct. I have the legal right to take this home and read it at my leisure.' Finally, he tore the disclosure material off the application form and handed it to me."

In general, Sherry says, "People are just very ill-informed on this particular subject. Even though I've seen it said that consumers are getting more savvy about credit cards, such as switching to the ones with the lowest interest rates, I still question whether they really know the ins and outs of responsible credit use."

According to Hoemann, educating young people about money management is mainly a parental responsibility. "Mothers and fathers need to recognize that personal financial skills learned at home will prepare their children for adult life. It's an old story. We teach our kids how to earn money, but not how to spend it." ■

BACKGROUND

The Biblical Word

The biblical injunction against usury helped shape modern Western views about credit. In biblical times, usury referred to charging any amount of interest on a loan, and it was branded a mortal sin, the harshest censure the church could deliver. The medieval poet Dante gave expression to this attitude in *The Divine Comedy,* which relegates usurers to one of the hottest circles of Hell.

During the Middle Ages, however, pressure for credit overwhelmed the church's efforts to restrain it. Merchants, lords and kings required loans, and their needs were met one way or another. The church itself, as one of Europe's richest institutions, entered into financial deals with the great Italian banking families — lending, borrowing and entangling itself in a practice it publicly condemned.

A turning point came in the latter half of the 16th century, when nonprofit pawnshops, jointly managed by clergymen and municipal officials, were established to benefit the poor. To cover their operating costs, papal sanction was obtained for charging low rates of interest on loans. This was a significant break in the rigid definition of usury as the taking of any interest for the loan of money. Theologians reasoned that the lender should be compensated not only for expenses but also for the cost of capital — the return that could have been earned by placing the funds in investments of similar risk. In effect, usury was redefined as the taking of excessive interest, rather than the taking of any interest.

Henry VII decided to set interest ceilings in England, capping the top rate at 10 percent; by 1714 the figure had been halved. The 13 American Colonies, except for New Hampshire, also set their own maximum interest rates. But they made them just enough higher than 5 percent to attract British investment in the Colonies.

Borrowing was an accepted fact of life in Colonial America, not just for the merchants and importers who relied heavily on credit from their British suppliers, but for their customers as well. Retail credit was available to farmers on a crop-to-crop basis, with the finance charge determined by the price the farmer eventually got for his crop. Thomas Jefferson, heavily in debt himself, wrote in 1787: "The maxim of buying nothing without the money in our pocket to pay for it would make of our country one of the happiest on Earth. . . . I look forward to the abolition of all credit as the only other remedy." [10] Yet even such an apostle of thrift as Benjamin Franklin is known to have extended credit liberally as a printer and bookseller.

A legal market for installment loans was effectively barred, however, by the usury laws that America had inherited from Britain, which prohibited moneylending at economically feasible rates. In 1834, more than 200 Boston businessmen signed a petition urging the repeal of Massachusetts usury laws, citing the trading difficulties they caused.

Many states deliberately weakened their usury laws, enabling high interest rates to prevail despite the strong opposition of Western and Southern farmers who, being chronic debtors,

Continued from p. 1018

Chronology

1910s-1920s

Banks and other commercial institutions begin lending to consumers in the years before and after World War I.

1910
The Fidelity Savings and Trust Company of Norfolk, Va., becomes the nation's first major commercial business devoted solely to personal lending.

1919
General Motors Corp. sets up its own financing agency in 1919. Ford Motor Co. follows suit in 1928.

1928
New York's National City Bank becomes the first major commercial bank to organize a personal loan department.

1940s

Consumer lending is tightly regulated during World War II but rebounds strongly with the return of peace.

1941
President Franklin D. Roosevelt issues an executive order establishing controls over consumer credit, such as minimum down payments. The Federal Reserve Board administers the controls throughout World War II.

Dec. 1, 1946
The Fed lifts credit controls on everything except a dozen consumer durables, including cars.

1949
The Diners' Club card, the first third-party, universal credit card, is introduced.

1950s-1960s

Credit card use explodes, giving rise to concern that consumers are ill-informed about the hazards of revolving debt.

1958
American Express and Carte Blanche are introduced.

1966
Several large bank credit departments are combined into two national credit card companies, BankAmericard and the Interbank Card Association (issuer of Master Charge cards).

1968
President Lyndon B. Johnson signs the Consumer Credit Protection Act, which requires creditors to give consumers printed information about credit matters.

1970s

Consumer borrowing continues to grow, as do efforts to protect consumers from questionable lending practices.

1970
President Richard M. Nixon signs legislation restricting unsolicited credit cards and limiting to $50 cardholders' liability for unauthorized use of their card.

1974
Nixon signs a measure amending the 1970 law to protect consumers against inaccurate and unfair credit billing and credit card practices and to ban discrimination on the basis of gender or marital status from any credit transaction.

1976
BankAmericard changes its name to Visa. Four years later, Master Charge becomes MasterCard.

1977
President Jimmy Carter signs legislation protecting consumers from harassment by debt collectors.

1980s-1990s

Banking deregulation fuels still more consumer lending.

1982
A banking-deregulation law signed by President Ronald Reagan frees traditional deposit-taking institutions to compete head-on with money-market funds. As a result, banks across the country are able to attract depositors by offering high interest on deposits and then passing those high rates on to borrowers — including holders of bank-issued credit cards.

1988
Reagan signs legislation requiring direct-mail solicitations for credit cards to clearly show such information as annual percentage interest rates, annual fees and minimum finance charges.

Jan. 6, 1996
President Clinton signs the Intelligence Authorization Act, giving the FBI access to credit-report information without a court order.

Sept. 30, 1996
Clinton signs legislation making it easier for consumers to find out if information in their credit report has been used against them; to contest incorrect report material; and to withhold their names from marketing lists sold to credit card issuers.

Gangs of 'Very, Very Slick' Con Men . . .

Attorney Mari J. Frank of Laguna Niguel, Calif., received a chilling phone call in August. "How come you haven't made any payments on your $11,000 Toys R Us bill?" someone from the Bank of New York (BNY) asked.

Frank thought it was a crank call. "Who would ever spend $11,000 at Toys R Us?" she replied. The bank representative explained, "These are charges on a Toys R Us credit card from Bank of New York that was issued to you last October." "I went, 'Oh, my God!' " Frank says. "At that point, both of us realized it was fraud."

Frank was luckier than most victims of credit-identity fraud, in which a person's name and Social Security number are used by crooks to obtain fraudulent credit cards. Her legal training had taught her where to find help, and in two days she had located the thief.

The culprit turned out to be a woman married to a policeman in Ventura, Calif., about a four-hour drive from Laguna Niguel. Posing as a private investigator, the woman, Tracey Lloyd, had gained access to Frank's credit report at Equifax Credit Information Services, one of the nation's three main credit bureaus, through a small service company with access to Equifax's database.[1] She had also visited Frank's law office, where she filched several business cards from a tray on the receptionist's desk. These enabled Lloyd to pose as an attorney-mediator when she sought to open new credit lines in Frank's name.

Federal law limits losses on fraudulent credit card debt to $50 per card. But that is often small consolation to victims. They must spend untold hours trying to determine the extent of their victimization: How many credit lines did the thief open in the victim's name? How much was charged, and where? Answers may not be forthcoming for months or years, if ever.

"Banks are quite a bit at fault," Frank says, because "there's really no punishment for issuing credit so haphazardly that it causes these problems."

Experts blame much credit-identity fraud on gangs of Nigerian con artists. After entering the United States on student visas, they say, the Nigerians hone their skills at "academies" run by their countrymen. "They are the pre-eminent credit card fraudsters in the world," says David Robertson, president of *The Nilson Report*, a credit card newsletter published in Oxnard, Calif. "They are very, very slick."

To carry out their schemes, according to *Forbes*, credit-identity thieves only need to "access one of the tens of thousands of computer terminals . . . wired to national credit data banks. Virtually every bank, insurance company, mortgage broker, stockbroker, auto dealer and department store in the country is on-line. The thieves can then punch up practically anyone's credit information — Social Security number, address and other personal data — including, of course, credit status. Then they're off to the races."[2]

In August, Federal Trade Commission staffers examined one such scam. It involved a man who went to a car dealer to test-drive a truck. The man had fake documents identifying himself as 'John Smith,' but he claimed to have forgotten his Social Security number. The salesman obligingly took the thief into his office, where he called up several John Smiths on his computer screen, each accompanied by a Social Security number. Randomly claiming one of the names as his own, the thief obtained a printout of the data about the man, who turned out to be a general contractor.

Continued from p. 1016

wanted "cheap money." The agrarian movement in American politics, especially during the second half of the 19th century, advocated low interest rates along with the free coinage of silver and the use of greenbacks as legal tender. The financial centers of the East, in contrast, favored the gold standard to maintain the value of currency and keep inflation down.

Rise of Consumer Credit

The industrialization and urbanization of America wrought significant changes in the consumer credit business. A class of wage earners emerged who had enough money left after buying family necessities to enter into credit transactions. In many states, so-called salary loans were made by assigning part of the borrower's earnings to the repayment of his debt. Lenders were virtually assured of repayment, since employers generally were firm believers in the sanctity of contracts and were apt to fire a worker who showed irresponsibility in his financial affairs.

Salary loans tended to plunge borrowers into debt for extended periods. Meanwhile, the creditor could claim exemption from the usury laws on the ground that he was not lending money but simply purchasing a salary, as one might purchase any other commodity.

The city worker's regular flow of wages, as compared with the farmer's or farm laborer's seasonal income, made possible regular payments on an installment purchase. Other new forces also were at work, as historian Daniel J. Boorstin has noted: "Industry was using newly improved metals (especially iron and steel) to turn out millions of durable objects, which nearly every citizen could imagine owning. Since a sewing machine could usually be reconditioned for the secondhand market, it did not seem imprudent for the retailer to allow a customer to use the machine while he paid for it."[11]

. . . Turn Credit Card Fraud Into Big Profits

Thus armed, the bogus Smith "began applying for credit cards, telling the credit card companies that his actual address was his 'new' address and that [the legitimate John] Smith's address was his 'old' address," according to *BNA's Banking Report.* "In this manner, the thief obtained more than $50,000 in goods and services charged in Smith's name, in addition to a [new] general contractor's license. Tracking down the discrepancies took [the real] Smith six months; correcting most of the discrepancies took a year." [3]

Robertson expects credit-identity fraud to persist, viewing it as an ongoing game of cat-and-mouse between criminals and the credit industry. "The criminals exploit an Achilles' heel, the industry patches it up and then the criminals locate another one." But the situation has improved somewhat, he says: "It used to be the industry was one step behind these guys, but now it's trying to stay one step ahead."

Newspaper and magazine articles on credit identity fraud have made the public more aware of the problem, as has the CBS-TV program "60 Minutes." But increased knowledge has not brought peace of mind: "Unfortunately, we're all going to be looking over our shoulder too much as we enter the next century."

Although credit-identity fraud may be impossible to stamp out, some precautions can be taken. Frank recommends that consumers write a letter to each of the three nationwide credit bureaus asking that they:

- "Provide me with a copy of my current credit report";
- "Remove my name from any and all mailing lists and promotions to any entity";
- "Do not change my mailing address or phone number without verification from me in writing"; and
- "Do not provide my credit report to anyone without my prior permission by phone, fax, or writing."

Frank says she's still "furious at the banks." In her view, they "just recoup their losses from credit-identity fraud by charging higher interest rates and higher annual fees. They consider it a cost of doing business, just like litigation is. It's a write-off for them."

At the personal level, moreover, Frank is consumed by uncertainty. "I still don't know what else [Lloyd] did. I don't know if she took money from people, saying she's an attorney, and then skipped out on them. I don't know if she did anything that will get me in trouble with the Internal Revenue Service. I don't know if she went to a casino or a racetrack, won some money and then put it on my Social Security number. You see what I'm saying? All kinds of insidious things could still happen."

Lloyd pleaded guilty in October to six counts of felony fraud. Sentencing is scheduled for Nov. 19. In the meantime, Frank is required to prepare a victim-impact statement.

"What's scary is that Lloyd gets a copy of it," Frank says. "Knowing that makes the thing hard to write. I'm worried that if I describe my fears, and my kids' fears, she may get ideas about retaliating after she leaves prison."

---

[1] The three nationwide credit bureaus are Equifax, Atlanta, Ga.; Experian Information Solutions Inc. (formerly TRW Information Systems and Services), Orange, Calif., and Trans Union Corp., Chicago, Ill.

[2] Brigid McMenamin, "Invasion of the Credit Snatchers," *Forbes*, Aug. 26, 1996, p. 256.

[3] "FTC Hears Testimony on 'Credit Theft;' Suggestions for Ways to Prevent Fraud," *BNA's Banking Report*, Aug. 26, 1996, p. 299.

Salary loans were generally very small — $10 to $40. The size of the sums involved forced lenders to charge high rates in order to cover their overhead and make a profit. An investigative study published by the Russell Sage Foundation in 1908 found that the average salary loan office in New York had only $10,000 out on loan but charged interest at an annual rate of 120-240 percent, or more. These rates were often accompanied by heavy-handed collection practices. A favorite tactic of loan offices was to send a female "bawlerout" to the delinquent debtor's workplace, where he would be loudly denounced in front of his colleagues as a liar and a cheat.

The flourishing loan offices, which by 1900 were operating in most large cities, bore witness to the need for government regulation of small installment loans. Many of the borrowers were genteel but impoverished civil servants and members of the middle class who were unable to live on their meager incomes, especially when faced with medical bills or funeral expenses. At that time, public opinion was almost as antagonistic toward the borrowers as toward the loan sharks who exploited them.

In addition to fighting the loan sharks, philanthropic organizations led by the Sage Foundation sought to convince the public that there was a pressing need for legal sources of consumer credit. Their efforts to attract responsible capital into the consumer finance field finally resulted in the drafting of a model Uniform Small Loan Act, eventually adopted by most states. To encourage lenders to make small loans, it allowed interest rates in excess of the limits set by usury laws.

Credit unions, which have become a leading source of consumer credit, began operating in 1909. Financial institutions entered the field much later. In 1928, New York's National City Bank became the first major commercial bank to organize a personal loan department.

It was the automobile that transformed installment buying into a dominant American institution. "Until automobiles came off the assembly lines

Consumer Advocates Urge School Courses on Credit Skills

Money-management skills are vital, but they get scant attention in the nation's schools, says consumer advocate Ruth E. Susswein. As the executive director of Bankcard Holders of America, in McLean, Va., she advocates a one-year course in personal finance in junior high school, since "college-bound high school students already are being targeted by credit card issuers. No matter what students major in, they will need information on personal finance. And they are not formally getting it anywhere now."

But schools must have help with the credit-education burden, Susswein says. "It's the parents' responsibility to pass that kind of information on to their children. Also, it's up to individuals to educate themselves, since this clearly affects them. And credit issuers bear some responsibility for educating cardholders, since they stand to gain by doing so."

Indeed, the credit industry already is involved in education programs aimed at the school-age population. Perhaps the best-known program is "Train the Trainers," run by the International Credit Association (ICA), whose members are credit executives.

"It's a two-day course in which high school teachers learn the fundamentals of consumer credit," says ICA President Howard Hoemann. "Those teachers pass on their knowledge to other teachers, who then deliver it to their students. We estimate that 400,000 high school students are trained each year through the program. And other organizations are doing similar things."

The National Foundation for Consumer Credit (NFCC) also promotes the wise use of credit. In 1995, the foundation's more than 1,100 member offices nationwide "conducted 43,778 live consumer education programs for more than 3.5 million people in an effort to help families prevent troubles associated with problem debt and to stress the importance of money management," the NFCC says. "Educational programs are conducted for a wide variety of organizations, including employee assistance programs, civic associations, schools and church groups."

Although Susswein regards "Train the Trainers" as a "terrific program," she notes that school districts generally regard consumer credit as an elective subject, at best. "Sometimes the information is incorporated into a business or consumer economics class. Individual school districts make those decisions. So, credit instruction is all voluntary and hit-and-miss at this point."

Recent research by Tahira K. Hira, a professor of human development and family studies at Iowa State University, raised the possibility that school-based credit education does little to change students' thinking. In a survey of 2,000 randomly selected Iowans, Hira asked: "Looking at your own money-management behavior, who had the most important influence on you?"

"I started with a hypothesis that younger people would say they were influenced primarily by outside forces, such as the media, peers and schools. I also expected the older respondents to say, 'My parents.'

"But to my great surprise, respondents in all age groups cited their parents as the primary source of their money-management knowledge. Often the knowledge was imparted through childrens' observation of their parents' behavior. Fewer than 10 percent of my respondents said schools had taught them most of what they knew about credit."

Nonetheless, Hira strongly believes that schools should teach children how to manage their own money. "It's not something that you can learn just by observing others. I say that because I see college students who write checks when they have blank ones in the checkbook but no money in the bank, and they don't understand why the checks bounce."

"It's easy to assume people know simple things like how to write a check," said Tonia Izzard, an assistant vice president at First National Bank of Platteville, Wis. "The perception is this is just something you know. Someone has to teach children how to tie their shoes. Financial services are the same way." [1]

---

[1] Quoted in "Combating Financial Illiteracy," *Northwestern Financial Review*, Aug. 24, 1996, p. 15

by the millions," wrote Boorstin, "there was no other object of universal use so costly as to require a scheme for time payments." [12] New techniques of buying and financing developed even more rapidly than the methods of automobile production, and provided both a mass market for cars and a remarkable increase in the volume of consumer credit.

General Motors Corp. set up its own financing agency in 1919, and Ford Motor Co. followed suit in 1928. (Henry Ford initially opposed time-payment plans, favoring instead the old-fashioned virtues of thrift and prudence.) As the auto industry became concentrated in a handful of companies, the risk that a manufacturer would go out of business before a car was paid for virtually disappeared.

The Soldiers' and Sailors' Civil Relief Act, which freed members of the armed forces from the need to make installment payments during World War II, led to fears among lenders that millions might interrupt their payments or turn in their installment-purchased cars. But few did, and this established installment buying even more firmly after the war. From 1919 to 1963, General Motors' Time Payment Plan financed nearly 50 million car buyers.

Credit Cards

The postwar credit boom grew out of consumer and business adaptation to a changing way of life. As Americans' expectations for the future rose, so did their willingness to incur debt.

Young married couples are heavy users of credit, and the number of young people was growing faster than any other age group. With home ownership came asset ownership — of stoves, refrigerators and television sets. And as more women moved into the labor force and the desire for leisure time increased, there was added demand for labor-saving devices such as vacuum cleaners, dishwashers and clothes dryers.

Young adults of the postwar period, with higher, more stable incomes than their parents had enjoyed at the same age, had few qualms about using credit. The credit industry responded by creating new lending instruments. Competing gasoline companies and large retailers not only offered credit but also made it portable and convenient by introducing the credit card. This was soon transformed into an all-purpose credit device. Starting in 1949 the Diners' Club, followed by Carte Blanche and American Express, made a profitable business out of supplying credit cards and assuming the risk on credit card accounts.

New York's Franklin National Bank offered the first bank credit card in 1951. In the late 1960s, in order to convince retailers that enough consumers held the cards to make it worthwhile to join their plan, banks began mailing unsolicited credit cards. By then, the wallet-sized squares of embossed plastic had worked a revolution in consumer finance, as Boorstin observed: "Credit, once closely tied to the character, honor and reputation of a particular person, one of a man's most precious possessions, was becoming a flimsy, plasticized, universal gadget." [13]

Action by Congress

Concern about mounting consumer indebtedness prompted demands in the 1960s for protective legislation. Capping almost a decade of debate on the issue, Congress in 1968 enacted the Consumer Credit Protection Act to help consumers make informed decisions when they obtained credit.

Known as the "truth-in-lending" law, it was one of the toughest and most far-reaching consumer bills passed by Congress since the securities disclosure laws of the 1930s. It required all buyers to be told the cost of loans and installment purchase plans in terms of an annual percentage rate calculated in a specified way. The resulting uniformity was designed to let consumers make valid cost comparisons between the lending rates or installment plans of different stores or lending institutions, just as they could compare the prices of similar products manufactured by different companies.

In 1970, Congress banned the issuance of unsolicited credit cards and limited to $50 cardholders' maximum liability for unauthorized use of their card. The same law regulated, for the first time, consumer reporting agencies. Further amendments in 1974 (the Fair Credit Reporting Act) sought to protect consumers against inaccurate and unfair credit-billing and credit card practices, and also banned discrimination in any credit transaction on the basis of gender or marital status.

Three years later, Congress turned its attention to abuses committed by agencies that collected other companies' overdue bills. Legislation signed by President Jimmy Carter on Sept. 8, 1977, established a nationwide system of controls for collection agencies. (Excluded from coverage were department stores, banks and other businesses that collected their own debts.) Before the law was enacted, debtors were frequently harassed by late-night phone calls, deceived by collectors posing as government agents and humiliated about their debt in front of neighbors and co-workers.

Laws to combat debt-collection abuse already were on the statute books of 37 states and the District of Columbia in 1977. However, supporters of a federal law argued that reliance on state laws had left about 80 million people wholly or partially vulnerable to collector abuse. Furthermore, increasing use of interstate phone lines was said to have undermined state-operated control programs.

A banking-deregulation law enacted in 1982 freed traditional deposit-taking institutions to compete head-on with money-market funds. As

Legislation signed by President Jimmy Carter on Sept. 8, 1977, established a nationwide system of controls for collection agencies. Before the law was enacted, debtors were frequently harassed by late-night phone calls, deceived by collectors posing as government agents and humiliated about their debt in front of neighbors and co-workers.

Are 'Instant' Bankruptcies the Latest Trend?

To a considerable extent, the English essayist and critic Charles Lamb reflected society's attitudes when he declared in an 1829 letter: "It has long been my deliberate judgment that all bankrupts, of whatsoever denomination, civil or religious, ought to be hanged."

Fast-forward to *The Wall Street Journal* of Aug. 28, 1996, and a story topped by a headline that sums up an increasingly common contemporary approach to personal finance: "Go Directly to Bankruptcy. Do Not Pass Delinquency."

For creditors, it's alarming enough that personal bankruptcies are expected to exceed 1 million in 1996 for the first time ever. Even more disturbing is the apparent willingness of some debtors to walk away from their financial obligations without any pangs of conscience.

"Historically, the pattern for personal bankruptcy has been more of a migration from a 30-day delinquency to a 180-day delinquency, which is [an accounting] charge-off," said Scott Calhoun, deputy comptroller for risk evaluation at the Office of the Comptroller of the Currency. But now, he says, increasing numbers of consumers are going directly from being solvent one day to filing for bankruptcy the next, without showing any of the traditional signals of imminent default.[1]

The modern U.S. bankruptcy system dates from the 1978 Bankruptcy Reform Act, which overhauled a structure that had remained virtually unchanged for 40 years. The measure gave individual debtors two bankruptcy options. They could file for "straight bankruptcy" under Chapter 7, which required them to liquidate their property in exchange for discharge of all their unsecured debts. In other words, they would be granted a "fresh start," free of all prior debt. The second option was filing under Chapter 13, which merely postpones repayment of all or part of the debt, according to a court-approved repayment plan extending over several years. Such arrangements do not require any property to be liquidated and distributed to creditors. The 1978 law also established a new, independent bankruptcy court system to be operated by judges appointed by the president for 14-year terms.

Critics blamed the changes for the sudden rise in bankruptcy filings, from fewer than 200,000 to 450,000 a year, which occurred after the law took effect on Oct. 1, 1979. They complained that consumers were taking undue advantage of the law to avoid paying their debts, in some cases going on credit-financed buying sprees just days before filing for bankruptcy.

The Supreme Court, in any event, declared the 1978 law unconstitutional in 1982. It held that Congress had given judges too much power. Two years later, Congress approved legislation that curtailed the power of bankruptcy judges but otherwise left the earlier statute largely intact.

Ten more years were to pass before Congress again made major changes in the bankruptcy system. Legislation signed by President Clinton on Oct. 26, 1994:

- Eliminated delays in bankruptcy cases by streamlining the judicial process;
- Made it easier for individual debtors to file for Chapter 13;
- Cleared the way for payment of income taxes with a credit card;
- Made it more difficult for spouses to declare bankruptcy to avoid alimony and child-support payments; and
- Authorized formation of a National Bankruptcy Review Commission to review and recommend changes in the bankruptcy code.

"Regrettably, the laws on bankruptcy won't change before the end of 1997, if in fact they ever do," says David Robertson, president of *The Nilson Report,* a credit card newsletter. "The bankruptcy commission won't report to Congress until the end of 1997, and its proposals obviously will become a political hot potato. No one in the industry is expecting anything to happen in terms of relief at the government level."

What the industry can do, Robertson says, is "remind consumers that if they do file for bankruptcy, their credit will be sullied. It will be difficult to get a home loan or a car loan. Also, I think you'll find more information-sharing on the part of card issuers.

"For instance, when Alpha Bank compares notes with Beta Bank, they may find that an individual withdrew a lot of cash from his ATM machine and bought a plane ticket to a nice tropical island later that day. They may also find that he spent all the rest of the cash advance on the island, and declared personal bankruptcy soon after returning home. Creditors are going to start putting two and two together and fighting that sort of thing."

---

[1] Quoted in *The Wall Street Journal,* Aug. 28, 1996, p. C1.

a result, banks across the country were able to attract depositors by offering high interest on deposits and then passing those high rates on to borrowers — including the holders of bank-issued credit cards.

"The banks learned an important lesson during this period: Consumers continue to incur debt no matter what the rate of interest charged," noted Medoff and Harless. "Thus, even when the federal funds rate (the interest rate that banks charge one another for overnight loans) fell from more than 14 percent to less than 9 percent between June and December of 1982, the interest rate on credit cards remained high. Moreover, between 1980 and 1992, as the federal funds rate fell from 13.4 percent to 3.5 percent, the average credit card interest rate rose from 17.3 percent to 17.8 percent. The ability of banks to borrow money at a fairly low interest rate and to relend it at a high interest rate further spurred the lenders' foray into the high-risk [consumer credit] markets."[14]

To enhance consumer awareness of credit card borrowing costs, Congress in 1988 mandated the disclosure of certain data. All direct-mail solicitations for credit cards, for example, had to clearly show annual interest rates and fees, the length of the grace period before interest begins to accrue and the minimum finance charges for cash advances and late payments.

A separate credit disclosure bill that cleared Congress in 1988 applied to home-equity loans, which had been made possible by sweeping tax-law changes approved two years earlier. Such loans proved immensely popular, since they were the only form of consumer borrowing on which interest payments remained fully tax-deductible. *

Most home-equity loans were open-ended, meaning they provided a line of credit against which individuals could borrow, often merely by writing a check. However, banks were not subject in most states to disclosure requirements for such loans, and they were free to alter the terms of loans — often to the detriment of borrowers — after they were made. The new law barred banks and other lenders from changing the terms of loans once they were established, except that interest rates could be variable, as on some conventional mortgages.

The fiscal 1996 intelligence authorization bill signed early this year by President Clinton contained a controversial provision enabling the FBI to obtain credit reports for counterintelligence investigations. Specifically, the measure allowed the bureau to obtain a court order to gain access to consumer credit files and find the names and addresses of the financial institutions where an individual had an account. The law also provided that the FBI would have to pay the credit reporting agency for the information it obtained and that all parties would face civil penalties if the FBI probe were disclosed.

"It is anticipated in Washington that the new law will be used in investigating suspected terrorists or potential terrorists," noted *Credit Card Management,* a monthly trade publication. "The number of requests is expected to be small."[15] ■

CURRENT SITUATION

Credit Bureau Law

A decidedly consumer-friendly credit-report law cleared Congress on Sept. 30, the final day of fiscal 1996. Enacted as Title II of the omnibus fiscal 1997 appropriations bill, the measure was designed to make it easier for consumers to examine and correct information in their credit bureau files.[16]

Among other provisions, the new law required credit bureaus to make their reports more intelligible and to include in them all the material in an individual's file. However, the bureaus were allowed to keep confidential any credit "scores" or similar data used to assess a consumer's creditworthiness.

The law also required the credit bureaus to:

- Set up toll-free numbers for consumers and make sure that callers are put in touch with a bureau employee, not just a recorded message.
- Investigate complaints within 30 days and inform the complainant of what happened as a result. Existing law also mandates such probes, but sets no deadline for their completion.
- Notify consumers of their right to have their names removed from marketing lists used by credit card issuers to prescreen potential customers.
- Inform consumers of their rights when an adverse action is taken against them. In such cases, consumers are entitled to a free copy of the report that triggered the action. They also are free to challenge any information contained in it.
- Take reasonable steps to ensure that erroneous information does not reappear in a consumer's file after it has been removed.

The law will not take effect until October 1997, giving the credit industry time to make any needed adjustments. Consumer groups praised the new safeguards, and industry representatives voiced no strong objections. "A lot of what it entails is what we had already adopted as an industry," said Norman Magnuson, public affairs director of Associated Credit Bureaus, a Washington-based trade group. "We don't see any problems with it."[17]

Indeed, credit card marketers had begun addressing consumers' privacy concerns well before the law cleared Congress. Last spring, for example, MBNA America Bank of Wilmington, Del., told prospects for its Platinum Plus card: "To help protect your privacy, we will not sell your name to other companies." And MasterCard International published a new brochure on credit privacy: "In the Driver's Seat: Steering your Financial and Consumer Information in the Right Direction."

Credit Card War

Meanwhile, though, fierce competition among credit card issuers assures that privacy will remain a volatile issue. "Marketing is getting much more aggressive, and credit card marketing is probably one of the most information-intensive forms of marketing you can find," says Martin E. Abrams, director of information policy

* Under the Tax Reform Act of 1986, deductions for interest on credit cards and other consumer purchases were phased out over five years, beginning in 1988.

and privacy at Experian Information Solutions Inc., one of the nation's three main credit bureaus.

The aggressiveness often takes the form of wooing ever-smaller segments of the consumer population. Just a few years ago, a typical mass mailing to credit card prospects comprised about 30 million pieces, each containing one of two or three different sales pitches. Today's mailings tend to be smaller and more tightly focused: 3 million pieces, say, with up to 25 "sells," each targeting a specific consumer subgroup.

Before long, even this approach may seem scattershot. The time is coming, says Robertson of *The Nilson Report,* when card issuers will be able to prepare a mass mailing that's individually tailored to each recipient: "Not one that's aimed at everybody in your ZIP code, but just at you."

Such customizing of sales appeals is called database marketing, which relies on detailed analysis of credit and demographic data culled from numerous sources. The same technique is expected to help creditors do a better job of identifying the brightest prospects in the subprime credit market. Since most borrowers with top-notch credit ratings already have at least one installment loan and one or more credit cards, lenders have turned their attention to the less creditworthy B and C groups.

To some extent, they were inspired by the performance of Fingerhut Cos., the consumer catalog marketing firm in Minnetonka, Minn. Fingerhut entered the credit card business in early 1995, focusing primarily on lower-income consumers. By the end of the year, it was the nation's 23rd-largest issuer of co-branded Visa and MasterCard cards, with $500 million in receivables on 750,000 accounts.

Fingerhut's success was hard-won, since conventional credit scoring formulas aren't designed to spot nuggets hidden in the tailings. Instead, they "are geared toward finding the cream of the crop and tossing away the rest," according to *Bank Technology News*. "Less effort is made to distinguish between the 'good-bads' and the 'bad-bads' — that is, applicants who exhibit positive signs of improvement vs. the ones with ongoing troubles." [18]

Determining who belongs in each group requires intense scrutiny of credit histories. The more promising candidates "include people who may have had credit skirmishes in the past, but who have cleaned the slate," the publication said. "Others may be young people who've maximized their lines of credit, but hold promise of paying them off. Still others are those with blemishes tied directly to a life event; for example, a divorce or a severe illness could suddenly alter the ability to repay, but not affect longer-term habits. The goal is to pick the candidates who truly want to improve their credit ratings, and weed out the ones who don't care." [19]

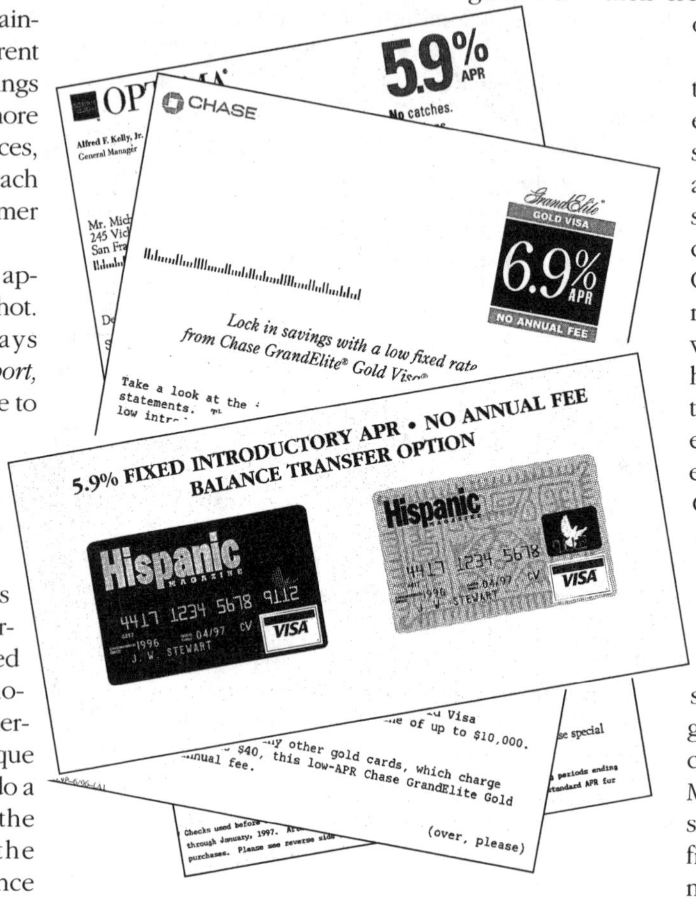

Ironically, at the very time that credit card issuers are re-examining their policies toward subprime credit risks, they are adopting a harder line toward some of their most responsible customers. On Sept. 10, GE Capital Corp. announced it was notifying holders of its GE Rewards MasterCard that they will have to pay a $25 annual fee if they pay off their balances every month, thus avoiding interest charges. Two weeks later, General Motors halved the maximum car rebate that holders of its gold MasterCard could earn over seven years from $7,000 to $3,500.

"The GM move underscores the fact that there are no guarantees with bank credit cards," commented Robert McKinley, president of RAM Research, a credit card tracking firm in Frederick, Md. "Once too many cardholders figure out how to beat the system, card issuers change the rules." [20]

Increasingly aggressive credit card marketing threatens consumers' privacy, consumer advocates say.

The 'Indebted Society'

In their recent book, Medoff and Harless pointed to a troubling change in consumer borrowing since the 1960s. They noted that the "classic model for consumer behavior is that when times are good, people borrow in the expectation of more good times." Today, in contrast,

Continued on p. 1026

At Issue:

Has the credit card industry made credit too easily available to teenagers and college students?

yes

KEN McELDOWNEY
Executive Director, Consumer Action

FROM TESTIMONY BEFORE THE HOUSE BANKING, FINANCE AND URBAN AFFAIRS SUBCOMMITTEE ON CONSUMER CREDIT AND INSURANCE, MARCH 10, 1994.

The dramatic increase of new players in the credit card field has saturated the market and led the industry to react in two ways that disturb us greatly: the first is to heavily stimulate usage of cards, such as by encouraging cardholders to use them to pay for groceries and other basic necessities; the second is to suspend the traditional criteria for cardholders and offer large amounts of easy credit to people who have no credit experience or familiarity with the credit world, namely college students. . . .

Many callers to our [consumer information line] are besieged by credit debts and are confused about how to handle them. . . . Most do not understand how to determine the true cost of credit or how much they really owe. A surprisingly large number . . . do not realize the implications of only making the minimum payment each month; a common statement we hear is that the bank must be making a mistake, because, "I make the minimum payment each month, but the balance I owe hardly goes down. . . ."

While most of the callers to our switchboard are adults, not college students, this fact tends to make us even more concerned about the plight of students using credit cards.

If so many adults lack a basic understanding of how to use credit wisely, how can we expect that their children will do any better? We do not believe college students are miraculously better at handling credit than their elders.

The following factors tend to mask the degree to which young people are incurring excessive credit card debt:

They make minimum payments, expecting that they will be able to wipe out their debts at some future time when they are employed at high salaries; they rely on their parents to step in whenever they have trouble paying debts; with credit so easily available to people who already have credit cards, they apply for more cards and use that additional credit to help them make ends meet.

Such patterns of behavior can only go on so long. For those students who do not graduate, or do not find immediate employment or high-paying jobs, their post-college lives as young adults may be burdened by the nightmare of an enormous debt load, both from credit cards and student loans.

We feel that the credit card industry must shoulder blame for this problem, especially for the aggressive ways in which it pushes credit card applications at students, without balancing messages of "easy credit" with explanations of how to use credit wisely. . . .

no

VISA U.S.A. INC.

FROM TESTIMONY BEFORE THE HOUSE BANKING, FINANCE AND URBAN AFFAIRS SUBCOMMITTEE ON CONSUMER CREDIT AND INSURANCE, MARCH 10, 1994.

There is a high demand for credit cards in the college student market. Like other members of modern society, students need a variety of payment methods, including credit cards. Indeed college students particularly benefit from credit cards because such cards enable them to time important purchases, such as books and tuition, rather than have such purchases subject to available savings or cash flow. . . .

Having and using a credit card as an alternative to cash and checks is a normal and accepted means of payment in our society. . . . As adults, college students have every right to have access to this payment option. Nearly half of the college students in this country live on their own and qualify as "heads of households." Old enough to vote and to serve in the armed forces, most students appreciate the opportunity to have and use credit cards. Most importantly, a young adult can legally enter into a contractual agreement at the age of 18. A majority of students view credit card ownership and management as another rung on the maturity ladder, offering not only a chance to access credit but an opportunity to establish a good credit history. . . .

Contrary to what is often presented in the mass media, the average college student uses a credit card responsibly. More than half of the 9 million full-time undergraduates in this country have a general purpose credit card — and the majority of them maintain a better payment record than the general public. Research shows that college students pay the balance in full half of the time. Indeed college students are less likely to carry balances on their credit cards than the population at large, and when they do carry a balance, the amount is about one-third that of the average non-college credit card holder.

In fact, the college market mirrors or performs better than the general population in all areas of performance. College students tend to handle their credit cards in the same way as adults in other age groups — their charge-off rates appear to be no worse than that for the cardholder population as a whole.

While the efforts of Visa and its members in marketing credit products to college students is a way of building brand loyalty and eventually establishing a profitable relationship, none of the marketing would be worthwhile if these students weren't responsible consumers. Much of the media coverage on this issue centers on the student who got in over his or her head and couldn't meet their financial obligations. These students are anomalies. Nine out of 10 college students with credit cards use them wisely — and Visa would not be satisfied with any other outcome.

FOR MORE INFORMATION

American Bankers Association, 1120 Connecticut Ave. N.W., Washington, D.C. 20036; (202) 663-5471. The ABA tracks credit card delinquencies on a quarterly basis.

Bankcard Holders of America, 6862 Elm St., Suite 300, McLean, Va. 22101; (703) 917-9805. BHA educates consumers about the prudent use of credit and their rights and responsibilities as credit users.

Consumer Action, 116 New Montgomery St., Suite 233, San Francisco, Calif. 94105; (415) 777-9648. This nonprofit advocacy and education group focuses on issues related to credit cards.

Credit Research Center, Krannert Graduate School of Management, Purdue University, West Lafayette, Ind.; (317) 494-4380. The center prepares and distributes studies on how the credit markets are working.

International Credit Association, 243 N. Lindbergh Blvd., St. Louis, Mo. 63141; (314) 991-3030. ICA represents credit industry executives and professionals; its "Train the Trainers" program teaches teachers how to incorporate credit education into the school curriculum.

Continued from p. 1024

"when times are bad, people borrow to make up the gap between expectation and reality.

"In itself, this pattern is not a problem, because over the business cycle, it is good that people continue to borrow during a recession. But the pattern becomes a problem when the economic downturn extends beyond a long-term trend (as it has). Over time, consumer borrowing starts to tie up more and more resources that could be better allocated to investment." [21]

According to Medoff and Harless, consumer debt forms only part of a much broader phenomenon affecting all sectors of the economy. "Families borrow to maintain lifestyles eroded by falling wages. Firms under pressure to service their current debt forgo investments in future productivity. And the government borrows solely to meet interest payments [on the national debt]. Today one can hardly imagine a world in which these three groups are not way over their heads in debt." [22]

To "reverse the vicious circles" of indebtedness "and move into a virtuous circle," the authors recommend such steps as higher taxes on the top one-fifth of U.S. households, tax-sheltered personal savings, extended jobless benefits and job protection for older workers. "Americans will spend some years in the wilderness before the promised land becomes visible," they concede. "Unfortunately for those hurting in the Indebted Society, we must pass through it before moving beyond it." [23]

"Debt," the TV Game Show

Television, meanwhile, has found a way to turn consumer debt into mass entertainment. The vehicle is a game show called "Debt," which debuted on the Lifetime cable channel in June. [24] The contestants compete not for cars, refrigerators and vacations in Hawaii but for liquidation of their personal debts, up to a limit of $10,000.

"The country's in debt!" cries Wink Martindale, the show's host. "You're probably in debt! But most importantly, these three players ... have come to us today with their real-life debt, and one of them might be lucky enough to get out of it by the end of the show." [25]

During the first two rounds of "Debt," contestants field questions on pop culture; each correct answer reduces the amount owed to the player's creditors. The contestant who sheds the most debt then moves on to a "lightning round" of 10 additional questions. The reward for a perfect score on these is a check for the contestant's total personal debt — up to $10,000.

Even then, the game isn't necessarily over. The winner can elect to field one final question. The correct answer doubles the jackpot; a wrong one sends the contestant home empty-handed.

After viewing "Debt," David J. Morrow of *The New York Times* reached some unsettling conclusions: "While most contestants know their trivia, don't expect them to know the interest rates on their credit cards or their monthly account balances. . . . What many of these contestants did say, however, was that their financial troubles were not their fault. The debt is just the price of their lifestyle, which by their definition is Spartan." [26] ■

OUTLOOK

Charging Ahead

Consumer advocates and credit industry officials foresee easing of the nation's consumer credit burden in the near future. Though credit card issuers continue to incur more losses, says Susswein, "they're still raking in record profits. But they also are tightening credit standards to cut their losses. We should see the results of that in the next 18 to 24 months."

Heller of Veribanc is even more optimistic. "Absent a severe downturn in the economy, we'll start seeing the effects of what the banks and card issuers are doing to restrain borrowing within a year."

Looking further ahead, credit experts are guarded about the role of so-called "smart cards" in the credit marketplace. Smart cards contain a computer chip that enables them to perform more than one function. The chip could, for example, combine the features of a credit card, debit card and stored-value card.

The most recent test of smart cards on a mass scale occurred in Atlanta during this year's Olympic Games. First Union Bank, NationsBank and Wachovia Bank of Georgia issued some 2 million stored-value cards in $10, $20, $50 and $100 denominations. About 50 Atlanta-area merchants, with a combined 1,500 retail outlets, agreed to accept the cards. But while the issuing banks termed the experiment a success, *Bank Advertising News* concluded that "the product was basically a dud, with only limited response from a handful of consumers." [27]

In Robertson's opinion, "It will be a long, long time before Visa and MasterCard cards have smart chips in them." However, he predicts that the government will provide welfare recipients with smart cards, so benefits-transfers can be made electronically. "This will eliminate the need to mail checks or distribute food stamps, for instance," Robertson says. "The idea makes tons of sense. Considering just the potential for reducing fraud, it would be a terrific change for the better."

However, adds Robertson, "There's no reason at all to think smart cards are going to transform the Visa-MasterCard world, because all those retail terminals now in use would have to be upgraded or replaced. And that would cost many billions of dollars."

For Susswein, the smart-card issue is a "classic chicken-or-egg situation. Does a store invest in new technology to accept these cards before people are using them? Conversely, why should people use the cards before stores can accept them? My hunch is that smart cards are going to emerge slowly over time. We'll probably see more growth in credit and debit cards and stored-value cards, which will then evolve into smart cards combining all those features and possibly others as well."

In the meantime, credit card use in such non-traditional venues as supermarkets and movie theaters is expected to continue growing. "That's because of the ease of using credit cards," says MasterCard's Shimmerine. "The consumer only has to pay one check at the end of the month. And since processing technology has improved, credit card transactions can be handled faster and more cheaply than before. Therefore, more merchants accept plastic."

Sherry agrees with Shimmerine's view of the future, but with some foreboding. "People are going out of their way to charge things like groceries, and it just seems like a really bad idea," she says. "You may be able to handle the charges now because you've got a good job. But suppose something catastrophic happens? Who will pay the credit card bills if you lose your job or fall seriously ill?" ■

Notes

[1] See "Why are consumers cutting back on spending?" *USA Today,* Nov. 4, 1996.

[2] James Medoff and Andrew Harless, *The Indebted Society: Anatomy of an Ongoing Disaster* (1996), p. 18. Medoff is a professor of labor and industry at Harvard University; Harless is an economic and financial consultant.

[3] *Loc. cit.*

[4] Testimony before House Committee on Banking and Financial Services, Sept. 12, 1996.

[5] *Loc. cit.*

[6] See Mary Geraghty, "Students, Wooed by Credit-Card Purveyors, Often Over-Commit Themselves, Colleges Find," *The Chronicle of Higher Education,* Nov. 8, 1996, p. A37.

[7] Testimony before Subcommittee on Consumer Credit and Insurance, House Committee on Banking, Finance and Urban Affairs, March 10, 1994.

[8] *Ibid.*

[9] *Ibid.*

[10] Quoted by Irving J. Michelman, *Consumer Finance: A Case History in American Business* (1966), p. 98.

[11] Daniel J. Boorstin, *The Americans: The Democratic Experience* (1973), p. 424.

[12] *Ibid.,* p. 423.

[13] *Ibid.,* p. 428.

[14] Medoff and Harless, *op. cit.,* p. 12.

[15] "A Green Light for FBI Snooping?" *Credit Card Management,* May 1996, p. 34.

[16] The three main nationwide credit bureaus are Equifax Credit Information Services, Experian Information Solutions Inc. (formerly TRW Information Systems and Services) and Trans Union Corp.

[17] Quoted in *The Washington Post,* Oct. 27, 1996, p. C1.

[18] Jackie Cohen, "Credit Scoring New Markets," *Bank Technology News,* July 1996, p. 38.

[19] *Loc. cit.*

[20] Quoted in *USA Today,* Sept. 24, 1996, p. 2B.

[21] Medoff and Harless, *op. cit.,* p. 17.

[22] *Ibid.,* p. 7.

[23] *Ibid.,* pp. 225-26..

[24] The ABC network has an option to move "Debt" into its prime-time lineup as early as next year.

[25] Quoted in *TV Guide,* Aug. 17, 1996.

[26] David J. Morrow, "The Hit Quiz Show for Those Who Owe," *The New York Times,* Aug. 11, 1996.

[27] "Smart Card Reception Lukewarm in Atlanta," *Bank Advertising News,* Aug. 12, 1996, p. 6.

Bibliography

Selected Sources Used

Books

Medoff, James, and Andrew Harless, *The Indebted Society: Anatomy of an Ongoing Disaster,* Little, Brown, 1996.

Though Medoff and Harless discuss consumer debt, they devote most of their book to corporate and public indebtedness. Rising debt, in their view, has distorted the economy and heightened feelings of economic insecurity among working Americans. Among other remedies, they recommend raising taxes on the top one-fifth of U.S. households, extending unemployment benefits and enacting laws to protect the jobs of older workers. "Americans will spend some years in the wilderness before the promised land becomes visible," they write. "Unfortunately for those hurting in the Indebted Society, we must pass through it before going beyond it."

Articles

Cocheo, Steve, "This Is Not Your Father's American Express," *ABA Banking Journal,* September 1996.

Cocheo, executive editor of the journal, details how American Express, a credit card pioneer, is working to regain lost market share through more aggressive and flexible marketing.

Daly, James J., "The Pressure Builds," *Credit Card Management,* May 1996.

Daly, the editor of *Credit Card Management,* looks at rising concern among lenders about credit card delinquencies and charge-offs. "Clearly, the credit card is still king of the banking hill," he writes. "But if the loss situation doesn't get back under control, plastic could find itself dethroned."

Frank, John N., "The Brouhaha Over Privacy," *Credit Card Management,* May 1996.

Contributing Editor Frank examines the reasons why many consumers worry about the privacy of their financial data. A major concern is the selling of names to direct-mail marketers without consumers' knowledge or permission.

Harden, Lisa, "Combatting Financial Illiteracy," *Northwestern Financial Review,* Aug. 24, 1996.

Harden surveys efforts by some bankers and educators in the upper Midwest to improve the financial savvy of young people.

Hudson, Michael, "Cashing In on Poverty: How Big Business Wins Every Time," *The Nation,* May 20, 1996.

Hudson shows how certain lenders prosper by catering to the nation's least affluent consumers. "Pawn shops, check-cashing outlets, rent-to-own stores, finance companies, high-interest mortgage lenders and many others are raking in big money by targeting people on the bottom third of the economic ladder — perhaps 60 million consumers who are virtually shut out by banks and other conventional merchants."

McMenamin, Brigid, "Invasion of the Credit Snatchers," *Forbes,* Aug. 26, 1996.

McMenamin examines consumer-identity fraud, which occurs when a crook obtains a person's Social Security number and credit card account numbers and uses the information to establish fraudulent credit lines. "Some imposters actually live under the names they steal," notes McMenamin. "They take out driver's licenses, sign leases, even give the stolen names to police when nabbed for other crimes."

Stark, Ellen, "Swamped by Debt? Here Are Six Ways to Get Out," *Money,* September 1995.

Climbing out of a debt swamp is never painless, but it can be done, Stark says.

Zizka, Robert, and Sanford Rose, "Who Wins in Consumer Lending — and Why?" *Journal of Retail Banking,* spring 1995.

The authors, both associated with First Manhattan Consulting Group, take a look at "customer data-base management," a strategy for separating the wheat from the chaff among credit risks.

Reports and Studies

American Bankers Association, *1995 Bank Card Industry Survey Report,* 1996.

The ABA, trade group of the U.S. banking industry, reviews key legislative and regulatory developments at the federal level in 1993-94, the first two years of the Clinton administration.

Subcommittee on Consumer Credit and Insurance, U.S. House Committee on Banking, Finance and Urban Affairs, *Kiddie Credit Cards* (published proceedings of hearing held March 10, 1994).

Representatives of consumer groups and credit card companies offer contrasting views on whether college students know enough about money management to be entrusted with credit cards of their own.

The Next Step

Additional information from UMI's Newspaper & Periodical Abstracts database

Consumer Debt

Bleakley, Fred R., "Consumer debt alarms some analysts," *The Wall Street Journal,* Sept. 11, 1995, p. A2.
Consumers are taking on so much debt that some economists are beginning to sound alarm bells, predicting that caution will set in, consumers will pull back and the economy will stall. Other economists are more optimistic, saying lenient credit terms allow consumers to carry their debt longer.

Browning, E S, "Heard on the street: Bank stocks fall on fears about cards," *The Wall Street Journal,* June 21, 1996, p. C1.
Investors clobbered bank and credit card stocks on June 20, 1996, as worries spread about mounting rates of personal bankruptcy and bad credit-card debt. The sell-off was triggered by Bank of New York's announcement on June 19 that it would boost credit card loss reserves by $350 million.

Coleman, Calmetta Y., "Consumer debt and charge-offs escalate," *The Wall Street Journal,* Feb. 12, 1996, p. A2.
Credit card issuers are finding that as they reach out for more customers, they are seeing higher charge-off rates, or accounts written off as uncollectable. The charge-off rates of a number of card issuers are examined.

"Easing in consumer debt," *The New York Times,* March 8, 1995, p. D2.
The Federal Reserve said on March 7, 1995, that consumer credit rose in January at the slowest rate in 20 months, led by a decline in borrowing to buy automobiles. Credit rose $3.7 billion compared with a gain of $6.6 billion in December 1994.

"Growth in consumer debt slows sharply," *Los Angeles Times,* July 9, 1996, p. D2.
The growth in consumer debt slowed sharply in May 1996, climbing at an annualized rate of just 4.9 percent, according to government data released on July 8, 1996. Some analysts attributed the slowdown to a tightening of credit standards by lenders worried about rising delinquency rates.

Gullo, Karen, "Worries rise over jump in consumer debt," *Boston Globe,* Oct. 29, 1995, p. 44.
The average American wallet holds seven different credit cards, contributing to an explosion of consumer debt, according to RAM Research, a consulting business that follows the credit card industry. Now, a rise in late payments has some analysts worried that consumers are overextended, and companies that lend money are headed for trouble.

Kaslow, Amy, "Consumer debt could slow 1996, economic engine," *The Christian Science Monitor,* Dec. 28, 1995, p. 1.
Although 1995 was a solid year for the American economy, top analysts predict slower growth in 1996, with the glum prospect that a recession could begin right around election day in November. Factors contributing to an economic slowdown are highlighted.

Lee, Louise, "Consumer debt crimps profit at Penney and Dillard as Wal-Mart net rises 12 percent," *The Wall Street Journal,* Aug. 14, 1996, p. A2.
Rising consumer debt levels led to lackluster results at J. C. Penney Co. and Dillard Department Stores during their second quarters, while Wal-Mart Stores Inc., the U.S.'s largest discounter, bounced back to post a double-digit gain in profit. Penney saw a 19 percent drop in profit in the period ended July 27, 1996, Dillard posted a slight increase for its quarter ended Aug. 3 and Wal-Mart reported a rise of 12 percent.

McGeehan, Patrick, "Consumer debt worries weigh on stocks," *USA Today,* Oct. 26, 1995, p. B3.
The Dow Jones industrial average fell 29.98 points to close at 4753.68 on Oct. 25, 1995, while the S&P 500 fell 4.07 to 582.47 and the Nasdaq composite fell 12.77 to 1026.47.

Montague, Bill, "Heavy credit card use pushes consumer debt up 8 percent in," *USA Today,* Sept. 10, 1996, p. B2.
Consumer credit rose at an 8 percent annual rate in July 1996, the biggest gain in three months. The consumer credit figure, reported Sept. 9 by the FRB, was slightly higher than analysts expected due to the fact that credit card debt soared in July at a 19.4 percent annual rate. Monthly consumer credit is depicted for July 1995—July 1996.

Shao, Maria, "Rising debt of consumers spurs worries," *Boston Globe,* June 21, 1996, p. 83.
From credit card late payments to mortgage delinquencies to personal bankruptcies, U.S. consumers seem stretched to the max in June 1996. While the overall economy has been humming along with low inflation, a number of signs have emerged that consumers, who account for two-thirds of economic activity, are under stress.

Tharpe, Gene, "Consumer debt piling up," *Atlanta Constitution,* June 10, 1996, p. E2.
Tharpe notes the burgeoning debt-collection business in America and offers advice on consumer protection rights concerning collections.

Vogel, Thomas T. Jr., "Consumer debt worries are overblown," *The Wall Street Journal,* Dec. 14, 1995, p. A2.

Worries about the surge in consumer debt may be overblown, a growing number of economists are concluding. The American Bankers Association reported Dec. 13, 1995, that while bank credit delinquencies have reached near record levels, there have not been similarly large increases for broader measures of consumer debt.

Credit Card Delinquencies

"Credit card delinquencies almost hit 15-year high," *The Wall Street Journal,* June 11, 1996, p. A16.

The American Bankers Association reported that credit card delinquencies reached an almost 15-year high in the first quarter of 1996. The percentage of overdue credit card accounts hit 3.53 percent in the quarter, up from 3.34 percent in the last quarter of 1995.

"Credit Card Delinquencies Reach a Record Level," *The New York Times,* Sept. 18, 1996, p. D4.

The rate of late payments on credit cards reached a record level in the second quarter of 1996, the ABA said on Sept. 17, citing the effect of loose lending standards. Delinquencies were reported on 3.66 percent of credit card accounts, up from 3.53 percent in the first quarter.

Hershey, Robert D. Jr., "Credit card delinquencies rise; Price report shows no inflation," *The New York Times,* March 15, 1996, p. D1.

The ranks of consumers who have fallen behind on credit card payments edged up to match a 10-year high in the final quarter of 1995, a sign of growing household distress that some economists argue threatens to bring the five-year-old economic expansion to an end. Meanwhile, prices paid to factories, farmers and other producers fell in February 1996 for the first time in eight months, easing fears that the big jump in new jobs might lead to higher inflation.

Matthews, Gordon, "Credit card delinquencies worry stock analysts," *American Banker,* June 13, 1996, p. 1.

Some Wall Street analysts are growing more worried about the impact of rising credit card losses on bank earnings and stock prices. Their concerns heightened the effect of news during the week of June 9 from the American Bankers Association that card account delinquencies reached a 15-year high in the first quarter.

Stark, Ellen, "Avoid these high credit card charges," *Money,* January, 1996, p. 38.

Credit card delinquency rates are at their highest mark since recessionary 1991. Card holders can avoid high credit card charges by grabbing a low-rate card, not overstepping their credit limit and avoiding late charges.

Credit-Identity Fraud

Dugas, Christine, "Credit card fraud is put to the test," *USA Today,* May 15, 1996, p. B1.

Biometric technologies, based on unique personal characteristics such as fingerprint, retina scan or voiceprint, are being tested by banks in an effort to stop credit card fraud .

McLeod, Ramon G., "Beyond credit card theft," *San Francisco Chronicle,* Aug. 30, 1996, p. A26.

Theft of identity may be one of the fastest-growing forms of credit card fraud today, according to a report issued on Aug. 29, 1996, by the California Public Interest Research Group. However, consumers can take some simple steps to protect themselves.

"U.S. invades privacy in Nevada credit card sting," *Denver Post,* Sept. 10, 1996, p. B8.

An editorial comments on a Las Vegas, Nev., case where the federal government, in an attempt to snare a computer operator who had expressed interest in illegally obtaining credit card information, and a major bank, gave a suspected crook the credit card numbers and personal histories of citizens, without their permission or knowledge.

Credit Card Marketing

Croghan, Lore, "The Avis of credit card data," *Financial World,* July 18, 1995, p. 56.

Total System Services is investing in cutting-edge technology to try to become number one in the credit card data-processing business. The $188 million-in-sales card processer hopes new software will win over banks.

"First USA to add 2 credit card processors," *The New York Times,* Aug. 26, 1995, p. A35.

First USA Inc. said on Aug. 25, 1995, that it would acquire the U.S.'s two largest independent direct-marketing credit card processors in separate stock and cash deals for undisclosed terms. Dallas-based First USA said it would offer stock to acquire Litle & Co. and pay cash for the DMGT Corp.

Fitzgerald, Kate, "In credit card business, relationships count," *Advertising Age,* Oct. 7, 1996, p. S18.

John D. Hayes is an advertising executive at American Express, and John Cochran is the chief marketing officer at MBNA America Bank. Cochran is a master of database and relational marketing. Hayes oversaw the launch of American Express' first global advertising campaign.

"Kmart Plans Nationwide Expansion of Credit Card," *The New York Times,* Aug. 28, 1996, p. D3.

The Kmart Corp. said on Aug. 27, 1996, that it would make its new credit card available in more than 2,100 stores across the U.S. The discount retailer had strong results in test-marketing of the credit card at 167 stores.

Murray, Matt, and Vanessa O'Connell, "Banc One to test credit card that lets holders borrow against 401(k) money," *The Wall Street Journal,* June 24, 1996, p. A7.

Banc One Corp has decided to proceed in fall 1996 with test-marketing a long-discussed credit card that would permit holders to borrow against their 401(k) retirement accounts.

Sheets, Ken, "Does your credit card match your style?" ***Kiplinger's Personal Finance Magazine,*** **January 1995, pp. 112-116.**
Credit cards that are tailored to match particular spending profiles are described. Consumers who carry a balance of less than $1,000 should get a no-annual-fee card.

Tharpe, Gene, "Credit card offers: Reality in the fine print," ***Atlanta Constitution,*** **Nov. 13, 1995, p. E2.**
Tharpe explains the realities behind some of the marketing lures used in preapproved credit card offers.

Personal Bankruptcy

de Senerpont Domis, Olaf, "Bankruptcy too easy an out, Visa exec. tells banking panel," ***American Banker,*** **Sept. 13, 1996, p. B2.**
Kenneth Crone, vice president of Visa U.S.A.'s risk management and security division, told a House Banking Committee hearing on consumer loan delinquencies Sept. 12, 1996, that the Bankruptcy Code "allows debtors to obtain more protection than they need." Crone argued that unless Congress legislates to curb the rate of bankruptcies, banks will be forced to restrict how much credit they offer.

Dugas, Christine, "Bankruptcy cases grow despite healthy economy," ***USA Today,*** **Aug. 9, 1996, p. B6.**
Despite good economic news, debt is a growing problem for many Americans, resulting in more bankruptcy filings, perhaps a 20 percent jump in 1996. The types of personal bankruptcy are examined, as well as other factors besides debt that can lead to bankruptcy.

Dutt, Jill, "Bank losses on credit cards rise," ***The Washington Post,*** **Sept. 12, 1996, p. D9.**
Bank credit card losses are at their highest level since 1992, the federal government reported Sept. 11, 1996, in what many analysts said is both a side effect of the surge in personal bankruptcy filings as well as fallout from years of corporate downsizing.

Frank, Stephen E., "Your money matters: Weekend report: Over your head in debt? Bankruptcy offers new start," ***The Wall Street Journal,*** **Aug. 23, 1996, p. 1.**
For many Americans mired in debt, bankruptcy can actually be good news. Indeed, the bankruptcy laws were intended to help people wipe the slate clean and start over. And for some people hopelessly over their heads in bills, a fresh start is just what they need. The pros and cons of claiming personal bankruptcy are examined.

Kogan, Rick, "The age of Aquarius," ***Chicago Tribune,*** **p. 13. June 30, 1996**
Theater producer Michael Butler is profiled as he emerges from personal bankruptcy. Although Butler produced the play and the film "Hair," he lost millions of dollars over his career.

Tharpe, Gene, "Going for broke," ***Atlanta Constitution,*** **Sept. 23, 1996, p. E1.**
Personal bankruptcies filed nationwide climbed to record numbers during the last two quarters, and estimates are they will top 1 million for 1996, the first time ever for a calendar year. The Atlanta and north Georgia district, for the 12 months ending June 30, recorded slightly fewer than 28,000 personal bankruptcies, the sixth-highest district total in the U.S.

Trumbull, Mark, "Rising bankruptcies show value of managing debts," ***The Christian Science Monitor,*** **Sept. 3, 1996, p. 9.**
In the year ending June 30, 1996, the number of bankruptcy filings totaled more than 1 million for the first time ever in a 12-month period. That's almost one person for every 100 U.S. households. If bankruptcy has lost some of its stigma, however, it hasn't lost its sting, both emotionally and in a tarnished credit record.

Students as Target of Credit Card Marketing

"American Express Co.: Credit card for the young is being test-marketed," ***The Wall Street Journal,*** **Aug. 15, 1995, p. A10.**
American Express Co. is test-marketing Personal Choice, a credit card targeted at younger people without a credit history. The new card allows holders to choose their own credit limit between $500 and $1,500.

Dugas, Christine, "Credit card firms recruit new users on campuses," ***USA Today,*** **May 28, 1996, p. B1.**
Credit card companies are aggressively pursuing college students, who haven't hesitated to accept the offers. In 1996, consumers under age 30 are more likely to carry a credit card balance and to be worried about the amount of debt they are carrying, according to an informal *USA Today* reader survey.

Meece, Mickey, "Star and student loan group sending credit card to school," ***American Banker,*** **Aug. 8, 1996, p. 10.**
College students on 31 campuses this fall will be able to pay for school-related expenses at selected merchants with CollegeCard, the brainchild of nonprofit, student-lending organization Southwest Student Services Corp of Mesa, Ariz., Star Banc Corp. of Cincinnati issues the private-label card and Total System Services Inc, Columbus, Ga., processes the transactions. Star Bank said the card is underwritten like a student loan, so it's no risk to the bank.

Shepardson, David, "U-M students can use school credit card off-campus," ***Detroit News,*** **April 26, 1995, p. B7W.**
With some kinks still to be worked out, 500 University of Michigan students and Ann Arbor merchants are testing a program that allows school credit card holders to make purchases at off-campus locations.

Back Issues

Great Research on Current Issues Starts Right Here...Recent topics covered by The CQ Researcher are listed below. Before May 1991, reports were published under the name of Editorial Research Reports.

MAY 1995
Assisted Suicide Controversy
Overhauling Social Security
Learning to Read
Mandatory Sentencing

JUNE 1995
Combating Infectious Disease
Property Rights
Repetitive Stress Injuries
Regulating the Internet

JULY 1995
War Crimes
Highway Safety
Combating Terrorism
Preventing Teen Drug Use

AUGUST 1995
Job Stress
Organ Transplants
United Nations at 50
Advances in Cancer Research

SEPTEMBER 1995
Catholic Church in the U.S.
Northern Ireland Cease-Fire
High School Sports
Teaching History

OCTOBER 1995
Quebec's Future
Revitalizing the Cities
Networking the Classroom
Indoor Air Pollution

NOVEMBER 1995
The Working Poor
The Jury System
Sex, Violence and the Media
Police Misconduct

DECEMBER 1995
Teens and Tobacco
Gene Therapy's Future
Global Water Shortages
Third-Party Prospects

JANUARY 1996
Emergency Medicine
Punishing Sex Offenders
Bilingual Education
Helping the Homeless

FEBRUARY 1996
Reforming the CIA
Campaign Finance Reform
Academic Politics
Getting Into College

MARCH 1996
The British Monarchy
Preventing Juvenile Crime
Tax Reform
Pursuing the Paranormal

APRIL 1996
Centennial Olympic Games
Managed Care
Protecting Endangered Species
New Military Culture

MAY 1996
Russia's Political Future
Marriage and Divorce
Year-Round Schools
Taiwan, China and the U.S.

JUNE 1996
Rethinking NAFTA
First Ladies
Teaching Values
Labor Movement's Future

JULY 1996
Recovered-Memory Debate
Native Americans' Future
Crackdown on Sexual Harassment
Attack on Public Schools

AUGUST 1996
Fighting Over Animal Rights
Privatizing Government Services
Child Labor and Sweatshops
Cleaning Up Hazardous Wastes

SEPTEMBER 1996
Gambling Under Attack
The States and Federalism
Civic Journalism
Reassessing Foreign Aid

OCTOBER 1996
Political Consultants
Insurance Fraud
Rethinking School Integration
Parental Rights

NOVEMBER 1996
Global Warming
Clashing Over Copyright

Back issues are available for $5.00 (subscribers) or $8.00 (non-subscribers). Quantity discounts apply to orders over ten. To order, call Congressional Quarterly Customer Service at (202) 887-8621.

Binders are available for $18.00. To order call 1-800-638-1710. Please refer to stock number 648.

Future Topics

- ***Governing Washington, D.C***
- ***Welfare, Work and the States***
- ***Volunteerism***

PUBLISHED BY CONGRESSIONAL QUARTERLY INC.

Governing Washington, D.C.

Are major changes needed, or simply more money?

The nation's capital is facing a political and fiscal crisis. Two decades after Congress granted the city limited home rule, public services are faltering, the government is in debt and residents and jobs are moving out. Congress last year created a financial control board with broad powers to override the decisions of the District of Columbia's elected government. Now the board is pressuring the District government to cut costs and reduce waste. This month, the board fired the school superintendent and appointed a new board of trustees to run the school system. Home rule supporters say the District needs more money and greater political autonomy, but Congress is in no mood to grant either one until more reforms are in place.

INSIDE THIS ISSUE

CQ Nov. 22, 1996 • Volume 6, No. 44 • Pages 1033-1056

Formerly Editorial Research Reports

GOVERNING WASHINGTON, D.C.

COVER: PROBLEMS WITH SNOW CLEARING ARE A PERENNIAL SORE POINT WITH D.C. RESIDENTS. REUTERS/MIKE THEILER

Nov. 22, 1996
Volume 6, No. 44

The CQ Researcher (ISSN 1056-2036). Formerly Editorial Research Reports. Published weekly (48 times per year, not printed March 1, May 31, Aug. 30, Nov. 29) by Congressional Quarterly Inc., 1414 22nd St., N.W., Washington, D.C. 20037. Annual subscription rate for libraries, businesses and government is $319. Additional rates furnished upon request. Periodicals postage paid at Washington, D.C. POSTMASTER: Send address changes to The CQ Researcher, 1414 22nd St., N.W., Washington, D.C. 20037.

Governing Washington, D.C.

By Kenneth Jost

The Issues

Gaping potholes crater the streets. School roofs leak. Police cars and fire trucks need repairs. Pushers and prostitutes sell their wares openly. Residents worry about trash in the alleys and bacteria in the water. And the only elected officials have no power to make final decisions for the government.

Welcome to the capital of the world's wealthiest nation and most powerful democracy — a hometown that residents ruefully compare with a slum-ridden city in the Third World.

Washington has the highest per capita income and the lowest unemployment rate of the country's 15 biggest cities. But it's also a city where services are faltering despite high taxes, and the budget is chronically in red ink.

"The city is financially bankrupt," community activist Dorothy Brizill says. "It has a high degree both of mismanagement and corruption."

"The current form of government just doesn't work," says John Tydings, president of the Greater Washington Board of Trade, an influential business group. "Some would say it is dysfunctional."

The District of Columbia ranks high in many of the problems that afflict U.S. cities today. Compared with the 50 states, Washington stands at or near the top in violent crime and at or near the bottom in educational achievement. It has the highest infant mortality rate, the highest percentage of single-parent families and the highest violent death rate among teenagers. And, despite the metropolitan area's growth and general prosperity, Washington itself is losing people and jobs — about 55,000 jobs in the last six years.

Washington's social and economic problems are exacerbated by a political crisis that now threatens the limited self-government that Congress granted the District only 23 years ago. Federal lawmakers are frustrated with Washington's inability to control spending and wary of Mayor Marion S. Barry Jr., who was re-elected to his fourth term in 1994 after serving a six-month sentence for drug possession three years earlier. (*See story, p. 1045.*)

"The loss of confidence in our political leadership is greater in Washington than in most other central cities," says James Gibson, executive director of D.C. Agenda, a civic reform group. "That's a serious, aggravating dimension to this problem."

Many District advocates place much of the blame for the city's problems on Congress, which retained final authority over the District when it approved home rule in 1973. Among other things, they say that federal lawmakers prevented the District from imposing a vitally needed commuter income tax; exempted nearly half the city's land from taxation; and skimped on the federal government's annual payment to the District.

In addition, District supporters accuse federal lawmakers of constantly meddling in local issues ranging from taxicab fares to the death penalty. "Washington has been an easy mark for members of Congress to exercise their will over us," Tydings says.

But critics blame the District government itself for the failure of home rule. "The city has gone from having a bright promise to being a total basket case," says Thomas Edmonds, a political consultant and one-time District resident. "They can play the blame game, but there's nobody responsible except themselves."

For its part, Congress last year agreed with the city's critics and voted to create a powerful, presidentially appointed control board to oversee the District. The board — officially, the District of Columbia Financial Responsibility and Management Assistance Authority — was empowered to reorganize city government, cut programs and reject union contracts if the city did not reduce spending.

In its first year, the control board has repeatedly lectured the mayor and 13-member City Council about the need to cut spending. This month, the board touched off a fierce controversy by reducing the powers of the elected Board of Education and replacing the school superintendent.

Supporters of the five-member board say it is forcing the district to manage its $4.5 billion budget.* For fiscal 1994 — the last full year before Barry took office — the District had a record budget deficit of $335 million. For the current fiscal year, a $74 million deficit is projected.

Rep. Thomas M. Davis III, a Republican from suburban Virginia and principal author of the law that created the control board, says the District government "is doing better than if

---

* The budget includes $3.4 billion in local funds, including the annual federal payment, and an additional $1.1 billion in federal program grants and other revenues. The District's total operating budget of $5.1 billion also includes self-sustaining "enterprise funds," such as the lottery and the water and sewer authority, which are considered as off-budget items.

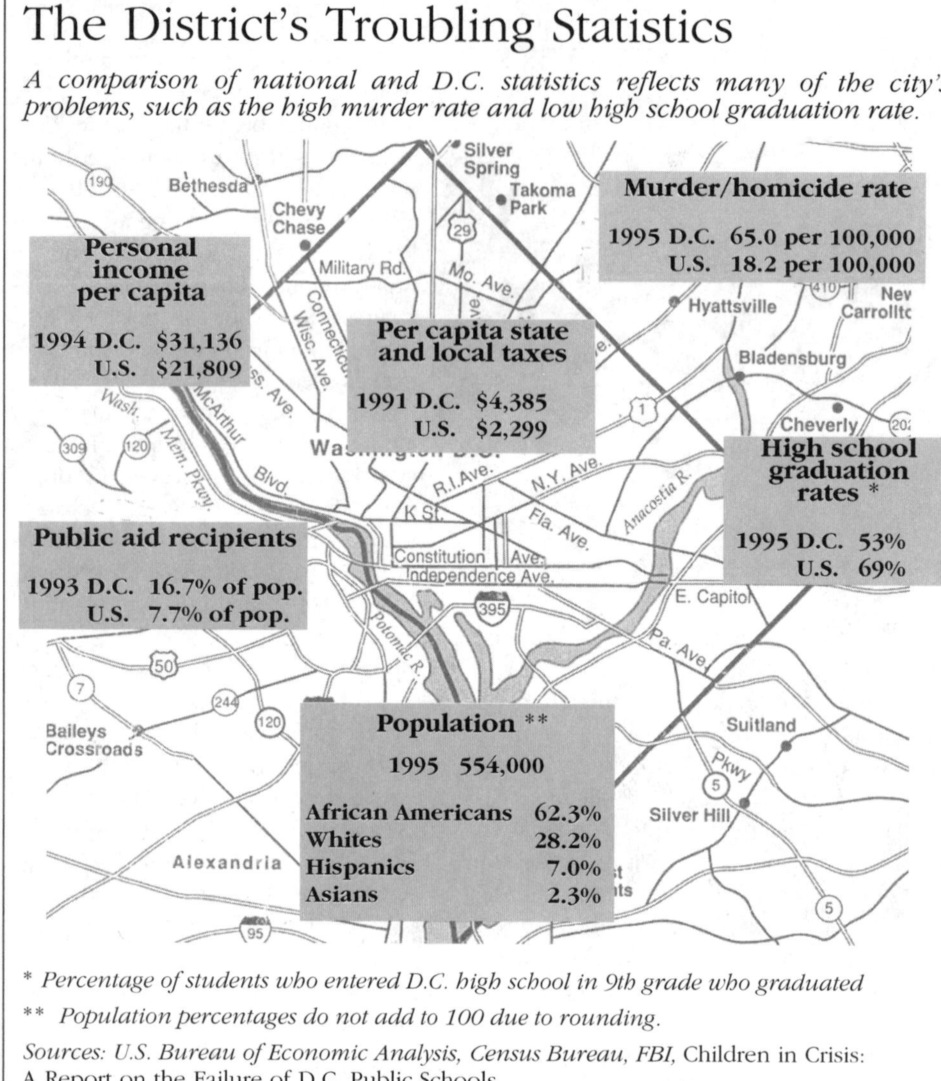

The District's Troubling Statistics

A comparison of national and D.C. statistics reflects many of the city's problems, such as the high murder rate and low high school graduation rate.

* *Percentage of students who entered D.C. high school in 9th grade who graduated*

** *Population percentages do not add to 100 due to rounding.*

Sources: U.S. Bureau of Economic Analysis, Census Bureau, FBI, Children in Crisis: A Report on the Failure of D.C. Public Schools

they didn't have the control board." But Davis, who chairs the House Government Oversight and Reform Subcommittee on the District of Columbia — the "District Subcommittee" — also says local officials do not fully recognize their precarious political standing in Congress. "Not a lot of people on either side of the aisle are willing to stand up and take a risk for the District," Davis says.

In Washington, however, many District supporters are disappointed with the control board. "It has done very good work in reining in overspending," says Del. Eleanor Holmes Norton, the District's non-voting representative in the House and the District Subcommittee's ranking Democrat. "Unfortunately, this is being done by emergency cuts, cuts as they come up, not through reforms of the agencies."

Arguments about the structure for governing Washington go back to the decision in 1790 to create the District of Columbia from land ceded by Maryland and Virginia for the new nation's permanent capital. Washingtonians have never had their own voting representatives in Congress, and the city was run by a congressionally created Board of Commissioners for nearly a century before home rule began in 1975. Even then, Congress retained authority to approve the District's budget and veto legislation approved by the City Council.

Many Washingtonians view the anomalous political situation as manifestly unfair. "D.C. residents do not share in the full self-government and congressional representation enjoyed by their fellow Americans," Edward M. Meyers writes in a new book on Washington's political status. [1]

But proposals to grant the District representation in Congress, statehood or increased home rule powers have repeatedly failed. And supporters of such changes concede that the District's financial and political crisis rules out expanded political rights for now.

In the meantime, the District government and the control board remain prickly partners in a reform process with no certain outcome. As efforts to rehabilitate the city continue, these are among the questions being debated:

Should Congress abolish or further limit home rule?

Home rule supporters are on the defensive nowadays. Critics, including a growing number of frustrated D.C. residents, blame the District's problems on home rule and want Congress to reassert control over local affairs.

"The 22-year experiment in home rule has failed miserably," writes James K. Glassman, a columnist for *The Washington Post*. "The District of Columbia is now, literally, out of control." [2]

Author Thomas Edmonds agrees that home rule has failed. "In any way you can measure, it's been an unqualified failure," says Edmonds, who compiled an array of negative statistics about the District for his recent book, *D.C. by the Numbers*. [3]

Supporters of home rule argue, however, that Washington was never given a fair chance at self-government, that Congress saddled the District with most of the responsibilities of a state government but denied it the resources to pay for public services.

"There are structural problems in the way the District of Columbia has been set up that Congress has failed to address and which, in some respects, the Congress has contributed to and aggravated," says Gibson of D.C. Agenda.

Home rule supporters also note that the District's budget must run a gauntlet that includes the federal Office of Management and Budget (OMB) and Appropriations committees in both chambers of Congress. "There is not a city in America that has had that degree of control" over it, says Board of Trade President Tydings.

Critics, however, say the District must take responsibility for the budget deficits and poor government services that led Congress to establish the control board last year. "City leaders had more than adequate resources and more than adequate control over their own affairs," Edmonds says.

Two former Barry aides, Julius Hobson Jr. and Dwight Cropp, stirred the debate over home rule this summer with an op-ed article in *The Washington Post* urging Congress to suspend home rule and appoint a receiver to run the District. "As overseer of the federal city, Congress has a constitutional duty to intervene," wrote Hobson, now an American Medical Association lobbyist, and Cropp, a George Washington University vice president. [4]

"I used to believe that someone could run for mayor on a campaign theme of cleaning [government] up and come in and do it," says Hobson, whose late father was a founder of the District Statehood Party. "I no longer believe that. You have to suspend home rule, put in a receiver for a few years and then change the charter to a city manager form of government."

Congress considered a receivership last year but created the control board instead as a less severe intrusion on home rule. Today, Rep. Davis says he hears increasing support for the more drastic approach. "Wherever I go, people are saying take [the city] over," Davis says. "And I hear the same thing from members [of Congress] on both sides of the aisle."

The proposal to change the District's charter from a strong mayor to a city manager form of government (with a weak, ceremonial mayor) appears to be picking up increasing support, even from home rule defenders. But most District advocates oppose receivership. "This organization would be right up there screaming that that would be unfair," Tydings says, referring to the Board of Trade.

For his part, Gibson would modify home rule to permit greater cooperation between the District and Congress. He cites as one example of such cooperation the District's zoning board, which is composed of three locally appointed members and two designated federal officials.

"Home rule ought to remain," Gibson says. "But that does not remove the necessity for Congress to address the [unique] fiscal status of the District. You have to adapt [home rule] further."

Should Congress increase the federal payment to the District?

The federal government has funded

Where the District's Money Goes

Expenditures for public safety and justice and health and human services account for more than half of Washington's $4.5 billion fiscal 1997 budget. Discretionary spending for such areas as education, public works and economic development comprises less than one-third of the total.

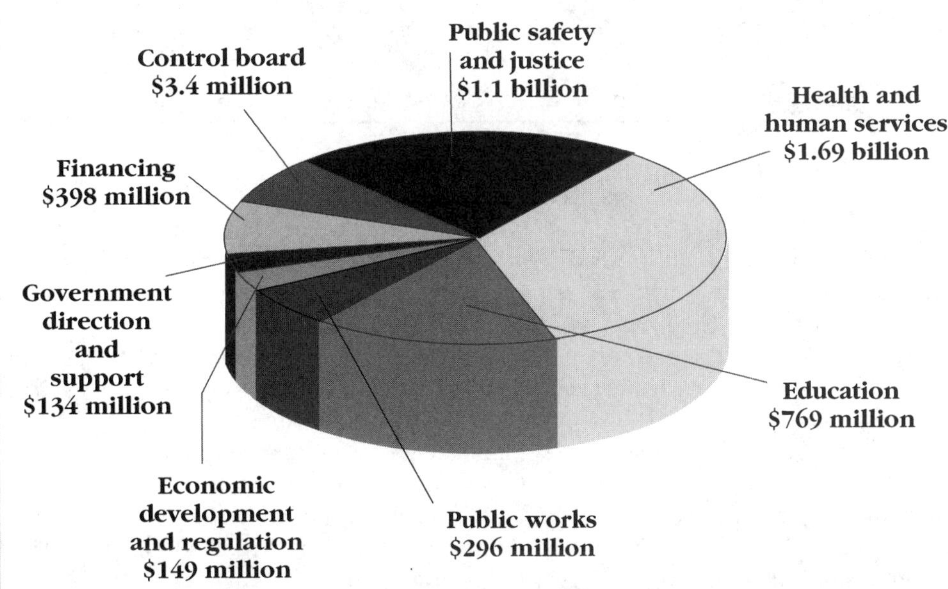

Note: The total does not include $600 million for self-supporting off-budget programs such as the D.C. lottery and water-sewer authority.

Source: District of Columbia budget

The Nation's Shrinking Capital

Washington's population has declined more than 30 percent since 1950. The city had more than half the metropolitan area's population at the beginning of the century but now has about one-seventh the total. The shift began in the 1940s and '50s, when the suburbs began to explode and the once-burgeoning city began losing residents.

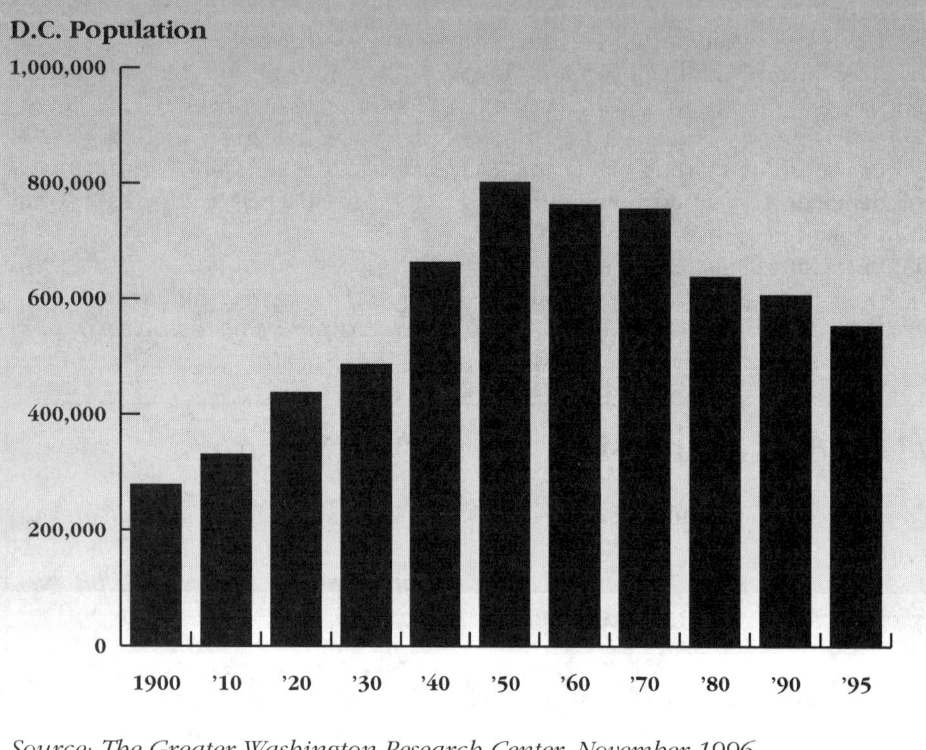

Source: The Greater Washington Research Center, November 1996

part of the District's budget ever since Washington became the capital in 1800. For many Americans outside Washington, the federal payment — $660 million last year — seems adequate, if not generous, to compensate for the costs of serving as the seat of government.

But District leaders say the compensation is inadequate. Moreover, they say Congress has restricted Washington's power to support itself by exempting much of the property within the District from taxation and prohibiting D.C. from imposing a so-called commuter income tax — commonplace in many large cities — on people from the suburbs who work in Washington. *

"We have an irrational structure with respect to revenue," Gibson says. "It is incapable of meeting the needs of the national capital."

But critics of the District government insist that Washington has sufficient revenues and needs instead to eliminate jobs, trim services and privatize some government functions. "This city has no shortage of revenue," Edmonds says. "That's just a bogus, bogus argument."

* Most commuters would not face larger tax bills with a commuter tax since they could deduct the tax paid to the District from their state taxes. But Maryland and Virginia could lose hundreds of millions of dollars in revenue.

Two reports issued as the District's fiscal crisis emerged lend support to both viewpoints. In 1990, a blue-ribbon commission headed by Alice M. Rivlin — then a fellow at the Brookings Institution and now vice chairman of the Federal Reserve System's Board of Governors — said the District's work force was far larger than those of other cities even after taking into account the District's responsibility for some functions usually handled by state governments. But the Rivlin Commission also called for increasing the federal payment to the District and considering new taxes, including a commuter tax or a special levy to help pay for regional transportation. [5]

Four years later, another study blamed about one-third of the District's financial problems on overspending but two-thirds on revenue shortfalls. "Debate over whether the solution lies in a leaner city government, a higher federal payment or help from regional governments is moot," the study concluded. "All will be necessary, and all will be appropriate." [6]

The federal government currently contributes about 15 percent of the District's general fund. But as late as 1922, the government paid for 40 percent or more of the budget. At the start of home rule in 1975, the contribution was 25 percent.

Today, congressional leaders are in no mood to raise the payment. "You tell the city they're going to get more money," Davis says, "and they'll just spend it."

Congress is even less likely to lift the restriction against a tax on commuters. "It's the nation's capital," Davis says. "If there's a shortfall, it's a national responsibility," not the obligation of Maryland or Virginia commuters.

With any general fiscal relief measure ruled out for now, District leaders have focused on discrete measures. In Congress, Norton proposed requiring the federal government to give more support to the pension system for D.C. workers that was transferred from federal responsibility to the District when home rule was established.

Norton also proposed a 15 percent federal income tax cut for D.C. residents. While the bill would not directly help the District's revenue problems, Norton says it would encourage individuals and businesses not to abandon the city.

The 104th Congress adjourned without acting on either measure. The Clinton administration and Davis both have indicated a willingness to consider ways of easing the city's pension burden. But outgoing White House Chief of Staff Leon E. Panetta said last summer that the administration opposed the tax cut. And Davis took a skeptical stance during a hearing on the bill in July.

For the moment, then, the District must focus on cutting spending. Critics say that is the right priority, but Gibson says Congress is being shortsighted. "You're continuing a situation of inadequate performance and inadequate revenue as opposed to an approach that corrects both the revenue deficiency and the performance deficiency," he says.

The District's Heavy Load

*Although Washington has just 15 percent of the metropolitan area's population, it accounts for a disproportionate share of the region's expenditures for social services and law enforcement. **

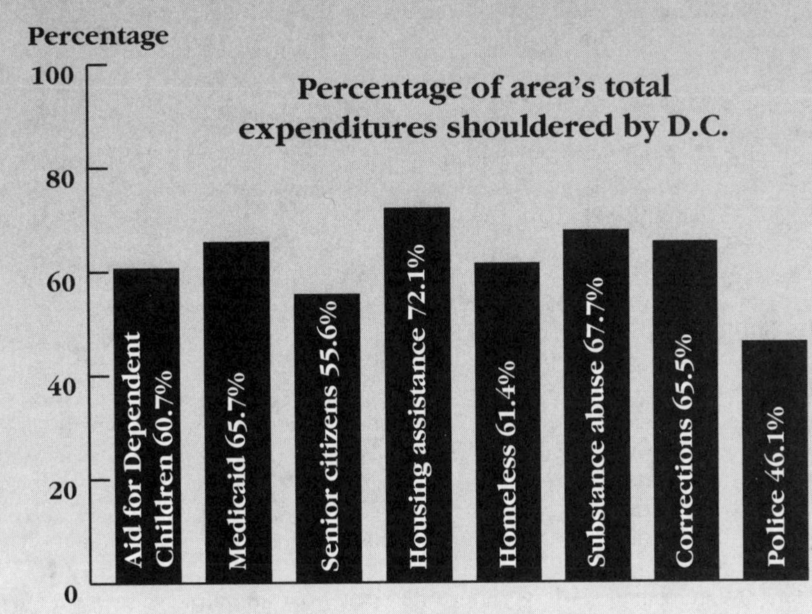

** The metropolitan area includes Washington; Montgomery and Prince George's counties, in Maryland; and the city of Alexandria and Arlington and Fairfax counties, in Virginia.*

Source: Edward M. Meyers, Public Opinion and the Future of the Nation's Capital *(1996)*

Should Washington be made a state or given voting representation in Congress?

Twice in the last 20 years, Washingtonians thought they were close to gaining a voice in Congress. But their efforts failed against a backdrop of race, politics and inertia. And today, there is widespread agreement that statehood or voting representation in Congress is unattainable for the foreseeable future.

"The District's not going to get statehood for some time," Norton says bluntly. Similarly, Tydings of the Board of Trade rules out gaining a voting representative in Congress. "There isn't any prospect for that in the near future," he says.

The District's anomalous condition stems in part from the Constitution, which gives Congress power to "exercise exclusive legislation" over the land — "not exceeding 10 miles square" — to be ceded for the nation's capital.[7] Originally, District residents voted for members of Congress from Virginia or Maryland. But in 1801, Congress abolished that practice and left D.C. residents with no vote for president or for a voting member of Congress.

The District's disenfranchisement extended into the middle of the 20th century, except for its brief period as a territory (1871-1874) when it had a non-voting delegate to the House of Representatives. The 23rd Amendment, ratified in 1961, gave Washingtonians a voice in presidential elections. And Washington got a non-voting delegate to the House in 1970. But a constitutional amendment approved by Congress in 1978 to allow the District two senators and one representative in Congress failed to win ratification.

With the voting rights amendment stalled in the states, District advocates adopted the more ambitious goal of

Advocates Say Congress Created D.C.'s Money Problems . . .

When President George Bush was asked about statehood for the District of Columbia in 1990, he said Washington "should remain a federal city" because "its funds come almost exclusively from the federal government." [1] Whatever his position on statehood, Bush was flatly wrong about the source of the District government's funds.

Washingtonians themselves pay for the great bulk of the District's budget through local taxes. And District leaders and advocacy groups say the federal payment — frozen at $660 million for the past three years — does not make up for the congressionally imposed limitations on the District's taxing powers.

"Congress established policies in the [home rule] charter that prohibit the District from collecting taxes on most of the employment in its borders," says James Gibson, president of the civic reform group D.C. Agenda. "And it has established a federal payment which is not fully responsive to the [costs of services and lost taxes] inherent in the national capital function, which are disproportionately borne by the residents." (*See graph, p. 1039.*)

The federal payment to the District, approved by Congress each year as part of the annual D.C. appropriations bill, currently amounts to about 15 percent of the city's $4.5 billion budget. The percentage is low by historic standards — it stood at 40-50 percent up to the 1920s — and has been falling since the District's first home rule government took office in 1975.

The District government and outside advocacy groups contend that the federal payment is far less than the revenue lost from two major limitations: the high percentage of tax-exempt property within the District and the congressional ban on a commuter income tax. By one recent estimate, the District loses more than $1.1 billion in potential revenue from these two sources — $500 million more than the federal payment.

The percentage of tax-exempt property in Washington — properties owned by the federal or District governments, foreign governments, nonprofit institutions or other exempt entities — is unusually high: about 57 percent of land area. The District government estimates that the exemptions for federal and foreign property alone cost it about $586 million in fiscal 1995. The D.C. Appleseed Center, a public interest group, reached a higher estimate: about $694 million.

Washington also has an unusually high percentage of its work force who live outside its borders. In fact, the District leads the nation's cities in the percentage of income earned by non-residents — about 64 percent. Yet, unlike almost all states and many cities, the District is prohibited by Congress from taxing the income of non-residents. Using a typical non-resident income tax rate of 2 percent, the Appleseed Center estimates that the ban on a commuter tax cost the District about $471 million in fiscal 1995.

Congress gave the District one other big-ticket liability at the start of home rule. It transferred responsibility but no money for a pension system for D.C. teachers, police, firefighters and judges. The federal government was operating the District's pension system on a pay-as-you-go basis — paying retirees with contributions from current workers. The federal government, because of its superior taxing ability, can afford to do that but state and local governments cannot.

The unfunded liability the District inherited with home

full statehood. D.C. voters approved a statehood initiative in 1980 by 53 percent to 47 percent. Under the initiative, a convention met in 1982 to draft a constitution for the state of "New Columbia."

Given the District's substantial black and Democratic majorities, the issues of statehood or voting rights have inevitably been tied up with race and politics. The Democratic Party platform has endorsed statehood since 1984, while Republicans have almost uniformly opposed it. Civil rights groups have rallied to one or the other of the goals, in part because the District, under either scenario, would almost certainly elect one or two blacks to the Senate.

Statehood advocates see the move as the only way to give D.C. residents full political equality. "We're simply asking for equal democratic rights [and] equal economic rights, nothing more, nothing less," says Timothy Cooper, president of the Statehood Solidarity Committee. "We pay our fair share of taxes. We send our sons and daughters to war. We bear all the burdens of citizenship. Yet we share in none of its rewards."

Republicans and other District critics scoff at the notion that Washington could stand on a par with the 50 existing states. "It's a ridiculous proposition," Davis says. "The city doesn't have the tax base to be a city, let alone a state."

Statehood supporters thought their goal was within reach after President Clinton took office in 1993. House Democratic leaders started the year with a rules change to give the District's delegate a vote on the floor. But when the House voted on statehood in December, the measure failed 153-277. Opponents included all but one of the Republican members and nearly 40 percent of the Democrats.

The obstacles to statehood or voting rights have led some D.C. residents to call for allowing Washingtonians to vote in congressional elections in Maryland. Others favor "retrocession" — ceding the District of Columbia back to Maryland. "This is a chance for District residents to be full citizens," says Lawrence Mirel, an

. . . by Curbing Federal Payments and D.C.'s Taxing Power

rule was estimated at $2 billion. The District government has been setting aside pension funds since home rule. In 1979, the federal government also began making an annual contribution of $52 million. But the unfunded liability has continued to grow and now equals about $5 billion, according to the General Accounting Office.[2] District advocates say the contribution needed to eliminate the unfunded liability — variously estimated at around $300 million per year — exceeds D.C.'s current budget deficit.

The District's critics minimize these financial handicaps. Instead, they say the District government's problems lie on the spending side. In his book *D.C. by the Numbers,* Republican political consultant Thomas Edmonds compiles statistics showing the District ranked higher than any of the 50 states in per pupil expenditures on education or per capita expenditures on corrections, health care, hospitals, police and fire protection.[3]

On education, for example, the District spends $9,549 per pupil in primary and secondary education — about $200 per pupil higher than the next ranking jurisdiction, New York State. "How can you spend nearly $10,000 per pupil and not have textbooks or smoke detectors that work?" Edmonds asks.

District leaders and advocates, however, contend that spending comparisons are misleading because of Washington's ambiguous status as a city that provides two expensive services — corrections and Medicaid — normally run and paid for by state governments.

"The District shouldn't be taking on those responsibilities," says Albert "Butch" Hopkins Jr., president of the Anacostia Economic Development Corporation, a nonprofit community development organization. "The federal government should serve as the state to the District of Columbia."

Some District advocacy groups and experts acknowledge that the D.C. government also allowed spending to get out of control during the 1980s and early '90s. "The boom of the '80s raised government spending and expectations," says Philip Dearborn, a municipal finance expert at the Greater Washington Research Center, a business-supported think tank. "The recession of the '90s hit Washington hard, and the District was slow to adjust its budget to reflect the changed conditions."

Nevertheless, the District's spending, adjusted for inflation, was essentially flat from 1988 to 1993 and has declined by more than 10 percent since that time. The efforts to control spending have not been enough, however, to eliminate the District's budget deficit. But key members of Congress — including House District Subcommittee Chairman Thomas M. Davis III, a Republican from suburban Virginia — warn that increased federal support will not be coming until the District shows greater budget discipline.

In setting up the financial control board, Congress provided that it would stay in power until the District had balanced its budget for four consecutive years. "That will be some time to come," says Dearborn. "The hole the District is in is pretty deep. It won't be easy to recover."

[1] Quoted in *The Washington Post,* March 24, 1990, p. A1.

[2] U.S. General Accounting Office, "District Pensions: Federal Options for Sharing Burden to Finance Unfunded Liability," December 1994. See also D.C. Appleseed Center, "The District of Columbia's Pension Dilemma — An Immediate and Lasting Solution," June 26, 1996.

[3] Thomas N. Edmonds and Raymond J. Keating, *D.C. by the Numbers: A State of Failure* (1996).

attorney who heads the pro-retrocession Committee for the Capital City.

Elected leaders on both sides of the District's borders, however, oppose the idea. Rep. Constance A. Morella, a moderate Republican from Maryland, dismisses the idea as "ridiculous." Norton agrees. "My constituents don't want to be part of Maryland," she says. "We have our own identity."

Most recently, a prominent Washington law professor has proposed a federal lawsuit challenging the disenfranchisement of District voters. "The right to an equal vote is a fundamental one that the government may not deny without a compelling interest," Jamin Raskin, associate dean of American University's law school, argued in September.[8] (*See story, p. 1047.*)

Despite the current stalemate, even many District critics agree that Washingtonians should have some voice in Congress. "I personally favor giving the District a voting member on the House floor," Davis says. Republicans stripped Norton and the other delegates of their votes when they gained control of Congress in 1995, but some GOP leaders have indicated a willingness to reconsider the issue.

As for statehood, author Meyers remains optimistic. For his book, Meyers conducted focus groups around the country. He found that most of the people did not understand the District's political status and, when it was explained, overwhelmingly favored voting rights and greater self-rule. "Most of the panelists," Meyers wrote, "could not accept the unequal division of America's cake."[9] ■

BACKGROUND

The Federal City

The District of Columbia originally conformed to the dimensions specified in the Constitution: a square, 10 miles on a side. The site, ceded by Maryland and Virginia, consisted in 1790 mostly of farms and forests and swampy river bottom lands. The only communities of note were two developing port cities, Georgetown and Alexandria. [10]

George Washington and the other founders had grand plans to construct an elegant capital. The French architect and engineer Pierre Charles L'Enfant mapped out a federal district with diagonal avenues criss-crossing a standard grid and the Capitol and Executive Mansion situated a mile and a half apart at the center.

But when the government arrived in 1800, the Capitol and White House were unfinished, business establishments were scarce and members of Congress had to live in crowded boardinghouses.

For the people of Washington, the government's arrival brought a disheartening jolt. The first legislation proposed for governing the new city called for giving the residents no voice in local government. Alexandria and Georgetown were to continue as self-governing cities, but Washington itself would be run by presidential appointees. A flurry of opposition arose, and Congress shelved the bill. Two years later, Congress reconsidered and granted Washington a charter permitting residents to elect a city council but no representatives in Congress. For their part, Alexandria and Georgetown also chafed under their new status and sought to return to their states of origin.

The government continued treating the District as a stepchild until after the Civil War. The federal government paid for about 40 percent of Washington's local budget, but it begrudged the funds needed to continue with L'Enfant's master plan. "They were trying to get a capital built with as little investment as possible," says Barbara Franco, executive director of the Columbia Historical Society. Alexandria and Georgetown continued to clamor for retrocession. In 1846, Congress finally granted Alexandria's pleas, voting to return to Virginia the parts of the District west of the Potomac — more than one-third of the original area.

The District's population grew, slowly but steadily, throughout the antebellum period. By 1860, it stood at about 75,000 — including nearly 61,000 whites, 11,000 free blacks and some 3,000 slaves. [11] Although the District recognized slavery, authorities and residents showed no interest in enforcing fugitive slave laws, and the District became a refuge for fleeing slaves.

The influx stirred conflicting sentiments. In 1861, *The Washington Star* warned that the newcomers could render Washington "uninhabitable to the white man." But after the Civil War, in the early rush of Reconstruction, some Republicans saw a chance to make Washington a model of political freedom and economic progress. Sen. Charles Sumner of Massachusetts declared that Washington should be "not only the seat of freedom, but shall also be occupied and surrounded by a prosperous, enterprising and progressive population." [12]

Monuments and Decay

Washington began to emerge as a modern city in the decade after the Civil War and as a monumental capital in the early 20th century. It also enjoyed a taste of somewhat enhanced self-government during three years as a territory. But territorial government crashed into a sea of debt left from an ambitious public works program. And the city's growth spawned urban blight that lay, largely neglected, within the shadows of the capital's marble edifices.

The first of the two modern builders of Washington was Alexander "Boss" Shepherd, who rose in a period of four years from alderman to public works commissioner to territorial governor before losing power and retiring to obscurity. As alderman, Shepherd was the most prominent advocate of the 1870 legislation creating the "Territory of the District of Columbia." The measure was weaker than Washingtonians preferred. Instead of a popularly elected governor and legislature, as originally proposed, the act provided for the president to appoint the governor; voters would only elect members of one of the two chambers of the territorial legislature and a non-voting delegate to Congress.

President Ulysses S. Grant named Shepherd to the territory's Board of Public Works. From that position, Shepherd presided over a costly program that graded and paved city streets, laid sewers, planted trees and cleared unsightly buildings. [13] He brooked no opposition. When some residents obtained a court injunction to block a bond issue, Shepherd persuaded the legislature to authorize a tax increase and then borrowed against the anticipated revenues. Later, after the second of two congressional investigations disclosed that he had run well past the territory's debt limit of $10 million, Shepherd tacitly admitted that he had counted on Congress to make up the difference.

The two investigations also disclosed evidence of favoritism among contractors and lucrative referral fees. Local officials defended Shepherd, but the scandals provoked outrage in the nation. Congress pronounced territorial government a failure, replacing it in 1874 with a temporary board of three presidentially appointed commissioners. Four years later, Congress passed the Organic Act of 1878 making the commission form of government permanent.

The building of monumental Washington began a quarter-century later after a senator from Michigan, James McMillan, authored legislation in 1901 creating an advisory Park Commission for the District. The commission laid out the now familiar heart of official Washington: the two-mile long National Mall between the Capitol and a planned memorial to President Abraham Lincoln. The plan called for the Mall to be lined with museums, public galleries and government buildings.

Continued on p. 1044

Chronology

1790-1870

Washington is selected as the nation's capital in 1790, but plans for a splendid, elegant city go largely unrealized.

1800
The federal government moves to Washington from Philadelphia, but the capital has few permanent residents until Civil War.

1846
Congress approves "retrocession" of about one-third of the District's land area to Virginia.

1871-1960

Washington becomes a city of monuments, but residents have no voice in local government.

1871
Congress establishes territorial government for the District of Columbia; President Grant appoints Alexander 'Boss' Shepherd to the new territory's Board of Public Works.

1874
Territorial government is abolished after Shepherd's lavish public works program results in huge deficit and accusations of favoritism and corruption. Three-member, presidentially appointed commission is created to govern District; it survives until 1967.

1960
Washington has majority black population for first time, according to federal census.

1961-1980 ***Congress passes home rule legislation, granting D.C. residents partial self-government for first time since the 1870s.***

1961
The 23rd Amendment is ratified, giving D.C. residents the right to vote in presidential elections.

1967
President Lyndon B. Johnson reorganizes District government, replacing board of commissioners with a single mayor-commissioner, Walter E. Washington.

1971
D.C. is given non-voting delegate in U.S. House of Representatives.

December 1973
Limited home rule for the District of Columbia is approved by wide margin in Congress and signed into law Dec. 24 by President Richard M. Nixon.

May 7, 1974
District voters overwhelmingly approve home rule charter; Walter Washington wins Democratic primary in September and general election in November to become city's first elected mayor since 1871.

Sept. 12, 1978
Marion S. Barry Jr. narrowly wins three-way Democratic mayoral primary and goes on to win general election Nov. 7.

1980s ***Washington prospers from a real estate boom and seemingly well-managed government, but bids for statehood or voting representation in Congress fail. Mayor Barry is convicted of drug possession.***

Aug. 22, 1985
Constitutional amendment to give District of Columbia voting representation in Congress dies; only 16 states voted to ratify within seven-year deadline.

Jan. 18, 1990
Mayor Barry is arrested for cocaine possession after videotaped federal sting operation. He is convicted on Aug. 10 of a single misdemeanor count after a two-month trial and given a six-month sentence.

Nov. 20, 1990
The Rivlin Commission report says Washington faces a fiscal crisis and calls for budget cuts and increased aid from the federal government.

1990s ***Washington's fiscal crisis worsens, Barry is re-elected mayor and Congress creates financial control board.***

Nov. 21, 1993
House of Representatives rejects D.C. statehood bill, 153-277.

Sept. 13, 1994
Barry wins Democratic nomination for mayor; he defeats Republican opponent in November and begins his fourth term on Jan. 1, 1995, inheriting a projected budget shortfall of more than $700 million.

April 17, 1995
President Clinton signs congressional legislation creating financial review board.

Nov. 15, 1996
Control board replaces school superintendent and establishes a new panel to run the schools.

Continued from p. 1042

The plan gave the nation the capital L'Enfant had dreamed of, but at the city's expense. It created what Howard Gillette, a historian at George Washington University, calls a "white marble monumental core" divorced from "the undifferentiated brick wilderness" where most Washingtonians lived. The layout of the Mall confirms, Gillette says, "that the federal government was going to set itself apart physically as well as psychologically from the city."

The building of Washington shoved aside issues of social and economic justice for Washingtonians — in particular, African Americans. Anti-discrimination laws passed by the City Council and territorial legislature during Reconstruction were repealed or went unenforced. For some whites, losing voting rights was a mixed blessing because it shut blacks out of political influence.

Some urban advocates did win attention for the "alleyway" slums behind the city's stately avenues. Indeed, Congress in 1934 created the Alley Dwelling Authority, the country's first public housing agency, to tear down the alleyways and build low-cost housing for the displaced families. But the agency accomplished little, beaten down by lawsuits and rising land prices.

After World War II, the government cleared out slums from the southwest quadrant to make room for freeways and better housing. But, as Gillette notes, the project brought no benefits for black Washingtonians. Developers bought up the cleared land for upscale apartments, while the displaced families simply carried the problems of urban blight with them into what had been middle-class, black neighborhoods.

Home Rule

Washingtonians won a measure of political rights in the 1960s and '70s, but Congress kept control over the District's budget and reserved the right to veto laws passed by the City Council. And a constitutional amendment to give the District voting representation in Congress failed to win ratification from the states.

Civil rights forces played a crucial part in bringing the District's anomalous political condition to the nation's attention. By 1960, the migration of middle- and upper-income whites to the suburbs gave Washington a majority-black population for the first time. Yet, in the quarter-century before home rule, the most powerful man in District affairs was a white congressman from South Carolina, Democrat John L. McMillan, who chaired the House District of Columbia Committee from 1941-53 and 1955-73. McMillan was, as recently described by *The Washington Post,* "a jowly segregationist" who "fixed parking tickets," "padded the city payroll," "creamed off kickbacks for himself" and "year after dismal year" bottled up bills to grant the District home rule.[14]

McMillan's opposition forced Washington residents to content themselves with half-steps toward political rights. They won the right to vote in presidential elections with ratification of the 23rd Amendment in 1961, which granted the District three votes in the Electoral College. But even President Lyndon B. Johnson could not get home rule through the legislative thicket. In 1967, however, Johnson circumvented congressional opposition through an executive order reorganizing the District government. He replaced the three-member Board of Commissioners with a single mayor-commissioner and a nine-member appointed City Council.

Another half-step followed three years later, when Congress voted to give the District a non-voting delegate in the House. Voters in 1971 chose Walter E. Fauntroy, a black minister and civil rights leader, for the post. For the first time in nearly a century, Washingtonians had a voice, though not a vote, in the national legislature.

The next year, McMillan was an unexpected loser in a Democratic primary for renomination to Congress. Black voters cast ballots against him, urged on by civil rights groups who explained McMillan's role in disenfranchising Washington's black majority. With McMillan's defeat, chairmanship of the House District Committee passed to Rep. Charles C. Diggs Jr., a black Democrat from Michigan.

Diggs convened hearings on home rule in February 1973; a subcommittee completed a draft measure by June. The Senate, which had backed home rule eight times since 1949, prepared its own bill. Originally, the Senate and House bills gave the District substantial autonomy. But Diggs accepted crucial modifications in his bill to avert a possible defeat on the House floor, including a line-item congressional veto over the District budget and a mandatory 30-day waiting period on any council-passed legislation to give Congress an opportunity to disapprove it.

The final measure cleared Congress in December. It provided that, subject to voter approval, the District would have an elected mayor and 13-member city council exercising governmental power subject to congressional approval of the District budget, a congressional veto over legislation and other restrictions. Home rule advocates cheered, though a leading advocate of statehood, Julius Hobson Sr., ridiculed the measure as "home fool."

Two decisions in the transition to home rule — the ban on a commuter income tax and the transfer of an unfunded pension system — were to emerge as ticking time-bombs for the District's financial well-being. No clouds, however, were allowed to darken Washingtonians' celebration of their hard-won self-rule. Voters went to the polls in May 1974 to give their blessing to the new city charter. In September, Mayor Walter E. Washington, the black lawyer who had been appointed by President Johnson, won the Democratic nomination — tantamount to election in the heavily Democratic city — to become the city's first elected mayor in more than 100 years.

Washington's 'Mayor for Life' Defies the Oddsmakers

To his critics, Washington's four-term mayor, Marion S. Barry Jr., embodies the political and fiscal crisis in the nation's capital: excessive government largess, racial divisiveness and personal amorality.

But to his supporters, Barry remains a positive figure: defender of home rule for the District of Columbia, advocate for the poor, symbol of racial pride and personal example of the capacity for redemption and rehabilitation.

Admirers and detractors agree, however, that for Americans inside and outside the Washington Beltway, Barry has become personally identified with the city and its political problems.

"America looks at Washington, and they see a predominantly black city with a crack-smoking mayor and a government that can't manage its budget," says Lawrence Guyot, an official in the District's Youth Services Administration and a friend of Barry's since the 1960s, when they were in the civil rights movement together.

"So much of the District's current status and maybe future is tied up with Marion Barry," says community activist Dorothy Brizill. "We've got to break that umbilical cord."

Mayor Marion S. Barry Jr.

Barry has held elective office in Washington continuously since 1971 except for a two-year hiatus that included a six-month federal prison sentence for possession of cocaine. Critics mock him as "mayor for life," but the title attests to his personal stamina and political appeal, especially in the city's poorest neighborhoods.

Born in 1936 in a tiny Mississippi Delta town, Barry began his political career in the 1960s in Tennessee with the Student Non-Violent Coordinating Committee (SNCC), one of the more radical groups in the civil rights movement. Ambitious and well-educated (he has a degree in chemistry), he moved to Washington in 1965 to become head of the local SNCC office. He gained visibility first with the pro-home rule organization Free D.C. and then with a federally funded inner-city jobs program, Pride Inc.

Barry won his first election to the District's pre-home rule school board in 1971. From there, he advanced to an at-large seat on the first elected city council in 1975 and then to the mayor's office in 1979.

After easily winning re-election to a second and third term, Barry hit a political pothole in January 1990 when a federal sting operation caught him on camera smoking crack cocaine furnished him by a former lover turned informant. He decided not to seek re-election. But after a jury convicted him in August on only one misdemeanor count, Barry mounted an eleventh-hour bid for an at-large council seat. He lost — his only electoral defeat in a quarter-century of D.C. politics.

Released from a federal prison in April 1992, Barry promptly re-entered politics as a candidate for the City Council from the District's poorest ward. He won and immediately began using the post as a launching pad for what became a successful campaign in 1994 to recapture the mayor's office.

Today, Barry's power is substantially reduced because of the congressionally created financial control board. His 15-day "retreat" in May also touched off speculation that he had resumed drinking or using drugs. Barry denied the rumors. Today, his friend Guyot says Barry still has "relentless energy and relentless empathy."

Immediately after the mayor's absence, a *Washington Post* poll found indications of weakening political support for Barry. A significant minority of those surveyed — 36 percent — said Barry should resign before completing his term. And two-thirds of those questioned — including 59 percent of black Washingtonians and 88 percent of whites — said Barry should not seek re-election in 1998.[1]

So far, Barry has declined to tell his political plans, but Guyot predicts that he will run and win despite "an unrelenting attack from the federal government and from business interests." Brizill also expects a fifth Barry term, but sees it as only compounding the District's problems. "I don't think the District of Columbia will survive if you have another Marion Barry term," she says. "That's the bottom line. It will not survive."

[1] *The Washington Post,* May 22, 1996, p. D1.

'Mayor for Life'

Washington got a new mayor in 1978 when Marion Barry, a civil rights activist turned establishment politician, defeated Mayor Washington in a three-way race by 1,400 votes. Barry has dominated Washington politics ever since — so much so that the local *City Paper* has dubbed him "Mayor for Life."

Barry reached the mayor's office after winning two previous Districtwide elections, for the school board in 1971 and an at-large council seat in 1974. On the council, he used his post as chairman of the Finance

Committee to win support from white leaders by opposing tax increases and criticizing waste in Mayor Washington's administration. When he ran for mayor against Washington and City Council Chairman Sterling Tucker in 1978, he used his reputation as an energetic pragmatist — and his considerable personal skills — to win a critical editorial endorsement from the Post. With the city's black vote divided, the Post's support was widely credited with giving Barry the white votes he needed to win.

Barry's first two terms as mayor were viewed as largely successful. But by the mid-1980s, his image was seriously tarnished by allegations of wasteful spending and corruption. In addition, the U.S. attorney's office was conducting an intensive investigation of Barry's alleged use of drugs. The investigation climaxed with his arrest on Jan. 18, 1990, when a federal sting investigation videotaped Barry in a downtown hotel room smoking crack cocaine given him by a former lover, Rasheeda Moore.

Barry responded with a dual strategy of promising to seek help for his drug dependency and blasting prosecutors for interfering in Washington politics. He won substantial vindication when a jury — which included 10 blacks and two whites — convicted him of only a single count, a misdemeanor for possession of cocaine. He was sentenced to six months in prison.

Barry stayed out of the 1990 mayor's race but filed after the verdict as an independent candidate for an at-large council seat. On Aug. 30, the Post endorsed a political novice for mayor: Sharon Pratt Dixon, a black utility company executive who promised to "clean house, not with a broom but a shovel." As in Barry's first election, white votes made the difference in Dixon's victory in the Democratic primary on Sept. 7.

Barry lost his bid for the council in the November general election. A year later, after losing an appeal of his conviction, Barry reported to a minimum security federal prison to begin serving his sentence. But when he was released in April 1992, Barry quickly returned to District politics as a candidate in the Democratic primary to represent the poorest, and most neglected, of the city's wards — Anacostia.

Redemption and Return

Barry presented himself as a redeemed drug and alcohol abuser who could use his skills to vitalize a blighted neighborhood. He won, easily beating the ward's longtime council member. Over the next two years, Barry used his council seat to cement his political support from the city's lower-income blacks to prepare for a campaign against his successor, who had remarried and was now Mayor Sharon Pratt Kelly.

The new mayor had enjoyed a honeymoon of sorts for her first year in office, but quickly proved to be an ineffectual manager and an artless politician. Barry launched his campaign in May 1994. Kelly garnered little support in her bid for a second term, but it was enough to take away votes from Barry's strongest challenger, veteran councilman John Ray.

On Sept. 13, Barry won the three-way runoff race with 47 percent of the vote. Two months later, he turned back an energetic challenge from the Republican nominee, former council and school board member Carol Schwartz. On Jan. 2, 1995, Barry was sworn in for his fourth term, backed by a minority of the city's black population, strongly opposed by the city's white voters and facing a fiscal crisis.

Fiscal Crisis

As Mayor Barry left office in 1990, the blue-ribbon Rivlin Commission he had created three years earlier warned that the District government was confronting "an immediate fiscal crisis." The commission said the deficit would be $200 million for the coming fiscal year and possibly $700 million by 1996. It recommended the elimination of 6,000 government jobs along with a substantially higher federal payment, a commuter income tax and a regional transportation levy. [15]

Despite the grim assessment, the new mayor took office in a buoyant mood — encouraged by her reform mandate and heartened by a warm reception on Capitol Hill. Her good relations with Congress tangibly paid off. The perennially stingy lawmakers voted the District a supplemental appropriation of $100 million and then increased the federal payment for fiscal 1992 to a record $630 million, up from $430 million in the previous year. [16]

By the end of Kelly's term in 1994, however, her good will was gone, and the red ink was increasing. [17] Her supporters insisted she had started to trim expenditures and institute reforms. But almost all of the 2,000 payroll positions eradicated came through attrition and retirement. And she "balanced" the books only by accounting gimmicks. In fiscal 1993, for example, she erased the deficit by crediting $170 million in property tax payments due the next fiscal year.

In June 1994, a federal audit warned that the District was almost out of cash. To maintain cash flow, the District government had already started delaying payments to vendors and contractors. Congress, under Democratic control, ordered Kelly to make $140 million in budget cuts. In October, a new report on the District's finances warned that without spending cuts and revenue increases the budget deficit could rise to $1 billion in 2000. [18]

In his 1994 campaign, Barry described himself as a "financial wizard." After taking office in 1995, he promised a "miracle budget" to deal with a multiyear budget shortfall newly projected at $722 million. And he began with the good wishes of the new Republican-controlled Congress. GOP

Framing a Court Case for a Vote in Congress

Washingtonians have gone to court repeatedly since the 1800s, attacking their peculiar constitutional status. They argue, essentially, that it is wrong to tax them if they have no representation in Congress. But the courts have turned a deaf ear. "No taxation without representation" was only a Revolutionary War slogan, the courts said, not a constitutional principle.

Now, an activist law professor is framing a different legal challenge to try to win residents of the District of Columbia voting representation in Congress. Jamin Raskin, associate dean of American University's Washington College of Law, says the established practice of denying Washingtonians a voice in Congress is itself a violation of the Constitution.

"We're saying that American citizens cannot be denied the right of voting representation in Congress," Raskin says.

Raskin's theory collides with a structure that has been treated heretofore as an integral part of the Constitution itself. The new capital was formed from land ceded by Maryland and Virginia to be a federal district, not a state. And Congress was given the power under the Constitution to "exercise exclusive legislation" over what became the District of Columbia.

But Raskin says the so-called District Clause does not require that Washingtonians be denied representation in Congress.

"The purpose was to give Congress the assurance that it could govern the District internally and maintain the military and physical security of federal government buildings," Raskin says. "That interest in no way collides with the equally compelling interest of guaranteeing the right to vote."

Raskin first aired his theory in an article in *The Washington Post's* Sunday opinion section in September. He argued that courts have previously recognized that Washingtonians cannot be denied other constitutional rights, such as the right to trial by jury. "The Bill of Rights applies with undiluted force to American citizens living in the District," he wrote. [1]

In an accompanying article, the section's deputy editor heartily embraced the idea of challenging the District's disenfranchisement in court. "[T]he woes that I and my fellow D.C. citizens have been experiencing," Brian Kelly wrote, "all stem from Congress's mismanagement of the District." The Constitution, he continued, "never intended this to be so." [2]

Raskin, who most recently represented Reform Party candidate Ross Perot in an unsuccessful court suit to be admitted to the presidential debates, says both he and Kelly have received "very enthusiastic" encouragement about the possible suit from District residents and leaders. Raskin says he has met with lawyers to begin mapping out a possible legal strategy, with an eye toward filing a suit sometime next year.

The trickiest part of the suit, Raskin says, would be the question of what remedy the courts would order if the challenge was accepted. The idea of the Supreme Court telling Congress to seat new members from the District of Columbia seems far-fetched. But Raskin says the court might simply require Congress to come up with some solution from a number of possible options.

The simplest solution, he says, would be a statute giving District residents the right to vote either in their native states or in Maryland. He notes that military personnel and foreigners living abroad currently are allowed to vote in their home states. In addition, he says that for the District of Columbia's first 10 years, residents were allowed to vote in congressional elections in either Maryland or Virginia.

Alternatively, Raskin says, Congress could approve the District's effort to win statehood. Or it could approve "retrocession" — returning the land to the state of Maryland, just as part of the District was returned to Virginia in 1846. And Raskin says it would not be out of the question for Congress to give D.C. an official seat in the House or the Senate.

"The District has been treated like a 'state' for many constitutional and statutory purposes," Raskin says. "What could be more important than the interest in representation?"

Raskin concedes the court case faces an uphill road. "Every great constitutional case looks completely absurd when it's first conceived," Raskin says. But he says the issue is important whatever the outcome. "This is an opportunity to try to articulate a constitutional critique of a regime of injustice that governs hundreds of thousands of American citizens," he concludes.

---

[1] Jamin Raskin, "Hear Ye, Hear Ye . . ." *The Washington Post,* Sept. 22, 1996, p. C1.

[2] Brian Kelly, "Let's Sue Congress," *The Washington Post,* Sept. 22, 1996, p. C1.

leaders, including House Speaker Newt Gingrich, R-Ga., said the District's problems offered an opportunity to show that their free-enterprise, tax-cutting philosophy could improve public services even in the most challenging of inner-city environments.

Control Board Established

The lawmakers' solution, however, came at the expense of home rule. Congress completed work in April 1995 on legislation to establish a powerful five-member control board to oversee the District. The bill, signed by President Clinton April 17, gave the board broad power to reorganize city government, slash programs and reject union contracts if city officials did not cut spending.

"Our capital city is a powerful symbol of America," District Subcommittee Chairman Davis, principal author of the bill, declared. "This symbol has been tarnished by the current crisis. It needs to be polished."

The act provided that the board would remain in existence until the District presented balanced budgets over four consecutive years. To head the board, Clinton picked Andrew F. Brimmer, a black economist, longtime Washington resident and former member of the Federal Reserve System's Board of Governors. Also named to the unpaid posts were Joyce A. Ladner, a professor at Howard University, the historically black college in Washington; Constance Berry Newman, under secretary of the Smithsonian Institution; Edward A. Singletary, a retired telephone company executive; and Stephen D. Harlan, a real estate executive. All of the board members except Harlan are black.

After a private, two-hour session with Barry, Brimmer, in his first public comments about his new post, played down the board's role in helping the city. "I do not anticipate, do not expect and have no intention of engaging in any day-to-day decision-making in this city to either hire or fire or cancel or make contracts or anything of that sort," Brimmer said. "The mayor is responsible for administration of this city, and the mayor with the council is responsible for fiscal affairs." [19] ■

CURRENT SITUATION

Control Board Politics

One day after Washingtonians went to the polls in November to elect a half-dozen school board members, they awoke to read some startling news. The control board had hatched a plan to fire the school superintendent, hire a replacement, create a new panel to oversee the school system and reduce the elected school board to a strictly advisory role. [20]

Officials and D.C. residents reacted angrily. Outgoing school board President Karen Shook called the move "a slap in the face" to the board and voters. Board member Jay Silberman used a racially laden metaphor: "the lynching of home rule." Del. Norton met privately with Brimmer to convey her opposition. "I made it clear," Norton said afterward, "that I opposed any downgrading of an elected school board on the heels of their election."

Control board officials delayed any immediate comment, but the next week they released a scathing critique of the school system. The 56-page report began by labeling the school system "a failure," recited a litany of "bleak" assessments of educational performance and blamed the system's waste and mismanagement on the school board and Superintendent Franklin W. Smith. [21]

Three days later — despite pleas for modifications from Norton, the school board and the City Council — the control board voted, unanimously and without debate, to establish a new, nine-member board of trustees for the school system and hire a retired Army general, Julius W. Becton Jr., as the new "chief executive officer-superintendent." The school board president was given a seat on the new board, but otherwise the board's role was reduced to advisory. Ladner bluntly answered critics of the overhaul plan: "The bottom line is that it is undemocratic to permit the kind of educational abuse and neglect that we have today."

The episode illustrated the tricky balancing act the control board faces in trying to effect major changes in a District government widely regarded as dysfunctional while respecting the authority of elected officials and the principle of home rule. The board's first-year report, completed on Oct. 30, put its role in a positive light. "The [control board's] assistance, for the most part, has been provided to the District government in a participatory and cooperative manner," the report began. [22]

In fact the board clashed repeatedly with Barry during its first 18 months. Board members grumbled in September 1995 about Barry's choice of Anthony Williams, a high-ranking Agriculture Department official, for the newly created post of chief financial officer. It rejected his first choice for a second newly created position, inspector general, and then, after ratifying his second choice, privately upbraided her in March for moving too slowly against waste and fraud in Barry's administration. In June, the board forced Barry to fire a longtime ally, Vernon Hawkins, as head of the District's Human Services Department. And in September, it forced Barry to back away from naming another political ally to be a federally financed advocate for the city's disabled residents. [23]

The board clashed with other D.C. officials. It vetoed 12 acts passed by the D.C. council, jarred city employee unions by announcing plans to review all existing labor contracts with the District and had a dramatic showdown with the District's Lottery Board after an investigation uncovered possible corruption. When the Lottery Board sought to fire its executive director, who was helping the probe, the control board blocked the move and, for good measure, directed the council to abolish the lottery board altogether.

For its part, the control board's annual report stressed its accomplishments in a handful of seven-figure cost-saving items, such as helping negotiate a lower interest rate on the construction of a new sports arena. The board claimed credit for helping reduce the District's work force by almost one-fourth to 33,000 full-time equivalent positions. It cited Williams' work as chief financial officer in straightening out vendor payment schedules and adopting other finan-

Continued on p. 1050

At Issue:

Should Congress enact a federal income tax cut for D.C. residents?

yes

James L. Prost
Economic consultant, Basile Baumann Prost & Associates, Inc.

WRITTEN FOR *THE CQ RESEARCHER*, NOVEMBER 1996.

The District of Columbia is losing its middle-income wage earners. This contributes to the District's fiscal crises by reducing the tax base, increasing taxes for those remaining and generating a higher proportion of residents needing governmental services. From 1990 to 1995, the District lost over 22,500 middle-income households. The recent census projection forecasts an even bleaker fiscal future for the District.

Something must be done to stop the "bleeding" of middle-income wage earners leaving Washington. This action must directly benefit middle-income wage earners, not directly fund the District government, and encourage reinvestment within the District.

The District of Columbia Economic Recovery Act, introduced by Delegate Eleanor Holmes-Norton, will have such a dramatic impact. It has broad bipartisan support and is structured to target benefits to the middle class and encourage investment and job creation in the district.

The act has been referred to by some as a "progressive tax." While this may be perceived as an oxymoron, the act is carefully structured to target benefits to encourage middle-income people to work, live and invest within the District.

The act encourages small business investment and venture capital into Washington by eliminating the capital gains tax for District residents for capital gains earned within the District. The act avoids tax abuse by applying its lower tax rate only to wages and salaries earned in the metropolitan region and investment income earned within the District. Higher income households, with significant earnings from investments, wages and salaries earned outside the District, will pay taxes on this outside income two to three times higher than on their District earnings.

The act reduces the federal income tax of moderate-income residents significantly more than that of upper-income filers — those with adjusted gross incomes over $100,000. The proportional tax burden is shifted from middle-income to higher-income filers.

Obviously, the act needs to be matched by improvements in district services, schools and public safety. But dramatic steps to retain the middle class offer the best hope of achieving these other turnarounds. By encouraging investments and increasing disposable income, the act will do much to facilitate neighborhood revitalization and small/minority business development.

The act represents an innovative, balanced and targeted approach, offering the opportunity to immediately change market perception, encourage the middle class to remain in Washington and achieve broad bipartisan support.

no

Stephen S. Fuller
Professor of Public Policy, George Mason University

WRITTEN FOR *THE CQ RESEARCHER*, NOVEMBER 1996.

The 15 percent flat federal income tax proposed for district residents would not lead to the revitalization of the D.C. economy. This is not because of some flaw in the tax concept. It is just the wrong answer to the District's economic problems.

Taxes are not the issue facing residential and business investment decisions in the District. The federal income tax is not responsible for the District's loss of 50,000 residents and 50,000 jobs over the last five years.

The problem is the District's deteriorating infrastructure, growing fears for personal safety, declining market conditions and government mismanagement. The reputation of the District of Columbia as a good place to live and do business has been seriously diminished over the past decade. Reducing the federal income tax with the hope that this taxpayer subsidy would ameliorate these fundamental problems or make them less important to current and future residents and investors ignores the factors that shape these important personal and business decisions.

Research has shown that the most important factors in determining residential location are proximity to place of work, quality of public facilities and services, community reputation and image, housing conditions and costs, neighborhood amenities and familiarity with the jurisdiction. Taxes are not a primary factor. In fact, residents are willing to pay higher taxes if they feel that the investment value of their house will grow and be protected because of the city's strong commitment to high quality of local public facilities. It is not that taxes are unimportant. It is just that other factors are more important.

Tax-based incentives are far too indirect a means for influencing the District's economy. The windfall benefits from lower federal tax rates, which would accrue primarily to households with incomes above $100,000, would not generate significant levels of new spending in the District. Rather, these tax savings would be spent or invested elsewhere in the national economy. Accordingly, there would be no direct job growth or business development generated in the district.

The Office of Management and Budget has estimated that this tax cut would cost the nation's taxpayers $700 million a year. With funding of that magnitude, improvements having direct impacts on the District's quality of life, ones that correct the problems discouraging business investment and residential location decisions, could be undertaken. Such an approach would have much more certain results than can be hoped for from a tax cut where the benefits to the District of Columbia cannot be focused on its real problems.

FOR MORE INFORMATION

D.C. Agenda, 1155 15th St. N.W., Washington, D.C. 20005; (202) 223-2598. An influential business group, the Federal City Council, established this organization to spearhead civic reform in collaboration with other constituencies and interest groups.

D.C. Appleseed Center, 733 15th St. N.W., Suite 700, Washington, D.C. 20005; (202) 393-1158. This public interest group has published reports on selected fiscal issues.

District of Columbia Financial Responsibility and Management Assistance Authority, 1 Thomas Circle N.W., Suite 900, Washington, D.C. 20005; (202) 504-3400. The congressionally created financial control board, established in June 1995, has broad power to reorganize and oversee the District's elected government.

Greater Washington Board of Trade, 1129 20th St. N.W., Washington, D.C. 20036; (202) 857-5900. The Board of Trade is an influential regional business organization.

Greater Washington Research Center, 1129 20th St. N.W., 2nd floor, Washington, D.C. 20036; (202) 466-6680. This business-sponsored think tank conducts research on social and economic trends in Washington.

cial management improvements. And, most significantly, the board said it had played a critical part in allowing the District to return to private markets for a $170 million bond issue last month.

Some advocates and observers applauded the board for some of its moves. "The control board's evolving role has been positive," says Board of Trade President Tydings. But others are more critical. "I'd give it a D-plus," says Gibson of D.C. Agenda. He said the board had been "far less productive" than similar agencies Congress had created to bail out two other troubled cities, New York City and Philadelphia.

Norton says she is "distressed" at the confrontational relationship between the board and the District government, but blames both parties. "I blame the District because they know they're going to lose every fight," Norton says. "I blame the control board because they should have known it was going to be like this."

More broadly, Norton says the board has concentrated too much on "ad hoc, crisis problem-solving" rather than systematic changes. "The only way to bring finances into permanent stability," she says, "is to systematically reform city services and operations."

Control board officials acknowledge some fault for the early confrontations with the District government but say relations are better now. "The early part of the control board relationship with the mayor was marred by having issues come up and not resolving them quickly," says Executive Director John W. Hill Jr. The board is settling issues faster now, he says, quickly adding: "That doesn't mean we always will agree."

A City Manager?

Within days of his election, Barry held back-to-back press conferences on two issues that had vexed his past administrations: snow removal and police protection. But Barry's initiatives did little to dispel questions about his performance as mayor or about the future of the mayor's office altogether.

The control board significantly reduced Barry's influence. In addition, he and some of his close associates are subjects of a continuing federal probe into alleged financial wrongdoing. [24] Moreover, a growing number of advocates and observers are proposing to amend the home rule charter by reducing the powers of the mayor and giving principal administrative responsibility to a professional city manager.

For Washingtonians, Barry's news conferences Nov. 7 and 8 offered reassurances about city services that ranked high on the list of criticisms of the District government. Many residents had waited for weeks during the record January blizzard for city snow plows to reach their streets. Some gave up and hired private plows. And crime remained a pervasive concern even though the District in recent years had seen some reductions in crime from the period in the late 1980s and early '90s when its 400-plus homicides per year earned it the title "Murder Capital of the U.S."

Barry had a cloudy record on both issues. During a previous severe snowstorm in 1987, he was conspicuously away from the city — at the Super Bowl in Pasadena, Calif. As for crime, he had come under increasing criticism during the year for doing little about the issue. The critics included the chief federal law enforcement officer for the District, U.S. Attorney Eric H. Holder Jr., who warned in a pair of op-ed articles earlier this year of a crisis in the police department and implicitly blamed Barry for the problems. [25]

Holder returned to the issue in a forum on crime sponsored by the Heritage Foundation last month. "Quite frankly, we are not getting the leadership that is necessary, leadership from the top," Holder said at the Oct. 15 session. Asked who he was referring to, Holder said simply: "The mayor."

Barry's actions on both issues illustrated the limits the District faces in trying to improve city services while under a fiscal crisis. On snow, Barry said residential streets would be given priority in snow clearance operations over major commuter thoroughfares. In effect, the move signaled to the federal government that it would have to pitch in if a major snowstorm threatened to keep workers away from their jobs.

As for crime, Barry's plan — modeled after a program in New York City — calls for more emphasis on community-oriented policing, greater emphasis on gang-related violence and a stricter approach to so-called quality-of-life crimes such as public drunkenness or urination. But in contrast to the New York program, which included the hiring of 8,000 additional officers, Barry said Washington would be hiring no new police.

Many other public services were faltering under a poorly managed, financially strapped District government. For the second year in row, several D.C. public schools were blocked by a local judge from opening because of fire code violations. The city's water supply was found to have excessive levels of bacteria, apparently the result of poorly maintained water mains. A fire at the Treasury Department in June called attention to the fire department's equipment problems: The assigned ladder truck was out of service for repairs.

Congress has been moved at times to provide a dose of quick relief. Lawmakers in March voted a $15 million supplemental appropriation for the police department. In September, Congress provided $12 million for school repairs but directed the money to go to the control board instead of the school board.

Courts also have stepped in to remedy deficiencies in government services. Judges have appointed receivers to take over the District's housing agency and child welfare system and ordered broad changes in the mental health and correctional systems.

As the District's woes mount, many residents are being drawn to the idea of a city manager. In their proposal in the Post in July, the two former Barry aides, Hobson and Cropp, cited the standard arguments for a city manager: greater technical expertise and political neutrality. They also said Washington's unique political situation created a particular reason for believing a city manager would perform better than an elected mayor.

With no political posts to offer beyond the mayor's office, Hobson and Cropp wrote, the District government did not attract "the best and the brightest" people into office. But as the nation's capital, Washington would offer a "quite attractive" opportunity to "an aspiring municipal expert," they said.[26]

The proposal drew a hefty share of critical letters to the Post. Kathryn Pearson-West, a Democratic committeewoman, called the idea of a receiver "foolish," while longtime resident Philomena Jurey said any change to a city manager should be subject to referendum by District voters.[27] But in interviews this fall, the proposed change to a city manager drew favorable responses from a range of people, including community activist Brizill, political consultant Edmonds and Board of Trade President Tydings. Unlike some other changes, Tydings says, "a city manager form of government preserves [the people's] prerogatives to elect their own government."

The District's highest-ranking elected officials, however, both threw cold water on the idea. Barry minimized the potential benefits, telling reporters that a city manager was "not a panacea." Norton cautions, "You don't restructure home rule until the District government itself is fixed." ■

OUTLOOK

Frustration and Hope

Frustration runs deep among the people of Washington — frustration with the District government, with the congressionally created control board and with Congress itself. But Albert "Butch" Hopkins Jr., an Anacostia community development executive, blames the District's plight mainly on the American people themselves.

"I wish Americans would take a greater interest in how the nation's capital is structured, how it's governed and what its responsibilities are to its citizens," Hopkins says. "If the people in the rest of the country understood that, they would pressure their officials to take a more humane interest in the District of Columbia to see if it could be the best that it could be."

Control board officials maintain things are getting better. Rep. Davis, the principal author of the law, also sees progress, but he says the District still has far to go. "We've moved the ball off the goal line," Davis says. "We've had our backs to the goal line for five or six years. We've moved the ball to the 25-yard line. We've got a long way to go. We've got to get it to field goal range before we can claim success."

Delegate Norton urges District officials and residents to avoid confrontations with the control board. Instead, she says, the board should be pressured to move more quickly on broad, systemic reforms. "Those who oppose the control board or want greater democratic powers for the District should be the first to want [the control board] to be proactive, so it can be gone," she says.

Norton and Davis both say that despite some disagreements, they try to work on the District's problems on a bipartisan basis. Both lawmakers stress that the District's problems stem in part from the exodus of the middle class to the suburbs. Davis says that requires the District to cut back: "You have to give the city services it can afford." Norton says the solution is her tax-cut bill, which "would offer an incentive for people to remain in the District and thus provide the revenue stream that other jurisdictions have."

Whatever legislative action is taken,

an expert on Washington's demographics says the flight to the suburbs is likely to continue. "There is nothing to indicate that the population in the District is about to stabilize or increase," says George Grier, a fellow with the Greater Washington Research Center.

On Capitol Hill, the prospects for legislative action to help the District are uncertain. The proposal with the best chance for action is relief from the unfunded pension liability. "We're going to have to work out something different than we have today," Davis says. The Clinton administration is considering offering a proposal for the federal government to pay for most of the cost, according to Carol Thompson Cole, who heads the administration's task force on the District.

Even though many District advocates have written it off, Norton also believes her tax cut has a chance of passage in the new Congress. "The 105th Congress, like the 104th Congress, is likely to be far more disposed to tax cuts than they are to tax increases or to increases in programs or increases in federal payment for a single jurisdiction," she says. Norton also believes President Clinton would sign the bill if it reached his desk. "The president was far more inclined toward my bill than his financial advisers," she says.

Meanwhile, in the District itself thoughts are already turning to the 1998 mayor's race — and Barry's political future. Barry renewed concerns about whether he is up to the job this spring when he took a 15-day "retreat" for what he described as spiritual and physical renewal. A poll afterward showed a slim majority of Washingtonians approved of his performance, but more than two-thirds — 68 percent — said he should not run for re-election. [28]

So far, Barry has declined to answer questions about 1998. A handful of council members already are jockeying for position in the race, but many observers expect Barry to run — and to be the favorite. "Marion has a 25 percent base," Hobson says. "And he has the ability to add to that base during the course of a campaign, depending on what's going on."

Whatever happens in the mayor's race, the control board is to remain in place until the District presents four consecutive balanced budgets — which means at least through the rest of the century. Confrontations of the sort that marked the board's first year seem all but certain to continue. The open question is whether the board can fulfill its stated goal of giving the District enough financial and management assistance to recover from its deep fiscal and political crisis.

The past offers reasons for discouragement about finding a solution, according to historian Gillette. "Until the structural issues are resolved, it doesn't matter who's mayor or who's in the council," he says. "You're going to continue to have budget shortfalls, and the middle class is going to continue to leave."

But Gibson of D.C. Agenda says Washington's status as the national capital will force Congress ultimately to craft a solution. "Things will deteriorate only so far before federal initiatives move in," Gibson says. "This is the national capital, for which Congress and the federal government have responsibility." ■

Notes

[1] Edward M. Meyers, *Public Opinion and the Political Future of the Nation's Capital* (1996).

[2] *The Washington Post,* June 4, 1996, p. A17.

[3] Thomas N. Edmonds and Raymond J. Keating, *D.C. by the Numbers* (1995).

[4] Julius Hobson Jr. and Dwight Cropp, "It's Time to Suspend Home Rule," *The Washington Post,* July 7, 1996, p. C1.

[5] Commission on Budget and Financial Priorities of the District of Columbia, "Financing the Nation's Capital," November 1990.

[6] McKinsey & Company/The Urban Institute, "Assessing the District of Columbia's Financial Future," October 1994. The report was commissioned by the Federal City Council, a business group.

[7] U.S. Constitution, Art. I, Section 8.

[8] Jamin Raskin, "Hear Ye, Hear Ye," *The Washington Post,* Sept. 22, 1996, p. C3.

[9] Meyers, *op. cit.,* p. 195.

[10] For background, see Howard Gillette Jr., *Between Justice and Beauty: Race, Planning, and the Failure of Urban Policy in Washington, D.C.* (1995); Junior League of Washington, *The City of Washington: An Illustrated History* (1977); and Constance McLoughlin Green, *Washington: Village and Capital, 1800-1878* [vol I]; *Capital City, 1879-1950* [vol II]; (1962, 1963).

[11] See Green, *op. cit.,* p. 21.

[12] Quoted in Gillette, *op. cit.,* p. 42.

[13] See Green, *op. cit.,* pp. 339-362.

[14] "A City in Transition: D.C., Where Home Rule Flew and Faltered," *The Washington Post,* June 18, 1995, p. A1.

[15] Commission on Budget and Financial Priorities of the District of Columbia, *op. cit.,* p. A1.

[16] *1991 Congressional Quarterly Almanac,* p. 190.

[17] See *The Washington Post,* Dec. 31, 1994, p. A1.

[18] McKinsey & Co./The Urban Institute, *op. cit.*

[19] *The Washington Post,* June 7, 1995, p. B1.

[20] *The Washington Post,* Nov. 6, 1996, p. D1. *The Post* had an earlier speculative story about the plan on Oct. 10, p. A1.

[21] District of Columbia Financial Responsibility and Management Assistance Authority, "Children in Crisis: A Report on the Failure of D.C.'s Public Schools," November 1996.

[22] District of Columbia Financial Responsibility and Management Assistance Authority, "Report to the Congress," Oct. 30, 1995, p. 1.

[23] See *The Washington Post,* Sept. 13, 1995, p. B1; March 3, 1996, p. B3.

[24] See *The Washington Post,* Sept. 17, 1996, P. A1.

[25] Eric H. Holder Jr., "911 for the Police," *The Washington Post,* Jan. 31, 1996, p. A15; Feb. 1, 1996, p. A21.

[26] Hobson and Cropp, *op. cit.*

[27] See *The Washington Post,* July 14, 1996, p. C3.

[28] *The Washington Post,* May 22, 1996, p. D1.

Bibliography

Selected Sources Used

Books

Bowling, Kenneth R., *The Creation of Washington, D.C.: The Idea and Location of the American Capital*, George Mason University Press, 1991.

Bowling, a historian with the First Federal Congress Project at George Washington University in Washington, details the intricate politics behind the compromise decision in 1790 to locate the national capital in what was to become Washington, D.C. The book includes detailed source notes. An illustrated version of parts of the book was published under the title *Creating the Federal City, 1774-1800: Potomac Fever* by the American Institute of Architects Press in 1988.

Edmonds, Thomas N., and Raymond J. Keating, *D.C. by the Numbers: A State of Failure*, University Press of America, 1995.

Edmonds, a Republican political consultant, and Keating, an economist and tax-reduction activist, compile an array of statistics about government expenditures and services to argue that Washington's "experiment" in home rule has produced "social and economic chaos." *The Washington Times* published a five-part series of opinion pieces by Edmonds and Keating based on the book, Jan. 23-27, 1995.

Gillette, Howard, Jr., *Between Justice and Beauty: Race, Planning, and the Failure of Urban Policy in Washington, D.C.*, Johns Hopkins University Press, 1995.

Gilette, a professor at George Washington University in Washington, argues that Washington's urban needs have been neglected by Congress throughout its history. The book includes detailed source notes and an eight-page bibliographical note.

Green, Constance McLaughlin, *Washington: Village and Capital, 1800-1878* [vol. 1]; *Capital City, 1879-1950* [vol. II], Princeton University Press, 1962, 1963.

This two-volume history comprehensively traces Washington's political history from its founding as a tiny village in 1800 through its development as a city of monuments and international stature after the Civil War and up to 1950. Each volume includes a detailed bibliography and separate bibliographical note.

Jaffe, Harry S., and Tom Sherwood, *Dream City: Race, Power, and the Decline of Washington, D.C.*, Simon & Schuster, 1994.

Journalists Jaffe and Sherwood draw a sharply critical portrait of Mayor Marion S. Barry Jr., faulting him for failing to deal with the District's social and economic problems while exploiting racial tensions to further his political career. The book includes a three-page bibliography.

Junior League of Washington, *The City of Washington: An Illustrated History*, Wings Books, 1977.

This coffee-table volume provides a celebratory overview of Washington's city from its founding into the 1970s. The book includes nearly 700 illustrations and a one-page bibliography.

Lesoff, Alan, *The Nation and Its City: Politics, "Corruption," and Progress in Washington, D.C., 1861-1902*, Johns Hopkins University Press, 1994.

Lesoff, a professor at Texas A&M University in Corpus Christi, gives a detailed account of a crucial period in Washington's history: the controversial rule of Alexander "Boss" Shepherd from 1871-1874 and the resulting decision by Congress to create an appointed commission form of government, which continued until 1967. The book includes detailed source notes and a five-page bibliographical note.

Meyers, Edward M., *Public Opinion and the Future of the Nation's Capital*, Georgetown University Press, 1996.

Meyers, a member of the D.C. Public Service Commission, uses five focus groups from across the country to explore public opinion about proposals to change the District of Columbia's political status. The book, which includes an 11-page bibliography, is an expanded version of a doctoral dissertation Meyers wrote at Georgetown University.

Articles

"A City in Transition: D.C., Where Home Rule Flew and Faltered," *The Washington Post*, June 18, 1995, p. A1.

The 8,700-word article — written by a team of reporters headed by Blaine Harden — thoroughly reviews the history of home rule from its approval by Congress in 1973 through the creation of a financial control board by Congress in 1995.

Reports and Studies

Commission on Budget and Financial Priorities of the District of Columbia, *Financing the Nation's Capital*, November 1990.

To avert what it termed a "fiscal crisis," the so-called Rivlin Commission recommended a series of cost savings, including a cutback of 6,000 jobs, and revenue enhancements, including a commuter income tax and a larger payment from the federal government. The blue-ribbon commission was named after its chair, Alice M. Rivlin, then a senior fellow at the Brookings Institution and now vice chair of the Federal Reserve System's Board of Governors.

The Next Step

Additional information from UMI's Newspaper & Periodical Abstracts database

Financial Control Board

Horwitz, Sari, and Valerie Strauss, "D.C. school superintendent dismisses 21 administrators," *The Washington Post,* Oct. 18, 1996, p. A1.

Washington, D.C., school Superintendent Franklin L. Smith, under pressure from the District's financial control board to improve the management of city schools, fired 21 administrators Oct. 17, 1996.

Loeb, Vernon, "Control board hires law firm that's suing D.C.," *The Washington Post,* May 27, 1996, p. B1.

The Washington, D.C., financial control board has hired Hunton & Williams, a large Richmond, Va., law firm to represent the district government in a complex financial transaction involving delinquent tax accounts even though the firm is suing the city for $80 million in a separate case.

Loeb, Vernon, "Control board joins consensus on D.C. budget," *The Washington Post,* June 14, 1996, p. B1.

The Washington, D.C., financial control board approved and sent to Congress a $5.1 billion 1997 "consensus" budget supported by Mayor Marion Barry and the City Council that would boost spending on public safety but sharply curtail social programs and continue downsizing the city work force.

Spears, LaWanza, "D.C. Control Board is not the real problem," *Afro-American,* June 15, 1996, p. A5.

Spears questions whether the control board of Washington, D.C., is the real enemy of the community. Spears notes that Mayor Marion Barry is calling for citizens to support the removal of the board after the board attempted to fire long-time city employee Vernon Hawkins.

Vise, David A., and Vernon Loeb, "D.C. control board cuts schools, social spending," *The Washington Post,* Feb. 24, 1996, p. A1.

The financial control board voted to close six school buildings and slash $67.8 million from the Department of Human Services, but boosted spending on police and public works.

Vise, David A., "Norton joins GOP in urging D.C. to hasten reform," *The Washington Post,* July 10, 1996, p. B1.

Washington, D.C., Delegate Eleanor Holmes Norton said she agrees with congressional Republicans that the financial control board and city officials are moving too slowly to adopt major financial and management reforms.

Fiscal Problems

Barry, Marion, "What makes the financial condition of D.C. so fragile?," *Afro-American,* July 13,1996, p. A5.

Mayor Marion Barry discusses the district's fragile financial condition and some ways to address its problems.

Kemp, Jack F., "Okay, D.C., let's get radical," *The Washington Post,* June 4, 1995, p. C1.

Kemp says that while the imposition of fiscal responsibility is a vital first step, there has been no effort to solve Washington's real problems of a fleeing middle class and shrinking job base.

Pyatt, Rudolph A. Jr., "Quick-fix remedies won't cure anemic tax revenue in D.C.," *The Washington Post,* Feb. 27, 1995, p. WBIZ3.

Pyatt asserts that the financial control board will only offer a short-term solution to one aspect of the District's money problems and outlines the various financial concerns of the District.

Pyatt, Rudolph A. Jr., "In D.C., the tax base shrivels and the fiscal problems grow," *The Washington Post,* July 11, 1996, p. D10.

Pyatt states that a crippling revenue drain is at the core of Washington's fiscal problems, commenting that both jobs and taxes continue to be sucked from the city's economy.

Spayd, Liz, "D.C.'s diminishing options: If Barry and the board fail, what comes next?" *The Washington Post,* Feb. 11, 1996, p. C1.

Spayd comments on the diminishing number of options to bring Washington, D.C., out of fiscal ruin, noting the possibility of a receiver being appointed to control the city's spending.

Williams, Vanessa, "D.C. Council is seen as part of problem," *The Washington Post,* Sept. 8, 1996, p. B1.

The view that the Washington, D.C., Council is incapable of fixing its broken government has underscored what a number of politicians and analysts describe as a fundamental failure of the council.

Marion Barry

Behr, Peter, "Barry seeks tax break to keep firm in D.C.," *The Washington Post,* Aug. 22, 1996, p. D8.

The Barry administration is trying to work out a unique tax deferment agreement with one of Washington, D.C.'s largest non-government employers, the Bureau of National Affairs Inc., that would keep the newsletter publisher from moving to the suburbs.

Boo, Katherine, and Howard Schneider, "Barry's security costs anger D.C. Council," ***The Washington Post,*** **May 5, 1995, p. D1.**
Washington, D.C., Council members criticized as excessive the amount of money being spent on Mayor Marion Barry's security detail.

Buckley, Stephen, "What crisis in D.C.?: Barry defends spending on his security," ***The Washington Post,*** **May 6, 1995, p. A1.**
Mayor Marion Barry deflected criticism over spending on his personal security and said his 10-day trip to West Africa for the 1995 African-African-American Summit is appropriate because the district is not in a state of crisis.

Stone, Andrea, "D.C.'s Barry says he's rested, ready to go," ***USA Today,*** **May 14, 1996, p. A6.**
Mayor Marion Barry returned to work from two weeks of "personal renewal," denying rumors that he had relapsed into "drinking and drugging" or considered resigning from office.

Twomey, Steve, "The only way out for Barry, for D.C.," ***The Washington Post,*** **May 2, 1996, p. B1.**
Twomey asserts that Washington, D.C., Mayor Marion Barry should resign after announcing his need to go on a retreat to renew his health and spirit.

"D.C. exodus and Mr. Barry's plan," ***The Washington Post,*** **Jan. 30, 1996, p. A14.**
An editorial questions whether Washington, D.C., Mayor Marion Barry is serious about altering the way the city does business in light of the fact that census estimates confirm that more and more District residents are leaving the city and heading for the suburbs.

Williams, Vanessa, "Barry, 54 other D.C. officials go on West Virginia retreat," ***The Washington Post,*** **Sept. 28, 1996, p. B3.**
Mayor Marion Barry and dozens of city officials piled onto a bus Sept. 27, 1996, and set out for the Coolfont Resort in Berkeley Springs, W.Va., for a two-day retreat at which they will seek ways to improve district government.

Social Conditions

Brossard, Mario A., and Hamil R. Harris, "D.C. residents ask: Should I stay or go?" ***The Washington Post,*** **March 31, 1996, p. B1.**
As Washington, D.C., staggers under the weight of a deep financial crisis and widespread problems with basic services, polls and statistics show that many district residents are wondering whether they should join the thousands moving away.

Brown, DeNeen L., "Divided D.C. school board backs cuts, closings," ***The Washington Post,*** **March 6, 1996, p. C1.**
The D.C. school board, under pressure from the financial control board and Mayor Marion Barry to cut millions from the school system's budget, voted to close 12 schools, cut summer school and increase class sizes by laying of hundreds of teachers.

Jeter, Jon, "With city at low ebb, some in D.C. see resurgence ahead," ***The Washington Post,*** **May 5, 1996, p. A24.**
In spite of Washington's difficulties, a number of residents say the District has endured the worst, and they believe better times lie ahead.

Lipton, Eric, "D.C., suburbs reach pact on Blue Plains," ***The Washington Post,*** **Oct. 13, 1995, p. A1.**
The District's government has agreed to turn over its Blue Plains sewage treatment plant to an independent authority under a pact with suburban governments aimed at ending financial and environmental problems at the Southwest Washington facility that serves about two-thirds of the area's residents.

Milloy, Courtland, "Focusing on the good in D.C.," ***The Washington Post,*** **Aug. 11, 1996, p. B1.**
Milloy relates what he likes about Washington, D.C., commenting that despite the bad press the district is a metropolitan area of tremendous resources and goodwill, a family of neighborhoods that make up the nation's capital.

Statehood

"Congress's next bailout: Washington, D.C.," ***U.S. News & World Report,*** **Feb. 13, 1995, p. 10.**
The dream of statehood for Washington, D.C., has been elusive because of the city's financial credibility in Congress. Its credibility crumbled last week when Mayor Marion Barry made it clear that the nation's capital no longer can take care of itself.

Harris, Charles W., "Bringing democracy to the folks in D.C.," ***The Wall Street Journal,*** **Nov. 22, 1995, p. A11.**
Harris, a professor at Howard University, responds to the Oct. 12, 1995, review of his book, *Congress and the Governance of the Nation's Capital,* by Fred Siegel. Harris clarifies his position on the issue of statehood, saying he believes that Washington, D.C., should remain a district, but be treated like a state.

Jenkins, Kent Jr., "D.C. home rule, statehood take shape in draft platform," ***The Washington Post,*** **Aug. 27, 1996, p. A14.**
The delegates who control the Democratic National Convention are poised to go on record with the Democratic Party's strongest endorsement ever of locally elected, home-rule government for Washington, D.C., and of making it America's 51st state.

Back Issues

Great Research on Current Issues Starts Right Here...Recent topics covered by The CQ Researcher are listed below. Before May 1991, reports were published under the name of Editorial Research Reports.

MAY 1995
Assisted Suicide Controversy
Overhauling Social Security
Learning to Read
Mandatory Sentencing

JUNE 1995
Combating Infectious Disease
Property Rights
Repetitive Stress Injuries
Regulating the Internet

JULY 1995
War Crimes
Highway Safety
Combating Terrorism
Preventing Teen Drug Use

AUGUST 1995
Job Stress
Organ Transplants
United Nations at 50
Advances in Cancer Research

SEPTEMBER 1995
Catholic Church in the U.S.
Northern Ireland Cease-Fire
High School Sports
Teaching History

OCTOBER 1995
Quebec's Future
Revitalizing the Cities
Networking the Classroom
Indoor Air Pollution

NOVEMBER 1995
The Working Poor
The Jury System
Sex, Violence and the Media
Police Misconduct

DECEMBER 1995
Teens and Tobacco
Gene Therapy's Future
Global Water Shortages
Third-Party Prospects

JANUARY 1996
Emergency Medicine
Punishing Sex Offenders
Bilingual Education
Helping the Homeless

FEBRUARY 1996
Reforming the CIA
Campaign Finance Reform
Academic Politics
Getting Into College

MARCH 1996
The British Monarchy
Preventing Juvenile Crime
Tax Reform
Pursuing the Paranormal

APRIL 1996
Centennial Olympic Games
Managed Care
Protecting Endangered Species
New Military Culture

MAY 1996
Russia's Political Future
Marriage and Divorce
Year-Round Schools
Taiwan, China and the U.S.

JUNE 1996
Rethinking NAFTA
First Ladies
Teaching Values
Labor Movement's Future

JULY 1996
Recovered-Memory Debate
Native Americans' Future
Crackdown on Sexual Harassment
Attack on Public Schools

AUGUST 1996
Fighting Over Animal Rights
Privatizing Government Services
Child Labor and Sweatshops
Cleaning Up Hazardous Wastes

SEPTEMBER 1996
Gambling Under Attack
The States and Federalism
Civic Journalism
Reassessing Foreign Aid

OCTOBER 1996
Political Consultants
Insurance Fraud
Rethinking School Integration
Parental Rights

NOVEMBER 1996
Global Warming
Clashing Over Copyright
Consumer Debt

Back issues are available for $5.00 (subscribers) or $8.00 (non-subscribers). Quantity discounts apply to orders over ten. To order, call Congressional Quarterly Customer Service at (202) 887-8621.

Binders are available for $18.00. To order call 1-800-638-1710. Please refer to stock number 648.

Future Topics

- ***Welfare, Work and the States***
- ***Volunteerism***
- ***Implementing the Disabilities Act***

THE CQ Researcher

PUBLISHED BY CONGRESSIONAL QUARTERLY INC.

Welfare, Work and the States

Can states move welfare recipients into jobs?

In one bold stroke, the federal government has terminated its 61-year-old welfare program and given the states the leading role in charting welfare policy. But Washington also has made clear that it expects the states to help many more welfare recipients go to work. This adds up to an enormous challenge for states. Welfare-to-work efforts and public employment traditionally have cost more than simply writing benefit checks for welfare recipients. But federal spending for training and welfare promises to decline over time. Moreover, states will have to face the prospect that many welfare recipients could eventually lose welfare benefits completely, even though they may be unable to find jobs that pay enough for them to become self-sufficient.

INSIDE THIS ISSUE

Dec. 6, 1996 • Volume 6, No. 45 • Pages 1057-1080

Formerly Editorial Research Reports

WELFARE, WORK AND THE STATES

COVER: MISSOURI'S "BEYOND WELFARE" PROGRAM HAS MOVED 42,000 PEOPLE OFF WELFARE AND INTO JOBS SINCE 1993, INCLUDING LAROY JENKINS, AT WORK AS A CHEF AT WESTPORT BREWERY CO. IN KANSAS CITY. (BOB HULSEY/MISSOURI DEPARTMENT OF SOCIAL SERVICES)

THE CQ Researcher

Dec. 6, 1996
Volume 6, No. 45

Bibliographic records and abstracts included in The Next Step section of this publication are from UMI's Newspaper and Periodical Abstracts database, and are used with permission.

The CQ Researcher (ISSN 1056-2036). Formerly Editorial Research Reports. Published weekly (48 times per year, not printed March 1, May 31, Aug. 30, Nov. 29) by Congressional Quarterly Inc., 1414 22nd St., N.W., Washington, D.C. 20037. Annual subscription rate for libraries, businesses and government is $319. Additional rates furnished upon request. Periodicals postage paid at Washington, D.C. POSTMASTER: Send address changes to The CQ Researcher, 1414 22nd St., N.W., Washington, D.C. 20037.

Welfare, Work and the States

By Christopher Conte

The Issues

It's a cold, blustery morning in Des Moines, and a group of welfare applicants are attending a rather chilling orientation session at the state Department of Employment Services.

"Don't confuse the state with big-hearted, warm, kind individuals," Todd McGee, an interviewer for the department, tells them. "Welfare reform means nothing else but 'Get off welfare and get a job.'"

That may oversimplify Iowa's Family Investment Program, one of the nation's longest-running and most comprehensive welfare-reform efforts. But it does capture the spirit of welfare reform in the 1990s. Across the country, policy-makers of all political stripes have come to agree that welfare recipients not only *can* but *must* work — and without a great deal of delay.

Now, the federal government has raised the stakes. The new Personal Responsibility and Work Opportunity Reconciliation Act of 1996, which President Clinton reluctantly signed in August, requires that in six years at least half of each state's adult welfare recipients must be working. States that fail could lose up to 21 percent of their federal welfare funding.

Individual recipients also will feel the heat. They generally will be expected to work — either in paid employment or community service — within two years of the time they go on welfare. And no one will be allowed to collect welfare for more than five years over a lifetime.

States must meet the new work requirements in the context of a fundamentally changed relationship with the federal government — one that poses some opportunities, but also considerable risks. In the past, Washington set most of the rules for welfare and then helped states pay benefits to all eligible

recipients. But now, states will receive federal money in the form of block grants, which will remain essentially unchanged for the next six years, regardless of what happens to welfare caseloads. While fewer strings will be attached to the federal money, states will have to bear the burden if, for any reason, they fail to contain costs and trim the welfare roles.

They also will have to bear much of the cost of any additional job training and counseling required to make welfare recipients more employable. That's because the federal government, even while requiring more welfare recipients to go to work, hasn't increased its support for job training. In fact, spending on the basic training programs that could benefit welfare recipients has declined steadily over the last several years, according to the Congressional Budget Office (CBO).

In 1994, the federal government provided $5 billion for job training under the Job Training and Partnership Act (JTPA), plus another $1.1 billion for the basic welfare-to-work program, the Job Opportunity and Basic Skills (JOBS) program. In fiscal 1997, which began Oct. 1, the government is providing just $4.7 billion for the JTPA, and the new welfare-reform law eliminated the JOBS program altogether.

How will states react? Will they feel emboldened to take advantage of their new flexibility, or will they become reluctant to take chances because of their greater fiscal exposure? Will they invest in efforts to make welfare recipients more employable, or will they slash benefits and services in a "race to the bottom" designed to make sure that they don't attract welfare families from other, less generous states?

Nobody knows for sure. Reform advocates hope most states will follow the lead of Iowa and others who have converted welfare into more of a jobs program. But there is no guarantee all will follow this course. "There are real questions about whether states will convert their welfare programs to work," concedes a House aide who worked on the legislation. "It's hard to do, and for some states, the money will be tight."

Indeed, money will be a pivotal issue. So far, the most successful welfare-reform efforts have required states to increase spending, at least initially. When Iowa launched its reform program, for instance, it more than doubled its outlays for employment programs, from $9.7 million in fiscal 1993 to $25.7 million in fiscal 1996. The additional funds paid for more counselors to help welfare recipients seek — and prepare for — work.

The hope, of course, is that this up-front investment eventually will pay off. Again, there are indications that it can — at least modestly. In Iowa, the welfare caseload dropped from 39,536 to 33,800 in the first two years after the reform program went into effect, and the portion of welfare recipients who work jumped to 35 percent, compared with 18 percent for a control group. With the caseload down, and more of those who remain on welfare earning outside income,

Welfare Block Grants Vary Greatly From State to State

The 1996 welfare reform law creates block grants for Temporary Assistance for Needy Families to replace Aid to Families with Dependent Children (AFDC) and several related programs. States must convert to block grants no later than July 1, 1997. Money will be distributed to each state based on its federal funding for AFDC and related programs in fiscal 1995, fiscal 1994 or the average of fiscal 1992-94, whichever is higher.

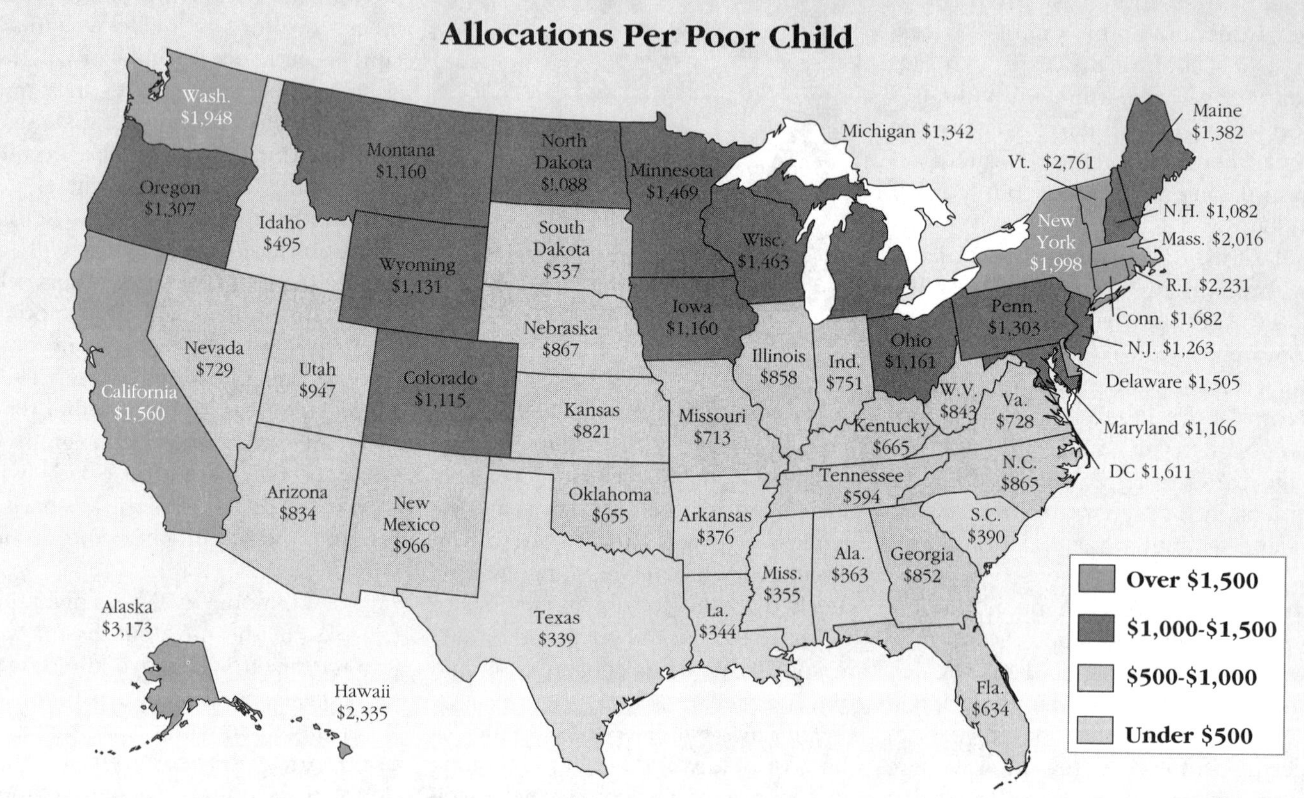

Source: Center for Law and Social Policy, citing Congressional Research Service calculations based on data from Census Bureau March Current Population Surveys (CPS). Numbers of children in poverty were computed using 3-year averages for 1992-94. Estimates for smaller states are of lower reliability due to sample sizes.

monthly cash assistance payments dropped from $14.1 million in January 1994 to $11.2 million two years later.

Still, Iowa had to curtail some training options — for instance, it limited the number of postsecondary education slots — to contain its costs. While some reform advocates argue that education hasn't proven to be an effective tool for reducing the welfare rolls anyway, critics of the work-no-matter-what approach say the lack of post-high school training opportunities consigns many welfare families to dead-end jobs that don't pay enough for them to achieve self-sufficiency.

To some, the debate over how much to provide in the way of training points to a fundamental contradiction in the goals of welfare reformers. "We want to reduce dependency on welfare and reduce poverty — and we want to do it all at low cost," says David Butler, a welfare analyst at Manpower Demonstration Research Corp. (MDRC) in New York. "We can't have it all."

If helping welfare families climb beyond the bottom rung of the career ladder would require increased spending, some of the alternatives for handling welfare recipients who won't be able to find private-sector jobs or won't be able to support themselves when their benefits run out won't be cheap either. Workfare — that is, requiring welfare recipients to perform community services — costs about $6,000 a year more per recipient than simply handing out benefit checks, according to Wendell Primus, who resigned as deputy assistant secretary of the Department of Health and Human Services when President Clinton decided to sign the tough, new welfare law.

The extra cost includes $3,000 for child care, about $700 for transportation and $2,000-$2,500 to arrange and supervise the jobs. And that investment wouldn't make welfare recipients any better off financially than when they were simply receiving welfare checks. To create a full-time public-sector job that would provide health and other benefits and offer a chance of economic advancement probably would cost $3,000-$6,000 more per recipient than a workfare job, Primus says.

Few people expect Washington or the states to come up with that kind of money. Indeed, far from increasing spending, the new law will cut federal welfare outlays by $54.2 billion, according to the CBO. While the bulk of those cuts reflects reductions in food stamps and a controversial provision making legal immigrants ineligible for most federal welfare benefits, the CBO estimates that the states will have to spend $13 billion more than Congress has authorized for welfare-to-work programs over the next six years to meet the employment targets set by the new law.

The $13 billion doesn't count child-care costs. Even though the new law increases federal spending for child care by $3.5 billion, to a total of $14 billion, the CBO says that still falls about $1.8 billion short of what would be needed if states are to meet the law's work targets. In light of those projections and the strong public pressure to reduce, rather than increase, spending on welfare, "We don't think states will meet the work requirements," says CBO analyst Sheila Dacey.

On top of the federal spending cuts, the new law will allow states to reduce their own welfare spending by $40 billion between 1997 and 2002 without penalty.

Balancing a desire to restrain welfare spending against the needs of many welfare recipients isn't the only tough choice states face. They also will have to reconcile the public's insistence that welfare recipients work with its desire to make sure that children are sheltered from severe poverty.

Unfortunately for reformers, "children and their parents are a package," notes MDRC President Judith M. Gueron. "You cannot help one without helping the other." [1]

The Urban Institute concluded that the new law will push 1.1 million more children below the poverty line, in addition to the 9.7 million already there. About 20 percent of all families with children would lose an average of $1,300 a year, it said. [2] Proponents of the new law argue that this analysis underestimates how many adults will be prompted by the work requirements to find jobs. And, they say, it fails to recognize the demoralizing effect of welfare dependency on children.

Only time will tell who is right. Meanwhile, the key issue in welfare reform for the years ahead will be whether states can achieve the ambitious work objectives set by the new law — and whether welfare families can become self-sufficient in the process.

Can states meet the work targets the new law sets for welfare recipients?

At first glance, there appear to be plenty of jobs. For decades, the U.S. economy has been an impressive job-creation machine. In the 1960s, for instance, employment grew 19.6 percent, or by 12.9 million jobs, even though the population grew just 16.9 percent. In the 1970s, employment increased 26.2 percent, while the population rose 22.4 percent. And in the 1980s, the total number of jobs jumped 18.7 percent, again outstripping the 12.1 percent growth in population. [3] This pattern has continued in the 1990s; the unemployment rate in October stood at 5.2 percent, a rate that most economists consider at or near "full employment" given normal turnover in the work force.

But Rebecca Blank, an economist at Northwestern University, argues that "the aggregate numbers are very deceptive." For one thing, there is relatively less demand for poorly educated workers than for people who have had more schooling. The unemployment rate among people who don't have high school degrees is double that of people who graduated from high school, and five times that of people with college degrees, according to Blank. [4]

Those figures suggest welfare recipients may face tougher going in the labor market than most people. Almost 47 percent of the people on welfare have less than a high school education, and 39 percent had amassed no work experience at all for a year before they first began receiving assistance. [5] Besides lacking the basic skills needed for many jobs today, many welfare recipients don't have the necessary "soft" skills, such as knowledge about personal grooming, basic language abilities and an ability to function smoothly in workplace settings. Others face chronic health or emotional problems, are victims of violence or sexual abuse, or have histories of drug or alcohol abuse.

Given these problems, what can welfare reformers realistically expect to achieve? Iowa, which has been working at moving welfare recipients into jobs longer and harder than most states, hasn't been able to get more than 35 percent of its adult welfare caseload working. Doug Howard, administrator of the state Division of Economic Assistance, says there seems to be a "cellophane ceiling" — perhaps not as hard to break as a glass ceiling, but still a barrier — that has prevented the state from going beyond that.

Reforms Target Food Stamp Users, Immigrants . . .

President Clinton has vowed to seek changes in two controversial provisions of the Personal Responsibility and Work Opportunity Reconciliation Act of 1996 that he says "have nothing to do with welfare reform." But his task will be complicated because the two provisions have much to do with the $54.2 billion the new law is expected to save the federal government over the next six years.

As signed by Clinton Aug. 22, the law will cut spending on the food stamp program by $23.3 billion. It will save almost $24 billion by making legal immigrants ineligible for most welfare benefits, including food stamps, Medicaid and Supplemental Security Income (SSI), a cash benefit program for the low-income aged, blind and disabled.

Critics say the changes will seriously fray the federal safety net — simply to save the government money. Sandy Clark, a policy analyst at the Urban Institute, says that "unlike the major fundamental changes in AFDC [Aid to Families with Dependent Children], changes in the food stamp program amount to cutting benefits, plain and simple."

But reformers argue that the food stamp program was shot through with waste, fraud and abuse. They insist that welfare reform, not just budget cuts, was at the heart of reductions in both food stamps and benefits for immigrants.

The Center on Budget and Policy Priorities estimates that food stamp benefits will be reduced almost 20 percent — from the current 80 cents per person per meal to 66 cents per person per meal. According to the center, 6.7 million families with children (the primary beneficiaries of food stamps) will lose, on average, $435 in 1998, the first year that cuts take effect. The very poorest families — those with annual incomes at or below $6,250, or one-half the official poverty level for a family of three — will lose $655 each in 1998. By 2002, the cuts will cost them $790 a year.

In what the center calls "probably the single, harshest provision written into a major safety net program in at least 30 years," the law allows unemployed adults between 18 and 50 who have no dependent children to receive food stamps for just three months every three years, unless they are working at least half-time. Despite imposing this requirement, the bill provides no new money for workfare or training slots.

The Congressional Budget Office predicts that in an average month 1 million unemployed Americans who are willing to work but cannot find a job or a slot in workfare or job training programs will be affected. About 40 percent of them will be women, and nearly one-third will be over 40, an age at which it is particularly difficult for unskilled workers to find jobs. Because people in this group have no dependent children, they don't qualify for other welfare benefits.

Projected Cuts in Welfare Spending

The 1996 welfare overhaul law will cut federal spending by $58.4 billion over six years, mainly by scaling back food stamps and making legal immigrants ineligible for most welfare benefits. The law also includes modest increases in family support payments and other programs, bringing the net savings to $54.2 billion.

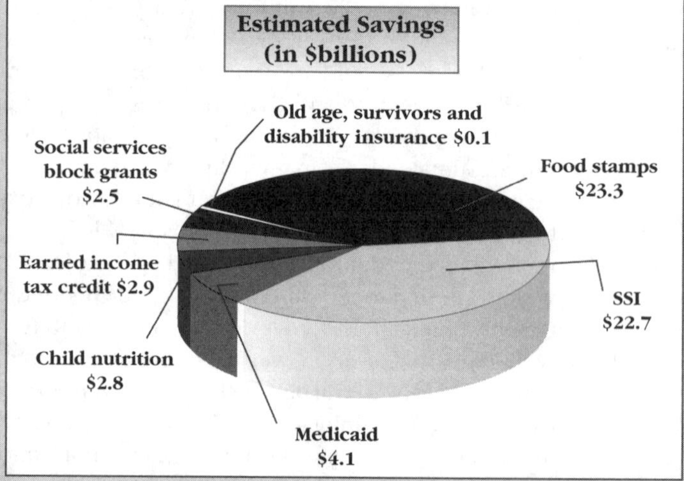

Rep. Pat Roberts, R-Kan., chairman of the House Agriculture Committee, defends the cuts, arguing that the food stamp program has been on "automatic pilot" for too long, more than doubling in cost over the past 10 years. He says that under the new law, adjustments in benefits will be tied to increases in the actual cost of food. The law also tightens controls on waste and fraud while increasing penalties for illegal trafficking in food stamps. And, to help promote private-sector jobs for people moving from welfare to work, the law allows states to transfer food stamp allotments to private employers who can use them to supplement salaries for welfare recipients who take jobs.

Roberts, who declared July 31 on the House floor that "food stamps must not be a disincentive to work," says only a handful of food stamp recipients will be affected by the three-month restriction on benefits for the unemployed. For those who cannot find work because there are no jobs

Utah, which has been even more aggressive about moving welfare recipients into the labor force, reports similar results, although officials there appear a bit more optimistic. "About one-third [of the welfare caseload] can be moved into the job market fairly easily," says Connie Cowley, program specialist for the state's Family Employment Program. "A middle third have more difficult issues to resolve, but we think we can [get them working] with

. . . But Clinton Vows to Seek Changes

available, and for areas where the unemployment rate is 10 percent or higher, the states will have flexibility to make exceptions to the three-month rule, he contends.

The immigration provisions of the welfare-reform law are contested just as vehemently as the food stamp ones. The National Immigration Law Center in Los Angeles says that legal immigrants are "by far the biggest losers in the final bill." Even though most legal immigrants to the U.S. pay taxes, have the right to vote and can join — or be drafted into — the armed forces, the law denies them eligibility for all welfare benefits except emergency medical treatment.

According to the National Conference of State Legislatures, approximately 600,000 legal immigrants may lose access to Medicaid, 1 million will be ineligible for food stamps and 500,000 elderly, blind and disabled legal immigrants will lose SSI benefits if the new law is enforced to the letter. [1]

That seems fair enough to those who support the change. "There ought to be meaningful distinctions between citizens and non-citizens, and this [welfare reform] can be one of them," says John J. Miller, vice president of the Center for Equal Opportunity, which says it is dedicated to establishing a color-blind, pro-assimilation society. Miller argues that welfare is destructive because it breeds dependency. "You want [immigrants] to come here and stay and succeed, and I don't think welfare helps them do that," he argues. "It may help them stay, but it does not help them succeed."

The old welfare system bred dependency and the presumption that entitlements are a natural part of the family budget, says Daniel Stein, executive director of the Federation for American Immigration Reform. New Chinese immigrants in California, for example, have "acculturated and assimilated into welfare and have evolved an understanding that [SSI] is part of a family entitlement," Stein says.

According to Stein, elderly Chinese immigrants who come to the United States commonly transfer their assets to children already here so that they can qualify for welfare benefits as indigents. Stein says the Government Accounting Office has identified a 500 percent increase in the use of SSI by elderly aliens in the last 15 years. "We cannot be the retirement home for the world's indigent elderly," Stein argues.

He also contends America can't afford to continue letting a relatively uneducated, unskilled and more dependent immigrant population move to the U.S. just because some businesses want cheap labor. This is especially so because average taxpayers, not employers, cover the cost of welfare for such immigrants when they fall upon hard times, he says.

Jana Mason, a government liaison for Immigration and Refugee Services of America, argues that the law does an injustice to many of the immigrants and refugees whom the organization helps to settle in this country. Even though working-age immigrants are among the least likely welfare beneficiaries, she says, they can encounter the same difficulties and setbacks that any native-born or naturalized worker faces. "They can have an illness or they can have abuse in their families," she notes. "They also can have a falling out with people who sponsored them" and who are responsible for helping them stay off welfare if they are injured, lose their jobs or can't find work.

In the absence of any changes in the law, states may use their own funds to help legal immigrants living below the poverty line. In Maryland, for instance, Democratic Gov. Parris N. Glendening has pledged that the state will allocate almost $8 million to continue some welfare benefits to immigrants. [2]

Clinton, for his part, already has issued a directive saying that the administration will grant waivers to encourage extending the period that legal immigrants are eligible for food stamps to the maximum time allowed by law. He also said that legal immigrants should not be denied access to soup kitchens or emergency medical and child protection services. And to ensure access to full benefits as quickly as possible, Clinton directed Attorney General Janet Reno and the Immigration and Naturalization Service to "remove the bureaucratic roadblocks to citizenship to all eligible, legal immigrants." Partly as a result of the months-long debate over welfare reform, nearly 1.1 million immigrants were naturalized during fiscal 1996, more than double the record-breaking number of naturalizations in fiscal 1995. [3]

The welfare bill is "a great inducement to naturalize," Stein concludes. "In this sense, [it's] the greatest civics education we've had in 50 years. Suddenly, citizenship means something again."

---

[1] Most of the other savings in the SSI program will come from a provision that makes it harder for children to be considered disabled to qualify for SSI. The Congressional Budget Office estimates that about 300,000 children — or 22 percent — who would be receiving SSI in 2002 would lose their eligibility as a result of this change. See *CQ Weekly Report*, Aug. 3, 1996, p. 2193.

[2] See Jon Jeter, "Md. to Continue Some Welfare for Legal Immigrants," *The Washington Post*, Sept. 17, 1996, pp. D1, D6.

[3] The Associated Press, "Clinton Moves to Protect Legal Aliens' Welfare Benefits," *The Washington Post*, Aug. 24, 1996, p. A6; and Sam Howe Verhovek, "Immigrants' Anxieties Spur a Surge in Naturalizations," *The New York Times*, Sept. 13, 1996.

some short-term intervention."

But the final third have "multiple barriers" to employment — including alcohol or drug-abuse problems, family members who require regular care, histories of physical and sexual abuse and low IQs — that will greatly complicate efforts to move them from welfare to employment, Cowley says. Because the federal law allows states to exempt only 20 percent of welfare recipients from time limits, that sug-

Welfare Cases Began to Drop Before Welfare Reform

After rising for more than three decades, the number of families receiving Aid to Families with Dependent Children (AFDC) fell 13 percent between 1994 and August 1996 — the month Congress passed a welfare reform bill replacing AFDC with a system of block grants to the states. The total number of welfare recipients, including children, dropped 14 percent in the past two years, reflecting a continuing decline in the average size of families on welfare.

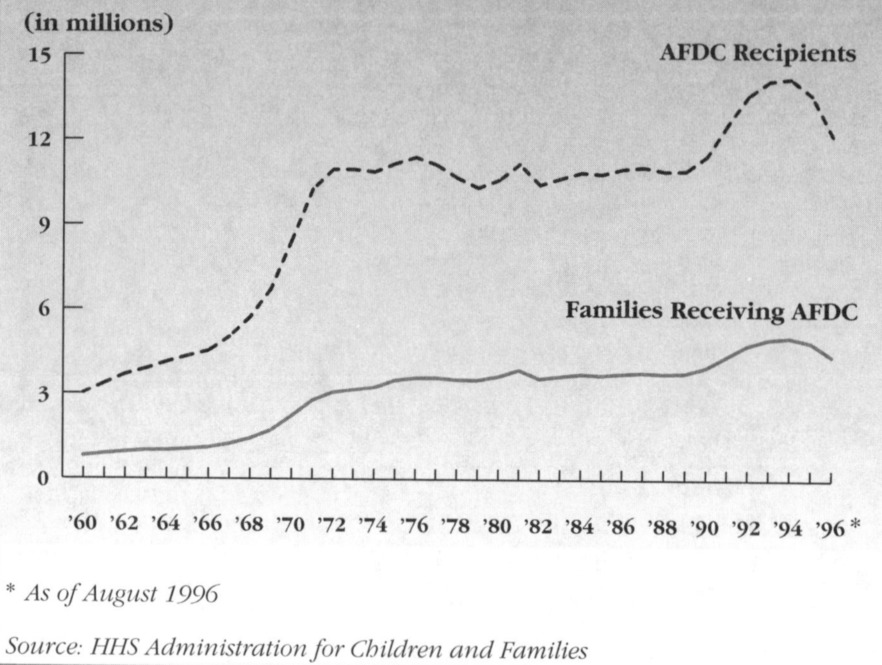

* *As of August 1996*

Source: HHS Administration for Children and Families

gests some people could be cut off from welfare even though they have serious obstacles to finding work.

There also are geographic pockets where jobs are particularly hard to find even in today's strong economy. In parts of West Virginia, for instance, the unemployment rate exceeds 17 percent; faced with such labor market conditions, Susan Sergi, commissioner of the state's Bureau for Children and Families, told *The Wall Street Journal* in August that she doubted the state will meet the employment targets in the new law. [6]

Inner cities, where many welfare recipients live, are an even tougher problem. For them, the long-term exodus of manufacturing jobs to the suburbs makes the welfare-to-work transition appear particularly daunting. Philadelphia, which has a welfare caseload of 70,000 adults, would have to put 15,000 welfare recipients to work in 1997 under the new law. But it actually lost 32,000 jobs between 1993 and 1996, according to Mark Alan Hughes, vice president of Public-Private Ventures, a public policy research organization in Philadelphia.

Hughes notes that other cities face similar challenges. New York, which has 285,000 adults on welfare, gained just 46,000 jobs between 1993 and 1996. Chicago picked up 12,000 jobs between 1993 and 1996, but it has 100,000 adults on welfare. Detroit, which has a welfare population of 65,000 adults, added just 14,000 jobs during the three-year period.

"The need is so great that unless we come up with some kind of public-sector employment and stop deluding ourselves that we can make a transition to private-sector employment, [welfare reform] won't work," says Hughes. In a recent op-ed article in *The Washington Post,* he predicted that time limits on welfare could create a "welfare dust bowl" in major American cities. [7]

Harvard sociologist William Julius Wilson describes the dismal labor market many urban blacks face in a new book, *When Work Disappears: The World of the New Urban Poor.* "For the first time in the 20th century," Wilson writes, "most adults in many inner-city ghetto neighborhoods are not working in a typical week." In 1950, according to Wilson, 69 percent of all males 14 and over who lived in three of Chicago's predominantly black South Side communities worked in a typical week. In 1960, the figure was still 64 percent. But by 1990, it had plummeted to just 37 percent. [8]

According to Wilson, the disappearance of high-paying manufacturing jobs from these inner-city areas was a major contributor to their social decline. Inner-city ghetto residents who continue to be employed — primarily in the kind of low-wage, service-sector jobs that remain in these neighborhoods — "are, in effect, working against all odds," Wilson argues. "They somehow manage to work steadily despite the lack of work-support networks (car pools, informal job information networks), institutions (good schools and training programs), and systems (child care and transportation) that most of the employed population of this country rely on. Moreover, the travel costs, child care costs and other employment-related expenses consume a significant portion of their already meager incomes." [9]

Many of Wilson's critics counter that he has mistaken the chicken for the egg — that the loss of manufacturing jobs in the inner cities was a response to social decline, rather than a cause of it. [10]

But whoever is right, there's no doubt that addressing the widespread joblessness in inner cities will be a crucial challenge for state welfare programs. Consider the case of Wisconsin, a state considered in the vanguard of welfare reform. Between 1990 and 1994, its welfare rolls dropped 6.3 percent statewide. But the number of welfare recipients actually climbed 0.4 percent in predominantly urban Milwaukee County. [11]

Will the new welfare law lead to a permanent reduction in dependency?

It's one thing to get a welfare recipient a job. But it may be something else altogether to help that person become truly self-sufficient.

"The presumption that a transition from welfare to work represents a move toward self-sufficiency or economic well-being ignores the fact that low-wage jobs neither pay enough to remove a family from poverty nor guarantee future access to better paying jobs," writes sociologist Kathryn J. Edin of Rutgers University. [12]

In a study of 214 recipients of Aid to Families with Dependent Children (AFDC) and 165 low-wage workers in four U.S. cities, Edin found frustration among welfare mothers. Most generally are eager to work, but the only jobs they can find — mostly in the fast-food business — pay very low wages, seldom offer benefits, often don't even guarantee a regular number of hours of work per week and are subject to frequent layoffs.

"Most of the welfare mothers interviewed believed they could eventually get a job if they tried, particularly if they were willing to do minimum-wage work," Edin writes. "However, they also believed that a minimum-wage job would get them nowhere." [13]

Edin estimates that a single mother would have to hold a full-time job paying between $8-$9 an hour to cover all her expenses — including the additional cost of clothing, transportation and day care associated with working — to be better off than when she was on welfare. Yet many welfare mothers can only find work at $5-$6 an hour, and often for less than 40 hours a week.

Faced with these realities, a significant number of women see welfare as part of a "broader strategy to improve their human capital," according to Edin. They opt for welfare in place of low-wage work, she explains, in the hope it will buy them the time and resources to receive training that will qualify them for jobs that will pay enough for them to become self-sufficient.

In spite of the obvious demand, critics of past welfare-to-work programs argue that financing education or training hasn't proven a cost-effective way to reduce welfare rolls. "Education and training are very ineffective because this population is not good at learning new skills," says Lawrence Mead, a professor of politics at New York University. "They accomplish more with work experience."

The new federal law, reflecting this view, says states can't count welfare recipients who are enrolled in post-secondary education toward satisfying their obligation to enroll a growing portion of their caseload in work programs. Further, it allows states to count only a limited number of people enrolled in vocational education classes.

Even if the lack of training opportunities consigns welfare families to low-wage jobs with little hope, Mead contends that this is an improvement over being on welfare. Having a job confers on a person a certain respectability and a right to claim other social benefits, such as earned-income tax credits and unemployment and disability insurance, he says.

While many analysts agree the welfare system can't be expected to solve the problem of declining wages for unskilled workers, they concede it is a serious concern. Between 1979 and 1995, according to a new study from the Economic Policy Institute, wages for people with less than a high school education fell a stunning 23 percent after adjustment for inflation — to an average of just $8.16 an hour. High school graduates saw their wages drop 11.8 percent, to $10.46 an hour. While people with college or advanced degrees didn't fare particularly well by historical standards either, their wages at least rose somewhat — 4.3 percent and 12.1 percent, respectively. [14]

Brookings Institution economist Gary Burtless adds a worrisome footnote to the well-documented deterioration in wages for low-skilled workers. If welfare reform succeeds in pushing 2 million more unskilled workers into the labor force, the likely result, he says, would be a further decline in wages. According to Burtless, "With fierce competition for unskilled and semiskilled jobs, wage rates would be driven down, at least modestly, and [welfare] recipients would face worse job prospects than those . . . who left the rolls during the 1980s." [15] ■

BACKGROUND

From Welfare to Work

It wasn't always assumed that welfare mothers should work. When Congress enacted the first modern welfare program in 1935, most mothers stayed home with their children, and Aid to Dependent Children, as the program established by Title IV of the Social Security Act of 1935 was then known, provided cash benefits to help needy widows care for their children at home.

As late as 1962, when Congress amended the Social Security Act at the behest of President John F. Kennedy, work was not a particular focus of welfare-reform strategies. The amendments approved that year instead stressed providing more social services to needy families. In particular, they provided funds to send welfare caseworkers into the neighborhoods and homes of welfare recipients.

Mary Jo Bane and David Ellwood,

welfare experts at Harvard University who later would serve in the first Clinton administration, describe in their book *Welfare Realities* how the rising cost of welfare quickly led policy-makers to grow disenchanted with the social services approach. Conservatives, including Gov. Ronald Reagan of California, complained that caseworkers were driving up welfare costs by overlooking violations of welfare rules and advocating more services to address problems such as inadequate housing and child care, alcoholism and domestic violence. [16]

As a result of such criticism, welfare agencies were encouraged to concentrate on determining eligibility and processing welfare payments, rather than on providing services. Neighborhood visits were stopped, and standards for proving eligibility were toughened.

At the same time, with more and more women entering the work force, policy-makers increasingly began seeking ways to encourage welfare mothers to work. In 1967, House Ways and Means Committee Chairman Wilbur D. Mills, D-Ark., bemoaned a rising welfare caseload in terms that would be echoed almost 30 years later. "For five years, this load has gone up and up and up, with no end in sight," Mills said. "We are not going to put federal funds into states for the benefit of parents when they refuse to get out of the house and try to earn something." [17]

Mills helped steer one of the first welfare-to-work efforts through Congress that year. Under the Work Incentive (WIN) program, AFDC recipients with no preschool children were required to register for state work-training and employment services. The program was a disappointment, though. In 1986, according to Bane and Ellwood, 1.6 million AFDC recipients were registered with the program, but only about 220,000 actually were receiving services. And only 130,000 had worked their way off welfare — most of them without help from WIN. [18]

Bane and Ellwood attribute the lackluster results partly to inadequate funding. But they also cite a lack of coordination between state welfare and employment programs. "Welfare workers typically felt no obligation to require or encourage more active employment-directed activity," they said. "Employment service workers found welfare clients difficult to place, and saw no reason not to focus their activities on more promising clients." [19]

Family Support Act

By the 1980s, politicians were becoming increasingly adamant that welfare recipients should be required to work — or at least participate in activities that would prepare them for jobs. President Reagan and the Democratic-controlled Congress agreed in 1988 to a new version of welfare reform that combined some of the social service concepts of the 1960s with tougher work requirements.

In the Family Support Act of 1988, conservatives won language stating that adult welfare recipients were to be "encouraged, assisted and required to fulfill their responsibilities to support their children by preparing for, accepting and retaining such employment as they are capable of performing."

But liberals won support for provisions that required states to offer welfare recipients, in addition to job readiness and placement services, opportunities to attain both basic literacy and high school or equivalent degrees, job skills training and help with child care and transportation expenses. States also could help pay for postsecondary education for welfare recipients interested in improving their skills, as well as provide community work experience slots — essentially public service employment — for those who otherwise couldn't find work. And the new law extended child-care and medical benefits to families of people who left the welfare roles for jobs.

"In return for having a work requirement and work as a goal, the government would provide support for education, training, health care and child care," said A. Sidney Johnson III, then-executive director of the American Public Welfare Association. "There was a concept of a reciprocal agreement." [20]

The grand left-right compromise failed to quell demands for welfare reform, however. States, free to determine for themselves which welfare recipients would be required to participate in the JOBS program, came up with widely differing figures. As late as fiscal 1994, Arizona exempted all but 19 percent of its AFDC adults, while Rhode Island said 70 percent of its adult caseload were eligible.

Nationwide, only 43.5 percent of AFDC recipients were designated as able to participate. But only a small portion of that group actually was required to participate. That's because sponsors of the new law, aware that JOBS would be more difficult and expensive than simply passing out benefit checks, set very low participation targets. Even when the law was fully phased in, states were required to enroll just 20 percent of eligible adults in work activities.

To make matters worse, the Family Support Act was staggered at the outset by a recession that sent welfare rolls surging 25 percent between 1989 and 1992. The weakened economy also drained state coffers, further undermining the new law. In fiscal 1992, for instance, states were able to claim only $750 million of the $1 billion in federal JOBS funds available, according to the Department of Health and Human Services.

State Experiments

From its inception, welfare had been a shared responsibility between the federal government and the states. But

Continued on p. 1068

Chronology

1930s The Depression throws millions of Americans into poverty, with no comprehensive policy in place for delivering aid and services to the needy.

1935
Title IV of the landmark Social Security Act creates Aid to Dependent Children (ADC) program, giving states matching federal funds "to assist, broaden and supervise existing mothers' aid programs."

1960s The nation focuses anew on poverty with the goal of helping Americans get off welfare and become self-sufficient.

1962
President John F. Kennedy persuades Congress to amend the Social Security Act to fight poverty with larger welfare payments and to encourage more vocational training for welfare recipients. The ADC program is renamed Aid to Families with Dependent Children (AFDC). States are permitted to require unemployed adults to participate in community work and training programs as a condition to receiving AFDC benefits.

1967
Concerned about rising welfare caseloads, Congress enacts the Work Incentive (WIN) program, which requires states to offer worker training and work incentives to AFDC recipients.

1970s States curtail efforts to bring social services to welfare recipients and focus instead on controlling costs by reducing fraud and policing eligibility more closely. Some states initiate demonstration programs that require AFDC recipients to work in exchange for welfare benefits.

1971
WIN is amended to require all able-bodied AFDC recipients to register for the program.

1980s President Reagan advocates strict work requirements for AFDC recipients. A number of states start experimenting with welfare-to-work programs.

1981
Congress rejects Ronald Reagan's proposal to require states to operate Community Work Experience Programs as a condition of receiving AFDC. But lawmakers give states greater latitude in administering WIN and in imposing work requirements.

1988
Reagan and the Democratic-controlled Congress agree to the Family Support Act. The law creates the Job Opportunities and Basic Skills (JOBS) program, which offers welfare recipients a variety of options for work and training designed to lead them to self-sufficiency, and it requires that only 7 percent of eligible adults participate initially.

1990s A recession hinders state efforts to implement the new JOBS program. States begin exploring new options for reforming welfare, ranging from letting welfare recipients keep more of their earnings before losing benefits to time limits on benefits to "family caps" limiting benefits to people who have more children while on welfare.

1992
President George Bush pledges in his State of the Union address to support state experimentation on welfare. The Department of Health and Human Services grants nine waivers from AFDC rules for state reform experiments.

Jan. 21, 1993
Sen. Daniel Patrick Moynihan, D-N.Y., proposes legislation to provide full federal funding for the JOBS program, but it fails to advance.

June 14, 1994
President Clinton unveils his $9.3 billion welfare-reform proposal limiting welfare recipients to two years but providing community jobs for those who can't find work in the private sector. The plan gets a lukewarm reception from congressional Democrats and opposition from Republicans.

November 1994
Republicans vow to enact their "Contract with America," including a proposal to end entitlement status for AFDC.

Aug. 22, 1996
Following his earlier veto of two Republican welfare-reform bills, Clinton signs the Personal Responsibility and Work Opportunity Reconciliation Act of 1996.

Recent Studies Offer Clues . . .

Advocates of the new welfare reform law say it will end welfare dependency, substitute work for passivity, reduce the size of welfare families, discourage out-of-wedlock births and teenage parenthood and reduce government costs. While it will take some years to test these theories, there is substantial data that may provide clues to what the future may bring.

The Twentieth Century Fund, a nonpartisan foundation that sponsors research on economic, social and political issues, summarized much of these data in a 1995 report, *Welfare Reform: A Twentieth Century Fund Guide to the Issues*. In addition, LaDonna Pavetti, a research associate at the Urban Institute and an authority on welfare dynamics, has summarized her research in the institute's 1996 report, *Welfare Reform: An Analysis of the Issues*.

Here are some of their findings:

How many people will be affected by the two-year work requirement and the five-year time limit on welfare benefits?

Advocates of time limits contend that welfare should provide temporary assistance, rather than be a way of life. In fact, half of all welfare recipients already stop receiving public assistance within a year, 70 percent leave within two years and almost 90 percent leave within five years. [1]

"It is commonly imagined that there is a large, stagnant Aid to Families with Dependent Children (AFDC) population for whom welfare has become a way of life," the Twentieth Century Fund report says. "But the data show a very dynamic welfare population, with many different women entering and leaving [and] only a small percentage remaining on welfare continuously."

There is, however, a difference between *getting* off welfare and *staying* off. While 30 percent of welfare recipients stop receiving welfare permanently in less than two years, fully 42 percent return within that time frame. That's partly because the earnings of many who escape remain so low, and their foothold in the labor market is so tenuous, that relatively minor problems — loss of a car or the breakdown of a day-care arrangement, for instance — can send them back to the welfare office. Some 40 percent of the women who leave welfare because they get jobs don't earn enough to escape poverty, according to the Twentieth Century Fund.

With so many people cycling on and off welfare, how many people are likely to bump up against the five-year lifetime limit on federal welfare benefits?

Only about one-third of the women who ever use welfare spend more than five years on it, according to Pavetti. Still, she estimates that if past patterns continue, 1.4 million families will hit the five-year time limit in 2001, the first year anybody could be thrown off welfare as a result of the controversial new provision. By 2005, she says, just under 2 million families could be affected. [2]

What distinguishes welfare recipients who are likely to use up their lifetime welfare benefits from those who give up public aid relatively quickly?

According to Pavetti, most long-term welfare recipients are women with limited job prospects. "Recipients who first receive welfare when they are young, have never married, have low levels of education and have no recent work experience are all overrepresented among recipients with longer stays on welfare," she told the House Ways and Means Subcommittee on Human Resources last May. "When these factors are considered simultaneously, the strongest predictors of whether a recipient will leave welfare for work in a given month are recent work experience and educational attainment, including mastery of basic skills." [3]

Fully 62.8 percent of long-term welfare recipients have less than a high school education, compared with 34.8 percent of those who spend two years on public assistance. Half of the long-term recipients had no work experience in the year before they first received welfare, compared with 30.2 percent of the short-stayers.

Continued from p. 1066

beginning in the 1980s, as federal officials battled over welfare reform — and frequently came up with compromise solutions that seemed to please nobody — they began unleashing the states to try their own reform experiments. [21]

In 1981, for instance, President Reagan battled with Congress to require states to operate Community Work Experience Programs as a condition to receiving AFDC. Opponents of the idea ultimately succeeded in thwarting it, but its advocates managed to win for the states greater latitude in administering WIN and imposing work requirements of their own.

Several notable experiments were launched by state welfare departments under federal waivers of WIN rules. The Massachusetts ET (education and training) Program, for instance, used case managers to work with welfare recipients to develop plans for becoming self-sufficient. Clients were exposed to job listings and recruiters and were offered opportunities for basic education, skills training, job search assistance or subsidized employment. The voluntary program claimed modest successes in increasing employment.

In 1988, the Reagan administration launched a new phase in welfare reform experimentation by granting Wisconsin a waiver from federal AFDC rules to reduce welfare benefits to parents who failed to prevent truancy among their teenage children. Reagan's successor, George Bush, granted Ohio a waiver in 1989, allow-

. . . About Future Impact of Welfare Reform

The number of children a welfare mother has is a poor predictor of how long she will stay on welfare, however. Although many believe that welfare mothers tend to have large families, Pavetti's figures show that 57.2 percent of all welfare mothers had just one child at the time they first went on welfare. Even among mothers who stayed on welfare five years or more, 59.1 percent have just one child. By the same token, just 9.7 percent of welfare mothers had three children when they first went on welfare, and just 10.4 percent of long-term recipients did. [4]

Did AFDC encourage women to have more children?

A few states, including New Jersey, have approved "family caps," which limit benefits to women who have children while on welfare. But the Twentieth Century Fund concluded from its review of research data that there is no evidence that welfare encourages women to have more children.

"Ten major studies on welfare and non-marital childbearing have been done over the past six years, and not one has found a direct effect of welfare-benefit levels on subsequent births to women on welfare," it says. Overall, the fund reports, 72.7 percent of all AFDC families have two or fewer children. And the average size of a family on AFDC decreased from 4.0 to 2.9 persons between 1969 and 1992. [5]

The evidence is more ambiguous on the correlation between welfare and out-of-wedlock births generally. White women appear to be more likely to have children out of wedlock if they live in high-benefit states, although illegitimacy among black and Hispanic women doesn't seem to rise as welfare benefits go up, the Twentieth Century Fund reports. Out-of-wedlock births are rising among all women, not just those on welfare, though. In 1960, just 5.3 percent of unmarried women of childbearing age gave birth; by 1990, that figure had risen fivefold, to 28 percent.

Still, the fund reports that welfare mothers who have never married tend to stay on welfare much longer than those who have married. Some 39 percent of welfare mothers who never married receive welfare payments during a 10-year period or longer, compared with just 14 percent of divorced mothers, 24 percent of separated mothers and 10 percent of widowed mothers. [6]

Does welfare encourage teenage pregnancy?

Finally, while teenage pregnancy is a particular concern of welfare reformers, the data show that it is a relatively small part of the welfare problem — and thus successes in averting it will have only a minor impact on the welfare system overall.

In 1992, only 7.6 percent of AFDC mothers were teenagers, the Twentieth Century Fund reports. And, contrary to widespread belief, teenage motherhood has *declined,* not increased, over the past 30 years. In 1960, 89 out of every 1,000 teenagers ages 15-19 bore a child; but in 1992, only 61 out of every 1,000 teenagers in that age bracket bore a child.

At the same time, however, far fewer teenagers are getting married now than 20 years ago. In 1960, 14 percent of all girls ages 15-19 were married, while in 1992, just 5 percent were. [7]

---

[1] LaDonna Pavetti, "Time on Welfare and Welfare Dependency," testimony before House Ways and Means Subcommittee on Human Resources, May 23, 1996. Available online at http://www.urban.org/welfare/pavtes.html

[2] LaDonna Pavetti, "Who is Affected by Time Limits?" in *Welfare Reform, An Analysis of the Issues* (1996), p. 32.

[3] Pavetti, "Time on Welfare and Welfare Dependency," *op. cit.*

[4] Pavetti, "Who is Affected by Time Limits?" *op. cit.*, p. 33.

[5] Twentieth Century Fund, *Welfare Reform, A Twentieth Century Fund Guide to the Issues* (1996), p. 6.

[6] *Ibid.*, p. 7.

[7] *Ibid.*, p. 5.

ing it to require all teen parents on AFDC to attend school.

But the idea of waiving AFDC rules really caught on in 1992, when Bush touted the idea in his State of the Union address. "States throughout the country are beginning to operate with new assumptions: that when able-bodied people receive government assistance, they have responsibilities to the taxpayer, a responsibility to seek work, education or job training, a responsibility to get their lives in order; a responsibility to hold their families together and refrain from having children out of wedlock — and a responsibility to obey the law," Bush said. "We are going to help this movement."

Waiver requests came flooding in — a process that gained momentum when Bill Clinton, himself a former governor and vigorous welfare-reform advocate, took office in 1993. The waivers reflected a wide range of ideas about how best to reform welfare. A majority of states, hoping to increase incentives to work, received permission to allow families to earn more before having their AFDC benefits reduced. But many also won approval to impose time limits on welfare benefits.

Numerous states were allowed to begin experimenting with the idea of using AFDC grants to subsidize wages, employ welfare recipients to rehabilitate public housing, help welfare families set up their own small businesses and to create subsidized jobs. But a handful also were trying "family caps," which seek to prevent families from receiving additional cash grants — or even cut the grants they receive — if they have addi-

Big Companies See Big Profits in Welfare

If the era of big government is over, then the era of big welfare contracts for private companies is ready for takeoff.

"I see this as the future of welfare reform," said Gerald H. Miller, former director of the Michigan Family Independence Agency and former president of the American Public Welfare Association. "The private sector will ultimately run these programs," added Miller, who announced in September that he would leave his post to direct for-profit welfare initiatives for the $30 billion defense company Lockheed Martin. "The era of big government is over." [1]

Along with other large companies, such as Electronic Data Systems (EDS), IBM and the Arthur Andersen accounting firm, Lockheed Martin has positioned itself to become a major player in the competition for what promise to be lucrative welfare contracts with states and counties across the country.

Advocates of more private-sector involvement in welfare reform contend that corporations are quicker than government bureaucracies to respond to change and new demands. Unlike welfare bureaucracies, which are geared toward delivering benefits, private corporations are governed by a work ethic that makes them better suited to reward employees who help welfare recipients find jobs, supporters suggest.

Private-sector boosters also predict that states and counties, whose welfare budgets will be capped under the new federal block-grant system, will be happy to embrace fixed-price contracts with large companies that can absorb the shock of government penalties, if need be. Finally, they say contracting out welfare services will help states reduce their own administrative costs.

Those who oppose privatization, however, say that profit-driven companies will use the harshest provisions of the new law to remove welfare recipients from the roles just to boost their profits. "We have people who are in tremendous need on the one hand, and on the other side we have people [private contractors] who are making a profit, and it looks like they're going to make more of a profit if they serve fewer people in need," argues Henry A. Freedman, executive director of the Center on Social Welfare Policy and Law in New York City.

The first big prize in welfare privatization will be Texas, where Lockheed, EDS and Andersen are competing for a $563 million contract to reform and administer cash assistance, Medicaid, food stamps and nutrition programs for women, infants and children.

Some smaller companies have made significant headway into the welfare-to-work marketplace. One company, America Works, has won praise from Mayor Rudolph W. Giuliani, R-N.Y., and former Gov. Mario M. Cuomo, D-N.Y., for its jobs-placement programs in New York City and Albany. It also has won accolades from admirers of its Indianapolis, Ind., program.

But Deborah A. Merrifield, commissioner of social services for the Erie County Department of Social Services in New York, predicts that if states require private enterprises to train and find jobs for all welfare clients regardless of how employable they are, the new welfare entrepreneurs are unlikely to realize huge profits.

"I think it's pretty risky business for a private, for-profit company to say, 'I shall ensure that I give someone all their benefits and get them into a job and I won't need any more [public] money,' " says Merrifield. "That's a big risk for anyone to take at this point."

[1] Quoted in "Welfare Reform Leader Makes Corporate Move: Ex-Official Predicts Privately Run Programs," *The Washington Post*, Sept. 17, 1996.

tional children while on welfare.

By 1996, waivers had become so widespread that states effectively had seized the initiative in setting welfare policy. Douglas Besharov, a resident scholar at the American Enterprise Institute, was widely quoted in April as declaring that President Clinton, in his generous approval of waiver requests, "can justifiably claim he has ended welfare as we know it." In effect, Besharov argued, the waiver requests had ended the idea of welfare as a "personal entitlement."

Unlike Besharov, Mark Greenberg, a lawyer at the liberal Center for Law and Social Policy (CLASP), sees the easy waiver policy as harmful. But he agrees that it undermined the idea of strong federal action on welfare reform. "Once the Bush and Clinton administrations conveyed a willingness to grant waivers of federal requirements freely, the way to become a high-prestige state was to announce that you were departing from federal law rather than effectively implementing federal law," he says. "As all the attention shifted to whoever had submitted the most dramatic waiver, it became increasingly difficult for a state to say it was implementing welfare reform by a thoughtful implementation of the Family Support Act."

The Clinton Plan

President Clinton may have approved so many waivers partly because of difficulties he was having resolving conflicts over welfare within his own administration. One issue was the age-old tension between a desire to help welfare recipients and a belief it would be better to get tough with them. Straddling the issue, Clinton had talked during his 1992 campaign about "empowering" Americans to leave welfare by giving them education, training and child care, and he said Americans should receive universal health insurance. But he also said welfare benefits should be cut off after a two-year transitional period.

The administration also was ambivalent about the respective roles of the federal government and the states. Harvard's Ellwood, in a December 1992 working paper on welfare reform written shortly before he joined the administration, suggested that welfare reform should be phased in gradually, beginning "in a modest number of states," and that it should be extended to others "over time." But later, Ellwood noted that gradualism would open the president to criticism that he was backing off his sweeping campaign promises. And, after travelling around the country to see what states were doing, Ellwood came to favor strong federal action. Too many states, he said, had "lost sight of the values of welfare," and the "broad framework" of a strong, national policy was needed. [22]

While wrestling with this and other issues, the administration also made a crucial strategic decision. Health-care reform, along with crime and trade legislation, would be the administration's top priority. Welfare reform would have to wait. As a result, the White House didn't even present a welfare reform proposal until June 14, 1994. And even then, it was introduced with little fanfare, and, coming just five months before congressional elections, was given little chance.

As expected, the plan would have required welfare recipients to find work within two years of accepting their benefits. To ease the transition to work, the government would spend more on job training and child care. And those who still couldn't find jobs were to be placed in federally subsidized jobs.

To control costs — Clinton had promised he wouldn't seek new taxes to pay for his plan — the administration proposed applying the plan only to people born after 1971. Even at that, it would have cost $9.3 billion more over five years than the current welfare system.

The president didn't find much support in Congress for his recommendations. Liberals were cool to the idea of a two-year limit, and to a proposal that would let states limit benefit increases to parents who had more children while on welfare. Republicans denounced the White House plan even more strenuously, complaining that it would cover only part of the welfare caseload, provide too much flexibility in administering time limits, do little to discourage illegitimate births and, unlike their own plan, continue providing welfare assistance to immigrants. [23]

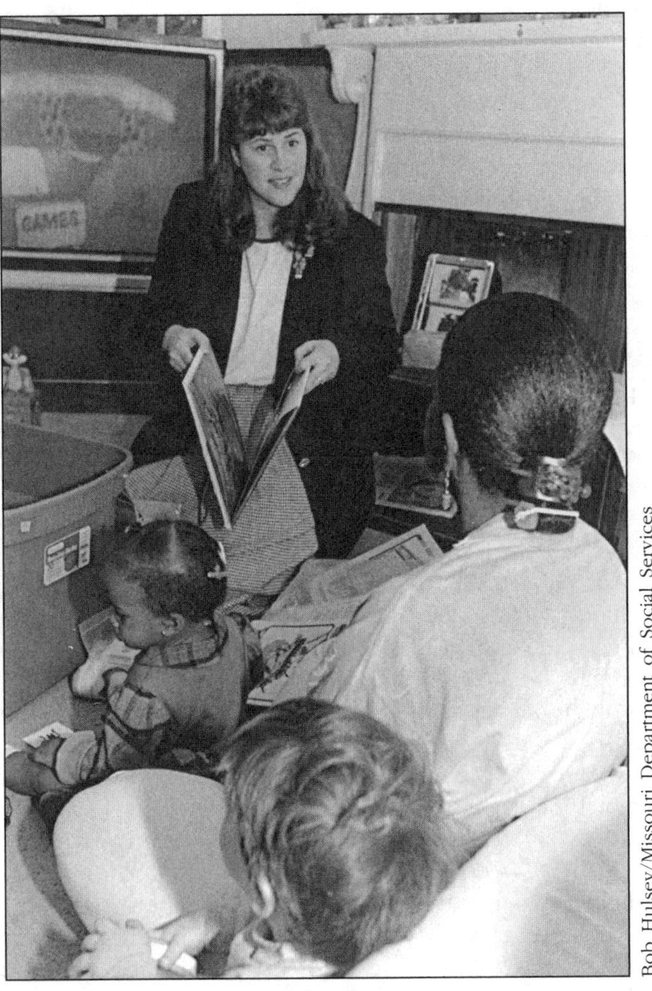

Bob Hulsey/Missouri Department of Social Services

Educating and nurturing low-income children is a key component of Missouri's "Beyond Welfare" reform strategy.

Republican Plans Vetoed

The 1994 elections gave Republicans control of Congress, and with it, the initiative in charting federal welfare policy. The new majority brought together several disparate groups, including reformers who sought to impose tougher work requirements, states'-rights advocates who hoped to shift power from the federal government to the states [24] and budget cutters who were eager to reduce domestic social spending.

This coalition produced a welfare-reform proposal far bolder than anything the Republicans had proposed during the first two years of the Clinton administration. Earlier GOP proposals would have preserved the federal entitlement to welfare benefits while providing states more money to move welfare recipients into jobs. But the new Republican plan sought to eliminate the federal entitlement altogether and convert federal welfare spending to block grants. There was no promise of jobs for those who sought work and couldn't find it. And where the Republican welfare-overhaul legislation of 1993 would have saved taxpayers $19.5 billion over five years, the new plan would have reduced federal spending $102 billion over seven years.

President Clinton vetoed one version of the Republican welfare plan on Dec. 6, 1995, and a second one Jan. 6, 1996. But with the November 1996 elections drawing nearer, Republicans knew that Clinton would find it increasingly difficult to block welfare-reform legislation since he had promised during his 1992 campaign to "end welfare as we know it." Jack Howard, an aide to House Speaker Newt Gingrich, R-Ga., urged Republicans to send the president as tough a bill as possible because, "I believe the White House will sign just about anything we send them, so we should make them eat as much as they can." [25]

'Hit by a Freight Train'

The Republican Congress sent Clinton a third welfare reform measure in late July 1996, less than four months before the presidential election. Sen. Daniel Patrick Moynihan, D-N.Y., author of the Family Support Act of 1988 and one of the Senate's leading experts on welfare reform, watched the Republican juggernaut in dismay. The president, he said, was trapped by his own 1992 rhetoric. "He keeps his promise and he abandons his principles — or he keeps his principles and abandons his promise," Moynihan said. [26]

Clinton signed the measure on Aug. 22, 1996, despite staunch opposition from liberals, among them Children's Defense Fund President Marian Wright Edelman, a longstanding friend of the president. Edelman had said the legislation "makes a mockery of his pledge not to hurt children. . . . It will leave a moral blot on his presidency and on our nation that will never be forgotten. [27]

Ellwood decided to leave the administration after Clinton said he would sign the bill. He complained that Republicans had seized on the president's rhetoric — in particular, his pledge to "end welfare as we know it" — while ignoring the president's other pledge to provide jobs to those who can't find them. Acknowledging that the administration had lost control of the issue after the Republicans took control of Congress in 1994, Ellwood said glumly, "We got hit by a freight train, in part, of course, because our own train moved too sluggishly." [28] ■

CURRENT SITUATION

Maneuvering Room

As yet, it is unclear what states will do with the newfound freedom — and responsibility — that welfare reform affords them. "I don't think there's a definitive picture of what states are going to do at this point," says Andrea Kane, senior policy analyst at the National Governors' Association. "I don't think there's any state that knows exactly what they're going to do about all the provisions."

States may have a bit of time to prepare for their new role, though. Just as a recession set back efforts to put the Family Support Act into effect, the chances of success with the new law will be improved, at least initially, by the currently strong economy.

Sustained growth and low unemployment helped push the number of families on welfare down 13 percent between 1994 and August 1996, from just over 5 million to about 4.4 million; the number of recipients, including children, dropped 14 percent, from 14.2 million to 12.2 million. (*See graph, p. 1064.*) Because the new welfare block grants are based on state expenditures in the early 1990s, when caseloads were higher, that means most states actually will receive more in general welfare assistance this year than last year.

Moreover, the decline in the welfare rolls will make it easier for states to meet their initial requirements for moving welfare recipients into work. The law allows states to reduce their required work participation rate by 1 percentage point for every like decline in its total caseload. That means a state whose caseload has fallen 10 percent would have to get only 15 percent of its AFDC adults working this year, not the official 25 percent target in the law. New York, for instance, will have to have only about 20 percent of its welfare recipients working in the current fiscal year, instead of 25 percent. Mississippi, meanwhile, faces a requirement of just 15 percent — a rate it effectively has achieved already.

Because of this "caseload-reduction credit," Robert Rector, senior policy analyst at the Heritage Foundation, estimates that a typical state will have to have just 18 percent of its AFDC caseload working by 1999, not 35 percent as prescribed in the law.

Rector sees this at once as a vindication of the tough approach to welfare reform and as a "loophole" that will keep the new law from being everything it could be. "If you sincerely say that welfare will no longer be free income and that you must actually work for the benefits, all of a sudden you change the desirability of welfare, and people now have a very strong incentive to go elsewhere," he argues. "The number of people who even bother to apply to get onto welfare will go down very substantially."

Isabel Sawhill, a senior fellow at the Urban Institute, agrees that there is "anecdotal evidence" suggesting that work requirements are turning some welfare applicants away. But it's difficult to separate that effect from the impact of economic growth. For instance, while the welfare caseload in reform-minded Wisconsin dropped 37 percent between 1993 and last summer, Mississippi and Alabama, which generally aren't considered to be in the forefront of welfare reform, posted declines that were almost as substantial — 30 percent and 29 percent, respectively.

Other provisions of the law give states more room to maneuver — at least in the short run — than headlines have suggested. For one thing, states

Continued on p. 1074

At Issue:

Will the new federal welfare law hurt needy children?

Mark E. Courtney
Assistant professor of social work, University of Wisconsin-Madison

FROM A PAPER PRESENTED AT A CONFERENCE ON CHILDREN AND WELFARE REFORM FUNDED BY THE CARNEGIE CORPORATION, OCT. 11, 1996.

yes

There are a number of ways that the federal welfare reform law and its implementation at the state level could substantially increase the number of children living in poverty.

First, the Congressional Budget Office has estimated that between 2.5 million and 3.5 million children could be affected by the five-year time limit on assistance when the law is fully implemented. Second, an unknown, but potentially large, number of families will lose cash and other benefits due to non-compliance with work requirements. Third, the Urban Institute has estimated that elimination of Supplemental Security Income (SSI) and food stamp benefits for non-citizens will move approximately 450,000 children into poverty. Fourth, some parents, and future parents, will be banned from program participation for life because of drug-related crimes. This provision may have a serious impact on the child welfare system, given the large proportion of families currently involved with the system that suffer from substance abuse problems. Lastly, since the individual entitlement to support has been eliminated, some states may simply cut off benefits when economic or political circumstances result in inadequate funds to continue assistance. . . .

Growth in child poverty is likely to lead to an increase in child maltreatment and a corresponding increase in demand for child welfare services including substitute care. . . . Some families who under current law would use SSI, Aid to Families with Dependent Children and/or food stamps to house and feed their children will lose all such aid. . . .

The expansion of work requirements could also contribute to a movement of children into foster care, particularly if it is not accompanied by an adequate expansion of subsidized child care. The Congressional Budget Office estimates that by 2002 federal child care funding will fall $1.8 billion short of what will be needed to provide child care for low-income working families if states meet work participation goals by placing participants in work programs. Many parents may be faced with the choice of either losing benefits due to non-compliance with work requirements in order to care for their children or leaving their children unsupervised.

In either case, the children in these families are at increased risk of neglect. Moreover, many of the families who are most likely to be unable or unwilling to find work are, by and large, already at relatively high risk of neglecting or abusing their children. Elimination or reduction of benefits to these families will heighten that risk.

Robert Rector
Senior analyst, The Heritage Foundation

FROM AN INTERVIEW WITH THE CQ RESEARCHER, OCTOBER 1996.

no

The impact of the current welfare system on children is overwhelmingly and abusively negative. The reform has many key provisions that should reduce dependence as well as out-of-wedlock births, which are the two most harmful factors in terms of destroying children's future. By reducing dependence through work requirements and time limits, and by reducing illegitimacy through a number of incentives, the [law] should have the most profound positive effect on children's well-being.

Most of the debate on this suffers from the liberal myopia of the last 30 years, which sees the principal problem facing children as a lack of material resources and then simply tries to stuff resources into families. That approach has catastrophically failed, and everyone except the most troglodyte leftist realizes it has failed.

A child's success or well-being in future life is not really dependent upon its family's bank account status. The liberal hypothesis is if we raise family income then these kids are going to graduate from high school and the crime rate is going to go down and drug use is going to go down. But everything we've learned in the last 30 years shows that that is absolutely untrue. Trying to raise family income by giving them handouts doesn't have any beneficial consequences, but in fact has negative consequences.

If material resources were the critical reason kids fall into crime or why they drop out of school and so forth, then this country should have been awash in crime and drug abuse and so forth back in 1950, when close to a third of the population was poor. But it was not. The reality is that what's critical to children's success are the values that they receive in their communities and inside their families, not just the family's bank account level. Welfare destroys those values — the very things that are most necessary for children's success. That's why welfare harms kids.

If you can reduce dependency and reduce illegitimacy, you will actually raise the living standards of poor families. They're not getting rich by being on welfare. But that's really a secondary concern. The real problem is that the values the child acquires living in a single-parent dependent home are values that will cripple that child in its quest to become a member of American society. It's the worst environment for children that you can possibly imagine.

that were operating under waivers from the old AFDC rules can continue with those programs until the waivers expire. That includes a majority of states; 43 states had waivers to conduct some 78 welfare experiments when the new law was adopted.

Besides allowing for some continuity in previously launched state welfare-reform experiments, the decision to let existing waiver arrangements continue could provide an early indication of whether provisions of the federal law will work. At least 10 states, for instance, have imposed shorter time limits on welfare benefits than the five-year limit in the federal law.

States, meanwhile, may be able to soften the impact of the federal law by using their own funds to maintain benefits for which federal money no longer can be used.

Disparities Among States

Still, while most states are currently enjoying a windfall in their federal welfare payments, it's clear that they are beginning the new era in welfare policy with widely differing financial situations. Because the federal block grants are calculated on the basis of welfare spending in the early 1990s, states that were relatively generous, or that invested in welfare reform early in hopes of reaping benefits later, will be better off than others.

Vermont, for instance, will be in a relatively good position. Besides already having a waiver to operate its own welfare-reform program — one that focuses heavily on providing social services to needy families — the state's relatively high spending level in the past means it will collect $2,761 for every poor child in the state, according to the Center for Law and Social Policy. Texas, on the other hand, which has been considerably less generous, will get just $339 per poor child. *(See map, p. 1060.)*

"States with a high level of resources have a number of alternatives, but states at the bottom have fewer alternatives because they have so much less to work with," says CLASP's Greenberg.

Supporters of the federal law say they hope that legislatures in states like Texas will be willing to make a bigger investment now. But that would require a break with their previous practices. Wisconsin, a relatively high benefit state which is operating under a series of federal AFDC waivers, illustrates the potential up-front costs that may be required.

Under its program, all welfare recipients are required to choose between four options: finding regular employment; taking trial jobs in which the state subsidizes the wages; holding community service jobs to develop the work habits and skills needed to land a private-sector job; or, for those with particularly low levels of ability, participation in "transition" work activities such as sheltered workshops.

The state expects it will have to create almost 30,000 community-service positions, roughly one for every two adults currently on welfare. Overall, it anticipates spending about 13 percent more initially under its plan, called "Wisconsin Works," than it did previously. Its child-care spending is projected to soar from $48 million to $158 million. [29]

Welfare Magnets

Some analysts worry that if other states don't make comparable investments, the disparity between states could widen. That, they say, could trigger a harmful "race to the bottom," in which states feel compelled to slash benefits in order to avoid becoming "magnets" that attract poor people from other states.

"Clearly, states are going to worry more about the magnet effect," says Thomas Corbett, acting director of the Institute for Research on Poverty at the University of Wisconsin in Madison. "The fear is that compassion, however defined — it could include subsidizing employers and providing training, not just paying more in benefits — might become too costly if there's any suspicion that low-income people are being attracted to a state."

Officials in states that have been generous in the past admit privately to some concerns about becoming welfare magnets, but publicly they play the issue down. "If a governor does not make welfare reform work, it's going to be a pretty bad mark against him or her when re-election comes around," says Amy Tucci, spokesperson for the American Public Welfare Association. "So it's incumbent on legislatures and governors to make welfare reform work."

Modest Solutions

The New Republic magazine predicted that the new welfare law will unleash a period of "radical state experimentation." [30] But so far, many states are looking instead at relatively modest ways to reduce their welfare rolls.

Oregon and Arkansas, for instance, are considering incentive plans that would pay bonuses to welfare recipients who find jobs. Maine is bringing back the 1960s-era idea of sending caseworkers to visit welfare applicants in their homes. New Jersey is considering consolidating transportation programs for the elderly into a single system that also helps welfare recipients get to jobs. [31]

In Kentucky, meanwhile, a task force is studying a proposal to provide "relocation assistance" to help unemployed welfare recipients move to places where jobs may be more abundant. And the Clinton administration is experimenting with ways to link inner-city people with jobs. In September, it awarded five cities $17 million to help 3,100 welfare recipients commute to suburban jobs over the next four years. Officials say they will ask for $75 million more next year to expand the program to at least 75 cities.

Utah, meanwhile, is empowering state welfare officials to intercept people with short-term problems and help them before they are forced onto welfare. That could include helping a prospective welfare applicant fix a car so he or she can continue getting to work, or paying for clothing that would improve an applicant's chances of getting a job, for instance.

At the opposite end of the spectrum, New York has initiated a large-scale public-jobs program. There, some 34,000 people already are required to work in cleanup and other jobs in exchange for their benefits. Under a new plan, the number of workfare slots could grow to 100,000 within two years. By 2002, the number may be as large as New York City's current municipal payroll — 204,000 — and could cost more than $1 billion a year. [32]

But most states may follow the lead of Iowa and others, which rather than dramatically revising their welfare programs have sought to convert them somewhat more gradually — emphasizing the importance of work and the idea that welfare is a temporary, not permanent, benefit, but taking individual circumstances into consideration.

In Iowa, for instance, caseworkers help clients develop individualized Family Investment Plans spelling out what steps they will take to become self-sufficient. The state, which stands to collect $1,161 for every poor child within its borders, even believes that it will be able to enhance its educational offerings, which have been limited in past years because of budget pressures. State welfare administrator Howard says state officials are working with community college officials on ways to provide welfare recipients with carefully targeted training.

And in Arizona, caseworkers manage portfolios on each welfare recipient, listing the benefits they receive for child care, public assistance, child support, earned income and other services. The workers then seek ways to increase clients' income and reduce their dependence on cash assistance from the government. As in Iowa and Utah, failure to comply can bring swift sanctions.

"The idea is to change behavior and get mutual responsibility going — to make sure people are living up to their contracts," says Linda J. Blessing, director of the Arizona Department of Economic Security. ■

OUTLOOK

Private-Sector Help?

While many state officials are relatively sanguine about the near-term prospects for welfare reform, they say the longer-term outlook is more clouded. In part, that's because current, positive trends such as declining caseloads and moderating costs could be reversed quite rapidly in the event of a recession.

"At least for the first few years, when caseloads remain low or shrink further, most states think they'll have adequate resources," says Kane of the governors' association.

The new law establishes a $2 billion contingency fund for states to tap in the event of a rise in unemployment. But that's only one-third the actual run-up in welfare costs that occurred during the last recession, from 1990 to 1992, according to the Center for Budget and Policy Priorities.

Moreover, there's good reason to believe that getting welfare recipients off assistance will become more difficult with time. States that have had the most experience with welfare-to-work efforts have found that once the most employable welfare recipients move into the labor force, caseloads will tend to become more heavily weighted with people who have the most serious obstacles to employment.

Utah, for one, already has started encountering this law of diminishing returns; it has responded by hiring more caseworkers with master's degrees in social work or counseling. "The era of rapid caseload depletions is over," warned Edward L. Schilling, director of the department of social services in Fond du Lac County, Wis. [33]

Politicians, meanwhile, are unlikely to let the welfare issue lie untouched. President Clinton, along with many Democrats, would like to reverse the steep cuts in spending on food stamps and immigrants. That may prove difficult, however, since Republicans retained control of Congress, and balancing the budget remains a major priority of both parties.

The president may have more luck with proposals designed to facilitate welfare recipients' transition to work. When Clinton signed the 1996 reform law, he sought to mollify his liberal critics by promising to seek legislation in his new term to establish a $3 billion job placement program designed to help 1 million welfare recipients find work. The president also said he would seek a $400 million tax credit for businesses that hire welfare recipients. And he promised to encourage business development in depressed urban areas by proposing more tax-favored "empowerment zones" and the creation of more community-development banks.

"Welfare is no longer a political football to be kicked around," said Clinton, who himself rode the welfare issue into office in 1992, only to find himself outflanked by Republicans two years later. "It's a personal responsibility of every American who ever criticized the welfare system to help poor people now to move from welfare to work." [34]

Republicans, for their part, say they plan to scrutinize the administration closely to make sure officials don't seek to undermine the tough work provisions of the new law. But they, too, have further reform proposals.

FOR MORE INFORMATION

American Public Welfare Association, 810 First St. N.E., Suite 500, Washington, D.C. 20002; (202) 682-0100. APWA monitors federal and state legislation and regulations and disseminates information to its membership of social welfare administrators and professionals.

Center for Law and Social Policy, 1616 P St. N.W., Suite 150, Washington, D.C. 20036; (202) 328-5140; http://epn.org/clasp.html. A public interest law firm, CLASP engages in educational activities, policy research and advocacy on behalf of low-income families.

Center on Budget and Policy Priorities, 820 First St. N.E., Suite 510, Washington, D.C. 20002; (202) 408-1080; http://www.cbpp.org/. This nonpartisan research organization and policy institute conducts research and analysis on a range of government policies and programs, with an emphasis on those affecting low- and moderate-income people.

Heritage Foundation, 214 Massachusetts Ave. N.E., Washington, D.C. 20002; (202) 546-4400; http://www.townhall.com/heritage/. This conservative think tank promotes the ideas of free enterprise, limited government and "traditional" American values.

Institute for Research on Poverty, 1180 Observatory Dr., 3412 Social Science Building, University of Wisconsin-Madison, Madison, Wisc. 53706; (608) 262-6358; http://www.ssc.wisc.edu/irp/. IRP is a national, nonpartisan center for research into the causes and consequences of poverty and social inequality in the United States.

Sen. Daniel R. Coats, R-Ind., has proposed providing a tax credit for contributions to private charities. Others seek to relax a prohibition on providing federal funds to religious organizations that seek to help the poor.

These and other proposals reflect a belief that future stages of welfare reform will further diminish the role of government. "The end of poverty doesn't lie with government," says Michael Tanner, director of health and welfare studies at the Cato Institute and author of *The End of Welfare* (1996). "No amount of restructuring, budget cutting or micromanagement of individual moral behavior can make a government-spawned welfare system work. Only a civil society, one based on voluntary cooperation and persuasion, not force or coercion — a society built upon revitalized social institutions such as the family, church and charities — can break the cycle of dependency and give the poor what they really need to become independent, whole and free."

President Clinton continues to argue for a more assertive role for government, but he concedes that, for the foreseeable future, the fate of welfare may lie more in private hands. "The most important thing," Clinton says, "is establishing a state- and then a community-based partnership with the private sector and with others who have to fill the needs of people who are trying to move from welfare to work."[35] ■

Christopher Conte is a freelancer in the Washington, D.C., area.

Notes

[1] Judith M. Gueron, "A Research Context for Welfare Reform," *Journal of Policy Analysis and Management*, fall 1996, p. 548.

[2] Sheila Zedlewski et al, "Potential Effects of Congressional Welfare Reform Legislation on Family Incomes," *The Urban Institute*, July 26, 1996. p. 1.

[3] Rebecca Blank, "Outlook for the U.S. Labor Market and Prospects for Low-Wage Entry Jobs," *The Work Alternative* (1995), p. 35.

[4] *Ibid.*, p. 39.

[5] LaDonna Pavetti, "Who is Affected by Time Limits?" *Welfare Reform: An Analysis of the Issues* (1995), p. 33. For background, see "Welfare Reform," *The CQ Researcher*, April 10, 1992, pp. 313-336.

[6] Dana Milbank, "Welfare Law's Work Rules Worry States," *The Wall Street Journal*, Aug. 5, 1996, p. A2.

[7] *The Washington Post*, Sept. 25, 1996.

[8] William Julius Wilson, *When Work Disappears: The World of the New Urban Poor* (1996), pp. xiii, 19-20.

[9] *Ibid.*, p. 53.

[10] See Marvin Kosters, "Looking for Jobs in All the Wrong Places," *The Public Interest*, fall 1996, pp. 125-131; Joe Klein, "The True Disadvantage," *The New Republic*, Oct. 26, 1996, pp. 32-36.

[11] Michael Wiseman, "State Strategies for Welfare Reform: The Wisconsin Story," *Journal of Policy Analysis and Management, op. cit.*, p. 540.

[12] Kathryn J. Edin, "The Myths of Dependence and Self-Sufficiency: Women, Welfare and Low-Wage Work," *Focus*, fall/winter 1995, pp. 1-2, published by University of Wisconsin-Madison Institute for Research on Poverty.

[13] *Ibid.* For background, see "The Working Poor," *The CQ Researcher*, Nov. 3, 1995, pp. 969-992.

[14] Lawrence Mishel, Jared Bernstein and John Schmitt, *The State of Working America, 1996-1997* (1996), p. 167, published by Economic Policy Institute.

[15] Gary Burtless, "Employment Prospects of Welfare Recipients," *The Work Alternative, op. cit.*, p. 89.

[16] Mary Jo Bane and David T. Ellwood, *Welfare Realities: From Rhetoric to Reform* (1994), p. 15.

[17] Quoted in *ibid.*, p. 12.

[18] *Ibid.*, pp. 20-21.

[19] *Ibid.*, p. 21.

[20] Quoted in *1993 CQ Almanac*, p. 373.

[21] For background, see "Welfare Experiments," *The CQ Researcher*, Sept. 16, 1994, pp. 793-816.

[22] Quoted in Bane and Ellwood, *op. cit.*, pp. 805-807.

[23] See *1994 CQ Almanac*, pp. 364-365.

[24] For background, see "The States and Federalism," *The CQ Researcher*, Sept. 13, 1996, pp. 793-816.

[25] Quoted in *Congressional Quarterly Weekly Report*, July 27, 1996, p. 2117.

[26] Quoted in Jason DeParle, "The New Contract with America's Poor," *The New York Times*, July 28, 1996.

[27] Quoted in *Facts on File*, Aug. 1, 1996, p. 526.

[28] David Ellwood, "Welfare Reform as I Knew It: When Bad Things Happen to Good Policies," *The American Prospect*, May-June 1996, pp. 22-29.

[29] See Mickey Kaus, "Adopt the Wisconsin Plan," *The Washington Post*, July 9, 1996.

[30] Editorial in *The New Republic*, Aug. 12, 1996, p. 8.

[31] Barbara Vobejda and Judith Havemann, "States Take Variety of Paths to Welfare Reform," *The Washington Post*, Oct. 6, 1996, p. A4.

[32] David Firestone, "New York Girding for Surge in Workfare Jobs," *The New York Times*, Aug. 13, 1996, p. B1.

[33] Quoted in "The Silent Welfare Reforms," *Business Week*, May 20, 1996, p. 73.

[34] Remarks at bill signing ceremony, Aug. 22, 1996.

[35] Remarks to the Southern Governors Association, Kansas City, Mo., Sept. 10, 1996.

Bibliography

Selected Sources Used

Books

Bane, Mary Jo, and David T. Ellwood, *Welfare Realities: From Rhetoric to Reform,* Harvard University Press, 1994.
This collection represents nearly a decade in the work of the two experts President Clinton selected to shape his welfare proposals — and who resigned from their posts after Clinton signed the Republican-sponsored Personal Responsibility and Work Opportunity Reconciliation Act of 1996. Compiled while Bane and Ellwood were teaching at Harvard, the chapters discuss the history of welfare and set out various policy proposals.

Murray, Charles, *Losing Ground: American Social Policy, 1950-1980,* Basic Books, 1984.
This book played a key role in sparking the conservative revolution against government social programs that culminated in 1996 with the termination of the federal government's 61-year-old welfare experiment and the decision to turn federal welfare money over to the states.

Nightingale, Demetra Smith, and Robert H. Haveman, eds., *The Work Alternative: Welfare Reform and the Realities of the Job Market,* Urban Institute Press, 1995.
In this volume, based on a 1994 conference, leading authorities on welfare and labor markets explore the prospects for moving large numbers of people from welfare to work.

Wilson, William Julius, *When Work Disappears: The World of the New Urban Poor,* Alfred A. Knopf, 1996.
In this widely acclaimed, though controversial, book, Harvard sociologist Wilson attributes social deterioration in America's inner cities to the exodus of high-paying jobs to the suburbs. Wilson's critics say he fails to recognize how behavioral changes helped prompt the disappearance of jobs, but few question his description of the devastating consequences of widespread joblessness.

Articles

Conte, Christopher, "Will Workfare Work?" *Governing,* April 1996, pp. 19-23.
This article describes the experience of one state, Iowa, which was among the first to convert welfare into a jobs program. Its successes have been limited by budget constraints and the near disappearance of high-paying manufacturing jobs for low-skilled workers.

Gueron, Judith M., "A Research Context for Welfare Reform," *Journal of Policy Analysis and Management,* Vol. 15, No. 4, fall 1996, pp. 547-561.
Gueron, president of the Manpower Demonstration Research Corp. in New York, looks at previous welfare-reform efforts and how they have sought to balance the goals of putting welfare recipients to work, protecting their children from severe poverty and controlling costs. The article is one of five in the journal that discuss welfare reform.

"Sign It," *The New Republic,* Aug. 12, 1996, pp. 7-8.
This article, written before President Clinton decided to sign the 1996 welfare-reform law, captures the concerns that led commentators once considered liberal to support the new block-grant approach. "The continuing agony of the underclass is destroying our cities, our race relations, our sense of civility, our faith in the possibilities of government," the magazine's editors said. "It's worth taking some risks to end it."

Reports and Studies

Edin, Kathryn J., "The Myths of Dependence and Self-Sufficiency: Women, Welfare, and Low-Wage Work," *Focus,* Institute for Research on Poverty, University of Wisconsin, fall/winter 1995; on-line: gopher://gopher.ssc.wisc.edu:70/11/irpgopher/publications/focus.
Edin, an assistant professor at Rutgers University, summarizes data from interviews with welfare recipients and low-wage workers in four U.S. cities. She reports that welfare benefits in most states are so low that recipients must supplement them with other income, and that low-wage jobs don't pay enough to move families from poverty or guarantee future access to better-paying jobs. She says many unskilled single mothers use welfare as part of a broader strategy to improve their education and skills.

Sawhill, Isabel V., ed., *Welfare Reform: An Analysis of the Issues,* Urban Institute Press, 1995; on-line: http://www.urban.org/welfare/overview.htm
Written before the new welfare-reform law was enacted, this volume explores the myriad issues that surround welfare, including the federal role in maintaining a social safety net, the possibility there will be a "race to the bottom," the role of food stamps in providing a safety net and the debate over whether immigrants should receive public benefits.

Super, David A., et al, *The New Welfare Law,* Center on Budget and Policy Priorities, Aug. 13, 1996; on-line: http://www.epn.org/cbpp/wconfbl2.html
This analysis of the welfare reform act concludes that its overriding effect "is likely to be a large increase in poverty, especially among children and legal immigrants."

The Next Step

Additional information from UMI's Newspaper & Periodical Abstracts database

Welfare Reform Law

Jouzaitis, Carol, "Welfare poor face life without a net," *Chicago Tribune,* Aug. 5, 1996, P. 3.

For the last 60 years, the nation's social safety net has been secured by a fundamental guarantee: If one is needy and eligible, the federal government will help. But under the Personal Responsibility and Work Opportunity Act of 1996, which President Clinton is expected to sign, that basic principle will be erased July 1, 1997.

Katz, Jeffrey L., "Welfare overhaul law," *Congressional Quarterly Weekly Report,* Sept. 21, 1996, P. 8.

The provisions of the Personal Responsibility and Work Opportunity Reconciliation Act of 1996, signed into law by President Clinton Aug. 22, 1996, are presented. The welfare legislation replaces six decades of federal policy with a new reliance on states.

Page, Susan, "Welfare overhaul a dramatic shift," *USA Today,* Aug. 1, 1996, p. A1.

The Personal Responsibility and Work Opportunity Act is expected to slide through the Senate Aug. 1, 1996, and President Clinton says he will sign it. With that, the government will end a 61-year guarantee that poor children and their families are entitled to federal benefits, reflecting a sea change in public attitudes about society's obligations to its neediest citizens and those citizens' responsibilities in return.

Children and Welfare

Freeman, Edith M., "Welfare reforms and services for children and families: Setting a new practice, research and policy agenda," *Social Work,* September 1996, pp. 521-532.

Freeman discusses barriers to family and community self-sufficiency. Many of the barriers have resulted from policy-makers' biased definitions of self-sufficiency and related social program reforms.

Jacobson, Linda, "Advocates fear harmful effects of welfare law," *Education Week,* Oct. 2, 1996, p. 1.

Although the new welfare law that takes effect this week is kinder to children than previous drafts, advocates for poor children say the shift in social policy could have damaging effects. The impact on children largely depends on how states implement the measure, Jacobson says.

Loose, Cindy, "Children of the working poor called invisible in welfare debate," *The Washington Post,* June 3, 1996, p. D3.

Social scientists call the impoverished children of working parents the "invisible poor," and they say the nation's recent focus on getting welfare recipients off the rolls and into the work force is pushing such children even further into the background.

"No, welfare reform hasn't made the sky fall," *Atlanta Journal,* Oct. 16, 1996, p. A12.

An editorial notes that despite the claims of critics of the 1996 federal welfare reform law, none of the plans submitted by 26 states as of mid-October will in any way jeopardize the welfare of children. Georgia's plan has not been submitted yet, but there will be no attempt to supplant a system of cash grants with other methods of helping the poor.

"Welfare warning: Study warns of reform's effect on children," *Detroit News & Free Press,* Nov. 5, 1995, p. E2.

A *Detroit Free Press* editorial says that by apparently withholding a study showing that the Senate's version of welfare "reform" would push 1.1 million children into poverty, the Clinton administration has compromised its moral authority and cast doubt on its own standards for reform.

Whitman, David, "A reality check on welfare reform," *U.S. News & World Report,* Nov. 13, 1995, pp. 46-48.

Half of all single parents on Aid to Families with Dependent Children would be required to work 35 hours a week within a matter of years under the welfare reform bills passed by the House and the Senate. However, the experience of Detroit's ambitious welfare-to-work program shows that locating jobs for welfare recipients is difficult for several reasons.

Impact on States

Havemann, Judith, "Some states are hobbled in race to welfare reform," *The Washington Post,* Oct. 22, 1996, p. A4.

Although every state will face the same work requirements for resident welfare recipients, each state will not receive the same amount of federal funds to implement welfare reform. Anticipated problems with this funding disparity are highlighted.

Kilborn, Peter T., "With Welfare Overhaul Now Law, States Grapple with the Consequences," *The New York Times,* Aug. 23, 1996, p. A22.

The impact of the new welfare reform bill on the states is assessed. Even as President Clinton signed the bill, launching the biggest shift in social policy since the Depression, many state officials across the U.S. say they are nowhere near ready to assume the greater control the measure grants them of the nation's welfare system.

Vobejda, Barbara, and Judith Havemann, "States take variety of paths to welfare reform," ***The Washington Post,*** **Oct. 6, 1996, p. A4.**
Energized by the far-reaching federal welfare law, state officials across the U.S. are churning out ideas that go well beyond the traditional notion of giving a monthly check to those who need it. The new law has created a vast market for novel approaches to helping the poor become self-sufficient.

"Welfare reform: Just who's going to create all the jobs?" ***Los Angeles Times,*** **Aug. 27, 1996, p. B6.**
An editorial comments on the new federal welfare law, which will require millions of welfare recipients to seek jobs, and questions where the jobs will come from in hard-hit urban areas like Southern California.

Job Training for Welfare Recipients

Hill, James, "Graduation from welfare is moms' goal in job training," ***Chicago Tribune,*** **June 2, 1995, Sec. 2, p. 1.**
Eighteen mothers on public assistance received their certificates for completing the Vocational Skills Training Program at the College of Lake County, Ill. The free, state-funded venture provides 16 weeks of vocational and educational training to help Lake County public aid recipients find employment and become self-sufficient.

Kleiman, Carol, "Waging the uphill pay battle after welfare reform," ***Chicago Tribune,*** **Aug. 27, 1996, p. 3.**
Kleiman examines employment training programs for women affected by the federal welfare reform initiative.

Sullivan, Leon H., "Welfare reform: The final payoff?" ***Chicago Defender,*** **Sept. 12, 1996, p. 12.**
Sullivan discusses the accomplishments of the Opportunities Industrialization Centers of America, the largest self-help training program in the U.S., in preparing more than 2 million Americans for jobs.

Welfare-to-Work Programs in Individual States

Eggleston, Richard, "Wisconsin riding wave of welfare reform," ***USA Today,*** **May 20, 1996, p. A5.**
Wisconsin's welfare-to-work law, endorsed by President Clinton, is designed to do away with welfare in the state by requiring able-bodied parents to work or begin job training.

Moskowitz, Eric, "Second-chance homes clear welfare-to-work path," ***The Christian Science Monitor,*** **Oct. 2, 1995, p. 4.**
The Island Family Inn, a privately run but government-funded program in New York City that provides job training, education and child care instruction to single parents on welfare, is featured. Such programs provide a model for helping welfare mothers achieve greater self-sufficiency.

Poe, Janita, "City's schools turn to welfare moms as tutors," ***Chicago Tribune,*** **Oct. 20, 1996, Sec. 4, p. 1.**
Parents as Teachers First is a new Chicago Public Schools program that is trying to provide tutoring for large numbers of impoverished children. It calls for mothers who use the program to serve as tutor-mentors after they get job training under state initiatives designed to get them off welfare. At least one local watchdog group has publicly expressed doubts about the program, and some local and national education experts question the qualifications of the tutor-mentors.

"State must set bar higher to reform welfare system," ***Atlanta Journal,*** **Sept. 27, 1996, p. A20.**
An editorial says the new U.S. welfare bill is so lax that Georgia should set higher standards in order to move the poor from dependency to work. Some of the points where the new federal law is lax are noted.

Mothers on Welfare

Christian, Sue Ellen, "Welfare reform puts mom in middle," ***Chicago Tribune,*** **Oct. 31, 1996, p. 1.**
An Illinois welfare reform measure, the so-called "family cap," takes effect on Nov. 1, 1996, denying additional cash assistance to mothers who have a baby while on welfare. The impact on Chicagoan Ollivette Reeves, an unemployed single mother who is expecting twins, is discussed.

Folbre, Nancy, "Venomous tide in welfare reform," ***The Boston Globe,*** **Oct. 15, 1996, p. D4.**
Folbre describes her struggles to convince the hosts of radio talk shows that welfare recipients do not have eight children and eat steak and lobster every night. Folbre questions what welfare reforms will do to the average, but poor, mothers and children who receive it.

Goodwin, Joanne L., "Employable mothers and suitable work: A re-evaluation of welfare and wage-earning for women in the twentieth-century United States," ***Journal of Social History,*** **Winter 1995, pp. 253-274.**
The evolution of welfare policies for impoverished, mother-only families is discussed. These welfare policies can best be explained by considering the public sector's relationship to both families and markets in the U.S.

Strausberg, Chinta, "Welfare moms demand jobs," ***Chicago Defender,*** **May 18, 1995, p. 3.**
Several mothers on welfare in Chicago have claimed the welfare system is "unfair" to women who want to get off Aid to Families with Dependent Children (AFDC) and enter the work force, that the system fails to provide an education or job training and that AFDC will eventually be abolished without replacement.

Back Issues

Great Research on Current Issues Starts Right Here...Recent topics covered by The CQ Researcher are listed below. Before May 1991, reports were published under the name of Editorial Research Reports.

MAY 1995
Assisted Suicide Controversy
Overhauling Social Security
Learning to Read
Mandatory Sentencing

JUNE 1995
Combating Infectious Disease
Property Rights
Repetitive Stress Injuries
Regulating the Internet

JULY 1995
War Crimes
Highway Safety
Combating Terrorism
Preventing Teen Drug Use

AUGUST 1995
Job Stress
Organ Transplants
United Nations at 50
Advances in Cancer Research

SEPTEMBER 1995
Catholic Church in the U.S.
Northern Ireland Cease-Fire
High School Sports
Teaching History

OCTOBER 1995
Quebec's Future
Revitalizing the Cities
Networking the Classroom
Indoor Air Pollution

NOVEMBER 1995
The Working Poor
The Jury System
Sex, Violence and the Media
Police Misconduct

DECEMBER 1995
Teens and Tobacco
Gene Therapy's Future
Global Water Shortages
Third-Party Prospects

JANUARY 1996
Emergency Medicine
Punishing Sex Offenders
Bilingual Education
Helping the Homeless

FEBRUARY 1996
Reforming the CIA
Campaign Finance Reform
Academic Politics
Getting Into College

MARCH 1996
The British Monarchy
Preventing Juvenile Crime
Tax Reform
Pursuing the Paranormal

APRIL 1996
Centennial Olympic Games
Managed Care
Protecting Endangered Species
New Military Culture

MAY 1996
Russia's Political Future
Marriage and Divorce
Year-Round Schools
Taiwan, China and the U.S.

JUNE 1996
Rethinking NAFTA
First Ladies
Teaching Values
Labor Movement's Future

JULY 1996
Recovered-Memory Debate
Native Americans' Future
Crackdown on Sexual Harassment
Attack on Public Schools

AUGUST 1996
Fighting Over Animal Rights
Privatizing Government Services
Child Labor and Sweatshops
Cleaning Up Hazardous Wastes

SEPTEMBER 1996
Gambling Under Attack
The States and Federalism
Civic Journalism
Reassessing Foreign Aid

OCTOBER 1996
Political Consultants
Insurance Fraud
Rethinking School Integration
Parental Rights

NOVEMBER 1996
Global Warming
Clashing Over Copyright
Consumer Debt
Governing Washington, D.C.

Back issues are available for $5.00 (subscribers) or $8.00 (non-subscribers). Quantity discounts apply to orders over ten. To order, call Congressional Quarterly Customer Service at (202) 887-8621.

Binders are available for $18.00. To order call 1-800-638-1710. Please refer to stock number 648.

Future Topics

- ***Volunteerism***
- ***Implementing the Disabilities Act***
- ***America's Pampered Pets***

THE CQ Researcher

PUBLISHED BY CONGRESSIONAL QUARTERLY INC.

The New Volunteerism

Is America poised for a surge in good works?

Feed the hungry, teach the illiterate, transport the elderly, staff the museums — the quintessentially American willingness to lend a hand is demonstrated annually by 93 million volunteers. Giving of oneself has long been a way to build civic-mindedness and learn about the world beyond one's back yard. But in the current climate of shrinking government, volunteerism is emerging as more than just a conscience-comforting avocation. Lawmakers are counting on a new burst of commitment to offset pending cuts in social service, education and community development programs. But what is the proper role for government in promoting volunteerism? Conservatives are wary of too much bureaucracy and a "politicized" agenda. Liberals see government as a necessary catalyst that plugs holes in the social safety net.

INSIDE THIS ISSUE

Dec. 13, 1996 • Volume 6, No. 46 • Pages 1081-1104

Formerly Editorial Research Reports

THE NEW VOLUNTEERISM

COVER: AMERICORPS VOLUNTEERS JOIN COMMUNITY MEMBERS IN CLEANING UP MERIDIAN HILL PARK IN WASHINGTON, D.C. (JOCELYN AUGUSTINO/AMERICORPS)

Dec. 13, 1996
Volume 6, No. 46

The CQ Researcher (ISSN 1056-2036). Formerly Editorial Research Reports. Published weekly (48 times per year, not printed March 1, May 31, Aug. 30, Nov. 29) by Congressional Quarterly Inc., 1414 22nd St., N.W., Washington, D.C. 20037. Annual subscription rate for libraries, businesses and government is $319. Additional rates furnished upon request. Periodicals postage paid at Washington, D.C. POSTMASTER: Send address changes to The CQ Researcher, 1414 22nd St., N.W., Washington, D.C. 20037.

The New Volunteerism

By Charles S. Clark

The Issues

It's Christmastime, and phone calls to the homeless shelter come thick and fast. "I'd like to bring some cookies around," says a typical first-time caller. Judy Caitland, executive director of the 80-bed Carpenter's Shelter in Alexandria, Va., has grown accustomed to the seasonal rise in altruism. It dramatizes a key distinction between "one-shot" volunteers and the long-term, committed volunteers the facility depends upon. "Both groups are welcome and have lots to offer," she says, "but we are more appreciative of those who stay and build a relationship and learn more about why we're here."

Carpenter's is blessed with a large group of community volunteers who serve on a regular schedule, staffing the shelter's reception area, passing out supplies, preparing meals and bringing in new volunteers when "others burn out or move away," Caitland adds. The shelter's Rolodex of volunteers lists some 800 church members, retirees and idealistic 20-somethings, many who help homeless clients with health care or résumé writing. The community support is indispensable, Caitland says.

Reliance on unpaid service may soon be more common — and necessary — in communities around the country. In a time of shrinking government and skepticism toward bureaucratic social programs, volunteer groups both public and private are banking on a new surge of activists. Their help is needed in everything from literacy tutoring and home renovation to transporting the elderly and collecting door-to-door for cancer research. [1]

"If the era of big government is over, then the era of the big citizen must begin," says former Sen. Harris L. Wofford, D-Pa., chief executive officer of the federal government's Corporation for National Service. Its AmeriCorps program is leading an effort to recruit more than 10 million new volunteers to pitch in around the nation.

"Now is the right time for a fresh look at how we Americans give our money and our time," says recent Republican presidential candidate Lamar Alexander, who heads the new National Commission on Philanthropy and Civic Renewal, which is funded by the conservative Lynde and Harry Bradley Foundation.

Interest in volunteerism clearly crosses party lines: President Clinton and first lady Hillary Rodham Clinton, along with former Presidents Jimmy Carter and Gerald R. Ford, plan to attend a two-day summit on volunteerism in February. The meeting in Philadelphia is sponsored by the Corporation for National Service and the private Points of Light Foundation. *

* The Points of Light Foundation was founded in 1990 to encourage volunteerism and takes its name from President George Bush's reference to volunteers as "a thousand points of light." The foundation receives 40 percent of its funding from the appropriation for the Corporation for National Service; the rest comes from foundations and corporations.

Boosters of the new volunteerism begin with a sizable effort already in progress. Some 93 million Americans performed some type of volunteer effort in 1995 for an average of 4.2 hours a week, according to a survey conducted by the Gallup Organization for Independent Sector, a national coalition of nearly 800 voluntary organizations, foundations and corporate-giving programs. A total of 20.3 billion volunteer hours were logged in 1995, a billion more than in 1993.

Volunteering is a part of family life in 36 percent of households, according to a 1994 Gallup survey conducted for the Points of Light Foundation. And charitable giving, which helps support many volunteer programs, in 1995 rose by 5 percent over the previous year. [2]

The business community is stepping up its workplace volunteer organizing. As many as 82 percent of corporations surveyed last year by Boston College's Center for Corporate Community Relations sponsor volunteer programs, while 26 percent give employees time off to volunteer.

Volunteer spirit is particularly evident among the young. Nearly two-thirds of 240,000 college freshmen surveyed in September 1995 said they had performed volunteer work in the past year. [3] And even further down the age scale, the "Big Help" campaign sponsored by the children's cable television channel Nickelodeon recently received 8.5 million calls from youngsters promising 92.5 million hours of community service.

Historians assert that Americans have long alternated between inward-looking and outward-looking moods. If so, observers at both ends of the political spectrum are predicting a swing of the national mood to outward-looking, public-purpose activism. "Rather than just increased volunteerism, we're trying to find a way to really solve problems," Wofford says. "We need the twin engines of [government-sustained] full-

Who Are America's Volunteers

Americans who are college-educated, white, middle-aged, married and high-earners are most likely to volunteer, according to a recent survey. Nearly three-quarters of the respondents who went to college said they volunteer compared with about a third of those who didn't go past high school.

Demographic characteristic	Percentage of group who volunteered
All respondents	49%
Gender	
Male	45%
Female	52%
Race	
White	52%
Non-White	36%
Black	35%
Hispanic	40%
Age	
18-24	38%
25-34	51%
35-44	55%
45-54	55%
55-64	48%
65-74	45%
75+	34%
Income	
Under $10,000	35%
$10,000-$19,999	34%
$20,000-$29,999	45%
$30,000-$39,999	46%
$40,000-$49,999	53%
$50,000-$74,999	60%
$75,000-$99,999	65%
$100,000 and over	69%
Religion	
Catholic	49%
Protestant	49%
Other	58%
None	40%
Marital status	
Married	56%
Single	40%
Divorced, separated, widowed	41%
Education	
High school or less	36%
Technical, trade school or some college	54%
College graduate	71%

Source: Survey for Independent Sector conducted by The Gallup Organization, May 4-June 16, 1996.

time service and millions of casual volunteers. We want to do what has never been done in these complicated modern times but was commonplace in frontier times in small towns, such as raising barns or building schools" with citizen labor.

No one says that increasing the ranks of volunteers will be easy. Data show that while many Americans indeed do contribute to the common good, most volunteer work is done by an elite of "influentials" working mainly at nonprofit groups. Since the 1940s, pollsters regularly have asked Americans if they have ever done three or more of the following: attended a public meeting; written to their member of Congress; served on a local committee; served as a local organization's officer; attended a political rally; written a letter to the editor; made a speech; worked for a political party; belonged to a better-government group; held or run for elected office; or written an article.

On average, only 10 percent of the population answer "yes" each year the survey is taken.[4]

What's more, the kind of volunteering that some say is most needed — aid to the poor, for example — isn't particularly popular. "Giving to public television is up, but we haven't had the same response for human services, which are more expensive," says David Beckmann, president of the anti-hunger group Bread for the World in Silver Spring, Md. Indeed, volunteering for human services came in sixth in a ranking of volunteers' most common areas of emphasis in a recent poll conducted by the University of Chicago's National Opinion Research Center.

Why are many potential volunteers reluctant to commit to helping in the human services area? Experts say that such problems often require more inspiration, time and will power than most Americans can summon. "Acting with compassion is not doing good because we think we ought to," write international activists Ram Dass and

Mirabai Bush. "It is being drawn to action by heartfelt compassion. It is giving ourselves into what we are doing, being present in the moment — no matter how difficult, sad or even boring it feels, no matter how much it demands." [5]

The factors that do encourage volunteers, according to Virginia Hodgkinson, vice president for research at Independent Sector, include experience volunteering as a youth; spending time socially with people in volunteer organizations; recent experience giving time to a friend or loved one; a high education level; regular religious activity; and membership in a youth group.

People are also more likely to volunteer if they give money to charities, and if someone has asked them to volunteer. Those least likely to volunteer, according to current data, are people ages 18-24, who are single, black or Hispanic, and who have incomes under $20,000. (*See table, p. 1084.*)

Many volunteers are motivated by a combination of selflessness and self-interest — such as the Washington, D.C., woman who helps at an art museum: "I wanted to learn about art," she said, "but it's also my responsibility to give something back" to the community. [6]

To skeptics, particularly some political conservatives, the movement for volunteerism reflects a certain naiveté, a refusal to make hardheaded calculations about whether good works actually work. "Today," says neoconservative scholar Irving Kristol, "an idealist is someone who, in the spirit of compassion, gives away other people's money." [7] Similarly, syndicated columnist George F. Will warns against "the danger of being earnest in an era when that attribute seems like evidence of an itch to be an improver, which voters nowadays consider a synonym for nuisance." [8]

But other conservatives, as well as many liberals, embrace volunteerism as a higher level of living. Author and conservative columnist Ariana Huffington, who works with disadvantaged children in the nation's capital on weekends, says the naysayers are "missing a fundamental point about life. Every major philosopher and religious leader has stressed the importance of serving. The Constitution's language about the pursuit of happiness refers not to seeking pleasure but doing good."

Habitat for Humanity

Since 1976, Habitat for Humanity volunteers have worked with community members in need to build more than 50,000 low-income homes worldwide.

As debate over the new volunteerism unfolds, these are among the key issues that are likely to be debated:

Should government play a strong role in promoting volunteerism?

"Americans have lost patience with the Great Society," Republican presidential candidate Bob Dole said last summer. "But they have not lost their compassion for the poor and their commitment to the common good." [9]

The heady days of the 1960s, when President John F. Kennedy inspired many with his stirring "ask what you can do" call to public service, have given way in the '90s to wariness toward ambitious government programs. But feelings toward volunteering remain positive. That was one of the calculations behind the administration's 1994 launch of AmeriCorps, which President Clinton has called the "transcendent idea" of his presidency.

AmeriCorps planners have a vision far beyond the 25,000 full-time corps members who currently do community work in 438 localities (and who receive stipends and education benefits). To push volunteerism to a new level, planners at the so-called "Domestic Peace Corps" want to recruit more than 10 million part-time volunteers to tutor children with reading problems, provide companionship for the elderly and renovate low-income housing. AmeriCorps estimates that just from July-September 1995 alone, its members recruited 73,000 new volunteers who gave 700,000 hours of service.

"The challenge is how to split the atom of civic power," CEO Wofford says. "National service can be a kind of research and development operation into what works and what doesn't. It can be a school for volunteerism, citizenship and teamwork."

The new push for volunteers, of course, would not replace the role government has long played in the nonprofit sector. In addition to the government's impact on volunteerism through tax and labor policy and tort liability regulation, there are the myriad

Fail to Volunteer and You Might Fail High School

"It is in giving ourselves to others that we find ourselves," Bernie Noe, upper school principal at Sidwell Friends School in Washington, D.C., assures his teenage students. He is instructing them in the Quaker tradition of community service, lived out in such activities as cleaning up the C&O Canal, picking vegetables for the poor or renovating a low-income house for the national program Christmas in April.

As a private school, Sidwell has long had the unchallenged right to require its graduates to volunteer. But in recent years, such service requirements for academic credit have been implemented in taxpayer-supported public high schools. After the idea got rolling in the mid-1980s, it was endorsed by President George Bush and then spread in some form to nearly a quarter of all public U.S. high schools, according to the Educational Research Service. [1]

"To make a contribution to the community, and learning from that contribution, helps one to become a lifelong learner," says Maryland Superintendent of Schools Nancy S. Grasmick, whose state in 1992 became the first to make community service a graduation requirement. [2] The idea of having Maryland high schoolers give 75 hours to serving in soup kitchens, removing graffiti from school property or performing other charitable services was the pet project of Maryland Lt. Gov. Kathleen Kennedy Townsend, the niece of Peace Corps champion John F. Kennedy.

An idea that sounds rosy in theory, however, is not without its thorns. Maryland recently reported that of the program's first group affected by the new requirement, the Class of '97, nearly 5,000 seniors, or 40 percent statewide, have yet to fulfill the minimum number of hours.

What's more, several conservative political and legal groups have challenged the program on constitutional grounds, using the same arguments many use against community-service requirements for convicts and pro bono work that some attorneys are required to perform. Some parents warn that the program is unfair to lower-income students who already have after-school jobs.

"The assumption is often made that if something is good for some it must be good for all, and should be practiced by all," says a spokesman for the National Center for Effective Secondary Schools, which has studied teen service. "Service freely entered into may not even be the same thing, nor have the same effect, as service mandated by a higher authority, which calls up the image of reluctant teenagers trudging resentfully through their service assignment." [3]

In Chapel Hill, N.C., the parents of two students sued the local Board of Education to challenge the schools' service requirement, citing the 13th Amendment's ban on involuntary servitude. A federal appeals court in North Carolina this July upheld the school district. "Freedom from compulsory charitable service is not among the rights" identified by courts, said the 4th Circuit judges. "More importantly, the community-service requirement is in no way comparable to the horrible injustice of human slavery." The Institute for Justice, a conservative group in Washington, filed an appeal with the Supreme Court in November. [4]

In the volunteer community, graduation requirements for service draw mixed reviews. "I have no problem with a law firm requiring its attorneys to do pro bono work because the lawyers can choose whether to work there," says University of Texas history Professor Marvin Olasky. "But high school students? The question is, are they getting a good education academically? Will they start doing other things instead?"

Harris L. Wofford, CEO of the Corporation for National Service, which sponsors AmeriCorps, says he would back the idea if he were on a local school board. "All Catholic and prep schools require it, and you can connect service with the curriculum, so that students are not just talking about civics and reading the Constitution, but they're going out and *doing* civics and citizenship," he says. Wofford does not, however, favor Congress stepping into a local education issue and mandating community service requirements nationwide.

"I don't think coerced volunteerism works," says Princeton University social scientist Julian Wolpert. "It is a good idea to train students to live civically in society where others' needs are important, but a better approach is to recruit the best students or the most athletic students to serve as examples."

About the same percentage of schools that require volunteerism have programs that merely encourage it, says Virginia Hodgkinson, vice president for research at Independent Sector. "And giving students a chance to volunteer through a course they're taking is not the same as requiring it."

---

[1] *Utne Reader*, May-June 1996, p. 14.

[2] *The Washington Post*, Sept. 25, 1996.

[3] Quoted in Jill K. Cunningham, "What You Can Do For Your Country," *Alternatives in Philanthropy*, Capital Research Center, August 1992.

[4] For background, see *The Chronicle of Higher Education*, July 25, 1996, p. 14.

state and municipal commissions and councils on volunteerism and the hundreds of volunteer coordinators at federal facilities around the country.

Government's interest in a healthy volunteer pool is also clear from the fact that many local government programs, though taxpayer-funded, are designed with a built-in dependency on volunteers. In Portland, Maine, the city's chauffeuring service for incapacitated elderly residents includes 15 volunteer drivers in its team of 20; in Los Angeles, the Child Advocates Office of the welfare department counts on 275 unpaid child-abuse investigators. [10]

Most significant, much of the training, direction and materials provided to volunteers by nonprofits is funded by government. In 1995, some 600,000 charitable organizations received 37 percent of their estimated $575 billion in expenses from different levels of government, according to an Independent Sector study. [11]

There is some evidence of past success in government efforts to build volunteerism, even without the galvanizing push of a clear national crisis on the order of World War II. During the 1980s, for example, a special office for volunteers set up by North Carolina prompted fully 70 percent of all adults in the state to perform volunteer work worth an estimated $300 million. [12]

But in the current climate of budget-balancing and government cutbacks, philosophical opponents of active government have been vocal in warning of wasteful bureaucracy and taxpayer-subsidized partisan politics. AmeriCorps itself often has been slammed as "coerced volunteerism" by House Speaker Newt Gingrich, R-Ga., and as an "outrageous boondoggle" by Sen. Charles E. Grassley, R-Iowa. [13] And in 1995, soon after congressional Republicans began pursuing federal budget cuts under their "Contract with America," a group of leftist activists from ACORN (the Association of Community Organizations for Reform Now) staged a protest at an event where Gingrich had been scheduled to speak. Gingrich stayed away, but he later made much of the fact that ACORN was an AmeriCorps grant recipient.

Other critics argue that government efforts actually stifle the volunteer sector. "All of us should have a responsibility to our family and community, and if we shrink the government sector, we can resuscitate that spirit among ourselves," says Jessica Gavora, director of programs for the conservative New Citizenship Project. "Many will want to work in the community if given the opportunity, and their self-interest combines with genuine concern for their fellow man. When government tries to come in as an equal partner, it's so big and unwieldy that it overshadows the private sector with its easily accessible funding. Government is not accountable or controlled like the business and nonprofit sectors, which have to sustain themselves."

Youth Service America

Young volunteers help clean-up Waterfront Park in Washington, D.C.'s Anacostia neighborhood during last year's National Youth Service Day. In 1997, service day will be April 15.

Hudson Institute President Leslie Lenkowski, a board member of the Corporation for National Service, says: "The notion that government can stimulate volunteerism is the kind of arrogance that gives national service a bad name. I believe there is a role for public policy in encouraging volunteerism, but we should keep it modest. Local charities can benefit from grants-in-aid that provide a full-time staff. That way, when the volunteers come in on a Saturday, the materials [for home building, for example] are there, and the site is clear for the eager bodies who want to help."

Similar distinctions are made by Marvin Olasky, a professor of history and journalism at the University of Texas who has written widely on philanthropy. "The Preamble to the Constitution says we should promote the general welfare," he says. "But there is a big difference between providing and promoting. In the past, government has been in the habit of providing."

As an example of proper promoting, Olasky cites the state's capital, Austin, which provides free maintenance for baseball fields used by the Optimist Club for youth programs in disadvantaged neighborhoods. "If the government tries to pick the places that are eligible, as AmeriCorps does, you get into some First Amendment problems" with volunteers from religious groups that want to incorporate a spiritual dimension to their work, he says. "I'd be happy if government encouraged it with a tax credit, but I don't want [Health and Human Services Secretary] Donna Shalala to make the calls" as to who gets services.

Clinton-appointee Wofford sees too much ideology in such criticism. "If your primary interest is getting government out of people's lives, then close down the government; that drastic tactic was already tried," he says, referring to last December's budget

Continued on p. 1089

Strategies for Mobilizing Suburban Volunteers

As America has suburbanized, so has its philanthropy. For decades, lifestyles built around well-tended lawns and detached tranquility have moved the nation's affluence outside its urban centers, creating distance between the pool of most likely volunteers and their urban clients and organizations.

"Donors generally target their contributions on their own communities," notes Julian Wolpert, a professor at Princeton University's Woodrow Wilson School of Public and International Affairs. "Thus, only about 10 percent of charitable contributions are directed to the poor, and most charities lack the mechanisms to reallocate donations where they are needed most."[1] Compounding the problem is the time-crunch experienced by today's two-income families.

Increasingly, however, urban activists are arriving at new strategies for tapping into suburban volunteers. "Clever organizations are offering flexible time, so instead of having the same person come to the same event every week, they split it among two or three," says Virginia Hodgkinson, vice president for research at Independent Sector. "Parents who have kids in Girl Scouts already know this."

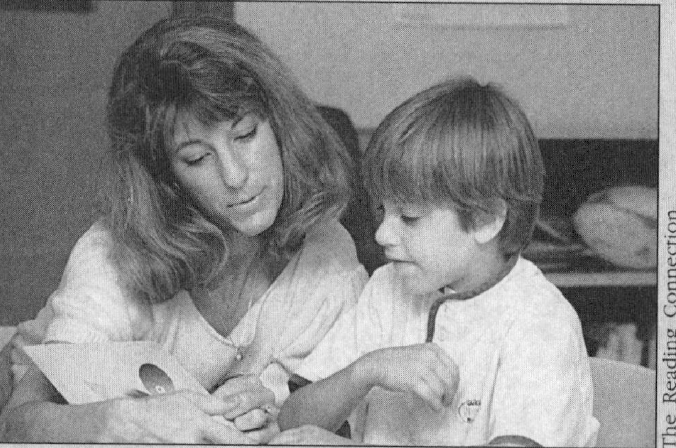

The Reading Connection

Beth Reese and other volunteers at The Reading Connection in Arlington, Va., read to youngsters in local shelters.

The problem of how to lure suburbanites from backyard cookouts to needy neighborhoods may be a question of assuring their personal safety, says Marvin Olasky, author of *The Tragedy of American Compassion.* "If you approach a person in the suburbs and simply say, 'Go to this inner-city area at this time to meet these people,' they won't respond," he says. "But if you say, 'Here's a group of us who work in this area, and we're an organization that's been around for a while, let's go together in a van during daylight and meet these people,' quite a few will be willing to come and then come back."

One group that has demonstrated a shrewd ability to turn out suburban volunteers is The Reading Connection, a children's literacy organization based in Arlington, Va. Founded in 1989 with 10 volunteers, the group schedules volunteers to read aloud to children at homeless shelters and shelters for battered women. "It's based on something people do naturally with their own children or grandchildren," says organization Chairwoman Beth Reese, a mother of three and former teacher who spent seven years as the group's unpaid executive director. "Because so many of these children have never been read to, it opens the world of books to them in a way that is so real, so right, so basic."

Growing by word-of-mouth and through business and nonprofit donations, the Connection now mobilizes 450 volunteers — and a paid director — serving seven Northern Virginia shelters, some discreetly operating in residential areas. "Many of our volunteers at first are shocked to learn that there are homeless children in their neighborhood," Reese says. Unlike the generation-to-generation poverty of many inner-city poor, she adds, the suburban homeless are often middle-class people who faced a marital, health or job crisis and exhausted their network of friends and extended families.

When confronting such people "living on the edge," potential volunteers often feel overwhelmed, Reese says. "The initial call is answered by the volunteer because that's part of being human. But many get discouraged or even depressed because it all seems so big and distant, particularly if they don't already belong to a church or work with an organization."

The key to attracting volunteers, Reese says, is to offer a range of opportunities. "Some people are affiliation-motivated, meaning they like belonging to a group. Some are more achievement-motivated, meaning they want a task with a beginning, middle and end. They would prefer to work at home maintaining our database or sewing the welcome bags [for the books, paper and crayons that are given to the children]. Then there are those who are power-oriented, meaning that they are ready for more responsibility."

Training for The Reading Connection is completed after a single session, and the once-a-month commitment can be fulfilled conveniently in the evening. Burnout and apathy, says Reese, can be averted "if people are given the right job and are given the resources to do it. If the commitment is hard to get to, if the volunteers are not scheduled right, if they feel they don't have the needed skills, then what may look like apathy" could actually be frustration.

"People don't want to be pressured by guilt," Reese says. But once a volunteer is involved, the work "brings out the best of human nature, and people find a side of someone they never knew about. Many volunteers learn that they are helping children who may be in their own children's school. They call to thank us for helping them find something that was missing between the carpool and the job."

---

[1] Julian Wolpert, "What Charity Can and Cannot Do," report from the Twentieth Century Fund, February 1996, p. 19.

Continued from p. 1087
stalemate between Congress and the White House. "But if you want to solve problems, government can be one of the central elements."

Wofford points to the partnership between government and Millard Fuller, founder of the home-building group Habitat for Humanity. "He is a religious conservative who at first didn't want government or AmeriCorps," Wofford says. "But he agreed to work with AmeriCorps because he wants all American families to have housing, and he knows that without some full-time staff, there won't be anyone to organize or recruit the volunteers.

"Conservatives haven't realized that they won on the issue of how we structured AmeriCorps," Wofford continues. "[Back in the 1960s], the Peace Corps was centrally controlled, and it told its volunteers where they would go. AmeriCorps, by contrast, is much more like a voucher system." In other words, "volunteers choose the organizations where they want to work, and the organizations receive funding to carry out their mission."

As for the complaint that government-funded volunteers can veer off into lobbying or partisan politics, many veterans of nonprofits accept that possibility as inevitable. Nathaniel Winship, a long-time volunteer community nutrition activist in Massachusetts, says that most anti-hunger activists "realize that volunteering is at best a stopgap measure. The educated volunteer soon realizes that we need to translate this work into getting the whole system to take care of things. It's no secret that some of the best advocates have gotten federal money over the years, which has always been controversial. In the end, the cure for poverty is money."

Beckmann of Bread for the World agrees, noting that his group's work against hunger is affected by the government's "macroeconomic and education policies, the earned-income tax credit, the minimum wage and jobs growth."

Huffington, who runs the Center for Effective Compassion, an education and advocacy group, says: "The mistake my friends on the left make is that they think advocacy is the way to spend time. But advocacy is an inferior involvement to being in the trenches. The conservative mistake is to assume that cuts in government will be enough to restore citizen participation.

"People should quit arguing over the role of government and program cuts and increase their giving of money and time. We're in a crisis, and if we don't make big changes, we will all have to deal with the social breakdown."

Hodgkinson says that studies of volunteers show that they are more realistic about social problems once they get involved, and that most believe that both government and the nonprofit sector have roles to play. "If conservative means the goal is self-help, then volunteers are with that," she says. "But most see it as a co-responsibility."

The question of whether government can spend money effectively on behalf of volunteerism is "a valid one," says Julian Wolpert, a professor at Princeton University's Woodrow Wilson School of Public and International Affairs. "Simply passing out funds through a bureaucracy, without any direct contact with the needy," certainly has not worked very well, he says. But it is also true, he adds, that areas with active governments — Minneapolis, Minn., Pittsburgh, Pa., Cleveland, Ohio, for example — are the same areas that also have active volunteer sectors. [14]

It is questionable, Wolpert says, whether the self-appointed volunteer and religious groups can do the job well. It might be better to have an active government that provides people with the skills, backgrounds and relationships with professionals than to rely on "well-meaning but not knowledgeable volunteers who want to impose their own beliefs on people." Most of the clients, he adds, "don't need advice. They simply don't have enough money for food or shelter."

Can volunteers make up for what the poor may lose from welfare reform?

"Give a man a fish, and you've given him a meal. Teach him to fish, and he'll have food for a lifetime."

The old adage — invoked by people of all political stripes in the volunteer community — acquired new significance this year when Congress passed, and President Clinton signed, the massive overhaul of the nation's 61-year-old welfare program. The plan is to reduce federal welfare and nutrition spending by $54 billion over the next six years and give states responsibility for managing federal funding in the form of block grants. [15] To reassure those who worry that the poor may suffer, backers of the plan promise, among other things, that the charitable and volunteer community will step into the breach, taking advantage of a provision in the new law that allows religious groups to receive public funds. But many leaders of nonprofits anticipate disaster.

"We're almost certain to see increases in hunger or poverty in the next three to 10 years, and kids sleeping under bridges," says Beckmann of Bread for the World. "Volunteer groups are not equipped to redistribute goods from one part of the country to another," he adds. "They will be forced into rationing and triage." To compensate for the cuts, he calculates that each of the country's 350,000 churches and synagogues would have to raise an additional $150,000 over the next six years.

Princeton's Wolpert says the amount of money needed for welfare is so great that "if the states don't compensate for the federal cuts, we won't be able to maintain the social safety net." As for volunteers, the need is greatest in places where they are most absent, and many of them prefer to volunteer in education and the arts rather than human services, "where the problems seem too long-term and massive."

Independent Sector's Hodgkinson

cautions that it is too early to be certain how states will alter their current welfare programs in reaction to the federal changes. But judging from progress in states that tackled welfare reform early, such as New Jersey and Wisconsin, she predicts that many in the volunteer community "will feel overwhelmed" by an increase in "the working poor" — people newly released from welfare benefits who are struggling at jobs just above the poverty line. [16]

"Volunteers are needed," Hodgkinson says, "but we can't assume that they come for free." In day care, nursing-home staffing and alcohol and drug counseling, volunteers can be useful, but they need guidance and training from professionals. "There's always been a partnership between government and volunteer organizations," she says. "If you take that contract away, you have a diminished capacity."

As a backer of welfare reform, Olasky at the University of Texas agrees only partially, arguing that it's worth a try to see whether the overall welfare burden declines. "Some welfare recipients' behavior will change, and some will get jobs," he says. "Churches will do something, the community will do something, and the Odd Fellows, Elks and Optimist clubs will do something. It's unclear, but it's not something we have to know going in. We should push it as far as it goes, and then see if there's a new government role."

Olasky adds that volunteers will be more successful if they emphasize a one-on-one personal bonding with needy people, challenging their past habits and working from a "spiritual base." The government approach emphasizes entitlement, he says. "You need some people who are well-trained in management, but volunteers who bond one-on-one will do better because they will have responsibility for just a few people. I would rather have five volunteers working for stipends than one master of social work."

Yet even backers of privatizing welfare warn that volunteer religious groups have much to learn. "Unfortunately, many churches and synagogues, mosques and other places of worship basically copy the government's approach: They provide the poor with food, clothing and emergency financial aid, but with little personal attention or follow-up," writes Amy Sherman, a visiting fellow at the conservative Ethics and Public Policy Center. "Clearly, welfare reform inside churches must accompany the welfare reforms emerging from state capitals." [17]

Gavora acknowledges geographical mismatches between suburban volunteers and the inner-city poor who need help, but points out that there are many inner-city black churches around to sustain declining urban communities. "We do believe that civil and religious society can step in and perform many of the functions, but we don't assume that the burden shifts to the private sector unchanged," she says. "If we didn't address the attitudes and habits of mind and body that come with the welfare state, we would simply be repositioning the deck chairs on the *Titanic*."

Wolpert says there is no evidence that this approach works. "The average person neither knows nor greatly cares about the organization chart of safety-net programs of government and private agencies," he writes. "Few are even aware of the sources of support for the social services provided in their communities, and most probably have no opinion on whether government or private charity is inherently best at providing assistance to the poor. The public at large, therefore, has not discerned a necessity for private charity to displace government welfare programs. The advocacy for that shift emanates solely from the right, acting on the basis of ideology." [18]

Though predicting the worst, Beckmann acknowledges that welfare reform will create new opportunities among charitable groups for helping welfare beneficiaries move to jobs. "Quite a few middle-class church people will have the experience of helping, say, 100-200 welfare mothers, which is good for the 100-200, but it carries the danger of false consciousness," he says. "People will tell themselves, 'Hey, we're reforming welfare,' but it doesn't really make a dent."

Even so, Beckmann, an ordained minister, says the volunteer community is not likely to allow the welfare changes to demoralize them. "Religious people expect to end up on the cross," he says. "They didn't get into this expecting to win." ■

BACKGROUND

De Tocqueville's Vision

Philosophical debates over American volunteerism frequently invoke the insights of the French writer and politician Alexis de Tocqueville. In the 1830s, after a trip to study the U.S. penal system, he wrote *Democracy in America*. The collection of observations on the new nation's behaviors and institutions to this day continues to hold a mirror up to America's identity.

"I have often seen Americans make really great sacrifices for the common good," he wrote, "and I have noticed a hundred cases in which, when help was needed, they hardly ever failed to give each other trusty support."

What's more, he noted in an often-repeated observation, Americans are joiners. They are in the habit of forming voluntary associations to create schools, hospitals and churches, and also "if they want to proclaim a truth or propagate some feeling by the encouragement of a great example. . . . In every case, at the head of any new undertaking, where in France you would find the government or in England some territorial magnate, in the

Continued on p. 1092

Chronology

1800s ***Volunteer and charitable groups are mostly private and religious.***

1878
The Salvation Army is founded by street missionaries in England.

1881
Clara Barton founds American Red Cross to bring aid in times of war and national disaster.

1897
Forerunner of National PTA is founded in Washington, D.C.

1900s-1950s ***Economic swings spawn talk of national service.***

1906
Psychologist William James calls for "moral equivalent of war" in which youth would be conscripted to serve the nation.

1933
President Franklin D. Roosevelt creates Civilian Conservation Corps, sending unemployed men to work in rural areas.

1960s ***Government service inspires volunteers.***

1961
President John F. Kennedy creates Peace Corps to enable Americans to volunteer overseas.

1964
President Lyndon B. Johnson creates Volunteers in Service to America (VISTA), a domestic version of the Peace Corps.

1970s ***Success of Great Society programs is questioned.***

1971
Congress creates ACTION to coordinate Peace Corps and VISTA.

1976
Habitat for Humanity is founded by Millard and Linda Fuller in Americus, Ga., to build housing for low-income families.

1980s ***Domestic hunger and homelessness become issues among volunteers.***

1980
Independent Sector is founded in Washington as coalition of voluntary organizations.

1986
Youth Service America is founded to promote ideals of service in National Youth Service Day.

1988
Congress creates Student Literacy Corps for college student volunteers.

Aug. 18, 1988
In his acceptance speech at Republican Convention, presidential candidate George Bush coins phrase "1,000 points of light."

1990s ***Non-governmental anti-hunger volunteers top 900,000. Debate over national service comes to fore.***

1990
Points of Light Foundation is founded in Washington. President Bush signs National Community Service Act creating a commission to study national service.

Sept. 21, 1993
President Clinton signs National and Community Service Trust Act, which provides educational awards to individuals who perform community service.

September 1994
First class of AmeriCorps volunteers goes to work.

January 1995
In his State of the Union address, President Clinton calls AmeriCorps the "essence" of his "new covenant" with the American people.

May 1995
Republican congressional budget resolutions call for huge cuts in Clinton's AmeriCorps program.

September 1995
Sen. Daniel R. Coats, R-Ind., and former Education Secretary William J. Bennett introduce Project for American Renewal to encourage volunteers.

December 1995
Following Clinton vetoes of GOP budgets, AmeriCorps funding survives, though at 44 percent less than Clinton requested.

Oct. 26, 1996
Nearly a million Americans volunteer on national "Make a Difference Day."

Feb. 17-18, 1997
Current and former presidents and first ladies are scheduled to gather in Philadelphia for summit on service sponsored by Corporation for National Service and Points of Light Foundation.

Does Trend Toward Bowling Alone . . .

The 80 million Americans who go bowling every year are taking time for some recreation, not making statements about civic involvement. But last year, they became a metaphor for a lively debate in the political and volunteer communities.

It began when Robert D. Putnam, a professor of international affairs at Harvard University, published "Bowling Alone: America's Declining Social Capital." His research and polling data from the past three decades pointed to a dramatic drop in the membership of civic, recreational and educational organizations. For example, membership in the PTA fell from 12 million in 1964 to 5 million in 1982, before inching up; women's club membership dropped by more than 59 percent since 1964; Elks Clubs are off by 18 percent since 1979; Boy Scouts are down 26 percent since 1970; and the number of Americans bowling *in leagues* decreased by 40 percent between 1980 and 1993.[1]

According to Putnam, such signs of "civic disengagement" threaten the quality of public life and the performance of social institutions. Society's progress in such areas as education, urban poverty, unemployment, crime and health care, he argues, depends on "norms and networks of civic engagement." Such "dense networks of interaction probably broaden the participants' sense of self, developing the 'I' into a 'we,' or [enhance] the participants' 'taste' for collective benefits," he writes.

Putnam's thesis drew positive reactions from President Clinton and from many in the press, particularly among a cohort of politically liberal baby-boomers perhaps eager to preserve the social activism they recall from the 1960s.[2]

But soon an array of critics weighed in. Many took issue with Putnam's numbers, arguing with his interpretations of the General Social Survey taken by the University of Chicago's National Opinion Research Center.

The theory is "mostly bunk," wrote syndicated economics columnist Robert Samuelson. Only in church-related organizations is membership dramatically down, he notes, while the same survey shows that membership in sports clubs, fraternities and hobbies has actually grown. Besides, Samuelson argues, Putnam's touted "community" of the past "was more compartmentalized and less compassionate than today's. Blacks were segregated in schools and jobs. Most married women stayed at home. There was little federal 'safety net' for the old and poor."[3]

Other critics added examples of increased citizen involvement. There was a Gallup Poll showing that attendance at school board meetings rose from 16 percent in 1969 to 39 percent in 1995. There was a report from the Amateur Softball Association that the number of softball teams participating in leagues has grown from 19,000 to 261,000 since 1967. Pollsters such as Roper's Everett Ladd argue that while voter turnout (49 percent in November) is certainly down, philanthropy and volunteering has been rising for a decade and a half. "Civic engagement isn't disappearing but reinventing itself," wrote Richard Stengel of *Time* magazine.[4]

Finally, Putnam's implicit call for government to reconnect America's citizenry has grated against political conservatives. Because of their emphasis on individualism, freedom and

Falling PTA Membership

The decline in National PTA membership since 1962 reflects the "civic disengagement" that Harvard University Professor Robert Putnam sees in American society.

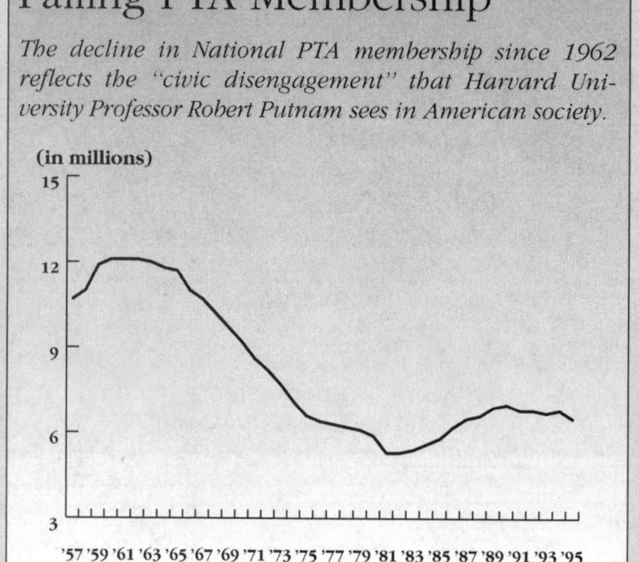

Source: National PTA

Continued from p. 1090

United States you are sure to find an association."[19]

This tradition of mutual aid and belonging unprompted by government would persist through the 19th century as Americans formed the great voluntary associations of the modern era — the American Red Cross, the Salvation Army and the National PTA. Though the work of such groups often intersected with government, the motivations of the members were moralistic and often religious.

In her study of poverty and compassion during the Victorian era, historian Gertrude Himmelfarb comments that the ethos of the times required that volunteers focus not just on giving money but on effective character building. The approach was "neither sentimental or utopian," she writes. "It was stern not only in the personal demands it made upon its missionaries — the commitment in time, labor and energy it exacted from philanthropists and reformers — but also in

. . . Really Mean Civic Ethic Is Dying?

the desire to preserve volunteerism that arises "naturally," many conservatives reject Putnam's implication that government and any of its offshoots are automatically worthy of a citizen's trust.

"Any discussion of civic engagement is necessarily riddled with value judgments about whether a particular activity is a good form of membership, a bad form of trust, or whatever," writes Hudson Institute researcher John Clark. "Measures taken to enhance civic engagement could well backfire and serve only to increase tendencies toward the fragmentation of American society by strengthening communities of narrow interest, ethnicity and religion." [5]

Putnam offers a potpourri of possible explanations for the putative decline in civic connection: the distractions of television (and the VCR); the movement of women into the work force; the increased mobility of American families; the rise in divorce; the takeover of local small businesses by impersonal conglomerates; and the retirement of the civic-minded generation that came together to win World War II. [6]

But his message about a role for government is loud and clear. "Past initiatives such as the county agriculture-agent system, community colleges and tax deductions for charitable contributions illustrate that government can encourage social-capital formation," he says. "Even a recent proposal in San Luis Obispo, Calif., to require that all new houses have front porches illustrates the power of the government to influence where and how networks are formed." [7]

Many who work for volunteer organizations are inclined toward the "bowling alone" thesis. Indeed, fully 90 percent of volunteer leaders surveyed by the Points of Light Foundation last July agreed that many social problems are a direct result of disintegration and disconnection among people and their communities.

"Many of the attacks on Putnam were petty, from people picking at him over the numbers," says Harris L. Wofford, CEO of the Corporation for National Service. "His fundamental point is still important, that with women in the work force, things in the volunteer sector have gotten more complicated."

Virginia Hodgkinson, vice president for research at Independent Sector, a Washington-based coalition that supports voluntary action, says: "Putnam hit on the pulse of Americans who are seeking meaning in community. This comes in cycles. And while we have not seen a decline in the volunteer sector, there is a clear disconnect in the political process as seen in the absence of campaign participation. One reason we've seen the volunteer sector strengthening is because that is an area where people's contributions have demonstrated meaning."

Putnam himself says he has learned a great deal from his critics' reactions, and though he issued one small correction on a set of numbers, he stands by his overall thesis. "I still feel passionate about the underlying issue of what we can do to encourage a rebirth of civic engagement," he says.

Whether or not civic engagement had faded, a *Time*-CNN Poll last July showed that 77 percent of Americans wish they could have more contact with other members of their community.

And in November, following a presidential election in which turnout sank to the lowest level since 1924, a new bipartisan commission was launched by retiring Sen. Sam Nunn, D-Ga., and former Education Secretary William J. Bennett to study civic indifference. With $1 million from the Pew Charitable Trusts, the National Commission on Civic Renewal will spend the next year taking the measure of "our social fabric," cataloging civic initiatives nationwide and making recommendations for enhancing civic life.

The commission will be directed by William Galston, a University of Maryland public policy professor and former Clinton White House official, who expressed concern about the "noticeable drop in Americans' trust in government and each other" in the past 30 years.

---

[1] Robert D. Putnam, "Bowling Alone: America's Declining Social Capital," *Journal of Democracy*, Vol. 6, No. 1, January 1995, p. 65.

[2] See Nicholas Lemann, "Kicking in Groups: Alleged Decline of America's Communal Capital," *The Atlantic Monthly*, April 1, 1996. p. 22.

[3] Robert Samuelson, "Harvard Scholar Misses the Point of 'Real Life,'" *Chicago Tribune*, April 12, 1996.

[4] Richard Stengel, "Bowling Together," *Time*, July 22, 1996, p. 35.

[5] John Clark, "Shifting Engagements: Lessons from the 'Bowling Alone' Debate," *Hudson Briefing Report*, October 1996, p. 12.

[6] Robert D. Putnam, "Tuning in, Tuning Out: The Strange Disappearance of Social Capital in America," *PS: Political Science and Politics*, December 1995, pp. 664-665.

[7] *Journal of Democracy, op. cit.*

---

the nature of that commitment. Compassion had its reasons of mind as well as of the heart." [20]

Olasky, in his history of American philanthropy, sees similar commitments to relationship-building in the work of the "female charitable societies" and "ladies benevolent societies" that operated in New York and other cities in the early 1800s. "These groups emphasized personal contact with the poor, even when some of their members were stunned by the firsthand experience," he writes. "They refused to settle for the feed-and-forget principle or its equally depersonalizing but harsher opposite, the forget-and-don't-feel standard." [21]

The perception of a conflict between the charitable impulse and government policy was not prevalent until well into the 20th century, when conservatives began resisting the government anti-poverty activism of President Franklin D. Roosevelt's New Deal in the 1930s and President Lyndon B. Johnson's Great Society in the 1960s.

One such critique, Richard C.

Cornuelle's *Reclaiming the American Dream: The Role of Private Individuals and Voluntary Associations,* appeared in 1965 amid the flurry of Great Society legislation and the expansion of government cooperation with foundations and nonprofits. Denouncing the charitable world's growing reliance on bureaucratic organizations and middlemen, Cornuelle hearkened back to de Tocqueville.

"We wanted, from the beginning, a free society, free in the sense that each man was his own supervisor and the architect of his own ambitions," Cornuelle wrote. "We wanted as well, with equal fervor, a good society — a humane, responsible society in which helping hands reached out to people in honest distress, in which common needs were met freely and fully. . . . In pursuit of this ambition, Americans used remarkable imagination." [22]

Motivating Volunteers

People perform volunteer work for complex reasons. As Harvard University psychiatrist Robert Coles has written, the inner conflicts of the "call to service" are seldom clean or settled. "In medical school, I was always on the verge of dropping out because I felt utterly inadequate. . . . I went to visit [Catholic anti-poverty crusader] Dorothy Day's community on the Lower East Side more as a refuge from my own life than in response to what she and her co-workers were doing." Day had a simple answer to his confusion about service to others. "'If I were going to forbid hypocrites to work here with us,'" she told him, "'there'd be no one to do the work, and no one to do the forbidding!' " [23]

Clearly, some individuals are drawn to volunteering out of a need to shock the establishment. An extreme example was the "Digger" movement in San Francisco, Calif., in the mid-1960s. Described in the media as a "hippie, philanthropic, do-gooder organization," the anarchistic Diggers "are hip to property," wrote one of its founders. "Everything is free, do your own thing. Human beings are the means of exchange. Food, machines, clothing, materials, shelter and props are merely there. . . . If someone asks to see the manager, tell him he's the manager." [24]

"Visionaries," a recent public television documentary about middle-class people who abandon secure jobs to find fulfillment in service to the poor and sick, boiled the motives down to a strong ability to empathize. "The more you examine the common traits of today's visionaries," writes the documentary's producer, "the more you begin to see that a key component of their personalities is a belief in the power of human emotion." [25]

Others acknowledge that service can be a way to distract oneself from life's rougher patches. Nutrition activist Winship, a small farmer, says: "I never wanted to get rich, and so I'm proud that my family has made do despite my having been laid off many times due to the uncertainty of the social service world. But sometimes I take an existential point of view that says life isn't everything it's cracked up to be. My way of dealing with it is doing something for others. My life is good compared to that of the poor people I try to help, so I share the wealth."

Tips for Recruiting

The main barriers to volunteering, according to a Red Cross study, are language and cultural differences, economic hardships, physical handicaps, time constraints, distance from sites and too few opportunities for family togetherness. [26] An astonishing 74 percent of respondents to a recent Wirthlin Group survey said they don't volunteer simply because they don't know how to get started.

The key to recruiting volunteers, according to Independent Sector, is to get them while they're young. Some 44 percent of teenage volunteers surveyed said they got started before their 11th birthday, often through a church youth group or a school program such as Kids in Action in Baltimore, Md.

Most significantly, the most fertile fields for recruiters are among people who are active in organized religion. A 1995 Independent Sector poll found that among religious respondents, 76 percent give money and 55 percent volunteer; by comparison, among those not involved in a religion only 50 percent give and 34 percent volunteer. People who vote in presidential elections are also more likely to volunteer.

Though many people cite a lack of time as the reason for not volunteering, studies of Americans' daily routines point to a surprising conclusion: The way to get something done is to ask a busy person. "Employed people belong to somewhat more groups than those outside the paid labor force," writes Harvard scholar Robert D. Putnam. Even more striking is the fact that among workers, longer hours are linked to more civic engagement, not less. [27] *(See story, p. 1092.)*

Most volunteering, adds University of Maryland time-use specialist John Robinson, is done by people with either the shortest or the longest work weeks and does not decline with marriage or the arrival of children. Volunteering is most prevalent in rural areas, and on weekends, particularly Sunday. "Far more altruistic activity," he writes in a forthcoming book, "appears in the form of personal help than [is] done through a formal organization, reflecting the presence of those 'thousand points of light' we keep hearing about but almost never see."

A 1995 survey by the Points of Light Foundation found that women volunteers are more likely to work with children with learning disabilities, teen mothers and pregnant teenagers. Men are more likely to work with programs related to alcohol and drug abuse.

Need for Training

One reason nonprofits prefer committed volunteers to casuals is the need for training. At Princeton, says Wolpert, the 500-600 students who've been working with underprivileged children are trained not to invest their own egos in keeping a needy, often minority child dependent on a relationship with a middle-class white. "We teach them to avoid making statements like, 'You've got to be like me,' and we train them to listen, to know what to do if a kid tells you he witnessed a crime or speaks of abuse at home. We train them in when to call in the professionals."

Similarly, managers of nonprofits are taught how to deal effectively with volunteers. Jerry Poggi, senior director of training at the United Way of America's National Academy of Voluntarism in Alexandria, Va., says his group is sensitive to the criticism advanced by many conservatives that nonprofits are hidebound in bureaucracy and large budgets. He gives the United Way professionals, volunteers and corporate executives he trains a thorough grounding in "tools and techniques of good management, fund-raising and community development. We're into state-of-the-art on how to interact in the appropriate manner with all groups. This requires professional training."

The notion that inspired volunteers can serve the poor more effectively than trained professionals is not borne out by research, according to Johns Hopkins University scholar Lester A. Salamon. He found that the alienation that often accompanies steady contact with poverty is more apt to discourage volunteers than professionals. He also discovered that nonprofits staffed with the highest proportion of professionals spent more time actually addressing problems of the poor than those staffed more by volunteers. His surveys of nonprofit professionals, not surprisingly, found that 80 percent rejected the suggestion that "volunteers can be substituted extensively for paid professionals in nonprofit organizations without any significant decline in quality." [28]

Jocelyn Augustino/AmeriCorps

An AmeriCorps member tutors a child in a reading program in Baltimore, Md.

Politics a Turnoff

One reason offered for the recent rise in volunteerism is the fact that many Americans who crave civic involvement appear turned off by politics. A Points of Light Foundation survey of 240 volunteer leaders in June found that 76 percent viewed the political process as ineffective in helping citizens change their communities. The same percentage said volunteers could help make politics better. This "confirms for us that volunteer engagement is not just nice, it's extremely necessary," says foundation President Robert K. Goodwin. "Getting people volunteering together on issues they care about is a way to build trust."

The belief that the volunteer movement can enhance the political process is the basis of the "civic volunteerism model" put forward recently by a trio of political scientists. "The resources of money, time and civic skills derive from involvements in family, job, organizations and religious institutions," they write. "If we can link political activity back to resources, and resources, in turn, back to their institutional origins, we shall thus be able to establish the roots of citizen activity in the basic institutions of civil society." [29]

Conservatives, says columnist Huffington, have a lot of catching up to do when it comes to volunteering to tackle social problems. "There's an enormous complacency in the world of politics," she says, "and the role models are such that there is more cachet in giving to the arts, prestigious colleges and teaching hospitals. But I don't see how you can justify refurbishing an opera house when there are poor people 10 minutes away."

Liberals think too narrowly in viewing action as either paid or charitable, says George Washington University social scientist Amitai Etzioni, who helped found the communitarian movement to improve community life. "The image of volunteerism and doing good is very American and very important, but it isn't really community," he says.

"Community means that in, say, crime watch, you watch my house and I watch yours. This is what can restore the fabric of society. You don't want to base it completely on altruism, which is too frail a base. Rather than making it sound negative, there should be joy involved, like friendship or good sex. It's not something that someone has to give up or put up with." ■

CURRENT SITUATION

Attacking AmeriCorps

Just before the September 1993 passage of the bill launching AmeriCorps, a national service prototype dubbed the "Summer of Service" by President Clinton went into action. Funded with $10 million, the program put some 1,500 young adults to work in 16 projects in community improvement and inner-city health counseling.

Conservative critics were quick to pounce. *(See "At Issue," p. 1097.)* Jill K. Cunningham, managing editor of *Philanthropy, Culture and Society,* described the summer project she visited in Baltimore as a "Potemkin village" where, for $130 a week and $1,000 in education benefits, the young workers performed calisthenics, ate buffet dinners and visited theme parks under the watch of TV news cameras, but spent very little time ministering to underprivileged youth. [30]

"Recruiters for the program placed a high priority on racial, ethnic and class 'diversity' in choosing participants," added another critic. "Predictably, a training session held near San Francisco quickly balkanized into black, Hispanic, Native American and gay/lesbian/bisexual caucuses, leading *The Washington Monthly* to dub the program the 'P.C. Corps.' " [31]

By 1994, AmeriCorps was up and running, awarding grants administered by the Corporation for National Service. The corporation now administers the old VISTA program and the National Civilian Community Corps, as well as a college-tutoring program called Learn and Serve America and the National Senior Service Corps, which handles programs for foster grandparents and senior companions. In 1994-95, more than 600 businesses and foundations gave more than $41 million in funds and in-kind resources to AmeriCorps.

"You'll be surprised by what one year of service does for your country, your résumé and your future," AmeriCorps bus ads tell the nation's youth. Many youngsters who sign up are attracted by the annual stipend, currently $7,500 for full-time workers, plus $4,725 in education benefits and health- and child-care services.

But in 1995, when the Republicans took over Congress, there were proposals to zero out AmeriCorps' funding — which prompted President Clinton to threaten to veto a major appropriations bill. Critics such as Sen. Grassley complained that too many AmeriCorps hirees were simply working for federal agencies. He produced figures arguing that the cost of an AmeriCorps volunteer was as high as $42,000, far more than the $17,000 estimated by the first CEO of the Corporation for National Service, Eli Segal. (Spokesmen for conservative groups testifying before Congress put the figure at $30,000, while a General Accounting Office study said that when state and local government contributions were added in, the average AmeriCorps volunteer cost some $27,000. [32])

"AmeriCorps' premise was flawed, and it was an unhealthy development in volunteerism," says Gavora of the New Citizenship Project. "Having the government pay people to volunteer won't spark civic renewal because the incentives are all wrong. It has a corrupting effect for charities that get the grants. Habitat for Humanity, for example, does great things, but now it has lobbying offices in Washington, D.C." *

AmeriCorps Gets Reprieve

As things turned out, the Republicans didn't kill off AmeriCorps. Last spring, Grassley and AmeriCorps' CEO Wofford agreed to give the program new life. The agency has promised to reduce costs from $17,629 per member to $15,000 by 1999. It also will discontinue grants to federal agencies while better policing against lobbying and partisan political activity; seek more private funds, tapping into existing civic and religious groups; boost state autonomy in running AmeriCorps programs; and resurrect the "Points of Light" awards, which have lain dormant since the Bush administration.

Wofford was plainly pleased that Congress, toward the end of this year's election-year session, restored nearly $200 million to the appropriation that funds AmeriCorps and other key National Service Corporation programs in fiscal 1997. ** This will finance as many as 11,000 new slots for the program, particularly in its work-study program for college student tutors who can implement President Clinton's campaign promise that all the nation's third-graders will get help learning to read.

The Hudson Institute's Lenkowski is dubious about AmeriCorps' goal of spearheading a new volunteerism. "I know of community volunteers who haven't even heard of the Corporation for National Service," he says. "We will know whether it's working when it's been helpful to lots of people who right now are doing things below the public's radar screen."

Continued on p. 1098

---

* Habitat for Humanity, which since 1976 has built more than 50,000 low-income homes worldwide, opened the Washington office in 1993, it says, to build relationships with other U.S. nonprofits and with the embassies of the 40 countries where it works.

** The total fiscal 1997 budget for the Corporation for National Service is $616.5 million.

At Issue:

Should the federal government try to stimulate volunteerism through its national service program?

yes

HARRIS WOFFORD
CEO, Corporation for National Service

FROM AN ADDRESS TO AMERICORPS RENEWAL CONFERENCE, OCT. 30, 1996.

Consensus has emerged at the highest levels that the problems we face — crime, drugs, teen pregnancy, illiteracy, school dropouts — can't be solved by government alone. It is only through citizens acting together that we can solve these problems.

If the era of big government is over, then the era of big citizens must begin. If we're not going to have large new government programs to create a Great Society, then we'd better have Great Citizens, who can act on the problems that are mounting and festering in our midst. . . .

When Martin Luther King saw that the battle to get the vote and end legal segregation was won, he did not rest on the victory. He raised his sights to the bigger mountain of race and class and urban problems. We too must open our eyes to the next challenge — the higher mountains we have to climb in national service. . . .

The greatest challenge is to bring national service to scale, making it truly national, unleashing the power of service on a scale large enough to really solve some of the most important problems facing our country. . . . The strategic plan adopted by our board has some big plans and big goals for the next three years: Expand the Senior Corps to at least 1 million volunteers by the year 2000; help make service part of the ethic and practice of every school and college in America; double the number of community volunteers recruited and organized through our programs; dramatically increase the number of people performing service through AmeriCorps and all the other programs of the Corporation [for National Service].

But doubling or even tripling our programs is not enough. Our vision goes far beyond that. We want a nation where service is valued and known throughout the country because it touches millions of Americans. A nation where people look first to themselves and one another to improve their lives. A nation where service is a rite of passage for every young person, a routine part of life for Americans of every age. To make this quantum leap in service, we must look beyond our own programs. National service should be a catalyst for unleashing a much larger service movement. . . . [W]e will take the best of what works around the country and try to make it contagious. We need to find the pilot programs that are working and throw the spotlight on them. What is the purpose of the pilot of a furnace? It's to ignite the whole furnace. AmeriCorps has started all kinds of pilots, some wonderful pilots, and now our job must be to ignite the whole.

no

JOHN P. WALTERS
President, The New Citizenship Project

MEMORANDUM ON "REPUBLICANS AND THE POLITICS OF MEANING," May 29, 1996.

Over the past 18 months, we've had a lot to say about the president's national service program, principally that it represents an unnecessary and corrupting intrusion of government into the voluntary sector. Our critics have scoffed, calling us narrowly partisan, or worse. But here we are, just three years after President Clinton signed into law the National and Community Service Act, and its pernicious effects are being felt. Republicans and Democrats alike are seriously at work constructing a "new paradigm" of voluntarism based not on the institutions of civil society but the institution of government. . . .

Gone is the old Tocquevillian ethic of citizens coming together voluntarily for no more compensation than the sense of satisfaction that comes from bettering the lives of themselves and their communities. In its stead . . . we are fostering a new kind of "voluntarism" that takes its direction from government, not citizens.

The reinvention of voluntarism claims to privatize the welfare state while in fact extending the reach of government into private charity, turning citizens into government-subsidized workers. . . .

This new vision of volunteerism goes hand in hand with calls for compulsory-service requirements in public high schools. And where government cannot mandate service, it will subsidize and direct it through programs like AmeriCorps. In this way, not only will our social needs be met, but individuals will be transformed into citizens by the benevolent, guiding hand of the state. . . .

Supporters of AmeriCorps have always defended the program as a new kind of bureaucratic animal, a hybrid somewhere between the private sector and the state, that would use the resources of government to strengthen the non-governmental sector. But . . . . in its three years of existence, AmeriCorps has been revealed to be riddled with bureaucracy, cost overruns and financial mismanagement — that is, with all the problems of big government. . . .

We predict that AmeriCorps will have more success transforming our understanding of voluntarism than in transforming itself. . . . [V]oluntarism cannot be bought. Giving oneself costs something; it must cost something or it is meaningless. Anything less is essentially a job. And government programs that fund such activity are called jobs programs.

New Initiatives

As an alternative to an activist government approach to social action, many in the volunteer community are backing new tax credits. In September 1995, Sen. Daniel R. Coats, R-Ind., and former Education Secretary William J. Bennett introduced the Project for American Renewal, a legislative proposal to give tax credits to individuals. The goal was to keep money needed for good works in the hands of community volunteers, rather than taxing it for redistribution by the government.

In June 1996, Coats and Rep. John R. Kasich, R-Ohio, expanded the plan into a 16-plank legislative package "pursuing a bold new definition of public compassion and fulfilling our responsibilities to the disadvantaged." It was organized around themes of effective compassion, community empowerment, fathering, mentoring and family. In May, the Senate approved one of the new planks, which permits doctors, nurses and other health professionals to provide volunteer care to poor people without risk of malpractice suits. The Coats-sponsored provision was attached to the Kennedy-Kassebaum health insurance reform bill signed by Clinton in August.

The president has expressed some interest in the Coats package. And Wofford calls it "a very constructive approach. But I'm in favor of a balanced budget, so I want to understand the full costs." Libertarians, however, have attacked the tax credits as more "social engineering." [33]

Private Efforts

In the debate over government and volunteering, it is easy to lose sight of the fact that most volunteering is orchestrated privately. In October, Youth Service America, a 7,000-group coalition founded to promote community service, opened its SERVnet site on the Internet. Like AmeriCorps, it hopes to recruit 10 million new volunteers, by offering online "chat rooms" about volunteering and matching potential volunteers with organizations.

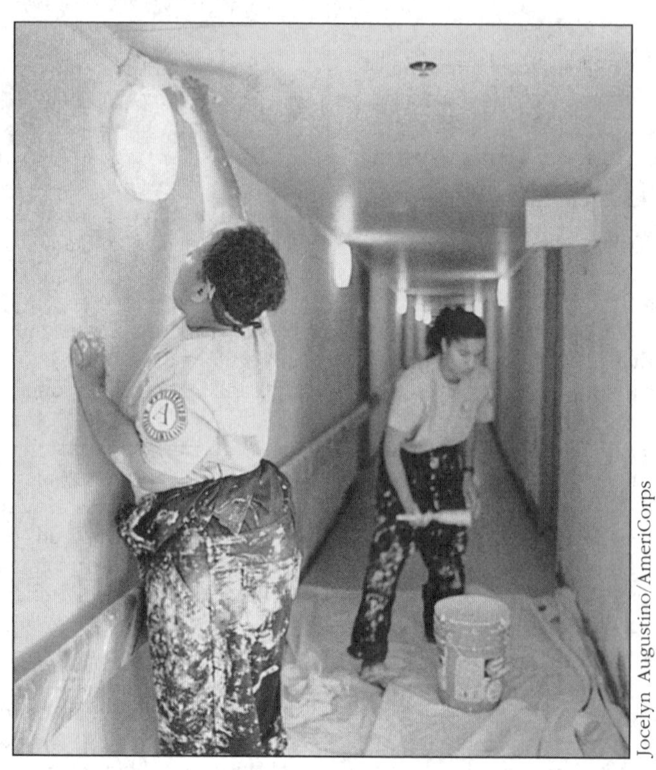

Jocelyn Augustino/AmeriCorps

AmeriCorps members help renovate an apartment for senior citizens in Washington, D.C.

In October, on National Make a Difference Day, organized by Gannett Co.'s *USA Weekend* magazine, thousands of church groups, scout troops and individual volunteers around the country turned out for such projects as painting community centers, planting shrubbery and stabilizing historic buildings.

Every April, the Share Our Strength anti-hunger group sponsors "Taste of the Nation" food and wine tastings to raise money in more than 100 cities. This fall, it joined with Second Harvest, Bread for the World and other like-minded groups to form an umbrella organization that will coordinate anti-hunger strategy under the theme "Hunger Has a Cure."

In the corporate world, AT&T inaugurated a new volunteerism policy in November, becoming the largest U.S. company to guarantee all its employees (127,000 nationwide) a day off to do volunteer work. Though volunteers must clear their day off with supervisors, they will not be required to provide proof of the activity. A company spokesman said employees had expressed rising frustration with the absence of time for volunteer work, and that next year's experiment with the plan, if successful, could be continued. [34]

Overall, fully 77 percent of the companies polled in 1993 by The Conference Board, a New York-based business group, agreed that volunteer programs benefit corporate strategic goals; and 90 percent said they build teamwork, improve morale and attract better employees.

On campuses, some 15,000 students have signed up for "Break Away," a program launched at Vanderbilt University in 1991, in which students devote their between-semester breaks to helping migrant workers or children in Head Start programs on Indian reservations. [35] At American University in Washington, the Freshman Service Experience program organizes students in such activities as serving at soup kitchens and weeding lawns at undermaintained public schools. And at Harvard, some 1,700 students work in food pantries and homeless shelters under the auspices of the Phillips Brooks House Association, a campus nonprofit that has a full-time administrative staff funded by the university.

"There's been a volunteerism boom among students in the past five years," says Roy Bahat, treasurer of the group. "And though Harvard doesn't offer academic credit for service like some schools do, there are courses in which service learning is integrated." ■

OUTLOOK

Fighting Cynicism

"I believe that the genius of the United States is basically humanitarian," novelist James Michener wrote in a recent essay. "We are idealists who have always been willing to experiment with new social orders and new solutions to old problems. We are not a horde of people who will march backward." [36]

Indeed, a recent Points of Light Foundation survey found that half of the adults not currently volunteering say they probably will in the future. But mobilizing a great army of the unpaid could be a tall order. As Lamar Alexander points out, "For every hour we volunteer, we watch TV for six hours." And many average Americans feel uncomfortable around "do-gooders." A recent review of a new biography of Pearl S. Buck, the legendary author and U.S. missionary in China, makes the discouraging but all-too-human assertion that "she got on people's nerves. She did too many good deeds." [37]

There is also the great enemy of those who give themselves to service: cynicism. It shows itself as the letdown that sets in when problems seem intractable, when the energy required by selflessness burns out. Veteran volunteers know better than anyone the challenges of sorting one's true motivations. "Guilt about the homeless on the New York streets led one woman to work long hours at a job she hated in a soup kitchen, where she came to resent the very people she hoped to serve," write activists Dass and Bush. "In the long run, guilt, as does self-gratification, often turns out to be unsatisfying as a motivator." [38]

The solace that religion offers to so many Americans suggests that religion, with its emphasis on good works, may grow in its influence on volunteerism. "Religious volunteers are a great untapped pool," says the University of Texas' Olasky. Without much fanfare, "millions of volunteers just go out and do what they can, many of them even full time. They go to their church and say, 'Here's the budget I need; will you each give me $25 a month?' "

Beckmann of Bread for the World, by contrast, says that his God wants him to be working to connect people of goodwill to the machinery of public policy in order to help poor people. "When volunteers also get directly involved in education and advocacy," he says, "they can have huge impact."

Hudson's Lenkowski prescribes a more subdued approach, citing the admonition of 12th-century Jewish theologian Maimonides that people should give quietly. "Not getting publicity is not a bad thing," he says.

Conservative activist Huffington sees volunteering as an imperative, warning that "the middle class can't be insulated from the breakdown of urban America. Giving time is critical to rebuilding the broken connection," she says. "Having an adult visit with at-risk children for an hour a week is the single most significant factor in reducing violence."

Wofford of the Corporation for National Service sees a landscape ripe for change. "Most people need to be needed for something other than

FOR MORE INFORMATION

Capital Research Center, 727 15th St. N.W., Suite 800, Washington, D.C. 20005; (202) 393-2600. This conservative, nonprofit center analyzes foundation activities and publishes newsletters reporting on issues affecting charities and volunteering.

Corporation for National Service, 1201 New York Ave. N.W., Washington, D.C. 20525; (202) 606-5000. Created in 1993 to administer the AmeriCorps program, this agency took over the existing government volunteer programs known as ACTION and the National Civilian Community Corps. It also administers the Learn and Serve program for college volunteers and the National Senior Service Corps.

Independent Sector, 1828 L St. N.W., Suite 1200, Washington, D.C. 20036; (202) 223-8100. This coalition of corporations and voluntary, charitable and philanthropic organizations promotes nonprofit-sector activities through research and advocacy.

The New Citizenship Project, 1150 17th St. N.W., Suite 510, Washington, D.C. 20036; (202) 822-8333. Chaired by conservative political strategist William Kristol, this advocacy group offers sustained criticism of the "failures" of governmental efforts to solve problems of poverty, crime and poor-quality education, promoting instead citizen-led alternatives.

Youth Service America, 1101 15th St. N.W., Suite 200, Washington, D.C. 20005. (202) 296-2992. Internet: http://www.SERVEnet.org. Founded in 1988, this alliance of organizations committed to community development and national service coordinates projects that help young people get involved in service to towns and cities.

doing for themselves," he says. "This is especially [true] in the years between adolescence and one's career, when people want to go on adventures, to test themselves and make a difference. If the volunteer world doesn't rise to this new challenge, if it just keeps pointing out that there are 90 million volunteers but doesn't mobilize them, then the cynicism about whether we can govern ourselves will deepen." ■

Notes

[1] For background, see "The Homeless," *The CQ Researcher,* Aug. 7, 1992, pp. 675-698, and "Parents and Schools," *The CQ Researcher,* Jan. 20, 1995, pp. 49-72.

[2] Annual survey of nonprofits by *The Chronicle of Philanthropy,* Oct. 31, 1996, p. 1. For background, see "Charitable Giving," *The CQ Researcher,* Nov. 12, 1993, pp. 985-1008; and "National Service," *The CQ Researcher,* June 15, 1993, pp. 553-576.

[3] Higher Education Research Institute, University of California, Los Angeles, "The American Freshman: National Norms for Fall 1995," December 1995. In addition, a 1996 study by Independent Sector found that the total number of teenagers ages 12-17 volunteering in the U.S. increased by 7 percent between 1992 and 1996, from 12.4 million to 13.3 million.

[4] *American Demographics,* June 1996, p. 4.

[5] Ram Dass and Mirabai Bush, *Compassion in Action: Setting Out on the Path of Service* (1992), p. 5.

[6] Quoted in *The Washington Post,* Oct. 21, 1996, p. B4.

[7] Quoted in *The New Yorker,* Oct. 21/28, 1996, p. 180.

[8] Column in *The Washington Post,* Oct. 24, 1996.

[9] Quoted in *Time,* June 3, 1996, p. 24.

[10] *Los Angeles Times,* Nov. 15, 1996, p. B2.

[11] Virginia Hodgkinson, Thomas H. Pollak and Lester M. Salamon, "The Impact of Federal Budget Proposals Upon the Activities of Charitable Organizations and the People They Serve, 1996-2002: The 100 Nonprofit Organizations Study," *Independent Sector,* June 15, 1995, p. 3.

[12] Jeremy Rifkin, *The End of Work* (1995), p. 263.

[13] Grassley spoke in the Senate, April 3, 1995.

[14] Julian Wolpert, "What Charity Can and Cannot Do," *Twentieth Century Fund Report,* February 1996, p. 18.

[15] For details, see "Welfare, Work and the States," *The CQ Researcher,* Dec. 6, 1996, pp. 1057-1080

[16] For background, see "The Working Poor," *The CQ Researcher,* Nov. 3, 1995, pp. 969-992.

[17] *The Chronicle of Philanthropy,* May 16, 1996. p. 44.

[18] Wolpert, *op. cit.,* p. 29.

[19] Alexis de Tocqueville, *Democracy in America* (1969 edition), edited by J.P. Mayer, pp. 512-513.

[20] Gertrude Himmelfarb, *Poverty and Compassion* (1991), p. 4.

[21] Marvin Olasky, *The Tragedy of American Compassion* (1992), p. 219.

[22] Quoted in Daniel T. Oliver, "Restoring American Voluntarism," *Alternatives in Philanthropy,* March 1994. Cornuelle's book was reissued in 1993, as the debate on national service got under way.

[23] Robert Coles, *The Call of Service: A Witness to Idealism* (1993), p. xxv.

[24] Emmett Grogan, *Ringolevio* (1990), p. 301.

[25] Bill Mosher, *Visionaries: A Companion to the Public Television Series* (1995), p. 113.

[26] American Red Cross, "Taking Volunteerism into the 21st Century," March 1990.

[27] Robert D. Putnam, "Tuning in, Tuning Out: The Strange Disappearance of Social Capital in America," *PS: Political Science and Politics,* December 1995, pp. 664-665.

[28] Lester M. Salamon, *Partners in Public Service: Government-Nonprofit Relations in the Modern Welfare State* (1995), p. 136.

[29] Sidney Verba, Kay Lehman Schlozman and Henry E. Brady, *Voice and Equality: Civic Voluntarism in American Politics* (1995), p. 334.

[30] "Adrift in Uptopia," *Philanthropy, Culture and Society,* Capital Research Center, November 1993.

[31] Jessica Gavora, "P.C. Corps," *Heterodoxy,* February 1996, Vol. 4, No. 2, published by the Center for the Study of Popular Culture, Los Angeles, Calif.

[32] See U.S. General Accounting Office, "National Service Programs: AmeriCorps USA — Early Program Resource and Benefit Information," August 1995.

[33] David Boaz, "Expensive Solutions," op-ed, *The Washington Post,* Sept. 27, 1996.

[34] *The Washington Post,* Nov. 15, 1996.

[35] *The New York Times,* "Education Life" section, Nov. 3, 1996, p. 7.

[36] James Michener, "Will the U.S. Prevail?" *Parade,* Oct. 27, 1996, p. 6.

[37] Carolyn See, writing in *The Washington Post,* Nov. 8, 1996.

[38] Dass and Bush, *op. cit.,* p. 226.

Bibliography

Selected Sources Used

Books

Coles, Robert, *The Call of Service: A Witness to Idealism,* Houghton Mifflin, 1993.

A noted Harvard University psychiatrist and children's advocate recalls his lifetime experiences as a volunteer and civil rights worker, examining such issues as "burn-out" and the portrayal of volunteerism in literature.

Dass, Ram, and Mirabai Bush, *Compassion in Action: Setting Out on the Path of Service,* Crown, 1992.

A Harvard University psychiatrist-turned-meditation guru teamed up with the head of an international service foundation to write this essay on the meaning of volunteerism in humanity's search for identity.

Garr, Robin, *Reinvesting in America: The Grassroots Movements That Are Feeding the Hungry, Housing the Homeless and Putting Americans Back to Work,* Addison-Wesley, 1995.

A Kentucky journalist-turned-anti-hunger activist traveled the country to profile dozens of local volunteer groups working in food pantries, job training programs and drug and alcohol counseling.

Himmelfarb, Gertrude, *Poverty and Compassion: The Moral Imagination of the Late Victorians,* Alfred A. Knopf, 1991.

A historian at the City University of New York examines the role of charity, social conditions and moral attitudes in 19th-century England, arguing for Victorian-style compassion as a model for modern volunteer efforts to instill character and self-sufficiency in the needy.

Mosher, Bill, *Visionaries: A Companion to the Public Television Series,* Orbis Books, 1995.

A television producer and active volunteer profiles people who committed themselves to hunger relief, anti-poverty work and comfort for the dying both in and outside the United States.

Moskos, Charles, *A Call to Civic Service: National Service for Country and Community,* The Free Press, 1988.

A Northwestern University sociologist and longtime student of the U.S. military outlined his proposal for a national service program before the Clinton administration pushed through AmeriCorps.

Olasky, Marvin, *The Tragedy of American Compassion,* Regnery, 1992.

A professor of history and journalism at the University of Texas caught the attention of House Speaker Newt Gingrich, R-Ga., with this history of American charity and volunteerism. He argues for direct involvement between volunteers and the needy rather than cash payments from government or nonprofit bureaucracies.

Salamon, Lester M., *Partners in Public Service: Government-Nonprofit Relations in the Modern Welfare State,* Johns Hopkins University Press, 1995.

A Johns Hopkins University policy professor examines cooperation between government and nonprofits in addressing social problems, arguing against current proposals to dismantle much of government's contribution.

Verba, Sidney, Kay Lehman Schlozman and Henry E. Brady, *Voice and Equality: Civic Voluntarism in American Politics,* Harvard University Press, 1995.

Political scientists from Harvard University, Boston College and the University of California at Berkeley provide mounds of data in this effort to examine why Americans get interested in politics, charities, affinity groups and volunteer organizations. They discuss the quality of each type of experience, arguing that politics allows the least amount of active participation.

Reports and Studies

Wolpert, Julian, *What Charity Can and Cannot Do,* Twentieth Century Fund, February 1996.

The conservative argument for defunding government social services and turning them over to charity is made for ideological rather than practical reasons, argues a professor at Princeton's Woodrow Wilson School of Public and International Affairs. Government is needed, he says, to bridge the geographical mismatch between needs and available resources.

The Next Step

Additional information from UMI's Newspaper & Periodical Abstracts database

AmeriCorps Program

"Any volunteers?" *The Economist,* Jan. 21, 1995, p. 32.

House Speaker Newt Gingrich, R-Ga., has made his attack on government personal by going after President Clinton's pet program, AmeriCorps. While Gingrich views AmeriCorps as coerced voluntarism, Clinton sees it as reward for good work.

Cheakalos, Christina, "Volunteers put spark in eyes of children," *Atlanta Constitution,* April 26, 1995, p. B1.

Volunteers at Benteen Elementary, near the Atlanta federal penitentiary in Grant Park, are members of AmeriCorps, President Clinton's domestic version of the Peace Corps. In the nine months they've spent at the school, AmeriCorps volunteers have painted huge, multicultural murals and quilts, built reading lofts in each of the first-grade classrooms, planted flowers, started gardens and chased hookers and drug dealers from an adjacent park.

Hamber, Fredric, "AmeriCorps' 'paid volunteers'," *San Francisco Chronicle,* July 27, 1995, p. A21.

Hamber contends that Congress should abolish AmeriCorps and says that needing to justify one's life by performing altruistic acts is a distinctly un-American notion.

Johnson, Stephen, "Volunteer work becomes priority," *Houston Chronicle,* Dec. 29, 1995, p. A34.

Midway through his 10-month tour of volunteer duty with the federal AmeriCorps program, Houstonian Daniel Sanborn, an honors student, has remained enthusiastic about interrupting his academic career to help his country.

Katz, Nancie L., "AmeriCorps program boosts needy volunteers," *Atlanta Journal Constitution,* Nov. 26, 1995, p. D3.

Katz comments on the impact AmeriCorps volunteers have had on communities such as Atlanta in light of congressional Republicans' efforts to eliminate the program.

Sanchez, Rene, "It's 'volunteer' service, but what does it cost?" *The Washington Post,* July 20, 1995, p. A25.

Few government programs have faced as many skeptical questions from the GOP as AmeriCorps, President Clinton's national service initiative. The battle over how to figure out exactly what it costs to give the 20,000 AmeriCorps members a minimum-wage salary and up to $9,500 for college tuition in exchange for the 1,700 hours of community service work they perform is discussed.

Sekhar, Anjali J., "Volunteers help 'Make a Difference' for a day," *Detroit News & Free Press,* Oct. 27, 1996, p. B1.

In Detroit, local organizations and Michigan neighborhood AmeriCorps program volunteers participated in the Oct. 26, 1996, 6th annual National Make a Difference Day. Sponsored by *USA Weekend* magazine, the event encourages volunteer work in the community.

Walters, John P., "Don't call them volunteers," *The New York Times,* Feb. 10, 1996, p. A23.

Walters discusses what he views as the failings of President Clinton's AmeriCorps national service program, and contends that the program has shown itself, in the year and a half of its existence, to be everything that is wrong with big government.

Zagaroli, Lisa, "Schools, families count on Americorps volunteers," *Detroit News & Free Press,* March 12, 1995, p. B1.

The value of the AmeriCorps program is discussed as Congress begins debate on whether the federal government should fund programs offered by AmeriCorps, President Clinton's national service project.

Volunteering as an Academic Requirement

Bacon-Blood, Littice, "Mandatory volunteerism earns both A's, F's," *New Orleans Times-Picayune,* April 1, 1996, p. A1.

Community service as a graduation requirement in St. John the Baptist and Jefferson parishes in Louisiana is part of a growing national trend. Supporters and opponents express their thoughts on the idea.

Bunce, Alan, "Mandatory volunteering: An oxymoron or a valuable lesson?" *The Christian Science Monitor,* April 26, 1996, p. 11.

Volunteerism in high school is a longstanding tradition, but a contentious aspect of it is being debated around the country in 1996: mandatory community service.

Hayes, Karen, "In a growing number of schools, volunteerism is making the grade," *The Boston Globe,* Feb. 19, 1995, p. SW1.

Despite a spate of lawsuits nationally over what some call compulsory volunteerism, administrators in public school systems in southern Massachusetts are leaning toward required community service for their students.

Hlotke, Suzanne G., "College orientation steers students to volunteerism," *Chicago Tribune,* Sept. 11, 1995, p. D3.

The 330 freshmen at North Central College in Naperville, Ill., took part in a one-day program, "Into the Streets," working at 18 different sites in the Naperville area, as well as a few in Chicago, doing some heavy lifting, a little painting and some outdoor maintenance.

Kirka, Danica, "Requiring volunteer work defeats the purpose," *Los Angeles Times,* Feb. 4, 1995, p. B7.
Comments are provided from Southern California students on a move by some area high schools to require at least a few hours of community volunteer work as a requirement for graduation.

Shen, Fern, "Md. students are failing to volunteer," *The Washington Post,* Sept. 25, 1996, p. D3.
The first class of high school students obligated to meet Maryland's community service requirement is approaching graduation. According to a state progress report, which places Montgomery County among the jurisdictions with the highest numbers of students in danger of not receiving diplomas, nearly 5,000 seniors are far from meeting their "service learning" goal by late September 1996.

Nonprofits' Response to Welfare Reform

Brunner, Lincoln, "States, nonprofits shoulder welfare-reform burden," *Christianity Today,* Feb. 5, 1996, pp. 100-101.
Wisconsin has a plan that would restructure welfare systems by requiring all able-bodied participants to work in order to receive benefits.

Sirico, Robert A., "Putting private charity back into welfare," *Detroit News & Free Press,* May 28, 1995, p. B3.
Sirico says the nation's largest non-profit groups are lobbying Washington, D.C,. with the goal of scuttling the shift from government welfare to the private sector, adding that the welfare lobby offers false choices.

Souder, Mark E., "Make giving less taxing," *The Wall Street Journal,* July 10, 1995, p. A14.
Rep. Souder, R-Ind., comments on welfare reform, suggesting that the real answer to the problem may be private charities and other nonprofit organizations. Souder says he has introduced the Giving Incentive and Volunteer Empowerment Act, which would expand tax code incentives to give and encourage more volunteer involvement in private relief efforts.

"The dependent sector," *Detroit News,* June 30, 1995, p. A8.
An editorial states that any effort to "end welfare as we know it" must resurrect the principles of independence and responsibility, which guided fraternal societies, adding that to do so will be impossible while government-funded charities with a vested interest in perpetuating themselves stay in business.

Williams, Bett A., "Positive steps," *Atlanta Journal Constitution,* Jan. 22, 1995, p. B6.
In a letter to the editor, Williams of Support To Employment Project Inc., suggests that the public should instruct Congress to consult nonprofit organizations that have been working through job training programs to break down the barriers that poverty imposes, rather than place emphasis on "welfare" reform.

Volunteering in the U.S.

Bryant, Kathryn A., "Volunteering is good citizenship," *Michigan Chronicle,* April 5, 1995, p. A9.
Bryant discusses the benefits of volunteering and comments that corporate America is demonstrating a solid commitment to volunteerism, stating that big companies are gaining an understanding of the relationship between corporate strength and corporate citizenship.

Ditmer, Joanne, "America's volunteer spirit is alive and well in Colorado," *Denver Post,* April 7, 1996, p. D1.
Ditmer discusses the extent of volunteerism in the U.S. in general and in Colorado in particular.

Gardner, Marilyn, "Families find unity volunteering together," *The Christian Science Monitor,* Nov. 9, 1995, p. 1.
A growing movement across the U.S. in 1995 involves entire families volunteering together. By including children and teenagers, parents are instilling a sense of community responsibility and enjoying family time together.

Krieger, Gary F., "Volunteerism — it's the 'in' thing — but will it work?" *American Medical News,* Feb. 20, 1995, p. 17.
Thousands of doctors volunteer their efforts in political campaigns to make their voices heard in shaping public policy. Whether this wave of physician volunteerism will have an impact is discussed.

Lee, Henry K., "Legions of volunteers serve holiday feasts to the needy," *San Francisco Chronicle,* Dec. 26, 1995, p. A18.
Christmas cheer and good tidings were plentiful on Dec. 25, 1995, as churches, soup kitchens and community groups throughout the Bay Area served holiday meals to thousands of homeless and needy families.

O'Connor, James V., "Volunteers ever vigilant to peril on the Hudson," *The New York Times,* Jan. 28, 1996, p. WC1.
The United States Volunteer Life Saving Corps has rescued people from sinking boats, put out fires and dragged the muddy river bottoms for drowning victims since 1870. Volunteers from New York's Yonkers district are described.

Puckett, Patti, "Fewer volunteers aid shelters for homeless," *Atlanta Constitution,* Nov. 15, 1995, p. B1.
The pool of people willing to work at night at homeless shelters is shrinking. This problem is so serious at two metro Atlanta shelters, the Central Night Shelter downtown and the Holy Trinity Shelter in Decatur, Ga., that organizers say the shelters may be forced to shut down.

Back Issues

Great Research on Current Issues Starts Right Here...Recent topics covered by The CQ Researcher are listed below. Before May 1991, reports were published under the name of Editorial Research Reports.

JUNE 1995
Combating Infectious Disease
Property Rights
Repetitive Stress Injuries
Regulating the Internet

JULY 1995
War Crimes
Highway Safety
Combating Terrorism
Preventing Teen Drug Use

AUGUST 1995
Job Stress
Organ Transplants
United Nations at 50
Advances in Cancer Research

SEPTEMBER 1995
Catholic Church in the U.S.
Northern Ireland Cease-Fire
High School Sports
Teaching History

OCTOBER 1995
Quebec's Future
Revitalizing the Cities
Networking the Classroom
Indoor Air Pollution

NOVEMBER 1995
The Working Poor
The Jury System
Sex, Violence and the Media
Police Misconduct

DECEMBER 1995
Teens and Tobacco
Gene Therapy's Future
Global Water Shortages
Third-Party Prospects

JANUARY 1996
Emergency Medicine
Punishing Sex Offenders
Bilingual Education
Helping the Homeless

FEBRUARY 1996
Reforming the CIA
Campaign Finance Reform
Academic Politics
Getting Into College

MARCH 1996
The British Monarchy
Preventing Juvenile Crime
Tax Reform
Pursuing the Paranormal

APRIL 1996
Centennial Olympic Games
Managed Care
Protecting Endangered Species
New Military Culture

MAY 1996
Russia's Political Future
Marriage and Divorce
Year-Round Schools
Taiwan, China and the U.S.

JUNE 1996
Rethinking NAFTA
First Ladies
Teaching Values
Labor Movement's Future

JULY 1996
Recovered-Memory Debate
Native Americans' Future
Crackdown on Sexual Harassment
Attack on Public Schools

AUGUST 1996
Fighting Over Animal Rights
Privatizing Government Services
Child Labor and Sweatshops
Cleaning Up Hazardous Wastes

SEPTEMBER 1996
Gambling Under Attack
The States and Federalism
Civic Journalism
Reassessing Foreign Aid

OCTOBER 1996
Political Consultants
Insurance Fraud
Rethinking School Integration
Parental Rights

NOVEMBER 1996
Global Warming
Clashing Over Copyright
Consumer Debt
Governing Washington, D.C.

DECEMBER 1996
Welfare, Work and the States

Back issues are available for $5.00 (subscribers) or $8.00 (non-subscribers). Quantity discounts apply to orders over ten. To order, call Congressional Quarterly Customer Service at (202) 887-8621.

Binders are available for $18.00. To order call 1-800-638-1710. Please refer to stock number 648.

Future Topics

- ***Implementing the Disabilities Act***
- ***America's Pampered Pets***
- ***Combating Scientific Misconduct***

PUBLISHED BY CONGRESSIONAL QUARTERLY INC.

Implementing the Disabilities Act

Should the scope of the ADA be narrowed?

Five years after it took effect, the Americans with Disabilities Act (ADA) has done much to make life easier for persons with physical and mental impairments. But businesses favor amending ADA, claiming that the law imposes unfair financial burdens on them. They favor limiting the number of protected disabilities and possibly also placing a cap on the money businesses must spend to accommodate the disabled. Advocates for the disabled defend the law's case-by-case approach, arguing that no single formula could meet the myriad needs of disabled persons. The architecture profession, meanwhile, is beginning to embrace the principles of "universal design." The concept enables structures to be both attractive and readily accessible to disabled and able-bodied people alike.

INSIDE THIS ISSUE

 Dec. 20, 1996 • Volume 6, No. 47 • Pages 1105-1128

Formerly Editorial Research Reports

Implementing The Disabilities Act

COVER: SALLY GROVE MAY, A PROFESSIONAL BENEFITS SPECIALIST FOR ARLINGTON COUNTY, VA., USES AN ENLARGED WORK STATION TO ACCOMMODATE HER WHEELCHAIR AND A VOICE MAIL BOX THAT ALLOWS CALLERS MORE TIME TO RESPOND. (ARLINGTON COUNTY, VA.)

THE CQ Researcher

Dec. 20, 1996
Volume 6, No. 47

The CQ Researcher (ISSN 1056-2036). Formerly Editorial Research Reports. Published weekly (48 times per year, not printed March 1, May 31, Aug. 30, Nov. 29) by Congressional Quarterly Inc., 1414 22nd St., N.W., Washington, D.C. 20037. Annual subscription rate for libraries, businesses and government is $319. Additional rates furnished upon request. Periodicals postage paid at Washington, D.C. POSTMASTER: Send address changes to The CQ Researcher, 1414 22nd St., N.W., Washington, D.C. 20037.

Implementing the Disabilities Act

BY RICHARD L. WORSNOP

THE ISSUES

When Patricia Wangsness and her husband decided to open a bagel shop in Vienna, Va., two years ago, they budgeted $70,000 for renovations.

Their plans included an oversized restroom for disabled patrons, which they thought would meet the access requirements of the Americans with Disabilities Act of 1990 (ADA). Not even close, inspectors told them. They needed *two* wheelchair-accessible restrooms — one for men, one for women.

In addition to costing $7,000 more than they had budgeted, the additional restroom displaced several seats. "Half a dozen seats may not sound like much," Wangsness says, "but we have a very small shop." In her opinion, the ADA "is not written clearly enough."

Wangsness' views are widely shared by others in the business community. "Smaller employers don't have the time and expertise to determine how to comply with the regulations, which are voluminous," says Peter Eide, manager of labor law policy for the U.S. Chamber of Commerce.

Moreover, Eide says, the law makes small businesses spend more to comply with ADA than is reasonable. "One of our big concerns is that we don't think those [ADA] regulations have been subjected to cost-benefit analysis," he says. Indeed, Wangsness noted that of her first 15,000 customers, only one used a wheelchair. [1]

Disability-rights advocates challenge the notion that ADA imposes unfair burdens on business. In a July op-ed column in *The Wall Street Journal,* Attorney General Janet Reno and former Attorney General Dick Thornburgh asserted that the law "encourages low-cost ways to solve a problem. Restaurants do not have to provide menus in Braille; waiters can read them to blind customers. A business located on the second floor of an older building need not install an elevator; it would be enough to offer curbside service to customers with disabilities." [2]

ADA's reach extends well beyond public accommodations. The statute also safeguards the rights of handicapped people in employment, public service and telecommunications (*see p. 1118*). And the ADA and older laws benefiting the disabled have added features to the urban landscape that have long since lost their novelty — sidewalk curb cuts, wheelchair lifts on buses, Braille instruction plates on everything from elevator panels to ATM machines.

Retrofitting buildings for the disabled also has raised the general public's consciousness about handicapped Americans. "Able-bodied people are getting more used to the idea of somebody with a disability being their neighbor, or the person they meet every day at the bus stop, or the co-worker in the next office," says Linda Kilb, an attorney at the Disability Rights Education and Defense Fund in San Francisco. "There is even a sense now of expecting to see people with all kinds of disabilities."

That sense is especially keen among those who have attended school since the Education for All Handicapped Children Act became law in 1975 and encouraged the "mainstreaming" of disabled children into classrooms with able-bodied children.

Nonetheless, Kilb says, "A lot of people without disabilities are still surprised by how competent disabled persons can be. They may have the abstract notion that a person with disabilities is fine, but if the person turns out to be their banker, doing a great job for them, they're somewhat shocked."

The recent national elections may also have helped to change popular perceptions of the disabled. At the Republican National Convention in San Diego, GOP presidential nominee Bob Dole spoke of the World War II wounds that crippled his right arm. In Chicago two weeks later, the Democratic National Convention heard from actor Christopher Reeve, who was paralyzed from the neck down in a 1995 riding accident. Reeve noted that President Franklin D. Roosevelt's paralysis had been concealed from the public, and urged Americans to confront the problems of the disabled.

Among the victorious Senate candidates on Nov. 5 was Georgia Democrat Max Cleland. Cleland, who won the seat being vacated by Democrat Sam Nunn, lost an arm and both legs in the Vietnam War. He visited Washington in mid-November to discuss wheelchair access issues with the Architect of the Capitol's staff and to see how fast he could make it to the Senate floor from his office. "I took it slowly, step by step, as it were," he reported. "It's very doable." [3]

Kathi Wolf, a blind writer in Falls Church, Va., is ambivalent about the attention lavished on disabled celebrities. "Americans want to admire us — to be inspired by our personal stories," she wrote recently. "But they

Work Status of Americans With Disabilities

More than 14 million of the nearly 50 million Americans with disabilities were employed in 1992, including 2.9 million with severe disabilities, according to a Census Bureau survey.

Americans with Disabilities

U.S. total	48.9 million
Under age 15	6%
Between age 15-64	60%
Between age 21-64	56%
65 and over	34%
Men	22.9 million
Women	26.0 million
People with severe disabilities	
Men	9.9 million
Women	14.2 million

Employed Persons Age 21 to 64

U.S. total	108.7 million
People with disabilities	14.3 million
Men	7.9 million
Women	6.4 million
People with a severe disability	2.9 million
Men	1.3 million
Women	1.6 million

Note: The survey sampled about 30,000 households; people with disabilities living in institutions are not included. A person with a disability is defined as having difficulty performing one or more daily living tasks; individuals completely unable to perform a task are considered to have a severe disability.

Source: National Organization on Disability, "Americans With Disabilities, 1991-1992," U.S. Census Bureau, January 1994

don't want to hear about us as people with civil rights — or who need health care, or some accommodation to toil alongside others in the workplace."[4]

There is disagreement about the number of disabled Americans. A 1994 Census Bureau report, based on data gathered in 1991-92, placed the figure at 48.9 million, or 19.4 percent of the nation's then-251.8 million population. But the Disability Statistics Rehabilitation, Research and Training Center at the University of California-San Francisco said in July that there were about 61 million disabled Americans in 1992, or 24 percent of the population.

The disparity in the survey results largely reflects differences in defining the term "disabled." Essentially, the center used a broader definition, including 2.8 million persons with "symptoms, signs and ill-defined conditions," such as "dizziness and giddiness, malaise and fatigue, nervousness and perinatal conditions and other unknown and unspecified causes."

Indeed, much of the debate over disabled rights centers on just such issues of definition. Many business executives would focus aid efforts on deaf and blind persons and those with restricted mobility. But advocates for the disabled retort that persons with mental and emotional handicaps also merit protection under the law.

As lawmakers, rights advocates and business interests consider changes in the major disability-rights laws, these are some of the questions being asked:

Should Congress narrow the scope of the Americans with Disabilities Act?

Critics of the ADA contend that it is too vague and too sweeping. Even before the measure became law, beginning in 1992, they complained about the impreciseness of its call for "reasonable accommodation" of disabled persons, or its assertion that "undue hardship" would not be required of those having to make the accommodations. At the same time, critics stressed their support of the measure's overall objectives.

Zachary D. Fasman, a lawyer representing the U.S. Chamber of Commerce, told a congressional committee that the business group "shares the goals of the authors of this act .... Full participation in our economic life by people with disabilities is essential as we face global economic challenges, as well as important for the dignity of the individuals in question."[5]

Fasman asserted, however, that the bill's definition of "reasonable accommodation" of disabled employees and job applicants is "overly broad, unclear and unnecessary." "Does the bill require employers to alter production methods to suit the needs of every disabled employee or applicant? If so, how broad must the modification be?"

Rep. Tom DeLay, R-Texas, made a similar point before another panel. "A concrete formula must be developed so that an employer can know precisely how much would have to be spent in order to 'reasonably' accommodate employees with physical and/or mental impairments," he declared. "At present, an uncertain legal standard exists, as businesses must demonstrate to the satisfaction of bureaucrats or the courts that reasonable accommodation would pose an undue hardship. Each case will have to be decided upon individually, at untold costs, not to mention time consumption." [6]

Despite such concerns, Congress did little to further clarify the standards set forth in the final versions of ADA. Steven B. Epstein, director of legal writing at the University of Illinois College of Law, has suggested four reasons for Congress' decision to turn aside business groups' objections:

- "Congress anticipated that, for the most part, reasonably accommodating employees with disabilities would not require employers to make anything more than trivial expenditures."
- "Congress believed that the undue hardship concept, as it had come to exist under the [1973] Rehabilitation Act, had worked well for 17 years. It concluded that any ambiguity which initially existed regarding its meaning and scope had been sufficiently clarified by judicial decisions."
- "[T]o the extent that the ADA undue hardship standard is not sufficiently precise, Congress decided that courts would be better able to define the standards on a case-by-case basis than it could do in one fell swoop."
- "Congress concluded that, because of the infinite permutations of disabilities, needs for accommodation and levels of employer resources, a fixed standard could not possibly be applied fairly in all situations." [7]

The debate over ADA's loosely worded standards continues unabated to this day. "The more precise the language is, the better," says the Chamber of Commerce's Eide. "Reasonable accommodation is the phrase? Well, okay, what's reasonable? That is just so unspecific, so nebulous, and there are so many factors that have to be considered that it's actually unreasonable — especially for a smaller employer."

Marriott Foundation

This young man with Down's syndrome works as a coat room attendant at a Marriott Hotel. He participated in the Bridges school-to-work transition program established by the Marriott Foundation for People with Disabilities.

A company with 100 or fewer employees "probably doesn't have somebody who spends more than a half-day per week on human resources issues — making sure that notices are posted, doing the payroll, stuff like that," he says. "So how is the company supposed to find the time and staff needed to determine what ADA says, and the regulations say, and figure out how to comply with them? That's the real problem."

Adds Mary Reed, ADA expert for the National Federation of Independent Business: "Most of our members feel they will never really know whether they're in compliance with the law, so they often end up in court."

Another problem, in Eide's view, is that former substance abusers are covered by ADA. "The ADA regulations need to be reassessed in light of cost-benefit analysis and other regulatory-review procedures," he says. "Congress should enlarge and level the playing field for the disabled people who need help the most — those who require special equipment to be mobile and to work. And we have to ask ourselves, 'To what extent is being a former abuser of drugs or alcohol a genuine disability?' "

Supporters of ADA insist that no sweeping changes are needed. "The law was very carefully crafted, and in fact was considered by two Congresses before passage," says Kilb of the disability rights fund. "There were extensive hearings, at which members of the business community and coalitions representing business groups presented their views. The law is very carefully balanced to include things like different requirements for new construction and alterations in existing facilities, which is intended to recognize the cost problem of altering existing facilities. That's just one example of the many balancings in the law."

As for the "undue hardship" standard, Kilb notes that the term "was taken directly out of Section 504 of the

Hearing and Vision Problems Most Common

*Nearly four times as many disabled Americans have vision and hearing problems as use wheelchairs or have difficulty walking, according to the Census Bureau.**

■ Used a wheelchair	1.5 million
Women	919,000
Men	575,000
■ Used a cane, walker or crutches for six months or longer	4.0 million
■ Even when wearing corrective lenses, had difficulty seeing words or letters in ordinary newsprint	8.1 million
■ Even when wearing corrective lenses, could not see the words and letters in newsprint at all	1.6 million
■ Had difficulty hearing a normal conversation with another person	10.0 million
■ Could not hear what is said in a normal conversation	924,000

* *The data cover individuals age 15 and over not living in institutions.*

Source: National Organization on Disability, "Americans With Disabilities, 1991-1992," U.S. Census Bureau, January 1994

1973 Rehabilitation Act, where we had both the regulatory history and almost 20 years of judicial interpretation. So, I think the complaints that the term is vague stem from the lack of a formulaic rule. That is, there's no provision saying you have to spend $100 per employee, or something like that.

"But the absence of a formula doesn't mean 'undue hardship' is vague, because the factors that are to be considered are very clearly set out," Kilb says. "Also, there has been a lot of case law under 504, interpreting how those factors have been applied to various situations."

As Kilb sees it, the point of ADA "is to create an atmosphere for thoughtful consideration of access. That can never be formulaic. If it does become formulaic, I think the purpose of the law would be defeated. That's because what works in one employment environment may be utterly inappropriate in another."

Reed strongly disagrees. "We'd like to see the law amended to include a dollar cap for terms like undue hardship," she says. "We'd also like to see a list of all the specific disabilities that are covered by the law. Right now there is no such comprehensive list, so there is a vast number of potentially protected conditions that an employer has to make sure he is covered for.

"For most people, 'disability' means wheelchairs, blindness or deafness. But it can also mean mental illness, alcoholism or obesity — conditions that are much more difficult for a small business to deal with."

Defenders of ADA contend that many complaints about the law's requirements are baseless. For example, Reno and Thornburgh noted that critics often claim the law demands "extensive renovation of all state and local government buildings." Actually, "ADA requires all government programs, not all government buildings, to be accessible. Local governments need not do anything that would result in an undue financial burden. A town library . . . need not provide elevators to reach upper floors, so long as librarians are available to retrieve books for patrons who use wheelchairs." [8]

Another "myth," says the President's Committee on Employment of People with Disabilities, is that ADA forces business and government to hire unqualified people. In fact, according to the committee, "No unqualified job applicant or employee with a disability can claim employment discrimination under the ADA. Employees or job applicants must meet all the necessary requirements of the job and perform the essential functions of the job with or without reasonable accommodation. No accommodation must be provided if it would result in an undue hardship on the employer." [9]

John Palenicek, senior legislative and federal affairs officer for the American Psychological Association, says concerns about the scope of ADA coverage are overblown. "The ADA clearly states that employees must be capable of fulfilling the requirements of their job," he says. "So if an individual has a personality disorder, and nothing else, they are not protected under the law — a confusing point for some employers.

"For instance, if a person is defiant,

chronically late or otherwise difficult to deal with, that behavior is not, by itself, protected by ADA," Palenicek says. "However, if the personality disorder stems from an underlying medical condition, such as traumatic brain injury, the individual is protected. The Equal Employment Opportunity Commission's guidelines clearly state that undesirable personality traits are not disabilities covered under the ADA unless they are the result of some sort of underlying impairment."

Jay Cutler, director of government relations for the American Psychiatric Association, also opposes proposals to limit ADA's coverage to those with physical impairments. "We are absolutely, unequivocally opposed" to such proposals, Cutler says. "We cannot understand why you would separate out mental illness from physical illness. It is beyond anyone's comprehension, unless it reflects ignorance based on fear, stigma and a refusal to deal with the realities of life."

Have job opportunities improved for disabled people since passage of the Americans with Disabilities Act?

Because a chief aim of the ADA was to prohibit job discrimination against the severely disabled (*see p. 1117*), it was hoped that employment opportunities for qualified persons with disabilities would expand.

ADA supporters argued, and continue to argue, that hiring the handicapped makes bottom-line sense. "Each year, the federal government spends 40 times more money to support [unemployed] people with disabilities . . . than it spends to assist them to prepare for or find employment," the President's Committee on Employment of People with Disabilities asserted. "The lack of labor-force participation [by] people with disabilities costs our nation's economy over $200 billion annually." [10]

In the years since ADA went into effect, the law appears to have helped to open more employment doors to the disabled. According to Census Bureau data released in July, the number of employed persons with severe disabilities increased from 2.9 million in 1991 (23.3 percent of all severely disabled individuals of working age) to 3.7 million in 1994 (26.1 percent) — a gain of 800,000 persons. The number of employed persons with non-severe disabilities rose more modestly during the same period, from 11.4 million (76 percent of the working-age total) to 11.7 million (76.9 percent). [11]

Dole Foundation for Employment of People with Disabilities

Minor changes in his work station enabled Todd Gauchet to become an accomplished data entry clerk.

Tony Coelho, chairman of the President's Committee on Employment of People with Disabilities, hailed the findings as "the first true measure of the ADA's impact" on employment of the disabled. "We must renew our confidence in this unalterable assertion of human rights," he said, "and move vigorously ahead with the implementation of the principles of the ADA in the workplace." [12]

Equal Employment Opportunity Commission Commissioner Paul Steven Miller also voiced satisfaction with the survey results, but he added a caveat. "Although these numbers are encouraging," he said, "we clearly have a long way to go before ADA's vision of inclusion, empowerment and independence is realized." [13]

A Sept. 3 report by the General Accounting Office (GAO), the congressional watchdog agency, cited reasons why it may be difficult to put significant numbers of the severely disabled to work. Persons with disabilities who rely on federal income-support programs such as Social Security Disability Insurance (DI) or Supplemental Security Income (SSI), the report stated, may "be discouraged from attempting to work by the prospect of losing their benefits, particularly their health insurance coverage. Disability advocates and rehabilitation counselors believe that the fear of losing medical coverage is one of the most significant barriers to the participation of SSI and DI beneficiaries in the Vocational Rehabilitation program, their return to work, or both." [14]

Lack of coordination among the 26 federal programs providing employment aid to the disabled dilutes their effectiveness, according to GAO. "Many of the agencies administering these 26 employment-focused programs did not require or collect data on program outcomes — specifically, data on whether participants got jobs and kept them, what wages they received and

The Etiquette of Offering Help

"Excuse me. Would you mind hailing me a cab?" The request comes from a blind man standing at a busy intersection with his guide dog. Naturally, you are happy to oblige. Moments later a cab stops, the man and his dog get in, and you congratulate yourself for having done something nice.

But encounters between disabled and able-bodied persons may not go so smoothly. Suppose, say, that a person using a wheelchair was at that same intersection, poised to cross the street. Many bystanders would hesitate to offer help, for fear of bungling the job or of being rebuffed.

"This fear is not entirely unrealistic," according to public health specialists Chalda Maloff and Susan MacDuff Wood. Indeed, they write, it is "definitely possible for a well-meaning helper to do more harm than good." [1]

Most would-be Good Samaritans, they note, are unfamiliar with wheelchair operation. "Persons accustomed to pushing shopping carts tend not to realize that wheelchairs are less steady, and that hitting even a small bump in the ground can send the occupant face down onto the pavement." [2]

Before extending a helping hand to a person with limited mobility, the authors advise, "Consider whether you can cope with the consequences if it turns out that your gusto has outstripped your physical prowess. If you pop your football knee carrying your friend up a flight of steps, will you be able to find two people to carry you both back down?"

Similarly, they suggest that able-bodied persons dining with a mobility-impaired person in a restaurant volunteer their services before ordering. "Your dinner companion may opt to forgo the beef stew and order the barbecued ribs if he knows ahead of time that someone is available to help engineer his attack." [3]

For the visually impaired, they write, "the single most useful thing a friend or stranger can do . . . is to furnish relevant information about the immediate surroundings, such as showing where the towel dispenser or hand drier is located in a restroom." Hearing-impaired people, they note, prefer to be addressed in a moderately loud voice, but not a shout — "shouting makes words sound less distinct and tends to contort lip movements." Above all, "Take care not to drop your voice at the end of a sentence, since the last two or three words can be the most important." [4]

Wood, an epidemiologist at the University of California-Berkeley School of Public Health, says that able-bodied Americans "don't necessarily feel more comfortable about knowing what to do when they're with a disabled person than they did before passage of the Americans with Disabilities Act in 1990. It's certainly true that more handicapped people are able to participate in mainstream activities. But I don't think it follows that the able-bodied world has become more at ease with them."

In her view, able-bodied people are more aware that a disabled person "might need to use the bathroom, or the changing room, more urgently than they do. But that's not the same as pursuing friendship with disabled people, or having them over for dinner."

---

[1] Chalda Maloff and Susan MacDuff Wood, *Business and Social Etiquette With Disabled People* (1988), pp. 7-8.

[2] *Ibid.*, p. 11.

[3] *Ibid.*, p. 21.

[4] *Ibid.*, p. 97.

---

whether they received employee benefits such as health insurance." [15]

Moreover, the GAO reported, the lack of coordination made disabled job seekers needlessly jump through extra hoops. "Because disabled people with disabilities often face multiple barriers to employment, including insufficient job training, lack of transportation and employer discrimination, they may require services from more than one program to make employment feasible," the GAO said. "However, each program has its own eligibility requirements, and applicants must often establish eligibility separately because no effective mechanism exists to promote or ensure coordination." [16]

Are architects and building owners meeting their legal obligations to the disabled?

Since the Architectural Barriers Act (ABA) became law in 1968, businesses and governments have been required to make many new buildings accessible to the disabled and to retrofit existing structures. Nonetheless, complaints still surface about violations of the ABA and of subsequent laws that broadened its scope.

Last February, for instance, the Justice Department filed civil suits against Days Inns of America Inc. and its parent company, Hospitality Franchise Systems Inc., accusing them of ignoring the ADA in building five hotels. The alleged violations included overly steep wheelchair ramps, failure to provide visual fire alarms for the hearing impaired and restrooms too small for wheelchairs.

"Not only do these violations impede access, in many cases it is unsafe for guests with disabilities to stay at these hotels," said Deval L. Patrick, assistant attorney general for civil rights. "We just cannot ignore a blatant disregard for the law. . . . These hotels were built well after the [ADA] was passed" in 1990. [17]

In a similar case, the Paralyzed Veterans of America recently sued the owners, operators and architects of a sports facility under construction in downtown Washington. The group alleged that the MCI Arena, scheduled to open for next year's National Basketball Association and National Hockey League games, falls short of ADA standards because fans in wheelchairs will have obstructed views. A ruling in the recently concluded U.S. District Court trial is expected shortly.

Stuart Binstock, vice president for federal affairs at the American Institute of Architects (AIA), argues that violations of ADA standards often are inadvertent. "Our members tell us they don't know if they've complied with the ADA until a project is completed, and they either get sued or don't get sued by the Justice Department or a private individual," he says. "In its current form, the law isn't clear enough."

Indeed, just three months before the U.S. Holocaust Memorial was to open in Washington, D.C., in 1993, officials discovered that ADA requirements had not been met in several cases, requiring expensive adjustments. There were bathrooms that didn't meet access requirements, missing handrails and auditorium seating and water fountains that needed alterations. The most complicated problem was the Hall of Remembrance, which had not been equipped with a wheelchair lift.[18]

Another factor that contributes to ADA-linked litigation, Binstock feels, is that "architectural education is not keeping up with architectural practice." But Martin Moeller, executive director of the Association of Collegiate Schools of Architecture, says that laws like the ADA "pretty much have permeated the architectural curriculum."

Moeller notes that architecture schools "must address disability issues in their programs in order to maintain their accreditation." As a result, "You'll find that disability shows up, at least implicitly, in virtually everything that happens in the design studio — and in a lot of other courses as well." Moeller adds that almost every architecture student is assigned a renovation or retrofitting project in which the needs of the disabled are spotlighted.

At present, it's difficult to accurately assess how knowledgeable practicing architects are about accommodating the disabled. Thomas Lowther, AIA's director of continuing education, notes that the continuing-education requirements for the AIA's 57,000 members will not be fully phased in until the end of 1997.

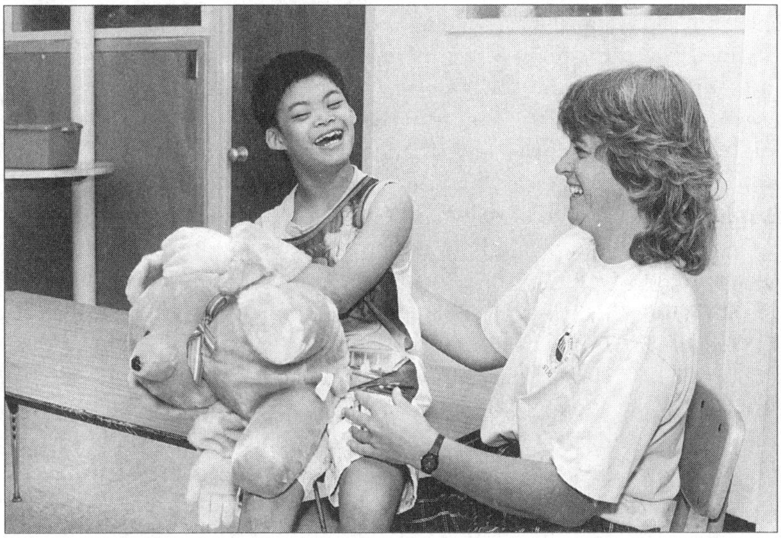

As the education data accumulate in AIA computer files, researchers will be able to tell how much time member architects spent on courses dealing with disability rights. "At this point, we're just in the infancy of being able to do that," Lowther says. "Lots of architects may have signed up for courses in the last year or two and didn't report it, because they didn't have to. But two years from now, I'll be able to supply hard data on any continuing-ed programs our members have taken." ■

Arlington County, Va.

Molly McDonald, a hearing-impaired recreation specialist for Arlington County, Va., uses an amplified telephone and a portable telephone-teletype (TTY) machine.

BACKGROUND

Early Initiatives

As recently as the 1950s, popular attitudes toward disability were tinged with ignorance, fear and superstition.

"Age-old beliefs that the birth of a disabled child was a form of divine retribution still persisted, especially amongst the older generation," British television producers Steve Humphries and Pamela Gordon wrote. "Some believed that disability represented a curse on the family, God's punishment for evil deeds committed in the past. A few were of the opinion that children with disabilities — often those who had epileptic fits — were possessed by the devil. This kind of myth and folklore had a long history reaching back to ancient civilization and the early days of Christianity, when physical disability was closely associated with spiritual uncleanliness and evil."[19]

Mental disability stirred similar feelings. During the Middle Ages, for instance, the mentally retarded and the mentally ill were lumped together and often persecuted. But in the late 15th and early 16th centuries, custodial facilities for mentally deficient persons were organized in France by St. Vincent de Paul.[20]

Programs of care for the disabled developed slowly in the United States. For the most part, the task was left to family members and a small band of social reformers. Prominent among this group were Thomas Hopkins Gallaudet, who established a school for the deaf in Hartford, Conn., in 1817, and John Dix Fischer, who started the New England Asylum for the Blind in Boston in 1829.[21]

These private initiatives stood in sharp contrast to the government's hands-off stance. Indeed, after crusader Dorothea Dix persuaded Congress to authorize funds for public mental hospitals, President Franklin Pierce vetoed the measure in 1854. Caring for the physically and mentally disabled, declared the president, was not a federal responsibility.

Disabled Veterans Prompt Smith-Fess Act

Pierce's hands-off policy remained conventional wisdom in Washington until just after World War I. As thousands of disabled veterans returned to the United States, demands rose for federal aid to the handicapped. Congress responded by approving the Vocational Rehabilitation Act of 1920, popularly known as the Smith-Fess Act, which established the first broad-based federal program to assist disabled persons.[22]

Services available under Smith-Fess included job training, counseling and guidance, job placement and the provision of artificial limbs and other prosthetic devices. However, it did not include medical services designed to restore physical capacities. States were required to match federal grants dollar-for-dollar.

At the time the act was passed, only 12 states had their own rehabilitation laws. By 1938, however, all of the then-48 states had set up programs and were receiving federal funds. Meanwhile, the original legislation, enacted on an experimental basis, had been made permanent by the Social Security Act of 1935.

The World War II manpower shortage and the discovery of new methods for treating servicemen disabled in battle inspired the first major changes in Smith-Fess. The vehicle was the Barden-LaFollette Act of 1943, which authorized state agencies in the rehabilitation program to offer medical services aimed at reducing or even eliminating disabilities. Previously, the approach had been to accept the disability and "train around" it.

Other innovations under the 1943 law included help for the blind and for persons suffering psychiatric illness. Barden-LaFollette also made a change in the 50-50 financing formula, requiring the federal government to reimburse the states for their entire costs of administering vocational rehabilitation programs. Other costs were to be shared equally, as before, by the states and the federal governments.

In 1947, a special President's Committee on the Handicapped was established at the suggestion of President Harry S Truman. The committee called attention to the job needs and capabilities of disabled persons; encouraged businesses to hire the disabled; and coordinated the efforts of federal, state and private agencies in helping disabled Americans find suitable employment. In 1962 the committee was reconstituted by President John F. Kennedy as the President's Committee on Employment of the Handicapped (now the President's Committee on Employment of People with Disabilities).

The Vocational Rehabilitation Amendments of 1954, proposed by President Dwight D. Eisenhower, represented another milestone in disability-rights legislation. The measure greatly expanded the existing vocational rehabilitation program, authorizing, for example, the creation of clinics for the treatment of speech, hearing, cardiac and other disorders. The House and the Senate approved the bill by voice vote.

Sweeping New Laws

As the civil rights movement gained force in the early 1960s, it not only improved prospects for African-Americans but also began to reshape the outlook of disability-rights groups. For 40 years, advocates for the disabled had focused primarily on bread-and-butter issues, primarily jobs. Increasingly, though, they came to view their cause as a struggle for equal opportunity, not just rehabilitation.

Thus, disability-rights activists turned their attention to the architectural barriers that frustrated handicapped people. Most cities and towns were virtually inaccessible to the disabled, especially those using wheelchairs. Curbs, stairs, narrow doors, telephone booths, high elevator buttons, tight corners in hallways, narrow restroom stalls and high drinking fountains were constant reminders to the handicapped that they were discriminated against.

Mounting awareness of the problem spurred Congress to approve the Architectural Barriers Act in 1968. The measure required all public buildings financed wholly or in part with federal funds to be built or remodeled to be accessible to the physically handicapped. Similarly, the Urban Mass Transportation Act of 1970 required all public transportation services to be accessible to the disabled in order to qualify for federal funding.

Education for All Handicapped Children Act

As the idea of "mainstreaming" the disabled into society gained currency, so did initiatives to educate disabled children in the public schools. Prodded by a rising number of court verdicts giving handicapped children the right to be educated, Congress in 1975 passed the Education for All Handicapped Children Act. * It required the

Continued on p. 1116

* When it was amended in 1992, the law was renamed the Individuals with Disabilities Education Act (IDEA).

Chronology

19th Century

Attending to disabled persons is generally considered the responsibility of family members.

1817
Thomas Hopkins Gallaudet opens a school for the deaf in Hartford, Conn.

1854
President Franklin Pierce vetoes a bill to allocate federal funds to public mental hospitals.

1920s-1930s

Disabled servicemen returning to the U.S. after World War I spur demands for government action to aid all handicapped individuals.

1920
Disabled American Veterans (DAV) is founded.

1920
President Woodrow Wilson signs the Vocational Rehabilitation Act, which authorizes grants to the states for rehabilitation activities.

1935
President Franklin D. Roosevelt signs the Social Security Act, which specifies income-support benefits for disabled workers and authorizes vocational rehabilitation programs on a permanent basis.

1940s-1950s

World War II gives fresh impetus to efforts on behalf of the nation's disabled population.

1943
Roosevelt signs the Barden-LaFollette Act, which authorizes state agencies providing vocational rehabilitation services to offer medical treatments aimed at reducing or eliminating disabilities.

1945
President Harry S Truman signs legislation designating the first week in October of each year as National Employ the Physically Handicapped Week. (Under 1988 legislation, each October is now National Disability Employment Awareness Month.)

1947
The President's Committee on the Handicapped (now called the President's Committee on Employment of People with Disabilities) is established.

1954
President Dwight D. Eisenhower signs the Vocational Rehabilitation Amendments, greatly enlarging the existing rehab program.

1960s-1970s

The federal government becomes increasingly active in safeguarding the rights of the disabled.

1968
President Lyndon B. Johnson signs the Architectural Barriers Act, aimed at removing obstacles to disabled persons in federal buildings.

1970
President Richard M. Nixon signs the Urban Mass Transportation Act, which requires that public transportation be accessible to the disabled in order to qualify for federal funding.

1973
Nixon signs the Rehabilitation Act. Among other provisions, the measure requires federal contractors to take affirmative action to employ the disabled.

1975
President Gerald R. Ford signs the Education for All Handicapped Children Act.

1980s-1990s

The most far-reaching disability rights law yet enacted ignites a controversy.

1988
President Ronald Reagan signs the Fair Housing Act Amendments, adding persons with disabilities to those protected from discrimination in housing.

1990
President George Bush signs the Americans with Disabilities Act (ADA), describing it as "one of the most important pieces of legislation to ever reach Capitol Hill."

1991
Bush signs the Civil Rights Act of 1991, which enables disabled workers to bring cases alleging intentional discrimination under the ADA.

1992
The Education for All Handicapped Children Act is renamed the Individuals with Disabilities Education Act (IDEA).

1996
Failure to revise IDEA leaves existing disciplinary policies for disabled students in place.

Giving a Boost to Disabled Test Takers

Not all test takers are born equal. That's why youngsters certified as learning disabled can get extra time to finish exams.

Under the 1990 Americans with Disabilities Act (ADA), students with a wide range of impairments, including learning disability (LD) and attention-deficit disorder (ADD) as well as limited sight or hearing, are eligible for special accommodation when taking college-admissions exams such as the Scholastic Assessment Test (SAT). LD students can receive additional (or sometimes unlimited) time to complete the test.

Just how much of a marginal boost the extra time confers is open to question. According to some experts, coping with the pressure of a timed test forms part of the challenge of getting a high score. Others say that a firm grasp of the test material is paramount. If the test taker doesn't know the answer to a question, this reasoning holds, a few more minutes won't help him find it.

Some media accounts give the impression that college admissions testers are being overwhelmed by suspect applications for LD status. "With a note from a doctor and some documentation from the high school, the teen [claiming ADD] can qualify for an extended or untimed Scholastic [Assessment] Test in a private, distraction-free room," *Forbes* magazine reported this summer. [1]

In fact, it's not that simple, says June Zumoff, associate program director of SAT services for students with disabilities at the Educational Testing Service (ETS) in Princeton, N.J. "Our requirements are that a student has to have a documented disability on file at the school, and that they are receiving similar accommodations in classroom tests for what they're asking for on the SAT," she says. "For example, if a student says she wants a large-type test, we ask whether she usually gets to take large-type tests at her school. The same applies to extra time and other test-taking accommodations."

However, Zumoff adds, students without a documented history of disability can still qualify for special consideration in taking the SAT. Private schools that receive no public funding, she notes, are not required to cater to the needs of their disabled pupils. "We can't deny these kids just because their school doesn't give them accommodation."

College applicants seeking special accommodation on the SAT may appeal to ETS, which refers such requests to a three-member review panel. "By far the majority of cases are denied," Zumoff says, "because the documentation does not support the stated need."

[1] Dyan Machan and Luisa Kroll, "An Agreeable Affliction," *Forbes*, Aug. 12, 1996, p. 148.

Continued from p. 1114

states to provide free education to all disabled children.

The legislation also stipulated that federal funds could be used to pay the "excess" costs of educating disabled children after state and local school districts spent as much money on each handicapped child as they did on other children.

Although he hinted at a veto, President Gerald R. Ford signed the bill after both houses of Congress approved a conference report with enough votes to guarantee a veto override. "Unfortunately, this bill promises more than it can deliver," Ford said. "Even the strongest supporters of this measure know as well as I that they are falsely raising the expectations of the groups affected by claiming authorization levels which are excessive and unrealistic." [23] In particular, Ford criticized the measure's "vast array of detailed, complex and costly administrative requirements, which would unnecessarily assert federal control over traditional state and local government functions."

In expanding the federal government's role in handicapped education, the act significantly changed national policy in the field. In the same spirit, Congress set an ambitious schedule of increasing levels of assistance to states and local schools to help handicapped education. The idea was that the federal commitment would expand along with the national requirements for educating all handicapped children.

Civil Rights Act for the Disabled

In 1973, meanwhile, Congress had passed the Rehabilitation Act, hailed as the "civil rights act for the disabled." The measure barred discrimination against the handicapped by any program or activity receiving federal funds. But progress in implementing the law was stalled for nearly four years. Regulations were drawn up by the Ford administration, but President Jimmy Carter in 1977 called for more study before putting them into effect.

Organizations supporting the disabled staged demonstrations across the country to pressure the Carter administration to implement the law, and the strategy evidently worked. In April 1977, Secretary of Health, Education and Welfare Joseph A. Califano Jr. signed the regulations. The law, he said, "represents the first federal civil rights law protecting the rights of handicapped persons and reflects a national commitment to end discrimination on the basis of handicap. The language . . . is almost identical to the comparable non-discrimination provisions of Title VI of the Civil Rights Act of 1964 and Title IX of the Education Amendments of 1972 [applying to racial discrimination and discrimination in education on the basis of sex.] It establishes a mandate to . . . bring handicapped persons into the mainstream of American life."

Under the regulations, schools receiving federal funds had to ensure that all programs in existing buildings were accessible. If program accessibility could not be accomplished, existing buildings had to be modified within three years. In addition, the regulations required that all handicapped children be provided with a free education, in their neighborhood school if possible. Universities were prohibited from discriminating against handicapped persons in any area of campus life. *

In the past, disabled children often had been placed in segregated, special schools. But such arrangements, it was argued, had profoundly negative effects on children's self-image as well as their ability to learn. Like civil rights legislation of the 1960s, civil rights laws for the disabled rejected segregated education.

One of the most controversial provisions of the Rehabilitation Act was Section 504, which directed federally funded institutions, including schools, to make all their facilities physically accessible to the handicapped. Specific changes were to be determined by the facts of each situation. In general, schools had to provide elevators for students in wheelchairs, Braille markers for blind students and adjustable-volume telephones for the hearing-impaired.

However, schools did not have to make every room handicapped-accessible. But they had to make sure that all educational and extracurricular programs were accessible. In other words, schools were not required to have an elevator in every building. But they did have to make sure that the only calculus course, for example, did not meet in an inaccessible classroom.

When Congress extended the Education for All Handicapped Children Act in 1986, it included a new program for the estimated 70,000 disabled children ages 3-5 who were still not receiving special education. Though states were not required to provide for those preschoolers, the law authorized significantly higher grants to those that did.

Under separate legislation enacted the same year, parents were allowed to recover the legal cost of defending the education rights of handicapped children. The bill was drafted in response to the 1984 Supreme Court ruling in *Smith v. Robinson,* in which the court held that nothing in existing law allowed parents to recover their attorneys' fees when they prevailed in court cases brought under the Education for All Handicapped Children Act.

Dole Foundation

Hearing-impaired students learn the airline catering business at the Lexington Center for Vocational Services in Jackson Heights, N.Y., funded by the Dole Foundation for Employment of People with Disabilities.

Fair Housing Act Amendments of 1988

In approving the Fair Housing Act Amendments of 1988, Congress supplied a missing link in the chain of civil rights available to the disabled. As originally enacted in 1968, the act had barred discrimination in the sale or rental of housing based on race, color, religion, sex or national origin.

As amended in 1988, the law was broadened to prohibit housing discrimination against the handicapped and families with young children. It also empowered the Department of Housing and Urban Development (HUD) to penalize those who discriminated in the sale or rental of housing. Specifically, the law:

• Required newly constructed dwellings with four or more units to include features such as wheelchair accessibility, reinforced bathroom walls to accommodate grab bars and accessible light switches, electrical outlets and thermostats.

• Required landlords to treat people with disabilities just as they treated the able-bodied.

• Prohibited landlords from asking current tenants or people applying for housing about their age, health, or ability to live independently.

• Required landlords to make reasonable accommodations in rules and procedures, and to allow reasonable modification of the premises, at the request of tenants with disabilities. *

* Under the regulations, "handicapped" was defined as any mental or physical impairment that limited at least one "major life activity," such as walking, seeing, hearing, speaking and performing manual tasks; alcoholism and drug addiction were included in the definition.

* A reasonable accommodation could include posting of large-print notices for a vision-impaired tenant; a reasonable modification could mean installing a wheelchair ramp at the building entrance.

Tearing Down Obstacles to Recreation

Consider the picnic table. For able-bodied Americans, it's an integral part of summertime, and no problem. For the disabled, it's an almost insurmountable barrier.

But picnicking is beginning to get easier for people with disabilities. Just as handicapped-access laws have made it possible for millions of disabled Americans to work and travel, changes in the recreation scene are enabling people with disabilities to take part in a wide array of outdoor activities.

Picnic tables, for example, are being designed to stretch a foot longer at one end or with cut-out sections in their benches to accommodate picnickers in wheelchairs.

"You can picnic, and it doesn't look like some big ugly obstacle," said Cindy Walsh, access supervisor for the Fairfax County (Va.) Park Authority. "We're trying to keep it as natural as possible." [1]

Similarly, some paths and trails in public recreation areas have been paved over for wheelchair users and persons who use canes or walkers. These and other innovations were inspired largely by the 1990 Americans with Disabilities Act (ADA), which barred discrimination against the disabled in employment, telecommunications, public services and public accommodations.

Other federal laws also have expanded recreational opportunities for the disabled. The Amateur Sports Act of 1978 sought to "encourage and provide assistance to amateur athletic programs and competition for handicapped individuals, including . . . the expansion of opportunities for meaningful participation by handicapped individuals in programs of athletic competition for able-bodied individuals."

The United States Olympic Committee (USOC) now supports seven sports organizations for disabled athletes, including the Special Olympics. "I think we've done a lot to generate awareness and understanding for the disabled athlete at all levels," says Mark Shepherd, the USOC's director of disabled sports services. [2]

The USOC's efforts on behalf of disabled athletes were showcased in Atlanta, Ga., in July and August. Lighting the Olympic flame at the opening ceremonies of the centennial Summer Games was former Olympic and world heavyweight boxing champion Muhammad Ali, his hand trembling from Parkinson's disease.

At the Paralympic Games, held in Atlanta later that month, the flame-lighting honors fell to Mark Wellman, 36, an American mountain climber who is paralyzed from the waist down. This did not prevent him from scaling the 184-foot Olympic tower hand over hand while carrying a lighted torch between his legs. After Wellman ignited the flame, paralyzed actor Christopher Reeve pronounced the Games open. [3]

"We are poised to do even more in the future," Shepherd says. "As we integrate disabled sports into non-disabled sports at various levels of competition, I think we have a golden opportunity to validate the disabled athlete's quest for excellence."

The Paralympics, Shepherd feels, did that to some degree, notwithstanding the limited media coverage. In his view, disabled athletes "are going through the painstaking process of proving they are a part of society in all its facets — employment, sport, recreation — and not just rehabilitation."

[1] Quoted by Patricia Davis, "Less of An Obstacle Course and a Lot More Fun," *The Washington Post*, July 27, 1996, p. A16.

[2] For background, see "Centennial Olympic Games," *The CQ Researcher*, April 5, 1996, p. 306.

[3] Reeve, who was paralyzed from the neck down in a riding accident, also participated in this year's Wall Street Challenge Cup sailing benefit for the disabled.

The 1988 legislation also safeguarded landlords' rights by specifying that the law didn't require a dwelling to be made available to an individual whose residency "would constitute a direct threat to the health or safety of other individuals" or "would result in substantial physical damage to the property of others."

ADA Extends Rights

Rewarding years of effort by disability-rights and public health groups, Congress in 1990 approved the Americans with Disabilities Act, designed to extend civil rights protections to an estimated 43 million persons. ADA was notable more for its sweep than its novelty. In essence, it codified many regulatory concepts and guidelines from Section 504 of the Rehabilitation Act of 1973 and other predecessor laws and extended the Section 504 prohibition against discrimination in the private sector. [24]

ADA barred discrimination against the disabled in employment, public services and public accommodations, and required that telecommunications be made accessible to those with speech and hearing impairments through the use of special relay systems.

Moreover, the measure required employers to make "reasonable accommodations" for disabled workers, but not changes that would involve "undue hardship" — language borrowed from existing disability-rights legislation. The employment provisions were to take effect in two years for employers of 25 or more people and in four years (1994) for employers of 15-24.

Although it was modeled after the 1964 Civil Rights Act, ADA went well beyond that landmark statute. Its public accommodations section applied not only to the restaurants, lodgings, places of entertainment and gas stations covered by the earlier law but also to museums, sports stadiums and arenas, doctors' offices and hospitals, dry cleaners, drug stores and other retail and service establishments.

Furthermore, businesses were required to make new facilities accessible to the disabled and to make whatever "readily achievable" modifications in existing facilities were needed to accommodate the disabled. ADA also required all new buses and rail cars to be accessible to the disabled, but it did not mandate the retrofitting of existing vehicles.

ADA commanded unusually broad support for a measure opposed by many business groups, sweeping through the House by a vote of 377-28 and the Senate by 76-8.

"Let the shameful wall of exclusion finally come tumbling down," President George Bush said on signing the bill into law on July 26, 1990. "Every man, woman and child with a disability can now pass through once-closed doors into a bright new era of equality, independence and freedom."

Three months later, on Oct. 30, Bush signed a bill reauthorizing the 1975 law on education of the handicapped, broadening the definition of "children with disabilities" to embrace those with traumatic brain injury. The category joined a list that comprised hearing, speech, visual and orthopedic impairments; mental retardation; serious emotional disturbances; autism; and other health problems and learning disabilities. [25]

Furthermore, the reauthorization law effectively reversed a 1989 Supreme Court ruling that children with disabilities who were denied an appropriate, free public education by a state were not entitled to reimbursement for tuition paid for an alternative program. The 11th Amendment, the court declared in *Dellmuth v. Muth,* protected states from federal court suits arising from the handicapped children law. The reauthorization clarified that Congress had indeed meant to allow litigants to sue in federal court to enforce their rights under the act. ■

CURRENT SITUATION

IDEA Revision Fails

The most significant disabilities-rights legislation considered by Congress in 1996 would have revised the Individuals with Disabilities Education Act (IDEA), which requires that all disabled children receive a "free, appropriate public education." Courts interpreting the law have ruled that such education be provided in "the least restricted environment" — for the most part, in schools and classrooms with able-bodied students. This "mainstreaming" of disabled youngsters was thought to enhance their educational and emotional development. [26]

According to education researchers, disabled children can absorb the language and social skills of their non-disabled classmates more readily at an early age. Moreover, they say, disabled students who are mainstreamed from preschool onward tend to be less disruptive in class as they grow older. As an added benefit, able-bodied pupils reportedly gain insights into the nature of disability. [27]

The chief point of contention during House and Senate debate on reauthorizing IDEA concerned what to do about disruptive disabled students. Alarmed by reports of violence committed on school property, Republicans in both chambers proposed giving school officials more authority to discipline troublemakers.

Democrats on the House Economic and Educational Opportunities Employer-Employee Relations Subcommittee, which handled the reauthorization bill, opposed a provision allowing disabled students to be expelled without educational services when the offense was unrelated to disability and involved the use of weapons or illegal drugs. Under existing law, states cannot deny an education to disabled students regardless of the misconduct's nature.

However, the expulsion language was softened before the bill came to a floor vote; "assault and battery" was eliminated as grounds for expelling a student without alternative educational services. The House approved the IDEA reauthorization measure by voice vote on June 10. In a statement issued the same day, the Clinton administration expressed support for the bill but also "significant concerns" about the disciplinary provisions.

The Senate version of the reauthorization bill never reached the Senate floor in 1996, and the legislation died with the 104th Congress. However, supporters of the existing law applauded when Congress voted Sept. 30 to spend $4 billion on IDEA programs in fiscal 1997, or $790.6 million more than in fiscal 1996. Most of the money is earmarked for basic grants to the states to carry out programs under the law. The House had sought to freeze IDEA spending, while President Clinton had requested a modest increase, to $3.6 billion.

The failure to reauthorize IDEA in 1996 means that existing disciplinary policies for disabled students remain in place. Under current regulations, schools may not suspend, expel or change the placement of a disabled student for more than 10 days without parental consent or a court order. If the misconduct involves firearms, the suspension can be as long as 45 days. This "stay-put" provision seeks to ensure that disabled students are not arbitrarily denied an education.

Other sanctions under IDEA depend on whether the misconduct is found to be disability-related. If it is, the student must be returned to the classroom. The student could be placed in a more restrictive classroom or another school only with parental consent or a court order.

If the misconduct is not disability-related, the student is subject to the same disciplinary standards as able-bodied classmates — except that the student must still receive treatment for the disability. A deaf student who brandishes a knife in school, for instance, could receive the same punishment as a non-disabled student committing that offense. The difference is that the deaf student would continue to receive an education tailored to impaired hearing.

Some educators feel that IDEA should address the question of who should attend to the needs of students with such disabilities as allergies, asthma, diabetes and attention-deficit disorder. Such students require monitoring and medication, ideally by a health professional. In many cases, though, hard-pressed schools turn the job over to classroom teachers, who rarely possess the training to perform delicate medical procedures or cope with health emergencies.

And the situation is sure to get worse, according to Arthur Caplan, director of the University of Pennsylvania's Center for Bioethics. "Who would have thought 10 years ago that we'd have kids coming to school who needed to be tube-fed or catheterized?" he said. "Are more coming? Yes. With technology and the push to mainstream, you're going to see more of them coming to your schools." [28] ■

OUTLOOK

'Universal Design'

No major disability-rights legislation is on the horizon in 1997. "There are several issues we'd like to see addressed by Congress, but disability rights is not one of them," says Eide of the Chamber of Commerce. "Our members are more concerned about the Occupational Safety and Health Act [OSHA] and the Family Medical Leave Act than about the Americans with Disabilities Act."

However, Binstock says the AIA intends to press for a change in the ADA that will help eliminate confusion about the regulations. Under current law, the Justice Department is only permitted to certify that state statutes are in ADA compliance.

AIA favors amending the law to give Justice authority to certify model building codes as well as applicable statutes. "Then the state can adopt a code with that certification and know in advance that it is in compliance with ADA," Binstock says. "That small change would create a great deal more certainty than presently exists."

Meanwhile, the architecture profession is taking steps of its own to help the disabled by promoting the use of "universal design." In essence, universal design enables structures to be both esthetically pleasing and readily accessible to disabled and able-bodied people alike.

"Universal design goes beyond the Americans with Disabilities Act or the Fair Housing Act in some ways, in that it suggests that housing has to be adaptable — whether it's single-family or multi-unit," says Jon Pynoos, a professor of gerontology, public policy and urban planning at the University of Southern California.

Pynoos expects universal design principles to gain greater acceptance as rising land costs result in the construction of more multilevel homes. "There are only two ways a two-story house can work for someone in a wheelchair," he says. "One is to design the first floor in such a way that someone could live there all the time. That requires accessibility to the entrance, a kitchen, a bathroom and a living space that doubles as sleeping space — all on the first floor.

"The other approach is to provide better access to the second floor through chair lifts or some other apparatus that can carry a disabled person to the second floor. But the second-floor rooms also have to be made accessible, which is more difficult than with the first floor."

The guiding principle of universal design, Pynoos says, is that architectural features accommodating the needs of the disabled "are features that should be useful for anybody. They should be attractive and unobtrusive. Universal design is a worldwide movement, and architects are leading it."

Pynoos credits disability-rights activists with persuading architects that many of the problems disabled persons face aren't their fault — "it's the environment that's creating the problem. That change in mindset is clearly going to affect designers in the future."

Moreover, he believes that much remains to be done in terms of designing buildings accessible to people with disabilities not involving mobility, sight or hearing. "What do we do about people in a building who have dementia? Do we redo the signage to help them find their way? Do we try to enclose the walking space so that they don't get lost if they wander off? We haven't thought through these issues in terms of our existing building stock."

Architecture schools "are doing a better job about meeting the minimal standards" for accommodating the disabled that are set forth in legislation and local building codes, Pynoos says. But now the schools "are starting to get the sense that there are broader goals that architects can strive for to create an even better environment for disabled people of all ages."

All members of the Association of Collegiate Schools of Architecture "are having to address universal design in some way," Moeller says. "Regardless of its being a requirement for main-

Continued on p. 1122

At Issue:

Does the Americans with Disabilities Act impose unreasonable burdens on business?

yes

Andrew Ferguson
Senior editor, **The Weekly Standard**

FROM "DISABLING AMERICA," *THE WASHINGTONIAN*, AUGUST 1995.

Most everyone agrees that easing the way of the disabled into the mainstream of American life amounts to an ethical injunction. Compassion and empathy demand nothing less. The authors of the Americans with Disabilities Act (ADA), however, made empathy irrelevant. Concern for the disabled is no longer an ethical injunction but a government mandate, and failure to meet it is punishable to the point of bankruptcy.

[T]he ADA is the single greatest expansion of federal power in the country's history. Its supporters call it a civil rights law. It is this and much more. The ADA is a building code, a public transit code, a private transit code, a workplace code, a food-handling code . . . and it is still more than this. Thanks to the ADA, the federal government, through the courts or regulatory mechanisms, can now dictate everything from how wide hallways are in a private office to where you can display merchandise in your store. . . .

And most miraculous of all, it can do this without spending any money! Most legislation in this age of deficits is trumpeted as a cost-cutting measure, and the ADA was no exception. President Bush pointed out that taxpayers now spend almost $200 billion a year to support Americans with disabilities — the implication being that the ADA would save us all $200 billion a year.

The cost, like the responsibility, has merely been shifted. There are no hard data on the costs to private parties engendered by the ADA. The costs are too diffuse, and come in too many forms, like revenue lost to private parking garages that must set aside handicapped spaces whether or not they have handicapped customers. . . .

The ADA was passed and is being enforced in an atmosphere in which reasonable questions are considered off the point. For the point of the ADA is a demonstration of good feeling and virtue, and those who question its wisdom are deemed guilty of bad faith at least and bad character at worst. Though it is the greatest unfunded mandate ever conceived, the ADA is exempt from the recent ban on unfunded federal mandates because it is technically a civil rights law. So it proceeds undeterred, cowing employers, employees, homeowners, architects, bureaucrats, public policy experts — all of them held hostage to the accusation that they may be insensitive, a cold-hearted . . . bad person.

no

Edward B. Bennett III
President, Archimedes Group, a nonprofit disability information organization in New Haven, Conn., and co-chair of the American Civil Liberties Union's National Disability Rights Task Force

FROM "DON'T STRAITJACKET THE LAW," *LOS ANGELES TIMES*, JULY 21, 1995.

The Americans with Disabilities Act (ADA) is under attack. Despite its successes, the ADA confronts a small but determined group bent on its repeal or weakening. Critics argue that it costs too much, creates frivolous litigation, enjoys no business support and mandates federal intrusion while discouraging negotiation and ignoring market forces. They are wrong on all accounts.

The ADA is a market sensitive civil rights act. It explicitly permits businesses to spend only what they can afford. It requires "reasonable" expenditures as it balances legitimate cost concerns with the ideal of integration. The balance works. The ADA's ideal can often be realized simply and inexpensively. A ramp, a sign or a telephone will do. According to the Job Accommodation Network, fully one-third of workplace accommodations cost nothing; another third averages less than $500.

All buildings "accommodate" someone. Architects design structures to accommodate those who typically use them. The ADA simply insists that we accommodate everyone, not just those who walk or see.

Discrimination and segregation in the pre-ADA world taxed everyone heavily. Americans with disabilities suffer an unemployment rate of 69 percent (as against 17 percent in the former West Germany, where employment policies aggressively promote jobs), and we spend billions on welfare programs for people who would rather work and pay taxes than collect government checks.

People with disabilities — I am one of them — want to create the wealth that makes access possible. We want a bigger pie for everybody, not a larger slice of a shrinking pie. We believe that a rising tide lifts all boats, but we need to be able to board the ship. . . .

Critics argue that the business community opposes the ADA. A July Harris Poll forcefully says otherwise: 82 percent of executives agree that the law is worth its costs, and 70 percent said it should not be changed.

We need the ADA because of the enduring power of these myths. Critics suffer from the problem the law tries to cure. They hold a distorted view of the capacities of people with disabilities, the discrimination they suffer and the cost of curbing that discrimination. Fortunately, the ADA educates as much as it prescribes.

FOR MORE INFORMATION

Disability Rights Education and Defense Fund, 2212 6th St., Berkeley, Calif. 94710; (510) 644-2555. The fund seeks to advance the rights and opportunities of disabled persons by educating the public and policymakers about issues affecting the handicapped.

National Federation of Independent Business, 600 Maryland Ave. S.W., Suite 700, Washington, D.C. 20024; (202) 554-9000. NFIB tracks laws and policy issues affecting small businesses, particularly disability-rights legislation.

President's Committee on Employment of People With Disabilities, 1331 F St. N.W., Suite 300, Washington, D.C. 20004-1107; (202) 376-6200. The committee promotes training, rehabilitation and job opportunities for the disabled.

U.S. Chamber of Commerce, 1615 H St. N.W., Washington, D.C. 20062-2000; (202) 463-5682. The chamber is a federation of business, trade and professional groups that monitors laws and regulations affecting business, including those involving disability rights.

Continued from p. 1120

taining accreditation, most every school is going to want to cover that. It's a major issue, something that has received a lot of attention in the last few years."

Kilb of the Disability Rights Education and Defense Fund is cautiously optimistic about such developments. "There is still a latent expectation that people with disabilities are disabled in every way," she says. But she also senses that perceptions are changing.

"If you see a disabled person every day at the bus stop," she says, "it seeps into your consciousness that they're going somewhere to do something. And then it may occur to you that if they can board the bus, they probably are just as competent at performing whatever task awaits them at the end of the bus ride." ■

Notes

[1] For background, see Michael Barrier, "Unfunded and Unloved," *Nation's Business*, April 1995, p. 40.

[2] Janet Reno and Dick Thornburgh, "ADA — Not a Disabling Mandate," *The Wall Street Journal*, July 26, 1996, p. A12. Thornburgh served under President George Bush, who signed ADA into law in July 1990.

[3] Quoted in *The Washington Post*, Nov. 15, 1996, p. D3. Cleland served as head of the Veterans Administration (now the Department of Veterans Affairs) under President Jimmy Carter. Before his election to the Senate, he served 13 years as Georgia secretary of state.

[4] Kathi Wolf, "Disability Politics," *The Washington Post*, Sept. 1, 1996, p. C5.

[5] Testimony prepared for hearing of the Senate Labor and Human Resources Subcommittee on the Handicapped, May 9, 1989.

[6] Testimony prepared for hearing of the House Committee on Small Business, Feb. 22, 1990.

[7] Steven B. Epstein, "In Search of a Bright Line: Determining When an Employer's Financial Hardship Becomes 'Undue' Under the Americans with Disabilities Act," *Vanderbilt Law Review*, March 1995, p. 427.

[8] Reno and Thornburgh, *loc. cit.*

[9] President's Committee on Employment of People with Disabilities, "Dispelling Myths About the Americans with Disabilities Act," Fact Sheet, July 1996.

[10] President's Committee on Employment of People with Disabilities, Fact Sheet, October 1995.

[11] U.S. Census Bureau, "Survey of Income Program and Participation (SIPP)," July 1996.

[12] President's Committee on Employment of People with Disabilities, Press release, July 22, 1996.

[13] *Ibid.*

[14] U.S. General Accounting Office, "People With Disabilities: Federal Programs Could Work Together More Efficiently to Promote Employment," Sept. 3, 1996, p. 13.

[15] *Ibid.*, p. 22.

[16] *Ibid.*, p. 3.

[17] Quoted in *The Washington Post*, Feb. 9, 1996, p. A2.

[18] Judith Weinraub, "How a New Museum Has to Be Retrofitted for the Disabled," *The Washington Post*, Aug. 21, 1994, p. G8.

[19] Steve Humphries and Pamela Wright, *Out of Sight: The Experience of Disability, 1900-1950* (1992), p. 12.

[20] For background, see "Mental Illness," *The CQ Researcher*, Aug. 6, 1993, pp. 673-696.

[21] In 1856, Gallaudet's son Edward founded Gallaudet College (now university) in Washington, D.C., for hearing-impaired students. Another Gallaudet son, Thomas, established a home for aged and infirm deaf mutes near Poughkeepsie, N.Y.

[22] See "Vocational Rehabilitation," *Congress and the Nation, Vol. I* (1965), p. 1216.

[23] Statement released by the White House, Dec. 2, 1975.

[24] For background, see "The Disabilities Act," *The CQ Researcher*, Dec. 27, 1991, pp. 993-1016.

[25] For background, see "Learning Disabilities," *The CQ Researcher*, Dec. 10, 1993, pp. 1081-1104.

[26] For background, see Jeffrey L. Katz, "Policy on Disabled Is Scrutinized Over Discipline Problems, Cost," *CQ Weekly Report*, May 11, 1996, pp. 1295-1299.

[27] Tara Mack, "Making the Grade, All Together," *The Washington Post*, Sept. 23, 1996, p. B1.

[28] Quoted by Marlene Cimons, "Bad Medicine: Health Care Crisis in Schools," *Los Angeles Times*, Nov. 17, 1996, pp. A1-A2.

Bibliography

Selected Sources Used

Books

Humphries, Steve, and Pamela Gordon, *Out of Sight: The Experience of Disability, 1900-1950,* Northcote House, 1992.

Humphries and Gordon, British television producers, recreate the lonely and anguished world of disability in Britain in the first half of the century. They do so through lengthy excerpts from interviews with disabled people who came of age during the period.

Maloff, Chalda, and Susan MacDuff Wood, *Business and Social Etiquette With Disabled People,* Charles C. Thomas, 1988.

Many people hesitate to offer help to disabled individuals in public, for fear of bungling the job or of being rebuffed. "This fear is not entirely unrealistic; it is definitely possible for a well-meaning helper to do more harm than good," Maloff and Wood write. They dispense tips on when and how to lend aid.

Pope, Andrew M., and Alvin R. Tarlov, eds., *Disability in America: Toward a National Agenda for Prevention,* National Academy Press, 1991.

The contributors to this study examine ways of preventing a potentially disabling condition from developing into full-blown disability and on minimizing the effects of such conditions on a person's productivity and quality of life. "In one sense," co-editor Tarlov notes, "disability frequently results from the failure of our successes — for example, success in saving the lives of low-birthweight babies and persons with traumatic injuries or chronic disease."

Reedy, Joel, *Marketing to Consumers With Disabilities,* Probus Publishing, 1993.

A population segment comprising 40-plus million people obviously represents a sales opportunity, and Reedy suggests ways of making the most of it.

Articles

Blaser, Arthur, "A Brilliant Future With Disabilities," *The Futurist,* September-October 1996.

Blaser, assistant dean of the Chapman University School of Law in Orange, Calif., envisions a future with many more disabled people than today. "A society that does not value people with disabilities tends not to value anyone," he writes, "for it is increasingly likely that *everyone* will at some point be living with a disability."

Borow, Zev, "The Learning-Disability Scam," *New York*, March 18, 1996.

Borow details how many academically gifted high school students strive to be classified as learning-disabled under the provisions of the Americans with Disabilities Act. The reason is that youngsters certified as "LD" can demand additional time to complete the Scholastic Assessment Test, possibly gaining an edge on getting into the college of their choice.

Epstein, Steven B., "In Search of a Bright Line: Determining When an Employer's Financial Hardship Becomes 'Undue' Under the Americans With Disabilities Act," *Vanderbilt Law Review,* March 1995.

Epstein, director of legal writing at the University of Illinois College of Law, examines the Americans with Disabilities Act — notably the concepts of "reasonable accommodation" and "undue hardship" — and suggests ways to make the language more concrete.

Parmet, Wendy E., et al., "The Physician's Role in Helping Smoke-Sensitive Patients to Use the Americans with Disabilities Act to Secure Smoke-Free Workplaces and Public Spaces," *The Journal of the American Medical Association*, Sept. 18, 1996.

The ADA, note the authors, may give people who are sensitive to environmental tobacco smoke a legal right to a smoke-free environment. They go on to suggest ways by which doctors can advise such patients on how to obtain the clean air they are entitled to.

Wong, Mei-lan E., "The Implications of School Choice for Children With Disabilities," *Yale Law Journal*, December 1993.

According to Wong, a "choice school system that does not provide special education at every choice school does not provide children with disabilities equal access to the same educational opportunities as their non-disabled peers."

Zuriff, G.E., "Medicalizing Character," *The Public Interest*, spring 1996.

Zuriff, a clinical psychologist, argues that "new regulations must clarify and . . . limit the definition of mental disability" under the ADA. Otherwise, he contends, individuals with personality disorders could overwhelm a system designed to accommodate persons with more conventional disabilities.

Reports and Studies

U.S. General Accounting Office, *People With Disabilities: Federal Programs Could Work Together More Efficiently to Promote Employment*, September 1996.

This report by the congressional watchdog agency asserts that programs aimed at enhancing the job prospects of people with disabilities are scattered among several federal agencies, blunting their collective impact.

The Next Step

Additional information from UMI's Newspaper & Periodical Abstracts database

Americans with Disabilities Act

Appel, Alan, "Requirements and rewards of the Americans with Disabilities Act," *Corrections Today,* April 1995, pp. 84-86.

All corrections administrators share the concern of complying with the Americans with Disabilities Act (ADA). Advancements in this area are discussed.

Fram, David K., "Manager's journal: What employers should know about the ADA," *The Wall Street Journal,* Sept. 16, 1996, p. A18.

Fram addresses common questions about the Americans with Disabilities Act.

Jacoby, Jeff, "Americans with Disabilities Act: A ticket to sue," *The Boston Globe,* March 21, 1995, p. 15.

Jacoby suggests that the Disability Law Center exists for the express purpose of using lawsuits as blunt weapons with which to reshape society to fit its views. He argues that the Americans with Disabilities Act is a dangerous law that is being exploited by stop-at-nothing zealots.

Miller, Susan H., "Americans with Disabilities Act opens doors for everyone," *Michigan Chronicle,* May 17, 1995, p. A7.

Miller comments on the importance of the American with Disabilities Act and encourages citizens to support it.

Silvers, Anita, "(In)equality, (ab)normality, and the Americans with Disabilities Act," *Journal of Medicine & Philosophy,* April 1996, pp. 209-224.

The 1990 Americans with Disabilities Act (ADA) codified the understanding of "disability" as a defective state of society that disadvantages disabled individuals. In order to liberate social thought from the medical model and thus move the disabled from being socially marginalized to being socially enabled, current practice must be reconceptualized by adopting the ADA's conceptual framework.

Sixel, L. M., "Law on disabled read differently," *Houston Chronicle,* July 5, 1996, p. C1.

Sixel discusses the lack of uniformity among employers in the implementation of the Americans with Disabilities Act.

Debate Over Designation of Certain Medical and Emotional Disorders as Protected Disabilities

Banta, Carol J., "The impact of the Americans with Disabilities Act on state bar examiners' inquiries into the psychological history of bar applicants," *Michigan Law Review,* October 1995, pp. 167-190.

It is argued that the use of any questions based upon an applicants' psychological history in the state bar application process violates the Americans with Disabilities Act.

Doherty, Brian, "Unreasonable accommodation: The case against the Americans with Disabilities Act," *Reason,* August 1995, p. 18-26.

Doherty discusses the Americans with Disabilities Act of 1990, which was passed by Congress with runaway bipartisan support. Five years later, the law has created an industry of people to interpret the law.

Jacobs, Margaret A., "Legal beat: Women seek infertility benefits under disabilities law," *The Wall Street Journal,* June 12, 1996, p. B7.

Like a growing number of infertile women, some of whom delayed child-bearing to pursue careers, Lynn Gansar filed a lawsuit against her employer, WDSU-Television Inc., claiming her discharge, which allegedly occurred after the TV station learned she was having fertility treatments, violated the Americans with Disabilities Act. Since the act went into effect, at least a dozen suits have been filed by women who say employers illegally refused to reduce their hours during the costly, debilitating treatments or illegally failed to provide insurance coverage.

Levine, Susan, "A case for alternative care: Advocates want brain-injured patients out of Md. mental hospitals," *The Washington Post,* Sept. 8, 1996, p. B1.

A federal trial set to begin Sept. 9, 1996, in Baltimore, Md., will test the bounds of the sweeping Americans with Disabilities Act, which prohibits unnecessary segregation of the disabled. The Maryland Disability Law Center, an advocacy group, sued the state in 1994, for "dumping and warehousing" people with traumatic brain injury in mental institutions.

Nealon, Patricia, "Court to hear suit from patient with HIV," *Boston Globe,* Nov. 8, 1996, p. B1.

The lawsuit of Sidney Abbott, who is HIV-positive, against Bangor, Maine, dentist Randon Bragdon who refused to fill a cavity in her tooth in the fall of 1994, in his office, insisting that the procedure be done in a hospital operating room where he felt safer, is detailed. A federal appeals court in Boston will hear the case Nov. 8, 1996, becoming the first federal appellate court in the U.S. to consider whether a dentist who refuses to treat a patient with HIV out of fear of becoming infected is violating the Americans with Disabilities Act of 1990.

Whitaker, Barbara, "Infertility is a New Focus of Workplace Lawsuits," *The New York Times,* April 21, 1996, p. 12.
A lawsuit filed by Charline Pacourek against Inland Steel Industries concerning her treatment for infertility is being watched closely by employers and insurers because the Americans with Disabilities Act of 1990 could come into play in deciding whether fertility treatments must be included in insurance plans.

Will, George F., "Protection for the personality-impaired," *The Washington Post,* April 4, 1996, p. A31.
Will comments on the regulations pertaining to mental illness in the Americans with Disabilities Act of 1990.

Efforts to Make Commercial and Residential Buildings Accessible

Berenson, Alex, "Lottery enforcing ADA," *Denver Post,* June 11, 1996, p. C1.
On July 1, 1996, the Colorado lottery will begin enforcing the Americans with Disabilities Act at all 2,700 retailers that sell its tickets. Vendors who don't provide accessibility for people with disabilities to buy tickets, may lose their licenses.

Bertelson, Christine, "Activist orders up wheelchair access at House of Pancakes," *St. Louis Post-Dispatch,* Sept. 5, 1996, p. B1.
Bertelson comments on Michelle Steger's activism to bring restaurants, stores and public buildings into compliance with the Americans with Disabilities Act.

Feldman, Claudia, "A home for Allison," *Houston Chronicle,* March 27, 1996, p. D1.
The Rosenberg family of Bellaire, Texas, is suing the city and the board of adjustments for a variance that would allow them to build a home that would accommodate the needs of their disabled daughter Allison. The board denied their original request on Feb. 20, 1996. The Rosenbergs argue that federal disability laws state that reasonable accommodations must be made to help the handicapped.

Haggerty, Maryann, "Pollin sued over design of MCI Center," *The Washington Post,* June 15, 1996, p. C1.
A group of paralyzed veterans on June 14, 1996, filed suit alleging that the MCI Center sports arena under construction in downtown Washington, D.C., is not properly designed to accommodate wheelchair users and violates the Americans with Disabilities Act.

Harmon, Brian, "Paralyzed veterans sue over lack of access to businesses," *Detroit News & Free Press,* July 4, 1996.
Six southeast Michigan businesses are being sued by the Michigan Paralyzed Veterans of America for not complying with the 1990 Americans with Disabilities Act. Any money won will finance litigation against other businesses that refuse to accommodate the disabled, according to MPVA president Clark Schule.

Helliker, Kevin, "Gaining access: Catering to the disabled at convention time is a lucrative niche," *The Wall Street Journal,* Sept. 19, 1996, p. A1.
To comply with the 1990 Americans with Disabilities Act, much of the hotel industry is grudgingly improving accessibility to the disabled. Other hotels aren't doing much of anything, prompting a flurry of federal lawsuits for alleged non-compliance. But a growing number of hotels are making their facilities extraordinarily hospitable. These hotels have discovered that conventions of people with disabilities represent a lucrative niche, worth tens of million of dollars.

Ilka, Douglas, "U.S. bureaucracy delaying tots' play equipment," *Detroit News,* May 8, 1996, p. D5.
Parks and Recreation Director Bruce Austin of Rochester, Mich., says he may have to wait until 1998 before he gets detailed instructions on what equipment for three of the city's tot lots will qualify as "handicap accessible" under guidelines being drafted to comply with the Americans with Disabilities Act. The guidelines were supposed to be set in September 1993.

Morton, Joann B., and Judy C. Anderson, "Implementing the Americans with Disabilities Act for inmates," *Corrections Today,* October 1996, pp. 86-90.
Discussions concerning the Americans with Disabilities Act's (ADA's) implications for correctional agencies have focused on how implementation of the act's provisions affect correctional personnel. Issues of applying ADA provisions to the offender population are reviewed, and some actions correctional personnel might take to avoid or minimize their liability under the act are suggested.

"Obey law, and common sense," *Los Angeles Times,* Sept. 24, 1996, p. B6.
An editorial comments on equipping prisons to meet the needs of disabled prisoners following a federal court ruling that the provisions of the 1990 Americans with Disabilities Act apply to California state prisons.

Roswal, Glenn, Martin E. Block and Shannon Cooper, "The Americans with Disabilities Act: Camp compliance," *Camping Magazine,* September 1996, p. 8
The Americans with Disabilities Act is designed to facilitate the integration of individuals with disabilities into every aspect of society by offering a clear and comprehensive national mandate that eliminates discrimination against people with disabilities. Examples of how the act impacts camp programs and practical steps camps can take to comply are presented.

Skrzycki, Cindy, "Mirror, mirror on the wall, what's the fairest reg. of all?" *The Washington Post,* July 12, 1996, p. D1.
Skrzycki states that five years after passage of the Americans with Disabilities Act, a committee is about to issue recommendations that would rewrite thousands of standards that often are duplicated or contradicted in the numerous state and local building codes.

"United Artists agrees to make its theaters handicapped-friendly," *The Wall Street Journal,* April 17, 1996, p. B9.
United Artists Theater Circuit Inc., resolving a lawsuit filed by the government and others, agreed to make its theaters fully accessible to handicapped customers in compliance with the 1990 Americans with Disabilities Act.

Wade, Betsy, "Disabled Access to Inns at Issue," *The New York Times,* April 14, 1996, p. 4.
Days Inns of America and the Justice Department are going to court over the Americans with Disabilities Act, which bars discrimination in areas such as employment, public attractions and public accommodation. The Justice Department says Days Inn is not requiring motels bearings its name to meet requirements on safety and access for the disabled.

Wilhelmus, David W., "Perspectives on the Americans with Disabilities Act: Accessibility of Academic libraries to visually impaired patrons," *Journal of Academic Librarianship,* September 1996, pp. 366-370.
Wilhelmus reviews the recent history of academic libraries' responses to the needs of visually impaired patrons and offers suggestions to ease the impact of libraries' enforcement of the Americans with Disabilities Act.

"Work week: Disabled Americans," *The Wall Street Journal,* April 2, 1996, p. A1.
A citizens' advisory committee is debating thorny revisions to the Americans with Disabilities Act. Private work spaces, now exempt from the ADA, are a sore point. For example, advocates for the hearing-impaired seek strobe-light fire alarms, but groups representing epileptics say strobes could trigger seizures.

Impact of ADA on Job Opportunities for the Disabled

DiCesare, Constance B., "Americans with Disabilities Act," *Monthly Labor Review,* July 1995, p. 78.
A federal judge ruled in *McKay v. Toyota Motor Manufacturing, U.S.A., Inc.* that an automobile worker's inability to perform repetitive factory work, which resulted in her being fired, did not meet the criteria for impairment under the Americans with Disabilities Act.

Finn, Peter, "Disabled becoming a work force to be reckoned with," *The Washington Post,* Sept. 2, 1996, B1.
The number of people with severe disabilities in the work force continues to rise, driven by the Americans with Disabilities Act, new technology, increasing openness on the part of employers and, most importantly, the determination of the disabled to stake their claim to a place in the work force.

Higginbotham, Mickey, "Jobs a growing worry for the disabled," *Atlanta Constitution,* Aug. 15, 1996, p. G3.
Advocates attending the Paralympic Congress in Atlanta in August 1996, are troubled by reports that fewer disabled persons may be in the work force since the Americans with Disabilities Act was passed in 1990.

Mathews, Jay, "More disabled hired, census study shows," *The Washington Post,* July 26, 1996, p. F3.
New federal statistics show for the first time a rise in the employment of severely disabled Americans under the Americans with Disabilities Act (ADA), and a private survey shows the act having a significant impact on American lives.

Rubin, Paula N., "The Americans with Disabilities Act's impact on corrections," *Corrections Today,* April 1995, pp. 114-120.
The Americans with Disabilities Act (ADA) impacts every aspect of society. The ADA will have a significant impact on how corrections facilities hire personnel.

Slack, James D., "The Americans with Disabilities Act and the workplace: Management's responsibilities in AIDS-related situations," *Public Administration Review,* July 1995, pp. 365-370.
The dynamics involved with applying the protections of the Americans with Disabilities Act of 1990 to those individuals in the HIV spectrum is examined.

Individuals with the Disabilities Education Act

Alpert, Bruce, "Tougher penalties needed, but don't unduly weaken special-ed. law," *Atlanta Journal Constitution,* June 9, 1996, p. B2.
Alpert examines the problems that the Individuals with Disabilities Education Act (IDEA) has created for special education teachers and school administrators who are angry that their hands are tied when it comes to disciplinary measures against unruly and violent special education students.

"Balance on special education," *The Christian Science Monitor,* June 10, 1996, p. 20.
An editorial agrees that Congress should search for a fair revision to the 1975 Individuals with Disabilities Education Act and asserts that putting some boundaries around cost and giving school officials more leeway on discipline are driving the congressional revision. The editorial states that the revision probably won't go as far as critics of the law hope, nor should it be as slight as many advocates for special education might like.

Heumann, Judith, "Educating disabled good IDEA," ***USA Today,*** **June 25, 1996, p. A12.**

In a letter to the editor, Heumann of the U.S. Department of Education defends the Individuals with Disabilities Education Act against attacks in a June 17, 1996, *USA Today* article, "Special ed.: Is the price too high?"

Heumann, Judith E., "Dispelling the myths about special education," ***Exceptional Parent,*** **September 1996, pp. 54-57.**

The Individuals with Disabilities Education Act has been the subject of recent controversy in the media. Several myths surrounding the provision of special education services to children and youth with disabilities are addressed.

"Issue: Individuals with Disabilities Education Act," ***Congressional Quarterly Weekly Report,*** **Aug. 31, 1996, p. 2451.**

House and Senate bills to revamp the Individuals with Disabilities Education Act are running out of time in the 104th Congress. The House has passed HR 3268, but Senate floor action is still pending on S 1578.

Long, Richard, "Key issues remain unresolved as election nears," ***Reading Today,*** **October 1996, p. 6.**

Long examines the key issues that remain unresolved in Congress. These include the funding issue, the possible reauthorization of IDEA (Individuals with Disabilities Education Act) and issues affecting immigrants.

Schnaiberg, Lynn, "Rifts stymie efforts to retool special ed. law," ***Education Week,*** **Oct. 16, 1996, p. 19.**

Congress had approved bills to reauthorize the Individuals with Disabilities Education Act, but completion of the law's renewal was hindered by lukewarm support from outside groups and internal disagreements among lawmakers over a wide range of issues. School discipline and safety were major concerns.

"Schools for disabled children," ***The Washington Post,*** **July 10, 1996, p. A16.**

An editorial discusses parallel bills in Congress to address some of the long-festering issues resulting from the 21-year-old Individuals with Disabilities Education Act, which deals with such issues as how much of their limited money school districts are obliged to lay out for disabled students.

Zirkel, Perry A., and Ivan B. Gluckman, "Full inclusion of students with disabilities, part 2," ***NASSP Bulletin,*** **September 1996, pp. 91-93.**

Zirkel and Gluckman provide a recent illustrative case and a question-and-answer discussion about accompanying court decisions under the "least restrictive environment" language of the Individuals with Disabilities Education Act .

Impact of ADA on Sports Eligibility of Disabled Individuals

Block, Martin E., "Ensuring the quality of life through activity — Americans with Disabilities Act: Its impact on youth sports," ***Journal of Physical Education, Recreation & Dance,*** **January 1995, pp. 28-32.**

The Americans with Disabilities Act is described, and an explanation of how it affects youth sports programs is offered.

Lane, George, "Team, ex-player deal," ***Denver Post,*** **March 22, 1996, p. B5.**

The Denver Broncos and former lineman Kenny Walker reached a settlement in March 1996, over Walker's allegation that the Broncos violated the Americans with Disabilities Act when they cut him from the team. A "confidential settlement agreement" was reached that stipulates the details not be made public.

Nicholson, Kieran, "Feds examine ruling against grid hopeful," ***Denver Post,*** **Sept. 21, 1996, p. B2.**

Gabriel Lane, the 20-year-old high school senior with Down's syndrome who was barred from playing varsity football at Greeley Central High School in Colorado, may have a new champion, the U.S. Justice Department, which is looking at whether the actions of the Colorado High School Activities Association may have violated the Americans with Disabilities Act.

Wieberg, Steve, "Michigan State, hopeful, fights eligibility ruling," ***USA Today,*** **Aug. 14, 1996, p. C1.**

Despite an NCAA ruling that Chad Ganden, a learning-disabled swimmer planning to enter Michigan State University, must sit out his freshman year for failing to meet academic requirements, his family is intent on getting him to swim. The family and the U.S. Department of Justice, which is trying to determine whether the NCAA violated the Americans with Disabilities Act, are awaiting details of the association's decision before proceeding.

Back Issues

Great Research on Current Issues Starts Right Here...Recent topics covered by The CQ Researcher are listed below. Before May 1991, reports were published under the name of Editorial Research Reports.

JUNE 1995
Combating Infectious Disease
Property Rights
Repetitive Stress Injuries
Regulating the Internet

JULY 1995
War Crimes
Highway Safety
Combating Terrorism
Preventing Teen Drug Use

AUGUST 1995
Job Stress
Organ Transplants
United Nations at 50
Advances in Cancer Research

SEPTEMBER 1995
Catholic Church in the U.S.
Northern Ireland Cease-Fire
High School Sports
Teaching History

OCTOBER 1995
Quebec's Future
Revitalizing the Cities
Networking the Classroom
Indoor Air Pollution

Back issues are available for $5.00 (subscribers) or $8.00 (non-subscribers). Quantity discounts apply to orders over ten. To order, call Congressional Quarterly Customer Service at (202) 887-8621.

Binders are available for $18.00. To order call 1-800-638-1710. Please refer to stock number 648.

NOVEMBER 1995
The Working Poor
The Jury System
Sex, Violence and the Media
Police Misconduct

DECEMBER 1995
Teens and Tobacco
Gene Therapy's Future
Global Water Shortages
Third-Party Prospects

JANUARY 1996
Emergency Medicine
Punishing Sex Offenders
Bilingual Education
Helping the Homeless

FEBRUARY 1996
Reforming the CIA
Campaign Finance Reform
Academic Politics
Getting Into College

MARCH 1996
The British Monarchy
Preventing Juvenile Crime
Tax Reform
Pursuing the Paranormal

APRIL 1996
Centennial Olympic Games
Managed Care
Protecting Endangered Species
New Military Culture

MAY 1996
Russia's Political Future
Marriage and Divorce
Year-Round Schools
Taiwan, China and the U.S.

JUNE 1996
Rethinking NAFTA
First Ladies
Teaching Values
Labor Movement's Future

JULY 1996
Recovered-Memory Debate
Native Americans' Future
Crackdown on Sexual Harassment
Attack on Public Schools

AUGUST 1996
Fighting Over Animal Rights
Privatizing Government Services
Child Labor and Sweatshops
Cleaning Up Hazardous Wastes

SEPTEMBER 1996
Gambling Under Attack
The States and Federalism
Civic Journalism
Reassessing Foreign Aid

OCTOBER 1996
Political Consultants
Insurance Fraud
Rethinking School Integration
Parental Rights

NOVEMBER 1996
Global Warming
Clashing Over Copyright
Consumer Debt
Governing Washington, D.C.

DECEMBER 1996
Welfare, Work and the States
The New Volunteerism

Future Topics

- ***America's Pampered Pets***
- ***Combating Scientific Misconduct***
- ***Deregulating Electric Power***

THE CQ Researcher

PUBLISHED BY CONGRESSIONAL QUARTERLY INC.

America's Pampered Pets

Has our love affair with pets gone too far?

Nearly six out of 10 U.S. households own a pet, and while cats and dogs are still the most popular animal companions, fish, reptiles and even more exotic creatures are increasingly common. Our love affair with pets is fueling a booming industry. Americans spent more than $9.3 billion last year just on food for Fluffy and Fido, and billions more on toys, grooming tools and myriad other pet accessories — from preservative-free pet food and organic flea treatments to carpet-covered gym sets for cats and plastic exercise ramps for gerbils. But there's a darker side to pet ownership. Animal shelters still euthanize millions of "throw-away" pets each year. Meanwhile, local officials are worried about controlling vicious dogs, banning ownership of more exotic animals and balancing the rights of pet owners and the rest of the community.

INSIDE THIS ISSUE

Dec. 27, 1996 • Volume 6, No. 48 • Pages 1129-1152

Formerly Editorial Research Reports

America's Pampered Pets

Cover: Nearly four out of 10 U.S. households own at least one dog. (Humane Society of the United States)

The CQ Researcher

Dec. 27, 1996
Volume 6, No. 48

The CQ Researcher (ISSN 1056-2036). Formerly Editorial Research Reports. Published weekly (48 times per year, not printed March 1, May 31, Aug. 30, Nov. 29) by Congressional Quarterly Inc., 1414 22nd St., N.W., Washington, D.C. 20037. Annual subscription rate for libraries, businesses and government is $319. Additional rates furnished upon request. Periodicals postage paid at Washington, D.C. POSTMASTER: Send address changes to The CQ Researcher, 1414 22nd St., N.W., Washington, D.C. 20037.

America's Pampered Pets

BY MARY H. COOPER

THE ISSUES

Before a hushed crowd of anxious onlookers, a long-haired cat stands on a brightly lit table. The immaculately groomed, blue-cream Persian remains calm as a man lifts and scrutinizes it, looking for some invisible deviation from breed standards. To enthusiastic applause, the man declares the cat flawless and returns the fluffy animal to its cage.

Crowded into two large rooms at the Montgomery County Fairgrounds in the Maryland suburbs of Washington, some 315 cats and their owners are vying for recognition at the Capital Cat Fanciers' all-breed show. In addition to the pug-nosed, fluffy Persians, there are sleek, rust-colored Abyssinians, long-haired, blue-eyed Birmans and more than a dozen other breeds.

"These cat shows are just like Little League," says Karen Hess, a veterinarian from Allentown, Pa., who breeds and shows ocicats, an unusual spotted variety that originated from interbreeding American Shorthair, Siamese and Abyssinian cats. "The cats are our children, and there's a show every weekend within driving distance. It's like a social event, where we all get together and talk about them."

Most cat owners, of course, will never take their pets to a cat show. The vast majority of pet felines are not show quality, or even recognizable as specific breeds. * Not to mention the fact that few pet cats would put up with the frequent bathing, blow-drying, combing and claw-clipping that come with life on the show circuit.

But that is not to say that Americans have lost their affection for felines. In fact, cats have surpassed dogs as the nation's favorite pet. According to the

Pet Food Institute, the dog population has grown only slightly in recent years, rising from 54.6 million in 1987 to 54.9 million in 1995. Over the same period, the institute reports, the number of pet cats rose from 57.3 million to 65.8 million. [1] *(See graph, p. 1132.)*

The growing popularity of cats fits in with recent changes in the way Americans live. "Many more people are working today, and most don't have big yards," says Mark Hannon, a Cat Fanciers' Association board member who breeds Persians as a hobby at his home in Reston, Va. "For someone living alone in an apartment who wants companionship, a dog won't fit into the lifestyle. Dogs will not thrive without you around. Cats are more independent."

While cats may be more popular, dogs retain their faithful following. "We register more dogs than ever before," says Wayne Cavanaugh, spokesman for the American Kennel Club (AKC), the world's largest purebred dog registry. The AKC, which recognizes more than 140 breeds, registered about 1.3 million purebreds last year. "There may be more cats as pets today, but there are more dog-owning households than cat-owning households," Cavanaugh says. *(See chart, p. 1134.)*

Dog owners say their pets meet the same basic needs cats and other animals do for their owners, only in slightly different ways. "Pets give us what we need, and some of us are terribly needy," says Roger Caras, president of the American Society for the Prevention of Cruelty to Animals (ASPCA) and the proud owner of 12 dogs and "27 or 28" other assorted pets. "I would hate my home if there weren't dogs in it. I would not want to come home and not have a whole phalanx of [them] jumping up on me and wagging their tails, telling me how much they love me."

Nearly six out of 10 U.S. households own a pet of some type, and while cats and dogs are the most popular animal companions, Americans share their homes with everything from potbellied pigs to iguanas. The third most popular pets are freshwater fish, including goldfish. According to the American Pet Products Manufacturing Association, one in 10 households owns freshwater fish, a 38 percent increase since 1990. [2]

More exotic pets enjoy a small but loyal following. Entire magazines are devoted to the enjoyment and care of snakes, spiders, hedgehogs and other unusual creatures. A Web site on the Internet offers tarantula owners solutions to all sorts of problems. "What can I do about hair loss on my tarantula's abdomen?" one owner asks. "My tarantula has unexpectedly laid an eggsac," another writes, "and I don't have the time or knowledge to raise the spiderlings. What should I do?" (Not to worry: The hair will grow back "after the next molt." To avoid the "extremely time-consuming prospect of raising" spiderlings, just sell the eggsac. "A good eggsac ... may provoke a bidding war among potential buyers.") [3]

Supplying this seemingly boundless

---

* The Cat Fanciers' Association recognizes more than 35 breeds of pedigreed cats.

The Truth About Cats and Dogs

Cats have surpassed dogs as the nation's favorite pet. According to the Pet Food Institute, the dog population has grown only slightly in recent years, rising from 54.6 million in 1987 to 54.9 million in 1995. Over the same period, the number of pet cats rose from 57.3 million to 65.8 million.

Source: Pet Food Institute, "Pet Incidence Trend Report," Sept. 18, 1996

— if not bizarre — desire of Americans to keep pets is a booming industry producing specialized food, toys, cages, grooming tools and even clothing. Pet food is the industry's core product. "We now have seven zillion types of designer pet food, which makes it all a lot more expensive," says Cavanaugh, who attributes owners' willingness to splurge on their pets to the healthy economy and growing concern over their own health. "People are more conscious about what they are eating now, and as a result they are more concerned with what their dogs are eating. A lot of the new pet foods are preservative-free and even organic. They're also a lot more expensive than traditional [pet] food."

While many Americans lavish money and affection on their pets, there is a dark side of pet ownership — the willingness of some people to mistreat, abuse and dispose of domestic animals as though they were inanimate objects.

Weeks before the November release of Walt Disney Co.'s remake of the children's classic "101 Dalmatians," Dalmatian breeders launched a publicity blitz warning parents not to buy their kids a puppy because Dalmatians are often hard to live with. Puppies purchased impulsively often end up in animal shelters when they prove too much trouble to keep.

As many as 20 million dogs and cats are euthanized each year, according to the ASPCA. "It is true that a good percentage of them must be put down for humane reasons," Caras says. "Either they are so sick or injured, often by a car or truck, or they have such gross social ineptitude that they are dangerous. Vicious people — it's the people who are vicious — convert perfectly nice dogs into ferocious dogs."

Most animals suffer abuse and die in silence. But when it comes to dogs, the abuse often makes victims of people as well. The Centers for Disease Control and Prevention in Atlanta estimates that there were some 4.5 million dog bites in 1994, resulting in 15 fatalities and 800,000 injuries requiring medical treatment. [4]

A rash of attacks by people wielding vicious dogs as weapons has prompted many cities to ban or muzzle pit bulls (*see p. 1144*). In response to one well-publicized incident in Washington, D.C., in which a teenage girl was severely mauled by a pit bull after the dog's owner sicked it on her for refusing to take off her clothes, the City Council took extraordinary steps to restrict ownership of the mix-breed dogs. The council passed a law requiring owners of pit bulls to muzzle their dogs when in public, register them as dangerous dogs and buy extra insurance to pay for injuries if the dogs bite someone.

Critics of such breed restrictions say they are unfair to responsible dog owners. "The issue that prompted this response was not a dangerous dog issue," says Randall Lockwood, vice president for training initiatives at the Humane Society of the United States (HSUS). "It was an urban-crime issue. It's just that the criminal's weapon of choice happened to be a pit bull instead of a .38. Breed-specific laws like this one are a very narrowly focused, shortsighted Band-Aid being applied to the much larger cancer of urban violence, disenfranchisement and a host of other issues."

But Mark Sobo, who wrote the D.C. law as legislative assistant for council member Frank Smith Jr., says it was the only solution to a relentless problem. "Some of these owners should be put on a leash," he says. "Someone testified at the hearings on our bill that he looks on his dogs like his children. Well, that's tough. What about all those senior citizens who can't even sit down in the park because they're so scared of pit bulls and Rottweilers? Don't they have rights, too?"

Clearly, regulating pet ownership is sparking an emotional debate. As local jurisdictions wrestle with pet-related problems, they must come to grips with a few fundamental issues:

Are there too many pets in the United States?

In their fundraising campaigns, the Humane Society of the United States and other animal protection organizations point to the millions of dogs and cats that are humanely killed, or euthanized, each year. Because there is no national organization representing animal shelters across the country, the exact number is unknown. But commonly cited estimates range from 10 million to 20 million. "Pet overpopulation continues to be a major concern of all humane groups," says Lockwood.

Some experts question these numbers, however. "The people who are decrying an animal overpopulation of 20 million are using the same numbers that have been used since 1901," says Alan Beck, director of the Center for Applied Ethology and Human-Animal Interaction at Purdue University's School of Veterinary Medicine. "It probably was exaggerated even then."

In Beck's view, national humane organizations such as HSUS have an interest in inflating the statistics because they base their fundraising campaigns on the need to help finance the operations of animal shelters. "Anyone who really looks at this objectively, as opposed to the pet industry or the humane societies that might have a certain agenda, knows that the dog population [in shelters] has fallen," Beck says. "In fact, there may not be any dog and cat overpopulation at all."

Humane Society of the United States

Pets help children learn to be nurturers.

That is not to say that animal shelters do not euthanize large numbers of unwanted animals. Many shelter residents are strays, often animals that were abandoned by their owners at the side of a road. These "throwaway pets" often are the result of impulse purchases of puppies or kittens by people who underestimate the time required to properly train and care for a pet or the expense of feeding that five-pound St. Bernard puppy when he grows into a 150-pound adult.

An important key to reducing the number of throwaway pets, experts agree, is consumer education. The AKC, for example, strongly advises prospective dog owners to take the time to study the different breeds to find the right match for their expectations and lifestyles before buying a puppy. Equally important, they say, is to buy from a reputable breeder who guarantees the puppies' health or freedom from genetic disorders that may be common to different breeds. Deafness runs in Dalmatians, for example, collies are prone to blindness, while German Shepherds and other large breeds are susceptible to hip dysplasia, a crippling joint disorder. Responsible breeders carefully avoid breeding dogs that carry genetic disorders and screen puppies for symptoms when possible.

Cat and dog breeders and associations also warn consumers against buying their puppies and kittens from pet shops, which often obtain them from breeders who are in the business purely to make a profit. Because they often fail to ascertain their animals' genetic soundness or keep them in unsanitary conditions, puppy and kitten "mills" tend to produce poor prospects for pet ownership.

Breed registry clubs also warn prospective owners against buying puppies or kittens from "backyard breeders," poorly informed owners anxious to sell off the products of the family pet's unintentional mating. When genetic diseases or behavior problems resulting from poor socialization in early life crop up as the animal grows,

Pets and Their Owners

Nearly six out of 10 U.S. households own a pet of some type, and while cats and dogs are the most popular animal companions, Americans share their homes with everything from potbellied pigs to iguanas.

Type of Pet	Percentage of U.S. households that own at least one	Characteristics of owners
Any Pet	59%	
Dogs	37%	Tend to be married, have smaller households, have no children living at home, own their own home and earn moderate-to-high incomes (above $25,000)
Cats	32%	Tend to be older, a quarter are single or previously married, tend to own their own home and tend not to have children at home
Freshwater and saltwater fish	12%	Tend to be younger, married, from larger households, rent rather than own, have moderate incomes, live in metropolitan areas and have children
Birds	6%	Tend to be married (but with 25 percent previously married/single), more likely to rent in urban areas and tend not to have children
Small animals	5%	Tend to be younger, married, have children at home, have larger households, have higher incomes and own their own home
Reptiles	3%	Tend to be younger, from larger households, tend to have children, own their home and live in metropolitan areas

Source: American Pet Products Manufacturers Association, 1996 APPMA National Pet Owners Survey

it often ends up in the local shelter and, most likely, another statistic in the long list of euthanized pets.

While the AKC and other breed clubs agree that there are too many unwanted pets in the United States, they adamantly defend the right of responsible breeders to produce quality cats and dogs. "We think that breeding good, healthy dogs responsibly is a right that we'd like to maintain for all the right reasons," says the AKC's Cavanaugh. "Dogs still work on farms in America, and they still herd and hunt. They are still used for hearing assistance, guiding eye and other important uses. The top-winning Labrador in our sport last year was bred by the guiding eye foundation."

In any case, breeders who register and show their animals say they are not the cause of pet overpopulation because they are not in the business to make money. "You shouldn't be easily making a profit at this," says Pennsylvania veterinarian Hess. "The breeders who do it as a business show one cat in order to sell 20 kittens. I never bring kittens to a show because for me it's an adoption, not a sale."

It's not the purebred dogs or cats that make up most of the shelter population, Cavanaugh says, but rather strays — specifically, stray cats. "In some shelters there are almost no dogs to adopt out, but there are lots and lots of stray cats," he says. "We know that the dogs that belong to our club members don't end up in shelters, and the cat fanciers are even worse. Their cats are never even allowed to go outside. So they're definitely not contributing to the [overpopulation] problem. However, the feral cat population is going up."

Does animal companionship benefit the physical and emotional well-being of humans?

People have kept pets for so long that the practice has become a fundamental part of human experience. "Name one single thing that we do, aside from our own biology, that our far, far distant ancestors did in a cave 15,000 years ago," says ASPCA President Caras. "We do one thing: We keep companion animals. It is the most natural single thing and the oldest single thing, older by far than any group relationships that we understand."

Bolstering this argument, recent research shows that pets have a measurable calming effect on their owners. In one study of dog-owning married couples, stress levels — measured by blood pressure and heart rate — fell most drastically when the subjects were accompanied by their dogs alone when performing stressful tasks. Stress levels were highest when the subjects were in the company of their spouses alone. [5]

Pets offer something for just about everyone. Domestic animals, especially dogs and cats, offer a kind of predictably loyal companionship that their owners say they don't find in other people. "People have bad days — animals don't," says Hess. "They don't care if you don't get out of your sweats all day. They don't judge you like people do."

Families often get pets for the children. "There is almost twice as much animal ownership once there is a child over 6 in the family because of the perception that animals are good for children," says veterinarian Beck. "And, in fact, they are. One of the ways that children learn to be nurturers is by being parents, and pets are our children's children."

Pets can help institutionalized people, such as autistic children and the elderly, relate with the world around them. "The most devastating thing you can do to an elderly person is ask them why they are getting up today," says Caras. "But if they have a companion animal, they are relevant, they are needed, they're wanted. They have to get out of bed because the pet must be seen to. It brings people back into the circle of relevance and gives their lives meaning."

People with emotional difficulties often respond to animals far more quickly than to other people. Linda Buel, a boarding kennel owner in Rockville, Md., hires people with drug and alcohol problems from a local halfway house. "These people had been stripped of everything — their families, their work, everything," she says of three employees who have stayed on the job for at least four years without relapsing into substance abuse. "They are permanent employees now. Working with the animals has kept them on the straight and narrow."

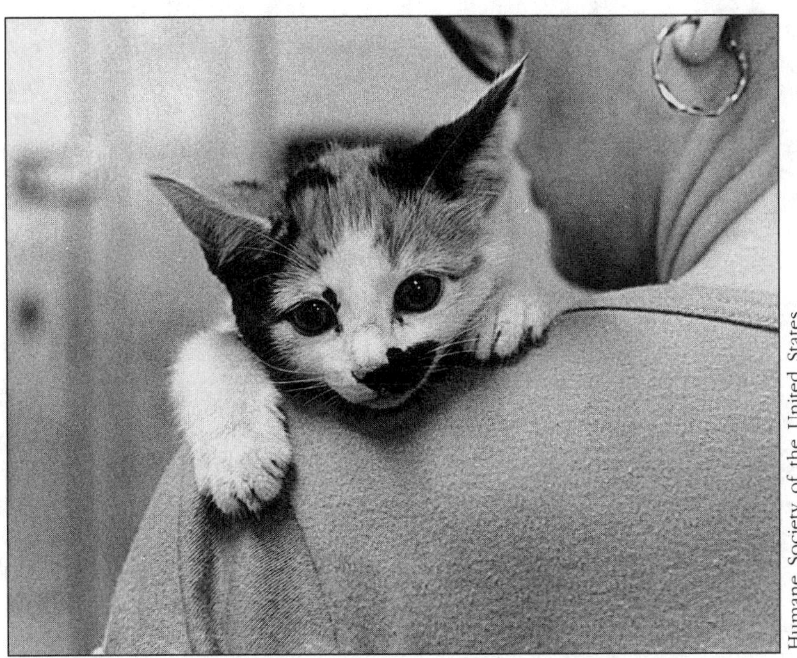

Humane Society of the United States

Recent research indicates that pets have a measurable calming effect on their owners.

Critics of the view that pet ownership is sanctioned by history point out that some people, especially dog owners, may use their pets inappropriately to compensate for perceived shortcomings in their own personalities. "Many pit bull owners are teenagers who like to fight with [the animals] or look tough," says District of Columbia legislative assistant Sobo. "It's a power trip for some people, including women, who think the dog will protect them from being victims of rape or a mugging."

Some critics of pet ownership say it is morally wrong. "It's a freedom issue for me," says Colman McCarthy, a columnist for *The Washington Post* and a pacifist who teaches college and high-school courses on non-violence. "These are living, sentient beings that have the same right to live and grow as humans do."

Adopting an animal at the shelter may save the life of one animal, but it hurts many others, McCarthy says, because "we're out there killing cows and pigs and chickens to feed the animals at home." McCarthy calls for a 20-year phaseout to gradually end pet ownership altogether. In the meantime, he says, "The only way to deal with this problem effectively is to make ownership so costly that people will think twice" before obtaining a pet.

Cavanaugh rejects claims that pet ownership is exploitative or a sign of mental imbalance. "The human-canine bond goes back to the beginning of recorded history," he says. "It's a fact that dogs lower your blood pressure when they walk into the room. If that's bad, then I guess I exploit my dog. There's so much that we don't even understand about these relationships that it's hard to say that anybody is exploiting anybody. I certainly know

Top Dog

Labrador Retrievers have been the most popular dogs in the United States for the past five years, according to the American Kennel Club.

United Kennel Club

Most Popular Breeds for 1995*

1. Labrador Retriever
2. Rottweiler
3. German Shepherd
4. Golden Retriever
5. Beagle
6. Poodle
7. Cocker Spaniel
8. Dachshund
9. Pomeranian
10. Yorkshire Terrier

* *Rankings are based on the number of purebred dogs registered with the AKC in 1995 from the 141 breeds it currently recognizes.*

Source: American Kennel Club press release, April 1, 1996

who's the boss in our house, and he weighs 12 pounds."

Occupying the middle ground on people's need for pets is Beck. "We may actually have a hard-wired need for contact, not necessarily with dogs and cats, but with nature," he says. "When I was growing up in Brooklyn, my contact with nature was to walk to the Jamaica Bay dump and watch the rats. With urbanization we have brought some nature indoors, either with plants or domestic animals. We all know the individual whose dog is their child, who may love animals in a misanthropic way, instead of loving people. There are extremes in every human behavior. But I don't think the person like myself, who really finds great comfort with a dog, is that much more out of sync than a person who enjoys a good book, watches PBS or goes camping."

The idea that pets are a healthy link with nature was sharply challenged by the late Paul Shepard, who was a professor of human ecology at Pitzer College and the Claremont Graduate School. (*See "At Issue," p. 1145.*) "What is wrong at the heart of the keeping of pets is that they are deficient animals in whom we have invested the momentum of 2 million years of love . . . ," Shepard wrote in a book published shortly before he died earlier this year. "They are monsters of the order invented by Frankenstein except that they are engineered to conform to our wishes, biological slaves who cringe and fawn or perform or whatever we wish. As embodiments of trust, dependence, companionship, esthetic beauty, vicarious power, innocence or action by command, they are wholly unlike the wild world. In effect, they are organic machines conforming to our needs." [6]

Should certain species be banned as pets?

There are more than 45 kinds of domestic animals, ranging from common dogs and cats and barnyard chickens and cows to South American llamas and Asian water buffalo. What distinguishes these animals from their wild cousins, explains the ASPCA's Caras, is that "their genes have been sufficiently under the control of man for long enough that natural selection is not a factor, but selective breeding is."

While farmers have at times made pets of all domesticated animals, few of them have proved suitable for life in urban or suburban areas. "Dogs and cats are clearly suitable," Caras says. "So are those caged birds that were not captured in the wild but bred in captivity, and of course fish."

He cautions consumers about getting so-called "shelf pets," small mammals such as gerbils, hamsters, rats or guinea pigs, because they are so vulnerable to mistreatment. "You have to take care of them, keep them clean, feed them and give them water because once you put them in that 10-gallon aquarium and clamp on the screened lid, they're trapped," he says. "They're there forever and will live whatever life you give them. They can't ask you for anything."

Caras draws the line at what he calls "fad animals," unusual pets that often sell at exorbitant prices. "Right now it's the European hedgehog," he says. "These are just get-rich-quick schemes, where somebody imports and breeds them for a while, like chinchillas, gets them selling at absurd prices and then takes his money and gets out of it."

Most jurisdictions permit only certain common animals to be kept as pets. Some specifically prohibit the capture of wild animals or hybrids, such as the wolf-dog. (*See story, p. 1140.*) Many, including the state of California, ban ferrets, small weasel-like animals, because they consider them to be wild and because they have been known to bite, causing serious injury to children.

Caras says such bans are inappropriate, however. "The so-called ferret is actually a European stoat," he says. "It's not a ferret at all, and it's been domesticated for about 2,000 years. I wouldn't have one because they really do stink. But they're interesting little animals and kind of nice, though I would never leave one loose with an infant in a crib."

When it comes to deciding whether it's a good idea to take in an exotic animal as a pet, Beck offers some advice. "There's absolutely no good reason to keep any animal unless you are really skilled in caring for it or if it could really hurt someone if it escapes," he says. That rules out poisonous snakes, scorpions and other venomous creatures. "It's also wrong to keep animals for which our understanding of disease transmission is inadequate," he says. That rules out monkeys and other primates because they can spread tuberculosis and other diseases to people. "Finally," he says, "it is wrong to take in animals for which our own veterinary skills are somewhat limited. That's just cruel." ■

BACKGROUND

Domesticating Animals

Humans are thought to have begun taming animals around the end of the last Ice Age in Egypt's Nile Valley and other parts of the Near East. It was around the same time that humans, armed with fire and the first rudely fashioned tools, began to migrate from the tropics where they originated to the colder climes of the Northern Hemispheres.

The range of animals that people have domesticated over the millennia is vast. Many, such as the dog, domestic sheep and goats, cattle and horses, have been literally created by man, who gradually shaped these animals into creatures that are visibly different from their wild forebears. Other domestic animals, such as camels, llamas, reindeer, elephants and even cats, have been tamed but not radically changed from their wild counterparts.

What all these species have in common is a series of traits that Francis Galton, a 19th-century English biologist, identified as essential for the successful domestication of wild animals: "They should be hardy; they should have an inborn liking for man; they should be comfort-loving; they should be found useful to the savages; they should breed freely; and they should be easy to tend." [7]

Wolves — the progenitors of today's dogs — lent themselves to early association with people because of all these qualities, in addition to their highly developed social behavior as members of packs. Initially lured to human camps in search of food, wolves are believed to have been tamed and used to protect their new masters from attack by other predators and to assist them in hunting. Archaeological evidence suggests that people began taming wolves at least 12,000 years ago, around the same time they began domesticating sheep and goats. [8]

Selective breeding of wild animals during the domestication process has produced a wide range of breeds, or groups with distinct, inherited characteristics, of the same species. Breeding has led to certain consistent changes within species, however. All breeds of domestic horses, for example, have longer manes and tails than wild horses, while even the biggest dogs have smaller teeth than wolves. Pigs are fatter than boars, their wild counterparts. Likewise, domestic animals that return to the wild, or become feral, often quickly shed the physical and behavioral characteristics of the domestic animal. After a few generations, stray pigs begin to develop the bristles, tusks and lean bodies typical of the boar.

Dogs are farther removed genetically from their ancestor, the wolf. Today there are more than 400 recognized dog breeds around the world, and dogs can be found in virtually every part of the world where people live. But a pack of stray dogs of widely differing breeds, such as Pekinese, Great Danes and Dalmatians, would within a few years lose their specific breed traits and produce litters of medium-sized dogs of similar size and shape.

Cats came under human control much later than dogs, beginning around 4,000 years ago. Prized for their ability to keep rodents at bay, wild cats were domesticated by ancient Egyptians and transformed into a smaller, less ferocious variety. The Egyptians worshiped their cats, mummified them at death and forbade the killing of cats.

But over the centuries, cats have undergone less of a transformation from the wild state than have dogs. Although there are numerous recognized breeds of cats around the world — more than 35 in the United States alone — there are fewer than dog breeds and the differences in size and behavior are far less distinct. Feral cats readily adapt to the wild environment.

Cultural Differences

Of all the domestic animals, dogs and cats came to be Americans' favorite pets. But these animals have not always enjoyed their elevated status. Cats were reviled in medieval Europe, where they were associated with witchcraft and often executed along with their owners.

At the same time that dogs were prized in much of Europe, North America and other parts of the world as hunting companions, herders and sentinels, they were despised as unclean vermin in the Muslim world. In East Asia and North America dogs have been kept both as pets and as sources of protein. In journals documenting their quest for a river passage to the Pacific Ocean in the early 1800s, explorers Meriwether Lewis and William Clark say they dined frequently on dog meat provided by the Nez Percé Indians in the Pacific Northwest. [9]

Even today, animals that are cherished as pets by Americans are treated as pests in other cultures. Beijing and other Chinese cities, where dog meat is still considered to be a delicacy, have from time to time imposed total bans on pet dogs. Just last year, the Beijing government banned all big dogs in an effort to quash their growing popularity as pets. [10] Earlier this year, the government of Quito, Ecuador, launched a "decaninization" campaign in which any dog caught at large was killed on the spot in an effort to quell a rabies epidemic. [11]

But dogs and cats fare better in some countries than they do in the United States. Six out of 10 households in France own a pet of some kind; nearly half include a dog or a cat. In fact, there are almost as many pets in that country (42 million) as there are people (58 million). [12] While few communities in the United States allow pets in public buildings, dogs have long been welcomed in restaurants and other businesses in France, Belgium and many other European countries. And while some 100,000 dogs and 80,000 cats are abandoned each year in France, other European countries — notably Britain and the Scandinavian nations — have such a long tradition of humane care of their pets that euthanasia is far less frequent than in the United States.

Regulating Ownership

In the United States, the earliest regulations related to domestic animals focused on their humane treatment. The first Societies for the Prevention of Cruelty to Animals were created in the 1860s in New York, Boston and Philadelphia to protect horses from abuse and overwork. In 1869, Caroline Earl White opened a second Philadelphia chapter directed and run entirely by women. The group established one of the first pet shelters in the country. [13]

For the most part, however, national humane organizations were founded to promote considerate treatment of all animals, not just pets. The oldest of these, the American Society for the Prevention of Cruelty to Animals, was founded in 1866 "to alleviate pain, fear and suffering in animals." Until its current president, Roger Caras, ended the practice in 1994, the ASPCA also ran animal control shelters in New York City.

Later groups include the American Humane Association (AHA), which is concerned with the welfare of children as well as animals, and the Humane Society of the United States, which split off from the AHA in 1954 to focus more specifically on animal rights. [14] None of the national groups are involved in running shelters, however. Although many local animal shelters are called humane societies or SPCAs, the vast majority are independently run and unaffiliated with any larger organization.

Pet ownership mushroomed after World War II, with the arrival of the baby boom children and suburban development. The sudden appearance of single-family homes with back yards surrounding the nation's cities created an especially hospitable environment for cats and dogs. Regulations governing ownership of these pets developed almost exclusively at state and local levels. (The only federal law, the 1966 Animal Welfare Act, focused on ways to ensure humane treatment of all animals, including livestock, animals in zoos and lab animals, as well as pets.)

Continued on p. 1141

Chronology

1860s-90s ***The first animal protection groups are formed in major U.S. cities to protect horses from abuse.***

1866
American Society for the Prevention of Cruelty to Animals (ASPCA) is founded in New York City "to alleviate pain, fear and suffering in animals."

1869
Caroline Earl White opens a chapter of the ASPCA in Philadelphia; it establishes one of the first pet shelters in the country.

1894
The Robinson-Danforth Commission Co. is founded. Renamed Ralston Purina in 1902, the company will later become a leader in the multibillion-dollar pet food and supply industry.

1950s ***As pet ownership mushrooms with the postwar "baby boom" and suburban development, animal rights groups concentrate their efforts on protecting domestic animals.***

1954
The Humane Society of the United States breaks away from the American Humane Association — dedicated to protecting children as well as animals — to focus more specifically on animal rights.

1960s-70s ***Regulation of household pets, especially dogs, becomes stricter, especially in cities where complaints of animal waste and noise prompt many pet bans and "scoop laws" requiring dog owners to clean up after their pets.***

1966
Congress passes the Animal Welfare Act aimed at ensuring the humane treatment of all animals, including livestock, animals in zoos and lab animals, as well as pets.

Aug. 1, 1978
One of the country's first "scoop laws" goes into effect in New York City, requiring all dog owners to clean up after their animals in city streets and parks.

1980s ***Research indicating the health benefits of pet ownership results in the reversal of pet bans in many jurisdictions.***

1981
The White House Conference on Aging adopts a resolution calling on federal, state and local governments to support legislation allowing the elderly to keep their companion animals. California, Maryland, New York and other states later enact laws protecting the rights of elderly tenants to own pets.

1990s ***With more Americans choosing "low-maintenance" pets, cats for the first time surpass dogs as the country's most popular pet.***

1996
The Pet Food Institute estimates that there are now 66 million pet cats in the United States, far outnumbering the pet dog population, estimated at 55 million. But many cat owners have more than one pet, and there continue to be more dog-owning households overall. At the same time, as many as 20 million cats and dogs are expected to be euthanized at shelters around the country.

April 1996
Washington, D.C., passes ordinance requiring pit bull owners to muzzle their dogs in public, joining a growing number of jurisdictions that ban or restrict specific dog breeds that have been implicated in vicious attacks. The temporary measure expires in November.

1997
The National Pet Council, a group of humane, veterinary and breed associations, plans to release the first nationwide animal-shelter survey, which is expected to show that stray cats far outnumber stray dogs.

Ignore the Call of the Wild

Experts in animal care are virtually unanimous in their recommendation to stick to domesticated animals when choosing a pet. Although wild animals may be cute and cuddly in the early months of life, they tend to become less and less suitable as human companions as they mature. The characteristics that have helped their species survive over the millennia are rarely compatible for life in captivity.

In no instance is this more poignant than with wolves and wolf-dog hybrids. Although wolf-dog hybrids have long been common among Native Alaskan sled dog teams, it's only been in the past decade or so that the practice of breeding dogs with wolves has spread to other parts of the country.

"Some people think that these are going to be some kind of cool, macho watchdog, which is totally wrong," says Randall Lockwood, an animal behaviorist and vice president for training initiatives of the Humane Society of the United States. "Then there are the wolf groupies, who see owning a wolf or hybrid almost as part of a spiritual or religious quest, as their link to the wild. They have their wolf artwork and medallions, and while they may see something in the animal on a spiritual level, they often are ill-equipped to meet the animal's basic biological needs."

Many of those needs are quite different from a dog's. "We spent at least 12,000 years turning a wild animal — the wolf — into an animal that can fit well into human society," says Lockwood. "We've taken one of the most powerful predators on the planet and through thousands of generations of selection produced animals that for the most part can live in our homes without hurting or eating us."

Even the biggest dogs have smaller teeth than wolves, and they tend to look to a person — not another dog — as their pack leader, or master. While wolves roam vast territories in search of food, dogs have been bred to stay much closer to home. But in addition to breeding some of the characteristics of wolves out of their dogs, people have also bred into domestic dogs a kind of territorial aggressiveness needed to make good watchdogs that is absent in their wild cousins.

Wolf hybrids contain an unpredictable mix of these features. "Usually you have an animal that's quite a bit larger than either wolves or dogs, that is naturally selected for traveling miles and miles every day, that's now essentially relegated to living on a chain in someone's back yard or pickup truck," Lockwood says. "It still has the predatory instincts of the wolf and yet at the same time might have some heightened aggression that we've bred for in dogs."

Lockwood, who has studied problems related to wolf hybrids around the country, says these animals are less apt to become vicious toward people than they are to cause other problems that often land them in local animal shelters. "They get bored, and because they're very strong, they almost always escape, injuring themselves or others in the process," he says. "They go after neighbors' dogs, they jump fences and get hit by cars, they jump out of windows, they eat your house."

This destructive behavior typically lasts longer than the normal "adolescent" phase in dogs because it takes two or three years for wolves to mature, at least twice as long as dogs. "Many people get these animals naively, thinking they are cute or will make interesting and different pets," Lockwood says. "Then they call us when they realize that what they have is something they can't control. They don't realize that this is essentially a wild animal that is further hampered by having lost some of the instinctive controls on aggressions that are there in the wolf. Instead of having the best of both worlds, often hybrids have the worst."

If wolf hybrids often turn out to be a disappointment for their owners, they pose a real threat to the wild wolf population. Exterminated throughout most of the country decades ago, wolves are just beginning to make a comeback, thanks to the determined efforts of wildlife groups and a gradual shifting of public opinion in favor of restoring natural habitats. Small numbers of wolves have migrated from Canada to remote areas of Minnesota and Montana, and a controversial reintroduction effort has restored healthy wolf populations to remote areas in Idaho and near Yellowstone National Park in Wyoming and Montana.[1]

Wolf-hybrid owners, often among the strongest supporters of wolf reintroduction projects, may do more harm than good to their cause. "A lot of people who get hybrids think they can help defuse the 'Little Red Riding Hood' myth in their community," Lockwood says. "And yet the first time their animal bites somebody or gets into other trouble, they've just made things much worse." Owners who give up in frustration and abandon their fertile hybrids in the woods in areas inhabited by wolves cause even greater harm by contaminating the wild population with dog genes.

The most vocal opponents of wolf reintroduction projects are ranchers, who fear the wolves will kill their livestock. Free-roaming dog packs have long been a nuisance to ranchers in the West, so much so that ranchers maintain the right to shoot on sight dogs they find on their land. Wolves tend to favor their natural prey — deer, elk and smaller mammals — to sheep or cattle. "We have plenty of instances of dogs and wolf-dog hybrids that have attacked livestock," Lockwood says. "Often it's the local coyote and recovering wolf populations that get blamed."

For anyone who yearns to own a piece of the wild, Lockwood has simple advice: "If you want to get a wolf hybrid or a wolf because you want to help the wolves, save the $15,000 you'll spend buying the animal and a high fence and give it to one of the groups that are working for wolf recovery."

---

[1] For background, see "Environmental Movement at 25," *The CQ Researcher*, March 31, 1995, pp. 286-287.

Continued from p. 1138

For many years, oversight of pet ownership was lax, especially in the suburbs. Although dog owners were routinely required to inoculate their pets against rabies, a viral disease fatal to animals and humans alike, pet dogs and cats roamed freely in most parts of the country well into the 1960s. In the cities, however, where apartment living made it hard to keep large pets, nuisance complaints about barking dogs, yowling cats and the unsanitary environment caused by animal waste prompted some jurisdictions and building owners to impose sweeping bans on all types of pets.

After heart-breaking news stories about the suffering caused when elderly residents were forced to give up their pets, participants at the 1981 White House Conference on Aging adopted a resolution calling on federal, state and local governments to support legislation allowing the elderly to keep their companion animals because of their "measurable therapeutic effects on their [owners'] physical and emotional health." Maryland, California, New York and other states have since enacted laws aimed at protecting the rights of elderly tenants to own pets. [15]

But restrictions on pet ownership grew more rigid for other Americans with the continued growth in the population of both animals and people. Leash laws, long a standard requirement in large cities, spread in an effort to force dog owners to keep their pets from overturning garbage cans, roving in aggressive packs and being killed on the nation's rapidly expanding roadways. Licensing requirements became more strictly enforced, and animal control workers began picking up not just nuisance animals but any dog running at large. Finally, beginning in the late 1970s, local jurisdictions began imposing "scoop laws," requiring dog owners to clean up after their pets when off their property. ■

CURRENT SITUATION

Cats vs. Dogs

The difficulty of properly caring for dogs in today's urban environment has prompted many Americans to turn to cats for companionship — so much so that by one measure cats have recently bumped dogs out of their traditional status as the country's favorite pet.

Dog owners may still prevail, however. Four in 10 households include at least one dog, compared with three in 10 for cats. [16] But because many cat-owners have more than one, cats now are thought to outnumber dogs by some 10 million. "There have not been any dramatic increases in the dog and cat populations in the past few years," says Bob Wilbur, spokesman for the Pet Food Institute in Washington, D.C. "But there was a pretty sharp increase in pet cats during the 1980s."

Stricter dog ordinances, coupled with the increase in two-earner households, may explain the shift. "I used to be a dog person, but we live in an apartment where dogs aren't allowed," says Scott Butler, a bartender who lives with his wife in Silver Spring, Md. "So we compromised and bought an Abyssinian at a pet store. They're intelligent and have a dog-like temperament." Butler was so enchanted with his lively, red-coated cat that he began breeding Abyssinians as a hobby three years ago and now owns eight of them.

There seems to be a different cat breed for every lifestyle. "Cats have become more popular among everyone as people have become more metropolitan and a lot of places only accept small pets," says Judy Stap, who has bred Persians at her home on Maryland's Eastern Shore since 1968. She says women often are drawn to the less-demanding personalities typical of Persians and other long-haired cats. "Men tend to prefer the shorthairs, which are more active," Stap says. "Women like longhairs because they enjoy grooming and caring for them. Also, these cats are docile. Persians gravitate to the lap."

Some experts see an even more significant shift away from dog ownership. "We're really seeing a shift to what you might call low-maintenance animals," says Beck. "The cat population has gone up, but the bird population has grown proportionally higher than any pet species, by about 21 percent over the past five years."

Beck foresees a continuation of this trend. "There are more families in which both parents work, as well as single-parent households," he says. "Presumably, all this means that people are leading busier lives. Also, more middle-class and high-income Americans, who are the biggest animal owners, are moving into condos. All these things have been cited in explaining why people who want to keep a pet may not want to have to run home by 5 o'clock to walk the dog."

Pet Products Boom

Americans may want pets that are easy to live with, but many pet owners treat their "low-maintenance" companions as though they were children.

The manufacturers of pet products couldn't be happier. *The Whole Kitty Catalog* lists more than 800 products for cats alone. One featured item, described as a "deluxe kitty climbing aerie," is a collection of six-foot tall posts and platforms that resembles a carpet-covered children's gym set and would fill a small room. The set sells for $1,250, plus shipping and handling. [17] In addition to traditional sup-

The High Cost of Pet Ownership

If cost is a consideration in choosing a pet, you may want to think twice before getting a dog.

Breeders, who supply about a third of the pet dogs in the United States, charge anywhere from $100 for a pet-quality animal to $1,000 or more for a show-quality female; females often cost more than males because of their breeding potential.

Even if your dog is a gift from a friend or relative, or you adopt a shelter animal or a stray, the cost of dog ownership is high. Unless you qualify for services at one of the low-income veterinary clinics that are beginning to appear in some large cities, spaying or neutering will run around $200-$300. The cost of basic obedience training — a key investment — can range from a nominal fee for a local-government-sponsored course to hundreds of dollars for one-on-one professional training.

Even after puppyhood, dogs tend to be expensive pets, costing owners on average between $500 and $840 a year, depending on the animal's size. According to the American Pet Products Manufacturers Association, the biggest outlays are for non-surgical veterinary expenses (about $140 a year on average), food ($200) and grooming ($100). Flea and tick products, toys and other supplies run about $50 a year.[1]

Cats typically are much less expensive pets than dogs. The vast majority of cat-owners get their pets free of charge, as kittens from household litters, as strays or from friends. It costs about $390 a year to care for a cat. The biggest expense is food ($165 a year on average), followed by veterinary bills ($87) and supplies such as kitty litter ($48).

Smaller mammals are not necessarily a bargain compared with Fido and Fluffy. A pet chinchilla runs about $380 to buy and $200 a year to keep. Ferrets — where they are permitted — cost $120 each and over $200 to care for. The real bargains among so-called "shelf pets" — at least the warm-blooded variety — are mice and rats, which can be had for less than $5 each and cost about $60 a year to keep.

The cost of keeping other types of animals varies widely. People who own saltwater fish, such as angel and butterfly fish, spend about twice as much each year ($180) as owners of freshwater fish, which include tropical fish such as neons and cardinals as well as goldfish. The biggest items in all fish owners' budgets are equipment and lighting. Birds, which sell on average for $120 at pet stores, cost about $130 a year to care for.

If your tastes run to the reptilian, turtles are the real bargain, costing on average $20 to buy and $87 a year to maintain. Iguanas are about twice as expensive to purchase and keep ($220) as lizards ($110). Of all the common reptile pets, snakes are the most expensive, running on average $160 each to buy. Snake owners then pay about $275 a year to keep their pets, mostly for food. But for that they get to watch them eat it. While it squirms.

---

[1] American Pet Products Manufacturers Association, Inc., *1996 APPMA National Pet Owners Survey*, p. 55. Other figures sited in this sidebar are from pp. 101, 224-225, 142-143, 185 and 261.

plies, such as rawhide bones and catnip-scented toys, pet stores now offer a wide range of expensive grooming tools, collars, flea treatment kits — not to mention such esoteric items as pet clothing, exercise ramps for gerbils, live crickets for tarantulas and plastic toys for parrots.

For the truly doting pet-owner, there are specialized providers, including exercise gyms where overweight dogs and people can trot off their excess calories together, bed and breakfasts that cater to the traveling pooch and lawn companies that will periodically rid your back yard of unwanted deposits.

But the real bonanza is found in dog and cat food sales, which amounted to $9.3 billion in 1995, according to the Pet Food Institute. The institute does not say how much of that revenue translated into profits for its member companies. "Even we don't know that," says Wilbur. "Most of the companies are divisions of integrated corporations, and they don't release profits by division."

But there is little doubt that upscale pet owners are paying top dollar to ensure that their dogs and cats are eating quality fare. "Premium cat and dog foods are more likely to contain more highly digestible protein," Wilbur says. "They also carry a higher average price than traditional brands sold in grocery stores." Premium brands such as Iams and Hills typically are sold exclusively by veterinary clinics and pet stores.

The demand for premium food at more reasonable prices has fueled the phenomenal success of warehouse-style chain stores. Nationwide chains, such as Phoenix-based PetsMart and Petco of San Diego, which already have more than 100 stores across the country, offer premium foods and a vast array of other products at prices that traditional pet stores can't match. Although most of the estimated 18,000 pet stores in the United States are still small, independent operations, many go out of business when a chain store moves into the neighborhood.[18]

Pet owners also are spending more to secure veterinary care for their pets. In addition to the basic rabies shots and puppy worming medications, routine care now includes monthly doses of heartworm medicine to protect dogs from this deadly parasite and vaccination and screening for feline leukemia and feline immunodeficiency virus, an AIDS-like affliction that has become prevalent throughout the country. And these are just the basics: Canine psychotherapists will prescribe Prozac and other psychoactive drugs to help Fido behave, [19] while holistic health practitioners will use massage, acupuncture and herbal medicines to bring Fluffy back to health.

In addition, owners are seeking specialists' care to treat injuries and illnesses that only a few years ago would have made pets candidates for euthanasia. Although the cost of veterinary treatment is far less than the corresponding costs of human health care, the gap is closing. Repair of a torn anterior cruciate ligament for a large dog at one suburban Washington clinic, for example, exceeds $2,000, including anesthesia and post-operative care.

The cost of veterinary care — and pet owners' reluctance to have Fido put to sleep until all treatment options have been exhausted — are driving demand for a nascent pet health insurance industry. "It's not something that's broadly available yet," says Brad Gehrke, a research analyst at the American Veterinary Medical Association in Schaumburg, Ill. "There are only two or three companies in the country that are offering any kind of pet insurance."

Owners who are eager to reduce their veterinary bills should be aware, however, that the same kinds of limits that are common to human coverage apply to pets as well: no pre-existing conditions for the previous six months, no routine preventive care and no elective treatment. But the premiums are much lower. Veterinary Pet Insurance of Anaheim, Calif., charges $89 for a puppy or a kitten and $134 for a 5-year-old pet. [20]

Spay-Neuter Campaigns

The pet industry and veterinarians are joining local animal shelters, advocacy groups and breeders throughout the country in their efforts to reduce the number of animals that end up in shelters, often to die by lethal injection. Though no one knows for sure how many abandoned pets are euthanized each year, estimates reach as high as 20 million.

To stem the tide of unwanted animals, animal welfare groups strongly encourage people to neuter their animals (a procedure called spaying in the case of females) before they have a chance to reproduce. "We've been yelling spay-neuter from the rooftops since day one," says Caras of the ASPCA, whose shelters in New York City euthanized 38,000 animals during their last year of operation in 1994. "Spay or neuter your animals, stop breeding them and don't let them breed on their own. With fewer dogs and cats out there, there would be homes for a much higher percentage of the ones that are left."

Most animal shelters require new owners when adopting pets to spay or neuter them. As an additional incentive, many jurisdictions charge more when they issue dog licenses for unneutered animals. In Washington, D.C., for example, dog owners who spay or neuter their pets pay just $10 a year to license them, compared with $35 for unneutered animals.

Breed registry clubs encourage owners of purebred dogs and cats who are not professional breeders to neuter their pets by emphasizing the improvement in behavior neutering often brings. "Neutering reduces the destructive side that tomcats exhibit," writes one cat fancier. "Most intact males are overly aggressive, fight with other cats and spray urine to mark their territory." [21] Likewise, both male and female dogs tend to be less aggressive after they are neutered.

© 1992 Stephen Cooper, AllStock, PNI Ltd.

A Web site on the Internet offers tarantula owners solutions to all sorts of problems.

Prospective owners who want to adopt rather than buy a purebred pet can do so through breed-specific rescue organizations that provide foster care for animals of that breed that would otherwise be euthanized in shelters. "Most rescue pets are older and therefore housebroken, are more independent and calm or beyond many destructive habits," reads a pamphlet issued by Somali/Abyssinian Breed Rescue & Education (SABRE), based in Cary, Ill. "Nevertheless, these older animals can be just as loving and gentle as a kitten or puppy raised in your home." By adopting a breed rescue pet, the group says, "you are making a contribution to both the breed and the homeless animal."

Campaigns to adopt shelter animals and limit pet reproduction are paying off. According to Cavanaugh of the AKC, the number of animals that are euthanized in the nation's shelters has fallen by half over the past two decades, and even more dramatically in the past five years. "We think this is due to educational efforts encouraging responsible pet ownership, including spaying and neutering pets," he says. "Also shelters are carrying out much more aggressive adoption policies. Shelters that once had no money and just waited for people to come to them to adopt a pet are now aggressively raising money and selling their product, as they say in marketing."

One way shelters and humane groups are pushing adoption is through local newsletters distributed free of charge in veterinary clinics and pet stores. The Animal Welfare League of Arlington, Va., for example, issues a 20-page newsletter — *Pawpourri* — four times a year in which local shelters and breed rescue groups feature dogs and cats that are up for adoption. Advertisements for pet stores, pet sitters and other service providers help defray the cost of publication.

Vicious-Dog Laws

The use of dogs as offensive weapons has prompted some local jurisdictions to restrict or even ban certain breeds or types. In Washington, D.C., for example, reports of dog bites by pit bulls and Rottweilers have escalated in recent years, as drug dealers and other criminals have trained these animals to attack on command.

After a man sicked his pit bull on a teenage girl last April, the D.C. City Council passed emergency legislation that singled out the two breeds as "dangerous dogs" subject to special restrictions. Owners of pit bulls and Rottweilers were required to muzzle their dogs when off their property and buy special liability insurance to pay for any injuries they might cause. When Rottweiler owners protested that the breed was not inherently dangerous, the new law was changed to apply only to mixed-breed pit bulls. *

United Kennel Club

Many dog owners and breed registry clubs challenge the assertion that bull terrier breeds are naturally violent and aggressive.

"Pit bulls have been determined all over the place as dangerous because of their character traits," says Sobo, the legislative assistant who drafted the bill. "Pit bulls have a natural tendency to be very short-tempered, very strong and very, very aggressive. It has the unique quality, if you can call it that, to lock its jaws when it bites. It cannot open its jaws to let go of the victim, so it has to tear off flesh. It's very gory, I can tell you that."

Many dog owners and breed clubs criticize such breed-specific restrictions as unfair and ineffective. "We oppose individual breed restrictions but we strongly support vicious dog laws that cover all types of dogs," says the AKC's Cavanaugh. "If the dog shows vicious tendencies like growling or snapping, it should be muzzled, insured and locked, regardless of the breed. But to punish an entire breed rather than the deed that the dog commits is unfortunate."

The United Kennel Club (UKC), the world's second largest purebred dog registry, also opposes breed-specific ordinances. "Victims of dog bites do not care what breed of dog has caused their injury — they want laws to protect them against all vicious dogs and their owners," says UKC President Fred T. Miller. "The community of responsible dog owners wants strong legislation against vicious dogs — not breeds."

Pit bulls are not recognized by the UKC or AKC because they are mixed-breed dogs. The term is sometimes misapplied to the American Pit Bull Terrier, also called the American Staffordshire Terrier, and related bull terrier breeds. And, according to Miller, the term is often misused by the media to describe any mongrel dog involved in a violent incident. "The

Continued on p. 1146

* Washington's emergency pit bill restriction expired in November 1996. The City Council failed to pass a permanent measure after the D.C. Control Board argued that the city lacked the funds to enforce it.

At Issue:

Are pets a healthy link with nature?

PET INDUSTRY JOINT ADVISORY COUNCIL
The pet industry's legislative advocate based in Washington, D.C.

FROM *OUR PETS, OUR HEALTH,* A PAMPHLET ISSUED IN 1996.

yes

Animal companionship has always been important to people. Every society has lived with some sort of animal.

Why this human-animal bond exists has long been a source of speculation. Beginning in the 1980s, serious research into the advantages of animal companionship has documented a wide range of benefits to humans. Lower stress, better socialization with others and the comfort of physical contact are just a few of the ways that animals enrich our lives.

During the past decade, Dr. Alan Beck, now at the School of Veterinary Medicine, Purdue University, has been a leading force in the research of how animal companionship facilitates the mental and physical well-being of humans. . . .

How does interacting with animals improve our health? All the reasons are not clear, but Dr. Beck says we modify our behavior in the presence of animals. People talking to their companion dogs, cats and birds speak more slowly, softly and with a more relaxed mode, which, in itself, tends to reduce blood pressure. . . . Additionally, when we are with animals, we focus our attention on them rather than on the problems that are causing our stress.

Many studies have shown that animal contact lessens feelings of loneliness and depression for older people, especially when the people have a sense of attachment to their animals. . . .

As today's increasingly urban, fast paced life-style seems to take us further and further from nature, stress, alienation and tension are generated by our separation from the "living environment." Keeping in touch with nature is an important part of our natural needs, especially for city dwellers and suburbanites. While there is no clearly identified *single* explanation for the positive effect pets have on their owners, there is growing epidemiologic evidence that people who feel an attachment for nature or companion animals have lessened risks of disease and disease processes compared with people without such experiences.

After conducting numerous research projects on the human-animal bond, Dr. Beck believes that in addition to the love and companionship they offer, pets also serve as our link with nature. They act as a natural barometer to tell us that all is right with the world. When we come home and the cat rubs against us or the guinea pig squeals for lettuce, we are reassured by their constant and predictable behavior.

Not only are our own pets an important link with nature, but even viewing animals in general affects us positively. In fact, our innate need to be with animals is such an important part of human nature that more people visit zoos each year than attend all sporting events combined.

PAUL SHEPARD
Professor of human ecology, Pitzer College and the Claremont Graduate School; Shepard died in 1996

FROM THE OTHERS: HOW ANIMALS MADE US HUMAN (1996).

no

Animals were present at the center of human life for thousands of centuries before anyone thought of taking them captive, making them companions, forming the "friendship loops" of which animal-facilitation therapists and ethicists speak. . . .

Pets are not part of human evolution or the biological context out of which our ecology comes. They are civilized paraphernalia whose characteristic combination of accompaniment and accommodation is tangled in an ambiguous tyranny. Constance Perrin, an anthropologist, calls it "attachment theory." The animal triggers nurturant behavior and serves as a kind of intermediate object between the owner and a more or less alien world, but at the same time it is dragged about like a tattered security blanket. Indeed, the domestication of animals has never ensured their tender care. . . . Pets are deliberately abandoned by the millions and necessitate city-run slaughterhouses, shelters and "placement" services." This paradox of frenetic emotion and casual dismissal reveals our deep disappointment in the pet's ability to do something, be something, that we cannot quite identify. . . .

Domestic animals were "created" by humans by empirical genetic engineering over the past 10 thousand years. They are vestiges and fragments from a time of deep human respect for animals, whose abundance dazzled us in their many renditions of life, helping us to know ourselves by showing all that we had not become. The pet cannot restore us to that wholeness any more than an artificial limb renews the original; nor can it do more than simulate the Others among whom our ancestors lived for so long, the Others that constituted for them a cosmos. They and all captive animals are like organ transplants: healthy for us but cut out of their own organic fabric.

What is wrong at the heart of the keeping of pets is that they are deficient animals in whom we have invested the momentum of 2 million years of love of the Others. They are monsters of the order invented by Frankenstein except that they are engineered to conform to our wishes, biological slaves who cringe and fawn or perform or whatever we wish. As embodiments of trust, dependence, companionship, esthetic beauty, vicarious power, innocence, or action by command, they are wholly unlike the wild world. In effect, they are organic machines conforming to our needs.

Continued from p. 1144

name gets more TV news attention and sells more newspapers," he says.

Miller also challenges the assertion that bull terrier breeds are naturally violent and aggressive, and have jaws that have a tendency to lock and tear human flesh. "All dog jaws work in the same manner. . . . Likewise, all dog bites tear flesh in exactly the same manner, regardless of the breed of dog," he says. "The extent of the injuries is based solely on the size and strength of the dog involved."

Apart from the fairness issue, many experts say pit bull bans simply won't work. "Do you really think that somebody who is cutting drugs in his basement is not going to get another dog that will do the same thing?" asks Caras. "He'll take a Doberman, which is a lovely dog today, and turn that into a killer. Or a German Shepherd or a Belgian Malinois or a Great Pyrenees. I could list 50 breeds that would be perfectly willing to take on that role. Problems with animals are really problems with people, and animals are just the instruments." ■

OUTLOOK

More Regulations?

Ingrained as pet ownership is in the American way of life, it's probably safe to say that cats, dogs and other companion animals are here to stay. But owners are likely to face continuing calls to restrict their pets' impact on the surrounding community. These restrictions will fall most heavily on dogs — and their owners.

In local jurisdictions across the country, heated debates are arising over the rights of dog owners and the rest of the community. Bans on certain breeds of dog perceived to be dangerous may be designed to protect citizens from vicious and potentially lethal dog bites. But owners of non-aggressive animals of the targeted breeds are fighting back — in some cases with success. Last April's muzzle law against pit bulls and Rottweilers in Washington, D.C., for example, was subsequently changed after Rottweiler owners and breeders persuaded the City Council to drop that breed from the measure.

But restrictions on certain dog breeds are winning converts, even among humane groups. When the D.C. City Council was considering its ordinance requiring the muzzling of pit bulls earlier this year, local animal welfare groups were among the most vocal critics. "Our primary concern was whether mandatory muzzling would be detrimental to the animals and also whether it would actually address the problem," says Mary C. Healey, executive director of the Washington Humane Society, which runs the city's animal shelters.

But because the D.C. ordinance stopped short of banning pit bulls, as nearby Baltimore and many other jurisdictions are doing, and enabled animal control workers to better monitor the treatment of these dogs, Healey has changed her mind. "After six months of working with it," she says, "it actually turns out that it was a fairly decent law."

In addition to restricting ownership of certain types of dogs, some local jurisdictions are making it harder for dog owners to exercise their pets off leash. Urban dog owners often find isolated areas in local parks where they let their pets run around with other dogs. While this practice may violate local leash laws, it often has been ignored as long as the dogs don't disturb passersby. But as more and more dog owners work outside the home, these informal "dog parks" have become more crowded before and after work. In response to complaints by other park users, who say the dogs threaten their children and dirty public grounds, local authorities are more strictly enforcing leash laws.

Dog owners are not giving up without a fight. When New York City authorities cracked down on leash-law violations in Central Park last spring by issuing fines to owners of free-running dogs, they faced a barrage of criticism — and sometimes physical abuse — from enraged owners. [22]

Dog owners in Redondo Beach, Calif., offer a less confrontational approach to the problem that may serve as a model for other localities. When the local government instituted a leash law in parks, dog owners convinced city officials to hand over a three-acre abandoned dump, helped plant trees and grass over the lot and opened the first park in Southern California set aside exclusively for dogs. The Redondo Beach Dog Park, which has separate areas for large and small dogs to run free, water troughs and plastic "scooper" bags, is such a success that other jurisdictions are taking note. The Los Angeles City Council recently approved a plan to create a 10-acre dog park, which would be the largest in the county. [23]

Dogs are bearing the brunt of new pet ordinances. But cat owners used to letting their pets prowl the neighborhood at will may soon be in for a rude awakening. "Every once in a while we run into someone who thinks their dog should be allowed to run down the street free and happy, but the majority of people don't," Healey says. "However, people do think it's OK for their cats to be let out and run loose, and they've become a problem now. Cats don't bark, but they can create a lot of problems in terms of property damage."

They are also are a growing problem for shelter operators. Healey says cats have outnumbered dogs in D.C. shelters for the past 15 years or so.

Calls for a crackdown on free-roaming cats may gain momentum next year, when the first-ever national census of animal shelters is expected to be completed. "What we're finding out in the preliminary data is what we knew all along — it's stray cats that are the problem," says the AKC's Cavanaugh, a member of the board of the National Pet Council, a group of humane, veterinary and breed associations that has commissioned the survey. "In some shelters the ratio is huge, with almost no dogs to adopt out, but lots and lots of stray cats."

Although the survey is not expected to be completed until next year, humane societies are already studying ways to stem the number of stray cats that end up in their care, including bans on free-roaming cats. "We, as animal welfare organizations, have really neglected cats," says Healey. "But hopefully, cats are on our list of priorities now, and we'll do something about it." ■

FOR MORE INFORMATION

American Kennel Club, 51 Madison Ave., New York, N.Y. 10010; (212) 696-8200. The largest dog registry in the world provides information on dog breeds and on the choice and care of canine pets.

American Veterinary Medical Association, 1931 N. Meacham Rd., Suite 100, Schaumburg, Ill. 60173; (847) 925-8070. The national association representing veterinarians publishes information on the profession as well as dog and cat ownership.

American Society for the Prevention of Cruelty to Animals, 424 E. 92nd St., New York, N.Y. 10128; (212) 876-7700. The oldest humane society in the Western Hemisphere supports efforts to improve the lives of all animals.

Humane Society of the United States, 2100 L St. N.W., Washington, D.C. 20037; (202) 452-1100. The largest animal protection organization in the United States focuses on wildlife, farm animals and laboratory animals, as well as pets.

Notes

[1] Pet Food Institute, Fact Sheet 1996, April 3, 1996, p. 3. Also see "Dog and Cat Ownership, 1991-1998," *Journal of the American Veterinary Medical Association* (JAVMA), April 15, 1994, pp. 1166-1167.

[2] American Pet Products Manufacturers Association, *1996 APPMA National Pet Owners Survey,* 1996, pp. 2-3.

[3] American Tarantula Society Web site at http://www.cowboy.net/~spider/faq.html.

[4] See Anne Colden, "Suits over Dog Bites Are Ripping a Hole in Insurers' Pockets," *The Wall Street Journal,* March 11, 1996.

[5] See "Everybody's Best Friend," *American Health,* September 1996, p. 46.

[6] Paul Shepard, *The Others: How Animals Made Us Human* (1996), p. 151.

[7] Quoted by Juliet Clutton-Brock in *Domesticated Animals from Early Times* (1981), p. 10.

[8] *Ibid,* p. 34.

[9] See Stephen E. Ambrose, *Undaunted Courage* (1996), p. 350.

[10] See Kathy Chen, "Tough Rules for Dogs in Beijing Have Some Pet Owners Howling," *The Wall Street Journal,* June 20, 1995.

[11] See Gabriel Escobar, "On Ecuadoran Streets, All Dogs Must Die; To Stem Rabies Outbreak, Government Orders Decanınization," *The Washington Post,* April 2, 1996.

[12] See "Alouette, Gentile Alouette," *The Economist,* Aug. 24, 1996, p. 41.

[13] See Alan Beck and Aaron Katcher, *Between Pets and People* (1996), pp. 258-259.

[14] For background, see "Fighting Over Animal Rights," *The CQ Researcher,* Aug. 2, 1996, pp. 673-696.

[15] Beck and Katcher, *op. cit.,* p. 257.

[16] American Pet Products Manufacturers Association, *op. cit.,* p. 2.

[17] John Analon Reed, *The Whole Kitty Catalog* (1996).

[18] See Greg Johnson, "Dog-Eat-Dog World," *Los Angeles Times,* May 23, 1995.

[19] For background, see "Prozac Controversy," *The CQ Researcher,* Aug. 19, 1994, p. 734.

[20] See Reed Abelson, "When the Best Policy May Be No Policy At All," *The New York Times,* Nov. 3, 1996.

[21] Sandra Toney, "Factoring Your Feline's Personality: The Real Reasons Behind Your Cat's Behavior," *Cats,* February 1996, p. 41.

[22] See Douglas Martin, "Free-Range Canines," *The New York Times,* April 27, 1996.

[23] See Tracy Johnson, "Bark Park," *Los Angeles Times,* Nov. 18, 1996.

Bibliography

Selected Sources Used

Books

Beck, Alan, and Aaron Katcher, *Between Pets and People: The Importance of Animal Companionship*, Purdue University Press, 1996.

Beck and Katcher, veterinarians and experts in human-animal interaction, first described the ways pets benefit their owners' mental and physical health more than a decade ago. In this updated volume, they offer even more evidence of this symbiotic relationship.

Budiansky, Stephen, *The Covenant of the Wild: Why Animals Chose Domestication,* William Morrow and Co., Inc., 1992.

In this response to the animal-rights movement, the author argues that domestication has benefited animals as much as man, by presenting a vehicle for certain species to survive and thrive at the cost of losing some of their wild traits.

Clutton-Brock, Juliet, *Domesticated Animals from Early Times,* University of Texas Press and British Museum (Natural History), 1981.

The author, a zoologist at the British Museum of Natural History, traces the history of domestication for a broad range of animals from the end of the last Ice Age 10,000 years ago.

Robinson, I., ed., *The Waltham Book of Human-Animal Interaction: Benefits and Responsibilities of Pet Ownership,* Pergamon, 1995.

This collection of articles deals with the benefits of pet ownership for children, the elderly and other people, and examines the differences among dogs and cats and other domestic animals.

Serpell, James, *In the Company of Animals: A Study of Human-Animal Relationships,* Basil Blackwell, 1986.

According to this animal behaviorist at Cambridge University, man has created an artificial separation in his treatment of animals by elevating certain animal species to the status of pets while continuing to eat others.

Shepard, Paul, *The Others: How Animals Made Us Human,* Island Press/Shearwater Books, 1996.

A noted scholar in the field of human ecology and evolution examines the ways different cultures treat and interact with animals. Humans both despise and admire these "others" in their midst, Shepard concludes, and have yet to discover ways to allow animals and humans alike to flourish.

Smith, Carin A., *101 Training Tips for Your Cat,* Dell Publishing, 1994.

A veterinarian offers solutions to feline behavior problems ranging from trash can raids to bullying the new kitten in the house. She also provides health and general care information for cat owners.

Thomas, Elizabeth Marshall Thomas, *The Hidden Life of Dogs,* Houghton Mifflin Co., 1993.

The author closely examined the behavior of her dogs, following them as they roamed the streets of Cambridge, Mass., and concluded that dogs have many of the same emotions as people but prefer the company of their kind.

Articles

Glenn, Joshua, "Wild At Heart," *Utne Reader*, January-February 1996, pp. 51-67.

Four animal experts examine the relationship between people and their pets. Their conclusions range from endorsement of pet ownership as a healthy link to nature to its condemnation as an immoral act of enslavement.

Caras, Roger, "Heavy Petting," *The Washingtonian,* November 1996, pp. 72-75.

The author, president of the American Society for the Prevention of Cruelty to Animals, describes the way politicians use their pets to gain support among voters. They are able to do this because people tend to view favorably people who love animals.

Kaufman, Margo, "Animal Crackers," *Los Angeles Times Magazine,* March 7, 1993, pp. 34-36, 48-50.

The author draws a clear distinction between pet owners and "pet parents," people who treat their pets more like children than animals, lavishing luxuries of all descriptions on their companion animals. Pet suppliers couldn't be happier.

Klein, Richard, "The Power of Pets," *The New Republic,* July 10, 1995, pp. 18-23.

Americans are obsessed with their pets, the author contends, to the point of ignoring the central fact of their animal nature. But turning pets into surrogate humans, he writes, hurts both sides of the relationship.

Reports and Studies

American Kennel Club, *The Complete Dog Book,* 1996.

The AKC's official guide includes detailed descriptions of some 140 breeds that it recognizes in addition to tips on the care and feeding of dogs.

American Pet Products Manufacturers Association, *APPMA National Pet Owners Survey,* 1996.

Every two years the association updates its exhaustive information about the ownership and care of dogs, cats, fish, birds, small animals and reptiles.

The Next Step

Additional information from UMI's Newspaper & Periodical Abstracts database

Vicious Dogs

Kates, Joan Giangrasse, "U.S. postal campaign to snap back at dogs," *Chicago Tribune,* June 16, 1995, Sec. 2C, p. 3.

In 1994, more than 2,700 of the nation's 274,000 letter carriers were bitten by dogs. In a $15 million nationwide campaign, the U.S. Postal Service and the U.S. Humane Society have joined to promote responsible pet ownership.

Gardner, Janice Merrifield, "The canine legislative beat," *Dog World,* November 1995, pp. 52-54.

Rottweilers and Akitas are the latest dog breeds to prompt legislation because of their "dangerousness." Previously, it was pit bulls that received the most notoriety.

Gorman, Tom, "Pets land in insurance doghouse," *Los Angeles Times,* March 20, 1995, p. A3.

Owners of pit bulls, Rottweilers and other dog breeds with reputations for aggressiveness, are finding it harder to get homeowners insurance in California. Some insurance companies deem owners of such dogs too risky to insure.

Wheeler, Linda, "In turbulent hearing, dog lovers protest regulating pit bulls, Rottweilers," *The Washington Post,* April 24, 1996, p. D6.

About 40 angry animal lovers put Washington, D.C. City Council member Frank Smith Jr. in the political doghouse, staging a noisy protest of a new city law that requires all pit bull terriers and Rottweilers to be muzzled and registered as dangerous.

Pet Abuse and Mistreatment

Green, Chuck, "Cruelty to pets an issue for legislature," *Denver Post,* Feb. 23, 1996, p. B1.

Green supports a new law proposed in Colorado that would increase the penalty for intentionally causing serious injury to someone's household pet. Green highlights the case of Dan Winter, who poisoned two dogs in October 1995, as a reason for a tougher law.

Selby, Gardner, "Will bark of judge's pets be worse than their bite?" *The Houston Post,* Jan. 25, 1995, p. A19.

Judge Steve Mansfield of Texas, already under scrutiny amid questions he lied about his qualifications before winning election on Nov. 8, 1995, is also running into trouble with the Austin Humane Society because he leaves his two dogs in his car in an underground garage while he is in court.

Shapiro, Kenneth, "Violence and animal abuse: All in the family," *Animals' Agenda,* July 1996, pp. 55-56.

Many people say that they consider their pets to be members of the family. While this relationship has benefits to both humans and animals, when violence occurs within a family, pets can also get hurt.

Stewart, Richard, "No more pets. Pair collared at puppy farm," *Houston Chronicle,* April 2, 1995, p. D1.

Authorities of Jasper County, Texas, raided a pet farm, seizing 165 dogs, nine cats, seven turtles, two Shetland ponies, three rheas, a pair of hamsters and a potbellied pig that has "adopted" a short-eared rabbit. Sharon and Bobby James, the owners of the pet farm, pleaded guilty to animal cruelty charges.

Stroup, Sheila, "Pet abuse too common," *Times-Picayune,* April 20, 1995, p. B1.

Stroup reflects on the story of Snoops, the dog Charles Childers of Los Angeles, Calif., hanged in March 1995. Stroup says this incident epitomizes the larger, sadder story of pet abuse.

Emotional Benefits of Pet Ownership

"Activity therapy," *Mayo Clinic Health Letter,* August 1995, p. 6.

Hobbies can be the tickets to better mental and physical health. The benefits of pet ownership, gardening and listening to music are discussed.

"Canine caregivers cheer up patients," *American Journal of Nursing,* December 1995, p. 9.

Canine caregivers are cheering up patients in intensive care units at one California hospital. Several studies have documented the benefits to health and well-being of interaction with animals in therapeutic settings.

Nicholas, Anna Katherine, "Here, there & everywhere," *Dog World,* November 1995, pp. 111-113.

Nicholas discusses the special affinity between dogs and children.

Sable, Pat, "Pets, attachment, and well-being across the life cycle," *Social Work,* May 1995, pp. 334-341.

The ways in which family pets, especially dogs and cats, provide certain components of attachment that contribute to emotional and social well-being throughout the life cycle are explored. Pets supply ongoing comfort and reduce feelings of loneliness in times of stress.

Voelker, Rebecca, "Puppy love can be therapeutic, too," *JAMA: The Journal of the American Medical As-*

***sociation,* Dec. 27, 1995, p. 4.**
The health benefits of pet ownership have long been touted, but now more evidence is surfacing that pets can also be helpful in rehabilitation therapy. Animal-assisted therapy programs are discussed.

"Welfare group joins seniors, pets," *Dog World,* November 1996, p. 53.
Researchers have found that patients with coronary disease have increased survival rates if they own pets. The health benefits of owning a pet may be greatest on older Americans, who often find themselves alone.

Pet Adoption Programs

Conover, Kirsten A. "A cat-by-cat solution to homeless pets," *The Christian Science Monitor,* March 25, 1996, p. 14.
Sheera Kahn is a Boston travel agent who devotes much of her free time to rescuing and rehabilitating homeless cats and placing them in loving families. A typical day in her home is featured.

Gray, Madison J., "'Pets for People' program allows seniors to adopt felines for free," *Detroit News,* April 10, 1996, p. K3.
In a program underwritten by the Ralston Purina Corp. of Dunkirk, N.Y., senior citizens can adopt a cat from a Michigan Humane Society shelter for free. However, before seniors can adopt cats and kittens, they must be screened by Humane Society counselors to prove they can provide decent homes.

Johnson, Stephen, "Shelter for cast-off pets may soon be homeless, too," *Houston Chronicle,* Jan. 4, 1995, p. A16.
Facing the impending loss of their animal shelter in Houston, Texas, officials of Special Pals Inc. continue their search for a new facility to care for homeless animals. The organization, which receives about 3,000 dogs and cats a year for adoption, must vacate the premise by the end of January 1995, because its lease ends.

Van Dine, Lynn, "Animal rescue agencies go online to find pets a home," *Detroit News,* May 29, 1996, p. J3.
Dogs, cats and even gerbils can be adopted online through a number of Web sites hosted by humane societies, animal rescue leagues and smaller organizations. The Michigan Greyhound Connection in Mt. Clemens has a World Wide Web site for people interested in adopting retired racing greyhounds.

Exotic Pets

Antosh, Nelson, "Exotic animals finding home on, off Texas range," *Houston Chronicle,* September 10, 1996, p. C5.
More and more, Texas is becoming a home where the buffalo roam, where the deer and the antelope play. A survey released by the Texas Agriculture Statistics Service in September 1996 found that the state is home to nearly 200,000 exotic hoofed animals.

Curley, Tom, "Boom in exotic pets breeds concerns," *USA Today,* Oct. 13, 1995, p. A3.
The exotic pet trade has flourished in the U.S. The federal government sharply restricts trade in endangered species, but there is less monitoring of trade for animals that aren't endangered.

Lamb, Rachel, "Unfair to exotic pets," *The Washington Post,* Oct. 28, 1995, p. A26.
Lamb, director of the U.S. Humane Society's Companion Animal Care program, responds in a letter to *The Washington Post's* Oct. 15, 1995, profile of veterinarian Hanna Siemering, saying it glossed over the serious problems that arise when exotic animals are kept as pets.

Lev, Michael A., "Exotic animals often pet peeves in suburbs," *Chicago Tribune,* April 29, 1995, Sec. 1D, p. 1.
The past decade has brought an explosion of interest in exotic and unusual pets. With it has come some fairly unusual discussions around Chicago-area village halls as officials must decide whether to change local laws to reflect changing tastes in pets.

Mason, Jim, and Jim Brewer, "A lion in every back yard: The mass marketing of exotic animals," *Animals' Agenda,* July 1996, pp. 26-27.
Today, in most states, almost anyone can buy, breed and sell just about any kind of animal. A new industry of importers, breeders, dealers, suppliers, veterinarians, auctions, trade associations and lobby groups is hustling to cater to such buyers.

Merrill, Cristina, "Doris Duke's pets put U.S. Trust to the camel test," *American Banker,* Aug. 8, 1995, p. 12.
As a preliminary co-executor of the estate of billionaire Doris Duke, an ardent animal lover and conservationist, the U.S. Trust Company, an investment management bank, has become responsible for and enmeshed in litigation involving the care of such animals as camels, miniature horses and dogs. The unusual story is recounted.

Nakashima, Ellen, "Caring for that special pet: Veterinarian is one of few specializing in exotic animals," *The Washington Post,* Oct. 15, 1995, p. B1.
Veterinarian Hanna Siemering is among a small but growing number of vets who treat exotic pets. Siemering, who runs the Exotic Pet Clinic in Springfield, Va., was the first veterinarian in Northern Virginia to devote herself exclusively to such animals.

Sorter, Amy, "Big cats, bad pets," *Cats Magazine,* October 1996, pp. 32-35.
Reasons why large exotic cats do not make good pets are discussed. Large cats are dangerous, and it is impossible

for private owners to satisfy the psychological and physical needs of these animals.

Struman, Maryann, "Once-popular porkers lose their appeal as pets," *Detroit News,* Jan. 10, 1996, p. D1.
Vietnamese potbellied pigs, one of the trendiest pets of the last decade, are going to the dogs, literally. Lucky pigs are landing at Detroit area animal shelters. The less fortunate are ending up in dog food. Many owners expected the pigs to be like dogs, but the animals act like pigs.

Van Matre, Lynn, "Exotic animals don't stay cute for long," *Chicago Tribune,* July 7, 1996, Sec. 4D, p. 1.
A 3-foot-long American alligator that turned up in Woodridge, Ill., was probably dumped by its owners, who no longer thought the reptile they brought back from Florida was as cute as when it was tiny. The peril of abandoned animals is discussed.

Yaqub, Reshma Memon, "Exotic pets may have exotic needs," *The Washington Post,* Sept. 20, 1996, p. D5.
Guidelines for evaluating a pet store and answers to questions about uncommon animals are presented.

Spay-Neuter Campaigns

Bell, Rhonda, "SNIP cuts into number of strays," *Times-Picayune,* Aug. 18, 1996, p. B1.
The Southern Animal Foundation's Spay-Neuter Intervention Program (SNIP), which aggressively attacks the overpopulation of cats and dogs in the New Orleans area, is featured. The foundation works in cooperation with area animal shelters.

Duplessis, Kim, "Clinic on wheels gives animal sterilizations," *Times-Picayune,* Aug. 15, 1996, Sec. OTB, p. 1.
The Southern Animal Foundation's Spay-Neuter van will visit St. Bernard Church in Los Angeles, Calif., on Aug. 21, 1996, to provide free sterilizations for pets of needy residents. Friends of the Animal Shelter has donated $300 to cover the cost of the van's visit.

Stroup, Sheila, "SNIP helps pets in need," *Times-Picayune,* Oct. 22, 1996, p. B1.
Stroup comments on the pet overpopulation problem in the New Orleans area, with colonies of cats living under raised shotgun houses and packs of dogs running wild in the woods. Stroup details the efforts of the Spay-Neuter Intervention Program.

Maintaining a Happy and Healthy Pet

"Enzyme supplements can keep pets healthy," *Better Nutrition for Today's Living,* December 1995, p. 28.
Pets need enzymes to enhance their digestive processes. Enzyme supplements that can help preserve the health of pets include a powdered green barley supplement rich in natural enzymes and raw, natural foods.

"Home-prepared meals plus supplements best for pets," *Better Nutrition for Today's Living,* October 1995, p. 36.
Pets are healthiest when they eat wholesome foods that are prepared at home, as some pet foods may not have the required nutrients. Supplements can also help pets maintain healthy nutrition levels.

Marder, Amy, "Solving the problem of home-alone pets," *Prevention,* December 1995, pp. 121-124.
Professional pet sitters are now offering a wider array of services that are tailored to meet the needs of working people who want their pets to be happy. Marder discusses pet-sitting options and choosing a sitter.

Back Issues

Great Research on Current Issues Starts Right Here...Recent topics covered by The CQ Researcher are listed below. Before May 1991, reports were published under the name of Editorial Research Reports.

JUNE 1995
Combating Infectious Disease
Property Rights
Repetitive Stress Injuries
Regulating the Internet

JULY 1995
War Crimes
Highway Safety
Combating Terrorism
Preventing Teen Drug Use

AUGUST 1995
Job Stress
Organ Transplants
United Nations at 50
Advances in Cancer Research

SEPTEMBER 1995
Catholic Church in the U.S.
Northern Ireland Cease-Fire
High School Sports
Teaching History

OCTOBER 1995
Quebec's Future
Revitalizing the Cities
Networking the Classroom
Indoor Air Pollution

NOVEMBER 1995
The Working Poor
The Jury System
Sex, Violence and the Media
Police Misconduct

DECEMBER 1995
Teens and Tobacco
Gene Therapy's Future
Global Water Shortages
Third-Party Prospects

JANUARY 1996
Emergency Medicine
Punishing Sex Offenders
Bilingual Education
Helping the Homeless

FEBRUARY 1996
Reforming the CIA
Campaign Finance Reform
Academic Politics
Getting Into College

MARCH 1996
The British Monarchy
Preventing Juvenile Crime
Tax Reform
Pursuing the Paranormal

APRIL 1996
Centennial Olympic Games
Managed Care
Protecting Endangered Species
New Military Culture

MAY 1996
Russia's Political Future
Marriage and Divorce
Year-Round Schools
Taiwan, China and the U.S.

JUNE 1996
Rethinking NAFTA
First Ladies
Teaching Values
Labor Movement's Future

JULY 1996
Recovered-Memory Debate
Native Americans' Future
Crackdown on Sexual Harassment
Attack on Public Schools

AUGUST 1996
Fighting Over Animal Rights
Privatizing Government Services
Child Labor and Sweatshops
Cleaning Up Hazardous Wastes

SEPTEMBER 1996
Gambling Under Attack
The States and Federalism
Civic Journalism
Reassessing Foreign Aid

OCTOBER 1996
Political Consultants
Insurance Fraud
Rethinking School Integration
Parental Rights

NOVEMBER 1996
Global Warming
Clashing Over Copyright
Consumer Debt
Governing Washington, D.C.

DECEMBER 1996
Welfare, Work and the States
The New Volunteerism
Implementing the Disabilities Act

Back issues are available for $5.00 (subscribers) or $8.00 (non-subscribers). Quantity discounts apply to orders over ten. To order, call Congressional Quarterly Customer Service at (202) 887-8621.

Binders are available for $18.00. To order call 1-800-638-1710. Please refer to stock number 648.

Future Topics

- ***Combating Scientific Misconduct***
- ***Deregulating Electric Power***
- ***The New Immigrants***

The CQ Researcher

Subject-Title Index

January 1991-December 1996

NOTE: Weekly CQ Researcher reports are indexed by title under boldface subject headings. Titles are followed by the date of the report and the number of the first page. Page numbers followed by asterisks refer to sidebars or the "At Issue" pro/con feature. Issues dated before May 10, 1991, were published under the name of Editorial Research Reports.